THE

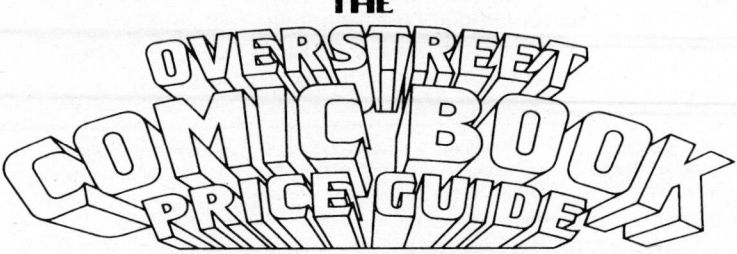

OVERSTREET COMIC BOOK PRICE GUIDE

27th Edition

BOOKS FROM 1897 - PRESENT INCLUDED
CATALOGUE & EVALUATION GUIDE - ILLUSTRATED

By
Robert M. Overstreet

SPECIAL CONTRIBUTORS TO THIS EDITION

Jerry Robinson, Murphy Anderson, Joe Mannarino, Jerry Weist,
Tom Inge, Michael Renegar, Arnold T. Blumberg, Scott Braden,
Robert J. Roter, Robert L. Beerbohm, Steven Fishler

SPECIAL ADVISORS TO THIS EDITION

Bruce Hamilton • Hugh O'Kennon • Ron Pussell • Gary M. Carter • John Snyder
Terry Stroud • Michael Naiman • Steve Geppi • James Payette
Harry Matetsky • Jerry Weist • John Verzyl • Mark Wilson • Joe Mannarino
Gary Guzzo • John Hone • Joe Dungan • David T. Alexander • Jon Berk
Larry Curcio • Gary Dolgoff • Richard Evans • Steve Fishler • Steve Gentner
Michael Goldman • Jamie Graham • Daniel Greenhalgh • John Hauser
Bill Hughes • Rob Hughes • Philip J. Gaudino • Joseph Koch • Phil Levine
•Keif Fromm • Richard Olson • Raymond S. True • Bruce Ellsworth
John Chruscinski • Vincent Zurzolo, Jr. • Todd Reznik • Robert Rogovin • Rory Root
Robert Roter • Chuck Rozanski • Tony Starks • Joe Verenault • Harley Yee

The CONFIDENT COLLECTOR™

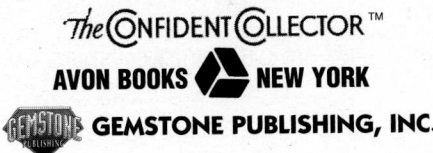

AVON BOOKS NEW YORK

GEMSTONE GEMSTONE PUBLISHING, INC.

Serious Comic Book Collectors, Don't Miss
THE OVERSTREET COMIC BOOK GRADING GUIDE
By Robert M. Overstreet and Gary M. Carter
A Confident Collector Title from Avon Books

Important Notice. All of the information, including valuations, in this book has been compiled from the most reliable sources, and every effort has been made to eliminate errors and questionable data. Nevertheless, the possibility of error always exists in a work of such immense scope. The publisher will not be held responsible for losses which may occur in the purchase, sale, or other transaction of items because of information contained herein. Readers who feel they have discovered errors are invited to *write* and inform us so that the errors may be corrected in subsequent editions.

Front cover art: All Characters are trademarks of DC Comics and are used with permission. Copyright 1997 DC Comics. All rights reserved.
Spine art: Action Comics #1 and Detective Comics #27 © DC Comics
Amazing Spider-Man #1 and X-Men #1 © Marvel Entertainment Group

Cover Illustration and logo design by Alex Ross; logo inks by John K. Snyder III

THE OVERSTREET COMIC BOOK PRICE GUIDE (27th Edition) is an original publication of Gemstone Publishing, Inc. and Avon Books. This edition has never before appeared in book form.

AVON BOOKS
A division of
The Hearst Corporation
1350 Avenue of the Americas
New York, New York 10019

First Avon Books Trade Printing: May 1997
AVON TRADEMARK REG. U.S. PAT. OFF. AND IN OTHER COUNTRIES, MARCA REGISTRADA, HECHO EN U.S.A.

Printed in the U.S.A.
10 9 8 7 6 5 4 3 2 1

TABLE OF CONTENTS

ACKNOWLEDGEMENTS

Mark Arnold (Harvey data); Larry Bigman (Frazetta-Williamson data); Glenn Bray (Kurtzman data); Gary Carter (DC data); J. B. Clifford Jr. (E. C. data); Gary Coddington (Superman data); Wilt Conine (Fawcett data); Dr. S. M. Davidson (Cupples & Leon data); Al Dellinges (Kubert data); David Gerstein (Walt Disney Comics data); Kevin Hancer (Tarzan data); Charles Heffelfinger and Jim Ivey (March of Comics listing); R. C. Holland and Ron Pussell (Seduction and Parade of Pleasure data); Grant Irwin (Quality data); Richard Kravitz (Kelly data); Phil Levine (giveaway data); Dan Malan & Charles Heffelfinger (Classic Comics data); Fred Nardelli (Frazetta data); Michelle Nolan (love comics); Mike Nolan (MLJ, Timely, Nedor data); George Olshevsky (Timely data); Richard Olson (LOA & R. F. Outcault data); Scott Pell ('50s data); Greg Robertson (National data); Don Rosa (Late 1940s to 1950s data); Matt Schiffman (Bronze Age data); Frank Scigliano (Little Lulu data); Gene Seger (Buck Rogers data); Rick Sloane (Archie data); David R. Smith, Archivist, Walt Disney Productions (Disney data); Tony Starks (Silver and Bronze Age data); Don and Maggie Thompson (Four Color listing); Mike Tiefenbacher & Jerry Sinkovec (Atlas and National data); Raymond True (Classic Comics data); Jim Vadeboncoeur Jr. (Williamson and Atlas data); Kim Weston (Disney and Barks data); Cat Yronwode (Spirit data); Andrew Zerbe and Gary Behymer (M. E. data).

My appreciation must also be extended to Bruce Hamilton, Jerry Weist, John Verzyl, James Payette, Robert Rotor, Ron Pussell, Joe Mannarino, Terry Stroud, Conrad Eschenberg, Eric Groves, Dave Anderson (OK), Gary Colabuono, Rod Dyke, Gary Guzzo, Harley Yee, John Snyder, Matt Hawkins, Lou Bank, Jeff Mariotte, Donna Sava, Maureen McTigue, Marty Stever, Gale Young, Steve Geppi, Hugh O'Kennon and Don Maris, for their continued support and help; to Steven Fishler and Marc Patten for their "How to Sell Your Comic Collection"; to Dr. Richard Olson for grading and Yellow Kid information; to Tom Inge for his "Chronology of the American Comic Book"; to Robert Beerbohm for his introduction to the Platinum Age as well as for supplying much needed data for the listings; to Bill Blackbeard of the San Francisco Academy of Comic Art for his Platinum Age cover photos; to Jerry Robinson and Murphy Anderson for providing some of their valuable time for interviews just for this edition; to Bill Spicer and Zetta DeVoe (Western Publishing Co.) for their contribution of data; and especially to Bill for his kind permission to reprint portions of his and Jerry Bails' America's Four Color Pastime;

Special Credit is due our talented staff for their assistance with this 27th edition and for their help at the conventions last year; to Arnold T. Blumberg (Production Manager), Scott Braden (Research Editor), Brenda Busick (Art Director), Jeffrey Dillon (Senior Graphic Artist), Cathy Disbrow (Graphic Artist), Todd M. Hoffer (Managing Editor), Benn Ray (Associate Editor), J. Patrick Rybandt (Copy Editor), Jennifer Unglesbee (Customer Service), J. C. Vaughn (Marketing), Christopher Woodward (Copy Editor); and Dave Noah (research and statistical data) for their valuable contributions to this edition and the continuing success of the Annual Price Guide.

Finally, thanks is due to my wife Caroline Overstreet and my editor Michael Renegar for their inspiration, advice and hard work in getting this reference work to the printer on time. Thanks to all who placed ads in this 27th edition.

Acknowledgement is also due to the following people who generously contributed much needed data for this edition:

C. Arnedo	Jim Grimwood	Bill Lest	Eric Reynolds
Mark Arnold	Doug Haines	Dr. Michael J. S. Levine	Rick Roden
Ian Auld	Cully Hamner	Philip M. Levine	John Romita, Jr.
Stephen Baer	Terry Harms	Boyd Magers	Alex Ross
Jonathan Bennett	Tom Hayes	Don Maris	Steve Schanes
Michael Brewster	Carl Horak	Jeff Matsuda	Frank Simmons
Richard M. Brown	Adam Hughes	Mike Mignola	Tony Starks
Quinton Clem	Wayne Jacques	John Mlachnik	Ray Storch
Anthony F. De Maria	Dan Jurgens	Rich Morrissey	Karl Story
David Gerstein	Jeff Keffer	Michael Naiman	Steve Treiber
Keif A. Fromm	Dave Kuhl	David Noah	John K. Vavra
Dwight Fuhro	Lynne Keith	Hugh O'Kennon	Lee Weeks
Lyndon F. Fuller	Chris Khalaf	Jerry Ordway	Travis Wetzel
Tom Garcia	Tony Kowalik	Leo Pando	Doug Wheeler
Ron Garney	Andy Kubert	Dennis K. Petilli	Mark Wilson
David Gerstein	Dan Kurdilla	Ron Pussell	Garth & Kelly Wood
Dennis Grimm	David LaBelle	Mike Randolph	

INTRODUCTION

Congratulations! We at Gemstone welcome you to the hobby of comic books. This book is the most comprehensive reference work available on comics. It is also respected and used by dealers and collectors everywhere. The Overstreet price is the accepted price around the world, and we have not earned this privilege easily. Through hard work, diligence and constant contact with the market for decades, Overstreet has become the most trusted name in comics.

HOW TO USE THIS BOOK

This volume is an accurate, detailed alphabetical list of comic books and their retail values. Comic books are listed by title, regardless of company. Prices listed are shown in Good, Fine and Near Mint condition with many key books priced in an additional Very Fine grade. Comic books that fall in between the grades listed can be priced simply with the following procedure: Very Good is half way between Good and Fine; Very Fine is half way between Fine and Near Mint (unless a VF price is already shown). The older true Mint books usually bring a premium over the Near Mint price. Books in Fair bring 50 to 70% of the Good price. Some books only show a Very Fine price as the highest grade. The author has not been able to determine if these particular books exist in better than Very Fine condition, thus the omission of a Near Mint price. Most comic books are listed in groups, i.e., 11-20, 21-30, 31-50, etc. The prices listed opposite these groupings represent the value of each issue in that group. More detailed information is given for individual comic books. If you are looking for a particular character, consult the first appearance indexes which will help you locate the correct title and issue. This book also contains hundreds of ads covering all aspects of this hobby. Whether you are buying or selling, the advertising sections can be of tremendous benefit to you.

COMIC BOOK VALUES LISTED

All values listed in this book are in U.S. currency and are retail prices based on (but not limited to) reports from our extensive network of experienced advisors which include convention sales, mail order, auctions, unpublished personal sales and stores. Overstreet, with several decades of market experience, has developed a unique and comprehensive system for gathering, documenting, averaging and pricing data on comic books. The end result is a true fair market value for your use. We have earned the reputation for our cautious, conservative approach to pricing comic books. You, the collector, can be assured that the prices listed in this volume are the most accurate and useful in print.

IMPORTANT NOTE: This book is not a dealer's price list, although some dealers may base their prices on the values listed. The true value of any comic book is what you are willing to pay. Prices listed herein are an indication of what collectors (not dealers) would probably pay. For one reason or another, these collectors might want certain books badly, or else need specific issues to complete their runs and so are willing to pay more.

DEALERS POSITION: Dealers are not in a position to pay the full prices listed, but work on a percentage depending largely on the amount of investment required and the quality of material offered. Usually they will pay from 20 to 70% of the list price depending on how long it will take them to sell the collection after making the investment; the higher the demand and better the condition, the more the percentage. Most dealers are faced with expenses such as advertising, travel, telephone and mailing, rent, employee salaries, plus convention costs. These costs all go in before the books are sold. The high demand books usually sell right away but there are many other titles that are difficult to sell due to low demand. Sometimes a dealer will have cost tied up in this type of material for several years before finally moving it. Remember, his position is that of handling, demand, and overhead. Most dealers are victims of these economics.

HOW COMIC BOOKS ARE LISTED

Comic books are listed alphabetically by title. The true title of a comic book can be found listed with the publisher's information, or indicia, usually found at the bottom of the inside front cover. Titles that appear on the front cover can vary from the official title listed inside.

Comic book titles, sequence of issues, dates of first and last issues, publishing companies, origin and special issues are listed when known. Prominent and collectible artists are also pointed out (usually in footnotes). Page counts will always include covers. Most comic books began with a #1, but occasionally many titles began with an odd number. There is a reason for this. Publishers had to register new titles with the post office for 2nd class permits. The registration fee was expensive. To avoid this expense, many publishers would continue the numbering of new titles from old defunct titles. For instance, **Weird Science** #12 (1st issue) was continued from the defunct **Saddle Romances** #11 (the last issue). In doing this, the publishers hoped to avoid having to register new titles. However, the post office would soon discover the new title and force the publisher to pay the registration fee as well as to list the correct number. For instance, the previous title mentioned began with #12 (1st issue). Then #13 through #15 were published. The next issue became #5 after the Post Office correction. Now the sequence of published issues (see the listings) is #12-15, 5-on. This created a problem in early fandom for the collector because the numbers 12-15 in this title were duplicated.

WHAT COMIC BOOKS ARE LISTED

The Guide will be listing primarily American comic books due to space limitations. The earliest comic books date back to 1897 and are included in their own section under The Platinum Age. These books basically reprinted newspaper strips and were published in varying sizes, usually with cardboard covers, but sometimes as hardbacks. The format of **Funnies On Parade**, published in 1933 (saddle-stitched), soon became the standard for the modern comic book, although square-bound versions were also published. Most of these formats that appeared on newsstands will be included.

POLICY OF LISTING NEW COMIC BOOKS

The 1980s and '90s has experienced an explosion of publishers with hundreds of new titles appearing in black and white and color. Many of these comics are listed in this book, but not all due to space limitation. We will attempt to list complete information only on those titles that show some collector interest. The selection of titles to include is constantly being monitored by our board of advisors who work on our monthly magazine. Of course a much better coverage of recent books will be made in the monthly throughout the year. Please do not contact us to list your new comic books. Listings are determined by the marketplace. However, we are interested in receiving review copies of all new comic books published.

GRADING COMIC BOOKS

GET THE TOOLS

For complete, detailed information on grading and restoration, consult the **Overstreet Comic Book Grading Guide**. Copies are available through all normal distribution channels or can be ordered direct from the publisher by sending $12 plus $2 postage and handling. You can also call Gemstone toll free at 1-888-375-9800.

The Overstreet Comic Book Grading Card, known as the **ONE** and **OWL Card** is also available. This card has two functions. The **ONE Card** (Overstreet's Numerical Equivalent) is used to convert grading condition terms to the new numerical grading system. The **OWL Card** (Overstreet's Whiteness Level) is used for grading the whiteness of paper. The color scale on the **OWL Card** is simply placed over the interior comic book paper. The paper color is matched with the color on the card to get the **OWL** number. The **ONE/OWL Card** may be ordered direct from the publisher by sending $1.30 per card.

HOW TO GRADE

Before a comic book's true value can be assessed, its condition or state of preservation must be determined. In all comic books, the better the condition the more desirable and valuable the book. Comic books in **MINT** condition will bring several times the price of the same book in **POOR** condition. Therefore it is very important to be able to properly grade your books. Comics should be graded from the inside out, so the following comic book areas should be examined before assigning a final grade.

Check inside pages, inside spine and covers and outside spine and covers for any tears, markings, brittleness, tape, soiling, chunks out or other defects that would affect the grade. After all the above steps have been taken, then the reader can begin to consider an overall grade for his or her book. The grading of a comic book is done by simply looking at the book and describing its condition, which may range from absolutely perfect newsstand condition **MINT** to extremely worn, dirty, and torn **POOR**.

Numerous variables influence the evaluation of a comic book's condition and all must be considered in the final evaluation. As grading is the most subjective aspect of determining a comic's value, it is very important that the grader be careful not to allow wishful thinking to influence what the eyes see. It is also very important to realize that older comics in **MINT** condition are extremely scarce and are rarely advertised for sale; most of the higher grade comics advertised range from

GRADING DEFINITIONS

Note: This edition uses both the traditional grade abbreviations and the **ONE** number throughout the listings. The Overstreet Numerical Equivalent (**ONE**) spread range is given with each grade.

MINT (MT) (ONE 100-98): Near perfect in every way. Only the most subtle bindery or printing defects are allowed. Cover is flat with no surface wear. Cover inks are bright with high reflectivity and minimal fading. Corners are cut square and sharp. Staples are generally centered, clean with no rust. Cover is generally well centered and firmly secured to interior pages. Paper is supple and fresh. Spine is tight and flat.

NEAR MINT (NM) (ONE 97-90): Nearly perfect with only minor imperfections such as tiny corner creases or staple stress lines, a few color flecks, bindery tears, tiny impact creases or a combination of the above where the overall eye appeal is less than Mint. Only the most subtle binding and/or printing defects allowed. Cover is flat with no surface wear. Cover inks are bright with high reflectivity and minimum fading. Corners are cut square and sharp with ever so slight blunting permitted. Staples are generally centered, clean with no rust. Cover is well centered and firmly secured to interior pages. Paper is supple and like new. Spine is tight and flat.

VERY FINE (VF) (ONE 89-75): An excellent copy with outstanding eye appeal. Sharp, bright and clean with supple pages. Cover is relatively flat with minimal surface wear beginning to show. Cover inks are generally bright with moderate to high reflectivity. Slight wear beginning to show including some minute wear at corners. Staples may show some discoloration. Spine may have a few transverse stress lines but is relatively flat. A light 1/2 inch crease is acceptable. Pages and covers can be yellowish/tannish (at the least, but not brown and will usually be off-white to white).

FINE (FN) (ONE 74-55): An exceptional, above-average copy that shows minor wear but is still relatively flat and clean with no major creasing or other serious defects. Eye appeal is somewhat reduced because of noticeable surface wear and the accumulation of smaller defects, especially on the spine and edges. A Fine condition comic book appears to have been read many times and has been handled with moderate care. Compared to a VF, cover inks are beginning to show a significant reduction in reflectivity but it is still a highly collectible and desirable book.

VERY GOOD (VG) (ONE 54-35): The average used comic book. A comic in this grade shows moderate wear, can have a reading or center crease or a rolled spine, but has not accumulated enough total defects to reduce eye appeal to the point that it is not a desirable copy. Some discoloration, fading and even minor soiling is allowed. No chunks can be missing but a small piece can be out at the corner or edge. Store stamps, name stamps, arrival dates, initials, etc. have no effect on this grade. Cover and interior pages can have minor tears and folds and the centerfold may be loose or detached. One or both staples might be loose, but cover is not completely detached. Common bindery and printing defects do not affect grade. Pages and inside covers may be brown but not brittle. Tape should never be used for comic book repair, however many VG condition comics have minor tape repair.

GOOD (GD) (ONE 34-15): A copy in this grade has all pages and covers, although there may be small pieces missing. Books in this grade are commonly creased, scuffed, abraded and soiled, but completely readable. Often paper quality is low but not brittle. Cover reflectivity is low and in some cases completely absent. Most collectors consider this the lowest collectible grade because comic books in lesser condition are usually incomplete and/or brittle. This grade can have a large accumulation of defects but still maintains its basic structural integrity.

FAIR (FR) (ONE 14-5): A copy in this grade has all pages and most of the covers, is soiled, ragged and unattractive. Creases and folds are prevalent and paper quality may be very low. The centerfold may be missing if it does not affect a story. Spine may be completely split its entire length. Staples may be gone, and/or cover completely detached. Corners are commonly severely rounded or absent. Coupons may be cut from front cover and/or back cover and/or interior pages. These books are mostly readable although soiling, staining, tears, markings or chunks missing may interfere with reading the complete story. Very often paper quality is low and may even be brittle around the edges but not in the central portion of the pages.

POOR (PR) (ONE 4-1): Most comic books in this grade have been sufficiently degraded to the point that there is no longer any collector value. Copies in this grade typically have pages and/or approximately 1/3 or more of the front cover missing. They may have extremely severe stains, mildew or heavy cover abrasion to the point that cover inks are indistinct/absent. They may have been defaced with paints, varnishes, glues, oil, indelible markers or dyes. Other defects often include severe rips, tears, folding and creasing. Another common defect in this grade is moderate to severe brittleness, often to the point that the comic book literally "falls apart" when examined.

DUST JACKETS

Many of the early strip reprint comics were printed in hardback with dust jackets. Books with dust jackets are worth more. The value can increase from 20 to 50 percent depending on the rarity of book. Usually, the earlier the book, the greater the percentage. Unless noted, prices listed are without dust jackets. The condition of the dust jacket should be graded independently of the book itself.

RESTORED COMICS

Our board of advisors suggests that **professionally restored comic books** are an accepted component of the comic book market, but only if the following criteria are met: 1–Must be professional work. 2–Complete disclosure of the extent and type of restoration. 3–Both parties are informed. 4–Priced accordingly depending on availability and demand. **Note:** A professionally restored book, reasonably priced, while not worth as much as the same book unrestored, will increase in value at the same rate. However, if you pay the unrestored price for a restored book, you would be paying a premium, which of course may not be a good investment.

Initial indications on sales and auction results suggests the following: Unrestored key books in Fine or better condition may prove in the future to be better investments as their availability decreases, and should not be restored to an apparent higher grade. Restoration should be concentrated on books in less than Fine condition. **Warning:** Before getting restoration done, seek advice from a professional and avoid doing it yourself.

Many rare and expensive books are being repaired and restored by professionals and amateurs alike. If the book is expensive, there is a strong likelihood that some type of repair, cleaning or restoration has been done. In most cases, after restoration, these books are not actually higher grades but are altered lower grade books. **Note:** Expert restoration is always preferable to amateur work and is sometimes very difficult to spot and can be easily missed when grading. In some cases, the work done is so good that it is impossible to spot. Depending upon the extent and type of restoration and the quality of what was done, you will have to decide whether the value has increased or decreased. In many cases we have observed in the market that the value has been increased on certain books that were originally in low grade before restoration where the appearance and structural integrity was greatly improved afterwards. Restoration on higher grade copies may or may not affect value depending on what is done. Of course, when a comic book is graded, everything must be taken into account in the final grade given.

To the novice grading will appear difficult at first, but as experience is gained accuracy will improve. Whenever in doubt (after using *The Overstreet Comic Book Grading Guide*), consult with a reputable dealer or experienced collector in your area. The following grading information is given to further aid the collector:

SCARCITY OF COMIC BOOKS RELATED TO GRADE

1897-1933 Comics: Most of these books are bound with thick cardboard covers and are very rare to non-existent in VF or better condition. Due to their extreme age, paper browning is very common. Brittleness could be a problem.

1933-1940 Comics: There are many issues from this period that are very scarce in any condition, especially from the early to mid-1930s. Surviving copies of any particular issue range from a handful to several hundred. Near Mint to Mint copies are virtually non-existent with known examples of any particular issue limited to five or fewer copies. Most surviving copies are in FN-VF or less condition. Brittleness or browning of paper is fairly common and could be a problem.

A-13

A-15

1941-1952 Comics: Surviving comic books would number from less than 100 to several thousand copies of each issue. Near Mint to Mint copies are a little more common but are still relatively scarce with only a dozen or so copies in this grade existing of any particular issue. Exceptions would be recent warehouse finds of most Dell comics (6-100 copies, but usually 30 or less), and Harvey comics (1950s-1970s) surfacing. Due to low paper quality of the late 1940s and 1950s, many comics from this period are rare in Near Mint to Mint condition. Most remaining copies are VF or less. Browning of paper could be a problem.

1953-1959 Comics: As comic book sales continued to drop during the 1950s, production values were lowered resulting in cheaply printed comics. For this reason, high grade copies are extremely rare. Many Atlas and Marvel comics have chipping along the trimmed edges (Marvel chipping) which reduces even more the number of surviving high grade copies.

1960-1970 Comics: Early '60s comics are rare in Near Mint to Mint condition. Most copies of early '60s Marvels and DCs grade no higher than VF. Many early keys in NM or MT exist in numbers less than 10-20 of each. Mid- to late-'60s books in high grade are more common due to the hoarding of comics that began in the mid-'60s.

1970-Present: Comics of today are common in high grade. VF to NM is the standard rather than the exception.

When you consider how few Golden and Silver Age books exist compared to the current market, you will begin to appreciate the true rarity of these early books. In many cases less than 5-10 copies exist of a particular issue in Near Mint to Mint condition, while most of the 1930s books do not exist in this grade at all.

KNOW THE BUZZ WORDS

Many of the following terms and abbreviations are used in the comic book market and are explained here: (Note: Consult the **Overstreet Comic Book Grading Guide** for a more detailed list of terms.)

a-Story art; **a(i)**-Story art inks; **a(p)**-Story art pencils; **a(r)**-Story art reprint.

Adult Material-Contains story and/or art for "mature" readers. Re: sex, violence, strong language.

Adzine-A magazine primarily devoted to the advertising of comic books and collectibles as its first publishing priority as opposed to written articles.

Annual-A book that is published yearly.

Arrival Date-Markings on a comic book cover (usually in pencil) made by either the newsstand dealer or the distributor. These markings denote the date the book was placed on the newsstand. Usually the arrival date is one to two months prior to the cover date.

Ashcan-A prepublication facsimile or dummy issue of an intended title usually prepared to show advertisers. Part or all of the pages may be blank or from a different book with a new cover. Black and white ashcans are common.

B&W-Black and white art.

Bad Girl Art (BGA)-A term coined in 1993 to describe an attitude as well as a style of art that portrays women in a sexually implicit way.

Baxter paper-A high quality, white, heavy paper used in the printing of some comic books.

Bi-Monthly-Published every two months.

Bi-Weekly-Published every two weeks.

Bondage Cover-Usually denotes a female in restraints.

Brittleness-The final stage of paper deterioration.

c-Cover art; **c(i)**-Cover inks; **c(p)**-Cover pencils; **c(r)**-Cover reprint.

Bronze Age-(1) Non-specific term not in general acceptance by collectors which denotes comics published from approximately 1970 through 1980, (2) Term which describes "the Age" of comic books after the Silver Age.

Browning-Paper aging between tanning and brittleness.

Cameo-When a character appears briefly.

CCA-Comics Code Authority.

CCA Seal-An emblem that was placed on the cover of all CCA approved comics beginning in April-May, 1955.

Center Crease- (see Subscription Crease)

Centerfold-The stapled, four page middle sheet of a comic or magazine.

CFO-Abbreviation for "Centerfold out."

Chromium Cover-A special Chromium foil used on covers

Church, Edgar Collection-A large high grade comic book collection discovered by Mile High Comics in Colorado (over 22,000 books).

Classic Cover-A cover highly prized by collectors as a prime or matchless example of its kind.

Cleaning-A process in which dirt and dust is removed.

Color Touch-A restoration process by which colored ink is used to hide color flecks, flakes and larger areas

Colorist-An artist who paints the color guides for comics. Many modern colorists

use computer technology.

Comic Book Dealer-(1) A seller of comic books. (2) One who makes a living buying and selling comic books.

Comic Book Repair-When a tear, loose staple or centerfold has been mended without changing or adding to the original finish of the book. Repair may involve tape, glue or nylon gossamer and is easily detected. It is considered a defect

Comic Book Restoration-Any attempt, whether professional or amateur, to enhance the appearance of a comic book. These procedures may include any or all of the following techniques: recoloring, adding missing paper, stain, ink, dirt, tape removal, whitening, pressing out wrinkles, staple replacement, trimming, re-glossing, etc. Note: Unprofessional work can lower the value of a book. In all cases, except for some simple cleaning procedures, a restored book can never be worth the same as an unrestored book in the same condition.

Comics Code Authority-In 1954 the major publishers joined together and formed a committee which set up guidelines for acceptable comic contents. It was their task to approve the contents of comics before publication.

Complete Run-All issues of a given title.

Con-A Convention or public gathering of fans.

Condition-The state of preservation of a comic book.

Cosmic Aeroplane-Refers to a large collection discovered by Cosmic Aeroplane

Books.

Costumed Hero–A costumed crime fighter with "developed" powers instead of "super" powers.

Coupon Cut–Comic book missing a coupon.

Cover Loose–Cover is detached from staple or staples

Cover Trimmed–Cover has been reduced in size through trimming.

Crease–A paper fold that occurs in comic books from misuse

Crossover–When one character or characters appears briefly in another character's story.

Deacidification–The process of reducing acid in paper.

Debut–The first time that a character appears anywhere.

Defect–Any fault or flaw that detracts from perfection.

Denver Collection–A collection of early '40s high grade #1s bought at auction in Pennsylvania by a Denver, Colorado dealer.

Die-Cut Cover–When areas of a cover are precut by a printer to a special shape or to create a desired effect.

Distributor Painted Stripes–Color brushed or sprayed on the edges of comic book stacks as special coding by distributors (not a defect).

Double–A duplicate copy.

Double Cover–An error in the binding process which results in two or more covers being bound to a single book. Multiple covers are not considered a defect.

Drug Propaganda Story–Where comic makes an editorial stand about drug abuse.

Drug Use Story–Shows the actual use of drugs: shooting, taking a trip, harmful effects, etc.

Dust Shadow–Usually the fore-edge of a comic cover exposed to the gathering of dust creating a dark stripe.

Embossed Cover–When a pattern is embossed onto the cover creating a raised area.

Eye Appeal–A term used to describe the overall appeal of a comic's apparent condition.

Fanzine–An amateur fan publication.

File Copy–A comic originating from the publisher's file. Not all file copies are in pristine condition. **Note:** An arrival date on the cover of a comic indicates that it is not a file copy though a copyright date may.

First App.–Same as debut.

Flashback–When a previous story is being recalled.

Foil Cover–A thin metallic foil that is hot stamped on comic covers.

Four Color–A printing process in which the three primary colors plus black are used. Also refers to the Four Color series published by Dell.

Foxing–Tiny orange-brown spots on the cover or pages of a comic book caused by mold growth.

G. A.–Golden Age period.

Gatefold Cover–A double cover folded in itself.

Genre–Categories of comic book subject matter grouped as to type.

Giveaway–Type of comic book used as a premium for promotional purposes.

Golden Age (G.A.)–The period beginning with **Action** #1 (June, 1938) and ending with World War II in 1945.

Good Girl Art (GGA)–A term coined in 1977 to describe a style of art that portrays women in a sexually implicit way.

Headlights–Women's breasts, usually provocative.

Hologram Cover–True 3-D holograms are prepared and affixed to comic book covers and cards for special effect.

Hot Stamping–The process of pressing foil, prism paper and inks on cover stock.

i-Art inks.

Indicia–Publishers title, issue number, date, copyright and general information statement usually located on the inside front facing pages or inside back cover.

Infinity Cover–Shows the same scene within a scene repeated into infinity.

Inker–Artist that does the inking.

Intro–Same as debut.

JLA–Justice League of America.

JLI–Justice League International.

JSA–Justice Society of America.

Key Issue–An important issue in a run.

Lamont Larson–Refers to a large high grade collection of comics. Many of the books have Lamont or Larson written on the cover.

Lenticular Covers (aka flicker covers)– Images move when viewed at different angles specially prepared and affixed to cover.

Logo–The title of a strip or comic book as it appears on the cover or title page.

LSH–Legion of Super-Heroes.

Marvel Chipping–A defect that occurred during the trimming process of 1950s and 1960s Marvels which produced a ragged edge around the comic cover. Usually takes the form of a tiny chip or chips along the right hand edge of the cover.

Mile High–Refers to a large NM-Mint collection of comics originating from Denver, Colorado (Edgar Church collection).

Modern Age–Period from 1980 to the present.

Mylar ™–An inert, very hard, space age plastic used to make high quality protective bags and sleeves used for comic storage. Mylar ™ is a trademark of the DuPont Company.

nd–No date.

nn–No number.

N. Y. Legis. Comm.–New York Legislative Committee to Study the Publication of Comics (1951).

One-Shot–When only one issue is published of a title or the title is published on an infrequent or irregular schedule, whether or not as part of a numbered series (such as Dell's Four Color).

Origin–When the story of the character's creation is given.

Over Guide–When a comic book is priced at a value over Guide list.

p–Art pencils.

Painted Cover–Cover taken from an actual painting instead of a line drawing.

Paper Cover–Comic book cover made from the same newsprint as interior pages (self cover). These books are extremely rare in high grade.

Pedigree–A book from a famous collection, e.g. Allentown, Larson, Church/Mile High, Denver, San Francisco, Cosmic Aeroplane, etc. Note: Beware of non-pedigree collections being promoted as pedigree books. Only outstanding high grade collections similar to those listed qualify.

Penciler–Artist that does the pencils.

Photo Cover–Made from a photograph instead of a line drawing or painting.

POP–Parade of Pleasure, book about the censorship of comics.

Post-Code–Comic books published with the CCA seal.

Post-Golden Age–Comic books published between 1945 and 1950.

Post-Silver Age–Comic books published from 1969 to present.

Poughkeepsie–Refers to a large collection of Dell Comics' file copies believed to have originated from the warehouse of Western Publishing in Poughkeepsie, N.Y.

Pre-Code–Comic books published before the CCA seal.

Pre-Golden Age–Comic books published prior to **Action** #1 (June, 1938).

Pre-Hero–A term that describes the issues in a run prior to a superhero entering the run.

Pre-Silver Age–Comic books published between 1950 and **Showcase** #4 (1956).

Printing Defect–A defect caused by the printing process. Examples would include paper wrinkling, miscut edges, misfolded spine, untrimmed pages, off-registered color, off-centered trimming, misfolded and misbound pages. It should be noted that these are defects that lower the grade of the book.

Prism Cover–Special reflective foil material with 3-dimensional repeated designs. Used for special effect.

Provenance-When the owner of a book is known and is stated for the purpose of authenticating and documenting the history of the book. Example: A book from the Stan Lee or Forrest Ackerman collection would be an example of a value-adding provenance.

Quarterly-Published every three months (four times a year).

R or r-Reprint.

Rare-10 to 20 copies estimated to exist.

Rat Chew–Damage caused by gnawing rats or mice.

Reprint Comics-Comic books that contain newspaper strip reprints.

Restoration–The fine art of repairing a comic book to look as close as possible to its original condition.

Rice Paper-A thin, transparent paper commonly used by restorers to repair tears and replace small pieces on covers and pages of comic books.

Rolled Spine–A spine condition caused by folding back pages while reading.

S. A.-Silver Age.

Saddle Stitch–The staple binding of comic books.

S&K-Joe Simon and Jack Kirby (artists).

Scarce-20 to 100 copies estimated to exist.

Semi-Monthly-Published twice a month, as distinguished from bi-weekly.

Silver Age-Officially begins with **Showcase** #4 in 1956 and ends in 1969.

Silver Proof-A black & white actual size print on thick glossy paper hand painted by an artist to indicate colors to the engraver.

SOTI-Seduction of the Innocent, book about the censorship of comics. Refer to listing in this Guide.

Spine-The area representing the folded and stapled part of a comic book.

Spine Roll-A defect caused by improper storage which results in uneven pages and the shifting or bowing of the spine.

Splash Panel-A large panel that usually appears at the front of a comic story.

Squarebound-A comic book glue-bound with a square spined cover, aka perfect bound.

Store Stamp-Store name stamped in ink on cover.

Stress Lines-Light, tiny wrinkles occuring along the spine, projecting from the staples or appearing anywhere on the covers of a comic book.

Subscription Crease-A center crease caused by the folding of comic books for mailing to subscribers. This is considered a defect.

Sun Shadow–A darkened strip along the fore-edge of a comic cover caused by prolonged exposure to light, unlike the dust shadow which can often be removed. A serious defect.

Superhero–A costumed hero crime fighter with powers beyond those of mortal man.

Supervillain–A costumed criminal with powers beyond those of mortal man.

Swipe–A panel, sequence, or story obviously stolen or copied from previously published material.

3-D Comic-Comic art that is drawn and printed in two mismatched colors, producing a 3-D effect when viewed through special glasses.

3-D Effect Comic-Comic art that is drawn to appear 3-D, but isn't.

Title Page–The first page showing the title of a story.

Under Guide-When a comic book is priced at a value less than Guide list.

Variant Cover-a different cover image used on the same issue of a comic title.

Very Rare-1 to 10 copies estimated to exist.

Warehouse Copy-Originating from a publisher's warehouse; similar to file copy.

X-Over-When one character crosses over into another's strip.

Zine-See Fanzine.

COLLECTING COMIC BOOKS

HOW TO START COLLECTING

New comic books are available in many different kinds of stores. Grocery stores, drug stores, Wal-Mart, K-Mart, book stores, comic book stores and card and comics specialty shops are a few examples. Local flea markets and, of course, comic book conventions in your area are excellent sources for new and old comic books.

Most collectors begin by buying new issues in mint condition directly off the newsstand or from their local comic store. (Subscription copies are available from several mail-order services, and often the publishers themselves.) Each week new comics appear on the stands that are destined to become true collectors' items. The trick is to locate a store that carries a complete line of comics. In several localities this may be difficult. Most collectors frequent several magazine stands in order not to miss something they want. Even then, it pays to keep in close contact with collectors in other areas. Sooner or later, nearly every collector has to rely upon a friend in Fandom or a dealer to obtain for him an item that is unavailable locally (see ads in this book).

Before you buy any comic to add to your collection, you should carefully inspect its condition. Unlike stamps and coins, defective comics are generally not highly prized. The cover should be properly cut and printed. Remember that every blemish or sign of wear depreciates the beauty and value of your comics.

The serious collector usually buys extra copies of popular titles. He may trade these multiples for items unavailable locally (for example, foreign comics), or he may store the multiples for resale at some future date. Such speculation is, of course, a gamble. Selecting the right investment books is tricky business that requires special knowledge. With experience, the beginner will improve his buying skills. Remember, if you play the new comics market, be prepared to buy and sell fast as values rise and fall rapidly.

COLLECTING IN THE 1990s

Comic book collecting has become more fun and exciting than ever before. The stands are filled with a broad selection of every type of comic book imaginable, but look closely. There is something new about today's comic book. The inside pages are printed on slick paper that makes the colors jump. The covers are beautiful, exciting and dazzling. Most comic book companies, especially Marvel, DC, and Image, are placing these eye-catching specialty covers on their comic books.

Gimmicks to encourage sales abound. Take your pick. Holograms, prism, foil, embossed, die-cut, 3-D, posters, cards, talking covers, scratch and sniff, you name it. Check out **Green Lantern** #80 with the foil cover from DC, the **Generation X** #1 Chromium cover from Marvel, not to mention all the specialty covers from Chaos! Comics. Almost every company produces a variant cover for special releases these days.

Polybagged comics–It is the official policy of this Guide to grade comics regardless of whether they are still sealed in their polybag or not. Sealed comics in bags are not always in mint condition and could even be damaged. The value should not suffer as long as the bag (opened) and all of its original manufactured contents are preserved and kept together.

Collecting on a budget–Collectors check out their local newsstand or comic specialty store for the latest arrivals. Hundreds of brand new comic books are displayed each week for the collector–much more than anyone can afford to purchase. Due to this, today's reader must be careful and budget his money wisely in choosing what to buy.

Collecting artists–Many collectors enjoy favorite artists and follow their work from issue to issue, title to title, company to company. In recent years, some artists have achieved stardom status. Autograph signings occur at all major comic conventions as well as special promotions with local stores. Fans line up by the hundreds at such events to meet these super stars. Some of the current top artists of new comics are: Todd McFarlane, Rob Liefeld, Jim Lee, Joe Quesada, Whilce Portacio, Billy Tucci, Sam Kieth, Marc Silvestri, and Steven Hughes. Original artwork from these artists have been bringing record prices at auctions and from dealers' lists.

Collecting by companies–Some collectors become loyal to a particular company and only collect its titles. It is another way to specialize and collect in a market that expands faster than your pocket book.

Collecting number ones–For decades, comic enthusiasts have always collected number ones. It is yet another way to control spending and build a very interesting collection for the future. Number ones have everything going for them. Some introduce new characters. Other issues are sometimes underprinted, creating a rarity factor. A number one collection crosses many subjects, as well as companies, and makes an intriguing display.

COLLECTING BACK ISSUES

A back issue is any comic currently not available on the stands. Collectors of current titles often want to find the earlier issues in order to complete the run. Thus a back issue collector is born. Comic books have been published and collected for over 100 years. However, the earliest known comic book dealers didn't appear until the late 1930s. But today, there are hundreds of dealers that sell old comic books (See ads in this book).

Locating back issues–The first place to begin, of course, is with your collector friends who may have unwanted back issues or duplicates for sale. Look in the yellow pages, or call the Comic Shop Locator Service at 1-888-COMIC-BOOK, to see if you have a comic book store available. If you do, they would know of other collectors in your area. Advertising in local papers could get good results. Go to regional markets and look for comic book dealers. There are many trade publications in the hobby that would put you in touch with out-of-town dealers. **Overstreet's FAN** and, of course, this Annual Guide have ads buying and selling old comic books. Some dealers publish regular price lists of old comic books for sale. Get on their mailing list.

Putting a quality collection of old comics together takes a lot of time, effort and money. Many old comics are not easy to find. Persistence and luck play a big part in acquiring needed issues. Most quality collections are put together over a long period of time by placing mail orders with dealers and other collectors.

Comics of early vintage are extremely expensive if they are purchased through a regular dealer or collector. Unless you have unlimited funds to invest in your hobby, you will find it necessary to restrict your collecting in certain ways. However you define your collection, you should be careful to set your goals well within affordable limits.

PROPER HANDLING OF COMIC BOOKS

Comic books are fragile and easy to damage. Most dealers and collectors hesitate to let anyone personally handle their rare comics. It is common courtesy to ask permission before handling another person's comic book. Most dealers would prefer to remove the comic from its bag and show it to the customer themselves. In this way, if the book is damaged, it would be the dealer's responsibility–not the customer's. Remember, the slightest crease or chip could render an otherwise Mint book to Near Mint or even Very Fine.

Consult the **Overstreet Comic Book Grading Guide** and learn the proper way to hold a comic book. The following steps are provided to aid the novice in the proper handling of comic books: 1. Remove the comic from its protective sleeve or bag very carefully. 2. Gently lay the comic (unopened) in the palm of your hand so that it will stay relatively flat and secure. 3. You can now leaf through the book by carefully rolling or flipping the pages with the thumb and forefinger of your other hand. Caution: Be sure the book always remains relatively flat or slightly rolled. Avoid creating stress points on the covers with your fingers and be particularly cautious in bending covers back too far on Mint books. 4. After examining the book, carefully insert it back into the bag or protective sleeve. Watch corners and edges for folds or tears as you replace the book (also watch the tape).

STORAGE OF COMIC BOOKS

Comic books should be protected from the elements as well as the dangers of light, heat, and humidity. This can easily be achieved with proper storage. Improper storage methods will be detrimental to the "health" of your collection, and may even quicken its deterioration.

Comic books should be stored away from direct light sources, especially florescent which contains high levels of ultra-violet (UV) radiation. UV lights are like sunlight, and will quickly fade the cover inks. Tungsten filament lighting is safer than florescent but should still be used at brief intervals. Remember, exposure to light accumulates damage, so store your collection in a cool, dark place away from windows.

Temperatures must also be carefully regulated. Fungus and mold thrives in higher temperatures, so the lower the temperature, the longer the life of your collection. Paper life doubles with every 10° F drop in temperature. A constant temperature of 68-72° F is best.

Atmospheric pollution is another problem associated with long term storage of paper. Sulfuric dioxide which can occur from automobile exhaust will cause paper to turn yellow over a period of time. For this reason, it is best not to store your valuable comics close to a garage. Some of the best preserved comic books known were protected from exposure to the air such as the Gaines EC collection. These books were carefully wrapped in paper at time of publication, and completely sealed from the air. Each package was then sealed in a box and stored in a closet in New York. After over 40 years of storage when the packages were opened, you could instantly catch the odor of fresh newsprint; the paper was snow white and supple, and the cover inks were as brilliant as the day they were printed. This illustrates how important it is to protect your comics from the atmosphere.

Like UV, high relative humidity (rh) can also be damaging to paper. Maintaining a low and stable relative humidity, around 50%, is crucial; varying humidity will only damage your collection.

Care must be taken when choosing materials for storing your comics. Many common items such as plastic bags, boards, and boxes may not be as safe as they seem. Some bags and boards contain chemicals that will actually help to destroy your collection rather than save it. Always purchase materials designed for long-term storage, such as Mylar type "D" sleeves and acid-free boards and boxes. Polypropylene and polyethylene bags, while safe for temporary storage, should be changed every three to five years.

Comics are best stored vertically in boxes. For shelving, make sure that the comic books do not come into direct contact with the shelving surface. Use acid-free boards as a buffer between the shelves and the comic books. Also, never store comics directly on the floor; elevate them 6-10 inches to allow for flooding. Similarly, never store your collection directly against a wall, particularly an outside wall. Condensation and poor air circulation will encourage mold and fungus growth.

When handling your high grade comics, wash your hands first, eliminating harmful oils from the skin before coming into contact with the books. Lay the comic on a flat surface and slowly turn the pages. This will minimize the stress to the staples and spine.

With these guidelines, your collection should enjoy a long life and maintain a reasonable condition and value.

HOW TO SELL YOUR COMIC COLLECTION

By purchasing this Guide, you have begun the long process necessary to successfully sell your comics. Before you can proceed, however, you must decide what category listed below best describes your collection. As a rule of thumb, the lower categories will need less detail provided in your inventory list. A collection of key late '30s DCs will require you to list exact titles, numbers, and grades, as well as possible restoration information. If, however, you have 20,000 miscellaneous '80s and '90s comics for sale, a rough list of the number of books and publishers should be enough. The categories are:

1. Platinum Age (pre-1933)--The supply is very scarce. More people are becoming interested in these early books due to comics passing their 100th birthday. Moderate interest among average dealers, but high interest with dealers that specialize in this material. A detailed list will be necessary paying attention to brittleness, damage and pages missing. Dealers will pay up to a high percentage of Guide list for key titles.

2. Golden Age, All Grades (1933 - pre-1956)--The most desirable. A detailed inventory will be necessary. Key higher grade books are easier to sell, but lower grades in most titles show the best selling potential, due to the fact that many collectors cannot afford a $20,000 VF book but may be able to afford a GD for only $2,000. Highest demand is for the superhero titles such as **Batman**, **Superman**, **Human Torch**, etc. The percentage of Guide that dealers will pay for your collection will vary depending on condition and contents. A collection of low demand titles will not bring the same percentage as a collection of prime titles.

3. High Grade Silver Age (1956-mid 1960s) --A detailed inventory will be necessary. There are always investors looking for VF or better books from this period. Dealers will usually pay a high percentage of Guide list for these high grade books. Silver Age below VF will fall into category #4.

4. Low Grade Silver Age--Spanning books lower than VF from the late '50s to 1970, this category exhibits the average grade of most collections. Consequently, the supply of this material is much more common than category #2. This means that you could be competing with many other similar collections being offered at the same time. You will have to shop this type of collection to get the best price, and be prepared to sell at a significant discount if you find a willing buyer with good references.

5. Modern Age (post-1970)--Certain titles from the early 1970s in high grade are showing increasing demand. However, many books from the 1980s to the 1990s are in low demand with the supply for the most part always being of high grade books. These collections are typified by long runs of certain titles and/or publishers. A detailed inventory will not be necessary. Contact local comic stores or buyers first to gauge their level of interest. Dealing with buyers outside your area should be avoided if possible.

6. Bulk (post-1980 in quantities greater than 5,000)--These collections usually contain multiple copies of the same issues. It is advisable to price on a per-book basis (2¢ and 20¢ each). Do NOT attempt an inventory list, and only contact buyers who advertise buying in bulk quantity.

You should never deal with a buyer without fully checking their references. For additional verification, consult The Better Business Bureau; the local BBB may be able to help you in establishing a buyer's credibility, as well as assisting in resolving any disputes. **The Overstreet Comic Book Price Guide**, **Overstreet's FAN**, and **Comic Book Marketplace** are also recognized authorities. Advertised dealers will likely have a more established reputation.

Potential buyers will be most concerned with the retail value of your entire collection, which may be more or less than Guide depending what you have and their current demand. Some rare books in VF or NM may bring a price over Guide list while other titles in lower grade may sell for a price under Guide list. Most books, however, will sell for around the Guide price. You must then decide on what percentage you would be willing to accept for your collection, taking into account how the collection breaks down into fast, moderate and slow moving books. To expect someone to pay full retail is unrealistic. You will have to be flexible in order to close a deal.

Many buyers may want to purchase only certain key or high grade books from your collection, almost always favoring the buyer. While you may be paid a high percentage of retail, you will find that "cherry-picked" collections are much more difficult to sell. Furthermore, the percentage of retail that you will receive for a "cherry-picked" collection will be much lower than if the collection had been left intact. Remember, key issues and/or high grade issues make or break a collection. Selling on consignment, another popular option in today's market, could become a breeding ground for cherry-pickers, so again, always check a dealer's references thoroughly.

Some collectors may choose to sell their comic books on a piecemeal basis, requiring much greater care and detail in preparing an inventory list and grading comics for sale. You will be able to realize a higher percentage of retail by selling your collection this way, but the key books will certainly sell first, leaving a significant portion of the collection unsold. You will need to keep repricing and discounting your books to encourage buyers.

You can advertise your collection in trade publications or through mass mailings. If you sell books through the mail, you must also establish a reasonable return policy, as some books will unquestionably be returned. Check the local post office and/or UPS regarding the various rates and services available for shipping your books. Marketing your books at conventions is another option. As a dealer, you will also incur overhead expenses such as postage, mailing and display supplies, advertising costs, etc.

In all cases, be willing to establish trust with a prospective buyer. By following the procedures outlined here, you will be able to sell your collection successfully, for a fair price, with both parties walking away satisfied. After all, collecting comic books is supposed to be fun; it only becomes a chore if you let it.

WHERE TO BUY AND SELL

Throughout this book you will find the advertisements of many reputable dealers who sell back-issue comics magazines. If you are an inexperienced collector, be sure to compare prices before you buy. When a dealer is selected (ask for references), send him a small order (under $100) first to check out his grading accuracy, promptness in delivery, guarantees of condition advertised, and whether he will accept returns when dissatisfied. Never send cash through the mail. Send money orders or checks for your personal protection. Beware of bargains, as the items advertised sometimes do not exist but are only a fraud to get your money.

The Price Guide is indebted to everyone who placed ads in this volume. Your mentioning this book when dealing with the advertisers would be greatly appreciated.

COMIC BOOK CONVENTIONS

The first comic book conventions, or cons, were originally conceived as the comic book counterpart to science fiction fandom conventions. There were many attempts to form successful national cons, but they were all stillborn. It is interesting that after only three relatively organized years of existence, the first comic con was held. Of course, its magnitude was nowhere near as large as most established cons held today.

What is a comic con? Dealers, collectors, fans, publishers, distributors, manufacturers, whatever they call themselves can be found trading, selling, and buying the adventures of their favorite characters for hours on end. Additionally most cons have guests of honor, usually professionals in the field of comic art, either writers, artists, or editors. The committees put together panels for the con attendees in which the assembled pros talk about certain areas of comics, most of the time fielding questions from the assembled audience. At cons one can usually find displays of various and sundry things, usually toys, thousands of comic books, original art, and more. There can be the showing of movies or videos. Of course there is always the chance to get together with friends at cons and just talk about comics. One also has a good opportunity to make new friends who have similar interests and with whom one can correspond after the con.

It is difficult to describe accurately what goes on at a con. The best way to find out is to go to one and see for yourself. The largest cons are WonderCon (April), Pittsburgh (April), San Diego (July), Chicago (July), and Atlanta (July). For accurate dates and addresses, consult ads in this edition as well as some of the adzines. Please remember when writing for convention information to include a self addressed, stamped envelope for reply.

COVER BAR CODES FOR NEW COMIC BOOKS

Today's comic books are cover-coded for the direct sales (comic shop, newsstand, and foreign markets). They are all first printings, with the special coding being the only difference. The comics sold to the comic shops have to be coded differently, as they are sold on a no-return basis while newsstand comics are not. The Price Guide has not detected any price difference between these versions. Currently, the difference is easily detected by looking at the front cover bar code (a box located at the lower left). The bar code used to be filled in for newsstand sales and left blank or contain a character for comic shop sales. Now, as you can see above, direct sale editions are clearly marked, both versions containing the bar code.

Newsstand

Direct Sales (DC)

Direct Edition (Marvel)

MARVEL REPRINTS

In recent years Marvel has reprinted some of their comics. There has been confusion in identifying the reprints from the originals. However, in 99 percent of the cases, the reprints have listed "reprint," or "2nd printing," etc. in the indicia, along with a later copyright date in some cases. Some Marvel 2nd printings will have a gold logo. The only known exceptions are a few of the movie books such as **Star Wars**, the **Marvel Treasury Editions**, and tie-in books such as **G.I. Joe**. These books were reprinted and not identified as reprints. The **Star Wars** reprints have a large diamond with no date and a blank UPC symbol on the cover. The other reprints had some cover variation such as a date missing, different colors, etc. Beginning in mid-1990, all Marvel 2nd printings have a gold logo.

Gold Key and other comics were also sold with a Whitman label. There are collectors who prefer the regular labels to Whitman, although the Price Guide does not differentiate in the price. Beginning in 1980, all comics produced by Western carried the Whitman label.

COMIC BOOK PUBLISHERS' CODES–
The following abbreviations are used with the cover reproductions throughout the book for copyright credit purposes. The companies they represent are listed here:

AC-(Americomics)	**EP**-Elliott Publications	**QUA**-Quality Comics Group
ACE-Ace Periodicals	**ERB**-Edgar Rice Burroughs	**REAL**-Realistic Comics
ACG-American Comics Group	**FAW**-Fawcett Publications	**RH**-Rural Home
AJAX-Ajax-Farrell	**FC**-First Comics	**S & S**-Street and Smith Publishers
AP-Archie Publications	**FF**-Famous Funnies	**SKY**-Skywald Publications
ATLAS-Atlas Comics (see below)	**FH**-Fiction House Magazines	**STAR**-Star Publications
AVON-Avon Periodicals	**FOX**-Fox Features Syndicate	**STD**-Standard Comics
BP-Better Publications	**GIL**-Gilberton	**STJ**-St. John Publishing Co.
C & L-Cupples & Leon	**GK**-Gold Key	**SUPR**-Superior Comics
CC-Charlton Comics	**GP**-Great Publications	**TC**-Tower Comics
CEN-Centaur Publications	**HARV**-Harvey Publications	**TM**-Trojan Magazines
CCG-Columbia Comics Group	**H-B**-Hanna-Barbera	**TOBY**-Toby Press
CG-Catechetical Guild	**HILL**-Hillman Periodicals	**TOPS**-Tops Comics
CHES-Harry 'A' Chesler	**HOKE**-Holyoke Publishing Co.	**UFS**-United Features Syndicate
CLDS-Classic Det. Stories	**KING**-King Features Syndicate	**VAL**-Valiant
CM-Comics Magazine	**LEV**-Lev Gleason Publications	**VITL**-Vital Publications
DC-DC Comics, Inc.	**MAL**-Malibu Comics	**WDC**-The Walt Disney Company
DEF-Defiant Comics	**ME**-Magazine Enterprises	**WEST**-Western Publishing Co.
DELL-Dell Publishing Co.	**MEG**-Marvel Ent. Group	**WHIT**-Whitman Publishing Co.
DH-Dark Horse	**MLJ**-MLJ Magazines	**WHW**-William H. Wise
DMP-David McKay Publishing	**MS**-Mirage Studios	**WMG**-William M. Gaines (E. C.)
DS-D. S. Publishing Co.	**NOVP**-Novelty Press	**WP**-Warren Publishing Co.
EAS-Eastern Color Printing Co.	**PG**-Premier Group	**YM**-Youthful Magazines
EC-E. C. Comics	**PINE**-Pines	**Z-D**-Ziff-Davis Publishing Co.
ECL-Eclipse Comics	**PMI**-Parents' Magazine Institute	
ENWIL-Enwil Associates	**PRIZE**-Prize Publications	

TIMELY/MARVEL/ATLAS COMICS
"A Marvel Magazine" and "Marvel Group" was the symbol used between December 1946 and May 1947 (not used on all titles/issues during period). The Timely Comics symbol was used between July 1942 and September 1942 (not used on all titles/issues during period). The round "Marvel Comic" symbol was used between February 1949 and June 1950. Early comics code symbol (star and bar) was used between April 1952 and February 1955. The Atlas globe symbol was used between December 1951 and September 1957. The M over C symbol (beginning of Marvel Comics) was used between July 1961 until the price increased to 12 cents on February 1962.

MARVEL/TIMELY/ATLAS PUBLISHERS' ABBREVIATION CODES

ACI-Animirth Comics, Inc.	**FCI**-Fantasy Comics, Inc.	**OMC**-Official Magazine Corp.
AMI-Atlas Magazines, Inc.	**FPI**-Foto Parade, Inc.	**OPI**-Olympia Publications, Inc.
ANC-Atlas News Co., Inc.	**GPI**-Gem Publishing, Inc.	**PPI**-Postal Publications, Inc.
BPC-Bard Publishing Corp.	**HPC**-Hercules Publishing Corp.	**PrPI**-Prime Publications, Inc.
BFP-Broadcast Features Pubs.	**IPS**-Interstate Publishing Corp.	**RCM**-Red Circle Magazines, Inc.
CBS-Crime Bureau Stories	**JPI**-Jaygee Publications, Inc.	**SAI**-Sports Actions, Inc.
CLDS-Classic Detective Stories	**LBI**-Lion Books, Inc.	**SePI**-Select Publications, Inc.
CCC-Comic Combine Corp.	**LCC**-Leading Comic Corp.	**SnPC**-Snap Publishing Co.
CDS-Current Detective Stories	**LMC**-Leading Magazine Corp.	**SPC**-Select Publishing Co.
CFI-Crime Files, Inc.	**MALE**-Male Publishing Corp.	**SPI**-Sphere Publications, Inc.
CmPI-Comedy Publications, Inc.	**MAP**-Miss America Publishing Corp.	**TCI**-Timely Comics, Inc.
CmPS-Complete Photo Story	**MCI**-Marvel Comics, Inc.	**TP**-Timely Publications
CnPC-Cornell Publishing Corp.	**MgPC**-Margood Publishing Corp.	**20 CC**-20th Century Comics Corp.
CPC-Chipiden Publishing Corp.	**MjMC**-Marjean Magazine Corp.	**USA**-U.S.A. Publications, Inc.
CPI-Crime Publications, Inc.	**MMC**-Mutual Magazine Corp.	**VPI**-Vista Publications, Inc.
CPS-Canam Publishing Sales Corp.	**MPC**-Medalion Publishing Corp.	**WFP**-Western Fiction Publishing
CSI-Classics Syndicate, Inc.	**MPI**-Manvis Publications, Inc.	**WPI**-Warwick Publications, Inc.
DCI-Daring Comics, Inc.	**NPI**-Newsstand Publications, Inc.	**YAI**-Young Allies, Inc.
EPC-Euclid Publishing Co.	**NPP**-Non-Pareil Publishing Corp.	**ZPC**-Zenith Publishing Co., Inc.
EPI-Emgee Publications, Inc.	**OCI**-Official Comics, Inc.	

GOTHAM KNIGHTS

A CONVERSATION WITH JERRY ROBINSON

*Jerry Robinson's work on **Batman** laid the groundwork for one of the most enduring comic book characters, and since then, he has distinguished himself as editorial director and founder of Cartoonists & Writers Syndicate and CartoonArts International; author of The Comics: An Illustrated History of Comic Strip Art, as well as author and illustrator of over 30 others; President of both the Association of American Editorial Cartoonists and the National Cartoonists Society; and member of the Board of Trustees of the International Museum of Cartoon Art (IMCA) in Boca Raton, Florida. In this interview, Jerry reminisces about **Batman** and the characters that would become pop culture icons...*

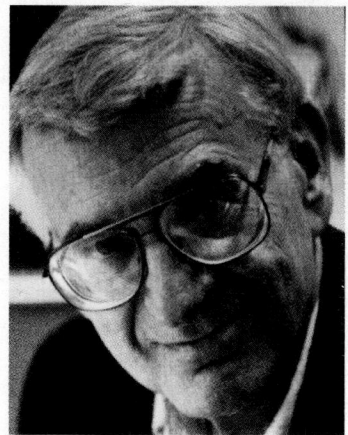

The man himself, Jerry Robinson.

When did you first meet Bob Kane?

JR- I was living in Trenton, New Jersey in the summer of 1939. I'd just graduated high school, intending to study journalism. I had a job selling ice cream in the suburbs, and we didn't have motorized carts, so I had to work peddling a bicycle to earn any money. You'd get a commission of one or two cents for each sale, and I saved up all summer. I was on the 98-pound track team, but by the end of the summer I could make the 76-pound track team (laughter), and I was also playing a lot of tennis, which was a passion of mine.

A very strenuous regimen.

Yes, so my mother persuaded me to take twenty-five dollars, which I was loathe to do, and go to the Poconos to fatten up, because she didn't think I'd

survive my first semester at college. On my first day, I went to the tennis court wearing a painter's jacket that I'd decorated with various cartoons, which was a fad at the time. Somebody tapped me on the shoulder and asked who drew the cartoons. I said I did, and he said they were pretty good. It was Bob Kane, who was also taking a vacation. He had just started **Batman**, and asked if I'd heard of it. I'd never seen a comic book before, although I'd enjoyed the newspaper strips, so we strolled down to a village store to find a copy of **Batman**. He learned I planned to go to college, and by this time I'd decided on Syracuse University. He said that if I was in New York, he'd give me a job assisting on **Batman** and pay twenty-five dollars a week. At age seventeen, it was a step up from selling ice cream!

That's enough for another vacation.

Yes (laughter). So I quickly switched to Columbia, where I had also been accepted, called home, told them about the job, and went straight from the mountains to New York. I started at Columbia, found a place in the Bronx a couple of blocks from Bob, and started working on **Batman**. I met Bill Finger, the writer, and there we had our team.

What was it like working on *Batman* in the beginning?

It was tough. I was going to classes and working all night, so instead of gaining weight, I think I lost more (laughter). At first it was a way of earning money for college, but it seemed I had an ability to copy anything I could see, and soon I realized I could create characters. So I got excited about the prospect of writing and drawing, and realized this

BY ARNOLD T. BLUMBERG

could be a career.

What were your responsibilities?

I started inking and lettering, and soon I was inking the whole strip. As I got more proficient, Bob did sketchier outlines, so it became more of a challenge. It was an exciting time, it was a new medium, and it must've been like the early days of film where you were doing things that were never done before. It was also a time of learning, because neither one of us had any academic training. I think that was fortunate because we drew more expressionistical-ly—we weren't hung up on anatomy We tried to draw accurately, but we could stretch things a bit. Of course, we were struggling in the beginning. We used to slave over the art for hours to get it right, and it was nothing to work two or three days in a row without sleep, but it was exciting too. I actually did go to art school for a month, and on the first day they put my drawings up on the wall. So I figured I wasn't going to learn anything there (laughter).

And Bill?

He was a very genial open guy, and he became a cultural mentor to me. He took me downtown to the first foreign films, Fritz Lang's *Metropolis*, and *The Cabinet of Dr. Caligari*, and these were fantastic to see for the first time. We were all influenced by that, and I tried to use that black and white surreal effect on the things that I inked.

Tell us about the creation of the Joker.

Batman began to take off, and we got word from Whit Ellsworth, the editor, that they were planning to put out a whole Batman book in addition to **Detective Comics**. Suddenly we were doing five stories a month instead of just one for **Detective**, and I soon realized I had to give up college. It was a tremendous burden for the three of us, and it was hard for Bill to write this much. He was a visual writer, and he always knew what would work graph-ically. He would do an enormous amount of research for locales, like a movie script. He would attach clips right to the script so we could visualize the story. Bill plotted them very carefully. He was a very detailed, dedicated craftsman, but he wasn't prolific. He really sweated those stories out.

Now there were too many to write.

Yes, so I volunteered to do one. I wanted to be a writer, and this was a great opportunity--I could get credit for the story in my creative writing class and get paid as well! That night, I went back to my room and was very excited. I decided to start with the villain, because all great heroes have an antagonist, from David and Goliath to Sherlock Holmes and Moriarty. I thought that was lacking in **Batman**. Like all the comics of the '30s, the villains were the Dillingers and Pretty Boy Floyds. Some with more flair, but the same type.

You wanted a larger-than-life character.

Yes, and I'd always loved the humor and twists in short stories by de Maupessant and O'Henry. Those were the stories I was trying to write in high school and college. All kind of great characters had an internal contradiction that made them more inter-esting, so I thought a villain with a sense of humor would be intriguing. First, I needed a name to build on, and the Joker came fairly quickly. I always loved cards, even though I wasn't in the same league as my mother and brother, who were expert champion bridge players. As soon as I thought of the Joker, I searched frantically and found a deck of cards with the classic joker image, from which I kept the white face, which I thought added a macabre note. The next day, I brought in a character sketch of the Joker and his calling card, along with the concept of the character, and when I showed it to Bob and Bill, they loved it immediately. There was only some trep-idation that if the villain was too strong he would overpower Batman. Dick Tracy was probably influ-ential, because that proved how popular bizarre characters were. The Joker had that bizarre touch.

What was the next step?

Everyone loved it so much, they decided it would be the first story in **Batman** #1, so Bob persuaded me to let Bill write it. I was heartbroken giving up my brainchild, but I had to acknowledge that Bill was the best writer for the story, as we were on a dead-line. I'm sure it would've taken me weeks, but Bill could write it in a few days for Bob and myself to start drawing, with Bob doing the layouts and me on inking, lettering and backgrounds. That persuaded me to give it up. I must credit Bill for taking the idea and running with it. The basis of the first story, the closed room, was the familiar writer's test of how to write yourself out of that situation, like the challenge of a humor cartoonist to do another varia-tion of the desert island gag.

Soon after, another crucial element fell into the place with the introduction of Robin.

The Boy? Yes, I'm pretty sure that was Bill's idea, because all the innovative ideas really came from Bill and he never got his due. Bob was able to trans-late those beautifully and he deserves all the initial credit, but I'm convinced that Batman was a joint effort, much like the Siegel and Shuster collabora-tion. Unfortunately, Bill died before he was really recognized.

So Bill came in with the idea for Robin?
When I came in one day, Bill and Bob were already discussing introducing a boy. So we immediately set out to name him, and we sat down and wrote long lists of names. I remember specifically names like Mercury, and other mythological choices. None of us felt comfortable with any of them. Suddenly, Robin Hood popped into my head, and although it's been written that Robin came from my last name, that was the furthest thing from my mind. As Batman didn't have super powers, nor would the boy, I felt the name should have a contemporary feel.

You weren't trying to name him after yourself.
I certainly wouldn't have been so presumptuous, particularly after they called him the Boy Wonder. I was kidded about that by people in the field later, but I hated it. I was the youngest of the artists at that time, and at that age you want to be older. You don't want to be thought of as a kid, but they called me the Boy Wonder. Now you can call me that anytime you like, I don't object at all (laughter).

We'll be sure to do that (laughter). The Robin Hood motif extended to the costume design too.
As soon as we had the name, Bob sat down at the drawing board, and I took a sketch pad, and we sketched ideas for the costume. I knew the basic design of Robin Hood, and if you look at it, you can see the jacket and the mail-like shorts. Bob put in that little thing on the heel of the shoe, and I remember specifically that I added the R on the chest. Even before Robin, I had adopted this style of a decorative letter as the first letter in the captions. We already had the symbol on Batman's chest, so Robin's "R" was a counterpoint.

With these two characters, you opened up new avenues for *Batman* stories.
There was no boy hero in the books up to that time. Batman was a character a lot of teenaged readers identified with, but with Robin, younger readers could identify with someone too. Afterwards, everywhere you looked there were sidekick characters. Robin also expanded the story possibilities—now he could be in trouble, and Batman would have to rescue him. And the Joker started off the whole rogues' gallery that Bill subsequently created. Bill gave Bob credit for creating Two-Face, but the other major characters were Bill's. Bob and Bill were really the driving forces behind **Batman**. Our sessions were for the most part as a team.

It sounds like you were an incredible team for that short period of time.
It didn't last long, maybe two or three years. I

Original concept art for the Joker's calling card.

should also mention George Roussos. He was originally hired to assist me in the inking and took over most of the backgrounds. He added a lot to the look of **Batman**. After **Batman** became successful, Bill and I had offers from other publishers who tried to persuade us to leave. When DC heard about that, they hired us, and thereafter we worked directly for them, moving up to DC headquarters. That broke up the team. I worked with Whit Ellsworth, and he was a great art director. He really gave me my freedom to design the covers and do complete stories--pencil, ink, and even on occasion, color.

There were some very striking covers.
We gave a lot of attention to them to attract the eye. I particularly enjoyed doing symbolic covers, like the one for "Slay Me With Flowers," for which I also drew the story, of the Joker growing out of a flower, or "A Crime A Day," with a huge Joker tearing pages off a calendar. Among my other favorites are **Detective** #62, I believe the first Joker cover, #68, #69, #70, #71, and **Batman** #10 and #13.

I guess you never thought these characters would become such icons.
No, I don't think any of us could've foreseen that. We all knew we'd write more stories about them, and that it had a definite future, but fifty years later? Never. In a way it's a tribute to the genre itself. The sequential narrative is such a unique storytelling medium that it has the potential for lasting this length of time. A character like Batman lasts because he's not static. He grows and evolves, as do his readers. In this case, it's a combination of the medium, and the unique striking character of the Batman.

I'm sure there was a little magic involved too.
I'm sure there was.

STATE OF THE ART ACTION!

State of the art adventure!

STATE OF THE ART TERROR!

Critics agree! There haven't been comics like the ones that inspired HBO's *Tales From The Crypt* since the advent of the Comics Code Authority... but you can still get these classics at today's prices!

EC Comics

Just like the originals! All 32 pages (with new letters). We begin with the first issue of each title and reprint them all in chronological order. Relive those fond memories of your youth, or discover them for the first time!

EC Annuals

The same 32-page EC comics you know and love conveniently packaged in squarebound format. Each hefty annual contains five complete EC comics, including covers.

EC Library Sets

Own the best of the best! For just a fraction of what they'd cost you on the back issue market, you can get a complete run of your favorite EC titles. Each set of annotated, smythe-sewn library albums reprints the entire run of a featured series in crystal clear black and white (including all text, ads, and letters pages) with full-color covers.

To order call toll free 1-800-EC-Crypt.

GEMSTONE
PUBLISHING

AN ENTERTAINING EC COMIC

STRANGE ADVENTURES

A CONVERSATION WITH MURPHY ANDERSON

Collector, illustrator, and storyteller Murphy Anderson spent years bringing new and wonderful worlds to countless fans. His realistic and detailed pencils sent the reader spiraling into the comics themselves, challenging the imagination with every stroke of his brush. Now, Mr. Anderson, who many consider "the gentleman of comics", paints a clearer picture of just what inspired him in his successful comics career, as well as what may have been behind the characters and creations we've all grown to love. Strange adventures indeed.

Murphy, what would you consider to be the biggest influence on your work in comics?
That's a hard thing to say. If I had to pick one single influence, though, I would probably say it was Buck Rogers, not just for the art, but for the whole concept of my work. I also liked other characters in that vein, such as Alex Raymond's **Flash Gordon**—when I could get it—and **Mandrake the Magician**, which I read fairly regularly because it was part of the **New York Daily Journal-American's Saturday Color Comics Section** (Tabloid-Size). I could pick those up for a nickel at the local newsstand the week before they were normally to appear, so I kept up with them. Back in those days, Lee Falk wrote quite a bit of science fiction type material for his Mandrake. Anyway, those strips definitely had an effect on my work.

When you did Buck Rogers yourself for the newspapers, did you look to Buck's early adventures in telling your own stories?
Oh sure (laughter). I had Buck involved in that business of walking through walls, which I used in the first stuff I did. I also had Buck falling through a floor and whatnot (laughter).

When I first took on the character, I had a lot of talks with John Flint Dille, who was really the guy that started Buck's adventures in comics. When Phillip Francis Nowlan's story in the August, 1928 issue of **Amazing Stories** titled "Armageddon—2419 A.D." appeared, he saw the potential of it as a comic strip, partly because Frank R. Paul illustrated it and Paul had several small pictures throughout the story, some of which were the size and shape of a newspaper comic strip panel. I think that must've turned on a light, because Dille got in touch with Nowlan and the rest is history. Both Nowlan and Dille were very much ahead of their time.

Someone else who was ahead of his time was Captain Easy creator Roy Crane. What was it about his work that appealed to you?
I loved his stuff! It was very adventurous. His characterization was great, and he really had a way of getting you to read the next day's strip—you could hardly wait! He had these things that were just beautifully staged and of course, Captain Easy was almost out before he finally triumphed. Crane put enthusiasm, characterization, and just fun in his strips. Not political fun, but just good rollicking adventure—that's

Murphy Anderson creating new art as Price Guide guru Bob Overstreet looks on.

BY SCOTT BRADEN

what attracted me to Crane, I guess. But you know, other strips had a similar effect. Even the **Mickey Mouse** that Gottfriedson drew and Segar's **Popeye** had a lot of stuff that was very similar.

Now isn't it true that Superman owes something to Crane's Captain Easy?
Yeah. I had suspected that Superman was designed using the body of Harold Foster's Tarzan and Captain Easy's head. It was obvious that Joe Shuster was a big fan of Roy Crane. You could see that in his drawing approach, the way he articulated figures, the action and all of that kind of thing. I once asked Jerry Siegel about that. I never knew Shuster, I met him once, briefly in San Diego, but I knew Jerry quite well because we worked together at Ziff-Davis. Years later, he'd come into DC very quietly and I'd find him in the coffee shop where we'd sit around and talk. I asked him once about my suspicions, and he confirmed them. I said, "It seems to me he got his storytelling from Crane, and the figure treatment of Superman was very much from Tarzan." Jerry laughed and agreed, and said, "Yes, that's exactly right."

What can you tell us about some of our other favorite heroes? For instance, most people don't know that you're a big fan of Blackhawk and the other Quality heroes. Can you tell us what the inspiration was behind the character of Blackhawk? Where did he come from?
Well, you can get into a big fight over that one. If you ever meet Chuck Cuidera, just tell him that Will Eisner created it, and you'll have a fight on your hands. Chuck is a pretty spunky guy, and he's quick to tell you what he thinks. I really don't know who actually thought up the idea of the characters, sort of grouped together like that or who thought up the central character of Blackhawk himself, but I'm sure that once it was decided to do it, there was a contribution from both Will and Chuck.

Well, Blackhawk's a terrific hero...
Yes, he is. There was a movie that Errol Flynn made back in the late '30s, in which they did a very **Blackhawk** kind of thing. Alan Hale, Sr. is in it, and he's just like the Blackhawk character called Henderson. The movie revolves around Errol Flynn's character, who's an American that joins the British Air Force during World War II. His bomber and crew are shot down over Germany, and they're captured by the Nazis, but they break out and have this madcap chase through Europe. In France, Flynn and his crew find the identical bomber that they were shot down in, and learn that the Germans are setting it up for a surprise raid on England, since it wouldn't be detected until too late. They then steal the restored bomber from the Germans and escape. It's a real Blackhawk story. I'm trying to think who else was in that thing. Alan Hale, Sr., Errol Flynn and William Kennedy were in it. But it was that era, you know...the late '30s. I've often felt that it had to be some sort of a catalyst for the **Blackhawk** concept.

What about the Black Condor and The Ray? Do you by chance know where they came from?
They were more or less products of Will Eisner's brain. Will thought up an awful lot of that stuff, or if he didn't come up with the actual spark, he and his studio would sort of brainstorm an idea and then work it up.

I know you're a big fan of these characters as well. Is it because they were based in science fiction?
Well, it's basically because Lou Fine was drawing them that I liked them so much. I'm sure he had an input into the stories, though just how much I don't know. He and Will collaborated so much that a lot of things I've always thought were purely Lou's I've later learned Will was involved in. I can now detect it knowing that they worked together. Will would often lay things out, and Lou would finish them. They would be the roughest kind of a thumbnails sometimes, but enough to see it was Eisner's thinking.

What about Buck? Any secrets you can tell us about him?
There's an idea that I have had floating around that Buck's "ray gun" was named after former president Ronald Reagan. You see, John Dille was from Dixon, Illinois and he knew Reagan as a young man. As a matter of fact, Dille's oldest son was probably about the same age as Reagan. Anyhow, one of the fanzines used to have a column that would trace the origins of things, such as the "ray gun," and that got me thinking about the association between Reagan and the "ray gun." It just became an idea of mine that the term "ray gun" doesn't appear in **Buck Rogers** in the earliest strips, I don't know when it was introduced, but in the beginning, they had the rocket pistol and they had the disintegrator, but they didn't use the term "ray gun." It seems to me that it would've been natural for it to have occurred to Dille knowing Reagan as he did.

Changing tracks again, we've talked about science fiction and movies influencing comics. What about other works such as the Bible?
That's kind of an indirect thing. I'm sure the Bible has influenced every form of literature, but going beyond that, as a kid, I was exposed to the Dore

drew most of the early stories, was a big fan of Raymond's, and he would imitate him, and in some cases, try to draw exactly like he did. Shelly's very underrated as an artist, I think. He drew quite well. And he knew all the stuff so well that he could take a Hal Foster or a Milton Caniff or an Alex Raymond, any of those guys who were well-known artists of the period, and he could work up drawings so that they fit with his. It didn't look like he'd "swiped" them for use with the story because they worked in the way he did it.

Bringing up Hawkman, let's talk a little bit about your work for DC. As an illustrator, was there ever a time when you wanted to say, "Hey Carmine Infantino, how about letting me pencil for awhile?"

(Laughter) No, no. I had been in and out, and I was just doing covers for Julie during the mid '50s, and then after I'd worked on the **Buck Rogers** strip, I tried to get Julie to help me on **Buck**, on the writing of the thing, and he said he wasn't a writer, he was an editor, and we went back and forth on that. And that was about the time I worked up the first **Adam Strange** cover, and I couldn't handle it, I couldn't do any work on it because I'd taken on **Buck Rogers**. Then when I gave up **Buck** and came back a year later, the whole comic field had shrunk so much, it became very hard to find work. Julie, Sol Harrison, and others at DC wanted to give me work, but the only thing they could scrounge up at the time was inking, and that was because Frank Giacoia at the time had decided to go over to Marvel, so that left a hole for an inker. They were giving me a little bit of work when Julie would turn up an SF story, but they had an obligation to keep Gil, Carmine, and the others busy. It wasn't right for them to dismiss them just to give me work. They were very paternalistic back in those days is what I'm trying to say. They'd get a guy and they'd really try their best to keep him busy and keep him on. You weren't technically an employee, but you had just as much security as any syndicated artist would have. Still, I always considered myself not just an inker, but a guy doing the whole job.

Murphy is still doing "the whole job" with his recreation of classic covers that have made him, and others such as Lou Fine, legends in an industry that so many love. But while recreating these beautiful covers of comics past, he still looks towards the hobby's future. "As far as I'm concerned, comics have just gotten off the ground. I see comics going to even greater heights!"

Bible. My grandmother had one, and I'd pour over the thing. I was fascinated by the drawings in it. Gustav Dore was prodigious, he produced so much stuff. He wanted to be a painter, but he had little success painting, so he was really one of our first cartoonists. You'd have to call anyone a cartoonist who would lay out all of these pictures. He had a crew of people working with him that engraved this stuff, and each engraver would spend weeks on a picture, but he would supervise everything. Dore also came up with the concept, as far as I know, for the angels that appear in the Dore Bible. In his bible, almost every page had an illustration, and he often showed angels and most of which looked just like Alex Raymond's Hawkmen from **Flash Gordon**. I'm sure that Raymond was aware of Dore's work, although I don't know that he swiped it directly by any means. But some of the scenes, particularly one, where Raymond took a full Sunday page of Hawkmen swooping down on Flash Gordon, looked as if he did copy Dore. I think there were three panels on the page, one in the upper right hand corner, one in the lower left hand corner, and the rest of it was taken up by the Hawkmen swooping down.

In turn, when National created their Hawkman, do you think that they were looking to Raymond's Hawkmen from *Flash Gordon*?

Aw, sure. I'm sure they were. Sheldon Moldoff, who

COMIC BOOK ARTISTS

Many of the popular artists are pointed out in the listings. When more than one artist worked on a story, their names are separated by a (/). The first name did the pencil drawings and the second the inks. When two or more artists work on a story, only the most prominent will be noted in some cases. We wish all good artists could be listed, but due to space limitation, only the most popular can. The following list of artists are considered to be either the most collected in the comic field or are historically significant. Artists designated below with an (*) indicate that only their most noted work will be listed. The rest will eventually have all their work shown as the information becomes available. This list could change from year to year as new artists come into prominence.

Adams, Arthur	*Elder, Bill	*Kane, Gil	Moreira, Ruben	Silvestri, Marc
Adams, Neal	Evans, George	Kelly, Walt	*Morisi, Pete	Simon & Kirby (S&K)
Bagley, Mark	Everett, Bill	Kieth, Sam	*Newton, Don	*Simonson, Walt
Baker, Matt	Feldstein, Al	Kinstler, E. R.	Nostrand, Howard	Smith, Barry Windsor
Barks, Carl	Fine, Lou	Kirby, Jack	Orlando, Joe	Smith, Paul
Beck, C. C.	Foster, Harold	Krenkel, Roy	Pakula, Mac	Stanley, John
*Brunner, Frank	Fox, Matt	Krigstein, Bernie	*Palais, Rudy	*Starlin, Jim
*Buscema, John	Frazetta, Frank	Kubert, Adam & Andy	*Perez, George	Steranko, Jim
Byrne, John	Gibbons, Dave	*Kubert, Joe	Portacio, Whilce	Stevens, Dave
Campbell, J. Scott	*Giffen, Keith	Kurtzman, Harvey	Powell, Bob	Texeira, Mark
Capullo, Greg	Golden, Michael	Lapham, Dave	Quesada, Joe	Thibert, Art
*Check, Sid	Gottfredson, Floyd	Larsen, Erik	Raboy, Mac	Torres, Angelo
Cole, Jack	*Guardineer, Fred	Lee, Jae	Ramos, Humberto	Toth, Alex
Cole, L. B.	Gustavson, Paul	Lee, Jim	Raymond, Alex	Tuska, George
Craig, Johnny	*Heath, Russ	Liefeld, Rob	Ravielli, Louis	Ward, Bill
Crandall, Reed	Howard, Wayne	Manning, Russ	*Redondo, Nestor	Williamson, Al
Darrow, Geof	*Infantino, Carmen	McFarlane, Todd	Rogers, Marshall	Woggon, Bill
Davis, Jack	Ingels, Graham	McWilliams, Al	Ross, Alex	Wolverton, Basil
Disbrow, Jayson	Jones, Jeff	Meskin, Mort	Schomburg, Alex	Wood, Wallace
*Ditko, Steve	Kamen, Jack	Mignola, Mike	Sears, Bart	Wrightson, Bernie
Eisner, Will	Kane, Bob	Miller, Frank	Siegel & Shuster	Zeck, Mike

COMIC BOOK ARTISTS
& THEIR FIRST WORK

Adams, Neal - (1 pg.) **Archie's Jokebook Mag.** #41, 9/59; (1st on Batman, cvr only) **Detective Comics** #370, 12/67; (1st Warren art) **Creepy** #14

Balent, Jim - **Sgt. Rock** #393, 10/84

Barks, Carl - (art only) **Donald Duck Four Color** #9, 8/42; (scripts only) **Large Feature Comic** #7, ca. Spring 1942

Broderick, Pat - (cover & art) **Planet of Vampires** #1, 2/75

Brunner, Frank - (fan club sketch) **Creepy** #10, 1965

Buckler, Rich - **Flash Gordon** #10, 11/67

Burnley, Jack - (cover & art) **NY World's Fair** nn, '40

Buscema, John - (1st at Marvel) **Strange Tales** #150, 11/66

Byrne, John - **Nightmare** #20, 8/74; (1st at DC) **Untold Legend of the Batman** #1, 7/80; (1st at Marvel) **Giant-Size Dracula** #5, 6/75

Capullo, Greg - (1st on X-Force) **X-Force Annual** #1, '92

Cole, Jack - (1 pg.) **Star Comics** #11, 4/38

Crandall, Reed - **Hit Comics** #10, 4/41

Davis, Jack - (cartoon) **Tip Top Comics** #32, 12/38

Ditko, Steve - (1st publ.) **Black Magic** V4#3, 11-12/53 (1st drawn story), **Fantastic Fears** #5, 1-2/54

Ellison, Harlan - (1st pro story) **Weird Science-Fantasy** #24, 6/54

Everett, Bill - **Amazing Mystery Funnies** V1#2,9/38

Fine, Lou - (1st cvr) **Wonder Comics** #2, 6/39; **Jumbo Comics** #4, 12/38

Frazetta, Frank - **Tally-Ho Comics** nn, 12/44

Garney, Ron - **G. I. Joe, A Real American Hero** #110, 3/91

Giffen, Keith - (1 pg.) **Deadly Hands of Kung-Fu** #17, 11/75; (1st story) **Deadly Hands of Kung-Fu** #22, 4?/76; (tied w/Deadly Hands) **Amazing Adventures** #35, 3/76

Golden, Michael - **Marvel Classics Comics** #28, '77

Grell, Mike - **Adventure Comics** #435, 9-10/74

Hamner, Cully - **Green Lantern: Mosaic** #1, 6/92

Hughes, Adam - **Blood of Dracula** #1, 11/87

Ingels, Graham art at E.C. - **Saddle Justice** #4, Sum '48

Jurgens, Dan - **Warlord** #53, 1/82

Kaluta, Michael - **Teen Confessions** #59, 12/69

Kelly, Walt - **New Comics** #1, 12/35

Keown, Dale - **Nth Man the Ultimate Ninja** #8, 1/90; (1st at Marvel) **Samurai** #13, ?/87; (1st on Hulk) **Incredible Hulk** #367, 3/90

Kieth, Sam - **Primer** #5, 11?/83

Kirby, Jack - **Jumbo Comics** #1, 9/38;

Kubert, Adam/Andy/Joe art - **Sgt. Rock** #422, 7/88

Kurtzman, Harvey - **Tip Top Comics** #36, 4/39; (1st at E.C.) **Lucky Fights It Through** nn, 1949

Larsen, Erik - **Megaton** #1, 11/83

Lee, Jae - **Marvel Comics Presents** #85, '91

Lee, Jim - (1st at Marvel) **Alpha Flight** #51, 10/87; (1st on X-Men) **X-Men** #248?, ?/89; (art on Punisher) **Punisher War Journal** #1, 11/88

Liefeld, Rob - (1st at DC) **Warlord** #131, 9/88; (1st at Marvel) **X-Factor** #40, 4?/89; (1st full story) **Megaton** #8, 8/87; (inside

front cover only) **Megaton** #5, 6/86; (art on New Mutants)
   New Mutants Annual #5, '89
Lim, Ron - (art on Silver Surfer) **Silver Surfer Ann.** #1, '88
Matsuda, Jeff - **Brigade** #0, 9/93
Mayer, Sheldon - **New Comics** #1, 12/35
McFarlane, Todd - **Coyote** #11, ?/85; (1st full story) **All Star**
   Squadron #47, 7/85; (1st on Hulk) **Incredible Hulk** #330, 4/87
Medina, Angel - (pin-up only) **Megaton** #3, 2/86
Mignola, Mike - **Marvel Fanfare** #15, 5/83
Miller, Frank - (1st on Batman) **DC Special Series** #21, Spr '80;
   (1st on Daredevil) **Spectacular Spider-Man** #27, 2/79
Newton, Don - **Many Ghosts of Dr. Graves** #45, 5/74
Perez, George - (1st at DC) **Flash** #289, 9/80; (2 pgs.)
   Astonishing Tales #25, 8/74
Portacio, Whilce - (1st on X-Men) **X-Men** #201, 1/86
Pulido, Brian - **Evil Ernie** #1, 12/91
Quesada, Joe - (1st on X-Factor) **X-Factor Ann.** #7, '92
Raboy, Mac - (1st cover for Fawcett) **Master Comics** #21, 12/41
Ramos, Humberto - (1st U.S. work) **Hardwire** #15, 6/94
Romita, John - **Daredevil** #12, 1/66
Romita, John Jr. - (1st complete story) **Iron Man** #115, 10/78
Ross, Alex - **The Terminator: The Burning Earth** V2#1, 3/90
Shuster, Joe - (cover) **New Adv. Comics** #16, 6/37

Siegel & Shuster - **New Fun Comics** #6, 10/35
Simon & Kirby - **Blue Bolt** #2, 7/40
Simonson, Walter - **Magnus, Robot Fighter** #10, 5/65
Smith, Barry - **X-Men** #53, 2/69
Smith, Paul - (1 pg. pin-up) **King Conan** #7, 9/81; (1st full story)
   Marvel Fanfare #1, 3/82
Steranko, Jim - **Spyman** #1, Sep '66; (1st at Marvel) **Strange**
   Tales #151, 12/66
Swan, Curt - **Dick Cole** #1, 12-1/48-49
Talbot, Bryan - (1st U.S. work) **Hellblazer Annual** #1,
   Summer '89
Thomas, Roy - (scripts) **Son of Vulcan** #50, 1/66
Torres, Angelo - **Crime Mysteries** #13, 5/54
Turner, Mike - **Cyberforce Origins-Stryker**, 2/95
Weeks, Lee - **Tales of Terror** #5, 11/85
Weiss, Alan - (illo) **Blue Beetle** #5, 3-4/65
Williamson, Al - (1st at E.C.) **Tales From the Crypt** #31, 9/52;
   (text illos) **Famous Funnies** #169, 8/48
Wood, Wally - (art at E.C.) **Saddle Romances** #10, 1-2/50
Wrightson, Bernie - **House of Mystery** #179, 4/68; (1st at
   Marvel) **Chamber of Darkness** #7, 10/70; (1st cover) **Web of**
   Horror #3, 4/70; (fan club sketch) **Creepy** #9
Zeck, Mike - (illos) **Barney and Betty Rubble** #11, 2/75

KEY COMICS SOLD IN 1996

The following list of books sold were reported to Gemstone during the year and represent only a small portion of the total amount of important books that have sold.

GOLDEN-POST GOLDEN AGE
ACTUAL SALES OF PEDIGREE AND OTHER HIGH GRADE BOOKS
Allentown (AT), Bethlehem (BH), File (File copy), Denver (DEN), Larson (LR),
Mile High (MH),Pennsylvania (PA), Restored (R), San Francisco (SF), Traded (T), White
Mountain (WM); trade (tr)

Action #1VG+	#110,000	All Star #36VF+	$1,925	Captain America #59VF	$1,550
Action #1VG+	#100,000	All Top #8NM	$1,200	Captain Marvel #26 (MH)	$1,265
Action #1FN+	$100,000	All Winners #1NM	$20,000	Captain Science #7 (WM)	$435
Action #1FN68(R)	$63,250	All Winners #1VF+	$11,000	Catman #1 (DEN)	$4,250
Action #1VF84(R)	$62,100	All Winners #7VF	$800	Catman #1VG	$1,000
Action #1VG	$38,000	All Winners #19Vf+	$2,500	Catman #31FN+	$825
Action #1GD+	$65,000 with tr	America's Best #10 (MH)	$1,100	Classic Comics #3(o)FN+	$875
Action #2VG	$9,000	America's Best #18 (MH)	$1,100	Classic Comics #17(o)VF	$455
Action #7FN73	$4,830	Archie #1VG	$3,750	Classic Comics #31(o)VF	$245
Action #7VG+	$7,000	Batman #1FN(R)	$10,000	Classic Comics #34(o)VF	$300
Adventure #40FN+	$22,000	Batman #9VF+	$4,400	Classic Comics #46NM+	$110
Adventure #48 (LR)	$30,000	Batman #41VF	$600	Classic Comics #56NM+	$120
Adventure #48VF	$13,500	Batman #58VF	$650	Classic Comics #60NM+	$95
Adventure #61FN+	$5,000	Batman #64NM	$605	Crime Must Stop #1VF+	$350
Adventure #93VF+	$550	Batman #78FN+	$425	Dell Giant #43NM+	$300
Adventure #94VF+	$800	Big Book of Fun #1VG	$11,000	Detective #1 (MH)	$150,000
Adventure #149VF+	$265	Big Book of Fun #1FR+	$3,500		mostly tr
All American #16VF(R)	$21,000	Blackhawk #71VF	$155	Detective #2VG+	$4,400
All American #19VF	$13,000	Blackhawk #99VF+	$110	Detective #5GD	$1,760
All Amer. Western #114 (MH)	$640	Blackhawk #100VF+	$120	Detective #9GD+	$1,700
All Flash #1VF+	$13,500	Bold Stories VF	$1,850	Detective #21VG	$1,300
All Flash #1FN+	$9,800	Boy's Ranch #1 (MH)	$1,320	Detective #27VF(R)	$65,000
All Select #1VF+	$9000	Boy's Ranch #6 (MH)	$430	Detective #27VF(R)	$60,000
All Star #1 (MH)	$34,500	Buzzy #5 S(MH)	$220	Detective #27FN+(R)	$50,000
All Star #3 (MH)	85,000	Captain Aero #22VF+	$380	Detective #27VG	$60,000
All Star #3FN+	$21,000	Captain America #1VF+	$65,000	Detective #29FR	$2,100
All Star #8VF+	$45,000	Captain America #2VF83	$4,700	Detective #33GD+	$4,500
All Star #8FN+	$20,000	Captain America #5VF+	$3,500	Detective #84 (PA)	$2,530
All Star #20 (MH)	$5,500	Captain America #8VF+	$2,800	Detective #88 (PA)	$2,530

Title	Price	Title	Price	Title	Price
Detective #106 (MH)	$3,050	More Fun #27FN	$1,200	Star Spangled #112VF	$220
Detective #110VF+	$440	More Fun #52 & 53 (LR)	$148,000	Star Spang. War #19VF+	$135
Detective #155 (MH)	$2,560	More Fun #52FN+(R)	$15,300	Star Spang. War #24VF+	$145
Detective #168VF	$900	More Fun #52VG+(R)	$12,000	Startling #16VF+	$290
Detective #170 (MH)	$2,800	More Fun #53VF(R)	$9,000	Startling #36 (MH)	$660
Detective #174 (MH)	$2,800	More Fun #54VF	$7,500	Startling #49NM	$2,000
Dick Tracy #49 (File)	$165	More Fun #56VF	$3,000	Startling #49FN	$1,350
Eerie #9VF+	$165	More Fun #73VF(R)	$5,500	Strange Adventures #7FN+	$305
EH! #6NM	$110	More Fun #73FN+	$4,950	Strange Adventures #23VF+	$275
Exciting #19 (MH)	$1,000	More Fun #73VG+	$6,500	Sub-Mariner #1NM	$25,000
Exciting #21 (MH)	$770	More Fun #101 (MH)	$60,000	Superboy #3NM	$1,650
Exciting #49 (MH)	$1,100		with tr	Superboy #7VF	$470
Exciting #50 (MH)	$1,100	More Fun #101VF	$7,150	Superboy #19VF+	$415
Famous Funnies #102VF	$165	More Fun #101FN+	$3,630	Superboy #25VF+	$275
Famous Funnies #210VF+	$605	Mot. Pic. Funn. Wkly #1NM (pay		Superman #1 (MH)	$170,000
Famous Funnies #211VF+	$765	copy)	$42,000	Superman #1VG+	$45,000 with tr
Fantastic #11VF+	$650	My Great. Adv. #24VF+	$220	Superman #1VG	
Fighting Yank #8 (MH)	$1,375	My Great. Adv. #28VF+	$305		plus $12,000 tr
Flash #1FN+	$14,500	My Great. Adv. #42NM+	$220	Superman #1FN65(R)	$11,500
Flash #58VF	$425	My Great. Adv. #56NM+	$205	Superman #1VG	$26,000
Flash #103FN+	$1,600	My Great. Adv. #60NM+	$220	Superman #14VF+	$4,500
Flippity and Flop #1NM	$165	Mystery In Space #55VF	$195	Superman #24FN+	$1,250
Friendly Ghost Casper #1NM	$220	Mystery Men #1VF(R)	$4,000	Superman #32VFd+	$650
Frontline Combat #7 (Gaines)	$470	Mystery Men #5 (AT)	$2,250	Superman #50VF	$500
Gangbusters #15 (MH)	$330	Mystery Men #11FN+	$750	Superman #53FN+	$800
Gangbusters #18 (MH)	$250	Mystic #1VF+	$10,000	Superman #75VF	$360
Gangbusters #21 (MH)	$305	Mystic #2VF+(2nd)	$750	Superman #76VF+	$700
Ghost Comics #6 (BH)	$330	National #13VF+	$550	Suspense #3FN	$12,000
Great Comics #1VF+('45)	$220	National #14VF	$440	Suspense Comics #3FR	$2,500
Green Lantern #1VF80(R)	$5,175	National #16VF+	$500	Suspense Comics #11VF+	$2,750
Green Lantern #20VF+	$700	Nellie The Nurse #16 (MH)	$205	Tales From/Crypt #23VF+	$360
Green Lantern #38VF+	$1,100	New Adventure #24 (MH)	$4,000	Tales From/Crypt #24VF	$265
Hangman #8VF	$1,100	New Comics #8VF+	$3,025	Tales of/Unexpected #17NM	$305
Haunt of Fear #8VF+	$210	New Fun #1VF(R)	$55,000	Tales to Astonish #32 (WM)	$275
Haunt of Fear #12VF+	$160	New Fun #1VG	$40,000 tr	Terrors of/Jungle #10VF+	$170
Haunted Thrills #5VF	$100	New Fun #2GD	$7,000	Terrors of/Jungle #10VF+	$230
Human Torch #1FN+	$10,000	New Fun #2FR	$3,300	Terrors of/Jungle #18VF+	$195
Human Torch #8FN	$1,200	N.Y. World's Fair '40VF+	$15,000	Terrors of/Jungle #21VF	$220
Humbug #1NM+	$300	Out of This World #14 (WM)	$85	Terrors of/Jungle #18VF	$165
Humbug #2NM+	$110	Pep Comics #53 (MH)	$715	Thing #17VF+	$300
Jackpot #6VF+	$850	Pep Comics #54 (MH)	$550	Torchy #5VF+	$800
Journey Into. Myst. #43 (c8)	$220	Phantom Lady #4VF+	$330	Tough Kid Squad #1VF	$7,500
Journey Into Myst. #55NM	$140	Phantom Lady #13FN+	$1,050	Two-Fisted Tales #34 (Gaines)	$470
Jumbo #1VG+	$5,500	Phantom Lady #17VF+	$4,500	Vault of Horror #18VF	$230
Looney Tunes #1VF+	$20,000	Pic. Stories/Science #1(Gaines)	$210	Vault of Horror #28VF	$145
Looney Tunes #3VF+	$950	Planet #1VF	$12,000	Vault of Horror #34 (Gaines)	$660
MAD #1-24 (Gaines)	$44,850	Power Comics #2VF	$1,320	Walt Disney's C&S #1VF+	$25,000 tr
MAD #1VF	$2,200	Power Comics #4VF	$715	Weird Fantasy #13VF('50)	$660
MAD #7NM	$635	Reform School Girl FN+	$1,350	Weird Fantasy #17VF('51)	$275
MAD #26VF	$180	Sensation #1 (MH)	$90,000	Weird Fantasy #7VF	$205
Marvel #1VF+ (AT) tr	$115,000		mostly tr	Weird Science-Fant. #26VF+	$165
Marvel #1FN+(R)	$52,000	Sensation #1NM	$30,000	Weird Tales/Future #2VF+	$1,430
Marvel #1VG+	$37,000	Sensation #1VF+	$23,000	Weird Tales/Future #5FN+	$1,200
Marvel Mystery #5NM (LR)	$25,000	Sensation #1VF	$20,000 tr	Western Comics #26 (MH)	$415
Marvel Mystery #32VF	$900	Sensation #1FN+	$7,600	Woman Outlaws #1VF	$160
Marvel Mystery #65VF+	$800	Sensation #22VF+	$450	Wonder Woman #1VF+	$21,000
Marvel Mystery #65VF+	$625	Sensation #71VF+	$650	Wonder Woman #1VF+	$28,000 tr
Marvel Mystery #71VF+	$650	Shock SuspenStories #1VF+	$385	Wonder Woman #1VF	$14,000
Marvel Myst. Annual GD+	$6,000	Shock SuspenStories #12VF+	$250	Wonder Woman #2NM+	$5,000
Marvel Myst. Annual GD	$3,715	Smash #40 (MH)	$605	Wonder Woman #4VF+	$1,700
Marvel Tales #120 (WM)	$470	Speed #43 (File)	$210	Wonder Woman #45 (MH)	$3,000
Marvel Tales #143 (WM)	$260	Special Edition #1VF	$6,500	World's Finest #7NM	$1,760
Master #15VF	$425	Star Spangled #23VF	$470	World's Finest #7VF+	$950
Master #23VF	$1,200	Star Spangled #35 (MH)	$1,650	World's Finest #8NM	$1,100
Mickey Mouse FC#16VF	$9,500	Star Spangled #49 (MH)	$1,540		

SILVER AGE
REPORTED SALES OF HIGH GRADE BOOKS

Title	Price	Title	Price	Title	Price
Adventure #224VF+	$260	Amazing Fantasy #15VF	$14,000	Amaz. Spider-Man #2VF+	$2,800
Amazing Fantasy #15VF+	$30,000	Amaz. Spider-Man #1NM	$25,000	Amaz. Spider-Man #3NM	$2,500
Amazing Fantasy #15VF+	$20,000	Amaz. Spider-Man #1VF+	$18,000	Amaz. Spider-Man #3VF+	$1,400
Amazing Fantasy #15 VF84	$17,500	Amaz. Spider-Man #1VF+	$14,000	Amaz. Spider-Man #4VF+	$1,233

Amaz. Spider-Man #4VF+	$1,150	Fant. Four #5VF+	$2,800	Showcase #4VF+	$24,500
Amaz. Spider-Man #5NM	$1,450	Fant. Four #6VF+	$1,400	Showcase #4VF+	$17,000
Amaz. Spider-Man #6NM	$1,000	Fant. Four #10VF+	$647	Showcase #4VF(R)	$5,500
Amaz. Spider-Man #7NM	$950	Fant. Four $12VF+	$1,800	Showcase #6VF+	$2,900
Amaz. Spider-Man #7VF+	$850	Fant. Four #12VF+	$1,600	Showcase #7NM	$1,425
Amaz. Spider-Man #7VF+	$600	Fant. Four #13VF+	$565	Showcase #8VF+	$10,000
Amaz. Spider-Man #8VF+	$875	Fant. Four #48NM+	$1,250	Showcase #8VF76	$4,025
Amaz. Spider-Man #9NM	$1,000	Fant. Four #48VF+	$750	Showcase #9VF+	$11,000
Amaz. Spider-Man #9VF+	$825	Fant. Four Annual #1NM	$665	Showcase #10NM91	$6,900
Amaz. Spider-Man #10NM	$900	Flash #105NM93	$9,775	Showcase #10VF+	$7,000
Amaz. Spider-Man #13NM	$750	Flash #105VF+	$7,500	Showcase #13 (MV)	$3,300
Amaz. Spider-Man #13VF+	$500	Flash #108VF+	$605	Showcase #14VF84	$5,750
Amaz. Spider-Man #13VF+	$475	Flash #109VF+	$840	Showcase #14VF+	$3,630
Amaz. Spider-Man #14VF+	$1,600	Flash #122VF+	$250	Showcase #19NM93	$4,370
Amaz. Spider-Man #14VF+	$1,350	Flash #132VF+	$120	Showcase #20VF	$700
Amaz. Spider-Man #15VF+	$415	Flash #143VF+	$70	Showcase #22VF+	$7,500
Amaz. Spider-Man #16VF+	$305	Flash #146NM	$110	Showcase #28NM	$580
Amaz. Spider-Man #17NM	$750	F-Troop #1NM	$101	Silver Surfer #1VF+	$415
Amaz. Spider-Man #28VF+	$700	Frankenstein Jr. #1NM	$60	Silver Surfer #4VF+	$360
Amaz. Spider-Man #28VF+	$415	Giant Size X-Men #1NM	$385	Snagglepuss #1NM	$120
Amaz. Spider-Man #30NM+	$170	Green Lantern #1VF+	$5,000	Star Trek #1VF+	$415
Amaz. Spider-Man #38NM+	$195	Green Lantern #13NM	$220	Star Trek #6NM+	$165
Amaz. Spider-Man #43	$110	Green Lantern #40NM	$495	Star Trek #8NM+	$140
Amaz. Spider-Man #50NM+	$380	Green Lantern #76VF+	$160	Superboy #44VF	$125
The Atom #4VF+	$180	H-B Super Heroes #1NM	$125	Superboy #46VF	$140
The Atom #6NM	$205	Hawkman #10VF+	$85	Superboy #84NM	$130
The Atom #10NM	$205	Hawkman #12VF+	$70	Superboy #85NM	$150
Augie Doogie #1NM	$180	Hawkman #13VF+	$85	Superman #103VF	$210
The Avengers #1NM+	$6,500	Honey West #1NM	$150	Superman #144VF+	$110
The Avengers #1NM90	$2,990	I Dream of Jeannie #2NM	$120	Superman #148NM+	$195
The Avengers #1NM	$2,000	Incre. Hulk #1,2,4,5 VF76	$6,900	Superman Annual #2VF+	$275
The Avengers #2NM	$900	Incre. Hulk #1VF+	$14,000	Tales of Suspense #40VF	$1,100
The Avengers #4VF+	$1,250	Incre. Hulk #1VF+	$6,875	Teen Titans #1VF+	$110
The Avengers #5NM	$270	Incre. Hulk #1FN+	$3,800	Thor #158NM	$100
The Avengers #6VF+	$195	Incre. Hulk #4VF	$540	Top Cat #1NM	$230
The Avengers #7NM	$200	Incre. Hulk #105NM	$60	Wonder Woman #105NM	$3,000
The Avengers #8NM	$210	Incre. Hulk #181FN+	$275	World's Finest #75VF	$530
Barbie & Ken #5NM	$315	Incre. Hulk #181FN+	$155	World's Finest #86VF	$120
Batman #167NM	$110	Jetsons #1NM	$285	World's Finest #105NM	$180
Batman Annual #4VF	$95	Journey Into Myst. #83NM	$8,000	X-Men #1NM	$10,500
Beverly Hillbillies #1NM	$203	Journey Into Myst. #83VF	$2,420	X-Men #1VF+	$8,000
Blackhawk #133VF	$60	Justice League #1VF+ (BH)	$6,000	X-Men #1VF	$4,000
Brave & the Bold #34NM+	$4,730	Justice League #1FN+	$1,320	X-Men #2VF+	$635
Bullwinkle(GK) #1NM	$180	Lois Lane #1VF+	$6,000	X-Men #3VF+	$380
Conan #2NM+	$100	Lois Lane #11VF+	$165	X-Men #5VF+	$330
Daredevil #1VF+	$1,000	Mighty Hercules #1NM	$128	X-Men #19NM	$105
Detective #225VF+	$8,000	The Monkees #1NM	$120	X-Men #22NM+	$85
Detective #287VF+	$90	The Munsters #1NM	$250	X-Men #27NM+	$85
Detective #298VF+	$250	New Terrytoons #2NM	$60	X-Men #30NM+	$100
Fant. Four #1NM	$27,000	Pebbles Flintstone #1NM	$90	X-Men #62VF+	$60
Fant. Four #1VF+	$12,000	Richie Rich #9NM	$125	X-Men #94VF+	$285
Fant. Four #1VF+	$11,000	Sea Devils #1VF+	$360	X-Men #95NM+	$100
Fant. Four #4VF+	$2,300	Sgt. Fury #1VF	$750	Young Men #24VG	$700

NEW PRICE GUIDE LISTINGS

The following is a quick reference list of selected Gold and Silver Age books showing last year's price, this year's price and the rate of change.

PLATINUM AGE

Title	1997 price	% change	1996 price	Title	1997 price	% change	1996 price
Advs of Detective Ace King #1	$1,000	33%	$750	Katzenjammer Kids 1903	$1,400	27%	$1,100
Buster Brown & His Resolutions 1903				Little Nemo 1906	3,000	11%	2,700
	3,500	9%	3,200	Little Nemo 1909	2,500	9%	2,300
Buster Brown, His Dog Tige & Their Jolly Times 1906				Little Sammy Sneeze 1905	2,800	12%	2,500
	1,400	8%	1,300	Mickey Mouse Book	10,000	0%	10,000
...& Their Troubles 1904	1,700	6%	1,600	Mickey Mouse Comic #1	1,500	9%	1,375
Buster Brown's Blue Ribbon Book of Jokes and Jingles #1				Mickey Mouse Comic #3	1,500	9%	1,375
	3,400	6%	3,200	Pore Li'l Mose 1902	1,400	33%	1,050
Buster Brown's BRBJJ #2	1,400	0%	1,400	Tarzan of the Apes #988	1,600	0%	1,600
Buster Brown's BRBJJ #3	1,400	0%	1,400	Yellow Kid #1	FN 1,650	3%	1,600
Buster Brown's BRBJJ #4	1,400	0%	1,400	Yellow Kid nn, 1897	FN 6,500	44%	4,500
Dreams of the Rarebit Fiend	2,600	8%	2,400				

GOLDEN AGE

Title	1997 price	% change	1996 price
Action Comics #1	$160,000	10%	$145,000
Action Comics #23	5,000	4%	4,800
Adventure Comics #40	32,000	14%	28,000
Adventure Comics #48	20,000	18%	17,000
Adventure Comics #72	10,000	11%	9,000
All-American Comics #16	60,000	7%	56,000
All-American Comics #25	8,000	9%	7,300
All Flash #1	11,500	17%	9,800
All Select #1	7,000	17%	6,000
All Star Comics #3	30,000	0%	30,000
All Star Comics #8	24,000	9%	22,000
All Winners #1	14,000	17%	12,000
Archie Comics #1	9,000	6%	8,500
Batman #1	60,000	9%	55,000
Big All-American #1	10,500	5%	10,000
Big Book of Fun Comics #1	20,000	11%	18,000
Blue Beetle #1	3,200	14%	2,800
Captain America Comics #1	56,000	4%	54,000
Captain Marvel Adv. #1	27,000	8%	25,000
Captain Marvel Jr. #1	4,000	11%	3,600
Comic Calvacade #1	7,500	7%	7,000
Daredevil #1	8,500	6%	8,000
Daring Mystery #1	16,500	10%	15,000
Detective Comics #1	83,000	0%	83,000
Detective Comics #27	150,000	7%	140,000
Detective Comics #33	32,000	10%	29,000
Donald Duck 4-Color #4	10,000	0%	10,000
Exciting Comics #9	6,000	20%	5,000
Fantastic Comics #1	3,300	18%	2,800
Flash Comics #1	50,000	11%	45,000
Funnies On Parade	11,000	10%	10,000
Gene Autry #1	5,800	11%	5,200
Green Lantern #1	25,000	9%	23,000
Hit Comics #1	4,800	14%	4,200
Hopalong Cassidy #1	4,000	11%	3,600
Human Torch #1	21,000	11%	19,000
King Comics #1	$11,250	25%	$9,000
Looney Tunes #1	9,500	12%	8,500
Jumbo Comics #1	19,200	14%	16,800
Mad #1	4,800	9%	4,400
Marvel Comics #1	98,000	6%	92,000
Marvel Mystery Comics #2	19,000	6%	18,000
Marvel Mystery Comics #9	16,000	14%	14,000
More Fun Comics #14	19,000	12%	17,000
More Fun Comics #52	47,000	7%	44,000
More Fun Comics #73	10,500	5%	10,000
Mystery Men Comics #1	9,400	10%	8,500
Mystic Comics #1	12,000	9%	11,000
National Comics #1	4,200	10%	3,800
New Book Of Comics #1	18,000	9%	16,500
New Comics #1	24,000	7%	22,500
New Fun Comics #1	61,500	9%	56,500
New Fun Comics #6	29,000	9%	26,500
N.Y. World's Fair 1939	24,000	9%	22,000
Pep Comics #22	8,000	7%	7,500
Phantom Lady #17	3,800	8%	3,500
Planet Comics #1	9,000	10%	8,200
Police Comics #1	5,800	5%	5,500
Sensation #1	20,000	0%	20,000
Silver Streak Comics #1	9,500	12%	8,500
Silver Streak Comics #6	10,500	10%	9,500
Sub-Mariner Comics #1	20,000	11%	18,000
Superman #1	110,000	10%	100,000
Suspense Comics #3	9,000	12%	8,000
USA Comics #1	9,000	12%	8,000
Walt Disney's C&S #1	16,000	7%	15,000
Whiz #1	60,000	9%	55,000
Wonder Comics #1	13,500	13%	12,000
Wonder Woman #1	16,500	10%	15,000
Wonderworld #3	5,700	14%	5,000
World's Best #1	12,500	9%	11,500
Young Allies #1	9,200	12%	8,200

SILVER AGE

Title	1997 price	% change	1996 price
Action Comics #242	$1,100	11%	$990
Action Comics #252	1,300	18%	1,100
Adventure Comics #210	2,800	12%	2,500
Adventure Comics #247	4,000	11%	3,600
Amazing Fantasy #15	27,000	4%	26,000
Amazing Spider-Man #1	19,000	5%	18,000
Amazing Spider-Man #14	1,400	8%	1,300
Aquaman #1	600	9%	550
Atom #1	750	3%	725
Avengers #1	2,400	4%	2,300
Avengers #4	1,400	4%	1,350
Batman #92	425	6%	400
Batman #171	400	0%	400
Brave & The Bold #28	4,800	12%	4,300
Brave & The Bold #29	2,200	5%	2,100
Brave & The Bold #34	1,800	9%	1,650
Captain America #100	325	8%	300
Chall. Of The Unknown #1	2,000	11%	1,800
Daredevil #1	1,800	9%	1,650
Detective Comics #225	5,000	9%	4,600
Detective Comics #233	1,100	10%	1,000
Fantastic Four #1	18,000	6%	17,000
Fantastic Four #4	2,600	8%	2,400
Fantastic Four #5	2,800	8%	2,600
Fantastic Four #48	850	6%	800
Flash #105	4,800	7%	4,500
Flash #110	1,150	9%	1,050
Flash #123	1,000	13%	850
Green Lantern #1	2,400	20%	2,000
Green Lantern #40	490	5%	465
Hawkman #1	525	7%	490
Incredible Hulk #1	11,000	10%	10,000
Incredible Hulk #102	150	-14%	175
Iron Man #1	375	0%	375
Jimmy Olsen #1	3,400	13%	3,000
Journey Into Mystery #1	2,300	15%	2,000
Journey Into Mystery #83	4,200	5%	4,000
Justice League Of America #1	2,900	3%	2,800
Lois Lane #1	2,200	16%	1,900
Mystery in Space #53	1,500	11%	1,350
Our Army at War #81	2,000	25%	1,600
Sgt. Fury #1	900	6%	850
Showcase #4	25,000	2%	24,500
Showcase #6	3,200	10%	2,900
Showcase #8	11,250	7%	10,500
Showcase #9	5,000	4%	4,800
Showcase #14	4,300	10%	3,900
Showcase #22	4,600	4%	4,400
Showcase #34	1,300	8%	1,200
Strange Tales #1	2,300	15%	2,000
Strange Tales #101	850	6%	800
Tales Of Suspense #1	1,350	12%	1,200
Tales Of Suspense #39	3,800	12%	3,400
Tales Of The Unexpected #40	850	6%	800
Tales To Astonish #1	1,400	8%	1,300
Tales To Astonish #27	3,100	7%	2,900
X-Men #1	5,000	11%	4,500

ANNUAL REPORT
by Bob Overstreet

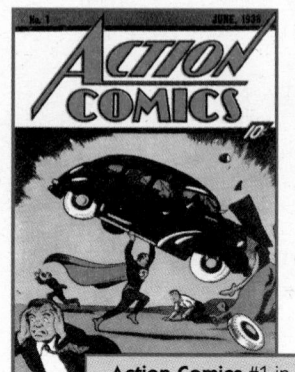

Action Comics #1 in apparent VG+ sells at $110,000!!

As interest rates remained steady and the Dow Jones soared to new record heights, Golden Age collecting trends recognized in the 1996 Guide continued unabated throughout the year. Although prices were not accelerating as quickly as prior years, there were still many record sales noted for Gold, Silver and Bronze Age books. Although the Golden Age market was reported as being strong by most dealers, prices paid for vintage material, especially in the lower grades, were showing signs of taking on a more conservative posture. This is reasonable and perfectly normal when considering the huge price increases that occurred in the marketplace last year. Both Silver and Golden Age books in high grade continued to command prices that were multiples of Guide list as in previous years. Sales at the auction houses showed mixed results with vintage DC material doing very well in both Gold and Silver. Restored books however, showed more price resistance than in previous years. Current reported values in the marketplace are beginning to stabilize on the lower grades but are still experiencing upward pressure in the VF to NM category. Gains posted in the comic marketplace once again outstripped national price indexes. As the supply of quality material continues to decline, one would expect this trend to continue.

All Star #8 Mile High copy gets $85,000!

GOLDEN AGE/POST-GOLDEN AGE: Still the hottest area in collecting. Collections surfaced a bit more frequently with the new, higher prices, but demand still far outstripped supply, particularly with DC, Timely, Fox, Nedor and MLJ comics. Dealers reported difficulty stocking most titles printed prior to the end of WWII. The Mile High copy of **All Star** #8 sold for $85,000! A NM copy of **Marvel Comics** #1 brought $115,000 (all trade!); An **Action** #1VG+ sold for an unbelievable $110,000! Covers by Schomburg and L.B.

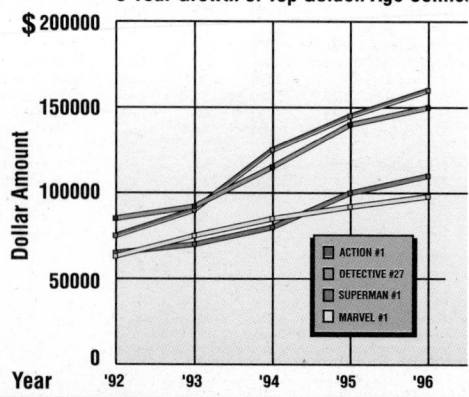

Marvel #1 in NM (Allentown copy) trades at $115,000!

5 Year Growth of Top Golden Age Comics

Legend:
- ACTION #1
- DETECTIVE #27
- SUPERMAN #1
- MARVEL #1

Dollar Amount (Year: '92, '93, '94, '95, '96)

The top four Golden Age books have shown strong growth over the past five years with **Action Comics** #1 taking the lead.

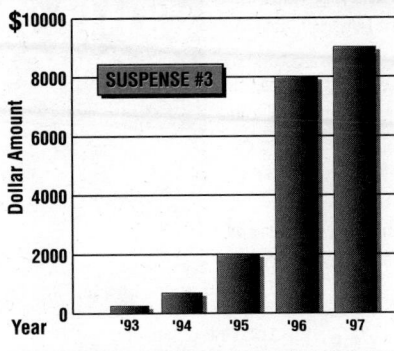

SUSPENSE #3

Dollar Amount $10000 / 8000 / 6000 / 4000 / 2000 / 0

Year '93 '94 '95 '96 '97

Schomburg covers are hot! This rare book has come out of nowhere to become one of the market's hottest books!

Cole were in high demand as were covers by classic artists such as Simon and Kirby, Lou Fine and Will Eisner. There was also growth in demand for lesser known artists such as Walter Johnson, who drew interesting covers for some of the more obscure publishers, such as Fox. A resurgence of interest in certain Frazetta covers was noted. Every title has certain outstanding covers currently being sought more and more by collectors. These are listed as "Classic covers," and as collectors and dealers report sales to us, more of these "gems" are pointed out in the listings. Other areas of increased demand were Disney, SOTI, early Archies, good girl art books as well as crime, science fiction and horror comics of the 1940s-1950s.

A LOOK AT SOME OF THE HOTTEST COMIC BOOK TITLES IN 1996:

1897-1920s Titles - Demand for these titles increased as more collectors began to focus on the fact that comics are now over 100 years old. Original cartoon art from this period is now accepted abroad as a true art form along with Rembrandts and Picassos. In fact, a large auction company from Japan began offering original art from this period to wealthy Japanese investors through a chain of exclusive department stores similar to Bloomingdale's or Macy's here in this country. Titles remained scarce and continued to enjoy steady growth with increased demand for key books such as **Buster Brown** and **The Yellow Kid**. Sotheby's June auction featured a collection of rare Yellow Kid items which all sold briskly for record prices. A copy of **Yellow Kid in McFadden's Flats** in GD+ sold for $7,500.

1930s Titles - Demand for books from this period increased as supplies continued to dry up. All pre-1946 titles such as **Famous Funnies, The Funnies, King, Tip Top, Popular** were in demand. These books sold very well in all grades due to their scarcity with copies above Fine condition seldom offered for sale. The early issues of **Detective, Adventure, New Fun**, and other DC titles continued to be in high demand. A **New Fun** #2 in GD brought $7,000. Most copies that surface today are in the lower grades however, but dealers reported no problem moving them to anxious buyers. A copy of **Big Book of Fun Comics** in VG sold for $11,000 and in FR+ for $3,500. Other sales: **Famous Funnies** #35FN $200, #102VF $165, #210VF+ $605, #211VF+ $765. A **Don Winslow** #2(1937) sold for $1,000. **Phantom** and **Mandrake** were also hot.

Extremely rare **Yellow Kid** book in GD/VG brings $7,500!!

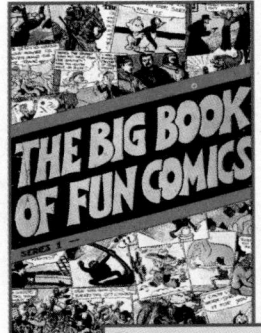

© DC
Big Book of Fun in VG sells for $11,000!!

1940s Titles - Superhero titles remained the backbone of the market, representing the largest amount of revenue collected from comic book sales. All mainstream publishers' books were in demand, especially DC, Timely, Nedor, Fox, Quality, Gleason and MLJ. L.B. Cole, Lou Fine, Matt Baker and Simon & Kirby covers. Classic cover issues by Lou Fine, Schomburg and L.B. Cole, including **Suspense** #3 & 8, **Startling** #49, **Fantastic**

#3 and **Mystery Men** #3 were still being sought by collectors. Most western titles remained steady while late 1940s good girl art (**Phantom Lady**, etc.), crime and horror enjoyed increased sales.

<u>1950s Titles</u> - The most collected publishers were DC, Atlas, Fox, Charlton, Star (L.B. Cole covers), Ziff Davis, Avon, ACG as well as many of the more obscure publishers such as St. John, Fawcett, Ajax, Superior, Story, Premier, Avon, etc. Pre-Marvel hero books sold very well with high demand for all prototype issues. Simon & Kirby art books of all genres including love were in high demand. L.B. Cole covers were hot. All covers and stories with bizarre themes, including all Seduction books, sold well. ECs remained popular, and were selling at current levels indicating no need for price increases.

GOLDEN AGE/POST-GOLDEN AGE REPORT (BY COMPANIES):

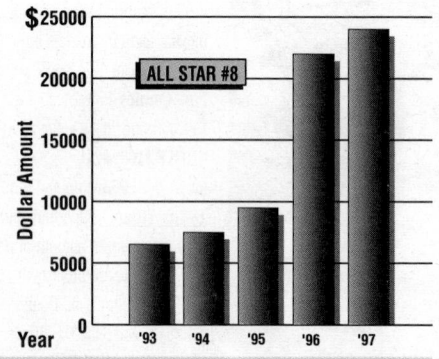

Lou Fine covers are highly collected such as this **Fantastic** #3.

© FOX

DC - All main-line superhero titles were selling at up to 250% of Guide list, depending on the grade. Best selling were **Batman**, **Superman**, **Flash**, **All Star**, **Green Lantern** and their related titles. Good gains by offbeat titles. The Mile High copy of **All Star** #8 brought a staggering $85,000! Another copy in VF+ sold for $45,000 and another copy in FN+ sold for $20,000. An **All Star** #3FN+ brought $21,000. The Mile High copy of **Sensation** #1 went for $90,000 (mostly all trade). Another copy in VF+ sold for

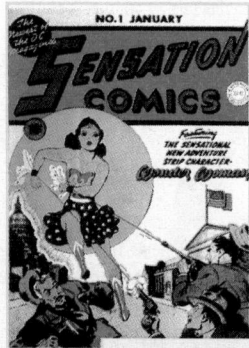

$23,000 while still another copy in VF traded at $20,000. The Mile High copy of **Detective** #1 went for $150,000 (mostly trade). A **Superman** #1VG sold for $26,000 while a VG copy with heavy restoration sold for $10,000. Early **Action Comics**, including #1, were very strong during the year. An **Action** #1 in VG+ sold for $110,000! Another copy in GD+ brought $65,000! Sotheby's offered a unique original owner set of the first nine issues of **Action Comics** in their summer auction which created a lot of excitement on the auction floor as bidding reached and passed Guide list for all issues! Demand for almost all of this company's titles remained very high. DC continues to be the leader in the Golden Age market, commanding the highest amount of money paid for comic books. A **Detective** #27 in VG sold for $60,000! Other copies in VF(R) brought $65,000 and $60,000 respectively. Another copy in VF(R, tape) sold for $38,500 and a copy in FN+(R) went for $50,000. The hottest titles were **Action**, **Adventure**, **All American**, **All-Flash**, **Batman**, **Detective** and **Green Lantern**. An **All Flash** #1VF+ sold for $13,500 and an **Adventure** #40FN+ went for $22,000 and a VG(R) got $5,200. **Adventure** #48VF (Nova Scotia) sold for

© DC

Sensation #1
Mile High copy
trades at $90,000!

© DC

Superman #1 in VG
sells for $26,000!

This book contains the 1st app. of Wonder Woman and is one of the most sought-after books from the 1940s!

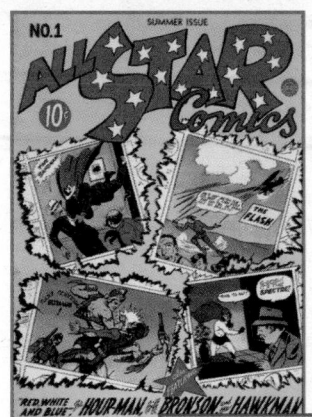

All Star #1
Mile High copy
brings $34,500!

$13,500! An **All-American** #16VF(R) fetched $21,000. Our survey of the market indicated increased interest in **Sensation** and **Wonder Woman**. This was due in part to the market undervaluing these titles for years, and now waking up to that fact. A **Sensation** #1 in NM sold for $30,000 and a **Wonder Woman** #1 in VF+ went for $28,000 (trade), another copy in VF+ sold for $21,000 and a VF brought $14,000! **All Star Comics** are holding at current price levels with certain keys still achieving multiples of Guide list. The Mile High copy of **All Star** #1 sold at auction for $34,500! Later issues of this title remained scarce. The early square bound issues of **Comic Cavalcade** and **World's Finest** were in high demand. DC's first comic book, **New Fun**, remained very rare with a copy in VF(R) selling for $55,000. Another copy in VG went for $40,000 (trade). **More Fun** is still a very popular title that seldom turns up. Spectre issues are very hot, which is reflected in the high values listed. The Mile High copy of **More Fun** #101 traded at $60,000(cash/trade)! The Larson copies of #52 & 53 sold as a set for $148,000! The early issues of **Star Spangled** with classic covers and interior art by Simon & Kirby enjoyed good sales while **Boy Commandos** held its own. The classic Kubert covers on the later issues of **Flash Comics** were hot with few copies turning up. Some of the sales for 1996 include: **Action** *#1VF84(R) $62,100, VG $38,000, VG+(R) $28,600, FR $22,000, #2FN55 $16,100, VG $9,000, #3VG+ $6,500, VF(R) $5,000, #4VF+(R) $3,500, VF+(R) $3,800, #6VG+ $4,500, #7FN58 $12,650, VG+ $7,000, #8VG+ $5,000, #7VF(R) $5,900, #11VG+ $1,500, #13 & #7FN66 $9,200;* **Adventure** *#48 (Larson) $30,000, PR $1,100, #61FN+ $5,000, #93VF+ $550, #94VF+ $800, #149VF+ $265;.* **All American** *#8GD $220, #16GD+ $10,000, #18FR+ $650, #19VF $13,000, VG+ $2,500, #27FN+ $1,000, #53VF $500;* **All Flash** *#1VG $3,750, VG 2,200, FR $775, #12VG+ $180, #13FN $225, #14FN $225;* **All Star Comics** *#3VG $5,500, #4VG+ $1,100, #5GD $775, #8FN $7,000, #12VG+ $675, #14FR+ $175, #16GD $175, #18VG+ $450, #20(MH) $5500, #29VG $165, #36VF+ $1,925, VG+ $700; #50GD $115, #52VG+ $275, #55GD+ $135;* **Batman** *#1VF79(R)*

Flash Comics #1
in FN+ restored
sells for $14,500!

$7,600, FN+(R) $10,000, FN+(R) $11,000, #2VF(R) $6,500, VG+ $2,000, #7VG $600, #9VF+ $4,400, #13GD $350, #25GD $180, #30GD+ $190, #31GD $90, #36VF+ $1,925, #41VF $600, #58VF $650, #64NM $605, #70VG $90, #78FN+ $425; **Blackhawk** *#71VF $155, #99VF+ $110, #100VF+ $120;* **Detective** *#2VG(R) $4,400, #5GD $1,760, #7FR $750, #9GD+ $1,700, #18VF(R) $3,800, #19VF(R) $2,200, #21VG $1,300, #27VF(R) $60,000, $65,000, VF(R, tape) $38,500, FN+(R) $50,000, VG $50,000, #28FN74(R) $4,025, #29FR $2,100, #32GD+ $1,000, #33GD+ $4,500, #41FN+ $950, #46VG $525, #84NM+(PA) $2,530, #106(MH) $3,050, #110VF+ $440, #155(MH) $2,560, #170(MH) $2,800* **Flash Comics** *#1FN+(R) $14,500, #2VG+ $1,900, #24VF(R) $1,000, #58VF $425, #63GD+ $100, #76FN $225, #83GD+ $125, #87VG $200, #91GD $220, #101VF(R) $750, #103FN+ $1,600, $700;* **Green Lantern** *#1VF(R) $5,175, #8VF $675, #9VF $750, #13GD+ $165, #14VF $650 + $150 trade, #20VF $700, #32VF $550, #38VF+ $1,100;* **More Fun** *#52FN+(R) $15,300, VG+(R)*

Wonder Woman #1VF
gets $14,000!!

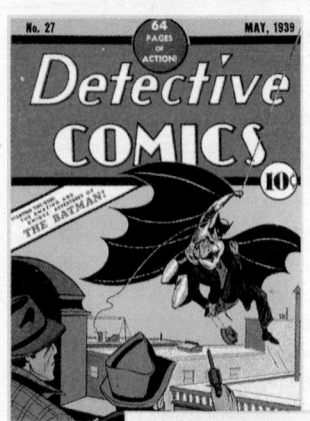

No. 27 | 64 PAGES of ACTION! | MAY, 1939

Detective COMICS 10¢

© DC

$12,000, #53VF(R) $9,000, #54VF $7,500, #56VF $3,000, #60VG+ $750, #57 GD+ $400, #73VF(R) $5,500, FN $6,500, FN+ $4,950, #101VF $7,150, FN+ $3,630 **Mutt & Jeff** #2VG+ $250; **New Adventure** #13VG $1,750, #14GD+ $1,000, #23GD $375, #24(MH) $4,000, VG+ $575, #30GD+ $600; **New Book of Comics** #8VF+ $3,025; **New Comics** #1FN(R) $3,500; **New Fun** #2FR $3,300; **New York World's Fair** 1940VF+ $15,000, VF $7,260; **Sensation Comics** #7VG+ $235, #22VF+ $490, #71VF+ $650, #80FN $100, #108FN+ $180 **Star Spangled Comics** #23VF $470, #35(MH) $1,650, #49(MH) $1,540, #59FN+ $230, #112VF $220; **Superboy** #1GD $880, #2VG+ $440, #2VG+ $410, #3VG+ $275, #3NM $1,650, #4VG+ $200, #4FN $255, #6VG+ $195, #7VF $470, #12VG+ $155, #19VF+ $415, #25VF+ $275; **Superman** #1FN+ $19,000, FN65(R) $11,500, VG (Nova Scotia) $30,000 ($12,000 trade), FN(R)

$12,650, $10,000, VG $26,000, VG(R) $10,000, #2FN(R) $1,650, 3VG+ $2,200, #4VG+ $800, #5FR $330, #5VG+ $1,100, #6FN+ $800, VG $525, #8VG $450, #14VF+ $4,500, #20FN $400, #24FN+ $1,250, VG $350, #32VF+ $650, #37FN+ $305, #43VG+ $200, #50VF $500, #53FN+ $800, VG $430, #54VG+ $125, #60FN $190, #71FN+ $155, #73FN+ $275, #75VF $360, #76FN+ $700, FN $500, #79FN $155, #94FN $150; **Wonder Woman** #1VF $14,000, #2NM+ $5,000, #2VG+ $605, #4VF+ $1,700, #45(MH) $3,000 **World's Best** #1FN+ $4,000, VG $3,500; **World's Finest Comics** #7NM $1,760, VF+ $950, #8NM $1,100, #9VG $330, #18GD $80, #31FN+ $190, #35VG+ $165.

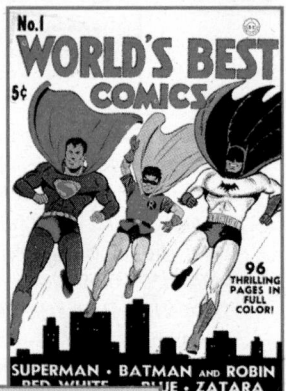

No.1 | 5¢ | WORLD'S BEST COMICS | 96 THRILLING PAGES IN FULL COLOR! | SUPERMAN · BATMAN AND ROBIN RED WHITE... BLUE · ZATARA

© DC

TIMELY - All superhero titles were hot and represented one of the top collected companys of the 1940s. Traditionally collected titles such as **Captain America, Human Torch, Sub-Mariner, All Winners, All Select, Miss Fury, Sun Girl, Namor, Mystic** and **Young Allies** remained the strongest. Because of scarcity of product, prices remained high and books sold quickly for up to 250% of Guide list regardless of condition. A **Captain America** #1VF sold for $65,000! A **Sub-Mariner** #1NM sold for $25,000! An **All Winners** #1VF+ sold for $11,000! However, **Marvel Mystery**, Timely's flagship title, with its magnificent covers,

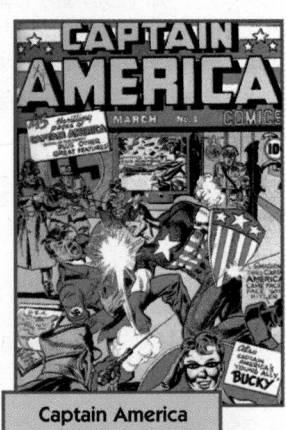

CAPTAIN AMERICA COMICS | MARCH No. 1 | 10¢ | BUCKY

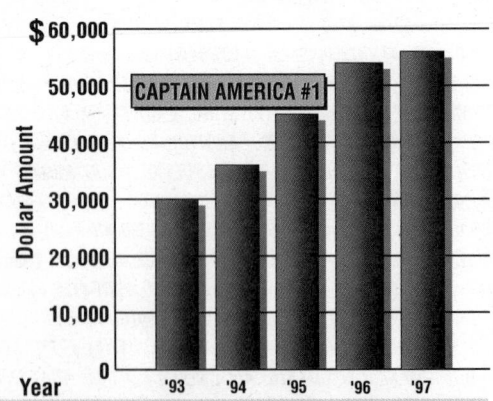

CAPTAIN AMERICA #1

Dollar Amount | Year: '93 '94 '95 '96 '97
$60,000 / 50,000 / 40,000 / 30,000 / 20,000 / 10,000 / 0

First appearance of one of America's most popular patriotic heroes has shown excellent growth over the past 5 years!

reached a plateau due to large price increases over the past few years. Key issues in high grade were still selling for over-Guide prices however. A #5NM Larson copy brought $25,000! The Allentown **Marvel** #1NM went for $115,000 (all trade), another copy in FN+(R) brought $52,000, a VG+ sold for $37,000 and a VF(heavy restoration) went for $20,000. The pay copy of **Motion Picture Funnies Weekly** sold for $42,000! A copy of the 128pg. **Annual** in GD+ sold for $6,000! **Miss America** #1 was hot with renewed interest in **Sub-Mariner**. Several leaders in the market reported that copies of **Red Raven** seemed to be drying up. Some of the post-Golden Age late 1940s titles such as **Millie The Model**, **The Witness**, etc. showed increased interest. Many of these later issues contain classic "Hey Look" by Kurtzman which were also in demand. Some of the sales for 1996 include: **All Select** #1VF+ $9,000, VG+ $2,000; **All Winners** #1NM $20,000, VG $2,100, #7VF $800, #10FN $715, #19VF+(Overstreet) $2,500; **Captain America** #2VF83 $4,700, #5VF+ $3,500, GD+ $600, #8VF+

$2,800, #13VG $950, #17GD+ $600, #20FR+ $235, #25FN(R) $300, #33FR+ $125, #36VG+ $900, #37VG+ $600, #59VF $1,550, #75FN+ $1,000; **Human Torch** #2(#1)FN+ $10,000, #2GD $2,000, #8FN+ $1,250, FN $1,200, #29FN+ #265; **Kid Komics** #1VG $750; **Marvel Comics** #1FN72 $18,250; **Marvel Mystery** #1FN+(R) $52,000, VG+ $37,000, VF(R) $20,000, #4FN $1,500, GD $700, #6VG $650, #7FN(R) $2,800, #10GD+ $950, #17FN $800, #32VF $900, #33FN+ $775, #48VG+(R) $275, #63VG+ $385, #65VF+ $800, $625, #71VF+ $650, #76VG+ $250, #92VG $550, **Annual** GD $3715; **Mystic** (1st) #1VF+ (Nova Scotia) $10,000, #3FN $925, #4FN $800, #5VG+ $800; **Mystic** (2nd) #2VF+ $750; **Nellie The Nurse** #16(MH) $205; **Sub-Mariner** #18GD+ $220, #20VG $205; **Sun Girl** #1VG+ $195; **Tough Kid Squad** #1VF $7,500; **Young Allies** #1VG+ $2,420.

FAWCETT - Very good sales overall. During the 1940s Captain Marvel and company ruled supreme and out-sold almost all comic books of that period. His fan club had over a million members! For many years Fawcetts have taken a back seat to the two giants, DC and Marvel, yet many dealers reported Fawcetts to be steady and reliable sellers.

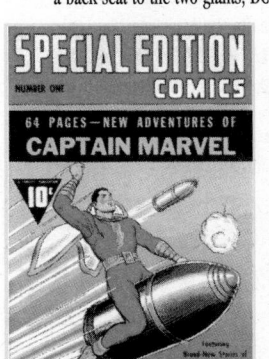

Traditionally, the best selling title is **Captain Marvel**. Compared to DC and Timely issues of the same period, the early issues of this title are undervalued. The same can be said for early issues of **Captain Marvel Jr.** and **Master Comics**. Some of the most beautiful covers ever published on comics were drawn by Mac Raboy who worked for Fawcett. His covers are consistently sought, even in average grade, with Nazi themes the most popular. **Bulletman** has a solid following with beautiful Mac Raboy covers on early issues. A **Special Edition** #1VF sold for $6,500. **Whiz** was reported as a steady seller with the higher numbers more commonly turning up. **America's Greatest** was reported as a hot title, and so was **Mary Marvel**, due to the continuing recent high demand for classic female characters. The **Gene Autry** Fawcett issues remained scarce and began to appear on a number of want lists. Early issues of **Master** were also very difficult to locate. Other titles such as **Marvel Family, Captain Midnight, Gift** and **Holiday** enjoyed slow to moderate sales. A few selected sales are: **Captain Marvel Adventures** #2VG+ $700, #18FN+ $650, 26NM+ $1,265;

Captain Marvel Jr. #10VG+ $250; **Marvel Family** #1FN+ $440; **Master** #1VG $1,000, #21VF $1,250, #22VF $1,250, #23VF $1,200; **Marvel Family** #1FN+ $440; **Master** #15VF $425; **Special Edition** #1VG+ $1,200; **Whiz** #1FR $3,850.

QUALITY - This company's books were becoming more scarce with a pickup in demand, especially for the lower numbers of **Crack, Hit, Military, National** and **Smash**. Demand for the work of Lou Fine was getting stronger all the time. Some of his best covers appear on titles from this company. Sales reported for **Blackhawk** and **Modern** were slow to moderate while other titles such as **Police, Plastic Man, Feature** and **Dollman** enjoyed moderate sales. **Police** #103 and up, as well as later issues of **Smash**, picked up in demand. Jack Cole was brilliant with **Plastic Man**, which is long overdue for a comeback in demand. All offbeat titles showed good gains. Reported sales: **Hit** #5VG+ $1,925; **National** #5VG+ $275, #13VF+ $550, #14VF $440, #16VF+ $500; **Smash** #40(MH) $605.

FICTION HOUSE - There was a solid demand for early issues of **Jumbo, Planet** and **Wings**, with the early issues of **Jumbo** still very difficult to obtain. **Planet** remained the most popular title, although some collectors were beginning to complain about prices. A **Planet** #1VF sold for $12,000. Good gains were reported on most offbeat titles. The good girl art covers by Matt Baker, Celardo, Zolnerowich and others continued to be in high demand. These covers appeared on issues of **Fight, Jumbo, Jungle, Planet, Rangers** and **Wings**. The individually great covers showing bondage, etc. sold very well. **Kaanga** was reported slow while **Sheena** sold well. Reported

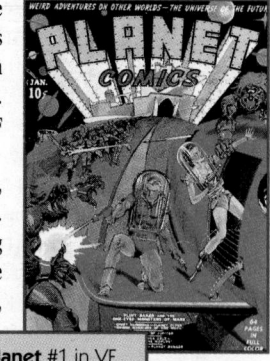

Planet #1 in VF
brings $12,000!

© FH

sales: **Jumbo** #1VG+ $5,500; **Planet** #1VF(R) $4,500, VG+ $2,700.

FOX - Since this company didn't publish superhero titles very long after the war years, titles like **Fantastic, Mystery Men, Science, Weird** and **Wonderworld** remained very difficult to find in all conditions due to the paper drive efforts. Even with the large price increases given this company's key books last year, there was still a solid demand for #1s and classic cover issues such as **Wonder** #1 & 2, **Mystery Men** #1, **Science** #1, **Wonderworld** #3, **Weird** #1 and **Fantastic** #1 & 3. It was reported that Lou Fine artwork was still in high demand, driving the prices paid for the early issues to even higher levels. Very hot in 1996 was this company's good girl art issues published in the late 1940s. All issues of **Phantom Lady** were sizzling red hot with many dealers asking prices way over Guide list.

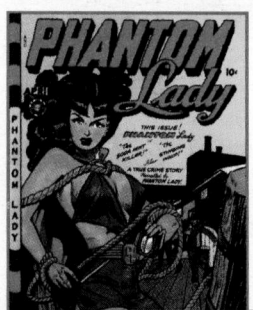

© FOX

Phantom Lady #17 in
VF sells for $4,500!

Other hot titles include **All Top, Rulah, Zegra, Zoot,** and the later issues of **Blue Beetle**. The offbeat titles continued to sell at or slightly over current Guide levels. Some sales in 1996 include: **Fantastic** #11VF+ $650, #4FN $605; **Mystery Men** #1VF(R) $4,000, #5NM (Allentown) $2,250, #10VG+ $450, #11FN+ $750; **Phantom Lady** #13FN+ $1,050, #15GD+ $275, #17VF (Overstreet) $4,500, #4VF+ $330; **Planet** #56VG+ $140; **Woman Outlaws** #1VF $160.

NEDOR - All titles and issues sold very fast, especially issues by Schomburg with a World War II theme. Demand in this company's titles was due primarily to the beautiful Schomburg covers which gives them the same look as those

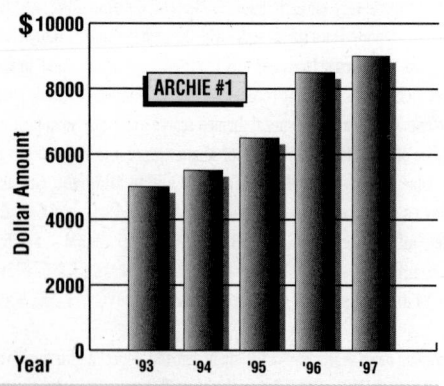

This rare comic book has shown remarkable growth over the past five years and should continue to be a good investment in the years ahead.

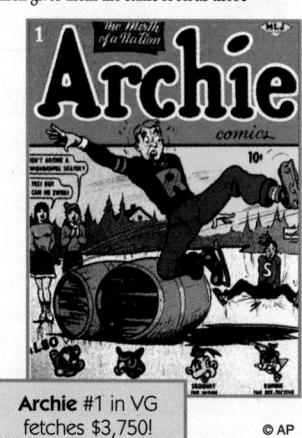

Archie #1 in VG
fetches $3,750!

© AP

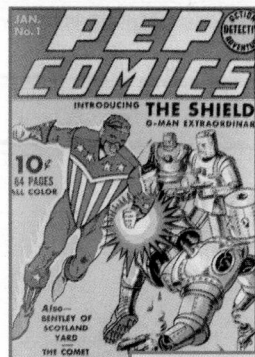

© WDC

Pep #1VG+ brings $1,250!

titles produced by Timely. However, contents of the comics are not comparable to the Timely look-alikes. It has been observed that covers are playing a more important role in collecting demand and this company's titles are a good example. **America's Best**, **Black Terror**, **Exciting**, **Fighting Yank**, **Startling**, **Thrilling** were all sought after. The Miss Masque issues were expecially hot. Some sales are: **America's Best** #10(MH) $1,100; #18(MH) $1,100; **Exciting Comics** #19(MH) $1,000, #21(MH) $770, #49(MH) $1,100, #50(MH) $1,100; **Fighting Yank** #8(MH) $1,375; **Startling Comics** #16VF+ 290, #36(MH) $660, #49NM $2,000, FN $1,350; **Thrilling** #1VG+ $440.

MLJ/ARCHIE - All early issues of the hero titles were hot, selling quickly in all grades. **Pep**, **Jackpot**, **Top Notch**, **Blue Ribbon** and **Hangman** were among the most popular titles. Although most of the characters except for Archie didn't last, most runs exhibit beautiful covers. Reports are that low number **Archies** were in big demand and sold easily at and above current price levels. **Betty and Veronica** were also requested. Other related titles such as **Pep** (Archie issues) and **Laugh** were slower. The late 1940s titles such as **Suzie**, **Katy Keene** and **Wilbur** have reported slow sales. A few reported sales: **Archie** #1VG $3,750; **Hangman** #8VF $1,100; **Jackpot** #6VF+ $850; **Pep Comics** #1VG+ $1,250, #53(MH) $715, #54(MH) $550; **Top Notch** #1VG $1,015.

HARVEY - Solid sales for most titles with **Green Hornet** and **Speed** leading the way. An ashcan copy of **Champion** #1 surfaced from the copyright office in 1996 which may account for this title starting with #2. **All New**, **Black Cat** and **Speed** enjoyed steady demand. Demand did not increase for **Dick Tracy**, **Terry and the Pirates**, **Joe Palooka**, **Steve Canyon** or **Kerry Drake**. Interest remained high, however, in Kirby's **Boy Explorers**, **Boy's Ranch** and **Stuntman**. Some reported sales: **Boy's Ranch** #1(MH) $1,320, #6(MH) $430; **Dick Tracy** #49(file copy) $165; **Speed** #37FN+(File) $100, #38VF(File) $165, #40FN+ $100, #43VF+(File) $210.

DISNEY - After many years of stability, Disney books began to show considerable demand in 1996 as you will note by the increased prices in this edition. The supply of various 1930s books of this genre, as well as the early issues of **Comics & Stories**, were drying up with demand on the increase. There was still a strong demand for high grade Duck one-shots which are not available at prices near Guide. This is one of the few areas in Golden Age collecting that does need to be in higher grade to sell well. **Comics and Stories** above #100 were reported to be slow by some dealers. Some sales in 1994 include: **Mickey Mouse Four Color** #16VF $9,500; **Merry Christmas From Mickey Mouse** VF $1,500; **Walt Disney's Comics & Stories** #1VG $2,300.

Walt Disney's Comics & Stories #1 in VF+ trades at $25,000!

© WDC

CENTAUR - Due to the scarcity of most titles produced, collectors always have trouble locating specific issues. Many important artists worked on these early books and created great covers and quality contents. Being the forerunner of Timely Comics, there was a solid demand for them. A few reported sales: **Amazing Mystery Funnies** V2#7GD+ $825; **Funny Pages** #42GD+(repair) $200.

© DELL

Looney Tunes #1VF+ sells for record $20,000!

LEV GLEASON - Current reports indicated a slight increase in demand for early issues of **Boy**, **Daredevil**, **Silver Streak** and **Crime Does Not Pay**. Iron Jaw cover appearances were still in high demand. Prices realized were at or slightly above Guide list. Reported sales: **Silver Streak** #6VG+ $2,400.

A-45

DELLS-DISNEY - Early issues of **Walt Disney's Comics & Stories** remained scarce, especially in grade. As this title developed, issues were selling in the millions by the late 1940s into the 1950s. Consequently there was a supply of these books in most grades available in the marketplace. Carl Barks, who wrote and drew the Donald Duck stories, has become very popular in Europe and elsewhere, bringing new collectors into the market all the time. For this reason, quite a lot of the Barks issues were being sold overseas. The Duck one-shots by Barks are scarce in NM+ condition and were slow to moderate sellers in the other grades. **FC #223** (Lost in the Andes) has shown increased demand; **Uncle Scrooge** enjoyed moderate demand as did the **Mickey Mouse Four Colors**. However, **Mickey Mouse FC #16** (The Phantom Blot) was a solid book with many collectors looking for FN or better copies. **Dell Giants** were selling at current Guide levels, and a **Walt Disney's Comics & Stores** #1VF+ was traded at $25,000.

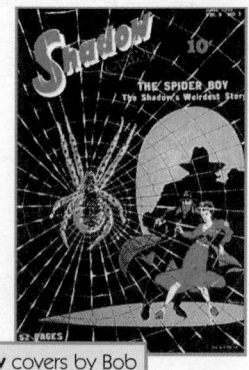

DELLS-NON-DISNEY - Overall slow to moderate sales were reported by many dealers. Compared to superhero sales, this may be true, but there were dealers who reported excellent sales when the books were in NM+ condition. File copies also sold well at over Guide prices. The **Four Color** series, with all its hidden #1s, diversity and photo covers, were selling well at current Guide levels. Other titles in this run such as **Rawhide**, **Ricky Nelson**, **John Wayne**, etc. were at a temporary plateau with all the price increases of a few years ago. **Lulus** were reportedly selling moderately. There was renewed interest in **Looney Tunes**, especially #1, due to its historical importance and the perception in the market of being under valued. A **Looney Tunes** #1VF+ sold for $20,000! **Tarzan**s under #20 and **Felix** were hot. Reported sales: **Dell Giant** #43NM+ $300; **Looney Tunes** #3VF+ $950; **Tarzan** #1GD+ $250.

STREET and SMITH - Interest in this company was volatile! The classic Powell covers on **Shadow** issues sold very quickly. **Doc Savage** was still revered by crossover pulp collectors as well as comic book collectors. But the real sleeper was **Supersnipe**, a character that was historically undervalued and underappreciated. When collectors discovered copies of this title, they bought them up. **Red Dragon** (esp. 2nd series) sold very well.

CATMAN #1

This book has increased in value 400% over the past five years!

Classic Comics #33VF
sells for $875!

© GIL

HOLYOKE-CONTINENTAL - Catman was sizzling hot! All issues were in high demand, especially the L.B. Cole cover issues. Other titles that were still on fire, carrying over from previous years, were **Power Comics, Suspense** and **Terrific Comics**, again with a mix of L.B. Cole and Schomburg covers. A **Suspense** #3 in FN sold for $12,000! **Captain Aero** was also enjoying excellent demand. Reported sales: **Captain Aero** #22VF+ $380; **Catman** #1VF+ (Denver) $4,250, VG $1,000, #31FN+ $825; **Power Comics** #2VF $1,320, #3VG+ $660, #4VF $715; **Suspense Comics** #3FR $2,500, #8GD $400, #11VF+ $2,750, #12GD $220.

CLASSIC COMICS - The demand for original editions as well as early reprints increased with reports of a strong market for 1996. It was reported that any edition in Fine or better condition sold quickly. Line drawn covers were in high demand in all grades. Early originals (#1-50) sold at multiples of Guide list in the VF/NM grade. Steady growth is predicted for these books in the years ahead. **Sherlock Holmes** #33 in VF88 sold for $800. At the Chicago Con a FN copy of #1 was priced at $5,000 while **Classic Giants** were priced at $900 to $1,400 for VF copies. A #8VF was priced at $560. Reported sales are: #3 (o)FN+ $875, #7 (o)VG+ $250, #17 (o)VF $455, #13 (o)GD+ $200, #18 (o)VG+ $225, #19 (o)FN+ $270, #24 (o)FN+ $240, #31 (o)VF $245, #34 (o)VF $300, #45 (o)VF $70, #46NM $110, #49 (o) $105, #56NM $120, #60NM+ $95, #133 VF+ $35, #157 (o)VF $35, #166(o) FN $32, #169 (o)VF+ $70.

FUNNY ANIMAL - The demand was mostly for Timely and DC titles, otherwise most other publishers enjoyed slow to average sales. Early **Looney Tunes** were scarce while Jay Ward and Hanna Barbera titles continued to be popular.

MISC. 1940s - There were a lot of hot books here. **All New Comics, Big Shot, Capt. Flight, Contact, Dynamic, Frankenstein, Green Lama, Punch, Red Seal, Spotlight** and early issues of **Target.**

1950s TITLES - Most horror, crime, war, western and science fiction comics were collected from this period with heavy demand for DC, Atlas, EC, Charlton, ACG as well as a host of small obscure publishers such as Aragon, Ajax and Superior. The pedigree books (known as Mile High, Bethlehem, White Mountain and others) were sill breaking price barriers as they have in years past. Interest in pre-code books continued to increase across-the-board.

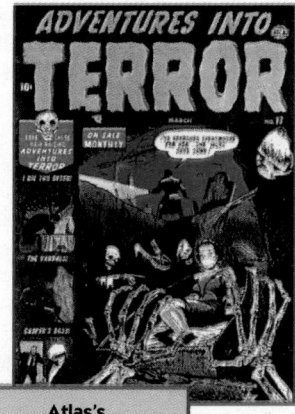

Atlas's
Adventures Into Terror
#17 in NM brings $260!

© MEG

ATLAS - Collector interest for this company's late 1940s and 1950s comics increased significantly across a broad spectrum. Not only were the pre-code horror comics such as **Journey Into Unknown Worlds, Journey Into Mystery, Marvel Tales, Menace, Spellbound, Uncanny Tales,** etc. in high demand, but so were the crime and war issues. The so-called prototype appearances of later important Marvel characters, usually in the pre-hero issues, were crackling hot! Since most of these books are rare in high grade due to lower quality paper and Marvel chipping, look for new record price levels to be achieved in the future. Some recorded sales are: **Adventure Into Mystery** #2VF $135, #5VF+ $105; **Adventures Into Terror** #17NM $260; **Journey Into Mystery** #43NM (Circle 8) $220, #55NM $140; **Journey Into Unknown Worlds** #14FN+ $275; **Marvel Tales** #120NM+(WM) $470, #143NM+(WM) $260.

EC - Most pre-trend titles were selling at around Guide list with collector interest for the transition issues to the New Trend (the first Vault

Mad #1 in VF
sells for $2,200!

© EC

Vault Of Horror #12 (#1) goes for $660 in VG!

and Crypt Keeper issues). Inexpensive and readily available reprints continued to suppress demand for most new trend titles, but collectors still wanted and continued to seek out the original items. The demand seemed highest for horror followed by science fiction with crime and war somewhere in between. Reports indicate that **MAD** continued to be EC's hottest selling title but leveled off due to past price hikes. It's interesting to see how an ongoing title helps the collectibility of the back issues. A Gaines file copy set of #1-23 sold at auction in the summer for a record price of $44,850! The New Directional titles basically held their own. **M.D.** and **Psychoanalysis** were seen as esoteric by some collectors in the market. Reported sales are: **Crime SuspenStories** #27FN $60; **Frontline Combat** #7(Gaines) $470; **Haunt of Fear** #6FN $125, #8FN+ $180, VF+ $210, #12VF+ $160, #21VG+ $60, #26FN+ $85; **Mad** #1VF $2,200, #4VG+ $205, #5VG $250, #7NM(WM) $635, #8VG $110, #9VG+ $180, #24FN $330, #26VF $180; **Picture Stories From American History** #2(Gaines) $230; **Picture Stories From Science** #2(Gaines) $310; **Shock SuspenStories** #1VF+ $385, #3VG+ $85, #12VF+ $250, #16VF+ $80; **Tales From The Crypt** #22FN $195, #23VF+ $360, #24VF $265, #30VF $265, #46VG $100; **Two-Fisted Tales** #21FN $95, #22FN $90, #23FN+ $85, #34(Gaines) $470, FN $60, #35(Gaines) $415; **Vault Of Horror** #12VG $660, #16FN $140, #17VG+ $85, #18VF $230, FN+ $120, #19VG+ $85, #20VG+ $70, #21VG+ $70, #23FN $100, #24VG+ $70, #28VF $145, #32FN+ $100, #34(Gaines) $660, #38FN+ $100, #40FN $100; **Annual** 1953 FN $175; **Weird Fantasy** #13VF $660, #17VF $275, #6VF $165, #7VF $205, #12FN+ $550, #16VG+ $75, #21FN+ $155; **Weird Science Fantasy** #24FN $105, #26VF+ $165, #28VF $165.

AVON - With the recent focus in the market on 1950s horror, crime, science fiction and esoteric titles, this company's books have enjoyed an increase in demand. The Crime and science fiction titles are the best sellers. A few sales reported: **Eerie** #9VF+ $165, #13VF+ $140.

GOLDEN AGE/POST-GOLDEN AGE REPORT (BY GENRE):

HORROR - The comic book marketplace simply cannot buy enough pre-code horror comics. There seems to be no price resistance anywhere across the board. The more bizarre the cover – electrocution, injury to the eye, head-

Phantom Ladys were too hot to touch!! #16 shown

Terrors Of The Jungle #10 in VF sells for $230!

lights, hanging, decapitation, etc. – the better they sold. After EC, Atlas led the way with DC right behind. The Harvey titles, such as **Black Cat Mystery**, also sold well. The more obscure company's titles, such as **Chilling Tales, Blue Bolt Weird, Dark Mysteries, Journey into Fear, Mister Mystery, Strange Fantasy, Strange Mysteries, Strange Suspense Stories, Strange Terrors, The Thing!, This Magazine is Haunted, Weird Chills, Weird Mysteries, Witche's Tales,** etc., were all very hot. Reported sales: **Ghost** comics #6(Bethlehem) $330; **Haunted Thrills** #5VF $100; **Terrors Of The Jungle** #10VF+ $230, $170, #18VF+ $195, VF $165, #19FN $165, #21VF $220; **Thing** #1FN $160, #7VG+ $165, #17VF+ $300.

WAR - EC produced the classic war comics of all time, **Frontline Combat** and **Two-Fisted Tales,** which were selling well at around Guide list levels. Of course, NMs and books from pedigree collections sold above Guide. DC war titles have long been known for their desirability and collectibility; however, there now seems to be long overdue appreciation for the Atlas titles. Reported sales: **Star Spangled War Stories** #133FN+ $175, #5FN+ $100,

#19VF+ $135, #24VF+ $145.

COMIC STRIP REPRINTS - Earlier issues of **Ace, King, Super, Popular, Funnies** and **Crackajack** were becoming very scarce, and some collectors were looking for them. Usually these books were in used condition when they turned up, but they sold quickly. The early issues of **Famous Funnies** remained scarce while later issues were available in the market. **Funnies on Parade**, the first modern age format comic book and **Century of Comics** also remained scarce.

GOOD GIRL ART - Sizzling red hot! Fox titles led by **Phantom Lady, All Top, Zoot, Jo-Jo, Rulah** and later **Blue Beetle** remained in highest demand. Atlas titles also had a solid following. **Bold Stories, Candid Tales, Brenda Starr, Crimes By Women, Seven Seas, Meet Corliss Archer, Reform School Girl, Sunny, Women Outlaws** were all on fire! A large demand for all the recognized cover classics was evident. Sales in all categories from **All Top** to **Zoot** were over Guide, some as much as 300%. The most requested artists were Matt Baker, Jack Kamen and Al Feldstein.

ROMANCE - There was a large increase in demand reported last year. There has been a focus on good girl art comics in recent years with Matt Baker as the leading artist. Simon and Kirby's art has become more popular and so has L.B. Cole's. These artists also worked on many romance comics. Matt Baker's covers for such comics as **Teenage Temptations** are sensational and probably underpriced. It was reported that all of the Simon and Kirby titles sold very well. Earlier Quality romance titles, with well-composed covers, photo or drawn, were also selling. All L.B. Cole romance covers were also hot. All this adds up to increased interest in this genre. This is also one area where a collector or dealer can buy a sizeable stack of books for only a few hundred dollars.

WESTERNS - Fawcetts featuring the more popular B-western stars, such as **Hopalong Cassidy** and **Lash LaRue**, sold at a steady pace, particularly with photo covers, although Saunders painted covers also did well. DC **All American Western** and **Hopalongs** were hot. Certain titles remained scarce, such as **Whip Wilson, Sunset Carson** and **Hoot Gibson**, and sold easily when available. M.E. 's **Ghost Rider** is popular year in and year out. On the other hand, Dell westerns in low grade were slow, while high grade still sold well. The only exception to this rule are the lower number Four Color issues of **Roy Rogers** which are not turning up as often. Earlier Atlas westerns were increasingly popular. Reported sales: **All-American Western** #114(MH) $640, #117(MH) $465, #121(MH) $520, #122(MH) $465, #125(MH) $245; **Western Comics** #26(MH) $415.

Ghost Rider is still very popular! #1 shown

© ME

HUMOROUS AND FUNNY ANIMAL - Certain DC funny titles remained steady, selling at current price levels. **Fox and Crow** sold well, as did Sheldon Mayer's **Sugar and Spike** and **Scribbley**. Harvey's **Casper** titles, **Little Dot, Little Audrey, Little Lotta, Richie Rich** and **Spooky** also did well. Dell funny animal issues were in abundant supply, with no greater demand than usual, except for earlier numbers of **Looney Tunes**. Some characters and titles were underappreciated and overdue for attention, such as **Mighty Mouse, Pogo, Popeye** and **Felix**. Reported sales: **Buzzy** #5(MH) $220, #8(MH) $175; **Flippity and Flop** #1NM $165; **Friendly Ghost Casper** #1NM $220; **Humbug** #1NM+ $300, $305, #2NM+ $110; **Scribbly** #1VG+ $250.

Torchy is sizzling hot! #5 in VF sells for $800!

© QUA

MISCELLANEOUS AND ESOTERIC - Collectors continued to uncover interesting out-of-the-mainstream titles and bought them up. Books like **Juke Box Comics** were in demand. True-to-life comics, such as **Heroic, Real Life Comics**, etc. were collected for specific issues, personalities, or artists. The comic book marketplace has begun to recognize the distinctive qualities of certain Chesler comics, such as **Punch** and **Dynamic**, which became red hot due to their covers. Other titles like **All New, Big Shot,**

Captain Flash, Captain Flight, Contact, Dynamic, Frankenstein, Green Lama, Red Seal, Spotlight and comic books featuring UFOs were also hot. A few Sales: **Purple Claw** #1FN $85; **Torchy** #5VF+ sold for $800.

CRIME - There was increased demand for late 1940s and 1950s titles. Atlas crime comics and covers brimming with activity were in demand. Lev Gleason's **Crime Does Not Pay**, particularly early issues with gory covers, sold very well. **Justice Traps the Guilty**, with Simon and Kirby covers, were hot. **Authentic Police Cases**, **Crime Mysteries**, **Ken Shannon**, **Manhunt**, **True Crime Comics** were also in demand. Individual hot issues were **Teen-Age Dope Slaves** and **Giant Comics Edition** #12 (Baker prostitute cover). Post-code crime comics sold slowly to moderately. Avon crime comics with sensational photo covers were steady sellers. Reported sales: **Complete Book of True Crime** VG+ $165; **Crime Must Stop** #1VF+ $350; **Gangbusters** #15(MH) $330, #18(MH) $250, #21(MH) $305; **Law Breakers Suspense Stories** #11GD+ $225; **Racket Squad In Action** #12VF $160; **Reform School Girl** FN+ $1,350.

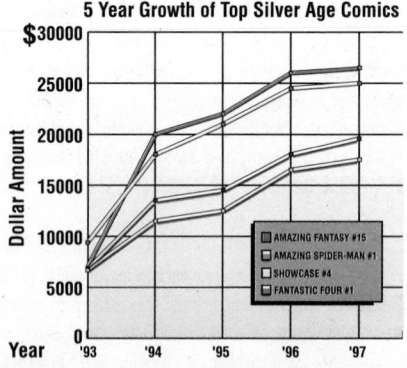

Strange Adventures #1 in VG sells for $500!

© DC

SCIENCE FICTION - Many titles sold at over Guide list prices. The most popular were EC's **Weird Fantasy** and **Weird Science**, which were selling well at current Guide levels, followed by DC's **Strange Adventures** and **Mystery In Space.** All Atlas titles, such as **Space Man** and **Space Squadron**, etc. sold very well. Off-beat titles like **Weird Mysteries** and **Weird Tales of the Future** were also in demand. Reported sales: **Captain Science** #7(WM) $435; **Out Of This World** #14VF+(WM) $85; **Strange Adventures** #1VG $500, #2FN+ $660, #7FN+ $305, #20FN+ $275, #23VF+ $275, #145VF+ $60; **Weird Tales Of The Future** #2VF+ $1,430, #5VF+ $1,200.

Get Smart #5 NM still strong at $60!

© Talent Associates

TV AND MOVIE TIE-INS - There was slower demand for Dell movie titles, but TV related titles remained fairly strong from a year earlier. The supply of NM file copies of specific hot titles historically offered by Diamond Int'l Galleries in the past were no longer in inventory. In fact, years ago when the Dell load was purchased, many of the key titles and issues sold out early on. DC titles such as **Jackie Gleason**, **Sgt Bilko**, **Dennis The Menace**, **Ozzie and Harriet** and **Bob Hope** were consistent sellers. Reported sales: **Aristocats** #1NM $87; **Astro Boy** #1FN+ $244; **Augie Doggie** #1NM $180; **Bamm Bamm & Pebbles** #1NM $60; **The Beverly Hillbillies** #1NM $203; **Bewitched** #1NM $150, #3NM $60, #10NM $60; **Bullwinkle** #1NM $150; **Bullwinkle** (Gold Key) #1NM $180; **Daniel Boone** #1VF+ $90;

Lois Lane #1VF+ fetches $6,000!!

© DC

5 Year Growth of Top Silver Age Comics

Dollar Amount / Year '93 '94 '95 '96 '97

- AMAZING FANTASY #15
- AMAZING SPIDER-MAN #1
- SHOWCASE #4
- FANTASTIC FOUR #1

The top Silver Age books have leveled off after tremendous growth over the past five years, even though record prices in high grade are still occurring in isolated cases.

Amazing Fantasy #15 in NM jolts the comic market, bringing $30,000!

© MEG

Dr. Who #1 $143; **Family Affair** #1NM $42; **Frankenstein Jr.** #1NM $60; **F-Troop** #1NM $101; **Get Smart** #5NM $60; **Gomer Pyle** #1NM $68; **Hanna Barbera Super Heroes** #1NM $125; **Have Gun Will Travel** #931NM $158; **Hawaiian Eye** #1NM $45; **Honey West** #1NM $150; **I Dream of Jeannie** #2NM $120; **Jetsons** #1NM $285, #2NM $135, #4VF+ $93; **The Lucy Show** #1NM $150; **McHale's Navy** #1NM $50; **Mighty Hercules** #1NM $128, #2NM $128; **Mighty Heroes** #1NM $158; **The Monkees** #1NM $120; **The Munsters** #1NM $250; **New Terrytoons** #2NM $60; **Peanuts** #1NM $150; **Pebbles Flintstone** #1NM $90; **Snagglepuss** #1NM $120; **Space Family Robinson** #1VG+ $65; **Star Trek** #1VF+ $415, #6NM+ $165, #8NM+ $140; **Top Cat** #1NM $230; **Wonderful World of Brothers Grimm** #1NM $50.

SILVER AGE: Early issues in FN to NM and later issues in VF to NM did well and remained strong from the previous year. Prices achieved for NM mainstream DC and Marvel books priced in the Guide at $30 to $100 were consistently sold at multiples of Guide list. **Amazing Spider-Man** and **X-Men** led the way, but all Marvel superhero sold well in this grade. However, the Silver Age boom of the early 1990s which drove prices to high levels had an impact on the lower grades, which sold at and under Guide list values. With the recent increases in the Golden Age market taking place over the past three years, the Silver Age may be poised for the next cycle of growth. Record prices are still occurring, for example a copy of **Amazing Fantasy** #15NM brought $30,000 and a **Showcase** #4 in VF+ went for $24,500 in 1996! Many more sales of key issues are listed under each company.

DC: Dealers reported a noticeable increase in demand for this company's books with record prices paid for many key issues. This trend was also apparent at auctions during the year. Probably one of the hottest books in 1996 was **Wonder Woman** #105, where a NM copy sold for $3,000! **Flash** #105 was red hot! A copy in NM93 sold for $9,775, while a VF+ copy went for $7,500! **Batman** and **Detective** were hot! A **Detective** #225VF+ sold for $8,000! **Lois Lane** #1, which is very rare in high grade, sold in VF+ for $6,000! Key books in top grade still continued to bring high prices with **Showcase** remaining the hottest title. A

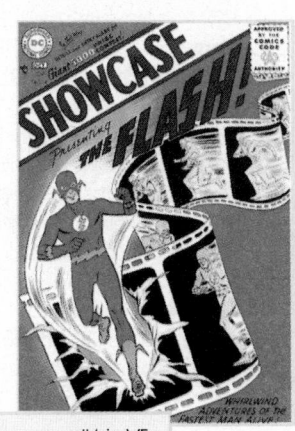

Showcase #4 in VF+ goes for $24,500!

© DC

Showcase #4VF+ went for $17,000, #14VF84 brought $5,750, #8VF+ got $10,000, #9VF $10,000, #10VF+ $7,000, #19NM93 $4,370, #22NM $7,500! Demand for **Brave and the Bold**, **Action** and **Adventure** followed. Certain issues appeared to be hard to find in condition. For example, **Batman** #80 to #100 and **Superman** #90 to #100. There was renewed interest in **My Greatest Adventure**, **Mystery in Space** and **Strange Adventures** as well as **House of Mystery** and **House of Secrets**. **Wonder Woman** was hot with many reported sales over Guide list. Demand for **Justice League** slowed while **The Flash** was steady with high demand for issues #105-120. A **Justice League** #1VF+(Bethlehem) sold for $6,000! **Green Lantern** held its own and **Worlds Finest** showed increased demand. A **Green Lantern** #1NM brought $5,000! The superhero titles from 1952 to 1957 sold very well and were probably the toughest period to fill out after the pre-1940 issues. These books were all difficult to find, with many of them qualifying as scarce. Reported sales are: **Adventure** #210VG+ $550, #224VF+ $260,

Showcase #22NM gets $7,500!!

© DC

Amazing Spider-Man #1 in NM fetches $25,000!

#232VF+ $220, #239VF $195, #247VG+ $500, #266VF+ $100; **Atom** #4 VF+ $180, #6NM $205, #10NM $205, VG $36; **Batman** #167NM $110; **Annual** #4VF $95; **Blackhawk** #108VG $165, #133VFN $60; **Brave & the Bold** #34NM+ $4,730; **Detective** #287VF+ $90, #298VF+ $250; **Flash** #108VF+ $605, #109VF+ $840, #114VG $65, #122VF+ $250, #132VF+ $120, #143VF+ $70, #146NM $110, #147VF+ $95; **Green Lantern** #2NM $220, #40NM $495, #76VF+ $160; **Hawkman** #9VF $70, #10VF+ $85, #12 VF+ $70, #13VF+ $85; **House of Secrets** #92VG+ $110; **Justice League** #1FN+ $1320, #2FN+ $360; **My Greatest Adventure** #23FN+ $80, #24VF+ $220, #25NM $250, #28VF+ $305, #30VF+ $195, #31VF+ $125, #39VF+ $90, #40VF+ $165, #42NM+ $220, #43NM+ $215, #51VF+ $80, #56NM+ $205, #57NM $205, #60NM+ $220; **Mystery In Space** #55VF $195; **Sea Devils** #1VF+ $360; **Showcase** #3VF+ $500, #5VF+ $675, #6VF+ $2,900, #7NM $1,425, #13VF+(Mohawk) $3,300, #14VF+ $3,630, #15FN+ $500, #28NM $580; **Superboy** #40FN $90, #42FN+ $125, #44VF $125, #46VF $140, #49VG+ $100, #84NM $130, #85NM $150; **Superman** #96VG+ $85, #97FN $115, #98VG+ $165, #102VG+ $85, #103VF $210, #104VG+ $110, #106FN $110, #114VG+ $110, #115FN $140, #118FN $110, #129VG+ $95, #137FN $60, #138FN $65, #140FN $60, #144VF+ $110, #148NM+ $195; **Annual** #2VF+ $275; **Superman's Girl Friend Lois Lane** #11VF+ $165; **Tales Of The Unexpected** #17NM $305; **Teen Titans** #1VF+ $110; **World's Finest** #75VF $530, #79VG+ $100, #85FN $100, #86VF(Biljo White) $120, #88VG+ $70, #105NM(Biljo White) $180.

MARVEL: This company's books have traditionally been the back bone of the Silver Age market since its inception, but due to recent developments at Marvel over the past two years that has impacted tremendously on the market, dealers have reported a slight shift in collector demand from Marvel to DC. This also may be due, in part, to the recent blockbuster movies and television shows based on Batman and Superman produced by Time Warner, placing the DC characters square in the public eye. Key Marvels in top condition were still fetching over-Guide prices though, but the lower grades remained slow, selling at and below Guide. An **Amazing Fantasy** #15NM sold for $30,000! A **Fantastic Four** in NM sold for a record $27,000! **Amazing Spider-Man** #1 in NM brought $25,000! **The Incredible**

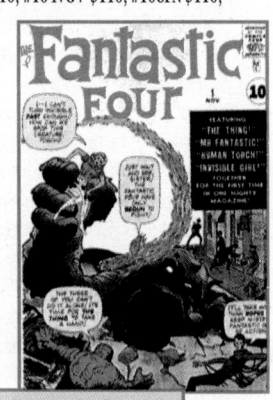

Fantastic Four #1 in NM goes for $30,000!

Hulk #1NM went for $14,000! Reported sales are: **Amazing Fantasy** #15VF+ $20,000, VF $14,000, FN71 $6,325, VG+ $4,500, VG $2,000, FR+ $900; **Amazing Spider-Man** #1VF+ $9,500, GD+$1,000, #2VF+ $2,800, #3VF+ $2,500, $1,400, #4VF+ $1,233, $1,150, #6NM $1,000, #7NM $950, VF+ $850, $600, #8VF+ $875, #9NM $1,000, VF+ $825, #10NM $900, #13VF+ $750, #14VF+ $1,600, $1,350, VF $800, #17NM $750, VF+ $600, $533, VG $119, #18VG $87, #19VG $92, #22VG $60, #27VG+ $65, #28VF+ $700, #50 VF+ $550, **Annual** #1VF+ $530; **Avengers** #1NM+ $6,500, $2,000, #4VF+ $1,250, $900, #5NM $270, #6VF+ $95, #7NM $200, #8NM $210; **Conan** #2NM+ $100; **Daredevil** #1VF+ $1,000, #5VG $55, #6VG+ $45, #8VG+ $45; **Fantastic Four** #1VF+ $18,000, VF $14,000, VG+ $1,570, GD $715, #4VF+ $2,300, #5VF+ $2,800, #6VF+ $1,400, #10VF+ $647, #12VF+ $1,800, $1,600, #13VF+ $565, #26VF+ $550, #48NM+ $1,250, VF+ $750, **Annual** #1NM $665; **Human Torch** #36VG+ $215, #38VG $165; **Incredible Hulk** #1VF+ $6,875, FN+ $3,800, GD+ $600, #2VG+ $440, #4VF $540, #6GD+ $160, #105NM $60; **Journey Into Mystery** #83VF+ $8,000, VF $2420, GD $330, #109VF $80;

X-Men #1 in NM, a red hot book, goes for $10,500!

Men's Adventures #27VG $250; Silver Surfer #1VF+ $415, #4VF+ $360; Sub-Mariner #42GD+ $195; Tales Of Suspense #39FN $750, #40GD+ $135, #49FN $70; Tales To Astonish #27FN+ $700, #32VF+(WM) $275; Thor #158NM+ $100; X-Men #1NM $10,500, VF+ $8,000, FN $1,100, #2VF+ $635, VG $260, #3VF+ $380, FN+ $250, #5VF+ $330, #19NM $105, #22NM+ $85, #27NM+ $85, #30NM+ $100, #62VF+ $60; Young Men #24VG $700, #28FN $340, VG+ $250.

DELL-GOLD KEY - Average sales overall. TV titles such as **Twilight Zone** and cartoon titles like **Atom Ant** and **Astro Boy** were hot. UFO and flying saucer books were also hot.

BRONZE AGE: The 1970s books are now over 20 years old and the marketplace is beginning to focus on numerous titles from this period. Increased demand was reported for '70s oversize books such as **DC 100 Page Giants**, their 52-page 25 cent cover books, and Treasury size books from both Marvel & DC. A **DC 100 Page Super Spectacular** #5 (Love Stories) in VG+ sold for $45 and a VF+ copy brought $125! This indicates that some of the scarce and obscure books from this period are on the move. Other hot books are **Weird War Tales** #1-10 (a #1 in VF+ sold for $90!), **Weird Western Tales**, **Witching Hour**, **Dark Mansion of Forbidden Love** #1-4, **Secrets Of Sinister House**, **Sinister House of Secret Love**, **DC Super Special** (especially S-13 & the romance issues), and **Night Nurse**. **Hot Wheels** and **All Star Western** #10 (1st Johan Hex) were very hot! The last 5 issues of **Adventures Of Jerry Lewis** were also requested as well as **Leave It To Binky** and the non reprint issues (#11-16) of **Outlaw Kid**. Other titles that sold in high grade were: **Combat Kelly**, **Crazy**, **Creatures On The Loose**, **Monsters On The Prowl**, **Red Wolf**, **Western Gunfighters**, **Where Monsters Dwell**, etc. The two most noted books from this period were **Giant Size X-Men** #1 and **X-Men #94** with **Incredible Hulk** #181 not far behind. NM copies of **GS X-Men** brought $500 with no resistance. **All Star Western** #10 (Jonah Hex), **Adventure** #381, #428(Supergirl & Black Orchid), **Ghosts** #1, later issues of **House of Mystery** and **House of Secrets**, and **Superman** #233, were also hot books. It seems the Bronze Age is finally coming of age! Reported sales: **Giant Size X-Men** #1NM $385, $330; **Incredible Hulk** #181VF $220, FN+ $275, FN+ $155; **X-Men** #94VF+ $285, #95NM+ $100.

SUMMATION: It is becoming more evident that the availability of certain Golden Age titles and issues is clearly diminishing and demand far outstrips supply. This has been true of many early superhero comics for several years, but now the phenomenon is occurring elsewhere. For example, early pre-Barks editions of **Walt Disney's Comics and Stories**, particularly in higher grades, were not showing up on the market as often. The same may be said of strip reprint comics such as **Crackajack**, **The Funnies**, **Super** and **Popular**.

It has been reported to us that the public's perception of collectible comics can be interesting. Most people who discover a cache of old books, and who offer them for sale, first purchase **Overstreet** and research the value of what they have. Unfortunately, some sellers do not understand that market demand varies dramatically from title to title. They do not realize that one will hold **Porky Pig** for sale much longer than **Superman** and that a dealer cannot pay the same percentage of the Guide for slow movers as he may for books that sell quickly. Unfortunately, in some cases the seller decides not to sell due to the low offer created by slow movers in their collection. Another problem with the uninitiated is with grading.

Later issues of **House of Mystery** are HOT, HOT, HOT!
© DC

Giant Size X-Men #1 is a top Bronze Age book!
© MEG

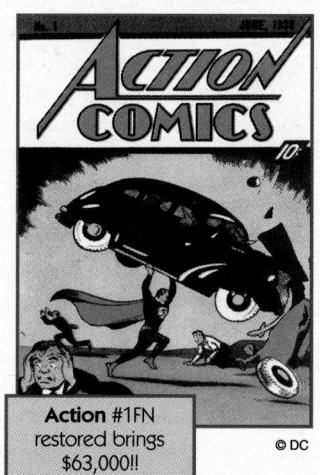

Action #1FN restored brings $63,000!!
© DC

They expect to get a value based on the Near Mint price listed in the Guide when the collection is usually in lower grade.

Flash #105NM
brings $9,775!!
© DC

CHRISTIE'S COMIC COLLECTIBLES SALE A HIT!
by Joe Mannarino

Christie's held its sixth Comic Collectibles Sale on November 1, 1996 at its New York showroom. The sale was a huge success as all segments of the market scored with big hits. Silver Age comics, Golden Age comics, Silver Age art, Golden Age art, Disney, comic strip art, fantasy/sci-fi and premiums did exceptionally well. Much of the success can be attributed to Christie's policy of limiting the number of lots, choosing to emphasize a balanced sale without the overkill that tends to dilute interest and prices. As opposed to other concerns, Christie's feels that when sales surpass four hours in length and offer an excessive number of lots and items within those lots, pre-sale publicity is diffused, advertising resources are quickly exhausted, duplicate and similar items compete with each other and consigners are left with poor results. The publicity that follows affects market prices, which can be misrepresented. This of course impacts all collectors and the field. With this in mind, Christie's has endeavored in all the areas of collectibles in which they are involved--posters, Hollywood and pop memorabilia, animation, toys and sports--to limit the number of items while increasing quality and focus. These decisions were substantiated as the attention and excitement created by 400 lots created intense interest. The result was superior prices across the entire spectrum.

Highlights include: Golden Age books: **Action** #1 in FN (68) moderate rest. est. $40,000-50,000-$63,000. Silver Age books: **Flash** #105 estimated at $2,500-$3,500 in NM (93) - $9,775. Golden Age art: Schomburg recreation **Captain America** #28 est. $3,000-5000-$11,500. Silver Age art:

Gottfredson **"Mickey Mouse in the Race For Riches"** painting fetches $29,900!!
© WDC

Jack Kirby splash page est. $6,000-8,000, **Fantastic Four** #51-$14,950. Comic strip art: Winsor McCay, **Little Nemo** 1910 - $21,850. Disney: Floyd Gottfredson's painting "Mickey Mouse in the Race for Riches"- $29,900. Fantasy/ Sci-Fi: Frazetta Arcanum book, pencil illustration-$11,500. Premiums: Gold Collection, **Three Stooges** promotion est. $3,000-4000 - $13,225.

Golden Age Comics: Action #1 restored FN (68) realized $63,000; Mile High **All Star** #1 NM (94) $34,500; **Action Comics** #7 restored FN+(73) estimated at $2,000-2,500 brought $4,830; **Superboy** #1 restored FN+(69) $1,700; **Detective Comics** #58,60,61 and 62 overall FN+(61) estimated $2,000-2,500 sold for $3,450; **The Submariner** #1 VG (44) $3,220; **Green Lantern** #1 VG (45) $4,025; **Batman** #33,73 and **Green Lantern** #10 estimated at $1,000-1,500 brought $2,070; **Superman** #53-58,65,66 and 76 offered with **Superboy** #10,17 and 20 overall FN+(69) $3,450 and **Batman** #3,4,5 and 6 overall GD-

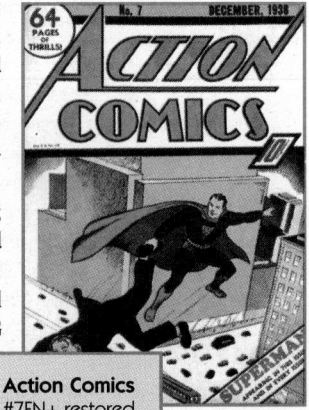

Action Comics
#7FN+ restored
brings $4,830!
© DC

A-54

$1,840.

Overview: The Golden Age market remained strong with high grade books from DC still topping well-heeled collectors' lists. **Superman** regained his position atop the world of comics with **Batman** close behind. Interest continued to sway between these behemoths with the release of feature films. Interestingly, low grade books which have historically performed well seem to have slowed; opportunities available here. The sale also featured one of the few offerings at a major auction of a DC first from the Edgar Church (Mile High) collection of comics. **All Star Comics** #1 realized $34,500, over three times Guide and likely a record price for the book.

Silver Age Comics: Christie's was pleased to offer property from a Big Apple Collection. The collection included Silver Age books, many in unread condition. Interestingly, not all the books were of similar condition as some, including the **Flash** #105 and **Showcase** #19, were stored in manila envelopes, while others were simply stacked in a closet exposing them to light. The results reflected condition: **Showcase** #19 NM (93) estimated at $1,500-2,000 realized $4,370; **Flash** #105 NM (93) estimated at $2,500-3,500 sold for a whopping $9,775; **Showcase** #14 VF (84) estimated at $2,000-2,500 sold for $5,750; **Amazing Fantasy** #15 FN+ (70) $5,750; **Showcase** #8 VF -(76) $4,025; **The Incredible Hulk** #1,2,4, and 5 overall VF- (76) $6,900; **Tales of Suspense** #1 and 2 VF- (77)

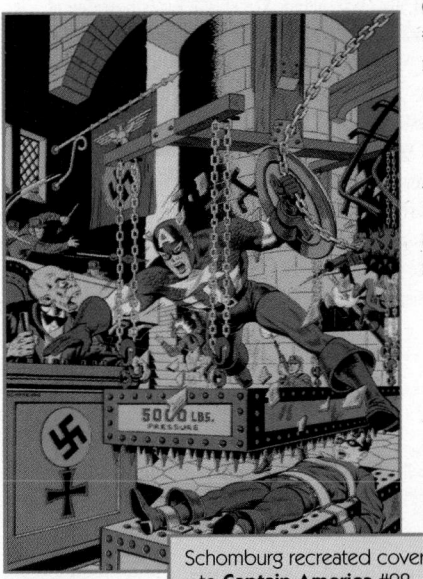

© MEG

Schomburg recreated cover to **Captain America** #28 brings $11,500!!

estimated at $800-$1,200 brought $1,955; **Showcase** #23, 29, 38 and 39 overall VF- (77) $1,150. Other prices realized include: **Fantastic Four** #2-10 overall FN- (60) $4,370; Bethlehem copy of **Strange Tales** #1 FN+ (73) $2,530; the Bethlehem copy of **Showcase** #10 NM (91) $6,900; **Adventure Comics** #103 NM (94) $5,750; **Amazing Spider-Man** #9, 10, 13 and 14 estimated at $2,500-3,000 sold for $4,025; 30 issues of **Amazing Spider-Man** beginning with #15 overall VF (82) $5,060; **Showcase** #4 VG (52) $3,450; **The Avengers** #1 NM (90) $2,990; **Amazing Spider-Man** #1 restored FN +(70) $2,530 and **Amazing Fantasy** #15 restored FN+ (70) $2,300.

Overview: As seems obvious by these results, the Silver Age market remained very strong for fresh, high grade material among knowledgeable collectors. Evidence of the downturn in the new comic market finally seemed to manifest itself in some back issues. In past years, sales of restored or mid-grade Marvels were brisk as current readers looked to fill in the key books with solid copies that did not have to be in the stratosphere of price or condition. With the current decline of modern titles, this segment of the market has also withdrawn. There seems little doubt that it should bounce back when we ride out this malaise.

Golden Age Art: Some highlights from the newly discovered Kozlak collection included: The Kubert Flash page from **Flash Comics** #72 realized $4,025; Jack Burnley page from **All Star** #9 sold for $4,025; Splash from **All American Comics** #55 brought $2,530; Alex Schomburg recreation from **Captain America** #28 estimated at $3,000-5,000 realized $11,500.

Overview: This segment of the market has yet to really take off. With a lack of material available, collectors have not really explored Golden Age art. The historical significance is undeniable. The campy quality of much of this early work was of course the predecessor of the slicker more realistic art of the Silver Age and today. Perhaps as more collectors continue to explore the roots of comics, they will come to better appreciate the rarity and significance of this enchanting era.

Silver Age Art : Jack Kirby began his career in the late 1930s at the inception of the comic industry. He was one of the chief architects of the genre leading it through its Golden Age, engineering its Silver Age and pioneering

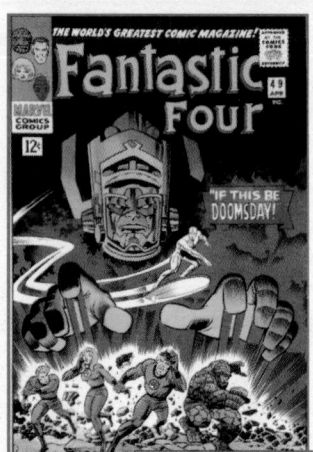

THE WORLD'S GREATEST COMIC MAGAZINE!

Fantastic Four

"IF THIS BE DOOMSDAY!"

© MEG

Original recreated cover art to **Fantastic Four** by Joe Sinnot sells for $3,680!

its Modern Age. Key examples of Marvel art lead by Jack Kirby and Steve Ditko continue to perform extraordinarily well. Jack Kirby's splash page to **Fantastic Four** #51 inked by Joe Sinnott, estimated at $6,000-8,000 realized $14,950; Steve Ditko's splash page **Amazing Spider-Man** #8 realized $12,650; pages #4,5,11 and 12 also from **Amazing Spider-Man** #8 sold for $6,325; eight other pages sold for $10,800; page #20 from **Amazing Spider-Man** #21 sold for $3,680. Cover recreations rendered by the original Silver Age artists out-performed all expectations. Jim Steranko's recreation of **Nick Fury Agent Of Shield** #6 cover estimated at $4,000-6,000 realized $10,350. Dick Ayers' recreation with coloring by the original colorist, Stan Goldberg, of **Fantastic Four** #3 estimated at $1,000-1,500 brought $2,990. Joe Sinnott's recreation with coloring by Marie Severin, estimated at $2,000-3,000 realized $3,680 . Chic Stone's recreation of **Sgt. Fury and his Howling Commandos** #13 estimated at $1,500-2,000 sold for $2,990. Gil Kane's recreation of **Showcase** #22 brought $3,220. Kirby's original art for the National Cartoonists Portfolio sold for $6,900; pages #14 and 17 from **Avengers** #6 estimated at $800-1,200 realized $2,300; page #12 from **Fantastic Four** #15 $1,725; page #11 from **Journey Into Mystery** #112 estimated at $800-1,200 realized $1,725; Neal Adams cover, **Detective** #418, $3,680; a specialty piece by Steranko realized $3,680; a Wally Wood splash from **Daredevil** #11, $2,300.

Overview: The market for Marvel art adjusted from where it was just two years ago. In past years few examples became available to the average collector. As pieces came to market they were quickly scooped up with little regard as to content and significance. As prices rose, more loose pages became available, and collectors became more selective. The result is that better examples realized a premium price, while the price for average or below average pages dipped.

Strip Art: Winsor McCay, one of the fathers of the comic art form, was an undisputed genius whose work influenced all those who have followed. **Little Nemo**, considered by many the greatest fantasy cartoon ever created, embodies the restless imagination within all of us. Each week his exploits would send the reader on a wondrous roller coaster journey, rich in color, wrought with design and enthralling in its beauty and originally published in the **New York Herald** The legendary William Randolph Hearst added another gem to his crown of noted cartoonists when in 1911, he persuaded McCay to join his **New York America**. We were proud to present examples directly from the McCay estate. A Winsor McCay **Little Nemo In Slumberland** dated 1910 from the classic airship sequence, in excellent condition sold for $21,850, a second partial page dating back to 1906 brought $9,775. Two **Dreams of the Rarebit Fiends** fetched $2,875 each and a third brought $3,220; an editorial car-

Little Nemo original from 1910 hammers at $21,850!!

toon realized $1,725. Other newspaper comic strip original art performed equally well. Charles Schulz's **Peanuts** remains very hot. A specialty drawing by Schulz estimated at $700-900 sold for $1,265; two **Peanuts** Sundays, one from 1956 sold for $4,600 and the other from 1978 sold for $5,175 and a **Peanuts** daily from 1964 estimated at $1,000-1,500 brought $2,530. Also offered were two Hogarth Sundays, both from 1944. One estimated at $2,500-3,000 went for $4,370, while the other estimated at $2,000-2,500 sold for $4,140. An early, Al Taliaferro **Silly Symphony** Sunday realized $5,175 while a Floyd Gottfredson **Mickey Mouse** daily from 1937 sold for $5,750. A **Krazy Kat** Sunday from 1943 estimated at $2,000-3,000 brought $5,520 while a daily from 1941 estimated at $1,200-1,500 sold for $2,415. Al Capp's **Li'l Abner** was very popular! Examples from 1940 (8 dailies) estimated at $1,200-1,800 realized $2,070; examples from 1950 (10 dailies) sold for $1,840 and examples from 1944, 1945 and 1948 (9 dailies) sold for $2,530. A Frazetta **Johnny Comet** daily from the first year of the strip sold for $1,840.

Overview: The market for newspaper comic strip art was the strongest that it has been in years. In the past, a handful of collectors dominated the market, focusing on Raymond, Foster and Herriman, pushing prices to lofty levels. When one or two of these major players departed, the market followed. Today there is a broader base of collectors with interest in many features and artists. While the prices for Raymond and Foster have not returned to those heady days, artists such as McCay, Schulz, Herriman, Gould, Gottfredson, Hogarth, Segar and a dozen more were very much in demand.

Disney: Floyd Gottfredson's "Mickey Mouse in the Race for Riches," a 1980 commissioned piece, sold for $29,900. A Carl Barks pencil drawing depicting **Uncle Scrooge** in the money bin with his nephews sold for $2,875. A Barks cover rough for an **Uncle Scrooge** comic estimated at $1,000-1,500 sold for $2,530. A pencil on tissue depicting Uncle Scrooge fleeing from the Beagle Boys sold for $1,495. Another pencil on tissue depicting Donald, Daisy, Pluto and one of the nephews estimated at $700-900 sold for $2,990. A Bibo and Lang Mickey Mouse book sold for $2,185.

Fantasy and Sci-Fi Art: The first ever offering from Frank Frazetta's Arcanum book, pencil on paper sold for $11,500 as well as a Frazetta pen and ink depicting **The Phantom** brought $3,220. Boris Vallejo's painting, "Tarzan The Untamed" from the 1978 Tarzan calendar, sold for $3,220 while Vallejo's "Tarzan and the Golden Lion" brought $5,750. J. Allen St. John's cover art for "Tarzan and the Lion Man" fetched $8,625. John R. Neil's original art for "The Patchwork God Of Oz" estimated at $3,500-4,000 sold for $4,830.

Premiums: The Gordon K. Gold premium collection was a big success. Gordon Gold and his father, Sam Gold, were the originators and producers of radio, cereal and movie premiums, displays and innovative children's books in the United States from 1920 through 1974. Many holes in the history of premiums were filled with the unveiling of this treasure trove. The Golds were creators of many ingenious books including the rare **Mickey Mouse** and **Wizard Of Oz** waddle books as well as the innovative comic character pop up books. It was with this knowledge of cleverly engineered lithography that Sam Gold, in the 1930s, pioneered promotions for radio and cereal companies in the form of bonuses or premiums. It all began with radio shows such as **Radio Orphan Annie** sponsored by Ovaltine and moved into films with the **Three Stooges**. Cereal companies quickly followed, creating an industry and a pop-culture phenomenon. In the early 1940s they created what is considered the most popular premium campaign of all time - an 86 button comic character pin-back button set produced for Kellogg's Pep cereal. By the 1950s the Golds pioneered the traffic builder, an incentive program for major manufactures such as Sylvania TV and General Electric. What made this collection so unique is that aside from the rare premiums that were included, Gold maintained original art, mock-ups and rare one of a kind display items. Posters, window cards, die cut standees and counter displays were all there. Some highlights: **Superman Pep** pin art offered with a **Pep** pin die-cut display sold for $5,175; **Hopalong Cassid**y trading cards promotion estimated at $2,000-3,000 realized $2,990; **Superman** full color display poster $4,025; two lots of **The Three Stooges** Moving Picture Machine Promotion estimated at $3,000-4,000 realized $13,225 each; a **Funny Face** National Premium promotion estimated at $1,500-2,000 sold for $3,105; **Buck Rogers Space Ranger** promotion realized $3,220; a **Davy Crockett** patches promotion sold for $1,610. It was very obvious that premiums that featured comic characters had tremendous cross-over appeal.

Sotheby's Sixth Comic Book and Comic Art Auction, June 28th and 29th, 1996
by Jerry Weist, Sotheby's comic book consultant

Sotheby's sixth comic book and comic art auction was another two day affair with 707 lots representing the entire history of the comic book medium. This auction featured total sales of $1,797,363, falling short of the over two million dollar figure realized with Sotheby's fifth comic book auction. However it stands as the second largest sale of its kind and in many ways represents important changes for our market.

First and foremost the Golden Age comic book market finally came down to earth, and prices for restored comics and especially restored key issues slipped from their high orbits into a LEO (lower earth orbit), or for those who need a clearer description - prices realized were down! Examples abound and a few are listed here. Two years ago a Fine restored copy of **All Winners** #1 sold for $4,600 while this year a FN restored copy of the same book hammered at $2,300. Two years ago a VF- restored **Sub-Mariner** #1 sold for $4,600 and this year an apparent restored FN copy of **Sub-Mariner** #1 hammered at $1,725! The most remarkable example took place within the Silver Age section when a copy of **Showcase** #4 restored to FN+, along with a copy of **Amazing Fantasy** #15 restored to FN- sold for an amazing $2,300! These three examples represent specifics for an overview that unfolded on the second day Saturday auction. Does this mean that comics are going to "crash," or does it mean that no one should ever again have any comic book restored? Several factors are involved here, and it should be stated for the public record

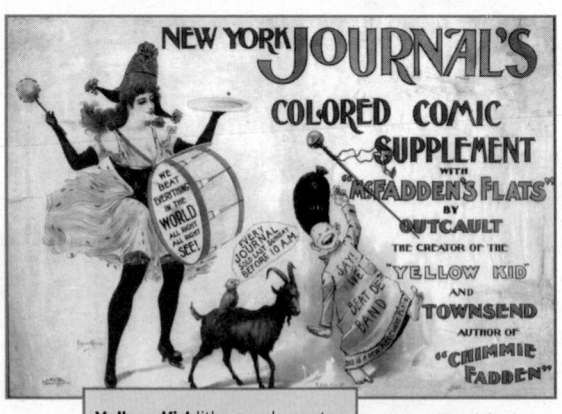

Yellow Kid lithograph poster, late 1890s sells for $5,750!

that Sotheby's comic book auction was pushed further into the summer because of the Jackie Kennedy Auction that held court for the better part of three weeks during May of 1996. In addition to this later date of June 28th and 29th, the Chicago Comic book convention was moved up in time, because the Republican National Convention had pushed San Diego out of their traditional August date. So hard core fans had to fly to Chicago, fly back to NYC, and then fly out to San Diego to attend the three major events of the summer. Few people made all three events, and several had burned out by the Sotheby's auction. Too much of a good thing within too short of a time made for a smaller bidding crowd at this particular auction.

Despite these facts however, what is important to note about the prices for Golden Age and Silver Age comics is the following. During the "boom" of the past five years, many dealers were selling out of the more common GA titles (such as **Superman** #4-13, **Batman** #5-20, etc.) and they were having an especially hard time locating the rarer titles and numbers (such as **Adventure** #40-45, or **More Fun** #53-63) in any kind of condition. This situation caused the market to witness higher and higher prices for lower grade copies, and fundamentally silly prices for restored keys. This particular trend was reinforced at public auctions where the public was pushing prices for key Golden Age titles and certain Silver Age books up and up . The best remembered examples for un-restored books were the sales for **Amazing Fantasy** #15 from the White Mountain collection for $39,000, and the un-restored copy of **Detective Comics** #27 in VG49 with a small tear to the spine hammering for $69,000. The best remembered examples for restored comics were for **Action Comics** #1 in apparent restored VF- selling for $75,900, and a copy of **Marvel Comics** #1 restored with a tear to cover spine, selling for $41,400.

In today's market "both" of the restored books would sell for less, and in addition, the White Mountain copy of **Amazing Fantasy** #15 would sell for less and the un-restored copy of **Detective Comics** #27 would most likely sell for more. This defines our market exactly and where it is headed in the future. In other words, as the market slows down the lower grade copies and especially restored books come under fire. Within the Silver Age, restored books are especially taking a beating. The extreme highs of the late 1980s and early 1990s with Silver Age keys may be in for a

Yellow Kid composition head squeaker doll sells for $1,150!

short term adjustment, however the prime Golden Age comic books in UN-RESTORED condition are still climbing! Basically with a little bit of sobriety, and a short fall of money, the market comes back into a more realistic focus. What is really rare, and what do collectors "really" want? They want early Golden Age comic books in VG+to VF unrestored condition; this is what they feel most secure with and this is where the savvy and experienced collectors are still putting their money. There is really nothing new or novel with this defined trend; simply, collectors want value for money and they are through spending impossible sums of cash chasing the illusion of rarity.

Once we get past analyzing this important trend, the fact remains that Sotheby's sixth auction was remarkable for a number of reasons. Long time comic art collector Pete Koch recently said that he had never in his life seen so much quality original artwork offered for sale at one time. Not only did this sale host some important original Golden Age covers from the collection of Roy Thomas, but the real surprise took place on Friday when the collection of Didier Moiselet's Robert Crumb originals were brought to sale.

Friday began with the once-in-a-lifetime opportunity for collectors to bid on the early premiums from the collection of Craig Koste, featuring the **Yellow Kid**, the first comic book character. Total sales for the first 31 lots (most of these collectibles were from 1895 to 1901!) were just over $50,000. There were European buyers as well as American for the **Yellow Kid** pins, toys, and posters, and bid-

Li'l Folks original Sunday page dated 7/24/49 by Schulz sells for $17,250!!

Fritz the Cat cover original by R. Crumb sells for an unbelieveable $56,350!

ding was spirited. After **YK** came the newspaper strip original artwork and some of the biggest surprises were with unexpected originals. A daily **Barney Google** dated 8/20/31 by Billy DeBeck estimated at $750-$1,000 sold for an unprecedented $7,475! A rare and early Charles Schulz **Li'l Folks** Sunday format original estimated at $2,500-$4,500 hammered for $17,250. And the crowd was surprised by a late offering of a rare hand-colored Sunday by Waterson for **Calvin & Hobbs** which sold for $7,475. A Windsor McCay bottom tier to a **Little Nemo in Slumberland** estimated at $2,000-$4,000 went down on the block for $8,575. All this took place while a full Sunday Raymond **Flash Gordon** failed at its $14,000 reserve and an absolutely "killer" Sunday Foster **Tarzan** estimated at $5,000-$7,000 sold for a mere $5,750.

After newspaper strip original artwork came premiums, and some sales of note follow. A standing **Popeye** Pipe Display from 1934, in FN, sold for $1,150. The **Buck Rogers** Repeller Ray Premium Ring in FN sold for $1,495. After premiums, a short selection of science fiction and fantasy artwork was auctioned and the first lot offered was Frank Frazetta's original oil painting for "Savage World," selling for $74,750. A small preliminary Frazetta watercolor for a King Kong painting sold for $5,460. Virgil Finlay originals did well, however originals by H. R. Giger, Basil Gogos, and Roy Krenkel failed to meet their reserve prices.

The Friday session was brought to a close by the Robert Crumb artwork offered from the collection of Didier Moiselet, a French collector who had built his collection in the early 1970s and 1980s. Estimates were high and no one knew where the bidding was headed, and additionally there was a very large offering. The first important offering was Crumb's original cover for **Zap** #0 from 1967 estimated at $20,000 to $30,000 (collectors should keep in mind that this estimate is higher than any estimate for any previous Golden Age comic book cover from "any" Sotheby's auction). The bidding climbed to an amazing $46,000. However, a few lots later, the room was shocked into a hushed

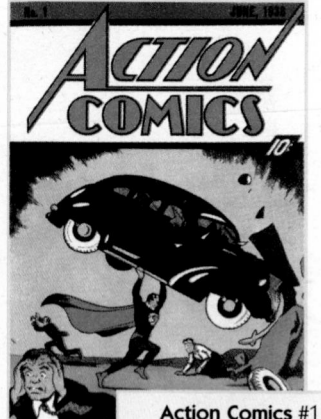

Rare **Superman** war bond poster brings $14,950!

© DC

reverence when the cover for **Fritz The Cat** from the 1969 Ballantine paperback book (this original was unsigned!), estimated at an incredible $35,000-$45,000, sold for $56,350! This price stands as a world record for any comic book cover, and is a price most likely to stand for quite some time. By the time the bidding was over for the 22 lots of R. Crumb artwork, just over $250,000 had been spent! A remarkable day at auction for a single artist.

The Friday session, with just the **Yellow Kid** collection, the newspaper strip artwork, premiums, SF and fantasy artwork, and the R. Crumb collection, had totaled $692,725, and not one comic book had yet been sold.

Saturday began with a bigger crowd and prices began briskly with a **Superman** War Bond Savings Poster from the 1940s in VG condition estimated at $8,000-$10,000 selling for $14,950, and a

Action Comics #1 in apparent VF84 (restored) sells at $62,100!

© DC

All Star cover art to #50 hammers at $6,900!

restored copy of **Superman** #1 in apparent FN65 selling for $11,500. Then prices began to settle in for the restored comics with the following examples taking place. **Green Lantern** #1 in apparent VF80 sold for $5,175, while **Detective Comics** #28 in restored FN74 sold for $4,025. **Batman** #1 in apparent restored VF79, estimated at $7,000-$9000, sold for $7,600 and a restored copy of **Action Comics** #1 in apparent VF84 sold for $62,100, down from the high $70,000+ price of the previous year. However, among this adjustment the following examples still tell us where unrestored high grade important Golden Age books are headed... and the direction is UP! **Action Comics** #2 in unrestored FN55, estimated at $4,000-$8,000, sold for $16,100!! **Action Comics** #7 in unrestored FN58 estimated at $2,500-$5,500 sold for $12,650! All of the **Action Comics** copies from #2 through #9 in unrestored condition sold for very healthy prices. Then a lot that seemed buried in the auction, **Action Comics** #13 and **Superman** #7 in unrestored FN66 estimated at $1,500-$2,500 sold for $9,200! The signal here is apparent (no pun intended).

The remainder of the Golden Age offering, which was deep and ran across many different publishers, saw mixed results, with the unrestored lots faring well above estimates for the most part.

Virtually every Golden Age original cover offered on Saturday sold. The cover for **All Star Comics** #54 by Peddy and Sachs from the collection of Roy Thomas sold for $8,625, and the cover for **All Star Comics** #50 by Peddy and Sachs from the collection of Roy Thomas sold for $6,900. The finest example of Lou Fine's work ever brought to auction, the cover for **Hit** #5, sold for $16,675, and Schomburg covers for **All New** #10 sold for $4025, while the cover for **Green Hornet** #20 brought $4,312. Even **Wonder Woman** flew on this day with an unpublished cover circa 1940s bringing $5,750.

Sotheby's ended its first Saturday session with EC pre-trend covers, and began its second session with EC artwork. This offering will most likely be the last "large" offering of EC artwork from the Gaines Vault to be brought to Sotheby's

Cover art to **Hit Comics** #5 by Lou Fine gets $16, 675!

since Russ Cochran has started up again with his own EC comic art auctions. EC comics and original artwork have always been BLUE CHIP investments from the very beginnings of comic fandom. Anyone buying an original Wally Wood **Weird Science** cover from the first few Cochran auctions and then selling in the current Sotheby's 1990 market would experience a jump from $1,500 to $25,000! What bond or stock can boast such a performance? This year the EC highlights were many, Al Feldstein's cover for **3-D Tales From The Crypt Of Terror**, sold for $6,037; Wally Wood's cover for **Tales From The Crypt** #26 sold for $8,575; Reed Crandall's cover for the Picto Fiction **Terror Illustrated** #1 sold for $8,500; and Al Feldstein's pre-trend cover for **War Against Crime** #11 sold for $4,025. All pre-trend covers and stories did quite well, and some other exceptional works were Frank Frazetta's cover painting for **Tales From The Crypt** selling at $27,600, while a Frazetta original inking from "Pellucidar" brought $14,950 and an Al Williamson inking

Original cover for **Superman** #170 sells for $5,750!

for a **Flash Gordon** scene hammered at $12,650. The real star of the day for EC however was reserved for the Gaines File Copy set of **Mad** comics #1-23. This **Mad** lot was estimated at $25,000-$35,000 and brought the house down with a final price of $44,850! Again it

must be noted that a normal run of **Mad** in VF (nothing to scoff at) would sell for most likely $7,500 to $8,500 at auction - look what happened with the Gaines file copies in an A.C.G. grade of NM93.

EC was followed by the Silver Age collections which closed the sixth auction out on Saturday. There were some VF groups of Silver Age comics, but in point of fact no really remarkable high grade runs or key issues in this auction. The Bethlehem copy of **Showcase** #8 was the exception to this rule, and it failed to sell at its reserve of just under $17,000. Runs of **Superman, Batman, Detective, Blackhawk**, and other DC titles did very well when condition held, when it did not the results were soft. Marvel pre-hero groups in lower grades sold for very little money, and a very curious result was a high grade run of unrestored pre-hero titles selling for under the low end! An unrestored copy of **Amazing Fantasy** #15 in FN71 sold for $6,325, and this sums up the recent Silver Age market!

Silver Age original artwork, on the other hand, is another story! The cover for Murphy Anderson's **Brave And The Bold** #61 sold for $17,250, much higher than most Golden Age covers sell for, and Murphy's cover for **Hawkman** #1 sold for $11,500! A Jack Kirby pre-hero splash page sold for $4,312, and the Jack Kirby/Joe Sinnott

Fantastic Four cover for #65 sold for $12,650, with a splash page from **Fantastic Four** #17 by Kirby and Ayers selling for $9,775! But the top was really blown off the market when the original artwork for Don Heck and Jack Kirby (concept pencils) to **Tales Of Suspense** #39, the origin story for Iron Man, sold for an amazing $46,000! This lot included the re-creation cover that Jack did for **Suspense** #39, but it must be stated that if any other origin story from Marvel were to appear at Sotheby's the roof would most likely be blown off again.

PACIFIC COMIC EXCHANGE, INC.
1996 Year in Review
by Robert J. Roter

Pacific Comic Exchange, Inc. ("PCE") specializes exclusively in vintage comic books and operates in the same manner as a real estate brokerage house. Prices are negotiable between buyer and seller and all sales are documented through the PCE Monthly Listing Report.

1996 saw a slow-down in the comic market from the previous record year. It was the first year in the last five

All Select #1VG+
sells for $2,000!

© MEG

that sales actually declined. The comic market had continued to expand at a record pace until late 1995. Though the market was relatively slow it was still healthy overall. Many good sales were recorded and high quality books tended to sell quickly if priced competitively.

In general, Golden Age books tended to sell at Guide in low to mid grades. In high grades these books would bring premiums over Guide ranging from 10-50%. Golden Age books in NM would still bring 1.5 to 2 times Guide. Silver Age books would sell at 70-80% of Guide in low to mid grade and 80-100% of Guide in high grade. NM Silver Age would bring full-1.5 times Guide.

Sample sales for 1996 (prices include the 10% buyers commission) are listed below. All books are reported in the Comic Grading Standard of America ("CGSA") grading scale with the Page Quality (PQ) rating: (Terms: S: slight, L: light, M: moderate, E: extensive,a: appearance , t: trimmed.)

All Top #8NM
brings $1,200!

© FOX

Action Comics #1, Fr 6 (5.5) $22,000; **Action Comics** #1, M taFN-35(5.5) $28,600; **Action Comics** #4, VG/FN 30 (5.5) $4,620; **Action Comics** #6, M aVG 20 (5.5) $1,800; **Action Comics** #7, Jerry Siegel collection, Fr 6 (5.5) $1,875; **Action Comics** #8, VG/FN 30 (5.0) $5,000; **Action Comics** #9, Court Case copy, VG 20 (5.0) $2,530; **Action Comics** #10, Jerry Siegel collection, Fr 6 (6.0), $1,375; **Action Comics** #11, Court Case copy, VG+ 25 (4.5), $1,925; **Action Comics** #14, VG 20 (5.0), $1,000; **All Star Comics** #8, VG 20 (5.5) $3,850; **All Star Comics** #20, Mile High copy, NM/M 90 (1.0) $5,500; **All Star Comics** #36, VFN+ 65 (3.5) $1,925; **All Top Comics** #8, NM 80 (2.5) $1,200; **All-American Western** #114, Mile High copy, NM 80 (1.0) $64; **All Select Comics** #1, VG/FN 30 (4.5) $2,000; **Amazing Spider-Man** #1, VG/FN 30 (4.0) $1,815; **America's Best Comics** #10, Mile High copy, NM/M 90 (3.3) $1,100; **America's Best Comics** #18, Mile High copy, NM+ 85 (3.0) $1,100; **Batman** #6, FN+ 45 (4.0) $1,330; **Batman** #9, VFN+ 65 (3.0) $4,400; **Batman** #10, FN/VFN 50 (5.0)

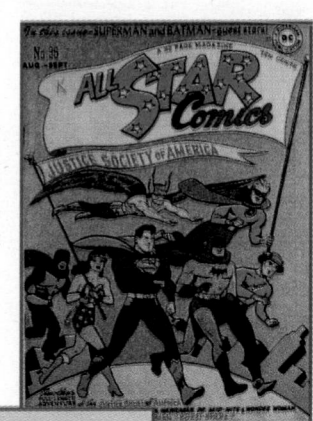

All Star #36VF+
goes for $1,925!

© DC

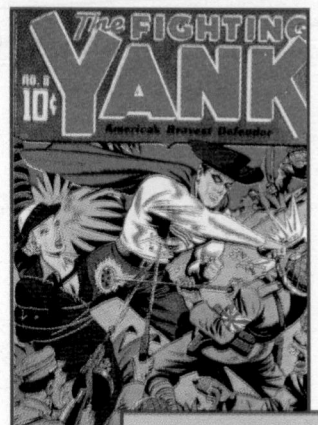

© NEDOR

Fighting Yank #8 (Mile High copy) sells for $1375!

$1,100; **Boy's Ranch** #1, Mile High copy, NM+ 85 (3.3) $1,320; **Brave And The Bold** #34, NM++ 88 (3.5) $4,730; **Captain America Comics** #1, VG+ 25 (5.0) $11,000; **Captain America's Weird Tales** #75, FN+ 45 (4.5) $1,000; **Captain Marvel-Adventures** #26, Mile High copy, NM++ 88 (3.3) $1,265; **Catman Comics** #31, FN/VFN 50 (4.0) $825; **Detective Comics** #2, M aVG/FN 30 (6.0) $4,400; **Detective Comics** #5, G 10 (5.0) $1,760; **Detective Comics** #29, Fr 6 (5.0) $2,100; **Detective Comics** #32, G/VG 15 (5.0) $1,000; **Detective Comics** #84, Pennsylvania copy, NM++ 88 (3.3) $2,530; **Detective Comics** #88, Pennsylvania copy, NM++ 88 (3.0) $2,530; **Detective Comics** #106, Mile High copy, NM/M 90 (3.0) $3,050; **Detective Comics** #155, Mile High copy, NM++ 88 (3.5) $2,560; **Detective Comics** #170, Mile High copy, NM/M 90 (2.5) $2,800; **Detective Comics** #174, Mile High copy, NM++ 88 (3.0) $2,800; **Exciting Comics** #19, Mile High copy, NM++ 88 (2.0) $1,000; **Exciting Comics** #49, Mile High copy, NM/M 90 (3.3) $1,100; **Fighting Yank** #8, Mile High copy, NM+ 85 (2.5) $1,375; **Flash Comics** 104, E aVFN 60 (3.5) $1,375; **Hit Comics** #5, VG/FN 30 (7.0) $1,925; **Human Torch** #2(#1), G 10 (7.0) $2,000; **Incredible Hulk** #1, VFN+ 65 (4.0), $6,875; **Marvel Mystery Comics Annual**, G 10 (4.5) $3,715; **More Fun Comics** #73, FN+ 45 (4.5) $4,950; **More Fun Comics** #101, FN/VFN 50 (4.5) $3,630; **New Adventure Comics** #24, Mile High copy, VF/NM 70 (3.3) $4,000; **New Comics** #8, VFN+ 65 (5.0) $3,025; **New Fun Comics** #2, Fr 6 (8.0) $3,300; **New York World's Fair** 1940, VFN 60 (4.5) $7,260; **Phantom Lady** #17, Overstreet Collection, VFN+ 65 (3.5) $4,500; **Power Comics** #2, VFN 60 (5.0) $1,320; **Showcase** #13, Mohawk Valley copy, VF/VF+ 63 (5.5) $3,300; **Showcase** #14, VFN+ 65 (3.5) $3,630; **Star Spangled Comics** #35, Mile High copy, NM++ 88 (3.0) $1,650; **Superboy** #3, NM 75 (4.5) $1,650; **Superman** #1, M aFN+ 45 (6.0) $12,650; **Superman** #2, Jerry Siegel Collection, G 10 (5.0) $1,000; **Superman** #3, FN- 35 (3.3) $2,200; **Suspense Comics** #11, VFN++ 68 (3.5) $2,750; **Vault Of Horror** #34, Gaines File copy, NM++ 88 (3.3) $660; **Weird Tales Of The Future** #2, VF/NM 70 (4.5) $1,430; **Whiz Comics** #1, Fr 6 (7.5) $3,850; **Wonder Woman** #45, Mile High copy, NM 80 (3.0) $3,000; **Young Allies Comics** #1, VG/FN 30 (4.5) $2,420.

Showcase #14 VF+ sells for $3,630! © DC

In summary, there appeared to be no clear reason as to why the comic market would slow down, given that the overall economy is strong. One theory may be that the stock market has taken money away from the comic market. All year the Dow Jones Industrials and other market indicators continued to set new highs. Nevertheless, we remain very optimistic over the long-term outlook for the comic market.

© SPM

Weird Tales Of The Future #2 VF+ sells for $1,430!

The following tables denote the rate of appreciation of the top Golden Age books and the top Silver Age books, as well as selected genres over the past year and the past six years (1992-1997). The retail value for a NM copy of each book in 1997 is compared to its value in 1996 and 1992. The rate of return for 1997 over 1996 is given. The place in rank is given for each comic by year, with its corresponding NM value. These tables can be very useful in forecasting trends in the market place. For instance, the investor might want to know which book is yielding the best dividend from one year to the next, or one might just be interested in seeing how the popularity of books changes from year to year. For instance, *Adventure Comics* #40 was in 16th place in 1996 and has increased to 13th place in 1997.

The following tables are meant as a guide to the investor. However, it should be pointed out that trends may change at anytime and that some books can meet market resistance with a slowdown in price increases, while others can develop into real comers from a presently dormant state. In the long run, if the investor sticks to the books that are appreciating steadily each year, he shouldn't go very far wrong.

TOP GOLDEN AGE BOOKS
1997 OVER 1996 GUIDE VALUES

Issue No.	1997 Rank	1997 NM Price	1996 Rank	1996 NM Price	$ Incr.	% Incr.
Action Comics #1	1	$160,000	1	$145,000	$15,000	10%
Detective Comics #27	2	$150,000	2	$140,000	$10,000	7%
Superman #1	3	$110,000	3	$100,000	$10,000	10%
Marvel Comics #1	4	$98,000	4	$92,000	$6,000	6%
Detective Comics #1	5	$83,000	5	$83,000	$0	0%
New Fun Comics #1	6	$61,500	6	$56,500	$5,000	9%
All-American Comics #16	7	$60,000	7	$56,000	$4,000	7%
Batman #1	8	$60,000	8	$55,000	$5,000	9%
Whiz Comics #2 (#1)	9	$60,000	9	$55,000	$5,000	9%
Captain America Comics #1	10	$56,000	10	$54,000	$2,000	4%
Flash Comics #1	11	$50,000	11	$45,000	$5,000	11%
More Fun Comics #52	12	$47,000	12	$44,000	$3,000	7%
Adventure Comics #40	13	$32,000	16	$28,000	$4,000	14%
Detective Comics #33	14	$32,000	15	$29,000	$3,000	10%
More Fun Comics #53	15	$32,000	14	$30,000	$2,000	7%
All Star Comics #3	16	$30,000	13	$30,000	$0	0%
New Fun Comics #6	17	$29,000	17	$26,500	$2,500	9%
Detective Comics #38	18	$28,000	18	$26,000	$2,000	8%
Captain Marvel Adventures #1	19	$27,000	19	$25,000	$2,000	8%
New Fun Comics #2	20	$26,000	21	$23,000	$3,000	13%
Green Lantern #1	21	$25,000	20	$23,000	$2,000	9%
All Star Comics #8	22	$24,000	23	$22,000	$2,000	9%
New Comics #1	23	$24,000	22	$22,500	$1,500	7%
New York World's Fair 1939	24	$24,000	24	$22,000	$2,000	9%
Detective Comics #2	25	$23,000	32	$20,000	$3,000	15%
Detective Comics #29	26	$23,000	25	$21,000	$2,000	10%
Detective Comics #31	27	$23,000	26	$21,000	$2,000	10%
Famous Funnies-Series 1 #1	28	$21,000	29	$19,000	$2,000	11%
Human Torch #2 (#1)	29	$21,000	30	$19,000	$2,000	11%
Adventure Comics #48	30	$20,000	35	$17,000	$3,000	18%
Big Book of Fun Comics #1	31	$20,000	31	$18,000	$2,000	11%
Sensation Comics #1	32	$20,000	28	$20,000	$0	0%
Sub-Mariner Comics #1	33	$20,000	34	$18,000	$2,000	11%
Jumbo Comics #1	34	$19,200	27	$16,800	$2,400	14%
Marvel Mystery Comics #2	35	$19,000	33	$18,000	$1,000	6%
More Fun Comics #14	36	$19,000	36	$17,000	$2,000	12%
Action Comics #2	37	$18,000	37	$16,000	$2,000	13%
New Book Of Comics #1	38	$18,000	40	$16,500	$1,500	9%
Century Of Comics nn	39	$17,500	38	$16,000	$1,500	9%
Daring Mystery #1	40	$16,500	39	$15,000	$1,500	10%
Detective Comics #3	41	$16,500	47	$15,000	$1,500	10%
Wonder Woman #1	42	$16,500	42	$15,000	$1,500	10%
Marvel Mystery Comics #9	43	$16,000	43	$14,000	$2,000	14%
Walt Disney's Comics & Stories #1	44	$16,000	41	$15,000	$1,000	7%
Motion Picture Funnies Weekly #1	45	$15,000	44	$14,000	$1,000	7%
Amazing Man #5	46	$14,500	46	$13,500	$1,000	7%
Famous Funnies #1	47	$14,500	48	$13,500	$1,000	7%
All Winners #1	48	$14,000	51	$12,000	$2,000	17%
Detective Comics #28	49	$14,000	49	$13,000	$1,000	8%
Four Color Ser. 1 (Mickey Mouse) #16	50	$14,000	45	$13,600	$400	3%
Marvel Mystery Comics #5	51	$14,000	50	$12,500	$1,500	12%
Wonder Comics #1	52	$13,500	53	$12,000	$1,500	13%

Issue No.	1997 Rank	1997 NM Price	1996 Rank	1996 NM Price	$ Incr.	% Incr.
New Fun Comics #3	53	$13,000	61	$12,000	$1,000	8%
New Fun Comics #4	54	$13,000	62	$12,000	$1,000	8%
New Fun Comics #5	55	$13,000	63	$12,000	$1,000	8%
New York World's Fair 1940	56	$13,000	52	$12,000	$1,000	8%
World's Best #1	57	$12,500	54	$11,500	$1,000	9%
Wow Comics #1	58	$12,500	55	$11,500	$1,000	9%
Action Comics #3	59	$12,000	67	$10,000	$2,000	20%
All-American Comics #17	60	$12,000	70	$10,000	$2,000	20%
All-American Comics #19	61	$12,000	56	$11,000	$1,000	9%
All Star Comics #1	62	$12,000	64	$10,500	$1,500	14%
Comics Magazine #1	63	$12,000	57	$11,000	$1,000	9%
Mystic Comics #1	64	$12,000	60	$11,000	$1,000	9%
All Flash #1	65	$11,500	77	$9,800	$1,700	17%
More Fun Comics #55	66	$11,500	59	$11,000	$500	4%
King Comics #1	67	$11,250	83	$9,000	$2,250	25%
Adventure Comics #61	68	$11,000	68	$10,000	$1,000	10%
Adventure Comics #73	69	$11,000	69	$10,000	$1,000	10%
Double Action #2	70	$11,000	71	$10,000	$1,000	10%
Funnies on Parade nn	71	$11,000	73	$10,000	$1,000	10%
Mickey Mouse Magazine #1	72	$11,000	58	$11,000	$0	0%
Batman #2	73	$10,500	78	$9,500	$1,000	10%
Big All-American #1	74	$10,500	74	$10,000	$500	5%
Four Color Ser. 1 (Donald Duck) #4	75	$10,500	72	$10,000	$500	5%
More Fun Comics #73	76	$10,500	76	$10,000	$500	5%
Silver Streak #6	77	$10,500	79	$9,500	$1,000	10%
Action Comics #7	78	$10,000	91	$8,000	$2,000	25%
Adventure Comics #72	79	$10,000	80	$9,000	$1,000	11%
Captain America Comics #2	80	$10,000	81	$9,000	$1,000	11%
Looney Tunes #1	81	$9,500	86	$8,500	$1,000	12%
Silver Streak #1	82	$9,500	88	$8,500	$1,000	12%
Mystery Men #1	83	$9,400	87	$8,500	$900	10%
Red Raven #1	84	$9,400	82	$9,000	$400	4%
Superman #2	85	$9,200	84	$8,700	$500	6%
Young Allies Comics #1	86	$9,200	90	$8,200	$1,000	12%
New Book of Comics #2	87	$9,150	97	$7,800	$1,350	17%
Archie Comics #1	88	$9,000	85	$8,500	$500	6%
Planet Comics #1	89	$9,000	89	$8,200	$800	10%
Suspense Comics #3	90	$9,000	94	$8,000	$1,000	12%
USA Comics #1	91	$9,000	95	$8,000	$1,000	12%
Daredevil #1	92	$8,500	93	$8,000	$500	6%
Green Giant #1	93	$8,000	100	$7,500	$500	7%
More Fun Comics #54	94	$8,000	96	$7,800	$200	2%
Special Edition Comics #1	95	$8,000	101	$7,500	$500	7%
Famous Funnies-Carnival of Comics nn	96	$7,500	98	$7,500	$0	0%
Four Color (Donald Duck) #9	97	$7,500	99	$7,500	$0	0%
Exciting Comics #9	98	$6,000	--	$5,000	$1,000	20%
Feature Book (Dick Tracy) nn (#1)	99	$6,000	65	$6,000	$0	0%
Feature Book (Popeye) nn (#1)	100	$6,000	66	$6,000	$0	0%

Note: The above chart includes books where the highest grade in the listings is a VF price. A NM price has been estimated in each case for the purpose of this chart.

TOP 10 SILVER AGE BOOKS
1997 OVER 1996 GUIDE VALUES

Issue No.	1997 Rank	1997 NM Price	1996 Rank	1996 NM Price	$ Incr.	% Incr.
Amazing Fantasy #15	1	$27,000	1	$26,000	$1,000	4%
Showcase #4	2	$25,000	2	$24,500	$500	2%
Amazing Spider-Man #1	3	$19,000	3	$18,000	$1,000	5%
Fantastic Four #1	4	$18,000	4	$17,000	$1,000	6%
Showcase #8	5	$11,250	5	$10,500	$750	7%
Incredible Hulk #1	6	$11,000	6	$10,000	$1,000	10%
Detective Comics #225	7	$5,000	8	$4,600	$400	9%
X-Men #1	8	$5,000	10	$4,500	$500	11%
Brave And The Bold #28	9	$4,800	12	$4,300	$500	12%
Flash #105(#1)	10	$4,800	9	$4,500	$300	7%

(Genre charts begin on next page)

TOP 10 HORROR COMICS
1997 OVER 1996 AND 1992 GUIDE VALUE

Title Issue#	1997	1996	% change '96 to '97	1992
Vault of Horror 12	$3,500	$3,500	0%	$2,000
Tales of Terror Annual 1	$3,000	$3,000	0%	$2,000
Journey into Mystery 1	$2,300	$2,000	15%	$600
Strange Tales 1	$2,300	$2,000	15%	$750
Crypt of Terror 17	$1,900	$1,900	0%	$1,100
Haunt of Fear 15	$1,900	$1,900	0%	$1,100
Eerie 1	$1,800	$1,500	2%	$350
Crime Patrol 15	$1,700	$1,700	0%	$800
House of Mystery 1	$1,550	$1,400	11%	$500
Tales to Astonish 1	$1,400	$1,300	8%	$450

TOP 10 '50s SCI-FI COMICS
1997 OVER 1996 AND 1992 GUIDE VALUE

Title Issue#	1997	1996	% change '96 to '97	1992
Mystery In Space 1	$2,500	$2,200	14%	$1,300
Strange Adventures 1	$2,200	$2,100	5%	$1,050
Showcase (Adam Strange) 17	$1,950	$1,800	8%	$650
Showcase (Space Ranger) 15	$1,550	$1,400	11%	$400
Fawcett Movie (Man From Planet X) 15	$1,500	$1,400	7%	$1,050
Journey Into Unknown Worlds 36	$1,400	$1,200	17%	$400
Strange Adventures 9	$1,300	$1,200	8%	$700
Weird Fantasy 13	$1,300	$1,300	0%	$700
Weird Science 12	$1,300	$1,300	0%	$725
Weird Science-Fantasy Annual 1952	$1,300	$1,300	0%	$900

TOP 10 WESTERN COMICS
1997 OVER 1996 AND 1992 GUIDE VALUE

Title Issue#	1997	1996	% change '96 to '97	1992
Gene Autry 1	$5,800	$5,200	11%	$1,200
Hopalong Cassidy 1	$4,000	$3,600	11%	$1,000
Lone Ranger Ice Cream 1939	$3,800	$3,500	8%	$1,500
Red Ryder Victory Patrol	$3,400	$3,200	6%	$1,200
Tom Mix Ralston 1	$2,500	$2,200	14%	$850
Red Ryder Comics 1	$2,200	$1,800	22%	$650
Roy Rogers Four Color 38	$1,600	$1,400	14%	$420
Western Picture Stories 1	$1,200	$1,000	20%	$675
Tomahawk 1	$1,150	$900	27%	$475
Gene Autry 2	$935	$850	10%	$450

TOP 10 PREMIUM COMICS
1997 OVER 1996 AND 1992 GUIDE VALUE

Title Issue#	1997	1996	% change '96 to '97	1992
Century of Comics	$17,500	$16,000	9%	$5,000
Motion Picture Funnies Weekly	$15,000	$14,000	7%	(no NM listed)
Funnies on Parade	$11,000	$10,000	1%	$4,500
Famous Funnies-Carnival of Comics	$7,500	$7,500	0%	$4,500
March of Comics #4	$7,000	$6,800	3%	$5,000
Skippy's Own Book of Comics	$5,000	$5,000	0%	$4,500
March of Comics #20	$4,000	$3,800	5%	$2,500
Lone Ranger Ice Cream 1939	$3,800	$3,500	8%	$1,500
Superman Christmas Adventure 1940	$3,500	$3,400	3%	$1,500
Buster Brown 1904	$3,400	$3,200	6%	(no NM listed)

Selected samplings from particular genres. Note the proximity of the starting points (prices) of these selected books.

THE OVERSTREET COMIC BOOK HALL OF FAME
(1933 - 1997)

For decades, historians, collectors and bibliofiles have tried to identify, list and document all the important, trend-setting comic books of the past century. This interesting topic continues to be debated and discussed by experts everywhere. In an attempt to answer these questions, Overstreet would like to nominate the following books to Overstreet's Hall Of Fame. The author invites your critique, comments and ideas concerning the accuracy of this list for future editions. Remember, only the very top books will be considered for inclusion.

PLATINUM AGE
1897 - 1932

Yellow Kid in McFadden's Flats, The, 1897, Dillingham Co. (1st comic book)
Funny Folk, 1899, E.P. Dutton (2nd comic book)
Vaudeville and Other Things, 1900, Blandiard Co. (3rd comic book)
Blackberries, The, 1901, R.H. Russell (Ties as 4th comic book)
Foxy Grandpa, 1901, F.A. Stokes Co. (Ties as 4th comic book)
Pore Li'l Mose, 1902, Cupples & Leon (1st satire book) (1st Cupples & Leon book)
Alphonse & Gaston & Leon, 1903, Hearst's New York American
Buster Brown and His Resolutions, 1903, F.A. Stokes Co. (1st nationally distr. comic)
Happy Hooligan, 1903, Hearst's New York American (1st comic book app.)
Katzenjammer Kids, 1903, Hearst's New York American (1st comic book app.)
Brown's Blue Ribbon Book of Jokes and Jingles, 1904, Brown Shoe Co. (1st comic book premium)
Dreams of the Rarebit Fiend, 1905, Doffield & Co. (Ties as 1st Windsor McCay book)
Little Sammy Sneeze, 1905, New York Herald Co. (Ties as 1st Winsor McCay book)
Buster Brown, 1906, Cupples & Leon (1st C&L series comic)
Little Nemo, 1906, Doffield & Co. by Winsor McCay
3 Funmakers, 1908, Stokes (1st comic to feature more than one character)
Mutt & Jeff, 1910, Ball Publ. (1st

comic book app.)
Comic Monthly, 1922, Embee Dist. Co. (1st monthly newsstand comic)
Funnies, The, 1929, Dell Publ. Co. (1st four-color comic newsstand publ.)
Mickey Mouse Book, 1930, Bibo & Lang (1st Disney licensed book)
Thimble Theatre Starring Popeye, 1931, Sonnet Publ. Co. (1st Popeye book)

PRE-GOLDEN AGE
1933 - May, 1938

Funnies On Parade #nn, 1933, Eastern Color (1st GA comic book)
Century Of Comics #nn, 1933, Eastern Color (2nd GA comic book, 1st 100 pgs.)
Famous Funnies-Carnival Of Comics, nn, 1933, Eastern Color, (3rd GA comic book)
Detective Dan, 1933, Humor Publ. Co. (the book that helped bridge the gap between the PA and SA)
Famous Funnies-Series 1, 1934, Eastern Color, (1st 10 cent comic book)
Famous Funnies #1, 7/34, Eastern Color (1st newsstand comic book)
New Fun Comics #1, 2/35, DC (1st DC comic book)
Big Book Of Fun Comics #1, Spr/35, DC, (1st annual in comics)
New Fun Comics #6, 10/35, DC (1st siegel & Shuster work in comics)
More Fun Comics #14, 10/36, DC (1st Superman prototype at DC, 1st in color)
Detective Comics #1, 3/37, DC (1st issue of title that launched Batman)

GOLDEN AGE
June, 1938 - 1945

Action Comics #1, 6/38, DC (1st Superman and Lois Lane)
Funny Pages #V2#10, 9/38, Centaur (1st Arrow, 1st costumed hero)
Jumbo Comics #1, 9/38, Fiction House (1st Sheena, 1st Fiction House comic book)
Movie Comics #1, 4/39, DC (1st movie comic)
New York World's Fair 1939, 4/39, DC (1st published Sandman story)
Detective Comics #27, 5/39, DC (1st Batman)
Wonder Comics #1, 5/39, Fox (1st Wonderman, 1st Superman imitator)
Superman #nn (#1), Summer/39, DC (1st issue, 1st hero to get his own book)
Adventure Comics #40, 7/39, DC (1st conceived Sandman story)
Marvel Comics #1, 10/39, Timely (1st newsstand Sub-Mariner, 1st Human Torch, 1st Marvel comic)
Silver Streak #1, 12/39, Lev Gleason (1st Gleason comic book, 1st Claw)
Flash Comics #1, 1/40, DC (1st Flash, Hawkman, & Johnny Thunder)
Pep Comics #1, 1/40, MLJ/Archie (1st Shield, 1st patriotic hero)
Planet Comics #1, 1/40, Fiction House (1st all science fiction comic book)
More Fun Comics #52, 2/40, DC (1st Spectre)
Whiz Comics #2 (#1), 2/40, Fawcett (1st Captain Marvel & Spy Smasher, 1st Fawcett comic book)
Adventure Comics #48, 3/40, DC (1st Hourman)
More Fun Comics #53, 3/40, DC (Part II of 1st Spectre story)

Special Edition Comics #1 © FAW

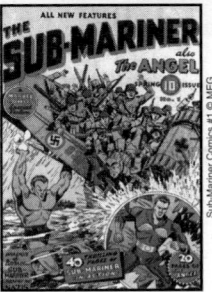

Sub-Mariner Comics #1 © MEG

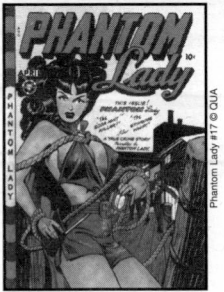

Phantom Lady #17 © QUA

Four Color Ser. 1 (Donald Duck) #4, 3?/40, (1st four color Donald Duck)

Action Comics #23, 4/40, DC (1st Lex Luthor)

Detective Comics #38, 4/40, DC (1st Robin)

Batman #1, Spring/40, DC (1st issue of DC's 2nd most important character; 1st 2 Joker stories; 1st Catwoman)

More Fun Comics #55, 5/40, DC (1st Dr. Fate)

All American Comics #16, 7/40, DC (1st Green Lantern)

Blue Bolt #3, 7/40, Fox (1st Simon & Kirby story art)

Marvel Mystery Comics #9, 7/40, Timely (1st superhero battle; key battle issue)

Red Raven #1, 8/40, Timely (Early Kirby art)

Special Edition Comics #1, 8/40, Fawcett (1st comic book devoted to Captain Marvel)

Silver Streak #6, 9/40, Lev Gleason (1st Daredevil)

Batman #3, Fall/40, DC (1st Catwoman in costume)

Human Torch #2 (#1), Fall/40, Timely (1st issue of early Marvel star)

Walt Disney's Comics & Stories #1, 10/40, Dell (1st funny animal comic book series)

All American Comics #19, 10/40, DC (1st Atom)

All Star Comics #3, Winter/40-41, DC (1st super hero group)

Adventure Comics #72, 3/41, DC (1st Simon & Kirby Sandman)

Captain America Comics #1, 3/41, Timely (1st Captain America)

Captain Marvel Adventures #1, 3/41, Fawcett (1st issue of Fawcett's top character)

Sub-Mariner Comics #1, Spring/41, Timely (1st issue of Marvel's important character)

Adventure Comics #61, 4/41, DC (1st Starman)

All Flash #1, Summer/41, DC (1st issue of top DC character)

Daredevil #1, 7/41, Lev Gleason (1st issue of top character)

Military Comics #1, 8/41, Quality (1st Blackhawk)

Famous Funnies #100, 10/41, Eastern (1st comic book to reach 100)

Green Lantern #1, Fall/41, DC (1st issue of top DC character)

More Fun Comics #73, 11/41, DC (1st Aquaman)

Pep Comics #22, 12/41, MLJ/Archie (1st Archie)

Four Color Ser. 1 (Mickey Mouse) #16, 1941, (1st comic book devoted to Mickey Mouse)

Looney Tunes #1, Fall/41, Dell (1st Bugs Bunny, Porky Pig & Elmer Fudd in comics)

All Star Comics #8, 12-1/41-42, DC (1st Wonder Woman)

Animal Comics #1, 12-1/41-42, Dell (1st Pogo by Walt Kelly)

Sensation Comics #1, 1/42, DC (1st series to star Wonder Woman)

Crime Does Not Pay #22, 6/42, Gleason (1st Crime comic book series)

Wonder Woman #1, Summer/42, DC (1st issue of top DC character)

Four Color (Donald Duck) #9, 8/42 Dell (1st Barks story/art on Donald Duck)

Archie Comics #1, Winter/42-43, MLJ/ Archie, (1st Teenage comic)

Capt Marvel Adventures #22, 3/43, Fawcett, (Begins Mr. Mind serial)

Plastic Man #1, Summer/43, Quality (1st issue of top Quality

character)

Big All-American Comic Book #1, 1944, DC, (1st annual of **All-American Comics**)

More Fun Comics #101, 1/2/45, DC (1st Superboy)

Molly O'Day #1, 2/45, Avon (1st Avon comic)

Terry Toones #38, 11/45, Timely (1st Mighty Mouse)

POST GOLDEN AGE
1946 - 1949

Romantic Picture Novelette #1, 1946, ME (one shot)(1st love comic theme)

All Winners #19, Fall/46, Timely (1st All Winners Squad, 1st Marvel group)

All Winners #21, Winter/46-47, Timely (2nd All Winners Squad)

Eerie #1, 1/47, Avon (1st horror comic)

Young Romance Comics #1, 9-10/47, Prize (1st romance series)

Four Color (Uncle Scrooge) #178, 12/47, Dell (1st Uncle Scrooge)

Phantom Lady #17, 4/48, Fox (Classic cover issue–good girl art)

Adventures Into The Unknown #1, Fall/48, ACG (1st horror series)

Moon Girl #5, Winter/48, EC (1st E.C. horror story)

Casper #1, 9/49, St John (1st Baby Huey)

Crime Patrol #15, 12-1/49-50, EC (1st Crypt Keeper)

War Against Crime #10, 12-1/49-50, EC (1st Vault Keeper)

PRE-SILVER AGE
1950 - Aug, 1956

Howdy Doody #1, 1/50, Dell (1st TV comic book)

Archie Annual #1, 1950, Archie

Captain America Comics #1 © MEG

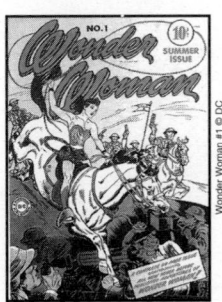

Wonder Woman #1 © DC

Crime Patrol #15 © WMG

Weird Science #12 (#1) © WMG

Superman's Girlfriend Lois Lane #1 © DC

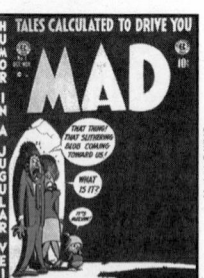
Fantastic Four #1 © MEG

(1st **Archie** annual)

Crypt Of Terror #17, 4-5/50, EC
(1st issue of Crypt Keeper tales,
EC horror)

Haunt Of Fear #15 (#1), 5-6/50, EC
(1st issue of EC horror, trend-
setting)

Weird Fantasy #13 (#1), 5-6/50, EC
(1st issue of EC science fiction,
trend-setting)

Weird Science #12 (#1), 5-6/50, EC
(1st issue of EC science fiction,
trend-setting)

Strange Tales #1, 6/51, Marvel
(1st issue of top Marvel title)

Mad #1, 10-11/52, EC
(1st satire comic)

Journey Into Mystery #1, 6/52,
Marvel (1st issue of top Marvel
title)

Little Dot #1, 9/53, Harvey
(1st Richie Rich)

Young Men #24, 12/53, Marvel
(Revival of Capt. America, Human
Torch & Sub-Mariner)

World's Finest Comics #71, 7-8/54,
DC (1st Superman/Batman team
issue)

Superman's Pal, Jimmy Olsen #1,
9-10/54, DC, (1st issue of top DC
title)

My Greatest Adventure #1,
1-2/55, DC (1st issue of top DC
fantasy title)

Brave And The Bold #1, 8-9/55, DC
(1st issue of top DC showcase
title)

Superman #100, 9-10/55, DC
(Landmark issue)

Detective Comics #225, 11/55, DC
(1st Martian Manhunter)

Tales Of The Unexpected #1,
2-3/56, DC (1st issue of top DC
fantasy title)

Showcase #1, 3-4/56, DC
(1st issue of top DC showcase

title)

Sugar & Spike #1, 4-5/56, DC
(1st issue of top title by Sheldon
Mayer)

Batman #100, 6/56, DC
(Landmark issue)

Detective Comics #233, 7/56, DC
(1st Batwoman)

SILVER AGE
Sept, 1956 - 1969

House Of Secrets #1, 11-12/56, DC
(1st issue of top DC horror title)

Showcase #4, 9-10/56, DC
(1st Silver Age book) (The Flash)

Showcase #6, 1-2/57, DC (1st Silver
Age group)(Challengers)

Showcase #9, 7-8/57, DC
(1st Lois Lane book)

**Superman's Girl Friend, Lois Lane
#1**, 3-4/58, DC (1st issue of top
character)

Adventure Comics #247, 4/58, DC
(1st Legion of Superheroes)

Challengers Of The Unknown #1,
4-5/58, DC, (1st issue of 1st Silver
Age group)

Showcase #15, 7-8/58, DC
(1st Space Ranger)

Showcase #17, 11-12/58, DC
(1st Adam Strange)

Tales Of Suspense #1, 1/59, Marvel
(1st issue of top fantasy title)

Tales To Astonish #1, 1/59, Marvel
(1st issue of top fantasy title)

Flash #105 (#1), 2-3/59, DC
(1st issue of top DC title)

Our Army At War #81, 4/59, DC
(1st Sgt. Rock)

Action Comics #252, 5/59, DC
(1st Supergirl)

Showcase #20, 5-6/59, DC
(1st Rip Hunter)

Double Life Of Private Strong #1,
6/59, Archie (1st Silver Age

Shield, 1st Fly)

Mystery In Space #53, 8/59, DC
(1st Adam Strange)

Tales Of The Unexpected #40,
8/59, DC (1st Space Ranger in
own title)

Adventures of the Fly #1, 8/59,
Archie (1st issue of top Archie
title)

Showcase #22, 9-10/59, DC
(1st Silver Age Green Lantern)

Flash #110, 12-1/59/60, DC
(1st Kid Flash)

Brave And The Bold #28, 2/3/60,
DC (1st Justice League of
America)

Green Lantern #1, 7-8/60, DC
(1st issue of top DC character)

Showcase #27, 7-8/60, DC
(1st Sea Devils)

Brave And The Bold #31, 8-9/60,
DC (1st Cave Carson)

Justice League Of America #1,
10-11/60, DC (1st issue of top DC
title)

Showcase #30, 1-2/61, DC
(1st Silver Age Aquaman)

Brave And The Bold #34, 2-3/61,
DC (1st Silver Age Hawkman)

Amazing Adventures #1, 6/61,
Marvel (1st Dr. Droom, the 1st
Marvel-Age superhero)

Flash #123, 9/61, DC
(1st G.A. Flash in Silver Age)

Showcase #34, 9-10/61, DC
(1st Silver Age Atom)

Fantastic Four #1, 11/61, Marvel
(1st Fantastic Four)

Amazing Adult Fantasy #7, 12/61,
Marvel (1st issue of title that leads
to Spider-Man)

Tales To Astonish #27, 1/62,
Marvel (1st Antman)

Showcase #37, 3-4/62, DC
(1st Metal Men)

Fantastic Four #4, 5/62, Marvel

Mad #1 © WMG

Flash #105 (#1) © DC

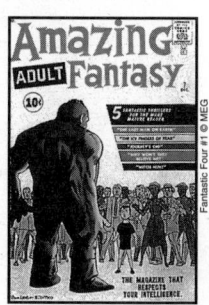

Fantastic Four #1 © MEG

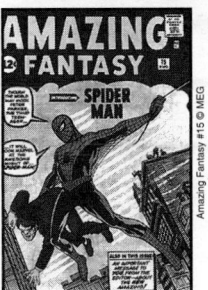

(1st Silver Age Sub-Mariner)
Incredible Hulk #1, 5/62, Marvel
  (1st Hulk)
Mystery In Space #75, 5/62, DC
  (Early JLA cross-over in Adam
  Strange story)
Fantastic Four #5, 7/62, Marvel
  (1st Dr. Doom)
Journey Into Mystery #83, 8/62,
  Marvel (1st Thor)
Amazing Fantasy #15, 8-9/62,
  Marvel (1st Spider-Man)
Tales To Astonish #35, 9/62,
  Marvel (2nd Antman, 1st in cos
  tume)
Strange Tales #101, 10/62, Marvel
  (1st S.A. Human Torch solo story)
Amazing Spider-Man #1, 3/63,
  Marvel (1st Spider-Man in own
  title)
Tales Of Suspense #39, 3/63,
  Marvel (1st Iron Man)
Strange Tales #110, 7/63, Marvel
  (1st Dr. Strange)
Avengers #1, 9/63, Marvel
  (1st Avengers)
X-Men #1, 9/63, Marvel
  (1st X-Men)
Mystery In Space #87, 11/63, DC
  (1st Hawkman in title)
Avengers #4, 3/64, Marvel
  (1st Silver Age Captain America)
Daredevil #1, 4/64, Marvel
  (1st Daredevil)
Amazing Spider-Man #14, 7/64,
  Marvel (1st Green Goblin)
Fantastic Four #48, 3/66, Marvel
  (1st Silver Surfer)
Strange Tales #135, 7/65, Marvel
  (Origin & 1st app. Nick Fury)
Strange Adventures #205, 10/67,
  DC (1st Deadman)

POST SILVER AGE
1970 - 1979

Detective Comics #400, 6/70, DC
  (1st Man-Bat)
Star Spangled War Stories #151,
  6-7/70, DC (1st Unknown Soldier)
**Superman's Pal, Jimmy Olsen
  #133**, 10/70, DC (1st Silver Age
  Newsboy Legion)
Forever People #1, 2-3/71, DC
  (1st Forever People)
New Gods #1, 3/71, DC
  (1st New Gods)
Mister Miracle #1, 3/71, DC
  (1st Mister Miracle)
Savage Tales #1, 5/71, Marvel
  (1st Man-Thing)
House of Secrets #92, 6/71, DC
  (1st app. Swamp Thing by Bernie
  Wrightson)
Amazing Spider-Man #101, 10/71,
  Marvel (1st Morbius the Living
  Vampire)
Marvel Feature #1, 12/71, Marvel
  (Origin and 1st app. Defenders)
All Star Western #10, 2-3/72, DC
  (1st Jonah Hex)
Tomb of Dracula #1, 4/72, Marvel
  (1st app. Dracula)
Marvel Spotlight #2, 6/72, Marvel
  (1st app. Werewolf by Night)
Marvel Spotlight #5, 8/72, Marvel
  (Origin and 1st app. new Ghost
  Rider)
**Kamandi: The Last Boy on Earth
  #1**, 10/72, DC (Origin and 1st
  app. Kamandi)
Iron Man #55, 2/73, Marvel (1st.
  app. Thanos & Drax the Destroyer)
Marvel Spotlight #12, 10/73, Marvel
  (1st solo Son of Satan)
Marvel Special Edition #15, 12/73,
  Marvel (1st Master of Kung Fu)

Amazing Spider-Man #129, 2/74,
  Marvel (1st Punisher)
Astonishing Tales #25, 8/74,
  Marvel (1st Deathlok)
Incredible Hulk #181, 11/74,
  Marvel (1st app. of Wolverine)
  (story)
Giant Size X-Men #1, Summer/75,
  Marvel (1st New X-Men; intro
  Nightcrawler, Storm, Colossus &
  Thunderbird)
X-Men #94, 8/75, Marvel
  (New X-Men team begins)
All Star Comics #58, 1-2/76, DC
  (1st Power Girl)
Marvel Spotlight #32, 2/77, Marvel
  (1st Spider-Woman)
Black Lightning #1, 4/77, DC
  (1st Black Lightning)
Cerebus #1, 12/77, Aardvark-
  Vanaheim (1st app. Cerebus)
  (B&W)

MODERN AGE
1980 - PRESENT

Detective Comics #327, 5/84, DC
  (New Batman) (Silver Age/
  Modern)
Teenage Mutant Ninja Turtles #1,
  pre 6/84, Mirage, (1st app.
  Teenage Mutant Ninja Turtles)
Amazing Spider-Man #300, 5/88,
  Marvel (1st venom) (full app &
  story)
Sandman #1, 1/89, DC (1st app.
  new Sandman)
Youngblood #1, 4/92, Image
  (1st Image comic)
Spawn #1, 5/92, Image (1st app.
  Spawn)
Superman (2nd Series) #75, 1/93,
  DC (Death of Superman) (Huge
  Media Coverage)

HISTORIC FIRSTS
(First comic book of a genre, publisher, theme or type, etc.)

Aviation Comic–Wings Comics #1, 9/40
Comic Book Annual–Big Book Of Fun Comics #1,
  Spr, 1936
Comic Book–Funnies On Parade nn, 1933
Comic Book to go into endless reprints–Classic
  Comics #1, 10/41
**Comic Book to kill off a super
  hero**–Pep Comics #17, 7/41 (The Comet)
Comic Book with metallic logo–Silver Streak #1, 12/39
Comic Book with original material–New Fun Comics
  #1, 2/35
Costumed Hero Battle comic–Marvel Mystery #9, 7/40
Costumed Hero Comic (Strip)–Ace Comics #11, 2/38
  (The Phantom)

Costumed Hero Comic (Original material)–Funny Pages
  V2/10 9/38 (The Arrow)(3 months after Superman)
Costumed Hero sidekick comic–
  Detective Comics #38, 4/40 (Robin)
Crime–Crime Does Not Pay #22, 6/42
Detective comic–Detective Picture Stories #1, 12/36
Disney Single Character comic book–
  Donald Duck nn, 1938
Disney Single Character comic book in color–Donald
  Duck 4-Color #4, 3/40
Educational theme comic–Classic Comics #1, 10/41
5 cent comic–Nickel Comics #1, 1938
15 cent comic–New York World's Fair, 1940
Flying Saucer comic–Spirit Section 9/28/47 (3 months

after 1st sighting in Idaho on 6/25/47
Funny Animal Series–Walt Disney's Comics & Stories #1, 10/40
Funny Animal single character comic–Donald Duck nn, 1938
Giveaway comic–Funnies On Parade nn, 1933
Golden Age comic–Action Comics #1, 6/38
Heroine Single Theme comic–Sheena, Queen of the Jungle #1, Spr, 1942
Horror comic (one shot)–Eerie Comics #1, 1/47
Horror comic (series)–Adventures Into The Unknown #1, Fall, 1948
Jungle comic–Jumbo Comics #1, 9/38
Large Sized comic–New Fun Comics #1, 2/35
Love comic (One Shot)–Romantic Picture Novelettes #1, 1946 (Mary Worth strip-r)
Love comic (series)–Young Romance Comics #1, 10/47
Magician comic–Super Magic Comics #1, 5/41
Magician comic series–Super Magician Comics #2, 9/41
Masked Hero–Funny Pages #6, 11/36(The Clock)
Movie comic–Movie Comics #1, 4/39
Negro comic–Negro Heroes, Spr, 1947
Newsstand comic–Famous Funnies #1, 7/34
#2 in comics–Famous Funnies #2, 8/34
100 page comic–Century of Comics nn, 1933
100th issue–Famous Funnies #100, 11/43
One Shot Series–Feature Book nn, 1937
Patriotic Hero comic–Pep Comics #1, 1/40 (The Shield)
Prototype comic–The Comics Magazine #1, 5/36 (Superman)
Public Event comic–New York World's Fair 1939
Religious Theme series–Topix Comics #1, 11/42
Reprint comic–Funnies On Parade nn, 1933
Satire comic–Mad #1, 10-11/52
Science Fiction comic–Planet Comics #1, 1/40
Sidekick group comic–Young Allies #1, Sum, 1941
Silver Age Archie comic–Double Life of Private Strong #1, 6/59
Silver Age comic–Showcase #4, 9-10/56
Silver Age DC Annual–Superman Annual #1, 10/60
Silver Age Marvel Annual–Strange Tales Annual #1, 1962
Silver Age Marvel comic–Fantastic Four #1, 11/61
Single Character comic–Skippy's Own Book Of Comics, 1934
Single original character comic–Superman #1, Sum, 1939

Single Strip Reprint Character comic–Mutt and Jeff #1, Sum, 1939
Single Theme comic–Detective Picture Stories #1, 12/36
Single Theme comic, the first important–Detective Comics #1, 3/37
Single Theme Reprint Strip comic–Mutt and Jeff #1, Sum, 1939
Small-sized comic–Little Giant Comics #1, 7/38
Sports comic–Champion Comics #2, 12/39
Squarebound comic–New Book Of Comics #1, 1937
Squarebound series–World's Best #1, Spr, 1941
Super Hero comic–Action Comics #1, 6/38 (Superman)
Super Hero Team–All Star Comics #3, Wint, 1940-41
Super Heroine comic–All Star Comics #8, 11-12/41
Super Heroine comic series–Sensation Comics #1, 1/42
Superman imitator–Wonder Comics #1, 5/39 (Wonder Man)
Teen-age comic–Pep Comics #22, 12/41
Teen-age comic series–Archie Comics #1, Wint, 1942-43
10 cent comic–Famous Funnies Series 1, 3-5/34
3-D comic–Mighty Mouse 3-D #1, 9/53
T.V. comic–Howdy Doody #1, 1/50
25 cent comic–New York World's Fair, 1939
True Life comic–Sport Comics #1, 10/40
Villain cover (Fu Manchu)–Detective Comics #1, 3/37
Villain Story (Fu Manchu)–Detective Comics #17, 7/38
Villain Cover/story (Original to comics)– Silver Streak #1, 12/39 (The Claw)
War comic–War Comics #1, 5/40
Weekly comic book–The Spirit #1, 6/2/40
Western comic–Western Picture Stories #1, 2/37 & Star Ranger #1, 2/37
Western of one character–The Lone Ranger Comics nn, 1939
Western run of one character (Giveaway)–Tom Mix #1, 9/40
Western newsstand run of one character–Red Ryder Comics #1, 8/41
Western with photo cover–Roy Rogers 4-color #38, 4/44
X-Over comic–Marvel Mystery #9, 7/40

Showcase #4
© DC

A Chronology of the Development of THE AMERICAN COMIC BOOK

By M. Thomas Inge

Precursors: The facsimile newspaper strip reprint collections constitute the earliest "comic books." The first of these was a collection of Richard Outcault's **Yellow Kid** from the Hearst New York American in March 1897. Commercial and promotional reprint collections, usually in cardboard covers, appeared through the 1920s and featured such newspaper strips as **Mutt and Jeff, Foxy Grandpa, Buster Brown**, and **Barney Google**. During 1922 a reprint magazine, **Comic Monthly**, appeared with each issue devoted to a separate strip, and from 1929 to 1930 George Delacorte published 36 issues of **The Funnies** in tabloid format with original comic pages in color, becoming the first four-color comic newsstand publication.

1933: The Ledger syndicate published a small broadside of their Sunday comics on 7" by 9" plates. Employees of Eastern Color Printing Company in New York, sales manager Harry I. Wildenberg and salesman Max C. Gaines, saw it and figured that two such plates would fit a tabloid page, which would produce a book about 7-1/2" x 10" when folded. Thus 10,000 copies of **Funnies on Parade**, containing 32 pages of Sunday newspaper reprints, was published for Proctor and Gamble to be given away as premiums. Some of the strips included were: **Joe Palooka**, **Mutt and Jeff**, **Hairbreadth Harry**, and **Reg'lar Fellas**. M. C. Gaines was very impressed with this book and convinced Eastern Color that he could sell a lot of them to such big advertisers as Milk-O-Malt, Wheatena, Kinney Shoe Stores, and others to be used as premiums and radio give-aways. So, Eastern Color printed **Famous Funnies: A Carnival of Comics**, and then **Century of Comics**, both as before, containing Sunday newspaper reprints. Mr. Gaines sold these books in quantities of 100,000 to 250,000. Although slightly larger in size than **Famous Funnies**, Humor Publications produced two one-issue magazines, **Detective Dan** and **The Adventures of Detective Ace King**, which contained original comic art and sold for ten cents per copy.

1934: The give-away comics were so successful that Mr. Gaines believed that youngsters would buy comic books for ten cents like the "Big Little Books" coming out at that time. So, early in 1934, Eastern Color ran off 35,000 copies of **Famous Funnies, Series 1**, 64 pages of reprints for Dell Publishing Company to be sold for ten cents in chain stores. Since it sold out promptly on the stands, Eastern Color, in May 1934, issued **Famous Funnies** No. 1 (dated July 1934) which became, with issue No. 2 in July, the first monthly comic magazine. The title continued for over 20 years through 218 issues, reaching a circulation peak of over 400,000 copies a month. At the same time, Mr. Gaines went to the sponsors of Percy Crosby's **Skippy**, who was on the radio, and convinced them to put out a Skippy book, advertise it on the air, and give away a free copy to anyone who bought a tube of Phillip's toothpaste. Thus 500,000 copies of **Skippy's Own Book of Comics** was run off and distributed through drug stores everywhere. This was the first four-color comic book of reprints devoted to a single character.

1935: Major Malcolm Wheeler-Nicholson's National Periodical Publications issued in February a tabloid-sized comic publication called **New Fun**, which became **More Fun** after the sixth issue and was converted to the normal comic-book size after issue eight. **More Fun** was the first comic book of a standard size to publish original material, and it continued publication until 1949. **Mickey Mouse Magazine** began in the summer, to become **Walt Disney's Comics and Stories** in 1940, and combined original material with reprinted newspaper strips in most issues.

1936: In the wake of the success of **Famous Funnies**, other publishers, in conjunction with the major newspaper strip syndicates, inaugurated more reprint comic books: **Popular Comics** (News Tribune, February), **Tip Top Comics** (United Features, April), **King Comics** (King Features, April), and **The Funnies** (new series, NEA, October). Four issues of **Wow Comics**, from David McKay and Henle Publications, appeared, edited by S. M. Iger and including early art by Will Eisner, Bob Kane, and Alex Raymond. The first non-reprint comic book devoted to a single theme was **Detective Picture Stories** issued in December by The Comics Magazine Company.

1937: The second single theme title, **Western Picture Stories**, came in February from The Comics Magazine Company, and the third was **Detective Comics**, an offshoot of **More Fun**, which began in March to be published to the present. The book's initials, "D.C.," have long served to refer to National Periodical Publications, which was purchased from Major Nicholson by Harry Donenfeld late this year.

1938: "DC" copped a lion's share of the comic book market with the publication of **Action Comics** No. 1 in June which contained the first appearance of Superman by writer Jerry Siegel and artist Joe Shuster, a discovery of Max C. Gaines. The "man of steel" inaugurated the "Golden Era" in comic book history. Fiction House, a pulp publisher, entered the comic book field in September with **Jumbo Comics**, featuring Sheena, Queen of the Jungle, and appearing in over-sized format for the first eight issues.

1939: The continued success of "DC" was assured in May with the publication of **Detective Comics** No. 27 containing the first episode of Batman by artist Bob Kane and writer Bill Finger. **Superman Comics** appeared in the summer. Also, during the summer, a black and white premium comic titled **Motion Picture Funnies Weekly** was published to be given away at motion picture theatres. The plan was to issue it weekly and to have continued stories so that the kids would come back week after week not to miss an episode. Four issues were planned but only one came out. This book contains the first appearance and origin of the Sub-Mariner by Bill Everett (8 pages) which was later reprinted in **Marvel Comics**. In November, the first issue of **Marvel Comics** came out, featuring the Human Torch by Carl Burgos and the Sub-Mariner reprint with color added.

1940: The April issue of **Detective Comics** No. 38 introduced Robin the Boy Wonder as a sidekick to Batman, thus establishing the "Dynamic Duo" and a major precedent for later costumed heroes who would also have boy companions. **Batman Comics** began in the spring. Over 60 different comic book titles were being issued, including **Whiz Comics** begun in February by Fawcett Publications. A creation of writer Bill Parker and artist C. C. Beck, Whiz's Captain Marvel was the only superhero ever to surpass Superman in comic book sales. Drawing on their own popular pulp magazine heroes, Street and Smith Publications introduced **Shadow Comics** in March and **Doc Savage Comics** in May. A second trend was established with the summer appearance of the first issue of **All Star Comics**, which brought several superheroes together in one story and in its third issue that winter would announce the establishment of the Justice Society of America.

1941: Wonder Woman was introduced in the spring issue of **All Star Comics** No. 8, the creation of psychologist William Moulton Marston and artist Harry Peter. **Captain Marvel Adventures** began this year. By the end of 1941, over 160 titles were being published, including **Captain America** by Jack Kirby and Joe Simon, **Police Comics** with Jack Cole's Plastic Man and later Will Eisner's Spirit, **Military Comics** with Blackhawk by Eisner and Charles Cuidera, **Daredevil Comics** with the original character by Charles Biro, **Air Fighters** with Airboy also by Biro, and **Looney Tunes & Merrie Melodies** with Porky Pig, Bugs Bunny, and Elmer Fudd, reportedly created by Bob Clampett for the Leon Schlesinger Productions animated films and drawn for the comics by Chase Craig. Also, Albert Kanter's Gilberton Company initiated the **Classics Illustrated** series with The Three Musketeers.

1942: Crime Does Not Pay by editor Charles Biro and publisher Lev Gleason, devoted to factual accounts of criminals' lives, began a different trend in realistic crime stories. **Wonder Woman** appeared in the summer. John Goldwater's character Archie, drawn by Bob Montana, first published in **Pep Comics**, was given his own magazine **Archie Comics**, which has remained popular over 40 years. The first issue of **Animal Comics** contained Walt Kelly's "Albert Takes the Cake," featuring the new character of Pogo. In mid-1942, the undated Dell Four Color title, No. 9, **Donald Duck Finds Pirate Gold**, appeared with art by Carl Barks and Jack Hannah. Barks, also featured in **Walt Disney's Comics and Stories**, remained the most popular delineator of Donald Duck and later introduced his greatest creation, Uncle Scrooge, in **Christmas on Bear Mountain** (Dell Four Color No. 178). The fantasy work of George Carlson appeared in the first issue of **Jingle Jangle Comics**, one of the most imaginative titles for children ever to be published.

1945: The first issue of **Real Screen Comics** introduced the Fox and the Crow by James F. Davis, and John Stanley began drawing the **Little Lulu** comic book based on a popular feature in the **Saturday Evening Post** by Marjorie Henderson Buell from 1935 to 1944. Bill Woggon's Katy Keene appears in issue No. 5 of **Wilbur Comics** to be followed by appearances in **Laugh, Pep, Suzie** and her own comic book in 1950. The popularity of Dick Briefer's satiric version of the Frankenstein monster, originally drawn for **Prize Comics** in 1941, led to the publication of **Frankenstein Comics** by Prize publications.

1950: The son of Max C. Gaines, William M. Gaines, who earlier had inherited his father's firm Educational Comics (later Entertaining Comics), began publication of a series of well-written and masterfully drawn titles which would establish a "New Trend" in comics magazines: **Crypt of Terror** (later **Tales from the Crypt**, April), **The Vault of Horror** (April), **The Haunt of Fear** (May), **Weird Science** (May), **Weird Fantasy** (May), **Crime SuspenStories** (October), and **Two Fisted Tales** (November), the latter stunningly edited by Harvey Kurtzman.

1952: In October EC published the first number of **Mad** under Kurtzman's creative editorship, thus establishing a style of humor which would inspire other publications and powerfully influence the underground comic book movement of the 1960s.

1953: All Fawcett titles featuring Captain Marvel were ceased after many years of litigation in the courts during which National Periodical Publications claimed that the superhero was an infringement on the copyrighted Superman. In December, Captain America, Human Torch, and Sub-Mariner were revived by Atlas Comics.

1954: The appearance of Fredric Wertham's book **Seduction of the Innocent** in the spring was the culmination of a continuing war against comic books fought by those who believed they corrupted youth and debased culture. The U. S. Senate Subcommittee on Juvenile Delinquency investigated comic books and in response the major publishers banded together in October to create the Comics Code Authority and adopted, in their own words, "the most stringent code in existence for any communications media." Before the Code took effect, more than 1,000,000,000 issues of comic books were being sold annually.

1955: In an effort to avoid the Code, EC launched a "New Direction" series of titles, such as **Impact, Valor, Aces High, Extra, M.D.,** and **Psychoanalysis**, none of which lasted beyond the year. **Mad** was changed into a larger magazine format with issue No. 24 in July to escape the Comics Code entirely, and EC closed down its line of comic books altogether.

1956: Beginning with the Flash in **Showcase** No. 4, Julius Schwartz began a popular revival of DC superheroes which would lead to the Silver Age in comic book history.

1957: Atlas reduced the number of titles published by two-thirds, with **Journey into Mystery** and **Strange Tales** surviving, while other publishers did the same or went out of business. Atlas would survive as a part of the Marvel Comics Group.

1960: After several efforts at new satire magazines (**Trump** and **Humbug**), Harvey Kurtzman, no longer with Gaines, issued in August the first number of another abortive effort, **Help!**, where the early work of underground cartoonists Jay Lynch, Skip Williamson, Gilbert Shelton, and Robert Crumb appeared.

1961: Stan Lee edited in November the first **Fantastic Four**, featuring Mr. Fantastic, the Human Torch, the Thing, and the Invisible Girl, and inaugurated an enormously popular line of titles from Marvel Comics featuring a more contemporary style of superhero.

1962: Lee introduced **The Amazing Spider-Man** in August, with art by Steve Ditko, **The Hulk** in May and **Thor** in August, the last two produced by Dick Ayers and Jack Kirby.

1963: Marvel's **The X-Men**, with art by Jack Kirby, began a successful run in November, but the title would experience a revival and have an even more popular reception in the 1980s.

1965: James Warren issued **Creepy**, a larger black and white comic book, outside Comics Code's control, which emulated the EC horror comic line. Warren's **Eerie** began in September and **Vampirella** in September 1969.

1967: Robert Crumb's **Zap** No. 1 appeared, the first underground comic book to achieve wide popularity, although the undergrounds had begun in 1962 with **Adventures of Jesus** by Foolbert Sturgeon (Frank Stack) and 1964 with **God Nose** by Jack Jackson.

1970: Editor Roy Thomas at Marvel begins **Conan the Barbarian** based on fiction by Robert E. Howard with art by Barry Smith, and Neal Adams began to draw for DC a series of **Green Lantern/Green Arrow** stories which would deal with relevant social issues such as racism, urban poverty, and drugs.

1972: The Swamp Thing by Berni Wrightson begins in November from DC.

1973: In February, DC revived the original **Captain Marvel** with new art by C. C. Beck and reprints in the first issue of **Shazam** and in October **The Shadow** with scripts by Denny O'Neil and art by Mike Kaluta.

1974: DC began publication in the spring of a series of over-sized facsimile reprints of the most valued comic books of the past under the general title of "Famous First Editions," beginning with a reprint of **Action** No. 1 and including afterwards **Detective Comics** No. 27, **Sensation Comics** No. 1, **Whiz Comics** No. 2, **Batman** No. 1, **Wonder Woman** No. 1, **All-Star Comics** No. 3, **Flash Comics** No. 1, and **Superman** No. 1. Mike Friedrich, an independent publisher, released **Star★Reach** with work by Jim Starlin, Neal Adams, and Dick Giordano, with ownership of the characters and stories invested in the creators themselves.

1975: In the first collaborative effort between the two major comic book publishers of the previous decade, Marvel and DC produced together an over-sized comic book version of MGM's **Marvelous Wizard of Oz** in the fall, and then the following year, in an unprecedented crossover, produced **Superman vs. the Amazing Spider-Man**, written by Gerry Conway, drawn by Ross Andru, and inked by Dick Giordano.

1976: Frank Brunner's Howard the Duck, who had appeared earlier in Marvel's **Fear** and **Man-Thing**, was given his own book in January, which because of distribution problems became an overnight collector's item. After decades of litigation, Jerry Siegel and Joe Shuster were given financial recompense and recognition by National Periodical Publications for their creation of Superman, after several friends of the team made a public issue of the case.

1977: Stan Lee's **Spider-Man** was given a second birth, fifteen years after his first, through a highly successful newspaper comic strip, which began syndication on January 3 with art by John Romita. This invasion of the comic strip by comic book characters continued with the appearance on June 6 of Marvel's **Howard the Duck**, with story by Steve Gerber and visuals by Gene Colan. In an unusually successful collaborative effort, Marvel began publication of the comic book adaption of the George Lucas film **Star Wars**, with script by Roy Thomas and art by Howard Chaykin, at least three months before the film was released nationally on May 25. The demand was so great that all six issues of **Star Wars** were reprinted at least seven times, and the installments were reprinted in two volumes of an over-sized Marvel Special Edition and a single paperback volume for the book trade. Dave Sim, with an issue dated December, began self-publication of his **Cerebus the Aardvark**, the success of which would help establish the independent market for non-traditional black-and-white comics.

1978: In an effort to halt declining sales, Warner Communications drastically cut back on the number of DC titles and overhauled its distribution process in June. The interest of the visual media in comic book characters reached a new high with the Hulk, Spider-Man, and Doctor Strange, the subjects of television shows; with various projects begun to produce film versions of Flash Gordon, Dick Tracy, Popeye, Conan, The Phantom, and Buck Rogers; and with the movement reaching an outlandish peak of publicity with the release of **Superman** in December. Two significant applications of the comic book format to traditional fiction appeared this year: **A Contract with God and Other Tenement Stories** by Will Eisner and **The Silver Surfer** by Stan Lee and Jack Kirby. Eclipse Enterprises published Don McGregor and Paul Gulacy's **Sabre**, the first graphic album produced for the direct sales market, and initiated a policy of paying royalties and granting copyrights to comic book creators. Wendy and Richard Pini's **Elfquest**, a self-publishing project begun this year, eventually became so popular that it achieved bookstore distribution. The magazine **Heavy Metal** brought to American attention the avant-garde comic book work of European artists.

1980: Publication of the November premiere issue of **The New Teen Titans**, with art by George Perez and story by Marv Wolfman, brought back to widespread popularity a title originally published by DC in 1966.

1981: Distributor Pacific Comics began publishing titles for direct sales through comic shops with the first issue of Jack Kirby's **Captain Victory and the Galactic Rangers** and offered royalties to artists and writers on the basis of sales. DC would do the same for regular newsstand comics in November (with payments retroactive to July 1981), and Marvel followed suit by the end of the year. The first issue of **Raw**, irregularly published by Art Spiegelman and Francoise Mouly, carried comic book art into new extremes of experimentation and innovation with work by European and American artists. With issue No. 158, Frank Miller began to write and draw Marvel's **Daredevil** and brought a vigorous style of violent action to comic book pages.

1982: The first slick format comic book in regular size appeared, **Marvel Fanfare** No. 1, with a March date. Fantagraphics Books began publication in July of **Love and Rockets** by Mario, Gilbert, and Jaime Hernandez and brought a new ethnic sensibility and sophistication in style and content to comic book narratives for adults.

1983: More comic book publishers, aside from Marvel and DC, issued more titles than had existed in the past 40 years, most small independent publishers relying on direct sales, such as Americomics, Capital, Eagle, Eclipse, First, Pacific, and Red Circle, and with Archie, Charlton, and Whitman publishing on a limited scale. Frank Miller's mini-series **Ronin** demonstrated a striking use of sword play and martial arts typical of Japanese comic book art, and Howard Chaykin's stylish but controversial **American Flagg** appeared with an October date on its first issue.

1984: A publishing, media, film, and merchandising phenomenon began with the first issue of **Teenage Mutant Ninja Turtles** from Mirage Studios by Kevin Eastman and Peter Laird.

1985: Ohio State University's Library of Communication and Graphic Arts hosted the first major exhibition devoted to the comic book May 19 through August 2. In what was billed as an irreversible decision, the Silver Age superheroine Supergirl was killed in the seventh (October) issue of **Crisis on Infinite Earths**, a limited series intended to reorganize and simplify the DC universe on the occasion of the publisher's 50th anniversary.

1986: In recognition of its twenty-fifth anniversary, Marvel began publishing several new ongoing titles comprising Marvel's "New Universe", a self-contained fictional world. DC attracted extensive publicity and media coverage with its revisions of the character of **Superman** by John Byrne and of **Batman** in the **Dark Knight** series by Frank Miller. **Watchmen**, a limited-series graphic novel by Alan Moore and artist Dave Gibbons, began publication with a September issue from DC and Marvel's **The `Nam**, written by Vietnam veteran Doug Murray and penciled by Michael Golden, began with its December issue. DC issued guidelines in December for labelling their titles either for mature readers or for readers of all ages; in response, many artists and writers publicly objected or threatened to resign.

1987: Art Spiegelman's **Maus: A Survivor's Tale** was nominated for the National Book Critics Circle Award in biography, the first comic book to be so honored. A celebration of Superman's fiftieth Birthday began with the opening of an exhibition on his history at the Smithsonian's Museum of American History in Washington, D.C., in June and a symposium on "The Superhero in America" in October.

1988: Superman's birthday celebration continued with a public party in New York and a CBS television special in February, a cover story in **Time Magazine** in March (the first comic book character to appear on the cover), and an international exposition in Cleveland in June. With issue number 601 for May 24, **Action Comics** became the first modern weekly comic book, which ceased publication after 42 issues with the December 13 issue. In August, DC initiated a new policy of allowing creators of new characters to retain ownership of them rather than rely solely on work-for-hire.

1989: The fiftieth anniversary of Batman was marked by the release of the film **Batman**, starring Michael Keaton as Bruce Wayne and Jack Nicholson as the Joker; it grossed more money in its opening weekend than any other motion picture in film history to that time.

1990: The publication of a new **Classics Illustrated** series began in January from Berkley/First with adaptations of Poe's **The Raven and Other Poems** by Gahan Wilson, Dickens' **Great Expectations** by Rick Geary, Carroll's **Through the Looking Glass** by Kyle Baker, and Melville's **Moby Dick** by Bill Sienkiewicz, with extensive media attention. The adaptation of characters to film continued with the most successful in terms of popularity and box office receipts being **Teenage Mutant Ninja Turtles** and Warren Beatty's **Dick Tracy**. In November, the engagement of Clark Kent and Lois Lane was announced in **Superman** No. 50 which brought public fanfare about the planned marriage.

1991: One of the first modern comic books to appear in the former Soviet Union was a Russian version of **Mickey Mouse** published in Moscow on May 16 in a printing of 200,000 copies which were sold out within hours. The first issue of **Bone**, written, drawn, and published by Jeff Smith, appeared with a July cover date. Issue number one of a new series of Marvel's **X-Men**, with story and art by Chris Claremont and Jim Lee, was published in October in five different editions with a print run of eight million copies, the highest number in the history of the comic book. On December 18, Sotheby's of New York held its first auction of comic book material.

1992: In April, Image Comics debuts with **Youngblood** #1, changing the comic book industry by widening the playing field and legitimizing independent comics. The opening weekend for **Batman Returns** in June was the biggest in film box office history, bringing in over 46 million dollars, exceeding the record set by **Batman** in 1989, and not to be topped until the release of **Jurassic Park** a year later. At the second Sotheby auction in September, **Action Comics** No. 1 brought $82,500, a world record for a single comic book sold at auction. In November the death of Superman generated considerable media attention, with **Superman** No. 75 selling in excess of 4 million copies, the second best-selling issue in comic book history. A record number of over one hundred publishers of comic books and graphic albums issued titles this year.

1993: In April, for the first time since 1987, DC Comics surpassed Marvel in sales, primarily because of interest in the titles devoted to the return of Superman.

1994: Overproduction, changes in marketing practices, and publisher mergers and collapses triggered an apparent crisis in comic book publishing—which some have read as a sign of its influence and presence in American commerce and culture.

1995: Batman Forever, released in June with Val Kilmer in the lead role, grossed in its opening weekend over $53 million, the largest return in film box office history, exceeding the similar records set by the first two Batman films in 1989 and 1992. Writer Neil Gaiman decided after seven years to retire his popular and literate version of **Sandman**, the second revival of a Golden Age DC superhero first created in 1939.

1996: The longest-running give-away title ended after issue No. 467 of **The Adventures of the Big Boy** in September. In a long anticipated event coordinated between several comic book titles, the ABC television series **Lois & Clark: The New Adventures of Superman**, and the publication of **Superman: The Wedding Album**, Lois Lane and Clark Kent were married in October.

FOREIGN COMIC BOOKS

COLLECTING FOREIGN COMICS AND AMERICAN REPRINTS

One extremely interesting source of early vintage comics–one which is not necessarily expensive–is the foreign market. Many American newspaper and magazine strips are reprinted abroad (in English and in other languages) months and even years after they appear in the States. By arranging trades with foreign collectors, one can obtain, for practically cover price, substantial runs of American comic book reprints and newspaper strips dating back five, ten, and even twenty or more years. These reprints are often in black and white, and sometimes the reproduction is poor, but this is not always the case. Once interest in foreign-published comics has been piqued, a collector might become interested in original strips from these countries. Many are excellent, with a broader appeal than American comic books.

COMIC BOOK FANDOM

THE HISTORY OF COMICS FANDOM

It is possible to discern two distinct and largely unrelated movements in the history of Comics Fandom. The first began about 1953 as a response to the the the trend-setting EC lines of comics. The first true comics fanzines of this movement were short-lived. Bob Stewart's **EC FAN BULLETIN** was a hectographed newsletter that ran two issues about six months apart; Jimmy Taurasi's **FANTASY COMICS**, a newsletter devoted to all science-fiction comics of the period, was a monthly that ran for about six months. These were followed by other newsletters such as Mike May's **EC FAN JOURNAL**, and George Jennings' **EC WORLD PRESS**. EC fanzines of a wider and more critical scope appeared somewhat later. Two of the finest were **POTRZEBIE**, from a number of fans, and Ron Parker's **HOOHAH**. Gauging from the response that **POTRZEBIE** received from an EC letter column plug, Ted White estimated the average age of EC fans at 9 to 13, while many were actually in their mid-teens. This was discouraging to many fanzine editors hoping to reach an older audience. Consequently, many gave up their efforts on behalf of Comics Fandom, especially with the demise of the EC groups, and turned to SF (science fiction) fandom with its longer tradition and older membership. While the flourish of fan activity in response to the EC comics was certainly noteworthy, it never developed into a full-fledged, independent, and self-sustaining movement.

The second comics fan movement began in 1960, largely as a response to (and later stimulus for) the reappearance of the costumed hero and the Second Heroic Age of Comics. Most historians date the Second Heroic Age from **Flash** #105, February 1959. The letter departments of Julius Schwartz (editor at National Periodicals), and later those of Stan Lee (Marvel Group) and Bill Harris (Gold Key) were influential in bringing comics readers into Fandom. Sparks were lit among SF fans first, when experienced fan writers, who were part of an established tradition, produced the first in a series of articles on '40s comics–ALL IN COLOR FOR A DIME. The series was introduced in **XERO** No. 1 (September 1960), a general SF fanzine edited and published by Dick Lupoff.

Meanwhile, outside SF fandom, Jerry Bails and Roy Thomas, two comics fans of long-standing, conceived the first true comics fanzine in response to the Second Heroic Age, **ALTER EGO**, appearing in March 1961. The first issues were widely circulated, and profoundly influenced the comics fan movement, attracting many fans in their twenties and thirties, unlike the earlier EC fan following. Many of these older fans had been collectors for years but were largely unknown to each other. Joined by scores of new, younger fans, this group formed the nucleus of a movement that is still growing and shows every sign of being self-sustaining. Although it has borrowed a few appropriate SF terms, Comics Fandom of the '60s was an independent if fledging movement without the advantages and disadvantages of a longer tradition. What Comics Fandom did derive from SF fans was largely thanks to fanzines produced by so-called double fans, the most notable being **COMIC ART**, edited and published by Don and Maggie Thompson.

The **ROCKET'S BLAST COMIC COLLECTOR** by G.B. Love was the first sucessful adzine in the early 1960s and was instrumental in the early development of the comics market. G.B. remembers beginning his fanzine **THE ROCKET'S BLAST** in late 1961. Only six copies of the first 4 page issue were printed. Soon after Mr. Love had a letter published in **MYSTERY IN SPACE**, telling all about his new fanzine. His circulation began to grow. Buddy Saunders, a well known comic book store owner, designed the first **ROCKET'S BLAST** logo, and was an artist on the publication for many years thereafter. With issue #29 he took over **THE COMICOLLECTOR** fanzine from Biljo White and combined it with **ROCKET'S BLAST** to form the **RBCC**. He remembers that the **RBCC** hit its highest circulation of 2500 around 1971. Many people who wrote, drew or otherwise contributed to the **RBCC** went on to become well known writers, artists, dealers and store-owners in the comics field.

COLLECTING STRIPS

Collecting newspaper comic strips is somewhat different than collecting comic books, although it can be equally satisfying. Obviously, most strip collectors begin by clipping strips from their local paper, but soon branch out to out-of-town papers. Naturally this can become more expensive and more frustrating, as it is easy to miss out-of-town editions. Consequently, most strip collectors work out trade agreements with collectors in other cities to get the strips they want. This usually means saving local strips for trade purposes only.

Back issues of strips dating back several decades are also occasionally available from dealers. Prices per panel vary greatly depending on the age, condition, and demand for the strip. When the original strips are unavailable, it is sometimes possible to get photostatic copies from collectors, libraries, or newspaper morgues.

COLLECTING ORIGINAL ART

In addition to comic books and strips, some enthusiasts also collect original comic book and strip art. These mostly black and white, inked drawings are usually done on illustration paper at about 30 percent up (30 percent larger than the original printed panels). Because original art is a one-of-a-kind article, it is highly prized and can be difficult to obtain.

Interest in original comic art has increased tremendously in the past few years. One of the reasons more current art is available is that companies now return originals to the artists, who then either sell the work themselves at cons, or through agents and dealers. The best way to find the piece you want is to scour cons and get on as many art dealers' mailing lists as possible. As with any other area of collecting, rarity and demand govern value. Although the masters' works from the Golden and Silver Ages bring fine art prices, most current work is available at moderate prices, with something for everyone at various costs, from Kirby to McFarlane, Ditko to Steve Dillon, Heath to Chris Bachalo. The art is there for fans to seek out.

Why buy from World's Finest?

• *ACCURATE GRADING*

Our company is considered by many to be among the most conservative graders in the business. We were chosen as an advisor to the Overstreet Grading Guide because of this.

• *COMPETITIVE PRICING*

We price fairly. Our pricing is based on the Overstreet Guide value, and the price we paid for the book. We cater to the collector first & foremost. Investors generally find our pricing to good to be true.

• *GREAT SELECTION*

We spend a great deal of our time tracking down collections. And always seem to come up with many great items. Whether you are searching for a Batman #1 or an X-Men #100, chances are that we will get it in. We deal in all types of comic books from 1900 - 1980. **Also:** Cartoon Posters, Movie Posters, Premiums, Original Art, Superman items, Animation cels, and much more!

• *QUARTERLY CATALOG*

We consistently put out the best catalog in the business. Not a list, but a **huge** (11" x 14") photo illustrated catalog that averages 80 pages each issue. At a cost of only $3.00 per issue (1st class post paid), it's an incredible bargain!

• *ORDER YOUR COPY TODAY* •

• *FULLY GUARANTEED*

We are the safest way to buy: Why? We offer a seven day return privilege, which takes the pressure off. If we made a mistake, give us a call. We're here to talk. If after talking to us you decide not to keep the book you ordered, simply return it for a full refund. Remember: I want you as a customer for many years. It is good business to satisfy your collecting needs.

WORLD'S FINEST COMICS & COLLECTIBLES
"THE RIGHT CHOICE"

Call: (360) 274-9163   **Write:** P.O. Box 340 Castle Rock, WA 98611

Just the Facts.

<u>Fact 1:</u> **Absolutely no other comic dealer buys more golden and silver age comics than we do.**

Although the pages of this guide are filled with other dealers offering to pay "top dollar", the simple truth is that Metropolis spends more money on more quality comic book collections, year in and year out, than any other dealer in the country. We have the funds and the expertise to back up our words. The fact is that we have spent nearly 2 million dollars on rare comic books and movie posters over the last year. If you have books to sell, call us toll-free at 1-800-229-6387. If you know of any comic book or movie poster collection, call us today for a generous finder's fees. All calls will be kept strictly confidential.

<u>Fact 2:</u> **Absolutely no other comic dealer sells more golden and silver books than we do.**

We simply have the best stock of golden and silver age comic books in the country. The thousands of collectors familiar with our strict grading standards and excellent service can attest to this. Chances are, if you want it, we have it.

METROPOLIS COMICS

873 Broadway Suite 201, New York, NY 10003
1-800-229-6387
1-212-260-4147
Fax: 212-260-4304

Thank You!

For Making 1996-1997 Our Most Successful Year Yet.

We will continue to strive for the best in 1997-1998 by providing you with the highest grade, non-restored books, correct grading and personable service.

Time and time again, you've told us how our honesty and integrity have set us apart from all the rest. We owe our success to you, our valued friends and customers!

Sincerely,

Marnin & Scott

COLLECTORS ASSEMBLE!

A-115

PACIFIC COMIC EXCHANGE, INC.

http://www.pcei.com/ E-Mail: Sales@pcei.com

™ The Pacific Comic Exchange, Inc. (PCE) founded in 1990 is the largest "on-line comic book trading company specializing in Golden and Silver Age comics from 1933-1969. All comics listed on "The Exchange" have been graded using the Comic Grading Standard of America (CGSA), a standardized numerical grading system that ensures an unprecedented degree of accuracy and consistency.

CGSA	M	NM/M	NM	VFN/NM	VFN	FN/VFN	FN	VG/FN	VG	G/VG	G	Fr	Pr
	100-91	90	88,85,80,75	70	65,60,55	50	45,40,35	30	25,20	15	10	6	3
PgQ	0,1,2,2.5	3	3.3	4	5	6	6.5	7	7.5	8	8.5	9	9.5	10

LIQUIDITY

❖ PCE is an international network of dealers, collectors, and retailers.
❖ Consignments are listed on the Exchange in as little as one day..
❖ Negotiable prices, prompt payment to sellers.
❖ Sellers enjoy the lowest brokerage commissions (7% to 13%) in the industry.

ACCESS

❖ "The Exchange" is accessible via phone, computer, mail, and now the **Internet**.
❖ Detailed monthly reports (available through subscription) of sales data, updated listings, special market analyses, etc., help Buyers and Sellers make informed decisions.
❖ Buyers have access to the largest selection of (over One Million Dollars) Golden and Silver age comics at negotiable prices.

CONFIDENCE AND PROTECTION

❖ CGSA certified books are guaranteed to be in stated condition.
❖ Full disclosure of any restoration is certified by such respected experts as **Susan Ciccone** of **The Restoration Lab**, and **Jef Hinds** of the **Comic Conservation Co.**
❖ All books are uniquely identified and catalogued - Buyers and Sellers are protected from fraudulent substitution or damage.
❖ All books are fully insured

COMPREHENSIVE ON-LINE SERVICE

❖ All statistics available "on-line":
new listings, prices, grading, restoration information, etc.
❖ "Want Lists" link Sellers with interested Buyers.
❖ Buyers and Sellers can utilize extended "after hours" trading.

CONSIGNMENTS ACCEPTED
Sell Retail Not Wholesale

Call or write for more information about opening a free trading account, viewing a demonstration of the PCE "on-line" service, or selling comics on "The Exchange."

Meeting and consultations are arranged by appointment only.

Pacific Comic Exchange, Inc.
P.O. Box 34849 Los Angeles, CA 90034
❖Tel: (310) 836-7234(PCEI) ❖Fax: (310) 836-7127 ❖Modem: (310) 836-3076
World Wide Web page at *http://www.pcei.com/* E-Mail: *Sales@pcei.com*

DET27 25$29850 MFC52 15$3575 S1 20$7700 B1 15$5500 BB28 65$2750 SHO4 25$2300 AMZ15 40$2200

PACIFIC COMIC EXCHANGE, INC.

P.O. BOX 34849, Los Angeles, CA 90034 ◆ 337 S. Robertson Blvd. Suite 203, Beverly Hills, CA 90211 ◆ Tel: (310) 836-7234 (PCEI) Fax: (310) 836-7127

http://www.pcei.com/   E-Mail: sales@pcei.com

Instructions: The following books are currently listed on the Exchange and are available for sale at the prices specified. Prices are subject to change without notice. All orders are subject to a 10% buyers commission. The grade listed is the CGSA grade (see diagram below).
a: Appears, R: Restored (C: Color Touch, S: Slight (e.g. tear sealed,cover cleaned; etc), L: Light, M: Moderate, E: Extensive)
PgQ: Page Quality (0.0, 1, 2, 2.5, 3: White; 3.3: Near White; 3.5: Off-White; 4: Beige or Cream Color, 4.5-6.5: Light to Dark Tan).
California residents please add 8 1/4% sales tax. * Prices may be NEGOTIABLE

Consignments Accepted Immediately!

CGSA	M					NM/M	NM		VFN/NM	VFN	FN/VFN	FN		VG/FN	VG	G/VG	G	Fr.	Pr
	100.99.98.97.96.95.94.93.92.91					90	88.85.80.75		70	65.60.55	50	45.40.35		30	25.20	15	10	6	3
PgQ	0	1	2	2.5		3	3.3	4		5		6.5		7.5		8	8.5	9	9.5	10

DC Action Comics 5
Scarce
FN-- 32 (5.0) $7,000

DC Action Comics 23
1stApp Luthor (W/Red Hair)
VG/FN 30 (5.0) $3,400

DC All Star Comics 3
Origin/1stApp J.S.A.
FN/VFN 50 (3.5) $25,000

DC All Flash 1
Recil Macon Copy/Cvr Pressed
VF/NM 70 (3.5) $15,000

MVL Amazing Fantasy 15
Origin/1stApp Spider-Man
VFN++ 68 (3.5) $20,000

NEDOR America's Best 9
Mile High/Schomburg-C
NM/M 90 (2.5) $1,600

FWCT America's Greatest 1
Mile High/White Pages
NM+ 85 (2.0) $8,000

DC Batman 1
Origin Batman/1stApp Joker
VG/FN 30 (3.3) $20,000

DC Batman 5
1stApp Batmobile W/Bat-Head
NM 75 (3.3) $7,500

FWCT Bulletman 3
Mile High
NM/M 90 (3.0) $3,250

TIM CaptainAmerica 3
Murphy Anderson
FN+ 45 (5.5) $5,500

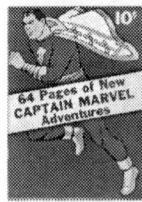

FWCT Capt. Marvel Adv. 1
Captain Marvel By Jack Kirby
E aVG+ 25 (4.5) $6,500

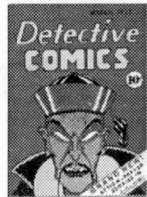

DC Detective Comics 1
(Scarce) / Fu-Manchu-C
M aFN 35 (5.0) $22,500

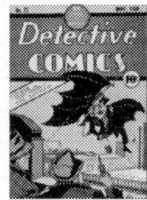

DC Detective Comics 27
1stApp Batman
M aVG/FN 30 (4.5) $45,000

DC Flash Comics 1
Origin/1stApp Flash
VG 20 (5.0) $14,000

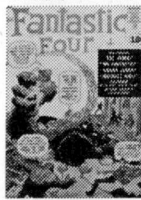

MVL Fantastic Four 1
White Mountain
NM- 85 (2.0) $60,000

TIM Human Torch 2 (#1)
Intro/Origin Toro
VG+ 25 (3.5) $5,000

DC More Fun Comics 52
Mod. Restored By S. Cicconne
M aVFN 60 (4.0) $17,500

DC Sensation Comics 2
Etta Candy Begins
VF/NM 70 (3.5) $5,500

DC Showcase 4
O./1stApp Flash (Ohio Copy)
VFN++ 68 (3.0) $37,500

DC Showcase 8
2nd App Flash (Ohio Copy)
FN/VFN 50 (3.5) $9,000

DC Superman 1
Moderate Restoration
M aVG/FN 30 (6.5) $22,000

DC Superman 3
2nd Story-R From Action #5
VFN- 55 (5.0) $6,000

FWCT Whiz Comics 1
Origin/1stApp Capt. Marvel
Fr 6 (4.0) $9,500

DC Wonder Woman 1
Origin Wonder Woman Retold
NM++ 88 (3.0) $75,000

Ideals™

TRUE Archival Quality
100% Mylar® D Sleeves

IN A CATEGORY BY THEMSELVES
They'll last for centuries, not just a few years.

Ideals® 4ml Classic Open Top	Size	Singles	25	50	100	500	1000
1A Modern Comic (fits 1970 on)	7.25" x 11.25"	.80	12.95	20.95	36.95	169.00	319.00
1B Silver Comic (fits 1950 to 1969)	7.75" x 11.25"	.85	14.95	22.95	39.95	175.00	329.00
1C Gold Comic (fits 1935 to 1949)	8.25" x 11.25"	.90	15.95	24.95	41.95	179.00	339.00
4A Magazine/Photo	9.25" x 12"	.95	17.95	29.95	49.95	229.00	425.00
5A Card/POG/Stamp/Coin	3" x 4"	.30	5.95	9.95	16.95	78.95	99.00
5K Record/Laser Disc	13 1/8" square	3.00			195.00		
5L Original Art/Newspapers	15" x 23.5"	3.50			249.00		

Idealocks® 4ml "E-Z" Fold Lock Top							
Z1 Modern Comic (fits in long comic boxes!)	7.25" x 10.75"	.90	15.95	28.95	55.95	249.00	449.00
Z2 Silver Comic (fits 1950 to 1969)	7.75" x 11.25"	.95	16.95	29.95	55.95	249.00	449.00
Z3 Gold Comic (fits 1935 to 1949)	8 3/8" x 11.25"	.99	17.95	32.95	59.95	259.00	459.00
Please add shipping and handling		3.00	4.00	4.00	5.00	9.00	18.00

Idealites® 1ml Mylar D Comic Bags	Size	Singles	100	500	1000	3000	
6A Modern Comic (fits 1970 on)	7" x 10.75"	.30	18.95	78.95	134.95	129.00 per 1000	
6B Silver Comic (fits 1950 to 1969)	7.30" x 10.75"	.30	18.95	79.95	136.95	129.00 per 1000	
6C Gold Comic (fits 1935 to 1949)	7.75" x 10.75"	.30	19.95	81.95	138.95	129.00 per 1000	
Please add shipping and handling		3.00	4.00	6.00	9.00	18.00	

Buffer Boards The only kind of board worth using.			Singles	100	500	1000
X1 – Modern, X2 – Silver, X3 – Gold 30ml 3% CaCo3 pH 8.5 (acid neutralizer)			.30	19.95	94.95	189.00
Please add shipping and handling			3.00	5.00	9.00	18.00

Phone or Fax 24 Hour Order Line

 1-608-277-8775

or send check or money order to:
Comic Conservation Co.
P.O. Box 44803
Madison, WI 53744-4803

Please include
phone number and
street address.

Orders shipped within
24 hours weekdays
unless otherwise notified.
(Checks must clear.)

Wisconsin residents add
5.5% sales tax.

PRICES SUBJECT TO CHANGE WITHOUT NOTICE.

Mylar ™ Dupont. Ideals, Idealites, Idealocks are ™ Comic Conservation Co. World's Finest ™ DC.

A-121

A-130

GRAB THE BEST IN GOLD
AND SILVER AGE COMICS
AT

BEDROCK CITY
COMIC COMPANY

6521 Westheimer
(at Hillcroft)
Houston, Texas 77057
(713) 780-0675

2204-D FM 1960 W.
(at Kuykendahl)
Houston, Texas 77090
(713) 444-9763

Fax (713) 780-2366

GOTHAM CITY COLLECTIBLES

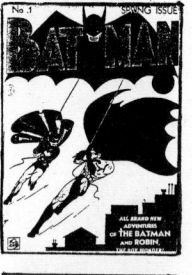

FRUSTRATED?
HAVE YOU SPENT WAY TOO MUCH TIME
AND MONEY TRYING TO FILL THE HOLES
IN YOUR COLLECTION?

WELL, LOOK NO FURTHER! WE, AT MORE FUN
COMICS SIMPLY STOCK MORE GOLDEN AGE
AND SILVER AGE COMICS THAN ANYONE ELSE
IN THE SOUTH. WE PROVIDE SOME OF THE BEST
GRADING AND PRICING ANYWHERE, OUR BUSI-
NESS IS BUILT ON THE PREMISE THAT WE
ARE HERE TO SERVE THE COLLECTING INDUS-
TRY IN THE FAIREST, MOST COURTEOUS, AND
TIMELIEST WAY POSSIBLE. THERE IS NO GUESS-
WORK WITH US!
CALL OR WRITE:

BILL PONSETI
GOTHAM CITY COLLECTIBLES
760 MAGAZINE ST., SUITE #205
NEW ORLEANS, LA 70130
OFFICE: (504) 523-8134
FAX: (504) 865-1869

WHEN YOU ARE READY TO DEAL WITH HONEST,
KNOWLEDGEABLE PROFESSIONALS GIVE US
A CALL OR DROP US A LINE. YOU'LL BE HAPPY
YOU DID!

LOOKING TO SELL?
WE'LL BE HAPPY TO BUY YOUR COMICS OR
COLLECTION. NO COLLECTION IS TOO BIG OR
SMALL; IN 1995 WE WERE RESPONSIBLE FOR
THE LARGEST CASH PURCHASE EVER OF A
SINGLE COLLECTION!

LOOKING TO BUY?
WHEN DEALING WITH US, UNLIKE MANY
OTHER DEALERS, YOU'LL FIND THAT WE
GRADE THE SAME WAY WHEN WE BUY AS
WHEN WE SELL! SO, IF YOU ARE LOOKING
FOR THAT HARD TO FIND GOLDEN AGE PIECE
OR TRYING TO COMPLETE ONE OF YOUR RUNS,
WE ARE HERE TO HELP.

WANT LISTS ARE A SPECIALTY

SENIOR ADVISOR
TO THE OVERSTREET PRICE GUIDE

HEROES
Aren't Hard To Find ™
AMERICA'S COMICS SOURCE

P.O. Box 9181 Charlotte NC 28299
704-375-7463•fax 704-375-7464
www.heroesonline.com

Spider-Man Illustration by Mike Wieringo
© & tm 1997 Marvel Characters Inc. All Rights Reserved.

HEROES CONVENTION™
CHARLOTTE

JUNE 13-15, 1997

Host Hotel
The Westin Hotel
222 East Third Street
HeroesCon Rate $99
704-377-1500

Strangers In Paradise® & tm 1997 Terry Moore

Strangers In Paradise
creator TERRY MOORE'S
only East Coast appearance in '97

NEIL GAIMAN* & CHARLES VESS
preview their next big Vertigo project
STARDUST
Neil will read Saturday Night
for a special CBLDF Benefit.

Sandman tm & ™1997 DC Comics
Stardust tm & ® 1997 Neil Gaiman & Charles Vess. All Rights Reserved.

The Darkness tm & ®1997 TOP COW Productions Inc. All Rights Reserved.

TOP COW'S Top Bulls
come home to HeroesCon '97!
Meet
Marc Silvestri (The Darkness) Batt
Michael Turner (Witchblade) D-Tron

More Fun...Featuring...
Old & New Comics for Sale
Toys • Cards • Gaming
CCG's • Contests
Art Exhibits & Auctions
Creator Workshops
Tons-O-Freebies

THE COMIC BOOK LEGAL DEFENSE FUND
*Neil Gaiman's
Appearance Benefits
The Comic Book Legal
Defense Fund

A-138

Remember The Good Old Days?

Remember when you bought new comics to read and enjoy, not for an investment? Do you remember the days when you walked into a comic shop looking for that certain back issue, you could actually find it there or they would have the resources to obtain it for you? If you do, come to **Tropic Comics**. We have over one million back issues in stock and four locations to serve you. With our computerized stock listing we can accomodate all your want list needs, just mail or fax us. **Tropic Comics** also has a convenient subscription service so you don't have to worry about missing the latest titles or newest issues.

Convenience, Service, Selection, **Tropic Comics.**

Tropic Comics

Main 313 South State Road Seven, Plantation, Florida 33317 (954) 587-8878 fax (954) 587-0409
East 5439 North Federal Hwy., Ft. Lauderdale, Florida 33308 (954) 351-0001 fax (954) 351-0002
South 742 Northeast 167th St., N. Miami Beach, Florida 33162 (305) 940-8700 fax (305) 940-1551

Come visit us on the net
http://www.tropiccomics

A-142

Let us introduce you to an exciting source for those hard-to-find Character Collectibles you want to add to your collection . . . Hake's mail & phone bid auctions.

FREE CATALOG OFFER
Write or Call—
just specify offer #356
to receive your introductory
auction catalog
FREE!
(A $7.50 value.)

ILLUSTRATION BY BILL NELSON

Five times a year, Hake's publishes a catalog of 3200+ items available for sale by mail & phone bid auction. All items are fully photo illustrated (many in color) and thoroughly described in careful detail. Each catalogue contains 1000 or more quality character collectibles.

Forget about the frustrating waste of time, energy and dollars scouring those endless toy shows and flea markets. Enjoy the ease and convenience of shopping from the privacy and comfort of your home or office. Simply submit your advance bids by mail or phone. On auction days, you can check on the current status of your bids by telephone.

You Can Buy from Hake's with confidence because . . .
- All items are original—NO reproductions.
- No hidden buyer's premium or credit card surcharges.
- In keeping with Hake's 30 year reputation for fair and honest dealing, the accuracy of each item's description is satisfaction guaranteed.
- We take extreme care and pride in the packing and shipping of your valued collectibles—so you can receive your delicate items in a safe and timely manner.

Don't miss that special addition to your collection! Call or write today—for your FREE sample catalog for Hake's current or next auction. **Specify offer #356.**

Hake's Americana & Collectibles
POB 1444 ● York, PA 17405
Phone 717-848-1333 ● FAX 717-852-0344

THE HOTTEST SHOW AROUND

WHERE THE SUPERHEROES MEET
BIMONTHLY IN NEW YORK CITY
JOIN US
COLLECTOR & DEALER HOTLINE
718-275-1567

BIG APPLE CONVENTIONS INC. 67-53 WOODHAVEN BLVD. REGO PARK, NY 11374

http://www.digdomdes.com/bigapple

A-149

A-150

Sold.

That is all you will be able to say when you are dealing with Harley Yee. My prices paid out are among the highest. You are always able to receive cash immediately. There is no collection that is too small because I will travel anywhere to view your collection.

I have over 14 years experience and I'm also a senior advisor to the *Overstreet Price Guide*. You will always receive prompt, professional service. I specialize in the Golden and Silver Age.

HARLEY YEE

P.O. Box 51758
Livonia, MI 48151-5758
voice: 800.731.1029 or 313.421.7921
fax: 313.421.7928

Call or write for a free catalog.

A-153

J & S COMICS
BUYING

AT J & S COMICS, WE BUY:

★ <u>ALL</u> COMICS BEFORE 1966

★ ENTIRE COLLECTIONS, ANY SIZE

★ GOLDEN AGE KEY ISSUES

★ SILVER AGE KEY ISSUES

★ WAREHOUSES

★ INVENTORIES

★ ESTATES

★ SPORT AND NON-SPORT CARDS

GET YOUR BEST OFFER, THEN CALL US !
OR SHIP US YOUR COMICS *NOW* FOR
AN IMMEDIATE, NO OBLIGATION OFFER!
(Write first before shipping any 1970-1994 comics)

A-156

A-157

TO ALL OF THE WRITERS, ALL OF THE
ARTISTS, ALL OF THE STORE OWNERS,
ALL OF THE DISTRIBUTORS, AND ALL OF
THE READERS WHO HAVE MADE THE
FIRST TEN YEARS POSSIBLE:

THANKS!

YOUR CONTINUED SUPPORT HAS MADE THESE
FIRST TEN YEARS A TERRIFIC ADVENTURE!

FROM MIKE RICHARDSON AND
EVERYONE AT DARK HORSE COMICS

COMING IN JUNE 1997...

THE
NEXT
COMIC

HEAVEN

AUCTION

OVER 5,000 GOLDEN AND SILVER
AGE COMIC BOOKS WILL BE OFFERED

Comic Heaven
John and Nanette Verzyl
P.O. Box 900
Big Sandy, TX 75755
1-903-636-5555

A-170

A BRIEF HISTORICAL NOTE ABOUT "COMIC HEAVEN"

John Verzyl started collecting comic books in 1965, and within ten years, he had amassed thousands of Golden and Silver Age comic books. In 1979, with his wife Nanette, he opened "COMIC HEAVEN", a retail store devoted entirely to the buying and selling of comic books.

Over the years, John Verzyl has come to be recognized as an authority in the field of comic books,. He has served as an advisor to the "Overstreet Price Guide". Thousands of his "mint" comics were photographed for Ernst Gerbers newly-released "Photo-Journal Guide To Comic Books". His tables and displays at the annual San Diego Comic Convention draw customers from all over the country.

The first COMIC HEAVEN AUCTION was held in 1987, and today his Auction Catalogs are mailed out to more then ten thousand interested collectors (and dealers).

Comic Heaven
John and Nanette Verzyl
P.O. Box 900
Big Sandy, TX 75755
1-903-636-5555

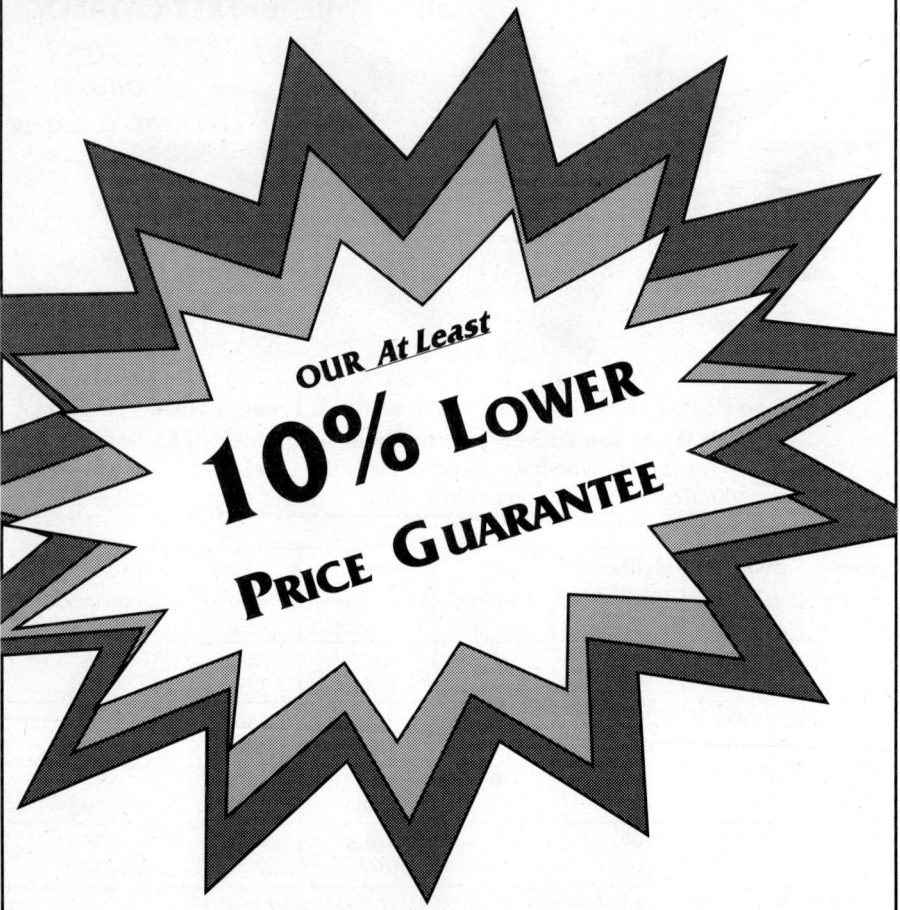

The American Comic Book: 1897-1932

The Beginning:*

THE PLATINUM AGE

Robert L. Beerbohm

Historians cannot agree on exactly what a "comic book" is, nor when the first one actually appeared. There are ongoing debates in some circles over what constitutes a "comic strip"as well. Many argue that comic strips and books must have a narrative continuity of recurring characters accompanied by word balloons that speak to the reader. I will not bore the reader by digging back to the Ice Age's cave paintings or by discussing the differences of opinion about whether the "modern" comic strip was invented in Germany, England or the United States.

There is much essential background material to consider, however. I learned a great deal about the early incarnations of

Comicon line to see George McManus in Toronto, 1923

comic books from the earliest collector I ever had the good fortune to meet, back in 1970, when I was 18 years old and he was then in his early 80s. By his own count, Ernie McGee began collecting comics in 1914 when **The Yellow Kid** was already twenty years old. Ernie was the only person in the country who had the vision to carefully preserve the only known complete run of every appearance of Richard Felton Outcault's creation. He collected comics until the day he died, and when he went, the greatest repository of comics lore I ever knew died with him.

The beginnings of the American comic book can be traced to the first single panel cartoon published in America, generally considered one entitled "God Helps Those Who Help Themselves," appearing in Benjamin Franklin's newspaper **Plain Truth** in 1747. Many later "political" cartoons in his **Gazette** started appearing in the 1750s, with its early calls for a separation from King George's England. One hundred and fifty years would pass before what we recognize today as a true comic strip finally evolved. Where each evolutionary step originates is ultimately less important than the fact that late 19th Century American story tellers elevated it to an art form wholly unique to this country, a distinction it shares with jazz music.

The scope of most comic book collectors these days unfortunately centers shortsightedly on the format invented by Harry I. Wildenberg and Maxwell Charles ("M. C.") Gaines; a saddle-stitched or glue bound four-color or black & white magazine, printed on newsprint or better paper, usually with a slick cover. After Wildenberg made a promotional booklet for the **Philadelphia Ledger** by folding a

*Excerpts from **Comic Book Store Wars** by Robert L. Beerbohm. ©1996 Robert L. Beerbohm. All rights reserved.

standard newspaper tabloid comic section in half and putting two reduced Sunday pages side by side, it was thought that maybe this "new" format would be of interest as a promotional giveaway.

Lee Whittlesey wrote in a seminal article published in a mid-1960s **RBCC** that Morris Margolis was brought in from Charlton Publications of Derby, Connecticut to solve binding problems centered on getting the pages in proper numerical sequence on that last fold to "modern" comic book size. Ten years later, Charlton itself became a very prolific comic book publisher. Sol Harrison worked on the color separations. Decades later, he became President of DC Comics, and signed Phil Seuling's original "direct sales" contract. Once Wildenberg and Gaines interested companies like Kinney Shoes, Procter & Gamble and others with the idea, they went to George Janosik, then President of Eastern Color, who gave the "OK" to begin production. After all, they were salesmen working on a commission, and if one does not "sell", one does not eat.

The format for what we today call the "modern comic book" had its first humble marketing trial with a title called **Funnies On Parade** in 1933. It had a small print run of 10,000 and only 32 pages for that first issue, and was utilized as a premium for the customers of Procter & Gamble. The entire print run was given away in just a couple of weeks. This was very encouraging to the young entrepreneurs. Prior to **Funnies On Parade**, comic strips in books appeared in a multitude of styles and shapes for over 35 years. These earliest comic books would grow to be quite popular in their day. They captured the imagination of the general public in the decades before radio and then television. The field is still vibrant and active to this day.

Words, phrases and slang from these earliest comic strips quickly passed into daily speech all over the country. There were immensely popular songs of **The Yellow Kid** as early as 1896. **Katzenjammer Kids, Happy Hooligan** and **Foxy Grandpa** began appearing in sheet music one could play on the piano as early as 1902. This new-found energy was then used to influence the circulation of competing newspapers in a very popular way. Early on, comics were also influencing the fashions of their day as comic strips began to permeate most levels of society. Women dressed like Polly, Maggie, Toots, Tillie, and a growing host of other "girl" strips paying homage to the "fairer" sex. Mothers were even dressing their babies to look like **The Yellow Kid** as early as 1897. One is pictured in Bill Blackbeard's new **Yellow Kid** book (Kitchen Sink, 1995), which utilized Ernie McGee's complete run of this seminal comic strip.

By early 1897, William Randolph Hearst's **New York Journal** gave permission to the G. W. Dillingham Company of New York to collect **The Yellow Kid's** bonafide first sequential comic strip appearances, appear-

ing since October 25, 1896, with "The Yellow Kid and His New Phonograph," in a 5x7 format. This first comic book in America was actually **Dillingham's American Authors Library** #24, March, 1897, with extra text by E. W. Townsend telling the story of **The Yellow Kid in McFadden's Flats**. This also gives it the honor of being the first "origin" comic book. Indeed, it even says "comic book" on its back cover.

Dillingham's original market for this "comic book" were the millions of train commuters who had to endure the long rides between Boston and Philadelphia by way of New York City. The comic was available on commuter trains and in the train stations that dotted the land. These tracks were the freeways of the day, hauling millions of people where in many cases there were no paved roads yet made. In fact, David A. Kyle (author of **A Pictorial History of Science Fiction**), who put out the first comics fanzine as a teenager in February 1936, called **Phantasy World**, recently told me that when he was a youngster in the '20s, his parents would purchase a comic book for him at the train station to keep him quiet while on the way to visiting relatives or simply on vacation.

Dillingham's comic book never sold out of the New York area. Numbers 1 through 23 and 25 onwards were books of a completely different nature, but it was definitely a comic book with a cover price of 50 cents. Sadly, only a handful are still known to exist today. The contents of the book are © 1897 Richard F. Outcault. Indeed, Outcault submitted his copyright notification to the Library of Congress in Sept. of 1896. In those days the publisher of newspaper art, by law, usually owned the rights to the title and the use of the characters to promote the newspaper, while the creator also retained the rights to write and draw what had been created. In any event, it would be a couple of years before the next comic book was to appear.

A format of publishing called "pulps" dominated the newsstands for decades prior to the arrival of the modern comic book. The standard "pulp" format started in the early 1880s. Usually published monthly, these had a slick full color process painted cover that grabbed the attention of the potential reader, with the text contents printed on the cheapest paper available so it could be marketed for the "common man" to afford to purchase it. Spot illustrations were scattered throughout. There were "pulps" for every genre imaginable. By the 1930s, there were so many different pulps vying for newsstand space that some of the marginal, newer publishers had to resort to risqué sensationalism to grab the attention of a potential reader in order to acquire that dime.

Long before the pulps, there were what was known as "Dime Novels," and prior to that there were the "Popular Story papers" in a newspaper format. The latter publications can date their origins to these publications, which came out around 1830. The Popular Story weeklies initially rode the second class mailing permits that were then granted to newspapers to encourage subscriptions. This was before the newsstand was to start permeating the land in a couple of decades.

THE FIVE CENT
WIDE AWAKE LIBRARY

FRANK READE AND HIS STEAM HORSE.
By "NONAME."

The Five Cent Wide Awake Library
© Frank Tousey

These early weeklies looked and felt like a newspaper, with an occasional illustration to go along with the story. Some of the titles were **Street and Smith's New York Weekly**, **New York Ledger**, **Saturday Night**, **Banner Weekly**, **Saturday Journal**, **Cassel's Illustrated Family Paper**, **Family Story Paper**, **Harper's Magazine**, **Fireside Companion**, and many more. They lasted until the 1890s, with most of their sales being mainly by mail subscription for almost fifty years, until the modern newsstand grew to sufficient numbers to influence their evolution into magazines with color covers to better attract attention. With the advent of literacy, the audience was becoming more sophisticated as well.

The Dime Novel slapped a cover on these "popular stories," usually with a lurid yellow color. The same product was simply reformatted with eye-catching artwork to compete, and found its way onto the urban newsstands of the largest metropolitan centers in the 1860s as well as by mail subscription. The first one is generally credited as "Malaeska" by Mrs. Ann Stephens and appeared in June 1860. The Dime Novels were the precursors of what we generally call "the pulps" in this day and age. Later titles include **Buffalo Bill's Wild West Adventures**, **Beadle's Dime Library**, **Beadle's Pocket Library**, **Beadle's New Dime Novels**, **Frank Starrs American Novels**, **Old Cap. Collier Library**, **Deadwood Dick**, **Nick Carter Weekly**, **Pluck and Luck**, **Old Sleuth Library** and literally hundreds of others. Distribution lines into "small town" America were firmly entrenched by this time . In the years after the Civil War, transportation of goods and services increased dramatically. Cover art was essential to attract attention as the number of titles increased to "glut" proportions.

All these earlier formats telling the fantastic exploits of America's "popular" heroes and heroines are important to understand in context as they build on one another. Beginning with straight text, they moved on to a combination of comic art with interior illustrations coupled with a text story until we arrive at the comic strip, with its intertwined usage of words and pictures in a panel format as devised by Outcault with **The Yellow Kid** in 1896. Eventually in 1933, those two visionary printer's salesmen hit upon the winning formula that has been essentially the same ever since. However, there have been many varied formats employed over the last 100 years. Chris Ware's **Acme Novelty Library** rests my case.

The public fell in love with their comic strips. They became the most popular form of entertainment in the land, with a combined readership that exceeded 100 million people for many decades in the USA alone. By the early '30s the entire Board of Directors of U. S. Steel were quoted in print about what fervent comics fans they were as a comics fever swept the country.

Scores of "how-to" cartoonists' schools sprung up in every major city, with promises of "easy" wealth that could be had by entertaining the country with a comic strip if it became popular. Early on, many of these first comic strips were translated into live-action vaudeville-type plays that traveled the country, playing in many a small town as far-flung as Texarkana, Texas, including **The Yellow Kid**, **Buster Brown**, **Little Nemo**, **Mutt & Jeff.** At one point, there were four separate **Mutt & Jeff** troupes traversing the country. There was also a multitude of merchandise created that fans could collect, from pinback buttons, collector cards, cookies, cigarettes and much more.

With the advent of the animated cartoon, some of the earliest characters utilized were **Little Nemo**, **The Katzenjammer Kids**, **Krazy Kat**, **Mutt and Jeff,** and other famous comic strip superstars. It was simply a matter of time before collections of comic strips started appearing in book form on a regular basis as well, starting with the break-out from the original "Big Six" pioneers of Outcault, Swinnerton, Dirks, Opper, McCay and McManus.

The earliest "standard" format was borrowed from **Funny Folks** by F. M. Howarth, a book of cartoons from **Puck Magazine** published in 1899 by E. P. Dutton and Co. with a 12x16 format. There are some interior colored pages, but this is not yet a comic strip, so it may not be a true comic book. It is a series of illustrations with textual captions running underneath the art. Howarth soon went on to be a very famous comic strip storyteller just a few years later.

A company called Isaac H. Blanchard Company brought out **Vaudeville and Other Things** by "Bunny" (otherwise known as Carl

E. Schultze) in 1900 which measured 10x13 or so. The first of many **Foxy Grandpa** volumes by Schultze came out at the same time. These two strips began on January 7th, 1900, with the first book printings in November 1900, just in time for Christmas sales. From the New York Herald, they copied the basic format which the Dutton company had first introduced. This became the industry standard for many years to come.

The following year, copying the Dutton format, Cupples & Leon ushered in their first comic book. It was a compilation of Outcault's extremely racist look at black life in America, **Pore Li'l Mose**, a short-lived strip for which the artist encountered tremendous flak, and rightfully deserved. This book probably soured Cupples & Leon on doing more comic books for a while, as it was four years before they ventured into the field again. **The Blackberries** by E. W. Kemble from the R. H. Russell Company also premiered that year.

As early as 1903, Sears, Roebuck and Co. was offering some of the earliest comic reprint books through their definitive mail order catalog. In November of 1902, Hearst's **New York American & Journal** issued these five large (10x15) semi-hard cover comic books: **The Katzenjammer Kids** by Dirks, **Happy Hooligan** and **Alphonse and Gaston and Leon** by Opper, and **Tigers** and **On and Off Mount Ararat** by Swinnerton. These last two volumes were the two very first "funny animal" comic books

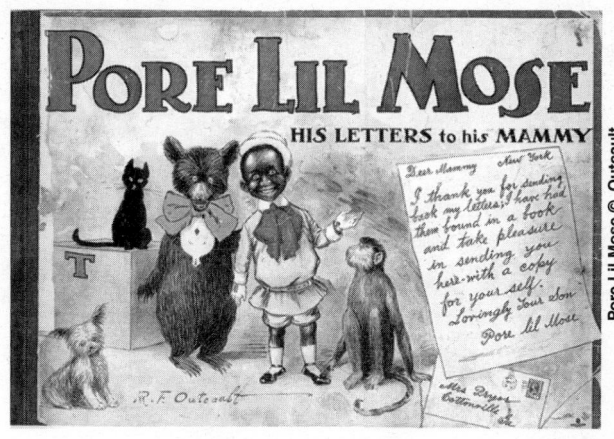

ever issued. The more popular ones underwent a number of reprintings as the new artform slowly invaded the consciousness of America with its polychromatic sequential humor. They were for sale at fifty cents each either by mail order catalog or in book stores in the larger cities, sometimes from the newspaper itself as a promotional tool.

Shortly thereafter, the first of many other **Katzenjammer Kids** (1903) volumes started appearing in comic strip fans' libraries all over the country. This Rudolph Dirks creation, along with **Buster Brown**, was probably the most popular of the early comic books. **The Katzenjammer Kids** is also the oldest strip in existence, beginning in 1897, and is still drawn today by Hy Eisman.

Opper's **Hooligan** began in 1900 and by 1903 almost all of Frederic Opper's major creations saw their very own comic books competing in the stores, including other volumes of **Happy Hooligan**, **And Her Name Was Maud** and **Alphonse & Gaston & Leon**.

Buster Brown debuted in 1902 and began showing up as the first comic premiums as early as 1904 for the Brown Shoe Company as well as for The Buster Brown Bread Company, The Buster Brown Stocking Company, Collins Baking Company and other early licenses to help these companies sell their products such as stoves, facial cream, etc. In 1903, regular large size comic book editions began appearing, with the very first one titled **Buster Brown and His Resolutions**. **Buster Brown** as a licensed commodity really took off with the founding in 1910 of the Outcault Advertising Agency. Buster and Tige stand as the longest continuously licensed comic characters, long after the strip stopped running with the death of Outcault in 1928.

The comic book business soon experienced its first major boom in these early years (1903-1910) as the reading of comics soon became a national pastime, dominating the consciousness of the country until the dawn of the TV era almost fifty years later. Many of these earliest comic books were published by William Randolph Hearst, who, to his ever lasting credit, loved comic strips, and carried many of his favorites for many years after their economic viability had worn out simply because he liked them, the most famous example being **Krazy Kat** by the genius George Herriman.

The main publishers prior to World War One were Hearst Publishing, New York Herald Company, and the Frederic A. Stokes Company, which picked up all the titles that Hearst had been publishing, bringing out many new ones as well as reprinting earlier ones. Stokes was followed by the M. A. Donahue Company and eventually the Cupples & Leon Company, which would grow to dominate the comics business a couple of decades later.

There were many volumes of the early great comic strips issued in 1905, including a very beautiful **Little Sammy Sneeze** with a breath-taking cover by Winsor McCay that contrasts greatly in quality with the offerings of the next early McKay comics publisher chronicled here. It was this year as well that comics pioneer James Swinnerton saw his first collected **Jimmy** comic book in book stores from coast to coast.

Willie Westinghouse Edison Smith, The Boy Inventor by Frank Crane was another early favorite in the Sunday newspaper comic section that made play on two famous inventors who were busily transforming America with many a technological advance. A collected comic book was published by Stokes in 1906. One can see a distinct influence on later Rube Goldberg creations.

The Doffield Company brought out Winsor McCay's **Little Nemo in Slumberland** and **Dreams of a Rare-bit Fiend** in 1906, reprinting strips from the previous year. It published just these two comic books, and they are extremely rare to find these days. The covers are rather lack-luster, with a minimal amount of artwork by McKay. The luscious, colored fine lines of Winsor McKay are obscured by slightly off registered printing, blurring the art a bit in the process. Likewise, **Sam and His Laugh** by Swinnerton debuted from the Frederick A. Stokes company.

Also in 1906, collections of **Peck's Bad Boy** by one of the grand old men of the early comics scene, Walt McDougall, started appearing. McDougall had been doing pantomime comic strips that had all the essential elements of a true comic strip sans word balloons in **Puck** since the late 1880s. Some think it was this gent who invented the comic strip in America. When the last piece of the puzzle had finally been invented by Outcault, McDougall was quick to pick up on the concept and get on the band wagon. In the 1920s, McDougall brought comics fans a new daily strip called **The Radio Buggs**, which poked hilarious fun at those who were crazed about the (then) brand-new medium of, you guessed it, radio.

The Cupples & Leon company, which was a major force in children's textual story books for much of this decade, started getting into serious comics publishing as well in 1906. They started with their large size **Buster Brown** series, which came out concurrently with the books from Stokes, as well as another short lived Outcault Sunday feature called **Buddy Tucker,** which was a kind of a cross between **Buster Brown** and Outcault's earlier **Yellow Kid**. Buster was a spoiled rich kid and Buddy was from a more "common" environment and a far cry from Outcault's abortive **Li'l Mose**, which caused quite a stir among people who found such subject matter quite vulgar. **The Katzenjammer Kids** had continuing new editions to follow as well soon thereafter.

By 1907, Cupples & Leon introduced a new 6x7 format that reprinted three Sunday pages with a twist. Each panel occupied one page, but this time they also printed on both sides of the paper. The color textures were deep and rich, with a lot of care going into the printing. One of the series was a set of ten **Buster Brown** and **Buddy Tucker** comics by Richard Outcault that had on its back covers the earliest known usage of the term "funny book" to describe their new format book of comic strips. **Buster Brown Goes Swimming** had a nude Buster cavorting with his dog, Tige, on the front cover as another youngster was seen stealing his clothes from the side of a creek. Such was the early "funny" book.

In the same basic size and single panel format, Cupples & Leon, with help from Saalfield Publishing Company, brought out a series of cloth "muslin" for **Buster Brown** and **Foxy Grandpa** in the same year for little kids who still chewed more of their comic book than actually read it.

(The Outbursts of) Everett True by A. D. Condo appears to be Saalfield Publishing Company's first comic book published by themselves, collecting these zany mis-adventures in 1907 as well. Condo helped pioneer the concept of the daily comic strip with the first **Everett True,** appearing on July 22. 1905, not too long after the 1904 abortive start-up of **A. Piker Clerk** by Clare Briggs, the first "true" attempt at an on-going daily comics strip. **Clerk** might have enjoyed a much longer run than a few months if "The Boss," William Randoplh Hearst, hadn't found it "vulgar" and pulled the plug. Condo delighted readers for more than two decades with the antics of a man who wasted no time informing those around him exactly what he thought of them, usually followed by "outbursts" of a violent temper. The panels were stacked on top of each other running from two to four, depending on the gag. The character was popular enough for this volume to undergo various reprintings through the 1920s, again from Saalfield.

In that same year, Saalfield brought George McManus's **The Newlyweds** to the public in a 13x10 format. "Baby Snookums" was the little tyke the newlywed couple tried raising and was a big hit, sparking character merchandise that included a five inch tall cold cast statue in 1909 that says "© George McManus" on its base. Around this time, **The Newlyweds** was also the earliest known comic strip to make the transition to the silver screen in a series of live action shorts for which I have so far unearthed two lobby cards.

By 1908, the first comic book with more than one strip in it appeared exactly 25 years before **Funnies On Parade**. It was a major evolutionary step. Published by Stokes, **The Three Funmakers** were "The Katzenjammer Kids" by Rudolph Dirks, "...And Her Name Was Maud" and "Happy Hooligan" by Fredric Opper. The characters of these three strips all appeared together on the cover of **The Three Funmakers** in a beautiful jam cover by the two now world-renowned artists. It is in the pre-World War I standard size of 10x15, with full color board covers as well as full color pages printed on one side only .

In 1909, Cupples & Leon brought out a number of the large "standard" Dutton size comics of major favorites that it slowly captured from the other early publishers, including one volume of **Little Nemo in Slumberland** with a front cover much better than the lack-lustre earlier effort, and **The Monkeyshines of Marseleen** by Norman Jennet. Cupples & Leon would grow to dominate the comic book market during the 1920s with an innovative format size introduced ten years later that led to the elimination of most other formats.

In 1910, the daily newspaper comic strip was being ingrained in the consciousness of the American reader, and the Ball Company introduced yet another size variant format with **Mutt & Jeff**. Measuring 5x15 with 68 daily newspaper strips and printing on both sides of each page, it had hard covers and clear, crisp reproduction of the art. The strips in these books were larger than the work originally appeared in the newspapers. In #2, Ball printed **Mutt & Jeff's** misadventures while trying to partake in the Mexican Revolution, including Jeff smoking opium in a Chinese opium den. Bud Fisher spent time hanging out with

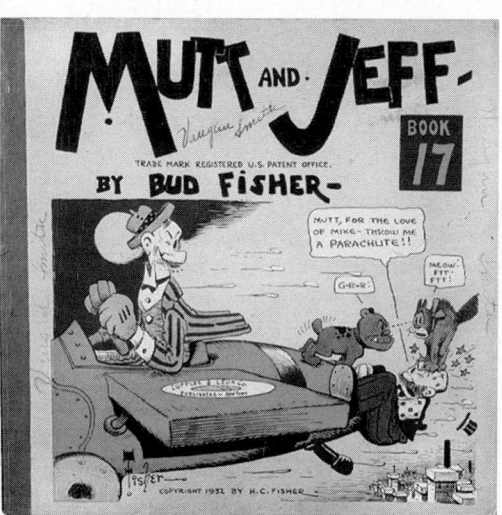

Pancho Villa while legal issues were being settled with Hearst as to who owned the copyright to his creation.

With issue #5 in 1916, just prior to America's entry into The Great War, Ball was reprinting the duo's misadventures in the trenches of World War I in Europe. Each of the first four issues underwent various reprintings and were immensely popular. There are editions from all over the country, noting the newspaper from a particular town as well as variants of the covers. The war-oriented fifth number is the rarest and hardest to find today, even though all of them are increasingly difficult to uncover as time marches on.

This format was quite popular in presenting a collected daily strip. The M. A. Donahue Company in 1912 came out with a 6x15 version of **Silk Hat Harry's Divorce Suit** by Thomas "TAD" Dorgan which, in typical TAD style, wreaked havoc with social conventions of married life with the characters regularly cheating on their wives, hanging out in saloons all night, and ending up in front of a judge to explain their actions away. The judge of the court was always telling the arresting officers to "put that boob in the cooler for a month." TAD invented hundreds of expressions and slang-words that quickly found their way into everyday usage, many of which are still present in today's jargon.

There wasn't too much comic book activity during the World War years of 1914 to 1917, with just a few comic books published. The 5x16 format was tried out by Hearst's Star Company (later King Features) in 1917 when they brought to bookstores a whopping, 100 page **Bringing Up Father** edition.

That same year the M. A. Donahue Company brought out a series of E.C. Segar collections of his **Charlie Chaplin** Sunday page, including **Comic Capers**, **In the Movies**, **Up in the Air**, **In the Army** and **Funny Stunts**, with this last volume in full color. They were in the basic Dutton format, sans a hard cover, which went on for some years before the superior Cupples & Leon formula forced it out. The books Donohue put out at this time were consequently rather flimsy to handle, and are now incredibly rare in high grade condition. Segar would introduce "**The Thimble Theater**" just a couple of years later through Hearst's King Feature Syndicate and bring us **Popeye** a decade after that in 1929.

Also in 1917, Saalfield published two separate issues of Gus Mager's very funny Sherlock Holmes spoof, **Hawkshaw the Detective**, and **Adventures of Hawkshaw**, in black & white with color covers and printing on both sides of the paper, cutting Sunday pages in half and making them face one another. In addition, Saalfield came out with a couple **Captain & The Kids** collections called **Hans and Fritz**, plus an edition of **S'Matter Pop?** by Charlie Payne. Again, they all measured 10x13 1/2 inches to 14 inches. In addition, Saalfield became the first publisher to use the term "comic book" on the front cover to describe the contents. Titled simply **Comic Book**, it was dated 1917, and featured early **Clancy the Cop** by VEP on the full-color cover with black & white interiors.

Prior to starting **Skippy**, Lieut. P. L. Crosby produced a strip called **That Rookie From the 13th Squad,** starting in 1917 for the McClure Syndicate, which focused on humorous aspects of surviving "boot" camp in the Army. In 1918, Harper & Row came out with a collected version in hard cover measuring 8x9. It floated between single panel jokes and four panel continuities with many of the punch lines still holding up after all these years.

With **Mutt & Jeff** #6, Cupples and Leon scored a coup in 1919 with the series that had originated with Ball. They quickly switched it to their (then) brand new 10x10, 52 page black & white format, slicing a daily strip into a four panel box as well as starting up a brand new **Bringing Up Father** series taken from the dailies. Each ran until at least 1933 with a standard 10x10, 52 page format, and were reprinted over and over. (**Funnies On Parade,** and later **Famous Funnies,** were to pull **Mutt & Jeff** away. The adventures of Jiggs and Maggie by the comics genius George McManus were to find a home in **King Comics** starting in 1936. Black & white has always had to try harder to compete with full color). In those fifteen years, in addition to the above two series, they brought out **Joe Palooka**, **Barney Google and Sparkplug**, **The Gumps**, **Keeping Up With The Jones**, **The**

Nebbs, **Moon Mullins**, **Harold Teen**, **Reg'lar Fellers**, **Tillie the Toiler**, and **Toonerville Trolley** among others. These were some of the most popular comics of their day.

The Cupples & Leon Company's many comic strip titles were to dominate the comic book field all through the Roaring Twenties, publishing the last numbers of their many titles with the dawn of the Wildenburg and Gaines creation. Most of these are now incredibly hard to find, even more so if trying to collect a complete set of all the titles together. I am, however, getting a little ahead of myself. It wasn't until 1934 or so that they got out of the comic book business.

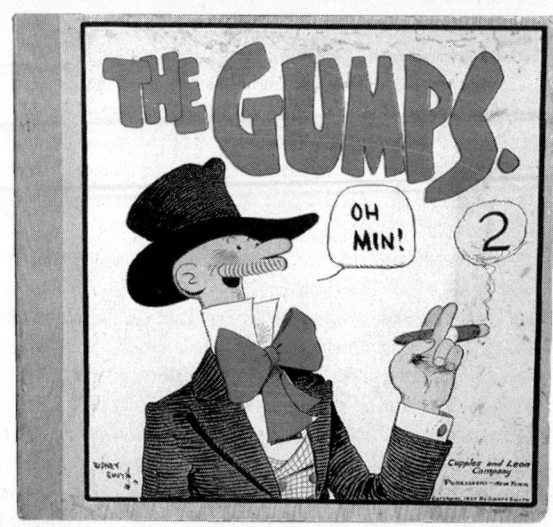

The Gumps #2
© C&L

Between 1918 and 1922, the Landfield-Kupfer Printing Co. of Chicago came out with a series of **The Gumps** in a 8x13 format that was extremely flimsy. It lasted at least six issues. The world's only known copy of #1 turned up this year in Omaha, Nebraska. At one point, **The Gumps** was America's most beloved dysfunctional family. On March 15, 1922, Robert Sydney Smith signed the first million dollar comics contract in history. He was guaranteed $100,000 a year for ten years to bring his famous creation to the public for **The Chicago Tribune**. By 1924, Cupples & Leon added **The Gumps** to their stable of popular comic books, publishing the antics of these superior characters until at least 1931.

The Embee Company was partially funded and half-owned by George McManus, who had become quite wealthy with the success of **Bringing Up Father**. The other owner was Rudolph Block Jr, hence the name "eM-Bee". George McManus was a very early self-promoter, getting comic books into the hands of casual readers at the newsstand. A 1923 issue of Hearst's internal industry house organ (ala **Diamond Dialogue**), **Circulation**, had a two page spread of George McManus attending a comics fair in his honor in Toronto, Canada, with a title blurb that read, "George McManus Outdraws the Prince of Wales." There is a photograph included of thousands of people waiting in line.

Hans und Fritz
© Saalfield Publ.

Rudolph Block Jr. managed the business end of Embee and McManus gathered the talent together. Both worked for Hearst's King Features Syndicate. Rudolph's father was Block Sr., who had been the editor of the New York American's Sunday supplement since the turn of the century, part of the flagship of the Hearst empire. His father had been around for the development of virtually all of Hearst's comic strips, starting with the first one originated there, **The Katzenjammer Kids**, in 1897. Obviously, a love of the comics rubbed off on the son.

Their first product came out in 1919. It was a **Bringing Up Father** board game that was advertised in the Cupples & Leon **Bringing Up Father** series as "easy to learn, hard to quit, impossible to beat." One was to send $1.50 directly to Embee

Distributing at 141-155 East 25th St. in New York, which also just happened to be an address of the Hearst Empire. One wonders how many they sold. It is quite rare today.

Acquiring their own office space at 1493 Broadway in New York City by 1921, Embee then tried to introduce the first newsstand comic book twelve years before **Famous Funnies,** called **Comic Monthly,** with 28 pages and a two color cover for 10¢ in the basic Cupples & Leon format, albeit less than half the price and half the page count of strips. Such a bargain. It was to last a full year with one issue coming out each month. Today, these are some of the rarest comics to try to collect. Hearst most likely gave a couple of friends his permission to see if those who didn't read his papers would fall in love with the comics. It was a noble experiment.

Embee reprinted a different newspaper comic strip each month, including **Polly & Her Pals** by Cliff Sterrett, **Barney Google** by Billy DeBeck, **Little Jimmy** by Jimmy Swinnerton, **Mike & Ike** and **Foolish Questions** by Rube Goldberg, **Indoor Sports** by "TAD" Dorgan as well as **S'Matter Pop, Tillie the Toiler** and **Toots & Casper,** all in a slightly smaller 8 1/2x9, basic Cupples & Leon size. What I have always found rather puzzling is that there is no obvious **Bringing Up Father** issue as part of the series, considering that Mr. McManus owned half the company.

This pioneering company was extremely innovative for its day, but in 1921-22 the right formula for competing on the newsstand had yet to be found. The talent Embee had gathered together was awesome, so it should have flown. Unfortunately, the production values were low, as they unwisely utilized a rather flimsy paper. Considering the times, its cover price of 10¢ for 28 black & white pages was rather high when one considers that a decade later one got 64 full color pages for the same entry fee.

Besides **Comic Monthly,** Embee did bring out a 9x15 collection of **Bringing Up Father** Sunday pages in full color in 1921 for sale in book stores, which might make George McManus the first comic book self-publisher on record. A separate 10x16 full color volume of **The Katzenjammer Kids** by Knerr also came out, marking the last appearance of Hearst's copyrighted version in a collected book, until the few pages that appeared in each issue of **King Comics** some fifteen years later.

In 1922, Whitman tried the same basic format on a couple of Clare Brigg's creations, but with a twist: **Mr. and Mrs.** and **Ain't It A Grand and Glorious Feeling** came out in both full color and black & white editions. Two years later, The Prairie Farmer Publishing Company brought out **The Adventures of Slim and Spud** in a 100 page, 4x10 comic book of newspaper reprints. 1924 also saw Cupples & Leon snag **The Gumps** into its stable of super-stars. The M.S. Publishing Company brought out Harry Tuthill's **Home, Sweet Home** the following year. This strip evolved into **The Bungle Family**. That same year, M.S. snagged **Reg'lar Fellers** for one issue before C&L won it back.

Starting in 1926, Cupples & Leon added several other formats of size and thickness, including their famous 7x9 dust-jacketed 60¢ hard covers that included the yearly **Little Orphan Annie** as well as **Smitty, Bobby Thatcher, Harold Teen, Tailspin Tommy** and **Reg'lar Fellers**. These were available in finer book stores everywhere or through the mails directly from Cupples & Leon's own catalog that appeared somewhere in most of their books. These books were later reissued as 25¢ soft bounds.

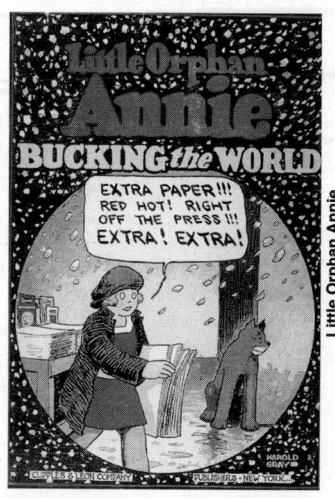

Little Orphan Annie saw a new edition every year from 1926 through 1934 as the public soaked them up, fully identifying with the orphan waif's misadventures through hard times and Daddy Warbuck's many rescues. These were personally edited by Harold Gray to condense his Annie storylines, which usually ran a minimum of eight months, into a nice, concise package.

Cupples & Leon next came out with "The Big Book" format, containing 142 pages of newspaper reprint comics for 75¢ in a hard cover while still measuring 10x10. Tried out for size were **Bringing Up Father**, **Mutt & Jeff** and **Moon Mullins**. The first two titles were reprinted several times as well as having a second volume appear. The following year, **Felix the Cat** entered the fray with a 52 page comic book of reprints from the McLoughlin Brothers. Measuring 8x16 inches, it presented half the strips in color and half in black & white. Reissued in 1931, it was changed to look almost like the by-then standard Cupples & Leon 10x10 size, dropping some of the pages in the process.

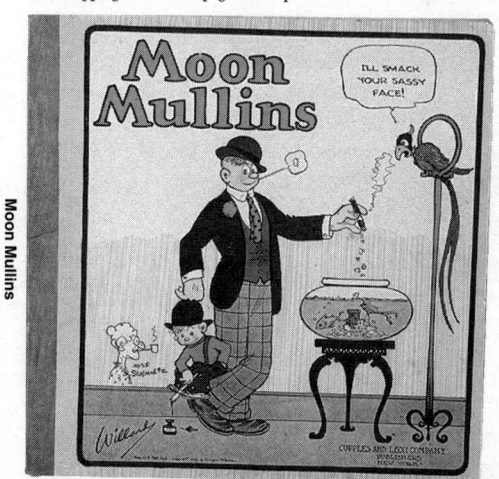

In 1929, **The Funnies**, a weekly tabloid from the Dell Publishing, gave original, never-before-published comics a try by utilizing a lot of unknown artists and strips, except for the tired **Foxy Grandpa**, who had been into his second childhood by then for thirty years. The slapstick humor of the earliest comics since the turn of the century was wearing a bit thin on an increasingly sophisticated audience; they wanted a continued action series with a more complex plot than the same old, tired, rehashed jokes. **The Funnies** also contained original work by a young Boody Rogers, called **Deadwood Gulch**, a humorous western strip, as well as **Tack Knight's My Big Brudder**.

The comics reading public had just been introduced to **Buck Rogers**, **Tarzan**, **Popeye** and quite a few others a few months before **The Funnies** had started, and were beginning to embrace strong narrative adventure continuity, which **The Funnies** simply did not contain. The second Golden Age of Comics was just beginning to unfold in this country. Four years later, **Buck Rogers** would be the star beginning in the 3rd issue of the first successful newsstand comic magazine, **Famous Funnies**, which was a direct outgrowth of the format first devised for **Funnies On Parade**. They tried it for 36 issues between 1929 and 1930 before throwing in the towel. It was 16 tabloid pages for 10¢ at first, with the last dozen or so reduced to a nickel. It didn't help. My guess is that the competition was too great to sustain interest, as there was nothing to really compel the reader to get the next one. Weekly was probably just too frequent a publication schedule for many people caught in the early throes of the "Great Depression," which also coincided with the launch of this noble experiment.

Tarzan Book No. 1 © ERB

Dell would later be the third newsstand comic book publisher in the new format, jumping in with **Popular Comics** and growing in a short while to be the largest comic book publisher in the world, a position they held for more than twenty years. **Walt Disney's Comics & Stories** would top five million copies sold a month. (According to the June 14, 1947 issue of **Editor & Publisher**, Dell would also be the first comic book company to call other publishers together to try and form some sort of "Comics Code," called the Association of Comics Magazine Publishers. Elected as its first President was George Delecorte, with M. C. Gaines as Vice President. The latter was killed in a tragic boating accident in August, and Delecorte seems to have resigned shortly thereafter.)

Towards the end of 1929, Grosset & Dunlap entered the fray with a 50¢ compilation of Hal Foster's initial **Tarzan of the Apes** daily strips, which had begun on January 7th, in the same 7x9 dust-wrapped hard-cover format Cupples & Leon had introduced three years before with their famous **Little Orphan Annie** series. Hal Foster would later attain world-wide fame in his own right with one of the greatest of all comic strips, **Prince Valiant**, a "must-read" for all collectors. This same **Tarzan** book was also reprinted by 1934 with less pages for only a quarter, sans the cloth hard-cover and dust-wrapper. This "origin" story is much cruder than Foster's later work on the companion **Tarzan** Sunday page, which he took up in 1931 and continued through 1937.

1929 marked a new beginning in the era of the adventure strip when one considers that **Buck Rogers** debuted the same day as Tarzan. Shortly thereafter, Popeye showed up in **Thimble Theatre** and **Captain Easy** walked into Roy Crane's seminal **Wash Tubbs**. That same year saw Reilly & Lee (**Wizard of Oz** publishers) abandon their textual format with art by Frank King on **Gasoline Alley**. They had been putting out the adventures of Uncle Walt and Skeezix without presenting the entire comic strip through the '20s, so it was only a matter of time before they brought out books of strip reprints that followed the same basic size as the Grosset & Dunlap **Tarzan**, complete with hard covers.

Dell Publishing Company took the plunge once again in 1930, bringing out two volumes in Cupples & Leon's 10x10 industry standard format of non reprint material of a strip by VEP called **Clancy the Cop**. It did not sell very well. In 1930, they also tried

Thimble Theatre Starring Popeye #2
© Sonnet

a volume of Boody Rogers' **Deadwood Gulch**. These strips had first seen print in the abortive **Funnies** that Dell had just canceled earlier that year

He Done Her Wrong by the late, great Milt Gross was first published this same year. It is "The Great American Novel Told Without Words" that saw printings through at least 1963, and is truly the first original graphic novel published in this country. Running well over 100 pages, it is extremely easy to follow without the use of a single word, balloon or otherwise, as this genius created a new experiment that moved The New York Times to write, "Milt Gross exhibits as wild a fancy, as prodigal an imagination as one could wish...crammed with action, coincidence, villainy, love..." This is comics genius at one of its all-time heights of glory, and I have never tired of re-reading it over the decades since I first discovered this gem.

Other publishers like David McKay (**Mickey Mouse**) and Sonnet (**Thimble Theatre Starring Popeye**) followed in 1931 with Cupples & Leon's innovative 10x10 format, placing their publications in many book stores across the country. The Mickey

12

Mouse compilations underwent several printings and were extremely popular as "The Mouse" took the world by storm. McKay released one **Mickey Mouse** each year from 1931 to 1934 with the third issue in beautiful full-process color.

The Henry Altemus Company entered comic book publishing in 1931 with three **Felix the Cat** dust-wrapped hard-cover books in the basic C&L **Little Orphan Annie** style. By the early '30s, this format was quite popular as the books would fit nicely on a library shelf, thereby "legitimizing" having a comic "book" for that segment of the population who worried about such things. They also came out with two **Bobby Thatcher** volumes, the second one being a hard-cover with a dust-wrapper.

Just Kids, by Arthur Carter, was collected in 1932 by the McLoughlin Brothers, which was trying to compete with the Gene Byrne's **Reg'lar Fellers** and Walter Berndt's **Smitty** books that Cupples & Leon had been issuing. Kid strips have been immensely popular long before the advent of **Peanuts**, **Dennis the Menace** or **Calvin & Hobbes.**

In late 1932 Whitman Publishing of Racine, Wisconsin invented the "Big Little Book," bringing out **The Adventures of Dick Tracy** by Chester Gould as the first one, closely followed by **Mickey Mouse** and **Little Orphan Annie**. Whitman went on to produce many hundreds of these compact 3x4 comic books with an alternating page of text and art work that at first were mainly newspaper strip reprints, soon followed by many original in-house creations that didn't need to have royalties paid to other companies. They soon had many competitors from the likes of Saalfield, Lynn Publishing and others. Big Little Books sold in the millions and were for sale in many finer department stores since they had great eye appeal as well as fitting nicely on store shelves. "Big

Reg'lar Fellers © C & L

Little Books" went toe to toe with the soon to be made "modern" comic book for about ten years before being slowly squeezed off the shelves as the public embraced what they wanted to spend that dime on. They lasted until the late 1940s, undergoing several minor format changes along the way, including a name change to "Better" Little Books.

Later, Whitman also introduced "The Big Big Book," which was a 7x10 version of the Big Little Book. There were several dozen of these as well, including **Buck Rogers**, **Mickey Mouse**, **Popeye**, **Buck Jones**, **Tarzan**, etc. They also manufactured what is known as the "Penny Comic Book," measuring 2x2 inches and usually sold in boxed sets of six at a time, with the most important groupings including **Mickey Mouse** and **Little Orphan Annie**.

Cupples & Leon added **Dick Tracy** to its over-whelming stable of stars in 1933, with two 7x8 1/2 dust-wrapped hard-covers explaining **How Dick Tracy & Dick Tracy Jr Captured "Stooge" Viller** and **How Dick Tracy & Dick Tracy it Caught The Racketeers**. These were quite popular and were reprinted several times in the next year or so. **Dick Tracy** captured the public's imagination when it debuted a couple years earlier with its no-nonsense approach to crime fighting as well as the most eclectic assortment of villains comics had ever seen up to this point. **Dick Tracy** was incredibly violent right from its inception in 1931, and his creator, Chester Gould, merely said it was realistic, capturing what was happening in American society during the height of the "bootleg" era. I personally think 1933 was a pivotal year in the publishing business because Prohibition was repealed and many "gangster-types" wished to go as legit as possible.

Rare 1933 club pinback; probably the first comic book club.

Detective Dan, Secret Op. 48 debuted in 1933 as well in a 9 1/2x12 inch format from the Humor Publishing Company. A precursor to **Dan Dunn**, it was a **Dick Tracy** knockoff. Incredibly, Humor Publishing has been overlooked all these years, and unfairly so. They published original newsstand material at least two years before **New Fun** #1 debuted on the stands. As far as I know, there was only one other comic book Humor ever put out, called **Adventures of the Detective Ace King**, in the same basic format as well as another Tracy knock-off. One might say that these are yet another "missing link" in the development of the comic book as we know it today. Two other titles mentioned as "coming soon" are **Happy Mulligan** and **Bob Scully, Two-Fisted Hick Detective**, as well as second issues of the two known titles. So far, none of these have surfaced.

As a pivotal footnote in history, within a short time of the publication of these historically important comic books, two teenagers from Cleveland, Ohio met with the owners of Humor when they were in town to show them their first version of **Superman**. They worked up a complete cover, borrowing elements from both of the current Humor titles such as the phrase

"A...story in cartoons" as well as the use of "double Os" in the word "cartoons," which in turn finds its origin in the cover of the legendary **Cartoons Magazine** that began before World War I. Very rare today, **Cartoons** ran for many years and covered all facets of comic strips and political cartoons in depth. At first agreeing to the **Superman** concept, a short time later the still-unknown owners of the Humor Publishing Company reneged, sending the original art back, thereby becoming the first comics companies to reject what would grow into comics greatest success story.

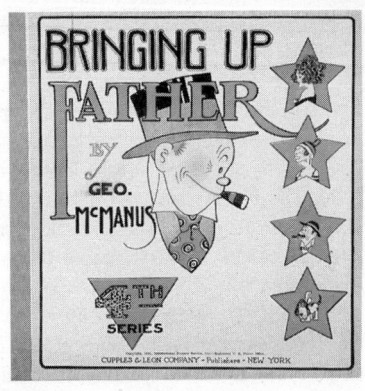

1933 also saw two separate giveaway **Mickey Mouse Magazine** series, with one of them lasting until 1935. The long-running **Mickey Mouse Magazine** newsstand series eventually became **Walt Disney's Comics & Stories** from Dell in 1940, which grew to be the best-selling comic book series of all time, topping over 5.5 million copies an issue. The first two series were giveaways for all kinds of stores to build a customer base. By the summer of 1935, and with the obvious presence of **Famous Funnies** on newsstands nationwide, the corporate heads realized people would gladly pay money for these books. The first newsstand issue was a large 13x10 that retailed for a quarter, with all subsequent smaller issues for a dime. They all contained some comic strip material with a portion of each mag given over to puzzles & games for kids. Finding an unused **MM** mag with nothing written in it is extremely difficult these days.

Comic Cuts from the H. L. Baker Co., Inc. made a stab at garnering a newsstand market in early 1934, with a weekly 24 page full-color 5 cent tabloid of all original material. This folded after nine issues during the summer when **Famous Funnies** debuted on the newsstand comics market with its superior format. With a lackluster roster that included no recognizable superstars as well as being unwieldy on the stands to boot, **Comic Cuts** unfortunately didn't stand as much of a chance as the earlier ill-fated Dell effort, **The Funnies**, from five years previous.

David McKay Publishers came out in 1934 with two **Secret Agent X-9** compilations in a 8x7 1/2 soft bound format, with world famous "pulp" writer Dashiell Hammett getting all the glory on the front cover. Inside is where we learn of "Illustrations by Alex Raymond," almost an after-thought on the part of the publishers. Mr. Raymond had yet to come into super-stardom in his own right.

It took a couple of years for the artwork on **Flash Gordon** and **Jungle Jim**, which had debuted on January 7, 1934 along with **X-9** a couple of months later, to gel into what most people remember today as some of the most beautifully rendered work ever to grace the comics. **Flash Gordon** would soon eclipse **Buck Rogers** in popularity. The "Class of '34" was a seminal one in the history of all comics. Not only did **Famous Funnies** debut on the newsstand, with **Buck Rogers** starting with the third issue, and Alex Raymond start three sensational comic strips that would grow into true works of art that were a wonder to behold, but many other famous strips started that year as well, providing much inspiration for the comic books that were yet to come. The three other most famous classics of this year were **Terry And The Pirates** by Milton Caniff, **Li'l Abner** by Al Capp and **Mandrake the Magician** by Lee Falk and Phil Davis. **Red Barry** by Will Gould, yet another Tracy knockoff, **Radio Patrol** by Sullivan & Schmidt, **Don Winslow of the Navy** by Frank Martinek, USN, & Leon Beroth, USN, with assistance from Frank Knox, Secretary of the Navy, and **The Little King** by Otto Soglow entered the fray as well.

The adventure strip, as well as the science fiction and character pulps, plus the explosion of increasingly sophisticated sound movies and radio adventure programming, captured the public's imagination. Many fertile creative minds would soon be pumping out so many new, innovative (yet inspired by previously produced material) comic book heroes by 1940. Saalfield jumped in again and experimented with yet another size format that same year with the appearance of the **Popeye Cartoon Book**. It measured a bizarre 8 1/2x13 in glorious full-process color, appearing as both a 40 page edition and one with only 12 pages. One has to read the pages across the paper fold, otherwise one wonders what is going on., unlike almost every other comic book ever produced, which are complete on each page before venturing on to the next. This is another comic book that is very rare today, and due to its exceedingly odd, flimsy size, it is rarely found in high grade.

Also in 1934, Whitman made an appearance with a reprint of Mckay's #3 full color **Mickey Mouse** from the previous year, as well as two series called **Famous Comics** and **Famous Comics Cartoon Books**. The former was a smaller, oblong 3 1/2x8 1/2 book that came in a 100 page, multi-character three issue box set, containing **Polly & Her Pals**, **Barney Google**, **Katzenjammer Kids**, and **Little Jimmy**. The latter was a larger 8x7 series of 72 page, single-character hardbacks that included **The Captain & The Kids**, **Captain Easy**, **Ella Cinders** and **Freckles & His Friends**. These books reprinted daily comic strips without resorting to cutting them and re-pasting to fit. I rather like this format and it is too bad it never caught on.

Barney Google and Spark Plug #2
© C&L

The once great comics powerhouse of Cupples & Leon issued their last comics in 1934 with the final volumes of **Bringing Up Father** and **Little Orphan Annie**, then got out of the comic book business after almost thirty years of producing many fine collections. Change was clearly in the air. In 1935, David McKay (Philadelphia) brought out the last known 10x10 inch, 52 page comic book in the old Cupples & Leon format. **Popeye #1** debuted without the "Thimble Theatre" moniker to distract from the book's star. This issue is most difficult to find. There was also a second issue later in the year which is quite rare as well.

By the end of 1935, with the **Famous Funnies'** new format firmly entrenched, still somewhat recognizable in today's comic books, the standard 10x10 comic book of color board covers with black & white interiors for a quarter, as well as almost all of the other formats we have discussed, was gone. Original material began once again in 1935 when Major Malcolm Wheeler-Nicholson's first pioneering publishing efforts that eventually became DC Comics finally started to proliferate along with more publishers who entered the field. It was indeed a watershed year.

The comics in "book" form had started at 50 cents for those pre World War I, large-size editions. As we moved into the '20s, Cupples & Leon pioneered the 25 cent concept, plus a better, "user friendly" format, albeit in black & white. With **Famous Funnies** debuting in the middle of a bad economic depression, the page count went way up, full color was added and the price came down to a thin dime. Each time the price dropped, the circulation went up and up. More people could afford to purchase and read more than one or two comic books every once in a while than they ever could before.

Distribution of magazines, as pioneered in 1860 with the American News Company, was by this time as exact a science as the times permitted. Regularly ID distributors proliferated by the hundreds, with each having their own territories. Many of the largest cities had multiple competitors vying for the rack space of many a dealer. The world was soon to witness a publishing phenomenon the likes of which it had never seen before. The industry's combined circulation of comics would soar to over one billion copies sold a year, a figure that will most likely never be duplicated again.

Major corporations have lined up by the hundreds to have their products endorsed by comics characters. Untold thousands of comics premiums have been manufactured and given away in the last 100 years, with a veritable explosion of them beginning in the 1930s. This cross-pollination of corporate effort has created a vast body of modern mythology that many thousands of people now treasure and archive for posterity.

Robert L. Beerbohm has been a student of comic books since acquiring his first one in 1956. He began selling comics through the pages of G. B. Love's legendary RBCC in 1966. Along with Bud Plant and John Barrett, he co-founded Comics & Comix in 1972, the first retail comic book chain store in the country, as well as being intimately involved in helping to set up the "direct sales" market for comic book distribution. His book, *Comic Book Store Wars*, is a 600 page, definitive 100 year history of the business of comics in America, to be published later in 1997.

Barney Google and Spark Plug #1 © C&L   Bringing Up Father #2 © C&L   Bringing Up Father #5 © C&L

	GD25	FN65	VF82

	GD25	FN65	VF82

ADVENTURES OF DETECTIVE ACE KING, THE (See Detective Dan)
No date (1933) (9-1/2x12"; 36 pgs., B&W, paper-c)
Humor Publ. Co.

Book 1-Not reprints; Ace King by Martin Nadle (The American Sherlock Holmes)

	167.00	500.00	1000.00

ADVENTURES OF HAWKSHAW (See Hawkshaw The Detective)
1917 (9-3/4x13-1/2", 48 pgs., Color & two-tone)
The Saalfield Publishing Co.

nn-By Gus Mager (only 24 pgs. of strips, reverse of each pg. is blank)

	35.00	140.00	250.00

ADVENTURES OF MICKEY MOUSE, THE
Book I, 1931 - Book II, 1932 (5-1/2"x8-1/2", 32 pgs.)
David McKay Co., Inc.

Book I-First Disney book, by strict definition (1st printing-50,000 copies)(see Mickey Mouse Book by Bibo & Lang). Illustrated text refers to Clarabelle Cow as "Carolyn" and Horace Horsecollar as "Henry". The name "Donald Duck" appears with a non-costumed generic duck on back cover & inside, not in the context of the character that later debuted in the Wise Little Hen.

Hardback w/characters on back-c	71.00	285.00	500.00
Softcover w/characters on back-c	36.00	145.00	250.00
Version without characters on back-c	43.00	172.00	300.00

Book II-Less common than Book I. Character development brought into conformity with the Mickey Mouse cartoon shorts and syndicated strips. Captain Church Mouse, Tanglefoot, Peg-Leg Pete and Pluto appear with Mickey & Minnie

	18.00	72.00	125.00

ADVENTURES OF SLIM AND SPUD, THE
1924 (3-3/4x 9-3/4", 104 pgs., B&W strip reprints)
Prairie Farmer Publ. Co.

nn

	35.00	140.00	250.00

ADVENTURES OF WILLIE GREEN, THE
1915 (50¢, 8-1/2X16", B&W, soft-c)
Frank M. Acton Co.

Book 1-By Harris Brown; strip-r

	35.00	140.00	250.00

AIN'T IT A GRAND & GLORIOUS FEELING? (Also see Mr. & Mrs.)
1922 (9x9-3/4", 52 pgs., stiff cardboard-c)
Whitman Publishing Co.

nn-1921 daily strip-r; B&W, color-c; Briggs-a

	35.00	140.00	250.00

nn-(9x9-1/2", 28pgs., stiff cardboard-c)-Sunday strip-r in color (inside front-c says "More of the Married Life of Mr. & Mrs".)

	21.00	85.00	150.00

ALL THE FUNNY FOLKS
1926 (11-1/2x8-1/2", 112 pgs., color, hard-c)
World Press Today, Inc.

nn-Barney Google, Spark Plug, Jiggs & Maggie, Tillie The Toiler, Happy Hooligan, Hans & Fritz, Toots & Casper, etc.

	85.00	340.00	600.00

ALONG THE FIRING LINE WITH ROGER BEAN
1916 (6x17", 66 pgs., B&W, hard-c)
Chas. B. Jackson

3-By Chic Jackson (1915 daily strips)

	45.00	180.00	315.00

ALPHONSE & GASTON & LEON
1903 (15x10", Sunday strip reprints in color)
Hearst's New York American & Journal

nn-By Fred Opper

	115.00	460.00	825.00

ANGELIC ANGELINA
1909 (11-1/2x17", 30 pgs., 2 colors)
Cupples & Leon Company

nn-By Munson Paddock

	35.00	140.00	250.00

BANANA OIL
1924 (52 pgs., B&W)
MS Publ. Co.

nn-Milt Gross-a; not reprints

	42.00	168.00	300.00

BARNEY GOOGLE AND SPARK PLUG (See Comic Monthly & Giant Comic Album)
1923 - No. 6, 1928 (52 pgs., B&W, daily strip-r)
Cupples & Leon Co.

1-By Billy DeBeck	50.00	200.00	350.00
2-6	35.00	140.00	250.00

NOTE: Started in 1918 as newspaper strip; Spark Plug began 1922, 1923.

BLACKBERRIES, THE
1901 (9"x12", color, hard-c)
R. H. Russell

nn-By E. W. Kemble

	93.00	372.00	650.00

BOBBY THATCHER & TREASURE CAVE
1932 (7x9", 86 pgs., B&W, hard-c)
Altemus Co.

nn-Reprints; Storm-a

	20.00	80.00	140.00

BOBBY THATCHER'S ROMANCE
1931 (7x8-3/4")
The Bell Syndicate/Henry Altemus Co.

nn-By Storm

	20.00	80.00	140.00

BRINGING UP FATHER
1917 (16-1/2x5-1/2", 100 pgs., B&W, cardboard-c)
Star Co. (King Features)

nn-(Rare)-Daily strip reprints by George McManus (no price on-c)

	111.00	445.00	775.00

BRINGING UP FATHER
1919 - No. 26, 1934 (10x10", 52 pgs., B&W, stiff cardboard-c) (No. 22 is 9-1/4x9-1/2")
Cupples & Leon Co.

1-Daily strip-r by George McManus in all	75.00	300.00	525.00
2-10	36.00	145.00	255.00
11-26 (Scarcer)	45.00	180.00	315.00
The Big Book 1(1926)-Thick book (hardcover); 10-1/4x10-1/4", 142 pgs.	111.00	445.00	775.00
The Big Book 2(1929)	89.00	355.00	625.00

NOTE: The Big Books contain 3 regular issues rebound and probably w/dust jackets.

BUDDY TUCKER & HIS FRIENDS (Also see Buster Brown)
1906 (11x17", color)
Cupples & Leon Co.

nn-1905 Sunday strip-r by R. F. Outcault

	100.00	400.00	700.00

BUDDY TUCKER VISITS THE HOUSE THAT JACK BUILT
1907
Cupples & Leon Co.

nn

	28.00	112.00	200.00

BUFFALO BILL'S PICTURE STORIES
1909 (Soft cardboard cover)
Street & Smith Publications

nn

	35.00	140.00	265.00

BUGHOUSE FABLES
1921 (10¢, 4x4-1/2", 48 pgs.)
Embee Distributing Co. (King Features)

1-Barney Google

	25.00	100.00	180.00

BUG MOVIES
1931 (52 pgs., B&W)
Dell Publishing Co.

nn-Not reprints; Stookie Allen-a

	20.00	80.00	140.00

BUSTER BROWN (Also see Brown's Blue Ribbon Book of Jokes and Jingles & Buddy Tucker & His Friends)
1903 - 1916 (Daily strip-r in color)
Frederick A. Stokes Co.

(1)...& His Resolutions (1903, 11-1/4x16", 66 pgs.) by R. F. Outcault (Rare)-1st nationally distributed comic. Distr. through Sears & Roebuck(Rare)

	643.00	2570.00	4500.00

Buster Brown, His Dog Tige and Their Troubles © C&L

Buster Brown The Fun Maker © Frederick A. Stokes

Buster Brown's Book of Travels © Brown Shoe Co.

	GD25	FN65	VF82

(2)...His Dog Tige & Their Troubles (1904, 11-1/4x16-1/4", 66 pgs.)(Rare)
242.00 970.00 1700.00
(3)...Pranks (1905, 11-1/4x16-3/8", 66 pgs.)(Rare)
200.00 800.00 1400.00
(4)...Antics (1906, 11x16-3/8", 66 pgs.)(Rare) 200.00 800.00 1400.00
(5)...And Company (1906, 11x16-1/2", 66 pgs.)(Scarce)
165.00 660.00 1150.00
(6)...Mary Jane & Tige (1906, 11-1/4x16, 66 pgs.)(Scarce)
165.00 660.00 1150.00
(7) Collection of Buster Brown Comics (1908)(Scarce)
135.00 540.00 950.00
(8)...Up to Date (1910, 10-1/8x15-3/4", 66 pgs.)(Rare)
135.00 540.00 950.00
(9)... Fun And Nonsense (1911, 10-1/8x15-3/4", 62 pgs.)
135.00 540.00 950.00
(10)...The Fun Maker (1912, 10-1/8x15-3/4", 66 pgs.)(Rare)-Yellow Kid (4 pgs.)
135.00 540.00 950.00
(11)...At Home (1913, 10-1/8x15-3/4", 56 pgs.)
120.00 480.00 850.00
(12)...The Little Rogue (1916, 10-1/8x15-3/4", 62 pgs.) (Rare)
120.00 480.00 850.00
(13)...And Tige Here Again 115.00 460.00 800.00
(14)...The Real Buster Brown 115.00 460.00 800.00
NOTE: Rarely found in fine or mint condition.

BUSTER BROWN
1904 - 1912 (3x5" to 5x7"; sizes vary)(Advertising premium booklets)
Various Publishers

The Brown Shoe Company, St. Louis, USA
Set of five books (5x7", 16 pgs., color)
Brown's Blue Ribbon Book of Jokes and Jingles Book 1 (nn, 1904)-By R. F. Outcault; Buster Brown & Tige, Little Tommy Tucker, Jack & Jill, Little Boy Blue, Dainty Jane; The Yellow Kid app. on back-c
(1st comic book premium) 485.00 1940.00 3400.00
Buster Brown's Blue Ribbon Book of Jokes and Jingles Book 2 (1905)-Original color art by Outcault 200.00 800.00 1400.00
Buster's Book of Jokes & Jingles Book 3 (1909)-r/Blue Ribbon post cards not signed by R.F. Outcault 200.00 800.00 1400.00
Buster's Book of Instructive Jokes and Jingles Book 4 (1910)-Original color art not signed by R.F. Outcault 200.00 800.00 1400.00
...Book of Travels nn (1912, 3x5")-Original color art not signed by Outcault
85.00 340.00 600.00
NOTE: Estimated 5 to 6 known copies exist of books #1-4.
The Buster Brown Bread Company
"Buster Brown" Bread Book of Rhymes, The nn (1904, 4x6", 12 pgs.)-Original color art not signed by R.F. Outcault 120.00 480.00 850.00
The Buster Brown Stocking Company
Buster Brown Drawing Book, The nn (nd, 5x6", 20 pgs.)-B&W reproductions of 1903 R.F. Outcault art to trace 60.00 240.00 425.00
Collins Baking Company
Buster Brown Drawing Book nn (1904, 3x5", 12 pgs.)-Original B&W art to trace not signed by R.F. Outcault 60.00 240.00 425.00
C. H. Morton, St. Albans, VT
Merry Antics of Buster Brown, Buddy Tucker & Tige nn (nd, 3-1/2x5-1/2", 16 pgs.)-Original B&W art by R.F. Outcault 60.00 240.00 425.00
Frederick A. Stokes Co.
...Abroad (1904, 8x10-1/4, 86 pgs., B&W, hard-c)-R. F. Outcault-a (Rare)
135.00 540.00 950.00
...Abroad (1904, B&W, 67 pgs.)-R.F. Outcault-a 135.00 540.00 950.00
...My Resolutions (1906, 10x8", B&W, 68 pgs.)-R.F. Outcault-a (Rare)
165.00 660.00 1150.00
Ivan Frank & Company
Buster Brown nn (1904, 3x5", 12 pgs.)-B&W repros of R. F. Outcault Sunday pages (First premium to actually reproduce Sunday comic pages – may be first premium comic book?) 60.00 240.00 425.00
Pond's Extract
Buster Brown's Experiences With Pond's Extract nn (1904, 4-1/2x6-3/4",

---

	GD25	FN65	VF82

28 pgs.)-Original color art by R.F. Outcault 120.00 480.00 850.00
Ringen Stove Company
Quick Meal Steel Ranges nn (nd, 3x5", 16 pgs.)-Original B&W art not signed by R.F. Outcault 55.00 220.00 400.00
Saalfield Company Muslin Books
(1)...Goes Fishing (1907, 6-7/8x6-1/8", 24 pgs., color)-r/1905 Sunday comics page by Outcault(Rare) 28.00 84.00 200.00
(2)...Plays Indian (1907, 6-7/8x6-1/8", 24 pgs., color)-r/1905 Sunday comics page by Outcault(Rare) 21.00 84.00 150.00
(3)...Plays Cowboy (1907, 6-7/8x6-1/8", 24 pgs., color)-r/1905 Sunday comics page by Outcault(Rare) 21.00 84.00 150.00
(4)...And The Donkey (1907, 6-7/8x6-1/8", 24 pgs., color)-r/1905 Sunday comics page by Outcault (Rare) 21.00 84.00 150.00
No Publisher Listed
The Drawing Book nn (1906, 3-9/16x5", 8 pgs.)-Original B&W art to trace not signed by R.F. Outcault 55.00 220.00 400.00

BUSTER BROWN
1906 - 1917 (11x17", color, strip-r)
Cupples & Leon Co./N. Y. Herald Co.
(By R. F. Outcault)

	GD25	FN65	VF82

(1A)...His Dog Tige & Their Jolly Times (1906, 11x16, 46 pgs.)
200.00 800.00 1400.00
(1B)...His Dog Tige And Their Jolly Times (1906, 11-3/8x16-5/8", 68 pgs.)

(2)...Latest Frolics (1906, 11-3/8x16-5/8", 66 pgs.)
118.00 472.00 825.00
(3)...Amusing Capers (1908, 58 pgs.) 89.00 355.00 625.00
(4)...The Busy Body (1909, 11-3/8x16-5/8", 62 pgs.)
(5)...On His Travels (1910, 11x16", 46 pgs.) 89.00 355.00 625.00
(6)...Happy Days (1911, 11-3/8x16-5/8", 58 pgs.) 89.00 355.00 625.00
(7)...In Foreign Lands (1912) 89.00 355.00 625.00
(8)...And His Pets (1913, 11x16", 46 pgs.) 89.00 355.00 625.00
(9)...Funny Tricks (1914, 11-3/8x16-5/8", 58 pgs.) 89.00 355.00 625.00
(10)...And the Cat (1917) 89.00 355.00 625.00
NOTE: Rarely found in fine or mint condition.
BUSTER BROWN NUGGETS
1907 (1905, 7-1/2x6-1/2", 36 pgs., color, strip-r, hard-c)(By R. F. Outcault)
Cupples & Leon Co./N.Y.Herald Co.
(1) Buster Brown Goes Fishing 29.00 115.00 200.00
(2) Buster Brown Goes Swimming 29.00 115.00 200.00
(3) Buster Brown Plays Indian 29.00 115.00 200.00
(4) Buster Brown Goes Shooting 29.00 115.00 200.00
(5) Buster Brown Plays Cowboy 29.00 115.00 200.00
(6) Buster Brown On Uncle Jack's Farm 29.00 115.00 200.00
(7) Buster Brown Tige And The Bull 29.00 115.00 200.00
(8) Buster Brown And Uncle Buster 29.00 115.00 200.00
(9) Buddy Tucker Meets Alice in Wonderland 29.00 115.00 200.00
(10) Buddy Tucker Visits The House That Jack Built 29.00 115.00 200.00
BUSTER BROWN'S AUTOBIOGRAPHY
1907 (B&W, 10x8", 71 pgs.) (16 color plates & 36 B&W illos)
Frederick A. Stokes Co.
nn 42.00 130.00 300.00
BUTTONS & FATTY IN THE FUNNIES
nd (1927)(10-1/4"x15-1/2", 28pg., color)
Whitman Publishing Co.
W936-Signed "M.E.B.", probably Merrill Blosser; strips in color copyright The Brooklyn Daily Eagle; thought to be one of the first two western Publ. Co. books (very rare) 53.00 212.00 375.00
CHARLIE CHAPLIN
1917 (9x16", B&W, large size soft-c)
Essanay/M. A. Donohue & Co.
Series 1, #315-Comic Capers (9-3/4x15-3/4")-18pgs. by Segar; Series 1, #316-In the Movies 200.00 800.00 1400.00
Series 1, #317-Up in the Air, #318-In the Army 200.00 800.00 1400.00

Charlie Chaplin #317 © Essanay

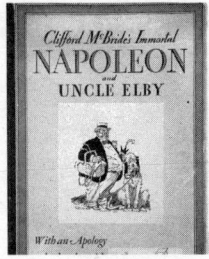

Clifford McBride's Immortal Napoleon & Uncle Elby © The Castle Press

Foxy Grandpa: The Latest Adventures of... © Frederick A. Stokes

	GD25	FN65	VF82

Funny Stunts-(12-1/2x16-3/8", color) — 165.00 — 660.00 — 1150.00
NOTE: All contain Segar -a; pre-Thimble Theatre.

CHASING THE BLUES
1912 (7-1/2x10", 52 pgs., B&W, hard-c)
Doubleday Page

nn-by Rube Goldberg — 100.00 — 400.00 — 700.00

CLANCY THE COP
1930 - No. 2, 1931 (10x10", 52 pgs., B&W, cardboard-c) (not-r)
Dell Publishing Co.

1,2-Vep-a — 34.00 — 136.00 — 240.00

CLIFFORD MCBRIDE'S IMMORTAL NAPOLEON & UNCLE ELBY
1932 (12x17"; soft-c cartoon book)
The Castle Press

nn-Intro. by Don Herod — 32.00 — 128.00 — 225.00

COMIC MONTHLY
Jan, 1922 - No. 12, Dec, 1922 (10¢, 8-1/2"x9", 28 pgs., 2-color covers)
(1st monthly newsstand comic publication) (Reprints 1921 B&W dailies)
Embee Dist. Co.

1-Polly & Her Pals — 143.00 — 570.00 — 1000.00
2-Mike & Ike by Rube Goldberg — 71.00 — 285.00 — 500.00
3-S'Matter, Pop? — 50.00 — 200.00 — 350.00
4-Barney Google — 78.00 — 315.00 — 550.00
5-Tillie the Toiler — 44.00 — 116.00 — 310.00
6-12: 6-Indoor Sports. 7-Little Jimmy. 8-Toots and Casper. 9,10-Foolish
Questions. 11-Barney Google & Spark Plug in the Abadaba Handicap.
12-Polly & Her Pals — 16.00 — — — 280.00

COMIC PAINTING AND CRAYONING BOOK
1917 (10x13-1/2", 32 pgs.) (No price on-c)
Saalfield Publ. Co.

nn-Tidy Teddy by F. M. Follett, Clarence the Cop, Mr. & Mrs. Butt-In;
regular comic stories to read or color — 33.00 — 132.00 — 230.00

DAFFYDILS
1911 (6x8", 52 pgs., B&W, hard-c)
Cupples & Leon Co.

nn-By Tad — 34.00 — 136.00 — 240.00

DEADWOOD GULCH
1931 (52 pgs., B&W)
Dell Publishing Co.

nn-By Charles "Boody" Rogers — 20.00 — 80.00 — 135.00

DICK TRACY & DICK TRACY JR. CAUGHT THE RACKETEERS, HOW
1933 (7x8-1/2", 88pgs., hard-c) (See Treasure Box of Famous Comics)
Cupples & Leon Co.

2-(Numbered on pg. 84)-Continuation of Stooge Viller book (daily strip reprints
from 8/3/33 thru 11/8/33)(Rarer than #1) — 78.00 — 312.00 — 550.00
With dust jacket... — 117.00 — 470.00 — 825.00

DICK TRACY & DICK TRACY JR. AND HOW THEY CAPTURED "STOOGE" VILLER
1933 (7x8-1/2", 100 pgs., hard-c, one-shot)
Reprints 1932 & 1933 Dick Tracy daily strips
Cupples & Leon Co.

nn(No.1)-1st app. of "Stooge" Viller — 45.00 — 180.00 — 315.00
with dust jacket... — 78.00 — 312.00 — 550.00

DOINGS OF THE DOO DADS, THE
1922 (50¢, 7-3/4x7-3/4", 34 pgs, B&W, red & white-c, square binding)
Detroit News (Universal Feat. & Specialty Co.)

nn-Reprints 1921 newspaper strip "Text & Pictures" given away as prize in the
Detroit News Doo Dads contest; by Arch Dale — 34.00 — 136.00 — 240.00

DOLLY DIMPLES & BOBBY BOONCE'
1933
Cupples & Leon Co.

nn — 15.00 — 60.00 — 110.00

DREAMS OF THE RAREBIT FIEND
1905
Doffield & Co.?

nn-By Winsor McCay (Very Rare) (Three copies known to exist)
Estimated value.... — 500.00 — 2000.00 — 3500.00

FELIX
1931 (6-1/2"x8-1/4", 52 pgs., color, hard-c w/dust jacket)
Henry Altemus Company

1-3-Sunday strip reprints of Felix the Cat by Otto Messmer. Book No. 2 r/1931
Sunday panels mostly two to a page in a continuity format oddly arranged so
each tier of panels reads across two pages, then drops to the next tier.
(Books 1 & 3 have not been documented.)(Rare)
Each — 78.00 — 312.00 — 550.00
With dust jacket — 128.00 — 512.00 — 900.00

FELIX THE CAT BOOK
1927 (8"x15-3/4", 52 pgs, half in color-half in B&W)
McLoughlin Bros.

nn-Reprints 23 Sunday strips by Otto Messmer from 1926 & 1927, every other
one in color, two pages per strip. (Rare)
— 170.00 — 680.00 — 1200.00
260-Reissued (1931), reformatted to 9-1/2"x10-1/4" (same color plates, but one
strip per every three pages), retitled ("Book" dropped from title) and abridged
(only eight strips repeated from first issue, 28 pgs.).(Rare)
— 78.00 — 312.00 — 550.00

FOXY GRANDPA (Also see The Funnies, 1st series)
1901 - 1916 (Strip-r in color, hard-c)
N. Y. Herald/Frederick A. Stokes Co./M. A. Donahue & Co./Bunny Publ.
(L. R. Hammersly Co.)

1901-9x15" in color-N. Y. Herald — 128.00 — 512.00 — 900.00
1902- "Latest Larks of...", 32 pgs., 9-1/2x15-1/2" — 92.00 — 368.00 — 650.00
1902- "The Many Advs. of...", 9x12", 148 pgs. (Hammersly)
— 100.00 — 400.00 — 700.00
1903- "Latest Advs.", 9x15", 24 pgs., Hammersly Co.
— 92.00 — 368.00 — 650.00
1903- "...'s New Advs.", 10x15", 32 pgs., Stokes — 92.00 — 368.00 — 650.00
1904- "Up to Date", 10x15", 28 pgs., Stokes — 92.00 — 368.00 — 650.00
1905- "& Flip Flaps", 9-1/2x15-1/2", 52 pgs. — 92.00 — 368.00 — 650.00
1905- "The Latest Advs. of", 9x15", 28, 52, & 66 pgs., M.A. Donahue
Co.; re-issue of 1902 issue — 70.00 — 280.00 — 490.00
1905- "Merry Pranks of", 9-1/2x15-1/2", 52 pgs., Donahue
— 70.00 — 280.00 — 490.00
1905- "Latest Larks of", 9-1/2x15-1/2", 52 pgs., Donahue; re-issue
of 1902 issue — 70.00 — 280.00 — 490.00
1905- "Latest Larks of", 9-1/2x15-1/2", 24 pg. edition, Donahue;
re-issue of 1902 issue — 70.00 — 280.00 — 490.00
1906- "Frolics", 10x15", 30 pgs., Stokes — 70.00 — 280.00 — 490.00
1907 — 70.00 — 280.00 — 490.00
1908?- "Triumphs", 10x15" — 70.00 — 280.00 — 490.00
1908?- "...& Little Brother", 10x15" — 70.00 — 280.00 — 490.00
1911- "Latest Tricks", r-1910,1911 Sundays-Stokes Co.
— 70.00 — 280.00 — 490.00
1914-(9-1/2x15-1/2", 24 pgs.)-6 color cartoons/page, Bunny Publ.
— 62.00 — 248.00 — 440.00
1916- "Merry Book", 10x15", Stokes — 62.00 — 248.00 — 440.00

FOXY GRANDPA SPARKLETS SERIES
1908 (9-1/2x7", 24 pgs., color)
M. A. Donahue & Co.

"... Rides the Goat", "...& His Boys", "...Playing Ball", "...Fun on the Farm",
"...Fancy Shooting", "...Show the Boys Up Sports",... "Plays Santa Claus"
each.... — 75.00 — 300.00 — 525.00
900- "Playing Ball"; Bunny illos; 8 pgs.; linen like pgs., no date
— 60.00 — 240.00 — 425.00

Foxy Grandpa''s Triumphs © Fredserick A. Stokes

The Gumps #6 © C&L

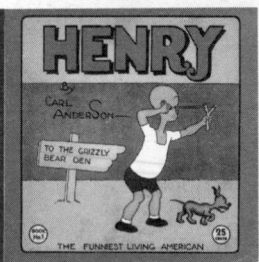

Henry Book 1 © DMP

FUNNIES, THE (Also see Comic Cuts)
1929 - No. 36, 10/18/30 (10¢; 5¢ No. 22 on) (16 pgs.)
Full tabloid size in color; not reprints; published every Saturday
Dell Publishing Co.

1-My Big Brudder, Johnathan, Jazzbo & Jim, Foxy Grandpa, Sniffy, Jimmy Jams & other strips begin; first four-color comic newsstand publication; also contains magic, puzzles & stories	100.00	400.00	700.00
2-21 (1930, 30¢)	36.00	145.00	250.00
22(nn-7/12/30-5¢)	27.00	108.00	190.00
23(nn-7/19/30-5¢), 24(nn-7/26/30-5¢), 25(nn-8/2/30), 26(nn-8/9/30), 27(nn-8/16/30), 28(nn-8/23/30), 29(nn-8/30/30), 30(nn-9/6/30), 31(nn-9/13/30), 32(nn-9/20/30), 33(nn-9/27/30), 34(nn-10/4/30), 35(nn-10/11/30), 36(nn, no date-10/18/30) each….	27.00	108.00	190.00

FUNNY FOLK
1899 (12"x16-1/2", half in color-half in B&W, hard-c) (Reprints cartoons from Puck)
E. P. Dutton

nn	170.00	680.00	1200.00

GASOLINE ALLEY (Also see Popular Comics & Super Comics)
1929 (7x8-3/4", B&W daily strip-r, hard-c)
Reilly & Lee Publishers

nn-By King (96 pgs.)	42.00	168.00	300.00

GUMPS, THE
No. 1, 1918 - No. 6, 1921; 1924 - No. 8, 1931 (10x10", 52 pgs., B&W)
Landfield-Kupfer/Cupples & Leon No. 2

Book No. 1(1918)(Rare)-cardboard-c, 5-1/4x13-1/3", 64 pgs., daily strip-r by Sidney Smith	114.00	456.00	800.00
Book No.2(1918)-(Rare); 5-1/4x13-1/3"; paper cover; 36 pgs. daily strip reprints by Sidney Smith	78.00	312.00	550.00
Book No. 3-6 (Rare)	50.00	200.00	350.00
nn(1924)-By Sidney Smith	52.00	208.00	365.00
2,3	36.00	145.00	250.00
4-7	31.00	124.00	220.00
8-(10x14"); 36 pgs.; B&W; National Arts Co.	31.00	124.00	220.00

GUMPS, ANDY AND MIN, THE
nd (1920s)(Giveaway, 5-1/2"x14", 20 pgs., B&W, soft-c)
Landfield-Kupfer Printing Co., Chicago/Morrison Hotel

nn-Strip-r by Sidney Smith; art & logo embossed on cover w/hotel restaurant menu on back-c or a hotel promo ad; 4 diff. issues known	17.00	68.00	125.00

HANS UND FRITZ
1929 (10x13-1/2", 28 pgs., B&W)
The Saalfield Publishing Co.

193-(Rare)-By R. Dirks; contains 1916 Sunday strip reprints of Katzenjammer Kids & Hawkshaw the Detective	100.00	400.00	700.00
…The Funny Larks Of (1929)	78.00	312.00	550.00

HAPPY HOOLIGAN (See Alphonse…)
1903 (18 pgs., Sunday strip reprints in color)
Hearst's New York American-Journal

Book 1-By Fred Opper	117.00	468.00	825.00
50 Pg. Edition(1903)-10x15" in color	125.00	500.00	875.00

HAPPY HOOLIGAN (Handy…) (See The Travels of…)
1908 (10x15", 32 pgs, color, cardboard-c)
Frederick A. Stokes Co.

nn	78.00	312.00	550.00

HAPPY HOOLIGAN (Story of…)
No. 281, 1932 (9-1/2x12", 16 pgs., soft-c)
McLoughlin Bros.

281-Three-color text, pictures on heavy paper	37.00	148.00	265.00

HAROLD TEEN (Adventures of…)
1929-31 (52 pgs., cardboard-c)

Cupples & Leon Co.

nn-B&W daily strip reprints by Carl Ed	34.00	136.00	240.00

HAWKSHAW THE DETECTIVE (See Advs. of…, Hans Und Fritz & Okay)
1917 (10-1/2x13-1/2", 24 pgs., B&W Sunday strip-r)
The Saalfield Publishing Co.

nn-By Gus Mager	34.00	136.00	240.00

HENRY
1935 (25¢, soft-c)
David McKay Co.

Book 1-By Carl Anderson	45.00	180.00	300.00

HOME, SWEET HOME
1925 (10-1/4x10")
M.S. Publishing Co.

nn-By Tuthill	28.00	112.00	200.00

IT HAPPENS IN THE BEST FAMILIES
1920 (52 pgs., B&W Sunday strip-r)
Powers Photo Engraving Co.

nn-By Briggs	23.00	92.00	165.00
Special Railroad Edition (30¢)-r/strips from 1914-1920	20.00	80.00	140.00

JIMMY (James Swinnerton)
1905 (10x15", 40 pgs., color)
N. Y. American & Journal

nn	82.00	328.00	575.00

JOE PALOOKA
1933 (52 pgs., B&W daily strip-r)
Cupples & Leon Co.

nn-(Scarce)-by Fisher	103.00	412.00	725.00

JUST KIDS
No. 283, 1932 (9-1/2x12", 16 pgs., paper-c)
McLoughlin Bros.

283-Three-color text, pictures on heavy paper	15.00	60.00	110.00

KATZENJAMMER KIDS, THE (Also see Hans Und Fritz)
1903 (10x15-1/4", 50 pgs., color)
New York American & Journal (By Rudolph Dirks; strip 1st appeared in 1898)

1903 (Rare)	200.00	800.00	1400.00
1905	121.00	485.00	850.00
1905-A Series of Comic Pictures, 10x15", 40 pgs. in color	121.00	485.00	850.00
1905-Tricks of…(10x15)	121.00	485.00	850.00
1906-Stokes-10x16", 32 pgs. in color	110.00	440.00	775.00
1910-The Komical…(10x15)	75.00	300.00	525.00
1921-Embee Dist. Co., 10x16", 20 pgs. in color	60.00	240.00	425.00

KEEPING UP WITH THE JONESES
1920 - No. 2, 1921 (9-1/4x9-1/4", 52 pgs., B&W daily strip-r)
Cupples & Leon Co.

1,2-By Pop Momand	30.00	120.00	215.00

LADY BOUNTIFUL
1917 (10-1/4x13-1/2", 24 pgs., B&W, cardboard-c)
Saalfield Publ. Co./Press Publ. Co.

nn-By Gene Carr; 2 panels per page	30.00	120.00	215.00

LIFE'S LITTLE JOKES
No date (1924) (52 pgs., B&W)
M.S. Publ. Co.

nn-By Rube Goldberg	50.00	200.00	350.00

LILY OF THE ALLEY IN THE FUNNIES
No date (1927) (10-1/4x15-1/2", 28 pgs., color)
Whitman Publishing Co.(one of their first two books)

Little Orphan Annie © C&L

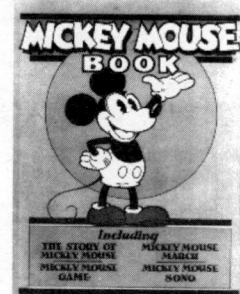

Mickey Mouse Book © WDC

Moon Mullins © C&L

	GD25	FN65	VF82
W936 - By T. Burke (Rare)	45.00	180.00	325.00

LITTLE ANNIE ROONEY
1935 (25¢, soft-c)
David McKay Co.

Book 1	45.00	180.00	300.00

LITTLE JOHNNY & THE TEDDY BEARS
1907 (10x14", 32 pgs., color)
Reilly & Britton Co.

nn-By J. R. Bray	37.00	148.00	265.00

LITTLE NEMO (…in Slumberland)
1906, 1909 (Sunday strip-r in color, cardboard covers)
Doffield & Co.(1906)/Cupples & Leon Co.(1909)

1906-11x16-1/2" by Winsor McCay; 30 pgs. (Rare)

	430.00	1720.00	3000.00

1909-10x14" by Winsor McCay (Rare)

	357.00	1428.00	2500.00

LITTLE ORPHAN ANNIE (See Treasure Box of Famous Comics)
1926 - 1934 (7x8-3/4", 100 pgs., B&W daily strip-r, hard-c)
Cupples & Leon Co.

1(1926)-Little Orphan Annie	45.00	180.00	315.00
1(1926)-softback (see Treasure Box...)			
2('27)-In the Circus	33.00	132.00	230.00
2('28)-softback (36 pgs.)	27.00	108.00	190.00
3('28)-The Haunted House	33.00	132.00	230.00
3('28)-softback (36 pgs.)	27.00	108.00	190.00
4('29)-Bucking the World	33.00	132.00	230.00
5('30)-Never Say Die	27.00	108.00	190.00
6('31)-Shipwrecked	27.00	108.00	190.00
7('32)-A Willing Helper	21.00	84.00	150.00
8('33)-In Cosmic City	21.00	84.00	150.00
9('34)-Uncle Dan	27.00	108.00	190.00

NOTE: Each book reprints dailies from the previous year.

LITTLE SAMMY SNEEZE
1905 (11x16-1/2", 28 pgs., color)
New York Herald Co.

nn-By Winsor McCay (Rare)	429.00	1715.00	3000.00

NOTE: Rarely found in fine to mint condition.

MAUD
1906 (10x15-1/2", 32 pgs., color, cardboard-c)
Frederick A. Stokes Co.

nn-By Fred Opper	57.00	230.00	400.00

MICKEY MOUSE BOOK
1930 (9"x12", stapled-c, 20 pgs., 4 printings)
Bibo & Lang

nn-First Disney licensed publication in magazine format, despite "book" used in title. (see first book: Adventures of Mickey Mouse.) Contains story of how Mickey met Walt and got his name. contains games, cartoons & song "Mickey Mouse (You Cute Little Feller)," written by Irving Bibo. Minnie, Clarabelle Cow, Horace Horsecollar & caricature of Walt shaking hands with Mickey appear. 4/15/30 Mickey strip by Win Smith appears on page 8 and some printings have 4/17/30 strip on back cover. Printings with both strips are more desirable to comic book collectors. One known copy has a Xmas-New Year greeting & Dec. 27,1930 printed on inside front-c; all other printings have blank inside front-c. **NOTE:** Most copies are missing pages 9 & 10 which had a puzzle to be cut out. Ub Iwerks-c

1st--4th printings (complete)	1430.00	6500.00	10,000.00

(Estimated up to 75 total copies exist)
NOTE: Rare variations add 10%. Puzzle (pages 9 and 10) cut out or missing, subtract 60% to 75%.

MICKEY MOUSE COMIC

1931 - No. 4, 1934 (10"x9-3/4", 52 pgs., cardboard-c) (Later reprints exist)
David McKay Co.

1(1931)-Reprints Floyd Gottfredson daily strips in black & white from 1930 & 1931, including the famous two week sequence in which Mickey tries to commit suicide

	215.00	860.00	1500.00

2(1932)-1st app. of Pluto reprinted from 7/8/31 daily. All pgs. from 1931

	165.00	660.00	1150.00

3(1933)-Reprints 1932 & 1933 Sunday pages in color, one strip per page, including the "Lair of Wolf Barker" continuity pencilled by Gottfredson and inked by Al Taliaferro & Ted Thwaites. First app. Mickey's nephews, Morty & Ferdie, one identified by name of Mortimer Fieldmouse, not to be confused with Uncle Mortimer Mouse who is introduced in the Wolf Barker story

	215.00	860.00	1500.00

4(1934)-1931 dailies, include the only known reprint of the infamous strip of 2/4/31 where the villainous Kat Nipp snips off the end of Mickey's tail with a pair of scissors

	121.00	485.00	850.00

MILITARY WILLY
1907 (7x9-1/2", 14 pgs., every other page in color, stapled)
J. I. Austen Co.

nn-By F. R. Morgan	34.00	136.00	240.00

MISCHIEVOUS MONKS OF CROCODILE ISLE, THE
1908 (8-1/2x11-1/2", 12 pgs., 4 pgs. in color)
J. I. Austen Co., Chicago

nn-By F. R. Morgan; reads longwise	38.50	155.00	270.00

MR. & MRS. (Also see Ain't It A Grand and Glorious Feeling?)
1922 (9x9-1/2", 52 & 28 pgs., cardboard-c)
Whitman Publishing Co.

nn-By Briggs (B&W, 52 pgs.)	27.00	108.00	190.00
nn-28 pgs.-(9x9-1/2")-Sunday strips-r in color	31.00	125.00	220.00

MONKEY SHINES OF MARSELEEN
1909 (11-1/2x17", 28 pgs. in two colors)
Cupples & Leon Co.

nn-By Norman E. Jennett	30.00	120.00	215.00

MOON MULLINS
1927 - 1933 (52 pgs., B&W daily strip-r)
Cupples & Leon Co.

Series 1('27)-By Willard	53.50	215.00	375.00
Series 2('28), Series 3('29), Series 4('30)	36.00	145.00	250.00
Series 5('31), 6('32), 7('33)	31.00	124.00	215.00
Big Book 1('30)-B&W	45.00	180.00	315.00

MUTT & JEFF (…Cartoon, The)
1910 - No. 5, 1916 (5-3/4x15-1/2", B&W, hard-c)
Ball Publications

1(1910)(68 pgs., 50¢)	165.00	660.00	1150.00
2,3: 2(1911, 68 pgs.)-Opium den panels; Jeff smokes opium (pipe dreams). 3(1912, 68 pgs.)	89.00	356.00	625.00
4(1915)(68 pgs., 50¢)(Rare)	89.00	356.00	625.00
5(1916)(68 pgs.)-(Rare)-Photos of Fisher, 1st pg.	118.00	355.00	825.00

NOTE: Mutt & Jeff first appeared in newspapers in 1908. Cover variations exist showing Mutt & Jeff reading various newspapers; i.e., The Oregon Journal, The American, and The Detroit News. Reprinting of each issue began soon after publication. No. 5 may not have been reprinted. Values listed include the reprints.

MUTT & JEFF
No. 6, 1919 - No. 22, 1933? (9-1/2x9-1/2", B&W dailies, stiff-C)
Cupples & Leon Co.

6-22-By Bud Fisher	54.00	215.00	375.00

NOTE: Later issues are somewhat rarer.

nn(1920)-(Advs. of...) 16x11"; 20 pgs.; reprints 1919 Sunday strips			
	89.00	356.00	625.00
Big Book nn(1926, 144 pgs., hardcovers)	110.00	440.00	775.00
w/dust jacket	186.00	745.00	1300.00
Big Book 1(1928)-Thick book (hardcovers)	110.00	440.00	775.00

Mutt & Jeff #11 © C&L

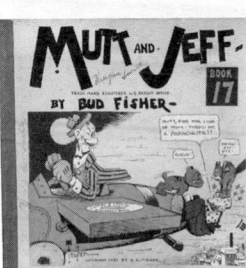
Mutt & Jeff #17 © C&L

Skeezix and Pal © Reilly & Lee Co.

	GD25	FN65	VF82
w/dust jacket (rare)	179.00	715.00	1250.00
Big Book 2(1929)-Thick book (hardcovers)	110.00	440.00	775.00
w/dust jacket (rare)	179.00	715.00	1250.00

NOTE: *The Big Books contain three previous issues rebound.*

MUTT & JEFF
1921 (9x15")
Embee Publ. Co.

nn-Sunday strips in color (Rare)	128.00	512.00	900.00

NEBBS, THE
1928 (52 pgs., B&W daily strip-r)
Cupples & Leon Co.

nn-By Sol Hess; Carlson-a	34.00	136.00	240.00

NEWLYWEDS
1907; 1917 (cardboard-c)
Saalfield Publ. Co.

...& Their Baby' by McManus; Saalfield, (1907, 13x10", 52 pgs.); daily strips in full color	92.00	368.00	650.00
...& Their Baby's Comic Pictures, The, by McManus, Saalfield, (1917, 14x10", 22 pgs, oblong, cardboard-c); reprints 'Newlyweds' (Baby Snookums stips) mainly from 1916; blue cover; says for painting & crayoning, but some pages in color. (Scarce)	70.00	280.00	485.00

NIPPY'S POP
1917 (10-1/2x13-1/2", B&W, Sunday strip-r)
The Saalfield Publishing Co.

nn-32 pgs.	31.00	124.00	215.00

OH, MAN (A Bully Collection of Those Inimitable Humor Cartoons)
1919 (8-1/2x12")
P.F. Volland & Co.

nn-By Briggs	31.00	124.00	215.00

OH SKIN-NAY!
1913 (8-1/2x13")
P.F. Volland & Co.

nn-The Days Of Real Sport by Briggs	31.00	124.00	215.00

ON THE LINKS
Dec, 1926 (9x10", 48 pgs.)
Associated Feature Service

nn-Daily strip-r	19.00	76.00	135.00

OUTBURSTS OF EVERETT TRUE
1921 (32 pgs., B&W)
Saalfield Publ. Co.

1907 (2-panel strips reprint)	30.00	120.00	210.00

PECKS BAD BOY
1906 - 1908 (11-1/4x15-3/4", strip-r)
Thompson of Chicago (by Walt McDougal)

...& Cousin Cynthia(1907)-In color	50.00	200.00	350.00
...& His Chums (1908)-Hardcover; in full color; 16 pgs.	50.00	200.00	350.00
Advs. of...And His Country Cousins (1906)-In color, 18 pgs., oblong	50.00	200.00	350.00
Advs. of...in Pictures (1908)-In color; Stanton & Van V. Liet Co.	50.00	200.00	350.00

PERCY & FERDIE
1921 (10x10", 52 pgs., B&W dailies, cardboard-c)
Cupples & Leon Co.

nn-By H. A. MacGill (Rare)	50.00	200.00	350.00

PETER RABBIT
1922 - 1923 (9-1/4x6-1/4", paper-c)
John H. Eggers Co. The House of Little Books Publishers

B1-B4-(Rare)-(Set of 4 books which came in a cardboard box)-Each book

reprints half of a Sunday page per page and contains 8 B&W and 2 color pages; by Harrison Cady

each....	41.00	165.00	290.00
Box only	56.00	225.00	390.00

PINK LAFFIN
1922 (9x12")(Strip-r)
Whitman Publishing Co.

...the Lighter Side of Life, ...He Tells 'Em, ...His Family, ...Knockouts; Ray Gleason-a (All rare)

each...	23.00	92.00	165.00

PORE LI'L MOSE
1902 (10-1/2x15", 30 pgs., color)
New York Herald Publ. by Grand Union Tea
Cupples & Leon Co.

nn-By R. F. Outcault; 1 pg. strips about early Negroes

	257.00	1030.00	1800.00

REG'LAR FELLERS (See All-American Comics, Popular Comics & Treasure Box of Famous Comics)
1921 - 1929
Cupples & Leon Co./MS Publishng Co.

1(1921)-52 pgs. B&W dailies (Cupples & Leon, 10x10")	35.00	140.00	250.00
1925, 48 pgs. B&W dailies (MS Publ.)	33.00	132.00	230.00
Hardcover (1929, 96 pgs.)-B&W reprints	45.00	180.00	315.00

ROGER BEAN, R. G. (Regular Guy)
1915 - No. 5, 1917 (4-3/4x16", 34 pgs., B&W, cardboard-c)
(No. 1 & 4 bound on side, No. 3 bound at top)
The Indiana News Co.

1-By Chic Jackson (48 pgs.)(Scarce)	35.00	140.00	250.00
2-5 (Scarce)	23.00	92.00	165.00

SILK HAT HARRY'S DIVORCE SUIT
1912 (5-3/4x15-1/2", B&W)
M. A. Donoghue & Co.

Newspaper-r by Tad (Thomas Dorgan)	20.00	80.00	140.00

SKEEZIX (Also see Gasoline Alley)
1925 - 1928 (Strip-r, soft covers) (pictures & text)
Reilly & Lee Co.

...and Uncle Walt (1924)-Origin	23.00	92.00	165.00
...and Pal (1925)	18.00	72.00	130.00
...at the Circus (1926)	18.00	72.00	130.00
...& Uncle Walt (1927)	18.00	72.00	130.00
...Out West (1928)	18.00	72.00	130.00
Hardback Editions...	30.00	120.00	215.00

SKIPPY
Circa 1920s (10x8", 16 pgs., color/B&W cartoons)
No publisher listed

nn-By Percy Crosby	75.00	300.00	525.00

S'MATTER POP?
1917 (10x14", 44 pgs., B&W, cardboard-c)
Saalfield Publ. Co.

nn-By Charlie Payne; in full color; pages printed on one side

	32.00	128.00	230.00

SMITTY (See Treasure Box of Famous Comics)
1928 - 1933 (9-1/2x9-1/2", 52 pgs., B&W strip-r, cardboard-c)
Cupples & Leon Co.

1928-(96 pgs. 7x8-3/4")	37.00	148.00	265.00
1929-At the Ball Game, 1930-The Flying Office Boy, 1931-The Jockey, 1932-In the North Woods each...	27.00	108.00	190.00
1933-At Military School	27.00	108.00	190.00
Hardback Editions-(7x8-1/4", 100 pgs.)(Rare)-With dust jacket each...	34.00	136.00	240.00

Thimble Theatre Starring Popeye #1 © Sonnet

Tillie The Toiler #6 © C & L

Willie Westinghouse Edison Smith The Boy Inventor © William A. Stokes

	GD25	FN65	VF82

STRANGE AS IT SEEMS
1932 (64 pgs., B&W, square binding)
Blue-Star Publishing Co.

1-Newspaper-r	30.00	120.00	210.00

NOTE: Published with and without No. 1 and price on cover.
Ex-Lax giveaway(1936, B&W, 24 pgs., 5x7")-McNaught Synd.

	10.00	40.00	65.00

TAILSPIN TOMMY STORY & PICTURE BOOK
No. 266, 1931? (nd) (10-1/2x10", color strip-r)
McLoughlin Bros.

266-By Forrest	34.00	136.00	240.00

TAILSPIN TOMMY (Also see Famous Feature Stories & The Funnies)
1932 (100 pgs., hard-c)
Cupples & Leon Co.

nn-(Rare)-B&W strip reprints from 1930 by Hal Forrest & Glenn Claffin	35.00	140.00	250.00

TARZAN BOOK (The Illustrated…)
1929 (7x9", 80 pgs.)
Grosset & Dunlap

1(Rare)-Contains 1st B&W Tarzan newspaper comics from 1929.
Cloth reinforced spine & dust jacket (50¢); Foster-c

with dust jacket…	82.00	328.00	575.00
without dust jacket…	33.00	132.00	230.00

2nd Printing(1934, 25¢, 76 pgs.)-4 Foster pgs. dropped; paper spine, circle in lower right hand corner over 25¢ price. The 25¢ is barely visible on some copies

	31.00	124.00	220.00

1967-House of Greystoke reprint-7x10", using the complete 300 illustrations/text from the 1929 edition minus the original indicia, foreword, etc. Initial version bound in gold paper & sold for $5.00. Officially titled **Burroughs Bibliophile #2**. A very few additional copies were bound in heavier blue paper.

Gold binding…	3.60	9.00	18.00
Blue binding…	4.00	12.00	24.00

TARZAN OF THE APES TO COLOR
No. 988, 1933 (10-3/4x15-1/4", 24 pgs)(Coloring book)
Saalfield Publishing Co.

988-(Very Rare)-Contains 1929 daily reprints with some new art by Hal Foster. Two panels blown up large on each page with one at the top of opposing pages on every other double-page spread. Believed to be the only time these panels appeared in color. Most color panels are reproduced a second time in b&w to be colored

	229.00	915.00	1600.00

THIMBLE THEATRE STARRING POPEYE
1931 - No. 2, 1932 (25¢, B&W, 52 pgs.)(Rare)
Sonnet Publishing Co.

1-Daily strip serial-r in both by Segar	150.00	600.00	1050.00
2	132.00	528.00	925.00

NOTE: The very first Popeye reprint book. Popeye first entered Thimble Theatre in 1929.

3 FUNMAKERS, THE
1908 (10x15", 64 pgs., color) (1904-06 Sunday strip-r)
Stokes and Company

nn-Maude, Katzenjammer Kids, Happy Hooligan	93.00	370.00	650.00

"TIGE" HIS STORY
1905 (10x8", 63 pgs., B&W) (63 illos.)
Frederick A. Stokes Co.

nn	71.00	285.00	500.00

TILLIE THE TOILER
1925 - No. 8, 1933 (52 pgs., B&W, daily strip-r)
Cupples & Leon Co.

nn (#1)	42.00	168.00	300.00
2-8	31.00	124.00	215.00

NOTE: First strip appearance was January, 1921.

TOM SAWYER & HUCK FINN
1925 (10-3/4x10", 52 pgs, stiff covers)(Sunday strips in color)

Stoll & Edwards Co.

nn-By Dwiggins; 1923, 1924-r	30.00	120.00	210.00

TOONERVILLE TROLLEY
1921 (52 pgs., B&W, daily strip-r)
Cupples & Leon Co.

1-By Fontaine Fox	40.00	160.00	285.00

TRAVELS OF HAPPY HOOLIGAN, THE
1906 (10-1/4x15-3/4", 32 pgs., cardboard covers)
Frederick A. Stokes Co.

nn-Contains reprints from 1905	55.00	220.00	390.00

TREASURE BOX OF FAMOUS COMICS
Mid 1930's (6-7/8x8-1/2", 36 pgs, soft covers)(Boxed set of 5 books)
Cupples & Leon Co.

Little Orphan Annie (1926)	20.00	80.00	140.00
Reg'lar Fellers (1928)	17.00	68.00	120.00
Smitty (1928)	17.00	68.00	120.00
Harold Teen (1931)	17.00	68.00	120.00
How Dick Tracy & Dick Tracy Jr. Caught The Racketeers (1933)	25.00	100.00	175.00
Softcover set of five books in box	157.00	625.00	1100.00
Box only	50.00	200.00	350.00

NOTE: Dates shown are copyright dates; all books actually came out in 1934 or later. The softcovers are abbreviated versions of the hardcover editions listed under each character.

TRIALS OF LULU AND LEANDER, THE
1906 (10x16", 32 pgs. in color)
William A. Stokes Co.

nn-By F. M. Howarth	31.00	125.00	220.00

TROUBLE OF BRINGING UP FATHER, THE
1921 (9x15", Sunday-r in color)
Embee Publ. Co.

nn-(Rare)	66.00	265.00	465.00

VAUDEVILLE AND OTHER THINGS
1900 (10-1/2x13", 18+ pgs., color)
Isaac H. Blandiard Co.

nn-By Bunny	64.00	256.00	450.00

WILLIE WESTINGHOUSE EDISON SMITH THE BOY INVENTOR
1906 (10x16", 36 pgs. in color)
William A. Stokes Co.

nn-By Frank Crane	52.00	208.00	365.00

WINNIE WINKLE
1930 - No. 4, 1933 (52 pgs., B&W daily strip-r)
Cupples & Leon Co.

1	33.00	132.00	235.00
2-4	22.00	88.00	160.00

YELLOW KID, THE (Magazine)
1897 - #6, June 5, 1897 (5¢, B&W w/color covers)
Howard Ainslee & Co., N.Y.

1-Outcault Yellow Kid on-c only #1-6	550.00	2200.00	-
2	300.00	1200.00	-
3-6 (#5, 5/22/97)	230.00	920.00	-

NOTE: Richard Outcault's Yellow Kid from the Hearst New York American represents the very first successful comic strip in America. Eventually the first prototype comic books appeared reprinting these early strips. This magazine is listed here due to historical importance but is not a comic book.

YELLOW KID IN MCFADDEN'S FLATS, THE
1897 (50¢, 5 1/2x7 1/2", 196 pgs., B&W, squarebound)
G. W. Dillingham Company, New York

nn-The first "comic" book; E. W. Townsend narrative w/R. F. Outcault Sunday comic page art-r & some original drawings   3500.00   6500.00

The American Comic Book: 1933-Present

THE GOLDEN AGE AND BEYOND:
THE MODERN COMIC BOOK

Richard D. Olson, Ph.D.

The birth of the modern American comic book occurred in 1933, with the publication of Harry I. Wildenberg and Max Gaines' **Funnies on Parade.** It had a small print run of 10,000, and was only 32 pages. Just another experimental format at the time of its issue for reprinting newspaper comics, it rapidly became the seminal model of comic books for the next 50 years! The reasons the new format proved to be so successful included the total use of color, packaging a variety of characters in one book, and the cost--it was free, a premium given by Proctor and Gamble. The great success of

Funnies On Parade © EAS

Funnies on Parade quickly led Gaines to publish additional giveaway books in the same format, including **A Century of Comics, A Carnival of Comics**, and **Skippy's Own Book of Comics**. After several of these comics magazine premiums were successfully produced and distributed, Max Gaines stickered 10¢ on several dozen copies of the latest premium, titled **Famous Funnies,** as a test, and talked a couple newsstands into trying this experiment out. The copies sold out over the weekend and the newsies asked for more. George Janosik, the president of Eastern Color, then called on George Delacorte to go into a possible partnership. The later publisher had already tried out a weekly comics publication a few years earlier, however, and together they went to American News in early 1933 with a proposal which was promptly turned down. They then interested a few chain stores into buying 35,000 copies of what became known as **Famous Funnies, Series 1,** with a 10¢ price on the cover.

In early 1934, another Eastern Color employee named Harold A. Moore read an account from a prominent New York newspaper while riding the train that they owed much of their circulation success to their comics section. Mr. Moore went back to American News with the article in hand. He succeeded in acquiring a print order of 200,000 for a proposed monthly comics magazine. In May of 1934, **Famous Funnies** #1 (with a July cover date) hit the newsstands with Steven A. Douglass as its only editor till it ceased publication some 20 years later. It was a 64-page version of the 32-page giveaways, and more importantly, it sold for a dime! The first issue lost $4,150.60. Delacorte got cold feet and sold back his interest to Eastern even though the 7th issue cleared a profit of $2,664.25. The second issue was published in September and came out monthly through July, 1955, ending with issue #218. **Famous Funnies** also began carrying some original material, apparently as early as the second issue!

New Fun Comics #1 © DC

After Max Gaines did a successful half million copy promo with a **Skippy** premium for Philips Dental that was given away during the Skippy radio program, he convinced Delacorte to try a new title called **Popular Comics** in late 1935. Packaged by Gaines and his youthful assistant Sheldon Mayer, it became the 2nd continuing series of the modern newsstand comic books as we know them today.

The first modern comic book to contain only original material, however, was **New Fun Comics** #1, published by National in February, 1935. **New Fun Comics**, a large tabloid became **More Fun Comics** with issue #7, and adopted the modern format with issue #9. **New Fun Comics** #6 is now famous for introducing Siegel and Shuster's Dr. Occult, later to become the first superhero.

And the race was on! New publishers entered the arena with a variety of titles, and the comic book market exploded. DC published **Detective Comics** #1 in March, 1937, and **Action Comics** #1 in June, 1938. Centaur, Fiction House, Timely, and Lev Gleason were all publishing their own titles before 1940. Within a year, MLJ, Fawcett, Fox, and Dell, had also joined the market, as well as numerous smaller companies. The comic book had become an integral part of society.

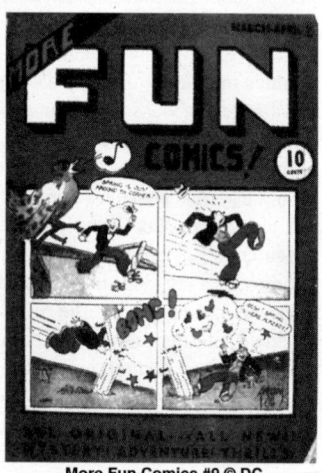

More Fun Comics #9 © DC

Over the years, the comic book downsized, reduced paper quality, printed more ads, and increased its cover price, but it has survived. There have been several developmental periods that collectors now recognize: (1) Pre-Golden Age, 1933-(May)1936, reprint comics dominate the period; (2) Golden Age, June, 1938-1945, the superhero through WW II; (3) Post Golden Age, 1946-1949, the waning years of early titles; (4) Pre-Silver Age, 1950-(August)1956, experimentation with new titles and themes; (5) Silver Age, (September)1956-1969, clear change in contents and themes, including the Marvel books; Post Silver Age or Bronze Age, 1970-1979, sales decrease as comics stagnate; and (7) Modern Age, 1980-Present, DC and Marvel are challenged by the Independents, all are threatened by overproduction.

A final few notes of personal interest. First, many of the early comic artists and writers toiled in virtual anonymity. One of the great changes in the field is that today there are annual awards and everyone in the production line is recognized in each issue. Second, as in so many hobbies, condition is king!

The prices of all comic books have to reflect the marketplace, and the marketplace issues the greatest premiums on the most perfect books. Third, enjoy the books you collect. I have a run of **Green Arrow** that has little investment potential, but I really like the scripts and art. Collecting comics can be and is a great hobby… enjoy.

additional material by Robert L. Beerbohm

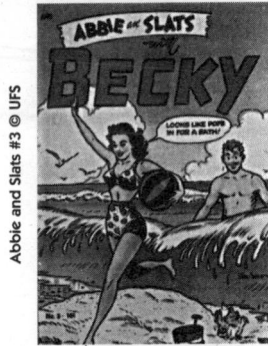

Abbie and Slats #3 © UFS

Ace Comics #110 © DMP

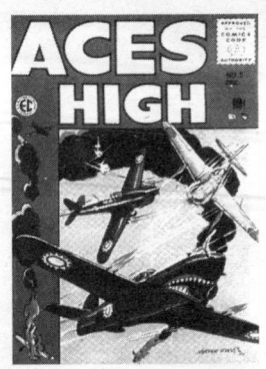

Aces High #5 © WMG

	GD25	FN65	NM94

The correct title listing for each comic book can be determined by consulting the indicia (publication data) on the beginning interior pages of the comic. The official title is determined by those words of the title in capital letters only, and not by what is on the cover.

Titles are listed in this book as if they were one word, ignoring spaces, hyphens, and apostrophes, to make finding titles easier. Comic books listed should be assumed to be in color unless noted "B&W".

Comic publishers are invited to send us sample copies for possible inclusion in future guides.

Near Mint is the highest value listed in this price guide. True mint books from the 1970s and 1990s do exist, so the Near Mint value listed should be interpreted as a Mint value for those books.

A-1 (See A-One)

ABBIE AN' SLATS (...With Becky No. 1-4) (See Comics On Parade, Fight for Love, Giant Comics Edition 2, Giant Comics Editions #1, Sparkler Comics, Tip Topper, Treasury of Comics, & United Comics)
1940; March, 1948 - No. 4, Aug, 1948 (Reprints)
United Features Syndicate

	GD25	FN65	NM94
Single Series 25 ('40)	34.00	103.00	240.00
Single Series 28	29.00	86.00	200.00
1 (1948)	16.00	47.00	110.00
2-4: 3-r/Sparkler #68-72	9.15	27.50	55.00

ABBOTT AND COSTELLO (...Comics)(See Giant Comics Editions #1 & Treasury of Comics)
Feb, 1948 - No. 40, Sept, 1956 (Mort Drucker-a in most issues)
St. John Publishing Co.

1	45.00	135.00	360.00
2	23.00	69.00	160.00
3-9 (#8, 8/49; #9, 2/50)	15.00	45.00	105.00
10-Son of Sinbad story by Kubert (new)	20.00	60.00	140.00
11,13-20 (#11, 10/50; #13, 8/51; #15, 12/52)	10.00	30.00	70.00
12-Movie issue	12.00	36.00	85.00
21-30: 28-r/#8. 30-Painted-c	9.15	27.50	55.00
31-40: 33,38-Reprints	7.50	22.50	45.00
3-D #1 (11/53, 25¢)-Infinity-c	33.00	99.00	230.00

ABBOTT AND COSTELLO (TV)
Feb, 1968 - No. 22, Aug, 1971 (Hanna-Barbera)
Charlton Comics

1	7.00	21.50	50.00
2	3.60	11.00	25.00
3-10	3.25	9.50	22.00
11-22	2.30	6.75	16.00

ABC (See America's Best TV Comics)

ABRAHAM LINCOLN LIFE STORY (See Dell Giants)

ABSENT-MINDED PROFESSOR, THE
Apr, 1961 (Disney)
Dell Publishing Co.

Four Color #1199-Movie, photo-c	7.00	21.00	70.00

ABSOLUTE VERTIGO
Winter, 1995 (99¢, mature)
DC Comics (Vertigo)

nn-Previews upcoming titles including Jonah Hex: Riders of the Worm, etc., The Invisibles (King Mob), The Eaters, Ghostdancing & Preacher

		7.50	18.00

ABYSS, THE (Movie)
June, 1989 - No. 2, July, 1989 ($2.25, limited series)
Dark Horse Comics

1,2-Adaptation of film; Kaluta & Moebius-a		.90	2.25

ACE COMICS
Apr, 1937 - No. 151, Oct-Nov, 1949 (All contain some newspaper strip reprints)
David McKay Publications

1-Jungle Jim by Alex Raymond, Blondie, Ripley's Believe It or Not, Krazy Kat begin (1st app. of each)	300.00	900.00	2400.00
2	85.00	250.00	675.00
3-5	56.25	170.00	450.00
6-10	40.00	120.00	325.00
11-The Phantom begins (1st app., 2/38) (in brown costume)	60.00	180.00	475.00
12-20	36.00	107.00	250.00
21-25,27-30	31.00	94.00	220.00
26-Origin & 1st app. Prince Valiant (5/39); begins series?	78.00	235.00	625.00
31-40: 37-Krazy Kat ends	21.00	64.00	150.00
41-60	17.00	51.00	120.00
61-64,66-76-(7/43; last 68 pgs.)	15.00	45.00	105.00
65-(8/42)-Flag-c	16.00	47.00	110.00
77-84 (3/44; all 60 pgs.)	12.00	36.00	85.00
85-99 (52 pgs.)	10.00	30.00	70.00
100 (7/45; last 52 pgs.)	11.50	34.00	80.00
101-134: 128-(11/47)-Brick Bradford begins. 134-Last Prince Valiant (all 36 pgs.)	9.15	27.50	55.00
135-151: 135-(6/48)-Lone Ranger begins	8.00	24.00	48.00

ACE KELLY (See Tops Comics & Tops In Humor)

ACE KING (See Adventures of Detective...)

ACES
Apr, 1988 - No. 5, Dec, 1988 ($2.95, B&W, magazine)
Acme Press (Eclipse Comics)

1-5		1.20	3.00

ACES HIGH
Mar-Apr, 1955 - No. 5, Nov-Dec, 1955
E.C. Comics

1-Not approved by code	19.00	58.00	135.00
2	12.00	36.00	85.00
3-5	10.00	30.00	70.00

NOTE: All have stories by *Davis, Evans, Krigstein,* and *Wood. Evans c-1-5.*

ACTION ADVENTURE (War) (Formerly Real Adventure)
V1#2, June, 1955 - No. 4, Oct, 1955
Gillmor Magazines

V1#2-4	4.00	11.00	22.00

ACTION COMICS (...Weekly #601-642) (Also see The Comics Magazine #1, More Fun #14-17 & Special Edition)
6/38 - No. 583, 9/86; No. 584, 1/87 - Present
National Periodical Publ./Detective Comics/DC Comics

	GD25	FN65	VF82	NM94
1-Origin & 1st app. Superman by Siegel & Shuster, Marco Polo, Tex Thompson, Pep Morgan, Chuck Dawson & Scoop Scanlon; 1st app. Zatara & Lois Lane; Superman story missing 4 pgs. which were included when reprinted in Superman #1; Clark Kent works for Daily Star; story continued in #2	30,000.00	70,000.00	100,000.00	160,000.00

(Estimated up to 75+ total copies exist, 4 in NM/Mint)
(Issues 1 through 10 are all scarce to rare)

1-Reprint, Oversize 13-1/2x10". **WARNING:** This comic is an exact reprint of the original except for its size. DC published it in 1974 with a second cover titling it as a Famous First Edition. There have been many reported cases of the outer cover being removed and the interior sold as the original edition. The reprint with the new outer cover removed is practically worthless. See Famous First Edition for value.

	GD25	FN65	NM94
1(1976,1983)-Giveaway; paper cover, 16pgs. in color; reprints complete Superman story from #1 ('38)	2.40	6.00	12.00
1(1987 Nestle Quik giveaway; 1988, 50¢)	.80	2.00	

Action Comics #4 © DC

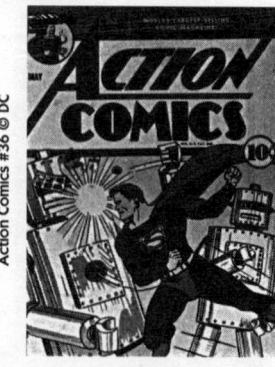
Action Comics #36 © DC

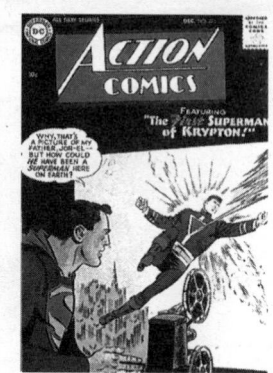
Action Comics #223 © DC

	GD25	FN65	NM94
1(1993)-Came w/Reign of Superman packs	.30	.75	1.50
2	1800.00	5400.00	18000.00
3 (Scarce)-Superman apps. in costume in only one panel	1200.00	3600.00	12000.00
4-6: 6-1st Jimmy Olsen (called office boy)	700.00	2100.00	7000.00
7-2nd Superman cover	1000.00	3000.00	10000.00
8,9	555.00	1670.00	5500.00
10-3rd Superman cover by Siegel & Shuster	850.00	2550.00	8500.00
11,14: 14-Clip Carson begins, ends #41; Zatara-c	300.00	900.00	2800.00
12-Has 1 pg. Batman ad for Det. #27 (5/39); Zatara sci-fi cover	325.00	975.00	3000.00
13-Guardineer Superman-c; last Scoop Scanlon	450.00	1350.00	4500.00
15-Guardineer Superman-c	400.00	1200.00	4000.00
16	225.00	675.00	2000.00
17-Superman cover; last Marco Polo	350.00	1050.00	3200.00
18-Origin 3 Aces; 1st X-Ray Vision?	225.00	675.00	2000.00
19-Superman covers begin; has full pg. ad for New York World's Fair 1939	312.00	938.00	2800.00
20-The 'S' left off Superman's chest; Clark Kent works at 'Daily Star'	300.00	900.00	2700.00
21-Has 2 ads for More Fun #52 (1st Spectre)	212.00	638.00	1800.00
22,24,25: 24-Kent at Daily Planet. 25-Last app. Gargantua T. Potts, Tex Thompson's sidekick	175.00	525.00	1600.00
23-1st app. Luthor (w/red hair) & Black Pirate; Black Pirate by Moldoff; 1st mention of The Daily Planet (4/40)-Has 1 panel ad for Spectre in More Fun	535.00	1600.00	5000.00
26-28,30	150.00	450.00	1350.00
29-1st Lois Lane-c (10/40)	175.00	525.00	1600.00
31,32: 32-Intro/1st app. Krypto Ray Gun in Superman story by Burnley	94.00	285.00	850.00
33-Origin Mr. America; Superman by Burnley	125.00	375.00	1000.00
34-40: 37-Origin Congo Bill. 40-(9/41)-Intro/1st app. Star Spangled Kid & Stripesy	94.00	285.00	850.00
41	88.00	265.00	800.00
42-1st app./origin Vigilante; Bob Daley becomes Fat Man; origin Mr. America's magic flying carpet; The Queen Bee & Luthor app; Black Pirate ends; not in #41	125.00	375.00	1100.00
43-46,48-50: 44-Fat Man's i.d. revealed to Mr. America. 45-1st app. Stuff (Vigilante's oriental sidekick)	88.00	265.00	800.00
47-1st Luthor cover in comics (4/42)	125.00	370.00	1100.00
51-1st app. The Prankster	100.00	300.00	800.00
52-Fat Man & Mr. America become the Ameri-commandos; origin Vigilante retold	109.00	327.00	875.00
53-60: 56-Last Fat Man. 57-2nd Lois Lane-c in Action (3rd anywhere, 2/43). 59-Kubert Vigilante begins?, ends #70. 60-First app. Lois Lane as Super-woman	65.00	196.00	525.00
61-63,65-70: 63-Last 3 Aces	59.00	160.00	475.00
64-Intro Toyman	69.00	206.00	550.00
71-79: 74-Last Mr. America	56.00	168.00	450.00
80-2nd app. & 1st Mr. Mxyzptlk-c (1/45)	84.00	225.00	675.00
81-90: 83-Intro Hocus & Pocus	56.00	150.00	450.00
91-99: 93-Xmas-c. 99-1st small logo (8/46)	53.00	141.00	425.00
100	112.00	300.00	900.00
101-Nuclear explosion-c	112.00	300.00	900.00
102-120: 105,117-X-Mas-c	45.00	135.00	400.00
121-126,128-140: 135,138-Zatara by Kubert	42.00	125.00	375.00
127-Vigilante by Kubert; Tommy Tomorrow begins (12/48, see Real Fact #6)	50.00	150.00	450.00
141-157,159-161: 151-Luthor/Mr. Mxyztplk/Prankster team-up. 156-Lois Lane as Super Woman. 160- Last 52 pgs.	40.00	120.00	350.00
158-Origin Superman retold	94.00	285.00	850.00
162-180: 168,176-Used in POP, pg. 90	30.00	90.00	275.00
181-201: 191-Intro. Janu in Congo Bill. 198-Last Vigilante. 201-Last pre-code issue	30.00	90.00	275.00
202-220: 212-(1/56)-Includes 1956 Superman calender that is part of story.			

	GD25	FN65	NM94
	32.00	96.00	250.00
221-240: 221-1st S.A. issue. 224-1st Golden Gorilla story. 228-(5/57)-Kongorilla in Congo Bill story (Congorilla try-out)	25.00	75.00	190.00
241,243-251: 241-Batman x-over. 248-Origin/1st app. Congorilla; Congo Bill renamed Congorilla. 251-Last Tommy Tomorrow	21.00	62.00	160.00
242-Origin & 1st app. Brainiac (7/58); 1st mention of Shrunken City of Kandor	110.00	330.00	1100.00
252-Origin & 1st app. Supergirl (5/59); intro new Metallo	130.00	390.00	1300.00
253-2nd app. Supergirl	34.00	103.00	350.00
254-1st meeting of Bizarro & Superman-c/story	31.00	94.00	230.00
255-1st Bizarro Lois Lane-c/story & both Bizarros leave Earth to make Bizarro World	22.00	66.00	165.00
256-261: 259-Red Kryptonite used. 261-1st X-Kryptonite which gave Streaky his powers; last Congorilla in Action; origin & 1st app. Streaky The Super Cat	13.50	41.00	100.00
262,264-266,268-270	12.00	36.00	90.00
263-Origin Bizarro World	16.00	47.00	115.00
267(8/60)-3rd Legion app; 1st app. Chameleon Boy, Colossal Boy, & Invisible Kid, 1st app. of Supergirl as Superwoman.	44.00	132.00	360.00
271-275,277-282: 274-Lois Lane as Superwoman; 282-Last 10¢ issue	10.00	30.00	75.00
276(5/61)-6th Legion app; 1st app. Brainiac 5, Phantom Girl, Triplicate Girl, Bouncing Boy, Sun Boy, & Shrinking Violet; Supergirl joins Legion	22.00	66.00	160.00
283(12/61)-Legion of Super-Villains app.	11.00	33.00	80.00
284(1/62)-Mon-el app.	11.00	33.00	80.00
285(2/62)-12th Legion app; Brainiac 5 cameo; Supergirl's existence revealed to world; JFK & Jackie cameos	11.00	33.00	80.00
286(3/62)-Legion of Super Villains app.	6.50	19.50	50.00
287(4/62)-14th Legion app.(cameo)	6.50	19.50	50.00
288-Mon-el app.; r-origin Supergirl	6.50	19.50	50.00
289(6/62)-16th Legion app. (Adult); Lightning Man & Saturn Woman's marriage 1st revealed	6.50	19.50	50.00
290(7/62)-17th Legion app. (cameo); Phantom Girl app. 290-1st Supergirl emergency squad	6.50	19.50	50.00
291,292,294-299: 291-1st meeting Supergirl & Mr. Mxyzptlk. 292-2nd app. Superhorse (see Adv. #293). 297-Mon-el app. 298-Legion cameo	6.25	19.00	50.00
293-Origin Comet (Superhorse)	11.00	33.00	78.00
300-(5/63)	6.50	19.50	50.00
301-303,305-308,310-320: 306-Brainiac 5, Mon-el app. 307-Saturn Girl app. 314-r-origin Supergirl; J.L.A. x-over. 317-Death of Nor-Kan of Kandor. 319-Shrinking Violet app.	2.85	8.50	22.00
304-Origin & 1st app. Black Flame (9/63)	4.00	12.00	30.00
309-(2/64)-Legion app.; Batman & Robin-c & cameo; JFK app. (he died 11/22/63; on stands same time as death?)	3.75	11.25	30.00
321-333,335,337-340: 336-Origin Akvar (Flamebird). 340-Origin, 1st app. Parasite	2.30	6.70	16.00
334-Giant G-20; origin Supergirl, Streaky, Superhorse & Legion (all-r)	5.00	15.00	40.00
341-346,348-359: 344-Batman x-over. 350-Batman, Green Arrow & Green Lantern app. in Supergirl back-up story	1.85	5.50	13.00
347,360-Giant Supergirl G-33,G-45; 347-Origin Comet-r plus 3 Bizarro stories. 360-Legion-r; r/origin Supergirl	3.75	11.25	27.00
361-372,374-380: 361-2nd app. Parasite. 365-Legion app. 370-New facts about Superman's origin. 376-Last Supergirl in Action. 377-Legion begins.	1.65	4.20	10.00
373-Giant Supergirl G-57; Legion-r	3.75	11.25	30.00
381-402: 392-Last Legion in Action; Saturn Girl gets new costume. 393-402-All Superman issues	1.30	3.25	8.00
403-413: All 52 pg. issues. 411-Origin Eclipso-(r). 413-Metamorpho begins, ends #418	1.70	5.00	12.00
414-424: 419-Intro. Human Target. 421-Intro Capt. Strong; Green Arrow			

Action Comics #726 © DC

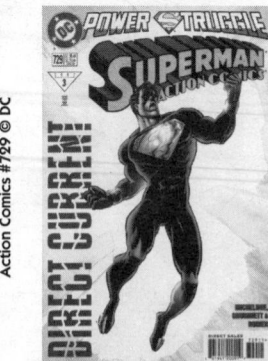
Action Comics #729 © DC

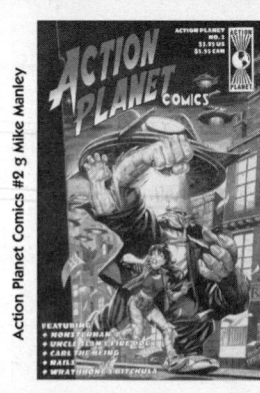
Action Planet Comics #2 g Mike Manley

	GD25	FN65	NM94

begins. 422,423-Origin Human Target
| | | |
425-Neal Adams-a(p); The Atom begins 1.30 | 3.25 | 8.00 |
426-436,438,439: 432-Toyman app (2/74). 2.00 | 6.00 | 14.00 |
437,443-(100 pg. giants) 1.20 | 3.00 | 7.00 |
440-1st Grell-a on Green Arrow 2.00 | 6.00 | 14.00 |
441-Grell-a on Green Arrow continues 1.00 | 2.60 | 6.00 |
  1.00 | 2.00 | 5.00

442,444-499: 449-(68 pgs.). 454-Last Atom. 458-Last Green Arrow. 484-Earth II Superman & Lois Lane wed; 40th anniversary issue (6/78). 487,488-(44 pgs.). 487-Origin & 1st app. Microwave Man; origin Atom retold
  1.40   3.50

500-($1.00, 68 pgs.)-Infinity-c; Superman life story; shows Legion statues in museum 1.00 2.00 5.00
501-551,554-582: 511-514-Airwave II solo stories. 513-The Atom begins. 517-Aquaman begins; ends #541. 521-1st app. The Vixen. 532,536-New Teen Titans cameo. 535,536-Omega Men app. 544-(Mando paper, 68 pgs.)-Origins new Luthor & Brainiac; Omega Men cameo. 544-Shuster-a (pin-up); article by Siegel. 546-J.L.A., New Teen Titans app. 551-Starfire becomes Red-Star
  .80 2.00
552,553-Animal Man-c & app. (2/84 & 3/84) 1.60 4.00
583-Alan Moore scripts; last Earth 1 Superman story (cont'd from Superman #423) 1.65 4.20 10.00
584-Byrne-a begins; New Teen Titans app. .80 2.00
585-599: 586-Legends x-over. 596-Millennium x-over; Spectre app. 598-1st app. Checkmate .60 1.50
600-($2.50, 84 pgs., 5/88) 1.00 2.00 5.00
601-642-Weekly issues ($1.50, 52 pgs.): 601-Re-intro The Secret Six. 611-614-: Catwoman stories (new costume in #611). 613-618-Nightwing stories
  .70 1.75
643-Superman & monthly issues begin again; Perez-c/a/scripts begins; swipes cover to Superman #1 .70 1.75
644-649,651,661,663-666,668-673,675-679: 645-1st app. Maxima. 654-Part 3 of Batman storyline. 655-Free extra 8 pgs. 660-Death of Lex Luthor. 661-Begin $1.00-c. 675-Deathstroke cameo. 679-Last $1.00 issue 1.25
650-($1.50, 52 pgs.)-Lobo cameo (last panel) 1.60 4.00
662-Clark Kent reveals i.d. to Lois Lane; story continued in Superman #53
  1.00 2.60 6.00
667-($1.75, 52 pgs.) .80 2.00
674-Supergirl logo & c/story (reintro) 1.20 3.00
680-682 1.50
683-Doomsday cameo 1.60 4.00
683-2nd & 3rd printings 1.25
684-Doomsday battle issue 1.60 4.00
685,686-Funeral for a Friend issues; Supergirl app. 1.00 2.50
685-2nd & 3rd printings 1.25
687-($1.95)-Collector's Edition with die-cut-c .90 2.25
687-($1.50)-Newsstand Edition with mini-poster .70 1.70
688-694,696-699,701-703-($1.50): 688-Guy Gardner-c/story. 697-Bizarro-c/story. 703-(9/94)-Zero Hour 1.50
695-($1.50)-Collector's Edition w/embossed foil-c 1.00 2.50
700-($2.95, 68 pgs.)-Fall of Metropolis Pt 1; Pete Ross marries Lana Lang; Curt Swan & Murphy Anderson inks 1.20 3.00
700-Platinum 1.30 3.25 8.00
0,704-709: 0-(10/94). 704-(11/94) 1.50
710-735: 710-Begin $1.95-c. 714-Joker app. 718-Batman-c/app. 720-2nd print. 721-Mr. Mxyzptlk app. 723-Brainiac as Superman; Dave Johnson-c. 727-Final Night x-over .80 2.00
720-Lois breaks off engagement w/Clark 1.20 3.00
Annual 1(1987)-Art Adams-c/a(p); Batman app. 1.10 2.70 6.50
Annual 2(1989, $1.75, 68 pgs.)-Perez-c/a(i) .80 2.00
Annual 3(1991, $2.00, 68 pgs.)-Armageddon 2001 1.00 2.50
Annual 4(1992, $2.50, 68 pgs.)-Eclipso vs. Shazam 1.00 2.50
Annual 5(1993, $2.50, 68 pgs.)-Bloodlines; 1st app. Loose Cannon.
  1.00 2.50
Annual 6(1994, $2.95)-Elseworlds story 1.20 3.00

	GD25	FN65	NM94

Annual 7(1995, $3.95)-Year One story 1.60 4.00
Annual 8(1996, $2.95)-Legends of the Dead Earth story 3.00
Theater Giveaway (1947, 32 pgs., 6-1/2 x 8-1/4", nn)-Vigilante story based on Columbia Vigilante serial; no Superman-c or story
  70.00 210.00 500.00
NOTE: *Supergirl's* origin in 262, 280, 285, 291, 305, 309. **N. Adams**-c-356, 358, 359, 361-364, 366, 367, 370-374, 377-379i, 398-400, 402, 404-406, 419p, 466, 468, 473i, 485. **Aparo** a-642. **Austin** c/a-682i. **Baily** a-24, 25. **Burnley** a-28-33; c-487, 53-55, 58, 59?, 60-63, 65, 66p, 67p, 70p, 71p, 79p, 82p, 84-86p, 90-92p, 93p?, 94p, 107p, 108p. **Byrne** a-584-598p, 599i, 600p; c-584-591, 596-600. **Ditko** a-642. **Giffen** a-560, 563, 565, 577, 579; c-539, 580, 563, 565, 577, 579. **Grell** a-440-442, 444-446, 450-452, 456-458; c-456. **Guardineer** a-25; c-8, 11, 12, 14-16, 18, 25. **Guice** a(p)-676-681, 683-698, 700; c-683, 685, 686, 687(direct), 688-693i, 694-696, 697i, 698-700. **Infantino** a-642. **Kaluta** c-613. **Bob Kane's** Clip Carson-14-41. **Gil Kane** a-443r, 493r, 539-541, 544-549, 551-554, 601-605, 642; c-535p, 540, 541, 544p, 545-549, 551-554, 580, 627. **Kirby** c-638. **Meskin** a-42-121(most), **Mignola** a-600, Annual 2; c-c-614. **Moldoff** a-23-25, 443r. **Mooney** a-667p. **Mortimer** c-153, 154, 159-172, 174, 178-181, 184, 186-189, 191-193, 196, 200, 206. **Orlando** a-617p; c-621. **Perez** a-600i, 643-652p, Annual 2p; c-529p, 602, 643-651, Annual 2p. **Quesada** c-Annual 4p. **Fred Ray** c-34, 36-46, 50-52. **Siegel & Shuster** a-1-27. **Paul Smith** c-608. **Starlin** a-509; c-631. **Leonard Starr** a-597(part), **Staton** a-525p, 526p, 531p, 535p, 536p. **Swan/Moldoff** c-281, 286, 287, 293, 298, 334. **Thibert** c-676, 677p, 678-681, 684. **Toth** a-406, 407, 413, 431; c-616. **Tuska** a-486p, 550. **Williamson** a-568i. **Zeck** c-Annual 5

ACTION FORCE (Also see G.I. Joe European Missions)
Mar, 1987 - No. 40?, 1988 ($1.00, weekly, magazine)
Marvel Comics Ltd. (British)
1-40: British G.I. Joe series. 3-w/poster insert 1.00

ACTION GIRL
Oct, 1994 - Present ($2.50/$2.75, B&W)
Slave Labor Graphics
1-3 1.00 2.50
4-8: 4-Begin $2.75-c 1.10 2.75
1-4 ($2.75, 2nd printings): All read 2nd Print in indicia. 1-(2/96). 2-(10/95). 3-(2/96). 4-(7/96) 1.10 2.75

ACTION PLANET COMICS
1996 - Present ($3.95, B&W, 44 pgs.)
Action Planet
1-3: 1-Intro Monster Man by Mike Manley & other stories 2.00 4.00

ACTUAL CONFESSIONS (Formerly Love Adventures)
No. 13, Oct, 1952 - No. 14, Dec, 1952
Atlas Comics (MPI)
13,14 4.00 11.00 22.00

ACTUAL ROMANCES (Becomes True Secrets #3 on?)
Oct, 1949 - No. 2, Jan, 1950 (52 pgs.)
Marvel Comics (IPS)
1 9.15 27.50 55.00
2-Photo-c 5.35 16.00 32.00

ADAM AND EVE
1975,1978 (35¢/49¢)
Spire Christian Comics (Fleming H. Revell Co.)
nn-By Al Hartley 1.00

ADAM STRANGE (Also see Green Lantern #132, Mystery In Space #53 & Showcase #17)
1990 - No. 3, 1990 ($3.95, 52 pgs, limited series, squarebound)
DC Comics
Book One - Three: Andy & Adam Kubert-c/a 1.60 4.00

ADAM-12 (TV)
Dec, 1973 - No. 10, Feb, 1976 (Photo-c)
Gold Key
1 6.00 18.00 60.00
2-10 2.25 6.75 22.00

ADDAMS FAMILY (TV cartoon)
Oct, 1974 - No. 3, Apr, 1975 (Hanna-Barbera)

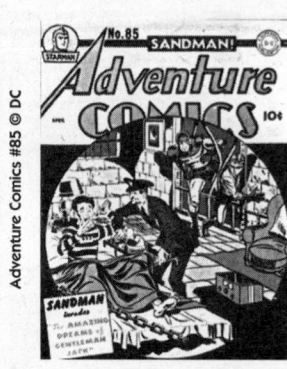

Advanced Dungeons & Dragons #5 © TSR

Adventure Comics #42 © DC

Adventure Comics #85 © DC

	GD25	FN65	NM94

	GD25	FN65	NM94

Gold Key

		GD25	FN65	NM94
1		7.00	21.00	70.00
2,3		3.20	9.60	32.00

ADLAI STEVENSON
Dec, 1966
Dell Publishing Co.

	GD25	FN65	NM94
12-007-612-Life story; photo-c	2.50	7.50	25.00

ADOLESCENT RADIOACTIVE BLACK BELT HAMSTERS (See Clint)
1986 - No. 9, Jan, 1988 ($1.50, B&W)
Comic Castle/Eclipse Comics

1-9: 1st & 2nd printings exist			1.00
1-Limited Edition		1.60	4.00
1-In 3-D (7/86)		.70	1.80
2-4 ($2.50)		1.00	2.50
Massacre The Japanese Invasion #1 (8/89, $2.00)		.80	2.00

ADULT TALES OF TERROR ILLUSTRATED (See Terror Illustrated)

ADVANCED DUNGEONS & DRAGONS (Also see TSR Worlds)
Dec, 1988 - No. 36, Dec, 1991 (Newsstand #1 is Holiday, 1988-89)
($1.25/$1.50/$1.75)
DC Comics

1-Based on TSR role playing game	1.30	3.25	8.00
2	1.00	2.60	6.00
3		1.60	4.00
4-10: Later issues $1.50-c		1.20	3.00
11-15		.80	2.00
16-24			1.50
24-36: 25-$1.75-c begins		.70	1.80
Annual 1 (1990, $3.95, 68 pgs.)		1.60	4.00

ADVENTURE BOUND
Aug, 1949
Dell Publishing Co.

Four Color 239	4.80	14.40	48.00

ADVENTURE COMICS (Formerly New Adventure)(...Presents Dial H For
Hero #479-490)
No. 32, 11/38 - No. 490, 2/82; No. 491, 9/82 - No. 503, 9/83
National Periodical Publications/DC Comics

32-Anchors Aweigh (ends #52), Barry O'Neil (ends #60, not in #33), Captain
Desmo (ends #47), Dale Daring (ends #47), Federal Men (ends #70), The
Golden Dragon (ends #36), Rusty & His Pals (ends #52) by Bob Kane, Todd
Hunter (ends #38) and Tom Brent (ends #39) begin

	466.00	1400.00	2800.00
33-38: 37-Cover used on Double Action #2	216.00	650.00	1300.00
39(6/39):-Jack Wood begins, ends #42; 1st mention of Marijuana in comics	216.00	650.00	1300.00

	GD25	FN65	VF82	NM94
40-(Rare, 7/39, on stands 6/10/39)-The Sandman begins by Bert Christman				
(who died in WWII); believed to be 1st conceived story (see N.Y. World's				
Fair for 1st published app.); Socko Strong begins, ends #54				
	2900.00	8700.00	18,850.00	32,000.00

	GD25	FN65	NM94
41	425.00	1275.00	3800.00
42,44-Sandman-c by Flessel. 44-Opium story	545.00	1630.00	4900.00
43,45	290.00	860.00	2300.00
46,47-Sandman covers by Flessel. 47-Steve Conrad Adventurer begins,			
ends #76	370.00	1100.00	3300.00

	GD25	FN65	VF82	NM94
48-Intro & 1st app. The Hourman by Bernard Bailey; Baily-c				
(Hourman c-48,50,52-59)	1890.00	5670.00	11,830.00	20,000.00
(Estimated up to 80 total copies exist, 8 in NM/Mint)				

	GD25	FN65	NM94
49,50: 50-Cotton Carver by Jack Lehti begins, ends #64			

		GD25	FN65	NM94
		212.00	640.00	1700.00
51,60-Sandman-c: 51-Sandman-c by Flessel.	262.00	790.00	2100.00
52-59: 53-1st app. Jimmy "Minuteman" Martin & the Minutemen of America			
in Hourman; ends #78. 58-Paul Kirk Manhunter begins (1st app.), ends #72			
	175.00	525.00	1400.00

	GD25	FN65	VF82	NM94
61-1st app. Starman by Jack Burnley (4/41); Starman c-61-72; Starman by				
Burnley in #61-80	1100.00	3335.00	6675.00	11,000.00
(Estimated up to 100+ total copies exist, 7 in NM/Mint)				

	GD25	FN65	NM94
62-65,67,68,70: 67-Origin & 1st app. The Mist. 70-Last Federal Men			
	150.00	450.00	1200.00
66-Origin/1st app. Shining Knight (9/41)	190.00	565.00	1500.00
69-1st app. Sandy the Golden Boy (Sandman's sidekick) by Paul Norris (in a			
Bob Kane style); Sandman dons new costume	170.00	505.00	1350.00
71-Jimmy Martin becomes costume aide to the Hourman; 1st app.Hourman's			
Miracle Ray machine	135.00	412.00	1100.00

	GD25	FN65	VF82	NM94
72-1st Simon & Kirby Sandman (3/42), 1st DC work)				
	1000.00	3000.00	6000.00	10,000.00
(Estimated up to 100+ total copies exist, 8 in NM/Mint)				
73-Origin Manhunter by Simon & Kirby; begin new series; Manhunter-c				
	1100.00	3335.00	6675.00	11,000.00
(Estimated up to 100+ total copies exist, 7 in NM/Mint)				

	GD25	FN65	NM94
74-80: 74-Thorndyke replaces Jimmy, Hourman's assistant; new Sandman-			
c begin by S&K. 75-Thor app. by Kirby; 1st Kirby Thor (see Tales of the			
Unexpected #16). 77-Origin Genius Jones; Mist story. 79-Manhunter-c.			
80-Last S&K Manhunter & Burnley Starman	175.00	525.00	1400.00
81-90: 83-Last Hourman. 84-Mike Gibbs begins, ends #102			
	112.00	335.00	900.00
91-Last Simon & Kirby Sandman	95.00	280.00	750.00
92-99,101,102: 92-Last Manhunter. 102-Last Starman, Sandman, & Genius			
Jones; most-S&K-c (Genius Jones cont'd in More Fun #108)			
	90.00	270.00	725.00
100-S&K-c	120.00	360.00	950.00
103-Aquaman, Green Arrow, Johnny Quick & Superboy all move over from			
More Fun Comics #107; 8th app. Superboy; Superboy-c begins; 1st small			
logo (4/46)	262.00	790.00	2100.00
104	95.00	280.00	750.00
105-110	62.00	190.00	500.00
111-120: 113-X-Mas-c	60.00	180.00	475.00
121-126,128-130: 128-1st meeting Superboy & Lois Lane			
	52.00	160.00	420.00
127-Brief origin Shining Knight retold	55.00	165.00	440.00
131-141,143-149: 132-Shining Knight 1st return to King Arthur time; origin			
aide Sir Butch	44.00	132.00	350.00
142-Origin Shining Knight & Johnny Quick retold	50.00	145.00	385.00
150,151,153,155,157,159,161,163-All have 6 pg. Shining Knight stories by			
Frank Frazetta. 159-Origin Johnny Quick	50.00	150.00	400.00
152,154,156,158,160,162,164-169: 166-Last Shining Knight. 168-Last 52 pg.			
issue	40.00	120.00	290.00
170-180	39.00	116.00	270.00
181-199: 189-B&W and color illo in **POP**	37.00	111.00	260.00
200 (5/54)	44.00	145.00	290.00
201-208: 207-Last Johnny Quick (not in 205)	36.00	109.00	265.00
209-Last pre-code issue; origin Speedy	38.00	114.00	275.00

	GD25	FN65	VF82	NM94
210-1st app. Krypto (Superdog)-c/story (3/55)				
	254.00	765.00	1780.00	2800.00

	GD25	FN65	NM94
211-213,215-220: 220-Krypto app.	30.00	90.00	230.00
214-2nd app. Krypto	40.00	120.00	350.00
221-246: 229-1st S.A. issue. 237-1st Intergalactic Vigilante Squadron (6/57)			

Adventure Comics #986 © DC

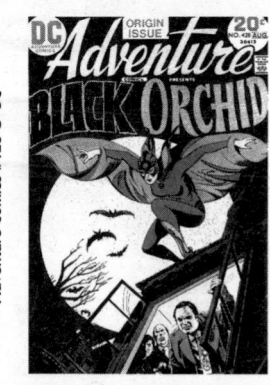

Adventure Comics #426 © DC

Adventure Comics #474 © DC

	GD25	FN65	NM94
	25.00	75.00	190.00
	GD25	**FN65**	**VF82**
247(4/58)-1st Legion of Super Heroes app.; 1st app. Cosmic Boy, Lightning Boy (later Lightning Lad in #267), & Saturn Girl (origin)	360.00	1080.00	2540.00 **NM94** 4000.00
	GD25	**FN65**	**NM94**
248-252,254,255-Green Arrow in all: 255-Intro. Red Kryptonite in Superboy (used in #252 but with no effect)	19.00	58.00	150.00
253-1st meeting of Superboy & Robin; Green Arrow by Kirby in #250-255 (also see World's Finest #96-99)	27.00	81.00	210.00
256-Origin Green Arrow by Kirby	66.00	197.00	550.00
257-259: 258-Green Arrow x-over in Superboy	18.00	54.00	125.00
260-1st Silver-Age origin Aquaman (5/59)	70.00	210.00	600.00
261-266,268,270: 262-Origin Speedy in Green Arrow. 266-(11/59)-Origin & 1st app. Aquagirl (tryout, not same as later character). 270-Congorilla begins, ends #281,283	13.00	39.00	100.00
267(12/59)-2nd Legion of Super Heroes app.; Lightning Boy now called Lightning Lad; new costumes for Legion	111.00	333.00	750.00
269-Intro. Aqualad (2/60); last Green Arrow (not in #206)	26.00	79.00	200.00
271-Origin Luthor retold	28.00	84.00	215.00
272-274,277-280: 279-Intro White Kryptonite in Superboy. 280-1st meeting Superboy-Lori Lemaris	11.00	33.00	80.00
275-Origin Superman-Batman team retold (see World's Finest #94)	24.00	71.00	175.00
276-(9/60) Re-intro Metallo (3rd app?); story similar to Superboy #49	11.00	33.00	80.00
281,284,287-289: 281-Last Congorilla. 284-Last Aquaman in Adv. 287,288-Intro Dev-Em, the Knave from Krypton. 287-1st Bizarro Perry White & J. Olsen. 288-Bizarro-c. 289-Legion cameo (statues)	11.00	33.00	80.00
282(3/61)-5th Legion app; intro/origin Star Boy	20.00	60.00	155.00
283-Intro. The Phantom Zone	22.00	66.00	155.00
285-1st Tales of the Bizarro World-c/story (ends #299) in Adv. (see Action #255)	17.00	49.00	130.00
286-1st Bizarro Mxyzptlk; Bizarro-c	15.00	45.00	105.00
290(11/61)-8th Legion app; origin Sunboy in Legion (last 10¢ issue)	20.00	60.00	155.00
291,292,295-298: 292-1st Bizarro Lana Lang & Lucy Lane. 295-Bizarro-c; 1st Bizarro Titano	8.00	23.50	60.00
293(2/62)-13th Legion app; Mon-el & Legion Super Pets (1st app./origin) app. (1st Superhorse). 1st Bizarro Luthor & Kandor	13.00	39.00	100.00
294-1st Bizarro Marilyn Monroe, Pres. Kennedy.	13.00	39.00	100.00
299-1st Gold Kryptonite (8/62)	9.30	28.00	70.00
300-Tales of the Legion of Super-Heroes series begins (9/62); Mon-el leaves Phantom Zone (temporarily), joins Legion	44.00	132.00	350.00
301-Origin Bouncing Boy	17.00	49.00	115.00
302-305: 303-1st app. Matter Eater Lad. 304-Death of Lightning Lad in Legion	11.00	33.00	75.00
306-310: 306-Intro. Legion of Substitute Heroes. 307-1st app. Element Lad in Legion. 308-1st app. Lightning Lass in Legion	8.50	26.00	65.00
311-320: 312-Lightning Lad back in Legion. 315-Last new Superboy story; Colossal Boy app. 316-Origins & powers of Legion given. 317-Intro. Dream Girl in Legion; Lightning Lass becomes Light Lass; Hall of Fame series begins. 320-Dev-Em 2nd app.	7.00	21.50	55.00
321-Intro Time Trapper	6.50	19.50	50.00
322-330: 327-Intro/1st app. Lone Wolf in Legion. 329-Intro The Bizarro Legionnaires	5.50	16.50	42.00
331-340: 337-Chlorophyll Kid & Night Girl app. 340-Intro Computo in Legion	4.30	13.00	32.00
341-Triplicate Girl becomes Duo Damsel	3.75	11.25	28.00
342-345,347,350,351: 345-Last Hall of Fame; returns in 356,371. 351-1st app. White Witch	2.60	7.50	18.00
346,348,349: 346-1st app. Karate Kid, Princess Projectra, Ferro Lad, & Nemesis Kid. 348-Origin Sunboy; intro Dr. Regulus in Legion. 349-Intro			

	GD25	FN65	NM94
Universo & Rond Vidar	2.60	7.50	18.00
352,354-360: 355-Insect Queen joins Legion (4/67)	1.65	4.70	12.00
353-Death of Ferro Lad in Legion	3.60	11.00	25.00
361-364,366,368-370: 369-Intro Mordru in Legion	1.65	4.70	11.00
365,367,371,372: 365-Intro Shadow Lass; lists origins & powers of L.S.H. 367-New Legion headquarters. 371-Intro. Chemical King. 372-Timber Wolf & Chemical King join. 374-Article on comics fandom	1.65	4.70	11.00
373,374,376-380: Last Legion in Adventure	1.65	4.20	11.00
375-Intro Quantum Queen & The Wanderers	1.65	4.70	11.00
381-Supergirl begins; 1st full length supergirl story & her 1st solo book (6/69)	4.50	13.00	35.00
382-389,391-400: 399-Unpubbed G.A. Black Canary story. 400-New costume for Supergirl	1.60		4.00
390-Giant Supergirl G-69	2.15	6.50	15.00
401,402,404-410: 409-415,417-420-(52 pg. issues)	1.00	2.00	5.00
403-68pg. Giant G-81; Legion-r/#304,305,308,312	2.00	6.00	14.00
411,413: 413-Hawkman by Kubert r/B&B #44; G.A. Robotman-r/Det. #178; Zatanna by Morrow			1.50
412-Reprints origin/1st app. Animal Man/Strange Adventures #180	1.00	2.00	5.00
414-Reprints 2nd Animal Man/Strange Advs. #184	1.00	1.20	3.00
415,420-Animal Man reprints from Strange Adventures #190 (origin recap) & #195	.80		2.00
416-Giant DC-100 Page Super Spect. #10; GA-r; r/1st app. Black Canary from Flash #86; no Zatanna	1.00		2.50
417-Morrow Vigilante; Frazetta Shining Knight-r/Adv. #161; origin The Enchantress; no Zatanna	.80		2.00
418,419,421-424: Last Supergirl in Adventure. 418-Previously unpublished Dr. Mid-Nite story from 1948; No Zatanna			1.25
425-New look, content change to adventure; Kaluta-c; Toth-a, origin Capt. Fear	1.00	2.00	5.00
426,427,441-458: 426-1st Adventurers Club. 427-Last Vigilante. 441-452-Aquaman app. 450-Weather Wizard app. in Aquaman story. 443-Re-intro Clay Face. 445-447-The Creeper app. 446-Flag-c. 449-451-Martian Manhunter app. 453-458-Super-boy app. 453-Intro Mighty Girl. 457,458-Eclipso app.	.80		2.00
428-Origin/1st app. Black Orchid (c/story, 6-7/73)	2.15	6.50	15.00
429,430-Black Orchid-c/stories	1.30	3.25	8.00
431-Spectre by Aparo begins, ends #440.	2.15	6.50	15.00
432-440-Spectre app. 433-437-Cover title is Weird Adv. Comics. 436-Last 20¢ issue. 440-New Spectre origin.	1.20	3.00	7.00
459,460-New Gods/Darkseid storyline concludes from New Gods #19 (#459 is dated 9-10/78) without missing a month	1.65	4.20	11.00
461,462: 461-Justice Society begins; ends 466. 461,462-Death Earth II Batman (both $1.00, 68 pgs.)	1.00	2.00	5.00
463-466($1.00 size, 68 pgs.): 459-Flash (ends #466), Deadman (ends #466), Wonder Woman (ends #464), Green Lantern (ends #460), 460-Aquaman begins; ends #478			1.50
467-Starman by Ditko & Plastic Man begins; 1st app. Prince Gavyn (Starman).	1.70	5.00	12.00
468-490: 469,470-Origin Starman. 478-Last Starman & Plastic Man. 479-Dial 'H' For Hero begins, ends #490			1.25
491-503: 488,489-Deathstroke-c/cameos. 491-100pg. Digest size begins; r/ Legion of Super Heroes/Adv. #247,267; Spectre, Aquaman, Superboy, S&K Sandman, Bl. Canary-r & new Shazam by Newton begin. 493-Challengers of the Unknown begins by Tuska w/brief origin. 492,495,496,499-S&K Sandman-r/Adventure in all; 494-499-Spectre-r/Spectre 1-3, 5-7. 493-495,497-499-G.A. Captain Marvel-r. 498-Plastic Man-r begin; origin Bouncing Boy-r/#301. 500-All Legion-r (Digest size, 148 pgs.). 501-503: G.A.-r	1.20		3.00

NOTE: *Bizarro covers-285, 286, 288, 294, 295, 329. Vigilante app.-420, 426, 427. **N. Adams** a(r)-495i-498i; c-365-369, 371-373, 375-379, 381-383. **Aparo** a-431-433, 434i, 435, 436, 437i, 438i, 439-452, 503r; c-431-452. **Austin** a-449i 451i. **Bernard Baily** c-48, 50, 52-59. **Bolland** c-475. **Burnley** c-61-72, 116-120p. **Chaykin** a-438. **Ditko** a-467-478p; c-467p. **Craig Flessel** c-32, 33, 40, 42, 44, 46, 47, 51, 60. **Giffen** c-491p-494p, 500p. **Grell** a-435-437, 440. **Guardineer** c-34, 35, 45. **Infantino** a-416r. **Kaluta** c-425. **Bob Kane** a-38. **G. Kane** a-414r, 425; c-496-499,*

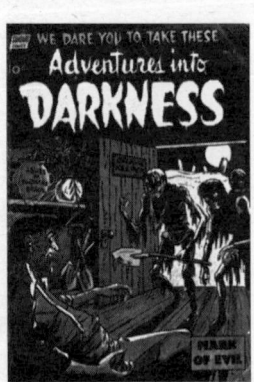

Adventure Into Darkness #8 © STD

Adventures Into Terror #17 © MEG

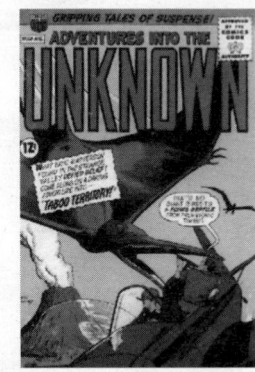

Adventure Into The Unknown #150 © ACG

	GD25	FN65	NM94

537. **Kirby** a-250-256. **Kubert** a-413. **Meskin** a-81,127. **Moldoff** a-494i; c-49. **Morrow** a-413-415, 417, 422, 502r, 503r. **Netzer/Nasser** a-449-451. **Newton** a-459-461, 464-466, 491p, 492p. **Paul Norris** a-69. **Orlando** a-457p, 458p. **Perez** c-484-486, 490p. **Simon/Kirby** a-503r; c-73-97, 100-102. **Starlin** c-471. **Staton** a-445-447l, 456-458p, 459, 460, 461p-465p, 466,467p-478p, 502p(r); c-458, 461(back). **Toth** a-418, 419, 425, 431, 495p-497p. **Tuska** a-494p.

ADVENTURE COMICS
No date (early 1940s) (Paper-c, 32 pgs.)
IGA

Two diff.issues; Super-Mystery-r from 1941	23.00	69.00	160.00

ADVENTURE IN DISNEYLAND
May, 1955 (Giveaway, soft-c, 16 pgs)
Walt Disney Productions (Dist. by Richfield Oil)

nn	10.00	30.00	60.00

ADVENTURE INTO MYSTERY
May, 1956 - No. 8, July, 1957
Atlas Comics (BFP No. 1/OPI No. 2-8)

1-Powell s/f-a; Forte-a; Everett-c	31.00	94.00	220.00
2-Flying Saucer story	18.00	54.00	125.00
3,6-Everett-c	14.00	43.00	100.00
4-Williamson-a, 4 pgs; Powell-a	16.00	47.00	110.00
5-Everett-c/a, Orlando-a	16.00	47.00	110.00
7-Torres-a; Everett-c	16.00	47.00	110.00
8-Moriera, Sale, Torres, Woodbridge-a, Severin-c	14.00	43.00	100.00

ADVENTURE IS MY CAREER
1945 (44 pgs.)
U.S. Coast Guard Academy/Street & Smith

nn-Simon, Milt Gross-a	18.00	54.00	125.00

ADVENTURERS, THE
Aug, 1986 - No. 10, 1987? ($1.50, B&W)
V2#1, 1987 - V2#9, 1988; V3#1, Oct, 1989 - V3#6, 1990
Aircel Comics/Adventure Publ.

1-Peter Hsu-a	1.00	2.00	5.00
1-Cover variant, limited ed.	1.65	4.20	10.00
1-2nd print (1986); 1st app. Elf Warrior		1.20	3.00
2,3		1.00	2.50
0 (#4, 12/86)-Origin		.80	2.00
4-10			1.60
Book II, regular & limited ed. #1			1.60
Book II, #2,3,0,4-9			1.60
Book III, #1 (10/89, $2.25)-Regular & limited-c		.90	2.25
Book III, #2-6		.90	2.25

ADVENTURES (No. 2 Spectacular... on cover)
Nov, 1949 - No. 2, Feb, 1950 (No. 1 ...in Romance on cover)
St. John Publishing Co. (Slightly large size)

1(Scarce); Bolle, Starr-a(2)	23.00	69.00	160.00
2(Scarce)-Slave Girl; China Bombshell app.; Bolle, L. Starr-a	39.00	116.00	270.00

ADVENTURES FOR BOYS
Dec, 1954
Bailey Enterprises

nn-Comics, text, & photos	4.70	14.00	28.00

ADVENTURES IN PARADISE (TV)
Feb-Apr, 1962
Dell Publishing Co.

Four Color#1301	4.50	13.50	45.00

ADVENTURES IN ROMANCE (See Adventures)

ADVENTURES IN SCIENCE (See Classics Illustrated Special Issue)

ADVENTURES IN 3-D
Nov, 1953 - No. 2, Jan, 1954 (25¢)

Harvey Publications

1-Nostrand, Powell-a, 2-Powell-a	17.00	49.00	115.00

ADVENTURES INTO DARKNESS (See Seduction of the Innocent 3-D)
No. 5, Aug, 1952 - No. 14, 1954
Better-Standard Publications/Visual Editions

5-Katz-c/a; Toth-a(p)	25.00	75.00	175.00
6-Tuska, Katz-a	14.00	43.00	100.00
7-Katz-c/a	16.00	47.00	110.00
8,9-Toth-a(p)	17.00	51.00	120.00
10,11-Jack Katz-a	13.50	41.00	95.00
12-Toth-a?; lingerie panels	13.50	41.00	95.00
13-Toth-a(p); Cannibalism story cited by T. E. Murphy articles	17.00	49.00	115.00
14	11.00	33.00	75.00

NOTE: **Fawcette** a-13. **Moriera** a-5. **Sekowsky** a-10, 11, 13(2).

ADVENTURES INTO TERROR (Formerly Joker Comics)
No. 43, Nov, 1950 - No. 31, May, 1954
Marvel/Atlas Comics (CDS)

43(#1)	50.00	150.00	400.00
44(#2, 2/51)-Sol Brodsky-c	39.00	118.00	275.00
3(4/51), 4	21.00	64.00	150.00
5-Wolverton-c panel/Mystic #6; Rico-c panel also; Atom Bomb story	26.00	77.00	180.00
6,8: 8-Wolverton text illo r-/Marvel Tales #104	20.00	60.00	140.00
7-Wolverton-a "Where Monsters Dwell", 6 pgs.; Tuska; Maneely-c panels	45.00	130.00	340.00
9,10,12-Krigstein-a. 9-Decapitation panels	18.00	54.00	125.00
11,13-20	14.00	43.00	100.00
21-24,26-31	13.00	39.00	90.00
25-Matt Fox-a	17.00	51.00	120.00

NOTE: **Ayers** a-21. **Colan** a-3, 5, 14, 21, 24, 25, 28, 29; c-27. **Colletta** a-30. **Everett** c-13, 21, 25. **Fass** a-28, 29. **Forte** a-28. **Heath** a-43, 44, 4-6, 22, 24, 26; c-43, 9, 11. **Lazarus** a-7. **Maneely** a-7(3 pg.), 10, 11, 21., 22 c-15, 29. **Don Rico** a-4, 5(3 pg.). **Sekowsky** a-43, 3, 4. **Sinnott** a-8, 9, 11, 28. **Tuska** a-14; c-7.

ADVENTURES INTO THE UNKNOWN
Fall, 1948 - No. 174, Aug, 1967 (No. 1-33: 52 pgs.)
American Comics Group

(1st continuous series horror comic; see Eerie #1)

1-Guardineer-a; adapt. of 'Castle of Otranto' by Horace Walpole	150.00	450.00	1200.00
2	62.00	190.00	500.00
3-Feldstein-a (9 pgs)	65.00	195.00	515.00
4,5: 5-'Spirit Of Frankenstein' series begins, ends #12 (except #11)	34.00	101.00	235.00
6-10	26.00	77.00	180.00
11-16,18-20: 13-Starr-a	20.00	60.00	140.00
17-Story similar to movie 'The Thing'	25.00	75.00	175.00
21-26,28-30	17.00	51.00	120.00
27-Williamson/Krenkel-a (8 pgs.)	21.00	64.00	150.00
31-50: 38-Atom bomb panels	13.50	41.00	95.00
51-(1/54)-(3-D effect-c/story)-Only white cover	26.00	77.00	200.00
52-58: (3-D effect-c/stories with black covers). 52-E.C. swipe/Haunt Of Fear #14	24.00	73.00	190.00
59-3-D effect story only; new logo	19.00	58.00	150.00
60-Woodesque-a by Landau	8.50	26.00	65.00
61-Last pre-code issue (1-2/55)	8.30	25.00	60.00
62-70	5.50	16.50	40.00
71-90	4.00	12.00	30.00
91,96(#95 on inside),107,116-All have Williamson-a	5.50	16.50	42.00
92-95,97-99,101-106,108-115,117-127: 109-113,118-Whitney painted-c	3.75	11.25	28.00
100	4.00	12.00	30.00

Adventures Into Weird Worlds #7 © MEG

Adventures of Captain America #1 © MEG

Advs. of Cyclops & Phoenix #4 © MEG

	GD25	FN65	NM94
128-Williamson/Krenkel/Torres-a(r)/Forbidden Worlds #63; last 10¢ issue			
	3.75	11.25	28.00
129-152	3.40	10.00	24.00
153, 157-Magic Agent app.	3.25	9.50	22.00
154-Nemesis series begins (origin), ends #170	3.75	11.25	28.00
155,156,158-167,169-174: 169-Nemesis battles Hitler			
	2.85	8.50	20.00
168-Ditko-a(p)	3.75	11.25	28.00

NOTE: "Spirit of Frankenstein" series in 5, 6, 8-10, 12, 16. **Buscema** a-100, 106, 108-110, 158r, 165r. **Cameron** a-34. **Craig** a-152, 160. **Goode** a-45, 47, 60. **Landau** a-51, 59-63. **Lazarus** a-34, 48, 51, 52, 56, 58, 79, 87; c-31-56, 58. **Reinman** a-102, 111, 112, 115-118, 124, 130, 137, 141, 145, 164. **Whitney** c-12-30, 57, 59-on (most.) **Torres/Williamson** a-116.

ADVENTURES INTO WEIRD WORLDS
Jan, 1952 - No. 30, June, 1954
Marvel/Atlas Comics (ACI)

1-Atom bomb stories	42.00	130.00	340.00
2-Sci/fic stories (2); one by Maneely	30.00	90.00	210.00
3-10: 7-Tongue ripped out. 10-Krigstein, Everett-a	20.00	60.00	140.00
11-21: 21-Hitler in Hell story	16.00	47.00	110.00
22-26: 24-Man holds hypo & splits in two	13.50	41.00	95.00
27-Matt Fox end of world story-a; severed head-c	29.00	86.00	200.00
28-Atom bomb story; decapitation panels	16.00	47.00	110.00
29,30	11.00	33.00	75.00

NOTE: **Ayers** a-8, 26. **Everett** a-4, 5; c-6, 8, 10-13, 18, 19, 22, 24, 25; a-4, 25. **Fass** a-7. **Forte** a-21, 24. **Al Hartley** a-2. **Heath** a-1, 4, 17, 22; c-7, 9, 20. **Maneely** a-2, 3, 11, 20, 22, 23, 25; c-1, 3, 22, 25-27, 29. **Reinman** a-24, 28. **Rico** a-13. **Robinson** a-13. **Sinnott** a-25, 30. **Tuska** a-1, 2, 12, 15. **Whitney** a-28. Bondage c-22.

ADVENTURES IN WONDERLAND
April, 1955 - No. 5, Feb, 1956 (Jr. Readers Guild)
Lev Gleason Publications

1-Maurer-a	7.50	22.50	45.00
2-4	4.70	14.00	28.00
5-Christmas issue	5.35	16.00	32.00

ADVENTURES OF ALAN LADD, THE
Oct-Nov, 1949 - No. 9, Feb-Mar, 1951 (All 52 pgs.)
National Periodical Publications

1-Photo-c	88.00	262.00	700.00
2-Photo-c	47.00	141.00	375.00
3-6: Last photo-c	40.00	120.00	280.00
7-9	31.00	94.00	220.00

NOTE: **Dan Barry** a-1. **Moreira** a-3-7.

ADVENTURES OF ALICE
1945 (Also see Alice in Wonderland & ...at Monkey Island)
Civil Service Publ./Pentagon Publishing Co.

1	10.00	30.00	65.00
2-Through the Magic Looking Glass	9.15	27.50	55.00

ADVENTURES OF BARON MUNCHAUSEN, THE
July, 1989 - No. 4, Oct, 1989 ($1.75, limited series)
Now Comics

1-4: Movie adaptation		.70	1.80

ADVENTURES OF BAYOU BILLY, THE
Sept, 1989 - No. 5, June, 1990 ($1.00)
Archie Comics

1-5: Esposito-c/a/s. 5-Kelley Jones-c			1.00

ADVENTURES OF BOB HOPE, THE (Also see True Comics #59)
Feb-Mar, 1950 - No. 109, Feb-Mar, 1968 (#1-10: 52pgs.)
National Periodical Publications

1-Photo-c	135.00	412.00	1100.00
2-Photo-c	68.00	205.00	550.00
3,4-Photo-c	41.00	124.00	330.00
5-10	39.00	118.00	275.00

11-20	21.00	64.00	150.00
21-31 (2-3/55; last precode)	13.50	41.00	95.00
32-40	11.00	33.00	80.00
41-50	8.50	26.00	65.00
51-70	6.00	18.00	45.00
71-93,95-105: 95-1st app. Super-Hip & 1st monster issue (11/65)			
	3.40	10.00	24.00
94-Aquaman cameo	3.75	11.25	27.00
106-109-All monster-c/stories by N. Adams-c/a	5.00	15.00	40.00

NOTE: Buzzy in #34. Kitty Karr of Hollywood in #15, 17-20, 23, 28. Liz in #26, 109. Miss Beverly Hills of Hollywood in #7, 8, 10, 13, 14. Miss Melody Lane of Broadway in #15. Rusty in #23, 25. Tommy in #24. No 2nd feature in #2-4, 6, 8, 11, 12, 28-108.

ADVENTURES OF CAPTAIN AMERICA
Sept, 1991 - No. 4, Jan, 1992 ($4.95, 52 pgs., squarebound, limited series)
Marvel Comics

1-4: 1-Embossed-c; Fabian Nicieza scripts; Kevin Maguire-c/a(p) begins, ends #3. 2-4-Austin-c/a(i)	1.00	2.00	5.00

ADVENTURES OF CYCLOPS AND PHOENIX (Also See Askani'son & The Further Adventures of Cyclops And Phoenix)
May, 1994 - No. 4, Aug, 1994 ($2.95, limited series)
Marvel Comics

1-Characters from X-Men	1.00	2.00	5.00
2-4		1.80	4.50
Trade paperback ($14.95)-reprints #1-4			15.00

ADVENTURES OF DEAN MARTIN AND JERRY LEWIS, THE
(The Adventures of Jerry Lewis #41 on) (See Movie Love #12)
July-Aug, 1952 - No. 40, Oct, 1957
National Periodical Publications

1	81.00	245.00	650.00
2	40.00	120.00	325.00
3-10: 3-3 pg origin on how they became a team; I Love Lucy text featurette			
	20.00	60.00	140.00
11-19: Last precode (2/55)	11.50	34.00	90.00
20-30	10.00	30.00	70.00
31-40	7.50	22.50	50.00

ADVENTURES OF DETECTIVE ACE KING, THE (See Detective Dan)
No date (1933) (36 pgs., 9-1/2x12") (10¢, B&W, one-shot) (paper-c)
Humor Publ. Corp.

Book 1-Along with Detective Dan, the first comic w/original-a; Not reprints; Ace King by Martin Nadle (The American Sherlock Holmes). A Dick Tracy look-a-like	500.00	1500.00	3000.00

ADVENTURES OF FELIX THE CAT, THE
May, 1992 ($1.25)
Harvey Comics

1-Messmer-r			1.25

ADVENTURES OF FORD FAIRLANE, THE
May, 1990 - No. 4, Aug, 1990 ($1.50, limited series, mature)
DC Comics

1-4: Movie tie-in; Don Heck inks			1.50

ADVENTURES OF G. I. JOE
1969 (3-1/4x7") (20 & 16 pgs.)
Giveaways

First Series: 1-Danger of the Depths. 2-Perilous Rescue. 3-Secret Mission to Spy Island. 4-Mysterious Explosion. 5-Fantastic Free Fall. 6-Eight Ropes of Danger. 7-Mouth of Doom. 8-Hidden Missile Discovery. 9-Space Walk Mystery. 10-Fight for Survival. 11-The Shark's Surprise. **Second Series:** 5-Flying Space Adventure. 4-White Tiger Hunt. 7-Capture of the Pygmy Gorilla. 12-Secret of the Mummy's Tomb. Third Series: Reprinted surviving titles of First Series. Fourth Series: 13-Adventure Team Headquarters. 14-Search For the Stolen Idol.

each....	1.00	2.00	5.00

ADVENTURES OF HOMER COBB, THE
Sept, 1947 (Oversized)

Adventures of Pinky Lee #1 © DC

Adventures of Rex The Wonder Dog #44 © DC

Adventures of Superman #428 © DC

	GD25	FN65	NM94

Say/Bart Prod. (Publ. in the U.S., but printed in Canada)

	GD25	FN65	NM94
1-(Scarce)-Feldstein-c/a	26.00	77.00	180.00

ADVENTURES OF HOMER GHOST (See Homer The Happy Ghost)
June, 1957 - No. 2, Aug, 1957
Atlas Comics

V1#1,2	5.35	16.00	32.00

ADVENTURES OF JERRY LEWIS, THE (Adventures of Dean Martin & Jerry Lewis No. 1-40)(See Super DC Giant)
No. 41, Nov, 1957 - No. 124, May-June, 1971
National Periodical Publications

41	6.25	19.00	50.00
42-60	5.50	17.00	45.00
61-80; 68,74-Photo-c	4.30	13.00	32.00
81-91,93-96,98-100: 89-Bob Hope app.	2.85	8.50	20.00
92-Superman cameo	3.75	11.25	26.00
97-Batman/Robin/Joker-c/story; Riddler & Penguin app; Dick Sprang-c.			
	4.50	13.00	35.00
101,103,104-Neal Adams-c/a	4.00	12.00	32.00
102-Beatles app.; Neal Adams c/a	5.00	15.00	39.00
105-Superman x-over	3.60	11.00	25.00
106-111,113-116	1.65	4.20	10.00
112-Flash x-over	3.60	11.00	25.00
117-Wonder Woman x-over	1.85	5.50	13.00
118-124	1.30	3.25	8.00

ADVENTURES OF JO-JOY, THE (See Jo-Joy)

ADVENTURES OF LUTHER ARKWRIGHT, THE
Oct, 1987 - No. 9, Jan, 1989 ($2.00, B&W)
V2, #1, Mar, 1990 - V2#9, 1990 ($1.95, B&W)
Valkyrie Press/Dark Horse Comics

1-9: 1-Alan Moore intro.		.80	2.00
V2#1-9 (Dark Horse): Reprints 1st series; new-c		.80	2.00

ADVENTURES OF MARGARET O'BRIEN, THE
1947 (20 pgs. in color, slick-c, regular size) (Premium)
Bambury Fashions (Clothes)

In "The Big City" movie adaptation (scarce)	19.00	58.00	135.00

ADVENTURES OF MIGHTY MOUSE (Mighty Mouse Adventures No. 1)
No. 2, Jan, 1952 - No. 18, May, 1955
St. John Publishing Co.

2	23.00	69.00	160.00
3-5	11.50	34.00	80.00
6-18	9.15	27.50	55.00

ADVENTURES OF MIGHTY MOUSE (2nd Series)
(Two No. 144's; formerly Paul Terry's Comics; No. 129-137 have nn's)
(Becomes Mighty Mouse No. 161 on)
No. 126, Aug, 1955 - No. 160, Oct, 1963
St. John/Pines/Dell/Gold Key

126(8/55), 127(10/55), 128(11/55)-St. John	7.50	22.50	45.00
nn(129, 4/56)-144(8/59)-Pines	6.35	19.00	38.00
144(10-12/59)-155(7-9/62) Dell	5.00	15.00	30.00
156(10/62)-160(10/63) Gold Key	5.00	15.00	30.00

NOTE: Early issues titled "Paul Terry's Adventures of ....".

ADVENTURES OF MIGHTY MOUSE (Formerly Mighty Mouse)
No. 166, Mar, 1979 - No. 172, Jan, 1980
Gold Key

166-172		.65	2.00	6.50

ADVS. OF MR. FROG & MISS MOUSE (See Dell Junior Treasury No. 4)

ADVENTURES OF OZZIE AND HARRIET, THE (Radio)
Oct-Nov, 1949 - No. 5, June-July, 1950
National Periodical Publications

1-Photo-c	81.00	245.00	650.00
2	44.00	132.00	350.00
3-5	40.00	120.00	280.00

ADVENTURES OF PATORUZU
Aug, 1946 - Winter, 1946
Green Publishing Co.

nn's-Contains Animal Crackers reprints	4.15	12.50	25.00

ADVENTURES OF PINKY LEE, THE (TV)
July, 1955 - No. 5, Dec, 1955
Atlas Comics

1	24.00	73.00	170.00
2-5	16.00	47.00	110.00

ADVENTURES OF PIPSQUEAK, THE (Formerly Pat the Brat)
No. 34, Sept, 1959 - No. 39, July, 1960
Archie Publications (Radio Comics)

34	5.00	15.00	30.00
35-39	4.00	10.00	20.00

ADVENTURES OF QUAKE & QUISP, THE (See Quaker Oats "Plenty of Glutton")

ADVENTURES OF REX THE WONDER DOG, THE (Rex...No. 1)
Jan-Feb, 1952 - No. 45, May-June, 1959; No. 46, Nov-Dec, 1959
National Periodical Publications

1-(Scarce)-Toth-c/a	100.00	300.00	800.00
2-(Scarce)-Toth-c/a	48.00	145.00	390.00
3-(Scarce)-Toth-a	40.00	120.00	310.00
4,5	31.00	94.00	220.00
6-10	23.00	69.00	160.00
11-Atom bomb-c/story	25.00	75.00	175.00
12-19: 19-Last precode (1-2/55)	13.00	39.00	90.00
20-46	10.00	30.00	65.00

NOTE: Infantino, Gil Kane art in 5-19 (most)

ADVENTURES OF ROBIN HOOD, THE (Formerly Robin Hood)
No. 7, 9/57 - No. 8, 11/57 (Based on Richard Greene TV Show)
Magazine Enterprises (Sussex Publ. Co.)

7,8-Richard Greene photo-c. 7-Powell-a	13.50	41.00	95.00

ADVENTURES OF ROBIN HOOD, THE
Mar, 1974 - No. 7, Jan, 1975 (Disney cartoon) (36 pgs.)
Gold Key

1(90291-403)-Part-r of $1.50 editions	.50	1.50	5.00
2-7: 1-7 are part-r	.30	1.00	3.00

ADVENTURES OF SPIDER-MAN, THE (TV cartoon)
Apr, 1996 - Present (99¢)
Marvel Comics

1-12: Based on animated television show.			1.00

ADVENTURES OF STUBBY, SANTA'S SMALLEST REINDEER, THE
nd (early 1940s) (Giveaway, 12 pgs.)
W. T. Grant Co.

nn	4.00	11.00	22.00

ADVENTURES OF SUPERBOY, THE (See Superboy, 2nd Series)

ADVENTURES OF SUPERMAN (Formerly Superman)
No. 424, Jan, 1987 - No. 499, Feb, 1993; No. 500, Early June, 1993 - Present
DC Comics

424		.90	2.25
425-449: 426-Legends x-over. 432-1st app. Jose Delgado who becomes Gangbuster in #434. 436-Byrne scripts begin. 436,437-Millennium x-over. 438-New Brainiac app. 440-Batman app. 449-Invasion		.80	2.00
450-462: 457-Perez plots		.70	1.75
463-Superman/Flash race; cover swipe/Superman #199			
	1.00	2.00	5.00
464-Lobo-c & app. (pre-dates Lobo #1)		1.60	4.00

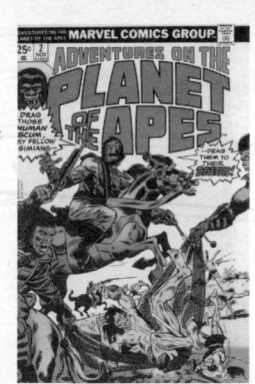

Adventures of Superman #517 © DC

Adventures of Superman #541 © DC

Adventures on the Planet of the Apes #2 © MEG

	GD25	FN65	NM94

465-479,481-491: 467-Part 2 of Batman story. 473-Hal Jordan, Guy Gardner x-over. 477-Legion app. 491-Last $1.00-c — — — 1.25
480-($1.75, 52 pgs.) — .80 2.00
492-495: 495-Forever People-c/story; Darkseid app. — — 1.50
496-Doomsday cameo — 1.00 2.00 5.00
496,497-2nd printings — — 1.25
497-Doomsday battle issue — 1.00 2.00 5.00
498,499-Funeral for a Friend; Supergirl app. — — 1.20 3.00
498-2nd & 3rd printings — — 1.25
500-($2.95, 68 pgs.)-Collector's edition w/card — — 1.30 3.25
500-($2.50, 68 pgs.)-Regular edition w/different-c — — 1.10 2.75
500-Platinum edition — 3.75 11.25 30.00
501-($1.95)-Collector's edition with die-cut-c — — .80 2.00
501-($1.50)-Regular edition w/mini-poster & diff.-c — — 1.50
502-517: 502-Supergirl-c/story. 508-Challengers of the Unknown app. 510-Bizarro-c/story. 517-(9/94)-Zero Hour — — — 1.50
505-($2.50)-Holo-grafx foil-c edition — — 1.00 2.50
0,518-523: 0-(10/94). 518-(11/94) — — — 1.50
524-545: 524-Begin $1.95-c. 527-Return of Alpha Centurion from Zero Hour. 533-Impulse c/app. 535-Luthor-c/app. 536-Brainiac app. 537-Parasite app. 540-Final Night x-over — .80 2.00
Annual 1 (1987, $1.25, 52 pgs.)-Starlin-c & scripts — — 1.50
Annual 2,3 (1990, 1991, $2.00, 68 pgs.): 2-Byrne-c/a(i); Legion '90 (Lobo) app. 3-Armageddon 2001 x-over — .90 2.25
Annual 4,5 (1992, 1993, $2.50, 68 pgs.): 4-Guy Gardner/Lobo-c/story; Eclipso storyline; Quesada-c(p). 5-Bloodlines storyline — 1.10 2.75
Annual 6 (1994, $2.95, 68 pgs.)-Elseworlds story — — 1.20 3.00
Annual 7 (1995, $3.95)-Year One story — — 1.60 4.00
Annual 8 (1996, $2.95)-Legends of the Dead Earth story — — 3.00
NOTE: **Erik Larsen** a-431.

ADVENTURES OF THE BIG BOY
1956 - No. 466, 1996? (Giveaway) (East & West editions of early issues)
Timely Comics/Webs Adv. Corp./Illus. Features

1-Everett-a	65.00	195.00	525.00
2-Everett-a	27.00	81.00	190.00
3-5	10.00	30.00	70.00
6-10: 6-Sci/fic issue	6.35	19.00	38.00
11-20	4.00	10.00	20.00
21-30	2.40	6.00	12.00
31-50	1.20	3.00	6.00
51-100		1.20	3.00
101-150		.80	2.00
151-240			1.00
241-466: 266-Superman x-over. 417-(1992)			.20
1-50 ('76-'84,Paragon Prod.)			.20
Summer, 1959 issue, large size	4.15	12.50	25.00

NOTE: No. 467 was completed but never published.

ADVENTURES OF THE DOVER BOYS
September, 1950 - No. 2, 1950 (No month given)
Archie Comics (Close-up)

1-38	6.25	19.00	50.00

ADVENTURES OF THE FLY (The Fly #1-6; Fly Man No. 32-39; See The Double Life of Private Strong, The Fly, Laugh Comics & Mighty Crusaders)
Aug, 1959 - No. 30, Oct, 1964; No. 31, May, 1965
Archie Publications/Radio Comics

1-Shield app.; origin The Fly; S&K-c/a	56.00	170.00	500.00
2-Williamson, S&K-a	34.00	107.00	275.00
3-Origin retold; Davis, Powell-a	27.00	84.00	215.00
4-Neal Adams-a(p)(1 panel); S&K-c; Powell-a; 2 pg. Shield story	14.00	43.00	110.00
5-10: 7-1st S.A. app. Black Hood (7/60). 8-1st S.A. app. Shield (9/60). 9-Shield app. 9-1st app. Cat Girl. 10-Black Hood app.	10.00	30.00	80.00
11-13,15-20: 13-1st app. Fly Girl w/o costume. 16-1st app 10¢ issue. 20-Origin Fly Girl retold	6.25	19.50	50.00

	GD25	FN65	NM94

14-Origin & 1st app. Fly Girl in costume	8.00	26.00	65.00
21-30: 23-Jaguar cameo. 27-29-Black Hood 1 pg. strips. 30-Comet x-over (1st S.A. app.) in Fly Girl	4.00	13.00	32.00
31-Black Hood, Shield, Comet app.	4.50	14.00	35.00

NOTE: **Simon** c-2-4. **Tuska** a-1. Cover title to #31 is Flyman; Advs. of the Fly inside.

ADVENTURES OF THE JAGUAR, THE (See Blue Ribbon Comics, Laugh Comics & Mighty Crusaders)
Sept, 1961 - No. 15, Nov, 1963
Archie Publications (Radio Comics)

1-Origin Jaguar (1st app.) by J.Rosenberger	19.00	60.00	155.00
2,3: 3-Last 10¢ issue	10.00	30.00	80.00
4-6-Catgirl app. (#4's-c is same as splash pg.)	7.50	22.00	60.00
7-10	5.60	17.00	45.00
11-15:13,14-Catgirl,Black Hood app. in both	4.50	14.00	35.00

ADVENTURES OF THE MASK (TV cartoon)
Jan, 1996 - No. 12, Dec, 1996 ($2.50)
Dark Horse Comics

1-12: Based on animated series		1.00	2.50

ADVENTURES OF THE OUTSIDERS, THE (Formerly Batman & The Outsiders; also see The Outsiders)
No. 33, May, 1986 - No. 46, June, 1987
DC Comics

33-46: 39-45-r/Outsiders #1-7 by Aparo			1.00

ADVENTURES OF THE SUPER MARIO BROTHERS (Also see Super Mario Bros.)
1990 - No. 9?, 1990? ($1.50)
Valiant

V2#1-9			1.50

ADVENTURES OF THE THING, THE (Also see The Thing)
Apr, 1992 - No. 4, July, 1992, ($1.25, limited series)
Marvel Comics

1-4: 1-r/Marvel Two-In-One #50 by Byrne; Kieth-c. 2-4-r/Marvel Two-In-One #80,51 & 77; 2-Ghost Rider-c/story. 3-Miller-r			1.25

ADVENTURES OF THE X-MEN, THE (TV cartoon)
Apr, 1996 - Present (99¢)
Marvel Comics

1-12: Based on television show.			1.00

ADVENTURES OF TINKER BELL (See Tinker Bell, 4-Color No. 896 & 982)

ADVENTURES OF TOM SAWYER (See Dell Junior Treasury No. 10)

ADVENTURES OF YOUNG DR. MASTERS, THE
Aug, 1964 - No. 2, Nov, 1964
Archie Comics (Radio Comics)

1,2	1.00	2.50	6.00

ADVENTURES ON OTHER WORLDS (See Showcase #17 & 18)

ADVENTURES ON THE PLANET OF THE APES
Oct, 1975 - No. 11, Dec, 1976
Marvel Comics Group

1-Planet of the Apes-r in color; Starlin-c		1.60	4.00
2-5		1.20	3.00
6-11		.80	2.00

NOTE: **Alcala** a-6-11r. **Buckler** c-2p. **Nasser** c-7. **Starlin** c-6. **Tuska** a-1-5r.

ADVENTURES WITH SANTA CLAUS
No date (early 50's) (9-3/4x 6-3/4", 24 pgs., giveaway, paper-c)
Promotional Publ. Co. (Murphy's Store)

nn-Contains 8 pgs. ads	4.00	12.00	24.00
16 pg. version	4.00	12.00	24.00

AFRICA
1955

Agents of Law #4 © DH

Age of Heroes #1 © Halloween Comics

Airboy #12 © ECL

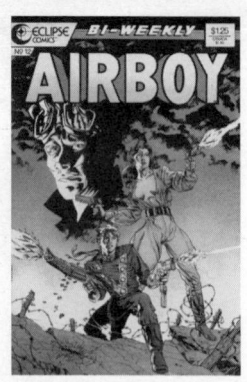

	GD25	FN65	NM94
Magazine Enterprises			
1(A-1#137)-Cave Girl,Thun'da;Powell-c/a(4)	20.00	60.00	140.00
AFRICAN LION (Disney movie)			
Nov, 1955			
Dell Publishing Co.			
Four Color #665	5.40	16.00	54.00
AFTER DARK			
No. 6, May, 1955 - No. 8, Sept, 1955			
Sterling Comics			
6-8-Sekowsky-a in all	7.00	21.00	42.00
AGAINST BLACKSHARD 3-D (Also see SoulQuest)			
August, 1986 ($2.25)			
Sirius Comics			
1		1.00	2.50
AGENT LIBERTY SPECIAL (See Superman, 2nd Series)			
1992 ($2.00, 52 pgs, one-shot)			
DC Comics			
1-1st solo adventure; Guice-c/a(i)		.80	2.00
AGENT THREE-ZERO			
Sept, 1993 ($3.95, 52 pgs.)			
Galaxinovels, Inc.			
1-Polybagged with card & mini-poster; Platt-c/a(1st work)			
		1.60	4.00
AGENT THREE-ZERO: THE BLUE SULTANS QUEST/ BLUE SULTAN-GALAXI FACT FILES			
1994 ($2.95, color w/text-no comics, limited series)			
Galaxi Novels			
1-($2.95)-Flip book w/Blue Sultan	1.20		3.00
1-($3.95)-Polybagged w/trading card; flip book w/Blue Sultan.			
		1.60	4.00
1-($5.95)-Platinum embossed edition; flip book w/ Blue Sultan			
	1.00	2.50	6.00
AGENTS OF LAW (Also see Comic's Greatest World)			
Mar, 1995 - No.6, Sept, 1995 ($2.50)			
Dark Horse Comics			
1-6: 5-Predator app. 6-Predator app.; death of Law	1.00		2.50
AGE OF APOCALYPSE: THE CHOSEN			
Apr, 1995 ($2.50, one-shot)			
Marvel Comics			
1-Wraparound-c	1.40		3.50
AGE OF HEROES, THE			
1996 - Present ($2.95, B&W)			
Halloween Comics			
1-3: James Hudnall scripts; John Ridgway-c/a			3.00
AGE OF INNOCENCE: THE REBIRTH OF IRON MAN			
Feb, 1996 ($2.50, one-shot)			
Marvel Comics			
1-New origin of Tony Stark	1.00		2.50
AGE OF REPTILES			
Nov, 1993 - No. 4, Feb, 1994 ($2.50, limited series)			
Dark Horse Comics			
1-4: Delgado-c/a/scripts in all	1.00		2.50
AGE OF REPTILES: THE HUNT			
May, 1996 - No. 5, Sept, 1996 ($2.95, limited series)			
Dark Horse Comics			
1-5: Delgado-c/a/scripts in all; wraparound-c			3.00

	GD25	FN65	NM94
AGGIE MACK			
Jan, 1948 - No. 8, Aug, 1949			
Four Star Comics Corp./Superior Comics Ltd.			
1-Feldstein-a, "Johnny Prep"	25.00	75.00	175.00
2,3-Kamen-c	13.00	39.00	90.00
4-Feldstein "Johnny Prep"; Kamen-c	18.00	54.00	125.00
5-8-Kamen-c/a	14.00	43.00	100.00
AGGIE MACK			
Apr - Jun, 1962			
Dell Publishing Co.			
Four Color #1335	3.60	11.00	36.00
AIR ACE (Formerly Bill Barnes No. 1-12)			
V2#1, Jan, 1944 - V3#8(No. 20), Feb-Mar, 1947			
Street & Smith Publications			
V2#1	19.00	58.00	135.00
V2#2-12: 7-Powell-a	10.00	30.00	65.00
V3#1-6	8.35	25.00	50.00
V3#7-Powell bondage-c/a; all atomic issue	17.00	51.00	120.00
V3#8 (V5#8 on-c)-Powell-c/a	10.00	30.00	60.00
AIRBOY (Also see Airmaidens, Skywolf, Target: Airboy & Valkyrie)			
July, 1986 - No. 50, Oct, 1989 (#1-8, 50¢, 20 pgs., bi-weekly; #9-on, 36pgs.; #34-on monthly)			
Eclipse Comics			
1		1.20	3.00
2-4,6-8: 2-1st Marisa; Skywolf gets new costume. 3-The Heap begins		.80	2.00
5-Valkyrie returns; Dave Stevens-c		1.20	3.00
9-32: 9-Begin $1.25-c; Skywolf begins. 11-Origin of G.A. Airboy & his plane Birdie. 28-Mr. Monster vs. The Heap.			1.60
33-41: 33-Begin $1.75-c. 38-40-The Heap-r by Infantino. 41-r/1st app. Valkyrie from Air Fighters			1.75
42-49: 42-Begin $1.95-c. 46,47-part-r/Air Fighters. 48-Black Angel-r/A.F		.80	2.00
50 ($4.95, 52 pgs.)-Kubert-c	1.00	2.00	4.95
NOTE: **Evans** c-21. **Gulacy** c-7, 20. **Spiegle** a-34, 35, 37. **Ken Steacy** painted c-17, 33.			
AIRBOY COMICS (Air Fighters Comics No. 1-22)			
V2#11, Dec, 1945 - V10#4, May, 1953 (No V3#3)			
Hillman Periodicals			
V2#11	60.00	180.00	475.00
12-Valkyrie app.	40.00	120.00	290.00
V3#1,2(no #3)	34.00	103.00	240.00
4-The Heap app. in Skywolf	31.00	94.00	220.00
5-8,10,11: 6-Valkyrie app.	26.00	77.00	180.00
9-Origin The Heap	31.00	94.00	220.00
12-Skywolf & Airboy x-over; Valkyrie app.	36.00	107.00	250.00
V4#1-Iron Lady app.	30.00	90.00	210.00
2,3,12: 2-Rackman begins	21.00	62.00	145.00
4-Simon & Kirby-c	24.00	71.00	165.00
5-11-All S&K-a	22.00	66.00	155.00
V5#1-4,6-11: 4-Infantino Heap. 10-Origin The Heap	14.00	43.00	100.00
5-Skull-c.	17.00	49.00	115.00
12-Krigstein-a(p)	17.00	51.00	120.00
V6#1-3,5-12: 6,8-Origin The Heap	14.00	43.00	100.00
4-Origin retold	19.00	56.00	130.00
V7#1-12: 7,8,10-Origin The Heap	14.00	43.00	100.00
V8#1-3,5-12	13.50	41.00	95.00
4-Krigstein-a	14.00	43.00	100.00
V9#1-4,6-12: 2-Valkyrie app. 7-One pg. Frazetta ad	11.00	33.00	75.00
5(#100)	12.00	36.00	85.00
V10#1-4	10.00	30.00	70.00
NOTE: **Barry** a-V2#3, 7. **Bolle** a-V4#12. **McWilliams** a-V3#7, 9. **Powell** a-V7#2, 3, V8#1, 6. **Starr** a-V5#1, 12. **Dick Wood** a-V4#12. Bondage-c V5#8.			

Airboy Meets the Prowler #1 © ECL

Akiko on the Planet Smoo #12 © Mark Crilley

Akira #26 © Mash Room

AL

	GD25	FN65	NM94
AIRBOY MEETS THE PROWLER			
Aug, 1987 ($1.95, one-shot)			
Eclipse Comics			
1-John Snyder, III-c/a	.35	1.00	1.95
AIRBOY-MR. MONSTER SPECIAL			
Aug, 1987 ($1.75, one-shot)			
Eclipse Comics			
1	.30	.90	1.80
AIRBOY VERSUS THE AIR MAIDENS			
July, 1988 ($1.95)			
Eclipse Comics			
1	.35	1.00	1.95
AIR FIGHTERS CLASSICS			
Nov, 1987 - No. 6, May, 1989 ($3.95, 68 pgs., B&W)			
Eclipse Comics			
1-6: Reprints G.A. Air Fighters #2-7. 1-Origin Airboy	1.60	4.00	
AIR FIGHTERS COMICS (Airboy Comics #23 (V2#11) on)			
Nov, 1941; No. 2, Nov, 1942 - V2#10, Fall, 1945			
Hillman Periodicals			
V1#1-(Produced by Funnies, Inc.); Black Commander only app.			
	180.00	545.00	1450.00
2(11/42)-(Produced by Quality artists & Biro for Hillman); Origin & 1st app.			
Airboy & Iron Ace; Black Angel (1st app.), Flying Dutchman & Skywolf			
(1st app.) begin, Fuje-a; Biro-c/a	285.00	860.00	2300.00
3-Origin/1st app. The Heap; origin Skywolf	135.00	412.00	1100.00
4	95.00	290.00	775.00
5,6	75.00	225.00	600.00
7-12	60.00	190.00	500.00
V2#1,3-9: 5-Flag-c; Fuje-a. 7-Valkyrie app.	55.00	170.00	450.00
2-Skywolf by Giunta; Flying Dutchman by Fuje; 1st meeting Valkyrie & Air-			
boy (she worked for the Nazis in beginning); 1st app. Valkyrie (11/43)			
	70.00	205.00	550.00
10-Origin The Heap & Skywolf	60.00	190.00	500.00
NOTE: Fuje a-V1#2, 5, 7, V2#2, 3, 5, 7-9. Giunta a-V2#2, 3, 7, 9.			
AIRFIGHTERS MEET SGT. STRIKE SPECIAL, THE			
Jan, 1988 ($1.95, one-shot, stiff-c)			
Eclipse Comics			
1-Airboy, Valkyrie, Skywolf app.	.80	2.00	
AIR FORCES (See American Air Forces)			
AIRMAIDENS SPECIAL			
August, 1987 ($1.75, one-shot, Baxter paper)			
Eclipse Comics			
1-Marisa becomes La Lupina (origin)	.70	1.80	
AIR POWER (CBS TV & the U.S. Air Force Presents)			
1956 (5-1/4x7-1/4", 32 pgs., giveaway, soft-c)			
Prudential Insurance Co.			
nn-Toth-a? Based on 'You Are There' TV program by Walter Cronkite			
	10.00	30.00	60.00
AIR RAIDERS			
Nov, 1987 - No. 5, Mar, 1988 ($1.00)			
Marvel Comics (Star Comics)/Marvel Comics #3 on			
1-5		1.00	
AIRTIGHT GARAGE, THE			
July, 1993 - No. 4, Oct, 1993 ($2.50, limited series)			
Marvel Comics (Epic Comics)			
1-4: Moebius-c/a/scripts	1.00	2.50	
AIR WAR STORIES			
Sept-Nov, 1964 - No. 8, Aug, 1966			

	GD25	FN65	NM94
Dell Publishing Co.			
1-Painted-c; Glanzman-c/a begins	2.60	8.00	26.00
2-8: 2-Painted-c (all painted?)	1.60	5.00	16.00
AKIKO ON THE PLANET SMOO			
Dec, 1995 - Present ($3.95/$2.50, B&W)			
Sirius			
1-($3.95)-Crilley-c/a/scripts; gatefold-c	1.00	2.00	5.00
1-4: Crilley-c/a/scripts		1.20	3.00
Hardcover V1#1 (12/95, $19.95, B&W, 40 pgs.)			20.00
AKIRA			
Sept, 1988 - No. 38, Dec, 1995 ($3.50/$3.95/$6.95, deluxe, 68 pgs.)			
Marvel Comics (Epic Comics)			
1	2.85	8.50	20.00
1,2-2nd printings (1989, $3.95)		1.60	4.00
2-5	1.30	3.25	8.00
6-16	1.00	2.60	6.00
17-33: 17-$3.95-c begins	1.00	2.00	5.00
34-38: 34-(1994)-$6.95-c begins. 35-37: 35-(1995). 37-Texieira back-up,			
Gibbons, Williams pin-ups. 38-Moebius, Allred, Pratt, Toth, Romita, Van			
Fleet, O'Neill, Madureira pin-ups.	1.20	3.00	7.00
ALADDIN & HIS WONDERFUL LAMP (See Dell Jr Treasury #2)			
ALAN LADD (See The Adventures of...)			
ALARMING ADVENTURES			
Oct, 1962 - No. 3, Feb, 1963			
Harvey Publications			
1-Crandall/Williamson-a	9.15	27.50	55.00
2,3: 2-Williamson/Crandall-a	5.35	16.00	32.00
NOTE: Bailey a-1, 3. Crandall a-1p, 2l. Powell a-2(2). Severin c-1-3. Torres a-2? Tuska a-1.			
Williamson a-1i, 2p.			
ALARMING TALES			
Sept, 1957 - No. 6, Nov, 1958			
Harvey Publications (Western Tales)			
1-Kirby-c/a(4); Kamandi prototype story by kirby	17.00	51.00	120.00
2-Kirby-a(4)	14.00	43.00	100.00
3,4-Kirby-a. 4-Powell, Wildey-a	10.00	30.00	65.00
5-Kirby/Williamson-a; Wildey-a; Severln-c	11.00	33.00	75.00
6-Williamson-a?; Severin-c	10.00	30.00	60.00
ALBEDO			
Apr, 1985 - No. 14, Spring, 1989 (B&W)			
Thoughts And Images			
0-Yellow cover; 50 copies	5.00	15.00	40.00
0-White cover, 450 copies	3.75	11.25	30.00
0-Blue, 1st printing, 500 copies	1.70	5.00	12.00
0-Blue, 2nd printing, 1000 copies	1.30	3.25	8.00
0-3rd printing		.80	2.00
0-4th printing			1.20
1-Dark red; 1st app. Usagi Yojimbo	1.70	5.00	12.00
1-Bright red	1.60	3.80	9.75
2	1.00	2.50	6.00
3-14		.80	2.00
ALBEDO ANTHROPOMORPHICS			
Spring, 1994			
Antartic Press			
V3#1-Steve Gallacci-c/a		1.20	3.00
ALBERTO (See The Crusaders)			
ALBERT THE ALLIGATOR & POGO POSSUM			
No. 105, Apr, 1946; No. 148, May, 1947			
Dell Publishing Co.			
Four Color #105 (#1)-Kelly-c/a	68.00	205.00	675.00

Alf #29 © Alien Productions

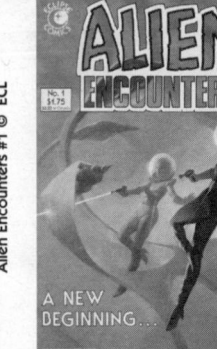
Alien Encounters #1 © ECL

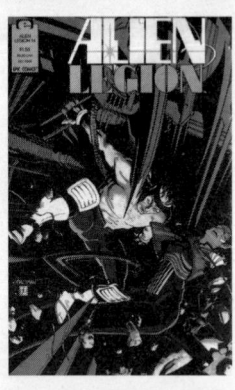
Alien Legion #14 © MEG

	GD25	FN65	NM94
Four Color #148 (#2)-Kelly-c/a	60.00	180.00	600.00
ALBUM OF CRIME (See Fox Giants)			
ALBUM OF LOVE (See Fox Giants)			
AL CAPP'S DOGPATCH (Also see Mammy Yokum)			
No. 71, June, 1949 - No. 4, Dec, 1949			
Toby Press			
71(#1)-Reprints from Tip Top #112-114	24.00	72.00	165.00
2-4: 4-Reprints from Li'l Abner #73	16.00	48.00	110.00
AL CAPP'S SHMOO (Also see Oxydol-Dreft & Washable Jones & Shmoo)			
July, 1949 - No. 5, Apr, 1950 (None by Al Capp)			
Toby Press			
1	33.00	99.00	230.00
2-5: 3-Sci-fi trip to moon. 4-X-Mas-c; origin/1st app. Super-Shmoo			
	24.00	71.00	165.00
AL CAPP'S WOLF GAL			
1951 - No. 2, 1952			
Toby Press			
1,2-Edited-r from Li'l Abner #63,64	32.00	96.00	225.00
ALEXANDER THE GREAT (Movie)			
No. 688, May, 1956			
Dell Publishing Co.			
Four Color 688-Buscema-a; photo-c	7.00	20.00	68.00
ALF (TV) (See Star Comics Digest)			
Mar, 1988 - No. 50, Feb, 1992 ($1.00)			
Marvel Comics			
1-49: 1-Photo-c. 22-X-Men parody			1.00
50-($1.75, 52 pgs.)-Final issue; photo-c	.70	1.75	
Annual 1-3: 2-Sienkiewicz-c	.70	1.75	
...Comics Digest 1 (1988)-Reprints Alf #1,2			1.50
Holiday Special 1 (1988, $1.75, 68 pgs.)	.70	1.75	
Holiday Special 2 (Winter, 1989, $2.00, 68 pgs.)	.80	2.00	
Spring Special 1 (Spr/89, $1.75, 68 pgs.)	.70	1.75	
ALFRED HARVEY'S BLACK CAT			
1995 ($3.50, B&W/color)			
Lorne-Harvey Productions			
1-Origin by Mark Evanier & Murphy Anderson; contains history of Alfred Harvey & Harvey Publications; 5 pg. B&W Sad Sack story; Hildebrandts-c			
	0.70	1.40	3.50
ALGIE			
Dec, 1953 - No. 3, 1954			
Timor Publ. Co.			
1-Teenage	4.00	12.00	24.00
1-Misprint exists w/Secret Mysteries #19 inside	4.70	14.00	28.00
2,3	3.60	9.00	18.00
Accepted Reprint #2(nd)	2.40	6.00	12.00
Super Reprint #15	2.00	5.00	10.00
ALIAS:			
July, 1990 - No. 5, Nov, 1990 ($1.75)			
Now Comics			
1-5: 1-Sienkiewicz-c	.70	1.80	
ALICE (New Adventures in Wonderland)			
No. 10, 7-8/51 - No. 2, 11-12/51			
Ziff-Davis Publ. Co.			
10-Painted-c; Berg-a	19.00	56.00	130.00
11-Dave Berg-a	10.00	30.00	65.00
2-Dave Berg-a	9.15	27.50	55.00
ALICE AT MONKEY ISLAND (See The Adventures of Alice)			
No. 3, 1946			

	GD25	FN65	NM94
Pentagon Publ. Co. (Civil Service)			
3	7.50	22.50	45.00
ALICE IN BLUNDERLAND			
1952 (Paper cover, 16 pgs. in color)			
Industrial Services			
nn-Facts about big government waste and inefficiency			
	12.00	36.00	84.00
ALICE IN WONDERLAND (Disney; see Advs. of Alice, Dell Jr. Treasury #1, The Dreamery, Movie Comics, Walt Disney Showcase #22, and World's Greatest Stories)			
No. 24, 1940; No. 331, 1951; No. 341, July, 1951			
Dell Publishing Co.			
Single Series 24 (#1)(1940)	40.00	120.00	300.00
Four Color 331, 341-"Unbirthday Party w/...	14.50	44.00	145.00
ALICE IN WONDERLAND			
1965; 1982			
Western Printing Company/Whitman Publ. Co.			
Meets Santa Claus(1950s), nd, 16 pgs.	4.00	11.00	22.00
Rexall Giveaway(1965, 16 pgs., 5x7-1/4) Western Printing (TV, Hanna-Barbera)			
	2.85	8.50	20.00
Wonder Bakery Giveaway(16 pgs, color, nn, nd) (Continental Baking Company, 1969)	2.85	8.50	20.00
1-(Whitman; 1982)-r/4-Color #331			1.20
ALICE IN WONDERLAND MEETS SANTA			
nd (6-5/8x9-11/16", 16 pgs., giveaway, paper-c)			
No publisher			
nn	10.00	30.00	65.00
ALIEN ENCOUNTERS (Replaces Alien Worlds)			
June, 1985 - No. 14, Aug, 1987 ($1.75, Baxter paper, mature readers)			
Eclipse Comics			
1-14: Nudity, strong language in all. 9-Snyder-a	.70	1.75	
ALIEN LEGION (See Epic & Marvel Graphic Novel #25)			
Apr, 1984 - No. 20, Sept, 1987 ($2.00/$1.50)			
Marvel Comics (Epic Comics)			
1-High quality paper	.80	2.00	
2-20: 2-$1.50-c			1.50
ALIEN LEGION (2nd Series)			
Aug, 1987 (indicia) (10/87 on-c) - No. 18, Aug, 1990 ($1.25)			
Marvel Comics (Epic Comics)			
V2#1-6			1.25
7-18: 7-Begin $1.50-c			1.50
ALIEN LEGION: BINARY DEEP			
1993 ($3.50, one-shot, 52 pgs.)			
Marvel Comics (Epic Comics)			
nn-With bound-in trading card	1.40	3.50	
ALIEN LEGION: JUGGER GRIMROD			
Aug, 1992 ($5.95, one-shot, 52 pgs.)			
Marvel Comics (Epic Comics)			
Book One	1.00	2.50	6.00
ALIEN LEGION: ONE PLANET AT A TIME			
May, 1993 - Book 3, July, 1993 ($4.95, squarebound, 52 pgs.)			
Marvel Comics (Epic Comics)			
Book 1-3: Hoang Nguyen-a	1.00	2.00	5.00
ALIEN LEGION: ON THE EDGE (The... #2 & 3)			
Nov, 1990 - No. 3, Jan, 1991 ($4.50, limited series, 52 pgs.)			
Marvel Comics (Epic Comics)			
1-3		1.80	4.50

Aliens: Mondo Heat © 20th Century Fox

Aliens/Predator: Deadliest of the Species #2 © 20th Century Fox

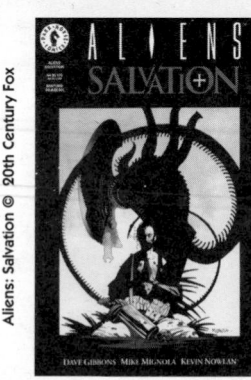

Aliens: Salvation © 20th Century Fox

AL

	GD25	FN65	NM94

ALIEN LEGION: TENNANTS OF HELL
1991 - No. 2, 1991 ($4.50, squarebound, 52 pgs.)
Marvel Comics (Epic Comics)

Book 1,2-Stroman-c/a(p)		1.80	4.50

ALIEN NATION (Movie)
Dec, 1988 ($2.50; 68 pgs.)
DC Comics

1-Adaptation of film; painted-c		1.00	2.50

ALIENS, THE (Captain Johner and...)(Also see Magnus Robot Fighter...)
Sept-Dec, 1967; No. 2, May, 1982
Gold Key

1-Reprints from Magnus #1,3,4,6-10; Russ Manning-a in all	1.50	4.50	15.00
2-Same contents as #1	1.60	4.00	

ALIENS (Movie) (See Alien: The Illustrated..., Dark Horse Comics & Dark Horse Presents #24)
May, 1988 - No. 6, July, 1989 ($1.95, B&W, limited series)
Dark Horse Comics

1-Based on movie sequel;1st app. Aliens in comics	3.60	11.00	25.00
1-2nd printing	1.00	2.00	5.00
1-3rd - 6th printings; 4th w/new inside front-c		.80	2.00
2	2.15	6.50	15.00
2-2nd printing		1.20	3.00
2-3rd printing w/new inside front-c		.80	2.00
3	1.50	3.75	9.00
4	1.00	2.60	6.00
5,6	1.00	2.00	5.00
3-6-2nd printings		.80	2.00
Mini Comic #1 (2/89, 4x6")-Was included with Aliens Portfolio	1.30	3.25	8.00
Collection 1 ($10.95,)-r/#1-6 plus Dark Horse Presents #24 plus new-a	1.65	4.20	10.00
Collection 1-2nd printing (1991, $11.95)-Printed on higher quality paper than 1st print; Dorman painted-c	1.70	5.00	12.00
Hardcover ('90, $24.95, B&W)-r/1-6, DHP #24	3.60	10.75	25.00
Platinum Edition (See Dark Horse Presents: Aliens Platinum Edition)			

ALIENS (Movie)
V2#1, Aug, 1989 - No. 4, 1990 ($2.25, limited series)
Dark Horse Comics

V2#1-Adapts sequel	1.30	3.25	8.00
1-2nd printing (1990, $2.25)		.90	2.25
2-4	1.00	2.00	5.00

ALIENS: BERSERKERS
Jan, 1995 - No. 4, Apr, 1995 ($2.50, limited series)
Dark Horse Comics

1-4		1.00	2.50

ALIENS: COLONIAL MARINES
Jan, 1993 - No. 10, July, 1994 ($2.50, limited series)
Dark Horse Comics

1-10		1.00	2.50

ALIENS: EARTH ANGEL
Aug, 1994 ($2.95, one-shot)
Dark Horse Comics

1-Byrne-a/story; wraparound-c		1.20	3.00

ALIENS: EARTH WAR
June, 1990 - No. 4, Oct, 1990 ($2.50, limited series)
Dark Horse Comics

1-All have Sam Kieth-a & Bolton painted-c	1.30	3.25	8.00
1-2nd printing		1.00	2.50

	GD25	FN65	NM94
2	1.20	3.00	7.00
3,4	1.00	2.00	5.00

ALIENS: GENOCIDE
Nov, 1991 - No. 4, Feb, 1992 ($2.50, limited series)
Dark Horse Comics

1-4-Arthur Suydam painted-c. 4-Wraparound-c, poster		1.00	2.50

ALIENS: HIVE
Feb, 1992 - No. 4, May, 1992 ($2.50, limited series)
Dark Horse Comics

1-4: Kelley Jones-c/a in all		1.00	2.50

ALIENS: LABYRINTH
Sept, 1993 - No. 4, Jan, 1994 ($2.50, limited series)
Dark Horse Comics

1-4: 1-Painted-c		1.00	2.50

ALIENS: MONDO HEAT
Feb, 1996 ($2.50, one-shot)
Dark Horse Comics

nn-Sequel to Mondo Pest		1.00	2.50

ALIENS: MONDO PEST
Apr, 1995 ($2.95, one-shot, 44 pgs.)
Dark Horse Comics

nn-Reprints Dark Horse Comics #22-24			3.00

ALIENS: MUSIC OF THE SPEARS
Jan, 1994 - No. 4, Apr, 1994 ($2.50, limited series)
Dark Horse Comics

1-4		1.00	2.50

ALIENS/PREDATOR: THE DEADLIEST OF SPECIES
July, 1993 - No. 12, Aug, 1995 ($2.50, limited series)
Dark Horse Comics

1-Bolton painted-c; Guice-a(p)		1.60	4.00
2-12: Bolton painted-c. 2,3-Guice-a(p)		1.00	2.50
1-Embossed foil platinum edition	2.85	8.50	20.00

ALIENS: ROGUE
Apr, 1993 - No. 4, July, 1993 ($2.50, limited series)
Dark Horse Comics

1-4: Painted-c		1.00	2.50

ALIENS: SACRIFICE
May, 1993 ($4.95, one-shot, 52 pgs.)
Dark Horse Comics

nn-Peter Milligan scripts; painted-c/a	1.00	2.00	5.00

ALIENS: SALVATION
Nov, 1993 ($4.95, one-shot, 52 pgs.)
Dark Horse Comics

nn-Mike Mignola-c/a(p); Dave Gibbons script	1.00	2.00	5.00

ALIENS: STRONGHOLD
May, 1994 - No. 4, Sept, 1994 ($2.50, limited series)
Dark Horse Comics

1-4		1.00	2.50

ALIENS VS. PREDATOR (See Dark Horse Presents #36)
June, 1990 - No. 4, Dec, 1990 ($2.50, limited series)
Dark Horse Comics

1-Painted-c	1.65	4.20	10.00
1-2nd printing		1.00	2.50
0-(7/90, $1.95, B&W)-r/Dark Horse Pres. #34-36	1.70	5.00	12.00
2,3	1.30	3.30	8.00
4-Dave Dorman painted-c	1.00	2.00	5.00

CLAREMONT · GUICE · BARRETO

DAVE GIBBONS   MIKE MIGNOLA   KEVIN NOWLAN

Aliens Vs. Predator: War #4 © 20th Century Fox

All-American Comics #41 © DC

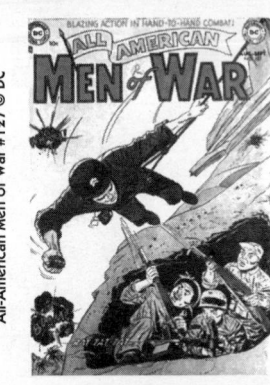

All-American Men of War #127 © DC

	GD25	FN65	NM94

ALIENS VS. PREDATOR: BOOTY
Jan, 1996 ($2.50, one-shot)
Dark Horse Comics

		GD25	NM94
nn-painted-c		1.00	2.50

ALIENS VS. PREDATOR: DUEL
Mar, 1995 - No. 2, Apr, 1995 ($2.50, limited series)
Dark Horse Comics

1,2	1.00	2.50

ALIENS VS. PREDATOR: WAR
No. 0, May, 1995 - No. 4, Aug, 1995 ($2.50, limited series)
Dark Horse Comics

0-4: Corben painted-c	1.00	2.50

ALIEN TERROR (See 3-D Alien Terror)

ALIEN: THE ILLUSTRATED STORY (Also see Aliens)
1980 ($3.95, soft-c, 8X11")
Heavy Metal Books

nn-Movie adaptation; Simonson-a	1.60	4.00

ALIEN³ (Movie)
June, 1992 - No. 3, July, 1992 ($2.50, limited series)
Dark Horse Comics

1-3: Adapts 3rd movie; Suydam painted-c	1.00	2.50

ALIEN WORLDS (Also see Eclipse Graphic Album #22)
Dec, 1982 - No. 9, Jan, 1985
Pacific Comics/Eclipse

1		1.50
2-9: 2,4-Dave Stevens-c/a		1.00
3-D No. 1-Art Adams 1st published art	1.20	3.00

ALISTER THE SLAYER
Oct, 1995 ($2.50)
Midnight Press

1-Boris-c	1.00	2.50

ALL-AMERICAN COMICS (...Western #103-126, ...Men of War #127 on; also
see The Big All-American Comic Book)
April, 1939 - No. 102, Oct, 1948
All-American/National Periodical Publications

1-Hop Harrigan (1st app.), Scribbly by Mayer (1st app.), Toonerville Folks, Ben Webster, Spot Savage, Mutt & Jeff, Red White & Blue (1st app.), Adv. in the Unknown, Tippie, Reg'lar Fellers, Skippy, Bobby Thatcher, Mystery Men of Mars, Daiseybelle, Wiley of West Point begin	830.00	2500.00	5000.00
2-Ripley's Believe It or Not begins, ends #24	230.00	700.00	1400.00
3-5: 5-The American Way begins, ends #10	165.00	500.00	1000.00
6,7: 6-Last Spot Savage; Popsicle Pete begins, ends #26, 28. 7-Last Bobby Thatcher	140.00	425.00	850.00
8-The Ultra Man begins & 1st-c app.	210.00	625.00	1250.00
9,10: 10-X-Mas-c	130.00	400.00	800.00
11-15: 11-Ultra Man-c. 12-Last Toonerville Folks. 15-Last Tippie & Reg'lar Fellars; Ultra Man-c	125.00	375.00	750.00

	GD25	FN65	VF82	NM94
16-(Rare)-Origin/1st app. Green Lantern by Sheldon Moldoff (c/a)(7/40) & begin series; appears in costume on-c & only one panel inside; created by Martin Nodell. Inspired in 1940 by a switchman's green lantern that would give trains the go ahead to proceed.	8,000.00	24,000.00	42,000.00	60,000.00

(Estimated up to 35+ total copies exist, 3 in NM/Mint)

	GD25	FN65		NM94
17-2nd Green Lantern	1222.00	3670.00		12,000.00
18-N.Y. World's Fair-c/story	800.00	2400.00		8000.00

	GD25	FN65	VF82	NM94
19-Origin/1st app. The Atom (10/40); last Ultra Man				

	1222.00	3670.00	7835.00	12,000.00

(Estimated up to 80 total copies exist, 5 in NM/Mint)

	GD25	FN65		NM94
20-Atom dons costume; Ma Hunkle becomes Red Tornado (1st app.)(1st DC costumed heroine, before Wonder Woman, 11/40); Rescue on Mars begins, ends #25; 1 pg. origin Green Lantern	365.00	1100.00		3300.00
21-23: 21-Last Wiley of West Point & Skippy. 23-Last Daiseybelle; 3 Idiots begin, end #82	235.00	712.00		1900.00
24-Sisty & Dinky become the Cyclone Kids; Ben Webster ends; origin Dr. Mid-Nite & Sargon, The Sorcerer in text with app.	300.00	900.00		2400.00

	GD25	FN65	VF82	NM94
25-Origin 1st story app. Dr. Mid-Nite by Stan Asch; Hop Harrigan becomes Guardian Angel; last Adventure in the Unknown	811.00	2433.00	4866.00	8000.00

(Estimated up to 120 total copies exist, 6 in NM/Mint)

	GD25	FN65		NM94
26-Origin/1st story app. Sargon, the Sorcerer	310.00	930.00		2800.00
27-#27-32 are misnumbered in indicia with correct No. appearing on-c. Intro. Doiby Dickles, Green Lantern's sidekick	330.00	990.00		3000.00
28-Hop Harrigan gives up costumed i.d.	138.00	415.00		1100.00
29,30	138.00	415.00		1100.00
31-40: 35-Doiby learns Green Lantern's i.d.	106.00	320.00		850.00
41-50: 50-Sargon ends	91.00	275.00		725.00
51-60: 59-Scribbly & the Red Tornado ends	78.00	235.00		625.00
61-Origin/1st app. Solomon Grundy (11/44)	378.00	1134.00		3400.00
62-70: 70-Kubert Sargon; intro Sargon's helper, Maximillian O'Leary	72.00	215.00		575.00
71-88: 71-Last Red White & Blue. 72-Black Pirate begins (not in #74-82); last Atom. 73-Winky, Blinky & Noddy begins, ends #82. 79,83-Mutt & Jeff-c.	62.00	185.00		500.00
89-Origin & 1st app. Harlequin	88.00	265.00		700.00
90-99: 90-Origin/1st app. Icicle. 99-Last Hop Harrigan	75.00	225.00		600.00
100-1st app. Johnny Thunder by Alex Toth (8/48); western theme begins (Scarce)	145.00	430.00		1150.00
101-Last Mutt & Jeff (Scarce)	106.00	320.00		850.00
102-Last Green Lantern, Black Pirate & Dr. Mid-Nite (Scarce)	175.00	525.00		1400.00

NOTE: No Atom in 47, 62-69. **Kinstler** Black Pirate-89. **Stan Aschmeier** a (Dr. Mid-Nite) 25-84; c-7. **Mayer** c-1, 2(part), 6, 10. **Moldoff** c-16-23. **Nodell** a-31. **Paul Reinman** a (Green Lantern)-53-55p, 56-84, 87; (Black Pirate)-83-88, 90; c-52, 55-76, 78, 80, 81, 87. **Toth** a-88, 92, 96, 98-102; c(p)-92, 96-102. Scribbly by Mayer in #1-59. Ultra Man by Mayer in #8-19.

ALL-AMERICAN MEN OF WAR (Previously All-American Western)
No. 127, Aug-Sept, 1952 - No. 117, Sept-Oct, 1966
National Periodical Publications

127 (#1, 1952)	85.00	255.00	675.00
128 (1952)	55.00	170.00	450.00
2(12-1/'52-53)-5	48.00	145.00	385.00
6-10	38.00	114.00	265.00
11-18: Last precode (2/55)	34.00	103.00	240.00
19-28	24.00	71.00	165.00
29,30,32-Wood-a	25.00	75.00	175.00
31,33-40: 38-1st S.A. issue	20.00	60.00	140.00
41-50	17.00	49.00	115.00
51-66	11.00	33.00	80.00
67-1st Gunner & Sarge by Andru & Esposito	29.00	86.00	220.00
68-70	11.50	34.00	85.00
71-80	7.00	21.50	55.00
81,83-88: 88-Last 10¢ issue	6.50	19.50	50.00
82-Johnny Cloud begins(1st app.), ends #111,114,115,117	11.00	33.00	85.00
89-100	4.30	13.00	32.00
101-117: 112-Balloon Buster series begins, ends #114,116. 117-Johnny Cloud-c & 3-part story	3.60	11.00	25.00

NOTE: **Colan** a-112. **Drucker** a-47, 65, 71, 74, 77. **Grandenetti** c(p)-127, 128, 2-17(most).

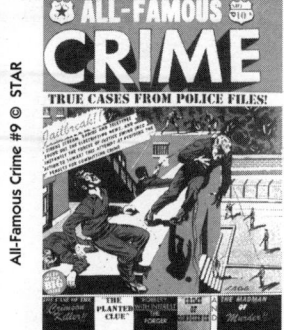

All-American Western #120 © DC

All-Famous Crime #9 © STAR

All-Flash #25 © DC

AL

	GD25	FN65	NM94

Heath *a-27, 32, 47, 71, 95, 111, 112; c-85, 91, 94-96, 100, 101, 112, others?* **Kirby** *a-29.* **Krigstein** *a-128('52), 2, 3, 5.* **Kubert** *a-29, 36, 38, 41, 43, 47, 49, 50, 52, 53, 55, 56, 60, 63, 65, 69, 71-73, 102, 103, 105, 106, 108, 114; c-41, 77, 102, 103, 105, 106, 108, 114, others?* Tank Killer in 69, 71, 76 by **Kubert**. **P. Reinman** *c-55, 57, 61, 62, 71, 72, 74-76, 80.*

ALL-AMERICAN SPORTS
Oct, 1967
Charlton Comics

1	1.65	4.20	10.00

ALL-AMERICAN WESTERN (Formerly All-American Comics; Becomes All-American Men of War)
No. 103, Nov, 1948 - No. 126, June-July, 1952 (103-121: 52 pgs.)
National Periodical Publications

103-Johnny Thunder & his horse Black Lightning continues by Toth, ends #126; Foley of The Fighting 5th, Minstrel Maverick, & Overland Coach begin; Captain Tootsie by Beck; mentioned in Love and Death

	GD25	FN65	NM94
	44.00	132.00	350.00
104-Kubert-a	34.00	103.00	240.00
105,107-Kubert-a	29.00	86.00	200.00
106,108-110,112: 112-Kurtzman's "Pot-Shot Pete" (1 pg.)			
	21.00	64.00	150.00
111,114-116-Kubert-a	24.00	71.00	165.00
113-Intro. Swift Deer, J. Thunder's new sidekick (4-5/50); classic Toth-c; Kubert-a	26.00	77.00	180.00
117-126: 121-Kubert-a; bondage-c	17.00	51.00	120.00

NOTE: **G. Kane** *c(p)-119, 120, 123.* **Kubert** *a-103-105, 107, 111, 112(1 pg.), 113-116, 121.* **Toth** *a 103-126; c(p)-103-116, 121, 122, 124-126.* Some copies of #125 have #12 on-c.

ALL COMICS
1945
Chicago Nite Life News

1	11.00	33.00	75.00

ALLEGRA
Aug, 1996 - Present ($2.50)
Image Comics (Wildstorm Productions)

1-4			2.50

ALLEY OOP (See The Comics, The Funnies, Red Ryder and Super Book #9)
No. 3, 1942
Dell Publishing Co.

Four Color 3 (#1)	48.00	145.00	475.00

ALLEY OOP
Nov, 1955 - No. 3, Mar, 1956 (Newspaper reprints)
Argo Publ.

1	16.00	47.00	110.00
2,3	11.00	33.00	75.00

ALLEY OOP
12-2/62-63 - No. 2, 9-11/63
Dell Publishing Co.

1,2	4.50	13.50	45.00

ALLEY OOP
No. 10, 1947 - No. 18, Oct, 1949
Standard Comics

10	21.00	64.00	150.00
11-18: 17,18-Schomburg-c	17.00	49.00	115.00

ALL-FAMOUS CRIME (Formerly Law Against Crime #1-3; becomes All-Famous Police Cases #6 on)
No. 4, 2/50 - No. 5, 5/50; No. 8, 5/51 - No. 10, 11/51
Star Publications

4 (#1-1st series)-Formerly Law-Crime	19.00	56.00	130.00
5 (#2)	11.50	34.00	80.00
8 (#3-2nd series)	13.00	39.00	90.00

9 (#4)-Used in **SOTI**, illo- "The wish to hurt or kill couples in lovers' lanes is a not uncommon perversion;" L.B. Cole-c/a(r)/Law-Crime #3

	23.00	69.00	160.00
10 (#5)-Becomes All-Famous Police Cases #6	11.00	33.00	75.00

NOTE: *All have* **L.B. Cole** *covers.*

ALL FAMOUS CRIME STORIES (See Fox Giants)

ALL-FAMOUS POLICE CASES (Formerly All Famous Crime #10 [#5])
No. 6, Feb, 1952 - No. 16, Sept, 1954
Star Publications

6	12.00	36.00	85.00
7,8: 7-Baker story; . 8-Marijuana story	11.00	33.00	75.00
9-16	10.00	30.00	65.00

NOTE: **L.B. Cole** *c-all; a-15, 1pg.* **Hollingsworth** *a-15.*

ALL-FLASH (...Quarterly No. 1-5)
Summer, 1941 - No. 32, Dec-Jan, 1947-48
National Periodical Publications/All-American

	GD25	FN65	VF82	NM94
1-Origin The Flash retold by E. E. Hibbard; Hibbard c-1-10,12-14,16,31p.				
	1150.00	3270.00	6533.00	11,500.00

(Estimated up to 200 total copies exist, 11 in NM/Mint)

	GD25	FN65	NM94
2-Origin recap	275.00	825.00	2200.00
3,4	145.00	430.00	1150.00
5-Winky, Blinky & Noddy begins (1st app.), ends #32			
	100.00	300.00	800.00
6-10	87.00	262.00	700.00
11-13: 12-Origin/1st The Thinker. 13-The King app.	75.00	225.00	600.00
14-Green Lantern cameo	87.00	262.00	700.00
15-20: 18-Mutt & Jeff begins, ends #22	68.00	205.00	550.00
21-31	56.00	170.00	450.00
32-Origin/1st app. The Fiddler; 1st Star Sapphire	81.00	245.00	650.00

NOTE: *Book length stories in 2-13, 16. Bondage c-31, 32.* **Martin Nodell** *c-15, 17-28.*

ALL FOR LOVE (Young Love V3#5-on)
Apr-May, 1957 - V3#4, Dec-Jan, 1959-60
Prize Publications

V1#1	8.35	25.00	50.00
2-6: 5-Orlando-c	4.70	14.00	28.00
V2#1-5(1/59), 5(3/59)	3.60	9.00	18.00
V3#1(5/59), 1(7/59)-4: 2-Powell-a	2.40	6.00	12.00

ALL FUNNY COMICS
Winter, 1943-44 - No. 23, May-June, 1948
Tilsam Publ./National Periodical Publications (Detective)

1-Genius Jones (1st app.), Buzzy (1st app., ends #4), Dover & Clover (see More Fun #93) begin; Bailey-a	45.00	140.00	365.00
2	21.00	64.00	150.00
3-10	13.50	41.00	95.00
11-13,15,18,19-Genius Jones app.	13.00	39.00	90.00
14,17,20-23	10.00	30.00	60.00
16-DC Super Heroes app.	30.00	90.00	210.00

ALL GOOD
Oct, 1949 (50¢, 260 pgs.)
St. John Publishing Co.

nn-(8 St. John comics bound together)	56.00	170.00	450.00

NOTE: *Also see L'il Audrey Yearbook & Treasury of Comics.*

ALL GOOD COMICS (See Fox Giants)
No.1, Spring, 1946 (36 pgs.)
Fox Features Syndicate

1-Joy Family, Dick Transom, Rick Evans, One Round Hogan			
	19.00	56.00	130.00

ALL GREAT (See Fox Giants)
1946 (36 pgs.)

All Humor Comics #15 © QUA

All-Out War #1 © DC

Alpha Flight #89 © MEG

	GD25	FN65	NM94

Fox Feature Syndicate

1-Crazy House, Bertie Benson Boy Detective, Gussie the Gob

	19.00	56.00	130.00

ALL GREAT
nd (1945?) (132 pgs.)
William H. Wise & Co.

nn-Capt. Jack Terry, Joan Mason, Girl Reporter, Baron Doomsday; Torture

scenes	34.00	103.00	240.00

ALL GREAT COMICS (Formerly Phantom Lady #13? Dagar, Desert Hawk No. 14 on)
No. 14, Oct, 1947 - No. 13, Dec, 1947 (Newspaper strip reprints)
Fox Features Syndicate

14(#12)-Brenda Starr & Texas Slim-r (Scarce)	42.00	125.00	340.00
13-Origin Dagar, Desert Hawk; Brenda Starr (all-r); Kamen-c; Dagar covers			
begin	40.00	120.00	300.00

ALL-GREAT CONFESSIONS (See Fox Giants)

ALL GREAT CRIME STORIES (See Fox Giants)

ALL GREAT JUNGLE ADVENTURES (See Fox Giants)

ALL HALLOW'S EVE
1991 ($4.95, 52 pgs.)
Innovation Publishing

1-Painted-c/a	1.00	2.00	5.00

ALL HERO COMICS
Mar, 1943 (100 pgs., cardboard-c)
Fawcett Publications

1-Capt. Marvel Jr., Capt. Midnight, Golden Arrow, Ibis the Invincible, Spy			
Smasher, Lance O'Casey; 1st Banshee O'Brien; Raboy-c	138.00	412.00	1100.00

ALL HUMOR COMICS
Spring, 1946 - No. 17, December, 1949
Quality Comics Group

1	17.00	49.00	115.00
2-Atomic Tot story; Gustavson-a	9.15	27.50	55.00
3-9: 3-Intro Kelly Poole who is cover feature #3 on. 5-1st app. Hickory?			
8-Gustavson-a	4.70	14.00	28.00
10-17	4.00	10.00	20.00

ALLIANCE, THE
Aug, 1995 - No. 3, Nov, 1995 ($2.50)
Image Comics (Shadowline Ink)

1-3: 2-(9/95)		1.00	2.50

ALL LOVE (…Romances No. 26)(Formerly Ernie Comics)
No. 26, May, 1949 - No. 32, May, 1950
Ace Periodicals (Current Books)

26 (No. 1)-Ernie, Lily Belle app.	7.50	22.50	45.00
27-L. B. Cole-a	10.00	30.00	65.00
28-32	4.00	12.00	24.00

ALL-NEGRO COMICS
June, 1947 (15¢)
All-Negro Comics

1 (Rare)	300.00	900.00	2400.00

NOTE: Seldom found in fine or mint condition; many copies have brown pages.

ALL-NEW COLLECTORS' EDITION (Formerly Limited …)
Jan, 1978 - Vol. 8, No. C-62, 1979 (No. 54-58: 76 pgs.)
DC Comics, Inc.

C-53-Rudolph the Red-Nosed Reindeer		1.20	3.00
C-54-Superman Vs. Wonder Woman	1.00	2.60	6.00
C-55-Superboy & the Legion of Super-Heroes; marriage of Lightning Lad &			
Saturn Girl	1.00	2.60	6.00
C-56-Superman Vs. Muhammad Ali; story & wraparound N. Adams-c			

	1.20	3.00	7.00
C-58-Superman Vs. Shazam	1.00	2.00	5.00
C-60-Rudolph's Summer Fun(8/78)		1.20	3.00
C-61-See Famous First Edition			
C-62-Superman the Movie (68 pgs.; 1979)-Photo-c from movie plus photos			
inside (also see DC Special Series #25)		1.20	3.00

NOTE: Buckler a-C-58; c-C-58

ALL-NEW COMICS (…Short Story Comics No. 1-3)
Jan, 1943 - No. 14, Nov, 1946; No. 15, Mar-Apr, 1947 (10 x 13-1/2")
Family Comics (Harvey Publications)

1-Steve Case, Crime Rover, Johnny Rebel, Kayo Kane, The Echo, Night			
Hawk, Ray O'Light, Detective Shane begin (all 1st app.?); Red Blazer on			
cover only; Sultan-a	212.00	635.00	1700.00
2-Origin Scarlet Phantom by Kubert	85.00	250.00	675.00
3	62.00	190.00	500.00
4,5	52.00	155.00	415.00
6-The Boy Heroes & Red Blazer (text story) begin, end #12; Black Cat app.;			
intro. Sparky in Red Blazer	55.00	165.00	440.00
7-Kubert, Powell-a; Black Cat & Zebra app.	55.00	165.00	440.00
8,9: 8-Shock Gibson app.; Kubert, Powell-a; Schomburg bondage-c. 9-Black			
Cat app.; Kubert-a	55.00	165.00	440.00
10-12: 10-The Zebra app. (from Green Hornet Comics); Kubert-a(3). 11-Girl			
Commandos, Man In Black app. 12-Kubert-a	50.00	150.00	400.00
13-Stuntman by Simon & Kirby; Green Hornet, Joe Palooka, Flying Fool app.;			
Green Hornet-c	53.00	160.00	425.00
14-The Green Hornet & The Man in Black Called Fate by Powell, Joe			
Palooka app.; J. Palooka-c by Ham Fisher	50.00	150.00	400.00
15-(Rare)-Small size (5-1/2x8-1/2"; B&W; 32 pgs.). Distributed to mail sub-			
scribers only. Black Cat and Joe Palooka app. Estimated value….$250-350			

NOTE: Also see Boy Explorers No. 2, Flash Gordon No. 5, and Stuntman No. 3. Powell a-11. Schomburg c-5, 7-11. Captain Red Blazer & Spark on c-5-11 (w/Boy Heroes #12).

ALL NEW COMICS
Oct, 1993 (Giveaway, no cover price, 16 pgs.) (Hanna-Barbera)
Harvey Comics

1-Flintstones, Scooby Doo, Jetsons, Yogi Bear & Wacky Races previews for			
upcoming Harvey's new Hanna-Barbera line-up			1.00

NOTE: Material previewed in Harvey giveaway was eventually published by Archie.

ALL-OUT WAR
Sept-Oct, 1979 - No. 6, Aug, 1980 ($1.00, 68 pgs.)
DC Comics

1-6: 1-The Viking Commando (origin), Force Three (origin), & Black Eagle			
Squadron begin			1.00

NOTE: Ayers a(p)-1-6. Elias r-2. Evans a-1-6. Kubert c-16.

ALL PICTURE ADVENTURE MAGAZINE
Oct, 1952 - No. 2, Nov, 1952 (100 pg. Giants, 25¢, squarebound)
St. John Publishing Co.

1-War comics	23.00	69.00	160.00
2-Horror-crime comics	36.00	107.00	250.00

NOTE: Above books contain three St. John comics rebound; variations possible. Baker art known in both.

ALL PICTURE ALL TRUE LOVE STORY
October, 1952 (100 pgs., 25¢)
St. John Publishing Co.

1-Canteen Kate by Matt Baker	40.00	120.00	325.00

ALL-PICTURE COMEDY CARNIVAL
October, 1952 (100 pgs., 25¢)(Contains 4 rebound comics)
St. John Publishing Co.

1-Contents can vary; Baker-a	40.00	120.00	300.00

ALL REAL CONFESSION MAGAZINE (See Fox Giants)

ALL ROMANCES (Mr. Risk No. 7 on)
Aug, 1949 - No. 6, June, 1950

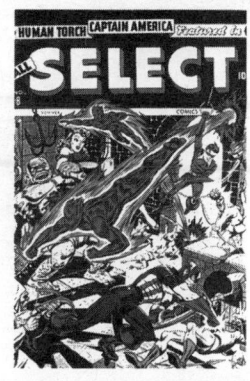

All-Select Comics #8 © MEG

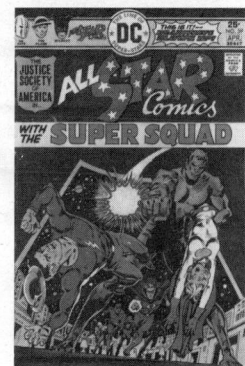

All Star Comics #59 © DC

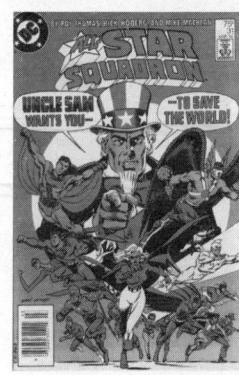

All-Star Squadron #31 © DC

	GD25	FN65	NM94

A. A. Wyn (Ace Periodicals)

		GD25	FN65	NM94
1		7.50	22.50	45.00
2		4.00	10.00	20.00
3-6		3.60	9.00	18.00

ALL-SELECT COMICS (Blonde Phantom No. 12 on)
Fall, 1943 - No. 11, Fall, 1946
Timely Comics (Daring Comics)

	GD25	FN65	NM94
1-Capt. America (by Rico #1), Human Torch, Sub-Mariner begin; Black Widow story (4 pgs.); Classic Schomburg-c	700.00	2100.00	7000.00
2-Red Skull app.	275.00	825.00	2200.00
3-The Whizzer begins	180.00	540.00	1450.00
4,5-Last Sub-Mariner	125.00	375.00	1000.00
6-9: 6-The Destroyer app. 8-No Whizzer	103.00	309.00	825.00
10-The Destroyer & Sub-Mariner app.; last Capt. America & Human Torch issue	103.00	309.00	825.00
11-1st app. Blonde Phantom; Miss America app.; all Blonde Phantom-c by Shores	190.00	560.00	1500.00

NOTE: **Schomburg** c-1-10. **Sekowsky** a-7. #7 & 8 show 1944 in indicia, but should be 1945.

ALL SPORTS COMICS (Formerly Real Sports Comics; becomes All Time Sports Comics No. 4 on)
No. 2, Dec-Jan, 1948-49; No. 3, Feb-Mar, 1949
Hillman Periodicals

	GD25	FN65	NM94
2-Krigstein-a(p), Powell, Starr-a	29.00	86.00	200.00
3-Mort Lawrence-a	20.00	60.00	140.00

ALL STAR COMICS (All Star Western No. 58 on)
Sum, '40 - No. 57, Feb-Mar, '51; No. 58, Jan-Feb, '76 -No. 74, Sept-Oct, '78
National Periodical Publ./All-American/DC Comics

	GD25	FN65	VF82	NM94
1-The Flash (#1 by E.E. Hibbard), Hawkman(by Shelly), Hourman(by Bernard Baily), The Sandman(by Creig Flessel), The Spectre(by Baily), Biff Bronson, Red White & Blue(ends #2) begin; Ultra Man's only app. (#1-3 are quarterly; #4 begins bi-monthly issues)	1200.00	3600.00	7200.00	12,000.00
(Estimated up to 200+ total copies exist, 6 in NM/Mint)				

	GD25	FN65		NM94
2-Green Lantern figure by Martin Nodell; Johnny Thunder begin; Green Lantern figure swipe from the cover of All-American Comics #16; Flash figure swipe from the cover of Flash Comics #8; Moldoff/Bailey/Flessel (cut & paste-c.)	467.00	1400.00		4500.00

	GD25	FN65	VF82	NM94
3-Origin & 1st app. The Justice Society of America (Win/40); Dr. Fate & The Atom begin, Red Tornado cameo 3000.00 9000.00 19,500.00 30,000.00				
(Estimated up to 150+ total copies exist, 6 in NM/Mint)				

3-Reprint, Oversize 13-1/2x10". **WARNING:** This comic is an exact reprint of the original except for its size. DC published it in 1974 with a second cover titling it as a Famous First Edition. There have been many reported cases of the outer cover being removed and the interior sold as the original edition. The reprint with the new outer cover removed is practically worthless. See Famous First Edition for value.

	GD25	FN65		NM94
4-1st adventure for J.S.A.	439.00	1317.00		4200.00
5-1st app. Shiera Sanders as Hawkgirl (1st costumed super-heroine, 6-7/41)	422.00	1267.00		3800.00
6-Johnny Thunder joins JSA	288.00	863.00		2300.00
7-Batman, Superman, Flash cameo; last Hourman; Doiby Dickles app.	338.00	1012.00		2700.00

	GD25	FN65	VF82	NM94
8-Origin & 1st app. Wonder Woman (12-1/41-42)(added as 9pgs. making book 76 pgs.; origin cont'd in Sensation #1; see W.W. #1 for more detailed origin); Dr. Fate dons new helmet; Hop Harrigan text stories & Starman begin; Shiera app.; Hop Harrigan JSA guest; Starman & Dr. Midnite become members 2400.00 6600.00 15,300.00 24,000.00				
(Estimated up to 150 total copies exist, 6 in NM/Mint)				

	GD25	FN65		NM94
9,10: 9-JSA's girlfriends cameo; Shiera app.; J. Edgar Hoover of FBI made associate member of JSA. 10-Flash, Green Lantern cameo; Sandman new				

	GD25	FN65	NM94
costume	269.00	806.00	2150.00
11-Wonder Woman begins; Spectre cameo; Shiera app. Classic Moldoff Hawkman-c	275.00	825.00	2200.00
12-Wonder Woman becomes JSA Secretary	250.00	750.00	2000.00
13-15: Sandman w/Sandy in #14 & 15. 15-Origin & 1st app. Brain Wave; Dr. Fate app.	238.00	712.00	1900.00
16-20: 19-Sandman w/Sandy. 20-Dr. Fate & Sandman cameo	175.00	525.00	1400.00
21-23: 21-Spectre & Atom cameo; Dr. Fate by Kubert; Dr. Fate, Sandman end.			
22-Last Hop Harrigan; Flag-c. 23-Origin/1st app. Psycho Pirate; last Spectre & Starman	156.00	470.00	1250.00
24-Flash & Green Lantern cameo; Mr. Terrific only app.; Wildcat, JSA guest; Kubert Hawkman begins	156.00	470.00	1250.00
25-27: 25-Flash & Green Lantern start again. 26-Robot-c. 27-Wildcat, JSA guest (#24-26: only All-American imprint)	131.00	394.00	1050.00
28-32	119.00	356.00	950.00
33-Solomon Grundy & Doiby Dickles app.; classic Solomon Grundy cover. Last Solomon Grundy G.A. app.	262.00	788.00	2100.00
34,35-Johnny Thunder cameo in both	110.00	330.00	875.00
36-Batman & Superman JSA guests	262.00	788.00	2100.00
37-Johnny Thunder cameo; origin & 1st app. Injustice Society; last Kubert Hawkman	144.00	431.00	1150.00
38-Black Canary begins; JSA Death issue	169.00	506.00	1350.00
39,40: 39-Last Johnny Thunder	105.00	320.00	850.00
41-Black Canary joins JSA; Injustice Society app. (2nd app.?)	105.00	320.00	850.00
42-Atom & the Hawkman don new costumes	105.00	320.00	850.00
43-49,51-56: 43-New logo. 55-Sci/Fi story	105.00	320.00	850.00
50-Frazetta art, 3 pgs.	120.00	355.00	950.00
57-Kubert-a, 6 pgs. (Scarce); last app. G.A. Green Lantern, Flash & Dr. Mid-Nite	125.00	375.00	1000.00
V12#58-74(1976-78)-Flash, Hawkman, Dr. Mid-Nite, Wildcat, Dr. Fate, Green Lantern, Star Spangled Kid, & Robin app.; intro Power Girl. 58-JSA app.			
69-1st modern app. Huntress (see Sensation)			1.50

NOTE: *No Atom-27, 36; no Dr. Fate-13; no Flash-8, 9, 11-23; no Green Lantern-8, 9,11-23; Hawkman in 1-57 (only one to app. in all 57 issues); no Johnny Thunder-5, 36; no Wonder Woman-9, 10, 33. Book length stories in 4-9, 11-14, 18-22, 25, 26, 29, 30, 32-36, 42, 43. Johnny Peril in #42-46, 48, 49, 51, 52,54-57. **Baily** a-1-10, 12, 13, 14, 15-20. **Burnley** Starman-8-13; c-12, 13. **Grell** c-58. **E.E. Hibbard** c-3, 4, 6-10. **Infantino** c-40. **Kubert** Hawkman-24-30, 33-37. **Lampert/Baily/Flessel** c-1, 2. **Moldoff** Hawkman-3-23; c-11. **Mart Nodell** c-25i, 26i, 27-32. **Purcell** c-5. **Simon & Kirby** Sandman 14-17, 19. **Staton** a-66-74p; c-74p. **Toth** a-37(2), 38(2), 40, 41; c-38, 41. **Wood** a-58i-63i, 64, 65; c-63i, 64, 65. Issues 1-7, 9-16 are 68 pgs.; #8 is 76 pgs.; #17-19 are 60 pgs.; #20-57 are 52 pgs.*

ALL STAR INDEX, THE
Feb, 1987 ($2.00, Baxter paper)
Independent Comics Group (Eclipse)

1		.80	2.00

ALL-STAR SQUADRON (See Justice League of America #193)
Sept, 1981 - No. 67, Mar, 1987
DC Comics

1-Original Atom, Hawkman, Dr. Mid-Nite, Robotman (origin), Plastic Man, Johnny Quick, Liberty Belle, Shining Knight begin			1.00
2-24: 4, 5-Spectre app. 5-Danette Reilly becomes new Firebrand. 8-Re-intro Steel, the Indestructible Man. 12-Origin G.A. Hawkman retold. 23-Origin/1st app. The Amazing Man. 24-Batman app.			1.00
25-1st app. Infinity, Inc. (9/83)			1.00
26-Origin Infinity, Inc. (2nd app.); Robin app.			1.00
27-46,48,49: 27-Dr. Fate vs. The Spectre. 30-35-Spectre app. 33-Origin Freedom Fighters of Earth-X. 36,37-Superman vs. Capt. Marvel; Ordway-c. 41-Origin Starman			1.00
47-Origin Dr. Fate; McFarlane-a (1st full story)/part-c (7/85)		1.60	4.00
50-Double size; Crisis x-over			1.00
51-67: 51-56-Crisis x-over. 61-Origin Liberty Belle. 62-Origin The Shining Knight. 63-Origin Robotman. 65-Origin Johnny Quick. 66-Origin Tarantula			1.00

All-Star Western #3 © DC

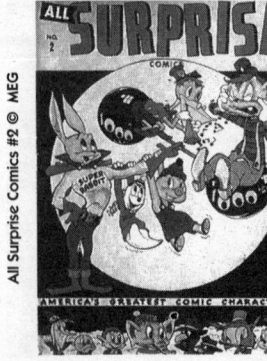

All Surprise Comics #2 © MEG

All Top Comics #4 © FOX

	GD25	FN65	NM94

Annual 1-3: 1(11/82)-Retells origin of G.A. Atom, Guardian & Wildcat; Jerry
  Ordway's 1st pencils for DC.(1st work was inking Carmine Infantino in House
  of Mystery #94) 2(11/83)-Infinity, Inc. app. 3(9/84)

			1.00

NOTE: **Buckler** a-1-5; c-1, 3-5, 51. **Kubert** c-2, 7-18. JLA app. in 14, 15. JSA app. in 4, 14, 15, 19, 27, 28.

ALL-STAR STORY OF THE DODGERS, THE
Apr, 1979 ($1.00)
Stadium Communications

1			1.00

ALL STAR WESTERN (Formerly All Star Comics No. 1-57)
No. 58, Apr-May, 1951 - No. 119, June-July, 1961
National Periodical Publications

	GD25	FN65	NM94
58-Trigger Twins (ends #116), Strong Bow, The Roving Ranger & Don Caballero begin	40.00	125.00	315.00
59,60: Last 52 pgs.	21.00	64.00	150.00
61-66: 61-64-Toth-a	17.00	51.00	120.00
67-Johnny Thunder begins; Gil Kane-a	21.00	64.00	150.00
68-81: Last precode (2-3/55)	10.00	30.00	65.00
82-98: 97-1st S.A. issue	9.15	27.50	60.00
99-Frazetta-r/Jimmy Wakely #4	10.00	30.00	65.00
100	10.00	30.00	65.00
101-107,109-116,118,119	6.35	19.00	42.00
108-Origin J. Thunder; J. Thunder logo begins	16.00	47.00	120.00
117-Origin Super Chief	10.00	30.00	70.00

NOTE: **Gil Kane** c(p)-58, 59, 61, 63, 64, 68, 69, 70-95(most), 97-99(most). **Infantino** art in most issues. Madame .44 app.-#117-119.

ALL-STAR WESTERN (Weird Western Tales No. 12 on)
Aug-Sept, 1970 - No. 11, Apr-May, 1972
National Periodical Publications

1-Pow-Wow Smith-r; Infantino-a	2.00	6.00	14.00
2-8: 2-Outlaw begins; El Diablo by Morrow begins; has cameos by Williamson, Torres, Gil Kane, Giordano & Phil Seuling. 3-Origin El Diablo. 5-Last Outlaw issue. 6-Billy the Kid begins, ends #8	1.00	2.60	6.00
9-Frazetta-a, 3pgs.(r)	1.20	3.00	7.00
10-Jonah Hex begins (1st app., 2-3/72)	15.00	45.00	120.00
11-2nd app. Jonah Hex	8.00	24.50	65.00

NOTE: **Neal Adams** c-1-5; **Aparo** a-3, 4, 6, 8. **Kubert** a-4r, 7-9r. **Morrow** a-2-4, 10, 11. No. 7-11 have 52 pgs..

ALL SURPRISE (Becomes Jeanie #13 on) (Funny animal)
Fall, 1943 - No. 12, Winter, 1946-47
Timely/Marvel (CPC)

1-Super Rabbit, Gandy & Sourpuss begin	24.00	73.00	170.00
2	11.00	33.00	75.00
3-10,12	9.15	27.50	55.00
11-Kurtzman "Pigtales" art	10.00	30.00	70.00

ALL TEEN (Formerly All Winners; All Winners & Teen Comics No. 21 on)
No. 20, January, 1947
Marvel Comics (WFP)

20-Georgie, Mitzi, Patsy Walker, Willie app.; Syd Shores-c	8.35	25.00	50.00

ALL-TIME SPORTS COMICS (Formerly All Sports Comics)
V2No. 4, Apr-May, 1949 - V2No. 7, Oct-Nov, 1949 (All 52 pgs.)
Hillman Periodicals

V2#4	20.00	60.00	140.00
5-7: 5-(V1#5 inside)-Powell-a; Ty Cobb sty. 7-Krigstein-p; Walter Johnson & Knute Rockne sty	14.00	43.00	100.00

ALL TOP
1944 (132 pgs.)
William H. Wise Co.

Capt. V, Merciless the Sorceress, Red Robbins, One Round Hogan, Mike the
  M.P., Snooky, Pussy Katnip app.

	27.00	81.00	190.00

	GD25	FN65	NM94

ALL TOP COMICS (My Experience No. 19 on)
1945; No. 2, Sum, 1946 - No. 18, Mar, 1949; 1957 - 1959
Fox Features Synd./Green Publ./Norlen Mag.

1-Cosmo Cat & Flash Rabbit begin (1st app.)	19.00	58.00	135.00
2 (#1-7 are funny animal)	10.00	30.00	60.00
3-7	7.50	22.50	45.00
8-Blue Beetle, Phantom Lady, & Rulah, Jungle Goddess begin (11/47); Kamen-c	175.00	525.00	1400.00
9-Kamen-c	93.00	280.00	750.00
10-Kamen bondage-c	100.00	300.00	800.00
11-13,15-17: 15-No Blue Beetle	80.00	240.00	650.00
14-No Blue Beetle; used in **SOTI**, illo- "Corpses of colored people strung up by their wrists"	93.00	280.00	750.00
18-Dagar, Jo-Jo app; no Phantom Lady or Blue Beetle	55.00	160.00	435.00
6(1957-Green Publ.)-Patoruzu the Indian; Cosmo Cat on cover only	3.60	9.00	18.00
6(1958-Literary Ent.)-Muggy Doo; Cosmo Cat on cover only	3.60	9.00	18.00
6(1959-Norlen)-Atomic Mouse; Cosmo Cat on cover only	3.60	9.00	18.00
6(1959)-Little Eva	3.60	9.00	18.00
6(Cornell)-Supermouse on-c	3.60	9.00	18.00

NOTE: Jo-Jo by **Kamen**-12,18.

ALL TRUE ALL PICTURE POLICE CASES
Oct, 1952 - No. 2, Nov, 1952 (100 pgs.)
St. John Publishing Co.

1-Three rebound St. John crime comics	40.00	120.00	285.00
2-Three comics rebound	29.00	86.00	200.00

NOTE: Contents may vary.

ALL-TRUE CRIME (...Cases No. 26-35; formerly Official True Crime Cases)
No. 26, Feb, 1948 - No. 52, Sept, 1952
Marvel/Atlas Comics(OFI #26,27/CFI #28,29/LCC #30-46/LMC #47-52)

26(#1)-Syd Shores-c	24.00	71.00	165.00
27(4/48)-Electric chair-c	17.00	49.00	115.00
28-41,43-48,50-52: 35-37-Photo-c	7.50	22.50	45.00
42,49-Krigstein-a. 49-Used in **POP**, Pg 79	9.15	27.50	55.00

NOTE: **Robinson** a-47, 50. **Shores** c-26. **Tuska** a-48a(3).

ALL-TRUE DETECTIVE CASES (Kit Carson No. 5 on)
Feb-Mar, 1954 - No. 4, Aug-Sept, 1954
Avon Periodicals

1	20.00	60.00	140.00
2-Wood-a	17.00	51.00	120.00
3-Kinstler-c	9.15	27.50	55.00
4-r/Gangsters And Gun Molls #2; Kamen-a	14.00	43.00	100.00
nn(100 pgs.)-7 pg. Kubert-a, Kinstler back-c	33.00	99.00	230.00

ALL TRUE ROMANCE (...Illustrated No. 3)
3/51 - No. 20, 12/54; No. 22, 3/55 - No. 30?, 7/57; No. 3(#31), 9/57;
No. 4(#32), 11/57; No. 33, 2/58 - No. 34, 3/58
Artful Publ. #1-3/Harwell(Comic Media) #4-20?/Ajax-Farrell(Excellent Publ.)
No. 22 on/Four Star Comic Corp.

1 (3/51)	12.00	36.00	85.00
2 (10/51; 11/51 on-c)	6.35	19.00	38.00
3(12/51) - #5(5/52)	5.00	15.00	30.00
6-Wood-a, 9 pgs. (exceptional)	14.00	43.00	100.00
7-10	4.15	12.50	25.00
11-13,16-19 (2/54)	3.60	9.00	18.00
14-Marijuana story	4.00	11.00	22.00
20,22: Last precode issue (Ajax, 3/55)	3.00	7.50	15.00
23-27,29,30	2.40	6.00	12.00
28 (9/56)-L.B. Cole, Disbrow-a	6.70	20.00	40.00
3,4,33,34 (Farrell, '57- '58)	1.80	4.50	9.00

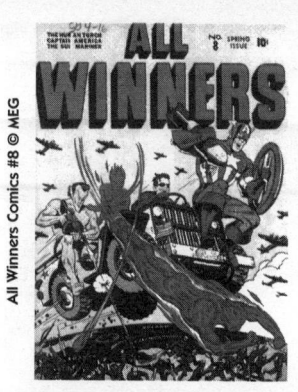

All Winners Comics #8 © MEG

Alpha Centurion #1 © DC

Alter Ego #2 © FC

	GD25	FN65	NM94

ALL WESTERN WINNERS (Formerly All Winners; becomes Western Winners with No. 5; see Two-Gun Kid No. 5)
No. 2, Winter, 1948-49 - No. 4, April, 1949
Marvel Comics(CDS)

	GD25	FN65	NM94
2-Black Rider (origin & 1st app.) & his horse Satan, Kid Colt & his horse Steel, & Two-Gun Kid & his horse Cyclone begin; Shores c-2-4			
	61.00	180.00	490.00
3-Anti-Wertham editorial	36.00	107.00	250.00
4-Black Rider i.d. revealed; Heath, Shores-a	36.00	107.00	250.00

ALL WINNERS COMICS (All Teen #20)
Summer, 1941 - No. 19, Fall, 1946; No. 21, Winter, 1946-47
(No #20) (No. 21 continued from Young Allies No. 20)
USA No. 1-7/WFP No. 10-19/YAI No. 21

	GD25	FN65	VF82	NM94
1-The Angel & Black Marvel only app.; Capt. America by Simon & Kirby, Human Torch & Sub-Mariner begin (#1 was advertised as All Aces); 1st app. All-Winners Squad in text story by Stan Lee				
	1400.00	4200.00	8400.00	14,000.00

	GD25	FN65		NM94
2-The Destroyer & The Whizzer begin; Simon & Kirby Captain America				
	390.00	1170.00		3500.00
3	250.00	750.00		2000.00
4-Classic War-c by Al Avison	275.00	825.00		2200.00
5	155.00	470.00		1250.00
6-The Black Avenger only app.; no Whizzer story; Hitler, Hirohito & Mussolini-c	175.00	525.00		1400.00
7-10	135.00	412.00		1100.00
11,13-18: 11-1st Atlas globe on-c (Winter, 1943-44; also see Human Torch #14). 14-16-No Human Torch	112.00	336.00		900.00
12-Red Skull story; last Destroyer; no Whizzer story				
	125.00	375.00		1000.00
19-(Scarce)-1st story app. & origin All Winners Squad (Capt. America & Bucky, Human Torch & Toro, Sub-Mariner, Whizzer, & Miss America); r-in Fantasy Masterpieces #10	310.00	930.00		2800.00
21-(Scarce)-All Winners Squad; bondage-c	300.00	900.00		2400.00

NOTE: *Everett* Sub-Mariner-1, 3, 4; *Burgos* Torch-1, 3, 4. *Schomburg* c-1, 7-18. *Shores* c-19p, 21.

(2nd Series - August, 1948, Marvel Comics (CDS))
(Becomes All Western Winners with No. 2)

	GD25	FN65		NM94
1-The Blonde Phantom, Capt. America, Human Torch, & Sub-Mariner app.				
	200.00	600.00		1600.00

ALL YOUR COMICS (See Fox Giants)
Spring, 1946 (36 pgs.)
Fox Feature Syndicate (R. W. Voight)

1-Red Robbins, Merciless the Sorceress app.	14.00	43.00		100.00

ALMANAC OF CRIME (See Fox Giants)
AL OF FBI (See Little Al of the FBI)

ALPHA AND OMEGA
1978 (49¢)
Spire Christian Comics (Fleming H. Revell)

nn				1.00

ALPHA CENTURION (See Superman, 2nd Series & Zero Hour)
1996 ($2.95, one-shot)
DC Comics

1				3.00

ALPHA FLIGHT (See X-Men #120,121 & X-Men/Alpha Flight)
Aug, 1983 - No. 130, Mar, 1994 (#52-on are direct sales only)
Marvel Comics Group

1-Byrne-a begins (52pgs.)-Wolverine & Nightcrawler cameo				
			.80	2.00
2-12: 2-Vindicator becomes Guardian; origin Marrina & Alpha Flight. 3-Con-				

cludes origin Alpha Flight. 6-Origin Shaman. 7-Origin Snowbird. 10,11-Origin Sasquatch. 12-(52 pgs.)-Death of Guardian

			1.50
13-Wolverine app.		1.00	2.50
14-16,18-28: 16-Wolverine cameo. 20-New headquarters. 25-Return of Guardian. 28-Last Byrne issue			1.25
17-X-Men x-over (70% reprinted from X-Men #109); Wolverine cameo			
		.80	2.00
29-32,35-49: 39-47,49-Portacio-a(i)			1.00
33,34: 33-X-Men (Wolverine) app. 34-Origin Wolverine		1.00	2.50
50-Double size; Portacio-a(i)			1.25
51-Jim Lee's 1st work at Marvel (10/87); Wolverine cameo; 1st Jim Lee Wolverine; Portacio-a(i)	1.00	2.00	5.00
52,53-Wolverine app.; Lee-a on Wolverine; Portacio-a(i); 53-Lee/Portacio-a			
		1.00	2.50
54,63,64-No Jim Lee-a; 54-Portacio-a(i)			1.00
55-62-Jim Lee-a(p)		1.00	2.50
65-74,76-86: 65-Begin $1.50-c. 71-Intro The Sorcerer (villain). 74-Wolverine, Spider-Man & The Avengers app. 89-Original Guardian returns			
			1.25
75-Double size ($1.95, 52 pgs.)		.80	2.00
87-90-Wolverine 4 part story w/Jim Lee covers	1.20	3.00
91-99,101-104: 91-Dr. Doom app. 94-F.F. x-over. 99-Galactus, Avengers app. 102-Intro Weapon Omega. 104-Last $1.50-c		1.50
100-($2.00, 52 pgs.)-Avengers & Galactus app.	.80	2.00
105,107-119,121-129: 107-X-Factor x-over. 110-112-Infinity War x-overs. 110, 111-Wolverine app. (brief). 111-Thanos cameo		1.50
106-Northstar revelation issue	.80	2.00
106-2nd printing (direct sale only)		1.25
120-($2.25)-Polybagged w/Paranormal Registration Act poster		
	.90	2.25
130-($2.25, 52 pgs.)	.90	2.25
Annual 1 (9/86, $1.25)		1.25
Annual 2(12/87, $1.25)		1.25
Special V2#1(6/92, $2.50, 52 pgs.)-Wolverine-c/story	1.00	2.50

NOTE: *Austin* c-1i, 2i, 53i. *Byrne* c-81, 82. *Guice* c-85, 91-99. *Jim Lee* a(p)-51, 53, 55-62, 64; c-53, 87-90. *Mignola* a-29-32p. *Whilce Portacio* a(i)-39-47, 49-54.

ALPHA FLIGHT SPECIAL
July, 1991 - No. 4, Oct, 1991 ($1.50, limited series)
Marvel Comics

1-3: Reprints Flight #97-99 w/covers			1.50
4 ($2.00, 52 pgs.)-Reprints Alpha Flight #100		.80	2.00

ALPHA KORPS
Sept, 1996 - Present ($2.50, limited series)
Diversity Comics

1-Origin/1st app. Alpha Korps			2.50

ALPHA WAVE
Mar, 1987 ($1.75, 36pgs.)
Darkline Comics

1			1.50

ALTER EGO
May, 1986 - No. 4, Nov, 1986 (Mini-series)
First Comics

1		.70	1.80
2-4			1.40

ALVIN (TV) (See Four Color Comics No. 1042)
Oct-Dec, 1962 - No. 28, Oct, 1973
Dell Publishing Co.

12-021-212 (#1)	11.00	33.00	110.00
2	6.30	21.00	63.00
3-10	4.50	15.00	45.00
11-28	3.80	12.00	36.00

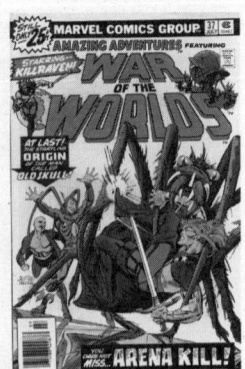

Amazing Adventures #37 © MEG

Amazing High Adventure #3 © MEG

Amazing Fantasy #17 © MEG

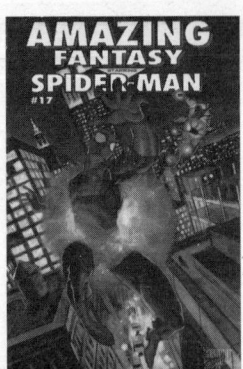

	GD25	FN65	NM94
Alvin For President (10/64)	2.40	9.00	24.00

...& His Pals in Merry Christmas with Clyde Crashcup & Leonardo 1
(02-120-402)-(12-2/64), reprinted in 1966 (12-023-604)

	5.40	18.00	54.00

ALVIN & THE CHIPMUNKS
July, 1992 - No. 5, May, 1994
Harvey Comics

1			1.25
2-5			1.50

AMALGAM AGE OF COMICS, THE: THE DC COMICS COLLECTION
1996 ($12.95, trade paperback)
DC Comics

nn-r/Amazon, Assassins, Doctor Strangefate, JLX, JLX, Legends of the Dark Claw, & Super Soldier			13.00

AMAZING ADULT FANTASY (Formerly Amazing Adventures #1-6; becomes Amazing Fantasy #15)
No. 7, Dec, 1961 - No. 14, July, 1962
Marvel Comics Group (AMI)

7-Ditko c/a begins, ends #14	66.00	197.00	550.00
8-Last 10¢ issue	53.00	158.00	450.00
9-13: 12-1st app. Mailbag. 13-Anti-communist story	47.00	141.00	400.00
14-Prototype issue (Professor X)	50.00	150.00	450.00

AMAZING ADVENTURE FUNNIES (Fantoman No. 2 on)
June, 1940 - No. 2, Sept. 1940
Centaur Publications

1-The Fantom of the Fair by Gustavson (r/Amaz. Mystery Funnies V2#7,V2#8), The Arrow, Skyrocket Steele From the Year X by Everett (r/AMF #2); Burgos-a	175.00	525.00	1400.00
2-Reprints; Published after Fantoman #2	112.00	335.00	900.00

NOTE: *Burgos* a-1(2). *Everett* a-1(3). *Gustavson* a-1(5), 2(3). *Pinajian* a-2.

AMAZING ADVENTURES (Also see Boy Cowboy & Science Comics)
1950; No. 1, Nov, 1950 - No. 6, Fall, 1952 (Painted covers)
Ziff-Davis Publ. Co.

1950 (no month given) (8-1/2x11) (8 pgs.) Has the front & back cover plus Schomburg story used in Amazing Advs. #1 (Sent to subscribers of Z-D s/f magazines & ordered through mail for 10¢. Used to test market) Estimated value...			280.00
1-Wood, Schomburg, Anderson, Whitney-a	60.00	180.00	475.00
2-5: 2-Schomburg-a. 2,4,5-Anderson-a. 3,5-Starr-a	29.00	86.00	200.00
6-Krigstein-a	32.00	96.00	225.00

AMAZING ADVENTURES (Becomes Amazing Adult Fantasy #7 on)
June, 1961 - No. 6, Nov, 1961
Atlas Comics (AMI)/Marvel Comics No. 3 on

1-Origin Dr. Droom (1st Marvel-Age Superhero) by Kirby; Kirby/Ditko-a (5 pgs.) Ditko & Kirby-a in all; Kirby monster c-1-6	111.00	333.00	1100.00
2	53.00	160.00	450.00
3-6: 6-Last Dr. Droom	47.00	141.00	385.00

AMAZING ADVENTURES
Aug, 1970 - No. 39, Nov, 1976
Marvel Comics Group

1-Inhumans by Kirby(p) & Black Widow (1st app. in Tales of Suspense #52) double feature begins	3.75	11.25	30.00
2-4: 2-F.F. brief app. 4-Last Kirby Inhumans	1.65	4.20	10.00
5-8: Neal Adams-a(p); 8-Last Black Widow	2.60	7.50	18.00
9,10: Magneto app. 10-Last Inhumans (origin-r by Kirby)	1.65	4.20	10.00
11-New Beast begins(1st app. in mutated form; origin in flashback); X-Men cameo in flashback (#11-17 are X-Men tie-ins)	5.00	15.00	40.00
12-17: 13-Brotherhood of Evil Mutants x-over from X-Men. 15-X-Men app.			

17-Last Beast (origin); X-Men app.	1.65	4.20	10.00
18-War of the Worlds begins (5/73); 1st app. Killraven; Neal Adams-a(p)	1.65	4.20	10.00
19-39: 35-Giffen's first published story (art), along with Deadly Hands of Kung-Fu #22 (3/76)	1.00	2.00	5.00

NOTE: *N. Adams* c-6-8. *Buscema* a-1p, 2p. *Colan* a-3-5p, 26p. *Ditko* a-24r. *Everett* a(i)3-5, 7-9. *Giffen* a-35i, 38p. *G. Kane* c-11, 25p, 29p. *Ploog* a-12i. *Russell* a-27-32, 34-37, 39; c-28, 30-32, 33i, 34, 35, 37, 39i. *Starlin* a-17. *Starlin* c-15p, 16, 17, 27. *Sutton* a-11-15p.

AMAZING ADVENTURES
Dec, 1979 - No. 14, Jan, 1981
Marvel Comics Group

V2#1-Reprints story/X-Men #1 & 38 (origins)		1.70	4.25
2-14: 2-6-Early X-Men-r. 7,8-Origin Iceman		1.30	3.25

NOTE: *Byrne* c-6p, 9p. *Kirby* a-1-14r; c-7, 9. *Steranko* a-12r. *Tuska* a-7-9.

AMAZING ADVENTURES
July, 1988 ($4.95, squarebound, one-shot, 80 pgs.)
Marvel Comics

1-Anthology; Austin, Golden-a	1.00	2.00	5.00

AMAZING ADVENTURES OF CAPTAIN CARVEL AND HIS CARVEL CRUSADERS, THE, (See Carvel Comics)

AMAZING CHAN & THE CHAN CLAN, THE (TV)
May, 1973 - No. 4, Feb, 1974 (Hanna-Barbera)
Gold Key

1-Warren Tufts-a in all	1.40	6.00	14.00
2-4	.80	3.25	8.00

AMAZING COMICS (Complete Comics No. 2)
Fall, 1944
Timely Comics (EPC)

1-The Destroyer, The Whizzer, The Young Allies (by Sekowsky), Sergeant Dix; Schomburg-c	170.00	505.00	1350.00

AMAZING DETECTIVE CASES (Formerly Suspense No. 2?)
No. 3, Nov, 1950 - No. 14, Sept, 1952
Marvel/Atlas Comics (CCC)

3	20.00	60.00	140.00
4-6	12.00	36.00	85.00
7-10	10.00	30.00	70.00
11,14: 11-(3/52)-Changes to horror	13.50	41.00	95.00
12-Krigstein-a	12.00	36.00	85.00
13-(Scarce)-Everett-a; electrocution-c/story	18.00	54.00	125.00

NOTE: *Colan* a-9. *Maneely* c-13. *Sekowsky* a-12. *Sinnott* a-13. *Tuska* a-13.

AMAZING FANTASY (Formerly Amazing Adult Fantasy #7-14)
#15, Aug, 1962 (Sept, 1962 shown in indicia); #16, Dec, 1995 - #18, Feb, 1996
Marvel Comics Group (AMI)

	GD25	FN65	VF82	NM94
15-Origin/1st app. of Spider-Man by Ditko (11 pgs.); 1st app. Aunt May & Uncle Ben; Kirby/Ditko-c	1733.00	5200.00	15,600.00	27,000.00

	GD25	FN65	NM94
16-18 ($3.95): Kurt Busiek scripts; painted-c/a		1.60	4.00

AMAZING GHOST STORIES (Formerly Nightmare)
No. 14, Oct, 1954 - No. 16, Feb, 1955
St. John Publishing Co.

14-Pit & the Pendulum story by Kinstler; Baker-c	23.00	69.00	160.00
15-r/Weird Thrillers #5; Baker-c, Powell-a	16.00	47.00	110.00
16-Kubert reprints of Weird Thrillers #4; Baker-c; Roussos, Tuska-a; Kinstler-a (1 pg.)	17.00	49.00	115.00

AMAZING HIGH ADVENTURE
8/84; No. 2, 10/85; No. 3, 10/86 - No. 5, 1987 ($2.00)
Marvel Comics

1-5: 3,4-Baxter paper		.80	2.00

NOTE: *Bissette* a-4. *Bolton* c/a-4. *Severin* a-1, 3. *Paul Smith* a-2. *Williamson* a-2l.

Amazing-Man Comics #13 © CEN

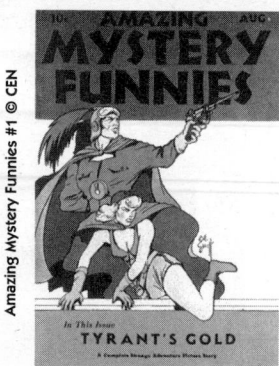

Amazing Mystery Funnies #1 © CEN

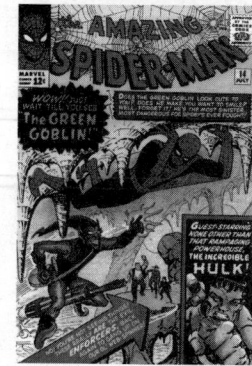

Amazing Spider-Man #14 © MEG

GD25 FN65 NM94 | **GD25 FN65 NM94**

AMAZING-MAN COMICS (Formerly Motion Picture Funnies Weekly?)
(Also see Stars And Stripes Comics)
No. 5, Sept, 1939 - No. 26, Jan, 1942
Centaur Publications

	GD25	FN65	VF82	NM94
5(#1)(Rare)-Origin/1st app. A-Man the Amazing Man by Bill Everett; The Cat-Man by Tarpe Mills (also #8), Mighty Man by Filchock, Minimidget & sidekick Ritty, & The Iron Skull by Burgos begins	1500.00	4500.00	9000.00	14,500.00

(Estimated up to 60 total copies exist, 3 in NM/Mint)

	GD25	FN65		NM94
6-Origin The Amazing Man retold; The Shark begins; Ivy Menace by Tarpe Mills app.	325.00	975.00		2600.00
7-Magician From Mars begins; ends #11	190.00	560.00		1500.00
8-Cat-Man dresses as woman	130.00	390.00		1050.00
9-Magician From Mars battles the 'Elemental Monster,' swiped into The Spectre in More Fun #54 & 55	130.00	390.00		1050.00
10,11: 11-Zardi, the Eternal Man begins; ends #16; Amazing Man dons costume; last Everett issue	112.00	335.00		900.00
12,13	100.00	300.00		800.00
14-Reef Kinkaid, Rocke Wayburn (ends #20), & Dr. Hypno (ends #21) begin; no Zardi or Chuck Hardy	85.00	250.00		675.00
15,17-20: 15-Zardi returns; no Rocke Wayburn. 17-Dr. Hypno returns; no Zardi	70.00	205.00		550.00
16-Mighty Man's powers of super strength & ability to shrink & grow explained; Rocke Wayburn returns; no Dr. Hypno; Al Avison (a character) begins, ends #18 (a tribute to the famed artist)	71.00	215.00		575.00
21-Origin Dash Dartwell (drug-use story); origin & only app. T.N.T.	70.00	205.00		550.00
22-Dash Dartwell, the Human Meteor & The Voice app; last Iron Skull & The Shark; Silver Streak app.	65.00	195.00		525.00
23-Two Amazing Man stories; intro/origin Tommy the Amazing Kid; The Marksman only app.	70.00	205.00		550.00
24-King of Darkness, Nightshade, & Blue Lady begin; end #26; 1st app. Super-Ann	65.00	195.00		525.00
25,26 (Scarce): Meteor Martin by Wolverton in both; 26-Electric Ray app.	105.00	320.00		850.00

NOTE: *Everett* a-5-11; c-5-11. *Gilman* a-14-20. *Giunta/Mirando* a-7-10. *Sam Glanzman* a-14-16, 18-21, 23. *Louis Glanzman* a-6, 9-11, 14-21; c-13-19, 21. *Robert Golden* a-9. *Gustavson* a-6; c-22, 23. *Lubbers* a-14-21. *Simon* a-10. *Frank Thomas* a-6, 9-11, 14, 15, 17-21.

AMAZING MYSTERIES (Formerly Sub-Mariner Comics No. 31)
No. 32, May, 1949 - No. 35, Jan, 1950 (1st Marvel Horror Comic)
Marvel Comics (CCC)

32-The Witness app.	70.00	205.00	550.00
33-Horror format	26.00	79.00	185.00
34,35: Changes to Crime. 34,35-Photo-c	15.00	45.00	105.00

AMAZING MYSTERY FUNNIES
Aug, 1938 - No. 24, Sept, 1940 (All 52 pgs.)
Centaur Publications

V1#1-Everett-c(1st); Dick Kent Adv. story; Skyrocket Steele in the Year X on cover only	312.00	935.00	2500.00
2-Everett 1st-a (Skyrocket Steele)	150.00	450.00	1200.00
3(#4, 12/38)-nn on cover, #3 on inside; bondage-c	81.00	240.00	650.00
V2#1-4,6: 2-Drug use story. 3-Air-Sub DX begins by Burgos. 4-Dan Hastings, Hastings, Sand Hog begins (ends #5). 6-Last Skyrocket Steele	71.00	215.00	575.00
	65.00	195.00	525.00
5-Classic Everett-c	81.00	240.00	650.00
7 (Scarce)-Intro. The Fantom of the Fair & begins; Everett, Gustavson, Burgos-a	312.00	935.00	2500.00
8-Origin & 1st app. Speed Centaur	112.00	335.00	900.00
9-11: 11-Self portrait and biog. of Everett; Jon Linton begins; early Robot cover (11/39)	65.00	195.00	525.00

12 (Scarce)-1st Space Patrol; Wolverton-a (12/39); new costume Phantom of the Fair	170.00	505.00	1350.00
V3#1(#17, 1/40)-Intro. Bullet; Tippy Taylor serial begins, ends #24 (continued in The Arrow #2)	65.00	195.00	525.00
18,20: 18-Fantom of the Fair by Gustavson	62.00	190.00	500.00
19,21-24: Space Patrol by Wolverton in all	88.00	263.00	700.00

NOTE: *Burgos* a-V2#3-9. *Eisner* a-V1#2, 3(2). *Everett* a-V1#2-4, V2#1, 3-6; c-V1#1-4,V2#3, 5, 18. *Filchock* a-V2#9. *Flessel* a-V2#6. *Guardineer* a-V1#4, V2#4-6; *Gustavson* a-V2#4, 5, 9-12, V3#1, 18, 19; c-V2#7, 9, 12, V3#1, 21, 22; *McWilliams* a-V2#9, 10. *TarpeMills* a-V2#2, 4-6, 9-12, V3#1. *Leo Morey*(Pulp artist) c-V2#10; text illo-V2#11. *FrankThomas* a-6-V2#11. *Webster* a-V2#4.

AMAZING SAINTS
1974 (39¢)
Logos International

nn-True story of Phil Saint .40

AMAZING SCARLET SPIDER
Nov, 1995 - No. 4, Jan, 1996 ($1.95, limited series)
Marvel Comics

1-4: Replaces "Amazing Spider-Man" for four issues .80 2.00

AMAZING SPIDER-MAN, THE (See All Detergent Comics, Amazing Fantasy, America's Best TV Comics, Aurora, Deadly Foes of Spider-Man, Giant-Size Spider-Man, Giant Size Super-Heroes Featuring..., Marvel Collectors Item Classics, Marvel Fanfare, Marvel Graphic Novel, Marvel Spec. Ed., Marvel Tales, Marvel Team-Up, Marvel Treasury Ed., Nothing Can Stop the Juggernaut, Official Marvel Index To..., Power Record Comics, Spectacular..., Spider-Man, Spider-Man Digest, Spider-Man Saga, Spider-Man 2099, Spider-Man Vs. Wolverine, Spidey Super Stories, Strange Tales Annual #2, Superman Vs. ..., Try-Out Winner Book, Web of Spider-Man & Within Our Reach)

AMAZING SPIDER-MAN, THE
March, 1963 - Present
Marvel Comics Group

	GD25	FN65	VF82	NM94
1-Retells origin by Steve Ditko; 1st Fantastic Four x-over (ties w/F.F. #12 as first Marvel x-over); intro. John Jameson & The Chameleon; Spider-Man's 2nd app.; Kirby/Ditko-c; Ditko-c/a #1-38	1000.00	3000.00	10,000.00	19,000.00
	GD25	FN65		NM94
1-Reprint from the Golden Record Comic set with record (1966)	26.00	77.00		180.00
	37.00	111.00		260.00
2-1st app. the Vulture & the Terrible Tinkerer	250.00	750.00		2800.00
3-1st full-length story; Human Torch cameo; intro. & 1st app. Doc Octopus;	200.00	600.00		1950.00
4-Origin & 1st app. The Sandman (see Strange Tales #115 for 2nd app.); Intro. Betty Brant & Liz Allen	150.00	450.00		1600.00
5-Dr. Doom app.	130.00	390.00		1400.00
6-1st app. Lizard	120.00	360.00		1100.00
7,8,10: 7-Vs. The Vulture; 1st monthly issue. 8-Fantastic Four app. in back-up story by Kirby/Ditko. 10-1st app. Big Man & The Enforcers	85.00	255.00		775.00
9-Origin & 1st app. Electro (2/64)	95.00	285.00		850.00
11,12: 11-1st app. Bennett Brant. 12-Doc Octopus unmasks Spider-Man-c/story	53.00	160.00		450.00
13-1st app. Mysterio	80.00	240.00		600.00
	GD25	FN65	VF82	NM94
14-(7/64)-1st app. The Green Goblin (c/story)(Norman Osborn); Hulk x-over	200.00	600.00	900.00	1400.00
	GD25	FN65		NM94
15-1st app. Kraven the Hunter; 1st mention of Mary Jane Watson (not shown)	75.00	225.00		550.00
16-Spider-Man battles Daredevil (1st x-over 9/64); still in old yellow costume	40.00	120.00		350.00
17-2nd app. Green Goblin (c/story); Human Torch x-over (also in #18 & #21)	63.00	189.00		550.00
18-1st app. Ned Leeds who later becomes Hobgoblin; Fantastic Four back-up story; 3rd app. Sandman	40.00	120.00		350.00
19-Sandman app.	37.00	111.00		285.00

Amazing Spider-Man #47 © MEG

Amazing Spider-Man #136 © MEG

Amazing Spider-Man #278 © MEG

	GD25	FN65	NM94
20-Origin & 1st app. The Scorpion	40.00	120.00	345.00
21-2nd app. The Beetle (see Strange Tales #123)	30.00	90.00	230.00
22-1st app. Princess Python	27.00	81.00	210.00
23-3rd app. The Green Goblin-c/story; Norman Osborn app.	40.00	120.00	320.00
24	24.00	73.00	175.00
25-(6/65)-1st app. Mary Jane Watson (cameo; face not shown); 1st app. Spencer Smythe; Norman Osborn app.	30.00	90.00	230.00
26-4th app. The Green Goblin-c/story; 1st app. Crime Master; dies in #27	33.00	99.00	250.00
27-5th app. The Green Goblin-c/story; Norman Osborn app.	31.00	92.00	235.00
28-Origin & 1st app. Molten Man (9/65, scarcer in high grade)	40.00	120.00	335.00
29,30	20.00	60.00	145.00
31-38: 31-1st app. Harry Osborn who later becomes 2nd Green Goblin, Gwen Stacy & Prof. Warren. 34-2nd app. Kraven the Hunter. 36-1st app. Looter. 37-Intro. Norman Osborn. 38-(7/66)-2nd app. Mary Jane Watson (cameo; face not shown); last Ditko issue	16.50	49.50	145.00
39-The Green Goblin-c/story; Green Goblin's i.d. revealed as Norman Osborn; Romita-a begins (8/66; see Daredevil #16 for 1st Romita-a on Spider-Man)	25.00	75.00	200.00
40-1st told origin The Green Goblin-c/story	39.00	118.00	300.00
41-1st app. Rhino	19.00	56.00	145.00
42-(11/66)-3rd app. Mary Jane Watson (cameo in last 2 panels); 1st time face is shown	17.00	51.00	130.00
43-49: 44,45-2nd & 3rd app. The Lizard. 46-Intro. Shocker. 47-M. J. Watson & Peter Parker 1st date. 47-Green Goblin cameo; Harry & Norman Osborn app. 47,49-3rd & 4th app. Kraven the Hunter	11.50	34.00	90.00
50-1st app. Kingpin (7/67)	43.00	130.00	400.00
51-2nd app. Kingpin	19.00	56.00	150.00
52-60: 52-1st app. Joe Robertson & 3rd app. Kingpin. 56-1st app. Capt. George Stacy. 57,58-Ka-Zar app. 59-1st app. Brainwasher (alias Kingpin); 1st-c app. M. J. Watson	9.30	28.00	70.00
61-74: 67-1st app. Randy Robertson. 69-Kingpin-c. 69,70-Kingpin app. 73-1st app. Silvermane. 74-Last 12¢ issue	7.00	21.00	50.00
75-89,91-93,95,99: 78,79-1st app. The Prowler. 83-1st app. Schemer & Vanessa. 84,85-Kingpin-c/story. 86-Re-intro & origin Black Widow in new costume. 93-1st app. Arthur Stacy	5.70	17.00	45.00
90-Death of Capt. Stacey	6.00	18.00	45.00
94-Origin retold	8.50	25.00	60.00
96-98-Green Goblin app. (97,98-Green Goblin-c); drug books not approved by CCA	11.00	32.00	80.00
100-Anniversary issue (9/71); Green Goblin cameo (2 pgs.)	24.00	73.00	175.00
101-1st app. Morbius the Living Vampire; Wizard cameo; last 15¢ issue (10/71)	19.00	56.00	150.00
101-Silver ink 2nd printing (9/92, $1.75)		.80	2.00
102-Origin & 2nd app. Morbius (25¢, 52 pgs.)	13.00	38.00	100.00
103-118: 104,111-Kraven the Hunter-c/stories. 108-1st app. Sha-Shan. 109-Dr. Strange-c/story (6/72). 110-1st app. Gibbon. 113-1st app. Hammerhead. 116-118-reprints story from Spectacular Spider-Man Mag. in color with some changes	3.75	11.25	26.00
119,120-Spider-Man vs. Hulk (4 & 5/73)	5.50	16.50	42.00
121-Death of Gwen Stacy (6/73) (killed by Green Goblin) (reprinted in Marvel Tales #98 & 192)	16.00	47.00	120.00
122-Death of The Green Goblin-c/story (7/73) (reprinted in Marvel Tales #99 & 192)	19.00	56.00	135.00
123-128: 123-Cage app. 124-1st app. Man-Wolf (9/73), origin in #125. 127-1st mention of Harry Osborn becoming Green Goblin	3.40	10.00	24.00
129-1st app. Jackal & The Punisher (2/74)	28.00	83.00	250.00
130-133,138-141,152-160: 131-Last 20¢ issue. 139-1st app. Grizzly. 140-1st app. Glory Grant. 159-Last 25¢ issue	2.15	6.50	15.00
134-Punisher cameo (7/74); 1st app. Tarantula; Harry Osborn discovers Spider-Man's id	3.25	9.50	22.00

	GD25	FN65	NM94
135-2nd full Punisher app. (8/74)	9.00	28.00	65.00
136-Reappearance of The Green Goblin (Harry Osborn; Norman Osborn's son)	5.70	17.00	45.00
137-Green Goblin-c/story (2nd Harry Osborn)	5.70	17.00	45.00
142,143-Gwen Stacy clone cameos: 143-1st app. Cyclone	3.40	10.00	24.00
144-Full app. of Gwen Stacy clone	2.60	7.50	18.00
145,146-Gwen Stacy clone storyline continues	2.60	7.50	18.00
147-Spider-Man learns Gwen Stacy is clone	2.60	7.50	18.00
148-Jackal revealed	3.90	11.50	27.00
149-Spider-Man clone story begins, clone dies (?); origin of Jackal	11.50	34.00	70.00
150-Spider-Man decides he is not the clone	8.00	23.50	40.00
151-Spider-Man disposes of clone body	4.85	14.50	34.00
161-Nightcrawler app. from X-Men; Punisher cameo; Wolverine & Colossus app.	1.70	5.00	12.00
162-Punisher, Nightcrawler app.; 1st Jigsaw	2.60	7.50	18.00
163-173,181-190: 167-1st app. Will O' The Wisp. 169-Clone story recapped. 171-Nova app. 181-Origin retold; gives life history of Spidey; Punisher cameo in flashback (1 panel). 182-(7/78)-Peter proposes to Mary Jane for 1st time, but she refuses	1.30	3.25	8.00
174,175-Punisher app.	2.60	7.50	18.00
176-180-Green Goblin app	2.70	8.00	19.00
191-193,195-199,203-208,210-219: 193-Peter & Mary Jane break up. 196-Faked death of Aunt May. 203-2nd app. Dazzler. 209-1st app. Calypso (Kraven's girlfriend). 210-1st app. Madame Web. 212-1st app. Hydro Man; origin Sandman	1.30	3.25	8.00
194-1st app. Black Cat	2.60	7.50	18.00
200-Giant origin issue (1/80)	4.30	13.00	30.00
201,202-Punisher app.	2.85	8.50	20.00
209-Origin & 1st app. Calypso (10/80)	1.30	3.25	8.00
220-237: 225-(2/82)-Foolkiller-c/story. 226,227-Black Cat returns. 236-Tarantula dies. 234-Free 16 pg. insert "Marvel Guide to Collecting Comics". 235-Origin Will-'O-The-Wisp	1.20	3.00	7.00
238-(3/83)-1st app. Hobgoblin (Ned Leeds); came with skin "Tattooz" decal	11.50	34.00	80.00
238-Without tattooz decal	3.60	10.75	25.00
239-2nd app. Hobgoblin & 1st battle w/Spidey	6.50	19.50	45.00
240-243,246-248: 241-Origin The Vulture. 243-Reintro Mary Jane Watson after 4 year absence	1.30	3.25	8.00
244-3rd app. Hobgoblin (cameo)	1.40	4.20	10.00
245-(10/83)-4th app. Hobgoblin (cameo); Lefty Donovan gains powers of Hobgoblin & battles Spider-Man	2.15	6.50	15.00
249-251: 3 part Hobgoblin/Spider-Man battle. 249-Retells origin & death of 1st Green Goblin. 251-Last old costume	2.00	6.00	14.00
252-Spider-Man dons new black costume (5/84); ties with Marvel Team-Up #141 & Spectacular Spider-Man #90 for 1st new costume (see Marvel S-H Secret Wars #8)	5.00	15.00	35.00
253-1st app. The Rose	1.50	3.75	9.00
254	1.20	3.00	7.00
255,263,264,266-273,277-280,282,283: 277-Vess back-up art. 279-Jack O'Lantern-c/story. 282-X-Factor x-over	1.00	2.00	5.00
256-1st app. Puma	1.00	2.00	5.00
257-Hobgoblin cameo; 2nd app. Puma; M. J. Watson reveals she knows Spidey's i.d.	1.65	4.20	10.00
258-Hobgoblin app. (minor)	1.65	4.70	11.00
259-Full Hobgoblin app.; Spidey back to old costume; origin Mary Jane Watson	3.75	11.25	28.00
260-Hobgoblin	1.65	4.20	10.00
261-Hobgoblin-c/story; painted-c by Vess	1.85	5.50	13.00
262-Spider-Man unmasked; photo-c	1.65	4.20	10.00
265-1st app. Silver Sable (6/85)	1.65	4.20	10.00
265-Silver ink 2nd printing ($1.25)		1.20	3.00
274-Zarathos (The Spirit of Vengeance) app. (3/86)	1.00	2.00	5.00

Amazing Spider-Man #290 © MEG

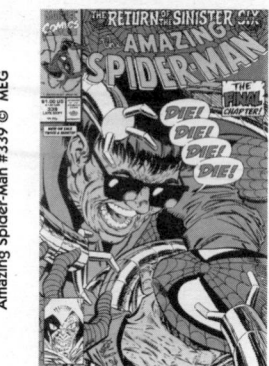

Amazing Spider-Man #339 © MEG

Amazing Spider-Man #417 © MEG

	GD25	FN65	NM94
275-($1.25, 52 pgs.)-Hobgoblin-c/story; origin-r by Ditko			
	2.15	6.50	15.00
276-Hobgoblin app.	1.70	5.00	12.00
281-Hobgoblin battles Jack O'Lantern	1.85	5.50	13.00
284-Punisher cameo; Gang War story begins; Hobgoblin-c/story			
	1.65	4.20	10.00
285-Punisher app.; minor Hobgoblin app.	2.15	6.50	15.00
286,287: 286-Hobgoblin-c & app. (minor). 287-Hobgoblin app. (minor)			
	1.00	2.60	6.00
288-Full Hobgoblin app.; last Gang War	1.50	3.75	9.00
289-(6/87, $1.25, 52 pgs.)-Hobgoblin's i.d. revealed as Ned Leeds; death of Ned Leeds; Macendale (Jack O'Lantern) becomes new Hobgoblin (1st app.)	3.40	10.00	24.00
290-292: 290-Peter proposes to Mary Jane. 292-She accepts; leads into Amazing Spider-Man Annual #21	1.00	2.00	5.00
293,294-Part 2 & 5 of Kraven story from Web of Spider-Man. 294-Death of Kraven	1.50	3.75	9.00
295-297	1.00	2.60	6.00
298-Todd McFarlane-c/a begins (3/88); 1st app. Eddie Brock who becomes Venom; (cameo on last pg.)	7.00	21.00	47.00
299-1st app. Venom with costume (cameo)	4.30	13.00	30.00
300 ($1.50, 52 pgs.)-25th Anniversary)-1st full Venom app.; last black costume (5/88)	11.50	34.00	85.00
301-305: 301 ($1.00 issues begin). 304-1st bi-weekly issue			
	2.15	6.50	15.00
306-311,313,314: 306-Swipes-c from Action #1. 315-317-Venom app.			
	1.65	4.20	10.00
312-Hobgoblin battles Green Goblin	3.25	9.50	22.00
315-317-Venom app.	2.85	8.50	20.00
318-323,325: 319-Bi-weekly begins again	1.30	3.25	8.00
324-Sabretooth app.; McFarlane cover only	2.30	6.70	16.00
326,327,329: 327-Cosmic Spidey continues from Spectacular Spider-Man (no McFarlane-c/a)	1.60	4.00	
328-Hulk x-over; last McFarlane issue	1.70	5.00	12.00
330,331-Punisher app. 331-Minor Venom app.	1.60	4.00	
332,333-Venom-c/story	1.65	4.20	10.00
334-336,338-343: 341-Tarantula app.	1.20	3.00	
337-Hobgoblin app.	1.60	4.00	
344-1st app. Cletus Kasady (Carnage)	1.70	5.00	8.00
345-1st full app. Cletus Kasady; Venom cameo on last pg.			
	1.65	4.20	10.00
346,347-Venom app.	1.65	4.20	10.00
348,349,351-359: 348-Avengers x-over. 351,352-Nova of New Warriors app. 353-Darkhawk app.; brief Punisher cameo & Nova, Night Thrasher (New Warriors), Darkhawk & Moon Knight app. 357,358-Punisher, Darkhawk, Moon Knight, Night Thrasher, Nova x-over. 358-3 part gatefold-c; last $1.00-c. 360-Carnage cameo	1.00	2.50	
350-($1.50, 52pgs.)-Origin retold; Spidey vs. Dr. Doom; pin-ups; Uncle Ben app.			
	1.20	3.00	
360-Carnage cameo	1.50	3.80	9.00
361-Intro Carnage (the Spawn of Venom); begin 3 part story; recap of how Spidey's alien costume became Venom	2.15	6.50	15.00
361-($1.25)-2nd printing; silver-c		.80	2.00
362,363-Carnage & Venom-c/story	1.50	3.75	9.00
362-2nd printing			1.50
364,366-374,376-387: 364-The Shocker app. (old villain). 366-Peter's parents-c/story. 369-Harry Osborn back-up (Gr. Goblin II). 373-Venom back-up. 374-Venom-c/story. 376-Cardiac app. 378-Maximum Carnage part 3. 381,382-Hulk app. 383-The Jury app. 384-Venom/carnage app. 387-New costume Vulture		.70	1.75
365-($3.95, 84 pgs.)-30th anniversary issue w/silver hologram on-c; Spidey/ Venom/Carnage pull-out poster; contains 5 pg. preview of Spider-Man 2099 (1st app.); Spidey's origin retold; reintro Peter's parents in Stan Lee 3 pg. text w/illo (story continues thru #370).	1.00	2.00	5.00

	GD25	FN65	NM94
365-Second printing; gold hologram on-c		1.60	4.00
375-($3.95, 68 pgs.)-Holo-grafx foil-c; vs. Venom story; ties into Venom: Lethal Protector #1; Pat Olliffe-a.	1.00	2.00	5.00
388-($2.25, 68 pgs.)-Newsstand edition; Venom back-up & Cardiac & chance back-up		.90	2.25
388-($2.95, 68 pgs.)-Collector's edition w/foil-c		1.20	3.00
389-396,398,399,401-430: 389-$1.50-c begins; bound-in trading card sheet; Green Goblin app. 394-Power & Responsibility Pt. 2. 396-Daredevil-c & app. 403-Carnage app. 406-1st New Doc Octopus. 407-Human Torch, Silver Sable, Sandman app. 409-Kaine, Rhino app. 410-Carnage app. 414-The Rose app. 415-Onslaught story; Spidey vs. Sentinels. 416-Epilogue to Onslaught; Garney-a(p); Williamson-a(i)		.70	1.75
390-($2.95)-Collector's edition polybagged w/16 pg. insert of new animated Spidey TV show plus animation cel		1.20	3.00
394-($2.95, 48 pgs.)-Deluxe edition; flip book w/Birth of a Spider-Man Pt. 2; silver foil both-c	1.00	2.00	5.00
397-($2.25)-Flip book w/Ultimate Spider-Man		.90	2.25
400-($2.95)-Death of Aunt May	1.00	2.00	5.00
400-($3.95)-Death of Aunt May; embossed double-c			
	1.00	2.60	6.00
400-Collector's Edition; white-c	2.15	6.50	15.00
Annual 1 (1964, 72 pgs.)-Origin Spider-Man; 1st app. Sinister Six (Dr. Octopus, Electro, Kraven the Hunter, Mysterio, Sandman, Vulture) (41 pg. story); plus gallery of Spidey foes	59.00	178.00	550.00
Annual 2 (1965, 25¢, 72 pgs.)-Reprints from #1,2,5 plus new Doctor Strange story	33.00	99.00	250.00
Special 3 (11/66, 25¢, 72 pgs.)-Avengers & Hulk x-over; Doctor Octopus-r from #11,12; Romita-a	12.00	36.00	90.00
Special 4 (11/67, 25¢, 68 pgs.)-Spidey battles Human Torch (new 41 pg. story)	11.50	34.00	85.00
Special 5 (11/68, 25¢, 68 pgs.)-New 40 pg. Red Skull story; 1st app. Peter Parker's parents; last annual with new-a	11.00	34.00	80.00
Special 6 (11/69, 25¢, 68 pgs.)-Reprints 41 pg. Sinister Six story from annual #1 plus 2 Kirby/Ditko stories (r)	4.00	12.00	30.00
Special 7 (12/70, 25¢, 68 pgs.)-All-r(#1,2)	4.00	12.00	30.00
Special 8 (12/71)-All-r	4.00	12.00	30.00
King Size 9 ('73)-Reprints Spectacular Spider-Man (mag.) #2; 40 pg. Green Goblin-c/story (re-edited from 58 pgs.)	4.00	12.00	28.00
Annual 10 (1976)-Origin Human Fly (vs. Spidey); new-a begins			
	1.30	3.00	8.00
Annual 11,12: 11 (1977). 12 (1978)-Spider-Man vs. Hulk-r/#119,120			
	1.30	3.00	8.00
Annual 13 (1979)-Byrne/Austin-a (new)	1.30	3.00	8.00
Annual 14 (1980)-Miller-c/a(p), 40pgs.	1.50	3.80	9.00
Annual 15 (1981)-Miller-c/a(p); Punisher app.	2.15	6.50	15.00
Annual 16-20: 16 (1982)-Origin-1st app. Capt. Marvel (female heroine). 17 (1983). 18 (1984). 19 (1985). 20 (1986)-Origin Iron Man of 2020	1.20	2.90	7.00
Annual 21 (1987)-Special wedding issue; newsstand & direct sale versions exist & are worth same	1.50	3.80	9.00
Annual 22 (1988, $1.75, 68 pgs.)-1st app. Speedball; Evolutionary War x-over; Daredevil app.	1.30	3.00	8.00
Annual 23 (1989, $2.00, 68 pgs.)-Atlantis Attacks; origin Spider-Man retold; She-Hulk app.; Byrne-c; Liefeld-a(p), 23 pgs.	1.00	2.60	6.00
Annual 24 (1990, $2.00, 68 pgs.)-Ant-Man app.	1.00	1.60	4.00
Annual 25 (1991, $2.00, 68 pgs.)-3 pg. origin recap; Iron Man app.; 1st Venom solo story; Ditko-a (6 pgs.)	1.65	4.20	10.00
Annual 26 (1992, $2.25, 68 pgs.)-New Warriors-c/story; Venom solo story cont'd in Spectacular Spider-Man Annual #12	1.20	2.90	7.00
Annual 27 (1993, $2.95, 68 pgs.)-Bagged w/card; 1st app. Annex			
	1.20	3.00	
Annual 28 (1994, $2.95, 68 pgs.)-Carnage-c/story; Rhino & Cloak and Dagger back-ups	1.20	3.00	
Super Special 1 (4/95, $3.95)-Flip Book			4.00

Amazing Spider-Man: Soul of the Hunter © MEG

Amazing X-Men #3 © MEG

Amazon Woman #4 (2nd Series) © FantaCo

CURSE OF THE AMAZON!

	GD25	FN65	NM94

...: Skating on Thin Ice 1(1990, $1.25, Canadian)-McFarlane-c; anti-drug
issue — 1.00 — 2.00 — 5.00
...: Skating on Thin Ice 1 (2/93, $1.50, American) — .80 — 2.00
...: Double Trouble 2 (1990, $1.25, Canadian) — 1.20 — 3.00
...: Double Trouble 2 (2/93, $1.50, American) — .80 — 2.00
...: Hit and Run 3 (1990, $1.25, Canadian)-Ghost Rider-c/story
— 1.20 — 3.00
...: Hit and Run 3 (2/93. $1.50, American) — .80 — 2.00
... : Carnage (6/93, $6.95)-r/ASM #344,345,359-363 1.20 — 3.00 — 7.00
...: Chaos in Calgary 4 (Canadian edition exist? part of 5 part series)
...: Chaos in Calgary 4 (2/93, $1.50, American) — .80 — 2.00
...: Deadball 5 (1993, $1.60, Canadian)-Green Goblin-c/story; features
Montreal Expos — — 1.50
... : Soul of the Hunter nn (8/92, $5.95, 52 pgs.)-Zeck-c/a(p)
— 1.00 — 2.50 — 6.00
Parallel Lives (1990, $8.95,68pgs.)-Graphic novel 1.50 — 3.75 — 9.00
Aim Toothpaste Giveaway (36 pgs., reg. size)-1 pg. origin recap; Green
Goblin-c/story — 1.00 — 2.50 — 6.00
Aim Toothpaste Giveaway (16 pgs., reg. size)-Dr. Octopus app.
— 1.00 — 2.00 — 5.00
All Detergent Giveaway (1979, 36 pgs.), nn-Origin-r
— 1.65 — 4.00 — 10.00
GiveawayY-Acme & Dingo Children's Boots (1980)-Spider-Woman app.
— 1.60 — 4.00
Amazing Spider-Man nn (1990, 6-1/8x9", 28 pgs.)-Shan-Lon giveaway; r/
Amazing Spider-Man #303 w/McFarlane-c/a — — 1.00
...& Power Pack (1984, nn)(Nat'l Committee for Prevention of Child Abuse
(two versions, mail offer & store giveaway)-Mooney-a; Byrne-c
— — 1.00
...& The Hulk (Special Edition)(6/8/80; 20 pgs.)-Supplement to Chicago
Tribune (giveaway) — 1.30 — 3.25 — 8.00
...& The Incredible Hulk (1981, 1982; 36 pgs.)-Sanger Harris supplement
to Dallas Times, Dallas Herald, Denver Post, Kansas City Star, Tulsa World;
Foley's supplement to Houston Chronicle (1982, 16 pgs.)-"Great Rodeo Rob-
bery"; The Jones Store-giveaway (1983, 16 pgs.) 1.65 — 4.00 — 10.00
...and the New Mutants Featuring Skids nn (National Committee for
Prevention of Child Abuse/K-Mart giveaway)-Williams-c(i) — — 1.00
...Captain America, The Incredible Hulk, & Spider-Woman (1981)
(7-11 Stores giveaway; 36 pgs.) — 1.00 — 2.00 — 5.00
...: Christmas in Dallas (1983) (Supplement to Dallas Times Herald)
giveaway — 1.00 — 2.00 — 5.00
..., Fire-Star, And Ice-Man at the Dallas Ballet Nutcracker (1983; supplement to
Dallas Times Herald)-Mooney-a — 1.00 — 2.00 — 5.00
Giveaway-Esquire & Eye Magazines (2/69)-Miniature-Still attached
— 9.00 — 26.00 — 60.00
..., Storm & Powerman (1982; 20 pgs.)(American Cancer Society)
giveaway — 1.00 — 2.00 — 5.00
...Vs. The Hulk (Special Edition; 1979, 20 pgs.)(Supplement to Columbus
Dispatch)-Giveaway — 1.00 — 2.00 — 5.00
...Vs. The Prodigy (Giveaway, 16 pgs. in color (1976, 5x6-1/2")-Sex
education; (1 million printed; 35-50¢)
NOTE: **Austin** a(i)-248, 335, 337, Annual 13; c(i)-188, 241, 242, 248, 331, 334, 343, Annual 25.
J. Buscema a(i)-72, 73, 76-81, 84, 85. **Byrne** a-189p, 190p, 206p, Annual 3r, 6r; 7r, 13p; c-
189p, 268, 296, Annual 12. **Ditko** a-1-38, Annual 1, Special 3(r), 2, 24(2); c-1i, 2-38. **Guice** c/a-
Annual 18i. **Gil Kane** a(p)-89-105, 120-124, 150, Annual 10, 12i, 24p; c-90p, 96, 98, 99, 101-
105p, 129p, 131p, 132p, 137-140p, 143p, 148p, 149p, 151p, 153p, 160p, 161p, Annual 10p, 24.
Kirby a-8. **Erik Larsen** a-324, 327, 329-350; c-327, 329-350, 354i, Annual 25. **McFarlane** a-
298p, 299p, 300-303, 304-323p, 325p, 328; c-298-325, 328. **Miller** c-218, 219. **Mooney** a-65i,
67-82i, 84-88i, 173i, 178i, 189i, 190i, 192i, 193i, 196-202i, 207i, 211-219i, 221i, 222i, 226i, 227i,
229-233i, Annual 11i, 17i. **Nasser** c-228p. **Nebres** a-Annual 24i. **Russell** c-357i. **Simonson** c-
222, 337i. **Starlin** a-113i, 114i, 187p. **Williamson** a-365i.

AMAZING WILLIE MAYS, THE
No date (Sept, 1954)
Famous Funnies Publ.

nn — 62.00 — 190.00 — 500.00

AMAZING WORLD OF SUPERMAN (See Superman)

AMAZING X-MEN
Mar, 1995 - No.4, July, 1995 ($1.95, limited series)
Marvel Comics

1-Age of Apocalypse — 1.20 — 3.00
2-4 — .80 — 2.00

AMAZON
Mar, 1989 - No. 3, May, 1989 ($1.95, limited series)
Comico

1-3: Ecological theme — .80 — 2.00

AMAZON (Also see Marvel Versus DC #3 & DC Versus Marvel #4)
Apr, 1996 ($1.95, one-shot)
DC Comics (Amalgam)

1-John Byrne-c/a/scripts — — 2.00

AMAZON ATTACK 3-D
Sept, 1990 ($3.95, 28 pgs.)
The 3-D Zone

1-Chaykin-a — 1.60 — 4.00

AMAZON WOMAN (1st Series)
Summer, 1994 - No. 2, Fall, 1994 ($2.95, B&W, limited series, mature)
FantaCo

1,2: Tom Simonton-c/a/scripts — 1.20 — 3.00

AMAZON WOMAN (2nd Series)
Feb, 1996 - No. 4, May, 1996 ($2.95, B&W, limited series, mature)
FantaCo

1-4: Tom Simonton-a/scripts — — 3.00

AMBUSH (See Zane Grey, Four Color 314)

AMBUSH BUG (Also see Son of...)
June, 1985 - No. 4, Sept, 1985 (75¢, limited series)
DC Comics

1-4: Giffen-c/a in all — — 1.00
Nothing Special 1 (9/92, $2.50, 68pg.)-Giffen-c/a — 1.00 — 2.50
Stocking Stuffer (2/86, $1.25)-Giffen-c/a — — 1.25

AMERICA IN ACTION
1942; Winter, 1945 (36 pgs.)
Dell(Imp. Publ. Co.)/Mayflower House Publ.

1942-Dell-(68 pgs.) — 14.00 — 43.00 — 100.00
1-(1945)-Has 3 adaptations from American history; Kiefer, Schrotter &
Webb-a — 10.00 — 30.00 — 70.00

AMERICA MENACED!
1950 (Paper-c)
Vital Publications

nn-Anti-communism — estimated value... — — 200.00

AMERICAN, THE
July, 1987 - No. 8, 1989 ($1.50/$1.75, B&W)
Dark Horse Comics

1-8: ($1.50) — — .80 — 2.00
Collection ($5.95, B&W)-Reprints — 1.00 — 2.50 — 6.00
Special 1 (1990, $2.25, B&W) — — .90 — 2.25

AMERICAN AIR FORCES, THE (See A-1 Comics)
Sept-Oct, 1944 - No. 4, 1945; No. 5, 1951 - No. 12, 1954
William H. Wise(Flying Cadet Publ. Co./Hasan(No.1)/Life's Romances/
Magazine Ent. No. 5 on)

1-Article by Zack Mosley, creator of Smilin' Jack
— 12.00 — 36.00 — 85.00
2-4 — 8.35 — 25.00 — 50.00
NOTE: All part comic, part magazine. Art by Whitney, Chas. Quinlan, H. C. Kiefer, and Tony
Dipreta.

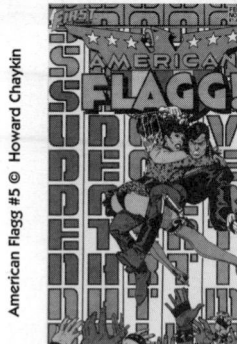
American Flagg #5 © Howard Chaykin

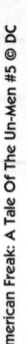
American Freak: A Tale Of The Un-Men #5 © DC

America Vs. The Justice Society #1 © DC

	GD25	FN65	NM94

5(A-1 45)(Formerly Jet Powers), 6(A-1 54), 7(A-1 58), 8(A-1 65), 9(A-1 67),
10(A-1 74), 11(A-1 79), 12(A-1 91)   5.35   16.00   32.00
NOTE: *Powell* c/a-5-12.

AMERICAN COMICS
1940's
Theatre Giveaways (Liberty Theatre, Grand Rapids, Mich. known)
Many possible combinations. "Golden Age" superhero comics with new cover added and given away at theaters. Following known: Superman #59, Capt. Marvel #20, Capt. Marvel Jr. #5, Action #33, Classics Comics #8, Whiz #39. Value would vary with book and should be 70-80 percent of the original.

AMERICAN FLAGG! (See First Comics Graphic Novel 3,9,12,21 & Howard Chaykin's..)
Oct, 1983 - No. 50, Mar, 1988
First Comics

1-Chaykin-c/a begins   1.20   3.00
2-50: 21-27-Alan Moore scripts. 31-Origin Bob Violence   1.00
Special 1 (11/86)-Introduces Chaykin's Time²   1.50

AMERICAN FREAK: A TALE OF THE UN-MEN
Feb, 1994 - No. 5, June, 1994 ($1.95, limited series, mature readers)
DC Comics (Vertigo)

1-5   .80   2.00

AMERICAN GRAPHICS
No. 1, 1954; No. 2, 1957 (25¢)
Henry Stewart

1-The Maid of the Mist, The Last of the Eries (Indian Legends of Niagara)
(sold at Niagara Falls)   9.15   27.50   55.00
2-Victory at Niagara & Laura Secord (Heroine of the War of 1812)
   5.85   17.50   35.00

AMERICAN INDIAN, THE (See Picture Progress)

AMERICAN LIBRARY
1943 - No. 6, 1944 (15¢, 68 pgs., B&W, text & pictures)
David McKay Publications

nn (#1)-Thirty Seconds Over Tokyo (movie)   33.00   99.00   230.00
nn (#2)-Guadalcanal Diary; painted-c (only 10¢)   26.00   77.00   180.00
3-6: 3-Look to the Mountain. 4-Case of the Crooked Candle (Perry Mason).
5-Duel in the Sun. 6-Wingate's Raiders   11.50   34.00   80.00

AMERICAN: LOST IN AMERICA, THE
July, 1992 - No. 4, Oct, 1992 ($2.50, limited series)
Dark Horse Comics

1-4: 1-Dorman painted-c. 2-Joe Phillips painted-c. 3-Mignola-c. 4-Jim Lee-c.
   1.00   2.50

AMERICAN SPLENDOR: COMIC-CON COMICS
Aug, 1996 ($2.95, B&W, one-shot)
Dark Horse Comics

1-H. Pekar script   3.00

AMERICAN SPLENDOR SPECIAL: A STEP OUT OF THE NEST
Aug, 1994 ($2.95, B&W, one-shot)
Dark Horse Comics

1-H. Pekar script   1.20   3.00

AMERICAN SPLENDOR: WINDFALL
Sept, 1995 - No. 2, 1995 ($3.95, B&W, limited series)
Dark Horse Comics

1,2-Pekar script   4.00

AMERICAN TAIL: FIEVEL GOES WEST, AN
Early Jan, 1992 - No. 3, Early Feb, 1992 ($1.00, limited series)
Marvel Comics

1-Adapts Universal animated movie; Wildman-a   1.00

AMERICA'S BEST COMICS

Feb, 1942; No. 2, Sept, 1942 - No. 31, July, 1949 (New logo with #9)
Nedor/Better/Standard Publications

1-The Woman in Red, Black Terror, Captain Future, Doc Strange, The
Liberator, & Don Davis, Secret Ace begin   175.00   525.00   1400.00
2-Origin The American Eagle; The Woman in Red ends
   71.00   215.00   575.00
3-Pyroman begins (11/42, 1st app.); also see Startling Comics #18, 12/42)
   56.00   170.00   450.00
4-6: 5-Last Capt. Future (not in #4); Lone Eagle app. 6-American Crusader
app.   44.00   132.00   350.00
7-Hitler, Mussolini & Hirohito-c   53.00   160.00   425.00
8-Last Liberator   40.00   120.00   315.00
9-The Fighting Yank begins; The Ghost app.   46.00   140.00   375.00
10-21: 10-Flag-c. 11-Hirohito & Tojo-c. (10/44) 14-American Eagle ends.
21-Infinity-c.   40.00   120.00   280.00
22-Capt. Future app.   34.00   103.00   240.00
23-Miss Masque begins; last Doc Strange   40.00   120.00   315.00
24-Miss Masque bondage-c   40.00   120.00   305.00
25-Last Fighting Yank; Sea Eagle app.   34.00   101.00   235.00
26-31: 26-The Phantom Detective & The Silver Knight app.; Frazetta text illo
& some panels in Miss Masque. 27,28-Commando Cubs. 27-Doc Strange.
28-Tuska Black Terror. 29-Last Pyroman   34.00   101.00   235.00
NOTE: *American Eagle* not in 3, 8, 9, 13. *Fighting Yank* not in 10, 12. *Liberator* not in 2, 6, 7. *Pyroman* not in 9, 11, 14-16, 23, 25-27. *Schomburg (Xela)* c-5, 7-31. Bondage c-18, 24.

AMERICA'S BEST TV COMICS (TV)
1967 (25¢, 68 pgs.)
American Broadcasting Company (Produced by Marvel Comics)

1-Spider-Man, Fantastic Four (by Kirby/Ayers), Casper, King Kong, George
of the Jungle, Journey to the Center of the Earth stories (promotes new TV
cartoon show)   8.75   26.00   70.00

AMERICA'S BIGGEST COMICS BOOK
1944 (196 pgs., one-shot)
William H. Wise

1-The Grim Reaper, The Silver Knight, Zudo, the Jungle Boy, Commando
Cubs, Thunderhoof app.   40.00   120.00   285.00

AMERICA'S FUNNIEST COMICS
1944 - No. 2, 1944 (15¢, 80 pgs.)
William H. Wise

nn(#1), 2   25.00   75.00   175.00

AMERICA'S GREATEST COMICS
May?, 1941 - No. 8, Summer, 1943 (15¢, 100 pgs., soft cardboard-c)
Fawcett Publications

1-Bulletman, Spy Smasher, Capt. Marvel, Minute Man & Mr. Scarlet begin;
Mac Raboy-c   250.00   750.00   2000.00
2   125.00   375.00   1000.00
3   93.00   280.00   750.00
4,5: 4-Commando Yank begins; Golden Arrow, Ibis the Invincible & Spy
Smasher cameo in Captain Marvel   70.00   205.00   550.00
6,7: 7-Balbo the Boy Magician app.; Captain Marvel, Bulletman cameo in Mr.
Scarlet   62.00   190.00   500.00
8-Capt. Marvel Jr. & Golden Arrow app.; Spy Smasher x-over in Capt.
Midnight; no Minute Man or Commando Yank   62.00   190.00   500.00

AMERICA'S SWEETHEART SUNNY (See Sunny, ...)

AMERICA VS. THE JUSTICE SOCIETY
Jan, 1985 - No. 4, Apr, 1985 ($1.00, limited series)
DC Comics

1-Double size; Alcala-a(i) in all   .30   .75   1.50
2-4: 3,4-Spectre cameo   .50   1.00

AMERICOMICS
April, 1983 - No. 6, Mar, 1984 ($2.00, Baxter paper/slick paper)

Amethyst #13 © DC

Angela #2 © Todd McFarlane

Anima #4 © DC

	GD25	FN65	NM94

	GD25	FN65	NM94

Americomics

1-Intro/origin The Shade; Intro. The Slayer, Captain Freedom and The Liberty Corps; Perez-c		1.00	2.50
1,2-2nd printings ($2.00)		.80	2.00
2-6: 2-Messenger app. & 1st app. Tara on Jungle Island. 3-New & old Blue Beetle battle. 4-Origin Dragonfly & Shade. 5-Origin Commando D. 6-Origin the Scarlet Scorpion		1.00	2.50
Special 1 (8/83, $2.00)-Sentinels of Justice (Blue Beetle, Captain Atom, Nightshade & The Question)		1.00	2.50

AMETHYST
Jan, 1985 - No. 16, Aug, 1986 (75¢)
DC Comics

1-16: 8-Fire Jade's i.d. revealed			1.00
Special 1 (10/86, $1.25)			1.25

AMETHYST
Nov, 1987 - No. 4, Feb, 1988 ($1.25, limited series)
DC Comics

1-4			1.25

AMETHYST, PRINCESS OF GEMWORLD
May, 1983 - No. 12, Apr, 1984 (Maxi-series)
DC Comics

1-(60¢)			1.00
1,2-(35¢)-Comic book tested in Austin & Kansas City	1.65	4.20	10.00
2-12: Perez-c(p) #6-11			1.00
Annual 1(9/84)			1.25

NOTE: *Perez* c-4i, 5-11p.

ANARCHO DICTATOR OF DEATH (See Comics Novel)

ANCHORS ANDREWS (The Saltwater Daffy)
Jan, 1953 - No. 4, July, 1953 (Anchors the Saltwater... No. 4)
St. John Publishing Co.

1-Canteen Kate by Matt Baker (9 pgs.)	17.00	51.00	120.00
2-4	5.00	15.00	30.00

ANDY & WOODY (See March of Comics No. 40, 55, 76)

ANDY BURNETT (TV, Disney)
Dec, 1957
Dell Publishing Co.

Four Color 865-Photo-c	10.00	30.00	100.00

ANDY COMICS (Formerly Scream Comics; becomes Ernie Comics)
No. 20, June, 1948 - No. 21, Aug, 1948
Current Publications (Ace Magazines)

20,21: Archie-type comic	5.35	16.00	32.00

ANDY DEVINE WESTERN
Dec, 1950 - No. 2, 1951
Fawcett Publications

1	50.00	150.00	400.00
2	40.00	120.00	300.00

ANDY GRIFFITH SHOW, THE (TV)(1st show aired 10/3/60)
#1252, Jan-Mar, 1962 - #1341, Apr-Jun, 1962
Dell Publishing Co.

Four Color 1252(#1), 1341-Photo-c	25.00	74.00	245.00

ANDY HARDY COMICS (See Movie Comics #3 by Fiction House)
April, 1952 - No. 6, Sept-Nov, 1954
Dell Publishing Co.

Four Color 389(#1)	3.60	11.00	36.00
Four Color 447,480,515,5,6	2.70	8.00	27.00
...& the New Automatic Gas Clothes Dryer (1952, 5x7-1/4", 16 pgs.) Bendix Giveaway (soft-c)	2.80	8.50	28.00

ANDY PANDA (Also see Crackajack Funnies #39, The Funnies, New Funnies & Walter Lantz...)
1943 - No. 56, Nov-Jan, 1961-62 (Walter Lantz)
Dell Publishing Co.

Four Color 25(#1, 1943)	48.00	145.00	475.00
Four Color 54(1944)	29.00	87.00	290.00
Four Color 85(1945)	16.00	48.00	155.00
Four Color 130(1946),154,198	10.00	30.00	100.00
Four Color 216,240,258,280,297	6.80	21.00	68.00
Four Color 326,345,358	3.80	12.00	38.00
Four Color 383,409	3.00	9.00	30.00
16(11-1/52-53) - 30	1.20	3.60	12.00
31-56	.80	2.40	8.00

(See March of Comics #5, 22, 79, & Super Book #4, 15, 27.)

ANGEL
Aug, 1954 - No. 16, Nov-Jan, 1958-59
Dell Publishing Co.

Four Color 576(#1, 8/54)	2.70	9.00	27.00
2(5-7/55) - 16	1.20	5.00	12.00

ANGELA
Dec, 1994 - No. 3, Feb, 1995 ($2.95, limited series)
Image Comics (Todd McFarlane Productions)

1-Gaiman scripts & Capullo-c/a in all; Spawn app.	2.00	6.00	14.00
2,3	1.65	4.20	10.00
Special Edition (1995)-Pirate Spawn-c			30.00
Special Edition (1995)-Angela-c			35.00
Trade paperback ($9.95, 1995) reprints #1-3 & Special Ed. w/additional pin-ups.			10.00

ANGEL AND THE APE (Meet Angel No. 7) (See Limited Collector's Edition C-34 & Showcase No. 77)
Nov-Dec, 1968 - No. 6, Sept-Oct, 1969
National Periodical Publications

1-(11-12/68)-Not Wood-a	3.75	11.25	30.00
2-6-Wood inks in all	2.60	7.50	18.00

ANGEL AND THE APE (2nd Series)
Mar, 1991 - No. 4, June, 1991 ($1.00, limited series)
DC Comics

1-4			1.00

ANGEL LOVE
Aug, 1986 - No. 8, Mar, 1987 (75¢, limited series)
DC Comics

1-8			1.00
Special 1 (1987, $1.25, 52 pgs.)			1.25

ANGEL OF LIGHT, THE (See The Crusaders)

ANIMA
Mar, 1994 - No. 15, July, 1995 ($1.75/$1.95/$2.25)
DC Comics

1-6		.70	1.75
7-(9/94)-Begin $1.95-c; Zero Hour x-over		.80	2.00
0,8-14: 0-(10/94). 8-(11/94)		.80	2.00
15-Begin $2.25-c			2.25

ANIMAL ADVENTURES
Dec, 1953 - No. 3, May?, 1954
Timor Publications/Accepted Publications (reprints)

1-Funny animal	4.35	13.00	26.00
2,3: 2-Featuring Soopermutt (2/54)	3.20	8.00	16.00
1-3 (reprints, nd)	1.60	4.00	8.00

ANIMAL ANTICS (Movie Town... No. 24 on)
Mar-Apr, 1946 - No. 23, Nov-Dec, 1949 (All 52 pgs.?)

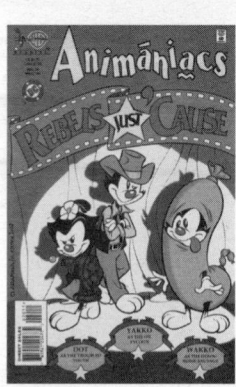
Animaniacs #20 © Warner Bros.

Morrison, Truog & Hazlewood
Animal Man #6 © DC

Annex #1 © MEG

	GD25	FN65	NM94

National Periodical Publications

1-Raccoon Kids begins by Otto Feur; some-c by Grossman; Seaman Sy			
Wheeler by Kelly in some issues	40.00	120.00	325.00
2	24.00	71.00	165.00
3-10: 10-Post-c/a	14.00	43.00	100.00
11-23: 14,15,18,19-Post-a	10.00	30.00	65.00

ANIMAL COMICS
Dec-Jan, 1941-42 - No. 30, Dec-Jan, 1947-48
Dell Publishing Co.

1-1st Pogo app. by Walt Kelly (Dan Noonan art in most issues)			
	95.00	283.00	850.00
2-Uncle Wiggily begins	47.00	142.00	425.00
3,5	34.00	102.00	310.00
4,6,7-No Pogo	21.00	63.00	190.00
8-10	25.00	75.00	225.00
11-15	16.00	50.00	140.00
16-20	11.00	32.00	95.00
21-30: 25-30- "Jigger" by John Stanley	8.00	24.00	70.00

NOTE: **Dan Noonan** a-18-30. **Gollub** art in most later issues; c-29, 30. **Kelly** c-7-26.

ANIMAL CRACKERS (Also see Adventures of Patoruzu)
1946; No. 31, July, 1950; No. 9, 1959
Green Publ. Co./Norlen/Fox Feat.(Hero Books)

1-Super Cat begins (1st app.)	13.00	39.00	90.00
2	8.35	25.00	50.00
3-10 (Exist?)	4.00	11.00	22.00
31(Fox)-Formerly My Love Secret	5.35	16.00	32.00
9(1959-Norlen)-Infinity-c	3.00	7.50	15.00
nn, nd ('50s), no publ.; infinity-c	3.00	7.50	15.00

ANIMAL FABLES
July-Aug, 1946 - No. 7, Nov-Dec, 1947
E. C. Comics (Fables Publ. Co.)

1-Freddy Firefly (clone of Human Torch), Korky Kangaroo, Petey Pig, Danny			
Demon begin	36.00	107.00	250.00
2-Aesop Fables begin	23.00	69.00	160.00
3-6	19.00	58.00	135.00
7-Origin Moon Girl	50.00	150.00	400.00

ANIMAL FAIR (Fawcett's…)
Mar, 1946 - No. 11, Feb, 1947
Fawcett Publications

1	23.00	69.00	160.00
2	11.00	33.00	75.00
3-6	8.70	26.00	52.00
7-11	6.35	19.00	38.00

ANIMAL FUN
1953 (25¢, came w/glasses)
Premier Magazines

1-(3-D)-Ziggy Pig, Silly Seal, Billy & Buggy Bear	33.00	99.00	230.00

ANIMAL MAN (See Action Comics #552, 553, DC Comics Presents #77, 78,
Secret Origins #39, Strange Adventures #180 & Wonder Woman #267, 268)
Sept, 1988 - No. 89, Nov, 1995 ($1.25/$1.50/$1.75/$1.95/$2.25, mature)
DC Comics (Vertigo imprint #57 on)

1-Grant Morrison scripts begin, ends #26	1.65	4.20	10.00
2-Superman cameo	1.30	3.25	8.00
3,4	1.00	2.00	5.00
5-10: 6-Invasion tie-in. 9-Manhunter-c/story		1.60	4.00
11-26: 11-Begin $1.50-c; 24-Arkham Asylum story; Bizarro Superman			
app. 25-Inferior Five app. 26-Morrison apps. in story; part photo-c (of			
Morrison?)		1.00	2.50
27-49,51-55,57-59: 41-Begin $1.75-c, end #59		.80	2.00
50-($2.95, 52 pgs.)-Last issue w/Veitch scripts	1.20		3.00

56-($3.50, 68 pgs.)		1.40	3.50
60-82: 60-Begin $1.95-c. 68-Photo-c. 71-Sutton-a(i)		.80	2.00
83-89: 83-Begin $2.25-c			2.25
Annual 1 (1993, $3.95, 68 pgs.)-Bolland-c; Children's Crusade Pt. 3			
		1.60	4.00

NOTE: **Bolland** c-1-63.

ANIMAL MYSTIC
1993 - Present ($2.95?/$3.50, B&W)
CFD/Sirius

1	7.00	20.50	55.00
1-Alternate	11.50	34.00	85.00
1-2nd printing	2.85	8.50	20.00
2	6.50	19.50	50.00
2,3-2nd prints (Sirius)	1.65	4.20	10.00
3	2.85	8.50	20.00
4-Color poster insert		1.60	4.00

ANIMAL MYSTIC WATER WARS
1996 ($2.95, limited series)
Sirius

1-Dark One-c/a/scripts		1.20	3.00

ANIMAL WORLD, THE (Movie)
No. 713, Aug, 1956
Dell Publishing Co.

Four Color 713	5.00	15.00	50.00

ANIMANIACS (TV)
May, 1995 - Present ($1.50/$1.75)
DC Comics

1-12			1.50
13-24: 13-Manga issue. 19-X-Files parody; Miran Kim-c; Adlard-a (4 pgs.)			
			1.17
A Christmas Special (12/94, $1.50, "1" on-c)			1.50

ANIMATED COMICS
No date given (Summer, 1947?)
E. C. Comics

1 (Rare)	64.00	193.00	500.00

ANIMATED FUNNY COMIC TUNES (See Funny Tunes)

ANIMATED MOVIE-TUNES (Movie Tunes No. 3)
Fall, 1945 - No. 2, Sum, 1946
Margood Publishing Corp. (Timely)

1,2-Super Rabbit, Ziggy Pig & Silly Seal	17.00	51.00	120.00

ANIMAX
Dec, 1986 - No. 4, June, 1987
Marvel Comics (Star Comics)

1-4: Based on toys			1.00

ANNE RICE'S THE MUMMY OR RAMSES THE DAMNED
Oct, 1990 - No. 12, 1991 ($2.50, high quality, limited series)
Millennium Publications

1-12: Adapts novel; Mooney-p in all		1.00	2.50

ANNETTE (Disney, TV)
No. 905, May, 1958; No. 1100, May, 1960 (Mickey Mouse Club)
Dell Publishing Co.

Four Color 905-Annette Funicello photo-c	26.00	78.00	260.00
Four Color 1100-…'s Life Story (Movie); A. Funicello photo-c			
	20.00	60.00	200.00

ANNEX
Aug, 1994 - No. 4, Nov, 1994 ($1.75)
Marvel Comics

1-4: 1-Spider-Man app.		.70	1.75

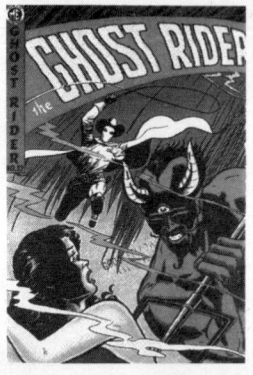

A-1 #1 © MEG

A-1 #32 © ME

A-1 #80 © ME

	GD25	FN65	NM94

ANNIE
Oct, 1982 - No. 2, Nov, 1982 (60¢)
Marvel Comics Group

1,2-Movie adaptation			1.00
Treasury Edition ($2.00, tabloid size)		.80	2.00

ANNIE OAKLEY (See Tessie The Typist #19, Two-Gun Kid & Wild Western)
Spring, 1948 - No. 4, 11/48; No. 5, 6/55 - No. 11, 6/56
Marvel/Atlas Comics(MPI No. 1-4/CDS No. 5 on)

1 (1st Series, 1948)-Hedy Devine app.	40.00	120.00	285.00
2 (7/48, 52 pgs.)-Kurtzman-a, "Hey Look", 1 pg; Intro. Lana; Hedy Devine app; Captain Tootsie by Beck	24.00	71.00	165.00
3,4	19.00	58.00	135.00
5 (2nd Series, 1955)-Reinman-a ; Maneely-c	13.00	39.00	90.00
6-9: 6,8-Woodbridge-a. 9-Williamson-a (4 pgs.)	10.00	30.00	70.00
10,11: 11-Severin-a	10.00	30.00	60.00

ANNIE OAKLEY AND TAGG (TV)
1953 - No. 18, Jan-Mar, 1959; July, 1965 (Gail Davis photo-c #3 on)
Dell Publishing Co./Gold Key

Four Color 438 (#1)	13.00	40.00	130.00
Four Color 481,575 (#2,3)	7.50	23.00	75.00
4(7-9/55)-10	6.80	21.00	68.00
11-18(1-3/59)	5.80	18.00	58.00
1(7/65-Gold Key)-Photo-c (c-r/#6)	4.50	15.00	45.00
NOTE: *Manning* a-13. Photo back c-4, 9, 11.

ANOTHER WORLD (See Strange Stories From...)

ANTHRO (See Showcase #74)
July-Aug, 1968 - No. 6, July-Aug, 1969
National Periodical Publications

1-(7-8/68)-Howie Post-a in all	5.50	16.50	40.00
2-6: 6-Wood-c/a (inks)	3.40	10.00	24.00

ANTONY AND CLEOPATRA (See Ideal, a Classical Comic)

ANYTHING GOES
Oct, 1986 - No. 6, 1987 ($2.00, #1-5 color & B&W/#6 B&W, limited series)
Fantagraphics Books

1-Flaming Carrot app. (1st in color?); G. Kane-c	1.20		3.00
2-6: 2-Miller-c(p); Alan Moore scripts; early Sam Kieth-a (2 pgs.). 3-Capt. Jack, Cerebus app.; Cerebus-c by N. Adams. 4-Perez-c. 5-2nd color Teenage Mutant Ninja Turtles app.		.80	2.00

A-1
1992 - No. 4, 1993 ($5.95, limited series, mature)
Marvel Comics (Epic Comics)

1-4: 3-Bisley-c	1.00	2.50	6.00

A-1 COMICS (A-1 appears on covers No. 1-17 only)(See individual title listings.)
(1st two issues not numbered.)
1944 - No. 139, Sept-Oct, 1955 (No #2)
Life's Romances Publ.-No. 1/Compix/Magazine Ent.
(See Individual Alphabetical listings for prices)

nn-Kerry Drake, Johnny Devildog, Rocky, Streamer Kelly (slightly large size)	1-Dotty Dripple (1 pg.), Mr. Ex, Bush Berry, Rocky, Lew Loyal (20 pgs.)
9-Texas Slim (all)	2-8,10-Texas Slim & Dirty Dalton, The Corsair, Teddy Rich, Dotty Dripple, Inca Dinca, Tommy Tinker, Little Mexico & Tugboat Tim, The Masquerader & others. 7-Corsair-c/s. 8-Intro. Rodeo Ryan
11-Teena; Ogden Whitney-c	
12,15-Teena	
13-Guns of Fact & Fiction (1948). Used in SOTI, pg. 19; Ingels & Johnny Craig-a	
16-Vacation Comics; The Pixies, Tom Tom, Flying Fredd, & Koko & Kola	14-Tim Holt Western Adventures #1 (1948)
18,20-Jimmy Durante; photo covers	17-Tim Holt #2; photo-c; last issue to carry A-1 on cover (9-10/48)
19-Tim Holt #3; photo-c	21-Joan of Arc (1949)-Movie adapta

22-Dick Powell (1949)-Photo-c	tion; Ingrid Bergman photo-covers & interior photos; Whitney-a
23-Cowboys and Indians #6; Doc Holiday-c/story	24-Trail Colt #1-Frazetta-r in-Manhunt #13; Ingels-c; L. B. Cole-a
25-Fibber McGee & Molly (1949) (Radio)	27-Ghost Rider #1(1950)-Origin
26-Trail Colt #2-Ingels-c	29-Ghost Rider #2-Frazetta-c (1950)
28-Christmas-(Koko & Kola #6) ("50)	31-Ghost Rider #3-Frazetta-c & origin ('51)
30-Jet Powers #1('51)	
32-Jet Powers #2	34-Ghost Rider #4-Frazetta-c (1951)
33-Muggsy Mouse #1('51)	36-Muggsy Mouse #2; Racist-c
35-Jet Powers #3-Williamson/Evans-a	38-Jet Powers #4-Williamson/Wood-a
37-Ghost Rider #5-Frazetta-c (1951)	40-Dogface Dooley #1('51)
39-Muggsy Mouse #3	42-Best of the West #1-Powell-a
41-Cowboys 'N' Indians #7	44-Ghost Rider #6
43-Dogface Dooley #2	46-Best of the West #2
45-American Air Forces #5-Powell-c/a	48-Cowboys 'N' Indians #8
47-Thun'da, King of the Congo #1-Frazetta-c/a('52)	49-Dogface Dooley #3
50-Danger Is Their Business #11 ('52)-Powell-a	51-Ghost Rider #7 ('52)
	52-Best of the West #3
53-Dogface Dooley #4	54-American Air Forces #6(8/52)-Powell-a
55-U.S. Marines #5-Powell-a	57-Ghost Rider #8
56-Thun'da #2-Powell-c/a	59-Best of the West #4
58-American Air Forces #7-Powell-a	61-Space Ace #5(1953)-Guardineer-a
60-The U.S. Marines #6-Powell-a	63-Manhunt #13-Frazetta
62-Starr Flagg, Undercover Girl #5 (#1) reprinted from A-1 #24	64-Dogface Dooley #5
65-American Air Forces #8-Powell-a	66-Best of the West #5
67-American Air Forces #9-Powell-a	68-U.S. Marines #7-Powell-a
69-Ghost Rider #9(10/52)	70-Best of the West #6
71-Ghost Rider #10(12/52)-Vs. Frankenstein	72-U.S. Marines #8-Powell-a(3)
74-American Air Forces #10-Powell-a	73-Thun'da #3-Powell-c/a
76-Best of the West #7	75-Ghost Rider #11(3/52)
78-Thun'da #4-Powell-c/a	77-Manhunt #14
80-Ghost Rider #12(6/52)-One-eyed Devil-c	79-American Air Forces #11-Powell-a
83-Thun'da #5-Powell-c/a	81-Best of the West #8
84-American Air Forces #13(7-8/53)	82-Cave Girl #11(1953)-Powell-c/a; origin (#1)
86-Thun'da #6-Powell-a	85-Best of the West #9
88-Bobby Benson's B-Bar-B Riders #20	87-Best of the West #10(9-10/53)
90-Red Hawk #11(1953)-Powell-c/a	89-Home Run #3-Powell-a; Stan Musial photo-c
91-American Air Forces #9-Powell-a	92-Dream Book of Romance #5-Photo-c; Guardineer-a
93-Great Western #8('54)-Origin The Ghost Rider; Powell-a	94-White Indian #11-Frazetta-a(r); Powell-c
95-Muggsy Mouse #4	97-Best of the West #11
96-Cave Girl #12, with Thun'da; Powell-c/a	98-Undercover Girl #6-Powell-c
99-Muggsy Mouse #5	100-Badmen of the West #1-Meskin-a(?)
101-White Indian #12-Frazetta-a(r)	103-Best of the West #12-Powell-a
101-Dream Book of Romance #6 (4-6/54); Marlon Brando photo-c; Powell, Bolle, Guardineer-a	104-White Indian #13-Frazetta-a(r) ('54)
105-Great Western #9-Ghost Rider app.; Powell-a, 6 pgs.; Bolle-c	106-Dream Book of Love #1 (6-7/54) -Powell, Bolle-a; Montgomery Clift, Donna Reed photo-c
107-Hot Dog #1	109-Dream Book of Romance #7 (7-8/54). Powell-a; movie photo-c
108-Red Fox #15 (1954)-L.B. Cole c/a; Powell-a	111-I'm a Cop #1 ('54); drug mention story; Powell-a
110-Dream Book of Romance #8 (10/54)-Movie photo-c	113-Great Western #10; Powell-a
112-Ghost Rider #14 ('54)	115-Hot Dog #3
114-Dream Book of Love #2-Guardineer, Bolle-a; Piper Laurie, Victor Mature photo-c	116-Cave Girl #13-Powell-c/a
	117-White Indian #14
118-Undercover Girl #7-Powell-c	119-Straight Arrow's Fury #1 (origin);

Aquaman (1st Limited Series) #2 © DC

Aquaman #1 (2nd Series) © DC

Aquaman (3rd Series) #7 © DC

	GD25	FN65	NM94			GD25	FN65	NM94

120-Badmen of the West #2
121-Mysteries of Scotland Yard #1;
reprinted from Manhunt (5 stories)
124-Dream Book of Romance #8
(10-11/54)
126-I'm a Cop #2-Powell-a
128-I'm a Cop #3-Powell-a
130-Strongman #1-Powell-a (2-3/55)
132-Strongman #2
134-Strongman #3
136-Hot Dog #4
138-The Avenger #4-Powell-c/a

Fred Meagher-c/a
122-Black Phantom #1 (11/54)
123-Dream Book of Love #3
(10-11/54)-Movie photo-c
125-Cave Girl #14-Powell-c/a
127-Great Western #11('54)-Powell-a
129-The Avenger #1('55)-Powell-a
131-The Avenger #2('55)-Powell-a
133-The Avenger #3-Powell-c/a
135-White Indian #15
137-Africa #1-Powell-c/a(4)
139-Strongman #4-Powell-a

NOTE: *Bolle* a-110. Photo-c-17-22, 89, 92, 101, 106, 109, 110, 114, 123, 124.

APACHE
1951
Fiction House Magazines

1	18.00	54.00	125.00
I.W. Reprint No. 1-r/#1 above	2.80	7.00	14.00

APACHE HUNTER
1954 (18 pgs. in color) (promo copy) (saddle stitched)
Creative Pictorials

nn-Severin, Heath stories	16.00	48.00	110.00

APACHE KID (Formerly Reno Browne; Western Gunfighters #20 on)
(Also see Two-Gun Western & Wild Western)
No. 53, 12/50 - No. 10, 1/52; No. 11, 2/54 - No. 19, 4/56
Marvel/Atlas Comics(MPC No. 53-10/CPS No. 11 on)

53(#1)-Apache Kid & his horse Nightwind (origin), Red Hawkins by Syd Shores begins	27.00	81.00	190.00
2(2/51)	13.00	39.00	90.00
3-5	10.00	30.00	60.00
6-10 (1951-52): 7-Russ Heath-a	7.50	22.50	45.00
11-19 (1954-56)	5.85	17.50	35.00

NOTE: *Heath* a-7. c-11, 13. *Maneely* a-53; c-53(#1), 12, 14-16. *Powell* a-14. *Severin* c-17.

APACHE MASSACRE (See Chief Victorio's...)

APACHE TRAIL
Sept, 1957 - No. 4, June, 1958
Steinway/America's Best

1	9.15	27.50	55.00
2-4: 2-Tuska-a	5.00	15.00	30.00

APPARITION
1995 ($3.95, 52 pgs., B&W)
Caliber Comics

1 ($3.95)		1.60	4.00
1 ($2.95)			3.00
Visitations		1.60	4.00

APPLESEED
Sept, 1988 - Book 4, Vol. 4, Aug, 1991 ($2.50/$2.75/$3.50, 52/68 pgs, B&W)
Eclipse Comics

Book One, Vol. 1 ($2.50)	1.65	4.00	10.00
Book One, Vol. 2-5 (1/89, $2.75 cover)		1.20	3.00
Book Two, Vol. 1(2/89) -5(7/89): Art Adams-c		1.20	3.00
Book Three, Vol. 1(8/89) -4 ($2.75)		1.20	3.00
Book Three, Vol. 5 ($3.50)		1.20	3.00
Book Four, Vol. 1 (1/91) - 4 (8/91) ($3.50, 68 pgs.)		1.20	3.00

APPLESEED DATABOOK
Apr, 1994 - No. 2, May, 1994 ($3.50, B&W, limited series)
Dark Horse Comics

1,2: 1-Flip book format		1.40	3.50

APPROVED COMICS

March, 1954 - No. 12, Aug, 1954 (All painted-c)
St. John Publishing Co. (Most have no c-price)

1-The Hawk #5-r	9.15	27.50	55.00
2-Invisible Boy (3/54)-Origin; Saunders-c	14.00	43.00	100.00
3-Wild Boy of the Congo #11-r (4/54)	9.15	27.50	55.00
4,5: 4-Kid Cowboy-r. 5-Fly Boy-r	9.15	27.50	55.00
6-Daring Adv.-r (5/54); Krigstein-a(2); Baker-c	10.00	30.00	70.00
7-The Hawk #6-r	9.15	27.50	55.00
8-Crime on the Run (6/54); Powell-a; Saunders-c	9.15	27.50	55.00
9-Western Bandit Trails #3-r, with new-c; Baker-c/a	10.00	30.00	70.00
11-Fightin' Marines #3-r (8/54); Canteen Kate app; Baker-c/a	11.00	33.00	75.00
12-North West Mounties #4-r(8/54); new Baker-c	11.00	33.00	75.00

AQUAMAN (See Adventure #260, Brave & the Bold, DC Comics Presents #5, DC Special #28, DC Special Series #1, DC Super Stars #7, Detective, Justice League of America, More Fun #73, Showcase #30-33, Super DC Giant, Super Friends, and World's Finest Comics)

AQUAMAN (1st Series)
Jan-Feb, 1962 - #56, Mar-Apr, 1971; #57, Aug-Sept,1977 - #63, Aug-Sept, 1978
National Periodical Publications/DC Comics

1-(1-2/62)-Intro. Quisp	69.00	206.00	600.00
2	34.00	101.00	250.00
3-5	19.00	56.00	140.00
6-10: 9-Sea Devils app.	12.00	36.00	90.00
11-20: 11-1st app. Mera. 18-Aquaman weds Mera; JLA cameo	10.00	30.00	75.00
21-32,34-40: 23-Birth of Aquababy. 26-Huntress app.(3-4/66). 29-1st app. Ocean Master, Aquaman's step-brother. 30-Batman & Superman-c & cameo. 40-Jim Aparo's 1st DC work (8/68).	8.00	23.50	60.00
33-1st app. Aqua-Girl (see Adventure #266)	10.00	30.00	75.00
41-47,49	4.00	12.00	30.00
48-Origin reprinted	4.50	14.00	35.00
50-52-Deadman by Neal Adams	6.00	18.00	45.00
53-56('71): 56-1st app. Crusader	1.70	5.00	12.00
57('77)-63: 58-Origin retold	1.30	3.25	8.00

NOTE: *Aparo* a-40-45, 46p, 47-59; c-58-63. *Nick Cardy* c-1-39. *Newton* c-60-63.

AQUAMAN (1st limited series)
Feb, 1986 - No. 4, May, 1986 (75¢, limited series)
DC Comics

1-New costume; 1st app. Nuada of Thierna Na Oge.		1.60	4.00
2-4: 3-Retelling of Aquaman & Ocean Master's origins.		.80	2.00
Special 1 (1988, $1.50, 52 pgs.)		.80	2.00

NOTE: *Craig Hamilton* c/a-1-4p. *Russell* c-2-4i.

AQUAMAN (2nd limited series)
June, 1989 - No. 5, Oct, 1989 ($1.00, limited series)
DC Comics

1-5: Giffen plots/breakdowns; Swan-a(p).			1.25
Special 1 (Legend of..., $2.00, 1989, 52 pgs.)-Giffen plots/breakdowns; Swan-a(p).		.80	2.00

AQUAMAN (2nd Series)
Dec, 1991 - No. 13, Dec, 1992 ($1.00/$1.25)
DC Comics

1-5			1.25
6-13: 6-Begin $1.25-c. 9-Sea Devils app.			1.50

AQUAMAN (3rd Series)(Also see Atlantis Chronicles)
Aug, 1994 - Present ($1.50/$1.75)
DC Comics

1-(8/94)-Peter David scripts begin; reintro Dolphin		1.60	4.00
2-(9/94)-Aquaman loses hand	1.00	2.00	5.00
0,3-8: 0- (10/94)-Aquaman replaces lost hand w/hook.			
3-(11/94)-Superboy-c/app. 4-Lobo app. 6-Deep Six app.			1.50

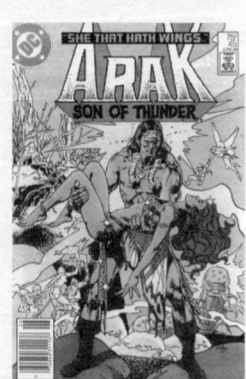
Arak/Son of Thunder #45 © DC

Arcana Annual #1 © DC

Archangel #1 © MEG

	GD25	FN65	NM94

9-35: 9-Begin $1.75-c. 10-Green Lantern app. 11-Reintro Mera.
15-Reintro Kordax. 16-vs. JLA. 18-Reintro Ocean Master & Atlan (Aquaman's father). 19-Reintro Garth (Aqualad). 23-1st app. Deep Blue (Neptune Perkins & Tsunami's daughter). 23,24-Neptune Perkins, Nuada, Tsunami, Arion, Power Girl, & The Sea Devils app. ... 1.75

	GD25	FN65	NM94
Annual 1 (1995, $3.50)-Year One story	1.40	3.50	
Annual 2 (1996, $2.95)-Legends of the Dead Earth story		3.00	

NOTE: **Mignola** c-6. **Simonson** c-15.

AQUAMAN: TIME & TIDE (3rd limited series) (Also see Atlantis Chronicles)
Dec, 1993 - No. 4, Mar, 1994 ($1.50, limited series)
DC Comics

	GD25	FN65	NM94
1-4: Peter David scripts; origin retold.	.80	2.00	
Trade paperback ($9.95)		10.00	

AQUANAUTS (TV)
May - July, 1961
Dell Publishing Co.

	GD25	FN65	NM94
Four Color 1197-Photo-c	6.30	19.00	63.00

ARABIAN NIGHTS (See Cinema Comics Herald)

ARACHNOPHOBIA (Movie)
1990 ($5.95, 68 pg. graphic novel)
Hollywood Comics (Disney Comics)

	GD25	FN65	NM94
nn-Adaptation of film; Spiegle-a	1.00	2.50	6.00
Comic edition ($2.95, 68 pgs.)	1.20	3.00	

ARAKNIS
1995 - No. 4, 1996 ($2.50, limited series)
Mushroom Comics

	GD25	FN65	NM94
1,2	1.60	4.00	
3,4: 3-w/pin-ups	1.00	2.50	

ARAKNIS
No. 0, Apr, 1996 - Present ($2.95/$2.50)
Mushroom Comics

	GD25	FN65	NM94
0-(4/96, $2.95)			3.00
0-Special Edition			5.00
1			2.50
1-Special Edition; polybagged w/certificate			10.00

ARAK/SON OF THUNDER (See Warlord #48)
Sept, 1981 - No. 50, Nov, 1985
DC Comics

1-50: 1-Origin; 1st app. Angelica, Princess of White Cathay. 3-Intro Valda, The Iron Maiden. 12-Origin Valda. 20-Origin Angelica. 24,50-(52 pgs.)

	GD25	FN65	NM94
			1.00
Annual 1(10/84)			1.00

ARCANA (Also see Books of Magic limited & ongoing series and Mister E)
1994 ($3.95, 68 pgs., annual)
DC Comics (Vertigo)

	GD25	FN65	NM94
1-Bolton painted-c; Children's Crusade/Tim Hunter story			
	1.60	4.00	

ARCHANGEL (See Uncanny X-Men, X-Factor & X-Men)
Feb, 1996 ($2.50, B&W, one-shot)
Marvel Comics

	GD25	FN65	NM94
1-Milligan story			2.50

ARCHER & ARMSTRONG
July (June inside), 1992 - No. 25, Sept, 1994 ($2.50)
Valiant

	GD25	FN65	NM94
0-(7/92)-B. Smith-c/a; Reese-i assists		1.60	4.00
0-(Gold Logo)	2.15	6.50	15.00
1-(8/92)-Origin & 1st app. Archer; Miller-c; B. Smith/Layton-a			
	1.20	3.00	

2-7: 2-2nd app. Turok(c/story); Smith/Layton-a; Simonson-c. 3,4-Smith-c&a(p) & scripts ... 1.20 ... 3.00
8-($4.50, 52 pgs.)-Combined with Eternal Warrior #8; B. Smith-c/a & scripts; 1st app. Ivar the Time Walker ... 1.80 ... 4.50
9-25: 10-2nd app. Ivar. 10,11-B. Smith-c. 21,22-Shadowman app. 22-w/bound-in trading card. 25-Eternal Warrior app. ... 1.00 ... 2.50

ARCHIE AMERICANA SERIES, BEST OF THE SIXTIES
1995 ($9.95, trade paperback)
Archie Publications

V3-r/strips from Archie #167; Betty & Veronica #67,101,105,135,138,142,156; Laugh #162; Life w/Archie #78, 84; Jughead #154; Pep #219,225,229; introduction by Frankie Avalon. ... 1.65 ... 4.20 ... 10.00

ARCHIE AND BIG ETHEL
1982 (69¢)
Spire Christian Comics (Fleming H. Revell Co.)

	GD25	FN65	NM94
nn			1.00

ARCHIE & FRIENDS
Dec, 1992 - Present ($1.25/$1.50, quarterly)
Archie Comics

	GD25	FN65	NM94
1-13			1.25
14-25: 14-Begin $1.50-c			1.50

ARCHIE AND ME (See Archie Giant Series Mag. #578, 591, 603, 616, 626)
Oct, 1964 - No. 161, Feb, 1987
Archie Publications

	GD25	FN65	NM94
1	13.50	54.00	135.00
2	6.50	26.00	65.00
3-5	3.20	14.00	32.00
6-10	1.80	7.50	18.00
11-20	.90	3.75	9.00
21-30: 26-X-Mas-c	.60	2.60	6.00
31-63: 43-63-(All Giants)		1.20	3.00
64-161-(Regular size)			1.20

ARCHIE AND MR. WEATHERBEE
1980 (59¢)
Spire Christian Comics (Fleming H. Revell Co.)

	GD25	FN65	NM94
nn			.60

ARCHIE...ARCHIE ANDREWS, WHERE ARE YOU? (...Comics Digest #9, 10; ...Comics Digest Mag. No. 11 on)
Feb, 1977 - Present (Digest size, 160-128 pgs., published 6 times a year)
Archie Publications

	GD25	FN65	NM94
1		1.80	4.50
2,3,5,7-9-N. Adams-a; 8-r-/origin The Fly by S&K. 9-Steel Sterling-r		1.30	3.20
4,6,10-50 ($1.00/$1.50): 17-Katy Keene story		.85	2.20
51-103		.80	2.00

ARCHIE AS PUREHEART THE POWERFUL (Also see Archie Giant Series #142, Jughead as Captain Hero, Life With Archie & Little Archie)
Sept, 1966 - No. 6, Nov, 1967
Archie Publications (Radio Comics)

	GD25	FN65	NM94
1-Super hero parody	6.00	26.00	60.00
2	4.00	17.00	40.00
3-6	3.00	13.00	30.00

NOTE: Evilheart cameos in all. Title: Archie As Pureheart the Powerful #1-3; ...As Capt. Pureheart-#4-6.

ARCHIE AT RIVERDALE HIGH (See Archie Giant Series Magazine #573, 586, 604 & Riverdale High)
Aug, 1972 - No. 113, Feb, 1987
Archie Publications

	GD25	FN65	NM94
1	3.80	16.50	38.00

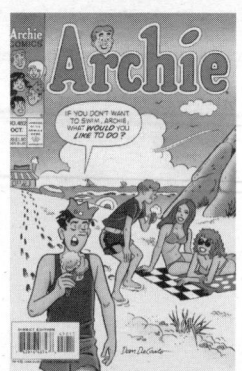

Archie Comics #38 © Archie Publ.

Archie Comics #452 © Archie publ.

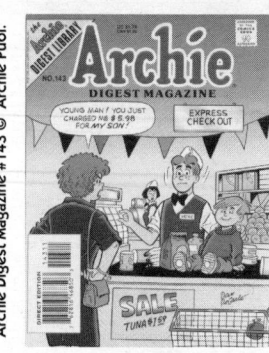

Archie Digest Magazine #143 © Archie Publ.

	GD25	FN65	NM94
2	1.60	6.70	16.00
3-5	.80	3.25	8.00
6-10		1.80	4.50
11-30		.80	2.00
31-114: 96-Anti-smoking issue			1.00

ARCHIE COMICS (Also see Christmas & Archie, Everything's..., Explorers of the Unknown, Jackpot, Little..., Oxydol-Dreft, Pep, Riverdale High, Teenage Mutant Ninja Turtles Adventures & To Riverdale and Back Again)

ARCHIE COMICS (Archie #158 on; 1st Teen-age comic; Radio show aired 6/2/45 by NBC)
Winter, 1942-43 - No. 19, 3-4/46; No. 20, 5-6/46 - Present
MLJ Magazines No. 1-19/Archie Publ.No. 20 on

	GD25	FN65	VF82	NM94
1 (Scarce)-Jughead, Veronica app.; 1st app. Mrs. Andrews	945.00	2833.00	5667.00	9000.00

(Estimated up to 50+ total copies exist, 5 in NM/Mint)

	GD25	FN65	NM94
2	275.00	825.00	2200.00
3 (60 pgs.)(scarce)	200.00	600.00	1600.00
4,5: 4-Article about Archie radio series	105.00	320.00	850.00
6-10: 6-X-Mas-c. 7-1st definitive love triangle story	75.00	225.00	600.00
11-20: 15,17,18-Dotty & Ditto by Woggon. 16-Woggon-a	50.00	150.00	400.00
21-30: 23-Betty & Veronica by Woggon. 25-Woggon-a. 30-Coach Piffle app., a Coach Kleets prototype. 34-Pre-Dilton try-out (named Dilbert)	33.00	100.00	265.00
31-40	18.00	54.00	145.00
41-50	13.00	38.00	100.00
51-60: (1954) 51-Katy Keene app.	9.00	27.00	70.00
61-70 (1954): 65-70, Katy Keene app.	8.00	24.00	55.00
71-80: 72-74-Katy Keene app.	5.50	17.00	45.00
81-99: 94-1st Coach Kleets	4.50	13.00	35.00
100	5.50	17.00	44.00
101-130 (1962)	2.00	8.50	20.00
131-160	1.00	3.00	10.00
161-200	.60	1.80	6.00
201-240		1.00	2.50
241-282		.70	1.75
283-Cover/story plugs "International Children's Appeal" which was a fraudulent charity, according to TV's 20/20 news program broadcast July 20, 1979		1.00	2.50
284-445: 300-Anniversary issue. 393-Infinity-c; 1st comic book printed on recycled paper. 423-Dan DeCarlo-c			1.25
446-465			1.50
Annual 1('50)-116 pgs. (Scarce)	162.00	490.00	1300.00
Annual 2('51)	81.00	240.00	650.00
Annual 3('52)	50.00	150.00	400.00
Annual 4,5(1953-54)	37.00	111.00	260.00
Annual 6-10(1955-59)	20.00	60.00	140.00
Annual 11-15(1960-65)	7.00	20.00	55.00
Annual 16-20(1966-70)	2.85	8.50	20.00
Annual 21-26(1971-75)	1.30	3.25	8.00
Annual Digest 27('75)-65('83-'94, $1.50-1.75)(...Magazine #35 on)		1.00	2.50
...All-Star Specials(Winter '75, $1.25)-6 remaindered Archie comics rebound in each; titles: "The World of Giant Comics", "Giant Grab Bag of Comics", "Triple Giant Comics" & "Giant Spec. Comics	1.00	2.00	5.00
...And His Friends Help Raise Literacy Awareness In Mississippi nn (3/94)-Giveaway			1.00
...And the History of Electronics nn (5/90, 36 pgs.)-Radio Shack giveaway; Howard Bender-c/a			1.00
Mini-Comics (1970-Fairmont Potato Chips Giveaway-Miniature)(8 issues-nn's, 8 pgs. each)	1.70	5.00	12.00

	GD25	FN65	NM94
Official Boy Scout Outfitter (1946, 9-1/2x6-1/2, 16 pgs.)-B. R. Baker Co. (Scarce)	44.00	132.00	350.00
Shoe Store giveaway (1948, Feb?)	15.00	45.00	105.00
...Vacation Special 1 (Summer 1994, $2.00, 52 pgs. plus poster)			2.00

NOTE: *Al Fagly* c-17-35. *Bob Montana* c-38, 41-50, 58, Annual 1-4. *Bill Woggon* c-53, 54.

ARCHIE COMICS DIGEST (...Magazine No. 37-95)
Aug, 1973 - Present (Small size, 160-128 pgs.)
Archie Publications

	GD25	FN65	NM94
1	3.60	15.50	36.00
2	1.80	7.50	18.00
3-5	.90	3.75	9.00
6-10	.55	2.50	5.50
11-33: 32,33-The Fly-r by S&K		1.00	2.50
34-140: 36-Katy Keene story		.70	1.75
141-155			1.79

NOTE: *Neal Adams* a-1, 2, 4, 5, 19-21, 24, 25, 27, 29, 31, 33. X-mas c-88, 94, 100, 106.

ARCHIE COMICS PRESENTS: THE LOVE SHOWDOWN COLLECTION
1994 ($4.95, squarebound)
Archie Publications

	GD25	FN65	NM94
nn-r/Archie #429, Betty #19, Betty & Veronica #82, & Veronica #39	1.00	2.00	5.00

ARCHIE GETS A JOB
1977
Spire Christian Comics (Fleming H. Revell Co.)

nn			1.00

ARCHIE GIANT SERIES MAGAZINE
1954 - No. 632, July, 1992 (No No. 36-135, no No. 252-451)(#1 not code approved)
Archie Publications

	GD25	FN65	NM94
1-Archie's Christmas Stocking	105.00	320.00	850.00
2-Archie's Christmas Stocking('55)	65.00	195.00	525.00
3-6-Archie's Christmas Stocking('56 - '59)	45.00	140.00	365.00
7-10: 7-Katy Keene Holiday Fun(9/60); Bill Woggon-c. 8-Betty & Veronica Summer Fun(10/60). 9-The World of Jughead (12/60). 10-Archie's Christmas Stocking(1/61)	34.00	102.00	240.00
11,13,16,18: 11-Betty & Veronica Spectacular (6/61). 13-Betty & Veronica Summer Fun (10/61). 16-Betty & Veronica Spectacular (6/62). 18-Betty & Veronica Summer Fun (10/62)	25.00	75.00	175.00
12,14,15,17,19,20: 12-Katy Keene Holiday Fun (9/61). 14-The World of Jughead (12/61). 15-Archie's Christmas Stocking (1/62). 17-Archie's Jokes (9/62); Katy Keene app. 19-The World of Jughead (12/62). 20-Archie's Christmas Stocking (1/63)	11.50	34.50	115.00
21,23,26,28: 21-Betty & Veronica Spectacular (6/63). 23-Betty & Veronica Summer Fun (10/63). 26-Betty & Veronica (6/64). 28-Betty & Veronica Summer Fun (9/64)	8.00	24.00	80.00
22,24,25,27,29,30: 22-Archie's Jokes (9/63). 24-The World of Jughead (12/63). 25-Archie's Christmas Stocking (1/64). 27-Archie's Jokes (8/64). 29-Around the World with Archie (10/64). 30-The World of Jughead (12/64)	5.00	16.50	55.00
31-35,136-141: 31-Archie's Christmas Stocking (1/65). 32-Betty & Veronica Spectacular (6/65). 33-Archie's Jokes (8/65). 34-Betty & Veronica Summer Fun (9/65). 35-Around the World with Archie (10/65). 136-The World of Jughead (12/65). 137-Archie's Christmas Stocking (1/66). 138-Betty & Veronica Spectacular (6/66). 139-Archie's Jokes (8/66). 140-Betty & Veronica Summer Fun (8/66). 141-Around the World with Archie (9/66)	4.00	12.00	40.00
142-Archie's Super-Hero Special (10/66)-Origin Capt. Pureheart, Capt. Hero, and Evilheart	4.00	12.00	40.00
143-160: 143-The World of Jughead (12/66). 144-Betty & Veronica Summer Fun (1/67). 145-Betty & Veronica Spectacular (6/67). 146-Archie's Jokes (6/67). 147-Betty & Veronica Summer Fun (8/67) 148-World of Archie (9/67). 149-World of Jughead (10/67). 150-Archie's Christmas Stocking (1/68). 151-			

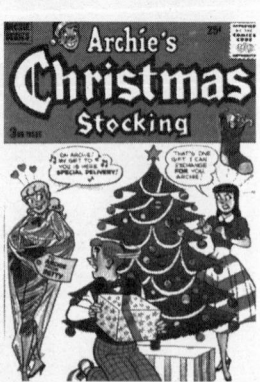

Archie Giant Series #1 © Archie Publ.

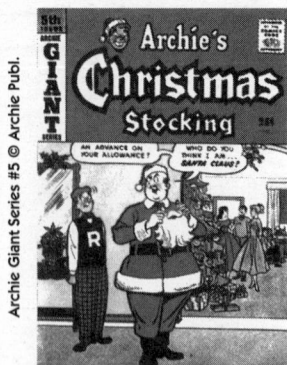

Archie Giant Series #5 © Archie Publ.

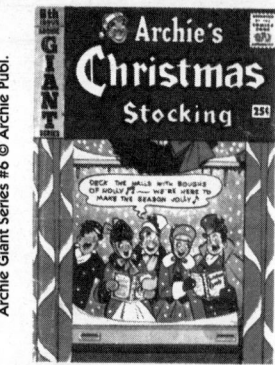

Archie Giant Series #6 © Archie Publ.

| | GD25 | FN65 | NM94 | | GD25 | FN65 | NM94 |

World of Archie (2/68). 152-World of Jughead (2/68). 153-Betty & Veronica Spectacular (6/68). 154-Archie Jokes (6/68). 155-Betty & VeronicaSummer Fun (6/68). 156-World of Archie (10/68). 157-World of Jughead (12/68). 158-Archie's Christmas Stocking (1/69). 159-Betty & Veronica Christmas Spectacular (1/69). 160-World of Archie (2/69) . . . . 1.80 . . . 5.50 . . 18.00

161-200: 161-World of Jughead (2/69). 162-Betty & Veronica Spectacular (6/69). 163-Archie's Jokes(8/69). 164-Betty & Veronica Summer Fun (9/69). 165-World of Archie (9/69). 166-World of Jughead (9/69). 167-Archie's Christmas Stocking (1/70). 168-Betty & Veronica Christmas Spect. (1/70). 169-Archie's Christmas Love-In (1/70). 170-Jughead's Eat-Out Comic Book Mag. (12/69). 171-World of Archie (2/70). 172-World of Jughead (2/70). 173-Betty & Veronica Spectacular (6/70). 174-Archie's Jokes (8/70). 175-Betty & Veronica Summer Fun (9/70). 176-Li'l Jinx Giant Laugh-Out (8/70). 177-World of Archie (9/70). 178-World of Jughead (9/70). 179-Archie's Christmas Stocking (12/71). 180-Betty & Veronica Christmas Spect. (1/71). 181-Archie's Christmas Love-In (1/71). 182-World of Archie (2/71). 183-World of Jughead (2/71). 184-Betty & Veronica Spectacular (6/71). 185-Li'l Jinx Giant Laugh-Out (6/71). 186-Archie's Jokes (8/71). 187-Betty & Veronica Summer Fun (9/71). 188-World of Archie (9/71). 189-World of Jughead (9/71). 190-Archie's Christmas Stocking (12/71). 191-Betty & Veronica Christmas Spectacular (2/72). 192-Archie's Christmas Love-In (1/72). 193-World of Archie (3/72). 194-World of Jughead (4/72). 195-Li'l Jinx Christmas Bag (1/72). 196-Sabrina's Christmas Magic (1/72). 197-Betty & Veronica Spectacular (6/72). 198-Archie's Jokes (8/72). 199-Betty & Veronica Summer Fun (9/72). 200-World of Archie (10/72) . . . . 1.20 . . . 3.00 . . . 7.00

201-251: 201-Betty & Veronica Spectacular (10/72). 202-World of Jughead (11/72). 203-Archie's Christmas Stocking (12/72). 204-Betty & Veronica Christmas Spectacular (2/73). 205-Archie's Christmas Love-In (1/73). 206-Li'l Jinx Christmas Bag (12/72). 207-Sabrina's Christmas Magic (12/72). 208-World of Archie (3/73). 209-World of Jughead (4/73). 210-Betty & Veronica Spectacular (6/73). 211-Archie's Jokes (8/73). 212-Betty & Veronica Summer Fun (9/73). 213-World of Archie (10/73). 214-Betty & Veronica Spectacular (10/73). 215-World of Jughead (11/73). 216-Archie's Christmas Stocking (12/73). 217-Betty & Veronica Christmas Spectacular (2/74). 218-Archie's Christmas Love-In (1/74). 219-Li'l Jinx Christmas Bag (12/73). 220-Sabrina's Christmas Magic (12/73). 221-Betty & Veronica Spectacular (Advertised as World of Jughead) (6/74). 222-Archie's Jokes (advertised as World of Jughead) (8/74). 223-Li'l Jinx (8/74). 224-Betty & Veronica Summer Fun (9/74). 225-World of Archie (9/74). 226-Betty & Veronica Spectacular (10/74). 227-World of Jughead (10/74). 228-Archie's Christmas Stocking (12/74). 229-Betty & Veronica Christmas Spectacular (2/74). 230-Archie's Christmas Love-In (1/75). 231-Sabrina's Christmas Magic (1/75). 232-World of Archie (3/75). 233-World of Jughead (4/75). 234-Betty & Veronica Spectacular (6/75). 235-Archie's Jokes (8/75). 236-Betty & Veronica Summer Fun (9/75). 237-World of Archie (9/75) 238-Betty & Veronica Spectacular (10/75). 239-World of Jughead (10/75). 240-Archie's Christmas Stocking (12/75). 241-Betty & Veronica Christmas Spectacular (12/75). 242-Archie's Christmas Love-In (1/76). 243-Sabrina's Christmas Magic (1/76). 244-World of Archie (3/76). 245-World of Jughead (4/76). 246-Betty & Veronica Spectacular (6/76). 247-Archie's Jokes (8/76). 248-Betty & Veronica Summer Fun (9/76). 249-World of Archie (9/76). 250-Betty & Veronica Spectacular (10/76). 251-World of Jughead each. . . . . 1.30 . . . 3.25

452-500: 452-Archie's Christmas Stocking (12/76). 453-Betty & Veronica Christmas Spectacular (12/76). 454-Archie's Christmas Love-In (1/77). 455-Sabrina's Christmas Magic (1/77). 456-World of Archie (3/77). 457-World of Jughead (4/77). 458-Betty & Veronica Spectacular (6/77). 459-Archie's Jokes (8/77)-Shows 8/76 in error. 460-Betty & Veronica Summer Fun (9/77). 461-World of Jughead (10/77). 462-Betty & Veronica Spectacular (10/77). 463-World of Jughead (10/77). 464-Archie's Christmas Stocking (12/77). 465-Betty & Veronica Christmas Spectacular (12/77). 466-Archie's Christmas Love-In (1/78). 467-Sabrina's Christmas Magic (1/78). 468-World of Archie (2/78). 469-World of Jughead (2/78). 470-Betty & Veronica Spectacular(6/78). 471-Archie's Jokes (8/78). 472-Betty & Veronica Summer Fun (9/78). 473-World of Archie (9/78). 474-Betty & Veronica

Spectacular (10/78). 475-World of Jughead (10/78). 476-Archie's Christmas Stocking (12/78). 477-Betty & Veronica Christmas Spectacular (12/78). 478-Archie's Christmas Love-In (1/79). 479-Sabrina Christmas Magic (1/79). 480-The World of Archie (3/79). 481-World of Jughead (4/79). 482-Betty & Veronica Spectacular (6/79). 483-Archie's Jokes (8/79). 484-Betty & Veronica Summer Fun(9/79). 485-The World of Archie (9/79). 486-Betty & Veronica Spectacular(10/79). 487-The World of Jughead (10/79). 488-Archie's Christmas Stocking (12/79). 489-Betty & Veronica Christmas Spectacular (1/80). 490-Archie's Christmas Love-in (1/80). 491-Sabrina's Christmas Magic (1/80).492-The World of Archie (2/80). 493-The World of Jughead (4/80). 494-Betty & Veronica Spectacular (6/80). 495-Archie's Jokes (8/80). 496-Betty & Veronica Summer Fun (9/80). 497-The World of Archie (9/80). 498-Betty & Veronica Spectacular (10/80). 499-The World of Jughead (10/80). 500-Archie's Christmas Stocking (12/80) each. . . . . .80 . . . 2.00

501-550: 501-Betty & Veronica Christmas Spectacular (12/80). 502-Archie's Christmas Love-in (1/81). 503-Sabrina Christmas Magic (1/81). 504-The World of Archie (3/81). 505-The World of Jughead (4/81). 506-Betty & Veronica Spectacular (6/81). 507-Archie's Jokes (8/81). 508-Betty & Veronica Summer Fun (9/81). 509-The World of Archie (9/81). 510-Betty & Veronica Spectacular (9/81). 511-The World of Jughead (10/81). 512-Archie's Christmas Stocking (12/81). 513-Betty & Veronica Christmas Spectacular (12/81). 514-Archie's Christmas Love-in (1/82). 515-Sabrina's Christmas Magic (1/82). 516-The World of Archie (2/80). 517-The World of Jughead (4/82). 518-Betty & Veronica Spectacular (6/82). 519-Archie's Jokes (8/82). 520-Betty & Veronica Summer Fun (9/82). 521-The World of Archie (9/82). 522-Betty & Veronica Spectacular (10/82). 523-The World of Jughead (10/82). 524-Archie's Christmas Stocking (1/83). 525-Betty and Veronica Christmas Spectacular (1/83). 526-Betty and Veronica Spectacular (5/83). 527-Little Archie (8/83). 528-Josie and the Pussycats (8/83). 529-Betty and Veronica Summer Fun (8/83). 530-Betty and Veronica Spectacular (9/83). 531-The World of Jughead (9/83). 532-The World of Archie (10/83). 533-Space Pirates by Frank Bolling (10/83). 534-Little Archie (1/84). 535-Archie's Christmas Stocking (1/84). 536-Betty and Veronica Christmas Spectacular (1/84). 537-Betty and Veronica Spectacular (6/84). 538-Little Archie (8/84). 539-Betty and Veronica Summer Fun (8/84). 540-Josie and the Pussycats (8/84). 541-Betty and Veronica Spectacular (9/84). 542-The World of Jughead (9/84). 543-The World of Archie (10/84). 544-Sabrina the Teen-Age Witch (10/84). 545-Little Archie (12/84). 546-Archie's Christmas Stocking (12/84). 547-Betty and Veronica Christmas Spectacular (12/84). 548-? 549-Little Archie. 550-Betty and Veronica Summer Fun each. 1.50

551-600: 551-Josie and the Pussycats. 552-Betty and Veronica Spectacular. 553-The World of Jughead. 554-The World of Archie. 555-Betty's Diary. 556-Little Archie (1/86). 557-Archie's Christmas Stocking (1/86). 558-Betty & Veronica Christmas Spectacular (1/86). 559-Betty & Veronica Spectacular. 560-Little Archie. 561-Betty & Veronica Summer Fun. 562-Josie and the Pussycats. 563-Betty & Veronica Spectacular. 564-World of Jughead. 565-World of Archie. 566-Little Archie. 567-Archie's Christmas Stocking. 568-Betty & Veronica Christmas Spectacular. 569-Betty & Veronica Spring Spectacular. 570-Little Archie. 571-Josie & the Pussycats. 572-Betty & Veronica Summer Fun. 573-Archie At Riverdale High. 574-World of Archie. 575-Betty & Veronica Spectacular. 576-Pep. 577-World of Jughead. 578-Archie And Me. 579-Archie's Christmas Stocking. 580-Betty and Veronica Christmas Spectacular. 581-Little Archie Christmas Special. 582-Betty & Veronica Spring Spectacular. 583-Little Archie. 584-Josie and the Pussycats. 585-Betty & Veronica Summer Fun. 586-Archie At Riverdale High. 587-The World of Archie (10/88); 1st app. Explorers of the Unknown. 588-Betty & Veronica Spectacular. 589-Pep (10/88). 590-The World of Jughead. 591-Archie & Me. 592-Betty & Veronica Christmas Spectacular. 593-Betty & Veronica Spectacular. 594-Little Archie. 595-Betty & Veronica Spring Spectacular. 596-Little Archie. 597-Josie and the Pussycats. 598-Betty & Veronica Summer Fun. 599-The World of Archie (10/89); 2nd app. Explorers of the Unknown. 600-Betty and Veronica Spectacular

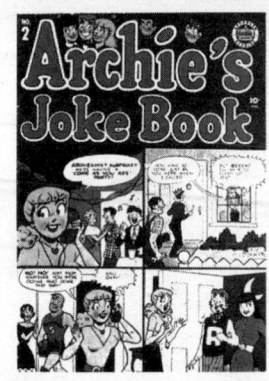

	GD25	FN65	NM94

	GD25	FN65	NM94

each.... 1.50

601-632: 601-Pep. 602-The World of Jughead. 603-Archie and Me. 604-Archie at Riverdale High. 605-Archie's Christmas Stocking. 606-Betty and Veronica Christmas Spectacular. 607-Little Archie. 608-Betty and Veronica Christmas Spectacular. 609-Little Archie. 610-Josie and the Pussycats. 611-Betty and Veronica Summer Fun. 612-The World of Archie. 613-Betty and Veronica Spectacular. 614-Pep (10/90). 615-Veronica's Summer Special. 616-Archie and Me. 617-Archie's Christmas Stocking. 618-Betty & Veronica Christmas Spectacular. 619-Little Archie. 620-Betty and Veronica Spectacular. 621-Betty and Veronica Summer Fun. 622-Josie & the Pussycats; not published. 623-Betty and Veronica Spectacular. 624-Pep Comics. 625-Veronica's Summer Special. 626-Archie and Me. 627-World of Archie. 628-Archie's Pals 'n' Gals Holiday Special. 629-Betty & Veronica Christmas Spectacular. 630-Archie's Christmas Stocking. 631-Archie's Pals 'n' Gals. 632-Betty & Veronica spectacular   each.... 1.50

ARCHIE MEETS THE PUNISHER (Same contents as The Punisher Meets Archie)
Aug, 1994 ($2.95, 52 pgs., one-shot)
Marvel Comics & Archie Comics Publications

1-Batton Lash story, J. Buscema-a on Punisher, S. Goldberg-a on Archie   1.20   3.00

ARCHIE'S ACTIVITY COMICS DIGEST MAGAZINE
1985 - No. 4? (Annual, 128 pgs., digest size)
Archie Enterprises

1-4   1.50

ARCHIE'S CAR
1979 (49¢)
Spire Christian Comics (Fleming H. Revell co.)

nn   1.00

ARCHIE'S CHRISTMAS LOVE-IN (See Archie Giant Series Mag. No. 169, 181,192, 205, 218, 230, 242, 454, 466, 478, 490, 502, 514)

ARCHIE'S CHRISTMAS STOCKING (See Archie Giant Series Mag. No. 1-6,10, 15, 20, 25, 31, 137, 144, 150, 158, 167, 179, 190, 203, 216, 228, 240, 452, 464, 476, 488, 500, 512, 524, 535, 546, 557, 567, 579, 592, 605, 617, 630)

ARCHIE'S CHRISTMAS STOCKING
1993 -1995 ($2.00, 52 pgs.)(Bound-in calender poster in all)
Archie Comics

1-3: 1-Dan DeCarlo-c/a   .80   2.00

ARCHIE'S CLEAN SLATE
1973 (35/49¢)
Spire Christian Comics (Fleming H. Revell Co.)

1(Some issues have nn)   1.00

ARCHIE'S DATE BOOK
1981
Spire Christian comics (Fleming H. Revell co.)

nn   1.00

ARCHIE'S DOUBLE DIGEST QUARTERLY MAGAZINE
1981 - Present ($1.95/$2.75, 256pgs.) (A.D.D. Magazine No. 10 on)
Archie Comics

1-100: 6-Katy Keene story. 29-Pureheart story   1.20   3.00

ARCHIE'S FAMILY ALBUM
1978 (39¢, 36 pgs.)
Spire Christian Comics (Fleming H. Revell Co.)

nn   1.00

ARCHIE'S FESTIVAL
1980 (49¢)
Spire Christian Comics (Fleming H. Revell Co.)

nn   1.00

ARCHIE'S GIRLS, BETTY AND VERONICA (Becomes Betty & Veronica)(Also see Veronica)
1950 - No. 347, Apr, 1987
Archie Publications (Close-Up)

1	127.00	375.00	1150.00
2	69.00	188.00	550.00
3-5	40.00	120.00	325.00
6-10: 6-Dan DeCarlo's 1st Archie work; Betty's 1st ponytail. 10-Katy Keene app. (2 pgs.)	36.00	107.00	250.00
11-20: 11,13,14,17-19-Katy Keene app. 17-Last pre-code issue (3/55). 20-Debbie's Diary (2 pgs.)	26.00	77.00	180.00
21-30: 27,30-Katy Keene app.	17.00	51.00	120.00
31-50: 44-Elvis Presley 1 pg. photo & bio. 45-Fabian 1 pg. photo & bio. 46-Bobby Darin 1 pg. photo & bio	9.50	28.00	75.00
51-74: 73-Sci-fi-c	5.50	16.50	55.00
75-Betty & Veronica sell souls to Devil	10.00	30.00	100.00
76-99: Bobby Rydell 1 pg. illustrated bio	2.80	8.40	28.00
100	3.80	11.40	38.00
101-140: 118-Origin Superteen (see Betty & Me #3). 119-Last Superteen story	1.20	3.60	12.00
141-180	1.00	2.00	5.00
181-220		1.00	2.50
221-347: 300-Anniversary issue			1.50
Annual 1 (1953)	72.00	216.00	650.00
Annual 2(1954)	33.00	100.00	300.00
Annual 3-5 (1955-1957)	28.00	83.00	220.00
Annual 6-8 (1958-1960)	18.00	53.00	140.00

ARCHIE SHOE-STORE GIVEAWAY
1944-49 (12-15 pgs. of games, puzzles, stories like Superman-Tim books, No nos. - came out monthly)
Archie Publications

(1944-47)-issues	12.00	36.00	85.00
2/48-Peggy Lee photo-c	10.00	30.00	65.00
3/48-Marylee Robb photo-c	10.00	30.00	60.00
4/48-Gloria De Haven photo-c	10.00	30.00	60.00
5/48,6/48,7/48	10.00	30.00	60.00
8/48-Story on Shirley Temple	10.00	30.00	65.00
10/48-Archie as Wolf on cover	10.00	30.00	65.00
5/49-Kathleen Hughes photo-c	7.50	22.50	45.00
7/49	7.50	22.50	45.00
8/49-Archie photo-c from radio show	11.00	33.00	75.00
10/49-Gloria Mann photo-c from radio show	10.00	30.00	65.00
11/49,12/49	7.50	22.50	45.00

ARCHIE'S JOKEBOOK COMICS DIGEST ANNUAL (See Jokebook...)

ARCHIE'S JOKE BOOK MAGAZINE (See Joke Book ...)
1953 - No. 3, Sum, 1954; No. 15, Fall, 1954 - No. 288, 11/82
Archie Publications

1953-One Shot (#1)	75.00	225./00	600.00
2	40.00	120.00	325.00
3 (no #4-14)	31.00	93.00	250.00
15-20: 15-Formerly Archie's Rival Reggie #14; last pre-code issue (Fall/54).			
15-17-Katy Keene app.	18.00	56.00	150.00
21-30	12.00	36.00	85.00
31-40,42,43: 43-story about guitarist Duane Eddy	7.00	20.00	55.00
41-1st professional comic work by Neal Adams (9/59), 1 pg.	17.00	50.00	135.00
44-47-N. Adams-a in all, 1-3 pgs.	8.75	26.00	70.00
48-Four pgs. N. Adams-a	9.50	28.00	75.00
49-60 (1962)	2.00	6.00	20.00
61-80	1.20	3.60	12.00
81-100	1.00	2.00	5.00
101-140		1.20	3.00

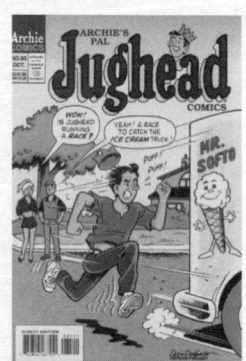

Archie's Pal Jughead #85 © Archie Publ.

Archie's Pals 'n' Gals Double Digest #20 © Archie

Archie's Rival Reggie #7 © Archie Publ.

	GD25	FN65	NM94
141-200		.80	2.00
201-288			1.50
Drug Store Giveaway (No. 39 w/new-c)	4.00	10.00	20.00

ARCHIE'S JOKES (See Archie Giant Series Mag. No. 17, 22, 27, 33, 139, 146, 154, 163, 174, 186, 198, 211, 222, 235, 247, 459, 471, 483, 495, 519)

ARCHIE'S LOVE SCENE
1973 (35¢/49¢)
Spire Christian Comics (Fleming H. Revell Co.)

1(Some copies have nn)			1.00

ARCHIE'S MADHOUSE (Madhouse Ma-ad No. 67 on)
Sept, 1959 - No. 66, Feb, 1969
Archie Publications

	GD25	FN65	NM94
1-Archie begins	24.00	73.00	200.00
2	13.00	38.00	100.00
3-5	7.50	22.50	65.00
6-10	5.50	17.00	45.00
11-17 (Last w/regular characters)	3.75	11.25	30.00
18-21,23-30 (New format): 25-1st app. Captain Sprocket (4/63)	1.20	3.60	12.00
22-1st app. Sabrina, the Teen-age Witch (10/62)	7.00	21.00	70.00
31-34,36-40: 34-Bordered-c begin.	1.00	2.60	6.00
35-Beatles cameo	1.30	3.25	8.00
41-66: 43-Mighty Crusaders cameo. 44-Swipes Mad #4 (Super-Duperman) in "Bird Monsters From Outer Space"		.80	2.00
Annual 1 (1962-63)	5.50	16.50	55.00
Annual 2 (1964)	2.80	8.40	28.00
Annual 3 (1965)-Origin Sabrina the Teen-Age Witch	1.50	4.50	15.00
Annual 4-6('66-69)(Becomes Madhouse Ma-ad Annual #7 on)	1.00	3.00	10.00

NOTE: Cover title to 61-65 is "Madhouse" and to 66 is "Madhouse Ma-ad Jokes".

ARCHIE'S MECHANICS
Sept, 1954 - No. 3, 1955
Archie Publications

	GD25	FN65	NM94
1-(15¢; 52 pgs.)	75.00	225.00	600.00
2-(10¢)-Last pre-code issue	46.00	137.00	365.00
3-(10¢)	40.00	120.00	300.00

ARCHIE'S ONE WAY
1972 (35/49¢, 36 pgs.)
Spire Christian Comics (Fleming H. Revell Co.)

nn			1.00

ARCHIE'S PAL, JUGHEAD (Jughead No. 122 on)
1949 - No. 126, Nov, 1965
Archie Publications

	GD25	FN65	NM94
1 (1949)-1st app. Moose (see Pep #33)	105.00	320.00	850.00
2 (1950)	53.00	150.00	425.00
3-5	33.00	100.00	265.00
6-10: 7-Suzie app.	22.00	66.00	175.00
11-20	14.00	41.00	110.00
21-30: 23-25,28-30-Katy Keene app. 28-Debbie's Diary app.	9.50	28.00	75.00
31-50	5.00	15.00	40.00
51-70	2.50	7.50	25.00
71-100	1.40	4.20	14.00
101-126	.80	2.40	8.00
Annual 1 (1953, 25¢)	44.00	133.00	400.00
Annual 2 (1954, 25¢)-Last pre-code issue	31.00	94.00	250.00
Annual 3-5 (1955-57, 25¢)	22.00	66.00	175.00
Annual 6-8 (1958-60, 25¢)	14.00	41.00	110.00

ARCHIE'S PAL JUGHEAD COMICS (Formerly Jughead #1-45)
No. 46, June, 1993 - Present ($1.25/$1.50/$1.75)
Archie Comic Publications

	GD25	FN65	NM94
46-64		.65	1.25
65-70, 76-82			1.50
71-95			1.75

ARCHIE'S PALS 'N' GALS (Also see Archie Giant Series Magazine #628)
1952-53 - No. 6, 1957-58; No. 7, 1958 - No. 224, Sept, 1991
Archie Publications

	GD25	FN65	NM94
1-(116 pgs., 25¢)	62.00	188.00	500.00
2(Annual)('54, 25¢)	39.00	118.00	275.00
3-5(Annual, '55-57, 25¢): 3-Last pre-code issue	27.00	81.00	190.00
6-10('58-'60)	16.00	47.00	110.00
11-20: 12-Harry Belafonte 2 pg. photo & bio	6.50	19.50	45.00
21-28,30-40	2.20	6.60	22.00
29-Beatles satire	4.00	12.00	40.00
41-60	.90	2.70	9.00
61-80		1.80	4.50
81-110		1.20	3.00
111-224: Later issues $1.00 cover. 197-G. Colan-a			1.50

ARCHIE'S PALS 'N' GALS DOUBLE DIGEST MAGAZINE
Nov, 1992 - Present ($2.50/$2.75)
Archie Comic Publications

1-3: 1-Capt. Hero story; Pureheart app. 2-Superduck story; Little Jinx in all		1.00	2.50
4-35: 4-Begin $2.75-c.		1.10	2.75

ARCHIE'S PARABLES
1973 (39/49¢, 36 pgs.)
Spire Christian Comics (Fleming H. Revell Co.)

nn-By Al Hartley			1.00

ARCHIE'S R/C RACERS
Sept, 1989 - No. 10, Mar, 1991
Archie Comics

1-10: Radio contol cars. 1,2-Begin 95¢-c. 3-Begin $1.00-c			1.00

ARCHIE'S RIVAL REGGIE (Reggie & Archie's Joke Book #15 on)
1950 - No. 14, Aug, 1954
Archie Publications

	GD25	FN65	NM94
1-Reggie 1st app. in Jackpot Comics #5	65.00	195.00	525.00
2	33.00	100.00	265.00
3-5	22.00	66.00	185.00
6-10	17.00	51.00	135.00
11-14: Katy Keene in No. 10-14, 1-2 pgs.	13.00	38.00	100.00

ARCHIE'S RIVERDALE HIGH (See Riverdale High)

ARCHIE'S ROLLER COASTER
1981 (69¢)
Spire Christian Comics (Fleming H. Revell Co.)

nn			1.00

ARCHIE'S SOMETHING ELSE
1975 (39/49¢, 36 pgs.)
Spire Christian Comics (Fleming H. Revell Co.)

nn			1.00

ARCHIE'S SONSHINE
1973, 1974 (39/49¢, 36 pgs.)
Spire Christian Comics (Fleming H. Revell Co.)

nn			1.00

ARCHIE'S SPORTS SCENE
1983
Spire Christian Comics (Fleming H. Revell Co.)

nn			1.00

ARCHIE'S SPRING BREAK
1996 ($2.00, 48 pgs.)

Argus #6 © DC

Arion The Immortal #6 © DC

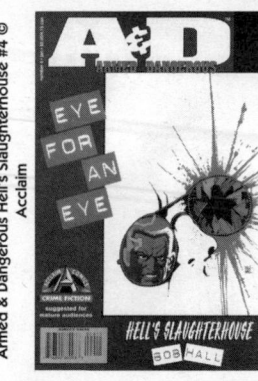

Armed & Dangerous Hell's Slaughterhouse #4 © Acclaim

	GD25	FN65	NM94

	GD25	FN65	NM94

Archie Comics
1-Dan DeCarlo-c 2.00

ARCHIE'S STORY & GAME COMICS DIGEST MAGAZINE
Nov, 1986 - No. 31, 1995? ($1.25/$1.35/$1.50, 128 pgs., digest-size)
Archie Enterprises
1-31 ..... 1.00 ..... 2.50

ARCHIE'S SUPER HERO SPECIAL (See Archie Giant Series Mag. No. 142)

ARCHIE'S SUPER HERO SPECIAL (...Comics Digest Mag. 2)
Jan, 1979 - No. 2, Aug, 1979 (95¢, 148 pgs.)
Archie Publications (Red Circle)
1-Simon & Kirby r-/Double Life of Pvt. Strong #1,2; Black Hood, The Fly, Jaguar, The Web app. ..... .80 ..... 2.00
2-Contains contents to the never published Black Hood #1; origin Black Hood; N. Adams, Wood, McWilliams, Morrow, S&K-a(r); N. Adams-c. The Shield, The Fly, Jaguar, Hangman, Steel Sterling, The Web, The Fox-r ..... .80 ..... 2.00

ARCHIE'S SUPER TEENS
1994 - No. 3, 1994 ($2.00, 52 pgs.)
Archie Comic Publications, Inc.
1-3: 1-Staton/Esposito-c/a; pull-out poster. 2-Fred Hembeck script; Bret Blevins/Terry Austin-a ..... .80 ..... 2.00

ARCHIE'S TV LAUGH-OUT
Dec, 1969 - No. 106, Apr, 1986
Archie Publications
1 ..... 3.20 ..... 9.60 ..... 32.00
2 ..... 1.20 ..... 3.60 ..... 12.00
3-5 ..... 1.00 ..... 2.60 ..... 6.00
6-10 ..... 1.00 ..... 2.50
11-20 ..... .80 ..... 2.00
21-106 ..... 1.25

ARCHIE'S VACATION SPECIAL
Winter, 1994? - Present ($2.00, annually)
Archie Publications
1,2 ..... .80 ..... 2.00

ARCHIE'S WORLD
1973, 1976 (39/49¢)
Spire Christian Comics (Fleming H. Revell Co.)
nn 1.00

ARCHIE 3000
May, 1989 - No. 16, July, 1991 (75¢/95¢/$1.00)
Archie Comics
1-16: 6-Begin $1.00-c; X-Mas-c 1.00

ARCOMICS PREMIERE
July, 1993 ($2.95)
Arcomics
1-1st lenticular-c on a comic (flicker-c) ..... 1.20 ..... 3.00

AREA 88
May 26, 1987 - No. 42, 1989 ($1.50/$1.75, B&W)
Eclipse Comics/VIZ Comics #37 on
1-36: 1,2-2nd printings exist 1.50
37-42: 37-Begin $1.75-c ..... .70 ..... 1.80

ARENA (Also see Marvel Graphic Novel)
Jan, 1990 ($1.50, 7x10-1/8", 20 pgs.)
Alchemy Studios
1-Science fiction 1.50
1-Signed & numbered ed. (500 copies) ..... 1.20 ..... 2.95

ARGUS (See Flash, 2nd Series) (Also see Showcase '95 #1,2)

Apr, 1995 - No. 6, Oct, 1995 ($1.50, limited series)
DC Comics
1-3 ..... 1.50
4-6: 4-Begin $1.75-c ..... .70 ..... 1.75

ARIANE AND BLUEBEARD (See Night Music #8)

ARIEL & SEBASTIAN (See Cartoon Tales & The Little Mermaid)

ARION, LORD OF ATLANTIS (Also see Warlord #55)
Nov, 1982 - No. 35, Sept, 1985
DC Comics
1-35: 1-Story cont'd from Warlord #62 ..... 1.00
Special #1 (11/85) 1.00

ARION THE IMMORTAL (Also see Showcase '95 #7)
July, 1992 - No. 6, Dec, 1992 ($1.50, limited series)
DC Comics
1-6: 4-Gustovich-a(i) 1.50

ARISTOCATS (See Movie Comics & Walt Disney Showcase No. 16)

ARISTOKITTENS, THE (...Meet Jiminy Cricket No. 1)(Disney)
Oct, 1971 - No. 9, Oct, 1975
Gold Key
1 ..... 2.60 ..... 7.80 ..... 26.00
2-9: 6-52 pgs. ..... 1.50 ..... 4.50 ..... 15.00

ARIZONA KID, THE (Also see The Comics & Wild Western)
Mar, 1951 - No. 6, Jan, 1952
Marvel/Atlas Comics(CSI)
1 ..... 19.00 ..... 58.00 ..... 135.00
2-4: 2-Heath-a(3) ..... 10.00 ..... 30.00 ..... 65.00
5,6 ..... 10.00 ..... 30.00 ..... 60.00
NOTE: **Heath** a-1-3; c-1-3. **Maneely** c-4-6. **Morisi** a-4-6. **Sinnott** a-6.

ARK, THE (See The Crusaders)

ARMAGEDDON: ALIEN AGENDA
Nov, 1991 - No. 4, Feb, 1992 ($1.00, limited series)
DC Comics
1-4 ..... 1.00

ARMAGEDDON FACTOR, THE
1987 - No. 2, 1987; No. 3, 1990 ($1.95)
AC Comics
1,2: Sentinels of Justice, Dragonfly, Femforce ..... .80 ..... 2.00
3-($3.95, color)-Almost all AC characters app. ..... 1.60 ..... 4.00

ARMAGEDDON: INFERNO
Apr, 1992 - No. 4, July, 1992 ($1.00, limited series)
DC Comics
1-4: Many DC heroes app. 3-A. Adams/Austin-a 1.00

ARMAGEDDON 2001
May, 1991 - No. 2, Oct, 1991 ($2.00, squarebound, 68 pgs.)
DC Comics
1-Features many DC heroes; intro Waverider ..... 1.00 ..... 2.50
1-2nd & 3rd printings; 3rd has silver ink-c ..... .70 ..... 1.75
2 ..... 1.00 ..... 2.50

ARMED & DANGEROUS
Apr, 1996 - No.4, July, 1996 ($2.95, B&W, limited series)
Acclaim Comics (Armada)
1-4-Bob Hall-c/a & scripts ..... 1.20 ..... 3.00
Special 1 (8/96, $2.95, B&W)-Hall-c/a & scripts. 3.00

ARMED & DANGEROUS HELL'S SLAUGHTERHOUSE
Oct, 1996 - No. 4, Jan, 1997 ($2.95, B&W, limited series)
Acclaim Comics (Armada)

Armorines #8 © Voyager Comm.

Arrgh! #1 © MEG

Artemis: Requiem #6 © DC

1-4: Hall-c/a/scripts.   3.00

ARMOR (AND THE SILVER STREAK)
Sept, 1985 - No.7, Mar, 1986 ($2.00)
Continuity Comics

1-7: 1-Intro/origin Armor & the Silver Streak; Neal Adams-c/a. 7-Origin Armor;
  Nebres-i   .80   2.00

ARMORED TROOPER VOTOMS (Manga)
July, 1996 - Present ($2.95, limited series)
CPM Comics

1   3.00

ARMORINES (See X-O Manowar #25)
June, 1994 - No. 12, June, 1995 ($2.25)
Valiant

1-12: 7-Wraparound-c. 12-Byrne-c/swipe (X-Men, 1st Series #138)
                                                       .90   2.25

ARMY AND NAVY COMICS (Supersnipe No. 6 on)
May, 1941 - No. 5, July, 1942
Street & Smith Publications

1-Cap Fury & Nick Carter   44.00   132.00 350.00
2-Cap Fury & Nick Carter   27.00   81.00 190.00
3,4   19.00   56.00 130.00
5-Supersnipe app.; see Shadow V2#3 for 1st app.; Story of Douglas
  MacArthur; George Marcoux-c/a   44.00   132.00 350.00

ARMY ATTACK
July, 1964 - No. 4, Feb, 1965; V2#38, July, 1965 - No. 47, Feb, 1967
Charlton Comics

V1#1   2.85   8.50   20.00
  2-4(2/65)   1.65   4.20   10.00
V2#38(7/65)-47 (formerly U.S. Air Force #1-37)
                                         1.65   4.20   10.00
NOTE: Glanzman a-1-3. Montes/Bache a-44.

ARMY AT WAR (Also see Our Army at War & Cancelled Comic Cavalcade)
Oct-Nov, 1978
DC Comics

1-Kubert-c   .80   2.00

ARMY OF DARKNESS (Movie)
Nov, 1992 - No. 2, Dec, 1992; No. 3, Oct, 1993 ($2.50, limited series)
Dark Horse Comics

1-3-Bolton painted-c/a   1.00   2.50

ARMY SURPLUS KOMIKZ FEATURING CUTEY BUNNY
1982 - No. 5, 1985 ($1.50, B&W)
Army Surplus Komikz/Eclipse Comics No. 5

1-Cutey Bunny begins   .80   2.00
2-5: 5-JLA/X-Men/Batman parody   1.50

ARMY WAR HEROES (Also see Iron Corporal)
Dec, 1963 - No. 38, June, 1970
Charlton Comics

1   2.85   8.50   20.00
2-38: 22-Origin & 1st app. Iron Corporal series by Glanzman. 24-Intro. Archer
  & Corp. Jack series   1.65   4.20   10.00
Modern Comics Reprint 36 ('78)   .80   2.00
NOTE: Montes/Bache a-1, 16, 17, 21, 23-25, 27-30.

AROUND THE BLOCK WITH DUNC & LOO (See Dunc and Loo)

AROUND THE WORLD IN 80 DAYS (Movie) (See A Golden Picture Classic)
Feb, 1957
Dell Publishing Co.

Four Color 784-Photo-c   6.30   18.00   63.00

AROUND THE WORLD UNDER THE SEA (See Movie Classics)

AROUND THE WORLD WITH ARCHIE (See Archie Giant Series Mag. #29, 35, 141)

AROUND THE WORLD WITH HUCKLEBERRY & HIS FRIENDS (See Dell
Giant No. 44)

ARRGH! (Satire)
Dec, 1974 - No. 5, Sept, 1975 (25¢)
Marvel Comics Group

1   1.20   3.00
2-5   .70   1.75
NOTE: Alcala a-2; c-3. Everett a-1r, 2r. Maneely a-4r. Sekowsky a-1p. Sutton a-1, 2.

ARROW, THE (See Funny Pages)
Oct, 1940 - No. 2, Nov, 1940; No. 3, Oct, 1941
Centaur Publications

1-The Arrow begins(r/Funny Pages)   250.00   750.00 2000.00
2,3: 2-Tippy Taylor serial continues from Amazing Mystery Funnies #24. 3-
  Origin Dash Dartwell, the Human Meteor; origin The Rainbow-r; bondage-c
                                        105.00   320.00 850.00
NOTE: Gustavson a-1, 2; c-3.

ARROWHEAD (See Black Rider and Wild Western)
April, 1954 - No. 4, Nov, 1954
Atlas Comics (CPS)

1-Arrowhead & his horse Eagle begin   13.00   39.00   90.00
2-4: 4-Forte-a   10.00   30.00   60.00
NOTE: Heath c-3. Jack Katz a-3. Maneely c-2. Pakula a-2. Sinnott a-1-4; c-1.

ARSENAL SPECIAL (See New Titans, Showcase '94 #7 & Showcase '95 #8)
1996 ($2.95, one-shot)
DC Comics

1   3.00

ARTEMIS: REQUIEM (Also see Wonder Woman, 2nd Series #90)
June, 1996 - No. 6, Nov, 1996 ($1.75, limited series)
DC Comics

1-6: Messner-Loebs scripts & Ed Benes-c/a in all. 1,2-Wonder Woman app.
                                                 .70   1.75

ART OF ZEN INTERGALACTIC NINJA, THE
1994 - No. 2, 1994 ($2.95)
Entity Comics

1,2   1.20   3.00

ARZACH (See Moebius...)
1996 ($6.95, one-shot)
Dark Horse Comics

nn-Moebius-c/a/scripts   7.00

ASH
Nov, 1994 - No. 6, Dec, 1995; No. 0, May, 1996 ($2.50/$3.00)
Event Comics

0-(5/96, $3.00)-Present & Future foil logo-c exist; w/pin-ups
                                                 1.60   4.00
0-Present Blue Foil logo-c & Future Blue Foil logo-c (1000 each)
                                                        12.00
0-Present Silver Prism logo-c & Future Silver Prism logo-c (500 each)
                                                        27.00
0-Present Red Prism logo-c & Future Red Prism logo-c (250 each)
                                                        37.00
0-Present Gold Hologram logo-c & Future Gold Hologram logo-c
  (1000 each)   22.00
1-Quesada-p/story; Palmiotti-i/story; Barry Windsor-Smith pin-up
                                         2.15   6.50   15.00
2-Mignola Hellboy pin-up   1.65   4.20   10.00
3,4: 3-Big Guy pin-up by Geoff Darrow. 4-Jim Lee pin-up
                                         1.30   3.25   8.00
4-Fahrenheit Gold   2.40   7.20   17.00

Assassins #1 © DC/MEG

Astonishing #32 © ATLAS

Astonishing X-Men #2 © MEG

AS

	GD25	FN65	NM94

	GD25	FN65	NM94
4-Fahrenheit Red	2.85	8.50	20.00
4-Fahrenheit White	4.30	13.00	30.00
5, 6-Double-c w/Hildebrandt Bros.-a, Quesada & Palmiotti. 6-Texiera-c		1.60	4.00
5-Fahrenheit Gold (2000)			12.00
5-Fahrenheit Red (1000)			17.00
5-Fahrenheit White (500)			27.00
6-Farenheit Gold (2000)			12.00
6-Farenheit Red (1000)			17.00
6-Farenheit White (500)			27.00
6-Farenheit White (500)-Texiera-c			27.00
Volume 1 (1996, $14.95, TPB)-r/#1-5, intro by James Robinson.			15.00

ASKANI'SON (Also see Adventures of Cyclops & Phoenix limited series)
Jan, 1996 - No. 4, May, 1996 ($2.95, limited series)
Marvel Comics

1-4: Lobdell/Loeb story; Gene Ha-c/a(p)	1.20	3.00

ASSASSINETTE
1994 -No.7, 1995? ($2.50, B&W)
Pocket Change Comics

1-7: 1-Silver foil-c	1.00	2.50

ASSASSINETTE HARDCORE
1995 - No.2, 1995 ($2.50, B&W, limited series)
Pocket Change Comics

1,2	1.00	2.50

ASSASSINS
Apr, 1996 ($1.95)
DC Comics (Amalgam)

1		2.00

ASSASSINS, INC.
1987 - No. 2, 1987 ($1.95)
Silverline Comics

1,2	.80	2.00

ASTER
Oct, 1994 - No. 4, 1995 ($2.95)
Entity Comics

0-4: 1,3,4-Foil Logo. 2-Foil-c. 3-Variant-c exists.	1.20	3.00

ASTER: THE LAST CELESTIAL KNIGHT
1995 - No. 3, 1996 ($2.50)
Entity Comics

1-3		2.50

ASTONISHING (Formerly Marvel Boy No. 1, 2)
No. 3, Apr, 1951 - No. 63, Aug, 1957
Marvel/Atlas Comics(20CC)

3-Marvel Boy continues; 3-5-Marvel Boy-c	80.00	240.00	635.00
4-6-Last Marvel Boy; 4-Stan Lee app.	51.00	155.00	415.00
7-10: 7-Maneely s/f story. 10-Sinnott s/f story	23.00	69.00	160.00
11,12,15,17,20	20.00	60.00	140.00
13,14,16,18,19-Krigstein-a. 18-Jack The Ripper sty			
	21.00	64.00	150.00
21,22,24	18.00	54.00	125.00
23-E.C. swipe "The Hole In The Wall" from Vault Of Horror #16			
	19.00	56.00	130.00
25,29: 25-Crandall-a. 29-Decapitation-c	16.00	47.00	110.00
26-28	14.00	43.00	100.00
30-Tentacled eyeball story	18.00	54.00	125.00
31-37-Last pre-code issue	13.00	39.00	90.00
38-43,46,48-52,56,58,59,61	10.00	30.00	70.00
44,45,47,53-55,57,60: 44-Crandall swipe/Weird Fantasy #22. 45,47-Krigstein-a.			

53-Ditko-a. 54-Torres-a, 55-Crandall, Torres-a. 57-Williamson/Krenkel-a			
(4 pgs.). 60-Williamson/Mayo-a (4 pgs.)	11.50	34.00	80.00
62,63: 62-Torres, Powell-a. 63-Woodbridge-a	10.00	30.00	65.00

NOTE: *Ayers* a-16. *Berg* a-36, 53, 56. *Cameron* a-50. *Gene Colan* a-12, 20, 29, 56. *Ditko* a-53. *Drucker* a-41, 62. *Everett* a-3-6(3), 6, 10, 12, 37, 47, 48, 58; c-3-5, 13,15, 16, 18, 29, 47, 49, 51, 53-55, 57, 59-63. *Fass* a-11, 34. *Forte* a-53, 58, 60. *Fuje* a-11. *Heath* a-8, 29; c-8, 9, 19, 22, 25, 26. *Kirby* a-56. *Lawrence* a-28, 37, 38, 42. *Maneely* a-7(2); c-7, 31, 33, 34, 56. *Moldoff* a-33. *Morisi* a-10, 60. *Morrow* a-52, 61. *Orlando* a-47, 58, 61. *Pakula* a-10. *Powell* a-43, 44, 48. *Ravielli* a-28. *Reinman* a-32, 34, 38. *Robinson* a-20. *J. Romita* a-7, 18, 24, 43, 57,61. *Roussos* a-35. *Sale* a-28, 38, 59; c-32. *Sekowsky* a-13. *Severin* c-46. *Shores* a-16, 60. *Sinnott* a-11, 30. *Whitney* a-13. *Ed Win* a-20. Canadian reprints exist.

ASTONISHING TALES (See Ka-Zar)
Aug, 1970 - No. 36, July, 1976 (#1-7: 15¢; #8: 25¢)
Marvel Comics Group

1-Ka-Zar (by Kirby(p) #1,2; by B. Smith #3-6) & Dr. Doom (by Wood #1-4; by Tuska #7,8) double feature begins; Kraven the Hunter-c/			
story; Nixon cameo	3.25	9.50	22.00
2-Kraven the Hunter-c/story; Kirby, Wood-a	1.65	4.20	10.00
3-6: B. Smith-p; Wood-a-#3,4. 5,6-Red Skull 2-part story			
	2.15	6.50	15.00
7,8: 8-(25¢, 52 pgs.)-Last Dr. Doom	1.65	4.20	10.00
9-Lorna-r/Lorna #14		1.20	3.00
10-B. Smith/Sal Buscema-a	1.00	2.60	6.00
11-Origin Ka-Zar & Zabu	1.00	2.50	6.00
12-Man-Thing by Neal Adams (apps. #13 also)	1.00	3.00	7.00
13-24: 14-Jann of the Jungle-r (1950s). 19-Starlin-a(p). 20-Last Ka-Zar. 21-It! the Living Colossus begins, ends #24		.80	2.00
25-1st app. Deathlok the Demolisher; full length stories begin, end #36; Perez's 1st work, 2 pgs. (8/74)	5.00	15.00	30.00
26-28,30	1.85	5.50	12.00
29-r/origin/1st app. Guardians of the Galaxy from Marvel Super-Heroes #18 plus-c w/4 pgs. omitted; no Deathlok story	2.15	6.50	15.00
31-36: 31-Watcher-r/Silver Surfer #3	1.65	4.20	10.00

NOTE: *Buckler* a-13i, 16p, 25, 26p, 27p, 28, 29p-36p; c-13, 25p, 26-30, 32-35p, 36. *John Buscema* a-9, 12p-14p, 16p; c-4-6p, 12p. *Colan* a-7p, 8p. *Ditko* a-21r. *Everett* a-6i. *G. Kane* a-11p, 15p; c-9, 10p, 11p, 14, 15p, 21p. *McWilliams* a-30i. *Starlin* a-19p; c-16p. *Sutton & Trimpe* a-8. *Tuska* a-5p, 6p, 8p. *Wood* a-1-4. *Wrightson* c-31i.

ASTONISHING X-MEN
Mar, 1995 - No.4, July, 1995 ($1.95, limited series)
Marvel Comics

1-Age of Apocalypse	1.20	3.00
2-4	.80	2.00

ASTRO BOY (TV) (See March of Comics #285 & The Original...)
August, 1965 (12¢)
Gold Key

1(10151-508)-Scarce;1st app. Astro Boy in comics 35.00	105.00	350.00

ASTRO CITY (See Kurt Busiek's Astro City)

ASTRO COMICS
1969 - 1979 (Giveaway)
American Airlines (Harvey)

nn-Harvey's Casper, Spooky, Hot Stuff, Stumbo the Giant, Little Audrey, Little Lotta, & Richie Rich reprints. 1970-r/Richie Rich #97. 1973-r/Richie Rich #122. 1977-r/Richie Rich & Casper #20. 1979-r/Richie Rich & Casper #30			
1		.60	4.00

ASYLUM
1993 ($2.50)
Millennium Publications

1-4: 1-Bolton-c/a; Russell 2-pg. illos	1.00	2.50

ASYLUM
Dec, 1995 - Present ($2.95, anthology) (#1-6 are flip books)
Maximum Press

1-10: 1-Warchild by Art Adams, Beanworld, Avengelyne, Battlestar

Atlantis Chronicles #6 © DC

Atom #3 © DC

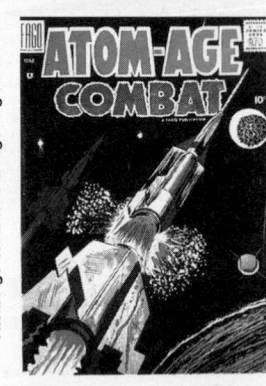

Atom-Age Combat #3 © Fago Magazines

	GD25	FN65	NM94

Galactica. 2-Intro Mike Deodato's Deathkiss; Cybrid story begins, ends #5.
4-1st app.Christian; painted Battlestar Galactica story begins. 5-Intro Black
Seed (formerly Black Flag) by Dan Fraga; B&W Christian story. 6-Intro Bionix
(Six Million Dollar Man & the Bionic Woman). 7-Don Simpson's Megaton Man;

	GD25	FN65	NM94
Black Seed pinup	1.20		3.00

ATARI FORCE
1982 - No. 5, 1983; Jan, 1984 - No. 20, Aug, 1985 (Mando paper)
DC Comics

1-3 (1982, 5X7", 52 pgs.)-Given away with Atari games			1.00
4,5 (1982-1983, 52 pgs.)-Given away with Atari games (scarcer)			1.00
			1.00
1-20: 1-(1/84)-Intro Tempest, Packrat, Babe, Morphea, & Dart			1.00
Special 1 (4/86)			1.00

NOTE: **Byrne** c-Special 1i. **Giffen** a-12p, 13i. **Rogers** a-18p, Special 1p.

A-TEAM, THE (TV)
Mar, 1984 - No. 3, May, 1984
Marvel Comics Group

1-3			1.00

ATLANTIS CHRONICLES, THE (Also see Aquaman, 3rd Series & Aquaman:
Time & Tide)
Mar, 1990 - No. 7, Sept, 1990 ($2.95, limited series, 52 pgs.)
DC Comics

1-7: 1-Peter David scripts. 7-True origin of Aquaman; nudity panels			
	1.30		3.25

ATLANTIS, THE LOST CONTINENT
May, 1961
Dell Publishing Co.

Four Color #1188-Movie, photo-c	10.00	30.00	100.00

ATLAS (See 1st Issue Special)

ATLAS
Feb, 1994 - No. 4, 1994 ($2.50, limited series)
Dark Horse Comics

1-4		1.00	2.50

ATOM, THE (See Action #425, All-American #19, Brave & the Bold, D.C. Special Series #1,
Detective, Flash Comics #80, Power Of The Atom, Showcase #34 -36 , Super Friends, Sword of
The Atom & World's Finest)

ATOM, THE (....& the Hawkman No. 39 on)
June-July, 1962 - No. 38, Aug-Sept, 1968
National Periodical Publ.

1-(6/7/62)-Intro Plant-Master; 1st app. Maya	80.00	242.00	750.00
2	40.00	120.00	320.00
3-1st Time Pool story; 1st app. Chronos (origin)	29.00	86.00	215.00
4,5: 4-Snapper Carr x-over	20.00	60.00	150.00
6,8-10: 8-Justice League, Dr. Light app.	17.00	49.00	120.00
7-Hawkman x-over (6-7/63; 1st Atom & Hawkman team-up); 1st app.			
Hawkman since Brave & the Bold tryouts	34.00	103.00	250.00
11-15: 13-Chronos-c/story	11.50	34.00	85.00
16-20: 19-Zatanna x-over	8.50	26.00	62.00
21-28,30: 28-Chronos-c/story	7.00	21.00	50.00
29-1st solo Golden Age Atom x-over in S.A.	18.00	54.00	140.00
31-35,37,38: 31-Hawkman x-over. 37-Intro. Major Mynah; Hawkman cameo			
	6.50	19.50	48.00
36-G.A. Atom x-over	8.50	26.00	65.00

NOTE: **Anderson** a-1-11i, 13i; c-inks-1-25, 31-35, 37. **Sid Greene** a-8i-37i. **Gil Kane** a-1p-37p;
c-1p-28p, 29, 33p, 34. **George Roussos** 38i **Mike Sekowsky** 38p Time Pool stories also in 6,
9,12, 17, 21, 27, 35.

ATOM AGE (See Classics Illustrated Special Issue)

ATOM-AGE COMBAT
June, 1952 - No. 5, Apr, 1953; Feb, 1958
St. John Publishing Co.

	GD25	FN65	NM94
1-Buck Vinson in all	40.00	120.00	300.00
2-Flying saucer story	24.00	71.00	165.00
3,5: 3-Mayo-a (6 pgs.). 5-Flying saucer-c/story	19.00	56.00	130.00
4 (Scarce)	24.00	71.00	165.00
1(2/58-St. John)	16.00	47.00	110.00

ATOM-AGE COMBAT
Nov, 1958 - No. 3, Mar, 1959
Fago Magazines

1-All have Dick Ayers-c/a	21.00	64.00	150.00
2,3: 2-A-Bomb explosion-c	16.00	47.00	110.00

ATOMAN
Feb, 1946 - No. 2, April, 1946
Spark Publications

1-Origin & 1st app. Atoman; Robinson/Meskin-a; Kidcrusaders, Wild Bill			
Hickok, Marvin the Great app.	47.00	141.00	375.00
2-Robinson/Meskin-a; Robinson c-1,2	39.00	118.00	275.00

ATOM & HAWKMAN, THE (Formerly The Atom)
No. 39, Oct-Nov, 1968 - No. 45, Oct-Nov, 1969
National Periodical Publications

39-45: 40-41- Kubert/Anderson-a. 43-Last 12¢ issue; 1st app. Gentleman			
Ghost, origin in #44	5.70	17.00	45.00

NOTE: **M. Anderson** a-39, 40i, 41i, 43, 44. **Sid Greene** a-40i-45i. **Kubert** a-40p, 41p; c-39-45.

ATOM ANT (TV) (See Golden Comics Digest #2)
January, 1966 (12¢)
Gold Key

1(10170-601)-Hanna-Barbera character	23.50	86.00	235.00

ATOM ANT & SECRET SQUIRREL
Nov, 1995 - Present ($1.50, bi-monthly)
Archie Publications

1-12-Hanna-Barbera characters			1.50

ATOMIC AGE
Nov, 1990 - No. 4, Feb, 1991 ($4.50, limited series, squarebound, 52 pgs.)
Marvel Comics (Epic Comics)

1-4: Williamson-a(i)		1.80	4.50

ATOMIC ATTACK (True War Stories; formerly Attack, first series)
No. 5, Jan, 1953 - No. 8, Oct, 1953 (1st story is sci/fi in all issues)
Youthful Magazines

5-Atomic bomb-c; science fiction stories in all	32.00	96.00	225.00
6-8	19.00	58.00	135.00

ATOMIC BOMB
1945 (36 pgs.)
Jay Burtis Publications

1-Airmale & Stampy	40.00	120.00	300.00

ATOMIC BUNNY (Formerly Atomic Rabbit)
No. 12, Aug, 1958 - No. 19, Dec, 1959
Charlton Comics

12	11.00	33.00	75.00
13-19	6.70	20.00	40.00

ATOMIC COMICS
Jan, 1946 (Reprints, one-shot)
Daniels Publications (Canadian)

1-Rocketman, Yankee Boy, Master Key app.	27.00	81.00	190.00

ATOMIC COMICS
Jan, 1946 - No. 4, July-Aug, 1946 (#1-4 were printed w/o cover gloss)
Green Publishing Co.

1-Radio Squad by Siegel & Shuster; Barry O'Neal app.; Fang Gow cover-r/			
Detective Comics (Classic-c)	125.00	375.00	1000.00
2-Inspector Dayton; Kid Kane by Matt Baker; Lucky Wings, Congo King,			

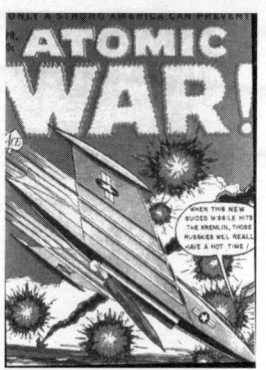
Atomic War! #4 © ACE

Atomik Angels #3 © William Tucci

Atom Special #2 © DC

AU

	GD25	FN65	NM94
Prop Powers (only app.) begin	53.00	160.00	425.00
3,4: 3-Zero Ghost Detective app.; Baker-a(2) each; 4-Baker-c			
	40.00	120.00	285.00

ATOMIC KNIGHTS (See Strange Adventures #117)
ATOMIC MOUSE (TV, Movies) (See Blue Bird, Funny Animals, Giant Comics Edition &Wotalife Comics)
3/53 - No. 54, 6/63; No. 1, 12/84; V2#10, 9/85 - No. 13, ?/86
Capitol Stories/Charlton Comics

1-Origin & 1st app.; Al Fago-c/a in all?	28.00	84.00	195.00
2	10.00	30.00	70.00
3-10: 5-Timmy The Timid Ghost app.; see Zoo Funnies			
	9.15	27.50	55.00
11-13,16-25	4.70	14.00	28.00
14,15-Hoppy The Marvel Bunny app.	7.00	21.00	42.00
26-(68 pgs.)	10.00	30.00	60.00
27-40: 36,37-Atom The Cat app.	4.00	12.00	24.00
41-54	2.60	6.50	13.00
1 (1984)			1.00
V2#10 (10/85) -13-Fago-r. #12(1/86)			1.00

ATOMIC RABBIT (Atomic Bunny #12 on; see Giant Comics #3 & Wotalife)
Aug, 1955 - No. 11, Mar, 1958
Charlton Comics

1-Origin & 1st app.; Al Fago-c/a in all?	25.00	75.00	175.00
2	10.00	30.00	65.00
3-10	7.00	21.00	42.00
11-(68 pgs.)	10.00	30.00	65.00

ATOMIC SPY CASES
Mar-Apr, 1950 (Painted-c)
Avon Periodicals

1-No Wood-a; A-bomb blast panels; Fass-a	26.00	77.00	180.00

ATOMIC THUNDERBOLT, THE
Feb, 1946 (one-shot)
Regor Company

1-Intro. Atomic Thunderbolt & Mr. Murdo	44.00	132.00	350.00

ATOMIC WAR!
Nov, 1952 - No. 4, Apr, 1953
Ace Periodicals (Junior Books)

1-Atomic bomb-c	75.00	225.00	600.00
2,3: 3-Atomic bomb-c	50.00	150.00	400.00
4-Used in POP, pg. 96 & illo.	50.00	150.00	400.00

ATOMIK ANGELS
May, 1996 - Present ($2.50)
Crusade Comics

1-3: 1-Freefall from Gen 13 app		1.20	3.00
1-Variant-c	1.30	3.25	8.00
Intrep-Edition (2/96, B&W, giveaway at launch party)-Previews Atomik Angels #1; includes Billy Tucci interview.			10.00

ATOM SPECIAL (See Atom & Justice League of America)
1993/1995 ($2.50/$2.95)
DC Comics

1-(1993, $2.50, 68 pgs.)-Dillon-c/a.		1.00	2.50
2-(1995, $2.95)-Dillon-c/a.		1.20	3.00

ATOM THE CAT (Formerly Tom Cat; see Giant Comics #3)
No. 9, Oct, 1957 - No. 17, Aug, 1959
Charlton Comics

9	7.50	22.50	45.00
10,13-17	4.35	13.00	26.00
11,12: 11(64pgs)-Atomic Mouse app. 12(100 pgs.)	10.00	30.00	60.00

	GD25	FN65	NM94

ATTACK
May, 1952 - No. 4, Nov, 1952; No. 5, Jan, 1953 - No. 5, Sept, 1953
Youthful Mag./Trojan No. 5 on

1-(1st series)-Extreme violence	21.00	64.00	150.00
2,3-Both Harrison-c/a; bondage, whipping	10.00	30.00	70.00
4-Krenkel-a (7 pgs.); Harrison-a (becomes Atomic Attack #5 on)			
	11.00	33.00	75.00
5-(#1, Trojan, 2nd series)	10.00	30.00	60.00
6-8 (#2-4), 5	6.70	20.00	40.00

ATTACK
No. 54, 1958 - No. 60, Nov, 1959
Charlton Comics

54 (25¢, 100 pgs.)	9.15	27.50	55.00
55-60	3.60	9.00	18.00

ATTACK!
1962 - No. 15, 3/75; No. 16, 8/79 - No. 48, 10/84
Charlton Comics

nn(#1)-('62) Special Edition	3.60	11.00	25.00
2('63), 3(Fall, '64)	2.00	6.00	14.00
V4#3(10/66), 4(10/67)-(Formerly Special War Series #2; becomes Attack At Sea V4#5)	1.65	4.20	10.00
1(9/71)		1.80	4.50
2-15(3/75): 4-American Eagle app.		.80	2.00
16(8/79) - 47			1.25
48(10/84)-Wood-r; S&K-c			1.50
Modern Comics 13('78)-r			1.00

ATTACK!
1975 (39¢/49¢, 36 pgs.)
Spire Christian Comics (Fleming H. Revell Co.)

nn			1.00

ATTACK AT SEA (Formerly Attack!, 1967)
V4#5, Oct, 1968
Charlton Comics

V4#5	1.65	4.20	10.00

ATTACK ON PLANET MARS (See Strange Worlds #18)
1951
Avon Periodicals

nn-Infantino, Fawcette, Kubert & Wood-a; adaptation of Tarrano the Conqueror by Ray Cummings	62.00	190.00	500.00

ATTITUDE LAD
Apr, 1994 - No. 3, Nov, 1994 ($2.95, B&W, limited series)
Slave Labor Graphics

1-3			3.00

AUDREY & MELVIN (Formerly Little...)(See Little Audrey & Melvin)
No. 62, Sept, 1974
Harvey Publications

62		.80	2.00

AUGIE DOGGIE (TV) (See Hanna-Barbera Band Wagon, Quick-Draw McGraw, Spotlight #2, Top Cat & Whitman Comic Books)
October, 1963 (12¢)
Gold Key

1-Hanna-Barbera character	13.00	47.00	130.00

AURORA COMIC SCENES INSTRUCTION BOOKLET
1974 (6-1/4x9-3/4," 8 pgs., slick paper) (Included with superhero model kits)
Aurora Plastics Co.

181-140-Tarzan; Neal Adams-a		1.60	4.00

182-140-Spider-Man. 183-140-Tonto(Gil Kane art). 184-140-Hulk. 185-140-Superman. 186-140-Superboy. 187-140-Batman. 188-140-The Lone

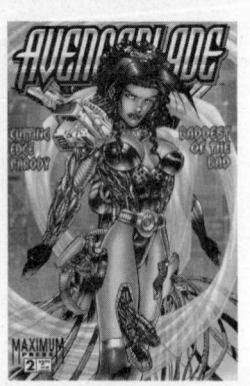
Avengeblade #2 © Rob Liefeld

Avengelyne #2 © Rob Liefeld

Avengers #7 © MEG

Ranger(1974-by Gil Kane). 192-140-Captain America(1975). 193-140-
Robin   each....   1.20   3.00

AUTHENTIC POLICE CASES
2/48 - No. 6, 11/48; No. 7, 5/50 - No. 38, 3/55
St. John Publishing Co.

1-Hale the Magician by Tuska begins	33.00	99.00	230.00
2-Lady Satan, Johnny Rebel app.	20.00	60.00	140.00
3-Veiled Avenger app.; blood drainage story plus 2 Lucky Coyne stories; used in SOTI, illo. from Red Seal #16	39.00	118.00	275.00
4,5: 4-Masked Black Jack app. 5-Late 1930s Jack Cole-a(r); transvestism story	21.00	64.00	150.00
6-Matt Baker-c; used in SOTI, illo- "An invitation to learning", r-in Fugitives From Justice #3; Jack Cole-a; also used by the N.Y. Legis. Comm.	40.00	120.00	285.00
7,8,10-14: 7-Jack Cole-a; Matt Baker begins #8, ends #?; Vic Flint in #10-14. 10-12-Baker-a(2 each)	17.00	49.00	115.00
9-No Vic Flint	13.00	39.00	90.00
15-Drug-c/story; Vic Flint app.; Baker-c	17.00	49.00	115.00
16,18,20,21,23: Baker-a(i)	10.00	30.00	68.00
17,19,22-Baker-c	11.00	33.00	75.00
24-28 (All 100 pgs.): 26-Transvestism	19.00	56.00	130.00
29,30	6.00	18.00	36.00
31,32	7.50	22.50	45.00
33-38: 33-Transvestism; Baker-c. 34-Baker-c/a(2); r/#95. 35-Baker-c/a(2); r/#10 36-r/#11; Vic Flint strip-r; Baker-c/a(2) unsigned. 37-Baker-c; r/#17. 38-Baker-c/a; r/#18	9.15	27.50	55.00

NOTE: Matt Baker c-6-16, 17, 19, 22, 27, 29, 31-38; a-13, 16. Bondage c-1, 3.

AUTUMN
1995 - Present ($2.95, B&W)
Caliber Comics

1-3		1.20	3.00

AUTUMN ADVENTURES (Walt Disney's...)
Autumn, 1990; No. 2, Autumn, 1991 ($2.95, 68 pgs.)
Disney Comics

1-Donald Duck-r(2) by Barks, Pluto-r, & new-a		1.30	3.25
2-D. Duck-r by Barks; new Super Goof story		1.30	3.25

AVATAR
Feb, 1991 - No. 3, Apr, 1991 ($5.95, limited series, 100 pgs.)
DC Comics

1-3: Based on TSR's Forgotten Realms	1.20	3.00	6.00

AVENGEBLADE
July, 1996 - No. 2, Aug, 1996 ($2.99, limited series)
Maximum Press

1,2: Bad Girls parody		1.20	3.00

AVENGELYNE
May, 1995 - No. 3, July, 1995 ($2.50/$3.50, limited series)
Maximum Press

1/2			15.00
1-Newstand ($2.50)-Photo-c; poster insert	1.00	2.00	5.00
1-Direct Market ($3.50)-Chromium-c; poster	1.30	3.25	8.00
1-Glossy edition	4.30	13.00	30.00
1-Gold	3.60	11.00	25.00
2-3: 2-Polybagged w/card		1.60	4.00
3-Variant-c; Deodato pin-up	1.00	2.00	5.00
...Swimsuit (8/95, $2.95)-Pin-ups/photos. 3-Variant-c exist (2 photo, 1 Liefeld-a)		1.20	3.00
...Swimsuit (1/96, $3.50, 2nd printing)-photo-c		1.40	3.50
Trade paperback (12/95, $9.95)			10.00

AVENGELYNE
V2#1, Apr, 1996 - Present ($2.95/$2.50)

Maximum Press

V2#1-4: 1-Four covers exist (2 photo-c). 2-Three covers exist (1 photo-c); flip book w/Darkchylde. 3-Flip book w/Priest preview. 4-Cybrid app; w/Darkchyld/Avengelyne poster. 5-Flip book w/Blindside. 6-Divinity-c/app.			3.00

AVENGELYNE: DEADLY SINS
Feb, 1996 - No. 2, Mar, 1996 ($2.95, limited series)
Maximum Press

1,2: 1-Two-c exist (1 photo, 1 Liefeld-a). 2-Liefeld-c; Pop Mhan-a(p).			3.00

AVENGELYNE/GLORY
Sept, 1995 ($3.95, one-shot)
Maximum Press

1-Chromium-c			4.00
1-Variant-c			5.00

AVENGELYNE/GLORY SWIMSUIT SPECIAL
June, 1996 ($2.95)
Maximum Press

1-Pin-ups & photos of Avengelyne and Glory; photo-c (variant illos-c. also exists)			3.00

AVENGELYNE/POWER
Nov, 1995 - No.3, Jan, 1996 ($2.95, limited series)
Maximum Press

1-3: 1,2-Liefeld-c. 3-Three variant-c. exist (1 photo-c)	1.00		2.50
1-Variant-c	1.40		3.50

AVENGELYNE • PROPHET
May, 1996 ($2.95, unfinished limited series)
Maximum Press

1-Liefeld-c/a(p)			3.00

AVENGER, THE (See A-1 Comics)
Feb-Mar, 1955 - No. 4, Aug-Sept, 1955
Magazine Enterprises

1(A-1 #129)-Origin	36.00	107.00	250.00
2(A-1 #131), 3(A-1 #133), 4(A-1 #138)	23.00	69.00	160.00
IW Reprint #9('64)-Reprints #1 (new cover)	4.00	11.00	22.00

NOTE: Powell a-2-4; c-1-4.

AVENGERS, THE (See Giant-Size..., Kree/Skrull War Starring..., Marvel Graphic Novel #27, Marvel Super Action, Marvel Super Heroes('66), Marvel Treasury Ed., Marvel Triple Action, Solo Avengers, Tales Of Suspense #49, West Coast Avengers & X-Men Vs....)

AVENGERS, THE (The Mighty Avengers on cover only #63-69)
Sept, 1963 - No. 402, Sept, 1996
Marvel Comics Group

	GD25	FN65	VF82	NM94
1-Origin & 1st app. The Avengers (Thor, Iron Man, Hulk, Ant-Man, Wasp); Loki app.	230.00	690.00	1495.00	2400.00

	GD25	FN65		NM94
2-Hulk leaves Avengers	68.00	204.00		610.00
3-1st Sub-Mariner x-over (outside the F.F.); Hulk & Sub-Mariner team-up & battle Avengers; Spider-Man cameo (1/64)	47.00	140.00		375.00
4-Revival of Captain America who joins the Avengers; 1st Silver Age app. of Captain America & Bucky (3/64)	135.00	405.00		1400.00
4-Reprint from the Golden Record Comic set With Record (1966)	13.50	41.00		95.00
	16.00	47.00		110.00
5-Hulk app.	32.00	96.00		250.00
6-8: 6-Intro/1st app. original Zemo & his Masters of Evil. 8-Intro Kang	24.00	73.00		175.00
9-Intro Wonder Man who dies in same story	26.00	77.00		180.00
10-Intro/1st app. Immortus; early Hercules app. (11/64)	21.00	64.00		150.00
11-Spider-Man-c & x-over (12/64)	25.00	75.00		180.00
12-15: 15-Death of original Zemo	14.00	43.00		110.00

Avengers #63 © MEG

Avengers #215 © MEG

Avengers Annual #23 © MEG

	GD25	FN65	NM94

16-New Avengers line-up (Hawkeye, Quicksilver, Scarlet Witch join; Thor, Iron Man, Giant-Man, Wasp leave) — 16.00 / 47.00 / 120.00

17-19: 19-Intro/1st app. Swordsman; origin Hawkeye (8/65) — 11.00 / 33.00 / 80.00

20-22: Wood inks — 7.00 / 21.50 / 55.00

23-30: 25-Dr. Doom-c/story. 28-Giant-Man becomes Goliath (5/66) — 5.30 / 16.00 / 40.00

31-40 — 3.90 / 11.50 / 30.00

41-52,54-56: 43,44-1st app. Red Guardian. 46-Ant-Man returns (re-intro, 11/67). 47-Magneto-c/story. 48-Origin/1st app. new Black Knight (1/68). 52-Black Panther joins; 1st app. The Grim Reaper. 54-1st app. new Masters of Evil. 56-Zemo app; story explains how Capt. America became imprisoned in ice during WWII, only to be rescued in Avengers #4. — 3.60 / 11.00 / 25.00

53-X-Men app. — 4.75 / 14.25 / 38.00

57-1st app. S.A. Vision (10/68) — 10.00 / 30.00 / 75.00

58-Origin The Vision — 6.50 / 19.50 / 50.00

59-67: 59-Intro. Yellowjacket. 60-Wasp & Yellowjacket wed. 63-Goliath becomes Yellowjacket; Hawkeye becomes the new Goliath. 65-Last 12¢ issue. 66,67-B. Smith-a — 2.85 / 8.50 / 20.00

68-70: 70-Nighthawk on cover — 2.00 / 6.00 / 14.00

71-1st app. The Invaders (12/69); 1st app. Nighthawk; Black Knight joins — 3.25 / 9.50 / 22.00

72-82,84-86,88-91: 80-Intro. Red Wolf (9/70). 82-Daredevil app. 88-Written by Harlan Ellison — 2.15 / 6.50 / 15.00

83-Intro. The Liberators (Wasp, Valkyrie, Scarlet Witch, Medusa & the Black Widow) — 1.70 / 5.00 / 12.00

87-Origin The Black Panther — 4.30 / 13.00 / 32.00

92-Last 15¢ issue; Neal Adams-c — 1.90 / 6.00 / 13.00

93-(52 pgs.)-Neal Adams-c/a — 7.00 / 21.50 / 52.00

94-96-Neal Adams-c/a — 4.50 / 14.00 / 32.00

97-G.A. Capt. America, Sub-Mariner, Human Torch, Patriot, Vision, Blazing Skull, Fin, Angel, & new Capt. Marvel x-over — 3.25 / 9.50 / 22.00

98,99: 98-Goliath becomes Hawkeye; Smith c/a(i). 99-Smith-c, Smith/Sutton-a — 3.90 / 11.50 / 27.00

100-(6/72)-Smith-c/a; featuring everyone who was an Avenger — 11.00 / 33.00 / 75.00

101-106,108,109: 101-Harlan Ellison scripts — 1.50 / 3.80 / 9.00

107-Starlin-a(p) — 1.65 / 4.20 / 10.00

110,111-X-Men app. — 2.85 / 8.50 / 20.00

112-1st app. Mantis — 1.70 / 5.00 / 12.00

113-124,126-130: 116-118-Defenders/Silver Surfer app. 123-Origin Mantis — 1.20 / 2.90 / 7.00

125-Thanos-c & brief app. — 2.15 / 6.50 / 15.00

131-140: 134,135-True origin Vision. 136-Ploog-r/Amazing Advs. #12 — 1.20 / 2.40 / 6.00

141-163: 144-Origin & 1st app. Hellcat. 146-25¢ & 30¢ variants exist. 150-Kirby-a(r); new line-up: Capt. America, Scarlet Witch, Iron Man, Wasp, Yellowjacket, Vision & The Beast. 151-Wonder Man returns w/new costume — 1.00 / 2.00 / 5.00

164-166: Byrne-a — 1.20 / 2.40 / 6.00

167-191: 168-Guardians of the Galaxy app. 174-Thanos cameo. 176-Starhawk app. 181-191-Byrne-a. 181-New line-up: Capt. America, Scarlet Witch, Iron Man, Wasp, Vision, Beast & The Falcon. 183-Ms. Marvel joins. 185-Origin Quicksilver & Scarlet Witch — 1.20 / 3.00 / 8.00

192-213,215-262: 195-1st app Taskmaster. 200-(10/80, 52 pgs.)-Ms. Marvel leaves. 211-New line-up: Capt. America, Iron Man, Tigra, Thor, Wasp & Yellowjacket. 213-Yellowjacket leaves. 215,216-Silver Surfer app. 216-Tigra leaves. 217-Yellowjacket & Wasp return. 221-Hawkeye & She-Hulk join. 227-Capt. Marvel (female) joins; origins of Ant-Man, Wasp, Giant-Man, Goliath, Yellowjacket, & Avengers. 230-Yellowjacket quits. 231-Iron Man leaves. 232-Starfox (Eros) joins. 234-Death Quicksilver, Scarlet Witch. 236-New logo. 238-Origin Blackout. 239-Avengers app. on David Letterman show. 240-Spider-Woman revived. 250-($1.00, 52 pgs.) — .90 / 2.25

214-Ghost Rider-c/story — 1.60 / 4.00

263-1st app. X-Factor (1/86)(story continues in Fantastic Four #286) — 1.00 / 2.60 / 6.00

264-299: 272-Alpha Flight app. 291-$1.00 issues begin. 297-Black Knight, She-Hulk & Thor resign. 298-Inferno tie-in — .80 / 2.00

300 (2/89, $1.75, 68 pgs.)-Thor joins; Simonson-a — 1.20 / 3.00

301-304,306-325,327,329-343: 302-Re-intro Quasar. 314-318-Spider-Man x-over. 320-324-Alpha Flight app. (320-cameo). 327-2nd app. Rage. 341, 342-New Warriors app. 343-Last $1.00-c — 1.50

305-Byrne scripts begin — .80 / 2.00

326-1st app. Rage (11/90) — 1.00 / 2.00 / 5.00

328-Origin Rage — 1.60 / 4.00

344-346,348,349,351-359,361,362,364,365,367: 365-Contains coupon for Hunt for Magneto contest — 1.50

347-($1.75, 56 pgs.) — .80 / 2.00

350-($2.50, 68 pgs.)-Double gatefold-c showing-c to #1; r/#53 w/cover in flip book format; vs. The Starjammers — 1.20 / 3.00

360-($2.95, 52 pgs.)-Embossed all-foil-c; 30th ann. — 1.00 / 2.00 / 5.00

363-($2.95, 52 pgs.)-All silver foil-c — 1.20 / 3.00

366-($3.95, 68 pgs.)-Embossed all gold foil-c — 1.60 / 4.00

368-Bloodties part 1; Avengers/X-Men x-over — 1.50

369-($2.95)-Foil embossed-c; Bloodties part 5 — 1.20 / 3.00

370-373 — 1.25

374,376-399: 374-$1.50-c begins; bound-in trading card sheet. 380-Deodato-a. 390,391-"The Crossing." 395-Death of "old" Tony Stark; wraparound-c. — 1.50

375-($2.00, 52 pgs.)-Regular ed.; Thunderstrike returns; leads into Malibu Comics' Black September. — .80 / 2.00

375-($2.50, 52 pgs.)-Collector's ed. w/bound-in poster; leads into Malibu Comics' Black September. — 1.00 / 2.50 / 1.50

400-Waid-s — 1.60 / 4.00

401,402: Waid's ed; 402-Deodato breakdowns; cont'd in X-Men #56 & Onslaught: Marvel Universe. — 1.00 / 2.50

Special 1(9/67, 25¢, 68 pgs.)-New-a; original & new Avengers team-up — 7.00 / 21.50 / 50.00

Special 2(9/68, 25¢, 68 pgs.)-New-a; original vs. new Avengers — 3.40 / 10.00 / 24.00

Special 3(9/69, 25¢, 68 pgs.)-r/Avengers #4 plus 3 Capt. America stories by Kirby (art); origin Red Skull — 4.00 / 12.00 / 28.00

Special 4(1/71, 25¢, 68 pgs.)-Kirby-r/Avengers #5,6 — 1.65 / 4.20 / 10.00

Special 5(1/72)-Spider-Man x-over — 1.50 / 3.75 / 9.00

Annual 6(11/76) — 1.00 / 2.60 / 6.00

Annual 7(11/77)-Starlin-c/a; Warlock dies; Thanos app. — 3.60 / 11.00 / 25.00

Annual 8(1978)-Dr. Strange, Ms. Marvel app. — 1.80 / 4.50

Annual 9(1979)-Newton-a(p) — 1.40 / 3.50

Annual 10(1981)-Golden-p; X-Men cameo; 1st app. Rogue & Madelyne Pryor — 3.60 / 11.00 / 25.00

Annual 11-16: 11(1982)-Vs. the Defenders. 12(1983). 13(1984). 14(1985). 15(1986). 16(1987) — 1.40 / 3.50

Annual 17(1988)-Evolutionary War x-over — 1.60 / 4.00

Annual 18(1989, $2.00, 68 pgs.)-Atlantis Attacks — 1.20 / 3.00

Annual 19,20(1990, 1991)(both $2.00, 68 pgs.) — 1.00 / 2.50

Annual 21(1992, $2.25, 68 pgs.) — .90 / 2.25

Annual 22(1993, $2.95, 68 pgs.)-Bagged w/card — 1.20 / 3.00

Annual 23(1994, $2.95, 68 pgs.) — 1.20 / 3.00

Marvel Double Feature...Avengers/Giant-Man #379 ($2.50, 52 pgs.)-Same as Avengers #379 w/Giant-Man flip book — 1.00 / 2.50

The Yesterday Quest ($6.95)-r/#181,182,185-187 — 1.20 / 3.00 / 7.00

NOTE: **Austin** c(i)-157, 167, 168, 170-177, 181, 183-188, 198-201, Annual 8. **John Buscema** a-41-44p, 46p, 47p, 49, 50, 51-62p, 74-77, 79-85, 87-91, 97, 105p; 121p, 124p,125p, 152, 153p, 255-279p, 281-302p; c-41-66, 68-71, 73-91, 97-99, 178, 256-259p, 261-279p, 281-302p. **Byrne** a-164-166p, 181-191p, 233p, Annual 13; 14p; c-186-190p, 233p, 260, 305p; scripts-305-312. **Colan** a(i)-155, 161, 206-208, 210, 211; c(p)-65, 206-208, 210, 211. **Ditko** a-Annual 13. **Guice** a-Annual 12p. **Don Heck** a-9-15, 17-40, 157. **Kane** c-37p, 159p. **Kane/Everett** c-97. **Kirby** a-1-8p, Special 3r, 4r(p); c-1-30, 148, 151-158; layouts-14-16. **Ron Lim** c(p)-335-341. **Miller** c-193p.

Avengers V2#1 © MEG

Avengers West Coast #64 © MEG

Azrael #25 © DC

Mooney a-86i, 179p, 180p. **Nebres** a-178i; c-179i. **Newton** a-204p, Annual 9p. **Perez** a(p)-141, 143, 144, 148, 150, 154, 155, 160, 161, 162, 167,168, 170, 171, 194-196, 198-202, Annual 6, 8; c(p)-160-162, 164-166, 170-174, 181,183-185, 191, 192, 194-201, 379-382, Annual 8. **Starlin** c-121, 135. **Staton** a-127-134i. **Tuska** a-47i,48i, 51i, 53i, 54i, 106p, 107p, 135p, 137-140p, 163p. Guardians of the Galaxy app. in #167, 168, 170, 173, 175, 181.

AVENGERS, THE (2nd Series)
V2#1, Nov, 1996 - Present ($2.95/$1.95) (Produced by Extreme Studios)
Marvel Comics

V2#1-($2.95)-Heroes Reborn begins; intro new team (Captain America, Swordsman, Scarlet Witch, Vision, Thor, Hellcat & Hawkeye); 1st app. Avengers Island; Loki & Enchantress app.; Rob Liefeld-p & plot; Chap Yaep-p; Jim Valentino scripts; variant-c exists			3.00
V2#2-12: 2-Begin $1.95-c; Jeph Loeb scripts begin. 2,3-Kang app.			2.00

AVENGERS, THE (TV)(Also see Steed and Mrs. Peel)
Nov, 1968 ("John Steed & Emma Peel" cover title) (15¢)
Gold Key

1-Photo-c	22.50	68.00	225.00

AVENGERS COLLECTOR'S EDITION, THE
1993 (Ordered through mail w/candy wrapper, 20 pgs.)
Marvel Comics

1-Contains 4 bound-in trading cards		.80	2.00

AVENGERS LOG, THE
Feb, 1994 ($1.95)
Marvel Comics

1-Gives history of all members; Perez-c		.80	2.00

AVENGERS SPOTLIGHT (Formerly Solo Avengers #1-20)
No. 21, Aug, 1989 - No. 40, Jan, 1991 (75¢/$1.00)
Marvel Comics

21 (75¢)-Byrne-c/a			1.00
22-40 ($1.00): 26-Acts of Vengeance story. 31-34-U.S. Agent series. 36-Heck-i. 37-Mortimer-i. 40-The Black Knight app.			1.00

AVENGERS STRIKEFILE
Jan, 1994 ($1.75, one-shot)
Marvel Comics

1		.70	1.75

AVENGERS: THE CROSSING
July, 1995 ($4.95, one-shot)
Marvel Comics

1-Deodato-c/a; 1st app. Thor's new costume	1.00	2.00	5.00

AVENGERS: THE LEGEND
Oct, 1996 ($3.95, one-shot)
Marvel Comics

1-Tribute issue			4.00

AVENGERS: THE TERMINATRIX OBJECTIVE
Sept, 1993 - No. 4, Dec, 1993 ($1.25, limited series)
Marvel Comics

1 ($2.50)-Holo-grafx foil-c		1.00	2.50
2-4-Old vs. new Avengers			1.25

AVENGERS: TIMESLIDE
Feb, 1996 ($4.95, one-shot)
Marvel Comics

1-Foil-c	1.00	2.00	5.00

AVENGERS/ULTRAFORCE (See Ultraforce/Avengers)
Oct, 1995 ($3.95, one-shot)
Marvel Comics

1-Wraparound foil-c by Perez		1.60	4.00

AVENGERS UNPLUGGED
Oct, 1995 - No. 6, Aug, 1996 (99¢, bi-monthly)
Marvel Comics

1-6			1.00

AVENGERS WEST COAST (Formerly West Coast Avengers)
No. 48, Sept, 1989 - No. 102, Jan, 1994 ($1.00/$1.25)
Marvel Comics

48,49: 48-Byrne-c/a & scripts continue thru #57			1.10
50-Re-intro original Human Torch			1.50
51-74,76-99,101,102: 54-Cover swipe/F.F. #1. 70-Spider-Woman app. 78-Last $1.00-c. 79-Dr. Strange x-over. 84-Origin Spider-Woman retold; Spider-Man app. (also in #85,86). 87,88-Wolverine-c/story. 93-95-Darkhawk app. 101-X-Men x-over			1.25
75-($1.50, 52 pgs.)-Fantastic Four x-over			1.50
100-($3.95, 68 pgs.)-Embossed all red foil-c		1.60	4.00
Annual 8 (1993, $2.95, 68 pgs.)-Bagged w/card		1.20	3.00

AVIATION ADVENTURES AND MODEL BUILDING
No. 16, Dec, 1946 - No. 17, Feb, 1947 (True Aviation Advs. ...No. 15)
Parents' Magazine Institute

16,17-Half comics and half pictures	5.85	17.50	35.00

AVIATION CADETS
1943
Street & Smith Publications

nn	13.00	39.00	90.00

A-V IN 3-D
Dec, 1984 ($2.00, 28 pgs. w/glasses)
Aardvark-Vanaheim

1-Cerebus, Flaming Carrot, Normalman & Ms. Tree		.80	2.00

AWFUL OSCAR (Formerly & becomes Oscar Comics with No. 13)
No. 11, June, 1949 - No. 12, Aug, 1949
Marvel Comics

11,12	6.70	20.00	40.00

AWKWARD UNIVERSE
12/95 ($9.95, graphic novel)
Slave Labor Graphics

nn			10.00

AXA
Apr, 1987 - No. 2, Aug, 1987 ($1.75)
Eclipse Comics

1,2		.70	1.80

AXEL PRESSBUTTON (Pressbutton No. 5; see Laser Eraser &...)
Nov, 1984 - No. 6, July, 1985 ($1.50/$1.75, Baxter paper)
Eclipse Comics

1-6: Reprints Warrior (British mag.). 1-Bolland-c; origin Laser Eraser & Pressbutton		.70	1.80

AXIS ALPHA
Feb, 1994 ($2.50, one-shot)
Axis Comics

V1-Previews Axis titles including, Tribe, Dethgrip, B.E.A.S.T.I.E.S. & more; Pitt app. in Tribe story.		1.00	2.50

AZRAEL (Also see Batman: Sword of Azrael)
Feb, 1995 - Present ($1.95)
DC Comics

1-Dennis O'Neill scripts begin	1.00	2.60	6.00
2,3		1.60	4.00
4-24: 5,6-Ras Al Ghul app. 13-Nightwing-c/app. 15-Contagion Pt. 5 (Pt. 4 on-c). 16-Contagion Pt. 10. 22-Batman-c/app..		.80	2.00
Annual 1 (1995, $3.95)-Year One story		1.60	4.00
Annual 2 (1996, $2.95)-Legends of the Dead Earth story		1.20	3.00

Aztek: The Ultimate Man #6 © DC

Babe #1 © John Byrne

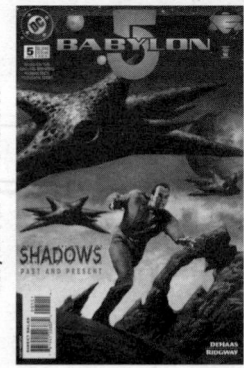

Babylon 5 #5 © Warner Bros.

BA

	GD25	FN65	NM94

AZTEC ACE
Mar, 1984 - No. 15, Sept, 1985 ($2.25/$1.50/$1.75, Baxter paper)
Eclipse Comics

		GD25	FN65	NM94
1-$2.25-c (52 pgs.)			.90	2.30
2,3: 2-Begin $1.50-c & 36 pgs.				1.50
4-15: ($1.75/$1.50-c)			.70	1.80

NOTE: *N. Redondo a-1i-8i, 10i. c-6-8i.*

AZTEK: THE ULTIMATE MAN
Aug, 1996 - Present ($1.75)
DC Comics

1-8: 1-1st app. Aztek & Synth; Grant Morrison & Mark Millar scripts in all.
2-Green Lantern app. 3-1st app. Death-Doll. 4-Intro The Lizard King.
5-Origin. 6-Joker app.; Batman cameo. 7-Batman app. 1.75
NOTE: *Breyfogle c-5p. N. Steven Harris a-1-5p. Porter c-1p. Wieringo c-2p.*

BABE (...Darling of the Hills, later issues)(See Big Shot and Sparky Watts)
June-July, 1948 - No. 11, Apr-May, 1950
Prize/Headline/Feature

		GD25	FN65	NM94
1-Boody Rogers-a		16.00	47.00	110.00
2-Boody Rogers-a		10.00	30.00	70.00
3-11-All by Boody Rogers		10.00	30.00	60.00

BABE
July, 1994 - No. 4, Jan, 1994 ($2.50, limited series)
Dark Horse Comics (Legend)

1-4: John Byrne-c/a/scripts; ProtoTykes back-up story .... 1.00 ... 2.50

BABE RUTH SPORTS COMICS (Becomes Rags Rabbit #11 on?)
April, 1949 - No. 11, Feb, 1951
Harvey Publications

		GD25	FN65	NM94
1-Powell-a		36.00	107.00	250.00
2-Powell-a		26.00	77.00	180.00
3-11: Powell-a in most		21.00	64.00	150.00

NOTE: *Baseball c-2-4, 9. Basketball c-1, 6. Football c-5. Yogi Berra c/story-8. Joe DiMaggio c/story-3. Bob Feller c/story-4. Stan Musial c-9.*

BABES IN TOYLAND (Disney, Movie) (See Golden Pix Story Book ST-3)
No. 1282, Feb-Apr, 1962
Dell Publishing Co.

Four Color 1282-Annette Funicello photo-c ... 11.50 ... 40.00 ... 115.00

BABES OF BROADWAY
May, 1996 ($2.95, one-shot)
Broadway Comics

1-Pin-ups of Broadway Comics' female characters; Alan Davis, Michael Kaluta,
J. G. Jones, Alan Weiss, Guy Davis & others-a; Giordano-c.
.... 3.00

BABE 2
Mar, 1995 - No. 2, May, 1995 ($2.50, limited series)
Dark Horse Comics (Legend)

1,2: John Byrne-c/a/scripts .... 1.00 ... 2.50

BABY ANGEL X
1995 ($2.95, B&W, mature)
Brainstorm Comics

		GD25	FN65	NM94
1			1.20	3.00
1-Gold ($5.00)	1.00		2.00	5.00

BABY HUEY
No. 100, Oct, 1990 - No. 101, Nov, 1990; No. 1, Oct, 1991 - No. 9, June, 1994
($1.00/$1.25/$1.50, quarterly)
Harvey Comics

100,101,1,2 ($1.00): 1-Cover says "Big Baby Huey" 1.00
3-7 ($1.25) 1.25
8,9 ($1.50) 1.50

BABY HUEY AND PAPA (See Paramount Animated...)
May, 1962 - No. 33, Jan, 1968 (Also see Casper The Friendly Ghost)
Harvey Publications

		GD25	FN65	NM94
1		14.00	43.00	140.00
2		6.00	18.00	60.00
3-5		4.00	12.00	40.00
6-10		2.00	6.00	20.00
11-20		1.00	3.00	10.00
21-33		.90	3.00	9.00

BABY HUEY DIGEST
June, 1992 (Digest-size, one-shot)
Harvey Publications

1-Reprints 1.00

BABY HUEY DUCKLAND
Nov, 1962 - No. 15, Nov, 1966 (25¢ Giants, 68 pgs.)
Harvey Publications

		GD25	FN65	NM94
1		10.00	30.00	100.00
2-5		4.00	12.00	40.00
6-15		2.00	6.00	20.00

BABY HUEY, THE BABY GIANT (Also see Big Baby Huey, Casper, Harvey
Hits #22, Harvey Comics Hits #60, & Paramount Animated Comics)
9/56 - #97, 10/71; #98, 10/72; #99, 10/80; #100, 10/90 - #102?
Harvey Publications

		GD25	FN65	NM94
1-Infinity-c		32.00	96.00	325.00
2		16.00	48.00	160.00
3-Baby Huey takes anti-pep pills		10.00	30.00	100.00
4,5		7.50	24.00	75.00
6-10		4.00	12.00	40.00
11-20		3.00	9.00	30.00
21-40		2.00	6.00	20.00
41-60		1.10	3.30	11.00
61-79 (12/67)		.90	3.00	9.00
80(12/68) - 95-All 68 pg. Giants		1.10	3.30	11.00
96,97-Both 52 pg. Giants		.90	3.00	9.00
98-99: Regular size			1.20	3.50
100-102 ($1.00)				1.00

BABYLON 5 (TV)
Jan, 1995 - No. 11, Dec, 1995 ($1.95/$2.50)
DC Comics

		GD25	FN65	NM94
1		2.85	8.50	20.00
2		2.15	6.50	15.00
3-6		1.65	4.20	10.00
7-11: 7-Begin $2.50-c		1.00	2.00	5.00

BABY SNOOTS (Also see March of Comics #359, 371, 396, 401, 419, 431,443,
450, 462, 474, 485)
Aug, 1970 - No. 22, Nov, 1975
Gold Key

		GD25	FN65	NM94
1		.90	2.70	9.00
2			1.60	4.00
3-22: 22-Titled Snoots, the Forgetful Elefink			.80	2.00

BACCHUS
1988 - No. 2, Aug, 1988 ($1.95, B&W)
Harrier Comics (New Wave)

1,2: Eddie Campbell-c/a/scripts. 2.00

BACHELOR FATHER (TV)
No. 1332, 4-6/62 - No. 2, 1962
Dell Publishing Co.

Four Color 1332 (#1), 2-Written by Stanley ... 8.00 ... 24.00 ... 80.00

BACHELOR'S DIARY

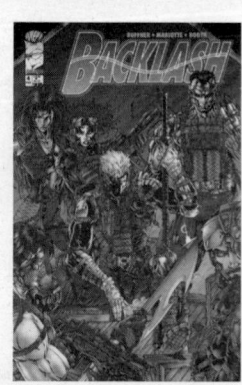

Backlash #4 © Aegis Entertainment

Bad Company #4 © Quality

Badger Shattered Minds #1 © Mike Baron

	GD25	FN65	NM94

1949 (15¢)
Avon Periodicals

1(Scarce)-King Features panel cartoons & text-r; pin-up, girl wrestling photos; similar to Sideshow	36.00	107.00	250.00

BACK DOWN THE LINE
1991 (Mature adults, 8-1/2 x 11", 52 pgs.)
Eclipse Books

nn (Soft-c, $8.95)-Bolton-c/a	1.50	3.75	9.00
nn (Limited Hard-c, $29.95)	4.30	13.00	30.00

BACKLASH (Also see The Kindred)
Nov,1994 - Present ($1.95/$2.50)
Image Comics (Wildstorm Productions)

1-Double-c; variant-double-c	1.00	2.00	5.00
2-6:5-Intro Mindscape; 2 pinups		1.20	3.00
7,9-30: 7-Begin $2.50-c. 19-Fire From Heaven Pt 2. 20-Fire From Heaven Pt 10		1.00	2.50
8-($1.95, newsstand)-Wildstorm Rising Pt. 8		.80	2.00
8-($2.50, direct market)-Wildstorm Rising Pt. 8	1.00		2.50

BACKLASH/SPIDER-MAN
Aug, 1996 - No. 2, Sept, 1996 ($2.50, limited series)
Image Comics (Wildstorm Productions)

1,2: Pike (villain from WildC.A.T.S) & Venom app.			2.50

BACK TO THE FUTURE (Movie, TV cartoon)
Nov, 1991 - No. 4, June, 1992 ($1.25)
Harvey Comics

1-4: 1,2-Gil Kane-c; based on animated cartoon			1.25
Special nn (1991, 20 pgs.)-Brunner-c; given away at Universal Studios in Florida			1.00

BACK TO THE FUTURE: FORWARD TO THE FUTURE
Oct, 1992 - No. 3, Feb, 1993 ($1.50 limited series)
Harvey Comics

1-3			1.50

BAD COMPANY
Aug, 1988 - No. 19?, 1990 ($1.50/$1.75, high quality paper)
Quality Comics/Fleetway Quality #15 on

1-15: 5,6-Guice-c			1.50
16-19: ($1.75-c)		.70	1.75

BAD EGGS, THE
June, 1995 - Present ($2.95)
Acclaim Comics (Armada)

1-8: Layton scripts; Perlin-a. 5-William Shatner app.			3.00

BADGE OF JUSTICE
No. 22, 1/55 - No. 23, 3/55; 4/55 - No. 4, 10/55
Charlton Comics

22(1/55)	8.35	25.00	50.00
23(3/55), 1	5.35	16.00	32.00
2-4	4.00	11.00	22.00

BADGER, THE
Dec, 1983 - No. 70, Apr, 1991; V2#1, Spring, 1991
Capital Comics(#1-4)/First Comics

1-4			1.50
5			1.50
6-49			1.00
50-($3.95, 52 pgs.)		1.60	4.00
51-70: 52-54-Tim Vigil-c/a		.80	2.00
V2#1 (Spring, 1991, $4.95)	1.00	2.00	5.00

BADGER GOES BERSERK
Sept, 1989 - No. 4, Dec, 1989 ($1.95, limited series, Baxter paper)

	GD25	FN65	NM94

First Comics

1-4: 2-Paul Chadwick-c/a(2pgs.)		.80	2.00

BADGER: SHATTERED MIRROR
July, 1994 - No. Oct, 1994 ($2.50, limited series)
Dark Horse Comics

1-4		1.00	2.50

BADGER: ZEN POP FUNNY-ANIMAL VERSION
July, 1994 - No. 2, Aug, 1994 ($2.50, limited series)
Dark Horse Comics

1,2		1.00	2.50

BAD GIRLS OF BLACKOUT
July, 1995 ($3.50)
Blackout Comics

1		1.40	3.50
Annual 1 (1995, $3.50)		1.40	3.50
Annual 1 Commemorative (1995, $9.95)	2.00	4.00	10.00

BADLANDS
May, 1990 ($3.00, glossy stock, mature)
Vortex Comics

1-Chaykin-c		1.20	3.00

BADLANDS
July, 1991 - No. 6, Dec, 1991 ($2.25, B&W, limited series, mature)
Dark Horse Comics

1-6: 1-John F. Kennedy-c		.90	2.30

BADMEN OF THE WEST
1951 (Giant) (132 pgs., painted-c)
Avon Periodicals

1-Contains rebound copies of Jesse James, King of the Bad Men of Deadwood, Badmen of Tombstone; other combinations possible. Issues with Kubert-a...	31.00	94.00	220.00

BADMEN OF THE WEST! (See A-1 Comics)
1953 - No. 3, 1954
Magazine Enterprises

1(A-1 100)-Meskin-a?	21.00	62.00	145.00
2(A-1 120), 3: 2-Larsen-a	13.00	39.00	90.00

BADMEN OF TOMBSTONE
1950
Avon Periodicals

nn	12.00	36.00	85.00

BADROCK (Also see Youngblood)
Mar, 1995 - Present ($1.75/$2.50)
Image Comics (Extreme Studios)

1-Variant-c (3)		.70	1.75
2-Liefeld-c/a & story; Savage Dragon app, flipbook w/Grifter/Badrock #2; variant-c exist			2.50
Annual 1(1995,$2.95)-Arthur Adams-c		1.20	3.00
Annual 1 Commemorative ($9.95)-Print run of 3,000	2.00	4.00	10.00
.../Wolverine (6/96, $4.95, squarebound)-Sauron app; pin-ups; variant-c exists			5.00
.../Wolverine (6/96)-Special Comicon Edition; variant-c exists			5.00

BADROCK AND COMPANY (Also see Youngblood)
Sept, 1994 - No.6, Feb, 1995 ($2.50, limited series)
Image Comics (Extreme Studios)

1-6: 6-Indicia reads "October 1994"; story cont'd in Shadowhawk #17		1.00	2.50

Ballistic #1 © Top Cow Productions

Ballistic Action #1 © Top Cow Productions

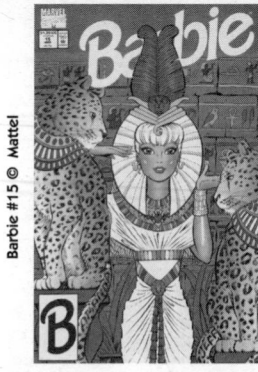

Barbie #15 © Mattel

	GD25	FN65	NM94

BAFFLING MYSTERIES (Formerly Indian Braves No. 1-4; Heroes of the
Wild Frontier No. 26-on)
No. 5, Nov, 1951 - No. 26, Oct, 1955
Periodical House (Ace Magazines)

5	26.00	79.00	185.00
6-24: 8-Woodish-a by Cameron. 10-E.C. Crypt Keeper swipe on-c. 24-Last			
pre-code issue	16.00	47.00	110.00
25-Reprints; surrealistic-c	13.00	39.00	90.00
26-Reprints	11.00	33.00	75.00

NOTE: *Cameron* a-8, 10, 16-18, 20-22. *Colan* a-5, 11, 25r/5. *Sekowsky* a-5, 6, 22. Bondage c-20, 23. Reprints in 18(1), 19(1), 24(3).

BALBO (See Master Comics #33 & Mighty Midget Comics)

BALDER THE BRAVE
Nov, 1985 - No. 4, 1986 (Limited series)
Marvel Comics Group

1-4: Simonson-c/a; character from Thor		1.00

BALLAD OF HALO JONES, THE
Sept, 1987 - No. 12, Aug, 1988 ($1.25/$1.50)
Quality Comics

1-12: Alan Moore scripts in all		1.50

BALLISTIC (Also See Cyberforce)
Sept, 1995 - No. 3, Dec, 1995 ($2.50, limited series)
Image Comics (Top Cow Productions)

1-3: Wetworks app, Turner-c/a	1.60	4.00

BALLISTIC ACTION
May, 1996 ($2.95, one-shot)
Image Comics (Top Cow Productions)

1-Pin-ups of Top Cow characters participating in outdoor sports.	
	3.00

BALLISTIC IMAGERY
Jan, 1996 ($2.50, anthology, one-shot)
Image Comics (Top Cow Productions)

1-Cyberforce app.	
	2.00

BALOO & LITTLE BRITCHES (Disney)
Apr, 1968
Gold Key

1-From the Jungle Book	3.40	10.00	24.00

BALTIMORE COLTS
1950 (Giveaway)
American Visuals Corp.

nn-Eisner-c	47.00	141.00	375.00

BAMBI (Disney) (See Movie Classics, Movie Comics, and Walt Disney
Showcase No. 31)
No. 12, 1942; No. 30, 1943; No. 186, Apr, 1948
Dell Publishing Co.

Four Color 12-Walt Disney's...	53.00	160.00	525.00
Four Color 30-Bambi's Children (1943)	53.00	160.00	525.00
Four Color 186-Walt Disney's...; reprinted as Movie Classic Bambi #3 (1956)			
	17.00	52.00	165.00

BAMBI (Disney)
1941, 1942, 1984
K. K. Publications (Giveaways)/Whitman Publ. Co.

1941-Horlick's Malted Milk & various toy stores; text & pictures; most copies			
mailed out with store stickers on-c	26.00	79.00	185.00
1942-Same as 4-Color #12, but no price (Same as '41 issue?) (Scarce)			
	40.00	120.00	300.00
1-(Whitman, 1984; 60¢)-r/4-Color #186		1.60	4.00

BAMBI (Disney)

1942 (50¢, 7"x8-1/2", 32pg, hard-c w/dust jacket)
Grosset & Dunlap

nn-Given away w/a copy of Thumper for a $2.00, 2-yr. subscription to WDC&S			
in 1942 (Xmas offer). Book only	15.00	45.00	125.00
w/dust jacket	29.00	86.00	200.00

BAMM BAMM & PEBBLES FLINTSTONE (TV)
Oct, 1964 (Hanna-Barbera)
Gold Key

1	5.00	15.00	50.00

BANANA SPLITS, THE (TV) (See Golden Comics Digest & March of Comics
No. 364)
June, 1969 - No. 8, Oct, 1971 (Hanna-Barbera)
Gold Key

1-Photo-c	5.00	15.00	50.00
2-8	2.80	8.50	28.00

BAND WAGON (See Hanna-Barbera Band Wagon)

BANDY MAN, THE
1996 ($2.95, B&W, one-shot)
Caliber

1-Stephan Petrucha scripts; Jill Thompson-a; Miran Kim-c		3.00

BANG-UP COMICS
Dec, 1941 - No. 3, June, 1942
Progressive Publishers

1-Cosmo Mann & Lady Fairplay begin; Buzz Balmer by Rick Yager in all			
(origin #1)	75.00	225.00	600.00
2,3	40.00	120.00	325.00

BANNER COMICS (Becomes Captain Courageous No. 6)
No. 3, Sept, 1941 - No. 5, Jan, 1942
Ace Magazines

3-Captain Courageous (1st app.) & Lone Warrior & Sidekick Dicky begin;			
Jim Mooney-c	87.00	262.00	700.00
4,5: 4-Flag-c	55.00	170.00	450.00

BARABBAS
Aug, 1986 - No. 2, Nov, 1986 ($1.50, B&W, limited series)
Slave Labor Graphics

1,2		1.50

BARBARIANS, THE
June, 1975
Atlas Comics/Seaboard Periodicals

1-Origin, only app. Andrax; Iron Jaw app.		1.00

BARBIE (Disney) (See Movie Classics, Movie Comics, and Walt Disney
Jan, 1991 - No. 66, Apr, 1996 ($1.00/$1.25/$1.50)
Marvel Comics

1-Polybagged w/Barbie Pink Card; Romita-c		.80	2.00
2-44: 14-$1.25 begins			1.25
45-66: 45-$1.50-c begins			1.50

BARBIE & KEN
May-July, 1962 - No. 5, Nov-Jan, 1963-64
Dell Publishing Co.

01-053-207(#1)-Based on Mattel toy dolls	33.00	100.00	335.00
2-4	24.00	72.00	240.00
5 (Rare)	27.00	81.00	285.00

BARBIE FASHION
Jan, 1991 - No. 63, Jan, 1996 ($1.00/$1.25/$1.50)
Marvel Comics

1-Polybagged w/doorknob hanger		.80	2.00
2-44-($1.25): 4-Contains preview to Sweet XVI. 14-Begin $1.25-c			

Barb Wire #2 © DH

Barker #1 © QUA

Barry Windsor-Smith: Storyteller #1 © Barry Windsor-Smith

	GD25	FN65	NM94

45-63: 45-Begin $1.50-c			1.25
			1.50

BARBI TWINS, THE
1995 ($2.50/$5.00)
Topps Comics

1-Razor app.	0.50	1.00	2.50
Swimsuit Art Calender ($5.00)-art by Linsner, Bradstreet, Hughes; Julie Bell-c			
	1.00	2.00	5.00

BARB WIRE (See Comics' Greatest World)
Apr, 1994 - No. 9, Feb, 1995 ($2.00/$2.50)
Dark Horse Comics

1-9: 1-Foil logo; 5-9-($2.50)		.80	2.00
Trade paperback (1996, $8.95)-r/#2,3,5,6 w/Pamela Anderson bio.			
			9.00

BARB WIRE: ACE OF SPADES
May, 1996 - No. 4, Sept, 1996 ($2.95, limited series)
Dark Horse Comics

1-4: Chris Warner-c/a(p)/scripts; Tim Bradstreet-c/a(i) in all	1.20		3.00

BARB WIRE COMICS MAGAZINE SPECIAL
May, 1996 ($3.50, B&W, magazine, one-shot)
Dark Horse Comics

nn-Adaptation of film; photo-c; poster insert.	1.40		3.50

BARB WIRE MOVIE SPECIAL
May, 1996 ($3.95, one-shot)
Dark Horse Comics

nn-Adaptation of film; photo-c; 1st app. new look	1.60		4.00

BARKER, THE (Also see National Comics #42)
Autumn, 1946 - No. 15, Dec, 1949
Quality Comics Group/Comic Magazine

1	17.00	49.00	115.00
2	9.15	27.50	55.00
3-10	6.35	19.00	38.00
11-14	4.15	12.50	25.00
15-Jack Cole-a(p)	5.35	16.00	32.00

NOTE: *Jack Cole* art in some issues.

BARNABY
1945 (25¢, 102 pgs., digest size)
Civil Service Publications Inc.

V1#1-r/Crocket Johnson strips from 1942	2.40	6.00	12.00

BARNEY AND BETTY RUBBLE (TV) (Flintstones' Neighbors)
Jan, 1973 - No. 23, Dec, 1976 (Hanna-Barbera)
Charlton Comics

1	3.40	10.00	24.00
2-10	1.65	4.00	10.00
11-23: 11(2/75)-1st Mike Zeck-a (illos)	1.20	2.40	6.00

BARNEY BAXTER (Also see Magic Comics)
1938 - No. 2, 1956
David McKay/Dell Publishing Co./Argo

Feature Books 15(McKay-1938)	26.00	78.00	260.00
Four Color 20(1942)	24.50	75.00	245.00
4,5	11.00	34.00	110.00
1,2 (1956-Argo)	5.00	15.00	50.00

BARNEY BEAR ...
1977-1981
Spire Christian Comics (Fleming H. Revell Co.)

...Home Plate nn-(1979, 49¢)			1.00
...Lost and Found nn-(1979, 49¢)			1.00
Out of The Woods nn-(1980, 49¢)			1.00

Sunday School Picnic nn-(1981, 69¢			1.00
The Swamp Gang!-(1977, 39¢)			1.00

BARNEY GOOGLE & SNUFFY SMITH
1942 - 1943; April, 1964
Dell Publishing Co./Gold Key

Four Color 19(1942)	38.00	114.00	370.00
Four Color 40(1944)	22.00	66.00	210.00
Large Feature Comic 11(1943)	23.50	70.00	235.00
1(10113-404)-Gold Key (4/64)	3.20	10.00	32.00

BARNEY GOOGLE & SNUFFY SMITH
June, 1951 - No. 4, Feb, 1952 (Reprints)
Toby Press

1	11.50	34.00	80.00
2,3	7.50	22.50	45.00
4-Kurtzman-a "Pot Shot Pete", 5 pgs.; reprints John Wayne #5			
	11.50	34.00	80.00

BARNEY GOOGLE AND SNUFFY SMITH
Mar, 1970 - No. 6, Jan, 1971
Charlton Comics

1	2.30	6.90	16.00
2-6	1.70	4.20	10.00

BARNYARD COMICS (Dizzy Duck No. 32 on)
June, 1944 - No. 31, Sept, 1950; No. 10, 1957
Nedor/Polo Mag./Standard(Animated Cartoons)

1 (nn, 52 pgs.)-Funny animal	17.00	51.00	120.00
2 (52 pgs.)	10.00	30.00	60.00
3-5	6.35	19.00	38.00
6-12,16	5.00	15.00	30.00
13-15,17,21,23,26,27,29-All contain Frazetta text illos			
	6.35	19.00	38.00
18-20,22,24,25-All contain Frazetta-a & text illos	10.00	30.00	70.00
28,30,31	3.60	9.00	18.00
10 (1957)(Exist?)	2.00	5.00	10.00

BARRY M. GOLDWATER
Mar, 1965 (Complete life story)
Dell Publishing Co.

12-055-503-Photo-c	2.60	8.00	26.00

BARRY WINDSOR-SMITH: STORYTELLER
Oct, 1996 - Present ($4.95, oversize)
Dark Horse Comics

1-4: 1-Intro Young Gods, Paradox Man & the Freebooters; Barry Smith-c/a/scripts			5.00

BAR SINISTER (Also see Shaman's Tears)
Jun, 1995 - No. 4, Sept, 1995 ($2.50, limited series)
Acclaim Comics (Windjammer)

1-4: Mike Grell-c/a/scripts		1.00	2.50

BARTMAN (Also see Simpson's Comics & Radioactive Man)
1993 - No. 6, 1994 ($1.95/$2.25)
Bongo Comics

1-($2.95)-Foil-c; bound-in jumbo Bartman poster		1.30	3.25
2		.80	2.00
3-6: 3-$2.25-c begins; w/trading card		.90	2.25

BASEBALL COMICS
Spring, 1949 (Reprinted later as a Spirit section)
Will Eisner Productions

1-Will Eisner-c/a	65.00	195.00	525.00

BASEBALL COMICS
1991 ($3.95, coated stock)

Baseball Thrills #10(#1) © Z-D

Basil #2 © STJ

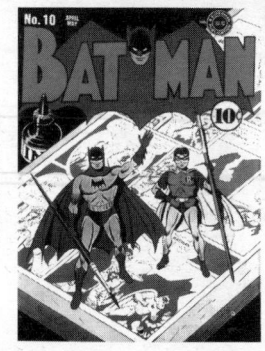

Batman #10 © DC

	GD25	FN65	NM94

Kitchen Sink Press
1-r/1949 ish. by Eisner; contains trading cards 　　1.60　4.00

BASEBALL HEROES
1952 (one-shot)
Fawcett Publications
nn (Scarce)-Babe Ruth photo-c; baseball's Hall of Fame biographies
　　70.00　205.00　550.00

BASEBALL'S GREATEST HEROES
Dec, 1991 - No. 2, May, 1992 ($1.75)
Magnum Comics
1-Mickey Mantle #1; photo-c; Sinnott-a(p) 　　.70　1.75
2-Brooks Robinson #1; photo-c; Sinnott-a(i) 　　.70　1.75

BASEBALL THRILLS
No. 10, Sum, 1951 - No. 3, Sum, 1952 (Saunders painted-c No.1,2)
Ziff-Davis Publ. Co.
10(#1)-Bob Feller, Musial, Newcombe & Boudreau stories
　　39.00　118.00　275.00
2-Powell-a(2)(Late Sum, '51); Feller, Berra & Mathewson stories
　　27.00　81.00　190.00
3-Kinstler-c/a; Joe DiMaggio story 　27.00　81.00　190.00

BASEBALL THRILLS 3-D
May, 1990 ($2.95, w/glasses)
The 3-D Zone
1-New L.B. Cole-c; life stories of Ty Cobb & Ted Williams 　1.20　3.00

BASICALLY STRANGE (Magazine)
Dec, 1982 ($1.95, B&W)
John C. Comics (Archie Comics Group)
1-(21,000 printed; all but 1,000 destroyed; pgs. out of sequence)
　　1.00　2.00　5.00
1-Wood, Toth-a; Corben-c; reprints & new art 　　.80　2.00

BASIC HISTORY OF AMERICA ILLUSTRATED
1976 (B&W) (Soft-c $1.50; Hard-c $4.50)
Pendulum Press
07-1999-America Becomes a World Power 1890-1920. 07-2251-The Industrial Era 1865-1915. 07-226x-Before the Civil War 1830-1860. 07-2278-Americans Move Westward 1800-1850. 07-2286-The Civil War 1850-1876; Redondo-a. 07-2294-The Fight for Freedom 1750-1783. 07-2308-The New World 1500-1750. 07-2316-Problems of the NewNation 1800-1830. 07-2324-Roaring Twenties and the Great Depression 1920-1940. 07-2332-The United States Emerges 1783-1800. 07-2340-America Today 1945-1976. 07-2359-World War II 1940-1945

BASIL (...the Royal Cat)
Jan, 1953 - No. 4, Sept, 1953
St. John Publishing Co.
1-Funny animal 　4.15　12.50　25.00
2-4　　3.20　8.00　16.00
I.W. Reprint 1 　1.40　3.50　7.00

BASIL WOLVERTON'S FANTASTIC FABLES
Oct, 1993 - No. 2 Dec, 1993 ($2.50, B&W, limited series)
Dark Horse Comics
1,2-Wolverton-c/a(r) 　　1.00　2.50

BASIL WOLVERTON'S GATEWAY TO HORROR
June, 1988 ($1.75, B&W, one-shot)
Dark Horse Comics
1-Wolverton-r 　　.70　1.80

BASIL WOLVERTON'S PLANET OF TERROR
Oct, 1987 ($1.75, B&W, one-shot)
Dark Horse Comics
1-Wolverton-r; Alan Moore-c 　　.70　1.80

	GD25	FN65	NM94

BATGIRL SPECIAL (See Teen Titans #50)
1988 ($1.50, one-shot, 52 pgs)
DC Comics
1　　1.00　2.50
NOTE: *Mignola* c-1.

BAT LASH (See DC Special Series #16, Showcase #76, Weird Western Tales)
Oct-Nov, 1968 - No. 7, Oct-Nov, 1969 (All 12¢ issues)
National Periodical Publications
1-(10-11/68)-2nd app. Bat Lash 　2.30　6.70　16.00
2-7　　1.65　4.20　10.00

BATMAN (See Arkham Asylum, Aurora, The Best of DC #2, Blind Justice, The Brave & the Bold, Cosmic Odyssey, DC 100-Page Super Spec. #14,20, DC Special, DC Special Series, Detective, Dynamic Classics, 80-Page Giants, Gotham By Gaslight, Gotham Nights, Greatest Batman Stories Ever Told, Greatest Joker Stories Ever Told, Heroes Against Hunger, The Joker, Justice League of America #250, Justice League Int., Legends of the Dark Knight, Limited Coll. Ed., Man-Bat, Power Record Comics, Real Fact #5, Saga of Ra's Al Ghul, Shadow of the..., Star Spangled, Super Friends, 3-D Batman, Untold Legend of..., Wanted... & World's Finest Comics)

BATMAN
Spring, 1940 - Present (#1-5 were quarterly)
National Periodical Publ./Detective Comics/DC Comics

	GD25	FN65	VF82	NM94
1-Origin The Batman reprinted (2 pgs.) from Det. #33 w/splash from #35 by Bob Kane; see Detective #33 for 1st origin; 1st app. Joker (2 stories intended for 2 separate issues of Det. Comics which would have been 1st & 2nd app.); splash pg. to 2nd Joker story is similar to cover of Det. #40 (story intended for #40); 1st app. The Cat (Catwoman)(1st villainess in comics); has Batman story (w/Hugo Strange) without Robin originally planned for Det. #38; mentions location (Manhattan) where Batman lives (see Det. #31). This book was created entirely from the inventory of Det. Comics; 1st Batman/Robin pin-up on back-c; has text piece & photo of Bob Kane	6,111.00	18,335.00	36,668.00	60,000.00

(Estimated up to 250+ total copies exist, 16 in NM/Mint)

1-Reprint, oversize 13-1/2x10". WARNING: This comic is an exact duplicate reprint of the original except for its size. DC published it in 1974 with a second cover titling it as a Famous First Edition. There have been many reported cases of the outer cover being removed and the interior sold as the original edition. The reprint with the new outer cover removed is practically worthless. See Famous First Edition for value.

	GD25	FN65	NM94
2-2nd app. The Joker; 2nd app. Catwoman (out of costume) in Joker story; 1st time called Catwoman			

NOTE: A 15¢-c for Canadian distr. exists.
　　1055.00　3167.00　10,500.00
3-3rd app Catwoman (1st in costume & 1st costumed villainess); 1st Puppet Master app. 　722.00　2166.00　6800.00
4-3rd app. The Joker (see Det. #45 for 4th); 1st mention of Gotham City in a Batman comic (on newspaper)(Win/40) 　578.00　1733.00　5600.00
5-1st app. the Batmobile with its bat-head front 　422.00　1267.00　4100.00
6,7: 7-Bullseye-c 　375.00　1130.00　3400.00
8-Infinity-c. 　360.00　1090.00　2900.00
9-10:9-1st Batman x-mas story; Burnley-c. 10-Catwoman story (gets new costume) 　340.00　1012.00　2700.00
11-Classic Joker-c by Ray/Robinson (3rd Joker-c, 6-7/42); Joker & Penguin app. 　555.00　1670.00　5000.00
12,15: 15-New costume Catwoman 　262.00　790.00　2100.00
13-Jerry Siegel (Superman's co-creator) appears in a Batman story. 　300.00　900.00　2400.00
14-2nd Penguin-c; Penguin app. (12-1/42-43) 　275.00　825.00　2200.00
16-Intro/origin Alfred (4-5/43); cover is a reverse of #9 cover by Burnley; 1st small logo 　472.00　1415.00　4250.00
17,19,20: 17-Penguin app. 20-1st Batmobile-c (12-1/43-44) 　162.00　490.00　1300.00
18-Hitler, Hirohito, Mussolini-c. 　205.00　620.00　1650.00
21,22,24,26,28-30: 21-1st skinny Alfred in Batman (2-3/44). 21,30-Penguin app. 22-1st Alfred solo-c/story (Alfred solo stories in 22-32,36); Catwoman & The Cavalier app. 　130.00　390.00　1050.00

Batman #64 © DC

Batman #127 © DC

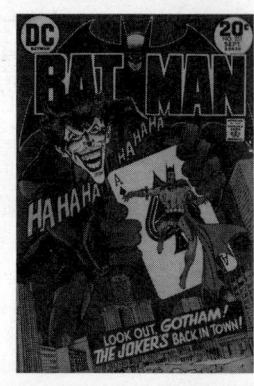

Batman #251 © DC

	GD25	FN65	NM94

23-Joker-c/story 175.00 525.00 1400.00
25-Only Joker/Penguin team-up; 1st team-up between two major villains
180.00 540.00 1450.00
27-Burnley Christmas-c; Penguin app. 162.00 490.00 1300.00
31,32,34-36,39: 32-Origin Robin retold. 35-Catwoman story (in new costume
w/o cat head mask). 36-Penguin app. 95.00 290.00 775.00
33-Christmas-c 112.00 335.00 900.00
37,40,44-Joker-c/stories 120.00 355.00 950.00
38-Penguin-c/story 103.00 309.00 825.00
41,45,46: 41-Penguin app. 45-Christmas-c/story; Catwoman story; Vicki Vale
app. (1st app?) 71.00 215.00 575.00
42,43: 42-2nd Catwoman-c (1st in Batman)(8-9/47); Catwoman story also.
43-Joker-c/story 90.00 270.00 720.00
47-1st detailed origin The Batman (6-7/48); 1st Bat-signal-c this title (see
Detective #108); Batman tracks down his parent's killer and reveals i.d. to
him 275.00 825.00 2400.00
48-1000 Secrets of the Batcave; r-in #203; Penguin story
90.00 270.00 725.00
49-Joker-c/story; 1st app. Mad Hatter; Vicki Vale app.
140.00 430.00 1150.00
50-Two-Face impostor app. 80.00 240.00 635.00
51,54,56,57,59: 57-Centerfold is a 1950 calendar. 59-1st app. Deadshot;
Batman in the future-c/story 70.00 205.00 550.00
52,55-Joker-c/stories 85.00 255.00 675.00
53,58,60,61: 58-Penguin-c. 61-Origin Batman Plane II
75.00 225.00 600.00
62-Origin Catwoman; Catwoman-c 95.00 290.00 775.00
63,80-Joker stories. 63-Flying saucer story(2-3/51) 62.00 185.00 500.00
64,67,70-72,74-77,79: 72-Last 52 pg. issue. 74-Used in POP, pg. 90.
79-Vicki Vale in "The Bride of Batman" 55.00 165.00 440.00
65,69,84-Catwoman-c/stories. 84-Two-Face app. 60.00 180.00 475.00
66,73-Joker-c/stories. 66-Pre-2nd Batman & Robin team try-out. 73-Vicki Vale
story 70.00 205.00 550.00
68,81-Two-Face-c/stories 55.00 170.00 450.00
78-(8-9/53)-Roh Kar, The Man Hunter from Mars story-the 1st lawman of Mars
to come to Earth (green skinned) 70.00 205.00 550.00
82,83,85-89: 86-Intro Batmarine (Batman's submarine). 89-Last pre-code
issue 53.00 160.00 425.00
90,91,93-99: 97-2nd app. Bat-Hound-c/story; Joker app. 99-(4/56)-Last S.A.
Penguin app. 40.00 120.00 340.00
92-1st app. Bat-Hound-c/story 50.00 150.00 425.00
100-(6/56) 170.00 510.00 1800.00
101-104,106-109: 103-1st S.A. issue; 3rd Bat-Hound-c/story
44.00 132.00 370.00
105-1st Batwoman in Batman (2nd anywhere) 51.00 154.00 425.00
110-Joker story 40.00 120.00 335.00
111-120: 112-1st app. Signalman (super villain). 113-1st app. Fatman; Batman
meets his counterpart on Planet X w/a chest plate similar to S.A. Batman's
design (yellow oval w/black design inside). 37.00 111.00 275.00
121- Origin/1st app. of Mr. Zero (Mr. Freeze). 37.00 111.00 275.00
122,124-126,128,130: 124-2nd app. Signal Man. 126-Batwoman-c/story.
128-Batwoman cameo. 130-Lex Luthor app. 24.00 73.00 180.00
123,127: 123-Joker story; Bat-Hound app. 127-(10/59)-Batman vs. Thor the
Thunder God-c/story; Joker story; Superman cameo
28.00 84.00 210.00
129-Origin Robin retold; bondage-c; Batwoman-c/story (reprinted in Batman
Family #8) 30.00 90.00 225.00
131-135,137-139,141-143: 131-Intro 2nd Batman & Robin series (see #66; also
in #135,145,154,159,163). 133-1st Bat-Mite in Batman (3rd app. anywhere).
134-Origin The Dummy. 139-Intro 1st original Bat-Girl; only app. Signalman
as the Blue Bowman. 141-2nd app. original Bat-Girl. 143-Last 10¢ issue.
19.00 58.00 145.00
136-Joker-c/stories 24.00 71.00 170.00
140,144-Joker stories. 140-Batwoman-c/story; Superman cameo. 144-3rd app.
original Bat-Girl 18.00 54.00 130.00

145,148-Joker-c/stories 21.00 62.00 150.00
146,147,149,150 14.00 43.00 110.00
151,152,153,154,156-158,160-162,164-168,170: 152-Joker story. 153-4th app.
original Bat-Girl. 156-Ant-Man/Robin team-up (6/63). 163-Original Bat-Girl as
Batwoman II. 164-New Batmobile (6/64); new Jokes & Mystery Analysts series
begins 11.50 34.00 85.00
155-1st S.A. app. The Penguin (5/63) 40.00 120.00 300.00
159,163-Joker-c/stories. 159-5th app. original Bat-Girl. 163-7th app. original
Bat-Girl & only app. as Batwoman II (last app. until Tales of the Teen Titans
#50) 13.00 39.00 100.00
169-2nd SA Penguin app. 17.00 49.00 125.00
171-1st Riddler app.(5/65) since Dec. 1948 50.00 150.00 400.00
172-175,177,178,180,184 8.00 23.50 60.00
176-(80-Pg. Giant G-17); Joker-c/story; Penguin app. in strip-r; Catwoman
reprint 9.30 28.00 70.00
179-2nd app. Silver Age Riddler 17.00 49.00 125.00
181-Batman & Robin poster insert; intro. Poison Ivy 13.00 39.00 100.00
182,187-(80 Pg. Giants G-24, G-30); Joker-c/stories 8.50 26.00 60.00
183-2nd app. Poison Ivy 9.50 28.00 75.00
185-(80 Pg. Giant G-27) 8.00 23.50 60.00
186-Joker-c/story 6.00 18.00 42.00
188,191,192,194-196,199 4.50 14.00 32.00
189-1st S.A. app. Scarecrow; retells origin of G.A. Scarecrow from World's
Finest #3(1st app.) 9.30 28.00 70.00
190-Penguin app. 5.70 17.00 45.00
193-(80-Pg. Giant G-37) 6.50 19.50 50.00
197-4th SA Catwoman app. cont'd from Det. #369; 1st new Batgirl app. in
Batman (5th anywhere) 9.30 28.00 70.00
198-(80-Pg. Giant G-43); Joker-c/story-r/World's Finest #61; Catwoman-r/
Det. #211; Penguin-r; origin-r/#47 11.50 34.00 85.00
200-(3/68)-Joker cameo; retells origin of Batman & Robin; 1st Neal Adams
work this title (cover only) 21.00 62.00 160.00
201-Joker story 3.75 11.25 28.00
202,204-207,209,210 2.15 6.50 15.00
203-(80 Pg. Giant G-49); r/#48, 61, & Det. 185; Batcave Blueprints
4.30 13.00 32.00
208-(80 Pg. Giant G-55); New origin Batman by Gil Kane plus 3 G.A. Batman
reprints w/Catwoman, Vicki Vale & Batwoman 4.30 13.00 32.00
211,212,214-217: 212-Last 12¢ issue. 214-Alfred given a new last name-
"Pennyworth" (see Detective #96). 2.30 6.75 16.00
213-(80-Pg. Giant G-61); 30th anniversary issue (7-8/69); origin Alfred
(r/Batman #16), Joker(r/Det. #168), Clayface; new origin Robin with new
facts 7.00 21.50 52.00
218-(80-Pg. Giant G-67) 4.30 13.00 32.00
219-Neal Adams-a 4.30 13.00 32.00
220,221,224-227,229-231 2.00 6.00 14.00
222-Beatles take-off; art lesson by Joe Kubert 4.50 14.00 35.00
223,228,233-(80-Pg. Giants G-73,G-79,G-85) 3.25 9.50 22.00
232-N. Adams-a. Intro/1st app. Ras Al Ghul; origin Batman & Robin retold.
9.50 28.00 75.00
234-1st S.A. app. Two-Face; N. Adams-a; 52 pg. issues begin, end #242
19.00 56.00 150.00
235,236,239-242: 239-XMas-c. 241-Reprint/#5 1.85 5.50 13.00
237-N. Adams-a. G.A. Batman-r/Det. #37; 1st app. The Reaper;
Wrightson/Ellison plots 5.00 15.00 38.00
238-DC-8 100 Page Super Spec.; G.A. Atom, Sargon (r/Sensation #57), Plastic
Man (r/Police #14) stories; Doom Patrol origin-r; Batman, Legion,
Aquaman-r; N. Adams wraparound-c 2.85 8.50 20.00
243-245-Neal Adams-a 3.60 11.00 25.00
246-250,252,253: 246-Scarecrow app. 253-Shadow-c & app.
2.00 6.00 14.00
251-(9/73)-N. Adams-c/a; Joker-c/story 6.50 19.50 45.00
254,256-259,261-All 100 pg. editions; part-r. 254-(2/74)-Man-Bat-c & app.
256-Catwoman app. 258-Joker & Penguin app.; The Cavalier-r.

Batman #493 © DC

Batman #516 © DC

Batman #526 © DC

	GD25	FN65	NM94
259-Shadow-c/app.	2.15	6.50	15.00
255-(100 pgs.)-N. Adams-c/a; tells of Bruce Wayne's father who wore bat cos tume & fought crime (r/Det. #235); r/story Batman #22			
	3.60	11.00	25.00
260-Joker-c/story (100 pgs.)	4.50	14.00	32.00
262-285,287-290,292,293,295-299: 262-(68pgs.). 266-Catwoman back to old costume	1.30	3.25	8.00
286,291,294,300: 294-Joker-c/stories. 300-Double-size			
	1.65	4.20	10.00
301-(7/78)-320,322-331,333-352: 304-(44 pgs.). 306-3rd app. Black Spider. 308-Mr. Freeze app. 310-1st modern app. The Gentleman Ghost in Batman; Kubert-c. 311-Batgirl-c/story; Batgirl reteams w/Batman. 313-2nd app. Calendar Man. 313,314,346-Two-Face-c/stories. 316-Robin returns. 318-Intro Firebug. 319-2nd modern age app. The Gentleman Ghost; Kubert-c. 322-324-Catwoman (Selina Kyle) app. 322,323-Cat-Man cameos (1st in Batman, 1 panel each). 323-1st meeting Catwoman & Cat-Man. 324-1st full app. Cat-Man this title. 344-Poison Ivy app. 345-1st app. new Dr. Death. 345,346,351-7 pg. Catwoman back-ups	1.65	4.20	10.00
321,353,359-Joker/stories.	1.70	4.20	10.00
332-Catwoman's 1st solo.	1.70	5.00	12.00
354-356,358,360-365,369,370: 358-1st app. Killer Croc. 361-1st app Harvey Bullock	1.10	2.70	6.50
357-1st app. Jason Todd (3/83); see Det. 524	1.00	2.00	5.00
366-Jason Todd 1st in Robin costume; Joker-c/story	2.15	6.50	15.00
368-1st new Robin in costume (Jason Todd)	1.00	2.00	5.00
371-399,401-403: 371-Cat-Man-c/story; brief origin Cat-Man (cont'd in Det. #538). 386,387-Intro Black Mask (villain). 380-391-Catwoman app. 398-Catwoman & Two-Face app. 401-2nd app. Magpie (see Man of Steel #3 for 1st). 403-Joker cameo		1.20	3.00

NOTE: Most issues between 397 & 432 were reprinted in 1989 and sold in multi-packs. Some are not identified as reprints but have newer ads copyrighted after cover dates. 2nd and 3rd print- ings exist.

	GD25	FN65	NM94
400 ($1.50, 68pgs.)-Dark Knight special; intro by Stephen King; Art Adams/ Austin-a	2.85	8.50	20.00
404-Miller scripts begin (end 407); Year 1; 1st modern app. Catwoman (2/87)			
	1.65	4.20	10.00
405-407: 407-Year 1 ends (See Det. Comics for Year 2)			
	1.00	2.00	5.00
408-410: New Origin Jason Todd (Robin)	1.00	2.00	5.00
411-416,421-425: 411-Two-face app. 412-Origin/1st app. Mime. 414-Starlin scripts begin, end #429. 416-Nightwing-c/story. 423-McFarlane-c			
	1.20	3.00	
417-420: "Ten Nights of the Beast" storyline	1.30	3.25	8.00
426-($1.50, 52 pgs.)- "A Death In The Family" storyline begins, ends #429			
	1.20	2.90	7.00
427,428: 427- "A Death In The Family" part 2. 428-Death of Robin (Jason Todd)	1.00	2.50	6.00
429-Joker-c/story; Superman app.	1.00	2.00	5.00
430-432		.80	2.00
433-435-Many Deaths of the Batman story by John Byrne-c/scripts			
	1.00		2.50
436-Year 3 begins (ends #439); origin original Robin retold by Nightwing (Dick Grayson); 1st app. Timothy Drake (8/89)	1.00	2.00	5.00
436-2nd printing			1.00
437-439: 437-Origin Robin continued		1.00	2.50
440,441: "A Lonely Place of Dying" Parts 1 & 3			1.25
442-1st app. Timothy Drake in Robin costume	1.50	3.75	9.00
443-456,458,459,462-464: 445-447-Batman goes to Russia. 448,449-The Penguin Affair Pts 1 & 3. 450-Origin Joker. 450,451-Joker-c/stories. 452-454-Dark Knight City storyline; Riddler app. 455-Alan Grant scripts begin, ends #466, 470. 464-Last solo Batman story; free 16 pg. preview of Impact Comics line			1.50
457-Timothy Drake officially becomes Robin & dons new costume			
	1.65	4.20	10.00

	GD25	FN65	NM94
457-Direct sale edition (has #000 in indicia)		1.60	4.00
460,461-Two part Catwoman story		1.00	2.50
465-487: 465-Robin returns to action with Batman. 470-War of the Gods x-over. 475,476-Return of Scarface-c/story. 476-Last $1.00-c.			
477,478-Photo-c			1.50
488-Cont'd from Batman: Sword of Azrael #4; Azrael-c & app.			
	1.50	3.75	9.00
489-Bane-c/story; 1st app. Azrael in Bat-costume	1.20	3.00	7.00
490-Riddler-c/story; Azrael & Bane app.	1.20	2.00	5.00
491,492: 491-Knightfall lead-in; Joker-c/story; Azrael & Bane app.; Kelley Jones-c begin. 492-Knightfall part 1; Bane app.	1.00	2.00	5.00
492-Platinum edition (promo copy)	1.65	4.20	10.00
493-Knightfall Pt. 3		1.20	3.00
494-Knightfall Pt. 5; Joker-c & app.		1.20	3.00
495,496: 495-Knightfall Pt. 7; brief Bane & Joker apps. 496-Knightfall Pt. 9; Joker-c/story; Bane cameo		1.20	3.00
497-(Late 7/93)-Knightfall Pt. 11; Bane breaks Batman's back; B&W outer-c; Aparo-a(p); Giordano-a(i)	1.00	2.00	5.00
497-499: 497-2nd printing. 497-Newsstand edition w/o outer cover. 498- Knightfall part 15; Bane & Catwoman-c & app. (see Showcase 93 #7 & 8)			
499-Knightfall Pt. 17; Bane app.		.80	2.00
500-($2.50, 68 pgs.)-Knightfall Pt. 19; Azrael in new Bat-costume; Bane-c/ story		1.00	2.50
500-($3.95, 68 pgs.)-Collector's Edition w/die-cut double-c w/foil by Joe Quesada & 2 bound-in post cards	1.80	4.50	
501-508,510,511: 501-Begin $1.50-c. 501-508-Knightquest. 503,504-Catwoman app. 507-Ballistic app.; Jim Balent-a(p). 510-KnightsEnd Pt. 7. 511-(9/94)- Zero Hour; Batgirl-c/story			1.50
509-($2.50, 52 pgs.)-KnightsEnd Pt. 1		1.00	2.50
0,512-514,516-520: 0-(10/94)-Origin retold. 512-(11/94)-Dick Grayson assumes Batman role			1.50
515-($2.50)-Kelley Jones-a begins; all black embossed-c; Troika Pt. 1			
		1.20	3.00
521-534,536-542: 521-Begin $1.95-c, return of Alfred, 522-Swamp Thing app. 525-Mr. Freeze app. 527,528-Two Face app. 529-Contagion Pt. 6. 530-532-Deadman app. 533-Legacy prelude. 534-Legacy Pt. 5. 536-Final Night x-over; Man-Bat-c/app.		.80	2.00
535-(10/96, $2.95)-1st app. The Ogre		1.20	3.00
535-(10/96, $3.95)-1st app. The Ogre; variant, cardboard, foldout-c			
		1.60	4.00
530-532 ($2.50)-Enhanced edition; glow-in-the-dark-c.	1.10	2.75	
Annual 1 (8-10/61)-Swan-c	60.00	180.00	600.00
Annual 2	31.00	92.00	275.00
Annual 3(Summer, '62)-Joker-c/story	32.00	95.00	285.00
Annual 4,5	16.00	47.00	125.00
Annual 6,7(7/64, 25¢, 80 pgs.)	12.00	36.00	95.00
Annual V5#8(1982)-Painted-c		1.80	4.50
Annual 9,10,12: 9(7/85). 10(1986). 12(1988, $1.50)	1.20	3.00	
Annual 11(1987, $1.25)-Penguin-c/story; Alan Moore scripts			
		1.60	4.00
Annual 13(1989, $1.75, 68 pgs.)-Gives history of Bruce Wayne, Dick Grayson, Jason Todd, Alfred, Comm. Gordon, Barbara Gordon (Batgirl) & Vicki Vale; Morrow-i		.90	2.25
Annual 14(1990, $2.00, 68 pgs.)-Origin Two-Face	.90	2.25	
Annual 15(1991, $2.00, 68 pgs.)-Armageddon 2001 x-over; Joker app.;			
		.90	2.25
Annual 15(2nd printing)		.80	2.00
Annual 16(1992, $2.50, 68 pgs.)-Joker-c/s; Kieth-a	1.00	2.50	
Annual 17(1993, $2.50, 68 pgs.)-Azrael in Bat-costume; intro Ballistic			
		1.00	2.50
Annual 18(1994, $2.95)		1.20	3.00
Annual 19(1995, $3.95)-Year One story; retells Scarecrow's origin			
		1.60	4.00
Annual 20(1996, $2.95)-Legends of the Dead Earth story; Moench script;			

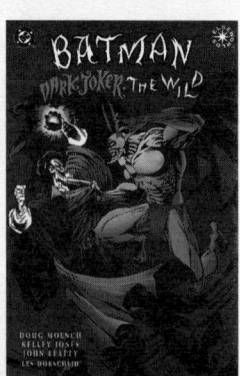

Batman: Dark Joker-The Wild © DC

Batman/Houdini: The Devil's Workshop © DC

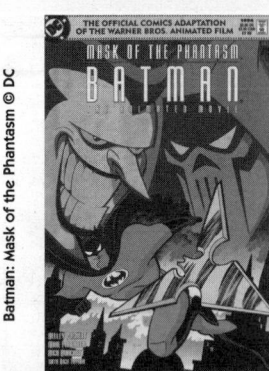

Batman: Mask of the Phantasm © DC

	GD25	FN65	NM94

	GD25	FN65	NM94
Giarrano-a.			3.00
Special 1 (4/84)-Mike W. Barr story; Golden-c/a	1.00	2.00	5.00
Pizza Hut giveaway(12/77)-exact-r of #122,123; Joker-c/story			
		1.20	3.00
Prell Shampoo giveaway(1966, 16 pgs.)- "The Joker's Practical Jokes"			
(6-7/8x3-3/8")	3.60	11.00	25.00

NOTE: **Art Adams** a-400p. **Neal Adams** c-200, 203, 210, 217, 219-222, 224-227, 229, 230, 232, 234, 236-241, 243-246, 251, 255, Annual 14. **Aparo** a-414-420, 426-435, 440-448, 450, 451, 480-483, 486-491, 494-500; c-414-416, 481, 482, 463i, 486, 487i. **Bolland** a-400; c-445-447. **Burnley** a-10, 12-18, 20, 22, 25, 27; c-9, 15, 16, 27, 28p, 40p, 42p. **Byrne** c-401, 433-435, 533-535, Annual 11. **Travis Charest** c-488-490p. **Colan** a-340p, 343-345p, 348-351p, 373p, 383p; c-343p, 345p, 350p. **J. Cole** a-238r. **Cowan** a-Annual 10p. **Golden** a-295p, 303p, 484, 485. **Alan Grant** scripts-455-466, 470, 474-476, 479, 480, Annual 16(part). **Grell** c-287, 288p, 289p, 290; c-287-290. **Infantino/Anderson** a-167, 173, 175, 181, 186, 191, 192, 194, 195, 198, 199. **Kelley Jones** a-513-519, 521-525, 527; c-491-499, 500(newstand), 501-510, 513. **Kaluta** c-242, 248, 253, Annual 12. **G. Kane/Anderson** c-178-180. **Bob Kane** a-1, 2, 5; c-1-5, 7, 17. **G. Kane** a-(r)-254, 255, 259, 261, 353i. **Kubert** a-238r, 400; c-310, 319p, 327, 328, 344. **McFarlane** c-423. **Mignola** c-426-429, 452-454, Annual 18. **Moldoff** c-101-140. **Moldoff/Giella** a-164-175, 177-181, 183, 184, 186. **Moldoff/Greene** a-169, 172-174, 177-179, 181, 184. **Mooney** a-255r. **Morrow** a-400i. **Newton** a-305, 306, 328p, 331p, 332p, 337p, 338p, 346p, 352-357p, 360-372p, 374-378p; c-374p, 378p. **Nino** a-Annual 9. **Irv Novick** c-201, 202. **Perez** a-400; c-436-442. **Fred Ray** c-8, 10; w/**Robinson**-11. **Robinson/Roussos** a-12-17, 20, 22, 24, 25, 27, 28, 31, 33, 37. **Robinson** a-12, 14, 18, 22-32,34, 36, 37, 255r, 260r, 261r; c-6, 8, 10, 12-15, 18, 21, 24, 26, 30, 37, 39. **Simonson** a-300p, 312p, 321p; c-300p, 312p, 366, 413i. **P. Smith** a-Annual 9. **Dick Sprang** c-19, 20, 22, 23, 25, 29, 31-36, 38, 51, 55, 66, 73, 76. **Starlin** c/a-402. **Staton** a-334. **Sutton** a-400. **Wrightson** a-265i, 400; c-320r. Bat-Hound app. in 92, 97, 103, 123, 125, 133, 156, 158. Bat-Mite app. in 133, 136, 144, 146, 158, 161. Batwoman app. in 105, 116, 122, 125, 128, 129, 131, 133, 139, 140, 141, 144, 145, 150, 151, 153, 154, 157, 159, 162, 163. **Zeck** c-417-420. Catwoman back-ups in 332, 345, 346, 348-351. Joker app. in 1, 2, 4, 5, 7-9, 11-13, 19, 20, 23, 25, 28, 32 & many more. Robin solo back-up stories in 337-339, 341-343.

BATMAN (Books and trade paperbacks)
...: A LONELY PLACE OF DYING (1990, $3.95, 132 pgs.)-r/Batman #440-442			
& New Titans #60,61; Perez-c		1.60	4.00
...AND DRACULA: RED RAIN nn (1991, $24.95)-Hard-c; Elseworlds storyline			
	5.70	17.00	40.00
...AND DRACULA: Red Rain nn (1992, $9.95)-SC	1.70	4.00	10.00
ARKHAM ASYLUM Hard-c (1989, $24.95)	3.60	10.75	25.00
ARKHAM ASYLUM Soft-c ($14.95)	2.15	6.50	15.00
BIRTH OF THE DEMON Hard-c (1992, $24.95)-Origin of Ra's al Ghul			
	3.60	10.75	25.00
BIRTH OF THE DEMON Soft-c (1993, $12.95)	1.85	5.50	13.00
BLIND JUSTICE nn (1992, $7.50)-r/Det. #598-600	1.25	3.00	7.50
BRIDE OF THE DEMON Hard-c (1990, $19.95)	3.20	8.00	20.00
BRIDE OF THE DEMON Soft-c ($12.95)	1.85	5.50	13.00
...: CASTLE OF THE BAT ($5.95)-Elseworlds story			6.00
...: COLLECTED LEGENDS OF THE DARK KNIGHT nn			
(1994, $12.95)-r/Legends of the Dark Knight #32-34,38,42,43			
	1.85	5.50	13.00
...: DARK JOKER-THE WILD (1993, $9.95)-Elseworlds story			
	1.70	4.00	10.00
DEATH IN THE FAMILY (1988, $3.95, trade paperback)-r/Batman #426-429 by			
Aparo	1.00	2.00	5.00
DEATH IN THE FAMILY: (2nd - 5th printings)		1.60	4.00
DIGITAL JUSTICE nn (1990, $24.95, Hard-c.)-Computer generated art			
	3.60	10.75	25.00
... FACES (1995, $9.95, TPB)			10.00
...GOTHIC (1992, $12.95, TPB)-r/Legends of the Dark Knight #6-10			
	1.85	5.50	13.00
GREATEST BATMAN STORIES Hard-c ($24.95)	7.00	21.50	50.00
GREATEST BATMAN STORIES Soft-c ($15.95)	2.30	6.90	16.00
GREATEST BATMAN STORIES Vol. 2 (1992, $16.95)	2.40	7.30	17.00
GREATEST JOKER STORIES Hard-c ($19.95)	3.75	11.25	30.00
GREATEST JOKER STORIES Soft-c ($14.95)	2.10	6.40	15.00
GREATEST JOKER STORIES (Stacked Deck...Expanded Edition)			
(1992, $29.95)-Longmeadow Press Publ.	5.00	15.00	35.00
...: THE MANY DEATHS OF THE BATMAN (1992, $3.95, 84 pgs.)-r/Batman			
#433-435 w/new Byrne-c		1.60	4.00
...: PREY (1992, $12.95)-Gulacy/Austin-a	1.85	5.50	13.00

	GD25	FN65	NM94
SHAMAN (1993, $12.95)-r/Legends/D.K. #1-5	1.85	5.50	13.00
...: SON OF THE DEMON Hard-c (9/87, $14.95)	7.00	21.50	50.00
...: SON OF THE DEMON limited signed & numbered Hard-c (1,700)			
	11.00	33.00	75.00
...: SON OF THE DEMON Soft-c w/new-c ($8.95)	1.50	3.75	9.00
...: SON OF THE DEMON Soft-c (1989, $9.95, 2nd printing - 4th printing)			
	1.65	4.00	10.00
...: TALES OF THE DEMON (1991, $17.95, 212 pgs.)-Intro by Sam Hamm;			
reprints by N. Adams(3) & Golden; contains Saga of Ra's Al Ghul #1			
	2.60	7.50	18.00
...: TEN NIGHTS OF THE BEAST (1994, $5.95)-r/Batman #417-420			
	1.00	2.60	6.00
...:THE LAST ANGEL (1994, $12.95, TPB)	1.85	5.50	13.00
...: VENOM (1993, $9.95, TPB)-r/Legends of the Dark Knight #16-20;			
embossed-c	1.65	4.00	10.00
YEAR ONE Hard-c (1988, $12.95)	1.85	5.50	13.00
YEAR ONE (1988, $9.95, TPB)-r/Batman #404-407 by Miller; intro by Miller			
	1.65	4.00	10.00
YEAR ONE (TPB, 2nd & 3rd printings)	1.65	4.00	10.00
YEAR TWO (1990, $9.95, TPB)-r/Det. 575-578 by McFarlane; wraparound-c			
	1.65	4.00	10.00

BATMAN (one-shots)
BATMAN AND OTHER DC CLASSICS 1 (1989, giveaway)-DC Comics/Diamon			
Comic Distributors; Batman origin-r/Batman #47, Camelot 3000-r by Bolland,			
Justice League-r('87), New Teen Titans-r by Perez.			1.00
...: CATWOMAN DEFIANT nn (1992, $4.95, prestige format)-Milligan scripts;			
cover interlocks w/Batman: Penguin Triumphant; special foil logo.			
	1.00	2.00	5.00
... FOREVER (1995, $5.95, direct market)			6.00
... FOREVER (1995, $3.95, newsstand)			4.00
BROTHERHOOD OF THE BAT (1995, $5.95)-Elseworlds story.			
	1.00	2.60	6.00
...: DARK ALLEGIANCES (1996, $5.95)-Elseworlds story, Chaykin-c/a.			
	1.00	2.60	6.00
...: DARK KNIGHT GALLERY (1995, $3.50)-Pin-ups by Pratt, Balent, & others.			
			3.50
.../DEMON (1996, $4.95)-Alan Grant scripts	1.00	2.00	5.00
FULL CIRCLE nn (1991, $5.95, stiff-c, 68 pgs.)-Sequel to Batman: Year Two			
	1.00	2.60	6.00
...GALLERY, The 1 (1992, $2.95)-Pin-ups by Miller, N. Adams & others			
		1.20	3.00
...GOTHAM BY GASLIGHT (1989, $3.95)		1.60	4.00
.../GREEN ARROW: THE POISON ARROW nn (1992, $5.95, squarebound,			
68 pgs.)-Netzer-c/a	1.00	2.60	6.00
HOLY TERROR nn (1991, $4.95, 52 pgs.)-Elseworlds story			
	1.00	2.00	5.00
.../HOUDINI: THE DEVIL'S WORKSHOP (1993, $5.95)			
	1.00	2.60	6.00
...: IN DARKEST KNIGHT nn (1994, $4.95, 52 pgs.)-Elseworlds story; Batman			
w/Green Lantern's ring.	1.00	2.50	5.00
...: JUDGE DREDD: JUDGEMENT ON GOTHAM nn			
(1991, $5.95, 68 pgs.)-Grant/Wagner scripts; Simon Bisley-c/a			
	1.00	2.60	6.00
...: JUDGE DREDD: JUDGEMENT ON GOTHAM nn (2nd printing)			
	1.00	2.60	6.00
...:JUDGE DREDD: THE ULTIMATE RIDDLE (1995, $4.95)			
	1.00	2.00	5.00
...:JUDGE DREDD: VENDETTA IN GOTHAM (1993, $5.95)			
	1.00	2.60	6.00
...: KNIGHTGALLERY (1995, $3.50)-Elseworlds sketchbook.			3.50
...: MASK OF THE PHANTASM ($2.95)-Movie adaptation			
		1.20	3.00
...: MASK OF THE PHANTASM ($4.95)-Movie adaptation			
	1.00	2.50	5.00

GD25 **FN**65 **NM**94

GD25 **FN**65 **NM**94

...: MASTER OF THE FUTURE nn (1991, $5.95, 68 pgs.)-Elseworlds storyline;
  sequel to Gotham By Gaslight; embossed-c 1.00 2.60 6.00
...: MITEFALL (1995, $4.95)-Alan Grant script, Kevin O'Neill-a
  1.00 5.00
...: PENGUIN TRIUMPHANT nn (1992, $4.95)-Staton-a(p); special foil logo
  1.00 2.00 5.00
.../PUNISHER: LAKE OF FIRE (1994, $4.95, DC/Marvel)
  1.00 2.00 5.00
...RETURNS MOVIE SPECIAL (1992, $3.95) 1.00 5.00
...RETURNS MOVIE PRESTIGE (1992, $5.95, squarebounded)-Dorman
  painted-c 1.00 2.60 6.00
...:RIDDLER-THE RIDDLE FACTORY (1995, $4.95)-Matt Wagner scripts
  5.00
...: SCAR OF THE BAT nn (1996, $4.95)-Elseworlds story; Max Allan Collins
  script; Barreto-a. 5.00
...: SEDUCTION OF THE GUN nn (1992, $2.50, 68 pgs.) 1.00 2.50
.../SPAWN: WAR DEVIL nn (1994, $4.95, 52 pgs.) 1.00 2.00 5.00
...: THE BLUE, THE GREY, & THE BAT nn
  (1992, $5.95, 68 pgs.)-Weiss/Lopez-a 1.00 2.60 6.00
...: THE KILLING JOKE (1988, deluxe 52 pgs., mature readers)-Bolland-c/a;
  Alan Moore scripts. 5.00
...: THE KILLING JOKE (2nd thru 8th printings) 3.50
...: THE OFFICIAL COMIC ADAPTATION OF THE WARNER BROS. MOTION
  PICTURE (1989, $2.50, regular format, 68 pgs.)-Ordway-c. 3.00
...: THE OFFICIAL COMIC ADAPTATION OF THE WARNER BROS. MOTION
  PICTURE (1989, $4.95, prestige format, 68 pgs.)-same interiors but
  different-c than regular format. 5.00
...: TWO-FACE-CRIME AND PUNISHMENT-(1995, $4.95)-Scott McDaniel-a
  1.00 2.00 5.00
...: VENGEANCE OF BANE SPECIAL 1 (1992, $2.50, 68 pgs.)-Origin & 1st app.
  Bane (see Batman #491) 3.20 8.00 20.00
...: VENGEANCE OF BANE SPECIAL 1 (2nd printing) 1.00 2.50
.....:VENGEANCE OF BANE II nn (1995, $3.95)-sequel 1.60 4.00
...Vs. THE INCREDIBLE HULK (1995, $3.95)-r/DC Special Series #27
  1.60 4.00

BATMAN (Kellogg's Poptarts comics)
1966 (Set of 6) (16 pgs.)
National Periodical Publications

"The Man in the Iron Mask", "The Penguin's Fowl Play", "The Joker's Happy Victims", "The
Catwoman's Catnapping Caper", "The Mad Hatter's Hat Crimes", "The Case of the Batman II"
  each.... 3.60 11.00 25.00
NOTE: All above were folded and placed in Poptarts boxes. Infantino art on Catwoman and
Joker issues.

BATMAN ADVENTURES, THE (TV)
Oct, 1992 - No. 36, Oct, 1995 ($1.25/$1.50) (Based on animated series)
DC Comics

1-Penguin-c/story 1.20 2.90 7.00
1 ($1.95, Silver Edition)-2nd printing .90 2.25
2-6,8-19: 2,12-Catwoman-c/story. 3-Joker-c/story. 5-Scarecrow-c/story.
  10-Riddler-c/story. 11-Man-Bat-c/story. 12-Batgirl & Catwoman-c/story.
  16-Joker-c/story; begin $1.50-c. 18-Batgirl-c/story. 19-Scarecrow-c/story.
  1.00 2.50
7-Special edition polybagged with Man-Bat trading card
  1.30 3.25 8.00
20-24,26-32: 26-Batgirl app. 1.50
25-($2.50, 52 pgs.)-Superman app. 1.00 2.50
33-36: 33-Begin $1.75-c .70 1.75
Mad Love nn (2/94, $3.95, 68 pgs.)-Joker-c/story 1.00 2.60 6.00
The Collected Adventures Vol. 1 (1993, $5.95) 1.00 2.60 6.00
The Collected Adventures Vol. 2 (1994, $5.95) 1.00 2.60 6.00
Annual 1 (1994, $2.95) 1.20 3.00
Annual 2 (1995, $3.50)-Demon-c/story; Ras al Ghul app.
  1.40 3.50
Holiday Special 1 (1995, $2.95) 1.20 3.00

BATMAN AND ROBIN ADVENTURES (TV)
Nov, 1995 - Present ($1.75) (Based on animated series)
DC Comics

1-Dini-s. 1.00 2.50
2-18: 2-4-Dini script. 4-Penguin-c/story. 5-Joker-c/story; Poison Ivy, Harley
  Quinn-c/app. 9-Batgirl & Talia-c/story. 10-Ra's Al Ghul-c/story
  .70 1.75

BATMAN AND THE OUTSIDERS (The Adventures of the Outsiders#33 on)
(Also see Brave & The Bold #200 & The Outsiders) (Replaces The Brave and the
Bold)
Aug, 1983 - No. 32, Apr, 1986 (Mando paper #5 on)
DC Comics

1-Batman, Halo, Geo-Force, Katana, Metamorpho & Black Lightning begin.
  1.00 2.50
2-32: 5-New Teen Titans x-over. 9-Halo begins. 11,12-Origin Katana. 18-
  More facts about Metamorpho's origin. 28-31-Lookers origin. 32-Team
  disbands 1.00
Annual 1 (9/84)-Miller/Aparo-c; Aparo-i 1.00
Annual 2 (9/85)-Metamorpho & Sapphire Stagg wed; Aparo-c
  1.00
NOTE: Aparo a-1-9, 11-13p, 16-20; c-1-4, 5i, 6-21. B. Kane a-3r. Layton a-19i, 20i. Lopez a-3p.
Perez c-5p. B. Willingham a-14p.

BATMAN: BLACK & WHITE
June, 1996 - No. 4, Sept, 1996 ($2.95, B&W, limited series)
DC Comics

1-4: 1-Stories by McKeever, Timm, Kubert, Chaykin, Goodwin; Jim Lee-c;
  Allred inside front-c. 2-Stories by Simonson, Corben,
  Bisley & Gaiman; Miller-c. 3-Stories by M. Wagner, Janson, Sienkiewicz,
  O'Neil & Kristiansen; B. Smith-c; Russell inside front-c. Silvestri inside back-c.
  4-Stories by Bolland, Goodwin & Gianni, Strnad & Nowlan, O'Neil &
  Stelfreeze; Toth-c; Neal Adams & Alex Ross pinups 3.00

BATMAN: CATWOMAN DEFIANT (See Batman one-shots)

BATMAN CHRONICLES, THE
Summer, 1995 - Present ($2.95, quarterly)
DC Comics

1-8: 1-Dixon/Grant/Moench script. 2-Bolland-a. 4-Contagion tie-in; Hitman
  story by Garth Ennis; Balent-c. 5-Oracle Year One story, Chaykin-c.
  6-Kaluta-c; Ra's Al Ghul story 1.20 3.00

BATMAN FAMILY, THE
Sept-Oct, 1975 - No. 20, Oct-Nov, 1978 (#1-4, 17-on: 68 pgs.)
(Combined with Detective Comics with No. 481)
National Periodical Publications/DC Comics

1-Origin/2nd app. Batgirl-Robin team-up (The Dynamite Duo); reprints plus one
  new story begins; N. Adams-a(r); r/1st app. Man-Bat from Det. #400
  1.20 3.00 7.00
2-5: 2-r/Det. #369. 3-Batgirl & Robin learn each's id.; r/Batwoman app. from
  Batman #105. 8-r/Batwoman app. 4-r/1st Fatman app. from Batman #113.
  5-r/1st Bat-Hound app. 1.10 2.75
6,9-Joker's daughter on cover (1st app?) 1.20 3.00
7,8,10,14-16: 10-1st revival Batwoman; Cavalier app.; 2nd app. Killer Moth.
  14-Batwoman app. 15-3rd app. Killer Moth. 16-Bat-Girl cameo (last app. in
  costume until New Teen Titans #47) 1.10 2.75
11-13-Rogers-a(p): 11-New stories begin; Man-Bat begins. 13-Batwoman
  cameo 1.00 2.00 5.00
17-($1.00 size)-Batman, Huntress begin; Batwoman & Catwoman meet
  1.10 2.75
18-20: Huntress by Staton in all. 20-Origin Ragman retold 1.50
NOTE: Aparo a-17; c-11-16. Austin a-12i. Chaykin a-14p. Michael Golden a-15-17,18-20p.
Grell a-1; c-1. Gil Kane a-3-r. Kaluta c-17, 19. Newton a-13. Robinson a-17r, 3i(r), 9r. Russell a-
18i, 19i. Starlin a-17; c-18, 20.

BATMAN FOREVER (See Batman one-shots)

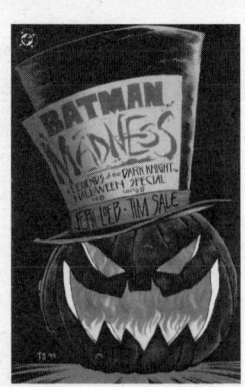

Batman Madness: LoDK Halloween Special #1 © DC

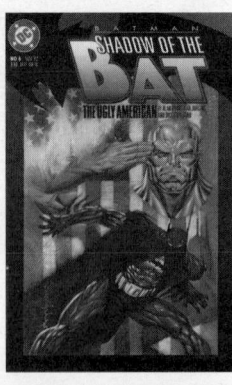

Batman: Shadow of the Bat #6 © DC

Batman: Sword of Azrael #1 © DC

	GD25	FN65	NM94

BATMAN: GCPD
Aug, 1996 - No. 4, Nov, 1996 ($2.25, limited series)
DC Comics

1-4: Features Jim Gordon; Aparo/Sienkiewicz-a			2.25

BATMAN: GOTHAM NIGHTS II (Also see Gotham Nights)
Mar, 1995 - No. 4, June, 1995 ($1.95, limited series)
DC Comics

1-4		.80	2.00

BATMAN/GRENDEL (1st limited series)
1993 - No. 2, 1993 ($4.95, limited series, squarebound; 52 pgs.)
DC Comics

1,2: Batman vs. Hunter Rose. 1-Devil's Riddle; Matt Wagner-c/a/scripts.			
2-Devil's Masque; Matt Wagner-c/a/scripts	1.00	2.50	5.50

BATMAN/GRENDEL (2nd limited series)
June, 1996 - No. 2, July, 1996 ($4.95, limited series, squarebound)
DC Comics

1,2: Batman vs. Grendel Prime. 1-Devil's Bones; Matt Wagner-c/a/scripts.			
	1.00	2.00	5.00

BATMAN: KNIGHTGALLERY (See Batman one-shots)

BATMAN: LEGENDS OF THE DARK KNIGHT (Legends of the Dark...#1-36)
Nov, 1989 - Present ($1.50/$1.75/$1.95)
DC Comics

1- "Shaman" begins, ends #5; outer cover has four different color variations,			
all worth same	1.00	2.00	5.00
2		1.20	3.00
3-5		.80	2.00
6-10- "Gothic" by Grant Morrison (scripts)		1.20	5.00
11-15,17,18: 11-15-Gulacy/Austin-a. 14-Catwoman app. 18-Last $1.50-c			
		.80	2.00
16-Intro drug Bane uses; begin Venom story	1.00	2.00	5.00
19-49,51-63: 38-Bat-Mite-c/story. 46-49-Catwoman app. w/Heath-c/a. 51-			
Ragman-story; Joe Kubert-c. 59,60-Knightquest x-over. 62,63-KnightsEnd			
Pt. 4 & 10		.80	2.00
50-($3.95, 68 pgs.)-Bolland embossed gold foil-c; Joker-c/story; pin-ups by			
Chaykin, Simonson, Williamson, Kaluta, Russell, others			
	1.00	2.00	5.00
64,0,65-95: 64-(9/94)-Begin $1.95-c. 0-(10/94)-Quesada/Palmiotti-c; various			
artists on story. 71-73-James Robinson scripts, J. Watkiss-c/a. 74,75-Ted			
McKeever-c/a/scripts. 76-78-Scott Hampton-c/a/scripts. 81-Card insert.			
83,84-Ellis scripts. 85-James Robinson script		.80	2.00
Annual 1 (1991, $3.95, 68 pgs.)-Joker app.		1.60	4.00
Annual 2 (1992, $3.50, 68 pgs.)-Netzer-c/a		1.40	3.50
Annual 3 (1993, $3.50, 68 pgs.)-New Batman (Azrael) app.		1.40	3.50
Annual 4 (1994, $3.50, 68 pgs.)-Elseworlds story		1.40	3.50
Annual 5 (1995, $3.95, 68 pgs.)		1.60	4.00
Annual 6 (1996, $2.95)-Legend of the Dead Earth story		1.20	3.00
Halloween Special 1 (12/93, $6.95, 84 pgs.)-Embossed & foil stamped-c			
	1.30	3.25	8.00
Batman Madness-...Halloween Special (1994, $4.95)			
	1.00	2.60	6.00
Bataman Ghosts-...Halloween Special (1995, $4.95) 1.00		2.60	6.00

NOTE: *Aparo* a-Annual 1. *Chaykin* scripts-24-26. *Giffen* a-Annual 1. *Golden* a-Annual 1. *Alan Grant* scripts-38, 52, 53. *Gil Kane* c/a-24-26. *Mignola* a-54; c-54, 62. *Morrow* a-Annual 3i. *Quesada* a-Annual 1. *James Robinson* scripts- 71-73. *Russell* c/a-42, 43. *Sears* a-21, 23; c-21, 23. *Zeck* a-71; c-69, 70.

BATMAN-LEGENDS OF THE DARK KNIGHT: JAZZ
Apr, 1995 - No. 3, June, 1995 ($2.50, limited series)
DC Comics

1-3		1.00	2.50

BATMAN: MANBAT
Oct, 1995 - No. 3, Dec, 1995 ($4.95, limited series)

DC Comics (Elseworlds)

1-3-Delano-script; Bolton-a.	1.00	2.00	5.00

BATMAN: MITEFALL (See Batman one-shots)
BATMAN MINIATURE (See Batman Kellogg's)
BATMAN: PENGUIN TRIUMPHANT (See Batman one-shots)
BATMAN RECORD COMIC
1966 (one-shot)
National Periodical Publications

1-With record (still sealed)	16.00	48.00	125.00
Comic only	10.00	30.00	70.00

BATMAN RETURNS MOVIE SPECIAL (See Batman one-shots)
BATMAN: RIDDLER-THE RIDDLE FACTORY (See Batman one-shots)
BATMAN: RUN, RIDDLER, RUN
1992 - Book 3, 1992 ($4.95, limited series)
DC Comics

Book 1-3: Mark Badger-a & plot	1.00	2.00	5.00

BATMAN: SCAR OF THE BAT (See Batman one-shots)
BATMAN: SHADOW OF THE BAT
June, 1992 - Present ($1.50/$1.75/$1.95)
DC Comics

1-The Last Arkham-c/story begins; Alan Grant scripts in all	1.20	3.00
1-($2.50)-Deluxe edition polybagged w/poster, pop-up & book mark			
	1.00	2.00	5.00
2-7: 4-The Last Arkham ends. 7-Last $1.50-c			1.50
8-28: 14,15-Staton-a(p). 16-18-Knightfall tie-ins. 19-28-Knightquest tie-ins			
w/Azrael as Batman. 19,20-Painted-c. 25-Silver ink-c; anniversary issue			
		.70	1.75
29-($2.95, 52 pgs.)-KnightsEnd Pt. 2		1.20	3.00
30,31,0,32-60: 30-KnightsEnd Pt. 8. 31-(9.94)-Begin $1.95-c; Zero			
Hour. 0-(10/94). 32-(11/94). 33-Robin-c. 35-Troika-Pt.2. 44-Cat-Man &			
Catwoman-c. 48-Contagion Pt. 1; card insert. 49-Contagion Pt.7.			
56,57-Poison Ivy-c/app.		.80	2.00
35-($2.95)-Variant embossed-c		1.20	3.00
Annual 1 (1993, $3.50, 68 pgs.)		1.40	3.50
Annual 2 (1994, $3.95, 68 pgs.)		1.60	4.00
Annual 3 (1995, $3.95)-Year One story; Poison Ivy app.			
		1.60	4.00
Annual 4 (1996, $2.95)-Legends of the Dead Earth story; Starman cameo			
			3.00

BATMAN-SPAWN: WAR DEVIL (See Batman one-shots)
BATMAN SPECTACULAR (See DC Special Series No. 15)
BATMAN: SWORD OF AZRAEL (Also see Azrael & Batman #488,489)
Oct, 1992 - No. 4, Jan, 1993 ($1.75, limited series)
DC Comics

1-Wraparound gatefold-c; Quesada-c/a(p) in all; 1st app. Azrael			
	2.15	6.50	15.00
2-4: 4-Cont'd in Batman #488	1.65	4.00	10.00
Silver Edition 1-4 (1993, $1.95)-Reprints #1-4		.80	2.00
Trade Paperback (1993, $9.95)-Reprints #1-4	1.65	4.00	10.00
Trade Paperback Gold Edition	2.15	6.50	15.00

BATMAN: THE CULT
1988 - No. 4, Nov, 1988 ($3.50, deluxe limited series)
DC Comics

1-Wrightson-a/painted-c in all	1.00	2.00	5.00
2-4		1.60	4.00
Trade Paperback ('91, $14.95)-New Wrightson-c	2.15	6.50	15.00

BATMAN: THE DARK KNIGHT
Mar, 1986 - No. 4, 1986 ($2.95, squarebound, limited series)

Batman Versus Predator II: Bloodmatch #4 © DC

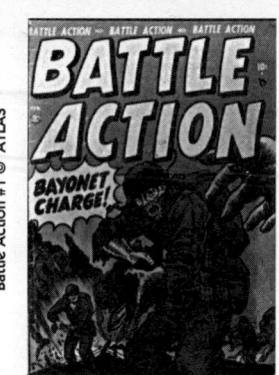
Battle Action #1 © ATLAS

Battle Cry #3 © Stanmor Publ.

BA

	GD25	FN65	NM94
DC Comics			
1-Miller story & c/a(p); set in the future	2.15	6.50	15.00
1-2nd & 3rd printings		1.20	3.00
2-Carrie Kelly becomes 1st female Robin	1.25	3.00	7.50
2-2nd & 3rd printings		1.20	3.00
3-Death of Joker; Superman app.	1.00	2.00	5.00
3-2nd printing		1.20	3.00
4-Death of Alfred; Superman app.		1.40	3.50
Hard-c, signed & numbered edition ($40.00)(4000 copies)			175.00
Hard-c, trade edition	4.30	13.00	30.00
Soft-c, trade edition (1st printing only)	1.65	4.00	10.00
Soft-c, trade edition (2nd thru 8th printings)	1.25	3.00	7.50

NOTE: The #2 second printings can be identified by matching the grey background colors on the inside front cover and c/a(p). The inside front cover of the second printing has a dark grey background which does not match the lighter grey of the facing page. On the true 1st printings, the backgrounds are both light grey. All other issues are clearly marked.

BATMAN: THE KILLING JOKE (See Batman one-shots)

BATMAN: THE OFFICIAL COMIC ADAPTATION OF THE WARNER BROS. MOTION PICTURE (See Batman one-shots)

BATMAN: THE ULTIMATE EVIL
1995 ($5.95, limited series, prestige format)
DC Comics

1,2-Barrett, Jr. adaptation of Vachss novel.			6.00

BATMAN 3-D (Also see 3-D Batman)
1990 ($9.95, w/glasses, 8-1/8x10-3/4")
DC Comics

nn-Byrne-a/scripts; Riddler, Joker, Penguin & Two-Face app. plus r/1953 3-D Batman; pin-ups by many artists	1.65	4.00	10.00

BATMAN: TWO-FACE-CRIME AND PUNISHMENT (See Batman one-shots)

BATMAN: TWO-FACE STRIKES TWICE
1993 - No. 2, 1993 ($4.95, 52 pgs.)
DC Comics

1,2-Flip book format w/Staton-a (G.A. side)	1.00	2.00	5.00

BATMAN VERSUS PREDATOR
1991 - No. 3, 1992 ($4.95/$1.95, limited series) (1st DC/Dark Horse x-over)
DC Comics/Dark Horse Comics

1 (Prestige format, $4.95)-1 & 3 contain 8 Batman/Predator trading cards; Andy & Adam Kubert-a; Suydam painted-c	1.00	2.50	5.50
1 (Regular format, $1.95)-No trading cards		1.00	2.50
2-(Prestige)-Extra pin-ups inside; Suydam-c	1.00	2.00	5.00
2-(Regular)-w/o cards		1.00	2.50
3-(Prestige)-Suydam-c	1.00	2.00	5.00
3-(Regular)-w/o cards		1.00	2.50
Trade paperback (1992, $5.95, 132pgs.)-r/#1-3 w/new introductions & forward plus new wraparound-c by Gibbons	1.00	2.50	6.00

BATMAN VERSUS PREDATOR II: BLOODMATCH
Late 1994 - No. 4, 1995 ($2.50, limited series)
DC Comics

1-4-Huntress app.; Moench scripts; Gulacy-a		1.00	2.50

BATMAN VS. THE INCREDIBLE HULK (See DC Special Series No. 27)

BAT MASTERSON (TV) (Also see Tim Holt #28)
Aug-Oct, 1959; Feb-Apr, 1960 - No. 9, Nov-Jan, 1961-62
Dell Publishing Co.

Four Color 1013 (#1) (8-10/59)	12.50	40.00	125.00
2-9: Gene Barry photo-c on all. 2-Two different back-c exist	7.50	24.00	75.00

BATS (See Tales Calculated to Drive You Bats)

BATS, CATS & CADILLACS
Oct, 1990 - No. 2, Nov, 1990 ($1.75)

	GD25	FN65	NM94
Now Comics			
1,2: 1-Gustovich-a(i); Snyder-c		.70	1.80
BATTLE			
Mar, 1951 - No. 70, June, 1960			
Marvel/Atlas Comics(FPI No. 1-62/Male No. 63 on)			
1	24.00	71.00	165.00
2	11.00	33.00	75.00
3-10: 4-1st Buck Pvt. O'Toole. 10-Pakula-a	8.35	25.00	50.00
11-20: 11-Check-a	6.35	19.00	38.00
21,23-Krigstein-a	8.00	24.00	48.00
22,24-36: 32-Tuska-a. 36-Everett-a	5.00	15.00	30.00
37-Kubert-a (Last precode, 2/55)	5.85	17.50	35.00
38-40,42-48	4.00	12.00	24.00
41-Kubert/Moskowitz-a	5.85	17.50	35.00
49-Davis-a	5.85	17.50	35.00
50-54,56-58	4.00	12.00	24.00
55-Williamson-a (5 pgs.)	6.35	19.00	38.00
59-Torres-a	5.00	15.00	30.00
60-62: 60,62-Combat Kelly app. 61-Combat Casey app.	4.00	11.00	22.00
63-Ditko-a.	7.50	22.50	45.00
64-66-Kirby-a. 66-Davis-a; has story of Fidel Castro in pre-Communism days (an admiring profile)	9.15	27.50	55.00
67,68: 67-Williamson/Crandall-a (4 pgs.). Kirby, Davis-a. 68-Kirby/ Williamson-a (4 pgs.); Kirby/Ditko-a	10.00	30.00	60.00
69,70: 69-Kirby-a. 70-Kirby/Ditko-a	8.35	25.00	50.00

NOTE: Andru a-37. Berg a-38, 14, 60-62. Colan a-33, 55. Everett a-36, 50, 70; c-56, 57. Heath a-6, 9, 13, 31, 69; c-6, 9, 12, 26, 35, 37. Kirby c-64-69. Maneely a-4, 6, 31, 61; c-4, 33, 59, 61. Orlando a-47. Powell a-53, 55. Reinman a-8, 9, 26, 32. Robinson a-9, 39. Romita a-26. Severin a-28, 32-34, 66-69; c-36, 55. Sinnott a-33, 37. Woodbridge a-52, 55.

BATTLE ACTION
Feb, 1952 - No. 12, 5/53; No. 13, 11/54 - No. 30, 8/57
Atlas Comics (NPI)

1-Pakula-a	19.00	58.00	135.00
2	10.00	30.00	60.00
3,4,6,7,9,10: 6-Robinson-c/a. 7-Partial nudity	5.70	17.00	34.00
5-Used in POP, pg. 93,94	6.70	20.00	40.00
8-Krigstein-a	7.50	22.50	45.00
11-15 (Last precode, 2/55)	5.70	17.00	34.00
16-26,28,29	5.00	15.00	30.00
27,30-Torres-a	5.00	15.00	30.00

NOTE: Battle Brady app. 5-7, 10-12. Berg a-3. Check a-11. Everett a-7; c-13, 25. Heath a-3, 8, 18; c-3,15, 18, 21. Maneely a-1; c-5. Reinman a-1. Robinson a-6, 7; c-6. Shores a-7(2). Sinnott a-3. Woodbridge a-28, 30.

BATTLE ATTACK
Oct, 1952 - No. 8, Dec, 1955
Stanmor Publications

1	8.35	25.00	50.00
2	4.70	14.00	28.00
3-8: 3-Hollingsworth-a	3.60	9.00	18.00

BATTLE BEASTS
Feb, 1988 - No. 4, 1988 ($1.50/$1.75, B&W/color)
Blackthorne Publishing

1-3 (B&W)-Based on Hasbro toys			1.50
4 ($1.75, color)		.70	1.80

BATTLE BRADY (Formerly Men in Action No. 1-9; see 3-D Action)
No. 10, Jan, 1953 - No. 14, June, 1953
Atlas Comics (IPC)

10: 10-12-Syd Shores-c	11.50	34.00	80.00
11-Used in POP, pg. 95 plus B&W & color illos	8.35	25.00	50.00
12-14	5.85	17.50	35.00

BATTLE CLASSICS (See Cancelled Comic Cavalcade)

Battlestar Galactica #13 © Universal Studios

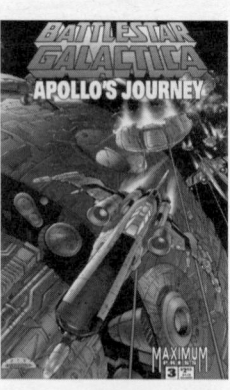

Battlestar Galactica: Apollo's Journey #3 © Universal Studios

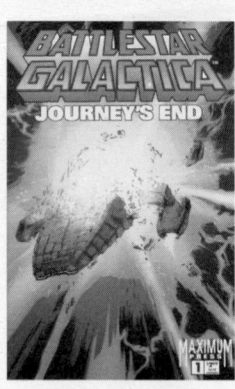

Battlesrtar Galactica: Journey's End #1 © Universal Studios

	GD25	FN65	NM94

Sept-Oct, 1978 (44 pgs.)
DC Comics

1-Kubert-r; new Kubert-c			1.00

BATTLE CRY
1952(May) - No. 20, Sept, 1955
Stanmor Publications

1	10.00	30.00	65.00
2	5.35	16.00	32.00
3,5-10: 8-Pvt. Ike begins, ends #13,17	4.00	10.00	20.00
4-Classic E.C. swipe	5.00	15.00	30.00
11-20	3.20	8.00	16.00

NOTE: *Hollingsworth* a-9; c-20.

BATTLEFIELD (War Adventures on the...)
April, 1952 - No. 11, May, 1953
Atlas Comics (ACI)

1-Pakula, Reinman-a	16.00	47.00	110.00
2-5: 2-Heath, Maneely, Pakula, Reinman-a	8.35	25.00	50.00
6-11	5.35	16.00	32.00

NOTE: *Colan* a-11. *Everett* a-8. *Heath* a-1, 2, 5p; c-2, 8, 9, 11. *Ravielli* a-11.

BATTLEFIELD ACTION (Formerly Foreign Intrigues)
No. 16, Nov, 1957 - No. 62, 2-3/66; No. 63, 7/80 - No. 89, 11/84
Charlton Comics

V2#16	4.70	14.00	28.00
17,20-30	3.00	7.50	15.00
18,19-Check-a (2 stories in #18)	3.60	9.00	18.00
31-62(1966)	1.80	4.50	9.00
63-89(1983-84)			1.00

NOTE: *Montes/Bache* a-43, 55, 62. *Glanzman* a-87r.

BATTLE FIRE
Apr, 1955 - No. 7, 1955
Aragon Magazine/Stanmor Publications

1	6.70	20.00	40.00
2	4.00	11.00	22.00
3-7	2.80	7.00	14.00

BATTLE FOR A THREE DIMENSIONAL WORLD
May, 1983 (20 pgs., slick paper w/stiff-c, $3.00)
3D Cosmic Publications

nn-Kirby c/a in 3-D; shows history of 3-D		1.20	3.00

BATTLEFORCE
Nov, 1987 - No. 2?, 1988 ($1.75, color/B&W)
Blackthorne Publishing

1,2: Based on game. 1-In color. 2-B&W		.70	1.75

BATTLE FOR INDEPENDENTS, THE (Also See Cyblade/Shi & Shi/Cyblade: The Battle For Independents)
1995 ($29.95)
Image Comics (Top Cow Productions)/Crusade Comics

nn-boxed set of all editions of Shi/Cyblade & Cyblade/Shi plus new variant.			
	5.00	15.00	40.00

BATTLE FOR THE PLANET OF THE APES (See Power Record Comics)

BATTLEFRONT
June, 1952 - No. 48, Aug, 1957
Atlas Comics (PPI)

1-Heath-c	21.00	64.00	150.00
2-Robinson-a(4)	10.00	30.00	70.00
3-5-Robinson-a(4) in each	9.15	27.50	55.00
6-10: Combat Kelly in No. 6-10	7.50	22.50	45.00
11-22,24-28: 14,16-Battle Brady app. 22-Teddy Roosevelt & His Rough Riders story. 28-Last pre-code (2/55)	5.00	15.00	30.00
23,43-Check-a	5.85	17.50	35.00
29-39,41,44-47	4.00	12.00	24.00
40,42-Williamson-a	6.70	20.00	40.00
48-Crandall-a	5.35	16.00	32.00

NOTE: *Ayers* a-19, 32. *Berg* a-44. *Colan* a-21, 22, 32, 33, 40. *Drucker* a-28, 29. *Everett* a-44. *Heath* c-23, 26, 27, 29, 32. *Maneely* a-22, 23; c-2, 13, 22, 35. *Morisi* a-42. *Morrow* a-41.*Orlando* a-47. *Powell* a-19, 21, 25, 29, 32, 40, 47. *Robinson* a-1-4, 5(4); c-4, 5. *Robert Sale* a-19. *Severin* a-32; c-40. *Woodbridge* a-45, 46.

BATTLEFRONT
No. 5, June, 1952
Standard Comics

5-Toth-a	12.00	36.00	85.00

BATTLE GROUND
Sept, 1954 - No. 20, Aug, 1957
Atlas Comics (OMC)

1	16.00	47.00	110.00
2-Jack Katz-a	9.15	27.50	55.00
3,4-Last precode (3/55)	5.85	17.50	35.00
5-8,10	5.35	16.00	32.00
9,11,13,18: 9-Krigstein-a. 11,13,18-Williamson-a in each	7.50	22.55	45.00
12,15-17,19,20	5.00	15.00	30.00
14-Kirby-a	7.50	22.55	45.00

NOTE: *Ayers* a-13. *Colan* a-11. *Drucker* a-7, 12, 13, 20. *Heath* c-2, 5, 13. *Maneely* a-19; c-1, 19. *Orlando* a-17.*Pakula* a-11. *Severin* a-5, 12, 19. c-20. *Tuska* a-11.

BATTLE HEROES
Sept, 1966 - No. 2, Nov, 1966 (25¢)
Stanley Publications

1,2	1.20	3.00	6.00

BATTLE OF THE BULGE (See Movie Classics)

BATTLE OF THE PLANETS (TV)
6/79 - No. 10, 12/80 (Based on syndicated cartoon by Sandy Frank)
Gold Key/Whitman No. 6 on

1		1.60	4.00
2-10: Mortimer a-1-4,7-10		.80	2.00

BATTLE REPORT
Aug, 1952 - No. 6, June, 1953
Ajax/Farrell Publications

1	6.70	20.00	40.00
2-6	4.15	12.50	25.00

BATTLE SQUADRON
April, 1955 - No. 5, Dec, 1955
Stanmor Publications

1	5.35	16.00	32.00
2-5: 3-Iwo Jima & flag-c	3.60	9.00	18.00

BATTLESTAR GALACTICA (TV) (Also see Marvel Comics Super Special #8)
Mar, 1979 - No. 23, Jan, 1981
Marvel Comics Group

1: 1-5 adapt TV episodes		1.40	3.50
2-23: 1-3-Partial-r		.80	2.00

NOTE: *Austin* c-9i, 10i. *Golden* c-18. *Simonson* a(p)-4, 5, 11-13, 15-20, 22, 23; c(p)-4, 5,11-13, 19, 20, 22, 23.

BATTLESTAR GALACTICA (TV) (Also see Asylum)
July, 1995 - No.4, Nov, 1995 ($2.50, limited series)
Maximum Press

1-4: Continuation of TV series		1.20	3.00
Trade paperback (12/95, $12.95)-reprints series			13.00

BATTLESTAR GALACTICA: APOLLO'S JOURNEY (TV)
Apr, 1996 - No. 3, June, 1996 ($2.95, limited series)
Maximum Press

Battlestar Galactica: The Enemy Within #3 © Universal Studios

Baywatch #2 © Acclaim

Beatles #1 © DELL

	GD25	FN65	NM94

1-3: Richard Hatch scripts — 1.20 — 3.00

BATTLESTAR GALACTICA: JOURNEY'S END (TV)
Aug, 1996 - No. 4, Nov, 1996 ($2.99, limited series)
Maximum Press

	GD25	FN65	NM94
1-4		1.20	3.00

BATTLESTAR GALACTICA: STARBUCK (TV)
Dec, 1995 - No. 3, Mar, 1996 ($2.50, limited series)
Maximum Press

1-3		1.00	2.50

BATTLESTAR GALACTICA: THE ENEMY WITHIN (TV)
Nov, 1995 - No. 3, Feb, 1996 ($2.50, limited series)
Maximum Press

1-3: 3-Indicia reads Feb, 1995 in error.		1.00	2.50

BATTLESTONE (Also see Brigade & Youngblood)
Nov, 1994 - No. 2, Dec, 1994 ($2.50, mini-series)
Image Comics (Extreme Studios)

1,2-Liefeld plots		1.00	2.50

BATTLE STORIES (See XMas Comics)
Jan, 1952 - No. 11, Sept, 1953
Fawcett Publications

1-Evans-a	11.00	33.00	75.00
2	6.35	19.00	38.00
3-11	4.70	14.00	28.00

BATTLE STORIES
1963 - 1964
Super Comics

Reprints #10-12,15-18: 10-r/U.S Tank Commandos #? 11-r/? 11, 12,17-r/Monty Hall #?; 13-Kintsler-a (1pg).15-r/American Air Forces #7 by Powell; Bolle-r.

18-U.S. Fighting Air Force #?		1.60	4.00

BATTLETECH (See Blackthorne 3-D Series #41 for 3-D issue)
Oct, 1987 - No. 6, 1988 ($1.75/$2.00)
Blackthorne Publishing\

1-6: Based on game. 1-Color. 2-Begin B&W		.70	1.75
Annual 1 ($4.50, B&W)		1.80	4.50

BATTLETECH
Feb, 1995 ($2.95)
Malibu Comics

0		1.20	3.00

BATTLETECH FALLOUT
Dec, 1994 - No. 4, Mar, 1995 ($2.95)
Malibu Comics

1-Two editions exist; normal logo and gold version w/foil logo stamped "Gold Limited Edition			3.00
1-Full-c holographic limited edition			15.00
2-4			3.00

BATTLETIDE (Death's Head II & Killpower...)
Dec, 1992 - No. 4, Mar, 1993 ($1.75, mini-series)
Marvel Comics UK, Ltd.

1-4: Wolverine, Psylocke, Dark Angel app.		.70	1.75

BATTLETIDE II (Death's Head II & Killpower...)
Aug, 1993 - No. 4, Nov, 1993 ($1.75, mini-series)
Marvel Comics UK, Ltd.

1-($2.95)-Foil embossed logo		1.20	3.00
2-4: 2-Hulk-c/story		.70	1.75

BATTLEZONES: DREAM TEAM 2 (See Dream Team)
Mar, 1996 ($3.95)
Malibu Comics (Ultraverse)

	GD25	FN65	NM94
1-pin-ups between Marvel & Malibu characters by Mike Wieringo, Phil Jimenez, Mike McKone, Cully Hamner, Gary Frank & others			4.00

BAYWATCH COMIC STORIES (TV) (Magazine)
May, 1996 - Present ($4.95) (Photo-c on all)
Acclaim Comics (Armada)

1-6: Photo comics based on TV show			5.00

BEACH BLANKET BINGO (See Movie Classics)

BEAGLE BOYS, THE (Walt Disney)(See The Phantom Blot)
11/64; No. 2, 11/65; No. 3, 8/66 - No. 47, 2/79 (See WDC&S #134)
Gold Key

1	2.50	7.50	25.00
2-5	1.20	3.60	12.00
6-10	.80	2.40	8.00
11-20: 11,14,19-r	1.00	2.00	5.00
21-47: 27-r		1.00	2.50

BEAGLE BOYS VERSUS UNCLE SCROOGE
Mar, 1979 - No. 12, Feb, 1980
Gold Key

1	.80	2.40	8.00
2-12: 9-r		1.60	4.00

BEANBAGS
Winter, 1951 - No. 2, Spring, 1952
Ziff-Davis Publ. Co. (Approved Comics)

1,2	8.35	25.00	50.00

BEANIE THE MEANIE
1958 - No. 3, May, 1959
Fago Publications

1-3	4.00	11.00	22.00

BEANY AND CECIL (TV) (Bob Clampett's...)
Jan, 1952 - 1955; July-Sept, 1962 - No. 5, July-Sept, 1963
Dell Publishing Co.

Four Color 368	25.00	75.00	250.00
Four Color 414,448,477,530,570,635(1/55)	17.00	51.00	170.00
01-057-209 (#1)	15.00	45.00	150.00
2-5	10.00	30.00	100.00

BEAR COUNTRY (Disney)
No. 758, Dec, 1956
Dell Publishing Co.

Four Color 758-Movie	5.40	16.00	54.00

B.E.A.S.T.I.E.S. (Also see Axis Alpha)
Apr, 1994 ($1.95)
Axis Comics

1-Javier Saltares-c/a/scripts		.80	2.00

BEATLES, THE (See Girls' Romances #109, Go-Go, Heart Throbs #101, Herbie #5, Howard the Duck Mag. #4, Laugh #166, Marvel Comics Super Special #4, My LittleMargie #54, Not Brand Echh, Strange Tales #130, Summer Love, Superman's Pal Jimmy Olsen #79, Teen Confessions #37, Tippy's Friends & Tippy Teen)

BEATLES, THE (Life Story)
Sept-Nov, 1964 (35¢)
Dell Publishing Co.

1-(Scarce)-Stories with color photo pin-ups	48.00	145.00	475.00

BEATLES EXPERIENCE, THE
Mar, 1991 - No. 8, 1991 ($2.50, B&W, limited series)
Revolutionary Comics

1-8: 1-Gold logo		1.00	2.50

BEATLES YELLOW SUBMARINE (See Movie Comics under Yellow...)

BEAUTIFUL PEOPLE

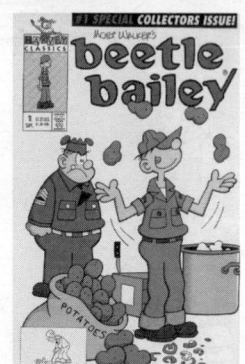
	GD25	FN65	NM94

Apr, 1994 ($4.95, 8-1/2x11", one-shot)
Slave Labor Graphics

nn			5.00

BEAUTIFUL STORIES FOR UGLY CHILDREN
1989 - No. 30, 1991 ($2.00/$2.50, B&W, mature)
DC Comics (Piranha Press)

V1-11		.80	2.00
12-30: 12-$2.50-c begins		1.00	2.50
A Cotton Candy Autopsy ($12.95, B&W)-Reprints 1st two volumes			
			13.00

BEAUTY AND THE BEAST, THE
Jan, 1985 - No. 4, Apr, 1985 (limited series)
Marvel Comics Group

1-4: Dazzler & the Beast from X-Men			1.50

BEAUTY AND THE BEAST (Graphic novel)(Also see Cartoon Tales & Disney's New Adventures of…)
1992
Disney Comics

nn-($4.95, prestige edition)-Adapts animated film	1.00	2.00	5.00
nn-($2.50, newsstand edition)		1.00	2.50

BEAUTY AND THE BEAST
Sept., 1992 - No. 2, 1992 ($1.50, limited series)
Disney Comics

1		.80	2.00
2			1.50

BEAUTY AND THE BEAST: PORTRAIT OF LOVE (TV)
May, 1989 - No. 2, Mar, 1990 ($5.95, 60 pgs., squarebound)
First Comics

1,2: 1-Based on TV show, Wendy Pini-a/scripts. 2-…: Night of Beauty; by Wendy Pini	1.00	2.60	6.00

BEAVER VALLEY (Movie)(Disney)
No. 625, Apr, 1955
Dell Publishing Co.

Four Color 625	7.00	21.00	70.00

BEAVIS AND BUTTHEAD (MTV's…)(TV cartoon)
Mar, 1994 - No. 28, June, 1996 ($1.95)
Marvel Comics

1-Silver ink-c. 1, 2-Punisher & Devil Dinosaur app.	1.00	2.00	5.00
1-2nd printing		.80	2.00
2,3: 2-Wolverine app. 3-Man-Thing, Spider-Man, Venom, Carnage, Mary Jane & Stan Lee cameos; John Romita, Sr. art (2 pgs.)	1.40		3.50
4-28: 5-War Machine, Thor, Loki, Hulk, Captain America & Rhino cameos. 6-Psylocke, Polaris, Daredevil & Bullseye app. 7-Ghost Rider & Sub-Mariner app. 8-Quasar & Eon app.9-Prowler & Nightwatch app. 11-Black Widow app. 12-Thujnderstrike & Bloodaxe app. 13-Night Thrasher app. 14-Spider-Man 2099 app. 15-Warlock app. 16-X-Factor app. 25-Juggernaut app.			
		.80	2.00

BECK & CAUL INVESTIGATIONS
Jan, 1994 - Present? ($2.95, B&W)
Gauntlet Comics (Caliber)

1-5		1.20	3.00
Special 1 ($4.95)	1.00	2.00	5.00

BEDKNOBS AND BROOMSTICKS (See Walt Disney Showcase No. 6 & 50)

BEDLAM!
Sept, 1985 - No. 2, Sept, 1985 (B&W-r in color)
Eclipse Comics

1,2-Bissette-a		.70	1.80

BEDTIME STORY (See Cinema Comics Herald)

BEELZELVIS
Feb, 1994 ($2.95, B&W, one-shot)
Slave Labor Graphics

1			3.00

BEEP BEEP, THE ROAD RUNNER (TV)(See Daffy & Kite Fun Book)
July, 1958 - No. 14, Aug-Oct, 1962; Oct, 1966 - No. 105, 1983
Dell Publishing Co./Gold Key No. 1-88/Whitman No. 89 on

Four Color 918 (#1, 7/58)	9.00	27.00	90.00
Four Color 1008,1046 (11-1/59-60)	4.50	13.50	45.00
4(2-4/60)-14(Dell)	3.60	10.00	36.00
1(10/66, Gold Key)	3.60	10.00	36.00
2-5	2.60	8.00	26.00
6-14 (1962)	1.80	5.50	18.00
15-18,20-40	1.30	4.00	13.00
19-With pull-out poster	2.60	8.00	26.00
41-50	1.00	2.60	6.00
51-70	.70	1.75	3.50
71-105			1.50

NOTE: *See March of Comics #351, 353, 375, 387, 397, 416, 430, 442, 455. #5, 8-10, 35, 53, 59-62, 68-r; 96-102, 104 are 1/3-r.*

BEETLE BAILEY (See Comics Reading Library, Giant Comic Album & Sarge Snorkel)
#459, 5/53 - #38, 5-7/62; #39, 11/62 - #53, 5/66; #54, 8/66 - #65, 12/67; #67, 2/69 - #119, 11/76; #120, 4/78 - #132, 4/80
Dell Publishing Co./Gold Key #39-53/King #54-66/Charlton #67-119/Gold Key #120-131/Whitman #132

Four Color 469 (#1)-By Mort Walker	10.00	30.00	100.00
Four Color 521,552,622	5.00	15.00	50.00
5(2-4/56)-10(5-7/57)	4.00	12.00	40.00
11-20(4-5/59)	3.00	9.00	30.00
21-38(5-7/62)	2.00	6.00	18.00
39-53(5/66)	1.00	3.00	9.00
54-119 (No. 66 publ. overseas only?)		1.20	3.00
120-132		.80	2.00
Bold Detergent Giveaway('69)-same as regular issue (#67) minus price			
		1.20	3.00
Cerebral Palsy Assn. Giveaway V2#71('69)-V2#73; (#1), 1/70 (Charlton)			
		1.20	3.00
Red Cross Giveaway-(1969, 5x7", 16 pgs., paper-c		1.20	3.00

BEETLE BAILEY
V2#1, Sept, 1992 - V2#9, Aug, 1994 ($1.25/$1.50)
Harvey Comics

V2#1-4			1.25
5-9-($1.50)			1.50
Big Book 1(11/92),2(5/93)(Both $1.95, 52 pgs.)		.80	2.00
Giant Size V2#1(10/92),2(3/93)(Both $2.25,68 pgs.)		.90	2.25

BEETLEJUICE (TV)
Oct, 1991 ($1.25)
Harvey Comics

1			1.25

BEETLEJUICE CRIMEBUSTERS ON THE HAUNT
Sept, 1992 - No. 3, Jan, 1993 ($1.50, limited series)
Harvey Comics

1-3			1.50

BEE 29, THE BOMBARDIER
Feb, 1945
Neal Publications

1-(Funny animal)	18.00	54.00	125.00

BEHIND PRISON BARS
1952

Beowulf #5 © DC

Berzerkers #2 © Rob Liefeld

Best From Boy's Life #1 © GIL

	GD25	FN65	NM94

Realistic Comics (Avon)

1-Kinstler-c ... 25.00 | 75.00 | 175.00

BEHOLD THE HANDMAID
1954 (Religious) (25¢ with a 20¢ sticker price)
George Pflaum

nn ... 3.20 | 8.00 | 16.00

BELIEVE IT OR NOT (See Ripley's...)

BEN AND ME (Disney)
No. 539, Mar, 1954
Dell Publishing Co.

Four Color 539 ... 3.20 | 9.50 | 32.00

BEN BOWIE AND HIS MOUNTAIN MEN
1952 - No. 17, Nov-Jan, 1958-59
Dell Publishing Co.

Four Color 443 (#1)	7.00	21.00	70.00
Four Color 513,557,599,626,657	3.40	10.00	34.00
7(5-7/56)-11: 11-Intro/origin Yellow Hair	3.40	10.00	34.00
12-17	2.70	9.00	27.00

BEN CASEY (TV)
June-July, 1962 - No. 10, June-Aug, 1965 (Photo-c)
Dell Publishing Co.

12-063-207 (#1)	4.00	12.00	40.00
2(10/62)-10: 4-Marijuana & heroin use story	3.00	9.00	30.00

BEN CASEY FILM STORY (TV)
Nov, 1962 (25¢) (Photo-c)
Gold Key

30009-211-All photos ... 7.00 | 21.00 | 70.00

BENEATH THE PLANET OF THE APES (See Movie Comics & Power Record Comics)

BEN FRANKLIN (See Kite Fun Book)

BEN HUR
No. 1052, Nov, 1959
Dell Publishing Co.

Four Color 1052-Movie, Manning-a ... 10.00 | 30.00 | 100.00

BEN ISRAEL
1974 (39¢)
Logos International

nn ... | | | 1.00

BEOWULF (Also see First Comics Graphic Novel #1)
Apr-May, 1975 - No. 6, Feb-Mar, 1976
National Periodical Publications

1			1.50
2-6: 5-Flying saucer-c/story			1.00

BERLIN
Apr, 1996 - Present ($2.50, B&W)
Black Eye Productions

1,2: Jason Lutes-c/a/scripts. ... | | | 2.50

BERNI WRIGHTSON, MASTER OF THE MACABRE
July, 1983 - No. 5, Nov, 1984 ($1.50, Baxter paper)
Pacific Comics/Eclipse Comics No. 5

1-5: Wrightson-c/a(r). 4-Jeff Jones-r (11 pgs.) ... | | | 1.50

BERRYS, THE (Also see Funny World)
May, 1956
Argo Publ.

1-Reprints daily & Sunday strips & daily Animal Antics by Ed Nofziger ... 5.00 | 15.00 | 30.00

BERZERKERS (See Youngblood V1#2)

Aug, 1995 - No. 3, Oct, 1995 ($2.50, limited series)
Image Comics (Extreme Studios)

1-3: Beau Smith scripts, Fraga-a ... | | 1.00 | 2.50

BEST COMICS
Nov, 1939 - No. 4, Feb, 1940 (Large size, reads sideways)
Better Publications

1-(Scarce)-Red Mask begins(1st app.) & c/s-all	65.00	195.00	525.00
2-4: 4-Cannibalism story	44.00	132.00	350.00

BEST FROM BOY'S LIFE, THE
Oct, 1957 - No. 5, Oct, 1958 (35¢)
Gilberton Company

1-Space Conquerors & Kam of the Ancient Ones begin, end #5	9.15	27.50	55.00
2,3,5	5.00	15.00	30.00
4-L.B. Cole-a	6.35	19.00	38.00

BEST LOVE (Formerly Sub-Mariner Comics No. 32)
No. 33, Aug, 1949 - No. 36, April, 1950 (Photo-c 33-36)
Marvel Comics (MPI)

33-Kubert-a	10.00	30.00	60.00
34	5.00	15.00	30.00
35,36-Everett-a	6.70	20.00	40.00

BEST OF BUGS BUNNY, THE
Oct, 1966 - No. 2, Oct, 1968
Gold Key

1,2-Giants ... 4.00 | 12.00 | 40.00

BEST OF DC, THE (Blue Ribbon Digest) (See Limited Coll. Ed. C-52)
Sept-Oct, 1979 - No. 71, Apr, 1986 (100-148 pgs; all reprints)
DC Comics

1-17,19-34,36-71: 11-The Year's Best Stories; 132 pgs. 28,29,41,47,58,65,68-Sugar & Spike. 28,29,39,45,70-Binky. 34-Has #497 on-c from Adv. Comics. 37,43,49,55-Funny Stuff. 60-Plop!; Wood-c(r) & Aragones-r (5/85). 63-Plop!		1.20	3.00
18-The New Teen Titans		1.60	4.00
35-The Year's Best Comics Stories(148 pgs.)		1.20	3.00

NOTE: **N. Adams** a-2r, 14r, 18r, 26, 51. **Aparo** a-9, 14, 26, 30; c-9, 14, 26. **Austin** a-51i. **Buckler** a-40p; c-16, 22. **Giffen** a-50, 52; c-33p. **Grell** a-33p. **Grossman** a-37. **Heath** a-26. **Infantino** a-10r, 18. **Kaluta** a-40. **G. Kane** a-10r, 18r; c-40, 44. **Kubert** a-10r, 21, 26. **Layton** a-21. **S. Mayer** c-29, 37, 41, 43, 47; a-28, 29, 37, 41, 43, 47, 58, 65, 68. **Moldoff** c-64p. **Morrow** a-40; c-40. **W. Mortimer** a-39p. **Newton** a-5, 51. **Perez** a-24, 50p; c-18, 21, 23. **Rogers** a-14, 51p. **Simonson** a-11r. **Spiegle** a-52. **Starlin** a-51. **Staton** a-5, 21. **Tuska** a-24. **Wolverton** a-60. **Wood** a-60, 63; c-60, 63. **Wrightson** a-60. New art in #14, 18, 24.

BEST OF DENNIS THE MENACE, THE
Summer, 1959 - No. 5, Spring, 1961 (100 pgs.)
Hallden/Fawcett Publications

1-All reprints; Wiseman-a	9.15	27.50	55.00
2-5	5.85	17.50	35.00

BEST OF DONALD DUCK, THE
Nov, 1965 (12¢, 36 pgs.)(Lists 2nd printing in indicia)
Gold Key

1-Reprints Four Color #223 by Barks ... 9.30 | 28.00 | 65.00

BEST OF DONALD DUCK & UNCLE SCROOGE, THE
Nov, 1964 - No. 2, Sept, 1967 (25¢ Giants)
Gold Key

1(30022-411)('64)-Reprints 4-Color #189 & 408 by Carl Barks; cover of F.C. #189 redrawn by Barks	7.00	21.00	70.00
2(30022-709)('67)-Reprints 4-Color #256 & "Seven Cities of Cibola" & U.S. #8 by Barks	7.00	21.00	70.00

BEST OF HORROR AND SCIENCE FICTION COMICS
1987 ($2.00)
Bruce Webster

Best of the Brave & the Bold #5 © DC

Bettie Page Comics #1 © DH

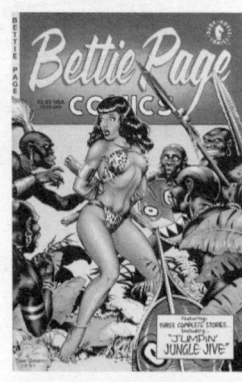

Betty and Veronica #10 © Archie

	GD25	FN65	NM94
1-Wolverton, Frazetta, Powell, Ditko-r		.80	2.00

BEST OF MARMADUKE, THE
1960
Charlton Comics

	GD25	FN65	NM94
1-Brad Anderson's strip reprints	4.00	11.00	22.00

BEST OF MS. TREE, THE
1987 - No. 4, 1988 ($2.00, B&W, limited series)
Pyramid Comics

		FN65	NM94
1-4		.80	2.00

BEST OF THE BRAVE AND THE BOLD, THE (See Super DC Giant)
Oct, 1988 - No. 6, Jan, 1989 ($2.50, limited series)
DC Comics

		FN65	NM94
1-6: Neal Adams-r, Kubert-r & Heath-r in all		1.00	2.50

BEST OF THE WEST (See A-1 Comics)
1951 - No. 12, April-June, 1954
Magazine Enterprises

	GD25	FN65	NM94
1(A-1 42)-Ghost Rider, Durango Kid, Straight Arrow, Bobby Benson begin	40.00	120.00	295.00
2(A-1 46)	19.00	58.00	135.00
3(A-1 52), 4(A-1 59), 5(A-1 66)	17.00	51.00	120.00
6(A-1 70), 7(A-1 76), 8(A-1 81), 9(A-1 85), 10(A-1 87), 11(A-1 97), 12(A-1 103)	12.00	36.00	85.00

NOTE: *Bolle* a-9. *Borth* a-12. *Guardineer* a-5, 12. *Powell* a-1, 12.

BEST OF UNCLE SCROOGE & DONALD DUCK, THE
Nov, 1966 (25¢)
Gold Key

	GD25	FN65	NM94
1(30030-611)-Reprints part 4-Color #159 & 456 & Uncle Scrooge #6,7 by Carl Barks	7.00	21.00	70.00

BEST OF WALT DISNEY COMICS, THE
1974 ($1.50, 52 pgs.) (Walt Disney)
(8-1/2x11" cardboard covers; 32,000 printed of each)
Western Publishing Co.

	GD25	FN65	NM94
96170-Reprints 1st two stories less 1 pg. each from 4-Color #62	2.50	11.00	25.00
96171-Reprints Mickey Mouse and the Bat Bandit of Inferno Gulch from 1934 (strips) by Gottfredson	2.50	11.00	25.00
96172-r/Uncle Scrooge #386 & two other stories	2.50	11.00	25.00
96173-Reprints "Ghost of the Grotto" (from 4-Color #159) & "Christmas on Bear Mountain" (from 4-Color #178)	2.50	11.00	25.00

BEST ROMANCE
No. 5, Feb-Mar, 1952 - No. 7, Aug, 1952
Standard Comics (Visual Editions)

	GD25	FN65	NM94
5-Toth-a; photo-c	10.00	30.00	70.00
6,7-Photo-c	4.15	12.50	25.00

BEST SELLER COMICS (See Tailspin Tommy)

BEST WESTERN (Formerly Terry Toons? or Miss America Magazine
V7#24(#57)?; Western Outlaws & Sheriffs No. 60 on)
No. 58, June, 1949 - No. 59, Aug, 1949
Marvel Comics (IPC)

	GD25	FN65	NM94
58,59-Black Rider, Kid Colt, Two-Gun Kid app.; both have Syd Shores-c	18.00	54.00	125.00

BETTIE PAGE COMICS
Mar, 1996 ($3.95)
Dark Horse Comics

			NM94
1-Dave Stevens-c; Bret Blevins & Russ Heath-a; Jaime Hernandez pin-up			4.00

BETTY (See Pep Comics #22 for 1st app.)
Sept, 1992 - Present ($1.25/$1.50)

Archie Comics

			NM94
1-24			1.25
25-45			1.50

BETTY AND HER STEADY (Going Steady with Betty No. 1)
No. 2, Mar-Apr, 1950
Avon Periodicals

	GD25	FN65	NM94
2	9.15	27.50	55.00

BETTY AND ME
Aug, 1965 - No. 200, Aug, 1992
Archie Publications

	GD25	FN65	NM94
1	8.50	25.50	85.00
2	4.20	12.50	42.00
3-5: 3-Origin Superteen. Superteen in new costume #4-7; dons new helmet in #5, ends #8 (see Archie's Girls #118)	2.50	7.50	25.00
6-10	1.40	4.20	14.00
11-30	.70	2.10	7.00
31-55 (52 pgs. #36-55)		1.30	3.25
56-100		.80	2.00
101-199: Later issues $1.00 cover			1.20
200-($1.50)-Last issue			1.50

BETTY AND VERONICA (Also see Archie's Girls...)
June, 1987 - Present (75¢ /$1.25/$1.50)
Archie Enterprises

		FN65	NM94
1-86		.60	1.25
87-115			1.50
Summer Fun 1 (1994, $2.00, 52 pgs. plus poster)		.80	2.00

BETTY & VERONICA ANNUAL DIGEST (...Digest Magazine #1-4, 44 on;
...Comics Digest Mag. #5-43)
Nov, 1980 - Present ($1.00/$1.50/$1.75, digest size)
Archie Publications

			NM94
1,2(11/81-Katy Keene story), 3(8/82)-70			1.50
70-84			1.75

BETTY & VERONICA ANNUAL DIGEST MAGAZINE
Sept, 1989 - Present ($1.50/$1.75, 128 pgs.)
Archie Comics

		FN65	NM94
1-20: 9-Neon ink logo		.70	1.75

BETTY & VERONICA CHRISTMAS SPECTACULAR (See Archie Giant Series
Magazine #159, 168, 180, 191, 204, 217, 229, 241, 453, 465, 477, 489, 501, 513, 525, 536, 547, 558, 568, 580, 593, 606, 618)

BETTY & VERONICA DOUBLE DIGEST MAGAZINE
1987 - Present ($2.25/$2.75/$1.50, digest size, 256 pgs.)(...Digest #12 on)
Archie Enterprises

		FN65	NM94
1-25: 5,17-Xmas-c. 16-Capt. Hero story		1.10	2.75
26-55			1.50

BETTY & VERONICA SPECTACULAR (See Archie Giant Series Mag. #11, 16, 21,
26, 32, 138, 145, 153, 162, 173, 184, 197, 201, 210, 214, 221, 226, 234, 238, 246, 250, 458,
462, 470, 482, 486, 494, 498, 506, 510, 518, 522, 526, 530, 537, 552, 559, 563, 569, 575, 582,
588, 600, 608, 613, 620, 623, and Betty & Veronica)

BETTY AND VERONICA SPECTACULAR
Oct, 1992 - Present ($1.25/$1.50)
Archie Comics

			NM94
1-10: 1-Dan DeCarlo-c/a			1.00
11-25			1.50

BETTY & VERONICA SPRING SPECTACULAR (See Archie Giant Series Magazine #569, 582, 595)

BETTY & VERONICA SUMMER FUN (See Archie Giant Series Mag. #8, 13, 18, 23,
28, 34, 140, 147, 155, 164, 175, 187, 199, 212, 224, 236, 248, 460, 484, 496, 508, 520,
529, 539, 550, 561, 572, 585, 598, 611, 621)

BETTY BOOP'S BIG BREAK

	GD25	FN65	NM94

1990 ($5.95, 52 pgs.)
First Publishing

nn-By Joshua Quagmire; 60th anniversary ish.	1.00	2.60	6.00

BETTY PAGE 3-D COMICS
1991 ($3.95, "7-1/2x10-1/4," 28pgs, no glasses)
The 3-D Zone

1-Photo inside covers; back-c nudity		1.60	4.00

BETTY'S DIARY (See Archie Giant Series Magazine No. 555)
April, 1986 - No. 40, Apr, 1991 (#1:65¢; 75¢/95¢)
Archie Enterprises

1-40			1.00

BEVERLY HILLBILLIES (TV)
4-6/63 - No. 18, 8/67; No. 19, 10/69; No. 20, 10/70; No. 21, Oct, 1971
Dell Publishing Co.

1-Photo-c	15.00	45.00	155.00
2-Photo-c	8.50	25.00	85.00
3-9: All have photo covers	5.85	17.50	55.00
10: No photo cover	3.60	9.00	35.00
11-21: All have photo covers. 18-Last 12¢ issue	4.50	13.00	45.00

NOTE: #1-9, 11-21 are photo covers. #19 reprints cover to #1, but not insides.

BEWARE (Formerly Fantastic; Chilling Tales No. 13 on)
No. 10, June, 1952 - No. 12, Oct, 1952
Youthful Magazines

10-E.A. Poe's Pit & the Pendulum adaptation by Wildey; Harrison/Bache-a;			
atom bomb and shrunken head-c	36.00	107.00	250.00
11-Harrison-a; Ambrose Bierce adapt.	25.00	75.00	175.00
12-Used in SOTI, pg. 388; Harrison-a	25.00	75.00	175.00

BEWARE
No. 13, 1/53 - No. 16, 7/53; No. 5, 9/53 - No. 15, 5/55
Trojan Magazines/Merit Publ. No. ?

13(#1)-Harrison-a	38.00	114.00	265.00
14(#2, 3/53)-Krenkel/Harrison-c; dismemberment, severed head panels			
	25.00	75.00	175.00
15,16(#3, 5/53; #4, 7/53)-Harrison-a	19.00	56.00	130.00
5,9,12,13	19.00	56.00	130.00
6-Ill. in SOTI- "Children are first shocked and then desensitized by all this brutality." Corpse on cover swipe/V.O.H. #26; girl on cover swipe/Advs. Into Darkness #10	40.00	120.00	285.00
7,8-Check-a	19.00	58.00	135.00
10-Frazetta/Check-c; Disbrow, Check-a	45.00	130.00	340.00
11-Disbrow-a; heart torn out, blood drainage	21.00	64.00	150.00
14,15: 14-Myron Fass-c. 15-Harrison-a	16.00	47.00	110.00

NOTE: Fass a-5, 6, 8; c-6, 11, 14. Forte a-8. Hollingsworth a-15(#3), 16(#4), 9; c-16(#4), 8, 9. Kiefer a-16(#4), 5, 6, 10.

BEWARE (Becomes Tomb of Darkness No. 9 on)
Mar, 1973 - No. 8, May, 1974 (All reprints)
Marvel Comics Group

1-Everett-c; Sinnott-r ('54)		1.80	4.50
2-8: 2-Forte, Colan-r. 6-Tuska-a. 7-Torres-r/Mystical Tales #7		.80	2.00

NOTE: Infantino a-4r. Gil Kane c-4. Wildey a-7r.

BEWARE TERROR TALES
May, 1952 - No. 8, July, 1953
Fawcett Publications

1-E.C. art swipe/Haunt of Fear #5 & Vault of Horror #26			
	36.00	107.00	250.00
2	21.00	64.00	150.00
3-8: 8-Tothish-a	17.00	51.00	120.00

NOTE: Andru a-2. Bernard Bailey a-1; c-1-5. Powell a-1, 2, 8. Sekowsky a-2.

BEWARE THE CREEPER (See Adventure, Best of the Brave & the Bold,

---

Brave & the Bold, 1st Issue Special, Flash #318-323, Showcase #73, World's Finest #249)
May-June, 1968 - No. 6, Mar-Apr, 1969 (All 12¢ issues)
National Periodical Publications

1-(5-6/68)-Classic Ditko-c; Ditko-a in all	8.50	26.00	60.00
2-6: 2-5-Ditko-c. 6-Gil Kane-c	5.70	17.00	40.00

BEWITCHED (TV)
4-6/65 - No. 11, 10/67; No. 12, 10/68 - No. 13, 1/69; No. 14, 10/69
Dell Publishing Co.

1-Photo-c	14.00	42.00	140.00
2-No photo-c	7.00	21.00	70.00
3-13-All have photo-c	5.00	15.00	50.00
14-No photo-c	3.35	10.00	32.00

BEYOND, THE
Nov, 1950 - No. 30, Jan, 1955
Ace Magazines

1-Bakerish-a(p)	32.00	96.00	225.00
2-Bakerish-a(p)	20.00	60.00	140.00
3-10: 10-Woodish-a by Cameron	12.00	36.00	85.00
11-20: 18-Used in POP, pgs. 81,82	10.00	30.00	65.00
21-26,28-30	10.00	30.00	60.00
27-Used in SOTI, pg. 111	10.00	30.00	70.00

NOTE: Cameron a-10, 11p, 12p, 15, 16, 21-27, 30; c-20. Colan a-6, 13, 17. Sekowsky a-2, 3, 5, 7, 11, 14, 27r. No. 1 was to appear as Challenge of the Unknown No. 7.

BEYOND THE GRAVE
July, 1975 - No. 6, June, 1976; No. 7, Jan, 1983 - No. 17, Oct, 1984
Charlton Comics

1-Ditko-a (6 pgs.); Sutton painted-c		1.60	4.00
2-6: 2-5-Ditko-a; Ditko c-2,3,6		.80	2.00
7-17: ('83-'84) Reprints. 13-Aparo-c(r). 15-Sutton-c			1.25
Modern Comics Reprint 2('78)			1.00

BIBLE TALES FOR YOUNG FOLK (...Young People No. 3-5)
Aug, 1953 - No. 5, Mar, 1954
Atlas Comics (OMC)

1	20.00	60.00	140.00
2-Everett, Krigstein-a	16.00	47.00	110.00
3-5: 4-Robinson-c	11.00	33.00	75.00

BIG (Movie)
Mar, 1989 ($2.00)
Hit Comics (Dark Horse Comics)

1-Adaptaiton of film; Paul Chadwick-a		.80	2.00

BIG ALL-AMERICAN COMIC BOOK, THE (See All-American Comics)
1944 (132 pgs., one-shot) (Early DC Annual)
All-American/National Per.l Publ.

	GD25	FN65	VF82	NM94
1-Wonder Woman, Green Lantern, Flash, The Atom, Wildcat, Scribbly, The Whip, Ghost Patrol, Hawkman by Kubert (1st on Hawkman), Hop Harrigan, Johnny Thunder, Little Boy Blue, Mr. Terrific, Mutt & Jeff app.; Sargon on cover only; cover by Kubert/Hibbard/Mayer/others				
	900.00	2700.00	6600.00	10,500.00

(Estimated up to 80+ total copies exist, 6 in NM/Mint)

BIG BABY HUEY (Also see Baby Huey)
Oct, 1991 - No. 4, Mar, 1992 ($1.00, quarterly)
Harvey Comics

	GD25	FN65	NM94
1-4			1.00

BIG BANG COMICS (Becomes Big Bang #4)
Spring, 1994 - No. 4, Feb, 1995 ($1.95, limited series)
Caliber Press

0-4: 0-Alex Ross-c.		.80	2.00

BIG BANG COMICS

Big Book of Conspiracies © DC

Big Bruisers #1 © Aegis Entertainment

Big Shot Comics #32 © CCG

	GD25	FN65	NM94
V2#1, May, 1996 - Present ($1.95)			
Image Comics (Highbrow Entertainment)			
V2#1-3: 1-Mighty Man app. 2-S.A. Shadowhawk app.			2.00
4-Begin $2.50-c			2.50

BIG BLOWN BABY (Also see Dark Horse Presents)
Aug, 1996 - No. 4, Nov, 1996 ($2.95, limited series, mature)
Dark Horse Comics

1-4: Bill Wray-c/a/scripts			3.00

BIG BOOK OF CONSPIRACIES, THE
1995 ($12.95, B&W, trade paperback)
DC Comics (Paradox Press)

nn	1.85	5.50	13.00

BIG BOOK OF DEATH, THE
1994 ($12.95, B&W, trade paperback)
DC Comics (Paradox Press)

nn	1.85	5.50	13.00

BIG BOOK OF FREAKS, THE
1996 ($14.95, B&W, trade paperback)
DC Comics (Paradox Press)

nn			15.00

BIG BOOK OF HOAXES
1996 ($14.95, B&W, trade paperback)
DC Comics (Paradox Press)

nn			15.00

BIG BOOK OF FUN COMICS (See New Book of Comics)
Spring, 1936 (Large size, 52 pgs.)(1st comic book annual & DC annual)

National Periodical Publications	GD25	FN65	VF82
1 (Very rare)-r/New Fun #1-5	2000.00	6000.00	12,000.00
(Estimated up to 15 total copies exist, none in NM/Mint)			

BIG BOOK OF LITTLE CRIMINALS, THE
1996 ($14.95, B&W, trade paperback)
DC Comics (Paradox Press)

nn			15.00

BIG BOOK OF URBAN LEGENDS, THE
1994 ($12.95, B&W, trade paperback)
DC Comics (Paradox Press)

nn	1.85	5.50	13.00

BIG BOOK OF WEIRDOS, THE
1995 ($12.95, B&W, trade paperback)
DC Comics (Paradox Press)

nn	1.85	5.50	13.00

BIG BOOK ROMANCES
Feb, 1950 (no date given) (148 pgs.)

Fawcett Publications	GD25	FN65	NM94
1-Contains remaindered Fawcett romance comics - several combinations possible	32.00	96.00	225.00

BIG BOY (See Adventures of the Big Boy)

BIG BRUISERS
July, 1996 ($3.50, one-shot)
Image Comics (Wildstorm Productions)

1-Features Maul from WildC.A.T.S, Impact from Cyberforce & Badrock from Youngblood; wraparound-c			3.50

BIG CHIEF WAHOO
July, 1942 - No. 23, 1945? (Quarterly)
Eastern Color Printing/George Dougherty (distr. by Fawcett)

1-Newspaper-r (on sale 6/15/42)	40.00	120.00	290.00

	GD25	FN65	NM94
2-Steve Roper app.	21.00	62.00	145.00
3-5: 4-Chief is holding a Katy Keene comic	15.00	45.00	105.00
6-10: 8-23-Exist?	10.00	30.00	70.00
11-23	7.50	22.50	45.00

NOTE: *Kerry Drake in some issues.*

BIG CIRCUS, THE (Movie)
No. 1036, Sept-Nov, 1959
Dell Publishing Co.

Four Color 1036-Photo-c	6.00	18.00	60.00

BIG COUNTRY, THE (Movie)
No. 946, Oct, 1958
Dell Publishing Co.

Four Color 946-Photo-c	7.00	21.00	70.00

BIG DADDY ROTH (Magazine)
Oct-Nov, 1964 - No. 4, Apr-May, 1965 (35¢)
Millar Publications

1-Toth-a	20.00	60.00	140.00
2-4-Toth-a	15.00	45.00	105.00

BIG GUY AND RUSTY THE BOY ROBOT, THE (Also See Madman Comics
#6,7 & Martha Washington Stranded In Space)
July, 1995 - No. 2, Aug, 1995 ($4.95, oversize, limited series)
Dark Horse (Legend)

1,2-Frank Miller scripts & Geoff Darrow-c/a	1.00	2.00	5.00
Trade paperback (10/96, $14.95)-r/1,2 w/cover gallery			15.00

BIG HERO ADVENTURES (See Jigsaw)

BIG JIM'S P.A.C.K.
No date (1975) (16 pgs.)
Mattel, Inc. (Marvel Comics)

nn-Giveaway with Big Jim doll; Buscema/Sinnott-c/a			1.00

BIG JON & SPARKIE (Radio)(Formerly Sparkie, Radio Pixie)
No. 4, Sept-Oct, 1952 (Painted-c)
Ziff-Davis Publ. Co.

4-Based on children's radio program	16.00	47.00	110.00

BIG LAND, THE (Movie)
No. 812, July, 1957
Dell Publishing Co.

Four Color 812-Alan Ladd photo-c	10.00	30.00	100.00

BIG RED (See Movie Comics)

BIG SHOT COMICS
May, 1940 - No. 104, Aug, 1949
Columbia Comics Group

	GD25	FN65	NM94
1-Intro. Skyman; The Face (1st app.; Tony Trent), The Cloak (Spy Master), Marvelo, Monarch of Magicians, Joe Palooka, Charlie Chan, Tom Kerry, Dixie Dugan, Rocky Ryan begin; Charlie Chan moves over from Feature Comics #31 (4/40).	162.00	490.00	1300.00
2	65.00	195.00	525.00
3-The Cloak called Spy Chief; Skyman-c	53.00	160.00	425.00
4,5	43.00	128.00	340.00
6-10: 8-Christmas-c	40.00	120.00	280.00
11-14: 14-Origin & 1st app. Sparky Watts (6/41)	36.00	107.00	250.00
15-Origin The Cloak	39.00	118.00	275.00
16-20	27.00	81.00	190.00
21-27,29,30: 24-Tojo-c. 29-Intro. Capt. Yank; Bo (a dog) newspaper strip-r by by Frank Beck begins, ends #104. 30-X-Mas-c	22.00	66.00	155.00
28-Hitler, Tojo & Mussolini-c	29.00	86.00	200.00
31,33-40	17.00	49.00	115.00
32-Vic Jordan newspaper strip reprints begin, ends #52; Hitler, Tojo & Mussolini-c	20.00	60.00	140.00
41-50: 42-No Skyman. 43,46-Hitler-c. 50-Origin The Face retold			

Big 3 #5 © FOX

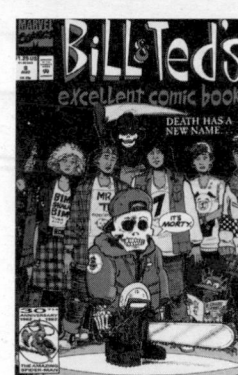
Bill & Ted's Excellent Comic Book #9 © MEG

Billi 99 #2 © DH

	GD25	FN65	NM94
	13.00	39.00	90.00
51-60	10.00	30.00	70.00
61-70: 63 on-Tony Trent, the Face	9.15	27.50	55.00
71-80: 73-The Face cameo. 74-(2/47)-Mickey Finn begins. 74,80-The Face			
app. in Tony Trent. 78-Last Charlie Chan strip-r	8.35	25.00	50.00
81-90: 85-Tony Trent marries Babs Walsh. 86-Valentines-c			
	6.70	20.00	40.00
91-99,101-104: 69-94-Skyman in Outer Space. 96-Xmas-c			
	5.85	17.50	35.00
100	7.50	22.50	45.00

NOTE: **Mart Bailey** art on "The Face" No. 1-104. **Guardineer** a-5. Sparky Watts by **Boody Rogers**-No. 14-42, 77-104, (by others No. 43-76). Others than Tony Trent wear "The Face" mask in No. 46-63, 93. Skyman by **Ogden Whitney**-No. 1, 2, 4, 12-37, 49, 70-101. Skyman covers-No. 1, 3, 7-12, 14, 16, 20, 27, 89, 95, 100.

BIG TEX
June, 1953
Toby Press

1-Contains (3) John Wayne stories-r with name changed to Big Tex			
	8.35	25.00	50.00

BIG-3
Fall, 1940 - No. 7, Jan, 1942
Fox Features Syndicate

1-Blue Beetle, The Flame, & Samson begin	175.00	525.00	1400.00
2	75.00	225.00	600.00
3-5	53.00	160.00	425.00
6,7: 6-Last Samson. 7-V-Man app.	44.00	132.00	350.00

BIG TOP COMICS, THE (TV's Great Circus Show)
1951 - No. 2, 1951 (No month)
Toby Press

1,2	7.50	22.50	45.00

BIG TOWN (Radio/TV) (Also see Movie Comics, 1946)
Jan, 1951 - No. 50, Mar-Apr, 1958 (No. 1-9: 52pgs.)
National Periodical Publications

1-Dan Barry-a begins	53.00	160.00	425.00
2	31.00	92.00	215.00
3-10	17.00	51.00	120.00
11-20	11.50	34.00	80.00
21-31: Last pre-code (1-2/55)	10.00	30.00	60.00
32-50	6.70	20.00	40.00

BIG VALLEY, THE (TV)
June, 1966 - No. 5, Oct, 1967; No. 6, Oct, 1969
Dell Publishing Co.

1: Photo-c #1-5	4.00	16.00	40.00
2-6: 6-Reprints #1	3.25	9.50	22.00

BIKER MICE FROM MARS (TV)
Nov, 1993 - No. 3, Jan, 1994 ($1.50, limited series)
Marvel Comics

1-3: 1-Intro Vinnie, Modo & Throttle. 2-Origin			1.50

BILL & TED'S BOGUS JOURNEY
Sept, 1991 ($2.95, squarebound, 84 pgs.)
Marvel Comics

1-Adapts movie sequel		1.20	3.00

"BILL AND TED'S EXCELLENT ADVENTURE" MOVIE ADAPTATION
1989 (No cover price)
DC Comics

nn-Torres-a.			1.00

BILL & TED'S EXCELLENT COMIC BOOK (Movie)
Dec, 1991 - No. 12, 1992 ($1.00/$1.25)
Marvel Comics

	GD25	FN65	NM94
1,2: 2-Last $1.00-c			1.00
3-12			1.25

BILL BARNES COMICS (...America's Air Ace Comics No. 2 on)
(Becomes Air Ace V2#1 on; also see Shadow Comics)
Oct, 1940(No. month given) - No. 12, Oct, 1943
Street & Smith Publications

1-23 pgs.-comics; Rocket Rooney begins	65.00	195.00	525.00
2-Barnes as The Phantom Flyer app.; Tuska-a	40.00	120.00	290.00
3-5	31.00	92.00	215.00
6-12	26.00	79.00	185.00

BILL BATTLE, THE ONE MAN ARMY (Also see Master Comics No. 133)
Oct, 1952 - No. 4, Apr, 1953 (All photo-c)
Fawcett Publications

1	10.00	30.00	60.00
2	5.85	17.50	35.00
3,4	4.25	13.00	28.00

BILL BLACK'S FUN COMICS
Dec, 1982 - No. 4, Mar, 1983 ($1.75, Baxter paper)(1st AC comic)
Paragon #1-3/Americomics #4

1-Intro. Capt. Paragon, Phantom Lady & Commando D (#1-3 are B&W fanzines; 8-1/2x11")		1.00	2.50
2-4: 4-($2.00, color)-Origin Nightfall (formerly Phantom Lady); Nightveil app.		.80	2.00

BILL BOYD WESTERN (Movie star; see Hopalong Cassidy & Western Hero)
Feb, 1950 - No. 23, June, 1952 (1-3,7,11,14-on: 36 pgs.)
Fawcett Publications

1-Bill Boyd & his horse Midnite begin; photo front/back-c			
	44.00	132.00	350.00
2-Painted-c	25.00	75.00	175.00
3-Photo-c begin, end #23; last photo back-c	19.00	58.00	135.00
4-6(52 pgs.)	16.00	47.00	110.00
7,11(36 pgs.)	11.50	34.00	80.00
8-10,12,13(52 pgs.)	12.00	36.00	85.00
14-22	11.00	33.00	75.00
23-Last issue	12.00	36.00	85.00

BILL BUMLIN (See Treasury of Comics No. 3)
BILL ELLIOTT (See Wild Bill Elliott)

BILLI 99
Sept, 1991 - No. 4, 1991 ($3.50, B&W, limited series, 52 pgs.)
Dark Horse Comics

1-4: Tim Sale-c/a		1.40	3.50

BILL STERN'S SPORTS BOOK
Spring-Summer, 1951 - V2#2, Winter, 1952
Ziff-Davis Publ. Co.(Approved Comics)

V1#10-(1951)	17.00	51.00	120.00
2-(Sum/52; reg. size)	13.00	39.00	90.00
V2#2-(1952, 96 pgs.)-Krigstein, Kinstler-a	17.00	51.00	120.00

BILL THE BULL: ONE SHOT, ONE BOURBON, ONE BEER
Dec, 1994 ($2.95, B&W, mature)
Boneyard Press

1		1.20	3.00

BILL THE CLOWN
Feb, 1992 ($2.50, one-shot)
Slave Labor Graphics

1			2.50
1-(2nd printing, 4/93, $2.95)			3.00
Comedy Isn't Pretty 1 (11/92, $2.50)			2.50
Death & Clown White 1 (9/93, $2.95)			3.00

Billy The Kid #5 © CC

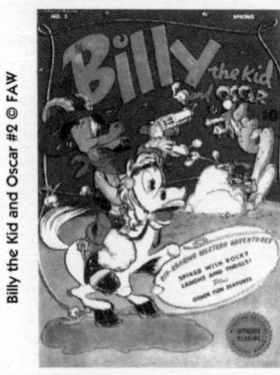

Billy the Kid and Oscar #2 © FAW

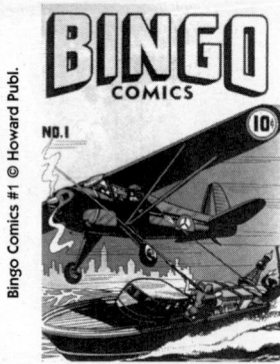

Bingo Comics #1 © Howard Publ.

	GD25	FN65	NM94

BILLY AND BUGGY BEAR (See Animal Fun)
1958; 1964
I.W. Enterprises/Super
I.W. Reprint #1, #7('58)-All Surprise Comics #?(Same issue-r for both)

		GD25	FN65	NM94
		1.00	2.00	5.00
Super Reprint #10(1964)		1.00	2.00	5.00

BILLY BUCKSKIN WESTERN (2-Gun Western No. 4)
Nov, 1955 - No. 3, Mar, 1956
Atlas Comics (IMC No. 1/MgPC No. 2,3)

1-Mort Drucker-a; Maneely-c/a	11.50	34.00	80.00
2-Mort Drucker-a	9.15	27.50	55.00
3-Williamson, Drucker-a	10.00	30.00	60.00

BILLY BUNNY (Black Cobra No. 6 on)
Feb-Mar, 1954 - No. 5, Oct-Nov, 1954
Excellent Publications

1	5.85	17.50	35.00
2	4.00	10.00	20.00
3-5	3.20	8.00	16.00

BILLY BUNNY'S CHRISTMAS FROLICS
1952 (25¢ Giant, 100 pgs.)
Farrell Publications

1	12.00	36.00	110.00

BILLY COLE
May, 1994 - No. 4, Aug, 1994 ($2.75, B&W, limited series)
Cult Press

1-4	1.10	2.75

BILLY MAKE BELIEVE
No. 14, 1939
United Features Syndicate

Single Series 14	26.00	77.00	180.00

BILLY NGUYEN, PRIVATE EYE
V2#1, 1990 ($2.50)
Caliber Press

V2#1	1.00	2.50

BILLY THE KID (Formerly The Masked Raider; also see Doc Savage Comics & Return of the Outlaw)
No. 9, Nov, 1957 - No. 121, Dec, 1976; No. 122, Sept, 1977 - No. 123, Oct, 1977; No. 124, Feb, 1978 - No. 153, Mar, 1983
Charlton Publ. Co.

9	9.15	27.50	55.00
10,12,14,17-19: 12-2 pg Check-sty	5.00	15.00	30.00
11-(68 pgs.)-Origin & 1st app. The Ghost Train	5.85	17.50	35.00
13-Williamson/Torres-a	6.35	19.00	38.00
15-Origin; 2 pgs. Williamson-a	6.35	19.00	38.00
16	6.35	19.00	38.00
20-26-Severin-a(3-4 each)	6.35	19.00	38.00
27-30	3.25	9.50	22.00
31-40	2.00	6.00	14.00
41-60	1.50	3.75	9.00
61-80: 66-Bounty Hunter series begins. Not in #79,82,84-863			
		1.80	4.50
81-99,101-123: 87-Last Bounty Hunter. 111-Origin The Ghost Train. 117-Gunsmith & Co., The Cheyenne Kid app.		1.20	3.00
100		.80	2.00
124(2/78)-153			1.50
Modern Comics 109 (1977 reprint)			1.20

NOTE: Severin a(r)-121-129, 134; c-23, 25. Sutton a-111.

BILLY THE KID ADVENTURE MAGAZINE
Oct, 1950 - No. 30, 1955

Toby Press

1-Williamson/Frazetta-a (2 pgs) r/from John Wayne Adventure Comics #2; photo-c	29.00	86.00	200.00
2-Photo-c	9.15	27.50	55.00
3-Williamson/Frazetta "The Claws of Death", 4 pgs. plus Williamson art	31.00	94.00	220.00
4,5,7,8,10: 4,7-Photo-c	5.85	17.50	35.00
6-Frazetta assist on "Nightmare"; photo-c	13.50	41.00	95.00
9-Kurtzman Pot-Shot Pete; photo-c	10.00	30.00	70.00
11,12,15-20: 11-Photo-c	5.00	15.00	30.00
13-Kurtzman-r/John Wayne #12 (Genius)	5.85	17.50	35.00
14-Williamson/Frazetta; r-of #1 (2 pgs.)	9.15	27.50	55.00
21,23-30	4.15	12.50	25.00
22-Williamson/Frazetta-r(1pg.)/#1; photo-c	5.35	16.00	32.00

BILLY THE KID AND OSCAR (Also see Fawcett's Funny Animals)
Winter, 1945 - No. 3, Summer, 1946 (Funny animal)
Fawcett Publications

1	12.00	36.00	85.00
2,3	9.15	27.50	55.00

BILLY WEST (Bill West No. 9,10)
1949 - No. 9, Feb, 1951; No. 10, Feb, 1952
Standard Comics (Visual Editions)

1	10.00	30.00	65.00
2	5.35	16.00	32.00
3-10: 7,8-Schomburg-c	4.00	11.00	22.00

NOTE: Celardo a-1-6, 9; c-1-3. Moreira a-3. Roussos a-2.

BING CROSBY (See Feature Films)

BINGO (...Comics) (H. C. Blackerby)
1945 (Reprints National material)
Howard Publ.

1-L. B. Cole opium-c	24.00	71.00	165.00

BINGO, THE MONKEY DOODLE BOY
Aug, 1951; Oct, 1953
St. John Publishing Co.

1(8/51)-By Eric Peters	5.00	15.00	30.00
1(10/53)	4.00	12.00	24.00

BINKY (Formerly Leave It to...)
No. 72, 4-5/70 - No. 81, 10-11/71; No. 82, Summer/77
National Periodical Publ./DC Comics

72-81: 78-1 pg. sty on Barry Williams of Brady Bunch			
	1.00	2.00	5.00
82 (1977, one-shot)		1.20	3.00

BINKY'S BUDDIES
Jan-Feb, 1969 - No. 12, Nov-Dec, 1970
National Periodical Publications

1	1.20	3.00	7.00
2-12		1.80	4.50

BIONEERS
Aug, 1994 ($2.75)
Mirage Publishing

1-w/bound-in trading card		1.10	2.75

BIONIC WOMAN, THE (TV)
Oct, 1977 - No. 5, June, 1978
Charlton Publications

1-5			1.25

BIRDS OF PREY: MANHUNT (See Black Canary/Oracle: Birds of Prey)
Sept, 1996 - No. 4, Dec, 1996 ($
DC Comics

Black & White #2 © Art Thibert

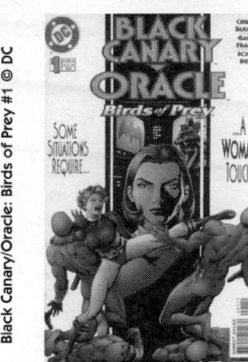

Black Canary/Oracle: Birds of Prey #1 © DC

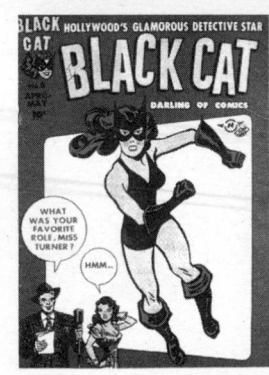

Black Cat Comics #5 © HARV

BL

	GD25	FN65	NM94

1,2: Features Black Canary, Oracle, Huntress, & Catwoman. Chuck Dixon
scripts; Gary Frank-c in all. 1-Catwoman cameo only .80 2.00
NOTE: *Gary Frank c-1-4. Matt Haley a-1-4p. Wade Von Grawbadger a-1i.*

BIRTH OF THE DEFIANT UNIVERSE, THE
May, 1993 (Giveaway)
Defiant Comics

nn-contains promotional artwork & text; limited print run of 1000 copies.
20.00

BISHOP (See Uncanny X-Men & X-Men)
Dec, 1994 - No.4, Mar, 1995 ($2.95, limited series)
Marvel Comics

1-4: Foil-c 1.20 3.00

BIZARRE ADVENTURES (Formerly Marvel Preview)
No. 25, 3/81 - No. 34, 2/83 (#25-33: Magazine-$1.50)
Marvel Comics Group

25-Lethal Ladies. 26-King Kull 1.50
27-Phoenix, Iceman & Nightcrawler app. 28-The Unlikely Heroes; Elektra by
Miller; Neal Adams-a 1.50
29-Horror. 30-Tomorrow. 31-After The Violence Stops; new Hangman
story; Miller-a. 32-Gods. 33-Horror; photo-c 1.50
34 ($2.00, Baxter paper, comic size)-Son of Santa; Christmas special; Howard
the Duck by Paul Smith .80 2.00
NOTE: *Alcala a-27i. Austin a-25i, 28i. J. Buscema a-27p, 29, 30p; c-26. Byrne a-31 (2 pg.).
Golden a-25p, 28p. Perez a-27p. Rogers a-25p. Simonson a-29; c-29. Paul Smith a-34.*

BLACK AND WHITE (See Large Feature Comic, Series I)

BLACK & WHITE (Also see Codename: Black & White)
Oct,1994 - No. 3, Jan,1995 ($1.95, limited series)
Image Comics (Extreme Studios)

1-3: Thibert-c/story .80 2.00

BLACK & WHITE MAGIC
1991 ($2.95, 98 pgs., B&W w/30 pgs. color, squarebound)
Innovation Publishing

1-Contains rebound comics w/covers removed; contents may vary
1.20 3.00

BLACKBALL COMICS
Mar, 1994 ($3.00)
Blackball Comics

1-Trencher-c/story by Giffen; John Pain by O'Neill 1.20 3.00

BLACKBEARD'S GHOST (See Movie Comics)

BLACK BEAUTY (See Son of Black Beauty)
No. 440, Dec, 1952
Dell Publishing Co.

Four Color 440 3.20 9.60 32.00

BLACK CANARY (See All Star Comics #38, Flash Comics #86, Justice League
of America #75 & World's Finest #244)
Nov, 1991 - No. 4, Feb, 1992 ($1.75, limited series)
DC Comics

1-4 .70 1.75

BLACK CANARY
Jan, 1993 - No. 12, Dec, 1993 ($1.75)
DC Comics

1-12: 8-The Ray-c/story. 9,10-Huntress-c/story .70 1.75

BLACK CANARY/ORACLE: BIRDS OF PREY (Also see Showcase '96 #3)
1996 ($3.95, one-shot)
DC Comics

1-Chuck Dixon scripts & Gary Frank-c/a. 1.80 4.50

BLACK CAT COMICS (...Western #16-19; ...Mystery #30 on)

	GD25	FN65	NM94

(See All-New #7,9, The Original Black Cat, Pocket & Speed Comics)
June-July, 1946 - No. 29, June, 1951
Harvey Publications (Home Comics)

1-Kubert-a; Joe Simon c-1-3 52.50 157.50 420.00
2-Kubert-a 31.00 94.00 220.00
3,4: 4-The Red Demons begin (The Demon #4 & 5)
24.00 73.00 170.00
5,6,7: 5,6-The Scarlet Arrow app. in ea. by Powell; S&K-a in both. 6-Origin
Red Demon. 7-Vagabond Prince by S&K plus 1 more story
32.00 96.00 225.00
8-S&K-a; Kerry Drake begins, ends #13 27.00 81.00 190.00
9-Origin Stuntman (r/Stuntman #1) 34.00 103.00 240.00
10-20: 14,15,17-Mary Worth app. plus Invisible Scarlet O'Neil-#15,20,24
20.00 60.00 140.00
21-26 17.00 51.00 120.00
27,28: 27-Used in **SOTI**, pg. 193; X-Mas-c; 2 pg. John Wayne story. 28-Intro.
Kit, Black Cat's new sidekick 19.00 58.00 135.00
29-Black Cat bondage-c; Black Cat stories 18.00 54.00 125.00

BLACK CAT MYSTERY (Formerly Black Cat; ...Western Mystery #54;
...Western #55,56;...Mystery #57; ...Mystic #58-62; Black Cat #63-65)
No. 30, Aug, 1951 - No. 65, Apr, 1963
Harvey Publications

30-Black Cat on cover only 20.00 60.00 140.00
31,32,34,37,38,40 14.00 43.00 100.00
33-Used in **POP**, pg. 89; electrocution-c 15.00 45.00 105.00
35-Atomic disaster cover/story 17.00 51.00 120.00
36,39-Used in **SOTI**: #36-Pgs. 270,271; #39-Pgs. 386-388
20.00 60.00 140.00
41-43 14.00 43.00 100.00
44-Eyes, ears, tongue cut out; Nostrand-a 15.00 45.00 105.00
45-Classic "Colorama" by Powell; Nostrand-a 24.00 71.00 165.00
46-49,51-Nostrand-a in all 15.00 45.00 105.00
50-Check-a; Warren Kremer?-c showing a man's face burning away
36.00 107.00 250.00
52,53 (r/#34 & 35) 10.00 30.00 70.00
54-Two Black Cat stories (2/55, last pre-code) 13.50 41.00 95.00
55,56-Black Cat app. 10.00 30.00 70.00
57(7/56)-Kirby-c 8.35 25.00 60.00
58-60-Kirby-a(4). 58,59-Kirby-c. 60,61-Simon-c 13.00 39.00 90.00
61-Nostrand-a; "Colorama" r/#45 11.00 33.00 75.00
62(3/58)-E.C. story swipe 9.15 27.50 55.00
63-Giant(10/62); Reprints; Black Cat app.; origin Black Kitten
11.50 34.00 80.00
64-Giant(1/63); Reprints; Black Cat app. 11.50 34.00 80.00
65-Giant(4/63); Reprints; Black Cat app.; 1 pg. Powell-a
11.50 34.00 80.00
NOTE: *Kremer a-37, 39, 43; c-36, 37, 47. Meskin a-51. Palais a-30, 31(2), 32(2), 33-35, 37-40.
Powell a-32-35, 36(2), 40, 41, 43-53, 57. Simon c-63-65. Sparling a-44. Bondage c-32, 34, 43.*

BLACK COBRA (Bride's Diary No. 4 on) (See Captain Flight #8)
No. 1, 10-11/54; No. 6(No. 2), 12-1/54-55; No. 3, 2-3/55
Ajax/Farrell Publications(Excellent Publ.)

1-Re-intro Black Cobra & The Cobra Kid (costumed heroes)
25.00 75.00 175.00
6(#2)-Formerly Billy Bunny 16.00 47.00 110.00
3-(Pre-code)-Torpedoman app. 14.00 43.00 100.00

BLACK CONDOR (Also see Crack Comics, Freedom Fighters & Showcase '94
#10,11)
June, 1992 - No. 12, May, 1993 ($1.25)
DC Comics

1-12: 1-10,12-Heath-c. 9,10-The Ray app. 12-Batman-c/scripts 1.25

BLACK CROSS SPECIAL (See Dark Horse Presents)
Jan, 1988 ($1.75, B&W, one-shot)(Reprints & new-a)

87

Blackhawk #19 © QUA

Blackhawk #257 © DC

Blackhawk #3 © DC

	GD25	FN65	NM94

Dark Horse Comics

1-1st & 2nd print; 2nd has 2pgs new-a		.70	1.75

BLACK DIAMOND
May, 1983 - No. 5, 1984 (no month)($2.00-$1.75, Baxter paper)
Americomics

1-3-Movie adapt.; 1-Colt back-up begins		1.00	2.50
4,5			1.50

NOTE: *Bill Black* a-1i; c-1. *Gulacy* c-2-5. Sybil Danning photo back-c-1.

BLACK DIAMOND WESTERN (Formerly Desperado No. 1-8)
No. 9, Mar, 1949 - No. 60, Feb, 1956 (No. 9-28: 52 pgs.)
Lev Gleason Publications

9-Black Diamond & his horse Reliapon begin; origin Black Diamond			
	17.00	51.00	120.00
10	9.15	27.50	55.00
11-15	6.70	20.00	40.00
16-28(11/49-11/51)-Wolverton's Bing Bang Buster	9.15	27.50	55.00
29-40: 31-One pg. Frazetta anti-drug ad	4.25	13.00	28.00
41-50,53-59	4.00	12.00	24.00
51-3-D effect-c/story	11.00	33.00	75.00
52-3-D effect story	10.00	30.00	70.00
60-Last issue	5.00	15.00	30.00

NOTE: *Biro* c-9-35?. *Fass* a-58, c-54-56, 58. *Guardineer* a-9, 15, 18. *Kida* a-9. *Maurer* a-10. *Ed Moore* a-16. *Morisi* a-55. *Tuska* a-10, 48.

BLACK DRAGON, THE
May, 1985 - No. 6, Oct, 1985 (Limited series, Baxter paper, mature)
Marvel Comics (Epic Comics)

1-Chris Claremont story & John Bolton-c/a in all.		.80	2.00
2-6			1.00

BLACK DRAGON, THE
Apr, 1996 ($17.95, B&W, trade paperback)
Dark Horse Comics

nn-Reprints Epic Comics limited series; intro by Anne McCaffrey.			
			18.00

BLACK FLAG (See Asylum #5)
Jan, 1995 - No.4, 1995; No. 0, July, 1995 ($2.50, B&W) (No. 0 in color)
Maximum Press

0-4: 0-(7/95)-Liefeld/Fraga-c. 1-(1/95). 2,4-Variant covers exist.			
		1.20	3.00
Preview Edition (6/94, $1.95, B&W)-Fraga/McFarlane-c.			
		.80	2.00

NOTE: *Fraga* a-0-4, Preview Edition; c-1-4. *Liefeld/Fraga* c-0. *McFarlane/Fraga* c-Preview Edition.

BLACK FURY (Becomes Wild West No. 58) (See Blue Bird)
May, 1955 - No. 57, Mar-Apr, 1966 (Horse stories)
Charlton Comics Group

1	5.85	17.50	35.00
2	3.20	8.00	16.00
3-10	2.40	6.00	12.00
11-15,19,20	1.60	4.00	8.00
16-18-Ditko-a	5.85	17.50	35.00
21-30	1.00	2.60	6.00
31-57		1.60	4.00

BLACK GOLD
1945? (8 pgs. in color)
Esso Service Station (Giveaway)

nn-Reprints from True Comics	5.00	15.00	30.00

BLACK GOLIATH
Feb, 1976 - No. 5, Nov, 1976
Marvel Comics Group

1: 1-3-Tuska-a(p)		1.70	4.25

	GD25	FN65	NM94

2-5		.90	2.25

BLACKHAWK (Formerly Uncle Sam #1-8; see Military & Modern Comics)
No. 9, Winter, 1944 - No. 243, 10-11/68; No. 244, 1-2/76 - No. 250, 1-2/77;
No. 251, 10/82 - No. 273, 11/84
Comic Magazines(Quality)No. 9-107(12/56); National Periodical Publications
No. 108(1/57)-250; DC Comics No. 251 on

9 (1944)	288.00	862.00	2400.00
10 (1946)	97.00	290.00	775.00
11-15: 14-Ward-a; 13,14-Fear app.	62.00	190.00	500.00
16-20: 20-Ward Blackhawk	51.00	155.00	415.00
21-30	40.00	120.00	310.00
31-40: 31-Chop Chop by Jack Cole	32.00	96.00	225.00
41-49,51-60	25.00	75.00	175.00
50-1st Killer Shark; origin in text	28.00	84.00	195.00
61,62: 61-Used in **POP**, pg. 91. 62-Used in **POP**, pg. 92 & color illo			
	23.00	69.00	160.00
63-70,72-80: 65-H-Bomb explosion panel. 66-B&W & color illos **POP**. 70-Return			
of Killer Shark; atomic explosion panel. 75-Intro. Blackie the Hawk			
	21.00	64.00	150.00
71-Origin retold; flying saucer-c; A-Bomb panels	25.00	75.00	175.00
81-86: Last precode (3/55)	20.00	60.00	140.00
87-92,94-99,101-107: 105-1st S.A. issue	16.00	47.00	110.00
93-Origin in text	17.00	49.00	115.00
100	20.00	60.00	140.00
108-1st DC issue (1/57); re-intro. Blackie, the Hawk, their mascot; not in #115			
	50.00	150.00	400.00
109-117	19.00	56.00	130.00
118-Frazetta-r/Jimmy Wakely #4 (3 pgs.)	19.00	58.00	135.00
119-130	12.00	36.00	85.00
131-140: 133-Intro. Lady Blackhawk	8.50	26.00	60.00
141-163,165,166: 143-Kurtzman-r/Jimmy Wakely #4. 166-Last 10¢ issue			
	6.00	18.00	45.00
164-Origin retold	6.00	18.00	45.00
167-180	2.60	7.50	18.00
181-190	2.00	6.00	14.00
191-197,199-202,204-210: 196-Combat Diary series begins. 197-New look for			
Blackhawks	1.65	4.70	11.00
198-Origin retold	1.70	5.00	12.00
203-Origin Chop Chop (12/64)	1.70	5.00	12.00
211-243(1968): 228-Batman, Green Lantern, Superman, The Flash cameos.			
230-Blackhawks become superheroes. 242-Return to old costumes			
	1.10	2.70	6.50
244 ('76) -250: 250-Chuck dies		.80	2.00
251-273: 251-Origin retold; Black Knights return. 252-Intro Domino. 253-Part			
origin Hendrickson. 258-Blackhawk's Island destroyed. 259-Part origin			
Chop-Chop. 265-273 (75¢ cover price)			1.50

NOTE: *Chaykin* a-260; c-257-260, 262. *Crandall* a-10, 11, 13, 167, 18-20, 22-26, 30-33, 35p, 36(2), 37, 387, 39-44, 46-50, 52-58, 60, 63, 64, 66, 67; c-14-20, 22-63(most except #28-33, 36, 37, 39). *Evans* a-244, 245,246i, 248-250i. *G. Kane* c-263, 264. *Kubert* c-244, 245. *Newton* a-266p. *Severin* a-257. *Spiegle* a-261-267, 269-273; c-265-272. *Toth* a-260p. *Ward* a-16-27(Chop Chop, 8pgs. ea.); pencilled stories-No. 17-63(approx.). *Wildey* a-268. Chop Chop solo stories in #10-95?

BLACKHAWK
Mar, 1988 - No. 3, May, 1988 ($2.95, limited series, mature)
DC Comics

1-3: Chaykin painted-c/a/scripts		1.20	3.00

BLACKHAWK
Mar, 1989 - No. 16, Aug, 1990 ($1.50, mature)
DC Comics

1-6,8-16: 16-Crandall-c swipe			1.50
7-($2.50, 52 pgs.)-Story-r/Military #1		1.00	2.50
Annual 1 (1989, $2.95, 68 pgs.)-Recaps origin of Blackhawk, Lady			
Blackhawk, and others		1.20	3.00
Special 1 (1992, $3.50, 68 pgs.)-Mature readers		1.40	3.50

Black Hood #10 © Impact

Black Lightning #1 © DC

Black Magic #3 © DC

	GD25	FN65	NM94

BLACK HEART ASSASSIN
Jan, 1994 ($2.95)
Iguana Comics

		GD25	FN65	NM94
1		1.20		3.00

BLACK HOLE (See Walt Disney Showcase #54) (Disney, movie)
Mar, 1980 - No. 4, Sept, 1980
Whitman Publishing Co.

11295(#1)-4: 1-Photo-c; Spiegle-a. 1,2-Movie adaptation. 2-4-Spiegle-a.
3-McWilliams-a; photo-c. 3,4-New stories — — 1.00

BLACK HOOD, THE (See Blue Ribbon, Flyman & Mighty Comics)
June, 1983 - No. 3, Oct, 1983 (Printed on Mandell paper)
Red Circle Comics (Archie)

1-Morrow, McWilliams, Wildey-a; Toth-c — — 1.50
2,3: MLJ's The Fox by Toth-c/a. 3-Morrow-a — — 1.00
(Also see Archie's Super-Hero Special Digest #2)

BLACK HOOD
Dec, 1991 - No. 12, Dec, 1992 ($1.00)
DC Comics (Impact Comics)

1-12: 11-Intro The Fox. 12-Origin Black Hood — — 1.00
Annual 1 (1992, $2.50, 68 pgs.)-w/Trading card — 1.00 2.50

BLACK HOOD COMICS (Formerly Hangman #2-8; Laugh Comics #20 on; also
see Black Swan, Jackpot, Roly Poly & Top-Notch #9)
No. 9, Winter, 1943-44 - No. 19, Summer, 1946 (on radio in 1943)
MLJ Magazines

	GD25	FN65	NM94
9-The Hangman & The Boy Buddies cont'd	87.00	262.00	700.00
10-Hangman & Dusty, the Boy Detective app.	47.00	141.00	375.00
11-Dusty app.; no Hangman	40.00	120.00	290.00
12-18: 14-Kinstler blood-c. 17-Hal Foster swipe from Prince Valiant; 1st			
issue with "An Archie Magazine" on-c	38.00	114.00	265.00
19-I.D. exposed	44.00	32.00	350.00

NOTE: Hangman by Fuje in 9, 10. Kinstler a-15, c-14-16.

BLACK JACK (Rocky Lane's...; formerly Jim Bowie)
No. 20, Nov, 1957 - No. 30, Nov, 1959
Charlton Comics

	GD25	FN65	NM94
20	8.35	25.00	50.00
21,27,29,30	4.25	13.00	28.00
22-(68 pgs.)	6.35	19.00	38.00
23-Williamson/Torres-a	6.70	20.00	40.00
24-26,28-Ditko-a	8.35	25.00	50.00

BLACK KNIGHT, THE
May, 1953; 1963
Toby Press

	GD25	FN65	NM94
1-Bondage-c	19.00	58.00	135.00
Super Reprint No. 11 (1963)-Reprints 1953 issue	2.60	7.50	18.00

BLACK KNIGHT, THE (Also see The Avengers #48, Marvel Super Heroes &
Tales To Astonish #52)
May, 1955 - No. 5, April, 1956
Atlas Comics (MgPC)

	GD25	FN65	NM94
1-Origin Crusader; Maneely-c/a	75.00	225.00	600.00
2-Maneely-c/a(4)	56.00	170.00	450.00
3-5: 4-Maneely-c/a. 5-Maneely-c, Shores-a	44.00	132.00	350.00

BLACK KNIGHT (Also see Avengers & Ultraforce)
June, 1990 - No. 4, Sept, 1990 ($1.50, limited series)
Marvel Comics

1-4: 1-Original Black Knight returns — — 1.50
NOTE: Buckler c-1-4p.

BLACK LAMB, THE
Nov, 1996 - No, 6, Apr, 1996 ($2.50, limited series)
DC Comics (Helix)

1-6: Tim Truman-c/a/scripts — — 2.50

BLACK LIGHTNING (See The Brave & The Bold, Cancelled Comic Cavalcade,
DC Comics Presents #16, Detective #490 and World's Finest #257)
Apr, 1977 - No. 11, Sept-Oct, 1978
National Periodical Publications/DC Comics

		GD25	FN65	NM94
1		1.20		3.00
2-11: 4-Intro Cyclotronic Man. 11-The Ray app.				1.00

NOTE: Buckler c-1-3p, 6-11p. #11 is 44 pgs.

BLACK LIGHTNING (2nd Series)
Feb, 1995 - No. 13, Feb, 1996 ($1.95/$2.25)
DC Comics

	GD25	FN65	NM94
1-5-Tony Isabella scripts begins, ends #8.	.80		2.00
6-13; 6-begin 2.25-c. 13-Batman-c/app.	.90		2.25

BLACK MAGIC (...Magazine) (Becomes Cool Cat V8#6 on)
10-11/50 - V4#1, 6-7/53; V4#2, 9-10/53 - V5#3, 11-12/54; V6#1, 9-10/57 -
V7#2, 11-12/58; V7#3, 7-8/60 - V8#5, 11-12/61
(V1#1-5, 52pgs.; V1#6-V3#3, 44pgs.)
Crestwood Publ. V1#1-4,V6#1-V7#5/Headline V1#5-V5#3,V7#6-V8#5

	GD25	FN65	NM94
V1#1-S&K-a, 10 pgs.; Meskin-a(2)	78.00	234.00	625.00
2-S&K-a, 17 pgs.; Meskin-a	40.00	120.00	295.00
3-6(8-9/51)-S&K, Roussos, Meskin-a	36.00	107.00	250.00
V2#1(10-11/51),4,5,7(#13),9(#15),12(#18)-S&K-a	26.00	77.00	180.00
2,3,6,8,10,11(#17)	17.00	49.00	115.00
V3#1(#19, 12/52) - 6(#24, 5/53)-S&K-a	19.00	58.00	135.00
V4#1(#25, 6-7/53), 2(#26, 9-10/53)-S&K-a(3-4)	21.00	62.00	145.00
3(#27, 11-12/53)-S&K-a; Ditko-a (2nd published-a); also see Captain 3-D,			
Daring Love #1, Strange Fantasy #9, & Fantastic Fears #5 (Fant. Fears was			
1st drawn, but not 1st publ.	40.00	120.00	285.00
4(#28)-Eyes ripped out/story-S&K, Ditko-a	29.00	86.00	200.00
5(#29, 3-4/54)-S&K, Ditko-a	22.00	66.00	155.00
6(#30, 5-6/54)-S&K, Powell?-a	17.00	49.00	115.00
V5#1(#31, 7-8/54 - 3(#33, 11-12/54)-S&K-a	13.50	41.00	95.00
V6#1(#34, 9-10/57), 2(#35, 11-12/57)	7.50	22.50	45.00
3(1-2/58) - 6(7-8/58)	7.50	22.50	45.00
V7#1(9-10/58) - 3(7-8/60)	7.50	22.50	45.00
4(9-10/60), 5(11-12/60)-Torres-a	5.85	17.50	35.00
6(1-2/61)-Powell-a(2)	5.85	17.50	35.00
V8#1(3-4/61)-Powell-c/a	5.85	17.50	35.00
2(5-6/61)-E.C. story swipe/W.F. #22; Ditko, Powell-a			
	7.50	22.50	45.00
3(7-8/61)-E.C. story swipe/W.F. #22; Powell-a(2)	7.50	22.50	45.00
4(9-10/61)-Powell-a(5)	5.85	17.50	35.00
5-E.C. story swipe/W.S.F. #28; Powell-a(3)	7.50	22.50	45.00

NOTE: Bernard Baily a-V4#6?, V5#3(2). Grandenetti a-V2#3, 11. Kirby c-V1#1-6, V2#1-12,
V3#1-6, V4#1, 2, 4-6; V5#1-3. McWilliams a-V3#2l. Meskin a-V1#1(2), 2, 3, 4(2), 5(2), 6, V2/1,
2, 3(2), 4(3), 5, 6(2), 7-9, 11, 12, V3#1(2), 5, 6, V5#1(2), 2. Orlando a-V6#1, 4, V7#2; c-V6/1-6.
Powell a-V5#1?, Roussos a-V1#3-5, 4(2), 5(2), 6, 8, 9, 10(2), 11, 12p, V3#1(2), 2i,
5, V5#2. Simon a-V2#12, V3#2, V7#5? c-V4#3?, V7#3?, 4, 5?, 6?, V8#1-5. Simon & Kirby a-
V1#1, 2(2), 3-6, V2#1, 4, 5, 7, 9, 12, V3#1-4, V4#1(3), 2(4), 3(2), 4(2), 5, 6, V5#1-3; c-V2#1.
Leonard Starr a-V1#1. Tuska a-V6#3, 4. Woodbridge a-V7#4.

BLACK MAGIC
Oct-Nov, 1973 - No. 9, Apr-May, 1975
National Periodical Publications

	GD25	FN65	NM94
1-S&K reprints		1.60	4.00
2-9-S&K reprints			1.50

BLACK MAGIC
Apr, 1990 - No. 4, Oct, 1990 ($2.75, B&W, mini-series, 52pgs.)
Eclipse International

	GD25	FN65	NM94
1-($3.50, 68pgs.)-Japanese manga		1.40	3.50
2-4 ($2.75)		1.10	2.80

BLACKMAIL TERROR (See Harvey Comics Library)

BLACK MASK

Black Ops #4 © Aegi Entertainment

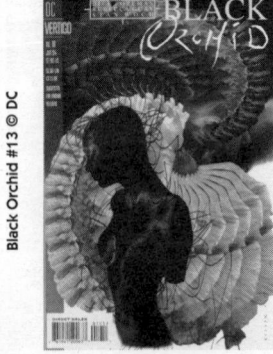

Black Orchid #13 © DC

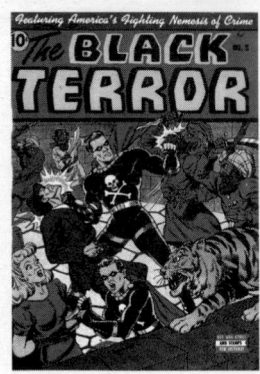

The Black Terror #2 © STD

	GD25	FN65	NM94

1993 - No. 3, 1994 ($4.95, limited series, 52 pgs.)
DC Comics

1-3	1.00	2.00	5.00

BLACK OPS
Jan, 1996 - No. 5, May, 1996 ($2.50, limited series)
Image Comics (Wildstorm Productions)

1-5			2.50

BLACK ORCHID (See Adventure Comics #428 & Phantom Stranger)
Holiday, 1988-89 - No. 3, 1989 ($3.50, limited series, prestige format)
DC Comics

Book 1,3: Neil Gaiman scripts & McKean-a in all	1.20	3.00	7.00
Book 2-Arkham Asylum story; Batman app.	1.30	3.25	8.00

BLACK ORCHID
Sept, 1993 - No. 22, June, 1995 ($1.95/$2.25)
DC Comics

1-10: Dave McKean-c #1-9		.80	2.00
1-Platinum Edition	2.85	8.50	20.00
11-20		.80	2.00
21,22		.90	2.25
Annual 1 (1993, $3.95, 68 pgs.)-Children's Crusade	1.60		4.00

BLACKOUTS (See Broadway Hollywood...)

BLACK PANTHER, THE (Also see Avengers #52, Fantastic Four #52, Jungle Action & Marvel Premiere #51-53)
Jan, 1977 - No. 15, May, 1979
Marvel Comics Group

1	1.65	4.20	10.00
2	1.00	2.00	5.00
3-10		1.00	2.50
11-15: 14,15-Avengers x-over		.80	2.00
NOTE: *J. Buscema c-15p. Kirby c/a & scripts-1-12. Layton c-13i.*

BLACK PANTHER
July, 1988 - No. 4, Oct, 1988 ($1.25)
Marvel Comics Group

1-4			1.25

BLACK PANTHER: PANTHER'S PREY
1991 - No. 4, 1991 ($4.95, squarebound, limited series, 52 pgs.)
Marvel Comics

1-4	1.00	2.00	5.00

BLACK, PEARL, THE
Sept, 1996 - No. 5, Jan, 1996 ($2.95, limited series)
Dark Horse Comics

1-5: Mark Hamill scripts			3.00

BLACK PHANTOM (See Tim Holt #25, 38)
Nov, 1954 (one-shot) (Female outlaw)
Magazine Enterprises

1 (A-1 #122)-The Ghost Rider story plus 3 Black Phantom stories; Headlight-c/a	35.00	105.00	245.00

BLACK PHANTOM
1989 - No. 3, 1990 ($2.50, B&W; #2 color)(Reprints & new-a)
AC Comics

1,2: 1-Ayers-r, Bolle-r/B.P. #1. 2-Redmask-r		1.00	2.50
3 ($2.75, B&W)-B.P., Redmask-r & new-a		1.10	2.75

BLACK PHANTOM, RETURN OF THE (See Wisco)

BLACK RIDER (Western Winners #1-7; Western Tales of Black Rider #28-31; Gunsmoke Western #32 on)(See All Western Winners, Best Western, Kid Colt, Outlaw Kid, Rex Hart, Two-Gun Kid, Two-Gun Western, Western Gunfighters, Western Winners, & Wild Western)

No. 8, 3/50 - No. 18, 1/52; No. 19, 11/53 - No. 27, 3/55
Marvel/Atlas Comics(CDS No. 8-17/CPS No. 19 on)

8 (#1)-Black Rider & his horse Satan begin; 36 pgs; Stan Lee photo-c as Black Rider)	40.00	120.00	280.00
9-52 pgs. begin, end #14	19.00	58.00	135.00
10-Origin Black Rider	23.00	69.00	160.00
11-14: 14-Last 52pgs.	13.50	41.00	95.00
15-19: 19-Two-Gun Kid app.	11.50	34.00	80.00
20-Classic-c; Two-Gun Kid app.	13.00	39.00	90.00
21-27: 21-23-Two-Gun Kid app. 24,25-Arrowhead app. 26-Kid Colt app. 27-Last issue; last precode. Kid Colt app. The Spider (a villain) burns to death	11.00	33.00	75.00
NOTE: *Ayers c-22. Jack Keller a-15, 26, 27. Maneely a-14; c-16, 17, 25, 27. Syd Shores a-19, 21, 22, 23(3), 24(3), 25-27; c-19, 21, 23. Sinnott a-24, 25. Tuska a-12, 19-21.*

BLACK RIDER RIDES AGAIN!, THE
Sept, 1957
Atlas Comics (CPS)

1-Kirby-a(3); Powell-a; Severin-c	20.00	60.00	140.00

BLACK SEPTEMBER (Also see Avengers/Ultraforce, Ultraforce (1st series) #10 & Ultraforce/Avengers)
1995 ($1.50, one-shot)
Malibu Comics (Ultraverse)

Infinity-Intro to the newUltraverse; variant-c exists.			1.50

BLACKSTONE (See Super Magician Comics & Wisco Giveaways)

BLACKSTONE, MASTER MAGICIAN COMICS
Mar-Apr, 1946 - No. 3, July-Aug, 1946
Vital Publications/Street & Smith Publ.

1	22.00	66.00	155.00
2,3	18.00	54.00	125.00

BLACKSTONE, THE MAGICIAN (...Detective on cover only #3 & 4)
No. 2, May, 1948 - No. 4, Sept, 1948 (No #1)(Cont'd from E.C. #1?)
Marvel Comics (CnPC)

2-The Blonde Phantom begins, ends #4	50.00	150.00	400.00
3,4: 3-Blonde Phantom by Sekowsky	39.00	118.00	275.00

BLACKSTONE, THE MAGICIAN DETECTIVE FIGHTS CRIME
Fall, 1947
E. C. Comics

1-1st app. Happy Houlihans	42.00	126.00	335.00

BLACK SWAN COMICS
1945
MLJ Magazines (Pershing Square Publ. Co.)

1-The Black Hood reprints from Black Hood No. 14; Bill Woggon-a; Suzie app.	19.00	58.00	135.00

BLACK TARANTULA (See Feature Presentations No. 5)

BLACK TERROR (See America's Best Comics & Exciting Comics)
Winter, 1942-43 - No. 27, June, 1949
Better Publications/Standard

1-Black Terror, Crime Crusader begin	219.00	650.00	1750.00
2	81.00	240.00	650.00
3	60.00	180.00	475.00
4,5	50.00	150.00	400.00
6-10: 7-The Ghost app.	44.00	132.00	350.00
11-20: 20-The Scarab app.	40.00	120.00	280.00
21-Miss Masque app.	40.00	120.00	300.00
22-Part Frazetta-a on one Black Terror story	40.00	120.00	280.00
23,25-27	39.00	116.00	270.00
24-Frazetta-a (1/4 pg.)	40.00	120.00	280.00
NOTE: *Schomburg (Xela) c-2-27; bondage c-2, 17, 24. Meskin a-27. Moreira a-27. Robinson/Meskin a-23, 24(3), 25, 26. Roussos/Mayo a-24. Tuska a-26, 27.*

The Black Terror #3 © ECL

Blasters Special #1 © DC

Blaze #2 © MEG

BL

	GD25	FN65	NM94		GD25	FN65	NM94

BLACK TERROR, THE (Also see Total Eclipse)
Oct., 1989 - No. 3, June, 1990 ($4.95, 52 pgs., squarebound, limited series)
Eclipse Comics

1-3: Beau Smith & Chuck Dixon scripts; Dan Brereton painted-c/a
            1.00   2.00   5.00

BLACKTHORNE 3-D SERIES
May, 1985 - No. 80, 1989 ($2.25/$2.50)
Blackthorne Publishing Co.

1-Sheena in 3-D #1. D. Stevens-c/retouched-a   1.00   2.50
2-10: 2-MerlinRealm in 3-D #1. 3-3-D Heroes #1. 4-Goldyn in 3-D #1. 5-Bizarre
3-D Zone #1. 6-Salimba in 3-D #1. 7-Twisted Tales in 3-D #1. 8-Dick Tracy in
3-D #1. 9-Salimba in 3-D #2. 10-Gumby in 3-D #1   1.00   2.50
11-20: 11-Betty Boop in 3-D #1. 12-Hamster Vice in 3-D #1. 13-Little Nemo in
3-D #1. 14-Gumby in 3-D #2. 15-Hamster Vice #6 in 3-D. 16-Laffin' Gas #6
in 3-D. 17-Gumby in 3-D #3. 18-Bullwinkle and Rocky in 3-D #1. 19-The
Flintstones in 3-D #1. 20-G.I. Joe in 3-D #1   1.00   2.50
21-30: 21-Gumby in 3-D #4. 22-The Flintstones in 3-D #2. 23-Laurel & Hardy in
3-D #1. 24-Bozo the Clown in 3-D #1. 25-The Transformers in 3-D #1. 26-G.I.
Joe in 3-D #2. 27-Bravestarr in 3-D #1. 28- Gumby in 3-D #5. 29-The
Transformers in 3-D #2. 30-Star Wars in 3-D #1   1.00   2.50
31-40: 31-The California Raisins in 3-D #1. 32-Richie Rich & Casper in 3-D #1.
33-Gumby in 3-D #6. 34-Laurel & Hardy in 3-D #2. 35-G.I. Joe in 3-D #3. 36-
The Flintstones in 3-D #3. 37-The Transformers in 3-D #3. 38-Gumby in 3-D
#7. 39-G.I. Joe in 3-D #4. 40-Bravestarr in 3-D #2   1.00   2.50
41-50: 41-Battletech in 3-D #1. 42-The Flintstones in 3-D #4. 43-Underdog in 3-
D #1. 44-The California Raisins in 3-D #2. 45-Red Heat in 3-D #1 (movie
adapt.). 46-The California Raisins in 3-D #3. 47. 48-Star Wars in
3-D #2,3. 49-Rambo in 3-D #1. 49-Sad Sack in 3-D #1. 50-Bullwinkle For
President in 3-D #1   1.00   2.50
51-60: 51-Kull in 3-D #1. 52-G.I. Joe in 3-D #5. 53-Red Sonja in 3-D #1. 54-Bozo
in 3-D #2. 55-Waxwork in 3-D #1 (movie adapt.). 56. 57-Casper in 3-D #1. 58-
Baby Huey in 3-D #1. 59-Little Dot in 3-D #1. 60-Solomon Kane in 3-D #1
            1.00   2.50
61-70: 61-Werewolf in 3-D #1. 62-G.I. Joe in 3-D Annual #1. 63-The California
Raisins in 3-D #4. 64-To Die For in 3-D #1. 65-Capt. Holo in 3-D #1. 66-
Playful Little Audrey in 3-D #1. 67-Kull in 3-D #2. 68. 69-The California
Raisins in 3-D#5. 70-Wendy in 3-D #1   1.00   2.50
71-80: 71. 72-Sports Hall of Shame #1. 73. 74-The Noid in 3-D #1. 75-
Moonwalker in 3-D #1 (Michael Jackson movie adapt.). 76-79. 80-The Noid in
3-D #2   2.50

BLACKWULF
June, 1994 - No. 10, Mar, 1995 ($1.50)
Marvel Comics

1-($2.50)-Embossed-c; Angel Medina-a   1.00   2.50
2-10   1.50

BLADE RUNNER (Movie)
Oct, 1982 - No. 2, Nov, 1982
Marvel Comics Group

1,2-r/Marvel Super Special #22; 1-Williamson-c/a. 2-Williamson-a
    .75

BLADE OF THE IMMORTAL (Manga)
June, 1996 - Present ($2.95, B&W, limited series)
Dark Horse Comics

1,2: 2-#1 on cover in error   3.00

BLADESMEN UNDERSEA
1994 ($3.50, B&W)
Blue Comet Press

1-Polybagged w/trading card   1.40   3.50

BLADE: THE VAMPIRE-HUNTER
July, 1994 - No. 10, Apr, 1995 ($1.95)

BLACK TERROR (column 2 header continues)
Marvel Comics

1-($2.95)-Foil-c   1.20   3.00
2-10   .80   2.00

BLAST (Satire Magazine)
Feb, 1971 - No. 2, May, 1971
G & D Publications

1-Wrightson & Kaluta-a   3.40   10.00   24.00
2-Kaluta-a   2.60   7.50   18.00

BLASTERS SPECIAL
1989 ($2.00, one-shot)
DC Comics

1-Peter David scripts; Invasion spin-off   .80   2.00

BLAST-OFF (Three Rocketeers)
October, 1965 (12¢)
Harvey Publications (Fun Day Funnies)

1-Kirby/Williamson-a(2); Williamson/Crandall-a; Williamson/Torres/
Krenkel-a; Kirby/Simon-c   3.75   11.25   28.00

BLAZE
Aug, 1994 - No. 12, July, 1995 ($1.95)
Marvel Comics

1-($2.95)-Foil embossed-c   1.20   3.00
2-12: 2-Man-Thing-c/story   .80   2.00

BLAZE CARSON (Rex Hart #6 on)(See Kid Colt, Tex Taylor, Wild Western,
Wisco)
Sept, 1948 - No. 5, June, 1949
Marvel Comics (USA)

1: 1,2-Shores-c   21.00   64.00   150.00
2,4,5: 4-Two-Gun Kid app. 5-Tex Taylor app.   17.00   49.00   115.00
3-Used by N.Y. State Legis. Comm. (injury to eye splash); Tex Morgan app.
        18.00   54.00   125.00

BLAZE: LEGACY OF BLOOD (See Ghost Rider & Ghost Rider/Blaze)
Dec, 1993 - No. 4, Mar, 1994 ($1.75, limited series)
Marvel Comics (Midnight Sons imprint)

1-4   .70   1.75

BLAZE THE WONDER COLLIE (Formerly Molly Manton's Romances #1?)
No. 2, Nov, 1949 - No. 3, Feb, 1950 (Both have photo-c)
Marvel Comics(SePI)

2(#1), 3-(Scarce)   21.00   64.00   150.00

BLAZING BATTLE TALES
July, 1975
Seaboard Periodicals (Atlas)

1-Intro. Sgt. Hawk & the Sky Demon; Severin, McWilliams, Sparling-a;
Thorne-c   1.25

BLAZING COMBAT (Magazine)
Oct, 1965 - No. 4, July, 1966 (35¢, B&W)
Warren Publishing Co.

1-Frazetta painted-c on all   16.00   47.00   110.00
2   3.75   11.25   28.00
3,4: 4-Frazetta half pg. ad   2.85   8.50   20.00
...Anthology (reprints from No. 1-4)   2.15   6.50   15.00
NOTE: *Above has art by Colan, Crandall, Evans, Morrow, Orlando, Severin, Torres, Toth,
Williamson,* and *Wood.*

BLAZING COMBAT: WORLD WAR I AND WORLD WAR II
Mar, 1994 ($3.75, B&W)
Apple Press

1,2: 1-r/Colan, Toth, Goodwin, Severin, Wood-a. 2-r/Crandall, Evans, Severin,
Torres, Williamson-a   1.60   4.00

BLAZING COMICS

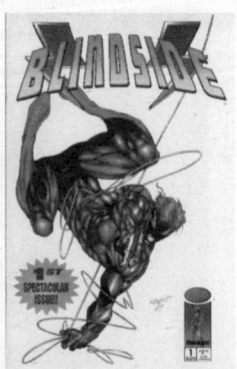

Blindside #1 © Rob Liefeld

Blitzkrieg #3 © DC

Blonde Phantom #16 © MEG

	GD25	FN65	NM94

6/44 - #3, 9/44; #4, 2/45; #5, 3/45; #5(V2#2), 3/55 - #6(V2#3), 1955?
Enwil Associates/Rural Home

	GD25	FN65	NM94
1-The Green Turtle, Red Hawk, Black Buccaneer begin; origin Jun-Gal			
	40.00	120.00	325.00
2-5: 3-Briefer.a. 5-(V2#2 inside)	29.00	86.00	200.00
5(3/55, V2#2-inside)-Black Buccaneer-c, 6(V2#3-inside, 1955)-Indian/			
Japanese-c	10.00	30.00	65.00

NOTE: No. 5 & 6 contain remaindered comics rebound and the contents can vary. Cloak & Daggar, Will Rogers, Superman 64, Star Spangled 130, Kaanga known. Value would be half of contents.

BLAZING SIXGUNS
Dec, 1952
Avon Periodicals

1-Kinstler-c/a; Larsen/Alascia-a(2), Tuska?-a; Jesse James, Kit Carson, Wild Bill Hickok app.	12.00	36.00	85.00

BLAZING SIXGUNS
1964
I.W./Super Comics

I.W. Reprint #1,8,9: 1-r/Wild Bill Hickok #26, Western True Crime #? & Blazing Sixguns #1 by Avon; Kinstler-c. 8-r/Blazing Western #?; Kinstler-c. 9-r/Blazing Western #1; Ditko-r; Kintsler-c reprinted from Dalton Boys #1.

	1.65	4.20	10.00
Super Reprint #10,11,15,16: 10,11-r/The Rider #2,1. 15-r/Silver Kid Western #?. 16-r/Buffalo Bill #?; Wildey-r; Severin-r. 17(1964)-r/Western True Crime #?			
	1.65	4.20	10.00
12-Reprints Bullseye #3; S&K-a	3.60	11.00	25.00
18-r/Straight Arrow #? by Powell; Severin-c	1.70	5.00	12.00

BLAZING SIX-GUNS (Also see Sundance Kid)
Feb, 1971 - No. 2, Apr, 1971 (52 pgs.)
Skywald Comics

1-The Red Mask, Sundance Kid begin; Avon's Geronimo reprint by Kinstler; Wyatt Earp app.	1.60		4.00
2-Wild Bill Hickok, Jesse James, Kit Carson-r plus M.E. Red Mask-r	.80		2.00

BLAZING WEST (Also see The Hooded Horseman)
Fall, 1948 - No. 22, Mar-Apr, 1952
American Comics Group (B&I Publ./Michel Publ.)

1-Origin & 1st app. Injun Jones, Tenderfoot & Buffalo Belle; Texas Tim & Ranger begins, ends #13	17.00	51.00	120.00
2,3	10.00	30.00	60.00
4-Origin & 1st app. Little Lobo; Starr-a	7.00	21.00	42.00
5-10: 5-Starr-a	6.35	19.00	38.00
11-13	4.70	14.00	28.00
14-Origin & 1st app. The Hooded Horseman	10.00	30.00	65.00
15-22: 15,16,18,19-Starr-a	7.00	21.00	42.00

BLAZING WESTERN
Jan, 1954 - No. 5, Sept, 1954
Timor Publications

1-Ditko-a (1st Western-a?); text story by Bruce Hamilton	12.00	36.00	85.00
2-4	5.00	15.00	30.00
5-Disbrow-a	5.85	17.50	35.00

BLEAT
Aug, 1995 ($2.95)
Slave Labor Graphics

1			3.00

BLESSED PIUS X
No date (Text/comics, 32 pgs., paper-c)
Catechetical Guild (Giveaway)

nn	3.60	9.00	18.00

BLIND JUSTICE (Also see Batman: Blind Justice)
1989 (Giveaway, squarebound)
DC Comics/Diamond Comic Distributors

nn-Contains Detective #598-600 by Batman movie writer Sam Hamm, w/covers; published same time as originals?	.80	2.00

BLINDSIDE
Aug, 1996 - Present ($2.50)
Image Comics (Extreme Studios)

1-Variant-c exists	2.50

BLITZKRIEG
Jan-Feb, 1976 - No. 5, Sept-Oct, 1976
National Periodical Publications

1-Kubert-c on all	1.25
2-5	.75

BLONDE PHANTOM (Formerly All-Select #1-11; Lovers #23 on)(Also see Blackstone, Marvel Mystery, Millie The Model #2, Sub-Mariner Comics #25 & Sun Girl)
No. 12, Winter, 1946-47 - No. 22, Mar, 1949
Marvel Comics (MPC)

12-Miss America begins, ends #14	118.00	355.00	950.00
13-Sub-Mariner begins (not in #16)	75.00	225.00	600.00
14,15: 15-Kurtzman's "Hey Look"	68.00	205.00	550.00
16-Captain America with Bucky story by Rico(p), 6 pgs.; Kurtzman's "Hey Look" (1 pg.)	96.00	290.00	775.00
17-22: 22-Anti Wertham editorial	65.00	195.00	525.00

NOTE: *Shores* c-12-18.

BLONDIE (See Ace Comics, Comics Reading Libraries, Dagwood, Daisy & Her Pups, Eat Right to Work…, King & Magic Comics)
1942 - 1946
David McKay Publications

Feature Books 12 (Rare)	60.00	180.00	600.00
Feature Books 27-29,31,34(1940)	17.00	51.00	120.00
Feature Books 36,38,40,42,43,45,47	16.00	47.00	110.00
…1944 (Hard-c, 1938, B&W, 128 pgs.)-1944 daily strip-r	13.00	39.00	90.00

BLONDIE & DAGWOOD FAMILY
Oct, 1963 - No. 4, Dec, 1965 (68 pgs.)
Harvey Publications (King Features Synd.)

1	1.60	4.80	16.00
2-4	1.00	3.00	10.00

BLONDIE COMICS (…Monthly No. 16-141)
Spring, 1947 - No. 163, Nov, 1965; No. 164, Aug, 1966 - No. 175, Dec, 1967; No. 177, Feb, 1969 - No. 222, Nov, 1976
David McKay #1-15/Harvey #16-163/King #164-175/Charlton #177 on

1	21.00	62.00	145.00
2	10.00	30.00	65.00
3-5	8.00	24.00	48.00
6-10	6.00	18.00	36.00
11-15	4.50	13.50	27.00
16-(3/50; 1st Harvey issue)	6.00	18.00	36.00
17-20: 20-(3/51)-Becomes Daisy & Her Pups #21 & Chamber of Chills #21			
	2.60	11.00	26.00
21-30	1.80	7.50	18.00
31-50	1.50	6.50	15.00
51-80	1.20	5.00	12.00
81-124,126-130	1.00	4.20	10.00
125 (80 pgs.)	1.80	6.50	18.00
131-136,138,139	.80	3.25	8.00
137,140-(80 pgs.)	1.20	4.20	12.00
141-167(#148,155,157-159,161-163 are 68 pgs.)	1.00	4.20	10.00

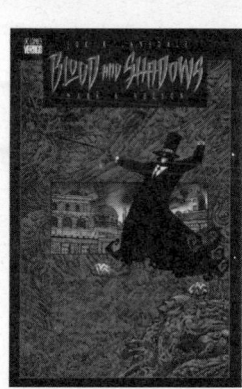

Blood and Shadows #4 © DC

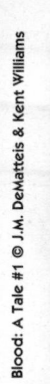

Blood: A Tale #1 © J.M. DeMatteis & Kent Williams

Bloodstone #2 © Rob Liefeld

	GD25	FN65	NM94
168-175,177-222 (no #176)	.50	1.50	5.00
Blondie, Dagwood & Daisy 1(100 pgs., 1953)	17.00	49.00	115.00
1950 Giveaway	4.00	10.00	20.00
1962,1964 Giveaway	1.30	3.25	8.00
N. Y. State Dept. of Mental Hygiene Giveaway-('50, '56, '61) Regular size			
(Diff. issues) 16 pgs.; no #	1.80	4.50	9.00

BLOOD
Feb, 1988 - No. 4, Apr, 1988 ($3.25, mature)
Marvel Comics (Epic Comics)

1-4: DeMatteis scripts & Kent Williams-c/a		1.40	3.50

BLOOD AND GLORY (Punisher & Captain America)
Oct, 1992 - No. 3, Dec, 1992 ($5.95, limited series)
Marvel Comics

1-3: 1-Embossed wraparound-c	1.00	2.50	6.00

BLOOD & ROSES: FUTURE PAST TENSE (Bob Hickey's...)
Dec, 1993 ($2.25)
Sky Comics

1-Silver ink logo		.90	2.25

BLOOD & ROSES: SEARCH FOR THE TIME-STONE (Bob Hickey's...)
Apr, 1994 ($2.50)
Sky Comics

1		1.00	2.50

BLOOD AND SHADOWS
1996 - Book 4, 1996 ($5.95, squarebound, limited series, mature)
DC Comics (Vertigo)

Books 1-4: Joe R. Lansdale scripts; Mark A. Nelson-c/a.	1.00	2.60	6.00

BLOOD: A TALE
Nov, 1996 - No. 4, Feb, 1997 ($2.95, limited series)
DC Comics (Vertigo)

1-4: Reprints Epic series w/new-c; DeMatteis scripts; Kent Williams-c/a			
		1.20	3.00

BLOODBATH
Early Dec, 1993 - No. 2, Late Dec, 1993 ($3.50, limited series, 68 pgs.)
DC Comics

1,2-Neon ink-c; Superman app.: 1-New Batman-c & app.		1.40	3.50

BLOODFIRE
June, 1993 - No. 12, May, 1994 ($2.95)
Lightning Comics

1-($3.50)-Foil-c; 1st app. Bloodfire	1.00	2.00	5.00
2-12: 2-Origin; contracts HIV virus via transfusion. 5-Polybagged w/card &			
collectors warning on bag. 12-(5/94)		1.20	3.00
0-(Indicia reads June 1994, MAY on-c, $3.50)		1.40	3.50
.../Hellina 1 (7/95, $3.00)		1.60	4.00
.../Hellina 1 (7/95, $9.95)-Nude edition; Deodato-c			
	1.70	5.00	12.00
.../Hellina (8/95, $9.95)-Commemorative edition			
	2.00	4.00	10.00

BLOOD IS THE HARVEST
1950 (32 pgs., paper-c)
Catechetical Guild

(Scarce)-Anti-communism (13 known copies)	93.00	280.00	750.00
Black & white version (5 known copies), saddle stitched			
	39.00	118.00	275.00

Untrimmed version (only one known copy); estimated value-$600
NOTE: *In 1979 nine copies of the color version surfaced from the old Guild's files plus the five black & white copies.*

BLOODLINES: A TALE FROM THE HEART OF AFRICA (See Tales From the Heart of Africa)

	GD25	FN65	NM94
1992 ($5.95, 52 pgs.)			
Marvel Comics (Epic Comics)			
1-Story cont'd from Tales From...	1.00	2.50	6.00

BLOOD OF DRACULA
Nov, 1987 - No. 20?, 1990 ($1.75/$1.95, B&W)($2.25 #14,16 on)
Apple Comics

1-13: 6-Begin $1.95-c. 10-Chadwick-c		.80	2.00
14,16-20 ($2.25): 14,16-19-Lost Frankenstein pgs. by Wrightson			
		.90	2.25
15-Contains stereo flexidisc ($3.75)		1.50	3.75

BLOOD OF THE INNOCENT (See Warp Graphics Annual)
1/7/86 - No. 4, 1/28/86 (Weekly mini-series, mature)
WaRP Graphics

1-4		.80	2.00

BLOODPACK
Mar, 1995 - No. 4, June,1995 ($1.50, limited series)
DC Comics

1-4			1.50

BLOODPOOL
Aug, 1995 - No. 4, Nov, 1995 ($2.50, limited series)
Image Comics (Extreme Studios)

1-4: Jo Duffy scripts in all		1.00	2.50
Special (3/96, $2.50)-Jo Duffy scripts		1.00	2.50
Trade Paperback (1996, $12.95)-r/#1-4			13.00

BLOOD REIGN SAGA
1996 ($3.00, B&W, mature)
London Night Studios

1-"Encore Edition"		1.20	3.00

BLOODSCENT
Oct, 1988 ($2.00, one-shot, Baxter paper)
Comico

1-Colan-p		.80	2.00

BLOODSEED
Oct, 1993 - No. 2, Nov, 1993 ($1.95, limited series)
Marvel Comics (Frontier Comics)

1,2: Sharp/Cam Smith-a		.80	2.00

BLOODSHOT (See Eternal Warrior #4 & Rai #0)
Nov, 1992 - No. 51, Aug, 1996 ($2.25/$2.50)
Valiant/Acclaim Comics (Valiant)

1-($3.50)-Chromium embossed-c by B. Smith w/poster	1.60	4.00
2-($2.50)		1.00	2.50
3-5,8-14: 3-$2.25-c begins; cont'd in Hard Corps #5. 4-Eternal Warrior-c/story.			
5-Rai & Eternal Warrior app. 14-(3/94)-Reese-c(i)		.90	2.25
6-1st app. Ninjak (out of costume)		1.20	3.00
7-1st app. Ninjak in costume		1.40	3.50
0-(3/94, $3.50)-Wraparound chromium-c by Quesada(p); origin			
		1.40	3.50
0-Gold variant	1.30	3.25	8.00
15-49: 15-(4/94). 16-w/bound-in trading card		.90	2.25
50,51: 50-$2.50-c begins. 51-Bloodshot dies?		1.00	2.50
Yearbook 1 (1994, $3.95)		1.60	4.00
Special 1 (3/94, $5.95)-Zeck-c/a(p)	1.20	2.40	6.00

BLOODSTRIKE (See Supreme V2#3)
1993 - No. 22, May, 1995; No. 25, May, 1994 ($1.95/$2.50)
Image Comics (Extreme Studios)

1-12, 25: Liefeld layouts in early issues. 1-Blood Brothers prelude. 2-1st app. Lethal. 5-1st app. Noble. 9-Black and White part 6 by Art Thibert; Liefeld pin-up. 9,10-Have coupon #3 & 7 for Extreme Prejudice #0. 10-(4/94). 11-(7/94).

Blood Syndicate #18 © Milestone Media

Bluebeard #1 © James Robinson

Blue Beetle #47 © FOX

25-(5/94) -Liefeld/Fraga-c		.80	2.00	6-Dynamite Thor begins (1st); origin Blue Beetle	50.00	150.00	400.00
13-22: 13-$2.50-c begins. 16:Platt-c; Prophet app. 17-19-polybagged				7,8-Dynamo app. in both. 8-Last Thor	47.00	141.00	375.00
w/card		1.00	2.50	9-12: 9,10-The Blackbird & The Gorilla app. in both. 10-Bondage/hypo-c			
NOTE: *Giffen* story/layouts-4-6. *Jae Lee* c-7, 8. *Rob Liefeld* layouts-1-3. *Art Thibert* c-6i.				11(2/42)-The Gladiator app. 12(6/42)-The Black Fury app.			
BLOODSTRIKE ASSASSIN					43.00	128.00	340.00
June, 1995 - No. 3, Aug, 1995; No. 0, Oct, 1995 ($2.50, limited series)				13-V-Man begins (1st app.), ends #18; Kubert-a	50.00	150.00	400.00
Image Comics (Extreme Studios)				14,15-Kubert-a in both. 14-Intro. side-kick (c/text only), Sparky (called			
0-3: 3-(8/95)-Quesada-c. 0-(10/95)-Battlestone app				Spunky #17-19)	44.00	132.00	350.00
		1.00	2.50	16-18: 17-Brodsky-c	39.00	118.00	275.00
BLOOD SWORD, THE				19-Kubert-a	40.00	120.00	290.00
Aug, 1988 - No. 44? 1991 ($1.50/$1.95, 68 pgs.)				20-Origin/1st app. Tiger Squadron; Arabian Nights begin			
Jademan Comics					40.00	120.00	310.00
1-8 ($1.50)-Kung Fu stories			1.50	21-26: 24-Intro. & only app. The Halo. 26-General Patton story & photo			
9-44: ($1.95)		.80	2.00		29.00	86.00	200.00
BLOOD SWORD DYNASTY				27-Tamaa, Jungle Prince app.	26.00	77.00	180.00
1989 - No. 30, 1991? ($1.25, 36 pgs.)				28-30(2/44)	24.00	71.00	165.00
Jademan Comics				31(6/44), 33,34,36-40: 34-38-"The Threat from Saturn" serial.			
1-30: Ties into Blood Sword			1.30		21.00	64.00	150.00
BLOOD SYNDICATE				32-Hitler-c	27.00	81.00	190.00
Apr, 1993 - No. 35, Feb, 1996 ($1.50/$1.75/$2.50/$3.50)				35-Extreme violence	26.00	77.00	180.00
DC Comics (Milestone)				41-45	19.00	56.00	130.00
1-($2.95)-Collector's Edition; polybagged with poster, trading card, & acid-free				46-The Puppeteer app.	21.00	64.00	150.00
backing board (direct sale only)		1.20	3.00	47-Kamen & Baker-a begin	93.00	281.00	750.00
1-9,11-17: 8-Intro Kwai. 15-Byrne-c. 16-Worlds Collide Pt. 6; Superman-c/app.				48-50	76.00	230.00	615.00
17-Worlds Collide Pt. 13			1.50	51,53	64.00	190.00	515.00
10-($2.50, 52 pgs.)-Simonson-c		1.00	2.50	52-Kamen bondage-c; true crime stories begin	96.00	290.00	775.00
18-27: 18-Begin $1.75-c		.70	1.75	54-Used in SOTI. Illo, "Children call these 'headlights' comics"			
25-($2.95, 52 pgs.)		1.20	3.00		109.00	320.00	875.00
28, 30-32: 28-Begin $2.50-c. 30-Long Hot Summer x-over				55-57: 56-Used in SOTI, pg. 145. 57(7/48)-Last Kamen issue; becomes			
		1.00	2.50	Western Killers?)	62.00	187.00	500.00
29, 33-34: 29-(99¢); Long Hot Summer x-over			1.00	58(4/50)-60-No Kamen-a	13.50	41.00	95.00
35-Kwai disappears		1.40	3.50	NOTE: *Kamen* a-47-51, 53, 55-57; c-47, 49-52. *Powell* a-4(2). Bondage-c 9-12, 46, 52.			
BLOODWULF				**BLUE BEETLE** (Unusual Tales #1-49; becomes Mr. Muscles No. 22 on)			
Feb, 1995 - No. 4, May, 1995 ($2.50, limited series)				(See Charlton Bullseye & Space Adventures)			
Image Comics (Extreme Studios)				No. 18, Feb, 1955 - No. 21, Aug, 1955			
1-4: 1-Liefeld-c w/4 different captions & alternate-c		1.00	2.50	Charlton Comics			
Summer Special (8/95, $2.50)-Jeff Johnson-c/a; Supreme app; story takes place				18,19-(Pre-1944-r). 18-Last pre-code issue. 19-Bouncer, Rocket Kelly-r			
between Legend of Supreme #3 & Supreme #23.		1.00	2.50		16.00	47.00	110.00
BLOODY MARY				20-Joan Mason by Kamen	20.00	60.00	140.00
Oct, 1996 - No. 4, Jan, 1997 ($2.25, limited series)				21-New material	13.50	41.00	95.00
DC Comics (Helix)				**BLUE BEETLE** (Unusual Tales #1-49; Ghostly Tales #55 on)(See Captain			
1-4: Garth Ennis scripts; Ezuerra-c/a in all			2.25	Atom & Charlton Bullseye)			
BLUEBEARD				V2#1, June, 1964 - V2#5, Mar-Apr, 1965; V3#50, July, 1965 - V3#54,			
Nov, 1993 - No. 3, Mar, 1994 ($2.95, B&W, limited series)				Feb-Mar, 1966; #1, June, 1967 - #5, Nov, 1968			
Slave Labor Graphics				Charlton Comics			
1-3: James Robinson scripts. 2-(12/93)			3.00	V2#1-Origin/1st S.A. app. Dan Garrett-Blue Beetle	7.00	21.50	50.00
Trade paperback (6/94, $9.95)			10.00	2-5: 5-Weiss illo; 1st published-a?	5.00	15.00	35.00
Trade paperback (2nd printing, 7/96, $12.95)-New-c			13.00	V3#50-54-Formerly Unusual Tales	5.00	15.00	35.00
BLUE BEETLE, THE (Also see All Top, Big-3, Mystery Men & Weekly Comic				1(1967)-Question series begins by Ditko	11.00	33.00	75.00
Magazine)				2-Origin Ted Kord-Blue Beetle (see Capt. Atom #83 for 1st Ted Kord Blue			
Winter, 1939-40 - No. 57, 7/48; No. 58, 4/50 - No. 60, 8/50				Beetle); Dan Garrett x-over	4.30	13.00	30.00
Fox Publ. No. 1-11, 31-60; Holyoke No. 12-30				3-5 (All Ditko-c/a in #1-5)	3.60	11.00	25.00
1-Reprints from Mystery Men 1-5; Blue Beetle origin; Yarko the Great-r/from				1,3(Modern Comics-1977)-Reprints			1.00
Wonder/Wonderworld 2-5 all by Eisner; Master Magician app.; (Blue Beetle				NOTE: *#6 only appeared in the fanzine 'The Charlton Portfolio.'*			
in 4 different costumes)	355.00	1065.00	3200.00	**BLUE BEETLE** (Also see Americomics, Crisis On Infinite Earths, Justice League			
2-K-51-r by Powell/Wonderworld 8,9	125.00	375.00	1000.00	& Showcase '94 #2-4)			
3-Simon-c	90.00	270.00	725.00	June, 1986 - No. 24, May, 1988			
4-Marijuana drug mention story	59.00	178.00	475.00	DC Comics			
5-Zanzibar The Magician by Tuska	53.00	160.00	425.00	1-Origin retold; intro. Firefist			1.00
				2-24: 2-Origin Firefist. 5-7-The Question app. 11-14-New Teen Titans x-over.			
				20-Justice League app. 20,21-Millennium tie-ins			1.00
				BLUEBERRY (See Lt. Blueberry & Marshal Blueberry)			

Blue Bolt #3 © NOVP

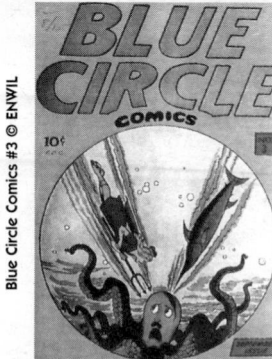

Blue Circle Comics #3 © ENWIL

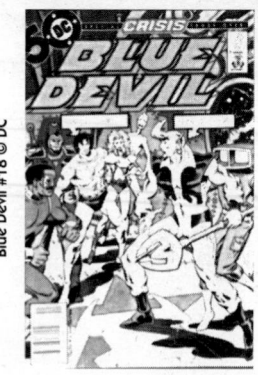

Blue Devil #18 © DC

	GD25	FN65	NM94

1989 - No. 5, 1990 ($12.95/$14.95, graphic novel)
Marvel Comics (Epic Comics)

1,3,4,5-($12.95)-Moebius-a in all	1.85	5.50	13.00
2-($14.95)	2.15	6.50	15.00

BLUE BIRD COMICS
Late 1940's - 1964 (Giveaway)
Various Shoe Stores/Charlton Comics

nn(1947-50)(36 pgs.)-Several issues; Human Torch, Sub-Mariner app. in some			
	11.50	34.00	80.00
1959-Li'l Genius, Timmy the Timid Ghost, Wild Bill Hickok (All #1)			
	2.00	5.00	10.00
1959-(6 titles; all #2) Black Fury #1,4,5, Freddy #4, Li'l Genius, Timmy the Timid Ghost #4, Masked Raider #4, Wild Bill Hickok (Charlton)			
	2.00	5.00	10.00
1959-(#5) Masked Raider #21	2.00	5.00	10.00
1960-(6 titles)(All #4) Black Fury #8,9, Masked Raider, Freddy #8,9, Timmy the Timid Ghost #9, Li'l Genius #7,9 (Charlt.)	2.00	5.00	10.00
1961,1962-(All #10's) Atomic Mouse #12,13,16, Black Fury #11,12, Freddy, Li'l Genius, Masked Raider, Six Gun Heroes, Texas Rangers in Action, Timmy the Ghost, Wild Bill Hickok, Wyatt Earp #3,11-13,16-18 (Charlton)			
	1.30	3.25	8.00
1963-Texas Rangers #17 (Charlton)	1.00	2.00	5.00
1964-Mysteries of Unexplored Worlds #18, Teenage Hotrodders #18, War Heroes #18 (Charlton)	1.20	3.00	7.00
1965-War Heroes #18	1.20	3.00	

NOTE: More than one issue of each character could have been published each year. Numbering is sporadic.

BLUE BIRD CHILDREN'S MAGAZINE, THE
V1#2, 1957 - No. 10 1958 (16 pgs., soft-c, regular size)
Graphic Information Service

V1#2-10: Pat, Pete & Blue Bird app.		1.60	4.00

BLUE BOLT
June, 1940 - No. 101 (V10#2), Sept-Oct, 1949
Funnies, Inc. No. 1/Novelty Press/Premium Group of Comics

V1#1-Origin Blue Bolt by Joe Simon, Sub-Zero Man, White Rider & Super Horse, Dick Cole, Wonder Boy & Sgt. Spook (1st app. of each)			
	262.00	790.00	2100.00
2-Simon & Kirby's 1st art & 1st super-hero (Blue Bolt)			
	118.00	355.00	950.00
3-1 pg. Space Hawk by Wolverton; 2nd S&K-a on Blue Bolt (same cover date as Red Raven #1); 1st time S&K names app. in a comic; Simon-c			
	100.00	300.00	800.00
4,5-S&K-a in each; 5-Everett-a begins on Sub-Zero			
	93.00	280.00	750.00
6,8-10-S&K-a	84.00	253.00	675.00
7-S&K-c/a	90.00	270.00	725.00
11,12: 11-Robot-c	87.00	262.00	700.00
V2#1-Origin Dick Cole & The Twister; Twister x-over in Dick Cole, Sub-Zero, & Blue Bolt; origin Simba Karno who battles Dick Cole thru V2#5 & becomes main support character V2#6 on; battle-c	29.00	86.00	200.00
2-Origin The Twister retold in text	21.00	64.00	150.00
3-5: 5-Intro. Freezum	19.00	56.00	130.00
6-Origin Sgt. Spook retold	16.00	47.00	110.00
7-12: 7-Lois Blake becomes Blue Bolt's costume aide; last Twister. 12-Textsty by Mickey Spillaine	13.50	41.00	95.00
V3#1-3	11.00	33.00	75.00
4-12: 4-Blue Bolt abandons costume	9.15	27.00	55.00
V4#1-Hitler, Tojo, Mussolini-c	12.00	36.00	85.00
V4#2-12: 3-Shows V4#3 on-c, V4#4 inside (9-10/43). 5-Infinity-c. 8-Last Sub-Zero	7.50	22.50	45.00
V5#1-8, V6#1-3,5-10, V7#1-12	6.70	20.00	40.00
V6#4-Racist cover	7.50	22.50	45.00

V8#1-6,8-12, V9#1-5,7,8	5.85	17.50	35.00
V8#7,V9#6,9-L. B. Cole-c	12.00	36.00	85.00
V10#1(#100)	5.85	17.50	35.00
V10#2(#101)-Last Dick Cole, Blue Bolt	5.85	17.50	35.00

NOTE: Everett c-V1#4, 11, V2#1, 2. Gustavson a-V1#1-12, V2#1-7. Kiefer c-V3#1. Rico a-V6#10, V7#4. Blue Bolt not in V9#8.

BLUE BOLT (Becomes Ghostly Weird Stories #120 on; continuation of Novelty Blue Bolt) (...Weird Tales #112-119)
No. 102, Nov-Dec, 1949 - No. 119, May-June, 1953
Star Publications

102-The Chameleon, & Target app.	26.00	77.00	180.00
103,104-The Chameleon app. 104-Last Target	24.00	73.00	170.00
105-Origin Blue Bolt (from #1) retold by Simon; Chameleon & Target app.; opium den story	40.00	120.00	300.00
106-Blue Bolt by S&K begins; Spacehawk reprints from Target by Wolverton begin, ends #110; Sub-Zero begins; ends #109	40.00	120.00	280.00
107-110: 108-Last S&K Blue Bolt reprint. 109-Wolverton-c(r)/inside Spacehawk splash. 110-Target app.	39.00	118.00	275.00
111,112: 111-Red Rocket & The Mask-r; last Blue Bolt; 1pg. L. B. Cole-a 112-Last Torpedo Man app.	36.00	109.00	255.00
113-Wolverton's Spacehawk-r/Target V3#7	39.00	116.00	270.00
114,116: 116-Jungle Jo-r	36.00	109.00	255.00
115-Sgt. Spook app.	39.00	118.00	275.00
117-Jo-Jo & Blue Bolt-r	37.00	111.00	260.00
118-"White Spirit" by Wood	39.00	118.00	275.00
119-Disbrow/Cole-c; Jungle Jo-r	37.00	111.00	260.00
Accepted Reprint #103(1957?, nd)	8.35	25.00	50.00

NOTE: L. B. Cole c-102-108, 110. Disbrow a-112(2), 113(3), 114(2), 115(2), 116-118. Hollingsworth a-117. Palais a-112r. Sci/Fi c-105-110. Horror c-111.

BLUE BULLETEER, THE (Also see Femforce Special)
1989 ($2.25, B&W, one-shot)
AC Comics

1-Origin by Bill Black; Bill Ward-a		1.00	2.50

BLUE CIRCLE COMICS (Also see Roly Poly Comic Book)
June, 1944 - No. 5, Mar, 1945; No. 6, 1950s
Enwil Associates/Rural Home

1-The Blue Circle begins (1st app.); origin & 1st app. Steel Fist			
	19.00	58.00	135.00
2,3: 3-Hitler parody-c	13.50	41.00	95.00
4-6: 5-Last Steel Fist. 6-(1950s)-Colossal Features-r			
	9.15	27.00	55.00

BLUE DEVIL (See Fury of Firestorm #24 & Underworld Unleashed)
June, 1984 - No. 31, Dec, 1986 (75¢/$1.25)
DC Comics

1-30: 4-Origin Nebiros. 7-Gil Kane-a. 8-Giffen-a. 17-19-Crisis x-over			
			1.00
31-($1.25, 52 pgs.)			1.25
Annual 1 (11/85)-Team-ups w/Black Orchid, Creeper, Demon, Madame Xanadu, Man-Bat & Phantom Stranger			1.25

BLUE PHANTOM, THE
June-Aug, 1962
Dell Publishing Co.

1(01-066-208)-by Fred Fredericks	2.40	7.25	24.00

BLUE RIBBON COMICS (...Mystery Comics No. 9-18)
Nov, 1939 - No. 22, Mar, 1942 (1st MLJ series)
MLJ Magazines

1-Dan Hastings, Richy the Amazing Boy, Rang-A-Tang the Wonder Dog begin (1st app. of each); Little Nemo app. (not by W. McCay); Jack Cole-a(3)			
	275.00	825.00	2400.00
2-Bob Phantom, Silver Fox (both in #3), Rang-A-Tang Club & Cpl. Collins begin (1st app. of each); Jack Cole-a	106.00	318.00	850.00

Blue Ribbon Comics #10 © MLJ

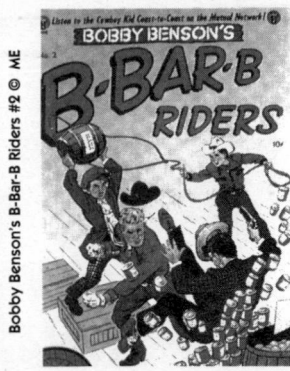

Bobby Benson's B-Bar-B Riders #2 © ME

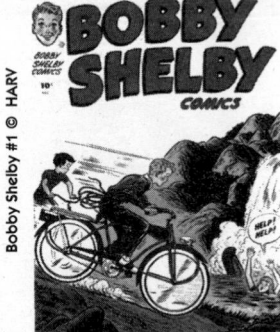

Bobby Shelby #1 © HARV

	GD25	FN65	NM94
3-J. Cole-a	75.00	225.00	600.00
4-Doc Strong, The Green Falcon, & Hercules begin (1st app. each); origin &			
1st app. The Fox & Ty-Gor, Son of the Tiger	81.00	243.00	650.00
5-8: 8-Last Hercules; 6,7-Biro, Meskin-a. 7-Fox app. on-c			
	56.00	168.00	450.00
9-(Scarce)-Origin & 1st app. Mr. Justice (2/41)	237.00	712.00	1900.00
10-13: 12-Last Doc Strong. 13-Inferno, the Flame Breather begins, ends #19;			
Devil-c	87.00	262.00	700.00
14,15,17,18: 15-Last Green Falcon	75.00	225.00	600.00
16-Origin & 1st app. Captain Flag (9/41)	150.00	450.00	1200.00
19-22: 20-Last Ty-Gor. 22-Origin Mr. Justice retold			
	75.00	225.00	600.00

NOTE: *Biro c-3-5; a-2 (Cpl. Collins & Scoop Cody). S. Cooper c-9-17. 20-22 contain "Tales From the Witch's Cauldron" (same strip as "Stories of the Black Witch" in Zip Comics). Mr. Justice c-9-18. Captain Flag c-16(w/Mr. Justice), 19-22.*

BLUE RIBBON COMICS (Becomes Teen-Age Diary Secrets #4)(See Heckle & Jeckle)
Feb, 1949 - No. 6, Aug, 1949
Blue Ribbon (St. John)

1,3-Heckle & Jeckle	7.50	22.50	45.00
2(4/49)-Diary Secrets; Baker-c	16.00	47.00	110.00
4(6/49)-Teen-Age Diary Secrets; Baker c/a(2)	17.00	49.00	115.00
5(8/49)-Teen-Age Diary Secrets; Oversize; photo-c; Baker-a(2)- Continues			
as Teen-Age Diary Secrets	21.00	64.00	150.00
6-Dinky Duck(8/49)	4.00	10.00	20.00

BLUE-RIBBON COMICS
Nov, 1983 - No. 14, Dec, 1984
Red Circle Prod./Archie Ent. No. 5 on

1-S&K-r/Advs. of the Fly #1,2; Williamson/Torres-r/Fly #2; Ditko-c			
			1.00
2-14: 2-Origin Steel Sterling. 5-S&K Shield-r. 6,7-The Fox app. 8-Toth			
centerspread. 8,11-Black Hood. 12-Thunder Agents. 13-Thunder Bunny.			
14-Web & Jaguar			1.00

NOTE: *N. Adams a(r)-8. Buckler a-4i. Nino a-2i. McWilliams a-8. Morrow a-8.*

BLUE STREAK (See Holyoke One-Shot No. 8)

BLYTHE (Marge's)
No. 1072, Jan-Mar, 1960
Dell Publishing Co.

Four Color 1072	5.00	15.00	50.00

B-MAN (See Double-Dare Adventures)

BO (Tom Cat #4 on) (Also see Big Shot #29 & Dixie Dugan)
June, 1955 - No. 3, Oct, 1955 (A dog)
Charlton Comics Group

1-3: Newspaper reprints by Frank Beck	7.00	21.00	42.00

BOATNIKS, THE (See Walt Disney Showcase No. 1)

BOB & BETTY & SANTA'S WISHING WELL
1941 (Christmas giveaway, 12 pgs.)
Sears Roebuck & Co.

nn	10.00	30.00	60.00

BOBBY BENSON'S B-BAR-B RIDERS (Radio) (See Best of the West, The Lemonade Kid & Model Fun)
May-June, 1950 - No. 20, May-June, 1953
Magazine Enterprises

1-The Lemonade Kid begins; Powell-a (Scarce)	40.00	120.00	300.00
2	13.50	41.00	95.00
3-5: 4,5-Lemonade Kid-c (#4-Spider-c)	11.00	33.00	75.00
6-8,10	11.00	30.00	65.00
9,11,13-Frazetta-c; Ghost Rider in #13-15 by Ayers-a. 13-Ghost Rider-c			
	28.00	84.00	195.00
12,17-20: 20-(A-1 #88)	10.00	30.00	60.00

14-Decapitation/Bondage-c & story; horror-c	16.00	47.00	110.00
15-Ghost Rider-c	13.00	39.00	90.00
16-Photo-c	11.00	33.00	75.00
...in the Tunnel of Gold-(1936, 5-1/4x8"; 100 pgs.) Radio giveaway by			
Hecker-H.O. Company(H.O. Oats); contains 22 color pgs. of comics,			
rest in novel form	9.15	27.50	55.00
...And The Lost Herd-same as above	9.15	27.50	55.00

NOTE: *Ayers a-13-15, 20. Powell a-1-12(4 ea.), 13(3), 14-16(Red Hawk only); c-1,8,1 0, 12. Lemonade Kid in most 1-13.*

BOBBY COMICS
May, 1946
Universal Phoenix Features

1-By S. M. Iger	7.00	21.00	42.00

BOBBY SHELBY COMICS
1949
Shelby Cycle Co./Harvey Publications

nn	3.20	8.00	16.00

BOBBY SHERMAN (TV)
Feb, 1972 - No. 7, Oct, 1972
Charlton Comics

1-Based on TV show "Getting Together"	3.60	11.00	25.00
2-7: 4-Photo-c	2.30	6.70	16.00

BOB COLT (Movie star)(See XMas Comics)
Nov, 1950 - No. 10, May, 1952
Fawcett Publications

1-Bob Colt, his horse Buckskin & sidekick Pablo begin; photo front/back-c			
begin	40.00	120.00	300.00
2	26.00	79.00	185.00
3-5	21.00	62.00	145.00
6-Flying Saucer story	18.00	54.00	125.00
7-10: 9-Last photo back-c	17.00	49.00	115.00

BOB HOPE (See Adventures of... & Calling All Boys #12)

BOB MARLEY, TALE OF THE TUFF GONG (Music star)
Aug, 1994 - No. 3, Nov, 1994 ($5.95, limited series)
Marvel Comics

1-3	1.00	2.60	6.00

BOB POWELL'S TIMELESS TALES
March, 1989 ($2.00, B&W)
Eclipse Comics

1-Powell-r/Black Cat #5 (Scarlet Arrow), 9 & Race for the Moon #1			
		.80	2.00

BOB SCULLY, TWO-FISTED HICK DETECTIVE
No date (1930's) (36 pgs., 9-1/2x12", B&W, paper cover)
Humor Publ. Co.

nn-By Howard Dell; not reprints	10.00	30.00	70.00

BOB SON OF BATTLE
No. 729, Nov, 1956
Dell Publishing Co.

Four Color 729	4.00	12.00	40.00

BOB STEELE WESTERN (Movie star)
Dec, 1950 - No. 10, June, 1952; 1990
Fawcett Publications/AC Comics

1-Bob Steele & his horse Bullet begin; photo front/back-c begin			
	50.00	150.00	400.00
2	29.00	86.00	200.00
3-5: 4-Last photo back-c	21.00	64.00	150.00
6-10: 10-Last photo-c	17.00	51.00	120.00
1 (1990, $2.75, B&W)-Bob Steele & Rocky Lane reprints; photo-c & inside			

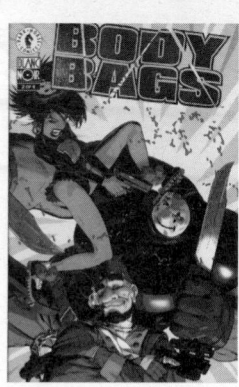

Body Bags #2 © Jason Pearson

Bone #15 © Jeff Smith

Boof #3 © Todd McFarlane

	GD25	FN65	NM94
covers	.55	1.60	2.75
BOB SWIFT (Boy Sportsman)			
May, 1951 - No. 5, Jan, 1952			
Fawcett Publications			
1	8.35	25.00	50.00
2-5: Saunders painted-c #1-5	4.25	13.00	28.00
BOB, THE GALACTIC BUM			
Feb, 1995 - No. 4, June, 1995 ($1.95, limited series)			
DC Comics			
1-4: 1-Lobo app.		.80	2.00
BODY BAGS			
Sept, 1996 - No. 4, Dec, 1996 ($2.95, mini-series, mature)(1st Blanc Noir series)			
Dark Horse Comics (Blanc Noir)			
1-4: Jason Pearson-c/a/scripts in all. 1-Intro Clownface & Panda.			
BODYCOUNT (Also see Casey Jones & Raphael)			
Mar, 1996 - No. 4, July, 1996 ($2.50, limited series)			
Image Comics (Highbrow Entertainment)			
1-4: Kevin Eastman-a(p)/scripts; Simon Bisley-c/a(i); Turtles app.			
			2.50
BOLD ADVENTURES			
Oct, 1983 - No. 3, June, 1984 ($1.50)			
Pacific Comics			
1-Time Force, Anaconda, & The Weirdling begin			1.50
2,3: 2-Soldiers of Fortune begins. 3-Spitfire			1.50
NOTE: *Kaluta* c-3. **Nebres** a-1-3. **Nino** a-2, 3. **Severin** a-3.			
BOLD STORIES (Also see Candid Tales & It Rhymes With Lust)			
Mar, 1950 - July, 1950 (Digest size, 144 pgs.)			
Kirby Publishing Co.			
Mar issue (Very Rare) - Contains "The Ogre of Paris" by Wood			
	100.00	300.00	800.00
May issue (Very Rare) - Contains "The Cobra's Kiss" by Graham			
Ingels (21 pgs.)	87.00	262.00	700.00
July issue (Very Rare) - Contains "The Ogre of Paris" by Wood			
	75.00	225.00	600.00
BOLT AND STAR FORCE SIX			
1984 ($1.75)			
Americomics			
1-Origin Bolt & Star Force Six		.80	2.00
Special 1 (1984, $2.00, 52pgs., B&W)		.80	2.00
BOMBARDIER (See Bee 29, the Bombardier & Cinema Comics Herald)			
BOMBAST			
1993 ($2.95, one-shot) (Created by Jack Kirby)			
Topps Comics			
1-Polybagged w/Kirbychrome trading card; Savage Dragon app.; Kirby-c;			
has coupon for Amberchrome Secret City Saga #0	1.20		3.00
BOMBA THE JUNGLE BOY (TV)			
Sept-Oct, 1967 - No. 7, Sept-Oct, 1968 (12¢)			
National Periodical Publications			
1-Intro. Bomba; Infantino/Anderson-c	2.40	7.20	17.00
2-7	1.65	4.20	10.00
BOMBER COMICS			
Mar, 1944 - No. 4, Winter, 1944-45			
Elliot Publ. Co./Melverne Herald/Farrell/Sunrise Times			
1-Wonder Boy, & Kismet, Man of Fate begin	44.00	132.00	350.00
2-4: 2-4-Have Classics Comics ad to HRN 20	32.00	96.00	225.00
BONANZA (TV)			
June-Aug, 1960 - No. 37, Aug, 1970 (All Photo-c)			

	GD25	FN65	NM94
Dell/Gold Key			
Four Color 1110 (6-8/60)	35.00	103.00	350.00
Four Color 1221,1283, & #01070-207, 01070-210	17.00	52.00	175.00
1(12/62-Gold Key)	17.00	52.00	175.00
2	7.50	22.50	75.00
3-10	6.50	19.50	65.00
11-20	5.50	16.50	55.00
21-37: 29-Reprints	5.00	15.00	50.00
BONE			
July, 1991 - Present ($2.95, B&W)			
Cartoon Books/Image Comics #21 on			
1-Jeff Smith-c/a in all	30.00	90.00	225.00
1-2nd printing	4.30	13.00	30.00
1-3rd thru 5th printings	1.20	3.00	7.00
2-1st printing	21.00	64.00	175.00
2-2nd & 3rd printings	1.20	3.00	7.00
3-1st printing	16.00	47.00	125.00
3-2nd thru 4th printings	1.20	3.00	7.00
4,5	6.50	19.50	45.00
6-8	4.30	13.00	30.00
9,10	2.15	6.50	15.00
11,12	1.20	3.00	7.00
13-20	1.00	2.00	5.00
13 1/2	2.15	6.50	15.00
13 1/2 (Gold)	2.85	8.50	20.00
21,22: 21-1st Image issue ($2.95)		1.20	4.00
23-25			3.00
1-9-($2.95): 1-Image reprints begin w/new-c. 2-Allred pin-up.			
		1.20	3.00
Holiday Special (1993, giveaway)	1.00	2.00	5.00
Sourcebook-San Diego Edition	1.20	3.00	7.00
Complete Bone Adventures Vol 1 (1993, $12.95, r/#1-6)			
	2.00	5.50	13.00
Complete Bone Adventures Vol 2 (1994, $12.95, r/#7-12)			
	2.00	5.50	13.00
Volume 1 Hardcover-($22.95)-reprints			23.00
Volume 2 Hardcover-($22.95)-reprints			23.00
NOTE: *Printings not listed sell for cover price.*			
BONGO (See Story Hour Series)			
BONGO & LUMPJAW (Disney, see Walt Disney Showcase #3)			
No. 706, June, 1956; No. 886, Mar, 1958			
Dell Publishing Co.			
Four Color 706 (#1)	4.50	13.50	45.00
Four Color 886	3.50	10.50	35.00
BON VOYAGE (See Movie Classics)			
BOOF			
July, 1994 - No. 6, Dec, 1994 ($1.95)			
Image Comics (Todd McFarlane Productions)			
1-6		.80	2.00
BOOF AND THE BRUISE CREW			
July, 1994 - No. 6, Dec, 1994 ($1.95)			
Image Comics (Todd McFarlane Productions)			
1-6		.80	2.00
BOOK AND RECORD SET (See Power Record Comics)			
BOOK OF ALL COMICS			
1945 (196 pgs.)(Inside f/c has Green Publ. blacked out)			
William H. Wise			
nn-Green Mask, Puppeteer & The Bouncer	34.00	103.00	240.00
BOOK OF BALLADS AND SAGAS, THE			

	GD25	FN65	NM94

Oct, 1995 - Present ($2.95/$3.50, B&W)
Green Man Press

1,2: 1-Vess-c/a; Gaiman story.		1.20	3.00
3-$3.50-c begins		1.40	3.50

BOOK OF COMICS, THE
No date (1944) (25¢, 132 pgs.)
William H. Wise

nn-Captain V app.	34.00	103.00	240.00

BOOK OF LOVE (See Fox Giants)

BOOK OF NIGHT, THE
July, 1987 - No. 3, 1987 ($1.75, B&W)
Dark Horse Comics

1-3: Reprints from Epic Illustrated; Vess-a		.75	1.80

BOOK OF THE DEAD
Dec, 1993 - No. 4, Mar, 1994 ($1.75, limited series, 52 pgs.)
Marvel Comics

1-4: 1-Ploog Frankenstein & Morrow Man-Thing-r begin; Wrightson-r/Chamber of Darkness #7. 2-Morrow new painted-c; Chaykin/Morrow Man-Thing; Krigstein-r/Uncanny Tales #54; r/Fear #10. 3-r/Astonishing Tales #10 & Starlin Man-Thing. 3,4-Painted-c		.70	1.75

BOOKS OF MAGIC
1990 - No. 4, 1991 ($3.95, 52 pgs., limited series, mature)
DC Comics

1-Bolton painted-c/a; Phantom Stranger app.; Gaiman scripts in all			
	1.70	5.00	12.00
2,3: 2-John Constantine, Dr. Fate, Spectre, Deadman app. 3-Dr. Occult app.; minor Sandman app.	1.30	3.25	8.00
4-Early Death-c/app. (early 1991)	1.65	4.20	10.00

BOOKS OF MAGIC
May, 1994 - Present ($1.95, mature)
DC Comics (Vertigo)

1-Charles Vess-c	1.00	2.50	5.50
1-Platinum	2.85	8.50	20.00
2,3		1.60	4.00
4-Death app.	1.00	2.00	5.00
5-14; Charles Vess-c			2.50
15-40: 15-$2.50-c begins. 22-Kaluta-c. 25-Death-c/app; Bachalo-c			
	1.00		2.50
Bindings (1995, $12.95, trade paperback)-r/#1-4			13.00
Summonings (1996, $17.50, trade paperback)-r/#5-13, Vertigo Rave #1			
			17.50

BOONDOGGLE
Mar, 1995 - Present ($2.95, B&W)
Knight Press

1-4: Stegelin-c/a/scripts			3.00

BOOSTER GOLD (See Justice League #4)
Feb, 1986 - No. 25, Feb, 1988 (75¢)
DC Comics

1-25: 4-Rose & Thorn app. 6-Origin. 6,7,23-Superman app. 8,9-LSH app. 22-JLI app. 24,25-Millennium tie-in			1.00
NOTE: *Austin* c-22l. *Byrne* c-23l.			

BOOTS AND HER BUDDIES
No. 5, 9/48 - No. 9, 9/49; 12/55 - No. 3, 1956
Standard Comics/Visual Editions/Argo (NEA Service)

5-Strip-r	14.00	43.00	100.00
6,8	10.00	30.00	65.00
7-(Scarce)-Spanking panels(3)	13.50	41.00	95.00
9-(Scarce)-Frazetta-a (2 pgs.)	24.00	73.00	170.00

	GD25	FN65	NM94

1-3(Argo-1955-56)-Reprints	4.25	13.00	28.00

BOOTS & SADDLES (TV)
No. 919, July, 1958; No. 1029, Sept, 1959; No. 1116, Aug, 1960
Dell Publishing Co.

Four Color 919 (#1)-Photo-c	9.00	27.00	80.00
Four Color 1029, 1116-Photo-c	6.00	18.00	54.00

BORDERLINE
June, 1992 ($2.25, B&W)
Friction Press

0-Ashcan edition; 1st app. of Cliff Broadway		.80	2.00
1-Painted-c		1.20	3.00
1-Special Edition (bagged w/ photo, S&N)	1.65	4.20	10.00

BORDER PATROL
May-June, 1951 - No. 3, Sept-Oct, 1951
P. L. Publishing Co.

1	10.00	30.00	65.00
2,3	7.50	22.50	45.00

BORDER WORLDS (Also see Megaton Man)
7/86 - No. 7, 1987; V2#1, 1990 - No. 4, 1990 ($1.95-$2.00, B&W, mature)
Kitchen Sink Press

1-7: ($1.95)-Donald Simpson-c/a/scripts		.80	2.00
V2#1-4 ($2.00)-Donald Simpson-c/a/scripts		.80	2.00

BORIS KARLOFF TALES OF MYSTERY (TV) (...Thriller No. 1,2)
No. 3, April, 1963 - No. 97, Feb, 1980
Gold Key

3-8,10-(Two #5's, 10/63,11/63): 5-(10/63)-11 pgs. Toth-a. 10-Orlando-a			
	2.85	8.50	20.00
9-Wood-a	3.40	10.00	24.00
11-Williamson-a, 8 pgs.; Orlando-a, 5 pgs.	3.40	10.00	24.00
12-Torres, McWilliams-a; Orlando-a(2)	2.60	7.50	18.00
13,14,16-20	2.00	6.00	14.00
15-Crandall	2.30	6.70	16.00
21-Jeff Jones-a(3 pgs.) "The Screaming Skull"	2.30	6.70	16.00
22-30: 23-Reprint; photo-c	1.65	4.20	10.00
31-50: 36-Weiss-a	1.00	2.60	6.00
51-74: 74-Origin & 1st app. Taurus		1.60	4.00
75-97: 80-86-(52 pgs.). 90-r/Torres, McWilliams-a/#12; Morrow-c			
		.80	2.00
Story Digest 1(7/70-Gold Key)-All text	1.30	3.25	8.00

(See Mystery Comics Digest No. 2, 5, 8, 11, 14, 17, 20, 23, 26)
NOTE: *Bolle* a-51-54, 56, 58, 59. *McWilliams* a-12, 14, 18, 19, 72, 80, 81, 93. *Orlando* a-11-15, 21. Reprints: 78, 81-86, 88, 90, 92, 95, 97.

BORIS KARLOFF THRILLER (TV) (Becomes Boris Karloff Tales...)
Oct, 1962 - No. 2, Jan, 1963 (80 pgs.)
Gold Key

1-Photo-c	5.50	16.50	55.00
2	4.00	12.00	40.00

BORIS THE BEAR INSTANT COLOR CLASSICS
July, 1987 - No. 3, 1987 ($1.75/$1.95)
Dark Horse Comics

1-3		.80	2.00

BORN AGAIN
1978 (39¢)
Spire Christian Comics (Fleming H. Revell Co.)

nn-Watergate, Nixon, etc.			1.00

BOUNCER, THE (Formerly Green Mask #9)
1944 - No. 14, Jan, 1945
Fox Features Syndicate

nn(1944, #10?)	21.00	64.00	150.00

Boy Comics #5 © LEV

Boy Commandos #17 © DC

Boy Meets Girl #23 © LEV

	GD25	FN65	NM94		GD25	FN65	NM94

11(#1)(9/44)-Origin; Rocket Kelly, One Round Hogan app.

	18.00	54.00	125.00
12-14: 14-Reprints no # issue	14.00	43.00	100.00

BOUNTY GUNS (See Luke Short's..., Four Color 739)

BOY AND HIS 'BOT, A
Jan, 1987 ($1.95)
Now Comics

1-A Holiday Special		.80	2.00

BOY AND THE PIRATES, THE (Movie)
No. 1117, Aug, 1960
Dell Publishing Co.

Four Color 1117-Photo-c	7.00	21.00	70.00

BOY COMICS (Captain Battle No. 1 & 2; Boy Illustories No. 43-108)
(Stories by Charles Biro)(Also see Squeeks)
No. 3, Apr, 1942 - No. 119, Mar, 1956
Lev Gleason Publications (Comic House)

3(No.1)-Origin Crimebuster, Bombshell & Young Robin Hood; Yankee
Longabo, Case 1001-1008, Swoop Storm, & Boy Movies begin; 1st app.
Iron Jaw; Crimebuster's pet monkey Squeeks begins

	250.00	750.00	2000.00
4-Hitler, Tojo, Mussolini-c	100.00	300.00	800.00
5	75.00	225.00	600.00
6-Origin Iron Jaw; origin & death of Iron Jaw's son; Little Dynamite begins,			
ends #39; 1st Iron Jaw-c	187.00	562.00	1500.00
7-Flag & Hitler, Tojo, Mussolini-c	68.00	206.00	550.00
8-Death of Iron Jaw; Iron Jaw-c	75.00	225.00	600.00
9-Iron Jaw-c	68.00	206.00	550.00
10-Return of Iron Jaw; classic Biro-c; Iron Jaw-c	100.00	300.00	800.00
11-Classic Iron Jaw-c	65.00	195.00	525.00
12,13	47.00	141.00	375.00
14-Iron Jaw-c	50.00	150.00	400.00
15-Death of Iron Jaw	62.00	187.00	500.00
16,18-20	31.00	94.00	220.00
17-Flag-c	36.00	107.00	250.00
21-29,31,32-(All 68 pgs.). 28-Yankee Longabo ends. 32-Swoop Storm			
& Young Robin Hood	22.00	66.00	155.00
30-(68 pgs.)-Origin Crimebuster retold	31.00	94.00	220.00
33-40: 34-Crimebuster story(2); suicide-c/story	16.00	47.00	110.00
41-50	13.50	41.00	95.00
51-59: 57-Dilly Duncan begins, ends #71	12.00	36.00	85.00
60-Iron Jaw returns	13.50	41.00	95.00
61-Origin Crimebuster & Iron Jaw retold	16.00	47.00	110.00
62-Death of Iron Jaw explained	14.00	43.00	100.00
63-73: 63-McWilliams-a. 73-Frazetta 1-pg. ad	10.00	30.00	70.00
74-88: 80-1st app. Rocky X of the Rocketeers; becomes "Rocky X" #101; Iron			
Jaw, Sniffer & the Deadly Dozen in 80-118	10.00	30.00	60.00
89-92-The Claw serial app. in all	10.00	30.00	65.00
93-Claw cameo; Rocky X by Sid Check	10.00	30.00	60.00
94-97,99	9.15	27.00	55.00
98-Rocky X by Sid Check	10.00	30.00	60.00
100	10.00	30.00	60.00
101-107,109,111,119: 111-Crimebuster becomes Chuck Chandler. 119-Last			
Crimebuster	7.50	22.50	45.00
108,110,112-118-Kubert-a	9.15	27.00	55.00

(See Giant Boy Book of Comics)
NOTE: Boy Movies in 3-5,40,41. Iron Jaw app.-3, 4, 6, 8, 10, 11, 13-15; returns-60-62, 68, 69,
72-79, 81-118. Biro c-all. Briefer a-5, 13, 14, 16-20 among others. Fuje a-55, 18 pgs. Palais a-
14, 16, 17, 19, 20 among others.

BOY COMMANDOS (See Detective #64 & World's Finest Comics #8)
Winter, 1942-43 - No. 36, Nov-Dec, 1949
National Periodical Publications

1-Origin Liberty Belle; The Sandman & The Newsboy Legion x-over in Boy

Commandos; S&K-a, 48 pgs.; S&K cameo? (classic-c)

	400.00	1200.00	4000.00
2-Last Liberty Belle; Hitler-c; S&K-a, 46 pgs.	125.00	375.00	1000.00
3-S&K-a, 45 pgs.	87.00	262.00	700.00
4-6: 6-S&K-a	62.00	187.00	500.00
7-10	44.00	132.00	350.00
11-Infinity-c	32.00	96.00	225.00
12-16,18-19-More S&K	25.00	75.00	175.00
17,20-Sci/fi-c/stories	27.00	81.00	190.00
21,22,24,25: 22-Judy Canova x-over. 24-1st costumed superhero satire-c.			
(11-12/47).	19.00	58.00	135.00
23-S&K-c/a(all)	23.00	69.00	160.00
26-Flying Saucer story (3-4/48)-4th of this theme	20.00	60.00	140.00
27,28,30: 30-Cleveland Indians story	19.00	56.00	130.00
29-S&K story (1)	21.00	62.00	145.00
31-35: 32-Dale Evans app. on-c & in story. 34-Intro. Wolf, their mascot			
	18.00	54.00	125.00
36-Intro The Atomobile c/sci-fi story (Scarce)	29.00	86.00	200.00

NOTE: Most issues signed by Simon & Kirby are not by them. S&K c-1-9, 13, 14, 17, 21, 23,
24, 30-32. Feller c-30.

BOY COMMANDOS
Sept-Oct, 1973 - No. 2, Nov-Dec, 1973 (G.A. S&K reprints)
National Periodical Publications

1,2: 1-Reprints story from Boy Commandos #1 plus-c & Detective #66 by			
S&K. 2-Infantino/Orlando-c		.80	2.00

BOY COWBOY (Also see Amazing Adventures & Science Comics)
1950 (8 pgs. in color)
Ziff-Davis Publ. Co.

nn-Sent to subscribers of Ziff-Davis mags. & ordered through mail for 10¢;			
used to test market for Kid Cowboy			
Estimated value		150.00	

BOY DETECTIVE
May-June, 1951 - No. 4, May, 1952
Avon Periodicals

1	15.00	45.00	105.00
2,3: 3-Kinstler-c	10.00	30.00	60.00
4-Kinstler-c	13.00	39.00	90.00

BOY EXPLORERS COMICS (Terry and The Pirates No. 3 on)
May-June, 1946 - No. 2, Sept-Oct, 1946
Family Comics (Harvey Publications)

1-Intro The Explorers, Duke of Broadway, Calamity Jane & Danny Dixon...			
Cadet; S&K-c/a, 24 pgs.	53.00	160.00	425.00
2-(Scarce)-Small size (5-1/2x8-1/2"; B&W; 32 pgs.) Distributed to mail			
subscribers only; S&K-a Estimated value		$250.00-$400.00	

(Also see All New No. 15, Flash Gordon No. 5, and Stuntman No. 3)

BOY ILLUSTORIES (See Boy Comics)

BOY LOVES GIRL (Boy Meets Girl No. 1-24)
No. 25, July, 1952 - No. 57, June, 1956
Lev Gleason Publications

25(#1)	5.85	17.50	35.00
26,27,29-33: 30-33-Serial, 'Loves of My Life	4.00	10.00	20.00
34-42: 39-Lingerie panels	3.60	9.00	18.00
28-Drug propaganda story	4.15	12.50	25.00
43-Toth-a	5.85	17.50	35.00
44-50: 50-Last pre-code (2/55)	2.80	7.00	14.00
51-57: 57-Ann Brewster-a	2.00	5.00	10.00

BOY MEETS GIRL (Boy Loves Girl No. 25 on)
Feb, 1950 - No. 24, June, 1952 (No. 1-17: 52 pgs.)
Lev Gleason Publications

1-Guardineer-a	7.50	22.50	45.00
2	4.15	12.50	25.00

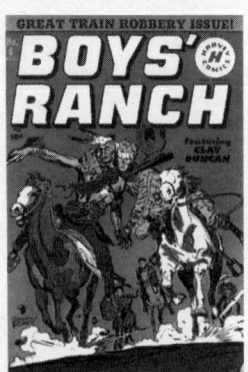

Boy's Ranch #4 © HARV

Bram Stoker's Dracula #1 © TOPPS

Brave and the Bold #33 © DC

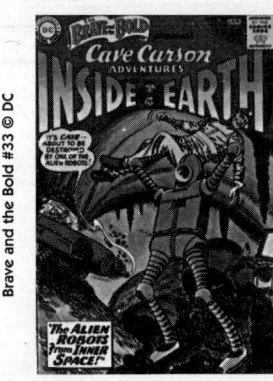

	GD25	FN65	NM94
3-10	4.00	11.00	22.00
11-24	3.60	9.00	18.00

NOTE: *Briefer* a-24. *Fuje* c-3,7. Painted-c 1-17. Photo-c 19-21, 23.

BOYS' AND GIRLS' MARCH OF COMICS (See March of Comics)

BOYS' RANCH (Also see Western Tales & Witches' Western Tales)
Oct, 1950 - No. 6, Aug, 1951 (No.1-3, 52 pgs.; No. 4-6, 36 pgs.)
Harvey Publications

	GD25	FN65	NM94
1-S&K-c/a(3)	53.00	160.00	425.00
2-S&K-c/a(3)	40.00	120.00	325.00
3-S&K-c/a(2); Meskin-a	40.00	120.00	290.00
4-S&K-c/a, 5 pgs.	36.00	107.00	250.00
5,6-S&K-c, splashes & centerspread only; Meskin-a	20.00	60.00	140.00
Shoe Store Giveaway #5,6 (Identical to regular issues except S&K centerfold replaced with ad)	19.00	56.00	130.00

BOZO (Larry Harmon's Bozo, the World's Most Famous Clown)
1992 ($6.95, 68 pgs.)
Innovation Publishing

	GD25	FN65	NM94
1-Reprints Four Color #285(#1)	1.20	3.00	7.00

BOZO THE CLOWN (TV) (Bozo No. 7 on)
July, 1950 - No. 4, Oct-Dec, 1963
Dell Publishing Co.

	GD25	FN65	NM94
Four Color 285(#1)	18.00	54.00	180.00
2(7-9/51)-7(10-12/52)	11.00	32.00	110.00
Four Color 464,508,551,594(10/54)	11.00	32.00	110.00
1(nn, 5-7/62) - 4(1963)	7.00	21.00	70.00
Giveaway-1961, 16 pgs., 3-1/2x7-1/4", Apsco Products	3.50	10.50	35.00

BOZZ CHRONICLES, THE
Dec, 1985 - No. 6, 1986 (Limited series, mature)
Marvel Comics (Epic Comics)

1-6			1.50

BRADY BUNCH, THE (TV)(See Kite Fun Book and Binky #78)
Feb, 1970 - No. 2, May, 1970
Dell Publishing Co.

	GD25	FN65	NM94
1,2	6.00	18.00	60.00

BRAIN, THE
Sept, 1956 - No. 7, 1958
Sussex Publ. Co./Magazine Enterprises

	GD25	FN65	NM94
1-Dan DeCarlo-a in all including reprints	6.70	20.00	40.00
2,3	4.00	11.00	22.00
4-7	3.20	8.00	16.00
I.W. Reprints #1-4,8-10('63),14: 2-Reprints Sussex #2 with new cover added	1.30	3.25	8.00
Super Reprint #17,18(nd)	1.30	3.25	8.00

BRAIN BOY
Apr-June, 1962 - No. 6, Sept-Nov, 1963 (Painted c-#5,6)
Dell Publishing Co.

	GD25	FN65	NM94
Four Color 1330(#1)-Gil Kane-a; origin	13.00	40.00	135.00
2(7-9/62),3-6: 4-Origin retold	7.00	21.00	75.00

BRAM STOKER'S BURIAL OF THE RATS (Movie)
Apr, 1995 - No.3, June, 1995 ($2.50)
Roger Corman's Cosmic Comics

1-3: Adaptation of film; Jerry Prosser scripts		1.00	2.50

BRAM STOKER'S DRACULA (Movie)(Also see Dracula: Vlad the Impaler)
Oct, 1992 - No. 4, Jan, 1993 ($2.95, limited series, polybagged)
Topps Comics

1-Adaptation of film begins; Mignola-c/a in all; 4 trading cards & poster;

	GD25	FN65	NM94
photo scenes of movie		1.20	3.00
1-2nd printing		1.20	3.00
1-Crimson foil edition (limited to 500)	3.50	11.00	25.00
2-Bound-in poster & cards		1.20	3.00
3,4: 4 trading cards in both. 3-Contains coupon to win 1 of 500 crimson foil-c edition of #1. 4-Contains coupon to win 1 of 500 uncut sheets of all 16 trading cards		1.20	3.00
3,4-Without coupon		1.20	3.00

BRAND ECHH (See Not Brand Echh)

BRAND OF EMPIRE (See Luke Short's...Four Color 771)

BRATS BIZZARE
1994 - No. 4, 1994 ($2.50, limited series)
Marvel Comics (Epic Comics/Heavy Hitters)

1-4: All w/bound-in trading cards		1.00	2.50

BRAVADOS, THE (See Wild Western Action)
Aug, 1971 (52 pgs., one-shot)
Skywald Publ. Corp.

	GD25	FN65	NM94
1-Red Mask, The Durango Kid, Billy Nevada-r	.30	.75	1.50

BRAVE AND THE BOLD, THE (See Best Of... & Super DC Giant) (Replaced Batman & The Outsiders)
Aug-Sept, 1955 - No. 200, July, 1983
National Periodical Publications/DC Comics

	GD25	FN65	NM94
1-Viking Prince by Kubert, Silent Knight, Golden Gladiator begin; part Kubert-c	230.00	690.00	2500.00
2	110.00	330.00	1100.00
3,4	66.00	197.00	575.00
5-Robin Hood begins (4-5/56, 1st DC app.), ends #15; see Robin Hood Tales #7	68.00	202.00	600.00
6-10: 6-Robin Hood by Kubert; last Golden Gladiator app.; Silent Knight; no Viking Prince. 8-1st S.A. issue	45.00	135.00	400.00
11-22,24: 12,14-Robin Hood-c. 18,21-23-Grey tone-c. 22-Last Silent Knight. 24-Last Viking Prince by Kubert (2nd solo book)	38.00	114.00	300.00
23-Viking Prince origin by Kubert; 1st B&B single theme issue & 1st Viking Prince solo book	45.00	135.00	400.00
25-1st app. Suicide Squad (8-9/59)	40.00	120.00	325.00
26,27-Suicide Squad	37.00	111.00	280.00

	GD25	FN65	VF82	NM94
28-(2-3/60)-Justice League intro./1st app.; origin/1st app. Snapper Carr	358.00	1075.00	2688.00	4800.00
29-Justice League (4-5/60)-2nd app.	210.00	630.00	1365.00	2200.00
30-Justice League (6-7/60)-3rd app.	170.00	510.00	1105.00	1800.00

	GD25	FN65	NM94
31-1st app. Cave Carson (8-9/60); scarce in high grade; 1st try-out series	39.00	118.00	300.00
32,33-Cave Carson	27.00	81.00	210.00

	GD25	FN65	VF82	NM94
34-Origin/1st app. Silver-Age Hawkman, Hawkgirl & Byth by Kubert (2-3/61); 1st S.A. Hawkman tryout series; all predate Hawkman #1	165.00	495.00	1073.00	1800.00

	GD25	FN65	NM94
35-Hawkman by Kubert (4-5/61)-2nd app.	60.00	180.00	485.00
36-Hawkman by Kubert; origin & 1st app. Shadow Thief (6-7/61)-3rd app.	51.00	153.00	410.00
37-Suicide Squad (2nd tryout series)	34.00	103.00	250.00
38,39-Suicide Squad. 38-Last 10¢ issue	30.00	90.00	220.00
40,41-Cave Carson Inside Earth (2nd try-out series). 40-Kubert-a. 41-Meskin-a	21.00	62.00	150.00
42-Hawkman by Kubert (2nd tryout series)	39.00	118.00	285.00
43-Hawkman by Kubert; more detailed origin	40.00	120.00	330.00
44-Hawkman by Kubert; grey-tone-c	32.00	96.00	230.00
45-49-Strange Sports Stories by Infantino	8.75	26.00	70.00

50-The Green Arrow & Manhunter From Mars (10-11/63); 1st Manhunter x-over

Brave And The Bold #44 © DC

Brave And The Bold #154 © DC

Brave And The Bold #195 © DC

	GD25	FN65	NM94
outside of Detective (pre-dates House of Mystery #143); team-ups begin	23.00	69.00	165.00
51-Aquaman & Hawkman (12-1/63-64); pre-dates Hawkman #1	32.00	96.00	235.00
52-(2-3/64)-3 Battle Stars; Sgt. Rock, Haunted Tank, Johnny Cloud, & Mlle. Marie team-up for 1st time by Kubert (c/a)	15.00	45.00	115.00
53-Atom & The Flash by Toth	8.50	26.00	65.00
54-Kid Flash, Robin & Aqualad; 1st app./origin Teen Titans (6-7/64)	35.00	105.00	260.00
55-Metal Men & The Atom	6.00	18.00	45.00
56-The Flash & Manhunter From Mars	6.00	18.00	45.00
57-Origin & 1st app. Metamorpho (12-1/64-65)	19.00	58.00	140.00
58-2nd app. Metamorpho by Fradon	9.30	28.00	70.00
59-Batman & Green Lantern; 1st Batman team-up in Brave and the Bold	13.50	41.00	100.00
60-Teen Titans (2nd app.)-1st app. new Wonder Girl (Donna Troy), who joins Titans (6-7/65)	11.00	33.00	80.00
61,62-Origin Starman & Black Canary by Anderson. 62-1st S.A. app. Wildcat (10-11/65); 1st S.A. app. of G.A. Huntress	13.00	39.00	100.00
63-Supergirl & Wonder Woman	4.50	13.00	35.00
64-Batman Versus Eclipso (see H.O.S. #61)	8.00	23.00	55.00
65-Flash & Doom Patrol (4-5/66)	2.30	6.70	20.00
66-Metamorpho & Metal Men (6-7/66)	2.85	8.50	20.00
67-Batman & The Flash by Infantino; Batman team-ups begin, end #200 (8-9/66)	5.00	15.50	40.00
68-Batman/Metamorpho/Joker/Riddler/Penguin-c/story; Batman as Bat-Hulk (Hulk parody)	8.00	24.00	58.00
69-Batman & Green Lantern	3.75	11.25	28.00
70-Batman & Hawkman; Craig-a(p)	3.75	11.25	28.00
71-Batman & Green Arrow	3.75	11.25	28.00
72-Spectre & Flash (6-7/67); 4th app. The Spectre; predates Spectre #1	3.75	11.25	28.00
73-Aquaman & The Atom	3.60	11.00	25.00
74-Batman & Metal Men	3.60	11.00	25.00
75-Batman & The Spectre (12-1/67-68); 6th app.; came out between Spectre #1 & #2	3.70	11.00	28.00
76-Batman & Plastic Man (2-3/68); came out between Plastic Man #8 & #9	3.60	11.00	25.00
77-Batman & The Atom	3.60	11.00	25.00
78-Batman, Wonder Woman & Batgirl	3.60	11.00	25.00
79-Batman & Deadman by Neal Adams (8-9/68); early Deadman app.	5.70	17.00	45.00
80-Batman & Creeper (10-11/68); N. Adams-a; early app. The Creeper; came out between Creeper #3 & #4	5.00	15.50	36.00
81-Batman & Flash; N. Adams-a	5.00	15.50	36.00
82-Batman & Aquaman; N. Adams-a; origin Ocean Master retold (2-3/69)	5.00	15.50	40.00
83-Batman & Teen Titans; N. Adams-a (4-5/69); last 12¢ issue	6.35	19.00	46.00
84-Batman (G.A., 1st S.A. app.) & Sgt. Rock; N. Adams-a	5.00	15.00	37.00
85-Batman & Green Arrow; 1st new costume for Green Arrow by Neal Adams (8-9/69)	5.00	15.00	37.00
86-Batman & Deadman (10-11/69); N. Adams-a; story concludes from Strange Adventures #216 (1-2/69)	5.00	15.00	38.00
87-Batman & Wonder Woman	3.25	9.50	22.00
88-Batman & Wildcat	3.25	9.50	22.00
89-Batman & Phantom Stranger (4-5/70); early Phantom Stranger app. (came out between Phantom Stranger #6 & 7	3.25	9.50	22.00
90-Batman & Adam Strange	3.25	9.50	22.00
91-Batman & Black Canary (8-9/70)	3.25	9.50	22.00
92-Batman; intro the Bat Squad			
93-Batman-House of Mystery; N. Adams-a	4.50	13.00	35.00
94-Batman-Teen Titans	2.15	6.50	15.00

	GD25	FN65	NM94
95-Batman & Plastic Man	2.00	6.00	14.00
96-Batman & Sgt. Rock	2.15	6.50	15.00
97-Batman & Wildcat; 52 pg. issues begin, end #102; reprints origin & 1st app. Deadman from Strange Advs. #205	1.70	5.00	12.00
98-Batman & Phantom Stranger; 1st Jim Aparo Batman-a?	1.70	5.00	12.00
99-Batman & Flash	1.70	5.00	12.00
100-(2-3/72, 25¢, 52 pgs.)-Batman-Gr. Lantern-Gr. Arrow-Black Canary-Robin; Deadman-r by Adams/Str. Advs. #210	4.50	13.00	35.00
101-Batman & Metamorpho; Kubert Viking Prince	1.00	2.60	6.00
102-Batman-Teen Titans; N. Adams-a(p)	1.65	4.20	10.00
103-110: Batman team-ups: 103-Metal Men. 104-Deadman. 105-Wonder Woman. 106-Green Arrow. 107-Black Canary. 108-Sgt. Rock. 109-Demon. 110-Wildcat	1.00	2.60	6.00
111-Batman/Joker-c/story	1.60	4.70	11.00
112-117: All 100 pgs.; Batman team-ups: 112-Mr. Miracle. 113-Metal Men; reprints origin/1st Hawkman from Brave and the Bold #34; r/origin Multi-Man/Challengers #14. 114-Aquaman. 115-Atom; r/origin Viking Prince from #23; r/Dr. Fate/Hourman/Solomon Grundy/Green Lantern from Showcase #55. 116-Spectre. 117-Sgt. Rock; last 100 pg. issue	1.30	3.25	8.00
118-Batman/Wildcat/Joker-c/story	1.70	5.00	12.00
119-128,132-140: Batman team-ups: 119-Man-Bat. 120-Kamandi(68 pgs.). 121-Metal Men. 122-Swamp Thing. 123-Plastic Man/Metamorpho. 124-Sgt. Rock. 125-Flash. 126-Aquaman. 127-Wildcat. 128-Mr. Miracle. 132-Kung-Fu Fighter. 133-Deadman. 134-Green Lantern. 135-Metal Men. 136-Metal Men/Green Arrow. 137-Demon. 138-Mr. Miracle. 139-Hawkman. 140-Wonder Woman	1.60		4.00
129,130-Batman/Green Arrow/Atom parts 1 & 2; Joker & Two Face-c/stories	1.70		12.00
131-Batman & Wonder Woman vs. Catwoman-c/sty	1.20	3.00	7.00
141-Batman/Black Canary vs. Joker-c/story	1.70	5.00	12.00
142-190,192-199: Batman team-ups: 142-Aquaman. 143-Creeper; origin Human Target (44 pgs.). 144-Green Arrow; origin Human Target part 2 (44 pgs.). 145-Phantom Stranger. 146-G.A. Batman/Unknown Soldier. 147-Supergirl. 148-Plastic Man. X-Mas-c. 149-Teen Titans. 150-Anniversary issue; Superman. 151-Flash. 152-Atom. 153-Red Tornado. 154-Metamorpho. 155-Green Lantern. 156-Dr. Fate. 157-Batman vs. Kamandi (ties into Kamandi #59). 158-Wonder Woman. 159-Ra's Al Ghul. 160-Supergirl. 161-Adam Strange. 162-G.A. Batman/Sgt. Rock. 163-Black Lightning. 164-Hawkman. 165-Man-Bat. 166-Black Canary; Nemesis (intro) back-up story begins, ends #192; Penguin-c/story. 167-G.A. Batman/Blackhawk; origin Nemesis. 168-Green Arrow. 169-Zatanna. 170-Nemesis. 171-Scalphunter. 172-Firestorm. 173-Guardians of the Universe. 174-Green Lantern. 175-Lois Lane. 176-Swamp Thing. 177-Elongated Man. 178-Creeper. 179-Legion. 180-Spectre. 181-Hawk & Dove. 182-G.A. Robin; G.A. Starman app.; 1st modern app. G.A. Batwoman. 183-Riddler. 184-Huntress. 185-Green Arrow. 186-Hawkman. 187-Metal Men. ,188,189-Rose & the Thorn. 190-Adam Strange. 192-Superboy vs. Mr. I.Q. 193-Nemesis. 194-Flash. 195-I... Vampire. 196-Ragman; origin Ragman retold. 197-Catwoman; Earth II Batman & Catwoman marry; 2nd modern app. of G.A. Batwoman. 198-Karate Kid. 199-Batman vs. The Spectre	1.40		3.50
191-Batman/Joker-c/story; Nemesis app.	1.30	3.25	8.00
200-Double-sized (64 pgs.); printed on Mando paper; Earth One & Earth Two Batman app. in separate stories; 1st app. Batman & The Outsiders	1.50	3.75	9.00

NOTE: **Neal Adams** a-79-86, 93, 100r, 102; c-75, 76, 79-86, 88-90, 93, 95, 99, 100r. **M. Anderson** a-115r; c-72i, 96i. **Andru/Esposito** c-25-27. **Aparo** a-98, 100-102, 104-125, 126i, 127-136, 138-145, 147, 148, 149-152, 154, 155, 157-162, 168-170, 173-178, 180-182, 184, 186i-189i, 191i-193i, 195, 196, 200; c-105-109, 111-136, 137i, 138-175, 177, 180-184, 186-200. **Austin** a-166i. **Bernard Baily** c-32, 33, 58. **Buckler** a-185, 186p; c-137, 178p, 185p, 186p. **Giordano** a-143, 144. **Infantino** a-67p, 72p, 97r, 98r, 115r, 172p, 183p, 190p, 194p; c-45-49, 67p, 69p, 70p, 72p, 96p, 98r. **Kaluta** c-51r; c-59, 64. **Kubert** a-52, 53, 58; **&/or Heath** a-124; reprints-101, 113, 115, 117. **Kubert** a-99r; c-22-24, 34-36, 40, 42-44, 52. **Mooney** a-114r. **Mortimer** a-54r. **Newton** a-153p, 156p, 165p. **Irv Novick** c-1(part), 2-21. **Fred Ray** a-78r. **Roussos** a-50, 76i, 114r. **Staton** 148p. 52pg.-97, 100; 68 pgs.-120; 100 pgs.-112-117.

BRAVE AND THE BOLD, THE

Campus Loves #3 © QUA

Buster Crabbe #5 © F..

Buddies in the U. S. Army #1 © AVON

Brigade #20 © Rob Liefeld

Ajax/Fi...

1-6: Post-c/a(p); f...

CAMP COMICS
Feb, 1942 - No. 3,
Dell Publishing Co...

1- "Seaman Sy W...
adaptation
2-Kelly-a, 12 pg...
3-(Scarce)-Dave...

CAMP RUNAMUC...
Apr, 1966
Dell Publishing Co...

1-Photo-c

CAMPUS LOVES...
Dec, 1949 - No. 5...
Quality Comics G...

1-Ward-c/a (9 pg...
2-Ward-c/a
3-5: 5-Spanking...
NOTE: **Gustavson a...**

CAMPUS ROMA...
Sept-Oct, 1949 -...
Avon Periodicals...

1-Walter Johnso...
2-Grandenetti-a...

3-c/Avon paper...
Realistic reprint...

CANADA DRY P...

CANCELLED C...
Summer, 1978 - ...
(Xeroxed pgs. o...
DC Comics, Inc...

1-(412 pgs.) Con...
14; The Deserter #...
2-(532 pgs.) Con...
#5; Shade #9 (ori...
Vixen #1; and cove...
Classics #3, Mr. M...
(Rare)
NOTE: In June, 19...
lished edition in gr...
buted. Only 35 cop...

CANDID TALE...
April, 1950; Jun...
Kirby Publishing...

nn-(Scarce) Co...
issue; Powe...
NOTE: Another ve...

CANDY
Fall, 1944 - No...
William H. Wis...

1-Two Scoop...
2,3-Scoop S...

CANDY (Teen...
Autumn, 1947...
Quality Comic...

1-Gustavson...
2-Gustavson...
3-10
11-30

Giant Mc...
cover...
NOTE: **Bo...**

BUSTE...
Nov, 19...
Famou...

1-1st...
Kid...
2-Will...

3-Will...
4-Fra...
5-Fra...

6,8
7-Fra...
9-One...
10-12...
NOTE: E...

BUSTE...
Dec, 19...
Lev Gle...

1,4: 1...
2,3-To...

June, 1...
Skywal...

1-Red...
2,3: 2...
Sun...

1-Lawrence...
2-Mort La...

1951
Avon P...

1-Kins...
NOTE: E...

BUTCH...

BUTCH...

June, 1...
DC Cor...

1-5: 1-...

BUZ SA...
June, 1...
Standa...

1-Roy...
2-Intro...
3

BUZ SA...
May, 1...
Horse F...

1-Paul...

BUZZY
Winter,...
Nationa...

1 (52...
Sept,...
Charlton...

BUCK R...
1990 - N...
TSR, Inc....

1-5 (199...
up sto...
Image...

BUCKSK...
No. 1011,...
Dell Publi...

Four Colo...
1988 ($5.9...
Continuity...

1-Michae...
Image...

BUCKY O...
Continuity...

1-6: 1-Mic...

BUDDIES...
Nov, 1952...
Avon Perio...

BUFFALO...
Dell Publish...

BUFFALO...
No. 2, Oct...
Youthful Ma...
Larg...
Four...

BUFFALO...
Dec,...
High...

BUFFALO...
Jan, 1956 -...
Dell Publishi...
1,2...
Holi...

BRID...
Four Color 6...
Four Color 7...

BRI...
1,2-Wildey...

BRI...

BRIDE...
Aug, 1...

BRIGA...
Image...

V2#1,...
Image...

V2#1...

BRIG...

1-Frank...
2
3-16:...

3-6: L...
7-11,...
12-Di...

BRIDE...

1-Lie...
3-Co...
4-Fli...

2-Wi...
3-Co...

1-Go...
2-Co...

Caged Heat 3000 #2 © Roger Corman

Captain America #278 © MEG

Captain America #453 © MEG

Captain America V2#1 © MEG

GD25 FN65 NM94

GD25 FN65 NM94

CAGE (Also s...
Apr, 1992 - N...
Marvel Comic...

1-($1.50)-Ha...
2-11,13-20:...
Rhino & H...
12-($1.75, 5...

CAGED HEA...
Nov, 1995 - ...
Roger Corma...

1-3: Adapta...

CAGES
1991 - No. 1...
Tundra Publ...

1-Dave Mc...
2-Misprint...
3-9: 5-$3.9...
10-($4.95)...

CAIN'S HU...
May-July, 1...
Dell Publis...

nn(01-094-...
2

CAIN/VAM...
Oct, 1994 ...
Harris Con...

nn-contain...
Fearbo...

CALIBER...
Jan, 1989...
Caliber Pr...

1-Antholo...
2-Deadwo...
3-14: 9-...
15-24 ($...

CALIBER...
1994 ($2...
Caliber P...

1

CALIBE...
May, 199...
Caliber F...

1-Kabu...

CALIBR...
1996 - F...
Caliber...

1,2: 1-...

CALIFO...
June, 1...
Eclipse...

1-8: A...

CALL I...
1952 (...
Catech...

nn

CALLI...
Jan, 19...

Team-Up, Marvel Treasury Special, Power Record Comics, USA Comics, Young Allies & Young Men)

CAPTAIN AMERICA (Formerly Tales of Suspense #1-99) (Captain America and the Falcon #134-223 & Steve Rogers: Captain America #444-454 appears on cover only)
No. 100, Apr, 1968 - No. 454, Aug, 1996
Marvel Comics Group

	GD25	FN65	NM94
100-Flashback on Cap's revival with Avengers & Sub-Mariner; story continued from Tales of Suspense #99; Kirby-c/a begins	40.00	120.00	325.00
101-The Sleeper-c/story; Red Skull app.	11.50	34.00	85.00
102-108: 102-Sleeper-c/s. 103,104-Red Skull-c/sty	6.15	18.50	45.00
109-Origin Capt. America retold	10.00	30.00	75.00
110,111,113-Classic Steranko-c/a: 110-Rick becomes Cap's partner; Hulk x-over; 1st app. Viper. 111-Death of Steve Rogers. 113-Cap's funeral	9.30	28.00	70.00
112-Origin retold; last Kirby-c/a	4.50	13.00	35.00
114-116,118-120: 115-Last 12¢ issue	3.60	11.00	25.00
117-1st app. The Falcon (9/69)	4.50	13.00	35.00
121-140: 121-Retells origin. 133-The Falcon becomes Cap's partner; origin Modok. 137,138-Spider-Man x-over. 140-Origin Grey Gargoyle retold	1.65	4.20	10.00
141-153,155-171,176-179: 142-Last 15¢ issue. 143-(52 pgs.) 144-New costume Falcon. 153-1st app. (cameo) Jack Monroe. 155-Origin; redrawn w/Falcon added; origin J. Monroe. 158-Cap's strength increased. 160-1st app. Solarr. 164-1st app. Nightshade. 176-End of Capt. America.	1.20	3.00	7.00
154-1st full app. Jack Monroe (Nomad)(10/72)	1.20	3.00	7.00
172-175-X-Men x-over	2.15	6.50	15.00
180-Intro/origin of Nomad (Steve Rogers)	1.30	3.25	8.00
181-Intro/origin new Cap.	1.00	2.60	6.00
182,184-200(8/76): 186-True origin The Falcon		1.60	4.00
183-Death of new Cap; Nomad becomes Cap	1.00	2.60	6.00
201-240,242-246: 215-Retells Cap's origin. 216-r/story from Strange Tales #114. 217-1st app. Marvel Man (later Quasar). 229-Marvel Man app. 230-Battles Hulk-c/story cont'd in Hulk #232. 233-Death of Sharon Carter. 234,235-Daredevil x-over; 235(7/79)-Miller-a(p). 244,245-Miller-c.	1.20		3.00
241-Punisher app.; Miller-c.	3.60	11.00	25.00
241-2nd print		.80	2.00
247-255-Byrne-a. 255-Origin; Miller-c.		1.40	3.50
256-281,284,285,289-322,324-326,329-331: 264-Old X-Men cameo in flashback. 265,266-Nick Fury & Spider-Man app. 267-1st app. Everyman. 269-1st Team America. 279-(3/83)-Contains Tattooz skin decals. 281-1950s Bucky returns. 284-Patriot (Jack Mace) app. 285-Death of Patriot. 298-Origin Red Skull		.80	2.00
282-Bucky becomes new Nomad (Jack Monroe)	1.30	3.25	8.00
282-Silver ink 2nd print ($1.75) w/original date (6/83)		.70	1.75
283-2nd print		1.60	4.00
286-288-Deathlok app.		1.00	2.50
323-1st app. new Super Patriot (see Nick Fury)		1.60	4.00
327-Captain America battles Super Patriot		1.20	3.00
328-Origin all app. D-Man		1.00	2.50
332-Old Cap resigns	1.30	3.25	8.00
333-Intro & origin new Captain (Super Patriot)	1.20	3.00	7.00
334-340: 339-Fall of the Mutants tie-in	1.00	2.00	5.00
341-343,345-349		.60	1.50
344-($1.50, 52 pgs.)-Ronald Reagan cameo		.80	1.90
350-($1.75, 68 pgs.)-Return of Steve Rogers (original Cap) to original costume	1.60		4.00
351-354: 351-Nick Fury app. 354-1st app. U.S. Agent (6/89, see Avengers West Coast)			1.50
355-382,384-396: 373-Bullseye app. 375-Daredevil app. 386-U.S. Agent app. 387-389-Red Skull back-up stories. 396-Last $1.00-c. 396,397-1st app. all new Jack O'Lantern			1.50
383-($2.00, 68 pgs.)-50th anniversary issue; Red Skull story; Jim Lee-c(i)			

	GD25	FN65	NM94
397-399,401-424,426: 402-Begin 6 part Man-Wolf story w/Wolverine in #403-407. 405-410-New Jack O'Lantern app. in back-up story. 406-Cable & Shatterstar cameo. 407-Capwolf vs. Cable-c/story. 408-Infinity War x-over; Falcon solo back-up. 423-Vs. Namor-c/story	1.60		4.00
			1.25
400-($2.25, 84 pgs.)-Flip book format w/double gatefold-c; r/Avengers #4 plus-c; contains cover pin-ups.	1.20		3.00
425-($2.95, 52 pgs.)-Embossed Foil-c edition; Fighting Chance Pt. 1	1.20		3.00
425-($1.75, 52 pgs.)-Regular edition	.75		1.80
427-443,446,447,449-454: 427-Begin $1.50-c; bound-in trading card sheet. 449-Thor app. 450-"Man Without A Country" storyline begins, ends #453; Bill Clinton app; variant-c exists. 451-1st app.Cap's new costume. 452-Machinesmith app. 453-Cap gets old costume back; Bill Clinton app.			1.50
444-Mark Waid scripts & Ron Garney-a(p) begins, ends #454; Avengers app.	1.00	2.00	5.00
445-Sharon Carter & Red Skull return.	1.60		4.00
448-($2.95, double-sized issue)-Waid script & Garney-c/a; Red Skull dies?	1.20		3.00
Special 1(1/71)-Origin retold	2.15	6.50	15.00
Special 2(1/72)-Colan-r/Not Brand Echh; all-r	1.70	5.00	12.00
Annual 3,5-7: 3(1976), 5('81, 52 pgs.). 6('82, 52 pgs.). 7('83, 52 pgs.)	1.00		2.50
Annual 4(1977, 52 pgs.)-Kirby-c/a(new); Magneto-c/story (34 pgs.)	1.00	2.00	5.00
Annual 8(9/86)-Wolverine-c/story	4.30	13.00	30.00
Annual 9(1990, $2.00, 68 pgs.)-Nomad back-up	1.60		4.00
Annual 10(1991, $2.00, 68 pgs.)-Origin retold (2 pgs.)	.80		2.00
Annual 11(1992, $2.25, 68 pgs.)-Falcon solo story	.90		2.25
Annual 12(1993, $2.95, 68 pgs.)-Bagged w/card	1.20		3.00
Annual 13(1994, $2.95, 68 pgs.)-Red Skull-c/story	1.20		3.00
...ASHCAN EDITION ('95, 75¢)			.75
...: DEATHLOK LIVES! (nn(10/93, $4.95)-r/#286-288	1.00	2.00	5.00
...DRUG WAR 1-(1994, $2.00, 52 pgs.)-New Warriors app.	.80		2.00
...MEDUSA EFFECT 1 (1994, $2.95, 68 pgs.)-Origin Baron Zemo	1.20		3.00
...OPERATION REBIRTH (1996, $9.95)-r/#445-448			10.00
...STREETS OF POISON ($15.95)-r/#372-378	2.30	6.90	16.00
...: THE MOVIE SPECIAL nn (5/92, $3.50, 52 pgs.)-Adapts movie; printed on coated stock; The Red Skull app.	1.20		3.00
...& THE CAMPBELL KIDS (1980, 36pg. giveaway, Campbell's Soup/U.S. Dept. of Energy)	.80		2.00
...GOES TO WAR AGAINST DRUGS (1990, no #, giveaway)-Distributed to direct sales shops; 2nd printing exists			1.00
...MEETS THE ASTHMA MONSTER (1987, no #, giveaway, Your Physician and Glaxo, Inc.)			1.00
...VS. ASTHMA MONSTER (1990, no #, giveaway, Your Physician & Allen & Hanbury's)			1.00

NOTE: *Austin* c-225i, 239i, 246i. *Buscema* a-115p, 217p; c-136p, 217, 297. *Byrne* c-223(part), 238, 239, 247p-254p, 290, 291, 313p; a-247-254p, 255, 313p, 350. *Colan* a(p)-116-137, 266. *Annual* 5; c(p)-116-123, 126, 129. *Everett* a-136i, 137i; c-126i. *Garney* a(p)-444-454. *Gil Kane* a-145p; c-147p, 149p, 150p, 170p, 172-174, 180, 181p, 183-190p, 215, 216, 220, 221. *Kirby* a(p)-100-109, 112, 193-214, 216, Special 1, 2(layouts), Annual 3, 4; c-100-109, 112, 126p, 193-214. *Ron Lim* a(p)-366, 368-378, 380-386; c-366p, 368-386, 379, 380-393p. *Miller* c-241p, 244p, 245p, 255p, Annual 5. *Mooney* a-149i. *Morrow* a-144. *Perez* c-243p, 246p. *Robbins* c/p-183-187, 189-192, 225. *Roussos* a-140i, 168i. *Starlin/Sinnott* c-162. *Sutton* a-244i. *Tuska* a(p)-112i, 215p, Special 2. *Waid* scripts-444-454. *Williamson* a-313i. *Wood* a-127i. *Zeck* a-263-289, c-300.

CAPTAIN AMERICA
V2#1, Nov, 1996 - Present ($2.95/$1.95) (Produced by Extreme Studios)
Marvel Comics

1-Heroes Reborn begins; Rob Liefeld-c; Jeph Loeb scripts; reintro Nick Fury			3.00
1-(Variant-c)-Liefeld-c/a			5.00
1-(Exclusive Comicon Edition)-Liefeld-c/a			5.00
2-12			2.00

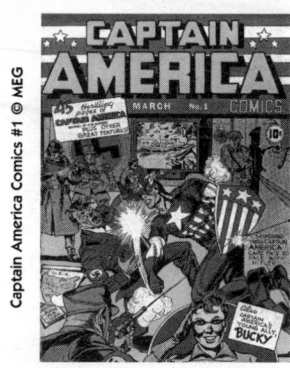
Captain America Comics #1 © MEG

Captain America Comics #57 © MEG

Captain Atom #11 © DC

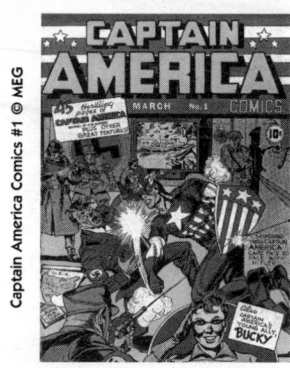

	GD25	FN65	NM94
	GD25	FN65	NM94

CAPTAIN AMERICA COMICS
Mar, 1941 - No. 75, Jan, 1950; No. 76, 5/54 - No. 78, 9/54
(No. 74 & 75 titled Capt. America's Weird Tales)
Timely/Marvel Comics (TCI 1-20/CmPS 21-68/MjMC 69-75/Atlas Comics (PrPl 76-78)

	GD25	FN65	VF82	NM94
1-Origin & 1st app. Captain America & Bucky by S&K; Hurricane, Tuk the Caveboy begin by S&K; 1st app. Red Skull; Hitler-c (by Simon?); intro of the "Capt. America Sentinels of Liberty Club" (advertised on inside front-c.; indicia reads Vol. 2, Number 1	6,000.00	18,000.00	36,000.00	56,000.00

(Estimated up to 180 total copies exist, 8 in NM/Mint)

	GD25	FN65	NM94
2-S&K Hurricane; Tuk by Avison (Kirby splash); classic Hitler-c	1000.00	3000.00	10,000.00
3-Classic Red Skull-c & app; Stan Lee's 1st text (1st work for Marvel)	811.00	2433.00	8000.00
4-1st full pg. panel in comics	480.00	1440.00	4800.00
5	450.00	1350.00	4500.00
6-Origin Father Time; Tuk the Caveboy ends	400.00	1200.00	4000.00
7-Red Skull app.; classic-c	450.00	1350.00	4500.00
8-10-Last S&K issue, (S&K centerfold #6-10)	355.00	1065.00	3200.00
11-Last Hurricane, Headline Hunter; Al Avison Captain America begins, ends #20; Avison-c(p)	311.00	933.00	2800.00
12-The Imp begins, ends #16; last Father Time	288.00	866.00	2600.00
13-Origin The Secret Stamp; classic-c	311.00	933.00	2800.00
14,15	288.00	866.00	2600.00
16-Red Skull unmasks Cap; Red Skull-c	350.00	1050.00	3100.00
17-The Fighting Fool only app.	275.00	825.00	2200.00
18-classic-c	250.00	750.00	2000.00
19-Human Torch begins #19	212.00	635.00	1700.00
20-Sub-Mariner app.; no H. Torch	212.00	635.00	1700.00
21-25: 25-Cap drinks liquid opium	200.00	600.00	1600.00
26-30: 27-Last Secret Stamp; last 68 pg. issue. 28-60 pg. issues begin.	188.00	562.00	1500.00
31-35,38-40: 34-Centerfold poster of Cap	162.00	487.00	1300.00
36-Classic Hitler-c	245.00	730.00	1950.00
37-Red Skull app.	188.00	562.00	1500.00
41-47: 41-Last Jap War-c. 46-German Holocaust-c. 47-Last German War-c.	143.00	431.00	1150.00
48-58,60	137.00	412.00	1100.00
59-Origin retold	275.00	825.00	2200.00
61-Red Skull-c/story	218.00	656.00	1750.00
62,64,65: 65-Kurtzman's "Hey Look"	143.00	431.00	1150.00
63-Intro/origin Asbestos Lady	150.00	450.00	1200.00
66-Bucky is shot; Golden Girl teams up with Captain America & learns his i.d; origin Golden Girl	155.00	468.00	1250.00
67-Captain America/Golden Girl team-up; Mxyztplk swipe; last Toro in Human Torch	143.00	431.00	1150.00
68,70-Sub-Mariner/Namora, and Captain America/Golden Girl team-up in each. 70-Science fiction-c/story	143.00	431.00	1150.00
69,71-73: 69-Human Torch/Sun Girl team-up. 71-Anti Wertham editorial; The Witness, Bucky app.	143.00	431.00	1150.00
74-(Scarce)(1949)-Titled "Captain America's Weird Tales"; Red Skull-c & app.; classic-c	375.00	1130.00	3400.00
75(2/50)-Titled "C.A.'s Weird Tales"; no C.A. app.; horror cover/stories	143.00	431.00	1150.00
76-78(1954): Human Torch/Toro stories; all have communist-c/stories	90.00	270.00	725.00
132-Pg. Issue (B&W-1942)(Canadian)-Has blank inside-c and back-c; contains Marvel Mystery #33 & Capt. America #18 w/cover from Capt. America #22; same contents as Marvel Mystery annual	1333.00	4000.00	12000.00
Shoestore Giveaway #77	53.00	160.00	425.00

NOTE: **Crandall** a-2i, 3i, 9i, 10i. **Kirby** c-8p. **Rico** c-69-71. **Romita** c-77, 78. **Schomburg** c-3, 4, 26-29, 31, 33, 37-39, 41, 42, 45-54, 58. **Sekowsky** c-55, 56. **Shores** c-1, 2, 5-7, 11i, 20-25, 30, 32, 34, 35, 40, 57, 59-67. **S&K** c-1, 3-6, 2, 5-7, 9, 10. Bondage c-3, 7, 15, 16, 34, 38.

CAPTAIN AMERICA/NICK FURY: BLOOD TRUCE
Feb, 1995 ($5.95, one-shot, squarebound)
Marvel Comics

nn-Chaykin story	1.00	2.60	6.00

CAPTAIN AMERICA SPECIAL EDITION
Feb, 1984 - No. 2, Mar, 1984 ($2.00, Baxter paper)
Marvel Comics Group

1,2: Steranko-c/a(r)		.80	2.00

CAPTAIN AMERICA: THE LEGEND
Sept, 1996 ($3.95, one-shot)
Marvel Comics

1-Tribute issue; wraparound-c		4.00

CAPTAIN AND THE KIDS, THE (See Famous Comics Cartoon Books)

CAPTAIN AND THE KIDS, THE (See Comics on Parade, Katzenjammer Kids,
Okay Comics & Sparkler Comics)
1938 -12/39; Sum, 1947 - No. 32, 1955; Four Color No. 881, Feb, 1958
United Features Syndicate/Dell Publ. Co.

Single Series 1(1938)	73.00	221.00	590.00
Single Series 1(Reprint)(12/39- "Reprint" on-c)	43.00	128.00	340.00
1(Summer, 1947-UFS)-Katzenjammer Kids	11.50	34.00	80.00
2	7.50	22.50	45.00
3-10	5.35	16.00	32.00
11-20	4.00	11.00	22.00
21-32(1955)	3.60	9.00	18.00
50th Anniversary issue-(1948)-Contains a 2 pg. history of the strip, including an account of the famous Supreme Court decision allowing both Pulitzer & Hearst to run the same strip under different names	7.50	22.50	45.00
Special Summer issue, Fall issue (1948)	5.85	17.50	35.00
Four Color 881 (Dell)	3.00	9.00	30.00

CAPTAIN ATOM
1950 - No. 7, 1951 (5¢, 5x7-1/4", 52 pgs.)
Nationwide Publishers

1-Sci/fic	29.00	86.00	200.00
2-7	16.00	47.00	110.00
...- Secret of the Columbian Jungle (16 pgs. in color, paper-c, 3-3/4x5-1/8")- Fireside Marshmallow giveaway	4.15	12.50	25.00

CAPTAIN ATOM (Formerly Strange Sus. Stories #77)(Also see Space Adv.)
V2#78, Dec, 1965 - V2#89, Dec, 1967
Charlton Comics

V2#78-Origin retold; Bache-a (3 pgs.)	8.50	26.00	60.00
79-82: 79-1st app. Dr. Spectro; 3 pg. Ditko cut & paste /Space Adventures #24. 82-Intro. Nightshade (9/66)	5.70	17.00	40.00
83-86: Ted Kord Blue Beetle in all. 83-(11/66)-1st app. Ted Kord. 84-1st app. new Captain Atom	5.00	15.00	35.00
87-89: Nightshade by Aparo in all	5.00	15.00	35.00
83-85(Modern Comics-1977)-reprints			1.00

NOTE: **Aparo** a-87-89. **Ditko** c/a(p) 78-89. **#90** only published in fanzine 'The Charlton Bullseye' #1, 2.

CAPTAIN ATOM (Also see Americomics & Crisis On Infinite Earths)
Mar, 1987 - No. 57, Sept, 1991 (Direct sales only #35 on)
DC Comics

1-(44 pgs.)-Origin/1st app. with new costume		.80	2.00
2-41,43-49: 5-Firestorm x-over. 6-Intro. new Dr. Spectro. 11-Millennium tie-in 14-Nightshade app. 16-Justice League app. 17-$1.00-c begins; Swamp Thing app. 20-Blue Beetle x-over. 24,25-Invasion tie-in			1.00
42		1.20	3.00
50-($2.00, 52 pgs.)		.80	2.00
51-57: 57-War of the Gods x-over			1.00
Annual 1 (1988, $1.25)-Intro Major Force			1.50

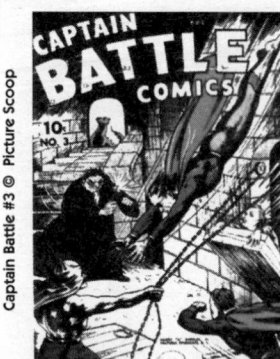

Captain Battle #3 © Picture Scoop

Captain Easy #14 © STD

Captain Fearless #2 © HOKE

	GD25	FN65	NM94

Annual 2 (1988, $1.50)   1.50

CAPTAIN BATTLE (Boy Comics #3 on) (See Silver Streak Comics)
Summer, 1941 - No. 2, Fall, 1941
New Friday Publ./Comic House

1-Origin Blackout by Rico; Captain Battle begins (1st appeared in Silver Streak #10, 5/41)	100.00	300.00	800.00
2	75.00	225.00	600.00

CAPTAIN BATTLE (2nd Series)
No. 3, Wint, 1942-43 - No. 5, Sum, 1943 (#3: 52pgs., nd)(#5: 68pgs.)
Magazine Press/Picture Scoop No. 5

3-Origin Silver Streak-r/SS#3; origin Lance Hale-r/Silver Streak; Simon-a(r)	62.00	187.00	500.00
4,5; 5-Origin Blackout retold	44.00	132.00	350.00

CAPTAIN BATTLE, JR.
Fall, 1943 - No. 2, Winter, 1943-44
Comic House (Lev Gleason)

1-The Claw vs. The Ghost	87.00	262.00	700.00
2-Wolverton's Scoop Scuttle; Don Rico c/a; The Green Claw story is reprinted from Silver Streak #6	75.00	225.00	600.00

CAPTAIN BEN DIX
1943 (Small size)
Bendix Aviation Corporation

nn	6.70	20.00	40.00

CAPTAIN BRITAIN (Also see Marvel Team-Up No. 65, 66)
Oct. 13, 1976 - No. 39, July 6, 1977 (Weekly)
Marvel Comics International

1-Origin; with Capt. Britain's face mask inside	1.65	4.20	10.00
2-Origin, part II; Capt. Britain's Boomerang inside	1.00	2.60	6.00
3-8; 3,8-Vs. Bank Robbers. 4-7-Vs. Hurricane		1.60	4.00
9-15; 9-13-Vs. Dr. Synne. 14,15-Vs. Mastermind		.80	2.00
16-20-With Capt. America; 17 misprinted & color section reprinted in #18		.70	1.80
21-23,25,26-With Capt. America		.70	1.80
24-With C.B.'s Jet Plane inside		1.45	3.60
27,33-35: 27-Origin retold. 33-35-More on origin		.70	1.80
28-32,36-39: 28-32-Vs. Lord Hawk. 36-Star Sceptre. 37-39-Vs. Highwayman & Munipulator			1.50
Annual (1978, Hardback, 64 pgs.)-Reprints #1-7 with pin-ups of Marvel characters	1.30	3.25	8.00
Summer Special (1980, 52 pgs.)-Reprints		.80	2.00

NOTE: No. 1, 2, & 24 are rarer in mint due to inserts. Distributed in Great Britain only. Nick Fury-r by **Steranko** in 1-20, 24-31, 35-37. Fantastic Four-r by **J. Buscema** in all. New **Buscema**-a in 24-30. Story from No. 39 continues in Super Spider-Man (British weekly) No. 231-247. Following cancellation of his series, new Captain Britain stories appeared in "Super Spider-Man" (British weekly) No. 231-247. Captain Britain stories which appear in Super-Spider-Man No 248-253 are reprints of Marvel Team-Up No. 65&66. Capt. Britain strips also appeared in Hulk Comic (weekly) 1, 3-30, 42-55, 57-60, in Marvel Superheroes (monthly) 377-388, in Daredevils (monthly) 1-11, Mighty World of Marvel (monthly) 7-16 & Captain Britain (monthly) 1-14. Issues 1-23 have B&W & color, paper-c, & are 32 pgs. Issues 24 on are all B&W w/glossy-c & are 36 pgs.

CAPTAIN CANUCK
7/75 - No. 4, 7/77; No. 4, 7-8/79 - No. 14, 3-4/81
Comely Comix (Canada) (All distr. in U. S.)

1-1st app. Bluefox		1.00	2.50
2-1st app. Dr. Walker, Redcoat & Kebec		.70	1.80
3(5-7/76)-1st app. Heather		.70	1.80
4(1st printing-2/77)-10x14-1/2''. (5.00); B&W; 300 copies serially numbered and signed with one certificate of authenticity	2.15	6.50	15.00
4(2nd printing-7/77)-11x17'', B&W; only 15 printed; signed by creator Richard Comely, serially #'d and two certificates of authenticity inserted; orange cardboard covers (Very Rare)	4.30	13.00	30.00
4-14: 4(7-8/79)-1st app. Tom Evans & Mr. Gold; origin The Catman. 5-Origin Capt. Canuck's powers; 1st app. Earth Patrol & Chaos Corps. 8-Jonn 'The		1.20	3.00

Final Chapter'. 9-1st World Beyond. 11-1st 'Chariots of Fire' story
   1.00

Summer Special 1(7-9/80, 95¢, 64 pgs.)			1.00

NOTE: 30,000 copies of No. 2 were destroyed in Winnipeg.

CAPTAIN CARROT AND HIS AMAZING ZOO CREW (Also see New Teen Titans & Oz-Wonderland War)
Mar, 1982 - No. 20, Nov, 1983
DC Comics

1-20: 1-Superman app. 3-Re-intro Dodo & The Frog. 9-Re-intro Three Mouseketeers, the Terrific Whatzit. 10,11- Pig Iron reverts back to Peter Porkchops. 20-The Changeling app.			1.00

CAPTAIN CARVEL AND HIS CARVEL CRUSADERS (See Carvel Comics)

CAPTAIN CONFEDERACY
Nov, 1991 - No. 4, Feb, 1992 ($1.95)
Marvel Comics (Epic Comics)

1-4: All new stories		.80	2.00

CAPTAIN COURAGEOUS COMICS (Banner #3-5; see Four Favorites #5)
No. 6, March, 1942
Periodical House (Ace Magazines)

6-Origin & 1st app. The Sword; Lone Warrior, Capt. Courageous app.; Capt. moves to Four Favorites #5 in May	65.00	195.00	525.00

CAPT'N CRUNCH COMICS (See Cap'n...)

CAPTAIN DAVY JONES
No. 598, Nov, 1954
Dell Publishing Co.

Four Color 598	4.00	12.00	40.00

CAPTAIN EASY (See The Funnies & Red Ryder #3-32)
1939 - No. 17, Sept, 1949; April, 1956
Hawley/Dell Publ./Standard(Visual Editions)/Argo

nn-Hawley(1939)-Contains reprints from The Funnies & 1938 Sunday strips by Roy Crane	93.00	280.00	650.00
Four Color 24 (1943)	41.00	123.00	410.00
Four Color 111(6-46)	15.00	45.00	145.00
10(Standard-10/47)	11.00	33.00	75.00
11-17: With content 1930s & '40s strip-r	9.15	27.00	55.00
Argo 1(4/56)-Reprints	6.70	20.00	40.00

NOTE: **Schomburg** c-13, 16.

CAPTAIN EASY & WASH TUBBS (See Famous Comics Cartoon Books)

CAPTAIN ELECTRON
Aug, 1986 ($2.25)
Brick Computer Science Institute

1-Disbrow-a		.90	2.25

CAPTAIN EO 3-D (Disney)
July, 1987 (Eclipse 3-D Special #18, $3.50, Baxter)
Eclipse Comics

1-Adapts 3-D movie		1.40	3.50
1-2-D limited edition	1.00	2.00	5.00
1-Large size (11x17'', 8/87)-Sold only at Disney Theme parks ($6.95)	1.20	3.00	7.00

CAPTAIN FEARLESS COMICS (Also see Holyoke One-Shot #6, Old Glory Comics & Silver Streak #1)
August, 1941 - No. 2, Sept, 1941
Helnit Publishing Co. (Holyoke Publishing Co.)

1-Origin Mr. Miracle, Alias X, Captain Fearless, Citizen Smith Son of the Unknown Soldier; Miss Victory (1st app.) begins (1st patriotic heroine? before Wonder Woman)	68.00	206.00	550.00
2-Grit Grady, Captain Stone app.	44.00	132.00	350.00

CAPTAIN FLAG (See Blue Ribbon Comics #16)

Captain Flight Comics #11 © Four Star

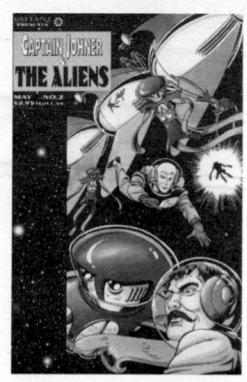

Captain Johner & the Aliens #2 © WEST

Captain Marvel #10 © MEG

CA

CAPTAIN FLASH
Nov, 1954 - No. 4, July, 1955
Sterling Comics

1-Origin; Sekowsky-a; Tomboy (female super hero) begins; only pre-code issue; atomic rocket-c	34.00	103.00	240.00
2-4: 4-Flying saucer invasion-c	20.00	60.00	140.00

CAPTAIN FLEET (Action Packed Tales of the Sea)
Fall, 1952
Ziff-Davis Publishing Co.

1-Painted-c	13.00	39.00	90.00

CAPTAIN FLIGHT COMICS
Mar, 1944 - No. 10, Dec, 1945; No. 11, Feb-Mar, 1947
Four Star Publications

nn	34.00	103.00	240.00
2-4: 4-Rock Raymond begins, ends #7	17.00	51.00	120.00
5-Bondage, classic torture-c; Red Rocket begins; the Grenade app. (scarce)	40.00	120.00	300.00
6	16.00	47.00	110.00
7-10: 7-L. B. Cole covers begin, end #11. 8-Yankee Girl begins; intro. Black Cobra & Cobra Kid & begins. 9-Torpedoman app.; last Yankee Girl; Kinstler-a. 10-Deep Sea Dawson, Zoom of the Jungle, Rock Raymond, Red Rocket, & Black Cobra app; bondage-c	32.00	96.00	225.00
11-Torpedoman, Blue Flame (Human Torch clone) app.; last Black Cobra, Red Rocket; classic L. B. Cole-c	40.00	120.00	300.00

CAPTAIN FORTUNE PRESENTS
1955 - 1959 (Giveaway, 3-1/4x6-7/8", 16 pgs.)
Vital Publications

"Davy Crockett in Episodes of the Creek War", "Davy Crockett at the Alamo", "In Sherwood Forest Tells Strange Tales of Robin Hood" ('57), "Meets Bolivar the Liberator" ('59), "Tells How Buffalo Bill Fights the Dog Soldiers" ('57), "Young Davy Crockett"	1.80	4.50	9.00

CAPTAIN GALLANT (...of the Foreign Legion) (TV) (Texas Rangers in Action No. 5 on?)
1955; No. 2, Jan, 1956 - No. 4, Sept, 1956
Charlton Comics

Heinz Foods Premium (#1?)(1955; regular size)-U.S. Pictorial; contains Buster Crabbe photos; Don Heck-a

	1.80	4.50	9.00

Non-Heinz version (same as above except pictures of show replaces ads)

(#1)-Buster Crabbe photo on-c; full page Buster Crabbe photo inside front-c	10.00	30.00	60.00
2-4: Buster Crabbe in all	8.35	25.00	50.00

CAPTAIN GLORY
Apr, 1993 ($2.95) (Created by Jack Kirby)
Topps Comics

1-Polybagged w/Kirbychrome trading card; Ditko-a & Kirby-c; has coupon for Amberchrome Secret City Saga #0	1.20		3.00

CAPTAIN HERO (See Jughead as...)

CAPTAIN HERO COMICS DIGEST MAGAZINE
Sept, 1981
Archie Publications

1-Reprints of Jughead as Super-Guy			1.00

CAPTAIN HOBBY COMICS
Feb, 1948 (Canadian)
Export Publication Ent. Ltd. (Dist. in U.S. by Kable News Co.)

1	5.85	17.50	35.00

CAPT. HOLO IN 3-D (See Blackthorne 3-D Series #65)

CAPTAIN HOOK & PETER PAN (Movie)(Disney)
No. 446, Jan, 1953

Dell Publishing Co.

Four Color 446	10.00	30.00	90.00

CAPTAIN JET (Fantastic Fears No. 7 on)
May, 1952 - No. 5, Jan, 1953
Four Star Publ./Farrell/Comic Media

1-Bakerish-a	16.00	47.00	110.00
2	10.00	30.00	65.00
3-5,6(?)	8.35	25.00	50.00

CAPTAIN JOHNER & THE ALIENS
May, 1995 - No. 2, May, 1995 ($2.95, limited series, shipped in same month)
Valiant

1,2: Reprints Magnus Robot Fighter 4000 A.D. back-up stories; new Paul Smith-c			3.00

CAPTAIN JUSTICE (TV)
Mar, 1988 - No. 2, Apr, 1988 (limited series)
Marvel Comics

1,2-Based on True Colors television series.			1.25

CAPTAIN KANGAROO (TV)
No. 721, Aug, 1956 - No. 872, Jan, 1958
Dell Publishing Co.

Four Color 721 (#1)-Photo-c	15.00	45.00	145.00
Four Color 780, 872-Photo-c	13.00	40.00	125.00

CAPTAIN KIDD (Formerly Dagar; My Secret Story #26 on)(Also see Comic Comics & Fantastic Comics)
No. 24, June, 1949 - No. 25, Aug, 1949
Fox Feature Syndicate

24,25: 24-Features Blackbeard the Pirate	12.00	36.00	85.00

CAPTAIN MARVEL (See All Hero, All-New Collectors' Ed., America's Greatest, Fawcett Miniature, Gift, Legends, Limited Collectors' Ed., Marvel Family, Master No. 21, Mighty Midget Comics, Shazam, Special Edition Comics, Whiz, Wisco, World's Finest #253 and XMas Comics)

CAPTAIN MARVEL (Becomes ...Presents the Terrible 5 No. 5)
April, 1966 - No. 4, Nov, 1966 (25¢ Giants)
M. F. Enterprises

nn-(#1 on pg. 5)-Origin; created by Carl Burgos	2.15	6.50	15.00
2-4: 3-(#3 on pg. 4)-Fights the Bat	1.30	3.25	8.00

CAPTAIN MARVEL (Marvel's Space-Born Super-Hero! Captain Marvel #1-6; see Giant-Size..., Life Of..., Marvel Graphic Novel #1, Marvel Spotlight V2#1 & Marvel Super-Heroes #12)
May, 1968 - No. 19, Dec, 1969; No. 20, June, 1970 - No. 21, Aug, 1970; No. 22, Sept, 1972 - No. 62, May, 1979
Marvel Comics Group

1	13.00	39.00	90.00
2-Super Skrull-c/story	4.50	13.00	35.00
3-5: 4-Captain Marvel battles Sub-Mariner	3.25	9.50	22.00
6-11: 11-Capt. Marvel given great power by Zo the Ruler; Smith/Trimpe-c; Death of Una	2.15	6.50	15.00
12-24: 14-Capt. Marvel vs. Iron Man; last 12¢ issue. 16,17-New costume. 21-Capt. Marvel battles Hulk; last 15¢ issue	1.65	4.20	10.00
25-Starlin-c/a begins; Starlin's 1st Thanos saga begins (3/73), ends #34; Thanos cameo (5 panels)	2.85	8.50	20.00
26-Minor Thanos app. (see Iron Man #55); 1st Thanos-c	3.60	11.00	25.00
27,28-1st & 2nd full app. Thanos. 28-Thanos-c/s	2.85	8.50	20.00
29,30-Thanos cameos. 29-C.M. gains more powers	1.00	4.00	10.00
31,32: Thanos app. 31-Last 20¢ issue. 32-Thanos-c	2.15	6.50	15.00
33-Thanos-c & app.; Capt. Marvel battles Thanos; 1st origin Thanos	3.60	11.00	25.00
34-1st app. Nitro; C.M. contracts cancer which eventually kills him; last Starlin-c/a	1.00	2.00	5.00

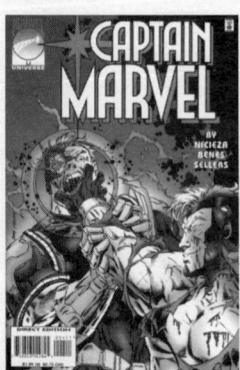

Captain Marvel #4 © MEG

Captain Marvel Adventures #18 © FAW

Captain Marvel, Jr. #9 © FAW

	GD25	FN65	NM94

35,37-56,58-62: 39-Origin Watcher. 41,43-Wrightson part inks; #43-c(i). 49-Starlin & Weiss-p assists. 58-Thanos cameo ... **1.50**

36-Reprints origin/1st app. Capt. Marvel from Marvel Super-Heroes #12; Starlin-a (3 pgs.) ... **1.00 2.00 5.00**

57-Thanos appears in flashback ... **1.00 2.00 5.00**

NOTE: **Alcala** a-35. **Austin** a-46i, 49-53i; c-52i. **Buscema** a-18p-21p. **Colan** a(p)-1-4, c(p)-1-4, 8, 9. **Heck** a-5-10p, 16p. **Gil Kane** a-17-21p; c-17-24p, 37p, 53. **McWilliams** a-40i. #25-34 were reprinted in The Life of Captain Marvel.

CAPTAIN MARVEL
Nov, 1989 ($1.50, one-shot, 52 pgs.)
Marvel Comics

1-Super-hero from Avengers; new powers ... **1.50**

CAPTAIN MARVEL
Feb, 1994 ($1.75, 52 pgs.)
Marvel Comics

1-(Indicia reads Vol 2 #2)-Minor Captain America app. ... **.70 1.75**

CAPTAIN MARVEL
Dec, 1995 - No. 6, May, 1996 ($2.95/$1.95)
Marvel Comics

1 ($2.95)-Advs. of Mar-Vell's son begins; Fabian Nicieza scripts; foil-c ... **1.00 3.00**

2-6: 2-Begin $1.95-c ... **.80 2.00**

CAPTAIN MARVEL ADVENTURES (See Special Edition Comics for pre #1)
1941 (March) - No. 150, Nov, 1953 (#1 on stands 1/16/41)
Fawcett Publications

	GD25	FN65	VF82	NM94

nn(#1)-Captain Marvel & Sivana by Jack Kirby. The cover was printed on unstable paper stock and is rarely found in Fine or Mint condition; blank bank inside-c ... **2500.00 7500.00 16,250.00 27,000.00**
(Estimated up to 140 total copies exist, 3 in NM/Mint)

	GD25	FN65	NM94

2-(Advertised as #3, which was counting Special Edition Comics as the real #1); Tuska-a ... **350.00 1050.00 3000.00**

3-Metallic silver-c ... **225.00 675.00 1800.00**

4-Three Lt. Marvels app. ... **150.00 450.00 1200.00**

5 ... **112.00 338.00 900.00**

6-10: 9-1st Otto Binder scripts on Capt. Marvel ... **87.00 262.00 700.00**

11-15: 12-Capt. Marvel joins the Army. 13-Two pg. Capt. Marvel pin-up. 15-Comic cards on back-c begin, end #26 ... **75.00 225.00 600.00**

16,17: 17-Painted-c ... **68.00 206.00 550.00**

18-Origin & 1st app. Mary Marvel & Marvel Family (12/11/42); painted-c; Mary Marvel by Marcus Swayze ... **156.00 468.00 1250.00**

19-Mary Marvel x-over; Christmas-c ... **56.00 168.00 450.00**

20,21-Attached to the cover, each has a miniature comic just like the Mighty Midget Comics #11, except that each has a full color promo ad on the back cover. Most copies were circulated without the miniature comic. These issues with miniatures attached are very rare, and should not be mistaken for copies with the similar Mighty Midget glued in its place. The Mighty Midgets had blank back covers except for a small victory stamp seal. Only the Capt. Marvel and Captain Marvel Jr. No. 11 miniatures have been positively documented as having been affixed tothese covers. Each miniature was only partially glued by its back cover to the Captain Marvel comic making it easy to see if it's the genuine miniature rather than a Mighty Midget.

    with comic attached.... ... **312.00 938.00 2800.00**

20-Without miniature ... **53.00 160.00 425.00**

21-Without miniature; Hitler-c ... **69.00 206.00 550.00**

22-Mr. Mind serial begins; 1st app. Mr. Mind ... **75.00 225.00 600.00**

23-25 ... **51.00 155.00 415.00**

26-30: 26-Flag-c. 29-1st Mr. Mind-c & 1st app. (his voice was heard over the radio before now)(11/43) ... **44.00 132.00 350.00**

31-35: 35-Origin Radar (5/44, see Master #50) ... **40.00 120.00 325.00**

36-40: 37-Mary Marvel x-over ... **39.00 118.00 275.00**

41-46: 42-Christmas-c. 43-Capt. Marvel 1st meets Uncle Marvel (1st app.); Mary Batson cameo. 46-Mr. Mind serial ends ... **31.00 94.00 220.00**

47-50 ... **29.00 86.00 200.00**

51-53,55-60: 51-63-Bi-weekly issues. 52-Origin & 1st app. Sivana Jr.; Capt.

	GD25	FN65	NM94

Marvel Jr. x-over ... **23.00 69.00 160.00**

54-Special oversize 68 pg. issue ... **24.00 71.00 165.00**

61-The Cult of the Curse serial begins ... **28.00 84.00 195.00**

62-66-Serial ends; Mary Marvel x-over in #65. 66-Atomic War-c. ... **24.00 71.00 165.00**

67-77,79: 69-Billy Batson's Christmas; Uncle Marvel, Mary Marvel, Capt. Marvel Jr. x-over. 71-Three Lt. Marvels app. 79-Origin Mr. Tawny ... **21.00 64.00 150.00**

78-Origin Mr. Atom ... **24.00 73.00 170.00**

80-Origin Capt. Marvel retold ... **40.00 120.00 300.00**

81-84,86-90: 81,90-Mr. Atom app. 82-Infinity-c. 86-Mr. Tawny app. ... **20.00 60.00 140.00**

85-Freedom Train issue ... **25.00 75.00 175.00**

91-99: 96-Mr. Tawny app. ... **20.00 60.00 140.00**

100-Origin retold; silver metallic-c ... **39.00 118.00 275.00**

101-115,117-120 ... **19.00 58.00 135.00**

116-Flying Saucer issue (1/51) ... **21.00 62.00 145.00**

121-Origin retold ... **26.00 77.00 180.00**

122-137,139-149: 141-Pre-code horror story "The Hideous Head-Hunter". 142-used in POP, pgs. 92,96 ... **19.00 56.00 130.00**

138-Flying Saucer issue (11/52) ... **21.00 64.00 150.00**

150-(Low distribution) ... **26.00 79.00 185.00**

Bond Bread Giveaways-(24 pgs.; pocket size-7-1/4x3-1/2"; paper cover): "...& the Stolen City" ('48), "The Boy Who Never Heard of Capt. Marvel", "Meets the Weatherman" -(1950)(reprint) each.... ... **26.00 77.00 180.00**

...Well Known Comics (1944; 12 pgs.; 8-1/2x10-1/2")-printed in red & in blue; soft-c; glued binding)-Bestmaid/Samuel Lowe Co. giveaway ... **17.00 51.00 120.00**

NOTE: **Swayze** a-12, 14, 15, 18, 19, 40; c-12, 15, 19.

CAPTAIN MARVEL ADVENTURES
1945 (6x8", full color, paper-c)
Fawcett Publications (Wheaties Giveaway)

nn- "Captain Marvel & the Threads of Life" plus 2 other stories (32 pgs.) ... **50.00 150.00 400.00**

NOTE: All copies were taped at each corner to a box of Wheaties and are never found in Fine or Mint condition. Prices listed for each grade include tape.

CAPTAIN MARVEL AND THE GOOD HUMOR MAN (Movie)
1950
Fawcett Publicationsnn-Partial photo-c w/Jack Carson & the Captain Marvel Club Boys ... **40.00 120.00 320.00**

CAPTAIN MARVEL AND THE LTS. OF SAFETY
1950 - 1951 (3 issues - no No.'s)
Ebasco Services/Fawcett Publications

	GD25	FN65	VF82

"Danger Flies a Kite" ('50, scarce), "Danger Takes to Climbing" ('50), "Danger Smashes Street Lights" ('51) ... **106.00 318.00 850.00**

CAPTAIN MARVEL COMIC STORY PAINT BOOK (See Comic Story...)

CAPTAIN MARVEL, JR. (See Fawcett Miniatures, Marvel Family, Master Comics, Mighty Midget Comics, Shazam & Whiz Comics)

CAPTAIN MARVEL, JR.
Nov, 1942 - No. 119, June, 1953 (No #34)
Fawcett Publications

1-Origin Capt. Marvel Jr. retold (Whiz No. 25); Capt. Nazi app. Classic Raboy-c ... **400.00 1200.00 4000.00**

2-Vs. Capt. Nazi; origin Capt. Nippon ... **156.00 468.00 1250.00**

3 ... **90.00 270.00 725.00**

4-Classic Raboy-c ... **96.00 290.00 775.00**

5-Vs. Capt. Nazi ... **84.00 253.00 675.00**

6-10: 8-Vs. Capt. Nazi. 9-Flag-c. 10-Hitler-c ... **62.00 187.00 500.00**

11,12,15-Capt. Nazi app. ... **53.00 160.00 425.00**

13,14,16-20: 13-Hitler-c. 14-X-Mas-c. 16-Capt. Marvel & Sivana x-over. 19-Capt. Nazi & Capt. Nippon app. ... **47.00 141.00 375.00**

21-30: 25-Flag-c ... **40.00 120.00 285.00**

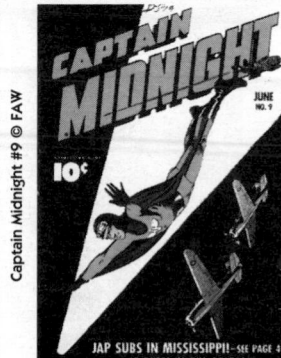

Captain Marvel Storybook #4 © FAW

Captain Midnight #9 © FAW

Captain Planet and the Planeteers #1 © MEG

CA

	GD25	FN65	NM94

31-33,36-40: 37-Infinity-c — 25.00 / 75.00 / 175.00
35-#34 on inside; cover shows origin of Sivana Jr. which is not on inside.
  Evidently the cover to #35 was printed out of sequence and bound with
  contents to #34 — 25.00 / 75.00 / 175.00
41-70: 53-Atomic Bomb-c/story — 19.00 / 56.00 / 130.00
71-99,101-104: 104-Used in POP, pg. 89 — 14.00 / 43.00 / 100.00
100 — 17.00 / 49.00 / 115.00
105-114,116-119: 116-Vampira, Queen of Terror app. 119-Electric chair-c
  — 13.50 / 41.00 / 95.00
115-Injury to eye-c; Eyeball story w/injury-to-eye panels
  — 19.00 / 56.00 / 130.00
..Well Known Comics (1944; 12 pgs.; 8-1/2x10-1/2")(Printed in blue; paper-c,
  glued binding)-Bestmaid/Samuel Lowe Co. giveaway
  — 13.00 / 40.00 / 80.00
NOTE: **Mac Raboy** c-1-28, 30-32, 57, 59 among others.

CAPTAIN MARVEL PRESENTS THE TERRIBLE FIVE
Aug, 1966; V2#5, Sept, 1967 (No #2-4) (25¢)
M. F. Enterprises

1 — 1.70 / 5.00 / 12.00
V2#5-(Formerly Captain Marvel) — 1.00 / 2.60 / 6.00

CAPTAIN MARVEL'S FUN BOOK
1944 (1/2" thick) (cardboard covers)
Samuel Lowe Co.

nn-Puzzles, games, magic, etc.; infinity-c — 32.00 / 96.00 / 225.00

CAPTAIN MARVEL SPECIAL EDITION (See Special Edition)

CAPTAIN MARVEL STORY BOOK
Summer, 1946 - No. 4, Summer?, 1948
Fawcett Publications

1-Half text — 50.00 / 150.00 / 400.00
2-4 — 39.00 / 118.00 / 275.00

CAPTAIN MARVEL THRILL BOOK (Large-Size)
1941 (B&W w/color-c)
Fawcett Publications

	GD25	FN65	VF82
1-Reprints from Whiz #8,10, & Special Edition #1 (Rare)	250.00	750.00	2500.00

NOTE: Rarely found in Fine or Mint condition.

CAPTAIN MIDNIGHT (TV, radio, films) (See The Funnies & Popular Comics)
(Becomes Sweethearts No. 68 on)
Sept, 1942 - No. 67, Fall, 1948 (#1-14: 68 pgs.)
Fawcett Publications

	GD25	FN65	NM94
1-Origin Captain Midnight; Captain Marvel cameo on cover	250.00	750.00	2000.00
2	112.00	338.00	900.00
3-5	81.00	243.00	650.00
6-10: 9-Raboy-c. 10-Raboy Flag-c	59.00	178.00	475.00
11-20: 11,17,18-Raboy-c	43.00	128.00	340.00
21-30	38.00	114.00	265.00
31-40	26.00	79.00	185.00
41-59,61-67: 50-Sci/fi theme begins?	21.00	64.00	150.00
60-Flying Saucer issue (2/48)-3rd of this theme; see Shadow Comics V7#10 & Boy Commandos #26	29.00	86.00	200.00

CAPTAIN NICE (TV)
Nov, 1967 (one-shot)
Gold Key

1(10211-711)-Photo-c — 6.50 / 19.50 / 65.00

CAPTAIN N: THE GAME MASTER (TV)
1990 - No. 6? ($1.95, thick stock, coated-c)
Valiant Comics

1-6: 4-6-Layton-c — .80 / 2.00

CAPTAIN PARAGON (See Bill Black's Fun Comics)
Dec, 1983 - No. 4, 1985
Americomics

1-4: 1-Intro/1st app. Ms. Victory — 1.50

CAPTAIN PARAGON AND THE SENTINELS OF JUSTICE
April, 1985 - No. 6, 1986 ($1.75)
AC Comics

1-6: 1-Capt. Paragon, Commando D., Nightveil, Scarlet Scorpion, Stardust &
  Atoman begin — .75 / 1.80

CAPTAIN PLANET AND THE PLANETEERS (TV cartoon)
Oct, 1991 - No. 12, Oct, 1992 ($1.00/$1.25)
Marvel Comics

1-12: 1-N. Adams painted-c. 3-Romita-c — 1.25

CAPTAIN POWER AND THE SOLDIERS OF THE FUTURE (TV)
Aug, 1988 - No. 2, 1988 ($2.00)
Continuity Comics

1,2: 1-Neal Adams-c/layouts/inks; variant-c exists. — .80 / 2.00

CAPTAIN PUREHEART (See Archie as...)

CAPTAIN ROCKET
Nov, 1951
P. L. Publ. (Canada)

1 — 36.00 / 107.00 / 250.00

CAPT. SAVAGE AND HIS LEATHERNECK RAIDERS (...And His Battlefield
Raiders #9 on)
Jan, 1968 - No. 19, Mar, 1970 (See Sgt. Fury No. 10)
Marvel Comics Group (Animated Timely Features)

1-Sgt. Fury & Howlers cameo — 1.65 / 4.20 / 10.00
2-10: 2-Origin Hydra. 1-5,7-Ayers/Shores-a. 7-Pre-"Thing" Ben Grimm story — 1.00 / 2.60 / 6.00
11-19 — 1.00 / 2.00 / 5.00

CAPTAIN SCIENCE (Fantastic No. 8 on)
Nov, 1950 - No. 7, Dec, 1951
Youthful Magazines

1-Wood-a; origin; 2 pg. text w/ photos of George Pal's "Destination Moon."
  — 68.00 / 206.00 / 550.00
2 — 39.00 / 118.00 / 275.00
3,6,7; 3,6-Bondage c-swipes/Wings #94,91 — 36.00 / 107.00 / 250.00
4,5-Wood/Orlando-c/a(2) each — 68.00 / 206.00 / 550.00
NOTE: Fass a-4. Bondage c-3, 6, 7.

CAPTAIN SILVER'S LOG OF SEA HOUND (See Sea Hound)

CAPTAIN SINBAD (Movie Adaptation) (See Fantastic Voyages of... & Movie Comics)

CAPTAIN STERNN: RUNNING OUT OF TIME
Sept, 1993 - No. 5, 1994 ($4.95, limited series, coated stock, 52 pgs.)
Kitchen Sink Press

1-5: Berni Wrightson-c/a/scripts — 1.00 / 2.00 / 5.00
1-Gold ink variant — 2.10 / 6.00 / 15.00

CAPTAIN STEVE SAVAGE (...& His Jet Fighters, No. 2-13)
1950 - No. 8, 1/53; No. 5, 9-10/54 - No. 13, 5-6/56
Avon Periodicals

nn(1st series)-Wood art, 22 pgs. (titled "...Over Korea")
  — 36.00 / 107.00 / 250.00
1(4/51)-Reprints nn issue (Canadian) — 15.00 / 45.00 / 105.00
2-Kamen-a — 10.00 / 30.00 / 60.00
3-11 (#6, 9-10/54, last precode) — 5.85 / 17.50 / 35.00
12-Wood-a (6 pgs.) — 10.00 / 30.00 / 70.00
13-Check, Lawrence-a — 7.50 / 22.50 / 45.00
NOTE: **Kinstler** c-2-5, 7-9, 11. **Lawrence** a-8. **Ravielli** a-5, 9.
5(9-10/54-2nd series)(Formerly Sensational Police Cases)

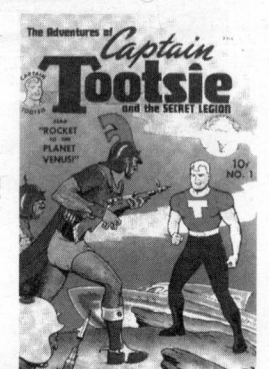

Captain Tootsie And The Secret Legion #1 © TOBY

Captain Victory And The Galactic Rangers #1 © Jack Kirby

Captain Video #4 © FAW

	GD25	FN65	NM94
	6.35	19.00	38.00
6-Reprints nn issue; Wood-a	10.00	30.00	60.00
7-13: 9,10-Kinstler-c. 10-r/cover #2 (1st series). 13-r/cover #8 (1st series)			
	4.00	12.00	24.00

CAPTAIN STONE (See Holyoke One-Shot No. 10)

CAPT. STORM (Also see G. I. Combat #138)
May-June, 1964 - No. 18, Mar-Apr, 1967 (Grey tone c-8)
National Periodical Publications

1-Origin	3.25	9.50	22.00
2-18: 3,6,13-Kubert-a. 4-Colan-a. 12-Kubert-c	1.85	5.50	13.00

CAPTAIN 3-D (Super hero)
December, 1953 (25¢, came with 2 pairs of glasses)
Harvey Publications

1-Kirby/Ditko-a (Ditko's 3rd published work tied with Strange Fantasy #9, see also Daring Love #1 & Black Magic V4 #3); shows cover in 3-D on inside;

Kirby/Meskin-c	10.00	30.00	60.00

CAPTAIN THUNDER AND BLUE BOLT
Sept, 1987 - No. 10, 1988 ($1.95)
Hero Comics

1-10: 1-Origin Blue Bolt. 3-Origin Capt. Thunder. 6-1st app. Wicket.

8-Champions x-over		.80	2.00

CAPTAIN TOOTSIE & THE SECRET LEGION (Advs. of...)(Also see Monte Hale #30,39 & Real Western Hero)
Oct, 1950 - No. 2, Dec, 1950
Toby Press

1-Not Beck-a; both have sci/fi covers	25.00	75.00	175.00
2-The Rocketeer Patrol app.; not Beck-a	16.00	47.00	110.00

CAPTAIN TRIUMPH (See Crack Comics #27)

CAPTAIN VENTURE & THE LAND BENEATH THE SEA (See Space Family Robinson)
Oct, 1968 - No. 2, Oct, 1969)
Gold Key

1,2: 1-r/Space Family Robinson serial; Spiegle-a in both

	3.50	11.00	35.00

CAPTAIN VICTORY AND THE GALACTIC RANGERS
11/81 - #13, 1/84 ($1.00, direct sales, 36-48 pgs.) (Created by Jack Kirby)
Pacific Comics

1-13: 1-1st app. Mr. Mind. 3-N. Adams-a			1.00
Special 1-(10/83)-Kirby c/a(p)			1.00

NOTE: Conrad a-10, 11. Ditko a-6. Kirby a-1-3p; c-1-13.

CAPTAIN VIDEO (TV) (See XMas Comics)
Feb, 1951 - No. 6, Dec, 1951 (No. 1,5,6-36pgs.; 2-4, 52pgs.) (All photo-c)
Fawcett Publications

1-George Evans-a(2)	93.00	281.00	750.00
2-Used in SOTI, pg. 382	62.00	187.00	500.00
3-6-All Evans-a except #5 mostly Evans	52.00	157.00	420.00

NOTE: Minor Williamson assists on most issues. Photo c-1, 5, 6; painted c-2-4.

CAPTAIN WILLIE SCHULTZ (Also see Fightin' Army)
No. 76, Oct, 1985 - No. 77, Jan, 1986
Charlton Comics

76,77			1.00

CAPTAIN WIZARD COMICS (See Meteor, Red Band & Three Ring Comics)
1946
Rural Home

1-Capt. Wizard dons new costume; Impossible Man, Race Wilkins app.

	23.00	69.00	160.00

CARDINAL MINDSZENTY (The Truth Behind the Trial of...)
1949 (24 pgs., paper cover)

	GD25	FN65	NM94

Catechetical Guild Education Society

nn-Anti-communism	5.85	17.50	35.00

Press Proof-(Very Rare)-(Full color, 7-1/2x11-3/4", untrimmed)

Only two known copies			150.00

Preview Copy (B&W, stapled), 18 pgs.; contains first 13 pgs. of Cardinal Mindszenty and was sent out as an advance promotion.

Only one known copy		150.00 - 200.00	

NOTE: Regular edition also printed in French. There was also a movie released in 1949 calle "Guilty of Treason" which is a fact-based account of the trial and imprisonment of Cardin Mindszenty by the Communist regime in Hungary.

CARE BEARS (TV, Movie)(See Star Comics Magazine)
Nov, 1985 - No. 20, Jan, 1989 ($1.00 #11 on)
Star Comics/Marvel Comics No. 15 on

1-20: Post-a begins			1.00

CAREER GIRL ROMANCES (Formerly Three Nurses)
June, 1964 - No. 78, Dec, 1973
Charlton Comics

V4#24-31,33-50		1.60	4.00
32-Elvis Presley, Hermans Hermits, Johnny Rivers line drawn-c			
	9.50	28.00	75.00
51-78		.80	2.00

CAR 54, WHERE ARE YOU? (TV)
Mar-May, 1962 - No. 7, Sept-Nov, 1963; 1964 - 1965 (All photo-c)
Dell Publishing Co.

Four Color 1257(#1, 3-5/62)	8.00	24.00	80.00
2(6-8/62)-7	4.00	12.00	40.00
2,3(10-12/64); 4(1-3/65)-Reprints #2,3,&4 of 1st series			
	3.00	9.00	30.00

CARL BARKS LIBRARY OF WALT DISNEY'S GYRO GEARLOOSE COMICS AND FILLERS IN COLOR, THE
1993 ($7.95, 8-1/2x11", limited series, 52 pgs.)
Gladstone

1-6: Carl Barks reprints	1.65	4.20	10.00

CARL BARKS LIBRARY OF WALT DISNEY'S COMICS AND STORIES IN COLOR, THE
Jan, 1992 - No. 51, Mar, 1996 ($8.95, 8-1/2x11", 60 pgs.)(51 ish. series)
Gladstone

1,2,6,8-51: 1-Barks Donald Duck-r/WDC&S #31-35; 2-r/#36,38-41; 6-r/#57-61; 8-r/#67-71; 9-r/#72-76; 10-r/#77-81; 11-r/#82-86; 12-r/#87-91; 13-r/#92-96; 14-r/#97-101; 15-r/#102-106; 16-r/#107-111; 17-r/#112,114,117,124,125; 18-r/#126-130; 19-r/#131,132(2),133,134; 20-r/#135-139; 21-r/#140-144; 22-r/#145-149; 23-r/#150-154; 24-r/#155-159; 25-r/#160-164; 26-r/#165-169; 27-r/#170-174;28-r/#175-179; 29-r/#180-184; 30-r/#185-189; 31-r/#190-194; 32-r/#195-199;33-r/#200-204; 34-r/#205-209; 35-r/#210-214; 36-r/#215-219; 37-r/#220-224; 38-r/#225-229; 39-r/#230-234; 40-r/#235-239; 41-r/#240-244; 42r/#245-249; 43-r/#250-254; 44-50; All contain one Heroes & Villains tradin card each

	1.65	4.20	10.00
3,4,7: 3-r/#42-46. 4-r/#47-51. 7-r/#62-66.	2.15	6.50	15.00
5-r/#52-56	2.85	8.50	20.00

CARL BARKS LIBRARY OF WALT DISNEY'S DONALD DUCK ADVENTURES IN COLOR, THE
1994 - Present ($7.95/$9.95, 44-68pgs., 8-1/2"x11")(25 issue series)
(all contain one Donald Duck trading card each)
Gladstone

1-16-Carl Barks-r: 1-r/FC #9; 2-r/FC #29; 3-r/FC #62; 4-r/FC #108; 5-r/FC #147 & #79(Mickey Mouse); 6-r/MOC #4, Cheerios "Atom Bomb," D.D. Tells Abou Kites; 7-r/FC #159. 8-r/FC #178 & 189. 9-r/FC #199 & 203; 10-r/FC 223 & 238; 11-r/Christmas Parade #1 & 2; 12-r/FC #296; 13-r/FC #263; 14-r/MOC #20 & 41; 15-r/FC 275 & 282; 16-r/FC #291&300; 17-r/FC #308 & 318; 18-r/Vac. Parade #1 & Summer Fun #2; 19-r/FC #328 & 367

	1.70	5.00	12.00

Carnage: Mind Bomb #1 © MEG

Casey-Crime Photographer #1 © MEG

Casey Jones #1 © Mirage Studios

CA

	GD25	FN65	NM94

CARL BARKS LIBRARY OF WALT DISNEY'S DONALD DUCK CHRISTMAS STORIES IN COLOR, THE
1992 ($7.95, 44pgs., one-shot)
Gladstone

	GD25	FN65	NM94
nn-Reprints Firestone giveaways 1945-1949	1.50	4.50	15.00

CARL BARKS LIBRARY OF WALT DISNEY'S UNCLE SCROOGE COMICS ONE PAGERS IN COLOR, THE
1992 - No. 2, 1993 ($8.95, limited series, 60 pgs., 8-1/2x11")
Gladstone

1-Carl Barks one pg. reprints	2.50	7.50	25.00
2-Carl Barks one pg. reprints	1.50	4.50	15.00

CARNAGE: IT'S A WONDERFUL LIFE
Oct, 1996 ($1.95, one-shot)
Marvel Comics

1-David Quinn scripts			2.00

CARNAGE: MIND BOMB
Feb, 1996 ($2.95, one-shot)
Marvel Comics

1-Warren Ellis script; Kyle Hotz-a			3.00

CARNATION MALTED MILK GIVEAWAYS (See Wisco)

CARNEYS, THE
Summer, 1994 ($2.00, 52 pgs)
Archie Comics

1-Bound-in pull-out poster		.80	2.00

CARNIVAL COMICS (Formerly Kayo #12; becomes Red Seal Comics #14)
1945
Harry 'A' Chesler/Pershing Square Publ. Co.

nn (#13)-Guardineer-a	13.50	41.00	95.00

CARNIVAL OF COMICS
1954 (Giveaway)
Fleet-Air Shoes

nn-Contains a comic bound with new cover; several combinations possible; Charlton's Eh! known	2.40	6.00	12.00

CAROLINE KENNEDY
1961 (one-shot)
Charlton Comics

nn-Interior photo covers of Kennedy family	9.50	28.00	75.00

CAROUSEL COMICS
V1#8, April, 1948
F. E. Howard, Toronto

V1#8	5.35	16.00	32.00

CARTOON KIDS
1957 (no month)
Atlas Comics (CPS)

1-Maneely-c/a; Dexter The Demon, Willie The Wise-Guy, Little Zelda app.			
	8.35	25.00	50.00

CARTOON TALES (Disney's...)
No date (1992) ($2.95, 6-5/8x9-1/2", 52 pgs.)
W.D. Publications (Disney)

nn-Ariel & Sebastian - Serpent Teen		1.20	3.00
nn-Beauty and the Beast - A Tale of Enchantment		1.20	3.00
nn-Darkwing Duck - Just Us Justice Ducks		1.20	3.00
nn-101 Dalmations - Canine Classics		1.20	3.00
nn-Tale Spin - Surprise in the Skies		1.20	3.00
nn-Uncle Scrooge - Blast to the Past		1.20	3.00

CARVEL COMICS (Amazing Advs. of Capt. Carvel)
1975 - No. 5, 1976 (25¢; #3-5: 35¢) (#4,5: 3-1/4x5")

Carvel Corp. (Ice Cream)

1-3			1.00
4,5(1976)-Baseball theme	1.00	2.50	6.00

CAR WARRIORS
June, 1991 - No. 4, Sept, 1991 ($2.25, limited series)
Marvel Comics (Epic Comics)

1-4: 1-Says April in indicia		.90	2.25

CASE OF THE SHOPLIFTER'S SHOE (See Perry Mason, Feature Book No.50)

CASE OF THE WASTED WATER, THE
1972? (Giveaway)
Rheem Water Heating

nn-Neal Adams-a	4.30	13.00	32.00

CASE OF THE WINKING BUDDHA, THE
1950 (132 pgs.; 25¢; B&W; 5-1/2x7-5-1/2x8")
St. John Publ. Co.

nn-Charles Raab-a; reprinted in Authentic Police Cases No. 25			
	23.00	69.00	160.00

CASEY-CRIME PHOTOGRAPHER (Two-Gun Western No. 5 on)(Radio)
Aug, 1949 - No. 4, Feb, 1950
Marvel Comics (BFP)

1-Photo-c; 52 pgs.	17.00	49.00	115.00
2-4: Photo-c	11.00	33.00	75.00

CASEY JONES (TV)
No. 915, July, 1958
Dell Publishing Co.

Four Color 915-Alan Hale photo-c	6.30	19.00	63.00

CASEY JONES & RAPHAEL (See Bodycount)
Oct, 1994 ($2.75, unfinished limited series)
Mirage Studios

1-Bisley-c; Eastman story & pencils		1.10	2.75

CASEY JONES: NORTH BY DOWNEAST
June, 1994? - No. 2, July, 1994 ($2.75, limited series)
Mirage Studios

1,2-Rick Veitch script & pencils; Kevin Eastman story & inks			
		1.10	2.75

CASPER ADVENTURE DIGEST
V2#1, Oct, 1992 - V2#8, Apr, 1994 ($1.75/$1.95, digest-size)
Harvey Comics

V2#1-8: Casper, Richie Rich, Spooky, Wendy		.70	1.75

CASPER AND...
Nov, 1987 - No. 12, June, 1990 (.75/$1.00, all reprints)
Harvey Comics

1-12: 1-Ghostly Trio. 2-Spooky; begin $1.00-c. 3-Wendy. 4-Nightmare. 5-Ghostly Trio. 6-Spooky. 7-Wendy. 8-Hot Stuff. 9-Baby Huey. 10-Wendy. 11-Ghostly Trio. 12-Spooky			1.00

CASPER AND FRIENDS
Oct, 1991 - No. 5, July, 1992 ($1.00/$1.25)
Harvey Comics

1-5: Nightmare, Ghostly Trio, Wendy, Spooky. 3-Begin $1.25-c.			
			1.25

CASPER AND NIGHTMARE (See Harvey Hits# 37, 45, 52, 56, 59, 62, 65, 68,71, 75)

CASPER AND NIGHTMARE (Nightmare & Casper 1-5)
No. 6, 11/64 - No. 44, 10/73; No. 45, 6/74 - No. 46, 8/74 (25¢)
Harvey Publications

6: 68 pg. Giants begin, ends #32	3.00	9.00	30.00
7-10	2.00	6.00	20.00

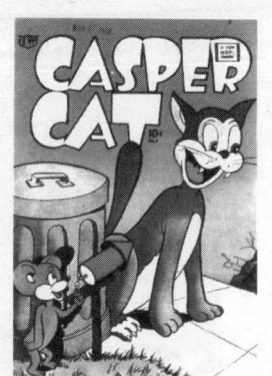

Casper Cat #1 © I. W. Publ.

Casper's Ghostland #1 © Paramount

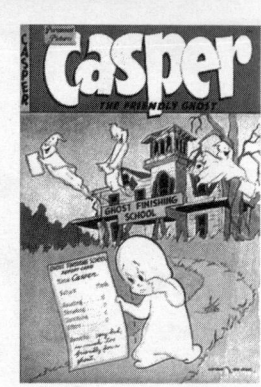

Casper The Friendly Ghost #1 © Paramount

	GD25	FN65	NM94

		GD25	FN65	NM94
11-20		1.30	3.25	10.00
21-46: 33-37-(52 pg. Giants)		1.60	4.00	
NOTE: Many issues contain reprints.				

CASPER AND SPOOKY (See Harvey Hits No. 20)
Oct, 1972 - No. 7, Oct, 1973
Harvey Publications

		GD25	FN65	NM94
1		1.20	3.60	12.00
2-7		1.00	2.00	5.00

CASPER AND THE GHOSTLY TRIO
Nov, 1972 - No. 7, Nov, 1973; No. 8, Aug, 1990 - No. 10, Dec, 1990
Harvey Publications

	GD25	FN65	NM94
1	1.20	3.60	12.00
2-7	1.00	2.00	5.00
8-10			1.50

CASPER AND WENDY
Sept, 1972 - No. 8, Nov, 1973
Harvey Publications

	GD25	FN65	NM94
1: 52 pg. Giant	1.20	3.60	12.00
2-8	1.00	2.00	5.00

CASPER BIG BOOK
V2#1, Aug, 1992 - No. 3, May, 1993 ($1.95, 52 pgs.)
Harvey Comics

	GD25	FN65	NM94
V2#1-3: 1-Spooky app.		.80	2.00

CASPER CAT (See Dopey Duck)
1958; 1963
I. W. Enterprises/Super

	GD25	FN65	NM94
1,7,1-Wacky Duck #?.7-Reprint, Super No. 14('63) 1.00		2.60	6.00

CASPER DIGEST (...Magazine #?; ...Halloween Digest #8, 10)
Oct, 1986 - No. 18, Jan, 1991 ($1.25/$1.75, digest-size)
Harvey Publications

	GD25	FN65	NM94
1-18: 11-Valentine-c. 18-Halloween-c		.70	1.75

CASPER DIGEST (...Magazine #? on)
V2#1, Sept, 1991 - V2#14, Nov, 1994 ($1.75/$1.95, digest-size)
Harvey Comics

	GD25	FN65	NM94
V2#1-14		.70	1.75

CASPER DIGEST STORIES
Feb, 1980 - No. 4, Nov, 1980 (95¢, 132 pgs., digest size)
Harvey Publications

	GD25	FN65	NM94
1		1.60	4.00
2-4		1.00	2.50

CASPER DIGEST WINNERS
Apr, 1980 - No. 3, Sept, 1980 (95¢, 132 pgs., digest size)
Harvey Publications

	GD25	FN65	NM94
1		1.00	2.50
2,3			1.50

CASPER ENCHANTED TALES DIGEST
May, 1992 - No. 10, Oct, 1994 ($1.75, digest-size, 98 pgs.)
Harvey Comics

	GD25	FN65	NM94
1-10-Casper, Spooky, Wendy stories		.70	1.75

CASPER GHOSTLAND
May, 1992 ($1.25)
Harvey Comics

	GD25	FN65	NM94
1			1.25

CASPER GIANT SIZE
Oct, 1992 - No. 4, Nov, 1993 ($2.25, 68 pgs.)
Harvey Comics

	GD25	FN65	NM94
V2#1-4-Casper, Wendy, Spooky stories		.90	2.25

CASPER HALLOWEEN TRICK OR TREAT
Jan, 1976 (52 pgs.)
Harvey Publications

	GD25	FN65	NM94
1		1.60	4.00

CASPER IN SPACE (Formerly Casper Spaceship)
No. 6, June, 1973 - No. 8, Oct, 1973
Harvey Publications

	GD25	FN65	NM94
6-8		1.00	2.00	5.00

CASPER'S GHOSTLAND
Winter, 1958-59 - No. 97, 12/77; No. 98, 12/79 (25¢)
Harvey Publications

	GD25	FN65	NM94
1-84 pgs. begin, ends #10	15.00	45.00	140.00
2	8.00	24.00	75.00
3-10	5.00	15.00	50.00
11-20: 11-68 pgs. begin, ends #61. 13-X-Mas-c	4.00	12.00	40.00
21-40	3.00	9.00	30.00
41-61	2.00	6.00	14.00
62-77: 62-52 pgs. begin	1.00	2.60	6.00
78-98: 94-X-Mas-c		1.60	4.00
NOTE: Most issues contain reprints w/new stories.			

CASPER SPACESHIP (Casper in Space No. 6 on)
Aug, 1972 - No. 5, April, 1973
Harvey Publications

	GD25	FN65	NM94
1: 52 pg. Giant	1.20	3.60	12.00
2-5	1.00	2.00	5.00

CASPER SPECIAL
nd (Dec, 1990) (Giveaway with $1.00 cover)
Target Stores (Harvey)

	GD25	FN65	NM94
Three issues-Given away with Casper video			1.00

CASPER STRANGE GHOST STORIES
October, 1974 - No. 14, Jan, 1977 (All 52 pgs.)
Harvey Publications

	GD25	FN65	NM94
1	.80	2.40	8.00
2-14		1.20	3.00

CASPER, THE FRIENDLY GHOST (See America's Best TV Comics, Famous TV Funday Funnies, The Friendly Ghost..., Nightmare &..., Richie Rich and..., Tastee-Freez, Treasury of Comics, Wendy the Good Little Witch & Wendy Witch World)

CASPER, THE FRIENDLY GHOST (Becomes Harvey Comics No. 61 (No. 6), and then continued with Harvey issue No. 7)(1st Series)
Sept, 1949 - No. 5, Aug, 1951
St. John Publishing Co.

	GD25	FN65	NM94
1(1949)-Origin & 1st app. Baby Huey & Herman the Mouse (1st time the name Casper app. in any media, even films)	137.00	412.00	1100.00
2,3 (2/50 & 8/50)	59.00	178.00	475.00
4,5 (3/51 & 8/51)	44.00	132.00	350.00

CASPER, THE FRIENDLY GHOST (Paramount Picture Star...)(2nd Series)
No. 7, Dec, 1952 - No. 70, July, 1958
Harvey Publications (Family Comics)
Note: No. 6 is Harvey Comics Hits No. 61 (10/52)

	GD25	FN65	NM94
7-Baby Huey begins, ends #9	27.00	81.00	265.00
8,9	15.00	45.00	145.00
10-Spooky begins (1st app., 6/53), ends #70?	16.50	50.00	160.00
11-18: Alfred Harvey app. in story	9.00	27.00	85.00
19-1st app. Nightmare (4/54)	11.00	32.00	110.00
20-Wendy the Witch begins (1st app., 5/54)	15.00	45.00	140.00
21-30: 24-Infinity-c	7.00	21.00	65.00
31-40	5.00	15.00	45.00
41-50	4.00	12.00	36.00
51-70 (Continues as Friendly Ghost... 8/58)	3.50	10.50	32.00
American Dental Association (Giveaways):			

Casual Heroes #1 © Motown

The Cat #4 © MEG

Catalyst: Agents of Change #4 © DH

	GD25	FN65	NM94

...'s Dental Health Activity Book-1977   1.40   3.50
...Presents Space Age Dentistry-1972   1.60   4.00
..., His Den, & Their Dentist Fight the Tooth Demons-1974
     1.60   4.00

CASPER THE FRIENDLY GHOST (Formerly The Friendly Ghost...)(3rd Series)
No. 254, July, 1990 - No. 260, Jan, 1991 ($1.00)
Harvey Comics
254-260   1.00

CASPER THE FRIENDLY GHOST (4th Series)
Mar, 1991 - No. 28, Nov, 1994 ($1.00/$1.25/$1.50)
Harvey Comics
1-14: 1-Casper becomes Mighty Ghost; Spooky & Wendy app. 7,8-Post-a.
   7-14-($1.25)   1.25
   15-28-($1.50)   1.50

CASPER T.V. SHOWTIME
Jan, 1980 - No. 5, Oct, 1980
Harvey Comics
1   .80   2.00
2-5   1.00

CASSETTE BOOKS
(Classics Illustrated)
1984 (48 pgs, b&w comic with cassette tape)
Cassette Book Co./I.P.S. Publ.
NOTE: This series was illegal. The artwork was illegally obtained, and the Classics Illustrated copyright owner, Twin Circle Publ. sued to get an injunction to prevent the continued sale of this series. Many C.I. collectors obtained copies before the 1987 injunction, but now they are already scarce. Here again the market is just developing, but sealed mint copies of com ic and tape should be worth at least $25.
   1001 (CI#1-A2)New-PC   1002(CI#3-A2)CI-PC   1003(CI#13-A2)CI-PC
   1004(CI#25)CI-LDC   1005(CI#10-A2)New-PC   1006(CI#64)CI-LDC

CASTILIAN (See Movie Classics)

CASUAL HEROES
Apr, 1996 ($2.25, unfinished limited series
Image Comics (Motown Machineworks)
1-Steve Rude-c   2.25

CAT, T.H.E. (TV) (See T.H.E. Cat)

CAT, THE (See Movie Classics)

CAT, THE
Nov, 1972 - No. 4, June, 1973
Marvel Comics Group
1-Origin & 1st app. The Cat (who later becomes Tigra); Mooney-a(i);
   Wood-c(i)/a(i)   2.15   6.50   15.00
2,3: 2-Marie Severin/Mooney-a. 3-Everett inks   1.30   3.25   8.00
4-Starlin/Weiss-a(p)   1.30   3.25   8.00

CATALYST: AGENTS OF CHANGE (Also see Comics' Greatest World)
Feb, 1994 - No.7, Nov, 1994 ($2.00, limited series)
Dark Horse Comics
1-7: 1-Foil stamped logo   .80   2.00

CAT & MOUSE
Dec, 1988 ($1.75, color w/part B&W)
EF Graphics (Silverline)
1-1st printing (12/88, 32 pgs.)   .70   1.75
1-2nd printing (5/89, 36 pgs.)   .70   1.75

CATFIGHT: DREAM INTO ACTION (Also see Hellina/Catfight)
Mar, 1996 ($2.75, B&W, one-shot)
Lightning Comics
1-Creed app.   2.75
1 Nude A & Nude B ($9.95)-Polybagged   10.00

---

1 Commemorative ($5.95)-Polybagged   6.00

CATFIGHT: DREAM WARRIOR (Also see Hellina/Catfight)
June, 1995 ($2.75, B&W, one-shot)
Insomnia Press
1-Hellina cameo   1.10   2.75

CAT FROM OUTER SPACE (See Walt Disney Showcase #46)

CATHOLIC COMICS (See Heroes All Catholic...)
June, 1946 - V3#10, July, 1949
Catholic Publications
1   24.00   71.00   165.00
2   12.00   36.00   85.00
3-13(7/47)   10.00   30.00   70.00
V2#1-10   6.70   20.00   40.00
V3#1-10: Reprints 10-part Treasure Island serial from Target V2#2-11
   (see Key Comics #5)   7.50   22.50   45.00

CATHOLIC PICTORIAL
1947
Catholic Guild
1-Toth-a(2) (Rare)   36.00   107.00   250.00

CATMAN COMICS (Formerly Crash Comics 1-5)
5/41 - No. 17, 1/43; No. 18, 7/43 - No. 22, 12/43; No. 23, 3/44 - No. 26,
11/44; No. 27, 4/45 - No. 30, 12/45; No. 31, 6/46 - No. 32, 8/46
Holyoke Publishing Co./Continental Magazines V2#12, 7/44 on
1(V1#6)-Origin The Deacon & Sidekick Mickey, Dr. Diamond & Rag-Man; The
   Black Widow app.; The Catman by Chas. Quinlan & Blaze Baylor begin
     288.00   862.00   2300.00
2(V1#7)   93.00   281.00   750.00
3(V1#8), 4(V1#9): 3-The Pied Piper begins   68.00   206.00   550.00
5(V2#10)-Origin Kitten; The Hood begins (c-redated), 6,7(V2#11,12)
     56.00   168.00   450.00
8(V2#13,3/42)-Origin Little Leaders; Volton by Kubert begins (his 1st comic
   book work)   68.00   206.00   550.00
9,10(V2#14,15): 10-Origin Blackout retold; Phantom Falcon begins
     45.00   136.00   365.00
11 (V3#1)-Kubert-a   45.00   136.00   365.00
12 (V3#2) - 15, 17, 18(V3#8, 7/43)   40.00   120.00   325.00
16 (V3#5)-Hitler, Tojo, Mussolini, Stalin-c   37.00   141.00   375.00
19 (V2#6)-Hitler, Tojo, Mussolini-c   37.00   141.00   375.00
20 (V2#7): 20-Hitler-c   37.00   141.00   375.00
21- 23 (V2#10, 3/44)   39.00   118.00   275.00
nn(V3#13, 5/44)-Rico-a; Schomburg bondage-c   38.00   114.00   265.00
nn(V2#12, 7/44)   38.00   114.00   265.00
nn(V3#1, 9/44)-Origin The Golden Archer; Leatherface app.
     38.00   114.00   265.00
nn(V3#2, 11/44)-L. B. Cole-c   53.00   160.00   425.00
27-Origin Kitten retold; L. B. Cole Flag-c   59.00   178.00   475.00
28-Catman learns Kitten's I.D.; Dr. Macabre, Deacon app.; L. B. Cole c/a
     62.00   187.00   500.00
29-32-L. B. Cole-c; bondage-#30   53.00   160.00   425.00
NOTE: Fuje a-11, 29(3), 30. Palais a-11, 29(2), 30(2), 32; c-25(7/44). Rico a-11(2).

CAT TALES (3-D)
Apr, 1989 ($2.95)
Eternity Comics
1-Felix the Cat-r in 3-D   1.20   3.00

CATWOMAN (Also see Action Comics Weekly #611, Batman #404-407,
Detective Comics, & Superman's Girlfriend Lois Lane #70, 71)
Feb, 1989 - No. 4, May, 1989 ($1.50, limited series, mature)
DC Comics
1   1.00   2.50   6.00
2   1.40   3.50

Catwoman #15 © DC

Caught #1 © ATLAS

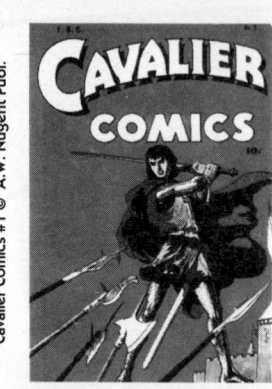

Cavalier Comics #1 © A.W. Nugent Publ.

	GD25	FN65	NM94
3,4: 3-Batman cameo. 4-Batman app.		1.00	2.50
Her Sister's Keeper (1991, $9.95, trade paperback)-r/#1-4			
		1.65	4.00	10.00

CATWOMAN (Also see Showcase '93, Showcase '95 #4, & Batman #404-407)
Aug, 1993 - Present ($1.50/$1.95)
DC Comics

		GD25	FN65	NM94
1-($1.95)-Embossed-c; Bane app.; Balent c-1-10; a-1-10p			
		1.00	2.00	5.00
2,3: 3-Bane flashback cameo		1.60	4.00
0,4-20, 26-35: 4-Brief Bane app. 6,7-Knightquest tie-ins; new Batman (Azrael)			
app. 8-1st app. Zephyr. 12-KnightsEnd Pt. 6. 13-KnightsEnd Aftermath.			
14-(9/94)-Zero Hour. 0-(10/94)-Origin retold		1.00	2.50
21-24, 26-36: 21-$1.95-c begins. 28,29-Penguin cameo app. 31-Contagion			
Pt. 4 (Reads Pt. 5 on-c). 32-Contagion Pt. 9. 36-Legacy Pt. 2. 38,39-Year			
Two; Batman, Joker, Penguin & Two-Face app.		.80	2.00
25-($2.95)-Robin app.		1.20	3.00
Annual 1 (1994, $2.95, 68 pgs.)-Elseworlds story; Batman app.; no Balent-a			
		1.20	3.00
Annual 2 (1995, $3.95)-Year One story		1.60	4.00
Annual 3 (1996, $2.95)-Legends of the Dead Earth story		1.20	3.00

CAUGHT
Aug, 1956 - No. 5, Apr, 1957
Atlas Comics (VPI)

	GD25	FN65	NM94
1	16.00	47.00	110.00
2,4: 4-Maneely-a (4 pgs.)	9.15	27.00	55.00
3-Maneely, Pakula, Torres-a	9.15	27.00	55.00
5-Crandall, Krigstein-a	10.00	30.00	65.00

NOTE: *Drucker* a-2. *Heck* a-4. *Severin* c-1, 2, 4, 5. *Shores* a-4.

CAVALIER COMICS
1945; 1952 (Early DC reprints)
A. W. Nugent Publ. Co.

	GD25	FN65	NM94
2(1945)-Speed Saunders, Fang Gow	17.00	49.00	115.00
2(1952)	9.15	27.00	55.00

CAVE GIRL (Also see Africa)
No. 11, 1953 - No. 14, 1954
Magazine Enterprises

	GD25	FN65	NM94
11(A-1 82)-Origin; all Cave Girl stories	40.00	120.00	300.00
12(A-1 96), 13(A-1 116), 14(A-1 125)-Thunda by Powell in each			
	29.00	86.00	200.00

NOTE: *Powell* c/a in all.

CAVE GIRL
1988 ($2.95, 44 pgs.) (16 pgs. of color, rest B&W)
AC Comics

	GD25	FN65	NM94
1-Powell-r/Cave Girl #11; Nyoka photo back-c from movie; Powell/Bill			
Black-c; Special Limited Edition on-c		1.20	3.00

CAVE KIDS (TV)
Feb, 1963 - No. 16, Mar, 1967 (Hanna-Barbera)
Gold Key

	GD25	FN65	NM94
1	4.00	12.00	40.00
2-5	2.00	6.00	20.00
6-16: 7,12-Pebbles & Bamm Bamm app.	1.70	5.00	12.00

CAVEWOMAN
Jan, 1994 - No. 6, 1995 ($2.95)
Caliber

	GD25	FN65	NM94
1-6		1.20	3.00

CAVEWOMAN: RAIN
1996 - Present ($2.95)
Caliber

	GD25	FN65	NM94
1-3		1.20	3.00

	GD25	FN65	NM94
CELESTINE (See Violator Vs. Badrock #1)			

May, 1996 - No. 2, June, 1996 ($2.50, limited series)
Image Comics (Extreme Studios)

		GD25	FN65	NM94
1,2: Warren Ellis scripts		1.00	2.50

CENTURION OF ANCIENT ROME, THE
1958 (no month listed) (B&W, 36 pgs.)
Zondervan Publishing House

	GD25	FN65	NM94
(Rare) All by Jay Disbrow	32.00	96.00	225.00

CENTURIONS (TV)
June, 1987 - No. 4, Sept, 1987 (75¢, limited series)
DC Comics

	GD25	FN65	NM94
1-4			1.00

CENTURY: DISTANT SONS
Feb, 1996 ($2.95, one-shot)
Marvel Comics

	GD25	FN65	NM94
1-Wraparound-c		1.20	3.00

CENTURY OF COMICS
1933 (100 pgs.) (Probably the 3rd comic book)
Eastern Color Printing Co.

Bought by Wheatena, Milk-O-Malt, John Wanamaker, Kinney Shoe Stores, &
others to be used as premiums and radio giveaways. No publisher listed.

	GD25	FN65	VF82
nn-Mutt & Jeff, Joe Palooka, etc. reprints	3400.00	10,200.00	17,500.00
(Estimated up to 20 total copies exist, none in NM-Mint)			

CEREBUS BI-WEEKLY
Dec. 2, 1988 - No. 26, Nov. 11, 1989 ($1.25, B&W)
Aardvark-Vanaheim

	GD25	FN65	NM94
1-26: Reprints Cerebus #1-26		.80	2.00

CEREBUS: CHURCH & STATE
Feb, 1991 - No. 30, Apr, 1992 ($2.00, B&W, bi-weekly)
Aardvark-Vanaheim

	GD25	FN65	NM94
1-30: r/Cerebus #51-80		1.00	2.50

CEREBUS: HIGH SOCIETY
Feb, 1990 - No. 25, 1991 ($1.70, B&W)
Aardvark-Vanaheim

	GD25	FN65	NM94
1-25: r/Cerebus #26-50		.90	2.25

CEREBUS JAM
Apr, 1985
Aardvark-Vanaheim

	GD25	FN65	NM94
1-Eisner, Austin, Dave Sim-a (Cerebus vs. Spirit)	1.00	2.00	5.00

CEREBUS THE AARDVARK (See A-V in 3-D, Nucleus, Power Comics)
Dec, 1977 - Present ($1.70/$2.00/$2.25, B&W)
Aardvark-Vanaheim

	GD25	FN65	NM94
0		1.20	3.00
0-Gold	4.30	13.00	30.00
1-1st app. Cerebus; 2000 print run; most copies poorly printed			
	32.00	96.00	225.00

Note: There is a counterfeit version known to exist. It can be distinguished from the original in the
following ways: inside cover is glossy instead of flat, black background on the front cover is blot-
ted or spotty. Reports show that a counterfeit #2 also exists.

	GD25	FN65	NM94
2-Dave Sim art in all	8.50	26.00	60.00
3-Origin Red Sophia	7.00	21.50	50.00
4-Origin Elrod the Albino	5.00	15.00	35.00
5,6	4.30	13.00	30.00
7-10	3.25	9.50	22.00
11,12: 11-Origin The Cockroach	2.85	8.50	20.00
13-15: 14-Origin Lord Julius	1.65	4.20	10.00
16-20	1.00	2.60	6.00
21-B. Smith letter in letter column	5.00	15.00	35.00

Cerebus #203 © Dave Sim

Chain Gang War #9 © DC

Chamber Of Chills #18 © MEG

	GD25	FN65	NM94
22-Low distribution; no cover price	2.15	6.50	15.00
23-30: 23-Preview of Wandering Star by Teri S. Wood. 26-High Society begins, ends #50	1.00	2.60	6.00
31-Origin Moonroach	1.30	3.25	8.00
32-40	1.00	2.00	5.00
41-50,52: 52-Church & State begins, ends #111; Cutey Bunny app.		1.60	4.00
51-Cutey Bunny app.	2.00	6.00	14.00
53-Intro. Wolveroach (cameo)	1.00	2.60	6.00
54-1st full Wolveroach story	1.30	3.25	8.00
55,56-Wolveroach app.; Normalman back-ups by Valentino	1.00	2.60	6.00
57-79: 61,62: Flaming Carrot app. 65-Gerhard begins		1.00	2.50
80-220: 104-Flaming Carrot app. 112/113-Double issue. 114-Jaka's Story begins, ends #136. 137-$2.25-c begins. 139-Melmoth begins, ends #150. 175-($2.25, 44 pgs). 151-Mothers & Daughters begins, ends #200 201-Guys storyline begins; Eddie Campbell's Bacchus app.		.90	2.25
151-153-2nd printings		.90	2.25
Free Cerebus (Giveaway, 1991-92?, 36 pgs.)-All-r			1.00

CHAIN GANG WAR
July, 1993 - No. 12, June, 1994 ($1.75)
DC Comics

	GD25	FN65	NM94
1-($2.50)-Embossed silver foil-c, Dave Johnson-c/a	1.00		2.50
2-4,6-12: 3-Deathstroke app. 4-Brief Deathstroke app. 6-New Batman (Azrael) cameo. 11-New Batman-c/story. 12-New Batman app.		.70	1.75
5-($2.50)-Foil embossed-c; Deathstroke app; new Batman cameo (1 panel).	1.00		2.50

CHAINS OF CHAOS
Nov, 1994 - No. 3, Jan, 1995 ($2.95, limited series)
Harris Comics

	GD25	FN65	NM94
1-3-Re-Intro of The Rook w/ Vampirella	1.20		3.00

CHALLENGE OF THE UNKNOWN (Formerly Love Experiences)
No. 6, Sept, 1950 (See Web Of Mystery No. 19)
Ace Magazines

	GD25	FN65	NM94
6- "Villa of the Vampire" used in N.Y. Joint Legislative Comm. Publ; Sekowsky-a	23.00	69.00	160.00

CHALLENGER, THE
1945 - No. 4, Oct-Dec, 1946
Interfaith Publications/T.C. Comics

	GD25	FN65	NM94
nn; nd; 32 pgs.; Origin the Challenger Club; Anti-Fascist with funny animal filler	29.00	86.00	200.00
2-4: Kubert-a; 4-Fuje-a	25.00	75.00	175.00

CHALLENGERS OF THE UNKNOWN (See Showcase #6, 7, 11, 12, Super DC Giant, and Super Team Family)
4-5/58 - No. 77, 12-1/70-71; No. 78, 2/73 - No. 80, 6-7/73;
No. 81, 6-7/77 - No. 87, 6-7/78
National Per. Publ./DC Comics

	GD25	FN65	NM94
1-(4-5/58)-Kirby/Stein-a(2); Kirby-c	200.00	600.00	2000.00
2-Kirby/Stein-a(2)	78.00	233.00	750.00
3-Kirby/Stein-a(2)	67.00	200.00	650.00
4-8-Kirby/Wood-a plus cover to #8	60.00	180.00	520.00
9,10	34.00	101.00	250.00
11-15: 11-Grey tone-c. 14-Origin/1st app. Multi-Man (villain)	23.00	69.00	170.00
16-22: 18-Intro. Cosmo, the Challengers Spacepet. 22-Last 10¢ issue	19.00	58.00	145.00
23-30	10.00	30.00	75.00
31-Retells origin of the Challengers	11.00	33.00	80.00
32-40	5.00	15.00	38.00
41-60: 43-New look begins. 48-Doom Patrol app. 49-Intro. Challenger Corps. 51-Sea Devils app. 55-Death of Red Ryan. 60-Red Ryan returns	2.60	7.50	18.00
61-73,75-77: 64,65-Kirby origin-r, parts 1 & 2. 66-New logo. 68-Last 12¢ issue. 69-1st app. Corinna	1.30	3.25	8.00
74-Deadman by Tuska/N. Adams; 1 pg. Wrightson-a	2.00	6.00	14.00
78-87: 82-Swamp Thing begins; Wrightson partial-i	1.60		4.00

NOTE: *N. Adams* c-67, 68, 70, 72, 74i, 81i. *Buckler* c-83-86p. *Giffen* a-83-87p. *Kirby* a-75-80r; c-75, 77, 78. *Kubert* c-64, 66, 69, 76, 79. *Nasser* c/a-81p, 82p. *Tuska* a-73. *Wood* r-76.

CHALLENGERS OF THE UNKNOWN
Mar, 1991 - No. 8, Oct, 1991 ($1.75, limited series)
DC Comics

	GD25	FN65	NM94
1-Jeph Loeb scripts & Tim Sale-a in all; Bolland-c	.80		2.00
2-8: 2-Superman app. 3-Dr. Fate app. 6-G. Kane-c(p). 7-Steranko-c swipe by Art Adams		.70	1.75

NOTE: *Art Adams* c-7. *Bolland* c-1. *Hempel* c-5. *Gil Kane* c-6p. *Sale* a-1-8; c-2, 3, 8. *Wagner* c-4.

CHALLENGE TO THE WORLD
1951 (10¢, 36 pgs.)
Catechetical Guild

	GD25	FN65	NM94
nn	3.60	9.00	18.00

CHAMBER OF CHILLS (Formerly Blondie Comics #20; ...of Clues No. 27 on)
No. 21, June, 1951 - No. 26, Dec, 1954
Harvey Publications/Witches Tales

	GD25	FN65	NM94
21 (#1)	33.00	99.00	230.00
22,24 (#2,3)	19.00	58.00	135.00
23 (#4)-Excessive violence; eyes torn out	22.00	66.00	155.00
5(2/52)-Decapitation, acid in face scene	22.00	66.00	155.00
6-Woman melted alive	21.00	62.00	145.00
7-Used in *SOTI*, pg. 389; decapitation/severed head panels	20.00	60.00	140.00
8-10: 8-Decapitation panels	17.00	49.00	115.00
11,12,14	11.50	34.00	80.00
13,15-24-Nostrand-a in all. 13,21-Decapitation panels. 18-Atom bomb panels.			
20-Nostrand-c	18.00	54.00	125.00
25,26	10.00	30.00	65.00

NOTE: *About half the issues contain bondage, torture, sadism, perversion, gore, cannabalism, eyes ripped out, acid in face, etc. Elias* c-4-11, 14-19, 21-26. *Kremer* a-12, 17. *Palais* a-21(?), 23. *Nostrand/Powell* a-13, 15, 16. *Powell* a-21, 23, 24('51), 5-8, 11, 13, 18-21, 23-25. Bondage-c-21, 24('51), 7. 25-r/#5; 26-r/#9.

CHAMBER OF CHILLS
Nov, 1972 - No. 25, Nov, 1976
Marvel Comics Group

	GD25	FN65	NM94
1-Harlan Ellison adaptation	1.00	2.00	5.00
2-25		.80	2.00

NOTE: *Adkins* a-1i, 2i. *Brunner* a-2-4; c-4. *Chaykin* a-4. *Ditko* r-14, 16, 19, 23, 24. *Everett* a-3i, 11r,21r. *Heath* a-1r. *Gil Kane* c-2p. *Powell* a-13r. *Russell* a-1p, 2p. *Williamson/Mayo* a-13r. *Robert E. Howard* horror story adaptation-2, 3.

CHAMBER OF CLUES (Formerly Chamber of Chills)
No. 27, Feb, 1955 - No. 28, April, 1955
Harvey Publications

	GD25	FN65	NM94
27-Kerry Drake-r/#19; Powell-a; last pre-code	10.00	30.00	60.00
28-Kerry Drake	6.35	19.00	38.00

CHAMBER OF DARKNESS (Monsters on the Prowl #9 on)
Oct, 1969 - No. 8, Dec, 1970
Marvel Comics Group

	GD25	FN65	NM94
1-Buscema-a(p)	4.30	13.00	30.00
2,3: 2-Neal Adams scripts. 3-Smith, Buscema-a	1.70	5.00	12.00
4-A Conanesque tryout by Smith (4/70); reprinted in Conan #16; Marie Severin/Everett-c	5.00	15.00	35.00
5,6,8: 5-H.P. Lovecraft adaptation	1.00	2.00	5.00

The Champions #12 © MEG

Chaos Quarterly #2 © Chaos! Comics

Charlemagne #1 © EEP

	GD25	FN65	NM94

	GD25	FN65	NM94
7-Wrightson-c/a, 7pgs. (his 1st work at Marvel); Wrightson draws himself in			
1st & last panels; Kirby/Ditko-r	1.65	4.20	10.00
1-(1/72; 25¢ Special)	1.00	2.60	6.00

NOTE: Adkins/Everett a-8. Buscema a-Special 1r. Craig a-5. Ditko a-6-8r. Heck a-1, 2, 8, Special 1r. Kirby a(p)-4, 5, 7r. Kirby/Everett c-5. Severin/Everett c-6. Shores a-2, 3i, Special 1r. Sutton a-1, 2i, 4, 7, Special 1r. Wrightson c-7, 8.

CHAMP COMICS (Formerly Champion No. 1-10)
No. 11, Oct, 1940 - No. 29, March, 1944
Worth Publ. Co./Champ Publ./Family Comics(Harvey Publ.)

	GD25	FN65	NM94
11-Human Meteor cont'd. from Champion	75.00	225.00	600.00
12-17,20: 14,15-Crandall-c. 20-The Green Ghost app.			
	53.00	160.00	425.00
18,19-Simon-c. 19-The Wasp app.	68.00	206.00	550.00
21-29: 22-The White Mask app. 23-Flag-c	44.00	132.00	350.00

CHAMPION (See Gene Autry's...)

CHAMPION COMICS (Formerly Speed Comics #1?; Champ Comics No. 11 on)
No. 2, Dec, 1939 - No. 10, Aug, 1940 (no No.1)
Worth Publ. Co.(Harvey Publications)

	GD25	FN65	NM94
2-The Champ, The Blazing Scarab, Neptina, Liberty Lads, Jungleman, Bill			
Handy, Swingtime Sweetie begin	118.00	356.00	950.00
3-7: 7-The Human Meteor begins?	62.00	187.00	500.00
8-10: 8-Simon-c. 9-1st S&K-c (1st collaboration together). 10-Bondage-c by			
Kirby	112.00	338.00	900.00

CHAMPIONS, THE
Oct, 1975 - No. 17, Jan, 1978
Marvel Comics Group

	GD25	FN65	NM94
1-Origin & 1st app. The Champions (The Angel, Black Widow, Ghost Rider,			
Hercules, Iceman); Venus x-over	2.15	6.50	15.00
2-17: 2,3-Venus x-over. 11-15,17-Byrne-a.	1.30	3.25	8.00

NOTE: Buckler/Adkins c-3. Byrne a-11-15, 17. Kane/Adkins c-1. Kane/Layton c-11. Tuska a-3p, 4p, 6p, 7p. Ghost Rider c-1-4, 7, 8, 10, 14, 16, 17 (4, 10, 14 are more prominent).

CHAMPIONS (Game)
June, 1986 - No. 6, Feb, 1987 (limited series)
Eclipse Comics

1-6: 1-Intro Flare; based on game. 5-Origin Flare			1.50

CHAMPIONS (Also see The League of Champions)
Sept, 1987 - No. 12, 1989 ($1.95)
Hero Comics

1-12: 1-Intro The Marksman & The Rose. 14-Origin Malice	.80		2.00
Annual 1(1988, $2.75, 52pgs.)-Origin of Giant	1.10		2.75

CHAMPION SPORTS
Oct-Nov, 1973 - No. 3, Feb-Mar, 1974
National Periodical Publications

1-3			1.50

CHAOS (See The Crusaders)

CHAOS BIBLE
Nov, 1995 ($3.30, one-shot)
Chaos! Comics

1-Profiles of characters & creators	1.40		3.50

CHAOS EFFECT, THE
1994
Valiant

Alpha (Giveaway w/trading card checklist)			1.00
Omega (11/94, $2.25)		.90	2.25
Epilogue Pt. 1, 2 (12/94, 1/95; $2.95)		1.20	3.00

CHAOS QUARTERLY
Oct, 1995 - Present ($4.95, quarterly)
Chaos! Comics

1-3: 1-anthology; Lady Death-c by Julie Bell. 2-Boris "Lady Demon"-c.

	GD25	FN65	NM94
	1.00	2.00	5.00
1-Premium Edition (7,500)			35.00

CHAPEL (Also see Youngblood & Youngblood Strikefile #1-3)
No. 1 Feb, 1995 - No. 2, Mar, 1995 ($2.50, limited series)
Image Comics (Extreme Studios)

1,2			2.50

CHAPEL (Also see Youngblood & Youngblood Strikefile #1-3)
V2 #1, Aug, 1995 - Present ($2.50)
Image Comics (Extreme Studios)

V2#1-7: 4-Babewatch x-over. 5-vs. Spawn. 7-Shadowhawk-c/app; Shadowhunt			
x-over		1.00	2.50
#1-Quesada & Palmiotti variant-c		1.20	3.00

CHARLEMAGNE (Also see War Dancer)
Mar, 1994 - No. 5, July, 1994 ($2.50)
Defiant Comics

1/2 (Hero Illustrated giveaway)-Adam Pollina-c/a.			
1-(3/94, $3.50, 52 pgs.)-Adam Pollina-c/a.		1.40	3.50
2,3,5: Adam Pollina-c/a. 2-War Dancer app. 5-Pre-Schism issue.			
		1.00	2.50
4-($3.25, 52 pgs.)		1.30	3.25

CHARLIE CHAN (See Big Shot Comics, Columbia Comics, Feature Comics & The New Advs. of...)

CHARLIE CHAN (The Adventures of...) (Zaza The Mystic No. 10 on) (TV)
6-7/48 - No. 5, 2-3/49; No.6, 6/55 - No. 9, 3/56
Crestwood(Prize) No. 1-5; Charlton No.6(6/55) on

	GD25	FN65	NM94
1-S&K-c, 2 pgs.; Infantino-a	62.00	187.00	500.00
2-5-S&K-c: 3-S&K-c/a	41.00	124.00	330.00
6 (6/55-Charlton)-S&K-c	29.00	86.00	200.00
7-9	14.00	43.00	100.00

CHARLIE CHAN
Oct-Dec, 1965 - No. 2, Mar, 1966
Dell Publishing Co.

	GD25	FN65	NM94
1-Springer-a	3.50	11.00	35.00
2	2.25	6.75	22.00

CHARLIE McCARTHY (See Edgar Bergen Presents...)
No. 171, Nov, 1947 - No. 571, July, 1954 (See True Comics #14)
Dell Publishing Co.

	GD25	FN65	NM94
Four Color 171	25.00	75.00	250.00
Four Color 196-Part photo-c; photo back-c	17.00	51.00	170.00
1(3-5/49)-Part photo-c; photo back-c	16.00	48.00	160.00
2-9(7/52; #5,6-52 pgs.)	7.00	21.00	70.00
Four Color 445,478,528,571	5.00	15.00	50.00

CHARLTON BULLSEYE
1975 - No. 5, 1976 ($1.50, B&W, bi-monthly, magazine format)
CPL/Gang Publications

1: 1 & 2 are last Capt. Atom by Ditko/Byrne intended for the never published			
Capt. Atom #90; Nightshade app.; Jeff Jones-a	2.00	6.00	14.00
2-Part 2 Capt. Atom story by Ditko/Byrne	1.65	4.70	11.00
3-Wrong Country by Sanho Kim	1.20	2.90	7.00
4-Doomsday + 1 by John Byrne	1.65	4.20	10.00
5-Doomsday + 1 by Byrne, The Question by Toth; Neal Adams back-c; Toth-c			
	2.00	6.00	14.00

CHARLTON BULLSEYE
June, 1981 - No. 10, Dec, 1982; Nov, 1986
Charlton Publications

1-Blue Beetle, The Question app.; 1st app. Rocket Rabbit			
		.80	2.00
2-10: 2-1st app. Neil The Horse; Rocket Rabbit app. 6-Origin & 1st app.			
Thunderbunny			1.50

Checkmate #33 © DC

Cheryl Blossom #1 © Archie

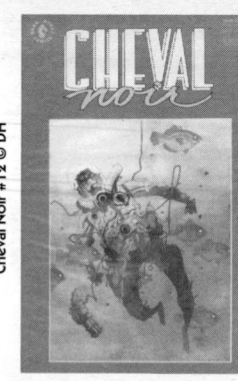
Cheval Noir #12 © DH

	GD25	FN65	NM94

	GD25	FN65	NM94
Special 1(11/86) (Half in B&W)		1.20	3.00
Special 2-Atomic Mouse app. (1987)		.80	2.00

CHARLTON CLASSICS
Apr, 1980 - No. 9, Aug, 1981
Charlton Comics

	GD25	FN65	NM94
1		.80	2.00
2-9			1.00

CHARLTON CLASSICS LIBRARY (1776)
V10 No.1, Mar, 1973 (one-shot)
Charlton Comics

	GD25	FN65	NM94
1776 (title) - Adaptation of the film musical "1776"; given away at movie theatres		1.60	4.00

CHARLTON PREMIERE (Formerly Marine War Heroes)
V1#19, July, 1967; V2#1, Sept, 1967 - No. 4, May, 1968
Charlton Comics

	GD25	FN65	NM94
V1#19-Marine War Heroes. V2#1-Trio; intro. Shape. Tyro Team. & Spookman. 2-Children of Doom. 3-Sinistro Boy Fiend; Blue Beetle & Peacemaker x-over. 4-Unlikely Tales; Aparo, Ditko-a	1.20	3.00	7.00

CHARLTON SPORT LIBRARY - PROFESSIONAL FOOTBALL
Winter, 1969-70 (Jan. on cover) (68 pgs.)
Charlton Comics

	GD25	FN65	NM94
1	1.70	5.00	12.00

CHECKMATE (TV)
Oct, 1962 - No. 2, Dec, 1962
Gold Key

	GD25	FN65	NM94
1,2-Photo-c	4.50	14.00	45.00

CHECKMATE! (See Action Comics #598)
Apr, 1988 - No. 33, Jan, 1991 ($1.25)
DC Comics

	GD25	FN65	NM94
1-12			1.25
13-33: $1.50/$2.00, new format			1.50

NOTE: *Gil Kane c-2, 4, 7, 8, 10, 11, 15-19.*

CHEERIOS PREMIUMS (Disney)
1947 (16 titles, pocket size, 32 pgs.)
Walt Disney Productions

Set "W"

	GD25	FN65	NM94
W1-Donald Duck & the Pirates	7.50	22.50	45.00
W2-Bucky Bug & the Cannibal King	4.00	11.00	22.00
W3-Pluto Joins the F.B.I.	4.00	11.00	22.00
W4-Mickey Mouse & the Haunted House	5.00	15.00	30.00

Set "X"

	GD25	FN65	NM94
X1-Donald Duck, Counter Spy	7.50	22.50	45.00
X2-Goofy Lost in the Desert	4.00	10.00	20.00
X3-Br'er Rabbit Outwits Br'er Fox	4.00	10.00	20.00
X4-Mickey Mouse at the Rodeo	5.00	15.00	30.00

Set "Y"

	GD25	FN65	NM94
Y1-Donald Duck's Atom Bomb by Carl Barks. Disney has banned reprinting this book	88.00	262.00	700.00
Y2-Br'er Rabbit's Secret	4.00	10.00	20.00
Y3-Dumbo & the Circus Mystery	4.70	14.00	28.00
Y4-Mickey Mouse Meets the Wizard	5.00	15.00	30.00

Set "Z"

	GD25	FN65	NM94
Z1-Donald Duck Pilots a Jet Plane (not by Barks)	7.50	22.50	45.00
Z2-Pluto Turns Sleuth Hound	4.00	10.00	20.00
Z3-The Seven Dwarfs & the Enchanted Mtn.	4.70	14.00	28.00
Z4-Mickey Mouse's Secret Room	5.00	15.00	30.00

CHEERIOS 3-D GIVEAWAYS (Disney)
1954 (24 titles, pocket size) (Glasses were cut-outs on boxes)
Walt Disney Productions

	GD25	FN65	NM94
Glasses only...	6.70	20.00	40.00

	GD25	FN65	NM94
(Set 1) 1-Donald Duck & Uncle Scrooge, the Firefighters			
2-Mickey Mouse & Goofy, Pirate Plunder			
3-Donald Duck's Nephews, the Fabulous Inventors			
4-Mickey Mouse, Secret of the Ming Vase			
5-Donald Duck with Huey, Dewey, & Louie; ...the Seafarers (title on 2nd page)			
6-Mickey Mouse, Moaning Mountain			
7-Donald Duck, Apache Gold			
8-Mickey Mouse, Flight to Nowhere (per book)	8.35	25.00	50.00
(Set 2) 1-Donald Duck, Treasure of Timbuktu			
2-Mickey Mouse & Pluto, Operation China			
3-Donald Duck in the Magic Cows			
4-Mickey Mouse & Goofy, Kid Kokonut			
5-Donald Duck, Mystery Ship			
6-Mickey Mouse, Phantom Sheriff			
7-Donald Duck, Circus Adventures			
8-Mickey Mouse, Arctic Explorers (per book)	8.35	25.00	50.00
(Set 3) 1-Donald Duck & Witch Hazel			
2-Mickey Mouse in Darkest Africa			
3-Donald Duck & Uncle Scrooge, Timber Trouble			
4-Mickey Mouse, Rajah's Rescue			
5-Donald Duck in Robot Reporter			
6-Mickey Mouse, Slumbering Sleuth			
7-Donald Duck in the Foreign Legion			
8-Mickey Mouse, Airwalking Wonder (per book)....	8.35	25.00	50.00

CHERYL BLOSSOM
Sept, 1995 - No. 3, Nov, 1995 ($1.50, limited series)
Archie Publications

	GD25	FN65	NM94
1-3			1.50
Special 1 (1995, $2.00)		.80	2.00
Special 2 (1995, $2.00)		.80	2.00

CHERYL BLOSSOM
July, 1996 - No. 3, Sept, 1996 ($1.50, limited series)
Archie Publications

	GD25	FN65	NM94
1-3: Dan DeCarlo-c/a			1.50

CHESTY AND COPTIE (Disney)
1946 (Giveaway, 4pgs.)
Los Angeles Community Chest

	GD25	FN65	NM94
nn-(One known copy) by Floyd Gottfredson	93.00	280.00	745.00

CHESTY AND HIS HELPERS (Disney)
1943 (Giveaway, 12 pgs., 5-1/2x7-1/4")
Los Angeles War Chest

	GD25	FN65	NM94
nn-Chesty & Coptie	62.00	188.00	500.00

CHESTY SANCHEZ
Nov, 1995 ($2.95, B&W)
Antarctic Press

	GD25	FN65	NM94
1		1.20	3.00

CHEVAL NOIR
1989 - No. 48, Nov, 1993 ($3.50, B&W, 68 pgs.)
Dark Horse Comics

	GD25	FN65	NM94
1-8,10 ($3.50): 6-Moebius poster insert		1.40	3.50
9,11,13,15,17,20,22 ($4.50, 84 pgs.)		1.80	4.50
12,18,19,21,23,25,26 ($3.95): 12-Geary-a; Mignola-c. 26-Moebius-a begins		1.60	4.00
14 ($4.95, 76 pgs.)(7 pgs. color)	1.00	2.00	5.00
16,24 ($3.75): 16-19-Contain trading cards		1.50	3.75
27-48 ($2.95): 33-Snyder III-c		1.20	3.00

NOTE: *Bolland a-2, 6, 7, 13, 14. Bolton a-2, 4, 45; c-4, 20. Chadwick c-13. Dorman painted c-16. Geary a-13, 14. Kelley Jones c-27. Kaluta a-6; c-6, 18. Moebius a-5, 9, 26. Dave Stevens*

Children's Big Book #1 © Dorene Publ. Co.

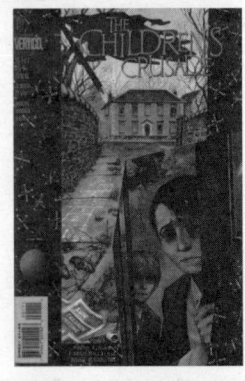

Children's Crusade #1 © DC

Chiller #1 © MEG

	GD25	FN65	NM94

	GD25	FN65	NM94

c-1, 7. Sutton painted c-36.

CHEYENNE (TV)
No. 734, Oct, 1956 - No. 25, Dec-Jan, 1961-62
Dell Publishing Co.

Four Color 734(#1)-Clint Walker photo-c	17.00	51.00	170.00
Four Color 772,803: Clint Walker photo-c	7.50	22.50	75.00
4(8-10/57) - 12: 4-9-Clint Walker photo-c. 10-12-Ty Hardin photo-c			
	5.00	15.00	50.00
13-25 (All Clint Walker photo-c)	5.00	15.00	50.00

CHEYENNE AUTUMN (See Movie Classics)

CHEYENNE KID (Formerly Wild Frontier No. 1-7)
No. 8, July, 1957 - No. 99, Nov, 1973
Charlton Comics

8 (#1)	5.85	17.50	35.00
9,15-19	4.00	10.00	20.00
10-Williamson/Torres-a(3); Ditko-c	9.15	27.50	55.00
11,12-Williamson/Torres-a(2) ea.; 11-(68 pgs.)-Cheyenne Kid meets Geronimo	10.00	30.00	60.00
13-Williamson/Torres-a (5 pgs.)	5.85	17.50	35.00
14-Williamson-a (5 pgs.?)	5.85	17.50	35.00
20-22,24,25-Severin c/a(3) each	3.25	9.50	22.00
23,27-29	1.65	4.20	10.00
26,30-Severin-a	2.30	6.70	16.00
31-59	1.00	2.60	6.00
60-99: 66-Wander by Aparo begins, ends #87. Apache Red begins #88, origin in #89		1.40	3.50
Modern Comics Reprint 87,89(1978)			1.00

CHIAROSCURO (THE PRIVATE LIVES OF LEONARDO DA VINCI)
July, 1995 - No. 10, Apr, 1996 ($2.50, limited series, mature)
DC Comics (Vertigo)

1-10		1.00	2.50

CHICAGO MAIL ORDER (See C-M-O Comics)

CHIEF, THE (Indian Chief No. 3 on)
No. 290, Aug, 1950 - No. 2, Apr-June, 1951
Dell Publishing Co.

Four Color 290(#1), 2	5.50	16.50	55.00

CHIEF CRAZY HORSE (See Wild Bill Hickok #21)
1950 (Also see Fighting Indians of the Wild West!)
Avon Periodicals

nn-Fawcette-c	18.00	54.00	125.00

CHIEF VICTORIO'S APACHE MASSACRE (See Fight Indians of/Wild West!)
1951
Avon Periodicals

nn-Williamson/Frazetta-a (7 pgs.); Larsen-a; Kinstler-c			
	39.00	118.00	275.00

CHILDREN OF FIRE
Nov, 1987 - No. 3, 1988 ($2.00, limited series)
Fantagor Press

1-3: by Richard Corben		.80	2.00

CHILDREN OF THE VOYAGER (See Marvel Frontier Comics Unlimited)
Sept, 1993 - No. 4, Dec, 1993 ($1.95, limited series)
Marvel Frontier Comics

1-($2.95)-Embossed glow-in-the-dark-c		1.20	3.00
2-4			1.50

CHILDREN'S BIG BOOK
1945 (25¢, stiff-c, 68 pgs.)
Dorene Publ. Co.

nn-Comics & fairy tales; David Icove-a	10.00	30.00	65.00

CHILDREN'S CRUSADE, THE
Dec, 1993 - No. 2, Jan, 1994 ($3.95, limited series, mature)
DC Comics (Vertigo)

1,2-Neil Gaiman scripts & Chris Bachalo-a; framing issues for Children's Crusade x-over	1.00	2.00	5.00

CHILD'S PLAY: THE SERIES (Movie)
May, 1991 - #3, 1991 ($2.50, 28pgs.)
Innovation Publishing

1-3		1.00	2.50

CHILD'S PLAY 2 THE OFFICIAL MOVIE ADAPTATION (Movie)
1990 - No. 3, 1990 ($2.50, bi-weekly limited series, high quality)
Innovation Publishing

1-3: Adapts movie sequel		1.00	2.50

CHILI (Millie's Rival)
5/69 - No. 17, 9/70; No. 18, 8/72 - No. 26, 12/73
Marvel Comics Group

1	2.85	8.50	20.00
2-5	1.65	4.20	10.00
6-17	1.20	3.00	7.00
18-26	1.00	2.00	5.00
Special 1(12/71)	1.65	4.20	10.00

CHILLER
Nov, 1993 - No. 2, Dec, 1993 ($7.95, limited series, 68 pgs.)
Marvel Comics (Epic Comics)

1,2	1.30	3.25	8.00

CHILLING ADVENTURES IN SORCERY (...as Told by Sabrina #1, 2)
(Red Circle Sorcery No. 6 on)
9/72 - No. 2, 10/72; No. 3, 10/73 - No. 5, 2/74
Archie Publications (Red Circle Productions)

1,2-Sabrina cameo in both	1.00	2.50	6.00
3-Morrow-c/a, all		1.40	3.50
4,5-Morrow-c/a (5 & 6 pgs)		1.40	3.50

CHILLING TALES (Formerly Beware)
No. 13, Dec, 1952 - No. 17, Oct, 1953
Youthful Magazines

13(No.1)-Harrison-a; Matt Fox-c/a	40.00	120.00	300.00
14-Harrison-a	26.00	79.00	185.00
15-Has #14 on-c; Matt Fox-c; Harrison-a	33.00	99.00	230.00
16-Poe adapt.- 'Metzengerstein'; Rudyard Kipling adapt.- 'Mark of the Beast,' by Kiefer; bondage-c	22.00	66.00	155.00
17-Matt Fox-c; Sir Walter Scott & Poe adapt.	29.00	86.00	200.00

CHILLING TALES OF HORROR (Magazine)
V1#1, 6/69 - V1#7, 12/70; V2#2, 2/71 - V2#5, 10/71 (50¢, B&W, 52 pgs.)
Stanley Publications

V1#1	2.85	8.50	20.00
2-7: 7-Cameron-a	2.00	6.00	14.00
V2#2,3,5: 2-Spirit of Frankenstein-r/Adventures into the Unknown #16			
	1.70	5.00	12.00
V2#4-r/9 pg. Feldstein-a from Adventures into the Unknown #3			
	2.00	6.00	14.00
NOTE: Two issues of V2#2 exist, Feb, 1971 and April, 1971.			

CHILLY WILLY
No. 740, Oct, 1956 - No. 1281, Apr-June, 1962 (Walter Lantz)
Dell Publishing Co.

Four Color 740 (#1)	4.00	12.00	40.00
Four Color 852 (2/58),967 (2/59),1017 (9/59), 1074 (2-4/60),1122 (8/60), 1177 (4-6/61), 1212 (7-9/61), 1281	3.00	9.00	30.00

CHINA BOY (See Wisco)

Choice Comics #1 © Grerat Publ.

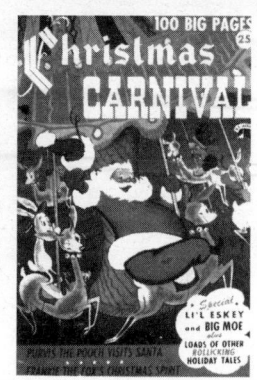

Christmas Carnival #2 © Z-D

Christmas Parade #6 © Gold Key

	GD25	FN65	NM94

CHIP 'N' DALE (Walt Disney)(See Walt Disney's C&S #204)
Nov, 1953 - No. 30, June-Aug, 1962; Sept, 1967 - No. 83, 1982
Dell Publishing Co./Gold Key/Whitman No. 65 on

Four Color 517(#1)	8.00	24.00	80.00
Four Color 581,636	5.00	15.00	50.00
4(12/55-2/56)-10	4.00	12.00	40.00
11-30	3.00	9.00	30.00
1(Gold Key, 1967)-Reprints	2.60	7.50	18.00
2-10	1.30	3.25	8.00
11-20		1.40	3.50
21-83			1.50

NOTE: *All Gold Key/Whitman issues have reprints except No. 32-35, 38-41, 45-47. No. 23-28, 30-42, 45-47, 49 have new covers.*

CHIP 'N DALE RESCUE RANGERS
June, 1990 - No. 19, Dec, 1991 ($1.50)
Disney Comics

1-19: New stories; 1,2-Origin			1.50

CHITTY CHITTY BANG BANG (See Movie Comics)

CHOICE COMICS
Dec, 1941 - No. 3, Feb, 1942
Great Publications

1-Origin Secret Circle; Atlas the Mighty app.; Zomba, Jungle Fight, Kangaroo Man, & Fire Eater begin	112.00	338.00	900.00
2	62.00	187.00	500.00
3-Double feature; Features movie "The Lost City" (classic cover); continued from Great Comics #3	93.00	281.00	750.00

CHOO CHOO CHARLIE
Dec, 1969
Gold Key

1-John Stanley-a (scarce)	9.00	27.00	90.00

CHRISTIAN HEROES OF TODAY
1964 (36 pgs.)
David C. Cook

nn	.80	2.00	4.00

CHRISTMAS (Also see A-1 Comics)
No. 28, 1950
Magazine Enterprises

A-1 28	4.25	13.00	28.00

CHRISTMAS ADVENTURE, A (See Classics Comics Giveaways, 12/69)

CHRISTMAS ADVENTURE, THE
1963 (16 pgs.)
S. Rose (H. L. Green Giveaway)

nn	1.20	3.00	6.00

CHRISTMAS ALBUM (See March of Comics No. 312)

CHRISTMAS & ARCHIE
Jan, 1975 ($1.00, 68 pgs., 10-1/4x13-1/4")
Archie Comics

1	1.20	3.60	12.00

CHRISTMAS AT THE ROTUNDA (Titled Ford Rotunda Christmas Book 1957 on) (Regular size)
1954 - 1961 (Given away every Christmas at one location)
Ford Motor Co. (Western Printing)

1954-56 issues (nn's)	5.00	15.00	30.00
1957-61 issues (nn's)	4.00	12.00	24.00

CHRISTMAS BELLS (See March of Comics No. 297)

CHRISTMAS CARNIVAL
1952 (25¢, one-shot, 100 pgs.)

Ziff-Davis Publ. Co./St. John Publ. Co. No. 2

nn	25.00	75.00	175.00
2-Reprints Ziff-Davis issue plus-c	16.00	47.00	110.00

CHRISTMAS CAROL, A (See March of Comics No. 33)

CHRISTMAS CAROL, A
No date (1942-43) (Giveaway, 32 pgs., 8-1/4x10-3/4", paper cover)
Sears Roebuck & Co.

nn-Comics & coloring book	14.00	43.00	100.00

CHRISTMAS CAROL, A
1940s ? (Christmas giveaway, 20 pgs.)
Sears Roebuck & Co.

nn-Comic book & animated coloring book	13.00	39.00	90.00

CHRISTMAS CAROLS
1959? (16 pgs.)
Hot Shoppes Giveaway

nn	3.60	9.00	18.00

CHRISTMAS COLORING FUN
1964 (20 pgs., slick-c, B&W)
H. Burnside

nn	1.60	4.00	8.00

CHRISTMAS DREAM, A
1950 (Kinney Shoe Store Giveaway, 16 pgs.)
Promotional Publishing Co.

nn	3.60	9.00	18.00

CHRISTMAS DREAM, A
1952? (Giveaway, paper cover, 16 pgs.)
J. J. Newberry Co.

nn	3.60	9.00	18.00

CHRISTMAS DREAM, A
1952 (Giveaway, 16 pgs., paper cover)
Promotional Publ. Co.

nn	3.60	9.00	18.00

CHRISTMAS EVE, A (See March of Comics No. 212)

CHRISTMAS FUN AROUND THE WORLD
No date (early 50's) (16 pgs., paper cover)
No publisher

nn	4.00	10.00	20.00

CHRISTMAS IN DISNEYLAND (See Dell Giants)

CHRISTMAS JOURNEY THROUGH SPACE
1960
Promotional Publishing Co.

nn-Reprints 1954 issue Jolly Christmas Book with new slick cover	4.15	12.50	25.00

CHRISTMAS ON THE MOON
1958 (Giveaway, 20 pgs., slick cover)
W. T. Grant Co.

nn	8.35	25.00	50.00

CHRISTMAS PARADE (See Dell Giant No. 26, Dell Giants, March of Comics No. 284, Walt Disney Christmas Parade & Walt Disney's...)

CHRISTMAS PARADE (Walt Disney's)
Jan, 1963 (no month) - No. 9, Jan, 1972 (#1,5: 80 pgs.; #2-4,7-9: 36 pgs.)
Gold Key

1 (30018-301)-Giant	9.00	27.00	90.00
2-6: 2-r/F.C. #367 by Barks. 3-r/F.C. #178 by Barks. 4-r/F.C. #203 by Barks. 5-r/Christ. Parade #1 (Dell) by Barks; giant. 6-r/Christmas Parade #2 (Dell) by Barks (64 pgs.); giant	7.00	21.00	70.00

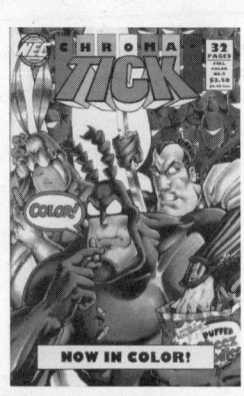

Chroma-Tick #5 © Ben Edlund

Chromium Man #0 © Triumphant

The Chronicles of Corum #4 © Michael Moorcock

	GD25	FN65	NM94
7,9: 7-Pull-out poster	4.00	12.00	40.00
8-r/F.C. #367 by Barks; pull-out poster	7.00	21.00	70.00
CHRISTMAS PARTY (See March of Comics No. 256)			
CHRISTMAS PLAY BOOK			
1946 (Giveaway, 16 pgs., paper cover)			
Gould-Stoner Co.			
nn	5.00	15.00	30.00
CHRISTMAS ROUNDUP			
1960			
Promotional Publishing Co.			
nn-Marv Levy-c/a	1.50	3.75	9.00
CHRISTMAS STORIES			
No. 959, 1951; No. 1062, 1959?			
Dell Publishing Co.			
Four Color #959 (Walt Scott's Little People 1951-56 strip-r.)			
	4.00	12.00	40.00
Four Color #1062 (Walt Scott's Little People strip-r	4.00	12.00	40.00
CHRISTMAS STORY (See March of Comics No. 326)			
CHRISTMAS STORY BOOK (See Woolworth's Christmas Story Book)			
CHRISTMAS STORY CUT-OUT BOOK, THE			
No. 393, 1951 (15¢, 36 pgs.)			
Catechetical Guild			
393-Half text & half comics	4.20	12.50	25.00
CHRISTMAS TREASURY, A (See Dell Giants & March of Comics No. 227)			
CHRISTMAS USA (Through 300 Years) (Also see Uncle Sam's...)			
1956 (Giveaway)			
Promotional Publ. Co.			
nn-Marv Levy-c/a	1.80	4.50	9.00
CHRISTMAS WITH ARCHIE			
1973, 1974 (49¢, 52 pgs.)			
Spire Christian Comics (Fleming H. Revell Co.)			
nn			1.00
CHRISTMAS WITH MOTHER GOOSE			
No. 90, Nov, 1945 - No. 253, Nov, 1949			
Dell Publishing Co.			
Four Color 90 (#1)-Kelly-a	17.00	51.00	170.00
Four Color 126 ('46), 172 (11/47)-By Walt Kelly	14.00	43.00	140.00
Four Color 201 (10/48), 253-By Walt Kelly	12.00	36.00	120.00
CHRISTMAS WITH SANTA (See March of Comics No. 92)			
CHRISTMAS WITH SNOW WHITE AND THE SEVEN DWARFS			
1953 (16 pgs., paper-c)			
Kobackers Giftstore of Buffalo, N.Y.			
nn	4.70	14.00	28.00
CHRISTMAS WITH THE SUPER-HEROES (See Limited Collectors' Edition)			
1988; No. 2, 1989 ($2.95)			
DC Comics			
1,2: 1-(100 pgs.)-All reprints; N. Adams-r, Byrne-c; Batman, Superman, JLA, LSH Christmas stories; r-Miller's 1st Batman/DC Special Series #21.			
2-(68 pgs.)-Superman by Chadwick; Batman, Wonder Woman, Deadman, Gr. Lantern, Flash app.; Morrow-a; Enemy Ace by Byrne; all new-a			
		1.40	3.50
CHRISTOPHERS, THE			
1951 (Giveaway, 36 pgs.) (Some copies have 15¢ sticker)			
Catechetical Guild			
nn-Stalin as Satan in Hell	23.00	69.00	160.00
CHROMA-TICK, THE (...Special Edition, #1,2) (Also see The Tick)			

	GD25	FN65	NM94
Feb, 1992 - No. 8, Nov, 1993 ($3.95/$3.50, 44 pgs.)			
New England Comics Press			
1,2-Includes serially numbered trading card set	1.00	2.00	5.00
3-8 ($3.50, 36 pgs.): 6-Bound-in card		1.60	4.00
CHROME			
1986 - No. 3, 1986 ($1.50, limited series)			
Hot Comics			
1-3			1.50
CHROMIUM MAN, THE			
Aug, 1993 - No.10, May, 1994 ($2.50)			
Triumphant Comics			
1-1st app. Mr. Death; all serially numbered		1.00	2.50
2-10: 2-1st app. Prince Vandal. 3-1st app. Candi, Breaker & Coil. 4,5-Triumphant Unleashed x-over. 8,9-(3/94). 10-(5/94)			
		1.00	2.50
0-(4/94)-Four color-c		1.00	2.50
0-All pink-c & all blue-c; no cover price		1.00	2.50
CHROMIUM MAN: VIOLENT PAST, THE			
Jan, 1994 - No. 2, Jan, 1994 ($2.50, limited series)			
Triumphant Comics			
1,2-Serially numbered to 22,000 each		1.00	2.50
CHRONICLES OF CORUM, THE (Also see Corum...)			
Jan, 1987 - No. 12, Nov, 1988 ($1.75/$1.95, deluxe series)			
First Comics			
1-12: Adapts Michael Moorcock's novel		.80	2.00
CHRONOWAR (Manga)			
Aug, 1996 - Present ($2.95, limited series)			
Dark Horse Comics			
1,2			3.00
CHUCKLE, THE GIGGLY BOOK OF COMIC ANIMALS			
1945 (132 pgs., one-shot)			
R. B. Leffingwell Co.			
1-Funny animal	17.00	52.00	120.00
CHUCK NORRIS (TV)			
Jan, 1987 - No. 3, May, 1987			
Marvel Comics (Star Comics)			
1-3: Ditko-a			1.00
CHUCK WAGON (See Sheriff Bob Dixon's...)			
CICERO'S CAT			
July-Aug, 1959 - No. 2, Sept-Oct, 1959			
Dell Publishing Co.			
1,2-Cat from Mutt & Jeff	3.50	11.00	35.00
CIMARRON STRIP (TV)			
Jan, 1968			
Dell Publishing Co.			
1-Stuart Whitman photo-c	3.00	9.00	30.00
CINDER AND ASHE			
May, 1988 - No. 4, Aug, 1988 ($1.75, limited series)			
DC Comics			
1-4: Mature readers		.70	1.75
CINDERELLA (Disney) (See Movie Comics)			
No. 272, Apr, 1950 - No. 786, Apr, 1957			
Dell Publishing Co.			
Four Color 272	10.00	30.00	100.00
Four Color 786-Partial-r 272	6.00	18.00	60.00
CINDERELLA			

Cinderella Love #11(#2) © Z-D

Cisco Kid #3 © DELL

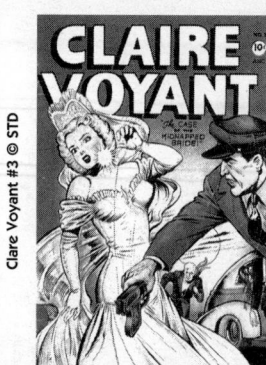

Clare Voyant #3 © STD

CL

	GD25	FN65	NM94		GD25	FN65	NM94

Apr, 1982
Whitman Publishing Co.

nn-Reprints 4-Color #272			1.00

CINDERELLA IN "FAIREST OF THE FAIR"
1955 (5x7-1/4", 16 pgs., soft-c) (Walt Disney)
American Dairy Association (Premium)

nn	10.00	30.00	65.00

CINDERELLA LOVE
No. 10, 1950; No. 11, 4-5/51; No. 12, 9/51; No. 4, 10-11/51 - No. 11, Fall, 1952;
No. 12, 10/53 - No. 15, 8/54; No. 25, 12/54 - No. 29, 10/55 (No #16-24)
Ziff-Davis/St. John Publ. Co. No. 12 on

10(#1)(1st Series, 1950)-Painted-c	10.00	30.00	70.00
11(#2, 4-5/51)-Crandall-a; Saunders painted-c	7.50	22.50	45.00
12(#3, 9/51)-Photo-c	5.35	16.00	32.00
4-8: 4,6,7-Photo-c	4.25	13.00	26.00
9-Kinstler-a; photo-c	6.35	19.00	38.00
10,11(Fall'52), 14: 10,11-Photo-c. 14-Baker-c	5.35	16.00	32.00
12(St. John-10/53)-#13:13-Painted-c.	4.00	12.00	24.00
15 (8/54)-Matt Baker-c	6.35	19.00	38.00
25(2nd Series)(Formerly Romantic Marriage)	4.00	12.00	24.00
26-Baker-c; last precode (2/55)	6.35	19.00	38.00
27,29-Matt Baker-c	6.35	19.00	38.00
28	4.00	10.00	20.00

CINDY COMICS (...Smith No. 39, 40; Crime Can't Win No. 41 on)(Formerly Krazy Komics) (See Junior Miss & Teen Comics)
No. 27, Fall, 1947 - No. 40, July, 1950
Timely Comics

27-Kurtzman-a, 3 pgs: Margie, Oscar begin	16.00	47.00	110.00
28-31-Kurtzman-a	10.00	30.00	65.00
32-40: 33-Georgie story; anti-Wertham editorial	6.70	20.00	40.00

NOTE: Kurtzman's "Hey Look"-#27(3), 29(2), 30(2), 31; "Giggles 'n' Grins"-28.

CINEMA COMICS HERALD
1941 - 1943 (4-pg. movie "trailers", paper-c, 7-1/2x10-1/2")(Giveaway)
Paramount Pictures/Universal/RKO/20th Century Fox/Republic

"Mr. Bug Goes to Town" (1941)	7.50	22.50	45.00
"Bedtime Story"	5.00	15.00	30.00
"Lady For A Night", John Wayne, Joan Blondell (1942)			
	11.50	34.00	80.00
"Reap The Wild Wind" (1942)	8.35	25.00	50.00
"Thunder Birds" (1942)	7.50	22.50	45.00
"They All Kissed the Bride"	7.50	22.50	45.00
"Arabian Nights" (nd)	7.50	22.50	45.00
"Bombardie" (1943)	7.50	22.50	45.00
"Crash Dive" (1943)-Tyrone Power	7.50	22.50	45.00

NOTE: The 1941-42 issues contain line art with color photos. 1943 issues are line art.

CIRCUS (...the Comic Riot)
June, 1938 - No. 3, Aug, 1938
Globe Syndicate

1-(Scarce)-Spacehawks (2 pgs.), & Disk Eyes by Wolverton (2 pgs.), Pewee Throttle by Cole (2nd comic book work; see Star Comics V1#11), Beau Gus, Ken Craig & The Lords of Crillon, Jack Hinton by Eisner, Van Bragger by Kane	750.00	2250.00	4500.00
2,3-(Scarce)-Eisner, Cole, Wolverton, Bob Kane-a in each	383.00	1150.00	2300.00

CIRCUS BOY (TV) (See Movie Classics)
No. 759, Dec, 1956 - No. 813, July, 1957
Dell Publishing Co.

Four Color 759 (#1)-The Monkees' Mickey Dolenz photo-c	11.00	33.00	110.00
Four Color 785 (4/57),813-Mickey Dolenz photo-c	11.00	33.00	110.00

CIRCUS COMICS
1945 - No. 2, June, 1945; Winter, 1948-49
Farm Women's Publishing Co./D. S. Publ.

1-Funny animal	10.00	30.00	65.00
2	7.00	21.00	42.00
1(1948)-D.S. Publ.; 2 pgs. Frazetta	21.00	64.00	150.00

CIRCUS OF FUN COMICS
1945 - No. 3, Dec, 1947 (A book of games & puzzles)
A. W. Nugent Publishing Company

1	11.00	33.00	75.00
2,3	8.35	25.00	50.00

CISCO KID, THE (TV)
July, 1950 - No. 41, Oct-Dec, 1958
Dell Publishing Co.

Four Color 292(#1)-Cisco Kid, his horse Diablo, & sidekick Pancho & his horse Loco begin; painted-c begin	22.00	66.00	220.00
2(1/51)-5	10.00	30.00	100.00
6-10	8.00	24.00	80.00
11-20	7.00	21.00	70.00
21-36-Last painted-c	5.00	15.00	50.00
37-41: All photo-c	10.00	30.00	100.00

NOTE: *Buscema* a-40. *Ernest Nordli* painted c-5-16, 20, 35.

CISCO KID COMICS
Winter, 1944 (one-shot)
Bernard Bailey/Swappers Quarterly

1-Illustrated Stories of the Operas: Faust; Funnyman by Giunta; Cisco Kid (1st app.) & Superbaby begin; Giunta-c	40.00	120.00	300.00

CITIZEN SMITH (See Holyoke One-Shot No. 9)

CITY OF THE LIVING DEAD (See Fantastic Tales No. 1)
1952
Avon Periodicals

nn-Hollingsworth-c/a	36.00	107.00	250.00

CITY SURGEON (Blake Harper...)
August, 1963
Gold Key

1(10075-308)-Painted-c	2.00	6.00	20.00

CIVIL WAR MUSKET, THE (Kadets of America Handbook)
1960 (25¢, half-size, 36 pgs.)
Custom Comics, Inc.

nn	2.85	8.50	20.00

CLAIRE VOYANT (Also see Keen Teens)
1946 - No. 4, 1947 (Sparling strip reprints)
Leader Publ./Standard/Pentagon Publ.

nn	48.00	144.00	385.00
2,4: 2-Kamen-c. 4-Kamen bondage-c	40.00	120.00	315.00
3-Kamen bridal-c; contents mentioned in Love and Death, a book by Gershom Legman(1949) referenced by Dr. Wertham in SOTI	45.00	135.00	360.00

CLAIRE VOYANTE
June, 1996 ($3.50, B&W)
Lightning Comics

1-Cleary-c		1.40	3.50
1-($9.95)-Platinum Edition			10.00
1-($9.95)-Nude A			10.00
1-($9.95)-Nude B			10.00

CLANDESTINE (Also see Marvel Comics Presents & X-Men: ClanDestine)
Oct, 1994 - No.12, Sept, 1995 ($2.95/$2.50)
Marvel Comics

ClanDestine #4 © MEG

ClanDestine Preview © MEG

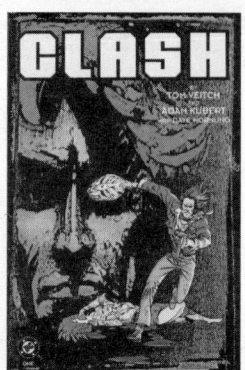

Clash #1 © Tom Veitch & Adam Kubert

	GD25	FN65	NM94

1-($2.95)-Alan Davis-c/a(p)/scripts & Mark Farmer-c/a(i) begin, ends #8; Modok app.; Silver Surfer cameo; gold foil-c ... 1.20 ... 3.00
2-12: 2-Wraparound-c. 2,3-Silver Surfer app. 5-Origin of ClanDestine.
6-Capt. America, Hulk, Spider-Man, Thing & Thor-c; Spider-Man cameo.
7-Spider-Man-c/app; Punisher cameo. 8-Invaders & Dr. Strange app.
9-12-Modok app. 10-Captain Britain-c/app. 11-Sub-Mariner app ... 1.00 ... 2.50

Preview (10/94, $1.50) ... 1.50

CLASH
1991 - No. 3, 1991 ($4.95, limited series, 52 pgs.)
DC Comics

Book One - Three: Adam Kubert-c/a ... 1.00 ... 2.00 ... 5.00

CLASSIC COMICS/ILLUSTRATED - INTRODUCTION
by Dan Malan

Further revisions have been made to help in understanding the **Classics** section. **Classics** reprint editions prior to 1963 had either incorrect dates or no dates listed. Those reprint editions should be identified only by the highest number on the reorder list (HRN). Past price guides listed what were calculated to be approximately correct dates, but many people found it confusing for the price guide to list a date not listed in the comic itself.

We have also attempted to clear up confusion about edition variations, such as color, printer, etc. Such variations will be identified by letters. Editions will now be determined by three categories. Original edition variations will be Edition 1A, 1B, etc. All reprint editions prior to 1963 will be identified by HRN only. All reprint editions from 9/63 on will be identified by the correct date listed in the comic.

We have also included new information on four recent reprintings of **Classics** not previously listed. From 1968-1976 Twin Circle, the Catholic newspaper, serialized over 100 **Classics** titles. That list can be found under non-series items at the end of this section. In 1972 twelve **Classics** were reissued as **Now Age Books Illustrated**. They are listed under **Pendulum Illustrated Classics**. In 1982, 20 **Classics** were reissued, adapted for teaching English as a second language. They are listed under **Regents Illustrated Classics**. Then in 1984, six **Classics** were reissued with cassette tapes. See the listing under **Cassette Books**.

UNDERSTANDING CLASSICS ILLUSTRATED
by Dan Malan

Since **Classics Illustrated** is the most complicated comic book series, with all its reprint editions and variations, with changes in covers and artwork, with a variety of means of identifying editions, and with the most extensive worldwide distribution of any comic-book series; therefore this introductory section is provided to assist you in gaining expertise about this series.
THE HISTORY OF CLASSICS

The **Classics** series was the brain child of Albert L. Kanter, who saw in the new comic-book medium a means of introducing children to the great classics of literature. In October of 1941 his Gilberton Co. began the **Classic Comics** series with **The Three Musketeers**, with 64 pages of storyline. In those early years, the struggling series saw irregular schedules and numerous printers, not to mention variable art quality and liberal story adaptations. With No.13 the page total was reduced to 56 (except for No. 33, originally scheduled to be No. 9), and with No. 15 the coming-next ad on the outside back cover moved inside. In 1945 the Jerry Iger Shop began producing all new CC titles, beginning with No. 23. In 1947 the search for a classier logo resulted in **Classics Illustrated**, beginning with No. 35, **Last Days of Pompeii**. With No. 45 the page total dropped again to 48, which was to become the standard.

Two new developments in 1951 had a profound effect upon the success of the series. One was the introduction of painted covers, instead of the old line drawn covers, beginning with No. 81, **The Odyssey**. The second was the switch to the major national distributor Curtis. They raised the cover price from 10 to 15 cents, making it the highest priced comic-book, but it did not slow the growth of the series, because they were marketed as books, not comics. Because of this higher quality image, **Classics** flourished during the fifties while other comic series were reeling from outside attacks. They diversified with their new **Juniors**, **Specials**, and **World Around Us** series.

Classics artwork can be divided into three distinct periods. The pre-Iger era (1941-44) was mentioned above for its variable art quality. The Iger era (1945-53) was a major improvement in art quality and adaptations. It came to be dominated by artists Henry Kiefer and Alex Blum, together accounting for some 50 titles. Their styles gave the first real personality to the series. The EC era (1954-62) resulted from the demise of the EC horror series, when many of their artists made the major switch to classical art.

But several factors brought the production of new CI titles to a complete halt in 1962. Gilberton lost its 2nd class mailing permit. External factors like television, cheap paperback books, and Cliff Notes were all eating away at their market. Production halted with No.167, **Faust**, even though many more titles were already in the works. Many of those found their way into foreign series, and are very desirable to collectors. In 1967, **Classics Illustrated** was sold to Patrick Frawley and his Catholic publication, Twin Circle. They issued two new titles in 1969 as part of an attempted revival, but succumbed to major distribution problems in 1971. In 1988, the trio: First Publishing, Berkley Press, and Classics Media Group acquired the u se rights for the old CI series art, logo, and name from the Frawley Group. So far they have used only the name in the new series, but do have plans to reprint the old CI.

One of the unique aspects of the **Classics Illustrated** (CI) series was the proliferation of reprint variations. Some titles had as many as 25 editions. Reprinting began in 1943. Some **Classic Comics** (CC) reprints (r) had the logo format revised to a banner logo, and added a motto under the banner. In 1947 CC titles changed to the CI logo, but kept their line drawn covers (LDC). In 1948, Nos. 13, 18, 29 and 41 received second covers (LDC2), replacing covers considered too violent, and reprints of Nos. 13-44 had pages reduced to 48, except for No. 26, which had 48 pages to begin with.

Starting in the mid-1950s, 70 of the 80 LDC titles were reissued with new painted covers (PC). Thirty of them also received new interior artwork (A2). The new artwork was generally higher quality with larger art panels and more faithful but abbreviated storylines. Later on, there were 29 second painted covers (PC2), mostly by Twin Circle. Altogether there were 199 interior art variations (169 (O)s and 30 A2 editions) and 272 different covers (169 (O)s, four LDC2s, 70 new PCs of LDC (O)s, and 29 PC2s). It is mildly astounding to realize that there are nearly 1400 different editions in the U.S. CI series.

FOREIGN CLASSICS ILLUSTRATED
If U.S. Classics variations are mildly astounding, the veritable plethora of foreign CI variations will boggle your imagination. While we still anticipate additional discoveries, we presently know about series in 25 languages and 27 countries. There were 250 new CI titles in foreign series, and nearly 400 new foreign covers of U.S. titles. The 1400 U.S. CI editions pale in comparison to the 4000 plus foreign editions. The very nature of CI lent itself to flourishing as an international series. Worldwide, they published over one billion copies! The first foreign CI series consisted of six Canadian Classic Comic reprints in 1946.

The following chart shows when CI series first began in each country:
1946: Canada. 1947: Australia. 1948: Brazil/The Netherlands. 1950: Italy. 1951: Greece/Japan/Hong Kong(?)/England/Argentina/Mexico. 1952: West Germany. 1954: Norway. 1955: New Zealand/South Africa. 1956: Denmark/Sweden/Iceland. 1957: Finland/France. 1962: Singapore(?). 1964: India (8 languages). 1971: Ireland (Gaelic). 1973: Belgium(?) /Philippines(?) & Malaysia(?).

Significant among the early series were Brazil and Greece. In 1950, Brazil was the first country to begin doing its own new titles. They issued nearly 80 new CI titles by Brazilian authors. In Greece in 1951 they actually had debates in parliament about the effects of Classics Illustrated on Greek culture, leading to the inclusion of 88 new Greek History & Mythology titles in the CI series.

But by far the most important foreign CI development was the joint European series which began in 1956 in 10 countries simultaneously. By 1960, CI had the largest European distribution of any American publication, not just comics! So when all the problems came up with U.S. distribution, they literally moved the CI operation to Europe in 1962, and continued producing new titles in all four CI series. Many of them were adapted and drawn in the U.S., the most famous of which was the British CI #158A. Dr. No, drawn by Norman Nodel. Unfortunately,

Classic Comics #1 © GIL

Classic Comics #2 © GIL

Classic Comics #3 © GIL

GD25 FN65 NM94

the British CI series ended in late 1963, which limited the European CI titles available in English to 15. Altogether there were 82 new CI art titles in the joint European series, which ran until 1976.

IDENTIFYING CLASSICS EDITIONS

HRN: This is the highest number on the reorder list. It should be listed in ( ) after the title number. It is crucial to understanding various CI editions.

ORIGINALS (O): This is the all-important First Edition. To determine (O)s, there is one primary rule and two secondary rules (with exceptions).

Rule No. 1: All (O)s and only (O)s have coming-next ads for the next number. **Exceptions:** No. 14(15) (reprint) has an ad on the last inside text page only. No. 14(O) also has a full-page outside back cover ad (also rule 2). Nos.55(75) and 57(75) have coming-next ads. (Rules 2 and 3 apply here). Nos. 168(O) and 169(O) do not have coming-next ads. No.168 was never reprinted; No. 169(O) has HRN (166). No. 169(169) is the only reprint.

Rule No. 2: On nos.1-80, all (O)s and only (O)s list 10c on the front cover. **Exceptions:** Nos. 37(62), 39(71), and 46(62) list 10c on the front cover. (Rules 1 and 3 apply here.)

Rule No. 3: All (O)s have HRN close to that title No. **Exceptions:** Some reprints also have HRNs close to that title number: a few CC(r)s, 58(62), 60(62), 149(149), 152(149) 153(149), and title nos. in the 160's. (Rules 1 and 2 apply here.)

DATES: Many reprint editions list either an incorrect date or no date. Since Gilberton apparently kept track of CI editions by HRN, they often left the (O) date on reprints. Often, someone with a CI collection for sale will swear that all their copies are originals. That is why we are so detailed in pointing out how to identify original editions. Except for original editions, which should have a coming-next ad, etc., all CI dates prior to 1963 are incorrect! So you want to go by HRN only if it is (165) or below, and go by listed date if it is 1963 or later. There are a few (167) editions with incorrect dates. They could be listed either as (167) or (62/3), which is meant to indicate that they were issued sometime between late 1962 and early 1963.

COVERS: A change from CC to LDC indicates a logo change, not a cover change; while a change from LDC to LDC2, LDC to PC, or from PC to PC2 does indicate a new cover. New PCs can be identified by HRN, and PC2s can be identified by HRN and date. Several covers had color changes, particularly from purple to blue.

Notes: If you see 15 cents in Canada on a front cover, it does not necessarily indicate a Canadian edition. Editions with an HRN between 44 and 75, with 15 cents on the cover are Canadian. Check the publisher's address. An HRN listing two numbers with a / between them indicates that there are two different reorder lists in the front and back covers. Official Twin Circle editions have a full-page back cover ad for their TC magazine, with no CI reorder list. Any CI with just a Twin Circle sticker on the front is not an official TC edition.

TIPS ON LISTING CLASSICS FOR SALE

It may be easy to just list Edition 17, but Classics collectors keep track of CI editions in terms of HRN and/or date, (O) or (r), CC or LDC, PC or PC2, A1 or A2, soft or stiff cover, etc. Try to help them out. For originals, just list (0), unless there are variations such as color (Nos. 10 and 61), printer (Nos. 18-22), HRN (Nos. 95, 108, 160), etc. For reprints, just list HRN if its (165) or below. Above that, list HRN and date. Also, please list type of logo/cover/art for the convenience of buyers. They will appreciate it.

CLASSIC COMICS (Also see Best from Boys Life, Cassette Books, Famous Stories, Fast Fiction, Golden Picture Classics, King Classics, Marvel Classics Comics, Pendulum Illustrated Classics, Picture Parade, Picture Progress, Regents III. Classics, Spitfire, Stories by Famous Authors, Superior Stories, and World Around Us.)

CLASSIC COMICS (Classics Illustrated No. 35 on)
10/41 - No. 34, 2/47; No. 35, 3/47 - No. 169, Spring 1969
(Reprint Editions of almost all titles 5/43 - Spring 1971)
(Painted Covers (0)s No. 81 on, and (r)s of most Nos. 1-80)
Elliot Publishing #1-3 (1941-1942)/Gilberton Publications #4-167 (1942-1967)/
Twin Circle Pub. (Frawley) #168-169 (1968-1971)

Abbreviations:
A–Art; C or c–Cover; CC–Classic Comics; CI–Classics Ill.; Ed–Edition; LDC–Line Drawn Cover; PC–Painted Cover; r–Reprint

GD25 FN65 NM94

1. The Three Musketeers

Ed	HRN	Date	Details	A	C	GD25	FN65	NM94
1	–	10/41	Date listed-1941; Elliot Pub; 68 pgs.	1	1	422.00	1267.00	4000.00
2	10	–	10¢ price removed on all (r)s; Elliot Pub; CC-r	1	1	31.00	94.00	220.00
3	15	–	Long Isl. Ind. Ed.; CC-r	1	1	23.00	69.00	160.00
4	18/20	–	Sunrise Times Ed.; CC-r	1	1	17.00	49.00	115.00
5	21	–	Richmond Courier Ed.; CC-r	1	1	15.00	45.00	105.00
6	28	1946	CC-r	1	1	11.50	34.00	80.00
7	36	–	LDC-r	1	1	6.35	19.00	38.00
8	60	–	LDC-r	1	1	4.25	13.00	26.00
9	64	–	LDC-r	1	1	3.60	9.00	18.00
10	78	–	C-price 15¢;LDC-r	1	1	3.20	8.00	16.00
11	93	–	LDC-r	1	1	3.20	8.00	16.00
12	114	–	Last LDC-r	1	1	2.40	6.00	12.00
13	134	–	New-c; old-a; 64 pg. PC-r	1	2	2.40	6.00	12.00
14	143	–	Old-a; PC-r; 64 pg.	1	2	2.00	5.00	10.00
15	150	–	New-a; PC-r; Evans/Crandall-a	2	2	2.40	6.00	12.00
16	149	–	PC-r	2	2	1.25	2.50	5.00
17	167	–	PC-r	2	2	1.25	2.50	5.00
18	167	4/64	PC-r	2	2	1.25	2.50	5.00
19	167	1/65	PC-r	2	2	1.25	2.50	5.00
20	167	3/66	PC-r	2	2	1.25	2.50	5.00
21	166	11/67	PC-r	2	2	1.25	2.50	5.00
22	166	Spr/69	C-price 25¢; stiff-c; PC-r	2	2	1.25	2.50	5.00
23	169	Spr/71	PC-r; stiff-c	2	2	1.25	2.50	5.00

2. Ivanhoe

Ed	HRN	Date	Details	A	C	GD25	FN65	NM94
1	(O)	12/41?	Date listed-1941; Elliot Pub; 68 pgs.	1	1	206.00	618.00	1650.00
2	10	–	Price & 'Presents' removed; Elliot Pub; CC-r	1	1	26.00	79.00	185.00
3	15	–	Long Isl. Ind. ed.; CC-r	1	1	19.00	56.00	130.00
4	18/20	–	Sunrise Times ed.; CC-r	1	1	17.00	49.00	115.00
5	21	–	Richmond Courier ed.; CC-r	1	1	15.00	45.00	105.00
6	28	1946	Last 'Comics'-r	1	1	11.50	34.00	80.00
7	36	–	1st LDC-r	1	1	6.70	20.00	40.00
8	60	–	LDC-r	1	1	4.15	12.50	25.00
9	64	–	LDC-r	1	1	4.00	10.00	20.00
10	78	–	C-price 15¢; LDC-r	1	1	3.20	8.00	16.00
11	89	–	LDC-r	1	1	2.80	7.00	14.00
12	106	–	LDC-r	1	1	2.40	6.00	12.00
13	121	–	Last LDC-r	1	1	2.40	6.00	12.00
14	136	–	New-c&a; PC-r	2	2	2.80	7.00	14.00
15	142	–	PC-r	2	2	1.25	2.50	5.00
16	153	–	PC-r	2	2	1.25	2.50	5.00
17	149	–	PC-r	2	2	1.25	2.50	5.00
18	167	–	PC-r	2	2	1.25	2.50	5.00

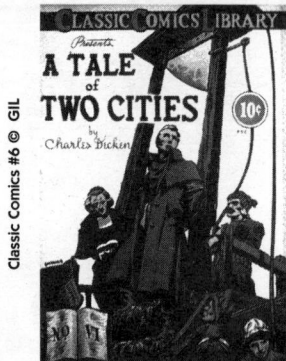

					GD25	FN65	NM94
19	167	5/64	PC-r	2 2	1.25	2.50	5.00
20	167	1/65	PC-r	2 2	1.25	2.50	5.00
21	167	3/66	PC-r	2 2	1.25	2.50	5.00
22A	166	9/67	PC-r	2 2	1.25	2.50	5.00
22B	166	–	Center ad for Children's Digest & Young Miss; rare; PC-r	2 2	10.00	30.00	60.00
23	166	R/68	C-Price 25¢; PC-r	2 2	1.25	2.50	5.00
24	169	Win/69	Stiff-c	2 2	1.25	2.50	5.00
25	169	Win/71	PC-r; stiff-c	2 2	1.25	2.50	5.00

3. The Count of Monte Cristo

Ed	HRN	Date	Details	A C	GD25	FN65	NM94
1	(O)	3/42	Elliot Pub; 68 pgs.	1 1	137.00	412.00	1100.00
2	10	–	Conray Prods; CC-r	1 1	26.00	77.00	180.00
3	15	–	Long Isl. Ind. ed.; CC-r	1 1	20.00	60.00	140.00
4	18/20		Sunrise Times ed.; CC-r	1 1	18.00	54.00	125.00
5	20	–	Sunrise Times ed.; CC-r	1 1	16.00	47.00	110.00
6	21	–	Richmond Courier ed.; CC-r	1 1	15.00	45.00	105.00
7	28	1946	CC-r; new Banner logo	1 1	11.50	34.00	80.00
8	36	–	1st LDC-r	1 1	6.70	20.00	40.00
9	60	–	LDC-r	1 1	4.15	12.50	25.00
10	62	–	LDC-r	1 1	5.00	15.00	30.00
11	71	–	LDC-r	1 1	3.60	9.00	18.00
12	87	–	C-price 15¢; LDC-r	1 1	3.20	8.00	16.00
13	113	–	LDC-r	1 1	2.40	6.00	12.00
14	135	–	New-c&a; PC-r; Cameron-a	2 2	2.40	6.00	12.00
15	143	–	PC-r	2 2	1.25	2.50	5.00
16	153	–	PC-r	2 2	1.25	2.50	5.00
17	161	–	PC-r	2 2	1.25	2.50	5.00
18	167	–	PC-r	2 2	1.25	2.50	5.00
19	167	7/64	PC-r	2 2	1.25	2.50	5.00
20	167	7/65	PC-r	2 2	1.25	2.50	5.00
21	167	7/66	PC-r	2 2	1.25	2.50	5.00
22	166	R/68	C-Price 25¢; PC-r	2 2	1.25	2.50	5.00
23	169		Win/71 Stiff-c; PC-r	2 2	1.25	2.50	5.00

4. The Last of the Mohicans

Ed	HRN	Date	Details	A C	GD25	FN65	NM94
1	(O)	8/42	Date listed-1942; Gilberton #4(0) on; 68 pgs.	1 1	115.00	345.00	925.00
2	12	–	Elliot Pub; CC-r	1 1	26.00	77.00	180.00
3	15	–	Long Isl. Ind. ed.; CC-r	1 1	20.00	60.00	140.00
4	20	–	Long Isl. Ind. ed.; CC-r; banner logo	1 1	17.00	51.00	120.00
5	21	–	Queens Home News ed.; CC-r	1 1	16.00	47.00	110.00
6	28	1946	Last CC-r; new	1 1	11.50	34.00	80.00
7	36	–	1st LDC-r	1 1	6.70	20.00	40.00
8	60	–	LDC-r	1 1	4.15	12.50	25.00
9	64	–	LDC-r	1 1	3.60	9.00	18.00
10	78	–	C-price 15¢; LDC-r	1 1	3.20	8.00	16.00
11	89	–	LDC-r	1 1	2.80	7.00	14.00
12	117	–	Last LDC-r	1 1	2.40	6.00	12.00
13	135	–	New-c; PC-r	1 2	2.40	6.00	12.00
14	141	–	PC-r	1 2	2.00	5.00	10.00
15	150	–	New-a; PC-r;	2 2	2.40	6.00	12.00

					GD25	FN65	NM94
			Severin, L.B. Cole-a				
16	161	–	PC-r	2 2	1.25	2.50	5.00
17	167	–	PC-r	2 2	1.25	2.50	5.00
18	167	6/64	PC-r	2 2	1.25	2.50	5.00
19	167	8/65	PC-r	2 2	1.25	2.50	5.00
20	167	8/66	PC-r	2 2	1.25	2.50	5.00
21	166	R/67	C-price 25¢; PC-r	2 2	1.25	2.50	5.00
22	169	Spr/69	Stiff-c; PC-r	2 2	1.25	2.50	5.00

5. Moby Dick

Ed	HRN	Date	Details	A C	GD25	FN65	NM94
1A	(O)	9/42	Date listed-1942; Gilberton; 68 pgs.	1 1	143.00	431.00	1150.00
1B			inside-c, rare free promo		206.00	618.00	1650.00
2	10	–	Conray Prods; Pg. 64 changed from 105 title list to letter from Editor; CC-r	1 1	27.00	81.00	190.00
3	15	–	Long Isl. Ind. ed.; Pg. 64 changed from Letter to the Editor to Ill. poem-Concord Hymn; CC-r	1 1	21.00	62.00	145.00
4	18/20		Sunrise Times ed.; CC-r	1 1	18.00	54.00	125.00
5	20	–	Sunrise Times ed.; CC-r	1 1	17.00	51.00	120.00
6	21	–	Sunrise Times ed.; CC-r	1 1	16.00	47.00	110.00
7	28	1946	CC-r; new banner logo	1 1	12.00	36.00	85.00
8	36	–	1st LDC-r	1 1	7.00	21.00	42.00
9	60	–	LDC-r	1 1	4.15	12.50	25.00
10	62	–	LDC-r	1 1	5.00	15.00	30.00
11	71	–	LDC-r	1 1	4.00	10.00	20.00
12	87	–	C-price 15¢; LDC-r	1 1	3.60	9.00	18.00
13	118	–	LDC-r	1 1	2.80	7.00	14.00
14	131	–	New c&a; PC-r	2 2	2.80	7.00	14.00
15	138	–	PC-r	2 2	1.25	2.50	5.00
16	148	–	PC-r	2 2	1.25	2.50	5.00
17	158	–	PC-r	2 2	1.25	2.50	5.00
18	167	–	PC-r	2 2	1.25	2.50	5.00
19	167	6/64	PC-r	2 2	1.25	2.50	5.00
20	167	7/65	PC-r	2 2	1.25	2.50	5.00
21	167	3/66	PC-r	2 2	1.25	2.50	5.00
22	166	9/67	PC-r	2 2	1.25	2.50	5.00
23	166	Win/69	New-c & c-price 25¢; Stiff-c; PC-r	2 3	2.00	5.00	10.00
24	169	Win/71	PC-r	2 3	2.00	5.00	10.00

6. A Tale of Two Cities

Ed	HRN	Date	Details	A C	GD25	FN65	NM94
1	(O)	10/42	Date listed-1942; 68 pgs. Zeckerberg c/a	1 1	112.00	338.00	900.00
2	14	–	Elliot Pub; CC-r	1 1	24.00	73.00	170.00
3	18	–	Long Isl. Ind. ed.; CC-r	1 1	19.00	58.00	135.00
4	20	–	Sunrise Times ed.; CC-r	1 1	17.00	51.00	120.00
5	28	1946	Last CC-r; new banner logo	1 1	11.50	34.00	80.00
6	51	–	1st LDC-r	1 1	6.35	19.00	38.00
7	64	–	LDC-r	1 1	4.00	11.00	22.00
8	78	–	C-price 15¢; LDC-r	1 1	3.60	9.00	18.00

Classic Comics #7 © GIL

Classic Comics #8 © GIL

Classic Comics #9 © GIL

Ed	HRN	Date	Details	A	C	GD25	FN65	NM94
9	89	–	LDC-r	1	1	2.40	6.00	12.00
10	117	–	LDC-r	1	1	2.40	6.00	12.00
11	132	–	New-c&a; PC-r; Joe Orlando-a	2	2	2.40	6.00	12.00
12	140	–	PC-r	2	2	1.25	2.50	5.00
13	147	–	PC-r	2	2	1.25	2.50	5.00
14	152	–	PC-r; very rare	2	2	17.00	49.00	115.00
15	153	–	PC-r	2	2	1.25	2.50	5.00
16	149	–	PC-r	2	2	1.25	2.50	5.00
17	167	–	PC-r	2	2	1.25	2.50	5.00
18	167	6/64	PC-r	2	2	1.25	2.50	5.00
19	167	8/65	PC-r	2	2	1.25	2.50	5.00
20	166	5/67	PC-r	2	2	1.25	2.50	5.00
21	166	Fall/68	New-c & 25¢; PC-r	2	3	2.40	6.00	12.00
22	169	Sum/70	Stiff-c; PC-r	2	3	2.40	6.00	12.00

7. Robin Hood

Ed	HRN	Date	Details	A	C	GD25	FN65	NM94
1	(O)	12/42	Date listed-1942; first Gift Box ad-bc; 68 pgs.	1	1	85.00	257.00	675.00
2	12	–	Elliot Pub; CC-r	1	1	24.00	71.00	165.00
3	18	–	Long Isl. Ind. ed.; CC-r	1	1	18.00	54.00	125.00
4	20	–	Nassau Bulletin ed.; CC-r	1	1	17.00	49.00	115.00
5	22	–	Queens Cty. Times ed.; CC-r	1	1	15.00	45.00	105.00
6	28	–	CC-r	1	1	11.50	34.00	80.00
7	51	–	LDC-r	1	1	6.35	19.00	38.00
8	64	–	LDC-r	1	1	4.00	11.00	22.00
9	78	–	LDC-r	1	1	3.20	8.00	16.00
10	97	–	LDC-r	1	1	2.80	7.00	14.00
11	106	–	LDC-r	1	1	2.40	6.00	12.00
12	121	–	LDC-r	1	1	2.40	6.00	12.00
13	129	–	New-c; PC-r	1	2	2.40	6.00	12.00
14	136	–	New-a; PC-r	2	2	2.40	6.00	12.00
15	143	–	PC-r	2	2	1.25	2.50	5.00
16	153	–	PC-r	2	2	1.25	2.50	5.00
17	164	–	PC-r	2	2	1.25	2.50	5.00
18	167	–	PC-r	2	2	1.25	2.50	5.00
19	167	6/64	PC-r	2	2	1.50	3.00	6.00
20	167	5/65	PC-r	2	2	1.25	2.50	5.00
21	167	7/66	PC-r	2	2	1.25	2.50	5.00
22	166	12/67	PC-r	2	2	1.50	3.00	6.00
23	169	Sum/69	Stiff-c; c-price 25¢; PC-r	2	2	1.25	2.50	5.00

8. Arabian Nights

Ed	HRN	Date	Details	A	C	GD25	FN65	NM94
1	(O)	2/43	Original; 68 pgs. Lilian Chestney-c/a	1	1	150.00	450.00	1200.00
2	17	–	Long Isl. ed.; pg. 64 changed from Gift Box ad to Letter from British Medical Worker; CC-r	1	1	53.00	161.00	430.00
3	20	–	Nassau Bulletin; Pg. 64 changed from letter to article-Three Men Named Smith; CC-r	1	1	43.00	128.00	340.00
4A	28	1946	CC-r; new banner logo, slick-c	1	1	31.00	94.00	220.00
4B	28	1946	Same, but w/stiff-c	1	1	31.00	94.00	220.00
5	51	–	LDC-r	1	1	21.00	64.00	150.00
6	64	–	LDC-r	1	1	18.00	54.00	125.00
7	78	–	LDC-r	1	1	17.00	49.00	115.00
8	164	–	New-c&a; PC-r	2	2	14.00	43.00	100.00

9. Les Miserables

Ed	HRN	Date	Details	A	C	GD25	FN65	NM94
1A	(O)	3/43	Original; slick paper cover; 68 pgs.	1	1	81.00	243.00	650.00
1B	(O)	3/43	Original; rough, pulp type-c; 68 pgs.	1	1	100.00	300.00	800.00
2	14	–	Elliot Pub; CC-r	1	1	26.00	77.00	180.00
3	18	3/44	Nassau Bul. Pg. 64 changed from Gift Box ad to Bill of Rights article; CC-r	1	1	21.00	62.00	145.00
4	20	–	Richmond Courier ed.; CC-r	1	1	17.00	51.00	120.00
5	28	1946	Gilberton; pgs. 60-64 rearranged/ illos added; CC-r	1	1	12.00	36.00	85.00
6	51	–	LDC-r	1	1	6.70	20.00	40.00
7	71	–	LDC-r	1	1	5.00	15.00	30.00
8	87	–	C-price 15¢; LDC-r	1	1	4.15	12.50	25.00
9	161	–	New-c&a; PC-r	2	2	4.00	12.00	24.00
10	167	9/63	PC-r	2	2	2.00	5.00	10.00
11	167	12/65	PC-r	2	2	2.00	5.00	10.00
12	166	R/1968	New-c & price 25¢; PC-r	2	3	2.80	7.00	14.00

10. Robinson Crusoe (Used in SOTI, pg. 142)

Ed	HRN	Date	Details	A	C	GD25	FN65	NM94
1A	(O)	4/43	Original; Violet-c; 68 pgs; Zuckerberg c/a	1	1	75.00	225.00	575.00
1B	(O)	4/43	Original; blue-grey-c, 68 pgs.	1	1	81.00	243.00	650.00
2A	14	–	Elliot Pub; violet-c; 68 pgs; CC-r	1	1	27.00	81.00	190.00
2B	14	–	Elliot Pub; blue-grey-c; CC-r	1	1	24.00	73.00	170.00
3	18	–	Nassau Bul. Pg. 64 changed from Gift Box ad to Bill of Rights article; CC-r	1	1	18.00	54.00	125.00
4	20	–	Queens Home News ed.; CC-r	1	1	16.00	47.00	110.00
5	28	1946	Gilberton; pg. 64 changes from Bill of Rights to WWII article-One Leg Shot Away; last CC-r	1	1	11.50	34.00	80.00
6	51	–	LDC-r	1	1	6.35	19.00	38.00
7	64	–	LDC-r	1	1	4.15	12.50	25.00
8	78	–	C-price 15¢; LDC-r	1	1	3.60	9.00	18.00
9	97	–	LDC-r	1	1	3.00	7.50	15.00
10	114	–	LDC-r	1	1	2.40	6.00	12.00
11	130	–	New-c; PC-r	1	2	2.80	7.00	14.00
12	140	–	New-a; PC-r	2	2	2.80	7.00	14.00
13	153	–	PC-r	2	2	1.25	2.50	5.00
14	164	–	PC-r	2	2	1.25	2.50	5.00
15	167	–	PC-r	2	2	1.25	2.50	5.00
16	167	7/64	PC-r	2	2	1.80	4.50	9.00
17	167	5/65	PC-r	2	2	1.80	4.50	9.00
18	167	6/66	PC-r	2	2	1.25	2.50	5.00
19	166	Fall/68	C-price 25¢; PC-r	2	2	1.25	2.50	5.00
20	166	R/68	(No Twin Circle ad)	2	2	1.50	3.00	6.00
21	169	Sm/70	Stiff-c; PC-r	2	2	1.50	3.00	6.00

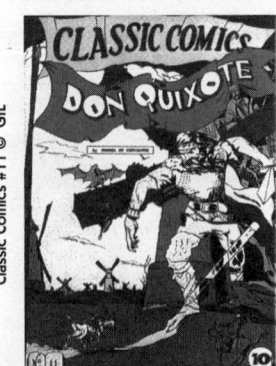
Classic Comics #11 © GIL

Classic Comics #12 © GIL

Classic Comics #14 © GIL

						GD25	**FN65**	**NM94**

11. Don Quixote

Ed	HRN	Date	Details	A	C	GD25	FN65	NM94
1	10	5/43	First (O) with HRN list; 68 pgs.	1	1	79.00	235.00	625.00
2	18	–	Nassau Bulletin ed.; CC-r	1	1	23.00	69.00	160.00
3	21	–	Queens Home News ed.; CC-r	1	1	18.00	54.00	125.00
4	28	–	CC-r	1	1	12.00	36.00	85.00
5	110	–	New-PC; PC-r	1	2	4.00	11.00	22.00
6	156	–	Pgs. reduced 68 to 52; PC-r	1	2	2.40	6.00	12.00
7	165	–	PC-r	1	2	1.75	3.50	7.00
8	167	1/64	PC-r	1	2	2.00	4.00	8.00
9	167	11/65	PC-r	1	2	1.75	3.50	7.00
10	166	R/1968	New-c & price 25¢; PC-r	1	3	3.20	8.00	16.00

12. Rip Van Winkle and the Headless Horseman

Ed	HRN	Date	Details	A	C	GD25	FN65	NM94
1	11	6/43	Original; 68 pgs.	1	1	79.00	235.00	600.00
2	15	–	Long Isl. Ind. ed.; CC-r	1	1	22.00	66.00	155.00
3	20	–	Long Isl. Ind. ed.; CC-r	1	1	17.00	51.00	120.00
4	22	–	Queens Cty. Times ed.; CC-r	1	1	15.00	45.00	105.00
5	28	–	CC-r	1	1	11.50	34.00	80.00
6	60	–	1st LDC-r	1	1	5.35	16.00	32.00
7	62	–	LDC-r	1	1	4.00	11.00	22.00
8	71	–	LDC-r	1	1	3.20	8.00	16.00
9	89	–	C-price 15¢; LDC-r	1	1	2.80	7.00	14.00
10	118	–	LDC-r	1	1	2.40	6.00	12.00
11	132	–	New-c; PC-r	1	2	2.40	6.00	12.00
12	150	–	New-a; PC-r	2	2	2.40	6.00	12.00
13	158	–	PC-r	2	2	1.25	2.50	5.00
14	167	–	PC-r	2	2	1.25	2.50	5.00
15	167	12/63	PC-r	2	2	1.25	2.50	5.00
16	167	4/65	PC-r	2	2	1.50	3.00	6.00
17	167	4/66	PC-r	2	2	1.25	2.50	5.00
18	166	R/1968	New-c&price 25¢; PC-r; stiff-c	2	3	2.00	5.00	10.00
19	169	Sm/70	PC-r; stiff-c	2	3	2.00	5.00	10.00

13. Dr. Jekyll and Mr. Hyde (Used in SOTI, pg. 143)(1st horror comic?)

Ed	HRN	Date	Details	A	C	GD25	FN65	NM94
1	12	8/43	Original 60 pgs.	1	1	109.00	328.00	875.00
2	15	–	Long Isl. Ind. ed.; CC-r	1	1	31.00	94.00	220.00
3	20	–	Long Isl. Ind. ed.; CC-r	1	1	21.00	64.00	150.00
4	28	–	No c-price; CC-r	1	1	17.00	49.00	115.00
5	60	–	New-c; Pgs. reduced from 60 to 52; H.C. Kiefer-c; LDC-r	1	2	5.70	17.00	34.00
6	62	–	LDC-r	1	2	4.35	13.00	26.00
7	71	–	LDC-r	1	2	4.00	10.00	20.00
8	87	–	Date returns (erroneous); LDC-r	1	2	3.60	9.00	18.00
9	112	–	New-c&a; PC-r; Cameron-a	2	3	4.00	10.00	20.00
10	153	–	PC-r	2	3	1.25	2.50	5.00
11	161	–	PC-r	2	3	1.25	2.50	5.00
12	167	–	PC-r	2	3	1.25	2.50	5.00
13	167	8/64	PC-r	2	3	1.25	2.50	5.00
14	167	11/65	PC-r	2	3	1.25	2.50	5.00
15	166	R/68	C-price 25¢; PC-r	2	3	1.50	3.00	6.00
16	169	Wn/69	PC-r; stiff-c	2	3	1.25	2.50	5.00

14. Westward Ho!

Ed	HRN	Date	Details	A	C	GD25	FN65	NM94
1	13	9/43	Original; last outside bc coming-next ad; 60 pgs.	1	1	175.00	525.00	1400.00
2	15	–	Long Isl. Ind. ed.; CC-r	1	1	52.00	157.00	420.00
3	21	–	Queens Home News; Pg. 56 changed from coming-next ad to Three Men Named Smith; CC-r	1	1	40.00	120.00	300.00
4	28	1946	Gilberton; Pg. 56 changed again to WWII article-Speaking for America; last CC-r	1	1	34.00	101.00	235.00
5	53	–	Pgs. reduced from 60 to 52; LDC-r	1	1	30.00	90.00	210.00

15. Uncle Tom's Cabin (Used in SOTI, pgs. 102, 103)

Ed	HRN	Date	Details	A	C	GD25	FN65	NM94
1	14	11/43	Original; Outside-bc ad: 2 Gift Boxes; 60 pgs.	1	1	65.00	195.00	525.00
2	15	–	Long Isl. Ind. listed- bottom inside-fc; also Gilberton listed bottom-pg. 1; CC-r	1	1	24.00	73.00	170.00
3	21	–	Nassau Bulletin ed.; CC-r	1	1	19.00	58.00	135.00
4	28	–	No c-price; CC-r	1	1	12.00	36.00	85.00
5	53	–	Pgs. reduced 60 to 52; LDC-r	1	1	6.00	18.00	36.00
6	71	–	LDC-r	1	1	4.15	12.50	25.00
7	89	–	C-price 15¢; LDC-r	1	1	4.00	12.00	24.00
8	117	–	New-c/lettering changes; PC-r	1	2	2.40	6.00	12.00
9	128	–	'Picture Progress' promo; PC-r	1	2	1.60	4.00	8.00
10	137	–	PC-r	1	2	1.25	2.50	5.00
11	146	–	PC-r	1	2	1.25	2.50	5.00
12	154	–	PC-r	1	2	1.25	2.50	5.00
13	161	–	PC-r	1	2	1.25	2.50	5.00
14	167	–	PC-r	1	2	1.25	2.50	5.00
15	167	6/64	PC-r	1	2	1.25	2.50	5.00
16	167	5/65	PC-r	1	2	1.25	2.50	5.00
17	167	5/67	PC-r	1	2	1.25	2.50	5.00
18	166	Wn/69	New-stiff-c; PC-r	1	3	2.00	5.00	10.00
19	169	Sm/70	PC-r; stiff-c	1	3	2.00	5.00	10.00

16. Gullivers Travels

Ed	HRN	Date	Details	A	C	GD25	FN65	NM94
1	15	12/43	Original-Lilian Chestney c/a; 60 pgs.	1	1	65.00	195.00	525.00
2	18/20	–	Price deleted; Queens Home News ed; CC-r	1	1	21.00	64.00	150.00
3	22	–	Queens Cty. Times ed.; CC-r	1	1	17.00	51.00	120.00
4	28	–	CC-r	1	1	11.50	34.00	80.00
5	60	–	Pgs. reduced to 48; LDC-r	1	1	5.00	15.00	30.00
6	62	–	LDC-r	1	1	4.00	11.00	22.00

Classic Comics #17 © GIL

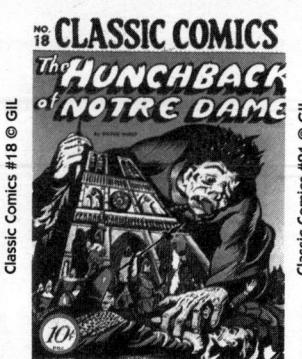

Classic Comics #18 © GIL

Classic Comics #21 © GIL

Ed	HRN	Date	Details	A	C	GD25	FN65	NM94
7	78	–	C-price 15¢; LDC-r	1	1	3.60	9.00	18.00
8	89	–	LDC-r	1	1	2.80	7.00	14.00
9	155	–	New-c; PC-r	1	2	2.80	7.00	14.00
10	165	–	PC-r	1	2	1.25	2.50	5.00
11	167	5/64	PC-r	1	2	1.25	2.50	5.00
12	167	11/65	PC-r	1	2	1.25	2.50	5.00
13	166	R/1968	C-price 25¢; PC-r	1	2	1.25	2.50	5.00
14	169	Wn/69	PC-r; stiff-c	1	2	1.25	2.50	5.00

17. The Deerslayer

Ed	HRN	Date	Details	A	C	GD25	FN65	NM94
1	16	1/44	Original; Outside-bc ad: 3 Gift Boxes; 60 pgs.	1	1	57.00	172.00	460.00
2A	18	–	Queens Cty Times (inside-fc); CC-r	1	1	22.00	66.00	155.00
2B	18	–	Gilberton (bottom-pg. 1); CC-r; Scarce	1	1	31.00	92.00	215.00
3	22	–	Queens Cty. Times ed.; CC-r	1	1	17.00	51.00	120.00
4	28	–	CC-r	1	1	11.50	34.00	80.00
5	60	–	Pgs. reduced to 52; LDC-r	1	1	5.00	15.00	30.00
6	64	–	LDC-r	1	1	4.00	10.00	20.00
7	85	–	C-price 15¢; LDC-r	1	1	2.80	7.00	14.00
8	118	–	LDC-r	1	1	2.40	6.00	12.00
9	132	–	LDC-r	1	1	2.40	6.00	12.00
10	167	11/66	Last LDC-r	1	1	2.00	5.00	10.00
11	166	R/1968	New-c & price 25¢; PC-r	1	2	2.80	7.00	14.00
12	169	Spr/71	Stiff-c; letters from parents & educators; PC-r	1	2	2.00	5.00	10.00

18. The Hunchback of Notre Dame

Ed	HRN	Date	Details	A	C	GD25	FN65	NM94
1A	17	3/44	Orig.; Gilberton ed; 60 pgs.	1	1	78.00	234.00	625.00
1B	17	3/44	Orig.; Island Pub. Ed.; 60 pgs.	1	1	68.00	206.00	550.00
2	18/20	–	Queens Home News ed.; CC-r	1	1	24.00	73.00	170.00
3	22	–	Queens Cty. Times ed.; CC-r	1	1	19.00	56.00	130.00
4	28	–	CC-r	1	1	14.00	43.00	100.00
5	60	–	New-c; 8pgs. deleted; Kiefer-c; LDC-r	1	2	5.35	16.00	32.00
6	62	–	LDC-r	1	2	4.00	10.00	20.00
7	78	–	C-price 15¢; LDC-r	1	2	3.60	9.00	18.00
8A	89	–	H.C.Kiefer on bottom right-fc; LDC-r	1	2	3.20	8.00	16.00
8B	89	–	Name omitted; LDC-r	1	2	4.00	12.00	24.00
9	118	–	LDC-r	1	2	2.80	7.00	14.00
10	140	–	New-c; PC-r	1	3	4.00	11.00	22.00
11	146	–	PC-r	1	3	3.20	8.00	16.00
12	158	–	New-c&a; PC-r; Evans/Crandall-a	2	4	3.20	8.00	16.00
13	165	–	PC-r	2	4	1.50	3.00	6.00
14	167	9/63	PC-r	2	4	1.50	3.00	6.00
15	167	10/64	PC-r	2	4	1.50	3.00	6.00
16	167	4/66	PC-r	2	4	1.25	2.50	5.00
17	166	R/1968	New price 25¢; PC-r	2	4	1.25	2.50	5.00
18	169	Sp/70	Stiff-c; PC-r	2	4	1.25	2.50	5.00

19. Huckleberry Finn

Ed	HRN	Date	Details	A	C	GD25	FN65	NM94
1A	18	4/44	Orig.; Gilberton ed.; 60 pgs.	1	1	50.00	150.00	385.00
1B	18	4/44	Orig.; Island Pub.; 60 pgs.	1	1	54.00	160.00	420.00
2	18	–	Nassau Bulletin ed.; fc-price 15¢-Canada; no coming-next ad; CC-r	1	1	23.00	69.00	160.00
3	22	–	Queens City Times ed.; CC-r	1	1	17.00	51.00	120.00
4	28	–	CC-r	1	1	11.50	34.00	80.00
5	60	–	Pgs. reduced to 48; LDC-r	1	1	5.00	15.00	30.00
6	62	–	LDC-r	1	1	4.00	11.00	22.00
7	78	–	LDC-r	1	1	3.20	8.00	16.00
8	89	–	LDC-r	1	1	2.80	7.00	14.00
9	117	–	LDC-r	1	1	2.40	6.00	12.00
10	131	–	New-c&a; PC-r	2	2	2.40	6.00	12.00
11	140	–	PC-r	2	2	1.25	2.50	5.00
12	150	–	PC-r	2	2	1.25	2.50	5.00
13	158	–	PC-r	2	2	1.25	2.50	5.00
14	165	–	PC-r (scarce)	2	2	2.00	5.00	10.00
15	167	–	PC-r	2	2	1.25	2.50	5.00
16	167	6/64	PC-r	2	2	1.25	2.50	5.00
17	167	6/65	PC-r	2	2	1.25	2.50	5.00
18	167	10/65	PC-r	2	2	1.25	2.50	5.00
19	166	9/67	PC-r	2	2	1.25	2.50	5.00
20	166	Win/69	C-price 25¢; PC-r; stiff-c	2	2	1.25	2.50	5.00
21	169	Sm/70	PC-r; stiff-c	2	2	1.25	2.50	5.00

20. The Corsican Brothers

Ed	HRN	Date	Details	A	C	GD25	FN65	NM94
1A	20	6/44	Orig.; Gilberton ed.; bc-ad: 4 Gift Boxes; 60 pgs.	1	1	41.00	124.00	330.00
1B	20	6/44	Orig.; Courier ed.; 60 pgs.	1	1	40.00	120.00	315.00
1C	20	6/44	Orig.; Long Island Ind. ed.; 60 pgs.	1	1	40.00	120.00	315.00
2	22	–	Queens Cty. Times ed.; white logo banner; CC-r	1	1	19.00	58.00	135.00
3	28	–	CC-r	1	1	17.00	51.00	120.00
4	60	–	Cl logo; no price; 48 pgs.; LDC-r	1	1	13.50	41.00	95.00
5A	62	–	LDC-r; Classics Ill. logo at top of pgs.	1	1	12.00	36.00	85.00
5B	62	–	w/o logo at top of pg. (scarcer)	1	1	13.50	41.00	95.00
6	78	–	C-price 15¢; LDC-r	1	1	11.50	34.00	80.00
7	97	–	LDC-r	1	1	10.00	30.00	70.00

21. 3 Famous Mysteries ("The Sign of the 4", "The Murders in the Rue Morgue", "The Flayed Hand")

Ed	HRN	Date	Details	A	C	GD25	FN65	NM94
1A	21	7/44	Orig.; Gilberton ed.; 60 pgs.	1	1	87.00	262.00	700.00
1B	21	7/44	Orig. Island Pub. Co.; 60 pgs.	1	1	91.00	275.00	735.00
1C	21	7/44	Original; Courier Ed.; 60 pgs.	1	1	79.00	236.00	630.00
2	22	–	Nassau Bulletin ed.; CC-r	1	1	35.00	105.00	245.00

Classic Comics #22 © GIL Classic Comics #23 © GIL Classic Comics #26 © GIL

						GD25	FN65	NM94
3	30	–	CC-r	1	1	28.00	84.00	195.00
4	62	–	LDC-r; 8 pgs. deleted; LDC-r	1	1	21.00	64.00	150.00
5	70	–	LDC-r	1	1	19.00	58.00	135.00
6	85	–	C-price 15¢; LDC-r	1	1	17.00	51.00	120.00
7	114	–	New-c; PC-r	1	2	17.00	51.00	120.00

22. The Pathfinder

Ed	HRN	Date	Details	A	C			
1A	22	10/44	Orig.; No printer listed; ownership statement inside fc lists Gilberton & date; 60 pgs.	1	1	43.00	129.00	315.00
1B	22	10/44	Orig.; Island Pub. ed.; 60 pgs.	1	1	39.00	116.00	270.00
1C	22	10/44	Orig.; Queens Cty Times ed. 60 pgs.	1	1	39.00	116.00	270.00
2	30	–	C-price removed; CC-r	1	1	11.50	34.00	80.00
3	60	–	Pgs. reduced to 52; LDC-r	1	1	4.15	12.50	25.00
4	70	–	LDC-r	1	1	4.00	10.00	20.00
5	85	–	C-price 15¢; LDC-r	1	1	3.20	8.00	16.00
6	118	–	LDC-r	1	1	2.80	7.00	14.00
7	132	–	LDC-r	1	1	2.40	6.00	12.00
8	146	–	LDC-r	1	1	2.40	6.00	12.00
9	167	11/63	New-c; PC-r	1	2	4.00	11.00	22.00
10	167	12/65	PC-r	1	2	2.80	7.00	14.00
11	166	8/67	PC-r	1	2	2.80	7.00	14.00

23. Oliver Twist (1st Classic produced by the Iger Shop)

Ed	HRN	Date	Details	A	C			
1	23	7/45	Original; 60 pgs.	1	1	40.00	120.00	295.00
2A	30	–	Printers Union logo on bottom left-fc same as 23(Orig.) (very rare); CC-r	1	1	29.00	86.00	200.00
2B	30	–	Union logo omitted; CC-r	1	1	11.50	34.00	80.00
3	60	–	Pgs. reduced to 48; LDC-r	1	1	4.25	13.00	28.00
4	62	–	LDC-r	1	1	4.00	11.00	22.00
5	71	–	LDC-r	1	1	3.60	9.00	18.00
6	85	–	C-price 15¢; LDC-r	1	1	3.20	8.00	16.00
7	94	–	LDC-r	1	1	2.60	6.50	13.00
8	118	–	LDC-r	1	1	2.60	6.50	13.00
9	136	–	New-PC, old-a; PC-r	1	2	2.60	6.50	13.00
10	150	–	Old-a; PC-r	1	2	2.00	5.00	10.00
11	164	–	Old-a; PC-r	1	2	3.00	7.50	15.00
12	164	–	New-a; PC-r; Evans/Crandall-a	2	2	4.00	10.00	20.00
13	167	–	PC-r	2	2	2.40	6.00	12.00
14	167	8/64	PC-r	2	2	1.25	2.50	5.00
15	167	12/65	PC-r	2	2	1.25	2.50	5.00
16	166	R/1968	New 25¢; PC-r	2	2	1.00	2.00	5.00
17	169	Win/69	Stiff-c; PC-r	2	2	1.25	2.50	5.00

24. A Connecticut Yankee in King Arthur's Court

Ed	HRN	Date	Details	A	C			
1	9/45	–	Original	1	1	37.00	111.00	260.00
2	30	–	No price circle; CC-r	1	1	11.00	33.00	75.00
3	60	–	8 pgs. deleted; LDC-r	1	1	4.15	12.50	28.00

						GD25	FN65	NM94
4	62	–	LDC-r	1	1	4.00	11.00	22.00
5	71	–	LDC-r	1	1	3.60	9.00	18.00
6	87	–	C-price 15¢; LDC-r	1	1	3.20	8.00	16.00
7	121	–	LDC-r	1	1	2.80	7.00	14.00
8	140	–	New-c&a; PC-r	2	2	3.20	8.00	16.00
9	153	–	PC-r	2	2	1.25	2.50	5.00
10	164	–	PC-r	2	2	1.25	2.50	5.00
11	167	–	PC-r	2	2	1.25	2.50	5.00
12	167	7/64	PC-r	2	2	1.25	2.50	5.00
13	167	6/66	PC-r	2	2	1.25	2.50	5.00
14	166	R/1968	C-price 25¢; PC-r	2	2	1.25	2.50	5.00
15	169	Spr/71	PC-r; stiff-c	2	2	1.25	2.50	5.00

25. Two Years Before the Mast

Ed	HRN	Date	Details	A	C			
1	10/45	–	Original; Webb/Heames-a&c	1	1	37.00	111.00	260.00
2	30	–	Price circle blank; CC-r	1	1	11.50	34.00	80.00
3	60	–	8 pgs. deleted; LDC-r	1	1	4.15	12.50	25.00
4	62	–	LDC-r	1	1	4.00	11.00	22.00
5	71	–	LDC-r	1	1	3.20	8.00	16.00
6	85	–	C-price 15¢; LDC-r	1	1	2.80	7.00	14.00
7	114	–	LDC-r	1	1	2.40	6.00	12.00
8	156	–	3 pgs. replaced by fillers; new-c; PC-r	1	2	2.80	7.00	14.00
9	167	12/63	PC-r	1	2	1.25	2.50	5.00
10	167	12/65	PC-r	1	2	1.25	2.50	5.00
11	166	9/67	PC-r	1	2	1.25	2.50	5.00
12	169	Win/69	C-price 25¢; stiff-c PC-r	1	2	1.25	2.50	5.00

26. Frankenstein (2nd horror comic?)

Ed	HRN	Date	Details	A	C			
1	26	12/45	Orig.; Webb/Brewster a&c; 52 pgs.	1	1	87.00	262.00	700.00
2A	30	–	Price circle blank; no indicia; CC-r	1	1	26.00	79.00	185.00
2B	30	–	With indicia; scarce; CC-r	1	1	31.00	94.00	220.00
3	60	–	LDC-r	1	1	8.00	24.00	48.00
4	62	–	LDC-r	1	1	11.50	34.00	80.00
5	71	–	LDC-r	1	1	5.00	15.00	30.00
6A	82	–	C-price 15¢; soft-c	1	1	4.15	12.50	25.00
6B	82	–	Stiff-c; LDC-r	1	1	5.35	16.00	32.00
7	117	–	LDC-r	1	1	3.20	8.00	16.00
8	146	–	New Saunders-c; PC-r	1	2	3.20	8.00	16.00
9	152	–	Scarce; PC-r	1	2	5.00	15.00	30.00
10	153	–	PC-r	1	2	1.25	2.50	5.00
11	160	–	PC-r	1	2	1.25	2.50	5.00
12	165	–	PC-r	1	2	1.25	2.50	5.00
13	167	–	PC-r	1	2	1.25	2.50	5.00
14	167	6/64	PC-r	1	2	1.25	2.50	5.00
15	167	6/65	PC-r	1	2	1.25	2.50	5.00
16	167	10/65	PC-r	1	2	1.25	2.50	5.00
17	166	9/67	PC-r	1	2	1.25	2.50	5.00
18	169	Fall/69	C-price 25¢; stiff-c PC-r	1	2	1.25	2.50	5.00
19	169	Spr/71	PC-r; stiff-c	1	2	1.25	2.50	5.00

27. The Adventures of Marco Polo

Ed	HRN	Date	Details	A	C			
1	4/46	–	Original	1	1	40.00	120.00	280.00

Classic Comics #28 © GIL

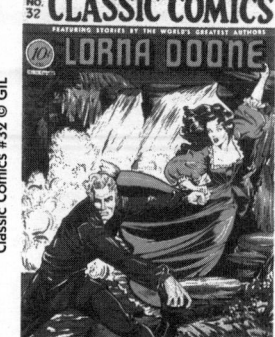

Classic Comics #32 © GIL

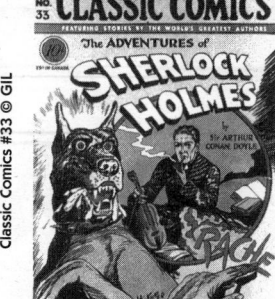

Classic Comics #33 © GIL

Ed	HRN	Date	Details	A	C	GD25	FN65	NM94
2	30	–	Last 'Comics' reprint; CC-r	1	1	11.00	33.00	75.00
3	70	–	8 pgs. deleted; no c-price; LDC-r	1	1	4.00	10.50	21.00
4	87	–	C-price 15¢; LDC-r	1	1	3.20	8.00	16.00
5	117	–	LDC-r	1	1	2.40	6.00	12.00
6	154	–	New-c; PC-r	1	2	2.40	6.00	12.00
7	165	–	PC-r	1	2	1.25	2.50	5.00
8	167	4/64	PC-r	1	2	1.25	2.50	5.00
9	167	6/66	PC-r	1	2	1.25	2.50	5.00
10	169	Spr/69	New price 25¢; stiff-c; PC-r	1	2	1.25	2.50	5.00

28. Michael Strogoff

Ed	HRN	Date	Details	A	C	GD25	FN65	NM94
1	6/46	–	Original	1	1	40.00	120.00	290.00
2	51	–	8 pgs. cut; LDC-r	1	1	11.50	34.00	80.00
3	115	–	New-c; PC-r	1	2	3.60	9.00	18.00
4	155	–	PC-r	1	2	1.80	4.50	9.00
5	167	11/63	PC-r	1	2	1.80	4.50	9.00
6	167	7/66	PC-r	1	2	1.80	4.50	9.00
7	169	Sm/69	C-price 25¢; stiff-c PC-r	1	3	2.20	5.50	11.00

29. The Prince and the Pauper

Ed	HRN	Date	Details	A	C	GD25	FN65	NM94
1	7/46	–	Orig.; "Horror"-c	1	1	52.00	157.00	420.00
2	60	–	8 pgs. cut; new-c by Kiefer; LDC-r	1	2	4.25	13.00	28.00
3	62	–	LDC-r	1	2	4.00	11.50	23.00
4	71	–	LDC-r	1	2	3.20	8.00	16.00
5	93	–	LDC-r	1	2	2.80	7.00	14.00
6	114	–	LDC-r	1	2	2.40	6.00	12.00
7	128	–	New-c; PC-r	1	3	2.40	6.00	12.00
8	138	–	PC-r	1	3	1.25	2.50	5.00
9	150	–	PC-r	1	3	1.25	2.50	5.00
10	164	–	PC-r	1	3	1.25	2.50	5.00
11	167	–	PC-r	1	3	1.25	2.50	5.00
12	167	7/64	PC-r	1	3	1.25	2.50	5.00
13	167	11/65	PC-r	1	3	1.25	2.50	5.00
14	166	R/68	C-price 25¢; PC-r	1	3	1.25	2.50	5.00
15	169	Sm/70	PC-r; stiff-c	1	3	1.25	2.50	5.00

30. The Moonstone

Ed	HRN	Date	Details	A	C	GD25	FN65	NM94
1	9/46	–	Original; Rico-c/a	1	1	40.00	120.00	280.00
2	60	–	LDC-r; 8pgs. cut	1	1	5.70	17.00	34.00
3	70	–	LDC-r	1	1	4.25	13.00	28.00
4	155	–	New L.B. Cole-c; PC-r	1	2	5.00	15.00	30.00
5	165	–	PC-r; L.B. Cole-a	1	2	3.20	8.00	16.00
6	167	1/64	PC-r; L.B. Cole-a	1	2	1.60	4.00	8.00
7	167	9/65	PC-r; L.B. Cole-a	1	2	1.50	3.00	6.00
8	166	R/1968	C-price 25¢; PC-r	1	2	1.25	2.50	5.00

31. The Black Arrow

Ed	HRN	Date	Details	A	C	GD25	FN65	NM94
1	10/46	–	Original	1	1	30.00	90.00	210.00
2	51	–	CI logo; LDC-r 8pgs. deleted	1	1	4.25	13.00	28.00
3	64	–	LDC-r	1	1	3.20	8.00	16.00
4	87	–	C-price 15¢; LDC-r	1	1	2.80	7.00	14.00
5	108	–	LDC-r	1	1	2.40	6.00	12.00
6	125	–	LDC-r	1	1	2.00	5.00	10.00
7	131	–	New-c; PC-r	1	2	2.40	6.00	12.00
8	140	–	PC-r	1	2	1.25	2.50	5.00
9	148	–	PC-r	1	2	1.25	2.50	5.00
10	161	–	PC-r	1	2	1.25	2.50	5.00
11	167	–	PC-r	1	2	1.25	2.50	5.00
12	167	7/64	PC-r	1	2	1.20	3.00	6.00
13	167	11/65	PC-r	1	2	1.25	2.50	5.00
14	166	R/1968	C-price 25¢; PC-r	1	2	1.25	2.50	5.00

32. Lorna Doone

Ed	HRN	Date	Details	A	C	GD25	FN65	NM94
1	12/46	–	Original; Matt Baker c&a	1	1	37.00	111.00	260.00
2	53/64	–	8 pgs. deleted; LDC-r	1	1	5.70	17.00	34.00
3	85	–	C-price 15¢; LDC-r;1 Baker c&a	1		4.15	12.50	25.00
4	118	–	LDC-r	1	1	3.20	8.00	16.00
5	138	–	New-c; old-c becomes new title pg.; PC-r	1	2	2.80	7.00	14.00
6	150	–	PC-r	1	2	1.25	2.50	5.00
7	165	–	PC-r	1	2	1.25	2.50	5.00
8	167	1/64	PC-r	1	2	1.60	4.00	8.00
9	167	11/65	PC-r	1	2	1.60	4.00	8.00
10	166	R/1968	New-c; PC-r	1	3	2.80	7.00	14.00

33. The Adventures of Sherlock Holmes

Ed	HRN	Date	Details	A	C	GD25	FN65	NM94
1	33	1/47	Original; Kiefer-c; contains Study in Scarlet & Hound of the Baskervilles; 68 pgs.	1	1	112.00	338.00	900.00
2	53	–	"A Study in Scarlet" (17 pgs.) deleted; LDC-r	1	1	40.00	120.00	315.00
3	71	–	LDC-r	1	1	34.00	101.00	235.00
4A	89	–	C-price 15¢; LDC-r	1	1	26.00	79.00	185.00
4B	89	–	Kiefer's name omitted from-c	1	1	29.00	86.00	200.00

34. Mysterious Island (Last "Classic Comic")

Ed	HRN	Date	Details	A	C	GD25	FN65	NM94
1	2/47	–	Original; Webb/ Heames-c/a	1	1	40.00	120.00	280.00
2	60	–	8 pgs. deleted; LDC-r	1	1	4.35	13.00	28.00
3	62	–	LDC-r	1	1	4.00	11.00	22.00
4	71	–	LDC-r	1	1	5.00	15.00	30.00
5	78	–	C-price 15¢ in circle; LDC-r	1	1	3.60	9.00	18.00
6	92	–	LDC-r	1	1	3.20	8.00	16.00
7	117	–	LDC-r	1	1	2.60	6.50	13.00
8	140	–	New-c; PC-r	1	2	2.60	6.50	13.00
9	156	–	PC-r	1	2	1.25	2.50	5.00
10	167	10/63	PC-r	1	2	1.25	2.50	5.00
11	167	5/64	PC-r	1	2	1.25	2.50	5.00
12	167	6/66	PC-r	1	2	1.25	2.50	5.00
13	166	R/1968	C-price 25¢; PC-r	1	2	1.25	2.50	5.00

35. Last Days of Pompeii (First "Classics Illustrated")

Ed	HRN	Date	Details	A	C	GD25	FN65	NM94
1	–	3/47	Original; LDC; Kiefer-c/a	1	1	40.00	120.00	285.00
2	161	–	New c&a; 15¢; PC-r; Kirby/Ayers-a	2	2	4.00	11.00	22.00
3	167	1/64	PC-r	2	2	2.00	5.00	10.00
4	167	7/66	PC-r	2	2	2.00	5.00	10.00
5	169	Spr/70	New price 25¢;	2	2	2.00	5.00	10.00

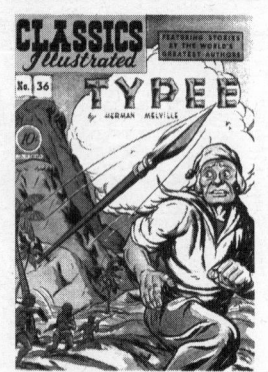

Classics Illustrated #36 © GIL

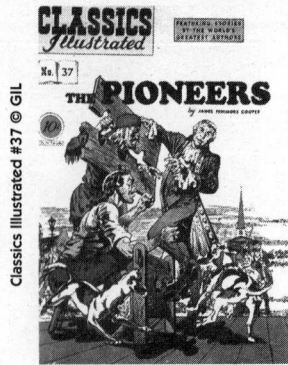

Classics Illustrated #37 © GIL

Classics Illustrated #42 © GIL

			GD25	FN65	NM94

stiff-c; PC-r

36. Typee
Ed	HRN	Date	Details	A	C			
1	4/47	–	Original	1	1	21.00	62.00	145.00
2	64	–	No c-price; 8 pg. ed.; LDC-r	1	1	5.35	16.00	32.00
3	155	–	New-c; PC-r	1	2	2.40	6.00	12.00
4	167	9/63	PC-r	1	2	1.40	3.50	7.00
5	167	7/65	PC-r	1	2	1.40	3.50	7.00
6	169	Sm/69	C-price 25¢; stiff-c PC-r	1	2	1.50	3.50	7.00

37. The Pioneers
Ed	HRN	Date	Details	A	C			
1	37	5/47	Original; Palais-c/a	1	1	15.00	45.00	105.00
2A	62	–	8 pgs. cut; LDC-r; price circle blank	1	1	4.00	11.00	22.00
2B	62	–	10¢; LDC-r;	1	1	24.00	71.00	165.00
3	70	–	LDC-r	1	1	2.80	7.00	14.00
4	92	–	15¢; LDC-r	1	1	2.40	6.00	12.00
5	118	–	LDC-r	1	1	2.00	5.00	10.00
6	131	–	LDC-r	1	1	2.00	5.00	10.00
7	132	–	LDC-r	1	1	2.00	5.00	10.00
8	153	–	LDC-r	1	1	1.80	4.50	9.00
9	167	5/64	LDC-r	1	1	1.40	3.50	7.00
10	167	6/66	LDC-r	1	1	1.40	3.50	7.00
11	166	R/1968	New-c; 25¢; PC-r	1	2	3.20	8.00	16.00

38. Adventures of Cellini
Ed	HRN	Date	Details	A	C			
1	6/47	–	Original; Froehlich c/a	1	1	26.00	79.00	185.00
2	164	–	New-c&a; PC-r	2	2	2.80	7.00	14.00
3	167	12/63	PC-r	2	2	1.60	4.00	8.00
4	167	7/66	PC-r	2	2	1.60	4.00	8.00
5	169	Spr/70	Stiff-c; new price 25¢; PC-r	2	2	1.60	4.00	8.00

39. Jane Eyre
Ed	HRN	Date	Details	A	C			
1	7/47	–	Original	1	1	26.00	77.00	180.00
2	60	–	No c-price; 8 pgs. cut; LDC-r	1	1	4.70	14.00	28.00
3	62	–	LDC-r	1	1	4.00	11.50	23.00
4	71	–	LDC-r; c-price 10¢	1	1	4.00	10.00	20.00
5	92	–	C-price 15¢; LDC-r	1	1	3.20	8.00	16.00
6	118	–	LDC-r	1	1	2.80	7.00	14.00
7	142	–	New-c; old-a; PC-r	1	2	3.60	9.00	18.00
8	154	–	Old-a; PC-r	1	2	2.80	7.00	14.00
9	165	–	New-a; PC-r	2	2	3.20	8.00	16.00
10	167	12/63	PC-r	2	2	3.20	8.00	16.00
11	167	4/65	PC-r	2	2	2.80	7.00	14.00
12	167	8/66	PC-r	2	2	2.80	7.00	14.00
13	166	R/1968	New-c; PC-r	2	3	5.85	17.50	35.00

40. Mysteries ("The Pit and the Pendulum", "The Advs. of Hans Pfall" & "The Fall of the House of Usher")
Ed	HRN	Date	Details	A	C			
1	8/47	–	Original; Kiefer-c/a, Froehlich, Griffiths-a	1	1	64.00	193.00	500.00
2	62	–	LDC-r; 8pgs. cut	1	1	26.00	79.00	185.00
3	75	–	LDC-r	1	1	23.00	69.00	160.00
4	92	–	C-price 15¢; LDC-r	1	1	18.00	54.00	125.00

41. Twenty Years After
Ed	HRN	Date	Details	A	C

1	9/47	–	Original; 'horror'-c	1	1	42.00	126.00	335.00
2	62	–	New-c; no c-price; 8 pgs. cut; LDC-r; Kiefer-c	1	2	4.35	13.00	28.00
3	78	–	C-price 15¢; LDC-r	1	2	4.00	10.00	20.00
4	156	–	New-c; PC-r	1	3	2.80	7.00	14.00
5	167	12/63	PC-r	1	3	1.20	3.00	6.00
6	167	11/66	PC-r	1	3	1.20	3.00	6.00
7	169	Spr/70	New price 25¢; stiff-c; PC-r	1	3	1.20	2.50	5.00

42. Swiss Family Robinson
Ed	HRN	Date	Details	A	C			
1	42	10/47	Orig.; Kiefer-c&a;	1	1	19.00	58.00	135.00
2A	62	–	8 pgs. cut; outside bc: Gift Box ad; LDC-r	1	1	4.25	13.00	28.00
2B	62	–	8 pgs.cut; outside-bc: Reorder list; scarce; LDC-r	1	1	8.70	26.00	52.00
3	75	–	LDC-r	1	1	3.60	9.00	18.00
4	93	–	LDC-r	1	1	3.20	8.00	16.00
5	117	–	LDC-r	1	1	2.80	7.00	14.00
6	131	–	New-c; old-a; PC-r	1	2	2.80	7.00	14.00
7	137	–	Old-a; PC-r	1	2	2.00	5.00	10.00
8	141	–	Old-a; PC-r	1	2	2.00	5.00	10.00
9	152	–	New-a; PC-r	2	2	2.40	6.00	12.00
10	158	–	PC-r	2	2	1.25	3.00	6.00
11	165	–	PC-r	2	2	2.40	6.00	12.00
12	167	12/63	PC-r	2	2	1.80	4.50	9.00
13	167	4/65	PC-r	2	2	1.50	3.00	6.00
14	167	5/66	PC-r	2	2	1.50	3.00	6.00
15	166	11/67	PC-r	2	2	1.25	2.50	5.00
16	169	Spr/69	PC-r; stiff-c	2	2	1.25	2.50	5.00

43. Great Expectations (Used in SOTI, pg. 311)
Ed	HRN	Date	Details	A	C			
1	11/47	–	Original; Kiefer-a/c	1	1	81.00	243.00	650.00
2	62	–	No c-price; 8 pgs. cut; LDC-r	1	1	45.00	136.00	365.00

44. Mysteries of Paris (Used in SOTI, pg. 323)
Ed	HRN	Date	Details	A	C			
1A	44	12/47	Original; 56 pgs.; Kiefer-c/a	1	1	62.00	187.00	500.00
1B	44	12/47	Orig.; printed on white/heavier paper; (rare)	1	1	68.00	206.00	550.00
2A	62	–	8 pgs. cut; outside-bc: Gift Box ad; LDC-r	1	1	26.00	79.00	185.00
2B	62	–	8 pgs. cut; outside-bc: reorder list; LDC-r	1	1	26.00	79.00	185.00
3	78	–	C-price 15¢; LDC-r	1	1	23.00	69.00	160.00

45. Tom Brown's School Days
Ed	HRN	Date	Details	A	C			
1	44	1/48	Original; 1st 48pg. issue	1	1	12.00	36.00	85.00
2	64	–	No c-price; LDC-r	1	1	5.00	15.00	30.00
3	161	–	New-c&a; PC-r	2	2	2.40	6.00	12.00
4	167	2/64	PC-r	2	2	1.60	4.00	8.00
5	167	8/66	PC-r	2	2	1.60	4.00	8.00
6	166	R/1968	C-price 25¢; PC-r	2	2	1.60	4.00	8.00

46. Kidnapped
Ed	HRN	Date	Details	A	C

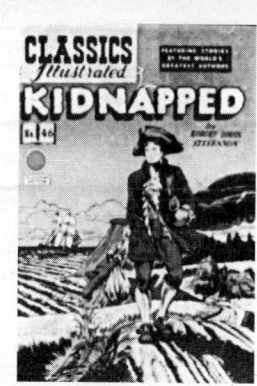

Classics Illustrated #46 © GIL

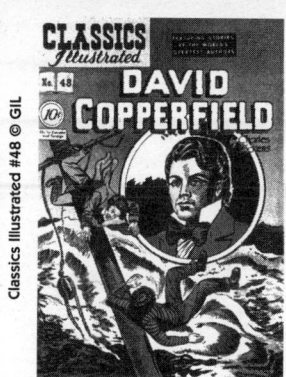

Classics Illustrated #48 © GIL

Classics Illustrated #52 © GIL

#	HRN	Date	Details	A	C	GD25	FN65	NM94
1	47	4/48	Original; Webb-c/a	1	1	11.50	34.00	80.00
2A	62	–	Price circle blank; LDC-r	1	1	4.00	12.00	24.00
2B	62	–	C-price 10¢; rare; LDC-r	1	1	26.00	77.00	180.00
3	78	–	C-price 15¢; LDC-r	1	1	3.60	9.00	18.00
4	87	–	LDC-r	1	1	2.80	7.00	14.00
5	118	–	LDC-r	1	1	2.40	6.00	12.00
6	131	–	New-c; PC-r	1	2	2.00	5.00	10.00
7	140	–	PC-r	1	2	1.25	2.50	5.00
8	150	–	PC-r	1	2	1.25	2.50	5.00
9	164	–	Reduced pg.width; PC-r	1	2	1.25	2.50	5.00
10	167	–	PC-r	1	2	1.25	2.50	5.00
11	167	3/64	PC-r	1	2	1.25	2.50	5.00
12	167	6/65	PC-r	1	2	1.25	2.50	5.00
13	167	12/65	PC-r	1	2	1.25	2.50	5.00
14	166	9/67	PC-r	1	2	1.25	2.50	5.00
15	166	Win/69	New price 25¢; stiff-c	1	2	1.25	2.50	5.00
16	169	Sm/70	PC-r; stiff-c	1	2	1.25	2.50	5.00

47. Twenty Thousand Leagues Under the Sea

Ed	HRN	Date	Details	A	C	GD25	FN65	NM94
1	47	5/48	Orig.; Kiefer-a&c;	1	1	11.50	34.00	80.00
2	64	–	No c-price; LDC-r	1	1	4.00	12.00	24.00
3	78	–	C-price 15¢; LDC-r	1	1	3.20	8.00	16.00
4	94	–	LDC-r	1	1	2.80	7.00	14.00
5	118	–	LDC-r	1	1	2.40	6.00	12.00
6	128	–	New-c; PC-r	1	2	2.40	6.00	10.00
7	133	–	PC-r	1	2	1.80	4.50	9.00
8	140	–	PC-r	1	2	1.25	2.50	5.00
9	148	–	PC-r	1	2	1.25	2.50	5.00
10	156	–	PC-r	1	2	1.25	2.50	5.00
11	165	–	PC-r	1	2	1.25	2.50	5.00
12	167	–	PC-r	1	2	1.25	2.50	5.00
13	167	3/64	PC-r	1	2	1.25	2.50	5.00
14	167	8/65	PC-r	1	2	1.25	2.50	5.00
15	167	10/66	PC-r	1	2	1.25	2.50	5.00
16	166	R/1968	C-price 25¢; new-c PC-r	1	3	2.00	5.00	10.00
17	169	Spr/70	Stiff-c; PC-r	1	3	2.40	6.00	12.00

48. David Copperfield

Ed	HRN	Date	Details	A	C	GD25	FN65	NM94
1	47	6/48	Original; Kiefer-c/a	1	1	11.50	34.00	80.00
2	64	–	Price circle replaced by motif of boy reading; LDC-r	1	1	4.00	11.00	22.00
3	87	–	C-price 15¢; LDC-r	1	1	2.80	7.00	14.00
4	121	–	New-c; PC-r	1	2	2.00	5.00	10.00
5	130	–	PC-r	1	2	1.50	3.00	6.00
6	140	–	PC-r	1	2	1.50	3.00	6.00
7	148	–	PC-r	1	2	1.50	3.00	6.00
8	156	–	PC-r	1	2	1.50	3.00	6.00
9	167	–	PC-r	1	2	1.25	2.50	5.00
10	167	4/64	PC-r	1	2	1.25	2.50	5.00
11	167	6/65	PC-r	1	2	1.25	2.50	5.00
12	166	5/67	PC-r	1	2	1.25	2.50	5.00
13	166	R/67	PC-r; C-price 25¢	1	2	2.00	5.00	10.00
14	166	Spr/69	C-price 25¢; stiff-c PC-r	1	2	1.25	2.50	5.00
15	169	Win/69	Stiff-c; PC-r	1	2	1.25	2.50	5.00

49. Alice in Wonderland

Ed	HRN	Date	Details	A	C	GD25	FN65	NM94
1	47	7/48	Original; 1st Blum a & c	1	1	16.00	47.00	115.00
2	64	–	No c-price; LDC-r	1	1	5.35	16.00	32.00
3A	85	–	C-price 15¢; soft-c LDC-r	1	1	4.00	12.00	24.00
3B	85	–	Stiff-c; LDC-r	1	1	4.25	13.00	28.00
4	155	–	New PC, similar to orig.; PC-r	1	2	4.00	12.00	24.00
5	165	–	PC-r	1	2	4.00	10.00	20.00
6	167	3/64	PC-r	1	2	3.20	8.00	16.00
7	167	6/66	PC-r	1	2	3.20	8.00	16.00
8A	166	Fall/68	New-c; soft-c; 25¢ c-price; PC-r	1	3	4.00	12.00	24.00
8B	166	Fall/68	New-c; stiff-c; 25¢ c-price; PC-r	1	3	7.50	22.50	45.00

50. Adventures of Tom Sawyer (Used in SOTI, pg. 37)

Ed	HRN	Date	Details	A	C	GD25	FN65	NM94
1A	51	8/48	Orig.; Aldo Rubano a&c	1	1	13.00	39.00	90.00
1B	51	9/48	Orig.; Rubano c&a	1	1	13.00	39.00	90.00
1C	51	9/48	Orig.; outside-bc: blue & yellow only; rare	1	1	19.00	56.00	130.00
2	64	–	No c-price; LDC-r	1	1	4.00	10.00	20.00
3	78	–	C-price 15¢; LDC-r	1	1	2.80	7.00	14.00
4	94	–	LDC-r	1	1	2.40	6.00	12.00
5	117	–	LDC-r	1	1	2.00	5.00	10.00
6	132	–	LDC-r	1	1	2.00	5.00	10.00
7	140	–	New-c; PC-r	1	2	2.00	5.00	10.00
8	150	–	PC-r	1	2	1.60	4.00	8.00
9	164	–	New-a; PC-r	2	2	2.40	6.00	12.00
10	167	–	PC-r	2	2	1.60	4.00	8.00
11	167	1/65	PC-r	2	2	1.25	2.50	5.00
12	167	5/66	PC-r	2	2	1.25	2.50	5.00
13	166	12/67	PC-r	2	2	1.25	2.50	5.00
14	169	Fall/69	C-price 25¢; stiff-c; PC-r	2	2	1.25	2.50	5.00
15	169	Win/71	PC-r	2	2	1.25	2.50	5.00

51. The Spy

Ed	HRN	Date	Details	A	C	GD25	FN65	NM94
1A	51	9/48	Original; inside-bc illo: Christmas Carol	1	1	11.00	33.00	75.00
1B	51	9/48	Original; inside-bc illo: Man in Iron Mask	1	1	11.00	33.00	75.00
1C	51	8/48	Original; outside-bc: full color	1	1	11.00	33.00	75.00
1D	51	8/48	Original; outside-bc: blue & yellow only; scarce	1	1	14.00	43.00	100.00
2	89	–	C-price 15¢; LDC-r	1	1	3.60	9.00	18.00
3	121	–	LDC-r	1	1	2.80	7.00	14.00
4	139	–	New-c; PC-r	1	2	2.40	6.00	12.00
5	156	–	PC-r	1	2	1.25	2.50	5.00
6	167	11/63	PC-r	1	2	1.25	2.50	5.00
7	167	7/66	PC-r	1	2	1.25	2.50	5.00
8A	166	Win/69	C-price 25¢; soft-c; scarce; PC-r	1	2	2.80	7.00	14.00
8B	166	Win/69	C-price 25¢; stiff-c; PC-r	1	2	1.25	2.50	5.00

52. The House of the Seven Gables

Ed	HRN	Date	Details	A	C	GD25	FN65	NM94
1	53	10/48	Orig.; Griffiths a&c	1	1	11.00	33.00	75.00

						GD25	FN65	NM94
2	89	–	C-price 15¢; LDC-r	1	1	3.60	9.00	18.00
3	121	–	LDC-r	1	1	2.80	7.00	14.00
4	142	–	New-c&a; PC-r; Woodbridge-a	2	2	2.80	7.00	14.00
5	156	–	PC-r	2	2	1.25	2.50	5.00
6	165	–	PC-r	2	2	1.25	2.50	5.00
7	167	5/64	PC-r	2	2	1.60	4.00	8.00
8	167	3/66	PC-r	2	2	1.25	2.50	5.00
9	166	R/1968	C-price 25¢; PC-r	2	2	1.25	2.50	5.00
10	169	Spr/70	Stiff-c; PC-r	2	2	1.25	2.50	5.00

53. A Christmas Carol

Ed	HRN	Date	Details	A	C	GD25	FN65	NM94
1	53	11/48	Original & only ed; Kiefer-c/a	1	1	13.50	41.00	95.00

54. Man in the Iron Mask

Ed	HRN	Date	Details	A	C	GD25	FN65	NM94
1	55	12/48	Original; Froehlich-a, Kiefer-c	1	1	10.00	30.00	70.00
2	93	–	C-price 15¢; LDC-r	1	1	4.00	10.00	20.00
3A	111	–	(O) logo lettering; scarce; LDC-r	1	1	4.25	13.00	28.00
3B	111	–	New logo as PC; LDC-r	1	1	3.60	9.00	18.00
4	142	–	New-c&a; PC-r	2	2	2.40	6.00	12.00
5	154	–	PC-r	2	2	1.25	2.50	5.00
6	165	–	PC-r	2	2	1.25	2.50	5.00
7	167	5/64	PC-r	2	2	1.25	2.50	5.00
8	167	4/66	PC-r	2	2	1.25	2.50	5.00
9A	166	Win/69	C-price 25¢; soft-c PC-r	2	2	3.20	8.00	16.00
9B	166	Win/69	Stiff-c	2	2	1.25	2.50	5.00

55. Silas Marner (Used in **SOTI**, pgs. 311, 312)

Ed	HRN	Date	Details	A	C	GD25	FN65	NM94
1	55	1/49	Original-Kiefer-c	1	1	11.00	33.00	75.00
2	75	–	Price circle blank; 'Coming Next' ad; LDC-r	1	1	4.00	12.00	24.00
3	97	–	LDC-r	1	1	2.80	7.00	14.00
4	121	–	New-c; PC-r	1	2	2.40	6.00	12.00
5	130	–	PC-r	1	2	1.25	2.50	5.00
6	140	–	PC-r	1	2	1.25	2.50	5.00
7	154	–	PC-r	1	2	1.25	2.50	5.00
8	165	–	PC-r	1	2	1.25	2.50	5.00
9	167	2/64	PC-r	1	2	1.25	2.50	5.00
10	167	6/65	PC-r	1	2	1.25	2.50	5.00
11	166	5/67	PC-r	1	2	1.25	2.50	5.00
12A	166	Win/69	C-price 25¢; soft-c PC-r	1	2	3.20	8.00	16.00
12B	166	Win/69	C-price 25¢; stiff-c PC-r	1	2	1.25	2.50	5.00

56. The Toilers of the Sea

Ed	HRN	Date	Details	A	C	GD25	FN65	NM94
1	55	2/49	Original; A.M. Froehlich-c/a	1	1	20.00	60.00	140.00
2	165	–	New-c&a; PC-r; Angelo Torres-a	2	2	4.15	12.50	25.00
3	167	3/64	PC-r	2	2	3.20	8.00	16.00
4	167	10/66	PC-r	2	2	2.80	7.00	14.00

57. The Song of Hiawatha

Ed	HRN	Date	Details	A	C	GD25	FN65	NM94
1	55	3/49	Original; Alex Blum-c/a	1	1	11.00	33.00	75.00
2	75	–	No c-price w/15¢	1	1	4.00	12.00	24.00

						GD25	FN65	NM94
			sticker; 'Coming Next' ad; LDC-r					
3	94	–	C-price 15¢; LDC-r	1	1	3.60	9.00	18.00
4	118	–	LDC-r	1	1	2.80	7.00	14.00
5	134	–	New-c; PC-r	1	2	2.40	6.00	12.00
6	139	–	PC-r	1	2	1.25	2.50	5.00
7	154	–	PC-r	1	2	1.25	2.50	5.00
8	167	–	Has orig.date; PC-r	1	1	1.25	2.50	5.00
9	167	9/64	PC-r	1	2	1.25	2.50	5.00
10	167	10/65	PC-r	1	2	1.25	2.50	5.00
11	166	F/1968	C-price 25¢; PC-r	1	2	1.25	2.50	5.00

58. The Prairie

Ed	HRN	Date	Details	A	C	GD25	FN65	NM94
1	60	4/49	Original; Palais c/a	1	1	11.00	33.00	75.00
2A	62	–	No c-price; no coming-next ad; LDC-r	1	1	6.35	19.00	38.00
2B	62	–	10¢ (rare)	1	1	14.00	43.00	100.00
3	78	–	C-price 15¢ in dbl. circle; LDC-r	1	1	3.60	9.00	18.00
4	114	–	LDC-r	1	1	2.80	7.00	14.00
5	131	–	LDC-r	1	1	2.40	6.00	12.00
6	132	–	LDC-r	1	1	2.40	6.00	12.00
7	146	–	New-c; PC-r	1	2	2.40	6.00	12.00
8	155	–	PC-r	1	2	1.25	2.50	5.00
9	167	5/64	PC-r	1	2	1.25	2.50	5.00
10	167	4/66	PC-r	1	2	1.25	2.50	5.00
11		Sm/69	New price 25¢; stiff-c; PC-r	1	2	1.25	2.50	5.00

59. Wuthering Heights

Ed	HRN	Date	Details	A	C	GD25	FN65	NM94
1	60	5/49	Original; Kiefer-c/a	1	1	12.00	36.00	85.00
2	85	–	C-price 15¢; LDC-r	1	1	4.25	13.00	28.00
3	156	–	New-c; PC-r	1	2	3.20	8.00	16.00
4	167	1/64	PC-r	1	2	1.75	3.50	7.00
5	167	10/66	PC-r	1	2	1.75	3.50	7.00
6	169	Sm/69	C-price 25¢; stiff-c; PC-r	1	2	1.25	2.50	5.00

60. Black Beauty

Ed	HRN	Date	Details	A	C	GD25	FN65	NM94
1	62	6/49	Original; Froehlich-c/a	1	1	11.50	34.00	80.00
2	62	–	No c-price; no coming-next ad; LDC-r (rare)	1	1	13.00	39.00	90.00
3	85	–	C-price 15¢; LDC-r	1	1	4.00	11.00	22.00
4	158	–	New L.B. Cole-c/a; PC-r	2	2	4.00	10.00	20.00
5	167	2/64	PC-r	2	2	2.40	6.00	12.00
6	167	3/66	PC-r	2	2	2.40	6.00	12.00
7	166	R/1968	New-c&price, 25¢; PC-r	2	3	6.70	20.00	40.00

61. The Woman in White

Ed	HRN	Date	Details	A	C	GD25	FN65	NM94
1A	62	7/49	Original; Blum-c/a fc-purple; bc: top illos light blue	1	1	12.00	36.00	85.00
1B	62	7/49	Original; Blum-c/a fc-pink; bc: top illos light violet	1	1	12.00	36.00	85.00
2	156	–	New-c; PC-r	1	2	3.60	9.00	18.00
3	167	1/64	PC-r	1	2	2.80	7.00	14.00
4	166	R/1968	C-price 25¢; PC-r	1	2	2.80	7.00	14.00

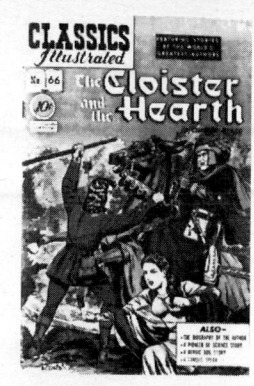

Classics Illustrated #66 © GIL

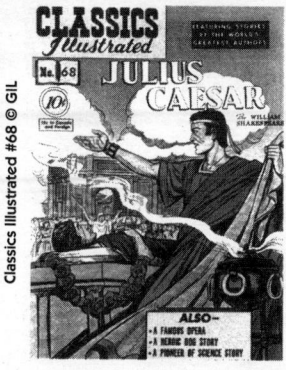

Classics Illustrated #68 © GIL

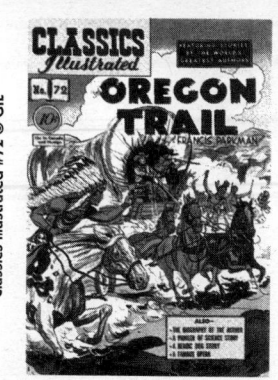

Classics Illustrated #72 © GIL

GD25   FN65   NM94   **GD25   FN65   NM94**

62. Western Stories ("The Luck of Roaring Camp" and "The Outcasts of Poker Flat")

Ed	HRN	Date	Details	A	C			
1	62	8/49	Original; Kiefer-c/a	1	1	10.00	30.00	70.00
2	89	–	C-price 15¢; LDC-r	1	1	4.00	11.00	22.00
3	121	–	LDC-r	1	1	3.20	8.00	16.00
4	137	–	New-c; PC-r	1	2	2.40	6.00	12.00
5	152	–	PC-r	1	2	1.50	3.00	6.00
6	167	10/63	PC-r	1	2	1.50	3.00	6.00
7	167	6/64	PC-r	1	2	1.25	2.50	5.00
8	167	11/66	PC-r	1	2	1.25	2.50	5.00
9	166	R/1968	New-c&price 25¢; PC-r	1	3	2.80	7.00	14.00

63. The Man Without a Country

Ed	HRN	Date	Details	A	C			
1	62	9/49	Original; Kiefer-c/a	1	1	11.00	33.00	75.00
2	78	–	C-price 15¢ in double circle; LDC-r	1	1	4.00	11.00	22.00
3	156	–	New-c, old-a; PC-r	1	2	3.20	8.00	16.00
4	165	–	New-a & text pgs.; PC-r; A. Torres-a	2	2	2.40	6.00	12.00
5	167	3/64	PC-r	2	2	1.25	2.50	5.00
6	167	8/66	PC-r	2	2	1.25	2.50	5.00
7	169	Sm/69	New price 25¢; stiff-c; PC-r	2	2	1.25	2.50	5.00

64. Treasure Island

Ed	HRN	Date	Details	A	C			
1	62	10/49	Original; Blum-c/a	1	1	11.00	33.00	75.00
2A	82	–	C-price 15¢; soft-c LDC-r	1	1	4.00	10.00	20.00
2B	82	–	Stiff-c; LDC-r	1	1	4.00	11.00	22.00
3	117	–	LDC-r	1	1	3.20	8.00	16.00
4	131	–	New-c; PC-r	1	2	2.40	6.00	12.00
5	138	–	PC-r	1	2	1.25	2.50	5.00
6	146	–	PC-r	1	2	1.25	2.50	5.00
7	158	–	PC-r	1	2	1.25	2.50	5.00
8	165	–	PC-r	1	2	1.25	2.50	5.00
9	167	–	PC-r	1	2	1.25	2.50	5.00
10	167	6/64	PC-r	1	2	1.25	2.50	5.00
11	167	12/65	PC-r	1	2	1.25	2.50	5.00
12A	166	10/67	PC-r	1	2	1.80	4.50	9.00
12B	166	10/67	w/Grit ad stapled in book	1	2	10.00	30.00	70.00
13	169	Spr/69	New price 25¢; stiff-c; PC-r	1	2	1.25	2.50	5.00
14	–	1989	Long John Silver's Seafood Shoppes; $1.95, First/Berkley Publ.; Blum-r	1	2	.40	1.00	2.00

65. Benjamin Franklin

Ed	HRN	Date	Details	A	C			
1	64	11/49	Original; Kiefer-c; Iger Shop-a	1	1	11.00	33.00	75.00
2	131	–	New-c; PC-r	1	2	2.80	7.00	14.00
3	154	–	PC-r	1	2	1.25	2.50	5.00
4	167	2/64	PC-r	1	2	1.25	2.50	5.00
5	167	4/66	PC-r	1	2	1.25	2.50	5.00
6	169	Fall/69	New price 25¢; stiff-c; PC-r	1	2	1.25	2.50	5.00

66. The Cloister and the Hearth

Ed	HRN	Date	Details	A	C			
1	67	12/49	Original & only ed;	1	1	24.00	71.00	165.00

67. The Scottish Chiefs
Kiefer-a & c

Ed	HRN	Date	Details	A	C			
1	67	1/50	Original; Blum-a&c	1	1	10.00	30.00	65.00
2	85	–	C-price 15¢; LDC-r	1	1	4.00	11.00	22.00
3	118	–	LDC-r	1	1	3.20	8.00	16.00
4	136	–	New-c; PC-r	1	2	2.40	6.00	12.00
5	154	–	PC-r	1	2	1.60	4.00	8.00
6	167	11/63	PC-r	1	2	2.00	5.00	10.00
7	167	8/65	PC-r	1	2	1.60	4.00	8.00

68. Julius Caesar (Used in SOTI, pgs. 36, 37)

Ed	HRN	Date	Details	A	C			
1	70	2/50	Original; Kiefer-c/a	1	1	10.00	30.00	60.00
2	85	–	C-price 15¢; LDC-r	1	1	4.00	10.00	20.00
3	108	–	LDC-r	1	1	3.20	8.00	16.00
4	156	–	New L.B. Cole-c; PC-r	1	1	3.60	9.00	18.00
5	165	–	New-a by Evans, Crandall; PC-r	2	2	3.60	9.00	18.00
6	167	2/64	PC-r	2	2	1.25	2.50	5.00
7	167	10/65	Tarzan books inside cover; PC-r	2	2	1.25	2.50	5.00
8	166	R/1967	PC-r	2	2	1.25	2.50	5.00
9	169	Win/69	PC-r; stiff-c	2	2	1.25	2.50	5.00

69. Around the World in 80 Days

Ed	HRN	Date	Details	A	C			
1	70	3/50	Original; Kiefer-c/a	1	1	10.00	30.00	60.00
2	87	–	C-price 15¢; LDC-r	1	1	4.00	10.00	20.00
3	125	–	LDC-r	1	1	3.20	8.00	16.00
4	136	–	New-c; PC-r	1	2	2.60	6.50	13.00
5	146	–	PC-r	1	2	1.25	2.50	5.00
6	152	–	PC-r	1	2	1.25	2.50	5.00
7	164	–	PC-r	1	2	1.25	2.50	5.00
8	167	–	PC-r	1	2	1.25	2.50	5.00
9	167	7/64	PC-r	1	2	1.25	2.50	5.00
10	167	11/65	PC-r	1	2	1.25	2.50	5.00
11	166	7/67	PC-r	1	2	1.25	2.50	5.00
12	169	Spr/69	C-price 25¢; stiff-c; PC-r	1	2	1.25	2.50	5.00

70. The Pilot

Ed	HRN	Date	Details	A	C			
1	71	4/50	Original; Blum-c/a	1	1	9.15	27.00	55.00
2	92	–	C-price 15¢; LDC-r	1	1	4.00	11.00	22.00
3	125	–	LDC-r	1	1	3.20	8.00	16.00
4	156	–	New-c; PC-r	1	2	2.80	7.00	14.00
5	167	2/64	PC-r	1	2	2.40	6.00	12.00
6	167	5/66	PC-r	1	2	1.80	4.50	9.00

71. The Man Who Laughs

Ed	HRN	Date	Details	A	C			
1	71	5/50	Original; Blum-c/a	1	1	15.00	45.00	105.00
2	165	–	New-c&a; PC-r	2	2	8.70	26.00	52.00
3	167	4/64	PC-r	2	2	8.70	26.00	52.00

72. The Oregon Trail

Ed	HRN	Date	Details	A	C			
1	73	6/50	Original; Kiefer-c/a	1	1	9.15	27.00	55.00
2	89	–	C-price 15¢; LDC-r	1	1	4.00	11.00	22.00
3	121	–	LDC-r	1	1	3.20	8.00	16.00
4	131	–	New-c; PC-r	1	2	2.60	6.50	13.00
5	140	–	PC-r	1	2	1.50	3.00	6.00
6	150	–	PC-r	1	2	1.25	2.50	5.00
7	164	–	PC-r	1	2	1.25	2.50	5.00
8	167	–	PC-r	1	2	1.25	2.50	5.00

					GD25	FN65	NM94
9	167	8/64	PC-r	1 2	1.25	2.50	5.00
10	167	10/65	PC-r	1 2	1.25	2.50	5.00
11	166	R/1968	C-price 25¢; PC-r	1 2	1.25	2.50	5.00

73. The Black Tulip

Ed	HRN	Date	Details	A C			
1	75	7/50	1st & only ed.; Alex Blum-c/a	1 1	30.00	90.00	210.00

74. Mr. Midshipman Easy

Ed	HRN	Date	Details	A C			
1	75	7/50	1st & only edition	1 1	29.00	86.00	200.00

75. The Lady of the Lake

Ed	HRN	Date	Details	A C			
1	75	9/50	Original; Kiefer-c/a	1 1	8.35	25.00	50.00
2	85	–	C-price 15¢; LDC-r	1 1	4.00	11.00	22.00
3	118	–	LDC-r	1 1	3.20	8.00	16.00
4	139	–	New-c; PC-r	1 2	2.40	6.00	12.00
5	154	–	PC-r	1 2	1.25	2.50	5.00
6	165	–	PC-r	1 2	1.25	2.50	5.00
7	167	4/64	PC-r	1 2	1.25	2.50	5.00
8	167	5/66	PC-r	1 2	1.25	2.50	5.00
9	169	Spr/69	New price 25¢; stiff-c; PC-r	1 2	1.25	2.50	5.00

76. The Prisoner of Zenda

Ed	HRN	Date	Details	A C			
1	75	10/50	Original; Kiefer-c/a	1 1	8.35	25.00	50.00
2	85	–	C-price 15¢; LDC-r	1 1	4.00	11.00	22.00
3	111	–	LDC-r	1 1	3.20	8.00	16.00
4	128	–	New-c; PC-r	1 2	2.80	7.00	14.00
5	152	–	PC-r	1 2	1.25	2.50	5.00
6	165	–	PC-r	1 2	1.25	2.50	5.00
7	167	4/64	PC-r	1 2	1.25	2.50	5.00
8	167	9/66	PC-r	1 2	1.25	2.50	5.00
9	169	Fall/69	New price 25¢; stiff-c; PC-r	1 2	1.25	2.50	5.00

77. The Iliad

Ed	HRN	Date	Details	A C			
1	78	11/50	Original; Blum-c/a	1 1	9.15	27.00	55.00
2	87	–	C-price 15¢; LDC-r	1 1	4.00	11.00	22.00
3	121	–	LDC-r	1 1	3.20	8.00	16.00
4	139	–	New-c; PC-r	1 2	2.40	6.00	12.00
5	150	–	PC-r	1 2	1.25	2.50	5.00
6	165	–	PC-r	1 2	1.25	2.50	5.00
7	167	10/63	PC-r	1 2	1.25	2.50	5.00
8	167	7/64	PC-r	1 2	1.25	2.50	5.00
9	167	5/66	PC-r	1 2	1.25	2.50	5.00
10	166	R/1968	C-price 25¢; PC-r	1 2	1.25	2.50	5.00

78. Joan of Arc

Ed	HRN	Date	Details	A C			
1	78	12/50	Original; Kiefer-c/a	1 1	8.35	25.00	50.00
2	87	–	C-price 15¢; LDC-r	1 1	4.00	11.00	22.00
3	113	–	LDC-r	1 1	3.20	8.00	16.00
4	128	–	New-c; PC-r	1 2	2.40	6.00	12.00
5	140	–	PC-r	1 2	1.25	2.50	5.00
6	150	–	PC-r	1 2	1.25	2.50	5.00
7	159	–	PC-r	1 2	1.25	2.50	5.00
8	167	–	PC-r	1 2	1.25	2.50	5.00
9	167	12/63	PC-r	1 2	1.25	2.50	5.00
10	167	6/65	PC-r	1 2	1.25	2.50	5.00
11	166	6/67	PC-r	1 2	1.25	2.50	5.00
12	166	Win/69	New-c&price, 25¢; PC-r; stiff-c	1 3	2.80	7.00	14.00

79. Cyrano de Bergerac

Ed	HRN	Date	Details	A C			
1	78	1/51	Orig.; movie promo inside front-c; Blum-c/a	1 1	8.35	25.00	50.00
2	85	–	C-price 15¢; LDC-r	1 1	4.00	11.00	22.00
3	118	–	LDC-r	1 1	3.20	8.00	16.00
4	133	–	New-c; PC-r	1 2	2.80	7.00	14.00
5	156	–	PC-r	1 2	2.00	5.00	10.00
6	167	8/64	PC-r	1 2	2.00	5.00	10.00

80. White Fang (Last line drawn cover)

Ed	HRN	Date	Details	A C			
1	79	2/51	Orig.; Blum-c/a	1 1	8.35	25.00	50.00
2	87	–	C-price 15¢; LDC-r	1 1	4.00	11.00	22.00
3	125	–	LDC-r	1 1	3.20	8.00	16.00
4	132	–	New-c; PC-r	1 2	2.40	6.00	12.00
5	140	–	PC-r	1 2	1.25	2.50	5.00
6	153	–	PC-r	1 2	1.25	2.50	5.00
7	167	–	PC-r	1 2	1.25	2.50	5.00
8	167	9/64	PC-r	1 2	1.25	2.50	5.00
9	167	7/65	PC-r	1 2	1.25	2.50	5.00
10	166	6/67	PC-r	1 2	1.25	2.50	5.00
11	169	Fall/69	New price 25¢; PC-r	1 2	1.25	2.50	5.00

81. The Odyssey (1st painted cover)

Ed	HRN	Date	Details	A C			
1	82	3/51	First 15¢ Original; Blum-c	1 1	8.00	24.00	48.00
2	167	8/64	PC-r	1 1	2.00	5.00	10.00
3	167	10/66	PC-r	1 1	2.00	5.00	10.00
4	169	Spr/69	New, stiff-c; PC-r	1 2	2.80	7.00	14.00

82. The Master of Ballantrae

Ed	HRN	Date	Details	A C			
1	82	4/51	Original; Blum-c	1 1	5.35	16.00	32.00
2	167	8/64	PC-r	1 1	2.40	6.00	12.00
3	166	Fall/68	New, stiff-c; PC-r	1 2	2.40	6.00	12.00

83. The Jungle Book

Ed	HRN	Date	Details	A C			
1	85	5/51	Original; Blum-c Bossert/Blum-a	1 1	5.00	15.00	30.00
2	110	–	PC-r	1 1	1.40	3.50	7.00
3	125	–	PC-r	1 1	1.25	2.50	5.00
4	134	–	PC-r	1 1	1.25	2.50	5.00
5	142	–	PC-r	1 1	1.25	2.50	5.00
6	150	–	PC-r	1 1	1.25	2.50	5.00
7	159	–	PC-r	1 1	1.25	2.50	5.00
8	167	–	PC-r	1 1	1.25	2.50	5.00
9	167	3/65	PC-r	1 1	1.25	2.50	5.00
10	167	11/65	PC-r	1 1	1.25	2.50	5.00
11	167	5/66	PC-r	1 1	1.25	2.50	5.00
12	166	R/1968	New c&a; stiff-c; PC-r	2 2	2.80	7.00	14.00

84. The Gold Bug and Other Stories ("The Gold Bug", "The Tell-Tale Heart", "The Cask of Amontillado")

Ed	HRN	Date	Details	A C			
1	85	6/51	Original; Blum-c/a Palais, Laverly-a	1 1	10.00	30.00	65.00
2	167	7/64	PC-r	1 1	10.00	30.00	60.00

85. The Sea Wolf

Ed	HRN	Date	Details	A C			
1	85	7/51	Original; Blum-c/a	1 1	4.00	10.00	20.00
2	121	–	PC-r	1 1	1.00	2.00	4.00
3	132	–	PC-r	1 1	1.00	2.00	4.00

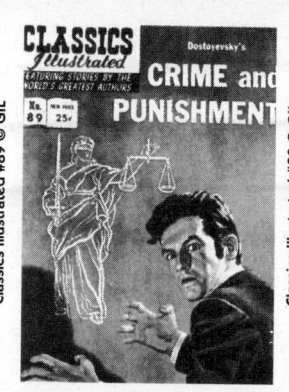

Classics Illustrated #89 © GIL

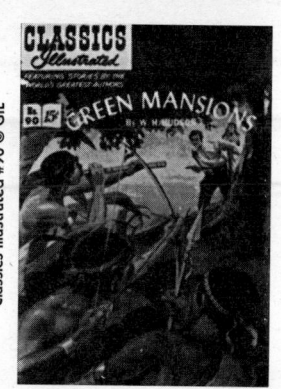

Classics Illustrated #90 © GIL

Classics Illustrated #95 © GIL

Ed	HRN	Date	Details	A	C	GD25	FN65	NM94
4	141	–	PC-r	1	1	1.00	2.00	4.00
5	161	–	PC-r	1	1	1.00	2.00	4.00
6	167	2/64	PC-r	1	1	1.00	2.00	5.00
7	167	11/65	PC-r	1	1	1.00	2.00	4.00
8	169	Fall/69	New price 25¢; stiff-c; PC-r	1	1	1.00	2.00	4.00

86. Under Two Flags

Ed	HRN	Date	Details	A	C			
1	87	8/51	Original; first delBourgo-a	1	1	4.00	10.00	20.00
2	117	–	PC-r	1	1	1.00	2.00	4.00
3	139	–	PC-r	1	1	1.00	2.00	4.00
4	158	–	PC-r	1	1	1.00	2.00	4.00
5	167	2/64	PC-r	1	1	1.00	2.00	4.00
6	167	8/66	PC-r	1	1	1.00	2.00	4.00
7	169	Sm/69	New price 25¢; stiff-c; PC-r	1	1	1.00	2.00	4.00

87. A Midsummer Nights Dream

Ed	HRN	Date	Details	A	C			
1	87	9/51	Original; Blum c/a	1	1	4.00	11.00	22.00
2	161	–	PC-r	1	1	1.25	2.50	5.00
3	167	4/64	PC-r	1	1	1.00	2.00	4.00
4	167	5/66	PC-r	1	1	1.00	2.00	4.00
5	169	Sm/69	New price 25¢; stiff-c; PC-r	1	1	1.00	2.00	4.00

88. Men of Iron

Ed	HRN	Date	Details	A	C			
1	89	10/51	Original	1	1	4.00	12.00	24.00
2	154	–	PC-r	1	1	1.25	2.50	5.00
3	167	1/64	PC-r	1	1	1.25	2.50	5.00
4	166	R/1968	C-price 25¢; PC-r	1	1	1.25	2.50	5.00

89. Crime and Punishment (Cover illo. in POP)

Ed	HRN	Date	Details	A	C			
1	89	11/51	Original; Palais-a	1	1	4.35	13.00	26.00
2	152	–	PC-r	1	1	1.00	2.00	4.00
3	167	4/64	PC-r	1	1	1.00	2.00	4.00
4	167	5/66	PC-r	1	1	1.00	2.00	4.00
5	169	Fall/69	New price 25¢; stiff-c; PC-r	1	1	1.00	2.00	4.00

90. Green Mansions

Ed	HRN	Date	Details	A	C			
1	89	12/51	Original; Blum-c/a	1	1	4.00	12.00	24.00
2	148	–	New L.B. Cole-c; PC-r	1	2	2.00	5.00	10.00
3	165	–	PC-r	1	2	1.00	2.00	4.00
4	167	4/64	PC-r	1	2	1.00	2.00	4.00
5	167	9/66	PC-r	1	2	1.00	2.00	4.00
6	169	Sm/69	New price 25¢; PC-r	1	2	1.00	2.00	4.00

91. The Call of the Wild

Ed	HRN	Date	Details	A	C			
1	92	1/52	Orig.; delBourgo-a	1	1	4.00	11.00	22.00
2	112	–	PC-r	1	1	1.25	2.50	5.00
3	125	–	'Picture Progress' on back-c; PC-r	1	1	1.00	2.00	4.00
4	134	–	PC-r	1	1	1.00	2.00	4.00
5	143	–	PC-r	1	1	1.00	2.00	4.00
6	165	–	PC-r	1	1	1.00	2.00	4.00
7	167	–	PC-r	1	1	1.00	2.00	4.00
8	167	4/65	PC-r	1	1	1.00	2.00	4.00
9	167	3/66	PC-r	1	1	1.00	2.00	4.00
10	166	11/67	PC-r	1	1	1.00	2.00	4.00
11	169	Spr/70	New price 25¢; stiff-c; PC-r	1	1	1.00	2.00	4.00

92. The Courtship of Miles Standish

Ed	HRN	Date	Details	A	C			
1	92	2/52	Original; Blum-c/a	1	1	4.00	11.00	22.00
2	165	–	PC-r	1	1	1.00	2.00	4.00
3	167	3/64	PC-r	1	1	1.00	2.00	4.00
4	166	5/67	PC-r	1	1	1.00	2.00	4.00
5	169	Win/69	New price 25¢; stiff-c; PC-r	1	1	1.00	2.00	4.00

93. Pudd'nhead Wilson

Ed	HRN	Date	Details	A	C			
1	94	3/52	Orig.; Kiefer-c/a;	1	1	4.00	12.00	24.00
2	165	–	New-c;	1	2	1.80	4.50	9.00
3	167	3/64	PC-r	1	2	1.40	3.50	7.00
4	166	R/1968	New price 25¢; soft-c; PC-r	1	2	1.40	3.50	7.00

94. David Balfour

Ed	HRN	Date	Details	A	C			
1	94	4/52	Original; Palais-a	1	1	4.00	12.00	24.00
2	167	5/64	PC-r	1	1	2.00	5.00	10.00
3	166	R/1968	C-price 25¢; PC-r	1	1	2.00	5.00	10.00

95. All Quiet on the Western Front

Ed	HRN	Date	Details	A	C			
1A	96	5/52	Orig.; del Bourgo-a	1	1	10.00	30.00	70.00
1B	99	5/52	Orig.; del Bourgo-a	1	1	8.70	26.00	52.00
2	167	10/64	PC-r	1	1	3.00	7.50	15.00
3	167	11/66	PC-r	1	1	3.00	7.50	15.00

96. Daniel Boone

Ed	HRN	Date	Details	A	C			
1	97	6/52	Original; Blum-a	1	1	4.00	10.00	20.00
2	117	–	PC-r	1	1	1.00	2.00	4.00
3	128	–	PC-r	1	1	1.00	2.00	4.00
4	132	–	PC-r	1	1	1.00	2.00	4.00
5	134	–	"Story of Jesus" on back-c; PC-r	1	1	1.00	2.00	4.00
6	158	–	PC-r	1	1	1.00	2.00	4.00
7	167	1/64	PC-r	1	1	1.00	2.00	4.00
8	167	5/65	PC-r	1	1	1.00	2.00	4.00
9	167	11/66	PC-r	1	1	1.00	2.00	4.00
10	166	Win/69	New-c; price 25¢; PC-r; stiff-c	1	2	2.00	5.00	10.00

97. King Solomon's Mines

Ed	HRN	Date	Details	A	C			
1	96	7/52	Orig.; Kiefer-a	1	1	4.00	10.00	20.00
2	118	–	PC-r	1	1	1.50	3.50	7.00
3	131	–	PC-r	1	1	1.00	2.00	4.00
4	141	–	PC-r	1	1	1.00	2.00	4.00
5	158	–	PC-r	1	1	1.00	2.00	4.00
6	167	2/64	PC-r	1	1	1.00	2.00	4.00
7	167	9/65	PC-r	1	1	1.00	2.00	4.00
8	169	Sm/69	New price 25¢; stiff-c; PC-r	1	1	1.25	2.50	5.00

98. The Red Badge of Courage

Ed	HRN	Date	Details	A	C			
1	98	8/52	Original	1	1	4.00	11.00	22.00
2	118	–	PC-r	1	1	1.00	2.00	4.00
3	132	–	PC-r	1	1	1.00	2.00	4.00
4	142	–	PC-r	1	1	1.00	2.00	4.00
5	152	–	PC-r	1	1	1.00	2.00	4.00
6	161	–	PC-r	1	1	1.00	2.00	4.00
7	167	–	Has orig.date; PC-r	1	1	1.00	2.00	4.00

Classics Illustrated #101 © GIL

Classics Illustrated #104 © GIL

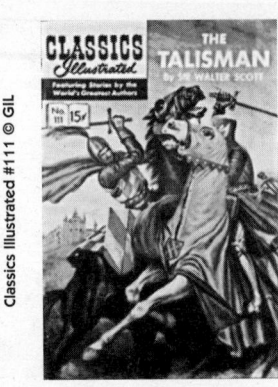

Classics Illustrated #111 © GIL

			GD25	**FN65**	**NM94**

			A	C			
8	167	9/64	PC-r	1	1	1.00	2.00	4.00
9	167	10/65	PC-r	1	1	1.00	2.00	4.00
10	166	R/1968	New-c&price 25¢; PC-r; stiff-c	1	2	2.80	7.00	14.00

99. Hamlet (Used in **POP**, pg. 102)

Ed	HRN	Date	Details	A	C			
1	98	9/52	Original; Blum-a	1	1	4.00	12.00	24.00
2	121	–	PC-r	1	1	1.00	2.00	4.00
3	141	–	PC-r	1	1	1.00	2.00	4.00
4	158	–	PC-r	1	1	1.00	2.00	4.00
5	167	–	Has orig.date; PC-r	1	1	1.00	2.00	4.00
6	167	7/65	PC-r	1	1	1.00	2.00	4.00
7	166	4/67	PC-r	1	1	1.00	2.00	4.00
8	169	Spr/69	New-c&price 25¢; PC-r; stiff-c	1	2	2.00	5.00	10.00

100. Mutiny on the Bounty

Ed	HRN	Date	Details	A	C			
1	100	10/52	Original	1	1	4.00	10.00	20.00
2	117	–	PC-r	1	1	1.00	2.00	4.00
3	132	–	PC-r	1	1	1.00	2.00	4.00
4	142	–	PC-r	1	1	1.00	2.00	4.00
5	155	–	PC-r	1	1	1.00	2.00	4.00
6	167	–	Has orig. date;PC-r	1	1	1.00	2.00	4.00
7	167	5/64	PC-r	1	1	1.00	2.00	4.00
8	167	3/66	PC-r	1	1	1.00	2.00	4.00
9	169	Spr/70	PC-r; stiff-c	1	1	1.00	2.00	4.00

101. William Tell

Ed	HRN	Date	Details	A	C			
1	101	11/52	Original; Kiefer-c delBourgo-a	1	1	4.00	10.00	20.00
2	118	–	PC-r	1	1	1.00	2.00	4.00
3	141	–	PC-r	1	1	1.00	2.00	4.00
4	158	–	PC-r	1	1	1.00	2.00	4.00
5	167	–	Has orig.date; PC-r	1	1	1.00	2.00	4.00
6	167	11/64	PC-r	1	1	1.00	2.00	4.00
7	166	4/67	PC-r	1	1	1.00	2.00	4.00
8	169	Win/69	New price 25¢; stiff-c; PC-r	1	1	1.00	2.00	4.00

102. The White Company

Ed	HRN	Date	Details	A	C			
1	101	12/52	Original; Blum-a	1	1	8.00	24.00	48.00
2	165	–	PC-r	1	1	3.60	9.00	18.00
3	167	4/64	PC-r	1	1	3.60	9.00	18.00

103. Men Against the Sea

Ed	HRN	Date	Details	A	C			
1	104	1/53	Original; Kiefer-c; Palais-a	1	1	4.00	12.00	24.00
2	114	–	PC-r	1	1	2.80	7.00	14.00
3	131	–	New-c; PC-r	1	2	2.00	5.00	10.00
4	158	–	PC-r	1	2	2.00	5.00	10.00
5	149	–	White reorder list; came after HRN-158; PC-r	1	2	4.00	10.00	20.00
6	167	3/64	PC-r	1	2	1.40	3.50	7.00

104. Bring 'Em Back Alive

Ed	HRN	Date	Details	A	C			
1	105	2/53	Original; Kiefer-c/a	1	1	3.60	9.00	18.00
2	118	–	PC-r	1	1	1.00	2.00	4.00
3	133	–	PC-r	1	1	1.00	2.00	4.00
4	150	–	PC-r	1	1	1.00	2.00	4.00
5	158	–	PC-r	1	1	1.00	2.00	4.00
6	167	10/63	PC-r	1	1	1.00	2.00	4.00

			A	C			
7	167	9/65	PC-r	1	1	1.00	2.00	4.00
8	169	Win/69	New price 25¢; stiff-c; PC-r	1	1	1.00	2.00	4.00

105. From the Earth to the Moon

Ed	HRN	Date	Details	A	C			
1	106	3/53	Original; Blum-a	1	1	3.60	9.00	18.00
2	118	–	PC-r	1	1	1.00	2.00	4.00
3	132	–	PC-r	1	1	1.00	2.00	4.00
4	141	–	PC-r	1	1	1.00	2.00	4.00
5	146	–	PC-r	1	1	1.00	2.00	4.00
6	156	–	PC-r	1	1	1.00	2.00	4.00
7	167	–	Has orig. date;	1	1	1.00	2.00	4.00
8	167	5/64	PC-r	1	1	1.00	2.00	4.00
9	167	5/65	PC-r	1	1	1.00	2.00	4.00
10A	166	10/67	PC-r	1	1	1.00	2.00	4.00
10B	166	10/67	w/Grit ad stapled in book	1	1	10.00	30.00	65.00
11	169	Sm/69	New price 25¢; stiff-c; PC-r	1	1	1.00	2.00	4.00
12	169	Spr/71	PC-r	1	1	1.00	2.00	4.00

106. Buffalo Bill

Ed	HRN	Date	Details	A	C			
1	107	4/53	Orig.; delBourgo-a	1	1	3.60	9.00	18.00
2	118	–	PC-r	1	1	1.00	2.00	4.00
3	132	–	PC-r	1	1	1.00	2.00	4.00
4	142	–	PC-r	1	1	1.00	2.00	4.00
5	161	–	PC-r	1	1	1.00	2.00	4.00
6	167	3/64	PC-r	1	1	1.00	2.00	4.00
7	166	7/67	PC-r	1	1	1.00	2.00	4.00
8	169	Fall/69	PC-r; stiff-c	1	1	1.00	2.00	4.00

107. King of the Khyber Rifles

Ed	HRN	Date	Details	A	C			
1	108	5/53	Original	1	1	4.00	10.00	20.00
2	118	–	PC-r	1	1	1.00	2.00	4.00
3	146	–	PC-r	1	1	1.00	2.00	4.00
4	158	–	PC-r	1	1	1.00	2.00	4.00
5	167	–	Has orig.date; PC-r	1	1	1.00	2.00	4.00
6	167	–	PC-r	1	1	1.00	2.00	4.00
7	167	10/66	PC-r	1	1	1.00	2.00	4.00

108. Knights of the Round Table

Ed	HRN	Date	Details	A	C			
1A	108	6/53	Original; Blum-a	1	1	4.00	12.00	24.00
1B	109	6/53	Original; scarce	1	1	5.70	17.00	34.00
2	117	–	PC-r	1	1	1.00	2.00	4.00
3	165	–	PC-r	1	1	1.00	2.00	4.00
4	167	4/64	PC-r	1	1	1.00	2.00	4.00
5	166	4/67	PC-r	1	1	1.00	2.00	4.00
6	169	Sm/69	New price 25¢; stiff-c; PC-r	1	1	1.00	2.00	4.00

109. Pitcairn's Island

Ed	HRN	Date	Details	A	C			
1	110	7/53	Original; Palais-a	1	1	4.00	12.00	24.00
2	165	–	PC-r	1	1	1.50	3.50	7.00
3	167	3/64	PC-r	1	1	1.50	3.50	7.00
4	166	6/67	PC-r	1	1	1.50	3.50	7.00

110. A Study in Scarlet

Ed	HRN	Date	Details	A	C			
1	111	8/53	Original	1	1	10.00	30.00	70.00
2	165	–	PC-r	1	1	9.15	27.50	55.00

111. The Talisman

Classics Illustrated #115 © GIL

Classics Illustrated #125 © GIL

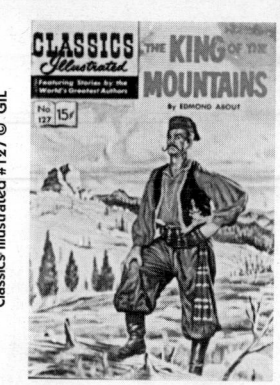

Classics Illustrated #127 © GIL

Ed	HRN	Date	Details	A	C	GD25	FN65	NM94
1	112	9/53	Original; last H.C. Kiefer-a	1	1	4.00	11.00	22.00
2	165	–	PC-r	1	1	1.25	2.50	5.00
3	167	5/64	PC-r	1	1	1.25	2.50	5.00
4	166	Fall/68	C-price 25¢; PC-r	1	1	1.25	2.50	5.00

112. Adventures of Kit Carson

Ed	HRN	Date	Details	A	C	GD25	FN65	NM94
1	113	10/53	Original; Palais-a	1	1	4.00	11.00	22.00
2	129	–	PC-r	1	1	1.00	2.00	4.00
3	141	–	PC-r	1	1	1.00	2.00	4.00
4	152	–	PC-r	1	1	1.00	2.00	4.00
5	161	–	PC-r	1	1	1.00	2.00	4.00
6	167	–	PC-r	1	1	1.00	2.00	4.00
7	167	2/65	PC-r	1	1	1.00	2.00	4.00
8	167	5/66	PC-r	1	1	1.00	2.00	4.00
9	166	Win/69	New-c&price 25¢; PC-r; stiff-c	1	2	2.00	5.00	10.00

113. The Forty-Five Guardsmen

Ed	HRN	Date	Details	A	C	GD25	FN65	NM94
1	114	11/53	Orig.; delBourgo-a	1	1	7.00	21.00	42.00
2	166	7/67	PC-r	1	1	4.00	11.00	22.00

114. The Red Rover

Ed	HRN	Date	Details	A	C	GD25	FN65	NM94
1	115	12/53	Original	1	1	7.00	21.00	42.00
2	166	7/67	PC-r	1	1	4.00	11.00	22.00

115. How I Found Livingstone

Ed	HRN	Date	Details	A	C	GD25	FN65	NM94
1	116	1/54	Original	1	1	8.70	26.00	52.00
2	167	1/67	PC-r	1	1	5.35	16.00	32.00

116. The Bottle Imp

Ed	HRN	Date	Details	A	C	GD25	FN65	NM94
1	117	2/54	Orig.; Cameron-a	1	1	8.70	26.00	52.00
2	167	1/67	PC-r	1	1	5.35	16.00	32.00

117. Captains Courageous

Ed	HRN	Date	Details	A	C	GD25	FN65	NM94
1	118	3/54	Orig.; Costanza-a	1	1	7.50	22.50	45.00
2	167	2/67	PC-r	1	1	3.20	8.00	16.00
3	169	Fall/69	New price 25¢; stiff-c; PC-r	1	1	3.20	8.00	16.00

118. Rob Roy

Ed	HRN	Date	Details	A	C	GD25	FN65	NM94
1	119	4/54	Original; Rudy & Walter Palais-a	1	1	8.70	26.00	52.00
2	167	2/67	PC-r	1	1	5.35	16.00	32.00

119. Soldiers of Fortune

Ed	HRN	Date	Details	A	C	GD25	FN65	NM94
1	120	5/54	Original Shaffenberger-a	1	1	6.35	19.00	38.00
2	166	3/67	PC-r	1	1	3.00	7.50	15.00
3	169	Spr/70	New price 25¢; stiff-c; PC-r	1	1	3.00	7.50	15.00

120. The Hurricane

Ed	HRN	Date	Details	A	C	GD25	FN65	NM94
1	121	6/54	Orig.; Cameron-a	1	1	6.35	19.00	38.00
2	166	3/67	PC-r	1	1	4.00	12.00	24.00

121. Wild Bill Hickok

Ed	HRN	Date	Details	A	C	GD25	FN65	NM94
1	122	7/54	Original	1	1	3.00	7.50	15.00
2	132	–	PC-r	1	1	1.00	2.00	4.00
3	141	–	PC-r	1	1	1.00	2.00	4.00
4	154	–	PC-r	1	1	1.00	2.00	4.00
5	167	–	PC-r	1	1	1.00	2.00	4.00
6	167	8/64	PC-r	1	1	1.00	2.00	4.00
7	166	4/67	PC-r	1	1	1.00	2.00	4.00
8	169	Win/69	PC-r; stiff-c	1	1	1.00	2.00	4.00

122. The Mutineers

Ed	HRN	Date	Details	A	C	GD25	FN65	NM94
1	123	9/54	Original	1	1	4.00	11.00	22.00
2	136	–	PC-r	1	1	1.00	2.00	4.00
3	146	–	PC-r	1	1	1.00	2.00	4.00
4	158	–	PC-r	1	1	1.00	2.00	4.00
5	167	11/63	PC-r	1	1	1.00	2.00	4.00
6	167	3/65	PC-r	1	1	1.00	2.00	4.00
7	166	8/67	PC-r	1	1	1.00	2.00	4.00

123. Fang and Claw

Ed	HRN	Date	Details	A	C	GD25	FN65	NM94
1	124	11/54	Original	1	1	4.00	11.00	22.00
2	133	–	PC-r	1	1	1.00	2.00	4.00
3	143	–	PC-r	1	1	1.00	2.00	4.00
4	154	–	PC-r	1	1	1.00	2.00	4.00
5	167	–	Has orig.date; PC-r	1	1	1.00	2.00	4.00
6	167	9/65	PC-r	1	1	1.00	2.00	4.00

124. The War of the Worlds

Ed	HRN	Date	Details	A	C	GD25	FN65	NM94
1	125	1/55	Original; Cameron-c/a	1	1	5.00	15.00	30.00
2	131	–	PC-r	1	1	1.40	3.50	7.00
3	141	–	PC-r	1	1	1.40	3.50	7.00
4	148	–	PC-r	1	1	1.40	3.50	7.00
5	156	–	PC-r	1	1	1.40	3.50	7.00
6	165	–	PC-r	1	1	1.80	4.50	9.00
7	167	–	PC-r	1	1	1.40	3.50	7.00
8	167	11/64	PC-r	1	1	1.60	4.00	8.00
9	167	11/65	PC-r	1	1	1.40	3.50	7.00
10	166	R/1968	C-price 25¢; PC-r	1	1	1.40	3.50	7.00
11	169	Sm/70	PC-r; stiff-c	1	1	1.40	3.50	7.00

125. The Ox Bow Incident

Ed	HRN	Date	Details	A	C	GD25	FN65	NM94
1	3/55	–	Original; Picture Progress replaces reorder list	1	1	3.00	7.50	15.00
2	143	–	PC-r	1	1	1.00	2.00	4.00
3	152	–	PC-r	1	1	1.00	2.00	4.00
4	149	–	PC-r	1	1	1.00	2.00	4.00
5	167	–	PC-r	1	1	1.00	2.00	4.00
6	167	11/64	PC-r	1	1	1.00	2.00	4.00
7	166	4/67	PC-r	1	1	1.00	2.00	4.00
8	169	Win/69	New price 25¢; stiff-c; PC-r	1	1	1.00	2.00	4.00

126. The Downfall

Ed	HRN	Date	Details	A	C	GD25	FN65	NM94
1	5/55	–	Orig.; 'Picture Progress' replaces reorder list; Cameron-c/a	1	1	4.00	11.00	22.00
2	167	8/64	PC-r	1	1	1.60	4.00	8.00
3	166	R/1968	C-price 25¢; PC-r	1	1	1.60	4.00	8.00

127. The King of the Mountains

Ed	HRN	Date	Details	A	C	GD25	FN65	NM94
1	128	7/55	Original	1	1	4.00	11.00	22.00
2	167	6/64	PC-r	1	1	1.60	4.00	8.00
3	166	F/1968	C-price 25¢; PC-r	1	1	1.60	4.00	8.00

Classics Illustrated #130 © GIL — Classics Illustrated #132 © GIL — Classics Illustrated #140 © GIL

				GD25	FN65	NM94

128. Macbeth (Used in **POP**, pg. 102)

Ed	HRN	Date	Details	A	C	GD25	FN65	NM94
1	128	9/55	Orig.; last Blum-a	1	1	4.00	12.00	24.00
2	143	–	PC-r	1	1	1.00	2.00	4.00
3	158	–	PC-r	1	1	1.00	2.00	4.00
4	167	–	PC-r	1	1	1.00	2.00	4.00
5	167	6/64	PC-r	1	1	1.00	2.00	4.00
6	166	4/67	PC-r	1	1	1.00	2.00	4.00
7	166	R/1968	C-Price 25¢; PC-r	1	1	1.00	2.00	4.00
8	169	Spr/70	Stiff-c; PC-r	1	1	1.00	2.00	4.00

129. Davy Crockett

Ed	HRN	Date	Details	A	C	GD25	FN65	NM94
1	129	11/55	Orig.; Cameron-a	1	1	10.00	30.00	65.00
2	167	9/66	PC-r	1	1	9.15	27.50	55.00

130. Caesar's Conquests

Ed	HRN	Date	Details	A	C	GD25	FN65	NM94
1	130	1/56	Original; Orlando-a	1	1	5.00	15.00	30.00
2	142	–	PC-r	1	1	1.25	2.50	5.00
3	152	–	PC-r	1	1	1.25	2.50	5.00
4	149	–	PC-r	1	1	1.25	2.50	5.00
5	167	–	PC-r	1	1	1.25	2.50	5.00
6	167	10/64	PC-r	1	1	1.25	2.50	5.00
7	167	4/66	PC-r	1	1	1.25	2.50	5.00

131. The Covered Wagon

Ed	HRN	Date	Details	A	C	GD25	FN65	NM94
1	131	3/56	Original	1	1	3.00	7.50	15.00
2	143	–	PC-r	1	1	1.00	2.00	4.00
3	152	–	PC-r	1	1	1.00	2.00	4.00
4	158	–	PC-r	1	1	1.00	2.00	4.00
5	167	–	PC-r	1	1	1.00	2.00	4.00
6	167	11/64	PC-r	1	1	1.00	2.00	4.00
7	167	4/66	PC-r	1	1	1.00	2.00	4.00
8	169	Win/69	New price 25¢; stiff-c; PC-r	1	1	1.00	2.00	4.00

132. The Dark Frigate

Ed	HRN	Date	Details	A	C	GD25	FN65	NM94
1	132	5/56	Original	1	1	4.00	12.00	24.00
2	150	–	PC-r	1	1	1.40	3.50	7.00
3	167	1/64	PC-r	1	1	1.40	3.50	7.00
4	166	5/67	PC-r	1	1	1.40	3.50	7.00

133. The Time Machine

Ed	HRN	Date	Details	A	C	GD25	FN65	NM94
1	132	7/56	Orig.; Cameron-a	1	1	5.00	15.00	30.00
2	142	–	PC-r	1	1	1.40	3.50	7.00
3	152	–	PC-r	1	1	1.40	3.50	7.00
4	158	–	PC-r	1	1	1.40	3.50	7.00
5	167	–	PC-r	1	1	1.40	3.50	7.00
6	167	6/64	PC-r	1	1	1.80	4.50	9.00
7	167	3/66	PC-r	1	1	1.40	3.50	7.00
8	166	12/67	PC-r	1	1	1.40	3.50	7.00
9	169	Win/71	New price 25¢; stiff-c; PC-r	1	1	1.40	3.50	7.00

134. Romeo and Juliet

Ed	HRN	Date	Details	A	C	GD25	FN65	NM94
1	134	9/56	Original; Evans-a	1	1	4.00	12.00	24.00
2	161	–	PC-r	1	1	1.00	2.00	4.00
3	167	9/63	PC-r	1	1	1.00	2.00	4.00
4	167	5/65	PC-r	1	1	1.00	2.00	4.00
5	166	6/67	PC-r	1	1	1.00	2.00	4.00
6	166	Win/69	New c&price 25¢; stiff-c; PC-r	1	2	3.60	9.00	18.00

135. Waterloo

Ed	HRN	Date	Details	A	C	GD25	FN65	NM94
1	135	11/56	Orig.; G. Ingels-a	1	1	4.00	11.00	22.00
2	153	–	PC-r	1	1	1.00	2.00	4.00
3	167	–	PC-r	1	1	1.00	2.00	4.00
4	167	9/64	PC-r	1	1	1.00	2.00	5.00
5	166	R/1968	C-price 25¢; PC-r	1	1	1.00	2.00	4.00

136. Lord Jim

Ed	HRN	Date	Details	A	C	GD25	FN65	NM94
1	136	1/57	Original; Evans-a	1	1	4.00	11.00	22.00
2	165	–	PC-r	1	1	1.00	2.00	4.00
3	167	3/64	PC-r	1	1	1.00	2.00	4.00
4	167	9/66	PC-r	1	1	1.00	2.00	4.00
5	169	Sm/69	New price 25 ¢; stiff-c; PC-r	1	1	1.00	2.00	4.00

137. The Little Savage

Ed	HRN	Date	Details	A	C	GD25	FN65	NM94
1	136	3/57	Original; Evans-a	1	1	4.00	11.00	22.00
2	148	–	PC-r	1	1	1.00	2.00	4.00
3	156	–	PC-r	1	1	1.00	2.00	4.00
4	167	–	PC-r	1	1	1.00	2.00	4.00
5	167	10/64	PC-r	1	1	1.00	2.00	5.00
6	167	8/67	PC-r	1	1	1.00	2.00	4.00
7	169	Spr/70	New price 25¢; stiff-c; PC-r	1	1			

138. A Journey to the Center of the Earth

Ed	HRN	Date	Details	A	C	GD25	FN65	NM94
1	136	5/57	Original	1	1	5.85	17.50	35.00
2	146	–	PC-r	1	1	1.25	2.50	5.00
3	156	–	PC-r	1	1	1.25	2.50	5.00
4	158	–	PC-r	1	1	1.25	2.50	5.00
5	167	–	PC-r	1	1	1.25	2.50	5.00
6	167	6/64	PC-r	1	1	1.40	3.50	7.00
7	167	4/66	PC-r	1	1	1.40	3.50	7.00
8	166	R/68	C-price 25¢; PC-r	1	1	1.25	2.50	5.00

139. In the Reign of Terror

Ed	HRN	Date	Details	A	C	GD25	FN65	NM94
1	139	7/57	Original; Evans-a	1	1	3.00	7.50	15.00
2	154	–	PC-r	1	1	1.00	2.00	4.00
3	167	–	Has orig.date; PC-r	1	1	1.00	2.00	4.00
4	167	7/64	PC-r	1	1	1.00	2.00	5.00
5	166	R/1968	C-price 25¢; PC-r	1	1	1.00	2.00	4.00

140. On Jungle Trails

Ed	HRN	Date	Details	A	C	GD25	FN65	NM94
1	140	9/57	Original	1	1	3.00	7.50	15.00
2	150	–	PC-r	1	1	1.00	2.00	4.00
3	160	–	PC-r	1	1	1.00	2.00	4.00
4	167	9/63	PC-r	1	1	1.00	2.00	5.00
5	167	9/65	PC-r	1	1	1.00	2.00	4.00

141. Castle Dangerous

Ed	HRN	Date	Details	A	C	GD25	FN65	NM94
1	141	11/57	Original	1	1	5.00	15.00	30.00
2	152	–	PC-r	1	1	1.50	3.00	6.00
3	167	–	PC-r	1	1	1.50	3.00	6.00
4	166	7/67	PC-r	1	1	1.50	3.00	6.00

142. Abraham Lincoln

Ed	HRN	Date	Details	A	C	GD25	FN65	NM94
1	142	1/58	Original	1	1	5.00	15.00	30.00
2	154	–	PC-r	1	1	1.00	2.00	4.00
3	167	–	PC-r	1	1	1.00	2.00	4.00
4	167	10/63	PC-r	1	1	1.00	2.00	5.00
5	167	7/65	PC-r	1	1	1.00	2.00	4.00
6	166	11/67	PC-r	1	1	1.00	2.00	4.00

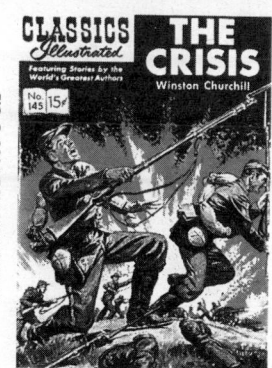

Classics Illustrated #135 © GIL

CLASSICS Illustrated — THE CRISIS — Winston Churchill — No.145 15¢

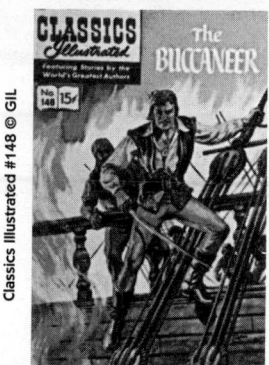

Classics Illustrated #148 © GIL

CLASSICS Illustrated — The Buccaneer — No.148 15¢

Classics Illustrated #149 © GIL

CLASSICS Illustrated — OFF ON A COMET — No.149 15¢

Ed	HRN	Date	Details	A	C	GD25	FN65	NM94
7	169	Fall/69	New price 25¢; stiff-c; PC-r	1	1	1.00	2.00	4.00

143. Kim

Ed	HRN	Date	Details	A	C			
1	143	3/58	Original; Orlando-a	1	1	4.00	11.00	22.00
2	165	–	PC-r	1	1	1.00	2.00	4.00
3	167	11/63	PC-r	1	1	1.00	2.00	5.00
4	167	8/65	PC-r	1	1	1.00	2.00	4.00
5	169	Win/69	New price 25¢; stiff-c; PC-r	1	1	1.00	2.00	4.00

144. The First Men in the Moon

Ed	HRN	Date	Details	A	C			
1	143	5/58	Original; Woodbridge/Williamson/Torres-a	1	1	4.00	12.00	24.00
2	152	–	(Rare)-PC-r	1	1	6.35	19.00	38.00
3	153	–	PC-r	1	1	1.25	2.50	5.00
4	161	–	PC-r	1	1	1.25	2.50	5.00
5	167	–	PC-r	1	1	1.25	2.50	5.00
6	167	12/65	PC-r	1	1	1.25	2.50	5.00
7	166	Fall/68	New-c&price 25¢; PC-r; stiff-c	1	2	2.00	5.00	10.00
8	169	Win/69	Stiff-c; PC-r	1	2	2.00	5.00	10.00

145. The Crisis

Ed	HRN	Date	Details	A	C			
1	143	7/58	Original; Evans-a	1	1	4.00	11.00	22.00
2	156	–	PC-r	1	1	1.00	2.00	4.00
3	167	10/63	PC-r	1	1	1.00	2.00	5.00
4	167	3/65	PC-r	1	1	1.00	2.00	4.00
5	166	R/68	C-price 25¢; PC-r	1	1	1.00	2.00	4.00

146. With Fire and Sword

Ed	HRN	Date	Details	A	C			
1	143	9/58	Original; Woodbridge-a	1	1	5.00	15.00	30.00
2	156	–	PC-r	1	1	1.40	3.50	7.00
3	167	11/63	PC-r	1	1	1.60	4.00	8.00
4	167	3/65	PC-r	1	1	1.40	3.50	7.00

147. Ben-Hur

Ed	HRN	Date	Details	A	C			
1	147	11/58	Original; Orlando-a	1	1	4.00	11.00	22.00
2	152	–	Scarce; PC-r	1	1	4.25	13.00	26.00
3	153	–	PC-r	1	1	1.00	2.00	5.00
4	158	–	PC-r	1	1	1.00	2.00	4.00
5	167	–	Orig.date; but PC-r	1	1	1.00	2.00	4.00
6	167	2/65	PC-r	1	1	1.00	2.00	4.00
7	167	9/66	PC-r	1	1	1.00	2.00	4.00
8A	166	Fall/68	New-c&price 25¢; PC-r; soft-c	1	2	2.80	7.00	14.00
8B	166	Fall/68	New-c&price 25¢; PC-r; stiff-c; scarce	1	2	4.25	13.00	26.00

148. The Buccaneer

Ed	HRN	Date	Details	A	C			
1	148	1/59	Orig.; Evans/Jenny-a; Saunders-c	1	1	4.00	11.00	22.00
2	568	–	Juniors list only PC-r	1	1	1.60	4.00	8.00
3	167	–	PC-r	1	1	1.00	2.00	4.00
4	167	9/65	PC-r	1	1	1.00	2.00	4.00
5	169	Sm/69	New price 25¢; PC-r; stiff-c	1	1	1.00	2.00	4.00

149. Off on a Comet

Ed	HRN	Date	Details	A	C	GD25	FN65	NM94
1	149	3/59	Orig.;G.McCann-a; blue reorder list	1	1	4.00	11.00	22.00
2	155	–	PC-r	1	1	1.00	2.00	4.00
3	149	–	PC-r; white reorder list; no coming-next ad	1	1	1.00	2.00	4.00
4	167	12/63	PC-r	1	1	1.00	2.00	5.00
5	167	2/65	PC-r	1	1	1.00	2.00	5.00
6	167	10/66	PC-r	1	1	1.00	2.00	4.00
7	166	Fall/68	New-c & price 25¢; PC-r	1	2	2.80	7.00	14.00

150. The Virginian

Ed	HRN	Date	Details	A	C			
1	150	5/59	Original	1	1	6.00	18.00	36.00
2	164	–	PC-r	1	1	2.80	7.00	14.00
3	167	10/63	PC-r	1	1	3.60	9.00	18.00
4	167	12/65	PC-r	1	1	2.80	7.00	14.00

151. Won By the Sword

Ed	HRN	Date	Details	A	C			
1	150	7/59	Original	1	1	5.00	15.00	30.00
2	164	–	PC-r	1	1	2.20	5.50	11.00
3	167	10/63	PC-r	1	1	2.40	6.00	12.00
4	166	7/67	PC-r	1	1	2.00	5.00	10.00

152. Wild Animals I Have Known

Ed	HRN	Date	Details	A	C			
1	152	9/59	Orig.; L.B. Cole c/a	1	1	6.00	18.00	36.00
2A	149	–	PC-r; white reorder list; no coming-next ad; IBC: Jr. list #572	1	1	1.25	2.50	5.00
2B	149	–	PC-r; inside-bc: Jr. list to #555	1	1	1.40	3.50	7.00
2C	149	–	PC-r; inside-bc: has World Around Us ad; scarce	1	1	3.20	8.00	16.00
3	167	9/63	PC-r	1	1	1.00	2.00	4.00
4	167	8/65	PC-r	1	1	1.00	2.00	4.00
5	169	Fall/69	New price 25¢; stiff-c; PC-r	1	1	1.00	2.00	4.00

153. The Invisible Man

Ed	HRN	Date	Details	A	C			
1	153	11/59	Original	1	1	6.00	18.00	36.00
2A	149	–	PC-r; white reorder list; no coming-next ad; inside-bc: Jr. list to #572	1	1	1.25	2.50	5.00
2B	149	–	PC-r; inside-bc: Jr. list to #555	1	1	1.40	3.50	7.00
3	167	–	PC-r	1	1	1.00	2.00	4.00
4	167	2/65	PC-r	1	1	1.00	2.00	4.00
5	167	9/66	PC-r	1	1	1.00	2.00	4.00
6	166	Win/69	New price 25¢; PC-r; stiff-c	1	1	1.00	2.00	4.00
7	169	Spr/71	Stiff-c; letters spelling 'Invisible Man' are 'solid' not 'invisible;' PC-r	1	1	1.00	2.00	4.00

154. The Conspiracy of Pontiac

Ed	HRN	Date	Details	A	C			
1	154	1/60	Original	1	1	6.00	18.00	36.00
2	167	11/63	PC-r	1	1	2.40	6.00	12.00
3	167	7/64	PC-r	1	1	2.40	6.00	12.00
4	166	12/67	PC-r	1	1	2.40	6.00	12.00

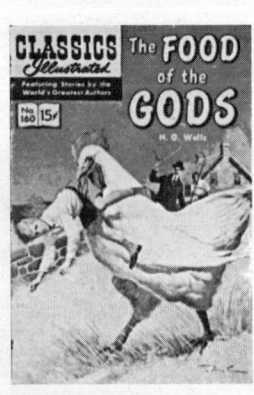

Classics Illustrated #160 © GIL

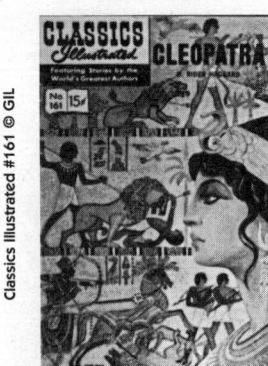

Classics Illustrated #161 © GIL

Classics Illustrated #168 © GIL

				GD25	FN65	NM94

155. The Lion of the North

Ed	HRN	Date	Details	A C			
1	154	3/60	Original	1 1	5.00	15.00	30.00
2	167	1/64	PC-r	1 1	2.00	5.00	10.00
3	166	R/1967	C-price 25¢; PC-r	1 1	1.80	4.50	9.00

156. The Conquest of Mexico

Ed	HRN	Date	Details	A C			
1	156	5/60	Orig.; Bruno Premiani-c/a	1 1	5.00	15.00	30.00
2	167	1/64	PC-r	1 1	1.40	3.50	7.00
3	166	8/67	PC-r	1 1	1.40	3.50	7.00
4	169	Spr/70	New price 25¢; stiff-c; PC-r	1 1	1.25	2.50	5.00

157. Lives of the Hunted

Ed	HRN	Date	Details	A C			
1	156	7/60	Orig.; L.B. Cole-c	1 1	6.00	18.00	36.00
2	167	2/64	PC-r	1 1	2.40	6.00	12.00
3	166	10/67	PC-r	1 1	2.40	6.00	12.00

158. The Conspirators

Ed	HRN	Date	Details	A C			
1	156	9/60	Original	1 1	5.35	16.00	32.00
2	167	7/64	PC-r	1 1	2.40	6.00	12.00
3	166	10/67	PC-r	1 1	2.40	6.00	12.00

159. The Octopus

Ed	HRN	Date	Details	A C			
1	159	11/60	Orig.; Gray Morrow-a; L.B. Cole-c	1 1	5.35	16.00	32.00
2	167	2/64	PC-r	1 1	2.00	5.00	10.00
3	166	R/1967	C-price 25¢; PC-r	1 1	2.00	5.00	10.00

160. The Food of the Gods

Ed	HRN	Date	Details	A C			
1A	159	1/61	Original	1 1	6.00	18.00	36.00
1B	160	1/61	Original; same, except for HRN	1 1	5.50	16.50	33.00
2	167	1/64	PC-r	1 1	2.20	5.50	11.00
3	166	6/67	PC-r	1 1	2.20	5.50	11.00

161. Cleopatra

Ed	HRN	Date	Details	A C			
1	161	3/61	Original	1 1	6.00	18.00	36.00
2	167	1/64	PC-r	1 1	2.80	7.00	14.00
3	166	8/67	PC-r	1 1	2.80	7.00	14.00

162. Robur the Conqueror

Ed	HRN	Date	Details	A C			
1	162	5/61	Original	1 1	5.35	16.00	32.00
2	167	7/64	PC-r	1 1	2.00	5.00	10.00
3	166	8/67	PC-r	1 1	2.00	5.00	10.00

163. Master of the World

Ed	HRN	Date	Details	A C			
1	163	7/61	Original; Gray Morrow-a	1 1	5.35	16.00	32.00
2	167	1/65	PC-r	1 1	2.00	5.00	10.00
3	166	R/1968	C-price 25¢; PC-r	1 1	2.00	5.00	10.00

164. The Cossack Chief

Ed	HRN	Date	Details	A C			
1	164	(1961)	Orig.; nd(10/61?)	1 1	5.00	15.00	30.00
2	167	4/65	PC-r	1 1	2.00	5.00	10.00
3	166	Fall/68	C-price 25¢; PC-r	1 1	2.00	5.00	10.00

165. The Queen's Necklace

Ed	HRN	Date	Details	A C			
1	164	1/62	Original; Morrow-a	1 1	5.00	15.00	30.00
2	167	4/65	PC-r	1 1	2.00	5.00	10.00
3	166	Fall/68	C-price 25¢; PC-r	1 1	2.00	5.00	10.00

166. Tigers and Traitors

Ed	HRN	Date	Details	A C			
1	165	5/62	Original	1 1	7.25	22.00	58.00
2	167	2/64	PC-r	1 1	3.60	9.00	18.00
3	167	11/66	PC-r	1 1	3.60	9.00	18.00

167. Faust

Ed	HRN	Date	Details	A C			
1	165	8/62	Original	1 1	12.00	36.00	85.00
2	167	2/64	PC-r	1 1	5.85	17.50	35.00
3	166	6/67	PC-r	1 1	5.85	17.50	35.00

168. In Freedom's Cause

Ed	HRN	Date	Details	A C			
1	169	Win/69	Original; Evans/Crandall-a; stiff-c; 25¢; no coming-next ad;	1 1	13.00	39.00	90.00

169. Negro Americans The Early Years

Ed	HRN	Date	Details	A C			
1	166	Spr/69	Orig. & last issue; 25¢; Stiff-c; no coming-next ad; other sources indicate publication date of 5/69	1 1	10.00	30.00	70.00
2	169	Spr/69	Stiff-c	1 1	6.35	19.00	38.00

NOTE: Many other titles were prepared or planned but were only issued in British/European series.

CLASSICS GIVEAWAYS (Arranged in chronological order)

12/41–Walter Theatre Enterprises (Huntington, WV) giveaway containing #2 (orig.) w/new generic-c (only 1 known copy) — 100.00 / 300.00 / 800.00

1942–Double Comics containing CC#1 (orig.) (diff. cover) (not actually a giveaway) (very rare) (also see Double Comics) (only one known copy) — 206.00 / 618.00 / 1650.00

12/42–Saks 34th St. Giveaway containing CC#7 (orig.) (diff. cover) (very rare; only 6 known copies) — 657.00 / 1970.00 / 4600.00

2/43–American Comics containing CC#8 (orig.) (Liberty Theatre giveaway) (different cover) (only one known copy) (see American Comics) — 137.00 / 412.00 / 1100.00

12/44–Robin Hood Flour Co. Giveaway - #7-CC(R) (diff. cover) (rare) (edition probably 5 [22]) — 275.00 / 825.00 / 2200.00

NOTE: How are above editions determined without CC covers? 1942 is dated 1942, and CC#1-first reprint did not come out until 5/43. 12/42 and 2/43 are determined by blue note at bottom of first text page only in original edition. 12/44 is estimated from page width each reprint edition had progressively smaller page width.

1951–Shelter Thru the Ages (C.I. Educational Series) (actually Giveaway by the Ruberoid Co.) (16 pgs.) (contains original artwork by H. C. Kiefer) (there are 5 diff. back cover ad variations: "Ranch" house ad, "Igloo" ad, "Doll House" ad, "Tree House" ad & blank)(scarce) — 75.00 / 225.00 / 600.00

1952–George Daynor Biography Giveaway (CC logo) (partly comic book/pictures/newspaper articles) (story of man who built Palace Depression out of junkyard swamp in NJ) (64 pgs.)(very rare; only 3 known copies, one missing-bc) — 857.00 / 2571.00 / 6000.00

1953–Westinghouse/Dreams of a Man (C.I. Educational Series) (Westinghouse bio./Westinghouse Co. giveaway) (contains original artwork by H. C. Kiefer) (16 pgs.) (also French/Spanish/Italian versions)(scarce) — 81.00 / 243.00 / 650.00

NOTE: Reproductions of 1951, 1952, and 1953 exist with color photocopy covers and black & white photocopy interior (W.C.N. Reprint) — 2.00 / 5.00 / 10.00

1951-53–Coward Shoe Giveaways (all editions very rare); 2 variations of back-c ad exist: With back-c photo ad: 5 (87), 12 (89), 22 (85), 49 (85), 69 (87), 72 (no

Classics Illustrated #503 © GIL

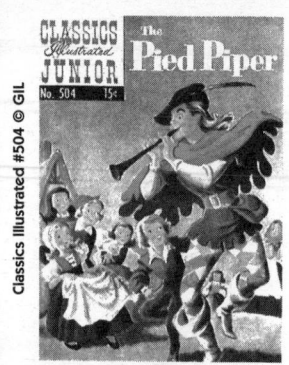

Classics Illustrated #504 © GIL

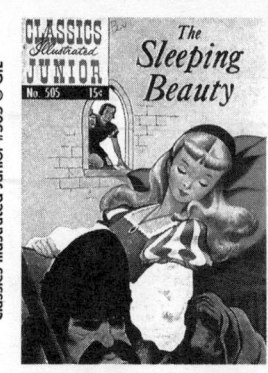

Classics Illustrated Junior #505 © GIL

GD25   FN65   NM94   **GD25   FN65   NM94**

HRN), 80 (0), 91 (0), 92 (0), 96 (0), 98 (0), 100 (0), 101 (0), 103-105 (all Os)	40.00	120.00	300.00
With back-c cartoon ad: 106-109 (all 0s), 110 (111), 112 (0)	44.00	132.00	350.00
1956—Ben Franklin 5-10 Store Giveaway (#65-PC with back cover ad) (scarce)	36.00	107.00	250.00
1956—Ben Franklin Insurance Co. Giveaway (#65-PC with diff. back cover ad) (very rare)	71.00	215.00	550.00
11/56—Sealtest Co. Edition - #4 (135) (identical to regular edition except for Sealtest logo printed, not stamped, on front cover) (only two copies known to exist)	40.00	120.00	300.00
1958—Get-Well Giveaway containing #15-CI (new cartoon-type cover)(Pressman Pharmacy) (only one copy known to exist)	39.00	118.00	275.00
1967-68—Twin Circle Giveaway Editions - all HRN 166, with back cover ad for National Catholic Press.			
2(R68), 4(R67), 10(R68), 13(R68)	4.25	13.00	26.00
48(R67), 128(R68), 535(576-R68)	5.35	16.00	32.00
16(R68), 68(R67)	7.50	22.50	45.00
12/69—Christmas Giveaway ("A Christmas Adventure") (reprints Picture Parade #4-1953, new cover) (4 ad variations)			
Stacy's Dept. Store	4.00	11.00	22.00
Anne & Hope Store	8.35	25.00	50.00
Gibson's Dept. Store (rare)	8.35	25.00	50.00
"Merry Christmas" & blank ad space	4.00	11.00	22.00

CLASSICS ILLUSTRATED GIANTS
October, 1949 (One-Shots - "OS")
Gilberton Publications

These Giant Editions, all with new Kiefer front and back covers, were advertised from 10/49 to 2/52. They were 50¢ on the newsstand and 60¢ by mail. They are actually fourclassics in one volume. All the stories are reprints of the Classics Illustrated Series. NOTE: There were also British hardback Adventure & Indian Giants in 1952, with the same covers but different contents: Adventure - 2, 7, 10; Indian - 17, 22, 37, 58. They are also rare.

"An Illustrated Library of Great Adventure Stories" - reprints of No. 6,7,8,10 (Rare); Kiefer-c	125.00	375.00	1000.00
"An Illustrated Library of Exciting Mystery Stories" - reprints of No. 30,21,40, 13 (Rare)	137.00	412.00	1100.00
"An Illustrated Library of Great Indian Stories" - reprints of No. 4,17,22,37 (Rare)	125.00	375.00	1000.00

INTRODUCTION TO CLASSICS ILLUSTRATED JUNIOR

Collectors of Juniors can be put into one of two categories those who want any copy of each title, and those who want all the originals. Those seeking every original and reprint edition are a limited group, primarily because Juniors have no changes in art or covers to spark interest, and because reprints are so low in value it is difficult to get dealers to look for specific reprint editions.

In recent years it has become apparent that most serious Classics collectors seek Junior originals. Those seeking reprints seek them for low cost. This has made the previous note about the comparative market value of reprints inadequate. Most dealers report difficulty in moving reprints for more than $2-$4 or mint copies. Some may be worth $5-$7, just because of the popularity of the title, such as Snow White, Sleeping Beauty, and Wizard of Oz. Others may be worth $5-$7, because of the scarcity of particular title nos., such as 514, 560, 562, 575 & 576. Three particular reprint editions are worth even more. For the 535-Twin Circle edition, see Giveaways. There are also reprint editions of 501 and 503 which have a full-page bc ad for the very rare Junior record. Those may sell as high as $10-$15 in mint. Original editions of 557 and 558 also have that ad.

There are no reprint editions of 577. The only edition, from 1969, is a 25 cent stiff-cover edition with no ad for the next issue. All other original editions have coming-next ad. But 577, like C.I. #168, was prepared in 1962 but not issued. Copies of 577 can be found in 1963 British/European series, which then continued with dozens of additional new Junior titles.

PRICES LISTED BELOW ARE FOR ORIGINAL EDITIONS, WHICH HAVE AN AD FOR THE NEXT ISSUE.

CLASSICS ILLUSTRATED JUNIOR
Oct, 1953 - Spring, 1971
Famous Authors Ltd. (Gilberton Publications)

501-Snow White & the Seven Dwarfs; Alex Blum-a	10.00	30.00	60.00
502-The Ugly Duckling	6.35	19.00	38.00
503-Cinderella	4.00	11.00	22.00
504-512: 504-The Pied Piper. 505-The Sleeping Beauty. 506-The Three Little Pigs. 507-Jack & the Beanstalk. 508-Goldilocks & the Three Bears. 509-Beauty and the Beast. 510-Little Red Riding Hood. 511-Puss-N Boots.			
512-Rumpelstiltskin	3.00	7.50	15.00
513-Pinocchio	4.00	11.00	22.00
514-The Steadfast Tin Soldier	5.35	16.00	32.00
515-Johnny Appleseed	3.00	7.50	15.00
516-Aladdin and His Lamp	4.00	11.00	22.00
517-519: 517-The Emperor's New Clothes. 518-The Golden Goose. 519-Paul Bunyan	3.00	7.50	15.00
520-Thumbelina	4.00	11.00	22.00
521-King of the Golden River	3.00	7.50	15.00
522-524,527,528,530: 522-The Nightingale. 523-The Gallant Tailor. 524-The Wild Swans. 527-The Golden-Haired Giant. 528-The Penny Prince. 530-The Golden Bird	2.40	6.00	12.00
525,526,529: 525-The Little Mermaid. 526-The Frog Prince. 529-The Magic Servants	2.60	6.50	13.00
531-Rapunzel	3.00	7.50	15.00
532-534: 532-The Dancing Princesses. 533-The Magic Fountain. 534-The Golden Touch	2.40	6.00	12.00
535-The Wizard of Oz	5.00	15.00	30.00
536,537: 536-The Chimney Sweep. 537-The Three Fairies.	2.80	7.00	14.00
538-Silly Hans	2.40	6.00	12.00
539-The Enchanted Fish	4.00	11.00	22.00
540-The Tinder-Box	4.00	11.00	22.00
541-Snow White & Rose Red	3.00	7.50	15.00
542-The Donkey's Tale	3.00	7.50	15.00
543-The House in the Woods	2.40	6.00	12.00
544-The Golden Fleece	5.00	15.00	30.00
545-The Glass Mountain	3.00	7.50	15.00
546-The Elves & the Shoemaker	3.00	7.50	15.00
547-The Wishing Table	2.80	7.00	14.00
548-551: 548-The Magic Pitcher. 549-Simple Kate. 550-The Singing Donkey. 551-The Queen Bee	2.40	6.00	12.00
552-The Three Little Dwarfs	3.00	7.50	15.00
553,556: 553-King Thrushbeard. 556-The Elf Mound	2.40	6.00	12.00
554,555: 554-The Enchanted Deer. 555-The Three Golden Apples	2.40	6.00	12.00
557-Silly Willy	4.00	10.50	21.00
558-The Magic Dish; L.B. Cole-c; soft and stiff-c exist on original	4.00	12.00	24.00
559-The Japanese Lantern; 1 pg. Ingels-a; L.B. Cole-c	4.00	12.00	24.00
560-The Doll Princess; L.B. Cole-c	4.25	13.00	26.00
561-Hans Humdrum; L.B. Cole-c	2.40	6.00	12.00
562-The Enchanted Pony; L.B. Cole-c	4.25	13.00	26.00
563-570: 563-The Wishing Well; L.B. Cole-c. 564-The Salt Mountain; L.B.Cole-c. 565-The Silly Princess; L.B. Cole-c. 566-Clumsy Hans; L.B. Cole-c. 567-The Bearskin Soldier; L.B. Cole-c. 568-The Happy Hedgehog; L.B. Cole-c. 569-The Three Giants. 570-The Pearl Princess	2.40	6.00	12.00
571-574: 571-How Fire Came to the Indians. 572-The Drummer Boy. 573-The Crystal Ball. 574-Brightboots	3.00	7.50	15.00
575-The Fearless Prince	3.60	9.00	18.00
576-The Princess Who Saw Everything	4.25	13.00	26.00
577-The Runaway Dumpling	5.35	16.00	32.00

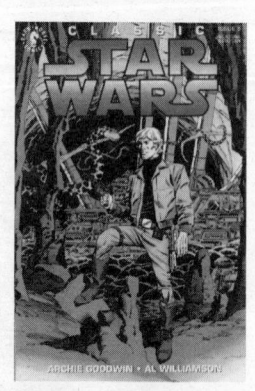

Classic Star Wars #5 © Lucasfilm

Classic X-Men #41 © MEG

Claw #5 © DC

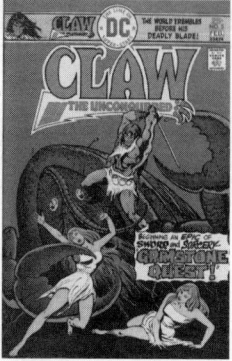

NOTE: Prices are for original editions. Last reprint - Spring, 1971. **Costanza** & **Shaffenberger** art in many issues.

CLASSICS ILLUSTRATED SPECIAL ISSUE
Dec, 1955 - July, 1962 (35¢, 100 pgs.)
Gilberton Co. (Came out semi-annually)

	GD25	FN65	NM94
129-The Story of Jesus (titled ...Special Edition) "Jesus on Mountain" cover	8.35	25.00	50.00
"Three Camels" cover (12/58)	10.00	30.00	70.00
"Mountain" cover (no date)-Has checklist on inside b/c to HRN #161 & different testimonial on back-c	7.50	22.50	45.00
"Mountain" cover (1968 re-issue; has white 50¢ circle)	6.00	18.00	36.00
132A-The Story of America (6/56); Cameron-a	6.35	19.00	38.00
135A-The Ten Commandments(12/56)	6.00	18.00	36.00
138A-Adventures in Science(6/57); HRN to 137	5.00	15.00	30.00
138A-(6/57)-2nd version w/HRN to 149	4.00	12.00	24.00
138A-(12/61)-3rd version w/HRN to 149	5.00	15.00	30.00
141A-The Rough Rider (Teddy Roosevelt)(12/57); Evans-a	6.00	18.00	36.00
144A-Blazing the Trails West(6/58)- 73 pgs. of Crandall/Evans plus Severin-a	6.00	18.00	36.00
147A-Crossing the Rockies(12/58)-Crandall/Evans-a	6.00	18.00	36.00
150A-Royal Canadian Police(6/59)-Ingels, Sid Check-a	6.00	18.00	36.00
153A-Men, Guns & Cattle(12/59)-Evans-a (26 pgs.); Kinstler-a	6.00	18.00	36.00
156A-The Atomic Age(6/60)-Crandall/Evans, Torres-a	6.00	18.00	36.00
159A-Rockets, Jets and Missiles(12/60)-Evans, Morrow-a	6.00	18.00	36.00
162A-War Between the States(6/61)-Kirby & Crandall/Evans-a; Ingels-a	12.00	36.00	85.00
165A-To the Stars(12/61)-Torres, Crandall/Evans, Kirby-a	6.00	18.00	36.00
166A-World War II('62)-Torres, Crandall/Evans, Kirby-a	10.00	30.00	60.00
167A-Prehistoric World(7/62)-Torres & Crandall/Evans-a; two versions exist (HRN to 165 & HRN to 167)	10.00	30.00	60.00
nn Special Issue-The United Nations (1964; 50¢; scarce); this is actually part of the European Special Series, which cont'd on after the U.S. series stopped issuing new titles in 1962. This English edition was prepared specifically for sale at the U.N. It was printed in Norway	31.00	94.00	220.00

NOTE: There was another U.S. Special Issue prepared in 1962 with artwork by **Torres** entitled World War I. Unfortunately, it was never issued in any English-language edition. It was issued in 1964 in West Germany, The Netherlands, and some Scandanavian countries, with another edition in 1974 with a new cover.

CLASSIC PUNISHER (Also see Punisher)
Dec, 1989 ($4.95, B&W, deluxe format, 68 pgs.)
Marvel Comics

1-Reprints Marvel Super Action #1 & Marvel Preview #2 plus new story	1.00	2.00	5.00

CLASSICS ILLUSTRATED
Feb, 1990 - No. 27, July?, 1991 ($3.75/$3.95, 52 pgs.)
First Publishing/Berkley Publishing

1-17: 1-Gahan Wilson-c/a. 4-Sienkiewicz painted-c/a. 6-Russell scripts/ layouts. 7-Spiegle-a. 9-Ploog-c/a. 16-Staton-a	1.50	3.75	
18-27: 18-Gahan Wilson-c/a; begin $3.95-c. 20-Geary-a. 26-Aesop's Fables (6/91). 26,27-Direct sale only	1.60	4.00	

CLASSICS LIBRARY (See King Classics)

CLASSIC STAR WARS (Also see Star Wars)
Aug, 1992 - No. 20, June, 1994 ($2.50)
Dark Horse Comics

1-19: Star Wars strip-r by Williamson; Williamson redrew portions of the panel to fit comic book format; Williamson c-1-5,7,9,10,14,15,20: 8-Polybagged w/ Star Wars Galaxy trading card. 8,17-M. Schultz-c. 13-Yeates-c. 19-Evans-c

		1.20	3.0
20-($3.50, 52 pg.)-Polybagged w/trading card		1.40	3.5
Trade paperback ($29.95, slip-cased)-Reprints all movie adaptations			30.0

CLASSIC STAR WARS: A NEW HOPE
June, 1994 - No. 2, July, 1994 ($3.95, limited series)
Dark Horse Comics

1-r/Star Wars #1-3, 7-9 pubbed Marvel Comics		1.60	4.0
2-r/Star Wars #4-6, 10-12 pubbed Marvel Comics		1.60	4.0

CLASSIC STAR WARS: RETURN OF THE JEDI
Oct, 1994 - No.2, Nov, 1994 ($3.50, limited series)
Dark Horse Comics

1,2: 1-r/1983-84 Marvel Comics series; polybagged with w/trading card		1.40	3.5

CLASSIC STAR WARS: THE EARLY ADVENTURES
Aug, 1994 - No. 9, Apr, 1995 ($2.50, limited series)
Dark Horse Comics

1-9		1.00	2.5

CLASSIC STAR WARS: THE EMPIRE STRIKES BACK
Aug, 1994 - No. 2, Sept, 1994 ($3.95, limited series)
Dark Horse Comics

1-r/Star Wars #39-44 pubbed by Marvel Comics		1.60	4.0

CLASSIC X-MEN (Becomes X-Men Classic #46 on)
Sept, 1986 - No. 45, Mar, 1990
Marvel Comics Group

1-Begins-r of New X-Men	1.00	2.00	5.0
2-4		1.60	4.0
5-9		1.20	3.0
10-Sabretooth app.		1.60	4.0
11-15: 11-1st origin of Magneto in back-up story		1.20	3.0
16,18-20		1.00	2.5
17-Wolverine-c		1.60	4.0
21-25,27-30: 27-r/X-Men #121; $1.25-c begins		.80	2.0
26-r/X-Men #120; Wolverine-c/app.		1.60	4.0
31-38,40-42,44,45: 35-r/X-Men #129		.80	2.0
39-New Jim Lee back-up story (2nd-a on X-Men)	1.00	2.00	5.0
43-Byrne-c/a(r); $1.75, double-size		.80	2.0

NOTE: **Art Adams** c(p)-1-10, 12-16, 18, 19, 25. **Austin** c-19i. **Bolton** back up stories in 1-28 least. **Williamson** c-12-14i.

CLAW (See Capt. Battle, Jr. Daredevil Comics & Silver Streak Comics)

CLAW THE UNCONQUERED (See Cancelled Comic Cavalcade)
5-6/75 - No. 9, 5/10/76; No. 10, 4-5/78 - No. 12, 8-9/78
National Periodical Publications/DC Comics

1-1st app. Claw		.80	2.0
2,3: 3-Nudity panel			1.5
4-12: 9-Origin			1.2

NOTE: **Giffen** a-8-12p. **Kubert** c-10-12. **Layton** a-9i, 12i.

CLAY CODY, GUNSLINGER
Fall, 1957
Pines Comics

1-Painted-c	4.25	13.00	26.0

CLEAN FUN, STARRING "SHOOGAFOOTS JONES"
1944 (10¢, B&W, oversized covers, 24 pgs.)
Specialty Book Co.

nn-Humorous situations involving Negroes in the Deep South White cover issue...	8.35	25.00	50.0

Clive Barker's Night Breed #21 © Clive Barker

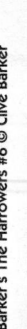

Clive Barker's The Harrowers #6 © Clive Barker

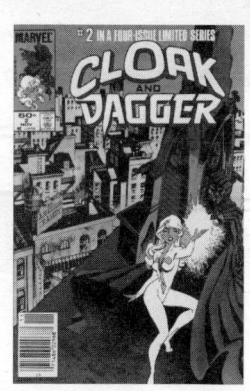

Cloak and Dagger #2 © MEG

CL

	GD25	FN65	NM94
Dark grey cover issue…	10.00	30.00	60.00

CLEMENTINA THE FLYING PIG (See Dell Jr. Treasury)

CLEOPATRA (See Ideal, a Classical Comic No. 1)

CLIFF MERRITT SETS THE RECORD STRAIGHT
Giveaway (2 different issues)
Brotherhood of Railroad Trainsmen

…and the Very Candid Candidate by Al Williamson	.60	1.50	3.00
…Sets the Record Straight by Al Williamson (2 different-c: one by Williamson, the other by McWilliams)	.60	1.50	3.00

CLIMAX! (Mystery)
July, 1955 - No. 2, Sept, 1955
Gillmor Magazines

1,2	11.50	34.00	80.00

CLINT (Also see Adolescent Radioactive Black Belt Hamsters)
Sept, 1986 - No. 2, Jan, 1987 ($1.50, B&W)
Eclipse Comics

1,2			1.50

CLINT & MAC (TV, Disney)
No. 889, Mar, 1958
Dell Publishing Co.

Four Color 889-Alex Toth-a, photo-c	13.00	40.00	130.00

CLIVE BARKER'S BOOK OF THE DAMNED: A HELLRAISER COMPANION
Oct, 1991 - No. 3, Nov, 1992 ($4.95, semi-annual, 52 pgs.)
Marvel Comics (Epic Comics)

Volume 1-3: 1-Simon Bisley-c. 2-(4/92). 3-(11/92)-McKean-a (1 pg.)	1.00	2.00	5.00

CLIVE BARKER'S HELLRAISER (Also see Epic, Hellraiser Nightbreed –Jihad, Revelations, Son of Celluloid, Tapping the Vein & Weaveworld)
1989 - No. 20, 1993 ($4.95, mature readers, quarterly, 68 pgs.)
Marvel Comics (Epic Comics)

Book 1-Based on Hellraiser & Hellbound movies; Bolton-c/a; Spiegle & Wrightson-a (graphic album)	1.00	2.00	5.00
Book 2-4,14-20: 20-By Gaiman/McKean	1.00	2.00	5.00
Book 5-9 ($5.95): 7-Bolton-a. 8-Morrow-a	1.00	2.50	6.00
Book 10,11,13($4.50, 52 pgs.): 10-Foil-c. 11-Guice-p	1.80		4.50
Book 12-Sam Kieth-a	1.80		4.50
…Dark Holiday Special ('92, $4.95)-Conrad-a	1.00	2.00	5.00
…Spring Slaughter 1 ('94, $6.95, 52 pgs.)-Painted-c	1.20	2.90	7.00
…Summer Special 1 ('92, $5.95, 68 pgs.)	1.00	2.50	6.00

CLIVE BARKER'S NIGHTBREED (Also see Epic)
Apr, 1990 - No. 24, Feb, 1993 ($1.95/$2.25/$2.50, mature readers)
Marvel Comics (Epic Comics)

1: 1-4-Adapt horror movie		.80	2.00
2-19: 5-New stories & $2.25-c begin; Guice-a(p)		.90	2.25
20-24: 20-Begin $2.50-c		1.00	2.50

CLIVE BARKER'S THE HARROWERS
Dec, 1993 - No. 9, May, 1994 ($2.50)
Marvel Comics (Epic Comics)

1-($2.95)-Glow-in-the-dark-c; Colan-c/a in all		1.20	3.00
2-9		1.00	2.50

NOTE: **Colan** a(p)-1-6; c-1-3, 4p, 5p. **Williamson** a(i)-2, 4, 5(part).

CLOAK AND DAGGER
Fall, 1952
Ziff-Davis Publishing Co.

1-Saunders painted-c	21.00	64.00	150.00

CLOAK AND DAGGER (Also see Marvel Fanfare)
Oct, 1983 - No. 4, Jan, 1984 (Mini-series)(See Spectacular Spider-Man #64)
Marvel Comics Group

	GD25	FN65	NM94
1-4-Austin-c/a(i) in all. 4-Origin			1.50

CLOAK AND DAGGER (Also see Marvel Graphic Novel #34, Mutant
Misadventures Of… & Strange Tales, 2nd Series)
July, 1985 - No. 11, Jan, 1987
Marvel Comics Group

1			1.50
2-8,10,11			1.00
9-Art Adams-p		.80	2.00
…And Power Pack (1990, $7.95, 68 pgs.)	1.30	3.25	8.00

NOTE: **Mignola** c-7, 8.

CLOBBERIN' TIME
Sept, 1995 ($1.95) (Based on card game)
Marvel Comics

nn-Overpower game guide; Ben Grimm story		.80	2.00

CLONEZONE SPECIAL
1989 ($2.00, B&W)
Dark Horse Comics/First Comics

1-Back-up series from Badger & Nexus		.80	2.00

CLOSE ENCOUNTERS (See Marvel Comics Super Special & Marvel Special Edition)

CLOSE SHAVES OF PAULINE PERIL, THE (TV?)
June, 1970 - No. 4, March, 1971 (Jay Ward?)
Gold.Key

1	1.00	3.00	10.00
2-4		1.80	6.00

CLOWN COMICS (No. 1 titled Clown Comic Book)
1945 - No. 3, Win, 1946
Clown Comics/Home Comics/Harvey Publ.

nn (#1)	9.15	27.00	55.00
2,3	5.85	17.50	35.00

CLUBHOUSE RASCALS (#1 titled …Presents?)
June, 1956 - No. 2, Oct, 1956 (Also see Three Rascals)
Sussex Publ. Co. (Magazine Enterprises)

1,2: The Brain app.	4.25	13.00	28.00

CLUB "16"
June, 1948 - No. 4, Dec, 1948
Famous Funnies

1-Teen-age humor	10.00	30.00	65.00
2-4	5.85	17.50	35.00

CLUE COMICS (Real Clue Crime V2#4 on)
Jan, 1943 - No. 15(V2#3), May, 1947
Hillman Periodicals

1-Origin The Boy King, Nightmare, Micro-Face, Twilight, & Zippo	87.00	262.00	700.00
2	41.00	124.00	330.00
3-5	32.00	96.00	225.00
6,8,9: 8-Palais-c/a(2)	24.00	71.00	165.00
7-Classic torture-c	36.00	107.00	250.00
10-Origin/1st app. The Gun Master & begin series; content changes to crime	24.00	71.00	165.00
11	17.00	49.00	115.00
12-Origin Rackman; McWilliams-a, Guardineer-a(2)	22.00	66.00	155.00
V2#1-Nightmare new origin; Iron Lady app.; Simon & Kirby-a	40.00	120.00	300.00
V2#2-S&K-a(2)-Bondage/torture-c; man attacks & kills people with electric iron. Infantino-a	40.00	120.00	300.00
V2#3-S&K-a(3)	40.00	120.00	300.00

CLUTCHING HAND, THE
July-Aug, 1954
American Comics Group

Codename: Firearm #3 © Malibu

Codename: Stryke Force #3 © Top Cow Productions

Colossial Features Magazine #3 © © FOX

	GD25	FN65	NM94
1	27.00	81.00	190.00

CLYDE BEATTY COMICS (Also see Crackajack Funnies)
October, 1953 (84 pgs.)
Commodore Productions & Artists, Inc.

	GD25	FN65	NM94
1-Photo front/back-c; movie scenes and comics	25.00	75.00	175.00
...African Jungle Book('56)-Richfield Oil Co. 16 pg. giveaway, soft-c	10.00	30.00	70.00

CLYDE CRASHCUP (TV)
Aug-Oct, 1963 - No. 5, Sept-Nov, 1964
Dell Publishing Co.

1-All written by John Stanley	11.00	33.00	110.00
2-5	10.00	30.00	100.00

C-M-O COMICS
1942 - No. 2, 1942 (68 pgs., full color)
Chicago Mail Order Co.(Centaur)

1-Invisible Terror, Super Ann, & Plymo the Rubber Man app. (all Centaur costume heroes)	78.00	234.00	625.00
2-Invisible Terror, Super Ann app.	50.00	150.00	400.00

COBALT BLUE (Also see Power Comics)
Sept, 1989 - No. 2, Oct, 1989 ($1.95, 28 pgs.)
Innovation Publishing

1,2-Gustovich-c/a/scripts		.80	2.00
The Graphic Novel ($6.95, color, 52 pgs.)-r/1,2	1.20	3.00	7.00

COCOMALT BIG BOOK OF COMICS
1938 (Regular size, full color, 52 pgs.)
Harry 'A' Chesler (Cocomalt Premium)

1-(Scarce)-Biro-c/a; Little Nemo by Winsor McCay Jr., Dan Hastings; Jack Cole, Guardineer, Gustavson, Bob Wood-a	200.00	600.00	1600.00

CODE NAME: ASSASSIN (See 1st Issue Special)

CODENAME: DANGER
Aug, 1985 - No. 4, May, 1986 ($1.50)
Lodestone Publishing

1-4			1.50

CODENAME: FIREARM (Also see Firearm)
June, 1995 - No. 5, Sept, 1995 ($2.95, bimonthly limited series)
Malibu Comics (Ultraverse)

0-5: 0-2-Alec Swan back-up story by James Robinson	1.20	3.00
NOTE: *Perez c-0.*

CODENAME: GENETIX
Jan, 1993 - No. 4, May, 1993 ($1.75, limited series)
Marvel Comics UK

1-4: 1-Wolverine in 4		.70	1.75

CODENAME SPITFIRE (Formerly Spitfire And The Troubleshooters)
No. 10, July, 1987 - No. 13, Oct, 1987
Marvel Comics Group

10-13: 10-Rogers-c/a			1.00

CODENAME: STRYKE FORCE (Also See Cyberforce V1#4 & Cyberforce/Stryke Force: Opposing Forces)
Jan, 1994 - No. 15, Sept, 1995 ($1.95/$2.25)
Image Comics (Top Cow Productions)

0		1.00	2.50
1-12-Silvestri stories, Peterson-a. 1-wraparound-c. 4-Stormwatch app.		.80	2.00
1-Gold			10.00
1-Blue			20.00
13-15: 13-$2.25-c begins. 15-Story continues in Cyberforce/Stryke Force: Opposing Forces.		.90	2.25

CODE NAME: TOMAHAWK
Sept, 1986 ($1.75, high quality paper)
Fantasy General Comics

1-Sci-fi		.70	1.7

CODY OF THE PONY EXPRESS (See Colossal Features Magazine)
Sept, 1950 - No. 3, Jan, 1951 (See Women Outlaws)
Fox Features Syndicate

1-3 (Actually #3-5). 1-Painted-c	11.00	33.00	75.0

CODY OF THE PONY EXPRESS (Buffalo Bill...) (Outlaws of the West #11 on; Formerly Bullseye)
No. 8, Oct, 1955; No. 9, Jan, 1956; No. 10, June, 1956
Charlton Comics

8-Bullseye on splash pg; not S&K-a	6.70	20.00	40.0
9,10: Buffalo Bill app. in all	4.25	13.00	26.0

CODY STARBUCK (1st app. in Star Reach #1)
July, 1978 (2nd printing exists)
Star Reach Productions

nn-Howard Chaykin-c/a		.80	2.0
NOTE: *Both printings say First Printing. True first printing is on lower-grade paper, somewhat off register, and snow in snow sequence has green tint.*

CO-ED ROMANCES
November, 1951
P. L. Publishing Co.

1	5.35	16.00	32.0

COFFEE WORLD
Oct, 1995 ($1.50, B&W, anthology)
World Comics

1-Shannon Wheeler's Too Much Coffee Man story			1.5

COLLECTORS DRACULA, THE
1994 - No. 2, 1994 ($3.95, color/B&W, 52 pgs., limited series)
Millennium Publications

1-Bolton-a (7 pgs.)		1.60	4.0

COLLECTORS ITEM CLASSICS (See Marvel Collectors Item Classics)

COLORS IN BLACK
Mar, 1995 - No. 4, June, 1995 ($2.95, limited series)
Dark Horse Comics

1-4		1.20	3.0

COLOSSAL FEATURES MAGAZINE (Formerly I Loved) (See Cody of the Pony Express)
No. 33, 5/50 - No. 34, 7/50; No. 3, 9/50 (Based on Columbia serial)
Fox Features Syndicate

33,34: Cody of the Pony Express begins. 33-Painted-c. 34-Photo-c	10.00	30.00	70.0
3-Authentic criminal cases	10.00	30.00	70.0

COLOSSAL SHOW, THE (TV)
October, 1969
Gold Key

1	3.20	9.60	32.0

COLOSSUS COMICS (See Green Giant & Motion Picture Funnies Weekly)
March, 1940
Sun Publications (Funnies, Inc.?)

1-(Scarce)-Tulpa of Tsang(hero); Colossus app.	266.00	800.00	2400.0
NOTE: *Cover by artist that drew Colossus in Green Giant Comics.*

COLOUR OF MAGIC, THE (Terry Pratchett's...)
1991 - No. 4, 1991 ($2.50, limited series)
Innovation Publishing

Combat #1 © ATLAS

Combat Kelly #3 © ATLAS

The Comet #18 © Impact

	GD25	FN65	NM94

1-4: Adapts 1st novel of the Discworld series 1.00 2.50

COLT .45 (TV)
No. 924, 8/58 - No. 1058, 11-1/59-60; No. 4, 2-4/60 - No. 9, 5-7/61
Dell Publishing Co.

Four Color 924(#1)-Wayde Preston photo-c on all	10.00	30.00	100.00
Four Color 1004,1058, #4,5,7-9: 1004-Photo-b/c	7.50	22.50	75.00
6-Toth-a	8.50	25.50	85.00

COLUMBIA COMICS
1943
William R. Wise Co.

1-Joe Palooka, Charlie Chan, Capt. Yank, Sparky Watts, Dixie Dugan app.	25.00	75.00	175.00

COLUMBUS
Sept, 1992 ($2.50, B&W, one-shot)
Dark Horse Comics

1-Yeates painted-c 1.00 2.50

COMANCHE (See Four Color No. 1350)

COMANCHEROS, THE
No. 1300, Mar-May, 1962
Dell Publishing Co.

Four Color 1300-Movie, John Wayne photo-c 15.00 45.00 150.00

COMBAT
June, 1952 - No. 11, April, 1953
Atlas Comics (ANC)

1	17.00	51.00	120.00
2-Heath-c/a	9.15	27.50	55.00
3,5-9,11: 9-Robert Q. Sale-a	5.85	17.50	35.00
4-Krigstein-a	7.50	22.50	45.00
10-B&W and color illos. in POP	6.70	20.00	40.00

NOTE: Combat Casey in 7-11. Heath c-1, 2, 9. Maneely a-1; c-3. Pakula a-1. Reinman a-1.

COMBAT
Oct-Nov, 1961 - No. 40, Oct, 1973 (No #9)
Dell Publishing Co.

1	5.70	17.00	40.00
2-5: 4-John F. Kennedy c/story (P.T. 109)	3.40	10.00	24.00
6,7,8(4-6/63), 8(7-9/63)	2.30	6.70	16.00
10-26	1.70	5.00	12.00
27-40(reprints #1-14). 30-r/#4	1.30	3.25	8.00

NOTE: Glanzman c/a-1-27, 28-40r.

COMBAT CASEY (Formerly War Combat)
No. 6, Jan, 1953 - No. 34, July, 1957
Atlas Comics (SAI)

6 (Indicia shows 1/52 in error)	11.00	33.00	75.00
7-Spanking panel	10.00	30.00	60.00
8-Used in POP, pg. 94	5.85	17.50	35.00
9	5.00	15.00	30.00
10,13-19-Violent art by R. Q. Sale; Battle Brady x-over #10	9.15	27.50	55.00
11,12,20-Last Precode (2/55)	5.00	15.00	30.00
21-34	4.25	13.00	26.00

NOTE: Everett a-6. Heath c-10, 17, 19, 30. Maneely c-6, 8. Powell a-29(5), 30(5), 34. Severin c-26, 33.

COMBAT KELLY
Nov, 1951 - No. 44, Aug, 1957
Atlas Comics (SPI)

1-1st app. Combat Kelly; Heath-a	21.00	64.00	150.00
2	10.00	30.00	70.00
3-10	7.50	22.50	45.00
11-Used in POP, pgs. 94,95 plus color illo.	5.85	17.50	35.00

12-Color illo. in POP	5.85	17.50	35.00
13-16	4.25	13.00	26.00
17-Violent art by R. Q. Sale; Combat Casey app.	9.15	27.50	55.00
18-20,22-44: 18-Battle Brady app. 28-Last precode (1/55). 38-Green Berets story (8/56)	4.25	13.00	26.00
21-Transvestism-c	5.85	17.50	35.00

NOTE: Berg a-8, 12-14, 16, 17, 19-23, 25, 26, 28, 31-36, 42-44; c-2. Colan a-4; c-2. Heath a-4; c-31. Lawrence a-23. Maneely a-4(2), 6, 7(3), 8; c-4, 5, 7, 8, 10, 25. R.Q. Sale a-17, 25. Severin c-41, 42. Whitney a-5.

COMBAT KELLY (...and the Deadly Dozen)
June, 1972 - No. 9, Oct, 1973
Marvel Comics Group

1-Intro & origin new Combat Kelly; Ayers/Mooney-a; Severin-c (20¢)	1.20	3.00	7.00
2-9			1.50

COMBINED OPERATIONS (See The Story of the Commandos)

COMEBACK (See Zane Grey 4-Color 357)

COMEDY CARNIVAL
no date (1950's) (100 pgs.)
St. John Publishing Co.

nn-Contains rebound St. John comics 31.00 94.00 220.00

COMEDY COMICS (1st Series) (Daring Mystery #1-8) (Becomes Margie Comics #35 on)
No. 9, April, 1942 - No. 34, Fall, 1946
Timely Comics (TCI 9,10)

9-(Scarce)-The Fin by Everett, Capt. Dash, Citizen V, & The Silver Scorn app.; Wolverton-a; 1st app. Comedy Kid; satire on Hitler & Stalin; The Fin, Citizen V & Silver Scorn cont. from Daring Mystery	250.00	750.00	2000.00
10-(Scarce)-Origin The Fourth Musketeer, Victory Boys; Monstro, the Mighty app.	188.00	562.00	1500.00
11-Vagabond, Stuporman app.	44.00	132.00	350.00
12,13	13.00	39.00	90.00
14-Origin/1st app. Super Rabbit (3/43) plus-c	44.00	132.00	350.00
15-20	11.00	33.00	75.00
21-32	9.15	27.00	55.00
33-Kurtzman-a (5 pgs.)	10.00	30.00	70.00
34-Intro Margie; Wolverton-a (5 pgs.)	17.00	49.00	115.00

COMEDY COMICS (2nd Series)
May, 1948 - No. 10, Jan, 1950
Marvel Comics (ACI)

1-Hedy, Tessie, Millie begin; Kurtzman's "Hey Look" (he draws himself)	29.00	86.00	200.00
2	10.00	30.00	70.00
3,4-Kurtzman's "Hey Look" (?&3)	12.00	36.00	85.00
5-10	6.35	19.00	38.00

COMET, THE (See The Mighty Crusaders & Pep Comics #1)
Oct, 1983 - No. 2, Dec, 1983
Red Circle Comics (Archie)

1,2: 1-Re-intro & origin The Comet; The American Shield begins. 2-Origin continues			1.00

COMET, THE
July, 1991 - No. 18, Dec, 1992 ($1.00/$1.25)
DC Comics (Impact Comics)

1-13: 4-Black Hood app. 6-Re-intro Hangman. 8-Web x-over. 10-Contains Crusaders trading card. 13-Last $1.00-c			1.00
14-18: 14-Origin. Netzer(Nasser) c(p)-11,14-17			1.25
Annual 1 (1992, $2.50, 68 pgs.)-Contains Impact trading card; Shield back-up story		1.00	2.50

COMET MAN, THE (Movie)
Feb, 1987 - No. 6, July, 1987 (limited series)

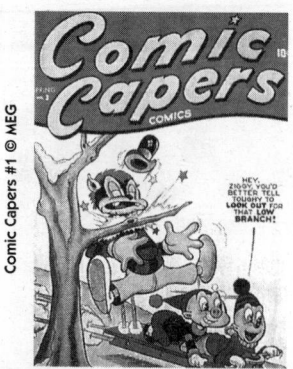

Comic Capers #1 © MEG

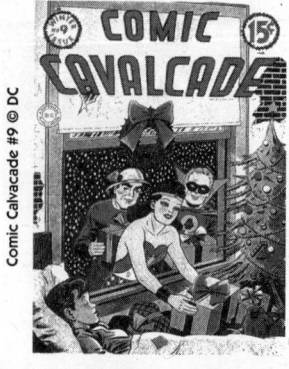

Comic Cavalcade #9 © DC

Comic Land #1 © Fact & Fiction Publ.

	GD25	FN65	NM94

Marvel Comics Group

| 1-6 | | | 1.00 |

NOTE: *Kelley Jones* a-1-6p.

COMIC ALBUM (Also see Disney Comic Album)
Mar-May, 1958 - No. 18, June-Aug, 1962
Dell Publishing Co.

1-Donald Duck	8.00	24.00	80.00
2-Bugs Bunny	4.00	12.00	40.00
3-Donald Duck	6.00	18.00	60.00
4-6,8,10: 4-Tom & Jerry. 5-Woody Woodpecker. 6,10-Bugs Bunny. 8-Tom & Jerry. 9-Woody Woodpecker	3.00	9.00	30.00
7,11: 7-Popeye (9-11/59). 11-Popeye (9-11/60)	4.00	12.00	40.00
12-14: 12-Tom & Jerry. 13-Woody Woodpecker. 14-Bugs Bunny	3.00	9.00	30.00
15-Popeye	4.00	12.00	40.00
16-Flintstones (12-2/61-62)-3rd app.	7.00	21.00	70.00
17-Space Mouse (3rd app.)	4.00	12.00	40.00
18-Three Stooges; photo-c	7.00	21.00	70.00

COMIC BOOK (Also see Comics From Weatherbird)
1954 (Giveaway)
American Juniors Shoe

Contains a comic rebound with new cover. Several combinations possible. Contents determines price.

COMIC BOOK
1995 ($6.95, oversize)
Marvel Comics

| 1-Spumco characters by John K. | 1.20 | 3.00 | 7.00 |

COMIC BOOK MAGAZINE
1940 - 1943 (Similar to Spirit Sections)(7-3/4x10-3/4"; full color; 16-24 pgs. ea.)
Chicago Tribune & other newspapers

1940 issues	5.85	17.50	35.00
1941, 1942 issues	4.70	14.00	28.00
1943 issues	4.00	12.00	24.00

NOTE: *Published weekly. Texas Slim, Kit Carson, Spooky, Josie, Nuts & Jolts, Lew Loyal, Brenda Starr, Daniel Boone, Captain Storm, Rocky, Smokey Stover, Tiny Tim, Little Joe, Fu Manchu appear among others. Early issues had photo stories with pictures from the movies; later issues had comic art.*

COMIC BOOKS (Series 1)
1950 (16 pgs.; 5-1/4x8-1/2"; full color; bound at top; paper cover)
Metropolitan Printing Co. (Giveaway)

1-Boots and Saddles; intro The Masked Marshal	5.00	15.00	30.00
1-The Green Jet; Green Lama by Raboy	29.00	86.00	200.00
1-My Pal Dizzy (Teen-age)	2.80	7.00	14.00
1-New World; origin Atomaster (costumed hero)	9.15	27.50	55.00
1-Talullah (Teen-age)	2.80	7.00	14.00

COMIC CAPERS
Fall, 1944 - No. 6, Summer, 1946
Red Circle Mag./Marvel Comics

1-Super Rabbit, The Creeper, Silly Seal, Ziggy Pig, Sharpy Fox begin	20.00	60.00	140.00
2	10.00	30.00	70.00
3-6	9.15	27.00	55.00

COMIC CAVALCADE
Winter, 1942-43 - No. 63, June-July, 1954
(Contents change with No. 30, Dec-Jan, 1948-49 on)
All-American/National Periodical Publications

	GD25	FN65	VF82	NM94
1-The Flash, Green Lantern, Wonder Woman, Wildcat, The Black Pirate by Moldoff (also #2), Ghost Patrol, and Red White & Blue begin; Scribbly app.; Minute Movie	778.00	2333.00	4667.00	7500.00
(Estimated up to 175 total copies exist, 6 in NM/Mint)				

	GD25	FN65	NM94
2-Mutt & Jeff begin; last Ghost Patrol & Black Pirate; Minute Movies	206.00	618.00	1650.00
3-Hop Harrigan & Sargon, the Sorcerer begin; The King app.	150.00	450.00	1200.00
4,5: 4-The Gay Ghost, The King, Scribbly, & Red Tornado app. 5-Christmas-c. 5-Prints ad for Jr. JSA membership kit that includes "The Minute Man Answers The Call"	125.00	375.00	1000.00
6-10: 7-Red Tornado & Black Pirate app.; last Scribbly. 9-Fat & Slat app.; X-Mas-c	96.00	290.00	775.00
11,12,14-20: 12-Last Red White & Blue. 15-Johnny Peril begins (1st app., 6-7/46), ends #29. 19-Christmas-c	81.00	243.00	650.00
13-Solomon Grundy app.; X-Mas-c	125.00	375.00	1000.00
21-23: 23-Harry Lampert-c (Toth swipes)	81.00	243.00	650.00
24-Solomon Grundy x-over in Green Lantern	93.00	281.00	750.00
25-28: 25-Black Canary app.; X-Mas-c. 26-28-Johnny Peril app. 28-Last Mutt & Jeff	62.00	187.00	500.00
29-(10/-11/48)-Last Flash, Wonder Woman, Green Lantern & Johnny Peril; Wonder Woman invents "Thinking Machine"; 1st computer in comics?; Leave It to Binky story (early app.)	68.00	206.00	550.00
30-(12-1/48-49)-The Fox & the Crow, Dodo & the Frog & Nutsy Squirrel begin	40.00	120.00	300.00
31-35	21.00	64.00	150.00
36-49	15.00	45.00	105.00
50-62(Scarce)	19.00	58.00	135.00
63(Rare)	32.00	96.00	225.00
Giveaway (1944, 8 pgs., paper-c, in color)-One Hundred Years of Co-operation-r/Comic Cavalcade #9	68.00	206.00	550.00
Giveaway (1945, 16 pgs., paper-c, in color)-Movie "Tomorrow The World" (Nazi theme); r/Comic Cavalcade #10	93.00	281.00	750.00
Giveaway (c. 1944-45; 8 pgs, paper-c, in color)-The Twain Shall Meet-r/Comic Cavalcade #8	81.00	243.00	650.00

NOTE: *Grossman a-30-63. E.E. Hibbard c-(Flash only)-1-4, 7-14, 16-19, 21. Sheldon Mayer a(2-3)-40-63. Moulson c(G.L.)-7, 15. Nodell c(G.L.)-9. H.G. Peter a(W. Woman only)-1, 3-21, 24. Post a-31, 36. Purcell c(G.L.)-2-5, 10. Reinman a(Green Lantern)-4-6, 8, 9, 13, 15-21; c(Green Lantern)-6, 8, 19. Toth a(Green Lantern)-26-28; c-27. Atom app.-22, 23.*

COMIC COMICS
Apr, 1946 - No. 10, Feb, 1947
Fawcett Publications

| 1-Captain Kidd; Nutty Comics #1 in indicia | 10.00 | 30.00 | 70.00 |
| 2-10-Wolverton-a, 4 pgs. each. 5-Captain Kidd app. Mystic Moot by Wolverton in #2-10? | 11.50 | 34.00 | 80.00 |

COMIC CUTS (Also see The Funnies)
5/19/34 - 7/28/34 (5¢, 24 pgs.) (Tabloid size in full color)
(Not reprints; published weekly; created for newsstand sale)
H. L. Baker Co., Inc.

| V1#1 - V1#7(6/30/34), V1#8(7/14/34), V1#9(7/28/34)-Idle Jack strips | 10.00 | 30.00 | 60.00 |

COMIC LAND
March, 1946
Fact and Fiction Publ.

| 1-Sandusky & the Senator, Sam Stupor, Sleuth, Marvin the Great, Sir Passer, Phineas Gruff app.; Irv Tirman & Perry Williams art | 11.00 | 33.00 | 75.00 |

COMICO CHRISTMAS SPECIAL
Dec, 1988 ($2.50, 44pgs.)
Comico

| 1-Rude/Williamson-a; Dave Stevens-c | 1.00 | 2.50 | |

COMICO PRIMER (See Primer)

COMIC PAGES (Formerly Funny Picture Stories)
V3#4, July, 1939 - V3#6, Dec, 1939
Centaur Publications

The Comics #7 © DELL

Comics Greatest World V3#2 © DH

Comics On Parade #19 © UFS

	GD25	FN65	NM94

	GD25	FN65	NM94
V3#4-Bob Wood-a	62.00	187.00	500.00
5,6: 6-Schwab-c	47.00	141.00	375.00

COMICS (See All Good)

COMICS, THE
March, 1937 - No. 11, Nov, 1938 (Newspaper strip-r; bi-monthly)
Dell Publishing Co.

	GD25	FN65	NM94
1-1st app. Tom Mix in comics; Wash Tubbs, Tom Beatty, Myra North, Arizona Kid, Erik Noble & International Spy w/Doctor Doom begin	150.00	450.00	1200.00
2	71.00	215.00	575.00
3-11: 3-Alley Oop begins	56.00	168.00	450.00

COMICS AND STORIES (See Walt Disney's Comics and Stories)

COMICS & STORIES (Also see Wolf & Red) (Created by Tex Avery)
Apr, 1996 - No. 3, June, 1996 ($2.95, limited series)
Dark Horse Comics

1-3: Wolf & Red app; reads Comics and Stories on-c. 1-Terry Moore-a. 2-Reed Waller-a.	1.20	3.00	

COMICS CALENDAR, THE (The 1946…)
1946 (25¢, 116 pgs.)(Stapled at top)
True Comics Press (ordered through the mail)

nn-(Rare) Has a "strip" story for every day of the year in color	38.00	114.00	265.00

COMICS DIGEST (Pocket size)
Winter, 1942-43 (B&W, 100 pgs)
Parents' Magazine Institute

1-Reprints from True Comics (non-fiction World War II stories)	9.15	27.50	55.00

COMIC SELECTIONS (Shoe store giveaway)
1944-46 (Reprints from Calling All Girls, True Comics, True Aviation, & Real Heroes)
Parents' Magazine Press

1	4.00	10.00	20.00
2-5	3.20	8.00	16.00

COMICS EXPRESS
Nov, 1989 - No. 2, Jan, 1990 ($2.95, B&W, 68pgs.)
Eclipse Comics

1,2: Collection of strip-r; 2(12/89-c, 1/90 inside)	1.20	3.00	

COMICS FOR KIDS
1945 (no month); No. 2, Sum, 1945 (Funny animal)
London Publishing Co./Timely

1,2-Puffy Pig, Sharpy Fox	11.00	33.00	75.00

COMICS FROM WEATHER BIRD (Also see Comic Book, Edward's Shoes, Free Comics to You & Weather Bird)
1954 - 1957 (Giveaway)
Weather Bird Shoes
Contains a comic bound with new cover. Many combinations possible. Contents would determine price. Some issues do not contain complete comics, but only parts of comics.Value equals 40 to 60 percent of contents.

COMICS' GREATEST WORLD
June, 1993 - V4#4, Sept, 1993 ($1.00, weekly, limited series)
Dark Horse Comics

Arcadia (Week 1)

V1#1,2,4: 1-X: Frank Miller-c. 2-Pit Bulls. 4-Monster.	1.20	3.00	
1-B&W Press Proof Edition (1500 copies)	2.15	6.50	15.00
1-Silver-c; distr. retailer bonus w/print & cards.	1.40	4.00	10.00
3-Ghost, Dorman-c; Hughes-a	1.00	2.00	5.00
Retailer's Premium Embossed Silver Foil Logo-r/V1#1-4.	2.15	6.50	15.00

Golden City (Week 2)

V2#1-4: 1-Rebel; Ordway-c. 2-Mecha; Dave Johnson-c. 3-Titan; Walt Simonson-c. 4-Catalyst; Perez-c.		.80	2.00
1-Gold-c; distr. retailer bonus w/print & cards.	1.30	3.25	8.00
Retailer's Premium Embossed Gold Foil Logo-r/V2#1-4.	1.65	4.20	10.00

Steel Harbor (Week 3)

V3#1-4: 1-The Machine; Mignola-a(p). 3-Wolfgang; Warner-c. 4-Motorhead	1.00	2.00	5.00
2-4: 2-The Machine; Mignola-a(p). 3-Wolfgang; Warner-c. 4-Motorhead			1.00
1-Silver-c; distr. retailer bonus w/print & cards	1.65	4.20	10.00
Retailer's Premium Embossed Red Foil Logo-r/V3#1-4.	2.15	6.50	15.00

Vortex (Week 4)

V4#1-4: 1-Division 13; Dorman-c. 2-Hero Zero; Art Adams-c. 3-King Tiger; Chadwick-a(p); Darrow-c. 4-Vortex; Miller-c.		.80	2.00
1-Gold-c; distr. retailer bonus w/print & cards.	1.30	3.25	8.00
Retailer's Premium Embossed Blue Foil Logo-r/V4#1-4.	1.65	4.20	10.00

COMICS' GREATEST WORLD: OUT OF THE VORTEX (See Out of The Vortex)

COMICS HITS (See Harvey Comics Hits)

COMICS MAGAZINE, THE (…Funny Pages #3)(Funny Pages #6 on)
May, 1936 - No. 5, Sept, 1936 (Paper covers)
Comics Magazine Co.

	GD25	FN65	VF82
1-Dr. Mystic, The Occult Detective (Later known as Dr. Occult, the 1st Superman prototype & 1st super hero) by Siegel & Shuster (1st episode of "The Koth and the Seven"; continues in More Fun #14; originally scheduled for publication at DC). 1 pg. Kelly-a; Sheldon Mayer-a	1285.00	3850.00	9000.00
(Estimated up to 10 total copies exist)			

	GD25	FN65	NM94
2-Federal Agent (a.k.a. Federal Men) by Siegel & Shuster; 1 pg. Kelly-a	212.00	637.00	1700.00
3-5	168.00	506.00	1350.00

COMICS NOVEL (Anarcho, Dictator of Death)
1947
Fawcett Publications

1-All Radar; 51 pg anti-fascism story	26.00	79.00	185.00

COMICS ON PARADE (No. 30 on are a continuation of Single Series)
Apr, 1938 - No. 104, Feb, 1955
United Features Syndicate

1-Tarzan by Foster; Captain & the Kids, Little Mary Mixup, Abbie & Slats, Ella Cinders, Broncho Bill, Li'l Abner begin	300.00	900.00	2700.00
2 (Tarzan & others app. on-c of #1-3,17)	118.00	356.00	950.00
3	93.00	281.00	750.00
4,5	71.00	215.00	575.00
6-10	47.00	141.00	375.00
11-16,18-20	40.00	120.00	300.00
17-Tarzan-c	44.00	132.00	350.00
21-29: 22-Son of Tarzan begins. 22,24,28-Tailspin Tommy-c. 29-Last Tarzan issue	34.00	101.00	235.00
30-Li'l Abner	21.00	64.00	150.00
31-The Captain & the Kids	15.00	45.00	105.00
32-Nancy & Fritzi Ritz	12.00	36.00	85.00
33-Li'l Abner	19.00	56.00	130.00
34-The Captain & the Kids (10/41)	15.00	45.00	105.00
35-Nancy & Fritzi Ritz	12.00	36.00	85.00
36-Li'l Abner	19.00	56.00	130.00
37-The Captain & the Kids (6/42)	15.00	45.00	105.00
38-Nancy & Fritzi Ritz; infinity-c	12.00	36.00	85.00
39-Li'l Abner	19.00	56.00	130.00
40-The Captain & the Kids (3/43)	15.00	45.00	105.00
41-Nancy & Fritzi Ritz	10.00	30.00	65.00

Commando Adventures #1 © ATLAS

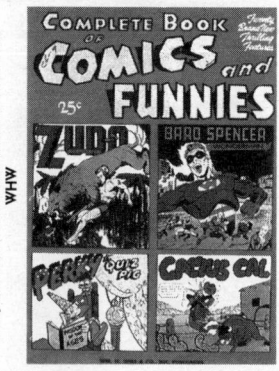

Complete Book Of Comics And Funnies #1 © WHW

Complete Love Magazine V26#2 © ACE

	GD25	FN65	NM94
42-Li'l Abner	19.00	56.00	130.00
43-The Captain & the Kids	15.00	45.00	105.00
44-Nancy & Fritzi Ritz (3/44)	10.00	30.00	65.00
45-Li'l Abner	15.00	45.00	105.00
46-The Captain & the Kids	12.00	36.00	85.00
47-Nancy & Fritzi Ritz	10.00	30.00	65.00
48-Li'l Abner (3/45)	15.00	45.00	105.00
49-The Captain & the Kids	12.00	36.00	85.00
50-Nancy & Fritzi Ritz	10.00	30.00	65.00
51-Li'l Abner	13.00	39.00	90.00
52-The Captain & the Kids (3/46)	10.00	30.00	60.00
53-Nancy & Fritzi Ritz	10.00	30.00	60.00
54-Li'l Abner	13.00	39.00	90.00
55-Nancy & Fritzi Ritz	10.00	30.00	60.00
56-The Captain & the Kids (r/Sparkler)	10.00	30.00	60.00
57-Nancy & Fritzi Ritz	10.00	30.00	60.00
58-Li'l Abner; continues as Li'l Abner #61?	13.00	39.00	90.00
59-The Captain & the Kids	8.00	24.00	48.00
60-70-Nancy & Fritzi Ritz	8.00	24.00	48.00
71-76-Nancy only	5.85	17.50	35.00
77-99,101-104-Nancy & Sluggo	5.85	17.50	35.00
100-Nancy & Sluggo	7.50	22.50	45.00
Special Issue, 7/46; Summer, 1948 - The Captain & the Kids app.			
	5.85	17.50	35.00

NOTE: Bound Volume (Very Rare) includes No. 1-12; bound by publisher in pictorial comic boards & distributed at the 1939 World's Fair and through mail order from ads in comic books (also see Tip Top). 237.00 712.00 1900.00
NOTE: Li'l Abner reprinted from Tip Top.

COMICS READING LIBRARIES (Educational Series)
1973, 1977, 1979 (36 pgs. in color) (Giveaways)
King Features (Charlton Publ.)

R-01-Tiger, Quincy		.80	2.00
R-02-Beetle Bailey, Blondie & Popeye		.80	2.00
R-03-Blondie, Beetle Bailey		.80	2.00
R-04-Tim Tyler's Luck, Felix the Cat	1.65	4.00	10.00
R-05-Quincy, Henry		.80	2.00
R-06-The Phantom, Mandrake	2.30	6.75	16.00
1977 reprint(R-04)	1.00	2.00	5.00
R-07-Popeye, Little King	1.00	2.00	5.00
R-08-Prince Valiant(Foster), Flash Gordon	3.40	10.00	24.00
1977 reprint	1.30	3.25	8.00
R-09-Hagar the Horrible, Boner's Ark		.80	2.00
R-10-Redeye, Tiger		.80	2.00
R-11-Blondie, Hi & Lois		.80	2.00
R-12-Popeye-Swee'pea, Brutus	1.00	2.50	6.00
R-13-Beetle Bailey, Little King		.80	2.00
R-14-Quincy-Hamlet		.80	2.00
R-15-The Phantom, The Genius	2.30	6.75	16.00
R-16-Flash Gordon, Mandrake	3.40	10.00	24.00
1977 reprint	1.30	3.25	8.00
Other 1977 editions....		.50	1.00
1979 editions(68pgs.)		.50	1.00

NOTE: Above giveaways available with purchase of $45.00 in merchandise. Used as a reading skills aid for small children.

COMICS REVUE
June, 1947 - No. 5, Jan, 1948
St. John Publ. Co. (United Features Synd.)

1-Ella Cinders & Blackie	10.00	30.00	60.00
2-Hap Hopper (7/47)	6.70	20.00	40.00
3-Iron Vic (8/47)	5.85	17.50	35.00
4-Ella Cinders (9/47)	6.70	20.00	40.00
5-Gordo No. 1 (1/48)	5.85	17.50	35.00

COMIC STORY PAINT BOOK
1943 (Large size, 68 pgs.)

Samuel Lowe Co.
1055-Captain Marvel & a Captain Marvel Jr. story to read & color; 3 panels in color per pg. (reprints) 60.00 180.00 600.00

COMIX BOOK
1974 - No. 5, 1976 ($1.00, B&W, magazine)
Marvel Comics Group/Krupp Comics Works No. 4,5

1-Underground comic artists; 2 pgs. Wolverton-a	1.20	2.90	7.00
2-Wolverton-a (1 pg.)		1.40	3.50
3-Low distribution (3/75)	1.00	2.00	5.00
4(2/76), 4(5/76), 5		1.20	3.00

NOTE: Print run No. 1-3: 200-250M; No. 4&5: 10M each.

COMIX INTERNATIONAL
July, 1974 - No. 5, Spring, 1977 (Full color)
Warren Magazines

1-Low distribution; all Corben story remainders from Warren			
	5.35	16.00	32.00
2-Wood, Wrightson-r	3.00	7.50	15.00
3-5: 4-Crandall-a. 5-Spirit story	2.00	5.00	10.00

NOTE: No. 4 had two printings with extra Corben story in one. No. 3 may also have a variation. No. 3 has two Jeff Jones reprints from Vampirella.

COMMANDER BATTLE AND THE ATOMIC SUB
July-Aug, 1954 - No. 7, Aug-Sept, 1955
American Comics Group (Titan Publ. Co.)

1 (3-D effect)-Moldoff flying saucer-c	40.00	120.00	310.00
2,4-7: 2-Moldoff-c. 4-(1-2/55)-Last pre-code; Landau-a. 5-3-D effect story			
(2 pgs.). 6,7-Landau-a. 7-Flying saucer-c	26.00	77.00	180.00
3-H-Bomb-c; Atomic Sub becomes Atomic Spaceship			
	27.00	81.00	190.00

COMMANDMENTS OF GOD
1954, 1958
Catechetical Guild

300-Same contents in both editions; diff-c	2.00	5.00	10.00

COMMANDO ADVENTURES
June, 1957 - No. 2, Aug, 1957
Atlas Comics (MMC)

1,2-Severin-c. 2-Drucker-a?	7.50	22.50	45.00

COMMANDO YANK (See The Mighty Midget Comics & Wow Comics)

COMPLETE BOOK OF COMICS AND FUNNIES
1944 (25¢, one-shot, 196 pgs.)
William H. Wise & Co.

1-Origin Brad Spencer, Wonderman; The Magnet, The Silver Knight by Kinstler, & Zudo the Jungle Boy app.	39.00	118.00	275.00

COMPLETE BOOK OF TRUE CRIME COMICS
No date (Mid 1940's) (25¢, 132 pgs.)
William H. Wise & Co.

nn-Contains Crime Does Not Pay rebound (includes #22)			
	81.00	243.00	650.00

COMPLETE COMICS (Formerly Amazing Comics No. 1)
No. 2, Winter, 1944-45
Timely Comics (EPC)

2-The Destroyer, The Whizzer, The Young Allies & Sergeant Dix; Schomburg-c	137.00	412.00	1100.00

COMPLETE LOVE MAGAZINE (Formerly a pulp with same title)
V26#2, May-June, 1951 - V32#4(#191), Sept, 1956
Ace Periodicals (Periodical House)

V26#2-Painted-c (52 pgs.)	4.70	14.00	28.00
V26#3-6(2/52), V27#1(4/52)-6(1/53)	4.00	10,.00	20.00
V28#1(3/53), V28#2(5/53), V29#3(7/53)-6(12/53)	3.20	8.00	16.00

Conan #1 © MEG

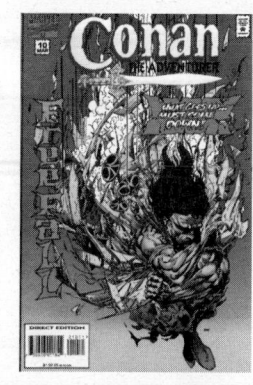

Conan The Adventurer #10 © MEG

Conan The Barbarian #62 © MEG

	GD25	FN65	NM94
V30#1(2/54), V30#1(#176, 4/54),2,4-6(#181, 1/55)	3.20	8.00	16.00
V30#3(#178)-Rock Hudson photo-c	4.00	12.00	24.00
V31#1(#182, 3/55)-Last precode	3.20	8.00	16.00
V31#2(5/55)-6(#187, 1/56)	2.00	5.00	10.00
V32#1(#188, 3/56)-4(#191, 9/56)	2.00	5.00	10.00

NOTE: (34 total issues). Photo-c V27#5-on. Painted-c V26#3.

COMPLETE MYSTERY (True Complete Mystery No. 5 on)
Aug, 1948 - No. 4, Feb, 1949 (Full length stories)
Marvel Comics (PrPI)

	GD25	FN65	NM94
1-Seven Dead Men	40.00	120.00	300.00
2-Jigsaw of Doom!	39.00	118.00	275.00
3-Fear in the Night; Burgos-c/a (28 pgs.)	39.00	118.00	275.00
4-A Squealer Dies Fast	39.00	118.00	275.00

COMPLETE ROMANCE
1949
Avon Periodicals

1-(Scarce)-Reprinted as Women to Love	34.00	103.00	240.00

COMPLIMENTARY COMICS
No date (1950's) (Giveaway)
Sales Promotion Publ.

1-Strongman by Powell, 3 stories	6.35	19.00	38.00

CONAN (See Chamber of Darkness #4, Giant-Size..., Handbook of..., King Conan, Marvel Graphic Novel #19, 28, Marvel Treasury Ed., Power Record Comics, Robert E. Howard's..., Savage Sword of Conan, and Savage Tales)

CONAN
Aug, 1995 - No. 11, June, 1996 ($2.95)
Marvel Comics

1-11: 4-Malibu Comic's Rune app.		1.20	3.00

CONAN CLASSIC
June, 1994 - No. 11, Apr, 1995 ($1.50)
Marvel Comics

1-11: 1-r/Conan #1 by B. Smith, r/covers w/changes. 2-11-r/Conan #2-11 by Smith			1.50
2-Bound w/cover to Conan The Adventurer #2 by mistake			1.50

CONAN SAGA, THE
June, 1987 - No. 97, Apr, 1995 ($2.00/$2.25, B&W, magazine)
Marvel Comics

1-Barry Smith-r 1-9,11; new Barry Smith-c 1-9		.80	2.00
2-27: 13,15-Boris-c. 17-Adams-r. 18,25-Chaykin-r. 22-r/Giant-Size Conan 1,2		.80	2.00
28-97 ($2.25): 31-Red Sonja by N. Adams/SSOC #1; 1 pg. Jeff Jones-r. 32-Newspaper strip-r begin by Buscema. 33-Smith/Conrad-a. 39-r/Kull #1('71) by Andru/Wood. 44-Swipes-c/Savage Tales #1. 57-Brunner-a/SSOC #30. 66-r/Conan Annual #2 by Buscema. 79-r/Conan #43-45 w/Red Sonja. 85-Based on Conan #57-63		.90	2.25

NOTE: J. Buscema r-32-on; c-86. Chaykin r-34. Chiodo painted c-63, 65, 66, 82. G. Colan a-47p. Jusko painted c-64, 83. Kaluta c-84. Nino a-37. Ploog a-50. N. Redondo painted c-48, 50, 51, 53, 57, 62. Simonson r-50-54, 56. B. Smith r-51. Starlin c-34. Williamson r-50i.

CONAN THE ADVENTURER
June, 1994 - No. 14, July, 1995 ($1.50)
Marvel Comics

1-($2.50)-Embossed foil-c; Kayaran-a		1.00	2.50
2-14			1.50
2-Contents are Conan Classics #2 by mistake			1.50

CONAN THE BARBARIAN
Oct, 1970 - No. 275, Dec, 1993
Marvel Comics

1-Origin/1st app. Conan (in comics) by Barry Smith; Kull app.; #1-9 are 15¢ issues	32.00	96.00	225.00

	GD25	FN65	NM94
2	12.50	37.00	87.00
3-(Low distribution in some areas)	24.00	73.00	170.00
4,5	8.50	26.00	60.00
6-9: 8-Hidden panel message, pg. 14	5.70	17.00	40.00
10,11 (25¢ giants): 10-Black Knight-r; Kull story by Severin	7.00	21.50	50.00
12,13: 12-Wrightson-c(i)	3.90	11.60	27.00
14,15-Elric app.	6.50	19.50	45.00
16,19,20: 16-Conan-r/Savage Tales #1	3.40	10.00	24.00
17,18-No Barry Smith-a	1.60	5.00	11.00
21,22: 22-Has reprint from #1	3.30	10.00	23.00
23-1st app. Red Sonja (2/73)	5.00	15.00	35.00
24-1st full Red Sonja story; last Smith-a	4.30	13.00	30.00
25-John Buscema-c/a begins	1.70	4.20	10.00
26-30	1.00	2.00	5.00
31-36,38-40		1.20	3.00
37-Neal Adams-c/a; last 20¢ issue; contains pull-out subscription form	1.20	3.00	7.00
41-57,59,60: 44,45-N. Adams-i(Crusty Bunkers). 45-Adams-c. 48-Origin retold. 59-Origin Belit		.80	2.00
58-2nd Belit app. (see Giant-Size Conan #1)		1.20	3.00
61-99: 68-Red Sonja story cont'd from Marvel Feature #7. 84-Intro. Zula. 85-Origin Zula. 87-r/Savage Sword of Conan #3 in color			1.25
100-(52 pg. Giant)-Death of Belit		1.20	3.00
101-114,116-199: 116-r/Power Record Comic PR31			1.25
115-Double size			1.50
200,250 ($1.50): 200-(52 pgs.). 250-(60 pgs.)			1.70
201-249,251,252: 232-Young Conan storyline begins; Conan is born. 244-Return of Zula. 252-Last $1.00-c			1.25
253-274: 262-Adapted from R.E. Howard story			1.35
275-($2.50, 68 pgs.)-Final issue; painted-c		1.00	2.50
King Size 1(1973, 35¢)-Smith-r/#2,4; Smith-c	1.65	4.20	10.00
Annual 2(1976, 50¢)-New full length story		1.50	3.75
Annual 3(1978)-Chaykin/N. Adams-r/SSOC #2		.90	2.25
Annual 4-6: 4(1978)-New full length story. 5(1979)-New full length Buscema story & part-c, 6(1981)-Kane-c/a		.70	1.75
Annual 7-12: 7(1982)-Based on novel "Conan of the Isles" (new-a). 8(1984). 9(1984), 10(1986). 12(1987)			1.35
Special Edition 1 (Red Nails)		1.50	3.75

NOTE: Arthur Adams c-248, 249. Neal Adams a-116r(i); c-49i. Austin a-125, 126; c-125i, 126i. Brunner c-17i. c-40. Buscema a-25-36p, 38, 39, 41-56p, 58-63p, 65-67p, 68, 70-78p, 84-86p, 88-91p, 93-126p, 136p, 140, 141-144p, 146-158p, 159, 161, 162, 163p, 165-185p, 187-190p, Annual 2(3pgs.). 3-5p, 7p; c(p)-26, 36, 44, 46, 52, 56, 58, 59, 64, 65, 72, 78-80, 83-91, 93-103, 105-126, 136-151, 155-159, 161, 162, 168, 169, 171, 172, 174, 175, 178-185, 188, 189, Annual 4, 5, 7. Chaykin a-79-83. Golden c-152. Kaluta c-167. Gil Kane a-12p, 17p, 18p, 127-130, 131-134p; c-12p, 17p, 18p, 23, 25, 27-32, 34, 35, 38, 39, 41-43, 45-51, 53-55, 57, 60-63, 65-71, 73p, 76p, 127-134. Jim Lee c-242. McFarlane c-241p. Ploog a-57. Russell a-21; c-251i. Simonson c-135. B. Smith a-1-11p, 12, 13-15p, 16, 19-21, 23, 24; c-1-11, 13-16, 19-24p. Starlin a-64. Wood a-47i. Issue Nos. 3-5, 7-9, 11, 16-18, 21, 23, 25, 27-30, 35, 37, 38, 42, 45, 52, 57, 58, 65, 69-71, 73, 79-83, 99, 100, 104, 114, Annual 2 have original Robert E. Howard stories adapted. Issues #32-34 adapted from Norvell Page's novel Flame Winds.

CONAN THE BARBARIAN MOVIE SPECIAL (Movie)
Oct, 1982 - No. 2, Nov, 1982
Marvel Comics Group

1,2-Movie adaptation; Buscema-a			1.00

CONAN THE DESTROYER (Movie)
Jan, 1985 - No. 2, Mar, 1985
Marvel Comics Group

1,2-r/Marvel Super Special			1.00

CONAN THE KING (Formerly King Conan)
No. 20, Jan, 1984 - No. 55, Nov, 1989
Marvel Comics Group

20-55: 48-55 ($1.50)			1.50

NOTE: Kaluta c-20-23, 24i, 26, 27, 30, 50, 52. Williamson a-37i; c-37i, 38i.

Concrete: Fragile Creature #1 © DH

Concrete: Killer Smile #4 © DH

Congorilla #2 © DC

	GD25	FN65	NM94

CONAN THE SAVAGE
Aug, 1995 - No. 10, May, 1996 ($2.95, B&W, Magazine)
Marvel Comics

		GD25	FN65	NM94
1-10: 1-Bisley-c. 4-vs. Malibu Comic's Rune. 5,10-Brereton-c		1.20		3.00

CONAN VS. RUNE (Also See Conan #4)
Nov, 1995 ($2.95, one-shot)
Marvel Comics

1-Barry Smith-c/a/scripts	1.20		3.00

CONCRETE (Also see Dark Horse Presents & Within Our Reach)
March, 1987 - No. 10, Nov, 1988 ($1.50, B&W)
Dark Horse Comics

1-Paul Chadwick-c/a in all	1.70	5.00	12.00
1-2nd print		1.20	3.00
2	1.00	2.60	6.00
3-Origin		1.60	4.00
4-10		1.20	3.00
A New Life 1 (1989, $2.95, B&W)-r/#3,4 plus new-a (11 pgs.)		1.40	3.50
Celebrates Earth Day 1990 ($3.50, 52 pgs.)		1.60	4.00
Color Special 1 (2/89, $2.95, 44 pgs.)-r/1st two Concrete apps. from Dark Horse Presents #1,2 plus new-a		1.40	3.50
Land And Sea 1 (2/89, $2.95, B&W)-r/#1,2		1.20	3.00
Odd Jobs 1 (7/90, $3.50)-r/5,6 plus new-a		1.40	3.50

CONCRETE: ECLECTICA
Apr, 1993 - No. 2, May, 1993 ($2.95, limited series)
Dark Horse Comics

1,2	1.20		3.00

CONCRETE: FRAGILE CREATURE
June, 1991 - No. 4, Feb, 1992 ($2.50, limited series)
Dark Horse Comics

1-4	1.00		2.50

CONCRETE: KILLER SMILE
July, 1994 - No. 4, Oct, 1994 ($2.95, limited series)
Dark Horse Comics (Legend)

1-4: 1st Concrete limited series under Legend Imprint	1.20		3.00

CONCRETE: THINK LIKE A MOUNTAIN
Mar, 1996 - No. 6, Aug, 1996 ($2.95, limited series)
Dark Horse Comics (Legend)

1-6: Chadwick-a/scripts & Darrow-c in all	1.20		3.00

CONDORMAN (Walt Disney)
Oct, 1981 - No. 3, Jan, 1982
Whitman Publishing

1-3: 1,2-Movie adaptation; photo-c			1.00

CONEHEADS
June, 1994 - No. 4, 1994 ($1.75, limited series)
Marvel Comics

1-4		.70	1.75

CONFESSIONS ILLUSTRATED (Magazine)
Jan-Feb, 1956 - No. 2, Spring, 1956
E. C. Comics

1-Craig, Kamen, Wood, Orlando-a	13.00	39.00	90.00
2-Craig, Crandall, Kamen, Orlando-a	11.50	34.00	80.00

CONFESSIONS OF LOVE
Apr, 1950 - No. 2, July, 1950 (25¢, 7-1/4x5-1/4", 132 pgs.)
Artful Publ.

1-Bakerish-a	24.00	71.00	165.00
2-Art & text; Bakerish-a	12.00	36.00	85.00

	GD25	FN65	NM94

CONFESSIONS OF LOVE (Formerly Startling Terror Tales #10; becomes Confessions of Romance No. 7 on)
No. 11, 7/52 - No. 14, 1/53; No. 4, 3/53- No. 6, 8/53
Star Publications

11-13: 12,13-Disbrow-a	10.00	30.00	70.00
14,5,6	7.50	22.50	45.00
4-Disbrow-a	9.15	27.00	55.00

NOTE: All have **L. B. Cole** covers.

CONFESSIONS OF ROMANCE (Formerly Confessions of Love)
No. 7, Nov, 1953 - No. 11, Nov, 1954
Star Publications

7	10.00	30.00	70.00
8	7.50	22.50	45.00
9-Wood-a	11.00	33.00	75.00
10,11-Disbrow-a	9.15	27.00	55.00

NOTE: All have **L. B. Cole** covers.

CONFESSIONS OF THE LOVELORN (Formerly Lovelorn)
No. 52, Aug, 1954 - No. 114, June-July, 1960
American Comics Group (Regis Publ./Best Synd. Features)

52 (3-D effect)	24.00	73.00	170.00
53,55	5.85	17.50	35.00
54 (3-D effect)	24.00	73.00	170.00
56-Anti-communist propaganda story, 10 pgs; last pre-code (2/55)	8.35	25.00	50.00
57-90	4.00	12.00	24.00
91-Williamson-a	7.00	21.00	42.00
92-99,101-114	3.60	9.00	18.00
100	4.00	11.00	22.00

NOTE: **Whitney** a-most issues; c-52, 53. Painted c-106, 107.

CONFIDENTIAL DIARY (Formerly High School Confidential Diary; Three Nurses #18 on)
No. 12, May, 1962 - No. 17, Mar, 1963
Charlton Comics

12-17	1.30	3.25	8.00

CONGO BILL (See Action Comics & More Fun Comics #56)
Aug-Sept, 1954 - No. 7, Aug-Sept, 1955
National Periodical Publication

	GD25	FN65	VF82
1 (Scarce)	78.00	234.00	625.00
2,7 (Scarce)	62.00	187.00	500.00
3-6 (Scarce). 4-Last pre-code issue	56.00	168.00	450.00

NOTE: (Rarely found in fine to mint condition.) Nick Cardy c-1-7.

CONGORILLA (Also see Actions Comics #224)
Nov, 1992 - No. 4, Feb, 1993 ($1.75, limited series)
DC Comics

	GD25	FN65	NM94
1-4: 1,2-Brian Bolland-c		.70	1.75

CONNECTICUT YANKEE, A (See King Classics)

CONQUEROR, THE
No., 690, Mar, 1956
Dell Publishing Co.

Four Color 690-Movie, John Wayne photo-c	14.50	43.50	145.00

CONQUEROR COMICS
Winter, 1945
Albrecht Publishing Co.

nn	15.00	45.00	105.00

CONQUEROR OF THE BARREN EARTH (See The Warlord #63)
Feb, 1985 - No. 4, May, 1985 (Limited series)
DC Comics

1-4: Back-up series from Warlord			1.00

CONQUEST

Contact Comics #11 © Aviation Press

Convocations: A Magic The Gathering Gallery © Wizards of the Coast

Corum #1 © FC

	GD25	FN65	NM94

1953 (6¢)
Store Comics

1-Richard the Lion Hearted, Beowulf, Swamp Fox	4.15	12.50	25.00

CONQUEST
Spring, 1955
Famous Funnies

1-Crandall-a, 1 pg.; contains contents of 1953 ish.	4.00	11.00	22.00

CONSTRUCT
1996 - No. 6, 1997 ($2.95, B&W, limited series)
Caliber (New Worlds)

1-6: Paul Jenkins scripts	1.20	3.00

CONTACT COMICS
July, 1944 - No. 12, May, 1946
Aviation Press

nn-Black Venus, Flamingo, Golden Eagle, Tommy Tomahawk begin	40.00	120.00	300.00
2-5: 3-Last Flamingo. 3,4-Black Venus by L. B. Cole. 5-The Phantom Flyer app.	32.00	96.00	225.00
6,11-Kurtzman's Black Venus; 11-Last Golden Eagle, last Tommy Tomahawk; Feldstein-a	36.00	107.00	250.00
7-10	29.00	86.00	200.00
12-Sky Rangers, Air Kids, Ace Diamond app.	31.00	92.00	215.00

NOTE: *L. B. Cole* a-3, 9; c-1-12. *Giunta* a-3. *Hollingsworth* a-5, 7, 10. *Palais* a-11, 12.

CONTEMPORARY MOTIVATORS
1977 - 1978 ($1.45, 5-3/8x8", 31 pgs., B&W)
Pendelum Press

14-3002 The Caine Mutiny; 14-3010 Banner in the Sky; 14-3029 God Is My Co-Pilot;14-3037 Guadalcanal Diary; 14-3045 Hiroshima; 14-3053 Hot Rod; 14-3061 Just Dial a Number; 14-307x Star Wars; 14-3088 The Diary of Anne Frank; 14-3096 Lost Horizon		1.50

NOTE: *Also see Now Age Illustrated. Above may have been distributed the same.*

CONTEST OF CHAMPIONS (See Marvel Super-Hero...)

CONTRACTORS
June, 1987 ($2.00, B&W, one-shot)
Eclipse Comics

1-Funny animal	.80	2.00

CONVOCATIONS: A MAGIC THE GATHERING GALLERY
Jan, 1996 ($2.50, one-shot)
Acclaim Comics (Armada)

1-pin-ups by various artists including Kaluta, Vess, and Dringenberg.	1.00	2.50

COO COO COMICS (...the Bird Brain No. 57 on)
Oct, 1942 - No. 62, Apr, 1952
Nedor Publ. Co./Standard (Animated Cartoons)

1-Origin/1st app. Super Mouse & begin series (cloned from Superman); the first funny animal super hero series (see Looney Tunes #5 for 1st funny animal super hero)	26.00	77.00	180.00
2	11.50	34.00	80.00
3-10: 10-(3/44)	6.70	20.00	40.00
11-33: 33-1 pg. Ingels-a	5.00	15.00	30.00
34-40,43-46,48-Text illos by Frazetta in all. 36-Super Mouse covers begin	7.50	22.50	45.00
41-Frazetta-a (6-pg. story & 3 text illos)	14.00	43.00	100.00
42,47-Frazetta-a & text illos.	10.00	30.00	65.00
49-(1/50)-3-D effect story; Frazetta text illo	9.15	27.00	55.00
50,51-3-D effect-c only. 50-Frazetta text illo	8.35	25.00	50.00
52-62: 56-Last Supermouse?	4.00	11.00	22.00

"COOKIE" (Also see Topsy-Turvy)
Apr, 1946 - No. 55, Aug-Sept, 1955
Michel Publ./American Comics Group(Regis Publ.)

1-Teen-age humor	19.00	58.00	135.00
2	10.00	30.00	65.00
3-10	7.50	22.50	45.00
11-20	5.85	17.50	35.00
21-23,26,28-30	4.25	13.00	26.00
24,25,27-Starlet O'Hara stories	5.00	15.00	30.00
31-34,37-55	4.00	12.00	24.00
35,36-Starlett O'Hara stories	4.25	13.00	26.00

COOL CAT (Formerly Black Magic)
V8#6, Mar-Apr, 1962 - V9#2, July-Aug, 1962
Prize Publications

V8#6, nn(V9#1, 5-6/62), V9#2	4.00	12.00	24.00

COOL WORLD (Movie)
Apr, 1992 - No. 4, Sept, 1992 ($1.75, limited series)
DC Comics

1-4: Prequel to animated/live action movie by Ralph Bakshi. 1-Bakshi-c. Bill Wray inks in all		.70	1.75
Movie Adaptation nn ('92, $3.50, 68pg.)-Bakshi-c		1.40	3.50

COPPER CANYON (See Fawcett Movie Comics)

COPS (TV)
Aug, 1988 - No. 15, Aug, 1989 ($1.00)
DC Comics

1 ($1.50, 52 pgs.)-Based on Hasbro Toys		1.50
2-15: 14-Orlando-c(p)		1.00

COPS: THE JOB
June, 1992 - No. 4, Sept, 1992 ($1.25, limited series)
Marvel Comics

1-4: All have Jusko scripts & Golden-c		1.25

CORBEN SPECIAL, A
May, 1984 (one-shot)
Pacific Comics

1-Corben-c/a; E.A. Poe adaptation	.80	2.00

CORKY & WHITE SHADOW (Disney, TV)
No. 707, May, 1956 (Mickey Mouse Club)
Dell Publishing Co.

Four Color 707-Photo-c	8.00	24.00	70.00

CORLISS ARCHER (See Meet Corliss Archer)

CORMAC MAC ART (Robert E. Howard's...)
1990 - No. 4, 1990 ($1.95, B&W, mini-series)
Dark Horse Comics

1-4: All have Bolton painted-c; Howard adapts.	.80	2.00

CORPORAL RUSTY DUGAN (See Holyoke One-Shot #2)

CORPSES OF DR. SACOTTI, THE (See Ideal a Classical Comic)

CORSAIR, THE (See A-1 Comics No. 5, 7, 10)

CORTEZ AND THE FALL OF THE AZTECS
1993 ($2.95, B&W, limited series)
Tome Press

1,2	1.20	3.00

CORUM: THE BULL AND THE SPEAR (See Chronicles Of Corum)
Jan, 1989 - No. 4, July, 1989 ($1.95)
First Comics

1-4: Adapts Michael Moorcock's novel	.80	2.00

COSMIC BOOK, THE
Dec, 1986 - No. 1, 1987 ($1.95)
Ace Comics

Cosmic Boy #4 © DC

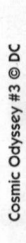
Cosmic Odyssey #3 © DC

Cowboy Love #1 © FAW

	GD25	FN65	NM94		GD25	FN65	NM94
1-(44pgs.)-Wood, Toth-a		.80	2.00	**1945**			
2-(B&W)			1.60	J. Edward Slavin			
				1,2,77	9.15	27.50	55.00

COSMIC BOY (Also see The Legion of Super-Heroes)
Dec, 1986 - No. 4, Mar, 1987 (limited series)
DC Comics

	GD25	FN65	NM94
1-4: Legends tie-ins all issues			1.00

COSMIC ODYSSEY
1988 - No. 4, 1988 ($3.50, limited series, squarebound)
DC Comics

	GD25	FN65	NM94
1-4: Reintro. New Gods into DC continuity; Superman, Batman, Green Lantern (John Stewart) app; Starlin scripts, Mignola-c/a in all. 2-Darkseid merges Demon & Jason Blood (seperated in Demon limited series #4); John Stewart responsible for the death of a star system.		1.40	3.50
Trade paperback-r/#1-4.			19.95

COSMIC POWERS
Mar, 1994 - No. 6, Aug, 1994 ($2.50, limited series)
Marvel Comics

	GD25	FN65	NM94
1-6: 1-Ron Lim-c/a(p). 1,2-Thanos app. 2-Terrax. 3-Ganymede & Jack of Hearts app.		1.00	2.50

COSMIC POWERS UNLIMITED
May, 1995 - No. 4, Feb, 1996 ($3.95, quarterly)
Marvel Comics

	GD25	FN65	NM94
1-4		1.60	4.00

COSMO CAT (Becomes Sunny #11 on; also see All Top & Wotalife Comics)
July-Aug, 1946 - No. 10, Oct, 1947; 1957; 1959
Fox Publications/Green Publ. Co./Norlen Mag.

	GD25	FN65	NM94
1	24.00	73.00	170.00
2	12.00	36.00	85.00
3-Origin (11-12/46)	16.00	47.00	110.00
4-10	7.50	22.50	45.00
2-4(1957-Green Publ. Co.)	4.00	11.00	22.00
2-4(1959-Norlen Mag.)	3.00	7.50	15.00
I.W. Reprint #1	1.60	4.00	8.00

COSMO THE MERRY MARTIAN
Sept, 1958 - No. 6, Oct, 1959
Archie Publications (Radio Comics)

	GD25	FN65	NM94
1-Bob White-a in all	13.50	41.00	95.00
2-6	10.00	30.00	65.00

COTTON WOODS
No. 837, Sept, 1957
Dell Publishing Co.

	GD25	FN65	NM94
Four Color 837	5.00	15.00	45.00

COUGAR, THE (Cougar No. 2)
April, 1975 - No. 2, July, 1975
Seaboard Periodicals (Atlas)

	GD25	FN65	NM94
1,2: 1-Adkins-a(p). 2-Origin; Buckler-c(p)			1.00

COUNTDOWN (See Movie Classics)

COUNT DUCKULA (TV)
Nov, 1988 - No. 15, Jan, 1991 ($1.00)
Marvel Comics

	GD25	FN65	NM94
1-15: Dangermouse back-ups. 8-Geraldo Rivera photo-c; Sienkiewicz-a(i)			1.00

COUNT OF MONTE CRISTO, THE
No. 794, May, 1957
Dell Publishing Co.

	GD25	FN65	NM94
Four Color 794-Movie, Buscema-a	10.00	30.00	90.00

COURAGE COMICS

COURTSHIP OF EDDIE'S FATHER (TV)
Jan, 1970 - No. 2, May, 1970
Dell Publishing Co.

	GD25	FN65	NM94
1,2-Bill Bixby photo-c	3.00	9.00	30.00

COVERED WAGONS, HO (Disney, TV)
No. 814, June, 1957 (Donald Duck)
Dell Publishing Co.

	GD25	FN65	NM94
Four Color 814-Mickey Mouse app.	6.00	18.00	60.00

COWBOY ACTION (Formerly Western Thrillers No. 1-4; Becomes Quick-Trigger Western No. 12 on)
No. 5, March, 1955 - No. 11, March, 1956
Atlas Comics (ACI)

	GD25	FN65	NM94
5	10.00	30.00	70.00
6-10: 6-8-Heath-c	7.50	22.50	45.00
11-Williamson-a (4 pgs.); Baker-a	9.15	27.00	55.00

NOTE: *Ayers a-8. Drucker a-6. Maneely c/a-5, 6. Severin c-10. Shores a-7.*

COWBOY COMICS (Star Ranger #12, Stories #14)(Star Ranger Funnies #15)
No. 13, July, 1938 - No. 14, Aug, 1938
Centaur Publishing Co.

	GD25	FN65	NM94
13-(Rare)-Ace and Deuce, Lyin Lou, Air Patrol, Aces High, Lee Trent, Trouble Hunters begin	106.00	318.00	850.00
14-Filchock-c	78.00	234.00	625.00

NOTE: *Guardineer a-13, 14. Gustavson a-13, 14.*

COWBOY IN AFRICA (TV)
Mar, 1968
Gold Key

	GD25	FN65	NM94
1(10219-803)-Chuck Connors photo-c	3.50	10.50	35.00

COWBOY LOVE (Becomes Range Busters?)
7/49 - V2#10, 6/50; No. 11, 1951; No. 28, 2/55 - No. 31, 8/55
Fawcett Publications/Charlton Comics No. 28 on

	GD25	FN65	NM94
V1#1-Rocky Lane photo back-c	16.00	47.00	110.00
2	5.00	15.00	30.00
V1#3,4,6 (12/49)	4.25	13.00	26.00
5-Bill Boyd photo back-c (11/49)	6.35	19.00	38.00
V2#7-Williamson/Evans-a	8.35	25.00	50.00
V2#8-11	4.00	12.00	24.00
V1#28 (Charlton)-Last precode (2/55) (Formerly Romantic Story?)	4.00	12.00	24.00
V1#29-31 (Charlton; becomes Sweetheart Diary #32 on)	4.00	11.00	22.00

NOTE: *Powell a-10. Marcus Swayze a-2, 3. Photo c-1-11. Nos. 1-3, 5-7, 9, 10 are 52 pgs.*

COWBOY ROMANCES (Young Men No. 4 on)
Oct, 1949 - No. 3, Mar, 1950 (All photo-c & 52 pgs.)
Marvel Comics (IPC)

	GD25	FN65	NM94
1-Photo-c	19.00	56.00	130.00
2-William Holden, Mona Freeman "Streets of Laredo" photo-c	12.00	36.00	85.00
3-Photo-c	10.00	30.00	70.00

COWBOYS 'N' INJUNS (...and Indians No. 6 on)
1946 - No. 5, 1947; No. 6, 1949 - No. 8, 1952
Com No. 1-5/Magazine Enterprises No. 6 on

	GD25	FN65	NM94
1	10.00	30.00	60.00
2-5-All funny animal western	5.85	17.50	35.00
6(A-1 23)-Half violent, half funny; Ayers-a	8.35	25.00	50.00
7(A-1 41, 1950), 8(A-1 48)-All funny	5.85	17.50	35.00
I.W. Reprint No. 1,7 (Reprinted in Canada by Superior, No. 7)			

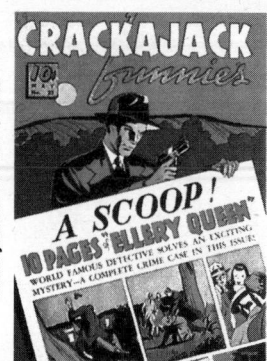

Cowgirl Romances #12 © FH

Crackajack Funnies #24 © DELL

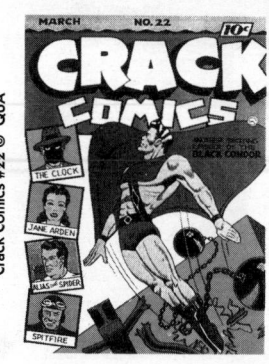

Crack Comics #22 © QUA

	GD25	FN65	NM94

	GD25	FN65	NM94

	1.30	3.25	8.00
Super Reprint #10 (1963)	1.30	3.25	8.00

COWBOY WESTERN COMICS (TV)(Formerly Jack In The Box; Becomes Space Western No. 40-45 & Wild Bill Hickok & Jingles No. 68 on; title:Cowboy Western Heroes No. 47 & 48; Cowboy Western No. 49 on)
No. 17, 7/48 - No. 39, 8/52; No. 46, 10/53; No. 47, 12/53; No. 48, Spr, '54; No. 49, 5-6/54 - No. 67, 3/58 (nn 40-45)
Charlton (Capitol Stories)

17-Jesse James, Annie Oakley, Wild Bill Hickok begin; Texas Rangers app.			
	16.00	47.00	110.00
18,19-Orlando-c/a. 18-Paul Bunyan begins. 19-Wyatt Earp story			
	10.00	30.00	65.00
20-25: 21-Buffalo Bill story. 22-Texas Rangers-c/story. 24-Joel McCrea photo-c & adaptation from movie "Three Faces West". 25-James Craig photo-c & adaptation from movie "Northwest Stampede"			
	9.15	27.00	55.00
26-George Montgomery photo-c and adaptation from movie "Indian Scout"; 1 pg. bio on Will Rogers	10.00	30.00	70.00
27-Sunset Carson photo-c & adapts movie "Sunset Carson Rides Again" plus 1 other Sunset Carson story	52.00	157.00	420.00
28-Sunset Carson line drawn-c; adapts movies "Battling Marshal" & "Fighting Mustangs" starring Sunset Carson	30.00	90.00	210.00
29-Sunset Carson line drawn-c; adapts movies "Rio Grande" with Sunset Carson & "Winchester '73" w/James Stewart plus 5 pg. life history of Sunset Carson featuring Tom Mix	30.00	90.00	210.00
30-Sunset Carson photo-c; adapts movie "Deadline" starring Sunset Carson plus 1 other Sunset Carson story	52.00	157.00	420.00
31-34,38,39,47-50 (no #40-45): 50-Golden Arrow, Rocky Lane & Blackjack (r?) stories	6.70	20.00	40.00
35,36-Sunset Carson-c/stories (2 in each). 35-Inside front-c photo of Sunset Carson plus photo on-c	31.00	92.00	215.00
37-Sunset Carson stories (2)	19.00	56.00	130.00
46-(Formerly Space Western)-Space western story	17.00	51.00	120.00
51-57,59-66: 51-Golden Arrow(r?) & Monte Hale-r renamed Rusty Hall. 53,54-Tom Mix-r. 55-Monte Hale story(r?). 66-Young Eagle story. 67-Wild Bill Hickok and Jingles-c/story	4.25	13.00	28.00
58-(1/56, 15¢, 68 pgs.)-Wild Bill Hickok, Annie Oakley & Jesse James stories; Forgione-a	5.35	16.00	32.00
67-(15¢, 68 pgs.)-Williamson/Torres-a, 5 pgs.	9.15	27.00	55.00

NOTE: Many issues trimmed 1" shorter. Maneely a-67(5). Inside front/back photo c-29.

COWGIRL ROMANCES (Young Men No. 4 on)
No. 28, Jan, 1950 (52 pgs.)
Marvel Comics (CCC)

28(#1)-Photo-c	18.00	54.00	125.00

COWGIRL ROMANCES
1950 - No. 12, Winter, 1952-53 (No. 1-3: 52 pgs.)
Fiction House Magazines

1-Kamen-a	29.00	86.00	200.00
2	14.00	43.00	100.00
3-5: 5-12-Whitman-c (most)	13.00	39.00	90.00
6-9,11,12	11.50	34.00	80.00
10-Frazetta?/Williamson?-a; Kamen?/Baker-a; r/Mitzi story from Movie Comics #4 w/all new dialogue	29.00	86.00	200.00

COW PUNCHER (...Comics)
Jan, 1947 - No. 2, Sept, 1947 - No. 7, 1949
Avon Periodicals

1-Clint Cortland, Texas Ranger, Kit West, Pioneer Queen begin; Kubert-a; Alabam stories begin	36.00	107.00	250.00
2-Kubert, Kamen/Feldstein-a; Kamen-c	29.00	86.00	200.00
3-5,7: 3-Kiefer story	19.00	58.00	135.00
6-Opium drug mention story; bondage, headlight-c; Reinman-a			
	25.00	75.00	175.00

COWPUNCHER

1953 (nn) (Reprints Avon's No. 2)			
Realistic Publications			
nn-Kubert-a	10.00	30.00	65.00

COWSILLS, THE (See Harvey Pop Comics)

COYOTE
June, 1983 - No. 16, Mar, 1986
Marvel Comics (Epic Comics)

1-16: 11-1st McFarlane-a. 12-14-McFarlane-a			1.25

CRACKAJACK FUNNIES (Giveaway)
1937 (Full size, soft-c, full color, 32 pgs.)(Before No. 1?)
Malto-Meal

nn-Features Dan Dunn, G-Man, Speed Bolton, Freckles, Buck Jones, Clyde Beatty, The Nebbs, Major Hoople, Wash Tubbs	87.00	262.00	700.00

CRACKAJACK FUNNIES (Also see The Owl)
June, 1938 - No. 43, Jan, 1942
Dell Publishing Co.

1-Dan Dunn, Freckles, Myra North, Wash Tubbs, Apple Mary, The Nebbs, Don Winslow, Tom Mix, Buck Jones, Major Hoople, Clyde Beatty, Boots begin	212.00	637.00	1700.00
2	90.00	270.00	725.00
3	62.00	187.00	500.00
4,5: 5-Nude woman on cover	48.00	144.00	385.00
6-8,10: 8-Speed Bolton begins (1st app.)	40.00	120.00	300.00
9-(3/39)-Red Ryder strip-r begin by Harman; 1st app. in comics & 1st cover app.	106.00	318.00	850.00
11-14	39.00	118.00	275.00
15-Tarzan text feature begins by Burroughs (9/39); not in #26,35			
	40.00	120.00	300.00
16-24: 18-Stratosphere Jim begins (1st app., 12/39). 23-Ellery Queen begins plus-c (1st comic book app., 5/40)	30.00	90.00	210.00
25-The Owl begins (1st app., 7/40); in new costume #26 by Frank Thomas (also see Popular Comics #72)	62.00	187.00	500.00
26-30: 28-Part Owl-c	45.00	136.00	365.00
31-Owl covers begin, end #42	44.00	132.00	350.00
32-Origin Owl Girl	51.00	155.00	415.00
33-38: 36-Last Tarzan issue. 37-Cyclone & Midge begin (1st app.)			
	40.00	120.00	285.00
39-Andy Panda begins (intro/1st app., 9/41)	44.00	132.00	350.00
40-42: 40-Last Owl-c.	39.00	118.00	275.00
43-Terry & the Pirates-r	34.00	101.00	235.00

NOTE: McWilliams art in most issues.

CRACK COMICS (Crack Western No. 63 on)
May, 1940 - No. 62, Sept, 1949
Quality Comics Group

1-Origin & 1st app. The Black Condor by Lou Fine, Madame Fatal, Red Torpedo, Rock Bradden & The Space Legion; The Clock, Alias the Spider (by Gustavson), Wizard Wells & Ned Brant begin; Powell-a; Note: Madame Fatal is a man dressed as a woman	410.00	1230.00	3700.00
2	200.00	600.00	1600.00
3	131.00	393.00	1050.00
4	118.00	356.00	950.00
5-10: 5-Molly The Model begins. 10-Tor, the Magic Master begins			
	87.00	262.00	700.00
11-20: 13-1 pg. J. Cole-a. 18-1st app. Spitfire?	75.00	225.00	600.00
21-24: 23-Pen Miller begins; continued from National Comics #22. 24-Last Fine Black Condor	59.00	178.00	475.00
25,26: 26-Flag-c	48.00	144.00	385.00
27-(1/43)-Intro & origin Captain Triumph by Alfred Andriola (Kerry Drake artist) & begin series	87.00	262.00	700.00
28-30	40.00	120.00	300.00
31-39: 31-Last Black Condor	25.00	75.00	175.00

Crack Western #75 © QUA

Crash Comics #3 © Tem Publ.

Crazy #4 © ATLAS

	GD25	FN65	NM94
40-46	17.00	51.00	120.00
47-57,59,60-Capt. Triumph by Crandall	19.00	58.00	135.00
58,61,62-Last Captain Triumph	13.00	39.00	90.00

NOTE: *Black Condor by Fine: No. 1, 2, 4-6, 8, 10-24; by Sultan: No. 3, 7; by Fugitani: No. 9. Cole a-34. Crandall a-61(unsigned); c-48, 49, 51-61. Guardineer a-17. Gustavson a-1, 13, 17. McWilliams a-15-27. Black Condor c-2, 4, 6, 8, 10, 12, 14, 16, 18, 20-26. Capt. Triumph c-27-62. The Clock c-1, 3, 5, 7, 9, 11, 13, 15, 17, 19.*

CRACKED (Magazine) (Satire) (Also see The 3-D Zone #19)
Feb-Mar, 1958 - Present
Major Magazines(#1-212)/Globe Communications (#213 on)

1-One pg. Williamson-a	17.00	51.00	120.00
2-1st Shut-Ups & Bonus Cut-Outs	8.35	25.00	50.00
3-6	5.00	15.00	30.00
7-10: 7-Reprints 6 covers on-c	3.40	10.00	24.00
11-12, 13(nn,3/60), 14-17, 18(nn,2/61), 19,20	3.25	9.50	22.00
21-27(11/62), 27(No.28, 2/63; mis-#d), 29(5/63)	2.60	7.50	18.00
31-60	1.85	5.50	13.00
61-98,100	1.50	3.75	9.00
99-Alfred E. Neuman on-c	3.75	11.25	28.00
101-200: 131-Bill Ward-a. 234-Don Martin-a begins ($1.75 #? on)	1.00	2.00	5.00
201-341	1.00		2.50
Biggest... (Winter, 1977)	1.70	5.00	12.00
Biggest, Greatest... nn('65)	3.75	11.25	26.00
Biggest, Greatest... 2('66) - #12('76)	2.30	6.75	16.00
...Blockbuster 1,2 ('88)		1.20	3.00
...Digest 1(Fall, '86, 148 pgs.) - #5		1.00	2.50
...Collectors' Edition 4 ('73; formerly ...Special)	1.50	3.75	9.00
5-70: 23-Ward-a		1.40	3.50
71-84: 83-Elvis, Batman parodies		1.60	4.00
...Party Pack 1,2('88)		1.60	4.00
...Shut-Ups (2/72-'72; Cracked Spec. #3) 1,2	1.20	3.00	7.00
...Special 3('73; formerly Cracked Shut-Ups; ...Collectors' Edition#4 on)			
	1.20	3.00	7.00
Extra Special... 1('76), 2('76)		1.60	4.00
Giant... nn('65)	3.75	11.25	30.00
Giant... 2('66)-12('76), nn(9/77)-48('87)	2.60	7.50	18.00
King Sized... 1('67)	4.50	13.00	35.00
King Sized... 2('68)-11('77)	3.25	9.50	22.00
King Sized... 12-22 (Sum/'86)		.80	2.00
Super... 1('68)	3.75	11.25	30.00
Super... 2('69)-24('88)	3.25	9.50	22.00
Super... 1('87, 100 pgs.)-Severin & Elder-a	1.10		2.75

NOTE: *Burgos a-1-10. Colan a-257. Davis a-5, 11-17, 24, 40, 80; c-12-14, 16. Elder a-5, 6, 10-13; c-10. Everett a-1-10, 23-25, 61; c-1. Heath a-1-3, 6, 13, 14, 17, 110; c-6. Jaffee a-5, 6. Don Martin a-235, 244, 247, 259, 261, 264. Morrow a-8-10. Reinman a-1-4. Severin c/a-in most all issues. Shores a-3-7. Torres a-7-10. Ward a-22-24, 27, 35, 40, 143, 144, 149, 150, 152, 153, 156. Williamson a-1 (1 pg.). Wolverton a-10 (2 pgs.), Giant nn('65). Wood a-27, 35, 40. Alfred E. Neuman c-177, 200, 202. Batman c-234, 248, 249, 256. Captain America c-256. Christmas c-234, 243. Spider-Man c-260. Star Trek c-127, 169, 207, 228. Star Wars c-145, 146, 148, 149, 152, 155, 173, 174, 199. Superman c-183, 233. #144, 146 have free full-color pre-glued stickers. #145, 147, 155, 163 have free full-color postcards. #123, 137, 154, 157 have free iron-ons.*

CRACKED MONSTER PARTY
July, 1988 - No. 26, 1990?
Globe Communications

1-26		.80	2.00

CRACKED'S FOR MONSTERS ONLY
Sept, 1969 - No. 9, Sept, 1969
Major Magazines

1-9		1.20	3.00

CRACKED SPACED OUT
Fall, 1993 - No. 4, 1994?
Globe Communications

1-4		.80	2.00

	GD25	FN65	NM94

CRACK WESTERN (Formerly Crack Comics; Jonesy No. 85 on)
No. 63, Nov, 1949 - No. 84, May, 1953 (36 pgs., 63-68,74-on)
Quality Comics Group

63(#1)-Ward-c; Two-Gun Lil (origin & 1st app.)(ends #84), Arizona Ames, his horse Thunder (with sidekick Spurs & his horse Calico), Frontier Marshal (ends #70), & Dead Canyon Days (ends #69) begin; Crandall-a

	20.00	60.00	140.00
64,65: 64-Ward-c. Crandall-a in both.	15.00	45.00	105.00
66,68-Photo-c. 66-Arizona Ames becomes A. Raines (ends #84)			
	13.00	39.00	90.00
67-Randolph Scott photo-c; Crandall-a	15.00	45.00	105.00
69(52pgs.)-Crandall-a	13.50	41.00	95.00
70(52pgs.)-The Whip (origin & 1st app.) & his horse Diablo begin (ends #84); Crandall-a	13.50	41.00	95.00
71(52pgs.)-Frontier Marshal becomes Bob Allen F. Marshal (ends #84); Crandall-c/a	15.00	45.00	105.00
72(52pgs.)-Tim Holt photo-c	12.00	36.00	85.00
73(52pgs.)-Photo-c	7.25	22.00	58.00
74-76,78,79,81,83-Crandall-c. 83-Crandall-a(p)	11.00	33.00	75.00
77,80,82	7.50	22.50	45.00
84-Crandall-c/a	12.00	36.00	85.00

NOTE: *Crandall c-71p, 74-81, 83p(w/Cuidera-i).*

CRASH COMICS (Catman Comics No. 6 on)
May, 1940 - No. 5, Nov, 1940
Tem Publishing Co.

1-The Blue Streak, Strongman (origin), The Perfect Human, Shangra begin (1st app. of each); Kirby-a	262.00	787.00	2100.00
2-Simon & Kirby-a	125.00	375.00	1000.00
3,5-Simon & Kirby-a	112.00	338.00	900.00
4-Origin & 1st app. The Catman; S&K-a	218.00	656.00	1750.00

NOTE: *Solar Legion by Kirby No. 1-5 (5 pgs. each). Strongman c-1-4. Catman c-5.*

CRASH DIVE (See Cinema Comics Herald)

CRASH RYAN (Also see Dark Horse Presents #44)
Oct, 1984 - No. 4, Jan, 1985 (Baxter paper, limited series)
Marvel Comics (Epic Comics)

1-4			1.50

CRAZY (Also see This Magazine is Crazy)
Dec, 1953 - No. 7, July, 1954
Atlas Comics (CSI)

1-Everett-c/a	21.00	64.00	150.00
2	17.00	51.00	120.00
3-7: 4-I Love Lucy satire. 5-Satire on censorship	14.00	43.00	100.00

NOTE: *Ayers a-5. Berg a-1, 2. Burgos c-5, 6. Drucker a-4. Everett a-1-4. Al Hartley a-4. Heath a-3, 7; c-7. Maneely a-1-7, c-3, 5. Post a-3-6. Funny monster c-1-4.*

CRAZY (Satire)
Feb, 1973 - No. 3, June, 1973
Marvel Comics Group

1-3-Not Brand Echh-r. 1-Beatles cameo (r)			1.00

CRAZY MAGAZINE (Satire)
Oct, 1973 - No. 94, Apr, 1983 (40-90¢, B&W magazine)
(#1, 44 pgs; #2-90, reg. issues, 52 pgs; #92-95, 68 pgs)'
Marvel Comics Group

1-Wolverton(1 pg.), Bode-a; 3 pg. photo story of Neal Adams & Dick Giordano		.80	2.00
2-Kurtzman's "Hey Look" 2 pg. reprint			1.50
3-16: 8-Casper parody. 9-Has 1st 8 covers on-c			1.00
17-29,31-36,38-41,43,48,50,51,53,54,56,57,59,60: 20-Superheroes song sheet. 41-Kiss-c. 43-E.C. swipe from Mad #131. 60,92-Star Trek parodies			
			1.00
30,37,42,49,52,55,61,64,67,70,73,76,85,88: Super Specials ($1.00, all 84 pgs). 85-Flintstones. 88-X-Men			1.50

	GD25	FN65	NM94

58-Super Special ($1.25); contains free Crazy #1 (2/73) comic reprint

			1.50
62,63,65,66,68,69,71,72,74,75,77,78,80,81,83,84,86,87,89,90: 62-Kiss-c			
& 2 pg. story. 63-Obnoxio app. 69-Richie Rich. 80-X-Men. 81-Wolverine/			
Hulk. 87-Obnoxio origin			1.25
79-Super Special ($1.25)-Full color looney labels			1.50
82-Super Special ($1.25); X-Men on-c			1.50
91-94: ($1.25) 91-Super Special; Black Knight by Maneely. 93-E.T.-c, &			
parody. 94-Avengers parody			1.50
Super Special 1(Summer, 1975, 100 pgs.)-Ploog, Neal Adams-r		.80	2.00

NOTE: N. Adams a-2, 61r, 94p. Austin a-82i. Buscema a-2, 82. Byrne c-82p. Nick Cardy c-7, 8, 10, 12-16, Super Special 1. Crandall a-76r. Ditko a-68r, 79r, 82r. Drucker a-3. Eisner a-9-16. Kelly Freas c-1-6, 9, 11; a-7. Kirby/Wood a-66r. Ploog a-1, 4, 7, 67r, 73r. Rogers a-82. Sparling a-92. Wood a-65r. Howard the Duck in 36, 50, 51, 53, 54, 59, 63, 65, 66, 68, 69, 71, 72, 74, 75, 77. Hulk in 46, c-42, 46, 57, 73. Star Wars in 32, 66; c-37.

CRAZYMAN
Apr, 1992 - No. 5, 1992 ($2.50, high quality paper)
Continuity Comics

1-($3.95, 52 pgs.)-Embossed-c; N. Adams part-i		1.60	4.00
2-5 ($2.50): 2-N. Adams/Bolland-c		1.00	2.50

CRAZYMAN
V2#1, May, 1993 - No. 4, Jan, 1994 ($2.50, high quality paper)
Continuity Comics

V2#1-($2.50)-Entire book is die-cut		1.00	2.50
2-4: 2-(12/93)-Adams-c(p) & part scripts. 3-(12/93). 4-Indicia says #3, Jan.			
1993		1.00	2.00

CRAZY, MAN, CRAZY (Magazine) (Becomes This Magazine is...?)
(Formerly From Here to Insanity)
V2#1, Dec, 1955 - V2#2, June, 1956 Humor Magazines (Charlton)

V2#1,V2#2-Satire; Wolverton-a, 3 pgs.	11.50	34.00	80.00

CREATURE, THE (See Movie Classics)

CREATURES OF THE ID
1990-? ($2.95, B&W)
Caliber Press

1-?; 1-Frank Einstein (Madman) app.; Allred-a			15.00

CREATURES ON THE LOOSE (Formerly Tower of Shadows No. 1-9)(See Kull)
No. 10, March, 1971 - No. 37, Sept, 1975 (New-a & reprints)
Marvel Comics Group

10-(15¢)-1st King Kull story; see Monsters on the Prowl (next app.?);			
Wrightson-a	3.60	11.00	25.00
11-29,31-37: 16-Origin Warrior of Mars (begins): ends #21). 21,22-Steranko-c.			
22-29-Thongor-c/stories.		1.00	2.50
30-Manwolf begins	1.00	2.00	5.00

NOTE: Crandall a-13. Ditko r-11, 15, 17, 18, 20, 22, 24, 27, 28. Everett a-16i(new). Matt Fox r-21i. Howard a-26i. Gil Kane a-16p, 17p, 19i; c-16, 17, 19, 20, 25, 29, 33p, 35p, 36p. Kirby a-10r, 16(2)r, 17r, 19r. Morrow a-20, 21. Perez a-33-37; c-34p. Sinnott r-21. Sutton c-10. Tuska a-31p, 32p.

CREED
Dec, 1994 - No. 2, Jan, 1995 ($2.50, B&W)
Hall of Heroes Comics

1	4.30	13.00	30.00
2	3.90	11.50	27.00

CREED
June, 1995 - Present ($2.75/$3.00, B&W/color)
Lightning Comics

1-($2.75)		1.60	4.00
1-($3.00, color)			4.50
1-($9.95)-Commemorative Edition	2.85	8.50	20.00
1-Twin Variant Edition (1250? print run)			25.00
1-Special Edition; polybagged w/certificate			5.00

1 Gold Collectors Edition; polybagged w/certificate			3.00
2,3-($3.00, color)-Butt Naked Edition & regular-c			3.00
3-($9.95)-Commemorative Edition; polybagged w/certificate & card			
			10.00

CREED/TEENAGE MUTANT NINJA TURTLES
May, 1996 ($3.00, one-shot)
Lightning Comics

1-Kaniuga-a(p)/scripts; Laird-c; variant-c exists			3.00
1-($9.95)-Platinum Edition			10.00
1-Special Edition; polybagged w/certificate			5.00

CREEPER, THE (See Beware... & 1st Issue Special)

CREEPSVILLE
V2#1, Winter, 1995 ($4.95)
Laughing Reindeer Press

V2#1-Comics w/text			5.00

CREEPY (See Warren Presents)
1964 - No. 146, Feb, 1983; No. 146, 1985 (B&W, magazine)
Warren Publishing Co./Harris Publ. #146

1-Frazetta-a (his last story in comics?); Jack Davis-c; 1st Warren all comics			
magazine	11.00	33.00	75.00
2: 2-Frazetta-c & 1 pg. strip	5.70	17.00	40.00
3-13: 3-7,9-11-Frazetta-c. 7-Frazetta 1 pg. strip. 9-Creepy fan club sketch by			
Wrightson (1st published-a); has 1/2 pg. anti-smoking strip by Frazetta. 10-			
Brunner fan club sketch (1st published work)	2.60	7.50	18.00
14-Neal Adams 1st Warren work	3.00	9.00	21.00
15-25: 15-17-Frazetta-c	2.00	6.00	14.00
26-40: 27,32-Frazetta-c. 32-Harlan Ellison story	1.70	5.00	12.00
41-47,49-54,56-61: 61-Wertham parody	1.65	4.20	10.00
48,55,65-(1973, 1974, 1975 Annuals)	1.70	5.00	12.00
62-64,66-112,114-145: 93-Sports issue. 96-Aliens issue. 102-All monster issue.			
121-All Severin-r issue. 125-All N. Adams-r issue. 137-All Williamson-r issue.			
139-All Toth-r issue. 144-Giant, $2.25; Frazetta-c	1.50	3.75	9.00
113-All Wrightson-r issue	1.70	5.00	12.00
146 ($2.95)-1st from Harris; resurrection issue	5.00	15.00	40.00
Year Book 1968, 1969	1.65	4.20	10.00
Year Book 1970-Neal Adams, Ditko-a(r)	1.65	4.20	10.00
Annual 1971,1972	1.65	4.20	10.00
1993 Fearbook ($3.95)-Harris Publications	1.00	2.00	5.00

NOTE: All issues contain many good artists works: Neal Adams, Brunner, Corben, Craig (Taycee), Crandall, Ditko, Evans, Frazetta, Heath, Jeff Jones, Krenkel, McWilliams, Morrow, Nino, Orlando, Ploog, Severin, Torres, Toth, Williamson, Wood, & Wrightson; others by Crandall, Davis, Frazetta, Morrow, San Julian, Todd/Bode; Otto Binder's "Adam Link" stories in No. 2, 4, 6, 8, 9, 12, 13, 15 with Orlando art. Frazetta c-2-7, 9-11, 15-17, 27, 32, 83r, 89r, 91r. E.A. Poe adaptations in 66, 69, 70.

CREEPY THINGS
July, 1975 - No. 6, June, 1976
Charlton Comics

1			1.50
2-6: Ditko-a in 3,5. Sutton c-3,4			1.00
Modern Comics Reprint 2-6(1977)			1.00

CRIME AND JUSTICE (Rookie Cop) No. 27 on)
March, 1951 - No. 26, Sept, 1955
Capitol Stories/Charlton Comics

1	25.00	75.00	175.00
2	8.35	25.00	50.00
3-8,10-13: 6-Negligee panels	7.00	21.00	42.00
9-Classic story "Comics Vs. Crime"	17.00	49.00	115.00
14-Color illos in POP; gory story of man who beheads women			
	12.00	36.00	85.00
15-17,19-26: 15-Negligee panels	4.25	13.00	28.00
18-Ditko-a	19.00	58.00	135.00

NOTE: Alascia c-20. Ayers a-17. Shuster a-19-21; c-19. Bondage c-11, 12.

Crime And Punishment #45 © LEV

Crime Can't Win #4 © MEG

Crime Detector #5 © Timor Publ.

	GD25	FN65	NM94

CRIME AND PUNISHMENT (Title inspired by 1935 film)
April, 1948 - No. 74, Aug, 1955
Lev Gleason Publications

1-Mr. Crime app. on-c	25.00	75.00	175.00
2	13.00	39.00	90.00
3-Used in **SOTI**, pg. 112; injury-to-eye panel; Fuje-a			
	17.00	49.00	115.00
4,5	10.00	30.00	60.00
6-10	8.70	26.00	52.00
11-20	7.50	22.50	45.00
21-30	5.85	17.50	35.00
31-38,40-44,46: 46-One pg. Frazetta-a	4.25	13.00	28.00
39-Drug mention story "The 5 Dopes"	8.35	25.00	50.00
45- "Hophead Killer" drug story	8.35	25.00	50.00
47-57,60-65,70-74:	4.25	13.00	28.00
58-Used in **POP**, pg. 79	5.00	15.00	30.00
59-Used in **SOTI**, illo "What comic-book America stands for"			
	23.00	69.00	160.00
66-Toth-c/a(4); 3-D effect issue (3/54); 1st "Deep Dimension" process			
	31.00	94.00	220.00
67- "Monkey on His Back" heroin story; 3-D effect issue			
	25.00	75.00	175.00
68-3-D effect issue; Toth-c (7/54)	23.00	69.00	160.00
69- "The Hot Rod Gang" dope crazy kids	9.15	27.00	55.00

NOTE: *Biro c-most. Everett a-31. Fuje a-3, 4, 12, 13, 17, 18, 20, 26, 27. Guardineer a-2-4, 10, 14, 17, 18, 20, 26-28, 32, 38-44. Kinstler c-69. McWilliams a-41, 48, 49. Tuska a-28, 30, 51, 64, 70.*

CRIME AND PUNISHMENT: MARSHALL LAW TAKES MANHATTAN
1989 ($4.95, 52 pgs., direct sales only, mature readers)
Marvel Comics (Epic Comics)

nn-Graphic album featuring Marshall Law	1.00	2.00	5.00

CRIME CAN'T WIN (Formerly Cindy Smith)
No. 41, 9/50 - No. 43, 2/51; No. 4, 4/51 - No. 12, 9/53
Marvel/Atlas Comics (TCI 41/CCC 42,43,4-12)

41(#1)	20.00	60.00	140.00
42(#2)	11.50	34.00	80.00
43(#3)-Horror story	13.00	39.00	90.00
4(4/51),5-12: 10-Possible use in **SOTI**, pg. 161	9.15	27.00	55.00

NOTE: *Robinson a-9-11. Tuska a-43.*

CRIME CASES COMICS (Formerly Willie Comics)
No. 24, 8/50 - No. 27, 3/51; No. 5, 5/51 - No. 12, 7/52
Marvel/Atlas Comics(CnPC No.24-8/MJMC No.9-12)

24 (#1, 52 pgs.)-True police cases	12.00	36.00	85.00
25-27(#2-4): 27-Morisi-a	9.15	27.00	55.00
5-12: 11-Robinson a. 12-Tuska-a	7.50	22.50	45.00

CRIME CLINIC
No. 10, July-Aug, 1951 - No. 5, Summer, 1952
Ziff-Davis Publishing Co.

10(#1)-Painted-c; origin Dr. Tom Rogers	21.00	62.00	145.00
11(#2),4,5: 4,5-Painted-c	14.00	43.00	100.00
3-Used in **SOTI**, pg. 18	16.00	47.00	110.00

NOTE: *All have painted covers by Saunders. Starr a-10.*

CRIME CLINIC
May, 1995 - No. 2, Oct, 1995 ($2.95, B&W, limited series)
Slave Labor Graphics

1,2		1.20	3.00

CRIME DETECTIVE COMICS
Mar-Apr, 1948 - V3#8, May-June, 1953
Hillman Periodicals

V1#1-The Invisible 6, costumed villains app; Fuje-c/a, 15 pgs.			
	20.00	60.00	140.00

2,5: 5-Krigstein-a	9.15	27.00	55.00
3,4,6,7,10-12: 6-McWilliams-a	7.50	22.50	45.00
8-Kirbyish-a by McCann	7.50	22.50	45.00
9-Used in **SOTI**, pg. 16 & "Caricature of the author in a position comic book publishers wish he were in permanently" illo.	29.00	86.00	200.00
V2#1,4,7-Krigstein-a: 1-Tuska-a	8.35	25.00	50.00
2,3,5,6,8-12 (1-2/52)	5.00	15.00	30.00
V3#1-Drug use-c	5.35	16.00	32.00
2-8	4.15	12.50	25.00

NOTE: *Briefer a-11, V3#1. Kinstlerish-a by McCann-V2#7, V3#2. Powell a-10, 11. Starr a-10.*

CRIME DETECTOR
Jan, 1954 - No. 5, Sept, 1954
Timor Publications

1	13.00	39.00	90.00
2	7.50	22.50	45.00
3,4	6.70	20.00	40.00
5-Disbrow-a (classic)	13.50	41.00	95.00

CRIME DOES NOT PAY (Formerly Silver Streak Comics No. 1-21)
No. 22, June, 1942 - No. 147, July, 1955 (1st crime comic)
Comic House/Lev Gleason/Golfing (Title inspired by film)

22(23 on cover, 22 on indicia)-Origin The War Eagle & only app.; Chip Gardner begins; #22 was rebound in Complete Book of True Crime (Scarce)	175.00	525.00	1400.00
23 (Scarce)	109.00	328.00	875.00
24-Intro. & 1st app. Mr. Crime (Scarce)	81.00	243.00	650.00
25-30	48.00	144.00	385.00
31-40	31.00	94.00	220.00
41-Origin & 1st app. Officer Common Sense	22.00	66.00	155.00
42-Electrocution-c	26.00	77.00	180.00
43-46,48-50: 44,45,50 are 68 pg. issues	14.00	43.00	100.00
47-Electric chair-c	25.00	75.00	175.00
51-70: 63,64-Possible use in **SOTI**, pg. 306.-Contains Biro & Gleason's self censorship code of 12 listed restrictions (5/48)	13.00	39.00	90.00
71-99: 87-Chip Gardner begins, ends #100	10.00	30.00	65.00
100	10.00	30.00	70.00
101-104,107-110: 102-Chip Gardner app	8.35	25.00	50.00
105-Used in **POP**, pg. 84	10.00	30.00	60.00
106,114-Frazetta-a, 1 pg.	8.35	25.00	50.00
111-Used in **POP**, pgs. 80 & 81; injury-to-eye sty illo	8.35	25.00	50.00
112,113,115-130	5.85	17.50	35.00
131-140	4.25	13.00	28.00
141,142-Last pre-code issue; Kubert-a(1)	8.35	25.00	50.00
143,147-Kubert-a, one story each	8.35	25.00	50.00
144-146	4.25	13.00	28.00
1(Golfing-1945)	5.85	17.50	35.00
The Best of...(1944, 128 pgs.)-Series contains 4 rebound issues			
	75.00	225.00	600.00
...1945 issue	56.00	168.00	450.00
...1946-48 issues	41.00	124.00	330.00
...1949-50 issues	40.00	120.00	285.00
...1951-53 issues	32.00	96.00	225.00

NOTE: *Many issues contain violent covers and stories. Who Dunnit by Guardineer-39-42, 44-105, 108-110; Chip Gardner by Bob Fujitani (Fuje)-88-103. Alderman a-29, 41-44, 49. Dan Barry a-75. Biro a-1-76, 122, 142. Briefer a-29(2), 30, 31, 33, 37, 39. G. Colan a-105. Fuje c-88, 89, 91-94, 96, 98, 99, 102, 103. Guardineer a-57, 71. Kubert c-143. Landau a-118. Maurer a-29, 39, 41, 42. McWilliams a-91, 93, 95, 100-103. Palais a-30, 33, 37, 39, 41-43, 44(2), 46, 49. Powell a-146, 147. Tuska a-48, 50(2), 51, 52, 56, 57(2), 60-64, 66, 67, 71. Painted c-87-102. Bondage c-43, 62, 98.*

CRIME EXPOSED
June, 1948; Dec, 1950 - No. 14, June, 1952
Marvel Comics (PPI)/Marvel Atlas Comics (PrPl)

1(6/48)	25.00	75.00	175.00
1(12/50)	15.00	45.00	105.00
2	10.00	30.00	65.00

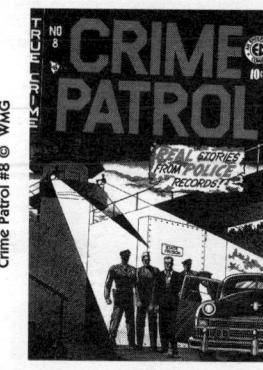

Crime Must Stop #1 © HILL

Crime Mysteries #2 © TM

Crime Patrol #8 © WMG

	GD25	FN65	NM94
3-9,11,14	8.35	25.00	50.00
10-Used in POP, pg. 81	9.15	27.00	55.00
12-Krigstein & Robinson-a	9.15	27.00	55.00
13-Used in POP, pg. 81; Krigstein-a	10.00	30.00	65.00

NOTE: *Maneely* c-8. *Robinson* a-11, 12. *Tuska* a-3, 4.

CRIMEFIGHTERS
Apr, 1948 - No. 10, Nov, 1949
Marvel Comics (CmPS 1-3/CCC 4-10)

1-Some copies are undated & could be reprints	20.00	60.00	140.00
2,3: 3-Morphine addict story	10.00	30.00	65.00
4-10: 6-Anti-Wertham editorial. 9,10-Photo-c	9.15	27.00	55.00

CRIME FIGHTERS (...Always Win)
No. 11, Sept, 1954 - No. 13, Jan, 1955
Atlas Comics (CnPC)

11-13: 11-Maneely-a,13-Pakula, Reinman, Severin-a			
	10.00	30.00	60.00

CRIME-FIGHTING DETECTIVE (Shock Detective Cases No. 20 on; formerly Criminals on the Run)
No. 11, Apr-May, 1950 - No. 19, June, 1952 (Based on true crime cases)
Star Publications

11-L. B. Cole-c/a (2 pgs.); L. B. Cole-c on all	12.00	36.00	85.00
12,13,15-19: 17-Young King Cole & Dr. Doom app.	10.00	30.00	60.00
14-L. B. Cole-c/a, r/Law-Crime #2	11.00	33.00	75.00

CRIME FILES
No. 5, Sept, 1952 - No. 6, Nov, 1952
Standard Comics

5-1pg. Alex Toth-a; used in SOTI, pg. 4 (text)	20.00	60.00	140.00
6-Sekowsky-a	10.00	30.00	70.00

CRIME ILLUSTRATED (Magazine)
Nov-Dec, 1955 - No. 2, Spring, 1956 (25¢, Adult Suspense Stories on-c)
E. C. Comics

1-Ingels & Crandall-a	12.00	36.00	85.00
2-Ingels & Crandall-a	10.00	30.00	70.00

NOTE: *Craig* a-1, 2; c-2. *Evans* a-1. *Davis* a-2. *Ingels* a-1, 2. *Krigstein/Crandall* a-1. *Orlando* a-1, 2; c-1.

CRIME INCORPORATED (Formerly Crimes Incorporated)
No. 2, Aug, 1950 - No. 3, Aug, 1951
Fox Features Syndicate

2	20.00	60.00	140.00
3(1951)-Hollingsworth-a	14.00	43.00	100.00

CRIME MACHINE (Magazine)
Feb, 1971 - No. 2, May, 1971 (B&W)
Skywald Publications

1-Kubert-a(2)(r)(Avon)	3.25	9.50	22.00
2-Torres, Wildey-a; violent-c/a	2.60	7.50	18.00

CRIME MUST LOSE! (Formerly Sports Action?)
No. 4, Oct, 1950 - No. 12, April, 1952
Sports Action (Atlas Comics)

4-Ann Brewster-a in all; c-used in N.Y. Legis. Comm. documents			
	14.00	43.00	100.00
5-10,12: 9-Robinson-a	10.00	30.00	60.00
11-Used in POP, pg. 89	10.00	30.00	65.00

CRIME MUST PAY THE PENALTY (Formerly Four Favorites; Penalty #47, 48)
No. 33, Feb, 1948; No. 2, June, 1948 - No. 48, Jan, 1956
Ace Magazines (Current Books)

33(#1, 2/48)-Becomes Four Teeners #34?	24.00	73.00	170.00
2(6/48)-Extreme violence; Palais-a?	16.00	47.00	110.00
3- "Frisco Mary" story used in Senate Investigation report, pg. 7			
	11.50	34.00	80.00

	GD25	FN65	NM94
4,8-Transvestism stories	13.00	39.00	90.00
5-7,9,10	7.50	22.50	45.00
11-20-Drug story "Dealers in White Death"	6.70	20.00	40.00
21-32,34-40,42-48	5.00	15.00	30.00
33(7/53)- "Dell Fabry-Junk King" drug story; mentioned in Love and Death			
	7.50	22.50	45.00
41-reprints "Dealers in White Death"	7.50	22.50	45.00

NOTE: *Cameron* a-29-31, 34, 35, 39-41. *Colan* a-20, 31. *Kremer* a-3, 37r. *Larsen* a-32. *Palais* a-57,37.

CRIME MUST STOP
October, 1952 (52 pgs.)
Hillman Periodicals

V1#1(Scarce)-Similar to Monster Crime; Mort Lawrence, Krigstein-a			
	50.00	150.00	400.00

CRIME MYSTERIES (Secret Mysteries #16 on; combined with Crime Smashers #7 on)
May, 1952 - No. 15, Sept, 1954
Ribage Publishing Corp. (Trojan Magazines)

1-Transvestism story; crime & terror stories begin	40.00	120.00	325.00
2-Marijuana story (7/52)	32.00	96.00	225.00
3-One pg. Frazetta-a	26.00	77.00	180.00
4-Cover shows girl in bondage having her blood drained; 1 pg. Frazetta-a			
	39.00	118.00	275.00
5-10	20.00	60.00	140.00
11,12,14	19.00	56.00	130.00
13-(5/54)-Angelo Torres 1st comic work (inks over Check's pencils); Check-a			
	24.00	71.00	165.00
15-Acid in face-c	29.00	86.00	200.00

NOTE: *Fass* a-13; c-4, 10. *Hollingsworth* a-10-13, 15; c-2, 12, 13, 15. *Kiefer* a-4. *Woodbridge* a-13? Bondage-c-1, 8, 12.

CRIME ON THE RUN (See Approved Comics #8)

CRIME ON THE WATERFRONT (Formerly Famous Gangsters)
No. 4, May, 1952 (Painted cover)
Realistic Publications

4	24.00	73.00	170.00

CRIME PATROL (Formerly International #1-5; International Crime Patrol #6; becomes Crypt of Terror #17 on)
No. 7, Summer, 1948 - No. 16, Feb-Mar, 1950
E. C. Comics

7-Intro. Captain Crime	50.00	150.00	400.00
8-14: 12-Ingels-a	44.00	132.00	350.00
15-Intro. of Crypt Keeper (inspired by Witches Tales radio show) & Crypt of Terror (see Tales From the Crypt #33 for origin); used by N.Y. Legis. Comm.; last pg. Feldstein-a	212.00	638.00	1700.00
16-2nd Crypt Keeper app.; Roussos-a	138.00	412.00	1100.00

NOTE: *Craig* c/a in most issues. *Feldstein* a-9-16. *Kiefer* a-8, 10, 11. *Moldoff* a-7.

CRIME PHOTOGRAPHER (See Casey...)

CRIME REPORTER
Aug, 1948 - No. 3, Dec, 1948 (Indicia shows Oct.)
St. John Publ. Co.

1-Drug club story	40.00	120.00	285.00
2-Used in SOTI; illo- "Children told me what the man was going to do with the red-hot poker;" r/Dynamic #17 with editing; Baker-c; Tuska-a	58.00	174.00	465.00
3-Baker-c; Tuska-a	31.00	92.00	215.00

CRIMES BY WOMEN
June, 1948 - No. 15, Aug, 1951; 1954 (True crime cases)
Fox Features Syndicate

1-True story of Bonnie Parker	100.00	300.00	800.00
2,3: 3-Used in SOTI, pg. 234	53.00	159.00	425.00
4,5,7-9,11-15: 8-Used in POP.14-Spanking panel r/from All Famous Crime			

Crime Smasher #1 © FAW

Crime SuspenStories #19 © WMG

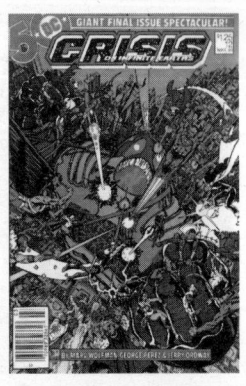

Crisis On Infinite Earths #12 © DC

	GD25	FN65	NM94
Stories (1949) (Fox Giant)	48.00	146.00	390.00
6-Classic girl fight-c; acid-in-face panel	53.00	159.00	425.00
10-Used in SOTI, pg. 72; girl fight-c	45.00	136.00	365.00
54(M.S. Publ.-'54)-Reprint; (formerly My Love Secret)			
	22.00	66.00	155.00

CRIMES INCORPORATED (Formerly My Past)
No. 12, June, 1950 (Crime Incorporated No. 2 on)
Fox Features Syndicate

12	11.50	34.00	80.00

CRIMES INCORPORATED (See Fox Giants)

CRIME SMASHER (See Whiz #76)
Summer, 1948 (one-shot)
Fawcett Publications

1-Formerly Spy Smasher	39.00	118.00	275.00

CRIME SMASHERS (Becomes Secret Mysteries No. 16 on)
Oct, 1950 - No. 15, Mar, 1953
Ribage Publishing Corp.(Trojan Magazines)

1-Used in SOTI, pg. 19,20, & illo "A girl raped and murdered;" Sally the Sleuth			
begins	62.00	187.00	500.00
2-Kubert-c	36.00	107.00	250.00
3,4	26.00	79.00	185.00
5-Wood-a	34.00	103.00	240.00
6,8-11	20.00	60.00	140.00
7-Female heroin junkie story	21.00	62.00	145.00
12-Injury to eye panel; 1 pg. Frazetta-a	21.00	64.00	150.00
13-Used in POP, pgs. 79,80; 1 pg. Frazetta-a	21.00	64.00	150.00
14,15	18.00	54.00	125.00

NOTE: Hollingsworth a-14. Kiefer a-15. Bondage c-7, 9.

CRIME SUSPENSTORIES (Formerly Vault of Horror No. 12-14)
No. 15, Oct-Nov, 1950 - No. 27, Feb-Mar, 1955
E. C. Comics

15-Identical to #1 in content; #1 printed on outside front cover. #15 (formerly "The Vault of Horror") printed and blackened out on inside front cover with Vol. 1, No. 1 printed over it. Evidently, several of No. 15 were printed before a decision was made not to drop the Vault of Horror and Haunt of Fear series. The print run was stopped on No. 15 and continued on No. 1. All of No. 15 were changed as described above.

	119.00	356.00	950.00
1	94.00	281.00	750.00
2	49.00	146.00	390.00
3-5: 3-Poe adaptation. 3-Old Witch stories begin	38.00	114.00	265.00
6-10	30.00	90.00	210.00
11,12,14,15: 15-The Old Witch guest stars	23.00	69.00	160.00
13,16-Williamson-a	26.00	77.00	180.00
17-Williamson/Frazetta-a (6 pgs.)	28.00	84.00	195.00
18,19: 19-Used in SOTI, pg. 235	19.00	58.00	135.00
20-Cover used in SOTI, illo "Cover of a children's comic book"			
	26.00	77.00	180.00
21,24-27: 24- "Food For Thought" similar to "Cave In" in Amazing Detective Cases #13 (1952)	13.50	41.00	95.00
22,23-Used in Senate investigation on juvenile delinquency. 22-Ax decapitation-c	20.00	60.00	140.00

NOTE: Craig a-1-21; c-1-18, 20-22. Crandall a-18-26. Davis a-4, 5, 7, 9-12, 20. Elder a-17,18. Evans a-15, 19, 21, 23, 25, 27; c-23, 24. Feldstein c-19. Ingels a-1-12, 14, 15, 27. Kamen a-2, 4-18, 20-27; c-25-27. Krigstein a-22, 24, 25, 27. Kurtzman a-1, 3. Orlando a-16, 22, 24, 26. Wood a-1, 3. Issues No. 11-15 have E.C. "quickie" stories. No. 25 contains the famous "Are You a Red Dupe?" editorial. Ray Bradbury adaptations-15, 17.

CRIME SUSPENSTORIES
Nov, 1992 - Present ($1.50/$2.00/$2.50)
Russ Cochran/Gemstone Publishing

1-3: 1,2-r/Crime SuspenStories #1,2			1.50
4-15-($2.00)		.80	2.00
16-20-($2.50)			2.50

CRIMINALS ON THE RUN (Formerly Young King Cole)

	GD25	FN65	NM94
(Crime Fighting Detective No. 11 on)			
V4#1, Aug-Sept, 1948 - #10, Dec-Jan, 1949-50			

Premium Group (Novelty Press)

V4#1-Young King Cole continues	23.00	69.00	160.00
2-6: 6-Dr. Doom app.	19.00	56.00	130.00
7-Classic "Fish in the Face" c by L. B. Cole	40.00	120.00	300.00
V5#1,2 (#8,9): 9-L. B. Cole-c	17.00	49.00	115.00
10-L. B. Cole-c	17.00	49.00	115.00

NOTE: Most issues have L. B. Cole covers. McWilliams a-V4#6, 7, V5#2; c-V4#5.

CRIMSON AVENGER, THE (See Detective Comics #20 for 1st app.)(Also see Leading Comics #1 & World's Best/Finest Comics)
June, 1988 - No. 4, Sept, 1988 ($1.00, limited series)
DC Comics

1-4		.50	1.00

CRISIS ON INFINITE EARTHS (Also see Official... Index)
Apr, 1985 - No. 12, Mar, 1986 (maxi-series)
DC Comics

1-1st DC app. Blue Beetle & Detective Karp from Charlton; Perez-c on all		1.60	4.00
2-6, 9-11: 6-Intro Charlton's Capt. Atom, Nightshade, Question, Judomaster, Peacemaker & Thunderbolt into DC Universe. 7-Double size; death of Supergirl 9-Intro. Charlton's Ghost into DC Universe. 10-Intro. Charlton's Banshee, Dr. Spectro, Image, Punch & Jewellee into DC Universe; Starman (Prince Gavyn) dies.		1.60	4.00
8-Death of Flash (Barry Allen)	1.00	2.00	5.00
12-(52 pgs.)-Deaths of Dove, Kole, Lori Lemaris, Sunburst, G.A. Robin & Huntress; Kid Flash becomes new Flash; 3rd & final DC app. of the 3 Lt. Marvels; Green Fury gets new look (becomes Green Flame in Infinity, Inc. #32)		1.60	4.00

CRITICAL MASS (See A Shadowline Saga: Critical Mass)

CRITTERS (Also see Usagi Yojimbo Summer Special)
1986 - No. 50, 1990 ($1.70/$2.00, B&W)
Fantagraphics Books

1-Cutey Bunny, Usagi Yojimbo app.		1.00	2.50
2-11: 3,6,7,10,11-Usagi Yojimbo app. 11-Christmas Special (68 pgs.); Usagi Yojimbo		.80	2.00
12-22,24-49: 14,38-Usagi Yojimbo app. 22-Watchmen parody; two diff. covers exist		.70	1.75
23-With Alan Moore Flexi-disc ($3.95)		1.60	4.00
50 ($4.95, 84 pgs.)-Neil the Horse, Capt. Jack, Sam & Max & Usagi Yojimbo app.; Quagmire, Shaw-a	1.00	2.00	5.00
Special 1 (1/88, $2.00)		.80	2.00

CROSLEY'S HOUSE OF FUN (Also see Tee and Vee Crosley...)
1950 (Giveaway, paper cover, 32 pgs.)
Crosley Div. AVCO Mfg. Corp.

nn-Strips revolve around Crosley appliances	4.35	13.00	26.00

CROSS
No. 0, Oct, 1995 - No. 6, Apr, 1995 ($2.95, limited series, mature)
Dark Horse Comics

0-6: Darrow-c & Vachss scripts in all		1.20	3.00

CROSS AND THE SWITCHBLADE, THE
1972 (35-49¢)
Spire Christian Comics (Fleming H. Revell Co.)

1-Some issues have nn			1.00

CROSSFIRE
1973 (39/49¢)
Spire Christian Comics (Fleming H. Revell Co.)

nn			1.00

CROSSFIRE (Also see DNAgents)

Crossfire #12 © ECL

Crossroads #3 © ECL

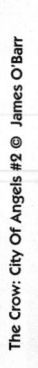
The Crow: City Of Angels #2 © James O'Barr

	GD25	FN65	NM94

5/84 - No. 17, 3/86; No. 18, 1/87 - No. 26, 2/88 ($1.50, Baxter paper)
Eclipse Comics

		GD25	FN65	NM94
1-17: 1-DNAgents x-over; Spiegle-c/a begins. 12-Dave Stevens-c.				
12,13-Death of Marilyn Monroe.				1.50
18-26-(B&W)			.70	1.80

CROSSFIRE AND RAINBOW (Also see DNAgents)
June, 1986 - No. 4, Sept, 1986 ($1.25, deluxe format)
Eclipse Comics

1-3: Spiegle-a		1.30
4-Dave Stevens-c	.80	2.00

CROSSING THE ROCKIES (See Classics Illustrated Special Issue)

CROSSROADS
July, 1988 - No. 5, Nov, 1988 ($3.25, limited series, deluxe format)
First Comics

1-5	1.20	3.25

CROW, THE (Also see Caliber Presents)
Feb, 1989 - No. 4, 1989 ($1.95, B&W, limited series)
Caliber Press

1-James O'Barr-c/a/scripts	11.00	33.00	75.00
1-3-2nd printing	1.70	5.00	12.00
2,4	5.70	17.00	40.00
2-3rd printing	1.65	4.20	10.00
3	6.00	18.00	42.00

CROW, THE
Jan, 1992 - No. 3, 1992 ($4.95, B&W, 68 pgs.)
Tundra Publishing, Ltd.

1-3: 1-r/#1,2 of Caliber series. 2-r/#3 of Caliber series w/new material. 3-All			
new material	1.70	5.00	12.00

CROW, THE
Jan, 1996 - No. 3, Mar, 1996 ($2.95, B&W, limited series)
Kitchen Sink Press

1-3: James O'Barr-c/scripts	1.20	3.00

CROW, THE: CITY OF ANGELS (Movie)
July, 1996 - No. 3, Sept, 1996 ($2.95, limited series)
Kitchen Sink Press

1-3: Adaptation of film; two-c (photo & illos.). 1-Vincent Perez interview		
	1.20	3.00

CROW, THE: FLESH AND BLOOD
May, 1996 - No. 3, July, 1996 ($2.95, limited series)
Kitchen Sink Press

1-3: O'Barr-c	1.20	3.00

CROWN COMICS
Winter, 1944-45; No. 2, Sum, 1945 - No. 19, July, 1949
Golfing/McCombs Publ.

1- "The Oblong Box" E.A. Poe adaptation	30.00	90.00	210.00
2,3-Baker-a; 3-Voodah by Baker	19.00	56.00	130.00
4-6-Baker-c/a; Voodah app. #4,5	20.00	60.00	140.00
7-Feldstein, Baker, Kamen-a; Baker-c	19.00	56.00	130.00
8-Baker-a; Voodah app.	17.00	51.00	120.00
9-11,13-19: Voodah in #10-19. 13-New logo	10.00	30.00	65.00
12-Master Marvin by Feldstein, Starr-a; Voodah-c	10.00	30.00	70.00

NOTE: *Bolle* a-11, 13-16, 18, 19; c-11p, 15. *Powell* a-19. *Starr* a-11-13; c-11i.

CRUCIBLE
Feb, 1993 - No. 6, July, 1993 ($1.25, limited series)
DC Comics (Impact Comics)

1-(99¢)-Quesada-c(p) & layouts begin; neon ink-c	1.00
2-6: 2-Last Quesada-c. 4-Last Quesada layouts	1.25

CRUSADER FROM MARS (See Tops in Adventure)
Jan-Mar, 1952 - No. 2, Fall, 1952 (Painted-c)
Ziff-Davis Publ. Co.

1-Cover is dated Spring	59.00	178.00	475.00
2-Bondage-c	48.00	144.00	385.00

CRUSADER RABBIT (TV)
No. 735, Oct, 1956 - No. 805, May, 1957
Dell Publishing Co.

Four Color 735 (#1)	29.00	87.00	290.00
Four Color 805	23.00	70.00	230.00

CRUSADERS, THE (Religious)
1974 - Vol. 16, 1985 (39/69¢, 36 pgs.)
Chick Publications

Vol.1-Operation Bucharest ('74). Vol.2-The Broken Cross ('74). Vol.3-Scarface		
('74). Vol.4-Exorcists ('75). Vol.5-Chaos ('75)		1.00
Vol.6-Primal Man? ('76)-(Disputes evolution theory). Vol.7-The Ark-(claims		
proof of existence, destroyed by Bolsheviks). Vol.8-The Gift-(Life story of		
Christ). Vol.9-Angel of Light-(Story of the Devil). Vol.10-Spellbound?-(Tells		
how rock music is Satanical & produced by witches). 11-Sabotage?. 12-		
Alberto. 13-Double Cross. 14-The Godfathers. (No. 6-14 low in distribution;		
loaded in religious propaganda.). 15-The Force. 16-The Four Horsemen		
		1.00

CRUSADERS (Southern Knights No. 2 on)
1982 (B&W, magazine size)
Guild Publications

1-1st app. Southern Knights	1.00	2.00	5.00

CRUSADERS, THE (Also see Black Hood, The Jaguar, The Comet, The Fly,
Legend of the Shield, The Mighty... & The Web)
May, 1992 - No. 8, Dec, 1992 ($1.00/$1.25)
DC Comics (Impact Comics)

1-Contains 3 Impact trading cards	1.25
2-8	1.00

CRUSH, THE
Jan, 1996 - No. 5, July, 1996 ($2.25, limited series)
Image Comics (Motown Machineworks)

1-5: Baron scripts	2.25

CRY FOR DAWN
1989 - No. 9 ($2.25, B&W, mature)
Cry For Dawn Pub.

1	29.00	86.00	200.00
1-2nd printing	14.00	43.00	100.00
1-3rd printing	11.00	33.00	75.00
2	18.00	54.00	125.00
2-2nd printing	5.00	15.00	35.00
3	11.00	33.00	75.00
4-6	6.50	19.50	45.00
5-2nd printing			
7-9	3.60	11.00	25.00
4-9-Signed & numbered editions	7.00	21.50	50.00
...Calender (1993)			47.00

CRYIN' LION COMICS
Fall, 1944 - No. 3, Spring, 1945
William H. Wise Co.

1-Funny animal	13.50	41.00	95.00
2-Hitler app.	11.00	33.00	75.00
3	10.00	30.00	60.00

CRYPT
Aug, 1995 - No.2, Oct. 1995 ($2.50, limited series)
Image Comics (Extreme Studios)

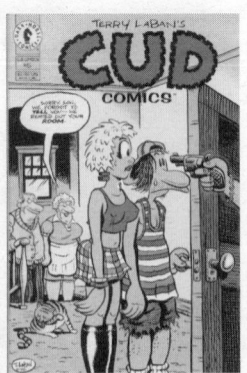

Cud Comics #5 © Terry LaBan

Curse of Spawn #1 © Todd McFarlane

Cyberforce #22 © Top Cow Productions

	GD25	FN65	NM94		GD25	FN65	NM94

1,2-Prophet app. — 1.00 — 2.50

CRYPT OF SHADOWS
Jan, 1973 - No. 21, Nov, 1975 (#1 & 2 are 20¢)
Marvel Comics Group

1-Wolverton-r/Advs. Into Terror #7 — 1.60 — 4.00
2-21: 2-Starlin/Everett-c — .80 — 2.00
NOTE: *Briefer* a-2r. *Ditko* a-13r, 18-20r. *Everett* a-6, 14r; c-2i. *Heath* a-1r. *Gil Kane* c-1, 6. *Mort Lawrence* a-1r, 8r. *Maneely* a-2r. *Moldoff* a-8. *Powell* a-12r, 14r. *Tuska* a-2r.

CRYPT OF TERROR (Formerly Crime Patrol; Tales From the Crypt No. 20 on)
No. 17, Apr-May, 1950 - No. 19, Aug-Sept, 1950
E. C. Comics

17-1st New Trend to hit stands — 238.00 — 712.00 — 1900.00
18,19 — 138.00 — 412.00 — 1100.00
NOTE: *Craig* c/a-17-19. *Feldstein* a-17-19. *Ingels* a-19. *Kurtzman* a-18. *Wood* a-18. Canadian reprints known; see Table of Contents.

CUD
Aug, 1992 - No. 8, Dec, 1994 ($2.25/$2.50/$2.75, B&W, mature)
Fantagraphics Books

1($2.25)-Terry LaBan scripts & art in all — 1.00 — 2.50
2-7 ($2.50): 6-1st Eno & Plum — 1.10 — 2.75
8 ($2.75) — 1.20 — 3.00

CUD COMICS
Jan, 1995 - Present ($2.95, B&W)
Dark Horse Comics

1-8: Terry LaBan-c/a/scripts. 5-Nudity; marijuana story
.60 — 1.20 — 3.00

CUPID
Dec, 1949 - No. 2, Mar, 1950
Marvel Comics (U.S.A.)

1-Photo-c — 11.00 — 33.00 — 75.00
2-Betty Page ('50s pin-up queen) photo-c; Powell-a (see My Love #4)
24.00 — 73.00 — 170.00

CURIO
1930's(?) (Tabloid size, 16-20 pgs.)
Harry 'A' Chesler

nn — 17.00 — 51.00 — 120.00

CURLY KAYOE COMICS (Boxing)
1946 - No. 8, 1950; Jan, 1958
United Features Syndicate/Dell Publ. Co.

1 (1946)-Strip-r (Fritzi Ritz); biography of Sam Leff, Kayoe's artist
14.00 — 43.00 — 100.00
2 — 8.35 — 25.00 — 50.00
3-8 — 5.85 — 17.50 — 35.00
United Presents...(Fall, 1948) — 5.00 — 15.00 — 30.00
Four Color 871 (Dell, 1/58) — 2.70 — 8.00 — 27.00

CURSE OF DREADWOLF
Sept, 1994 ($2.75, B&W)
Lightning Comics

1 — 1.10 — 2.75

CURSE OF RUNE (Becomes Rune, 2nd Series)
May, 1995 - No. 4, Aug, 1995 ($2.50, limited series)
Malibu Comics (Ultraverse)

1-4: 1-Two covers form one image — 1.00 — 2.50

CURSE OF THE SPAWN
Sept, 1996 - Present ($1.95)
Image Comics (Todd McFarlane Productions)

1-3: Dwayne Turner-a(p) — 2.00

CURSE OF THE WEIRD

Dec, 1993 - No. 4, Mar, 1994 ($1.25, limited series)(Pre-code horror-r)
Marvel Comics

1-4: 1,3,4-Wolverton-r(1-Eye of Doom; 3-Where Monsters Dwell; 4-The End of the World). 2-Orlando-r. 4-Zombie-r by Everett; painted-c — 1.25
NOTE: *Briefer* r-2. *Jack Davis* a-4r. *Ditko* a-1r, 2r, 4r; c-1r. *Everett* r-1. *Heath* r-1-3. *Kubert* r-3. *Wolverton* a-1r, 3r, 4r.

CUSTER'S LAST FIGHT
1950
Avon Periodicals

nn-Partial reprint of Cowpuncher #1 — 16.00 — 47.00 — 110.00

CUTEY BUNNY (See Army Surplus Komikz Featuring...)

CUTIE PIE
May, 1955 - No. 3, Dec, 1955; No. 4, Feb, 1956; No. 5, Aug, 1956
Junior Reader's Guild (Lev Gleason)

1 — 5.00 — 15.00 — 30.00
2-5: 4-Misdated 2/55 — 3.60 — 9.00 — 18.00

CUTTING EDGE
Dec, 1995 ($2.95)
Marvel Comics

1-Hulk-c/story; Messner-Loebs scripts — 1.20 — 3.00

CYBERCITY
Sept, 1995- Present ($2.95, bi-monthly)
CPM Comics

Part One #1,2 — 1.20 — 3.00
Part Two #1,2 — 1.20 — 3.00
Part Three #1,2 — 1.20 — 3.00

CYBERELLA
Sept, 1996 - Present ($2.25)(1st Helix series)
DC Comics (Helix)

1-6: Chaykin scripts & Cameron-a in all. 1,2-Chaykin-c. 3-5-Cameron-c/a
2.25

CYBERFORCE
Oct, 1992 - No. 4, 1993; No. 0, Sept, 1993 ($1.95, limited series)
Image Comics (Top Cow Productions)

1-Silvestri-c/a in all; coupon for Image Comics #0; 1st Top Cow Productions title. — 1.20 — 3.00 — 7.00
1-With coupon missing — .80 — 2.00
2-4: 2(3/93). 3-Pitt-c/story. 4-Codename: Stryke Force back-up (1st app.); foil-c — .80 — 2.00
0-(9/93)-Walt Simonson-c/a/scripts — 1.00 — 2.50

CYBERFORCE
V2#1, Nov, 1993 - Present ($1.95)
Image Comics (Top Cow Productions)/Top Cow Comics No. 28 on

V2#1-24: 1-7-Marc Silvestri/Keith Williams-c/a. 8-McFarlane-c/a. 10-Painted variant-c exists. 18-Variant-c exists. 23-Velocity-c. — .80 — 2.00
1-3: 1-Gold Logo-c. 2-Silver embossed-c. 3-Gold embossed-c — 10.00
1-(99¢, 3/96, 2nd printing) — 1.00
25-($3.95)-Wraparound, foil-c — 4.00
26-35: 26-Begin $2.50-c. 27-Quesada & Palmiotti's Ash app. 28-(11/96)-1st Top Cow Comics issue; Quesada & Palmiotti's Gabriel app. — 2.50
Annual 1 (3/95, $2.50) — 2.50
Annual 2 (8/96, $2.95) — 3.00
NOTE: Annuals read Volume One in the indica.

CYBERFORCE ORIGINS
Jan, 1995 - No. 3, Nov, 1995 ($2.50)
Image Comics (Top Cow Productions)

1-Cyblade (1/95) — 1.20 — 3.00 — 7.00
1-Cyblade (3/96, 99¢, 2nd printing) — 1.00
2-Stryker (2/95)-1st Mike Turner-a — 1.00 — 2.50

Cyberfrog #1 © Ethan Van Sciver

Cybernary #1 © Aegis Entertainment

Cyberpunx #1 © Rob Liefeld

DA

	GD25	FN65	NM94

	GD25	FN65	NM94
3-Impact		1.00	2.50

CYBERFORCE/STRYKEFORCE: OPPOSING FORCES (See Codename: Stryke Force #15)
Sept, 1995 - No.2, Oct, 1995 ($2.50, limited series)
Image Comics (Top Cow Productions)

1,2: 2-Stryker disbands Strykeforce.		1.00	2.50

CYBERFORCE UNIVERSE SOURCEBOOK
Aug, 1994/Feb, 1995 ($2.50)
Image Comics (Top Cow Productions)

1-Silvestri-c (8/94)		1.00	2.50
2-Silvestri-c (2/95)		1.00	2.50

CYBERFROG
June, 1994 - No. 2, Dec, 1994 ($2.50, B&W, limited series)
Hall of Heroes

1,2			2.50

CYBERFROG
Feb, 1996 - No. 3, Apr, 1996 ($2.95)
Harris Comics

1-3: Van Sciver-c/a/scripts. 2-Variant-c exists			3.00

CYBERFROG: RESERVOIR FROG
Sept, 1996 - No. 2, Oct, 1996 ($2.95, limited series)
Harris Comics

1,2: Van Sciver-c/a/scripts; wraparound-c			3.00

CYBERNARY (See Deathblow #1)
Nov, 1995 - No.5, Mar, 1996 ($2.50, limited series)
Image Comics (Wildstorm Productions)

1-5		1.00	2.50

CYBERPUNK
Sept, 1989 - No. 2, Oct, 1989 ($1.95, limited series, 28 pgs.)
Book 2, #1, May, 1990 - No. 2, 1990 ($2.25, 28 pgs.)
Innovation Publishing

1,2-Both have Ken Steacy painted-c (Adults)		.80	2.00
Book 2, #1,2		.90	2.30

CYBERPUNK: THE SERAPHIM FILES
Nov, 1990 - No. 2, Dec, 1990 ($2.50, 28 pgs., mature)
Innovation Publishing

1,2: 1-Painted-c; story cont'd from Seraphim		1.00	2.50

CYBERPUNX
Mar, 1996 ($2.50)
Image Comics (Extreme Studios)

1			2.50

CYBERRAD
1991 - No. 7, 1992 ($2.00)(Direct sale & newsstand-c variations)
V2#1 - V2#5, 1993? ($2.50/$2.00)
Continuity Comics

1-7: 5-Glow-in-the-dark-c by N. Adams (direct sale only). 6-Contains 4 pg. fold-out poster; N. Adams layouts		.80	2.00
V2#1-($2.95, direct sale ed.)-Die-cut-c w/B&W hologram on-c; Neal Adams sketches		1.20	3.00
V2#1-($2.50, newsstand ed.)-Without sketches		1.00	2.50
V2#2-5: 2-N. Adams-c		.80	2.00

CYBERRAD DEATHWATCH 2000 (Becomes CyberRad w/#2, 7/93)
Apr, 1993 - No. 2, 1993? ($2.50)
Continuity Comics

1,2: 1-Bagged w/2 cards; Adams-c & layouts & plots. 2-Bagged w/card; Adams scripts		1.00	2.50

CYBER 7

	GD25	FN65	NM94

Mar, 1989 - #7, Sept, 1989; V2#1, Oct, 1989 - #10, 1990 ($2.00, B&W)
Eclipse Comics

1-7: Stories translated from Japanese		.80	2.00
Book Two, #1-10		.80	2.00

CYBLADE/SHI (Also see Battle For The Independents & Shi/Cyblade: The Battle For The Independents)
1995 ($2.95, one-shot)
Image Comics (Top Cow Productions)

San Diego Preview			30.00
1-($2.95)-1st app. Witchblade	2.60	7.50	18.00
1-($2.95)-variant-c; Tucci-a	2.85	8.50	20.00

CYBRID
July, 1995 ($2.95)
Maximum Press

1		1.20	3.00

CYCLONE COMICS (Also see Whirlwind Comics)
June, 1940 - No. 5, Nov, 1940
Bilbara Publishing Co.

1-Origin Tornado Tom; Volton (the human generator), Tornado Tom, Kingdom of the Moon, Mister Q begin (1st app. of each)	106.00	318.00	850.00
2,3	57.00	172.00	460.00
4,5	47.00	141.00	375.00

CYCLOPS: RETRIBUTION
1994 ($5.95, trade paperback)
Marvel Comics

nn-r/Marvel Comics Presents #17-24	1.00	2.60	6.00

CYNDER
1995 - No. 3, 1996 ($2.50, B&W)
Immortelle Studios

1-3: 2-Tucci centerfold		1.00	2.50
Annual 1-(5/96, $2.95, color)			3.00

CYNDER/NIRA X
1996 ($2.95, one-shot)
Immortelle Studios

1-w/centerfold			3.00
1-Hughes variant-c.			3.00
1 (Gold)-Hughes-c.			10.00

CYNTHIA DOYLE, NURSE IN LOVE (Formerly Sweetheart Diary)
No. 66, Oct, 1962 - No. 74, Feb, 1964
Charlton Publications

66-74		.80	2.00	4.00

DAFFY (Daffy Duck No. 18 on)(See Looney Tunes)
#457, 3/53 - #30, 7-9/62; #31, 10-12/62 - #145, 1983 (No #132,133)
Dell Publishing Co./Gold Key No. 31-127/Whitman No. 128 on

Four Color 457(#1)-Elmer Fudd x-overs begin	9.00	27.00	90.00
Four Color 536,615('55)	4.50	13.50	45.00
4(1-3/56)-11('57)	2.70	8.00	27.00
12-19(1958-59)	2.00	6.00	18.00
20-40(1960-64)	1.50	3.75	9.00
41-60(1964-68)	1.00	2.00	5.00
61-90(1969-74)-Road Runner in most		1.40	3.50
91-131,134-145(1974-83)			1.75
Mini-Comic 1 (1976: 3-1/4x6-1/2")			1.00

NOTE: *Reprint issues-No.41-46, 48, 50, 53-55, 58, 59, 65, 67, 69, 73, 81, 96, 103-108; 136-142, 144, 145(1/3-2/3-r). (See March of Comics No. 277, 288, 303, 313, 331, 347, 357,375, 387, 397, 402, 413, 425, 437, 460).*

DAFFY TUNES COMICS
June, 1947; No. 12, Aug, 1947
Four-Star Publications

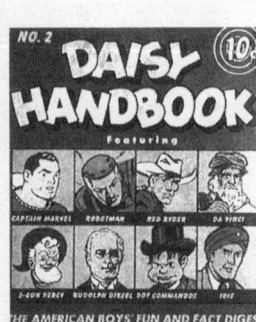

Daisy Handbook #2 © Daisy Manufacturing Co.

Dakkon Blackblade On The World Of Magic: The Gathering © Wizards of the Coast

Dale Evans #2 © DC

	GD25	FN65	NM94
nn	7.50	22.50	45.00
12-Al Fago-c/a; funny animal	6.35	19.00	38.00

DAGAR, DESERT HAWK (Captain Kidd No. 24 on; formerly All Great)
No. 14, Feb, 1948 - No. 23, Apr, 1949 (No #17,18)
Fox Features Syndicate

14-Tangi & Safari Cary begin; Good bondage-c/a	62.00	187.00	500.00
15,16-E. Good-a; 15-Bondage-c	40.00	120.00	300.00
19,20,22: 19-Used in SOTI, pg. 180 (Tangi)	37.00	111.00	260.00
21- "Bombs & Bums Away" panel in "Flood of Death" story used in SOTI	40.00	120.00	285.00
23-Bondage-a	39.00	118.00	275.00

NOTE: *Tangi by Kamen*-14-16, 19, 20; c-20, 21.

DAGAR THE INVINCIBLE (Tales of Sword & Sorcery...) (Also see Dan Curtis Giveaways & Gold Key Spotlight)
Oct, 1972 - No. 18, Dec, 1976; No. 19, Apr, 1982
Gold Key

1-Origin; intro. Villains Olstellon & Scor	1.70	5.00	12.00
2-5: 3-Intro. Graylin, Dagar's woman; Jarn x-over	1.00	2.50	6.00
6-1st Dark Gods story	1.00	2.00	5.00
7-10: 9-Intro. Torgus. 10-1st Three Witches story		1.60	4.00
11-18: 13-Durak & Torgus x-over; story continues in Dr. Spektor #15. 14-Dagar's origin retold. 18-Origin retold		1.00	2.50
19-Origin-r/#18			1.20

NOTE: *Durak app. in 7, 12, 13. Tragg app. in 5, 11.*

DAGWOOD (Chic Young's) (Also see Blondie Comics)
Sept, 1950 - No. 140, Nov, 1965
Harvey Publications

1	10.00	30.00	90.00
2	5.00	15.00	45.00
3-10	4.00	12.00	36.00
11-20	3.00	9.00	27.00
21-30	2.20	7.50	22.00
31-50	2.00	9.00	18.00
51-70	1.80	4.50	16.00
71-100	1.50	3.75	9.00
101-128,130,135	1.20	3.00	7.00
129,131-134,136-140-All are 68-pg. issues	1.50	3.75	9.00

NOTE: *Popeye and other one page strips appeared in early issues.*

DAGWOOD SPLITS THE ATOM (Also see Topix V8#4)
1949 (Science comic with King Features characters) (Giveaway)
King Features Syndicate

nn-Half comic, half text; Popeye, Olive Oyl, Henry, Mandrake, Little King, Katzenjammer Kids app.	4.00	12.00	36.00

DAI KAMIKAZE!
June, 1987 - No. 12, Aug, 1988 ($1.75)
Now Comics

1-12: 1st app. Speed Racer; 2nd print exists		.70	1.80

DAISY AND DONALD (See Walt Disney Showcase No. 8)
May, 1973 - No. 59, 1984 (no No. 48)
Gold Key/Whitman No. 42 on

1-Barks-r/WDC&S #280,308	3.20	8.00	16.00
2-5: 4-Barks-r/WDC&S #224	1.30	3.25	8.00
6-10	1.00	2.00	5.00
11-20		1.60	4.00
21-47,49,50: 32-r/WDC&S #308. 50-r/#3		1.20	3.00
51-Barks-r/4-Color #1150		1.20	3.00
52-59: 52-r/#2. 55-r/#5			1.50

DAISY & HER PUPS (Blondie's Dogs)(Formerly Blondie Comics #20)
No. 21, 7/51 - No. 27, 7/52; No. 8, 9/52 - No. 25, 7/55
Harvey Publications

	GD25	FN65	NM94
21-27 (#1-7): 26,27 have No. 6 & 7 on cover but No. 26 & 27 on inside	1.50	4.50	12.00
8-25: 19-25-Exist?	1.150	3.50	10.00

DAISY COMICS
Dec, 1936 (5-1/4x7-1/2")
Eastern Color Printing Co.

nn-Joe Palooka, Buck Rogers (2 pgs. from Famous Funnies No. 18), Napoleon Flying to Fame, Butty & Fally	31.00	94.00	220.00

DAISY DUCK & UNCLE SCROOGE PICNIC TIME (See Dell Giant #33)

DAISY DUCK & UNCLE SCROOGE SHOW BOAT (See Dell Giant #55)

DAISY DUCK'S DIARY (See Dynabrite Comics, & Walt Disney's C&S #298)
No. 600, Nov, 1954 - No. 1247, Dec-Fef, 1961-62 (Disney)
Dell Publishing Co.

Four Color 600 (#1)	6.00	18.00	60.00
Four Color 659, 743 (11/56)	5.00	15.00	50.00
Four Color 858 (11/57), 948 (11/58), 1247 (12-2/61-62)	4.00	12.00	40.00
Four Color 1055 (11-1/59-60), 1150 (12-1/60-61)-By Carl Barks	10.00	30.00	100.00

DAISY HANDBOOK
1946; No. 2, 1948 (10¢, pocket-size, 132 pgs.)
Daisy Manufacturing Co.

1-Buck Rogers, Red Ryder; Wolverton-a(2 pgs.)	38.00	114.00	265.00
2-Captain Marvel & Ibis the Invincible, Red Ryder, Boy Commandos & Robotman; Wolverton-a (2 pgs.); contains 8 pg. color catalog	38.00	114.00	265.00

DAISY LOW OF THE GIRL SCOUTS
1954, 1965 (16 pgs., paper-c)
Girl Scouts of America

1954-Story of Juliette Gordon Low	4.00	10.00	20.00
1965	1.60	4.00	8.00

DAISY MAE (See Oxydol-Dreft)

DAISY'S RED RYDER GUN BOOK
1955 (25¢, pocket-size, 132 pgs.)
Daisy Manufacturing Co.

nn-Boy Commandos, Red Ryder; 1pg. Wolverton-a	25.00	75.00	175.00

DAKKON BLACKBLADE ON THE WORLD OF MAGIC: THE GATHERING
June, 1996 ($5.95, one-shot)
Acclaim Comics (Armada)

1-Jerry Prosser scripts; Rags Morales-c/a.			6.00

DAKOTA LIL (See Fawcett Movie Comics)

DAKOTA NORTH
June, 1986 - No. 5, Feb, 1987
Marvel Comics Group

1-5			1.00

DAKTARI (Ivan Tors) (TV)
July, 1967 - No. 3, Oct, 1968; No. 4, Sept, 1969 (All have photo-c)
Dell Publishing Co.

1	3.25	9.50	22.00
2-4	2.15	6.50	15.00

DALE EVANS COMICS (Also see Queen of the West...)
Sept-Oct, 1948 - No. 24, July-Aug, 1952 (No. 1-19: 52 pgs.)
National Periodical Publications

1-Dale Evans & her horse Buttermilk begin; Sierra Smith begins by Alex Toth	87.00	262.00	700.00
2-Alex Toth-a	40.00	120.00	325.00

Damage #0 © DC

Damage Control #4 © MEG

Danger Trail #4 © DC

DA

	GD25	FN65	NM94

	GD25	FN65	NM94
3-11-Alex Toth-a	29.00	86.00	200.00
12-24: 12-Target-c	13.50	41.00	95.00

NOTE: Photo-c-1, 2, 4-14.

DALGODA
Aug, 1984 - No. 8, Feb, 1986 (High quality paper)
Fantagraphics Books

1-($2.25); Fujitake-c/a in all		.90	2.25
2-8-($1.50). 2,3-Debut Grimwood's Daughter. 8-Alan Moore story			1.50

DALTON BOYS, THE
1951
Avon Periodicals

1-(Number on spine)-Kinstler-c	14.00	43.00	100.00

DAMAGE
Apr, 1994 - No. 20, Jan, 1996 ($1.75/$1.95)
DC Comics

1-4			.70	1.75
5,6,0,7-12: 5-Begin $1.95-c. 6-(9/94)-Zero Hour. 0-(10/94). 7-(11/94)			.80	2.00
13-20: 13-Begin $2.25-c. 14-Ray app.			.90	2.25

DAMAGE CONTROL (See Marvel Comics Presents #19)
5/89 - No. 4, 8/89, V2#1, 12/89 - No. 4, 2/90 ($1.00)
V3#1, 6/91 - No. 4, 9/91 ($1.25, all are limited series)
Marvel Comics

V1#1-4,V2#1,3: V1#4-Wolverine app.	1.00
V2#2,4-Punisher app.	1.00
V3#1-4: 1-Spider-Man app. 2-New Warriors app. 3,4-Silver Surfer app.	
4-Infinity Gauntlet parody	1.25

DANCES WITH DEMONS (See Marvel Frontier Comics Unlimited)
Sept, 1993 - No. 4, Dec, 1993 ($1.95, limited series)
Marvel Frontier Comics

1-($2.95)-Foil embossed-c	1.20	3.00
2-4	.80	2.00

DAN CURTIS GIVEAWAYS
1974 (3x6", 24 pgs., reprints)
Western Publishing Co.

1-Dark Shadows, 2-Star Trek, 3-The Twilight Zone, 4-Ripley's Believe It or Not!, 5-Turok, Son of Stone (partial-r/Turok #78), 6-Star Trek, 7-The Occult Files of Dr. Spektor, 8-Dagar the Invincible, 9-Grimm's Ghost Stories

Set-	3.00	9.00	30.00

DANDEE
1947
Four Star Publications

nn	5.85	17.50	35.00

DAN DUNN (See Crackajack Funnies, Detective Dan, Famous Feature Stories & Red Ryder)

DANDY COMICS (Also see Happy Jack Howard)
Spring, 1947 - No. 7, Spring, 1948
E. C. Comics

1-Funny animal; Vince Fago-a in all; Dandy in all	30.00	90.00	210.00
2	23.00	69.00	160.00
3-7: 3-Intro Handy Andy who is c-feature #3 on	17.00	49.00	115.00

DANGER
Jan, 1953 - No. 11, Aug, 1954
Comic Media/Allen Hardy Assoc.

1-Heck-c/a	13.00	39.00	90.00
2,3,5,7,9-11:	7.50	22.50	45.00
6- "Narcotics" story; begin spy theme	8.35	25.00	50.00
4-Marijuana cover/story	10.00	30.00	60.00
8-Bondage/torture/headlights panels	10.00	30.00	70.00

NOTE: Morisi a-2, 5, 6(3), 10; c-2. Contains some reprints from Danger & Dynamite.

DANGER (Jim Bowie No. 15 on) (Formerly Comic Media title)
No. 12, June, 1955 - No. 14, Oct, 1955
Charlton Comics Group

12(#1)	7.50	22.50	45.00
13,14: 14-r/#12	5.85	17.50	35.00

DANGER
1964
Super Comics

Super Reprint #10-12 (Black Dwarf; #10-r/Great Comics #1 by Novack. #11-r/Johnny Danger #1. #12-r/Red Seal #14), #15-r/Spy Cases #26. #16-Unpublished Chesler material (Yankee Girl), #17-r/Scoop #8 (Capt. Courage & Enchanted Dagger), #18(nd)-r/Guns Against Gangsters #5 (Gun-Master, Annie Oakley, The Chameleon; L.B. Cole-r).

	1.50	3.75	9.00

DANGER AND ADVENTURE (Formerly This Magazine Is Haunted; Robin Hood and His Merry Men No. 28 on)
No. 22, Feb, 1955 - No. 27, Feb, 1956
Charlton Comics

22-Ibis the Invincible-c/story; Nyoka app.; last pre-code issue; Ditko-a in all	10.00	30.00	65.00
23-Lance O'Casey-c/story; Nyoka app.	10.00	30.00	65.00
24-27: 24-Mike Danger & Johnny Adventure begin	6.35	19.00	38.00

DANGER IS OUR BUSINESS!
1953(Dec.) - No. 10, June, 1955
Toby Press

1-Captain Comet by Williamson/Frazetta, 6 pgs. (science fiction)	40.00	120.00	300.00
2	10.00	30.00	65.00
3-10	9.15	27.00	55.00
I.W. Reprint #9('64)-Williamson/Frazetta-r/#1; Kinstler-c			
	10.00	30.00	65.00

DANGER IS THEIR BUSINESS (Also see A-1 Comic)
No. 50, 1952
Magazine Enterprises

A-1 50-Powell-a	11.00	33.00	75.00

DANGER MAN (TV)
No. 1231, Sept-Nov, 1961
Dell Publishing Co.

Four Color 1231-Patrick McGoohan photo-c	10.00	30.00	100.00

DANGER TRAIL (Also see Showcase #50, 51)
July-Aug, 1950 - No. 5, Mar-Apr, 1951 (52 pgs.)
National Periodical Publications

1-King Faraday begins, ends #4; Toth-a in all	96.00	290.00	775.00
2	71.00	215.00	575.00
3-(Rare) one of the rarest early '50s DCs	96.00	290.00	775.00
4,5: 5-Johnny Peril-c/story (moves to Sensation Comics #107); new logo	59.00	178.00	475.00

DANGER TRAIL
Apr, 1993 - No. 4, July, 1993 ($1.50, limited series)
DC Comics

1-4: Gulacy-c on all			1.50

DANGER UNLIMITED (See San Diego Comic Con Comics #2 & Torch of Liberty Special)
Feb, 1994 - No. 4, May, 1994 ($2.00, limited series)
Dark Horse Comics (Legend)

1-4: Byrne-c/a/scripts in all; origin stories of both original team (Doc Danger, Thermal, Miss Mirage, & Hunk) & future team (Thermal, Belebet, & Caucus).
1-Intro Torch of Liberty & Golgotha (cameo) in back-up story. 4-Hellboy & Torch of Liberty cameo in lead story.
		.80	2.00
Trade paperback (1995, $14.95)-r/#1-4; includes last pg. originally cut from #4

Daredevil #7 © MEG

Daredevil #156 © MEG

Daredevil #191 © MEG

	GD25	FN65	NM94
			15.00

DAN HASTINGS (See Syndicate Features)

DANIEL BOONE (See The Exploits of…, Fighting… Frontier Scout…,The Legends of… & March of Comics No. 306)
No. 1163, Mar-May, 1961
Dell Publishing Co.

	GD25	FN65	NM94
Four Color 1163-Marsh-a	6.00	18.00	60.00

DAN'L BOONE
Sept, 1955 - No. 8, Sept, 1957
Sussex Publ. Co.

1	14.00	43.00	100.00
2	9.15	27.00	55.00
3-8	6.70	20.00	40.00

DANIEL BOONE (TV) (See March of Comics No. 306)
Jan, 1965 - No. 15, Apr, 1969 (All have Fess Parker photo-c)
Gold Key

1	8.00	24.00	80.00
2	4.00	12.00	40.00
3-5	3.60	11.00	25.00
6-15	2.30	6.75	16.00

DANNY BLAZE (…Firefighter) (Nature Boy No. 3 on)
Aug, 1955 - No. 2, Oct, 1955
Charlton Comics

1,2	6.70	20.00	40.00

DANNY DINGLE (See Sparkler Comics)
No. 17, 1940
United Features Syndicate

Single Series 17	21.00	64.00	150.00

DANNY KAYE'S BAND FUN BOOK
1959 (Giveaway)
H & A Selmer

nn	5.85	17.50	35.00

DANNY THOMAS SHOW, THE (TV)
No. 1180, Apr-June, 1961 - No. 1249, Dec-Feb, 1961-62
Dell Publishing Co.

Four Color 1180-Toth-a, photo-c	15.00	45.00	153.00
Four Color 1249-Manning-a, photo-c	15.00	45.00	153.00

DARBY O'GILL & THE LITTLE PEOPLE (Movie)(See Movie Comics)
1959 (Disney)
Dell Publishing Co.

Four Color 1024-Toth-a; photo-c.	11.00	33.00	110.00

DAREDEVIL (…& the Black Widow #92-107 on-c only; see Giant-Size…,Marvel Advs., Marvel Graphic Novel #24, Marvel Super Heroes, '66 & Spider-Man &…)
Apr, 1964 - Present
Marvel Comics Group

	GD25	FN65	VF82	NM94
1-Origin/1st app. Daredevil; reprinted in Marvel Super Heroes #1 (1966); death of Battling Murdock; intro Foggy Nelson & Karen Page; Everett-c/a	180.00	540.00	1170.00	1800.00

	GD25	FN65		NM94
2-Fantastic Four cameo; 2nd app. Electro (Spidey villain); Thing guest star;	59.00	178.00		510.00
3-Origin & 1st app. The Owl (villain)	40.00	120.00		345.00
4	40.00	120.00		320.00
5-Minor costume change; Wood-a begins	29.00	86.00		215.00
6,8-10: 8-Origin/1st app. Stilt-Man	21.00	62.00		155.00
7-Daredevil battles Sub-Mariner & dons new red costume (4/65)	34.00	101.00		250.00
11-15: 12-Romita's 1st work at Marvel; 1st app. Plunderer; Ka-Zar app.				

	GD25	FN65	NM94
13-Facts about Ka-Zar's origin; Kirby-a	10.00	30.00	75.00
16,17-Spider-Man x-over. 16-1st Romita-a on Spider-Man (5/66)	12.00	36.00	90.00
18-20: 18-Origin & 1st app. Gladiator	7.00	21.50	54.00
21-26,28-30: 24-Ka-Zar app.	5.00	15.00	38.00
27-Spider-Man x-over	5.50	16.50	40.00
31-40: 38-Fantastic Four x-over; cont'd in F.F. #73. 39-1st Exterminator (later becomes Death-Stalker)	3.75	11.25	28.00
41-49: 41-Death Mike Murdock. 42-1st app. Jester. 43-Daredevil battles Captain America; origin partially retold. 45-Statue of Liberty photo-c	2.85	8.50	20.00
50-52-B. Smith-a	3.25	9.50	22.00
53-Origin retold; last 12¢ issue	3.40	10.00	24.00
54-56,58-60: 54-Spider-Man cameo. 56-1st app. Death's Head (9/69); story cont'd in #57 (not same as new Death's Head)	1.65	4.70	11.00
57-Reveals i.d. to Karen Page; Death's Head app.	1.70	5.00	12.00
61-99: 79-Stan Lee cameo. 81-Oversize issue; Black Widow begins (11/71). 83-B. Smith layouts/Weiss-p. 87-Electro-c/story	1.65	4.20	10.00
100-Origin retold	3.60	11.00	25.00
101-104,106,108-113,115-120: 113-1st app. Deathstalker (cameo)	1.20	3.00	7.00
105-Origin Moondragon by Starlin (12/73); Thanos cameo in flashback (early app.)	1.65	4.20	10.00
107-Starlin-c; Thanos cameo	1.00	2.60	6.00
114-1st full app. Deathstalker	1.20	3.00	7.00
121-130,133-137: 124-1st app. Copperhead; Black Widow leaves. 126-1st new Torpedo		1.60	4.00
131-Origin/1st app. new Bullseye (see Nick Fury #15)	3.60	11.00	25.00
132-Bullseye app.	1.00	2.60	6.00
138-Ghost Rider-c/story; Death's Head is reincarnated; Byrne-a	1.65	4.20	10.00
139-157: 142-Nova cameo. 146-Bullseye app. 148-(30 & 35¢ issues exist). 150-1st app. Paladin. 151-Reveals i.d. to Heather Glenn. 155-Black Widow returns. 156-The 1960s Daredevil cameo.		1.60	4.00
158-Frank Miller art begins (5/79); origin/death of Deathstalker (see Captain America #235 & Spectacular Spider-Man #27	5.70	17.00	40.00
159	2.60	7.50	18.00
160,161	1.30	3.00	8.00
162-Ditko-a; no Miller-a		1.20	3.00
163,164: 163-Hulk cameo. 164-Origin retold	1.20	2.90	7.00
165-167,170	1.00	2.60	6.00
168-Origin/1st app. Elektra	3.90	11.50	27.00
169-Elektra app.	1.30	3.25	8.00
171-175: 174,175-Elektra app.	1.00	2.00	5.00
176-180-Elektra app. 178-Cage app. 179-Anti-smoking issue mentioned in the Congressional Record		1.60	4.00
181-184: 181-(52 pgs.)-Death of Elektra; Punisher cameo out of costume 182-184-Punisher app. by Miller (drug issues)	1.30	3.25	8.00
185-191: 187-New Black Widow. 189-Death of Stick. 190-($1.00, 52 pgs.)-Elektra returns, part origin. 191-Last Miller Daredevil		1.20	3.00
192-195,197-210: 197,200-Bullseye app. 208-Harlan Ellison scripts borrowed from Avengers TV episode "House that Jack Built"			1.75
196-Wolverine app.	1.65	4.20	10.00
211-225: 219-Miller-c & story.			1.25
226-Frank Miller plots begin		.90	2.25
227-Miller scripts begin		1.60	4.00
228-233-Last Miller scripts		1.20	3.00
234-237,239,240,242-247			1.25
238-Mutant Massacre; Sabretooth app.	1.20	3.00	7.00
241-Todd McFarlane-a(p)		1.60	4.00
248,249-Wolverine app.	1.00	2.00	5.00
250,251,253,256,258: 250-1st app. Bullet. 258-Intro The Bengal (a villain)			1.25

Daredevil #358 © MEG

Daredevil #32 © LEV

Daredevil: The Man Without Fear #4 © MEG

	GD25	FN65	NM94
252-(52 pgs.); Fall of the Mutants		1.20	3.00
254-Origin & 1st app. Typhoid Mary (5/88)	1.65	4.20	10.00
255-2nd app. Typhoid Mary	1.00	2.00	5.00
256-3rd app. Typhoid Mary		1.60	4.00
257-Punisher app. (x-over w/Punisher #10)	1.65	4.20	10.00
259,260-Typhoid Mary app. 260-(52 pgs.)		1.20	3.00
261-291,294,296-299: 270-1st app. Black Heart. 272-Intro Shotgun (villain). 282-Silver Surfer app. (cameo in #281). 283-Capt. America app. 297-Typhoid Mary app.; Kingpin storyline begins. 299-Last $1.00-c			1.25
292,293,295: 293-Punisher app. 292-D. G. Chichester scripts begin. 295-Ghost Rider app.		.80	2.00
300-($2.00, 52 pgs.)-Kingpin story ends		1.00	2.50
301-318: 301-303-Re-intro the Owl. 304-Garney-c/a. 305,306-Spider-Man-c. 309-Punisher-c; Terror app. 310-Calypso-c.			1.25
319-Prologue to Fall From Grace; Elektra returns	1.00	2.00	5.00
319-2nd printing w/black-c			1.25
320-Fall From Grace Pt 1	1.00	2.00	5.00
321-Fall From Grace regular ed.; Pt 2; new costume; Venom app.		.80	2.00
321-($2.00)-Wraparound Glow-in-the-dark-c ed.		1.60	4.00
322-Fall From Grace Pt 3; Eddie Brock app.		1.60	4.00
323,324-Fall From Grace Pt. 4 & 5: 323-Vs. Venom-c/story. 324-Morbius-c/story		.70	1.75
325-($2.50, 52 pgs.)-Fall From Grace ends; contains bound-in poster		1.00	2.50
326,327: 326-New logo			1.25
328-343: 328-$1.50-c begins; bound-in trading card sheet. 330-Gambit app.			1.50
344-349, 351-353: 344-Begin $1.95-c. 348-1st Cary Nord art in DD (1/96); "Dec" on-c. 353-Karl Kesel scripts; Nord-c/a begins; Mr. Hyde-c/app.			2.00
350-($2.95)-Double-sized			2.00
350-($3.50)-Double-sized; gold ink-c			3.00
354-368: Kesel scripts, Nord-c/a in all. 354-$1.50-c begins. 355-Larry Hama layouts; Pyro app. 358-Mysterio-c/app. 359-Absorbing Man cameo			1.50
Special 1(9/67, 25¢, 68 pgs.)-New art/story	4.50	14.00	32.00
Special 2,3: 2(2/71, 25¢, 52 pgs.)-Entire book has Powell/Wood-r; Wood-c. 3(1/72)-Reprints	2.00	6.00	14.00
Annual 4(10/76)	.90	2.00	5.50
Annual 4(#5)(1989, $2.00, 68 pgs.)-Atlantis Attacks	1.00	2.00	5.50
Annual 6(1990, $2.00, 68 pgs.)-Sutton-a		.80	2.00
Annual 7(1991, $2.00, 68 pgs.)-Guice-a (7 pgs.)		.80	2.00
Annual 8(1992, $2.25, 68 pgs.)-Deathlok-c/story		.90	2.25
Annual 9(1993, $2.95, 68 pgs.)-Polybagged w/card		1.20	3.00
Annual 10(1994, $2.95, 68 pgs.)		1.20	3.00
.../PUNISHER TPB (1988, $4.95)-r/D.D. #182-184	1.00	2.00	5.00
.../PUNISHER TPB, 2nd & 3rd printings	1.00	2.00	5.00
...:FALL FROM GRACE TPB ($19.95)-r #319-325			20.00
...VS. VAPORA 1(Engineering Show Giveaway, 1993, 16 pg.)-Intro Vapora			1.25

NOTE: **Art Adams** c-238p, 239. **Austin** a-191i; c-151i, 200i. **John Buscema** a-136, 137p, 234p, 235p; c-86p, 136i, 137p, 142, 219. **Byrne** a-200p, 201, 203, 223. **Capullo** a-286p. **Colan** a(p)-20-49, 53-82, 84-98, 100, 110, 112, 124, 153, 154, 156, 157, Spec. 1p; c(p)-20-42, 44-49, 53-60, 71, 92, 98, 138, 153, 154, 156, 157, Annual 1. **Craig** a-50i, 52i. **Ditko** a-162, 234p, 235p, 264p; c-162. **Everett** c/a-1i; inks-21, 83. **Garney** c/a-304. **Gil Kane** a-141p, 146-148p, 151p; c(p)-85, 90, 91, 93, 94, 115, 116, 119, 120, 125-128, 133, 139, 147, 152. **Kirby** c-2-4, 5p, 12p, 13p, 43, 136p. **Layton** c-207, 208. **Miller** scripts-168-182, 183(part), 184-191, 219, 227-233; a-158-161p, 163-184p, 191p; c-158-161p, 163-184p, 185-189, 190p, 191. **Orlando** a-2-4p. **Powell** a-9p, 11p, Special 1r. **Simonson** c-199, 236p. **B. Smith** a-236p; c-51p, 52p. **Starlin** a-105p. **Steranko** c-44i. **Tuska** a-39i, 145p. **Williamson** a(i)-237, 239, 240, 243, 248-257, 259-263, 283(part), 284, 285, 287, 288(part), 289(part), 293-300; c(i)-237, 243, 244, 248-257, 259-263, 265-278, 280-289, Annual 8. **Wood** a-5-8, 9, 10, 11i, Spec. 2i; c(i)-5, 6-11, 164i.

DAREDEVIL COMICS (See Silver Streak Comics)
July, 1941 - No. 134, Sept, 1956 (Charles Biro stories)

Lev Gleason Publications (Funnies, Inc. No. 1)

	GD25	FN65	VF82	NM94
1-No. 1 titled "Daredevil Battles Hitler"; The Silver Streak, Lance Hale, Cloud Curtis, Dickey Dean, Pirate Prince team up w/Daredevil and battle Hitler; Daredevil battles the Claw; Origin of Hitler feature story. Hitler photo app. on-c	889.00	2667.00	5333.00	8500.00

(Estimated up to 215 total copies exist, 12 in NM/Mint)

	GD25	FN65		NM94
2-London, Pat Patriot (by Reed Crandall), Nightro, Real American No. 1 (by Briefer #2-11), Dickie Dean, Pirate Prince, & Times Square begin; intro. & only app. The Pioneer, Champion of America	288.00	862.00		2300.00
3-Origin of 13	162.00	487.00		1300.00
4	143.00	431.00		1150.00
5-Intro. Sniffer & Jinx; Ghost vs. Claw begins by Bob Wood, ends #20	115.00	346.00		925.00
6-(#7 in indicia)	96.00	290.00		775.00
7-10: 8-Nightro ends	82.00	247.00		660.00
11-London, Pat Patriot end; classic bondage/torture-c	87.00	262.00		700.00
12-Origin of The Claw; Scoop Scuttle by Wolverton begins (2 pgs.), ends #22, not in #21	125.00	375.00		1000.00
13-Intro. Little Wise Guys (10/42)	112.00	338.00		900.00
14	56.00	168.00		450.00
15-Death of Meatball	83.00	251.00		670.00
16,17	52.00	157.00		420.00
18-New origin of Daredevil (not same as Silver Streak #6)	115.00	346.00		925.00
19,20	45.00	135.00		360.00
21-Reprints cover of Silver Streak #6 (on inside) plus intro. of The Claw from Silver Streak #1	75.00	225.00		600.00
22-30: 27-Bondage/torture-c	37.00	111.00		260.00
31-Death of The Claw	68.00	206.00		550.00
32-37,39,41: 35-Two Daredevil stories begin, end #68 (35-41 are 64 pgs.	25.00	75.00		175.00
38-Origin Daredevil retold from #18	40.00	120.00		300.00
42-50: 42-Intro. Kilroy in Daredevil; 1 panel Steranko-a	20.00	60.00		140.00
51-69-Last Daredevil issue (12/50)	14.00	43.00		100.00
70-Little Wise Guys take over book; McWilliams-a; Hot Rock Flanagan begins, ends #80	11.00	33.00		75.00
71-79,81: 79-Daredevil returns	10.00	30.00		60.00
80-Daredevil x-over	10.00	30.00		65.00
82,90-One pg. Frazetta ad in both	10.00	30.00		60.00
83-89,91-99,101-134	8.35	25.00		50.00
100	14.00	30.00		60.00

NOTE: **Wolverton's** Scoop Scuttle-12-20, 22. **Biro** c/a-all? **Bolle** a-125. **Maurer** a-75. **McWilliams** a-73, 75, 79, 80.

DAREDEVIL THE MAN WITHOUT FEAR
Oct, 1993 - No. 5, Feb, 1994 ($2.95, limited series)(foil embossed covers)
Marvel Comics

		GD25	FN65	NM94
1-5: Miller scripts; Romita, Jr./Williamson-c/a			1.60	4.00
Hardcover				100.00
Trade paperback				20.00

DARING ADVENTURES (Also see Approved Comics)
Nov, 1953 (25¢, 3-D, came w/glasses)
St. John Publishing Co.

	GD25	FN65	NM94
1 (3-D)-Reprints lead story from Son of Sinbad #1 by Kubert	35.00	105.00	245.00

DARING ADVENTURES
1963 - 1964
I.W. Enterprises/Super Comics

	GD25	FN65	NM94
I. W. Reprint #8-r/Fight Comics #53; Matt Baker-a	6.70	20.00	40.00
I.W. Reprint #9-r/Blue Bolt #115; Disbrow-a(3)	6.70	20.00	40.00

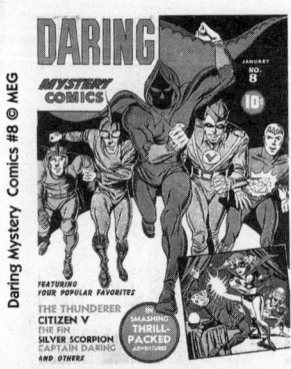

Daring Mystery Comics #8 © MEG

Darkchylde #1 © Randy Queen

Dark Dominion #9 © EEP

	GD25	FN65	NM94
Super Reprint #10,11('63)-r/Dynamic #24,16; 11-Marijuana story; Yankee Boy app.; Mac Raboy-a	2.85	8.50	20.00
Super Reprint #12('64)-Phantom Lady from Fox (r/#14 only? w/splash pg. omitted); Matt Baker-a	14.00	43.00	100.00
Super Reprint #15('64)-r/Hooded Menace #1	8.00	23.50	60.00
Super Reprint #16('64)-r/Dynamic #12	2.30	6.70	16.00
Super Reprint #17('64)-r/Green Lama #3 by Raboy	4.30	13.00	30.00
Super Reprint #18-Origin Atlas from unpublished Atlas Comics #1	3.25	9.50	22.00

DARING COMICS (Formerly Daring Mystery) (Jeanie Comics No. 13 on)
No. 9, Fall, 1944 - No. 12, Fall, 1945
Timely Comics (HPC)

9-Human Torch, Toro & Sub-Mariner begin	103.00	309.00	825.00
10-The Angel only app.	89.00	268.00	715.00
11,12-The Destroyer app.	89.00	268.00	715.00

NOTE: *Schomburg c-9-11. Sekowsky c-12? Human Torch, Toro & Sub-Mariner c-9-12.*

DARING CONFESSIONS (Formerly Youthful Hearts)
No. 4, 11/52 - No. 7, 5/53; No. 8, 10/53
Youthful Magazines

4-Doug Wildey-a; Tony Curtis story	10.00	30.00	70.00
5-8-Ray Anthony photo on-c. 6,8-Wildey-a	8.35	25.00	50.00

DARING LOVE (Radiant Love No. 2 on)
Sept-Oct, 1953
Gilmor Magazines

1—Steve Ditko's 1st published work (1st drawn was Fantastic Fears #5)(Also See Black Magic #27)(scarce)	29.00	86.00	200.00

DARING LOVE (Formerly Youthful Romances)
No. 15, 12/52; No. 16, 2/53-c, 4/53-Indicia; No. 17-4/53-c & indicia
Ribage/Pix

15	8.70	26.00	52.00
16,17: 17-Photo-c	7.00	21.00	42.00

NOTE: *Colletta a-15. Wildey a-17.*

DARING LOVE STORIES (See Fox Giants)

DARING MYSTERY COMICS (Comedy Comics No. 9 on; title changed to Daring Comics with No. 9)
1/40 - No. 5, 6/40; No. 6, 9/40; No. 7, 4/41 - No. 8, 1/42
Timely Comics (TPI 1-6/TCI 7,8)

	GD25	FN65	VF82	NM94
1-Origin The Fiery Mask (1st app.) by Joe Simon; Monako, Prince of Magic (1st app.), John Steele, Soldier of Fortune (1st app.), Doc Doyle (1st app.) begin; Flash Foster & Barney Mullen, Sea Rover only app; bondage-c	1667.00	5000.00	10,000.00	16,500.00

(Estimated up to 60 total copies exist, 5 in NM/Mint)

	GD25	FN65	NM94
2-(Rare)-Origin The Phantom Bullet (1st & only app.); The Laughing Mask & Mr. E only app.; Trojak the Tiger Man begins, ends #6; Zephyr Jones & K-4 & His Sky Devils app., also #4	578.00	1733.00	5700.00
3-The Phantom Reporter, Dale of FBI, Breeze Barton, Captain Strong & Marvex the Super-Robot only app.; The Purple Mask begins	356.00	1067.00	3500.00
4-Last Purple Mask; Whirlwind Carter begins; Dan Gorman, G-Man app.	275.00	825.00	2200.00
5-The Falcon begins (1st app.); The Fiery Mask, Little Hercules app. by Sagendorf in the Segar style; bondage-c	275.00	825.00	2200.00
6-Origin & only app. Marvel Boy by S&K; Flying Flame, Dynaman, & Stuporman only app.; The Fiery Mask by S&K; S&K-c	325.00	975.00	2900.00
7-Origin The Blue Diamond, Captain Daring by S&K, The Fin by Everett, The Challenger, The Silver Scorn & The Thunderer by Burgos; Mr. Millions app	288.00	862.00	2500.00
8-Origin Citizen V; Last Fin, Silver Scorn, Capt. Daring by Borth, Blue Diamond & The Thunderer; Kirby & part solo Simon-c; Rudy the Robot only			

	GD25	FN65	NM94
app.; Citizen V, Fin & Silver Scorn continue in Comedy #9	240.00	656.00	1925.00

NOTE: *Schomburg c-1-4, 7. Simon a-2, 3, 5. Cover features: 1-Fiery Mask; 2-Phantom Bullet; 3-Purple Mask; 4-G-Man; 5-The Falcon; 6-Marvel Boy; 7, 8-Multiple characters.*

DARING NEW ADVENTURES OF SUPERGIRL, THE
Nov, 1982 - No. 13, Nov, 1983 (Supergirl No. 14 on)
DC Comics

1-Origin retold; Lois Lane back-ups in #2-12			1.50
2-13: 8,9-Doom Patrol app. 13-New costume; flag-c			1.00

NOTE: *Buckler c-1p, 2p. Giffen c-3p, 4p. Gil Kane c-6, ,8, 9, 11-13.*

DARK, THE
Nov, 1990 - No. 4, Feb, 1993; V2#1, May, 1993 - V2#7, Apr?, 1994 ($1.95)
Continum Comics

1-($2.00)-Bright-p; Panosian, Hanna-i; Stroman-c	.80	2.00
2-(1/92, $2.25)-Stroman-c/a(p)	.90	2.25
3,4-($2.50): 4-Perez-c & part-i	1.00	2.50
V2#1-Red foil Bart Sears-c	.80	2.00
V2#1-Red non-foil variant-c	.80	2.00
V2#1-2nd printing w/blue foil Bart Sears-c	.80	2.00
V2#2-6: 2-Stroman/Bryant-a. 3-Perez-c(i). 3-6-Foil-c. 4-Perez-c & part-i; bound-in trading cards. 5,6-(2/3/94)-Perez-c(i)	.80	2.00
V2#7-(B&W)-Perez-c(i)	.80	2.00
Convention Book 1 (Fall/94, $2.00)-Perez-c	.80	2.00
Convention Book 2 (10/94, $2.00)-Perez-c(i)	.80	2.00

DARK ANGEL (Formerly Hell's Angel)
No. 6, Dec, 1992 - No. 16, Dec, 1993 ($1.75)
Marvel Comics UK, Ltd.

6-16: 6-Excalibur-c/story. 8-Psylocke app.	.70	1.75

DARKCHYLDE
June, 1996 - Present ($2.95)
Maximum Press

1-3: Randy Queen-c/a/scripts		5.00
1-Special Comicon Edition (contents & cover same as #1)		5.00
		5.00
1-(American Entertainment Edition)-wraparound-c		5.00
1-Variant-c (3)		3.00
2-Variant-c		5.00
3-Variant-c		4.00

DARK CRYSTAL, THE (Movie)
April, 1983 - No. 2, May, 1983
Marvel Comics Group

1,2-Adaptation of film	.50	1.00

DARK DOMINION
Oct, 1993 - No. 10, July, 1994 ($2.50)
Defiant

1-9-Len Wein scripts begin. 4-Free extra 16 pgs. 7-9-J.G. Jones-c/a	1.00	2.50
10-Pre-Schism issue; Shooter/Wein script; John Ridgway-a	1.00	2.50

DARKER IMAGE (Also see Deathblow, The Maxx, & Bloodwulf)
Mar, 1993 ($1.95, one-shot)
Image Comics

1-The Maxx by Sam Kieth begins; Bloodwulf by Rob Liefeld & Deathblow by Jim Lee begin (both 1st app.); polybagged w/1 of 3 cards by Kieth, Lee or Liefeld		2.50
1-B&W interior pgs. w/silver foil logo		10.00

DARKEWOOD
1987 - No. 5, 1988 ($2.00, 28pgs, limited series)
Aircel Publishing

1-5	.80	2.00

Darkhold #16 © MEG

Dark Horse Comics #19 © DH

Dark Horse Presents #62 © DH

	GD25	FN65	NM94

DARK FANTASIES
1994 - No. 6, 1995 ($2.95)
Dark Fantasy

1-Test print Run (3,000)-Linsner-c			15.00
1-Linsner-c	1.20	3.00	7.00
2-4 (Deluxe): 4-($3.95)	1.00	2.00	5.00
2-4 (Regular)		1.20	3.00
5,6 (Deluxe; $3.95)		1.60	4.00
5,6 (Regular; $3.50)		1.40	3.50

DARK GUARD
Oct, 1993 - No. 4, Jan, 1994 ($1.75)
Marvel Comics UK

1-($2.95)-Foil stamped-c		1.20	3.00
2-4		.70	1.75

DARKHAWK
Mar, 1991 - No. 50, Apr, 1995 ($1.00/$1.25/$1.50)
Marvel Comics

1-Origin/1st app. Darkhawk; Hobgoblin cameo		1.20	3.00
2-14: 2-Spider-Man & Hobgoblin app. 3-Spider-Man & Hobgoblin app. 6-Capt. America & Daredevil x-over. 9-Punisher app. 11-Last $1.00-c. 11,12-Tombstone app. 13,14-Venom-c/story		.80	2.00
15-24,26-38: 19-Spider-Man & Brotherhood of Evil Mutants-c/story. 20-Spider-Man app. 22-Ghost Rider-c/story. 23-Origin begins, ends #25. 27-New Warriors-c/story. 35-Begin 3 part Venom story			1.25
25-($2.95, 52 pgs.)-Red holo-grafx foil-c w/double gatefold poster; origin of Darkhawk armor revealed		1.20	3.00
39-49: 39-Begin $1.50-c; bound-in trading card sheet			1.50
50-($2.50, 52 pgs)		1.00	2.50
Annual 1 (1992, $2.25, 68 pgs.)-Vs. Iron Man		1.00	2.50
Annual 2 (1993, $2.95, 68 pgs.)-Polybagged w/card		1.20	3.00
Annual 3 (1994, $2.95)		1.20	3.00

DARKHOLD: PAGES FROM THE BOOK OF SINS (See Midnight Sons Unlimited)
Oct, 1992 - No. 16, Jan, 1994 ($1.75)
Marvel Comics (Midnight Sons imprint #15 on)

1-($2.75, 52 pgs.)-Polybagged w/poster by Andy & Adam Kubert; part 4 of Rise of the Midnight Sons storyline	1.10		2.75
2-10,12-16: 3-Reintro Modred the Mystic (see Marvel Chillers #1). 5-Punisher & Ghost Rider app. 15-Spot varnish-c. 15,16-Siege of Darkness part 4&12		.70	1.75
11-($2.25)-Outer-c is a Darkhold envelope made of black parchment w/gold ink		.90	2.25

DARK HORSE CLASSICS
1992 ($3.95, B&W, 52 pgs.)
Dark Horse Comics

nn's: The Last of the Mohicans. 20,000 Leagues Under the Sea

		1.60	4.00

DARK HORSE COMICS
Aug, 1992 - No. 25, Sept, 1994 ($2.50)
Dark Horse Comics

1-Dorman double gategold painted-c; Predator, Robocop, Timecop (3-part) & Renegade stories begin; 1st app. of Timecop	1.20		3.00
2-6,11-25: 2-Mignola-a. 3-Begin 3-part Aliens story; Aliens-c. 4-Predator-c. 6-Begin 4 part Robocop story. 12-Begin 2-part Aliens & 3-part Predator stories. 13-Thing From Another World begins w/Nino-a(i). 15-Begin 2-part Aliens: Cargo story. 16-Begin 3-part Predator story. 17-Begin 3-part Star Wars: Droids story 3-part Aliens: Alien story; Droids-c. 19-Begin 2-part X story; X cover		.50	1.25	2.50
7-Begin Star Wars: Tales of the Jedi 3-part story	1.20	3.00	7.00
8-1st app. X and begins; begin 4-part James Bond	1.00	2.00	5.00
9,10: 9-Star Wars ends. 10-X ends; Begin 3-part Predator & Godzilla stories			

NOTE: *Art Adams c-11.*

	1.60	4.00

DARK HORSE DOWN UNDER
June, 1994 - No. 3, Oct, 1994 ($2.50, B&W, limited series)
Dark Horse Comics

1-3		1.00	2.50

DARK HORSE PRESENTS
July, 1986 - Present ($1.50/$1.75/$1.95/$2.25/$2.50, B&W)
Dark Horse Comics

1-1st app. Concrete by Paul Chadwick	2.15	6.50	15.00
1-2nd printing (1988, $1.50)		1.00	2.50
1-Silver ink 3rd printing (1992, $2.25)-Says 2nd printing inside		.90	2.25
2-Concrete app.	1.20	3.00	7.00
3-Concrete app.	1.00	2.00	5.00
4,5-Concrete app.		1.60	4.00
6-10: 6,8,10-Concrete app. 10-1st app. The Mask		1.20	3.00
11-19,21-23: 11-19,21-Mask stories. 12,14,16,18,22-Concrete app. 15(2/88)			
17-All Roachmill issue		.80	2.00
20-($2.95, 68 pgs.)-Concrete, Flaming Carrot, Mask		1.20	3.00
24-Origin Aliens-c/story (11/88); Mr. Monster app.	2.90	8.60	20.00
25-31,33: 28-($2.95, 52 pgs.)-Concrete app.; Mr. Monster story (homage to Graham Ingels). 33-($2.25, 44 pgs.)		1.20	3.00
32-($3.50, 68 pgs.)-Annual; Concrete, American		1.60	4.00
34-Aliens-c/story	1.00	2.00	5.00
35-Predator-c/story; begin $1.95-c	1.00	2.00	5.00
36-1st Aliens Vs. Predator story; painted-c	1.30	3.25	8.00
36-Same as above, but line drawn-c	1.00	2.60	6.00
37-39,41,44,45,47-50: 38-Concrete. 44-Crash Ryan. 48-50-Contain 2 trading cards. 50-S/F story by Perez		.80	2.00
40-($2.95, 52 pgs.)-1st Argosy story		1.20	3.00
42,43-Aliens-c/stories	1.00	2.00	5.00
46-Prequel to new Predator II mini-series		1.20	3.00
51-53-Sin City by Frank Miller, parts 2-4; 51,53-Miller-c		1.60	4.00
54-The Next Men begins(1st app.) by Byrne(9/91); Miller-a	1.20	3.00	7.00
55-2nd app. The Next Men; parts 5 & 6 of Sin City by Miller; Homicide by Morrow in both. 54-Morrow-c; begin $2.25-c. 55-Miller-c	1.60		4.00
56-($3.95, 68 pg. annual)-2-part prologue to Aliens: Genocide; part 7 of Sin City by Miller; Next Men by Byrne		1.60	4.00
57-($3.50, 52 pgs.)-Part 8 of Sin City by Miller; Next Men by Byrne; Byrne & Miller-c; Alien Fire story; swipes cover to Daredevil #1	1.40		3.50
58-66,68-84-($2.25): 58,59-Part 9,10 Sin City by Miller; Alien Fire stories. 60,61-Part 11,12 Sin City by Miller. 62-Last Sin City (entire book by Miller, c/a;52 pgs.). 64-Dr. Giggles begins (1st app.), ends #66; Boris the Bear story. 66-New Concrete-c/story by Chadwick. 71-Begin 3 part Dominque story by Jim Balent; Balent-c. 72-(3/93)-Begin 3-part Eudaemon (1st app.) story by Nelson. 80-Art Adams-c/a (Monkeyman & O'Brien)		.90	2.25
67-($3.95, 68 pgs.)-Begin 3-part prelude to Predator: Race War mini-series; Oscar Wilde adapt. by Russell		1.60	4.00
85-99,101-120: 85-Begin $2.50-c. 88-91-Hellboy by Mignola. 92, 93, 95-Too Much Coffee Man. 101-Aliens c/a by Wrightson, story by Paul Pope. 103-Kirby gatefold-c. 106-Big Blown Baby by Bill Wray. 107-Mignola-c/a. 110-Ed Brubaker-a/scripts		1.00	2.50
100-1-Intro Lance Blastoff by Miller; Milk & Cheese by Evan Dorkin.		1.00	2.50
100-2-Hellboy-c by Wrightson; Hellboy story by Mignola; includes Roberta Gregory & Paul Pope stories		1.00	2.50
100-3-Darrow-c, Concrete by Chadwick; Pekar story		1.00	2.50
100-4-Gibbons-c; Miller story, Geary story/a		1.00	2.50
100-5-Allred-c, Adams, Dorkin, Pope		1.00	2.50
...Aliens Platinum Edition (1992)-r/DHP #24,43,43,56 & Special	2.90	8.60	20.00

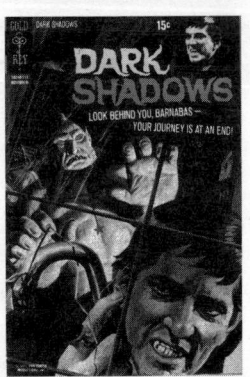

	GD25	FN65	NM94

...Fifth Anniversary Special nn (4/91, $9.95)-Part 1 of Sin City by Frank Miller (c/a); Aliens, Aliens vs. Predator, Concrete, Roachmill, Give Me Liberty & The American stories ... 2.15 ... 6.50 ... 15.00
NOTE: *Geary* a-59, 60. *Miller* a-Special, 51-53, 55-62; c-59-62, 100-1; c-51, 53, 55, 59-62, 100-1. *Moebius* a-63; c-63, 70. *Vess* a-78; c-75, 78.

DARK KNIGHT (See Batman: The Dark Knight & Legends of the...)

DARKLON THE MYSTIC (Also see Eerie Magazine #79,80)
Oct, 1983 (one-shot)
Pacific Comics

1-Starlin-c/a(r)		.80	2.00

DARKMAN (Movie)
Sept, 1990; Oct, 1990 - No. 3, Dec, 1990 ($1.50)
Marvel Comics

1 (9/90, $2.25, B&W mag., 68 pgs.)-Adaptation of film		.90	2.25
1-3: Reprints B&W magazine			1.50

DARKMAN
V2#1, Apr, 1993 -No. 6, Sept, 1993 ($2.95, limited series)
Marvel Comics

V2#1 ($3.95, 52 pgs.)		1.60	4.00
2-6		1.20	3.00

DARK MANSION OF FORBIDDEN LOVE, THE (Becomes Forbidden Tales of Dark Mansion No. 5 on)
Sept-Oct, 1971 - No. 4, Mar-Apr, 1972 (52 pgs.)
National Periodical Publications

1	3.75	11.25	30.00
2-4: 2-Adams-c. 3-Jeff Jones-c	1.70	5.00	12.00

DARK MYSTERIES (Thrilling Tales of Horror & Suspense)
June-July, 1951 - No. 25?, 1955
"Master" - "Merit" Publications

1-Wood-c/a (8 pgs.)	75.00	225.00	600.00
2-Wood/Harrison-c/a (8 pgs.)	51.00	153.00	410.00
3-9: 7-Dismemberment, hypo blood drainage stys	26.00	77.00	180.00
10-Cannibalism story; witch burning-c	27.00	81.00	190.00
11-13,15-18: 11-Severed head panels. 13-Dismemberment-c/story. 17-The Old Gravedigger host	20.00	60.00	140.00
14-Several E.C. Craig swipes	21.00	62.00	145.00
19-Injury-to-eye panel; E.C. swipe; torture-c	26.00	79.00	185.00
20-Female bondage, blood drainage story	24.00	71.00	165.00
21,22-Last pre-code issue, misdated 3/54 instead of 3/55	14.00	43.00	100.00
23-25 (#25-Exist?)	12.00	36.00	85.00

NOTE: *Cameron* a-1, 2. *Myron Fass* c/a-21. *Harrison* a-3, 7; c-3. *Hollingsworth* a-7-17, 20, 21, 23. *Wildey* a-5. *Woodish art by Fleishman*-9; c-10, 14-17. Bondage c-10, 18, 19.

DARKNESS, THE
1996
Top Cow Comics

Special Preview Edition-Garth Ennis script; Silvestri-a(p)			10.00

DARK ONE'S THIRD EYE
1996 ($4.95, squarebound, one-shot)
Sirius Entertainment

nn-Dark One-a; pinups			5.00

DARKSEID VS. GALACTUS: THE HUNGER
1995 ($4.95, one-shot)
DC Comics

nn-John Byrne-c/a/scripts	1.00	2.00	5.00

DARK SHADOWS
Oct, 1957 - No. 3, May, 1958
Steinway Comic Publications (Ajax)(America's Best)

1	13.50	41.00	95.00

	GD25	FN65	NM94
2,3	10.00	30.00	70.00

DARK SHADOWS (TV) (See Dan Curtis Giveaways)
Mar, 1969 - No. 35, Feb, 1976 (Photo-c: 1-7)
Gold Key

1(30039-903)-With pull-out poster (25¢)	23.50	70.50	235.00
1-With poster missing	8.50	25.50	85.00
2	8.00	24.00	80.00
3-With pull-out poster	11.00	33.00	110.00
3-With poster missing	6.00	18.00	60.00
4-7: 7-Last photo-c	7.00	21.00	70.00
8-10	5.50	16.50	55.00
11-20	4.50	13.50	45.00
21-35: 30-Last painted-c	3.50	10.50	35.00
Story Digest 1 (6/70)-Photo-c	5.50	16.50	55.00

DARK SHADOWS (TV) (See Nightmare on Elm Street)
June, 1992 - No. 4, Spring, 1993 ($2.50, limited series, coated stock)
Innovation Publishing

1-Based on 1991 NBC TV mini-series; painted-c		1.20	3.00
2-4		1.00	2.50

DARK SHADOWS: BOOK TWO
1993 - No. 4, July, 1993 ($2.50, limited series)
Innovation Publishing

1-4-Painted-c. 4-Maggie Thompson scripts		1.00	2.50

DARK SHADOWS: BOOK THREE
Nov, 1993 ($2.50)
Innovation Publishing

1-(Whole #9)		1.00	2.50

DARKSTARS, THE
Oct, 1992 - No. 38, Jan, 1996 ($1.75/$1.95)
DC Comics

1-1st app. The Darkstars		.80	2.00
2-21: 5-Hawkman & Hawkwoman app. 18-20-Flash app.		.70	1.75
22-24: 22-Begin $1.95-c. 24-(9/94)-Zero Hour		.80	2.00
0,25-30: 0-(10/94). 25-(11/94). 30-Green Lantern app.		.80	2.00
31-38: 31-...vs, Darkseid. 32-Green Lantern app.		.90	2.25

NOTE: *Travis Charest* a(p)-4-7; c(p)-2-5; c-6-11. *Stroman* a-1-3; c-1.

DARK TOWN
1995 ($3.95, magazine-size, quarterly)
Mad Monkey Press

1-Kaja Blackley scripts; Vanessa Chong-a		1.60	4.00

DARKWING DUCK (TV cartoon) (Also see Cartoon Tales)
Nov, 1991 - No. 4, Feb, 1992 ($1.50, limited series)
Disney Comics

1-4: Adapts hour-long premiere TV episode			1.50

DARLING LOVE
Oct-Nov, 1949 - No. 11, 1952 (no month) (52 pgs.)(All photo-c?)
Close Up/Archie Publ. (A Darling Magazine)

1-Photo-c	11.50	34.00	80.00
2-Photo-c	8.35	25.00	50.00
3-8,10,11: 3-6-photo-c	6.70	20.00	40.00
9-Krigstein-a	8.35	25.00	50.00

DARLING ROMANCE
Sept-Oct, 1949 - No. 7, 1951 (All photo-c)
Close Up (MLJ Publications)

1-(52 pgs.)-Photo-c	19.00	58.00	135.00
2	8.35	25.00	50.00

Dazzler #27 © MEG

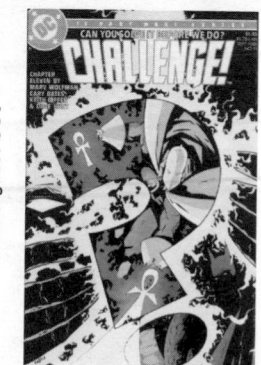

DC Challenge #11 © DC

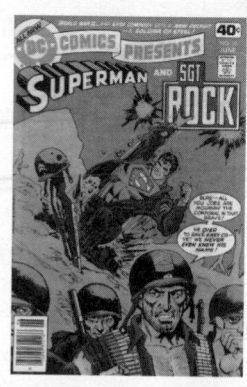

DC Comics Presents #10 © DC

	GD25	FN65	NM94
3-7	7.50	22.50	45.00

DART (Also see Freak Force & Savage Dragon)
Feb, 1996 - No. 3, May, 1996 ($2.50, limited series)
Image Comics (Highbrow Entertainment)

1-3			2.50

DASTARDLY & MUTTLEY (See Fun-In No. 1-4, 6 and Kite Fun Book)

DATE WITH DANGER
No. 5, Dec, 1952 - No. 6, Feb, 1953
Standard Comics

5,6-Secret agent stories	6.35	19.00	38.00

DATE WITH DEBBI (Also see Debbi's Dates)
Jan-Feb, 1969 - No. 17, Sept-Oct, 1971; No. 18, Oct-Nov, 1972
National Periodical Publications

1-Teenage	1.70	5.00	12.00
2-5	1.20	3.00	7.00
6-18	1.00	2.00	5.00

DATE WITH JUDY, A (Radio/TV, and 1948 movie)
Oct-Nov, 1947 - No. 79, Oct-Nov, 1960 (No. 1-25: 52 pgs.)
National Periodical Publications

1-Teenage	26.00	79.00	185.00
2	12.00	36.00	85.00
3-10	10.00	30.00	65.00
11-20	6.35	19.00	38.00
21-40	5.00	15.00	30.00
41-45: 45-Last pre-code (2-3/55)	4.25	13.00	26.00
46-79: 79-Drucker-c/a	4.00	11.00	22.00

DATE WITH MILLIE, A (Life with Millie No. 8 on)(Teenage)
Oct, 1956 - No. 7, Aug, 1957; Oct, 1959 - No. 7, Oct, 1960
Atlas/Marvel Comics (MPC)

1(10/56)-(1st Series)-Dan DeCarlo-a in #1-7	20.00	60.00	140.00
2	10.00	30.00	70.00
3-7	7.50	22.50	45.00
1(10/59)-(2nd Series)	10.00	30.00	70.00
2-7	7.50	22.50	45.00

DATE WITH PATSY, A (Also see Patsy Walker)
September, 1957 (One-shot)
Atlas Comics

1-Starring Patsy Walker	10.00	30.00	60.00

DAVID AND GOLIATH (Movie)
No. 1205, July, 1961
Dell Publishing Co.

Four Color 1205-Photo-c	6.00	18.00	60.00

DAVID CASSIDY (TV)(See Partridge Family, Swing With Scooter #33 & Time For Love #30)
Feb, 1972 - No. 14, Sept, 1973
Charlton Comics

1	2.85	8.50	20.00
2-14: 5,7,9,14-Photo-c	2.00	6.00	14.00

DAVID LADD'S LIFE STORY (See Movie Classics)

DAVY CROCKETT (See Dell Giants, Fightin'..., Frontier Fighters, It's Game Time, Power Record Comics, Western Tales & Wild Frontier)

DAVY CROCKETT (Frontier Fighter...)
1951
Avon Periodicals

nn-Tuska?, Reinman-a; Fawcette-c	16.00	47.00	110.00

DAVY CROCKETT (...King of the Wild Frontier No. 1,2)(TV)
5/55 - No. 671, 12/55; No. 1, 12/63; No. 2, 11/69 (Walt Disney)

	GD25	FN65	NM94

Dell Publishing Co./Gold Key

Four Color 631(#1)-Fess Parker photo-c	14.00	42.00	140.00
Four Color 639-Photo-c	14.00	42.00	140.00
Four Color 664,671(Marsh-a)-Photo-c	13.00	40.00	130.00
1(12/63-Gold Key)-Fess Parker photo-c; reprints	13.00	40.00	130.00
2(11/69)-Fess Parker photo-c; reprints	4.00	12.00	40.00
...Christmas Book (no date, 16 pgs., paper-c)-Sears giveaway	5.85	17.50	35.00
...In the Raid at Piney Creek (1955, 16 pgs., 5x7-1/4")-American Motors giveaway; slick, photo-c	7.50	22.50	45.00
...Safety Trails (1955, 16pgs, 3-1/4x7")-Cities Service giveaway	7.50	22.50	45.00

DAVY CROCKETT (...Frontier Fighter #1,2; Kid Montana #9 on)
Aug, 1955 - No. 8, Jan, 1957
Charlton Comics

1	8.35	25.00	50.00
2	5.00	15.00	30.00
3-8	4.00	11.00	22.00
Hunting With... nn ('55, 16 pgs.)-Ben Franklin Store giveaway (Publ.-S. Rose)	3.75	11.25	28.00

DAWN
June, 1995 - Present ($2.95)
Sirius Entertainment

1/2-w/certificate			15.00
1/2-Variant-c			35.00
1-Linsner-a	1.65	4.20	10.00
1-White Trash Edition			40.00
1-Black Light Edition			30.00
1-Look Sharp Edition			45.00
2-4: Linsner-c/a	1.00	2.60	6.00
2-Variant-c			30.00
3-Limited Edition			30.00
4-Vibrato-c			30.00

DAYS OF THE MOB (See In the Days of the Mob)

DAZEY'S DIARY
June-Aug, 1962
Dell Publishing Co.

01-174-208: Bill Woggon-c/a	3.00	9.00	30.00

DAZZLER, THE (Also see Marvel Graphic Novel & X-Men #130)
Mar, 1981 - No. 42, Mar, 1986
Marvel Comics Group

1,2-X-Men app.		.80	2.00
3-37,39-42: 10,11-Galactus app. 21-Double size; photo-c. 42-The Beast app.			1.00
38-Wolverine-c/app.; X-Men app.		.90	2.30	5.50

NOTE: No. 1 distributed only through comic shops. Alcala a-1i, 2i. Chadwick a-38-42p; c(p)-39, 41, 42. Guice a-38i, 42i; c-38, 40.

DC CHALLENGE
Nov, 1985 - No. 12, Oct, 1986 ($1.25, maxi-series)
DC Comics

1-11: 1-Colan-a. 2,8-Batman-c/app. 4-Gil Kane-c/a			1.25
12-($2.00)-Ordway-c		.80	2.00

NOTE: Batman app. in 1-4, 6-12. Joker app. in 7. Giffen c/a-11. Infantino a-3. Ordway c-12. Swan/Austin c-10.

DC COMICS PRESENTS
July-Aug, 1978 - No. 97, Sept, 1986 (Superman team-ups in all)
DC Comics

1-25, 27-40,42-71,73-76,79-84,86-97: 1,2-4th & final Superman/Flash race 4-Metal Men. 9-Wonder Woman. 19-Batgirl. 13,43,80-Legion of Super Heroes. 31,58-Robin. 35-Man-Bat. 42,47-Sandman. 52-Doom Patrol.

DC 100 Page Super Spectacular #19 © DC

DC Special #17 © DC

DC Special Series #16 © DC

82-Adam Strange. 83-Batman & Outsiders. 86-88-Crisis x-over. 88-Creeper
.80   2.00

26-(10/80)-Green Lantern; intro Cyborg, Starfire, Raven (1st app. New Teen
Titans in 16 pg. preview); Starlin-c/a; Sargon the Sorcerer back-up
1.20   3.00   7.00

41,72,77,78,85: 41-Superman/Joker-c/story. 72-Joker/Phantom Stranger-
c/story. 77,78-Animal Man app. (77-cover app. also). 85-Swamp Thing; Alan
Moore scripts. 1.20   3.00

Annual 1-4: 1(9/82)-G.A. Superman. 2(7/83)-Intro/origin Superwoman.
3(9/84)-Shazam. 4(10/85)-Superwoman .80   2.00
NOTE: **Adkins** a-54; c-2. **Buckler** a-33, 34; c-30, 33, 34. **Giffen** a-39; c-59. **Gil Kane** a-28, 35, Annual 3; c-48p, 56, 58, 60, 62, 64, 68, Annual 2, 3. **Kirby** c/a-84. **Kubert** c/a-66. **Morrow** c/a-65. **Newton** c/a-54p. **Orlando** c-53i. **Perez** a-26p, 61p; c-38, 61, 94. **Starlin** a-26-29p, 36p, 37p; c-26-29, 36, 37, 93. **Toth** a-84. **Williamson** i-79, 85, 87.

DC GRAPHIC NOVEL (Also see DC Science Fiction...)
Nov, 1983 - No. 7, 1986 ($5.95, 68 pgs.)
DC Comics

1-5,7: 1-Star Raiders. 2-Warlords; not from regular Warlord series. 3-The
Medusa Chain; Ernie Colon story/a. 4-The Hunger Dogs by Kirby; Darkseid
kills Himon from Mister Miracle & destroys New Genesis. 5-Me and
Joe Priest; Chaykin-c. 7-Space Clusters; Nino-c/a.
1.00   2.50   6.00
6-Metalzoic; Sienkiewicz-c. ($6.95) 1.20   3.00   7.00

DC/MARVEL: ALL ACCESS (Also see DC Versus Marvel & Marvel Versus DC)
1996 - No. 4, 1997 ($2.95, limited series)
DC Comics

1-4: 1-Superman & Spider-Man app. 3.00

DC 100 PAGE SUPER SPECTACULAR
(Title is 100 Page... No. 14 on)(Square bound) (Reprints, 50¢)
No. 4, Summer, 1971 - No. 13, 6/72; No. 14, 2/73 - No. 22, 11/73 (No #1-3)
National Periodical Publications

4-Weird Mystery Tales; Johnny Peril & Phantom Stranger; cover & splashes
by Wrightson; origin Jungle Boy of Jupiter 2.85   8.50   20.00
5-Love Stories; Wood inks (7 pgs.)(scarcer) 5.50   17.00   45.00
6- "World's Greatest Super-Heroes"; JLA, JSA, Spectre, Johnny Quick,
Vigilante & Hawkman; contains unpublished Wildcat story; N. Adams
wrap-around-c; r/JLA #21,22 2.70   6.75   16.00
7-13: 7-(See Superman #245). 8-(See Batman #238). 9-(See Our Army at
War #242). 10-(See Adventure #416). 11-(See Flash #214).12-(See
Superboy #185). 13-(See Superman #252). 1.30   3.25   8.00
14-Batman-r/Detective #31,32,156; Atom-r/Showcase #34
1.65   4.20   10.00
15-22: 15-r/2nd Boy Commandos/Det. #65. 17-JSA-r/All Star #37 (10-11/47,
38 pgs.), Sandman-r/Adv. #65 (8/41), JLA #23 (11/63) & JLA #43 (3/66).
20-Batman-r/Det. #66,68, Spectre; origin Two-Face. 21-r/Brave &
Bold #54. 22-r/All-Flash #13. 1.00   2.00   5.00
NOTE: **Anderson** r-11, 14, 18i, 22. **B. Baily** r-18, 20. **Burnley** r-18, 20. **Crandall** r-14p, 20. **Drucker** r-4. **Grandenetti** a-22(2)r. **Heath** a-22r. **Infantino** r-17, 20, 22. **G. Kane** r-18. **Kubert** r-6, 7, 16, 17; c-16, 19. **Manning** a-19r. **Meskin** r-4, 22. **Mooney** r-15, 21. **Toth** r-17, 20.

DC SCIENCE FICTION GRAPHIC NOVEL
1985 - No. 7, 1987 ($5.95)
DC Comics

SF1-SF7: SF1-Hell on Earth by Robert Bloch; Giffen-p. SF2-Nightwings by
Robert Silverberg; G. Colan-p. SF3-Frost & Fire by Bradbury. SF4-Mer-
chants of Venus by Ellison; M. Rogers-a. SF5-Demon With A Glass Hand
by Ellison; M. Rogers-a. SF6-The Magic Goes Away by Niven. SF7-Sandkings by George R.R.
Martin 1.00   2.50   6.00

DC SILVER AGE CLASSICS
1992 ($1.00, all reprints)
DC Comics

...Action Comics #252; r/1st Supergirl; Adventure Comics #247; r/1st Legion of
S.H....The Brave and the Bold #28; r/1st JLA; Detective Comics #225; r/1st

Martian Manhunter; Detective Comics #327; r/1st new look Batman; Green
Lantern #76; r/Green Lantern/Gr. Arrow; House of Secrets #92; r/1st Swamp
Thing; Showcase #4; r/1st S.A. Flash; Showcase #22; r/1st S.A. Green
Lantern; Sugar and Spike #99; 2 unpublished stories 1.00

DC SPECIAL (Also see Super DC...)
10-12/68 - No. 15, 11-12/71; No. 16, Spr/75 - No. 29, 8-9/77
National Periodical Publications

1-All Infantino issue; Flash, Batman, Adam Strange-r; begin 68 pg. issues,
end #21 2.15   6.50   15.00
2-13: 2-Teen humor. 5-All Kubert issue; Viking Prince, Sgt. Rock-r. 12-Viking
Prince; Kubert-c/a(r/B&B almost entirely). 1.50   3.75   9.00
14,15: 15-G.A. Plastic Man origin-r/Police #1; origin Woozy by Cole; 14,15-
(52 pgs.) 1.20   3.00   7.00
16-29: 16-Super Heroes Battle Super Gorillas; r/Capt. Storm #1, 1st Johnny
Cloud/All-Amer. Men of War #82. 17-Early S.A. Green Lantern-r. 22-Robin
Robin Hood. 26-Enemy Ace on-c only. 27-Captain Comet story. 28-Earth
Shattering Disaster Stories; Legion of Super-Heroes story.
29-The Untold Origin of the Justice Society 1.00   2.00   5.00
NOTE: **N. Adams** c-3, 4, 6, 11, 29. **Grell** a-20; c-17, 20. **Heath** a-12r. **G. Kane** a-6p, 13r, 17r, 19-21r. **Kubert** a-6r, 12r, 22. **Meskin** a-10. **Moreira** a-10. **Staton** a-29p. **Toth** a-13, 20r. #1-15: 25¢; 16-27: 50¢; 28, 29: 60¢. #1-13, 16-21: 68 pgs.; 14, 15: 52 pgs. 25-27: oversized.

DC SPECIAL BLUE-RIBBON DIGEST
Mar-Apr, 1980 - No. 24, Aug, 1982
DC Comics

1-24: All reprints? 1.00
NOTE: **N. Adams** a-16(6)r, 17r, 23r; c-16. **Aparo** a-6r, 24r; c-23. **Grell** a-8, 10; c-10. **Heath** a-14. **Infantino** a-15r. **Kaluta** a-15r, 22r. **Kirby** a-23r. **Kubert** a-3, 18r, 21r; c-7, 12, 14, 17, 18, 21, 24. **Morrow** a-24r. **Orlando** a-17r, 22r; c-1, 20. **Perez** c-19p. **Toth** a-21r, 24r. **Wood** a-3, 17r, 24r. **Wrightson** a-16r, 17r, 24r.

DC SPECIAL SERIES
9/77 - No. 16, Fall, 1978; No. 17, 8/79 - No. 27, Fall, 1981
(No. 19, 23, 24 - digest size, 100 pgs. No. 25-27 - over-sized)
National Periodical Publications/DC Comics

1,2(#1)-Five-Star Super-Hero Spectacular; Atom, Flash, Green Lantern,
Aquaman,Batman, Kobra app.; N. Adams-c. 2(#1)-The Original Swamp
Thing Saga (1977)-r/Swamp Thing #1&2 by Wrightson; Wrightson
wraparound-c. 1.60   4.00
3-15,17-20,22-24: 5-New 63pg. Superman vs. Brainiac & Lex Luthor. 6-Jones-
a. 7-Ghosts Special. 10-Origin Dr. Fate, Lightray & Black Canary. 14,17,20-
Original Swamp Thing Saga; r/Swamp Thing #3-10 by Wrightson (52-68
pgs.). 15-Batman Spectacular. 19-Secret Origins of Super-Heroes; origins
Wonder Woman (new-a), Robin, & Batman-Superman team. 22-G.I. Combat
1.00   2.50
16-Jonah Hex Spectacular; death of Jonah Hex; Bat Lash story
2.15   6.50   15.00
21-Frank Miller a-in "Batman--Wanted Dead or Alive" (1st Batman story, Spring,
1980). 1.70   5.00   12.00
V5#5-($2.95, Sum/81)-Superman II the Adventure Continues; photos from
movie & photo-c (see All-New Coll. Ed. C-62) 1.30   3.25
26-($2.95, Sum/81)-Superman and His Incredible Fortress of Solitude
1.20   3.00
27-($2.50)-Batman vs. The Incredible Hulk 2.15   6.50   15.00
NOTE: **Aparo** c-8. **Golden** a-15. **Heath** a-12i, 16. **Infantino** a-19r. **Kubert** c-13, 19r. **Nasser/Netzer** a-1, 10i, 15. **Newton** a-10. **Rogers** a-16. **Starlin** a-1. **Staton** a-1. **Tuska** a-19r. #25 & 26. #26 was advertised as All-New Collectors' Edition C-63, C-64. #26 was originally planned as All-New Collectors' Ed. C-30?; has C-630 & A.N.C.E. on cover.

DC SPOTLIGHT
1985 (50th anniversary special) (giveaway)
DC Comics

1-Includes profiles on Batman:The Dark Knight &The Watchmen.
1.20

DC SUPER-STARS
March, 1976 - No. 18, Winter, 1978 (No.3-18: 52 pgs.)

DC Super-Stars #1 © DC

DC Versus Marvel #4 © DC

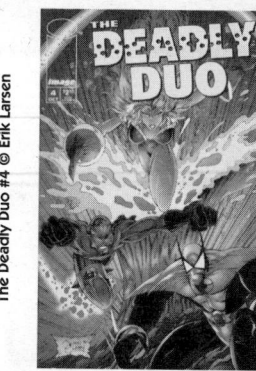

The Deadly Duo #4 © Erik Larsen

National Periodical Publications/DC Comics

1-(68 pgs.)-Re-intro Teen Titans (predates T. T. #44 (11/76); tryout iss.) plus r/Teen Titans; W.W. as girl was original Wonder Girl

1.00	2.00	5.00

2-7,9,11-14,16,18: 2,4-6,8-Adam Strange; 2-(68 pgs.)-r/1st Adam Strange/ Hawkman team-up from Mystery in Space #90 plus Atomic Knights origin-r. 3-Legion issue. 4-r/Tales/Unexpected #45. 13-Sergio Aragones Special

		1.50

8-r/1st Space Ranger from Showcase #15, Adam Strange-r/Mystery in Space #89 & Star Rovers-r/M.I.S. #80

	1.60	4.00

10-Strange Sports Stories; Batman/Joker-c/story — 1.80 — 4.50
15-Batman Spectacular; Golden & Rogers-a — 1.20 — 3.00
17-Secret Origins of Super-Heroes (origin of The Huntress); origin Green Arrow by Grell; Legion app.; Earth II Batman & Catwoman marry (1st revealed; also see B&B #197 & Superman Family #211) 1.00 2.50
NOTE: **M. Anderson** r-2, 4, 6. **Aparo** c-7, 14, 18. **Austin** a-11i. **Buckler** a-14p; c-10. **Grell** a-17. **G. Kane** a-1r, 10r. **Kubert** c-15. **Layton** a-16i, 17i. **Mooney** a-4r, 6r. **Morrow** c/a-11r. **Nasser** a-11. **Newton** c/a-16p. **Staton** a-17; c-17. No. 10, 12-18 contain all new material; the rest are reprints. #1 contains new and reprint material.

DC UNIVERSE: TRINITY
Aug, 1993 - No. 2, Sept, 1993 ($2.95, 52 pgs, limited series)
DC Comics

1,2-Foil-c; Green Lantern, Darkstars, Legion app. 1.20 3.00

DC VERSUS MARVEL (See Marvel Versus DC) (Also see Amazon, Assassins, Bruce Wayne: Agent of S.H.I.E. L.D., Bullets & Bracelets, Doctor Strangefate, JLX, Legend of the Dark Claw, Magneto & The Magnetic Men, Speed Demon, Spider-Boy, Super Soldier, X-Patrol)
No. 1, 1996, No. 4, 1996 ($3.95, limited series)
DC Comics

1,4: 1-Marz script, Jurgens-a(p); 1st app. of Access. .80 1.60 4.00

D-DAY (Also see Special War Series)
Sum/63; No. 2, Fall/64; No. 4, 9/66; No. 5, 10/67; No. 6, 11/68
Charlton Comics (no No. 3)

1(1963)-Montes/Bache-c 2.60 7.50 18.00
2(Fall,'64)-Wood-a(4) 2.85 8.50 20.00
4-6('66-'68)-Montes/Bache-a #5 2.00 6.00 14.00

DEAD AIR
July, 1989 ($5.95, graphic novel)
Slave Labor Graphics

nn-Mike Allred's 1st published work 6.00

DEAD END CRIME STORIES
April, 1949 (52 pgs.)
Kirby Publishing Co.

nn-(Scarce)-Powell, Roussos-a; painted-c 43.00 128.00 340.00

DEAD-EYE WESTERN COMICS
Nov-Dec, 1948 - V3#1, Apr-May, 1953
Hillman Periodicals

V1#1-(52 pgs.)-Krigstein, Roussos-a 14.00 43.00 100.00
V1#2,3-(52 pgs.) 8.35 25.00 50.00
V1#4-12-(52 pgs.) 5.00 15.00 30.00
V2#1,2,5-8,10-12: 1-7-(52 pgs.) 4.00 12.00 24.00
3,4-Krigstein-a 6.70 20.00 40.00
9-One pg. Frazetta ad 4.00 12.00 24.00
V3#1 4.00 11.00 22.00
NOTE: **Briefer** a-V1#8. Kinstleresque stories by McCann-12, V2#1, 2, V3#1. **McWilliams** a-V1#5. **Ed Moore** a-V1#4.

DEADFACE: DOING THE ISLANDS WITH BACCHUS
July, 1991 - No. 3, Sept, 1991 ($2.95, B&W, limited series, 52 pgs.)
Dark Horse Comics

1-3: By Eddie Campbell 1.20 3.00

DEADFACE: EARTH, WATER, AIR, AND FIRE
July, 1992 - No. 4, Oct, 1992 ($2.50, B&W, limited series; British-r)
Dark Horse Comics

1-4: By Eddie Campbell 1.00 2.50

DEAD IN THE WEST
Oct, 1993 - No. 2, Mar, 1994 ($3.95, B&W, 52 pgs.)
Dark Horse Comics

1,2-Timothy Truman-c 1.60 4.00

DEADLIEST HEROES OF KUNG FU (Magazine)
Summer, 1975
Marvel Comics Group

1 .70 1.80

DEADLINE USA
Apr, 1992 - No. 8, Nov, 1992 ($3.95, B&W, 52 pgs.)
Dark Horse Comics

1-8: Johnny Nemo w/Milligan scripts in all 1.60 4.00

DEADLY DUO, THE
Nov, 1994 - No. 3, Jan, 1995 ($2.50, limited series)
Image Comics (Highbrow Entertainment)

1-3: 1-1st app. of Kill Cat 1.00 2.50

DEADLY DUO, THE
June, 1995 - No. 4, Oct, 1995 ($2.50, limited series)
Image Comics (Highbrow Entertainment)

1-4: 1-Spawn app. 2-Savage Dragon app. 3-Gen 13 app.

1.00	2.50	

DEADLY FOES OF SPIDER-MAN (See Lethal Foes of...)
May, 1991 - No. 4, Aug, 1991 ($1.00, limited series)
Marvel Comics

1-4: 1-Punisher, Kingpin, Rhino app. 1.00

DEADLY HANDS OF KUNG FU, THE (See Master of Kung Fu)
April, 1974 - No. 33, Feb, 1977 (75¢, B&W, magazine)
Marvel Comics Group

1(V1#4 listed in error)-Origin Sons of the Tiger; Shang-Chi, Master of Kung Fu begins (ties w/Master of Kung Fu #17 as 3rd app. Shang-Chi); Bruce Lee photo pin-up 1.20 3.00 7.00
2,3,5 .80 2.00
4-Bruce Lee painted-c by Neal Adams; 8 pg. biog of Bruce Lee 1.20 3.00
6-14 .80 2.00
15-(Annual 1, Summer '75)-Origin Iron Fist retold (predates Iron Fist #1) 1.00 2.50
16-19,21-27,29-33: 17-1st Giffen-a (1 pg.; 11/75). 19-1st White Tiger. 22-1st app. Jack of Hearts; 1st Giffen story-a (along with Amazing Adventures #35, 3/76) 1.50
20-Origin The White Tiger; Perez-a .80 2.00
28-Origin Jack of Hearts; Bruce Lee life story 1.20 3.00
Special Album Edition 1(Summer, '74)-Iron Fist-c/story (very early app., 3rd?); Adams-i 1.00 2.60 6.00
NOTE: **N. Adams** a-1i(part), 27i; c-1, 2-4, 11, 12, 14, 17. **Giffen** a-22p, 24p. **G. Kane** a-23p. **Kirby** a-5r. **Nasser** a-27p, 28. **Perez** a(p)-6-14, 16, 17, 19, 21. **Rogers** a-26, 32, 33. **Starlin** a-1, 2r, 15r. **Staton** a-28p, 31, 32. Iron Fist in #10, 15, 18-24. Shang Chi, Master of Kung Fu in #1-9, 11-18, 33. Sons of the Tiger in #1, 3, 4, 6-14, 16-19 (White Tiger #20-24, 26, 27, 29-31).

DEADMAN (See The Brave and the Bold & Phantom Stranger #39)
May, 1985 - No. 7, Nov, 1985 ($1.75, Baxter paper)
DC Comics

1-Deadman-r by Infantino, N. Adams in all .70 1.75
2-7: 5-Batman-c/story-r/Str. Advs. 7-Batman-r .70 1.75

DEADMAN
Mar, 1986 - No. 4, June, 1986 (75¢, limited series)

Deadman: Love After Death #1 © DC

Dead of Night #11 © MEG

Deathblow #29 © Aegis Entertainment

	GD25	FN65	NM94

DC Comics

1-4: Lopez-c/a. 4-Byrne-c(p)			1.00

DEADMAN: EXORCISM
1992 - No. 2, 1992 ($4.95, limited series, 52 pgs.)
DC Comics

1,2: Kelley Jones-c/a in all.	1.00	2.00	5.00

DEADMAN: LOVE AFTER DEATH
1989 - No. 2, 1990 ($3.95, 52 pgs., limited series, mature)
DC Comics

Book One, Two: Kelley Jones-c/a in all. 1-contains nudity.

		1.60	4.00

DEAD OF NIGHT
Dec, 1973 - No. 11, Aug, 1975
Marvel Comics Group

1-Horror reprints		1.20	3.00
2-11: 11-Intro Scarecrow; Kane/Wrightson-c		.80	2.00

NOTE: *Ditko* r-7, 10. *Everett* c-2. *Sinnott* r-1.

DEADPOOL (See New Mutants #98)
Aug, 1994 - No. 4, Nov, 1994 ($2.50, limited series)
Marvel Comics

1: Mark Waid scripts in all.	1.00	2.00	5.00
2-4		1.20	3.00

DEADPOOL: THE CIRCLE CHASE (See New Mutants #98)
Aug, 1993 - No. 4, Nov, 1993 ($2.00, limited series)
Marvel Comics

1-($2.50)-Embossed-c		1.00	2.50
2-4		.80	2.00

DEADSHOT (See Batman #59, Detective Comics #474, & Showcase '93 #8)
Nov, 1988 - No. 4, Feb, 1989 ($1.00, limited series)
DC Comics

1-4			1.00

DEAD WHO WALK, THE (See Strange Mysteries, Super Reprint #15, 16)
1952 (one-shot)
Realistic Comics

nn	41.00	124.00	330.00

DEADWORLD (Also see The Realm)
Dec, 1986 - No. 28? ($1.50/$1.95/#15-28: $2.50, B&W, mature)
Arrow Comics/Caliber Comics

1		1.20	3.00
2		.80	2.00
3,4			1.50
5-11: Graphic covers			1.50
5-11: Tame covers		.70	1.75
12-28: Graphic covers, 12-28: Tame covers		.70	1.75
...Archives 1 (1992, $2.50)		1.00	2.50

DEAN MARTIN & JERRY LEWIS (See Adventures of...)

DEAR BEATRICE FAIRFAX
No. 5, Nov, 1950 - No. 9, Sept, 1951 (Vern Greene art)
Best/Standard Comics (King Features)

5-All have Schomburg air brush-c	7.00	21.00	42.00
6-9	4.25	13.00	28.00

DEAR HEART (Formerly Lonely Heart)
No. 15, July, 1956 - No. 16, Sept, 1956
Ajax

15,16	4.25	13.00	28.00

DEAR LONELY HEART (...Illustrated No. 1-6)
Mar, 1951; No. 2, Oct, 1951 - No. 8, Oct, 1952

Artful Publications

1	12.00	36.00	85.00
2	6.35	19.00	38.00
3-Matt Baker Jungle Girl story	13.00	39.00	90.00
4-8	5.85	17.50	35.00

DEAR LONELY HEARTS (Lonely Heart #9 on)
Aug, 1953 - No. 8, Oct, 1954
Harwell Publ./Mystery Publ. Co. (Comic Media)

1	6.70	20.00	40.00
2-8	4.00	11.00	22.00

DEARLY BELOVED
Fall, 1952
Ziff-Davis Publishing Co.

1-Photo-c	12.00	36.00	85.00

DEAR NANCY PARKER
June, 1963 - No. 2, Sept, 1963
Gold Key

1,2-Painted-c	1.80	5.40	18.00

DEATHBLOW (Also see Darker Image)
May, 1993 - No. 29, Aug, 1996 ($1.75/$1.95/$2.50)
Image Comics (Wildstorm Productions)

0-(8/96, $2.95, 32 pgs.)-r/Darker Image w/new story & art; Jim Lee & Trevor Scott-a; new Jim Lee-c			3.00
1-($2.50)-Red foil stamped logo on black varnish-c; Jim Lee-c/a; flip-book side has Cybernary -c/story (#2 also)		1.20	3.00
1-($1.95)-Newsstand version w/o foil-c & varnish		.80	2.00
2,4: 2-(8/93)-Lee-a; with bound-in poster. 4-Jim Lee-c.		.70	1.75
2-($1.75)-Newsstand version w/o poster		.70	1.75
3	1.00	2.00	5.00
5-9: Jim Lee-c in all. 5-Begin $1.95-c		.80	2.00
5-Alternate Portacio-c (Forms larger picture when combined with alternate-c for Gen 13 #5, Kindred #3, Stormwatch #10, Team 7 #1, Union #0, Wetworks #2 & WildC.A.T.S # 11)	1.65	4.20	10.00
10-14,15,19-30: 10-Begin $2.50-c. 13-W/pinup poster by Tim Sale & Jim Lee. 17-Variant "Chicago Comicon" edition exists. 20,21-Gen 13 app. 23-Backlash-c/app. 24,25-Grifter-c/app; Gen 13 & Dane from Wetworks app. 28-Deathblow dies. 29-Memorial issue		1.00	2.50
16 ($1.95, Newsstand)-Wildstorm Rising Pt. 6		.80	2.00
16 ($2.50, Direct Market)-Wildstorm Rising Pt. 6		1.00	2.50

DEATHDEALER
July, 1995 - Present ($5.95)
Verotik

1-Frazetta-c; Bisley-a	1.30	3.25	8.00
1-2nd print	1.00	2.60	6.00
2-($6.95)-Frazetta-c; embossed logo	1.20	3.00	7.00

DEATHLOK (Also see Astonishing Tales #25)
July, 1990 - No. 4, Oct, 1990 ($3.95, limited series, 52 pgs.)
Marvel Comics

1-4: 1,2-Guice-a(p). 3,4-Denys Cowan-a, c-4		1.60	4.00

DEATHLOK
July, 1991 - No. 34, Apr, 1994 ($1.75)
Marvel Comics

1-Silver ink cover; Denys Cowan-c/a(p) begins		.80	2.00
2-5: 2-Forge (X-Men) app. 3-Vs. Dr. Doom. 5-X-Men & F.F. x-over		1.00	2.50
6-10: 6,7-Punisher x-over. 9,10-Ghost Rider-c/story		.70	1.75
11-18,20-24,26-34: 16-Infinity War x-over. 17-Jae Lee-c. 22-Black Panther app. 27-Siege app.		.70	1.75

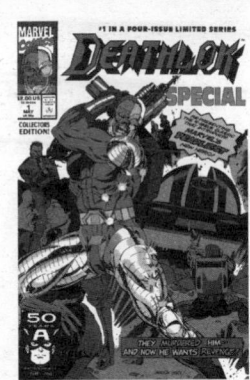
Deathlok Special #1 © MEG

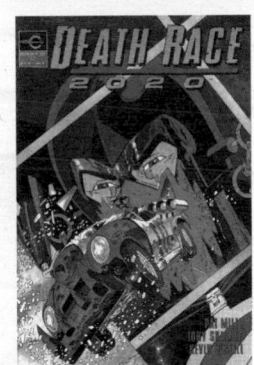
Death Race 2020 #2 © Roger Corman

Deathstroke The Terminator #60 © DC

DE

	GD25	FN65	NM94

19-($2.25)-Foil-c .90 2.25
25-($2.95)-Holo-grafx foil-c 1.20 3.00
Annual 1 (1992, $2.25, 68 pgs.)-Guice-p; Quesada-c(p) 1.00 2.50
Annual 2 (1993, $2.95, 68 pgs.)-Bagged w/card; intro Tracer 1.20 3.00
NOTE: **Denys Cowan** a(p)-9-13, 15, Annual 1; c-9-12, 13p, 14. **Guice/Cowan** c-8.

DEATHLOK SPECIAL
May, 1991 - No. 4, Late-June, 1991 ($2.00, bi-weekly limited series)
Marvel Comics

1-4: r/1-4(1990) w/new Guice-c #1,2; Cowan c-3,4 .80 2.00
1-2nd printing w/white-c .80 2.00

DEATHMARK
Dec, 1994 ($2.95, B&W)
Lightning Comics

1 1.20 3.00

DEATHMATE
Sept, 1993 - Epilogue (#6), Feb, 1994 ($2.95/$4.95, limited series)
Valiant (Prologue/Yellow/Blue)/Image Comics (Black/Red/Epilogue)

Preview-(7/93, 8 pgs.) 1.00
Prologue (#1)-Silver foil; Jim Lee/Layton-c; B. Smith/Lee-a; Liefeld-a(p)
1.20 3.00
Prologue-Special gold foil ed. of silver ed. 1.40 4.00 10.00
Black (#2)-(9/93, $4.95, 52 pgs.)-Silvestri/Jim Lee-c; pencils by Peterson/
Silvestri/Capullo/Jim Lee/Portacio; 1st app. Gen 13
1.30 3.25 8.00
Black-Special gold foil edition 2.85 8.50 20.00
Yellow (#3)-(10/93, $4.95, 52 pgs)-Yellow foil-c; Indicia says Prologue Sept 1993
by mistake; 3rd app. Ninjak; Thibert-c(i) 1.60 4.00
Yellow-Special gold foil edition 1.40 4.00 10.00
Blue (#4)-(10/93, $4.95, 52 pgs.)-Thibert blue foil-c(i); Reese-a(i)
1.60 4.00
Blue-Special gold foil edition 1.40 4.00 10.00
Red (#5) 1.60 4.00
Epilogue (#6)-(2/94, $2.95)-Silver foil Quesada/Silvestri-c; Silvestri-a(p)
1.20 3.00

DEATH METAL
Jan, 1994 - No. 4, Apr, 1994 ($1.95, limited series)
Marvel Comics UK

1-4: 1-Silver ink-c. Alpha Flight app. .80 2.00

DEATH METAL VS. GENETIX
Dec, 1993 - No. 2, Jan, 1994 (Limited series)
Marvel Comics UK

1-($2.95)-Polybagged w/2 trading cards 1.20 3.00
2-($2.50)-Polybagged w/2 trading cards 1.00 2.50

DEATH OF CAPTAIN MARVEL (See Marvel Graphic Novel #1)

DEATH OF MR. MONSTER, THE (See Mr. Monster #8)

DEATH OF LADY VAMPRE
1995 ($2.95, bi-monthly)
Blackout Comics

1-Mignola, Colan flip-c 1.20 3.00

DEATH OF SUPERMAN (See Superman, 2nd Series)

DEATH RACE 2020
Apr, 1995 - No. 8, Nov, 1995 ($2.50)
Roger Corman's Cosmic Comics

1-8: Sequel to the Movie 1.00 2.50

DEATH RATTLE (Formerly an Underground)
V2#1, 10/85 - No. 18, 1988, 1994 ($1.95, Baxter paper, mature)
Kitchen Sink Press

V2#1-7,9-18: 1-Corben-c. 2-Unpubbed Spirit story by Eisner. 5-Robot Woman-r

by Wolverton. 6-B&W issues begin. 10-Savage World-r by by Williamson/
Torres/ Krenkel/Frazetta from Witzend #1. 16-Wolverton Spacehawk-r
.80 2.00
8-(12/86)-1st app. Mark Schultz's Xenozoic Tales/Cadillacs & Dinosaurs
1.00 2.00 5.00
8-(1994)-r plus interview w/Mark Schultz 1.20 3.00

DEATH'S HEAD (See Daredevil #56, Dragon's Claws #5 & Incomplete...)
Dec, 1988 - No. 10, Sept, 1989 ($1.75)
Marvel Comics

1-Dragon's Claws spin-off 1.00 2.00 5.00
2-Fantastic Four app.; Dragon's Claws x-over 1.60 4.00
3,4 .80 2.00
5-10: 8-Dr. Who app. 9-F. F. x-over; Simonson-c(p) .80 2.00
...Gold 1 (1/94, $3.95, 68 pgs.)-Gold foil-c 1.60 4.00

DEATH'S HEAD II (Also see Battletide)
Mar, 1992 - No. 4, June (May inside), 1992 ($1.75, color, limited series)
Marvel Comics UK, Ltd.

1 1.00 2.00 5.00
1,2-Silver ink 2nd printings .70 1.75
2-4: 2-Fantastic Four app. 4-Punisher, Spider-Man , Daredevil, Dr. Strange,
Capt. America & Wolverine in the year 2020 .80 2.00

DEATH'S HEAD II (Also see Battletide)
Dec, 1992 - Present ($1.75/$1.95)
Marvel Comics UK, Ltd.

V2#1-5: 1-Gatefold-c. 1-4-X-Men app. .70 1.75
6-13,15,16 ($1.95): 15-Capt. America & Wolverine app. .80 2.00
14-($2.95)-Foil flip-c w/Death's Head II Gold #0 1.20 3.00

DEATH'S HEAD II & THE ORIGIN OF DIE CUT
Aug, 1993 - No. 2, Sept, 1993 (color, limited series)
Marvel Comics UK, Ltd.

1-($2.95)-Embossed-c 1.20 3.00
2 ($1.75) .70 1.75

DEATHSTROKE: THE TERMINATOR #0-47 (Deathstroke: The Hunted 48-60)
Deathstroke #48-60) (Also see Marvel & DC Present, New Teen Titans #2,
New Titans, Showcase '93 #7,9 & Tales of the Teen Titans #42-44)
Aug, 1991 - No. 60, June, 1996 ($1.75/$1.95/$2.25)
DC Comics

1-New Titans spin-off; Mike Zeck c-1-28 1.00 2.00 5.00
1-Gold ink 2nd printing ($1.75) .80 2.00
2 1.20 3.00
3-5 .80 2.00
6-37: 6,8-Batman cameo. 7,9-Batman-c/story. 9-1st new Vigilante (female) in
cameo. 10-1st full app. new Vigilante; Perez-i. 13-Vs. Justice League; Team
Titans cameo on last pg. 14-Total Chaos, part 1; Team Titans-c/story cont'd
in New Titans #90. 15-Total Chaos, part 4 .70 1.75
38-40: 38-Begin $1.95-c. 40-(9/94) .80 2.00
0 (10/94)-Begin Deathstroke, The Hunted, ends #47. .80 2.00
41 (11/94) - 47 .80 2.00
48,49,51-60: 48-Begin 2.25-c. .90 2.25
50 ($3.50) 1.40 3.50
Annual 1,2 (1992, 1993, $3.50, 68 pgs.): 1-Nightwing & Vigilante app.; minor
Eclipso app. 2-Bloodlines Deathstorm; 1st app. Gunfire.
1.40 3.50
Annual 3 (1994, $3.95, 68 pgs.)-Elseworlds story 1.60 4.00
Annual 4 (1995, $3.95)-Year One story 1.60 4.00
NOTE: **Golden** a-12. **Perez** a-11i. **Zeck** c-Annual 1, 2.

DEATH: THE HIGH COST OF LIVING (See Sandman #8) (Also see the Books
of Magic limited & ongoing series)
Mar, 1993 - No. 3, May, 1993 ($1.95, limited series)
DC Comics (Vertigo)

1-Bachalo/Buckingham-a; Dave McKean-c; Neil Gaiman scripts in all

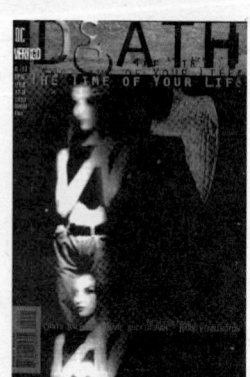

Death the Time of Your Life #2 © DC

Decade of Dark Horse #1 © DH

Defcon 4 #1 © Aegis Entertainment

	GD25	FN65	NM94
	1.20	2.90	7.00
1-Platinum edition	7.00	21.50	50.00
2	1.30	3.25	8.00
3-Pgs. 19 & 20 had wrong placement		1.60	4.00
3-Corrected version w/pgs. 19 & 20 facing each other; has no-c price plus has ads for Sebastion O & The Geek added		1.60	4.00
Hardcover (1994, $19.95)-r/#1-3 & Death Talks About Life; intro. by Tori Amos.			20.00
Trade paperback (6/94, $12.95, Titan Books)-r/#1-3 & Death Talks About Life; prism-c	1.85	5.50	13.00

DEATH: THE TIME OF YOUR LIFE (See Sandman #8)
Apr, 1996 - No. 3, July, 1996 ($2.95, limited series)
DC Comics (Vertigo)

1-3: Neil Gaiman story & Bachalo/Buckingham-a; Dave McKean-c. 2-(5/96).		1.20	3.00

DEATH 3
Sept, 1993 - No. 4, Dec, 1993 ($1.75, limited series)
Marvel Comics UK

1-($2.95)-Embossed-c		1.20	3.00
2-4		.70	1.75

DEATH VALLEY (Cowboys and Indians)
Oct, 1953 - No. 6, Aug, 1954?
Comic Media

1-Billy the Kid; Morisi-a; Andru/Esposito-c/a	8.35	25.00	50.00
2-Don Heck-c	5.00	15.00	30.00
3-6: 3,5-Morisi-a. 5-Discount-a	4.15	12.50	25.00

DEATH VALLEY (Becomes Frontier Scout, Daniel Boone No.10-13)
No. 7, 6/55 - No. 9, 10/55 (Cont'd from Comic Media series)
Charlton Comics

7-9: 8-Wolverton-a (half pg.)	4.70	14.00	28.00

DEATHWISH
Dec, 1994 - No. 4, Mar, 1995 (2.50, limited series)
DC Comics (Milestone Media)

1-4		1.00	2.50

DEATH WRECK
Jan, 1994 - No. 4, Apr, 1994 ($1.95, color, limited series)
Marvel Comics UK

1-4: 1-Metallic ink logo; Death's Head II app.		.80	2.00

DEBBIE DEAN, CAREER GIRL
April, 1945 - No. 2, July, 1945
Civil Service Publ.

1,2-Newspaper reprints by Bert Whitman	12.00	36.00	85.00

DEBBI'S DATES (Also see Date With Debbi)
Apr-May, 1969 - No. 11, Dec-Jan, 1970-71
National Periodical Publications

1	1.70	5.00	12.00
2,3,5,7-11	1.00	2.60	6.00
4,6: 4-Neal Adams text illo, 6-Superman cameo	1.30	3.25	8.00

DECADE OF DARK HORSE, A
July, 1996 - No. 4, Oct, 1996 ($2.95, B&W/color, limited series)
Dark Horse Comics

1-4: 1-Sin City-c/story by Miller; Grendel by Wagner; Predator. 2-Star Wars wraparound-c. 3-Aliens-c/story; Nexus, Mask stories			3.00

DEEP, THE (Movie)
Nov, 1977
Marvel Comics Group

1-Infantino-c/a			1.50

DEEP DARK FANTASIES

	GD25	FN65	NM94
Oct, 1995 ($4.50/$4.95, B&W)			

Dark Fantasy Productions

1-($4.50)-Clive Barker-c, anthology		1.80	4.50
1-($4.95)-Red foil logo-c	1.00	2.00	5.00

DEFCON 4
Feb, 1996 - No. 4, Sept, 1996 ($2.50, limited series)
Image Comics (Wildstorm Productions)

1/2			10.00
1/2 Gold-(1000 printed)			15.00
1-4: 1-Main Cover by Mat Broome & Edwin Rosell			2.50
1-Hordes of Cymulants variant-c by Michael Golden			3.00
1-Backs to the Wall variant-c by Humberto Ramos & Alex Garner			5.00
1-Defcon 4-Way variant-c by Jim Lee			10.00

DEFENDERS, THE (TV)
Sept-Nov, 1962 - No. 2, Feb-Apr, 1963
Dell Publishing Co.

12-176-211(#1), 12-176-304(#2)	2.60	7.80	26.00

DEFENDERS, THE (Also see Giant-Size…, Marvel Feature, Marvel Treasury Edition, Secret Defenders & Sub-Mariner #34, 35; The New…#140-on)
Aug, 1972 - No. 152, Feb, 1986
Marvel Comics Group

1-The Hulk, Doctor Strange, Sub-Mariner begin	9.30	28.00	65.00
2-Silver Surfer x-over	4.30	13.00	30.00
3-5: 3-Silver Surfer x-over. 4-Valkyrie joins	2.85	8.50	20.00
6-9: 6,8-Silver Surfer x-over. 9-Avengers app.	2.15	6.50	15.00
10-Hulk vs. Thor battle; Avengers app.	3.90	11.50	27.00
11-14: 11-Silver Surfer x-over. 12-Last 20¢ issue	1.50	3.75	9.00
15,16-Magneto & Brotherhood of Evil Mutants app. from X-Men	2.15	6.50	15.00
17-20: 17-Power Man x-over (11/74)	1.20	3.00	7.00
21-25: 24,25-Son of Satan app.	1.00	2.60	6.00
26-29-Guardians of the Galaxy app. (#26 is 8/75; pre-dates Marvel Presents #3): 28-1st full app. Starhawk (cameo #27). 29-Starhawk joins Guardians	1.65	4.20	10.00
30-50: 31,32-Origin Nighthawk. 35-Intro New Red Guardian. 44-Hellcat joins. 45-Dr. Strange leaves. 47-49-Early Moon Knight app. (5/77)		1.80	4.50
51-60: 53-1st app. Lunatik (cameo, Lobo lookalike). 55-Origin Red Guardian; Lunatik cameo. 56-1st full Lunatik story		1.60	4.00
61-75: 61-Lunatik & Spider-Man app. 70-Lunatik (origin #71). 73-75-Foolkiller II app. (Greg Salinger). 74-Nighthawk resigns		1.40	3.50
76-95,97-124,126-149,151: 77-Origin Omega. 78-Original Defenders return thru #101. 94-1st Gargoyle. 100-(52 pgs.)-Hellcat (Patsy Walker) revealed as Satan's daughter. 101-Silver Surfer-c & app. 104-The Beast joins. 105-Son of Satan joins. 106-Death of Nighthawk. 120,121-Son of Satan-c/ stories. 122-Final app. Son of Satan (2 pgs.). 129-New Mutants cameo (3/84, early x-over)		.90	2.25
96-Ghost Rider app.		1.80	4.50
125,150,152: 125-(52 pgs.)-Intro new Defenders. 150-(52 pgs.)-Origin Cloud. 152-(52 pgs.)-Ties in with X-Factor & Secret Wars II	1.20	3.00	
Annual 1 (1976, 52 pgs.)-New book-length story		1.60	4.00

NOTE: **Art Adams** c-142p. **Austin** a-53i; c-65i, 119i, 145i. **Frank Bolle** a-7i, 10i, 11i. **Buckler** c(p)-34, 38, 76, 77, 79-86, 90, 91. **J. Buscema** c-66. **Giffen** a-42-49p, 50, 51-54p. **Golden** c-53p, 54p; c-94, 96. **Gulce** c-129. **G. Kane** c(p)-13, 16, 18, 19, 21-26, 31-33, 35-37, 40, 41, 55. **Kirby** c-42-45. **Mooney** a-3i, 31-34i, 62i, 63i, 85i. **Nasser** c-88p. **Perez** c(p)-51, 53, **Rogers** c-98. **Starlin** c-110. **Tuska** a-57p. Silver Surfer in No. 2, 3, 6, 8-11, 92, 98-101, 112-115, 122-125.

DEFENDERS OF DYNATRON CITY
Feb, 1992 - No. 6, July, 1992 ($1.25, limited series)
Marvel Comics

1-6-Lucasarts characters. 2-Origin			1.25

Abraham Lincoln Life Story #1 © DELL

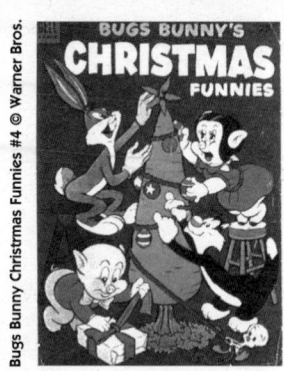

Bugs Bunny Christmas Funnies #4 © Warner Bros.

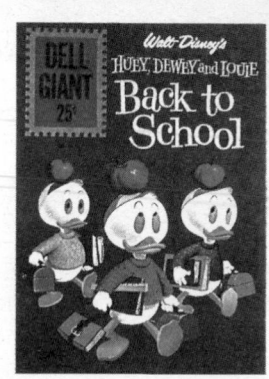

Huey, Dewie & Louie Back To School #1 © WDC

	GD25	FN65	NM94

DEFENDERS OF THE EARTH (TV)
Jan, 1987 - No. 5, Sept, 1987
Marvel Comics (Star Comics)

1-5: The Phantom, Mandrake The Magician, Flash Gordon begin

			1.00

DEFINITIVE DIRECTORY OF THE DC UNIVERSE, THE (See Who's Who...)
DELECTA OF THE PLANETS (See Don Fortune & Fawcett Miniatures)
DELLA VISION (...The Television Queen) (Patty Powers #4 on)
April, 1955 - No. 3, Aug, 1955
Atlas Comics

1-Al Hartley-c	12.00	36.00	85.00
2,3	10.00	30.00	60.00

DELL GIANT COMICS
    Dell Publishing began to release square bound comics in 1949 with a 132-page issue called Christmas Parade #1. The covers were of a heavier stock to accommodate the increased number of pages. The books proved profitable at 25 cents, but the average number of pages was quickly reduced to 100. Ten years later they were converted to a numbering system similar to the Four Color Comics, for greater ease in distribution and the page counts cut back to mostly 84 pages. The label "Dell Giant" began to appear on the covers in 1954. Because of the size of the books and the heavier, less pliant cover stock, they are rarely found in high grade condition, and with the exception of a small quantity of copies released from Western Publishing's warehouse–are almost never found in near mint.

Abraham Lincoln Life Story 1(3/58)	6.50	20.00	47.00	100.00
Bugs Bunny Christmas Funnies 1(11/50, 116pg)				
	17.00	52.00	121.00	260.00
...Christmas Funnies 2(11/51, 116pp)	11.50	34.00	79.00	170.00
...Christmas Funnies 3-5(11/52-11/54,)-Becomes Christmas Party #6				
	10.50	31.00	72.00	155.00
...Christmas Funnies 7-9(12/56-12/58)	9.50	28.00	65.00	140.00
...Christmas Party 6(11/55)-Formerly Bugs Bunny Christmas Funnies				
	7.50	23.00	54.00	115.00
...County Fair 1(9/57)	11.50	34.00	79.00	170.00
...Halloween Parade 1(10/53)	10.50	32.00	75.00	160.00
...Halloween Parade 2(10/54)-Trick 'N' Treat Halloween Fun #3 on				
	9.50	28.00	65.00	140.00
...Trick 'N' Treat Halloween Fun 3,4(10/55-10/56)-Formerly Halloween Parade				
#2	10.00	30.00	70.00	150.00
...Vacation Funnies 1(7/51, 112pg)	17.00	52.00	121.00	260.00
...Vacation Funnies 2('52)	14.00	42.00	98.00	210.00
...Vacation Funnies 3-5('53-'55)	10.50	31.00	72.00	155.00
...Vacation Funnies 6-9('54-6/59)	9.50	28.00	65.00	140.00
Cadet Gray of West Point 1(4/58)-Williamson-a, 10pgs.; Buscema-a; photo-c				
	5.50	17.00	39.00	85.00
Christmas In Disneyland 1(12/57)-Barks-a, 18 pgs.				
	25.00	76.00	177.00	380.00
Christmas Parade 1(11/49)(132 pgs.)(1st Dell Giant)-Donald Duck (25pgs. by Barks, r-in G.K. Christmas Parade #5); Mickey Mouse & other film oriented stories; Cinderella (prior to movie), 7 Dwarfs, Bambi & Thumper, So Dear To My Heart, Flying Mouse, Dumbo, Cookieland & others				
	56.00	170.00	396.00	850.00
Christmas Parade 2('50)-Donald Duck (132 pgs.)(25 pgs. by Barks, r-in G.K. Christmas Parade #6). Mickey, Pluto, Chip & Dale, etc. Contents shift to a holiday expansion of W.D. C&S type format				
	43.00	130.00	303.00	650.00
Christmas Parade 3-7('51-'55, #3-116pgs.; #4-7, 100 pgs.)				
	12.50	38.00	88.00	190.00
Christmas Parade 8(12/56)-Barks-a, 8 pgs.				
	21.50	64.00	149.00	320.00
Christmas Parade 9(12/58)-Barks-a, 20 pgs.				
	25.00	76.00	177.00	380.00

Christmas Treasury, A 1(11/54)	8.50	25.00	58.00	125.00
Davy Crockett, King Of The Wild Frontier 1(9/55)-Fess Parker photo-c;				
Marsh-a	16.00	48.00	112.00	240.00
Disneyland Birthday Party 1(10/58)-Barks-a, 16 pgs. r-by Gladstone				
	25.00	76.00	177.00	380.00
Donald and Mickey In Disneyland 1(5/58)11.50	34.00	79.00	170.00
Donald Duck Beach Party 1(7/54)-Has an Uncle Scrooge story (not by Barks) that prefigures the later rivalry with Flintheart Glomgold and tells of Scrooge's wild rivalry with another millionaire	14.50	44.00	103.00	220.00
...Beach Party 2(1955)-Lady & Tramp sty10.50	32.00	75.00	160.00
...Beach Party 3-5(1956-58)	10.50	32.00	75.00	160.00
...Beach Party 6(8/59, 84pp)-Stapled	7.50	22.00	51.00	110.00
Donald Duck Fun Book 1,2(1953 & 10/54)-Games, puzzles, comics & cut-outs (very rare in unused condition)(most copies commonly have defaced interior pgs.)	37.00	110.00	257.00	550.00
Donald Duck In Disneyland 1(9/55)-1st Disneyland Dell Giant				
	13.00	39.00	91.00	195.00
Golden West Rodeo Treasury 1(10/57)	8.00	24.00	56.00	120.00
Huey, Dewey and Louie Back To School 1(9/58)				
	8.50	26.00	61.00	130.00
Lady and The Tramp 1(6/55)	18.00	54.00	126.00	270.00
Life Stories of American Presidents 1(11/57)-Buscema-a				
	4.65	14.00	32.50	70.00
Lone Ranger Golden West 3(8/55)-Formerly Lone Ranger Western Treasury				
	16.50	50.00	117.00	250.00
Lone Ranger Movie Story nn(3/56)-Origin Lone Ranger in text; Clayton Moore photo-c	32.00	96.00	224.00	480.00
...Western Treasury 1(9/53)-Origin Lone Ranger, Silver, & Tonto; painted cover	18.00	54.00	126.00	270.00
...Western Treasury 2(8/54)-Becomes Lone Ranger Golden West #3				
	11.00	33.00	77.00	165.00
Marge's Little Lulu & Alvin Story Telling Time 1(3/59)-r/#2,5,3,11,30,10,21,17,8, 14,16; Stanley-a	12.50	37.00	86.00	185.00
...& Her Friends 4(3/56)-Tripp-a	10.50	32.00	75.00	160.00
...& Her Special Friends 3(3/55)-Tripp-a	12.50	38.00	88.00	190.00
...& Tubby At Summer Camp 5(10/57)-Tripp-a				
	10.50	32.00	75.00	160.00
...& Tubby At Summer Camp 2(10/58)-Tripp-a				
	10.50	32.00	75.00	160.00
...& Tubby Halloween Fun 6(10/57)-Tripp-a				
	10.50	32.00	75.00	160.00
...& Tubby Halloween Fun 2(10/58)-Tripp-a				
	10.50	32.00	75.00	160.00
...& Tubby In Alaska 1(7/59)-Tripp-a	10.50	32.00	75.00	160.00
...On Vacation 1(7/54)-r/4C-110,14,4C-146,5,4C-97,4,4C-158,3,1;Stanley-a				
	23.00	70.00	163.00	350.00
...& Tubby Annual 1(3/53)-r/4C-165,4C-74,4C-146,4C-158, 4C-139, 4C -131; Stanley-a (1st Lulu Dell Gnt)	28.00	85.00	198.00	425.00
...& Tubby Annual 2('54)-r/4C-139,6,4C-115,4C-74,5,4C-97,3,4C-146,18; Stanley-a	25.00	76.00	177.00	380.00
Marge's Tubby & His Clubhouse Pals 1(10/56)-1st app. Gran'pa Feeb;1st app. Janie; written by Stanley; Tripp-a	12.50	37.00	86.00	185.00
Mickey Mouse Almanac 1(12/57)-Barks-a, 8pgs.				
	26.00	78.00	182.00	390.00
...Birthday Party 1(9/53)-r/entire 48pgs. of Gottfredson's "Mickey Mouse in Love Trouble" from WDC&S 36-39. Quality equal to original. Also reprints one story each from 4-Color 27, 29, & 181 plus 6 panels of highlights in the career of Mickey Mouse	31.00	94.00	219.00	470.00
...Club Parade 1(12/55)-r/4-Color 16 with some death trap scenes redrawn by Paul Murry & recolored with night turned into day; quality less than original	25.00	76.00	177.00	380.00
...In Fantasy Land 1(5/57)	12.50	38.00	88.00	190.00
...In Frontier Land 1(5/56)-Mickey Mouse Club issue				
	12.50	38.00	88.00	190.00

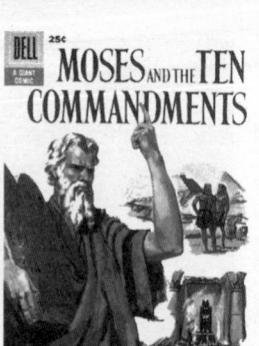

	GD25	FN65	NM94

...Summer Fun 1(8/58)-Mobile cut-outs on back-c; becomes Summer
Fun with #2 .... 12.50 38.00 88.00 190.00
Moses & The Ten Commandments 1(8/57)-Not based on movie; Dell's
adaptation; Sekowsky-a 5.50 16.00 37.00 80.00
Nancy & Sluggo Travel Time 1(9/58) 7.00 21.00 49.00 105.00
Peter Pan Treasure Chest 1(1/53, 212pp)-Disney; contains 54-page movie adap-
tation & other P. Pan stories; plus Donald & Mickey stories w/P. Pan; a 32-
page retelling of "D. Duck Finds Pirate Gold" with yellow beak, called "Capt.
Hook & the Buried Treasure" 100.00 300.00 700.00 1500.00
Picnic Party 6,7(7/55-5/56)(Formerly Vacation Parade)-UncleScrooge,
Mickey & Donald 10.50 32.00 75.00 160.00
Picnic Party 8(7/57)-Barks-a, 6pgs 21.00 64.00 149.00 320.00
Pogo Parade 1(9/53)-Kelly-a(r-Pogo from Animal Comics in this order:
#11,13,21,14,27,16,23,9,18,15,17) 28.00 85.00 198.00 425.00
Raggedy Ann & Andy 1/2(2/55) 15.50 47.00 110.00 235.00
Santa Claus Funnies 1(11/52)-Dan Noonan -A Christmas Carol adaptation
.... 8.50 25.00 58.00 125.00
Silly Symphonies 1(9/52)-Redrawing of Gotfredson's Mickey Mouse strip of "The
Brave Little Tailor"; 2 Good Housekeeping pages (from 1943); Lady and the
Two Siamese Cats, three years before "Lady & the Tramp;" a retelling of
Donald Duck's first app. in "The Wise Little Hen" & other stories based on
1930's Silly Symphony cartoons 28.00 85.00 198.00 425.00
Silly Symphonies 2(9/53)-M. Mouse in "The Sorcerer's Apprentice", 2 Good
Housekeeping pages (from 1944); The Pelican & the Snipe, Elmer Elephant,
Peculiar Penguins, Little Hiawatha, & others
.... 25.00 76.00 177.00 380.00
Silly Symphonies 3(2/54)-r/Mickey & The Beanstalk (4-Color #157, 39pgs.),
Little Minnehaha, Pablo, The Flying Gauchito, Pluto, & Bongo, & 2 Good
Housekeeping pages (1944) 21.00 64.00 149.00 320.00
Silly Symphonies 4(8/54)-r/Dumbo (4-Color 234), Morris The Midget
Moose, The Country Cousin, Bongo, & Clara Cluck
.... 21.00 64.00 149.00 320.00
Silly Symphonies 5(2/55)-r/Cinderella (4-Color 272), Bucky Bug, Pluto,
Little Hiawatha, The 7 Dwarfs & Dumbo, Pinocchio
.... 17.50 52.00 121.00 260.00
Silly Symphonies 6(8/55)-r/Pinocchio(WDC&S 63), The 7 Dwarfs &
Thumper (WDC&S 45), M. Mouse "Adventures With Robin Hood" (40 pgs.),
Johnny Appleseed, Pluto & Peter Pan, & Bucky Bug; Cut-out on back-c
.... 17.50 52.00 121.00 260.00
Silly Symphonies 7(2/57)-r/Reluctant Dragon, Ugly Duckling, M. Mouse &
Peter Pan, Jiminy Cricket, Peter & The Wolf, Brer Rabbit, Bucky Bug; Cut-out
on back-c 17.50 52.00 121.00 260.00
Silly Symphonies 8(2/58)-r/Thumper Meets The 7 Dwarfs (4-Color #19), Jiminy
Cricket, Niok, Brer Rabbit; Cut-out on back-c
.... 17.50 52.00 121.00 260.00
Silly Symphonies 9(2/59)-r/Paul Bunyan, Humphrey Bear, Jiminy Cricket, The
Social Lion, Goliath II; cut-out on back-c
.... 15.50 47.00 110.00 235.00
Sleeping Beauty 1(4/59) 28.00 85.00 198.00 425.00
Summer Fun 2(8/59, 84pp, stapled binding)(Formerly Mickey Mouse...)-Barks-
a(2), 24 pgs. 25.00 76.00 177.00 380.00
Tarzan's Jungle Annual 1(8/52)-Lex Barker photo on-c of #1,2
.... 12.50 38.00 89.00 190.00
...Annual 2(8/53) 9.50 29.00 68.00 145.00
...Annual 3-7('54-9/58)(two No. 5s)-Manning-a No. 3,5-7; Marsh-a in
No. 1-7 plus painted-c 1-7 8.00 24.00 56.00 120.00
Tom And Jerry Back To School 1(9/56) 13.50 41.00 95.00 205.00
...Picnic Time 1(7/58) 10.50 31.00 72.00 155.00
...Summer Fun 1(7/54)-Droopy written by Barks
.... 16.00 48.00 112.00 240.00
...Summer Fun 2-4(7/55-7/57) 7.00 21.00 49.00 105.00
...Toy Fair 1(6/58) 10.50 31.00 72.00 155.00
...Winter Carnival 1(12/52)-Droopy written by Barks
.... 21.00 64.00 149.00 320.00

	GD25	FN65	NM94

...Winter Carnival 2(12/53)-Droopy written by Barks
.... 17.50 53.00 124.00 265.00
...Winter Fun 3(12/54) 7.00 21.00 49.00 105.00
...Winter Fun 4-7(12/55-11/58) 6.00 18.00 42.00 90.00
Treasury of Dogs, A 1(10/56) 5.50 17.00 40.00 85.00
Treasury of Horses, A (9/55) 5.50 17.00 40.00 85.00
Uncle Scrooge Goes To Disneyland 1(8/57p)-Barks-a, 20pgs.r-by Gladstone
.... 25.00 76.00 177.00 380.00
Vacation In Disneyland 1(8/58) 11.50 34.00 79.00 170.00
Vacation Parade 1(7/50, 132pp)-Donald Duck & Mickey Mouse; Barks-a,
55 pgs. 80.00 240.00 560.00 1200.00
Vacation Parade 2(7/51,116pp) 28.00 85.00 198.00 425.00
Vacation Parade 3-5(7/52-7/54)-Becomes Picnic Party No. 6 on. #4-Robin
Hood Advs. 14.00 42.00 98.00 210.00
Western Roundup 1(6/52)-Photo-c; Gene Autry, Roy Rogers, Johnny Mack
Brown, Rex Allen, & Bill Elliott begin; photo back-c begin, and No. 14,16,18
.... 21.50 65.00 152.00 325.00
Western Roundup 2(2/53)-Photo-c 12.50 38.00 89.00 190.00
Western Roundup 3-5(7-9/53 - 1-3/54)-Photo-c
.... 10.00 30.00 70.00 150.00
Western Roundup 6-10(4-6/54 - 4-6/55)-Photo-c
.... 9.50 28.00 65.00 140.00
Western Roundup 11-13,16,17-Photo-c; Manning-a. 11-Flying A's Range
Rider, Dale Evans begin 8.50 25.00 58.00 125.00
Western Roundup 14,15,25(1-3/59)-Photo-c
.... 8.50 25.00 58.00 125.00
Western Roundup 18-Toth-a; last photo-c; Gene Autry ends
.... 8.50 26.00 60.00 130.00
Western Roundup 19-24-Manning-a. 19-Buffalo Bill Jr. begins (7-9/57; early
app.). 19,20,22-Toth-a. 21-Rex Allen, Johnny Mack Brown end. 22-Jace Pear-
son's Texas Rangers, Rin Tin Tin, Tales of Wells Fargo (2nd app., 4-6/58) &
Wagon Train (2nd app.) begin 7.50 23.00 54.00 115.00
Woody Woodpecker Back To School 1(10/52)
.... 10.00 30.00 70.00 150.00
...Back To School 2-4,6('53-10/57)-County Fair No. 5
.... 7.00 21.00 49.00 105.00
...County Fair 5(9/56)-Formerly Back To School
.... 7.00 21.00 49.00 105.00
...County Fair 2(11/58) 6.00 18.00 42.00 90.00

DELL GIANTS (Consecutive numbering)
No. 21, Sept, 1959 - No. 55, Sept, 1961 (Most 84 pgs., 25¢)
Dell Publishing Co.

	GD25	FN65	VF82	NM94

21-(#1)-M.G.M.'s Tom & Jerry Picnic Time (84pp, stapled binding)-Painted-c
.... 11.50 34.00 79.00 170.00
22-Huey, Dewey & Louie Back to School (Disney; 10/59, 84pp, square
binding begins) 8.50 26.00 61.00 130.00
23-Marge's Little Lulu & Tubby Halloween Fun (10/59)-Tripp-a
.... 10.50 32.00 75.00 160.00
24-Woody Woodpecker's Family Fun (11/59)(Walter Lantz)
.... 8.50 25.00 58.00 125.00
25-Tarzan's Jungle World(11/59)-Marsh-a; painted-c
.... 10.50 32.00 75.00 160.00
26-Christmas Parade(Disney; 12/59)-Barks-a, 16pgs.; Barks draws himself on
wanted poster pg. 13 21.50 64.00 149.00 320.00
27-Man in Space r-/4-Color 716,866, & 954 (100 pgs., 35¢)(Disney)(TV)
.... 10.50 31.00 72.00 155.00
28-Bugs Bunny's Winter Fun (2/60) 10.50 31.00 72.00 155.00
29-Marge's Little Lulu & Tubby in Hawaii (4/60)-Tripp-a
.... 10.50 32.00 75.00 160.00
30-Disneyland USA(Disney; 6/60) 10.50 32.00 75.00 160.00
31-Huckleberry Hound Summer Fun (7/60)(TV)(HannaBarbera)-Yogi Bear &
Pixie & Dixie app. 13.50 41.00 96.00 205.00
32-Bugs Bunny Beach Party 6.50 19.00 44.00 95.00

The Demon (Limited Series) #3 © DC

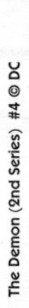

The Demon (2nd Series) #4 © DC

Demon Gun #1 © Gary Cohn

	GD25	FN65	NM94

	GD25	FN65	NM94

33-Daisy Duck & Uncle Scrooge Picnic Time (Disney; 9/60)
   9.50 28.00 65.00 140.00
34-Nancy & Sluggo Summer Camp (8/60)
   7.50 22.00 51.00 110.00
35-Huey, Dewey & Louie Back to School (Disney; 10/60)-1st app. Daisy Duck's
  Nieces, April, May & June 10.50 32.00 75.00 160.00
36-Marge's Little Lulu & Witch Hazel Halloween Fun (10/60)-Tripp-a
   10.50 32.00 75.00 160.00
37-Tarzan, King of the Jungle (11/60)-Marsh-a; painted-c
   9.50 29.00 68.00 145.00
38-Uncle Donald & His Nephews Family Fun (Disney; 11/60)-Cover painting
  based on a pencil sketch by Barks 13.50 41.00 96.00 205.00
39-Walt Disney's Merry Christmas (Disney; 12/60)-Cover painting based on a
  pencil sketch by Barks 13.50 41.00 96.00 205.00
40-Woody Woodpecker Christmas Parade (12/60)(Walter Lantz)
   6.50 19.00 44.00 95.00
41-Yogi Bear's Winter Sports (12/60)(TV)(Hanna-Barbera)-Huckleberry Hound
  & Top Cat app. 13.50 40.00 93.00 200.00
42-Marge's Little Lulu & Tubby in Australia (4/61)
   10.50 32.00 75.00 160.00
43-Mighty Mouse in Outer Space (5/61) 20.00 61.00 142.00 305.00
44-Around the World with Huckleberry and His Friends (7/61)(TV)(Hanna-
  Barbera)-Yogi Bear app. 13.50 40.00 93.00 200.00
45-Nancy & Sluggo Summer Camp (8/61)
   6.50 19.00 44.00 95.00
46-Bugs Bunny Beach Party (8/61) 9.50 19.00 44.00 95.00
47-Mickey & Donald in Vacationland (Disney; 8/61)
   8.50 26.00 61.00 130.00
48-The Flintstones (No. 1)(Bedrock Bedlam)(7/61)(TV)(Hanna-Barbera)
   18.00 54.00 126.00 270.00
49-Huey, Dewey & Louie Back to School (Disney; 9/61)
   8.50 26.00 61.00 130.00
50-Marge's Little Lulu & Witch Hazel Trick 'N' Treat (10/61)
   10.50 32.00 75.00 160.00
51-Tarzan, King of the Jungle by Jesse Marsh (11/61)-Painted-c
   7.50 23.00 54.00 115.00
52-Uncle Donald & His Nephews Dude Ranch (Disney; 11/61)
   7.50 22.00 51.00 110.00
53-Donald Duck Merry Christmas (Disney; 12/61)
   7.50 22.00 51.00 110.00
54-Woody Woodpecker's Christmas Party (12/61)-Issued after No. 55
   7.50 22.00 51.00 110.00
55-Daisy Duck & Uncle Scrooge Showboat (Disney; 9/61)
   8.50 26.00 61.00 130.00
NOTE: All issues printed with & without ad on back cover.

DELL JUNIOR TREASURY
June, 1955 - No. 10, Oct, 1957 (15¢) (All painted-c)
Dell Publishing Co.

	GD25	FN65	NM94
1-Alice in Wonderland; r/4-Color #331 (52 pgs.)	9.50	28.50	95.00
2-Aladdin & the Wonderful Lamp	6.00	18.00	60.00
3-Gulliver's Travels (1/56)	5.00	15.00	50.00
4-Adventures of Mr. Frog & Miss Mouse	5.50	16.50	55.00
5-The Wizard of Oz (7/56)	6.00	18.00	60.00
6-Heidi (10/56)	5.00	15.00	50.00
7-Santa and the Angel	5.00	15.00	50.00
8-Raggedy Ann and the Camel with the Wrinkled Knees			
	5.00	15.00	50.00
9-Clementina the Flying Pig	5.00	15.00	50.00
10-Adventures of Tom Sawyer	5.00	15.00	50.00

DEMOLITION MAN
Nov, 1993 - No. 4, Feb, 1994 ($1.75, color, limited series)
DC Comics

1-4-Movie adaptation .70 1.75

DEMON, THE (See Detective Comics No. 482-485)
Aug-Sept, 1972 - V3#16, Jan, 1974
National Periodical Publications

1-Origin; Kirby-c/a in all	5.00	15.00	35.00
2-5	2.85	8.50	20.00
6-16	2.15	6.50	15.00

DEMON, THE (1st limited series)(Also see Cosmic Odyssey #2)
Jan, 1987 - No. 4, Apr, 1987 (75¢, color, limited series)(#2 has #4 of 4 on-c)
DC Comics

1-4: Matt Wagner-a(p) & scripts in all. 4-Demon & Jason Blood become
  seperate entities. .80 2.00

DEMON, THE (2nd Series)
July, 1990 - No. 57, May, 1995 ($1.50/$1.75/$1.95, color)
DC Comics

1-Grant scripts begin, ends #39: 1-4-Painted-c .70 1.80
2-18,20-27: 3,8-Batman app. (cameo #4). 12-Bisley painted-c. 12-15,21-Lobo
  app. (1 pg. cameo #11). 23-Robin app. .65 1.60
19-($2.50, 44 pgs.)-Lobo poster stapled inside 1.20 3.00
28-42,46,47: 28-Superman-c/story; begin $1.75-c. 29-Superman app. 31,33-39-
  Lobo app. 40-Garth Ennis scripts begin. 46-48 Return of The Haunted Tank-c/s.
   .70 1.75
43-45-Hitman app. 1.65 4.20 10.00
48,49,51: 48-Begin $1.95-c. 51-(9/94) .80 2.00
50 ($2.95, 52 pgs.) 1.20 3.00
0,52-57: 0-(10/94) .80 2.00
Annual 1 (1992, $3.00, 68 pgs.)-Eclipso-c/story 1.20 3.00
Annual 2 (1993, $3.50, 68 pgs.)-1st app. of Hitman 1.70 5.00 12.00
NOTE: **Alan Grant** scripts in #1-16, 20, 21, 23-25, 30-39, Annual 1. **Wagner** a/scripts-22.

DEMON DREAMS
Feb, 1984 - No. 2, May, 1984
Pacific Comics

1,2-Mostly r-/Heavy Metal 1.50

DEMONGATE
May, 1996 - Present ($2.50, B&W)
Sirius Entertainment

1-4 2.50

DEMON GUN
June, 1996 - No. 3, 1996 ($2.95, B&W, limited series)
CrusadeEntertainment

1-3: Gary Cohn scripts. 2-(10/96). 3.00

DEMON-HUNTER
Sept, 1975
Seaboard Periodicals (Atlas)

1-Origin; Buckler-c/a 1.00

DEMONIQUE
1994 - No. 4, 1995 ($3.00, B&W, limited series)
London Night Studios

1-4 1.20 3.00

DEMONIQUE
No. 0, Aug, 1996 - Present ($3.00, mature)
London Night Studios

0,1 3.00
1-($6.00)-Nude Edition 6.00

DEMON KNIGHT: A GRIMJACK GRAPHIC NOVEL
1990 ($8.95, 52 pgs.)
First Publishing

nn-Flint Henry-a 1.50 3.75 9.00

DENNIS THE MENACE (TV with 1959 issues) (Becomes ...Fun Fest Series;

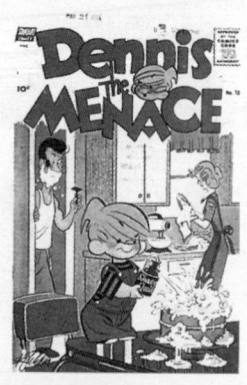

Dennis The Menace #10 © KFS

Dennis The Menace #14 © KFS

Dennis The Menace And His Pal Joey #1 © KFS

See The Best of... & The Very Best of...)(...Fun Fest on-c only to #156-166)
8/53 - #14, 1/56; #15, 3/56 - #31, 11/58; #32, 1/59 - #166, 11/79
Standard Comics/Pines No.15-31/Hallden (Fawcett) No.32 on

	GD	FN	NM
1-1st app. Dennis, Mr. & Mrs. Wilson, Ruff & Dennis' mom & dad; Wiseman-a, written by Fred Toole-most issues	49.00	148.00	395.00
2	25.00	75.00	175.00
3-10: 8-Last pre-code issue	14.00	43.00	100.00
11-20	11.00	33.00	75.00
21-30: 22-1st app. Margaret w/blonde hair	8.35	25.00	50.00
31-40: 31-1st app. Joey. 37-A-Bomb blast panel. 39-1st app. Gina (11/59)	5.00	15.00	30.00
41-60	2.85	8.50	20.00
61-90	1.70	5.00	12.00
91-166	1.00	2.50	6.00
...& Dirt('59,'68)-Soil Conservation giveaway; r-# 36; Wiseman-c/a	1.20	3.00	6.00
...Away We Go('70)-Caladayl giveaway	1.20	3.00	6.00
...Coping with Family Stress-giveaway	.80	2.00	4.00
...Takes a Poke at Poison('61)-Food & Drug Assn. giveaway; Wiseman-c/a	1.20	3.00	6.00
...Takes a Poke at Poison-Revised 1/66, 11/70, 1972, 1974, 1977, 1981	1.60		4.00

NOTE: *Wiseman c/a-1-46, 53, 68, 69.*

DENNIS THE MENACE (Giants) (No. 1 titled Giant Vacation Special; becomes Dennis the Menace Bonus Magazine No. 76 on)
(#1-8,18,23,25,30,38: 100 pgs.; rest to #41: 84 pgs.; #42-75: 68 pgs.)
Summer, 1955 - No. 75, Dec, 1979
Standard/Pines/Hallden(Fawcett)

	GD	FN	NM
nn-Giant Vacation Special(Summ/55-Standard)	17.00	51.00	120.00
nn-Christmas issue (Winter '55)	14.00	43.00	100.00
2-Giant Vacation Special (Summer '56-Pines)			
3-Giant Christmas issue (Winter '56-Pines)			
4-Giant Vacation Special (Summer '57-Pines)			
5-Giant Christmas issue (Winter '57-Pines)			
6-In Hawaii (Giant Vacation Special)(Summer '58-Pines)			
6-In Hawaii (Summer '59-Hallden)-2nd printing; says 3rd large printing on-c			
6-In Hawaii (Summer '60)-3rd printing; says 4th large printing on-c			
6-In Hawaii (Summer '62)-4th printing; says 5th large printing on-c			
6-Giant Christmas issue (Winter '58) each....	11.00	33.00	75.00
7-In Hollywood (Winter '59-Hallden)			
7-In Hollywood (Summer '61)-2nd printing			
8-In Mexico (Winter '60, 100 pgs.-Hallden/Fawcett)			
8-In Mexico (Summer '62, 2nd printing)			
9-Goes to Camp (Summer '61, 84 pgs.)-1st CCA approved issue			
9-Goes to Camp (Summer '62)-2nd printing			
10-X-Mas issue (Winter '61)			
11-Giant Christmas issue (Winter '62)			
12-Triple Feature (Winter '62) each....	9.15	27.50	55.00
13-Best of Dennis the Menace (Spring '63)-Reprints			
14-And His Dog Ruff (Summer '63)			
15-In Washington, D.C. (Summer '63)			
16-Goes to Camp (Summer '63)-Reprints No. 9			
17-& His Pal Joey (Winter '63)			
18-In Hawaii (Reprints No. 6)			
19-Giant Christmas issue (Winter '63)			
20-Spring Special (Spring '64) each....	3.60	11.00	25.00
21-40: 30-r/#6	1.70	5.00	12.00
41-75: 68-Partial-r/#6	1.30	3.25	8.00

NOTE: *Wiseman c/a-1-8, 12, 14, 15, 17, 20, 22, 27, 28, 31, 35, 36, 41, 49.*

DENNIS THE MENACE

Nov, 1981 - No. 13, Nov, 1982
Marvel Comics Group

	GD	FN	NM
1-13: 1,2-New art. 3-Part-r. 4,5-r. 5-X-Mas-c & issue			1.00

NOTE: *Hank Ketcham c-most; a-3, 12. Wiseman a-4, 5.*

DENNIS THE MENACE AND HIS DOG RUFF
Summer, 1961
Hallden/Fawcett

	GD	FN	NM
1-Wiseman-c/a	6.70	20.00	40.00

DENNIS THE MENACE AND HIS FRIENDS
1969; No. 5, Jan, 1970 - No. 46, April, 1980 (All reprints)
Fawcett Publications

	GD	FN	NM
Dennis the Menace & Joey No. 2 (7/69)	1.70	5.00	12.00
Dennis the Menace & Ruff No. 2 (9/69)	1.65	4.20	10.00
Dennis the Menace & Mr. Wilson No. 1 (10/69)	1.70	5.00	12.00
Dennis & Margaret No. 1 (Winter '69)	1.00	2.60	6.00
5-20: 5-Dennis the Menace & Margaret. 6-...& Joey. 7-...& Ruff. 8-...& Mr. Wilson		1.60	4.00
21-37		1.20	3.00
38-46 (Digest size, 148 pgs., 4/78, 95¢)		1.60	4.00

NOTE: *Titles rotate every four issues, beginning with No. 5.*

DENNIS THE MENACE AND HIS PAL JOEY
Summer, 1961 (10¢) (See Dennis the Menace Giants No. 45)
Fawcett Publications

	GD	FN	NM
1-Wiseman-c/a	6.70	20.00	40.00

DENNIS THE MENACE AND THE BIBLE KIDS
1977 (36 pgs.)
Word Books

	GD	FN	NM
1-10: 1-Jesus. 2-Joseph. 3-David. 4-The Bible Girls. 5-Moses. 6-More About Jesus. 7-The Lord's Prayer. 8-Stories Jesus told. 9-Paul, God's Traveller. 10-In the Beginning			1.00

NOTE: *Ketcham c/a in all.*

DENNIS THE MENACE BIG BONUS SERIES
No. 10, Feb, 1980 - No. 11, Apr, 1980
Fawcett Publications

	GD	FN	NM
10,11			1.50

DENNIS THE MENACE BONUS MAGAZINE (Formerly Dennis the Menace Giants Nos. 1-75)
No. 76, 1/70 - No. 194, 10/79; (No. 76-124: 68 pgs.; No. 125-163: 52 pgs.; No. 164 on: 36 pgs.)
Fawcett Publications

	GD	FN	NM
76-90		1.60	4.00
91-110		1.20	3.00
111-194: 166-Indicia printed backwards			1.20

DENNIS THE MENACE COMICS DIGEST
April, 1982 - No. 3, Aug, 1982 ($1.25, digest-size)
Marvel Comics Group

	GD	FN	NM
1-3-Reprints		.80	2.00

NOTE: *Ketcham c-all. Wiseman a-all. A few thousand #1's were published with a DC emblem on cover.*

DENNIS THE MENACE FUN BOOK
1960 (100 pgs.)
Fawcett Publications/Standard Comics

	GD	FN	NM
1-Part Wiseman-a	9.15	27.00	55.00

DENNIS THE MENACE FUN FEST SERIES (Formerly Dennis the Menace #166)
No. 16, Jan, 1980 - No. 17, Mar, 1980 (40¢)
Hallden (Fawcett)

	GD	FN	NM
16,17-By Hank Ketcham			1.00

DENNIS THE MENACE POCKET FULL OF FUN!

Desperado #6 © LEV

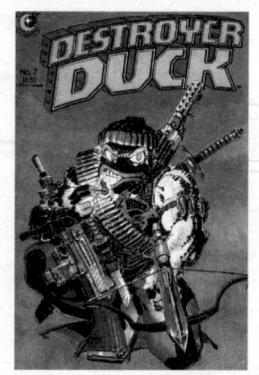

Destroyer Duck #7 © ECL

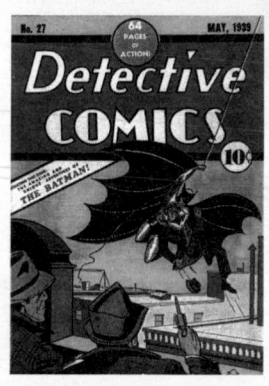

Detective Comics #27 © DC

	GD25	FN65	NM94

Spring, 1969 - No. 50, March, 1980 (196 pgs.) (Digest size)
Fawcett Publications (Hallden)

1-Reprints in all issues	1.70	5.00	12.00
2-10	1.00	2.60	6.00
11-28		1.60	4.00
29-50: 35,40,46-Sunday strip-r		.80	2.00

NOTE: No. 1-28 are 196 pgs.; No. 29-36: 164 pgs.; No. 37: 148 pgs.; No. 38 on: 132 pgs. No. 8, 11, 15, 21, 25, 29 all contain strip reprints.

DENNIS THE MENACE TELEVISION SPECIAL
Summer, 1961 - No. 2, Spring, 1962 (Giant)
Fawcett Publications (Hallden Div.)

1	8.35	25.00	50.00
2	4.25	13.00	28.00

DENNIS THE MENACE TRIPLE FEATURE
Winter, 1961 (Giant)
Fawcett Publications

1-Wiseman-c/a	8.35	25.00	50.00

DEPUTY, THE (TV)
No. 1077, Feb-Apr, 1960 - No. 1225, Oct-Dec, 1961 (all-Henry Fonda photo-c)
Dell Publishing Co.

Four Color 1077 (#1)-Buscema-a	13.00	40.00	130.00
Four Color 1130 (9-11/60)-Buscema-a,1225	10.00	30.00	100.00

DEPUTY DAWG (TV) (Also see New Terrytoons)
Oct-Dec, 1961 - No. 1299, 1962; No. 1, Aug, 1965
Dell Publishing Co./Gold Key

Four Color 1238,1299	11.00	33.00	110.00
1(10164-508)(8/65)-Gold Key	10.00	30.00	100.00

DEPUTY DAWG PRESENTS DINKY DUCK AND HASHIMOTO-SAN (TV)
August, 1965
Gold Key

1(10159-508)	7.50	22.50	75.00

DESERT GOLD (See Zane Grey 4-Color 467)

DESIGN FOR SURVIVAL (Gen. Thomas S. Power's...)
1968 (36 pgs. in color) (25¢)
American Security Council Press

nn-Propaganda against the Threat of Communism-Aircraft cover; H-Bomb panel	4.00	10.00	20.00
Twin Circle Edition-Cover shows panels from inside	2.40	6.00	12.00

DESPERADO (Becomes Black Diamond Western No. 9 on)
June, 1948 - No. 8, Feb, 1949 (All 52 pgs.)
Lev Gleason Publications

1-Biro-c on all; contains inside photo-c of Charles Biro, Lev Gleason & Bob Wood	11.00	33.00	75.00
2	6.35	19.00	38.00
3-Story with over 20 killings	7.50	22.50	45.00
4-8	4.25	13.00	28.00

NOTE: Barry a-2. Fuje a-4, 8. Guardineer a-5-7. Kida a-3-7. Ed Moore a-4, 6.

DESTINATION MOON (See Fawcett Movie Comics, Space Adventures #20, 23, & Strange Adventures #1)

DESTROY!!
1986 ($4.95, B&W, magazine-size, one-shot)
Eclipse Comics

1	1.00	2.00	5.00
3-D Special 1-r-/#1 ($2.50)		1.00	2.50

DESTROYER, THE
Nov, 1989 - No. 9, June, 1990 ($2.25, B&W, magazine, 52 pgs.)
Marvel Comics

1-Based on Remo Williams movie, paperbacks		.90	2.25

2-9: 2-Williamson part inks. 4-Ditko-a		.90	2.25

DESTROYER, THE
V2#1, March, 1991 ($1.95, 52 pgs.)
V3#1, Dec, 1991 - No. 4, Mar, 1992 ($1.95, mini-series)
Marvel Comics

V2#1,V3#1-4: Based on Remo Williams paperbacks. V3#1-4-Simonson-c. 3-Morrow-a		.80	2.00

DESTROYER, THE (Also see Solar, Man of the Atom)
Apr, 1995 ($2.95, color, one-shot)
Valiant

0-Indicia indicates #1		1.20	3.00

DESTROYER DUCK
Feb, 1982 - No. 7, May, 1984 (#2-7: Baxter paper) ($1.50)
Eclipse Comics

1-Origin Destroyer Duck; 1st app. Groo	1.00	2.00	5.00
2-7: 2-Starling back-up begins			1.25

NOTE: Neal Adams c-1i. Kirby c/a-1-5p. Miller c-7.

DESTRUCTOR, THE
February, 1975 - No. 4, Aug, 1975
Atlas/Seaboard

1-Origin; Ditko/Wood-a; Wood-c(i)			1.50
2-4: 2-Ditko/Wood-a. 3,4-Ditko-a(p)			1.00

DETECTIVE COMICS (Also see Batman, Batman:Shadow of the Bat & Special Edition)
Mar, 1937 - Present
National Periodical Publications/DC Comics

	GD25	FN65	VF82
1-(Scarce)-Slam Bradley & Spy by Siegel & Shuster, Speed Saunders by Guardineer, Flat Foot Flannigan by Gustavson, Cosmo, the Phantom of Disguise, Buck Marshall, Bruce Nelson begin; Chin Lung in 'Claws of the Red Dragon' serial begins; Vincent Sullivan-c.			
	8,333.00	25,000.00	50,000.00

(Estimated up to 30 total copies exist, 3 in NM/Mint)

2 (Rare)-Creig Flessel-c begin; new logo	2333.00	6999.00	14,000.00
3 (Rare)	1666.00	5000.00	10,000.00

	GD25	FN65	NM94
4,5: 5-Larry Steele begins	1033.00	3099.00	6200.00
6,7,9,10	750.00	2250.00	4500.00
8-Mister Chang-c; classic-c	1133.00	3399.00	6800.00
11-17,19: 17-1st app. Fu Manchu in Det.	566.00	1700.00	3400.00
18-Fu Manchu; last Flessel-c	950.00	2850.00	5700.00
20-The Crimson Avenger begins (1st app.)	866.00	2600.00	5200.00
21,23-25	450.00	1350.00	2700.00
22-1st & only Crimson Avenger-c (12/38)	583.00	1749.00	3500.00
26	400.00	1200.00	2400.00

	GD25	FN65	VF82	NM94
27-The Bat-Man & Commissioner Gordon begin (1st app.), created by Bill Finger & Bob Kane (5/39); Batman-c (1st)(by Kane). Bat-Man's secret identity revealed as Bruce Wayne in 6pg. sty. Signed Rob't Kane				
	25,000.00	65,000.00	100,000.00	150,000.00

(Estimated up to 50+ total copies exist, 3 in NM/Mint)

27-Reprint, Oversize 13-1/2x10". WARNING: This comic is an exact duplicate reprint of the original except for its size. DC published it in 1974 with a second cover titling it as Famous First Edition. There have been many reported cases of the outer cover being removed and the interior sold as the original edition. The reprint with the new outer cover removed is practically worthless; see Famous First Edition for value.

	GD25	FN65	NM94
27(1984)-Oreo Cookies giveaway (32 pgs., paper-c, r-/Det. 27, 38 & Batman No. 1 (1st Joker)	4.00	12.00	28.00
28-2nd app. The Batman (6 pg. story); non-Bat-Man-c; signed Rob't Kane			
	1444.00	4333.00	14,000.00

	GD25	FN65	VF82	NM94
29-1st app. Doctor Death-c/story, Batman's 1st name villain. 1st 2 part story (10 pgs.). 2nd Batman-c by Kane	2100.00	6300.00	13,650.00	23,000.00

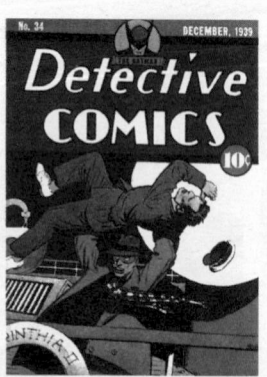

Detective Comics #34 © DC

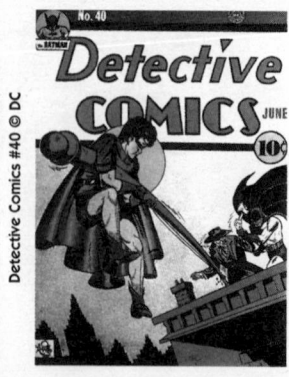

Detective Comics #40 © DC

Detective Comics #164 © DC

	GD25	FN65	NM94

(Estimated up to 75+ total copies exist, 6 in NM/Mint)

	GD25	FN65	NM94

30-Dr. Death app. Story concludes from issue #29. Classic Batman splash panel.

	500.00	1500.00	5000.00

	GD25	FN65	VF82	NM94

31-Classic Batman over castle-c; 1st app. The Monk & 1st Julie Madison (Bruce Wayne's 1st love interest); 1st Batplane (Bat-Gyro) and Batarang; 2nd 2-part Batman adventure. Gardner Fox takes over script from Bill Finger. 1st mention of Locale (New York City) where Batman lives

	2100.00	6300.00	13,650.00	23,000.00

(Estimated up to 75+ total copies exist, 6 in NM/Mint)

32-Batman story concludes from issue #31. 1st app. Dala (Monk's assistant). Batman uses gun for 1st time to slay The Monk and Dala. This was the 1st time a costumed hero used a gun in comic books. 1st Batman head logo on cover

	GD25	FN65	NM94
	500.00	1500.00	5000.00

	GD25	FN65	VF82	NM94

33-Origin The Batman (2 pgs.)(1st told origin); Batman w/smoking gun holster-c; Batman w/smoking gun panel at end of story. Batman story now 12 pgs. Classic Batman-c

	2900.00	8700.00	18,850.00	32,000.00

(Estimated up to 75+ total copies exist, 7 in NM/Mint)

	GD25	FN65	NM94

34-2nd Crimson Avenger-c by Creig Flessel and last non Batman-c. Story from issue #32 x-over as Bruce Wayne sees Julie Madison off to America from Paris. Classic Batman splash panel used later in Batman #1 for origin story. Steve Malone begins

	400.00	1200.00	3900.00

35-Classic Batman hypodermic needle-c that reflects story in issue #34. Classic Batman with smoking .45 automatic splash panel. Last time a costumed hero used a gun in comic books. Batman-c begin

	700.00	2100.00	6900.00

36-Batman-c that reflects adventure in issue #35. Origin/1st app. of Dr. Hugo Strange (1st major villain, 2/40). 1st finned-gloves worn by Batman

	500.00	1500.00	5000.00

37-Last solo Golden-Age Batman adventure in Detective Comics. Panel at end of story reflects solo Batman adventure in Batman #1 that was originally planned for Detective #38. Cliff Crosby begins

	500.00	1500.00	5000.00

	GD25	FN65	NM94

38-Origin/1st app. Robin the Boy Wonder (4/40); Batman and Robin-c begin; cover by Kane & Robinson taken from splash pg.

	2600.00	7800.00	16,900.00	28,000.00

(Estimated up to 85+ total copies exist, 9 in NM/Mint)

	GD25	FN65	NM94

39-Opium story

	450.00	1350.00	4500.00

40-Origin & 1st app. Clay Face (Basil Karlo); 1st Joker cover app. (6/40); Joker story intended for this issue was used in Batman #1 instead; cover is similar to splash pg. in 2nd Joker story in Batman #1

	578.00	1733.00	5500.00

41-Robin's 1st solo

	300.00	900.00	2600.00

42-44: 44-Crimson Avenger-new costume

	212.00	636.00	1700.00

45-1st Joker story in Det. (3rd book app. & 4th story app. over all, 11/40)

	300.00	900.00	2600.00

46-50: 46-Death of Hugo Strange. 48-1st time car called Batmobile (2/41); Gotham City 1st mention in Det. (1st mentioned in Wow #1; also see Batman #4). 49-Last Clay Face

	188.00	562.00	1500.00

51-57

	131.00	393.00	1050.00

58-1st Penguin app. (12/41); last Speed Saunders; Fred Ray-c

	350.00	1050.00	3000.00

59-Last Steve Malone; 2nd Penguin; Wing becomes Crimson Avenger's aide

	150.00	450.00	1200.00

60-Intro. Air Wave; Joker app. (2nd in Det.)

	150.00	450.00	1200.00

61,63: 63-Last Cliff Crosby; 1st app. Mr. Baffle

	131.00	393.00	1050.00

62-Joker-c/story (2nd Joker-c, 4/42)

	206.00	618.00	1650.00

64-Origin & 1st app. Boy Commandos by Simon & Kirby (6/42); Joker app.

	350.00	1050.00	3000.00

65-1st Boy Commandos-c (S&K-a on Boy Commandos & Ray/Robinson-a on

Batman & Robin on-c; 4 artists on one-c)

	281.00	843.00	2250.00

66-Origin & 1st app. Two-Face

	288.00	862.00	2500.00

67-1st Penguin-c (9/42)

	188.00	562.00	1500.00

68-Two-Face-c/story; 1st Two-Face-c

	150.00	450.00	1200.00

69-Joker-c/story

	143.00	431.00	1150.00

70

	103.00	309.00	825.00

71-Joker-c/story

	116.00	350.00	935.00

72,74,75: 74-1st Tweedledum & Tweedledee plus-c; S&K-a

	93.00	281.00	750.00

73-Scarecrow-c/story (1st Scarecrow-c)

	109.00	328.00	875.00

76-Newsboy Legion & The Sandman x-over in Boy Commandos; S&K-a; Joker-c/story

	156.00	468.00	1250.00

77-79: All S&K-a

	103.00	309.00	825.00

80-Two-Face app.; S&K-a

	111.00	333.00	890.00

81,82,84,86-90: 81-1st Cavalier-c & app. 89-Last Crimson Avenger; 2nd Cavalier-c & app.

	81.00	243.00	650.00

83-1st "skinny" Alfred (2/44)(see Batman #21; last S&K Boy Commandos. (also #92,128); most issues #84 on signed S&K are not by them

	91.00	275.00	735.00

85-Joker-c/story; last Spy; Kirby/Klech Boy Commandos

	106.00	318.00	850.00

91,102-Joker-c/story

	100.00	300.00	800.00

92-98: 96-Alfred's last name 'Beagle' revealed, later changed to 'Pennyworth' in #214

	70.00	211.00	565.00

99-Penguin-c

	106.00	318.00	850.00

100 (6/45)

	111.00	333.00	890.00

101,103-108,110-113,115-117,119: 108-1st Bat-signal-c (2/46). 114-1st small logo (8/46)

	67.00	202.00	540.00

109,114,118-Joker-c/stories

	91.00	273.00	730.00

120-Penguin-c (white-c, rare above fine)

	137.00	412.00	1100.00

121,123,125,127,129,130

	68.00	206.00	550.00

122-1st Catwoman-c (4/47)

	111.00	333.00	890.00

124,128-Joker-c/stories

	83.00	251.00	670.00

126-Penguin-c

	90.00	271.00	725.00

131-136,139: 135-Frankenstein-c/story

	55.00	165.00	440.00

137-Joker-c/story; last Air Wave

	70.00	210.00	560.00

138-Origin Robotman (see Star Spangled #7 for 1st app.); series ends #202

	103.00	311.00	830.00

140-The Riddler-c/story (1st app., 10/48)

	360.00	1080.00	3600.00

141,143-148,150: 150-Last Boy Commandos

	60.00	181.00	485.00

142-2nd Riddler-c/story

	103.00	309.00	825.00

149-Joker-c/story

	75.00	225.00	600.00

151-Origin & 1st app. Pow Wow Smith, Indian lawman (9/49) & begins series

	66.00	200.00	535.00

152,154,155,157-160: 152-Last Slam Bradley

	56.00	168.00	450.00

153-1st app. Roy Raymond TV Detective (11/49) ; origin The Human Fly

	63.00	191.00	510.00

156(2/50)-The new classic Batmobile

	76.00	228.00	610.00

161-167,169,170,172-176: Last 52 pg. issue

	64.00	193.00	515.00

168-Origin the Joker

	312.00	938.00	2800.00

171-Penguin-c/story

	83.00	251.00	670.00

177-179,181-186,188,189,191,192,194-199,201,202,204,206-210,212,214-216: 184-1st app. Fire Fly. 185-Secret of Batman's utility belt. 187-Two-Face app. 202-Last Robotman & Pow Wow Smith. 215-1st app. of Batmen of all Nations. 216-Last precode (2/55)

	47.00	141.00	375.00

180,193-Catwoman-c/stories

	50.00	150.00	400.00

187-Two-Face-c/story

	50.00	150.00	400.00

190-Origin Batman retold

	67.00	202.00	540.00

200 (10/53)

	63.00	191.00	510.00

203,211-Catwoman-c/stories

	50.00	150.00	400.00

205-Origin Batcave

	63.00	191.00	510.00

213-Origin & 1st app. Mirror Man

	55.00	165.00	440.00

217-224: 218-Batman Jr. & Robin Sr. app.

	40.00	120.00	310.00

	GD25	FN65	VF82	NM94

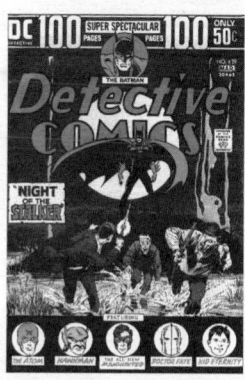

Detective Comics #439 © DC

Detective Comics #490 © DC

Detective Comics #586 © DC

	GD25	FN65	NM94

225-(11/55)-1st app. Martian Manhunter, John Jones; later changed to J'onn J'onzz; origin begins; also see Batman #78

	385.00	1155.00	2875.00	5000.00
		GD25	FN65	NM94

226-Origin Martian Manhunter cont'd (2nd app.) 129.00 386.00 1200.00
227-229: Martian Manhunter stories in all 50.00 150.00 450.00
230-1st app. Mad Hatter; brief recap origin of Martian Manhunter 53.00 160.00 475.00
231-Brief origin recap Martian Manhunter 39.00 118.00 300.00
232,234,237-240: 232-Batwoman app. 239-Early DC grey tone-c 37.00 111.00 285.00
233-Origin & 1st app. Batwoman (7/56) 125.00 375.00 1100.00
235-Origin Batman & his costume; tells how Bruce Wayne's father (Thomas Wayne) wore Bat costume & fought crime (reprinted in Batman #255) 60.00 170.00 525.00
236-1st S.A. issue; J'onn J'onzz talks to parents and Mars-1st since being stranded on Earth; 1st app. Bat-Tank? 40.00 120.00 330.00
241-260: 246-Intro. Diane Meade, John Jones' girl. 249-Batwoman-c/app. 253-1st app. The Terrible Trio. 254-Bat-Hound-c/story. 257-Intro. & 1st app. Whirly Bats. 259-1st app. The Calendar Man 30.00 90.00 230.00
261-J. Jones tie-in to sci/fi movie "Incredible Shrinking Man" 23.00 69.00 175.00
262-264,266,269,270: 261-1st app. Dr. Double X. 262-Origin Jackal 23.00 69.00 175.00
265-Batman's origin retold with new facts 36.00 107.00 275.00
267-Origin & 1st app. Bat-Mite (5/59) 32.00 96.00 240.00
268,271-Manhunter origin recap 22.00 66.00 170.00
272,274-280: 276-2nd app. Bat-Mite 17.00 51.00 135.00
273-J'onn J'onzz i.d. revealed for 1st time 19.00 56.00 145.00
281-292, 294-297: 286,292-Batwoman-c/app. 287-Origin J'onn J'onzz retold.
289-Bat-Mite-c/story. 292-Last Roy Raymond. 297-Last 10¢ issue (11/61) 13.50 41.00 105.00
293-(7/61)-Aquaman begins (pre #1); ends #300 15.00 45.00 115.00
298-(12/61)-1st modern Clayface (Matt Hagen) 27.00 81.00 210.00
299,300: 300-(2/62)-Aquaman ends 11.00 33.00 80.00
301-(3/62)-J'onn J'onzz returns to Mars (1st since stranded on Earth 6 years before) 10.00 30.00 76.00
302-326,329,330: 302,311,318,321-Batwoman-c/app. 311-Intro. Zook in John Jones; 1st app. Cat-Man. 318,325-Cat-Man-c/story (2nd & 3rd app.); also 1st & 2nd app. Batwoman as the Cat-Woman. 321-2nd Terrible Trio. 322-Bat-Girl's 1st/only app. in Det. (6th in all); Batman cameo in J'onn J'onzz (only hero to app. in series). 326-Last J'onn J'onzz, story cont'd in H.O.M. #143; intro. Idol-Head of Diabolu 8.00 23.50 60.00
327-(5/64)-Elongated Man begins, ends #383; 1st new look Batman with new costume; Infantino/Giella new look-a begins; Batman with gun 13.50 41.00 105.00
328-Death of Alfred; Bob Kane biog, 2 pgs. 12.00 36.00 90.00
331,333-340,342-358,360-364,366-368,370: 334-1st app. The Outsider. 345-Intro Block Buster. 347-"What If" theme story (1/66). 351-Elongated Man new costume. 355-Zatanna x-over in Elongated Man. 356-Alfred brought back in Batman, 1st SA app.? 359-1st app. Killer Moth. 362,364-S.A. Riddler app. (early). 363-2nd app. new Batgirl. 370-1st Neal Adams-a on Batman (cover only, 12/67) 5.70 17.00 42.00
332,341,365-Joker-c/stories 7.00 21.50 52.00
359-Intro/origin new Batgirl-c/story (1/67) 10.50 31.50 85.00
369(11/67)-N. Adams-a (Elongated Man); 3rd app. S.A. Catwoman (cameo); leads into Batman #197); 4th app. new Batgirl 8.00 23.50 60.00
371-1st new Batmobile from TV show (1/68) 5.70 17.00 45.00
372-386,389,390: 375-New Batmobile-c. 377-S.A. Riddler app. 4.30 13.00 32.00
387-r/1st Batman story from #27 (30th anniversary, 5/69); Joker-c 8.00 23.50 60.00
388-Joker-c/story; last 12¢ issue 5.70 17.00 45.00
391-394,396,398,399,401,403,405,406,409: 392-1st app. Jason Bard.

401-2nd Batgirl/Robin team-up 2.15 6.50 15.00
395,397,402,404,407,408,410-Neal Adams-a. 404-Tribute to Enemy Ace 3.40 10.00 24.00
400-(6/70)-Origin & 1st app. Man-Bat; 1st Batgirl/Robin team-up (cont'd in #401); Neal Adams-a 7.00 20.50 55.00
411-420: 413-Last 15¢ issue. 414-25¢, 52 pgs. begin, end #424.
418-Creeper x-over 1.85 5.50 13.00
421-436: 424-Last Batgirl. 426,430,436-Elongated Man app. 428,434-Hawkman begins, ends #467 1.70 5.00 12.00
437-New Manhunter begins (10-11/73, 1st app.) by Simonson, ends #443 2.15 6.50 15.00
438-445 (All 100 Page Super Spectaculars): 438-Kubert Hawkman-r. 440-Origin Manhunter. 440-G.A. Manhunter(Adv. #79) by S&K, Hawkman, Dollman, Gr. Lantern; Toth-a. 441-G.A. Plastic Man, Ibis-r. 442-G.A. Newsboy Legion, Bl. Canary, Elongated Man, Dr. Fate-r. 443-Origin The Creeper-r; death of Manhunter; G.A. Green Lantern, Spectre-r; Batman-r/Batman #18.
444-G.A. Kid Eternity-r. 445-G.A. Dr. Midnite-r 3.60 11.00 25.00
446-460: 457-Origin retold & updated 1.30 3.00 7.50
461-465,469,470,480: 480-(44 pgs.). 463-1st app. Black Spider. 464-2nd app. Black Spider 1.20 2.40 6.00
466-468,471-474,478,479-Rogers-a in all: 466-1st app. Signalman since Batman #139. 469-Intro/origin Dr. Phosphorous. 470,471-1st modern app. Hugo Strange. 474-1st app. new Deadshot. 478-1st app. 3rd Clayface (Preston Payne). 479-(44 pgs.)-Clayface app. 2.15 6.50 15.00
475,476-Joker-c/stories; Rogers-a 3.60 11.00 25.00
477-Neal Adams-a(r); Rogers-a (3 pgs.) 2.60 7.50 18.00
481-(Combined with Batman Family, 12-1/78-79, begin $1.00, 68 pg. issues, ends #495); 481-495-Batgirl, Robin begin 1.70 5.00 12.00
482-Starlin/Russell, Golden-a; The Demon begins (origin-r), ends #485 (by Ditko #483-485) 1.30 3.00 7.50
483-40th Anniversary issue; origin retold; Newton Batman begins 1.65 4.20 10.00
484-499: 484-Origin Robin. 485-Death of Batwoman. 487-The Odd Man by Ditko. 489-Robin/Batgirl team-up. 490-Black Lightning begins. 491-(#492 on inside) 1.00 2.00 5.00
500-($1.50, 52 pgs.)-Batman/Deadman team-up; new Hawkman story by Joe Kubert; incorrectly says 500th anniv. of Det. 1.60 5.00 11.00
501-503,505-523: 512-2nd app. new Dr. Death. 519-Last Batgirl. 521-Green Arrow series begins. 523-Solomon Grundy app. 1.00 2.00 5.00
504-Joker-c/story 1.20 2.90 7.00
524-2nd app. Jason Todd (cameo)(3/83) 1.40 3.50
525-3rd app. Jason Todd (See Batman #357) 1.70 4.00
526-Batman's 500th app. in Detective Comics ($1.50, 68 pgs.); Death of Jason Todd's parents, Joker-c/story (55 pgs.); Bob Kane pin-up 2.40 7.20 17.00
527-531,533,534,536-568,571,573: 538-Cat-Man-c/story cont'd from Batman #371. 542-Jason Todd quits as Robin (becomes Robin again #547). 549, 550-Alan Moore scripts (Gr. Arrow). 554-1st new Black Canary (9/85). 566-Batman villains profiled. 567-Harlan Ellison scripts 1.20 3.00
532,569,570-Joker-c/stories 1.20 2.40 6.00
535-Intro new Robin (Jason Todd)-1st appeared in Batman 1.60 4.00
572-(3/87, $1.25, 60 pgs.)-50th Anniv. of Det. Comics 1.60 4.00
574-Origin Batman & Jason Todd retold 1.00 2.00 5.00
575-Year 2 begins, ends #578 2.00 6.00 14.00
576-578: McFarlane-c/a. 578-Clay Face app. 1.70 5.00 12.00
579-597,601-610: 579-New bat wing logo. 583-1st app. villains Scarface & Vintriloquist. 589-595-(52 pgs.)-Each contain free 16 pg. Batman stories. 604-607-Mudpack storyline. 604,607-Contain Batman mini-posters. 610-Faked death of Penguin; artists names app. on tombstone on-c 1.50
598-($2.95, 84 pgs.)- "Blind Justice" storyline begins by Batman movie writer Sam Hamm, ends #600 1.60 4.00
599 1.20 3.00

Detective Comics #645 © DC

Detective Comics #690 © DC

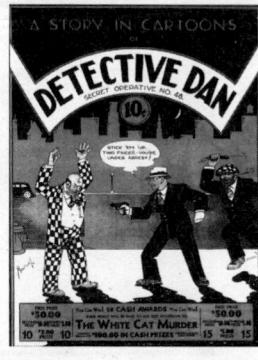

Detective Dan, Secret Operative 48 © Norman Marsh

	GD25	FN65	NM94

600-(5/89, $2.95, 84 pgs.)-50th Anniv. of Batman in Det.; 1 pg. Neal Adams
pin-up, among other artists .... 1.00 ... 2.60 ... 6.00
611-626,628-658: 612-1st new look Cat-Man; Catwoman app. 615- "The
Penguin Affair" part 2 (See Batman #448,449). 617-Joker-c/story. 624-1st
new Catwoman (w/death) & 1st new Batwoman. 626-Batman's 600th app. in
Det. 642-Return of Scarface, part 2. 644-Last $1.00-c. 652,653-Huntress-c/
story w/new costume plus Travis Charest-c on both 1.25
627-($2.95, 84 pgs.)-Batman's 601st app. in Det.; reprints 1st story/#27 plus 3
versions (2 new) of same story .... 1.40 ... 3.50
659,660: 659-Knightfall part 2; Kelley Jones-c. 660-Knightfall part 4; Bane-c by
Sam Kieth .... 1.00 ... 2.00 ... 5.00
661-664: 661-Knightfall part 6; brief Joker & Riddler app. 662-Knightfall part 8;
Riddler app.; Sam Kieth-c. 663-Knightfall part 10; Kelley Jones-c. 664-
Knightfall part 12; Bane-c/story; Joker app.; continued in Showcase 93 #7
& 8; Jones-c .... 1.60 ... 4.00
665,666-Knightfall parts 16 & 18; 666-Bane-c/story .... 1.00 ... 2.50
667,668: 667-Knightquest: The Crusade & new Batman begins (1st app. in
Batman #500) .... .70 ... 1.75
669-675: 669-Begin $1.50-c; Knightquest, cont'd in Robin #1. 671,673-Joker
app. .... .70 ... 1.75
675-($2.95)-Collectors edition w/foil-c .... 1.20 ... 3.00
676-($2.50, 52 pgs.)-KnightsEnd Pt. 3 .... 1.00 ... 2.50
677,678: 677-KnightsEnd Pt. 9. 678-(9/94)-Zero Hour tie-in.
.... 1.50
0,679-684: 0-(10/94). 679-(11/94). 682-Troika Pt. 3
.... 1.50
682-($2.50) Embossed-c Troika Pt. 3 .... 1.00 ... 2.50
686-699,701-715: 686-Begin $1.95-c. 693,694-Poison Ivy-c/story.
695-Contagion Pt. 2; Catwoman, Penguin app. 696-Contagion Pt. 8.
698-Two-Face-c/app. 701-Legacy Pt. 6; Batman vs. Bane-c/app. 702-Legacy
Epilogue. 703-Final Night x-over 2.00
700-($4.95, Collectors Edition)-Legacy Pt. 1; Ra's Al Ghul-c/app.; Talia &
Bane app; book displayed at shops in envelope 1.00 ... 2.00 ... 5.00
700-($2.95, Regular Edition)-Different-c .... 1.20 ... 3.00
Annual 1 (1988, $1.50) .... 1.00 ... 2.00 ... 5.00
Annual 2 (1989, $2.00, 68 pgs.) .... 1.60 ... 4.00
Annual 3 (1990, $2.00, 68 pgs.) .... .80 ... 2.00
Annual 4 (1991, $2.00, 68 pgs.)-Painted-c .... .80 ... 2.00
Annual 5 (1992, $2.50, 68 pgs.)-Joker-c/story (54 pgs.) continued in Robin
Annual #1; Sam Kieth-c; Eclipso app. .... 1.00 ... 2.50
Annual 6 (1993, $2.50, 68 pgs.)-Azrael as Batman in new costume; intro Geist
the Twilight Man; Bloodlines storyline .... 1.00 ... 2.50
Annual 7 (1994, $2.95, 68 pgs.)-Elseworlds story .... 1.20 ... 3.00
Annual 8 (1995, $3.95, 68 pgs.)-Year One story .... 1.60 ... 4.00
Annual 9 (1996, $2.95)-Legends of the Dead Earth story 3.00
NOTE: Neal Adams c-370, 372, 383, 385, 389, 391, 392, 394-422, 439. Aparo a-437, 438, 444-
446, 500, 625-632p, 638-643p; c-430, 437, 444-448, 468-470, 480, 484(back), 492-
502,508, 509, 515, 518-522, 641. Austin a(i)-450, 451, 463-468, 471-476; c(i)-474-476, 478.
Baily a-443r. Buckler a-434, 446p, 479p; c(p)-467, 482, 505-507, 511, 513-516, 518. Burnley
a(Batman)-65, 75, 78, 83, 100, 103, 125; c-62i, 63i, 64, 73i, 78, 83p, 96p, 103p, 105p, 106, 108,
121p, 123p, 125p. Chaykin a-441. Colan a(p)-510, 512, 517, 523, 528-538, 540-546, 555-567;
c(p)-510, 512, 528, 530-535, 537, 538, 540, 541, 543-545, 556-558, 560-564. J. Craig a-488.
Ditko a-443r, 483-485, 487. Golden a-482p; c-625, 626, 628-631, 633, 644-646. Alan Grant
scripts-584-597, 601-621, 641, 642, Annual 5. Grell a-445, 455, 463p, 464p; c-455. Guardineer
c-23, 24, 26, 28, 30, 32. Gustavson a-441r. Infantino a-442(2)r, 500, 572. Infantino/Anderson
c-333, 337-340, 343, 344, 347, 351, 352, 359, 361-368, 371. Kelley Jones c-651, 657i, 658i,
659, 661, 663-675. Kaluta c-423, 424, 426-428, 431, 434, 438, 484, 486, 572. Bob Kane a-Most
early issues #27 on, 297r, 356r, 438-440r, 442r, 443r. Kane/Robinson c-33. Gil Kane a(p)-368,
370-374, 384, 385, 388-407, 438r, 439r, 520. Kane/Anderson c-369. Sam Kieth c-654-656
(657, 658 w/Kelley Jones), 660, 662, Annual #5. Kubert a-438r, 439r, 500; c-348, 350.
McFarlane c/a(p)-576-578. Meskin a-420r. Mignola c-583. Moldoff c-233-354, 259, 266, 267,
275, 287, 289, 290, 310. Moldoff/Giella a-328, 330, 332, 334, 336, 338, 340, 342, 344, 346,
346, 348, 350, 352, 354, 356. Mooney a-444r. Moreira a-153-300, 419r, 444r, 445r.
Nasser/Netzer a-654, 655, 657, 658. Newton a(p)-480, 481, 483-499, 501-509, 511, 513-516,
518-520, 524, 526, 539; c-526p. Irv Novick c-375-377. Robbins a-426p, 429p. Robinson a-
part: 66, 68, 71-73; all: 74-76, 79, 80; c-62, 64, 66, 68-74, 76, 79, 82, 86, 88, 442r, 443r. Rogers
a-466-468, 471-479p, 481p; c-471p, 472p, 473, 474-479p. Roussos Airwave-76-105(most); c(i)-
71, 72, 74-76, 79, 107. Russell a-481i, 482i. Simon/Kirby a-440r, 442r. Simonson a-437-443,
450, 469, 470, 500. Dick Sprang c-77, 82, 84, 85, 87, 89-93, 95-100, 102, 103i, 104i, 106, 108,

114, 117, 118, 122, 123, 128, 129, 131, 133, 135, 141, 148, 149, 168, 622-624. Starlin a-481p,
482p; c-503, 504, 567p. Starr a-444r. Toth a-442; r-414, 416, 418, 424, 440-441, 443, 444.
Tuska a-486p, 490p. Matt Wagner c-647-649. Wrightson c-425.

DETECTIVE DAN, SECRET OP. 48 (Also see Advs. of Detective Ace King)
1933 (10¢, 10x13", 36 pgs., B&W, one-shot) (3 color, cardboard-c)
Humor Publ. Co. (Norman Marsh)

	GD	FN	VF

nn-By Norman Marsh, 1st comic w/ original-a; 1st news-stand-c; Dick Tracy
look-alike; forerunner of Dan Dunn. (Title and Wu Fang character
inspired Detective #1 four years later.) ... 916.00 ... 2750.00 ... 5500.00

DETECTIVE EYE (See Keen Detective Funnies)
Nov, 1940 - No. 2, Dec, 1940
Centaur Publications

	GD	FN	NM

1-Air Man (see Keen Detective) & The Eye Sees begins; The Masked Marvel
& Dean Denton app. .... 181.00 ... 543.00 ... 1450.00
2-Origin Don Rance and the Mysticape; Binder-a; Frank Thomas-c
.... 125.00 ... 375.00 ... 1000.00

DETECTIVE PICTURE STORIES (Keen Detective Funnies No. 8 on?)
Dec, 1936 - No. 5, Apr, 1937 (1st comic of a single theme)
Comics Magazine Company

1 .... 550.00 ... 1650.00 ... 3300.00
2-The Clock app. (1/37, early app.) .... 233.00 ... 699.00 ... 1400.00
3,4: 4-Eisner-a .... 150.00 ... 450.00 ... 900.00
5-The Clock-c/story (4/37); Kane-a; .... 166.00 ... 500.00 ... 1000.00

DETECTIVES, THE (TV)
No. 1168, Mar-May, 1961 - No. 1240, Oct-Dec, 1961
Dell Publishing Co.

Four Color 1168 (#1)-Robert Taylor photo-c ... 10.00 ... 30.00 ... 100.00
Four Color 1219-Robert Taylor, Adam West photo-c ... 8.00 ... 24.00 ... 80.00
Four Color 1240-Tufts-a; Robert Taylor photo-c ... 8.00 ... 24.00 ... 80.00

DETECTIVES, INC. (See Eclipse Graphic Album Series)
Apr, 1985 - #2, Apr, 1985 ($1.75, both w/April dates)
Eclipse Comics

1,2: 2-Nudity .... .70 ... 1.80

DETENTION COMICS
Oct, 1996 ($3.50, 56 pgs., one-shot)
DC Comics

1-Robin story by Dennis O'Neil & Norm Breyfogle; Superboy story by Ron Marz
& Ron Lim; Warrior story by Ruben Diaz & Joe Phillips; Phillips-c
.... 3.50

DETONATOR
Dec, 1994 - No. 2, 1995 ($2.95, limited series)
Chaos! Comics

1,2-Brian Pulido scripts; Steven Hughes-a .... 1.20 ... 3.00

DEVIL DINOSAUR
Apr, 1978 - No. 9, Dec, 1978
Marvel Comics Group

1-Kirby/Royer-a in all; all have Kirby-c ... 1.00 ... 2.00 ... 5.00
2-9 .... 1.20 ... 3.00

DEVIL-DOG DUGAN (Tales of the Marines No. 4 on)
July, 1956 - No. 3, Nov, 1956
Atlas Comics (OPI)

1-Severin-c .... 10.00 ... 30.00 ... 60.00
2-Iron Mike McGraw x-over; Severin-c ... 6.70 ... 20.00 ... 40.00
3 .... 5.00 ... 15.00 ... 30.00

DEVIL DOGS
1942
Street & Smith Publishers

Devil Man #1 © Go Nagai

Diary Loves #8 © QUA

Dick Cole #6 © STAR

	GD25	FN65	NM94
1-Boy Rangers, U.S. Marines	25.00	75.00	175.00

DEVLIN (See Avengelyne/Glory)
Apr, 1996 ($2.50, one-shot)
Maximum Press

1-Avengelyne app.			2.50

DEVILINA (Magazine)
Feb, 1975 - No. 2, May, 1975 (B&W)
Atlas/Seaboard

1,2: 1-Reese-a		1.20	3.00

DEVIL KIDS STARRING HOT STUFF
July, 1962 - No. 107, Oct, 1981 (Giant-Size #41-55)
Harvey Publications (Illustrated Humor)

1 (12¢ cover price #1-#41-9/69)	12.00	36.00	120.00
2	6.00	18.00	60.00
3-10 (1/64)	4.00	12.00	40.00
11-20	2.85	8.50	20.00
21-30	2.30	6.75	16.00
31-40: 40-(6/69)	1.70	5.00	12.00
41-50: All 68 pg. Giants	2.00	6.00	14.00
51-55: All 52 pg. Giants	1.70	5.00	12.00
56-70	1.00	2.60	6.00
71-90		1.60	4.00
91-107		.80	2.00

DEVILMAN
June, 1995 - Present ($2.95, mature)
Verotik

1-3: Go Nagai story and art. 3-Bisley-c		1.20	3.00

DEXTER COMICS
Summer, 1948 - No. 5, July, 1949
Dearfield Publ.

1-Teen-age humor	7.00	21.00	42.00
2-Junie Prom app.	5.00	15.00	30.00
3-5	4.00	11.00	22.00

DEXTER THE DEMON (Formerly Melvin The Monster)(See Cartoon Kids & Peter the Little Pest)
No. 7, Sept, 1957
Atlas Comics (HPC)

7	4.25	13.00	26.00

DHAMPIRE: STILLBORN
1996 ($5.95, one-shot, mature)
DC Comics (Vertigo)

1-Nancy Collins script; Paul Lee-c/a			6.00

DIARY CONFESSIONS (Formerly Ideal Romance)
No. 9, May, 1955 - No. 14, Apr, 1955
Stanmor/Key Publ.(Medal Comics)

9	5.00	15.00	30.00
10-14	4.00	10.00	20.00

DIARY LOVES (Formerly Love Diary #1; G. I. Sweethearts #32 on)
No. 2, Nov, 1949 - No. 31, April, 1953
Quality Comics Group

2-Ward-c/a, 9 pgs.	13.00	39.00	90.00
3 (1/50)-Photo-c begin, end #27?	4.25	13.00	28.00
4-Crandall-a	7.00	21.00	42.00
5-7,10	4.00	10.00	20.00
8,9-Ward-a 6,8 pgs. 8-Gustavson-a	10.00	30.00	60.00
11,13,14,17-20	4.00	10.00	20.00
12,15,16-Ward-a 9,7,8 pgs.	9.15	27.00	55.00
21-Ward-a, 7 pgs.	7.00	21.00	42.00

	GD25	FN65	NM94
22-31: 31-Whitney-a	2.60	6.50	13.00

NOTE: *Photo c-3-10, 12-27.*

DIARY OF HORROR
December, 1952
Avon Periodicals

1-Hollingsworth-c/a; bondage-c	31.00	92.00	215.00

DIARY SECRETS (Formerly Teen-Age Diary Secrets)
No. 10, Feb, 1952 - No. 30, Sept, 1955
St. John Publishing Co.

10-Baker-c/a most issues	12.00	36.00	85.00
11-16,18,19	10.00	30.00	60.00
17,20: Kubert-r/Hollywood Confessions #1. 17-r/Teen Age Romances #9	10.00	30.00	62.00
21-30: 22,27-Signed stories by Estrada. 28-Last precode (3/55)	6.35	19.00	38.00
(See Giant Comics Edition for Annual)			

DIATOM
Apr, 1995 ($4.95, unfinished limited series)
Photographics

1-Photo/computer-a	1.00	2.00	5.00

DICK COLE (Sport Thrills No. 11 on)(See Blue Bolt & Four Most #1)
Dec-Jan, 1948-49 - No. 10, June-July, 1950
Curtis Publ./Star Publications

1-Sgt. Spook; L. B. Cole-c; McWilliams-a; Curt Swan's 1st work	21.00	64.00	150.00
2,5	10.00	30.00	70.00
3,4,6-10: All-L.B. Cole-c. 10-Joe Louis story	12.00	36.00	85.00
Accepted Reprint #7(V1#6 on-c)(1950's)-Reprints #7; L.B. Cole-c	5.85	17.50	35.00
Accepted Reprint #9(nd)-(Reprints #9 & #8-c)	5.85	17.50	35.00

NOTE: *L. B. Cole c-1, 3, 4, 6-10. Al McWilliams a-6. Dick Cole in 1-9. Baseball c-10. Basketball c-9. Football c-8.*

DICKIE DARE
1941 - No. 4, 1942 (#3 on sale 6/15/42)
Eastern Color Printing Co.

1-Caniff-a, Everett-c	36.00	107.00	250.00
2	24.00	71.00	165.00
3,4-Half Scorchy Smith by Noel Sickles who was very influential in Milton Caniff's development	27.00	81.00	190.00

DICK POWELL (Also see A-1 Comics)
No. 22, 1949 (one shot)
Magazine Enterprises

A-1 22-Photo-c	24.00	71.00	165.00

DICK QUICK, ACE REPORTER (See Picture News #10)

DICK'S ADVENTURES IN DREAMLAND
No. 245, Sept, 1949
Dell Publishing Co.

Four Color 245	5.00	15.00	50.00

DICK TRACY (See Famous Feature Stories, Harvey Comics Library, Limited Collectors' Ed., Mammoth Comics, Merry Christmas, The Original..., Popular Comics, Super Book No. 1, 7, 13, 25, Super Comics & Tastee-Freez)

DICK TRACY
May, 1937 - Jan, 1938
David McKay Publications

Feature Books nn - 100 pgs., partially reprinted as 4-Color No. 1 (appeared before Large Feature Comics, 1st Dick Tracy comic book) (Very Rare-three known copies) Estimated Value....	600.00	1800.00	6000.00
Feature Books 4 - Reprints nn ish. w/new-c	110.00	330.00	1100.00
Feature Books 6,9	80.00	240.00	800.00

DICK TRACY (...Monthly #1-24)

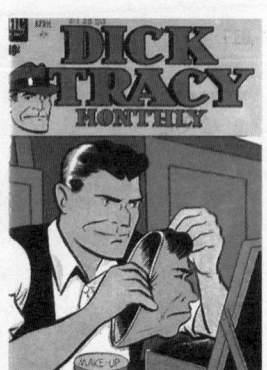
Dick Tracy #16 © Tribune Media Services

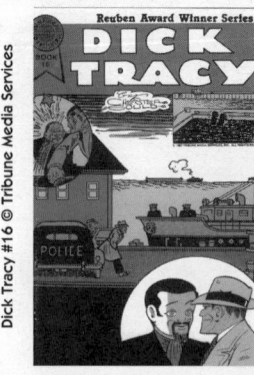
Dick Tracy #16 © Tribune Media Services

Dick Tracy Special #1 © Tribune Media Services

	GD25	FN65	NM94

1939 - No. 24, Dec, 1949
Dell Publishing Co.

Large Feature Comic 1 (1939) -Dick Tracy Meets The Blank

	GD25	FN65	NM94
	130.00	390.00	1300.00
Large Feature Comic 4,8	65.00	195.00	650.00
Large Feature Comic 11,13,15	75.00	225.00	750.00

	GD25	FN65	VF82	NM94
Four Color 1(1939)('35-r)	650.00	1950.00	3900.00	6500.00

(Estimated up to 75+ total copies exist, 5 in NM/Mint)

	GD25	FN65	NM94
Four Color 6(1940)('37-r)-(Scarce)	145.00	435.00	1450.00
Four Color 8(1940)('38-'39-r)	72.50	217.50	725.00
Large Feature Comic 3(1941, Series II)	64.00	192.00	640.00
Four Color 21('41)('38-r)	61.50	184.50	615.00
Four Color 34('43)('39-'40-r)	41.00	123.00	410.00
Four Color 56('44)('40-r)	33.00	99.00	330.00
Four Color 96('46)('40-r)	24.50	73.50	245.00
Four Color 133('47)('40-'41-r)	21.00	63.00	210.00
Four Color 163('47)('41-r)	16.50	49.50	165.00
Four Color 215('48)-Titled "Sparkle Plenty", Tracy-r	10.00	30.00	100.00
1(1/48)('34-r)	43.00	130.00	390.00
2,3	24.00	73.00	210.00
4-10	22.00	65.00	200.00
11-18: 13-Bondage-c	15.00	45.00	135.00
19-1st app. Sparkle Plenty, B.O. Plenty & Gravel Gertie in a 3-pg. strip not			
by Gould	16.00	48.00	145.00
20-1st app. Sam Catchem; c/a not by Gould	12.00	36.00	110.00
21-24-Only 2 pg. Gould-a in each	12.00	36.00	110.00

NOTE: No. 19-24 have a 2 pg. biography of a famous villain illustrated by **Gould**: 19-Little Face; 20-Flattop; 21-Breathless Mahoney; 22-Measles; 23-Itchy; 24-The Brow.

DICK TRACY (Continued from Dell series)(...Comics Monthly #25-140)
No. 25, Mar, 1950 - No. 145, April, 1961
Harvey Publications

	GD25	FN65	NM94
25-Flat Top-c/story (also #26,27)	16.50	49.50	165.00
26-28,30; 28-Bondage-c. 28,29-The Brow-c/stories	11.50	34.50	115.00
29-1st app. Gravel Gertie in a Gould-r	15.50	46.50	155.00
31,32,34,35,37-40: 40-Intro/origin 2-way wrist radio (6/51)			
	10.50	31.50	105.00
33- "Measles the Teen-Age Dope Pusher"	11.50	34.50	115.00
36-1st app. B.O. Plenty in a Gould-r	11.50	34.50	115.00
41-50	8.50	25.50	85.00
51-56,58-80: 51-2pgs Powell-a	7.50	22.50	75.00
57-1st app. Sam Catchem in a Gould-r	9.50	28.50	95.00
81-99,101-140	5.80	17.40	58.00
100	6.50	19.50	65.00
141-145 (25¢)(titled "Dick Tracy")	5.80	17.40	58.00

NOTE: **Powell** a(1-2pgs.)-43, 44, 104, 108, 109, 145. No. 110-120, 141-145 are all reprints from earlier issues.

DICK TRACY
12/84 - No. 24, 6/89 (1-12: $5.95; 13-24: $6.95, B&W, 76 pgs.)
Blackthorne Publishing

1-3-1st printings; hard-c ed. ($14.95)	2.15	6.50	15.00
1-3-1st printings; squarebound. thick-c	1.00	2.60	6.00
1-3-2nd printings, 1986; hard-c ed.	2.15	6.50	15.00
1-3-2nd printings, 1986; squarebound, thick-c	1.00	2.60	6.00
4-8-Hardcover ed. ($14.95)	2.15	6.50	15.00
4-12: Squarebound, thick-c	1.00	2.60	6.00
13-24 ($6.95): 21,22-Regular-c & stapled	1.20	3.00	7.00

NOTE: **Gould** daily & Sunday strip-r in all. 1-12 r-12/31/45-4/5/49; 13-24 r-7/13/41-2/20/44.

DICK TRACY (Disney)
1990 - No. 3, 1990 (color) (Book 3 adapts 1990 movie)
WD Publications

Book One ($3.95, 52pgs.)-Kyle Baker-c/a		1.60	4.00

Book Two, Three ($5.95, 68pgs.)-Direct sale	1.00	2.60	6.00
Book Two, Three ($2.95, 68pgs.)-Newsstand		1.20	3.00

DICK TRACY ADVENTURES
May, 1991 ($4.95, 76 pgs.)
Gladstone Publishing

1-Reprints strips 2/1/42-4/18/42	1.00	2.00	5.00

DICK TRACY, EXPLOITS OF
1946 ($1.00, hard-c strip reprints)
Rosdon Books, Inc.

1-Reprints the near complete case of "The Brow" from 6/12/44 to 9/24/44			
(story starts a few weeks late)	25.00	75.00	175.00
with dust jacket...	40.00	120.00	300.00

DICK TRACY GIVEAWAYS
1939 - 1958; 1990

Buster Brown Shoes Giveaway (1940s?, 36 pgs. in color); 1938-39-r by			
Gould	34.00	101.00	235.00

Gillmore Giveaway (See Superbook)

...Hatful of Fun (No date, 1950-52, 32pgs.; 8-1/2x10")-Dick Tracy hat promotion; Dick Tracy games, magic tricks. Miller Bros. premium			
	16.00	47.00	110.00

Motorola Giveaway (1953)-Reprints Harvey Comics Library #2; "The Case of the Sparkle Plenty TV Mystery"	5.00	15.00	30.00

Original Dick Tracy by Chester Gould, The (Aug, 1990, 16 pgs., 5-1/2x8-1/2")- Gladstone Publ.; Bread Giveaway	4.00	10.00	20.00

Popped Wheat Giveaway (1947, 16 pgs. in color)-1940-r; Sig Feuchtwanger Publ.; Gould-a	2.00	5.00	10.00

...Presents the Family Fun Book; Tip Top Bread Giveaway (1940, Fawcett Publ., 16 pgs. in color)-Spy Smasher, Ibis, Lance O'Casey app.	56.00	168.00	450.00
Same as above but without app. of heroes & Dick Tracy on cover only	11.00	33.00	75.00

Service Station Giveaway (1958, 16 pgs. in color)(regular size, slick cover)- Harvey Info. Press	3.60	9.00	18.00

Shoe Store Giveaway (Weatherbird)(1939, 16 pgs.)-Gould-a	13.50	41.00	95.00

DICK TRACY MONTHLY/WEEKLY
May, 1986 - No. 99, 1989 ($2.00, B&W) (Becomes Weekly #26 on)
Blackthorne Publishing

1-99; Gould-r. 30,31-Mr. Crime app.	.40	1.00	2.00

NOTE: #1-10 reprint strips 3/10/40-7/13/41; #10(pg.8)-51 reprint strips 4/6/49-12/31/55; #52-99 reprint strips 12/26/56-4/26/64.

DICK TRACY SHEDS LIGHT ON THE MOLE
1949 (16 pgs.) (Ray-O-Vac Flashlights giveaway)
Western Printing Co.

nn-Not by Gould	6.70	20.00	40.00

DICK TRACY SPECIAL
Jan, 1988 - No. 3, Aug. (no month), 1989 ($2.95, B&W)
Blackthorne Publishing

1-3: 1-Origin D. Tracy; 4/strips 10/12/31-3/30/32		1.20	3.00

DICK TRACY: THE EARLY YEARS
Aug, 1987 - No. 4, Aug (no month) 1989 ($6.95, B&W, 76 pgs.)
Blackthorne Publishing

1-3: 1-4-r/strips 10/12/31(1st daily)-8/31/32 & Sunday strips 6/12/32-8/28/32; Big Boy apps. in #1-3	1.20	3.00	7.00
4 ($2.95, 52pgs.)		1.20	3.00

DICK TRACY UNPRINTED STORIES
Sept, 1987 - No. 4, June, 1988 ($2.95, B&W)
Blackthorne Publishing

1-4: Reprints strips 1/1/56-12/25/56		1.20	3.00

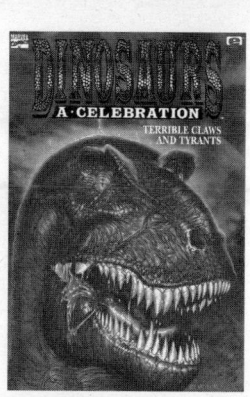

Dinosaurs, A Celebration #1 © MEG

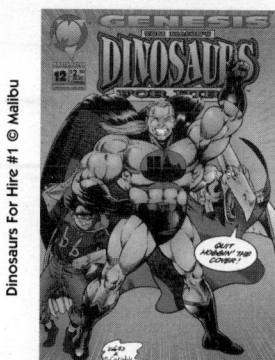

Dinosaurs For Hire #1 © Malibu

Dirty Pair: Fatal But Not Serious #1 © DH

DI

DICK TURPIN (See Legend of Young...)
DICK WINGATE OF THE U.S. NAVY
1951; 1953 (no month)
Superior Publ./Toby Press

nn-U.S. Navy giveaway		2.40	6.00	12.00
1(1953, Toby)-Reprints nn issue? (same-c)	4.00	10.00	20.00

DIE-CUT
Nov, 1993 - No. 4, Feb, 1994 ($1.75, limited series)
Marvel Comics UK, Ltd

1-($2.50)-Die-cut-c; The Beast app.		1.00	2.50
2-4		.70	1.75

DIE-CUT VS. G-FORCE
Nov, 1993 - No. 2, Dec, 1993 ($2.75, limited series)
Marvel Comics UK, Ltd

1,2-($2.75)-Gold foil-c on both		1.10	2.75

DIE, MONSTER, DIE (See Movie Classics)
DIG 'EM
1973 (2-3/8x6", 16 pgs.)
Kellogg's Sugar Smacks Giveaway

nn-4 different issues	1.00	2.00	5.00

DIGITEK
Dec, 1992 - No. 4, Mar, 1993 ($1.95/$2.25, mini-series)
Marvel Comics UK, Ltd

1,2 ($1.95)		.80	2.00
3,4 ($2.25): 3-Deathlock-c/story		.90	2.25

DILLY (Dilly Duncan from Daredevil Comics; see Boy Comics #57)
May, 1953 - No. 3, Sept, 1953
Lev Gleason Publications

1-Teenage; Biro-c	5.00	15.00	30.00
2,3-Biro-c	4.00	10.00	20.00

DILTON'S STRANGE SCIENCE (See Pep Comics #78)
May, 1989 - No. 5, May, 1990 (75¢/$1.00)
Archie Comics

1-5			1.00

DIME COMICS
1945; 1951
Newsbook Publ. Corp.

1-Silver Streak-c/story; L. B. Cole-c	39.00	118.00	275.00
1(1951), 5	4.00	10.00	20.00

DINGBATS (See 1st Issue Special)
DING DONG
Summer?, 1946 - No. 5, 1947 (52 pgs.)
Compix/Magazine Enterprises

1-Funny animal	16.00	47.00	110.00
2 (9/46)	9.15	27.00	55.00
3 (Wint '46-'47) - 5	7.50	22.50	45.00

DINKY DUCK (Paul Terry's...) (See Blue Ribbon, Giant Comics Edition #5A & New Terrytoons)
Nov, 1951 - No. 16, Sept, 1955; No. 16, Fall, 1956; No. 17, May, 1957 - No. 19, Summer, 1958
St. John Publishing Co./Pines No. 16 on

1-Funny animal	10.00	30.00	70.00
2	5.85	17.50	35.00
3-10	4.00	11.00	22.00
11-16(9/55)	3.20	8.00	16.00
16(Fall, '56) - 19	2.40	6.00	12.00

DINKY DUCK & HASHIMOTO-SAN (See Deputy Dawg Presents...)

DINO (TV)(The Flintstones)
Aug, 1973 - No. 20, Jan, 1977 (Hanna-Barbera)
Charlton Publications

1	1.10	2.70	6.50
2-20		1.40	3.50

DINO ISLAND
Feb, 1994 - No. 2, Mar, 1994 ($2.75, limited series)
Mirage Studios

1,2-By Jim Lawson		1.10	2.75

DINO RIDERS
Feb, 1989 - No. 3, 1989 ($1.00)
Marvel Comics

1-3: Based on toys			1.00

DINOSAUR REX
1986 - No. 3, 1986 ($2.00, limited series)
Upshot Graphics (Fantagraphics Books)

1-3		.80	2.00

DINOSAURS, A CELEBRATION
Oct, 1992 - No. 4, Oct, 1992 ($4.95, limited series, 52 pgs.)
Marvel Comics (Epic Comics)

1-4: 2-Bolton painted-c	1.00	2.00	5.00

DINOSAURS ATTACK! THE GRAPHIC NOVEL
1991 - Book 3, 1992 ($3.95, limited series, coated stock, stiff-c)
Eclipse Comics

Book One - Three: Based on Topps trading cards	1.60	4.00

DINOSAURS FOR HIRE
Feb, 1993 - No. 12, Feb, 1994 ($1.95/$2.50)
Malibu Comics

1-Flip book		.80	2.00
2-12: 8-($2.50)-Bagged w/Skycap; Staton-c. 10-Flip book	1.00	2.50

DINOSAURS GRAPHIC NOVEL (TV)
1992 - No. 2, 1993 ($2.95, 52 pgs.)
Disney Comics

1,2-Staton-a; based on Dinosaurs TV show		1.20	3.00

DINOSAURUS
No. 1120, Aug, 1960
Dell Publishing Co.

Four Color 1120-Movie, painted-c	7.00	21.00	70.00

DIPPY DUCK
October, 1957
Atlas Comics (OPI)

1-Maneely-a; code approved	7.00	21.00	42.00

DIRECTORY TO A NONEXISTENT UNIVERSE
Dec, 1987 ($2.00, B&W)
Eclipse Comics

1		.80	2.00

DIRTY DOZEN (See Movie Classics)
DIRTY PAIR (Manga)
Dec, 1988 - No. 4, Apr, 1989 ($2.00, B&W, limited series)
Eclipse Comics

1-4: Japanese manga with original stories		.80	2.00

DIRTY PAIR: FATAL BUT NOT SERIOUS (Manga)
July, 1995 - No. 5, Nov, 1995 ($2.95, limited series)
Dark Horse Comics

1-5		1.20	3.00

DIRTY PAIR: SIM HELL (Manga)

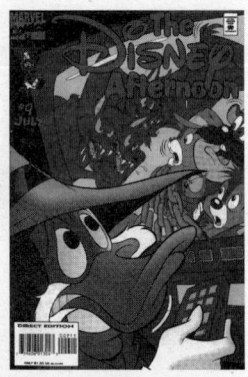
Disney Afternoon #9 © WDC

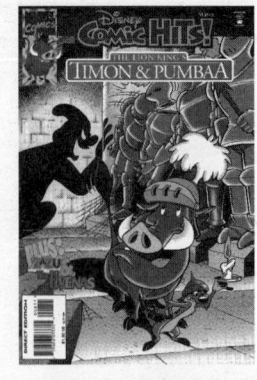
Disney Comics Hits! #8 © WDC

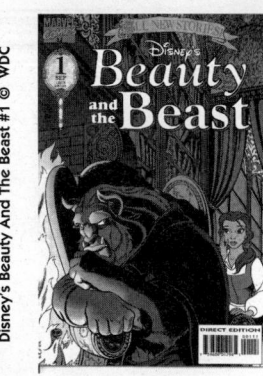
Disney's Beauty And The Beast #1 © WDC

	GD25	FN65	NM94

May, 1993 - No. 4, Aug, 1993 ($2.50, B&W, limited series)			
Dark Horse Comics			
1-4		1.00	2.50
DIRTY PAIR II (Manga)			
June, 1989 - No. 5, Mar, 1990 ($2.00, B&W, limited series)			
Eclipse Comics			
1-5: 3-Cover is misnumbered as #1		.80	2.00
DIRTY PAIR III, THE (A Plague of Angels) (Manga)			
Aug, 1990 - No. 5, Aug, 1991 ($2.00, B&W, limited series)			
Eclipse Comics			
1,2	.40	1.00	2.00
3-5: ($2.25)	.45	1.15	2.25
DISHMAN			
Sept, 1988 ($2.50, B&W, 52 pgs.)			
Eclipse Comics			
1		1.00	2.50
DISNEY AFTERNOON, THE (TV)			
Nov, 1994 - No. 10?, Aug, 1995 ($1.50)			
Marvel Comics			
1-10: 3-w/bound-in Power Ranger Barcode Card			1.50
DISNEY COMIC ALBUM			
1990(no month, year) - No. 8, 1991 ($6.95/$7.95)			
Disney Comics			
1,2 ($6.95): 1-Donald Duck and Gyro Gearloose by Barks(r). 2-Uncle Scrooge			
by Barks(r); Jr. Woodchucks app.	1.20	3.00	7.00
3-8: 3-Donald Duck-r/F.C. 308 by Barks; begin $7.95-c. 4-Mickey Mouse			
Meets the Phantom Blot; r/M.M Club Parade(censored 1956 version of story).			
5-Chip `n' Dale Rescue Rangers; new-a. 6-Uncle Scrooge. 7-Donald Duck in			
Too Many Pets; Barks-r(4) including F.C. #29. 8-Super Goof; r/S.G. #1, D.D.			
#102	1.30	3.25	8.00
DISNEY COMIC HITS			
Oct, 1995 - Present ($1.50/$2.50)			
Marvel Comics			
1-9,11-15: 4-Toy Story. 6-Aladdin. 7-Pocahontas. 13-Aladdin and the Forty			
Thieves			1.50
10-(7/96, $2.50)-The Hunchback of Notre Dame (Same story in Disney's The			
Hunchback of Notre Dame)			2.50
DISNEY COMICS			
June, 1990			
Disney Comics			
Boxed set of #1 issues includes Donald Duck Advs., Ducktales, Chip 'n Dale			
Rescue Rangers, Roger Rabbit, Mickey Mouse Advs. & Goofy Advs.; limited			
to 10,000 sets	1.00	2.60	6.00
DISNEYLAND BIRTHDAY PARTY (Also see Dell Giants)			
Aug, 1985 ($2.50)			
Gladstone Publishing Co.			
1-Reprints Dell Giant with new-photo-c	1.65	4.20	10.00
...Comics Digest #1-(Digest)	1.30	3.25	8.00
DISNEYLAND MAGAZINE			
Feb. 15, 1972 - ? (10-1/4"x12-5/8", 20 pgs, weekly)			
Fawcett Publications			
1-One or two page painted art features on Dumbo, Snow White, Lady & the			
Tramp, the Aristocats, Brer Rabbit, Peter Pan, Cinderella, Jungle Book, Alice			
& Pinocchio. Most standard characters app.	3.00	9.00	20.00
DISNEYLAND, USA (See Dell Giant No. 30)			
DISNEY MOVIE BOOK			
1990 ($7.95, 8-1/2"x11", 52 pgs.)(w/pull-out poster)			
Walt Disney Productions (Gladstone)			

	GD25	FN65	NM94

1-Roger Rabbit in Tummy Trouble; from the cartoon film strips adapted to the			
comic format. Ron Dias-c	1.70	5.00	12.00
DISNEY'S ALADDIN (Movie)			
Oct, 1994 - No. 11, 1995 ($1.50)			
Marvel Comics			
1-11			1.50
DISNEY'S BEAUTY AND THE BEAST (Movie)			
Sept, 1994 - No. 13, 1995 ($1.50)			
Marvel Comics			
1-13			1.50
DISNEY'S COLOSSAL COMICS COLLECTION			
1991 - No. 10, 1993 ($1.95, digest-size, 96/132 pgs.)			
Disney Comics			
1-10: Ducktales, Talespin, Chip 'n Dale's Rescue Rangers. 4-r/Darkwing			
Duck #1-4. 6-Goofy begins. 8-Little Mermaid		.80	2.00
DISNEY'S COMICS IN 3-D			
1992 ($2.95, w/glasses, polybagged)			
Disney Comics			
1-Infinity-c; Barks, Rosa, Gottfredson-r		1.20	3.00
DISNEY'S NEW ADVENTURES OF BEAUTY AND THE BEAST (Also see			
Beauty and the Beast & Disney's Beauty and the Beast)			
1992 - No. 2, 1992 ($1.50, limited series)			
Disney Comics			
1,2-New stories based on movie			1.50
DISNEY'S POCAHONTAS (Movie)			
1995 ($4.95, one-shot)			
Marvel Comics			
1-Movie adaptation			5.00
DISNEY'S TALESPIN LIMITED SERIES: "TAKE OFF" (TV) (See Talespin)			
Jan, 1991 - No. 4, Apr, 1991 ($1.50, limited series, 52 pgs.)			
W. D. Publications (Disney Comics)			
1-4: Based on animated series; 4 part origin			1.50
DISNEY'S THE LION KING (Movie)			
July, 1994 - No. 2, July, 1994 ($1.50, limited series)			
Marvel Comics			
1,2: 2-part movie adaptation			1.50
1-($2.50, 52 pgs.)-Complete story		1.00	2.50
DISNEY'S THE LITTLE MERMAID (Movie)			
Sept, 1994 - No. 12, 1995 ($1.50)			
Marvel Comics			
1-12			1.50
DISNEY'S THE LITTLE MERMAID LIMITED SERIES (Movie)			
Feb, 1992 - No. 4, May, 1992 ($1.50, limited series)			
Disney Comics			
1-4: Peter David scripts			1.50
DISNEY'S THE HUNCHBACK OF NOTRE DAME (Movie)(See Disney's Comic			
Hits #10)			
July, 1996 ($4.95, squarebound, one-shot)			
Marvel Comics			
1-Movie adaptation.			5.00
NOTE: A different edition of this series was sold at Wal-Mart stores with new covers depicting			
scenes from the 1989 feature film. Inside contents and price were identical.			
DISNEY'S THE THREE MUSKETEERS (Movie)			
Jan, 1994 - No. 2, Feb, 1994 ($1.50, limited series)			
Marvel Comics			
1,2-Morrow-c; Spiegle-a; Movie adaptation			1.50
DISNEY'S TOY STORY (Movie)			

A Distant Soil #13 © Colleen Doran

Doc Samson #1 © MEG

Doc Savage Annual #1 © Conde Nast

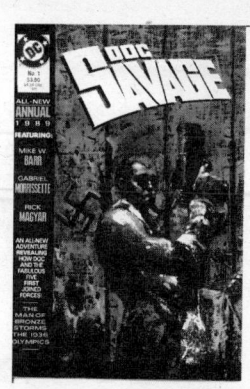

	GD25	FN65	NM94

Dec, 1995 ($4.95, one-shot)
Marvel Comics

nn-Adaptation of film			5.00

DISTANT SOIL, A (1st Series)
Dec, 1983 - No. 9, Mar 1986 ($1.50, B&W)
WaRP Graphics

1-9			1.50

NOTE: Second printings exist of #1, 2, 3 & 6.

DISTANT SOIL, A
Mar, 1989 ($12.95, trade paperback)
Donning (Star Blaze)

nn-new material			13.00

DISTANT SOIL, A (2nd Series)
June, 1991 - Present ($1.75/$2.50/$2.95, B&W)
Aria Press/Image Comics (Highbrow Entertainment) #15 on

1-8			
9-12: 9-$2.50-c begins			2.50
13-15: 13-$2.95-c begins. 15-(8/96)-1st Image issue.			3.00

NOTE: Second printings exist for #1 and are clearly marked. Second printings exist of #2-4 and are also clearly marked.

A DISTANT SOIL: IMMIGRANT SONG
Aug, 1987 ($6.95, trade paperback)
Donning (Star Blaze)

nn-new material			7.00

DIVER DAN (TV)
Feb-Apr, 1962 - No. 2, June-Aug, 1962
Dell Publishing Co.

Four Color 1254(#1), 2	6.00	18.00	60.00

DIVISION 13 (See Comic's Greatest World)
Sept, 1994 - Jan, 1995 ($2.50, color)
Dark Horse Comics

1-4: Giffen story in all. 1-Art Adams-c		1.00	2.50

DIXIE DUGAN (See Big Shot, Columbia Comics & Feature Funnies)
July, 1942 - No. 13, 1949 (Strip reprints in all)
McNaught Syndicate/Columbia/Publication Ent.

1-Joe Palooka x-over by Ham Fisher	26.00	79.00	185.00
2	14.00	43.00	100.00
3	11.00	33.00	75.00
4,5(1945-46)-Bo strip-r	8.35	25.00	50.00
6-13(1/47-49): 6-Paperdoll cut-outs	6.35	19.00	38.00

DIXIE DUGAN
V3#1, Nov, 1951 - V4#4, Feb, 1954
Prize Publications (Headline)

V3#1	7.50	22.50	45.00
2-4	5.00	15.00	30.00
V4#1-4(#5-8)	4.00	12.00	24.00

DIZZY DAMES
Sept-Oct, 1952 - No. 6, July-Aug, 1953
American Comics Group (B&M Distr. Co.)

1-Whitney-c	9.15	27.00	55.00
2	5.35	16.00	32.00
3-6	4.00	12.00	24.00

DIZZY DON COMICS
1942 - No. 22, 1946; No. 3, Apr, 1947 (Most B&W)
F. E. Howard Publications/Dizzy Don Ent. Ltd (Canada)

1 (B&W)	8.35	25.00	50.00
2 (B&W)	4.00	12.00	24.00
4-21 (B&W)	4.00	11.00	22.00

22-Full color, 52 pgs.	9.15	27.00	55.00
3 (4/47)-Full color, 52 pgs.	7.00	21.00	42.00

DIZZY DUCK (Formerly Barnyard Comics)
No. 32, Nov, 1950 - No. 39, Mar, 1952
Standard Comics

32-Funny animal	7.50	22.50	45.00
33-39	4.00	12.00	24.00

DNAGENTS (The New DNAgents V2/1 on)(Also see Surge)
March, 1983 - No. 24, July, 1985 ($1.50, Baxter paper)
Eclipse Comics

1-Origin		1.20	3.00
2-10: 4-Amber app. 9-Spiegle-a		1.00	2.50
11-24: 18-Infinity-c. 24-Dave Stevens-c		.80	2.00

DOBERMAN (See Sgt. Bilko's Private...)

DOBIE GILLIS (See The Many Loves of...)

DOC CARTER VD COMICS
1949 (16 pgs. in color) (Paper-c)
Health Publications Institute, Raleigh, N. C. (Giveaway)

nn	19.00	58.00	135.00

DOC CHAOS: THE STRANGE ATTRACTOR
Apr, 1990 - #3, 1990 ($3.00, 32 pgs.)
Vortex Comics

1-3: The Lust For Order		1.20	3.00

DOC SAMSON (Also see Incredible Hulk)
Jan, 1996 - No. 4, Apr, 1996 ($1.95, limited series)
Marvel Comics

1-4: 1-Hulk c/app. 2-She-Hulk-c/app. 3-Punisher-c/app. 4-Polaris-c/app.			
		.80	2.00

DOC SAVAGE
Nov, 1966
Gold Key

1-Adaptation of the Thousand-Headed Man; James Bama c-r/1964 Doc Savage paperback	8.50	25.50	85.00

DOC SAVAGE (Also see Giant-Size...)
Oct, 1972 - No. 8, Jan, 1974
Marvel Comics Group

1	1.30	3.25	8.00
2-8: 2,3-Steranko-c	1.00	2.00	5.00

NOTE: Gil Kane c-5, 6. Mooney a-1i. No. 1, 2 adapts pulp story "The Man of Bronze"; No. 3, 4 adapts "Death in Silver"; No. 5, 6 adapts "The Monsters"; No. 7, 8 adapts "The Brand of The Werewolf".

DOC SAVAGE (Magazine)
Aug, 1975 - No. 8, Spring, 1977 ($1.00, B&W)
Marvel Comics Group

1-Cover from movie poster; Ron Ely photo-c	1.00	2.00	5.00
2-8: 1,3-Buscema-a. 5-Adams-a(1 pg.), Rogers-a(1 pg)		1.20	3.00

DOC SAVAGE
Nov, 1987 - No. 4, Feb, 1988 ($1.75, limited series)
DC Comics

1-4		.70	1.75

DOC SAVAGE
Nov, 1988 - No. 24, Oct, 1990 ($1.75/$2.00: #13-24)
DC Comics

1-24		.80	2.00
Annual 1 (1989, $3.50, 68 pgs.)		1.40	3.50

DOC SAVAGE COMICS (Also see Shadow Comics)
May, 1940 - No. 20, Oct, 1943 (1st app. in Doc Savage pulp, 3/33)

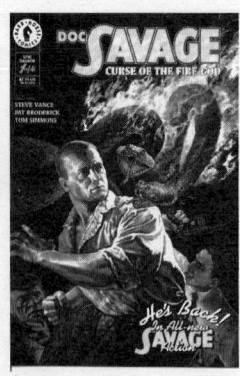

Doc Savage Comics #1 © S&S

Doc Savage: Curse Of The Fire God #1 © Conde Nast

Dr. Fate #2 © DC

	GD25	FN65	NM94

	GD25	FN65	NM94

Street & Smith Publications

1-Doc Savage, Cap Fury, Danny Garrett, Mark Mallory, The Whisperer, Captain Death, Billy the Kid, Sheriff Pete & Treasure Island begin; Norgil, the Magician app.	360.00	1080.00	3600.00
2-Origin & 1st app. Ajax, the Sun Man; Danny Garrett, The Whisperer end	131.00	393.00	1050.00
3	106.00	318.00	850.00
4-Treasure Island ends; Tuska-a	87.00	262.00	700.00
5-Origin & 1st app. Astron, the Crocodile Queen, not in #9 & 11; Norgi the Magician app.	65.00	195.00	525.00
6-10: 6-Cap Fury ends; origin & only app. Red Falcon in Astron story. 8-Mark Mallory ends; Charlie McCarthy app. on-c plus true life story. 9-Supersnipe app. 10-Origin & only app. The Thunderbolt	53.00	159.00	425.00
11,12	47.00	141.00	375.00
V2#1-8(#13-20): 16-The Pulp Hero, The Avenger app.; Fanny Brice story. 17-Sun Man ends; Nick Carter begins; Duffy's Tavern part photo-c & story. 18-Huckleberry Finn part-c/story. 19-Henny Youngman part photo-c & life story. 20-Only all funny-c w/Huckleberry Finn	47.00	141.00	375.00

DOC SAVAGE: CURSE OF THE FIRE GOD
Sept, 1995 - No. 4, Dec, 1995 ($2.95, limited series)
Dark Horse Comics

1-4		1.20	3.00

DOC SAVAGE: THE MAN OF BRONZE
1991 - No. 4, 1991 ($2.50, limited series)
Millennium Publications

1-4: 1-Bronze logo		1.00	2.50
...: The Manual of Bronze 1 ($2.50, B&W, color, one-shot)-Unpublished proposed Doc Savage strip in color, B&W strip-r		1.00	2.50

DOC SAVAGE: THE MAN OF BRONZE, DOOM DYNASTY
1992 (Says 1991) - No. 2, 1992 ($2.50, limited series)
Millennium Publications

1,2		1.00	2.50

DOC SAVAGE: THE MAN OF BRONZE - REPEL
1992 ($2.50)
Innovation Publishing

1-Dave Dorman painted-c		1.00	2.50

DOC SAVAGE: THE MAN OF BRONZE THE DEVIL'S THOUGHTS
1992 (Says 1991) - No. 2, 1992 ($2.50, limited series)
Millennium Publications

1,2		1.00	2.50

DOC STEARN...MR. MONSTER (See Mr. Monster)

DR. ANTHONY KING, HOLLYWOOD LOVE DOCTOR
1952(Jan) - No. 3, May, 1953; No. 4, May, 1954
Minoan Publishing Corp./Harvey Publications No. 4

1	10.00	30.00	70.00
2-4: 4-Powell-a	6.70	20.00	40.00

DR. ANTHONY'S LOVE CLINIC (See Mr. Anthony's...)

DR. BOBBS
No. 212, Jan, 1949
Dell Publishing Co.

Four Color 212	3.60	10.80	36.00

DOCTOR BOOGIE
1987 ($1.75)
Media Arts Publishing

1-Airbrush waparound-c; Nick Cuti-i		.70	1.80

DOCTOR CHAOS
Nov, 1993 - No. 6, Mar, 1994 ($2.50)
Triumphant Comics

1-6: 1,2-Triumphant Unleashed x-over. 2-1st app. War Dancer in pin-up. 3-Intro The Cry		1.00	2.50

DR. DOOM'S REVENGE
1989 (Came w/computer game from Paragon Software)
Marvel Comics

V1#1-Spider-Man & Captain America fight Dr. Doom			1.00

DR. FATE (See 1st Issue Special, The Immortal..., Justice League, More Fun #55, & Showcase)

DOCTOR FATE
July, 1987 - No. 4, Oct, 1987 ($1.50, limited series, Baxter paper)
DC Comics

1-4: Giffen-c/a in all			1.50

DOCTOR FATE
Winter, 1988-`89 - No. 41, June, 1992 ($1.25/$1.50 #5 on)
DC Comics

1-31: 15-Justice League app. 25-1st new Dr. Fate		.75	1.50
32-41: 32-Begin $1.75-c. 36-Original Dr. returns		.70	1.75
Annual 1(1989, $2.95, 68 pgs.)-Sutton-a		1.20	3.00

DR. FU MANCHU (See The Mask of...)
1964
I.W. Enterprises

1-r/Avon's "Mask of Dr. Fu Manchu"; Wood-a	9.00	27.00	65.00

DR. GIGGLES (See Dark Horse Presents #64-66)
Oct., 1992 - No. 2, Oct, 1992 ($2.50, limited series)
Dark Horse Comics

1,2-Based on movie		1.00	2.50

DOCTOR GRAVES (Formerly The Many Ghosts of...)
No. 73, Sept, 1985 - No. 75, Jan, 1986
Charlton Comics

73-75			1.00

DR. JEKYLL AND MR. HYDE (See A Star Presentation & Supernatural Thrillers #4)

DR. KILDARE (TV)
No. 1337, 4-6/62 - No. 9, 4-6/65 (All Richard Chamberlain photo-c)
Dell Publishing Co.

Four Color 1337(#1, 1962)	7.00	21.00	70.00
2-9	5.00	15.00	50.00

DR. MASTERS (See The Adventures of Young...)

DOCTOR SOLAR, MAN OF THE ATOM (Also see The Occult Files of Dr. Spektor #14 & Solar)
10/62 - No. 27, 4/69; No. 28, 4/81 - No. 31, 3/82 (1-27 have painted-c)
Gold Key/Whitman No. 28 on

1-(#10000-210)-Origin/1st app. Dr. Solar (1st original Gold Key character)	40.00	120.00	280.00
2-Prof. Harbinger begins	13.00	40.00	90.00
3,4	9.00	26.00	60.00
5-Intro. Man of the Atom in costume	10.00	32.00	75.00
6-10	5.70	17.00	40.00
11-14,16-20	4.70	14.00	33.00
15-Origin retold	7.00	21.00	50.00
21-27	3.00	9.40	22.00
28-31: 29-Magnus Robot Fighter begins. 31-The Sentinel app.	1.70	4.20	10.00

NOTE: **Frank Bolle** a-6-19, 29-31; c-29i, 30i. **Bob Fugitani** a-1-5. **Spiegle** a-29-31. **Hal McWilliams** a-20-23.

DOCTOR SOLAR, MAN OF THE ATOM
1990 - No. 2, 1991 ($7.95, card stock-c, high quality, 96 pgs.)
Valiant Comics

1,2: Reprints Gold Key series	1.30	3.25	8.00

Doctor Strange #13 © MEG

Doctor Strange Sorcerer Supreme #76 © MEG

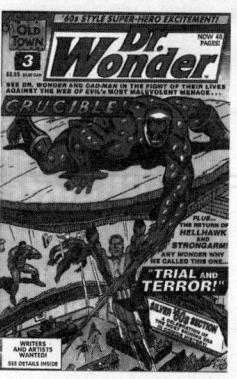

Dr. Wonder #3 © Old Town Publ.

	GD25	FN65	NM94

DOCTOR SPEKTOR (See The Occult Files of..., & Spine-Tingling Tales)

DOCTOR STRANGE (Formerly Strange Tales #1-168) (Also see The Defenders, Giant-Size..., Marvel Fanfare, Marvel Graphic Novel, Marvel Premiere, Marvel Treasury Edition & Strange Tales, 2nd Series)
No. 169, 6/68 - No. 183, 11/69; 6/74 - No. 81, 2/87
Marvel Comics Group

	GD25	FN65	NM94
169(#1)-Origin retold; panel swipe/M.D. #1-c	19.00	56.00	130.00
170-176	6.50	19.50	45.00
177-New costume	5.70	17.00	40.00
178-183: 178-Black Knight app. 179-Spider-Man story-r. 180-Photo montage-c.			
181-Brunner-c(part-i)	5.00	15.00	35.00
1(6/74, 2nd series)-Brunner-c/a	4.60	14.00	32.00
2	2.40	7.30	17.00
3-5	1.30	3.00	8.00
6-10	1.00	2.50	6.00
11-20: 14-Dracula app.	1.00	2.00	5.00
21-26: 21-Origin-r/Doctor Strange #169		1.60	4.00
27-77,79-81: 31-Sub-Mariner-c/story. 56-Origin retold. 58-Re-intro Hannibal			
King (cameo). 59-Hannibal King full app. 59-62-Dracula app. (Darkhold			
storyline). 61,62-Doctor Strange, Blade, Hannibal King & Frank Drake team-			
up to battle Dracula. 62-Death of Dracula & Lilith	.80		2.00
78-New costume		1.00	2.50
Annual 1(1976, 52 pgs.)-New Russell-a (35 pgs.)	1.60		4.00
.../Silver Dagger Special Edition 1 (3/83, $2.50)-r/#1,2,4,5; Wrightson-c			
	1.00		2.50
NOTE: **Adkins** a-169, 170, 171i; c-169-171, 172i, 173. **Adams** a-4i. **Austin** a(i)-48-60, 66, 68, 70, 73; c(i)-38, 47-53, 55, 58-60, 70. **Brunner** a-1-5p; c-1-6, 22, 28-30, 33. **Colan** a(p)-172-178, 180-183, 6-18, 36-45, 47; c(p)-172, 174-183, 11-21, 23, 27, 35, 36, 47. **Ditko** a-179r, 3r. **Everett** c-183i. **Golden** a-46p, 55p; c-42-44, 46, 55p. **G. Kane** c(p)-8-10. **Miller** c-46p. **Nebres** a-20, 22, 23, 24i, 26i, 32i; c-32i, 34. **Rogers** a-48-53p; c-47p-53p. **Russell** a-34i, 46i, Annual 1. **B. Smith** c-179. **Paul Smith** a-54p, 56p, 65, 66p, 68p, 69, 71-73; c-56, 65, 66, 68, 71. **Starlin** a-23p, 26; c-25, 26. **Sutton** a-27-29p, 31i, 33, 34p. Painted c-62, 63.

DOCTOR STRANGE CLASSICS
Mar, 1984 - No. 4, June, 1984 ($1.50 cover price; Baxter paper)
Marvel Comics Group

1-4: Ditko-r; Byrne-a. 4-New Golden pin-up		.80	2.00
NOTE: **Byrne** c-1i, 2-4.

DOCTOR STRANGEFATE (See Marvel Versus DC #3 & DC Versus Marvel #4)
Apr, 1996 ($1.95)
DC Comics (Amalgam)

1-Ron Marz script w/Jose Garcia-Lopez-(p) & Kevin Nowlan-(i). Access &			
Charles Xavier app.			2.00

DOCTOR STRANGE, SORCERER SUPREME
Nov, 1988 - No. 90, June, 1996 ($1.25/$1.50/$1.75/$1.95, direct sales only, Mando paper)
Marvel Comics (Midnight Sons imprint #60 on)

1 ($1.25)		1.20	3.00
2-9,12-14,16-27,29,30 ($1.50): 3-New Defenders app. 5-Guice-96c/a begins.			
14-18-Morbius story line. 26-Werewolf by Night app.			1.50
10-Re-intro Morbius w/new costume (11/89)		.80	2.00
11-Hobgoblin app.		1.60	4.00
15-Unauthorized Amy Grant photo-c	1.00	2.00	5.00
28-Ghost Rider story cont'd from G.R. #12; same book published at same time			
as Doctor Strange/Ghost Rider Special #1 (4/91)		1.60	4.00
31-36-Infinity Gauntlet x-overs: 31-Silver Surfer app. 33-Thanos-c & cameo.			
36-Warlock app.		1.20	3.00
37-49,51-64: 37-Silver Surfer app. 38-Begin $1.75-c. 40-Daredevil x-over. 41-			
Wolverine-c/story. 42-47-Infinity War x-overs. 47-Gamora app. 52,53-			
Morbius-c/stories. 60,61-Siege of Darkness pt. 7 & 15. 60-Spot varnish-c.			
61-New Doctor Strange begins (cameo, 1st app.). 62-Dr. Doom & Morbius			
app.		.70	1.75
50-($2.95, 52 pgs.)-Holo-grafx foil-c; Hulk, Ghost Rider & Silver Surfer app.;			
leads into new Secret Defenders series		1.20	3.00

65-74, 76-90: 65-Begin $1.95-c; bound-in card sheet. 72-Silver ink-c. 80-82-Ellis			
story. 84-DeMatteis story begins. 87-Death of Baron Mordo.			
75 ($2.50)		.80	2.00
75 ($3.50)-Foil-c		1.00	2.50
Annual 2 ('92, $2.25, 68 pgs.)-Return of Defenders		1.40	3.50
Annual 3 ('93, $2.95, 68 pgs.)-Polybagged w/card		.90	2.25
Annual 4 ('94, $2.95)		1.20	3.00
.../Ghost Rider Special 1 (4/91, $1.50)-Same book as D.S.S.S. #28		1.20	3.00
...Vs. Dracula 1 (3/94, $1.75, 52 pgs.)-r/Tomb of Dracula #44 & Dr. Strange #14		.80	2.00
		.70	1.75
NOTE: **Colan** c/a-19. **Golden** c-28. **Guice** a-5-16, 18, 20-24; c-5-12, 20-24. See 1st series for Annual #1.

DR. TOM BRENT, YOUNG INTERN
Feb, 1963 - No. 5, Oct, 1963
Charlton Publications

1	1.80	4.50	9.00
2-5	1.00	2.50	5.00

DR. VOLTZ (See Mighty Midget Comics)

DR. WEIRD SPECIAL
Feb, 1994 ($3.95, B&W, 68 pgs.)
Big Bang Comics

1-Origin-r by Starlin; Starlin-c.		1.60	4.00

DOCTOR WHO (Also see Marvel Premiere #57-60)
Oct, 1984 - No. 23, Aug, 1986 ($1.50, color, direct sales, Baxter paper)
Marvel Comics Group

1-23-British-r.			1.50

DR. WHO & THE DALEKS (See Movie Classics)

DR. WONDER
June, 1996 - Present ($2.95, B&W)
Old Town Publishing

1-3: 1-Intro & origin of Dr. Wonder; Dick Ayers-c/a; Irwin Hasen-a; contains			
profiles of the artists			3.00

DOCTOR ZERO
Apr, 1988 - No. 8, Aug, 1989 ($1.25/$1.50)
Marvel Comics (Epic Comics)

1-8: 1-Sienkiewicz-a. 6,7-Spiegle-a			1.50
NOTE: **Sienkiewicz** a-3i, 4i; c-1. **Spiegle** a-6, 7.

DO-DO (Funny Animal Circus Stories)
1950 - No. 7, 1951 (5¢, 5x7-1/4" Miniature)
Nation Wide Publishers

1 (52 pgs.)	15.00	45.00	105.00
2-7	9.15	27.00	55.00

DODO & THE FROG, THE (Formerly Funny Stuff; also see It's Game Time #2)
No. 80, 9-10/54 - No. 88, 1-2/56; No. 89, 8-9/56; No. 90, 10-11/56;
No. 91, 9/57; No. 92, 11/57 (See Comic Cavalcade)
National Periodical Publications

80-1st app. Doodles Duck by Sheldon Mayer	20.00	60.00	140.00
81-91: Doodles Duck by Mayer in #81,83-90	13.00	39.00	90.00
92-(Scarce) Doodles Duck by S. Mayer	17.00	51.00	120.00

DOGFACE DOOLEY
1951 - No. 5, 1953
Magazine Enterprises

1(A-1 40)	5.85	17.50	35.00
2(A-1 43), 3(A-1 49), 4(A-1 53), 5(A-1 64)	4.25	13.00	26.00
I.W. Reprint #1('64), Super Reprint #17	2.00	5.00	10.00

DOG MOON
1996 ($6.95, one-shot)

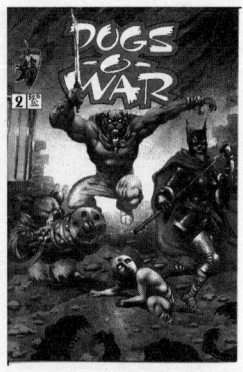

Dog Moon © Robert Hunter & Tim Truman

Dog's O'War #2 © William Tucci

Doll Man Quarterly #40 © QUA

	GD25	FN65	NM94

DC Comics (Vertigo)

1-Robert Hunter-scripts; Tim Truman-c/a.			7.00

DOG OF FLANDERS, A
No. 1088, Mar, 1960
Dell Publishing Co.

Four Color 1088-Movie, photo-c	5.00	15.00	50.00

DOGPATCH (See Al Capp's... & Mammy Yokum)

DOGS OF WAR (Also see Warriors of Plasm)
Apr, 1994 - No. 5, Aug, 1994 ($2.50)
Defiant

1-5		1.00	2.50

DOGS O' WAR
June, 1996 - Present ($2.95, B&W, limited series)
Crusade Entertainment

1,2: Photo-c			3.00

DOLLFACE & HER GANG (Betty Betz'...)
No. 309, Jan, 1951
Dell Publishing Co.

Four Color 309	5.00	15.00	50.00

DOLLMAN (Movie)
Sept, 1991 - No. 4, Dec, 1991 ($2.50, limited series)
Eternity Comics

1-4: Adaptation of film		1.00	2.50

DOLL MAN QUARTERLY, THE (Doll Man #17 on; also see Feature Comics #27 & Freedom Fighters)
Fall, 1941 - No. 7, Fall, '43; No. 8, Spring, '46 - No. 47, Oct, 1953
Quality Comics Group

1-Dollman (by Cassone), Justin Wright begin	250.00	750.00	2000.00
2-The Dragon begins; Crandall-a(5)	103.00	309.00	825.00
3,4	75.00	225.00	600.00
5-Crandall-a	58.00	176.00	470.00
6,7(1943)	44.00	132.00	350.00
8(1946)-1st app. Torchy by Bill Ward	75.00	225.00	600.00
9	40.00	120.00	325.00
10-20	34.00	103.00	240.00
21-30: 28-Vs. The Flame	29.00	86.00	200.00
31-36,38,40: 31-(12/50)-Intro Elmo, the wonder dog (Dollman's faithful dog).	24.00	71.00	165.00
32-34-Jeb Rivers app.; 34 by Crandall(p)	24.00	71.00	165.00
37-Origin & 1st app. Dollgirl; Dollgirl bondage-c	34.00	103.00	240.00
39- "Narcotics...the Death Drug" c-/story	22.00	66.00	155.00
41-47	17.00	51.00	120.00
Super Reprint #11('64, r/#20),15(r/#23),17(r/#28): 15,17-Torchy app.; Andru/ Esposito-c	3.25	9.50	22.00

NOTE: *Ward* Torchy in 8, 9, 11, 12, 14-24, 26, 27; by Fox-#30, 35-47. *Crandall* a-2, 5, 10, 13 & Super #11, 17, 18. *Crandall/Cuidera* c-40-42. *Guardineer* a-3. Bondage c-27, 37, 38, 39.

DOLLS
June, 1996 ($2.95, B&W, one-shot)
Sirius

1		1.20	3.00

DOLLY
No. 10, July-Aug, 1951 (Funny animal)
Ziff-Davis Publ. Co.

10-Painted-c	4.35	13.00	28.00

DOLLY DILL
1945
Marvel Comics/Newsstand Publ.

1	13.50	41.00	95.00

DOMINION (Manga)

Dec, 1990 - No. 6., July, 1990 ($2.00, B&W, limited series)
Eclipse Comics

1-6		.80	2.0

DOMINION: CONFLICT 1 (Manga)
Mar, 1996 - Present ($2.95, B&W, limited series)
Dark Horse Comics

1-5: Shirow-c/a/scripts			3.0

DOMINIQUE: KILLZONE
May, 1995 ($2.95, B&W)
Caliber Comics

1		1.20	3.0

DOMINO CHANCE
May-June, 1982 - No. 9, May, 1985 (B&W)
Chance Enterprises

1	1.00	2.00	5.0
1-Reprint, May, 1985		1.00	2.5
2-6,9			1.0
7-1st app. Gizmo, 2 pgs.		1.60	4.0
8-1st full Gizmo story	1.00	2.00	5.0

DONALD AND MICKEY IN DISNEYLAND (See Dell Giants)

DONALD AND MICKEY MERRY CHRISTMAS (Formerly Famous Gang Book Of Comics)
1943 - 1949 (Giveaway, 20 pgs.) Put out each Christmas; 1943 issue titled "Firestone Presents Comics" (Disney)
K. K. Publ./Firestone Tire & Rubber Co.

1943-Donald Duck-r/WDC&S #32 by Carl Barks	60.00	180.00	650.0
1944-Donald Duck-r/WDC&S #35 by Barks	60.00	180.00	650.0
1945- "Donald Duck's Best Christmas", 8 pgs. Carl Barks; intro. & 1st app. Grandma Duck in comic books	80.00	240.00	875.0
1946-Donald Duck in "Santa's Stormy Visit", 8 pgs. Carl Barks	65.00	195.00	700.0
1947-Donald Duck in "Three Good Little Ducks", 8 pgs. Carl Barks	55.00	165.00	600.0
1948-Donald Duck in "Toyland", 8 pgs. Carl Barks	55.00	165.00	600.0
1949-Donald Duck in "New Toys", 8 pgs. Barks	55.00	165.00	600.0

DONALD AND SCROOGE
1992 ($8.95, squarebound, 100 pgs.)
Disney Comics

nn-Don Rosa reprint special; r/U.S., D.D. Advs.	1.65	4.20	10.0
1-3 (1992, $1.50)-r/D.D. Advs. (Disney) #1,22,24 & U.S. #261-263,269		.80	2.0

DONALD AND THE WHEEL (Disney)
No. 1190, Nov, 1961
Dell Publishing Co.

Four Color 1190-Movie, Barks-c	7.00	21.00	70.0

DONALD DUCK (See Adventures of Mickey Mouse, Cheerios, Donald & Mickey, Ducktales, Dynabrite Comics, Gladstone Comic Album, Mickey & Donald, Mickey Mouse Mag., Story Hour Series, Uncle Scrooge, Walt Disney's Comics & Stories, W. D.'s Donald Duck, Wheaties & Whitman Comic Books, Wise Little Hen, The)

DONALD DUCK
1935, 1936 (All pages on heavy linen-like finish cover stock in color;1st book ever devoted to Donald Duck; see Advs. of Mickey Mouse for 1st app.)
(9-1/2x13")
Whitman Publishing Co./Grosset & Dunlap/K.K.

978(1935)-16 pgs.; Illustrated text story book	300.00	900.00	2000.0
nn(1936)-36 pgs.plus hard cover & dust jacket. Story completely rewritten with B&W illos added. Mickey appears and his nephews are named Morty & Mont			
Book only	300.00	900.00	2000.0
Dust jacket only....	80.00	240.00	500.0

DONALD DUCK (Walt Disney's) (10¢)

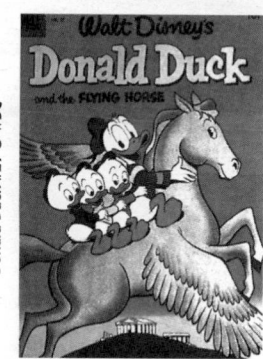

Donald Duck #27 © WDC

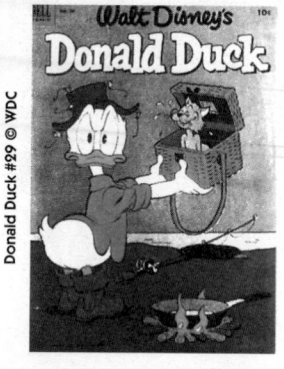

Donald Duck #29 © WDC

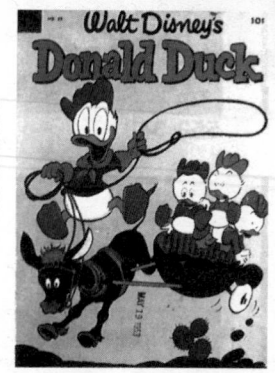

Donald Duck #34 © WDC

	GD25	FN65	NM94

1938 (8-1/2x11-1/2", B&W, cardboard-c)(Has D. Duck with bubble pipe on-c)
Whitman/K.K. Publications

	GD25	FN65	VF82	NM94
nn-The first Donald Duck & Walt Disney comic book; 1936 & 1937 Sunday strip-r(in B&W); same format as the Feature Books; 1st strips with Huey, Dewey & Louie from 10/17/37	250.00	750.00	1500.00	2250.00

DONALD DUCK (Walt Disney's...#262 on; see 4-Color listings for titles & Four Color No. 1109 for origin story)
1940 - No. 84, Sept-Nov, 1962; No. 85, Dec, 1962 - No. 245, 1984; No. 246, Oct, 1986 - No. 279, May, 1990; No. 280, Sept, 1993 - Present
Dell Publishing Co./Gold Key #85-216/Whitman #217-245/
Gladstone #246 on

	GD25	FN65	VF82	NM94
Four Color 4(1940)-Daily 1939 strip-r by Al Taliaferro	875.00	2625.00	6562.00	10,500.00
(Estimated up to 175 total copies exist, 9 in NM/Mint)				
Large Feature Comic 16(1/41?)-1940 Sunday strips-r in B&W	333.00	1000.00	2500.00	4000.00
Large Feature Comic 20('41)-Comic Paint Book, r-single panels from Large Feature #16 at top of each pg. to color; daily strip-r across bottom of each pg.	417.00	1250.00	3125.00	5000.00
Four Color 9('42)- "Finds Pirate Gold"; 64 pgs. by Carl Barks & Jack Hannah (pgs. 1,2,5,12-40 are by Barks, his 1st Donald Duck comic book art work; © 8/17/42)	600.00	1875.00	4688.00	7500.00
(Estimated up to 270 total copies exist, 18 in NM/Mint)				
Four Color 29(9/43)- "Mummy's Ring" by Barks; reprinted in Uncle Scrooge & Donald Duck #1('65), W. D. Comics Digest #44('73) & Donald Duck Advs. #14	485.00	1500.00	3750.00	6000.00
(Estimated up to 300 total copies exist, 14 in NM/Mint)				

	GD25	FN65	NM94
Four Color 62(1/45)- "Frozen Gold"; 52 pgs. by Barks, reprinted in The Best of W.D. Comics & Donald Duck Advs. #4	167.00	500.00	2000.00
Four Color 108(1946)- "Terror of the River"; 52 pgs. by Carl Barks; reprinted in Gladstone Comic Album #2	121.00	362.00	1450.00
Four Color 147(5/47)-in "Volcano Valley" by Barks	83.00	250.00	1000.00
Four Color 159(8/47)-in "The Ghost of the Grotto";52 pgs. by Carl Barks; reprinted in Best of Uncle Scrooge & Donald Duck #1 ('66) & The Best of W.D. Comics & D.D. Advs. #9; two Barks stories	67.00	200.00	800.00
Four Color 178(12/47)-1st app. Uncle Scrooge by Carl Barks; reprinted in Gold Key Christmas Parade #2 & The Best of Walt Disney Comics	100.00	300.00	1200.00
Four Color 189(6/48)-by Carl Barks; reprinted in Best of Donald Duck & Uncle Scrooge #1('64) & D.D. Advs. #19	62.00	188.00	750.00
Four Color 199(10/48)-by Carl Barks; mentioned in Love and Death; r/in Gladstone Comic Album #5	62.00	188.00	750.00
Four Color 203(12/48)-by Barks; reprinted as Gold Key Christmas Parade #4	47.00	140.00	560.00
Four Color 223(4/49)-by Barks; reprinted as Best of Donald Duck #1 & Donald Duck Advs. #3	62.00	188.00	750.00
Four Color 238(8/49)-in "Voodoo Hoodoo" by Barks	47.00	140.00	560.00
Four Color 256(12/49)-by Barks; reprinted in Best of Donald Duck & Uncle Scrooge #2('67), Gladstone Comic Album #16 & W.D. Comics Digest #44('73)	33.00	100.00	400.00
Four Color 263(2/50)-Two Barks stories; r-in D.D. #278	33.00	100.00	400.00
Four Color 275(5/50), 282(7/50), 291(9/50), 300(11/50)-All by Carl Barks; 275, 282 reprinted in W.D. Comics Digest #44('73). #275 r/in Gladstone Comic Album #10. #291 r/in D. Duck Advs. #16	31.00	94.00	375.00
Four Color 308(1/51), 318(3/51)-by Barks; #318-reprinted in W.D. Comics Digest #34 & D.D. Advs. #2,19	27.00	81.00	325.00
Four Color 328(5/51)-by Carl Barks	29.00	88.00	350.00
Four Color 339(7-8/51), 379-2nd Uncle Scrooge-c; art not by Barks.	8.00	24.00	80.00
Four Color 348(9-10/51), 356,394-Barks-c only	17.00	50.00	200.00

	GD25	FN65	NM94
Four Color 367(1-2/52) by Barks; reprinted as Gold Key Christmas Parade #2 & #8	27.00	80.00	320.00
Four Color 408(7-8/52), 422(9-10/52)-All by Carl Barks. #408-r-in Best of Donald Duck & Uncle Scrooge #1('64) & Gladstone Comic Album #13	27.00	80.00	320.00
26(11-12/52)-In "Trick or Treat" (Barks-a, 36pgs.) 1st story r-in Walt Disney Digest #16 & Gladstone C.A. #23	27.00	82.00	330.00
27-30-Barks-c only	12.00	36.00	120.00
31-44,47-50	5.50	16.50	55.00
45-Barks-a (6 pgs.)	14.00	43.00	135.00
46- "Secret of Hondorica" by Barks, 24 pgs.; reprinted in Donald Duck #98 & 154	23.00	69.00	235.00
51-Barks-a,1/2 pg.	5.50	16.50	55.00
52- "Lost Peg-Leg Mine" by Barks, 10 pgs.	14.00	43.00	145.00
53,55-59	4.50	13.50	45.00
54- "Forbidden Valley" by Barks, 26 pgs. (10¢ & 15¢ versions exist)	14.00	43.00	145.00
60- "Donald Duck & the Titanic Ants" by Barks, 20 pgs. plus 6 more pgs.	14.00	43.00	145.00
61-67,69,70	3.25	9.75	32.00
68-Barks-a, 5 pgs.	11.00	32.00	115.00
71-Barks-r, 1/2 pg.	3.25	9.75	32.00
72-78,80,82-97,99,100: 96-Donald Duck Album	3.25	9.75	32.00
79,81-Barks-a, 1pg.	3.25	9.75	32.00
98-Reprints #46 (Barks)	3.25	9.75	32.00
101-133: 102-Super Goof. 112-1st Moby Duck	2.10	6.50	20.00
134-Barks-r/#52 & WDC&S 194	2.10	6.50	20.00
135-Barks-a/WDC&S 198, 19 pgs.	2.10	6.50	20.00
136-153,155,156,158	1.70	4.20	12.00
154-Barks-r/#46	1.70	5.00	15.00
157,159,160,164: 157-Barks-r(#45). 159-Reprints/WDC&S #192 (10 pgs.). 160-Barks-r(#26). 164-Barks-r(#479)	1.70	5.00	12.00
161-163,165-173,175-187,189-191: 187-Barks r/#68.	1.30	3.25	8.00
174,188: 174-r/4-Color #394.	1.65	4.20	10.00
192-Barks-r(40 pgs.) from Donald Duck #60 & WDC&S #226,234 (52 pgs.)	1.65	4.20	10.00
193-200,202-207,209-211,213-218: 217 has 216 on-c1.00		2.00	5.00
201,208,212: 201-Barks-r/Christmas Parade #26, 16pgs. 208-Barks-r/#60 (6 pgs.). 212-Barks-r/WDC&S #130	1.00	2.00	5.00
219-Barks-r/WDC&S #106,107, 10 pgs. ea.	1.00	2.00	5.00
220-227,231-245		1.60	4.00
228-230: 228-Barks-r/F.C. #275. 229-Barks-r/F.C. #282. 230-Barks-r/ #52 & WDC&S #194	1.00	2.00	5.00
246-(1st Gladstone issue)-Barks-r/FC #422	2.15	6.50	15.00
247-249,251: 248,249-Barks-r/DD #54 & 26. 251-Barks-r/1945 Firestone	1.65	4.20	10.00
250-($1.50, 68 pgs.)-Barks-r/4-Color #9	1.70	5.10	12.00
252-279: 254-Barks-r/FC #328. 256-Barks-r/FC #147. 257-($1.50, 52 pgs.)-Barks-r/Vacation Parade #1. 261-Barks-r/FC #300. 275-Kelly-r/FC #92. 278-($1.95, 68 pgs.)-Rosa-a; Barks-r/FC #263. 279-($1.95, 68 pgs.)-Rosa-c; Barks-r/MOC #1	1.00	2.00	5.00
280, 286: 280 (#1, 2nd Series). 286-Rosa-a.	1.00	2.00	5.00
281,282,284		1.60	4.00
283,285,287-291: 283-Don Rosa-a, part-c & scripts	.80	2.00	5.00
286 ($2.95, 68 pgs.)-Happy Birthday, Donald	1.20		3.00
Mini-Comic #1(1976)-(3-1/4x6-1/2"); r/D.D. #150			1.00

NOTE: **Carl Barks** wrote all issues he illustrated, but #117, 126, 138 contain his script only. Issues 4-Color #189, 199, 203, 223, 238, 256, 263, 275, 282, 308, 348, 356, 367, 394, 408, 422, 26-30, 35, 44, 46, 52, 55, 57, 60, 65, 70-73, 77-80, 83, 101, 103, 105, 106, 111, 126, 246r, 266r, 268r, 271r, 275r, 278r(F.C. 263) all have **Barks** covers. **Barks** r-263-267, 269-278-282, 284, 285. #96 titled "Comic Album", #99-"Christmas Album". New art issues (not reprints)-106-46, 148-63, 167, 169, 170, 172, 173, 175, 178, 179, 196, 209, 223, 225, 236. **Taliaferro** daily newspaper strips #258-260, 264, 284, 285; Sunday strips #247, 280-283.

DONALD DUCK

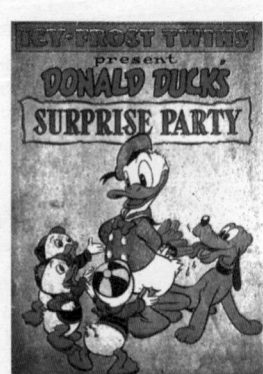
Donald Duck's Surprise Party #1 © WDC

Don Fortune Magazine #5 © Don Fortune Publ.

Don Simpson's Bizarre Heroes #4 © Don Simpson

	GD25	FN65	NM94

1944 (Christmas giveaway, paper-c, 16 pgs.)(2 versions)
K. K. Publications

	GD25	FN65	NM94
nn-Kelly cover reprint	65.00	195.00	650.00

DONALD DUCK ALBUM (See Comic Album No. 1,3 & Duck Album)
5-7/59 - F.C. No. 1239, 10-12/61; 1962; 8/63 - No. 2, Oct, 1963
Dell Publishing Co./Gold Key

	GD25	FN65	NM94
Four Color 995 (#1)	5.00	15.00	50.00
Four Color 1182, 01204-207 (1962-Dell)	4.00	12.00	40.00
Four Color 1099,1140,1239-Barks-c	6.00	18.00	60.00
1(8/63-Gold Key)-Barks-c	5.00	15.00	50.00
2(10/63)	4.00	12.00	40.00

DONALD DUCK AND THE BOYS (Also see Story Hour Series)
1948 (5-1/4x5-1/2", 100pgs., hard-c; art & text)
Whitman Publishing Co.

	GD25	FN65	NM94
845-(49) new illos by Barks based on his Donald Duck 10-pager in WDC&S #74, Expanded text not written by Barks; Cover not by Barks	48.00	143.00	475.00

(Prices vary widely on this book)

DONALD DUCK AND THE CHRISTMAS CAROL
1960 (A Little Golden Book, 6-3/8"x7-5/8", 28 pgs.)
Whitman Publishing Co.

nn-Story book pencilled by Carl Barks with the intended title "Uncle Scrooge's Christmas Carol." Finished art adapted by Norman McGary. (Rare)-Reprinted in Uncle Scrooge in Color.			75.00

DONALD DUCK AND THE RED FEATHER
1948 (8-1/2x11", 4 pgs., B&W)
Red Feather Giveaway

	GD25	FN65	NM94
nn	13.50	41.00	95.00

DONALD DUCK BEACH PARTY (Also see Dell Giants)
Sept, 1965 (12¢)
Gold Key

	GD25	FN65	NM94
1(#10158-509)-Barks-r/WDC&S #45; painted-c	5.50	16.50	55.00

DONALD DUCK BOOK (See Story Hour Series)

DONALD DUCK COMIC PAINT BOOK
No. 20, 1941 (B&W)
Dell Publishing Co.

	GD25	FN65	NM94
Large Feature Comic 20	417.00	1250.00	5200.00

DONALD DUCK COMICS DIGEST
Nov, 1986 - No. 5, July, 1987 ($1.25/$1.50, 96 pgs.)
Gladstone Publishing

	GD25	FN65	NM94
1,3: 1-Barks-c/a-r	1.00	2.00	5.00
2,4,5: 4,5-$1.50-c		1.20	3.00

DONALD DUCK FUN BOOK (See Dell Giants)
DONALD DUCK IN DISNEYLAND (See Dell Giants)
DONALD DUCK IN "THE LITTERBUG"
1963 (5x7-1/4", 16 pgs., soft-c) (Disney giveaway)
Keep America Beautiful

	GD25	FN65	NM94
nn	5.00	15.00	30.00

DONALD DUCK MARCH OF COMICS (See March of Comics #4,20,41,56,69,263)
DONALD DUCK MERRY CHRISTMAS (See Dell Giant No. 53)
DONALD DUCK PICNIC PARTY (See Picnic Party listed under Dell Giants)
DONALD DUCK "PLOTTING PICNICKERS" (Also see Ludwig Von Drake & Mickey Mouse)
1962 (3-1/4x7", soft-c, 16 pgs.) (Disney)
Fritos Giveaway

	GD25	FN65	NM94
nn	5.70	17.00	40.00

DONALD DUCK'S SURPRISE PARTY

1948 (16 pgs.) (Giveaway for Icy Frost Twins Ice Cream Bars)
Walt Disney Productions

	GD25	FN65	NM94
nn-(Rare)-Kelly-c/a	285.00	857.00	2100.0

DONALD DUCK TELLS ABOUT KITES (See Kite Fun Book)
DONALD DUCK, THIS IS YOUR LIFE (Disney, TV)
No. 1109, Aug-Oct, 1960
Dell Publishing Co.

	GD25	FN65	NM94
Four Color 1109-Gyro flashback to WDC&S #141; origin Donald Duck (1st told)	17.00	51.00	170.00

DONALD DUCK XMAS ALBUM (See regular Donald Duck No. 99)
DONALD IN MATHMAGIC LAND (Disney)
No. 1051, Oct-Dec, 1959 - No. 1198, May-July, 1961
Dell Publishing Co.

	GD25	FN65	NM94
Four Color 1051 (#1)-Movie	10.00	30.00	100.00
Four Color 1198-Reprint of above	7.00	21.00	70.00

DONATELLO, TEENAGE MUTANT NINJA TURTLE
Aug, 1986 ($1.50, B&W, one-shot, 44 pgs.)
Mirage Studios

	GD25	FN65	NM94
1	1.00	2.00	5.00

DONDI
No. 1176, Mar-May, 1961 - No. 1276, Dec, 1961
Dell Publishing Co.

	GD25	FN65	NM94
Four Color 1176 (#1)-Movie; origin, photo-c	5.00	15.00	50.00
Four Color 1276	4.00	12.00	40.00

DON FORTUNE MAGAZINE
Aug, 1946 - No. 6, Feb, 1947
Don Fortune Publishing Co.

	GD25	FN65	NM94
1-Delecta of the Planets by C. C. Beck in all	17.00	51.00	120.00
2	11.50	34.00	80.00
3-6: 3-Bondage-c	9.15	27.00	55.00

DONNA MATRIX
Aug, 1993 ($2.95, 52 pgs.)
Reactor, Inc.

	GD25	FN65	NM94
1-Computer generated-c/a by Mike Saenz; 3-D effects		1.20	3.00

DONNA MIA
Oct, 1995 - Present ($3.95/$4.95, limited series, mature)
Dark Fantasy Productions

	GD25	FN65	NM94
1,2-($4.95): 1-Kaluta-c-red foil; fold-out centerfold. 2-(9/96)-Kaluta blue foil-c; nudity	1.00	2.00	5.00
1,2-($3.95): Kaluta-c on both. 2-(9/96)-Nudity		1.60	4.00

DON NEWCOMBE
1950 (Baseball)
Fawcett Publications

	GD25	FN65	NM94
nn-Photo-c	39.00	116.00	270.00

DON ROSA CLASSICS
0-14: 0-r/Bizarre Heroes #1(1990). 1,2-Megaton Man-c/story 1.20 3.00

DON SIMPSON'S BIZARRE HEROES (Also see Megaton Man)
May, 1990 - Present ($2.50/$2.95, B&W)
Fiasco Comics

1-10			$2.5
0,11-17: 0-Begin $2.95-c; r/Bizarre Heroes #1. 17-(9/96)-Indicia also reads Megaton Man #0; intro Megaton Man and the Fiascoverse to new readers			3.00

DON'T GIVE UP THE SHIP
No. 1049, Aug, 1959
Dell Publishing Co.

	GD25	FN65	NM94
Four Color 1049-Movie, Jerry Lewis photo-c	7.00	21.00	70.00

Doom Patrol #44 © DC

Doomsday #1 © DC

Doom 2099 #44 © MEG

	GD25	FN65	NM94

DON WINSLOW OF THE NAVY
Apr, 1937 - No. 2, May, 1937 (96 pgs.)(A pulp/comic book cross; stapled spine)
Merwil Publishing Co.

	GD	FN	VF
V1#1-Contains 16 pgs. comics in color. Captain Colorful & Jupiter Jones by Sheldon Mayer; complete Don Winslow novel	850.00	1700.00	3400.00
2-Sheldon Mayer-a	100.00	300.00	800.00

DON WINSLOW OF THE NAVY (See Crackajack Funnies, Famous Feature Stories, Popular Comics & Super Book #5,6)
No. 1, Nov, 1939 - No. 22, 1941
Dell Publishing Co.

Four Color 2 (#1)-Rare	126.00	377.00	1250.00
Four Color 22	31.00	94.00	300.00

DON WINSLOW OF THE NAVY (See TV Teens; Movie, Radio, TV)
(Fightin' Navy No. 74 on)
2/43 - #64, 12/48; #65, 1/51 - #69, 9/51; #70, 3/55 - #73, 9/55
Fawcett Publications/Charlton No. 70 on

	GD	FN	NM
1-(68 pgs.)-Captain Marvel on cover	87.00	262.00	700.00
2	44.00	132.00	350.00
3	36.00	107.00	250.00
4-6: 6-Flag-c	27.00	81.00	190.00
7-10: 8-Last 68 pg. issue?	19.00	56.00	130.00
11-20	14.00	43.00	100.00
21-40	10.00	30.00	65.00
41-64: 51,60-Singapore Sal (villain) app. 64-(12/48)	9.15	27.00	55.00
65(1/51)-Flying Saucer attack; photo-c	10.00	30.00	70.00
66 - 69(9/51): All photo-c. 66-sci-fi story	10.00	30.00	70.00
70(3/55)-73: 70-73 r/#26,58 & 59	7.50	22.50	45.00

DOOM FORCE SPECIAL
July, 1992 ($2.95, 68 pgs., one-shot, mature) (X-Force parody)
DC Comics

1-Grant Morrison scripts; Simonson, Steacy, & others-a; Giffen/Mignola-c.	1.20		3.00

DOOM PATROL, THE (Formerly My Greatest Adventure No. 1-85; see Brave and the Bold, DC Special Blue Ribbon Digest 19, Official… Index & Showcase No. 94-96)
No. 86, 3/64 - No. 121, 9-10/68; No. 122, 2/73 - No. 124, 6-7/73
National Periodical Publications

86-1 pg. origin (#86-121 are 12¢ issues)	14.00	41.00	110.00
87-99: 88-Origin The Chief. 91-Intro. Mento. 99-Intro. Beast Boy (later becomes the Changeling in New Teen Titans	10.00	30.00	75.00
100-Origin Beast Boy; Robot-Maniac series begins (12/65)			
	11.00	33.00	80.00
101-110: 102-Challengers of the Unknown app. 105-Robot-Maniac series ends. 106-Negative Man begins (origin)	5.00	15.00	40.00
111-120	3.90	11.50	30.00
121-Death of Doom Patrol; Orlando-c.	11.00	33.00	80.00
122-124: All reprints	1.20		3.00

DOOM PATROL
Oct, 1987 - No. 87, Feb, 1995 (75¢/$1.00/$1.50/$1.75/$1.95, new format)
DC Comics (Vertigo imprint on #64 on)

1-75¢-c begins.		.80	2.00
2-18: 3-1st app. Lodestone. 4-1st app. Karma. 8,15,16-Art Adams-c(i). 10-$1.00-c begins. 18-Invasion tie-in.			1.00
19-(2/89)-Grant Morrison scripts begin, ends #63; 1st app Crazy Jane; $1.50-c & new format begins.	1.65	4.20	10.00
20-25	1.00	2.60	6.00
26-30: 29-Superman app. 30-Night Breed fold-out	1.60		4.00
31-40: 35-1st app. of Flex Mentallo (cameo). 36-1st full app. of Flex Mentallo. 39-World Without End preview.		.80	2.00
41-49,51-56,58-60: 42-Origin of Flex Mentallo.		.80	2.00

50,57 ($2.50, 52 pgs.)		1.00	2.50
61-65: 61-$1.75-c begins; photo-c. 63-(1/93).		.70	1.80
66-87: 66-$1.95-c begins. 70-Photo-c. 73-Death cameo (2 panels).			
		.80	2.00
…And Suicide Squad 1 (3/88, $1.50, 52 pgs.)-Wraparound-c		.65	1.60
Annual 1 (1988, $1.50, 52 pgs.)		.65	1.60
Annual 2 (1994, $3.95, 68 pgs.)-Children's Crusade tie-in.			
		1.60	4.00

NOTE: *Simon Bisley* painted c-26-48, 55-58. **Bolland** c-64, 75. **Dringenberg** a-42(p). **Steacy** a-53.

DOOMSDAY
1995 ($3.95, one-shot)
DC Comics

1-Year One story by Jurgens, L. Simonson, Ordway, and Gil Kane; Darkseid, Superman app.		1.60	4.00

DOOMSDAY + 1 (Also see Charlton Bullseye)
July, 1975 - No. 6, June, 1976; No. 7, June, 1978 - No. 12, May, 1979
Charlton Comics

1: #1-5 are 25¢ issues	1.50	3.75	9.00
2	1.00	2.00	5.00
3-6: 4-Intro Lor. 5-Ditko-a(1 pg.) 6-Begin 30¢ issues	1.60		4.00
V3#7-12 (reprints #1-6)		.65	1.60
5 (Modern Comics reprint, 1977)			1.00
NOTE: **Byrne** c/a-1-12; Painted covers-2-7.

DOOMSDAY SQUAD, THE
Aug, 1986 - No. 7, 1987 ($2.00)
Fantagraphics Books

1-7: Byrne-a in all. 1-3-New Byrne-c. 3-Usagi Yojimbo app. (1st in color).4-N Adams-c. 5-7-Gil Kane-c		.80	2.00

DOOM'S IV
July, 1994 - No.4, Oct, 1994 ($2.50, limited series)
Image Comics (Extreme Studios)

1-4-Liefeld story		1.00	2.50
1,2-Two alternate Liefeld-c each, 4 covers form 1 picture			
	1.00	2.00	5.00

DOOM 2099 (See Marvel Comics Presents #118 & 2099: World of Tomorrow)
Jan, 1993 - No. 44, Aug, 1996 ($1.25/$1.50/$1.95)
Marvel Comics

1-($1.75)-Metallic foil stamped-c		.80	2.00
1-2nd printing		.70	1.75
2-16: 14-Ron Lim-c(p)			1.25
17-24, 26-28: 17-Begin $1.50-c; bound-in trading card sheet			
			1.50
25 ($2.25, 52 pgs.)		1.30	3.25
25 ($2.95, 52pgs.) Foil embossed cover		1.20	3.00
29-44: 29-Begin $2.95-c. 40-Namor & Doctor Strange app. 41-Daredevil app., Namor-c/app. 44-Intro The Emissary; story contin'd in 2099: World of Tomorrow.		.80	2.00
29 ($3.50)-acetate-c.		1.40	3.50

DOORWAY TO NIGHTMARE (See Cancelled Comic Cavalcade)
Jan-Feb, 1978 - No. 5, Sept-Oct, 1978
DC Comics

1-5-Madame Xanadu in all. 4-Craig-a			1.00
NOTE: **Kaluta** covers on all. Merged into The Unexpected with No. 190.

DOPEY DUCK COMICS (Wacky Duck No. 3) (See Super Funnies)
Fall, 1945 - No. 2, Apr, 1946
Timely Comics (NPP)

1,2-Casper Cat, Krazy Krow	17.00	49.00	115.00

DORK
June, 1993 - No. 3, 1995 ($2.50/$2.75, B&W, mature)

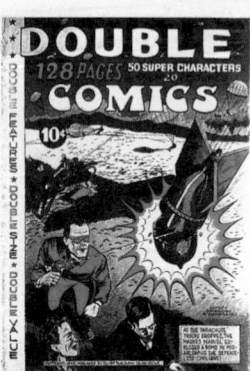

Double Comics #1 © EP

Double Dragon #3 © Technos Japan Corp.

Double Impact #5 © High Impact Studios

	GD25	FN65	NM94

Slave Labor

1-3: Evan Dorkin-c/a/scripts in all. 3-$2.75-c 1.10 2.75
1,2-(2nd printing, $2.75): 1-(8/95). 2-(1/96)-Reads 2nd Print on bottom inside-c
  1.10 2.75

DOROTHY LAMOUR (Formerly Jungle Lil)(Stage, screen, radio)
No. 2, June, 1950 - No. 3, Aug, 1950
Fox Features Syndicate

2,3-Wood-a(3) each, photo-c 21.00 64.00 150.00

DOT AND DASH AND THE LUCKY JINGLE PIGGIE
1942 (Christmas giveaway, 12 pgs.)
Sears Roebuck Co.

nn-Contains a war stamp album and a punch out Jingle Piggie bank
  6.70 20.00 40.00

DOT DOTLAND (Formerly Little Dot Dotland)
No. 62, Sept, 1974 - No. 63, Nov, 1974
Harvey Publications

62,63 .80 2.00

DOTTY (...& Her Boy Friends)(Formerly Four Teeners; Glamorous
Romances No. 41 on)
No. 35, June, 1948 - No. 40, May, 1949
Ace Magazines (A. A. Wyn)

35-Teen-age 5.85 17.50 35.00
36,38-40 3.60 9.00 18.00
37-Transvestism story 4.00 10.00 20.00

DOTTY DRIPPLE (Horace & Dotty Dripple No. 25 on)
1946 - No. 24, June, 1952 (Also see A-1 No. 3-8, 10)
Magazine Ent.(Life's Romances)/Harvey No. 3 on

A-1 #1 (1pg. D. Dripple; Mr. Ex, Bush Berry, Rocky, Lew Loyal (20 pgs.)
  10.00 30.00 70.00
1 (nd) (10¢) 4.15 12.50 25.00
2 2.40 6.00 12.00
3-10: 3,4-Powell-a 1.60 4.00 8.00
11-24 1.20 3.00 6.00

DOTTY DRIPPLE AND TAFFY
No. 646, Sept, 1955 - No. 903, May, 1958
Dell Publishing Co.

Four Color 646 (#1) 4.00 12.00 40.00
Four Color 691,718,746,801,903 3.00 9.00 30.00

DOUBLE ACTION COMICS
No. 2, Jan, 1940 (68 pgs., B&W)
National Periodical Publications

2-Contains original stories(?); pre-hero DC contents; same cover as
Adventure No. 37. (six known copies) (not an ashcan)
  Estimated value.... 11,000.00
NOTE: The cover to this book was probably reprinted from Adventure #37. #1 exists as an ash
can copy with B&W cover; contains a coverless comic on inside with 1st & last page missing.

DOUBLE COMICS
1940 - 1944 (132 pgs.)
Elliot Publications

1940 issues; Masked Marvel-c & The Mad Mong vs. The White Flash covers
known 193.00 581.00 1550.00
1941 issues; Tornado Tim-c, Nordac-c, & Green Light covers known
  137.00 412.00 1100.00
1942 issues 106.00 318.00 850.00
1943,1944 issues 84.00 253.00 675.00
NOTE: Double Comics consisted of an almost endless combination of pairs of remaindered,
unsold issues of comics representing most publishers and usually mixed publishers in the same
book; e.g., a Captain America with a Silver Streak, or a Feature with a Detective, etc., could
appear inside the same cover. The actual contents would have to determine its price. Prices listed are for average contents. Any containing rare origin or first issues are worth much more.

	GD25	FN65	NM94

Covers also vary in same year. Value would be approximately 50 percent of contents.

DOUBLE-CROSS (See The Crusaders)

DOUBLE-DARE ADVENTURES
Dec, 1966 - No. 2, Mar, 1967 (35¢/25¢, 68 pgs.)
Harvey Publications

1-Origin Bee-Man, Glowing Gladiator, & Magic-Master; Simon/Kirby-a (last
S&K art as a team?) 5.00 15.00 40.00
2-Williamson/Crandall-a; r/Alarming Adv. #3('63) 3.75 11.25 30.00
NOTE: Powell a-1. Simon/Sparling c-1, 2.

DOUBLE DRAGON
July, 1991 - No. 6, Dec, 1991 ($1.00, limited series)
Marvel Comics

1-6: Based on video game. 2-Art Adams-c 1.00

DOUBLE EDGE
Alpha, 1995; Omega, 1995 ($4.95, limited series)
Marvel Comics

Alpha ($4.95)- Punisher story, Nick Fury app. 1.00 2.00 5.00
Omega ($4.95)-Punisher, Daredevil, Ghost Rider app. Death of Nick Fury
  1.00 2.00 5.00

DOUBLE IMPACT (Double Impact Blondage #3 & Double Impact Buttshots #6
on cover only)
Mar, 1995 - No. 7, 1996 ($3.95/$2.95/$3.00)
High Impact Studios

1 (Chromium-c.)-Intro Jazz & China. 1.60 4.00
1 (Rainbow-c.) 2.60 7.50 18.00
2-7 (Regular-c.): 4-variant-c. w/no logo exists. 5-fold out back-c. 6-3 variant-c
exist. 7-Intro Nikki Blade. 1.20 3.00
2,3 (Nude-c.) (limited to 5000) 2.15 6.50 15.00
San Diego Special (Limited to 5000) 2.30 6.75 16.00

DOUBLE IMPACT
V2#1, 1996 - Present ($3.00)
High Impact Studios

V2#1-Wraparound-c 3.00
1-($4.00)-Deluxe Edition; wraparound-foil-c 4.00
1-Wraparound, prism, foil-c 7.00
1-Gold foil logo 5.00
1-Variant-c 5.00

DOUBLE IMPACT/HELLINA (See Hellina/Double Impact)
Mar, 1996 ($3.00, one-shot)
High Impact Studios

1 3.00

DOUBLE LIFE OF PRIVATE STRONG, THE
June, 1959 - No. 2, Aug, 1959
Archie Publications/Radio Comics

1-Origin & re-intro The Shield; Simon & Kirby-c/a, their re-entry into the super
hero genre; intro./1st app. The Fly; 1st S.A. super-hero for Archie Publ.
  62.00 188.00 550.00
2-S&K-c/a; Tuska-a; The Fly app. (2nd or 3rd?) 40.00 120.00 300.00

DOUBLE TALK (Also see Two-Faces)
No date (1962?) (32 pgs., full color, slick-c)
Christian Anti-Communism Crusade (Giveaway)
Feature Publications

nn-Sickle with blood-c 10.00 30.00 70.00

DOUBLE TROUBLE
Nov, 1957 - No. 2, Jan-Feb, 1958
St. John Publishing Co.

1,2 4.25 13.00 28.00

DOUBLE TROUBLE WITH GOOBER

Dracula Versus Zorro #2 © TOPPS

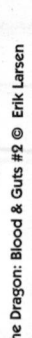

The Dragon: Blood & Guts #2 © Erik Larsen

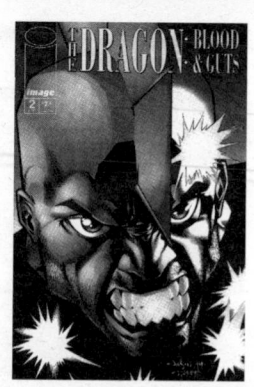

Dragon Chiang #1 © ECL

	GD25	FN65	NM94

No. 417, Aug, 1952 - No. 556, May, 1954
Dell Publishing Co.

Four Color 417	3.00	9.00	30.00
Four Color 471,516,556	2.00	6.00	20.00

DOUBLE UP
1941 (Pocket size, 200 pgs.)
Elliott Publications

1-Contains rebound copies of digest sized issues of Pocket Comics, Speed Comics, & Spitfire Comics	70.00	210.00	565.00

DOVER & CLOVER (See All Funny & More Fun Comics #93)

DOVER BOYS (See Adventures of the…)

DOVER THE BIRD
Spring, 1955
Famous Funnies Publishing Co.

1-Funny animal; code approved	4.25	13.00	26.00

DOWN WITH CRIME
Nov, 1952 - No. 7, Nov, 1953
Fawcett Publications

1	24.00	71.00	165.00
2,4,5: 2,4-Powell-a in each. 5-Bondage-c	12.00	36.00	85.00
3-Used in **POP**, pg. 106; "H is for Heroin" drug story	13.50	41.00	95.00
6,7: 6-Used in **POP**, pg. 80	10.00	30.00	65.00

DO YOU BELIEVE IN NIGHTMARES?
Nov, 1957 - No. 2, Jan, 1958
St. John Publishing Co.

1-Mostly Ditko-c/a	39.00	116.00	270.00
2-Ayers-a	21.00	62.00	145.00

D.P. 7
Nov, 1986 - No. 32, June, 1989 (26 on: $1.50)
Marvel Comics Group (New Universe)

1-32			1.25
Annual #1 (11/87)-Intro. The Witness			1.25

DRACULA (See Bram Stoker's Dracula, Giant-Size…, Little Dracula, Marvel Graphic Novel, Requiem for Dracula, Spider-Man Vs…., Tomb of… & Wedding of…; also see Movie Classics under Universal Presents as well as Dracula)

DRACULA (See Movie Classics for #1)(Also see Frankenstein & Werewolf)
No. 2, 11/66 - No. 4, 3/67; No. 6, 7/72 - No. 8, 7/73 (No #5)
Dell Publishing Co.

2-Origin & 1st app. Dracula (11/66) (super hero)	2.30	6.70	16.00
3,4: 4-Intro. Fleeta ('67)	1.65	4.20	10.00
6-('72)-r/#2 w/origin	1.00	2.60	6.00
7,8-r/#3, #4	1.00	2.00	5.00

DRACULA (Magazine)
1979 (120 pgs., full color)
Warren Publishing Co.

Book 1-Maroto art; Spanish material translated into English	1.65	4.20	10.00

DRACULA CHRONICLES
Apr, 1995 - No. 3, June, 1995 ($2.50, limited series)
Topps Comics

1-3-Linsner-c			2.50

DRACULA LIVES! (Magazine)(Also see Tomb of Dracula)
1973(no month) - No. 13, July, 1975 (75¢, B&W)
Marvel Comics Group

1	1.00	2.50	6.00
2,3: 2-Origin; Starlin-a		1.80	4.50

	GD25	FN65	NM94
4-Ploog-a		1.20	3.00
5(V2#1)-13: 5-Dracula series begins		1.00	2.50
Annual 1(Summer, 1975, $1.25)-Morrow painted-c		1.00	2.50

NOTE: **N. Adams** a-2, 3i, 10i, Annual 1r(2, 3i). **Alcala** a-9. **Buscema** a-3p, 6p, Annual 1p. **Colan** a(p)-1, 2, 5, 6, 8. **Evans** a-7. **Heath** a-1r, 13. **Pakula** a-6r. **Weiss** r-Annual 1p.

DRACULA: RETURN OF THE IMPALER
July, 1993 - No. 4, Oct, 1994 ($2.95, limited series)
Slave Labor Graphics

1-4			3.00

DRACULA VERSUS ZORRO
Oct, 1993 - No. 2, Nov, 1993 ($2.95, limited series)
Topps Comics

1,2: 1-Spot varnish & red foil-c. 2-Polybagged w/16 pg. Zorro #0		1.20	3.00

DRACULA: VLAD THE IMPALER (Also see Bram Stoker's Dracula)
Feb, 1993 - No. 3, Apr, 1993 ($2.95, limited series)
Topps Comics

1-3-Polybagged with 3 trading cards each; Maroto-c/a		1.20	3.00

DRAFT, THE
1988 ($3.50, one-shot, squarebound)
Marvel Comics

1-Sequel to "The Pitt"		1.40	3.50

DRAG 'N' WHEELS (Formerly Top Eliminator)
No. 30, Sept, 1968 - No. 59, May, 1973
Charlton Comics

30-40-Scot Jackson begins	2.60	7.50	18.00
41-50	1.70	5.00	12.00
51-59: Scot Jackson	1.20	3.00	7.00
Modern Comics Reprint 58('78)		1.60	4.00

DRAGON, THE (Also see The Savage Dragon)
Mar, 1996 - No. 5, July, 1996 (99¢, limited series)
Image Comics (Highbrow Entertainment)

1-5: Reprints Savage Dragon series w/new story & art. 5-Youngblood app; includes 5 pg. Savage Dragon story from 1984			1.00

DRAGON, THE: BLOOD & GUTS (Also see The Savage Dragon)
Mar, 1995 - No. 3, May, 1995 ($2.50, limited series)
Image Comics (Highbrow Entertainment)

1-3: Jason Pearson-c/a/scripts		1.00	2.50

DRAGON CHIANG
1991 ($3.95, B&W, squarebound, 52 pgs.)
Eclipse Books

nn -Timothy Truman-c/a(p)		1.60	4.00

DRAGONFLIGHT
Feb, 1991 - No. 3, 1991 ($4.95, 52 pgs.)
Eclipse Books

Book One - Three: Adapts 1968 novel	1.00	2.00	5.00

DRAGONFLY (See Americomics #4)
Sum, 1985 - No. 8, 1986 ($1.75/$1.95)
Americomics

1		1.20	3.00
2-8		.80	2.00

DRAGONFORCE
1988 - No. 13, 1989 ($2.00)
Aircel Publishing

1-Dale Keown-c/a/scripts in #1-12		1.60	4.00
2-13: 13-No Keown-a		.80	2.00
…Chronicles Book 1-5 ($2.95, B&W, 60 pgs.): Dale Keown-r/Dragonring &			

Drama #1 © Joseph Michael Linsner

Dreadstar #31 © Jim Starlin

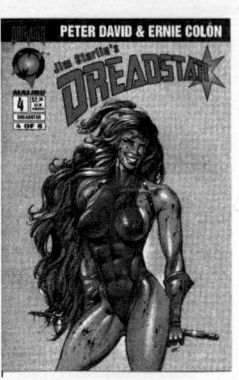
PETER DAVID & ERNIE COLÓN
Dreadstar #4 © Jim Starlin

	GD25	FN65	NM94

	GD25	FN65
Dragonforce	1.20	3.00

DRAGONHEART (Movie)
May, 1996 - No. 2, June, 1996 ($2.95/$4.95, limited series)
Topps Comics

1-($2.95, 24 pgs.)-Adaptation of the film; Hildebrandt Bros-c; Lim-a.		3.00
2-($4.95, 64 pgs.)		5.00

DRAGONLANCE (Also see TSR Worlds)
Dec, 1988 - No. 34, Sept, 1991 ($1.25/$1.50, Mando paper)
DC Comics

1-Based on TSR game	1.60	4.00
2	1.20	3.00
3-15: 6-Begin $1.50-c	.80	2.00
16-34: 25-Begin $1.75-c. 30-32-Kaluta-c	.70	1.80
Annual 1 (1990, $2.95, 68 pgs.)	1.20	3.00

DRAGON LINES
May, 1993 - No. 4, Aug, 1993 ($1.95, limited series)
Marvel Comics (Epic Comics/Heavy Hitters)

1-($2.50)-Embossed-c; Ron Lim-c/a in all	1.00	2.50
2-4	.80	2.00

DRAGON LINES: WAY OF THE WARRIOR
Nov, 1993 - No. 2, Jan, 1994 ($2.25, limited series)
Marvel Comics (Epic Comics/ Heavy Hitters)

1,2-Ron Lim-c/a(p)	.90	2.25

DRAGONQUEST
Dec, 1986 - No. 3, 1987 ($1.50, B&W, 28 pgs.)
Silverwolf Comics

1-3-Tim Vigil-c/a in all	1.00	2.00	5.00

DRAGONRING
1986 - V2#15, 1988 ($1.70/$2.00, B&W/color)
Aircel Publishing

1	1.20	3.00
2-6: 6-Last B&W issue	.80	2.00
V2#1-($2.00, color)	.80	2.00
2-15	.70	1.80

DRAGON'S CLAWS
July, 1988 - No. 10, Apr, 1989 ($1.25/$1.50/$1.75, British)
Marvel Comics UK, Ltd.

1-4: 2-Begin $1.50-c. 3-Death's Head 1 pg. strip on back-c (1st app.). 4- Silhouette of Death's Head on last pg.		1.50
5-1st full app. new Death's Head; begin $1.75-c	1.60	4.00
6-10	.70	1.75

DRAGONSLAYER (Movie)
October, 1981 - No. 2, Nov, 1981
Marvel Comics Group

1,2-Paramount Disney movie adaptation		1.00

DRAGON'S STAR 2
1994 ($2.95, B&W)
Caliber Press

1	1.20	3.00

DRAGON STRIKE
Feb, 1994 ($1.25)
Marvel Comics

1-Based on TSR role playing game		1.25

DRAGOON WELLS MASSACRE
No. 815, June, 1957
Dell Publishing Co.

	GD25	FN65	NM94
Four Color 815-Movie, photo-c	9.00	27.00	90.0

DRAGSTRIP HOTRODDERS (World of Wheels No. 17 on)
Sum, 1963; No. 2, Jan, 1965 - No. 16, Aug, 1967
Charlton Comics

1	4.30	13.00	32.0
2-5	3.25	9.50	22.0
6-16	2.30	6.75	16.0

DRAMA
June, 1994 ($2.95, mature)
Sirius

1-1st full color Dawn app. in comics	2.40	7.20	17.0
1-Limited edition (1400 copies); signed & numbered; fingerprint authenticity	7.00	20.50	55.0

NOTE: Dawn's 1st full color app. was a pin-up in Amazing Heroes' Swimsuit Special #5.

DRAMA OF AMERICA, THE
1973 ($1.95, 224 pgs.)
Action Text

1- "Students' Supplement to History"		1.20	3.0

DREADLANDS (Also see Epic)
1992 - No. 4, 1992 ($3.95, limited series, 52 pgs.)
Marvel Comics (Epic Comics)

1-4: Stiff-c		1.60	4.0

DREADSTAR
Nov, 1982 - No. 64, Mar, 1991
Marvel Comics (Epic Comics)/First Comics No. 27 on

1-64: 1-Starlin-a begins			1.2
Annual 1 (12/83)-r/The Price		.70	1.7

DREADSTAR
Apr, 1994 - No.6, Jan, 1995 ($2.50, limited series)
Malibu Comics (Bravura)

1-6-Peter David scripts: 1,2-Starlin-c		1.00	2.5

NOTE: Issues 1-6 contain Bravura stamps.

DREADSTAR AND COMPANY
July, 1985 - No. 6, Dec, 1985
Marvel Comics (Epic Comics)

1-6: Reprints of Dreadstar series			1.

DREAM BOOK OF LOVE (Also see A-1 Comics)
No. 106, June-July, 1954 - No. 123, Oct-Nov, 1954
Magazine Enterprises

A-1 106 (#1)-Powell, Bolle-a; Montgomery Clift, Donna Reed photo-c	10.00	30.00	60.
A-1-114 (#2)-Guardineer, Bolle-a; Piper Laurie, Victor Mature photo-c	8.35	25.00	50.
A-1 123 (#3)-Movie photo-c	6.70	20.00	40.0

DREAM BOOK OF ROMANCE (Also see A-1 Comics)
No. 92, 1954 - No. 124, Oct-Nov, 1954
Magazine Enterprises

A-1 92 (#5)-Guardineer-a; photo-c	9.15	27.00	55.
A-1 101 (#6)(4-6/54)-Marlon Brando photo-c; Powell, Bolle, Guardineer0a	16.00	47.00	110.
A-1 109 (#7)(7-8/54)-Powell-a; movie photo-c	6.70	20.00	40.
A-1 110 (#8)(1/54)-Movie photo-c	6.70	20.00	40.0
A-1 124 (#8)(10-11/54)	6.70	20.00	40.0

DREAMERY, THE
Dec, 1986 - No. 14, Feb, 1989 ($2.00, B&W, Baxter paper)
Eclipse Comics

1-14: 2-7-Alice In Wonderland adapt.		.80	2.

DREAMING, THE (See Sandman, 2nd Series)

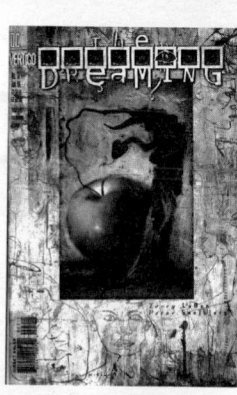
The Dreaming #3 © DC

Druid #4 © MEG

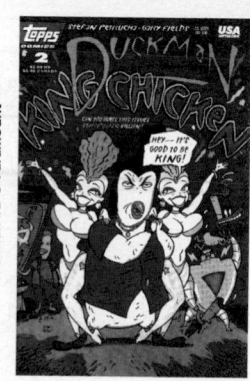
Duckman #2 © Paramount

	GD25	FN65	NM94

June, 1996 - Present ($2.50)
DC Comics (Vertigo)

1-10: McKean-c on all. 1-3-LaBan scripts & Snejbjerg-a. 4-7-Hogan scripts;
    Parkhouse-a   2.50

DREAM OF LOVE
1958 (Reprints)
I. W. Enterprises

1,2,8: 1-r/Dream Book of Love #1; Bob Powell-a. 2-r/Grest Lovers Romances
    #10. 8-Great Lover's Romances #1; also contains 2 Jon Juan stories by
    Siegel & Schomburg; Kinstler-c.   1.30   3.25   8.00
9-Kinstler-c; 1pg. John Wayne interview & Frazetta illo from John Wayne Adv.
    Comics #2   1.20   3.00   7.00

DREAM TEAM (See Battlezones: Dream Team 2)
July, 1995 ($4.95, one-shot)
Malibu Comics (Ultraverse)

1-Pin-ups teaming up Marvel & Ultraverse characters by various artists
    including Allred, Hamner, Romita, Darrow, Balent, Quesada & Palmiotti.
    1.00   2.00   5.00

DRIFT FENCE (See Zane Grey 4-Color 270)

DRIFT MARLO
May-July, 1962 - No. 2, Oct-Dec, 1962
Dell Publishing Co.

01-232-207(#1), 2(12-232-212)   3.00   9.00   30.00

DRISCOLL'S BOOK OF PIRATES
1934 (B&W, hardcover; 124 pgs, 7x9")
David McKay Publ. (Not reprints)

nn-By Montford Amory   20.00   60.00   140.00

DROIDS (Also see Dark Horse Comics)
April, 1986 - No. 8, June, 1987 (Based on Saturday morning cartoon)
Marvel Comics (Star Comics)

1-8: R2D2, C-3PO from Star Wars app.   1.20   3.00
NOTE: **Romita** a-3p. **Williamson** a-2i, 5i, 7i, 8i. **Sinnott** a-3i.

DROPSIE AVENUE: THE NEIGHBORHOOD
June, 1995 ($15.95/$24.95, B&W)
Kitchen Sink Press

nn-Will Eisner (softcover)   2.30   6.70   16.00
nn-Will Eisner (hardcover)   3.60   11.00   25.00

DROWNED GIRL, THE
1990 ($5.95, 52 pgs, mature)
DC Comics (Piranha Press)

nn   1.00   2.50   6.00

DRUG WARS
1989 ($1.95)
Pioneer Comics

1-Grell-c.   .80   2.00

DRUID
May, 1995 - No. 4, Aug, 1995 ($2.50, limited series)
Marvel Comics

1-4-Warren Ellis scripts.   1.00   2.50

DRUM BEAT
No. 610, Jan, 1955
Dell Publishing Co.

Four Color 610-Movie, Alan Ladd photo-c   10.00   30.00   100.00

DRUNKEN FIST
Aug, 1988 - Present? ($1.50/$1.95, 68 pgs.)
Jademan Comics

1-8-($1.50)   1.50

9-44-($1.95)   .80   2.00

DUCK ALBUM (See Donald Duck Album)
No. 353, Oct, 1951 - No. 840, Sept, 1957
Dell Publishing Co.

Four Color 353 (#1)-Barks-c; 1st Uncle Scrooge-c (also appears on back-c).
    8.00   24.00   80.00
Four Color 450-Barks-c   6.00   18.00   60.00
Four Color 492,531,560,586,611,649,686   5.00   15.00   50.00
Four Color 726,782,840   5.00   15.00   50.00

DUCKMAN
Sept, 1990 ($1.95, B&W, one-shot)
Dark Horse Comics

1-Story & art by Everett Peck   .80   2.00

DUCKMAN
Nov, 1994 - No. 5, May, 1995; No. 0, Feb, 1996 ($2.50, bi-monthly)
Topps Comics

0 (2/96, $2.95, B&W)-r/Duckman #1 from Dark Horse Comics.
    1.20   3.00
1-5: 1-w/ coupon #A for Duckman trading card. 2-w/Duckman 1st season
    episode guide   1.00   2.50

DUCKMAN: THE MOB FROG SAGA
Nov, 1994 - No. 3, Feb, 1995 ($2.50, limited series)
Topps Comics

1-3: 1-w/coupon #B for Duckman tradiing card, S. Shaw!-c   1.00   2.50

DUCKTALES
Oct, 1988 - No. 13, May, 1990 (1,2,9-11: $1.50; 3-8: 95¢)
Gladstone Publishing

1-Barks-r   1.00   2.60   6.00
2,10,11: Barks-r   1.60   4.00
3-9:4-6,9-Barks-r. 7-Barks-r(1 pg.)   1.20   3.00
12,13 ($1.95, 68 pgs.)-Barks-r; 12-r/F.C. #495   1.00   2.00   5.00

DUCKTALES
June, 1990 - No. 18, Nov, 1991 ($1.50)
Disney Comics

1-All new stories   1.10   2.75
2-18   .65   1.60
The Movie nn (1990, $7.95, 68 pgs.)-Graphic novel adapting animated movie
    1.30   3.25   8.00

DUDLEY (Teen-age)
Nov-Dec, 1949 - No. 3, Mar-Apr, 1950
Feature/Prize Publications

1-By Boody Rogers   13.50   41.00   95.00
2,3   10.00   30.00   65.00

DUDLEY DO-RIGHT (TV)
Aug, 1970 - No. 7, Aug, 1971 (Jay Ward)
Charlton Comics

1   6.00   18.00   42.00
2-7   4.00   12.00   28.00

DUKE OF THE K-9 PATROL
Apr, 1963
Gold Key

1 (10052-304)   2.85   8.50   20.00

DUMBO (Disney; see Movie Comics, & Walt Disney Showcase #12)
No. 17, 1941 - No. 668, Jan, 1958
Dell Publishing Co.

Four Color 17 (#1)-Mickey Mouse, Donald Duck, Pluto app.
    170.00   510.00   1700.00
Large Feature Comic 19 ('41)-Part-r 4-Color 17   250.00   750.00   2500.00

Durango Kid #1 © AC

DV8 #1 © Aegis Entertainment

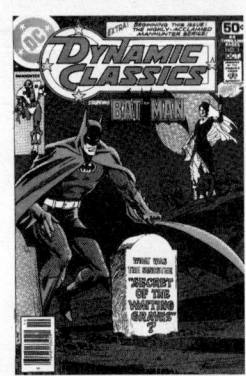
Dynamic Classics #1 © DC

	GD25	FN65	NM94

Four Color 234 ('49)   10.00   30.00   100.00
Four Color 668 (12/55)-1st of two printings. Dumbo on-c with starry sky.
Reprints Four Color 234? same-c as 234   8.00   24.00   80.00
Four Color 668 (1/58)-2nd printing. Same cover altered with Timothy Mouse
added. Same contents as above   6.00   18.00   60.00

DUMBO (Walt Disney's..., The Flying Elephant)
1941 (K.K. Publ. Giveaway)
Weatherbird Shoes/Ernest Kern Co.(Detroit)

nn-16 pgs., 9x10" (Rare)   40.00   120.00   325.00
nn-52 pgs., 5-1/2x8-1/2", slick cover in color; B&W interior; half text, half
reprints 4-Color No. 17   25.00   75.00   175.00

DUMBO COMIC PAINT BOOK (See Dumbo, Large Feature Comic No. 19)

DUMBO WEEKLY
1942 (Premium supplied by Diamond D-X Gas Stations)
Walt Disney Productions

1   40.00   120.00   350.00
2-16   13.00   39.00   100.00
Binder only   275.00
NOTE: A cover and binder came separate at gas stations. Came with membership card.

DUNC AND LOO (#1-3 titled "Around the Block with Dunc and Loo")
Oct-Dec, 1961 - No. 8, Oct-Dec, 1963
Dell Publishing Co.

1   9.00   27.00   90.00
2   5.50   16.50   55.00
3-8   4.00   12.00   40.00
NOTE: Written by John Stanley; Bill Williams art.

DUNE (Movie)
Apr, 1985 - No. 3, June, 1985
Marvel Comics

1-3-r/Marvel Super Special; movie adaptation   1.00

DURANGO KID, THE (Also see Best of the West, Great Western & White
Indian) (Charles Starrett starred in Columbia's Durango Kid movies)
Oct-Nov, 1949 - No. 41, Oct-Nov, 1955 (36 Pgs.)
Magazine Enterprises

1-Charles Starrett photo-c; Durango Kid & his horse Raider begin; Dan Brand
& Tipi (origin) begin by Frazetta & continue through #16
  62.00   187.00   500.00
2-Starrett photo-c.   33.00   99.00   230.00
3-5-All have Starrett photo-c.   31.00   94.00   220.00
6-10: 7-Atomic weapon-c/story   16.00   47.00   110.00
11-16-Last Frazetta issue   11.00   33.00   75.00
17-Origin Durango Kid   16.00   47.00   110.00
18-Fred Meagher-a on Dan Brand begins   10.00   30.00   60.00
19-30: 19-Guardineer-c/a(3) begins, end #41. 23-Intro. The Red Scorpion
  10.00   30.00   60.00
31-Red Scorpion returns   9.15   27.00   55.00
32-41-Bolle/Frazettaish-a (Dan Brand; true in later issues?)
  9.15   27.00   55.00
NOTE: #6, 8, 14, 15 contain Frazetta art not reprinted in White Indian. Ayers
a(3)-19-41; c-19-41. Fred Meagher a-18-29 at least.

DURANGO KID, THE
1990 - #2, 1990 ($2.50, half-color)
AC Comics

1-Starrett photo front/back-c; Guardineer-r   1.00   2.50
2-($2.75, B&W)-Starrett photo-c; White Indian-r by Frazetta; Guardineer-r (50th
anniversary of films)   1.10   2.75

DV8 (See Gen 13)
Aug, 1996 - Present ($2.50)
Image Comics (Wildstorm Productions)

1-4: Warren Ellis scripts & Humberto Ramos-c/a(p)   2.50

1-Seven variant-c exist based on the seven deadly sins
      5.00
Rave-(7/96, $1.75)-Ramos-c; pinups & interviews   1.75

DWIGHT D. EISENHOWER
December, 1969
Dell Publishing Co.

01-237-912 - Life story   2.00   6.00   20.00

DYNABRITE COMICS
1978 - 1979 (69¢, 10x7-1/8", 48 pgs., cardboard-c)
(Blank inside covers)
Whitman Publishing Co.

11350 - Walt Disney's Mickey Mouse & the Beanstalk (4-C 157). 11350-1 - Mickey Mouse
Album (4-C 1057,1151,1246). 11351 - Mickey Mouse & His Sky Adventure (4-C 214, 343)
11352 - Donald Duck (4-C 408, Donald Duck 45,52)-Barks-a. 11352-1 - Donald Duck (4-C 318,
10 pg. Barks/WDC&S 125,128)-Barks-c(r). 11353 - Daisy Duck's Diary (4-C 1055,1150) Barks-
a. 11354 - Goofy: A Gaggle of Giggles. 11354-1 - Super Goof Meets Super Thief. 11355 - Uncle
Scrooge (Barks-a/U.S. 12,33). 11355-1 - Uncle Scrooge (Barks-a/U.S. 13,16) - Barks-c(r). 11356
- (?). 11357 - Star Trek (r/-Star Trek 33,41). 11358 - Star Trek (r/-Star Trek 34,36). 11359 - Bugs
Bunny-r. 11360 - Winnie the Pooh Fun and Fantasy (Disney-r). 11361 - Gyro Gearloose & the
Disney Ducks (r/4-C 1047,1184)-Barks-c(r)
each....   1.00

DYNAMIC ADVENTURES
No. 8, 1964 - No. 9, 1964
I. W. Enterprises

8-Kayo Kirby-r by Baker?/Fight Comics 53.   2.00   6.00   14.00
9-Reprints Avon's "Escape From Devil's Island"; Kinstler-c
  2.30   6.70   16.00
nn (no date)-Reprints Risks Unlimited with Rip Carson, Senorita Rio; r/Fight #53
  2.00   6.00   14.00

DYNAMIC CLASSICS (See Cancelled Comic Cavalcade)
Sept-Oct, 1978 (44 pgs.)
DC Comics

1-Neal Adams Batman, Simonson Manhunter-r   1.00   2.50

DYNAMIC COMICS (No #4-7)
Oct, 1941 - No. 3, Feb, 1942; No. 8, 1944 - No. 25, May, 1948
Harry 'A' Chesler

1-Origin Major Victory by Charles Sultan (reprinted in Major Victory #1),
Dynamic Man & Hale the Magician; The Black Cobra only app.; Major
Victory & Dynamic Man begin   137.00   412.00   1100.00
2-Origin Dynamic Boy & Lady Satan; intro. The Green Knight & sidekick
Lance Cooper   65.00   195.00   525.00
3   53.00   159.00   425.00
8-Dan Hastings, The Echo, The Master Key, Yankee Boy begin; Yankee
Doodle Jones app.; hypo story   53.00   159.00   425.00
9-Mr. E begins; Mac Raboy-c   56.00   168.00   450.00
10   40.00   120.00   325.00
11-15: 15-The Sky Chief app.   40.00   120.00   280.00
16-Marijuana story   40.00   120.00   290.00
17(1/46)-Illustrated in SOTI, "The children told me what the man was going to
do with the hot poker," but Wertham saw this in Crime Reporter #2
  47.00   141.00   375.00
18,19,21,22,24,25   29.00   86.00   200.00
20-Bare-breasted woman-c   40.00   120.00   325.00
23-Yankee Girl app.   29.00   86.00   200.00
I.W. Reprint #1,8('64): 1-r/#23. 8-Exist?   2.60   7.50   18.00
NOTE: Kinstler c-IW #1. Tuska art in many issues, #3, 9, 11, 12, 16, 19. Bondage c-16.

DYNAMITE (Becomes Johnny Dynamite No. 10 on)
May, 1953 - No. 9, Sept, 1954
Comic Media/Allen Hardy Publ.

1-Pete Morisi-a; Don Heck-c; r-as Danger #6   14.00   43.00   100.00
2   9.15   27.00   55.00
3-Marijuana story; Johnny Dynamite (1st app.) begins by Pete Morisi(c/a);

Dynamite #3 © Comic Media

Dynamo Joe #11 © FC

Eagle #1 © RH

	GD25	FN65	NM94

Heck text-a; man shot in face at close range 10.00 30.00 70.00
4-Injury-to-eye, prostitution; Morisi-c/a 11.50 34.00 80.00
5-9-Morisi-c/a in all. 7-Prostitute story plus reprints 8.35 25.00 50.00

DYNAMO (Also see Tales of Thunder & T.H.U.N.D.E.R. Agents)
Aug, 1966 - No. 4, June, 1967 (25¢)
Tower Comics

1-Crandall/Wood, Ditko/Wood-a; Weed series begins; NoMan & Lightning
cameos; Wood-c/a 5.70 17.00 45.00
2-4: Wood-c/a in all 4.00 12.00 30.00
NOTE: **Adkins/Wood** a-2. **Ditko** a-4?. **Tuska** a-2, 3.

DYNAMO JOE (Also see First Adventures & Mars)
May, 1986 - No. 15, Jan, 1988 (#12-15: $1.75)
First Comics

1-15: 4-Cargonauts begin 1.50
Special 1(1/87)-Mostly-r/Mars 1.50

DYNOMUTT (TV)(See Scooby-Doo (3rd series))
Nov, 1977 - No. 6, Sept, 1978 (Hanna-Barbera)
Marvel Comics Group

1-The Blue Falcon, Scooby Doo in all 1.10 2.75
2-6: 1.60

EAGLE, THE (1st Series) (See Science Comics & Weird Comics #8)
July, 1941 - No. 4, Jan, 1942
Fox Features Syndicate

1-The Eagle begins; Rex Dexter of Mars app. by Briefer; all issues feature
German war covers 162.00 487.00 1300.00
2-The Spider Queen begins (origin) 78.00 234.00 625.00
3,4: 2-Joe Spook begins (origin) 64.00 193.00 515.00

EAGLE (2nd Series)
Feb-Mar, 1945 - No. 2, Apr-May, 1945
Rural Home Publ.

1-Aviation stories 29.00 86.00 200.00
2-Lucky Aces 18.00 54.00 125.00
NOTE: **L. B. Cole** c/a in each.

EAGLE
Sept, 1986 - No. 26?, 1989 ($1.50/1.75/1.95, B&W)
Crystal Comics/Apple Comics #17 on

1 .80 2.00
1-Signed and limited 1.10 2.75
2-26: 12-Double size origin issue ($2.50) 1.50

EAGLES DARE
Aug, 1994 - Present? ($1.95, B&W, limited series)
Aager comics, Inc.

1,2 .80 2.00

EARTH MAN ON VENUS (An...) (Also see Strange Planets)
1951
Avon Periodicals

nn-Wood-a (26 pgs.); Fawcette-c 100.00 300.00 800.00

EARTHWORM JIM (TV, cartoon)
Dec, 1995 - No. 3?, Feb, 1996 ($2.25)
Marvel Comics

1-3: Based on video game and toys .90 2.25

EASTER BONNET SHOP (See March of Comics No. 29)

EASTER WITH MOTHER GOOSE
No. 103, 1946 - No. 220, Mar, 1949
Dell Publishing Co.

Four Color 103 (#1)-Walt Kelly-a 19.00 57.00 190.00
Four Color 140 ('47)-Kelly-a 15.50 46.50 155.00
Four Color 185 ('48),220-Kelly-a 13.00 39.00 130.00

	GD25	FN65	NM94

EAST MEETS WEST
Apr, 1990 - No. 2, 1990 ($2.50, limited series, mature)
Innovation Publishing

1,2: 1-Stevens part-i; Redondo-c(i). 2-Stevens-c(i); 1st app. Cheech & Chong
in comics 1.00 2.50

EAT RIGHT TO WORK AND WIN
1942 (16 pgs.) (Giveaway)
Swift & Company

Blondie, Henry, Flash Gordon by Alex Raymond, Toots & Casper, Thimble Theatre(Popeye),
Tillie the Toiler, The Phantom, The Little King, & Bringing up Father - original strips just for this
book -(in daily strip form which shows what foods we should eat and why)
20.00 60.00 240.00

E. C. CLASSIC REPRINTS
May, 1973 - No. 12, 1976 (E. C. Comics reprinted in color minus ads)
East Coast Comix Co.

1-The Crypt of Terror #1 (Tales from the Crypt #46) 1.00 2.50 6.00
2-Weird Science #15('52) 1.60 4.00
3-12: 3-Shock SuspenStories #12. 4-Haunt of Fear #12. 5-Weird Fantasy #13
('52). 6-Crime SuspenStories #25. 7-Vault of Horror #26. 8-Shock Suspen-
Stories #6. 9-Two-Fisted Tales #34. 10-Haunt of Fear #23. 11-Weird
Science #12(#1). 12-Shock SuspenStories #2 1.20 3.00

EC CLASSICS
Aug, 1985 - No. 12, 1986? (High quality paper; each-r 8 stories in color)
Russ Cochran (#2-12 were resolicited in 1990)($4.95, 56 pgs., 8x11")

1-12: 1-Tales From the Crypt. 2-Weird Science. 3-Two-Fisted Tales. 4-Shock
SuspenStories. 5-Weird Fantasy. 6-Vault of Horror. 7-Weird Science-Fantasy
(r/23,24). 8-Crime SuspensStories. 9-Haunt of Fear. 10-Panic (r/1,2). 11-
Tales From the Crypt (r/23,24). 12-Weird Science (r/20,22)
1.00 2.00 5.00

ECHO OF FUTUREPAST
May, 1984 - No. 9, Jan, 1986 ($2.95, color, 52 pgs.)
Pacific Comics/Continuity Comics

1-9: Neal Adams-c/a in all? 1.20 3.00
NOTE: **N. Adams** a-1-6,7i,9i; c-1-3, 5p,7i,8,9i. **Golden** a-1-6 (Bucky O'Hare); c-6. **Toth** a-6,7.

ECLIPSE GRAPHIC ALBUM SERIES
Oct, 1978 - Present (8-1/2x11") (B&W #1-5)
Eclipse Comics

1-Sabre (10/78, B&W, 1st print.); Gulacy-a; 1st direct sale graphic novel
1.30 3.25 8.00
1-Sabre (2nd printing, 1/79) 1.30 3.25 8.00
1-Sabre (3rd print, $5.95) 1.00 2.50 6.00
2-Night Music (11/79, B&W)-Russell-a 1.00 2.00 5.00
3-Detectives, Inc. (5/80, B&W)-Rogers-a 1.20 3.00 7.00
4-Stewart The Rat (1980, B&W)-G. Colan-a 1.20 3.00 7.00
5-The Price (10/81, B&W)-Starlin-a 1.70 5.00 12.00
6-I Am Coyote (11/84, color)-Rogers-c/a 1.30 3.25 8.00
7-The Rocketeer (9/85, color)-Dave Stevens-a (r/chapters 1-5)(see Pacific
Presents & Starslayer); has 7 pgs. new-a 1.30 3.25 8.00
7-The Rocketeer (2nd print, $7.95) 1.30 3.25 8.00
7-The Rocketeer (3rd print, 1991, $8.95) 1.50 3.75 9.00
7-The Rocketeer, signed & limited HC 9.00 26.00 60.00
7-The Rocketeer, hard-c (1986, $19.95) 4.00 10.00 20.00
7-The Rocketeer, unsigned HC (3rd, $32.95) 4.70 14.00 33.00
8-Zorro In Old California ('86, color) 1.30 3.25 8.00
8-Hardcover 1.70 5.00 12.00
9-Sacred And The Profane ('86)-Steacy-a 2.30 6.75 16.00
9-Hardcover ($24.95) 3.60 10.75 25.00
10-Somerset Holmes ('86, $15.95)-Adults, soft-c 2.30 6.75 16.00
10-Hardcover ($24.95) 3.60 10.75 25.00
11-Floyd Farland, Citizen of the Future ('87, $3.95, B&W) 1.60 4.00
12-Silverheels ('87, $8.95, color) 1.50 3.75 9.00

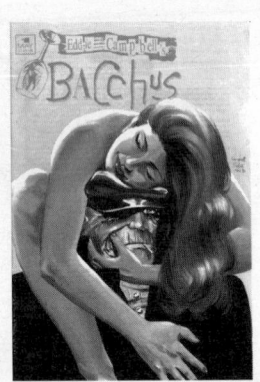

Eddie Campbell's Bacchus #1 © Eddie Campbell

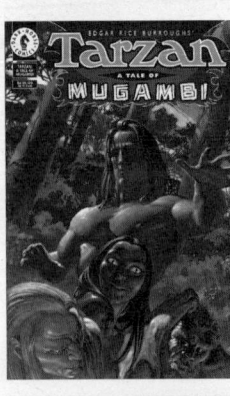

Edgar Rice Burroughs Tarzan: A Tale of Mugambi © ERB

Edge #2 © Steven Grant & Gil Kane

	GD25	FN65	NM94
12-Hardcover ($14.95)	2.15	6.50	15.00
12-Hardcover, signed & #'d ($24.95)	3.60	10.75	25.00
13-The Sisterhood of Steel ('87, $9.95, color)	1.65	4.00	10.00
14-Samurai, Son of Death ('87, $4.95, B&W)	1.00	2.00	5.00
14-Samurai, Son of Death ($3.95, 2nd printing)		1.60	4.00
15-Twisted Tales (11/87, color)-Dave Stevens-c		1.60	4.00
16-See Airfighters Classics #1			
17-Valkyrie, Prisoner of the Past ('88, $3.95, color)		1.60	4.00
18-See Airfighters Classics #2			
19-Scout: The Four Monsters ('88, $14.95, color)-r/Scout #1-7; soft-c			
	2.15	6.50	15.00
20-See Airfighters Classics #3		1.60	4.00
21-XYR-Multiple ending comic ('88, $3.95, B&W)		1.60	4.00
22-Alien Worlds #1 (5/88, $3.95, 52 pgs.)-Nudity		1.60	4.00
23-See Airfighters Classics #4		1.60	4.00
24-Heartbreak ($4.95, B&W)	1.00	2.00	5.00
25-Alex Toth's Zorro Vol. 1 ($10.95, B&W)	1.65	4.70	11.00
26-Alex Toth's Zorro Vol. 2 ($10.95, B&W)	1.65	4.70	11.00
27-Fast Fiction (She) ($5.95, B&W)	1.00	2.50	6.00
28-Miracleman Book I ($5.95)	1.00	2.50	6.00
29-Real Love: The Best of the Simon and Kirby Romance Comics (10/88, $12.95)	1.85	5.50	13.00
30-Brought To Light; Alan Moore scripts (1989)	1.65	4.70	11.00
30-Limited hardcover ed. ($29.95)	4.30	13.00	30.00
31-Pigeons From Hell by R. E. Howard (11/88)	1.30	3.25	8.00
31-Signed & Limited Edition ($29.95)	4.30	13.00	30.00

ECLIPSE MAGAZINE (Becomes Eclipse Monthly)
May, 1981 - No. 8, Jan, 1983 ($2.95, B&W, magazine)
Eclipse Publishing

1-8: 1-1st app. Cap'n Quick and a Foozle by Rogers, Ms. Tree by Beatty, and Dope by Trina Robbins. 2-1st app. I Am Coyote by Rogers. 7-1st app. Masked Man by Boyer	1.20	3.00

NOTE: Colan a-3, 5, 8. Golden c/a-2. Gulacy a-6, c-1, 6. Kaluta c/a-5. Mayerik a-2, 3. Rogers a-1-8. Starlin a-1. Sutton a-6.

ECLIPSE MONTHLY
Aug, 1983 - No. 10, July, 1984 (Baxter paper; 1-3, 52 pgs., $2.00)
Eclipse Comics

1-3: ($2.00)-Cap'n Quick and a Foozle by Rogers, Static by Ditko, Dope by Trina Robbins, Rio by Doug Wildey, The Masked Man by Boyer begin.		
3-Ragamuffins begins	.80	2.00
4-10: 4-8-$1.50-c. 9,10-$1.75-c	.70	1.80

NOTE: Boyer c-6. Ditko a-1-3. Rogers a-1-4; c-2, 4, 7. Wildey a-1, 2, 5, 9, 10; c-5, 10.

ECLIPSO (See Brave and the Bold #64, House of Secrets #61 & Phantom Stranger, 1987)
Nov, 1992 - No. 18, Apr, 1994 ($1.25)
DC Comics

1-14: 1-Giffen plots/breakdowns begin. 10-Darkseid app.		1.25
15-18: 15-Begin $1.50-c. Creeper in #3-6,9,11-13. 18-Spectre-c/s		1.50
Annual 1 (1993, $2.50, 68 pgs.)-Intro Prism	1.00	2.50

ECLIPSO: THE DARKNESS WITHIN
July, 1992 - No. 2, Oct, 1992 ($2.50, 68 pgs.)
DC Comics

1-With purple gem attached to-c	1.00	2.50
1-Without gem; Superman, Creeper app.	1.00	2.50
2-Concludes Eclipso storyline from annuals	1.00	2.50

E. C. 3-D CLASSICS (See Three Dimensional...)

ECTOKID (See Razorline)
Sept, 1993 - No. 9, May, 1994 ($1.75/$1.95)
Marvel Comics

1-($2.50)-Foil embossed-c; created by C. Barker	1.00	2.50
2-8: 2-Origin. 5-Saint Sinner x-over	.70	1.75

	GD25	FN65	NM94
9-Begin $1.95-c		.80	2.00
...: Unleashed 1 (10/94, $2.95, 52 pgs.)		1.20	3.00

EDDIE STANKY (Baseball Hero)
1951 (New York Giants)
Fawcett Publications

nn-Photo-c	29.00	86.00	200.00

EDDIE CAMPBELL'S BACCHUS
May, 1995 - Present ($2.95, B&W)
Eddie Campbell Comics

1-16: 1-Cerebus app. 9-Alex Ross back-c.		1.20	3.00

EDEN MATRIX, THE
1994 ($2.95)
Adhesive Comics

1,2-Two variant-c; alternate-c on inside back-c		1.20	3.00

EDGAR BERGEN PRESENTS CHARLIE McCARTHY
No. 764, 1938 (36 pgs.; 15x10-1/2"; in color)
Whitman Publishing Co. (Charlie McCarthy Co.)

764	68.00	206.00	550.00

EDGAR RICE BURROUGHS' TARZAN: A TALE OF MUGAMBI
1995 ($2.95, one-shot)
Dark Horse Comics

1		1.20	3.00

EDGAR RICE BURROUGHS' TARZAN: IN THE LAND THAT TIME FORGOT AND THE POOL OF TIME
1996 ($12.95, trade paperback)
Dark Horse Comics

nn-r/Russ Manning-a			13.00

EDGAR RICE BURROUGHS' TARZAN: THE LOST ADVENTURE
Jan, 1995 - No. 4, Apr, 1995 ($2.95, B&W, limited series)
Dark Horse Comics

1-4: ERB's last Tarzan story, adapted by Joe Lansdale		1.20	3.00
Limited Edition Hardcover ($99.95)-signed & numbered			100.00

EDGE
July, 1994 - No. 3, Apr, 1995 ($2.50, unfinished limited series)
Malibu Comics (Bravura)

1-3-S. Grant-story & Gil Kane-c/a; w/Bravura stamp		1.00	2.50

EDGE OF CHAOS
July, 1983 - No. 3, Jan, 1984 (Limited series)
Pacific Comics

1-3-Morrow c/a; all contain nudity		.80	2.00

EDWARD'S SHOES GIVEAWAY
1954 (Has clown on cover)
Edward's Shoe Store

Contains comic with new cover. Many combinations possible. Contents determines price, 50-60 percent of original. (Similar to Comics From Weatherbird & Free Comics to You)

ED WHEELAN'S JOKE BOOK STARRING FAT & SLAT (See Fat & Slat)

EERIE (Strange Worlds No. 18 on)
No. 1, Jan, 1947; No. 1, May-June, 1951 - No. 17, Aug-Sept, 1954
Avon Periodicals

1(1947)-1st horror comic; Kubert, Fugitani-a; bondage-c			
	225.00	675.00	1800.00
1(1951)-Reprints story from 1947 #1	45.00	136.00	365.00
2-Wood-c/a; bondage-c	53.00	159.00	425.00
3-Wood-c; Kubert, Wood/Orlando-a	53.00	159.00	425.00
4,5-Wood-c	43.00	130.00	345.00
6,8,13,14: 8-Kinstler-a; bondage-c; Phantom Witch Doctor story			
	24.00	71.00	165.00

Eerie #5 © I. W. Enterprises

Egypt #5 © Peter Milligan & Glyn Dillon

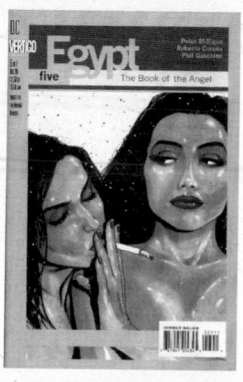

80 Page Giant #1 © DC

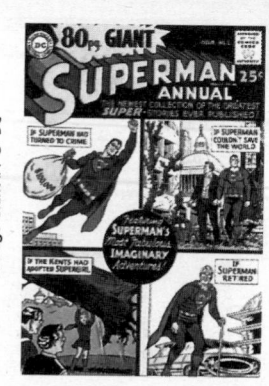

EI

	GD25	FN65	NM94

	GD25	FN65	NM94
7-Wood/Orlando-c; Kubert-a	39.00	116.00	270.00
9-Kubert-a; Check-c	27.00	81.00	190.00
10,11: 10-Kinstler-a. 11-Kinstlerish-a by McCann	21.00	64.00	150.00
12-Dracula story from novel, 25 pgs.	28.00	84.00	195.00
15-Reprints No. 1('51)minus-c(bondage)	17.00	49.00	115.00
16-Wood-a r-/No. 2	19.00	56.00	130.00
17-Wood/Orlando & Kubert-a; reprints #3 minus inside & outside Wood-c			
	24.00	71.00	165.00

NOTE: *Hollingsworth a-9-11; c-10, 11.*

EERIE
1964
I. W. Enterprises

I.W. Reprint #1('64)-Wood-c(r); r-story/Spook #1	3.25	9.50	22.00
I.W. Reprint #2,6,8: 8-Dr. Drew by Grandenetti from Ghost #9			
	2.30	6.70	16.00
I.W. Reprint #9-r/Tales of Terror #1(Toby); Wood-c	3.40	10.00	24.00

EERIE (Magazine)(See Warren Presents)
No. 1, Sept, 1965; No. 2, Mar, 1966 - No. 139, Feb, 1983
Warren Publishing Co.

1-24 pgs., black & white, small size (5-1/4x7-1/4"), low distribution; cover from inside back cover of Creepy No. 2; stories reprinted from Creepy No. 7, 8. At least three different versions exist.
First Printing - B&W, 5-1/4" wide x 7-1/4" high, evenly trimmed. On page 18, panel 5, in the upper left-hand corner, the large rear view of a bald headed man blends into solid black and is unrecognizable. Overall printing quality is poor.

	36.00	107.00	250.00

Second Printing - B&W, 5-1/4x7-1/4", with uneven, untrimmed edges (if one of these were trimmed evenly, the size would be less than as indicated). The figure of the bald headed man on page 18, panel 5 is clear and discernible. The staples have a 1/4" blue stripe.

	13.50	41.00	95.00

Other unauthorized reproductions for comparison's sake would be practically worthless. One known version was probably shot off a first printing copy with some loss of detail; the finer lines tend to disappear in this version which can be determined by looking at the lower right-hand corner of page one, first story. The roof of the house is shaded with straight lines. These lines are sharp and distinct on original, but broken on this version.

NOTE: *The Overstreet Comic Book Price Guide recommends that, before buying a 1st issue, you consult an expert.*

2-Frazetta-c (also #3,5,7,8)	7.00	21.00	50.00
3-Frazetta-c & half pg. ad (rerun in #4)	5.75	17.00	40.00
4-10: 4-Frazetta-a (1/2 pg. ad). 5,7,8-Frazetta-c. 9-Headlight-c			
	3.25	9.50	22.00
11-22,24,25: 25-Steranko-c	2.30	6.70	16.00
23-Frazetta-c	2.60	7.50	18.00
26-41,43-45	1.65	4.70	11.00
42,51-(1973 & 1974 Annuals)	1.65	4.70	11.00
46-50,52,53,56-59,61-78: 46-Dracula series by Sutton begins. 78-The Mummy-r			
	1.30	3.25	8.00
54,55-Color Spirit story by Eisner, reprints sections 12/21/47 & 6/16/46			
	1.65	4.70	11.00
60-Summer Giant (9/74, $1.25)	1.65	4.20	10.00
79,80-Origin Darklon the Mystic by Starlin (1st app.)	1.30	3.25	8.00
81,83-139: 84-All sports issue	1.00	2.60	6.00
82-1st app. The Rook	1.65	4.20	10.00
Year Book 1970, 1971-Reprints in both	2.00	5.00	12.00
Year Book 1972-Reprints	1.50	3.80	9.00

NOTE: *The above books contain art by many good artists: N. Adams, Brunner, Corben, Craig (Taycee), Crandall, Ditko, Eisner, Evans, Jeff Jones, Krenkel, McWilliams, Morrow, Orlando, Ploog, Severin, Starlin, Torres, Toth, Williamson, Wood, and Wrightson; covers by Bode', Corben, Davis, Frazetta, Morrow, and Orlando. Frazetta c-2, 3, 7, 8, 23. Annuals from 1973-on are included in regular numbering. 1970-74 Annuals are complete reprints. Annuals from 1975-on are in the format of the regular magazines.*

EERIE ADVENTURES (Also see Weird Adventures)
Winter, 1951 (Painted-c)
Ziff-Davis Publ. Co.

1-Powell-a(2), McCann-a; used in **SOTI**; bondage-c; Krigstein back-c			
	31.00	92.00	215.00

NOTE: *Title dropped due to similarity to Avon's Eerie & legal action.*

EERIE TALES (Magazine)
1959 (Black & White)
Hastings Associates

1-Williamson, Torres, Tuska-a, Powell(2), & Morrow(2)-a			
	9.15	27.00	55.00

EERIE TALES
1963-1964
Super Comics

Super Reprint No. 10,11,12,18: 10('63)-r/Spook #27. Purple Claw in #11,12			
('63); #12-r/Avon's Eerie #1('51)-Kida-r	1.70	5.00	12.00
15-Wolverton-a, Spacehawk-r/Blue Bolt Weird Tales #113; Disbrow-a			
	4.50	14.00	32.00

EGBERT
Spring, 1946 - No. 20, 1950
Arnold Publications/Quality Comics Group

1-Funny animal; intro Egbert & The Count	18.00	54.00	125.00
2	10.00	30.00	65.00
3-10	5.85	17.50	35.00
11-20	4.00	12.00	24.00

EGYPT
Aug, 1995 - No.7, Feb, 1996 ($2.50, limited series, mature)
DC Comics (Vertigo)

1-7: Milligan scripts in all.	1.00		2.50

EH! (...Dig This Crazy Comic) (From Here to Insanity No. 8 on)
Dec, 1953 - No. 7, Nov-Dec, 1954 (Satire)
Charlton Comics

1-Davisish-c/a by Ayers, Woodish-a by Giordano; Atomic Mouse app.			
	26.00	77.00	180.00
2-Ayers-c/a	17.00	49.00	115.00
3-7: 4,6-Sexual innuendo-c. 6-Ayers-a	14.00	43.00	100.00

EIGHTBALL
Oct, 1989 - Present ($2.75/$2.95/$3.95, semi-annually, mature)
Fantagraphics Books

1 ($2.95)	1.65	4.20	10.00
2-7 ($2.75)	1.20	3.00	7.00
8 ($2.95)	1.00	2.00	5.00
9,10,11,13-15 ($2.95)		1.20	3.00
12 ($2.75)		1.10	2.75
16,17 ($3.95): 17-(8/96)			4.00

EIGHT IS ENOUGH KITE FUN BOOK (See Kite Fun Book)

80 PAGE GIANT (...Magazine No. 2-15)
8/64 - No. 15, 10/65; No. 16, 11/65 - No. 89, 7/71 (25¢)(All reprints)
National Periodical Publications (#1-56: 84 pgs.; #57-89: 68 pgs.)

1-Superman Annual; originally planned as Superman Annual #9 (8/64)			
	35.00	105.00	420.00
2-Jimmy Olsen	19.00	57.00	230.00
3,4: 3-Lois Lane. 4-Flash-G.A.-r; Infantino-a	14.50	43.75	175.00
5-Batman; has Sunday newspaper strip; Catwoman-r; Batman's Life Story-r			
(25th anniversary special)	14.50	43.75	175.00
6-Superman	11.50	35.00	140.00
7-Sgt. Rock's Prize Battle Tales; Kubert-c/a	12.50	37.50	150.00
8-More Secret Origins-origins of JLA, Aquaman, Robin, Atom, & Superman;			
Infantino-a	28.00	85.00	340.00
9-11: 9-Flash r/Flash #106,117,123 & Showcase #14). Infantino-a. 10-			
Superboy. 11-Superman; all Luthor issue	11.25	33.75	135.00
12-Batman; has Sunday newspaper strip	11.25	33.75	135.00
13,14: 13-Jimmy Olsen. 14-Lois Lane	11.25	33.75	135.00
15-Superman and Batman; Joker-c/story	11.25	33.75	135.00

El Diablo #2 © DC

Elektra Megazine #1 © MEG

Elementals: Ghost Of A Chance © Comico

	GD25	FN65	NM94

Continued as part of regular series under each title in which that particular book came out, a Giant being published instead of the regular size. Issues No. 16 to No. 89 are listed for your information. See individual titles for prices.
16-JLA #39 (11/65), 17-Batman #176, 18-Superman #183, 19-Our Army at War #164, 20-Action #334, 21-Flash #160, 22-Superboy #129, 23-Superman #187, 24-Batman #182, 25-Jimmy Olsen #95, 26-Lois Lane #68, 27-Batman #185, 28-World's Finest #161, 29-JLA #48, 30-Batman #187, 31-Superman #193, 32-Our Army at War #177, 33-Action #347, 34-Flash #169, 35-Superboy #138, 36-Superman #197, 37-Batman #193, 38-Jimmy Olsen #104, 39-Lois Lane #77, 40-World's Finest #170, 41-JLA #58, 42-Superman #202, 43-Batman #198, 44-Our Army at War #190, 45-Action #360, 46-Flash #178, 47-Superboy #147, 48-Superman #207, 49-Batman #203, 50-Jimmy Olsen #113, 51-Lois Lane #86, 52-World's Finest #179, 53-JLA #67, 54-Superman #212, 55-Batman #208, 56-Our Army at War #203, 57-Action #373, 58-Flash #187, 59-Superboy #156, 60-Superman #217, 61-Batman #213, 62-Jimmy Olsen #122, 63-Lois Lane #95, 64-World's Finest #188, 65-JLA #76, 66-Superman #222, 67-Batman #218, 68-Our Army at War #216, 69-Adventure #390, 70-Flash #196, 71-Superboy #165, 72-Superman #227, 73-Batman #223, 74-Jimmy Olsen #131, 75-Lois Lane #104, 76-World's Finest #197, 77-JLA #85, 78-Superman #232, 79-Batman #228, 80-Our Army at War #229, 81-Adventure #403, 82-Flash #205, 83-Superboy #174, 84-Superman #239, 85-Batman #233, 86-Jimmy Olsen #140, 87-Lois Lane #113, 88-World's Finest #206, 89-JLA #93.

87TH PRECINCT (TV)
Apr-June, 1962 - No. 2, July-Sept, 1962
Dell Publishing Co.

Four Color 1309(#1)-Krigstein-a	10.00	30.00	100.00
2	8.00	24.00	80.00

EL BOMBO COMICS
1946
Standard Comics/Frances M. McQueeny

nn(1946)	10.00	30.00	65.00
1(no date)	10.00	30.00	65.00

EL CID
No. 1259, 1961
Dell Publishing Co.

Four Color 1259-Movie, photo-c	7.00	21.00	70.00

EL DIABLO (See All-Star Western #2 & Weird Western Tales #12)
Aug, 1989 - No. 16, Jan, 1991 ($1.50-$1.75, color)
DC Comics

1 ($2.50, 52pgs.)-Masked hero	1.00		2.50
2-6 ($1.50)			1.50
7-11: 7-Begin $1.75-c	.70		1.80
12-16: 12-Begin $2.00-c	.80		2.00

EL DORADO (See Movie Classics)

ELECTRIC UNDERTOW (See Strikeforce Morituri: Electric Undertow)

ELECTRIC WARRIOR
May, 1986 - No. 18, Oct, 1987 ($1.50, Baxter paper)
DC Comics

1-18			1.50

ELEKTRA (Also see Daredevil #319-325)
Mar, 1995 - No. 4, June, 1995 ($2.95, limited series)
Marvel Comics

1-4-Embossed-c; Scott McDaniel-a	1.20		3.00

ELEKTRA (Also see Daredevil)
Nov, 1996 - Present ($1.95)
Marvel Comics

1-Peter Milligan scripts; Deodato-c/a			2.00
1-Variant-c			3.00

ELEKTRA: ASSASSIN (Also see Daredevil)
Aug, 1986 - No. 8, June, 1987 (Limited series, mature)
Marvel Comics (Epic Comics)

1-Miller scripts in all; Sienkiewicz-c/a.	1.60		4.00
2	1.20		3.00
3-7	.80		2.00
8	1.60		4.00

ELEKTRA LIVES AGAIN (Also see Daredevil)
1990 ($24.95, oversize, hardcover, 76 pgs.)(Produced by Graphitti Designs)
Marvel Comics (Epic Comics)

nn-Frank Miller-c/scripts; Lynn Varley painted-a; Matt Murdock & Bullseye app.; Elektra dies			25.00

Signed & numbered hardcover (Graphittii Designs, $39.95, 2000 print run)-
reprints 1-8   50.00

ELEKTRA MEGAZINE
Nov, 1996 - No. 2, Dec, 1996 ($3.95, 96 pgs., reprints, limited series)
Marvel Comics

1,2: Reprints Frank Miller's Elektra stories in Daredevil			4.00

ELEKTRA SAGA, THE
Feb, 1984 - No. 4, June, 1984 ($2.00, limited series, Baxter paper)
Marvel Comics Group

1-4-r/Daredevil 168-190; Miller-c/a	1.20		3.00

ELEMENTALS, THE (See The Justice Machine & Morningstar Spec.)
June, 1984 - No. 29, Sept, 1988; V2#1, Mar, 1989 - No. 28, 1994? ($1.50/$2.50, Baxter paper); V3#1, Dec, 1995 - Present ($2.95)
Comico The Comic Co.

1-Willingham-c/a, 1-8	1.60		4.00
2	1.00		2.50
3-10: 9-Bissette-a(p). 10-Photo-c	.80		2.00
11-29			1.50
V2#1-28: 1-3-$1.95-c. 4-Begin $2.50-c. 16-1st app. Strike Force America. 18-Prelude to Avalon mini-series. 37-Prequel to Strike Force America series			
		.80	2.00
V3#1,2: 1-Daniel-a(p), bagged w/gaming card.	1.20		3.00
Special 1 (3/86)-Willingham-a(p)	.70		1.75
Special 2 (1/89, $1.95)	.80		2.00

ELEMENTALS: GHOST OF A CHANCE
Dec, 1995 ($5.95, graphic novel)
Comico

nn-Ross-c.			6.00

ELEVEN OR ONE
Apr, 1995 ($2.95)
Sirius

1-Linsner-c/a	2.15	6.50	15.00

ELFLORD
1986 - No. 30, 1989 ($1.70, B&W); V2#1- V2#30, 1995 ($2.00)
Aircel Publishing

1		1.60	4.00
1,2-2nd printings			1.50
2,3		1.00	2.50
4-6: Last B&W issue			1.60
V2#1-Color-a begins		1.00	2.50
2-20			1.60
21-Double size ($4.95)	1.00	2.00	5.00
22-30: 22-New cast. 25-Begin B&W, $1.95-c		.70	1.75

ELFLORD: DRAGON'S EYE
1993 ($2.50, B&W)
Night Wynd Enterprises

1		1.00	2.50

ELFQUEST (Also see Fantasy Quarterly & Warp Graphics Annual)
No. 2, Aug, 1978 - No. 21, Feb, 1985 (All magazine size)
No. 1, Apr, 1979
WaRP Graphics, Inc.
NOTE: **Elfquest** was originally published as one of the stories in **Fantasy Quarterly** #1. When the publisher went out of business, the creative team, Wendy and Richard Pini, formed WaRP

Elfquest: Blood of Ten Chiefs #9 © Richard & Wendy Pini

Elfquest: Jink #5 © Richard & Wendy Pini

Elfquest: The Rebels #8 © Richard & Wendy Pini

EL

	GD25	FN65	NM94

Graphics and continued the series, beginning with **Elfquest #2**. **Elfquest #1**, which reprinted the story from **Fantasy Quarterly**, was published about the same time **Elfquest #4** was released. Thereafter, most issues were reprinted as demand warranted, until Marvel announced it would reprint the entire series under its Epic imprint (Aug., 1985).

	GD25	FN65	NM94
1(4/79)-Reprints Elfquest story from Fantasy Quarterly No. 1			
1st printing ($1.00-c)	5.00	15.00	35.00
2nd printing ($1.25-c)	1.65	4.70	11.00
3rd printing ($1.50-c)	1.00	2.00	5.00
4th printing; different-c ($1.50-c)			1.50
2(8/78)-5: 1st printings ($1.00-c)	3.25	9.50	22.00
2nd printings ($1.25-c)	1.00	2.00	5.00
3rd & 4th printings ($1.50-c)(all 4th prints 1989)		1.20	3.00
6-9: 1st printings ($1.25-c)	1.50	3.75	9.00
2nd printings ($1.50-c)		1.60	4.00
3rd printings ($1.50-c)		.80	2.00
10-14: ($1.50-c); 16-8pg. preview of A Distant Soil	1.00	2.60	6.00
10-14: 2nd printings ($1.50)			1.50
15-21 (only one printing)	1.00	2.60	6.00

ELFQUEST
Aug, 1985 - No. 32, Mar, 1988
Marvel Comics (Epic Comics)

	GD25	FN65	NM94
1-Reprints in color the Elfquest epic by WaRP Graphics		1.60	4.00
2-32		.80	2.00

ELFQUEST
1989 - No. 4, 1989 ($1.50, B&W)
WaRP Graphics

	GD25	FN65	NM94
1-4: Reprints original Elfquest series			1.50

ELFQUEST: BLOOD OF TEN CHIEFS
July, 1993 - No. 20, Sept, 1995 ($2.00/$2.50)
WaRP Graphics

	GD25	FN65	NM94
1-15-By Richard & Wendy Pini		.90	2.25
16-20: 16-Begin $2.50-c			2.50

ELFQUEST:JINK
Nov, 1994 - No. 12, Feb, 1996 ($2.25/$2.50)
WaRP Graphics

	GD25	FN65	NM94
1-3-W. Pini and John Byrne collaborate on Back-c		.90	2.25
4-12: 4-Begin $2.50-c		1.00	2.50

ELFQUEST: KAHVI
Oct, 1995 - No. 6, Mar, 1996 ($2.25, B&W)
WaRP Graphics

	GD25	FN65	NM94
1-6		.90	2.25

ELFQUEST: KINGS OF THE BROKEN WHEEL
June, 1990 - No. 9, Feb, 1992 ($2.00, B&W) (3rd Elfquest saga)
WaRP Graphics

	GD25	FN65	NM94
1-9: By Richard & Wendy Pini; 1-Color insert	.80	2.00	
1-2nd printing	.80	2.00	

ELFQUEST: METAMORPHOSIS
Apr, 1996 - Present ($2.95, B&W)
WaRP Graphics

	GD25	FN65	NM94
1			3.00

ELFQUEST: NEW BLOOD (...Summer Special on-c #1 only)
Aug, 1992 - No. 35, Jan, 1996 ($2.00/$2.25/$2.50, color/B&W, bi-monthly)

	GD25	FN65	NM94
1-($3.95, 68 pgs.)-Byrne-a/scripts (16 pgs.)	1.60	4.00	
2-17: Barry Blair-a in all	.90	2.25	
18-26: 18-Begin $2.25-c	.90	2.25	
27-31: 27 begin $2.50-c.	1.00	2.50	
32-35 ($2.25)-B&W	.90	2.25	

ELFQUEST: SHARDS
Aug, 1994 - No. 16, Mar, 1996 ($2.25/$2.50)
WaRP Graphics

	GD25	FN65	NM94
1-8		.90	2.25
9-16:9-Begin $2.50-c		1.00	2.50

ELFQUEST: SIEGE AT BLUE MOUNTAIN
Mar, 1987 - No. 8, Dec, 1988 ($1.75/$1.95, B&W, limited series)
WaRP Graphics/Apple Comics

	GD25	FN65	NM94
1-Staton-a(i) in all; 2nd Elfquest saga	1.00	2.00	5.00
1-2nd printing		.80	2.00
2		1.40	3.50
2,3-2nd printings		.70	1.75
3-8		.80	2.00

ELFQUEST: THE REBELS
Nov, 1994 - No. 12, Mar, 1996 ($2.25/$2.50, B&W/color)
WaRP Graphics

	GD25	FN65	NM94
1-3			2.25
4-12: 4-Begin $2.50-c			2.50

ELFQUEST: TWO-SPEAR
Oct, 1995 - No. 5, Feb, 1996 ($2.25, B&W)
WaRP Graphics

	GD25	FN65	NM94
1-5			2.25

ELFQUEST: TWO-SPEAR
V2#1, May, 1996 - Present ($4.95, B&W)
WaRP Graphics

	GD25	FN65	NM94
V2#1-4: 1-3-Wendy Pini-c			5.00

ELFQUEST: WAVE DANCERS
Dec, 1993 - No. 6, Mar, 1996 ($2.00/$2.25)
WaRP Graphics

	GD25	FN65	NM94
1,2: 1-Foil-c & poster		1.00	2.50
3-6: 3-Begin 2.25-c		.90	2.25
Special 1 ($2.95)			3.00

ELF-THING
March, 1987 ($1.50, B&W, one-shot)
Eclipse Comics

	GD25	FN65	NM94
1			1.50

ELIMINATOR (Also see The Solution #16 & The Night Man #16)
Apr, 1995 - No. 3, July, 1995 ($2.95/$2.50, limited series)
Malibu Comics (Ultraverse)

	GD25	FN65	NM94
0-Mike Zeck-a in all		1.20	3.00
1-3:($2.50): 1-1st app. Siren		1.00	2.50
1-($3.95)-Black cover edition		1.60	4.00

ELIMINATOR FULL COLOR SPECIAL
Oct, 1991 ($2.95, one-shot)
Eternity Comics

	GD25	FN65	NM94
1-Dave Dorman painted-c		1.20	3.00

ELLA CINDERS (See Comics On Parade, Comics Revue #1,4, Famous Comics Cartoon Book, Giant Comics Editions, Sparkler Comics, Tip Top & Treasury of Comics)

ELLA CINDERS
1938 - 1940
United Features Syndicate

	GD25	FN65	NM94
Single Series 3(1938)	40.00	120.00	285.00
Single Series 21(#2 on-c, #21 on inside), 28('40)	34.00	103.00	240.00

ELLA CINDERS
Mar, 1948 - No. 5, Mar, 1949
United Features Syndicate

	GD25	FN65	NM94
1-(#2 on cover)	12.00	36.00	85.00

Ellery Queen #2 © SUPR

Elric: Sailor On The Sails Of Fate #4 © Michael Moorcock

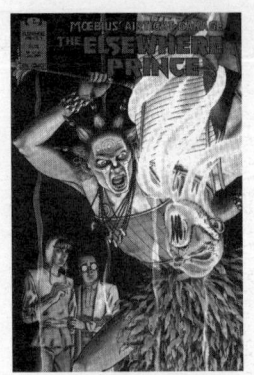

The Elsewhere Prince #3 © Moebius

	GD25	FN65	NM94
2	8.35	25.00	50.00
3-5	5.85	17.50	35.00

ELLERY QUEEN
May, 1949 - No. 4, Nov, 1949
Superior Comics Ltd.

1-Kamen-c; L.B. Cole-a; r-in Haunted Thrills	40.00	120.00	325.00
2-4: 3-Drug use stories(2)	34.00	101.00	235.00
NOTE: *Iger shop art in all issues.*

ELLERY QUEEN (TV)
1-3/52 (Spring on-c) - No. 2, Summer/52 (Saunders painted-c)
Ziff-Davis Publishing Co.

1-Saunders-c	40.00	120.00	290.00
2-Saunders bondage, torture-c	34.00	101.00	235.00

ELLERY QUEEN (Also see Crackajack Funnies No. 23)
No. 1165, Mar-May, 1961 - No.1289, Apr, 1962
Dell Publishing Co.

Four Color 1165 (#1)-	11.00	33.00	110.00
Four Color 1243 (11-1/61-61), 1289	9.00	27.00	90.00

ELMER FUDD (Also see Camp Comics, Daffy, Looney Tunes #1 & Super Book #10, 22)
No. 470, May, 1953 - No. 1293, Mar-May, 1962
Dell Publishing Co.

Four Color 470 (#1)	4.00	12.00	40.00
Four Color 558,628,689('56)	3.00	9.00	30.00
Four Color 725,783,841,888,938,977,1032,1081,1131,1171,1222,1293('62)	2.00	6.00	20.00

ELMO COMICS
Jan, 1948 (Daily strip-r)
St. John Publishing Co.

1-By Cecil Jensen	10.00	30.00	60.00

ELONGATED MAN (See Flash #112 & Justice League of America #105)
Jan, 1992 - No. 4, Apr, 1992 ($1.00, limited series)
DC Comics

1-4: 3-The Flash app.			1.00

ELRIC (Of Melnibone)(See First Comics Graphic Novel #6 & Marvel Graphic Novel #2)
Apr, 1983 - No. 6, Apr, 1984 ($1.50, Baxter paper)
Pacific Comics

1-6: Russell-c/a(i) in all			1.50

ELRIC
1996 ($2.95, one-shot)
Topps Comics

0--One Life: Russell-c/a; adapts Neil Gaiman's short story "One Life--Furnished in Early Moorcock."			3.00

ELRIC, SAILOR ON THE SEAS OF FATE
June, 1985 - No. 7, June, 1986 ($1.75, limited series)
First Comics

1-7: Adapts Michael Moorcock's novel		.80	2.00

ELRIC: THE BANE OF THE BLACK SWORD
Aug, 1988 - No. 6, June, 1989 ($1.75/$1.95, limited series)
First Comics

1-4: Adapts Michael Moorcock's novel		.80	2.00

ELRIC: THE VANISHING TOWER
Aug, 1987 - No. 6, June, 1988 ($1.75, limited series)
First Comics

1-6: Adapts Michael Moorcock's novel		.70	1.80

ELRIC: WEIRD OF THE WHITE WOLF

Oct, 1986 - No. 5, June, 1987 ($1.75, limited series)
First Comics

1-5: Adapts Michael Moorcock's novel		.70	1.80

EL SALVADOR - A HOUSE DIVIDED
March, 1989 ($2.50, B&W, Baxter paper, stiff-c, 52 pgs.)
Eclipse Comics

1-Gives history of El Salvador		1.00	2.50

ELSEWHERE PRINCE, THE (Moebius' Airtight Garage)
May, 1990 - No. 6, Oct, 1990 ($1.95, limited series)
Marvel Comics (Epic Comics)

1-6: Moebius scripts & back-up-a in all		.80	2.00

ELSIE THE COW
Oct-Nov, 1949 - No. 3, July-Aug, 1950
D. S. Publishing Co.

1-(36 pgs.)	21.00	64.00	150.00
2,3	17.00	51.00	120.00
Borden Milk Giveaway-(16 pgs., nn) (3 ishs) 1957)	13.00	39.00	90.00
Elsie's Fun Book(1950; Borden Milk)	13.00	39.00	90.00
Everyday Birthday Fun With... (1957; 20 pgs.)(100th Anniversary); Kubert-a	13.00	39.00	90.00

ELSON'S PRESENTS
1981 (100 pgs., no cover price)
DC Comics

Series 1-6: Repackaged 1981 DC comics; Superman, Action, Flash, DC Comics Presents & Batman known. Series I has a Batman/Joker-c.

Series 3-New Teen Titans #3('81)	1.00	2.00	5.00

ELVEN (Also see Prime)
Oct, 1994 - No. 4, Feb, 1995 ($2.50, limited series)
Malibu Comics (Ultraverse)

0 ($2.95)-Prime app.		1.20	3.00
1-4: 2,4-Prime app. 3-Primevil app.		1.00	2.50
1-Limited Foil Edition- no price on cover	1.00	2.00	5.00

ELVIRA MISTRESS OF THE DARK
May, 1993 - Present ($2.50, B&W)
Claypool Comics (Eclipse)

1-30-Photo-c: 1-Austin-a(i). 1-6-Spiegle-a		1.00	2.50

ELVIRA'S HOUSE OF MYSTERY
Jan, 1986 - No. 11, Jan, 1987
DC Comics

1-($1.50)			1.50
2-11: 9-Photo-c. 11-Dave Stevens-c			1.25
Special 1 (3/87, $1.25)			1.25

ELVIRA MISTRESS OF THE DARK
Oct, 1988 ($2.00, B&W, magazine size)
Marvel Comics

1-Movie adaptation		.80	2.00

ELVIS MANDIBLE, THE
1990 ($3.50, 52 pgs., B&W, mature)
DC Comics (Piranha Press)

nn		1.40	3.50

ELVIS PRESLEY (See Career Girl Romances #32, Go-Go, Howard Chaykin's American Flagg #10, Humbug #8, I Love You #60 & Young Lovers #18)

E-MAN
Oct, 1973 - No. 10, Sept, 1975 (Painted-c No. 7-10)
Charlton Comics

1-Origin & 1st app. E-Man; Staton c/a in all	1.70	5.00	12.00
2-4: 2,4-Ditko-a. 3-Howard-a	1.00	2.60	6.00

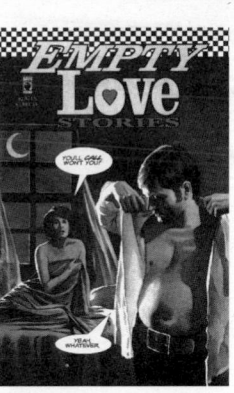

Empty Love Stories #1 © Steve Darnall

Enemy #5 © DH

Enigma #7 © Peter Milligan & Duncan Fegredo

	GD25	FN65	NM94

5-Miss Liberty Belle app. by Ditko — 1.00 — 2.00 — 5.00
6-10: Early Byrne-a in all (#6 is 1/75). 8-Full-length story; Nova begins as E-Man's partner — 1.20 — 3.00 — 7.00
1-4,9,10(Modern Comics reprints, '77) — — — 1.00
NOTE: *Killjoy* app.-No. 2, 4. *Liberty Belle* app.-No. 5. *Rog 2000* app.-No. 6, 7, 9, 10. *Travis* app.-No. 3. **Tom Sutton** a-1.

E-MAN (Also see Michael Mauser & The Original E-Man)
Apr, 1983 - No. 25, Aug, 1985 ($1.00/$1.25, direct sales only)
First Comics

1-25: 2-X-Men satire. 3-X-Men/Phoenix satire. 6-Origin retold. 8-Cutey Bunny app. 10-Origin Nova Kane. 24-Origin Michael Mauser — — — 1.00
NOTE: *Staton* a-1-5, 6-25p; c-1-25.

E-MAN
Sept, 1989 ($2.75, one-shot, no ads, high quality paper)
Comico

1-Staton-c/a; Michael Mauser story — — 1.10 — 2.80

E-MAN
V4#1, Jan, 1990 - No. 3, Mar, 1990 ($2.50, limited series)
Comico

1-3: Staton-c/a — — 1.00 — 2.50

E-MAN
Oct, 1993 ($2.75)
Alpha Productions

V5#1-Staton-c/a; 20th anniversary issue — — 1.10 — 2.75

E-MAN RETURNS
1994 ($2.75, B&W)
Alpha Productions

1-Joe Staton-c/a(p) — — 1.10 — 2.75

EMERALD DAWN
1991 ($4.95, trade paperback)
DC Comics

nn-Reprints Green Lantern: Emerald Dawn #1-6 — 1.00 — 2.00 — 5.00

EMERALD DAWN II (See Green Lantern...)

EMERGENCY (Magazine)
June, 1976 - No. 4, Jan, 1977 (B&W)
Charlton Comics

1-Neal Adams-c/a; Heath, Austin-a — — 1.00 — 2.50
2,4: 2-N. Adams-c. 4-Alcala-a — — .65 — 1.60
3-N. Adams-a — — .80 — 2.00

EMERGENCY (TV)
June, 1976 - No. 4, Dec, 1976
Charlton Comics

1-Staton-c; Byrne-a — 1.00 — 2.00 — 5.00
2-4: 2-Staton-c — — 1.20 — 3.00

EMERGENCY DOCTOR
Summer, 1963 (one-shot)
Charlton Comics

1 — — 1.20 — 3.00 — 6.00

EMIL & THE DETECTIVES (See Movie Comics)

EMMA PEEL & JOHN STEED (See The Avengers)

EMPEROR'S NEW CLOTHES, THE
1950 (10¢, 68 pgs.), 1/2 size, oblong)
Dell Publishing Co.

nn - (Surprise Books series) — 3.20 — 8.00 — 16.00

EMPIRE STRIKES BACK, THE (See Marvel Comics Super Special #16 & Marvel Special Edition)

EMPTY LOVE STORIES

	GD25	FN65	NM94

Nov, 1994 - Present ($2.95, B&W)
Slave Labor Graphics

1,2: Steve Darnall scripts in all. 1-Alex Ross-c. 2-(8/96)-Mike Allred-c — — — 3.00

ENCHANTED APPLES OF OZ, THE (See First Comics Graphic Novel #5)

ENCHANTER
Apr, 1987 - No. 3, Aug. 1987 ($2.00, B&W, limited series)
Eclipse Comics

1-3 — — .80 — 2.00

ENCHANTING LOVE
Oct, 1949 - No. 6, July, 1950 (All 52 pgs.)
Kirby Publishing Co.

1-Photo-c — 10.00 — 30.00 — 70.00
2-Photo-c; Powell-a — 6.70 — 20.00 — 40.00
3,4,6: 3-Jimmy Stewart photo-c — 5.35 — 16.00 — 32.00
5-Ingels-a, 9 pgs.; photo-c — 13.00 — 39.00 — 90.00

ENCHANTMENT VISUALETTES (Magazine)
Dec, 1949 - No. 5, Apr, 1950 (Painted c-1)
World Editions

1-Contains two romance comic strips each — 13.00 — 39.00 — 90.00
2 — 10.00 — 30.00 — 70.00
3-5 — 10.00 — 30.00 — 60.00

ENEMY
May, 1994 - No. 5, Sept, 1994 ($2.50, limited series)
Dark Horse Comics

1-5 — — 1.00 — 2.50

ENEMY ACE SPECIAL (Also see Our Army at War #151, Showcase #57, 58 & Star Spangled War Stories #138)
1990 ($1.00, one-shot)
DC Comics

1-Kubert-r/Our Army #151,153; c-r/Showcase 57 — — 1.20 — 3.00

ENIGMA
Mar, 1993 - No. 8, Oct, 1993 ($2.50, limited series)
DC Comics (Vertigo)

1-8: Milligan scripts — — 1.00 — 2.50
Trade paperback ($19.95)-reprints — — — 20.00

ENSIGN O'TOOLE (TV)
Aug-Oct, 1963 - No. 2, 1964
Dell Publishing Co.

1,2 — — 2.60 — 7.50 — 18.00

ENSIGN PULVER (See Movie Classics)

EPIC
1992 - Book 4, 1992 ($4.95, limited series, 52 pgs.)
Marvel Comics (Epic Comics)

Book One-Four: 2-Dorman painted-c — 1.00 — 2.00 — 5.00
NOTE: *Alien Legion* in #3. *Cholly & Flytrap* by **Burden**(scripts) & **Suydam**(art) in 3, 4. *Dinosaurs* in #4. *Dreadlands* in #1. *Hellraiser* in #1. *Nightbreed* in #2. *Sleeze Brothers* in #2. *Stalkers* in #1-4. *Wild Cards* in #1-4.

EPIC ILLUSTRATED (Magazine)
Spring, 1980 - No. 36, Feb, 1986 ($2.00/$2.50, B&W/color, mature)
Marvel Comics Group

1-Frazetta-c — — 1.20 — 3.00
2-26: 12-Wolverton Spacehawk-r edited & recolored w/article on him. 13-Bladerunner preview by Williamson. 14-Elric of Melnibone by Russell; Revenge of the Jedi preview. 15-Vallejo-c & interview; 1st Dreadstar story (cont'd in Dreadstar #1). 16-B. Smith-c/a(2). 20-The Sacred & the Profane begins by Ken Steacy. 26-Galactus series begins; Cerebus the Aardvark story by Dave Sim — — .80 — 2.00

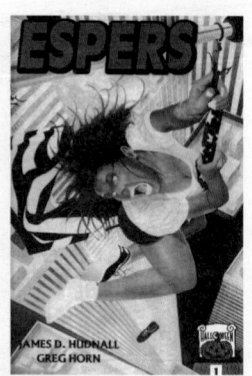

ESPers V2#1 © Halloween Comics

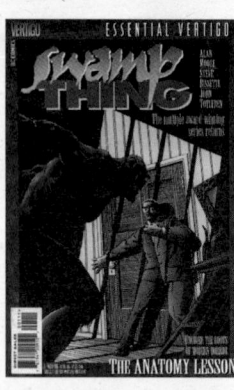

Essential Vertigo: The Swamp Thing #1 © DC

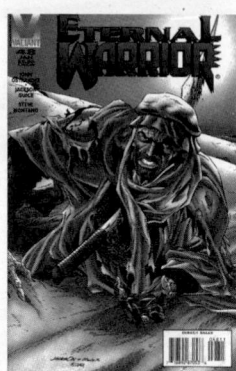

Eternal Warrior #42 © Acclaim

	GD25	FN65	NM94

27-36: ($2.50): 27-Groo. 28-Cerebus app. — 1.20 — 3.00

NOTE: **N. Adams** a-7; c-6. **Austin** a-15-20i. **Bode** a-19, 23, 27r. **Bolton** a-7, 10-12, 15, 18, 22-25; c-10, 18, 22, 23. **Boris** c/a-15. **Brunner** c-12. **Buscema** a-1p, 9p, 11-13p. **Byrne/Austin** a-26-34. **Chaykin** a-2; c-8. **Conrad** a-2-5, 7-9, 25-34; c-17. **Corben** a-15; c-2. **Frazetta** c-1. **Golden** a-3r. **Gulacy** c/a-3. **Jeff Jones** c-25. **Kaluta** a-17r, 21, 24r, 26; c-4, 28. **Nebres** a-1. **Reese** a-12. **Russell** a-2-4, 9, 14, 33; c-14. **Simonson** a-17. **B. Smith** c/a-7, 16. **Starlin** a-1-9, 14, 15, 34. **Steranko** c-19. **Williamson** a-13, 27, 34. **Wrightson** a-13p, 22, 25, 27, 34; c-30.

EPIC LITE
Sept, 1991 ($3.95, 52 pgs., one-shot)
Marvel Comics (Epic Comics)

1-Bob the Alien, Normalman by Valentino — 1.60 — 4.00

EPICURUS THE SAGE
Vol. 1, 1991 - Vol. 2, 1991 ($9.95, 8-1/8x10-7/8")
DC Comics (Piranha Press)

Volume 1,2-Sam Kieth-c/a — 1.65 — 4.00 — 10.00

EPSILON WAVE
Oct, 1985 - V2#2, 1987 ($1.50/$1.25/$1.75)
Independent Comics/Elite Comics No. 5 on

1-4: 1-3-($1.50)-Seadragon app. 4-$1.25-c — — — 1.50
5-8: 5-8-$1.75-c. 6-Seadragon app. — — .70 — 1.75
V2#1,2 (B&W) — — — 1.60

ERADICATOR
Aug, 1996 - No. 4, Nov, 1996 ($1.75, limited series)
DC Comics

1-4: Superman app. — — — 1.75

ERNIE COMICS (Formerly Andy Comics #21; All Love Romances #26 on)
No. 22, Sept, 1948 - No. 25, Mar, 1949
Current Books/Ace Periodicals

nn (9/48,11/48; #22,23)-Teenage humor — 5.70 — 17.00 — 34.00
24,25 — 4.00 — 12.00 — 24.00

ESCAPADE IN FLORENCE (See Movie Comics)

ESCAPE FROM DEVIL'S ISLAND
1952
Avon Periodicals

1-Kinstler-c; r/as Dynamic Adventures #9 — 31.00 — 94.00 — 220.00

ESCAPE FROM FEAR
1956, 1962, 1969 (Giveaway, 8 pgs. full color) (On birth control)
Planned Parenthood of America

1956 edition — 10.00 — 30.00 — 65.00
1962 edition — 7.50 — 22.50 — 45.00
1969 edition — 4.00 — 11.00 — 22.00

ESCAPE FROM THE PLANET OF THE APES (See Power Record Comics)

ESCAPE TO WITCH MOUNTAIN (See Walt Disney Showcase No. 29)

ESPERS
July, 1986 - No. 5, Apr, 1987 ($1.25/$1.75, Mando paper)
Eclipse Comics

1-3 ($1.25)-James Hudnall story & David Lloyd-a. — — — 1.30
4,5 ($1.75) — — .70 — 1.80

ESPERS
V2#1, 1996 - Present ($2.95, B&W)(1st Halloween Comics series)
Halloween Comics

V2#1-3; James D. Hudnall scripts. — — — 3.00

ESPIONAGE (TV)
May-July, 1964 - No. 2, Aug-Oct, 1964
Dell Publishing Co.

1,2 — 2.85 — 8.50 — 20.00

ESSENTIAL VERTIGO: THE SANDMAN

Aug, 1996 - Present ($1.95, reprints)
DC Comics (Vertigo)

1-6: Reprints Sandman, 2nd series — — — 2.00

ESSENTIAL VERTIGO: SWAMP THING
Nov, 1996 - Present ($1.95, reprints)
DC Comics

1-6: Reprints Alan Moore's Swamp Thing stories — — — 2.00

ETC
1989 - No. 5, 1990 ($4.50, 60 pgs., limited series, mature)
DC Comics (Piranha Press)

Book 1-5: Conrad scripts/layouts in all — — 1.80 — 4.50

ETERNAL BIBLE, THE
1946 (Large size) (16 pgs. in color)
Authentic Publications

1 — 11.50 — 34.00 — 80.00

ETERNALS, THE
July, 1976 - No. 19, Jan, 1978
Marvel Comics Group

1-Origin & 1st app. Eternals — 1.00 — 2.00 — 5.00
2-19: 2-1st app. Ajak & The Celestials; 25¢ & 30¢ issues exist. 14,15-Cosmic powered Hulk-c/story — — 1.20 — 3.00
Annual 1(10/77) — — 1.20 — 3.00

NOTE: **Kirby** c/a(p) in all. Price changed from 25¢ to 30¢ during run of #1.

ETERNALS, THE
Oct, 1985 - No. 12, Sept, 1986 (Maxi-series, mando paper)
Marvel Comics Group

1,12 ($1.25, 52 pgs.): 12-Williamson-a(i) — — — 1.25
2-11-(75¢) — — — 1.00

ETERNALS: THE HEROD FACTOR
Nov, 1991 ($2.50, 68 pgs.)
Marvel Comics

1 — — 1.00 — 2.50

ETERNAL WARRIOR (See Solar #10 & 11)
Aug, 1992 - No. 50, Mar, 1996 ($2.25/$2.50)
Valiant/Acclaim Comics (Valiant)

1-Unity x-over; Miller-c; origin Eternal Warrior & Armstrong — 1.00 — 2.00 — 5.00
1-Gold logo — 1.30 — 3.25 — 8.00
1-Gold foil logo — 1.65 — 4.20 — 10.00
2,3: 2-Unity x-over; Simonson-c. 3-Archer & Armstrong x-over — 1.20 — 3.00
4-1st app. Bloodshot (last pg. cameo); see Rai #0 for 1st full app.; Cowan-c — 1.00 — 2.00 — 5.00
5-2nd full app. Bloodshot (12/92; see Rai #0) — — 1.20 — 3.00
6,7: 6-2nd app. Master Darque — — 1.00 — 2.50
8-Flip book w/Archer & Armstrong #8 — — 1.80 — 4.50
9-25,27-37: 9-1st Book of Geomancer. 14-16-Bloodshot app. 18-Doctor Mirage cameo. 19-Doctor Mirage app. 22-W/bound-in trading card. 25-Archer & Armstrong app.; cont'd from A&A #25 — — .90 — 2.25
26-($2.75, 44 pgs.)-Flip book w/Archer & Armstrong — — 1.10 — 2.75
35-50: 35-Double-c; $2.50-c begins. 50-Geomancer app. — — 1.00 — 2.50

Special 1 (2/96, $2.50) — — 1.00 — 2.50
Yearbook 1 (1993, $3.95) — — 1.60 — 4.00
Yearbook 2 (1994, $3.95) — — 1.60 — 4.00

ETERNAL WARRIOR: FIST AND STEEL
May, 1996 - No. 2, June, 1996 ($2.50, limited series)
Acclaim Comics (Valiant)

1,2: Geomancer app. in both. 1-Indicia reads "June." 2-Bo Hampton-a — — 1.00 — 2.50

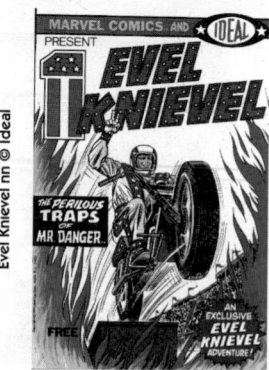

Evangeline #8 © FC

Evel Knievel nn © Ideal

The Everyman #1 © Mike Allred

EX

	GD25	FN65	NM94

ETERNITY SMITH
Sept, 1986 - No. 5, May, 1987 ($1.25/$1.50, 36 pgs.)
Renegade Press

1 ($1.25)-1st app. Eternity Smith			1.30
2-5 ($1.50): 5-Death of Jasmine			1.50

ETERNITY SMITH
Sept, 1987 - No. 9, 1988 ($1.95)
Hero Comics

V2#1-9: 8-Indigo begins		.80	2.00

ETTA KETT
No. 11, Dec, 1948 - No. 14, Sept, 1949
King Features Syndicate/Standard

11-Teenage	8.35	25.00	50.00
12-14	5.35	16.00	32.00

EUDAEMON, THE (See Dark Horse Presents #72-74)
Aug, 1993 - No. 3, Nov, 1993 ($2.50, limited series)
Dark Horse Comics

1-3: Nelson-a, painted-c & scripts	1.00		2.50

EVANGELINE (Also see Primer)
1984 - #2, 6/84; V2#1, 5/87 - V2#12, Mar, 1989 (Baxter paper)
Comico/First Comics V2#1 on/Lodestone Publ.

1		1.20	3.00
2		.80	2.00
V2#1 (5/87) - 12		.80	2.00
Special #1 (1986, $2.00)-Lodestone Publ.		.80	2.00

EVA THE IMP
1957 - No. 2, Nov, 1957
Red Top Comic/Decker

1,2	3.20	8.00	16.00

EVEL KNIEVEL
1974 (Giveaway, 20 pgs.)
Marvel Comics Group (Ideal Toy Corp.)

nn-Contains photo on inside back-c			1.00

EVERYBODY'S COMICS (See Fox Giants)

EVERYMAN, THE
Nov, 1991 ($4.50, one-shot, 52 pgs.)
Marvel Comics (Epic Comics)

1-Mike Allred-a	1.00	2.00	5.00

EVERYTHING HAPPENS TO HARVEY
Sept-Oct, 1953 - No. 7, Sept-Oct, 1954
National Periodical Publications

1	21.00	64.00	150.00
2	12.00	36.00	85.00
3-7	10.00	30.00	65.00

EVERYTHING'S ARCHIE
May, 1969 - No. 157, Sept, 1991 (Giant issues No. 1-20)
Archie Publications

1	5.50	16.50	55.00
2	2.60	11.00	26.00
3-5	2.00	6.00	16.00
6-10	1.65	4.20	10.00
11-20	1.00	2.60	6.00
21-50		1.20	3.00
51-157: 142,148-Gene Colan-a			1.25

EVERYTHING'S DUCKY (Movie)
No. 1251, 1961
Dell Publishing Co.

	GD25	FN65	NM94
Four Color 1251	5.00	15.00	50.00

EVIL ERNIE
Dec, 1991 - No. 5, 1992 ($2.50, B&W, limited series)
Eternity Comics

1-1st app. Lady Death by Steven Hughes (12,000 print run); Lady Death app. in all issues	18.00	54.00	135.00
2,3: 2-1st Lady Death-c. 2,3-(7,000 print run)	16.00	47.00	125.00
4-(8,000 print run)	11.00	33.00	80.00
5	6.50	19.50	50.00
Special Edition 1	8.00	24.50	65.00
Youth Gone Wild! ($9.95, trade paperback)-r/#1-5	1.65	4.20	10.00
Youth Gone Wild! Director's Cut ($4.95)-Limited to 15,000 copies, shows the making of the comic	1.00	2.00	5.00

EVIL ERNIE: THE RESURRECTION
1993 - No. 4, 1994 (Limited series)
Chaos! Comics

1	2.15	6.50	15.00
1A-Gold	6.25	19.00	50.00
2-4	1.65	4.20	10.00

EVIL ERNIE: REVENGE
Oct, 1994 - No.4, Feb, 1995 ($2.95, limited series)
Chaos! Comics

1: 1-Glow-in-the-dark-c; Lady Death app. 1-3-flip book w. Kilzone Preview (series of 3)	1.70	5.00	12.00
1-Commemorative-(4000 print run)			35.00
2-4	1.00	2.00	5.00
Trade paperback (10/95, $12.95)			13.00

EVIL ERNIE: STRAIGHT TO HELL
Oct, 1995 - No. 5, May, 1996 ($2.95, limited series)
Chaos! Comics

1-5: 1-fold-out-c		1.20	3.00
3-Chastity Chase Cover-(4000 print run)			17.00
Special Edition (10,000)	3.75	11.25	30.00

EVIL ERNIE VS. THE SUPER HEROES
Aug, 1995 ($2.95, one-shot)
Chaos! Comics

1-Lady Death poster		1.20	3.00
1-Foil-c variant (limited to 10,000)	3.75	11.25	30.00
1-Limited Edition (1000)			25.00

EWOKS (TV) (See Star Comics Magazine)
June, 1985 - No. 15?, Sept, 1987 (75¢/$1.00 #14 on) (Star Wars)
Marvel Comics (Star Comics)

1-15 (From Star Wars): 10-Williamson-a		.80	2.00

EXCALIBUR (Also see Marvel Comics Presents #31)
Apr, 1988; Oct, 1988 - Present ($1.50/$1.75)
Marvel Comics

Special Edition nn (The Sword is Drawn)(4/88, $3.25)-1st Excalibur comic	1.30	3.25	8.00
Special Edition nn (2nd print, 10/88, $3.50)		1.40	3.50
Special Edition nn (3rd print, 12/89, 4.50)		1.80	4.50
...The Sword is Drawn (Apr, 1992, $4.95)	1.00	2.00	5.00
1($1.50, 10/88)-X-Men spin-off; Nightcrawler, Shadowcat(Kitty Pryde), Capt. Britain, Phoenix & Meggan begin	1.20	3.00	7.00
2		1.40	3.50
3,4		1.00	2.50
5-10		.90	2.25
11-15: 10,11-Rogers/Austin-a		.80	2.00
16-23: 19-Austin-i. 21-Intro Crusader X. 22-Iron Man x-over			1.50
24-40,42-49,51-70,72-74,76: 32-($1.50). 24-John Byrne app. in story; $1.75-c begins. 26-Ron Lim-c/a. 27-B. Smith-a(p). 37-Dr. Doom & Iron Man app.			

Excalibur #102 © MEG

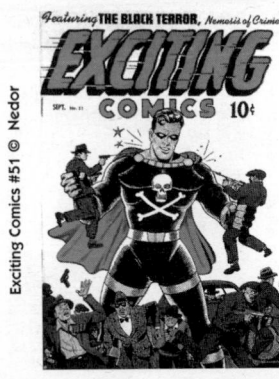
Exciting Comics #51 © Nedor

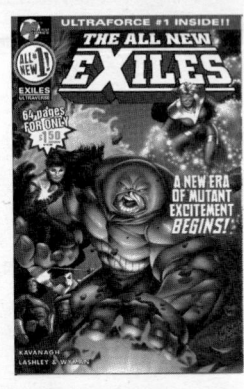
Exiles V2#1 © Malibu

49-Neal Adams c-swipe. 52,57-X-Men (Cyclops, Wolverine) app. 53-Spider-
Man-c/story. 58-X-Men (Wolverine, Gambit, Cyclops, etc.)-c/story.

61-Phoenix returns. 68-Starjammers-c/story			1.50
41-X-Men (Wolverine) app.; Cable cameo		.70	2.00
50-($2.75, 56 pgs.)-New logo		1.10	2.75
71-($3.95, 52 pgs.)-Hologram on-c; 30th anniversary			
	1.00	2.00	5.00
75-($3.50, 52 pgs.)-Holo-grafx foil-c	1.00	2.00	5.00
75-($2.25, 52 pgs.)-Regular edition		.90	2.25

77-81,83-86: 77-Begin $1.95-c; bound-in trading card sheet. 83-86-Deluxe
edition. 86-1st app. Pete Wisdom

		.80	2.00
82-($2.50)-Newsstand edition		1.00	2.50
82-($3.50)-Enhanced edition	1.00	2.00	5.00
	.80	2.00	
83-86-($1.50)-Standard edition			1.50

87-89,91-99,101-115: 87-Return from Age of Apocalypse. 92-Colossus-c/app.
94-Days of Future Tense 95-X-Man-c/app. 96-Sebastian Shaw & the Hellfire
Club app. 99-Onslaught app. 101-Onslaught tie-in. 102-w/card insert.

103-Last Warren Ellis scripts; Belasco app.		.80	2.00
90-($2.95)-double-sized		1.20	3.00
100-($2.95)-Onslaught tie-in; wraparound-c		1.40	3.50
Annual 1 (1993, $2.95)-1st app. Khaos		1.20	3.00
Annual 2 (1994, $2.95, 68 pgs.)-X-Men & Psylocke app.	1.20	3.00	
...Air Apparent nn (12/91, $4.95)-Simonson-c		1.60	4.00
...Mojo Mayhem nn (12/89, $4.50)-Art Adams/Austin-c/a	1.60	4.00	
...: The Possession nn (7/91, $2.95, 52 pgs.)		1.00	2.50
...: XX Crossing (7/92, 5/92-inside, $2.50)-vs. The X-Men	.80	2.00	

EXCITING COMICS
Apr, 1940 - No. 69, Sept, 1949
Nedor/Better Publications/Standard Comics

1-Origin & 1st app. The Mask, Jim Hatfield, Sgt. Bill King, Dan Williams begin; early Robot-c (see Smash #1)	266.00	800.00	2400.00
2-The Sphinx begins; The Masked Rider app.; Son of the Gods begins, ends #8	125.00	375.00	1000.00
3-Robot-c	87.00	262.00	700.00
4,5	58.00	174.00	465.00
6-Robot-c	71.00	215.00	575.00
7,8	45.00	136.00	365.00
9-Origin/1st app. of The Black Terror & sidekick Tim, begin series (5/41) (Black Terror c-9-52,54,55)	600.00	1800.00	6000.00
10-2nd app. Black Terror	212.00	637.00	1700.00
11	106.00	318.00	850.00
12,13	71.00	215.00	575.00
14-Last Sphinx, Dan Williams	47.00	141.00	375.00
15-The Liberator begins (origin)	50.00	150.00	400.00
16-20: 20-The Mask ends	40.00	120.00	300.00
21,23-27	38.00	114.00	265.00
22-Origin The Eaglet; The American Eagle begins	43.00	128.00	340.00
28-30: 28-Schomburg-c begin. 28-Crime Crusader begins, ends #58	44.00	132.00	350.00
31-38: 35-Liberator ends, not in 31-33	40.00	120.00	300.00
39-Origin Kara, Jungle Princess	47.00	141.00	375.00
40-50: 42-The Scarab begins. 45-Schomburg Robot-c. 49-Last Kara, Jungle Princess. 50-Last American Eagle	44.00	132.00	350.00
51-Miss Masque begins (1st app.)	48.00	146.00	390.00
52-54: Miss Masque ends. 53-Miss Masque-c	40.00	120.00	320.00
55-58: 55-Judy of the Jungle begins, ends #69; 1 pg. Ingels-a; Judy of the Jungle c-56-66. 56-58: All airbrush-c	44.00	132.00	350.00
59-Frazetta art in Caniff style; signed Frank Frazeta (one t), 9 pgs.			
	44.00	132.00	350.00
60-66: 60-Rick Howard, the Mystery Rider begins. 66-Robinson/Meskin-a	40.00	120.00	300.00
67-69-All western covers	16.00	47.00	110.00

NOTE: *Schomburg (Xela)* c-28-68; airbrush c-57-66. Black Terror by *R. Moreira*-#65. *Roussos*

a-62. Bondage-c 9, 12, 13, 20, 23, 25, 30, 59.

EXCITING ROMANCES
1949 (nd); No. 2, Spring, 1950 - No. 5, 10/50; No. 6 (1951, nd); No. 7, 9/51 -
No. 14, 1/53
Fawcett Publications

1(1949)	11.00	33.00	75.00
2,4,5-(1950)	6.70	20.00	40.00
3-Wood-a	11.50	34.00	80.00
6-14	5.00	15.00	30.00

NOTE: *Powell* a-8-10. *Marcus Swayze* a-5, 6, 9. Photo c-1-7, 10-12.

EXCITING ROMANCE STORIES (See Fox Giants)

EXCITING WAR (Korean War)
No. 5, Sept, 1952 - No. 8, May, 1953; No. 9, Nov, 1953
Standard Comics (Better Publ.)

5	6.70	20.00	40.00
6,7,9	4.00	11.00	22.00
8-Toth-a	6.70	20.00	40.00

EXILES (Also see Break-Thru)
Aug, 1993 - No. 4, Nov, 1993 ($1.95)
Malibu Comics (Ultraverse)

1,2,4: 1,2-Bagged copies of each exist. 2-Gustovich-c. 4-Team dies; story cont'd in Break-Thru #1		.80	2.00
3-($2.50, 40 pgs.)-Rune flip-c/story by B. Smith (3 pgs.)	1.00	2.50	
1-Holographic-c edition	2.85	8.50	20.00

EXILES (All New, The) (2nd Series) (Also see Black September)
Sept, 1995 - V2#11, Aug, 1996 ($1.50)
Malibu Comics (Ultraverse)

Infinity (9/95, $1.50)-Intro new team including Marvel's Juggernaut & Reaper.			1.50
Infinity (2000 signed)	1.65	4.20	10.00

V2#1-11: 1-(10/95, 64 pgs.)-Reprint of Ultraforce V2#1 follows lead story.
2-1st app. Hellblade. 5-Juggernaut returns to the Marvel Universe. 8-Intro

Maxis. 11-Vs. Maxis; Ripfire app.; cont'd in Ultraforce #12			1.50
V2#1 (2000 signed)	1.65	4.20	10.00

EX-MUTANTS
Nov, 1992 - No. 18, Apr, 1994 ($1.95/$2.25/$2.50)
Malibu Comics

1-10		.80	2.00
11-14 ($2.25): 11-Polybagged w/Skycap		.90	2.25
15-18 ($2.50)		1.00	2.50

EXORCISTS (See The Crusaders)

EXOSQUAD (TV)
No. 0, Jan, 1994 ($1.25)
Topps Comics

0-($1.00, 20 pgs.)-1st app.; Staton-a(p); wraparound-c			1.00

EXOTIC ROMANCES (Formerly True War Romances)
No. 22, Oct, 1955 - No. 31, Nov, 1956
Quality Comics Group (Comic Magazines)

22	7.50	22.50	45.00
23-26,29	4.00	12.00	24.00
27,31-Baker-c/a	8.35	25.00	50.00
28,30-Baker-a	7.50	22.50	45.00

EXPLOITS OF DANIEL BOONE
Nov, 1955 - No. 6, Oct, 1956
Quality Comics Group

1-All have Cuidera-c(i)	23.00	69.00	160.00
2	14.00	43.00	100.00
3-6	11.50	34.00	80.00

FA

EXPLOITS OF DICK TRACY (See Dick Tracy)

EXPLORER JOE
Winter, 1951 - No. 2, Oct-Nov, 1952
Ziff-Davis Comic Group (Approved Comics)

1-2: Saunders painted covers; 2-Krigstein-a	10.00	30.00	70.00

EXPLORERS OF THE UNKNOWN (See Archie Giant Series #587, 599)
June, 1990 - No. 6, Apr, 1991 ($1.00)
Archie Comics

1-6: Featuring Archie and the gang			1.00

EXPOSED (...True Crime Cases; ...Cases in the Crusade Against Crime #5-9)
Mar-Apr, 1948 - No. 9, July-Aug, 1949
D. S. Publishing Co.

1	17.00	51.00	120.00
2-Giggling killer story with excessive blood; two injury-to-eye panels; electrocution panel	19.00	58.00	135.00
3,8,9	9.15	27.00	55.00
4-Orlando-a	10.00	30.00	60.00
5-Breeze Lawson, Sky Sheriff by E. Good	10.00	30.00	60.00
6-Ingels-a; used in **SOTI**, illo. "How to prepare an alibi"			
	32.00	96.00	225.00
7-Illo. in **SOTI**, "Diagram for housebreakers;" used by N.Y. Legis. Committee	32.00	96.00	225.00

EXTRA!
Mar-Apr, 1955 - No. 5, Nov-Dec, 1955
E. C. Comics

1-Not code approved	16.00	47.00	110.00
2-5	11.00	33.00	75.00

NOTE: *Craig, Crandall, Severin art in all.*

EXTRA COMICS
1948 (25¢, 3 comics in one)
Magazine Enterprises

1-Giant; consisting of rebound ME comics. Two versions known; (1)-Funnyman by Siegel & Shuster, Space Ace, Undercover Girl, Red Fox by L.B. Cole, Trail Colt & (2)-All Funnyman	45.00	136.00	365.00

EXTREME
Aug, 1993 (Giveaway)
Image Comics (Extreme Studios)

0	1.00	2.00	5.00

EXTREME JUSTICE
Jan, 1995 - No. 18, July, 1996 ($1.50/$1.75)
DC Comics

1-5			1.50
6-18: 6-Begin $1.75-c	.70		1.75

EXTREME SACRIFICE
Jan, 1995 ($2.50, limited series)
Image Comics (Extreme Studios)

Prelude (#1)-Liefeld wraparound-c; polybagged w/ trading card			
		1.00	2.50
Epilogue (#2)-Liefeld wraparound-c; polybagged w/trading card			
		1.00	2.50
Trade paperback (6/95, $16.95)-Platt-a			17.00

EXTREME SUPER CHRISTMAS SPECIAL
Dec, 1994 ($2.95, one-shot)
Image Comics (Extreme Studios)

1		1.20	3.00

EXTREMIST, THE
Sept, 1993 - No. 4, Dec, 1993 ($1.95, limited series)
DC Comics (Vertigo)

1-4-Peter Milligan scripts; McKeever-c/a		1.00	2.50
1-Platinum Edition	1.65	4.20	10.00

EYE OF THE STORM
Dec, 1994 - No. 7, June, 1995? ($2.95)
Rival Productions

1-7: Computer generated comic		1.20	3.00

FACE
Jan, 1995 ($4.95, one-shot)
DC Comics (Vertigo)

1	1.00	2.00	5.00

FACE, THE (Tony Trent, the Face No. 3 on) (See Big Shot Comics)
1941 - No. 2, 1941?
Columbia Comics Group

1-The Face; Mart Bailey-c	68.00	206.00	550.00
2-Bailey-c	41.00	124.00	330.00

FACTOR X
Mar, 1995 - No. 4, July, 1995 ($1.95, limited series)
Marvel Comics

1-Age of Apocalypse		1.20	3.00
2-4		.80	2.00

FACULTY FUNNIES
June, 1989 - No. 5, May, 1990 (75¢/95¢ #2 on)
Archie Comics

1-5: 1,2-The Awesome Four app.			1.00

FAFHRD AND THE GREY MOUSER (Also see Sword of Sorcery & Wonder Woman #202)
Oct, 1990 - No. 4, 1991 ($4.50, 52 pgs., squarebound)
Marvel Comics

1-4: Mignola/Williamson-a; Chaykin scripts		1.80	4.50

FAIRY TALE PARADE (See Famous Fairy Tales)
June-July, 1942 - No. 121, Oct, 1946 (Most all by Walt Kelly)
Dell Publishing Co.

1-Kelly-a begins	130.00	390.00	1300.00
2(8-9/42)	55.00	165.00	550.00
3-5 (10-11/42 - 2-4/43)	38.00	114.00	380.00
6-9 (5-7/43 - 11-1/43-44)	29.00	87.00	290.00
Four Color 50('44),69('45), 87('45)	25.00	75.00	250.00
Four Color 104,114('46)-Last Kelly issue	19.00	57.00	190.00
Four Color 121('46)-Not by Kelly	11.00	33.00	110.00

NOTE: *#1-9, 4-Color #50, 69 have **Kelly** c/a; 4-Color #87, 104, 114-**Kelly** art only. #9 has a redrawn version of The Reluctant Dragon. This series contains all the classic fairy tales from Jack In The Beanstalk to Cinderella.*

FAIRY TALES
No. 10, Apr-May, 1951 - No. 11, June-July, 1951
Ziff-Davis Publ. Co. (Approved Comics)

10,11-Painted-c	14.00	43.00	100.00

FAITHFUL
Nov, 1949 - No. 2, Feb, 1950 (52 pgs.)
Marvel Comics/Lovers' Magazine

1,2-Photo-c	7.50	22.50	45.00

FALCON (See Marvel Premiere #49)(Also see Avengers #181 & Captain America #117 & 133)
Nov, 1983 - No. 4, Feb, 1984 (Mini-series)
Marvel Comics Group

1-4: 1-Paul Smith-c/a(p). 2-Paul Smith-c			1.00

FALLEN ANGEL ON THE WORLD OF MAGIC: THE GATHERING
May, 1996 ($5.95, one-shot)
Acclaim (Armada)

Falling In Love #1 © DC

Family Man #1 © DC

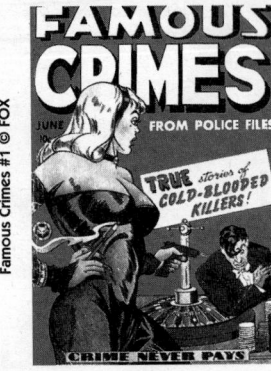

Famous Crimes #1 © FOX

	GD25	FN65	NM94

1-Nancy Collins story.			6.00

FALLEN ANGELS
April, 1987 - No. 8, Nov, 1987 (Limited series)
Marvel Comics Group

1		.80	2.00
2-8			1.40

FALLING IN LOVE
Sept-Oct, 1955 - No. 143, Oct-Nov, 1973
Arleigh Publ. Co./National Periodical Publications

1	36.00	107.00	250.00
2	17.00	51.00	120.00
3-10	10.00	30.00	70.00
11-20	8.35	25.00	50.00
21-40	5.85	17.50	35.00
41-47: 47-Last 10¢ issue?	4.25	13.00	26.00
48-100,108: 108-Wood-a (4 pgs., 7/69)	2.00	6.00	14.00
101-107,109-143	1.30	3.25	8.00
NOTE: *Colan* c/a-75, 81. 52 pgs.-#125-133.			

FALL OF THE HOUSE OF USHER, THE (See A Corben Special & Spirit section
8/22/48)

FALL OF THE ROMAN EMPIRE (See Movie Comics)

FAMILY AFFAIR (TV)
Feb, 1970 - No. 4, Oct, 1970 (25¢)
Gold Key

1-With pull-out poster; photo-c	3.80	11.40	38.00
1-With poster missing	1.60	4.80	16.00
2-4: 3,4-Photo-c	2.00	6.00	20.00

FAMILY FUNNIES
No. 9, Aug-Sept, 1946
Parents' Magazine Institute

9	4.00	11.00	22.00

FAMILY FUNNIES (Tiny Tot Funnies No. 9)
Sept, 1950 - No. 8, Apr, 1951
Harvey Publications

1-Mandrake (has over 30 King Feature strips)	6.35	19.00	38.00
2-Flash Gordon, 1 pg.	4.25	13.00	26.00
3-8: 4,5,7-Flash Gordon, 1 pg.	4.00	12.00	24.00
1(Black & white)	2.40	6.00	12.00

FAMILY MAN
1995 - No. 3, 1995 ($4.95, B&W, digest-size, limited series)
DC Comics (Paradox Press)

1-3	1.00	2.00	5.00

FAMOUS AUTHORS ILLUSTRATED (See Stories by...)

FAMOUS COMICS (Also see Favorite Comics)
No date; Mid 1930's (24 pgs., paper-c)
Zain-Eppy/United Features Syndicate

nn-Reprinted from 1933 & 1934 newspaper strips in color; Joe Palooka, Hairbreadth Harry, Napoleon, The Nebbs, etc. (Many different versions known)	40.00	120.00	310.00

FAMOUS COMICS
1934 (100 pgs., daily newspaper-r)
(3-1/2x8-1/2"; paper cover) (came in a box)
King Features Syndicate (Whitman Publ. Co.)

684(#1)-Little Jimmy, Katzenjammer Kids, & Barney Google	33.00	99.00	230.00
684(#2)-Polly, Little Jimmy, Katzenjammer Kids	33.00	99.00	230.00
684(#3)-Little Annie Rooney, Polly and her Pals, Katzenjammer Kids	33.00	99.00	230.00
....Box price....	31.00	92.00	215.00

FAMOUS COMICS CARTOON BOOKS
1934 (8x7-1/4", 72 pgs., B&W hard-c, daily strip-r)
Whitman Publishing Co.

1200-The Captain & the Kids (1st app?); Dirks reprints credited to Bernard Dibble	27.00	81.00	190.00
1202-Captain Easy (1st app?) & Wash Tubbs by Roy Crane; 2 slightly different versions of cover exist	33.00	99.00	230.00
1203-Ella Cinders (1st app?)	26.00	79.00	185.00
1204-Freckles & His Friends (1st app?)	24.00	71.00	165.00
NOTE: Called *Famous Funnies Cartoon Books* inside.			

FAMOUS CRIMES
June, 1948 - No. 19, Sept, 1950; No. 20, Aug, 1951; No. 51, 52, 1953
Fox Features Syndicate/M.S. Dist. No. 51,52

1-Blue Beetle app. & crime story-r/Phantom Lady #16	40.00	120.00	300.00
2-Has woman dissolved in acid; lingerie-c/panels	31.00	94.00	220.00
3-Injury-to-eye story used in **SOTI**, pg. 112; has two electrocution stories	39.00	118.00	275.00
4-6	15.00	45.00	105.00
7- "Tarzan, the Wyoming Killer" used in **SOTI**, pg. 44; drug trial/ possession story	33.00	99.00	230.00
8-20: 17-Morisi-a	12.00	36.00	85.00
51(nd, 1953)	12.00	36.00	85.00
52	6.70	20.00	40.00

FAMOUS FAIRY TALES
1942; 1943 (32 pgs.); 1944 (16 pgs.) (Giveaway, soft-c)
K. K. Publ. Co.

1942-Kelly-a	40.00	120.00	300.00
1943-r-/Fairy Tale Parade No. 2,3; Kelly-a	32.00	96.00	225.00
1944-Kelly-a	29.00	86.00	200.00

FAMOUS FEATURE STORIES
1938 (7-1/2x11", 68 pgs.)
Dell Publishing Co.

1-Tarzan, Terry & the Pirates, King of the Royal Mtd., Buck Jones, Dick Tracy, Smilin' Jack, Dan Dunn, Don Winslow, G-Man, Tailspin Tommy, Mutt & Jeff, Little Orphan Annie reprints - all illustrated text	65.00	195.00	525.00

FAMOUS FIRST EDITION (See Limited Collectors' Edition)
($1.00, 10x13-1/2", 72 pgs.) (No.6-8, 68 pgs.)
1974 - No. 8, Aug-Sept, 1975; C-61, 1979
National Periodical Publications/DC Comics

C-26-Action Comics #1; gold ink outer-c	1.20	4.00	12.00
C-28-Detective #27; silver ink outer-c	3.50	11.00	35.00
C-28-Hardbound edition	6.80	20.00	68.00
C-30-Sensation #1(1974); bronze ink outer-c	1.20	4.00	12.00
F-4-Whiz Comics #2(#1)(10-11/74)-Cover not identical to original (dropped "Gangway for Captain Marvel" from cover); gold ink on outer-c	1.20	4.00	12.00
F-5-Batman #1(F-6 inside); silver ink on outer-c	2.50	7.50	25.00
V2#F-6-Wonder Woman #1	1.20	4.00	12.00
F-7-All-Star Comics #3	1.20	4.00	12.00
F-8-Flash Comics #1(8-9/75)	1.20	4.00	12.00
V8#C-61-Superman #1(1979, $2.00)	1.20	4.00	12.00
Hardbound editions (w/dust jackets $5.00 extra) (Lyle Stuart, Inc.)			
C-26,C-30,F-4,F-6 known	2.00	6.00	17.00

Warning: The above books are almost **exact** reprints of the originals that they represent except for the Giant-Size format. None of the originals are Giant-Size. The first five issues and C-61 were printed with two covers. Reprint information can be found on the outside cover, but not the inside cover which was reprinted exactly like the original (inside and out).

FAMOUS FUNNIES
1933 - No. 218, July, 1955
Eastern Color

	GD25	FN65	VF82	NM94
A Carnival of Comics (probably the second comic book), 36 pgs., no date given, n				

Famous Funnies #4 © EAS

Famous Funnies #211 © EAS

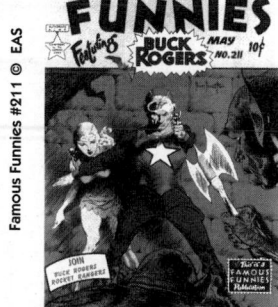

Famous Funnies #216 © EAS

GD25 FN65 NM94

publisher, no number; contains strip reprints of The Bungle Family, Dixie Dugan, Hairbreadth Harry, Joe Palooka, Keeping Up With the Jones, Mutt & Jeff, Reg'lar Fellers, S'Matter Pop, Strange As It Seems, and others. This book was sold by M. C. Gaines to Wheatena, Milk-O-Malt, John Wanamaker, Kinney Shoe Stores, & others to be given away as premiums and radio giveaways (1933).　750.00　2250.00　4875.00　7500.00

(Estimated up to 50 total copies exist, 2 in NM/Mint)

Series 1-(Very rare)(nd-early 1934)(68 pgs.) No publisher given (Eastern Color PrintingCo.); sold in chain stores for 10c. 35,000 print run. Contains Sunday strip reprints of Mutt & Jeff, Reg'lar Fellers, Nipper, Hairbreadth Harry, Strange As It Seems, Joe Palooka, Dixie Dugan, The Nebbs, Keeping Up With the Jones, and others. Inside front and back covers and pages 1-16 of Famous Funnies Series 1, #s 49-64 reprinted from **Famous Funnies, A Carnival of Comics**, and most of pages 17-48 reprinted from **Funnies on Parade**. This was the first comic book sold.
3000.00　9000.00　15,000.00　21,000.00

GD25 FN65 VF82

(Estimated up to 12 copies exist, 1 in NM/Mint)

No. 1 (Rare)(7/34-on stands 5/34) - Eastern Color Printing Co. First monthly newsstand comic book. Contains Sunday strip reprints of Toonerville Folks, Mutt & Jeff, Hairbreadth Harry, S'Matter Pop, Nipper, Dixie Dugan, Connie, Ben Webster, Tailspin Tommy, The Nebbs, Joe Palooka, & others.　2415.00　7250.00　10,865.00　14,500.00

(Estimated up to 30 total copies exist, 3 in NM/Mint)

GD25 FN65 NM94

2 (Rare, 9/34)　450.00　1350.00　2700.00
3-Buck Rogers Sunday strip-r by Rick Yager begins, ends at #218; not in #191-208; 1st comic book app. of Buck Rogers; the number of the 1st strip reprinted is pg. 190, Series No. 1　583.00　1750.00　3500.00
4　183.00　550.00　1100.00
5-1st Christmas-c on a newsstand comic　150.00　450.00　900.00
6-10　108.00　324.00　650.00

GD25 FN65 NM94

11,12,18-Four pgs. of Buck Rogers in each issue; completes stories in Buck Rogers #1 which lacks these pages. 18-Two pgs. of Buck Rogers reprinted in Daisy Comics #1　95.00　287.00　575.00
13-17,19,20: 14-has two Buck Rogers panels missing. 17-2nd Christmas-c on a newsstand comic (12/35)　73.00　219.00　440.00
21,23-30: 27-(10/36)-War on Crime begins (4 pgs.); 1st true crime in comics (reprints); part photo-c. 29-X-Mas-c (12/36)　52.00　157.00　315.00
22-Four pgs. of Buck Rogers needed to complete stories in Buck Rogers #1　56.00　170.00　340.00
31,33,34,36,37,39,40: 33-Careers of Baby Face Nelson & John Dillinger traced　40.00　120.00　240.00
32-(3/37) 1st app. the Phantom Magician (costume hero) in Advs. of Patsy　43.00　130.00　260.00
35-Two pgs. Buck Rogers omitted in Buck Rogers #2　43.00　130.00　260.00
38-Full color portrait of Buck Rogers　39.00　117.00　235.00
41-60: 41,53-X-Mas-cs. 55-Last bottom panel, pg. 4 in Buck Rogers redrawn in Buck Rogers #3-c　28.00　84.00　170.00
61,63,64,66,67,69,70　17.00　51.00　120.00
62,65,68-Two pgs. Kirby-a "Lightnin' & the Lone Rider". 65-X-Mas-c　20.00　60.00　140.00
71,73,77-80: 77-X-Mas-cs. 80-(3/41)-Buck Rogers story continues from Buck Rogers #5　13.50　41.00　95.00
72-Speed Spaulding begins by Marvin Bradley (artist), ends by #88. This series was written by Edmund Balmer & Philip Wylie (later appeared as film & book "When Worlds Collide")　14.00　43.00　100.00
74-76-Two pgs. Kirby-a in all　13.50　41.00　95.00
81-Origin & 1st app. Invisible Scarlet O'Neil (4/41); strip begins #82, ends #167; 1st non-funny-c (Scarlet O'Neil)　10.00　30.00　70.00
82-Buck Rogers-c　13.50　41.00　95.00
83-87,90: 86-Connie vs. Monsters on the Moon-c (sci/fi). 87 has last Buck Rogers full page-r. 90-Bondage-c　10.00　30.00　70.00
88-Buck Rogers in "Moon's End" by Calkins, 2 pgs.(not reprints). Beginning with #88, all Buck Rogers pgs. have rearranged panels　11.00　33.00　75.00
89-Origin & 1st app. Fearless Flint, the Flint Man　11.00　33.00　75.00
91-93,95,96,98-99,101,103-110: 105-Series 2 begins (Strip Page #1)　10.00　30.00　65.00
94-Buck Rogers in "Solar Holocaust" by Calkins, 3 pgs.(not reprints)

GD25 FN65 NM94

　　10.00　30.00　65.00
97-War Bond promotion, Buck Rogers by Calkins, 2 pgs.(not reprints)
　　10.00　30.00　65.00
100　10.00　30.00　65.00
102-Chief Wahoo vs. Hitler, Tojo & Mussolini-c (1/43)13.00　39.00　90.00
111-130: 115-X-Mas-c　7.50　22.50　45.00
131-150: 137-Strip page No. 110 omitted　5.35　16.00　32.00
151-162,164-168　4.70　14.00　28.00
163-St. Valentine's Day-c　5.85　17.50　35.00
169,170-Two text illos. by Williamson, his 1st comic book work　10.00　30.00　60.00
171-180: 171-Strip pgs. 227,229,230, Series 2 omitted. 172-Strip Pg. 232 omitted　4.35　13.00　26.00
181-190: 181-Buck Rogers ends with start of strip pg. 302, Series 2. 190-Oaky Doaks-c/story　4.35　13.00　26.00
191-197,199,201,203,206-208: No Buck Rogers. 191-Barney Carr, Space detective begins, ends #192.　4.00　12.00　24.00
198,202,205-One pg. Frazetta ads; no B. Rogers　4.35　13.00　26.00
200-Frazetta 1 pg. ad　4.35　13.00　26.00
204-Used in POP, pg. 79,99; war-c begin, end #208　4.70　14.00　28.00
209-Buck Rogers begins (12/53) with strip pg. 480, Series 2; Frazetta-c　65.00　195.00　525.00
210-216: Frazetta-c. 211-Buck Rogers ads by Anderson begins, ends #217. #215-Contains B. Rogers strip pg. 515-518, series 2 followed by pgs. 179-181, Series 3　65.00　195.00　525.00
217,218-B. Rogers ends with pg. 199, Series 3. 218-Wee Three-c/story　4.35　13.00　26.00

NOTE: **Rick Yager** did the Buck Rogers Sunday strips reprinted in Famous Funnies. The Sundays were formerly done by Russ Keaton and Lt. Dick Calkins did the dailies, but would sometimes assist Yager on a panel or two from time to time. Strip No. 169 is Yager's first full Buck Rogers page. Yager did the strip until 1958 when **Murphy Anderson** took over. **Tuska** art from 4/26/59 - 1965. Virtually every panel was rewritten for Famous Funnies. Not identical to the original Sunday page. The Buck Rogers reprints run continuously through Famous Funnies issue No. 190 (Strip No. 302) with no break in story line. The story line has no continuity after No. 190. The Buck Rogers newspaper strips came out in four series: Series 1, 3/30/30 - 9/21/41 (No. 1 - 600); Series 2, 9/28/41 -10/21/51 (No. 1 -525)(Strip No. 110-1/2 (1/2 pg.) published in only a few newspapers); Series 3, 10/28/51 -2/9/58 (No. 100-428)(No No.1-99); Series 4, 2/16/58 - 6/13/65 (No numbers, dates only). **Everett** c-85, 86. **Moulton** a-100. Chief Wahoo c-93, 97, 102, 116, 136, 139, 151. Dickie Dare c-83, 88. Fearless Flint c-89. Invisible Scarlet O'Neil c-81, 87, 95, 121(part), 132. Scorchy Smith c-84, 90.

FAMOUS FUNNIES
1964
Super Comics
Super Reprint Nos. 15-18:17-r/Double Trouble #1. 18-Space Comics #?
　　1.65　4.20　10.00

FAMOUS GANG BOOK OF COMICS (Becomes Donald & Mickey Merry Christmas 1943 on)
Dec, 1942 (Christmas giveaway, 32 pgs., paper-c)
Firestone Tire & Rubber Co.
nn-(Rare)-Porky Pig, Bugs Bunny, Mary Jane & Sniffles, Elmer Fudd; r/Looney Tunes　60.00　180.00　600.00

FAMOUS GANGSTERS (Crime on the Waterfront No. 4)
Apr, 1951 - No. 3, Feb, 1952
Avon Periodicals/Realistic No. 3
1-Capone, Dillinger; c-/Avon paperback #329　30.00　90.00　210.00
2-Dillinger Machine Gun Killer; Wood-c/a (1 pg.); r/Saint #7 & retitled "Mike Strong"　30.00　90.00　210.00
3-Lucky Luciano & Murder, Inc; c-/Avon paperback #66　30.00　90.00　210.00

FAMOUS INDIAN TRIBES
July-Sept, 1962; No. 2, July, 1972
Dell Publishing Co.
12-264-209(#1) (The Sioux)　1.00　3.00　10.00
2(7/72)-Reprints above　.80　2.00

Fantastic Comics #5 © FOX

Fantastic Force #7 © MEG

Fantastic Four #7 © MEG

	GD25	FN65	NM94

FAMOUS STARS
Nov-Dec, 1950 - No. 6, Spring, 1952 (All have photo-c)
Ziff-Davis Publ. Co.

1-Shelley Winters, Susan Peters, Ava Gardner, Shirley Temple;Jimmy			
Stewart & Shelley Winters photo-c; Whitney-a 26.00 77.00			180.00
2-Betty Hutton, Bing Crosby, Colleen Townsend, Gloria Swanson; Betty			
Hutton photo-c; Everett-a(2) 18.00 54.00			125.00
3-Farley Granger, Judy Garland's ordeal, Alan Ladd; Farley Granger &			
Judy Garland photo-c; Whitney-a 17.00 49.00			115.00
4-Al Jolson, Bob Mitchum, Ella Raines, Richard Conte, Vic Damone; Bob			
Mitchum photo-c; Crandall-a, 6pgs. 15.00 45.00			105.00
5-Liz Taylor, Betty Grable, Esther Williams, George Brent, Mario Lanza; Liz			
Taylor photo-c; Krigstein-a 20.00 60.00			140.00
6-Gene Kelly, Hedy Lamarr, June Allyson, William Boyd, Janet Leigh, Gary			
Cooper; Gene Kelly photo-c 13.50 41.00			95.00

FAMOUS STORIES (...Book No. 2)
1942 - No. 2, 1942
Dell Publishing Co.

1,2: 1-Treasure Island. 2-Tom Sawyer 28.00 84.00			195.00

FAMOUS TV FUNDAY FUNNIES
Sept, 1961
Harvey Publications

1-Casper the Ghost 3.00 9.00			30.00

FAMOUS WESTERN BADMEN (Formerly Redskin)
No. 13, Dec, 1952 - No. 15, Apr, 1953
Youthful Magazines

13-Redskin story 10.00 30.00			70.00
14,15: 15-The Dalton Boys story 7.50 22.50			45.00

FANGS OF THE WIDOW
Sept, 1995 - Present ($3.00, B&W)
London Night Studios/Ground Zero #5 on

1-9: 5-1st Ground Zero issue		1.20	3.00
1-Platinum 1.00 2.00			5.00

FANTASTIC (Formerly Captain Science; Beware No. 10 on)
No. 8, Feb, 1952 - No. 9, Apr, 1952
Youthful Magazines

8-Capt. Science by Harrison; decapitation, shrunken head panels			
	30.00	90.00	210.00
9-Harrison-a	21.00	64.00	150.00

FANTASTIC ADVENTURES
1963 - 1964 (Reprints)
Super Comics

9,10,12,15,16,18: 9-r/ 10-r/He-Man #2(Toby). 11-Disbrow-a. 12-Unpublished			
Chesler material? 15-r/Spook #23. 16-r/Dark Shadows #2(Steinway); Briefer-			
a.18-r/Superior Stories #1 2.00 6.00			14.00
11-Wood-a; r/Blue Bolt #118 3.75 11.25			28.00
17-Baker-a(2) r/Seven Seas #6 3.75 11.25			28.00

FANTASTIC COMICS
Dec, 1939 - No. 23, Nov, 1941
Fox Features Syndicate

1-Intro/origin Samson; Stardust, The Super Wizard, Sub Saunders (by			
Kiefer), Space Smith, Capt. Kidd begin 366.00 1100.00			3300.00
2-Powell text illos 175.00 525.00			1400.00
3-Classic Lou Fine Robot-c; Powell text illos 642.00 1928.00			4500.00
4,5: Last Lou Fine-c 150.00 450.00			1200.00
6,7-Simon-a 112.00 338.00			900.00
8-10: 10-Intro/origin David, Samson's aide 81.00 243.00			650.00
11-17,19,20,22: 16-Stardust ends 68.00 206.00			550.00
18-1st work Black Fury & sidekick Chuck; ends #23			

	GD25	FN65	NM94

	70.00	210.00	565.00
21,23: 21-The Banshee begins(origin); ends #23; Hitler-c. 22-Likeness of Hitler			
as furnace on cover. 23-Origin The Gladiator 70.00 210.00			565.00

NOTE: *Lou Fine* c-1-5. **Tuska** a-3-5, 8. Bondage c-6, 8, 9. Issue #11 has indicia to Mystery Men Comics #15. All issues feature Samson covers.

FANTASTIC COMICS (Fantastic Fears #1-9; Becomes Samson #12)
No. 10, Nov-Dec, 1954 - No. 11, Jan-Feb, 1955
Ajax/Farrell Publ.

10 (#1)	13.00	39.00	90.00
11-Robot-c	16.00	47.00	110.00

FANTASTIC FABLES
Feb, 1987 ($1.50, 28 pgs., B&W)
Silverwolf Comics

1-Tim Vigil-a (6 pgs.)		.80	2.00

FANTASTIC FEARS (Formerly Captain Jet) (Fantastic Comics #10 on)
No. 7, May, 1953 - No. 9, Sept-Oct, 1954
Ajax/Farrell Publ.

7(#1, 5/53)-Tales of Stalking Terror	32.00	96.00	225.00
8(#2, 7/53)	20.00	60.00	140.00
3,4	14.00	43.00	100.00
5-(1-2/54)-Ditko story (1st drawn) is written by Bruce Hamilton; r-in Weird			
V2#8 (1st pro work for Ditko but Daring Love #1 was published 1st)			
	62.00	188.00	500.00
6-Decapitation of girl's head w/paper cutter (classic)38.00 114.00			265.00
7(5-6/54), 9(9-10/54)	14.00	43.00	100.00
8(7-8/54)-Contains story intended for Jo-Jo; name changed to Kaza;			
decapitation story 17.00 49.00			115.00

FANTASTIC FORCE
Nov, 1994 - No. 18, Apr, 1996 ($1.75)
Marvel Comics

1-($2.50)-Foil wraparound-c; intro Fantastic Force w/Huntara, Delvor,			
Psi-Lord & Vibraxas 1.00			2.50
2-18: 13-She-Hulk app.		.70	1.75

FANTASTIC FOUR (See America's Best TV..., Giant- Size..., Giant Size Super- Stars, Marvel Collectors Item Classics, Marvel Milestone Edition, Marvel's Greatest,Marvel Treasury Edition, Marvel Triple Action, Official Marvel Index to... & Power Record Comics)

FANTASTIC FOUR (Created by Stan Lee & Jack Kirby)
Nov, 1961 - No. 416, Sept, 1996

Marvel Comics Group	GD25	FN65	VF82	NM94
1-Origin & 1st app. The Fantastic Four (Reed Richards: Mr. Fantastic, Johnny				
Storm: The Human Torch, Sue Storm: The Invisible Girl, & Ben Grimm: The				
Thing–Marvel's 1st super-hero group since the G.A.; 1st app. S.A. Human				
Torch); origin/1st app. The Mole Man.				
	950.00	2850.00	9500.00	18,000.00

		GD25	FN65	NM94
1-Golden Record Comic Set Reprint (1966)-cover not identical to original				
		26.00	77.00	180.00
with Golden Record		38.00	114.00	265.00
2-Vs. The Skrulls (last 10¢ issue)		300.00	900.00	3300.00
3-Fantastic Four don costumes & establish Headquarters; brief 1pg. origin;				
intro The Fantasti-Car; Human Torch drawn w/two left hands on-c				
		200.00	600.00	2200.00

	GD25	FN65	VF82	NM94
4-1st S. A. Sub-Mariner app. (5/62)				
	240.00	720.00	1560.00	2600.00
5-Origin & 1st app. Doctor Doom	260.00	780.00	1690.00	2800.00

	GD25	FN65	NM94
6-Sub-Mariner, Dr. Doom team up; 1st Marvel villain team-up (2nd S.A.			
Sub-Mariner app.)	135.00	405.00	1450.00
7-10: 7-1st app. Kurrgo. 8-1st app. Puppet-Master & Alicia Masters. 9-3rd			
Sub-Mariner app. 10-Stan Lee (1st app. in comics?) & Jack Kirby app. in			

Fantastic Four #12 © MEG

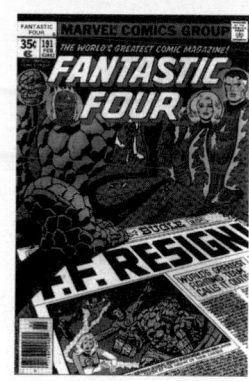

Fantastic Four #191 © MEG

Fantastic Four #239 © MEG

FA

	GD25	FN65	NM94
story	78.00	233.00	750.00
11-Origin/1st app. The Impossible Man (2/63)	67.00	200.00	585.00
12-Fantantic Four Vs. The Hulk (1st meeting); 1st Hulk x-over & ties w/Amazing Spider-Man #1 as 1st Marvel x-over; (3/63)	100.00	300.00	1000.00
13-Intro. The Watcher; 1st app. The Red Ghost	52.00	155.00	465.00
14-19: 14-Sub-Mariner x-over. 15-1st app. Mad Thinker. 16-1st Ant-Man x-over (7/63); Wasp cameo. 18-Origin/1st app. The Super Skrull. 19-Intro. Rama-Tut; Stan Lee & Jack Kirby cameo	38.00	114.00	280.00
20-Origin/1st app. The Molecule Man	40.00	120.00	300.00
21-Intro The Hate Monger; 1st Sgt. Fury x-over (12/63)	26.00	79.00	200.00
22-24: 22-Sue Storm gains more powers	17.00	51.00	135.00
25,26-The Hulk vs. The Thing (their 1st battle). 25-3rd Avengers x-over (1st time w/Capt. America)(cameo, 4/64); 2nd S.A. app. Cap (takes place between Avengers #4 & 5. 26-4th Avengers x-over	44.00	133.00	370.00
27-1st Doctor Strange x-over (6/64)	20.00	60.00	155.00
28-Early X-Men x-over (7/64); same date as X-Men #6	29.00	86.00	220.00
29,30: 30-Intro. Diablo	13.00	39.00	100.00
31-40: 31-Early Avengers x-over (10/64). 33-1st app. Attuma; part photo-c. 35-Intro/1st app. Dragon Man. 36-Intro/1st app. Madam Medusa & the Frightful Four (Sandman, Wizard, Paste Pot Pete). 39-Wood inks on Daredevil (early x-over)	11.50	34.00	90.00
41-47: 41-43-Frightful Four app. 44-Intro. Gorgon. 45-Intro/1st app. The Inhumans (c/story, 12/65); also see Incredible Hulk Special #1 & Thor #146, & 147. 46-1st Black Bolt-c (Kirby) & 1st full app.	8.00	23.50	60.00
48-Partial origin/1st app. The Silver Surfer & Galactus (3/66) by Lee & Kirby; Galactus cameo in last panel; 1st of 3 part story.	89.00	267.00	850.00
49-2nd app. Silver Surfer & Galactus	29.00	86.00	210.00
50-Silver Surfer battles Galactus	32.00	96.00	235.00
51,54- 54-Inhumans cameo	6.50	19.50	48.00
52-1st app. The Black Panther (7/66)	13.00	39.00	95.00
53-Origin & 2nd app. The Black Panther	11.50	34.00	85.00
55-Thing battles Silver Surfer; 4th app. Silver Surfer	10.00	30.00	75.00
56-60: Silver Surfer x-over. 59,60-Inhumans cameos	8.50	26.00	63.00
61-65,68-70: 61-Silver Surfer cameo; Sandman-c/s	5.70	17.00	42.00
66-Begin 2 part origin of Him (Warlock); does not app. (9/67)	13.00	39.00	95.00
67-Origin/1st app. Him (Warlock); 1 pg. cameo; see Thor #165,166 for 1st full app.	14.00	43.00	105.00
71,73-78,80: 73-Spider-Man, D.D., Thor x-over; cont'd from Daredevil #38	4.30	13.00	32.00
72-Silver Surfer-c/story (pre-dates Silver Surfer #1)	4.30	13.00	32.00
74-77: Silver Surfer app.(#77 is same date/S.S. #1)	4.30	13.00	33.00
81-88: 81-Crystal joins & dons costume. 82,83-Inhumans app. 84-87-Dr. Doom app. 88-Last 12¢ issue	3.40	10.00	24.00
89-99,101,102: 94-Intro. Agatha Harkness. 102,103-Fantastic Four vs. Sub-Mariner	2.60	7.50	14.00
100 (7/70)	9.30	28.00	70.00
103-111: 104-Magneto-c/story. 108-Last Kirby issue (not in #103-107). 110-Variant in cover color	2.00	6.00	14.00
112-Hulk Vs. Thing (7/71)	6.50	19.50	45.00
113-115: 115-Last 15¢ issue	1.85	5.50	13.00
116-120: 116-(52 pgs.)	1.65	4.20	10.00
121-123-Silver Surfer-c/stories. 122,123-Galactus	2.30	6.70	16.00
124,125,127,129-149: 129-Intro. Thundra. 130-Sue leaves F.F. 131-Quicksilver app. 132-Medusa joins. 133-Thundra Vs. Thing. 142-Kirbyish-a by Buckler begins. 143-Dr. Doom-c/story. 147-Sub-Mariner	1.50	3.75	9.00
126-Origin F.F. retold; cover swipe of F.F. #1	1.65	4.20	10.00
128-Four pg. insert of F.F. Friends & Foes	1.65	4.20	10.00
150-Crystal & Quicksilver's wedding	1.65	4.20	10.00

	GD25	FN65	NM94
151-154,158-160: 151-Origin Thundra. 159-Medusa leaves; Sue rejoins	1.30	3.25	8.00
155-157: Silver Surfer in all	1.50	3.75	9.00
161-180: 164-The Crusader (old Marvel Boy) revived (origin #165); 1st app.Frankie Raye. 168-170-Cage app. 176-Re-intro Impossible Man; Marvel artists app. 180-r/#101 by Kirby		1.60	4.00
181-199: 189-G.A. Human Torch app. & origin retold. 190,191-Fantastic Four break up		1.20	3.00
200-(11/78, 52 pgs.)-F.F. re-united vs. Dr. Doom	1.20	2.60	6.00
201-208,219,222-231: 207-Human Torch vs. Spider-Man-c/story. 211-1st app. Terrax		.80	2.00
209-216,218,220,221-Byrne-a. 209-1st Herbie the Robot. 220-Brief origin		1.00	2.50
217-Dazzler app. by Byrne		1.20	3.00
232-Byrne-a begins		1.60	4.00
233-235,237-249,251-260: All Byrne-a. 238-Origin Frankie Raye. 244-Frankie Raye becomes Nova, Herald of Galactus. 252-Reads sideways; Annihilus app.; contains skin "Tattooz" decals		1.20	3.00
236-20th Anniversary issue(11/81, 68 pgs., $1.00)-Brief origin F.F.; Byrne-c/a(p); new Kirby-a(p)		1.60	4.00
250-(52 pgs)-Spider-Man x-over; Byrne-a; Skrulls impersonate New X-Men		1.60	4.00
261-285: 261-Silver Surfer. 262-Origin Galactus; Byrne writes & draws himself into story. 264-Swipes-c of F.F. #1. 274-Spider-Man's alien costume app. (4th app., 1/85, 2 pgs.)		1.20	3.00
286-2nd app. X-Factor continued from Avengers #263; story continues in X-Factor #1	1.00	2.00	5.00
287-295: 292-Nick Fury app. 293-Last Byrne-a		.80	2.00
296-($1.50)-Barry Smith-c/a; Thing rejoins		1.20	3.00
297-318,320-330: 300-Johnny Storm & Alicia Masters wed. 306-New team begins (9/87). 311-Re-intro The Black Panther. 312-X-Factor x-over. 327-Mr. Fantastic & Invisible Girl return		.80	2.00
319-Double size		1.00	2.50
331-346,351-357,359,360: 334-Simonson-c/scripts begin. 337-Simonson-a begins. 342-Spider-Man cameo. 356-F.F. vs. the New Warriors; Paul Ryan-c/a begins. 360-Last $1.00-c			1.50
347-Ghost Rider, Wolverine, Spider-Man, Hulk-c/stories thru #349; Arthur Adams-c/a(p) in each		1.00	5.00
347-Gold 2nd printing		1.00	2.50
348,349		1.20	3.00
348-Gold 2nd printing			1.50
350-($1.50, 52 pgs.)-Dr. Doom app.		1.20	3.00
358-(11/91, $2.25, 88 pgs.)-30th anniversary issue; gives history of F.F.; die cut-c; Art Adams back-up story-a		1.20	3.00
361-368,370,372-374,376-380,382-386: 362-Spider-Man app. 367-Wolverine app. (brief). Infinity War x-over; Thanos & Magus app. 374-Secret Defenders (Ghost Rider, Hulk, Wolverine) x-over			1.50
369-Infinity War x-over; Thanos app.		1.00	2.50
371-All white embossed-c ($2.00)		1.60	4.00
371-All red 2nd printing		1.00	2.50
375-($2.95, 52 pgs.)-Holo-grafx foil-c; ann. issue		1.20	3.00
381-Death of Reed Richards (Mister Fantastic) & Dr. Doom		1.20	3.00
387-Newsstand ed. ($1.25)			1.25
387-($2.95)-Collector's Ed. w/Die-cut foil-c		1.20	3.00
388-393, 395-397: 388-Bagged $1.50-c; bound-in trading card sheet			1.50
394 ($2.95)-Polybagged w/16 pg. Marvel Action Hour book and acetate print; pink logo		1.20	3.00
398,399-Rainbow Foil-c		1.00	2.50
400-Rainbow-Foil-c		1.40	3.50
401-415: 401,402-Atlantis Rising. 407,408-Return of Reed Richards. 411-Inhumans app. 414-Galactus vs. Hyperstorm. 415-Onslaught tie-in; X-Men app.			1.50

Fantastic Four Annual #23 © MEG

Fantastic Four V2#2 © MEG

Fantastic Four Unlimited #4 © MEG

	GD25	FN65	NM94

	GD25	FN65	NM94
416-($2.50)-Onslaught tie-in; Dr. Doom app.; wraparound-c		1.00	2.50
Annual 1('63)-Origin F.F.; Ditko-i	52.00	156.00	625.00
Annual 2('64)-Dr. Doom origin & c/story	29.00	87.00	350.00
Annual 3('65)-Reed & Sue wed; r/#6,11	13.00	41.00	165.00
Special 4(11/66)-G.A. Torch x-over (1st S.A. app.) & origin retold; r/#25,26			
(Hulk vs. Thing); Torch vs. Torch battle	9.00	27.00	90.00
Special 5(11/67)-New art; Intro. Psycho-Man; early Black Panther, Inhumans			
& Silver Surfer (1st solo story) app.	10.00	30.00	100.00
Special 6(11/68)-Intro. Annihilus; birth of Franklin Richards; new 48 pg. movie			
length epic; last non-reprint annual	4.50	13.50	45.00
Special 7(11/69)-r/F.F. #1-5; Marvel staff photos	2.20	6.60	22.00
Special 8-10: All reprints. 8(12/70)-F.F. vs. Sub-Mariner plus gallery of F.F. foes.			
9(12/71). 10('73)	1.20	3.60	12.00
Annual 11-14: 11(1976)-New art begins again. 12(1978). 13(1978). 14(1979)			
	1.00	2.50	8.00
Annual 15-21: 15(1980). 16(1981). 17(1983)-Byrne-c/a. 18(1984). 19(1985).			
20(1987). 21(1988)-Evolutionary War x-over		1.60	4.00
Annual 22-24 (1989-91, $2.00, 68 pgs.): 22-Atlantis Attacks x-over; Sub-			
Mariner & The Avengers app.; Buckler-a. 23-Byrne-c; Guice-p. 24-2 pg.			
origin recap of Fantastic Four; Guardians of the Galaxy x-over			
	1.00	2.50
Annual 25(1992, $2.25, 68 pgs.)-Moondragon story	.90	2.25
Annual 26,27('93,'94, $2.95, 68 pgs.). 26-Bagged w/card	1.20	3.00
Special Edition 1(5/84)-r/Annual #1; Byrne-c/a	1.00	2.50
...: Monsters Unleashed nn (1992, $5.95)-r/F.F. #347-349 w/new Arthur			
Adams-c	1.00	2.50	6.00
...: Nobody Gets Out Alive (1994, $15.95) TPB r/ #387-392			
			16.00
Giveaway (nn, 1981, 32pgs., Young Model Builders Club)		.80	2.00
NOTE: *Arthur Adams* c/a-347-349p. *Austin* c(i)-232-236, 238, 240-242, 250i, 286i. *Buckler* c-168. *John Buscema* a(p)-107, 108(w/*Kirby* & *Romita*),109-130, 132, 134-141, 160, 173-175, 202, 296-309p, Annual 11, 13; c(p)-107-122, 124-129, 133-139, 202, Annual 12p, Special 10. *Byrne* a-209-218p, 220p, 221p, 232-235, 266i, 267-273, 274-293p, Annual 17, 19; c-211-214p, 220p, 232-236p, 237, 238p, 239, 240-242p, 243-249, 250p, 251-267, 269-277, 278-281p, 283p, 284, 285, 286p, 288-293, Annual 17, 18. *Ditko* a-13i, 14i(w/*Kirby*-p), Annual 16. G. *Kane* a-150p, 160p. *Kirby* a-1-102p, 108, 180i, 189r, 236p, Special 1-10; c-1-101, 164, 167, 171-177, 180, 181, 190, 200, Annual 11, Special 1-7, 9. *Marcos* a-Annual 14i. *Mooney* a-118i, 152i. *Perez* a(p)-164-167, 170-172, 176-178, 184-188, 191p, 192p, Annual 14p, 15p; c(p)-183-188, 191, 192, 194-197. *Simonson* a-337-341, 343, 344p, 345p, 346, 350p, 352-354; c-212, 334-341, 342p, 343-346, 350, 353, 354. *Steranko* c-130-132p. *Williamson* a-357i.			
FANTASTIC FOUR			
V2#1, Nov, 1996 - Present ($2.95/$1.95)(Produced by Wildstorm Productions)			
Marvel Comics			
1-($2.95)-Reintro Fantastic Four; Jim Lee-c/a; Brandon Choi scripts; Mole Man			
app.	1.20	3.00
1-($2.95)-Variant-c		5.00
2-12: 2-Begin $1.95-c; Namor-c/app. 3-Avengers-c/app.	.80	2.00
FANTASTIC FOUR: ATLANTIS RISING			
June, 1995 - No. 2, July, 1995 ($3.95, limited series)			
Marvel Comics			
1,2: Acetate-c	1.60	4.00
Collector's Preview (5/95, $2.25, 52 pgs.)	.90	2.25
FANTASTIC FOUR INDEX (See Official...)			
FANTASTIC FOUR ROAST			
May, 1982 (75¢, one-shot, direct sales)			
Marvel Comics Group			
1-Celebrates 20th anniversary of F.F.#1; X-Men, Ghost Rider & many others			
cameo; Golden, Miller, Buscema, Rogers, Byrne, Anderson art;			
Hembeck/Austin-c	1.60	4.00
FANTASTIC FOUR: THE LEGEND			
Oct, 1996 ($3.95, one-shot)			
Marvel Comics			
1-Tribute issue	1.60	4.00

FANTASTIC FOUR 2099			
Jan, 1996 - No. 8, Aug, 1996 ($3.95/$1.95)			
Marvel Comics			
1-($3.95)-Chromium-c; X-Nation preview		1.60	4.00
2-8: 4-Spider-Man 2099-c/app. 5-Doctor Strange app. 7-Thibert-c			
			2.00
NOTE: *Williamson* a-1i; c-1i.			
FANTASTIC FOUR UNLIMITED			
Mar, 1993 - No. 12, Dec, 1995 ($3.95, 68 pgs.)			
Marvel Comics			
1-12: 1-Black Panther app. 4-Thing vs. Hulk. 5-Vs. The Frightful Four. 6-Vs.			
Namor. 7, 9-12-Wraparound-c		1.60	4.00
FANTASTIC FOUR UNPLUGGED			
Sept, 1995 - No. 6, Aug 1996 (99¢, bi-monthly)			
Marvel Comics			
1-6			1.00
FANTASTIC FOUR VS. X-MEN			
Feb, 1987 - No. 4, June, 1987 (Limited series)			
Marvel Comics			
1		1.30	3.25
2-4: 4-Austin-a(i)		.90	2.25
FANTASTIC GIANTS (Formerly Konga #1-23)			
V2#24, Sept, 1966 (25¢, 68 pgs.)			
Charlton Comics			
V2#24-Special Ditko issue; origin Konga & Gorgo reprinted plus two new			
Ditko stories	6.50	19.50	50.00
FANTASTIC TALES			
1958 (no date) (Reprint, one-shot)			
I. W. Enterprises			
1-Reprints Avon's "City of the Living Dead"	3.40	10.00	24.00
FANTASTIC VOYAGE (See Movie Comics)			
Aug, 1969 - No. 2, Dec, 1969			
Gold Key			
1,2 (TV)	3.00	9.00	30.00
FANTASTIC VOYAGES OF SINDBAD, THE			
Oct, 1965 - No. 2, June, 1967			
Gold Key			
1,2-Painted-c	4.00	12.00	40.00
FANTASTIC WORLDS			
No. 5, Sept, 1952 - No. 7, Jan, 1953			
Standard Comics			
5-Toth, Anderson-a	30.00	90.00	210.00
6-Toth-c/a	25.00	75.00	175.00
7	16.00	47.00	110.00
FANTASY FEATURES			
1987 - No. 2, 1987 ($1.75)			
Americomics			
1,2		.70	1.80
FANTASY MASTERPIECES (Marvel Super Heroes No. 12 on)			
Feb, 1966 - No. 11, Oct, 1967; V2#1, Dec, 1979 - No. 14, Jan, 1981			
Marvel Comics Group			
1-Photo of Stan Lee (12¢-c #1,2)	5.50	16.50	38.00
2-r/1st Fin Fang Foom from Strange Tales #89	2.60	7.50	18.00
3-8: 3-G.A. Capt. America-r begin, end #11; 1st 25¢ Giant; Colan-r. 3-Kirby-c			
(p). 4-Kirby-c(p)(i). 7-Begin G.A. Sub-Mariner, Torch-r/M. Mystery. 8-Torch			
battles the Sub-Mariner-r/Marvel Mystery #9	2.60	7.50	18.00
9-Origin Human Torch-r/Marvel Comics #1	2.85	8.50	20.00
10,11: 10-r/origin & 1st app. All Winners Squad from All Winners #19.			

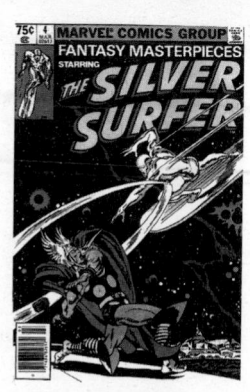

Fantasy Masterpieces V2#4 © MEG

Fatale #3 © Golden Books

Fate #4 © DC

	GD25	FN65	NM94

	GD25	FN65	NM94

11-r/origin of Toro (H.T. #1) & Black Knight #1 — 2.60 / 7.50 / 18.00
V2#1(12/79, 75¢, 52 pgs.)-r/origin Silver Surfer from Silver Surfer #1 with editing plus reprints cover; J. Buscema-a — 1.80 / 4.50
2-14-Reprints Silver Surfer #2-14 w/covers — 1.20 / 3.00
NOTE: Buscema c-V2#7-9(in part). Ditko r-1-3, 7, 9. Everett r-1,7-9. Matt Fox r-9i. Kirby r-1-11; c(p)-3, 4i, 5, 6. Starlin r-8-13. Some direct sale V2#14's had a 50¢ cover price. #3-11 contain Capt. America-r/Capt. America #3-10. #7-11 contain G.A.Human Torch & Sub-Mariner-r.

FANTASY QUARTERLY (Also see Elfquest)
Spring, 1978 (B&W) (2nd printing exist?)
Independent Publishers Syndicate

1-1st app. Elfquest; Dave Sim-a (6 pgs.) — 5.70 / 17.00 / 40.00

FANTOMAN (Formerly Amazing Adventure Funnies)
No. 2, Aug, 1940 - No. 4, Dec, 1940
Centaur Publications

2-The Fantom of the Fair, The Arrow, Little Dynamite-r begin; origin The Ermine by Filchock; Fantoman app. in 2-4; Burgos, J. Cole, Ernst, Gustavson-a — 118.00 / 356.00 / 950.00
3,4: Gustavson-a. 4-Red Blaze story — 100.00 / 300.00 / 800.00

FARGO KID (Formerly Justice Traps the Guilty)(See Feature Comics #47
V11#3(#1), June-July, 1958 - V11#5, Oct-Nov, 1958
Prize Publications

V11#3(#1)-Origin Fargo Kid; Severin-c/a; Williamson-a(2); Heath-a — 17.00 / 51.00 / 120.00
V11#4,5-Severin-c/a — 11.00 / 33.00 / 75.00

FARMER'S DAUGHTER, THE
Feb-Mar, 1954 - No. 3, June-July, 1954; No. 4, Oct, 1954
Stanhall Publ./Trojan Magazines

1-Lingerie, nudity panel — 17.00 / 51.00 / 120.00
2-4(Stanhall) — 11.00 / 33.00 / 75.00

FASHION IN ACTION
Aug, 1986 - Feb, 1987 (Baxter paper)
Eclipse Comics

Summer Special 1 ($1.75)-Snyder III-c/a — .70 / 1.80
Winter Special 1 (2/87, $2.00)-Snyder III-c/a — 1.00 / 2.00

FASTEST GUN ALIVE, THE (Movie)
No. 741, Sept, 1956 (one-shot)
Dell Publishing Co.

Four Color 741-Photo-c — 8.00 / 24.00 / 70.00

FAST FICTION (...Action) (Stories by Famous Authors Illustrated #6 on)
Oct, 1949 - No. 5, Mar, 1950 (All have Kiefer-c)(48 pgs.)
Seaboard Publ./Famous Authors Ill.

1-Scarlet Pimpernel; Jim Lavery-c/a — 34.00 / 103.00 / 240.00
2-Captain Blood; H. C. Kiefer-c/a — 31.00 / 94.00 / 220.00
3-She, by Rider Haggard; Vincent Napoli-a — 40.00 / 120.00 / 300.00
4-(1/50, 52 pgs.)-The 39 Steps; Lavery-c/a — 25.00 / 75.00 / 175.00
5-Beau Geste; Kiefer-c/a — 25.00 / 75.00 / 175.00
NOTE: Kiefer a-2, 5; c-2, 3,5. Lavery a/c-1, 4. Napoli a-3.

FAST FORWARD
1992 - No. 3, 1993 ($4.95, 68 pgs.)
DC Comics (Piranha Press)

1-3: 1-Morrison scripts; McKean-c/a. 3-Sam Kieth-a — 1.00 / 2.00 / 5.00

FAST WILLIE JACKSON
Oct, 1976 - No. 7, 1977
Fitzgerald Periodicals, Inc.

1-7 — 1.00

FAT ALBERT (...& the Cosby Kids) (TV)
Mar, 1974 - No. 29, Feb, 1979
Gold Key

1 — 1.20 / 3.00
2-29 — 1.00

FATALE (Also see Powers That Be #1 & Shadow State #1,2)
Jan, 1996 - No. 6, Aug, 1996 ($2.50)
Broadway Comics

1-6: J.G. Jones-c/a in all — 1.00 / 2.50
Preview Edition 1 (11/95, B&W) — 1.00 / 2.50

FAT AND SLAT (Ed Wheelan) (Becomes Gunfighter No. 5 on)
Summer, 1947 - No. 4, Spring, 1948
E. C. Comics

1-Intro/origin Voltage, Man of Lightning; "Comics" McCormick, the World's No. 1 Comic Book Fan begins, ends #4 — 28.00 / 84.00 / 195.00
2-4: 4-Comics McCormick-c feature — 20.00 / 60.00 / 140.00

FAT AND SLAT JOKE BOOK
Summer, 1944 (52 pgs., one-shot)
All-American Comics (William H. Wise)

nn-by Ed Wheelan — 23.00 / 69.00 / 160.00

FATE (See Hand of Fate & Thrill-O-Rama)

FATE
Oct, 1994 - No. 22, Sept, 1996 ($1.95/$2.25)
DC Comics

0-7 — .80 / 2.00
8-22: 8-Begin $2.25-c. 12-Alan Scott (Sentinel) app. 14-Zatanna app. 21-Phantom Stranger app. 22-Spectre app. — .90 / 2.25

FATHER & SON
July, 1995 ($2.75, B&W, limited series)
Kitchen Sink

1-Jeff Nicholson-s/a — 1.10 / 2.75

FATHER OF CHARITY
No date (32 pgs.; paper cover)
Catechetical Guild Giveaway

nn — 2.50 / 5.00 / 10.00

FATHOM
May, 1987 - No. 3, July, 1987 ($1.50, limited series)
Comico

1-3 — 1.50

FATIMA...CHALLENGE TO THE WORLD
1951, 36 pgs. (15¢)
Catechetical Guild

nn (not same as 'Challenge to the World') — 2.40 / 6.00 / 12.00

FATMAN, THE HUMAN FLYING SAUCER
April, 1967 - No. 3, Aug-Sept, 1967 (68 pgs.)
Lightning Comics(Milson Publ. Co.) (Written by Otto Binder)

1-Origin/1st app. Fatman & Tinman by Beck — 5.70 / 17.00 / 40.00
2-C. C. Beck-a — 3.90 / 11.50 / 27.00
3-(Scarce)-Beck-a — 6.50 / 19.50 / 45.00

FAUNTLEROY COMICS (Super Duck Presents...)
1950 - No. 3, 1952
Close-Up/Archie Publications

1-Super Duck-c/stories by Al Fagaly in all — 8.35 / 25.00 / 50.00
2,3 — 5.00 / 15.00 / 30.00

FAUST
1989 - Present ($2.00/$2.25, B&W, mature themes)
Northstar Publishing/Rebel Studios #7 on

1-Decapitation-c; Tim Vigil-c/a in all; Begin $2.00-c — 5.00 / 15.00 / 35.00
1-2nd printing — 1.65 / 4.20 / 10.00
1-3rd printing — 1.20 / 3.00

Fawcett Movie Comic-Destination Moon © FAW

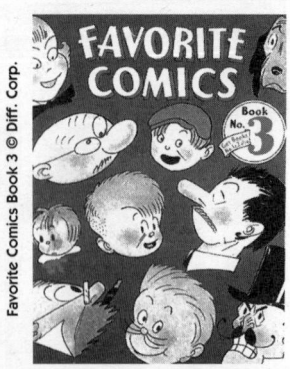

Favorite Comics Book 3 © Diff. Corp.

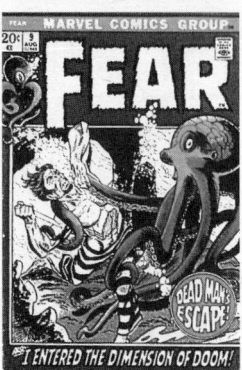

Fear #9 © MEG

	GD25	FN65	NM94
2	3.60	10.50	25.00
2-2nd & 3rd printings		1.20	3.00
3-Begin $2.25-c	2.10	6.40	15.00
3-2nd printing		1.20	3.00
4	1.00	2.00	5.00
5-10: 7-Begin Rebel Studios series		1.20	3.00
11-($2.25)		.90	2.25

FAVORITE COMICS (Also see Famous Comics)
1934 (36 pgs.)
Grocery Store Giveaway (Diff. Corp.) (detergent)

Book 1-The Nebbs, Strange As It Seems, Napoleon, Joe Palooka, Dixie Dugan, S'Matter Pop, Hairbreadth Harry, etc. reprints	56.00	168.00	450.00
Book 2,3	44.00	132.00	350.00

FAWCETT MINIATURES (See Mighty Midget)
1946 (3-3/4x5", 12-24 pgs.) (Wheaties giveaways)
Fawcett Publications

Captain Marvel "And the Horn of Plenty"; Bulletman story	11.50	34.00	80.00
Captain Marvel "& the Raiders From Space"; Golden Arrow story	11.50	34.00	80.00
Captain Marvel Jr. "The Case of the Poison Press!" Bulletman story	11.50	34.00	80.00
Delecta of the Planets; C. C. Beck art; B&W inside; 12 pgs.; 3 printing variations (coloring) exist	21.00	62.00	145.00

FAWCETT MOTION PICTURE COMICS (See Motion Picture Comics)

FAWCETT MOVIE COMIC
1949 - No. 20, Dec, 1952 (All photo-c)
Fawcett Publications

nn- "Dakota Lil"; George Montgomery & Rod Cameron (1949)	29.00	88.00	205.00
nn- "Copper Canyon"; Ray Milland & Hedy Lamarr (1950)	22.00	66.00	155.00
nn- "Destination Moon" (1950)	68.00	206.00	550.00
nn- "Montana"; Errol Flynn & Alexis Smith (1950)	23.00	69.00	160.00
nn- "Pioneer Marshal"; Monte Hale (1950)	23.00	69.00	160.00
nn- "Powder River Rustlers"; Rocky Lane (1950)	34.00	103.00	240.00
nn- "Singing Guns"; Vaughn Monroe, Ella Raines & Walter Brennan (1950)	20.00	60.00	140.00
7- "Gunmen of Abilene"; Rocky Lane; Bob Powell-a (1950)	26.00	77.00	180.00
8- "King of the Bullwhip"; Lash LaRue; Bob Powell-a(2/51; mis-dated 2/50)	39.00	116.00	270.00
9- "The Old Frontier"; Monte Hale; Bob Powell-a(2/51; mis-dated 2/50)	24.00	73.00	170.00
10- "The Missourians"; Monte Hale (4/51)	24.00	73.00	170.00
11- "The Thundering Trail"; Lash LaRue (6/51)	31.00	94.00	220.00
12- "Rustlers on Horseback"; Rocky Lane (8/51)	26.00	77.00	180.00
13- "Warpath"; Edmond O'Brien & Forrest Tucker (10/51)	17.,00	49.00	115.00
14- "Last Outpost"; Ronald Reagan (12/51)	40.00	120.00	280.00
15-(Scarce)- "The Man From Planet X"; Robert Clark; Shaffenberger-a (2/52)	187.00	562.00	1500.00
16- "10 Tall Men"; Burt Lancaster	13.00	39.00	90.00
17- "Rose of Cimarron"; Jack Buetel & Mala Powers	10.00	30.00	70.00
18- "The Brigand"; Anthony Dexter & Anthony Quinn; Shaffenberger-a	10.00	30.00	70.00
19- "Carbine Williams"; James Stewart; Costanza-a; James Stewart photo-c	11.50	34.00	80.00
20- "Ivanhoe"; Robert Taylor & Liz Taylor photo-c	17.00	51.00	120.00

FAWCETT'S FUNNY ANIMALS (No. 1-26, 80-on titled "Funny Animals"; becomes Li'l Tomboy No. 92 on?)
12/42 - #79, 4/53; #80, 6/53 - #83, 12?/53; #84, 4/54 - #91, 2/56

	GD25	FN65	NM94
Fawcett Publications/Charlton Comics No. 84 on			
1-Capt. Marvel on cover; intro. Hoppy The Captain Marvel Bunny, cloned from Capt. Marvel; Billy the Kid & Willie the Worm begin	48.00	146.00	390.00
2-Xmas-c	29.00	86.00	200.00
3-5: 3-Spirit of '43-c	18.00	54.00	125.00
6,7,9,10	11.50	34.00	80.00
8-Flag-c	12.00	36.00	85.00
11-20: 14-Cover is a 1944 calendar	10.00	30.00	60.00
21-40: 25-Xmas-c. 26-St. Valentines Day-c	6.35	19.00	38.00
41-87,90,91	4.35	13.00	28.00
87-89(10-54-2/55)-Merry Mailman ish (TV/Radio)-part photo-c	6.35	19.00	38.00

NOTE: Marvel Bunny in all issues to at least No. 68 (not in 49-54).

FAZE ONE FAZERS
1986 - No. 4, Sept, 1986 (Limited series)
Americomics (AC Comics)

..1-4			1.50

F.B.I., THE
Apr-June, 1965
Dell Publishing Co.

1-Sinnott-a	2.60	7.50	18.00

F.B.I. STORY, THE (Movie)
No. 1069, Jan-Mar, 1960
Dell Publishing Co.

Four Color 1069-Toth-a; James Stewart photo-c	11.00	33..00	110.00

FEAR (Adventure into…)
Nov, 1970 - No. 31, Dec, 1975 (No.1-6: Giant Size)
Marvel Comics Group

1-Fantasy & Sci-Fi reprints in early issues	1.30	3.25	8.00
2-6	1.00	2.00	5.00
7-9		1.20	3.00
10-Man-Thing begins (10/72, early app.), ends #19; see Savage Tales #1 for 1st app.; Chaykin/Morrow-c/a	1.30	3.25	8.00
11,12: 11-N. Adams-c. 12-Starlin/Buckler-a		1.60	4.00
13,14,16-18: 17-Origin/1st app. Wundarr		1.20	3.00
15-1st full-length Man-Thing story (8/73)	1.00	2.00	5.00
19-Intro. Howard the Duck; Val Mayerik-a (12/73)	1.65	4.20	10.00
20-Morbius, the Living Vampire begins, ends #31; has history recap of Morbius with X-Men & Spider-Man	2.85	8.50	20.00
21-25	1.65	4.20	10.00
26-31	1.30	3.25	8.00

NOTE: Bolle a-13i. Brunner c-15-17. Buckler a-11p, 12i. Chaykin a-10i. Colan a-23r. Craig a-10p. Ditko a-6-8r. Evans a-30. Everett a-9, 10i, 21r. Gulacy a-20p. Heath a-12r. Heck a-8r, 13r. Gil Kane a-21p; c(p)-20, 21, 23-28, 31. Kirby a-8r, 9r. Maneely a-24r. Mooney a-11i, 26r. Morrow a-11i. Paul Reinman a-14r. Robbins a(p)-25-27, 31. Russell a-23p, 24p. Severin c-8. Starlin c-12p.

FEARBOOK
April, 1986 ($1.75, one-shot, mature)
Eclipse Comics

..1-Scholastic Mag- r; Bissette-a		.90	1.80

FEAR IN THE NIGHT (See Complete Mystery No. 3)

FEARLESS FAGAN
No. 441, Dec, 1952 (one-shot)
Dell Publishing co.

Four Color 441	4.00	12.00	40.00

FEATURE BOOK (Dell) (See Large Feature Comic)

FEATURE BOOKS (Newspaper-r, early issues)
May, 1937 - No. 57, 1948 (B&W) (Full color, 68 pgs. begin #26 on)
David McKay Publications

Feature Books #5 © DMP

Feature Comics #101 © QUA

Felicia Hardy, The Black Cat #4 © MEG

	GD25	FN65	NM94

Note: See individual alphabetical listings for prices

nn-Popeye & the Jeep (#1, 100 pgs.); reprinted as Feature Books #3(Very Rare; only 3 known copies, 1-VF, 2-in low grade)

nn-Dick Tracy (#1)-Reprinted as Feature Book #4 (100 pgs.) & in part as 4-Color #1 (Rare, less than 10 known copies)

NOTE: *Above books were advertised together with different covers from Feat. Books #3 & 4.*

1-King of the Royal Mtd. (#1)
2-Popeye (6/37) by Segar
3-Popeye (7/37) by Segar;
4-Dick Tracy (8/37)-Same as nn issue but a new cover added same as nn issue but a new cover added
5-Popeye (5/37) by Segar
6-Dick Tracy (10/37)
7-Little Orphan Annie (#1, 11/37) (Rare)-Reprints strips from 12/31/34 to 7/17/35
8-Secret Agent X-9 (12/37) -Not by Raymond
9-Dick Tracy (1/38)
10-Popeye (2/38)
11-Little Annie Rooney (#1, 3/38)
12-Blondie (#1) (4/38) (Rare)
13-Inspector Wade (5/38)
14-Popeye (6/38) by Segar
15-Barney Baxter (#1) (7/38)
16-Red Eagle (8/38)
17-Gangbusters (#1, 9/38) (1st app.)
18,19-Mandrake
20-Phantom (#1, 12/38)
21-Lone Ranger
22-Phantom
23-Mandrake
24-Lone Ranger (1941)
25-Flash Gordon (#1)-Reprints not by Raymond
26-Prince Valiant (1941)-Hal Foster -c/a; newspaper strips reprinted, pgs. 1-28,30-63; color & 68 pg. issues begin; Foster cover is only original comic book artwork by him
27-29,31,34-Blondie
30-Katzenjammer Kids (#1, 1942)
32,35,41,44-Katzenjammer Kids
33(nn)-Romance of Flying; World War II photos
36('43),38,40('44),42,43, 45,47-Blondie
37-Katzenjammer Kids; has photo & biog. of Harold K.Knerr(1883-1949) who took over strip from Rudolph Dirks in 1914
39-Phantom
46-Mandrake in the Fire World-(58 pgs.)
48-Maltese Falcon by Dashiell Hammett('46)
49,50-Perry Mason; based on Gardner novels
51,54-Rip Kirby; Raymond-c/s; origin-#51
52,55-Mandrake
53,56,57-Phantom

NOTE: *All Feature Books through #25 are over-sized 8-1/2x11-3/8" comics with color covers and black and white interiors. The covers are rough, slick newsprint type stock. The page counts, including covers, are as follows: nn, #3, 4-100 pgs.; #1, 2-52 pgs.; #5-25 are all 76 pgs. #33 was found in bound set from publisher.*

FEATURE COMICS (Formerly Feature Funnies)
No. 21, June, 1939 - No. 144, May, 1950
Quality Comics Group

	50.00	150.00	400.00
21-The Clock, Jane Arden & Mickey Finn continue from Feature Funnies	50.00	150.00	400.00
22-26: 23-Charlie Chan begins (8/39, 1st app.)	40.00	120.00	280.00
26-(nn, nd)-Cover in one color, (10¢, 36 pgs.); issue No. blanked out. Two variations exist,each contain half of the regular(#26)	13.00	39.00	90.00
27-(Rare)-Origin/1st app. Doll Man by Eisner (scripts) & Lou Fine (art); Doll Man begins, ends #139	288.00	866.00	2600.00
28-2nd app. Doll Man by Lou Fine	137.00	412.00	1100.00
29,30: 30-1st Doll Man-c	80.00	240.00	640.00
31-Last Clock & Charlie Chan issue (4/40); Charlie Chan moves to Big Shot #1 following month (5/40)	65.00	195.00	520.00
32-37: 32-Rusty Ryan & Samar begin. 34-Captain Fortune app. 37-Last Fine Doll Man	45.00	135.00	360.00

Note: *A 15¢ Canadian version of Feature Comics #37, made in the US, exists.*

38-41: 38-Origin the Ace of Space. 39-Origin The Destroying Demon, ends #40; X-Mas-c. 40-Bruce Blackburn in costume	40.00	120.00	290.00
42,43,45-50: 42-USA, the Spirit of Old Glory begins. 46-Intro. Boyville Brigadiers in Rusty Ryan. 47-Fargo Kid begins. 48-USA ends	29.00	86.00	200.00
44-Doll Man by Crandall begins, ends #63; Crandall-a(2)	40.00	120.00	300.00
51-60: 56-Marijuana story in Swing Sisson strip. 57-Spider Widow begins.			

60-Raven begins, ends #71	21.00	64.00	150.00
61-68 (5/43)	20.00	60.00	140.00
69,70-Phantom Lady x-over in Spider Widow	22.00	66.00	155.00
71-80,100: 71-Phantom Lady x-over. 72-Spider Widow ends	14.00	43.00	100.00
81-99	13.00	39.00	90.00
101-144: 139-Last Doll Man & last Doll Man-c. 140-Intro. Stuntman Stetson (Stuntman Stetson c-140-144)	10.00	30.00	65.00

NOTE: *Celardo a-37-43. Crandall a-44-60, 62, 63-on(most). Gustavson a-(Rusty Ryan)- 32-134. Powell a-34, 64-73. The Clock c-25, 28, 29. Doll Man c-30, 32, 34, 36, 38, 40, 42, 44, 46, 48, 50, 52, 54, 56, 58, 60, 62, 64, 66, 68, 70, 72, 74, 77-139. Joe Palooka c-21, 24, 27.*

FEATURE FILMS
Mar-Apr, 1950 - No. 4, Sept-Oct, 1950 (All photo-c)
National Periodical Publications

1- "Captain China" with John Payne, Gail Russell, Lon Chaney & Edgar Bergen	59.00	178.00	475.00
2- "Riding High" with Bing Crosby	62.00	187.00	500.00
3- "The Eagle & the Hawk" with John Payne, Rhonda Fleming & D. O'Keefe	59.00	178.00	475.00
4- "Fancy Pants"; Bob Hope & Lucille Ball	62.00	187.00	500.00

FEATURE FUNNIES (Feature Comics No. 21 on)
Oct, 1937 - No. 20, May, 1939
Harry 'A' Chesler

1(V9#1-indicia)-Joe Palooka, Mickey Finn (1st app.), The Bungles, Jane Arden, Dixie Dugan (1st app.), Big Top, Ned Brant, Strange As It Seems, & Off the Record strip reprints begin	316.00	950.00	1900.00
2-The Hawk app. (11/37); Goldberg-c	145.00	437.00	875.00
3-Hawks of Seas begins by Eisner, ends #12; The Clock begins; Christmas-c	112.00	337.00	675.00
4,5	83.00	250.00	500.00
6-12: 11-Archie O'Toole by Bud Thomas begins, ends #22	62.00	187.00	375.00
13-Espionage, Starring Black X begins by Eisner, ends #20	70.00	210.00	420.00
14-20	50.00	150.00	300.00

NOTE: *Joe Palooka covers 1, 6, 9, 12, 15, 18.*

FEATURE PRESENTATION, A (Feature Presentations Magazine #6) (Formerly Women in Love) (Also see Startling Terror Tales #11)
No. 5, April, 1950
Fox Features Syndicate

5(#1)-Black Tarantula	37.00	111.00	260.00

FEATURE PRESENTATIONS MAGAZINE (Formerly A Feature Presentation #5; becomes Feature Stories Magazine #3 on)
No. 6, July, 1950
Fox Features Syndicate

6(#2)-Moby Dick; Wood-c	26.00	79.00	185.00

FEATURE STORIES MAGAZINE (Formerly Feature Presentations Mag. #6)
No. 3, Aug, 1950 - No. 4, Oct, 1950
Fox Features Syndicate

3-Jungle Lil, Zegra stories; bondage-c	27.00	81.00	190.00
4	21.00	64.00	150.00

FEDERAL MEN COMICS (See Adventure Comics #32, The Comics Magazine, New Adventure Comics, New Book of Comics, New Comics & Star Spangled Comics #91)
No. 2, 1945 (DC reprints from 1930's)
Gerard Publ. Co.

2-Siegel & Shuster-a; cover redrawn from Detective #9; spanking panel	31.00	92.00	215.00

FELICIA HARDY: THE BLACK CAT
July, 1994 - No. 4, Oct, 1994 ($1.50, limited series)
Marvel Comics

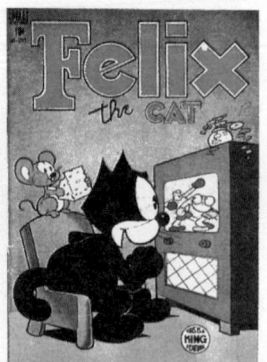

Felix The Cat #10 © DELL

Femforce #94 © AC

Ferret #6 © Malibu

	GD25	FN65	NM94

1-4: 1,4-Spider-Man app.   1.50

FELIX'S NEPHEWS INKY & DINKY
Sept, 1957 - No. 7, Oct, 1958
Harvey Publications

	GD25	FN65	NM94
1-Cover shows Inky's left eye with 2 pupils	8.35	25.00	50.00
2-7	4.00	11.00	22.00

NOTE: **Messmer** art in 1-6. **Oriolo** a-1-7.

FELIX THE CAT (See Cat Tales 3-D, The Funnies, March of Comics #24,36, 51, New Funnies & Popular Comics)
1943 - No. 118, Nov, 1961; Sept-Nov, 1962 - No. 12, July-Sept, 1965
Dell Publ. No. 1-19/Toby No. 20-61/Harvey No. 62-118/Dell No. 1-12

	GD25	FN65	NM94
Four Color 15	70.00	210.00	700.00
Four Color 46('44)	41.00	123.00	410.00
Four Color 77('45)	38.00	114.00	380.00
Four Color 119('46)-All new stories begin	32.50	97.50	325.00
Four Color 135('46)	24.00	72.00	240.00
Four Color 162(9/47)	18.00	54.00	180.00
1(2-3/48)(Dell)	25.00	75.00	250.00
2	13.50	40.50	135.00
3-5	10.50	31.50	105.00
6-19(2-3/51-Dell)	7.50	22.50	75.00
20-30,32,33,34,36,38-61(6/55)-All Messmer issues.(Toby): 28-(2/52)-Some copies have #29 on cover, #28 on inside (Rare in high grade)	19.00	57.00	190.00
31,34,35-No Messmer-a; Messmer-c only 31,34	6.00	18.00	60.00
37-(100 pgs., 25 ¢, 1/15/53, X-Mas-c, Toby; daily & Sunday-r (rare)	42.00	126.00	420.00
62(8/55)-100 (Harvey)	3.00	9.00	30.00
101-118(11/61): 101-117-Reprints. 118-All new-a	2.00	6.00	20.00
12-269-211(#1, 9-11/62)(Dell)-No Messmer	4.00	12.00	36.00
2-12(7-9/65)(Dell, TV)-No Messmer	3.00	9.00	27.00
3-D Comic Book 1(1953-One Shot, 25¢)-w/glasses	38.00	114.00	265.00
Summer Annual nn ('53, 25¢, 100 pgs., Toby)-Daily & Sunday-r	36.00	108.00	360.00
Winter Annual 2 ('54, 25¢, 100 pgs., Toby)-Daily & Sunday-r	36.00	108.00	360.00

(Special note: Despite the covers on Toby 37 and the Summer Annual above proclaiming "all new stories," they were actually reformatted newspaper strips)

NOTE: **Otto Messmer** went to work for Universal Film as an animator in 1915 and then worked for the Pat Sullivan animation studio in 1916. He created a black cat in the cartoon short, Feline Follies in 1919 that became known as Felix in the early 1920s. The Felix Sunday strip began Aug. 14, 1923 and continued until Sept. 19, 1943 whjen **Messmer** took the character to Dell (Western Publishing) and began doing Felix comic books, first adapting strips to the comic format. The first all new Felix comic was Four Color #119 in 1946 (#4 in the Dell run). The daily Felix was begun on May 9, 1927 by another artist, but by the following year, **Messmer** did it too. King Features took the daily away from **Messmer** in 1954 and he began to do some of his most dynamic art for Toby Press. The daily was continued by **Joe Oriolo** who drew it until it was discontinued Jan. 9, 1967. **Oriolo** was **Messmer's** assistant for many years and inked some of **Messmer's** pencils through the Toby run, as well as doing some of the stories by himself. Though **Messmer** continued to work for Harvey, his contribuitons were limited, and no all **Messmer** stories appeared after the Toby run until some early Toby reprints were published in the 1990s Harvey revival of the title. 4-Color No. 15, 46, 77 and the Toby Annuals are all daily or Sunday newspaper reprints from the 1930's-1940's drawn by **Otto Messmer**. #101-r/#64; 102-r/#65; 103-r/#67; 104-117-r/#68-81. **Messmer**-a in all Dell/Toby/Harvey issues except #31, 34, 35, 97, 98, 100, 118. **Oriolo** a-20, 31-on.

FELIX THE CAT (Also see The Nine Lives of...)
Sept, 1991 - No. 7, Jan, 1994 ($1.25/$1.50, bi-monthly)
Harvey Comics/Gladstone

1-5: Reprints 1950s Toby issues by Messmer. 1-Inky and Dinky back-up story (produced by Gladstone)			1.25
6,7-($1.50-c)			1.50
Big Book V2#1 (9/92, $1.95, 52 pgs.)		.80	2.00

FELIX THE CAT AND FRIENDS
1992 - No. 4, 1992 ($1.95)
Felix Comics

1-4: 1-Contains Felix trading cards		.80	2.00

FELIX THE CAT & HIS FRIENDS (Pat Sullivan's...)
Dec, 1953 - No. 3, 1954 (Indicia title for #2&3 as listed)
Toby Press

	GD25	FN65	NM94
1 (Indicia title, "Felix and His Friends," #1 only)	18.50	55.50	185.00
2-3	11.50	34.50	115.00

FELIX THE CAT DIGEST MAGAZINE
July, 1992 ($1.75, digest-size, 98 pgs.)
Harvey Comics

1-Felix, Richie Rich stories		.70	1.75

FELIX THE CAT KEEPS ON WALKIN'
1991 ($15.95, 8-1/2"x11", 132 pgs.)
Hamilton Comics

nn-Reprints 15 Toby Press Felix the Cat and Felix and His Friends stories in new computer color	2.30	6.90	16.00

FEM FANTASTIQUE
Aug, 1988 ($1.95, B&W)
AC Comics

V2#1-By Bill Black; Betty Page pin-up		1.10	2.75

FEMFORCE (Also see Untold Origin of the Femforce)
Apr, 1985 - Present (1.75/1.95/2.25/2.75/2.95, B&W #16-56)
Americomics

	GD25	FN65	NM94
1-Black-a in most; Nightveil, Ms. Victory begin	1.00	2.00	5.00
2		1.20	3.00
3-30: 12-15-$1.95-c. 16-19-2.25-c. 20-Begin $2.50-c, 44 pgs. 25-Origin/1st app. new Ms. Victory. 28-Colt leaves. 29,30-Camilla-r by Mayo from Jungle Comics		1.10	2.75
31-35,37-49,51-100: 31-Begin $2.75-c. 44-Contains mini-comic insert, Catman & Kitten #0. 51-Photo-c from movie. 57-Begin color issues.64-Re-intro Black Phantom. 95-Photo-c		1.10	2.75
36 (2.95, 52 pgs.)		1.20	3.00
50 (2.95, 52 pgs.)-Contains flexi-disc; origin retold; most AC characters app.		1.20	3.00
88 (2.95)		1.20	3.00
Special 1 (Fall, '84)(B&W, 52pgs.)-1st app. Ms. Victory, She-Cat, Blue Bulleteer, Rio Rita & Lady Luger		.80	2.00
Bad Girl Backlash-(12/95, $5.00)	1.00	2.00	5.00
Frightbook 1 ('92, $2.95, B&W)-Halloween special		1.20	3.00
In the House of Horror 1 (`89, 2.50, B&W)		1.00	2.50
Night of the Demon 1 ('90, 2.75, B&W)		1.10	2.75
Out of the Asylum Special 1 ('87, B&W, $1.95)		.80	2.00
Pin-Up Portfolio		.80	2.00

FEMFORCE UP CLOSE
Apr, 1992 - No. 4, 1993 ($2.75, quarterly)
AC Comics

1-4: 1-Stars Nightveil; inside f/c photo from Femforce movie. 2-Stars Stardust. 3-Stars Dragonfly. 4-Stars She-Cat		1.10	2.75

FERDINAND THE BULL (See Mickey Mouse Magazine V4#3)
1938 (10¢, large size, some color w/rest B&W)
Dell Publishing Co.

	GD25	FN65	NM94
nn	17.00	51.00	120.00

FERRET
Sept, 1992; May, 1993 - No. 10, Feb, 1994 ($1.95)
Malibu Comics

1-(1992, one-shot)		.80	2.00
1-($2.50)-Completely die-cut cover		1.00	2.50
2-4-($2.50)-Collector's Edition w/poster		1.00	2.50
2-4-($1.95)-Newsstand Edition w/different-c		.80	2.00
5-8($2.25): 5-Polybagged w/Skycap		.90	2.25

Feud #3 © MEG

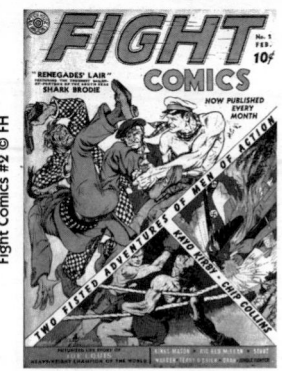

Fight Comics #2 © FH

Fighting American #3 © PRIZE

FI

	GD25	FN65	NM94
9,10: 9-Begin $2.50-c		1.00	2.50

FEUD
July, 1993 - No. 4, Oct, 1993 ($1.95, limited series)
Marvel Comics (Epic Comics/Heavy Hitters)

	GD25	FN65	NM94
1-($2.50)-Embossed-c		1.00	2.50
2-4		.80	2.00

FIBBER McGEE & MOLLY (Radio)(Also see A-1 Comics)
No. 25, 1949 (one-shot)
Magazine Enterprises

	GD25	FN65	NM94
A-1 25	9.15	27.50	55.00

55 DAYS AT PEKING (See Movie Comics)

FIGHT AGAINST CRIME (Fight Against the Guilty #22, 23)
May, 1951 - No. 21, Sept, 1954
Story Comics

	GD25	FN65	NM94
1-True crime stories #1-4	25.00	75.00	175.00
2	13.00	39.00	90.00
3,5: 5-Frazetta-a, 1 pg.; content change to horror & suspense	10.00	30.00	65.00
4-Drug story "Hopped Up Killers"	10.00	30.00	70.00
6,7: 6-Used in **POP**, pgs. 83,84	10.00	30.00	60.00
8-Last crime format issue	9.15	27.00	55.00

NOTE: No. 9-21 contain violent, gruesome stories with blood, dismemberment, decapitation, E.C. style plot twists and several E.C. swipes. Bondage c-4, 6, 18, 19.

	GD25	FN65	NM94
9-11,13	23.00	69.00	160.00
12-Morphine drug story "The Big Dope"	24.00	73.00	170.00
14-Tothish art by Ross Andru; electrocution-c	23.00	69.00	160.00
15-B&W & color illos in **POP**	22.00	66.00	155.00
16-E.C. story swipe/Haunt of Fear #19; Tothish-a by Ross Andru; bondage-c	24.00	73.00	170.00
17-Wildey E.C. swipe/Shock SuspenStories #9; knife through neck-c (1/54)	24.00	73.00	170.00
18,19: 19-Bondage/torture-c	22.00	66.00	155.00
20-Decapitation cover; contains hanging, ax murder, blood & violence	19.00	118.00	275.00
21-E.C. swipe	19.00	56.00	130.00

NOTE: Cameron a-4, 5, 8. Hollingsworth a-3-7, 9, 10, 13. Wildey a-6, 15, 16.

FIGHT AGAINST THE GUILTY (Formerly Fight Against Crime)
No. 22, Dec, 1954 - No. 23, Mar, 1955
Story Comics

	GD25	FN65	NM94
22-Tothish-a by Ross Andru; Ditko-a; E.C. story swipe; electrocution-c (Last pre-code)	19.00	56.00	130.00
23-Hollingsworth-a	14.00	43.00	100.00

FIGHT COMICS
Jan, 1940 - No. 83, 11/52; No. 84, Wint, 1952-53; No. 85, Spring, 1953;
No. 86, Summer, 1954
Fiction House Magazines

	GD25	FN65	NM94
1-Origin Spy Fighter, Starring Saber; Jack Dempsey life story; Shark Brodie & Chip Collins begin; Fine-c; Eisner-a	225.00	675.00	1800.00
2-Joe Louis life story; Fine/Eisner-c	96.00	290.00	775.00
3-Rip Regan, the Power Man begins (3/40)	68.00	206.00	550.00
4,5: 4-Fine-c	56.00	168.00	450.00
6-10: 6,7-Powell-c	43.00	128.00	340.00
11-14: Rip Regan ends	40.00	120.00	300.00
15-1st app. Super American plus-c (10/41)	53.00	159.00	425.00
16-Captain Fight begins (12/41); Spy Fighter ends	53.00	159.00	425.00
17,18: Super American ends	41.00	124.00	330.00
19-Captain Fight ends; Senorita Rio begins (6/42), origin & 1st app.); Rip Carson, Chute Trooper begins	41.00	124.00	330.00
20	38.00	114.00	265.00
21-30	26.00	77.00	180.00
31,33-50: 31-Decapitation-c. 44-Capt. Fight returns. 48-Used in Love and			

	GD25	FN65	NM94
Death by Legman. 49-Jungle-c begin, end #81	21.00	64.00	150.00
32-Tiger Girl begins (6/44, 1st app.?)	24.00	71.00	165.00
51-Origin Tiger Girl; Patsy Pin-Up app.	36.00	107.00	250.00
52-60,62-64-Last Baker issue	17.00	49.00	115.00
61-Origin Tiger Girl retold	21.00	64.00	150.00
65-78: 78-Used in **POP**, pg. 99	16.00	47.00	110.00
79-The Space Rangers app.	16.00	47.00	110.00
80-85: 81-Last jungle-c. 82-85-War-c/stories	13.50	41.00	95.00
86-Two Tigerman stories by Evans-r/Rangers Comics #40,41; Moreira-r/ Rangers Comics #45	13.50	41.00	95.00

NOTE: Bondage covers, Lingerie, headlights panels are common. Captain Fight by Kamen-51-66. Kayo Kirby by Baker-#43-64, 67(not by Baker). Senorita Rio by Kamen-#57-64; by Grandenetti-#65, 66. Tiger Girl by Baker-#36-60, 62-64; Eisner-c 1-3, 5, 10, 11. Kamen a-54?, 57? Tuska a-1, 5, 8, 10, 21, 29, 34. Whitman c-73-84. Zolnerwich c-16, 17, 22. Power Man c-5, 6, 9. Super American c-15-17. Tiger Girl c-49-81.

FIGHT FOR FREEDOM
1949, 1951 (Giveaway, 16 pgs.)
National Association of Mfgrs./General Comics

	GD25	FN65	NM94
nn-Dan Barry-c/a; used in **POP**, pg. 102	5.85	17.50	35.00

FIGHT FOR LOVE
1952 (no month)
United Features Syndicate

	GD25	FN65	NM94
nn-Abbie & Slats newspaper-r	10.00	30.00	60.00

FIGHTING AIR FORCE (See United States Fighting Air Force)

FIGHTIN' AIR FORCE (Formerly Sherlock Holmes?; Never Again? War and Attack #54 on)
No. 3, Feb, 1956 - No. 53, Feb-Mar, 1966
Charlton Comics

	GD25	FN65	NM94
V1#3	5.85	17.50	35.00
4-10	4.00	10.00	20.00
11(3/58, 68 pgs.)	4.00	11.00	22.00
12 (100 pgs.)	4.35	13.00	26.00
13-30: 13,24-Glanzman-a. 24-Glanzman-c	3.20	8.00	16.00
31-50: 50-American Eagle begins	2.20	5.50	11.00
51-53	1.40	3.50	7.00

FIGHTIN' ARMY (Formerly Soldier and Marine Comics) (See Captain Willy Schultz)
No. 16, 1/56 - No. 127, 12/76; No. 128, 9/77 - No. 172, 11/84
Charlton Comics

	GD25	FN65	NM94
16	5.85	17.50	35.00
17-19,21-23,25-30	3.60	9.00	18.00
20-Ditko-a	5.00	15.00	30.00
24 (3/58, 68 pgs.)	4.00	10.00	20.00
31-45	3.20	8.00	16.00
46-60	1.65	4.20	10.00
61-80: 75-92-The Lonely War of Willy Schultz	1.00	2.00	5.00
81-172: 89,90,92-Ditko-a; Devil Brigade in #79,82,83		1.00	2.50
108(Modern Comics-1977)-Reprint			1.50

NOTE: Aparo c-154. Montes/Bache a-48, 49, 51, 69, 75, 76, 170r.

FIGHTING AMERICAN
Apr-May, 1954 - No. 7, Apr-May, 1955
Headline Publications/Prize (Crestwood)

	GD25	FN65	NM94
1-Origin & 1st app. Fighting American & Speedboy (Capt. America & Bucky clones); S&K-c/a(3); 1st super hero satire series	150.00	450.00	1200.00
2-S&K-a(3)	75.00	215.00	575.00
3,4-S&K-a(3)	58.00	176.00	470.00
5-S&K-a(2); Kirby/?-a	58.00	176.00	470.00
6-Origin-r (4 pgs.) plus 2 pgs. by S&K	56.00	168.00	450.00
7-Kirby-a	50.00	150.00	400.00

NOTE: Simon & Kirby covers on all. 6 is last pre-code issue.

FIGHTING AMERICAN
Oct, 1966 (25¢)

Fighting Leathernecks #3 © TOBY

The Fighting Man #1 © AJAX

Fighting Yank #14 © Nedor

	GD25	FN65	NM94

Harvey Publications

1-Origin Fighting American & Speedboy by S&K-r; S&K-c/a(3); 1 pg. Neal Adams ad — 2.85 / 8.50 / 20.00

FIGHTING AMERICAN
Feb, 1994 - No. 6, 1994 ($1.50, limited series)
DC Comics

1-6			1.50

FIGHTING CARAVANS (See Zane Grey 4-Color 632)

FIGHTING DANIEL BOONE
1953
Avon Periodicals

nn-Kinstler-c/a, 22 pgs.	17.00	49.00	115.00
I.W. Reprint #1-Reprints #1 above; Kinstler-c/a; Lawrence/Alascia-a	1.70	5.00	12.00

FIGHTING DAVY CROCKETT (Formerly Kit Carson)
No. 9, Oct-Nov, 1955
Avon Periodicals

9-Kinstler-c	9.15	27.00	55.00

FIGHTIN' FIVE, THE (Fightin' 5 #40 on?; formerly Space War) (Also see The Peacemaker)
July, 1964 - No. 41, Jan, 1967; No. 42, Oct, 1981 - No. 49, Dec, 1982
Charlton Comics

V2#28-Origin & 1st app. Fightin' Five	3.75	11.25	30.00
29-39,41	2.60	7.50	18.00
40-Peacemaker begins (1st app.)	3.75	11.25	28.00
42-49: Reprints	.80		2.00

FIGHTING FRONTS!
Aug, 1952 - No. 5, Jan, 1953
Harvey Publications

1	7.50	22.50	45.00
2-Extreme violence; Nostrand/Powell-a	8.35	25.00	50.00
3-5: 3-Powell-a	4.00	12.00	24.00

FIGHTING INDIAN STORIES (See Midget Comics)

FIGHTING INDIANS OF THE WILD WEST!
Mar, 1952 - No. 2, Nov, 1952
Avon Periodicals

1-Geronimo, Chief Crazy Horse, Chief Victorio, Black Hawk begin; Larsen-a; McCann-a(2)	12.00	36.00	85.00
2-Kinstler-c & inside-c only; Larsen, McCann-a	9.15	27.00	55.00
100 Pg. Annual (1952, 25¢)-Contains three comics rebound; Geronimo, Chief Crazy Horse, Chief Victorio; Kinstler-c	26.00	77.00	180.00

FIGHTING LEATHERNECKS
Feb, 1952 - No. 6, Dec, 1952
Toby Press

1- "Duke's Diary"; full pg. pin-ups by Sparling	11.50	34.00	80.00
2- "Duke's Diary"	10.00	30.00	60.00
3-5- "Gil's Gals"; full pg. pin-ups	10.00	30.00	60.00
6-(Same as No. 3-5?)	6.70	20.00	40.00

FIGHTING MAN, THE (War)
May, 1952 - No. 8, July, 1953
Ajax/Farrell Publications(Excellent Publ.)

1	10.00	30.00	60.00
2	4.25	13.00	28.00
3-8	4.00	12.00	24.00
Annual 1 (1952, 25¢, 100 pgs.)	19.00	58.00	135.00

FIGHTIN' MARINES (Formerly The Texan; also see Approved Comics)
No. 15, 8/51 - No. 12, 3/53; No. 14, 5/55 - No. 132, 11/76; No. 133, 10/77 - No. 176, 9/84 (No #13?) (Korean war #1-3)

St. John(Approved Comics)/Charlton Comics No. 14 on

15(#1)-Matt Baker c/a "Leatherneck Jack"; slightly large size; Fightin' Texan No. 16 & 17?	34.00	103.00	240.00
2-1st Canteen Kate by Baker; slightly large size; partial Baker-c	37.00	111.00	260.00
3-9,11-Canteen Kate by Baker; Baker c-#2,3,5-11; 4-Partial Baker-c	19.00	56.00	130.00
10-Matt Baker-c	7.50	22.50	45.00
12-No Baker-a; Last St. John issue?	3.60	9.00	18.00
14 (5/55; 1st Charlton issue; formerly?)-Canteen Kate by Baker; all stories reprinted from #2	13.00	39.00	95.00
15-Baker-c	6.70	20.00	40.00
16,18-20-Not Baker-c	3.00	7.50	15.00
17-Canteen Kate by Baker	11.00	33.00	75.00
21-24	3.00	7.50	15.00
25-(68 pgs.)(3/58)-Check-a?	4.15	12.50	25.00
26-(100 pgs.)(8/58)-Check-a(5)	7.50	22.50	45.00
27-50	2.00	5.00	10.00
51-81,83-100: 78-Shotgun Harker & the Chicken series begin	1.00	2.00	5.00
82-(100 pgs.)	1.30	3.25	8.00
101-122: 122-Pilot issue for "War" title (Fightin' Marines Presents War)		1.20	3.00
123-176			1.50
120(Modern Comics reprint, 1977)			1.50

NOTE: No. 14 & 16 (CC) reprint St. John issues; No. 16 reprints St. John insignia on cover. Colan a-3, 7. Glanzman c/a-92, 94. Montes/Bache a-48, 53, 55, 64, 65, 72-74, 77-83, 176r.

FIGHTING MARSHAL OF THE WILD WEST (See The Hawk)

FIGHTIN' NAVY (Formerly Don Winslow)
No. 74, 1/56 - No. 125, 4-5/66; No. 126, 8/83 - No. 133, 10/84
Charlton Comics

74	5.00	15.00	30.00
75-81	3.20	8.00	16.00
82-Sam Glanzman-a	1.65	4.70	11.00
83-99,101-105,106-125('66)	1.20	3.00	7.00
100	1.30	3.25	8.00
126-133 (1984)			1.50

NOTE: Montes/Bache a-109. Glanzman a-82, 131r.

FIGHTING PRINCE OF DONEGAL, THE (See Movie Comics)

FIGHTIN' TEXAN (Formerly The Texan & Fightin' Marines?)
No. 16, Sept, 1952 - No. 17, Dec, 1952
St. John Publishing Co.

16,17: Tuska-a each. 17-Cameron-c/a	6.35	19.00	38.00

FIGHTING UNDERSEA COMMANDOS (See Undersea Fighting...)
May, 1952 - No. 5, April, 1953 (U.S. Navy frogmen)
Avon Periodicals

1-Cover title is Undersea Fighting... #1 only	10.00	30.00	65.00
2	7.00	21.00	42.00
3-5: 1,3-Ravielli-c. 4-Kinstler-c	6.35	19.00	38.00

FIGHTING WAR STORIES
Aug, 1952 - No. 5, 1953
Men's Publications/Story Comics

1	8.35	25.00	50.00
2-5	4.25	13.00	28.00

FIGHTING YANK (See America's Best Comics & Startling Comics)
Sept, 1942 - No. 29, Aug, 1949
Nedor/Better Publ./Standard

1-The Fighting Yank begins; Mystico, the Wonder Man app; bondage-c	175.00	525.00	1400.00
2	75.00	225.00	600.00
3,4: 4-Schomburg-c begin	59.00	178.00	475.00

Firearm #3 © Malibu

Firebrand #9 © DC

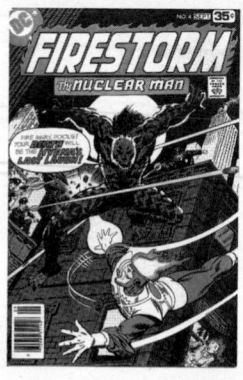

Firestorm #4 © DC

	GD25	FN65	NM94
5-10: 7-Grim Reaper app. 8,10-Bondage/torture-c	45.00	135.00	360.00
11-20: 11-The Oracle app. 12-Hirohito bondage-c. 15-Bondage/torture-c.			
18-The American Eagle app.	40.00	120.00	300.00
21,23,24: 21-Kara, Jungle Princess app. 24-Miss Masque app.			
	40.00	120.00	300.00
22-Miss Masque-c/story	45.00	135.00	360.00
25-Robinson/Meskin-a; strangulation, lingerie panel; The Cavalier app.			
	45.00	135.00	360.00
26-29: All-Robinson/Meskin-a. 28-One pg. Williamson-a			
	40.00	120.00	300.00

NOTE: Schomburg (Xela) c-4-29; airbrush-c 28, 29. Bondage c-1, 4, 8, 10, 11, 12, 15, 17.

FIGHTMAN
June, 1993 ($2.00, one-shot, 52 pgs.)
Marvel Comics

1		.80	2.00

FIGHT THE ENEMY
Aug, 1966 - No. 3, Mar, 1967 (25¢, 68 pgs.)
Tower Comics

1-Lucky 7 & Mike Manly begin	3.20	9.00	21.00
2-Boris Vallejo, McWilliams-a	2.40	7.25	17.00
3-Wood-a (1/2 pg.); McWilliams, Bolle-a	2.40	7.25	17.00

FILM FUNNIES
Nov, 1949 - No. 2, Feb, 1950 (52 pgs.)
Marvel Comics (CPC)

1-Krazy Krow, Wacky Duck	16.00	47.00	110.00
2-Wacky Duck	13.00	39.00	90.00

FILM STARS ROMANCES
Jan-Feb, 1950 - No. 3, May-June, 1950 (True life stories of movie stars)
Star Publications

1-Rudy Valentino & Gregory Peck stories; L. B. Cole-c; lingerie panels			
	38.00	114.00	265.00
2-Liz Taylor/Robert Taylor photo-c & true life story	31.00	94.00	220.00
3-Douglas Fairbanks story; photo-c	21.00	64.00	150.00

FINAL CYCLE, THE
July, 1987 - No. 4, 1988 (Limited series)
Dragon's Teeth Productions

1-4		.80	2.00

FIRE
1993 - No. 2, 1993 ($2.95, B&W, limited series, 52 pgs.)
Caliber Press

1,2-Photo-c		1.20	3.00

FIRE AND BLAST
1952 (Giveaway, 16 pgs., paper-c)
National Fire Protection Assoc.

nn-Mart Baily A-Bomb-c; about fire prevention	15.00	45.00	105.00

FIREARM (Also see Codename: Firearm, Freex #15, Night Man #4 & Prime #10)
Sept, 1993 - No. 18, Mar, 1995 ($1.95/$2.50)
Malibu Comics (Ultraverse)

0 ($14.95)-Came w/ video containing 1st half of story (comic contains 2nd half); 1st app. Duet			15.00
1,3-6: 1-James Robinson scripts begin; Cully Hamner-a; Howard Chaykin-c; 1st app Alec Swan. 3-Intro The Sportsmen; Chaykin-c. 4-Break-Thru x-over; Chaykin-c. 5-1st app. Ellen (Swan's girlfriend); 2 pg. origin of Prime. 6-Prime app. (story cont'd in Prime #10); Brereton-c		.80	2.00
1-($2.50)-Newsstand edition polybagged w/card		1.00	2.50
1-Ultra Limited silver foil-c	1.65	4.20	10.00
2 ($2.50, 44 pgs.)-Hardcase app.;Chaykin-c; Rune flip-c/story by B. Smith			

	GD25	FN65	NM94
(3 pgs.)		1.00	2.50
7-10,12-17: 12-The Rafferty Saga begins, ends #18; 1st app. Rafferty			
15-Night Man & Freex app. 17-Swan marries Ellen		.80	2.00
11-($3.50, 68 pgs.)-Flip book w/Ultraverse Premiere #5		1.40	3.50
18-Death of Rafferty; Chaykin-c		1.00	2.50

NOTE: Brereton c-6. Chaykin c-1-4, 14, 16, 18. Hamner a-1-4. Herrera a-12. James Robinson scripts-0-18.

FIRE BALL XL5 (See Steve Zodiac & The ...)

FIREBRAND (Also see Showcase '96 #4)
Feb, 1996 - No. 9, Oct, 1996 ($1.75)
DC Comics

1-9: Brian Augustyn scripts; Velluto-c/a in all. 9-Daredevil #319-c/swipe			
			1.75

FIRE CHIEF AND THE SAFE OL' FIREFLY, THE
1952 (16 pgs.) (Safety brochure given away at schools)
National Board of Fire Underwriters (produced by American Visuals Corp.) (Eisner)

nn-(Rare) Eisner-c/a	50.00	150.00	400.00

FIREHAIR COMICS (Formerly Pioneer West Romances #3-6; also see Rangers Comics)
Winter/48-49; No. 2, Wint/49-50; No. 7, Spr/51 - No. 11, Spr/52
Fiction House Magazines (Flying Stories)

1-Origin Firehair	47.00	141.00	375.00
2	24.00	73.00	170.00
7-11	17.00	51.00	120.00
I.W. Reprint 8-(nd)-Kinstler-c; reprints Rangers #57; Dr. Drew story by Grandenetti	2.85	8.50	20.00

FIRESTAR
Mar, 1986 - No. 4, June, 1986 (75¢)(From Spider-Man TV series)
Marvel Comics Group

1-X-Men & New Mutants app.		1.20	3.00
2-Wolverine-c (not real Wolverine?); Art Adams-a(p)			
	1.00	2.00	5.00
3,4: 3-Art Adams/Sienkiewicz-c. 4-B. Smith-c		.80	2.00

FIRESTONE (See Donald And Mickey Merry Christmas)

FIRESTORM (See Cancelled Comic Cavalcade, DC Comics Presents, Flash #289, The Fury of... & Justice League of America #179)
March, 1978 - No. 5, Oct-Nov, 1978
DC Comics

1-Origin & 1st app.		1.20	3.00
2-5: 2-Origin Multiplex. 3-Origin & 1st app. Killer Frost. 4-1st app. Hyena			
		.80	2.00

FIRESTORM, THE NUCLEAR MAN (Formerly Fury of Firestorm)
No. 65, Nov, 1987 - No. 100, Aug, 1990
DC Comics

65-99: 66-1st app. Zuggernaut; Firestorm vs. Green Lantern. 71-Death of Capt. X. 67,68-Millennium tie-ins. 83-1st new look			1.00
100-($2.00, 68 pgs.)		1.20	3.00
Annual 5 (10/87)-1st app. new Firestorm			1.25

FIRST ADVENTURES
Dec, 1985 - No. 5, Apr, 1986 ($1.25)
First Comics

..1-5: Blaze Barlow, Whisper & Dynamo Joe in all			1.30

FIRST AMERICANS, THE
No. 843, Sept, 1957
Dell Publishing Co.

Four Color 843-Marsh-a	10.00	30.00	100.00

FIRST CHRISTMAS, THE (3-D)

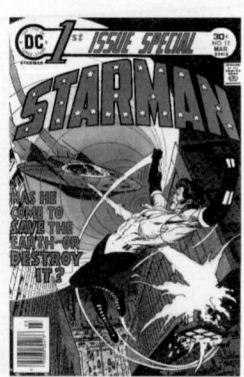

1st Issue Special #12 © DC

Fish Police #4 © MEG

The Flame #2 © FOX

	GD25	FN65	NM94

1953 (25¢, 8-1/4x10-1/4", oversize)(Came w/glasses)
Fiction House Magazines (Real Adv. Publ. Co.)

nn-(Scarce)-Kelly Freas painted-c; Biblical theme, birth of Christ; Nativity-c

	38.00	114.00	265.00

FIRST COMICS GRAPHIC NOVEL
Jan, 1984 - No. 20? (52pgs./176 pgs., high quality paper)
First Comics

1-Beowulf ($5.95)	1.00	2.50	6.00
1-2nd printing ($6.95)	1.20	3.00	7.00
2-Time Beavers ($5.95)	1.00	2.50	6.00
3($11.95, 100 pgs.)-American Flagg! Hard Times (2nd printing exists)			
	1.70	5.00	12.00
4-Nexus ($6.95)-r/B&W 1-3	1.30	3.25	8.00
5-The Enchanted Apples of Oz ($7.95, 52 pgs.)-Intro by Harlan Ellison (1986)			
	1.30	3.25	8.00
6-Elric of Melnibone ($14.95, 176 pgs.)-Reprints with new color			
	2.15	6.50	15.00
7-The Secret Island Of Oz ($7.95)	1.30	3.25	8.00
8-Teenage Mutant Ninja Turtles Book I ($9.95, 132 pgs.)-r/TMNT #1-3 in color			
w/12 pgs. new-a; origin	1.65	4.00	10.00
9-Time 2: The Epiphany by Chaykin (11/86, $7.95, 52pgs. - indicia says #8)			
	1.30	3.25	8.00
10-Teenage Mutant Ninja Turtles Book II ($9.95)-r/TMNT #4-6 in color			
	1.65	4.00	10.00
11-Sailor On The Sea of Fate ($14.95)	2.15	6.50	15.00
nn-Time 2: The Satisfaction of Black Mariah (9/87)	1.30	3.25	8.00
12-American Flagg! Southern Comfort (10/87, $11.95)			
	1.70	5.00	12.00
13-The Ice King Of Oz ($7.95)	1.30	3.25	8.00
14-Teenage Mutant Ninja Turtles Book III ($9.95)-r/TMNT #7,8 in color plus			
new 12 pg. story	1.65	4.00	10.00
15-Hex Breaker: Badger ($7.95, 68 pgs.)	1.30	3.25	8.00
16-The Forgotten Forest of Oz ($8.95)	1.50	3.75	9.00
17-Mazinger (68 pgs., $8.95)	1.50	3.75	9.00
18-Teenage Mutant Ninja Turtles Book IV ($9.95)-r/TMNT #10,11 plus 3 pg.			
fold-out	1.65	4.00	10.00
19-The Original Nexus Graphic Novel ($7.95, 104 pgs.)-Reprints First Comics			
Graphic Novel #4 ($7.95)	1.30	3.25	8.00
20-American Flagg!: State of the Union; r/A.F. 7-9 ($11.95, 96 pgs.)			
	1.70	5.00	12.00

NOTE: Most or all issues have been reprinted.

1ST FOLIO (The Joe Kubert School Presents...)
Mar, 1984 ($1.50, one-shot)
Pacific Comics

1-Joe Kubert-c/a(2 pgs.); Adam & Andy Kubert-a			1.50

1ST ISSUE SPECIAL
Apr, 1975 - No. 13, Apr, 1976 (Try out series)
National Periodical Publications

1-7,9-12: 1-Intro. Atlas; Kirby-c/a/script. 2-Green Team (see Cancelled Comic Cavalcade). 3-Metamorpho by Ramona Fraden. 4-Lady Cop. 5-Manhunter; Kirby-c/a/script. 6-Dingbats; Kirby-c/a/script. 7-The Creeper by Ditko(c/a). 9-Dr. Fate; Kubert-c; Simonson-a. 10-The Outsiders. 11-Code Name: Assassin; Grell-c. 12-Origin/1st app. "Blue" Starman (2nd app. in Starman, 2nd Series #3); Kubert-c.

		1.20	3.00

8,13: 8-Origin/1st app. The Warlord; Grell-c/a (11/75). 13-Return of the New Gods; Darkseid app.; 1st new costume Orion; predates New Gods #12 by more than a year

	1.30	3.25	8.00

FIRST KISS
Dec, 1957 - No. 40, Jan, 1965
Charlton Comics

V1#1	2.85	8.50	20.00
V1#2-10	1.65	4.20	10.00

		1.00	2.00	5.00
11-40		1.00	2.00	5.00

FIRST LOVE ILLUSTRATED
2/49 - No. 9, 6/50; No. 10, 1/51 - No. 86, 3/58; No. 87, 9/58 - No. 88, 11/58; No. 89, 11/62, No. 90, 2/63
Harvey Publications(Home Comics)(True Love)

1-Powell-a(2)	13.00	39.00	90.00
2-Powell-a	7.70	23.00	46.00
3-"Was I Too Fat To Be Loved" story	7.70	23.00	46.00
4-10	4.25	13.00	28.00
11-30: 13-"I Joined a Teen-age Sex Club" story. 30-Lingerie panel			
	4.00	10.50	21.00
31-34,37,39-49: 49-Last pre-code (2/55)	3.00	7.50	15.00
35-Used in SOTI, illo "The title of this comic book is First Love"			
	14.00	43.00	100.00
36-Communism story, "Love Slaves"	4.00	12.00	24.00
38-Nostrand-a	5.00	15.00	30.00
50-90	2.80	7.00	14.00

NOTE: Disbrow a-13. Orlando c-87. Powell a-1, 3-5, 7, 10, 11, 13-17, 19-24, 26-29, 33,35-41, 43, 45, 46, 50, 54, 55, 57, 58, 61-63, 65, 71-73, 76, 79r, 82, 84, 88.

FIRST MEN IN THE MOON (See Movie Comics)

FIRST ROMANCE MAGAZINE
8/49 - #6, 6/50; #7, 6/51 - #50, 2/58; #51, 9/58 - #52, 11/58
Home Comics(Harvey Publ.)/True Love

1	11.50	34.00	80.00
2	7.00	21.00	42.00
3-5	5.35	16.00	32.00
6-10	4.25	13.00	26.00
11-20	3.60	9.00	18.00
21-27,29-32: 32-Last pre-code issue (2/55)	3.00	7.50	15.00
28-Nostrand-a(Powell swipe)	4.25	13.00	26.00
33-52	2.40	6.00	12.00

NOTE: Powell a-1-5, 8-10, 14, 18, 20-22, 24, 25, 28, 36, 46, 48, 51.

FIRST TRIP TO THE MOON (See Space Adventures No. 20)

FISH POLICE (Inspector Gill of the...#2, 3)
Dec, 1985 - No. 11, Nov, 1987 ($1.50, B&W)
V2#5, April, 1988 - V2#17, May, 1989 ($1.75, color)
No. 18, Aug, 1989 - No. 26, Dec, 1990 ($2.25, B&W)
Fishwrap Productions/Comico V2#5-17/Apple Comics #18 on

1		1.20	3.00
1-2nd print (5/86)			1.50
2		1.00	2.00
2-2nd print			1.50
3-11			1.50
V2#5-17-(Color): V2#5-11. 12-17, new-a		1.25	2.50
18-26 ($2.25-c, B&W) 18-Origin Inspector Gill		1.00	2.00
Special 1($2.50, 7/87, Comico)		1.25	2.50
Graphic Novel: The Hairball Saga (r/1-4, color)	1.35	4.00	8.00

FISH POLICE
V2#1, Oct, 1992 - No. 6, Mar, 1993 ($1.25)
Marvel Comics

V2#1-6: 1-Hairballs Saga begins; r/#1 (1985)			1.25

5-STAR SUPER-HERO SPECTACULAR (See DC Special Series No. 1)

FLAME, THE (See Big 3 & Wonderworld Comics)
Summer, 1940 - No. 8, Jan, 1942 (#1,2: 68 pgs.; #3-8: 44 pgs.)
Fox Features Syndicate

1-Flame stories reprinted from Wonderworld #5-9; origin The Flame; Lou Fine-a (36 pgs.), r/Wonderworld #3,10

	287.00	862.00	2300.00
2-Fine-a(2); Wing Turner by Tuska	120.00	361.00	965.00
3-8: 3-Powell-a	80.00	240.00	640.00

FLAME, THE (Formerly Lone Eagle)

Flaming Carrot #15 © Bob Burden

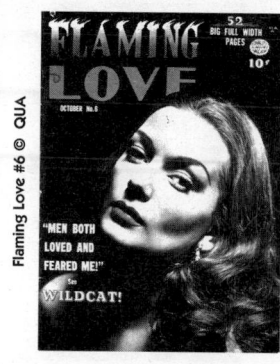

Flaming Love #6 © QUA

Flash #110 (1st Series) © DC

FL

	GD25	FN65	NM94

No. 5, Dec-Jan, 1954-55 - No. 3, April-May, 1955
Ajax/Farrell Publications (Excellent Publ.)

5(#1)-1st app. new Flame		34.00	103.00	240.00
2,3		24.00	71.00	165.00

FLAMING CARROT (...Comics #6? on; see Anything Goes, Cerebus, Teenage
Mutant Ninja Turtles/Flaming Carrot Crossover & Visions)
5/84 - No. 5, 1/85; No. 6, 3/85 - Present? ($1.70/$2.00, B&W)
Aardvark-Vanaheim/Renegade Press #6-17/Dark Horse #18 on

1-Bob Burden story/art		6.00	18.00	42.00
2		3.30	10.00	23.00
3		2.30	6.70	16.00
4-6		1.65	4.70	11.00
7-9		1.20	3.00	7.00
10-12		1.00	2.00	5.00
13-15			1.20	3.00
15-Variant without cover price		1.00	2.00	5.00
16-20: 18-1st Dark Horse issue			1.20	3.00
21-23,25: 25-Contains trading cards; TMNT app.			.80	2.00
24-(2.50, 52 pg.)-10th anniversary issue			1.00	2.50
26-28: 26-Begin $2.25-c. 26,27-Teenage Mutant Ninja Turtles x-over.				
27-Todd McFarlane-c			.90	2.25
29,31-(2.50-c)			1.00	2.50

FLAMING CARROT COMICS (Also see Junior Carrot Patrol)
Summer-Fall, 1981 ($1.95, one shot) (Large size, 8-1/2x11")
Killian Barracks Press

1-Bob Burden-c/a/scripts; serially numbered to 6500				
		9.30	28.00	65.00

FLAMING LOVE
Dec, 1949 - No. 6, Oct, 1950 (Photo covers #2-6) (52 pgs.)
Quality Comics Group (Comic Magazines)

1-Ward-c/a (9 pgs.)		31.00	94.00	220.00
2		13.00	39.00	90.00
3-Ward-a (9 pgs.); Crandall-a		22.00	66.00	155.00
4-6: 4-Gustavson-a		11.50	34.00	80.00

FLAMING WESTERN ROMANCES (Formerly Target Western Romances)
No. 3, Mar-Apr, 1950
Star Publications

3-Robert Taylor, Arlene Dahl photo on-c with biographies inside; L. B. Cole-c				
		34.00	103.00	240.00

FLARE (Also see Champions for 1st app. & League of Champions)
Nov, 1988 - No. 3, Jan, 1989 ($2.75, color, 52 pgs)
V2#1, Nov, 1990 - No. 7, Nov, 1991 ($2.95/$3.50, color, mature, 52 pgs.)
V2#8, Oct, 1992 - No. 16, Feb, 1994 ($3.50/$3.95, B&W, mature, 36 pgs.)
Hero Comics/Hero Graphics Vol. 2 on

1-3			1.10	2.75
V2#1-3,16 ($2.95)			1.20	3.00
V2#4-6,8-10: 4-Begin $3.50-c. 5-Eternity Smith returns. 6-Intro The Tigress				
			1.40	3.50
V2#7,11-15 ($3.50)			1.60	4.00
Annual 1(1992, $4.50, B&W, 52 pgs.)-Champions-r			1.80	4.50

FLARE ADVENTURES
Feb, 1992 - No. 12, 1993? ($3.50/$3.95)
Hero Graphics

1 (90¢, color, 20 pgs.)				1.00
2-7 ($3.50)-Flip books w/Champions Classics			1.40	3.50
8-12 ($3.95)-Flip books w/Champions Classics			1.60	4.00

FLASH, THE (See Adventure, The Brave and the Bold, Crisis On Infinite Earths, DC Comics
Presents, DC Special, DC Special Series, DC Super-Stars, Green Lantern, Justice League of
America, Showcase, Super Team Family, & World's Finest)

FLASH, THE (1st Series)(Formerly Flash Comics)(See Showcase #4,8,13,14)

(Also see Justice League of America)
No. 105, Feb-Mar, 1959 - No. 350, Oct, 1985
National Periodical Publ./DC

	GD25	FN65	VF82	NM94
105-(2-3/59)-Origin Flash(retold), & Mirror Master (1st app.)				
	375.00	1125.00	2812.00	4800.00

	GD25	FN65		NM94
106-Origin Grodd & Pied Piper; Flash's 1st visit to Gorilla City; begin Grodd				
the Super Gorilla trilogy (Scarce)	130.00	390.00		1300.00
107-Grodd trilogy, part 2	72.00	217.00		700.00
108-Grodd trilogy ends	68.00	202.00		600.00
109-2nd app. Mirror Master	53.00	160.00		450.00
110-Intro/origin The Weather Wizard & Kid Flash who later becomes Flash				
in Crisis On Infinite Earths #12; begin Kid Flash trilogy, ends #112 (also				
in #114,116,118)	115.00	345.00		1150.00
111-2nd Kid Flash tryout; Cloud Creatures	38.00	112.00		330.00
112-Origin & 1st app. Elongated Man (4-5/60); also apps. in #115,119,130				
	45.00	135.00		385.00
113-Origin & 1st app. Trickster	39.00	118.00		340.00
114-Captain Cold app. (see Showcase #8)	34.00	101.00		250.00
115,116,118-120: 119-Elongated Man marries Sue Dearborn. 120-Flash &				
Kid Flash team-up for 1st time	25.00	75.00		190.00
117-Origin & 1st app. Capt. Boomerang; 1st & only S.A. app. Winky Blinky &				
Noddy	34.00	103.00		260.00
121,122: 122-Origin & 1st app. The Top	18.00	54.00		140.00
123-(9/61)-Re-intro. Golden Age Flash; origins of both Flashes; 1st mention of				
an Earth II where DC G. A. heroes live	100.00	300.00		1000.00
124-Last 10¢ issue	16.00	47.00		120.00
125-128,130: 127-Return of Grodd-c/story. 128-Origin & 1st app. Abra Kadabra				
	15.00	45.00		115.00
129-2nd G.A. Flash x-over; J.S.A. cameo in flashback (1st S.A. app. G.A.				
Green Lantern, Hawkman, Atom, Black Canary & Dr. Mid-Nite)				
	36.00	109.00		270.00
131-136,138,140: 130-(7/62)-1st Gauntlet of Super-Villains (Mirror Master,				
Capt. Cold, The Top, Capt. Boomerang & Trickster). 131-Early Green				
Lantern x-over (9/62). 135-1st app. of Kid Flash's yellow costume (3/63).				
136-1st Dexter Miles. 140-Origin & 1st app. Heat Wave				
	15.00	45.00		115.00
137-G.A. Flash x-over; J.S.A. cameo (1st real app. since 2-3/51);				
1st S.A. app. Vandall Savage & Johnny Thunder; JSA team decides to re-				
form	47.00	141.00		400.00
139-Origin & 1st app. Prof. Zoom	17.00	51.00		125.00
141-150: 142-Trickster app.	11.00	33.00		80.00
151-Engagement of Barry Allen & Iris West; G.A. Flash vs. The Shade.				
	13.50	41.00		100.00
152-159	7.50	22.00		55.00
160-(80-Pg. Giant G-21); G.A. Flash & Johnny Quick-r				
	10.00	30.00		80.00
161-168,170: 165-Silver Age Flash weds Iris West. 167-New facts about				
Flash's origin. 168-Green Lantern-c/story. 170-Dr. Mid-Nite, Dr. Fate,				
G.A. Flash x-over	7.00	21.00		50.00
169-(80-Pg. Giant G-34)-New facts about origin	10.00	30.00		80.00
171-174,176,177,179,180: 171-JLA, Green Lantern, Atom flashbacks. 173-G.A.				
Flash x-over. 174-Barry Allen reveals I.D. to wife. 179-(5/68)-Flash travels to				
Earth -Prime and meets DC editor Julie Schwartz; 1st unnamed app.				
Earth-Prime (See Justice League of America #123 for 1st named app. & 3rd				
app. overall)	5.50	17.00		45.00
175-2nd Superman/Flash race (12/67) (See Superman #199 & World's Finest				
#198,199); JLA cameo; gold kryptonite used (on J'onn J'onzz impersonating				
Superman)	17.00	49.00		120.00
178-(80-Pg. Giant G-46)	7.50	22.50		65.00
181-186,188-195,197-200: 186-Re-intro. Sargon	3.75	11.25		28.00
187,196: (68-Pg. Giants G-58, G-70)	5.50	17.00		45.00
201-204,206-210: 201-New G.A. Flash story. 208-52 pg. begins, end #213,				
215,216. 206-Elongated Man app.	2.00	6.00		14.00
205-(68-Pg. Giant G-82)	3.75	11.25		30.00

229

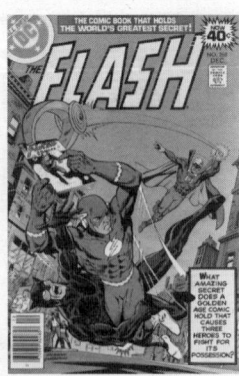

Flash #268 (1st Series) © DC

Flash #112 (2nd Series) © DC

Flash Annual #9 (2nd Series) © DC

	GD25	FN65	NM94

211-213,216,220: 211-G.A. Flash origin-r/#104. 213-Reprints #137. 220-1st app.
Turtle since Showcase 4 ... 1.70 ... 5.00 ... 14.00
214-DC 100 Page Super Spectacular DC-11; origin Metal Men-r/Showcase
#37; never before pubbed G.A. Flash story ... 3.60 ... 11.00 ... 25.00
215 (52 pgs.)-Flash-r/Showcase #4; G.A. Flash x-over, reprinted in #216
... 2.85 ... 8.50 ... 20.00
217-219: Neal Adams-a in all. 217-Green Lantern/Green Arrow series begins
(9/72); 2nd G.L. & G.A. team-up series (see Green Lantern #76). 219-Last
Green Arrow ... 2.15 ... 6.50 ... 15.00
221-225,227,228,230,231,233: 222-G. Lantern x-over. 228-(7-8/74)-Flash writer
Cary Bates travels to Earth-One & meets Flash, Iris West & Trickster; 2nd
unnamed app. Earth-Prime (See Justice League of America #123 for 1st
named app. & 3rd app. overall) ... 1.20 ... 3.00 ... 7.00
226-Neal Adams-a ... 1.65 ... 4.20 ... 10.00
229,232-(100 pg. issues)-G.A. Flash-r & new-a ... 1.70 ... 5.00 ... 12.00
234-288,290: 235-Green Lantern x-over. 243-Death of The Top. 245-Origin The
Floronic Man in Green Lantern back-up, ends #246. 246-Last Green Lantern
256-Death of The Top retold. 250-Intro Golden Glider. 265-267-(44 pgs.).
267-Origin of Flash's uniform. 270-Intro The Clown. 275,276-Iris West Allen
dies. 286-Intro/origin Rainbow Raider ... 1.40 ... 3.50
289-1st Perez DC art (Firestorm); new Firestorm back-up series begins (9/80),
ends #302 ... 1.20 ... 2.40 ... 6.00
291-299,301-305: 291-1st app. Saber-Tooth (villain). 295-Gorilla Grodd-c/story.
298-Intro/origin new Shade. 301-Atomic bomb-c. 303-The Top returns. 304-
Intro/origin Colonel Computron; 305-G.A. Flash x-over ... 1.20 ... 3.00
300-(52 pgs.)-Origin Flash retold; 25th ann. issue ... 1.00 ... 2.00 ... 5.00
306-Dr. Fate by Giffen begins, ends #313 ... 1.20 ... 3.00
307-349: 307-313-Giffen-a. 309-Origin Flash retold. 318-323-Creeper back-ups.
323,324-Two part Flash vs. Flash story. 324-Death of Reverse Flash (Prof.
Zoom). 328-Iris West Allen's death retold. 344-Origin Kid Flash
... 1.00 ... 2.50
350-Double size ($1.25) ... 1.00 ... 2.50
Annual 1(10-12/63, 84 pgs.)-Origin Elongated Man & Kid Flash-r; origin Grodd;
G.A. Flash-r ... 38.50 ... 115.50 ... 385.00

NOTE: **N. Adams** c-194, 195, 203, 204, 206-208, 211, 213, 215, 246. **M. Anderson** a-202i.
Austin a-233i, 234i, 246i. **Buckler** a-271p, 272p; c(p)-247-250, 252, 253p, 255, 256p, 258, 262,
265-267, 269-271. **Giffen** a-306-313p; c-310p, 315. **Sid Greene** a-167-174i, 229(r). **Grell** a-
237p, 238p, 240-243p; c-236. **Infantino/Anderson** a-135. c-135, 201. **Infantino/Giella** c-105-
112. **G. Kane** a-195p, 197-199p, 229r, 232r; c-197-199, 312p. **Kubert** a-108p, 215i(r); c-189-
191. **Lopez** c-272. **Meskin** a-229r, 232r. **Perez** a-289-293p; c-293. **Starlin** a-294-296p. **Staton**
c-263p, 264p. Green Lantern x-over-131, 143, 168, 171, 191.

FLASH (2nd Series)(See Crisis on Infinite Earths #12)(Also see Justice League
Europe)
June, 1987 - Present (75¢/$1.00/$1.50/$1.75)
DC Comics

1-Guice-c/a begins; New Teen Titans app. ... 1.00 ... 2.00 ... 5.00
2,3: 3-Intro. Kilgore ... 1.20 ... 3.00
4-10: 5-Intro. Speed McGee. 7-1st app. Blue Trinity. 8,9-Millennium tie-ins.
9-1st app. The Chunk ... 1.00 ... 2.50
11-65: 12-Free extra 16 pg. Dr. Light story. 19-Free extra 16 pg. Flash
story. 28-Capt. Cold app. 29-New Phantom Lady app. 40-Dr. Alchemy app.
50-($1.75, 52 pgs.). 62-Flash: Year One begins, ends #65. 65-Last $1.00-c
... .80 ... 2.00
66-78,80-84: 66-Aquaman app. 69,70-Green Lantern app. 70-Gorilla Grodd
story ends. 73-Re-intro Barry Allen & begin saga (Barry Allen revealed as
Reverse Flash in #78). 76-Re-intro of Max Mercury (Quality Comics's
Quicksilver). 80-Regular ed. 81,82-Nightwing & Starfire app. 84-Razer app.
... .80 ... 2.00
79-($2.50, 68 pgs.)-Barry Allen saga ends ... 1.10 ... 2.75
80-($2.50)-Foil-c edition ... 1.10 ... 2.75
0,85-91,93,101: 85-Begin $1.50-c. 94-Zero Hour. 95-"Terminal Velocity" begins,
ends #100. 96,98,99-Kobra app. 97-Origin Max Mercury; Chillblaine app.
... .80 ... 2.00
92-1st Impulse ... 1.30 ... 3.25 ... 8.00
100 ($2.50)-Newstand edition; Kobra & JLA app. ... 1.20 ... 3.00

100 ($3.50)-Foil-c edition; Kobra & JLA app. ... 1.60 ... 4.00
102-130: 102-Mongul app.; begin-$1.75-c. 105-Mirror Master app. 107-Shazam
app. 108-"Dead Heat" begins; 1st app. Savitar. 109-"Dead Heat" Pt. 2
(cont'd in Impulse #10). 110-"Dead Heat" Pt. 4 (cont'd in Impulse #11).
111-"Dead Heat" finale; Savitar disappears into the Speed Force; John Fox
cameo (2nd app.). 112-"Race Against Time" begins, ends #118; re-intro John
Fox; intro new Chillblaine. 113-Tornado Twins app. 119-Final Night x-over
... .70 ... 1.75
Annual 1 (1987, $1.25) ... .80 ... 2.00
Annual 2, 3: 2-(1988, $1.50) 3-(1989, $1.75, 68 pgs.)-Gives history of G.A.,
S.A., & Modern Age Flash in text. ... .70 ... 1.75
Annual 4 (1991, $2.00, 68 pgs.)-Armaggedon 2001 ... .80 ... 2.00
Annual 5 (1992, $2.50, 68 pgs.)-Eclipso-c/story ... 1.00 ... 2.50
Annual 6 (1993, $2.50, 68 pgs.) ... 1.00 ... 2.50
Annual 7 (1994, $2.95)-Elseworlds story ... 1.20 ... 3.00
Annual 8 (1995, $3.50)-Year One story ... 1.40 ... 3.50
Annual 9 (1996, $2.95)-Legends of the Dead Earth story; J.H. Williams-a(p);
Mick Gray-a(i) ... 3.00
Special 1 (1990, $2.95, 84 pgs.)-50th anniversary issue; Kubert-c; 1st Flash
story by Mark Waid; 1st app. John Fox (27th Century Flash).
... 1.20 ... 3.00
TV Special 1 (1991, $3.95, 76 pgs.)-Photo-c plus behind the scenes photos
of TV show; Saltares-a, Byrne scripts ... 1.60 ... 4.00
Terminal Velocity (1996, TPB)-r/#95-100.
The Return of Barry Allen (1996, $12.95, TPB)-r/#74-79. ... 13.00
NOTE: **Guice** a-1-9p, 11p, Annual 1p; c-1-9p, Annual 1p. **Perez** c-15-17, Annual 2i. **Travest
Charest** c/a-Annual 5p.

FLASH COMICS (Whiz Comics No. 2 on)
Jan, 1940 (12 pgs., B&W, regular size)
(Not distributed to newsstands; printed for in-house use)
Fawcett Publications

NOTE: Whiz Comics #2 was preceded by two books, Flash Comics and Thrill Comics, both
dated Jan, 1940, (12 pgs., B&W, regular size) and were not distributed. These two books are
identical except for the title and were sent out to major distributors as ad copies to promote
sales. It is believed that the complete 68 page issue of Fawcett's Flash and Thrill Comics #1
was finished and ready for publication with the January date. Since DC Comics was also about
to publish a book with the same date and title, Fawcett hurriedly printed up the black and white
version of Flash Comics to secure copyright before DC The inside covers are blank, with the
covers and inside pages printed on a high quality uncoated paper stock. The eight page origin
story of Captain Thunder is composed of pages 1-7 and 13 of the Captain Marvel story essentially as they appeared in the first issue of Whiz Comics. The balloon dialogue on page thirteen
was relettered to tie the story into the end of page seven in Flash and Thrill Comics to produce
a shorter version of the origin story for copyright purposes. Obviously, DC acquired the copyright
and Fawcett dropped Flash as well as Thrill and came out with Whiz Comics a month later.
Fawcett never used the cover to Flash and Thrill #1, designing a new cover for Whiz Comics.
Fawcett also must have discovered that Captain Thunder had already been used by another
publisher (Captain Terry Thunder by Fiction House). All references to Captain Thunder were
relettered to Captain Marvel before appearing in Whiz.

1 (nn or-c, #1 on inside)-Origin & 1st app. Captain Thunder. Eight copies of
Flash and three copies of Thrill exist. All 3 copies of Thrill sold in 1986 for
between $4,000-$10,000 each. A NM copy of Thrill sold in 1987 for
$12,000. A vg copy of Thrill sold in 1987 for $9000 cash; another copy
sold in 1987 for $2000 cash, $10,000 trade; cover by Leo O'Mealia

FLASH COMICS (The Flash No. 105 on) (Also see All-Flash)
Jan, 1940 - No. 104, Feb, 1949
National Periodical Publications/All-American

	GD25	FN65	VF82	NM94

1-The Flash (origin/1st app.) by Harry Lampert, Hawkman (origin/1st app.) by
Gardner Fox, The Whip, & Johnny Thunder (origin/1st app.) by Stan Asch;
Cliff Cornwall by Moldoff, Flash Picture Novelets (later Minute Movies w/#12)
begin; Moldoff (Shelly) cover; 1st app. Shiera Sanders who later becomes
Hawkgirl, #24; reprinted in Famous First Edition (on sale 11/10/39);
The Flash-c ... 5000.00 ... 15,000.00 ... 30,000.00 ... 50,000.00
(Estimated up to 75+ total copies exist, 7 in NM/Mint)
1-Reprint, Oversize 13-1/2x10". WARNING: This comic is an exact reprint of the
original except for its size. DC published it in 1974 with a second cover titling it as a Famous First

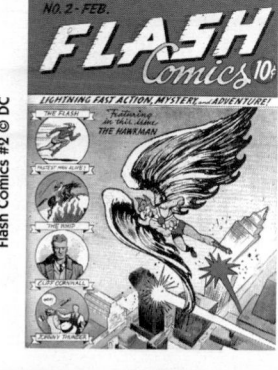

Flash Comics #2 © DC

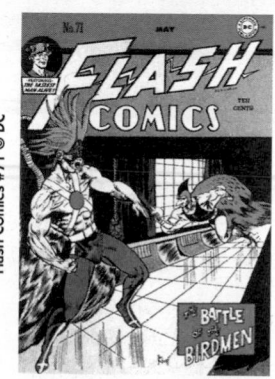

Flash Comics #71 © DC

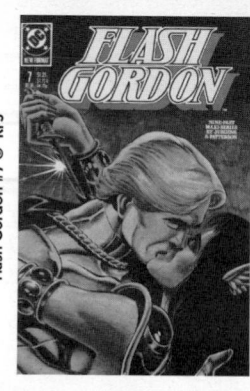

Flash Gordon #7 © KFS

	GD25	FN65	NM94

Edition. There have been many reported cases of the outer cover being removed and the interior sold as the original edition. The reprint with the new outer cover removed is practically worthless. See Famous First Edition for value.

	GD25	FN65	NM94
2-Rod Rian begins, ends #11; Hawkman	556.00	1667.00	5500.00
3-King Standish begins (1st app.), ends #41 (called The King #16-37,39-41); E.E. Hibbard-a begins on Flash	422.00	1267.00	4200.00
4-Moldoff (Shelly) Hawkman begins; The Whip-c	333.00	1000.00	3300.00
5-The King-c	325.00	975.00	2800.00
6-2nd Flash-c (alternates w/Hawkman #6 on)	389.00	1167.00	3800.00
7-2nd Hawkman-c; 1st Moldoff Hawkman	333.00	1000.00	3300.00
8-New logo begins	250.00	750.00	2000.00
9,10: 9-Classic Moldoff Hawkman-c; 10-Classic Moldoff Flash-c	267.00	800.00	2400.00
11-13,15-20: 12-Les Watts begins; "Sparks" #16 on. 17-Last Cliff Cornwall	162.00	487.00	1300.00
14-classic-c	200.00	600.00	1600.00
21-23	137.00	412.00	1100.00
24-Shiera becomes Hawkgirl (12/41); see All-Star Comics #5 for 1st app.	175.00	525.00	1400.00
25-28,30: 28-Last Les Sparks.	100.00	300.00	800.00
29-Ghost Patrol begins (origin/1st app.), ends #104.	112.00	338.00	900.00
31-40: 33-Origin Shade	89.00	268.00	715.00
41-50	82.00	247.00	660.00
51-61: 59-Last Minute Movies. 61-Last Moldoff Hawkman	71.00	215.00	575.00
62-Hawkman by Kubert begins	92.00	277.00	740.00
63-70: 66-68-Hop Harrigan in all. 70-Mutt & Jeff app.	71.00	215.00	575.00
71-85: 80-Atom begins, ends #104	71.00	215.00	575.00
86-Intro. The Black Canary in Johnny Thunder (8/47); see All-Star #38.	212.00	637.00	1700.00
87-90: 88-Origin Ghost. 89-Intro villain The Thorn	105.00	315.00	840.00
91,93-99: 98-Atom & Hawkman don new costumes	118.00	356.00	950.00
92-1st solo Black Canary plus-c; rare in Mint due to black ink smearing on white-c	275.00	825.00	2200.00
100 (10/48),103(Scarce)-52 pgs. each	275.00	825.00	2200.00
101,102(Scarce)	218.00	656.00	1750.00
104-Origin The Flash retold (Scarce)	556.00	1667.00	5500.00

NOTE: *Irwin Hasen a-Wheaties Giveaway. c-97, Wheaties Giveaway. E.E. Hibbard c-6, 12, 20, 24, 26, 28, 30, 44, 46, 48, 50, 62, 66, 68, 69, 72, 74, 76, 78, 80, 82. Infantino a-86p; 90, 93-95, 99-104; c-90, 92, 93, 97, 99, 101, 103. Kinstler a-87, 89(Hawkman); c-87. Chet Kozlak c-77, 79, 81. Krigstein a-94. Kubert a-62-76, 83, 85, 86, 88-104; c-63, 65, 67, 70, 71, 73, 75, 83, 85, 86, 88, 89, 91, 94, 96, 98, 100, 104. Moldoff a-3; c-3, 7-11, 13-17, plus odd #'s 19-61. Martin Naydell c-52, 54, 56, 58, 60, 64, 84.*

FLASH COMICS
1946 (6-1/2x8-1/4", 32 pgs.)
National Periodical Publications (Wheaties Giveaway)

nn-Johnny Thunder, Ghost Patrol, The Flash & Kubert Hawkman app.; Irwin Hasen-c/a .... 300.00 ... 900.00
NOTE: *All known copies have Wheaties boxes and are never found in mint condition. Copies with light tape residue bring the listed prices in all grades.*

FLASH DIGEST, THE (See DC Special Series #24)

FLASH GORDON (See Defenders Of The Earth, Eat Right to Work..., Giant Comic Album, King Classics, King Comics, March of Comics #118, 133, 142, The Phantom #18, Street Comix & Wow Comics, 1st series)

FLASH GORDON
No. 25, 1941; No. 10, 1943 - No. 512, Nov, 1953
Dell Publishing Co.

	GD25	FN65	NM94
Feature Books 25 (#1)(1941))-r-not by Raymond	70.00	210.00	700.00
Four Color 10(1943)-by Alex Raymond; reprints "The Ice Kingdom"	75.00	225.00	750.00
Four Color 84(1945)-by Alex Raymond; reprints "The Fiery Desert"			

	GD25	FN65	NM94
Four Color 173,190: 190-Bondage-c	37.50	112.50	375.00
Four Color 204,247	13.50	40.50	135.00
Four Color 424-Painted-c	10.50	31.50	105.00
2(5-7/53-Dell)-Painted-c; Evans-a?	8.50	25.50	85.00
Four Color 512-Painted-c	5.00	15.00	50.00
Macy's Giveaway(1943)-(Rare)-20 pgs.; not by Raymond	5.00	15.00	50.00
	56.00	168.00	450.00

FLASH GORDON (See Tiny Tot Funnies)
Oct, 1950 - No. 4, April, 1951
Harvey Publications

	GD25	FN65	NM94
1-Alex Raymond-a; bondage-c; reprints strips from 7/14/40 to 12/8/40	24.00	73.00	170.00
2-Alex Raymond-a; r/strips 12/15/40-4/27/41	18.00	54.00	125.00
3,4-Alex Raymond-a; 3-bondage-c; r/strips 5/4/41-9/21/41. 4-r/strips 10/24/37-3/27/38	16.00	47.00	110.00
5-(Rare)-Small size-5-1/2x8-1/2"; B&W; 32 pgs.; Distributed to some mail subscribers only. Estimated value		$200.00–$300.00	

(Also see All-New No. 15, Boy Explorers No. 2, and Stuntman No. 3)

FLASH GORDON
1951 (16 pgs. in color, regular size, paper-c)
Harvey Comics (Gordon Bread giveaway)

	GD25	FN65	NM94
1,2: r/strips 10/24/37 - 2/1/38. 2-r/strips 7/14/40 - 10/6/40; Reprints by Raymond....	1.50	4.50	10.00

NOTE: *Most copies have brittle edges.*

FLASH GORDON
June, 1965
Gold Key

	GD25	FN65	NM94
1 (1947 reprint)-Painted-c	2.85	8.50	28.00

FLASH GORDON (Also see Comics Reading Libraries)
9/66 - #11, 12/67; #12, 2/69 - #18, 1/70; #19, 10-11/78 - #37, 3/82 (Painted covers No. 19-30, 34)
King #1-11/Charlton #12-18/Gold Key #19-23/Whitman #28 on

	GD25	FN65	NM94
1-1st S.A. app Flash Gordon; Williamson c/a(2); E.C. swipe/Incredible S.F. #32; Mandrake story	4.30	13.00	30.00
1-8: 1-Army giveaway(1968)("Complimentary" on cover)(Same as regular #1 minus Mandrake story & back-c). 2-Bolle, Gil Kane-c; Mandrake story. 3-Williamson-c. 4-Secret Agent X-9 begins, Williamson-c/a(3). 5-Williamson-c/a(2). 6,8-Crandall-a. 7-Raboy-a (last in comics?). 8-Secret Agent X-9-r	2.85	8.50	20.00
9,10-Raymond-r. 10-Buckler's 1st pro work (11/67)	2.60	7.70	18.00
11-Crandall-a	1.90	6.00	13.00
12-Crandall-c/a	2.10	6.50	15.00
13-Jeff Jones-a (15 pgs.)	2.60	7.50	18.00
14-17: 17-Brick Bradford story	1.40	3.50	8.50
18-Kaluta-a (3rd pro work?)(see Teen Confessions)	1.65	4.20	10.00
19(9/78, G.K.), 20-30(10/80)		1.40	3.50
30-37: 30 (7/81; re-issue). 31-33: Movie adaptation; Williamson-a.			
34-37: Movie adaptation		.80	2.00

NOTE: *Aparo a-8. Bolle a-21, 22. Boyette a-14-18. Briggs c-10. Buckler a-10. Crandall c-6. Estrada a-3. Gene Fawcette a-29, 30, 34, 37. McWilliams a-31-33, 36.*

FLASH GORDON
June, 1988 - No. 9, Holiday, 1988-'89 ($1.25, mini-series)
DC Comics

1-9; 1,5-Painted-c			1.25

FLASH GORDON
June, 1995 - No. 2, July, 1995 ($2.95, limited series)
Marvel Comics

1,2: Schultz scripts; Williamson-a		1.20	3.00

FLASH GORDON THE MOVIE
1980 (8-1/4 x 11", $1.95, 68 pgs.)

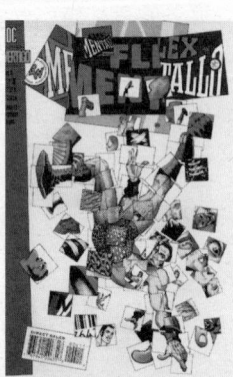

Flex Mentallo #4 © DC

The Flintstones V2#1 © H-B

The Fly #5 © AP

	GD25	FN65	NM94

Western Publishing Co.
| 11294-Williamson-c/a; adapts movie | | .80 | 2.00 |
| 13743-Hardback edition | 1.00 | 2.00 | 5.00 |

FLASH SPECTACULAR, THE (See DC Special Series No. 11)

FLAT-TOP
11/53 - No. 3, 5/54; No. 4, 3/55 - No. 7, 9/55
Mazie Comics/Harvey Publ.(Magazine Publ.) No. 4 on
1-Teenage; Flat-Top, Mazie, Mortie & Stevie begin	4.70	14.00	28.00
2,3	3.20	8.00	16.00
4-7	2.40	6.00	12.00

FLESH & BLOOD
Dec, 1995 ($2.95, B&W, mature)
Brainstorm Comics
| 1-Balent-c; foil-c. | 1.20 | | 3.00 |

FLESH AND BONES
June, 1986 - No. 4, Dec, 1986 (Limited series)
Upshot Graphics (Fantagraphics Books)
| 1-Dalgoda by Fujitake in all | | 1.25 | 2.50 |
| 2-4 Alan Moore scripts (r) in all | | 1.00 | 2.00 |

FLESH CRAWLERS
Aug, 1993 - No. 2, Jan, 1995 ($2.50, B&W, limited series, mature)
Kitchen Sink Press
| 1,2 | | 1.00 | 2.50 |

FLEX MENTALLO (Man of Muscle Mystery) (See Doom Patrol, 2nd Series)
June, 1996 - No. 4, Sept, 1996 ($2.50, limited series, mature)
DC Comics (Vertigo)
| 1-4: Grant Morrison scripts & Frank Quitely-c/a. | | | 2.50 |

FLINTSTONE KIDS, THE (TV) (See Star Comics Digest)
Aug, 1987 - No. 11, Apr, 1989
Star Comics/Marvel Comics #5 on
| 1-11 | | | 1.00 |

FLINTSTONES, THE (TV)(See Dell Giant #48 for No. 1)
No. 2, Nov-Dec, 1961 - No. 60, Sept, 1970 (Hanna-Barbera)
Dell Publ. Co./Gold Key No. 7 (10/62) on
2-2nd app. (TV show debuted on 9/30/60)	9.00	27.00	90.00
3-6(7-8/62): 2-5: 15¢. 6-Begin 12¢ issues	6.50	19.50	65.00
7 (10/62; 1st GK)	5.50	16.50	55.00
8-10: Mr. & Mrs. J. Evil Scientist begin?	4.50	13.50	45.00
11-1st app. Pebbles (6/63)	6.50	19.50	65.00
12-15,17-20	4.00	12.00	40.00
16-1st app. Bamm-Bamm (1/64)	5.50	16.50	55.00
21-30: 24-1st app. The Grusomes	3.20	9.60	32.00
31-33,35-40: 31-Xmas-c. 33-Meet Frankenstein & Dracula. 39-Reprints			
	3.30	9.90	30.00
34-1st app. The Great Gazoo	4.25	12.50	38.00
41-60: 45-Last 12¢ issue	3.15	9.35	28.00
At N. Y. World's Fair('64)-J.W. Books(25¢)-1st printing; no date on-c			
(29¢ version exists, 2nd print?)	5.00	15.00	45.00
At N. Y. World's Fair (1965 on-c; re-issue). NOTE: Warehouse find in 1984			
	1.20	3.00	7.00
Bigger & Boulder 1(#30013-211) (Gold Key Giant, 11/62, 25¢, 84 pgs.)			
	8.00	24.00	80.00
Bigger & Boulder 2-(1966, 25¢)-Reprints B&B No. 1			
	6.50	19.50	65.00
...With Pebbles & Bamm Bamm (100 pgs., G.K.)-30028-511 (paper-c, 25¢)			
(11/65)	7.00	21.00	70.00
NOTE: (See Comic Album #16, Bamm-Bamm & Pebbles Flintstone, Dell Giant 48, Golden Comics Digest, March of Comics #229, 243, 271, 289, 299, 317, 327, 341, Pebbles Flintstone, Top Comics #2-4, and Whitman Comic Books.)

FLINTSTONES, THE (TV)(...& Pebbles)
Nov, 1970 - No. 50, Feb, 1977 (Hanna-Barbera)
Charlton Comics
1	5.50	16.50	38.00
2	2.85	8.50	20.00
3-7,9,10	2.00	6.00	14.00
8- "Flintstones Summer Vacation" (Summer, 1971, 52 pgs.)			
	2.40	7.20	17.00
11-50: 36-Mike Zeck illos (early work). 37-Byrne text illos (early work; see Nightmare #20). 42-Byrne-a (2 pgs.)	1.70	5.00	12.00
(Also see Barney & Betty Rubble, Dino, The Great Gazoo, & Pebbles & Bamm-Bamm)			

FLINTSTONES, THE (TV)(See Yogi Bear, 3rd series)
October, 1977 - No. 9, Feb, 1979 (Hanna-Barbera)
Marvel Comics Group
| 1-9: Yogi Bear app. 4-The Jetsons app. | | .80 | 2.00 |

FLINTSTONES, THE (TV)
Sept, 1992 - No. 13, June, 1994 ($1.25/$1.50) (Hanna-Barbera)
Harvey Comics
V2#1-4			1.25
5-13: 5-Begin $1.50-c			1.50
...Big Book 1,2 (11/92, 3/93; both $1.95, 52 pgs.)		.80	2.00
...Giant Size 1-3 (10/92, 4/93, 11/93; $2.25, 68 pgs.)		.90	2.25

FLINTSTONES, THE (TV)
Sept, 1995 - Present ($1.50)
Archie Publications
| 1-20 | | | 1.50 |

FLINTSTONES CHRISTMAS PARTY, THE (See The Funtastic World of Hanna-Barbera No. 1)

FLIP
April, 1954 - No. 2, June, 1954 (Satire)
Harvey Publications
| 1,2-Nostrand-a each. 2-Powell-a | 21.00 | 62.00 | 145.00 |

FLIPPER (TV)
Apr, 1966 - No. 3, Nov, 1967 (All have photo-c)
Gold Key
| 1 | 5.00 | 15.00 | 50.00 |
| 2,3 | 3.50 | 11.00 | 35.00 |

FLIPPITY & FLOP
12-1/51-52 - No. 46, 8-10/59; No. 47, 9-11/60
National Periodical Publ. (Signal Publ. Co.)
1-Twiddle and Twaddle begin	24.00	73.00	170.00
2	14.00	43.00	100.00
3-5	11.00	33.00	75.00
6-10	10.00	30.00	65.00
11-20: 20-Last precode (3/55)	9.15	27.00	55.00
21-47	7.50	22.50	45.00

FLOATERS
Sept, 1993 - No. 5, Jan, 1994 ($2.50, B&W, limited series)
Dark Horse Comics
| 1-5 | | 1.00 | 2.50 |

FLOOD RELIEF
Jan, 1994 (36 pgs.)(Ordered thru mail w/$5.00 to Red Cross)
Malibu Comics (Ultraverse)
| 1-Hardcase, Prime & Prototype app. | 1.00 | 2.00 | 5.00 |

FLOYD FARLAND (See Eclipse Graphic Album Series #11)

FLY, THE (Also see Adventures of..., Blue Ribbon Comics & Flyman)
May, 1983 - No. 9, Oct, 1984
Archie Enterprises, Inc.

THe Fly #17 © Impact

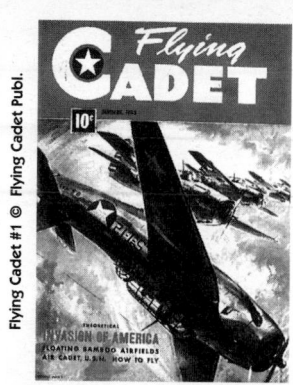

Flying Cadet #1 © Flying Cadet Publ.

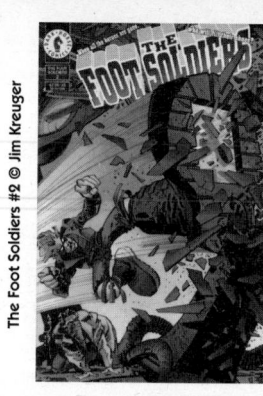

The Foot Soldiers #2 © Jim Kreuger

FO

1-9: 1-Mr. Justice app; origin Shield. 2-Flygirl app.   1.00
NOTE: *Buckler* a-1, 2. *Ditko* a-2-9; c-4-8p. *Nebres* c-3, 4, 5i, 6, 7i. *Steranko* c-1, 2.

FLY, THE
Aug, 1991 - No. 17, Dec, 1992 ($1.00)
Impact Comics (DC)

1-17: 4-Vs. The Black Hood. 9-Trading card inside			1.00
Annual 1 ('92, $2.50, 68 pgs.)-Impact trading card		1.00	2.50

FLYBOY (Flying Cadets)(Also see Approved Comics)
Spring, 1952 - No. 4, 1953
Ziff-Davis Publ. Co. (Approved)

1-Saunders painted-c	14.00	43.00	100.00
2-(10-11/52)-Saunders painted-c	11.00	33.00	75.00
3,4-Saunders painted-c	9.15	27.50	55.00

FLYING ACES (Aviation stories)
July, 1955 - No. 5, Mar, 1956
Key Publications

1	4.25	13.00	28.00
2-5: 2-Trapani-a	4.00	10.00	20.00

FLYING A'S RANGE RIDER, THE (TV) (See Western Roundup under Dell Giants)
#404, 6-7/52; #2, June-Aug, 1953 - #24, Aug, 1959 (All photo-c)
Dell Publishing Co.

Four Color 404(#1)-Titled "The Range Rider"	11.00	33.00	110.00
2	6.50	19.50	65.00
3-10	5.00	15.00	50.00
11-16,18-24	4.50	13.50	45.00
17-Toth-a	5.80	17.40	58.00

FLYING CADET (WW II Plane Photos)
Jan, 1943 - V2#8, 1947 (Half photos, half comics)
Flying Cadet Publishing Co.

V1#1-Painted-c	12.00	36.00	85.00
2	6.70	20.00	40.00
3-9 (Two #6's, Sept. & Oct.): 5,6a,6b-Photo-c	5.85	17.50	35.00
V2#1-7(#10-16)	4.25	13.00	28.00
8(#17)-Bare-breasted woman-c	14.00	43.00	100.00

FLYIN' JENNY
1946 - No. 2, 1947 (1945 strip-r)
Pentagon Publ. Co./Leader Enterprises #2

nn-Marcus Swayze strip-r (entire insides)	11.00	33.00	75.00
2-Baker-c; Swayze strip reprints	12.00	36.00	85.00

FLYING MODELS
V61#3, May, 1954 (5¢, 16 pgs.)
H-K Publ. (Health-Knowledge Publs.)

V61#3 (Rare)	7.50	22.50	45.00

FLYING NUN (TV)
Feb, 1968 - No. 4, Nov, 1968
Dell Publishing Co.

1-Sally Field photo-c	4.00	12.00	40.00
2-4: 2-Sally Field photo-c	2.50	7.50	25.00

FLYING NURSES (See Sue & Sally Smith...)

FLYING SAUCERS
1950; 1952; 1953
Avon Periodicals/Realistic

1(1950)-Wood-a, 21 pgs.; Fawcette-c	62.00	187.00	500.00
nn(1952)-Cover altered plus 2 pgs. of Wood-a not in original	40.00	120.00	315.00
nn(1953)-Reprints above	31.00	94.00	220.00

FLYING SAUCERS (Comics)

April, 1967 - No. 4, Nov, 1967; No. 5, Oct, 1969
Dell Publishing Co.

1	2.00	6.00	20.00
2-5	1.70	5.00	12.00

FLY MAN (Formerly Adventures of The Fly; Mighty Comics #40 on)
No. 32, July, 1965 - No. 39, Sept, 1966 (Also see Mighty Crusaders)
Mighty Comics Group (Radio Comics) (Archie)

32,33-Comet, Shield, Black Hood, The Fly & Flygirl x-over. 33-Re-intro Wizard, Hangman (1st S.A. appearances)	4.00	12.00	28.00
34-36: 34-Shield begins. 35-Origin Black Hood. 36-Hangman x-over in Shield; re-intro. & origin of Web (1st S.A. app.)	2.70	8.00	19.00
37-39: 37-Hangman, Wizard x-over in Flyman; last Shield issue. 38-Web story. 39-Steel Sterling story (1st S.A. app.)	2.70	8.00	19.00

FOES
1989 - No. 3, 1989 ($1.95, limited series)
Ram Comics

1-3		.80	2.00

FOLLOW THE SUN (TV)
May-July, 1962 - No. 2, Sept-Nov, 1962 (Photo-c)
Dell Publishing Co.

01-280-207(No.1), 12-280-211(No.2)	4.00	12.00	40.00

FOODANG
July, 1994 ($1.95, B&W, bi-monthly)
Continuum Comics

1		.80	2.00

FOODINI (TV)(The Great...; see Jingle Dingle & Pinhead &...)
March, 1950 - No. 5, 1950 (All have 52 pgs.)
Continental Publications (Holyoke)

1-Based on TV puppet show (very early TV comic)	14.00	43.00	100.00
2-Jingle Dingle begins	9.15	27.50	55.00
3-5: 4-(8/50)	6.70	20.00	40.00

FOOEY (Magazine) (Satire)
Feb, 1961 - No. 4, May, 1961
Scoff Publishing Co.

1	5.35	16.00	32.00
2-4	4.00	11.00	22.00

FOOFUR (TV)
Aug, 1987 - No. 6, June, 1988
Marvel Comics (Star Comics)/Marvel Comics No. 5 on

1-6			1.00

FOOLKILLER (Also see The Amazing Spider-Man #225, The Defenders #73 Man-Thing #3 & Omega the Unknown #8)
Oct, 1990 - No. 10, Oct, 1991 ($1.75, limited series)
Marvel Comics

1-10: 1-Origin 3rd Foolkiller; Greg Salinger app; DeZuniga-a(i) in 1-4. 8-Spider-Man x-over		.70	1.75

FOOTBALL THRILLS (See Tops In Adventure)
Fall-Winter, 1951-52 - No. 2, Fall, 1952 (Edited by "Red" Grange)
Ziff-Davis Publ. Co.

1-Powell a(2); Saunders painted-c; Red Grange, Jim Thorpe stories	26.00	79.00	185.00
2-Saunders painted-c	18.00	54.00	125.00

FOOT SOLDIERS, THE
Jan, 1996 - No. 4, Apr, 1996 ($2.95, limited series)
Dark Horse Comics

1-4: Jim Krueger story & Michael Avon Oeming-a. in all. 1-Alex Ross-c. 4-John K. Snyder, Ill-c.			3.00

Force Works #13 © MEG

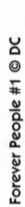

Forever People #1 © DC

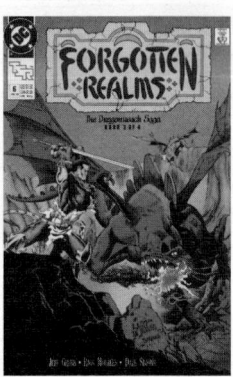

Forgotten Realms #6 © TSR

FOR A NIGHT OF LOVE
1951
Avon Periodicals

nn-Two stories adapted from the works of Emile Zola; Astarita, Ravielli; Kinstler-c	24.00	73.00	170.00

FORBIDDEN LOVE
Mar, 1950 - No. 4, Sept, 1950 (52 pgs.)
Quality Comics Group

1-(Scarce)-Classic photo-c; Crandall-a	59.00	178.00	475.00
2,3-(Scarce)-Photo-c	29.00	86.00	200.00
4-(Scarce)-Ward/Cuidera-a; photo-c	33.00	99.00	230.00

FORBIDDEN LOVE (See Dark Mansion of...)

FORBIDDEN PLANET
May, 1992 - No. 4, 1992 ($2.50, limited series)
Innovation Publishing

1-4: Adapts movie; painted-c		1.00	2.50

FORBIDDEN TALES OF DARK MANSION (Formerly Dark Mansion of Forbidden Love #1-4)
No. 5, May-June, 1972 - No. 15, Feb-Mar, 1974
National Periodical Publications

5-15: 5-(52 pgs.). 13-Kane/Howard-a	1.00	2.00	5.00

NOTE: *N. Adams* c-9. *Alcala* a-9-11, 13. *Chaykin* a-7,15. *Evans* a-14. *Heck* a-5. *Kaluta* a-7i, 8-12; c-7, 8, 13. *G. Kane* a-13. *Kirby* a-6. *Nino* a-8, 12, 15. *Redondo* a-14.

FORBIDDEN WORLDS
7-8/51 - No. 34, 10-11/54; No. 35, 8/55 - No. 145, 8/67
(No. 1-5: 52 pgs.; No. 6-8: 44 pgs.)
American Comics Group

1-Williamson/Frazetta-a (10 pgs.)	112.00	338.00	900.00
2	56.00	168.00	450.00
3-Williamson/Orlando-a (7 pgs.); Wood (2 panels); Frazetta (1 panel)	58.00	176.00	470.00
4	31.00	94.00	220.00
5-Krenkel/Williamson-a (8 pgs.)	45.00	136.00	365.00
6-Harrison/Williamson-a (8 pgs.)	40.00	120.00	310.00
7,8,10: 7-1st monthly issue	24.00	71.00	165.00
9-A-Bomb explosion story	26.00	79.00	185.00
11-20	17.00	49.00	115.00
21-33: 24-E.C. swipe by Landau	11.50	34.00	80.00
34(10-11/54)(Scarce)(becomes Young Heroes #35 on)-Last pre-code story; A-Bomb explosion story	11.50	34.00	80.00
35(8/55)-Scarce	10.00	30.00	65.00
36-62	7.50	22.50	45.00
63,69,76,78-Williamson-a in all; w/Krenkel #69	8.35	25.00	50.00
64,66-68,70-72,74,75,77,79-85,87-90	6.35	19.00	38.00
65-"There's a New Moon Tonight" listed in #114 as holding 1st record fan mail response	7.50	22.50	45.00
73-1st app. Herbie by Ogden Whitney	34.00	101.00	235.00
86-Flying saucer-c by Schaffenberger	5.70	17.00	40.00
91-93,95-100	3.40	10.00	24.00
94-Herbie app.	8.00	23.50	60.00
101-109,111-113,115,117-120	2.85	8.50	20.00
110,114,116-Herbie app. 114-1st Herbie-c; contains list of editor's top 20 ACG stories. 116-Herbie goes to Hell	5.00	15.00	40.00
121-124: 124-Magic Agent app.	3.25	9.50	22.00
125-Magic Agent app.; intro. & origin Magicman series, ends #141	3.75	11.25	28.00
126-130	3.25	9.50	22.00
131-139: 133-Origin/1st app. Dragonia in Magicman (1-2/66); returns in #138.			
136-Nemesis x-over in Magicman	2.85	8.50	22.00
140-Mark Midnight app. by Ditko	3.25	9.50	22.00
141-145	2.00	6.00	14.00

NOTE: *Buscema* a-75, 79, 81, 82, 140r. *Cameron* a-5. *Disbrow* a-10. *Ditko* a-137p, 138, 140. *Landau* a-24, 27-29, 31-34, 48, 86r, 96, 143-45. *Lazarus* a-18, 23, 24, 57. *Moldoff* a-27, 31, 139r. *Reinman* a-93. *Whitney* a-115, 116, 137; c-40, 46, 57, 60, 68, 78, 79, 90, 93, 94, 100, 102, 103, 106-108, 114, 129.

FORCE, THE (See The Crusaders)

FORCE OF BUDDHA'S PALM THE
Aug, 1988 - No. 46, June, 1992? ($1.50/$1.95, 68 pgs.)
Jademan Comics

1-8 ($1.50)-Kung Fu stories			1.50
9-46 ($1.95)		1.00	2.00

FORCE WORKS
July, 1994 - No. 22, Apr, 1996 ($1.50)
Marvel Comics

1-($3.95)-Fold-out pop-up-c; Iron Man, Wonder Man, Spider-Woman,U.S. Agent & Scarlet Witch (new costume)		1.60	4.00
2-11, 13-22: 5-Blue logo version & pink logo version. 9-Intro Dreamguard. 13-Avengers app.			1.50
5 Pink logo ($2.95)-polybagged w/ 16pg. Marvel Action Hour Preview & acetate print		1.20	3.00
12 ($2.50)-Flip book w/War Machine.		1.00	2.50

FORD ROTUNDA CHRISTMAS BOOK (See Christmas at the Rotunda)

FOREIGN INTRIGUES (Formerly Johnny Dynamite; becomes Battlefield Action #16 on)
No. 13, 1956 - No. 15, Aug, 1956
Charlton Comics

13-15-Johnny Dynamite continues	5.35	16.00	32.00

FOREMOST BOYS (See 4Most)

FOREST FIRE (Also see Smokey The Bear)
1949 (dated-1950) (16 pgs., paper-c)
American Forestry Assn.(Commerical Comics)

nn-Intro/1st app. Smokey The Forest Fire Preventing Bear; created by Rudy Wendelein; Wendelein/Sparling-a; 'Carter Oil Co.' on back-c of original	17.00	51.00	120.00

FOREVER, DARLING (Movie)
No. 681, Feb, 1956
Dell Publishing Co.

Four Color 681-w/Lucille Ball & Desi Arnaz; photo-c	11.00	33.00	110.00

FOREVER PEOPLE, THE
Feb-Mar, 1971 - No. 11, Oct-Nov, 1972 (Fourth World)
National Periodical Publications

1-1st app. Forever People; Superman x-over; Kirby-c/a begins; 1st full app. Darkseid (3rd anywhere, 3 weeks before New Gods #1); Darkseid storyline begins, ends #8(app. in 1-4,6,8; cameos in 5,11)	6.50	19.50	45.00
2-5: 4-G.A. reprints begin, end #9	4.30	13.00	30.00
6-11: 9,10-Deadman app.	2.15	6.50	15.00

NOTE: *Kirby* c/a(p)-1-11; #4-9 contain Sandman reprints from Adventure #85, 84, 75, 80, 77, 79 in that order. #1-3, 10-11 are 36pgs; #4-9 are 52pgs.

FOREVER PEOPLE
Feb, 1988 - No. 6, July, 1988 ($1.25, limited series)
DC Comics

1-6			1.25

FOR GIRLS ONLY
Nov, 1953 (100 pgs., digest size)
Bernard Bailey Enterprises

1-Half comic book, half magazine	11.50	34.00	80.00

FORGOTTEN FOREST OF OZ, THE (See First Comics Graphic Novel #16)

FORGOTTEN REALMS (Also see Avatar & TSR Worlds)
Sept, 1989 - No. 25, Sept, 1991 ($1.50/$1.75)
DC Comics

Four Color #2 (Series I) © DELL

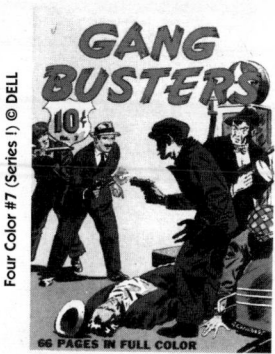

Four Color #7 (Series I) © DELL

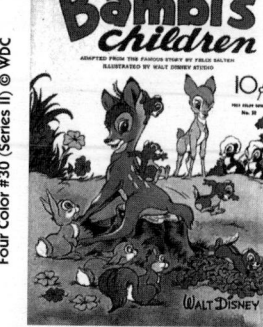

Four Color #30 (Series II) © WDC

	GD25	FN65	NM94
1-Based on TSR role-playing game		.80	2.00
2,3		.80	2.00
4-10		.75	1.80
11-15			1.50
16-25: 16-Begin $1.75-c. 18-Avatar story		.75	1.80
Annual 1 (1990, $2.95, 68 pgs.)		1.20	3.00

FORGOTTEN STORY BEHIND NORTH BEACH, THE
No date (8 pgs., paper-c)
Catechetical Guild

nn		2.40	6.00	12.00

FORLORN RIVER (See Zane Grey Four Color 395)

FOR LOVERS ONLY (Formerly Hollywood Romances)
No. 60, Aug, 1971 - No. 87, Nov, 1976
Charlton Comics

60-87: 73-Spanking scene-c/story			1.20

40 BIG PAGES OF MICKEY MOUSE
No. 945, Jan, 1936 (10-1/4x12-1/2", 44 pgs., cardboard-c)
Whitman Publishing Co.

945-Reprints Mickey Mouse Magazine #1, but with a different cover; ads were eliminated and some illustrated stories had expanded text. The book is 3/4" shorter than Mickey Mouse Mag. #1, but the reprints are the same size (Rare) 150.00 450.00 1200.00

48 FAMOUS AMERICANS
947 (Giveaway) (Half-size in color)
J. C. Penney Co. (Cpr. Edwin R. Stroh)

nn-Simon & Kirby-a 11.00 33.00 75.00

FOR YOUR EYES ONLY (See James Bond...)

FOUR COLOR
Sept?, 1939 - No. 1354, Apr-June, 1962 (Series I are all 68 pgs.)
Dell Publishing Co.

NOTE: Four Color only appears on issues #19-25, 1-99,101. Dell Publishing Co. filed these as Series I, #1-25, and Series II, #1-1354. Issues beginning with #710? were printed with and without ads on back cover. Issues without ads are worth more.

SERIES I:

	GD25	FN65	VF82	NM94
(nn)-Dick Tracy	650.00	1950.00	3900.00	6500.00

(Estimated up to 115 total copies exist, 5 in NM/Mint)

	GD25	FN65		NM94
2(nn)-Don Winslow of the Navy (#1) (Rare) (11/39?)				
	126.00	377.00		1250.00
3(nn)-Myra North (1/40?)	72.00	216.00		725.00

	GD25	FN65	VF82	NM94
4-Donald Duck by Al Taliaferro (1940)(Disney)(3/40?)				
	875.00	2625.00	6562.00	10,500.00

(Prices vary widely on this book)

	GD25	FN65		NM94
5-Smilin' Jack (#1) (5/40?)	58.00	174.00		585.00
6-Dick Tracy (Scarce)	145.00	435.00		1450.00
7-Gang Busters	35.00	105.00		350.00
8-Dick Tracy	72.50	217.50		725.00
9-Terry and the Pirates-r/Super #9-29	58.00	174.00		580.00
10-Smilin' Jack	52.00	156.00		525.00
1-Smitty (#1)	36.00	108.00		360.00
2-Little Orphan Annie; reprints strips from 12/19/37 to 6/4/38				
	48.50	145.50		485.00
3-Walt Disney's Reluctant Dragon-('41)-Contains 2 pgs. of photos from film; 2 pg. foreword to Fantasia by Leopold Stokowski; Donald Duck, Goofy, Baby Weems & Mickey Mouse (as the Sorcerer's Apprentice) app. (Disney)	160.00	480.00		1600.00
4-Moon Mullins (#1)	35.00	105.00		350.00

	GD25	FN65	NM94
15-Tillie the Toiler (#1)	35.00	105.00	350.00

	GD25	FN65	VF82
16-Mickey Mouse (#1) (Disney) by Gottfredson	800.00	2400.00	8500.00

	GD25	FN65	NM94
17-Walt Disney's Dumbo, the Flying Elephant (#1)(1941)-Mickey Mouse, Donald Duck, & Pluto app. (Disney)	170.00	510.00	1700.00
18-Jiggs and Maggie (#1)(1936-38-r)	39.00	117.00	390.00
19-Barney Google and Snuffy Smith (#1)-(1st issue with Four Color on the cover)	37.00	114.00	370.00
20-Tiny Tim	29.00	87.00	290.00
21-Dick Tracy	61.50	184.50	615.00
22-Don Winslow	31.00	94.00	300.00
23-Gang Busters	26.50	79.50	265.00
24-Captain Easy	41.00	129.00	410.00
25-Popeye (1942)	70.00	210.00	700.00

SERIES II:

	GD25	FN65	NM94
1-Little Joe (1942)	45.00	135.00	450.00
2-Harold Teen	25.00	75.00	250.00
3-Alley Oop (#1)	48.00	145.00	475.00
4-Smilin' Jack	43.00	129.00	435.00
5-Raggedy Ann and Andy (#1)	50.00	150.00	500.00
6-Smitty	21.00	63.00	210.00
7-Smokey Stover (#1)	32.00	96.00	320.00
8-Tillie the Toiler	22.00	66.00	220.00

	GD25	FN65	VF82	NM94
9-Donald Duck Finds Pirate Gold, by Carl Barks & Jack Hannah (Disney) (© 8/17/42)	600.00	1875.00	4688.00	7500.00

	GD25	FN65	NM94
10-Flash Gordon by Alex Raymond; reprinted from "The Ice Kingdom"	75.00	225.00	750.00
11-Wash Tubbs	29.00	87.00	290.00
12-Walt Disney's Bambi (#1)	53.00	171.00	525.00
13-Mr. District Attorney (#1)-See The Funnies #35 for 1st app.	28.00	84.00	280.00
14-Smilin' Jack	34.00	102.00	345.00
15-Felix the Cat (#1)	70.00	210.00	700.00
16-Porky Pig (#1)(1942)- "Secret of the Haunted House"	78.00	233.00	780.00
17-Popeye	52.50	157.50	525.00
18-Little Orphan Annie's Junior Commandos; Flag-c; reprints strips from 6/14/42 to 11/21/42	38.00	114.00	380.00
19-Walt Disney's Thumper Meets the Seven Dwarfs (Disney); reprinted in Silly Symphonies	55.00	165.00	550.00
20-Barney Baxter	24.50	75.00	245.00
21-Oswald the Rabbit (#1)(1943)	50.00	150.00	500.00
22-Tillie the Toiler	17.00	51.00	170.00
23-Raggedy Ann and Andy	37.00	111.00	370.00
24-Gang Busters	26.50	79.50	265.00
25-Andy Panda (#1) (Walter Lantz)	48.00	145.00	475.00
26-Popeye	52.50	157.50	525.00
27-Walt Disney's Mickey Mouse and the Seven Colored Terror	85.00	255.00	850.00
28-Wash Tubbs	21.00	63.00	210.00

	GD25	FN65	VF82	NM94
29-Donald Duck and the Mummy's Ring, by Carl Barks (Disney) (9/43)	485.00	1500.00	3750.00	6000.00

	GD25	FN65	NM94
30-Bambi's Children (1943)-Disney	53.00	171.00	525.00
31-Moon Mullins	18.00	54.00	180.00
32-Smitty	15.00	45.00	155.00
33-Bugs Bunny "Public Nuisance #1"	100.00	300.00	1000.00
34-Dick Tracy	41.00	123.00	410.00
35-Smokey Stover	16.00	48.00	160.00
36-Smilin' Jack	22.00	66.00	225.00

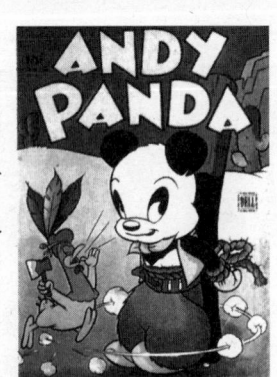

Four Color #54 (Series II) © Walter Lantz

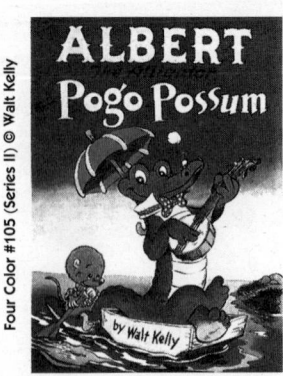

Four Color #105 (Series II) © Walt Kelly

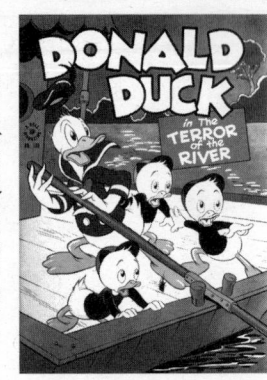

Four Color #108 (Series II) © WDC

	GD25	FN65	NM94
37-Bringing Up Father	18.50	55.50	185.00
38-Roy Rogers (#1, © 4/44)-1st western comic with photo-c			
	160.00	480.00	1600.00
39-Oswald the Rabbit (1944)	35.00	105.00	350.00
40-Barney Google and Snuffy Smith	21.00	66.00	210.00
41-Mother Goose and Nursery Rhyme Comics (#1)-All by Walt Kelly			
	22.00	65.00	220.00
42-Tiny Tim (1934-r)	16.00	48.00	160.00
43-Popeye (1938-'42-r)	31.00	93.00	315.00
44-Terry and the Pirates (1938-r)	39.50	118.50	395.00
45-Raggedy Ann	30.00	90.00	300.00
46-Felix the Cat and the Haunted Castle	41.00	123.00	410.00
47-Gene Autry (copyright 6/16/44)	40.00	120.00	400.00
48-Porky Pig of the Mounties by Carl Barks (7/44)	100.00	300.00	1000.00
49-Snow White and the Seven Dwarfs (Disney)	60.00	180.00	600.00
50-Fairy Tale Parade-Walt Kelly art (1944)	25.00	75.00	250.00
51-Bugs Bunny Finds the Lost Treasure	35.00	105.00	350.00
52-Little Orphan Annie; reprints strips from 6/18/38 to 11/19/38			
	30.00	90.00	300.00
53-Wash Tubbs	15.50	46.50	155.00
54-Andy Panda	29.00	87.00	290.00
55-Tillie the Toiler	13.00	40.00	130.00
56-Dick Tracy	33.00	99.00	330.00
57-Gene Autry	36.50	109.50	365.00
58-Smilin' Jack	22.00	66.00	225.00
59-Mother Goose and Nursery Rhyme Comics-Kelly-c/a			
	19.00	57.00	190.00
60-Tiny Folks Funnies	14.00	43.00	140.00
61-Santa Claus Funnies(11/44)-Kelly art	24.00	72.00	240.00
62-Donald Duck in Frozen Gold, by Carl Barks (Disney) (1/45)			
	167.00	500.00	2000.00
63-Roy Rogers; color photo-all 4 covers	47.00	141.00	465.00
64-Smokey Stover	12.00	36.00	120.00
65-Smitty	12.00	36.00	120.00
66-Gene Autry	36.50	109.50	365.00
67-Oswald the Rabbit	17.00	52.00	170.00
68-Mother Goose and Nursery Rhyme Comics, by Walt Kelly			
	19.00	57.00	190.00
69-Fairy Tale Parade, by Walt Kelly	25.00	75.00	250.00
70-Popeye and Wimpy	25.00	75.00	255.00
71-Walt Disney's Three Caballeros, by Walt Kelly (© 4/45)-(Disney)			
	79.00	237.00	790.00
72-Raggedy Ann	25.00	75.00	250.00
73-The Gumps (#1)	11.00	33.00	110.00
74-Marge's Little Lulu (#1)	96.00	288.00	960.00
75-Gene Autry and the Wildcat	29.00	87.00	290.00
76-Little Orphan Annie; reprints strips from 2/28/40 to 6/24/40			
	24.00	72.00	245.00
77-Felix the Cat	38.00	114.00	380.00
78-Porky Pig and the Bandit Twins	24.00	72.00	240.00
79-Walt Disney's Mickey Mouse in The Riddle of the Red Hat by Carl Barks			
(8/45)	105.00	315.00	1050.00
80-Smilin' Jack	15.00	45.00	155.00
81-Moon Mullins	10.00	30.00	100.00
82-Lone Ranger	42.50	127.50	425.00
83-Gene Autry in Outlaw Trail	29.00	87.00	290.00
84-Flash Gordon by Alex Raymond-Reprints from "The Fiery Desert"			
	37.50	112.50	375.00
85-Andy Panda and the Mad Dog Mystery	16.00	48.00	155.00
86-Roy Rogers; photo-c	32.00	96.00	325.00
87-Fairy Tale Parade by Walt Kelly; Dan Noonan-c	25.00	75.00	250.00
88-Bugs Bunny's Great Adventure (Sci/fi)	20.00	60.00	200.00
89-Tillie the Toiler	13.00	40.00	130.00
90-Christmas with Mother Goose by Walt Kelly (11/45)			

	GD25	FN65	NM94
	18.00	54.00	180.0
91-Santa Claus Funnies by Walt Kelly (11/45)	18.00	54.00	180.0
92-Walt Disney's The Wonderful Adventures Of Pinocchio (1945); Donald			
Duck by Kelly, 16 pgs. (Disney)	60.00	180.00	600.0
93-Gene Autry in The Bandit of Black Rock	25.00	75.00	250.0
94-Winnie Winkle (1945)	12.00	36.00	120.0
95-Roy Rogers Comics; photo-c	32.00	96.00	325.0
96-Dick Tracy	24.50	73.50	245.0
97-Marge's Little Lulu (1946)	45.00	135.00	450.0
98-Lone Ranger, The	31.00	93.00	310.0
99-Smitty	10.50	31.50	105.0
100-Gene Autry Comics; photo-c	25.00	75.00	250.0
101-Terry and the Pirates	27.00	81.00	270.0

NOTE: No. 101 is last issue to carry "Four Color" logo on cover; all issues beginning with
100 are marked "...O. S." (One Shot) which can be found in the bottom left-hand panel on t
first page; the numbers following "O. S." relate to the year/month date.

	GD25	FN65	NM94
102-Oswald the Rabbit-Walt Kelly art, 1 pg.	15.00	45.00	150.0
103-Easter with Mother Goose by Walt Kelly	19.00	57.00	190.0
104-Fairy Tale Parade by Walt Kelly	19.00	57.00	190.0
105-Albert the Alligator and Pogo Possum (#1) by Kelly (4/46)			
	67.50	205.00	675.0
106-Tillie the Toiler	10.00	30.00	100.0
107-Little Orphan Annie; reprints strips from 11/16/42 to 3/24/43			
	22.00	67.00	215.0
108-Donald Duck in The Terror of the River, by Carl Barks (Disney)			
(© 4/16/46)	121.00	362.00	1450.
109-Roy Rogers Comics; photo-c	25.00	75.00	255.
110-Marge's Little Lulu	33.00	99.00	325.
111-Captain Easy	15.00	45.00	145.0
112-Porky Pig's Adventure in Gopher Gulch	14.00	43.00	140.0
113-Popeye; all new Popeye stories begin	13.00	39.00	130.0
114-Fairy Tale Parade by Walt Kelly	19.00	57.00	190.0
115-Marge's Little Lulu	33.00	99.00	325.0
116-Mickey Mouse and the House of Many Mysteries (Disney)			
	24.00	72.00	235.0
117-Roy Rogers Comics; photo-c	18.00	54.00	180.0
118-Lone Ranger, The	31.00	93.00	310.0
119-Felix the Cat; all new Felix stories begin	32.50	97.50	325.0
120-Marge's Little Lulu	28.00	84.00	280.0
121-Fairy Tale Parade-(not Kelly)	11.00	33.00	110.0
122-Henry (10/46)	13.00	39.00	130.
123-Bugs Bunny's Dangerous Venture	15.00	43.00	150.
124-Roy Rogers Comics; photo-c	18.00	54.00	180.
125-Lone Ranger, The	21.00	63.00	210.
126-Christmas with Mother Goose by Walt Kelly (1946)			
	14.00	43.00	140.0
127-Popeye	13.00	39.00	130.0
128-Santa Claus Funnies- "Santa & the Angel" by Gollub; "A Mouse in the			
House" by Kelly	14.00	43.00	140.0
129-Walt Disney's Uncle Remus and His Tales of Brer Rabbit (#1) (1946)-			
Adapted from Disney movie "Song of the South"	28.00	86.00	280.0
130-Andy Panda (Walter Lantz)	10.00	30.00	100.0
131-Marge's Little Lulu	28.00	84.00	280.0
132-Tillie the Toiler (1947)	10.00	30.00	100.0
133-Dick Tracy	21.00	63.00	210.0
134-Tarzan and the Devil Ogre; Marsh-c/a	60.00	180.00	600.0
135-Felix the Cat	24.00	72.00	240.0
136-Lone Ranger, The	21.00	63.00	210.0
137-Roy Rogers Comics; photo-c	18.00	54.00	180.0
138-Smitty	9.00	27.00	90.
139-Marge's Little Lulu (1947)	26.00	78.00	260.
140-Easter with Mother Goose by Walt Kelly	15.50	46.50	155.
141-Mickey Mouse and the Submarine Pirates (Disney)			
	21.00	63.00	200.

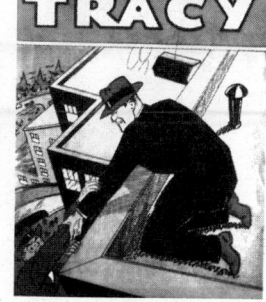
Four Color #163 © KFS

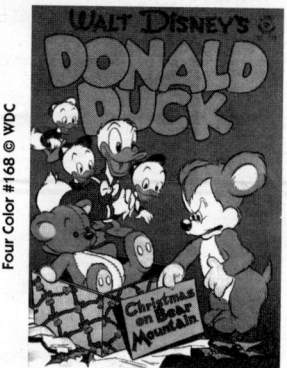
Four Color #168 © WDC

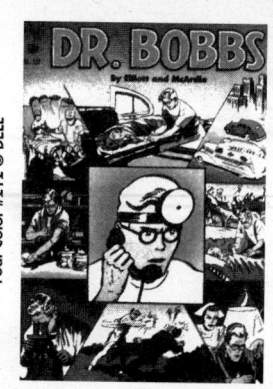
Four Color #212 © DELL

FO

	GD25	FN65	NM94
42-Bugs Bunny and the Haunted Mountain	15.00	43.00	150.00
43-Oswald the Rabbit & the Prehistoric Egg	9.00	27.00	90.00
44-Roy Rogers Comics (1947)-Photo-c	18.00	54.00	180.00
45-Popeye	13.00	39.00	130.00
46-Marge's Little Lulu	26.00	78.00	260.00
47-Donald Duck in Volcano Valley, by Carl Barks (Disney) (5/47)	83.00	250.00	1000.00
48-Albert the Alligator and Pogo Possum by Walt Kelly (5/47)	60.00	180.00	600.00
49-Smilin' Jack	10.00	30.00	100.00
50-Tillie the Toiler (6/47)	9.00	27.00	90.00
51-Lone Ranger, The	17.00	51.00	170.00
52-Little Orphan Annie; reprints strips from 1/2/44 to 5/6/44	14.00	45.00	140.00
53-Roy Rogers Comics; photo-c	15.50	46.50	155.00
54-Walter Lantz Andy Panda	10.00	30.00	100.00
55-Henry (7/47)	8.00	24.00	80.00
56-Porky Pig and the Phantom	10.00	30.00	100.00
57-Mickey Mouse & the Beanstalk (Disney)	21.00	63.00	200.00
58-Marge's Little Lulu	26.00	78.00	260.00
59-Donald Duck in the Ghost of the Grotto, by Carl Barks (Disney) (8/47)	67.00	200.00	800.00
60-Roy Rogers Comics; photo-c	16.00	48.00	155.00
61-Tarzan and the Fires Of Tohr; Marsh-c/a	52.50	157.50	525.00
62-Felix the Cat (9/47)	18.00	54.00	180.00
63-Dick Tracy	16.50	49.50	165.00
64-Bugs Bunny Finds the Frozen Kingdom	15.00	43.00	150.00
65-Marge's Little Lulu	26.00	78.00	260.00
66-Roy Rogers Comics (52 pgs.)-Photo-c	16.00	48.00	155.00
67-Lone Ranger, The	17.00	51.00	170.00
68-Popeye (10/47)	13.00	39.00	130.00
69-Woody Woodpecker (#1)- "Manhunter in the North"; drug use story	14.50	43.50	145.00
70-Mickey Mouse on Spook's Island (11/47)(Disney)-reprinted in Mickey Mouse #103	16.00	48.00	160.00
71-Charlie McCarthy (#1) and the Twenty Thieves	25.00	75.00	250.00
72-Christmas with Mother Goose by Walt Kelly (11/47)	14.00	43.00	140.00
73-Flash Gordon	13.50	40.50	135.00
74-Winnie Winkle	7.00	21.00	70.00
75-Santa Claus Funnies by Walt Kelly (1947)	14.00	43.00	140.00
76-Tillie the Toiler (12/47)	9.00	27.00	90.00
77-Roy Rogers Comics-(36 pgs.); Photo-c	16.00	48.00	155.00
78-Donald Duck "Christmas on Bear Mountain" by Carl Barks; 1st app. Uncle Scrooge (Disney)(12/47)	100.00	300.00	1200.00
79-Uncle Wiggily (#1)-Walt Kelly-c	16.00	48.00	160.00
80-Ozark Ike (#1)	10.00	30.00	100.00
81-Walt Disney's Mickey Mouse in Jungle Magic	16.00	48.00	160.00
82-Porky Pig in Never-Never Land (2/48)	10.00	30.00	100.00
83-Oswald the Rabbit (Lantz)	9.00	27.00	90.00
84-Tillie the Toiler	9.00	27.00	90.00
85-Easter with Mother Goose by Walt Kelly (1948)	13.00	39.00	130.00
86-Walt Disney's Bambi (4/48)-Reprinted as Movie Classic Bambi #3 (1956)	17.00	52.00	165.00
87-Bugs Bunny and the Dreadful Dragon	12.00	34.00	120.00
88-Woody Woodpecker (Lantz, 5/48)	10.00	30.00	100.00
89-Donald Duck in The Old Castle's Secret, by Carl Barks (Disney) (6/48)	62.00	188.00	750.00
90-Flash Gordon ('48)	13.50	40.50	135.00
91-Porky Pig to the Rescue	10.00	30.00	100.00
92-The Brownies (#1)-by Walt Kelly (7/48)	12.00	40.00	120.00
93-M.G.M. Presents Tom and Jerry (#1)(1948)	14.00	43.00	140.00
94-Mickey Mouse in The World Under the Sea (Disney)-Reprinted in Mickey Mouse #101	16.00	48.00	160.00

	GD25	FN65	NM94
195-Tillie the Toiler	6.00	18.00	60.00
196-Charlie McCarthy in The Haunted Hide-Out; part photo-c	17.00	51.00	170.00
197-Spirit of the Border (#1) (Zane Grey) (1948)	11.50	34.50	115.00
198-Andy Panda	10.00	30.00	100.00
199-Donald Duck in Sheriff of Bullet Valley, by Carl Barks; Barks draws himself on wanted poster, last page; used in Love & Death (Disney) (10/48)	62.00	188.00	750.00
200-Bugs Bunny, Super Sleuth (10/48)	12.00	34.00	120.00
201-Christmas with Mother Goose by W. Kelly	12.00	36.00	120.00
202-Woody Woodpecker	6.30	18.90	63.00
203-Donald Duck in the Golden Christmas Tree, by Carl Barks (Disney) (12/48)	47.00	140.00	560.00
204-Flash Gordon (12/48)	10.50	31.50	105.00
205-Santa Claus Funnies by Walt Kelly	13.00	40.00	130.00
206-Little Orphan Annie; reprints strips from 11/10/40 to 1/11/41	7.50	22.50	75.00
207-King of the Royal Mounted (#1) (12/48)	17.00	52.00	170.00
208-Brer Rabbit Does It Again (Disney) (1/49)	11.50	34.00	115.00
209-Harold Teen	4.00	12.00	40.00
210-Tippie and Cap Stubbs	4.00	12.00	40.00
211-Little Beaver (#1)	7.50	22.50	75.00
212-Dr. Bobbs	3.60	10.80	36.00
213-Tillie the Toiler	6.00	18.00	60.00
214-Mickey Mouse and His Sky Adventure (2/49)(Disney)-Reprinted in Mickey Mouse #105	14.00	43.00	140.00
215-Sparkle Plenty (Dick Tracy-r by Gould)	10.00	30.00	100.00
216-Andy Panda and the Police Pup (Lantz)	6.80	21.00	68.00
217-Bugs Bunny in Court Jester	12.00	34.00	120.00
218-3 Little Pigs and the Wonderful Magic Lamp (Disney) (3/49)(#1)	12.00	36.00	130.00
219-Swee'pe	9.00	27.00	100.00
220-Easter with Mother Goose by Walt Kelly	13.00	39.00	130.00
221-Uncle Wiggily-Walt Kelly cover in part	10.00	30.00	100.00
222-West of the Pecos (Zane Grey)	7.00	21.00	70.00
223-Donald Duck "Lost in the Andes" by Carl Barks (Disney-4/49) (square egg story)	62.00	188.00	750.00
224-Little Iodine (#1), by Hatlo (4/49)	9.00	27.00	90.00
225-Oswald the Rabbit (Lantz)	5.00	15.00	50.00
226-Porky Pig and Spoofy, the Spook	8.00	24.00	80.00
227-Seven Dwarfs (Disney)	11.00	33.00	110.00
228-Mark of Zorro, The (#1) (1949)	21.00	63.00	210.00
229-Smokey Stover	5.00	15.00	50.00
230-Sunset Pass (Zane Grey)	7.00	21.00	70.00
231-Mickey Mouse and the Rajah's Treasure (Disney)	14.00	43.00	140.00
232-Woody Woodpecker (Lantz, 6/49)	6.30	18.90	63.00
233-Bugs Bunny, Sleepwalking Sleuth	12.00	34.00	120.00
234-Dumbo in Sky Voyage (Disney)	10.00	30.00	100.00
235-Tiny Tim	5.00	15.00	50.00
236-Heritage of the Desert (Zane Grey) (1949)	7.00	21.00	70.00
237-Tillie the Toiler	6.00	18.00	60.00
238-Donald Duck in Voodoo Hoodoo, by Carl Barks (Disney) (8/49)	47.00	140.00	560.00
239-Adventure Bound (8/49)	4.80	14.40	48.00
240-Andy Panda (Lantz)	6.80	21.00	68.00
241-Porky Pig, Mighty Hunter	8.00	24.00	80.00
242-Tippie and Cap Stubbs	4.00	12.00	40.00
243-Thumper Follows His Nose (Disney)	10.00	30.00	100.00
244-The Brownies by Walt Kelly	11.00	34.00	110.00
245-Dick's Adventures in Dreamland (9/49)	5.00	15.00	50.00
246-Thunder Mountain (Zane Grey)	4.50	13.50	45.00
247-Flash Gordon	10.50	31.50	105.00
248-Mickey Mouse and the Black Sorcerer (Disney)	14.00	43.00	140.00

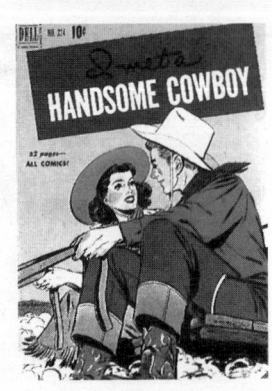

Four Color #255 © Zane Grey

Four Color #287 © Gene Autry

Four Color #324 © DELL

	GD25	FN65	NM94

249-Woody Woodpecker in the "Globetrotter" (10/49)
| | 6.30 | 18.90 | 63.00 |

250-Bugs Bunny in Diamond Daze; used in **SOTI**, pg. 309
| | 12.00 | 34.00 | 120.00 |

251-Hubert at Camp Moonbeam | 5.00 | 15.00 | 50.00
252-Pinocchio (Disney)-not by Kelly; origin | 10.00 | 30.00 | 100.00
253-Christmas with Mother Goose by W. Kelly | 12.00 | 36.00 | 120.00
254-Santa Claus Funnies by Walt Kelly; Pogo & Albert story by Kelly (11/49)
| | 13.00 | 40.00 | 130.00 |

255-The Ranger (Zane Grey) (1949) | 4.50 | 13.50 | 45.00
256-Donald Duck in "Luck of the North" by Carl Barks (Disney) (12/49)-Shows
#257 on inside | 33.00 | 100.00 | 400.00

257-Little Iodine | 7.00 | 21.00 | 70.00
258-Andy Panda and the Balloon Race (Lantz) | 6.80 | 21.00 | 68.00
259-Santa and the Angel (Gollub art-condensed from #128) & Santa at the
Zoo (12/49)-two books in one | 5.00 | 15.00 | 50.00

260-Porky Pig, Hero of the Wild West (12/49) | 8.00 | 24.00 | 80.00
261-Mickey Mouse and the Missing Key (Disney) | 14.00 | 43.00 | 140.00
262-Raggedy Ann and Andy | 7.00 | 21.00 | 70.00
263-Donald Duck in "Land of the Totem Poles" by Carl Barks (Disney)
(2/50)-Has two Barks stories | 33.00 | 100.00 | 400.00

264-Woody Woodpecker in the Magic Lantern (Lantz)
| | 6.30 | 18.90 | 63.00 |

265-King of the Royal Mounted (Zane Grey) | 10.00 | 30.00 | 100.00
266-Bugs Bunny on the "Isle of Hercules" (2/50)-Reprinted in Best of Bugs
Bunny #1 | 10.00 | 30.00 | 100.00

267-Little Beaver; Harman-c/a | 3.80 | 11.40 | 38.00
268-Mickey Mouse's Surprise Visitor (1950) (Disney)
| | 14.00 | 43.00 | 140.00 |

269-Johnny Mack Brown (#1)-Photo-c | 22.00 | 65.00 | 225.00
270-Drift Fence (Zane Grey) (3/50) | 4.50 | 13.50 | 45.00
271-Porky Pig in Phantom of the Plains | 8.00 | 24.00 | 80.00
272-Cinderella (Disney) (4/50) | 10.00 | 30.00 | 100.00
273-Oswald the Rabbit (Lantz) | 5.00 | 15.00 | 50.00
274-Bugs Bunny, Hare-brained Reporter | 10.00 | 30.00 | 100.00
275-Donald Duck in "Ancient Persia" by Carl Barks (Disney) (5/50)
| | 31.00 | 94.00 | 375.00 |

276-Uncle Wiggily | 8.00 | 24.00 | 80.00
277-Porky Pig in Desert Adventure (5/50) | 8.00 | 24.00 | 80.00
278-Bill Elliott Comics (#1)-Photo-c | 13.00 | 40.00 | 130.00
279-Mickey Mouse and Pluto Battle the Giant Ants (Disney); reprinted in
Mickey Mouse #102 & 245 | 11.00 | 33.00 | 110.00

280-Andy Panda in The Isle Of Mechanical Men (Lantz)
| | 6.80 | 21.00 | 68.00 |

281-Bugs Bunny in The Great Circus Mystery | 10.00 | 30.00 | 100.00
282-Donald Duck and the Pixilated Parrot by Carl Barks (Disney)
(© 5/23/50) | 31.00 | 94.00 | 375.00

283-King of the Royal Mounted (7/50) | 10.00 | 30.00 | 100.00
284-Porky Pig in The Kingdom of Nowhere | 8.00 | 24.00 | 80.00
285-Bozo the Clown & His Minikin Circus (#1) (TV) | 19.00 | 57.00 | 190.00
286-Mickey Mouse in The Uninvited Guest (Disney) | 11.00 | 33.00 | 110.00
287-Gene Autry's Champion in The Ghost Of Black Mountain; photo-c
| | 10.00 | 30.00 | 100.00 |

288-Woody Woodpecker in Klondike Gold (Lantz) | 6.30 | 18.90 | 63.00
289-Bugs Bunny in "Indian Trouble" | 10.00 | 30.00 | 100.00
290-The Chief (#1) (8/50) | 5.50 | 16.50 | 55.00
291-Donald Duck in "The Magic Hourglass" by Carl Barks (Disney) (9/50)
| | 31.00 | 94.00 | 375.00 |

292-The Cisco Kid Comics (#1) | 22.00 | 66.00 | 220.00
293-The Brownies-Kelly-c/a | 11.00 | 34.00 | 110.00
294-Little Beaver | 3.80 | 11.40 | 38.00
295-Porky Pig in President Porky (9/50) | 8.00 | 24.00 | 80.00
296-Mickey Mouse in Private Eye for Hire (Disney) | 11.00 | 33.00 | 110.00
297-Andy Panda in The Haunted Inn (Lantz, 10/50) | 6.80 | 21.00 | 68.00

298-Bugs Bunny in Sheik for a Day | 10.00 | 30.00 | 100.0
299-Buck Jones & the Iron Horse Trail (#1) | 15.00 | 45.00 | 150.0
300-Donald Duck in "Big-Top Bedlam" by Carl Barks (Disney) (11/50)
| | 31.00 | 94.00 | 375.0 |

301-The Mysterious Rider (Zane Grey) | 4.50 | 13.50 | 45.0
302-Santa Claus Funnies (11/50) | 4.00 | 12.00 | 40.0
303-Porky Pig in The Land of the Monstrous Flies | 5.00 | 15.00 | 50.0
304-Mickey Mouse in Tom-Tom Island (Disney) (12/50)
| | 9.00 | 27.00 | 90.0 |

305-Woody Woodpecker (Lantz) | 3.60 | 10.80 | 36.0
306-Raggedy Ann | 5.00 | 15.00 | 50.0
307-Bugs Bunny in Lumber Jack Rabbit | 7.50 | 24.00 | 75.0
308-Donald Duck in "Dangerous Disguise" by Carl Barks (Disney) (1/51)
| | 27.00 | 81.00 | 325.0 |

309-Betty Betz' Dollface and Her Gang (1951) | 5.00 | 15.00 | 50.0
310-King of the Royal Mounted (1/51) | 7.00 | 21.00 | 70.0
311-Porky Pig in Midget Horses of Hidden Valley | 5.00 | 15.00 | 50.0
312-Tonto (#1) | 12.00 | 36.00 | 120.0
313-Mickey Mouse in The Mystery of the Double-Cross Ranch (#1)
(Disney) (2/51) | 9.00 | 27.00 | 90.0

Note: Beginning with the above comic in 1951 Dell/Western began adding #1 in
small print on the covers of several long running titles with the evident intention
of switching these titles to their own monthly numbers, but when the conversion
were made, there was no connection. It is thought that the post office may have
stepped in and decreed the sequences should commence as though the first
four colors printed had each begun with number one, or the first issues sold by
subscription. Since the regular series' numbers don't correctly match to the numbers of earlier issues published, it's not known whether or not the numbering
was in error.

314-Ambush (Zane Grey) | 4.50 | 13.50 | 45.0
315-Oswald the Rabbit (Lantz) | 4.00 | 12.00 | 40.0
316-Rex Allen (#1)-Photo-c; Marsh-a | 16.00 | 48.00 | 160.0
317-Bugs Bunny in Hair Today Gone Tomorrow (1/51) | 7.50 | 24.00 | 75.0
318-Donald Duck in "No Such Varmint" by Carl Barks (#1)-Indicia shows #317
(Disney, © 1/23/51) | 27.00 | 81.00 | 325.0

319-Gene Autry's Champion; painted-c | 4.00 | 12.00 | 40.
320-Uncle Wiggily (#1) | 8.00 | 24.00 | 80.
321-Little Scouts (#1) (3/51) | 3.60 | 10.80 | 36.
322-Porky Pig in Roaring Rockets (#1 on-c) | 5.00 | 15.00 | 50.
323-Susie Q. Smith (#1) (3/51) | 4.00 | 12.00 | 40.0
324-I Met a Handsome Cowboy (3/51) | 9.00 | 27.00 | 90.0
325-Mickey Mouse in The Haunted Castle (#2) (Disney) (4/51)
| | 9.00 | 27.00 | 90.0 |

326-Andy Panda (#1) (Lantz) | 3.80 | 12.00 | 38.0
327-Bugs Bunny and the Rajah's Treasure (#2) | 7.50 | 24.00 | 75.0
328-Donald Duck in Old California (#2) by Carl Barks-Peyote drug issue
(Disney) (5/51) | 29.00 | 88.00 | 350.0

329-Roy Roger's Trigger (#1)(5/51)-Photo-c | 11.00 | 33.00 | 110.0
330-Porky Pig Meets the Bristled Bruiser (#2) | 5.00 | 15.00 | 50.0
331-Alice in Wonderland (Disney) (1951) | 14.50 | 44.00 | 145.0
332-Little Beaver | 3.80 | 11.40 | 38.0
333-Wilderness Trek (Zane Grey) (5/51) | 4.50 | 13.50 | 45.0
334-Mickey Mouse and Yukon Gold (Disney) (6/51) | 9.00 | 27.00 | 90.0
335-Francis the Famous Talking Mule (#1, 6/51)-1st Dell non animated movie
comic (all issues based on movie) | 10.00 | 30.00 | 100.

336-Woody Woodpecker (Disney) | 3.60 | 10.80 | 36.
337-The Brownies-not by Walt Kelly | 3.60 | 11.00 | 36.
338-Bugs Bunny and the Rocking Horse Thieves | 7.50 | 24.00 | 75.
339-Donald Duck and the Magic Fountain-not by Carl Barks (Disney) (7-8/51)
| | 8.00 | 24.00 | 80.0 |

340-King of the Royal Mounted (7/51) | 7.00 | 21.00 | 70.0
341-Unbirthday Party with Alice in Wonderland (Disney) (7/51)
| | 14.50 | 44.00 | 145.0 |

342-Porky Pig the Lucky Peppermint Mine | 4.00 | 12.00 | 40.0

Four Color #369 © DELL

Four Color #408 © WDC

Four Color #421 © Videofeatures

	GD25	FN65	NM94
343-Mickey Mouse in The Ruby Eye of Homar-Guy-Am (Disney)-Reprinted in Mickey Mouse #104	7.00	21.00	70.00
344-Sergeant Preston from Challenge of The Yukon (#1) (TV)	11.00	33.00	110.00
345-Andy Panda in Scotland Yard (8-10/51) (Lantz)	3.80	12.00	38.00
346-Hideout (Zane Grey)	4.50	13.50	45.00
347-Bugs Bunny the Frigid Hare (8-9/51)	7.50	24.00	75.00
348-Donald Duck "The Crocodile Collector"; Barks-c only (Disney) (9-10/51)	17.00	50.00	200.00
349-Uncle Wiggily	7.00	21.00	70.00
350-Woody Woodpecker (Lantz)	3.60	10.80	36.00
351-Porky Pig & the Grand Canyon Giant (9-10/51)	4.00	12.00	40.00
352-Mickey Mouse in The Mystery of Painted Valley (Disney)	7.00	21.00	70.00
353-Duck Album (#1)-Barks-c (Disney)	8.00	24.00	80.00
354-Raggedy Ann & Andy	5.00	15.00	50.00
355-Bugs Bunny Hot-Rod Hare	7.50	24.00	75.00
356-Donald Duck in "Rags to Riches"; Barks-c only	17.00	50.00	200.00
357-Comeback (Zane Grey)	3.60	10.80	36.00
358-Andy Panda (Lantz) (11-1/52)	3.80	12.00	38.00
359-Frosty the Snowman (#1)	8.00	24.00	80.00
360-Porky Pig in Tree of Fortune (11-12/51)	4.00	12.00	40.00
361-Santa Claus Funnies	4.00	12.00	40.00
362-Mickey Mouse and the Smuggled Diamonds	7.00	21.00	70.00
363-King of the Royal Mounted	6.00	18.00	60.00
364-Woody Woodpecker (Lantz)	3.40	10.20	34.00
365-The Brownies-not by Kelly	4.00	11.00	36.00
366-Bugs Bunny Uncle Buckskin Comes to Town (12-1/52)	7.50	24.00	75.00
367-Donald Duck in "A Christmas for Shacktown" by Carl Barks (Disney) (1-2/52)	27.00	80.00	320.00
368-Bob Clampett's Beany and Cecil (#1)	25.00	75.00	250.00
369-The Lone Ranger's Famous Horse Hi-Yo Silver (#1); Silver's origin	9.00	27.00	90.00
370-Porky Pig in Trouble in the Big Trees	4.00	12.00	40.00
371-Mickey Mouse in The Inca Idol Case (1952) (Disney)	7.00	21.00	70.00
372-Riders of the Purple Sage (Zane Grey)	3.60	10.80	36.00
373-Sergeant Preston (TV)	7.00	21.00	70.00
374-Woody Woodpecker (Lantz)	3.40	10.20	34.00
375-John Carter of Mars (E. R. Burroughs)-Jesse Marsh-a; origin	25.00	75.00	250.00
376-Bugs Bunny, "The Magic Sneeze"	7.50	24.00	75.00
377-Susie Q. Smith	3.50	10.50	35.00
378-Tom Corbett, Space Cadet (#1) (TV)-McWilliams-a	16.00	48.00	160.00
379-Donald Duck in "Southern Hospitality"; Not by Barks (Disney)	8.00	24.00	80.00
380-Raggedy Ann & Andy	5.00	15.00	50.00
381-Marge's Tubby (#1)	17.50	52.50	175.00
382-Snow White and the Seven Dwarfs (Disney)-origin; partial reprint of 4-Color #49 (Movie)	13.00	40.00	130.00
383-Andy Panda (Lantz)	3.00	9.00	30.00
384-King of the Royal Mounted (3/52)(Zane Grey)	6.00	18.00	60.00
385-Porky Pig in The Isle of Missing Ships (3-4/52)	4.00	12.00	40.00
386-Uncle Scrooge (#1)-by Carl Barks (Disney) in "Only a Poor Old Man" (3/52)	100.00	300.00	900.00
387-Mickey Mouse in High Tibet (Disney) (4-5/52)	7.00	21.00	70.00
388-Oswald the Rabbit (Lantz)	4.00	12.00	40.00
389-Andy Hardy Comics (#1)	3.60	11.00	36.00
390-Woody Woodpecker (Lantz)	3.40	10.20	34.00
391-Uncle Wiggily	7.00	21.00	70.00
392-Hi-Yo Silver	4.50	13.50	45.00

	GD25	FN65	NM94
393-Bugs Bunny	7.50	24.00	75.00
394-Donald Duck in Malayalaya-Barks-c only (Disney)	17.00	50.00	200.00
395-Forlorn River(Zane Grey)-First Nevada (5/52)	3.60	10.80	36.00
396-Tales of the Texas Rangers(#1)(TV)-Photo-c	11.00	33.00	110.00
397-Sergeant Preston of the Yukon (TV) (5/52)	7.00	21.00	70.00
398-The Brownies-not by Kelly	3.60	11.00	36.00
399-Porky Pig in The Lost Gold Mine	4.00	12.00	40.00
400-Tom Corbett, Space Cadet (TV)-McWilliams-c/a	10.00	30.00	100.00
401-Mickey Mouse and Goofy's Mechanical Wizard (Disney) (6-7/52)	5.00	15.00	50.00
402-Mary Jane and Sniffles	9.00	27.00	90.00
403-Li'l Bad Wolf (Disney) (6/52)(#1)	8.00	24.00	80.00
404-The Range Rider (#1) (TV)-Photo-c	11.00	33.00	110.00
405-Woody Woodpecker (Lantz) (6-7/52)	3.40	10.20	34.00
406-Tweety and Sylvester (#1)	7.00	21.00	70.00
407-Bugs Bunny, Foreign-Legion Hare	6.00	18.00	60.00
408-Donald Duck and the Golden Helmet by Carl Barks (Disney) (7-8/52)	27.00	80.00	320.00
409-Andy Panda (7-9/52)	3.00	9.00	30.00
410-Porky Pig in the Water Wizard (7/52)	4.00	12.00	40.00
411-Mickey Mouse and the Old Sea Dog (Disney) (8-9/52)	5.00	15.00	50.00
412-Nevada (Zane Grey)	3.60	10.80	36.00
413-Robin Hood (Disney-Movie) (8/52)-Photo-c (1st Disney movie four color book)	11.00	33.00	110.00
414-Bob Clampett's Beany and Cecil (TV)	17.00	51.00	170.00
415-Rootie Kazootie (#1) (TV)	11.00	33.00	110.00
416-Woody Woodpecker (Lantz)	3.40	10.20	34.00
417-Double Trouble with Goober (#1) (8/52)	3.00	9.00	30.00
418-Rusty Riley, a Boy, a Horse, and a Dog (#1)-Frank Godwin-a (strip reprints) (8/52)	5.00	15.00	50.00
419-Sergeant Preston (TV)	7.00	21.00	70.00
420-Bugs Bunny in The Mysterious Buckaroo (8-9/52)	6.00	18.00	60.00
421-Tom Corbett, Space Cadet(TV)-McWilliams-a	10.00	30.00	100.00
422-Donald Duck and the Gilded Man, by Carl Barks (Disney) (9-10/52) (#423 on inside)	27.00	80.00	320.00
423-Rhubarb, Owner of the Brooklyn Ball Club (The Millionaire Cat) (#1)-Painted cover	5.00	15.00	50.00
424-Flash Gordon-Test Flight in Space (9/52)	8.50	25.50	85.00
425-Zorro, the Return of	12.50	37.50	125.00
426-Porky Pig in The Scalawag Leprechaun	4.00	12.00	40.00
427-Mickey Mouse and the Wonderful Whizzix (Disney) (10-11/52)-Reprinted in Mickey Mouse #100	5.00	15.00	50.00
428-Uncle Wiggily	5.00	15.00	50.00
429-Pluto in "Why Dogs Leave Home" (Disney) (10/52)(#1)	9.50	28.50	95.00
430-Marge's Tubby, the Shadow of a Man-Eater	10.00	30.00	100.00
431-Woody Woodpecker (10/52) (Lantz)	3.40	10.20	34.00
432-Bugs Bunny and the Rabbit Olympics	6.00	18.00	60.00
433-Wildfire (Zane Grey) (11-1/52-53)	3.60	10.80	36.00
434-Rin Tin Tin "In Dark Danger" (#1) (TV) (11/52)-Photo-c	15.00	45.00	150.00
435-Frosty the Snowman (11/52)	4.00	12.00	40.00
436-The Brownies-not by Kelly (11/52)	3.20	9.50	32.00
437-John Carter of Mars (E. R. Burroughs)-Marsh-a	16.00	48.00	160.00
438-Annie Oakley (#1) (TV)	13.00	40.00	130.00
439-Little Hiawatha (Disney) (12/52)}(#1)	6.00	18.00	60.00
440-Black Beauty (12/52)	3.20	9.60	32.00
441-Fearless Fagan	4.00	12.00	40.00
442-Peter Pan (Disney) (Movie)	10.00	30.00	100.00
443-Ben Bowie and His Mountain Men (#1)	7.00	21.00	70.00

Four Color #486 © KFS

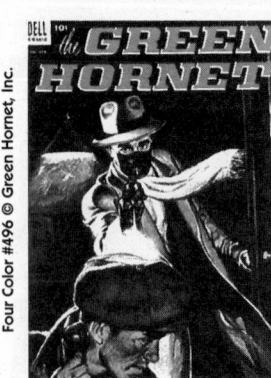

Four Color #496 © Green Hornet, Inc.

Four Color #512 © KFS

	GD25	FN65	NM94		GD25	FN65	NM94
444-Marge's Tubby	10.00	30.00	100.00	504-Krazy Kat; not by Herriman	4.00	12.00	40.00
445-Charlie McCarthy	5.00	15.00	50.00	505-The Sword and the Rose (Disney) (10/53)(Movie)-Photo-c			
446-Captain Hook and Peter Pan (Disney)(Movie)(1/53)					9.00	27.00	90.00
	10.00	30.00	90.00	506-The Little Scouts	1.80	5.40	18.00
447-Andy Hardy Comics	2.70	8.00	27.00	507-Oswald the Rabbit (Lantz)	3.00	9.00	30.00
448-Bob Clampett's Beany and Cecil (TV)	17.00	51.00	170.00	508-Bozo (10/53)	11.00	32.00	110.00
449-Tappan's Burro (Zane Grey) (2-4/53)	3.60	10.80	36.00	509-Pluto (Disney) (10/53)	6.00	18.00	60.00
450-Duck Album; Barks-c (Disney)	6.00	18.00	60.00	510-Son of Black Beauty	4.00	12.00	40.00
451-Rusty Riley-Frank Godwin-a (strip-r) (2/53)	4.00	12.00	40.00	511-Outlaw Trail (Zane Grey)-Kinstler-a	4.50	13.50	45.00
452-Raggedy Ann & Andy (1953)	5.00	15.00	50.00	512-Flash Gordon (11/53)	5.00	15.00	50.00
453-Susie Q. Smith (2/53)	3.50	10.50	35.00	513-Ben Bowie and His Mountain Men	3.40	10.00	34.00
454-Krazy Kat Comics; not by Herriman	4.00	12.00	40.00	514-Frosty the Snowman (11/53)	4.00	12.00	40.00
455-Johnny Mack Brown Comics(3/53)-Photo-c	6.00	18.00	60.00	515-Andy Hardy	2.70	8.00	27.00
456-Uncle Scrooge Back to the Klondike (#2) by Barks (3/53) (Disney)				516-Double Trouble With Goober	2.00	6.00	20.00
	61.00	183.00	550.00	517-Chip 'N' Dale (#1) (Disney)	8.00	24.00	80.00
457-Daffy (#1)	9.00	27.00	90.00	518-Rivets (11/53)	3.00	9.00	30.00
458-Oswald the Rabbit (Lantz)	3.00	9.00	30.00	519-Steve Canyon (#1)-Not by Milton Caniff	9.00	27.00	90.00
459-Rootie Kazootie (TV)	7.00	21.00	70.00	520-Wild Bill Elliott-Photo-c	5.00	15.00	50.00
460-Buck Jones (4/53)	5.50	16.50	55.00	521-Beetle Bailey (12/53)	5.00	15.00	50.00
461-Marge's Tubby	9.00	27.00	90.00	522-The Brownies	3.20	9.00	32.00
462-Little Scouts	1.80	5.40	18.00	523-Rin Tin Tin (TV)-Photo-c (12/53)	8.00	24.00	80.00
463-Petunia (4/53)	4.00	12.00	40.00	524-Tweety and Sylvester	3.50	10.00	35.00
464-Bozo (4/53)	11.00	32.00	110.00	525-Santa Claus Funnies	4.00	12.00	40.00
465-Francis the Famous Talking Mule	7.00	21.00	70.00	526-Napoleon	2.35	7.00	23.00
466-Rhubarb, the Millionaire Cat; painted-c	4.00	12.00	40.00	527-Charlie McCarthy	5.00	15.00	50.00
467-Desert Gold (Zane Grey) (5-7/53)	3.60	10.80	36.00	528-Queen of the West Dale Evans; photo-c	9.00	27.00	90.00
468-Goofy (#1) (Disney)	15.00	45.00	150.00	529-Little Beaver	3.50	10.50	35.00
469-Beetle Bailey (#1) (5/53)	10.00	30.00	100.00	530-Bob Clampett's Beany and Cecil (TV) (1/54)	17.00	51.00	170.00
470-Elmer Fudd	4.00	12.00	40.00	531-Duck Album (Disney)	5.00	15.00	50.00
471-Double Trouble with Goober	2.00	6.00	20.00	532-The Rustlers (Zane Grey) (2-4/54)	3.60	10.80	36.00
472-Wild Bill Elliott (6/53)-Photo-c	5.00	15.00	50.00	533-Raggedy Ann and Andy	5.00	15.00	50.00
473-Li'l Bad Wolf (Disney) (6/53)(#2)	5.00	15.00	50.00	534-Western Marshal(Ernest Haycox's)-Kinstler-a	6.00	18.00	60.00
474-Mary Jane and Sniffles	8.00	24.00	80.00	535-I Love Lucy (#1) (TV) (2/54)-Photo-c	47.50	142.50	475.00
475-M.G.M.'s The Two Mouseketeers (#1)	7.00	21.00	70.00	536-Daffy (3/54)	4.50	13.50	45.00
476-Rin Tin Tin (TV)-Photo-c	8.00	24.00	80.00	537-Stormy, the Thoroughbred... (Disney-Movie) on top 2/3 of each page;			
477-Bob Clampett's Beany and Cecil (TV)	17.00	51.00	170.00	Pluto story on bottom 1/3 of each page (2/54)	4.00	12.00	40.00
478-Charlie McCarthy	5.00	15.00	50.00	538-The Mask of Zorro; Kinstler-a	13.50	40.50	135.00
479-Queen of the West Dale Evans (#1)-Photo-c	20.00	60.00	200.00	539-Ben and Me (Disney) (3/54)	3.20	11.00	32.00
480-Andy Hardy Comics	2.70	8.00	27.00	540-Knights of the Round Table (3/54) (Movie)-Photo-c			
481-Annie Oakley and Tagg (TV)	7.50	23.00	75.00		7.00	21.00	70.00
482-Brownies-not by Kelly	3.20	9.50	32.00	541-Johnny Mack Brown; photo-c	6.00	18.00	60.00
483-Little Beaver (7/53)	3.50	10.50	35.00	542-Super Circus Featuring Mary Hartline (TV) (3/54)			
484-River Feud (Zane Grey) (8-10/53)	3.60	10.80	36.00		6.00	18.00	60.00
485-The Little People-Walt Scott (#1)	7.00	21.00	70.00	543-Uncle Wiggily (3/54)	5.00	15.00	50.00
486-Rusty Riley-Frank Godwin strip-r	4.00	12.00	40.00	544-Rob Roy (Disney-Movie)-Manning-a; photo-c	9.00	27.00	90.00
487-Mowgli, the Jungle Book (Rudyard Kipling's)	5.00	15.00	50.00	545-The Wonderful Adventures of Pinocchio-Partial reprint of 4-Color #92			
488-John Carter of Mars (Burroughs)-Marsh-a; painted-c				(Disney-Movie)	8.00	24.00	80.00
	16.00	48.00	160.00	546-Buck Jones	5.50	16.50	55.00
489-Tweety and Sylvester	3.50	10.00	35.00	547-Francis the Famous Talking Mule	5.00	15.00	50.00
490-Jungle Jim (#1)	7.00	21.00	70.00	548-Krazy Kat; not by Herriman	4.00	12.00	40.00
491-Silvertip (#1) (Max Brand)-Kinstler-a (8/53)	10.00	30.00	100.00	549-Oswald the Rabbit (Lantz)	3.00	9.00	30.00
492-Duck Album (Disney)	5.00	15.00	50.00	550-The Little Scouts	1.80	5.40	18.00
493-Johnny Mack Brown; photo-c	6.00	18.00	60.00	551-Bozo (4/54)	11.00	32.00	110.00
494-The Little King (#1)	10.00	30.00	100.00	552-Beetle Bailey	5.00	15.00	50.00
495-Uncle Scrooge (#3) (Disney)-by Carl Barks (9/53)				553-Susie Q. Smith	3.50	10.50	35.00
	50.00	150.00	450.00	554-Rusty Riley (Frank Godwin strip-r)	4.00	12.00	40.00
496-The Green Hornet; painted-c	25.00	75.00	250.00	555-Range War (Zane Grey)	3.60	10.80	36.00
497-Zorro (Sword of...)-Kinstler-a	13.50	40.50	135.00	556-Double Trouble With Goober (5/54)	2.00	6.00	20.00
498-Bugs Bunny's Album (9/53)	5.00	15.00	50.00	557-Ben Bowie and His Mountain Men	3.40	10.00	34.00
499-M.G.M.'s Spike and Tyke (#1) (9/53)	3.00	9.00	30.00	558-Elmer Fudd (5/54)	3.00	9.00	30.00
500-Buck Jones	5.50	16.50	55.00	559-I Love Lucy (#2) (TV)-Photo-c	32.50	97.50	325.00
501-Francis the Famous Talking Mule	5.00	15.00	50.00	560-Duck Album (Disney) (5/54)	5.00	15.00	50.00
502-Rootie Kazootie (TV)	7.00	21.00	70.00	561-Mr. Magoo (5/54)	10.00	30.00	100.00
503-Uncle Wiggily (10/53)	5.00	15.00	50.00	562-Goofy (Disney)(#2)	8.00	24.00	80.00

Four Color #578 © Field Enterprises

Four Color #596 © WEST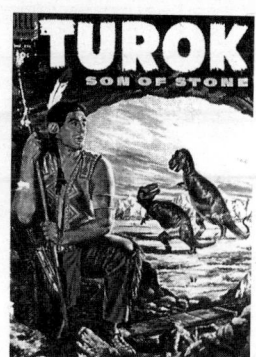

Four Color #617 © Johnston McCulley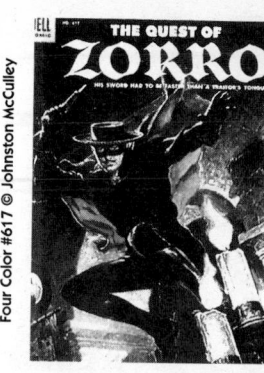

	GD25	FN65	NM94
563-Rhubarb, the Millionaire Cat (6/54)	4.00	12.00	40.00
564-Li'l Bad Wolf (Disney)(#3)	5.00	15.00	50.00
565-Jungle Jim	4.00	12.00	40.00
566-Son of Black Beauty	4.00	12.00	40.00
567-Prince Valiant (#1)-By Bob Fuje (Movie)-Photo-c	10.00	30.00	100.00
568-Gypsy Colt (Movie) (6/54)	5.00	15.00	50.00
569-Priscilla's Pop	4.00	12.00	40.00
570-Bob Clampett's Beany and Cecil (TV)	17.00	51.00	170.00
571-Charlie McCarthy	5.00	15.00	50.00
572-Silvertip (Max Brand) (7/54); Kinstler-a	5.00	15.00	50.00
573-The Little People by Walt Scott	4.00	12.00	40.00
574-The Hand of Zorro; Kinstler-a	13.50	40.50	135.00
575-Annie Oakley and Tagg (TV)-Photo-c	7.50	23.00	75.00
576-Angel (#1) (8/54)	2.70	8.10	27.00
577-M.G.M.'s Spike and Tyke	2.00	6.00	20.00
578-Steve Canyon (8/54)	5.00	15.00	50.00
579-Francis the Famous Talking Mule	5.00	15.00	50.00
580-Six Gun Ranch (Luke Short-8/54)	4.00	12.00	40.00
581-Chip 'N' Dale (#2) (Disney)	5.00	15.00	50.00
582-Mowgli Jungle Book (Kipling) (8/54)	4.00	12.00	40.00
583-The Lost Wagon Train (Zane Grey)	3.60	10.80	36.00
584-Johnny Mack Brown-Photo-c	6.00	18.00	60.00
585-Bugs Bunny's Album	5.00	15.00	50.00
586-Duck Album (Disney)	5.00	15.00	50.00
587-The Little Scouts	1.80	5.40	18.00
588-King Richard and the Crusaders (Movie) (10/54) Matt Baker-a; photo-c	10.00	30.00	100.00
589-Buck Jones	5.50	16.50	55.00
590-Hansel and Gretel; partial photo-c	6.00	18.00	60.00
591-Western Marshal(Ernest Haycox's)-Kinstler-a	6.00	18.00	60.00
592-Super Circus (TV)	6.00	18.00	60.00
593-Oswald the Rabbit (Lantz)	3.00	9.00	30.00
594-Bozo (10/54)	11.00	32.00	110.00
595-Pluto (Disney)	4.00	12.00	40.00
596-Turok, Son of Stone (#1)	67.00	201.00	675.00
597-The Little King	7.00	21.00	70.00
598-Captain Davy Jones	4.00	12.00	40.00
599-Ben Bowie and His Mountain Men	3.40	10.00	34.00
600-Daisy Duck's Diary (#1) (Disney) (11/54)	6.00	18.00	60.00
601-Frosty the Snowman	4.00	12.00	40.00
602-Mr. Magoo and Gerald McBoing-Boing	10.00	30.00	100.00
603-M.G.M.'s The Two Mouseketeers	4.00	12.00	40.00
604-Shadow on the Trail (Zane Grey)	3.60	10.80	36.00
605-The Brownies-not by Kelly (12/54)	3.20	9.50	32.00
606-Sir Lancelot (not TV)	9.00	27.00	90.00
607-Santa Claus Funnies	4.00	12.00	40.00
608-Silvertip- "Valley of Vanishing Men" (Max Brand)-Kinstler-a	5.00	15.00	50.00
609-The Littlest Outlaw (Disney-Movie) (1/55)-Photo-c	7.00	21.00	70.00
610-Drum Beat (Movie); Alan Ladd photo-c	11.00	33.00	110.00
611-Duck Album (Disney)	5.00	15.00	50.00
612-Little Beaver (1/55)	3.00	9.00	30.00
613-Western Marshal (Ernest Haycox's) (2/55)-Kinstler-a	6.00	18.00	60.00
614-20,000 Leagues Under the Sea (Disney) (Movie) (2/55)-Painted-c	9.00	27.00	90.00
615-Daffy	4.50	13.50	45.00
616-To the Last Man (Zane Grey)	3.60	10.80	36.00
617-The Quest of Zorro	12.50	37.50	125.00
618-Johnny Mack Brown; photo-c	6.00	18.00	60.00
619-Krazy Kat; not by Herriman	4.00	12.00	40.00
620-Mowgli Jungle Book (Kipling)	4.00	12.00	40.00

	GD25	FN65	NM94
621-Francis the Famous Talking Mule (4/55)	4.00	12.00	40.00
622-Beetle Bailey	5.00	15.00	50.00
623-Oswald the Rabbit (Lantz)	2.00	6.00	20.00
624-Treasure Island(Disney-Movie)(4/55)-Photo-c	9.00	27.00	90.00
625-Beaver Valley (Disney-Movie)	7.00	21.00	70.00
626-Ben Bowie and His Mountain Men	3.40	10.00	34.00
627-Goofy (Disney) (5/55)	8.00	24.00	80.00
628-Elmer Fudd	3.00	9.00	30.00
629-Lady and the Tramp with Jock (Disney)	6.00	18.00	60.00
630-Priscilla's Pop	4.00	12.00	40.00
631-Davy Crockett, Indian Fighter (#1) (Disney) (5/55) (TV)-Fess Parker photo-c	15.00	45.00	150.00
632-Fighting Caravans (Zane Grey)	3.60	10.80	36.00
633-The Little People by Walt Scott (6/55)	4.00	12.00	40.00
634-Lady and the Tramp Album (Disney) (6/55)	5.00	15.00	50.00
635-Bob Clampett's Beany and Cecil (TV)	17.00	51.00	170.00
636-Chip 'N' Dale (Disney)	5.00	15.00	50.00
637-Silvertip (Max Brand)-Kinstler-a	5.00	15.00	50.00
638-M.G.M.'s Spike and Tyke (8/55)	2.00	6.00	20.00
639-Davy Crockett at the Alamo (Disney) (7/55) (TV)-Fess Parker photo-c	15.00	45.00	150.00
640-Western Marshal(Ernest Haycox's)-Kinstler-a	6.00	18.00	60.00
641-Steve Canyon (1955)-by Caniff	5.00	15.00	50.00
642-M.G.M.'s The Two Mouseketeers	4.00	12.00	40.00
643-Wild Bill Elliott; photo-c	4.00	12.00	40.00
644-Sir Walter Raleigh (5/55)-Based on movie "The Virgin Queen"; photo-c	7.00	21.00	70.00
645-Johnny Mack Brown; photo-c	6.00	18.00	60.00
646-Dotty Dripple and Taffy (#1)	4.00	12.00	40.00
647-Bugs Bunny's Album (9/55)	5.00	15.00	50.00
648-Jace Pearson of the Texas Rangers (TV)-Photo-c	6.00	18.00	60.00
649-Duck Album (Disney)	5.00	15.00	50.00
650-Prince Valiant; by Bob Fuje	6.00	18.00	60.00
651-King Colt (Luke Short) (9/55)-Kinstler-a	4.00	12.00	40.00
652-Buck Jones	4.00	12.00	40.00
653-Smokey the Bear (#1) (10/55)	10.00	30.00	100.00
654-Pluto (Disney)	4.00	12.00	40.00
655-Francis the Famous Talking Mule	4.00	12.00	40.00
656-Turok, Son of Stone (#2) (10/55)	42.00	126.00	420.00
657-Ben Bowie and His Mountain Men	3.40	10.00	34.00
658-Goofy (Disney)	8.00	24.00	80.00
659-Daisy Duck's Diary (Disney)(#2)	5.00	15.00	50.00
660-Little Beaver	3.00	9.00	30.00
661-Frosty the Snowman	4.00	12.00	40.00
662-Zoo Parade (TV)-Marlin Perkins (11/55)	4.50	13.50	45.00
663-Winky Dink (TV)	7.00	21.00	70.00
664-Davy Crockett in the Great Keelboat Race (TV) (Disney) (11/55)-Fess Parker photo-c	14.00	42.00	140.00
665-The African Lion (Disney-Movie) (11/55)	5.40	16.00	54.00
666-Santa Claus Funnies	4.00	12.00	40.00
667-Silvertip and the Stolen Stallion (Max Brand) (12/55)-Kinstler-a	5.00	15.00	50.00
668-Dumbo (Disney) (12/55)-First of two printings. Dumbo on cover with starry sky. Reprints 4-Color #234?; same-c as #234	8.00	24.00	80.00
668-Dumbo (Disney) (1/58)-Second printing. Same cover altered, with Timothy Mouse added. Same contents as above	6.00	18.00	60.00
669-Robin Hood (Disney-Movie) (12/55)-Reprints 413 plus-c; photo-c	5.00	15.00	50.00
670-M.G.M.'s Mouse Musketeers (#1) (1/56)-Formerly the Two Mouseketeers	3.00	9.00	30.00
671-Davy Crockett and the River Pirates (TV) (Disney) (12/55)-Jesse Marsh-a; Fess Parker photo-c	14.00	42.00	140.00
672-Quentin Durward (1/56) (Movie)-Photo-c	7.00	21.00	70.00

Four Color #688 © DELL

Four Color #699 © KFS

Four Color #752 © KFS

	GD25	FN65	NM94
673-Buffalo Bill, Jr. (#1) (TV)-James Arness photo-c	6.30	19.00	63.00
674-The Little Rascals (#1) (TV)	7.00	21.00	70.00
675-Steve Donovan, Western Marshal (#1) (TV)-Kinstler-a; photo-c			
	8.00	24.00	80.00
676-Will-Yum!	2.70	8.00	27.00
677-Little King	7.00	21.00	70.00
678-The Last Hunt (Movie)-Photo-c	7.00	21.00	70.00
679-Gunsmoke (#1) (TV)-Photo-c	13.00	40.00	130.00
680-Out Our Way with the Worry Wart (2/56)	3.00	9.00	30.00
681-Forever, Darling (Movie) with Lucille Ball & Desi Arnaz (2/56)-; photo-c			
	11.00	33.00	110.00
682-When Knighthood Was in Flower (Disney-Movie)-Reprint of #505; Renamed			
the Sword & the Rose for the novel; photo-c	7.00	21.00	70.00
683-Hi and Lois (3/56)	3.00	9.00	30.00
684-Helen of Troy (Movie)-Buscema-a; photo-c	11.00	33.00	110.00
685-Johnny Mack Brown; photo-c	6.00	18.00	60.00
686-Duck Album (Disney)	5.00	15.00	50.00
687-The Indian Fighter (Movie)-Kirk Douglas photo-c	6.00	18.00	60.00
688-Alexander the Great (Movie) (5/56)-Buscema-a; photo-c			
	7.00	20.00	68.00
689-Elmer Fudd (3/56)	3.00	9.00	30.00
690-The Conqueror (Movie) - John Wayne	14.50	43.50	145.00
691-Dotty Dripple and Taffy	3.00	9.00	30.00
692-The Little People-Walt Scott	4.00	12.00	40.00
693-Song of the South (Disney) (1956)-Partial reprint of #129			
	10.00	30.00	100.00
694-Super Circus (TV)-Photo-c	6.00	18.00	60.00
695-Little Beaver	3.00	9.00	30.00
696-Krazy Kat; not by Herriman (4/56)	4.00	12.00	40.00
697-Oswald the Rabbit (Lantz)	2.00	6.00	20.00
698-Francis the Famous Talking Mule (4/56)	4.00	12.00	40.00
699-Prince Valiant-by Bob Fuje	6.00	18.00	60.00
700-Water Birds and the Olympic Elk (Disney-Movie) (4/56)			
	6.00	18.00	60.00
701-Jiminy Cricket (#1) (Disney) (5/56)	9.00	27.00	90.00
702-The Goofy Success Story (Disney)	8.00	24.00	80.00
703-Scamp (#1) (Disney)	9.00	27.00	90.00
704-Priscilla's Pop (5/56)	4.00	12.00	40.00
705-Brave Eagle (#1) (TV)-Photo-c	6.00	18.00	60.00
706-Bongo and Lumpjaw (Disney) (6/56)	4.50	13.50	45.00
707-Corky and White Shadow (Disney) (5/56)-Mickey Mouse Club (TV);			
photo-c	8.00	24.00	80.00
708-Smokey the Bear	5.00	15.00	50.00
709-The Searchers (Movie) - John Wayne photo-c	26.00	78.00	260.00
710-Francis the Famous Talking Mule	4.00	12.00	40.00
711-M.G.M's Mouse Musketeers	2.00	6.00	20.00
712-The Great Locomotive Chase (Disney-Movie) (9/56)-Photo-c			
	8.00	24.00	80.00
713-The Animal World (Movie) (8/56)	5.00	15.00	50.00
714-Spin and Marty (#1) (TV) (Disney)-Mickey Mouse Club (6/56); photo-c			
	11.00	33.00	110.00
715-Timmy (8/56)	4.00	12.00	40.00
716-Man in Space (Disney)(A science feature from Tomorrowland)			
	9.00	27.00	90.00
717-Moby Dick (Movie)-Gregory Peck photo-c	9.00	27.00	90.00
718-Dotty Dripple and Taffy	3.00	9.00	30.00
719-Prince Valiant; by Bob Fuje (8/56)	6.00	18.00	60.00
720-Gunsmoke (TV)-James Arness photo-c	7.00	21.00	70.00
721-Captain Kangaroo (TV)-Photo-c	15.00	45.00	145.00
722-Johnny Mack Brown-Photo-c	6.00	18.00	60.00
723-Santiago (Movie)-Kinstler-a (9/56); Alan Ladd photo-c			
	11.00	33.00	110.00
724-Bugs Bunny's Album	5.00	15.00	50.00
725-Elmer Fudd (9/56)	2.00	6.00	20.00

	GD25	FN65	NM94
726-Duck Album (Disney) (9/56)	5.00	15.00	50.0
727-The Nature of Things (TV) (Disney)-Jesse Marsh-a			
	7.00	21.00	70.0
728-M.G.M's Mouse Musketeers	2.00	6.00	20.0
729-Bob Son of Battle (11/56)	4.00	12.00	40.0
730-Smokey Stover	3.80	11.40	38.0
731-Silvertip and The Fighting Four (Max Brand)-Kinstler-a			
	5.00	15.00	50.0
732-Zorro, the Challenge of (10/56)	12.50	37.50	125.0
733-Buck Jones	4.00	12.00	40.
734-Cheyenne (#1) (TV) (10/56)-Clint Walker photo-c			
	17.00	51.00	170.0
735-Crusader Rabbit (#1) (TV)	29.00	87.00	290.0
736-Pluto (Disney)	4.00	12.00	40.0
737-Steve Canyon-Caniff-a	5.00	15.00	50.0
738-Westward Ho, the Wagons (Disney-Movie)-Fess Parker photo-c			
	10.00	30.00	100.0
739-Bounty Guns (Luke Short)-Drucker-a	4.00	12.00	40.0
740-Chilly Willy (#1) (Walter Lantz)	4.00	12.00	40.0
741-The Fastest Gun Alive (Movie)(9/56)-Photo-c	8.00	24.00	80.0
742-Buffalo Bill, Jr. (TV)-Photo-c	4.50	13.50	45.0
743-Daisy Duck's Diary (Disney) (11/56)	5.00	15.00	50.0
744-Little Beaver	3.00	9.00	30.0
745-Francis the Famous Talking Mule	4.00	12.00	40.0
746-Dotty Dripple and Taffy	3.00	9.00	30.0
747-Goofy (Disney)	8.00	24.00	80.0
748-Frosty the Snowman (11/56)	3.50	10.50	35.
749-Secrets of Life (Disney-Movie)-Photo-c	6.00	18.00	60.
750-The Great Cat Family (Disney-TV/Movie)-Pinocchio & Alice app.			
	6.00	18.00	60.
751-Our Miss Brooks (TV)-Photo-c	8.00	24.00	80.
752-Mandrake, the Magician	10.00	30.00	100.
753-Walt Scott's Little People (11/56)	4.00	12.00	40.
754-Smokey the Bear	5.00	15.00	50.
755-The Littlest Snowman (12/56)	3.60	11.00	36.
756-Santa Claus Funnies	4.00	12.00	40.
757-The True Story of Jesse James (Movie)-Photo-c			
	10.00	30.00	100.
758-Bear Country (Disney-Movie)	5.40	16.00	54.
759-Circus Boy (TV)-The Monkees' Mickey Dolenz photo-c (12/56)			
	11.00	33.00	110.
760-The Hardy Boys (#1) (TV) (Disney)-Mickey Mouse Club; photo-c			
	11.00	33.00	110.
761-Howdy Doody (TV) (1/57)	9.50	28.50	95.
762-The Sharkfighters (Movie) (1/57); Buscema-a; photo-c			
	10.00	30.00	100.
763-Grandma Duck's Farm Friends (#1) (Disney)	8.00	24.00	80.
764-M.G.M's Mouse Musketeers	2.00	6.00	20.
765-Will-Yum!	2.70	8.00	27.
766-Buffalo Bill, Jr. (TV)-Photo-c	4.50	13.50	45.
767-Spin and Marty (TV) (Disney)-Mickey Mouse Club (2/57)			
	10.00	30.00	100.
768-Steve Donovan, Western Marshal (TV)-Kinstler-a; photo-c			
	6.00	18.00	60.
769-Gunsmoke (TV)-James Arness photo-c	7.00	21.00	70.
770-Brave Eagle (TV)-Photo-c	4.00	12.00	40.
771-Brand of Empire (Luke Short)(3/57)-Drucker-a	4.00	12.00	40.
772-Cheyenne (TV)-Clint Walker photo-c	7.50	22.50	75.
773-The Brave One (Movie)-Photo-c	5.00	15.00	50.
774-Hi and Lois (3/57)	3.00	9.00	30.
775-Sir Lancelot and Brian (TV)-Buscema-a; photo-c			
	10.00	30.00	100.
776-Johnny Mack Brown; photo-c	6.00	18.00	60.
777-Scamp (Disney) (3/57)	7.00	21.00	70.

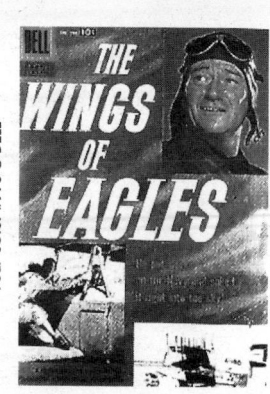

Four Color #790 © DELL

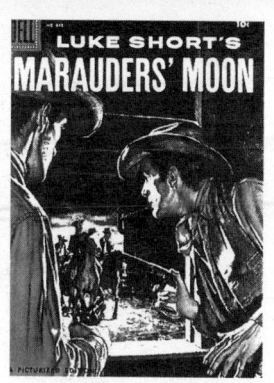

Four Color #848 © WDC

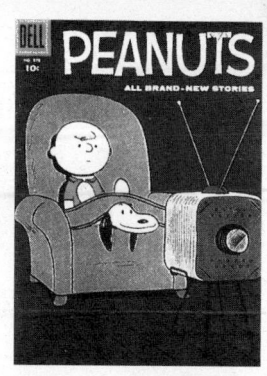

Four Color #878 © UFS

FO

	GD25	FN65	NM94
778-The Little Rascals (TV)	4.00	12.00	40.00
779-Lee Hunter, Indian Fighter (3/57)	5.00	15.00	50.00
780-Captain Kangaroo (TV)-Photo-c	13.00	40.00	125.00
781-Fury (#1) (TV) (3/57)-Photo-c	10.00	30.00	100.00
782-Duck Album (Disney)	5.00	15.00	50.00
783-Elmer Fudd	2.00	6.00	20.00
784-Around the World in 80 Days (Movie) (2/57)-Photo-c			
	6.30	18.00	63.00
785-Circus Boy (TV) (4/57)-The Monkees' Mickey Dolenz photo-c			
	11.00	33.00	110.00
786-Cinderella (Disney) (3/57)-Partial-r of #272	6.00	18.00	60.00
787-Little Hiawatha (Disney) (4/57)(#2)	5.00	15.00	50.00
788-Prince Valiant; by Bob Fuje	6.00	18.00	60.00
789-Silvertip-Valley Thieves (Max Brand) (4/57)-Kinstler-a			
	5.00	15.00	50.00
790-The Wings of Eagles (Movie) (John Wayne)-Toth-a; John Wayne photo-c; 10 & 15¢ editions exist			
	14.50	43.50	145.00
791-77th Bengal Lancers (TV)-Photo-c	7.00	21.00	70.00
792-Oswald the Rabbit (Lantz)	2.00	6.00	20.00
793-Morty Meekle	3.00	9.00	30.00
794-The Count of Monte Cristo (5/57) (Movie)-Buscema-a			
	10.00	30.00	100.00
795-Jiminy Cricket (Disney)(#2)	6.00	18.00	60.00
796-Ludwig Bemelman's Madeleine and Genevieve	4.00	12.00	40.00
797-Gunsmoke (TV)-Photo-c	7.00	21.00	70.00
798-Buffalo Bill, Jr. (TV)-Photo-c	4.50	13.50	45.00
799-Priscilla's Pop	4.00	12.00	40.00
800-The Buccaneers (TV)-Photo-c	6.30	19.00	63.00
801-Dotty Dripple and Taffy	3.00	9.00	30.00
802-Goofy (Disney) (5/57)	8.00	24.00	80.00
803-Cheyenne-Clint Walker photo-c	7.50	22.50	75.00
804-Steve Canyon-Caniff-a (1957)	5.00	15.00	50.00
805-Crusader Rabbit (TV)	23.00	70.00	230.00
806-Scamp (Disney) (6/57)	7.00	21.00	70.00
807-Savage Range (Luke Short)-Drucker-a	4.00	12.00	40.00
808-Spin and Marty (TV)(Disney)-Mickey Mouse Club; photo-c			
	10.00	30.00	100.00
809-The Little People (Walt Scott)	4.00	12.00	40.00
810-Francis the Famous Talking Mule	3.50	11.00	35.00
811-Howdy Doody (TV) (7/57)	9.50	28.50	95.00
812-The Big Land (Movie); Alan Ladd photo-c	10.00	30.00	100.00
813-Circus Boy (TV)-The Monkees' Mickey Dolenz photo-c			
	11.00	33.00	110.00
814-Covered Wagons, Ho! (Disney)-Donald Duck (TV) (6/57); Mickey Mouse app.			
	6.00	18.00	60.00
815-Dragoon Wells Massacre (Movie)-photo-c	9.00	27.00	90.00
816-Brave Eagle (TV)-photo-c	4.00	12.00	40.00
817-Little Beaver	3.00	9.00	30.00
818-Smokey the Bear (6/57)	5.00	15.00	50.00
819-Mickey Mouse in Magicland (Disney) (7/57)	4.00	12.00	40.00
820-The Oklahoman (Movie)-Photo-c	10.00	30.00	100.00
821-Wringle Wrangle (Disney)-Based on movie "Westward Ho, the Wagons"; Marsh-a; Fess Parker photo-c			
	9.00	27.00	90.00
822-Paul Revere's Ride with Johnny Tremain (TV) (Disney)-Toth-a			
	12.50	37.50	125.00
823-Timmy	3.00	9.00	30.00
824-The Pride and the Passion (Movie) (8/57)-Frank Sinatra & Cary Grant photo-c			
	9.00	27.00	90.00
825-The Little Rascals (TV)	4.00	12.00	40.00
826-Spin and Marty and Annette (TV) (Disney)-Mickey Mouse Club; Annette Funicello photo-c			
	24.00	72.00	240.00
827-Smokey Stover (8/57)	3.80	11.40	38.00
828-Buffalo Bill, Jr. (TV)-Photo-c	4.50	13.50	45.00
829-Tales of the Pony Express (TV) (8/57)-Painted-c	5.00	15.00	50.00

	GD25	FN65	NM94
830-The Hardy Boys (TV) (Disney)-Mickey Mouse Club (8/57); photo-c			
	10.00	30.00	100.00
831-No Sleep 'Til Dawn (Movie)-Karl Malden photo-c	7.00	21.00	70.00
832-Lolly and Pepper (#1)	4.00	12.00	40.00
833-Scamp (Disney) (9/57)	7.00	21.00	70.00
834-Johnny Mack Brown; photo-c	6.00	18.00	60.00
835-Silvertip-The False Rider (Max Brand)	4.50	13.50	45.00
836-Man in Flight (Disney) (TV) (9/57)	7.00	21.00	70.00
837-All-American Athlete Cotton Woods	5.00	15.00	50.00
838-Bugs Bunny's Life Story Album (9/57)	5.00	15.00	50.00
839-The Vigilantes (Movie)	7.00	21.00	70.00
840-Duck Album (Disney) (9/57)	5.00	15.00	50.00
841-Elmer Fudd	2.00	6.00	20.00
842-The Nature of Things (Disney-Movie) ('57)-Jesse Marsh-a (TV series)			
	8.00	24.00	80.00
843-The First Americans (Disney) (TV)-Marsh-a	10.00	30.00	100.00
844-Gunsmoke (TV)-Photo-c	7.00	21.00	70.00
845-The Land Unknown (Movie)-Alex Toth-a	14.50	44.00	145.00
846-Gun Glory (Movie)-by Alex Toth; photo-c	12.00	36.00	120.00
847-Perri (squirrels) (Disney-Movie)-Two different covers published			
	8.00	24.00	80.00
848-Marauder's Moon (Luke Short)	5.00	15.00	50.00
849-Prince Valiant; by Bob Fuje	6.00	18.00	60.00
850-Buck Jones	4.00	12.00	40.00
851-The Story of Mankind (Movie) (1/58)-Hedy Lamarr & Vincent Price photo-c			
	7.00	21.00	70.00
852-Chilly Willy (2/58) (Lantz)	3.00	9.00	30.00
853-Pluto (Disney) (10/57)	4.00	12.00	40.00
854-The Hunchback of Notre Dame (Movie)-Photo-c	13.00	40.00	130.00
855-Broken Arrow (TV)-Photo-c	5.40	18.00	54.00
856-Buffalo Bill, Jr. (TV)-Photo-c	4.50	13.50	45.00
857-The Goofy Adventure Story (Disney) (11/57)	8.00	24.00	80.00
858-Daisy Duck's Diary (Disney) (11/57)	4.00	12.00	40.00
859-Topper and Neil (TV) (11/57)	4.00	12.00	40.00
860-Wyatt Earp (#1) (TV)-Manning-a; photo-c	11.00	33.00	110.00
861-Frosty the Snowman	3.50	10.50	35.00
862-The Truth About Mother Goose (Disney-Movie) (11/57)			
	8.00	24.00	80.00
863-Francis the Famous Talking Mule	3.50	11.00	35.00
864-The Littlest Snowman	3.60	11.00	36.00
865-Andy Burnett (TV) (Disney) (12/57)-Photo-c	10.00	30.00	100.00
866-Mars and Beyond (Disney-TV)(A science feature from Tomorrowland)			
	10.00	30.00	90.00
867-Santa Claus Funnies	4.00	12.00	40.00
868-The Little People (12/57)	4.00	12.00	40.00
869-Old Yeller (Disney-Movie)-Photo-c	7.00	21.00	70.00
870-Little Beaver (1/58)	3.00	9.00	30.00
871-Curly Kayoe	2.70	8.00	27.00
872-Captain Kangaroo (TV)-Photo-c	13.00	40.00	125.00
873-Grandma Duck's Farm Friends (Disney)	6.00	18.00	60.00
874-Old Ironsides (Disney-Movie with Johnny Tremain) (1/58)			
	7.00	21.00	70.00
875-Trumpets West (Luke Short) (2/58)	4.00	12.00	40.00
876-Tales of Wells Fargo (#1)(TV)(2/58)-Photo-c	10.00	30.00	100.00
877-Frontier Doctor with Rex Allen (TV)-Alex Toth-a; Rex Allen photo-c			
	10.00	30.00	100.00
878-Peanuts (#1)-Schulz-c only (2/58)	14.00	43.00	135.00
879-Brave Eagle (TV) (2/58)-Photo-c	4.00	12.00	40.00
880-Steve Donovan, Western Marshal-Drucker-a (TV)-Photo-c			
	4.00	12.00	40.00
881-The Captain and the Kids (2/58)	3.00	9.00	30.00
882-Zorro (Disney)-1st Disney issue; by Alex Toth (TV) (2/58); photo-c			
	18.00	54.00	180.00
883-The Little Rascals (TV)	4.00	12.00	40.00

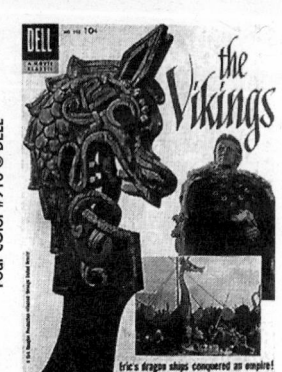

Four Color #910 © DELL

Four Color #911 © DELL

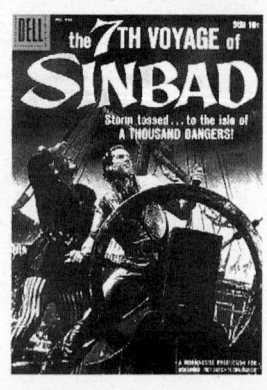

Four Color #944 © DELL

884-Hawkeye and the Last of the Mohicans (TV) (3/58); photo-c
| | 7.00 | 21.00 | 70.00 |
885-Fury (TV) (3/58)-Photo-c
| | 7.00 | 21.00 | 70.00 |
886-Bongo and Lumpjaw (Disney) (3/58)
| | 3.50 | 10.50 | 35.00 |
887-The Hardy Boys (Disney) (TV)-Mickey Mouse Club (1/58)-Photo-c
| | 10.00 | 30.00 | 100.00 |
888-Elmer Fudd (3/58)
| | 2.00 | 6.00 | 20.00 |
889-Clint and Mac (Disney) (TV) (3/58)-Alex Toth-a; photo-c
| | 14.00 | 43.00 | 140.00 |
890-Wyatt Earp (TV)-by Russ Manning; photo-c
| | 7.50 | 23.00 | 75.00 |
891-Light in the Forest (Disney-Movie) (3/58)-Fess Parker photo-c
| | 9.00 | 27.00 | 90.00 |
892-Maverick (#1) (TV) (4/58)-James Garner photo-c
| | 25.00 | 75.00 | 250.00 |
893-Jim Bowie (TV)-Photo-c
| | 6.00 | 18.00 | 60.00 |
894-Oswald the Rabbit (Lantz)
| | 2.00 | 6.00 | 20.00 |
895-Wagon Train (#1) (TV) (3/58)-Photo-c
| | 12.00 | 36.00 | 120.00 |
896-The Adventures of Tinker Bell (Disney)
| | 8.00 | 24.00 | 80.00 |
897-Jiminy Cricket (Disney)
| | 6.00 | 18.00 | 60.00 |
898-Silvertip (Max Brand)-Kinstler-a (5/58)
| | 5.00 | 15.00 | 50.00 |
899-Goofy (Disney) (5/58)
| | 5.00 | 15.00 | 50.00 |
900-Prince Valiant; by Bob Fuje
| | 6.00 | 18.00 | 60.00 |
901-Little Hiawatha (Disney)
| | 5.00 | 15.00 | 50.00 |
902-Will-Yum!
| | 2.70 | 8.00 | 27.00 |
903-Dotty Dripple and Taffy
| | 3.00 | 9.00 | 30.00 |
904-Lee Hunter, Indian Fighter
| | 4.00 | 12.00 | 40.00 |
905-Annette (Disney) (TV) (5/58)-Mickey Mouse Club; Annette Funicello photo-c
| | 26.00 | 78.00 | 260.00 |
906-Francis the Famous Talking Mule
| | 3.50 | 11.00 | 35.00 |
907-Sugarfoot (#1) (TV)Toth-a; photo-c
| | 13.00 | 40.00 | 125.00 |
908-The Little People and the Giant-Walt Scott (5/58)
| | 4.00 | 12.00 | 40.00 |
909-Smitty
| | 3.00 | 9.00 | 30.00 |
910-The Vikings (Movie)-Buscema-a; Kirk Douglas photo-c
| | 9.00 | 27.00 | 90.00 |
911-The Gray Ghost (TV)-Photo-c
| | 9.00 | 27.00 | 90.00 |
912-Leave It to Beaver (#1) (TV)-Photo-c
| | 18.00 | 54.00 | 180.00 |
913-The Left-Handed Gun (Movie) (7/58); Paul Newman photo-c
| | 11.00 | 33.00 | 110.00 |
914-No Time for Sergeants (Movie)-Andy Griffith photo-c; Toth-a
| | 10.00 | 30.00 | 100.00 |
915-Casey Jones (TV)-Alan Hale photo-c
| | 6.30 | 19.00 | 63.00 |
916-Red Ryder Ranch Comics (7/58)
| | 3.00 | 9.00 | 30.00 |
917-The Life of Riley (TV)-Photo-c
| | 12.00 | 36.00 | 120.00 |
918-Beep Beep, the Roadrunner (#1) (7/58)-Published with two different back covers
| | 9.00 | 27.00 | 90.00 |
919-Boots and Saddles (#1) (TV)-Photo-c
| | 9.00 | 27.00 | 90.00 |
920-Zorro (Disney) (TV) (6/58)Toth-a; photo-c
| | 12.50 | 37.50 | 125.00 |
921-Wyatt Earp (TV)-Manning-a; photo-c
| | 7.50 | 23.00 | 75.00 |
922-Johnny Mack Brown by Russ Manning; photo-c
| | 7.00 | 21.00 | 70.00 |
923-Timmy
| | 3.00 | 9.00 | 30.00 |
924-Colt .45 (#1) (TV) (8/58)-W. Preston photo-c
| | 10.00 | 30.00 | 100.00 |
925-Last of the Fast Guns (Movie) (8/58)-Photo-c
| | 7.00 | 21.00 | 70.00 |
926-Peter Pan (Disney)-Reprint of #442
| | 5.00 | 15.00 | 50.00 |
927-Top Gun (Luke Short) Buscema-a
| | 4.00 | 12.00 | 40.00 |
928-Sea Hunt (#1) (9/58) (TV)-Lloyd Bridges photo-c
| | 12.00 | 36.00 | 120.00 |
929-Brave Eagle (TV)
| | 4.00 | 12.00 | 40.00 |
930-Maverick (TV) (7/58)-James Garner photo-c
| | 11.00 | 33.00 | 110.00 |
931-Have Gun, Will Travel (#1) (TV)-Photo-c
| | 14.00 | 42.00 | 140.00 |
932-Smokey the Bear (His Life Story)
| | 5.00 | 15.00 | 50.00 |
933-Zorro (Disney, 9/58) (TV)-Alex Toth-a; photo-c
| | 12.50 | 37.50 | 125.00 |
934-Restless Gun (#1) (TV)-Photo-c
| | 11.00 | 33.00 | 110.00 |
935-King of the Royal Mounted
| | 4.00 | 12.00 | 40.00 |

936-The Little Rascals (TV)
| | 4.00 | 12.00 | 40.00 |
937-Ruff and Reddy (#1) (9/58) (TV) (1st Hanna-Barbera comic book)
| | 12.00 | 36.00 | 120.0 |
938-Elmer Fudd (9/58)
| | 2.00 | 6.00 | 20.0 |
939-Steve Canyon - not by Caniff
| | 5.00 | 15.00 | 50.0 |
940-Lolly and Pepper (10/58)
| | 3.00 | 9.00 | 30.0 |
941-Pluto (Disney) (10/58)
| | 3.50 | 10.00 | 35.0 |
942-Pony Express (TV)
| | 5.00 | 15.00 | 50.0 |
943-White Wilderness (Disney-Movie) (10/58)
| | 7.00 | 21.00 | 70.0 |
944-The 7th Voyage of Sinbad (Movie) (9/58)-Buscema-a; photo-c
| | 13.00 | 40.00 | 130.0 |
945-Maverick (TV)-James Garner/Jack Kelly photo-c
| | 11.00 | 33.00 | 110.0 |
946-The Big Country (Movie)-Photo-c
| | 7.00 | 21.00 | 70.0 |
947-Broken Arrow (TV)-Photo-c (11/58)
| | 4.50 | 15.00 | 45.0 |
948-Daisy Duck's Diary (Disney) (11/58)
| | 4.00 | 12.00 | 40.0 |
949-High Adventure(Lowell Thomas')(TV)-Photo-c
| | 5.00 | 15.00 | 50.0 |
950-Frosty the Snowman
| | 3.50 | 10.50 | 35.0 |
951-The Lennon Sisters Life Story (TV)-Toth-a, 32 pgs.; photo-c
| | 15.00 | 45.00 | 145.0 |
952-Goofy (Disney) (11/58)
| | 5.00 | 15.00 | 50.0 |
953-Francis the Famous Talking Mule
| | 3.50 | 11.00 | 35.0 |
954-Man in Space-Satellites (TV)
| | 7.00 | 21.00 | 70.0 |
955-Hi and Lois (11/58)
| | 3.00 | 9.00 | 30.0 |
956-Ricky Nelson (#1) (TV)-Photo-c
| | 20.00 | 60.00 | 200.0 |
957-Buffalo Bee (#1) (TV)
| | 9.00 | 27.00 | 90.0 |
958-Santa Claus Funnies
| | 3.50 | 10.50 | 35.0 |
959-Christmas Stories-(Walt Scott's Little People) (1951-56 strip reprints)
| | 4.00 | 12.00 | 40.0 |
960-Zorro (Disney) (TV) (12/58)-Toth art; photo-c | 12.50 | 37.50 | 125.0 |
961-Jace Pearson's Tales of the Texas Rangers (TV)-Spiegle-a; photo-c
| | 5.00 | 15.00 | 50.0 |
962-Maverick (TV) (1/59)-James Garner/Jack Kelly photo-c
| | 11.00 | 33.00 | 110.0 |
963-Johnny Mack Brown; photo-c
| | 6.00 | 18.00 | 60.0 |
964-The Hardy Boys (TV) (Disney) (1/59)-Mickey Mouse Club; photo-c
| | 10.00 | 30.00 | 100.0 |
965-Grandma Duck's Farm Friends (Disney)(1/59)
| | 5.00 | 15.00 | 50.0 |
966-Tonka (starring Sal Mineo; Disney-Movie)-Photo-c
| | 9.00 | 27.00 | 90.0 |
967-Chilly Willy (2/59) (Lantz)
| | 3.00 | 9.00 | 30.0 |
968-Tales of Wells Fargo (TV)-Photo-c
| | 9.00 | 27.00 | 90.0 |
969-Peanuts (2/59)
| | 10.00 | 30.00 | 100.0 |
970-Lawman (#1) (TV)-Photo-c
| | 13.00 | 39.00 | 130.0 |
971-Wagon Train (TV)-Photo-c
| | 6.50 | 19.50 | 65.0 |
972-Tom Thumb (Movie)-George Pal (1/59)
| | 10.00 | 30.00 | 100.0 |
973-Sleeping Beauty and the Prince(Disney)(5/59)
| | 13.00 | 40.00 | 130.0 |
974-The Little Rascals (TV) (3/59)
| | 4.00 | 12.00 | 40.0 |
975-Fury (TV)-Photo-c
| | 7.00 | 21.00 | 70.0 |
976-Zorro (Disney) (TV)-Toth-a; photo-c | 12.50 | 37.50 | 125.0 |
977-Elmer Fudd (3/59)
| | 2.00 | 6.00 | 20.0 |
978-Lolly and Pepper
| | 3.00 | 9.00 | 30.0 |
979-Oswald the Rabbit (Lantz)
| | 2.00 | 6.00 | 20.0 |
980-Maverick (TV) (4-6/59)-James Garner/Jack Kelly photo-c
| | 10.00 | 30.00 | 110.0 |
981-Ruff and Reddy (TV) (Hanna-Barbera)
| | 8.00 | 24.00 | 80.0 |
982-The New Adventures of Tinker Bell (TV) (Disney)
| | 8.00 | 24.00 | 80.0 |
983-Have Gun, Will Travel (TV) (4-6/59)-Photo-c | 8.00 | 24.00 | 80.0 |
984-Sleeping Beauty's Fairy Godmothers (Disney) | 10.00 | 30.00 | 100.0 |
985-Shaggy Dog (Disney-Movie)-Photo-all four covers; Annette on back-c(5/59)
| | 7.00 | 21.00 | 70.0 |
986-Restless Gun (TV)-Photo-c
| | 8.00 | 24.00 | 80.0 |
987-Goofy (Disney) (7/59)
| | 5.00 | 15.00 | 50.0 |

Four Color #1006 © DELL

HERCULES
The Strongest Man in the World

His mighty arms destroyed a throne, and launched the quest for the GOLDEN FLEECE!

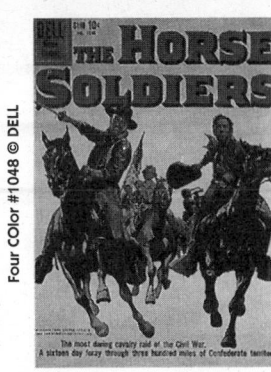

Four Color #1048 © Warner Bros.

THE HORSE SOLDIERS

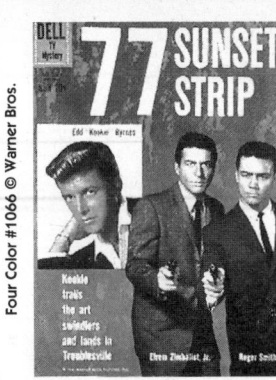

Four Color #1066 © Warner Bros.

77 SUNSET STRIP

FO

	GD25	FN65	NM94
988-Little Hiawatha (Disney)	5.00	15.00	50.00
989-Jiminy Cricket (Disney) (5-7/59)	6.00	18.00	60.00
990-Huckleberry Hound (#1)(TV)(Hanna-Barbera); 1st app. Huck, Yogi Bear, & Pixie & Dixie & Mr. Jinx	10.00	30.00	100.00
991-Francis the Famous Talking Mule	3.50	11.00	35.00
992-Sugarfoot (TV)-Toth-a; photo-c	13.00	40.00	125.00
993-Jim Bowie (TV)-Photo-c	6.00	18.00	60.00
994-Sea Hunt (TV)-Lloyd Bridges photo-c	8.50	26.00	85.00
995-Donald Duck Album (Disney) (5-7/59)(#1)	5.00	15.00	50.00
996-Nevada (Zane Grey)	3.20	9.60	32.00
997-Walt Disney Presents-Tales of Texas John Slaughter (#1) (TV) (Disney)-Photo-c; photo of W. Disney inside-c	7.00	21.00	70.00
998-Ricky Nelson (TV)-Photo-c	20.00	60.00	200.00
999-Leave It to Beaver (TV)-Photo-c	16.00	48.00	160.00
1000-The Gray Ghost (TV) (6-8/59)-Photo-c	9.00	27.00	90.00
1001-Lowell Thomas' High Adventure (TV) (8-10/59)-Photo-c	5.00	15.00	50.00
1002-Buffalo Bee	6.30	19.00	63.00
1003-Zorro (Disney)-Toth-a; photo-c	12.50	37.50	125.00
1004-Colt .45 (TV) (6-8/59)-Photo-c	7.50	22.50	75.00
1005-Maverick (TV)-James Garner/Jack Kelly photo-c	11.00	33.00	110.00
1006-Hercules (Movie)-Buscema-a; photo-c	11.00	33.00	110.00
1007-John Paul Jones (Movie)-Robert Stack photo-c	5.00	15.00	50.00
1008-Beep Beep, the Road Runner (7-9/59)	4.50	15.00	45.00
1009-The Rifleman (#1) (TV)-Photo-c	22.00	66.00	220.00
1010-Grandma Duck's Farm Friends (Disney)-by Carl Barks	14.00	43.00	135.00
1011-Buckskin (#1) (TV)-Photo-c	9.00	27.00	90.00
1012-Last Train from Gun Hill (Movie) (7/59)-Photo-c	9.00	27.00	90.00
1013-Bat Masterson (#1) (TV) (8/59)-Gene Barry photo-c	12.50	40.00	125.00
1014-The Lennon Sisters (TV)-Toth-a; photo-c	15.00	45.00	145.00
1015-Peanuts-Schulz-c	10.00	30.00	100.00
1016-Smokey the Bear Nature Stories	4.00	12.00	40.00
1017-Chilly Willy (Lantz)	3.00	9.00	30.00
1018-Rio Bravo (Movie)(6/59)-John Wayne; Toth-a; John Wayne, Dean Martin & Ricky Nelson photo-c	20.00	60.00	200.00
1019-Wagon Train (TV)-Photo-c	6.50	19.50	65.00
1020-Jungle Jim-McWilliams-a	3.00	9.00	30.00
1021-Jace Pearson's Tales of the Texas Rangers (TV)-Photo-c	5.00	15.00	50.00
1022-Timmy	3.00	9.00	30.00
1023-Tales of Wells Fargo (TV)-Photo-c	9.00	27.00	90.00
1024-Darby O'Gill and the Little People (Disney-Movie)-Toth-a; photo-c	14.00	43.00	125.00
1025-Vacation in Disneyland (8-10/59)-Carl Barks-a(24pgs.) (Disney)	20.00	60.00	200.00
1026-Spin and Marty (TV) (Disney) (9-11/59)-Mickey Mouse Club; photo-c	7.50	22.50	75.00
1027-The Texan (#1)(TV)-Photo-c	8.00	24.00	80.00
1028-Rawhide (#1) (TV) (9-11/59)-Clint Eastwood photo-c; Tufts-a	23.00	68.00	225.00
1029-Boots and Saddles (TV) (9/59)-Photo-c	6.00	18.00	60.00
1030-Spanky and Alfalfa, the Little Rascals (TV)	4.00	12.00	40.00
1031-Fury (TV)-Photo-c	7.00	21.00	70.00
1032-Elmer Fudd	2.00	6.00	20.00
1033-Steve Canyon-not by Caniff; photo-c	5.00	15.00	50.00
1034-Nancy and Sluggo Summer Camp (9-11/59)	3.00	9.00	30.00
1035-Lawman (TV)-Photo-c	7.00	21.00	70.00
1036-The Big Circus (Movie)-Photo-c	6.00	18.00	60.00
1037-Zorro (Disney) (TV)-Tufts-a; Annette Funicello photo-c	16.00	48.00	160.00
1038-Ruff and Reddy (TV)(Hanna-Barbera)(1959)	8.00	24.00	80.00

	GD25	FN65	NM94
1039-Pluto (Disney) (11-1/60)	3.50	10.00	35.00
1040-Quick Draw McGraw (#1) (TV) (Hanna-Barbera) (12-2/60)	11.00	33.00	110.00
1041-Sea Hunt (TV) (10-12/59)-Toth-a; Lloyd Bridges photo-c	9.00	27.00	90.00
1042-The Three Chipmunks (Alvin, Simon & Theodore) (#1) (TV) (10-12/59)	3.60	10.80	36.00
1043-The Three Stooges (#1)-Photo-c	18.00	54.00	180.00
1044-Have Gun, Will Travel (TV)-Photo-c	9.00	27.00	90.00
1045-Restless Gun (TV)-Photo-c	8.00	24.00	80.00
1046-Beep Beep, the Road Runner (11-1/60)	4.50	15.00	45.00
1047-Gyro Gearloose (#1) (Disney)-All Barks-c/a	17.50	52.50	175.00
1048-The Horse Soldiers (Movie) (John Wayne)-Sekowsky-a; painted cover featuring John Wayne	13.00	40.00	130.00
1049-Don't Give Up the Ship (Movie) (8/59)-Jerry Lewis photo-c	7.00	21.00	70.00
1050-Huckleberry Hound (TV) (Hanna-Barbera) (10-12/59)	7.00	21.00	70.00
1051-Donald in Mathmagic Land (Disney-Movie)	10.00	30.00	100.00
1052-Ben-Hur (Movie) (11/59)-Manning-a	10.00	30.00	100.00
1053-Goofy (Disney) (11-1/60)	5.00	15.00	50.00
1054-Huckleberry Hound Winter Fun (TV) (Hanna-Barbera) (12/59)	7.00	21.00	70.00
1055-Daisy Duck's Diary (Disney)-by Carl Barks (11-1/60)	10.00	30.00	100.00
1056-Yellowstone Kelly (Movie)-Clint Walker photo-c	5.40	16.00	54.00
1057-Mickey Mouse Album (Disney)	3.50	10.50	35.00
1058-Colt .45 (TV)-Photo-c	7.50	22.50	75.00
1059-Sugarfoot (TV)-Photo-c	9.00	27.00	90.00
1060-Journey to the Center of the Earth (Movie)-Pat Boone & James Mason photo-c	12.00	36.00	120.00
1061-Buffalo Bee (TV)	6.30	19.00	63.00
1062-Christmas Stories (Walt Scott's Little People strip-r)	4.00	12.00	40.00
1063-Santa Claus Funnies	3.50	10.50	35.00
1064-Bugs Bunny's Merry Christmas (12/59)	5.00	15.00	50.00
1065-Frosty the Snowman	3.50	10.50	35.00
1066-77 Sunset Strip (#1) (TV)-Toth-a (1-3/60)-Efrem Zimbalist, Jr. & Edd "Kookie" Byrnes photo-c	11.00	33.00	110.00
1067-Yogi Bear (#1) (TV) (Hanna-Barbera)	10.00	30.00	100.00
1068-Francis the Famous Talking Mule	3.50	11.00	35.00
1069-The FBI Story (Movie)-Toth-a; James Stewart photo on-c	11.00	33.00	110.00
1070-Solomon and Sheba (Movie)-Sekowsky-a; photo-c	10.00	30.00	100.00
1071-The Real McCoys (#1) (TV) (1-3/60)-Toth-a; Walter Brennan photo-c	10.00	30.00	100.00
1072-Blythe (Marge's)	5.00	15.00	50.00
1073-Grandma Duck's Farm Friends-Barks-c/a (Disney)	14.00	43.00	135.00
1074-Chilly Willy (Lantz)	3.00	9.00	30.00
1075-Tales of Wells Fargo (TV)-Photo-c	9.00	27.00	90.00
1076-The Rebel (#1) (TV)-Sekowsky-a; photo-c	10.00	30.00	100.00
1077-The Deputy (#1) (TV)-Buscema-a; Henry Fonda photo-c	13.00	40.00	130.00
1078-The Three Stooges (2-4/60)-Photo-c	10.00	30.00	100.00
1079-The Little Rascals (TV) (Spanky & Alfalfa)	4.00	12.00	40.00
1080-Fury (2-4/60)-Photo-c	7.00	21.00	70.00
1081-Elmer Fudd	2.00	6.00	20.00
1082-Spin and Marty (Disney) (TV)-Photo-c	7.50	22.50	75.00
1083-Men into Space (TV)-Anderson-a; photo-c	6.00	18.00	60.00
1084-Speedy Gonzales	3.00	9.00	30.00
1085-The Time Machine (H.G. Wells) (Movie) (3/60)-Alex Toth-a; Rod Taylor photo-c	15.00	45.00	150.00

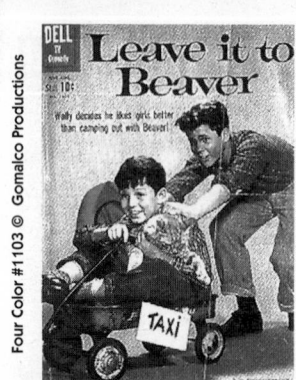
Four Color #1103 © Gomalco Productions

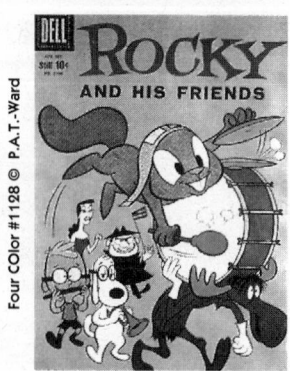
Four Color #1128 © P.A.T.-Ward

Four Color #1134 © DELL

	GD25	FN65	NM94
1086-Lolly and Pepper	3.00	9.00	30.00
1087-Peter Gunn (TV)-Photo-c	10.00	30.00	100.00
1088-A Dog of Flanders (Movie)-Photo-c	5.00	15.00	50.00
1089-Restless Gun (TV)-Photo-c	8.00	24.00	80.00
1090-Francis the Famous Talking Mule	3.50	11.00	35.00
1091-Jacky's Diary (4-6/60)	5.00	15.00	50.00
1092-Toby Tyler (Disney-Movie)-Photo-c	7.00	21.00	70.00
1093-MacKenzie's Raiders (Movie/TV)-Richard Carlson photo-c from TV show	7.00	21.00	70.00
1094-Goofy (Disney)	5.00	15.00	50.00
1095-Gyro Gearloose (Disney)-All Barks-c/a	11.00	33.00	110.00
1096-The Texan (TV)-Rory Calhoun photo-c	8.00	24.00	80.00
1097-Rawhide (TV)-Manning-a; Clint Eastwood photo-c	15.00	45.00	150.00
1098-Sugarfoot (TV)-Photo-c	9.00	27.00	90.00
1099-Donald Duck Album (Disney) (5-7/60)-Barks-c	6.00	18.00	60.00
1100-Annette's Life Story (Disney-Movie) (5/60)-Annette Funicello photo-c	20.00	60.00	200.00
1101-Robert Louis Stevenson's Kidnapped (Disney-Movie) (5/60); photo-c	7.00	21.00	70.00
1102-Wanted: Dead or Alive (#1) (TV) (5-7/60); Steve McQueen photo-c	12.00	36.00	125.00
1103-Leave It to Beaver (TV)-Photo-c	16.00	48.00	160.00
1104-Yogi Bear Goes to College (TV) (Hanna-Barbera) (6-8/60)	7.00	21.00	70.00
1105-Gale Storm (Oh! Susanna) (TV)-Toth-a; photo-c	12.50	37.50	125.00
1106-77 Sunset Strip(TV)(6-8/60)-Toth-a; photo-c	10.00	30.00	100.00
1107-Buckskin (TV)-Photo-c	7.00	21.00	70.00
1108-The Troubleshooters (TV)-Keenan Wynn photo-c	6.00	18.00	60.00
1109-This Is Your Life, Donald Duck (Disney) (TV) (8-10/60)-Gyro flashback to WDC&S #141; origin Donald Duck (1st told)	17.00	51.00	170.00
1110-Bonanza (#1) (TV) (6-8/60)-Photo-c	35.00	103.00	350.00
1111-Shotgun Slade (TV)-Photo-c	6.00	18.00	60.00
1112-Pixie and Dixie and Mr. Jinks (#1) (TV) (Hanna-Barbera) (7-9/60)	7.00	21.00	70.00
1113-Tales of Wells Fargo (TV)-Photo-c	9.00	27.00	90.00
1114-Huckleberry Finn (Movie) (7/60)-Photo-c	5.00	15.00	50.00
1115-Ricky Nelson (TV)-Manning-a; photo-c	15.00	45.00	150.00
1116-Boots and Saddles (TV) (8/60)-Photo-c	6.00	18.00	60.00
1117-Boy and the Pirates (Movie)-Photo-c	7.00	21.00	70.00
1118-The Sword and the Dragon (Movie) (6/60)-Photo-c	8.00	24.00	80.00
1119-Smokey the Bear Nature Stories	4.00	12.00	40.00
1120-Dinosaurus (Movie)-Painted-c	7.00	21.00	70.00
1121-Hercules Unchained (Movie) (8/60)-Crandall/Evans-a	10.00	30.00	100.00
1122-Chilly Willy (Lantz)	3.00	9.00	30.00
1123-Tombstone Territory (TV)-Photo-c	10.00	30.00	100.00
1124-Whirlybirds (#1) (TV)-Photo-c	9.00	27.00	90.00
1125-Laramie (#1) (TV)-Photo-c; G. Kane/Heath-a	10.00	30.00	100.00
1126-Sundance (TV) (8-10/60)-Earl Holliman photo-c	6.00	18.00	60.00
1127-The Three Stooges-Photo-c (8-10/60)	10.00	30.00	100.00
1128-Rocky and His Friends (#1) (TV) (Jay Ward) (8-10/60)	35.00	105.00	350.00
1129-Pollyanna (Disney-Movie)-Hayley Mills photo-c	10.00	30.00	100.00
1130-The Deputy (TV)-Buscema-a; Henry Fonda photo-c	10.00	30.00	100.00
1131-Elmer Fudd (9-11/60)	2.00	6.00	20.00
1132-Space Mouse (Lantz) (8-10/60)	4.00	12.00	40.00
1133-Fury (TV)-Photo-c	7.00	21.00	70.00

	GD25	FN65	NM94
1134-Real McCoys (TV)-Toth-a; photo-c	10.00	30.00	100.
1135-M.G.M.'s Mouse Musketeers (9-11/60)	2.00	6.00	20.
1136-Jungle Cat (Disney-Movie)-Photo-c	7.00	21.00	70.
1137-The Little Rascals (TV)	4.00	12.00	40.
1138-The Rebel (TV)-Photo-c	9.00	27.00	90.
1139-Spartacus (Movie) (11/60)-Buscema-a; Kirk Douglas photo-c	12.00	36.00	120.
1140-Donald Duck Album (Disney)-Barks-a	6.00	18.00	60.
1141-Huckleberry Hound for President (TV) (Hanna-Barbera) (10/60)	7.00	21.00	70.
1142-Johnny Ringo (TV)-Photo-c	8.00	24.00	80.
1143-Pluto (Disney) (11-1/61)	3.50	10.00	35.
1144-The Story of Ruth (Movie)-Photo-c	10.00	30.00	100.
1145-The Lost World (Movie)-Gil Kane-a; photo-c; 1 pg. Conan Doyle biograph by Torres	11.00	33.00	110.
1146-Restless Gun (TV)-Photo-c; Wildey-a	8.00	24.00	80.
1147-Sugarfoot (TV)-Photo-c	9.00	27.00	90.
1148-I Aim at the Stars-the Wernher Von Braun Story (Movie) (11-1/61)-Photo-c	7.00	21.00	70.
1149-Goofy (Disney) (11-1/61)	5.00	15.00	50.
1150-Daisy Duck's Diary (Disney) (12-1/61) by Carl Barks	10.00	30.00	100.
1151-Mickey Mouse Album (Disney) (11-1/61)	3.50	10.50	35.
1152-Rocky and His Friends (TV) (Jay Ward) (12-2/61)	25.00	75.00	250.
1153-Frosty the Snowman	3.50	10.50	35.
1154-Santa Claus Funnies	3.50	10.50	35.
1155-North to Alaska (Movie)-John Wayne photo-c	16.00	48.00	160.
1156-Walt Disney Swiss Family Robinson (Movie) (12/60)-Photo-c	7.00	21.00	70.
1157-Master of the World (Movie) (7/61)	6.00	18.00	60.
1158-Three Worlds of Gulliver (2 issues exist with different covers) (Movie)-Photo-c	6.00	18.00	60.
1159-77 Sunset Strip (TV)-Toth-a; photo-c	10.00	30.00	100.
1160-Rawhide (TV)-Clint Eastwood photo-c	15.00	45.00	150.
1161-Grandma Duck's Farm Friends (Disney) by Carl Barks (2-4/61)	14.00	43.00	135.
1162-Yogi Bear Joins the Marines (TV) (Hanna-Barbera) (5-7/61)	7.00	21.00	70.
1163-Daniel Boone (3-5/61); Marsh-a	6.00	18.00	60.
1164-Wanted: Dead or Alive (TV)-Steve McQueen photo-c	10.00	30.00	100.
1165-Ellery Queen (#1) (3-5/61)	11.00	33.00	110.
1166-Rocky and His Friends (TV) (Jay Ward)	25.00	75.00	250.
1167-Tales of Wells Fargo (TV)-Photo-c	8.00	24.00	80.
1168-The Detectives (TV)-Robert Taylor photo-c	10.00	30.00	100.
1169-New Adventures of Sherlock Holmes	16.00	48.00	160.
1170-The Three Stooges (3-5/61)-Photo-c	10.00	30.00	100.
1171-Elmer Fudd	2.00	6.00	20.
1172-Fury (TV)-Photo-c	7.00	21.00	70.
1173-The Twilight Zone (#1) (TV) (5/61)-Crandall/Evans-c/a; Crandall tribute to Ingles	19.00	58.00	190.
1174-The Little Rascals (TV)	3.00	9.00	30.
1175-M.G.M.'s Mouse Musketeers (3-5/61)	2.00	6.00	20.
1176-Dondi (Movie)-Origin; photo-c	5.00	15.00	50.
1177-Chilly Willy (Lantz) (4-6/61)	3.00	9.00	30.
1178-Ten Who Dared (Disney-Movie) (12/60)-Painted-c; cast member photo on back-c	7.00	21.00	70.
1179-The Swamp Fox (TV) (Disney)-Leslie Nielson photo-c	9.00	27.00	90.
1180-The Danny Thomas Show (TV)-Toth-a; photo-c	15.00	45.00	153.
1181-Texas John Slaughter (TV) (Disney) (4-6/61)-Photo-c	7.00	21.00	70.

Four Color #1192 © DELL

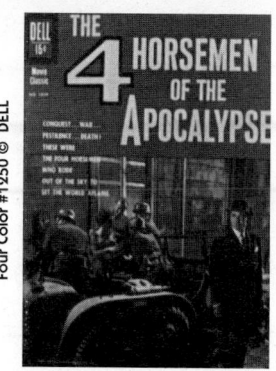

Four Color #1250 © DELL

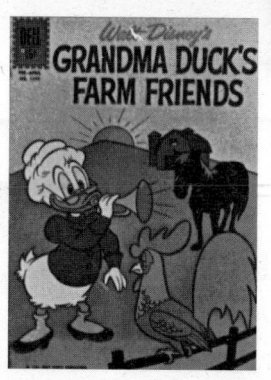

Four Color #1279 © WDC

	GD25	FN65	NM94
1182-Donald Duck Album (Disney) (5-7/61)	4.00	12.00	40.00
1183-101 Dalmatians (Disney-Movie) (3/61)	10.00	30.00	100.00
1184-Gyro Gearloose; All Barks-c/a (Disney) (5-7/61) Two variations exist	11.00	33.00	110.00
1185-Sweetie Pie	4.00	12.00	40.00
1186-Yak Yak (#1) by Jack Davis (2 versions - one minus 3-pg. Davis-c/a)	9.00	27.00	90.00
1187-The Three Stooges (6-8/61)-Photo-c	10.00	30.00	100.00
1188-Atlantis, the Lost Continent (Movie) (5/61)-Photo-c	10.00	30.00	100.00
1189-Greyfriars Bobby (Disney-Movie) (11/61)-Photo-c (scarce)	7.00	21.00	70.00
1190-Donald and the Wheel (Disney-Movie) (11/61); Barks-c	7.00	21.00	70.00
1191-Leave It to Beaver (TV)-Photo-c	16.00	48.00	160.00
1192-Ricky Nelson (TV)-Manning-a; photo-c	15.00	45.00	150.00
1193-The Real McCoys (TV) (6-8/61)-Photo-c	9.00	27.00	90.00
1194-Pepe (Movie) (4/61)-Photo-c	4.00	12.00	40.00
1195-National Velvet (#1) (TV)-Photo-c	7.00	21.00	70.00
1196-Pixie and Dixie and Mr. Jinks (TV) (Hanna-Barbera) (7-9/61)	5.00	15.00	50.00
1197-The Aquanauts (TV) (5-7/61)-Photo-c	6.30	19.00	63.00
1198-Donald in Mathmagic Land (Disney-Movie)-Reprint of #1051	7.00	21.00	70.00
1199-The Absent-Minded Professor (Disney-Movie) (4/61)-Photo-c	7.00	21.00	70.00
1200-Hennessey (TV) (8-10/61)-Gil Kane-a; photo-c	7.00	21.00	70.00
1201-Goofy (Disney) (8-10/61)	5.00	15.00	50.00
1202-Rawhide (TV)-Clint Eastwood photo-c	15.00	45.00	150.00
1203-Pinocchio (Disney) (3/62)	5.85	17.50	58.00
1204-Scamp (Disney)	3.50	10.50	35.00
1205-David and Goliath (Movie) (7/61)-Photo-c	6.00	18.00	60.00
1206-Lolly and Pepper (9-11/61)	3.00	9.00	30.00
1207-The Rebel (TV)-Sekowsky-a; photo-c	9.00	27.00	90.00
1208-Rocky and His Friends (Jay Ward) (TV)	25.00	75.00	250.00
1209-Sugarfoot (TV)-Photo-c (10-12/61)	9.00	27.00	90.00
1210-The Parent Trap (Disney-Movie) (8/61)-Hayley Mills photo-c	10.00	30.00	100.00
1211-77 Sunset Strip (TV)-Manning-a; photo-c	9.00	27.00	90.00
1212-Chilly Willy (Lantz) (7-9/61)	3.00	9.00	30.00
1213-Mysterious Island (Movie)-Photo-c	9.00	27.00	90.00
1214-Smokey the Bear	4.00	12.00	40.00
1215-Tales of Wells Fargo (TV) (10-12/61)-Photo-c	8.00	24.00	80.00
1216-Whirlybirds (TV)-Photo-c	8.00	24.00	80.00
1218-Fury (TV)-Photo-c	7.00	21.00	70.00
1219-The Detectives (TV)-Robert Taylor & Adam West photo-c	8.00	24.00	80.00
1220-Gunslinger (TV)-Photo-c	9.00	27.00	90.00
1221-Bonanza (TV) (9-11/61)-Photo-c	17.00	52.00	175.00
1222-Elmer Fudd (9-11/61)	2.00	6.00	20.00
1223-Laramie (TV)-Gil Kane-a; photo-c	6.00	18.00	60.00
1224-The Little Rascals (TV) (10-12/61)	3.00	9.00	30.00
1225-The Deputy (TV)-Henry Fonda photo-c	10.00	30.00	100.00
1226-Nikki, Wild Dog of the North (Disney-Movie) (9/61)-Photo-c	6.00	18.00	60.00
1227-Morgan the Pirate (Movie)-Photo-c	10.00	30.00	100.00
1229-Thief of Baghdad (Movie)-Crandall/Evans-a; photo-c	6.00	18.00	60.00
1230-Voyage to the Bottom of the Sea (#1) (Movie)-Photo insert on-c	10.00	30.00	100.00
1231-Danger Man (TV) (9-11/61)-Patrick McGoohan photo-c	10.00	30.00	100.00
1232-On the Double (Movie)	5.00	15.00	50.00
1233-Tammy Tell Me True (Movie) (1961)	7.00	21.00	70.00

	GD25	FN65	NM94
1234-The Phantom Planet (Movie) (1961)	7.00	21.00	70.00
1235-Mister Magoo (#1) (12-2/62)	9.00	27.00	90.00
1235-Mister Magoo (3-5/65) 2nd printing; reprint of 12-2/62 issue	5.00	15.00	50.00
1236-King of Kings (Movie)-Photo-c	8.00	24.00	80.00
1237-The Untouchables (#1) (TV)-Not by Toth; photo-c	22.00	66.00	220.00
1238-Deputy Dawg (TV)	11.00	33.00	110.00
1239-Donald Duck Album (Disney) (10-12/61)-Barks-c	6.00	18.00	60.00
1240-The Detectives (TV)-Tufts-a; Robert Taylor photo-c	8.00	24.00	80.00
1241-Sweetie Pie	4.00	12.00	40.00
1242-King Leonardo and His Short Subjects (#1) (TV) (11-1/62)	14.00	43.00	140.00
1243-Ellery Queen	9.00	27.00	90.00
1244-Space Mouse (Lantz) (11-1/62)	4.00	12.00	40.00
1245-New Adventures of Sherlock Holmes	16.00	48.00	160.00
1246-Mickey Mouse Album (Disney)	3.50	10.50	35.00
1247-Daisy Duck's Diary (Disney) (12-2/62)	4.00	12.00	40.00
1248-Pluto (Disney)	3.50	10.00	35.00
1249-The Danny Thomas Show (TV)-Manning-a; photo-c	15.00	45.00	153.00
1250-The Four Horsemen of the Apocalypse (Movie)-Photo-c	7.00	21.00	70.00
1251-Everything's Ducky (Movie) (1961)	5.00	15.00	50.00
1252-The Andy Griffith Show (TV)-Photo-c; 1st show aired 10/3/60	25.00	74.00	245.00
1253-Space Man (#1) (1-3/62)	8.00	24.00	80.00
1254-"Diver Dan" (#1) (2-4/62)-Photo-c	6.00	18.00	60.00
1255-The Wonders of Aladdin (Movie) (1961)	6.30	19.00	63.00
1256-Kona, Monarch of Monster Isle (#1) (2-4/62)-Glanzman-a	7.00	21.00	70.00
1257-Car 54, Where Are You? (#1) (TV) (3-5/62)-Photo-c	8.00	24.00	80.00
1258-The Frogmen (#1)-Evans-a	8.00	24.00	80.00
1259-El Cid (Movie) (1961)-Photo-c	7.00	21.00	70.00
1260-The Horsemasters (TV, Movie) (Disney) (12-2/62)-Annette Funicello photo-c	11.00	33.00	110.00
1261-Rawhide (TV)-Clint Eastwood photo-c	15.00	45.00	150.00
1262-The Rebel (TV)-Photo-c	9.00	27.00	90.00
1263-77 Sunset Strip (TV) (12-2/62)-Manning-a; photo-c	9.00	27.00	90.00
1264-Pixie and Dixie and Mr. Jinks (TV) (Hanna-Barbera)	5.00	15.00	50.00
1265-The Real McCoys (TV)-Photo-c	9.00	27.00	90.00
1266-M.G.M.'s Spike and Tyke (12-2/62)	1.80	5.50	18.00
1267-Gyro Gearloose; Barks-c/a, 4 pgs. (Disney) (12-2/62)	7.50	22.50	75.00
1268-Oswald the Rabbit (Lantz)	2.00	6.00	20.00
1269-Rawhide (TV)-Clint Eastwood photo-c	15.00	45.00	150.00
1270-Bullwinkle and Rocky (#1) (TV) (Jay Ward) (3-5/62)	19.00	58.00	190.00
1271-Yogi Bear Birthday Party (TV) (Hanna-Barbera) (11/61)	4.50	13.50	45.00
1272-Frosty the Snowman	3.50	10.50	35.00
1273-Hans Brinker (Disney-Movie)-Photo-c (2/62)	8.00	24.00	80.00
1274-Santa Claus Funnies (12/61)	3.50	10.50	35.00
1275-Rocky and His Friends (TV) (Jay Ward)	25.00	75.00	250.00
1276-Dondi	4.00	12.00	40.00
1278-King Leonardo and His Short Subjects (TV)	14.00	43.00	140.00
1279-Grandma Duck's Farm Friends (Disney)	5.00	15.00	50.00
1280-Hennessey (TV)-Photo-c	7.00	21.00	70.00
1281-Chilly Willy (Lantz) (4-6/62)	3.00	9.00	30.00

Four Favorites #3 © ACE

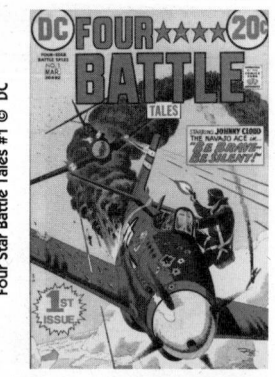

Four Star Battle Tales #1 © DC

Four Star Spectacular #5 © DC

	GD25	FN65	NM94

1282-Babes in Toyland (Disney-Movie) (1/62); Annette Funicello photo-c
                                       11.50   40.00   115.00
1283-Bonanza (TV) (2-4/62)-Photo-c   17.00   52.00   175.00
1284-Laramie (TV)-Heath-a; photo-c   6.00   18.00   60.00
1285-Leave It to Beaver (TV)-Photo-c   16.00   48.00   160.00
1286-The Untouchables (TV)-Photo-c   16.00   48.00   160.00
1287-Man from Wells Fargo (TV)-Photo-c 5.00   15.00   50.00
1288-Twilight Zone (TV) (4/62)-Crandall/Evans-c/a 11.00 34.00 115.00
1289-Ellery Queen   9.00   27.00   90.00
1290-M.G.M.'s Mouse Musketeers   2.00   6.00   20.00
1291-77 Sunset Strip (TV)-Manning-a; photo-c 9.00 27.00 90.00
1293-Elmer Fudd (3-5/62)   2.00   6.00   20.00
1294-Ripcord (TV)   7.00   21.00   70.00
1295-Mister Ed, the Talking Horse (#1) (TV) (3-5/62)-Photo-c
                                       13.00   40.00   130.00
1296-Fury (3-5/62)-Photo-c   7.00   21.00   70.00
1297-Spanky, Alfalfa and the Little Rascals (TV) 3.00 9.00 30.00
1298-The Hathaways (TV)-Photo-c   4.50   14.00   45.00
1299-Deputy Dawg (TV)   11.00   33.00   110.00
1300-The Comancheros (Movie) (1961)-John Wayne photo-c
                                       15.00   45.00   150.00
1301-Adventures in Paradise (TV) (2-4/62) 4.50 13.50   45.00
1302-Johnny Jason, Teen Reporter (2-4/62) 3.00 9.00   30.00
1303-Lad: A Dog (Movie)-Photo-c   4.00   12.00   40.00
1304-Nellie the Nurse (3-5/62)-Stanley-a 10.00 30.00   100.00
1305-Mister Magoo (3-5/62)   9.00   27.00   90.00
1306-Target: The Corruptors (#1) (TV) (3-5/62)-Photo-c
                                        5.00   15.00   50.00
1307-Margie (TV) (3-5/62)   4.00   12.00   40.00
1308-Tales of the Wizard of Oz (TV) (3-5/62) 10.00 30.00 100.00
1309-87th Precinct (#1) (TV) (4-6/62)-Krigstein-a; photo-c
                                       10.00   30.00   100.00
1310-Huck and Yogi Winter Sports (TV) (Hanna-Barbera) (3/62)
                                        7.00   21.00   70.00
1311-Rocky and His Friends (TV) (Jay Ward) 25.00 75.00 250.00
1312-National Velvet (TV)-Photo-c   4.00   12.00   40.00
1313-Moon Pilot (Disney-Movie) (1961)-Evans-a; photo-c
                                        7.00   21.00   70.00
1328-The Underwater City (Movie) (1961)-Evans-a; photo-c
                                        7.00   21.00   70.00
1329-See Gyro Gearloose #01329-207
1330-Brain Boy (#1)-Gil Kane-a   13.00   40.00   135.00
1332-Bachelor Father (TV)   8.00   24.00   80.00
1333-Short Ribs (4-6/62)   5.00   15.00   50.00
1335-Aggie Mack (4-6/62)   3.60   11.00   36.00
1336-On Stage; not by Leonard Starr   5.00   15.00   50.00
1337-Dr. Kildare (#1) (TV) (4-6/62)-Photo-c 7.00 21.00   70.00
1341-The Andy Griffith Show (TV) (4-6/62)-Photo-c 25.00 74.00 245.00
1348-Yak Yak (#2)-Jack Davis-c/a   9.00   27.00   90.00
1349-Yogi Bear Visits the U.N. (TV) (Hanna-Barbera) (1/62)-Photo-c
                                        9.00   27.00   90.00
1350-Comanche (Disney-Movie)(1962)-Reprints 4-Color #966 (title change
    from "Tonka" to "Comanche") (4-6/62)-Sal Mineo photo-c
                                        6.00   18.00   60.00
1354-Calvin & the Colonel (#1) (TV) (4-6/62) 7.00 21.00 70.00
NOTE: Missing numbers probably do not exist.

4-D MONKEY, THE (Adventures of... #? on)
1988 - No. 11, 1990 ($1.80/$2.00, 52 pgs.)
Leung's Publications
   1-Karate Pig, Ninja Flounder & 4-D Monkey (48 pgs., centerfold is a Christmas
      card)   1.80
   2-4 (52 pgs.)   1.80
   5-11 ($2.00-c)   .80   2.00

FOUR FAVORITES (Crime Must Pay the Penalty No. 33 on)
Sept, 1941 - No. 32, Dec, 1947

Ace Magazines
   1-Vulcan, Lash Lightning (formerly Flash Lightning in Sure-Fire), Magno the
      Magnetic Man & The Raven begin; flag-c   112.00 338.00 900.00
   2-The Black Ace only app.   45.00 136.00 365.00
   3-Last Vulcan   40.00 120.00 315.00
   4,5: 4-The Raven & Vulcan end; Unknown Soldier begins (see Our Flag), ends
      #28. 5-Captain Courageous begins (5/42), ends #28 (moves over from
      Captain Courageous #6); not in #6   40.00 120.00 280.00
   6-8: 6-The Flag app.; Mr. Risk begins (7/42)   34.00 103.00 240.00
   9-Kurtzman-a (Lash Lightning);   40.00 120.00 280.00
   10-Classic Kurtzman-c/a (Magno & Davey)   41.00 124.00 330.00
   11-Kurtzman-a; Hitler, Mussolini, Hirohito-c; L.B. Cole-a; Unknown Soldier by
      Kurtzman   40.00 120.00 315.00
   12-L.B. Cole-a   27.00   81.00 190.00
   13-20: 18,20-Palais-c/a   21.00   64.00 150.00
   21-No Unknown Soldier; The Unknown app.   16.00   47.00 110.00
   22-26: 22-Captain Courageous drops costume. 23-Unknown Soldier drops
      costume. 25-29-HapHazard app. 26-Last Magno 16.00 47.00 110.00
   27-32: 30-Funny-c begin (teen humor), end #32   11.50   34.00   80.00
NOTE: Dave Berg c-5. Jim Mooney a-6; c-1-3. Palais a-18-20; c-18-25. Torture chamber c-5.

FOUR HORSEMEN, THE (See The Crusaders)

FOUR HORSEMEN OF THE APOCALYPSE, THE (Movie)
No. 1250, Jan-Mar, 1962 (one-shot)
Dell Publishing co.
   Four Color 1250-Photo-c   7.00   21.00   70.00

4MOST (Foremost Boys No. 32-40; becomes Thrilling Crime Cases #41 on)
Winter, 1941-42 - V8#5(#36), 9-10/49; #37, 11-12/49 - #40, 4-5/50
Novelty Publications/Star Publications No. 37-on
   V1#1-The Target by Sid Greene, The Cadet & Dick Cole begin with origins
      retold; produced by Funnies Inc.; quarterly issues begin, end V6#3
                                                  96.00 290.00 775.00
   2-Last Target (Spr/42)   41.00 124.00 330.00
   3-Dan'l Flannel begins; flag-c   39.00 118.00 275.00
   4-1pg. Dr. Seuss (signed) (Aut/42)   33.00   99.00 230.00
   V2#1-3   10.00   30.00   60.00
   4-Hitler, Tojo & Mussolini app. as pumpkins on-c 13.00 39.00   90.00
   V3#1-4   10.00   30.00   60.00
   V4#1-4: 2-Walter Johnson-c   7.50   22.50   45.00
   V5#1-4: 1-The Target & Targeteers app.   6.35   19.00   38.00
   V6#1-4: 1-White Rider & Super Horse begin   6.35   19.00   38.00
      5-L. B. Cole-c   12.00   36.00   85.00
   V7#1,3,5, V8#1, 37   6.35   19.00   38.00
   2,4,6-L. B. Cole-c. 6-Last Dick Cole   12.00   36.00   85.00
   V8#2,3,5-L. B. Cole-c/a   14.00   43.00 100.00
   4-L. B. Cole-a   10.00   30.00   65.00
   38-40: 38-Johnny Weismuller (Tarzan) life story & Jim Braddock (boxer) life
      story. 38-40-L.B. Cole-a. 40-Last White Rider 11.50 34.00   80.00
   Accepted Reprint 38-40 (nd): 40-r/Johnny Weismuller life story; all have
      L.B. Cole-c   7.50   22.50   45.00

FOUR-STAR BATTLE TALES
Feb-Mar, 1973 - No. 5, Nov-Dec, 1973
National Periodical Publications
   1-reprints begin   1.60   4.00
   2-5   .80   2.00
NOTE: Drucker r-1, 3-5. Heath r-2, 5; c-1. Krigstein r-5. Kubert r-4; c-2.

FOUR STAR SPECTACULAR
Mar-Apr, 1976 - No. 6, Jan-Feb, 1977
National Periodical Publications
   1-6: Reprints in all. 2-Infinity cover   1.00
NOTE: All contain DC Superhero reprints. #1 has 68 pgs.. #2-6, 52 pgs.. #1, 4-Hawkman app.;
#2-Kid Flash app.; #3-Green Lantern app; #2, 4, 5-Wonder Woman, Superboy app; #5-Green
Arrow, Vigilante app; #6-Blackhawk G.A.-r.

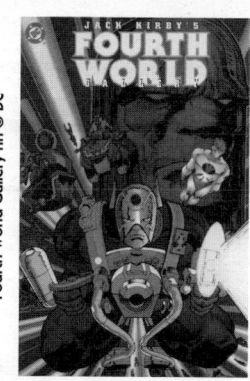

Fourth World Gallery nn © DC

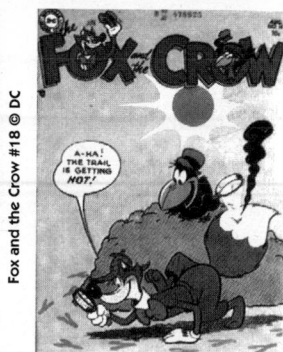

Fox and the Crow #18 © DC

Foxhole #3 © Mainline

	GD25	FN65	NM94

FOUR TEENERS (Formerly Crime Must Pay The Penalty; Dotty No. 35 on)
No. 34, April, 1948 (52 pgs.)
A. A. Wyn

34-Teen-age comic; Dotty app.; Curly & Jerry continue from Four Favorites

	5.00	15.00	30.00

FOURTH WORLD GALLERY, THE (Jack Kirby's...)
1996 (9/96) ($3.50, one-shot)
DC Comics

nn-Pin-ups of Jack Kirby's Fourth World characters (New Gods, Forever People & Mister Miracle) by John Byrne, Rick Burchett, Dan Jurgens, Walt Simonson & others 3.50

FOX AND THE CROW (Stanley & His Monster No. 109 on) (See Comic Cavalcade & Real Screen Comics)
Dec-Jan, 1951-52 - No. 108, Feb-Mar, 1968
National Periodical Publications

1	87.00	262.00	700.00
2(Scarce)	44.00	132.00	350.00
3-5	31.00	94.00	220.00
6-10	22.00	66.00	155.00
11-20	16.00	47.00	110.00
21-40: 22-Last precode issue (2/55)	10.00	30.00	70.00
41-60	8.00	24.00	48.00
61-80	5.35	16.00	32.00
81-94	3.40	10.00	24.00
95-Stanley & His Monster begins(origin)(1st app?)	3.75	11.25	26.00
96-99,101-108	1.70	5.00	12.00
100 (10-11/66)	2.15	6.50	15.00

NOTE: Many covers by Mort Drucker.

FOX AND THE HOUND, THE (Disney)(Movie)
Aug, 1981 - No. 3, Oct, 1981
Whitman Publishing Co.

11292(#1),2,3-Based on animated movie			1.00

FOXFIRE (See The Phoenix Resurrection)
Feb, 1996 - No. 4, May, 1996 ($1.50)
Malibu Comics (Ultraverse)

1-4: Sludge, Ultraforce app. 4-Punisher app.			1.50

FOX GIANTS
1944 - 1950 (25¢, 132 - 196 pgs.)
Fox Features Syndicate

Album of Crime nn(1949, 132p)	40.00	120.00	300.00
Album of Love nn(1949, 132p)	39.00	116.00	270.00
All Famous Crime Stories nn('49, 132p)	40.00	120.00	300.00
All Good Comics 1(1944, 132p)(R.W. Voigt)-The Bouncer, Purple Tigress,Rick Evans, Puppeteer, Green Mask; Infinity-c	38.00	114.00	265.00
All Great nn(1944, 132p)-Capt. Jack Terry, Rick Evans, Jaguar Man	38.00	114.00	265.00
All Great nn(Chicago Nite Life News)(1945, 132p)-Green Mask, Bouncer, Puppeteer, Rick Evans, Rocket Kelly	40.00	120.00	285.00
All-Great Confessions nn(1949, 132p)	36.00	107.00	250.00
All Great Crime Stories nn('49, 132p)	40.00	120.00	300.00
All Great Jungle Adventures nn('49, 132p)	45.00	135.00	360.00
All Real Confession Magazine 3 (3/49, 132p)	36.00	107.00	250.00
All Real Confession Magazine 4 (4/49, 132p)	36.00	107.00	250.00
All Your Comics 1(1944, 132p)-The Puppeteer, Red Robbins, & Merciless the Sorcerer	39.00	118.00	275.00
Almanac Of Crime nn(1948, 148p)-Phantom Lady	43.00	131.00	350.00
Almanac Of Crime 1(1950, 132p)	40.00	120.00	300.00
Book Of Love nn(1950, 132p)	34.00	103.00	240.00
Burning Romances 1(1949, 132p)	40.00	120.00	285.00
Crimes Incorporated nn(1950, 132p)	39.00	118.00	275.00
Daring Love Stories nn(1950, 132p)	34.00	103.00	240.00

	GD25	FN65	NM94

Everybody's Comics 1(1944, 50¢, 196p)-The Green Mask, The Puppeteer, The Bouncer, Rocket Kelly, Rick Evans	40.00	120.00	300.00
Everybody's Comics 1(1946, 196p)-Green Lama, The Puppeteer	34.00	101.00	235.00
Everybody's Comics 1(1946, 196p)-Same as 1945 Ribtickler	26.00	77.00	180.00
Everybody's Comics nn(1947, 132p)-Jo-Jo, Purple Tigress, Cosmo Cat, Bronze Man	33.00	99.00	230.00
Exciting Romance Stories nn(1949, 132p)	34.00	103.00	240.00
Famous Love nn(1950, 132p)	34.00	103.00	240.00
Intimate Confessions nn(1950, 132p)	34.00	103.00	240.00
Journal Of Crime nn(1949, 132p)	40.00	120.00	300.00
Love Problems nn(1949, 132p)	36.00	107.00	250.00
Love Thrills nn(1950, 132p)	36.00	107.00	250.00
March of Crime nn('48, 132p)-Female w/rifle-c	39.00	118.00	275.00
March of Crime nn('49, 132p)-Cop w/pistol-c	39.00	118.00	275.00
March of Crime nn(1949, 132p)-Coffin & man w/machine-gun-c	39.00	118.00	275.00
Revealing Love Stories nn(1950, 132p)	34.00	103.00	240.00
Ribtickler nn(1945, 50¢, 196p)-Chicago Nite Life News; Marvel Mutt, Cosmo Cat, Flash Rabbit, The Nebbs app.	31.00	94.00	220.00
Romantic Thrills nn(1950, 132p)	34.00	103.00	240.00
Secret Love nn(1949, 132p)	34.00	103.00	240.00
Secret Love Stories nn(1949, 132p)	34.00	103.00	240.00
Strange Love nn(1950, 132p)-Photo-c	40.00	120.00	285.00
Sweetheart Scandals nn(1950, 132p)	34.00	103.00	240.00
Teen-Age Love nn(1950, 132p)	34.00	103.00	240.00
Throbbing Love nn(1950, 132p)-Photo-c; used in POP, pg. 107	40.00	120.00	285.00
Truth About Crime nn(1950, 132p)	40.00	120.00	300.00
Variety Comics 1(1946, 132p)-Blue Beetle, Jungle Jo	34.00	103.00	240.00
Variety Comics nn(1950, 132p)-Jungle Jo, My Secret Affair(w/Harrison/ Wood-a), Crimes by Women & My Story	33.00	99.00	230.00
Western Roundup nn('50, 132p)-Hoot Gibson; Cody of the Pony Express app.	38.00	114.00	265.00

NOTE: Each of the above usually contain four remaindered Fox books minus covers. Since these missing covers often had the first page of the first story, most Giants therefore are incomplete. Approximate values are listed. Books with appearances of Phantom Lady, Rulah, Jo-Jo, etc. could bring more.

FOXHOLE (Becomes Never Again #8?)
9-10/54 - No. 4, 3-4/55; No. 5, 7/55 - No. 7, 3/56
Mainline/Charlton Comics No. 5 on

1-Classic Kirby-c	26.00	77.00	180.00
2-Kirby-c/a(2); Kirby scripts based on his war time experiences	20.00	60.00	140.00
3-5-Kirby-c only	11.00	33.00	75.00
6-Kirby-c/a(2)	17.00	51.00	120.00
7	4.00	12.00	24.00
Super Reprints #10-12,15-18: 10-r/? 11,12,18-r/Foxhole #1,2,3. 15,16-r/ United States Marines #5,8. 17-r/Monty Hall #?	1.30	3.25	8.00

NOTE: Kirby a(r)-Super #11, 12. Powell a(r)-Super #15, 16. Stories by actual veterans.

FOXY FAGAN COMICS
Dec, 1946 - No. 7, Summer, 1948
Dearfield Publishing Co.

1-Foxy Fagan & Little Buck begin	11.50	34.00	80.00
2	6.70	20.00	40.00
3-7: 6-Rocket ship-c	5.35	16.00	32.00

FRACTURED FAIRY TALES (TV)
Oct, 1962 (Jay Ward)
Gold Key

1 (10022-210)-From Bullwinkle TV show	10.00	30.00	100.00

FRAGGLE ROCK (TV)

Frankenstein #9 © MEG

The Frankenstein/Dracula War #3 © TOPPS

Freak Force #17 © Erik Larsen

	GD25	FN65	NM94

Apr, 1985 - No. 8, Sept, 1986; V2#1, Apr, 1988 - No. 6, Sept, 1988
Marvel Comics (Star Comics)/Marvel V2#1 on

	GD25	FN65	NM94
1-8 (75¢)			.75
V2#1-6-($1.00): Reprints 1st series			1.00

FRANCIS, BROTHER OF THE UNIVERSE
1980 (75¢, 52 pgs., one-shot)
Marvel Comics Group

nn-Buscema/Marie Severin-a; story of Francis Bernadone celebrating his 800th
birthday in 1982   1.00

FRANCIS THE FAMOUS TALKING MULE (All based on movie)
No. 335 (#1), June, 1951 - No. 1090, March, 1960
Dell Publishing Co.

	GD25	FN65	NM94
Four Color 335 (#1)	10.00	30.00	100.00
Four Color 465	7.00	21.00	70.00
Four Color 501,547,579	5.00	15.00	50.00
Four Color 621,655,698,710,745	4.00	12.00	40.00
Four Color 810,863,906,953,991,1068,1090	3.50	11.00	35.00

FRANK
Apr (Mar inside), 1994 - No. 4, 1994 ($1.75/$2.50, limited series)
Nemesis Comics (Harvey)

	GD25	FN65	NM94
1-4-($2.50, direct sale): 1-Foil-c Edition		1.00	2.50
1-4-($1.75)-Newsstand Editions; Cowan-a in all		.70	1.75

FRANK
Sept, 1996 - Present ($2.95, B&W)
Fantagraphics Books

	GD25	FN65	NM94
1-Woodring-c/a/scripts			3.00

FRANK BUCK (Formerly My True Love)
No. 70, May, 1950 - No. 3, Sept, 1950
Fox Features Syndicate

	GD25	FN65	NM94
70-Wood a(p)(3 stories)-Photo-c	30.00	90.00	210.00
71-Wood-a (9 pgs.); photo/painted-c	15.00	45.00	105.00
3: 3-Photo/painted-c	11.50	34.00	80.00
NOTE: Based on "Bring 'Em Back Alive" TV show.

FRANKENSTEIN (See Dracula, Movie Classics & Werewolf)
Aug-Oct, 1964; No. 2, Sept, 1966 - No. 4, Mar, 1967
Dell Publishing Co.

	GD25	FN65	NM94
1(12-283-410)(1964)	4.20	12.60	42.00
2-Intro. & origin super-hero character (9/66)	2.50	7.50	25.00
3,4	1.40	4.20	14.00

FRANKENSTEIN (The Monster of...; also see Monsters Unleashed #2,
Power Record Comics, Psycho & Silver Surfer #7)
Jan, 1973 - No. 18, Sept, 1975
Marvel Comics Group

	GD25	FN65	NM94
1-Ploog-c/a begins, ends #6	3.75	11.25	30.00
2-5,8,9: 8,9-Dracula app. 9-Death of Dracula	2.85	8.50	20.00
6,7,10	1.65	4.20	10.00
11-18	1.00	2.00	5.00
NOTE: **Adkins** c-17i. **Buscema** a-7-10p. **Ditko** a-12r. **G. Kane** c-15p. **Orlando** a-8r. **Ploog** a-1-3, 4p, 5p, 6; c-1-6. **Wrightson** c-18i.

FRANKENSTEIN COMICS (Also See Prize Comics)
Sum, 1945 - V5#5(#33), Oct-Nov, 1954
Prize Publications (Crestwood/Feature)

1-Frankenstein begins by Dick Briefer (origin); Frank Sinatra parody

	GD25	FN65	NM94
	90.00	270.00	725.00
2	45.00	135.00	360.00
3-5	36.00	107.00	250.00
6-10: 7-S&K a(r)-Headline Comics. 8(7-8/47)-Superman satire	31.00	92.00	215.00
11-17(1-2/49)-11-Boris Karloff parody-c/story. 17-Last humor issue			

	GD25	FN65	NM94
18(3/52)-New origin, horror series begins	36.00	107.00	250.00
19,20(V3#4, 8-9/52)	21.00	64.00	150.00
21(V3#5), 22(V3#6)	19.00	58.00	135.00
23(V4#1) - #28(V4#6)	19.00	58.00	135.00
29(V5#1) - #33(V5#5)	19.00	58.00	135.00
NOTE: **Briefer** c/a-all. **Meskin** a-21, 29.

FRANKENSTEIN/DRACULA WAR, THE
Feb, 1995 - No. 3, May, 1995 ($2.50, limited series)
Topps Comics

	GD25	FN65	NM94
1-3		1.00	2.50

FRANKENSTEIN, JR. (...& the Impossibles) (TV)
Jan, 1966 (Hanna-Barbera)
Gold Key

	GD25	FN65	NM94
1-Super hero	4.50	13.50	45.00

FRANKENSTEIN: OR THE MODERN PROMETHEUS
1994 ($2.95, one-shot)
Caliber Press

	GD25	FN65	NM94
1		1.20	3.00

FRANK FRAZETTA'S THUN'DA TALES
1987 ($2.00, one-shot)
Fantagraphics Books

	GD25	FN65	NM94
1-Frazetta-r		.80	2.00

FRANK FRAZETTA'S UNTAMED LOVE (Also see Untamed Love)
Nov, 1987 ($2.00, one-shot)
Fantagraphics Books

	GD25	FN65	NM94
..1-Frazetta-r from 1950's romance comics		.80	2.00

FRANKIE COMICS (...& Lana No. 13-15) (Formerly Movie Tunes;
becomes Frankie Fuddle No. 16 on)
No. 4, Wint, 1946-47 - No. 15, June, 1949
Marvel Comics (MgPC)

	GD25	FN65	NM94
4-Mitzi, Margie, Daisy app.	11.00	33.00	75.00
5-9	6.70	20.00	40.00
10-15: 13-Anti-Wertham editorial	5.35	16.00	32.00

FRANKIE DOODLE (See Sparkler, both series)
No. 7, 1939
United Features Syndicate

	GD25	FN65	NM94
Single Series 7	29.00	88.00	205.00

FRANKIE FUDDLE (Formerly Frankie & Lana)
No. 16, Aug, 1949 - No. 17, Nov, 1949
Marvel Comics

	GD25	FN65	NM94
16,17	5.85	17.50	35.00

FRANK LUTHER'S SILLY PILLY COMICS (See Jingle Dingle...)
1950 (10¢)
Children's Comics (Maltex Cereal)

	GD25	FN65	NM94
1-Characters from radio, records, & TV	5.00	15.00	30.00

FRANK MERRIWELL AT YALE (Speed Demons No. 5 on?)
June, 1955 - No. 4, Jan, 1956 (Also see Shadow Comics)
Charlton Comics

	GD25	FN65	NM94
1	4.25	13.00	28.00
2-4	4.00	11.00	22.00

FRANTIC (Magazine) (See Ratfink & Zany)
Oct, 1958 - V2#2, Apr, 1959 (Satire)
Pierce Publishing Co.

	GD25	FN65	NM94
V1#1,2	5.85	17.50	35.00
V2#1,2: 1-Burgos-a, Severin-c/a; Powell-a?	4.15	12.50	25.00

FREAK FORCE (Also see Savage Dragon)

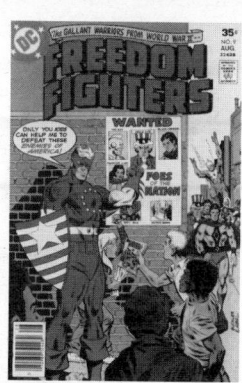

Freedom Fighters #9 © DC

Freedom Train © S&S

Freex #17 © Malibu

	GD25	FN65	NM94		GD25	FN65	NM94

Dec, 1993 - No. 18, July, 1995 ($1.95/$2.50)
Image Comics (Highbrow Entertainment)

1-7-Superpatriot & Mighty Man in all; Erik Larsen scripts in all. 4-Vanguard
app. .80 2.00
8-18: 8-Begin $2.50-c. 9-Cyberforce-c & app. 1.00 2.50

FRECKLES AND HIS FRIENDS (See Crackajack Funnies, Famous Comics Cartoon
Book, Honeybee Birdwhistle... & Red Ryder)

FRECKLES AND HIS FRIENDS
No. 5, 11/47 - No. 12, 8/49; 11/55 - No. 4, 6/56
Standard Comics/Argo

5-Reprints 6.70 20.00 40.00
6-12-Reprints. 7-9-Airbrush-c (by Schomburg?). 11-Lingerie panels
4.25 13.00 26.00
NOTE: Some copies of No. 8 & 9 contain a printing oddity. The negatives were elongated in the
engraving process, probably to conform to page dimensions on the filler pages. Those pages
only look normal when viewed at a 45 degree angle.
1(Argo,'55)-Reprints (NEA Service) 4.25 13.00 28.00
2-4 4.00 10.00 20.00

FREDDY (Formerly My Little Margie's Boy Friends) (Also see Blue Bird)
V2#12, June, 1958 - No. 47, Feb, 1965
Charlton Comics

V2#12 3.60 9.00 18.00
13-15 1.80 4.50 9.00
16-47 1.00 2.00 5.00
Schiff's Shoes Presents... #1 (1959)-Giveaway 1.00 2.00 5.00

FREDDY
May-July, 1963 - No. 3, Oct-Dec, 1964
Dell Publishing Co.

1-3 .90 2.70 9.00

FREDDY KRUEGER'S A NIGHTMARE ON ELM STREET
Oct, 1989 - No. 2, Dec, 1989 ($2.25, B&W, movie adaptation)
Marvel Comics

1,2: Origin Freddy Krueger; Buckler/Alcala-a .90 2.30

FREDDY'S DEAD: THE FINAL NIGHTMARE
Oct, 1991 - No. 3, Dec 1991 ($2.50, color mini-series, adapts movie)
Innovation Publishing

..1-3: Dismukes (film poster artist) painted-c 1.25 2.50

FRED HEMBECK DESTROYS THE MARVEL UNIVERSE
July, 1989 ($1.50, one-shot)
Marvel Comics

1-Punisher app.; Staton-i (5 pgs.) 1.50

FRED HEMBECK SELLS THE MARVEL UNIVERSE
Oct, 1990 ($1.25, one-shot)
Marvel Comics

1-Punisher, Wolverine parodies; Hembeck/Austin-c 1.25

FREE COMICS TO YOU FROM... (name of shoe store) (Has clown on cover
& another with a rabbit) (Like comics from Weather Bird & Edward's Shoes)
Circa 1956, 1960-61
Shoe Store Giveaway

Contains a comic bound with new cover - several combinations possible; some
Harvey titles known. Contents determines price.

FREEDOM AGENT (Also see John Steele)
Apr, 1963 (12¢)
Gold Key

1 (10054-304)-Painted-c 3.00 9.00 30.00

FREEDOM FIGHTERS (See Justice League of America #107,108)
Mar-Apr, 1976 - No. 15, July-Aug, 1978
National Periodical Publications/DC Comics

1-Uncle Sam, The Ray, Black Condor, Doll Man, Human Bomb, & Phantom
Lady begin (all former Quality characters) 1.60 4.00
2-14: 4,5-Wonder Woman x-over. 7-1st app. Crusaders. 10-Origin Doll Man;
Cat-Man-c/story (4th app; 1st revival since Det. #325). 11-Origin The Ray.
12-Origin Firebrand. 13-Origin Black Condor. 14-Batgirl & Batwoman app.
1.50
15-Batgirl & Batwoman app.; origin Phantom Lady 1.00 2.50
NOTE: Buckler c-5-11p, 13p, 14p.

FREEDOM TRAIN
1948 (Giveaway)
Street & Smith Publications

nn-Powell-c w/mailer 17.00 51.00 120.00

FREEX
July, 1993 - No. 18, Mar, 1995 ($1.95)
Malibu Comics (Ultraverse)

1-3,5-14,16-18: 1-Polybagged w/trading card. 2-Some were polybagged
w/card. 6-Nightman-c/story. 7-2 pg. origin Hardcase by Zeck. 17-Rune app.
.80 2.00
1-Holographic-c edition 2.85 8.50 20.00
1-Ultra 5,000 limited silver ink-c 1.65 4.20 10.00
4-($2.50, 48 pgs.)-Rune flip-c/story by B. Smith (3 pgs.); 3 pg. Night Man
preview 1.00 2.50
15 ($3.50)-w/Ultraverse Premiere #9 flip book; Alec Swan & Rafferty app.
1.40 3.50
Giant Size 1 (1994, $2.50)-Prime app. 1.00 2.50
NOTE: Simonson c-1.

FRENZY (Magazine) (Satire)
Apr, 1958 - No. 6, Mar, 1959
Picture Magazine

1 6.35 19.00 38.00
2-6 4.00 12.00 24.00

FRIDAY FOSTER
October, 1972
Dell Publishing Co.

1 2.30 6.70 16.00

FRIENDLY GHOST, CASPER, THE (Becomes Casper... #254 on)
Aug, 1958 - No. 224, Oct, 1982; No. 225, Oct, 1986 - No. 253, June, 1990
Harvey Publications

1-Infinity-c 22.00 67.00 220.00
2 10.00 30.00 100.00
3-10: 6-X-Mas-c 5.00 15.00 50.00
11-20: 18-X-Mas-c 3.50 10.50 35.00
21-30 2.00 6.00 20.00
31-50 1.70 5.00 14.00
51-100: 54-X-Mas-c 1.50 3.75 9.00
101-159 1.00 2.60 6.00
160-163: All 52 pg. Giants 1.10 2.70 6.50
164-237: 173,179,185-Cub Scout Specials. 230-X-mas-c. 232-Valentine's-c
1.00 2.50
238-253: 238-Begin $1.00-c. 238,244-Halloween-c. 243-Last new material
1.00
American Dental Assoc. giveaway-Small size (1967, 16 pgs.)
1.00 2.60 6.00

FRIENDS OF MAXX (Also see Maxx)
Apr, 1996 ($2.95)
Image Comics (I Before E)

1-Featuring Dude Japan; Sam Kieth-c/a/scripts 3.00

FRIGHT
June, 1975 (Aug on inside)
Atlas/Seaboard Periodicals

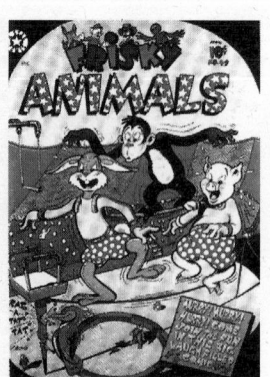
Frisky Animals #49 © STAR

Frisky Fables #2 © Premium Group

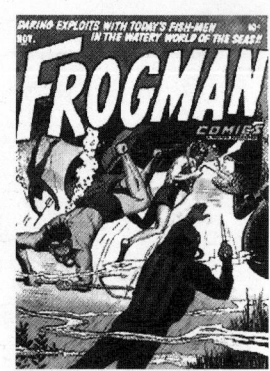
Frogman Comics #5 © HILL

	GD25	FN65	NM94
1-Origin The Son of Dracula; Frank Thorne-c/a			1.00

FRIGHT NIGHT
Oct, 1988 - No. 22, 1990 ($1.75)
Now Comics

		GD25	FN65	NM94
..1-22: 1-3 Adapts movie. 8, 9-Evil Ed horror photo-c from movie			.70	1.75

FRIGHT NIGHT II
1989 ($3.95, 52 pgs.)
Now Comics

	GD25	FN65	NM94
..1-Adapts movie sequel		1.60	4.00

FRISKY ANIMALS (Formerly Frisky Fables; Super Cat #56 on)
No. 44, Jan, 1951 - No. 55, Sept, 1953
Star Publications

	GD25	FN65	NM94
44-Super Cat; L.B. Cole	17.00	51.00	120.00
45-Classic L. B. Cole-c	26.00	77.00	180.00
46-51,53-55: Super Cat. 54-Super Cat-c.begin	16.00	47.00	110.00
52-L. B. Cole-c. 3 1/2 pgs.; X-Mas-c	17.00	51.00	120.00

NOTE: All have **L. B. Cole**-c. No. 47-No Super Cat. **Disbrow** a-49, 52. **Fago** a-51.

FRISKY ANIMALS ON PARADE (Formerly Parade Comics; becomes Superspook)
Sept, 1957 - No. 3, Dec-Jan, 1957-1958
Ajax-Farrell Publ. (Four Star Comic Corp.)

	GD25	FN65	NM94
1-L. B. Cole-c	14.00	43.00	100.00
2-No L. B. Cole-c	6.70	20.00	40.00
3-L. B. Cole-c	11.50	34.00	80.00

FRISKY FABLES (Frisky Animals No. 44 on)
Spring, 1945 - No. 43, Oct, 1950
Premium Group/Novelty Publ./Star Publ. V5#4 on

	GD25	FN65	NM94
V1#1-Funny animal; Al Fago-c/a #1-38	17.00	49.00	115.00
2,3(Fall & Winter, 1945)	8.35	25.00	50.00
V2#1(#4, 4/46) - 9,11,12(#15, 3/47): 4-Flag-c	5.85	17.50	35.00
10-Christmas-c	6.70	20.00	40.00
V3#1(#16, 4/47) - 12(#27, 3/48): 4-Flag-c. 7,9-Infinity-c. 10-X-Mas-c			
	5.00	15.00	30.00
V4#1(#28, 4/48) - 7(#34, 2-3/49)	5.00	15.00	30.00
V5#1(#35, 4-5/49) - 4(#38, 10-11/49)	5.00	15.00	30.00
39-43-L. B. Cole-c; 40-X-mas-c	15.00	45.00	105.00
Accepted Reprint No. 43 (nd); L.B. Cole-c	6.70	20.00	40.00

FRITZI RITZ (See Comics On Parade, Single Series #5, 1(reprint), Tip Top & United Comics)

FRITZI RITZ (United Comics No. 8-26)
Fall, 1948 - No. 7, 1949; No. 27, 3-4/53 - No. 36, 9-10/54; No. 42, 1/55; No. 43, 6/56 - No. 55, 9-11/57; No. 56, 12-2/57-58 - No. 59, 9-11/58
United Features Synd./St. John No. 37?-55/Dell No. 56 on

	GD25	FN65	NM94
nn(1948)-Special Fall issue; by Ernie Bushmiller	11.50	34.00	80.00
2	6.70	20.00	40.00
3-7(1949): 6-Abbie & Slats app.	5.35	16.00	32.00
27-29(1953): 29-Five pg. Abbie & Slats; 1 pg. Mamie by Russell Patterson	8.00	12.00	24.00
30-59: 31-Peanuts by Schulz (1st app.?, 11-12/53). 36-1 pg. Mamie by Patterson	4.00	11.00	22.00

NOTE: Abbie & Slats in #6,7, 27-31. Li'l Abner in #33, 35, 36. Peanuts in #31, 43, 58, 59.

FROGMAN COMICS
Jan-Feb, 1952 - No. 11, May, 1953
Hillman Periodicals

	GD25	FN65	NM94
1	10.00	30.00	70.00
2	5.85	17.50	35.00
3,4,6-11: 4-Meskin-a	4.25	13.00	28.00
5-Krigstein-a	6.70	20.00	40.00

FROGMEN, THE
No. 1258, Feb-Apr, 1962 - No. 11, Nov-Jan, 1964-65 (Painted-c)
Dell Publishing Co.

	GD25	FN65	NM94
Four Color 1258(#1)-Evans-a	8.00	24.00	80.00
2,3-Evans-a; part Frazetta inks in #2,3	6.00	18.00	60.00
4,6-11	3.00	9.00	30.00
5-Toth-a	4.00	12.00	40.00

FROM BEYOND THE UNKNOWN
10-11/69 - No. 25, 11-12/73 (No. 7-11: 64 pgs.; No. 12-17: 52 pgs.)
National Periodical Publications

	GD25	FN65	NM94
1	2.15	6.50	15.00
2-10: 7-Intro. Col. Glenn Merrit. 13-Wood-a(i)(r)	1.20	3.00	7.00
11-25: Star Rovers-r begin #18,19. Space Museum in #23-25	1.60		4.00

NOTE: **N. Adams** c-3, 6, 8, 9. **Anderson** c-2, 4, 5, 10, 11i, 15-17, 22; reprints-3, 4, 6-8, 10, 11, 13-16, 24, 25. **Infantino** r-1-5, 7-19, 23-25; c-11p. **Kaluta** c-18, 19. **Gil Kane** a-9r. **Kubert** c-1, 7, 12-14. **Toth** a-2r. **Wood** a-13i. Photo c-22.

FROM DUSK TILL DAWN (Movie)
1996 ($4.95, one-shot)
Big Entertainment

	GD25	FN65	NM94
nn-Adaptation of the film; Brereton-c			5.00

FROM HERE TO INSANITY (Satire) (Formerly Eh! #1-7)
(See Frantic & Frenzy)
No. 8, Feb, 1955 - V3#1, 1956
Charlton Comics

	GD25	FN65	NM94
8	12.00	36.00	85.00
9	10.00	30.00	70.00
10-Ditko-c/a (3 pgs.)	17.00	51.00	120.00
11,12-All Kirby except 4 pgs.	24.00	71.00	165.00
V3#1(1956)-Ward-c/a(2) (signed McCartney); 5 pgs. Wolverton-a; 3 pgs. Ditko-a; magazine format (cover says "Crazy, Man, Crazy" and becomes Crazy, Man, Crazy with V2#2)	38.00	114.00	265.00

FROM THE PIT
1994 ($4.95, one-shot, mature)
Fantagor Press

	GD25	FN65	NM94
1-R. Corben-a; HP Lovecraft back-up story	1.00	2.00	5.00

FRONTIER DAYS
1956 (Giveaway)
Robin Hood Shoe Store (Brown Shoe)

	GD25	FN65	NM94
1	3.20	8.00	16.00

FRONTIER DOCTOR (TV)
No. 877, Feb, 1958 (one-shot)
Dell Publishing Co.

	GD25	FN65	NM94
Four Color 877-Toth-a, Rex Allen photo-c	10.00	30.00	100.00

FRONTIER FIGHTERS
Sept-Oct, 1955 - No. 8, Nov-Dec, 1956
National Periodical Publications

	GD25	FN65	NM94
1-Davy Crockett, Buffalo Bill (by Kubert), Kit Carson begin (Scarce)	50.00	150.00	400.00
2	40.00	120.00	295.00
3-8	36.00	107.00	250.00

NOTE: Buffalo Bill by **Kubert** in all.

FRONTIER ROMANCES
Nov-Dec, 1949 - No. 2, Feb-Mar, 1950 (Painted-c)
Avon Periodicals/I. W.

	GD25	FN65	NM94
1-Used in **SOTI**, pg. 180(General reference) & illo. "Erotic spanking in a western comic book"	43.00	128.00	340.00
2 (Scarce)-Woodish-a by Stallman	33.00	99.00	230.00
I.W. Reprint #1-Reprints Avon's #1	4.30	13.00	30.00
I.W. Reprint #9-Reprints ?	2.60	7.50	18.00

FRONTIER SCOUT: DAN'L BOONE (Formerly Death Valley; The Masked Raider No. 14 on)

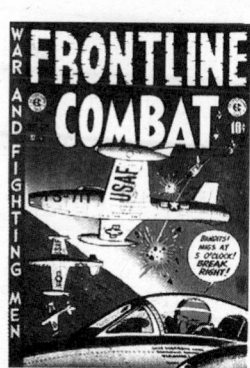

Frontline Combat #8 © WMG

Front Page Comic Book #1 © HARV

Fugitives From Justice #4 © STJ

FU

	GD25	FN65	NM94

No. 10, Jan, 1956 - No. 13, Aug, 1956; V2#14, Mar, 1965
Charlton Comics

	GD25	FN65	NM94
10	10.00	30.00	60.00
11-13(1956)	5.35	16.00	32.00
V2#14(3/65)	4.00	10.00	20.00

FRONTIER TRAIL (The Rider No. 1-5)
No. 6, May, 1958
Ajax/Farrell Publ.

6	4.25	13.00	26.00

FRONTIER WESTERN
Feb, 1956 - No. 10, Aug, 1957
Atlas Comics (PrPI)

1	16.00	47.00	110.00
2,3,6-Williamson-a, 4 pgs. each	11.00	33.00	75.00
4,7,9,10: 10-Check-a	6.70	20.00	40.00
5-Crandall, Baker, Davis-a; Williamson text illos	10.00	30.00	60.00
8-Crandall, Morrow, & Wildey-a	6.70	20.00	40.00

NOTE: *Baker* a-9. *Colan* a-2, 6. *Drucker* a-3, 4. *Heath* c-5. *Maneely* c/a-2, 7, 9. *Maurera* a-2. *Romita* a-7. *Severin* c-6, 8, 10. *Tuska* a-2. *Wildey* a-5, 8. Ringo Kid in No. 4.

FRONTLINE COMBAT
July-Aug, 1951 - No. 15, Jan, 1954
E. C. Comics

1-Severin/Kurtzman-a	56.00	168.00	450.00
2	37.00	111.00	260.00
3	26.00	79.00	185.00
4-Used in **SOTI**, pg. 257; contains "Airburst" by Kurtzman which is his personal all-time favorite story	24.00	71.00	165.00
5	20.00	60.00	140.00
6-10	17.00	49.00	115.00
11-15	12.00	36.00	85.00

NOTE: *Davis* a-in all; c-11, 12. *Evans* a-10-15. *Heath* a-1. *Kubert* a-14. *Kurtzman* a-1-5; c-1-9. *Severin* a-5-7, 9, 13, 15. *Severin/Elder* a-2-11; c-10. *Toth* a-8, 12. *Wood* a-1-4, 6-10, 12-15; c-13-15. Special issues: No. 7 (Iwo Jima), No. 9 (Civil War), No. 12 (Air Force). (Canadian reprints known; see Table of Contents.)

FRONTLINE COMBAT
Aug, 1995 - Present ($2.50)
Russ Cochran/Gemstone Publishing

1-4			2.00
5-9			2.50

FRONT PAGE COMIC BOOK
1945
Front Page Comics (Harvey)

1-Kubert-a; intro. & 1st app. Man in Black by Powell; Fuje-c	34.00	103.00	240.00

FROST AND FIRE (See DC Science Fiction Graphic Novel)

FROSTY THE SNOWMAN
No. 359, Nov, 1951 - No. 1272, Dec-Feb?/1961-62
Dell Publishing Co.

Four Color 359 (#1)	8.00	24.00	80.00
Four Color 435	4.00	12.00	40.00
Four Color 514,601,661	4.00	12.00	40.00
Four Color 748,861,950,1065,1153,1272	3.50	10.50	35.00

FRUITMAN SPECIAL
Dec, 1969 (68 pgs.)
Harvey Publications

1-Funny super hero	2.85	8.50	20.00

F-TROOP (TV)
Aug, 1966 - No. 7, Aug, 1967 (All have photo-c)
Dell Publishing Co.

	GD25	FN65	NM94
1	8.50	25.50	85.00
2-7	5.00	15.00	50.00

FUGITIVES FROM JUSTICE
Feb, 1952 - No. 5, Oct, 1952
St. John Publishing Co.

1	16.00	47.00	110.00
2-Matt Baker-r/Northwest Mounties #2; Vic Flint strip reprints begin	17.00	51.00	120.00
3-Reprints panel from Authentic Police Cases that was used in **SOTI** with changes; Tuska-a	17.00	51.00	120.00
4	7.50	22.50	45.00
5-Last Vic Flint-r; bondage-c	10.00	30.00	60.00

FUGITOID
1985 (B&W, magazine size, one-shot)
Mirage Studios

1-Ties into Teenage Mutant Ninja Turtles #5	1.00	2.00	5.00

FULL COLOR COMICS
1946
Fox Features Syndicate

nn	11.00	33.00	75.00

FULL OF FUN
Aug, 1957 - No. 2, Nov, 1957; 1964
Red Top (Decker Publ.)(Farrell)/ I. W. Enterprises

1(1957)-Funny animal; Dave Berg-a	5.00	15.00	30.00
2-Reprints Bingo, the Monkey Doodle Boy	4.00	11.00	22.00
8-I.W. Reprint('64)	1.30	3.25	8.00

FUN AT CHRISTMAS (See March of Comics No. 138)

FUN CLUB COMICS (See Interstate Theatres...)

FUN COMICS (Formerly Holiday Comics #1-8; Mighty Bear #13 on)
No. 9, Jan, 1953 - No. 12, Oct, 1953
Star Publications

9-(25¢ Giant)-L. B. Cole X-Mas-c; X-Mas issue	17.00	51.00	120.00
10-12-L. B. Cole-c. 12-Mighty Bear-c/story	14.00	43.00	100.00

FUNDAY FUNNIES (See Famous TV..., and Harvey Hits No. 35,40)

FUN-IN (TV)(Hanna-Barbera)
Feb, 1970 - No. 10, Jan, 1972; No. 11, 4/74 - No. 15, 12/74
Gold Key

1-Dastardly & Muttley in Their Flying Machines; Perils of Penelope Pitstop in #1-4; It's the Wolf in all	2.80	8.40	28.00
2-4,6-Cattanooga Cats in 2-4	1.40	3.50	14.00
5,7-Motormouse & Autocat, Dastardly & Muttley in both; It's the Wolf in #7	1.65	4.70	16.00
8,10-The Harlem Globetrotters, Dastardly & Muttley in #10	1.30	3.25	12.00
9-Where's Huddles?, Dastardly & Muttley, Motormouse & Autocat app.	1.65	4.70	16.00
11-15: 11-Butch Cassidy. 12,15-Speed Buggy. 13-Hair Bear Bunch. 14-Inch High Private Eye	.90	2.70	9.00

FUNKY PHANTOM, THE (TV)
Mar, 1972 - No. 13, Mar, 1975 (Hanna-Barbera)
Gold Key

1	2.00	6.00	22.00
2-5	1.20	3.00	12.00
6-13	.70	2.10	7.00

FUNLAND
No date (1940s) (25¢)
Ziff-Davis (Approved Comics)

nn-Contains games, puzzles, cut-outs, etc.	13.00	39.00	90.00

Funnies #57 © DELL

Funny Folks #20 © DC

Funnyman #6 © ME

	GD25	FN65	NM94

FUNLAND COMICS
1945
Croyden Publishers

1-Funny animal	13.00	39.00	90.00

FUNNIES, THE (New Funnies No. 65 on)
Oct, 1936 - No. 64, May, 1942
Dell Publishing Co.

1-Tailspin Tommy, Mutt & Jeff, Alley Oop (1st app?), Capt. Easy (1st app.), Don Dixon begin	325.00	975.00	1950.00
2-Scribbly by Mayer begins (1st app.)	137.00	412.00	825.00
3	110.00	330.00	660.00
4,5: 4-Christmas-c	83.00	249.00	500.00
6-10	62.00	187.00	375.00
11-20: 16-Christmas-c	56.00	170.00	340.00
21-29: 25-Crime Busters by McWilliams(4pgs.)	44.00	132.00	265.00
30-John Carter of Mars (origin/1st app.) begins by Edgar Rice Burroughs; Warner Bros.' Bosko-c (4/39)	90.00	270.00	725.00
31-44: 33-John Coleman Burroughs art begins on John Carter. 34-Last funny-c. 35-(9/39)-Mr. District Attorney begins; based on radio show	58.00	176.00	470.00
45-Origin/1st app. Phantasmo, the Master of the World (Dell's 1st super-hero, 7/40) & his sidekick Whizzer McGee	48.00	144.00	385.00
46-50: 48-The Black Knight begins, ends #62	39.00	114.00	275.00
51-56-Last ERB John Carter of Mars	38.00	114.00	265.00
57-Intro. & origin Captain Midnight (7/41)	100.00	300.00	800.00
58-60: 58-Captain Midnight-c begin, end #63	41.00	124.00	330.00
61-Andy Panda begins by Walter Lantz	41.00	124.00	330.00
62,63: 63-Last Captain Midnight-c; bondage-c	41.00	124.00	330.00
64-Format change; Oswald the Rabbit, Felix the Cat, Li'l Eight Ball app.; origin & 1st app. Woody Woodpecker in Oswald; last Capt. Midnight; Oswald, Andy Panda, Li'l Eight Ball-c	75.00	225.00	600.00

NOTE: **Mayer** c-26, 48. **McWilliams** art in many issues on "Rex King of the Deep". Alley Oop c-17, 20. Captain Midnight c-57(i/2), 58-63. John Carter c-35-37, 40. Phantasmo c-45-56, 57(1/2), 58-61(part). Rex King c-38, 39, 42. Tailspin Tommy c-41.

FUNNIES ANNUAL, THE
1959 ($1.00, approx. 7x10", B&W; tabloid-size)
Avon Periodicals

1-(Rare)-Features the best newspaper comic strips of the year: Archie, Snuffy Smith, Beetle Bailey, Henry, Blondie, Steve Canyon, Buz Sawyer, The Little King, Hi & Lois, Popeye, & others. Also has a chronological history of the comics from 2000 B.C. to 1959.	40.00	120.00	325.00

FUNNIES ON PARADE (Premium)
1933 (Probably the 1st comic book) (36 pgs., slick cover)
No date or publisher listed
Eastern Color Printing Co.

	GD25	FN65	VF82	NM94
nn-Contains Sunday page reprints of Mutt & Jeff, Joe Palooka, Hairbreadth Harry, Reg'lar Fellers, Skippy, & others (10,000 print run). This book was printed for Proctor & Gamble to be given away & came out before Famous Funnies or Century of Comics.	1111.00	3333.00	6667.00	11,000.00

(Estimated up to 50 total copies exist, 3 in NM/Mint)

FUNNY ANIMALS (See Fawcett's Funny Animals)
Sept, 1984 - No. 2, Nov, 1984
Charlton Comics

	GD25	FN65	NM94
1,2-Atomic Mouse-r			1.00

FUNNYBONE (... The Laugh-Book of Comical Comics)
1944 (25¢, 132 pgs.)
La Salle Publishing Co.

nn	25.00	75.00	175.00

FUNNY BOOK (...Magazine for Young Folks) (Hocus Pocus No. 9)
Dec, 1942 - No. 9, Aug-Sept, 1946 (Comics, stories, puzzles, games)
Parents' Magazine Press (Funny Book Publishing Corp.)

1-Funny animal; Alice In Wonderland app.	13.00	39.00	90.00
2-Gulliver in Giant-Land	7.50	22.50	45.00
3-9: 4-Advs. of Robin Hood. 9-Hocus-Pocus strip	5.35	16.00	32.00

FUNNY COMICS
1955 (7¢, 5x7", 36 pgs.)
Modern Store Publ.

1-Funny animal	1.60	4.00	8.00

FUNNY COMIC TUNES (See Funny Tunes)

FUNNY FABLES
Aug, 1957 - V2#2, Nov, 1957
Decker Publications (Red Top Comics)

V1#1	4.00	12.00	24.00
V2#1,2	3.20	8.00	16.00

FUNNY FILMS (Features funny animal characters from films)
Sept-Oct, 1949 - No. 29, May-June, 1954 (No. 1-4: 52 pgs.)
American Comics Group(Michel Publ./Titan Publ.)

1-Puss An' Boots, Blunderbunny begin	17.00	51.00	120.00
2	10.00	30.00	65.00
3-10: 3-X-Mas-c	6.35	19.00	38.00
11-20	4.25	13.00	28.00
21-29	4.00	10.50	21.00

FUNNY FOLKS (Hollywood... on cover only No. 16-26; becomes Hollywood Funny Folks No. 27 on)
April-May, 1946 - No. 26, June-July, 1950 (52 pgs., #16 on)
National Periodical Publications

1-Nutsy Squirrel begins (1st app.) by Rube Grossman	40.00	120.00	290.00
2	19.00	56.00	130.00
3-5: 4-1st Nutsy Squirrel-c	13.50	41.00	95.00
6-10: 6,9-Nutsy Squirrel-c begin	10.00	30.00	70.00
11-26: 16-Begin 52 pg. issues (10-11/48)	10.00	30.00	60.00

NOTE: **Sheldon Mayer** a-in some issues. **Post** a-18. Christmas c-12.

FUNNY FROLICS
Summer, 1945 - No. 5, Dec, 1946
Timely/Marvel Comics (SPI)

1-Sharpy Fox, Puffy Pig, Krazy Krow	19.00	56.00	130.00
2	10.00	30.00	65.00
3,4	8.00	24.00	48.00
5-Kurtzman-a	10.00	30.00	60.00

FUNNY FUNNIES
April, 1943 (68 pgs.)
Nedor Publishing Co.

1-Funny animals; Peter Porker app.	18.00	54.00	125.00

FUNNYMAN (Also see Cisco Kid Comics & Extra Comics)
Dec, 1947; No. 1, Jan, 1948 - No. 6, Aug, 1948
Magazine Enterprises

nn(12/47)-Prepublication B&W undistributed copy by Siegel & Shuster-(5-3/4x8"), 16 pgs.; Sold in San Francisco in 1976 for $300.00			
1-Siegel & Shuster-a in all; Dick Ayers 1st pro work (as assistant) on 1st few issues	38.00	114.00	265.00
2	24.00	73.00	170.00
3-6	21.00	62.00	145.00

FUNNY MOVIES (See 3-D Funny Movies)

FUNNY PAGES (Formerly The Comics Magazine)
No. 6, Nov, 1936 - No. 42, Oct, 1940
Comics Magazine Co./Ultem Publ.(Chesler)/Centaur Publications

V1#6 (nn, nd)-The Clock begins (2 pgs., 1st app.), ends #11; The Clock is the 1st masked comic book hero	143.00	431.00	1150.00

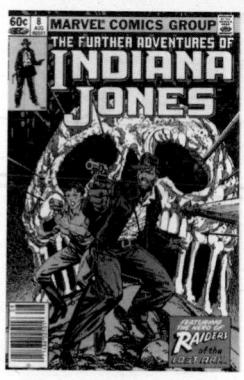

Funny Pages #41 © CHES

The Further Adventures Of Cyclops And Phoenix #3 © MEG

The Further Adventures of Indiana Jones #8 © Lucasfilm

	GD25	FN65	NM94
7-11	62.00	187.00	500.00
V2#1 (9/37)(V2#2 on-c; V2#1 in indicia)	41.00	124.00	330.00
V2#2 (10/37)(V2#3 on-c; V2#2 in indicia)	41.00	124.00	330.00
3(11/37)-5	41.00	124.00	330.00
6(1st Centaur, 3/38)	75.00	225.00	600.00
7-9	50.00	150.00	400.00
10(Scarce, 9/38)-1st app. of The Arrow by Gustavson (Blue costume)			
	225.00	675.00	1800.00
11,12	90.00	270.00	725.00
V3#1-6: 6,8-Last funny covers	87.00	262.00	700.00
7-1st Arrow-c (9/39)	156.00	468.00	1250.00
8,9: 9-Tarpe Mills jungle-c	90.00	270.00	725.00
10-2nd Arrow-c	125.00	375.00	1000.00
V4#1(1/40, Arrow-c)-(Rare)-The Owl & The Phantom Rider app.; origin Mantoka, Maker of Magic by Jack Cole. Mad Ming begins, ends #42; Tarpe Mills-a			
	156.00	468.00	1250.00
35-Classic Arrow-c	137.00	412.00	1100.00
36-38-Mad Ming-c	87.00	262.00	700.00
39-42-Arrow-c. 42-Last Arrow	112.00	338.00	900.00

NOTE: **Biro** c-V2#9. **Burgos** c-V3#10. **Jack Cole** a-V2#3, 7, 8, 10, 11, V3#2, 6, 9, 10, V4#1, 37; c-V3#2, 4. **Eisner** a-V1#7, 8?, 10. **Ken Ernst** a-V1#7, 8. **Everett** a-V2#11 (illos). **Filchock** c-V2#10, V3#6. **Gill Fox** a-V2#11. **Sid Greene** a-39. **Guardineer** a-V2#2, 3, 5. **Gustavson** a-V2#5, 11, 12, V3#1-10, 35, 38-42; c-V3#7, 35, 39-42. **Bob Kane** a-V3#1. **McWilliams** a-V2#12, V3#1, 3-6. **Tarpe Mills** a-V3#8-10, V4#1; c-V3#9. **Ed Moore** Jr. a-V2#12. **Schwab** c-V3#1. **Bob Wood** a-V2#2, 3, 8, 11, V3#6, 9, 10; c-V2#6, 7. Arrow c-V3#7, 10, V4#1, 35, 40-42.

FUNNY PICTURE STORIES (Comic Pages V3#4 on)
Nov, 1936 - V3#3, May, 1939
Comics Magazine Co./Centaur Publications

V1#1-The Clock begins (c-feature)(see Funny Pages for 1st app.)			
	275.00	825.00	2400.00
2	87.00	262.00	700.00
3-9: 4-Eisner-a; X-Mas-c. 7-Racial humor-c	62.00	187.00	500.00
V2#1 (9/37) (V1#10 on-c; V2#1 in indicia)-Jack Strand begins			
	41.00	124.00	330.00
2 (10/37, V1#11 on-c; V2#2 in indicia)	41.00	124.00	330.00
3-5: 4-Xmas-c	40.00	120.00	290.00
6(1st Centaur, 3/38)	68.00	206.00	550.00
7-11	40.00	120.00	290.00
V3#1-3	39.00	118.00	275.00
Laundry giveaway (16-20 pgs., 1930s)-slick-c	27.00	81.00	190.00

NOTE: **Biro** c-V2#1, 8, 9, 11. **Guardineer** a-V1#11; c-V2#6, V3#5. **Bob Wood** c/a-V1#11, V2#2; c-V2#3, 5.

FUNNY STUFF (Becomes The Dodo & the Frog No. 80)
Summer, 1944 - No. 79, July-Aug, 1954 (#1-7 are quarterly)
All-American/National Periodical Publications No. 7 on

1-The Three Mouseketeers (ends #28) & The "Terrific Whatzit" begin; Sheldon Mayer-a	87.00	262.00	700.00
2-Sheldon Mayer-a	41.00	124.00	330.00
3-5: 3-Flash parody. 5-All Mayer-a/scripts issue	30.00	90.00	210.00
6-10 10-(6/46)	20.00	60.00	140.00
11-17,19,20: 20-1st Dodo & the Frog-c (4/47)	15.00	45.00	105.00
18-The Dodo & the Frog (2/47, 1st app?) begin?; X-Mas-c			
	26.00	79.00	185.00
21,23-30: 24-Infinity-c	10.00	30.00	70.00
22-Superman cameo	40.00	120.00	300.00
31-79: 70-1st Bo Bunny by Mayer & begins	8.70	26.00	52.00

NOTE: **Mayer** a-1-8, 55, .57, 58, 61, 62, 64, 65, 68, 70, 72, 74-79; c-2, 5, 6, 8.

FUNNY STUFF
1946 (6-1/2x8-1/4")
National Periodical Publications (Wheaties Giveaway)

nn-(Scarce)-Dodo & the Frog, Three Mouseketeers, etc.; came taped to Wheaties box; never found in better than fine	67.00	200.00	—

FUNNY STUFF STOCKING STUFFER

Mar, 1985 ($1.25, 52 pgs.)
DC Comics

1-Almost every DC funny animal featured			1.25

FUNNY 3-D
December, 1953 (25¢, came with 2 pair of glasses)
Harvey Publications

1-Shows cover in 3-D on inside	11.00	33.00	75.00

FUNNY TUNES (Animated Funny Comic Tunes No. 16-22; Funny Comic Tunes No. 23, on covers only; formerly Krazy Komics #15; Oscar No. 24 on)
No. 16, Summer, 1944 - No. 23, Fall, 1946
U.S.A. Comics Magazine Corp. (Timely)

16-Silly Seal, Ziggy Pig, Krazy Krow begin	11.00	33.00	75.00
17 (Fall/44)-Becomes Gay Comics #18 on?	9.15	27.00	55.00
18-22: 21-Super Rabbit app.	7.00	21.00	42.00
23-Kurtzman-a	9.15	27.00	55.00

FUNNY TUNES (Becomes Space Comics #4 on)
July, 1953 - No. 3, Dec-Jan, 1953-54
Avon Periodicals

1-Space Mouse, Peter Rabbit, Merry Mouse, Spotty the Pup, Cicero the Cat begin; all continue in Space Comics	8.35	25.00	50.00
2,3	5.35	16.00	32.00

FUNNY WORLD
1947 - No. 3, 1948
Marbak Press

1-The Berrys, The Toodles & other strip-r begin	7.50	22.50	45.00
2,3	5.85	17.50	35.00

FUNTASTIC WORLD OF HANNA-BARBERA, THE (TV)
Dec, 1977 - No. 3, June, 1978 ($1.25, oversized)
Marvel Comics Group

1-3: 1-Flintstones Christmas Party(12/77). 2-Yogi Bear's Easter Parade(3/78). 3-Laff-a-lympics(6/78)	.90	2.30	5.50

FUN TIME
Spring, 1953; No. 2, Sum, 1953; No. 3(nn), Fall, 1953; No. 4, Wint, 1953-54
Ace Periodicals

1-(25¢, 100 pgs.)-Funny animal	6.35	19.00	38.00
2-4 (All 25¢, 100 pgs.)	11.00	33.00	75.00

FUN WITH SANTA CLAUS (See March of Comics No. 11, 108, 325)

FURTHER ADVENTURES OF CYCLOPS AND PHOENIX (Also see Adventures of Cyclops and Phoenix, Uncanny X-Men & X-Men)
June, 1996 - No. 4, Sept, 1996 ($1.95, limited series)
Marvel Comics

1-4: Origin of Mr. Sinister; Peter Milligan scripts; John Paul Leon-c/a(p). 2-4-Apocalypse app.			2.00

FURTHER ADVENTURES OF INDIANA JONES, THE (Movie) (Also see Indiana Jones and the Last Crusade & Indiana Jones and the Temple of Doom)
Jan, 1983 - No. 34, Mar, 1986
Marvel Comics Group

1-34: 1-Byrne/Austin-a; Austin-c. 2-Byrne/Austin-c/a			1.00

NOTE: **Austin** a-1i, 2i, 6i, 9i; c-1, 2i, 6i, 9i. **Byrne** a-1p, 2p; c-2p. **Chaykin** a-6p; c-6p, 8p-10p. **Ditko** a-21p, 25-28, 34. **Golden** c-24, 25. **Simonson** c-9. Painted c-14.

FURTHER ADVENTURES OF NYOKA, THE, JUNGLE GIRL, THE (See Nyoka)
1988 - No. 5, 1989 ($1.95, color; $2.25/$2.50, B&W)
AC Comics

1,2 ($1.95)-Bill Black-a plus reprints		.80	2.00
3,4 ($2.25, B&W); 3-Photo-c. 4-Krigstein-r		.90	2.30
5 ($2.50, B&W)-Reprints plus movie photos		1.00	2.50

FURY (Straight Arrow's Horse...) (See A-1 No. 119)

Fury #1 © MEG

Fury Of Firestorm #10 © DC

Fury Of S.H.I.E.L.D. #4 © MEG

FURY (TV) (See March Of Comics #200)
No. 781, Mar, 1957 - Nov, 1962 (All photo-c)
Dell Publishing Co./Gold Key

Four Color 781	10.00	30.00	100.00
Four Color 885,975,1031,1080,1133,1172,1218,1296, 01292-208(#1-'62)			
	7.00	21.00	70.00
10020-211(11/62-G.K.)	7.00	21.00	70.00

FURY
May, 1994 ($2.95, one-shot)
Marvel Comics

1-Ironman, Red Skull, FF, Hatemonger, Logan, Scorpio app.; Origin Nick
Fury   1.20   3.00

FURY OF FIRESTORM, THE (Becomes Firestorm The Nuclear Man #65 on)
(Also see Firestorm)
June, 1982 - No. 64, Oct, 1987 (75¢ on)
DC Comics

1-Intro The Black Bison; brief origin   .80   2.00
2-64: 4-JLA x-over. 17-1st app. Firehawk. 21-Death of Killer Frost. 22-Origin.
 23-Intro. Byte. 24-(6/84)-1st app. Blue Devil & Bug (origin); origin Byte. 34-
 1st app./origin Killer Frost II. 39-Weasel's i.d. revealed 41,42-Crisis x-over.
 48-Intro. Moonbow. 53-Origin/1st app. Silver Shade. 55,56-Legends x-over.
 58-1st app./origin Parasite   1.00
61-Test cover variant; Superman logo   4.50   13.00   35.00
Annual 1-4: 1(1983), 2(1984), 3(1985), 4(1986)   1.25
NOTE: *Colan a-19p, Annual 4p. Giffen a-Annual 4p. Gil Kane c-30. Nino a-37. Tuska a-(p)-17,
18, 32, 45.*

FURY OF HELLINA (Also see Hellina)
Jan, 1995 ($2.75, B&W)
Lightning Comics

1   1.10   2.75

FURY OF SHEILD
Apr, 1995 - No. 4, July, 1995 ($2.50/$1.95, limited series)
Marvel Comics

1 ($2.50)-Foil-c   1.00   2.50
2-4: 4-Bagged w/ decoder   .80   2.00

FUSION
Jan, 1987 - No. 17, Oct, 1989 ($2.00, B&W, Baxter paper)
Eclipse Comics

1-17: 11-The Weasel Patrol begins (1st app.?)   1.00   2.00

FUTURE COMICS
June, 1940 - No. 4, Sept, 1940
David McKay Publications

1-(6/40, 64 pgs.)-Origin The Phantom (4 pgs.); The Lone Ranger (8 pgs.) &
 Saturn Against the Earth (4 pgs.) begin   225.00   675.00   1800.00
2   109.00   328.00   875.00
3,4   90.00   270.00   725.00

FUTURETECH
Jan, 1996 - Present ($2.50, limited series)
Mushroom Comics

1-Flipbook w/SWARM   2.50

FUTURE WORLD COMICS
Summer, 1946 - No. 2, Fall, 1946
George W. Dougherty

1,2: H. C. Kiefer-c   20.00   60.00   140.00

FUTURE WORLD COMIX (Warren Presents...)
Sept, 1978
Warren Publications

1-Corben-a; Todd-c   1.50

FUTURIANS, THE (See Marvel Graphic Novel #9)
Sept, 1985 - No. 3, 1985 ($1.50)
Lodestone Publishing/Eternity Comics

1-3: Indicia title "Dave Cockrum's..."   1.50
Graphic Novel 1 ($9.95, Eternity)-r/#1-3, plus never published #4 issue
                                              1.70   5.00   10.00

FUTURIANS, THE (See Marvel Graphic Novel #9)
Aug, 1995 ($2.95, one-shot)
Aardwolf

1-Dave Cockrum   1.20   3.00

G-8 (See G-Eight)

GABBY (Formerly Ken Shannon) (Teen humor)
No. 11, July, 1953; No. 2, Sept, 1953 - No. 9, Sept, 1954
Quality Comics Group

11(#1)(7/53)   7.00   21.00   42.00
2   4.25   13.00   26.00
3-9   3.60   9.00   18.00

GABBY GOB (See Harvey Hits No. 85, 90, 94, 97, 100, 103, 106, 109)

GABBY HAYES ADVENTURE COMICS
Dec, 1953
Toby Press

1-Photo-c   13.50   41.00   95.00

GABBY HAYES WESTERN (Movie star) (See Monte Hale, Real Western
Hero & Western Hero!)
Nov, 1948 - No. 50, Jan, 1953; No. 51, Dec, 1954 - No. 59, Jan, 1957
Fawcett Publications/Charlton Comics No. 51 on

1-Gabby & his horse Corker begin; photo front/back-c begin
                                              47.00   142.00   380.00
2   22.00   66.00   155.00
3-5   14.00   43.00   100.00
6-10: 9-Young Falcon begins   12.00   36.00   85.00
11-20: 19-Last photo back-c   10.00   30.00   65.00
21-49: 20,22,24,26,28,29-(52 pgs.)   7.50   22.50   45.00
50-(1/53)-Last Fawcett issue; last photo-c?   9.15   27.00   55.00
51-(12/54)-1st Charlton issue; photo-c   9.15   27.00   55.00
52-59(1955-57): 53,55-Photo-c. 58-Swayze-a   4.25   13.00   28.00
Quaker Oats Giveaway nn's(#1-5, 1951, 2-1/2x7") (Kagran Corp.)-...In Tracks
 of Guilt, ...In the Fence Post Mystery, ...In the Accidental Sherlock, ...
 In the Frame-Up, ...In the Double Cross Brand known
                                              10.00   30.00   65.00

GAGS
July, 1937 - V3#10, Oct, 1944 (13-3/4x10-3/4")
United Features Synd./Triangle Publ. No. 9 on

1(7/37)-52 pgs.; 20 pgs. Grin & Bear It, Fellow Citizen
                                               5.85   17.50   35.00
V1#9 (36 pgs.) (7/42)   4.00   11.00   22.00
V3#10   3.60   9.00   18.00

GALACTIC GUARDIANS
July, 1994 - No. 4, Oct, 1994 ($1.50, limited series)
Marvel Comics

1-4   1.50

GALACTIC WAR COMIX (Warren Presents... on cover)
December, 1978
Warren Publications

nn-Wood, Williamson-r   1.50

GALLANT MEN, THE (TV)
Oct, 1963 (Photo-c)
Gold Key

Gambit #2 © MEG

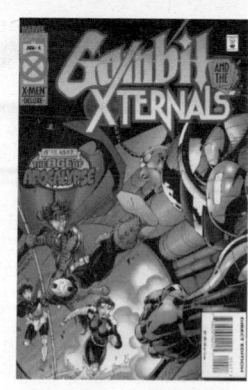
Gambit And The X-Ternals #4 © MEG

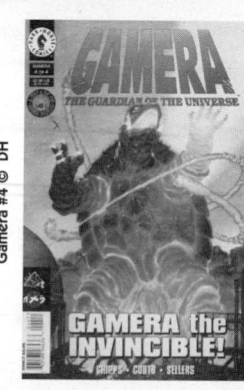
Gamera #4 © DH

	GD25	FN65	NM94
1(1008-310)-Manning-a	2.30	6.70	16.00

GALLEGHER, BOY REPORTER (Disney, TV)
May, 1965
Gold Key

	GD25	FN65	NM94
1(10149-505)-Photo-c	1.70	5.00	12.00

GAMBIT (See X-Men #266 & X-Men Annual #14)
Dec, 1993 - No. 4, Mar, 1994 ($2.00, limited series)
Marvel Comics

	GD25	FN65	NM94
1-($2.50)-Lee Weeks-c/a in all; gold foil stamped-c.			
	1.00	2.00	5.00
1 (Gold)	2.85	8.50	20.00
2-4		1.20	3.00

GAMBIT AND THE X-TERNALS
Mar, 1995 - No. 4, July, 1995 ($1.95, limited series)
Marvel Comics

	GD25	FN65	NM94
1-Age of Apocalypse		1.20	3.00
2-4		.80	2.00

GAMEBOY
1990 - No. 6? ($1.95, coated-c)
Valiant

	GD25	FN65	NM94
1-6: 3,4,6-Layton-a. 4-Morrow-a. 5-Layton-c(i)		.80	2.00

GAMMARAUDERS
Jan, 1989 - No. 10, Dec, 1989 ($1.25/$1.50/$2.00)
DC Comics

	GD25	FN65	NM94
1-10-Based on TSR game		.80	2.00

GAMERA
Aug, 1996 - No. 4, Nov, 1996 ($2.95, limited series)
Dark Horse Comics

	GD25	FN65	NM94
1-4			3.00

GAMORRA SWIMSUIT SPECIAL
June, 1996 ($2.50, one-shot)
Image Comics (Wildstorm Productions)

	GD25	FN65	NM94
1-Campbell wraparound-c; pinups			2.50

GANDY GOOSE (Movies/TV)(See All Surprise, Giant Comics Edition #5A &10,
Paul Terry's Comics & Terry-Toons)
Mar, 1953 - No. 5, Nov, 1953; No. 5, Fall, 1956 - No. 6, Sum/58
St. John Publ. Co./Pines No. 5,6

	GD25	FN65	NM94
1-All St. John issues are pre-code	9.15	27.00	55.00
2	4.25	13.00	26.00
3-5(1953)(St. John)	4.00	11.00	22.00
5,6(1956-58)(Pines)-CBS Televison Presents…	3.60	9.00	18.00

GANG BUSTERS (See Popular Comics #38)
1938 - 1943
David McKay/Dell Publishing Co.

	GD25	FN65	NM94
Feature Books 17(McKay)('38)-1st app.	52.50	157.50	525.00
Large Feature Comic 10('39)-(Scarce)	52.50	157.50	525.00
Large Feature Comic 17('41)	31.50	94.50	315.00
Four Color 7(1940)	35.00	105.00	350.00
Four Color 23,24('42-43)	26.50	79.50	265.00

GANG BUSTERS (Radio/TV)(Gangbusters #14 on)
Dec-Jan, 1947-48 - No. 67, Dec-Jan, 1958-59 (No. 1-23: 52 pgs.)
National Periodical Publications

	GD25	FN65	NM94
1	75.00	225.00	600.00
2	37.00	111.00	260.00
3-5	26.00	79.00	185.00
6-10: 9-Dan Barry-a. 9,10-Photo-c	20.00	60.00	140.00
11-13-Photo-c	17.00	51.00	120.00
14,17-Frazetta-a, 8 pgs. each. 14-Photo-c	36.00	107.00	250.00

	GD25	FN65	NM94
15,16,18-20	12.00	36.00	85.00
21-25,27-30	11.00	33.00	75.00
26-Kirby-a	11.50	34.00	85.00
31-44: 44-Last Pre-code (2-3/55)	10.00	30.00	65.00
45-67	8.35	25.00	50.00

NOTE: *Barry* a-6, 8, 10. *Drucker* a-51. *Moreira* a-48, 50, 59. *Roussos* a-8.

GANGSTERS AND GUN MOLLS
Sept, 1951 - No. 4, June, 1952 (Painted c-1-3)
Avon Periodical/Realistic Comics

	GD25	FN65	NM94
1-Wood-a, 1 pg; c/Avon paperback #292	40.00	120.00	300.00
2-Check-a, 8 pgs.; Kamen-a; Bonnie Parker story			
	30.00	90.00	210.00
3-Marijuana mention story; used in **POP**, pg. 84,85			
	27.00	81.00	190.00
4-Syd Shores-c	22.00	66.00	155.00

GANGSTERS CAN'T WIN
Feb-Mar, 1948 - No. 9, June-July, 1949 (All 52 pgs?)
D. S. Publishing Co.

	GD25	FN65	NM94
1-True crime stories	26.00	77.00	180.00
2	11.50	34.00	85.00
3-6: 4-Acid in face story	10.00	30.00	70.00
7-9	9.15	27.00	55.00

NOTE: *Ingles* a-5, 6. *McWilliams* a-5, 7. *Reinman* c-6.

GANG WORLD
No. 5, Nov, 1952 - No. 6, Jan, 1953
Standard Comics

	GD25	FN65	NM94
5-Bondage-c	14.00	43.00	100.00
6	11.50	34.00	80.00

GARGOYLE (See The Defenders #94)
June, 1985 - No. 4, Sept, 1985 (75¢, limited series)
Marvel Comics Group

	GD25	FN65	NM94
1-4: 1-Wrightson-c; character from Defenders			1.00

GARGOYLES (TV cartoon)
Feb, 1995 - No. 17, June, 1996 ($2.50)
Marvel Comics

	GD25	FN65	NM94
1-17: Based on animated series		1.00	2.50

GARRISON'S GORILLAS (TV)
Jan, 1968 - No. 4, Oct, 1968; No. 5, Oct, 1969 (Photo-c)
Dell Publishing Co.

	GD25	FN65	NM94
1	4.00	12.00	40.00
2-5: 5-Reprints #1	2.85	8.50	28.00

GASOLINE ALLEY (Top Love Stories No. 3 on?)
Sept-Oct, 1950 - No. 2, Dec, 1950 (Newspaper-r)
Star Publications

	GD25	FN65	NM94
1-Contains 1 pg. intro. history of the strip (The Life of Skeezix); reprints 15 scenes of highlights from 1921-1935, plus an adventure from 1935 and 1936 strips; a 2-pg. filler is included on the life of the creator Frank King, with photo of the cartoonist.			
	19.00	58.00	135.00
2-(1936-37 reprints)-L. B. Cole-c	22.00	66.00	155.00
(See Super Book No. 21)			

GASP!
Mar, 1967 - No. 4, Aug, 1967 (12¢)
American Comics Group

	GD25	FN65	NM94
1	3.30	9.90	23.00
2-4	2.00	6.00	14.00

GAY COMICS (Honeymoon No. 41)
Mar, 1944 (no month); No. 18, Fall, 1944 - No. 40, Oct, 1949
Timely Comics/USA Comic Mag. Co. No. 18-24

	GD25	FN65	NM94
1-Wolverton's Powerhouse Pepper; Tessie the Typist begins; 1st app. Willie (one shot)	40.00	120.00	310.00

Gene Autry Comics #11 © Gene Autry

Generation Next #2 © MEG

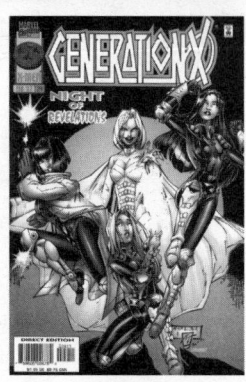

Generation X #24 © MEG

	GD25	FN65	NM94
18-(Formerly Funny Tunes #17?)-Wolverton-a	24.00	73.00	170.00
19-29: Wolverton-a in all. 21,24-6 pg., 7 pg. Powerhouse Pepper; additional 2 pg. story in 24). 23-7 pg Wolverton story & 2 two pg stories(total of 11pgs.).			
24,29-Kurtzman-a (24-"Hey Look"(2))	19.00	56.00	130.00
30,33,36,37-Kurtzman's "Hey Look"	8.35	25.00	50.00
31-Kurtzman's "Hey Look" (1), Giggles 'N' Grins (1-1/2)			
	8.35	25.00	50.00
32,35,38-40: 35-Nellie The Nurse begins?	5.85	17.50	35.00
34-Three Kurtzman "Hey Look"	9.15	27.00	55.00

GAY COMICS (Also see see Smile, Tickle, & Whee Comics)
1955 (7¢, 5x7-1/4", 52 pgs.)
Modern Store Publ.

1		1.60	4.00

GAY PURR-EE (See Movie Comics)

GEEK, THE (See Brother Power... & Vertigo Visions)

G-8 AND HIS BATTLE ACES
Oct, 1966
Gold Key

1 (10184-610)-Painted-c	3.75	11.25	28.00

G-8 AND HIS BATTLE ACES
1991 ($1.50, one-shot)
Blazing Comics

1-Glanzman-a; Truman-c			1.50

NOTE: Flip book format with "The Spider's Web" #1 on other side w/**Glanzman**-a, **Truman**-c.

GEM COMICS
Apr, 1945 (52 pgs, Bondage-c)
Spotlight Publishers

1-Little Mohee, Steve Strong app.	23.00	69.00	160.00

GENE AUTRY (See March of Comics No. 25, 28, 39, 54, 78, 90, 104, 120, 135, 150 & Western Roundup under Dell Giants)

GENE AUTRY COMICS (Movie, Radio star; singing cowboy)
(Dell takes over with No. 11)
1941 (On sale 12/31/41) - No. 10, 1943 (68 pgs.)
Fawcett Publications

1 (Rare)-Gene Autry & his horse Champion begin			
	580.00	1740.00	5800.00
2-(1942)	116.00	350.00	935.00
3-5: 3-(11/1/42)	82.00	247.00	660.00
6-10	68.00	206.00	550.00

GENE AUTRY COMICS (...& Champion No. 102 on)
No. 11, 1943 - No. 121, Jan-Mar, 1959 (TV - later issues)
Dell Publishing Co.

11 (1943, 60 pgs.)-Continuation of Fawcett series; photo back-c			
	54.00	162.00	540.00
12 (2/44, 60 pgs.)	48.00	144.00	480.00
Four Color 47(1944, 60 pgs.)	40.00	120.00	400.00
Four Color 57(11/44),66('45)(52 pgs. each)	36.50	109.50	365.00
Four Color 75,83('45, 36 pgs. each)	29.00	87.00	290.00
Four Color 93,100('45-46, 36 pgs. each): 100-Photo-c			
	25.00	75.00	250.00
1(5-6/46, 52 pgs.)	40.00	120.00	400.00
2(7-8/46)-Photo-c begin, end #111	22.00	66.00	220.00
3-5: 4-Intro Flapjack Hobbs	16.00	48.00	160.00
6-10	12.50	37.50	125.00
11-20: 20-Panhandle Pete begins	10.00	30.00	100.00
21-29(36pgs.)	8.00	27.00	80.00
30-40(52pgs.)	6.50	21.00	65.00
41-56(52pgs.)	6.00	18.00	50.00
57-66(36pgs.): 58-X-mas-c	5.00	15.00	35.00
67-80(52pgs.)	5.35	16.00	38.00

81-90(52pgs.): 82-X-mas-c. 87-Blank inside-c	4.35	13.00	30.00
91-99(36pgs. No. 91-on). 94-X-mas-c	3.25	10.00	22.00
100	4.00	12.00	28.00
101-111-Last Gene Autry photo-c	3.25	10.00	22.00
112-121-All Champion painted-c, most by Savitt	2.75	7.50	18.00
...Adventure Comics And Play-Fun Book ('47)-32 pgs., 8x6-1/2"; games, comics, magic (Pillsbury premium)	26.00	80.00	210.00
Quaker Oats Giveaway(1950)-2-1/2x6-3/4"; 5 different versions; "Death Card Gang", "Phantoms of the Cave", "Riddle of Laughing Mtn.", "Secret of Lost Valley", "Bond of the Broken Arrow" (came in wrapper)			
each...	12.00	36.00	85.00
3-D Giveaway(1953)-Pocket-size; 5 different	13.50	41.00	95.00

NOTE: Photo back covers 4-18, 20-45, 48-65. **Manning** a-118. **Jesse Marsh** art: 4-Color No. 66, 75, 93, 100, No. 1-25, 27-37, 39, 40.

GENE AUTRY'S CHAMPION (TV)
No. 287, 8/50; No. 319, 2/51; No. 3, 8-10/51 - No. 19, 8-10/55
Dell Publishing Co.

Four Color 287(#1)('50, 52pgs.)-Photo-c	10.00	30.00	100.00
Four Color 319(#2, '51), 3: 2-Painted-c begin, most by Sam Savitt			
	4.00	12.00	40.00
4-19: 19-Last painted-c	3.00	9.00	30.00

GENE AUTRY TIM (Formerly Tim) (Becomes Tim in Space)
1950 (Half-size) (B&W Giveaway)
Tim Stores

nn-Several issues (All Scarce)	10.00	30.00	70.00

GENE DOGS
Oct, 1993 - No. 4, Jan, 1994 ($1.75, limited series)
Marvel Comics UK

1-($2.75)-Polybagged w/4 trading cards		1.10	2.75
2-4: 2-Vs. Genetix		.70	1.75

GENERAL DOUGLAS MACARTHUR
1951
Fox Features Syndicate

nn-True life story	18.00	54.00	125.00

GENERIC COMIC, THE
Apr, 1984 (one-shot)
Marvel Comics Group

1			1.00

GENERATION NEXT
Mar, 1995 - No. 4, June, 1995 ($1.95, limited series)
Marvel Comics

1-Age of Apocalypse; Scott Lobdell scripts & Chris Bachalo-c/a			
	1.00	2.00	5.00
2-4		1.20	3.00

GENERATION X
Oct, 1994 - Present ($1.50/$1.95)
Marvel Comics

Collectors Preview ($1.75)		.80	2.00
"Ashcan" Edition			1.00
1/2 (San Diego giveaway)	1.20	3.00	7.00
1-($3.95)-Wraparound chromium-c; Scott Lobdell scripts & Chris Bachalo-c/a begins.	1.00	2.00	5.00
2-($1.95)-Deluxe edition, Bachalo-a		1.20	3.00
3,4-($1.95)-Deluxe Edition; Bachalo-a		1.00	2.50
2-4-Standard Edition; Bachalo-a		.80	2.00
5-30: 5-(7/95)-Returns from "Age of Apocalypse," begin $1.95-c. 6-Bachalo-a(p) ends, returns #17. 7-Roger Cruz-a(p). 10-Omega Red-c/app. 13,14-Bishop-app. 17-Stan Lee app. (Stan Lee scripts own dialogue); Bachalo/Buckingham-a; Onslaught update. 18-Toad cameo. 20-Franklin Richards app; Howard the Duck cameo. 21-Howard the Duck app.			

	GD25	FN65	NM94
'95 Special-($3.95)		.80	2.00
'96 Special-($2.95)-Wraparound-c; Jeff Johnson-c/a		1.60	4.00
			3.00

GENE RODDENBERRY'S LOST UNIVERSE
Apr, 1995 - No. 6, Dec, 1995 ($1.95)
Tekno Comix

		GD25	FN65	NM94
0 (11/95, $2.25)			.90	2.25
1-3-w/ bound-in game piece & trading card			.80	2.00
4-6: 4-bound-in trading card			.80	2.00

GENE RODDENBURY'S XANDER IN LOST UNIVERSE
Dec, 1995 - No. 8, July, 1996 ($2.25)
Tekno Comix

	GD25	FN65	NM94
1-8: 1-5-Jae Lee-c. 4-Polybagged. 8-Includes Pt. 5 of The Big Bang x-over.		.90	2.25

GENETIX
Oct, 1993 - No. 6, Mar, 1994 ($1.75, limited series)
Marvel Comics UK

	GD25	FN65	NM94
1-($2.75)-Polybagged w/4 cards; Dark Guard app.		1.10	2.75
2-6: 2-Intro Tektos. 4-Vs. Gene Dogs		.70	1.75

GENSAGA
1995 ($2.50/$6.75, one-shot)
Entity Comics

	GD25	FN65	NM94
1		1.00	2.50
1 ($6.75)-bagged w/PC Game	1.15	2.85	6.75

GEN 13
Feb, 1994 - No. 5, July 1994 ($1.95, limited series)
Image Comics (Wildstorm Productions)

	GD25	FN65	NM94
0 (8/95, $2.50)-Ch. 1 w/Jim Lee-p; Ch.4 w/Charest-p	1.30	3.25	8.00
1/2	4.30	13.00	30.00
1-($2.50)-Created by Jim Lee	5.70	17.00	40.00
1-2nd printing	1.65	4.20	10.00
2-($2.50)	5.50	16.50	38.00
3-Pitt-c & story	2.85	8.50	20.00
4-Pitt-c & story; wraparound-c	2.60	7.50	18.00
5	1.30	3.25	8.00
5-Alternate Portacio-c; see Deathblow #5	2.85	8.50	20.00
..Collected Edition ('94, $12.95)-r/#1-5			13.00
..Rave ($1.50, 3/95)-wraparound-c	1.20		3.00

NOTE: Issues 1-4 contain coupons redeemable for ashcan edition of Gen 13 #0. Price listed is for complete books.

GEN 13
Mar, 1995 - Present ($2.50)
Image Comics (Wildstorm Productions)

	GD25	FN65	NM94
1-A (Charge)-Campbell/Gardner-c	1.00	2.60	6.00
1-B (Thumbs Up)-Campbell/Gardner-c	1.00	2.60	6.00
1-C (Lil' GEN 13)-Art Adams-c	2.85	8.50	20.00
1-D (Barbari-GEN)-Simon Bisley-c	2.85	8.50	20.00
1-E (Your Friendly Neighborhood Grunge)-John Cleary-c			
	2.85	8.50	20.00
1-F (GEN 13 Goes Madison Ave.)-Michael Golden-c			
	2.85	8.50	20.00
1-G (Lin-GEN-re)-Michael Lopez-c	3.60	11.00	25.00
1-H (GEN-et Jackson)-Jason Pearson-c	3.60	11.00	25.00
1-I (That's the way we became GEN 13)-Campbell/Gibson-c			
	2.85	8.50	20.00
1-J (All Dolled Up)-Campbell/McWeeney-c	2.85	8.50	20.00
1-K (Verti-GEN)-Joe Dunn-c	2.85	8.50	20.00
1-L (Picto-Fiction)	3.25	9.50	22.00
1-M (Do it Yourself Cover)	2.85	8.50	20.00
2 ($1.95, Newsstand)-WildStorm Rising Pt. 4; bound-in card	1.20		3.00
2-12,14-20: 2-($2.50, Direct Market)-WildStorm Rising Pt. 4, bound-in card.			

	GD25	FN65	NM94
6,7-Jim Lee-c/a(p). 9-Ramos-a. 10-Fire From Heaven Pt. 3. 11-Fire From Heaven Pt. 9	1.00	2.00	5.00
11-($4.95)-Special European Tour Edition; chromium-c			20.00
13A,13B,13C-($1.30, 13 pgs.): 13A-Archie & Friends app. 13B-Bone-c/app.; Teenage Mutant Ninja Turtles, Madman, Spawn & Jim Lee app.			
			1.30
Variant Collection-Four editions (all 13 variants w/Chromium variant-limited, signed)	32.00	96.00	250.00

GEN 13/MAXX
Dec, 1995 ($3.50, one-shot)
Image Comics (Wildstorm Publications)

	GD25	FN65	NM94
1-Wm. Messner-Loebs story, 1st Tomm Coker-c/a.			3.50

GEN 13: ORDINARY HEROES
Feb, 1996 - No. 2, July, 1996 ($2.50, limited series)
Image Comics (Wildstorm Publications)

	GD25	FN65	NM94
1-Adam Hughes-c/a/scripts			2.50

GEN 13: THE UNREAL WORLD
July, 1996 ($2.95, one-shot)
Image Comics (Wildstorm Productions)

	GD25	FN65	NM94
1-Humberto Ramos-c/a			3.00

GENTLE BEN (TV)
Feb, 1968 - No. 5, Oct, 1969 (All photo-c)
Dell Publishing Co.

	GD25	FN65	NM94
1	3.60	11.00	25.00
2-5: 5-Reprints #1	2.00	6.00	14.00

GEOMANCER (Also see Eternal Warrior: Fist & Steel)
Nov, 1994 - No. 8, June, 1995 ($3.75/$2.25)
Valiant

	GD25	FN65	NM94
1 ($3.75)-Chromium wraparound-c; Eternal Warrior app.	1.50		3.75
2-8		.90	2.25

GEORGE OF THE JUNGLE (TV)(See America's Best TV Comics)
Feb, 1969 - No. 2, Oct, 1969 (Jay Ward)
Gold Key

	GD25	FN65	NM94
1	7.50	22.50	75.00
2	6.00	18.00	60.00

GEORGE PAL'S PUPPETOONS
Dec, 1945 - No. 18, Dec, 1947; No. 19, 1950
Fawcett Publications

	GD25	FN65	NM94
1-Captain Marvel-c	40.00	120.00	290.00
2	21.00	62.00	145.00
3-10	13.00	39.00	90.00
11-19	11.00	33.00	75.00

GEORGIE COMICS (...& Judy Comics #20-35?; see All Teen & Teen Comics)
Spring, 1945 - No. 39, Oct, 1952 (#1-3 are quarterly)
Timely Comics/GPI No. 1-34

	GD25	FN65	NM94
1-Dave Berg-a	18.00	54.00	125.00
2	10.00	30.00	60.00
3-5,7,8	7.50	22.50	45.00
6-Georgie visits Timely Comics	10.00	30.00	65.00
9,10-Kurtzman's "Hey Look" (1 & ?); Margie app.	9.15	27.00	55.00
11,12: 11-Margie, Millie app.	5.35	16.00	32.00
13-Kurtzman's "Hey Look", 3 pgs.	8.35	25.00	50.00
14-Wolverton-a(1 pg.); Kurtzman's "Hey Look"	10.00	30.00	60.00
15,16,18-20	4.25	13.00	28.00
17,29-Kurtzman's "Hey Look", 1 pg.	7.50	22.50	45.00
21-24,27,28,30-39: 21-Anti-Wertham editorial	4.00	12.00	24.00
25-Painted-c by classic pin-up artist Peter Driben	8.35	25.00	50.00
26-Logo design swipe from Archie Comics	4.25	13.00	28.00

GERALD McBOING-BOING AND THE NEARSIGHTED MR. MAGOO (TV)

Ghost #2 © FH

Ghost #2 © DH

Ghost/Hellboy #1 © DH/Mike Mignola

	GD25	FN65	NM94

	GD25	FN65	NM94

(Mr. Magoo No. 6 on)
Aug-Oct, 1952 - No. 5, Aug-Oct, 1953
Dell Publishing Co.

1	9.00	27.00	90.00
2-5	7.00	21.00	70.00

GERONIMO (See Fighting Indians of the Wild West!)
1950 - No. 4, Feb, 1952
Avon Periodicals

1-Indian Fighter; Maneely-a; Texas Rangers-r/Cowpuncher #1; Fawcette-c			
	14.00	43.00	100.00
2-On the Warpath; Kit West app.; Kinstler-c/a	10.00	30.00	60.00
3-And His Apache Murderers; Kinstler-c/a(2); Kit West-r/Cowpuncher #6			
	10.00	30.00	60.00
4-Savage Raids of; Kinstler-c & inside front-c; Kinstlerish-a by McCann(3)			
	8.35	25.00	50.00

GERONIMO JONES
Sept, 1971 - No. 9, Jan, 1973
Charlton Comics

1	1.00	2.00	5.00
2-9		1.00	2.50
Modern Comics Reprint #7('78)			1.50

GETALONG GANG, THE (TV)
May, 1985 - No. 6, Mar, 1986
Marvel Comics (Star Comics)

1-6: Saturday morning TV stars			1.00

GET LOST
Feb-Mar, 1954 - No. 3, June-July, 1954 (Satire)
Mikeross Publications/New Comics

1-Andru/Esposito-a in all?	24.00	71.00	165.00
2-Andru/Esposito-c; has 4 pg. E.C. parody featuring "The Sewer Keeper"			
	17.00	51.00	120.00
3-John Wayne 'Hondo' parody	13.00	39.00	90.00
1,2 (10,12/87-New Comics)-B&W r-original			1.00

GET SMART (TV)
June, 1966 - No. 8, Sept, 1967 (All have Don Adams photo-c)
Dell Publishing Co.

1	9.00	27.00	90.00
2-Ditko-a	5.50	16.50	55.00
3-8: 3-Ditko-a(p)	5.00	15.00	50.00

GHOST (...Comics #9)
1951(Winter) - No. 11, Summer, 1954
Fiction House Magazines

1-Most covers by Whitman	55.00	165.00	440.00
2-Ghost Gallery & Werewolf Hunter stories	29.00	86.00	200.00
3-9: 3,6,7,9-Bondage-c. 9-Abel, Discount-a	24.00	73.00	170.00
10,11-Dr. Drew by Grandenetti in each, reprinted from Rangers; 11-Evans-r/			
Rangers #39; Grandenetti-r/Rangers #49	29.00	86.00	200.00

GHOST (See Comic's Greatest World)
Apr, 1995 - Present ($2.50)
Dark Horse Comics

1-Adam Hughes-a	1.00	2.00	5.00
2,3-Hughes-a		1.20	3.00
4-27: 4-Barb Wire app. 5,6-Hughes-c. 12-Ghost/Hellboy preview. 15-X app.			
18-Barb Wire app.		1.00	2.50
Special 1 (7/94, $3.95, 48 pgs.)	1.20	3.00	7.00
...Nocturnes (1996, $9.95, trade paperback)-r/#1-3 & 5			10.00
...Stories (1995, $9.95, trade paperback)-r/Early Ghost app.			10.00

GHOST AND THE SHADOW
Dec, 1995 ($2.95, one-shot)

Dark Horse Comics

1-Moench scripts			3.0

GHOST/HELLBOY
May, 1996 - No. 2, June, 1996 ($2.50, limited series)
Dark Horse Comics

1,2: Mike Mignola-c/scripts & breakdowns; Scott Benefiel finished-a			
			2.5

GHOST BREAKERS (Also see Racket Squad in Action, Red Dragon & (CC)
Sherlock Holmes Comics)
Sept, 1948 - No. 2, Dec, 1948 (52 pgs.)
Street & Smith Publications

1-Powell-c/a (magician) app.	37.00	111.00	260.0
2-Powell-c/a(2); Maneely-a	29.00	86.00	200.0

GHOSTBUSTERS (TV) (Also, see Real...and Slimer)
Feb, 1987 - No. 6, Aug, 1987 ($1.25)
First Comics

1-6: Based on new animated TV series			1.3

GHOSTBUSTERS II
Oct, 1989 - No. 3, Dec, 1989 ($1.95, mini-series)
Now Comics

1-3: Movie Adaptation		1.00	2.0

GHOST CASTLE (See Tales of...)

GHOSTDANCING
Mar, 1995 - No. 6, Sept, 1995 ($1.95, limited series)
DC Comics (Vertigo)

1-6: Case-c/a		.80	2.0

GHOSTLY HAUNTS (Formerly Ghost Manor)
#20, 9/71 - #53, 12/76; #54, 9/77 - #55, 10/77; #56, 1/78 - #58, 4/78
Charlton Comics

20-58: 27-Dr. Graves x-over. 32-New logo. 33-Back to old logo. 39-Origin &			
1st app. Destiny Fox		1.20	3.0
40,41(Modern Comics-r, 1977, 1978)			1.5

NOTE: Ditko a-22-25, 27, 28, 31-34, 36-41, 43-48, 50, 52, 54, 56r; c-22-27, 30, 33-37, 47, 5
56. Glanzman a-20. Howard a-27, 30, 35, 42. Newton c/a-42. Staton a-35; c-28, 46. Sutton
33, 37, 39, 41.

GHOST IN THE SHELL (Manga)
Mar, 1995 - No. 8, Oct, 1995 ($3.95, B&W/color, limited series)
Dark Horse Comics

1-8		1.60	4.0

GHOSTLY TALES (Formerly Blue Beetle No. 50-54)
No. 55, 4-5/66 - No. 124, 12/76; No. 125, 9/77 - No. 169, 10/84
Charlton Comics

55-Intro. & origin Dr. Graves	1.40	3.50	8.5
56-70-Dr. Graves ends		1.80	4.5
71-169: 107-Sutton, Wood-a. 114-Newton-a		1.40	3.5

NOTE: Aparo a-65, 66, 68, 72, 141r, 142r; c-71, 72, 74-76, 81, 146r. Ditko a-55-58, 60, 61, €
69-73, 75-90, 92-95, 97, 99-118, 120-122, 125r, 126r, 131-133r, 136-141r, 143r, 144r, 152, 1€
161, 163; c-67, 69, 73, 77, 78, 83, 84, 86-90, 92-97, 99, 102, 109, 111, 118, 120-122, 125, 13
133, 163. Glanzman a-167. Howard a-95, 98, 99, 117; c-98, 107, 120, 121, 161. Morisi a-8
84, 86. Newton a-114; c-115(painted). Palais a-61. Staton a-161; c-117. Sutton a-107, 1
114; c-100, 106, 110, 113(painted). Wood a-107.

GHOSTLY WEIRD STORIES (Formerly Blue Bolt Weird)
No. 120, Sept, 1953 - No. 124, Sept, 1954
Star Publications

120-Jo-Jo-r	29.00	86.00	200.
121-124: 121-Jo-Jo-r. 122-The Mask-r/Capt. Flight #5; Rulah-r; has 1pg. story			
'Death and the Devil Pills'-r/Western Outlaws #17. 123-Jo-Jo; Disbrow-a(2)			
124-Torpedo Man	24.00	73.00	170.

NOTE: Disbrow a-120-124. L. B. Cole covers-all issues (#122 is a sci-fi cover).

Ghost Rider #1 © ME

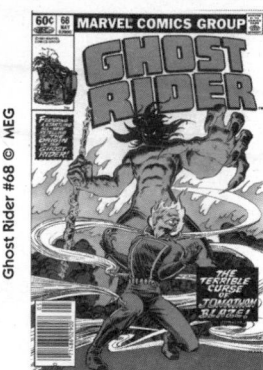

Ghost Rider #68 © MEG

Ghost Rider #82 © MEG

	GD25	FN65	NM94

HOST MANOR (Ghostly Haunts No. 20 on)
uly, 1968 - No. 19, July, 1971
harlton Comics

		1.65	4.20	10.00
2-5			1.80	4.50
6-12,17: 17-Morisi-a			1.40	3.50
3-16,18,19-Ditko-a; c-15,18,19			1.80	4.50

HOST MANOR (2nd Series)
ct, 1971 - No. 32, Dec, 1976; No. 33, Sept, 1977 - No. 77, 11/84
harlton Comics

		1.65	4.20	10.00
2-7,9,10			1.80	4.50
3-Wood-a		1.00	2.50	5.50
1-56,58-77: 18-Newton's 1st pro art. 19-20-Newton-a. 22-Newton-c/a. 21-
E-Man, Blue Beetle, Capt. Atom cameos. 28-Nudity panels. 40-Torture &
drug use. 77-Aparo-r/Space Adventures V3#60 (Paul Mann)			1.40	3.50
7-Wood, Ditko, Howard-a			1.80	4.50
9(Modern Comics reprint, 1977)				1.00

OTE: **Ditko** a-4, 8, 10, 11(2), 13, 14, 18, 20-22, 24-26, 28, 29, 31, 37r, 38r, 40r, 42-44r, 46r, 47,
r, 52r, 54r, 57, 60, 62(4), 64r, 71; c-2-7, 9-11, 14-16, 28, 31, 37, 38, 42, 43, 46, 47, 51, 52, 60,
, 64. **Howard** a-4, 8, 19-21, 57. **Newton** a-18-20, 22, 64. **Sutton** a-19;c-8, 18.

HOST RIDER (See A-1 Comics, Best of the West, Black Phantom, Bobby
enson, Great Western, Red Mask & Tim Holt)
950 - No. 14, 1954
agazine Enterprises
OTE: The character was inspired by Vaughn Monroe's "Ghost Riders in the Sky", and
sney's movie "The Headless Horseman".

(A-1 #27)-Origin Ghost Rider	59.00	178.00	475.00
2-5: 2(A-1 #29), 3(A-1 #31), 4(A-1 #34), 5(A-1 #37)-All Frazetta only	53.00	159.00	425.00
6,7: 6(A-1 #44)-Loco weed story, 7(A-1 #51)	23.00	69.00	160.00
8,9: 8(A-1 #57)-Drug use story, 9(A-1 #69)	19.00	58.00	135.00
0(A-1 #71)-Vs. Frankenstein	19.00	58.00	135.00
1-14: 11(A-1 #75). 12(A-1 #80)-Bondage-c; one-eyed Devil-c.13(A-1 #84).
14(A-1 #112)	17.00	49.00	115.00

OTE: **Dick Ayers** art in all; c-1, 6-14.

HOST RIDER, THE (See Night Rider & Western Gunfighters)
eb, 1967 - No. 7, Nov, 1967 (Western hero)(12¢)
arvel Comics Group

-Origin & 1st app. Ghost Rider; Kid Colt-reprints begin	5.70	17.00	40.00
7: 6-Last Kid Colt-r; All Ayers-c/a(p)	2.60	7.50	18.00
	2.15	6.50	15.00

HOST RIDER (See The Champions, Marvel Spotlight #5, Marvel Team-Up
5, 58, Marvel Treasury Edition #18, Marvel Two-In-One #8, The Original
host Rider & The Original Ghost Rider Rides Again)
ept, 1973 - No. 81, June, 1983 (Super-hero)
arvel Comics Group

| -Johnny Blaze, the Ghost Rider begins; 1st app. Daimon Hellstrom (Son of
Satan) in cameo	11.50	34.00	80.00
2-1st full app. Daimon Hellstrom; gives glimpse of costume (1 panel); story
continues in Marvel Spotlight #12	4.50	14.00	32.00
-5: 3-Ghost Rider gets new cycle; Son of Satan app.	3.30	10.00	23.00
-10: 10-Reprints origin/1st app. from Marvel Spotlight #5; Ploog-a	2.15	6.50	15.00
-19: 18-Spider-Man-c & app.	1.70	5.00	12.00
)-Daredevil x-over; ties into D.D. #138; Byrne-a	2.30	6.70	16.00
-30: 22-1st app. Enforcer. 29,30-Vs. Dr. Strange	1.20	3.00	7.00
-49	1.00	2.60	6.00
)-Double size	1.20	3.00	7.00

51-67,69-76,78-80: 80-Brief origin recap		1.80	4.50
68,77-Origin retold	1.00	2.60	6.00
81-Death of Ghost Rider (Demon leaves Blaze)	1.50	3.75	9.00

NOTE: **Anderson** c-64p. **Infantino** a(p)-43, 44, 51. **G. Kane** a-21p; c(p)-1, 2, 4, 5, 8, 9, 11-13,
19, 20, 24, 25. **Kirby** c-21-23. **Mooney** a-2-9p, 30i. **Nebres** c-26i. **Newton** a-23i. **Perez** c-26p.
Shores a-2i. **J. Sparling** a-62p, 64p, 65p. **Starlin** a(p)-35. **Sutton** a-1p, 44i, 64i, 65i, 66, 67i.
Tuska a-13p, 14p, 16p.

GHOST RIDER (Also see Doctor Strange/Ghost Rider Special, Marvel Comics
Presents & Midnight Sons Unlimited)
V2#1, May, 1990 - Present ($1.50/$1.75/$1.95/$1.50)
Marvel Comics (Midnight Sons imprint #44 on)

V2#1-($1.95, 52 pgs.)-Origin/1st app. new Ghost Rider; Kingpin app.			
	1.00	2.00	5.00
1-2nd printing (not gold)	.80	2.00	
2,3,5: 3-Kingpin app. 5-Punisher app.; Jim Lee-c			
	1.00	2.00	5.00
4-Scarcer		1.60	4.00
5-Gold background 2nd printing	.80	2.00	
6-Punisher app.		1.60	4.00
7-10: 9-X-Factor app. 10-Reintro Johnny Blaze on the last pg.			
	1.20	3.00	
11-14: 11-Stroman-c/a(p). 12,13-Dr. Strange x-over cont'd in D.S. #28. 13-
Painted-c. 14-Johnny Blaze vs. Ghost Rider; origin recap 1st Ghost
Rider (Blaze)	.90	2.25	
15-Glow in the dark-c; begin $1.75-c	1.20	3.00	
15-Gold background 2nd printing	.80	2.00	
16,17-Spider-Man/Hobgoblin-c/story	1.10	2.75	
18-24,29,30,32-39: 18-Painted-c by Nelson. 29-Wolverine-c/story. 32-Dr.
Strange x-over; Johnny Blaze app. 34-Williamson-a(i). 36-Daredevil app.
37-Archangel app.		1.50	
25-27: 25-($2.75)-Contains pop-up scene insert. 26,27-X-Men x-over;
Lee/Williams-c on both	.90	2.25	
28-($2.50, 52 pgs.)-Polybagged w/poster; part 1 of Rise of the Midnight
Sons storyline (see Ghost Rider/Blaze #1)	1.30	3.25	
31-($2.50, 52 pgs.)-Polybagged w/poster; part 6 of Rise of the Midnight
Sons	1.00	2.50	
40-Outer-c is Darkhold envelope made of black parchment w/gold
ink; Midnight Massacre; Demogoblin app.	.90	2.25	
41-48: 41-Lilith & Centurious app.; begin $1.75-c. 41-43-Neon ink-c. 43-Has
free extra 16 pg. insert on Siege of Darkness. 44,45-Siege of Darkness
parts 2 & 10. 44-Spot varnish-c. 46-Intro new Ghost Rider. 48-Spider-Man
app.	.70	1.75	
49,51-60,62-78: 49-Begin $1.95-c; bound-in trading card sheet; Hulk app.
55-Werewolf by Night app. 65-Punisher app. 67,68-Gambit app.
68-Wolverine app. 73,74-Blaze, Vengeance app. 78-New costume.	.80	2.00	
50-($2.50, 52 pgs.)-Regular edition	1.00	2.50	
50-($2.95, 52 pgs.)-Collectors ed. die cut foil-c	1.20	3.00	
61-($2.50)	1.00	2.50	
75-85: 75-Begin $1.50-c. 76-Vs. Vengeance. 77-Dr. Strange-c/app. 78-Dr.
Strange app.		1.50	
Annual 1 (1993, $2.95, 68 pgs.)-Bagged w/card	1.20	3.00	
Annual 2 (1994, $2.95, 68 pgs.)	1.20	3.00	
...And Cable 1 (9/92, $3.95, stiff-c, 68 pgs.)-Reprints Marvel
Presents #90-98 w/new Kieth-c	1.40	3.50	

NOTE: **Andy & Joe Kubert** c/a-28-31. **Quesada** c-21. **Williamson** a(i)-33-35; c-33i.

GHOST RIDER/BLAZE: SPIRITS OF VENGEANCE (Also see Blaze)
Aug, 1992 - No. 23, June, 1994 ($1.75)
Marvel Comics (Midnight Sons imprint #17 on)

| 1-($2.75, 52 pgs.)-Polybagged w/poster; part 2 of Rise of the Midnight Sons
storyline; Adam Kubert-c/a begins	1.10	2.75
2-11,14-21: 4-Art Adams & Joe Kubert-p. 5,6-Spirits of Venom parts 2 & 4
cont'd from Web of Spider-Man #95,96 w/Demogoblin. 14-17-Neon ink-c.
15-Intro Blaze's new costume & power. 17,18-Siege of Darkness parts 8 & | | |

Ghost Rider 2099 #25 © MEG

Ghosts #1 © DC

Giant Comics Edition #12 © STJ

	GD25	FN65	NM94

		GD25	FN65	NM94
13. 17-Spot varnish-c			.70	1.75
12-($2.95)-Glow-in-the-dark-c			1.20	3.00
13-($2.25)-Outer-c is Darkhold envelope made of black parchment w/gold ink; Midnight Massacre x-over			.90	2.25
22,23: 22-Begin $1.95-c; bound-in trading card sheet			.80	2.00

NOTE: Adam & Joe Kubert c-7, 8. Adam Kubert/Steacy c-6. J. Kubert a-13p(6 pgs.)

GHOST RIDER/CAPTAIN AMERICA: FEAR
Oct, 1992 ($5.95, 52 pgs.)
Marvel Comics

	GD25	FN65	NM94
nn-Wraparound gatefold-c; Williamson inks	1.00	2.50	6.00

GHOST RIDER 2099
May, 1994 - No. 25, May, 1996 ($1.50/$1.95)
Marvel Comics

	GD25	FN65	NM94
1 ($2.25)-Collector's Edition w/prismatic foil-c	1.00		2.50
1 ($1.50)-Regular Edition; bound-in trading card sheet			1.50
2-12: 7-Spider-Man 2099 app.			1.50
13-25 ($1.95)		.80	2.00

GHOST RIDER, WOLVERINE, PUNISHER: THE DARK DESIGN
Dec, 1994 ($5.95, one-shot)
Marvel Comics

	GD25	FN65	NM94
nn-Gatefold-c	1.00	2.60	6.00

GHOST RIDER; WOLVERINE; PUNISHER: HEARTS OF DARKNESS
Dec, 1991 ($4.95, one-shot, 52 pgs.)
Marvel Comics

	GD25	FN65	NM94
1-Double gatefold-c; John Romita, Jr.-c/a(p)	1.00	2.00	5.00

GHOSTS (Ghost No. 1)
Sept-Oct, 1971 - No. 112, May, 1982 (No. 1-5: 52 pgs.)
National Periodical Publications/DC Comics

	GD25	FN65	NM94
1-Aparo-a	3.60	11.00	25.00
2-Wood-a(i)	1.65	4.20	10.00
3-5	1.00	2.60	6.00
6-20		1.60	4.00
21-96: 40-(68 pgs.)		.80	2.00
97-99-The Spectre vs. Dr. 13 by Aparo. 97,98-Spectre-c by Aparo.		1.20	3.00
100-112: 100-Infinity-c			1.50

NOTE: B. Baily a-77. Buckler c-99, 100. J. Craig a-108. Ditko a-77, 111. Giffen a-104p, 106p, 111p. Glanzman a-2. Golden a-88. Infantino a-8. Kaluta c-7, 93, 101. Kubert a-8; c-89, 105-108, 111. Mayer a-111. McWilliams a-99. Win Mortimer a-89, 91, 94. Nasser/Netzer a-97. Newton a-92p, 94p. Nino a-35, 37, 57. Orlando a-74l; c-80. Redondo a-8, 13, 45. Sparling a(p)-90, 93, 94. Spiegle a-103, 105. Tuska a-2l. Dr. 13, the Ghostbreaker back-ups in 95-99, 101.

GHOSTS SPECIAL (See DC Special Series No. 7)

GHOST STORIES (See Amazing Ghost Stories)

GHOST STORIES
Sept-Nov, 1962; No. 2, Apr-June, 1963 - No. 37, Oct, 1973
Dell Publishing Co.

	GD25	FN65	NM94
12-295-211(#1)-Written by John Stanley	5.00	15.00	35.00
2	2.60	7.50	18.00
3-10: Two No. 6's exist with different c/a(12-295-406 & 12-295-503)	2.00	6.00	14.00
#12-295-503 is actually #9 with indicia to #6			
11-20	1.30	3.25	8.00
21-37	1.00	2.00	5.00

NOTE: #21-34, 36, 37 all reprint earlier issues.

GHOUL TALES (Magazine)
Nov, 1970 - No. 5, July, 1971 (52 pgs.) (B&W)
Stanley Publications

	GD25	FN65	NM94
1-Aragon pre-code reprints; Mr. Mystery as host; bondage-c	4.00	12.00	28.00
2,3: 2-(1/71)Reprint/Climax #1. 3-(3/71)	1.70	5.00	12.00

	GD25	FN65	NM94
4-(5/71)Reprints story "The Way to a Man's Heart" used in **SOTI**	3.60	11.00	25.00
5-ACG reprints	1.70	5.00	12.00

NOTE: No. 1-4 contain pre-code Aragon reprints.

GIANT BOY BOOK OF COMICS (Also see Boy Comics)
1945 (240 pgs., hard-c)
Newsbook Publications (Gleason)

	GD25	FN65	NM94
1-Crimebuster & Young Robin Hood; Biro-c	81.00	243.00	650.00

GIANT COMIC ALBUM
1972 (59¢, 11x14", 52 pgs., B&W, cardboard-c)
King Features Syndicate

Newspaper reprints: Little Iodine, Katzenjammer Kids, Henry, Mandrake the Magician ('59 Falk), Popeye, Beetle Bailey, Barney Google, Blondie, Flash Gordon ('68-69 Dan Barry), & Snuffy Smith

	GD25	FN65	NM94
each...	1.70	5.00	12.00

GIANT COMICS
Summer, 1957 - No. 3, Winter, 1957 (25¢, 100 pgs.)
Charlton Comics

	GD25	FN65	NM94
1-Atomic Mouse, Hoppy app.	19.00	58.00	135.00
2,3: 2-Romance. 3-Christmas Book; Atomic Mouse, Atomic Rabbit, Li'l Genius, Li'l Tomboy & Atom the Cat stories	14.00	43.00	100.00

NOTE: The above may be rebound comics; contents could vary.

GIANT COMICS (See Wham-O Giant Comics)

GIANT COMICS EDITION (See Terry-Toons)
1947 - No. 17, 1950 (25¢, 100-164 pgs.)
St. John Publishing Co.

	GD25	FN65	NM94
1-Mighty Mouse	40.00	120.00	400.00
2-Abbie & Slats	18.00	55.00	185.00
3-Terry-Toons Album; 100 pgs.	30.00	90.00	300.00
4-Crime comics; contains Red Seal No. 16, used & illo. in SOTI	47.50	142.50	475.00
5-Police Case Book (4/49, 132 pgs.)-Contents varies; contains remaindered St. John books - some volumes contain 5 copies rather than 4, with 160 pages; Matt Baker-c	45.00	135.00	450.00
5A-Terry-Toons Album (132 pgs.)-Mighty Mouse, Heckle & Jeckle, Gandy Goose & Dinky stories	28.00	84.00	280.00
6-Western Picture Stories; Baker-c/a(3); Tuska-a; The Sky Chief, Blue Monk, Ventrilo app., 132 pgs.	42.50	127.50	425.00
7-Contains a teen-age romance plus 3 Mopsy comics	25.00	75.00	250.00
8-The Adventures of Mighty Mouse (10/49)	28.00	84.00	280.00
9-Romance and Confession Stories; Kubert-a(4); Baker-a; photo-c (132 pgs)	44.00	132.00	440.00
10-Terry-Toons Album (132 pgs.)-Mighty Mouse, Heckle & Jeckle, Gandy Goose stories	28.00	84.00	280.00
11-Western Picture Stories-Baker-c/a(4); The Sky Chief, Desperado, & Blue Monk app.; another version with Son of Sinbad by Kubert (132 pgs.)	40.00	120.00	400.00
12-Diary Secrets; Baker prostitute-c; 4 St. John romance comics; Baker-a	70.00	210.00	700.00
13-Romances; Baker, Kubert-a	37.50	112.00	375.00
14-Mighty Mouse Album (132 pgs.)	28.00	84.00	280.00
15-Romances (4 love comics)-Baker-c	40.00	120.00	400.00
16-Little Audrey; Abbott & Costello, Casper	28.00	84.00	280.00
17(nn)-Mighty Mouse Album (nn, no date, but did follow No. 16); 100 pgs. on cover but has 148 pgs.	28.00	84.00	280.00

NOTE: The above books contain remaindered comics and contents could vary with each issue. No. 11, 12 have part photo magazine insides.

GIANT COMICS EDITIONS
1940's (132 pgs.)
United Features Syndicate

1-Abbie & Slats, Abbott & Costello, Jim Hardy, Ella Cinders, Iron Vic, Gordo

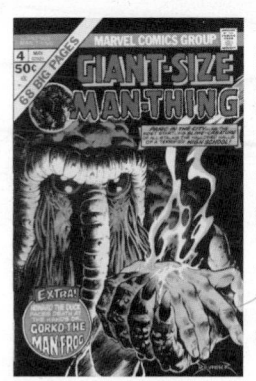

Giant Size Man-Thing #4 © MEG

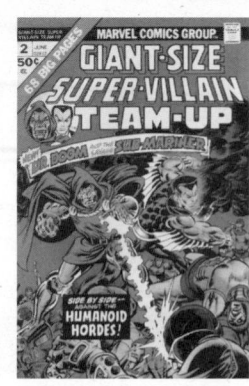

Ginat Size Super-Villain Team-Up #2 © MEG

G.I. Combat #5 © QUA

GI

	GD25	FN65	NM94
& Bill Bumlin	33.00	99.00	240.00
Jim Hardy, Ella Cinders, Elmo & Gordo	24.00	73.00	180.00
'E: Above books contain rebound copies; contents can vary.			

ANT GRAB BAG OF COMICS (See Archie All-Star Specials under Archie Comics)

ANTS (See Thrilling True Story of the Baseball…)

ANT-SIZE…
y, 1974 - Dec, 1975 (35/50¢, 52/68 pgs.)(Some titles quarterly)
rvel Comics Group

engers 1(8/74)-New-a plus G.A. H. Torch-r; 1st modern app. The Whizzer; 1st & only modern app. Miss America	1.65	4.20	10.00
engers 2,3: 2(11/74)-Death of the Swordsman. 3(2/75)			
	1.00	2.60	6.00
engers 4,5: 4(6/75)-Vision marries Scarlet Witch. 5(12/75)-Reprints Avengers Special #1	1.00	2.60	6.00
otain America 1(12/75)-r/stories T.O.S. 59-63 by Kirby (#63 reprints origin)	1.65	4.70	11.00
otain Marvel 1(12/75)-r/Capt. Marvel #17, 20 by Gil Kane (p)	1.50	3.75	9.00
llers 1(6/74, 52 pgs)-Curse of Dracula; origin/1st app. Lilith, Dracula's daughter; Heath-r; Colan-c/a(p); becomes Giant-Size Dracula #2 on	1.00	2.00	5.00
llers 1(2/75, 50¢, 68 pgs.)-Alacala-a	1.40		3.50
llers 2(5/75)-All-r; Everett-r from Advs. into Weird Worlds	1.20		3.00
llers 3(8/75)-Wrightson-c(new)/a(r); Colan, Kirby, Smith-r	1.60		4.00
nan 1(9/74)-B. Smith-r/#3; start adaptation of Howard's "Hour of the Dragon" (ends #4): 1st app. Belit; new-a begins	1.20	2.90	7.00
nan 2(12/74)-B. Smith-r/#5; Sutton-a(i) (#1 also); Buscema-a	1.00	2.50	6.00
nan 3-5: 3(4/75)-B. Smith-r/#6; Sutton-a(i). 4(6/75)-B. Smith-r/#7. 5(1975)-B. Smith-r/#14,15; Kirby-c	1.60		4.00
atures 1(5/74, 52 pgs.)-Werewolf app; 1st app. Tigra (formerly Cat); Crandall-a; becomes Giant-Size Werewolf w/#2	1.00	2.00	5.00
redevil 1(1975)	1.30	3.25	8.00
enders 1(7/74)-Silver Surfer app.; Starlin-a; Ditko, Everett & Kirby reprints	2.15	6.50	15.00
enders 2(10/74, 68 pgs.)-New G. Kane-c/a(p); Son of Satan app.; Sub-Mariner-r by Everett; Ditko-r/Strange Tales #119 (Dr. Strange); Maneely-r.	1.00	2.50	6.00
enders 3-5: 3(1/75)-1st app. Korvac.; Newton, Starlin-a; Ditko, Everett-r. 4(4/75)-Ditko, Everett-r; G. Kane-c. 5-(7/75)-Guardians app.	1.00	2.00	5.00
c Savage 1(1975, 68 pgs.)-r/#1,2; Mooney-r	1.60		4.00
ctor Strange 1(11/75)-Reprints stories from Strange Tales #164-168; Lawrence, Tuska-r	1.20	3.00	7.00
acula 1(9/74, 50¢)-Formerly Giant-Size Chillers	1.00	2.00	5.00
acula 3(12/74)-Fox-r/Uncanny Tales #6	1.60		4.00
acula 4(3/75)-Ditko-r(2)	1.20		3.00
acula 5(6/75)-1st Byrne art at Marvel	1.00	2.50	6.00
tastic Four 2-4: 2(8/74)-Formerly Giant-Size Super-Stars; Ditko-r. 3(11/74). 4(2/75)-1st Madrox; 2-4-All have Buscema-a	1.65	4.20	10.00
tastic Four 5,6: 5(5/75)-All-r; Kirby, G. Kane-r. 6(10/75)-All-r; Kirby-r	1.30	3.25	8.00
k 1(1975)	1.70	5.00	12.00
aders 1(6/75, 50¢, 68 pgs.)-Origin; G.A. Sub-Mariner-r/Sub-Mariner #1; intro Master Man	1.30	3.25	8.00
Man 1(1975)-Ditko reprint	1.50	3.80	9.00
Colt 1-3: 1(1/75). 2(4/75). 3(7/75)		1.60	4.00
n-Thing 1(8/74)-New Ploog-c/a (25 pg.); Ditko-r/Amazing Adv. #11; Kirby-r/Strange Tales Ann. #2 & T.O.S. #15; (#1-5 all have new Man-Thing stories, pre-hero-r & are 68 pgs.)	1.00	2.50	6.00
n-Thing 2,3: 2(11/74)-Buscema-c/a(p); Kirby, Powell-r. 3(2/75)-Alcala-a;			

	GD25	FN65	NM94
Ditko, Kirby, Sutton-r; Gil Kane-c		1.60	4.00
Man-Thing 4,5: 4(5/75)-Howard the Duck by Brunner-c/a; Ditko-r. 5(8/75)-Howard the Duck by Brunner (p); Dracula cameo in Howard the Duck; Buscema-a(p); Sutton-a(i); G. Kane-c	1.00	2.50	6.00
Marvel Triple Action 1,2: 1(5/75). 2(7/75)		1.20	3.00
Master of Kung Fu 1(9/74)-Russell-a; Yellow Claw-r in #1-4; Gulacy-a in #1,2	1.20	2.90	7.00
Master of Kung Fu 2(12/74)-r/Yellow Claw #1		1.70	4.25
Master of Kung Fu 3(3/75)-Gulacy-a		1.60	4.00
Master of Kung Fu 4(6/75)		1.60	4.00
Power Man 1(1975)	1.00	2.50	6.00
Spider-Man 1(7/74)-Kirby/Ditko, Byrne-r plus new-a (Dracula-c/story)	3.60	11.00	25.00
Spider-Man 2,3: 2(10/74). 3(1/75)-Byrne-r	1.65	4.20	10.00
Spider-Man 4(4/75)-3rd Punisher app.; Byrne, Ditko-r	7.00	21.50	50.00
Spider-Man 5,6: 5(7/75)-Byrne-r. 6(9/75)	1.50	3.75	9.00
Super-Heroes Featuring Spider-Man 1(6/74, 35¢, 52 pgs.)-Spider-Man vs. Man-Wolf; Morbius, the Living Vampire app.; Ditko-r; G. Kane-a(p); Spidey villains app.	5.70	17.00	40.00
Super-Stars 1(5/74, 35¢, 52 pgs.)-Fantastic Four; Thing vs. Hulk; Kirbyish-a by Buckler/Sinnott; F.F. villains profiled; becomes Giant-Size Fantastic Four #2 on	2.15	6.50	15.00
Super-Villain Team-Up 1(3/75, 68 pgs.)-Craig-r(i) (Also see Fantastic Four #6 for 1st super-villain team-up)	1.20	2.90	7.00
Super-Villain Team-Up 2(6/75, 68 pgs.)-Dr. Doom, Sub-Mariner app.; Spider-Man-r/Amazing Spider-Man #8 by Ditko; Sekowsky-a(p)	1.00	2.00	5.00
Thor 1(7/75)	1.20	3.00	7.00
Werewolf 2(10/74, 68 pgs.)-Formerly Giant-Size Creatures; Ditko-r; Frankenstein app.	1.00	2.00	5.00
Werewolf 3,5: 3(1/75, 68 pgs.). 5(7/75, 68 pgs.)	1.00	2.00	5.00
Werewolf 4(4/75, 68 pgs.)-Morbius the Living Vampire app.	1.00	2.60	6.00
X-Men 1(Summer, 1975, 50¢, 68 pgs.)-1st app. new X-Men; intro Nightcrawler, Storm, Colossus & Thunderbird; 2nd full app. Wolverine after Incredible Hulk #181	44.00	132.00	350.00
X-Men 2(11/75)-N. Adams-r (51 pgs)	5.70	17.00	40.00

GIANT SPECTACULAR COMICS (See Archie All-Star Special under Archie Comics)

GIANT SUMMER FUN BOOK (See Terry-Toons…)

G. I. COMBAT
Oct, 1952 - No. 43, Dec, 1956
Quality Comics Group

1-Crandall-c; Cuidera a-1-43i	47.00	141.00	375.00
2	24.00	71.00	165.00
3-5,10-Crandall-c/a	22.00	66.00	155.00
6-Crandall-a	20.00	60.00	140.00
7-9	16.00	47.00	110.00
11-20	12.00	36.00	85.00
21-31,33,35-43: 41-1st S.A. issue	10.00	30.00	70.00
32-Nuclear attack-c/story "Atomic Rocket Assault"	12.00	36.00	85.00
34-Crandall-a	11.00	33.00	75.00

G. I. COMBAT (See DC Special Series #22)
No. 44, Jan, 1957 - No. 288, Mar, 1987
National Periodical Publications/DC Comics

44-Grey tone-c	48.00	144.00	385.00
45	30.00	90.00	210.00
46-50	21.00	64.00	150.00
51-Grey tone-c	20.00	60.00	140.00
52-60	18.00	54.00	125.00
61-66,68-74: 68-Introduces "The Rock" (Sgt. Rock prototype?)	11.50	34.00	80.00

Giant Size Man-Thing #4 © MEG

Ginat Size Super-Villain Team-Up #2 © MEG

G.I. Combat #5 © QUA

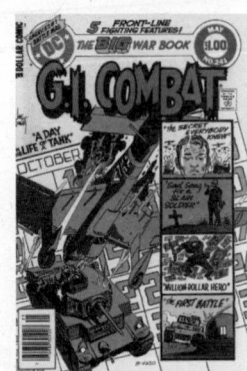

G. I Combat #241 © DC

G. I. Joe #10 © Hasbro

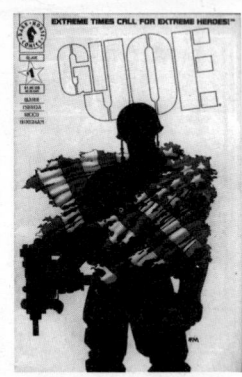

G. I. Joe #1 © Hasbro

	GD25	FN65	NM94
67-1st Tank Killer	16.00	47.00	110.00
75-80: 75-Greytone-c begin, end #109	10.50	32.00	85.00
81,82,84-86,88-90: 90-Last 10¢ issue	10.00	30.00	65.00
83-1st Big Al, Little Al, & Charlie Cigar	11.50	34.00	80.00
87-1st Haunted Tank	44.00	132.00	350.00
91-100: 91-1st Haunted Tank-c	9.15	27.00	55.00
101-108: 108-1st Sgt. Rock x-over.	7.00	21.00	42.00
109-Grey tone-c	8.00	24.00	55.00
110-113,115-120: 113-Grey tone-c	6.35	19.00	38.00
114-Origin Haunted Tank	10.00	30.00	70.00
121-137,139,140: 121-1st app. Sgt. Rock's father. 136-Last 12¢ issue	3.60	11.00	25.00
138-Intro. The Losers (Capt. Storm, Gunner/Sarge, Johnny Cloud) in Haunted Tank (10-11/69)	3.75	11.25	30.00
141-200: 146-148-(25¢, 68 pgs.). 149-154-(52 pgs.). 150-Ice Cream Soldier story (tells how he got his name). 151-Capt. Storm story. 151,153-Medal of Honor series by Maurer	1.00		6.00
201-281: 201-245,247-259 are $1.00 size. 232-Origin Kana the Ninja. 244-Death of Slim Stryker; 1st app. The Mercenaries. 246-(76 pgs., $1.50)-30th Anniversary issue. 257-Intro. Stuart's Raiders. 260-Begin $1.25, 52 pg. issues, end #281. 264-Intro Sgt. Bullet; origin Kana. 269-Intro. The Bravos of Vietnam	1.20		3.00
282-288 (75¢): 282-New advs. begin	1.20		3.00

NOTE: **N. Adams** c-168, 201, 202. **Check** a-168, 173. **Drucker** a-48, 61, 63, 66, 71, 72, 76, 134, 140, 141, 144, 147, 148, 153. **Evans** a-135, 138, 158, 164, 166, 201, 202, 204, 205, 215, 256. **Giffen** a-267. **Glanzman** a-most issues. **Kubert/Heath** a-most issues; **Kubert** covers most issues. **Morrow** a-159-161(2 pgs.). **Redondo** a-189, 240i, 243i. **Sekowsky** a-162p. **Severin** a-147, 152, 154. **Simonson** c-169. **Thorne** a-153. **Wildey** a-153. Johnny Cloud app.-112, 115, 120. **Mile. Marie** app.-123, 132, 200. **Sgt. Rock** app.-111-113, 115, 120, 125, 141, 146, 147, 149, 200. USS Stevens by **Glanzman**-145, 150-153, 157. **Grandenetti** c-44-48.

G. I. COMICS (Also see Jeep & Overseas Comics)
1945 - No. 73?, 1946 (Distributed to U. S. armed forces)
Giveaways

1-73-Contains Prince Valiant by Foster, Blondie, Smilin' Jack, Mickey Finn, Terry & the Pirates, Donald Duck, Alley Oop, Moon Mullins & Capt. Easy strip reprints (at least 73 issues known to exist)	4.00	12.00	28.00

GIDGET (TV)
Apr, 1966 - No. 2, Dec, 1966
Dell Publishing Co.

1,2: 1-Sally Field photo-c	5.50	16.50	55.00

GIFT (See The Crusaders)

GIFT COMICS
1942 - No. 4, 1949 (50¢/25¢, 324 pgs./152 pgs.)
Fawcett Publications

1-Captain Marvel, Bulletman, Golden Arrow, Ibis the Invincible, Mr. Scarlet, & Spy Smasher begin; not rebound, remaindered comics, printed at same time as originals; 50¢-c & 324 pgs. begin, end #3.	210.00	630.00	2100.00
2-Commando Yank, Phantom Eagle, others app.	150.00	450.00	1500.00
3	95.00	285.00	950.00
4-(25¢, 152 pgs.)-The Marvel Family, Captain Marvel, etc.; each issue can vary in contents	60.00	180.00	600.00

GIFTS FROM SANTA (See March of Comics No. 137)

GIGGLE COMICS (Spencer Spook No. 100) (Also see Ha Ha Comics)
Oct, 1943 - No. 99, Jan-Feb, 1955
Creston No.1-63/American Comics Group No. 64 on

1-Funny animal	27.00	81.00	190.00
2	13.00	39.00	90.00
3-5: Ken Hultgren-a begins?	10.00	30.00	65.00
6-10: 9-1st Superkatt (6/44)	8.35	25.00	50.00
11-20	6.35	19.00	38.00
21-40: 32-Patriotic-c. 37,61-X-Mas-c. 39-St. Valentine's Day-c			

	GD25	FN65	NM94
		5.00	15.00	30.
41-54,56-59,61-99: 95-Spencer Spook begins?	4.25	13.00	26.
55,60-Milt Gross-a	5.70	17.00	34.

G-I IN BATTLE (G-I No. 1 only)
Aug, 1952 - No. 9, July, 1953; Mar, 1957 - No. 6, May, 1958
Ajax-Farrell Publ./Four Star

1	8.35	25.00	50.
2	4.25	13.00	26.
3-9	4.00	11.00	22.
Annual 1(1952, 25¢, 100 pgs.)	21.00	64.00	150.
1(1957-Ajax)	5.00	15.00	30.
2-6	3.60	9.00	18.

G. I. JANE
May, 1953 - No. 11, Mar, 1955 (Misdated 3/54)
Stanhall/Merit No. 11

1-PX Pete begins; Bill Williams-c/a	10.00	30.00	65.
2-7(5/54)	5.35	16.00	32.
8-10(12/54, Stanhall)	4.25	13.00	26.
11 (3/55, Merit)	4.00	11.00	22.

G. I. JOE (Also see Advs. of..., Showcase #53, 54 & The Yardbirds)
No. 10, 1950; No. 11, 4-5/51 - No. 51, 6/57 (52pgs.: 10-14,6-17?)
Ziff-Davis Publ. Co. (Korean War)

10(#1, 1950)-Saunders painted-c begin	11.00	33.00	75
11-14(#2-5, 10/51): 11-New logo. 12-New logo	7.50	22.50	45
V2#6(12/51)-17-(11/52; Last 52 pgs.?)	6.70	20.00	40
18-(25¢, 100 pg. Giant, 12-1/52-53)	17.00	49.00	115
19-30: 20-22,24,28-31-The Yardbirds app.	5.35	16.00	32
31-47,49-51	5.00	15.00	30
48-Atom bomb story	5.35	16.00	32.

NOTE: **Powell** a-V2#7, 8, 11. **Norman Saunders** painted c-10-14, V2#6-14, 26, 30, 31, 35, 39. **Tuska** a-7. Bondage c-29, 35, 38.

G. I. JOE (America's Movable Fighting Man)
1967 (5-1/8x8-3/8", 36 pgs.)
Custom Comics

nn-Schaffenberger-a; based on Hasbro toy	1.65	4.20	10

G.I. JOE
Dec, 1995 - No. 4, Apr, 1996 ($1.95, limited series)
Dark Horse Comics

1-4: Mike W. Barr scripts. 1,2-Miller-c. 3-Simonson-c			2

G.I. JOE
V2#1, June, 1996 - V2#4, Sept, 1996 ($2.50)
Dark Horse Comics

V2#1-4: Mike W. Barr scripts. 4-Painted-c			2

G. I. JOE AND THE TRANSFORMERS
Jan, 1987 - No. 4, Apr, 1987 (Limited series)
Marvel Comics Group

1-4			1

G. I. JOE, A REAL AMERICAN HERO (...Starring Snake-Eyes on-c #135 on)
June, 1982 - No. 155, Dec, 1994
Marvel Comics Group

1-Printed on Baxter paper; based on Hasbro toy	1.00	2.00	5
2-Printed on reg. paper		1.80	4
3-10		1.20	3
11-20: 11-Intro Airborne		.70	1
21,22,26,27: 26,27-Origin Snake-Eyes parts 1 & 2		.80	2
23-25,28-30		.80	2
31-134,139-143: 33-New headquarters. 60-Todd McFarlane-a. 110-1st Ron Garney-a. 139-142-New Transformers app.		.70	1
135-138-($1.75)-Polybagged w/trading card		.70	1

264

G.. I. Joe special missions #16 © Hasbro

Girl #3 © Peter milligan & Duncan Fegredo

Girl Crazy #2 © Gilbert Hernandez

	GD25	FN65	NM94

	GD25	FN65	NM94
144-149,151-155-($1.25): 144-Origin Snake-Eyes			1.25
All 2nd printings			1.00
150-($2.00, 52 pgs.)		.80	2.00
Special Treasury Edition (1982)-r/#1		1.20	3.00
Yearbook 1 (3/85)-r/#1; Golden-c		.80	2.00
Yearbook 2 (3/86)-Golden-c/a , 3(3/87, 68 pgs.)		.80	2.00
Yearbook 4 (2/88)			1.50

NOTE: Garney a(p)-110. Golden c-23, 29, 34, 36. Heath a-24. Rogers a(p)-75, 77-82, 84, 86; -77.

G. I. JOE COMICS MAGAZINE
Dec, 1986 - No. 13, 1988 ($1.50, digest-size)
Marvel Comics Group

1-13: G.I. Joe-r			1.50

G.I. JOE EUROPEAN MISSIONS (Action Force in indicia)
June, 1988 - No. 15, Dec, 1989 ($1.50/$1.75 #12 on)
Marvel Comics Ltd. (British)

1-15: Reprints Action Force			1.50

G. I. JOE ORDER OF BATTLE, THE
Dec, 1986 - No. 4, Mar, 1987 (limited series)
Marvel Comics Group

1-4			1.00

G. I. JOE SPECIAL MISSIONS (Indicia title: Special Missions)
Oct, 1986 - No. 28, Dec, 1989 ($1.00)
Marvel Comics Group

1-28			1.00

G. I. JUNIORS (See Harvey Hits No. 86, 91, 95, 98, 101, 104, 107, 110, 112, 114, 116, 118, 120, 122)

GILGAMESH II
1989 - No. 4, 1989 ($3.95, limited series, prestige format, mature)
DC Comics

1-4: Starlin-c/a/scripts		1.60	4.00

GIL THORP
May-July, 1963
Dell Publishing Co.

1-Caniffish-a	2.60	7.50	26.00

GINGER
1951 - No. 10, Summer, 1954
Archie Publications

1-Teenage humor	9.50	28.50	95.00
2-(1952)	5.00	15.00	50.00
3-6: 6-(Sum/53)	3.50	10.50	35.00
7-10-Katy Keene app.	5.50	16.50	55.00

GINGER FOX (Also see The World of Ginger Fox)
Sept, 1988 - No. 4, Dec, 1988 ($1.75, limited series)
Comico

1-4: 1-4-part photo-c		.70	1.75

G. I. R.A.M.B.O.T.
Mar, 1987 - No. 2? ($1.95)
Wonder Color Comics/Pied Piper #2

1,2: 2-Exist?		.80	2.00

GIRL
July, 1996 - No. 3, 1996 ($2.50, limited series, mature)
DC Comics (Vertigo Verite)

1-3: Peter Milligan scripts; Fegredo-c/a			2.50

GIRL COMICS (Becomes Girl Confessions No. 13 on)
Dec, 1949 - No. 12, Jan, 1952 (#1-4: 52 pgs.)
Marvel/Atlas Comics(CnPC)

	GD25	FN65	NM94
1-Photo-c	16.00	47.00	110.00
2-Kubert-a; photo-c	10.00	30.00	65.00
3-Everett-a; Liz Taylor photo-c	13.00	39.00	90.00
4-11: 4-Photo-c. 10-12-Sol Brodsky-c	7.50	22.50	45.00
12-Krigstein-a; Al Hartley-c	9.15	27.00	55.00

GIRL CONFESSIONS (Formerly Girl Comics)
No. 13, Mar, 1952 - No. 35, Aug, 1954
Atlas Comics (CnPC/ZPC)

13-Everett-a	10.00	30.00	65.00
14,15,19,20	6.35	19.00	38.00
16-18-Everett-a	7.50	22.50	45.00
21-35: Robinson-a	4.00	12.00	24.00

GIRL CRAZY
May, 1996 - No. 3, July, 1996 ($2.95, B&W, limited series)
Dark Horse Comics

1-3: Gilbert Hernandez-a/scripts.			3.00

GIRL FROM U.N.C.L.E., THE (TV) (Also see The Man From...)
Jan, 1967 - No. 5, Oct, 1967
Gold Key

1-McWilliams-a; Stephanie Powers photo front/back-c & pin-ups (no ads, 12¢)	8.00	24.00	80.00
2-5-Leonard Swift-Courier No. 5	5.50	16.50	55.00

GIRLS' FUN & FASHION MAGAZINE (Formerly Polly Pigtails)
V5#44, Jan, 1950 - V5#47, July, 1950
Parents' Magazine Institute

V5#44	4.00	12.00	24.00
45-47	2.80	7.00	14.00

GIRLS IN LOVE
May, 1950 - No. 2, July, 1950
Fawcett Publications

1,2-Photo-c	8.35	25.00	50.00

GIRLS IN LOVE (Formerly G. I. Sweethearts No. 45)
No. 46, Sept, 1955 - No. 57, Dec, 1956
Quality Comics Group

46	5.85	17.50	35.00
47-53,55,56	4.00	12.00	24.00
54- 'Commie' story	4.25	13.00	28.00
57-Matt Baker-c/a	6.35	19.00	38.00

GIRLS IN WHITE (See Harvey Comics Hits No. 58)

GIRLS' LIFE (Patsy Walker's Own Magazine For Girls!)
Jan, 1954 - No. 6, Nov, 1954
Atlas Comics (BFP)

1	8.70	26.00	52.00
2-Al Hartley-c	4.25	13.00	28.00
3-6	4.00	12.00	24.00

GIRLS' LOVE STORIES
Aug-Sept, 1949 - No. 180, Nov-Dec, 1973 (No. 1-13: 52 pgs.)
National Comics(Signal Publ. No. 9-65/Arleigh No. 83-117)

1-Toth, Kinstler-a, 8 pgs. each; photo-c	48.00	144.00	385.00
2-Kinstler-a?	29.00	86.00	200.00
3-10: 1-9-Photo-c. 7-Infantino-c(p)	19.00	56.00	130.00
11-20	14.00	43.00	100.00
21-33: 21-Kinstler-a. 33-Last pre-code (1-2/55)	9.15	27.00	55.00
34-50	7.70	23.00	46.00
51-99: 83-Last true 10¢ issue	5.00	15.00	30.00
100	5.85	17.50	35.00
101-146: 113-117-April O'Day app.	2.30	6.75	16.00
147-151- "Confessions" serial	1.70	5.00	12.00
152-180: 161-170, 52 pgs.	1.20	3.00	7.00

Give Me Liberty #3 © Frank Miller & Dave Gibbons

Glory #13 © Rob Liefeld

Glory/Avengelyne #1 © Rob Liefeld

	GD25	FN65	NM94

GIRLS' ROMANCES
Feb-Mar, 1950 - No. 160, Oct, 1971 (No. 1-11: 52 pgs.)
National Periodical Publ.(Signal Publ. No. 7-79/Arleigh No. 84)

1-Photo-c	47.00	141.00	375.00
2-Photo-c; Toth-a	27.00	81.00	190.00
3-10: 3-6-Photo-c	19.00	56.00	130.00
11,12,14-20	13.00	39.00	90.00
13-Toth-c	14.00	43.00	100.00
21-31: 31-Last pre-code (2-3/55)	8.35	25.00	50.00
32-50	7.50	22.50	45.00
51-99: 80-Last 10¢ issue	5.00	15.00	30.00
100	5.85	17.50	35.00
101-108,110-120	4.00	10.00	20.00
109-Beatles-c/story	8.50	26.00	65.00
121-133,135-140	1.70	5.00	12.00
134-Neal Adams-c (splash pg. is same as-c)	2.00	6.00	14.00
141-160: 159,160-52 pgs.	1.20	3.00	7.00

G. I. SWEETHEARTS (Formerly Diary Loves; Girls In Love #46 on)
No. 32, June, 1953 - No. 45, May, 1955
Quality Comics Group

32	5.85	17.50	35.00
33-45: 44-Last pre-code (3/55)	4.00	12.00	24.00

G.I. TALES (Formerly Sgt. Barney Barker No. 1-3)
No. 4, Feb, 1957 - No. 6, July, 1957
Atlas Comics (MCI)

4-Severin-a(4)	6.35	19.00	38.00
5	4.25	13.00	26.00
6-Orlando, Powell, & Woodbridge-a	4.25	13.00	28.00

GIVE ME LIBERTY (Also see Dark Horse Presents Fifth Anniversary Special,
Dark Horse Presents #100-4, Happy Birthday Martha Washington, Martha
Washington Goes to War, Martha Washington Stranded In Space & San Diego
Comicon Comics #2)
June, 1990 - No. 4, 1991 ($4.95, limited series, 52 pgs.)
Dark Horse Comics

1-4: 1st app. Martha Washington; Frank Miller scripts, Dave Gibbons-c/a in all.	1.00	2.00	5.00

G. I. WAR BRIDES
Apr, 1954 - No. 8, June, 1955
Superior Publishers Ltd.

1	5.85	17.50	35.00
2	4.00	10.00	20.00
3-8: 4-Kamenesque-a; lingerie panels	3.20	8.00	16.00

G.I. WAR TALES
Mar-Apr, 1973 - No. 4, Oct-Nov, 1973
National Periodical Publications

1-4: Reprints. 2-N. Adams-a(r), 4-Krigstein-a(r)			1.00

NOTE: *Drucker* a-3r, 4r. **Heath** a-4r. **Kubert** a-2, 3; c-4r.

GIZMO (Also see Domino Chance)
May-June, 1985 (B&W, one-shot)
Chance Ent.

1	1.00	2.00	5.00

GIZMO
1986 - No. 6, July, 1987 ($1.50, B&W)
Mirage Studios

1		1.20	3.00
2-6		1.00	2.50

GLADSTONE COMIC ALBUM
1987 - No. 28, 1990 ($5.95/$9.95, 8-1/2x11")(All Mickey Mouse albums are by
Gottfredson)

Gladstone

1-10: 1-Uncle Scrooge; Barks-r; Beck-c. 2-Donald Duck; r/F.C. #108 by Bark			
3-Mickey Mouse-r by Gottfredson. 4-Uncle Scrooge; r/F.C. #456 by Barks			
unedited story. 5-Donald Duck Advs.; r/F.C. #199. 6-Uncle Scrooge-r by			
Barks. 7-Donald Duck-r by Barks. 8-Mickey Mouse-r. 9-Bambi; r/F.C. #186			
10-Donald Duck Advs.; r/F.C. #275	1.20	3.00	7.
11-20: 11-Uncle Scrooge; r/U.S. #4. 12-Donald And Daisy; r/F.C. #1055,			
WDC&S. 13-Donald Duck Advs.; r/F.C. #408. 14-Uncle Scrooge; Barks-r/			
U.S #21. 15-Donald And Gladstone; Barks-r. 16-Donald Duck Advs.; r/F.C.			
#238. 17-Mickey Mouse strip-r (The World of Tomorrow, The Pirate Ghost			
Ship). 18-Donald Duck and the Junior Woodchucks; Barks-r. 19-Uncle			
Scrooge; r/U.S. #12; Rosa-c. 20-Uncle Scrooge; r/F.C. #386; Barks-c/a(r)			
	1.20	3.00	7.
21-25: 21-Donald Duck Family; Barks-c/a(r). 22-Mickey Mouse strip-r.			
23-Donald Duck; Barks-r/D.D. #26 w/unedited story. 24-Uncle Scrooge;			
Barks-r; Rosa-c. 25-D. Duck; Barks-c/a-r/F.C. #367			
	1.20	3.00	7
26-28: All have $9.95-c. 26-Mickey and Donald; Gottfredson-c/a(r). 27-Donald			
Duck; r/WDC&S by Barks; Barks painted-c. 28-Uncle Scrooge & Donald			
Duck; Rosa-c/a (4 stories)	1.65	4.70	11
Special 1 (1989, $9.95)-Donald Duck Finds Pirate Gold; r/F.C. #9			
	1.65	4.70	11
Special 2 (1989, $8.95)-Uncle Scrooge and Donald Duck; Barks-r/Uncle			
Scrooge #5; Rosa-c	1.65	4.20	10
Special 3 (1989, $8.95)-Mickey Mouse strip-r	1.65	4.20	10
Special 4 (1989, $11.95)-Uncle Scrooge; Rosa-c/a-r/Son of the Sun from			
U.S. #219 plus Barks-r/U.S.	1.85	5.50	13
Special 5 (1990, $11.95)-Donald Duck Advs.; Barks-r/D. #282 & 422 plus			
Barks painted-c	1.85	5.50	13
Special 6 (1990, $12.95)-Uncle Scrooge; Barks-c/a-r/Uncle Scrooge			
	2.00	6.00	14
Special 7 (1990, $13.95)-Mickey Mouse; Gottfredson strip-r			
	2.15	6.50	15

GLADSTONE COMIC ALBUM (2nd Series)(Also see The Original Dick Tracy)
1990 ($5.95, 8-1/2 x 11," stiff-c, 52 pgs.)
Gladstone Publishing

1,2-The Original Dick Tracy. 2-Origin of the 2-way wrist radio.			
			6
3-D Tracy Meets the Mole-r by Bould ($6.95).			7

GLAMOROUS ROMANCES (Formerly Dotty)
No. 41, July, 1949 - No. 90, Oct, 1956 (Photo-c 68-90)
Ace Magazines (A. A. Wyn)

41-Dotty app.	6.70	20.00	40
42-72,74-80: 44-Begin 52 pg. issues, 45,50-61-Painted-c. 80-Last pre-code			
(2/55)	4.15	12.50	25
73-L.B. Cole-r/All Love #27	4.25	13.00	28
81-90	4.00	10.00	20

GLOBAL FORCE
1987 - No. 2? ($1.95)
Silverline Comics

1,2		1.00	2

GLORY
Mar, 1995 - Present ($2.50)
Image Comics (Extreme Studios)/Maximum Press

0-Deodato-c/a			2
1-(3/95)-Deodato-a		1.20	3
1A-Variant-c		1.20	3
2-11,13-20: 5-Bagged w/Youngblood gaming card. 7,8-Deodato-c/a(p).			
8-Babewatch x-over. 9-Cruz-c; Extreme Destroyer Pt. 5; polybagged w/ca			
10-Angela/c/app. 11-Deodato-c.		1.00	2
4-Variant-c by Quesada & Palmiotti		1.20	3
12-($3.50)-Photo-c			3

266

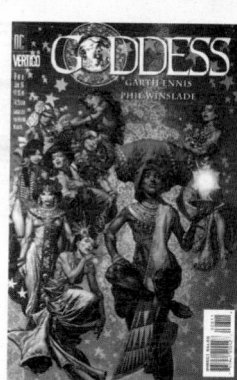

Goddess #8 © Garth Ennis & Phil Winslade

Godwheel #2 © Malibu

Godzilla #13 © DH

	GD25	FN65	NM94

	GD25	FN65	NM94

Trade Paperback (1995, $9.95)-r/#1-4 ... 10.00

GLORY & FRIENDS BIKINI FEST
Sept, 1995 - No. 2, Oct, 1995 ($2.50, limited series)
Image Comics (Extreme Studios)

1,2: 1-Photo-c; centerfold photo; pin-ups		1.00	2.50

GLORY & FRIENDS CHRISTMAS SPECIAL
Dec, 1995 ($2.50, one-shot)
Image Comics (Extreme Studios)

1-Deodato-c			2.50

GLORY & FRIENDS LINGIRIE SPECIAL
Sept, 1995 ($2.95, one-shot)
Image Comics (Extreme Studios)

1-Pin-ups w/photos; photo-c; varant-c exists			3.00

GLORY/ANGELA: ANGELS IN HELL (See Angela/Glory: Rage of Angels)
Apr, 1996 ($2.50, one-shot)
Image Comics (Extreme Studios)

1-Flip book w/Darkchylde #1			2.50

GLORY/AVENGELYNE
Oct, 1995 ($3.95, one-shot)
Image Comics (Extreme Studios)

1-Chromium-c		1.60	4.00
1-Regular-c		1.60	4.00

GNOME MOBILE, THE (See Movie Comics)

GOBBLEDYGOOK
1984 - No. 2, 1984 (B&W)(1st Mirage comic, published at same time)
Mirage Studios

1,2-(24 pgs.)-1st Teenage Mutant Ninja Turtles	29.00	86.00	200.00

GOBBLEDYGOOK
Dec, 1986 ($3.50, B&W, one-shot, 100 pgs.)
Mirage Studios

1-New 8 pg. TMNT story plus a Donatello/Michaelangelo 7 pg. story & a Gizmo story; Corben-i(r)/TMNT #7		1.60	4.00

GOBLIN, THE
June, 1982 - No. 4, Dec, 1982 (Magazine, $2.25)
Warren Publishing Co.

1-The Gremlin app; Golden-a(p)		.90	2.25
2-4: 2-1st Hobgoblin		.90	2.25

GODDESS
June, 1995 - No. 8, Jan, 1996 ($2.95, limited series)
DC Comics (Vertigo)

1-8: Garth Ennis scripts; Phil Winslade-c/a		1.20	3.00

GODFATHERS, THE (See The Crusaders)

GOD IS
1973, 1975 (35-49¢)
Spire Christian Comics (Fleming H. Revell Co.)

nn-By Al Hartley			1.00

GOD'S COUNTRY (Also see Marvel Comics Presents)
1994 ($6.95)
Marvel Comics

nn-P. Craig Russell-a; Colossus story; r/Marvel Comics Presents #10-17		1.20	3.00 ... 7.00

GODS FOR HIRE
Dec, 1986 - No. 3? ($1.50)
Slot Comics

1-3: Barry Crain-c/a(p)			1.50

GOD'S HEROES IN AMERICA
1956 (nn) (25¢/35¢, 68 pgs.)
Catechetical Guild Educational Society

307		1.60	4.00 ... 8.00

GOD'S SMUGGLER (Religious)
1972 (39¢/40¢)
Spire Christian Comics/Fleming H. Revell Co.

..1-Two variations exist			1.00

GODWHEEL
No. 0, Jan, 1995 - No. 3, Feb, 1995 ($2.50, limited series)
Malibu Comics (Ultraverse)

0-3: 0-Flip-c. 1-1st app. of Primevil; Thor cameo (1 panel). 3-Perez-a in Chapter 3, Thor app.		1.00	2.50

GODZILLA (Movie)
August, 1977 - No. 24, July, 1979 (Based on movie series)
Marvel Comics Group

1-Mooney-i		1.40	3.50 ... 8.50
2-24: 2-Tuska-i. 3-Champions app.(w/o Ghost Rider). 4,5-Sutton-a. 14-Shield app. 20-F.F. app. 21,22-Devil Dinosaur app.		1.00	2.00 ... 5.00

GODZILLA (Movie)
May, 1988 - No. 6, 1988 ($1.95, B&W, limited series) (Based on movie series)
Dark Horse Comics

1		1.00	2.60 ... 6.00
2-6		1.20	3.00
...Collection (1990, $10.95)-r/1-6 with new-c	1.65	4.70	11.00
...Color Special 1 (Sum, 1992, $3.50, color, 44 pgs.)-Arthur Adams wraparound-c/a & part scripts		1.60	4.00
...King Of The Monsters Special (8/87, $1.50)-Origin; Bissette-c/a		1.20	3.00
...Vs. Barkley nn (12/93, $2.95, color)-Dorman painted-c		1.20	3.00

GODZILLA (King of the Monsters) (Movie)
May, 1995 - Present ($2.50) (Based on movie series)
Dark Horse Comics

0-16: 0-r/Dark Horse Comics #10,11. 1-3-Kevin Maguire scripts. 3-8-Art Adams-c		1.00	2.50
...Vs. Hero Zero ($2.50)		1.00	2.50

GO-GO
June, 1966 - No. 9, Oct, 1967
Charlton Comics

1-Miss Bikini Luv begins; Rolling Stones, Beatles, Elvis, Sonny & Cher, Bob Dylan, Sinatra, parody; Herman's Hermits pin-ups; D'Agostino-c/a in #1-8	4.00	12.00	28.00
2-Ringo Starr, David McCallum & Beatles photos on cover; Beatles story and photos	4.00	12.00	28.00
3,4: 3-Blooperman begins, ends #6; 1 pg. Batman & Robin satire; full pg. photo pin-ups Lovin' Spoonful & The Byrds	2.60	7.50	18.00
5-9: 5 (2/67)-Super Hero & TV satire by Jim Aparo & Grass Green begins; Aparo's 1st published work. 6-8-Aparo-a. 6-Petula Clark photo-c. 7-Photo of Brian Wilson of Beach Boys on-c & Beach Boys photo inside f/b-c. 8-Monkees photo on-c & photo inside f/b-c; 9-Aparo-c/a.	2.60	7.50	18.00

GO-GO AND ANIMAL (See Tippy's Friends...)

GOING STEADY (Formerly Teen-Age Temptations)
No. 10, Dec, 1954 - No. 13, June, 1955; No. 14, Oct, 1955
St. John Publishing Co.

10(1954)-Matt Baker-c/a	16.00	47.00	110.00
11(2/55, last precode), 12(4/55)-Baker-c	9.15	27.00	55.00
13(6/55)-Baker-c/a	11.00	33.00	75.00
14(10/55)-Matt Baker-c/a, 25 pgs.	13.00	39.00	90.00

Golden Age #1 © DC

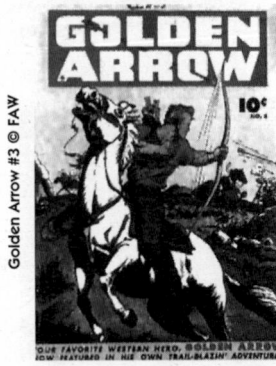

Golden Arrow #3 © FAW

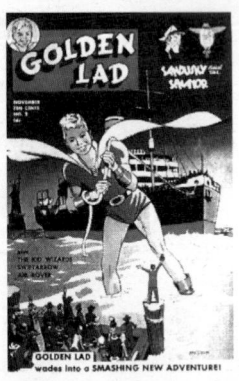

Golden Lad #2 © Spark

	GD25	FN65	NM94

GOING STEADY (Formerly Personal Love)
V3#3, Feb, 1960 - V3#6, Aug, 1960; V4#1, Sept-Oct, 1960
Prize Publications/Headline

	GD25	FN65	NM94
V3#3-6, V4#1	2.15	6.50	15.00

GOING STEADY WITH BETTY (Becomes Betty & Her Steady No. 2)
Nov-Dec, 1949
Avon Periodicals

1	11.50	34.00	80.00

GOLDEN AGE, THE
1993 - No. 4, 1994 ($4.95, limited series)
DC Comics (Elseworlds)

1-4: James Robinson scripts; Paul Smith-c/a; gold foil embossed-c.	1.00	2.60	6.00
Trade Paperback (1995, $19.95)	2.85	8.50	20.00

GOLDEN ARROW (See Fawcett Miniatures, Mighty Midget & Whiz Comics)
GOLDEN ARROW (...Western No. 6)
Spring, 1942 - No. 6, Spring, 1947 (68 pgs.)
Fawcett Publications

1-Golden Arrow begins	75.00	225.00	600.00
2-(1943)	39.00	118.00	275.00
3-5: 3-(Win/45-46). 4-(Spr/46). 5-(Fall/46)	29.00	86.00	200.00
6-Krigstein-a	32.00	96.00	225.00
...Well Known Comics (1944; 12 pgs.; 8-1/2x10-1/2"; paper-c; glued binding)-Bestmaid/Samuel Lowe giveaway; printed in green	8.35	25.00	50.00

GOLDEN COMICS DIGEST
May, 1969 - No. 48, Jan, 1976
Gold Key
NOTE: Whitman editions exist of many titles and are generally valued less.

1-Tom & Jerry, Woody Woodpecker, Bugs Bunny	2.60	6.50	13.00
2-Hanna-Barbera TV Fun Favorites; Space Ghost, Flintstones, Atom Ant, Jetsons, Yogi Bear, Banana Splits, others app.	2.40	7.20	17.00
3-Tom & Jerry, Woody Woodpecker	1.20	3.00	7.00
4-Tarzan; Manning & Marsh-a	2.40	7.20	17.00
5,8-Tom & Jerry, W. Woodpecker, Bugs Bunny	1.00	2.60	6.00
6-Bugs Bunny	1.00	2.60	6.00
7-Hanna-Barbera TV Fun Favorites	1.65	4.70	11.00
9-Tarzan	2.15	6.50	15.00
10-17: 10-Bugs Bunny. 11-Hanna-Barbera TV Fun Favorites. 12-Tom & Jerry, Bugs Bunny, W. Woodpecker Journey to the Sun. 13-Tom & Jerry. 14-Bugs Bunny Fun Packed Funnies. 15-Tom & Jerry, Woody Woodpecker, Bugs Bunny. 16-Woody Woodpecker Cartoon Special. 17-Bugs Bunny	1.00	2.60	6.00
18-Tom & Jerry; Barney Bear-r by Barks	1.20	3.00	7.00
19-Little Lulu	2.15	6.50	15.00
20-22: 20-Woody Woodpecker Falltime Funtime. 21-Bugs Bunny Showtime. 22-Tom & Jerry Winter Wingding	1.00	2.60	6.00
23-Little Lulu & Tubby Fun Fling	2.15	6.50	15.00
24-26,28: 24-Woody Woodpecker Fun Festival. 25-Tom & Jerry. 26-Bugs Bunny Halloween Hulla-Boo-Loo; Dr. Spektor article, also #25. 28-Tom & Jerry	1.00	2.60	6.00
27-Little Lulu & Tubby in Hawaii	1.70	5.00	12.00
29-Little Lulu & Tubby	1.70	5.00	12.00
30-Bugs Bunny Vacation Funnies	1.00	2.60	6.00
31-Turok, Son of Stone; r/4-Color #596,656; c-r/#9	2.00	6.00	14.00
32-Woody Woodpecker Summer Fun	1.00	2.60	6.00
33,36: 33-Little Lulu & Tubby Halloween Fun; Dr. Spektor app. 36-Little Lulu & Her Friends	2.15	6.50	15.00
34,35,37-39: 34-Bugs Bunny Winter Funnies. 35-Tom & Jerry Snowtime Funtime. 37-Woody Woodpecker County Fair. 38-The Pink Panther. 39-Bugs Bunny Summer Fun	1.00	2.60	6.00

40,43: 40-Little Lulu & Tubby Trick or Treat; all by Stanley. 43-Little Lulu in Paris	2.15	6.50	15.00
41,42,44,45,47: 41-Tom & Jerry Winter Carnival. 42-Bugs Bunny. 44-Woody Woodpecker Family Fun Festival. 45-The Pink Panther. 47-Bugs Bunny	1.00	2.00	5.00
46-Little Lulu & Tubby	1.70	5.00	12.00
48-The Lone Ranger	1.20	3.00	7.00
NOTE: #1-30, 164 pgs.; #31 on, 132 pgs..			

GOLDEN LAD
July, 1945 - No. 5, June, 1946 (#4, 5: 52 pgs.)
Spark Publications

1-Origin & 1st app. Golden Lad & Swift Arrow; Sandusky and the Senator begins	59.00	178.00	475.00
2-Mort Meskin-c/a	31.00	94.00	220.00
3,4-Mort Meskin-c/a	27.00	81.00	190.00
5-Origin/1st Golden Girl; Shaman & Flame app.	32.00	96.00	225.00
NOTE: All have Robinson, and Roussos art plus Meskin covers and art.			

GOLDEN LEGACY
1966 - 1972 (Black History) (25¢)
Fitzgerald Publishing Co.

1-Toussaint L'Ouverture (1966), 2-Harriet Tubman (1967), 3-Crispus Attucks & the Minutemen (1967), 4-Benjamin Banneker (1968), 5-Matthew Henson (1969), 6-Alexander Dumas & Family (1969), 7-Frederick Douglass, Part 1 (1969), 8-Frederick Douglass, Part 2 (1970), 9-Robert Smalls (1970), 10-J. Cinque & the Amistad Mutiny (1970), 11-Men in Action: White, Marshall J. Wilkins (1970), 12-Black Cowboys (1972), 13-The Life of Martin Luther King, Jr. (1972), 14-The Life of Alexander Pushkin (1971), 15-Ancient African Kingdoms (1972), 16-Black Inventors (1972) each....			1.50
1-10,12,13,15,16(1976)-Reprints			1.00

GOLDEN LOVE STORIES (Formerly Golden West Love)
No. 4, April, 1950
Kirby Publishing Co.

4-Powell-a; Glenn Ford/Janet Leigh photo-c	12.00	36.00	85.00

GOLDEN PICTURE CLASSIC, A
1956-1957 (Text stories w/illustrations in color; 100 pgs. each)
Western Printing Co. (Simon & Shuster)

CL-401: Treasure Island	8.35	25.00	50.00
CL-402: Tom Sawyer	7.00	21.00	42.00
CL-403: Black Beauty	7.00	21.00	42.00
CL-404: Little Women	7.00	21.00	42.00
CL-405: Heidi	7.00	21.00	42.00
CL-406: Ben Hur	4.70	14.00	28.00
CL-407: Around the World in 80 Days	4.70	14.00	28.00
CL-408: Sherlock Holmes	5.85	17.50	35.00
CL-409: The Three Musketeers	4.70	14.00	28.00
CL-410: The Merry Advs. of Robin Hood	4.70	14.00	28.00
CL-411: Hans Brinker	5.85	17.50	35.00
CL-412: The Count of Monte Cristo	5.85	17.50	35.00
(Both soft & hardcover editions are valued the same)			
NOTE: Recent research has uncovered new information. Apparently #s 1-6 were issued in 1956 and #7-12 in 1957. But they can be found in five different series listings: CL-1 to CL-12 (soft bound); CL-401 to CL-412 (also softbound); CL-101 to CL-112 (hardbound); plus two new series discoveries. A Golden Reading Adventure, publ. by Golden Press; edited down to 60 pages and reduced in size to 6x9"; only #s discovered so far are #381 (CL-4), #382 (CL-6) & #387 (CL-9). They have no reorder list and some have covers different from GPC. The fifth series is a found British hardbound editions of GPC with dust jackets. Copies of all five listed series vary from scarce to very rare. Some editions of some series have not yet been found at all.			

GOLDEN PICTURE STORY BOOK
Dec, 1961 (50¢, large size, 52 pgs.)(All are scarce)
Racine Press (Western)

ST-1-Huckleberry Hound (TV)	19.00	58.00	155.00
ST-2-Yogi Bear (TV)	19.00	58.00	155.00
ST-3-Babes in Toyland (Walt Disney's...)-Annette Funicello photo-c	24.00	73.00	220.00

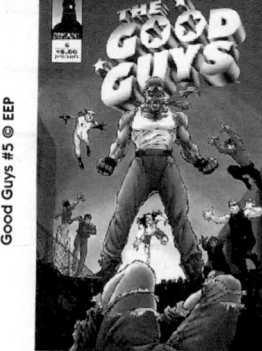

Gon #3 © Tanaka

Good Guys #5 © EEP

Goth #1 © Gleen Danzig

	GD25	FN65	NM94

ST-4-(...of Disney Ducks)-Walt Disney's Wonderful World of Ducks (Donald Duck, Uncle Scrooge, Donald's Nephews, Grandma Duck, Ludwig Von Drake, & Gyro Gearloose stories) — 24.00 73.00 220.00

GOLDEN RECORD COMIC (See Amazing Spider-Man #1, Avengers #4, Fantastic Four #1, Journey Into Mystery #83)

GOLDEN STORY BOOKS
1949 (Heavy covers, digest size, 128 pgs.) (Illustrated text in color)
Western Printing Co. (Simon & Shuster)

7-Walt Disney's Mystery in Disneyville, a book-length adventure starring Donald and Nephews, Mickey and Nephews, and with Minnie, Daisy and Goofy. Art by Dick Moores & Manuel Gonzales (scarce) — 24.00 73.00 185.00

10-Bugs Bunny's Treasure Hunt, a book-length adventure starring Bugs & Porky Pig, with Petunia Pig & Nephew, Cicero. Art by Tom McKimson (scarce) — 16.00 47.00 120.00

GOLDEN WEST LOVE (Golden Love Stories No. 4)
Sept-Oct, 1949 - No. 3, Feb, 1950 (All 52 pgs.)
Kirby Publishing Co.

1-Powell-a in all; Roussos-a; painted-c	17.00	49.00	115.00
2,3; Photo-c	11.00	33.00	75.00

GOLDEN WEST RODEO TREASURY (See Dell Giants)

GOLDILOCKS (See March of Comics No. 1)

GOLDILOCKS & THE THREE BEARS
1943 (Giveaway)
K. K. Publications

nn	10.00	30.00	70.00

GOLD KEY CHAMPION
Mar, 1978 - No. 2, May, 1978 (50¢, 52pgs.)
Gold Key

1-Space Family Robinson; half-r		.80	2.00
2-Mighty Samson; half-r		.80	2.00

GOLD KEY SPOTLIGHT
May, 1976 - No. 11, Feb, 1978
Gold Key

1-Tom, Dick & Harriet		1.60	4.00
2-5,710,11: 2-Wacky Advs. of Cracky. 3-Wacky Witch. 4-Tom, Dick & Harriet. 5-Wacky Advs. of Cracky. 7-Wacky Witch & Greta Ghost 10-O. G. Whiz. 11-Tom, Dick & Harriet		1.20	3.00
6,8,9: 6-Dagar the Invincible; Santos-a; origin Demonomicon. 8-The Occult Files of Dr. Spektor, Simbar, Lu-sai; Santos-a. 9-Tragg		1.60	4.00

GOLD MEDAL COMICS
1945 (25¢, one-shot, 132 pgs.)
Cambridge House

nn-Captain Truth by Fugitani, Crime Detector, The Witch of Salem, Luckyman, others app. — 24.00 73.00 170.00

GOMER PYLE (TV)
July, 1966 - No. 3, Jan, 1967
Gold Key

1-Photo front/back-c	6.00	18.00	60.00
2,3	4.50	13.50	45.00

GON
July, 1996 - No. 4, Oct, 1996 ($5.95, B&W, digest-size, limited series)
DC Comics (Paradox Press)

1-4: Misadventures of baby dinosaur; Tanaka-c/a/scripts in all
— 6.00

GOODBYE, MR. CHIPS (See Movie Comics)

GOOD GIRL ART QUARTERLY
Summer, 1990 - No. 16, 1992? (B&W/color, 52 pgs.)
AC Comics

1 ($3.50)-All have one new story (often FemForce) & rest reprints by Baker, Ward & other "good girl" artists		1.40	3.50
2 ($3.95)		1.60	4.00
3-16		1.40	3.50

GOOD GUYS, THE
Nov, 1993 - No. 9, July, 1994 ($2.50)
Defiant

1-($3.50, 52 pgs.)-Glory x-over from Plasm		1.40	3.50
2,3,5-9: 9-Pre-Schism issue		1.00	2.50
4-($3.25, 52 pgs.)		1.30	3.25

GOOFY (Disney)(See Dynabrite Comics, Mickey Mouse Magazine V4#7, Walt Disney Showcase #35 & Wheaties)
No. 468, May, 1953 - Sept-Nov, 1962
Dell Publishing Co.

Four Color 468 (#1)	15.00	45.00	150.00
Four Color 562,627,658,702,747,802,857	8.00	24.00	80.00
Four Color 899,952,987,1053,1094,1149,1201	5.00	15.00	50.00
12-308-211(Dell, 9-11/62)	5.00	15.00	50.00

GOOFY ADVENTURES
June, 1990 - No. 17, 1991 ($1.50)
Disney Comics

1-17: Most new stories. 2-Joshua Quagmire-a w/free poster. 7-WDC&S-r plus new-a. 9-Gottfredson-r. 14-Super Goof story. 15-All Super Goof issue. 17-Gene Colan-a(p) — 1.50

GOOFY ADVENTURE STORY (See Goofy No. 857)

GOOFY COMICS (Companion to Happy Comics)(Not Disney)
June, 1943 - No. 48, 1953
Nedor Publ. Co. No. 1-14/Standard No. 14-48 (Animated Cartoons)

1-Funny animal; Oriolo-c	23.00	69.00	160.00
2	11.50	34.00	80.00
3-10	10.00	30.00	60.00
11-19	6.70	20.00	40.00
20-35-Frazetta text illos in all	9.15	27.00	55.00
36-48	5.00	15.00	30.00

GOOFY SUCCESS STORY (See Goofy No. 702)

GOOSE (Humor magazine)
Sept, 1976 - No. 3, 1976 (75¢, 52 pgs.)
Cousins Publ. (Fawcett)

1-3			1.00

GORDO (See Comics Revue No. 5 & Giant Comics Edition)

GORGO (Based on M.G.M. movie) (See Return of...)
May, 1961 - No. 23, Sept, 1965
Charlton Comics

1-Ditko-a, 22 pgs.	24.00	70.00	170.00
2,3-Ditko-c/a	12.00	36.00	85.00
4-10: 4-Ditko-c	7.00	21.00	50.00
11,13-16-Ditko-a	5.70	17.00	40.00
12,17-23: 12-Reptisaurus x-over; Montes/Bache-a-No. 17-23. 20-Giordano-c	2.90	9.00	20.00
Gorgo's Revenge('62)-Becomes Return of...	5.00	15.00	35.00

GOSPEL BLIMP, THE
1973, 1974 (35¢/39¢, 36 pgs.)
Spire Christian Comics (Fleming H. Revell Co.)

nn			1.00

G.O.T.H.
Dec, 1995 - No. 3, June, 1996 ($2.95, limited series, mature)
Verotik

1-3: Danzig scripts; Liam Sharpe-a			3.00

Gravediggers #1 © Acclaim

Gravestone #7 © Malibu

Greatr Comics #1 © Novack

	GD25	FN65	NM94
GOTHAM BY GASLIGHT (A Tale of the Batman)(See Batman: Master of...)			
1989 ($3.95, one-shot, squarebound, 52 pgs.)			
DC Comics			
nn-Mignola/Russell-a; intro by Robert Bloch		1.60	4.00
GOTHAM NIGHTS (See Batman: Gotham Nights II)			
Mar, 1992 - No. 4, June, 1992 ($1.25, limited series)			
DC Comics			
1-4: Featuring Batman			1.25
GOTHIC ROMANCES			
Dec, 1974 (75¢, B&W, magazine)			
Atlas/Seaboard Publ.			
1-Text w/ illos by N. Adams, Chaykin, Heath (2 pgs. ea.)		.70	1.80
GOVERNOR & J. J., THE (TV)			
Feb, 1970 - No. 3, Aug, 1970 (Photo-c)			
Gold Key			
1	3.00	9.00	30.00
2,3	2.25	6.75	22.00
GRACKLE, THE			
Jan, 1997 - Present ($2.95, B&W)			
Acclaim Comics			
1-6: Mike Baron scripts & Paul Gulacy-c/a. 1-4-Doublecross	1.20		3.00
GRAFIK MUZIK			
Dec, 1989 - No. 3, May, 1990 ($2.95, 52 pgs.)			
Caliber Press			
1-3: Mike Allred-c/a/scripts	1.00	2.00	5.00
GRANDMA DUCK'S FARM FRIENDS(See Walt Disney's C&S 293 & Wheaties)			
No. 763, Jan, 1957 - No. 1279, Feb, 1962 (Disney)			
Dell Publishing co.			
Four Color 763 (#1)	8.00	24.00	80.00
Four Color 873	6.00	18.00	60.00
Four Color 965,1279	5.00	15.00	50.00
Four Color 1010,1073,1161-Barks-a; 1073,1161-Barks c/a			
	14.00	43.00	135.00
GRAND PRIX (Formerly Hot Rod Racers)			
No. 16, Sept, 1967 - No. 31, May, 1970			
Charlton Comics			
16-Features Rick Roberts	2.60	7.50	18.00
17-20	1.70	5.00	12.00
21-31	1.20	2.90	7.00
GRAVEDIGGERS			
Nov, 1996 - Present ($2.95, B&W)			
Acclaim Comics			
1-3: Moretti scripts			3.00
GRAVESTONE			
July, 1993 - No. 7, Feb, 1994 ($2.25)			
Malibu Comics			
1-6: 3-Polybagged w/Skycap		.90	2.25
7-($2.50)		1.00	2.50
GRAVE TALES (Also see Maggots)			
Oct, 1991 - No. 3, Feb, 1992 ($3.95, B&W, magazine, 52 pgs.)			
Hamilton Comics			
1-3: 1-Staton-c/a. 2-Staton-a; Morrow-c		1.60	4.00
GRAY GHOST, THE			
No. 911, July, 1958 - No. 1000, June-Aug, 1959			
Dell Publishing Co.			
Four Color 911 (#1)-Photo-c	9.00	27.00	90.00
Four Color 1000-Photo-c	9.00	27.00	90.00

	GD25	FN65	NM94
GREAT ACTION COMICS			
1958 (Reprints with new covers)			
I. W. Enterprises			
1-Captain Truth reprinted from Gold Medal #1	3.20	8.00	16.00
8,9-Reprints Phantom Lady #15 & 23	11.50	34.00	80.00
GREAT AMERICAN COMICS PRESENTS - THE SECRET VOICE			
1945 (10¢)			
Peter George 4-Star Publ./American Features Syndicate			
1-Anti-Nazi; "What Really Happened to Hitler"	21.00	64.00	150.00
GREAT AMERICAN WESTERN, THE			
1987 - No. 4, 1990? ($1.75/$2.95/$3.50, B&W with some color)			
AC Comics			
..1($1.75)-Western-r plus Bill Black-a		.90	1.80
..2,3 ($2.95)2-Tribute to ME comics; Durango Kid photo-c 3-Tribute to Tom Mix plus Roy Rogers, Durango Kid; Billy the Kid-r by Severin; photo-c			
		1.50	3.00
..4 ($3.50, 52 pgs., 16 pgs. color)-Tribute to Lash LaRue; photo-c & interior photos; Fawcett-r		1.75	3.50
GREAT CAT FAMILY, THE (Disney-TV/Movie)			
No. 750, Nov, 1956 (one-shot)			
Dell Publishing Co.			
Four Color 750-Pinocchio & Alice app.	6.00	18.00	60.00
GREAT COMICS			
Nov, 1941 - No. 3, Jan, 1942			
Great Comics Publications			
1-Origin/1st app. The Great Zarro; Madame Strange & Guy Gorham, Wizard of Science & The Great Zarro begin	103.00	309.00	825.00
2-Buck Johnson, Jungle Explorer app.; X-Mas-c	55.00	165.00	440.00
3-Futuro Takes Hitler to Hell-c/s; "The Lost City" movie story (starring William Boyd); continues in Choice Comics #3	103.00	309.00	825.00
GREAT COMICS			
1945			
Novack Publishing Co./Jubilee Comics/Barrel O' Fun			
1-(Novack)-The Defenders, Capt. Power app.; L. B. Cole-c			
	32.00	96.00	225.00
1-(Jubilee)-Same cover; Boogey Man, Satanas, & The Sorcerer & His Apprentice	24.00	71.00	165.00
1-(Barrel O' Fun)-L. B. Cole-c; Barrel O' Fun overprinted in indicia; Li'l Cactus, Cuckoo Sheriff (humorous)	13.50	41.00	95.00
GREAT DOGPATCH MYSTERY (See Mammy Yokum & the...)			
GREATEST BATMAN STORIES EVER TOLD, THE (See Batman)			
GREATEST JOKER STORIES EVER TOLD, THE (See Batman)			
GREAT EXPLOITS			
Oct, 1957			
Decker Publ./Red Top			
1-Krigstein-a(2) (re-issue on cover); reprints Daring Advs. #6 by Approved Comics	7.50	22.50	45.00
GREAT FOODINI, THE (See Foodini)			
GREAT GAZOO, THE (The Flintstones)(TV)			
Aug, 1973 - No. 20, Jan, 1977 (Hanna-Barbera)			
Charlton Comics			
1	1.20	2.90	7.00
2-20		1.60	4.00
GREAT GRAPE APE, THE (TV)(See TV Stars #1)			
Sept, 1976 - No. 2, Nov, 1976 (Hanna-Barbera)			
Charlton Comics			
1,2	1.10	2.70	6.5

Green Arrow # © DC

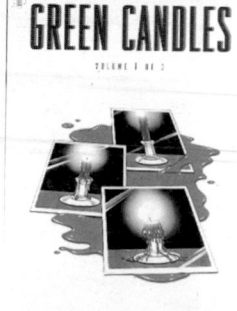

Green Candles #1 © Tom DeHaven & Robin Smith

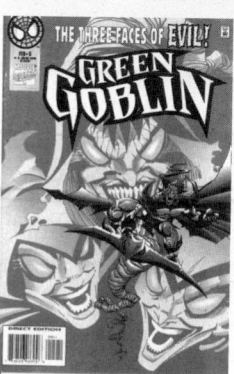

Green Goblin #5 © MEG

	GD25	FN65	NM94

GREAT LOCOMOTIVE CHASE, THE (Disney)
No. 712, Sept, 1956 (one-shot)
Dell Publishing Co.

Four Color 712-Movie, photo-c	8.00	24.00	80.00

GREAT LOVER ROMANCES (Young Lover Romances #4,5)
3/51; #2, 1951(nd); #3, 1952 (nd); #6, Oct?, 1952 - No. 22, May, 1955
Toby Press   (Photo-c #1-5, 10 ,13, 15, 17) (no #4, 5)

1-Jon Juan story-r/Jon Juan #1 by Schomburg; Dr. Anthony King app.			
	13.00	39.00	90.00
2-Jon Juan, Dr. Anthony King app.	7.50	22.50	45.00
3,7,9-14,16-22: 10-Rita Hayworth photo-c. 17-Rita Hayworth & Aldo Ray			
photo-c	4.15	12.50	25.00
6-Kurtzman-a (10/52)	7.50	22.50	45.00
8-Five pgs. of "Pin-Up Pete" by Sparling	7.50	22.50	45.00
15-Liz Taylor photo-c	9.15	27.00	55.00

GREAT PEOPLE OF GENESIS, THE
No date (Religious giveaway, 64 pgs.)
David C. Cook Publ. Co.

nn-Reprint/Sunday Pix Weekly	2.00	6.00	12.00

GREAT RACE, THE (See Movie Classics)

GREAT SACRAMENT, THE
1953 (Giveaway, 36 pgs.)
Catechetical Guild

nn	2.00	5.00	10.00

GREAT SCOTT SHOE STORE (See Bulls-Eye)

GREAT WEST (Magazine)
1969 (B&W, 52 pgs.)
M. F. Enterprises

V1#1		1.20	3.00

GREAT WESTERN
No. 8, Jan-Mar, 1954 - No. 11, Oct-Dec, 1954
Magazine Enterprises

8(A-1 93)-Trail Colt by Guardineer; Powell Red Hawk-r/Straight Arrow begins,			
ends #11; Durango Kid story	18.00	54.00	125.00
9(A-1 105), 11(A-1 127)-Ghost Rider, Durango Kid app. in each. 9-Red			
Mask-c, but no app.	10.00	30.00	70.00
10(A-1 113)-The Calico Kid by Guardineer-r/Tim Holt #8; Straight Arrow,			
Durango Kid app.	10.00	30.00	70.00
I.W. Reprint #1,2 9: 1,2-r/Straight Arrow #36,42. 9-r/Straight Arrow #?			
	2.30	6.70	16.00
I.W. Reprint #8-Origin Ghost Rider(r/Tim Holt #11); Tim Holt app.); Bolle-a			
	2.85	8.50	20.00

NOTE: *Guardineer c-8. Powell a(r)-8-11 (from Straight Arrow).*

GREEN ARROW (See Action #440, Adventure, Brave & the Bold, DC Super Stars #17, Detective #521, Flash #217, Green Lantern #76, Justice League of America #4, Leading, More Fun #73 (1st app.), Showcase '95 #9 & World's Finest Comics)

GREEN ARROW
May, 1983 - No. 4, Aug, 1983 (limited series)
DC Comics

1-Origin; Speedy cameo; Mike W. Barr scripts, Trevor Von Eeden-c/a.			
		1.20	3.00
2-4		.80	2.00

GREEN ARROW
Feb, 1988 - Present ($1.00/$1.50/$1.95/$2.25)(Painted-c #1-3)
DC Comics

1-Mike Grell scripts begin, ends #80		1.20	3.00
2		.90	2.25
3-49,51-74,76-86: 27,28-Warlord app. 35-38-Co-stars Black Canary; Bill			
Wray-i. 40-Grell-a. 47-Begin $1.50-c. 63-No longer has mature readers on-c.			

63-66-Shado app. 68-Last $1.50-c. 81-Aparo-a begins, ends #100; Nuklon			
app. 82-Intro & death of Rival. 83-Huntress-c/story. 84-Deathstroke cameo.			
85-Deathstroke-c/app. 86-Catwoman-c/story w/Jim Balent layouts			
		.60	1.50
50,75-($2.50, 52 pgs.): Anniversary issues. 75-Arsenal (Roy Harper) & Shado			
app.		1.00	2.50
0,87-86: 87-$1.95-c begins. 88-Guy Gardner, Martian Manhunter, &			
Wonder Woman-c/app.; Flash-c. 89-Anarky app. 90-(9/94)-Zero Hour tie-in.			
0-(10/94)-1st app. Connor Hawke; Aparo-a(p). 91-(11/94). 93-1st app.			
Camorouge. 95-Hal Jordan cameo. 96-Intro new Force of July; Hal Jordan			
(Parallax) app; Oliver Queen learns that Connor Hawke is his son			
			2.00
97-99,101-125: 97-Begin $2.25-c; no Aparo-a. 97-99-Arsenal app.			
101-Superman app. 101-Oliver Queen dies? 102,103-Underworld			
Unleashed x-over. 104-GL(Kyle Rainer)-c/app. 105-Robin-c/app.			
107-109-Thorn app. 109-Lois Lane cameo; Weeks-c. 110-Intro Hatchet.			
110,111-GL x-over. 114-Final Night x-over		.90	2.25
100-($3.95)-Foil-c; Superman app.		1.60	4.00
Annual 1(1988, $2.00)-No Grell scripts		.80	2.00
Annual 2(1989, $2.50, 68pgs.)-No Grell scripts; recaps origin Green Arrow,			
Speedy, Black Canary & others		1.00	2.50
Annual 3(1990, $2.95, 68pgs.)-Bill Wray-a		1.20	3.00
Annual 4(1991, $2.95, 68pgs.)-50th anniversary issue		.80	2.00
Annual 5(1992, $3.00, 68pgs.)-Batman, Eclipso app.		1.20	3.00
Annual 6(1993, $3.50, 68pgs.)-Bloodlines; Hook app.		1.40	3.50
Annual 7(1995, $3.95)-Year One story			3.95

NOTE: *Aparo a-0, 81-85, 86 (partial),87p, 88p, 91-95, 96i, 98-100p, 109p; c-81,98-100p. Austin c-96i. Balent layouts-86. Burchett c-91-95. Campanella a-100-108i, 110-113i; c-99i, 101-108i,110-113i. Denys Cowan a-39p, 41-43p, 47p, 48p, 60p; c-41-43. Damaggio a(p)-97p, 100-108p, 110-112p; c-97-99p, 101-108p, 110-113p. Mike Grell c-1-4, 10p, 11, 39, 40, 44, 45, 47-80, Annual 4, 5. Nasser/Netzer a-89, 96. Sienkiewicz a-109i. Springer a-67, 68. Weeks c-109.*

GREEN ARROW: THE LONG BOW HUNTERS
Aug, 1987 - No. 3, Oct, 1987 ($2.95, limited series, mature)
DC Comics

1-Grell-c/a in all	1.00	2.00	5.00
1,2-2nd printings		1.20	3.00
2,3		1.20	3.00
Trade paperback (1989, $12.95)-r/#1-3	1.85	5.50	13.00

GREEN ARROW: THE WONDER YEAR
Feb, 1993 - No. 4, May, 1993 ($1.75, limited series)
DC Comics

1-4: Mike Grell-a(p)/scripts & Gray Morrow-a(i)		.70	1.75

GREEN BERET, THE (See Tales of...)

GREEN CANDLES
Sept, 1995 - No. 3, Dec, 1995 ($5.95, B&W, limited series, digest size)
DC Comics (Paradox Press)

1-3	1.00	2.60	6.00

GREEN GIANT COMICS (Also see Colossus Comics)
1940 (No price on cover; distributed in New York City only)
Pelican Publ. (Funnies, Inc.)

	GD25	VF82	NM94
1-Dr. Nerod, Green Giant, Black Arrow, Mundoo & Master Mystic app.;			
origin Colossus (Rare)	888.00	2666.00	5330.00	8000.00
(Estimated up to 17 copies exist, 3 in NM/Mint)			

NOTE: *The idea for this book came from George Kapitan. Printed by Moreau Publ. of Orange, N.J. as an experiment to see if they could profitably use the idle time of their 40-page Hoe color press. The experiment failed due to the difficulty of obtaining good quality color registration and Mr. Moreau believes the book never reached the stands. The book has no price or date which lends credence to this. Contains five pages reprinted from Motion Picture Funnies Weekly.*

GREEN GOBLIN
Oct, 1995 - No. 13, Oct, 1996 ($2.95/$1.95)
Marvel Comics

1-($2.95)-Scott McDaniel-c/a begins, ends #7; foil-c		1.20	3.00

Green Hornet V2#33 © Now Comics

Green Lama #2 © PRIZE

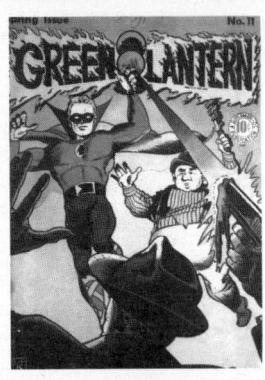
Green Lantern #11 © DC

	GD25	FN65	NM94

2-13: 2-Begin $1.95-c. 4-Hobgoblin-c/app; Thing app. 6-Daredevil-c/app.
8-Darrick Robertson-a; McDaniel-c. 10-Arcade app. 12,13-Onslaught x-over.
13-Green Goblin quits; Spider-Man app. .80 2.00

GREENHAVEN
1988 - No. 3, 1988 ($2.00, limited series, 28 pgs.)
Aircel Publishing
..1-3 1.00 2.00

GREEN HORNET, THE (TV)
Sept, 1953; Feb, 1967 - No. 3, Aug, 1967
Dell Publishing Co./Gold Key
Four Color 496-Painted-c. 25.00 75.00 250.00
1-All have Bruce Lee photo-c. 21.00 63.00 210.00
2,3 15.00 45.00 145.00

GREEN HORNET, THE (Also see Kato of the... & Tales of the...)
Nov, 1989 - No. 14, Feb, 1991 ($1.75)
V2#1, Sept, 1991 - V2#39, Dec, 1994 ($1.95)
Now Comics
1 ($2.95, double-size)-Steranko painted-c; G.A. Green Hornet
1.30 3.25 8.00
1-2nd printing ('90, $3.95)-New Butler-c 1.60 4.00
2 1.00 2.00 5.00
3-8: 5-Death of original (1930s) Green Hornet. 6-Dave Dorman painted-c
1.20 3.00
9-14: 11-Snyder-c .80 2.00
V2#1-11,13-21,24-26,28-30,32-37,39: 1-Butler painted-c. 9-Mayerik-c
.80 2.00
12-($2.50)-Color Green Hornet button polybagged inside 1.00 2.50
22,23-($2.95)-Bagged w/color hologravure card 1.20 3.00
27-($2.95)-Newsstand ed. polybagged w/multi-dimensional card (1993
Anniversary Special on cover) 1.20 3.00
27-($2.95)-Direct Sale ed. polybagged w/multi-dimensional card; cover
variations 1.20 3.00
31,38: 31-($2.50)-Polybagged w/trading card 1.00 2.50
1-($2.50)-Polybagged w/button (same as #12) 1.00 2.50
2,3-($1.95)-Same as #13 & 14 .80 2.00
Annual 1 (12/92, $2.50) 1.00 2.50
Annual 1994 (10/94, $2.95) 3.00

GREEN HORNET: SOLITARY SENTINEL, THE
Dec, 1992 - No. 3, 1993 ($2.50, limited series)
Now Comics
1-3 1.00 2.50

GREEN HORNET COMICS (...Racket Buster #44) (Radio, movies)
Dec, 1940 - No. 47, Sept, 1949 (See All New #13,14)(Early issues: 68 pgs.)
Helnit Pub. Co.(Holyoke) No. 1-6/Family Comics(Harvey) No. 7-on
1-1st app. Green Hornet & Kato; origin of Green Hornet on inside front-c; intro
the Black Beauty (Green Hornet's car); painted-c
360.00 1080.00 3600.00
2-Early issues based on radio adventures 137.00 412.00 1100.00
3 115.00 346.00 925.00
4-6: 6-(8/41) 87.00 262.00 700.00
7 (6/42)-Origin The Zebra & begins; Robin Hood, Spirit of '76, Blonde Bomber
& Mighty Midgets begin; new logo 75.00 225.00 600.00
8-10: 9-Kirby-c 64.00 193.00 515.00
11,12-Mr. Q in both 61.00 183.00 490.00
13-1st Nazi-c; shows Hitler poster on-c 52.00 157.00 420.00
14-20 47.00 141.00 375.00
21-23,25-30 40.00 120.00 300.00
24-Sci-Fi-c 40.00 120.00 325.00
31-The Man in Black Called Fate begins (11-12/41, early app.)
40.00 120.00 320.00
32-36 39.00 118.00 275.00

37-Shock Gibson app. by Powell; S&K Kid Adonis reprinted from
Stuntman #3 40.00 120.00 285.00
38-Shock Gibson, Kid Adonis app. 38.00 114.00 265.00
39-Stuntman story by S&K 43.00 128.00 340.00
40,41 29.00 86.00 200.00
42-47-Kerry Drake in all. 45-Boy Explorers on-c only. 46- "Case of the Marijuana Racket" cover/story; Kerry Drake app. 29.00 86.00 200.00
NOTE: *Fuje* a-23, 24, 26. *Henkle* c-7-9. *Kubert* a-20, 30. *Powell* a-7-10, 12, 14, 16-21, 30,
31(2), 32(3), 33, 34(3), 35, 36, 37(2), 38. *Robinson* a-27. *Schomburg* c-15, 17-23. Kirbyish c-7,
15. Bondage c-8, 14, 18, 26, 36.

GREEN JET COMICS, THE (See Comic Books, Series 1)

GREEN LAMA (Also see Comic Books, Series 1, Daring Adventures #17 &
Prize Comics #7)
Dec, 1944 - No. 8, Mar, 1946
Spark Publications/Prize No. 7 on
1-Intro. Lt. Hercules & The Boy Champions; Mac Raboy-c/a #1-8
112.00 338.00 900.00
2-Lt. Hercules borrows the Human Torch's powers for one panel
68.00 206.00 550.00
3,6,8: 7-X-mas-c; Raboy craft tint-c/a 55.00 165.00 440.00
4-Dick Tracy take-off in Lt. Hercules story by H. L. Gold (sci-fiction writer)
55.00 165.00 440.00
5-Lt. Hercules story; Little Qrphan Annie, Smilin' Jack & Snuffy Smith take-off
(5/45) 55.00 165.00 440.00
7-X-mas-c; Raboy craft tint-c/a (note: a small quantity of NM copies surfaced)
41.00 124.00 330.00
NOTE: *Robinson* a-3-5, 8. *Roussos* a-8. Formerly a pulp hero who began in 1940.

GREEN LANTERN (1st Series) (See All-American, All Flash Quarterly,
All Star Comics, The Big All-American & Comic Cavalcade)
Fall, 1941 - No. 38, May-June, 1949 (#1-18 are quarterly)
National Periodical Publications/All-American

	GD25	FN65	VF82	NM94
1-Origin retold	2,300.00	6,900.00	14,950.00	25,000.00

(Estimated up to 200 total copies exist, 8 in NM/Mint)

	GD25	FN65	NM94
2-1st book-length story	556.00	1667.00	5500.00
3-Classic German war-c by Mart Nodell	389.00	1167.00	3850.00
4-Green Lantern & Doiby Dickles join the Army	312.00	938.00	2750.00
5	225.00	675.00	1800.00
6,8: 8-Hop Harrigan begins	175.00	525.00	1400.00
7-Robot-c.	193.00	581.00	1550.00
9	162.00	487.00	1300.00
10-Origin/1st app. Vandal Savage	168.00	506.00	1350.00
11-17,19,20: 12-Origin/1st app. Gambler	125.00	375.00	1000.00
18-Christmas-c	137.00	412.00	1100.00
21-26,28-30: 30-Origin/1st app. Streak the Wonder Dog by Toth (2-3/48)	116.00	350.00	935.00
27-Origin/1st app. Sky Pirate	121.00	365.00	770.00
31-35: 35-Kubert-c. 35-38-New logo	96.00	288.00	770.00
36-38: 37-Sargon the Sorcerer app.	116.00	350.00	935.00

NOTE: *Book-length stories* #2-7. *Mayer/Moldoff* c-9. *Mayer/Purcell* c-8. *Purcell* c-1. *Mart
Nodell* c-2, 3, 7. *Paul Reinman* c-11, 12, 15-22. *Toth* a-28, 30, 31, 34-38; c-28, 30, 34p, 36-38.
Cover to #8 says Fall while the indicia says Summer Issue. Streak the Wonder Dog c-3
(w/Green Lantern), 34, 36, 38.

GREEN LANTERN (See Action Comics Weekly, Adventure Comics, Brave & the Bold, DC
Special, DC Special Series, Flash, Guy Gardner, Guy Gardner Reborn, Justice League of
America, Showcase, Showcase '93 #12 & Tales of The...Corps)

GREEN LANTERN (2nd Series) (Green Lantern Corps #206 on)
(See Showcase #22-24)
7-8/60 - No. 89, 4-5/72; No. 90, 8-9/76 - No. 205, 10/86
National Periodical Publ./DC Comics
1-(7-8/60)-Origin retold; Gil Kane c/a continues; 1st app. Guardians of the
Universe 200.00 600.00 1300.00 2400.00

	GD25	FN65	NM94

Green Lantern (2nd Series) #86 © DC

Green Lantern (2nd Series) #186 © DC

Green Lantern (3rd Series) #50 © DC

	GD25	FN65	NM94
2-1st Pieface	78.00	233.00	750.00
3-Contains readers poll	50.00	150.00	430.00
4,5: 5-Origin & 1st app. Hector Hammond	40.00	120.00	340.00
6-Intro Tomar-Re the alien G.L.	40.00	120.00	320.00
7-Origin/1st app. Sinestro (7-8/61)	36.00	107.00	265.00
8-10: 8-1st 5700 A.D. story; grey tone-c. 9-1st Jordan Brothers; last 10¢ issue	32.00	96.00	240.00
11,12	21.00	64.00	160.00
13-Flash x-over	26.00	79.00	195.00
14-20: 14-Origin/1st app. Sonar. 16-Origin & 1st app. Star Sapphire. 20-Flash x-over	19.00	58.00	145.00
21-30: 21-Origin & 1st app. Dr. Polaris. 23-1st Tattooed Man. 24-Origin & 1st app. Shark. 29-JLA cameo; 1st Blackhand	17.00	51.00	130.00
31-39: 37-1st app. Evil Star (villain)	14.00	43.00	105.00
40-1st app. Crisis (10/65); 2nd solo G.A. Green Lantern in Silver Age (see Showcase #55); origin The Guardians; Doiby Dickles app.	58.00	174.00	490.00
41-44,46-50: 42-Zatanna x-over. 43-Flash x-over	9.30	28.00	70.00
45-2nd S.A. app. G.A. Green Lantern in title (6/66)	17.00	49.00	125.00
51,53-58	7.00	21.50	52.00
52-G.A. Green Lantern x-over	10.00	30.00	75.00
59-1st app. Guy Gardner (3/68)	29.00	86.00	210.00
60,62-69: 69-Wood inks; last 12 cent issue	5.00	15.00	35.00
61-G.A. Green Lantern x-over	7.00	21.50	50.00
70-75	2.85	8.50	20.00
76-(4/70)-Begin Green Lantern/Green Arrow series (by Neal Adams #76-89) ends #122 (see Flash #217 for 2nd series)	19.00	58.00	150.00
77	7.00	21.50	50.00
78-80	5.50	16.50	40.00
81-84: 82-Wrightson-i(1 pg.). 83-G.L. reveals i.d. to Carol Ferris. 84-N. Adams/Wrightson-a(22 pgs.); last 15¢-c; partial photo-c	4.50	14.00	30.00
85,86-(52 pgs.)-Anti-drug issues. 86-G.A. Green Lantern-r; Toth-a	7.00	21.00	50.00
87-(52 pgs.): 2nd app. Guy Gardner (cameo); 1st app. John Stewart (12/1-71/72) (becomes 3rd Green Lantern in #182)	4.00	12.00	30.00
88-(2-3/72, 52 pgs.)-Unpubbed G.A. Green Lantern story; Green Lantern-r/Showcase #23. N. Adams-c/a (1 pg.)	1.65	4.20	10.00
89-(4-5/72, 52 pgs.)-G.A. Green Lantern-r; Green Lantern & Green Arrow move to Flash #217 (2nd team-up series)	2.15	6.50	15.00
90-99: 90-(8-9/76)-Begin 3rd Green Lantern/Green Arrow team-up series; Mike Grell-c/a begins, ends #111	1.00	2.00	5.00
100-(1/78, Giant)-Air Wave II	1.30	3.25	8.00
101-111,113-115,117-119: 107-1st Tales of the G.L. Corps story. 108-110-(44 pgs.)-G.A. Green Lantern back-ups in each. 111-Origin retold; G.A. Green Lantern app.		1.20	3.00
112-G.A. Green Lantern origin retold	1.20	3.00	7.00
116-1st app. Guy Gardner as a G.L. (5/79)	3.60	11.00	25.00
120,121,124-135,138-140,142-149: 130-132-Tales of the G.L. Corps. 132-Adam Strange series begins, ends 147. 142,143-Omega Men app. 144-Omega Men cameo. 148-Tales of the G.L. Corps begins, ends #173		.80	2.00
122-Last Green Lantern/Green Arrow team-up		1.20	3.00
123-Green Lantern back to solo action; 2nd app. Guy Gardner as Green Lantern	1.00	2.50	6.00
136,137-1st app. Citadel; Space Ranger app.		1.10	2.75
141-1st app. Omega Men (6/81)		1.10	2.75
150-Anniversary issue, 52 pgs.; no G.L. Corps		1.20	3.00
151-170: 159-Origin Evil Star. 160,161-Omega Men app. 181-Hal Jordan resigns as G.L. 182-John Stewart becomes new G.L.; origin recap of Hal Jordan as G.L.		.80	2.00
171-193,196-199,201-205: (75¢ cover). 185-Origin new G.L. (John Stewart). 188-I.D. revealed; Alan Moore back-up scripts. 191-Re-intro Star Sapphire (cameo). 192-Re-intro Star Sapphire (1st full app.). 194,198-Crisis x-over. 199-Hal Jordan returns as a member of G.L. Corps (3 G.L.s now). 201-Green			

	GD25	FN65	NM94
Lantern Corps begins (is cover title, says premiere issue)		.80	2.00
194-Hal Jordan/Guy Gardner battle; Guardians choose Guy Gardner to become new Green Lantern	1.00	2.50	6.00
195-Guy Gardner becomes Green Lantern; Crisis x-over	1.65	4.20	10.00
200-Double-size	1.10	2.75	
Annual 1 (See Tales Of The...)			
Annual 3 (See Green Lantern Corps Annual #3)			
Special 1 (1988), 2 (1989)-(Both $1.50, 52 pgs.)	1.00	2.50	

NOTE: **N. Adams** a-76, 77-87p, 89; c-63, 76-89p. **M. Anderson** a-137i. **Austin** a-93i, 94i, 171i. **Chaykin** c-196. **Greene** a-39-49i, 58-63i; c-54-58i. **Grell** a-90-106, 108-111; c-90-106, 108-112. **Gil Kane** a-1-49p, 50-57, 58-61p, 68-75p, 85p(r), 87p(r), 88p(r), 156, 177, 184p; c-1-52, 54-61p, 67-75, 123, 154, 156, 165-171, 177, 184. **Newton** a-148p, 149p, 181. **Perez** c-132p, 141-144. **Sekowsky** a-65p, 170p. **Simonson** c-200. **Sparling** a-63p. **Starlin** c-129, 133. **Staton** a-117p, 123-127p, 128, 129-131p, 132-139, 140p, 141-146, 147p, 148-150, 151-155p; c-107p, 117p, 135(i), 136p, 145p, 146, 147, 148-152p, 155p. **Toth** a-86r, 171p. **Tuska** a-166-168p, 170p.

GREEN LANTERN (3rd Series)
June, 1990 - Present ($1.00/$1.25/$1.50/$1.75)
DC Comics

	GD25	FN65	NM94
1-Hal Jordan, John Stewart & Guy Gardner return; Batman app.	1.20	3.00	
2,3	.80	2.00	
4-8		1.25	
9-12-Guy Gardner solo story	1.00	2.50	
13-($1.75, 52 pgs.)	.80	2.00	
14-18,20-24,26: 18-Guy Gardner solo story. 26-Last $1.00-c		1.00	
19-($1.75, 52 pgs.)-50th anniversary issue; Mart Nodell (original G.A. artist) part-p on G.A. Gr. Lantern; G. Kane-c	.70	1.75	
25-($1.75, 52 pgs.)-Hal Jordan/Guy Gardner battle	.80	2.00	
27-45,47: 30,31-Gorilla Grodd-c/story(see Flash #69). 38,39-Adam Strange-c/story. 42-Deathstroke-c/s. 47-Green Arrow x-over		1.25	
46-Superman app. cont'd in Superman #82	1.00	2.00	5.00
48,49: 48-Emerald Twilight part 1; begin $1.50-c	1.00	2.50	
50-($2.95, 52 pgs.)-Glow-in-the-dark-c	1.20	3.00	
0, 51-62: 51-1st app. New Green Lantern (Kyle Rayner) with new costume. 53-Superman-c/story. 55-(9/94)-Zero Hour. 0-(10/94). 56-(11/94).		1.50	
63-90: 63-Begin $1.75-c. 63,64-vs. Hal Jordan. 65-New Titans app. 66,67-Flash app. 71-Batman & Robin app. 72-Shazam! c/app. 73-Wonder Woman-c/app. 73-75-Adam Strange app. 76,77-Green Arrow x-over. 80-Final Night x-over. 81-(Regular Edition)-Memorial for Hal Jordan (Parallax); most DC heroes app.	.70	1.75	
81-($3.95, Deluxe Edition)-Embossed prism-c		4.00	
Annual 1 (1992, $2.50, 68 pgs.)-Eclipso app.	1.00	2.50	
Annual 2 (1993, $2.50, 68 pgs.)-Intro Nightblade	1.00	2.50	
Annual 3 (1994, $2.95)-Elseworlds story	1.20	3.00	
Annual 4 (1995, $3.50)-Year One story		3.50	
Annual 5 (1996, $3.95)-Legends of the Dead Earth		4.00	
...: Emerald Twilight nn (1994, $5.95)-r/#48-50	1.00	2.50	6.00
...: Ganthet's Tale nn (1992, $5.95, 68 pgs.)-Silver foil stamped logo;Larry Niven scripts; Byrne-c/a	1.00	2.50	6.00
.../Green Arrow Collection, Vol. 2-r/GI #84-87,89 & Flash #217-219 & GL/GA #5-7 by O'Neil/Adams/Wrightson	1.90	5.60	13.00
...The Road Back nn (1992, $8.95)-r/1-8 w/covers	1.50	3.75	9.00

NOTE: **Staton** a(p)-9-12; c-9-12.

GREEN LANTERN CORPS, THE (Formerly Green Lantern; see Tales of...)
No. 206, Nov. 1986 - No. 224, May, 1988
DC Comics

206-223: 220,221-Millennium tie-ins			1.00
224-Double-size last issue			1.50
...Corps Annual 2 (12/86)-Formerly Tales of ...Annual #1; Alan Moore scripts			1.50
...Corps Annual 3 (8/87)-Indicia says Green Lantern Annual #3; Moore scripts;			

The Green Mask #2 © FOX

Grendel #2 © Matt Wagner

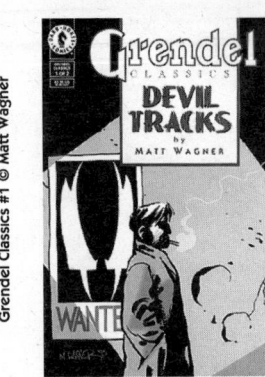

Grendel Classics #1 © Matt Wagner

	GD25	FN65	NM94

Byrne-a 1.50

NOTE: **Austin** a-Annual 3i. **Gil Kane** a-223, 224p; c-223, 224, Annual 2. **Russell** a-Annual 3i. **Staton** a-207-213p, 217p, 221p, 222p, Annual 3; c-207-213p, 217p, 221p, 222p. **Willingham** a-213p, 219p, 220p, 218p, 219p, Annual 2, 3p; c-218p, 219p.

GREEN LANTERN CORPS QUARTERLY
Summer, 1992 - No. 8, Spring, 1994 ($2.50/$2.95, 68 pgs.)
DC Comics

1-5: 1-Green Lantern story; Staton-a(p). 2-G.A. G.L.-c/story; Austin-c(i); Gulacy-a(p). 3-G.A. G.L. story. 4-Austin-i	1.00	2.50
6-8: 6-Begin $2.95-c. 7-Painted-c; Tim Vigil-a. 8-Lobo-c/s	1.20	3.00

GREEN LANTERN: EMERALD DAWN (Also see Emerald Dawn)
Dec, 1989 - No. 6, May, 1990 ($1.00, limited series)
DC Comics

1-Origin retold; Giffen plots in all	.80	2.00
2-6		1.50

GREEN LANTERN: EMERALD DAWN II (Emerald Dawn II #1 & 2)
Apr, 1991 - No. 6, Sept, 1991 ($1.00, limited series)
DC Comics

1		1.25
2-6		1.00

GREEN LANTERN/GREEN ARROW (Also see The Flash #217)
Oct, 1983 - No. 7, April, 1984 (52-60 pgs.)
DC Comics

1-7: Reprints Green Lantern #76-89	1.10	2.75

NOTE: **Neal Adams** r-1-7; c-1-4. **Wrightson** r-4, 5.

GREEN LANTERN: MOSAIC (Also see Cosmic Odyssey #2)
June, 1992 - No. 18, Nov, 1993 ($1.25)
DC Comics

1-18: Featuring John Stewart. 1-Painted-c by Cully Hamner		1.25

GREEN LANTERN/SILVER SURFER: UNHOLY ALLIANCES
1995 ($4.95, one-shot)(Prelude to DC Versus Marvel)
DC Comics

nn-Hal Jordan app.		5.00

GREEN MASK, THE (See Mystery Men)
Summer, 1940 - No. 9, 2/42; No. 10, 8/44 - No. 11, 11/44;
V2#1, Spring, 1945 - No. 6, 10-11/46
Fox Features Syndicate

V1#1-Origin The Green Mask & Domino; reprints/Mystery Men #1-3,5-7; Lou Fine-c	288.00	862.00	2500.00
2-Zanzibar The Magician by Tuska	112.00	338.00	900.00
3-Powell-a; Marijuana story	68.00	206.00	550.00
4-Navy Jones begins, ends #6	56.00	168.00	450.00
5	44.00	132.00	350.00
6-The Nightbird begins, ends #9; bondage/torture-c	40.00	120.00	280.00
7-9: 9(2/42)-Becomes The Bouncer #10(nn) on? & Green Mask #10 on	33.00	99.00	230.00
10,11: 10-Origin One Round Hogan & Rocket Kelly	26.00	77.00	180.00
V2#1	19.00	58.00	135.00
2-6	17.00	51.00	120.00

GREEN PLANET, THE
1962 (one-shot) (12¢)
Charlton Comics

nn-Giordano-c	8.35	25.00	50.00

GREEN TEAM (See Cancelled Comic Cavalcade & 1st Issue Special)

GREETINGS FROM SANTA (See March of Comics No. 48)

GRENDEL (Also see Primer #2 and Mage)
Mar, 1983 - No. 3, Feb, 1984 ($1.50, B&W)(#1 has indicia to Skrog #1)

Comico

1-Origin Hunter Rose	14.00	43.00	100.00
2,3: 2-Origin Argent	11.00	33.00	75.00

GRENDEL
Oct, 1986 - No. 40, Feb, 1991 ($1.50/$1.95/$2.50, mature)
Comico

1	1.00	2.00	5.00
1,2: 2nd printings		.80	2.00
2		1.20	3.00
3-10: 4-Dave Stevens-c(i)		.80	2.00
11-15: 13-15-Ken Steacy-c		.70	1.75
16-Re-intro Mage (series begins, ends #19)		1.60	4.00
17-32: 18-26-$1.75-c; 27-32-$1.95-c. 24-25, 27-28,30-31-Snyder-c/a; 26,29-Snyder-i		.80	2.00
33-($2.75, 44 pgs.)		1.20	3.00
34-40: 34-Begin $2.50 cover price		1.20	3.00
Devil by the Deed (Graphic Novel, 10/86, $5.95, 52 pgs.)-r/Grendel back-ups/ Mage 6-14; Alan Moore intro.	1.20	3.00	7.00
Devil's Legacy ($14.95, 1988, Graphic Novel)	2.15	6.50	15.00
Devil's Vagary (10/87, B&W & red)-No price; included in Comico Collection	1.70	5.00	12.00

GRENDEL CLASSICS
July, 1995 - Aug, 1995 ($3.95, limited series, mature)
Dark Horse Comics

1,2-reprints; new Wagner-c		1.60	4.00

GRENDEL CYCLE
Oct, 1995 ($5.95, one shot)
Dark Horse Comics

1-nn-history of Grendel by M. Wagner & others	1.00	2.60	6.00

GRENDEL: DEVIL BY THE DEED
July, 1993 ($3.95, one shot, spot varnish-c)
Dark Horse Comics

1-nn-M. Wagner-c/a/scripts; r/Grendel back-ups from Mage #6-14.	1.60	4.00

GRENDEL: DEVIL QUEST
Nov, 1995 ($4.95, one shot)
Dark Horse Comics

1-nn-Prequel to Batman/Grendel II; M. Wagner story & art; r/back-up story from Grendel Tales series.	1.00	2.00	5.00

GRENDEL: WAR CHILD
Aug, 1992 - No. 10, 1993 ($2.50, limited series, mature)
Dark Horse Comics

1-9: Bisley painted-c; Wagner-i & scripts		1.00	2.50
10-($3.50, 52 pgs.)		1.40	3.50
Limited Edition Hardcover ($99.95)			100.00

GRENDEL TALES: DEVILS AND DEATHS
Oct, 1994 - Nov, 1994 ($2.95, limited series, mature)
Dark Horse Comics

1,2 (10/94-11/94, $2.95, mature)		1.20	3.00

GRENDEL TALES: DEVIL'S CHOICES
Mar, 1995 - Jun, 1995 ($2.95, limited series, mature)
Dark Horse Comics

1-4		1.20	3.00

GRENDEL TALES: FOUR DEVILS, ONE HELL
Aug, 1993 - Jan, 1994 ($2.95, limited series, mature)
Dark Horse Comics

1-6-Wagner painted-c		1.20	3.00

GRENDEL TALES: HOMECOMING

Grendel Tales: The Devil May Care #4 © Matt Wagner

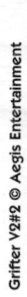

Grifter V2#2 © Aegis Entertainment

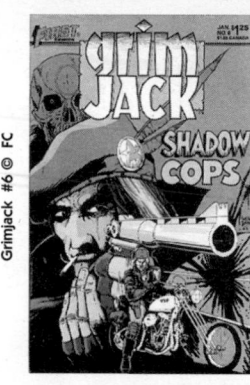

Grimjack #6 © FC

	GD25	FN65	NM94

	GD25	FN65	NM94

Dec, 1994 - Feb, 1995 ($2.95, limited series, mature)
Dark Horse Comics

1-3		1.20	3.00

GRENDEL TALES: THE DEVIL IN OUR MIDST
May, 1994 - Sep, 1995 ($2.95, limited series, mature)
Dark Horse Comics

1-5-Wagner painted-c. in all		1.20	3.00

GRENDEL TALES: THE DEVIL MAY CARE
Dec, 1995 - 1996 ($2.95, limited series, mature)
Dark Horse Comics

1-6-Terry LaBan scripts. 5-Batman/Grendel II preview		1.20	3.00

GRENDEL TALES: THE DEVIL'S HAMMER
Feb, 1994 - Apr, 1994 ($2.95, limited series, mature)
Dark Horse Comics

1-3		1.20	3.00

GREYFRIARS BOBBY (Disney)(Movie)
No. 1189, Nov, 1961 (one-shot)
Dell Publishing Co.

Four Color 1189-Photo-c (scarce)	7.00	21.00	70.00

GREYLORE
2/85 - No. 5, Sept, 1986 ($1.50/$1.75, high quality paper)
Sirius

1-5: Bo Hampton-a in all			1.50

GRIFFIN, THE
1991 - No. 6, 1992 ($4.95, limited series, 52 pgs.)
DC Comics

Book 1-6: Matt Wagner painted-c	1.00	2.00	5.00

GRIFTER (Also see Team 7 & WildC.A.T.S)
May, 1995 - No. 10, Mar, 1996 ($1.95)
Image Comics (Wildstorm Productions)

1 ($1.95, Newsstand)-WildStorm Rising Pt. 5		1.00	2.50
1 ($2.50, Direct Market)-WildStorm Rising Pt. 5, bound-in trading card			
		1.20	3.00
2-10		.80	2.00

GRIFTER
V2#1, July, 1996 - Present ($2.50)
Image Comics (Wildstorm Productions)

V2#1-6: Steven Grant scripts			2.50

GRIFTER AND THE MASK
Sept, 1996 - No. 2, Oct, 1996 ($2.50, limited series)
1st Dark Horse Comics/Image x-over)
Dark Horse Comics

1,2: Steve Seagle scripts			2.50

GRIFTER/BADROCK (Also see WildC.A.T.S & Youngblood)
Oct, 1995 - No.2, Nov, 1995 ($2.50, unfinished limited series)
Image Comics (Extreme Studios)

1,2: 2-Flip book w/Badrock #2			2.50

GRIFTER: ONE SHOT
Jan, 1995 ($4.95, one-shot)
Image Comics (Wildstorm Productions)

1-Flip-c	1.00	2.50	5.50

GRIFTER/SHI
Apr, 1996 - No. 2, May, 1996 ($2.95, limited series)
Image Comics (Wildstorm Productions)

1,2: 1-Jim Lee-c/a(p). 2-Billy Tucci-c/a(p); Travis Charest-a(p)			
Charest-a(p)			3.00

GRIM GHOST, THE
Jan, 1975 - No. 3, July, 1975
Atlas/Seaboard Publ.

1-3: 1-Origin. 3-Heath-c			1.00

GRIMJACK (Also see Demon Knight & Starslayer)
Aug, 1984 - No. 81, Apr, 1991 ($1.00/$1.95/$2.25)
First Comics

1-John Ostrander scripts & Tim Truman-c/a begins.			
		.80	2.00
2-25: 20-Sutton-c/a begins. 22-Bolland-a.			1.50
26-2nd color Teenage Mutant Ninja Turtles		.80	2.00
27-74,76-81 (Later issues $1.95, $2.25): 30-Dynamo Joe x-over; 31-Mandrake-			
c/a begins. 73,74-Kelley Jones-a			1.25
75-($5.95, 52 pgs.)-Fold-out map; coated stock	1.00	2.50	6.00

NOTE: *Truman* c/a-1-17.

GRIMJACK CASEFILES
Nov, 1990 - No. 5, Mar, 1991 ($1.95, limited series)
First Comics

1-5 Reprints 1st stories from Starslayer #10 on		1.00	2.00

GRIMM'S GHOST STORIES (See Dan Curtis)
Jan, 1972 - No. 60, June, 1982 (Painted-c #1-42,44,46-56)
Gold Key/Whitman No. 55 on

1	1.00	2.50	6.00
2-4,6,7,9,10		1.20	3.00
5,8-Williamson-a		1.60	4.00
11-35: 32,34-Reprints		.80	2.00
36-58,60: 43,44-(52 pgs.). 43,45-Photo-c			1.50
59-Williamson-a(r/#8)		.80	2.00
Mini-Comic No. 1 (3-1/4x6-1/2", 1976)			1.00

NOTE: *Reprints*-#32?, 34?, 39, 44, 477, 53; 56-60(1/3). *Bolle* a-8, 17, 22-25, 27, 29(2), 33, 35, 41, 43r, 45(2); 48(2), 50, 52. *Celardo* a-17, 26, 28p, 30, 31, 43(2), 45. *Lopez* a-24, 25. *McWilliams* a-33, 44r, 48, 54(2), 57, 58. *Win Mortimer* a-31, 33, 49, 51, 55, 56, 58(2), 59, 60. *Roussos* a-25, 30. *Sparling* a-23, 24, 28, 30, 31, 43r, 44, 45, 51(2), 52, 56, 58, 59(2), 60. *Spiegle* a-44.

GRIN (The American Funny Book) (Satire)
Nov, 1972 - No. 3, April, 1973 (Magazine, 52 pgs.)
APAG House Pubs

1		.80	2.00
2,3			1.00

GRIN & BEAR IT (See Gags)
No. 28, 1941
Dell Publishing Co.

Large Feature Comic 28	9.00	27.00	90.00

GRIPS (Extreme violence)
Sept, 1986 - No. 4, Dec, 1986 ($1.50, B&W, mature readers)
Silverwolf Comics

1-Tim Vigil-c/a in all	1.30	3.25	8.00
2-4	1.00	2.00	5.00

GRIT GRADY (See Holyoke One-Shot No. 1)

GROO (Sergio Aragones'...)
Dec, 1994 - No. 12, Dec, 1995 ($1.95)
Image Comics

1-12: 2-Indicia reads #1, Jan, 1995; Aragones-c/a in all		.80	2.00

GROO CARNIVAL, THE
Dec, 1991 ($8.95, trade paperback)
Marvel Comics (Epic Comics)

nn-Reprints Groo #9-12 by Aragones	1.50	3.75	9.00

GROO CHRONICLES, THE (Sergio Aragones)
June, 1989 - No. 6, Feb, 1990 ($3.50)

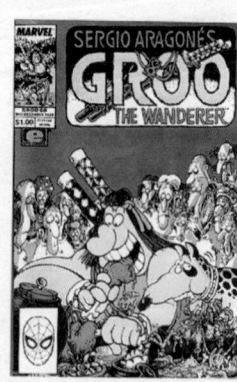

Groo The Wanderer #60 © Sergio Aragones

Guardians of the Galaxy #1 © MEG

Gumby Summer Fun Special #1 © Art Clokey

	GD25	FN65	NM94

Marvel Comics (Epic Comics)

Book 1-6: Reprints early Pacific issues		1.40	3.50

GROO SPECIAL
Oct, 1984 ($2.00, 52 pgs., Baxter paper)
Eclipse Comics

1-Aragones-c/a	4.30	13.00	30.00

GROO THE WANDERER (See Destroyer Duck #1, Marvel Graphic Novel #32 & & Starslayer #5)
Dec, 1982 - No. 8, Apr, 1984
Pacific Comics

1-Aragones-c/a(p) in all; Aragones biog., photo	4.00	12.00	28.00
2	2.60	7.70	18.00
3-7: 5-Deluxe paper (1.00-c)	2.10	6.50	15.00
8	1.70	5.10	12.00

GROO THE WANDERER (Sergio Aragones'...)
March, 1985 - No. 120, Jan, 1995
Marvel Comics (Epic Comics)

1-Aragones-c/a in all	1.65	4.20	10.00
2	1.00	2.60	6.00
3-10		1.60	4.00
11-20		1.00	2.50
21-30		.80	2.00
31-86: 50-($1.50, double size)			1.50
87-99,101-120: 87-Begin $2.25, direct sale only, high quality paper issues		1.00	2.50
100-($2.95, 52 pgs.)		1.20	3.00
Marvel Graphic Novel 32: Death of Groo	1.20	2.90	7.00
Death of Groo 2nd printing ($5.95)	1.00	2.50	6.00
Groo Garden, The (4/94, $10.95)-r/25-28	1.60	4.70	11.00

GROOVY (Cartoon Comics - not CCA approved)
March, 1968 - No. 3, July, 1968
Marvel Comics Group

1-Monkees, Ringo Starr, Sonny & Cher, Mamas & Papas photos	4.30	13.00	30.00
2,3	3.25	9.50	22.00

GROUP LARUE, THE
1989 - No. 4, 1990 ($1.95, mini-series)
Innovation Publishing

1-4 By Mike Baron; 4-Exist?		1.00	2.00

GUADALCANAL DIARY (See American Library)

GUARDIANS OF JUSTICE & THE O-FORCE
1990 (no date) ($1.50, 7-1/2 x10-1/4)
Shadow Comics

1-Super-hero group			1.50

GUARDIANS OF METROPOLIS
Nov, 1995 - Feb, 1995 ($1.50, limited series)
DC Comics

1-4: 1-Superman & Granny Goodness app.			1.50

GUARDIANS OF THE GALAXY (Also see The Defenders #26, Marvel Presents #3, Marvel Super-Heroes #18, Marvel Two-In-One #5)
June, 1990 - No. 62, July, 1995 ($1.00/$1.25)
Marvel Comics

1-16: 1-Valentino-c/a(p) begin. 2-Zeck-c(i). 5-McFarlane-c(i). 7-Intro Malevolence (Mephisto's daughter); Perez-c(i). 8-Intro Rancor (descendant of Wolverine) in cameo. 9-1st full app. Rancor; Rob Liefeld-c(i). 10-Jim Lee-c(i). 13,14-1st app. Spirit of Vengeance (futuristic Ghost Rider). 14-Spirit of Vengeance vs. The Guardians. 15-Starlin-c(i). 16-($1.50, 52 pgs.)-Starlin-c(i)		.80	2.00
17-23,26-38,40-47: 17-20-31st century Punishers storyline. 20-Last $1.00-c.			

21-Rancor app. 22-Reintro Starhawk. 26-Origin retold. 27-28-Infinity War x-over; 27-Inhumans app. 43-Intro Wooden (son of Thor)			1.2
24-Silver Surfer-c/story; Ron Lim-c		.80	2.0
25-($2.50)-Prism foil-c; Silver Surfer/Galactus-c/s		1.20	3.0
25-($2.50)-Without foil-c; newsstand edition		1.00	2.5
39-($2.95, 52 pgs.)-Embossed & holo-grafx foil-c; Dr. Doom vs. Rancor		1.20	3.0
48,49,51-62: 48-$1.50-c begins; bound-in trading card sheet			1.5
50-($2.00, 52 pgs.)-Newsstand edition		.80	2.0
50-($2.95, 52 pgs.)-Collectors ed. w/foil embossed-c		1.20	3.0
Annual 1 (1991, $2.00, 68 pgs.)-2 pg. origin		.80	2.*
Annual 2 (1992, $2.25, 68 pgs.)-Spirit of Vengeance-c/story			
		.90	2.2
Annual 3 (1993, $2.95, 68 pgs.)-Bagged w/card		1.20	3.
Annual 4 (1994, $2.95)		1.20	3.0

GUERRILLA WAR (Formerly Jungle War Stories)
No. 12, July-Sept, 1965 - No. 14, Mar, 1966
Dell Publishing Co.

12-14	1.70	5.00	12.

GUILTY (See Justice Traps the Guilty)

GULF FUNNY WEEKLY (Gulf Comic Weekly No. 1-4)
1933 - No. 422, 5/23/41 (in full color; 4 pgs.; tabloid size to 2/3/39; 2/10/39 on, regular comic book size)(early issues undated)
Gulf Oil Company (Giveaway)

1	56.00	168.00	450.00
2-5	19.00	56.00	130.0
6-30	10.00	30.00	65.0
31-100	7.50	22.50	45.0
101-196	5.00	15.00	30.0
197-Wings Winfair begins(1/29/37); by Fred Meagher beginning in 1938	25.00	75.00	175.0
198-300 (Last tabloid size)	13.00	39.00	90.0
301-350 (Regular size)	7.50	22.50	45.0
351-422	5.00	15.00	30.0

GULLIVER'S TRAVELS (See Dell Jr. Treasury No. 3)
Sept-Nov, 1965 - No. 3, May, 1966
Dell Publishing Co.

1	4.30	13.00	43.0
2,3	3.25	9.50	32.0

GUMBY'S SUMMER FUN SPECIAL
July, 1987 ($2.50)
Comico

1-Art Adams-c/a; B. Burden scripts		1.00	2.5

GUMBY'S WINTER FUN SPECIAL
Dec, 1988 ($2.50, 44 pgs.)
Comico

1-Art Adams-c/a		1.00	2.5

GUMPS, THE (See Merry Christmas..., Popular & Super Comics)
No. 73, 1945; Mar-Apr, 1947 - No. 5, Nov-Dec, 1947
Dell Publ. Co./Bridgeport Herald Corp.

Four Color 73 (Dell)(1945)	11.00	33.00	110.0
1 (3-4/47)	11.00	33.00	100.0
2-5	7.00	21.00	63.0

GUNFIGHTER (Fat & Slat #1-4) (Becomes Haunt of Fear #15 on)
No. 5, Summer, 1948 - No. 14, Mar-Apr, 1950
E. C. Comics (Fables Publ. Co.)

5,6-Moon Girl in each	41.00	124.00	330.0
7-14: 14-Bondage-c	34.00	101.00	235.0

Gunfire #6 © DC

Gun Runner #6 © MEG

Gunsmith Cats: The Return of Gray #4 © Kodansha, Ltd

GU

	GD25	FN65	NM94

OTE: *Craig & H. C. Kiefer* art in most issues. *Craig* c-5, 6, 13, 14. *Feldstein/Craig* a-10. *ldstein* a-7-11. *Harrison/Wood* a-13, 14. *Ingels* a-5-14; c-7-12.

UNFIGHTERS, THE
#63 - 1964
uper Comics (Reprints)

0-12,15,16,18: 10,11-r/Billy the Kid #s? 12-r/The Rider #5(Swift Arrow). 15-r/Straight Arrow #42; Powell-r. 16-r/Billy the Kid #?(Toby). 18-r/ The Rider #3; Severin-c	1.30	3.25	8.00

UNFIGHTERS, THE (Formerly Kid Montana)
0. 51, 10/66 - No. 52, 10/67; No. 53, 6/79 - No. 85, 7/84
narlton Comics

I,52	1.20	3.00	7.00
3-85: 53,54-Williamson/Torres-r/Six Gun Heroes #47,49. 56-Williamson/ Severin-c; Severin-r/Sheriff of Tombstone #1. 85-S&K-r/1955 Bullseye			
	1.20		3.00

UNFIRE (See Deathstroke Annual #2 & Showcase 94 #1,2)
ay, 1994 - No. 13, June, 1995 ($1.75)
C **Comics**

-4: 2-Ricochet-c/story. 5-(9/94)		.70	1.75
,0,6-12: 0-(10/94). 6-(11/94).		.80	2.00
3-$2.25-c begins.			2.25

UN GLORY (Movie)
0. 846, Oct, 1957 (one-shot)
ell **Publishing Co.**

ur Color 846-Toth-a, photo-c.	12.00	36.00	120.00

UNHAWK, THE (Formerly Whip Wilson)(See Wild Western)
0. 12, Nov, 1950 - No. 18, Dec, 1951 (Also see Two-Gun Western #5)
arvel Comics/Atlas (MCI)

2	14.00	43.00	100.00
3-18: 13-Tuska-a. 16-Colan-a. 18-Maneely-c	11.00	33.00	75.00

UNHAWKS (Gunhawk No. 7)
ct, 1972 - No. 7, October, 1973
arvel Comics Group

I-Reno Jones, Kid Cassidy; Shores-c/a(p)	1.00	2.00	5.00
2-7: 6-Kid Cassidy dies. 7-Reno Jones solo	1.60		4.00

UNHED
990 - No. 3, 1991? ($4.95, 7-1/8 x 9-1/8, 52 pgs., bi-monthly)
x **Comics**

I-3: Japanese sci-fi based on 1991 movie	2.50		5.00

UNMASTER (Becomes Judo Master #89 on)
64 - No. 4, 1965; No. 84, 7/65 - No. 88, 3-4/66; No. 89, 10/67
narlton Comics

I #1	3.20	8.00	20.00
2-4	1.70	5.00	12.00
5#84-86: 84-Formerly Six-Gun Heroes	1.70	5.00	12.00
5#87-89	1.20	3.00	7.00

OTE: *Vol. 5 was originally cancelled with #88 (3-4/66). #89 on, became Judo Master, then later 1967, Charlton issued #89 as a Gunmaster one-shot.*

UN RUNNER
ct, 1993 - No. 6, Mar, 1994 ($1.75, limited series)
arvel Comics UK

I-($2.75)-Polybagged w/4 trading cards; Spirits of Vengeance app.		1.10	2.75
2-6: 2-Ghost Rider & Blaze app.		.70	1.75

UNS AGAINST GANGSTERS (True-To-Life Romances #8 on)
ept-Oct, 1948 - No. 4, July-Aug, 1949; V2#1, Sept-Oct, 1949 - No. 2, 11-12/49
urtis **Publications/Novelty Press**

I-Toni & Greg Gayle begins by Schomburg; L.B. Cole-c			

	27.00	81.00	190.00
2-L.B. Cole-c	19.00	58.00	135.00
3-6, V2#1,2: 6-Toni Gayle-c	17.00	49.00	115.00

NOTE: *L. B. Cole* c-1-6, V2#1, 2; a-1, 2, 3(2), 4-6.

GUNSLINGER
No. 1220, Oct-Dec, 1961 (one-shot)
Dell Publishing Co.

Four Color 1220--Photo-c	9.00	27.00	90.00

GUNSLINGER (Formerly Tex Dawson…)
No. 2, Apr, 1973 - No. 3, June, 1973
Marvel Comics Group

2,3			1.00

GUNSMITH CATS: THE RETURN OF GRAY (Manga)
Aug, 1996 - No. 7, Feb, 1997 ($2.95, B&W, limited series)
Dark Horse Comics

1-7			3.00

GUNSMOKE (Blazing Stories of the West)
Apr-May, 1949 - No. 16, Jan, 1952
Western Comics (Youthful Magazines)

1-Gunsmoke & Masked Marvel begin by Ingels; Ingels bondage-c			
	38.00	114.00	265.00
2-Ingels-c/a(2)	24.00	71.00	165.00
3-Ingels bondage-c/a	19.00	56.00	130.00
4-6: Ingels-c	14.00	43.00	100.00
7-10	9.15	27.00	55.00
11-16: 15,16-Western/horror stories	6.70	20.00	40.00

NOTE: *Stallman* a-11, 14. *Wildey* a-15, 16.

GUNSMOKE (TV)
No. 679, Feb, 1956 - No. 27, June-July, 1961; Feb, 1969 - No. 6, Feb, 1970
Dell Publishing Co./Gold Key (All have James Arness photo-c)

Four Color 679(#1)	13.00	40.00	130.00
Four Color 720,769,797,844 (#2-5)	7.00	21.00	70.00
6(11-1/57-58), 7	7.00	21.00	70.00
8,9,11,12-Williamson-a in all, 4 pgs. each	8.00	24.00	80.00
10-Williamson/Crandall-a, 4 pgs.	8.00	24.00	80.00
13-27	6.00	18.00	60.00
Gunsmoke Film Story (11/62-G.K. Giant) No. 30008-211			
	8.00	24.00	80.00
1 (Gold Key)	4.50	13.50	45.00
2-6('69-70)	2.20	6.60	22.00

GUNSMOKE TRAIL
June, 1957 - No. 4, Dec, 1957
Ajax-Farrell Publ./Four Star Comic Corp.

1	9.15	27.00	55.00
2-4	5.35	16.00	32.00

GUNSMOKE WESTERN (Formerly Western Tales of Black Rider)
No. 32, Dec, 1955 - No. 77, July, 1963
Atlas Comics No. 32-35(CPS/NPI); **Marvel** No. 36 on

32-Baker & Drucker-a	13.50	41.00	95.00
33,35,36-Williamson-a in each: 5,6 & 4 pgs. plus Drucker-a #33. 33-Kinstler-a?			
	11.00	33.00	75.00
34-Baker-a, 4 pgs.; Kirby-c	8.35	25.00	50.00
37-Davis-a(2); Williamson text illo	9.15	27.00	55.00
38,39: 39-Williamson text illo (unsigned)	6.70	20.00	40.00
40-Williamson/Mayo-a (4 pgs.)	8.35	25.00	50.00
41,42,45,46,48,49,52-54,57,58,60: 49,52-Kid from Texas story. 57-1st Two Gun Kid by Severin. 60-Sam Hawk app. in Kid Colt			
	4.25	13.00	26.00
43,44-Torres-a	5.00	15.00	30.00
47-Kirby-a	5.00	15.00	30.00

Guy Gardner #42 © DC

The Hacker Files #6 © DC

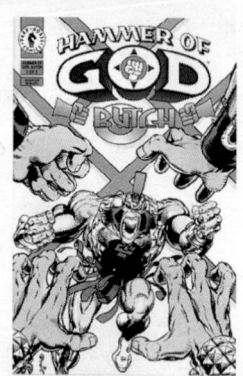

Hammer of God: Butch #1 © Mike Baron & Steve Rude

	GD25	FN65	NM94
50-Kirby, Crandall-a	6.70	20.00	40.00
51,59-Kirby-a	5.00	15.00	30.00
55,56-Matt Baker-a	5.85	17.50	35.00
61-Crandall-a	5.85	17.50	35.00
62-67,69,71,73,77-Kirby-a	4.15	12.50	25.00
68,70,74-76	3.25	9.50	22.00
72-Origin Kid Colt	3.75	11.25	28.00

NOTE: **Colan** a-35-37, 39, 72, 76. **Davis** a-37, 52, 54, 55; c-50, 54. **Ditko** a-66; c-56p. **Drucker** a-32-34. **Heath** c-33. **Jack Keller** a-35, 40, 60, 72; c-72. **Kirby** a-47, 50, 51, 59, 62(3), 63-67, 69, 71, 73, 77; c-56(w/Ditko),57, 58, 60, 61(w/Ayers), 62, 63, 66, 68, 69, 71-77. **Robinson** a-35. **Severin** a-35, 59-61; c-34, 35, 39, 42, 43. **Tuska** a-34. **Wildey** a-10, 37, 42, 56, 57. Kid Colt in all. Two-Gun Kid in No. 57, 59, 60-63. Wyatt Earp in No. 45, 48, 49, 52, 54, 55, 58.

GUNS OF FACT & FICTION (Also see A-1 Comics)
No. 13, 1948 (one-shot)
Magazine Enterprises

A-1 13-Used in **SOTI**, pg. 19; Ingels & J. Craig-a	25.00	75.00	175.00

GUN THAT WON THE WEST, THE
1956 (Giveaway, 24 pgs.)
Winchester-Western Division & Olin Mathieson Chemical Corp.

nn-Painted-c	4.70	14.00	28.00

GUY GARDNER (Guy Gardner: Warrior #17 on)(Also see Green Lantern #59)
Oct, 1992 - No. 44, July, 1996 ($1.25/$1.50/$1.75)
DC Comics

1-24,0,26-30: 1-Staton-c/a(p) begins. 6-Guy vs. Hal Jordan. 8-Vs. Lobo-c/story. 15-JLA x-over. 16-Begin $1.50-c. 18-Begin 4-part Emerald Fallout story; splash page x-over GL #50. 18-21-Vs. Hal Jordan. 24-(9/94)-Zero Hour. 0-(10/94)			1.50
25 (11/94, $2.50, 52 pgs.)		1.00	2.50
29 ($2.95)-Gatefold-c		1.20	3.00
29-Variant-c (Edward Hopper's Nighthawks)			1.50
31-44: 31-$1.75-c begins. 40-Gorilla Grodd-c/app. 44-Parallax-c/app. (1 pg.)			
Annual 1 (1995, $3.50)-Year One story		1.40	3.50
Annual 2 (1996, $2.95)-Legends of the Dead Earth story			3.00

GUY GARDNER REBORN
1992 - Book 3, 1992 ($4.95, limited series)
DC Comics

1-3: Staton-c/a(p). 1-Lobo-c/cameo. 2,3-Lobo-c/s	1.00	2.00	5.00

GYPSY COLT
No. 568, June, 1954 (one-shot)
Dell Publishing Co.

Four Color 568--Movie	5.00	15.00	50.00

GYRO GEARLOOSE (See Dynabrite Comics, Walt Disney's C&S #140 & Walt Disney Showcase #18)
No. 1047, Nov-Jan/1959-60 - May-July, 1962 (Disney)
Dell Publishing Co.

Four Color 1047 (No. 1)-All Barks-c/a	17.50	52.50	175.00
Four Color 1095,1184-All by Carl Barks	11.00	33.00	110.00
Four Color 1267-Barks c/a, 4 pgs.	7.50	22.50	75.00
01329-207 (#1, 5-7/62)-Barks-c only (intended as 4-Color 1329?)	5.00	15.00	50.00

HACKER FILES, THE
Aug, 1992 - No. 12, July, 1993 ($1.95)
DC Comics

1-12: 1-Sutton-a(p) begins; computer generated-c		.80	2.00

HAGAR THE HORRIBLE (See Comics Reading Libraries)

HA HA COMICS (Teepee Tim No. 100 on; also see Giggle Comics)
Oct, 1943 - No. 99, Jan, 1955
Scope Mag.(Creston Publ.) No. 1-80/American Comics Group

1-Funny animal	27.00	81.00	190.00
2	13.00	39.00	90.00

	GD25	FN65	NM94
3-5: Ken Hultgren-a begins?	10.00	30.00	65.
6-10	8.35	25.00	50.
11-20: 14-Infinity-c	6.35	19.00	38.
21-40	5.00	15.00	30.
41-94,96-99: 49-X-Mas-c	4.25	13.00	26.0
95-3-D effect-c	12.00	36.00	85.0

HAIR BEAR BUNCH, THE (TV) (See Fun-In No. 13)
Feb, 1972 - No. 9, Feb, 1974 (Hanna-Barbera)
Gold Key

1	1.40	4.20	14.0
2-9	.90	2.70	9.0

HALL OF FAME FEATURING THE T.H.U.N.D.E.R. AGENTS
May, 1983 - No. 3, Dec, 1983
JC Productions(Archie Comics Group)

1-3: Thunder Agents-r(Crandall, Tuska, Wood-a)			1.2

HALLOWEEN HORROR
Oct, 1987 (Seduction of the Innocent #7)($1.75)
Eclipse Comics

1-Pre-code horror-r		.75	1.8

HALLOWEEN MEGAZINE
Dec, 1996 ($3.95, one-shot, 96 pgs.)
Marvel Comics

1-Reprints Tomb of Dracula			4.0

HALO, AN ANGEL'S STORY
Apr, 1996 - No. 3, 1996 ($2.95, limited series)
Sirius Entertainment

1-3: Knowles-c/a/scripts			3.0

HALO JONES (See The Ballad of...)

HAMMERLOCKE
Sept, 1992 - No. 9, May, 1993 ($1.75, limited series)
DC Comics

1-($2.50, 52 pgs.)-Chris Sprouse-c/a in all		1.00	2.5
2-9		.70	1.7

HAMMER OF GOD (Also see Nexus)
Feb, 1990 - No. 4, May, 1990 ($1.95, limited series)
First Comics

1-4		1.00	2.0

HAMMER OF GOD: BUTCH
May, 1994 - No. 4, Aug, 1994 ($2.50, limited series)
First Comics

1-3		1.00	2.5

HAMMER OF GOD: PENTATHLON
Jan, 1994 ($2.50, one shot)
First Comics

1-character from Nexus		1.00	2.5

HAMMER OF GOD: SWORD OF JUSTICE
Feb 1991 - Mar 1991 ($4.95, limited series, squarebound, 52 pgs.)
First Comics

V2#1,2	1.00	2.50	5.0

HANDBOOK OF THE CONAN UNIVERSE, THE
June, 1985 ($1.25, one-shot)
Marvel Comics

1-Kaluta-c.			1.2

HAND OF FATE (Formerly Men Against Crime)
No. 8, Dec, 1951 - No. 26, March, 1955 (Weird/horror stories)(Two #25's)

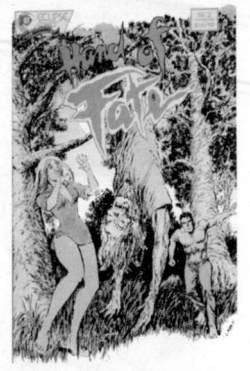
Hand of Fate #2 © ECL

Hangman Comics #4 © MLJ

Happy Birthday Martha Washington © Frank Miller & Dave Gibbons

	GD25	FN65	NM94
ce Magazines			
8-Surrealistic text story	30.00	90.00	210.00
9,10	17.00	51.00	120.00
1-18,20,22,23	13.50	41.00	95.00
9-Bondage, hypo needle scenes	15.00	45.00	105.00
1-Necronomicon story; drug belladonna used	17.00	51.00	120.00
4-Electric chair-c	21.00	64.00	150.00
5a(11/54), 25b(12/54)-Both have Cameron-a	10.00	30.00	75.00
6-Nostrand-a; exist?	13.50	41.00	95.00

NOTE: *Cameron a-9, 10, 19-25a, 25b; c-13. Sekowsky a-8, 9, 13, 14.*

AND OF FATE
eb, 1988 - No. 3, Apr, 1988 ($1.75/$2.00, Baxter paper)
clipse Comics

1,2		.90	1.75
3-$2.00-c; B&W		1.00	2.00

ANDS OF THE DRAGON
une, 1975
eaboard Periodicals (Atlas)

1-Origin; Mooney inks			1.00

ANGMAN COMICS (Special Comics No. 1; Black Hood No. 9 on)
Also see Flyman, Mighty Comics, Mighty Crusaders & Pep Comics)
o. 2, Spring, 1942 - No. 8, Fall, 1943
MLJ Magazines

2-The Hangman, Boy Buddies begin	150.00	450.00	1200.00
3-8: 3-Beheading splash pg.; 1st Nazi war-c. 5-1st Jap war-c. 8-2nd app. Super Duck (ties w/Jolly Jingles #11)	87.00	262.00	700.00

NOTE: *Fuje a-7(3), 8(3); c-3. Reinman c/a-3. Bondage c-3. Sahle c-6.*

ANK
946
entagon Publishing Co.

n-Coulton Waugh's newspaper reprint	7.00	21.00	42.00

ANNA-BARBERA (See Golden Comics Digest No. 2, 7, 11)

ANNA-BARBERA ALL-STARS
ct, 1995 - No. 6, Sept, 1996 ($1.50, bi-monthly)
rchie Publications

1-6			1.50

ANNA-BARBERA BAND WAGON (TV)
ct, 1962 - No. 3, Apr, 1963
old Key

1,2-Giants, 84 pgs. 1-Augie Doggie & Lippy the Lion app. (pre-#1's)	8.50	25.50	85.00
3-Regular size; Mr. & Mrs. J. Evil Scientist app. (pre-#1) & Snagglepuss app.	5.00	15.00	50.00

ANNA-BARBERA GIANT SIZE
ct, 1992 ($2.25, 68 pgs.)
arvey Comics

2#1-Flintstones, Yogi Bear, Magilla Gorilla, Huckleberry Hound, Quick Draw McGraw, Yakky Doodle & Chopper, Jetsons & others		.90	2.25

ANNA-BARBERA HI-ADVENTURE HEROES (See Hi-Adventure...)

ANNA-BARBERA PARADE (TV)
ept, 1971 - No. 10, Dec, 1972
harlton Comics

1	4.85	14.50	34.00
2-10: 7-(52 pgs.)- "Summer Picnic"	2.85	8.50	20.00

NOTE: *No. 4 (1/72) went on sale late in 1972 with the January 1973 issues.*

ANNA-BARBERA PRESENTS
ov, 1995 - Present ($1.50, bi-monthly)
rchie Publications

1-6: 2-Wacky Races. 4-Quick Draw McGraw & Magilla Gorilla. 5-A Pup Named Scooby-Doo			1.50

HANNA-BARBERA SPOTLIGHT (See Spotlight)

HANNA-BARBERA SUPER TV HEROES (TV)
Apr, 1968 - No. 7, Oct, 1969 (Hanna-Barbera)
Gold Key

1-The Birdman, The Herculoids(ends #6; not in #2), Moby Dick, Young Samson & Goliath(ends #2,4), and The Mighty Mightor begin; Spiegle-a in all	11.00	33.00	110.00
2-The Galaxy Trio app.; Shazzan begins; 12 & 15 cent versions exist	9.50	28.50	95.00
3-7: 3,6,7-The Space Ghost app.	9.00	27.00	90.00

HANNA-BARBERA TV FUN FAVORITES (See Golden Comics Digest #2,7,11)

HANNA-BARBERA (TV STARS) (See TV Stars)

HANS BRINKER (Disney)
No. 1273, Feb, 1962 (one-shot)
Dell Publishing Co.

Four Color 1273-Movie, photo-c	8.00	24.00	80.00

HANS CHRISTIAN ANDERSEN
1953 (100 pgs., Special Issue)
Ziff-Davis Publ. Co.

nn-Danny Kaye (movie)-Photo-c; fairy tales	16.00	47.00	110.00

HANSEL & GRETEL
No. 590, Oct, 1954 (one-shot)
Dell Publishing Co.

Four Color 590-Partial photo-c	6.00	18.00	60.00

HANSI, THE GIRL WHO LOVED THE SWASTIKA
1973, 1976 (39¢/49¢)
Spire Christian Comics (Fleming H. Revell Co.)

nn			1.00

HAP HAZARD COMICS (Real Love No. 25 on)
Summer, 1944 - No. 24, Feb, 1949 (#1-6 are quarterly issues)
Ace Magazines (Readers' Research)

1	11.00	33.00	75.00
2	6.35	19.00	38.00
3-10	4.25	13.00	26.00
11-13,15-24	4.00	10.00	20.00
14-Feldstein-c (4/47)	7.00	21.00	42.00

HAP HOPPER (See Comics Revue No. 2)

HAPPIEST MILLIONAIRE, THE (See Movie Comics)

HAPPINESS AND HEALING FOR YOU (Also see Oral Roberts'...)
1955 (36 pgs., slick cover) (Oral Roberts Giveaway)
Commercial Comics

nn	8.35	25.00	50.00

NOTE: *The success of this book prompted Oral Roberts to go into the publishing business himself to produce his own material.*

HAPPI TIM (See March of Comics No. 182)

HAPPY BIRTHDAY MARTHA WASHINGTON (Also see Give Me Liberty, Martha Washington Goes To War, & Martha Washington Stranded In Space)
Mar, 1995 ($2.95, one-shot)
Dark Horse Comics

1-Miller script; Gibbons-c/a		1.20	3.00

HAPPY COMICS (Happy Rabbit No. 41 on)
Aug, 1943 - No. 40, Dec, 1950 (Companion to Goofy Comics)
Nedor Publ./Standard Comics (Animated Cartoons)

1-Funny animal	22.00	66.00	155.00
2	11.50	34.00	80.00

Harbinger #41 © Yoyager Comm.

Hardcase #10 © Malibu

Hardware #36 © Millestone Media

	GD25	FN65	NM94
3-10	8.35	25.00	50.00
11-19	5.85	17.50	35.00
20-31,34-37-Frazetta text illos in all (2 in #34&35, 3 in #27,28,30). 27-Al Fago-a			
	7.50	22.50	45.00
32-Frazetta-a, 7 pgs. plus 2 text illos; Roussos-a	16.00	47.00	110.00
33-Frazetta-a(2), 6 pgs. each (Scarce)	23.00	69.00	160.00
38-40	4.00	12.00	24.00

HAPPY DAYS (TV)(See Kite Fun Book)
Mar, 1979 - No. 6, Feb, 1980
Gold Key

1-Photo-c of TV cast	1.00	2.60	6.00
2-6		1.60	4.00

HAPPY HOLIDAY (See March of Comics No. 181)

HAPPY HOULIHANS (Saddle Justice No. 3 on; see Blackstone, The Magician Detective)
Fall, 1947 - No. 2, Winter, 1947-48
E. C. Comics

1-Origin Moon Girl (same date as Moon Girl #1)	40.00	120.00	300.00
2	22.00	66.00	155.00

HAPPY JACK
Aug, 1957 - No. 2, Nov, 1957
Red Top (Decker)

V1#1,2	4.00	10.00	20.00

HAPPY JACK HOWARD
1957
Red Top (Farrell)/Decker

nn-Reprints Handy Andy story from E. C. Dandy Comics #5, renamed "Happy Jack"	4.00	12.00	24.00

HAPPY RABBIT (Formerly Happy Comics)
No. 41, Feb, 1951 - No. 48, April, 1952
Standard Comics (Animated Cartoons)

41-Funny animal	4.25	13.00	28.00
42-48	3.60	9.00	18.00

HARBINGER (Also see Unity)
Jan, 1992 - No. 41, June, 1995 ($1.95/$2.50)
Valiant

0-(Advance)	1.30	3.25	8.00
1-1st app.	1.00	2.00	5.00
2,3		1.60	4.00
4-Low print run	1.00	2.00	5.00
5-10: 8,9-Unity x-overs. 8-Miller-c. 9-Simonson-c. 10-1st app. H.A.R.D Corps (10/92)		1.20	3.00
11-16: 14-1st app. Stronghold		1.00	2.50
17-24,26-41: 18-Intro Screen. 19-1st app. Stunner. 22-Archer & Armstrong app. 24-Cover similar to #1. 26-Intro New Harbingers. 29-Bound-in trading card. 30-H.A.R.D. Corps app. 32-Eternal Warrior app. 33-Dr. Eclipse app.			
		1.00	2.50
25-($3.50, 52 pgs.)-Harada vs. Sting	1.40	3.50	
...Files 1,2 (8/94,2/95 $2.50)		1.00	2.50
Trade paperback nn (11/92, $9.95)-Reprints #1-4 & comes polybagged with a copy of Harbinger #0 w/new-c.	1.70	5.00	12.00

NOTE: Issues 1-6 have coupons with origin of Harada and are redeemable for Harbinger #0 .

HARD BOILED
9/90 - #3, 1992 ($4.95/$5.95, 8 1/2 x11", limited series, mature)
Dark Horse Comics

1-($4.95)-Miller scripts; Darrow-c/a; sexually explicit & violent			
		2.50	5.00
2,3-($5.95)		3.00	6.00

HARDCASE (See Break Thru, Flood Relief & Ultraforce, 1st Series)

June, 1993 - No. 26, Aug, 1995 ($1.95/$2.50)
Malibu Comics (Ultraverse)

1-Intro Hardcase; Dave Gibbons-c; has coupon for Ultraverse Premiere #0; Jim Callahan-a(p) begin, ends #3		1.60	4.0
1-With coupon missing			1.5
1-Platinum Edition	1.00	2.00	5.0
1-Holographic Cover Edition; 1st full-c holograph tied w/Prime 1 & Strangers			
	1.65	4.20	10.0
1-Ultra Limited silver foil-c	1.00	2.00	5.0
2,3-Callahan-a		1.10	2.7
2-($2.50)-Newsstand edition bagged w/trading card		1.00	2.5
4,6-15, 17-19: 4-Strangers app. 7-Break-Thru x-over. 8-Solution app. 9-Vs. Turf. 12-Silver foil logo, wraparound-c. 17-Prime app.	.80		2.0
5-($2.50, 48 pgs.)-Rune flip-c/story by B. Smith (3 pgs.)		1.00	2.5
16 ($3.50, 68 pgs.)-Rune pin-up		1.40	3.5
20-26: 20-$2.50-c begins. 23-Loki app.		1.00	2.5

NOTE: Perez a-8(2); c-20.

H.A.R.D. CORPS, THE (See Harbinger #10)
Dec, 1992 - No. 30, Feb, 1995 ($2.25) (Harbinger spin-off)
Valiant

1-(Advance)	1.00	2.00	5.0
1-($2.50)-Gatefold-c by Jim Lee & Bob Layton		1.00	2.5
1-Gold variant	1.00	2.00	5.0
2-6: 5-Bloodshot-c/story cont'd from Bloodshot #3		.90	2.2
5-Variant edition; came w/Comic Defense System		1.20	3.0
7-30: 10-Turok app. 17-vs. Armorines. 18-Bound-in trading card. 20-Harbinger app.		.90	2.2

HARDWARE
Apr, 1993 - Present ($1.50/$1.75/$2.50)
DC Comics (Milestone)

1-($2.95)-Collector's Edition polybagged w/poster & trading card (direct sale only)		1.20	3.0
1-Platinum Edition	1.00	2.00	5.0
1-15,17-19: 11-Shadow War x-over. 11,14-Simonson-c. 12-Buckler-a(p). 17-Worlds Collide Pt. 2. 18-Simonson-c; Worlds Collide Pt. 9. 15-1st Humberto Ramos DC work			1.5
16-($3.95, 52 pgs.)-Collector's Edition w/gatefold 2nd cover by Byrne; new armor; Icon app.		1.60	4.0
16-($2.50, 52 pgs.)-Newsstand Edition		1.00	2.5
20-24, 26-28: 20-Begin $1.75-c begins		.70	1.7
25-($2.95, 52 pgs.)		1.20	3.0
29-50: 29-Begin $2.50-c		1.00	2.5

HARDY BOYS, THE (Disney)
No. 760, Dec, 1956 - No. 964, Jan, 1959 (Mickey Mouse Club)
Dell Publishing Co.

Four Color 760 (#1)-Photo-c	11.00	33.00	110.0
Four Color 830(8/57), 887(1/58), 964-Photo-c	10.00	30.00	100.0

HARDY BOYS, THE (TV)
Apr, 1970 - No. 4, Jan, 1971
Gold Key

1	2.00	6.00	20.0
2-4	1.50	4.50	15.0

HARI KARI
No. 0, 1995 -No. 1, 1995 ($2.95)
Blackout Comics

0,1: Both have pin-ups. 1-Variant-c.			3.0
1 Commemorative ($9.95)-New-c; foil stamped; 2,500 copies.			10.0

HARI KARI PRIVATE GALLERY
No. 0, Feb, 1996 ($2.95, one-shot)
Blackout Comics

Hari Kari #0 © Blackout

Harlan Ellison's Dream Corridor Special © Harlan Ellison

Harriers #1 © Entity

	GD25	FN65	NM94

0-pin-ups   3.00
0 Commemorative ($9.95)   10.00

HARI KARI: THE BEGINNING
1996 ($2.95)
Blackout Comics

1-Origin   3.00

HARI KARI: THE SILENCE OF EVIL
No. 0, 1996 ($2.95, bi-monthly)
Blackout Comics

0   3.00

HARLAN ELLISON'S DREAM CORRIDOR
Mar, 1995 - No. 5, July, 1995 ($2.95, anthology)
Dark Horse Comics

1-5: Adaptation of Ellison stories. 1-4-Byrne-a.		1.20	3.00
Special (1/95, $4.95)	1.00	2.00	5.00
Trade paperback-(1996, $18.95, 192 pgs)-r/#1-5 & Special #1			
			19.00

HARLAN ELLISON'S DREAM CORRIDOR QUARTERLY
V2#1, Aug, 1996 ($5.95, anthology, squarebound)
Dark Horse Comics

V2#1-Adaptations of Ellison's stories w/new material; Neal Adams-a   6.00

HARLEM GLOBETROTTERS (TV) (See Fun-In No. 8, 10)
Apr, 1972 - No. 12, Jan, 1975 (Hanna-Barbera)
Gold Key

1	1.30	3.25	8.00
2-12		1.60	4.00

NOTE: #4, 8, and 12 contain 16 extra pages of advertising.

HAROLD TEEN (See Popular Comics, & Super Comics)
No. 2, 1942 - No. 209, Jan, 1949
Dell Publishing Co.

Four Color 2	25.00	75.00	250.00
Four Color 209	4.00	12.00	40.00

HARRIERS
June, 1995 - No. 3, 1995 ($2.50)
Entity Comics

1-Foil-c; polybagged w/PC game	1.20	3.00	7.00
1-3 ($2.50)		1.00	2.50

HARROWERS, THE (See Clive Barker's...)

HARSH REALM
1994 ($2.95, one-shot)
Harris Comics

1-4: Painted-c   1.20   3.00

HARVEY
Oct, 1970; No. 2, 12/70; No. 3, 6/72 - No. 6, 12/72
Marvel Comics

1	1.30	3.25	8.00
2-6		1.60	4.00

HARVEY COLLECTORS COMICS (Richie Rich Collectors Comics #10 on, cover title only)
Sept, 1975 - No. 15, Jan, 1978; No. 16, Oct, 1979 (52 pgs.)
Harvey Publications

1-Reprints Richie Rich #1,2	1.00	2.00	5.00
2-10: 7-Splash pg. shows-c to Friendly Ghost Casper #1			
		1.20	3.00
11-16: 16-Sad Sack-r			1.25

NOTE: All reprints: Casper-#2, 7, Richie Rich-#1, 3, 5, 6, 8-15, Sad Sack-#16. Wendy-#4. #6 titled 'Richie Rich...' on inside.

HARVEY COMICS HITS (Formerly Joe Palooka #50)
No. 51, Oct, 1951 - No. 62, Apr, 1953
Harvey Publications

51-The Phantom	24.00	73.00	170.00
52-Steve Canyon's Air Power(Air Force sponsored)	11.50	34.00	80.00
53-Mandrake the Magician	19.00	56.00	130.00
54-Tim Tyler's Tales of Jungle Terror	10.00	30.00	70.00
55-Love Stories of Mary Worth	5.35	16.00	32.00
56-The Phantom; bondage-c	21.00	62.00	145.00
57-Rip Kirby Exposes the Kidnap Racket; entire book by Alex Raymond			
	13.00	39.00	90.00
58-Girls in White (nurses stories)	5.00	15.00	30.00
59-Tales of the Invisible featuring Scarlet O'Neil	10.00	30.00	60.00
60-Paramount Animated Comics #1 (2nd app. Baby Huey); 1st Harvey app. Baby Huey & Casper the Friendly Ghost; 1st app. Herman & Catnip (c/story) & Buzzy the Crow (9/52)	37.00	111.00	260.00
61-Casper the Friendly Ghost #6 (2nd Harvey Casper, 10/52)-Casper-c			
	38.00	114.00	265.00
62-Paramount Animated Comics #2; Herman & Catnip, Baby Huey & Buzzy the Crow	11.00	33.00	75.00

HARVEY COMICS LIBRARY
Apr, 1952 - No. 2, 1952
Harvey Publications

1-Teen-Age Dope Slaves as exposed by Rex Morgan, M.D.; drug propaganda story; used in **SOTI**, pg. 27	68.00	206.00	550.00
2-Dick Tracy Presents Sparkle Plenty in "Blackmail Terror"			
	16.00	47.00	110.00

HARVEY COMICS SPOTLIGHT
Sept, 1987 - No. 4, Mar, 1988 (75¢/$1.00)
Harvey Comics

1-4: 1,2,4-All new material. 1-Begin 75¢-c, ends #3; Sad Sack. 2-Baby Huey. 3-Little Dot; contains reprints w/5 pg. new story. 4-$1.00-c; Little Audrey   1.00

NOTE: No. 5 was advertised but not published.

HARVEY HITS
Sept, 1957 - No. 122, Nov, 1967
Harvey Publications

1-The Phantom	29.00	86.00	200.00
2-Rags Rabbit (10/57)	4.00	10.00	20.00
3-Richie Rich (11/57)-r/Little Dot; 1st book devoted to Richie Rich; see Little Dot for 1st app.	87.00	262.00	700.00
4-Little Dot's Uncles (12/57)	17.00	51.00	120.00
5-Stevie Mazie's Boy Friend (1/58)	2.80	7.00	14.00
6-The Phantom (2/58); Kirby-c; 2pg. Powell-a	20.00	60.00	140.00
7-Wendy the Good Little Witch (3/58, pre-dates Wendy #1; 1st book devoted to Wendy)	20.00	60.00	140.00
8-Sad Sack's Army Life; George Baker-c	6.70	20.00	40.00
9-Richie Rich's Golden Deeds; reprints (2nd book devoted to Richie Rich)			
	43.00	128.00	340.00
10-Little Lotta's Lunch Box	11.50	34.00	80.00
11-Little Audrey Summer Fun (7/58)	9.15	27.00	55.00
12-The Phantom; Kirby-c; 2pg. Powell-a (8/58)	16.00	47.00	110.00
13-Little Dot's Uncles (9/58); Richie Rich 1pg.	10.00	30.00	70.00
14-Herman & Katnip (10/58, TV/movies)	3.60	9.00	18.00
15-The Phantom (12/58)-1 pg. origin	16.00	47.00	110.00
16-Wendy the Good Little Witch (1/59); Casper app.	10.00	30.00	70.00
17-Sad Sack's Army Life (2/59)	5.85	17.50	35.00
18-Buzzy & the Crow	4.00	10.00	20.00
19-Little Audrey (4/59)	5.85	17.50	35.00
20-Casper & Spooky	7.50	22.50	45.00
21-Wendy the Witch	6.70	20.00	40.00
22-Sad Sack's Army Life	5.00	15.00	30.00

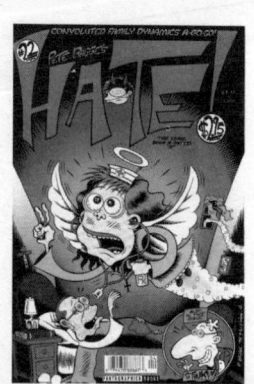

Hate #22 © Peter Bagge

Haunted #17 © CC

Haunted Love #8 © CC

	GD25	FN65	NM94
23-Wendy the Witch (8/59)	6.70	20.00	40.00
24-Little Dot's Uncles (9/59); Richie Rich 1pg.	9.15	27.00	55.00
25-Herman & Katnip (10/59)	2.80	7.00	14.00
26-The Phantom (11/59)	13.00	39.00	90.00
27-Wendy the Good Little Witch (12/59)	6.70	20.00	40.00
28-Sad Sack's Army Life (1/60)	3.60	9.00	18.00
29-Harvey-Toon (No.1)('60); Casper, Buzzy	4.70	14.00	28.00
30-Wendy the Witch (3/60)	6.70	20.00	40.00
31-Herman & Katnip (4/60)	1.80	4.50	9.00
32-Sad Sack's Army Life (5/60)	2.80	7.00	14.00
33-Wendy the Witch (6/60)	6.70	20.00	40.00
34-Harvey-Toon (7/60)	3.20	8.00	16.00
35-Funday Funnies (8/60)	1.80	4.50	9.00
36-The Phantom (1960)	11.00	33.00	75.00
37-Casper & Nightmare	5.00	15.00	30.00
38-Harvey-Toon	3.20	8.00	16.00
39-Sad Sack's Army Life (12/60)	2.80	7.00	14.00
40-Funday Funnies (1/61)	1.20	3.00	6.00
41-Herman & Katnip	1.60	4.00	8.00
42-Harvey-Toon (3/61)	2.40	6.00	12.00
43-Sad Sack's Army Life (4/61)	2.40	6.00	12.00
44-The Phantom (5/61)	10.00	30.00	70.00
45-Casper & Nightmare	4.00	11.00	22.00
46-Harvey-Toon (7/61)	2.00	5.00	10.00
47-Sad Sack's Army Life (8/61)	2.40	6.00	12.00
48-The Phantom (9/61)	10.00	30.00	70.00
49-Stumbo Harvey-Toon (1st app. in Hot Stuff)	10.00	30.00	60.00
50-Harvey-Toon (11/61)	2.00	5.00	10.00
51-Sad Sack's Army Life (12/61)	2.40	6.00	12.00
52-Casper & Nightmare	4.00	11.00	22.00
53-Harvey-Toons (2/62)	1.60	4.00	8.00
54-Stumbo the Giant	5.00	15.00	30.00
55-Sad Sack's Army Life (4/62)	2.40	6.00	12.00
56-Casper & Nightmare	4.00	11.00	22.00
57-Stumbo the Giant	5.00	15.00	30.00
58-Sad Sack's Army Life	2.40	6.00	12.00
59-Casper & Nightmare (7/62)	4.00	11.00	22.00
60-Stumbo the Giant (9/62)	5.00	15.00	30.00
61-Sad Sack's Army Life	2.00	5.00	10.00
62-Sad Sack's Army Life	3.60	9.00	18.00
63-Stumbo the Giant	4.70	14.00	28.00
64-Sad Sack's Army Life (1/63)	2.00	5.00	10.00
65-Casper & Nightmare	3.60	9.00	18.00
66-Stumbo The Giant (3/63)	4.70	14.00	28.00
67-Sad Sack's Army Life (4/63)	2.00	5.00	10.00
68-Casper & Nightmare	3.60	9.00	18.00
69-Stumbo the Giant (6/63)	4.70	14.00	28.00
70-Sad Sack's Army Life (7/63)	2.00	5.00	10.00
71-Casper & Nightmare (8/63)	2.40	6.00	12.00
72-Stumbo the Giant	4.70	14.00	28.00
73-Little Sad Sack (10/63)	2.00	5.00	10.00
74-Sad Sack's Muttsy… (11/63)	2.00	5.00	10.00
75-Casper & Nightmare	2.40	6.00	12.00
76-Little Sad Sack	2.00	5.00	10.00
77-Sad Sack's Muttsy…	2.00	5.00	10.00
78-Stumbo the Giant (3/64); JFK caricature	4.70	14.00	28.00
79-87: 79-Little Sad Sack (4/64). 80-Sad Sack's Muttsy… (5/64). 81-Little Sad Sack. 82-Sad Sack's Muttsy… 83-Little Sad Sack(8/64). 84-Sad Sack's Muttsy… 85-Gabby Gob (#1)(10/64). 86-G. I. Juniors (#1)(11/64). 87-Sad Sack's Muttsy… (12/64)	2.00	5.00	10.00
88-Stumbo the Giant (1/65)	4.70	14.00	28.00
89-122: 89-Sad Sack's Muttsy… 90-Gabby Gob. 91-G. I. Juniors. 92-Sad Sack's Muttsy… (5/65). 93-Sadie Sack (6/65). 94-Gabby Gob. 95-G. I. Juniors (8/65). 96-Sad Sack's Muttsy… (9/65). 97-Gabby Gob (10/65). 98-			

	GD25	FN65	NM94
G. I. Juniors (11/65). 99-Sad Sack's Muttsy… (12/65). 100-Gabby Gob(1/66) 101-G. I. Juniors (2/66). 102-Sad Sack's Muttsy… (3/66). 103-Gabby Gob. 104- G. I. Juniors. 105-Sad Sack's Muttsy… 106-Gabby Gob (7/66). 107-G. Juniors (8/66). 108-Sad Sack's Muttsy… 109-Gabby Gob. 110-G. I. Juniors (11/66). 111-Sad Sack's Muttsy… (12/66). 112-G. I. Juniors. 113-Sad Sack's Muttsy… 114-G. I. Juniors. 115-Sad Sack's Muttsy… 116-G. I. Juniors (5/67) 117-Sad Sack's Muttsy… 118-G. I. Juniors. 119-Sad Sack's Muttsy… (8/67) 120-G. I. Juniors (9/67). 121-Sad Sack's Muttsy… (10/67). 122-G. I. Juniors (11/67)	1.20	3.00	7.00

HARVEY HITS COMICS
Nov, 1986 - No. 6, Oct, 1987
Harvey Publications

1-6-Little Lotta, Little Dot, Wendy & Baby Huey: 3-Xmas-c			1.00

HARVEY POP COMICS (Teen Humor)
Oct, 1968 - No. 2, Nov, 1969 (Both are 68 pg. Giants)
Harvey Publications

1,2: 1-The Cowsills. 2-Bunny	2.30	6.70	23.00

HARVEY 3-D HITS (See Sad Sack)

HARVEY-TOON (…S) (See Harvey Hits No. 29, 34, 38, 42, 46, 50, 53)

HARVEY WISEGUYS (…Digest #? on)
Nov, 1987; #2, Nov, 1988; #3, Apr, 1989 - No. 4, Nov, 1989 (98 pgs., digest-size, $1.25/$1.75)
Harvey Comics

1,2: 1-Hot Stuff, Spooky, etc. 2 (68 pgs.)			1.20
3,4		.70	1.75

HATARI (See Movie Classics)

HATE
Spr, 1990 - Present ($2.50/$2.95, B&W/color)
Fantagraphics Books

1	2.85	8.50	20.00
2-3	2.15	6.50	15.00
4-10	1.30	3.25	8.00
11-15		1.60	4.00
16-24: 16-$2.95-c & color begins		1.20	3.00
Hate-Ball Special Edition ($3.95, giveaway)-reprints		1.60	4.00

HATHAWAYS, THE (TV)
No. 1298, Feb-Apr, 1962 (one-shot)
Dell Publishing Co.

Four Color 1298-Photo-c	4.50	14.00	45.00

HAUNTED (See This Magazine Is Haunted)

HAUNTED (Baron Weirwulf's Haunted Library #21 on)
9/71 - No. 30, 11/76; No. 31, 9/77 - No. 75, 9/84
Charlton Comics

1	1.30	3.25	8.00
2-5		1.60	4.00
6-21		1.20	3.00
22-75: 51-Reprints #1. 64,75-Reprints			1.50

NOTE: **Aparo** c-45. **Ditko** a-1-8, 11-16, 18, 23, 24, 28, 30, 34r, 36r, 39-42r, 47r, 49-51r, 57, 60, 74. c-1-7, 11, 13, 14, 16, 30, 41, 47, 49-51, 74. **Howard** a-18, 22, 32. **Morisi** a-13. **Newton** a-1 21, 59r; c-21, 22(painted). **Staton** a-18, 21, 22, 30, 33; c-18, 33. **Sutton** a-21, 22, 38; c-15, 17, 18, 23(painted), 24(painted), 64r. #49 reprints Tales of the Mysterious Traveler #4.

HAUNTED LOVE
Apr, 1973 - No. 11, Sept, 1975
Charlton Comics

1-Tom Sutton-a (16 pgs.)	1.30	3.25	8.00
2,3,6-11		.80	2.00
4,5-Ditko-a		1.00	2.50
Modern Comics #1(1978)			1.00

NOTE: **Howard** a-8i. **Newton** c-8, 9. **Staton** a-5.

Haunt of Fear #5 (1993) © WMG

Hawk and Dove #1 © DC

Hawkeye #2 © MEG

	GD25	FN65	NM94

HAUNTED THRILLS (Tales of Horror and Terror)
June, 1952 - No. 18, Nov-Dec, 1954
Ajax/Farrell Publications

1-r/Ellery Queen #1	34.00	103.00	240.00
2-L. B. Cole-a r-/Ellery Queen #1	21.00	64.00	150.00
3-5: 3-Drug use story	19.00	56.00	130.00
6-10,12: 7-Hitler story.	16.00	47.00	110.00
11-Nazi death camp story	17.00	51.00	120.00
13,16-18: 18-Lingerie panels	13.00	39.00	90.00
14-Jesus Christ apps. in story by Webb	13.00	39.00	90.00
15-Jo-Jo-r	13.00	39.00	90.00

NOTE: *Kamenish art in most issues. Webb a-12.*

HAUNT OF FEAR (Formerly Gunfighter)
No. 15, May-June, 1950 - No. 28, Nov-Dec, 1954
E. C. Comics

15(#1, 1950)(Scarce)-1st app. Old Witch	238.00	712.00	1900.00
16	94.00	281.00	750.00
17-Origin of Crypt of Terror, Vault of Horror, & Haunt of Fear; used in SOTI, pg. 43; last pg. Ingels-a used by N.Y. Legis. Comm.; story "Monster Maker" based on Frankenstein	94.00	281.00	750.00
4	65.00	197.00	525.00
5-Injury-to-eye panel, pg. 4 of Wood story	49.00	145.00	390.00
6-10: 8-Shrunken head cover. 10-Ingels biog.	36.00	109.00	255.00
11-13,15-18: 11-Kamen biog. 12-Feldstein biog. 16,18-Ray Bradbury adaptations. 18-Ray Bradbury biography	27.00	81.00	190.00
14-Origin Old Witch by Ingels	40.00	120.00	290.00
19-Used in SOTI, ill. "A comic book baseball game" & Senate investigation on juvenile delinq. bondage/decapitation-c	37.00	111.00	260.00
20-Feldstein-r/Vault of Horror #12	25.00	75.00	175.00
21,22,25,27: 27-Cannibalism story; Wertham cameo	17.00	49.00	115.00
23-Used in SOTI, pg. 241	17.00	51.00	120.00
24-Used in Senate Investigative Report, pg.8	16.00	47.00	110.00
26-Contains anti-censorship editorial, 'Are you a Red Dupe?'	16.00	47.00	110.00
28-Low distribution	17.00	51.00	120.00

NOTE: (Canadian reprints known; see Table of Contents). *Craig a-15-17, 5, 7, 10, 12, 13; c-15-17, 5-7. Crandall a-20, 21, 26, 27. Davis a-4-26, 28. Evans a-15-19, 22-25, 27. Feldstein a-15-17, 20; c-4, 8-10. Ingels a-16, 17, 4-28; c-11-28. Kamen a-16, 4, 6, 7, 9-11, 13-19, 21-28. Krigstein a-28. Kurtzman a-15(#1), 17(#3). Orlando a-9, 12. Wood a-15, 16, 4-6.*

HAUNT OF FEAR, THE
May, 1991 - No. 2, July, 1991 ($2.00, 68 pgs.)
Gladstone Publishing

1,2: 1-Ghastly Ingels-c(r); 2-Craig-c(r)		1.00	2.50

HAUNT OF FEAR
Sept, 1991 - No. 5, 1992 ($2.00, 68 pgs.)
Nov, 1992 - Present ($1.50/$2.00/$2.50)
Russ Cochran/Gemstone Publishing

1-Ingels-c(r)		1.00	2.50
2-5		.80	2.00
1-3: 1-3-r/HOF #15-17 with original-c			1.50
4-15: 4,5-r/HOF #4,5 with original-c		.80	2.00
16-20			2.50

HAUNT OF HORROR, THE (Magazine)
May, 1974 - No. 5, Jan, 1975 (75¢) (B&W)
Cadence Comics Publ. (Marvel)

1	1.00	2.50	6.00
2,4: 2-Origin & 1st app. Gabriel the Devil Hunter; Satana begins. 4-Neal Adams-a	1.00	2.00	5.00
3,5: 5-Evans-a(2)		1.60	4.00

NOTE: *Alcala a-2. Colan a-2p. Heath r-1. Krigstein r-3. Reese a-1. Simonson a-1.*

HAVE GUN, WILL TRAVEL (TV)

No. 931, 8/58 - No. 14, 7-9/62 (All Richard Boone photo-c)
Dell Publishing Co.

Four Color 931 (#1)	14.00	42.00	140.00
Four Color 983,1044 (#2,3)	9.00	27.00	90.00
4 (1-3/60) - 14	7.00	21.00	70.00

HAVOK & WOLVERINE - MELTDOWN (See Marvel Comics Presents #24)
Mar, 1989 - No. 4, Oct, 1989 ($3.50, mini-series, squarebound, mature)
Marvel Comics (Epic Comics)

1-4: Violent content		1.40	3.50

HAWAIIAN EYE (TV)
July, 1963 (Troy Donahue, Connie Stevens photo-c)
Gold Key

1 (10073-307)	4.00	12.00	40.00

HAWAIIAN ILLUSTRATED LEGENDS SERIES
1975 (B&W)(Cover printed w/blue, yellow, and green)
Hogarth Press

1-Kalelealuaka, the Mysterious Warrior			1.20
2,3(Exist?)			1.00

HAWK, THE (Also see Approved Comics #1, 7 & Tops In Adventure)
Wint/51 - No. 3, 11-12/52; No. 4, 1953 - No. 12, 5/55 (Painted c-1-4)
Ziff-Davis/St. John Publ. Co. No. 4 on

1-Anderson-a	19.00	56.00	130.00
2 (Sum, '52)-Kubert, Infantino-a	10.00	30.00	70.00
3-7,11: 11-Buckskin Belle & The Texan app.	9.15	27.00	55.00
8-Reprints #3 w/different-c by Baker	10.00	30.00	65.00
9-Baker-c/a; Kubert-a(r)/#2	10.00	30.00	65.00
10-Baker-c/a; r/one story from #2	10.00	30.00	65.00
12-Baker-c/a; Buckskin Belle app.	10.00	30.00	65.00
3-D 1(11/53, 25¢)-Came w/glasses; Baker-c	31.00	94.00	220.00

NOTE: *Baker c-8-12. Larsen a-10. Tuska a-1, 9, 12. Painted c-1, 4, 7.*

HAWK AND DOVE (2nd Series)
Oct, 1988 - No. 5, Feb, 1989 ($1.00, limited series)
DC Comics

1-Rob Liefeld-c/a(p) in all		1.20	3.00
2-5		.80	2.00
Trade paperback ('93, $9.95)-Reprints #1-5	1.65	4.00	10.00

HAWK AND DOVE
June, 1989 - No. 28, Oct, 1991 ($1.00)
DC Comics

1-28			1.00
Annual 1 (1990, $2.00)-Liefeld pin-up		.80	2.00
Annual 2 (1991)-Armageddon 2001 x-over		.80	2.00

HAWK AND THE DOVE, THE (See Showcase #75 & Teen Titans) (1st series)
Aug-Sept, 1968 - No. 6, June-July, 1969
National Periodical Publications

1-Ditko-c/a	6.50	19.50	45.00
2-6: 5-Teen Titans cameo	5.00	15.00	35.00

NOTE: *Ditko c/a-1, 2. Gil Kane a-3p, 4p, 5, 6p; c-3-6.*

HAWKEYE (See The Avengers #16 & Tales Of Suspense #57)
Sept, 1983 - No. 4, Dec, 1983 (limited series)
Marvel Comics Group

1-4: Mark Gruenwald-a/scripts. 1-Origin Hawkeye. 3-Origin Mockingbird. 4-Hawkeye & Mockingbird elope			1.00

HAWKEYE
Jan, 1994 - No. 4, Apr, 1994 ($1.75, limited series)
Marvel Comics

1-4		.70	1.75

HAWKEYE & THE LAST OF THE MOHICANS (TV)

Hawkman (2nd Series) #10 © DC

Hawkworld #3 © DC

Hazard #4 © Aegis Entertainment

	GD25	FN65	NM94

No. 884, Mar, 1958 (one-shot)
Dell Publishing Co.

Four Color 884-Photo-c	7.00	21.00	70.00

HAWKMAN (See Atom & Hawkman, The Brave & the Bold, DC Comics Presents, Detective, Flash Comics, Hawkworld, Justice League of America #31, Mystery in Space, Shadow War Of..., Showcase, & World's Finest #256)

HAWKMAN (1st Series) (Also see The Atom #7 & Brave & the Bold #34-36, 42-44, 51)
Apr-May, 1964 - No. 27, Aug-Sept, 1968
National Periodical Publications

1-(4-5/64)-Anderson-c/a begins, ends #21	61.00	185.00	525.00
2	26.00	77.00	180.00
3,5	17.00	49.00	115.00
4-Origin & 1st app. Zatanna (10-11/64)	19.00	56.00	150.00
6	14.00	43.00	100.00
7	13.00	39.00	90.00
8-10: 9-Atom cameo; Hawkman & Atom learn each other's I.D.; 2nd app. Shadow Thief	11.00	33.00	75.00
11-15	8.00	24.00	56.00
16-27: 18-Adam Strange x-over (cameo #19). 25-G.A. Hawkman-r by Moldoff. 27-Kubert-c	6.50	19.50	45.00

HAWKMAN (2nd Series)
Aug, 1986 - No. 17, Dec, 1987
DC Comics

1-17: 10-Byrne-c			1.00
Special #1 (1986, $1.25)			1.50
Trade paperback (1989, $19.95)-r/Brave and the Bold #34-36,42-44 by Kubert; Kubert-c	3.20	8.00	20.00

HAWKMAN (4th Series)(See both Hawkworld limited & ongoing series)
Sept, 1993 - No. 32, July, 1996 ($1.75/$1.95/$2.25)
DC Comics

1-($2.50)-Gold foil embossed-c; storyline cont'd from Hawkworld series; new costume & powers.	1.00		2.50
2-11: 2-Green Lantern x-over. 3-Airstryke app. 4,6-Wonder Woman app.		.70	1.75
12,13,0,14-20: 12-Begin $1.95-c. 13-(9/94)-Zero Hour. 0-(10/94). 14-(11/94). 15-Aquaman-c & begin.		.80	2.00
21-32: 21-Begin $2.25-c. 23-Wonder Woman app. 25-Kent Williams-c. 29,30-Chaykin-c. 32-Breyfogle-c		.90	2.25
Annual 1 (1993, $2.50, 68 pgs.)-Bloodlines Eathplague	1.00		2.50
Annual 2 (1995, $3.95)-Year One story	1.60		4.00

HAWKMOON: COUNT BRASS
Feb, 1989 - No. 4, Aug, 1989 ($1.95, limited series, Baxter paper)
First Comics

1-4: Adapts novel by Michael Moorcock	1.00		2.00

HAWKMOON: THE JEWEL IN THE SKULL
May, 1986 - No. 4, Nov, 1986 ($1.75, limited series, Baxter paper)
First Comics

1-4: Adapts novel by Michael Moorcock		.80	2.00

HAWKMOON: THE MAD GOD'S AMULET
Jan, 1987 - No. 4, July, 1987 ($1.75, limited series, Baxter paper)
First Comics

1-4: Adapts novel by Michael Moorcock		.80	2.00

HAWKMOON: THE RUNESTAFF
June, 1988 - No. 4, Dec, 1988 ($1.75-$1.95, limited series, Baxter paper)
First Comics

1-4: ($1.75) Adapts novel by Michael Moorcock. 3,4 ($1.95)	.80		2.00

HAWKMOON: THE SWORD OF DAWN
Sept, 1987 - No. 4, Mar, 1988 ($1.75, limited series, Baxter paper)

	GD25	FN65	NM94

First Comics

1-4: Dorman painted-c; adapts Moorcock novel		.80	2.00

HAWKWORLD
1989 - No. 3, 1989 ($3.95, prestige format, limited series)
DC Comics

Book 1-Tim Truman story & art in all; Hawkman dons new costume; reintro Byth.		1.60	4.00
Books 2,3		1.60	4.00

HAWKWORLD (3rd Series)
June, 1990 - No. 32, Mar, 1993 ($1.50/$1.75)
DC Comics

1-Hawkman spin-off; story cont'd from limited series.	1.00		2.50
2-32: 15,16-War of the Gods x-over. 22-J'onn J'onzz app.		.70	1.75
Annual 1-3 ('90-'92, $2.95, 68 pgs.)	1.20		3.00
Annual 2-2nd printing with silver ink-c	1.20		3.00
NOTE: *Truman* a-30-32; c-27-32, Annual 1.			

HAWTHORN-MELODY FARMS DAIRY COMICS
No date (1950's) (Giveaway)
Everybody's Publishing Co.

nn-Cheerie Chick, Tuffy Turtle, Robin Koo Koo, Donald & Longhorn Legends	1.60	4.00	8.00

HAYWIRE
Oct, 1988 - No. 13, Sept, 1989 ($1.25, mature)
DC Comics

1-13			1.30

HAZARD
June, 1996 - Present ($1.75)
Image Comics (Wildstorm Productions)

1-6: 1-Intro Hazard; Jeff Marriotte scripts begin; Jim Lee-c(p).			1.75

HEADLINE COMICS (...For the American Boy) (...Crime No. 32-39)
Feb, 1943 - No. 22, Nov-Dec, 1946; No. 23, 1947 - No. 77, Oct, 1956
Prize Publications

1-Junior Rangers-c/stories begin; Yank & Doodle x-over in Junior Rangers (Junior Rangers are Uncle Sam's nephews)	39.00	116.00	270.00
2	17.00	49.00	115.00
3-Used in POP, pg. 84	13.00	39.00	90.00
4-7,9,10: 4,9,10-Hitler stories in each	12.00	36.00	85.00
8-Classic Hitler-c	29.00	86.00	200.00
11,12	9.15	27.00	55.00
13-15-Blue Streak in all	10.00	30.00	65.00
16-Origin & 1st app. Atomic Man (11-12/45)	20.00	60.00	140.00
17,18,20,21: 21-Atomic Man ends (9-10/46)	10.00	30.00	65.00
19-S&K-a	22.00	66.00	155.00
22-Last Junior Rangers; Kiefer-c	6.70	20.00	40.00
23,24: (All S&K-a). 23-Valentine's Day Massacre story; content changes to true crime. 24-Dope-crazy killer story	21.00	62.00	145.00
25-35-S&K-c/a. 25-Powell-a	18.00	54.00	125.00
36-S&K-a; photo-c begin	13.50	41.00	95.00
37-1 pg. S&K, Severin-a; rare Kirby photo-c app.	14.00	43.00	100.00
38,40-Meskin-a	4.25	13.00	28.00
39,41,42,46-48,50,52-55: 41-J. Edgar Hoover 26th Anniversary Issue with photo on-c	4.00	10.00	20.00
43,49-Meskin-a	4.00	11.00	22.00
44-S&K-c; Severin/Elder, Meskin-a	9.15	27.00	55.00
45-Kirby-a	6.70	20.00	40.00
51-Kirby-c	4.25	13.00	26.00
56-S&K-a	9.15	27.00	55.00
57-77: 72-Meskin-c/a(i)	3.20	8.00	16.00
NOTE: *Hollingsworth* a-30. Photo c-36-43. **H. C. Kiefer** c-12-16, 22. Atomic Man c-17-19.			

Heartbreakers #1 © DH

Heart Of Darkness #1 © Hardline Studios

Heathcliff #55 © Geo Gately

	GD25	FN65	NM94

HEADMAN
1990 ($2.50, mature)
Innovation Publishing

1-Sci/fi		1.25	2.50

HEAP, THE
Sept, 1971 (52 pgs.)
Skywald Publications

1-Kinstler-r/Strange Worlds #8		1.20	3.00

HEART AND SOUL
April-May, 1954 - No. 2, June-July, 1954
Mikeross Publications

1,2	5.85	17.50	35.00

HEARTBREAKERS (Also see Dark Horse Presents)
Apr, 1996 - No. 4, July, 1996 ($2.95, limited series)
Dark Horse Comics

1-4: 1-W/paper doll & pin-up. 2-Ross pin-up. 3-Evan Dorkin pin-ups.			
4-Brereton-c; Matt Wagner pin-up			3.00

HEART OF DARKNESS
1994 ($2.95)
Hardline Studios

1-Brereton-c		1.20	3.00

HEART OF THE BEAST, THE
1994 ($19.95, hardcover, mature)
DC Comics (Vertigo)

1-Dean Motter scripts	3.00	8.60	20.00

HEARTS OF DARKNESS (See Ghost Rider; Wolverine; Punisher: Hearts of...)

HEART THROBS (Love Stories No. 147 on)
8/49 - No. 8, 10/50; No. 9, 3/52 - No. 146, Oct, 1972
Quality Comics/National Periodical #47(4-5/57) on (Arleigh #48-101)

1-Classic Ward-c, Gustavson-a, 9 pgs.	37.00	111.00	260.00
2-Ward-c/a (9 pgs); Gustavson-a	21.00	64.00	150.00
3-Gustavson-a	7.50	22.50	45.00
4,6,8-Ward-a, 8-9 pgs.	11.00	33.00	75.00
5,7	4.25	13.00	28.00
9-Robert Mitchum, Jane Russell photo-c	8.35	25.00	50.00
10,15-Ward-a	10.00	30.00	60.00
11-14,16-20: 12 (7/52)	4.00	12.00	24.00
21-Ward-c	8.35	25.00	50.00
22,23-Ward-a(p)	5.85	17.50	35.00
24-33: 33-Last pre-code (3/55)	4.00	11.00	22.00
34-39,41-46 (12/56; last Quality issue)	3.60	9.00	18.00
40-Ward-a; r-7 pgs.#21	5.35	16.00	32.00
47-(4-5/57); 1st DC issue)	31.00	94.00	220.00
48-60	11.00	33.00	75.00
61-70	8.35	25.00	50.00
71-100: 74-Last 10 cent issue	6.70	20.00	40.00
101-The Beatles app. on-c	11.50	34.00	80.00
102-120: 102-123-(Serial)-Three Girls, Their Lives, Their Loves. 120-Neal			
Adams-c	2.15	6.50	15.00
121-146: #133-142, 52 pgs.	1.30	3.25	8.00

NOTE: **Gustavson** a-8. **Tuska** a-128. Photo c-4, 5, 8-10, 15, 17.

HEATHCLIFF (See Star Comics Magazine)
Apr, 1985 - No. 56, Feb, 1991 (#16-on, $1.00)
Marvel Comics (Star Comics)/Marvel Comics No. 23 on

1-49,51-56: Post-a most issues. 43-X-Mas issue. 47-Batman parody			
(Catman vs. the Soaker)			1.00
50-($1.50, 52 pgs.)			1.50
Annual 1 ('87)			1.20

HEATHCLIFF'S FUNHOUSE

May, 1987 - No. 10, 1988
Marvel Comics (Star Comics)/Marvel Comics No. 6 on

1-10			1.00

HEAVY HITTERS
1993 ($3.75, 68 pgs.)
Marvel Comics (Epic Comics)

1-Bound w/trading card; Lawdog, Feud, Alien Legion, Trouble With Girls,			
& Spyke		1.50	3.75

HECKLE AND JECKLE (See Blue Ribbon, Giant Comics Edition #5A & 10,
Paul Terry's, Terry-Toons Comics)
10/51 - No. 24, 10/55; No. 25, Fall/56 - No. 34, 6/59
St. John Publ. Co. No. 1-24/Pines No. 25 on

1-Funny animal	25.00	75.00	175.00
2	13.00	39.00	90.00
3-5	10.00	30.00	70.00
6-10	7.50	22.50	45.00
11-20	5.85	17.50	35.00
21-34: 25-Begin CBS Television Presents on-c	4.35	13.00	26.00

HECKLE AND JECKLE (TV) (See New Terrytoons)
11/62 - No. 4, 8/63; 5/66; No. 2, 10/66; No. 3, 8/67
Gold Key/Dell Publishing Co.

1 (11/62; Gold Key)	6.00	18.00	60.00
2-4	2.40	7.20	24.00
1 (5/66; Dell)	3.00	9.00	30.00
2,3	2.20	6.60	22.00

(See March of Comics No. 379, 472, 484)

HECKLE AND JECKLE 3-D
1987 - No. 2?, 1987 ($2.50)
Spotlight Comics

1,2		1.25	2.50

HECTOR COMICS (The Keenest Teen in Town)
Nov, 1953 - No. 3, 1954
Key Publications

1-Teen humor	4.00	11.00	22.00
2,3	2.80	7.00	14.00

HECTOR HEATHCOTE (TV)
Mar, 1964
Gold Key

1 (10111-403)	4.50	14.00	45.00

HECTOR THE INSPECTOR (See Top Flight Comics)

HEDY DEVINE COMICS (Formerly All Winners #21? or Teen #22?(6/47);
Hedy of Hollywood #36 on; also see Annie Oakley, Comedy & Venus)
No. 22, Aug, 1947 - No. 50, Sept, 1952
Marvel Comics (RCM)/Atlas #50

22-1st app. Hedy Devine (also see Joker #32)	11.50	34.00	85.00
23,24,27-30: 23-Wolverton-a, 1 pg; Kurtzman's "Hey Look", 2 pgs. 24,27-30-			
"Hey Look" by Kurtzman, 1-3 pgs.	13.00	39.00	90.00
25-Classic "Hey Look" by Kurtzman, "Optical Illusion"			
	13.50	41.00	95.00
26- "Giggles 'n' Grins" by Kurtzman	10.00	30.00	60.00
31-34,36-50: 32-Anti-Wertham editorial	6.70	20.00	40.00
35-Four pgs. "Rusty" by Kurtzman	11.00	33.00	75.00

HEDY-MILLIE-TESSIE COMEDY (See Comedy Comics)

HEDY WOLFE (Also see Patsy & Hedy & Miss America Magazine V1#2)
Aug, 1957
Atlas Publishing Co. (Emgee)

1-Patsy Walker's rival; Al Hartley-c	9.15	27.00	55.00

HEE HAW (TV)

Hellblazer #60 © DC

Hellboy: Wake The Devil #5 © Mike Mignola

Hellina: Heart of Thorns #1 © Lightning Comics

	GD25	FN65	NM94		GD25	FN65	NM94

July, 1970 - No. 7, Aug, 1971
Charlton Press

1	2.30	6.75	16.00
2-7	1.65	4.20	10.00

HEIDI (See Dell Jr. Treasury No. 6)
HELEN OF TROY (Movie)
No. 684, Mar, 1956 (one-shot)
Dell Publishing Co.

Four Color 684-Buscema-a, photo-c 11.00 33.00 110.00

HELLBLAZER (John Constantine) (See Saga of Swamp Thing #37) (Also see Books of Magic limited series)
Jan, 1988 - Present ($1.25/$1.50/$2.25, mature)
DC Comics (Vertigo imprint #63 on)

1-(44 pgs.)-John Constantine 2.85 8.50 20.00
2-5 1.65 4.20 10.00
6-10: 9-X-over w/Swamp Thing #76. 9,10-Swamp Thing cameo
 1.00 2.00 5.00
11-20: 19-Dave McKean-c 1.60 4.00
21-26,28-30: 24-Contains bound-in Shocker movie poster. 25,26-Grant Morrison scripts. 1.20 3.00
27-Neil Gaiman scripts; Dave McKean-a; fold-out guide to Nightbreed
 1.65 4.20 10.00
31-39,41-49: 36-Preview of World Without End. 41-Ennis scripts begins; ends #83. 44-Delano $1.75-c. 44,45-Sutton-a(i) 1.00 2.50
40-($2.25, 52 pgs.)-Dave McKean-a & colors; preview of Kid Eternity
 1.40 3.50
50-($3.00, 52 pgs.) 1.60 4.00
51-65: 52-Glenn Fabry painted-c begin. 62-Special Death insert by McKean. 63-Silver metallic ink on-c .80 2.00
66-74,76-88: 66-Begin $1.95-c. 77-Totleben-c. 84-Sean Phillips-c/a begins; Delano story. 85-88-Eddie Campbell story. .80 2.00
75-($2.95, 52 pgs.) 1.20 3.00
89-99,101-120: 89-Paul Jenkins scripts begin; begin $2.25-c.
 .90 2.25
100 ($3.50, 48 pgs.) 1.40 3.50
Annual 1 (1989, $2.95, 68 pgs.)-Bryan Talbot's 1st work in American comics
 1.00 2.00 5.00
Special 1 (1993, $3.95, 68 pgs.)-Ennis story; w/pin-ups.
 1.00 2.00 5.00
NOTE: **Alcala** a-8i, 9i, 18-22i. **Gaiman** scripts-27. **McKean** a-27; c-19. **Sutton** a-44i, 45i. **Talbot** a-Annual 1.

HELLBOY: SEED OF DESTRUCTION (See Dark Horse Presents & San Diego Comic Con #2) (Also see Danger Unlimited #4 & Ghost/Hellboy)
Mar, 1994 - No. 4, June, 1994 ($2.50, limited series)
Dark Horse Comics (Legend)

1-4-Mignola-c/a w/Byrne scripts; Monkeyman & O'Brien back-up story (origin) by Art Adams. 1.60 4.00
Trade paperback (1994, $17.95)-collects all four issues plus r/Hellboy's 1st app. in San Diego Comic Con #2 & pin-ups 2.60 7.50 18.00
Limited edition hardcover (1995, $99.95)-includes everything in trade paperback plus additional material. 14.00 43.00 100.00
HELLBOY: THE CORPSE AND THE IRON SHOES
Jan, 1996 ($2.95, one-shot)
Dark Horse Comics (Legend)

nn-Mignola-c/a/scripts; reprints "The Corpse" serial from Advance Comics w/new story 3.00
HELLBOY: THE WOLVES OF ST. AUGUST
1995 ($4.95, squarebound, one-shot)
Dark Horse Comics (Legend)

nn-Mignola--c/a/scripts; r/Dark Horse Presents #88-91 with additional story.
 1.00 2.00 5.00

HELLBOY: WAKE THE DEVIL
June, 1996 - No. 5, Oct, 1996 ($2.95, limited series)(Sequel to Seed of Destruction)
Dark Horse Comics (Legend)

1-5: Mignola-c/a & scripts; The Monstermen back-up story by Gary Gianni.
 3.00

HELLHOUNDS (...: Panzer Cops #3-6)
1994 - No. 6, July, 1994 ($2.50, B&W, limited series)
Dark Horse

1,3-5: 1-Hamner-c. 3-(4/94) 1.00 2.50
2,6-($2.95, 52 pgs.): 2-Joe Phillips-c 1.20 3.00
HELLHOUND, THE REDEMPTION QUEST
Dec, 1993 - No. 4, Mar, 1994 ($2.25, limited series, coated stock)
Marvel Comics (Epic Comics)

1-4 .90 2.25
HELLINA
Sept, 1994 ($2.75/$9.95, B&W, one-shot)
Lightning Comics

1-Origin; pin-up gallery 1.20 3.00
1 ($9.95)-Nude Edition 1.65 4.20 10.00
HELLINA/CATFIGHT
Oct, 1995 ($2.75, B&W, one-shot)
Lightning Comics

1 2.75
1 ($9.95)-Nude Edition 10.00
HELLINA/DOUBLE IMPACT
Feb, 1996 ($3.00, one-shot)
Lightning Comics

1, 1b: 1b-Cleary-c. 3.00
1 ($9.95)-Nude edition; polybagged. 10.00
HELLINA: GENESIS
Apr, 1996 ($3.50, B&W, one-shot)
Lightning Comics

1-polybagged w/poster 3.50
1 ($9.95)-Nude Edition 10.00
1 ($20.00)-Platinum Edition 20.00
HELLINA: HEART OF THORNS
July, 1996 - No. 2, ($2.75/$3.00, limited series)
Lightning Comics

1-Flip book w/Moxi story 3.00
1,2A,2B-($9.95): All Nude Editions 10.00
2A,2B 2.75
2-($5.95)-Platinum Edition 6.00
HELLINA: KISS OF DEATH
July, 1995 ($2.75/$9.95/$20.00, B&W)
Lightning Comics

1 1.20 3.00
1 ($9.95)-Nude Edition 1.65 4.20 10.00
1 ($20.00)-Gold Edition 20.00
HELLINA: TAKING BACK THE NIGHT
Apr, 1995 ($2.75, B&W, one-shot)
Lightning Comics

1 1.20 3.00
HELLINA: WICKED WAYS
Nov, 1995 ($2.75/$9.95, B&W, one-shot)
Lightning Comics

1,1b: 1b-Trent Kaniuga-c; polybagged. 1.10 2.75

Hellshock #1 © Jae Lee

Herbie #1 © ACG

Hercules #3 © MEG

	GD25	FN65	NM94

1-($9.95)-Nude Edition 10.00

HELLO, I'M JOHNNY CASH
1976 (39/49¢)
Spire Christian Comics (Fleming H. Revell Co.)

nn 1.00

HELL ON EARTH (See DC Science Fiction Graphic Novel)

HELLO PAL COMICS (Short Story Comics)
Jan, 1943 - No. 3, May, 1943 (Photo-c)
Harvey Publications

1-Rocketman & Rocketgirl begin; Yankee Doodle Jones app.; Mickey Rooney photo-c	56.00	168.00	450.00
2-Charlie McCarthy photo-c (scarce)	47.00	142.00	380.00
3-Bob Hope photo-c	45.00	136.00	365.00

HELLRAISER/NIGHTBREED – JIHAD (Also see Clive Barker's...)
1991 - Book 2, 1991 ($4.50, 52 pgs.)
Epic Comics (Marvel Comics)

Book 1,2 .... 2.25 4.50

HELL-RIDER (Magazine)
Aug, 1971 - No. 2, Oct, 1971 (B&W)
Skywald Publications

1,2: 1-Origin & 1st app.; Butterfly & Wildbunch begins	1.00	2.00	5.00

NOTE: #3 advertised in Psycho #5 but did not come out. **Buckler** a-1, 2. **Morrow** c-3.

HELL'S ANGEL (Becomes Dark Angel #6 on)
July, 1992 - No. 5, Nov, 1993 ($1.75)
Marvel Comics UK

1-5: X-Men (Wolverine, Cyclops)-c/stories. 1-Origin. 3-Jim Lee cover swipe		.70	1.75

HELLSHOCK
July, 1994 - No. 4, Nov, 1994 ($1.95, limited series)
Image Comics

1-4-Jae Lee-c/a & scripts. 4-variant-c.		.80	2.00

HELLSTORM: PRINCE OF LIES (See Ghost Rider #1 & Marvel Spotlight #12)
Apr, 1993 - No. 21, Dec, 1994 ($2.00)
Marvel Comics

1-($2.95)-Parchment-c w/red thermographic ink		1.20	3.00
2-21: 14-Bound-in trading card sheet. 18-P. Craig Russell-c		.80	2.00

HE-MAN (See Masters Of The Universe)

HE-MAN (Also see Tops In Adventure)
Fall, 1952
Ziff-Davis Publ. Co. (Approved Comics)

1-Kinstler painted-c; Powell-a	12.00	36.00	85.00

HE-MAN
May, 1954 - No. 2, July, 1954 (Painted-c by B. Safran)
Toby Press

1	11.00	33.00	75.00
2	10.00	30.00	60.00

HENNESSEY (TV)
No. 1200, Aug-Oct, 1961 - No. 1280, Mar-May, 1962
Dell Publishing Co.

Four Color 1200-Gil Kane-a, photo-c	7.00	21.00	70.00
Four Color 1280-Photo-c	7.00	21.00	70.00

HENRY (Also see Little Annie Rooney)
1935 (52 pgs.) (Daily B&W strip reprints)(10"x10" cardboard-c)
David McKay Publications

1-By Carl Anderson	36.00	107.00	250.00

HENRY (See King Comics & Magic Comics)
No. 122, Oct, 1946 - No. 65, Apr-June, 1961
Dell Publishing Co.

Four Color 122-All new stories begin	13.00	39.00	130.00
Four Color 155 (7/47)	8.00	24.00	80.00
1 (1-3/48)-All new stories	8.00	24.00	80.00
2	3.60	10.80	36.00
3-10	3.20	9.60	32.00
11-20: 20-Infinity-c	2.60	7.50	18.00
21-30	2.00	6.00	14.00
31-40	1.50	3.75	9.00
41-65	1.20	3.00	7.00

HENRY (See Giant Comic Album and March of Comics No. 43, 58, 84, 101, 112, 129, 147, 162, 178, 189)

HENRY ALDRICH COMICS (TV)
Aug-Sept, 1950 - No. 22, Sept-Nov, 1954
Dell Publishing Co.

1-Part series written by John Stanley; Bill Williams-a	8.00	24.00	80.00
2	4.00	12.00	40.00
3-5	3.50	10.50	35.00
6-10	2.80	8.40	28.00
11-22	2.00	6.00	20.00
Giveaway (16 pgs., soft-c, 1951)-Capehart radio	4.00	11.00	22.00

HENRY BREWSTER
Feb, 1966 - V2#7, Sept, 1967 (All 25¢ Giants)
Country Wide (M.F. Ent.)

1	1.20	3.00	6.00
2-6(12/66)-Powell-a in most	.80	2.00	4.00
V2#7	.60	1.50	3.00

HERBIE (See Forbidden Worlds & Unknown Worlds)
April-May, 1964 - No. 23, Feb, 1967 (All 12¢)
American Comics Group

1-Whitney-c/a in most issues	18.00	54.00	135.00
2-4	9.30	28.00	70.00
5-Beatles, Dean Martin, F. Sinatra app.	11.00	33.00	85.00
6,7,9,10	7.00	20.00	50.00
8-Origin & 1st app. The Fat Fury	8.00	25.00	65.00
11-23: 14-Nemesis & Magicman app. 17-r/2nd Herbie from Forbidden Worlds #94. 23-r/1st Herbie from F.W. #73	4.60	14.00	35.00

HERBIE
Oct, 1992 - No. 12, 1993 ($2.50, limited series)
Dark Horse Comics

1-6: Whitney-r plus new-c/a. 1-Byrne-c/a & scripts. 3-Bob Burden-c/a. 4-Art Adams-c		1.00	2.50

HERBIE GOES TO MONTE CARLO, HERBIE RIDES AGAIN (See Walt Disney Showcase No. 24, 41)

HERCULES (See Hit Comics #1-21, Journey Into Mystery Annual, Marvel Graphic Novel #37, Marvel Premiere #26 & The Mighty...)

HERCULES
Oct, 1967 - No. 13, Sept, 1969; Dec, 1968
Charlton Comics

1-Thane of Bagarth series begins; Glanzman	1.65	4.20	10.00
2-13: 1-5,7,9,10-Aparo-a	1.20	3.00	7.00
8-(Low distribution)(12/68, 35¢, B&W); magazine format; new Hercules story plus-r story/#1; Thane-r/#1-3	2.85	8.50	20.00
Modern Comics reprint 10('77), 11('78)			1.00

HERCULES (Prince of Power) (Also see The Champions)
V1#1, 10/82 - V1#4, 12/82; V2#1, 3/84 - V2#4, 6/84 (color, both limited series)
Marvel Comics Group

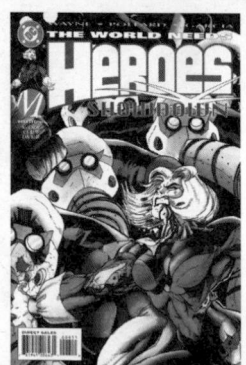
	GD25	FN65	NM94

1-4: Layton-c/a. .65 1.60
V2#1-4: Layton-c/a. 4-Death of Zeus. 1.00
NOTE: **Layton** a-1, 2, 3p, 4p, V2#1-4; c-1-4, V2#1-4.

HERCULES UNBOUND
Oct-Nov, 1975 - No. 12, Aug-Sept, 1977
National Periodical Publications

1-Wood inks begin .80 2.00
2-12: 10-Atomic Knights x-over 1.50
NOTE: **Buckler** c-7p. **Layton** inks-No. 9, 10. **Simonson** a-7-10p, 11, 12; c- 8p, 9-12. **Wood** a-1-8i; c-7i, 8i.

HERCULES (...Unchained #1121) (Movie)
No. 1006, June-Aug, 1959 - No.1121, Aug, 1960
Dell Publishing Co.

Four Color 1006-Buscema-a, photo-c 11.00 33.00 110.00
Four Color 1121-Crandall/Evans-a 10.00 30.00 100.00

HERCULES: THE LEGENDARY JOURNEYS (TV)
June, 1996 - Present ($2.95)
Topps Comics

1-5: 1-Golden-c. 3.00

HERE COMES SANTA (See March of Comics No. 30, 213, 340)

HERE IS SANTA CLAUS
1930s (16 pgs., 8 in color) (stiff paper covers)
Goldsmith Publishing Co. (Kann's in Washington, D.C.)

nn 9.15 27.00 55.00

HERE'S HOW AMERICA'S CARTOONISTS HELP TO SELL U.S. SAVINGS BONDS
1950? (16 pgs., giveaway, paper cover)
Harvey Comics

Contains: Joe Palooka, Donald Duck, Archie, Kerry Drake, Red Ryder, Blondie
& Steve Canyon 15.00 45.00 105.00

HERE'S HOWIE COMICS
Jan-Feb, 1952 - No. 18, Nov-Dec, 1954
National Periodical Publications

1 21.00 64.00 150.00
2 11.00 33.00 75.00
3-5: 5-Howie in the Army issues begin (9-10/52) 8.35 25.00 50.00
6-10 6.70 20.00 40.00
11-18 5.00 15.00 30.00

HERITAGE OF THE DESERT (See Zane Grey, 4-Color 236)

HERMAN & KATNIP (See Harvey Comics Hits #60 & 62, Harvey Hits #14,25,31,41 & Paramount Animated Comics #1)

HERMES VS. THE EYEBALL KID
Dec, 1994 - No. 3, Feb, 1995 ($2.95, B&W, limited series)
Dark Horse Comics

1-3: Eddie Campbell-c/a/scripts 1.20 3.00

HERO (Warrior of the Mystic Realms)
May, 1990 - No. 6, Oct, 1990 ($1.50, limited series)
Marvel Comics

1-6 1.50

HERO ALLIANCE, THE
Dec, 1985 - No. 2, Sept, 1986 (B&W)
Sirius Comics

1,2: 2-($1.50) 1.50
Special Edition 1 (7/86, color) 1.50

HERO ALLIANCE
May, 1987 ($1.95)
Wonder Color Comics

1-Ron Lim-a .80 2.00

HERO ALLIANCE
V2#1, Sept, 1989 - V2#18?, 1991 ($1.95, 28 pgs.)
Innovation Publishing

V2#1-18: 1,2-Ron Lim-a .80 2.00
Annual 1 (1990, $2.75, 36 pgs.)-Paul Smith-c/a 1.15 2.80
Special 1 (1992, $2.50, 32 pgs.)-Stuart Immonen-a (10 pgs.)

HERO ALLIANCE: END OF THE GOLDEN AGE
July, 1989 - No. 3, Aug, 1989 ($1.75, bi-weekly limited series)
Innovation Publishing

1-3: Bart Sears & Ron Lim-c/a; reprints & new-a .75 1.80

HEROES (Also see Shadow Cabinet & Static)
May, 1996 - No. 6, Nov, 1996 ($2.50, limited series)
DC Comics (Milestone)

1-6: 1-Intro Heroes (Iota, Donner, Blitzen, Starlight, Payback & Static)

HEROES AGAINST HUNGER
1986 ($1.50); one-shot for famine relief
DC Comics

1-Superman, Batman app.; Neal Adams-c(p); includes many artists work;
Jeff Jones assist (2 pg.) on B. Smith-a .80 2.00

HEROES ALL CATHOLIC ACTION ILLUSTRATED
1943 - V6#5, Mar 10, 1948 (paper covers)
Heroes All Co.

V1#1,2-(16 pgs., 8x11") 14.00 43.00 100.00
V2#1(1/44)-3(3/44)-(16 pgs., 8x11") 11.50 34.00 80.00
V3#1(1/45)-10(12/45)-(16 pgs., 8x11") 10.00 30.00 70.00
V4#1-35 (12/20/46)-(16 pgs.) 9.15 27.00 55.00
V5#1(1/10/47)-8(2/28/47)-(16 pgs.) 6.70 20.00 40.00
V5#9(3/7/47)-20(11/25/47)-(32 pgs.) 6.70 20.00 40.00
V6#1(1/10/48)-5(3/10/48)-(32 pgs.) 6.70 20.00 40.00

HEROES FOR HOPE STARRING THE X-MEN
Dec, 1985 ($1.50, one-shot, 52pgs., proceeds donated to famine relief)
Marvel Comics Group

1-Stephen King scripts; Byrne, Miller, Corben-a; Wrightson/J. Jones-a (3 pgs.);
Art Adams-c; Starlin back-c 1.20 3.00

HEROES, INC. PRESENTS CANNON
1969 - No. 2, 1976 (Sold at Army PX's)
Wally Wood/CPL/Gang Publ. No. 2

nn-Ditko, Wood-a; Wood-c; Reese-a(p) 1.60 4.00 8.00
2-Wood-c; Ditko, Byrne, Wood-a; 8-1/2x10-1/2"; B&W; $2.00
1.00 2.60 6.00
NOTE: First issue not distributed by publisher; 1,800 copies were stored and 900 copies were stolen from warehouse. Many copies have surfaced in recent years.

HEROES OF THE WILD FRONTIER (Formerly Baffling Mysteries)
No. 27, Jan, 1956 - No. 2, Apr, 1956
Ace Periodicals

27(#1),2-Davy Crockett, Daniel Boone, Buffalo Bill 4.00 12.00 24.00

HERO FOR HIRE (Power Man No. 17 on; also see Cage)
June, 1972 - No. 16, Dec, 1973
Marvel Comics Group

1-Origin & 1st app. Luke Cage; Tuska-a(p) 5.00 15.00 40.00
2-5: 2,3-Tuska-a(p). 3-1st app. Mace. 4-1st app. Phil Fox of the Bugle
1.70 5.00 12.00
6-10: 8,9-Dr. Doom app. 9-F.F. app. 1.00 2.50 6.00
11-16: 14-Origin retold. 15-Everett Subby-r('53). 16-Origin Stilletto; death of
Rackham 1.00 2.50 5.50

HERO HOTLINE (1st app. in Action Comics Weekly #637)
April, 1989 - No. 6, Sept, 1989 ($1.75, limited series)

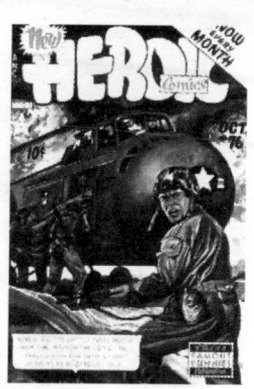

Heroic Comics #76 © EAS

Hex #6 © DC

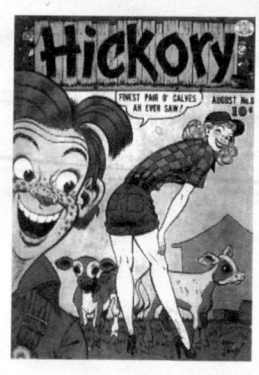

Hickory #6 © QUA

HI

	GD25	FN65	NM94

DC Comics

1-6: Super-hero humor; Schaffenberger-i   .90   1.80

HEROIC ADVENTURES (See Adventures)

HEROIC COMICS (Reg'lar Fellers...#1-15; New Heroic #41 on)
Aug, 1940 - No. 97, June, 1955
Eastern Color Printing Co./Famous Funnies(Funnies, Inc. No. 1)

	GD25	FN65	NM94
1-Hydroman (origin) by Bill Everett, The Purple Zombie (origin) & Mann of India by Tarpe Mills begins (all 1st apps.)	131.00	393.00	1050.00
2	65.00	195.00	520.00
3,4	43.00	128.00	340.00
5,6	39.00	116.00	270.00
7-Origin & 1st app. Man O'Metal (1 pg.)	40.00	120.00	300.00
8-10: 10-Lingerie panels	25.00	75.00	175.00
11,13: 13-Crandall/Fine-a	24.00	71.00	165.00
12-Music Master (origin/1st app.) begins by Everett, ends No. 31; last Purple Zombie & Mann of India	27.00	81.00	190.00
14,15-Hydroman x-over in Rainbow Boy. 14-Origin & 1st app. Rainbow Boy (super hero). 15-1st app. Downbeat	27.00	81.00	190.00
16-20: 16-New logo. 17-Rainbow Boy x-over in Hydroman. 19-Rainbow Boy x-over in Hydroman & vice versa	18.00	54.00	125.00
21-30:25-Rainbow Boy x-over in Hydroman. 28-Last Man O'Metal. 29-Last Hydroman	11.50	34.00	80.00
31,34,38	4.00	11.00	22.00
32,36,37-Toth-a (3-4 pgs. each)	5.85	17.50	35.00
33,35-Toth-a (8 & 9 pgs.)	6.35	19.00	38.00
39-42-Toth, Ingels-a	6.35	19.00	38.00
43,46,47,49-Toth-a (2-4 pgs.). 47-Ingels-a	4.70	14.00	28.00
44,45,50-Toth-a (6-9 pgs.)	5.35	16.00	32.00
48,53,54	4.00	10.00	20.00
51-Williamson-a	5.85	17.50	35.00
52-Williamson-a (3 pg. story)	4.35	13.00	26.00
55-Toth-c/a	5.00	15.00	30.00
56-60-Toth-c. 60-Everett-a	4.35	13.00	26.00
61-Everett-a	4.00	12.00	20.00
62,64-Everett-c/a	4.00	11.00	22.00
63-Everett-c	3.20	8.00	16.00
65-Williamson/Frazetta-a; Evans-a (2 pgs.)	7.00	21.00	42.00
66,75,94-Frazetta-a (2 pgs. each)	4.00	12.00	24.00
67,73-Frazetta-a (4 pgs. each)	4.70	14.00	28.00
68,74,76-80,84,85,88-93,95-97: 95-Last pre-code	3.20	8.00	16.00
69,72-Frazetta-a (6 & 8 pgs. each); 1st (?) app. Frazetta Red Cross ad	7.00	21.00	42.00
70,71,86,87-Frazetta, 3-4 pgs. each; 1 pg. ad by Frazetta in #70	4.00	12.00	24.00
81,82-Frazetta art (1 pg. each): 81-1st (?) app. Frazetta Boy Scout ad (tied w/ Buster Crabbe #9	3.20	8.00	16.00
83-Frazetta-a (1/2 pg.)	3.20	8.00	16.00

NOTE: *Evans a-64, 65. Everett a-(Hydroman-c/a-No. 1-9), 44, 60-64; c-1-9, 62-64. Harvey Fuller c-28-35. Sid Greene a-38-43, 46. Guardineer a-42(3), 43, 44, 45(2), 49(3), 50, 60, 61(2), 65, 67(2) 70-72. Ingels c-41. Kiefer a-46; c-19-22, 24, 44, 46, 48, 51-53, 65, 67-69, 71-74, 76, 77, 79, 80, 82, 85, 86, 88, 89, 94, 95. Mort Lawrence a-45. Tarpe Mills a-2(2), 3(2), 10. Ed Moore a-49, 52-54, 56-63, 65-69, 72-74, 76, 77. H.G. Peter a-58-74, 76, 77, 87. Paul Reinman a-49. Rico a-31. Captain Tootsie by Beck-31, 32. Painted-c #16 on Hydroman c-1-11. Music Master c-12, 13, 15. Rainbow Boy c-14.*

HERO ZERO (Also see Comics' Greatest World & Godzilla Versus Hero Zero)
Sept, 1994 ($2.50)
Dark Horse Comics

0		1.00	2.50

HEX (Replaces Jonah Hex)
Sept, 1985 - No. 18, Feb, 1987 (Story continues from Jonah Hex No. 92)
DC Comics

1-10,14-18: 1-Hex in post-atomic war world; origin. 6-Origin Stiletta		.80	2.00
11-13: All contain future Batman storyline. 13-Intro The Dogs of War (origin #15)		1.00	2.50

NOTE: *Giffen a(p)-15-18; c(p)-15,17,18. Texeira a-1, 2p, 3p, 5-7p, 9p, 11-14p; c(p)-1, 2, 4-7, 12.*

HEXBREAKER (See First Comics Graphic Novel #15)

HEY THERE, IT'S YOGI BEAR (See Movie Comics)

HI-ADVENTURE HEROES (TV)
May, 1969 - No. 2, Aug, 1969 (Hanna-Barbera)
Gold Key

	GD25	FN65	NM94
1-Three Musketeers, Gulliver, Arabian Knights	2.50	7.50	25.00
2-Three Musketeers, Micro-Venture, Arabian Knights	2.20	6.60	22.00

HI AND LOIS
No. 683, Mar, 1956 - No. 955, Nov, 1958
Dell Publishing Co.

Four Color 683 (#1)	3.00	9.00	30.00
Four Color 774(3/57),955	3.00	9.00	30.00

HI AND LOIS
Nov, 1969 - No. 11, July, 1971
Charlton Comics

1	2.00	6.00	14.00
2-11	1.20	2.90	7.00

HICKORY (See All Humor Comics)
Oct, 1949 - No. 6, Aug, 1950
Quality Comics Group

1-Sahl-c/a in all; Feldstein?-a	13.50	41.00	95.00
2	7.50	22.50	45.00
3-6	6.70	20.00	40.00

HIDDEN CREW, THE (See The United States Air Force Presents:...)

HIDE-OUT (See Zane Grey, Four Color No. 346)

HIDING PLACE, THE
1973 (39¢/49¢)
Spire Christian Comics (Fleming H. Revell Co.)

nn			1.00

HIGH ADVENTURE
Oct, 1957
Red Top(Decker) Comics (Farrell)

1-Krigstein-r from Explorer Joe (re-issue on-c)	4.00	11.00	22.00

HIGH ADVENTURE (TV)
No. 949, Nov, 1958 - No. 1001, Aug-Oct, 1959 (Lowell Thomas)
Dell Publishing Co.

Four Color 949 (#1)-Photo-c	5.00	15.00	50.00
Four Color 1001-Lowell Thomas'...(#2)	5.00	15.00	50.00

HIGH CHAPPARAL (TV)
Aug, 1968 (Photo-c)
Gold Key

1 (10226-808)-Tufts-a	4.00	12.00	40.00

HIGH SCHOOL CONFIDENTIAL DIARY (Confidential Diary #12 on)
June, 1960 - No. 11, Mar, 1962
Charlton Comics

1	2.85	8.50	20.00
2-11	1.50	3.75	9.00

HI-HO COMICS
nd (2/46?) - No. 3, 1946
Four Star Publications

1-Funny Animal; L. B. Cole-c	26.00	79.00	185.00
2,3: 2-L. B. Cole-c	16.00	47.00	110.00

Hilly Rose #7 © Astro Comics

Hit Comics #3 © QUA

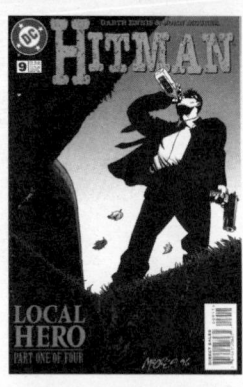
Hitman #9 © DC

	GD25	FN65	NM94

HI-JINX (Teen-age Animal Funnies)
1945; July-Aug, 1947 - No. 7, July-Aug, 1948
La Salle Publ. Co./B&I Publ. Co.(American Comics Group)/Creston

nn-(© 1945, 25 cents, 132 Pgs.)(La Salle)	18.00	54.00	125.00
1-Teen-age, funny animal	14.00	43.00	100.00
2,3	10.00	30.00	60.00
4-7-Milt Gross. 4-X-Mas-c	11.50	34.00	85.00

HI-LITE COMICS
Fall, 1945
E. R. Ross Publishing Co.

1-Miss Shady	13.00	39.00	90.00

HILLBILLY COMICS
Aug, 1955 - No. 4, July, 1956 (Satire)
Charlton Comics

1	7.00	21.00	42.00
2-4	4.25	13.00	26.00

HILLY ROSE'S SPACE ADVENTURES
May, 1995 - Present ($2.95, B&W)
Astro Comics

1-7		1.20	3.00
Trade Paperback (1996, $12.95)-r/#1-5			13.00

HIP-IT-TY HOP (See March of Comics No. 15)

HI-SCHOOL ROMANCE (...Romances No. 41 on)
Oct, 1949 - No. 5, June, 1950; No. 6, Dec, 1950 - No. 73, Mar, 1958;
No. 74, Sept, 1958 - No. 75, Nov, 1958
Harvey Publications/True Love(Home Comics)

1-Photo-c	11.50	34.00	80.00
2-Photo-c	6.70	20.00	40.00
3-9: 3,5-Photo-c	4.25	13.00	28.00
10-Rape story	6.70	20.00	40.00
11-20	3.20	8.00	16.00
21-31	2.80	7.00	14.00
32- "Unholy passion" story	4.25	13.00	28.00
33-36: 36-Last pre-code (2/55)	2.40	6.00	12.00
37-75	2.00	5.00	10.00

NOTE: *Powell* a-1-3, 5, 8, 12-16, 18, 21-23, 25-27, 30-34, 36, 37, 39, 45-48, 50-52, 57, 58, 60, 64, 65, 67, 69.

HI-SCHOOL ROMANCE DATE BOOK
Nov, 1962 - No. 3, Mar, 1963 (25¢ Giants)
Harvey Publications

1-Powell, Baker-a	3.40	10.00	24.00
2,3	1.70	5.00	12.00

HIS NAME IS SAVAGE (Magazine format)
June, 1968 (35¢, 52 pgs.)
Adventure House Press

1-Gil Kane-a	2.85	8.50	20.00

HI-SPOT COMICS (Red Ryder No. 1 & No. 3 on)
No. 2, Nov, 1940
Hawley Publications

2-David Innes of Pellucidar; art by J. C. Burroughs; written by Edgar Rice Burroughs	100.00	300.00	800.00

HISTORY OF THE DC UNIVERSE (Also see Crisis on Infinite Earths)
Sept, 1986 - No. 2, Nov, 1986 ($2.95, limited series)
DC Comics

1,2: 1-Perez-c/a		1.20	3.00
Limited Edition hardcover	6.50	19.50	45.00

HITCHHIKERS GUIDE TO THE GALAXY (See Life, the Universe and Everything & Restaraunt at the End of the Universe)
1993 - No. 3, 1993 ($4.95, limited series)

DC Comics

1-3: Adaptation of Douglas Adams book	1.00	2.00	5.00

HIT COMICS
July, 1940 - No. 65, July, 1950
Quality Comics Group

1-Origin/1st app. Neon, the Unknown & Hercules; intro. The Red Bee; Bob & Swab, Blaze Barton, the Strange Twins, X-5 Super Agent, Casey Jones & Jack & Jill (ends #7) begin	466.00	1400.00	4800.00
2-The Old Witch begins, ends #14	225.00	675.00	1800.00
3-Casey Jones ends; transvestism story "Jack & Jill"	200.00	600.00	1600.00
4-Super Agent (ends #17), & Betty Bates (ends #65) begin; X-5 ends	175.00	525.00	1400.00
5-Classic Lou Fine cover	422.00	1266.00	3800.00
6-10: 10-Old Witch by Crandall (4 pgs.); 1st work in comics (4/41)	162.00	487.00	1300.00
11-17: 13-Blaze Barton ends. 17-Last Neon; Crandall Hercules in all; Last Lou Fine-c	100.00	300.00	800.00
18-Origin & 1st app. Stormy Foster, the Great Defender (12/41); The Ghost of Flanders begins; Crandall-c	115.00	346.00	925.00
19,20	93.00	281.00	750.00
21-24: 21-Last Hercules. 24-Last Red Bee & Strange Twins	87.00	262.00	700.00
25-Origin & 1st app. Kid Eternity and begins by Moldoff (12/42); 1st app. The Keeper (Kid Eternity's aide)	131.00	393.00	1050.00
26-Blackhawk x-over in Kid Eternity	87.00	262.00	700.00
27-29	43.00	128.00	340.00
30,31- "Bill the Magnificent" by Kurtzman, 11 pgs. in each	40.00	120.00	300.00
32-40: 32-Plastic Man x-over. 34-Last Stormy Foster	21.00	64.00	150.00
41-50	14.00	43.00	100.00
51-60-Last Kid Eternity	13.00	39.00	90.00
61-63-Crandall-c/a; 61-Jeb Rivers begins	13.50	41.00	95.00
64,65-Crandall-a	13.00	39.00	90.00

NOTE: *Crandall* a-11-17(Hercules), 23, 24(Stormy Foster); c-18-20, 23, 24. *Fine* c-1-14, 16, 17(most). *Ward* c-33. Bondage c-7, 64. Hercules c-3, 10-17. Jeb Rivers c-61-65. Kid Eternity c-25-60 (w/Keeper-28-34, 36, 39-43, 45-55). Neon the Unknown c-2, 4, 8, 9. Red Bee c-1, 5-7. Stormy Foster c-18-24.

HITLER'S ASTROLOGER (See Marvel Graphic Novel #35)

HITMAN (Also see The Demon Annual #2)
May, 1996 - Present ($2.25)
DC Comics

1-10: 1-Garth Ennis scripts & John McCrea-c/a begins; Batman app. 2-Joker-c; Two Face, Mad Hatter, Mr. Zzz Zzz app; Batman cameo. 3-Batman-c/app.; Joker app. 4-1st app. Nightfist. 8-Final Night x-over			2.25

HI-YO SILVER (See Lone Ranger's Famous Horse... and also see The Lone Ranger and March of Comics No. 215)

HOBBIT, THE (See Lone Ranger's Famous Horse...)
1989 - No. 3, 1990 ($4.95, squarebound, 52 pgs.)
Eclipse Comics

Book 1-3: Adapts novel (#1has a 2nd printing)	1.00	2.00	5.00

HOCUS POCUS (Formerly Funny Book)
No. 9, Aug-Sept, 1946
Parents' Magazine Press

9	4.25	13.00	28.00

HOGAN'S HEROES (TV)
June, 1966 - No. 8, Sept, 1967; No. 9, Oct, 1969
Dell Publishing Co.

1: #1-7 photo-c	7.00	21.00	70.00
2,3-Ditko-a(p)	4.50	13.50	45.00

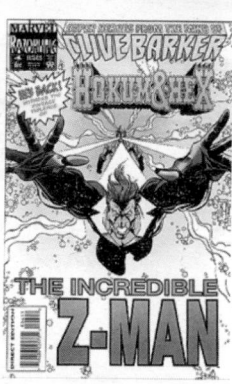

Hokum & Hex #4 © Clive Barker

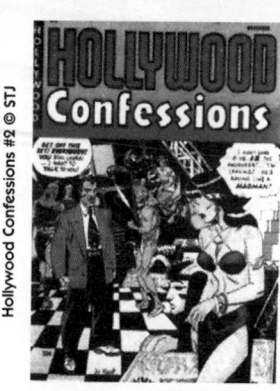

Hollywood Confessions #2 © STJ

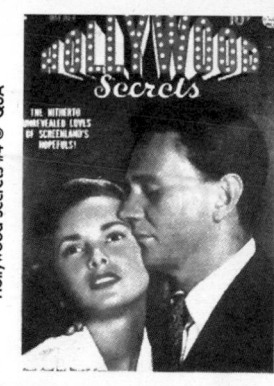

Hollywood Secrets #4 © QUA

	GD25	FN65	NM94
4-9: 9-Reprints #1	3.00	9.00	30.00

HOKUM & HEX (See Razorline)
Sept, 1993 - No. 9, May, 1994 ($1.75/$1.95)
Marvel Comics (Razorline)

1-($2.50)-Foil embossed-c; by Clive Barker		1.00	2.50
2-8: 5-Hyperkind x-over		.70	1.75
9-($1.95)		.80	2.00

HOLIDAY COMICS
1942 (25¢, 196 pgs.)
Fawcett Publications

1-Contains three Fawcett comics plus two page portrait of Captain Marvel; Capt. Marvel, Nyoka #1, & Whiz. Not rebound, remaindered comics; printed at the same time as originals	135.00	405.00	1350.00

HOLIDAY COMICS (Becomes Fun Comics #9-12)
Jan, 1951 - No. 8, Oct, 1952
Star Publications

1-Funny animal contents (Frisky Fables) in all; L. B. Cole X-Mas-c	27.00	81.00	190.00
2-Classic L. B. Cole-c	31.00	92.00	215.00
3-8: 5,8-X-Mas-c; all L.B. Cole-c	19.00	56.00	130.00
Accepted Reprint 4 (nd)-L.B. Cole-c	9.15	27.50	55.00

HOLIDAY DIGEST
1988 ($1.25, digest-size)
Harvey Comics

1			1.25

HOLIDAY PARADE (Walt Disney's...)
Winter, 1990-91(no yr. given) - No. 2, Winter, 1990-91 ($2.95, 68 pgs.)
W. D. Publications (Disney)

1-Reprints 1947 Firestone by Barks plus new-a		1.20	3.00
2-Barks-r plus other stories		1.20	3.00

HOLI-DAY SURPRISE (Formerly Summer Fun)
V2#55, Mar, 1967 (25¢ Giant)
Charlton Comics

V2#55	1.00	2.00	5.00

HOLLYWOOD COMICS
Winter, 1944 (52 pgs.)
New Age Publishers

1-Funny animal	16.00	47.00	110.00

HOLLYWOOD CONFESSIONS
Oct, 1949 - No. 2, Dec, 1949
St. John Publishing Co.

1-Kubert-c/a (entire book)	20.00	60.00	140.00
2-Kubert-c/a (entire book) (Scarce)	29.00	86.00	200.00

HOLLYWOOD DIARY
Dec, 1949 - No. 5, July-Aug, 1950
Quality Comics Group

1-No photo-c	14.00	43.00	100.00
2-Photo-c	10.00	30.00	65.00
3-5-Photo-c. 5-June Allyson/Peter Lawford photo-c	8.35	25.00	50.00

HOLLYWOOD FILM STORIES
April, 1950 - No. 4, Oct, 1950 (All photo-c; "Fumetti" type movie comic)
Feature Publications/Prize

1-June Allyson photo-c	14.00	43.00	100.00
2-4: 2-Lizabeth Scott photo-c. 3-Barbara Stanwick photo-c. 4-Betty Hutton photo-c	11.00	33.00	75.00

HOLLYWOOD FUNNY FOLKS (Formerly Funny Folks; Becomes Nutsy Squirrel #61 on)

No. 27, Aug-Sept, 1950 - No. 60, July-Aug, 1954
National Periodical Publications

27	12.00	36.00	85.00
28-40	9.15	27.00	55.00
41-60	7.50	22.50	45.00

NOTE: **Sheldon Mayer** a-27-35, 37-40, 43-46, 48-51, 53, 56, 57, 60.

HOLLYWOOD LOVE DOCTOR (See Doctor Anthony King...)

HOLLYWOOD PICTORIAL (...Romances on cover)
No. 3, Jan, 1950
St. John Publishing Co.

3-Matt Baker-a; photo-c	19.00	58.00	135.00

(Becomes a movie magazine - Hollywood Pictorial Western with No. 4.)

HOLLYWOOD ROMANCES (Formerly Brides In Love; becomes For Lovers Only #60 on)
V2#46, 11/66; #47, 10/67; #48, 11/68; V3#49, 11/69 - V3#59, 6/71
Charlton Comics

V2#46-Rolling Stones-c/story	6.25	19.00	50.00
V2#47-V3#59: 56- "Born to Heart Break" begins	1.00	2.60	6.00

HOLLYWOOD SECRETS
Nov, 1949 - No. 6, Sept, 1950
Quality Comics Group

1-Ward-c/a (9 pgs.)	26.00	79.00	185.00
2-Crandall-a, Ward-c/a (9 pgs.)	17.00	51.00	120.00
3-6: All photo-c. 5-Lex Barker (Tarzan)-c	9.15	27.00	55.00
...of Romance, I.W. Reprint #9; r/#2 above w/Kinstler-c	1.50	3.75	9.00

HOLLYWOOD SUPERSTARS
Nov, 1990 - No. 5, Apr, 1991 ($2.25)
Marvel Comics (Epic Comics)

1-($2.95, 52 pgs.)-Spiegle-c/a in all		1.50	3.00
2-5 ($2.25)		1.15	2.30

HOLO-MAN (See Power Record Comics)

HOLYOKE ONE-SHOT
1944 - No. 10, 1945 (All reprints)
Holyoke Publishing Co. (Tem Publ.)

1-Grit Grady (on cover only), Miss Victory, Alias X (origin)-All reprints from Captain Fearless	10.00	30.00	60.00
2-Rusty Dugan (Corporal); Capt. Fearless (origin), Mr. Miracle (origin) app.	10.00	30.00	60.00
3-Miss Victory; r/Crash #4; Cat Man (origin), Solar Legion by Kirby app.; Miss Victory on cover only (1945)	21.00	62.00	145.00
4-Mr. Miracle; The Blue Streak app.	8.35	25.00	50.00
5-U.S. Border Patrol Comics (Sgt. Dick Carter of the...), Miss Victory (story matches cover to #3), Citizen Smith, & Mr. Miracle app.	10.00	30.00	60.00
6-Capt. Fearless, Alias X, Capt. Stone (splash used as-c to #10); Diamond Jim & Rusty Dugan (splash from cover of #2)	8.35	25.00	50.00
7-Secret Agent Z-2, Strong Man, Blue Streak (story matches cover to #8); Reprints from Crash #2	10.00	30.00	60.00
8-Blue Streak, Strong Man (story matches cover to #7)-Crash reprints	8.35	25.00	50.00
9-Citizen Smith, The Blue Streak, Solar Legion by Kirby & Strongman, the Perfect Human app.; reprints from Crash #4 & 5; Citizen Smith on cover only-from story in #5 (1944-before #3)	13.00	39.00	90.00
10-Captain Stone; r/Crash; Solar Legion by S&K	13.00	39.00	90.00

HOMER COBB (See Adventures of...)

HOMER HOOPER
July, 1953 - No. 4, Dec, 1953
Atlas Comics

Homicide #1 © DH

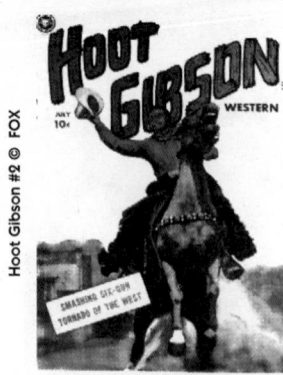

Hoot Gibson #2 © FOX

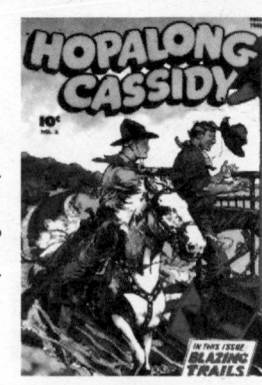

Hopalong Cassidy #3 © FAW

	GD25	FN65	NM94
1-Teenage humor	8.70	26.00	52.00
2-4	5.85	17.50	35.00

HOMER, THE HAPPY GHOST (See Adventures of…)
3/55 - No. 22, 11/58; V2#1, 11/69 - V2#5, 7/70
Atlas(ACI/PPI/WPI)/Marvel Comics

V1#1-Dan DeCarlo-c/a begins, ends #22	12.00	36.00	85.00
2-1st code approved issue	7.00	21.00	42.00
3-10	5.35	16.00	32.00
11-22	4.15	12.50	25.00
V2#1 - V2#5 (1969-70)	1.65	4.20	10.00

HOME RUN (Also see A-1 Comics)
No. 89, 1953 (one-shot)
Magazine Enterprises

A-1 89 (#3)-Powell-a; Stan Musial photo-c	10.00	30.00	65.00

HOMICIDE (Also see Dark Horse Presents)
Apr, 1990 ($1.95, B&W, one-shot)
Dark Horse Comics

1-Detective story		1.00	2.00

HONEYBEE BIRDWHISTLE AND HER PET PEPI (Introducing…)
1969 (Giveaway, 24 pgs., B&W, slick cover)
Newspaper Enterprise Association

nn-Contains Freckles newspaper strips with a short biography of Henry
Fornhals (artist) & Fred Fox (writer) of the strip 5.50 16.50 38.00

HONEYMOON (Formerly Gay Comics)
No. 41, Jan, 1950
A Lover's Magazine(USA) (Marvel)

41-Photo-c; article by Betty Grable	8.00	24.00	48.00

HONEYMOONERS, THE (TV)
Oct, 1986 ($1.50)
Lodestone

1-Photo-c			1.50

HONEYMOONERS, THE (TV)
Sept, 1987 - No. 13? ($2.00)
Triad Publications

1-13		.80	2.00

HONEYMOON ROMANCE
Apr, 1950 - No. 2, July, 1950 (25¢, digest size)
Artful Publications (Canadian)

1,2-(Rare)	31.00	92.00	215.00

HONEY WEST (TV)
Sept, 1966 (Photo-c)
Gold Key

1 (10186-609)	9.50	28.50	95.00

HONG KONG PHOOEY (TV)
June, 1975 - No. 9, Nov, 1976 (Hanna-Barbera)
Charlton Comics

1	2.85	8.50	20.00
2	1.30	3.25	8.00
3-9	1.00	2.60	6.00

HOODED HORSEMAN, THE (Also see Blazing West)
No. 21, 1-2/52 - No. 27, 1-2/53; No. 18, 12-1/54-55 - No. 27, 6-7/56
American Comics Group (Michel Publ.)

21(1-2/52)-Hooded Horseman, Injun Jones continue			
	13.00	39.00	90.00
22	9.15	27.00	55.00
23-25,27(1-2/53)	7.00	21.00	42.00
26-Origin/1st app. Cowboy Sahib by L. Starr	10.00	30.00	65.00

	GD25	FN65	NM94
18(11-12/54)(Formerly Out of the Night)	9.15	27.00	55.00
19-Last precode (1-2/55)	6.35	19.00	38.00
20-Origin Johnny Injun	8.00	24.00	48.00
21-24,26,27(6-7/56)	6.35	19.00	38.00
25-Cowboy Sahib on cover only; Hooded Horseman i.d. revealed			
	7.00	21.00	42.00

NOTE: *Whitney* c/a-21(`52), 20-22.

HOODED MENACE, THE (Also see Daring Adventures)
1951 (one-shot)
Realistic/Avon Periodicals

nn-Based on a band of hooded outlaws in the Pacific Northwest, 1900-1906;
reprinted in Daring Advs. #15 40.00 120.00 315.00

HOODS UP
1953 (15¢, distributed to service station owners, 16 pgs.)
Fram Corp.

1-(Very Rare; only 2 known); Eisner-c/a in all.	50.00	150.00	375.00
2-6-(Very Rare; only 1 known of #3, 4, 2 known of #2)			
	50.00	150.00	375.00

NOTE: *Convertible Connie gives tips for service stations, selling Fram oil filters.*

HOOK (Movie)
Early Feb, 1992 - No. 4, Late Mar, 1992 ($1.00, limited series)
Marvel Comics

1-4: Adapts movie; Vess-c; 1-Morrow-a(p)			1.00
nn (1991, $5.95, 84 pgs.)-Contains #1-4; Vess-c	1.00	2.50	6.00
1 (1991, $2.95, magazine, 84 pgs.)-Contains #1-4; Vess-c (same cover as nn issue)		1.20	3.00

HOOT GIBSON'S WESTERN ROUNDUP (See Western Roundup under Fox Giants)

HOOT GIBSON WESTERN (Formerly My Love Story)
No. 5, May, 1950 - No. 3, Sept, 1950
Fox Features Syndicate

5,6(#1,2): 5-Photo-c. 6-Photo/painted-c	24.00	71.00	165.00
3-Wood-a; painted-c	26.00	79.00	185.00

HOPALONG CASSIDY (Also see Bill Boyd Western, Master Comics, Real
Western Hero, Six Gun Heroes & Western Hero; Bill Boyd starred as H.
Cassidy in the movies; H. Cassidy in movies, radio & TV)
Feb, 1943; No. 2, Summer, 1946 - No. 85, Nov, 1953
Fawcett Publications

1 (1943, 68 pgs.)-H. Cassidy & his horse Topper begin (on sale 1/8/43)- Captain Marvel app. on-c	400.00	1200.00	4000.00
2-(Sum, '46)	58.00	171.00	525.00
3,4: 3-(Fall, '46, 52 pgs. begin)	28.00	86.00	260.00
5- "Mad Barber" story mentioned in **SOTI**, pgs. 308,309; photo-c			
	25.00	75.00	225.00
6-10: 8-Photo-c	20.00	60.00	180.00
11-19: 11,13-19-Photo-c	13.00	41.00	125.00
20-29 (52 pgs.)-Painted/photo-c	10.00	31.00	95.00
30,31,33,34,37-39,41 (52 pgs.)-Painted-c	8.25	25.00	58.00
32,40 (36pgs.)-Painted-c	6.85	20.50	48.00
35,42,43,45 (52 pgs.)-Photo-c	8.25	25.00	58.00
36,44,48 (36 pgs.)-Photo-c	6.85	20.50	48.00
46,47,49-51,53,54,56 (52 pgs.)-Photo-c	8.25	25.00	58.00
52,55,57-70 (36 pgs.)-Photo-c	5.75	17.00	40.00
71-84-Photo-c	4.50	13.75	32.00
85-Last Fawcett issue; photo-c	5.70	17.00	40.00

NOTE: *Line-drawn c-1-4, 6, 7, 9, 10, 12.*

Grape Nuts Flakes giveaway (1950,9x6")	12.00	36.00	85.00
…& the Mad Barber (1951 Bond Bread giveaway)-7x5"; used in **SOTI**, pgs. 308,309	20.00	60.00	140.00
…Meets the Brend Brothers Bandits (1951 Bond Bread giveaway, color, paper-c, 16pgs. 3-1/2x7")-Fawcett Publ.	10.00	30.00	60.00
…Strange Legacy (1951 Bond Bread giveaway)	10.00	30.00	60.00

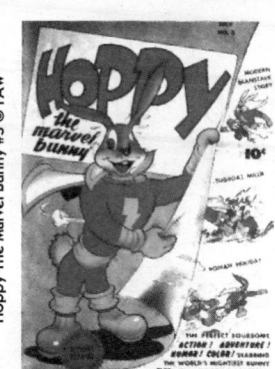
Hoppy The Marvel Bunny #3 © FAW

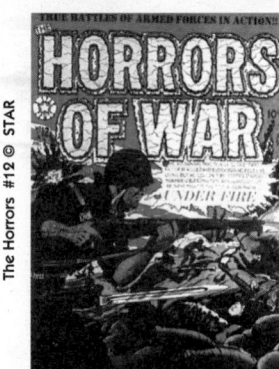
The Horrors #12 © STAR

Horseman #1 © Kevlar Studios

	GD25	FN65	NM94

	GD25	FN65	NM94
	1.00	2.60	6.00

White Tower Giveaway (1946, 16pgs., paper-c) — 10.00 / 30.00 / 60.00

HOPALONG CASSIDY (TV)
No. 86, Feb, 1954 - No. 135, May-June, 1959 (All-36 pgs.)
National Periodical Publications

	GD25	FN65	NM94
86-Gene Colan-a begins, ends #117; photo covers continue	34.00	103.00	240.00
87	19.00	56.00	130.00
88-91: 91-1 pg. Superboy-sty (6/54)	13.00	39.00	90.00
92-99 (98 has #93 on-c; last precode issue, 2/55). 95-Reversed photo-c to #52. 98-Reversed photo-c to #61. 99-Reversed photo-c to #60	11.00	33.00	75.00
100-Same cover as #50	12.00	36.00	85.00
101-108: 105-Same photo-c as #54. 107-Same photo-c as #51. 108-Last photo-c	9.75	30.00	58.00
109-135: 118-Gil Kane-a begins. 123-Kubert-a (2 pgs.). 124-Painted-c	8.00	24.00	48.00

HOPE SHIP
June-Aug, 1963
Dell Publishing Co.

	GD25	FN65	NM94
1	1.80	4.50	9.00

HOPPY THE MARVEL BUNNY (See Fawcett's Funny Animals)
Dec, 1945 - No. 15, Sept, 1947
Fawcett Publications

	GD25	FN65	NM94
1	26.00	79.00	185.00
2	13.00	39.00	90.00
3-15: 7-Xmas-c	11.00	33.00	75.00
Well Known Comics (1944,8-1/2x10-1/2", paper-c) Bestmaid/Samuel Lowe (printed in red or blue)	8.00	24.00	48.00

HORACE & DOTTY DRIPPLE (Dotty Dripple No. 1-24)
No. 25, Aug, 1952 - No. 43, Oct, 1955
Harvey Publications

	GD25	FN65	NM94
25-43	1.60	4.00	8.00

HORIZONTAL LIEUTENANT, THE (See Movie Classics)

HOROBI
1990 - No. 8, 1990 ($3.75, B&W, mature readers, 84 pgs.)
V2#1, 1990 - No. 7, 1991 ($4.25, B&W, 68 pgs.)
Viz Premiere Comics

		FN65	NM94
1-8: Japanese manga		1.60	4.00
Part Two, #1-7		1.80	4.50

HORRIFIC (Terrific No. 14 on)
Sept, 1952 - No. 13, Sept, 1954
Artful/Comic Media/Harwell/Mystery

	GD25	FN65	NM94
1	29.00	86.00	200.00
2	16.00	47.00	110.00
3-Bullet in head-c	26.00	79.00	185.00
4,5,7,9,10: 4-Shrunken head-c. 7-Guillotine-c	11.00	33.00	75.00
6-Jack The Ripper story	11.50	34.00	85.00
8-Origin & 1st app. The Teller (E.C. parody)	15.00	45.00	105.00
11-13: 11-Swipe/Witches Tales #6,27; Devil-c	10.00	30.00	60.00
NOTE: Don Heck a-8; c-3-13. Hollingsworth a-4. Morisi a-8. Palais a-5, 7-12.			

HORROR FROM THE TOMB (Mysterious Stories No. 2 on)
Sept, 1954
Premier Magazine Co.

	GD25	FN65	NM94
1-Woodbridge/Torres, Check-a; The Keeper of the Graveyard is host	29.00	88.00	205.00

HORRORIST, THE (Also see Hellblazer)
Dec, 1995 - No. 2, Jan, 1996 ($5.95, limited series, mature)
DC Comics (Vertigo)

1,2: Jamie Delano scripts, David Lloyd-c/a; John Constantine (Hellblazer) app.

HORRORS, THE (Formerly Startling Terror Tales #10)
No. 11, Jan, 1953 - No. 15, Apr, 1954
Star Publications

	GD25	FN65	NM94
11-Horrors of War; Disbrow-a(2)	21.00	64.00	150.00
12-Horrors of War; color illo in POP	20.00	60.00	140.00
13-Horrors of Mystery; crime stories	19.00	56.00	130.00
14,15-Horrors of the Underworld; crime stories	20.00	60.00	140.00
NOTE: All have L. B. Cole covers; a-12. Hollingsworth a-13. Palais a-13r.			

HORROR TALES (Magazine)
V1#7, 6/69 - V6#6, 12/74; V7#1, 2/75; V7#2, 5/76 - V8#5, 1977; V9#3, 8/78; (V1-V6: 52 pgs.; V7, V8#2: 112 pgs.; V8#4 on: 68 pgs.) (No V5#3, V8#1,3)
Eerie Publications

	GD25	FN65	NM94
V1#7	2.60	7.50	18.00
V1#8,9	1.70	5.00	12.00
V2#1-6('70), V3#1-6('71)	1.65	4.20	10.00
V4#1-3,5-7('72)	1.65	4.20	10.00
V4#4-LSD story reprint/Weird V3#5	2.85	8.50	20.00
V5#1,2,4,5(6/73),5(10/73),6(12/73),V6#1-6('74),V7#1,2,4('76),V7#3('76)-Giant issue,V8#2,4,5('77),V9#3(8/78, $1.50)	1.65	4.20	10.00
NOTE: Bondage-c-V6#1, 3, V7#2.			

HORSE FEATHERS COMICS
Nov, 1945 - No. 4, July(Summer on-c), 1948 (52 pgs.)
Lev Gleason Publications

	GD25	FN65	NM94
1-Wolverton's Scoop Scuttle, 2 pgs.	17.00	51.00	120.00
2	9.15	27.00	55.00
3,4: 3-(5/48)	6.35	19.00	38.00

HORSEMAN
Mar, 1996 - Present ($2.95)
Crusade Comics/Kevlar Studios

		FN65	NM94
0,1: 0-1st Kevlar Studios issue. 1-(3/96)-Crusade issue; Shi-c/app.		1.20	3.00

HORSEMASTERS, THE (Disney)(TV, Movie)
No. 1260, Dec-Feb, 1961/62
Dell Publishing Co.

	GD25	FN65	NM94
Four Color 1260-Annette Funicello photo-c	11.00	33.00	110.00

HORSE SOLDIERS, THE
No. 1048, Nov-Jan, 1959/60 (Movie-feat. John Wayne)
Dell Publishing Co.

	GD25	FN65	NM94
Four Color 1048-Painted-c, Sekowsky-a	13.00	40.00	130.00

HORSE WITHOUT A HEAD, THE (See Movie Comics)

HOT DOG
June-July, 1954 - No. 4, Dec-Jan, 1954-55
Magazine Enterprises

	GD25	FN65	NM94
1(A-1 #107)	6.35	19.00	38.00
2,3(A-1 #115),4(A-1 #136)	4.25	13.00	26.00

HOT DOG (See Jughead's Pal, Hotdog)

HOTEL DEPAREE - SUNDANCE (TV)
No. 1126, Aug-Oct, 1960 (one-shot)
Dell Publishing Co.

	GD25	FN65	NM94
Four Color 1126-Earl Holliman photo-c	6.00	18.00	60.00

HOT ROD AND SPEEDWAY COMICS
Feb-Mar, 1952 - No. 5, Apr-May, 1953
Hillman Periodicals

	GD25	FN65	NM94
1	21.00	64.00	150.00
2-Krigstein-a	17.00	49.00	115.00
3-5	9.15	27.00	55.00

Hot Shots: Avengers © MEG

Hot Stuff Sizzlers V2#1 © HARV

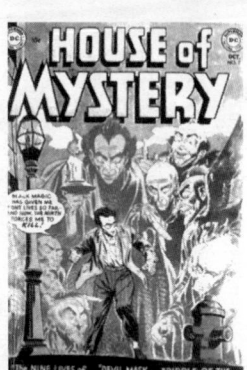

House of Mystery #7 © DC

	GD25	FN65	NM94

HOT ROD COMICS (...Featuring Clint Curtis) (See XMas Comics)
Nov, 1951 (no month given) - V2#7, Feb, 1953
Fawcett Publications

nn (V1#1)-Powell-c/a in all	25.00	75.00	175.00
2 (4/52)	15.00	45.00	105.00
3-6, V2#7	10.00	30.00	70.00

HOT ROD KING (Also see Speed Smith the Hot Rod King)
Fall, 1952
Ziff-Davis Publ. Co.

1-Giacoia-a; Saunders painted-c	21.00	62.00	145.00

HOT ROD RACERS (Grand Prix No. 16 on)
Dec, 1964 - No. 15, July, 1967
Charlton Comics

1	7.00	20.50	55.00
2-5	4.00	12.00	30.00
6-15	3.25	9.50	22.00

HOT RODS AND RACING CARS
Nov, 1951 - No. 120, June, 1973
Charlton Comics (Motor Mag. No. 1)

1-Speed Davis begins; Indianapolis 500 story	22.00	66.00	155.00
2	11.50	34.00	80.00
3-10	8.35	25.00	50.00
11-20	6.35	19.00	38.00
21-34,36-40	4.25	13.00	28.00
35 (6/58, 68 pgs.)	5.85	17.50	35.00
41-60	4.00	10.00	20.00
61-80	2.00	6.00	14.00
81-100	1.65	4.20	10.00
101-120	1.00	2.60	6.00

HOT SHOT CHARLIE
1947 (Lee Elias)
Hillman Periodicals

1	7.00	21.00	42.00

HOT SHOTS: AVENGERS
Oct, 1995 ($2.95, one-shot)
Marvel Comics

nn-pin-ups		1.20	3.00

HOTSPUR
June, 1987 - No. 3, Sept, 1987 ($1.75, color, limited series, Baxter paper)
Eclipse Comics

1-3		.90	1.80

HOT STUFF (See Stumbo Tinytown)
V2#1, Sept, 1991 - No. 12, June, 1994 ($1.00)
Harvey Comics

V2#1,2: 1-Stumbo back-up story			1.00
3-8 ($1.25)			1.25
9-12 ($1.50)			1.50
...Big Book 1 (11/92), 2 (6/93) (Both $1.95, 52 pgs.)		.80	2.00

HOT STUFF CREEPY CAVES
Nov, 1974 - No. 7, Nov, 1975
Harvey Publications

1	1.00	2.00	5.00
2-5		1.20	3.00
6,7			1.50

HOT STUFF DIGEST
July, 1992 - No. 5, Nov, 1993 ($1.75, digest-size)
Harvey Comics

V2#1-5: Hot Stuff, Stumbo, Richie Rich stories		.70	1.75

	GD25	FN65	NM94

HOT STUFF GIANT SIZE
Oct, 1992 - No. 3, Oct, 1993 ($2.25, 68 pgs.)
Harvey Comics

V2#1-3: Hot Stuff & Stumbo stories		.90	2.2

HOT STUFF SIZZLERS
July, 1960 - No. 59, Mar, 1974; V2#1, Aug, 1992
Harvey Publications

1: 84 pgs. begin, ends #5; Hot Stuff, Stumbo begin	9.00	27.00	90.
2-5	4.00	12.00	40.
6-10: 6-68 pgs. begin, ends #45	2.50	7.50	25.
11-20	1.80	5.40	18.
21-45	1.20	3.60	12.
46-52: 52 pgs. begin	.90	2.70	9.
53-59	.70	2.10	7.
V2#1-(8/92, $1.25)-Stumbo back-up			1.

HOT STUFF, THE LITTLE DEVIL (Also see Devil Kids & Harvey Hits)
10/57 - No. 141, 7/77; No. 142, 2/78 - No. 164, 8/82; No. 165, 10/86 -
No. 171, 11/87; No. 172, 11/88; No. 173, Sept, 1990 - No. 177, 1/91
Harvey Publications (Illustrated Humor)

1	28.50	85.50	285.
2-1st app. Stumbo the Giant (12/57)	14.00	43.00	140.
3-5	11.00	33.00	110.
6-10	6.00	18.00	60.
11-20	4.00	12.00	40.
21-40	2.50	7.50	25.
41-60	1.40	4.20	14.
61-105	.90	2.70	9.
106-112: All 52 pg. Giants	1.20	3.60	12.
113-125		1.60	4.
126-177: 172-177-($1.00)		.80	2.
Shoestore Giveaway('63)	1.20	3.60	12.

HOT WHEELS (TV)
Mar-Apr, 1970 - No. 6, Jan-Feb, 1971
National Periodical Publications

1	7.00	21.50	55.
2,4,5	3.25	9.50	22.
3-Neal Adams-c	4.30	13.00	32.
6-Neal Adams-c/a	5.00	15.50	38.

NOTE: *Toth* a-1p, 2-5; c-1p, 5.

HOURMAN (See Adventure Comics #48)

HOUSE OF MYSTERY (See Brave and the Bold #93, Elvira's House of Mystery,
Limited Collectors' Edition & Super DC Giant)

HOUSE OF MYSTERY, THE
Dec-Jan, 1951-52 - No. 321, Oct, 1983 (No. 199-203: 52 pgs.)
National Periodical Publications/DC Comics

1	193.00	581.00	1550.
2	84.00	253.00	675.
3	62.00	187.00	500.
4,5	47.00	141.00	375.
6-10	40.00	120.00	290.
11-15	34.00	101.00	235.
16(7/53)-25	25.00	75.00	175.
26-35(2/55)-Last pre-code issue; 30-Woodish-a	19.00	56.00	130.
36-49	14.00	41.00	110.
50-Text story of Orson Welles' War of the Worlds broadcast	14.00	41.00	110.
51-60: 55-1st S.A. issue	12.00	36.00	95.
61,63,65,66,70,72,76,84,85-Kirby-a	12.00	35.00	90.
62,64,67-69,71,73-75,77-83,86-99	8.50	26.00	70.
100 (7/60)	10.00	30.00	80.

House of Secrets #153 © DC

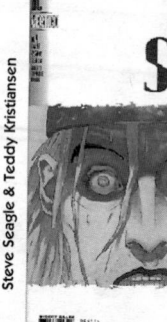

House of Secrets #4 ©
Steve Seagle & Teddy Kristiansen

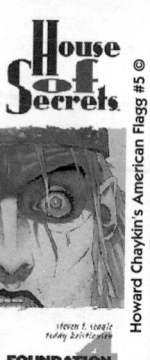

Howard Chaykin's American Flagg #5 ©
Howard Chaykin

	GD25	FN65	NM94
101-116: 109-Toth, Kubert-a. 116-Last 10¢ issue	7.50	22.50	60.00
117-130: 117-Swipes-c to HOS #20. 120-Toth-a	7.00	20.50	55.00
131-142	5.50	17.00	45.00
143-J'onn J'onzz, Manhunter begins (6/64), ends #173; story continues from Detective #326	34.00	101.00	235.00
144	18.00	54.00	125.00
145-155,157-159: 149-Toth-a. 155-The Human Hurrican app. (12/65), Red Tornado prototype. 158-Origin/1st app. Diabolu Idol-Head in J'onn J'onzz	10.50	32.00	85.00
156-Robby Reed begins (origin/1st app.), ends #173	13.50	41.00	95.00
160-(7/66)-Robby Reed becomes Plastic Man in this issue only; 1st S.A. app. Plastic Man; intro Marco Xavier (Martian Manhunter) & Vulture Crime Organization; ends #173	17.00	51.00	120.00
161-173: 169-Origin/1st app. Gem Girl	8.50	26.00	60.00
174-177,182: 174-Mystery format begins. 176-1st app. Cain (HOM host). 182-Toth-a	2.85	8.50	20.00
178-Neal Adams-a (2/68)	3.25	9.50	22.00
179-N. Adams/Orlando, Wrightson-a (1st pro work, 3 pgs.)	8.00	23.50	55.00
180,181,183: Wrightson-a (3,10, & 3 pgs.). 180-Last 12¢ issue; Kane/ Wood-a(2). 183-Wood-a	2.30	6.70	16.00
184-Kane/Wood, Toth-a	1.70	5.00	12.00
185-Williamson/Kaluta-a; Howard-a (3 pgs.)	1.85	5.50	13.00
186-N. Adams-a; Wrightson-a (10 pgs.)	2.00	6.00	14.00
187,190: 187-Toth-a. 190-Toth-a(r)	1.30	3.25	8.00
188,191,195-Wrightson-a (8, 3 & 10 pgs.). 195-Swamp creature story by Wrightson similar to Swamp Thing (10/71)	2.00	6.00	14.00
189,192,194,196,198: 189-Wood-a(i). 194-Toth, Kirby-a; 52 pg. issues begin, end #203	1.65	4.20	10.00
193-Wood-a (8pg.); Kirby-a	1.65	4.70	11.00
200-203-(25¢, 52 pg.)-One third-r. 200-(3/72)	1.65	4.20	10.00
204-Wrightson-c/a, 9 pgs.	1.30	3.25	8.00
205-223,225,227: 207-Wrightson, Starlin, Redondo act. 221-Wrightson/Kaluta-a (8 pgs.). 225-Spectre app.	1.00	2.60	6.00
224-Wrightson-r from Spectre #9; Dillin/Adams-r from House of Secrets #82; begin 100 pg. issues; Phantom Stranger-r	2.15	6.50	15.00
226-Wrightson-Redondo-a Phantom Stranger-r	1.65	4.20	10.00
228-N. Adams inks; Wrightson-r	1.65	4.20	10.00
229-Wrightson-a(r); Toth-r; last 100 pg. issue.	1.65	4.20	10.00
230-235,237-321: 230-(68 pgs.). 251-259-(84 pgs.). 251-Wood-a. 282-(68 pgs.)- Has extra story "The Computers That Saved Metropolis" Radio Shack give away by Jim Starlin	1.20	3.00	7.00
236-Ditko-a(p); N. Adams-i; Wrightson-c	1.20	3.00	7.00

NOTE: **Neal Adams** a-236i; c-175-192, 197, 199, 251-254. **Alcala** a-209, 217, 219, 224, 227. **M. Anderson** a-212; c/a-37. **Aparo** a-209. **Aragones** a-185, 186, 194, 196, 200, 202, 229, 251. **Bailey** a-279p. **Cameron** a-76, 79. **Colan** a-202r. **Craig** a-263, 275, 295, 300. **Dillin/Adams** r-224. **Ditko** a-236p, 247, 254, 258, 276; c-277. **Drucker** a-37. **Evans** c-218. **Fraden** a-251. **Giffen** a-247, 268, 273, 276, 284, 287, 288, 293-295, 300, 302, 304, 305, 309-319, 321. **Bob Kane** a-150, 161, 229r, 247i, 254, 279i. **Kaluta** a-195, 200, 250r; c-200-202, 210, 212, 233, 260, 261, 263, 267, 268, 273, 276, 284, 287, 288, 293-295, 300, 302, 304, 305, 309-319, 321. **Bob Kane** a-196p, 253p, 300p. **Gil Kane** a-196p, 253p, 300p. **Kirby** a-194r, 199r; c-65, 76, 78, 79, 85. **Kubert** a-282, 283, 286, 289-292, 297-299, 301, 303, 306-308. **Maneely** a-68, 227r. **Mayer** a-317p. **Meskin** a-144 (most); 195r; 224r; 229r; c-63, 66, 124, 127. **Mooney** a-24, 159, 160. **Moreira** a-3, 4, 20-58, 59, 62, 68, 77, 79, 90, 108, 113, 123, 201; c-4-28, 44, 47, 50, 54, 59, 62, 64, 68, 70, 72. **Morrow** a-192, 196, 255, 320. **Mortimer** a-204/3 pgs.). **Nasser** a-276. **Newton** a-259, 272. **Orlando** a-204, 212, 213, 220, 224, 225, 245, 250, 252-256, 283. **Orlando** a-175/2 pgs.), 178, 240i; 240, 258p, 262, 264p, 270p, 271, 272, 274, 275, 278, 296i. **Redondo** a-194, 195, 197, 202, 207, 211, 214, 217, 219, 226, 227, 229, 235, 241, 287(layout), 302p, 303i, 308; c-229. **Reese** a-195, 200, 205i. **Rogers** a-254, 274, 277. **Roussos** a-65, 84, 224i. **Sekowsky** a-282p. **Starling** a-203. **Starlin** a-207/2 pgs.), 282p; c-281. **Leonard Starr** a-9. **Staton** a-300p. **Sutton** a-271, 290, 291, 293, 295, 297-299, 302, 303, 306-309, 310-313i, 314. **Tuska** a-293p, 294p, 300p. **Wrightson** c-193-195, 204, 207, 209, 211, 213, 214, 217, 219, 221, 236, 255, 256; r-

HOUSE OF SECRETS (Combined with The Unexpected after #154)
12/56 - No. 80, 9-10/66; No. 81, 8-9/69 - No. 140, 2-3/76;
141, 8-9/76 - No. 154, 10-11/78
National Periodical Publications/DC Comics

	GD25	FN65	NM94
1-Drucker-a; Moreira-c	105.00	315.00	1050.00
2-Moreira-a	47.00	141.00	425.00
3-Kirby-c/a	40.00	120.00	350.00
4-Kirby-a	32.00	96.00	265.00
5-7	21.00	62.00	165.00
8-Kirby-a	25.00	75.00	205.00
9-11: 11-Lou Cameron-a (unsigned)	19.00	56.00	145.00
12-Kirby-c/a; Lou Cameron-a	20.00	60.00	155.00
13-15: 14-Flying saucer-c	13.00	39.00	105.00
16-20	11.50	34.00	90.00
21,22,24-30	11.00	33.00	85.00
23-1st app. Mark Merlin & begin series (8/59)	12.00	36.00	95.00
31-50: 48-Toth-a. 50-Last 10¢ issue	9.15	27.50	65.00
51-60: 58-Origin Mark Merlin	7.50	22.50	60.00
61-First Eclipso (7-8/63) and begin series	21.00	64.00	150.00
62	11.50	34.00	80.00
63-65,67-Toth-a on Eclipso (see Brave and the Bold #64)	9.30	28.00	65.00
66-1st Eclipso-c (also #67,70,78,79); Toth-a	12.00	36.00	85.00
68-80: 73-Mark Merlin becomes Prince Ra-Man (1st app.). 76-Prince Ra-Man vs. Eclipso. 80-Eclipso, Prince Ra-Man end	7.00	21.50	50.00
81-91: 81-Mystery format begins; 1st app. Abel (HOS host). 82-Neal Adams-c(i). 85-N. Adams-a(i). 87-Wrightson & Kaluta-a. 90-Buckler (early work)/ N. Adams-a(i)	1.65	4.20	10.00
92-1st app. Swamp Thing-c/story (8 pgs.)(6-7/71) by Berni Wrightson(p) w/Jeff Jones/Kaluta/Weiss ink assists; classic-c.	54.00	163.00	435.00
93-100: 94-Wrightson inks. 96-Wood-a	1.20	3.00	7.00
101-154: 140-Origin The Patchworkman	1.10	2.75	

NOTE: **Neal Adams** c-81, 82, 84-88, 90, 91. **Alcala** a-104-107. **Anderson** a-91. **Aparo** a-93, 97, 105. **B. Bailey** a-107. **Cameron** a-13, 15. **Colan** a-63. **Ditko** a-139p, 148. **Elias** a-58. **Evans** a-118. **Finlay** a-7r(Real Fact?). **Glanzman** a-91. **Golden** a-151. **Heath** a-31. **Heck** a-85. **Kaluta** a-87, 98, 99; c-98, 99, 101, 102, 105, 149, 151, 154. **Bob Kane** a-18, 21. **G. Kane** a-85p. **Kirby** c-3, 11, 12. **Kubert** a-39. **Meskin** a-2-68 (most), 94r; c-55-60. **Moreira** a-7, 8, 51, 54, 102-104, 106, 108, 113, 116, 118, 121, 123, 127; c-1, 2, 4-10, 13-20. **Morrow** a-86, 89, 90; c-89, 146-148. **Nino** a-101, 103, 106, 109, 115, 117, 126, 128, 131, 147, 153. **Redondo** a-95, 99, 102, 104p, 113, 116, 134, 136, 139, 140. **Reese** a-85. **Severin** a-91. **Starlin** c-150. **Sutton** a-154. **Toth** a-63-67, 83, 93r, 94r, 96r-98r, 123. **Tuska** a-90, 104. **Wrightson** a-134; c-92-94, 96, 100, 103, 106, 107, 135, 136, 139.

HOUSE OF SECRETS
Oct, 1996 - Present ($2.50) (Creator-owned series)
DC Comics (Vertigo)

1-4: Steven Seagle scripts & Teddy Kristiansen-c/a			2.50

HOUSE OF TERROR (3-D)
Oct, 1953 (25¢, came w/glasses)
St. John Publishing Co.

1-Kubert, Baker-a	29.00	86.00	200.00

HOUSE OF YANG, THE (See Yang)
July, 1975 - No. 6, June, 1976; 1978
Charlton Comics

1			1.50
2-6, Modern Comics #1,2(1978)			1.00

HOUSE II: THE SECOND STORY
Oct, 1987 (One-shot)
Marvel Comics

1-Adapts movie		.80	2.00

HOWARD CHAYKIN'S AMERICAN FLAGG (See American Flagg!)
V2#1, May, 1988 - V2#12, Apr, 1989 ($1.75/$1.95, Baxter paper)
First Comics

V2#1-5: ($1.75)-Chaykin-c(p) in all		.70	1.75
6-9,11,12: ($1.95)		.80	2.00
10-Elvis Presley photo-c		1.20	3.00

HOWARD THE DUCK (See Bizarre Adventures #34, Crazy Magazine, Fear,

Howard The Duck #3 © MEG

Howdy Doody #13 © DELL

How To Draw For The Comics © S&S

	GD25	FN65	NM94

Man-Thing, Marvel Treasury Edition & Sensational She-Hulk #14-17)
Jan, 1976 - No. 31, May, 1979; No. 32, Jan, 1986; No. 33, Sept, 1986
Marvel Comics Group

1-Brunner-c/a; Spider-Man x-over (low distr.)	1.00	2.60	6.00
2-11: 2-Brunner-c/a (low distr.). 3-Buscema-a(p)		.80	2.00
12-1st app. Kiss (cameo, 3/77)		1.20	3.00
13-Kiss app. (1st full story, 6/77); Daimon Hellstrom app. plus cameo of Howard as Son of Satan		1.60	4.00
14-33: 14-Howard as Son of Satan-c/story; Son of Satan app. 16-Album issue; 3 pgs. comics. 22,23-Man-Thing-c/stories. 30,32-P. Smith-a.			1.00
Annual 1(1977, 52 pgs.)-Mayerik-a			1.00

NOTE: *Austin* c-29l. *Bolland* c-33. *Brunner* a-1p, 2p; c-1. *Buckler* c-3p. *Buscema* a-3p. *Colan* a(p)-4-15, 17-20, 24-27, 30, 31; c(p)-4-31, Annual 1p. *Leialoha* a-1-13i; c(i)-3-5, 8-11. *Mayerik* a-22, 23, 33. *Paul Smith* a-30p, 32. Man-Thing app. in #22, 23.

HOWARD THE DUCK (Magazine)
Oct, 1979 - No. 9, Mar, 1981 (B&W, 68 pgs.)
Marvel Comics Group

1			1.50
2,3,5-9: 3-Xmas issue. 7-Has poster by Byrne			1.00
4-Beatles, John Lennon, Elvis, Kiss & Devo cameos; Hitler app.			1.20

NOTE: *Buscema* a-4p. *Colan* a-1-5p, 7-9p. *Jack Davis* c-3. *Golden* a(p)-1, 5, 6(51pgs.). *Rogers* a-7, 8. *Simonson* a-7.

HOWARD THE DUCK: THE MOVIE
Dec, 1986 - No. 3, Feb, 1987 (Limited series)
Marvel Comics Group

1-3: Movie adaptation; r/Marvel Super Special			1.00

HOW BOYS AND GIRLS CAN HELP WIN THE WAR
1942 (10¢, one-shot)
The Parents' Magazine Institute

1-All proceeds used to buy war bonds	23.00	69.00	160.00

HOWDY DOODY (TV)(See Poll Parrot)
1/50 - No. 38, 7-9/56; No. 761, 1/57; No. 811, 7/57
Dell Publishing Co.

1-(Scarce)-Photo-c; 1st TV comic	70.00	210.00	700.00
2-Photo-c	30.00	90.00	300.00
3-5: All photo-c	18.00	54.00	180.00
6-Used in SOTI, pg. 309; painted-c begin	15.00	45.00	150.00
7-10	12.00	36.00	125.00
11-20: 13-X-mas-c	10.00	30.00	100.00
21-38	8.50	25.50	85.00
Four Color 761,811	9.50	28.50	95.00

HOW IT BEGAN
No. 15, 1939 (one-shot)
United Features Syndicate

Single Series 15	29.00	88.00	205.00

HOW SANTA GOT HIS RED SUIT (See March of Comics No. 2)

HOW STALIN HOPES WE WILL DESTROY AMERICA
1951 (Giveaway, 16 pgs.)
Joe Lowe Co. (Pictorial News)

nn	46.00	137.00	365.00

HOW THE WEST WAS WON (See Movie Comics)

HOW TO DRAW FOR THE COMICS
No date (1942?) (10¢, 64 pgs., B&W & color, no ads)
Street and Smith

nn-Art by Winsor McCay, George Marcoux (Supersnipe artist), Vernon Greene (The Shadow artist), Jack Binder(with biog.), Thorton Fisher, Jon Small, & Jack Farr; has biographies of each artist	23.00	69.00	160.00

H. P. LOVECRAFT'S CTHULHU

Dec, 1991 - No. 3, Feb?, 1992 ($2.50, limited series)
Millennium Publications

1-3: 1-Contains trading cards on thin stock		1.00	2.[

H. R. PUFNSTUF (TV) (See March of Comics #360)
Oct, 1970 - No. 8, July, 1972
Gold Key

1-Photo-c (all have photo-c?)	14.00	42.00	140.[
2-8	6.00	18.00	60.[

HUBERT AT CAMP MOONBEAM
No. 251, Oct, 1949 (one shot)
Dell Publishing Co.

Four Color 251	5.00	15.00	50.[

HUCK & YOGI JAMBOREE (TV)
Mar, 1961 ($1.00, 6-1/4x9", 116 pgs., cardboard-c, high quality paper) (B&W original material)
Dell Publishing Co.

nn	8.00	24.00	80.[

HUCK & YOGI WINTER SPORTS (TV)
No. 1310, Mar, 1962 (Hanna-Barbera) (one-shot)
Dell Publishing Co.

Four Color 1310	7.00	21.00	70.[

HUCK FINN (See The New Adventures of... & Power Record Comics)

HUCKLEBERRY FINN (Movie)
No. 1114, July, 1960
Dell Publishing Co.

Four Color 1114-Photo-c	5.00	15.00	50.[

HUCKLEBERRY HOUND (See Dell Giant #31,44, Golden Picture Story Book, Kite Fun Book, March of Comics #199, 214, 235, Spotlight #1 & Whitman Comic Books)

HUCKLEBERRY HOUND (TV)
No. 990, 5-7/59 - No. 43, 10/70 (Hanna-Barbera)
Dell/Gold Key No. 18 (10/62) on

Four Color 990(#1)-1st app. Hucklebery Hound, Yogi Bear, & Pixie & Dixie & Mr. Jinx	10.00	30.00	105.[
Four Color 1050,1054 (12/59)	7.00	21.00	70.[
3(1-2/60) - 7 (9-10/60)	7.00	21.00	70.[
Four Color 1141 (10/60)	7.00	21.00	70.[
8-10	5.00	15.00	50.[
11-17 (6-8/62)	4.00	12.00	40.[
18,19 (84pgs.; 18-20 titled ...Chuckleberry Tales)	7.00	21.00	75.[
20-30: 20-Titled Chuckleberry Tales	3.00	9.00	30.[
31-43: 37-Reprints	2.20	6.60	22.[

HUCKLEBERRY HOUND (TV)
Nov, 1970 - No. 8, Jan, 1972 (Hanna-Barbera)
Charlton Comics

1	2.60	7.50	18.[
2-8	1.85	5.50	13.[

HUEY, DEWEY, & LOUIE (See Donald Duck, 1938 for 1st app. Also see Mickey Mouse Magazine V4#2, V5#7 & Walt Disney's Junior Woodchucks Limited Series)

HUEY, DEWEY, & LOUIE BACK TO SCHOOL (See Dell Giant #22, 35, 49 & Dell Giants)

HUEY, DEWEY AND LOUIE JUNIOR WOODCHUCKS (Disney)
Aug, 1966 - No. 81, 1984 (See Walt Disney's Comics & Stories #125)
Gold Key No. 1-61/Whitman No. 62 on

1	3.50	15.00	45[
2,3(12/68)	2.20	9.50	28[
4,5(4/70)-r/two WDC&S D.Duck stys by Barks	2.80	12.00	35[
6-17	3.50	15.00	45[
18,27-30	1.60	4.80	16[

Hulk 2099 #5 © MEG

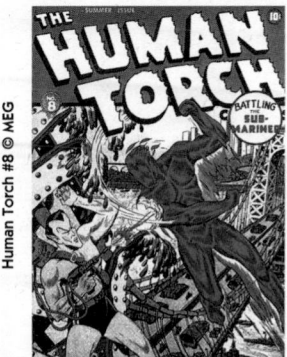
Human Torch #8 © MEG

Human Torch #24 © MEG

	GD25	FN65	NM94
9-23,25-New storyboarded scripts by Barks, 13-25 pgs. per issue			
	2.20	6.60	26.00
4,26: 26-r/Barks Donald Duck WDC&S stories	1.60	4.80	16.00
1-57,60-81: 35,41-r/Barks J.W. scripts	.80	2.40	8.00
8,59: 58-r/Barks Donald Duck WDC&S stories	1.00	3.00	10.00

UGGA BUNCH (TV)
ct, 1986 - No. 6, Aug, 1987
arvel Comics (Star Comics)

1-6			1.00

ULK (Magazine)(Formerly The Rampaging Hulk)(Also see The Incredible Hulk)
). 10, Aug., 1978 - No. 27, June, 1981 ($1.50)
arvel Comics

10-Bill Bixby interview	1.10	2.70	6.50
11-Moon Knight begins, ends 20	1.00	2.00	5.00
12-15: Moon Knight stories. 12-Lou Ferrigno interview	1.40		3.50
16,19,21,22,24-27: 24-Part color, Lou Ferrrigno interview. 25-Part color.			
26,27-are B&W		1.00	2.50
17,18,20: Moon Knight stories		1.30	3.25
23-Last full color issue; Banner is attacked		1.20	3.00

NOTE: **Alcala** a(i)-15, 17-20, 22, 24-27. **Buscema** a-23; c-26. **Chaykin** a(p)-11,
, 24-27. **Jusko** painted c-12. **Nebres** a-16. **Severin** a-19i. Moon Knight by **Sienkiewicz** in 13-
, 17, 18, 20. **Simonson** a-27; c-23. Dominic Fortune appears in #21-24.

ULK: FUTURE IMPERFECT
an, 1993 - No. 2, Dec, 1992 (In error) ($5.95, 52 pgs., squarebound, limited
eries)
arvel Comics

,2: Embossed-c; Peter David story & George Perez-c/a. 1-1st app. Maestro.			
	1.00	2.60	6.00

ULK 2099
ec, 1994 - No. 10, Sept, 1995 ($1.50/$1.95)
arvel Comics

1 ($2.50)-Green foil-c		1.00	2.50
2-6: 2-A. Kubert-c			1.50
7-10: 7-begin $1.95-c		.80	2.00

UMAN FLY
#63 - 1964 (Reprints)
W. Enterprises/Super

W. Reprint #1-Reprints Blue Beetle #44('46)	1.65	4.20	10.00
uper Reprint #10-R/Blue Beetle #46('47)	1.65	4.20	10.00

UMAN FLY, THE
ept, 1977 - No. 19, Mar, 1979
arvel Comics Group

1-Origin; Spider-Man x-over		1.20	3.00
2-Ghost Rider app.		1.60	4.00
3-19: 9-Daredevil x-over; Byrne-c(p)		.75	1.80

OTE: **Austin** c-4i, 9i. **Elias** a-1, 3p, 4p, 7p, 10-12p, 15p, 18p, 19p. **Layton** c-19.

UMAN TARGET SPECIAL (TV)
ov, 1991 ($2.00, 52 pgs., one-shot)
C Comics

		.80	2.00

UMAN TORCH, THE (Red Raven #1)(See All-Select, All Winners, Marvel
ystery, Men's Adventures, Mystic Comics (2nd series), Sub-Mariner, USA
Young Men)
). 2, Fall, 1940 - No. 15, Spring, 1944;
). 16, Fall, 1944 - No. 35, Mar, 1949 (Becomes Love Tales #36 on);
). 36, April, 1954 - No. 38, Aug, 1954
mely-Marvel Comics (TP 2,3/TCI 4-9/SePl 10/SnPC 11-25/CnPC
-35/Atlas Comics (CPC 36-38))

	GD25	FN65	VF82	NM94
(#1)-Intro & Origin Toro; The Falcon, The Fiery Mask, Mantor the Magician,				
& Microman only app.; Human Torch by Burgos, Sub-Mariner by Everett				

	GD25	FN65	NM94
begin (origin of each in text) 1900.00	5700.00	12,350.00	21,000.00
(Estimated up to 190 total copies exist, 10 in NM/Mint)			

	GD25	FN65	NM94
3(#2)-40pg. H.T. story; H.T. & S.M. battle over who is best artist in text-			
Everett or Burgos	422.00	1267.00	4200.00
4(#3)-Origin The Patriot in text; last Everett Sub-Mariner; 1st Nazi war-c this			
title (see Marvel Mystery #4); Sid Greene-a	322.00	967.00	3200.00
5(#4)-The Patriot app; Angel x-over in Sub-Mariner (Summer, 1941)			
	288.00	862.00	2400.00
5-Human Torch battles Sub-Mariner (Fall, '41); 60 pg. story			
	367.00	1100.00	3600.00
6,9	181.00	543.00	1450.00
7-1st Japanese war-c	193.00	581.00	1550.00
8-Human Torch battles Sub-Mariner; Wolverton-a, 1 pg.; 52 pg. story			
	288.00	862.00	2400.00
10-Human Torch battles Sub-Mariner; Wolverton-a, 1 pg.; 45 pg. story			
	231.00	693.00	1850.00
11,13-15: 14-1st Atlas Globe logo (Winter, 1943-44; see All Winners #11 also)			
	143.00	431.00	1150.00
12-classic-c	188.00	562.00	1500.00
16-20: 20-Last War issue	103.00	309.00	825.00
21,22,24-30:	96.00	288.00	770.00
23 (Sum/46)-Becomes Junior Miss 24? Classic Schomburg Robot-c			
	110.00	330.00	880.00
31-Namora x-over in Sub-Mariner (also #30); last Toro			
	81.00	243.00	650.00
32-Sungirl, Namora app.; Sungirl-c	81.00	243.00	650.00
33-Capt. America x-over	84.00	253.00	675.00
34-Sungirl solo	75.00	225.00	600.00
35-Captain America & Sungirl app. (1949)	84.00	253.00	675.00
36-38(1954)-Sub-Mariner in all	81.00	243.00	650.00

NOTE: **Ayers** Human Torch in 36(3). **Brodsky** c-25, 31-33?, 37, 38, **Burgos** c-36. **Everett** a-1-3,
27, 28, 30, 37, 38. **Powell** a-36(Sub-Mariner). **Schomburg** c-1-3, 5-8, 10-23. **Sekowsky** c-28,
34?, 35? **Shores** c-24, 26, 27, 29, 30. **Mickey Spillane** text 4-6. Bondage c-2, 12, 19.

HUMAN TORCH, THE (Also see Avengers West Coast, Fantastic Four, The
Invaders, Saga of the Original… & Strange Tales #101)
Sept, 1974 - No. 8, Nov, 1975
Marvel Comics Group

1: 1-8-r/stories from Strange Tales #101-108	1.00	2.00	5.00
2-8: 1st H.T. title since G.A. 7-vs. Sub-Mariner		1.20	3.00

NOTE: Golden Age & Silver Age Human Torch-r #1-8. **Ayers** r-6, 7. **Kirby/Ayers** r-1-5, 8.

HUMBUG (Satire by Harvey Kurtzman)
Aug, 1957 - No. 9, May, 1958; No. 10, June, 1958; No. 11, Oct, 1958
Humbug Publications

1-Wood-a (intro pgs. only)	23.00	69.00	160.00
2	11.00	33.00	75.00
3-9: 8-Elvis in Jailbreak Rock	10.00	30.00	60.00
10,11-Magazine format. 10-Photo-c	12.00	36.00	85.00
Bound Volume(#1-6)-Sold by publisher	38.00	114.00	265.00
Bound Volume(#7-11)	40.00	120.00	315.00

NOTE: **Davis** a-1-11. **Elder** a-2-4, 6-9, 11. **Heath** a-2, 4-8, 10. **Jaffee** a-2, 4-9. **Kurtzman** a-11.

HUMDINGER (Becomes White Rider and Super Horse #3 on?)
May-June, 1946 - V2#2, July-Aug, 1947
Novelty Press/Premium Group

1-Jerkwater Line, Mickey Starlight by Don Rico, Dink begin			
	26.00	79.00	185.00
2	11.50	34.00	80.00
3-6, V2#1,2	8.35	25.00	50.00

HUMOR (See All Humor Comics)

HUMPHREY COMICS (Joe Palooka Presents…; also see Joe Palooka)
Oct, 1948 - No. 22, Apr, 1952
Harvey Publications

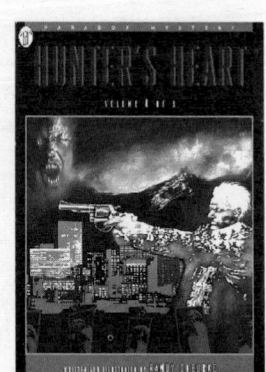
Hunter's Heart #1 © DC

Huntress #2 © DC

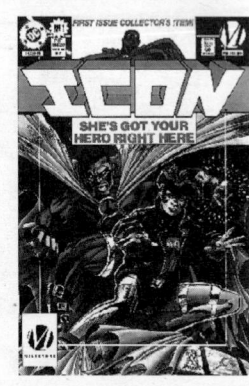
Icon #1 © Milestone Media

	GD25	FN65	NM94
1-Joe Palooka's pal (r); (52 pgs.)-Powell-a	11.00	33.00	75.00
2,3: Powell-a	5.85	17.50	35.00
4-Boy Heroes app.; Powell-a	6.70	20.00	40.00
5-8,10: 5,6-Powell-a. 7-Little Dot app.	4.35	13.00	26.00
9-Origin Humphrey	5.85	17.50	35.00
11-22	4.00	10.00	20.00

HUNCHBACK OF NOTRE DAME, THE
No. 854, Oct, 1957 (one shot)
Dell Publishing Co.

	GD25	FN65	NM94
Four Color 854-Movie, photo-c	13.00	40.00	130.00

HUNK
Aug, 1961 - No. 11, 1963
Charlton Comics

	GD25	FN65	NM94
1	2.85	8.50	20.00
2-11	1.65	4.20	10.00

HUNTED (Formerly My Love Memoirs)
No. 13, July, 1950 - No. 2, Sept, 1950
Fox Features Syndicate

	GD25	FN65	NM94
13(#1)-Used in SOTI, pg. 42 & illo. "Treating police contemptuously" (lower left); Hollingsworth bondage-c	28.00	84.00	195.00
2	11.00	33.00	75.00

HUNTER'S HEART
June, 1995 - No. 3, Aug, 1995 ($5.95, B&W, limited series)
DC Comics

	GD25	FN65	NM94
1-3	1.00	2.60	6.00

HUNTRESS, THE (See All-Star Comics #69, Batman Family, Brave & the Bold #62, DC Super Stars #17, Detective #652, Infinity, Inc. #1, Sensation Comics #68 & Wonder Woman #271)
Apr, 1989 - No. 19, Oct, 1990 ($1.00, mature)
DC Comics

1-19: Staton-c/a(p) in all. 17-19-Batman-c/stories			1.25

HUNTRESS, THE
June, 1994 - No. 4, Sept, 1994 ($1.50, limited series)
DC Comics

1-4-Netzer-c/a: 2-Batman app.		.70	1.75

HURRICANE COMICS
1945 (52 pgs.)
Cambridge House

	GD25	FN65	NM94
1-(Humor, funny animal)	19.00	56.00	130.00

HURRICANE KIDS, THE (Also See Magic Morro, The Owl, Popular Comics #45)
1941 (Giveaway, 7-1/2x5-1/4", soft-c)
R.S. Callender

	GD25	FN65	NM94
nn-Will Ely-a.	10.00	30.00	60.00

HYBRIDS
Jan, 1994 ($2.50, one-shot)
Continuity Comics

1-Neal Adams-c(p) & part-a(i); embossed-c.		1.00	2.50

HYBRIDS DEATHWATCH 2000
Apr, 1993 - No. 3, Aug, 1993 ($2.50)
Continuity Comics

0-(Giveaway)-Foil-c; Neal Adams-c(i) & plots (also #1,2)		1.00	2.50
1-5: 1-Polybagged w/card; die-cut-c. 2-Thermal-c. 3-Polybagged w/card; indestructible-c; Adams plot. 4,5-Valeria She-Bat; origin Hybrids; Adams-c(p)		1.00	2.50

HYBRIDS ORIGIN
1993 - No. 5, 1994? ($2.50)
Continuity Comics

	GD25	FN65	NM94
1-5: 2,3-Neal Adams-c. 4,5-Valeria the She-Bat app. Adams-c(i)		1.00	2.

HYDE-25
Apr, 1995 ($2.95, one-shot)
Harris Publications

0-coupon for poster; r/Vampirella's 1st app.		1.40	3.

HYDROMAN (See Heroic Comics)

HYPERKIND (See Razorline)
Sept, 1993 - No. 9, May, 1994 ($1.75/$1.95)
Marvel Comics

1-($2.50)-Foil embossed-c; by Clive Barker		1.00	2.
2-8		.70	1.
9-($1.95)		.80	2.

HYPERKIND UNLEASHED
Aug, 1994 ($2.95, 52 pgs., one-shot)
Marvel Comics

1		1.20	3.

HYPER MYSTERY COMICS
May, 1940 - No. 2, June, 1940 (68 pgs.)
Hyper Publications

	GD25	FN65	NM94
1-Hyper, the Phenomenal begins	162.00	487.00	1300
2	95.00	286.00	765

I AIM AT THE STARS (Movie)
No. 1148, Nov-Jan/1960-61 (one-shot)
Dell Publishing Co.

	GD25	FN65	NM94
Four Color 1148-The Werner Von Braun Sty-photo-c	7.00	21.00	70

I AM COYOTE (See Eclipse Graphic Album Series & Eclipse Magazine #2)

I AM LEGEND
1991 - No. 4, 1991 ($5.95, B&W, squarebound, 68 pgs.)
Eclipse Books

	GD25	FN65	NM94
1-4: Based on 1954 novel		1.00	2.60	6

IBIS, THE INVINCIBLE (See Fawcett Miniatures, Mighty Midget & Whiz)
1943 (Feb) - #2, 1943; #3, Wint, 1945 - #5, Fall, 1946; #6, Spring, 1948
Fawcett Publications

	GD25	FN65	NM94
1-Origin Ibis; Raboy-c; on sale 1/2/43	150.00	450.00	1200
2-Bondage-c	75.00	225.00	600
3-Wolverton-a #3-6 (4 pgs. each)	62.00	187.00	500
4-6: 5-Bondage-c	44.00	132.00	350

NOTE: *Mac Raboy c(p)-3-5.* **Shaffenberger** *c-6.*

I-BOTS (See Isaac Asimov's I-BOTS)

ICE AGE ON THE WORLD OF MAGIC: THE GATHERING (See Magic The Gathering)

ICE KING OF OZ, THE (See First Comics Graphic Novel #13)

ICEMAN (Also See The Champions & X-Men #94)
Dec, 1984 - No. 4, June, 1985 (Limited series)
Marvel Comics Group

1		.80	2
2,4		.70	1
3-The Defenders, Champions (Ghost Rider) & the original X-Men x-over		1.10	2

NOTE: *Zeck c-1-4.*

ICON
May, 1993 - Present ($1.50/$1.75/$2.50)
DC Comics (Milestone)

1-($2.95)-Collector's Edition polybagged w/poster & trading card (direct sale only)		1.20	3
1-14: 9-Simonson-c			1

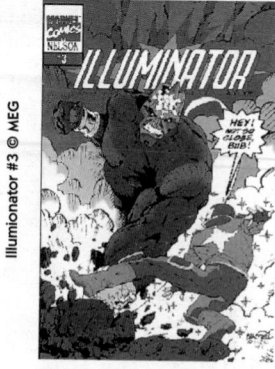

Idol #2 © MEG

Illuminator #3 © MEG.NELSON

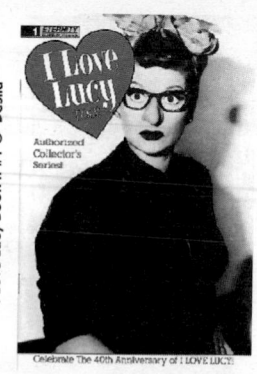

I Love Lucy Book II #1 © Desilu

Celebrate The 40th Anniversary of I LOVE LUCY!

IL

	GD25	FN65	NM94
15-24,26: 15-Begin $1.75-c. 15,16-Worlds Collide Pt. 4 & 11. 15-Superboy app.			
16-Superman-c/story		.70	1.75
25-($2.95, 52 pgs.)			3.00
27-30,32-45: Begin $2.50-c. 40-Vs. Blood Syndicate			2.50
31-(99¢)			1.00

IDAHO
June-Aug, 1963 - No. 8, July-Sept, 1965
Dell Publishing Co.

1	2.00	6.00	14.00
2-8: 5-7-Painted-c	1.30	3.25	8.00

IDEAL (... a Classical Comic) (2nd Series) (Love Romances No. 6 on)
July, 1948 - No. 5, March, 1949 (Feature length stories)
Timely Comics

1-Antony & Cleopatra	29.00	86.00	200.00
2-The Corpses of Dr. Sacotti	26.00	79.00	185.00
3-Joan of Arc; used in **SOTI**, pg. 308 'Boer War'	23.00	69.00	160.00
4-Richard the Lion-hearted; titled "...the World's Greatest Comics"; The Witness app.	40.00	120.00	285.00
5-Ideal Love & Romance; change to love; photo-c	14.00	43.00	100.00

IDEAL COMICS (1st Series) (Willie Comics No. 5 on)
Fall, 1944 - No. 4, Spring, 1946
Timely Comics (MgPC)

1-Funny animal; Super Rabbit in all	16.00	47.00	110.00
2	10.00	30.00	70.00
3,4	10.00	30.00	65.00

IDEAL LOVE & ROMANCE (See Ideal, A Classical Comic)

IDEAL ROMANCE (Formerly Tender Romance)
No. 3, April, 1954 - No. 8, Feb, 1955 (Diary Confessions No. 9 on)
Key Publications

3-Bernard Baily-c	5.85	17.50	35.00
4-8: 4,5-B. Baily-c	4.00	10.00	20.00

IDOL
1992 - No. 3, 1992 ($2.95, mini-series, 52 pgs.)
Marvel Comics (Epic Comics)

Book 1-3		1.20	3.00

I DREAM OF JEANNIE (TV)
Apr, 1965 - No. 2, Dec, 1966 (Photo-c)
Dell Publishing Co.

1-Barbara Eden photo-c, each	13.00	39.00	130.00
2	10.00	30.00	100.00

IF THE DEVIL WOULD TALK
1950; 1958 (32 pgs.; paper cover; in full color)
Roman Catholic Catechetical Guild/Impact Publ.

nn-(Scarce)-About secularism (20-30 copies known to exist); very low distribution	65.00	195.00	525.00
1958 Edition-(Impact Publ.); art & script changed to meet church criticism of earlier edition; 80 plus copies known to exist	32.00	96.00	225.00
Black & White version of nn edition; small size; only 4 known copies exist	30.00	90.00	200.00

NOTE: The original edition of this book was printed and killed by the Guild's board of directors. It is believed that a very limited number of copies were distributed. The 1958 version was a complete bomb with very limited, if any, circulation. In 1979, 11 original, 4 1958 reprints, and 4 B&W's surfaced from the Guild's old files in St. Paul, Minnesota.

ILLUMINATOR
1993 - No. 4, 1993 ($2.95, 52 pgs.)
Marvel Comics/Nelson Publ.

1,2-($4.99)	1.00	2.00	5.00
3,4		1.20	3.00

ILLUSTRATED GAGS

	GD25	FN65	NM94
No. 16, 1940 United Features Syndicate			
Single Series 16	15.00	45.00	105.00

ILLUSTRATED LIBRARY OF..., AN (See Classics Illustrated Giants)

ILLUSTRATED STORIES OF THE OPERAS
1943 (16 pgs.; B&W) (25 cents) (cover-B&W & red)
Baily (Bernard) Publ. Co.

nn-(Rare)-Faust (part-r in Cisco Kid #1)	50.00	150.00	400.00
nn-(Rare)-Aida	50.00	150.00	400.00
nn-(Rare)-Carmen; Baily-a	50.00	150.00	400.00
nn-(Rare)-Rigoleito	50.00	150.00	400.00

ILLUSTRATED STORY OF ROBIN HOOD & HIS MERRY MEN, THE
(See Classics Giveaways, 12/44)

ILLUSTRATED TARZAN BOOK, THE (See Tarzan Book)

I LOVED (Formerly Rulah; Colossal Features Magazine No. 33 on)
No. 28, July, 1949 - No. 32, Mar, 1950
Fox Features Syndicate

28	8.00	24.00	48.00
29-32	5.00	15.00	30.00

I LOVE LUCY
6/90 - No. 6, 1990;V2#1, 11/90 - No. 6, 1991 ($2.95, B&W, mini-series)
Eternity Comics

..1-6: Reprints 1950s comic strip; photo-c		1.50	3.00
Book II #1-6: Reprints comic strip; photo-c		1.50	3.00
...In Full Color 1 (1991, $5.95, 52 pgs.)-Reprints I Love Lucy Comics #4,5,8,16; photo-c with embossed logo (2 versions exist, one with pgs. 18 & 19 reversed, the other corrected)		3.00	6.00
...In 3-D 1 (1991, $3.95, w/glasses)-Reprints I Love Lucy Comics; photo-c sealed in plastic bag		2.00	4.00

I LOVE LUCY COMICS (TV) (Also see The Lucy Show)
No. 535, Feb, 1954 - No. 35, Apr-June, 1962 (All have Lucille Ball photo-c)
Dell Publishing Co.

Four Color 535(#1)	47.50	142.50	475.00
Four Color 559(#2, 5/54)	32.50	97.50	325.00
3 (8-10/54) - 5	19.00	57.00	190.00
6-10	15.00	45.00	150.00
11-20	11.00	33.00	110.00
21-35	8.50	25.50	85.00

I LOVE YOU
June, 1950 (one-shot)
Fawcett Publications

1-Photo-c	11.50	34.00	80.00

I LOVE YOU (Formerly In Love)
No. 7, 9/55 - No. 121, 12/76; No. 122, 3/79 - No. 130, 5/80
Charlton Comics

7-Kirby-c; Powell-a	10.00	30.00	65.00
8-10	4.00	12.00	24.00
11-16,18-20	2.80	7.00	14.00
17-(68 pg. Giant)	3.20	8.00	16.00
21-25,27-50	2.85	8.50	20.00
26-No Torres-a	1.65	4.20	10.00
51-59	1.00	2.60	6.00
60-(1/66)-Elvis Presley line drawn c/story	14.00	43.00	100.00
61-85		1.60	4.00
86-130			1.20

I, LUSIPHER (Becomes Poison Elves, 1st series #8 on)
1991 - No. 7, 1992 (B&W, magazine size)
Mulehide Graphics

1-Drew Hayes-c/a/scripts	8.50	26.00	60.00

Impact Comics #4 © WMG

Impulse #10 © DC

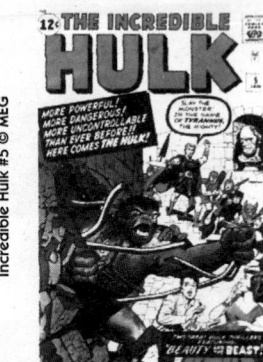

Incredible Hulk #5 © MEG

	GD25	FN65	NM94
2	5.70	17.00	40.00
3-Low print run	7.00	21.50	50.00
4,5	5.70	17.00	40.00
6,7	5.00	15.00	35.00

I'M A COP
1954 - No. 3, 1954?
Magazine Enterprises

1(A-1 #111)-Powell-c/a in all	11.00	33.00	75.00
2(A-1 #126), 3(A-1 #128)	6.70	20.00	40.00

IMAGE GRAPHIC NOVEL
1984 ($6.95)(Advertised as Pacific Comics Graphic Novel #1)
Image International

1-The Seven Samuroid; Brunner-c/a		3.50	7.00

IMAGES OF SHADOWHAWK (Also see Shadowhawk)
Sept, 1993 - No. 3, 1994 ($1.95, limited series)
Image Comics

1-3: 1-Keith Giffen-c/a; Trencher app.		.80	2.00

IMAGE ZERO
1993 (Received through mail w/coupons from Image books)
Image Comics

0-Savage Dragon, StormWatch, Shadowhawk, Strykeforce; 1st app. Troll; 1st app. McFarlane's Freak, Blotch, Sweat and Bludd			
	2.10	4.50	15.00

I'M DICKENS - HE'S FENSTER (TV)
May-July, 1963 - No. 2, Aug-Oct, 1963 (Photo-c)
Dell Publishing Co.

1,2	4.00	12.00	40.00

I MET A HANDSOME COWBOY
No. 324, Mar, 1951
Dell Publishing Co.

Four Color 324	9.00	27.00	90.00

IMMORTALIS (See Mortigan Goth: Immortalis)

IMMORTAL DOCTOR FATE, THE
Jan, 1995 - No. 3, Mar, 1985 ($1.25, limited series)
DC Comics

1-3: 1-Simonson-c/a. 2-Giffen-c/a(p)			1.30

IMPACT
Mar-Apr, 1955 - No. 5, Nov-Dec, 1955
E. C. Comics

1-Not code approved	15.00	45.00	105.00
2	11.00	33.00	75.00
3-5: 4-Crandall-a	10.00	30.00	58.00

NOTE: Crandall a-1-4. **Davis** a-2-4; c-1-5. **Evans** a-1, 4, 5. **Ingels** a-in all. **Kamen** a-3. **Krigstein** a-1, 5. **Orlando** a-2.

IMPACT CHRISTMAS SPECIAL
1991 ($2.50, 68 pgs.)
DC Comics (Impact Comics)

1-Gift of the Magi by Infantino/Rogers; The Black Hood, The Fly, The Jaguar, & The Shield stories	1.00		2.50

IMPOSSIBLE MAN SUMMER VACATION SPECTACULAR, THE
Aug, 1990; No. 2, Sept, 1991 ($2.00, 68 pgs.) (See Fantastic Four#11)
Marvel Comics

..1-Spider Man, Quasar, Dr. Strange, She-Hulk, Punisher & Dr. Doom stories; Barry Crain, Guice-a; Art Adams-c(i)		.80	2.00
..2-Ka Zar & Thor app.; Cable Wolverine-c app.		1.00	2.00

IMPULSE (See Flash #92, 2nd Series)
Apr, 1995 - Present ($1.50/$1.75)

DC Comics

	GD25	FN65	NM94
1-Mark Waid scripts & Humberto Ramos-c/a(p) begin; brief retelling of origin			
	1.00	2.60	6.00
2-4		1.40	3.50
5-20: 5-Begin $1.75-c. 9-XS from Legion (Impulse's cousin) comes to the 20th Century, returns to the 30th Century in #12. 10-Dead Heat Pt. 3 (cont'd in Flash #110). 11-Dead Heat Pt. 4 (cont'd in Flash #111); Johnny Quick dies. 14-Trickster app. 17-Zatanna-c/app.		.70	1.75
Annual 1 (1996, $2.95)-Legends of the Dead Earth; Ramos-c; Mike Parobeck-a			3.00

INCAL, THE
Nov, 1988 - No. 3, Jan, 1989 ($10.95/$12.95, mature)
Marvel Comics (Epic Comics)

1,3: Moebius-c/a in all; sexual content	1.65	4.70	11.00
2-($12.95)	1.85	5.50	13.00

INCOMPLETE DEATH'S HEAD (Also see Death's Head)
Jan, 1993 - No. 12, Dec, 1993 ($1.75, limited series)
Marvel Comics UK

1-($2.95, 56 pgs.)-Die-cut cover		1.20	3.00
2-11: 2-Re-intro original Death's Head. 3-Original Death's Head vs. Dragon's Claws		.70	1.75
12-($2.50, 52 pgs.)-She Hulk app.		1.00	2.50

INCREDIBLE HULK, THE (See Aurora, The Avengers #1, The Defenders #1, Giant-Size..., Hulk, Marvel Collectors Item Classics, Marvel Comics Presents #26, Marvel Fanfare, Marvel Treasury Edition, Power Record Comics, Rampaging Hulk, She-Hulk & 2099 Unlimited)

INCREDIBLE HULK, THE
May, 1962 - No. 6, Mar, 1963; No. 102, Apr, 1968 - Present

Marvel Comics Group	GD25	FN65	VF82	NM94
1-Origin & 1st app. (skin is grey colored); Kirby pencils begin, end #5				
	833.00	2500.00	6250.00	11,000.00
2-1st green skinned Hulk; Kirby/Ditko-a				
	180.00	540.00	1170.00	2300.00

	GD25	FN65	NM94
3-Origin retold; 1st app. Ringmaster & Hercules (9/62)			
	130.00	390.00	1400.00
4,5: 4-Brief origin retold	120.00	360.00	1300.00
6-Intro. Teen Brigade; all Ditko-a	180.00	540.00	1900.00
102-(Formerly Tales to Astonish)-Origin retold; story continued from Tales to Astonish #101	19.00	56.00	150.00
103	9.70	29.00	68.00
104-Rhino app.	9.00	26.50	62.00
105-108: 105-1st Missing Link. 107-Mandarin app.(9/68). 108-Mandarin & Nick Fury app. (10/68).	7.50	22.00	52.00
109,110: 109-Ka-Zar app.	5.00	15.00	35.00
111-117: 117-Last 12 cent issue	4.00	12.50	29.00
118-Hulk vs. Sub-Mariner	3.70	11.00	26.00
119-121,123-125	2.30	6.70	16.00
122-Hulk battles Thing (12/69)	4.85	14.50	34.00
126-140: 126-1st Barbara Norriss (Valkyrie). 131-Hulk vs. Iron Man; 1st Jim Wilson, Hulk's new sidekick. 136-1st Xeron, The Star-Slayer. 140-Written by Harlan Ellison; 1st Jarella, Hulk's love	1.60	4.20	10.00
141-1st app. Doc Samson (7/71)	2.15	6.50	25.00
142-144,146-157-161: 149-1st app. The Inheritor. 155-1st app. Shaper. 158-Warlock cameo(12/72). 161-The Mimic dies; Beast app.	1.00	2.60	6.00
145-(52 pgs.)-Origin retold	1.50	3.75	9.00
162-1st app. The Wendigo (4/73); Beast app.	1.30	3.00	8.00
163-171,173-175: 163-1st app. The Gremlin. 164-1st Capt. Omen & Colonel John D. Armbruster. 166-1st Zzzax. 168-1st The Harpy; nudity panels of Betty Brant. 169-1st app. Bi-Beast	1.00	2.50	6.00
165-Variant w/4 extra pgs. of ads on slick paper (7/73)			
	1.20	3.00	7.00

Incredible Hulk #224 © MEG

Incredible Hulk #300 © MEG

Incredible Hulk #444 © MEG

	GD25	FN65	NM94

172-X-Men cameo; origin Juggernaut retold — 1.50 / 3.75 / 9.00
176-Warlock cameo (2 panels only); same date as Strange Tales #178 (6/74) — 1.00 / 2.00 / 5.00
177-1st actual death of Warlock (last panel only) — 1.20 / 3.00 / 7.00
178-Rebirth of Warlock — 1.65 / 4.20 / 10.00
179-No Warlock — 1.00 / 2.00 / 5.00
180-(10/74)-1st app. Wolverine (cameo last pg.) — 10.00 / 30.00 / 70.00
181-(11/74)-1st full Wolverine story — 40.00 / 120.00 / 400.00
182-Wolverine cameo; see Giant-Size X-Men #1 for next app.; 1st Crackajack Jackson — 8.00 / 23.50 / 55.00
183-199: 185-Death of Col. Armbruster — 1.60 / 4.00
200-Silver Surfer app.; anniversary issue — 3.60 / 11.00 / 25.00
201-240: 212-1st app. The Constrictor. 227-Original Avengers app. 232-Capt. America x-over from C.A. #230. 233-Marvel Man app. 234-(4/79)-1st app. Quasar (formerly Marvel Man & changes name to Quasar) — 1.40 / 3.50
241-249,251-299: 243-Cage app. 271-Rocket Raccoon app. 272-Sasquatch & Wendigo app.; Wolverine & Alpha Flight cameo in flashback. 278,279-Most Marvel characters app. (Wolverine in both). 279-X-Men & Alpha Flight cameos. 282-284-She-Hulk app. 293-F.F. app. — 1.00 / 2.50
250-Giant size; Silver Surfer app. — 1.65 / 4.20 / 10.00
300-(11/84, 52 pgs.)-Spider-Man app in new black costume on-c & 2 pg. cameo — 1.00 / 2.00 / 5.00
301-313: 312-Origin Hulk retold — 1.20 / 3.00
314-Byrne-c/a begins, ends #319 — 1.00 / 2.00 / 5.00
315-319: 319-Bruce Banner & Betty Talbot wed — 1.20 / 3.00
320-323,325,327-329 — 1.00 / 2.50
324-1st app. Grey Hulk since #1 (c-swipe of #1) — 1.85 / 5.50 / 13.00
326-Grey vs. Green Hulk — 1.00 / 2.60 / 6.00
330-1st McFarlane issue (4/87); death of Thunderbolt Ross — 2.60 / 7.50 / 18.00
331-Grey Hulk series begins — 1.70 / 5.00 / 12.00
332-334,336-339: 336,337-X-Factor app. — 1.50 / 3.75 / 9.00
335-No McFarlane-a — 1.20 / 3.00
340-Hulk battles Wolverine by McFarlane — 5.70 / 17.00 / 40.00
341-344 — 1.20 / 3.00 / 7.00
345-($1.50, 52 pgs.) — 1.30 / 3.25 / 8.00
346-Last McFarlane issue — 1.00 / 2.60 / 6.00
347-349,351-358,360-366: 347-1st app. Marlo — 1.20 / 3.00
350-Hulk/Thing battle — 1.00 / 2.00 / 5.00
359-Wolverine app. (illusion only) — 1.80 / 4.50
367-1st app Dale Keown a on Hulk (3/90) — 2.15 / 6.50 / 15.00
368-Sam Kieth-c/a, 1st app. Pantheon — 1.85 / 5.50 / 13.00
369,370-Dale Keown-c/a. 370,371-Original Defenders app. — 1.65 / 4.70 / 11.00
371,373-376: Keown-c/a. 376-Green vs. Grey Hulk — 1.20 / 2.90 / 7.00
372-Green Hulk app.; Keown-c/a. — 2.15 / 6.50 / 15.00
377-1st all new Hulk; fluorescent-c; Keown-c/a — 2.40 / 7.20 / 17.00
377-Fluorescent green logo 2nd printing — 1.00 / 2.00 / 5.00
378,380,389: No Keown-a. 380-Doc Samson app. — 1.20 / 3.00
379-Keown-a — 1.00 / 2.00 / 5.00
381-388,390-392-Keown-a. 385-Infinity Gauntlet x-over. 389-Last $1.00-c. — 1.00 / 2.00 / 5.00
393-($2.50, 72 pgs.)-30th anniversary issue; green foil stamped-c; swipes-c to #1; has pin-ups of classic battles; Keown-c/a — 1.00 / 2.00 / 5.00
393-2nd printing — 1.20 / 3.00
394-397: 394-No Keown-c/a; intro Trauma. 395,396-Punisher-c/stories; Keown-c/a. 397-Begin "Ghost of the Past" 4-part sty; Keown c/a — .80 / 2.00
398,399: 398-Last Keown-c/a — .80 / 2.00
400-($2.50, 68 pgs.)-Holo-grafx foil-c & r/TTA #63 — 1.60 / 4.00
401-416: 402-Return of Doc Samson — .80 / 2.00
417-424: 417-Begin $1.50-c; Rick Jones' bachelor party; Hulk returns from "Future Imperfect"; bound-in trading card sheet. 418-(Regular edition)-Rick Jones marries Marlo; includes cameo apps of various Marvel characters

as well as DC's Death & Peter David. 420-Death of Jim Wilson. — .70 / 1.75
418-($2.50)-Collector's Edition w/gatefold die-cut-c — 1.20 / 3.00
425 ($2.25, 52 pgs.) — 1.00 / 2.50
425 ($3.50, 52 pgs.)-Holographic-c — 4.00
426-434, 436-460: 426-Begin $1.95-c. 427, 428-Man-Thing app. 431,432-Abomination app. 434-Funeral for Nick Fury. 436-Ghosts of the Future begins, ends #440. 439-Hulk becomes Maestro, Avengers app. 440-Thor-c/app. 441,442-She-Hulk-c/app. 442-Molecule Man app. — .90 / 2.00
435 ($2.50)-Rhino-app. — 1.00 / 2.50
443-445: 443-Begin $1.50-c. — 1.50
Special 1 (10/68, 25¢, 68 pg.)-New 51 pg. story, Hulk battles The Inhumans (early app.); Steranko-c. — 9.60 / 28.75 / 67.00
Special 2 (10/69, 25¢, 68 pg.)-Origin retold — 6.00 / 18.00 / 42.00
Special 3 (1/71, 25¢, 68 pg.) — 1.50 / 3.75 / 9.00
Special 4 (1/72) — 1.20 / 3.00 / 7.00
Annual 5 (1976) — 1.00 / 2.00 / 5.00
Annual 6 (1977) — 1.20 / 3.00
Annual 7 (1978)-Byrne/Layton-c/a; Iceman & Angel app. in book-length story — 1.60 / 4.00
Annual 8-17: 8('79)-Book-length Sasquatch-c/story. 9('80). 10('81). 11('82)-Doc Samson back-up by Miller(p)(5 pgs.); Spider-Man & Avengers app.; Buckler-a(p). 12 ('83). 13('84). 14('85). 15('86). 16('90, $2.00, 68 pgs.)-She-Hulk app. 17(1991, $2.00)-Origin retold — .80 / 2.00
Annual 18 (1992, $2.25, 68 pgs.)-Return of the Defenders, Pt. I; no Keown-a — .90 / 2.25
Annual 19 (1993, $2.95, 68 pgs.)-Bagged w/card — 1.20 / 3.00
Annual 20 (1994, $2.95, 68 pgs.) — 1.20 / 3.00
...And Wolverine 1 (10/86, $2.50)-r/1st app. #180-181.1.65 — 4.20 / 10.00
...Ground Zero ('95, $12.95) r/#340-346 — 1.85 / 5.50 / 13.00
...Versus Quasimodo 1 (3/83, one-shot)-Based on Saturday morning cartoon — .80 / 2.00
...Versus Venom 1 (4/94, $2.50, one-shot)-Embossed-c; red foil logo — 1.10 / 2.75

NOTE: Adkins a-111-116i. Austin a(i)-350, 351, 353, 354; c-302i, 350i. Ayers a-3-5i. Buckler a-Annual 5; c-252. John Buscema c-202p. Byrne a-314-319p; c-314-316, 318, 319, 359, Annual 14i. Colan c-363. Ditko a-2i, 6, 249, Annual 2r(5), 3r, 9p; c-2i, 6, 235, 249. Everett c-133i. Golden c-248, 251. Kane c(p)-193, 194, 196, 198. Dale Keown a(p)-367, 369-377, 379-388, 390-393, 395-398; c-369-377p, 381, 382p, 384, 385, 386, 387p, 388, 390p, 391-393, 395p, 396, 397p, 398. Kirby a-1-5p, Special 2, 3i; Annual 5p; c-1-5, Annual 5. McFarlane a-330-334p, 336-339p, 340-343, 344-346p; c-330p, 340p, 341-343, 344p, 345, 346p. Mignola c-302, 305, 313. Miller c-258p, 261, 264, 268. Mooney a-230p, 287i, 288i. Powell a-Special 3r(2). Romita a-Annual 17p. Severin a(i)-108-110, 131-133, 141-151, 153-155; c(i)-109, 110, 132, 142, 144-155. Simonson c-283, 364-367. Starlin a-222p; c-217. Staton a(i)-187-189, 191-209. Tuska a-102i, 105i, 106i, 218p. Williamson a-310i; c-310i, 311i. Wrightson c-197.

INCREDIBLE MR. LIMPET, The (See Movie Classics)

INCREDIBLE SCIENCE FICTION (Formerly Weird Science-Fantasy)
No. 30, July-Aug, 1955 - No. 33, Jan-Feb, 1956
E.C. Comics

30,33: 33-Story-r/Weird Fantasy #18 — 33.00 / 99.00 / 230.00
31-Williamson/Krenkel-a, Wood-a(2) — 35.00 / 105.00 / 245.00
32-Williamson/Krenkel-a — 35.00 / 105.00 / 245.00
NOTE: Davis a-30, 32, 33; c-30-32. Krigstein a-in all. Orlando a-30, 32, 33("Judgement Day" reprint). Wood a-30, 31, 33; c-33.

INDEPENDENCE DAY (Movie)
No. 0, June, 1996 - No. 2, Aug, 1996 ($1.95, limited series)
Marvel Comics

0-Special Edition; photo-c — 5.00
0-2 — 2.00

INDIANA JONES AND THE ARMS OF GOLD
Feb, 1994 - May, 1994 ($2.50, limited series)
Dark Horse Comics

1-4 — 1.00 / 2.50

Indiana Jones And The Last Crusade #1 © Lucasfilm

Indiana Jones And The Spear of Destiny #4 © Lucasfilm

Indiana Jones: Thunder In The Orient #2 © Lucasfilm

	GD25	FN65	NM94

INDIANA JONES AND THE FATE OF ATLANTIS
Mar, 1991 - Sep, 1991 ($2.50, limited series)
Dark Horse Comics

1-4-Dorman painted-c on all; contain trading cards (#1 has a 2nd printing, 10/91)		1.00	2.50

INDIANA JONES AND THE GOLDEN FLEECE
Jun, 1994 - July, 1994 ($2.50, limited series)
Dark Horse Comics

1,2		1.00	2.50

INDIANA JONES AND THE IRON PHOENIX
Dec, 1994 - Mar, 1995 ($2.50, limited series)
Dark Horse Comics

1-4		1.00	2.50

INDIANA JONES AND THE LAST CRUSADE
1989 - No. 4, 1989 ($1.00, limited series, movie adaptation)
Marvel Comics

1-4: Williamson-i assist			1.00
1-(1989, $2.95, B&W mag., 80 pgs.)		1.20	3.00

INDIANA JONES AND THE SHRINE OF THE SEA DEVIL
Sep, 1994 ($2.50, one shot)
Dark Horse Comics

1-Gary Gianni-a		1.00	2.50

INDIANA JONES AND THE SPEAR OF DESTINY
Apr, 1995 - Aug, 1995 ($2.50, limited series)
Dark Horse Comics

1-4		1.00	2.50

INDIANA JONES: THUNDER IN THE ORIENT
Sep, 1993 - 1994 ($2.50, limited series)
Dark Horse Comics

1-6: Dan Barry story & art in all; 1-Dorman painted-c		1.00	2.50

INDIANA JONES AND THE TEMPLE OF DOOM
Sept, 1984 - No. 3, Nov, 1984 (Movie adaptation)
Marvel Comics Group

1-3-r/Marvel Super Special; Guice-a			1.00

INDIAN BRAVES (Baffling Mysteries No. 5 on)
March, 1951 - No. 4, Sept, 1951
Ace Magazines

1-Green Arrowhead begins, ends #3	10.00	30.00	58.00
2	5.00	15.00	30.00
3,4	4.00	12.00	24.00
I.W. Reprint #1 (nd)-r/Indian Braves #4	1.50	3.75	9.00

INDIAN CHIEF (White Eagle...) (Formerly The Chief)
No. 3, July-Sept, 1951 - No. 33, Jan-Mar, 1959 (All painted-c)
Dell Publishing Co.

3	4.00	12.00	40.00
4-11: 6-White Eagle app.	3.00	9.00	30.00
12-1st White Eagle(10-12/53)-Not same as earlier character	4.00	12.00	40.00
13-29	2.00	6.00	20.00
30-33-Buscema-a	2.25	7.00	22.00

INDIAN CHIEF (See March of Comics No. 94, 110, 127, 140, 159, 170, 187)

INDIAN FIGHTER, THE (Movie)
No. 687, May, 1956 (one-shot)
Dell Publishing Co.

Four Color 687-Kirk Douglas photo-c	6.00	18.00	60.00

INDIAN FIGHTER
May, 1950 - No. 11, Jan, 1952

Youthful Magazines

1	10.00	30.00	65.00
2-Wildey-a/c(bondage)	5.85	17.50	35.00
3-11: 3,4-Wildey-a	4.15	12.50	25.00

NOTE: *Walter Johnson* c-1, 3, 4, 6. *Palais* a-10. *Stallman* a-7. *Wildey* a-2-4; c-2, 5.

INDIAN LEGENDS OF THE NIAGARA (See American Graphics)

INDIANS
Spring, 1950 - No. 17, Spring, 1953 (1-8: 52 pgs.)
Fiction House Magazines (Wings Publ. Co.)

1-Manzar The White Indian, Long Bow & Orphan of the Storm begin	22.00	66.00	155.00
2-Starlight begins	11.50	34.00	80.00
3-5: 5-17-Most-c by Whitman	10.00	30.00	65.00
6-10	8.35	25.00	50.00
11-17	6.70	20.00	40.00

INDIANS OF THE WILD WEST
Circa 1958? (no date) (Reprints)
I. W. Enterprises

9-Kinstler-c; Whitman-a; r/Indians #?	1.70	5.00	12.00

INDIANS ON THE WARPATH
No date (Late 40s, early 50s) (132 pgs.)
St. John Publishing Co.

nn-Matt Baker-c; contains St. John comics rebound. Many combinations possible	26.00	79.00	185.00

INDIAN TRIBES (See Famous Indian Tribes)

INDIAN WARRIORS (Formerly White Rider and Super Horse; becomes Western Crime Cases #9)
No. 7, June, 1951 - No. 8, Sept, 1951
Star Publications

7-White Rider & Superhorse continue; "Last of the Mohicans" serial begins; L.B. Cole-c	13.00	39.00	90.00
8-L. B. Cole-c	11.00	33.00	75.00
3-D 1(12/53, 25¢)-Came w/glasses; L. B. Cole-c	38.00	114.00	265.00
Accepted Reprint(nn)(inside cover shows White Rider & Superhorse #11)-r/ cover to #7; price w/print White Rider &...; L. B. Cole-c	5.00	15.00	30.00
Accepted Reprint #8 (nd); L.B. Cole-c (r-cover to #8)	5.00	15.00	30.00

INDOORS-OUTDOORS (See Wisco)

INDOOR SPORTS
nd (6x9", 64 pgs., B&W-r, hard-c)
National Specials Co.

nn-By Tad	5.00	15.00	30.00

INDUSTRIAL GOTHIC
Dec, 1995 - No. 5, Apr, 1996 ($2.50, limited series)
DC Comics (Vertigo)

1-5: Ted McKeever-c/a/scripts			2.50

INFERIOR FIVE, THE (Inferior 5 #11, 12) (See Showcase #62, 63, 65)
3-4/67 - No. 10, 9-10/68; No. 11, 8-9/72 - No. 12, 10-11/72
National Periodical Publications (#1-10: 12¢)

1-(3-4/67)-Sekowsky-a(p); 4th app.	5.00	15.00	35.00
2-Plastic Man, F.F. app.; Sekowsky-a(p)	2.70	8.00	19.00
3-12: 4-Thor app. 6-Stars DC staff. 10-Superman x-over; F.F., Spider-Man & Sub-Mariner app. 11,12-Orlando-c/a; both r/Showcase #62,63	2.00	6.00	14.00

INFERNO
1995 - Present ($2.95, B&W)
Caliber Comics

1-3		1.20	3.00

INFINITY CRUSADE

Infinity, Inc #10 © DC

Inhumans #1 © MEG

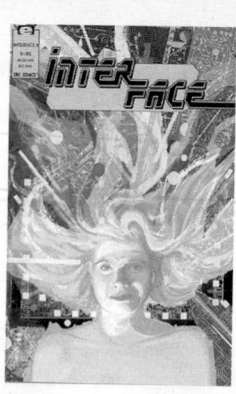
Interface#1 © James D. Hudnall

	GD25	FN65	NM94

June, 1993 - No. 6, Nov, 1993 ($2.50, limited series, 52 pgs.)
Marvel Comics

1-6: By Jim Starlin & Ron Lim		1.00	2.50

INFINITY GAUNTLET (The… #2 on; see Infinity Crusade, The Infinity War & Warlock & the Infinity Watch)
July, 1991 - No. 6, Dec, 1991 ($2.50, limited series)
Marvel Comics

1-Thanos-c/stories in all; Starlin scripts in all		1.60	4.00
2		1.10	2.75
3-6: 5,6-Ron Lim-c/a		1.00	2.50

NOTE: *Lim* a-3p(part), 5p, 6p; c-5i, 6i. *Perez* a-1-3p, 4p(part); c-1(painted), 2-4, 5i, 6i.

INFINITY, INC. (See All-Star Squadron #25)
Mar, 1984 - No. 53, Aug, 1988 ($1.25, Baxter paper, 36 pgs.)
DC Comics

1-Brainwave, Jr., Fury, The Huntress, Jade, Northwind, Nuklon, Obsidian, Power Girl, Silver Scarab & Star Spangled Kid begin			1.50
2-5: 2-Dr. Midnite, G.A. Flash, W. Woman, Dr. Fate, Hourman, Green Lantern, Wildcat app. 5-Nudity panels			1.20
6-13,38-49,51-53: 46,47-Millennium tie-ins			1.20
14-Todd McFarlane-a (5/85, 2nd full story)		1.20	3.00
15-37-McFarlane-a (20,23,24: 5 pgs. only; 33: 2 pgs.); 18-24-Crisis x-over. 21-Intro new Hourman & Dr. Midnight. 26-New Wildcat app. 31-Star Spangled Kid becomes Skyman. 32-Green Fury becomes Green Flame. 33-Origin Obsidian. 35-1st modern app. G.A. Fury		.70	1.80
50 ($2.50, 52 pgs.)		1.00	2.50
Annual 1,2: 1(12/85)-Crisis x-over. 2('88, $2.00)		.80	2.00
Special 1 (1987, $1.50)			1.50

NOTE: *Kubert* r-4. *McFarlane* a-14-37p, Annual 1p; c(p)-14-19, 22, 25, 26, 31-33, 37, Annual 1. *Newton* a-12p, 13p(last work 4/85). *Tuska* a-11p. *JSA* app. 3-10.

INFINITY WAR, THE (Also see Infinity Gauntlet & Warlock and the Infinity…)
June, 1992 - No. 6, Nov, 1992 ($2.50, mini-series)
Marvel Comics

1-Starlin scripts, Lim-c/a(p), Thanos app. in all		1.20	3.00
2-6: All have wraparound gatefold covers		1.00	2.50

INFORMER, THE
April, 1954 - No. 5, Dec, 1954
Feature Television Productions

1-Sekowsky-a begins	10.00	30.00	60.00
2	6.70	20.00	40.00
3-5	5.85	17.50	35.00

IN HIS STEPS
1973, 1977 (39/49¢)
Spire Christian Comics (Fleming H. Revell Co.)

nn			1.00

INHUMANOIDS, THE (TV)
Jan, 1987 - No. 4, July 1987
Marvel Comics (Star Comics)

1-4: Based on Hasbro toys			1.00

INHUMANS, THE (See Amazing Adventures, Fantastic Four #54 & Special #5, Incredible Hulk Special #1, Marvel Graphic Novel & Thor #146)
Oct, 1975 - No. 12, Aug, 1977
Marvel Comics Group

1: #1-4 are 25¢ issues	1.00	2.60	6.00
2-12: 9-Reprints Amazing Adventures #1,2('70)		1.20	3.00
Special 1(4/90, $1.50, 52 pgs.)-F.F. cameo		.80	2.00

NOTE: *Buckler* c-2-4p, 5. *Gil Kane* a-5-7p; c-1p, 7p, 8p. *Kirby* a-9r. *Mooney* a-11i. *Perez* a-1-4p, 8p.

INHUMANS: THE GREAT REFUGE
May, 1995 ($2.95, one-shot)
Marvel Comics

	GD25	FN65	NM94
1		1.20	3.00

INKY & DINKY (See Felix's Nephews…)

IN LOVE (…Magazine on-c; I Love You No. 7 on)
Aug-Sept, 1954 - No. 6, July, 1955 ('Adult Reading' on-c)
Mainline/Charlton No. 5 (5/55)-on

1-Simon & Kirby-a; book-length novel in all issues	26.00	77.00	180.00
2-S&K-a	15.00	45.00	105.00
3,4-S&K-a. 3-Last pre-code (12-1/54-55)	12.00	36.00	85.00
5-S&K-c only	7.50	22.50	45.00
6-No S&K-a	4.00	10.00	20.00

IN LOVE WITH JESUS
1952 (Giveaway, 36 pgs.)
Catechetical Educational Society

nn	3.60	9.00	18.00

INNOVATION SPECTACULAR
1991 - No. 2, 1991 ($2.95, squarebound, 100 pgs.)
Innovation Publishing

1,2: Contains rebound comics w/o covers		1.20	3.00

INNOVATION SUMMER FUN SPECIAL
1991 ($3.50, B&W/color, squarebound)
Innovation Publishing

1-Contains rebound comics (Power Factory)		1.40	3.50

INSANE
Feb, 1988 - No. 2? ($1.75, B&W)
Dark Horse Comics

1,2: 1-X-Men, Godzilla parodies. 2-Concrete		.70	1.80

IN SEARCH OF THE CASTAWAYS (See Movie Comics)

INSIDE CRIME (Formerly My Intimate Affair)
No. 3, July, 1950 - No. 2, Sept, 1950
Fox Features Syndicate (Hero Books)

3-Wood-a (10 pgs.); L. B. Cole-c	22.00	66.00	155.00
2-Used in **SOTI**, pg. 182,183; r/Spook #24	17.00	49.00	115.00
nn(no publ. listed, nd)	7.50	22.50	45.00

INSPECTOR, THE (TV) (Also see The Pink Panther)
July, 1974 - No. 19, Feb, 1978
Gold Key

1	1.30	3.25	8.00
2-5		1.60	4.00
6-19: 11-Reprints		.80	2.00

INSPECTOR GILL OF THE FISH POLICE (See Fish Police)

INSPECTOR WADE
No. 13, May, 1938
David McKay Publications

Feature Books 13	18.50	56.00	185.00

INSTANT PIANO
Aug, 1994 - No. 4, Feb, 1995 ($3.95, B&W, bimonthly, mature)
Dark Horse Comics

1-4		1.60	4.00

INTERFACE
Dec, 1989 - No. 8, Dec, 1990 ($1.95, mature, coated paper)
Marvel Comics (Epic Comics)

1-5: Based on ESPers; painted-c/a		1.00	2.00
6-8: 6-Begin $2.25-c		1.15	2.30

INTERNATIONAL COMICS (…Crime Patrol No. 6)
Spring, 1947 - No. 5, Nov-Dec, 1947
E. C. Comics

Intimate Confessions #7 © REAL

Invaders #34 © MEG

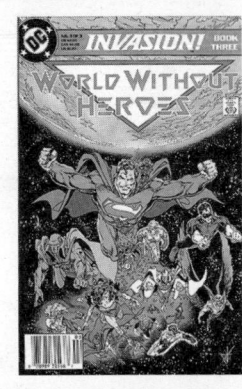

Invasion #3 © DC

	GD25	FN65	NM94
1-Schaffenberger-a begins, ends #4	51.00	154.00	410.00
2	40.00	120.00	285.00
3-5	34.00	103.00	240.00

INTERNATIONAL CRIME PATROL (Formerly International Comics #1-5; becomes Crime Patrol No. 7 on)
No. 6, Spring, 1948
E. C. Comics

6-Moon Girl app.	53.00	160.00	420.00

INTERSTATE THEATRES' FUN CLUB COMICS
Mid 1940's (10¢ on cover) (B&W cover) (Premium)
Interstate Theatres

Cover features MLJ characters looking at a copy of Top-Notch Comics, but contains an early Detective Comic on inside; many combinations possible 6.00 18.00 36.00

IN THE DAYS OF THE MOB (Magazine)
Fall, 1971 (B&W)
Hampshire Dist. Ltd. (National)

1-Kirby-a; John Dillinger wanted poster inside	3.60	11.00	25.00

IN THE PRESENCE OF MINE ENEMIES
1973 (35/49¢)
Spire Christian Comics/Fleming H. Revell Co.

nn			1.00

INTIMATE
Dec, 1957 - No. 3, May, 1958
Charlton Comics

1-3	2.40	6.00	12.00

INTIMATE CONFESSIONS (See Fox Giants)

INTIMATE CONFESSIONS
July-Aug, 1951 - No. 7, Aug, 1952; No. 8, Mar, 1953 (All painted-c)
Realistic Comics

1-Kinstler-c/a; c/Avon paperback #222	62.00	187.00	500.00
2	14.00	43.00	100.00
3-c/Avon paperback #250; Kinstler-c/a	17.00	51.00	120.00
4-6,8: 4-c/Avon paperback #304; Kinstler-a. 6-c/Avon paperback #120.			
8-c/Avon paperback #375; Kinstler-a	14.00	43.00	100.00
7-Spanking panel	14.00	43.00	100.00

INTIMATE CONFESSIONS
1964
I. W. Enterprises/Super Comics

I.W. Reprint #9,10	1.50	3.75	9.00
Super Reprint #12,18	1.50	3.75	9.00

INTIMATE LOVE
No. 5, 1950 - No. 28, Aug, 1954
Standard Comics

5	5.85	17.50	35.00
6-8-Severin/Elder-a	6.35	19.00	38.00
9	4.00	10.00	20.00
10-Jane Russell, Robert Mitchum photo-c	7.50	22.50	45.00
11-18,20,23,25,27,28	2.80	7.00	14.00
19,21,22,24,26-Toth-a	5.35	16.00	32.00

NOTE: **Celardo** a-8, 10. **Colletta** a-23. **Moreira** a-13(2). Photo-c-6, 7, 10, 12, 14, 15, 18-20, 24, 26, 27.

INTIMATE SECRETS OF ROMANCE
Sept, 1953 - No. 2, Apr, 1954
Star Publications

1,2-L. B. Cole-c	11.50	34.00	80.00

INTRIGUE
Jan, 1955
Quality Comics Group

	GD25	FN65	NM94
1-Horror; Jack Cole reprint/Web of Evil	24.00	73.00	170.00

INTRUDER
1990 - No. 10, 1991 ($2.95, 44 pgs.)
TSR, Inc.

1-10		1.50	3.00

INVADERS, THE (TV)
Oct, 1967 - No. 4, Oct, 1968 (All have photo-c)
Gold Key

1-Spiegle-a in all	9.50	28.50	95.00
2-4	7.00	21.00	70.00

INVADERS, THE (Also see The Avengers #71 & Giant-Size Invaders)
August, 1975 - No. 40, May, 1979; No. 41, Sept, 1979
Marvel Comics Group

1-Captain America & Bucky, Human Torch & Toro, & Sub-Mariner begin; cont'd. from Giant Size Invaders #1; #1-7 are 25¢ issues	2.15	6.50	15.00
2-10: 2-1st app. Mailbag & Brain-Drain. 3-Battle issue; Cap vs. Namor vs. Torch; intro U-Man. 6-Liberty Legion app; two cover prices, 25¢ & 30¢. 7-Intro Baron Blood & intro/1st app. Union Jack; Human Torch origin retold. 8-Union Jack-c/story. 9-Origin Baron Blood. 10-G.A. Capt. America-r/C.A #22	1.30	3.25	8.00
11-19: 11-Origin Spitfire; intro The Blue Bullet. 14-1st app. The Crusaders. 16-Re-intro The Destroyer. 17-Intro Warrior Woman. 18-Re-intro The Destroyer w/new origin. 19-Hitler-c/story	1.00	2.60	6.00
20-Reprints origin/1st app. Sub-Mariner from Motion Picture Funnies Weekly with color added & brief write-up about MPFW; 1st app. new Union Jack II	1.30	3.25	8.00
21-Reprints Marvel Mystery #10 (battle issue)	1.00	2.00	5.00
22-40: 22-New origin Toro. 24-r/Marvel Mystery #17 (team-up issue; all-r). 25-All new-a begins. 28-Intro new Human Top & Golden Girl. 29-Intro Teutonic Knight. 31-Frankenstein-c/story. 32,33-Thor app. 34-Mighty Destroyer joins. 35-The Whizzer app.	1.00	1.60	4.00
41-Double size last issue	1.00	2.00	5.00
Annual 1 (9/77)-Schomburg, Rico stories (new); Schomburg-c/a (1st for Marvel in 30 years); Avengers app.; re-intro The Shark & The Hyena	1.00	2.00	5.00

NOTE: **Buckler** a-5. **Everett** r-20(´39), 21(1940), 24, Annual 1. **Gil Kane** c(p)-13, 17, 18, 20-27. **Kirby** c(p)-3-12, 14-16, 32, 33. **Mooney** a-5i, 16, 22. **Robbins** a-1-4, 6-9, 10(3 pg.), 11-15, 17-21, 23, 25-28; c-28.

INVADERS (See Namor, the Sub-Mariner #12)
May, 1993 - No. 4, Aug, 1993 ($1.75, limited series)
Marvel Comics Group

1-4		.70	1.75

INVADERS FROM HOME
1990 - No. 6, 1990 ($2.50, mature)
DC Comics (Piranha Press)

1-6		1.25	2.50

INVASION
Holiday, 1988-'89 - No. 3, Jan, 1989 ($2.95, limited series, 84 pgs.)
DC Comics

1-McFarlane/Russell-a		1.20	3.00
2,3-McFarlane/Russell & Giffen/Gordon-a		1.20	3.00

INVINCIBLE FOUR OF KUNG FU & NINJA
April, 1988 - No. 12?, 1990 ($2.00)
Leung Publications

1-($2.75)		1.40	2.75
2-12: 2-Begin $2.00-c		1.00	2.00

INVISIBLE BOY (See Approved Comics)

INVISIBLE MAN, THE (See Superior Stories #1 & Supernatural Thrillers #2)

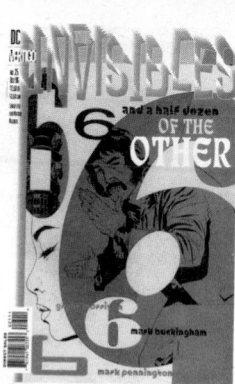

The Invisibles #25 © Grant Morrison

Iron Man #9 © MEG

Iron Man #268 © MEG

IR

INVISIBLES, THE
Sept, 1994 - No. 25, Oct, 1996 ($1.95/$2.50, mature)
DC Comics (Vertigo)

	GD25	FN65	NM94
1-($2.95, 52 pgs.)-Intro King Mob, Ragged Robin, Boy, Lord Fanny & Dane (Jack Frost); Grant Morrison scripts in all		1.40	3.50
2-8: 4-Includes bound-in trading cards. 5-1st app. Orlando; brown paper-c		.80	2.00
9-25: 9-Begin $2.50-c. 10-Intro Jim Crow. 13-15-Origin Lord Fanny. 19-Origin King Mob; polybagged. 20-Origin Boy. 21-Mister Six revealed. 25-Intro Division X			2.50
Say You Want A Revolution (1996, $17.50, TPB)-r/#1-8			17.50

NOTE: *Buckingham* a-25p. *Rian Hughes* c-1, 5. *Phil Jimenez* a-17p-19p. *Paul Johnson* a-16, 21. *Sean Phillips* c-2-4, 6-25. *Weston* a-10p. *Yeowell* a-1p-4p, 22p-24p.

INVISIBLE SCARLET O'NEIL (Also see Famous Funnies #81 & Harvey Comics Hits #59)
Dec, 1950 - No. 3, Apr, 1951
Famous Funnies (Harvey)(2-3 pgs. of Powell-a in each issue.)

	GD25	FN65	NM94
1-	12.00	36.00	85.00
2,3	10.00	30.00	65.00

IRON CORPORAL, THE (See Army War Heroes #22)
No. 23, Oct, 1985 - No. 25, Feb, 1986
Charlton Comics

23-25: Glanzman-a(r)			1.00

IRON FIST (See Deadly Hands of Kung Fu, Marvel Premiere & Power Man)
Nov, 1975 - No. 15, Sept, 1977
Marvel Comics

	GD25	FN65	NM94
1-Iron Fist battles Iron Man (#1-6: 25¢)	3.60	11.00	25.00
2	2.40	7.30	17.00
3-10: 8-Origin retold	1.60	4.20	10.00
11-13: 12-Capt. America app.	1.30	3.25	8.00
14-1st app. Sabretooth (8/77)(see Power Man)	21.00	64.00	150.00
15-X-Men app., Byrne-a (30¢ & 35¢ variants)	4.30	13.00	30.00

NOTE: *Adkins* a-8p, 10i, 13i; c-8i. *Byrne* a-1-15p; c-8p, 15p. *G. Kane* c-4-6p. *McWilliams* a-1i.

IRON FIST
Sept, 1996 - No. 2, Oct, 1996 ($1.50, limited series)
Marvel Comics

1,2			1.50

IRONHAND OF ALMURIC (Robert E. Howard's...)
Aug, 1991 - No. 4, 1991 ($2.00, B&W, mini-series)
Dark Horse Comics

1-4: 1-Conrad painted-c		1.00	2.00

IRON HORSE (TV)
March, 1967 - No. 2, June, 1967
Dell Publishing Co.

1,2-Dale Robertson photo covers	2.40	6.00	12.00

IRONJAW (Also see The Barbarians)
Jan, 1975 - No. 4, July, 1975
Atlas/Seaboard Publ.

1-1st app. Iron Jaw; Neal Adams-c; Sekowsky-a(p)			1.50
2-4: 2-Neal Adams-c. 4-Origin			1.50

IRON MAN (Also see The Avengers #1, Giant-Size..., Marvel Collectors Item Classics, Marvel Double Feature, Marvel Fanfare & Tales of Suspense #39)
May, 1968 - No. 332, Sept, 1996
Marvel Comics

	GD25	FN65	NM94
1-Origin; Colan-c/a(p); story continued from Iron Man & Sub-Mariner #1	47.00	141.00	375.00
2	16.00	47.00	110.00
3	11.00	33.00	75.00
4,5	8.00	23.50	55.00

	GD25	FN65	NM94
6-10: 9-Iron Man battles green Hulk-like android	6.00	18.00	42.00
11-15: 15-Last 12¢ issue	4.00	12.00	28.00
16-20	3.25	9.50	22.00
21-24,26-42: 22-Death of Janice Cord. 27-Intro Fire Brand. 33-1st app. Spymaster. 35-Nick Fury & Daredevil x-over. 42-Last 15¢ issue	2.15	6.50	15.00
25-Iron Man battles Sub-Mariner	3.30	10.00	23.00
43-Intro The Guardsman; 25¢ giant	2.15	6.50	15.00
44-46,48-50: 43-Giant-Man back-up by Ayers. 44-Ant-Man by Tuska. 46-The Guardsman dies. 50-Princess Python app.	1.65	4.70	11.00
47-Origin retold; Barry Smith-a(p)	2.00	6.00	15.00
51-53: 53-Starlin part pencils	1.20	2.90	7.00
54-Iron Man battles Sub-Mariner; 1st app. Moondragon (1/73) as Madame MacEvil; Everett part-c	2.15	6.50	15.00
55-1st app. Thanos (cameo), Drax the Destroyer, Mentor, Starfox & Kronos (2/73); Starlin-c/a	11.00	34.00	90.00
56-Starlin-a	3.00	7.20	18.00
57-67,69,70: 59-Firebrand returns. 65-Origin Dr. Spectrum. 70-Iron Man vs. Thor. 67-Last 20¢ issue	1.20	2.90	7.00
68-Sunfire & Unicorn app.; origin retold; Starlin-a	1.65	4.20	10.00
71-99: 72-Cameo portraits of N. Adams, 73-Rename Stark Industries to Stark International; Brunner. 76-r/#9. 86-1st app. Blizzard. 87-Origin Blizzard. 88-Thanos app. 89-Daredevil app.; last 25¢ issue. 96-1st app. new Guardsman	.80	2.10	5.00
100-(7/77)-Starlin-c	1.65	4.20	10.00
101-117: 101-Intro DreadKnight. 109-1st app. new Crimson Dynamo; 1st app. Vanguard. 110-Origin Jack of Hearts retold; death of Count Nefaria. 114-Avengers app.	1.00	2.50	5.50
118-Byrne-a(p); 1st app. Jim Rhodes	1.10	2.70	6.50
119,120,123-128-Tony Stark recovers from alcohol problem. 120,121-Sub-Mariner x-over. 125-Ant-Man app.	1.00	2.00	5.00
121,122,129-149: 122-Origin. 131,132-Hulk x-over		1.20	3.00
150-Double size		1.60	4.00
151-168: 152-New armor. 161-Moon Knight app. 167-Tony Stark alcohol problem starts again		1.00	2.50
169-New Iron Man (Jim Rhodes replaces Tony Stark)	1.50	3.75	9.00
170		1.80	4.50
171		1.60	4.00
172-199: 172-Captain America x-over. 186-Intro Vibro. 190-Scarlet Witch app. 191-198-Tony Stark returns as original Iron Man. 192-Both Iron Men battle		.90	2.25
200-(11/85, $1.25, 52 pgs.)-Tony Stark returns as new Iron Man (red & white armor) thru #230		1.90	4.75
201-224: 213-Intro new Dominic Fortune. 214-Spider-Woman apps. in new black costume (1/87)		.80	2.00
225-Double size ($1.25)		1.60	4.00
226-243,245-249: 228-vs. Capt. America. 231-Intro new Iron Man. 233-Ant-Man app. 234-Spider-Man x-over. 243-Tony Stark looses use of legs. 247-Hulk x-over		.80	2.00
244-($1.50, 52 pgs.)-New Armor makes him walk	1.60	4.00	
250-($1.50, 52 pgs.)-Dr. Doom-c/story		.80	2.00
251-274,276-281,283,285-287,289,291-299: 258-277-Byrne scripts. 271-Fin Fang Foom app. 276-Black Widow-c/story; last $1.00-c. 281-1st app. ;War Machine (cameo). 283-2nd full app. War Machine		.80	2.00
282-1st full app. War Machine (7/92)	1.00	2.00	5.00
275-($1.50, 52pgs.)		.80	2.00
284-Death of Iron Man (Tony Stark)		1.20	3.00
288-($2.50, 52pg.)-Silver foil stamped-c; Iron Man's 350th app. in comics		1.10	2.75
290-($2.95, 52pg.)-Gold foil stamped-c; 30th ann.		1.30	3.25
300-($3.95, 68 pgs.)-Collector's Edition w/embossed foil-c; anniversary issue; War Machine-c/story		1.70	4.25
300-($2.50, 68 pgs.)-Newsstand Edition		1.10	2.75
301-303: 302-Venom-c/story (cameo #301)			1.50

	GD25	FN65	NM94

304-316,318-324,326-332: 304-Begin $1.50-c; bound-in trading card sheet; Thunderstrike-c/story. 310-Orange logo. 312-w/bound-in Power Ranger Card. 319-Prologue to "The Crossing." 326-New Tony Stark; Pratt-c. 330-War Machine & Stockpile app; return of Morgan Stark. 332-Onslaught x-over. ... .70 ... 1.75

310 ($2.95)-Polybagged w/ 16 pg. Marvel Action Hour preview & acetate print; white logo. ... 3.00

317 ($2.50)-Flip book ... 1.00 ... 2.50

325-($2.95)-Wraparound-c ... 3.00

Special 1(8/70)-Sub-Mariner x-over; Everett-c ... 2.85 ... 8.50 ... 20.00

Special 2(11/71)-r/TOS #81,82,91 (all-r) ... 1.65 ... 4.20 ... 10.00

Annual 3(1976)-Man-Thing app. ... 1.60 ... 4.00

King Size 4(8/77)-The Champions (w/Ghost Rider) app.; Newton-a(i) ... 1.20 ... 3.00

Annual 5-9: 5(1982)-New-a. 6(1983)-New Iron Man (J. Rhodes) app. 7(1984). 8(1986)-X-Factor app. 9(1987) ... .90 ... 2.25

Annual 10(1989, $2.00, 68 pgs.)-Atlantis Attacks x-over; P. Smith-a; Layton/ Guice-a; Sub-Mariner app. ... 1.00 ... 2.50

Annual 11,12 ($2.00, 68 pgs.): 11-(1990)-Origin of Mrs. Arbogast by Ditko (p&i). 12-(1991)-1 pg. origin recap; Ant-Man back-up story ... .80 ... 2.00

Annual 13 (1992, $2.25, 68 pgs.)-Darkhawk & Avengers West Coast app.; Colan/Williamson-a ... .90 ... 2.25

Annual 14 (1993, $2.95, 68 pgs.)-Bagged w/card ... 1.20 ... 3.00

Annual 15 (1994, $2.95, 68 pgs.) ... 1.20 ... 3.00

Manual 1 (1993, $1.75)-Operations handbook ... .70 ... 1.75

Graphic Novel: Crash (1988, $12.95, Adults, 72 pgs?)-Computer generated art & color; violence & nudity ... 1.85 ... 5.50 ... 13.00

...Collector's Preview 1(11/94, $1.95)-wraparound-c; text & illos-no comics. ... 2.00

...Vs. Dr. Doom (12/94, $12.95)-r/#149-150, 249,250. J-Bell-c ... 13.00

.../X-O Manowar (10/96, $2.50)-Nicieza scripts; Pt. II of Iron Man/X-O Manowar x-over ... 2.50

NOTE: **Austin** c-105i, 109-111i, 151i. **Byrne** a-118p; c-109p, 197, 253. **Colan** a-1p, 253, Special 1p(3); c-1p. **Craig** a-1i, 2-4, 5-13i, 14, 15-19i, 24p, 25p, 26-28i; c-2-4. **Ditko** a-160p. **Everett** c-29. **Guice** a-233-241p. **G. Kane** c(p)-52-54, 63, 67, 72-75, 77-79, 88, 98. **Kirby** a-Special 1p; c-13, 80p, 90, 92-95. **Mooney** a-40i, 43i, 47i. **Perez** c-103p. **Simonson** c-Annual 8. **B. Smith** a-232p, 243i; c-232. **P. Smith** a-159p, 245p, Annual 10p; c-159. **Starlin** a-53p(part), 55p, 56p; c-55p, 160, 163. **Tuska** a-5-13p, 15-23p, 24i, 32p, 38-46p, 48-54p, 57-61p, 63-69p, 70-72p, 78p, 86-92p, 95-106p, Annual 4p. **Wood** a-Special 1i.

IRON MAN
V2#1, Nov, 1996 - Present ($2.95/$1.95)(Produced by Wildstorm Productions)
Marvel Comics

V2#1-12: 1-Scott Lobdell scripts & Whilce Portacio-c/a begin; new origin Hulk ... 3.00

1-Variant-c ... 5.00

IRON MAN & SUB-MARINER
Apr, 1968 (12¢, one-shot) (Pre-dates Iron Man #1 & Sub-Mariner #1)
Marvel Comics Group

1-Iron Man story by Colan/Craig continued from Tales of Suspense #99 & continued in Iron Man #1; Sub-Mariner story by Colan continued from Tales to Astonish #101 & continued in Sub-Mariner #1; Colan/Everett-c ... 18.00 ... 53.00 ... 140.00

IRON MAN: THE LEGEND
Sept, 1996 ($3.95, one-shot)
Marvel Comics

1-Tribute issue ... 4.00

IRON MAN 2020
June, 1994 ($5.95, one-shot)
Marvel Comics

nn ... 1.00 ... 2.50 ... 6.00

IRON MARSHALL
July, 1990 - No. 22, 1992 ($1.75, plastic coated-c)

	GD25	FN65	NM94

Jademan Comics

1-22: Kung Fu stories. 1-Poster centerfold ... .90 ... 1.80

IRON VIC (See Comics Revue No. 3 & Giant Comics Editions)
1940; Aug, 1947 - No. 3, 1947
United Features Syndicate/St. John Publ. Co.

Single Series 22 ... 29.00 ... 88.00 ... 205.00

2,3(St. John) ... 7.00 ... 21.00 ... 42.00

IRONWOLF
1986 ($2.00, one shot)
DC Comics

1-r/Weird Worlds 8-10; Chaykin story & art ... 1.00 ... 2.00

IRONWOLF: FIRES OF THE REVOLUTION (See Weird Worlds #8-10)
1992 ($29.95, hardcover)
DC Comics

nn-Chaykin/Moore story, Mignola-a w/Russell inks. ... 4.30 ... 13.00 ... 30.00

ISAAC ASIMOV'S I-BOTS
Dec, 1995 - No. 7, May, 1996 ($1.95)
Tekno Comix

1-7: 1-6-Perez-c/a. 2-Chaykin variant-c exists. 3-Polybagged. 7-Lady Justice-c/app. ... .80 ... 2.00

ISAAC ASIMOV'S I-BOTS
V2#1, June, 1996 - Present ($2.25)
BIG Entertainment

V2#1-6: 1-Lady Justice-c/app. 6-Gil Kane-c ... 2.25

ISIS (TV) (Also see Shazam)
Oct-Nov, 1976 - No. 8, Dec-Jan, 1977-78
National Periodical Publications/DC Comics

1-Wood inks ... 1.50

2-8: 5-Isis new look. 7-Origin ... 1.00

ISLAND AT THE TOP OF THE WORLD (See Walt Disney Showcase #27)

ISLAND OF DR. MOREAU, THE (Movie)
Oct, 1977 (52 pgs.)
Marvel Comics Group

1-Gil Kane-c ... 1.00

I SPY (TV)
Aug, 1966 - No. 6, Sept, 1968 (All have photo-c)
Gold Key

1-Bill Cosby, Robert Culp photo covers ... 22.00 ... 66.00 ... 220.00

2-6: 3,4-McWilliams-a ... 14.00 ... 42.00 ... 140.00

IS THIS TOMORROW?
1947 (One Shot) (3 editions) (52 pgs.)
Catechetical Guild

1-Theme of communists taking over the USA; (no price on cover) Used in POP, pg. 102 ... 13.00 ... 39.00 ... 90.00

1-(10¢ on cover) ... 18.00 ... 54.00 ... 125.00

1-Has blank circle with no price on cover ... 18.00 ... 54.00 ... 125.00

Black & White advance copy titled "Confidential" (52 pgs.)-Contains script and art edited out of the color edition, including one page of extreme violence showing mob nailing a Cardinal to a door; (only two known copies) ... 43.00 ... 130.00 ... 300.00

NOTE: The original color version first sold for 10 cents. Since sales were good, it was later printed as a giveaway. Approximately four million in total were printed. The two black and white copies listed plus two other versions as well as a full color untrimmed version surfaced in 1979 from the Guild's old files in St. Paul, Minnesota.

IT! (See Astonishing Tales No. 21-24 & Supernatural Thrillers No. 1)

ITCHY & SCRATCHY COMICS (Simpson's TV show)
1993 - No. 3, 1993 ($1.95)
Bongo Comics

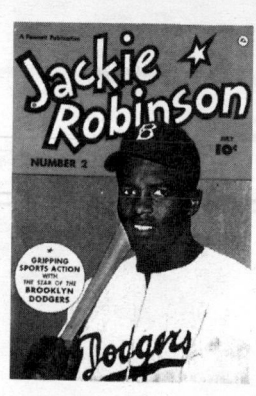

Jack Armstrong #12 © PMI

Jackie Gleason and The Honeymooner #10 © DC

Jackie Robinson #2 © FAW

	GD25	FN65	NM94
1-($2.25)-Bound-in jumbo poster		1.00	2.50
2		.80	2.00
3-($2.25)-w/decoder screen trading card		.90	2.25
Holiday Special ('94, $1.95)		.80	2.00

IT REALLY HAPPENED
1944 - No. 11, Oct, 1947
William H. Wise No. 1,2/Standard (Visual Editions)

1-Kit Carson & Ben Franklin stories	14.00	43.00	100.00
2	9.15	27.50	55.00
3,4,6,9,11: 6-Joan of Arc story. 9-Captain Kidd & Frank Buck stories			
	6.70	20.00	40.00
5-Lou Gehrig & Lewis Carroll stories	11.50	34.00	80.00
7-Teddy Roosevelt story	6.70	20.00	40.00
8-Story of Roy Rogers	13.50	41.00	95.00
10-Honus Wagner & Mark Twain stories	10.00	30.00	65.00

NOTE: *Guardineer* a-7(2), 8(2), 11. *Schomburg* c-1-7, 9-11.

IT RHYMES WITH LUST (Also see Bold Stories & Candid Tales)
1950 (Digest size, 128 pgs.)
St. John Publishing Co.

nn (Rare)-Matt Baker & Ray Osrin-a	44.00	132.00	350.00

IT'S ABOUT TIME (TV)
Jan, 1967
Gold Key

1 (10195-701)-Photo-c	3.50	10.50	35.00

IT'S A DUCK'S LIFE
Feb, 1950 - No. 11, Feb, 1952
Marvel Comics/Atlas(MMC)

1-Buck Duck, Super Rabbit begin	11.50	34.00	80.00
2	6.70	20.00	40.00
3-11	4.25	13.00	28.00

IT'S FUN TO STAY ALIVE
1948 (Giveaway, 16 pgs., heavy stock paper)
National Automobile Dealers Association

Featuring: Bugs Bunny, The Berrys, Dixie Dugan, Elmer, Henry, Tim Tyler, Bruce Gentry, Abbie & Slats, Joe Jinks, The Toodles, & Cokey; all art copyright 1946-48 drawn especially for this book.

	17.00	51.00	120.00

IT'S GAMETIME
Sept-Oct, 1955 - No. 4, Mar-Apr, 1956
National Periodical Publications

1-(Scarce)-Infinity-c; Davy Crockett app. in puzzle	62.00	187.00	500.00
2-4(Scarce): 2-Dodo & The Frog	53.00	159.00	425.00

IT'S LOVE, LOVE, LOVE
Nov, 1957 - No. 2, Jan, 1958 (10¢)
St. John Publishing Co.

1,2	4.00	11.00	22.00

IVANHOE (See Fawcett Movie Comics No. 20)

IVANHOE
July-Sept, 1963
Dell Publishing Co.

1 (12-373-309)	2.50	7.50	25.00

IWO JIMA (See Spectacular Features Magazine)

JACE PEARSON OF THE TEXAS RANGERS (Radio/TV)(4-Color #396 is titled Tales of the Texas Rangers; ...'s Tales of ... #11-on)(See Western Roundup under Dell Giants)
No. 396, 5/52 - No. 1021, 8-10/59 (No #10) (All-Photo-c)
Dell Publishing Co.

Four Color 396 (#1)	11.00	33.00	110.00
2(5-7/53) - 9(2-4/55)	6.00	18.00	60.00

	GD25	FN65	NM94
Four Color 648(#10, 9/55)	6.00	18.00	60.00
11(11-2/55-56) - 14,17-20(6-8/58)	5.00	15.00	50.00
15,16-Toth-a	6.00	18.00	60.00
Four Color 961, 1021: 961--Spiegle-a	5.00	15.00	50.00

NOTE: Joel McCrea photo c-1-9, F.C. 648 (starred on radio show only); Willard Parker photo c-11-on (starred on TV series).

JACK & JILL VISIT TOYTOWN WITH ELMER THE ELF
1949 (Giveaway, 16 pgs., paper cover)
Butler Brothers (Toytown Stores)

nn	3.20	8.00	16.00

JACK ARMSTRONG (Radio)(See True Comics)
Nov, 1947 - No. 9, Sept, 1948; No. 10, Mar, 1949 - No. 13, Sept, 1949
Parents' Institute

1-(scarce) (odd size)	39.00	118.00	275.00
2	16.00	47.00	110.00
3-5	12.00	36.00	85.00
6-13: 7-Vic Hardy's Crime Lab begins?	10.00	30.00	65.00
12-Premium version(distr. in Chicago only); Free printed on upper right-c; no price (Rare)	16.00	47.00	110.00

JACK HUNTER
July, 1987 - No. 4? ($1.25)
Blackthorne Publishing

1-4			1.25

JACKIE GLEASON (TV) (Also see The Honeymooners)
1948 - No. 2, 1948; Sept, 1955 - No. 4, Dec, 1955?
St. John Publishing Co.

1(1948)	65.00	195.00	525.00
2(1948)	50.00	150.00	400.00
1(1955)(TV)-Photo-c	53.00	160.00	425.00
2-4	40.00	120.00	290.00

JACKIE GLEASON AND THE HONEYMOONERS (TV)
June-July, 1956 - No. 12, Apr-May, 1958
National Periodical Publications

1-1st app. Ralph Kramden	78.00	234.00	625.00
2	50.00	150.00	400.00
3-11	40.00	120.00	300.00
12 (Scarce)	56.00	172.00	450.00

JACKIE JOKERS (Became Richie Rich &...)
March, 1973 - No. 4, Sept, 1973 (#5 was advertised, but not published)
Harvey Publications

1-4: 1-1st app. 2-President Nixon app.			1.00

JACKIE ROBINSON (Famous Plays of...) (Also see Negro Heroes #2 & Picture News #4)
May, 1950 - No. 6, 1952 (Baseball hero) (All photo-c)
Fawcett Publications

nn	75.00	225.00	600.00
2	48.00	144.00	385.00
3-6	40.00	120.00	310.00

JACK IN THE BOX (Formerly Yellowjacket Comics #1-10; becomes Cowboy Western Comics #17 on)
Feb, 1946; No. 11, Oct, 1946 - No. 16, Nov-Dec, 1947
Frank Comunale/Charlton Comics No. 11 on

1-Stitches, Marty Mouse & Nutsy McKrow	11.00	33.00	75.00
11-Yellowjacket (early Charlton comic)	13.00	39.00	90.00
12,14,15	5.35	16.00	32.00
13-Wolverton-a	18.00	54.00	125.00
16-12 pg. adapt. of Silas Marner; Kiefer-a	10.00	30.00	58.00

JACK KIRBY'S SECRET CITY SAGA
No. 0, Apr, 1993; No. 1, May, 1993 - No. 4, Aug, 1993 ($2.95, limited series)

	GD25	FN65	NM94		GD25	FN65	NM94

Topps Comics (Kirbyverse)

0-(No cover price, 20 pgs.)-Simonson-c/a 1.80 2.00

1-4-Bagged w/3 trading cards; Ditko-c/a: 1-Ditko/Art Adams-c. 2-Ditko/Byrne/c;
has coupon for Pres. Clinton holo-foil trading card. 3-Dorman poster; has
coupon for Gore holo-foil trading card. 4-Ditko/Perez-c 1.20 3.00
NOTE: Issues #1-4 contain coupons redeemable for Kirbychrome version of #1

JACK KIRBY'S SILVER STAR (Also see Silver Star)
Oct, 1993 ($2.95, intended as 4-issue limited series)
Topps Comics (Kirbyverse)

1-Silver ink-c; Austin-c/a(i); polybagged w/3 cards 1.20 3.00

JACK KIRBY'S TEENAGENTS (See Satan's Six)
Aug, 1993 - No. 3, Oct, 1993 ($2.95, intended as 4-issue limited series)
Topps Comics (Kirbyverse)

1-3-Polybagged with/3 trading cards; 1-3-Austin-c(i): 3-Liberty Project app.
.... 1.20 3.00

JACK OF HEARTS (Also see The Deadly Hands of Kung Fu #22 &
Marvel Premiere #44)
Jan, 1984 - No. 4, Apr, 1984 (60¢, limited series)
Marvel Comics Group

1-4 .... 1.00

JACKPOT COMICS (Jolly Jingles #10 on)
Spring, 1941 - No. 9, Spring, 1943
MLJ Magazines

1-The Black Hood, Mr. Justice, Steel Sterling & Sgt. Boyle begin; Biro-c
250.00 750.00 2000.00
2-S. Cooper-c 112.00 338.00 900.00
3-Hubbell-c 84.00 253.00 675.00
4-Archie begins (Win/41; on sale 12/41)-(also see Pep Comics #22); 1st app.
Mrs. Grundy, the principal; Novick-c 225.00 675.00 1800.00
5-Hitler-c by Montana; 1st definitive Mr. Weatherbee; 1st app. Reggie in 1
panel cameo 112.00 338.00 900.00
6-9: 6,7-Bondage-c by Novick. 8,9-Sahle-c 90.00 271.00 725.00

JACK Q FROST (See Unearthly Spectaculars)

JACK THE GIANT KILLER (See Movie Classics)

JACK THE GIANT KILLER (New Adventures of...)
Aug-Sept, 1953
Bimfort & Co.

V1#1-H. C. Kiefer-c/a 18.00 54.00 125.00

JACKY'S DIARY
No. 1091, Apr-June, 1960 (one-shot)
Dell Publishing Co.

Four Color 1091 5.00 15.00 50.00

JADEMAN COLLECTION
Dec, 1989 - No. 5?, 1990 ($2.50, plastic coated-c, 68 pgs.)
Jademan Comics

1-5: 1-Wraparound-c w/fold-out poster 1.00 2.50

JADEMAN KUNG FU SPECIAL
1988 ($1.50, 64 pgs.)
Jademan Comics

1 1.50

JAGUAR, THE (Also see The Adventures of...)
Aug, 1991 - No. 14, Oct, 1992 ($1.00)
Impact Comics (DC)

1-14: 4-The Black Hood x-over. 7-Sienkiewicz-c. 9-Contains Crusaders
trading card 1.00
Annual 1 (1992, $2.50, 68 pgs.)-With trading card 1.00 2.50

JAGUAR GOD

Mar, 1995 - Present ($2.95, mature)
Verotik

0 (2/96, $3.50)-Embossed Frazetta-c; Bisley-a; includes pin-ups. 3.5
1-4: 1,2-Frazetta-c. 3-Bisley-c. 1.00 2.00 5.0

JAKE THRASH
1988 - No. 3, 1988 ($2.00)
Aircel Publishing

1-3 1.00 2.0

JAM, THE (...Urban Adventure)
Nov, 1989 - Present ($1.95/$2.50/$2.95, B&W)
Slave Labor Nos. 1-5/Dark Horse Comics Nos. 6-8/Caliber Comics No. 9 on

1-5-Bernie Mireault-c/a/scripts .80 2.0
6-7: 6-1st Dark Horse issue; begin $2.50-c. 1.00 2.5
8-13: 8-Begin $2.95-c. 9-1st Caliber issue 1.20 3.0

JAMBOREE
Feb, 1946(no mo. given) - No. 3, Apr, 1946
Round Publishing Co.

1-Funny animal 19.00 56.00 130.0
2,3 11.00 33.00 75.0

JAMES BOND 007: A SILENT ARMAGEDDON
Mar, 1993 - Apr 1993 (limited series)
Dark Horse Comics/Acme Press

1,2 1.40 3.5

JAMES BOND 007: GOLDENEYE (Movie)
Jan, 1996 ($2.95, unfinished limited series)
Topps Comics

1-Movie adaptation; Stelfreeze-c 3.0

JAMES BOND 007: SERPENT'S TOOTH
July 1992 - Aug 1992 ($4.95, limited series)
Dark Horse Comics/Acme Press

1-3-Paul Gulacy-c/a 1.00 2.00 5.0

JAMES BOND 007: SHATTERED HELIX
Jun 1994 - July 1994 ($2.50, limited series)
Dark Horse Comics

1,2 1.20 3.0

JAMES BOND 007: THE QUASIMODO GAMBIT
Jan 1995 - May 1995 ($3.95, limited series)
Dark Horse Comics

1-3 1.80 4.5

JAMES BOND FOR YOUR EYES ONLY
Oct, 1981 - No. 2, Nov, 1981
Marvel Comics Group

1,2-Movie adapt.; r/Marvel Super Special #19 1.5

JAMES BOND JR. (TV)
Jan, 1992 - No. 12, Dec, 1992 (#1: $1.00, #2-on: $1.25)
Marvel Comics

1-12-Based on animated TV show 1.2

JAMES BOND: LICENCE TO KILL (See Licence To Kill)

JAMES BOND: PERMISSION TO DIE
1989 - No. 3, 1991 ($3.95, limited series, squarebound, 52 pgs.)
Eclipse Comics/ACME Press

1-3: Mike Grell-c/a/scripts in all. 3-($4.95) 1.00 2.00 5.0

**JAM, THE: SUPER COOL COLOR INJECTED TURBO ADVENTURE #1
FROM HELL!**
May, 1988 ($2.50, 44 pgs., one-shot)
Comico

Jeep Comics #2 © R. B. Leffingwell Co.

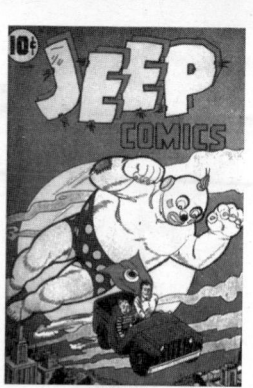

Jeff Jordan, U.S. Agent #1 © D. S. Publishing Co.

Jesse James #4 © AVON

	GD25	FN65	NM94
1		1.25	2.50

JANE ARDEN (See Feature Funnies & Pageant of Comics)
Mar, 1948 - No. 2, June, 1948
St. John (United Features Syndicate)

	GD25	FN65	NM94
1-Newspaper reprints	15.00	45.00	105.00
2	11.00	33.00	75.00

JANN OF THE JUNGLE (Jungle Tales No. 1-7)
No. 8, Nov, 1955 - No. 17, June, 1957
Atlas Comics (CSI)

8(#1)	25.00	75.00	175.00
9,11-15	13.00	39.00	90.00
10-Williamson/Colletta-c	13.50	41.00	95.00
16,17-Williamson/Mayo-a(3), 5 pgs. each	16.00	47.00	110.00

NOTE: *Everett c-15-17. Heck a-8, 15, 17. Maneely c-11. Shores a-8.*

JAR OF FOOLS
1994 ($5.95, B&W)
Penny Dreadful Press

1-Jason Lutes-c/a/scripts	1.00	2.60	6.00

JAR OF FOOLS
1994 - No. 2, 1994 ($6.95, B&W)
Black Eye Productions

1,2: 1-Reprints of earlier ed. Jason Lutesc/a/scripts	1.20	3.00	7.00

JASON & THE ARGONAUTS (See Movie Classics)

JASON GOES TO HELL: THE FINAL FRIDAY (Movie)
July, 1993 - No. 3, Sept, 1993 ($2.95, limited series)
Topps Comics

1-3: Adaptation of film. 1-Glow-in-the-dark-c	1.20		3.00

JASON'S QUEST (See Showcase #88-90)

JASON VS. LEATHERFACE
Oct, 1995 - No. 3, Jan, 1996 ($2.95, limited series)
Topps Comics

1-3: Collins scripts; Bisley-c	1.20		3.00

JAWS 2 (See Marvel Comics Super Special, A)

JAZZ (Also see Double Impact)
Mar, 1996 - No. 3, June, 1996 ($3.00, B&W, bi-monthly, limited series)
High Impact Studios

1-3			3.00
1-Gold foil logo (1000 print run)			20.00
2-($9.95)-Deluxe Edition; photo-c			10.00
3-Variant-c (1000 print run)			10.00

JCP FEATURES
Feb, 1982-c; Dec, 1981-indicia ($2.00, one-shot, B&W)
J.C. Productions (Archie)

1-T.H.U.N.D.E.R. Agents; Black Hood by Morrow & Neal Adams		.80	2.00

JEANIE COMICS (Formerly All Surprise; Cowgirl Romances #28)
No. 13, April, 1947 - No. 27, Oct, 1949
Marvel Comics/Atlas(CPC)

13-Mitzi, Willie begin	13.00	39.00	90.00
14,15	10.00	30.00	65.00
16-Used in Love and Death by Legman; Kurtzman's "Hey Look"	13.00	39.00	90.00
17-19,22-Kurtzman's "Hey Look", (1-3 pgs each)	10.00	30.00	60.00
20,21,23-27	7.00	21.00	42.00

JEEP COMICS (Also see G.I. Comics and Overseas Comics)
Winter, 1944 - No. 3, Mar-Apr, 1948
R. B. Leffingwell & Co.

	GD25	FN65	NM94
1-Capt. Power, Criss Cross & Jeep & Peep (costumed) begin	36.00	107.00	250.00
2	23.00	69.00	160.00
3-L. B. Cole dinosaur-c	32.00	96.00	225.00
1-46(Giveaways)-Strip reprints in all; Tarzan, Flash Gordon, Blondie, The Nebbs, Little Iodine, Red Ryder, Don Winslow, The Phantom, Johnny Hazard, Katzenjammer Kids; distr. to U.S. Armed Forces from 1945-1946	4.00	10.00	20.00

JEFF JORDAN, U.S. AGENT
Dec, 1947 - Jan, 1948
D. S. Publishing Co.

1	10.00	30.00	70.00

JEMM, SON OF SATURN
Sept, 1984 - No. 12, Aug, 1985 (Maxi-series, mando paper)
DC Comics

1-12: 3-Origin			1.00

NOTE: *Colan a-1-12p; c-1-5, 7-12p.*

JERRY DRUMMER (Formerly Soldier & Marine V2#9)
V2#10, Apr, 1957 - V3#12, Oct, 1957
Charlton Comics

V2#10, V3#11,12: 11-Whitman-c/a	4.25	13.00	26.00

JERRY IGER'S... (All titles, Blackthorne/First)(Value: cover or less)

JERRY LEWIS (See The Adventures of...)

JESSE JAMES (The True Story Of..., also see The Legend of...)
No. 757, Dec, 1956 (one shot)
Dell Publishing Co.

Four Color 757-Movie, photo-c	10.00	30.00	100.00

JESSE JAMES (See Badmen of the West & Blazing Sixguns)
8/50 - No. 9, 11/52; No. 15, 10/53 - No. 29, 8-9/56
Avon Periodicals

1-Kubert Alabam-r/Cowpuncher #1	16.00	47.00	110.00
2-Kubert-a(3)	13.00	39.00	90.00
3-Kubert Alabam-r/Cowpuncher #2	11.50	34.00	80.00
4,9-No Kubert	5.35	16.00	32.00
5,6-Kubert Jesse James-a(3); 5-Wood-a(1pg.)	11.50	34.00	80.00
7-Kubert Jesse James-a(2)	10.00	30.00	65.00
8-Kinstler-a(3)	7.00	21.00	42.00
15-Kinstler-r/#3	4.25	13.00	28.00
16-Kinstler-r/#3 & story-r/Butch Cassidy #1	5.00	15.00	30.00
17-19,21: 17-Jesse James-r/#4; Kinstler-c idea from Kubert splash in #6. 18-Kubert Jesse James-r/#5. 19-Kubert Jesse James-r/#6. 21-Two Jesse James-r/#4, Kinstler-r/#4	4.00	12.00	24.00
20-Williamson/Frazetta-a; r/Chief Vic. Apache Massacre; Kubert Jesse James-r/#6; Kit West story by Larsen	12.00	36.00	85.00
22,23-No Kubert	4.00	12.00	24.00
24-New McCarty strip by Kinstler; Kinstler-r	4.00	11.00	22.00
25-New McCarty Jesse James strip by Kinstler; Jesse James-r/#7,9	4.00	11.00	22.00
26,27-New McCarty Jesse James strip plus a Kinstler/McCann Jesse James-r	4.00	11.00	22.00
28,29: 28-Reprints most of Red Mountain, Featuring Quantrells Raiders	4.00	11.00	22.00
Annual nn (1952; 25¢, 100 pgs.)- "...Brings Six-Gun Justice to the West"- 3 earlier issues rebound; Kubert, Kinstler-a(3)	26.00	79.00	185.00

NOTE: *Mostly reprints #10 on. Fawcette c-1, 2. Kida a-5. Kinstler a-3, 4, 7-9, 15r, 16r(2), 21-27; c-3, 4, 9, 17-27. Painted covers c-5-8. 22 has 2 stories r/Sheriff Bob Dixon's Chuck Wagon #1 with name changed to Sheriff Bob Trent.*

JESSE JAMES
July, 1953
Realistic Publications

Jet Aces #2 © FH

Jet Fighters #7 © STD

Jetta of the 21st Century #6 © STD

	GD25	FN65	NM94
nn-Reprints Avon's #1; same-c, colors different	10.00	30.00	60.00
JEST (Formerly Snap; becomes Kayo #12)			
No. 10, 1944; No. 11, 1944			
Harry 'A' Chesler			
10-Johnny Rebel & Yankee Boy app. in text	12.00	36.00	85.00
11-Little Nemo in Adventure Land	12.00	36.00	85.00
JESTER			
No. 10, 1945			
Harry 'A' Chesler			
10	10.00	30.00	70.00
JESUS			
1979 (49¢)			
Spire Christian Comics (Fleming H. Revell Co.)			
nn			1.00
JET (See Jet Powers)			
JET ACES			
1952 - No. 4, 1953			
Fiction House Magazines			
1	11.00	33.00	75.00
2-4	7.50	22.50	45.00
JET DREAM (...and Her Stunt-Girl Counterspies)(See The Man from Uncle #7)			
June, 1968 (12¢)			
Gold Key			
1-Painted-c	2.85	8.50	28.00
JET FIGHTERS (Korean War)			
No. 5, Nov, 1952 - No. 7, Mar, 1953			
Standard Magazines			
5,7-Toth-a. 5-Toth-c	10.00	30.00	70.00
6-Celardo-a	4.25	13.00	28.00
JET POWER			
1963			
I.W. Enterprises			
I.W. Reprint 1,2-r/Jet Powers #1,2	3.25	9.50	22.00
JET POWERS (American Air Forces No. 5 on)			
1950 - No. 4, 1951			
Magazine Enterprises			
1(A-1 #30)-Powell-c/a begins	29.00	86.00	200.00
2(A-1 #32)	21.00	62.00	145.00
3(A-1 #35)-Williamson/Evans-a	34.00	103.00	240.00
4(A-1 #38)-Williamson/Wood-a; "The Rain of Sleep" drug story			
	34.00	103.00	240.00
JET PUP (See 3-D Features)			
JETSONS, THE (TV) (See March of Comics #276, 330, 348 & Spotlight #3)			
Jan, 1963 - No. 36, Oct, 1970 (Hanna-Barbera)			
Gold Key			
1	22.00	66.00	220.00
2	11.50	34.50	115.00
3-10	9.00	27.00	90.00
11-20	6.00	18.00	60.00
21-36	5.00	15.00	50.00
JETSONS, THE (TV) (Also see Golden Comics Digest)			
Nov, 1970 - No. 20, Dec, 1973 (Hanna-Barbera)			
Charlton Comics			
1	7.70	23.00	54.00
2	3.90	12.00	27.00
3-10	3.10	9.00	22.00
11-20	2.00	6.00	14.00

	GD25	FN65	NM94
JETSONS, THE (TV)			
V2#1, Sept, 1992 - No. 5, Nov, 1993 ($1.25/$1.50) (Hanna-Barbera)			
Harvey Comics			
V2#1-4			1.25
5 ($1.50)			1.50
...Big Book V2#1,2,3 ($1.95, 52 pgs.): 1-(11/92). 2-(4/93). 3-(7/93)			
		.80	2.00
...Giant Size 1,2,3 ($2.25, 68 pgs): 1-(10/92). 2-(4/93). 3-(10/93)			
		.90	2.25
JETSONS, THE (TV)			
Sept, 1995 - No. 17, Aug, 1996 ($1.50)			
Archie Comics			
1-12			1.50
JETTA OF THE 21ST CENTURY			
No. 5, Dec, 1952 - No. 7, Apr, 1953 (Teen-age Archie type)			
Standard Comics			
5	19.00	56.00	130.00
6,7	11.00	33.00	75.00
JEZEBEL JADE (Hanna-Barbara)			
Oct, 1988 - No. 3, Dec, 1988 ($2.00, mini-series)			
Comico			
1-3: Johnny Quest spin-off		.80	2.00
JIGGS & MAGGIE			
No. 18, 1941 (one shot)			
Dell Publishing Co.			
Four Color 18 (#1)-(1936-38-r)	39.00	117.00	390.00
JIGGS & MAGGIE			
No. 11, 1949(June) - No. 21, 2/53; No. 22, 4/53 - No. 27, 2-3/54			
Standard Comics/Harvey Publications No. 22 on			
11	10.00	30.00	65.00
12-15,17-21	5.35	16.00	32.00
16-Wood text illos.	7.00	21.00	42.00
22-25,27: 22-24-Little Dot app.	4.25	13.00	26.00
26-Four pgs. partially in 3-D	12.00	36.00	85.00
NOTE: Sunday page reprints by McManus loosely blended into story continuity. Based on Bringing Up Father strip. Advertised on covers as "All New."			
JIGSAW (Big Hero Adventures)			
Sept, 1966 - No. 2, Dec, 1966 (36 pgs.)			
Harvey Publications (Funday Funnies)			
1-Origin & 1st app.; Crandall-a (5 pgs.)	1.65	4.20	10.00
2-Man From S.R.A.M.	1.30	3.25	8.00
JIGSAW OF DOOM (See Complete Mystery No. 2)			
JIM BOWIE (Formerly Danger; Black Jack No. 20 on)			
No. 15, 1955? - No. 19, Apr, 1957			
Charlton Comics			
15	6.70	20.00	40.00
16-19	4.25	13.00	26.00
JIM BOWIE (TV, see Western Tales)			
No. 893, Mar, 1958 - No. 993, May-July, 1959			
Dell Publishing Co.			
Four Color 893 (#1), 993-Photo-c	6.00	18.00	60.00
JIM DANDY			
May, 1956 - No. 3, Sept, 1956 (Charles Biro)			
Dandy Magazine (Lev Gleason)			
1-Biro-c	6.35	19.00	38.00
2,3	4.00	12.00	24.00
JIM HARDY (See Giant Comics Eds., Sparkler & Treasury of Comics #2 & 5)			
1939; 1942; 1947 - No. 2, 1947			

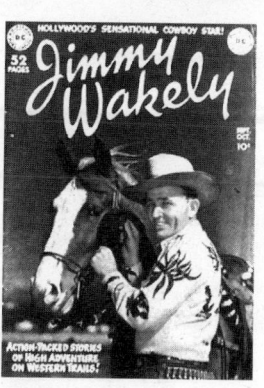

Jimmy Wakely #1 © DC

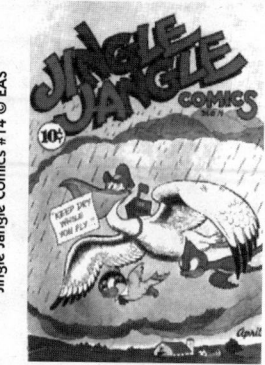

Jingle Jangle Comics #14 © EAS

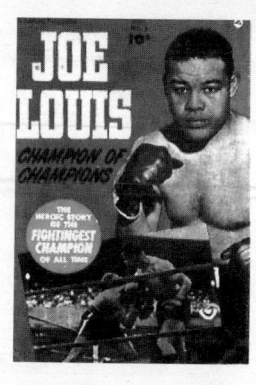

Joe Louis #2 © FAW

	GD25	FN65	NM94
United Features Syndicate/Spotlight Publ.			
Single Series 6 ('39)	39.00	118.00	275.00
Single Series 27('42)	31.00	92.00	215.00
1('47)-Spotlight Publ.	11.00	33.00	75.00
2	6.70	20.00	40.00

JIM HARDY
1944 (25¢, 132 pgs.) (Tip Top, Sparkler-r)
Spotlight/United Features Syndicate

nn-Origin Mirror Man; Triple Terror app.	38.00	114.00	265.00

JIMINY CRICKET (Disney,, see Mickey Mouse Mag. V5#3 & Walt Disney
Showcase #37)
No. 701, May, 1956 - No. 989, May-July, 1959
Dell Publishing Co.

Four Color 701	9.00	27.00	90.00
Four Color 795, 897, 989	6.00	18.00	60.00

JIMMY DURANTE (Also see A-1 Comics)
No. 18, 1949 - No. 20, 1949
Magazine Enterprises

A-1 18,20-Photo-c	36.00	107.00	250.00

JIMMY OLSEN (See Superman's Pal...)

JIMMY WAKELY (Cowboy movie star)
Sept-Oct, 1949 - No. 18, July-Aug, 1952 (1-13: 52pgs.)
National Periodical Publications

1-Photo-c, 52 pgs. begin; Alex Toth-a / Kit Colby Girl Sheriff begins	96.00	290.00	775.00
2-Toth-a	43.00	128.00	340.00
3,6,7-Frazetta-a in all, 3 pgs. each; Toth-a in all. 7-Last photo-c	44.00	133.00	355.00
4-Frazetta-a (3 pgs.); Kurtzman "Pot-Shot Pete", 1 pg; Toth-a	44.00	133.00	355.00
5,8-15,18-Toth-a; 12,14-Kubert-a (3 & 2 pgs.)	36.00	107.00	250.00
16,17	30.00	90.00	210.00

NOTE: *Gil Kane* c-10-19p.

JIM RAY'S AVIATION SKETCH BOOK
Mar-Apr, 1946 - No. 2, May-June, 1946
Vital Publishers

1,2-Picture stories about planes and pilots	22.00	66.00	155.00

JIM SOLAR (See Wisco/Klarer)

JINGLE BELLS (See March of Comics No. 65)

JINGLE BELLS CHRISTMAS BOOK
1971 (20 pgs., B&W inside, slick-c)
Montgomery Ward (Giveaway)

nn		.80	2.00

JINGLE DINGLE CHRISTMAS STOCKING COMICS (See Foodini #2)
V2#1, 1951 (no date listed) (25¢, 100 pgs.; giant-size)
Stanhall Publications (Publ. annually)

V2#1-Foodini & Pinhead, Silly Pilly plus games & puzzles	13.50	41.00	95.00

JINGLE JANGLE COMICS (Also see Puzzle Fun Comics)
Feb, 1942 - No. 42, Dec, 1949
Eastern Color Printing Co.

1-Pie-Face Prince of Old Pretzleburg, Jingle Jangle Tales by George Carlson, Hortense, & Benny Bear begin	39.00	118.00	275.00
2,3-No Pie-Face Prince	18.00	54.00	125.00
4-Pie-Face Prince cover	18.00	54.00	125.00
5	16.00	47.00	110.00
6-10: 8-No Pie-Face Prince	13.50	41.00	95.00
11-15	10.00	30.00	70.00

	GD25	FN65	NM94
16-30: 17,18-No Pie-Face Prince. 30-XMas-c	9.15	27.00	55.00
31-42: 36,42-Xmas-c	5.85	17.50	35.00

NOTE: *George Carlson* a-(2) in all except No. 2, 3, 8; c-1-6. *Carlson* 1 pg. puzzles in 9, 10, 12-15, 18, 20. *Carlson* illustrated a series of Uncle Wiggily books in 1930's.

JING PALS
Feb, 1946 - No. 4, Aug?, 1946 (Funny animal)
Victory Publishing Corporation

1-Wishing Willie, Puggy Panda & Johnny Rabbit begin	11.00	33.00	75.00
2-4	6.70	20.00	40.00

JINKS, PIXIE, AND DIXIE (See Kite Fun Book & Whitman Comic Books)

JINX
1996 - Present ($2.95, B&W, 32 pgs.)
Caliber Press

1,2: Brian Michael Bendis-c/a/scripts. 2-Photo-c			3.00

JLX
Apr, 1996 ($1.95)
DC Comics (Amalgam)

1-Mark Waid scripts			2.00

JOAN OF ARC (Also see A-1 Comics & Ideal a Classical Comic)
No. 21, 1949 (one shot)
Magazine Enterprises

A-1 21-Movie adaptation; Ingrid Bergman photo-covers & interior photos; Whitney-a	24.00	71.00	165.00

JOAN OF ARC
No date (28 pgs.)
Catechetical Guild (Topix) (Giveaway)

nn	10.00	30.00	60.00

NOTE: *Unpublished version exists which came from the Guild's files.*

JOE COLLEGE
Fall, 1949 - No. 2, Winter, 1950 (Teen-age humor, 52 pgs.)
Hillman Periodicals

1,2: Powell-a; 1-Briefer-a	9.15	27.00	55.00

JOE JINKS
No. 12, 1939
United Features Syndicate

Single Series 12	26.00	79.00	185.00

JOE LOUIS (See Fight Comics #2, Picture News #6 & True Comics #5)
Sept, 1950 - No. 2, Nov, 1950 (Photo-c) (Boxing champ)(See Dick Cole #10)
Fawcett Publications

1-Photo-c; life story	50.00	150.00	400.00
2-Photo-c	38.00	114.00	265.00

JOE PALOOKA (1st Series)(Also see Big Shot Comics, Columbia Comics &
Feature Funnies)
1942 - No. 4, 1944
Columbia Comic Corp. (Publication Enterprises)

1-1st to portray American president; gov't permission required	62.00	187.00	500.00
2 (1943)-Hitler-c	40.00	120.00	300.00
3,4: 3-Nazi Sub-c	29.00	86.00	200.00

JOE PALOOKA (2nd Series) (Battle Adv. #68-74; ...Advs. #75, 77-81, 83-85,
87; Champ of the Comics #76, 82, 86, 89-93) (See All-New)
Nov, 1945 - No. 118, Mar, 1961
Harvey Publications

1	42.00	125.00	335.00
2	21.00	64.00	150.00
3,4,6,7-1st Flyin' Fool, ends #25	13.00	39.00	90.00
5-Boy Explorers by S&K (7-8/46)	19.00	58.00	135.00

John Byrne's Next Men #16 © John Byrne

John Carter Warlord of Mars #18 © ERB

John Jakes Mullkon Empire #6 © Big Entertainment

	GD25	FN65	NM94
8-10	10.00	30.00	70.00
11-14,16-20: 19-Freedom Train-c	9.15	27.50	55.00
15-Origin & 1st app. Humphrey (12/47); Super heroine Atoma app. by			
Powell	13.00	39.00	90.00
21-30: 27-1st app. Little Max? (12/48). 30-Nude female painting			
	6.70	20.00	40.00
31-36: 35-Little Max-c/story. 36-Humphrey story. 39-Humphrey & Little Max			
begin (12/49). 41-Bing Crosby photo on-c. 44-Palooka marries Ann Howe.			
50-(11/51)-Becomes Harvey Comics Hits #51	5.00	15.00	30.00
62-S&K Boy Explorers-r	6.35	19.00	38.00
63-80: 66,67-'Commie' torture story	4.15	12.50	25.00
81-99,101-115	4.00	11.00	22.00
100	4.35	13.00	26.00
116-S&K Boy Explorers-r (Giant, '60)	6.35	19.00	38.00
117,118-Giants	5.35	16.00	32.00
...Body Building Instruction Book (1958 B&M Sports Toy giveaway, 16pgs.,			
5-1/4x7")-Origin	10.00	30.00	60.00
...Fights His Way Back (1945 Giveaway, 24 pgs.) Family Comics			
	17.00	51.00	120.00
...in Hi There! (1949 Red Cross giveaway, 12 pgs., 4-3/4x6")			
	9.15	27.50	55.00
...in It's All in the Family (1945 Red Cross giveaway, 16 pgs., regular size)			
	10.00	30.00	70.00
...Visits the Lost City nn (1945)(One Shot)(50¢)-164 page continuous story			
strip reprint. Has biography & photo of Ham Fisher; possibly the single			
longest comic book story published (159 pgs.?)	130.00	390.00	1300.00

NOTE: **Nostrand/Powell** a-73. **Powell** a-7, 8, 10, 12, 14, 17, 19, 26-45, 47-53, 70, 73 at least. Black Cat text stories #8, 12, 13, 19.

JOE YANK (Korean War)
No. 5, Mar, 1952 - No. 16, 1954
Standard Comics (Visual Editions)

	GD25	FN65	NM94
5-Toth, Celardo, Tuska-a	6.35	19.00	38.00
6-Toth, Severin/Elder-a	8.00	24.00	48.00
7	4.00	12.00	24.00
8-Toth-c	5.85	17.50	35.00
9-16: 9-Andru-a. 12-Andru-a	4.00	11.00	22.00

JOHN BOLTON'S HALLS OF HORROR
June, 1985 - No. 2, June, 1985 ($1.75, limited series)
Eclipse Comics

1,2-British-r; Bolton-c/a		.90	1.80

JOHN BYRNE'S NEXT MEN (See Dark Horse Presents #54)
Jan, 1992 - No. 30, Dec, 1994 ($2.50, mature)
Dark Horse Comics (Legend imprint #19 on)

1-Silver foil embossed-c; Byrne-c/a/scripts in all	1.00	2.00	5.00
1-2nd printing with gold ink logo		1.20	3.00
0-(2/92)-r/chapters 1-4 from DHP w/new Byrne-c	1.00	2.00	5.00
2		1.20	3.00
3,4		1.20	3.00
5-30: 7-10-MA #1-4 mini-series on flip side. 16-Origin of Mark IV. 17-Miller-c.			
19-22-Faith storyline. 23-26-Power storyline. 27-30-Lies storyline Pt. 1-4.			
	1.00		2.50
...Parallel, Book 2 ($16.95)-TPB; r/#7-12	2.40	7.30	17.00
...Fame, Book 3($16.95)-TPB r/#13-18			17.00
...Faith, Book 4($14.95)-TPB r/#19-22			15.00

NOTE: Issues 1 through 6 contain certificates redeemable for an exclusive Next Men trading card set by Byrne. Prices are for complete books. **Cody** painted c-23-26. **Mignola** a-21(part); c-21.

JOHN CARTER OF MARS (See The Funnies & Tarzan #207)
No. 375, Mar-May, 1952 - No. 488, Aug-Oct, 1953 (Edgar Rice Burroughs)
Dell Publishing Co.

	GD25	FN65	NM94
Four Color 375 (#1)-Origin; Jesse Marsh-a	25.00	75.00	250.00
Four Color 437, 488-Painted-c	16.00	48.00	160.00

JOHN CARTER OF MARS

Apr, 1964 - No. 3, Oct, 1964
Gold Key

		GD25	FN65	NM94
1(10104-404)-r/-4-Color #375; Jesse Marsh-a		4.00	12.00	40.00
2(407), 3(410)-r/-4-Color #437 & 488; Marsh-a		3.00	9.00	30.00

JOHN CARTER OF MARS
1970 (10-1/2x16-1/2", 72 pgs., B&W, paper-c)
House of Greystoke

	GD25	FN65	NM94
1941-42 Sunday strip reprints; John Coleman Burroughs-a			
	3.20	8.00	20.00

JOHN CARTER, WARLORD OF MARS (Also see Weird Worlds)
June, 1977 - No. 28, Oct, 1979
Marvel Comics

	GD25	FN65	NM94
1-28: 1-Origin. 11-Origin Dejah Thoris. 18-Frank Miller-a(p) (1st published			
Marvel work).		.80	2.00
Annuals 1-3: 1(1977). 2(1978). 3(1979)-All 52 pgs. with new book-length stories			
		.80	2.00

NOTE: **Austin** c-24i. **Gil Kane** a-1-10p; c-1p, 2p, 3, 4-9p, 10, 15p, Annual 1p. **Layton** a-17i. **Miller** c-25, 26p. **Nebres** a-24i, 8-16i; c(i)-6-9, 11-22, 25, Annual 1. **Perez** c-24p. **Simonson** a-15p. **Sutton** a-7i.

JOHN F. KENNEDY, CHAMPION OF FREEDOM
1964 (no month) (25¢)
Worden & Childs

	GD25	FN65	NM94
nn-Photo-c	8.00	24.00	48.00

JOHN F. KENNEDY LIFE STORY
Aug-Oct, 1964; Nov, 1965; June, 1966 (12¢)
Dell Publishing Co.

	GD25	FN65	NM94
12-378-410-Photo-c	3.20	9.60	32.00
12-378-511 (reprint, 11/65)	2.20	6.60	22.00
12-378-606 (reprint, 6/66)	2.00	6.00	20.00

JOHN FORCE (See Magic Agent)

JOHN HIX SCRAP BOOK, THE
Late 1930's (no date) (10¢, 68 pgs., regular size)
Eastern Color Printing Co. (McNaught Synd.)

	GD25	FN65	NM94
1-Strange As It Seems (resembles Single Series books)			
	31.00	94.00	220.00
2-Strange As It Seems	24.00	73.00	170.00

JOHN JAKES' MULLKON EMPIRE
Sept, 1995 - No. 6, Feb, 1996 ($1.95)
Tekno Comix

1-6		.80	2.00

JOHN LAW DETECTIVE(See Smash Comics #3)
April, 1983 ($1.50, Baxter paper)
Eclipse Comics

1-Three Eisner stories originally drawn in 1948 for the never published John			
Law #1; original cover pencilled in 1948 & inked in 1982 by Eisner			
		1.00	2.00

JOHNNY APPLESEED (See Story Hour Series)

JOHNNY CASH (See Hello, I'm...)

JOHNNY DANGER (See Movie Comics, 1946)
1950 (Based on movie serial)
Toby Press

	GD25	FN65	NM94
1-Photo-c; Sparling-a	13.50	41.00	95.00

JOHNNY DANGER PRIVATE DETECTIVE
Aug, 1954 (Reprinted in Danger #11 by Super)
Toby Press

	GD25	FN65	NM94
1-Photo-c; Opium den story	11.00	33.00	75.00

JOHNNY DYNAMITE (Formerly Dynamite #1-9; Foreign Intrigues #13 on)

Johnny Hazard #7 © STD

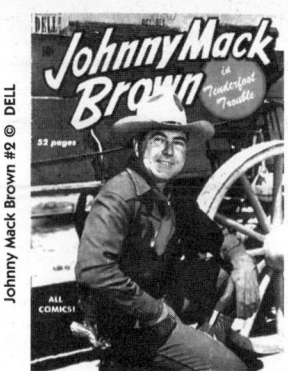

Johnny Mack Brown #2 © DELL

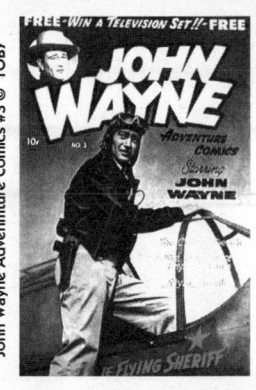

John Wayne Adventure Comics #3 © TOBY

	GD25	FN65	NM94

. 10, June, 1955 - No. 12, Oct, 1955
harlton Comics

0-12	6.35	19.00	38.00

OHNNY DYNAMITE
ept, 1994 - Dec, 1994 ($2.95, B&W & red, limited series)
ark Horse Comics

-4: Max Allan Collins scripts in all.		1.20	3.00

OHNNY HAZARD
. 5, Aug, 1948 - No. 8, May, 1949; No. 35, date?
est Books (Standard Comics) (King Features)

-Strip reprints by Frank Robbins (c/a)	12.00	36.00	85.00
,8-Strip reprints by Frank Robbins	10.00	30.00	65.00
"-New art, not Robbins	8.00	24.00	48.00
5	8.00	24.00	48.00

OHNNY JASON (...Teen Reporter)
eb-Apr, 1962 - No. 2, June-Aug, 1962
ell Publishing Co.

our Color 1302, 2(01380-208)	3.00	9.00	30.00

OHNNY JINGLE'S LUCKY DAY
56 (16 pgs.; 7-1/4x5-1/8") (Giveaway) (Disney)
merican Dairy Association

	4.00	12.00	24.00

OHNNY LAW, SKY RANGER
r, 1955 - No. 3, Aug, 1955; No. 4, Nov, 1955
ood Comics (Lev Gleason)

-Edmond Good-c/a	6.70	20.00	40.00
"-4	4.25	13.00	26.00

OHNNY MACK BROWN (TV western star; see Western Roundup under
ell Giants)
. 269, Mar, 1950 - No. 963, Feb, 1959 (All Photo-c)
ell Publishing Co.

our Color 269(#1)(3/50, 52pgs.)-Johnny Mack Brown & his horse Rebel begin;			
photo front/back-c begin; Marsh-a in #1-9	22.00	65.00	225.00
10-12/50, 52pgs.)	10.00	32.00	110.00
(1-3/51, 52pgs.)	9.00	30.00	100.00
10 (9-11/52)(36pgs.)	6.00	18.00	60.00
our Color 455,493,541,584,618	6.00	18.00	60.00
our Color 645,685,722,776,834,963	6.00	18.00	60.00
our Color 922-Manning-a	7.00	21.00	70.00

OHNNY NEMO
ept, 1985 - No. 3, Feb, 1986 (Mini-series)
clipse Comics

,2-($1.75)		.70	1.80
,3-($2.00)		.80	2.00

OHNNY PERIL (See Comic Cavalcade #15, Danger Trail #5, Sensation Comics #107 &
ensation Mystery)

OHNNY RINGO (TV)
. 1142, Nov-Jan, 1960/61 (one shot)
ell Publishing Co.

our Color 1142-Photo-c	8.00	24.00	80.00

OHNNY STARBOARD (See Wisco)

OHNNY THE HOMICIDAL MANIAC
g, 1995 - Present ($2.95, B&W)
ave Labor Graphics

			10.00
			7.00
",3: 2-(11/95). 3-(2/96)			
,5: 4-(5-96). 5-(8/96)		1.20	3.00

JOHNNY THUNDER
Feb-Mar, 1973 - No. 3, July-Aug, 1973
National Periodical Publications

1-3: Johnny Thunder & Nighthawk-r. 2-Trigger Twins app.			1.00

NOTE: All contain 1950s DC reprints from All-American Western. **Drucker** r-2, 3. **G. Kane** r-2, 3. **Moriera** r-1. **Toth** r-1, 3; c-1r, 3r. Also see All-American, All-Star Western, Flash Comics, Western Comics, World's Best & World's Finest.

JOHN PAUL JONES
No. 1007, July-Sept, 1959 (one-shot)
Dell Publishing Co.

Four Color 1007-Movie, Robert Stack photo-c	5.00	15.00	50.00

JOHN STEED & EMMA PEEL (See The Avengers, Gold Key series)

JOHN STEELE SECRET AGENT (Also see Freedom Agent)
Dec, 1964
Gold Key

1-Freedom Agent	8.50	25.50	85.00

JOHN WAYNE ADVENTURE COMICS (Movie star; See Big Tex,
Oxydol-Dreft, Tim McCoy, & With The Marines...#1)
Winter, 1949-50 - No. 31, May, 1955 (Photo-c: 1-12,17,25-on)
Toby Press

1 (36pgs.)-Photo-c begin (1st time in comics on-c)125.00		375.00	1000.00
2 (4/50, 36pgs.)-Williamson/Frazetta-a(2) 6 & 2 pgs. (one story-r/Billy the Kid			
#1); photo back-c	56.00	168.00	450.00
3 (36pgs.)-Williamson/Frazetta-a(2), 16 pgs. total; photo back-c			
	56.00	168.00	450.00
4 (52pgs.)-Williamson/Frazetta-a(2), 16 pgs. total	56.00	168.00	450.00
5 (52pgs.)-Kurtzman-a-(Alfred "L" Newman in Potshot Pete)			
	41.00	124.00	330.00
6 (52pgs.)-Williamson/Frazetta-a (10 pgs.); Kurtzman-a "Pot-Shot Pete",			
(5 pgs.); & "Genius Jones", (1 pg.)	52.00	157.00	420.00
7 (52pgs.)-Williamson/Frazetta-a (10 pgs.)	40.00	120.00	320.00
8 (36pgs.)-Williamson/Frazetta-a(2) (12 & 9 pgs.)	52.00	157.00	420.00
9-11: Photo western-c	32.00	96.00	225.00
12,14-Photo war-c. 12-Kurtzman-a(2 pg.) "Genius"	32.00	96.00	225.00
13,15: 13,15-Line-drawn-c begin, end #24	29.00	88.00	205.00
16-Williamson/Frazetta-r/Billy the Kid #1	31.00	92.00	215.00
17-Photo-c	32.00	96.00	225.00
18-Williamson/Frazetta-a (r/#4 & 8, 19 pgs.)	34.00	103.00	240.00
19-24: 23-Evans-a?	26.00	77.00	180.00
25-Photo-c resume; end #31; Williamson/Frazetta-r/Billy the Kid #3			
	34.00	103.00	240.00
26-28,30-Photo-c	30.00	90.00	210.00
29,31-Williamson/Frazetta-a in each (r/#4, 2)	31.00	94.00	220.00

NOTE: Williamsonish in later issues by **Gerald McCann.**

JO-JO COMICS (...Congo King #7-29; My Desire #30 on)
(Also see Fantastic Fears and Jungle Jo)
1945 - No. 29, July, 1949 (Two No.7's; no #13)
Fox Feature Syndicate

nn(1945)-Funny animal, humor	11.50	34.00	80.00
2(Sum,'46)-6(4-5/47): Funny animal. 2-Ten pg. Electro story (Fall/46)			
	7.00	21.00	42.00
7(7/47)-Jo-Jo, Congo King begins (1st app.); Bronze Man & Purlpe Tigress			
app.	70.00	210.00	565.00
7(#8) (9/47)	51.00	153.00	410.00
8-10(#9-11): 8-Tanee begins	40.00	120.00	315.00
11,12(#12,13),14,16: 11,16-Kamen bondage-c	39.00	116.00	270.00
15-Cited by Dr. Wertham in 5/47 Saturday Review of Literature			
	40.00	120.00	285.00
17-Kamen bondage-c	40.00	120.00	285.00
18-20	39.00	116.00	270.00
21-29: 21-Hollingsworth-a(4 pgs.; 23-1 pg.)	34.00	103.00	240.00

NOTE: Many bondage-c/a by **Baker/Kamen/Feldstein/Good.** No. 7's have Princesses

Jonah Hex #4 © DC

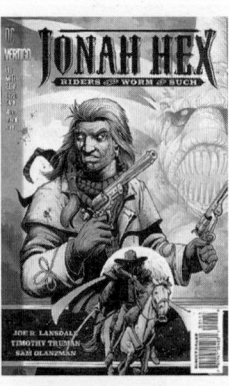

Jonah Hex: Riders Of The Worm And Such #1 © DC

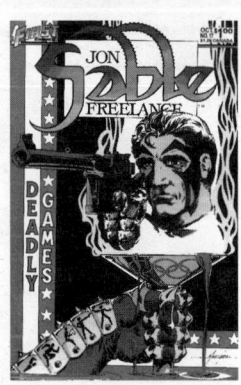

Jon Sable Freelance #17 © Mike Grell

	GD25	FN65	NM94

Gwenna, Geesa, Yolda, & Safra before settling down on Tanee.

JO-JOY (The Adventures of...)
1945 - 1953 (Christmas gift comic, 16 pgs., 7-1/16x10-1/4")
W. T. Grant Dept. Stores

1945-53 issues	4.35	13.00	26.00

JOKEBOOK COMICS DIGEST ANNUAL (...Magazine No. 5 on)
Oct, 1977 - No. 13, Oct, 1983 (Digest Size)
Archie Publications

1(10/77)-Reprints; Neal Adams-a		1.20	3.00
2(4/78)-13		1.20	3.00

JOKER, THE (See Batman #1, Batman: The Killing Joke, Brave & the Bold, Detective, Greatest Joker Stories & Justice League Annual #2)
May, 1975 - No. 9, Sept-Oct, 1976
National Periodical Publications

1-Two-Face app.	2.15	6.50	15.00
2,3: 3-The Creeper app.	1.30	3.25	8.00
4-6: 4-Green Arrow-c/sty. 6-Sherlock Holmes-c/sty	1.00	2.60	6.00
7-9: 7-Lex Luthor-c/story. 8-Scarecrow-c/story. 9-Catwoman-c/story			
	1.00	2.00	5.00

JOKER COMICS (Adventures Into Terror No. 43 on)
Apr, 1942 - No. 42, Aug, 1950
Timely/Marvel Comics No. 36 on (TCI/CDS)

1-(Rare)-Powerhouse Pepper (1st app.) begins by Wolverton; Stuporman app. from Daring Comics	200.00	600.00	1600.00
2-Wolverton-a; 1st app. Tessie the Typist & begin series			
	75.00	225.00	600.00
3-5-Wolverton-a	48.00	144.00	385.00
6-10-Wolverton-a. 6-Tessie-c begin	37.00	111.00	260.00
11-20-Wolverton-a	29.00	86.00	200.00
21,22,24-27,29,30-Wolverton cont'd. & Kurtzman's "Hey Look" in #23-27			
	24.00	73.00	170.00
23-1st "Hey Look" by Kurtzman; Wolverton-a	27.00	81.00	190.00
28,32,34,37-41: 28-Millie the Model begins. 32-Hedy begins. 41-Nellie the Nurse app.	6.70	20.00	40.00
31-Last Powerhouse Pepper; not in #28	17.00	51.00	120.00
33,35,36-Kurtzman's "Hey Look"	10.00	30.00	65.00
42-Only app. 'Patty Pinup,' clone of Millie the Model	8.35	25.00	50.00

JOKER: DEVIL'S ADVOCATE
1996 ($24.95/$12.95, one-shot)
DC Comics

nn-(Hardcover)-Dixon scripts			25.00
nn-(Softcover)			13.00

JOLLY CHRISTMAS, A (See March of Comics No. 269)

JOLLY CHRISTMAS BOOK (See Christmas Journey Through Space)
1951; 1954; 1955 (36 pgs.; 24 pgs.)
Promotional Publ. Co.

1951-(Woolworth giveaway)-slightly oversized; no slick cover; Marv Levy-c/a			
	6.70	20.00	40.00
1954-(Hot Shoppes giveaway)-regular size-reprints 1951 issue; slick cover added; 24 pgs.; no ads	6.70	20.00	40.00
1955-(J. M. McDonald Co. giveaway)-reg. size	4.25	13.00	28.00

JOLLY COMICS
1947
Four Star Publishing Co.

1	7.50	22.50	45.00

JOLLY JINGLES (Formerly Jackpot Comics)
No. 10, Sum, 1943 - No. 16, Wint, 1944/45
MLJ Magazines

10-Super Duck begins (origin & 1st app.); Woody The Woodpecker begins

	GD25	FN65	NM94

(not same as Lantz character)	34.00	103.00	240.0
11 (Fall, '43)-2nd Super Duck(see Hangman #8)	17.00	51.00	120.0
12-Hitler-c	13.50	41.00	95.
13-16: 13-Sahle-c. 15-Vigoda-c	10.00	30.00	70.

JONAH HEX (See All-Star Western, Hex and Weird Western Tales)
Mar-Apr, 1977 - No. 92, Aug, 1985
National Periodical Publications/DC Comics

1	5.00	15.00	35.0
2-6,9,10: 9-Wrightson-c.	1.60	4.20	10.
7,8-Explains Hex's face disfigurement (origin)	1.85	5.50	13.
11-20: 12-Starlin-c	1.00	2.60	6.
21-50: 31,32-Origin retold	1.00	2.00	5.
51-92: 89-Mark Texeira-a. 92-Story contd in Hex #1		1.60	4.

NOTE: **Ayers** a(p)-35-37, 40, 41, 44-53, 56, 58-82. **Buckler** a-11; c-11, 13-16. **Kubert** c-43-46. **Morrow** a-90-92; c-10. **Spiegle(Tothish)** a-34, 38, 40, 49, 52. **Texeira** a-89p. Batlash back-ups in 49, 52. El Diablo back-ups in 48, 56-60, 73-75. Scalphunter back-ups in 40, 41, 45-47.

JONAH HEX AND OTHER WESTERN TALES (Blue Ribbon Digest)
Sept-Oct, 1979 - No. 3, Jan-Feb, 1980 (100 pgs.)
DC Comics

1-3: 1-Origin Scalphunter-r, Ayers/Evans, Neal Adams-a.; painted-c. 2-Weird Western Tales-r; Neal Adams, Toth, Aragones-a	1.00	2.5

JONAH HEX: RIDERS OF THE WORM AND SUCH
Mar, 1995 - No. 5, July, 1995 ($2.95, limited series)
DC Comics (Vertigo)

1-5-Lansdale story, Truman -a		1.20	3.0

JONAH HEX SPECTACULAR (See DC Special Series No. 16)

JONAH HEX: TWO-GUN MOJO
Aug, 1993 - No. 5, Dec, 1993 ($2.95, limited series)
DC Comics (Vertigo)

1-Lansdale scripts in all;Truman/Glanzman-a in all w/Truman-c			
	1.20	2.90	7.
1-Silver ink edition with no price on cover	2.85	8.50	20.
2-5	1.00	2.00	5.

JONESY (Formerly Crack Western)
No. 85, Aug, 1953; No. 2, Oct, 1953 - No. 8, Oct, 1954
Comic Favorite/Quality Comics Group

85(#1)-Teen-age humor	5.85	17.50	35.
2	4.00	12.00	24.
3-8	3.20	8.00	16.

JON JUAN (Also see Great Lover Romances)
Spring, 1950
Toby Press

1-All Schomburg-a (signed Al Reid on-c); written by Siegel; used in **SOTI**, pg. 38 (Scarce)	53.00	159.00	425.

JONNI THUNDER (...A.K.A. Thunderbolt)
Feb, 1985 - No. 4, Aug, 1985 (75¢, limited series)
DC Comics

1-4: 1-Origin & 1st app.			1.

JONNY DEMON
May, 1994 - No. 3, July, 1994 ($2.50, limited series)
Dark Horse Comics

1-3		1.00	2.

JONNY QUEST (TV)
Dec, 1964 (Hanna-Barbera)
Gold Key

1 (10139-412)	30.00	90.00	300.

JONNY QUEST (TV)
June 1986 - No. 31, Dec, 1988 ($1.50/$1.75)(Hanna-Barbera)

Journey Into Mystery #16 © MEG

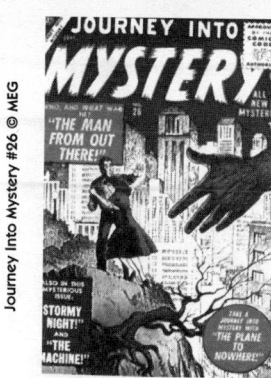

Journey Into Mystery #26 © MEG

Journey Into Mystery #96 © MEG

	GD25	FN65	NM94

	GD25	FN65	NM94

Comico

1	1.00	2.00	5.00
2		1.20	3.00
3,5-Dave Stevens-c		1.20	3.00
4,6-14			1.50
15-31: 15-Begin $1.75-c. 30-Adapts TV episode		.80	2.00
Special 1(9/88, $1.75), 2(10/88, $1.75)		.80	2.00

NOTE: **M. Anderson** a-9. **Mooney** a-Special 1. **Pini** a-2. **Quagmire** a-31p. **Rude** a-1; c-2i.
Siekiewicz c-11. **Spiegle** a-7, 12, 21; c-21 **Staton** a-2i, 11p. **Steacy** c-8. **Stevens** a-4l; c-3,5.
Wildey a-1, c-1, 7, 12. **Williamson** a-4l; c-4i.

JONNY QUEST CLASSICS (TV)
May, 1987 - No. 3, July, 1987 ($2.00) (Hanna-Barbera)
Comico

1-3: Wildey-c/a; 3-Based on TV episode		.80	2.00

JON SABLE, FREELANCE (Also see Mike Grell's Sable & Sable)
6/83 - No. 56, 2/88 (#1-17, $1; #18-33, $1.25, #34-on, $1.75)
First Comics

1-Mike Grell-c/a/scripts		1.40	3.50
2-5: 3-5-Origin, parts 1-3		1.00	2.50
6-10: 6-Origin, part 4		.80	2.00
11-20: 11-1st app. of Maggie the Cat. 14-Mando paper begins. 16-Maggie the Cat. app.		.75	1.80
21-33: 25-30-Shatter app.			1.50
34-56: 34-Deluxe format begins ($1.75)		.70	1.75

NOTE: **Aragones** a-33; c-33(part). **Grell** a-1-43;c-1-52, 53p, 54-56.

JOSEPH & HIS BRETHREN (See The Living Bible)

JOSIE (She's... #1-16) (...& the Pussycats #45 on) (See Archie Giant Series
Magazine #528, 540, 551, 562, 571, 584, 597, 610, 622)
Feb, 1963; No. 2, Aug, 1963 - No. 106, Oct, 1982
Archie Publications/Radio Comics

1	13.00	39.00	130.00
2	6.50	19.50	65.00
3-5	4.00	12.00	40.00
6-10	3.00	9.00	30.00
11-20	2.85	8.50	20.00
21-30: 22-Mighty Man & Mighty (Josie Girl) app.	2.00	6.00	14.00
31-54	1.30	3.25	8.00
55-74(52pg. issues)		1.60	4.00
75-106		.80	2.00

JOSIE & THE PUSSYCATS (TV)
1993 - No. 2, 1994 ($2.00, 52 pgs.)(Published annually)
Archie Comics

1,2-Bound-in pull-out poster in each. 2-(Spr/94)		.80	2.00

JOURNAL OF CRIME (See Fox Giants)

JOURNEY (Also see Journey: Wardrums)
1983 - No. 14, 9/84; No. 15, 4/85 - No. 27, 7/86 (B&W)
Aardvark-Vanaheim #1-14/Fantagraphics Books #15-on

1	1.00	2.00	5.00
2		1.20	3.00
3-27: 20-Sam Kieth-a			1.25

JOURNEY INTO FEAR
May, 1951 - No. 21, Sept, 1954
Superior-Dynamic Publications

1-Baker-r(2)	45.00	136.00	365.00
2	31.00	92.00	215.00
3,4	26.00	77.00	180.00
5-10,15: 15-Used in **SOTI**, pg. 389	18.00	54.00	125.00
11-14,16-21	17.00	49.00	115.00

NOTE: Kamenish 'headlight'-a most issues. **Robinson** a-10.

JOURNEY INTO MYSTERY (1st Series) (Thor Nos. 126-502)
6/52 - No. 48, 8/57; No. 49, 11/58 - No. 125, 2/66; 503, 11/96 - Present
Atlas(CPS No. 1-48/AMI No. 49-68/Marvel No. 69 (6/61) on)

1-Weird/horror stories begin	288.00	862.00	2300.00
2	90.00	270.00	725.00
3,4	68.00	206.00	550.00
5-11	44.00	132.00	350.00
12-20,22: 15-Atomic explosion panel. 22-Davisesque-a; last pre-code issue (2/55)	38.00	116.00	270.00
21-Kubert-a; Tothish-a by Andru	40.00	120.00	280.00
23-32,35-38,40: 24-Torres?-a. 38-Ditko-a	24.00	71.00	165.00
33-Williamson-a; Ditko-a (his 1st for Atlas?)	26.00	77.00	180.00
34,39: 34-Krigstein-a. 39-1st S.A. issue; Wood-a	24.00	73.00	170.00
41-Crandall-a; Frazettaesque-a by Morrow	21.00	62.00	145.00
42,48-Torres-a	21.00	62.00	145.00
43,44-Williamson/Mayo-a in both	23.00	69.00	160.00
45,47,52,53	19.00	58.00	135.00
46-Torres & Krigstein-a	21.00	62.00	145.00
49-Matt Fox, Check-a	21.00	64.00	150.00
50,54: 50-Davis-a. 54-Williamson-a	20.00	60.00	140.00
51-Kirby/Wood-a	24.00	71.00	165.00
55-61,63-65,67-69,71,72,74,75: 74-Contents change to Fantasy. 75-Last 10¢ issue	20.00	60.00	140.00
62-Prototype ish. (The Hulk); 1st app. Xemnu (Titan) called "The Hulk"	29.00	86.00	200.00
66-Prototype ish. (The Hulk)-Return of Xemnu "The Hulk"	29.00	86.00	200.00
70-Prototype ish. (The Sandman)(7/61); similar to Spidey villain	29.00	86.00	200.00
73-Prototype ish. (Spider-Man)	62.00	187.00	500.00
76,77,80-82: 80-Anti-communist propaganda story	17.00	49.00	115.00
78-The Sorceror (Dr. Strange prototype) app. (3/62)	29.00	86.00	200.00
79-Prototype issue. (Mr. Hyde)	25.00	75.00	175.00

	GD25	FN65	VF82	NM94
83-Origin & 1st app. The Mighty Thor by Kirby (8/62) and begin series; Thor-c also begin	333.00	1000.00	2500.00	4200.00

	GD25	FN65	NM94
83-Reprint from the Golden Record Comic Set with the record (1966)	17.00	49.00	115.00
84-2nd app. Thor	25.00	75.00	175.00
85-1st app. Loki & Heimdall; Odin cameo (1 panel)	100.00	300.00	900.00
86-1st full app. Odin	66.00	197.00	525.00
87-89: 89-Origin Thor retold	40.00	120.00	325.00
90-No Kirby-a	32.00	96.00	225.00
91,92,94-96-Sinnott-a	19.00	56.00	130.00
93,97-Kirby-a; Tales of Asgard series begins #97 (origin which concludes in #99)	17.00	49.00	115.00
98-100-Kirby/Heck-a. 98-Origin/1st app. The Human Cobra. 99-1st app. Surtur & Mr. Hyde	21.00	62.00	145.00
101-108,110: 101-1/2(2/64)-2nd Avengers x-over (w/o Capt. America); see Tales Of Suspense #49 for 1st x-over. 102-Intro Sif. 103-1st app. Enchantress. 105-109-Ten extra pgs. Kirby-a in each. 107-1st app. Grey Gargoyle. 108-(9/64)-Early Dr. Strange & Avengers x-over	16.00	47.00	110.00
	11.00	33.00	75.00
109-Magneto-c & app. (1st x-over, 10/64)	16.00	47.00	110.00
111,113,114,116-125: 114-Origin/1st app. Absorbing Man. 119-Intro Hogun, Fandrall, Volstagg. 124-Hercules-c/story	9.30	28.00	65.00
112-Thor Vs. Hulk (1/65). 112,113-Origin Loki	23.00	69.00	160.00
115-Origin Loki	12.00	36.00	85.00
503-510: 503-(11/96, $1.50)-The Lost Gods begin; Tom DeFalco scripts & Deodato Studios-c/a			1.50
Annual 1(1965, 25c, 72 pgs.)-New Thor vs. Hercules(1st app.)-c/story (see Incredible Hulk #3); Kirby-c/a; r/#85,93,95,97	21.00	62.00	145.00

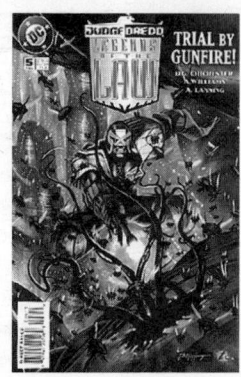

	GD25	FN65	NM94

NOTE: **Ayers** a-14, 39, 64i, 71i, 74i, 80i. **Bailey** a-43. **Briefer** a-5, 12. **Cameron** a-35. **Check** a-17. **Colan** a-23, 81; c-14. **Ditko** a-33, 38, 50-96; c-58, 67, 71, 88i. **Kirby/Ditko** a-50-83. **Everett** a-20, 48; c-4-7, 9, 36, 37, 39-42, 44, 45, 47. **Forte** a-19, 35, 40, 53. **Heath** a-4-6, 11, 14; c-1, 8, 11, 15, 51. **Heck** a-53, 73. **Kirby** a(p)-51, 52, 56, 57, 60, 62, 64, 66, 69, 71-74, 76, 79, 80-89, 93, 97, 98, 100(w/Heck), 101-125; c-50-57, 59-66, 68-70, 72-82, 88(w/Ditko), 83 & 84(w/Sinnott), 85-96(w/Ayers), 97-152p. **Leiber/Fox** a-93, 98-102. **Maneely** c-20-22. **Morisi** a-42. **Morrow** a-41, 42. **Orlando** a-30, 45, 57. **Mac Pakula** (Tothish) a-9, 35, 41. **Powell** a-20, 27, 34. **Reinman** a-39, 87, 92, 96i. **Robinson** a-9. **Roussos** a-39. **Robert Sale** a-14. **Severin** a-27; c-30. **Sinnott** a-41; c-50. **Tuska** a-11. **Wildey** a-16.

JOURNEY INTO MYSTERY (2nd Series)
Oct, 1972 - No. 19, Oct, 1975
Marvel Comics

1-Robert Howard adaptation; Starlin/Ploog-a	1.00	2.60	6.00
2,3,5-Bloch adaptation; 5-Last new story	1.20		3.00
4,6-19: 4-H. P. Lovecraft adaptation	.80		2.00

NOTE: **N. Adams** a-2i. **Ditko** r-7, 10, 12, 14, 15, 19; c-10. **Everett** r-9, 14. **G. Kane** a-1p, 2p; c-1-3p. **Kirby** r-7, 13, 18, 19; c-7. **Mort Lawrence** r-2. **Maneely** r-3. **Orlando** r-16. **Reese** a-1, 2i. **Starlin** a-1p, 3p. **Torres** r-16. **Wildey** r-9, 14.

JOURNEY INTO UNKNOWN WORLDS (Formerly Teen)
No. 36, 9/50 - No. 38, 2/51; No. 4, 4/51 - No. 59, 8/57
Atlas Comics (WFP)

36(#1)-Science fiction/weird; "End Of The Earth" c/story			
	175.00	525.00	1400.00
37(#2)-Science fiction; "When Worlds Collide" c/story; Everett-c/a; Hitler story			
	84.00	253.00	675.00
38(#3)-Science fiction	68.00	206.00	550.00
4-6,8,10-Science fiction/weird	44.00	132.00	350.00
7-Wolverton-a "Planet of Terror", 6 pgs; electric chair c-inset/story			
	71.00	215.00	575.00
9-Giant eyeball story	50.00	150.00	400.00
11,12-Krigstein-a	36.00	107.00	250.00
13,16,17,20	26.00	77.00	180.00
14-Wolverton-a "One of Our Graveyards Is Missing", 4 pgs; Tuska-a			
	53.00	161.00	430.00
15-Wolverton-a "They Crawl by Night", 5 pgs.; 2 pg. Maneely s/f story			
	53.00	161.00	430.00
18,19-Matt Fox-a	30.00	90.00	210.00
21-33: 21-Decapitation-c. 24-Sci/fic story. 26-Atom bomb panel. 27-Sid Check-a. 33-Last pre-code (2/55)	20.00	60.00	140.00
34-Kubert, Torres-a	15.00	45.00	105.00
35-Torres-a	14.00	43.00	100.00
36-42	13.00	39.00	90.00
43,44: 43-Krigstein-a. 44-Davis-a	13.00	39.00	90.00
45,55,59-Williamson-a in all; with Mayo #55,59. 55-Crandall-a			
	13.00	39.00	90.00
46,47,49,52,56-58	11.50	34.00	80.00
48,53-Crandall-a (4 pgs. #48). 48-Check-a	13.00	39.00	90.00
50-Davis, Crandall-a	13.00	39.00	90.00
51-Ditko, Wood-a	13.50	41.00	95.00
54-Torres-a	11.50	34.00	80.00

NOTE: **Ayers** a-24, 43, **Berg** a-38(#3), 43. **Lou Cameron** a-33. **Colan** a-37(#2), 6, 17, 19, 20, 23, 39. **Ditko** a-45, 51. **Drucker** a-35, 58. **Everett** a-37(#2), 11, 14, 41, 55, 56; c-37(#2), 11, 13, 14, 17, 22, 47, 48, 50, 53-55, 59. **Forte** a-49. **Fox** a-21i. **Heath** a-36(#1), 4, 6-8, 17, 20, 22, 36i; c-18. **Keller** a-15. **Mort Lawrence** a-38, 39. **Maneely** a-7, 8, 15, 16, 22, 49, 58; c-19, 25, 52. **Morrow** a-48. **Orlando** a-44, 57. **Pakula** a-36. **Powell** a-42, 53, 54. **Reinman** a-8. **Rico** a-21. **Robert Sale** a-24, 49. **Sekowsky** a-4, 5, 9. **Severin** a-38, 51; c-38, 48i, 56. **Sinnott** a-9, 21, 24. **Tuska** a-38(#3), 14. **Wildey** a-25, 43, 44.

JOURNEY OF DISCOVERY WITH MARK STEEL (See Mark Steel)

JOURNEY TO THE CENTER OF THE EARTH (Movie)
No. 1060, Nov-Jan, 1959/60 (one-shot)
Dell Publishing Co.

Four Color 1060-Pat Boone & James Madson photo-c	12.00	36.00	120.00

JUDE, THE FORGOTTEN SAINT
1954 (16 pgs.; 8x11"; full color; paper-c)
Catechetical Guild Education Society

nn	2.00	5.00	10.0

JUDGE COLT
Oct, 1969 - No. 4, Sept, 1970
Gold Key

1	1.30	3.25	8.
2-4	1.00	2.00	5.

JUDGE DREDD (...Classics #62 on; also see Batman - Judge Dredd, Dredd Rules, The Law of Dredd & 2000 A.D. Monthly)
Nov, 1983 - No. 35, 1986; V2#1, Oct, 1986 - No. 77, 1993
Eagle Comics/IPC Magazines Ltd./Quality Comics #34-35, V2#1-37/
Fleetway #38 on

1-Bolland-c/a	1.65	4.20	10.
2-35	1.00	2.00	5.
V2#1-77: 1-('86)-New look begins. 20-Begin $1.50-c. 21/22, 23/24-Two issue numbers in one. 28-1st app. Megaman (super-hero). 39-Begin $1.75-c. 51-Begin $1.95-c. 53-Bolland-a. 57-Reprints 1st published Judge Dredd story		.80	2.
Special 1		.80	2.

NOTE: **Bolland** a-1-6, 8, 10; c-1-10, 15. **Guice** c-V2#23/24, 26, 27.

JUDGE DREDD (3rd Series)
Aug, 1994 - No. 18, Jan, 1996 ($1.95)
DC Comics

1-11		.80	2.
12-18: 12-Begin $2.25-c		.90	2.
nn ($5.95)-Movie adaptation, Sienkiewicz-c	1.00	2.60	6.

JUDGE DREDD'S CRIME FILE
Aug, 1989 - No. 6, Feb, 1986 ($1.25, limited series)
Eagle Comics

1-6: 1-Byrne-a		.80	2.

JUDGE DREDD: LEGENDS OF THE LAW
Dec, 1994 - No. 13, Dec, 1995 ($1.95)
DC Comics

1-7: 1-5-Dorman-c		.80	2.
8-13: 8-Begin $2.25-c		.90	2.2

JUDGE DREDD: THE EARLY CASES
Feb, 1986 - No. 6, July, 1986 ($1.25, Mega-series, Mando paper)
Eagle Comics

1-6: 2000 A.D.-r			1.

JUDGE DREDD: THE JUDGE CHILD QUEST (Judge Child in indicia)
Aug, 1984 - No. 5, Oct, 1984 ($1.25, Limited series, Baxter paper)
Eagle Comics

1-5: 2000A.D.-r; Bolland-c/a			1.

JUDGE DREDD: THE MEGAZINE
1991 - Present ($4.95, stiff-c, squarebound, 52 pgs.)
Fleetway/Quality

1-3	1.00	2.60	6.

JUDGEMENT DAY
Sept, 1993 - No. 8, Apr, 1994 ($2.95)
Lightning Comics

1-($3.50)-Red foil-c		1.40	3.
1-Gold Prism Edition		1.20	3.
1-Purple-c Edition		1.20	3.
2-8: 2-Polybagged with trading card. 7-Origin		1.20	3.

JUDGE PARKER
Feb, 1956 - No. 2, 1956
Argo

1-Newspaper strip reprints	5.35	16.00	32.
2	4.00	11.00	22.

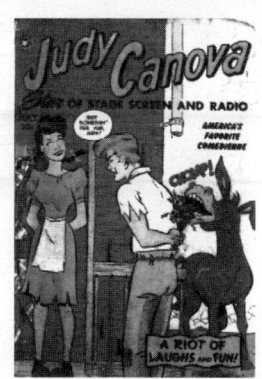

Judy Canova #2 © FOX

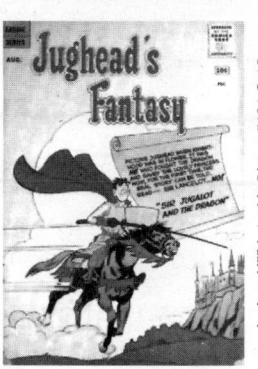

Jughead's Fantasy #1 © AP

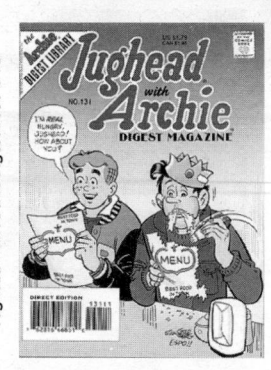

Jughead With Archie Digest #131 © AP

	GD25	FN65	NM94		GD25	FN65	NM94

DO JOE
g, 1953 - No. 3, Dec, 1953 (Judo lessons in each issue)
-Jay Corp.

		GD25	FN65	NM94
-Drug ring story		7.50	22.50	45.00
3: 3-Hypo needle story		5.00	15.00	30.00

DOMASTER (Gun Master #84-89) (Also see Crisis on Infinite Earths, Sarge
eel #6 & Special War Series)
. 89, May-June, 1966 - No. 98, Dec, 1967 (Two No. 89's)
arlton Comics

	GD25	FN65	NM94
-3rd app. Judomaster	3.25	9.50	22.00
-98: 91-Sarge Steel begins. 93-Intro. Tiger	2.60	7.50	18.00
,94,96,98(Modern Comics reprint, 1977)			1.25

TE: *Morisi* Thunderbolt #90. #91 has 1 pg. biography on writer/artist Frank McLoughlin.

DY CANOVA (Formerly My Experience) (Stage, screen, radio)
. 23, May, 1950 - No. 3, Sept, 1950
x Features Syndicate

	GD25	FN65	NM94
(#1)-Wood-a,a(p)?	17.00	51.00	120.00
-Wood-a(p)	17.00	51.00	120.00
Wood-c; Wood/Orlando-a	19.00	58.00	135.00

DY GARLAND (See Famous Stars)

DY JOINS THE WAVES
51 (For U.S. Navy)
by Press

	GD25	FN65	NM94
	5.35	16.00	32.00

GHEAD (Formerly Archie's Pal...)
. 127, Dec, 1965 - No. 352, June, 1987
hie Publications

	GD25	FN65	NM94
7-130	2.15	6.50	15.00
,133,135-160	1.70	5.00	12.00
2,134: 132-Shield-c; The Fly & Black Hood app.; Shield cameo. 134-			
Shield-c	1.85	5.50	13.00
-200	1.00	2.60	6.00
-240		.80	2.00
-352: 300-Anniversary issue; infinity-c			1.50

GHEAD (2nd Series)(Becomes Archie's Pal Jughead Comics #46 on)
g, 1987 - No. 45, May, 1993 (.75/$1.00/$1.25)
hie Enterprises

	GD25	FN65	NM94
45: 4-X-Mas issue. 17-Colan-c/a			1.25

GHEAD AS CAPTAIN HERO (See Archie as Purehear the Powerful,
hie Giant Series Magazine #142 & Life With Archie)
t, 1966 - No. 7, Nov, 1967
hie Publications

	GD25	FN65	NM94
-Super hero parody	3.20	9.60	32.00
	2.85	8.50	20.00
7	2.00	6.00	14.00

GHEAD JONES COMICS DIGEST, THE (...Magazine No. 10-64;
ghead Jones Digest Magazine #65)
he, 1977 - Present ($1.35/$1.50/$1.75, digest-size, 128 pgs.)
hie Publications

	GD25	FN65	NM94
Neal Adams-a; Capt. Hero-r	1.00	2.50	6.00
9/77)-Neal Adams-a		1.60	4.00
50: 7-Origin Jaguar-r; N. Adams-a. 13-r/1957 Jughead's Folly			
		.80	2.00
-94			1.50
-98		.70	1.75

GHEAD'S BABY TALES
ring, 1994 ($2.00, 52 pgs.)
hie Comics

	GD25	FN65	NM94
-Bound-in pull-out poster		.80	2.00

JUGHEAD'S DINER
Apr, 1990 - No. 7, Apr, 1991 ($1.00)
Archie Comics

	GD25	FN65	NM94
1-7			1.00

JUGHEAD'S DOUBLE DIGEST (...Magazine #5)
Oct, 1989 - Present ($2.25/$2.50/$2.75, quarterly, 256 pgs.)
Archie Comics

	GD25	FN65	NM94
1-25: 2,5-Capt. Hero stories		1.00	2.50
26-33		1.10	2.75

JUGHEAD'S EAT-OUT COMIC BOOK MAGAZINE (See Archie Giant Series
Magazine No. 170)

JUGHEAD'S FANTASY
Aug, 1960 - No. 3, Dec, 1960
Archie Publications

	GD25	FN65	NM94
1	14.50	43.50	145.00
2	10.00	30.00	100.00
3	8.50	25.50	85.00

JUGHEAD'S FOLLY
1957 (36 pgs.)(one-shot)
Archie Publications (Close-Up)

	GD25	FN65	NM94
1-Jughead a la Elvis (Rare) (1st reference to Elvis in comics?)			
	33.50	120.00	335.00

JUGHEAD'S JOKES
Aug, 1967 - No. 78, Sept, 1982
(No. 1-8, 38 on: reg. size; No. 9-23: 68 pgs.; No. 24-37: 52 pgs.)
Archie Publications

	GD25	FN65	NM94
1	5.00	15.00	50.00
2	2.60	7.80	26.00
3-5	2.00	6.00	14.00
6-10	1.20	3.00	7.00
11-30	1.00	2.00	5.00
31-50		1.00	2.50
51-78			1.50

JUGHEAD'S PAL HOT DOG (See Laugh #14 for 1st app.)
Jan, 1990 - No. 5, Oct, 1990 ($1.00)
Archie Comics

	GD25	FN65	NM94
1-5			1.00

JUGHEAD'S SOUL FOOD
1979 (49 cents)
Spire Christian Comics (Fleming H. Revell Co.)

	GD25	FN65	NM94
nn			1.00

JUGHEAD'S TIME POLICE
July, 1990 - No. 6, May, 1991 ($1.00, bi-monthly)
Archie Comics

	GD25	FN65	NM94
1-6: Colan a-3-6p; c-3-6			1.00

JUGHEAD WITH ARCHIE DIGEST (...Plus Betty & Veronica & Reggie Too
No. 1,2; ...Magazine #33-?, 101-on; ...Comics Digest Mag.)
March, 1974 - Present (Digest Size; $1.00/$1.25/$1.35/$1.50/$1.75)
Archie Publications

	GD25	FN65	NM94
1	2.60	7.50	18.00
2	1.30	3.25	8.00
3-10	1.00	2.00	5.00
11-20: Capt. Hero-r in #14-16; Pureheart the Powerful #18,21,22; Capt.			
Pureheart #17,19		1.40	3.50
21-50: 29-The Shield-r. 30-The Fly-r		1.00	2.50
51-121			1.50
122-150		.70	1.75

JUKE BOX COMICS

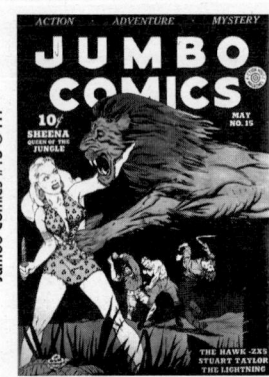

Jumbo Comics #15 © FH

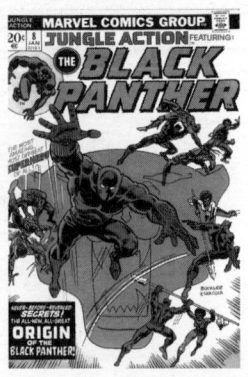

Jungle Action #8 © MEG

Jungle Adventures #2 © Skywald Comics

	GD25	FN65	NM94

Mar, 1948 - No. 6, Jan, 1949
Famous Funnies

1-Toth c/a; Hollingsworth-a	40.00	120.00	290.00
2-Transvestism story	24.00	73.00	170.00
3-6: 3-Peggy Lee story. 4-Jimmy Durante line drawn-c. 6-Features Desi Arnaz plus Arnaz line drawn-c	18.00	54.00	125.00

JUMBO COMICS (Created by S.M. Iger)
Sept, 1938 - No. 167, Mar, 1953 (No. 1-3: 68 pgs.; No. 4-8: 52 pgs.)
(No. 1-8 oversized-10-1/2x14-1/2"; black & white)
Fiction House Magazines (Real Adv. Publ. Co.)

	GD25	FN65	VF82
1-(Rare)-Sheena Queen of the Jungle(1st app.) by Meskin, Hawks of the Seas (The Hawk #10 on; see Feature Funnies #3) by Eisner, The Hunchback by Dick Briefer (ends #8), Wilton of the West (ends #24), Inspector Dayton (ends #67) & ZX-5 (ends #140) begin; 1st comic art by Jack Kirby (Count of Monte Cristo & Wilton of the West); Mickey Mouse appears (1 panel) with brief biography of Walt Disney; 1st app. Peter Pupp by Bob Kane. Note: Sheena was created by Iger for publication in England as a newspaper strip. The early issues of Jumbo contain Sheena strip-r; mutiple panel-c 1,2,7	1600.00	4800.00	16,000.00
(Estimated up to 45 total copies exist, 1 in NM/Mint)			
2-(Rare)-Origin Sheena. Diary of Dr. Hayward by Kirby (also #3) plus 2 other stories; contains strip from Universal Film featuring Edgar Bergen & Charlie McCarthy plus-c (preview of film)	520.00	1560.00	5200.00
3-Last Kirby issue	360.00	1080.00	3600.00
4-(Scarce)-Origin The Hawk by Eisner; Wilton of the West by Fine (ends #14)(1st comic work); Count of Monte Cristo by Fine (ends #15); The Diary of Dr. Hayward by Fine (cont'd #8,9)	345.00	1035.00	3450.00
5-Christmas-c	362.00	1087.00	2900.00
6-8-Last B&W issue. #8 was a 1939 N. Y. World's Fair Special Edition; Frank Buck's Jungleland story	288.00	862.00	2500.00
9-Stuart Taylor begins by Fine (ends #140); Fine-c; 1st color issue (8-9/39)-1st Sheena (jungle) cover; 8-1/4x10-1/4" (oversized in width only)	262.00	787.00	2100.00

	GD25	FN65	NM94
10-Regular size 68 pg. issues begin; Sheena dons new costume w/ origin costume; Stuart Taylor sci-fi-c; classic Lou Fine-c.	143.00	431.00	1150.00
11-13: 12-The Hawk-c by Eisner. 13-Eisner-c	112.00	338.00	900.00
14-Intro. Lightning (super-hero) on-c only	118.00	356.00	950.00
15,17-20: 15-1st Lightning story and begins, end #41. 17-Lightning part-c	68.00	206.00	550.00
16-Lightning-c	87.00	262.00	700.00
21-30: 22-1st Tom, Dick & Harry; origin The Hawk ends. 25-Midnight the Black Stallion begins, ends #65	55.00	165.00	440.00
31-40: 31-(9/41)-1st app. Mars God of War in Stuart Taylor story (see Planet Comics #15. 35-Shows V2#11 (correct number does not appear)	47.00	141.00	375.00
41-50: 42-Ghost Gallery begins, ends #167	40.00	120.00	300.00
51-60: 52-Last Tom, Dick & Harry	34.00	103.00	240.00
61-70: 68-Sky Girl begins, ends #130; not in #79	26.00	79.00	185.00
71-93,95-99: 89-ZX5 becomes a private eye.	21.00	64.00	150.00
94--Used in Love and Death by Legman	23.00	69.00	160.00
100	22.00	66.00	155.00
101-140,150-158	17.00	51.00	120.00
141-149-Two Sheena stories. 141-Long Bow, Indian Boy begins, ends #160	17.00	51.00	120.00
155-Used in POP, pg. 98	17.00	49.00	115.00
159-163: Space Scouts serial in all. 160-Last jungle-c (6/52). 161-Ghost Gallery covers begin, end #167. 163-Suicide Smith app.	14.00	43.00	100.00
164-The Star Pirate begins, ends #165	14.00	43.00	100.00
165-167: 165,167-Space Rangers app.	14.00	43.00	100.00

NOTE: Bondage covers, negligee panels, torture, etc. are common in this series. Hawks of the Seas, Inspector Dayton, Spies in Action, Sports Shorts, & Uncle Otto by Eisner, #1-7. Hawk by Eisner-#10-15. Eisner c-1-8, 12-14. 1pg. Patsy pin-ups in 92-97, 99-101. Sheena by Meskin-#1,

4; by Powell-#2, 3, 5-28; Powell c-14, 16, 17, 19. Powell/Eisner c-15. Sky Girl by Matt Bake #69-78, 80-130. ZX-5 & Ghost Gallery by Kamen-#90-130. Bailey a-3-8. Briefer a-1-8, 10. F a-14; c-9-11. Kamen a-101, 105, 123, 132; c-105, 121-145. Bob Kane a-1-8. Whitman c-14t 167(most). Jungle c-9, 13, 15, 17 on.

JUMPING JACKS PRESENTS THE WHIZ KIDS
1978 (In 3-D) with glasses (4 pgs.)
Jumping Jacks Stores giveaway

nn			1.

JUNGLE ACTION
Oct, 1954 - No. 6, Aug, 1955
Atlas Comics (IPC)

1-Leopard Girl begins by Al Hartley (#1,3); Jungle Boy by Forte; Maneely-a in all	29.00	88.00	205
2-(3-D effect cover)	33.00	99.00	230
3-6: 3-Last precode (2/55)	19.00	56.00	130

NOTE: Maneely c-1, 2, 5, 6. Romita a-3, 6. Shores a-3, 6; c-3, 4?.

JUNGLE ACTION (...& Black Panther #18-21?)
Oct, 1972 - No. 24, Nov, 1976
Marvel Comics Group

1-Lorna, Jann-r (All reprints in 1-4)	1.30	3.25	8
2-4		1.60	4
5-Black Panther begins (r- Avengers #62)-	1.65	4.20	10
6-18: 6-new stories begin; 8-Origin Black Panther. 9-Contains pull-out centerfold ad by Mark Jewelers		1.60	4
19-24: 19-23-KKK x-over. 23-r/#22. 24-1st Wind Eagle; sty contd in Marvel Premiere #51-#53		.80	2

NOTE: Buckler a-6-9p, 22; c-8p, 12p. Buscema a-5p; c-22. Byrne c-23. Gil Kane a-8p; c-2 10p, 11p, 13-17, 19, 24. Kirby c-18. Maneely r-1. Russell a-13i. Starlin c-3p.

JUNGLE ADVENTURES
1963 - 1964 (Reprints)
Super Comics

10,12,15: 10-r/Terrors of the Jungle #4 & #10(Rulah). 12-r/Zoot #14(Rulah). Kaanga from Jungle #152 & Tiger Girl	3.60	11.00	25
17-All Jo-Jo reprints	3.60	11.00	25
18-Reprints/White Princess of the Jungle #1; no Kinstler-a; origin of both White Princess & Cap'n Courage	3.60	11.00	25

JUNGLE ADVENTURES
Mar, 1971 - No. 3, June, 1971 (25¢, 52 pgs.)
Skywald Comics

1-Zangar origin; reprints of Jo-Jo, Blue Gorilla(origin)/White Princess #3, Kinstler-r/White Princess #2	1.30	3.25	8
2-Zangar, Sheena-r/Sheena #17 & Jumbo #162, Jo-Jo, origin Slave Girl Princess-r	1.30	3.25	8
3-Zangar, Jo-Jo, White Princess-r	1.30	3.25	8

JUNGLE BOOK (See King Louie and Mowgli, Movie Comics, Mowgli..., Walt Disney Showcase #45 & Walt Disney's The Jungle Book)

JUNGLE CAT (Disney)
No. 1136, Sept-Nov, 1960 (one shot)
Dell Publishing Co.

Four Color 1136-Movie, photo-c	7.00	21.00	70

JUNGLE COMICS
1/40 - No. 157, 3/53; No. 158, Spr, 1953 - No. 163, Summer, 1954
Fiction House Magazines

1-Origin The White Panther, Kaanga, Lord of the Jungle, Tabu, Wizard of the Jungle; Wambi, the Jungle Boy, Camilla & Capt. Terry Thunder begin (all 1st app.). Lou Fine-c	355.00	1066.00	340
2-Fantomah, Mystery Woman of the Jungle begins, ends #51; The Red Panther begins, ends #26	131.00	393.00	1050
3,4	115.00	346.00	925
5-Classic Eisner-c	122.00	367.00	940
6-10: 7,8-Powell-c	65.00	195.00	520

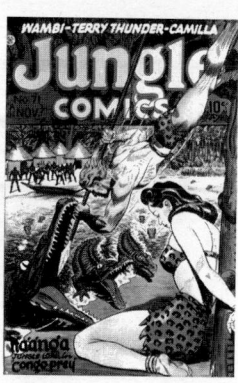

Jungle Comics #71 © FH

Jungle Jim #13 © STD

Jungle Jo #2 © FOX

	GD25	FN65	NM94
11-20: 13-Tuska-c	48.00	144.00	385.00
21-30: 25-Shows V2#1 (correct number does not appear). #27-New origin Fantomah, Daughter of the Pharoahs; Camilla dons new costume			
	41.00	124.00	330.00
31-40	33.00	99.00	230.00
41,43-50	29.00	86.00	200.00
42-Kaanga by Crandall, 12 pgs.	31.00	94.00	220.00
51-60	26.00	79.00	185.00
61-70: 67-Cover swipes Crandall splash pg. in #42	21.00	64.00	150.00
71-80: 79-New origin Tabu	19.00	58.00	135.00
81-97,99,101-110	19.00	56.00	130.00
98-Used in **SOTI**, pg. 185 & illo "In ordinary comic books, there are pictures within pictures for children who know how to look," used by N.Y. Legis. Comm.	31.00	92.00	215.00
100	21.00	64.00	150.00
111-163: 104-In Camilla story villain is Dr. Wertham. 118-Clyde Beatty app. 135-Desert Panther begins in Terry Thunder (origin), not in #137; ends (dies) #138. 139-Last 52 pg. issue. 143,145-Used in **POP**, pg. 99. 151-Last Camilla & Terry Thunder. 152-Tiger Girl begins. 158-Last Wambi; Sheena app.	17.00	49.00	115.00
.W. Reprint #1,9: 1-r/? 9-r/#151	3.25	9.50	22.00

NOTE: Bondage covers, negligee panels, torture, etc. are common to this series. Camilla by
Fran Hopper-#70-92; by Baker-#69, 100-113, 115, 116; by Lubbers-#97-99 by Tuska-#63, 65.
Kaanga by John Celardo-#80-113; by Larsen-#71, 75-79; by Moreira-#58, 60, 61, 63-70, 72-74;
by Tuska-#37, 62; by Whitman-#114-163. Tabu by Larsen-#59-75, 92-93; by Whitman-#93-
115. Terry Thunder by Hopper-#71, 72; by Celardo-#78, 79; by Lubbers-#80-85. Tiger Girl-r by
Baker-#152, 153, 155-157, 159. Wambi by Baker-#62-67, 74. Astarita c-45, 46. Celardo a-78;
-98-113. Crandall c-67 from splash pg. Eisner c-2, 5, 6. Fine c-1. Larsen a-65, 66, 71, 72, 74,
75, 79, 83, 84, 87-90. Moriera c-43, 44. Morisi c-51. Powell c-7, 8. Sultan c-3, 4. Tuska c-13.
Whitman c-132-163(most). Zolnerowich c-11, 12, 18-41.

UNGLE COMICS (May, 1988 - No.4? ($2.00, B&W/color)
Blackthorne Publishing

1-4: 1-Dave Stevens-c; B. Jones scripts in all. 2-B&W-a begins			
		.80	2.00

UNGLE GIRL (See Lorna, the...)

UNGLE GIRL (Nyoka, Jungle Girl No. 2 on)
Fall, 1942 (one-shot)(No month listed)
Fawcett Publications

1-Bondage-c; photo of Kay Aldridge who played Nyoka in movie serial app. on-c. Adaptation of the classic Republic movie serial Perils of Nyoka. 1st comic to devote entire contents to a movie serial adaptation			
	87.00	262.00	700.00

UNGLE GIRLS (1989 - No. 16, 1993 (B&W)
AC Comics

1-($1.95)-New story & "good girl" reprints		.80	2.00
2-($2.25)-New story & "good girl" reprints		.90	2.25
3-16: 3,4,10,13-16-New story & g.g. reprints. 5-9,11,12-All g.g. reprints (Baker, Powell, Lubbers, others)		1.00	2.50

UNGLE JIM (Also see Ace Comics)
No. 11, Jan, 1949 - No. 20, Apr, 1951
Standard Comics (Best Books)

1	7.50	22.50	45.00
2-20	4.25	13.00	26.00

UNGLE JIM
No. 490, 8/53 - No. 1020, 8-10/59 (Painted-c)
Dell Publishing Co.

Four Color 490(#1)	7.00	21.00	70.00
Four Color 565(#2, 6/54)	4.00	12.00	40.00
3(10-12/54)-5	3.75	11.50	37.00
6-19(1-3/59)	3.00	9.00	30.00
Four Color 1020(#20)	3.00	9.00	30.00

	GD25	FN65	NM94
JUNGLE JIM			

No. 5, Dec, 1967
King Features Syndicate

5-Reprints Dell #5; Wood-c	2.80	7.00	14.00

JUNGLE JIM (Continued from Dell series)
No. 22, Feb, 1969 - No. 28, Feb, 1970 (#21 was an overseas edition only)
Charlton Comics

22-Dan Flagg begins; Ditko/Wood-a	3.60	11.00	25.00
23-26: 23-Last Dan Flagg; Howard-c. 24-Jungle People begin	2.30	6.90	16.00
27,28: 27-Ditko/Howard-a. 28-Ditko-c	2.85	8.00	20.00

NOTE: Ditko cover of #22 reprints story panels

JUNGLE JO
Mar, 1950 - No. 6, Mar, 1951
Fox Feature Syndicate (Hero Books)

nn-Jo-Jo blanked out, leaving Congo King; came out after Jo-Jo #29 (intended as Jo-Jo #30?)	34.00	101.00	235.00
1-Tangi begins; part Wood-a	39.00	118.00	275.00
2	29.00	88.00	205.00
3-6	29.00	86.00	200.00

JUNGLE LIL (Dorothy Lamour #2 on; also see Feature Stories Magazine)
April, 1950
Fox Feature Syndicate (Hero Books)

1	30.00	90.00	210.00

JUNGLE TALES (Jann of the Jungle No. 8 on)
Sept, 1954 - No. 7, Sept, 1955
Atlas Comics (CSI)

1-Jann of the Jungle	30.00	90.00	210.00
2-7: 3-Last precode (1/55)	21.00	64.00	150.00

NOTE: Heath c-5. Heck a-6, 7. Maneely a-2; c-1, 3. Shores a-5-7; c-4, 6. Tuska a-2.

JUNGLE TALES OF TARZAN
Dec, 1964 - No. 4, July, 1965
Charlton Comics

1	4.00	12.00	28.00
2-4	3.25	9.50	22.00

NOTE: Giordano c-3p. Glanzman a-1-3. Montes/Bache a-4.

JUNGLE TERROR (See Harvey Comics Hits No. 54)

JUNGLE THRILLS (Formerly Sports Thrills; Terrors of the Jungle #17 on)
No. 16, Feb, 1952; Dec, 1953; No. 7, 1954
Star Publications

16-Phantom Lady & Rulah story-reprint/All Top No. 15; used in **POP**, pg. 98,99; L. B. Cole-c	40.00	120.00	325.00
3-D 1(12/53, 25¢)-Came w/glasses; Jungle Lil & Jungle Jo appear; L. B. Cole-c	43.00	130.00	345.00
7-Titled 'Picture Scope Jungle Adventures;' (1954, 36 pgs, 15¢)-3-D effect c/story; story & coloring book; Disbrow-a/script; L.B. Cole-c	40.00	120.00	315.00

JUNGLE TWINS, THE (Tono & Kono)
Apr, 1972 - No. 17, Nov, 1975; No. 18, May, 1982
Gold Key/Whitman No. 18

1	1.00	2.50	6.00
2-5		1.40	3.50
6-18: 18-Reprints		.80	2.00

NOTE: UFO c/story No. 13. Painted-c No. 1-17. Spiegle c-18.

JUNGLE WAR STORIES (Guerrilla War No. 12 on)
July-Sept, 1962 - No. 11, Apr-June, 1965 (Painted-c)
Dell Publishing Co.

01-384-209 (#1)	2.85	8.50	20.00
2-11	2.00	6.00	14.00

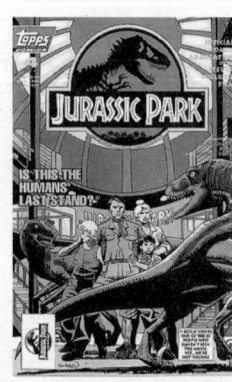

Jurassic Park # © Universal Studios & Amblin Entertainment

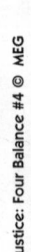

Justice: Four Balance #4 © MEG

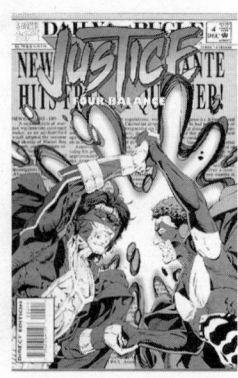

Justice, Inc. #4 © Conde Nast

	GD25	FN65	NM94

	GD25	FN65	NM94

JUNIE PROM (Also see Dexter Comics)
Winter, 1947-48 - No. 7, Aug, 1949
Dearfield Publishing Co.

1-Teen-age	10.00	30.00	70.00
2	6.35	19.00	38.00
3-7	4.25	13.00	26.00

JUNIOR CARROT PATROL (Jr. Carrot Patrol #2)
May, 1989; No. 2, Nov, 1990 ($2.00, B&W)
Dark Horse Comics

1,2-Flaming Carrot spin-off. 1-Bob Burden-c(i)		1.00	2.00

JUNIOR COMICS (Formerly Li'l Pan; becomes Western Outlaws with #17)
No. 9, Sept, 1947 - No. 16, July, 1948
Fox Feature Syndicate

9-Feldstein-c/a; headlights-c	62.00	187.00	500.00
10-16-Feldstein-c/a; headlights-c on all	56.00	170.00	450.00

JUNIOR FUNNIES (Formerly Tiny Tot Funnies No. 9)
No. 10, Aug, 1951 - No. 13, Feb, 1952
Harvey Publications (King Features Synd.)

10-Partial reprints in all; Blondie, Dagwood, Daisy, Henry, Popeye, Felix, Katzenjammer Kids	3.60	9.00	18.00
11-13	3.20	8.00	16.00

JUNIOR HOPP COMICS
Feb, 1952 - No. 3, July, 1952
Stanmor Publ.

1-Teenage humor	8.00	24.00	48.00
2,3: 3-Dave Berg-a	4.25	13.00	26.00

JUNIOR MEDICS OF AMERICA, THE
No. 1359, 1957 (15¢)
E. R. Squire & Sons

1359	2.80	7.00	14.00

JUNIOR MISS
Winter, 1944; No. 24, Apr, 1947 - No. 39, Aug, 1950
Timely/Marvel Comics (CnPC)

1-Frank Sinatra & June Allyson life story	21.00	64.00	150.00
24-Formerly The Human Torch #23?	10.00	30.00	60.00
25-38: 29,31,34-Cindy-c/stories (others?)	5.35	16.00	32.00
39-Kurtzman-a	7.50	22.50	45.00

NOTE: Painted-c 35-37. 35, 37-all romance. 36, 38-mostly teen humor.

JUNIOR PARTNERS (Formerly Oral Roberts' True Stories)
No. 120, Aug, 1959 - V3#12, Dec, 1961
Oral Roberts Evangelistic Assn.

120(#1)	5.35	16.00	32.00
2(9/59)	4.00	11.00	22.00
3-12(7/60)	2.80	7.00	14.00
V2#1(8/60)-5(12/60)	1.50	3.75	9.00
V3#1(1/61)-12	1.20	3.00	7.00

JUNIOR TREASURY (See Dell Junior...)

JUNIOR WOODCHUCKS GUIDE (Walt Disney's...)
1973 (8-3/4"x5-3/4", 214 pgs., hardcover)
Danbury Press

nn-Illustrated text based on the long-standing J.W. Guide used by Donald Duck's nephews Huey, Dewey & Louie by Carl Barks. The guidebook was a popular plot devise to enable the nephews to solve problems facing their uncle or Scrooge McDuck (scarce)

	4.20	12.50	25.00

JUNIOR WOODCHUCKS LIMITED SERIES (Walt Disney's...)
July, 1991 - No. 4, Oct, 1991 ($1.50, limited series; new & reprint-a)
W. D. Publications (Disney)

1-4: 1-The Beagle Boys app.; Barks-r			1.50

JUNIOR WOODCHUCKS (See Huey, Dewey & Louie...)

JURASSIC PARK
6/93 - No. 4, 8/93; #5, 10/94 - #10, 2/95
Topps Comics

1-($2.50)-Newsstand Edition; Kane/Perez-a in all; 1-4: movie adaptation

		1.20	3.
1-($2.95)-Collector's Ed.; polybagged w/3 cards	1.00	2.00	5.
1-Amberchrome Edition w/no price or ads	1.65	4.20	10.
2-4-($2.50)-Newsstand Edition		1.00	2.
2,3-($2.95)-Collector's Ed.; polybagged w/3 cards		1.20	3.
4-($2.95)-Collector's Ed.; polybagged w/1 of 4 different action hologram tradi card; Gil Kane/Perez-a		1.20	3.
5-10: 5-becomes Advs. of			2.
Annual 1 ($3.95, 5/95)		1.60	4.
Trade paperback (1993, $9.95)-r/#1-4; bagged w/#0			10.

JURASSIC PARK: RAPTOR
Nov, 1993 - No. 2, Dec, 1993 ($2.95, limited series)
Topps Comics

1,2: 1-Bagged w/3 trading cards & Zorro #0; Golden c-1,2		1.20	3.

JURASSIC PARK: RAPTORS ATTACK
Mar, 1994 - No. 4, June, 1994 ($2.50, limited series)
Topps Comics

1-4-Michael Golden-c/frontispiece		1.00	2

JURASSIC PARK: RAPTORS HIJACK
July, 1994 - No. 4, Oct, 1994 ($2.50, limited series)
Topps Comics

1-4: Michael Golden-c/front piece		1.00	2

JUSTICE
Nov, 1986 - No. 32, June, 1989
Marvel Comics Group (New Universe)

1-32: 26-32-$1.50-c			1.

JUSTICE COMICS (Formerly Wacky Duck; Tales of Justice #53 on)
No. 7, Fall/47 - No. 9, 6/48; No. 4, 8/48 - No. 52, 3/55
Marvel/Atlas Comics (NPP 7-9,4-19/CnPC 20-23/MjMC 24-38/Male 39-52

7(#1, 1947)	21.00	64.00	150.
8(#2)-Kurtzman-a "Giggles 'n' Grins" (3)	14.00	43.00	100.
9(#3, 6/48)	13.00	39.00	90.
4	11.50	34.00	85.
5-9: 8-Anti-Wertham editorial	10.00	30.00	60.
10-15-Photo-c	9.15	27.00	55.
16-30	7.00	21.00	42
31-40,42-47,49-52: Last precode. 35-Gene Colan-a	6.35	19.00	38
41-Electrocution-c	12.00	36.00	85
48-Pakula & Tuska-a	5.85	17.50	35

NOTE: Heath a-24. Maneely c-44, 52. Pakula a-43, 45, 48. Louis Ravielli a-39. Robinson a-22, 25, 41. Shores c-7(#1), 8(#2)? Tuska a-48. Wildey a-52.

JUSTICE: FOUR BALANCE
Sept, 1994 - No. 4, Dec, 1994 ($1.75, limited series)
Marvel Comics

1-4: 1-Thing & Firestar app.		.70	1.

JUSTICE, INC. (The Avenger) (Pulp)
May-June, 1975 - No. 4, Nov-Dec, 1975
National Periodical Publications

1-McWilliams-a, Kubert-c; origin			1
2-4: 2-4-Kirby-a(p), c-2,3p. 4-Kubert-c			1

NOTE: Adapted from Kenneth Robeson novel, creator of Doc Savage.

JUSTICE, INC. (Pulp)
1989 - No. 2, 1989 ($3.95, 52 pgs., squarebound, mature)

Justice League #7 © DC

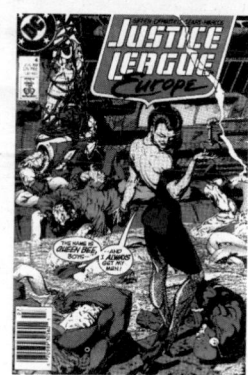

Justice League Europe #4 © DC

Justice League Europe #33 © DC

JU

DC Comics

1,2: Re-intro The Avenger; Andrew Helfer scripts & Kyle Baker-c/a
2.00 4.00

JUSTICE LEAGUE (...International #7-25; ...America #26 on)
May, 1987 - No. 113, Aug, 1996 (Also see Legends #6)
DC Comics

1-Batman, Green Lantern (Guy Gardner), Blue Beetle, Mr. Miracle, Capt. Marvel & Martian Manhunter begin	1.00	2.00	5.00
2		1.60	4.00
3-Regular-c (white background)		1.20	3.00
3-Limited-c (yellow background, Superman logo)			
	9.50	28.00	75.00
4-6: 4-Booster Gold joins. 5-Origin Gray Man; Batman vs. Guy Gardner; Creeper app.		1.00	2.50
7-($1.25, 52 pgs.)-Capt. Marvel & Dr. Fate resign; Capt. Atom & Rocket Red join	1.20		3.00
8-10: 9,10-Millennium x-over			1.50
11-23: 16-Bruce Wayne-c/story. 18-21-Lobo app.			1.25
24-($1.50)-1st app. Justice League Europe		.70	1.75
25-49,51-62: 31,32-Justice League Europe x-over. 58-Lobo app. 61-New team begins; swipes-c to JLA #1(10-11/60). 62-Last $1.00-c			1.25
50-($1.75, 52 pgs.)		.70	1.75
63-68,72-82: 80-Intro new Booster Gold. 82,83-Guy Gardner-c/stories			1.25
69-Doomsday tie-in; takes place between Superman: The Man of Steel #18 & Superman #74	1.65	4.20	10.00
69,70-2nd printings			1.25
70-Funeral for a Friend part 1; red 3/4 outer-c	1.30	3.25	8.00
70-Newsstand version w/o outer-c		1.60	4.00
71-Direct sales version w/black outer-c		.80	2.00
71-Newsstand version w/o outer-c			1.25
83-92: 83-$1.50-c begins. 92-(9/94)-Zero Hour x-over; Triumph app			
			1.50
0-(10/94)-New team begins (Hawkman, Wonder Woman, Metamorpho, Nuklon, Crimson Fox, Obsidian & Fire)			1.50
93-99: 93-(11/94)			1.50
100 ($3.95)-Foil-c; 52 pgs.		1.60	4.00
100 ($2.95)-Newsstand		1.20	3.00
101-113: 101-$1.75-c begins. 113-Flash, Green Lantern & Hawkman app			
		.70	1.75
Annual 1 (1987)		.80	2.00
Annual 2 (1988)-Joker-c/story; Batman cameo		.80	2.00
Annual 3 (1989, $1.75, 68 pgs.)		.80	2.00
Annual 4 (1990, $2.00, 68 pgs.)		.80	2.00
Annual 5 (1991, $2.00, 68 pgs.)-Armageddon 2001 x-over			
		.80	2.00
Annual 5-Silver ink 2nd printing		.80	2.00
Annual 6 (1992, $2.50, 68 pgs.)		1.00	2.50
Annual 7 (1993, $2.50, 68 pgs.)-Bloodlines x-over		1.00	2.50
Annual 8 (1994, $2.95, 68 pgs.)-Elseworlds story		1.20	3.00
Annual 9 (1995, $3.50)-Year One story		1.20	3.00
Special 1 (1990, $1.50, 52 pgs.)-Giffen plots			1.50
Special 2 (1991, $2.95, 52 pgs.)-Staton-a(p)		1.20	3.00
Spectacular 1 (1992, $1.50, 52 pgs.)-Intro new JLI & JLE teams; ties into JLI #61 & JLE #37			1.50
New Beginning Trade Paperback (1989, $12.95)-r/#1-7			
			13.00

NOTE: **Anderson** c-61i. **Austin** a-1i, 60i; c-1i. **Giffen** a-13; c-21p. **Guice** a-62i. **Maguire** a-1-12, 16-19, 22, 23. **Russell** a-Annual 1i; c-54i. **Willingham** a-30p, Annual 2.

JUSTICE LEAGUE: A MIDSUMMER'S NIGHTMARE
Sept, 1996 - No. 3, Nov, 1996 ($2.95, limited series, 38 pgs.)
DC Comics

1-3: Re-establishes Superman, Batman, Green Lantern, The Martian

Manhunter, Flash, Aquaman & Wonder Woman as the Justice League; Mark Waid & Fabian Nicieza co-scripts; Jeff Johnson & Darick Robertson-a(p); Kevin Maguire-c. 3.00

JUSTICE LEAGUE EUROPE (Justice League International #51 on)
Apr, 1989 - No. 68, Sept., 1994 (75¢/ $1.00/$1.25/$1.50)
DC Comics

1-Giffen plots in all, breakdowns in #1-8,13-30; Justice League #1-c/swipe			
		.80	2.00
2-49,51-57: 5-Begin $1.00-c. 7-9-Batman app. 7,8-JLA x-over. 8,9-Superman app. 12-Metal Men app. 20-22-Rogers-c/a(p). 33,34-Lobo vs. Despero. 37-New team begins; swipes-c to JLA #9; see JLA Spectacular.			1.25
50-($2.50, 68 pgs.)-Battles Sonar		1.00	2.50
58-68: 58-$1.50-c begins. 68-Zero Hour x-over; Triumph joins Justice League Task Force (See JLTF #17)			1.50
Annual 1 (1990, $2.00, 68 pgs.)-Return of the Global Guardians; Giffen plots/ breakdowns		.80	2.00
Annual 2 (1991, $2.00, 68pgs.)-Armageddon 2001; Giffen-a(p); Rogers-a(p); Golden-a(i)		.80	2.00
Annual 3 (1992, $2.50, 68 pgs.)-Eclipso app.		1.00	2.50
Annual 4 (1993, $2.50, 68 pgs.)-Intro Lionheart		1.00	2.50
Annual 5 (1994, $2.95)-Elseworlds story		1.20	3.00

NOTE: **Phil Jimenez** a-68p. **Rogers** a-20-22. **Sears** a-1-12, 14-19, 23-29; c-1-10, 12, 14-19, 23-29.

JUSTICE LEAGUE INTERNATIONAL (See Justice League Europe)

JUSTICE LEAGUE OF AMERICA (See Brave & the Bold #28-30, Mystery In Space #75 & Official... Index)
Oct-Nov, 1960 - No. 261, Apr, 1987 (#91-99,139-157: 52 pgs.)

National Periodical Publ./DC Comics	GD25	FN65	VF82	NM94
1-(10-11/60)-Origin & 1st app. Despero; Aquaman, Batman, Flash, Green Lantern, J'onn J'onzz, Superman & Wonder Woman continue from Brave and the Bold	280.00	840.00	1820.00	2900.00

	GD25	FN65		NM94
2	80.00	240.00		720.00
3-Origin/1st app. Kanjar Ro (see Mystery in Space #75)(scarce in high grade due to black-c)	69.00	206.00		600.00
4-Green Arrow joins JLA	47.00	141.00		400.00
5-Origin & 1st app. Dr. Destiny	40.00	120.00		300.00
6-8,10: 6-Origin & 1st app. Prof. Amos Fortune. 7-(10-11/61)-Last 10¢ issue. 10-(3/62)-Origin & 1st app. Felix Faust; 1st app. Lord of Time.	36.00	107.00		260.00
9-(2/62)-Origin JLA (1st story)	49.00	146.00		400.00
11-15: 12-(6/62)-Origin & 1st app. Dr. Light. 13-(8/62)-Speedy app. 14-(9/62)-Atom joins JLA	24.00	73.00		180.00
16-20: 17-Adam Strange flashback	21.00	62.00		150.00
21-(8/63)-"Crisis on Earth-One"; re-intro. of JSA in this title (see Flash #129)(1st S.A. app. Hourman & Dr. Fate)	40.00	120.00		300.00
22-"Crisis on Earth-Two"; JSA x-over (story continued from #21)	39.00	116.00		285.00
23-28: 24-Adam Strange app. 28-Robin app.	11.50	34.00		90.00
29-JSA x-over; 1st S.A. app. Starman; "Crisis on Earth-Three"	16.00	47.00		125.00
30-JSA x-over	13.50	41.00		100.00
31-Hawkman joins JLA, Hawkgirl cameo (11/64)	10.00	30.00		80.00
32-Intro & Origin Brain Storm	7.00	21.50		55.00
33,35,36,40,41: 40-3rd S.A. Penguin app. 41-Intro & origin The Key	8.00	23.50		60.00
34-Joker-c/story	7.00	21.50		55.00
37,38-JSA x-over (1st S.A. app. Mr. Terrific #37). 37-1st S.A. app. Mr. Terrific; Batman cameo. 38-"Crisis on Earth-A"	10.00	30.00		80.00
39-Giant G-16; r/B&B #28,30 & JLA #5	12.00	36.00		90.00
42-45: 42-Metamorpho app. 43-Intro. Royal Flush Gang	5.00	15.50		40.00
46-JSA x-over; 1st S.A. app. Sandman; 3rd S.A. app. of G.A. Spectre (8/66)				

Justice League of America #118 © DC

Justice League of America #138 © DC

Justice League of America #200 © DC

	GD25	FN65	NM94

	GD25	FN65	NM94
	11.00	33.00	85.00
47-JSA x-over; 4th S.A. app of G.A. Spectre.	5.70	17.00	45.00
48-Giant G-29; r/JLA #2,3 & B&B #29	5.00	15.50	40.00
49-54,57,59,60	4.50	14.00	35.00
55-Intro. Earth 2 Robin (1st G.A. Robin in S.A.)	7.00	21.00	50.00
56-JLA vs. JSA (1st G.A. Wonder Woman in S.A.)	4.50	14.00	35.00
58-Giant G-41; r/JLA #6,8,1	5.00	15.00	38.00
61-63,66,68-72: 69-Wonder Woman quits. 71-Manhunter leaves. 72-Last 12¢ issue	3.60	11.00	25.00
64,65-JSA story. 64-(8/68)-Origin/1st app. S.A. Red Tornado	3.75	11.25	30.00
67-Giant G-53; r/JLA #4,14,31	3.75	11.25	30.00
73-1st S.A. app. of G.A. Superman; 1st S.A. app. of Black Canary	2.85	8.50	20.00
74,77-80: 74-Black Canary joins; 1st meeting of G.A. & S.A. Superman. 78-Re-intro Vigilante (1st S.A. app?)	1.65	4.20	10.00
75-2nd app. Green Arrow in new costume (see Brave & the Bold #85)	1.70	5.00	12.00
76-Giant G-65	2.60	7.50	18.00
81-84,86-90: 82-1st S.A. app. of G.A. Batman (cameo). 83-Death of Spectre.	1.50	3.75	9.00
91,92: 91-1st meeting of the G.A. & S.A. Robin; begin 25¢, 52 pg. issues, ends #99. 92-S. A. Robin tries on costume that is similar to that of G.A. Robin in All Star Comics #58.	1.65	4.20	10.00
85,93-(Giant G-77,G-89; 68 pgs.)	2.60	7.50	18.00
94-Reprints 1st Sandman story (Adv. #40) & origin/1st app. Starman (Adv. #61); Deadman x-over; N. Adams-a (4 pgs.)	6.25	19.00	50.00
95-Reprint origin Dr. Fate & Dr. Midnight reprint (from More Fun #67, All-American #25)	1.85	5.50	13.00
96-Origin Hourman (Adv. #48); Wildcat-r	1.70	5.00	12.00
97-Origin JLA retold; Sargon, Starman-r	1.65	4.20	10.00
98,99: 98-G.A. Sargon, Starman-r. 99-G.A. Sandman, Starman, Atom-r; last 52 pg. issue	1.65	4.20	10.00
100-(8/72)-1st meeting of the G.A. & S.A. W. Woman	1.65	4.20	10.00
101,102: JSA x-overs. 102-Red Tornado dies	1.50	3.75	9.00
103-106,109: 103-Phantom Stranger joins. 105-Elongated Man joins. 106-New Red Tornado joins. 109-Hawkman resigns	1.60		4.00
107,108-J.A. Uncle Sam, Black Condor, The Ray, Dollman, Phantom Lady & The Human Bomb (JSA) x-over, 1st S.A. app.	1.20	3.00	5.00
110-116: All 100 pgs. 111-JLA vs. Scarecrow & Poison Ivy; Shining Knight, Green Arrow-r. 112-Amazo app; Crimson Avenger, Vigilante-r; origin Starman-r/Adv. #81. 115-Martian Manhunter app.	1.30	3.00	7.00
117-134,138-190: 117-Hawkman rejoins. 120,121,138-Adam Strange app. 123-(10/75)-1st named app. Earth-Prime (3rd app. overall) (See Flash; 1st Series #179 & 228); DC editor Julie Schwartz & JLA writers Cary Bates & Elliot S! Maggin appear in story as themselves. 123,124-JLA/JSA app. 125-Two-Face-c/story. 128-Wonder Woman rejoins. 129-Death of Red Tornado. 138-Adam Strange-c by Neal Adams; 1st app. Green Lantern of the 73rd Century. 139-Adam Strange app. 139-157-(52 pgs.). 144-Origin retold; origin J'onn J'onzz. 145-Red Tornado resurrected. 147,148-Legion x-over. 158-160-(44 pgs.). 161-Zatanna joins & new costume. 171-Mr. Terrific murdered. 178-Cover similar to #1; J'onn J'onzz app. 179-Firestorm joins. 181-Green Arrow leaves JLA	1.20		3.00
135-137-G.A. Bulletman, Bulletgirl, Spy Smasher, Mr. Scarlet, Pinky & Ibis x-over, 1st S.A. app. 137-Superman battles G.A. Capt. Marvel.	1.00	2.60	6.00
191-199: 192,193-Real origin Red Tornado. 193-1st app. All-Star Squadron as free 16 pg. insert		.90	2.25
200 ($1.50, Anniversary issue, 76pgs.)-JLA origin retold; Green Arrow rejoins; Bolland, Broderick, Aparo, Giordano, Gil Kane, Infantino, Kubert-a; Perez-c/a.		1.30	3.25
201-250: 203-Intro/origin new Royal Flush Gang. 207,208-JSA, JLA, & All-Star Squadron team-up. 219,220-True origin Black Canary. 228-Re-intro Martian			

	GD25	FN65	NM94
Manhunter. 228-230-War of the Worlds storyline; JLA Satellite destroyed by Martians. 233-Story cont'd from Annual #2. 243-Aquaman leaves.			
244,245-Crisis x-over. 250-Batman rejoins		.80	2.0
251-260: 253-Origin Despero. 258-Death of Vibe. 258-261-Legends x-over. 260-Death of Steel		1.25	
261-Last issue		1.20	3.0
Annual 1(1983)		1.10	2.7
Annual 2(1984)-Intro new J.L.A. (Aquaman, Martian Manhunter, Steel, Gypsy, Vixen, Vibe, Enlongated Man, & Zatanna)		.80	2.0
Annual 3(1985)-Crisis x-over		.80	2.0

NOTE: Neal Adams c-63, 66, 67, 70, 74, 79, 81, 82, 86-89, 91, 92, 94, 96-98, 138, 139. M. Anderson c-1-4, 6, 7, 10, 12-14. Aparo a-200. Austin a-200. Baily a-96r. Bolland a-200. Buckler c-158, 163, 164. Burnley r-94, 98, 99. Greene a-46-61, 64-73l, 110(r)r. Grell c-117, 122. Kaluta c-154z. Gil Kane a-200. Krigstein a-96(r/Sensation #84). Kubert a-200; c-72, 73. Nino a-228i, 230i. Orlando c-151i. Perez a-184-186p, 192-197p, 200p; c-184p, 186, 192-195, 196p, 197p, 199, 200, 201p, 202, 203-205p, 207-209, 212-215, 217, 219, 220. Reinman r-97. Roussos a-62i. Sekowsky a-37, 38, 44-63p, 110-112p(r); c-46-48p, 51p. Sekowsky/Anderso c-5, 8, 9, 11, 15. B. Smith c-185i. Starlin c-178-180, 183, 185p. Staton a-244p; c-157p, 244p. Toth r-110. Tuska a-153, 228p, 241-243p. JSA x-overs-21, 22, 29, 30, 37, 38, 46, 47, 55, 56, 64, 65, 73, 74, 82, 83, 91, 92, 100, 101, 102, 107, 108, 110, 113, 115, 123, 124, 135-137, 147, 148, 159, 160, 171, 172, 183-185, 195-197, 207-209, 219, 220, 231, 232, 244.

JUSTICE LEAGUE QUARTERLY (…International Quarterly #6 on)
Winter, 1990-91 - No. 17, Winter, 1994 ($2.95/$3.50, 84 pgs.)
DC Comics

1-6: 1-Intro The Conglomerate (Booster Gold, Praxis, Gypsy, Vapor, Echo, Maxi-Man, & Reverb); Justice League #1-c/swipe.			
1,2-Giffen plots/breakdowns. 3-Giffen plot; 72 pg. story.			
4-Rogers/Russell-a in back-up. 5,6-Waid scripts		1.20	3.0
7-17: 8,17-Global Guardians app. 12-Waid script			3.5

NOTE: Phil Jimenez a-17p. Sprouse a-1p.

JUSTICE LEAGUE TASK FORCE
June, 1993 - No. 37, Aug, 1996 ($1.25/$1.50/$1.75)
DC Comics

1-7: Aquaman, Nightwing, Flash, J'onn J'onzz, & Gypsy form team. 5,6-Knight quest tie-ins (new Batman cameo #5, 1 pg.)			1.2
8-16: 8-$1.50-c begins. 15-Triumph cameo. 16-(9/94)-Zero Hour x-over; Triumph app.			1.5
0,17-23: 0-(10/94). 17-(11/94)-Triumph becomes part of Justice League Task Force (See JLE #68)			1.5
24-35: 24-$1.75-c begins, 26-Impulse app. 35-Warlord app. 37-Triumph quits team		.70	1.7

JUSTICE MACHINE, THE
June, 1981 - No. 5, Nov, 1983 ($2.00, nos. 1-3 are magazine size)
Noble Comics

1-Byrne-c(p)	1.00	2.00	5.0
2-Austin-c(i)		1.60	4.0
3		1.20	3.0
4,5		1.00	2.5
Annual 1 (1/84, 68 pgs.)(published by Texas Comics); 1st app. The Elementals; Golden-c(p)		1.60	4.0

JUSTICE MACHINE (Also see The New Justice Machine)
Jan, 1987 - No. 29, May 1989 ($1.50/$1.75)
Comico/Innovation Publishing

1-29		.80	2.0
Annual 1(6/89, $2.50, 36 pgs.)-Last Comico ish.		1.25	2.5
Summer Spectacular 1 ('89, $2.75)-Innovation Publ.; Byrne/Gustovich cover		1.20	3.0

JUSTICE MACHINE, THE
1990 - No. 4, 1990 ($1.95/$2.25, deluxe format, mature)
Innovation Publishing

1-4: Gustovich-c/a in all		.90	2.2

JUSTICE MACHINE FEATURING THE ELEMENTALS
May, 1986 - No. 4, Aug, 1986 ($1.50, limited series)

Kabuki Gallery © David Mack

Kamandi, The Last Boy On Earth #29 © DC

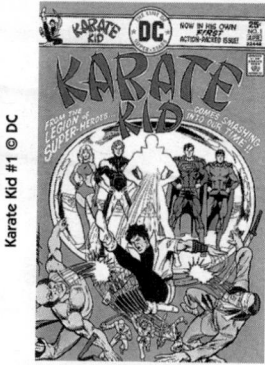

Karate Kid #1 © DC

KA

	GD25	FN65	NM94

Comico

1-4			1.50

JUSTICE SOCIETY OF AMERICA (See Adventure #461 & All-Star #3)
April, 1991 - No. 8, Nov, 1991 ($1.00, limited series)
DC Comics

1-8: 1-Flash. 2-Black Canary. 3-Green Lantern. 4-Hawkman. 5-Flash/			
Hawkman. 6-Gr. Lantern/Black Canary. 7-JSA			1.00

JUSTICE SOCIETY OF AMERICA (Also see Last Days of the... Special)
Aug, 1992 - No. 10, May, 1993 ($1.25)
DC Comics

1-10			1.25

JUSTICE TRAPS THE GUILTY (Fargo Kid V11#3 on)
Oct-Nov, 1947 - V11#2(#92), Apr-May, 1958 (True FBI Cases)
Prize/Headline Publications

V2#1-S&K-c/a; electrocution-c	43.00	128.00	340.00
2-S&K-c/a	27.00	81.00	190.00
3-5-S&K-c/a	25.00	75.00	175.00
6-S&K-c/a; Feldstein-a	27.00	81.00	190.00
7,9-S&K-c/a. 7-9-V2#1-3 in indicia; #7-9 on-c	21.00	64.00	150.00
8,10-Krigstein-a; S&K-c/a. 10-S&K-a	24.00	73.00	170.00
11,19-S&K-c	10.00	30.00	70.00
12,14-17,20-No S&K. 14-Severin/Elder-a (8pg.)	5.35	16.00	32.00
13-Used in SOTI, pg. 110-111	8.00	24.00	48.00
18-S&K-c, Elder-a	6.70	20.00	40.00
21,30-S&K-c/a	8.00	24.00	48.00
22,23,27-S&K-c	5.70	17.00	34.00
24-26,28,29,31-50: 28-Kirby-c. 32-Meskin story	4.00	10.00	20.00
51-55,57,59-70	3.60	9.00	18.00
56-Ben oda, Joe Simon, Joe Genola, Mort Meskin & Jack Kirby app. in			
police line-up on-c	4.15	12.50	25.00
58-Illo. in SOTI, "Treating police contemptuously" (top left); text on heroin			
	22.00	66.00	155.00
71-92: 76-Orlando-a	3.60	9.00	18.00

NOTE: **Bailey** a-12, 13. **Elder** a-8. **Kirby** a-19p. **Meskin** a-22, 27, 63, 64; c-45, 46. **Robinson/Meskin** a-5, 19. **Severin** a-8, 11p. Photo c-12, 15-17.

JUST MARRIED
January, 1958 - No. 114, Dec, 1976
Charlton Comics

1	5.00	15.00	30.00
2	3.00	7.50	15.00
3-10	1.60	4.00	9.00
11-30	.90	2.25	4.50
31-50	.40	1.00	2.00
51-114		.50	1.00

JUSTY
Dec 6, 1988 - No. 9, 1989 ($1.75, B&W, bi-weekly mini-series)
Viz Comics

1-9: Japanese manga		.90	1.80

KA'A'NGA COMICS (...Jungle King)(See Jungle Comics)
Spring, 1949 - No. 20, Summer, 1954
Fiction House Magazines (Glen-Kel Publ. Co.)

1-Ka'a'nga, Lord of the Jungle begins	45.00	136.00	365.00
2 (Winter, '49-'50)	24.00	73.00	170.00
3,4	18.00	54.00	125.00
5-Camilla app.	13.00	39.00	90.00
6-10: 7-Tuska-a. 9-Tabu, Wizard of the Jungle app. 10-Used in POP, pg. 99			
	11.00	33.00	75.00
11-15: 15-Camilla-r by Baker/Jungle #106	10.00	30.00	62.00
16-Sheena app.	10.00	30.00	68.00
17-20	10.00	30.00	58.00

	GD25	FN65	NM94

I.W. Reprint #1,8: 1-r/#18; Kinstler-c. 8-r/#10	2.15	6.50	15.00

NOTE: **Celardo** c-1. Whitman c-8-20(most).

KABUKI
Nov, 1994 ($3.50, B&W)
Caliber Press

1-Intro Kabuki	1.00	2.60	6.00
Color Special (1/96, $2.95)-Mack-c/a/scripts; pin-ups by Tucci, Harris &			
Quesada			3.00
Gallery (8/95, $2.95)- pinups from Mack, Paul Pope, Tim Bradstreet & others.			
		1.20	3.00

KABUKI: CIRCLE OF BLOOD
Jan, 1995 - Present
Caliber Press

1-David Mack story/a in all	1.00	2.00	5.00
2-5: 3-#1on inside indicia.		1.20	3.00

KABUKI: DANCE OF DEATH
Jan, 1995 ($3.00, B&W, one-shot)
London Night Studios

1-David Mack c/a/scripts-	1.00	2.60	6.00

KABUKI: DREAMS OF THE DEAD
July, 1996 ($2.95, one-shot)
Caliber

nn-David Mack-c/a/scripts			3.00

KABUKI: MASKS OF THE NOH
May, 1996 - No. 3, July, 1996 ($2.95, limited series)
Caliber

1-3: 1-Three-c (1A-Quesada, 1B-Buzz, &1C-Mack). 3-Terry Moore pin-up			
			3.00

KAMANDI: AT EARTH'S END
June, 1993 - No. 6, Nov, 1993 ($1.75, limited series)
DC Comics

1-6: Elseworlds storyline		.70	1.75

KAMANDI, THE LAST BOY ON EARTH (Also see Alarming Tales #1, Brave and the Bold #120 & 157 & Cancelled Comic Cavalcade)
Oct-Nov, 1972 - V7#59, Sept-Oct, 1978
National Periodical Publications/DC Comics

1-Origin & 1st app. Kamandi	5.70	17.00	40.00
2	3.60	11.00	25.00
3-5: 4-Intro. Prince Tuftan of the Tigers	2.15	6.50	15.00
6-10	1.60	4.20	10.00
11-20	1.20	3.00	7.00
21-40: 24-Last 20¢ issue. 29-Superman x-over. 31-Intro Pyra. 32-(68 pgs.)-r/			
origin from #1 plus one new story; 4 pg. biog. of Jack Kirby with B&W photos			
	1.00	2.00	5.00
41-59: 58-Karate Kid x-over from LSH. 59-(44 pgs.)-Cont'd in B&B #157; The			
Return of Omac back-up by Starlin-c/a(p)	1.20	3.00	3.00

NOTE: **Ayers** a(p)-48-59 (most). **Giffen** a-44p, 45p. **Kirby** a-1-40p; c-1-33. **Kubert** c-34-41. **Nasser** a-45p, 46p. **Starlin** a-59p; c-57, 59p.

KAMUI (Legend Of...#2 on)
May 12, 1987 - No. 37, Nov. 15, 1988 ($1.50, B&W, bi-weekly)
Eclipse Comics/Viz Comics

1-37: 1-3 have 2nd printings			1.50

KARATE KID (See Action, Adventure, Legion of Super-Heroes, & Superboy)
Mar-Apr, 1976 - No. 15, July-Aug, 1978 (Legion spin-off)
National Periodical Publications/DC Comics

1-15: 1-Meets Iris Jacobs; Estrada/Staton-a. 2-Major Disaster app. 15-			
Continued into Kamandi #58		.80	2.00

NOTE: **Grell** c-1-4, 5p, 6p, 7, 8. **Staton** a-1-9i. Legion x-over-No. 1, 2, 4, 6, 10, 12, 13. Princess Projectra x-over-#8, 9.

Katy Keene Special © AP

Ka-Zar #7 © MEG

Ka-Zar #12 © MEG

	GD25	FN65	NM94

KASCO KOMICS
1945; No. 2, 1949 (Regular size, paper-c)
Kasko Grainfeed (Giveaway)

1(1945)-Similar to Katy Keene; Bill Woggon-a; 28 pgs.; 6-7/8x9-7/8"			
	14.00	43.00	100.00
2(1949)-Woggon-c/a	11.50	34.00	80.00

KATHY
Sept, 1949 - No. 17, Sept, 1955
Standard Comics

1-Teen-age	8.70	26.00	52.00
2-Schomburg-c	5.35	16.00	32.00
3-5	4.00	11.00	22.00
6-17: 17-Code approved	3.00	7.50	15.00

KATHY (The Teenage Tornado)
Oct, 1959 - No. 27, Feb, 1964
Atlas Comics/Marvel (ZPC)

1-Teen-age	7.50	22.50	45.00
2	3.40	10.00	24.00
3-15	2.30	6.75	16.00
16-27	1.50	3.75	9.00

KAT KARSON
No date (Reprint)
I. W. Enterprises

1-Funny animals	1.50l	3.75	9.00

KATO OF THE GREEN HORNET (Also see The Green Hornet)
Nov, 1991 - No. 4, Feb, 1992 ($2.50, mini-series)
Now Comics

1-4: Brent Anderson-c/a		1.00	2.50

KATY AND KEN VISIT SANTA WITH MISTER WISH
1948 (Giveaway, 16 pgs., paper-c)
S. S. Kresge Co.

nn	4.00	12.00	24.00

KATY KEENE (Also see Kasco Komics, Laugh, Pep, Suzie, & Wilbur)
1949 - No. 4, 1951; No. 5, 3/52 - No. 62, Oct, 1961 (50-53-Adventures of…on-c)
Archie Publ./Close-Up/Radio Comics

1-Bill Woggon-c/a begins; swipes-c to Mopsy #1	91.00	272.00	725.00
2-(1950)	46.00	137.00	365.00
3-5: 3-(1951). 4-(1951)	39.00	118.00	275.00
6-10	33.00	99.00	230.00
11,13-21: 21-Last pre-code issue (3/55)	28.00	84.00	195.00
12-(Scarce)	31.00	94.00	220.00
22-40	20.00	60.00	140.00
41-62: 54-Wedding Album plus wedding pin-up	16.00	47.00	110.00
Annual 1('54, 25¢)-All new stories; last pre-code	44.00	132.00	350.00
Annual 2-6('55-59, 25¢)-All new stories	28.00	84.00	195.00
3-D 1(1953, 25¢, large size)-Came w/glasses	40.00	120.00	285.00
Charm 1(9/58)-Woggon-c/a; new stories, and cut-outs			
	26.00	79.00	185.00
Glamour 1(1957)-Puzzles, games, cut-outs	26.00	79.00	185.00
Spectacular 1('56)	26.00	79.00	185.00
NOTE: Debby's Diary in #45, 47-49, 52, 57.

KATY KEENE COMICS DIGEST MAGAZINE
1987 - No. 10, July, 1990 ($1.25/$1.35/$1.50, digest size)
Close-Up, Inc. (Archie Ent.)

1-10			1.50

KATY KEENE FASHION BOOK MAGAZINE
1955 - No. 13, Sum, '56 - N. 23, Wint, '58-59 (nn 3-10)
Radio Comics/Archie Publications

1-Bill Woggon-c/a	41.00	124.00	330.00

2	28.00	84.00	195.00
11-18: 18-Photo Bill Woggon	20.00	60.00	140.00
19-23	16.00	47.00	110.00

KATY KEENE HOLIDAY FUN (See Archie Giant Series Magazine No. 7, 12)
KATY KEENE PINUP PARADE
1955 - No. 15, Summer, 1961 (25¢)
Radio Comics/Archie Publications

1-Cut-outs in all?; last pre-code issue	41.00	124.00	330.00
2-(1956)	28.00	84.00	175.00
3-5: 3-(1957)	22.00	66.00	155.00
6-10,12-14: 8-Mad parody. 10-Bill Woggon photo	19.00	56.00	130.00
11-Story of how comics get CCA approved, narrated by Katy			
	24.00	73.00	170.00
15(Rare)-Photo artist & family	40.00	120.00	320.00

KATY KEENE SPECIAL (Katy Keene #7 on; see Laugh Comics Digest)
Sept, 1983 - No. 33, 1990 (Later issues published quarterly)
Archie Enterprises

1-33: 1-Woggon-r; new Woggon-c. 3-Woggon-r			1.00

KATZENJAMMER KIDS, THE (See Captain & the Kids & Giant Comic Album)
1945-1946; Summer, 1947 - No. 27, Feb-Mar, 1954
David McKay Publ./Standard No. 12-21(Spring/'50 - 53)/Harvey No. 22, 4/53 on

Feature Books 30	17.00	49.00	115.00
Feature Books 32,35('45),41,44('46)	15.00	45.00	105.00
Feature Book 37-Has photos & biography of Harold Knerr			
	17.00	49.00	115.00
1(1947)-All new stories begin	17.00	49.00	115.00
2	9.15	27.50	55.00
3-11	5.85	17.50	35.00
12-14(Standard)	4.35	13.00	26.00
15-21(Standard)	4.00	11.00	22.00
22-25,27(Harvey): 22-24-Henry app.	3.60	9.00	18.00
26-Half in 3-D	18.00	54.00	125.00

KAYO (Formerly Bullseye & Jest; becomes Carnival Comics)
No. 12, Mar, 1945
Harry 'A' Chesler

12-Green Knight, Capt. Glory, Little Nemo (not by McCay)			
	11.50	34.00	80.00

KA-ZAR (Also see Marvel Comics #1, Savage Tales #6 & X-Men #10)
Aug, 1970 - No. 3, Mar, 1971 (Giant-Size, 68 pgs.)
Marvel Comics Group

1-Reprints earlier Ka-Zar stories; Avengers x-over in Hercules; Daredevil, X-Men app.; hidden profanity-c	2.15	6.50	15.00
2,3-Daredevil-r. 2-r/Daredevil #12 w/Kirby layouts; Ka-Zar origin; Angel-r from X-Men by Tuska. 3-Romita & Heck-a (no Kirby)	1.65	4.20	10.00
NOTE: Buscema r-2. Colan a-1p(r). Kirby c/a-1, 2. #1-Reprints X-Men #10? & Daredevil #13?

KA-ZAR
Jan, 1974 - No. 20, Feb, 1977 (Regular Size)
Marvel Comics Group

1		1.20	3.00
2-20		1.00	2.50
NOTE: Alcala a-6i, 8i. Brunner c-4. J. Buscema a-6-10p; c-1, 5, 7. Heath a-12. G. Kane c(p)-3, 5, 8-11, 15, 20. Kirby c-12p. Reinman a-1p.

KA-ZAR THE SAVAGE (See Marvel Fanfare)
Apr, 1981 - No. 34, Oct, 1984 (Regular size) (Mando paper #10 on)
Marvel Comics Group

1-34: 11-Origin Zabu. 12-Two versions: With & without panel missing (1600 printed with panel). 20-Kraven the Hunter-c/story (also apps. in #21). 21-23,25,26-Spider-Man app. 26-Photo-c. 29-Double size; Ka-Zar & Shanna wed			1.00
NOTE: B. Anderson a-1-15p, 18, 19; c-1-17, 18p, 20(back). G. Kane a(back-up)-11, 12, 14.

Keen Detective Funnies V1#10 © CEN

Keen Teens #5 © ME

PERRY COMO...
writes for the record

Key Comics #1 © Consolidated Magazines

	GD25	FN65	NM94		GD25	FN65	NM94

KEEN DETECTIVE FUNNIES (Formerly Detective Picture Stories?)
No. 8, July, 1938 - No. 24, Sept, 1940
Centaur Publications

V1#8-The Clock continues-r/Funny Picture Stories #1; Roy Crane-a (1st?)			
	162.00	487.00	1300.00
9-Tex Martin by Eisner; The Gang Buster app.	71.00	215.00	575.00
10,11: 11-Dean Denton story (begins?)	62.00	187.00	500.00
V2#1,2-The Eye Sees by Frank Thomas begins; ends #23(Not in V2#3&5).			
2-Jack Cole-a	58.00	174.00	465.00
3-6: 3-TNT Todd begins. 4-Gabby Flynn begins. 5,6-Dean Denton story			
	54.00	163.00	435.00
7-The Masked Marvel by Ben Thompson begins (7/39, 1st app.)(scarce)			
	125.00	375.00	1000.00
8-Nudist ranch panel w/four girls	62.00	187.00	500.00
9-11	61.00	183.00	490.00
12(12/39)-Origin The Eye Sees by Frank Thomas; death of Masked Marvel's sidekick ZL	73.00	219.00	585.00
V3#1,2	58.00	174.00	465.00
18,19,21,22: 18-Bondage/torture-c	58.00	174.00	465.00
20-Classic Eye Sees-c by Thomas	78.00	234.00	625.00
23,24: 23-Air Man begins (intro). 23,24-Air Man-c			
	70.00	211.00	565.00

NOTE: *Burgos* a-V2#2. *Jack Cole* a-V2#2. *Eisner* a-10, V2#6. *Ken Ernst* a-V2#4-7, 9, 10, 19, 21; c-V2#4. *Everett* a-V2#6, 7, 9, 11, 12, 20. *Guardineer* a-V2#5, 66. *Gustavson* a-V2#4-6. *Simon* c-V3#1. *Thompson* c-V2#7, 9, 10, 22.

KEEN KOMICS
V2#1, May, 1939 - V2#3, Nov, 1939
Centaur Publications

V2#1(Large size)-Dan Hastings (s/f), The Big Top, Bob Phantom the Magician, The Mad Goddess app.	81.00	243.00	650.00
V2#2(Reg. size)-The Forbidden Idol of Machu Picchu; Cut Carson by Burgos begins	53.00	159.00	425.00
V2#3-Saddle Sniffl by Jack Cole, Circus Pays, Kings Revenge app.			
	53.00	159.00	425.00

NOTE: *Binder* a-V2#2. *Burgos* a-V2#2, 3. *Ken Ernst* a-V2#3. *Gustavson* a-V2#2. *Jack Cole* a-V2#3.

KEEN TEENS (Girls magazine)
1945 - No. 6, Aug-Sept, 1947
Life's Romances Publ./Leader/Magazine Enterprises

nn (#1)-14 pgs. Claire Voyant (cont'd. in other nn issue) movie photos, Dotty Dripple, Gertie O'Grady & Sissy; Van Johnson, Frank Sinatra photo-c			
	21.00	64.00	150.00
nn (#2, 1946)-16 pgs. Claire Voyant & 16 pgs. movie photos			
	21.00	64.00	150.00
3-6: 4-Glenn Ford photo-c. 5-Perry Como-c	7.00	21.00	42.00

KELLYS, THE (Formerly Rusty Comics; Spy Cases No. 26 on)
No. 23, Jan, 1950 - No. 25, June, 1950 (52 pgs.)
Marvel Comics (HPC)

23-Teenage	10.00	30.00	70.00
24,25: 24-Margie app.	7.50	22.50	45.00

KELVIN MACE
1986 - No. 2, 1986 ($2.00, B&W)
Vortex Publications

1,2: 1-(B&W). 2-(Color)		1.20	3.00
1-2nd print (1/87, $1.75)		.70	1.75

KEN MAYNARD WESTERN (Movie star)(See Wow Comics, 1936)
Sept, 1950 - No. 8, Feb, 1952 (All 36 pgs.; photo front/back-c)
Fawcett Publications

1-Ken Maynard & his horse Tarzan begin	53.00	159.00	425.00
2	36.00	107.00	250.00
3-8: 6-Atomic bomb explosion panel	27.00	81.00	190.00

KEN SHANNON (Becomes Gabby #11 on) (Also see Police Comics #103)
Oct, 1951 - No. 10, Apr, 1953 (A private eye)
Quality Comics Group

1-Crandall-a	31.00	94.00	220.00
2-Crandall c/a(2)	25.00	75.00	175.00
3-5-Crandall-a. 3-Horror-c	17.00	51.00	120.00
6-Crandall-c/a; "The Weird Vampire Mob"-c/s	19.00	56.00	130.00
7-Crandall-a	14.00	43.00	100.00
8,9: 8-Opium den drug use story	13.00	39.00	90.00
10-Crandall-c	14.00	43.00	100.00

NOTE: *Crandall/Cuidera* c-1-10. *Jack Cole* a-1-9. #1-15 published after title change to Gabby.

KEN STUART
Jan, 1949 (Sea Adventures)
Publication Enterprises

1-Frank Borth-c/a	8.00	24.00	48.00

KENT BLAKE OF THE SECRET SERVICE (Spy)
May, 1951 - No. 14, July, 1953
Marvel/Atlas Comics(20CC)

1-Injury to eye, bondage, torture; Brodsky-c	14.00	43.00	100.00
2-Drug use w/hypo scenes; Brodsky-c	10.00	30.00	65.00
3-14: 8-R.Q. Sale-a (2 pgs.)	6.70	20.00	40.00

NOTE: *Heath* c-5, 7, 8. *Infantino* c-12. *Maneely* c-3. *Sinnott* a-2(3). *Tuska* a-8(3pg.)

KERRY DRAKE (Also see A-1 Comics)
1944; Jan, 1956 - No. 2, March, 1956
Life's Romances Publ. nn/Argo

nn- (A-1 Comics on-c)(1944)Kerry Drake, Johnny Devildog, Rocky, Streamer Kelly (Slightly large size)	23.00	69.00	160.00
1,2-Newspaper-r	6.70	20.00	40.00

KERRY DRAKE DETECTIVE CASES (...Racket Buster No. 32,33)
(Also see Chamber of Clues & Green Hornet Comics #42-47)
1944 - No. 5, 1944; No. 6, Jan, 1948 - No. 33, Aug, 1952
Life's Romances/Com/Magazine Ent. No.1-5/Harvey No.6 on

nn(1944)(A-1 Comics)(slightly over-size)	23.00	69.00	160.00
2	14.00	43.00	100.00
3-5(1944)	11.00	33.00	75.00
6,8(1948): Lady Crime by Powell. 8-Bondage-c	7.00	21.00	42.00
7-Kubert-a; biog of Andriola (artist)	9.15	27.00	55.00
9,10-Two-part marijuana story; Kerry smokes marijuana in #10			
	11.50	34.00	80.00
11-15	6.35	19.00	38.00
16-33	5.00	15.00	30.00
...in the Case of the Sleeping City-(1951-Publishers Synd.)-16 pg. giveaway for armed forces; paper cover	4.00	12.00	24.00

NOTE: *Andiola* c-6-9. *Berg* a-5. *Powell* a-10-23, 28, 29.

KEWPIES
Spring, 1949
Will Eisner Publications

1-Feiffer-a; Kewpie Doll ad on back cover	40.00	120.00	300.00

KEY COMICS
Jan, 1944 - No. 5, Aug, 1946
Consolidated Magazines

1-The Key, Will-O-The-Wisp begin	30.00	90.00	210.00
2 (3/44)	16.00	47.00	110.00
3,4: 4-(5/46)-Origin John Quincy The Atom (begins); Walter Johnson c-3-5	13.00	39.00	90.00
5-4pg. Faust Opera adaptation; Kiefer-a; back-c advertises "Masterpieces Illustrated" by Lloyd Jacquet after he left Classic Comics (no copies of Masterpieces Illustrated known)	17.00	51.00	120.00

KEY COMICS
1951 - 1956 (32 pgs.) (Giveaway)

Kickers, Inc. #11 © MEG

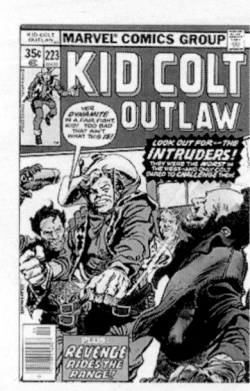

Kid Colt Outlaw #223 © MEG

Kid Eternity #11 © DC

	GD25	FN65	NM94

Key Clothing Co./Peterson Clothing
Contains a comic from different publishers bound with new cover. Cover changed each year. Many combinations possible. Distributed in Nebraska, Iowa, & Kansas. Contents would determine price, 40-60 percent of original.

KEY RING COMICS
1941 (16 pgs.; two colors) (sold 5 for 10¢)
Dell Publishing Co.

1-Sky Hawk	3.00	7.50	15.00
1-Viking Carter	3.00	7.50	15.00
1-Features Sleepy Samson	3.20	8.00	16.00
1-Origin Greg Gilday-r/War Comics #2	3.20	8.00	16.00
1-Radior(Super hero)	2.80	7.00	14.00

NOTE: Each book has two holes in spine to put in binder.

KICKERS, INC.
Nov, 1986 - No. 12, Oct, 1987
Marvel Comics Goup

1-12			1.00

KID CARROTS
September, 1953
St. John Publishing Co.

1-Funny animal	4.25	13.00	28.00

KID COLT OUTLAW (Kid Colt #1-4; ...Outlaw #5-on)(Also see All Western Winners, Best Western, Black Rider, Giant-Size..., Two-Gun Kid, Two-Gun Western, Western Winners, Wild Western, Wisco)
8/48 - No. 139, 3/68; No. 140, 11/69 - No. 229, 4/79
Marvel Comics(LCC) 1-16; Atlas(LMC) 17-102; Marvel 103-on

1-Kid Colt & his horse Steel begin.	78.00	234.00	625.00
2	40.00	120.00	290.00
3-5: 4-Anti-Wertham editorial; Tex Taylor app. 5-Blaze Carson app.	31.00	92.00	215.00
6-8: 6-Tex Taylor app; 7-Nimo the Lion begins, ends #10	20.00	60.00	140.00
9,10 (52 pgs.)	21.00	62.00	145.00
11-Origin	24.00	71.00	165.00
12-20	14.00	43.00	100.00
21-32	11.50	34.00	80.00
33-45: Black Rider in all	10.00	30.00	65.00
46,47,49,50	8.70	26.00	52.00
48-Kubert-a	7.25	22.00	58.00
51-53,55,56	7.00	21.00	42.00
54-Williamson/Maneely-c	8.00	24.00	48.00
57-60,66: 4-pg. Williamson-a in all. 59-Reprints Rawhide Kid #79; Colan text illo	8.70	26.00	52.00
61-63,67-78,80-86: 70-Severin-c. 73-Maneely-c. 86-Kirby-a(r).	5.00	15.00	30.00
64,65-Crandall-a	6.00	18.00	36.00
79,87: 79-Origin retold. 87-Davis-a(r)	5.85	17.50	35.00
88,89-Williamson-a in both (4 pgs.). 89-Redrawn Matt Slade #2	6.70	20.00	40.00
90-99,101: 91-Kirby/Ayers-c. 95-Kirby/Ayers-r/story. 101-Last 10¢ issue	4.00	10.00	20.00
100	4.00	10.00	22.00
101-120: 110-(5/63)-1st app Iron Mask (Iron Man type villian). 114-(1/64)-2nd app Iron Mask	2.40	6.00	12.00
121-140: 121-Rawhide Kid x-over. 125-Two-Gun Kid x-over. 130-132-68 pg. issues with one new story each. 130-Origin. 140-Reprints begin	1.30	3.25	8.00
141-160: 156-Giant; reprints (later issues all-r)	1.60	4.00	7.00
161-229: 170-Origin retold. 229-Rawhide Kid-r	.80	2.00	

...Album (no date; 1950's; Atlas Comics)-132 pgs.; random binding, cardboard cover, B&W stories; contents can vary (Rare) 71.00 212.00 565.00

NOTE: Ayers a-many. Colan a-52, 53; c(p)-223, 228, 229. Crandall a-140r, 167r. Everett a-90, 137i, 225i(r). Heath a-8(2); c-34, 35, 39, 44, 46, 48, 49, 57, 64. Heck a-135, 139. Jack Keller a-

25(2), 26-68(3-4), 78, 94p, 98, 99, 108, 110, 130, 132, 140-150r. Kirby a-86r, 93, 96, 119, 176(part); c-87, 92-95, 97, 99-112, 114-117, 121-123, 197r; w/Ditko c-89. Maneely a-12, 68, 81; c-17, 19, 40-43, 47, 52, 53, 62, 65, 68, 78, 81, 142r, 150r. Morrow a-173r, 216r. Rico a-13, 18. Severin c-58, 59, 143, 148, 149i. Shores a-39, 41-43, 143r; c-1-10(most), 24. Sutton a-136, 137p, 225p(r). Wildey a-47, 54, 82, 144r. Williamson r-147, 170, 172, 216. Woodbridge a-64, 81. Black Rider in #33-45, 74, 86. Iron Mask in #110, 114, 121, 127. Sam Hawk in #84, 101, 111, 121, 146, 174, 181, 188.

KID COWBOY (Also see Approved Comics #4 & Boy Cowboy)
1950 - No. 14, 1954 (Painted covers #1-10, 14)
Ziff-Davis Publ./St. John (Approved Comics)

1-Lucy Belle & Red Feather begin	11.00	33.00	75.00
2-Maneely-c	7.50	22.50	45.00
3-14: 5-Berg-a. 14-Code approved	5.85	17.50	35.00

KIDDIE KAPERS
1945?(nd); Oct, 1957; 1963 - 1964
Kiddie Kapers Co., 1945/Decker Publ. (Red Top-Farrell)

1(nd, 1945-46?, 36 pgs.)-Infinity-c; funny animal	6.70	20.00	40.00
1(10/57)(Decker)-Little Bit-r from Kiddie Karnival	4.00	11.00	22.00
Super Reprint #7, 10('63), 12, 14('63), 15,17('64), 18('64): 10, 14-r/Animal Adventures #1. 15-Animal Adventures #? 17-Cowboys 'N' Injuns #?	1.00	2.60	6.00

KIDDIE KARNIVAL
1952 (25¢, 100 pgs.) (One Shot)
Ziff-Davis Publ. Co. (Approved Comics)

nn-Rebound Little Bit #1,2; painted-c	31.00	94.00	220.00

KID DEATH & FLUFFY SPRING BREAK SPECIAL
July, 1996 ($2.50, B&W, one-shot)
Event Comics

1-Quesada & Palmiotti-c/scripts			2.50

KID ETERNITY (Becomes Buccaneers) (See Hit Comics)
Spring, 1946 - No. 18, Nov, 1949
Quality Comics Group

1	71.00	215.00	575.00
2	36.00	107.00	250.00
3-Mac Raboy-a	39.00	118.00	275.00
4-10	20.00	60.00	140.00
11-18	14.00	43.00	100.00

KID ETERNITY
1991 - No. 3, Nov, 1991 ($4.95, limited series)
DC Comics

1-3: Grant Morrison scripts	1.00	2.00	5.00

KID ETERNITY
May, 1993 - No. 16, Sept, 1994 ($1.95, mature)
DC Comics (Vertigo)

1-16: 1-Gold ink-c. 6-Photo-c. All Sean Phillips-c/a except #15 (Phillips-c/i only)		.80	2.00

KID FROM DODGE CITY, THE
July, 1957 - No. 2, Sept, 1957
Atlas Comics (MMC)

1-Don Heck-c	8.35	25.00	50.00
2-Everett-c	5.00	15.00	30.00

KID FROM TEXAS, THE (A Texas Ranger)
June, 1957 - No. 2, Aug, 1957
Atlas Comics (CSI)

1-Powell-a; Severin-c	9.15	27.00	55.00
2	5.00	15.00	30.00

KID KOKO
1958
I. W. Enterprises

Kid Supreme #3 © Rob Liefeld

The Killers #1 © ME

Killpower: The Early Years #3 © MEG

	GD25	FN65	NM94

	GD25	FN65	NM94

Reprint #1,2-(r/M.E.'s Koko & Kola #4, 1947) — 1.20 — 3.00 — 7.00

KID KOMICS (Kid Movie Komics No. 11)
Feb, 1943 - No. 10, Spring, 1946
Timely Comics (USA 1,2/FCI 3-10)

1-Origin Captain Wonder & sidekick Tim Mullrooney, & Subbie; intro the Sea-Going Lad, Pinto Pete, & Trixie Trouble; Knuckles & Whitewash Jones (from Young Allies) app.; Wolverton-a (7 pgs.)	325.00	975.00	2900.00
2-The Young Allies, Red Hawk, & Tommy Tyme begin; last Captain Wonder & Subbie	156.00	468.00	1250.00
3-The Vision, Daredevils & Red Hawk app.	115.00	346.00	925.00
4-The Destroyer begins; Sub-Mariner app.; Red Hawk & Tommy Tyme end	100.00	300.00	800.00
5,6: 5-Tommy Tyme begins, ends #10	76.00	230.00	615.00
7-10: 7,10-The Whizzer app. Destroyer not in #7,8. 10-Last Destroyer, Young Allies & Whizzer	70.00	211.00	565.00

NOTE: *Brodsky* c-5. *Schomburg* c-2-4, 6-10. *Shores* c-1. Captain Wonder c-1, 2. The Young Allies c-3-10.

KID MONTANA (Formerly Davy Crockett Frontier Fighter; The Gunfighters No. 51 on)
V2#9, Nov, 1957 - No. 50, Mar, 1965
Charlton Comics

V2#9	6.70	20.00	40.00
10	4.00	11.00	22.00
11,12,14-20	3.20	8.00	16.00
13-Williamson-a	4.00	11.00	22.00
21-35	1.50	3.75	9.00
36-50	1.00	2.00	5.00

NOTE: Title change to Montana Kid on cover only #44 & 45; remained Kid Montana on inside.

KID MOVIE KOMICS (Formerly Kid Komics; Rusty Comics #12 on)
No. 11, Summer, 1946
Timely Comics

11-Silly Seal & Ziggy Pig; 2 pgs. Kurtzman "Hey Look" plus 6 pg. "Pigtales" story	21.00	64.00	150.00

KIDNAPPED (Robert Louis Stevenson's...also see Movie Comics)(Disney)
No. 1101, May, 1960
Dell Publishcing Co.

Four Color 1101-Movie, photo-c	7.00	21.00	70.00

KIDNAP RACKET (See Harvey Comics Hits No. 57)

KID SLADE GUNFIGHTER (Formerly Matt Slade…)
No. 5, Jan, 1957 - No. 8, July, 1957
Atlas Comics (SPI)

5-Maneely, Roth, Severin-a in all; Maneely-c	10.00	30.00	65.00
6,8-Severin-c	5.00	15.00	30.00
7-Williamson/Mayo-a, 4 pgs.	8.35	25.00	50.00

KID SUPREME (See Supreme)
Mar, 1996 - Present ($2.50)
Image Comics (Extreme Studios)

1-3: Fraga-a/scripts. 3-Glory-c/app.			2.50

KID ZOO COMICS
July, 1948 (52 pgs.)
Street & Smith Publications

1-Funny Animal	22.00	66.00	155.00

KILLER (…Tales By Timothy Truman)
March, 1985 ($1.75, one-shot, Baxter paper)
Eclipse Comics

1-Timothy Truman-c/a		.70	1.75

KILLER INSTINCT (Video game)
June, 1996 - Present ($2.50, limited series)
Acclaim Comics

1-6: 1-Bart Sears-a(p). 4-Special #1. 5-Special #2. 6-Special #3			2.50

KILLERS, THE
1947 - No. 2, 1948 (No month)
Magazine Enterprises

1-Mr. Zin, the Hatchet Killer; mentioned in SOTI, pgs. 179,180; used by N.Y. Legis. Comm.; L. B. Cole-c	75.00	225.00	600.00
2-(Scarce)-Hashish smoking story; "Dying, Dying, Dead" drug story; Whitney, Ingels-a; Whitney hanging-c	65.00	195.00	525.00

KILLING JOKE, THE (See Batman: The Killing Joke under Batman one-shots)

KILLPOWER: THE EARLY YEARS
Sept, 1993 - No. 4, Dec, 1993 ($1.75, mini-series)
Marvel Comics UK

1-($2.95)-Foil embossed-c		1.20	3.00
2-4: 2-Genetix app. 3-Punisher app.		.70	1.75

KILLRAZOR
Aug, 1995 ($2.50, one-shot)
Image Comics (Top Cow Productions)

1		1.00	2.50

KILL YOUR BOYFRIEND
June, 1995 ($4.95, one-shot)
DC Comics (Vertigo)

1-Grant Morrison story	1.00	2.00	5.00

KILROY IS HERE
1995 ($2.95, B&W)
Caliber Press

1-4			3.00

KILROYS, THE
June-July, 1947 - No. 54, June-July, 1955
B&I Publ. Co. No. 1-19/American Comics Group

1	21.00	62.00	145.00
2	11.00	33.00	75.00
3-5: 5-Gross-a	9.15	27.00	55.00
6-10: 8-Milt Gross's Moronica	6.70	20.00	40.00
11-20: 14-Gross-a	5.85	17.50	35.00
21-30	4.25	13.00	26.00
31-47,50-54	4.00	12.00	24.00
48,49-(3-D effect-c/stories)	17.00	49.00	115.00

KILROY: THE SHORT STORIES
1995 ($2.95, B&W)
Caliber Press

1		1.20	3.00

KINDRED, THE
Mar, 1994 - No. 4, July, 1995 ($1.95, limited series)
Image Comics (Wildstorm Productions)

1-($2.50)-Grifter & Backlash app. in all; bound-in trading card.	1.20	3.00	7.00
2,3-($1.95)	1.00	2.00	5.00
2-Variant-c	1.30	3.25	8.00
3-Alternate-c by Portacio, see Deathblow #5	1.00	2.00	5.00
4-($2.50)		1.00	2.50
Trade paperback (2/95, $9.95)			10.00

NOTE: *Booth* c/a-1-4. The first four issues contain coupons redeemable for a Jim Lee Grifter/Backlash print.

KING ARTHUR AND THE KNIGHTS OF JUSTICE
Dec, 1993 - No. 3, Feb, 1994 ($1.25, limited series)
Marvel Comics UK

1-3: TV adaptation			1.25

King Conan #15 © MEG

Kingdom Come #1 © DC

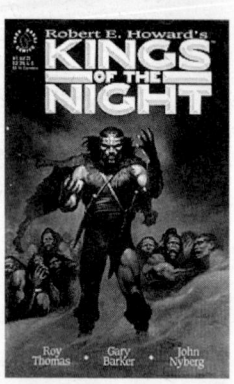

Kings Of The Night #1 © DH

KING CLASSICS
1977 (85¢, 36 pgs., cardboard-c)
King Features (Printed in Spain for U.S. distr.)

1-Connecticut Yankee, 2-Last of the Mohicans, 3-Moby Dick, 4-Robin Hood, 5-Swiss Family Robinson, 6-Robinson Crusoe, 7-Treasure Island, 8-20,000 Leagues, 9-Christmas Carol, 10-Huck Finn, 11-Around the World in 80 Days, 12-Davy Crockett, 13-Don Quixote, 14-Gold Bug, 15-Ivanhoe, 16-Three Musketeers, 17-Baron Munchausen, 18-Alice in Wonderland, 19-Black Arrow, 20-Five Weeks in a Balloon, 21-Great Expectations, 22-Gulliver's Travels, 23-Prince & Pauper, 24-Lawrence of Arabia (Originals, 1977-78)

each....		1.30	3.25	8.00
Reprints, 1979; HRN-24		1.00	2.50	6.00

NOTE: *The first eight issues were not numbered. Issues No. 25-32 were advertised but not published. The 1977 originals have HRN 32a; the 1978 originals have HRN 32b.*

KING COLT (Luke Short)
No. 651, Sept, 1955
Dell Publishing Co.

Four Color 651-Kinstler-a	4.00	12.00	40.00

KING COMICS (Strip reprints)
4/36 - No. 155, 11-12/49; No. 156, Spr/50 - No. 159, 2/52 (Winter on-c)
David McKay Publications/Standard #156-on

	GD25	FN65	VF82
1-1st app. Flash Gordon by Alex Raymond; Brick Bradford (1st app.), Popeye, Henry (1st app.) & Mandrake the Magician (1st app.) begin; Popeye-c begin	1125.00	3375.00	6750.00

(Estimated up to 25 total copies exist, none in NM/Mint)

	GD25	FN65	NM94
2	333.00	1000.00	2000.00
3	216.00	650.00	1300.00
4	175.00	525.00	1050.00
5	128.00	384.00	770.00
6-10: 9-X-Mas-c	91.00	275.00	550.00
11-20	70.00	212.00	425.00
21-30: 21-X-Mas-c	51.00	155.00	310.00
31-40: 33-Last Segar Popeye	41.00	125.00	250.00
41-50: 46-Little Lulu, Alvin & Tubby app. as text illos by Marge Buell.			
50-The Lone Ranger begins	31.00	94.00	220.00
51-60: 52-Barney Baxter begins?	21.00	64.00	150.00
61-The Phantom begins	19.00	56.00	135.00
62-80: 76-Flag-c. 79-Blondie begins	16.00	49.00	115.00
81-99	13.00	39.00	95.00
100	16.00	49.00	115.00
101-114: 114-Last Raymond issue (1 pg.); Flash Gordon by Austin Briggs begins, ends #155	12.00	36.00	85.00
115-145: 117-Phantom origin retold	10.00	30.00	62.00
146,147-Prince Valiant in both	8.00	24.00	48.00
148-155: 155-Flash Gordon ends (11-12/49)	8.00	24.00	48.00
156-159: 156-New logo begins (Standard)	7.00	21.00	42.00

NOTE: *Marge Buell text illos in No. 24-46 at least.*

KING CONAN (Conan The King No. 20 on)
Mar, 1980 - No. 19, Nov, 1983 (52 pgs.)
Marvel Comics Group

1		1.00	2.50
2-19: 4-Death of Thoth Amon. 7-1st Paul Smith-a, 1 pg. pin-up (9/81)		.70	1.75

NOTE: *J. Buscema a-1-9p, 17p; c(p)-1-5, 7-9, 14, 17. Kaluta c-19. Nebres a-17i, 18, 19i. Severin c-18. Simonson c-6.*

KINGDOM COME
1996 - No. 4, 1996 ($4.95, painted limited series)
DC Comics (Elseworlds)

1-4: Mark Waid scripts & Alex Ross-painted c/a in all; tells the last days of the DC Universe; 1st app. Magog. 2-Superman forms new Justice League.
5.00

KING KONG (See Movie Comics)

KING LEONARDO & HIS SHORT SUBJECTS (TV)

Nov-Jan, 1961-62 - No. 4, Sept, 1963
Dell Publishing Co./Gold Key

Four Color 1242,1278	14.00	43.00	140.00
01390-207(5-7/62)(Dell)	11.00	33.00	110.00
1 (10/62)	11.00	33.00	110.00
2-4	9.00	27.00	85.00

KING LOUIE & MOWGLI (See Jungle Book under Movie Comics)
May, 1968 (Disney)
Gold Key

1 (#10223-805)-Characters from Jungle Book	1.80	5.40	18.00

KING OF DIAMONDS (TV)
July-Sept, 1962
Dell Publishing Co.

01-391-209-Photo-c	3.00	9.00	30.00

KING OF KINGS (Movie)
No. 1236, Oct-Nov, 1961
Dell Publishing Co.

Four Color 1236-Photo-c	8.00	24.00	80.00

KING OF THE BAD MEN OF DEADWOOD
1950 (See Wild Bill Hickok #16)
Avon Periodicals

nn-Kinstler-c; Kamen/Feldstein-r/Cowpuncher #2	13.50	41.00	95.00

KING OF THE ROYAL MOUNTED (See Famous Feature Stories, King Comics, Red Ryder #3 & Super Book #2, 6)

KING OF THE ROYAL MOUNTED (Zane Grey's...)
No. 1, May, 1937; No. 9, 1940; No. 207, Dec, 1948 - No. 935, Sept-Nov, 1958
David McKay/Dell Publishing Co.

Feature Books 1 (5/37)(McKay)	67.50	202.00	675.00
Large Feature Comic 9 (1940)	36.50	109.00	365.00
Four Color 207(#1, 12/48)	17.00	52.00	170.00
Four Color 265,283	10.00	30.00	100.00
Four Color 310,340	7.00	21.00	70.00
Four Color 363,384	6.00	18.00	60.00
8(6-8/52)-10	6.00	18.00	60.00
11-20	4.00	12.00	40.00
21-28(3-5/58)	4.00	12.00	40.00
Four Color 935(9-11/58)	4.00	12.00	40.00

NOTE: *4-Color No. 207, 265, 283, 310, 340, 363, 384 are all newspaper reprints with Jim Gary art. No. 8 on are all Dell originals. Painted c No. 9-on.*

KING RICHARD & THE CRUSADERS
No. 588, Oct, 1954
Dell Publishing Co.

Four Color 588-Movie, Matt Baker-a, photo-c	10.00	30.00	100.00

KINGS OF THE NIGHT
1990 - No. 2, 1990 ($2.25, limited series)
Dark Horse Comics

1,2-Robert E. Howard adaptation; Bolton-c		1.15	2.30

KING SOLOMON'S MINES (Movie)
1951
Avon Periodicals

nn (#1 on 1st page)	34.00	103.00	240.00

KING TIGER & MOTORHEAD
Aug, 1996 - No. 2, Sept, 1996 ($2.95, limited series)
Dark Horse Comics

1,2: Chichester scripts		1.20	3.00

KIPLING, RUDYARD (See Mowgli, The Jungle Book)

KISS (See Crazy Magazine, Howard the Duck #12, 13, Marvel Comics Super Special #1, 5, Rock Fantasy Comics #10 & Rock N' Roll Comics #9)

Kissyfur #1 © Warner Bros.

Knightmare #4 © Rob Liefeld

Knights of Pendragon #4 © MEG

KN

	GD25	FN65	NM94

KISSYFUR (TV)
1989 (Sept.) ($2.00, 52 pgs., one-shot)
DC Comics

1-Based on Saturday morning cartoon		1.00	2.00

KIT CARSON (Formerly All True Detective Cases No. 4; Fighting Davy Crockett No. 9; see Blazing Sixguns & Frontier Fighters)
1950; No. 2, 8/51 - No. 3, 12/51; No. 5, 11-12/54 - No. 8, 9/55 (No #4)
Avon Periodicals

nn(#1) (1950)- "...Indian Scout"; r-Cowboys 'N' Injuns #?			
	11.50	34.00	80.00
2(8/51)	8.00	24.00	48.00
3(12/51)- "...Fights the Comanche Raiders"	6.70	20.00	40.00
5-6,8(11-12/54-9/55): 5-Formerly All True Detective Cases (last pre-code); titled "...and the Trail of Doom"	6.35	19.00	38.00
7-McCann-a?	6.70	20.00	40.00
I.W. Reprint #10('63)-r/Kit Carson #1; Severin-c	1.70	5.00	12.00

NOTE: *Kinstler* c-1-3, 5-8.

KIT CARSON & THE BLACKFEET WARRIORS
1953
Realistic

nn-Reprint; Kinstler-c	8.70	26.00	52.00

KITE FUN BOOK
1954 - 1981 (16pgs, 5x7-1/4", soft-c)
Pacific, Gas & Electric/Sou. California Edison/Florida Power & Light

1954-Donald Duck Tells About Kites-Fla. Power, S.C.E. & version with label issues-Barks pencils-8 pgs.; inks-7 pgs. (Rare)	400.00	1200.00	2800.00
1954-Donald Duck Tells About Kites-P.G.&E. issue -7th page redrawn changing middle 3 panels to show P.G.&E. in story line; (All Barks; last page Barks pencils only) Scarce	300.00	900.00	2100.00
1954-Pinocchio Learns About Kites (Disney)	44.00	132.00	350.00
1955-Brer Rabbit in "A Kite Tail" (Disney)	33.00	99.00	230.00
1956-Woody Woodpecker (Lantz)	13.50	41.00	95.00
1957-?			
1958-Tom And Jerry (M.G.M.)	8.00	23.50	55.00
1960-Porky Pig (Warner Bros.)	5.70	17.00	40.00
1960-Bugs Bunny (Warner Bros.)	5.70	17.00	40.00
1961-Huckleberry Hound (Hanna-Barbera)	7.00	21.50	50.00
1962-Yogi Bear (Hanna-Barbera)	4.50	14.00	32.00
1963-Rocky and Bullwinkle (TV)(Jay Ward)	13.50	41.00	95.00
1963-Top Cat (TV)(Hanna-Barbera)	6.70	20.00	40.00
1964-Magilla Gorilla (TV)(Hanna-Barbera)	4.30	13.00	30.00
1965-Jinks, Pixie and Dixie (TV)(Hanna-Barbera)	3.25	9.50	22.00
1965-Tweety and Sylvester (Warner); S.C.E. version with Reddy Kilowatt app.	1.50	3.75	9.00
1966-Secret Squirrel (Hanna-Barbera); S.C.E. version with Reddy Kilowatt app.	8.00	23.50	55.00
1967-Beep! Beep! The Road Runner (TV)(Warner)	2.60	7.50	18.00
1968-Bugs Bunny (Warner Bros.)	2.85	8.50	20.00
1969-Dastardly and Muttley (TV)(Hanna-Barbera)	4.30	13.00	30.00
1970-Rocky and Bullwinkle (TV)(Jay Ward)	9.30	28.00	65.00
1971-Beep! Beep! The Road Runner (TV)(Warner)	2.15	6.50	15.00
1972-The Pink Panther (TV)	1.65	4.20	10.00
1973-Lassie (TV)	3.40	10.00	24.00
1974-Underdog (TV)	2.30	6.70	16.00
1975-Ben Franklin	1.00	2.60	6.00
1976-The Brady Bunch (TV)	2.30	6.70	16.00
1977-Ben Franklin	1.00	2.60	6.00
1977-Popeye	1.70	5.00	12.00
1978-Happy Days (TV)	1.50	3.75	9.00
1979-Eight is Enough (TV)	1.70	5.00	12.00
1980-The Waltons (TV, released in 1981)	1.70	5.00	12.00

KIT KARTER

	GD25	FN65	NM94

May-July, 1962
Dell Publishing Co.

1	2.60	7.50	18.00

KITTY
Oct, 1948
St. John Publishing Co.

1-Teenage; Lily Renee-c/a	6.70	20.00	40.00

KITTY PRYDE AND WOLVERINE (Also see Uncanny X-Men & X-Men)
Nov, 1984 - No. 6, Apr, 1985 (Limited series)
Marvel Comics Group

1-Characters from X-Men		1.60	4.00
2-6		1.00	2.50

KLARER GIVEAWAYS (See Wisco)

KNIGHTHAWK
Sept, 1995 - No. 6, Nov, 1995 ($2.50, limited series)
Acclaim Comics (Windjammer)

1-6: 6-origin		1.00	2.50

KNIGHTMARE
Antarctic Press
July, 1994 ($2.75, B&W, mature readers)

1		1.10	2.75

KNIGHTMARE
Feb, 1995 - No. 5, June, 1995 ($2.50)
Image Comics (Extreme Studios)

0 ($3.50)		1.40	3.50
1-5: 5-Flip book w/Warcry		1.00	2.50
4-Quesada & Palmiotti variant-c		1.60	4.00

KNIGHTS OF PENDRAGON, THE (Also see Pendragon)
July, 1990 - No. 18, Dec, 1991 ($1.95)
Marvel Comics Ltd.

1-18: 1-Capt. Britain app. 2,8-Free poster inside. 9,10-Bolton-c. 11,18-Iron Man app.		.80	2.00

KNIGHTS OF THE ROUND TABLE
No. 540, Mar, 1954
Dell Publishing Co.

Four Color 540-Movie, photo-c	7.00	21.00	70.00

KNIGHTS OF THE ROUND TABLE
No. 10, April, 1957
Pines Comics

10	4.00	11.00	22.00

KNIGHTS OF THE ROUND TABLE
Nov-Jan, 1963-64
Dell Publishing Co.

1 (12-397-401)-Painted-c	2.50	7.50	25.00

KNIGHTSTRIKE (Also see Operation: Knightstrike)
Jan, 1996 ($2.50)
Image Comics (Extreme Studios)

1-Rob Liefeld & Eric Stephenson story; Extreme Destroyer Part 6.			
			2.50

KNOCK KNOCK (...Who's There?)
No. 801, 1936 (52 pgs.) (8x9", B&W)
Whitman Publ./Gerona Publications

801-Joke book; Bob Dunn-a	5.85	17.50	35.00

KNOCKOUT ADVENTURES
Winter, 1953-54
Fiction House Magazines

Kobalt #6 © Milestone Media

Kobra #6 © DC

Kong the Untamed #1 © DC

	GD25	FN65	NM94
1-Reprints Fight Comics #53 w/Rip Carson-c/s	13.00	39.00	90.00
KNOW YOUR MASS			
No. 303, 1958 (35¢, 100 Pg. Giant) (Square binding)			
Catechetical Guild			
303-In color	3.20	8.00	16.00
KNUCKLES' CHAOTIX			
Jan, 1996 ($2.00, annual)			
Archie Publications			
1			2.00
KOBALT			
June, 1994 - No. 15, Sept, 1995 ($1.75/$2.50)			
DC Comics (Milestone)			
1-12: 1-Byrne-c. 4-Intro Page		.70	1.75
13-15 ($2.50): 16-Kent Williams-c		1.00	2.50
KOBRA (See DC Special Series No. 1)			
Feb-Mar, 1976 - No. 7, Mar-Apr, 1977			
National Periodical Publications			
1-1st app.; Kirby-a redrawn by Marcos; only 25¢ issue		.80	2.00
2-7: (All 30¢ issues) 3-Giffen-a		.65	1.60
NOTE: *Austin* a-3i. *Buckler* a-5p; c-5p. *Kubert* c-4. *Nasser* a-6p, 7; c-7.			
KOKEY KOALA (...and the Magic Button)			
May, 1952			
Toby Press			
1	9.15	27.00	55.00
KOKO AND KOLA (Also see A-1 Comics #16 & Tick Tock Tales)			
Fall, 1946 - No. 5, May, 1947; No. 6, 1950			
Com/Magazine Enterprises			
1-Funny animal	10.00	30.00	58.00
2-X-mas-c	5.35	16.00	32.00
3-6: 6(A-1 28)	4.25	13.00	26.00
KO KOMICS			
Oct, 1945			
Gerona Publications			
1-The Duke of Darkness & The Menace (hero)	48.00	146.00	390.00
KOMIC KARTOONS			
Fall, 1945 - No. 2, Winter, 1945			
Timely Comics (EPC)			
1,2-Andy Wolf, Bertie Mouse	17.00	49.00	115.00
KOMIK PAGES (Formerly Snap; becomes Bullseye #11)			
Apr, 1945 (All reprints)			
Harry 'A' Chesler, Jr. (Our Army, Inc.)			
10(#1 on inside)-Land O' Nod by Rick Yager (2 pgs.), Animal Crackers, Foxy GrandPa, Tom, Dick & Mary, Cheerio Minstrels, Red Starr plus other 1-2 pg. strips; Cole-a	19.00	58.00	135.00
KONA (...Monarch of Monster Isle)			
Feb-Apr, 1962 - No. 21, Jan-Mar, 1967 (Painted-c)			
Dell Publishing Co.			
Four Color 1256 (#1)	7.00	21.00	70.00
2-10: 4-Anak begins	2.80	8.40	28.00
11-21	2.20	6.60	22.00
NOTE: *Glanzman* a-all issues.			
KONGA (Fantastic Giants No. 24) (See Return of...)			
1960; No. 2, Aug, 1961 - No. 23, Nov, 1965			
Charlton Comics			
1(1960)-Based on movie; Giordano-c	30.00	90.00	210.00
2-Giordano-c	15.00	45.00	105.00
3-5	11.50	34.00	80.00

	GD25	FN65	NM94
6-15	8.00	23.50	55.00
16-23	5.70	17.00	40.00
NOTE: *Ditko* a-1, 3-15; c-4, 6-9. *Glanzman* a-12. *Montes* & *Bache* a-16-23.			
KONGA'S REVENGE (Formerly Return of...)			
No. 2, Summer, 1963 - No. 3, Fall, 1964; Dec, 1968			
Charlton Comics			
2,3: 2-Ditko-c/a	5.70	17.00	40.00
1(12/68)-Reprints Konga's Revenge #3	2.85	8.50	20.00
KONG THE UNTAMED			
June-July, 1975 - V2#5, Feb-Mar, 1976			
National Periodical Publications			
1-1st app. Kong; Wrightson-c; Alcala-a		1.20	3.00
2-5: 2-Wrightson-c. 2,3-Alcala-a			1.00
KOOKIE			
Feb-Apr, 1962 - No. 2, May-July, 1962 (15 cents)			
Dell Publishing Co.			
1,2: Written by John Stanley; Bill Williams-a	6.50	19.50	65.00
KOOSH KINS			
Oct, 1991 - No. 3, Feb, 1992 ($1.00, bi-monthly, limited series)			
Archie Comics			
1-3			1.00
NOTE: No. 4 was planned, but cancelled.			
K. O. PUNCH, THE (Also see Lucky Fights It Through)			
1948 (Educational giveaway)			
E. C. Comics			
nn-Feldstein-splash; Kamen-a	125.00	375.00	750.00
KORAK, SON OF TARZAN (Edgar Rice Burroughs)(See Tarzan #139)			
Jan, 1964 - No. 45, Jan, 1972 (Painted-c No. 1-?)			
Gold Key			
1-Russ Manning-a	4.50	13.50	45.00
2-11-Russ Manning-a	2.70	8.00	27.00
12-21: 12,13-Warren Tufts-a. 14-Jon of the Kalahari ends. 15-Mabu, Jungle Boy begins. 21-Manning-a	1.80	5.40	18.00
22-30	1.20	3.60	12.00
31-45	.80	2.40	8.00
KORAK, SON OF TARZAN (Tarzan Family #60 on; see Tarzan #230)			
V9#46, May-June, 1972 - V12#56, Feb-Mar, 1974; No. 57, May-June, 1975 - No. 59, Sept-Oct, 1975 (Edgar Rice Burroughs)			
National Periodical Publications			
46-(52 pgs.)-Carson of Venus begins (origin), ends #56; Pellucidar feature; Weiss-a		1.60	4.00
47-59: 49-Origin Korak retold		.90	2.25
NOTE: *Kaluta* a-46-56. All have covers by *Joe Kubert. Manning* strip reprints-No. 57-59. *Frank Thorn* a-46-51.			
KOREA MY HOME (Also see Yalta to Korea)			
nd (1950s)			
Johnstone and Cushing			
nn-Anti-communist; Korean War	24.00	71.00	165.00
KORG: 70,000 B. C. (TV)			
May, 1975 - No. 9, Nov, 1976 (Hanna-Barbera)			
Charlton Publications			
1		1.80	4.50
2-9: 2-Painted-c; Byrne text illos		1.00	2.50
KORNER KID COMICS			
1947			
Four Star Publications			
1	5.75	17.25	40.00
KRAZY KAT			

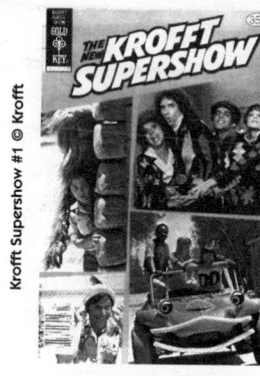

Krofft Supershow #1 © Krofft

Krull #1 © MEG

Kurt Busiek's Astro City #5 © Juke Box Productions

	GD25	FN65	NM94

1946 (Hardcover)			
Holt			
Reprints daily & Sunday strips by Herriman	64.00	193.00	450.00
dust jacket only	50.00	150.00	350.00

KRAZY KAT (See Ace Comics & March of Comics No. 72, 87)

KRAZY KAT COMICS (...& Ignatz the Mouse early issues)
May-June, 1951 - F.C. #696, Apr, 1956; Jan, 1964 (None by Herriman)
Dell Publishing Co./Gold Key

	GD25	FN65	NM94
1(1951)	8.00	24.00	80.00
2-5 (#5, 8-10/52)	5.00	15.00	50.00
Four Color 454,504	4.00	12.00	40.00
Four Color 548,619,696 (4/56)	4.00	12.00	40.00
1(10098-401)(1/64-Gold Key)(TV)	4.00	12.00	40.00

KRAZY KOMICS (1st Series) (Cindy Comics No. 27 on)
July, 1942 - No. 26, Spr, 1947 (Also see Ziggy Pig)
Timely Comics (USA No. 1-21/JPC No. 22-26)

	GD25	FN65	NM94
1-Toughy Tomcat, Ziggy Pig (by Jaffee) & Silly Seal begin			
	45.00	136.00	365.00
2	21.00	64.00	150.00
3-8,10	14.00	43.00	100.00
9-Hitler parody	16.00	47.00	110.00
11,13,14	10.00	30.00	70.00
12-Timely's entire art staff drew themselves into a Creeper story			
	19.00	58.00	135.00
15-(8-9/44)-Becomes Funny Tunes #16; has "Super Soldier" by Pfc. Stan Lee			
	10.00	30.00	70.00
16-24,26: 16-(10-11/44). 26-Super Rabbit-c/story	9.15	27.00	55.00
25-Wacky Duck-c/story & begin; Kurtzman-a (6pgs.)	10.00	30.00	70.00

KRAZY KOMICS (2nd Series)
Aug, 1948 - No. 2, Nov, 1948
Timely/Marvel Comics

	GD25	FN65	NM94
1-Wolverton (10 pgs.) & Kurtzman (8 pgs.)-a; Eustice Hayseed begins			
(Li'l Abner swipe)	39.00	118.00	275.00
2-Wolverton-a (10 pgs.); Powerhouse Pepper cameo			
	29.00	86.00	200.00

KRAZY KROW (Also see Dopey Duck, Film Funnies, Funny Frolics & Movie Tunes)
Summer, 1945 - No. 3, Wint, 1945/46
Marvel Comics (ZPC)

	GD25	FN65	NM94
1	14.00	43.00	100.00
2,3	10.00	30.00	70.00
I.W. Reprint #1('57), 2('58), 7	1.70	5.00	12.00

KRAZYLIFE (Becomes Nutty Life #2)
1945 (no month)
Fox Feature Syndicate

	GD25	FN65	NM94
1-Funny animal	11.50	34.00	80.00

KREE/SKRULL WAR STARRING THE AVENGERS, THE
Sept, 1983 - No. 2, Oct, 1983 ($2.50, 68 pgs., Baxter paper)
Marvel Comics Group

	GD25	FN65	NM94
1,2		1.00	2.50
NOTE: **Neal Adams** p-1r, 2. **Buscema** a-1r, 2r. **Simonson** a-1p; c-1p.

KRIM-KO KOMICS
5/18/35 - No. 6, 6/22/35; 1936 - 1939 (Giveaway, weekly)
Krim-ko Chocolate Drink

	GD25	FN65	NM94
1-(16 pgs., soft-c, Dairy giveaways)-Tom, Mary & Sparky Advs. by Russell Keaton, Jim Hawkins by Dick Moores, Mystery Island! by Rick Yager begin			
	13.00	39.00	90.00
2-6 (6/22/35)	10.00	30.00	65.00
Cola, Secret Agent; 184 issues, 4 pg. giveaways - all original series			

	GD25	FN65	NM94
each....	6.70	20.00	40.00

KROFFT SUPERSHOW (TV)
Apr, 1978 - No. 6, Jan, 1979
Gold Key

	GD25	FN65	NM94
1-Photo-c		1.20	3.00
2-6: 6-Photo-c			1.50

KRULL
Nov, 1983 - No. 2, Dec, 1983
Marvel Comics Group

	GD25	FN65	NM94
1,2-Adaptation of film; r/Marvel Super Special. 1-Photo-c from movie			
			1.00

KRUSTY COMICS
1995 - No. 3, 1995 ($2.25, limited series)
Bongo Comics

	GD25	FN65	NM94
1-3		.90	2.25

KRYPTON CHRONICLES
Sept, 1981 - No. 3, Nov, 1981
DC Comics

	GD25	FN65	NM94
1-Buckler-c(p)			1.50
2,3			1.00

KULL AND THE BARBARIANS
May, 1975 - No. 3, Sept, 1975 ($1.00, B&W, magazine, 84 pgs.)
Marvel Comics Group

	GD25	FN65	NM94
1-3: 1-Andru/Wood-r/Kull #1; 2 pgs. Neal Adams; Gil Kane(p), Marie & John Severin-a(r); Krenkel text illo. 2-Red Sonja by Chaykin begins; Soloman Kane by Weiss/N. Adams; Gil Kane-a. 3-Origin Red Sonja by Chaykin; N. Adams-a; Solomon Kane appr.			1.00

KULL THE CONQUEROR (...the Destroyer #11 on; see Creatures on the Loose #10 and Marvel Preview)
June, 1971 - No. 2, Sept, 1971; No. 3, July, 1972 - No. 15, Aug, 1974; No. 16, Aug, 1976 - No. 29, Oct, 1978
Marvel Comics Group

	GD25	FN65	NM94
1-Andru/Wood-a; origin Kull; 15¢ issue	1.50	3.75	9.00
2-5: 2-Last 15¢ issue. 3-13: 20¢ issues		1.70	4.25
6-10		1.30	3.25
11-29: 11-15-Ploog-a. 14-16: 25¢ issues		.90	2.25
NOTE: No. 1, 2, 7-9, 11 are based on Robert E. Howard stories. **Alcala** a-17p, 18-20i; c-24. **Ditko** a-12r, 15r. **Gil Kane** c-15p, 21. **Nebres** a-22i-27i; c-25i, 27i. **Ploog** c-11, 12p, 13. **Severin** a-2-9i; c-2-10i, 19. **Starlin** c-14.

KULL THE CONQUEROR
Dec, 1982 - No. 2, Mar, 1983 (52 pgs., Baxter paper)
Marvel Comics Group

	GD25	FN65	NM94
1,2: 1-Buscema-a(p)		1.00	2.00

KULL THE CONQUEROR (No. 9,10 titled "Kull")
5/83 - No. 10, 6/85 (52 pgs., Baxter paper)
Marvel Comics Group

	GD25	FN65	NM94
V3#1-10: Buscema-a in #1-3,5-10			1.00
NOTE: Bolton a-4. Golden painted c-3-8. Guice a-4p. Sienkiewicz a-4; c-2.

KUNG FU (See Deadly Hands of..., & Master of...)

KUNG FU FIGHTER (See Richard Dragon...)

KURT BUSIEK'S ASTRO CITY
Aug, 1995 - No. 6, Jan, 1996 ($2.25, limited series)
Image Comics (Juke Box Productions)

	GD25	FN65	NM94
1-Kurt Busiek scripts, Brent Anderson-a & Alex Ross front & back-c begins; 1st app. Samaritan & Honor Guard (Cleopatra, MHP, Beautie, The Black Rapier & N-Forcer)		1.20	3.00
2-6: 2-1st app. The Silver Agent, The Old Soldier, & the "orignal" Honor Guard (Max O'Millions, Starwoman, the "original" Cleopatra, the "original" N-Forcer,			

Kurt Busiek's Astro City V2#2 © Juke Box Productions

Lady Rawhide #3 © TOPPS

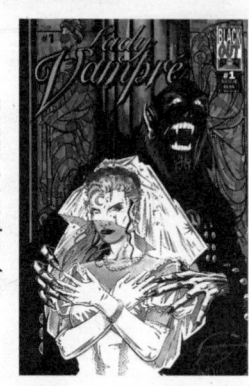

Lady Vampre #1 © Blackout

	GD25	FN65	NM94

the Bouncing Beatnik, Leopardman & Kitkat). 3-1st app. Jack-in-the-Box & The Deacon. 4-1st app. Winged Victory (cameo), The Hanged Man & The First Family. 5-1st app. Crackerjack, The Astro City Irregulars, Nightingale & Sunbird. 6-Origin Samaritan; 1st full app Winged Victory .90 2.25

KURT BUSIEK'S ASTRO CITY
V2#1, Sept, 1996 - Present ($2.50) (1st Homage Comics series)
Homage Comics

V2#1/2-(10/96)-The Hanged Man story; 1st app. The All-American & Slugger, The Lamplighter, The Time-Keeper & Eterneon		5.00
V2#1-8: Kurt Busiek scripts, Alex Ross-c, Brent Anderson-p & Will Blyberg-i begin; intro The Gentleman, Thunderhead & Helia. 2-Origin The First Family. 2,3-Astra story; The First Family app. 4-1st app. The Confessor		2.50
Life In The Big City-(8/96, $19.95, trade paperback)-r/Image Comics limited series w/sketchbook & cover gallery; Ross-c		20.00
Life In The Big City-(8/96, $49.95, hardcover, 1000 print run)-r/Image Comics limited series w/sketchbook & cover gallery; Ross-c		50.00

LABOR IS A PARTNER
1949 (32 pgs., paper-c)
Catechetical Guild Educational Society

nn-Anti-communism	19.00	56.00	130.00
Confidential Preview-(8-1/2x11", B&W, saddle stitched)-only one known copy; text varies from color version, advertises next book on secularism (If the Devil Would Talk)	36.00	107.00	250.00

LABYRINTH
Nov, 1986 - No. 3, Jan, 1987 (Limited series)
Marvel Comics Group

1-3: Movie adaptation; r/Marvel Super Special #40			1.00

LAD: A DOG (Movie)
1961 - No. 2, July-Sept, 1962
Dell Publishing Co.

Four Color 1303, 2	4.00	12.00	40.00

LADY AND THE TRAMP (Disney, See Dell Giants & Movie Comics)
No. 629, May, 1955 - No. 634, June, 1955
Dell Publishing Co.

Four Color 629 (#1)-..with Jock	6.00	18.00	60.00
Four Color 634-...Album	5.00	15.00	50.00

LADY AND THE TRAMP IN "BUTTER LATE THAN NEVER"
1955 (16 pgs., 5x7-1/4", soft-c) (Walt Disney)
American Dairy Association (Premium)

nn	11.00	33.00	75.00

LADY COP (See 1st Issue Special)

LADY DEATH (See Evil Ernie)
Jan, 1994 - No. 3, Mar, 1994 ($2.75, limited series)
Chaos! Comics

1/2: S. Hughes-c/a in all	3.60	11.00	25.00
1/2 Gold	5.00	15.00	40.00
1/2 Velvet	3.60	11.00	25.00
1-($3.50)-Chromium-c	9.50	28.00	75.00
1-Commemorative	8.00	24.50	65.00
2	5.50	17.00	45.00
3	3.60	11.00	25.00
...In Lingerie #1 (8/95, $2.95) pin-ups, wraparound-c		1.20	3.00
...In Lingerie #1-Leather Edition (10,000)	5.00	15.00	40.00
...In Lingerie #1-Micro Premium Edition; Lady Demon-c (2,000)	14.00	43.00	100.00
...Swimsuit Special #1-($2.50)-Wraparound-c	1.20	3.00	7.00
...Swimsuit Special #1-Red velvet-c	5.00	15.00	40.00
...: The Reckoning (7/94, $6.95)-r/#1-3	1.20	3.00	7.00
...: The Reckoning (8/95, $12.95)- new printing including Lady Death 1/2 &			

	GD25	FN65	NM94

Swimsuit Special	1.85	5.50	13.00

LADY DEATH: THE ODYSSEY
Apr, 1996 - No. 4, Aug, 1996 ($3.50/$2.95)
Chaos! Comics

1-($1.50)-Sneak Peek Preview			1.50
1-($1.50)-Sneak Peek Preview Micro Premium Edition (2500 print run)			20.00
1-($3.50)-Embossed, wraparound goil foil-c			6.00
1-Black Onyx Edition (200 print run)			125.00
1-($19.95)-Premium Edition (10,000 print run)			20.00
2-4-($2.95)			3.00

LADY DEATH II: BETWEEN HEAVEN & HELL
Mar, 1995 - No. 4, July, 1995 ($3.50, limited series)
Chaos! Comics

1-Chromium wraparound-c; Evil; Ernie cameo	1.30	3.25	8.00
1-Commemorative (4,000)	6.50	19.50	45.00
1-Black Velvet-c	5.00	15.00	40.00
1-"Refractor" edition (5,000)	7.00	21.50	50.00
2-4		1.20	3.00
4-Lady Demon variant-c	2.85	8.50	20.00
Trade paperback-($12.95)-r/#1-4			13.00

LADY FOR A NIGHT (See Cinema Comics Herald)
LADY JUSTICE (See Neil Gaiman's...)
LADY LUCK (Formerly Smash #1-85) (Also see Spirit Sections #1)
No. 86, Dec, 1949 - No. 90, Aug, 1950
Quality Comics Group

86(#1)	73.00	219.00	585.00
87-90	56.00	168.00	450.00

LADY PENDRAGON
Mar, 1996 ($2.50)
Maximum Press

1-Matt Hawkins script			2.50

LADY RAWHIDE
July, 1995 - No. 5, Mar, 1996 ($2.95, bi-monthly, limited series)
Topps Comics

1-5: Don McGregor scripts & Mayhew-a. in all. 2-Stelfreeze-a. 3-Hughes-c. 4-Golden-c. 5-Julie Bell-c.		1.20	3.00
Special Edition 1 (6/95, $3.95)-Reprints		1.60	4.00

LADY VAMPRE
June, 1995 - No. 1, 1995 ($2.95)
Blackout Comics

0,1		1.20	3.00

LADY VAMPRE: PLEASURES OF THE FLESH
1996 - Present ($2.95, B&W, limited series)
Blackout Comics

1-Wraparound-c			3.00

LAFF-A-LYMPICS (TV)(See The Funtastic World of Hanna-Barbera)
Mar, 1978 - No. 13, Mar, 1979 (Hanna-Barbera)
Marvel Comics

1-13: Yogi Bear, Scooby Doo, Pixie & Dixie, etc. 11-Jetsons x-over; 1 pg. illustrated bio of Mighty Mightor, Herculoids, Shazzan, Galaxy Trio & Space Ghost			1.00

LAFFY-DAFFY COMICS
Feb, 1945 - No. 2, Mar, 1945
Rural Home Publ. Co.

1,2-Funny animal	7.00	21.00	42.00

LANA (Little Lana No. 8 on)

Lance O'Casey #1© FAW

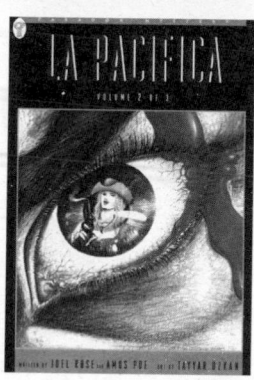

La Pacifica #2 © Joel Rose & Amos Poe

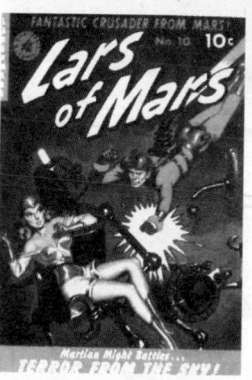

Lars of Mars #10 © Z-D

	GD25	FN65	NM94

Aug, 1948 - No. 7, Aug, 1949 (Also see Annie Oakley)
Marvel Comics (MjMC)

	GD25	FN65	NM94
1-Rusty, Millie begin	14.00	43.00	100.00
2-Kurtzman's "Hey Look" (1); last Rusty	10.00	30.00	65.00
3-7: 3-Nellie begins	7.00	21.00	42.00

LANCELOT & GUINEVERE (See Movie Classics)

LANCELOT LINK, SECRET CHIMP (TV)
Apr, 1971 - No. 8, Feb, 1973
Gold Key

1-Photo-c	1.60	4.80	16.00
2-8: 2-Photo-c	1.00	3.00	10.00

LANCELOT STRONG (See The Shield)

LANCE O'CASEY (See Mighty Midget & Whiz Comics)
Spring, 1946 - No. 3, Fall, 1946; No. 4, Summer, 1948
Fawcett Publications

1-Captain Marvel app. on-c	29.00	86.00	200.00
2	18.00	54.00	125.00
3,4	13.00	39.00	90.00

NOTE: The cover for the 1st issue was done in 1942 but was not published until 1946. The cover shows 68 pages but actually has only 36 pages.

LANCER (TV)(Western)
Feb, 1969 - No. 3, Sept, 1969 (All photo-c)
Gold Key

1	3.40	10.00	24.00
2,3	2.60	7.50	18.00

LAND OF THE GIANTS (TV)
Nov, 1968 - No. 5, Sept, 1969 (All have photo-c)
Gold Key

1	4.50	13.50	45.00
2-5	2.50	7.50	25.00

LAND OF THE LOST COMICS (Radio)
July-Aug, 1946 - No. 9, Spring, 1948
E. C. Comics

1	27.00	81.00	190.00
2	19.00	56.00	130.00
3-9	15.00	45.00	105.00

LAND UNKNOWN, THE (Movie)
No. 845, Sept, 1957
Dell Publishing Co.

Four Color 845-Alex Toth-a	14.50	44.00	145.00

LA PACIFICA
1994/1995 ($4.95, B&W, limited series, digest size, mature readers)
DC Comics (Paradox Press)

1-3	1.00	2.00	5.00

LARAMIE (TV)
Aug, 1960 - July, 1962 (All photo-c)
Dell Publishing Co.

Four Color 1125-Gil Kane/Heath-a	10.00	30.00	100.00
Four Color 1223,1284	6.00	18.00	60.00
4-418-207 (7/62)	6.00	18.00	60.00

LAREDO (TV)
June, 1966
Gold Key

1 (10179-606)-Photo-c	2.85	8.50	28.00

LARGE FEATURE COMIC (Formerly called Black & White in previous guides)
1939 - No. 13, 1943
Dell Publishing Co.

Note: See individual alphabetical listings for prices

1 (Series I)-Dick Tracy Meets the Blank
3-Heigh-Yo Silver! The Lone Ranger (text & ill.)(76 pgs.); also exists as a Whitman #710; based on radio
6-Terry & the Pirates & The Dragon Lady; reprints dailies from 1936
8-Dick Tracy the Racket Buster
9-King of the Royal Mounted (Zane Grey's...)
10-(Scarce)-Gang Busters (No. appears on inside front cover; first slick cover (based on radio program)
13-Dick Tracy and Scottie of Scotland Yard
15-Dick Tracy and the Kidnapped Princes
17-Gang Busters (1941)
18-Phantasmo (see The Funnies #45)
20-Donald Duck Comic Paint Book (rarer than #16) (Disney)
21,22: 21-Private Buck. 22-Nuts & Jolts
24-Popeye in "Thimble Theatre" by Segar
26-Smitty
28-Grin and Bear It
30-Tillie the Toiler
 2-Winnie Winkle (#1)
 3-Dick Tracy
 4-Tiny Tim (#1)
 6-Terry and the Pirates; Caniff-a
 8-Bugs Bunny (#1)('42)
 9-Bringing Up Father
10-Popeye (Thimble Theatre)
11-Barney Google and Snuffy Smith
13-(nn)-1001 Hours Of Fun; puzzles & games; by A. W. Nugent. This book was bound as #13 with Large Feature Comics in publisher's files

2-Terry and the Pirates (#1)
4-Dick Tracy Gets His Man
5-Tarzan of the Apes (#1) by Harold Foster (origin); reprints 1st Tarzan dailies from 1929
7-(Scarce, 52 pgs.)-Hi-Yo Silver the Lone Ranger to the Rescue; also exists as a Whitman #715, based on radio program
11-Dick Tracy Foils the Mad Doc Hump
12-Smilin' Jack; no number on-c
14-Smilin' Jack Helps G-Men Solve a Case!
16-Donald Duck; 1st app. Daisy Duck on back cover (6/41-Disney)
19-Dumbo Comic Paint Book (Disney); partial-r from 4-Color #17
23-The Nebbs
25-Smilin' Jack-1st issue to show title on-c
27-Terry and the Pirates; Caniff-c/a
29-Moon Mullins
 1 (Series II)-Peter Rabbit by Harrison Cady; arrival date-3/27/42
 5-Toots and Casper
 7-Pluto Saves the Ship (#1) (Disney)-Written by Carl Barks, Jack Hannah, & Nick George (Barks' 1st comic book work)
12-Private Buck

NOTE: The Black & White Feature Books are oversized 8-1/2x11-3/8" comics with color covers and black and white interiors. The first nine issues all have rough, heavy stock covers and, except for the #7, all have 76 pages, including covers. #7 and #10-on all has 52 pages. Beginning with #10 the covers are slick and thin and, because of their size, are difficult to handle without damaging. For this reason, they are seldom found in fine to mint condition. The paper stock, unlike Wow #1 and Capt. Marvel #1, is itself not unstable ...just thin.

LARRY DOBY, BASEBALL HERO
1950 (Cleveland Indians)
Fawcett Publications

nn-Bill Ward-a; photo-c	65.00	195.00	525.00

LARRY HARMON'S LAUREL AND HARDY (...Comics)
July-Aug, 1972 (Regular size)
National Periodical Publications

1		1.60	4.00

LARS OF MARS
No. 10, Apr-May, 1951 - No. 11, July-Aug, 1951 (Painted-c)
Ziff-Davis Publishing Co.

10-Origin; Anderson-a(3) in each	62.00	187.00	500.00
11-Gene Colan-a	50.00	150.00	400.00

LARS OF MARS 3-D
Apr, 1987 ($2.50)
Eclipse Comics

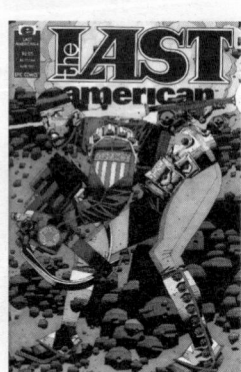

The Last American #4 © Alan Grant

The Last Avengers Story #2 © MEG

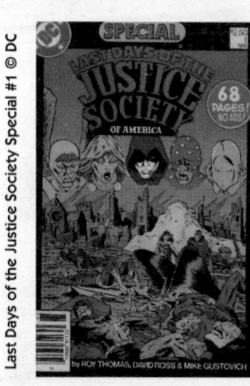

Last Days of the Justice Society Special #1 © DC

	GD25	FN65	NM94
1-r/Lars of Mars #10,11 in 3-D plus new story		1.25	2.50
2-D limited edition (B&W, 100 copies)	.85	2.50	5.00

LASER ERASER & PRESSBUTTON (See Axel Pressbutton & Miracle Man 9)
Nov, 1985 - No. 6, 1987 (95¢/$2.50, limited series)
Eclipse Comics

1-6: 5,6-(95¢)			1.00
...In 3-D 1 (8/86, $2.50)		1.00	2.50
2-D 1 (B&W, limited to 100 copies signed & numbered)			
		1.00	2.50

LASH LARUE WESTERN (Movie star; king of the bullwhip)(See Fawcett Movie Comic, Motion Picture Comics & Six-Gun Heroes)
Sum, 1949 - No. 46, Jan, 1954 (36pgs., 1-7,9,13,16-on)
Fawcett Publications

1-Lash & his horse Black Diamond begin; photo front/back-c begin			
	96.00	290.00	775.00
2(11/49)	40.00	120.00	315.00
3-5	38.00	114.00	265.00
6,7,9: 6-Last photo back-c; intro. Frontier Phantom (Lash's twin brother)			
	29.00	86.00	200.00
8,10 (52pgs.)	30.00	90.00	210.00
11,12,14,15 (52pgs.)	20.00	60.00	140.00
13,16-20 (36pgs.)	17.00	51.00	120.00
21-30: 21-The Frontier Phantom app.	15.00	45.00	105.00
31-45	13.00	39.00	90.00
46-Last Fawcett issue & photo-c	13.50	41.00	95.00

LASH LARUE WESTERN (Continues from Fawcett series)
No. 47, Mar-Apr, 1954 - No. 84, June, 1961
Charlton Comics

47-Photo-c	17.00	49.00	115.00
48	12.00	36.00	85.00
49-60	10.00	30.00	60.00
61-66,69,70: 52-r/#8; 53-r/#22	9.15	27.00	55.00
67,68-(68 pgs.). 68-Check-a	9.15	27.00	55.00
71-83	5.85	17.50	35.00
84-Last issue	7.50	22.50	45.00

LASH LARUE WESTERN
1990 ($3.50, 44 pgs) (24 pgs. of color, 16 pgs. of B&W)
AC Comics

| 1-Photo covers; r/Lash #6; r/old movie posters | | 1.75 | 3.50 |
| Annual 1 (1990, $2.95, B&W, 44 pgs.)-Photo covers | | 1.20 | 3.00 |

LASSIE (TV)(M-G-M's... #1-36; see Kite Fun Book)
June, 1950 - No. 70, July, 1969
Dell Publishing Co./Gold Key No. 59 (10/62) on

1 (52 pgs.)-Photo-c; inside lists One Shot #282 in error			
	14.00	42.00	140.00
2-Painted-c begin	6.00	18.00	60.00
3-10	3.80	11.40	38.00
11-19: 12-Rocky Langford (Lassie's master) marries Gerry Lawrence. 15-1st app. Timbu	2.80	8.40	28.00
20-22-Matt Baker-a	3.20	9.60	32.00
23-40: 33-Robinson-a. 39-1st app. Timmy as Lassie picks up her TV family			
	2.20	6.60	22.00
41-70: 63-Last Timmy (10/63). 64-r/#19. 65-Forest Ranger Corey Stuart begins, ends #69. 70-Forest Rangers Bob Ericson & Scott Turner app. (Lassie's new masters)	1.40	4.20	14.00
11193(1978, $1.95, 224 pgs., Golden Press)-Baker-r (92 pgs.)			
	1.00	2.60	6.00
The Adventures of... nn-(Red Heart Dog Food giveaway, 1949)-16 pgs, soft-c; 1st app. Lassie in comics	16.00	48.00	160.00

NOTE: Photo c-57, 63. (See March of Comics #210, 217, 230, 254, 278, 296, 308, 324, 334, 346, 358, 370, 381, 394, 411, 432)

	GD25	FN65	NM94

LAST AMERICAN, THE
Dec, 1990 - No. 4, March, 1991 ($2.25, mini-series)
Marvel Comics (Epic Comics)

| 1-4: Alan Grant scripts | | .90 | 2.2 |

LAST AVENGERS STORY, THE (Last Avengers #1)
Nov, 1995 - No. 2, Dec, 1995 ($5.95, painted, limited series)
Marvel Comics (Alterniverse)

| 1,2: Peter David story; acetate-c in all. 1-New team (Hank Pym, Wasp, Human Torch, Cannonball, She-Hulk, Hotshot, Bombshell, Tommy Maximoff, Hawkeye, & Mockingbird) forms to battle Ultron 59, Kang the Conqueror, The Grim Reaper & Oddball | 1.00 | 2.60 | 6. |

LAST DAYS OF THE JUSTICE SOCIETY SPECIAL
1986 ($2.50, one-shot, 68 pgs.)
DC Comics

| 1-62 pg. JSA story plus unpubbed G.A. pg. | | 1.00 | 2. |

LAST GENERATION, THE
1986 - No. 5, 1989 ($1.95, B&W, high quality paper)
Black Tie Studios

1		1.60	4.
2		1.20	3.
3-5		1.00	2.
Book 1 (1989, $6.95)-By Caliber Press	1.20	3.50	7.

LAST HUNT, THE
No. 678, Feb, 1956
Dell Publishing Co.

| Four Color 678-Movie, photo-c | 7.00 | 21.00 | 70. |

LAST KISS
1988 ($3.95, B&W, squarebound, 52 pgs.)
ACME Press (Eclipse)

| 1-One story adapts E.A. Poe's The Black Cat | | 1.60 | 4. |

LAST OF THE COMANCHES (Movie) (See Wild Bill Hickok #28)
1953
Avon Periodicals

| nn-Kinstler-c/a, 21pgs.; Ravielli-a | 13.00 | 39.00 | 90. |

LAST OF THE ERIES, THE (See American Graphics)

LAST OF THE FAST GUNS, THE
No. 925, Aug, 1958
Dell Publishing Co.

| Four Color 925-Movie, photo-c | 7.00 | 21.00 | 70. |

LAST OF THE MOHICANS (See King Classics & White Rider and...)

LAST OF THE VIKING HEROES, THE (Also see Silver Star #1)
Mar, 1987 - No. 12 ($1.50/$1.95)
Genesis West Comics

1-4: 4-Intro The Phantom Force		1.00	2.
1-Signed edition ($1.50)			1.
5A-Kirby/Stevens-c		1.30	3.
5B,6 ($1.95)		.80	2.
7-Art Adams-c		1.20	3.
8-12: 8-Kirby back-c. 9,10,12-($2.50)		1.00	2.
Summer Special 1-3: 1-(1988)-Frazetta-c & illos. 2(1990, $2.50)-A TMNT app.			
3 (1991, $2.50)-Teenage Mutant Ninja Turtles	1.20		3.
Summer Special 1-Signed edition (sold for $1.95)		.80	3.

NOTE: Art Adams c-7. Byrne c-3. Kirby c-1p, 5p. Perez c-2l. Stevens c-5Ai.

LAST ONE, THE
July, 1993 - No. 6, Dec, 1993 ($2.50, limited series, mature readers)
DC Comics (Vertigo)

| 1-6 | | 1.00 | 2. |

The Last Starfighter #2 © MEG

Laurel & Hardy #1 © Laurel & Hardy

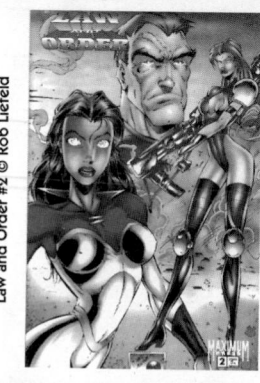

Law and Order #2 © Rob Liefeld

LA

	GD25	FN65	NM94

LAST STARFIGHTER, THE
Oct, 1984 - No. 3, Dec, 1984 (75¢, movie adaptation)
Marvel Comics Group

1-3: r/Marvel Super Special; Guice-c		1.00	

LAST TEMPTATION, THE
1994 - No. 3, 1994 ($4.95, limited series)
Marvel Comics

1-3: Alice Cooper story; Neil Gaiman scripts; McKean-c; Zulli-a			
	1.00	2.00	5.00

LAST TRAIN FROM GUN HILL
No. 1012, July, 1959
Dell Publishing Co.

Four Color 1012-Movie, photo-c	9.00	27.00	90.00

LATEST ADVENTURES OF FOXY GRANDPA (See Foxy Grandpa)

LATEST COMICS (Super Duper No. 3?)
Mar, 1945 - No. 2, 1945?
Spotlight Publ./Palace Promotions (Jubilee)

1-Super Duper	12.00	36.00	85.00
2-Bee-29 (nd); Jubilee in indicia blacked out	10.00	30.00	65.00

LAUGH
June, 1987 - No. 29, Aug, 1991 (75¢/$1.00)
Archie Enterprises

2#1-29: 5,19-X-Mas issues. 14-1st app. Hot Dog. 24-Re-intro Super Duck			
			1.00

LAUGH COMICS (Teenage) (Formerly Black Hood #9-19) (Laugh #226 on)
No. 20, Fall, 1946 - No. 400, Apr, 1987
Archie Publications (Close-Up)

20-Archie begins; Katy Keene & Taffy begin by Woggon; Suzie & Wilbur also begin; Archie covers begin	56.00	168.00	450.00
21-23,25	30.00	90.00	210.00
24- "Pipsy" by Kirby (6 pgs.)	32.00	96.00	225.00
26-30	16.00	47.00	110.00
31-40	11.50	34.00	80.00
41-60: 41,54-Debbi by Woggon	8.00	24.00	48.00
61-80: 67-Debbi by Woggon	5.35	17.50	35.00
81-99	3.75	11.25	28.00
100	4.50	14.00	32.00
101-126: 125-Debbi app.	2.60	7.50	18.00
127-144: Super-hero app. in all (see note)	2.85	8.50	20.00
145-160: 157-Josie app.	1.65	4.20	10.00
161-165,167-200	1.00	2.60	6.00
166-Beatles-c	2.60	7.50	18.00
201-240		1.20	3.00
241-280			1.50
281-400: 381-384-Katy Keene app.; by Woggon-381,382			1.00
NOTE: The Fly app. in 128, 129, 132, 134, 138, 139. Flygirl app. in 136, 137, 143. Flyman app. in 137. The Jaguar app. in 127, 130, 131, 133, 135, 140-142, 144. Josie app. in 145, 150, 164. Katy Keene app. in 20-125, 129, 130, 133. Many issues contain paper dolls. Al Fagaly 20-29. Montana c-33, 36, 37, 42. Bill Vigoda c-30, 50.			

LAUGH COMICS DIGEST (...Magazine #23-89; Laugh Digest Mag. #90 on)
Aug, 1974; No. 2, 9/75; No. 3, 3/76 - Present (Digest-size)
Archie Publications (Close-Up No. 1, 3 on)

1-Neal Adams-a	1.65	4.20	10.00
2,7,8,19-Neal Adams-a	1.00	2.00	5.00
3-6,9-18,20-50		1.20	3.00
51-116: Later issues $1.35,$1.50-c			1.50
117-130		.70	1.75
NOTE: Katy Keene in 23, 25, 27, 32-38, 40, 45-48, 50. The Fly-r in 19, 20. The Jaguar-r in 25, Mr. Justice-r in 21. The Web-r in 23.			

LAUGH COMIX (Formerly Top Notch Laugh; Suzie Comics No. 49 on)

	GD25	FN65	NM94

No. 46, Summer, 1944 - No. 48, Winter, 1944-45			
MLJ Magazines			
46-Wilbur & Suzie in all; Harry Sahle-c	18.00	54.00	125.00
47,48: 47-Sahle-c. 48-Bill Vigoda-c	13.50	41.00	95.00

LAUGH-IN MAGAZINE (TV)(Magazine)
Oct, 1968 - No. 12, Oct, 1969 (50¢) (Satire)
Laufer Publ. Co.

V1#1	2.60	7.70	18.00
2-12	1.50	3.75	9.00

LAUREL & HARDY (See Larry Harmon's... & March of Comics No. 302, 314)

LAUREL AND HARDY (...Comics)
3/49 - No. 3, 9/49; No. 26, 11/55 - No. 28, 3/56 (No #4-25)
St. John Publishing Co.

1	59.00	178.00	475.00
2	39.00	116.00	270.00
3	26.00	79.00	185.00
26-28 (Reprints)	14.00	43.00	100.00

LAUREL AND HARDY (TV)
Oct, 1962 - No. 4, Sept-Nov, 1963
Dell Publishing Co.

12-423-210 (8-10/62)	4.20	12.60	42.00
2-4 (Dell)	3.00	9.00	30.00

LAUREL AND HARDY (Larry Harmon's...)
Jan, 1967 - No. 2, Oct, 1967
Gold Key

1,2: 1-Photo back-c	2.60	7.80	26.00

LAW AGAINST CRIME (Law-Crime on cover)
April, 1948 - No. 3, Aug, 1948 (Real Stories from Police Files)
Essenkay Publishing Co.

1-(#1-3 are half funny animal, half crime stories)-L. B. Cole-c/a in all; electrocution-c	53.00	159.00	425.00
2-L. B. Cole-c/a	40.00	120.00	315.00
3-Used in SOTI, pg. 180,181 & illo "The wish to hurt or kill couples in lovers' lanes"; reprinted in All-Famous Crime #9	50.00	150.00	400.00

LAW AND ORDER
Sept, 1995 - No. 2, 1995 ($2.50, unfinished limited series)
Maximum Press

1,2		1.00	2.50

LAWBREAKERS (...Suspense Stories No. 10 on)
Mar, 1951 - No. 9, Oct-Nov, 1952
Law and Order Magazines (Charlton Comics)

1	24.00	73.00	170.00
2	12.00	36.00	85.00
3,5,6,8,9	10.00	30.00	60.00
4- "White Death" junkie story	11.50	34.00	80.00
7- "The Deadly Dopesters" drug story	11.50	34.00	80.00

LAWBREAKERS ALWAYS LOSE!
Spring, 1948 - No. 10, Oct, 1949
Marvel Comics (CBS)

1-2pg. Kurtzman-a, "Giggles 'n' Grins"	26.00	77.00	180.00
2	13.00	39.00	90.00
3-5: 4-Vampire story	10.00	30.00	65.00
6(2/49)-Has editorial defense against charges of Dr. Wertham	10.00	30.00	70.00
7-Used in SOTI, illo "Comic-book philosophy"	24.00	71.00	165.00
8-10: 9,10-Photo-c	9.15	27.00	55.00
NOTE: Brodsky c-4, 5. Shores c-1-3, 6-8.			

LAWBREAKERS SUSPENSE STORIES (Formerly Lawbreakers; Strange

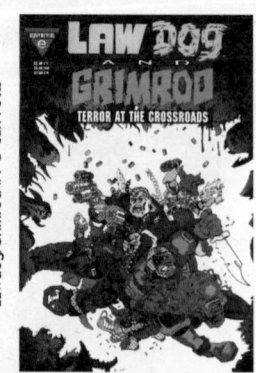

Lawdog/Grimrod #1 © Carl Potts

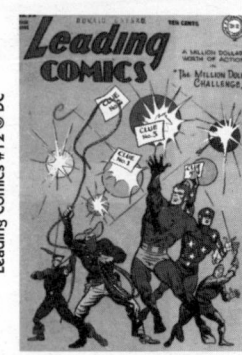

Leading Comics #12 © DC

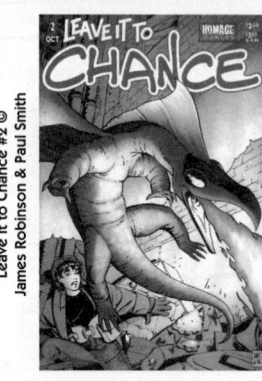

Leave it to Chance #2 ©
James Robinson & Paul Smith

	GD25	FN65	NM94
Suspense Stories No. 16 on)			
No. 10, Jan, 1953 - No. 15, Nov, 1953			
Capitol Stories/Charlton Comics			
10	21.00	64.00	150.00
11 (3/53)-Severed tongues-c/story & woman negligee scene			
	59.00	178.00	475.00
12-14: 13-Giordana-c begin, end #15	10.00	30.00	60.00
15-Acid-in-face-c/story; hands dissolved in acid sty	31.00	94.00	220.00

LAW-CRIME (See Law Against Crime)

LAWDOG/GRIMROD: TERROR AT THE CROSSROADS
Sept, 1993 ($3.50)
Marvel Comics (Epic Comics)

1		1.40	3.50

LAWMAN (TV)
No. 970, Feb, 1959 - No. 11, Apr-June, 1962 (All photo-c)
Dell Publishing Co.

Four Color 970(#1)	13.00	39.00	130.00
Four Color 1035('60)	7.00	21.00	70.00
3(2-4/60)-Toth-a	7.00	21.00	70.00
4-11	5.00	15.00	50.00

LAW OF DREDD, THE (Also see Judge Dredd)
1989 - No. 33, 1992 ($1.50/$1.75)
Quality Comics/Fleetway #8 on

1-8 ($1.50)-Bolland a-1-6,8,10-12,14(2 pg),15,19		.80	2.00
9-20,24-28: 9-Begin $1.75-c		.80	2.00
21-23,29-33)$1.95-c)		.90	2.25

LAWRENCE (See Movie Classics)

LAZARUS CHURCHYARD
June, 1992 - No. 3, 1992 ($3.95, 44 pgs., coated stock)
Tundra Publishing

1-3		1.60	4.00

LEADING COMICS (…Screen Comics No. 42 on)
Winter, 1941-42 - No. 41, Feb-Mar, 1950
National Periodical Publications

1-Origin The Seven Soldiers of Victory; Crimson Avenger, Green Arrow & Speedy, Shining Knight, The Vigilante, Star Spangled Kid & Stripesy begin; The Dummy (Vigilante villain) app.	338.00	1012.00	2900.00
2-Meskin-a;Fred Ray-c	125.00	375.00	1000.00
3	109.00	328.00	875.00
4,5	81.00	243.00	650.00
6-10	68.00	206.00	550.00
11-14(Spring, 1945)	47.00	141.00	375.00
15-(Sum,'45)-Contents change to funny animal	24.00	73.00	170.00
16-22,24-30: 16-Nero Fox-c begin, end #22	11.00	33.00	75.00
23-1st app. Peter Porkchops by Otto Feur & begins	25.00	75.00	175.00
31,32,34-41: 34-41-Leading Screen… on-c only	10.00	30.00	65.00
33-(Scarce)	19.00	58.00	135.00

NOTE: *Rube Grossman*-a(Peter Porkchops)-most #15-on; c-15-41. *Post* a-23-37, 39, 41.

LEADING SCREEN COMICS (Formerly Leading Comics)
No. 42, Apr-May, 1950 - No. 77, Aug-Sept, 1955
National Periodical Publications

42-Peter Porkchops-c/stories continue	10.00	30.00	65.00
43-77	9.15	27.00	55.00

NOTE: *Grossman* a-most. *Mayer* a-45-48, 50, 54-57, 60, 62-74, 75(3), 76, 77.

LEAGUE OF CHAMPIONS, THE (Also see The Champions)
Dec, 1990 - No. 3?, 1991 ($2.95, 52 pgs.)
Hero Graphics

1-3: 1-Flare app. 2-Origin Malice		1.20	3.00

LEAGUE OF JUSTICE

	GD25	FN65	NM94
1996 - No. 2, 1996 ($5.95, 48 pgs., limited series, squarebound)			
DC Comics (Elseworlds)			
1,2: Magic-based alternate DC Universe story; Giordano-i			6.0

LEATHERFACE
May (April on-c), 1991 ($2.75, painted-c)
Arpad Publishing

1-Based on Texas Chainsaw movie; Dorman-c		1.15	2.0

LEATHERNECK THE MARINE (See Mighty Midget Comics)

LEAVE IT TO BEAVER (TV)
No. 912, June, 1958; May-July, 1962 (All photo-c)
Dell Publishing Co.

Four Color 912	18.00	54.00	180.0
Four Color 999,1103,1191,1285, 01-428-207	16.00	48.00	160.0

LEAVE IT TO BINKY (Binky No. 72 on) (Super DC Giant) (No. 1-22: 52 pgs.)
2-3/48 - #60, 10/58; #61, 6-7/68 - #71, 2-3/70 (Teen-age humor)
National Periodical Publications

1-Lucy wears Superman costume	31.00	94.00	220.0
2	16.00	47.00	110.0
3,4	10.00	30.00	60.0
5-Superman cameo	14.00	43.00	100.0
6-10	8.35	25.00	50.0
11-14,16-20	6.70	20.00	40.0
15-Scribbly story by Mayer	10.00	30.00	65.0
21-28,30-45: 45-Last pre-code (2/55)	4.25	13.00	26.0
29-Used in POP, pg. 78	4.35	13.00	28.0
46-60: 60-(10/58)	4.00	10.00	20.0
61-71: 61-(6-7/68)	1.50	3.75	9.0

NOTE: *Drucker* a-28. *Mayer* a-1, 2, 15. Created by *Mayer*.

LEAVE IT TO CHANCE
Sept, 1996 - Present ($2.50)
Homage Comics

1-6: 1-Intro Chance Falconer & St. George; James Robinson scripts & Paul Smith-c/a begins			2.

LEE HUNTER, INDIAN FIGHTER
No. 779, Mar, 1957; No. 904, May, 1958
Dell Publishing Co.

Four Color 779 (#1)	5.00	15.00	50.0
Four Color 904	4.00	12.00	40.0

LEFT-HANDED GUN, THE (Movie)
No. 913, July, 1958
Dell Publishing Co.

Four Color 913-Paul Newman photo-c	11.00	33.00	110.0

LEGACY
Oct, 1993 - No. 2, Nov, 1993; No. 0, 1994 ($2.25)
Majestic Entertainment

1-2: 1-Glow-in-the-dark-c		.90	2.
0-Platinum	1.00	2.00	5.

LEGEND OF CUSTER, THE (TV)
Jan, 1968
Dell Publishing Co.

1-Wayne Maunder photo-c	1.70	5.00	12.

LEGEND OF JESSE JAMES, THE (TV)
Feb, 1966
Gold Key

10172-602-Photo-c	2.60	7.50	18.

LEGEND OF KAMUI, THE (See Kamui)
LEGEND OF LOBO, THE (See Movie Comics)

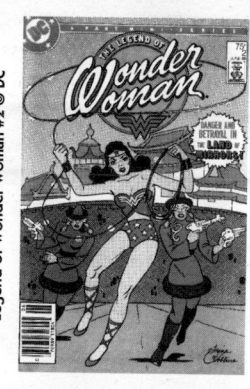

Legend of Wonder Woman #2 © DC

L.E.G.I.O.N. #9 © DC

Legionnaires #14 © DC

LE

	GD25	FN65	NM94

LEGEND OF MOTHER SARAH (Manga)
Apr, 1995 - No. 8, Nov, 1995 ($2.50, limited series)
Dark Horse Comics

1-8: Katsuhiro Otomo scripts	1.00	2.50

LEGEND OF MOTHER SARAH: CITY OF THE ANGELS (Manga)
Oct, 1996 - No. 9, June, 1997 ($3.95, B&W, limited series)
Dark Horse Comics

1-9: Otomo scripts	4.00

LEGEND OF MOTHER SARAH: CITY OF THE CHILDREN (Manga)
Jan, 1996 - No. 7, July, 1996 ($3.95, B&W, limited series)
Dark Horse Comics

1-7: Otomo scripts	4.00

LEGEND OF SUPREME
Dec, 1994 - No. 3, Feb, 1995 ($2.50, limited series)
Image Comics (Extreme Studios)

1-3	1.00	2.50

LEGEND OF THE SHIELD, THE
July, 1991 - No. 16, Oct, 1992 ($1.00)
DC Comics (Impact Comics)

1-16: 6,7-The Fly x-over. 12-Contains trading card		1.00
Annual 1 (1992, $2.50, 68 pgs.)-Snyder-a; w/trading card	1.00	2.50

LEGEND OF WONDER WOMAN, THE
May, 1986 - No. 4, Aug, 1986 (75¢, limited series)
DC Comics

1-4	1.00

LEGEND OF YOUNG DICK TURPIN, THE (Disney)(TV)
May, 1966
Gold Key

1 (10176-605)-Photo/painted-c	2.00	5.00	10.00

LEGEND OF ZELDA, THE (Link: The Legend… in indicia)
1990 - No. 4, 1990 ($1.95, coated stiff-c)
2#1, 1991 - No. 5, 1991 ($1.50)
Valiant Comics

1-4: 4-Layton-c(i)	.80	2.00
2#1-5		1.50

LEGENDS
Nov, 1986 - No. 6, Apr, 1987 (75¢, limited series)
DC Comics

1-Byrne-c/a(p) in all; 1st app. new Capt. Marvel	.90	2.25
2-5: 3-1st app. new Suicide Squad; death of Blockbuster	.80	2.00
6-1st app. new Justice League	1.00	2.50

LEGENDS OF DANIEL BOONE, THE (…Frontier Scout)
Oct-Nov, 1955 - No. 8, Dec-Jan, 1956-57
National Periodical Publications

1 (Scarce)-Nick Cardy c-1-8	56.00	168.00	450.00
2 (Scarce)	40.00	120.00	325.00
3-8 (Scarce)	40.00	120.00	285.00

LEGENDS OF NASCAR, THE
Nov, 1990 - No. 14, 1992? (#1 3rd printing (1/91) says 2nd printing inside)
Vortex Comics

1-Bill Elliott biog.; Trimpe-a ($1.50)	1.00	2.00	5.00
1-2nd printing (11/90, $2.00)		.80	2.00
1-3rd print; contains Maxx racecards ($3.00)		1.20	3.00
2-Richard Petty ($2.00)		.80	2.00
3-14: 3-Ken Schrader (7/91). 4-Bobby Allison; Spiegle-a(p); Adkins part-i.			

LEGENDS OF NASCAR, THE (continued at top of right column)

5-Sterling Marlin. 6-Bill Elliott. 7-Junior Johnson; Spiegle-c/a. 8-Benny Parsons; Heck-a		.70	1.80
1-13-Hologram cover versions. 2-Hologram shows Bill Elliott's car by mistake (all are numbered & limited)		1.60	4.00
2-Hologram corrected version		1.60	4.00
Christmas Special ($5.95)	1.00	2.50	6.00

LEGENDS OF THE DARK CLAW
Apr, 1996 ($1.95)
DC Comics (Amalgam)

1-Jim Balent-c/a		2.00

LEGENDS OF THE DARK KNIGHT (See Batman: …)

LEGENDS OF THE STARGRAZERS (See Vanguard Illustrated #2)
Aug, 1989 - No. 6, 1990 ($1.95, limited series, mature)
Innovation Publishing

1-6: 1-Redondo part inks	1.00	2.00

LEGENDS OF THE WORLD'S FINEST (See World's Finest)
1994 - No. 3, 1994 ($4.95, squarebound, limited series)
DC Comics

1-3: Simonson scripts; Brereton-c/a; embossed foil logos			
	1.00	2.00	5.00

L.E.G.I.O.N. (The # to right of title represents year of print)(Also see Lobo & R.E.B.E.L.S.)
Feb, 1989 - No. 70, Sept, 1994 ($1.50/$1.75)
DC Comics

1-Giffen plots/breakdowns in #1-12		.70	1.75
2-22,24-47: 3-Lobo app. #3 on. 4-1st Lobo-c this title. 5-Lobo joins L.E.G.I.O.N. 13-Lar Gand app. 16-Lar Gand joins L.E.G.I.O.N., leaves #19. 28-Giffen-c(p). 31-Capt. Marvel app. 35-L.E.G.I.O.N. '92 begins			1.50
23-($2.50, 52 pgs.)-L.E.G.I.O.N. '91 begins		1.00	2.50
48,49,51-69: 48-Begin $1.75-c. 63-L.E.G.I.O.N. '94 begins; Superman x-over		.70	1.75
50-($3.50, 68 pgs.)		1.40	3.50
70-($2.50, 52 pgs.)-Zero Hour		1.00	2.50
Annual 1-3 (1990-1992, $2.95, 68 pgs.): 1-Lobo, Superman app. 2-Alan Grant scripts		1.20	3.00
Annual 4 (1993, $3.50, 68 pgs.)		1.40	3.50
Annual 5 (1994, $3.50, 68 pgs.)-Elseworlds story; Lobo app.		1.40	3.50

NOTE: **Alan Grant** scripts in #1-39, 51, Annual 1, 2.

LEGIONNAIRES (See Legion of Super-Heroes #40, 41 & Showcase 95 #6)
Apr, 1992 - Present ($1.25/$1.50/$2.25)
DC comics

1-8: 1-Chris Sprouse-c/a; polybagged w/SkyBox trading card			1.50
0,9-25: 9-Begin $1.50-c. 11-Kid Quantum joins. 18-(9/94)-Zero Hour. 0-(10/94). 19-(11/94)			1.50
26-28: 26-Begin $1.75-c			1.75
29-49: 29-Begin $2.25-c. 37-Valor (Lar Gand) becomes M'onel (5/96). 43-Legion tryouts; reintro Princess Projectra, Shadow Lass & others		.90	2.25
Annual 1 (1994, $2.95)-Elseworlds story		1.20	3.00
Annual 2 (1995, $3.95)-Year One story		1.60	4.00
Annual 3 (1996, $2.95)-Legends of the Dead Earth story		1.20	3.00

LEGIONNAIRES THREE
Jan, 1986 - No. 4, May, 1986 (75¢, limited series)
DC comics

1-4	1.00

LEGION OF MONSTERS (Also see Marvel Premiere #28 & Marvel Preview #8)
September, 1975 ($1.00, B&W, magazine, 76 pgs.)
Marvel Comics Group

Legion of Super-Heroes #260 © DC

Legion of Super-Heroes #293 © DC

Legion of Super-Heroes #84 © DC

	GD25	FN65	NM94

1-Origin & 1st app. Legion of Monsters; Neal Adams-c; Morrow-a; origin &
only app. The Manphibian; Frankenstein by Mayerik; Bram Stoker's
Dracula adaptation; Reese-a; painted-c (#2 was advertised with Morbius
& Satana, but was never published) — 1.20 3.00 7.00

LEGION OF NIGHT, THE
Oct, 1991 - No. 2, Oct, 1991 ($4.95, 52 pgs.)
Marvel Comics

1,2-Whilce Portacio-c/a(p) — 1.00 2.00 5.00

LEGION OF SUBSTITUTE HEROES SPECIAL (See Adventure Comics #306)
July, 1985 ($1.25, one-shot, 52 pgs.)
DC Comics

1-Giffen-c/a(p) — 1.25

LEGION OF SUPER-HEROES (See Action, Adventure, All New Collectors
Edition, Limited Collectors Edition, Secrets of the…, Superboy & Superman)
Feb, 1973 - No. 4, July-Aug, 1973
National Periodical Publications

1-Legion & Tommy Tomorrow reprints begin — 1.30 3.25 8.00
2-4: 2-Forte-r. 3-r/Adv. #340. Action #240. 4-r/Adv. #341, Action #233;
Mooney-r — 1.00 2.50 5.50

LEGION OF SUPER-HEROES, THE (Formerly Superboy and…; Tales of The
Legion No. 314 on)
No. 259, Jan, 1980 - No. 313, July, 1984
DC Comics

259(#1)-Superboy leaves Legion — 1.20 3.00
260-270: 265-Contains 28 pg. insert "Superman & the TRS-80 Computer";
origin Tyroc; Tyroc leaves Legion — .80 2.00
271-284: 272-Blok joins; origin; 20pg. insert-Dial 'H' For Hero. 277-Intro
Reflecto. 280-Superboy re-joins Legion. 282-Origin Reflecto. 283-Origin
Wildfire — .70 1.75
285,286-Giffen back up story — .80 2.00
287-Giffen a-on Legion begins — 1.00 2.50
288-290: 290-294-Great Darkness saga — .80 2.00
291-293 — 1.50
294-Double size (52 pgs.); Giffen-a(p) — .70 1.75
295-299,301-305: 297-Origin retold. 298-Free 16pg. Amethyst preview
— 1.50
300-(68 pgs., Mando paper)-Anniversary issue; has c/a by almost everyone at
DC — .80 2.00
306-313 (75¢): 306-Brief origin Star Boy — 1.00
Annual 1(1982, 52 pgs.)-Giffen-c/a; 1st app./origin new Invisible Kid who joins
Legion — .80 2.00
Annual 2,3: 2(1983, 52 pgs.)-Giffen-c; Karate Kid & Princess Projectra wed
& resign. 3(1984, 52 pgs.) — 1.50
…The Great Darkness Saga (1989, $17.95, 196 pgs.)-r/LSH #287,290-294 &
Annual #3; Giffen-a/bk — 2.60 7.50 18.00
NOTE: Aparo c-282, 283, 300(part). Austin c-268l. Buckler c-273p, 274p, 276p. Colan a-311p.
Ditko a(p)-267, 268, 272, 274, 276, 281. Giffen a-285-313p, Annual 1p; c-287p, 288p, 289,
290p, 291p, 292, 293, 294-299p, 300, 301-313p, Annual 1p, 2p. Perez c-268p, 277-280, 281p.
Starlin a-265. Staton a-259p, 260p, 280. Tuska a-308p.

LEGION OF SUPER-HEROES (Reprinted in Tales of the Legion)
Aug, 1984 - No. 63, Aug, 1989 ($1.25/$1.75, deluxe format)
DC Comics

1-Silver ink logo — 1.50
2-10: 4-Death of Karate Kid. 5-Death of Nemesis Kid — 1.50
11-14: 12-Cosmic Boy, Lightning Lad, & Saturn Girl resign. 14-Intro new
members: Tellus, Sensor Girl, Quislet — 1.25
15-18: 15-17-Crisis tie-in. 18-Crisis x-over — 1.50
19-25: 25-Sensor Girl i.d. revealed as Princess Projectra — 1.25
26-36,39-44: 35-Saturn Girl rejoins. 40-$1.75-c. price begins. 42,43-
Millennium tie-ins. 44-Origin Quislet — 1.25
37,38-Death of Superboy — 1.65 4.20 10.00
45 ($2.95, 68 pgs.)-Anniversary issue — 1.20 3.00

46-49,51-62 — 1.2
50-Double size, $2.50 — 1.00 2.5
63-Final issue — 1.5
Annual 1 (10/85, 52 pgs.)-Crisis tie-in — .70 1.7
Annual 2,3: 2 (1986, 52 pgs.). 3 (1987, $2.25, 52 pgs.) — .90 2.2
Annual 4 (1988, $2.50, 52 pgs.) — 1.00 2.5
NOTE: Byrne c-36p. Giffen a(p)-1, 2, 50-55, 57-63, Annual 1p, 2; c-1-5p, 54p, Annual 1.
Orlando a-6p. Steacy c-45-50, Annual 3.

LEGION OF SUPER-HEROES
Nov, 1989 - Present ($1.75/$1.95/$2.25)
DC Comics

1-Giffen c/a(p)/scripts begin (4 pg.-a only #18) — .70 1.7
2-49,51-53,55-58: 4-Mon-El (Lar Gand) destroys Time Trapper, changes
reality. 5-Alt. reality story where Mordru rules all; Ferro Lad app. 6-1st app.
of Laurel Gand (Lar Gand's cousin). 8-Origin. 15-(7/91)-1st reference of Lar
Gand as Valor. 13-Free poster by Giffen showing new costumes.
21-24-Lobo & Darkseid storyline. 26-New map of headquarters. 34-Six pg.
preview of Timber Wolf mini-series. 40-Minor Legionnaires app.
41-(3/93)-Intro Legionnaires — .70 1.7
50-($3.50, 68 pgs.) — 1.40 3.5
54-($2.95)-Die-cut & foil stamped-c — 1.20 3.0
59-61: 59-Begin $1.95-c. 61-(9/94)-Zero Hour — .80 2.0
0,62-68: 0-(10/94). 62-(11/94) — .80 2.0
69-86: 69-Begin $2.25-c. 75-XS travels back to the 20th Century (cont'd in
Impulse #9). 77-Origin of Braniac 5. 81-Reintro Sun Boy — 2.2
Annual 1-5 (1990-1994, $3.50, 68 pgs.): 4-Bloodlines. 5-Elseworlds story
— 1.40 3.5
Annual 6 (1995,$3.95)-Year One story — 4.0
Annual 7 (1996, $3.50, 48 pgs.)-Legends of the Dead Earth story; intro 75th
Century Legion of Super-Heroes; Wildfire app. — 3.
NOTE: Giffen a-1-24; breakdowns-26-32, 34-36; c-1-7, 8(part), 9-24. Brandon Peterson a(p)
15(1st for DC), 16, 18, Annual 2(54 pgs.); c-Annual 2p. Swan/Anderson c-8(part).

LEMONADE KID, THE (See Bobby Benson's B-Bar-B Riders)
1990 ($2.50, 28 pgs.)
AC Comics

1-Powell-c(r); Red Hawk-r by Powell; Lemonade Kid-r/Bobby Benson by
Powell (2 stories) — 1.00 2.5

LENNON SISTERS LIFE STORY, THE
No. 951, Nov, 1958 - No. 1014, Aug, 1959
Dell Publishing Co.

Four Color 951 (#1)-Toth-a, 32pgs., photo-c — 15.00 45.00 145.0
Four Color 1014-Toth-a, photo-c — 15.00 45.00 145.0

LEONARD NIMOY'S PRIMORTALS
Mar, 1995 - No. 15, May, 1996 ($1.95)
Tekno Comix

1-15: Concept by Leonard Nimoy & Isaac Asimov 1-3-w/bound-in game piece
& trading card. 4-w/Teknophage Steel Edition coupon. 13,14-Art Adams-c.
15-Simonson-c — .80 2.

LEONARD NIMOY'S PRIMORTALS
V2#0, June, 1996 - Present ($2.25)
BIG Entertainment

V2#0-4: 0-Includes Pt. 9 of "The Big Bang" x-over. 0,1-Simonson-c. 3-Kelley
Jones-c — 2.

LEONARD NIMOY'S PRIMORTALS ORIGINS
Nov, 1995 - No. 2, Dec, 1995 ($2.95, limited series)
Tekno Comix

1,2: Nimoy scripts; Art Adams-c; polybagged — 1.20 3.

LEONARDO (Also see Teenage Mutant Ninja Turtles)
Dec, 1986 ($1.50, B&W, one-shot)
Mirage Studios

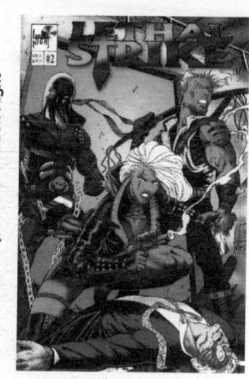

Lethal Stryke #2 © London Night

Lethargic Lad #3 © Greg Hyland

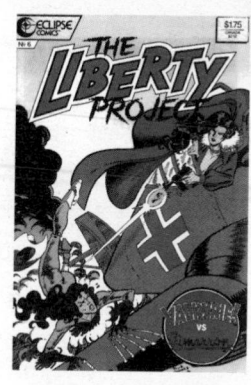

Liberty Project #6 © ECL

	GD25	FN65	NM94
1	1.00	2.00	5.00

LEO THE LION
No date(1960s) (10¢)
I. W. Enterprises

1-Reprint	1.30	3.25	8.00

LEROY (Teen-age)
Nov, 1949 - No. 6, Nov, 1950
Standard Comics

1	6.35	19.00	38.00
2-Frazetta text illo.	4.25	13.00	28.00
3-6: 3-Lubbers-a	4.00	11.00	22.00

LETHAL (Also see Brigade)
Feb, 1996 ($2.50, unfinished limited series)
Image Comics (Extreme Studios)

1-Marat Mychaels-c/a.			2.50

LETHAL FOES OF SPIDER-MAN (Sequel to Deadly Foes of Spider-Man)
Sept, 1993 - No. 4, Dec, 1993 ($1.75, limited series)
Marvel Comics

1-4		.70	1.75

LETHAL STRYKE
June, 1995 - Present ($3.00)
London Night Studios

0-(8/95, $5.95)-Collector's ed.	1.00	2.60	6.00
1/2, 1-3: 1-polybagged w/card		1.20	3.00
Annual 1-(1996, $3.00)			3.00
Annual 1-Platinum Edition			10.00
Trade paperback-(1996, $12.95)-r/#1/2-3			12.95

LETHAL STRYKE/DOUBLE IMPACT: LETHAL IMPACT
May, 1996 ($3.00, one-shot)
London Night Studios

1-Hartsoe/Lyon-a(p)			3.00
1-Natural Born Killers Edition			3.00

LETHARGIC LAD
June, 1996 - No. 3, Sept, 1996 ($2.95, B&W, limited series)
Crusade Entertainment

1-3: 3-Alex Ross-c/swipe (Kingdom Come)			3.00

LET'S PRETEND (CBS radio)
May-June, 1950 - No. 3, Sept-Oct, 1950
D. S. Publishing Co.

1	12.00	36.00	85.00
2,3	10.00	30.00	65.00

LET'S READ THE NEWSPAPER
1974
Charlton Press

nn-Features Quincy by Ted Sheares			1.00

LET'S TAKE A TRIP (TV) (CBS Television Presents)
Spring, 1958
Pines Comics

1-Marv Levy-c/a	4.00	10.00	20.00

LETTERS TO SANTA (See March of Comics No. 228)

LEX LUTHOR: THE UNAUTHORIZED BIOGRAPHY
1989 ($3.95, 52 pgs., one-shot, squarebound)
DC Comics

1-Painted-c; Clark Kent app.		1.60	4.00

LIBERTY COMICS (Miss Liberty No. 1)
No. 4, 1945 - No. 15, July, 1946 (MLJ & other reprints)

Green Publishing Co.

4	13.50	41.00	95.00
5 (5/46)-The Prankster app.; Starr-a	11.50	34.00	80.00
10-Hangman & Boy Buddies app.; Suzie & Wilbur begin; reprints Hangman story from Hangman #8	16.00	47.00	110.00
11(V2#2, 1/46)-Wilbur in women's clothes	13.50	41.00	95.00
12-Black Hood & Suzie app.	13.50	41.00	95.00
14,15-Patty of Airliner; Starr-a in both	9.15	27.00	55.00

LIBERTY GUARDS
No date (1946?)
Chicago Mail Order

nn-Reprints Man of War #1 with cover of Liberty Scouts #1; Gustavson-c			
	30.00	90.00	210.00

LIBERTY PROJECT, THE
June, 1987 - No. 8, May, 1988 ($1.75, color, Baxter paper)
Eclipse Comics

1-8: 6-Valkyrie app.		.90	1.80

LIBERTY SCOUTS (See Liberty Guards & Man of War)
No. 2, June, 1941 - No. 3, Aug, 1941
Centaur Publications

2(#1)-Origin The Fire-Man, Man of War; Vapo-Man & Liberty Scouts begin; intro Liberty Scouts; Gustavson-c/a in both	115.00	346.00	925.00
3(#2)-Origin & 1st app. The Sentinel	89.00	268.00	715.00

LICENCE TO KILL (James Bond 007) (Movie)
1989 ($7.95, slick paper, 52 pgs.)
Eclipse Comics

nn-Movie adaptation; Timothy Dalton photo-c	1.35	4.00	8.00
Limited Hardcover ($24.95)	4.15	12.50	25.00

LIDSVILLE (TV)
Oct, 1972 - No. 5, Oct, 1973
Gold Key

1-Photo-c	2.00	6.00	14.00
2-5	1.30	3.25	8.00

LIEUTENANT, THE (TV)
April-June, 1964
Dell Publishing Co.

1-Photo-c	2.00	6.00	14.00

LIEUTENANT BLUEBERRY (Also see Blueberry)
1991 - No. 3, 1991 (Graphic novel)
Marvel Comics (Epic Comics)

1,2 ($8.95)-Moebius-a in all	1.50	3.75	9.00
3 ($14.95)	2.15	6.50	15.00

LT. ROBIN CRUSOE, U.S.N. (See Movie Comics & Walt Disney Showcase #26)

LIFE OF CAPTAIN MARVEL, THE
Aug, 1985 - No. 5, Dec, 1985 ($2.00, Baxter paper)
Marvel Comics Group

1-5: 1-All reprint Starlin issues of Iron Man #55, Capt. Marvel #25-34 plus Marvel Feature #12 (all with Thanos). 4-New Thanos back-c by Starlin		.80	2.00

LIFE OF CHRIST, THE
No. 301, 1949 (35¢, 100 pgs.)
Catechetical Guild Educational Society

301-Reprints from Topix(1949)-V5#11,12	4.00	10.00	20.00

LIFE OF CHRIST: THE EASTER STORY, THE
1993 ($2.99, slick stock)
Marvel Comics/Nelson

nn		1.20	3.00

Life of Christ © ECL

Life Story #1 © FAW

Life With Snarky Parker #1 © FOX

	GD25	FN65	NM94
LIFE OF CHRIST VISUALIZED			
1942 - No. 3, 1943			
Standard Publishers			
1-3: All came in cardboard case	4.00	10.00	20.00
With case.....	8.35	25.00	50.00
LIFE OF CHRIST VISUALIZED			
1946? (48 pgs. in color)			
The Standard Publ. Co.			
nn	2.00	5.00	10.00
LIFE OF ESTHER VISUALIZED			
No. 2062, 1947 (48 pgs. in color)			
The Standard Publ. Co.			
2062	2.00	5.00	10.00
LIFE OF JOSEPH VISUALIZED			
No. 1054, 1946 (48 pgs. in color)			
The Standard Publ. Co.			
1054	2.00	5.00	10.00
LIFE OF PAUL (See The Living Bible)			
LIFE OF POPE JOHN PAUL II, THE			
Jan, 1983			
Marvel Comics Group			
1			1.50
LIFE OF RILEY, THE (TV)			
No. 917, July, 1958			
Dell Publishing Co.			
Four Color 917-Photo-c	12.00	36.00	120.00
LIFE OF THE BLESSED VIRGIN			
1950 (68pgs.) (square binding)			
Catechetical Guild (Giveaway)			
nn-Contains "The Woman of the Promise" & "Mother of Us All"			
rebound	4.00	10.00	20.00
LIFE'S LIKE THAT			
1945 (25¢, B&W, 68 pgs.)			
Croyden Publ. Co.			
nn-Newspaper Sunday strip-r by Neher	5.35	16.00	32.00
LIFE STORIES OF AMERICAN PRESIDENTS (See Dell Giants)			
LIFE STORY			
Apr, 1949 - V8#47, Jan, 1953; V8#47, Apr, 1953 (All have photo-c?)			
Fawcett Publications			
V1#1	10.00	30.00	70.00
2	5.00	15.00	30.00
3-6	4.25	13.00	26.00
V2#7-12	4.25	13.00	26.00
V3#13-Wood-a	11.00	33.00	75.00
V3#14-18, V4#19-24, V5#25-30, V6#31-35	4.00	11.00	22.00
V6#36- "I sold drugs" on-c	4.25	13.00	28.00
V7#37,40-42, V8#44,45	2.80	7.00	14.00
V7#38, V8#43-Evans-a	4.35	13.00	26.00
V7#39-Drug Smuggling & Junkie story	4.00	12.00	24.00
V8#46,47 (Scarce)	4.00	12.00	24.00

NOTE: **Powell** a-13, 23, 24, 26, 28, 30, 32, 39. **Marcus Swayze** a-1-3, 10-12, 15, 16, 20, 21, 23-25, 31, 35, 37, 40, 44, 46.

LIFE, THE UNIVERSE AND EVERYTHING (See Hitchhikers Guide to the Galaxy & Restaurant at the End of the Universe)
1996 - No. 3, 1996 ($6.95, squarebound, limited series)
DC Comics

1-3: Adaptation of novel by Douglas Adams.			7.00

	GD25	FN65	NM94
LIFE WITH ARCHIE			
Sept, 1958 - No. 285, 1991			
Archie Publications			
1	25.00	75.00	250.00
2-(9/59)	12.50	37.50	125.00
3-5: 3-(7/60)	8.50	25.50	85.00
6-10	5.00	15.00	50.00
11-20	3.00	9.00	30.00
21-30	2.60	7.80	26.00
31-41	1.60	4.80	16.00
42-45: 42-Pureheart begins (1st app., 1965?)	1.65	4.20	10.00
46-Origin Pureheart	2.30	6.70	16.00
47-59: 50-United Three begin: Pureheart (Archie), Superteen (Betty), Captain Hero (Jughead). 59-Pureheart ends	1.20	3.00	7.00
60-100: 60-Archie band begins		1.20	3.00
101-285: 208-Reintro Veronica. 238-(9/83)-25th anniversary issue; Ol' Betsy (jalopy) replaced. 279-Intro Mustang Sally ($1.00)			1.25

NOTE: **Gene Colan** a-272-279, 285, 286.

LIFE WITH MILLIE (Formerly A Date With Millie) (Modeling With Millie #21 on)
No. 8, Dec, 1960 - No. 20, Dec, 1962
Atlas/Marvel Comics Group

	GD25	FN65	NM94
8-Teenage	8.35	25.00	50.00
9-11	5.85	17.50	35.00
12-20	4.25	13.00	26.00

LIFE WITH SNARKY PARKER (TV)
Aug, 1950
Fox Feature Syndicate

1-Early TV comic; photo-c from TV puppet show	23.00	69.00	160.00

LIGHT AND DARKNESS WAR, THE
Oct, 1988 - No. 6, Dec, 1989 ($1.95, limited series)
Marvel Comics (Epic Comics)

1-6		.80	2.00

LIGHT FANTASTIC, THE (Terry Pratchett's)
June, 1992 - No. 4, Sept, 1992 ($2.50, mini-series)
Innovation Publishing

1-4: Adapts 2nd novel in Discworld series		1.00	2.50

LIGHT IN THE FOREST (Disney)
No. 891, Mar, 1958
Dell Publishing Co.

Four Color 891-Movie, Fess Parker photo-c	9.00	27.00	90.00

LIGHTNING COMICS (Formerly Sure-Fire No. 1-3)
No. 4, Dec, 1940 - No. 13(V3#1), June, 1942
Ace Magazines

4-Characters continue from Sure-Fire	87.00	262.00	700.00
5,6: 6-Dr. Nemesis begins	58.00	174.00	465.00
V2#1-6: 2- "Flash Lightning" becomes "Lash..."	45.00	136.00	365.00
V3#1-Intro. Lightning Girl & The Sword	45.00	136.00	365.00

NOTE: **Anderson** a-V2#6. **Mooney** c-V1#5, 6, V2#1-6, V3#1. Bondage c-V2#6. Lightning-c all.

LIGHTNING COMICS PRESENTS
May, 1994 ($3.50)
Lightning Comics

1-Red foil-c distributed by Diamond Distributors		1.40	3.50
1-Black/yellow/blue-c distrib. by Capital Distributors		1.40	3.50
1-Red/yellow-c distributed by H. World		1.40	3.50
1-Platinum		1.40	3.50

LI'L (See Little)

LIMITED COLLECTORS' EDITION (See Famous First Edition & Rudolph the Red Nosed Reindeer; becomes All-New Collectors' Edition)

Linda #1 © AJAX

Li'l Abner #65 © TOBY

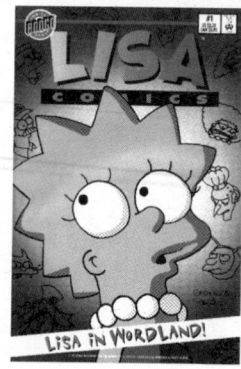

Lisa Comics #1 © Matt Groening

LI

(#21-34,51-59: 84 pgs.; #35-41: 68 pgs.; #42-50: 60 pgs.)
C-21, Summer, 1973 - No. C-59, 1978 ($1.00) (10x13-1/2")
National Periodical Publications/DC Comics

	GD25	FN65	NM94
nn(C-20)-Rudolph (date?)	1.65	4.20	10.00
C-21: Shazam (TV); r/Captain Marvel Jr. #11 by Raboy; C.C. Beck-c, biog. & photo	1.65	4.20	10.00
C-22: Tarzan; complete origin reprinted from #207-210; all Kubert-c/a; Joe Kubert biography & photo inside	1.65	4.20	10.00
C-23: House of Mystery; Wrightson, N. Adams/Orlando, G. Kane/Wood, Toth, Aragones, Sparling reprints	1.00	2.60	6.00
C-24: Rudolph The Red-nosed Reindeer		1.60	4.00
C-25: Batman; Neal Adams-c/a(r); G.A. Joker-r; Batman/Enemy Ace-r; has photos from TV show	1.65	4.20	10.00
C-26: See Famous First Edition C-26 (same contents)			
C-27: Shazam (TV); G.A. Capt. Marvel & Mary Marvel-r; Beck-r	1.00	2.00	5.00
C-29: Tarzan; reprints "Return of Tarzan" from #219-223 by Kubert; Kubert-c	1.20	3.00	7.00
C-31: Superman; origin-r; N. Adams-a; photos of George Reeves from 1950s TV show on inside b/c; Burnley, Boring-r	1.65	4.20	10.00
C-32: Ghosts (new-a)	2.15	6.50	15.00
C-33: Rudolph The Red-nosed Reindeer(new-a)		1.60	4.00
C-34: Christmas with the Super-Heroes; unpublished Angel & Ape story by Oksner & Wood; Batman & Teen Titans-r	1.50	3.75	9.00
C-35: Shazam (TV); photo cover features TV's Captain Marvel, Jackson Bostwick; Beck-r; TV photos inside b/c	1.00	2.60	6.00
C-36: The Bible; all new adaptation beginning with Genesis by Kubert, Redondo & Mayer; Kubert-c	1.00	2.60	6.00
C-37: Batman; r-1946 Sundays; inside b/c photos of Batman TV show villains (all villain issue; r/G.A. Joker, Catwoman, Penguin, Two-Face, & Scarecrow stories plus 1946 Sundays-r)	1.65	4.20	10.00
C-38: Superman; 1 pg. N. Adams; part photo-c; photos from TV show on inside back-c	1.30	3.25	8.00
C-39: Secret Origins of Super-Villains; N. Adams-i(r); collection reprints 1950's Joker origin, Luthor origin from Adv. Comics #271, Capt. Cold origin from Showcase #8 among others; G.A. Batman-r; Beck-r	1.00	2.50	6.00
C-40: Dick Tracy by Gould featuring Flattop; newspaper-r from 12/21/43 - 5/17/44; biog. of Chester Gould	1.00	2.50	6.00
C-41: Super Friends (TV); JLA-r(1965); Toth-c/a	1.30	3.25	8.00
C-42: Rudolph		1.60	4.00
C-43: Christmas with the Super-Heroes; Wrightson, S&K, Neal Adams-a	1.65	4.20	10.00
C-44: Batman; N. Adams-p(r) & G.A.-r; painted-c	1.65	4.20	10.00
C-45: More Secret Origins of Super-Villains; Flash-r/#105; G.A. Wonder Woman & Batman/Catwoman-r	1.20	3.00	7.00
C-46: Justice League of America(1963-r); 3 pgs. Toth-a	1.30	3.25	8.00
C-47: Superman Salutes the Bicentennial (Tomahawk interior); 2 pgs. new-a	1.00	2.60	6.00
C-48: Superman Vs. The Flash (Superman/Flash race); swipes-c to Superman #199; r/Superman #199 & Flash #175; 6 pgs. Neal Adams-a	1.30	3.25	8.00
C-49: Superboy & the Legion of Super-Heroes	1.00	2.60	6.00
C-50: Rudolph The Red-nosed Reindeer		1.60	4.00
C-51: Batman; Neal Adams-c/a	1.65	4.20	10.00
C-52: The Best of DC; Neal Adams-c/a; Toth, Kubert-a	1.65	4.20	10.00
C-57: Welcome Back, Kotter-r(TV)(5/78)	1.00	2.00	5.00
C-59: Batman's Strangest Cases; N. Adams-r; Wrightson-r/Swamp Thing #7; N. Adams/Wrightson-a	1.65	4.20	10.00

NOTE: All-r with exception of some special features and covers. Aparo a-52r; c-37. Grell c-49. Infantino a-25, 39, 44, 45, 52. Bob Kane r-25. Robinson r-25, 44. Sprang r-44. Issues #21-31, 35-39, 45, 48 have back cover cut-outs.

LINDA (Everybody Loves...) (Phantom Lady No. 5 on)
Apr-May, 1954 - No. 4, Oct-Nov, 1954
Ajax-Farrell Publ. Co.

	GD25	FN65	NM94
1-Kamenish-a	12.00	36.00	85.00
2-Lingerie panel	10.00	30.00	60.00
3,4	8.35	25.00	50.00

LINDA CARTER, STUDENT NURSE
Sept, 1961 - No. 9, Jan, 1963
Atlas Comics (AMI)

1-Al Hartley-c	4.50	14.00	32.00
2-9	3.40	10.00	24.00

LINDA LARK
Oct-Dec, 1961 - No. 8, Aug-Oct, 1963
Dell Publishing Co.

1	2.60	7.50	18.00
2-8	1.50	3.75	9.00

LINUS, THE LIONHEARTED (TV)
Sept, 1965
Gold Key

1 (10155-509)	6.50	19.50	65.00

LION, THE (See Movie Comics)

LION OF SPARTA (See Movie Classics)

LIPPY THE LION AND HARDY HAR HAR (TV)
Mar, 1963 (Hanna-Barbera) (12¢) (See Hanna-Barbera Band Wagon #1)
Gold Key

1 (10049-303)	7.50	22.50	75.00

LI'L ABNER (See Comics on Parade, Sparkle, Sparkler Comics, Tip Top Comics & Tip Topper)
1939 - 1940
United Features Syndicate

Single Series 4 ('39)	62.00	187.00	500.00
Single Series 18 ('40) (#18 on inside, #2 on-c)	53.00	159.00	425.00

LI'L ABNER (Al Capp's; continued from Comics on Parade #58)
No. 61, Dec, 1947 - No. 97, Jan, 1955 (See Oxydol-Dreft)
Harvey Publ. No. 61-69 (2/49)/Toby Press No. 70 on

61(#1)-Wolverton & Powell-a	31.00	94.00	220.00
62-65: 63-The Wolf Girl app. 65-Powell-a	19.00	56.00	130.00
66,67,69,70	16.00	47.00	110.00
68-Full length Fearless Fosdick-c/story	17.00	51.00	120.00
71-74,76,80	12.00	36.00	85.00
75,77-79,86,91-All with Kurtzman art; 91-r/#77	16.00	47.00	110.00
81-85,87-90,92-94,96,97: 93-reprints #71	11.00	33.00	75.00
95-Full length Fearless Fosdick story	13.50	41.00	95.00
...& the Creatures from Drop-Outer Space-nn (Job Corps giveaway; 36 pgs., in color)(entire book by Frank Frazetta)	29.00	86.00	200.00
...Joins the Navy (1950) (Toby Press Premium)	10.00	30.00	70.00
...by Al Capp Giveaway (Circa 1955, nd)	10.00	30.00	70.00

LI'L ABNER
1951
Toby Press

1	17.00	49.00	115.00

LI'L ABNER'S DOGPATCH (See Al Capp's...)

LISA COMICS
1995 ($2.25, color,annual)
Bongo Comics

1-Lisa in Wonderland		.90	2.25

LITTLE AL OF THE F.B.I.

Little Al of the Secret Service #2 © Z-D

Little Angel #6 © STD

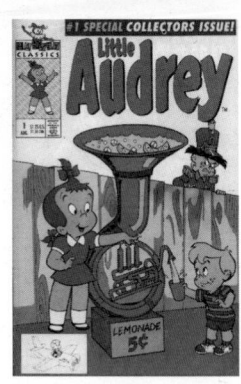

Little Audrey #1 © STJ

	GD25	FN65	NM94
No. 10, 1950 (no month) - No. 11, Apr-May, 1951 (Saunders painted-c)			
Ziff-Davis Publications			
10(1950)	12.00	36.00	85.00
11(1951)	10.00	30.00	65.00

LITTLE AL OF THE SECRET SERVICE
No. 10, 7-8/51; No, 2, 9-10/51; No. 3, Winter, 1951 (Saunders painted-c)
Ziff-Davis Publications

10(#1)-Spanking panels (2)	14.00	43.00	100.00
2,3	10.00	30.00	65.00

LITTLE ALONZO
1938 (B&W, 5-1/2x8-1/2")(Christmas giveaway)
Macy's Dept. Store

nn-By Ferdinand the Bull's Munro Leaf	7.50	22.50	45.00

LITTLE AMBROSE
September, 1958
Archie Publications

1-Bob Bolling-c	12.00	36.00	85.00

LITTLE ANGEL
No. 5, Sept, 1954; No. 6, Sept, 1955 - No. 16, Sept, 1959
Standard (Visual Editions)/Pines

5-Last pre-code issue	5.35	16.00	32.00
6-16	4.00	10.00	20.00

LITTLE ANNIE ROONEY (Also see Henry)
1935 (25¢, B&W dailies, 48 pgs.)(10"x10", cardboard-c)
David McKay Publications

Book 1-Daily strip-r by Darrell McClure	36.00	107.00	250.00

LITTLE ANNIE ROONEY (See King Comics & Treasury of Comics)
1938; Aug, 1948 - No. 3, Oct, 1948
David McKay/St. John/Standard

Feature Books 11 (McKay, 1938)	36.00	107.00	250.00
1 (St. John)	11.50	34.00	80.00
2,3	7.50	22.50	45.00

LITTLE ARCHIE (The Adventures of… #13-on) (See Archie Giant Series Mag.
#527, 534, 538, 545, 549, 556, 560, 566, 570, 583, 594, 596, 607, 609, 619)
1956 - No. 180, Feb, 1983 (Giants No. 3-84)
Archie Publications

1-(Scarce)	50.00	150.00	500.00
2 (1957)	21.00	63.00	210.00
3-5: 3-(1958)-Bob Bolling-c & giant issues begin	12.00	36.00	120.00
6-10	9.00	27.00	90.00
11-20	5.00	15.00	50.00
21-30	3.00	9.00	30.00
31-40: Little Pureheart apps. #40-42,44	2.60	7.50	18.00
41-60: 42-Intro The Little Archies. 59-Little Sabrina begins			
	1.70	5.00	12.00
61-84: 84-Last Giant-Size	1.20	3.00	7.00
85-100		1.20	3.00
101-180			1.50
…In Animal Land 1(1957)	14.00	43.00	100.00
…In Animal Land 17(Winter, 1957-58)-19(Summer,1958)-Formerly Li'l Jinx			
	8.35	25.00	50.00

LITTLE ARCHIE CHRISTMAS SPECIAL (See Archie Giant Series #581)

LITTLE ARCHIE COMICS DIGEST ANNUAL (…Magazine #5 on)
10/77 - No. 48, 5/91 (Digest-size, 128 pgs., later issues $1.35-$1.50)
Archie Publications

1(10/77)-Reprints		.80	2.00
2(4/78)-Neal Adams-a			1.40
3(11/78)-The Fly-r by S&K; Neal Adams-a			1.40

	GD25	FN65	NM94
4(4/79) - 48: 28,40,46-Christmas-c			1.40

NOTE: *Little Archie, Little Jinx, Little Jughead & Little Sabrina in most issues.*

LITTLE ARCHIE DIGEST MAGAZINE
July, 1991 - Present ($1.50, digest size, bi-annually)
Archie Comics

V2#1-10			1.50
11-14		.70	1.75

LITTLE ARCHIE MYSTERY
Aug, 1963 - No. 2, Oct, 1963 (12¢ issues)
Archie Publications

1	9.00	27.00	90.00
2	4.50	13.50	45.00

LITTLE ASPIRIN (See Little Lenny & Wisco)
July, 1949 - No. 3, Dec, 1949 (52 pgs.)
Marvel Comics (CnPC)

1-Oscar app.; Kurtzman-a (4 pgs.)	13.00	39.00	90.00
2-Kurtzman-a (4 pgs.)	8.35	25.00	50.00
3-No Kurtzman-a	4.25	13.00	26.00

LITTLE AUDREY (Also see Playful…)
Apr, 1948 - No. 24, May, 1952
St. John Publ.

1-1st app. Little Audrey	38.00	114.00	265.00
2	17.00	51.00	120.00
3-5	11.50	34.00	80.00
6-10	8.35	25.00	50.00
11-20: 16-X-Mas-c	5.00	15.00	30.00
21-24	4.00	12.00	24.00

LITTLE AUDREY (See Harvey Hits #11, 19)
No. 25, Aug, 1952 - No. 53, April, 1957
Harvey Publications

25-(Paramount Pictures Famous Star… on-c)	7.50	22.50	75.00
26-30: 26-28-Casper app.	4.00	12.00	40.00
31-40: 32-35-Casper app.	3.50	10.50	35.00
41-53	2.00	6.00	20.00
…Clubhouse 1 (9/61, 68 pg. Giant)-New stories & reprints			
	6.00	18.00	60.00

LITTLE AUDREY
Aug, 1992 - No. 8, July, 1993 ($1.25/$1.50)
Harvey Comics

V2#1-5			1.25
6-8 ($1.50)			1.50

LITTLE AUDREY (…Yearbook)
1950 (50¢, 260 pgs.)
St. John Publishing Co.

Contains 8 complete 1949 comics rebound; Casper, Alice in Wonderland, Little Audrey,
Abbott & Costello, Pinocchio, Moon Mullins, Three Stooges (from Jubilee), Little Annie
Rooney app. (Rare)   67.00   202.00   540.00

Rooney app. (Rare)	67.00	202.00	540.00

(Also see All Good & Treasury of Comics)
NOTE: *This book contains remaindered St. John comics; many variations possible.*

LITTLE AUDREY & MELVIN (Audrey & Melvin No. 62)
May, 1962 - No. 61, Dec, 1973
Harvey Publications

1	6.00	18.00	60.00
2-5	3.00	9.00	30.00
6-10	2.00	6.00	20.00
11-20	2.00	6.00	14.00
21-40: 22-Richie Rich app.	1.50	3.75	9.00
41-50,55-61	1.00	2.60	6.00
51-54: All 52 pg. Giants	1.20	3.00	7.00

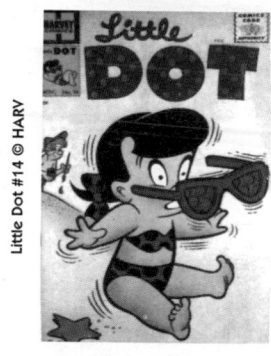
Little Dot #14 © HARV

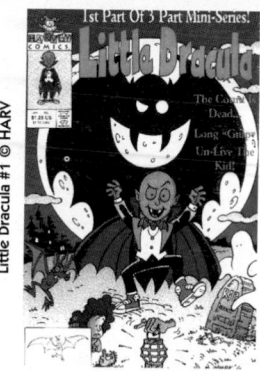
1st Part Of 3 Part Mini-Series!
Little Dracula #1 © HARV

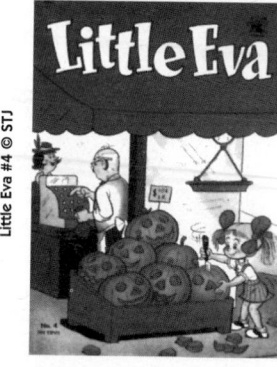
Little Eva #4 © STJ

	GD25	FN65	NM94

LITTLE AUDREY TV FUNTIME
Sept, 1962 - No. 33, Oct, 1971 (#1-31: 68 pgs.; #32,33: 52 pgs.)
Harvey Publications

1-Richie Rich app.	5.00	15.00	50.00
2,3: Richie Rich app.	3.80	11.40	38.00
4,5: 5-25¢ & 35¢ issues exist	3.00	9.00	30.00
6-10	1.70	5.00	12.00
11-20	1.30	3.25	8.00
21-33	1.00	2.60	6.00

LITTLE BAD WOLF (Disney; seeWalt Disney's C&S #52, Walt Disney
Showcase #21 & Wheaties)
No. 403, June, 1952 - No. 564, June, 1954
Dell Publishing Co.

Four Color 403 (#1)	8.00	24.00	80.00
Four Color 473 (6/53), 564	5.00	15.00	50.00

LITTLE BEAVER
No. 211, Jan, 1949 - No. 870, Jan, 1958 (All painted-c)
Dell Publishing Co.

Four Color 211('49)-All Harman-a	7.50	22.50	75.00
Four Color 267,294,332(5/51)	3.80	11.40	38.00
3(10-12/51)-8(1-3/53)	3.50	10.50	35.00
Four Color 483(8-10/53),529	3.50	10.50	35.00
Four Color 612,660,695,744,817,870	3.00	9.00	30.00

LITTLE BIT
Mar, 1949 - No. 2, June, 1949
Jubilee/St. John Publishing Co.

1,2	4.25	13.00	28.00

LITTLE DOT (See Humphrey, Li'l Max, Sad Sack, and Tastee-Freez Comics)
Sept, 1953 - No. 164, Apr, 1976
Harvey Publications

1-Intro./1st app. Richie Rich & Little Lotta	70.00	210.00	700.00
2-1st app. Freckles & Pee Wee (Richie Rich's poor friends)			
	30.00	90.00	300.00
3	19.00	57.00	185.00
4	14.00	42.00	140.00
5-Origin dots on Little Dot's dress	21.00	63.00	210.00
6-Richie Rich, Little Lotta, & Little Dot all on cover; 1st Richie Rich cover featured	17.00	51.00	170.00
7-10: 9-Last pre-code issue (1/55)	10.00	30.00	100.00
11-20	7.50	22.50	75.00
21-40	4.00	12.50	40.00
41-60	2.00	6.00	20.00
61-80	1.70	5.00	14.00
81-100	1.20	3.00	7.00
101-141	1.00	2.00	5.00
142-145: All 52 pg. Giants	1.20	3.00	7.00
146-164		.80	2.00
Shoe store giveaway 2	4.50	13.00	35.00
NOTE: Richie Rich & Little Lotta in all.			

LITTLE DOT
Sept, 1992 - No. 7, June, 1994 ($1.25/$1.50)
Harvey Comics

V2#1-3: Little Dot, Little Lotta, Richie Rich in all			1.25
4-7 ($1.50)			1.50

LITTLE DOT DOTLAND (Dot Dotland No. 62, 63)
July, 1962 - No. 61, Dec, 1973
Harvey Publications

1-Richie Rich begins	7.00	21.00	70.00
2,3	3.50	10.50	35.00
4,5	3.00	9.00	30.00

6-10	2.60	7.50	18.00
11-20	2.00	6.00	14.00
21-30	1.30	3.25	8.00
31-50,55-61	1.00	2.60	6.00
51-54: All 52 pg. Giants	1.50	3.75	9.00

LITTLE DOT'S UNCLES & AUNTS (See Harvey Hits No. 4, 13, 24)
Oct, 1961; No. 2, Aug, 1962 - No. 52, Apr, 1974
Harvey Enterprises

1-Richie Rich begins; 68 pgs. begin	8.00	24.00	80.00
2,3	4.00	12.00	40.00
4,5	3.00	9.00	30.00
6-10	2.85	8.50	20.00
11-20	2.00	6.00	14.00
21-37: Last 68 pg. issue	1.50	3.75	9.00
38-52: All 52 pg. Giants	1.30	3.25	8.00

LITTLE DRACULA
Jan, 1992 - No. 3, May, 1992 ($1.25, quarterly, mini-series)
Harvey Comics

1-3			1.25

LITTLE EVA
May, 1952 - No. 31, Nov, 1956
St. John Publishing Co.

1	10.00	30.00	70.00
2	5.85	17.50	35.00
3-5	4.00	11.00	22.00
6-10	3.20	8.00	16.00
11-31	2.80	7.00	14.00
3-D 1,2(10/53, 11/53, 25¢)-Both came w/glasses. 1-Infinity-c			
	16.00	47.00	110.00
I.W. Reprint #1-3,6-8: 1- r/Little Eva #28. 2- r/Little Eva #29. 3- r/Little Eva #24			
	1.00	2.00	5.00
Super Reprint #10,12('63),14,16,18('64): 18- r/Little Eva #25.			
	1.00	2.00	5.00

LITTLE FIR TREE, THE
nd (1942) (8-1/2x11") (12 pgs. with cover, color & B&W, heavy paper)
W. T. Grant Co. (Christmas giveaway)

nn-Story by Hans Christian Anderson; 8 pg. Kelly-r/Santa Claus Funnies (not signed); X-Mas-c
(One copy in Mint sold for $1750.00 in 1986 & another copy
in VF sold for $1000.00 in 1991)

LI'L GENIUS (Summer Fun No. 54) (See Blue Bird & Giant Comics #3)
1954 - No. 52, 1/65; No. 53, 10/65; No. 54, 10/85 - No. 55, 1/86
Charlton Comics

1	10.00	30.00	60.00
2	5.00	15.00	30.00
3-15,19,20	4.00	10.00	20.00
16,17-(68 pgs.)	4.25	13.00	26.00
18-(100 pgs., 10/58)	6.35	19.00	38.00
21-35	3.60	9.00	18.00
36-53	1.50	3.75	9.00
54,55			1.50

LI'L GHOST
Feb, 1958; Nov?, 1958 - No. 3, Mar, 1959
St. John Publishing Co./Fago No. 1 on

1(St. John)	7.00	21.00	42.00
1(Fago)-Fago-c/a begins	4.25	13.00	28.00
2,3: 2-(1/59)	4.00	11.00	22.00

LITTLE GIANT COMICS
7/38 - No. 3, 10/38; No. 4, 2/39 (132 pgs.) (6-3/4x4-1/2")
Centaur Publications

Li'l Jinx #1 © AP

Little Joe #1 © STJ

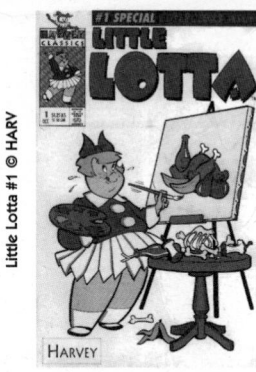

Little Lotta #1 © HARV

	GD25	FN65	NM94
1-B&W with color-c; stories, puzzles, magic	50.00	150.00	400.00
2,3-B&W with color-c	44.00	132.00	350.00
4 (6-5/8x9-3/8")(68 pgs., B&W inside)	45.00	136.00	365.00

NOTE: *Filchock* c-2, 4. *Gustavson* a-1. *Pinajian* a-4. *Bob Wood* a-1.

LITTLE GIANT DETECTIVE FUNNIES
Oct, 1938 - No. 4, Jan, 1939 (6-3/4x4-1/2", 132 pgs., B&W)
Centaur Publications

1-B&W with color-c	58.00	176.00	470.00
2,3	45.00	135.00	360.00
4(1/39, B&W; color-c; 68 pgs., 6-1/2x9-1/2")-Eisner-r	47.00	141.00	375.00

LITTLE GIANT MOVIE FUNNIES
Aug, 1938 - No. 2, Oct, 1938 (6-3/4x4-1/2", 132 pgs., B&W)
Centaur Publications

1-Ed Wheelan's "Minute Movies" reprints	58.00	176.00	470.00
2-Ed Wheelan's "Minute Movies" reprints	44.00	133.00	355.00

LITTLE GROUCHO (...the Red-Headed Tornado; ...Grouchy No. 2)
No. 16; Feb-Mar, 1955 - No. 2, June-July, 1955 (See Tippy Terry)
Reston Publ. Co.

16, 1 (2-3/55)	6.70	20.00	40.00
2(6-7/55)	4.25	13.00	26.00

LITTLE HIAWATHA (Disney; see Walt Disney's C&S #143)
No. 439, Dec, 1952 - No. 988, May-July, 1959
Dell Publishing Co.

Four Color 439 (#1)	6.00	18.00	60.00
Four Color 787 (4/57), 901 (5/58), 988	5.00	15.00	50.00

LITTLE IKE
April, 1953 - No. 4, Oct, 1953
St. John Publishing Co.

1	8.70	26.00	52.00
2	4.25	13.00	28.00
3,4	4.00	11.00	22.00

LITTLE IODINE (See Giant Comic Album)
No. 224, 4/49 - No. 257, 1949: 3-5/50 - No. 56, 4-6/62 (1-4: 52pgs.)
Dell Publishing Co.

Four Color 224-By Jimmy Hatlo	9.00	27.00	90.00
Four Color 257	7.00	21.00	70.00
1(3-5/50)	9.00	27.00	90.00
2-5	3.60	10.80	36.00
6-10	2.70	8.10	27.00
11-20	2.60	7.50	18.00
21-30: 27-Xmas-c	2.30	6.70	16.00
31-40	1.70	5.00	12.00
41-56	1.50	3.75	9.00

LITTLE JACK FROST
1951
Avon Periodicals

1	6.70	20.00	40.00

LI'L JINX (Little Archie in Animal Land #17) (Also see Pep Comics #62)
Nov, 1956 - No. 6, Sept, 1957
Archie Publications

1-By Joe Edwards	10.00	30.00	60.00
2-6	6.70	20.00	40.00

LI'L JINX (See Archie Giant Series Magazine No. 223)

LI'L JINX CHRISTMAS BAG (See Archie Giant Series Mag. No. 195, 206, 219)

LI'L JINX GIANT LAUGH-OUT (See Archie Giant Series Mag. No. 176, 185)
No. 33, Sept, 1971 - No. 43, Nov, 1973 (52 pgs.)
Archie Publications

	GD25	FN65	NM94
33-43		1.40	3.50

LITTLE JOE (See Popular Comics & Super Comics)
No. 1, 1942
Dell Publishing Co.

Four Color 1	45.00	135.00	450.00

LITTLE JOE
Apr, 1953
St. John Publishing Co.

1	4.00	10.00	20.00

LI'L KIDS (Also see Li'l Pals)
8/70 - No. 2, 10/70; No. 3, 11/71 - No. 12, 6/73
Marvel Comics Group

1	1.50	3.75	9.00
2-12: 10-12-Calvin app.		1.80	4.50

LITTLE KING
No. 494, Aug, 1953 - No. 677, Feb, 1956
Dell Publishing Co.

Four Color 494 (#1)	10.00	30.00	100.00
Four Color 597, 677	7.00	21.00	70.00

LITTLE KLINKER
Nov, 1960 (20 pgs.) (slick cover)
Little Klinker Ventures (Montgomery Ward Giveaway)

nn	1.70	5.00	12.00

LITTLE LANA (Formerly Lana)
No. 8, Nov, 1949; No. 9, Mar, 1950
Marvel Comics (MjMC)

8,9	5.85	17.50	35.00

LITTLE LENNY
June, 1949 - No. 3, Nov, 1949
Marvel Comics (CDS)

1-Little Aspirin app.	9.15	27.00	55.00
2,3	4.25	13.00	28.00

LITTLE LIZZIE
6/49 - No. 5, 4/50; 9/53 - No. 3, Jan, 1954
Marvel Comics (PrPl)/Atlas (OMC)

1	10.00	30.00	65.00
2-5	5.85	17.50	35.00
1 (9/53, 2nd series by Atlas)-Howie Post-c	6.70	20.00	40.00
2,3	4.25	13.00	28.00

LITTLE LOTTA (See Harvey Hits No. 10)
11/55 - No. 110, 11/73; No. 111, 9/74 - No. 120, 5/76
V2#1, Oct, 1992 - No. 4, July, 1993 ($1.25)
Harvey Publications

1-Richie Rich (r) & Little Dot begin	29.00	87.00	290.00
2,3	13.00	39.00	125.00
4,5	6.50	19.50	65.00
6-10	5.50	16.50	55.00
11-20	3.50	10.50	35.00
21-40	3.25	9.50	22.00
41-60	2.60	7.50	18.00
61-80	2.00	6.00	14.00
81-99	1.30	3.25	8.00
100-103: All 52 pg. Giants	1.50	3.75	9.00
104-120	1.00	2.00	5.00
V2#1-4 (1992-93)			1.25

NOTE: *No. 121 was advertised, but never released.*

LITTLE LOTTA FOODLAND
9/63 - No. 14, 10/67; No. 15, 10/68 - No. 29, Oct, 1972

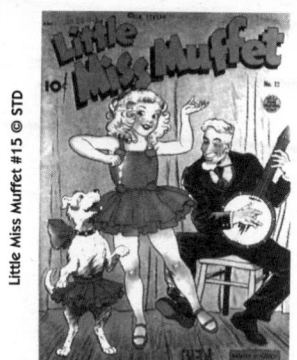
Little Miss Muffet #15 © STD

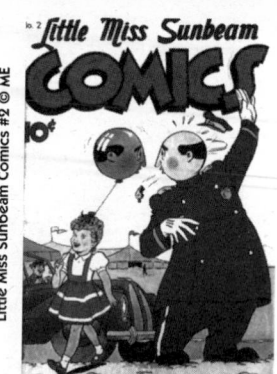
Little Miss Sunbeam Comics #2 © ME

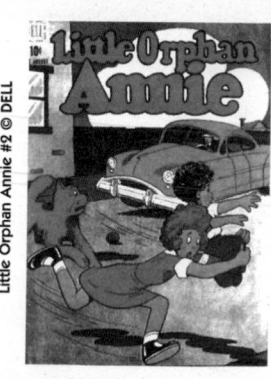
Little Orphan Annie #2 © DELL

	GD25	FN65	NM94

Harvey Publications

	GD25	FN65	NM94
1-Little Lotta, Little Dot, Richie Rich, 68 pgs. begin	10.00	30.00	100.00
2,3	6.00	18.00	60.00
4,5	4.00	12.00	40.00
6-10	3.00	9.00	30.00
11-20	2.00	6.00	20.00
21-26: 26-Last 68 pg. issue	1.70	5.00	14.00
27,28: Both 52 pgs.	1.70	5.00	14.00
29-(36 pgs.)	1.00	2.60	7.00

LITTLE LULU (Formerly Marge's...)
No. 207, Sept, 1972 - No. 268, April, 1984
Gold Key 207-257/Whitman 258 on

207,209,220-Stanley-r. 207-1st app. Henrietta	1.30	3.25	8.00
208,210-219: 208-1st app. Snobbly, Wilbur's brother	1.00	2.60	6.00
221-240,242-249, 250(r/#166), 251-254(r/#206)	1.60	4.00	
241,263,268-Stanley-r	1.60	4.00	
255-262,264-267: 256-r/#212	.80	2.00	

LITTLE MARY MIXUP (See Comics On Parade)
No. 10, 1939, - No. 26, 1940
United Features Syndicate

Single Series 10, 26	30.00	90.00	210.00

LITTLE MAX COMICS (Joe Palooka's Pal; see Joe Palooka)
Oct, 1949 - No. 73, Nov, 1961
Harvey Publications

1-Infinity-c; Little Dot begins; Joe Palooka on-c	15.00	45.00	105.00
2-Little Dot app.; Joe Palooka on-c	8.70	26.00	52.00
3-Little Dot app.; Joe Palooka on-c	6.00	18.00	36.00
4-10: 5-Little Dot app., 1pg.	4.00	12.00	24.00
11-20	3.60	9.00	18.00
21-73: 23-Little Dot app. 38-r/#20. 63,65,67,69-Include new five pg. Richie Rich stories 70-73-Little Lotta, Richie Rich app.	1.70	5.00	12.00

LI'L MENACE
Dec, 1958 - No. 3, May, 1959
Fago Magazine Co.

1-Peter Rabbit app.	6.35	19.00	38.00
2-Peter Rabbit (Vincent Fago's)	4.25	13.00	28.00
3	4.00	12.00	24.00

LITTLE MERMAID, THE (Walt Disney's...; also see Disney's...)
1990 (no date given)($5.95, no ads, 52 pgs.)
W. D. Publications (Disney)

n-Adapts animated movie	1.00	2.50	6.00
n-Comic version ($2.50)		1.00	2.50

LITTLE MERMAID, THE
1992 - No. 4, 1992 ($1.50, mini-series)
Disney Comics

1-4: Based on movie			1.50
1-4: 2nd printings sold at Wal-Mart w/different-c			1.50

LITTLE MISS MUFFET
No. 11, Dec, 1948 - No. 13, March, 1949
Best Books (Standard Comics)/King Features Synd.

11-Strip reprints; Fanny Cory-c/a	7.50	22.50	45.00
12,13-Strip reprints; Fanny Cory-c/a	5.00	15.00	30.00

LITTLE MISS SUNBEAM COMICS
June-July, 1950 - No. 4, Dec-Jan, 1950-51
Magazine Enterprises/Quality Bakers of America

1	11.50	34.00	80.00
2-4	6.70	20.00	40.00
..Advs. In Space ('55)	4.35	13.00	26.00
Bread Giveaway 1-4(Quality Bakers, 1949-50)-14 pgs. each			

	GD25	FN65	NM94
	4.00	12.00	24.00
Bread Giveaway (1957,61; 16pgs, reg. size)	4.00	11.00	22.00

LITTLE MONSTERS, THE (See March of Comics #423, Three Stooges #17)
Nov, 1964 - No. 44, Feb, 1978
Gold Key

1	3.60	9.00	18.00
2	1.80	4.50	9.00
3-10	1.40	3.50	7.00
11-20		1.40	3.50
21-44: 20,34-39,43-Reprints			1.50

LITTLE MONSTERS (Movie)
1989 - No. 6, June, 1990 ($1.75)
Now Comics

..1-6: Photo-c from movie		.90	1.80

LITTLE NEMO (See Cocomalt, Future Comics, Help, Jest, Kayo, Punch, Red Seal, & Superworld; most by Winsor McCay Jr., son of famous artist) (Other McCay books: see Little Sammy Sneeze & Dreams of the Rarebit Fiend)

LITTLE NEMO (...in Slumberland)
1945 (11x7-1/4", 28 pgs., B&W)
McCay Features/Nostalgia Press('69)

1905 & 1911 reprints by Winsor McCay	9.15	27.50	55.00
1969-70 (Exact reprint)	2.00	5.00	10.00

LITTLE ORPHAN ANNIE (See Annie, Famous Feature Stories, Marvel Super Special, Merry Christmas..., Popular Comics, Super Book #7, 11, 23 & Super Comics)

LITTLE ORPHAN ANNIE
No. 7, 1937 - No. 3, Sept-Nov, 1948; No. 206, Dec, 1948
David McKay Publ./Dell Publishing Co.

Feature Books(McKay) 7-(1937) (Rare)	85.00	255.00	850.00
Four Color 12(1941)	48.50	145.50	485.00
Four Color 18(1943)-Flag-c	38.00	114.00	380.00
Four Color 52(1944)	30.00	90.00	300.00
Four Color 76(1945)	24.00	72.00	245.00
Four Color 107(1946)	22.00	67.00	215.00
Four Color 152(1947)	14.00	45.00	140.00
1(3-5/48)-r/strips from 5/7/44 to 7/30/44	14.00	45.00	140.00
2-r/strips from 7/21/40 to 9/9/40	9.50	28.50	95.00
3-r/strips from 9/10/40 to 11/9/40	9.50	28.50	95.00
Four Color 206(12/48)	7.50	22.50	75.00
Junior Commandos Giveaway (same-c as 4-Color #18, K.K. Publ.)(Big Shoe Store); same back cover as '47 Popped Wheat giveaway; 16 pgs; flag-c; r/strips 9/7/42-10/10/42	31.00	92.00	215.00
Popped Wheat Giveaway ('47)-16 pgs. full color; reprints strips from 5/3/40 to 6/20/40	1.60	4.00	8.00
Quaker Sparkies Giveaway (1940)	18.00	54.00	125.00
Quaker Sparkies Giveaway (1941, full color, 20 pgs.); "LOA and the Rescue"; r/strips 4/13/39-6/21/39 & 7/6/39-7/17/39. "LOA and the Kidnappers"; r/strips 11/28/38-1/28/39	15.00	45.00	105.00
Quaker Sparkies Giveaway (1942, full color, 20 pgs.); "LOA and Mr. Gudge", r/strips 2/13/38-3/21/38 & 4/18/37-5/30/37. "LOA and the Great Am"	13.00	39.00	90.00

LI'L PALS (Also see Li'l Kids)
Sept, 1972 - No. 5, May, 1973
Marvel Comics Group

1-5		1.40	3.50

LI'L PAN (Formerly Rocket Kelly; becomes Junior Comics with #9)
No. 6, Dec-Jan, 1946-47 - No. 8, Apr-May, 1947 (Also see Wotalife Comics)
Fox Features Syndicate

6	7.50	22.50	45.00
7,8: 7-Atomic bomb story	5.00	15.00	30.00

LITTLE PEOPLE

The Living Bible #3 © Living Bible Corp.

Lobo #3 (Limited Series) #3 © DC

Lobo #33 © DC

	GD25	FN65	NM94

No. 485, Aug-Oct, 1953 - No. 1062, Dec, 1959 (Walt Scott's)
Dell Publishing Co.

	GD25	FN65	NM94
Four Color 485 (#1)	7.00	21.00	70.00
Four Color 573(7/54), 633(6/55)	4.00	12.00	40.00
Four Color 692(3/56),753(11/56),809(7/57),868(12/57),908(5/58), 959(12/58), 1062	4.00	12.00	40.00
Four Color 1024-Darby O'Gill &...-Movie, Toth-a, photo-c	13.00	40.00	125.00

LITTLE RASCALS
No. 674, Jan, 1956 - No. 1297, Mar-May, 1962
Dell Publishing Co.

Four Color 674 (#1)	7.00	21.00	70.00
Four Color 778(3/57),825(8/57)	4.00	12.00	40.00
Four Color 883(3/58),936(9/58),974(3/59),1030(9/59),1079(2-4/60),1137 (9-11/60)	4.00	12.00	40.00
Four Color 1174(3-5/61),1224(10-12/61),1297	3.00	9.00	30.00

LI'L RASCAL TWINS (Formerly Nature Boy)
No. 6, 1957 - No. 18, Jan, 1960
Charlton Comics

6-Li'l Genius & Tomboy in all	5.00	15.00	30.00
7-18	3.20	8.00	16.00

LITTLE ROQUEFORT COMICS (See Paul Terry's Comics #105)
June, 1952 - No. 9, Oct, 1953; No. 10, Summer, 1958
St. John Publishing Co.(all pre-code)/Pines No. 10

1-By Paul Terry	9.15	27.00	55.00
2	4.25	13.00	26.00
3-10: 10-CBS Television Presents on-c	4.00	10.00	20.00

LITTLE SAD SACK (See Harvey Hits No. 73, 76, 79, 81, 83)
Oct, 1964 - No. 19, Nov, 1967
Harvey Publications

1-Richie Rich app. on cover only	2.00	6.00	20.00
2-19	1.50	3.75	9.00

LITTLE SCOUTS
No. 321, Mar, 1951 - No. 587, Oct, 1954
Dell Publishing Co.

Four Color #321 (#1, 3/51)	3.60	10.80	36.00
2(10-12/51) - 6(10-12/52)	1.80	5.40	18.00
Four Color #462,506,550,587	1.80	5.40	18.00

LITTLE SHOP OF HORRORS SPECIAL (Movie)
Feb, 1987 ($2.00, 68 pgs.)
DC Comics

1-Colan-c/a		.80	2.00

LITTLE SPUNKY
No date (1963?) (10¢)
I. W. Enterprises

1-r/Frisky Fables #1	1.00	2.60	6.00

LITTLE STOOGES, THE (The Three Stooges' Sons)
Sept, 1972 - No. 7, Mar, 1974
Gold Key

1-Norman Maurer cover/stories in all	1.30	3.25	8.00
2-7		1.60	4.00

LITTLEST OUTLAW (Disney)
No. 609, Jan, 1955
Dell Publishing Co.

Four Color 609-Movie, photo-c	7.00	21.00	70.00

LITTLEST SNOWMAN, THE
No. 755, 12/56; No. 864, 12/57; 12-2/1963-64
Dell Publishing Co.

Four Color #755,864, 1(1964)	3.60	11.00	36.00

LI'L TOMBOY (Formerly Fawcett's Funny Animals; see Giant Comics #3)
V14#92, Oct, 1956; No. 93, Mar, 1957 - No. 107, Feb, 1960
Charlton Comics

V14#92	4.35	13.00	26.00
93-107: 97-Atomic Bunny app.	4.00	10.00	20.00

LITTLE TREE THAT WASN'T WANTED, THE
1960, (Color, 28 pgs.)
W. T. Grant Co. (Giveaway)

nn-Christmas giveaway	1.70	5.00	12.00

LI'L WILLIE COMICS (Formerly & becomes Willie Comics #22 on)
No. 20, July, 1949 - No. 21, Sept, 1949
Marvel Comics (MgPC)

20,21: 20-Little Aspirin app.	6.35	19.00	38.00

LITTLE WOMEN (See Power Record Comics)

LIVE IT UP
1973, 1976 (39-49 cents)
Spire Christian Comics (Fleming H. Revell Co.)

nn			1.00

LIVING BIBLE, THE
Fall, 1945 - No. 3, Spring, 1946
Living Bible Corp.

1-The Life of Paul; all have L. B. Cole-c	32.00	96.00	225.00
2-Joseph & His Brethren; Jonah & the Whale	20.00	60.00	140.00
3-Chaplains At War (classic-c)	33.00	99.00	230.00

LOBO
Dec, 1965; No. 2, Oct, 1966
Dell Publishing Co.

1,2-1st black character to have his own title.	1.00	3.00	10.00

LOBO (Also see Action #650, Adventures of Superman, Demon (2nd series), Justice League, L.E.G.I.O.N., Mister Miracle, Omega Men #3 & Superman #41)
Nov, 1990 - No. 4, Feb, 1991 ($1.50, color, limited series)
DC Comics

1-(99¢)-Giffen plots/Breakdowns in all		1.60	4.00
2-Legion '89 spin-off		.80	2.00
3,4: 1-4 have Bisley painted covers & art		1.00	2.50
...: Blazing Chain of Love 1 (9/92, $1.50)-Denys Cowan-c/a; Alan Grant scripts			1.50
...Convention Special 1 (1993, $1.75)		.70	1.75
...Paramilitary Christmas Special 1 (1991, $2.39, 52 pgs.)-Bisley-c/a		.80	2.50
...: Portrait of a Victim 1 (1993, $1.75)		.70	1.75

LOBO (Also see Showcase '95 #9)
Dec, 1993 - Present ($1.75/$1.95, mature)
DC Comics

1 ($2.95)-Foil enhanced-c; Alan Grant scripts begin		1.40	3.50
2-7-Alan Grant scripts		.70	1.75
0,8,-15: 8-Begin $1.95-c. 9-(9/94). 0-(10/94)-Origin retold		.80	2.00
16-40: 16-Begin $2.25-c			2.25
Annual 1 (1993, $3.50, 68 pgs.)-Bloodlines x-over		1.40	3.50
Annual 2 (1994, $3.50)-21 artists (20 listed on-c); Alan Grant script; Elseworlds story		1.40	3.50
Annual 3 (1995, $3.95)-Year One story			4.00
...Big Babe Spring Break Special (Spr, '95, $1.95)-Balent-a		.80	2.00
...Bounty Hunting for Fun and Profit ('95)-Bisley-c	1.00	2.00	5.00
...Lobocop 1 (2/94, $1.95)-Alan Grant scripts; painted-c		.80	2.00
.../Deadman: The Brave And The Bald (2/95, $3.50)		1.40	3.50
...Gallery (9/95, $3.50)-pin-ups.			3.50

Lobo Goes to Hollywood #1 © DC

Logan's Run #5 © MEG

Lois Lane #1 © DC

	GD25	FN65	NM94
...In the Chair 1 (8/94, $1.95, 36 pgs.)		.80	2.00
...I Quit-(12/95, $2.25)			2.25
.../Judge Dredd ('95, $4.95)-Alan Grant story.			5.00

LOBO: A CONTRACT ON GAWD
Apr, 1994 - July, 1994 ($1.75, mini-series, mature)
DC Comics

1-4: Alan Grant scripts. 3-Groo cameo		.70	1.75

LOBO: DEATH AND TAXES
Oct, 1996 - Jan, 1997 ($2.25, mini-series)
DC Comics

1-4-Giffen/Grant scripts			2.25

LOBO GOES TO HOLLYWOOD
Aug, 1996 ($2.25, one shot)
DC Comics

1-Grant scripts			2.25

LOBO: INFANTICIDE
Oct, 1992 - Jan, 1993 ($1.50, mini-series, mature)
DC Comics

1-4-Giffen-c/a; Alan Grant scripts			1.50

LOBO: UNAMERICAN GLADIATORS
Jun, 1993 - Sep, 1993 ($1.75, mini-series, mature)
DC Comics

1-4-Mignola-c; Grant/Wagner scripts		.70	1.75

LOBO'S BACK
May, 1992 - No. 4, Nov, 1992 ($1.50, mini-series, mature)
DC Comics

1-4: 1-Has 3 outer covers. Bisley painted-c 1,2; a-1-3. 3-Sam Kieth-c; all have			
Giffen plots/breakdown & Grant scripts			1.50
Trade paperback (1993, $9.95)-r/1-4	1.70	4.20	10.00

LOCKE!
1987 - No. 3, ($1.25, limited series)
Blackthorne Publishing

1-3			1.25

LOCO (Magazine) (Satire)
Aug, 1958 - V1#3, Jan, 1959
Satire Publications

1#1-Chic Stone-a	4.35	13.00	26.00
1#2,3-Severin-a, 2 pgs. Davis; 3-Heath-a	4.00	10.00	20.00

LOGAN: PATH OF THE WARLORD
Feb, 1996 ($5.95, one-shot)
Marvel Comics

1-John Paul Leon-a			6.00

LOGAN'S RUN
Jan, 1977 - No. 7, July, 1977
Marvel Comics Group

1: 1-5-Based on novel & movie		1.40	3.50
2-5,7: 6,7-New stories adapted from novel		.80	2.00
6-1st Thanos solo story (back-up) by Zeck (6/77)	1.65	4.20	10.00
NOTE: Austin a-6i. Gulacy c-6. Kane c-7p. Perez a-1-5p; c-1-5p. Sutton a-6p, 7p.			

LOIS & CLARK, THE NEW ADVENTURES OF SUPERMAN
1994 ($9.95, one-shot)
DC Comics

nn-r/Man of Steel #2, Superman Annual 1, Superman #9 & 11, Action #600 &			
655, Adventures of Superman #445, 462 & 466	1.70	4.20	10.00

LOIS LANE (Also see Daring New Adventures of Supergirl, Showcase #9,10 & Superman's Girlfriend...)
Aug, 1986 - No. 2, Sept, 1986 ($1.50, 52 pgs.)

	GD25	FN65	NM94
DC Comics			
1,2-Morrow-c/a in each			1.50

LOLLY AND PEPPER
No. 832, Sept, 1957 - July, 1962
Dell Publishing Co.

Four Color 832(#1)	4.00	12.00	40.00
Four Color 940,978,1086,1206	3.00	9.00	30.00
01-459-207 (7/62)	3.00	9.00	30.00

LOMAX (See Police Action)

LONDON NIGHT LINGERIE SPECIAL
1996 ($3.00/$10.00, one-shot)
London Night Studios

1-($3.00)-Nice Edition; JJ North photo-c			3.00

LONDON'S DARK
1989 ($8.95, B&W, graphic novel)
Escape/Titan

nn-James Robinson script; Paul Johnson-c/a			9.00

LONE EAGLE (The Flame No. 5 on)
Apr-May, 1954 - No. 4, Oct-Nov, 1954
Ajax/Farrell Publications

1	10.00	30.00	70.00
2-4: 3-Bondage-c	6.70	20.00	40.00

LONELY HEART (Formerly Dear Lonely Hearts; Dear Heart #15 on)
No. 9, Mar, 1955 - No. 14, Feb, 1956
Ajax/Farrell Publ. (Excellent Publ.)

9-Kamenesque-a; (Last precode)	7.00	21.00	42.00
10-14	4.25	13.00	26.00

LONE RANGER, THE (See Ace Comics, Aurora, Dell Giants, Future Comics, Golden Comics Digest #48, King Comics, Magic Comics & March of Comics #165, 174, 193, 208, 225, 238, 310, 322, 338, 350)

LONE RANGER, THE
No. 3, 1939 - No. 167, Feb, 1947
Dell Publishing Co.

Large Feature Comic 3(1939)-Heigh-Yo Silver; text with illus. by Robert Weisman; also exists as a Whitman #710	77.50	232.50	775.00
Large Feature Comic 7(1939)-Illustr. by Henry Vallely; Hi-Yo Silver the Lone Ranger to the Rescue; also exists as a Whitman #715	82.50	247.50	825.00
Feature Book 21(1940), 24(1941)	62.50	187.50	625.00
Four Color 82(1945)	42.50	127.50	425.00
Four Color 98(1945),118(1946)	31.00	93.00	310.00
Four Color 125(1946),136(1947)	21.00	63.00	210.00
Four Color 151,167(1947)	17.00	51.00	170.00

LONE RANGER, THE (Movie, radio & TV; Clayton Moore starred as Lone Ranger in the movies; No. 1-37: strip reprints)(See Dell Giants)
Jan-Feb, 1948 - No. 145, May-July, 1962
Dell Publishing Co.

1 (36 pgs.)-The Lone Ranger, his horse Silver, companion Tonto & his horse Scout begin	60.00	180.00	600.00
2 (52 pgs. begin, end #41)	28.00	84.00	280.00
3-5	21.00	63.00	210.00
6,7,9,10	17.50	52.50	175.00
8-Origin retold; Indian back-c begin, end #35	22.00	66.00	215.00
11-20: 11- "Young Hawk" Indian boy serial begins, ends #145	11.00	33.00	105.00
21,22,24-31: 51-Reprint. 31-1st Mask logo	9.00	27.00	90.00
23-Origin retold	12.00	36.00	115.00
32-37: 32-Painted-c begin. 36-Animal photo back-c begin, end #49. 37-Last newspaper-r issue; new outfit	7.00	21.00	70.00

	GD25	FN65	NM94
38-41 (All 52 pgs.)	6.50	19.50	63.00
42-50 (36 pgs.)	5.50	16.50	54.00
51-74 (52 pgs.): 56-One pg. origin story of Lone Ranger & Tonto. 71-Blank inside-c	5.50	16.50	54.00
75-99: 76-Flag-c. 79-X-mas-c	4.50	13.50	45.00
100	6.50	19.50	63.00
101-111: Last painted-c	4.50	13.50	45.00
112-Clayton Moore photo-c begin, end #145	17.00	52.00	165.00
113-117	8.00	24.00	90.00
118-Origin Lone Ranger, Tonto, & Silver retold; Special anniversary issue	24.00	72.00	240.00
119-145: 139-Last issue by Fran Striker	7.00	21.00	75.00
Cheerios Giveaways (1954, 16 pgs., 2-1/2x7", soft-c) #1- "The Lone Ranger, His Mask & How He Met Tonto". #2- "The Lone Ranger & the Story of Silver" each....	15.00	45.00	105.00
Doll Giveaways (Gabriel Ind.)(1973, 3-1/4x5")- "The Story of The Lone Ranger" & "The Carson City Bank Robbery"	1.65	4.20	10.00
How the Lone Ranger Captured Silver Book(1936)-Silvercup Bread giveaway	50.00	150.00	375.00
...In Milk for Big Mike (1955, Dairy Association giveaway), soft-c; 5x7-1/4", 16 pgs.	13.00	39.00	90.00
Merita Bread giveaway (1954, 16 pgs., 5x7-1/4")- "How to Be a Lone Ranger Health & Safety Scout"	14.00	43.00	100.00

NOTE: **Hank Hartman** painted c(signed)-65, 66, 70, 75, 82; unsigned-64?, 67-69?, 71, 72, 73?, 74?, 76-78, 80, 81, 83-91, 92?, 93-111. **Ernest Nordli** painted c(signed)-42, 50, 52, 53, 56, 59, 60; unsigned-39-41, 44-49, 51, 54, 55, 57, 58, 61-63?

LONE RANGER, THE
9/64 - No. 16, 12/69; No. 17, 11/72; No. 18, 9/74 - No. 28, 3/77
Gold Key (Reprints in #13-20)

1-Retells origin	2.50	7.50	25.00
2	1.40	4.20	14.00
3-10: Small Bear-r in #6-12	1.00	3.00	9.00
11-17	.75	2.25	7.00
18-28		2.00	6.00
Golden West 1(30029-610, 10/66)-Giant; r/most Golden West #3 including Clayton Moore photo front/back-c	6.00	18.00	60.00
Legend of The Lone Ranger (1969, 16 pgs., giveaway)-Origin The Lone Ranger	1.70	5.00	12.00

LONE RANGER AND TONTO, THE
Aug, 1994 - No. 4, Nov, 1994 ($2.50, limited series)
Topps Comics

1-4: 3-Origin of Lone Ranger; Tonto leaves; Lansdale story, Truman-c/a in all.		1.00	2.50
1-4: Silver logo	1.65	4.20	10.00
Trade paperback (1/95, $9.95)			10.00

LONE RANGER COMICS, THE
Book 1, 1939(inside) (shows 1938 on-c) (52 pgs. in color; regular size)
Lone Ranger, Inc. (Ice cream mail order)

	GD25	FN65	VF82
Book 1-(Scarce) The first western comic devoted to a single character; not by Vallely	633.00	1900.00	3800.00

(Estimated up to 20 total copies exist, none in NM/Mint)

LONE RANGER'S COMPANION TONTO, THE (TV)
No. 312, Jan, 1951 - No. 33, Nov-Jan/58-59 (All painted-c)
Dell Publishing Co.

	GD25	FN65	NM94
Four Color 312(#1, 1/51)	12.00	36.00	120.00
2(8-10/51),3; (#2 titled "Tonto")	6.00	18.00	56.00
4-10	4.50	13.50	45.00
11-20	3.60	10.80	36.00
21-33	2.70	8.10	27.00

NOTE: **Ernest Nordli** painted c(signed)-2, 7; unsigned-3-6, 8-11, 12?, 13, 14, 18?, 22-24? See Aurora Comic Booklets.

LONE RANGER'S FAMOUS HORSE HI-YO SILVER, THE (TV)

	GD25	FN65	NM94
No. 369, Jan, 1952 - No. 36, Oct-Dec, 1960 (All painted-c, most by Sam Savitt			

Dell Publishing Co.
Four Color 369(#1)-Silver's origin as told by The Lone Ranger

	9.00	27.00	90.
Four Color 392(#2, 4/52)	4.50	13.50	45.
3(7-9/52)-10(4-6/52)	3.60	10.80	36.
11-36	2.70	8.10	27.

LONE RIDER (Also see The Rider)
April, 1951 - No. 26, July, 1955 (#3-on: 36 pgs.)
Superior Comics(Farrell Publications)

1 (52 pgs.)-The Lone Rider & his horse Lightnin' begin; Kamenish-a begins	17.00	49.00	115.
2 (52 pgs.)-The Golden Arrow begins (origin)	9.15	27.00	55.
3-6: 6-Last Golden Arrow	7.50	22.50	45.
7-Golden Arrow becomes Swift Arrow; origin of his shield	9.15	27.00	55.
8-Origin Swift Arrow	10.00	30.00	65.
9,10	6.70	20.00	40.
11-14	5.00	15.00	30.
15-Golden Arrow origin-r from #2, changing name to Swift Arrow	6.70	20.00	40.
16-20,22-26: 23-Apache Kid app.	5.00	15.00	30.
21-3-D effect-c	11.50	34.00	80.

LONE WOLF AND CUB
May, 1987 - Jan, 1991 ($1.95-$3.25, B&W, deluxe size)
First Comics

1		1.60	4.
1-2nd print, 3rd print		.80	2.
2		1.00	2.
2-2nd print		.80	2.
3-25: 6-72 pgs. origin ish. 8-$2.50-c begins		1.00	2.
26-30,33 ($2.95)		1.00	2.
31,32,34-38,40,42 ($3.25): 40,42-Ploog-c		1.30	3.
39-($5.95, 120 pgs.)-Ploog-c	1.00	2.60	6.
41-($3.95, 84 pgs.)-Ploog-c		1.60	4.
Deluxe Edition ($19.95, B&W)	2.85	8.50	20

NOTE: **Miller** c-1-12p; intro 1-12. **Sienkiewicz** c-13-24. **Matt Wagner** c-25-30.

LONG BOW (...Indian Boy)(See Indians & Jumbo Comics #141)
1951 - No. 9, Wint, 1952/53
Fiction House Magazines (Real Adventures Publ.)

1-Most covers by Maurice Whitman	13.00	39.00	90.
2	10.00	30.00	60.
3-9	7.50	22.50	45.

LONG HOT SUMMER, THE
July, 1995 - No. 3, Sept, 1995 ($2.95/$2.50, limited series)
DC Comics (Milestone)

1 ($2.95)		1.20	3.
2,3 ($2.50)		1.00	2.

LONG JOHN SILVER & THE PIRATES (Formerly Terry & the Pirates)
No. 30, Aug, 1956 - No. 32, March, 1957 (TV)
Charlton Comics

30-32: Whitman-c	8.00	24.00	48.

LONGSHOT (Also see X-Men, 2nd Series #10)
Sept, 1985 - No. 6, Feb, 1986 (60¢, limited series)
Marvel Comics

1-Arthur Adams/Whilce Portacio-c/a in all	1.65	4.20	10.
2	1.50	3.75	9.
3-5: 4-Spider-Man app.	1.20	3.00	7.
6-Double size	1.30	3.25	8.
Trade Paperback (1989, $16.95)-r/#1-6	2.40	7.25	17.

Looney Tunes (3rd Series) #27 © Warner Bros.

Lord Pumpkin #1 © Malibu

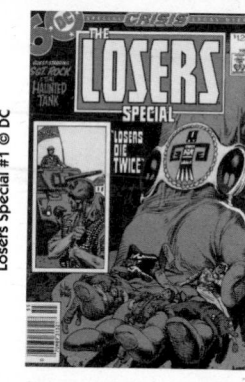

Losers Special #1 © DC

	GD25	FN65	NM94

LOONEY TUNES (2nd Series)
April, 1975 - No. 47, July, 1984
Gold Key/Whitman

1	1.00	2.00	5.00
2-47: Reprints: #1-4,16; 38-46(1/3-r)		1.20	3.00

LOONEY TUNES (3rd Series)
Apr, 1994 - Present ($1.50/$1.75)
DC Comics

1-22: 1-Marvin Martian-c/sty; Bugs Bunny, Roadrunner, Daffy, Tweety begin		
		1.50
23-30: 23-Begin $1.75-c		1.75

LOONEY TUNES AND MERRIE MELODIES COMICS ("Looney Tunes" #166 (8/55) on)(Also see Porky's Duck Hunt)
#941 - No. 246, July-Sept, 1962
Dell Publishing Co.

	GD25	FN65	VF82	NM94
1-Porky Pig, Bugs Bunny, Daffy Duck, Elmer Fudd, Mary Jane & Sniffles, Pat Patsy and Pete begin (1st comic book app. of each). Bugs Bunny story by Win Smith (early Mickey Mouse artist)				
	950.00	2850.00	5700.00	9500.00

(Estimated up to 171 total copies exist, 8 in NM/Mint)

	GD25	FN65	NM94
2 (11/41)	162.00	487.00	1300.00
3-Kandi the Cave Kid begins by Walt Kelly; also in #4-6,8,11,15			
	137.00	412.00	1100.00
4-Kelly-a	118.00	356.00	950.00
5-Bugs Bunny The Super-Duper Rabbit story (1st funny animal super hero, 3/42; also see Coo Coo); Kelly-a	106.00	318.00	850.00
6,8-Kelly-a	78.00	234.00	625.00
7,9,10: 9-Painted-c. 10-Flag-c	58.00	174.00	465.00
11,15-Kelly-a; 15-X-Mas-c	58.00	174.00	465.00
12-14,16-19	47.00	141.00	330.00
20-25: Pat, Patsy & Pete by Walt Kelly in all	40.00	120.00	290.00
26-30	30.00	90.00	210.00
31-40: 33-War bond-c. 39-X-Mas-c	18.00	56.00	170.00
41-50	15.00	46.00	140.00
51-60	10.00	31.00	95.00
61-80	7.25	22.00	65.00
90-99: 87-X-Mas-c	5.00	15.00	45.00
80	5.85	17.50	50.00
101-120	3.50	10.50	30.00
121-150	3.00	9.00	27.00
151-200: 159-X-Mas-c	2.30	6.70	16.00
201-246	1.70	5.00	12.00

LOONY SPORTS (Magazine)
Spring, 1975 (68 pgs.)
Strikes Publishing Co.

1-Sports satire		.80	2.00

LOOSE CANNON (Also see Action Comics Annual #5 & Showcase '94 #5)
June, 1995 - No. 4, Sept, 1995 ($1.75, limited series)
DC Comics

1-4: Adam Pollina-a. 1-Superman app.		.70	1.75

LOOY DOT DOPE
No. 13, 1939
United Features Syndicate

Single Series 13	26.00	79.00	185.00

LORD JIM (See Movie Comics)

LORD PUMPKIN
Oct, 1994 ($2.50, one-shot)
Malibu Comics (Ultraverse)

		1.00	2.50

LORD PUMPKIN/NECROMANTRA
Apr, 1995 - No. 4, July, 1995 ($2.95, limited series, flip book)
Malibu Comics (Ultraverse)

1-4		1.20	3.00

LORDS OF THE ULTRA-REALM
June, 1986 - No. 6, Nov, 1986 (Mini-series)
DC Comics

1		.80	2.00
2-6		.70	1.75
Special 1(12/87, $2.25)		.90	2.25

LORNA THE JUNGLE GIRL (...Jungle Queen #1-5)
July, 1953 - No. 26, Aug, 1957
Atlas Comics (NPI 1/OMC 2-11/NPI 12-26)

1-Origin & 1st app.	30.00	90.00	210.00
2-Intro. & 1st app. Greg Knight	14.00	43.00	100.00
3-5	11.50	34.00	80.00
6-11: 11-Last pre-code (1/55)	10.00	30.00	65.00
12-17,19-26: 14-Colletta & Maneely-c	8.35	25.00	50.00
18-Williamson/Colleta-c	9.15	27.00	55.00

NOTE: Brodsky c-1-3, 5, 9. Everett c-21, 23-26. Heath c-6, 7. Maneely c-12, 15. Romita a-20, 22, 24, 26. Shores a-14-16, 24, 26; c-11, 13, 16. Tuska a-6.

LOSERS SPECIAL (See Our Fighting Forces #123)(Also see G.I. Combat & Our Fighting Forces)
Sept, 1985 ($1.25, one-shot)
DC Comics

1-Capt. Storm, Gunner & Sarge; Crisis x-over			1.30

LOST CONTINENT
Sept, 1990 - No. 6, 1991 ($3.50, B&W, squarebound, 60 pgs.)
Eclipse International

1-6: Japanese story translated to English		1.40	3.50

LOST IN SPACE (TV)(Also see Space Family Robinson)
Aug, 1991 - No. 12, Jan, 1993 ($2.50, limited series)
Innovation Publishing

1-12: Bill Mumy (Will Robinson) scripts in #1-9. 9-Perez-c		1.00	2.50
1,2-Special Ed.; r/#1,2 plus new art & new-c		1.00	2.50
Annual 1,2 (1991, 1992, $2.95, 52 pgs.)		1.20	3.00

LOST IN SPACE: PROJECT ROBINSON (TV)
Nov, 1993 ($2.50, limited series intended)
Innovation Publishing

1-Takes place after #12		1.00	2.50

LOST IN SPACE: VOYAGE TO THE BOTTOM OF THE SOUL
No. 13, Aug, 1993 - No. 18, 1994 ($2.50, limited series)
Innovation Publishing

13(V1#1, $2.95)-Embossed silver logo edition; Bill Mumy scripts begin; painted-c		1.00	2.50
13(V1#1, $4.95)-Embossed gold logo edition bagged w/poster			
	1.00	2.00	5.00
14-18: Painted-c		1.00	2.50

NOTE: Originally intended to be a 12 issue limited series.

LOST PLANET
5/87 - No. 5, 2/88; No. 6, 3/89 ($1.75/$2.00, mini-series, Baxter paper)
Eclipse Comics

1,2 ($1.75)-Bo Hampton-c/a in all		.75	1.80
3-6 ($2.00)		.80	2.00

LOST WAGON TRAIN, THE (See Zane Grey Four Color 583)

LOST WORLD, THE
No. 1145, Nov-Jan, 1960-61
Dell Publishing Co.

Love and Rockets #50 © Hernandez Bros.

Love Classics #2 © MEG

Love Diary #1 © CC

	GD25	FN65	NM94		GD25	FN65	NM94

Four Color 1145-Movie, Gil Kane-a, photo-c; 1pg. Conan Doyle biography by
Torres   11.00   33.00   110.00

LOST WORLDS (Weird Tales of the Past and Future)
No. 5, Oct, 1952 - No. 6, Dec, 1952
Standard Comics

5- "Alice in Terrorland" by Alex Toth; J. Katz-a	36.00	107.00	250.00
6-Toth-a	30.00	90.00	210.00

LOTS 'O' FUN COMICS
1940's? (5¢, heavy stock, blue covers)
Robert Allen Co.

nn-Contents can vary; Felix, Planet Comics known; contents would determine value.
Similar to Up-To-Date Comics. Remainders - re-packaged.

LOU GEHRIG (See The Pride of the Yankees)

LOVE ADVENTURES (Actual Confessions #13)
Oct, 1949; No. 2, Jan, 1950; No. 3, Feb, 1951 - No. 12, Aug, 1952
Marvel (IPS)/Atlas Comics (MPI)

1-Photo-c	11.00	33.00	75.00
2-Powell-a; Tyrone Power, Gene Tierney photo-c	11.00	33.00	75.00
3-8,10-12: 8-Robinson-a	5.85	17.50	35.00
9-Everett-a	7.00	21.00	42.00

LOVE AND MARRIAGE
Mar, 1952 - No. 16, Sept, 1954
Superior Comics Ltd.

1	10.00	30.00	65.00
2	5.35	16.00	32.00
3-10	4.00	12.00	24.00
11-16	4.00	10.00	20.00
I.W. Reprint #1,2,8,11,14: 8-r/Love and Marriage #3. 11-r/Love and			
Marriage #11.	1.00	2.60	6.00
Super Reprint #10('63),15,17('64):15-Love and Marriage #?			
	1.00	2.60	6.00

NOTE: All issues have **Kamenish** art.

LOVE AND ROCKETS
July, 1982 - No. 50, May, 1996 ($2.95/$2.50/$4.95, B&W, mature)
Fantagraphics Books

1-B&W-c (6/82, $2.95; small size, publ. by Hernandez Bros.)(800 printed)			
	6.50	19.50	45.00
1 (Fall, '82; color-c)	3.60	11.00	25.00
1-2nd & 3rd printing		1.20	3.00
2	1.65	4.20	10.00
2-11, 29-31: 2nd printings ($2.50)		1.10	2.75
3-5	1.25	3.00	7.50
6-10		1.70	4.25
11-49: 30 ($2.95, 52 pgs.). 31-on: $2.50-c		1.20	3.00
50-($4.95)			5.00

LOVE AND ROMANCE
Sept, 1971 - No. 24, Sept, 1975
Charlton Comics

1		1.20	3.00
2-24			1.00

LOVE AT FIRST SIGHT
Oct, 1949 - No. 42, Aug, 1956 (Photo-c: 21-42)
Ace Magazines (RAR Publ. Co./Periodical House)

1-Painted-c	10.00	30.00	70.00
2-Painted-c	5.85	17.50	35.00
3-10: 4-Painted-c	4.00	12.00	24.00
11-20	4.00	10.00	20.00
21-33: 33-Last pre-code	3.00	7.50	15.00
34-42	2.20	5.50	11.00

LOVE BUG, THE (See Movie Comics)

LOVE CLASSICS
Nov, 1949 - No. 2, Feb, 1950 (Photo-c, 52 pgs.)
A Lover's Magazine/Marvel Comics

1,2: 2-Virginia Mayo photo-c; 30 pg. story "I Was a Small Town Flirt"			
	10.00	30.00	70

LOVE CONFESSIONS
Oct, 1949 - No. 54, Dec, 1956 (Photo-c: 3,4,6,7,9,11-18,21)
Quality Comics Group

1-Ward-c/a, 9 pgs; Gustavson-a	24.00	73.00	170
2-Gustavson-a; Ward-c	10.00	30.00	65
3	5.85	17.50	35
4-Crandall-a	7.50	22.50	45
5-Ward-a, 7 pgs.	10.00	30.00	58
6,7,9,11-13,15,16,18: 7-Van Johnson photo-c. 8-Robert Mitchum & Jane			
Russell photo-c	4.00	11.00	22
8,10-Ward-a(2 stories in #10)	10.00	30.00	60
14,17,19,22-Ward-a; 17-Faith Domerque photo-c	8.35	25.00	50
20-Ward-a(2)	10.00	30.00	60
21,23-28,30-38,40-42: Last precode, 4/55	3.00	7.50	15
29-Ward-a	8.00	24.00	48
39-Matt Baker-a	4.25	13.00	28
43,44,46-48,50-54: 47-Ward-c?	2.60	6.50	13
45-Ward-a	4.00	12.00	24
49-Baker-c/a	5.35	16.00	32

LOVE DIARY
July, 1949 - No. 48, Oct, 1955 (Photo-c: 1-24,27-29) (52 pgs. #1-11?)
Our Publishing Co./Toytown/Patches

1-Krigstein-a	13.00	39.00	90
2,3-Krigstein & Mort Leav-a in each	10.00	30.00	60
4-8	4.00	12.00	24
9,10-Everett-a	5.00	15.00	30
11-20: 16- Mort Leav-a, 3 pg. Baker-sty. Mort Leav-a			
	4.00	10.00	20
21-30,32-48: 45-Leav-a. 47-Last precode(12/54)	3.20	8.00	16
31-John Buscema headlights-c	4.00	11.00	22

LOVE DIARY (Diary Loves #2 on; title changed due to previously published
above?)
Sept, 1949
Quality Comics Group

1-Ward-c/a, 9 pgs.	24.00	73.00	170

LOVE DIARY
July, 1958 - No. 102, Dec, 1976
Charlton Comics

1	7.50	22.50	45
2	4.15	12.50	25
3-5,7-10: 10-Photo-c	3.00	7.50	15
6-Torres-a	4.00	10.00	20
11-20: 20-Photo-c	2.40	6.00	12
21-40	1.20	3.00	
41-60		1.40	
61-102			

LOVE DOCTOR (See Dr. Anthony King...)

LOVE DRAMAS (True Secrets No. 3 on?)
Oct, 1949 - No. 2, Jan, 1950
Marvel Comics (IPS)

1-Jack Kamen-a; photo-c	13.00	39.00	90
2	10.00	30.00	60

LOVE EXPERIENCES (Challenge of the Unknown No. 6)
Oct, 1949 - No. 5, June, 1950; No. 6, Apr, 1951 - No. 38, June, 1956

Lovelorn #49 © ACG

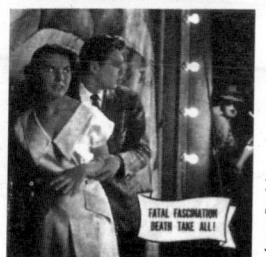

Love Mystery #3 © FAW

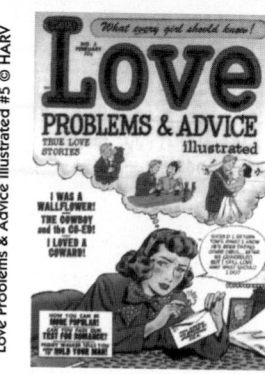

Love Problems & Advice Illustrated #5 © HARV

	GD25	FN65	NM94

Ace Periodicals (A.A. Wyn/Periodical House)

	GD25	FN65	NM94
1-Painted-c	10.00	30.00	60.00
2	4.25	13.00	28.00
3-5: 5-Painted-c	4.00	10.00	20.00
6-10	3.20	8.00	16.00
11-30: 30-Last pre-code (2/55)	2.40	6.00	12.00
31-38: 38-Indicia date-6/56; c-date-8/56	2.00	5.00	10.00

NOTE: *Anne Brewster* a-15. Photo c-4, 15-35, 38.

LOVE JOURNAL
No. 10, Oct, 1951 - No. 25, July, 1954
Our Publishing Co.

10	8.35	25.00	50.00
11-25: 19-Mort Leav-a	4.25	13.00	26.00

LOVELAND
Nov, 1949 - No. 2, Feb, 1950 (52 pgs.)
Mutual Mag./Eye Publ. (Marvel)

1,2-Photo-c	8.00	24.00	48.00

LOVE LESSONS
Oct, 1949 - No. 5, June, 1950
Harvey Comics/Key Publ. No. 5

1-Metallic silver-c printed over the cancelled covers of Love Letters #1; indicia title is "Love Letters"	10.00	30.00	65.00
2-Powell-a; photo-c	4.25	13.00	28.00
3-5: 3-Photo-c	4.00	12.00	24.00

LOVE LETTERS (10/49, Harvey; advertised but never published; covers were printed before cancellation and were used as the cover to Love Lessions #1)

LOVE LETTERS (Love Secrets No. 32 on)
1/49 - #6, 9/50; #7, 3/51 - #31, 6/53; #32, 2/54 - #51, 12/56
Quality Comics Group

1-Ward-c, Gustavson-a	19.00	58.00	135.00
2-Ward-c, Gustavson-a	15.00	45.00	105.00
3-Gustavson-a	10.00	30.00	65.00
4-Ward-a, 9 pgs.	13.50	41.00	95.00
5-8,10	4.00	12.00	24.00
9-One pg. Ward "Be Popular with the Opposite Sex"; Robert Mitchum photo-c	5.85	17.50	35.00
11-Ward-r/Broadway Romances #2 & retitled	6.35	19.00	38.00
12-15,18-20	4.00	10.00	20.00
16,17-Ward-a; 16-Anthony Quinn photo-c. 17-Jane Russell photo-c	9.15	27.00	55.00
21-29	3.60	9.00	18.00
30,31(6/53)-Ward-a	5.35	16.00	32.00
32(2/54)-39: 38-Crandall-a. 39-Last precode (4/55)	2.80	7.00	14.00
40-48	2.00	5.00	10.00
49,50-Baker-a	5.35	16.00	32.00
51-Baker-c	4.25	13.00	26.00

NOTE: *Photo-c* on most 3-28.

LOVE LIFE
Nov, 1951
L. Publishing Co.

	6.70	20.00	40.00

LOVELORN (Confessions of the Lovelorn #52 on)
Aug-Sept, 1949 - No. 51, July, 1954 (No. 1-26: 52 pgs.)
American Comics Group (Michel Publ./Regis Publ.)

1	11.00	33.00	75.00
2-10	6.35	19.00	38.00
11-20,22-48: 18-Drucker-a(2 pgs.). 46-Lazarus-a	4.25	13.00	28.00
21-Prostitution story	4.00	11.00	22.00
49-51-Has 3-D effect-c/stories	5.35	16.00	32.00
	13.00	39.00	90.00

LOVE MEMORIES
1949 (no month) - No. 4, July, 1950 (All photo-c)
Fawcett Publications

1	10.00	30.00	60.00
2-4: 2-(Win/49-50)	5.85	17.50	35.00

LOVE MYSTERY
June, 1950 - No. 3, Oct, 1950 (All photo-c)
Fawcett Publications

1-George Evans-a	17.00	51.00	120.00
2,3-Evans-a. 3-Powell-a	13.50	41.00	95.00

LOVE PROBLEMS (See Fox Giants)

LOVE PROBLEMS AND ADVICE ILLUSTRATED (Becomes Romance Stories of True Love No. 45 on)
June, 1949 - No. 6, Apr, 1950; No. 7, Jan, 1951 - No. 44, Mar, 1957
McCombs/Harvey Publ./Home Comics

V1#1	11.00	33.00	75.00
2	5.85	17.50	35.00
3-10: 7-9-Elias-c	4.25	13.00	28.00
11-13,15-23,25-31: 31-Last pre-code (1/55)	3.60	9.00	18.00
14,24-Rape scene	4.00	12.00	24.00
32-37,39-44	2.80	7.00	14.00
38-S&K-c	5.00	15.00	30.00

NOTE: *Powell* a-1, 2, 7-14, 17-25, 28, 29, 33, 40, 41. #3 has True Love... on inside.

LOVE ROMANCES (Formerly Ideal #5)
No. 6, May, 1949 - No. 106, July, 1963
Timely/Marvel/Atlas(TCI No. 7-71/Male No. 72-106)

6-Photo-c	10.00	30.00	65.00
7-Photo-c; Kamen-a	6.70	20.00	40.00
8-Kubert-a; photo-c	7.00	21.00	42.00
9-20: 9-12-Photo-c	4.25	13.00	28.00
21,24-Krigstein-a	7.00	21.00	42.00
22,23,25-35,37,39,40	4.00	12.00	24.00
36,38-Krigstein-a	6.35	19.00	38.00
41-44,46,47: Last precode (2/55)	4.00	12.00	24.00
45,57-Matt Baker-a	5.35	16.00	32.00
48,50-52,54-56,58-74	3.60	9.00	18.00
49,53-Toth-a, 6 & ? pgs.	6.70	20.00	40.00
75,77,82-Matt Baker-a	5.00	15.00	30.00
76,78-81,84,86-95: Last 10¢ issue? 80-Heath-c	3.60	9.00	18.00
83-Kirby, Severin-a	5.35	16.00	32.00
85,96-Kirby-c/a	5.85	17.50	35.00
97,100-104	3.20	8.00	16.00
98-Kirby-a(4)	8.35	25.00	50.00
99,105,106-Kirby-a	5.00	17.50	35.00

NOTE: *Anne Brewster* a-67, 72. *Colletta* a-37, 40, 42, 44, 67(2); c-42, 44, 49, 54, 80. *Everett* c-70. *Heath* a-87. *Kirby* c-80, 85, 88. *Robinson* a-29.

LOVERS (Formerly Blonde Phantom)
No. 23, May, 1949 - No. 86, Aug?, 1957
Marvel Comics No. 23,24/Atlas No. 25 on (ANC)

23-Photo-c begin, end #28	10.00	30.00	65.00
24-Tothish plus Robinson-a	5.35	16.00	32.00
25,30-Kubert-a; 7, 10 pgs.	6.35	19.00	38.00
26-29,31-36,39,40	4.00	12.00	24.00
37,38-Krigstein-a	7.00	21.00	42.00
41-Everett-a(2)	5.35	16.00	32.00
42,44-65: 65-Last pre-code (1/55)	4.00	11.00	22.00
43-Frazetta 1 pg. ad	4.00	11.00	22.00
66,68-86	3.60	9.00	18.00
67-Toth-a	5.00	15.00	30.00

NOTE: *Anne Brewster* a-86. *Colletta* a-54, 59, 62, 64, 65, 69, 85; c-61, 64, 65, 75. *Heath* a-61. *Maneely* a-57. *Powell* a-27, 30. *Robinson* a-54, 56.

LOVERS' LANE

Lovers Lane #1 © LEV

Love Scandals #2 © QUA

Love Secrets #1 © QUA

Oct, 1949 - No. 41, June, 1954 (No. 1-18: 52 pgs.)
Lev Gleason Publications

1-Biro-c	9.15	27.00	55.00
2-Biro-c	4.25	13.00	28.00
3-20: 3,4-Painted-c. 20-Frazetta 1 pg. ad	4.00	10.00	20.00
21-38,40,41	2.80	7.00	14.00
39-Story narrated by Frank Sinatra	4.25	13.00	26.00

NOTE: *Briefer a-6, 21. Fuje a-4, 16; c-many. Guardineer a-1. Kinstler c-41. Tuska a-6. Painted c-3-18. Photo c-19-22, 26-28.*

LOVE SCANDALS
Feb, 1950 - No. 5, Oct, 1950 (Photo-c #2-5) (All 52 pgs.)
Quality Comics Group

1-Ward-c/a, 9 pgs.	21.00	64.00	150.00
2,3: 2-Gustavson-a	8.00	24.00	48.00
4-Ward-a, 18 pgs; Gil Fox-a	17.00	49.00	115.00
5-C. Cuidera-a; tomboy story "I Hated Being a Woman"	8.00	24.00	48.00

LOVE SECRETS
Oct, 1949 - No. 2, Jan, 1950 (52 pgs., photo-c)
Marvel Comics(IPC)

1	10.00	30.00	65.00
2	7.00	21.00	42.00

LOVE SECRETS (Formerly Love Letters #31)
No. 32, Aug, 1953 - No. 56, Dec, 1956
Quality Comics Group

32	7.00	21.00	42.00
33,35-39	4.00	11.00	22.00
34-Ward-a	8.00	24.00	48.00
40-Matt Baker-c	5.00	15.00	30.00
41-43: 43-Last precode (3/55)	4.00	10.00	20.00
44,47-50,53,54	2.80	7.00	14.00
45,46-Ward-a. 46-Baker-a	5.85	17.50	35.00
51,52-Ward(r). 52-r/Love Confessions #17	4.00	12.00	24.00
55,56: 55-Baker-a. 56-Baker-c	4.25	13.00	26.00

LOVE STORIES (Formerly My Love Affair #5)
No. 6, 1950 - No. 12, 1951
Fox Feature Syndicate

6,8-Wood-a	14.00	43.00	100.00
7,9-12	6.70	20.00	40.00

LOVE STORIES (Formerly Heart Throbs)
No. 147, Nov, 1972 - No. 152, Oct-Nov, 1973
National Periodical Publications

147-152	1.00	2.00	5.00

LOVE STORIES OF MARY WORTH (See Harvey Comics Hits #55 & Mary Worth)
Sept, 1949 - No. 5, May, 1950
Harvey Publications

1-1940's newspaper reprints-#1-4	5.85	17.50	35.00
2	4.25	13.00	28.00
3-5: 3-Kamen/Baker-a?	4.25	13.00	26.00

LOVE TALES (Formerly The Human Torch #35)
No. 36, 5/49 - No. 58, 8/52; No. 59, date? - No. 75, Sept, 1957
Marvel/Atlas Comics (ZPC No. 36-50/MMC No. 67-75)

36-Photo-a	10.00	30.00	65.00
37	6.35	19.00	38.00
38-44,46-50: 39-41-Photo-c	4.25	13.00	26.00
45-Powell-a	4.25	13.00	28.00
51,69-Everett-a	5.00	15.00	30.00
52-Krigstein-a	5.35	16.00	32.00
53-60: 60-Last pre-code (2/55)	4.00	11.00	22.00

61-68,70-75: 75-Brewster, Cameron, Colletta-a	2.80	7.00	14.

LOVE THRILLS (See Fox Giants)

LOVE TRAILS (Western romance)
Dec, 1949 - No. 2, Mar, 1950 (52 pgs.)
A Lover's Magazine (CDS)(Marvel)

1,2: 1-Photo-c	10.00	30.00	60.

LOWELL THOMAS' HIGH ADVENTURE (See High Adventure)

LT. (See Lieutenant)

LUCIFER'S HAMMER (Larry Niven & Jerry Pournelle's...)
Nov, 1993 - No. 6, 1994 ($2.50, painted, limited series)
Innovation Publishing

1-6: Adaptatin of novel, painted-c & art		1.00	2.

LUCKY COMICS
Jan, 1944; No. 2, Summer, 1945 - No. 5, Summer, 1946
Consolidated Magazines

1-Lucky Starr & Bobbie begin	16.00	47.00	110.
2-5: 5-Devil-c by Walter Johnson	10.00	30.00	60.

LUCKY DUCK
No. 5, Jan, 1953 - No. 8, Sept, 1953
Standard Comics (Literary Ent.)

5-Funny animal; Irving Spector-a	10.00	30.00	70.
6-8-Irving Spector-a	9.15	27.50	55.

NOTE: Harvey Kurtzman tried to hire Spector for Mad #1.

LUCKY FIGHTS IT THROUGH (Also see The K. O. Punch)
1949 (Giveaway, 16 pgs. in color, paper-c)
Educational Comics

nn-(Very Rare)-1st Kurtzman work for E. C.; V.D. prevention	143.00	430.00	1000.
nn-Reprint in color (1977)		.80	2.

NOTE: Subtitled "The Story of That Ignorant, Ignorant Cowboy". Prepared for Communications Materials Center, Columbia University.

LUCKY "7" COMICS
1944 (No date listed)
Howard Publishers Ltd.

1-Pioneer, Sir Gallagher, Dick Royce, Congo Raider, Punch Powers; bondage-c	27.00	81.00	190.

LUCKY STAR (Western)
1950 - No. 7, 1951; No. 8, 1953 - No. 14, 1955 (5x7-1/4"; full color, 5¢)
Nation Wide Publ. Co.

nn (#1)-(5¢, 52 pgs.)-Davis-a	9.15	27.00	55.
2,3-(5¢, 52 pgs.)-Davis-a	5.85	17.50	35.
4-7-(5¢, 52 pgs.)-Davis-a	5.00	15.00	30.
8-14-(36 pgs.)	4.00	10.00	20.
Given away with Lucky Star Western Wear by the Juvenile Mfg. Co.			
	4.00	10.00	20.

LUCY SHOW, THE (TV) (Also see I Love Lucy)
June, 1963 - No. 5, June, 1964 (Photo-c: 1,2)
Gold Key

1	12.00	36.00	120.
2	6.00	18.00	60.
3-5: Photo back c-1,2,4,5	5.00	15.00	50.

LUCY, THE REAL GONE GAL (Meet Miss Pepper #5 on)
June, 1953 - No. 4, Dec, 1953
St. John Publishing Co.

1-Negligee panels	10.00	30.00	65.
2	5.85	17.50	35.
3,4: 3-Drucker-a	4.25	13.00	28.

LUDWIG BEMELMAN'S MADELEINE & GENEVIEVE

Luger #2 © ECL

Lunatik #3 © MEG

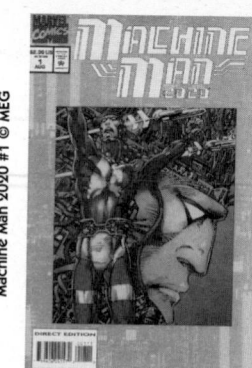

Machine Man 2020 #1 © MEG

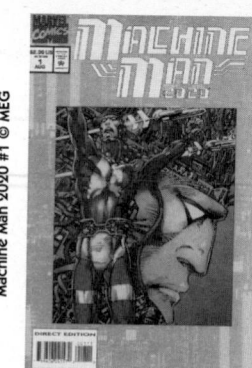

MA

	GD25	FN65	NM94

No. 796, May, 1957
Dell Publishing Co.

Four Color 796	4.00	12.00	40.00

LUDWIG VON DRAKE (TV)(Disney)(See Walt Disney's C&S #256)
Nov-Dec, 1961 - No. 4, June-Aug, 1962
Dell Publishing Co.

1	6.00	18.00	60.00
2-4	4.00	12.00	40.00
...Fish Stampede (1962, Fritos giveaway)-16 pgs., 3-1/4x7", soft-c; also see			
Donald Duck & Mickey Mouse	3.20	9.60	32.00

LUFTWAFFE: 1946
July, 1996 - Present ($2.95, B&W, limited series)
Antarctic Press

1			3.00

LUGER
Oct, 1986 - No. 3, Feb, 1987 ($1.75, mini-series, Baxter paper)
Eclipse Comics

1-3: Bruce Jones scripts; Yeates-c/a		.70	1.80

LUKE CAGE (See Cage & Hero for Hire)

LUKE SHORT'S WESTERN STORIES
No. 580, Aug, 1954 - No. 927, Aug, 1958
Dell Publishing Co.

Four Color 580(8/54)	4.00	12.00	40.00
Four Color 651(9/55)-Kinstler-a	4.00	12.00	40.00
Four Color 739,771,807,875,927	4.00	12.00	40.00
Four Color 848	5.00	15.00	50.00

LUNATIC FRINGE, THE
July, 1989 - No. 2, 1989 ($1.75, deluxe format)
Innovation Publishing

1,2			1.80

LUNATICKLE (Magazine) (Satire)
Feb, 1956 - No. 2, Apr, 1956
Whitstone Publ.

1,2-Kubert-a	3.00	7.50	15.00

LUNATIK
Dec, 1995 - No. 3, Feb, 1996 ($1.95, limited series)
Marvel Comics

1-3		.80	2.00

LYCANTHROPE LEO
1994 - No. 7($2.95, B&W, limited series, 44 pgs.)
Viz Communications

1-7		1.20	3.00

LYNCH MOB
June, 1994 - No. 4, Sept, 1994 ($2.50, limited series)
Chaos! Comics

1-4		1.00	2.50
1-Special edition full foil-c	1.00	2.00	5.00

LYNDON B. JOHNSON
Mar, 1965
Dell Publishing Co.

1-445-503-Photo-c	2.30	6.70	16.00

1990 - No. 4, 1991 ($4.95, painted, 52 pgs.)
Eclipse Books

1-Adapts movie; contains flexi-disc ($5.95)	1.00	2.60	6.00
1-4	1.00	2.00	5.00

MACHINE, THE
Nov, 1994 - Feb, 1995 ($2.50, color)
Dark Horse Comics

1-4		1.00	2.50

MACHINE MAN (Also see 2001, A Space Odyssey)
Apr, 1978 - No. 9, Dec, 1978; No. 10, Aug, 1979 - No. 19, Feb, 1981
Marvel Comics Group

1		1.30	3.25
2-17		.70	1.75
18-Wendigo, Alpha Flight-ties into X-Men #140	1.00	2.00	5.00
19-Intro/1st app. Jack O'Lantern (Macendale), later becomes 2nd Hobgoblin			
	1.70	5.00	12.00

NOTE: Austin c-7i, 19i. Buckler c-17p, 18p. Byrne c-14p. Ditko a-10-19; c-10-13, 14i, 15, 16. Kirby a-1-9p; c-1-5, 7-9p. Layton c-7i. Miller c-19p. Simonson c-6.

MACHINE MAN
Oct, 1984 - No. 4, Jan, 1985 (Limited-series)
Marvel Comics Group

1-Barry Smith-c/a(i) & colors in all			1.50
2-4			1.25

MACHINE MAN 2020
Aug, 1994 - Nov, 1994 ($2.00, 52 pgs., limited series)
Marvel Comics

1-4: Reprints Machine Man limited series; Barry Windsor-Smith-c/i(r)			
		.80	2.00

MACK BOLAN: THE EXECUTIONER (Don Pendleton's...)
July, 1993 ($2.50)
Innovation Publishing

1-($3.95)-Indestructible Cover Edition		1.60	4.00
1-($2.95)-Collector's Gold Edition; foil stamped		1.20	3.00
1-($3.50)-Double Cover Edition; red foil outer-c		1.40	3.50

MACKENZIE'S RAIDERS (Movie, TV)
No. 1093, Apr-June, 1960
Dell Publishing Co.

Four Color 1093-Richard Carlson photo-c from TV show			
	7.00	21.00	70.00

MACO TOYS COMIC
1959 (Giveaway, 36 pgs.)
Maco Toys/Charlton Comics

1-All military stories featuring Maco Toys	1.20	3.00	6.00

MACROSS (Becomes Robotech: The Macross Saga #2 on)
Dec, 1984 ($1.50)
Comico

1	1.00	2.00	5.00

MACROSS II
1992 - No. 10, 1993 ($2.75, B&W, limited series)
Viz Select Comics

1-10: Based on video series		1.10	2.75

MAD (Tales Calculated to Drive You...)
Oct-Nov, 1952 - Present (No. 24 on are magazine format)
(Kurtzman editor No. 1-28, Feldstein No. 29 - No. ?)
E. C. Comics (Educational Comics)

1-Wood, Davis, Elder start as regulars	489.00	1467.00	4800.00
2-Dick Tracy cameo	125.00	375.00	1000.00
3,4: 3-Stan Lee mentioned. 4-Reefer mention story "Flob Was a Slob" by			
Davis; Superman parody	78.00	234.00	625.00
5-Low distr.; W.M. Gaines biog.	128.00	384.00	1025.00
6-11: 6-Popeye cameo. 7,8- "Hey Look" reprints by Kurtzman. 11-Wolverton-a;			
Davis story was-r/Crime Suspenstories #12 w/new Kurtzman dialogue			

Mad #109 © WMG

Mad Dogs #3 © ECL

Mad Hatter #1 © O. W. Comics Corp.

	GD25	FN65	NM94
	59.00	178.00	475.00
12-15: 15,18-Pot Shot Pete-r by Kurtzman	47.00	141.00	375.00
16-23(5/55): 18-Alice in Wonderland by Jack Davis. 21-1st app. Alfred E. Neuman on-c in fake ad. 22-All by Elder plus photo-montages by Kurtzman.			
23-Special cancel announcement	40.00	120.00	290.00
24(7/55)-1st magazine issue (25¢); Kurtzman logo & border on-c; 1st "What? Me Worry?" on-c; 2nd printing exists	92.00	276.00	735.00
25-Jaffee starts as regular writer	40.00	120.00	310.00
26,27: 27-Jaffee starts as story artist; new logo	36.00	107.00	250.00
28-Last issue edited by Kurtzman; (three cover variations exist with different wording on contents banner on lower right of cover; value of each the same)			
	33.00	99.00	230.00
29-Kamen-a; Don Martin starts as regular; Feldstein editing begins			
	33.00	99.00	230.00
30-1st A. E. Neuman cover by Mingo; last Elder-a; Bob Clarke starts as regular; Disneyland & Elvis Presley spoof	45.00	135.00	360.00
31-Freas starts as regular; last Davis-a until #99	26.00	79.00	185.00
32,33: 32-Orlando, Drucker, Woodbridge start as regulars; Wood back-c.			
33-Orlando back-c	24.00	71.00	165.00
34-Berg starts as regular	19.00	56.00	130.00
35-Mingo wraparound-c; Crandall-a	19.00	56.00	130.00
36-40	12.00	36.00	85.00
41-50	10.00	30.00	70.00
51-60: 60-Two Clarke-c; Prohias starts as regular	10.00	30.00	60.00
61-70: 64-Rickard starts as regular. 68-Martin-c	7.50	22.50	45.00
71-80: 76-Aragones starts as regular	6.35	19.00	38.00
81-90: 86-1st Fold-in. 89-One strip by Walt Kelly. 90-Frazetta back-c; Beatles app.	5.35	16.00	32.00
91-100: 91-Jaffee starts as story artist. 99-Davis-a resumes			
	4.25	13.00	28.00
101-104,106-120: 101-Infinity-c. 106-Frazetta back-c			
	4.00	11.00	22.00
105-Batman TV show take-off	5.00	15.00	30.00
121-140: 121-Beatles app. 122-Ronald Reagan photo inside; Drucker & Mingo-c. 128-Last Orlando. 130-Torres begins as reg. 131-Reagan photo back-c. 135,139-Davis-c	2.15	6.50	15.00
141-170: 165-Martin-c. 169-Drucker-c	1.70	5.00	12.00
171-200: 182-Bob Jones starts as regular. 186-Star Trek take-off. 187-Harry North starts as regular. 196-Star Wars take-off	1.65	4.20	10.00
201-250: 203-Star Wars take-off. 204-Hulk TV show take-off. 208-Superman movie take-off. 245- Last Rikard-a.	1.00	2.60	6.00
251-300: 256-Last issue edited by Feldstein. 274-Last Martin-a. 289-Roger Rabbit-c/story. 289-Batman movie parody. 291-TMNT-c only.			
299-Simpson's-c/story		1.60	4.00
301-360: 306-TMNT III movie parody. 308-Terminator parody. 311-Addams Family-c/story. 314-Batman Returns-c/story. 315-Tribute to William Gaines. 316-Photo-c. 322-Batman animated series parody. 347-Broken Arrow & Mission Impossible parody. 350-Polybagged w/CD Rom disc			
		1.00	2.50
300-303 (1/91-6/91)-Special Hussein Asylum Editions; only distributed to the troops in the Middle East (see Mad Super Spec.)	1.00	2.00	5.00

NOTE: **Aragones** c-210, 293. **Davis** c-2, 27, 135, 139, 173, 178, 212, 213, 219, 246, 260, 296, 308. **Drucker** c-122, 169, 176, 225, 234, 264, 266, 274, 280, 285, 297, 299, 303, 314, 315, 321. **Elder** c-5, 259, 261, 268. **Elder/Kurtzman** a-258-274. **Jules Feiffer** a(r)-42. **Freas** c-39-59, 62-67, 69-70, 72, 74. **Heath** a-14, 27. **Jaffee** c-199, 217, 224, 258. **Kamen** a-29. **Krigstein** a-12, 17, 24, 26. **Kurtzman** c-1, 3, 4, 6-10, 13, 16, 18. **Martin** c-68, 165, 229. **Mingo** c-30-37, 61, 71, 75-80, 82-114, 117-124, 126, 129, 131, 133, 134, 136, 140, 143-148, 150-162, 164, 166-168, 171, 172, 174, 175, 177, 179, 181, 183, 185, 198, 206, 209, 211, 214, 218, 221, 222, 300. **John Severin** a-1-6, 9, 10. **Wolverton** c-11; a-11, 17, 29, 31, 36, 40, 82, 137. **Wood** a-24-45, 59; c-26, 28, 29. **Woodbridge** a-43. Issues 1-23 are 36 pgs.; 24-28 are 58 pgs.; 29 on are 52 pgs.

MAD (See Mad Follies, ...Special, More Trash from..., and The Worst from...)

MAD ABOUT MILLIE (Also see Millie the Model)
April, 1969 - No. 17, Dec, 1970
Marvel Comics Group

1-Giant issue	4.60	13.70	35.00

	GD25	FN65	NM94
2-17: 16,17-r	2.60	7.50	18.00
Annual 1(11/71)	1.70	5.00	12.00

MADAME XANADU
July, 1981 ($1.00, no ads, 36 pgs.)
DC Comics

1-Marshall Rogers-a(25 pgs.); Kaluta-c/a(2pgs.); pin-up of Madame Xanadu			
			1.00

MADBALLS
Sept, 1986 - No. 3, Nov, 1986; No. 4, June, 1987 - No. 10, June, 1988
Star Comics/Marvel Comics #9 on

1-10: Based on toys. 9-Post-a			1.00

MAD DISCO
1980 (one-shot, 36 pgs.)
E.C. Comics

1-Includes 30 minute flexi-disc of Mad disco music			
		.80	2.00

MAD DOGS
Feb, 1992 - No. 3, July, 1992 ($2.50, B&W, limited series)
Eclipse Comics

1-3		1.00	2.50

MAD 84 (Mad Extra)
1984 (84 pgs.)
E.C. Comics

1		.80	2.00

MAD FOLLIES (Special)
1963 - No. 7, 1969
E. C. Comics

nn(1963)-Paperback book covers	34.00	103.00	240.00
2(1964)-Calendar	26.00	77.00	180.00
3(1965)-Mischief Stickers	17.00	51.00	120.00
4(1966)-Mobile; Frazetta-r/back-c Mad #90	15.00	45.00	105.00
5(1967)-Stencils	10.00	30.00	70.00
6(1968)-Mischief Stickers	8.00	23.50	55.00
7(1969)-Nasty Cards	8.00	23.50	55.00

NOTE: **Clarke** c-4. **Frazetta** r-4, 6 (1 pg. ea.). **Mingo** c-1-3. **Orlando** a-5.

MAD HATTER, THE (Costumed Hero)
Jan-Feb, 1946; No. 2, Sept-Oct, 1946
O. W. Comics Corp.

1-Freddy the Firefly begins; Giunta-c/a	65.00	195.00	525.00
2-Has ad for E.C.'s Animal Fables #1	36.00	107.00	250.00

MADHOUSE
3-4/54 - No. 4, 9-10/54; 6/57 - No. 4, Dec?, 1957
Ajax/Farrell Publ. (Excellent Publ./4-Star)

1(1954)	24.00	71.00	165.00
2,3	13.00	39.00	90.00
4-Surrealistic-c	21.00	64.00	150.00
1(1957, 2nd series)	10.00	30.00	65.00
2-4	7.50	22.50	45.00

MAD HOUSE (Formerly Madhouse Glads; ...Comics #104? on)
No. 95, 9/74 - No. 97, 1/75; No. 98, 8/75 - No. 130, 10/82
Red Circle Productions/Archie Publications

95,96-Horror stories through #97		1.60	4.00
97-Intro. Henry Hobson; Morrow, Thorne-a		.80	2.00
98-130-Satire/humor stories		.80	2.00
Annual 8(1970-71)- 12(1974-75)-Formerly Madhouse Ma-ad Annual.			
11-Wood-a(r)		1.00	2.50
...Comics Digest 1('75-76)- 8(8/82)(...Mag. #5 on)		1.20	3.00

NOTE: **B. Jones** a-96. **McWilliams** a-97. **Morrow** a-96, 97; c-95-97. **Wildey** a-95, 96. See Archie Comics Digest #1, 13.

Madman Comics #11 © Mike Allred

Mage #11 © Matt Wagner

Magic Comics #17 © DMP

	GD25	FN65	NM94

MADHOUSE GLADS (Formerly ...Ma-ad; Madhouse #95 on)
No. 73, May, 1970 - No. 94, Aug, 1974 (No. 78-92: 52 pgs.)
Archie Publications

73	1.00	2.60	6.00
74-94	1.00	2.00	5.00

MADHOUSE MA-AD (...Jokes #67-70; ...Freak-Out #71-74)
(Formerly Archie's Madhouse) (Becomes Madhouse Glads on #75 on)
No. 67, April, 1969 - No. 72, Jan, 1970
Archie Publications

67-72	1.00	2.60	6.00
...Annual 7(1969-70)-Formerly Archie's Madhouse Annual; becomes Madhouse Annual	1.00	2.60	6.00

MADMAN (See Creatures of the Id #1)
Mar, 1992 - No. 3, 1992 ($3.95, duotone, high quality, limited series, 52 pgs.)
Tundra Publishing

1-Mike Allred-c/a in all	1.65	4.20	10.00
1-2nd printing	1.00	2.00	5.00
2,3	1.65	4.20	10.00

MADMAN ADVENTURES
1992 - No. 3, 1993 ($2.95, limited series)
Tundra Publishing

1-3-Mike Allred-c/a in all	1.20	3.00	7.00

MADMAN COMICS
Apr, 1994 - Present ($2.95, bi-monthly)
Dark Horse Comics (Legend No. 2 on)

1-Allred-c/a: 1-F. Miller back-c.	1.00	2.60	6.00
2-12: 3-Alex Toth back-c. 4-Dave Stevens back-c. 6,7-Miller/Darrow's Big Guy app. 6-Bruce Timm back-c. 7-Darrow back-c. 8-Origin?; Bagge back-c.			
10-Allred/Ross-c; Ross back-c. 11-Frazetta back-c	1.20	3.00	
Yearbook '95 (1996, $17.95, TPB)-r/#1-5, intro by Teller			18.00

MAD MONSTER PARTY (See Movie Classics)

MADNESS IN MURDERWORLD
1989 (Came with computer game from Paragon Software)
Marvel Comics

V1#1-Starring The X-Men			1.00

MADRAVEN HALLOWEEN SPECIAL
Oct, 1995 ($2.95, one-shot)
Hamilton Comics

nn-Morrow-a	1.20	3.00	

MAD SPECIAL (...Super Special)
Fall, 1970 - Present (84 - 116 pgs.)
E. C. Publications, Inc.

Fall 1970(#1)-Bonus-Voodoo Doll; contains 17 pgs. new material	10.00	30.00	70.00
Spring 1971(#2)-Wall Nuts; 17 pgs. new material	5.70	17.00	40.00
3-Protest Stickers	5.70	17.00	40.00
4-8: 4-Mini Posters. 5-Mad Flag. 6-Mad Mischief Stickers. 7-Presidential candidate posters, Wild Shocking Message posters. 8-TV Guise	5.00	15.00	35.00
9(1972)-Contains Nostalgic Mad #1 (28 pgs.)	3.60	11.00	25.00
10,11,13: 10-Nonsense Stickers (Don Martin). 11-33-1/3 RPM record. 13-Sickie Stickers; 3 pgs. Wolverton-r/Mad #137	3.60	11.00	25.00
12-Contains Nostalgic Mad #2 (36 pgs.); Davis, Wolverton-a	3.60	11.00	25.00
14-Vital Message posters & Art Depreciation paintings	2.00	6.00	14.00
15-Contains Nostalgic Mad #3 (28 pgs.)	2.40	7.20	17.00
16,17,19,20: 16-Mad-hesive Stickers. 17-Don Martin posters. 20-Martin Stickers	2.00	6.00	14.00

	GD25	FN65	NM94

18-Contains Nostalgic Mad #4 (36 pgs.)	2.00	6.00	14.00
21,24-Contains Nostalgic Mad #5 (28 pgs.) & #6 (28 pgs.)	2.00	6.00	14.00
22,23,25,27,29,30: 22-Diplomas. 23-Martin Stickers. 25-Martin Posters.27-Mad Shock-Sticks. 29-Mad Collectable-Correctables Posters. 30-The Movies	1.00	2.50	6.00
26-Has 33-1/3 RPM record	1.70	5.00	12.00
28-Contains Nostalgic Mad #7 (36 pgs.)	1.30	3.25	8.00
31,33-60: 36-Has 96 pgs. of comic book & comic strip spoofs: titles "The Comics" on-c	1.00	2.50	6.00
32-Contains Nostalgic Mad #8	1.30	3.25	8.00
61-88,90-100: 71-Batman parodies-r by Wood, Drucker. 72-Wolverton-c r-from 1st panel in Mad #11; Wolverton-s r/new dialogue. 83-All Star Trek spoof issue	1.40		3.50
76-(Fall, 1991)-Special Hussein Asylum Edition; distributed only to the troops in the Middle East (see Mad #300-303)	1.00	2.00	5.00
89-($3.95)-Polybaged w/1st of 3 Spy vs. Spy hologram trading cards (direct sale only issue)(other cards came w/card set)	1.60		4.00
100-120: 100?- ($3.99)	1.60		4.00

NOTE: #28-30 have no number on cover. **Freas** c-76. **Mingo** c-9, 11, 15, 19, 23.

MAGE (The Hero Discovered...; also see Grendel #16)
Feb, 1984 (no month) - No. 15, Dec, 1986 ($1.50, Mando paper)
Comico

1-Comico's 1st color comic	1.20	3.00	7.00
2	1.00	2.00	5.00
3-5: 3-Intro Edsel		1.20	3.00
6-Grendel begins (1st in color)	2.85	8.50	20.00
7-1st new Grendel story	2.15	6.50	15.00
8-14: 13-Grendel dies. 14-Grendel story ends	1.00	2.00	5.00
15-$2.95, Double size w/pullout poster	1.00	2.00	5.00

MAGGIE THE CAT (Also see Jon Sable, Freelance #11 & Shaman's Tears #12)
Jan, 1996 - No. 2, Feb, 1996 ($2.50, unfinished limited series)
Image Comics (Creative Fire Studio)

1,2: Mike Grell-c/a/scripts			2.50

MAGIC AGENT (See Forbidden Worlds & Unknown Worlds)
Jan-Feb, 1962 - No. 3, May-June, 1962
American Comics Group

1-Origin & 1st app. John Force	2.60	7.70	18.00
2,3	2.00	5.00	12.00

MAGIC COMICS
Aug, 1939 - No. 123, Nov-Dec, 1949
David McKay Publications

1-Mandrake the Magician, Henry, Popeye , Blondie, Barney Baxter, Secret Agent X-9 (not by Raymond), Bunky by Billy DeBeck & Thornton Burgess text stories illustrated by Harrison Cady begin; Henry covers begin	283.00	850.00	1700.00
2	100.00	300.00	600.00
3	77.00	232.00	465.00
4	66.00	200.00	400.00
5	50.00	150.00	300.00
6-10: 8-11,21-Mandrake/Henry-c	41.00	125.00	250.00
11-16,18,20: 12-Mandrake-c begin.	35.00	107.00	215.00
17-The Lone Ranger begins	38.00	114.00	230.00
19-Robot-c	41.00	125.00	250.00
21-30: 25-Only Blondie-c. 26-Dagwood-c begin	20.00	60.00	140.00
31-40: 36-Flag-c	14.00	42.00	100.00
41-50	11.00	34.00	80.00
51-60	10.00	30.00	70.00
61-70	7.50	22.50	45.00
71-99	6.35	19.00	38.00
100	7.50	22.50	45.00
101-106,109-123: 123-Last Dagwood-c	5.35	16.00	32.00

107,108-Flash Gordon app; not by Raymond	6.35	19.00	38.00

MAGICA DE SPELL (See Walt Disney Showcase #30)

MAGIC FLUTE, THE (See Night Music #9-11)

MAGIC MORRO (Also see see Super Comics #21, The Owl, & The Hurricane Kids)
1941 (7-1/2x5-1/4, giveaway, soft-c)
K. K. Publications

nn-Ken Ernst-a.	11.50	34.00	80.00

MAGIC OF CHRISTMAS AT NEWBERRYS, THE
1967 (Giveaway) (B&W, slick-c, 20 pgs.)
E. S. London

nn		1.20	3.00

MAGIC SWORD, THE (See Movie Classics)

MAGIC THE GATHERING: ANTIQUITIES WAR
Nov, 1995 - Feb, 1996 ($2.50, limited series)
Acclaim Comics (Armada)

1-4-Paul Smith-a(p). 1-Pratt-c.		1.00	2.50

MAGIC THE GATHERING: ARABIAN NIGHTS
Dec, 1995 - Jan, 1996 ($2.50, limited series)
Acclaim Comics (Armada)

1,2		1.00	2.50

MAGIC THE GATHERING: COLLECTION
1995 ($4.95, limited series)
Acclaim Comics (Armada)

1,2-polybagged	1.00	2.00	5.00

MAGIC THE GATHERING: CONVOCATIONS
1995 ($2.50, one shot)
Acclaim Comics (Armada)

1-nn-pin-ups		1.00	2.50

MAGIC THE GATHERING: ELDER DRAGONS
1995 ($2.50, limited series)
Acclaim Comics (Armada)

1,2-Doug Wheatley-a		1.00	2.50

MAGIC THE GATHERING: FALLEN ANGEL
1995 ($5.95, one shot)
Acclaim Comics (Armada)

nn	1.00	2.60	6.00

MAGIC THE GATHERING: FALLEN EMPIRES
Sep, 1995 - Oct, 1995 ($2.75, limited series)
Acclaim Comics (Armada)

1,2		1.10	2.75
...Collection ($4.95)-polybagged			5.00

MAGIC THE GATHERING: HOMELANDS
1995 ($5.95, one shot)
Acclaim Comics (Armada)

nn-polybagged w/card; Hildebrandts-c	1.00	2.60	6.00

MAGIC THE GATHERING: ICE AGE (On The World of...)
July, 1995 - Nov, 1995 ($2.50, limited series)
Acclaim Comics (Armada)

1-4: 1,2-bound in Magic Card. 3,4-bound-in insert		1.00	2.50

MAGIC THE GATHERING: LEGEND OF JEDIT OJANEN
1996 ($2.50, limited series)
Acclaim Comics (Armada)

1,2		1.00	2.50

MAGIC THE GATHERING: NIGHTMARE
1995 ($2.50, one shot)

Acclaim Comics (Armada)

1		1.00	2.50

MAGIC THE GATHERING: THE SHADOW MAGE
July, 1995 - Oct, 1995 ($2.50, limited series)
Acclaim Comics (Armada)

1-4--polybagged w/Magic The Gathering card		1.00	2.50
...Collection 1,2 (1995, $4.95)-Trade paperback; polybagged			
		1.00	2.00	5.00

MAGIC THE GATHERING: SHANDALAR
1996 ($2.50, limited series)
Acclaim Comics (Armada)

1,2		1.00	2.50

MAGIC THE GATHERING: WAYFARER
Nov, 1995 - Feb, 1996 ($2.50, limited series)
Acclaim Comics (Armada)

1-5		1.00	2.50

MAGIK (Illyana and Storm Limited Series)
Dec, 1983 - No. 4, Mar, 1984 (60¢, limited series)
Marvel Comics Group

1-Characters from X-Men; Inferno begins; X-Men cameo (Buscema pencils in #1,2; c-1p		1.60	4.00
2-4: 2-Nightcrawler app. & X-Men cameo		1.60	4.00

MAGILLA GORILLA (TV) (See Kite Fun Book)
May, 1964 - No. 10, Dec, 1968 (Hanna-Barbera)
Gold Key

1	6.00	18.00	60.00
2-10: 3-Vs. Yogi Bear for President	3.80	11.40	38.00

MAGILLA GORILLA (TV)(See Spotlight #4)
Nov, 1970 - No. 5, July, 1971 (Hanna-Barbera)
Charlton Comics

1	3.40	10.00	24.00
2-5	2.30	6.70	16.00

MAGNETO (See X-Men #1)
nd (Sept, 1993) (Giveaway) (one-shot)
Marvel Comics

0-Embossed foil-c by Sienkiewicz; r/Classic X-Men #19 & 12 by John Bolton			
	1.00	2.00	5.00

MAGNETO
Nov, 1996 - No. 4, Feb, 1997 ($1.95, limited series)
Marvel Comics

1-4: Peter Milligan scripts & Kelley Jones-a(p)			2.00

MAGNETO AND THE MAGNETIC MEN
Apr, 1996 ($1.95)
Marvel Comics (Amalgam)

1-Jeff Matsuda-a(p)			2.00

MAGNUS, ROBOT FIGHTER (...4000 A.D.)(See Doctor Solar)
Feb, 1963 - No. 46, Jan, 1977 (All Painted covers except #5)
Gold Key

1-Origin & 1st app. Magnus; Aliens (1st app.) series begins			
	33.00	99.00	250.00
2,3	17.00	51.00	120.00
4-10: 10-Simonson fan club illo (5/65, 1st-a?)	10.00	29.00	68.00
11-20	6.40	19.00	45.00
21,24-28: 28-Aliens ends	4.30	12.90	30.00
22,23-12¢ and 15¢ editions exist: 22-Origin-r/#1	3.90	12.00	27.00
29-46-Reprints	1.70	5.00	12.00

NOTE: **Manning** a-1-22, 28-43(r). **Spiegle** a-23, 44r.

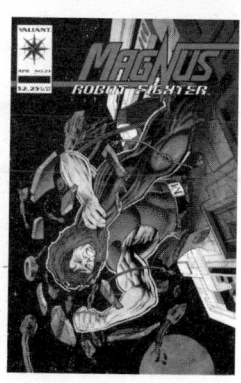

Magnus Robot Fighter #23 © WEST

Magnus RObot Fighter/Nexus #2 © WEST/Mike Baron & Steve rude

Man Against Time #2 © Motown

MAGNUS ROBOT FIGHTER (Also see Vintage Magnus)
May, 1991 - No. 64, Feb, 1996 ($1.75/$1.95/$2.25/$2.50)
Valiant Comics

1-Nichols/Layton-c/a; 1-8 have trading cards	1.50	3.75	9.00
2-5: 4-Rai cameo. 5-Origin & 1st full app. Rai (10/91); 5-8 are in flip book format and back-c & half of book are Rai #1-4 mini-series			
	1.20	3.00	7.00
6-8: 6-1st Solar x-over. 7-Magnus vs. Rai-c/story; 1st X-O Armor. 8-Begin $1.95-c			
		1.60	4.00
0-Origin issue; Layton-a; ordered through mail w/coupons from 1st 8 issues plus 50¢; B. Smith trading card	3.60	11.00	25.00
0-Sold thru comic shops without trading card	1.65	4.20	10.00
9-11: 11-Last $1.95-c		1.60	4.00
12-(3.25, 44 pgs.)-Turok-c/story (1st app. in Valiant universe, 5/92); has 8 pg. Magnus story insert	2.85	8.50	20.00
13-20,22-24,26-48, 50-63: 14-1st app. Isak. 15,16-Unity x-overs. 15-Miller-c. 16-Birth of Magnus. 24-Story cont'd in Rai & the Future Force #9. 33-Timewalker app.36-Bound-in trading cards. 37-Rai & Starwatchers app. 44-Bound-in sneak peek card		.90	2.25
21-New direction & new logo; Reese inks	1.00	2.50	
21-Gold ink variant	1.65	4.20	10.00
25-($2.95)-Embossed silver foil-c; new costume	1.20	3.00	
49, 64 ($2.50): 64-Magnus dies?		1.00	2.50
...Invasion (1994, $9.95)-r/Rai #1-4 & Magnus #5-8	1.65	4.20	10.00
Yearbook (1994, $3.95, 52 pgs.)		1.60	4.00

NOTE: *Ditko/Reese* a-18. *Layton* a(i)-5; c-6-9i, 25; back(i)-5-8. *Reese* a(i)-22, 25, 28; c(i)-22, 24, 28. *Simonson* c-16. Prices for issues 1-8 are for trading cards and coupons intact.

MAGNUS ROBOT FIGHTER 4000 A.D.
1990 - No. 2?, 1991 ($7.95, high quality paper, card stock-c, 96 pgs.)
Valiant Comics

1,2-Russ Manning-r. 1-Origin	1.30	3.25	8.00

MAGNUS ROBOT FIGHTER/NEXUS
Dec, 1993 - No. 2, Apr, 1994 ($2.95, limited series)
Valiant/Dark Horse Comics

1,2-Steve Rude painted-c & pencils	1.20	3.00	

MAID OF THE MIST (See American Graphics)

MAI, THE PSYCHIC GIRL
May 19, 1987 - No. 28, July, 1989 ($1.50, B&W, bi-weekly, 44pgs.)
Eclipse Comics

1		.80	2.00
1,2-2nd print			1.20
2-28			1.30

MAJOR HOOPLE COMICS (See Crackajack Funnies)
nd (Jan, 1943)
Nedor Publications

1-Mary Worth, Phantom Soldier app. by Moldoff	34.00	103.00	240.00

MAJOR INAPAK THE SPACE ACE
1951 (20 pgs.) (Giveaway)
Magazine Enterprises (Inapac Foods)

1-Bob Powell-c/a			1.00

NOTE: *Many warehouse copies surfaced in 1973.*

MAJOR VICTORY COMICS (Also see Dynamic Comics)
1944 - No. 3, Summer, 1945
H. Clay Glover/Service Publ./Harry 'A' Chesler

1-Origin Major Victory (patriotic hero) by C. Sultan (reprint from Dynamic #1); 1st app Spider Woman	47.00	141.00	375.00
2-Dynamic Boy app.	34.00	103.00	240.00
3-Rocket Boy app.	29.00	86.00	200.00

MALIBU ASHCAN: RAFFERTY (See Firearm #12)
Nov, 1994 (99¢, B&W w/color-c; one-shot)

Malibu Comics (Ultraverse)

1-Previews "The Rafferty Saga" storyline in Firearm; Chaykin-c.			
			1.00

MALTESE FALCON
No. 48, 1946
David McKay Publications

Feature Books 48-by Dashiell Hammett	65.00	195.00	520.00

MALU IN THE LAND OF ADVENTURE
1964 (See White Princess of Jungle #2)
I. W. Enterprises

1-r/Avon's Slave Girl Comics #1; Severin-c	5.85	17.50	35.00

MAMMOTH COMICS
1938 (84 pgs.) (B&W, 8-1/2x11-1/2")
Whitman Publishing Co.(K. K. Publications)

1-Alley Oop, Terry & the Pirates, Dick Tracy, Little Orphan Annie, Wash Tubbs, Moon Mullins, Smilin' Jack, Tailspin Tommy, Don Winslow, Dan Dunn, Smokey Stover & other reprints	137.00	412.00	1100.00

MAMMY YOKUM & THE GREAT DOGPATCH MYSTERY
1951 (Giveaway)
Toby Press

nn-Li'l Abner	18.00	54.00	125.00
nn-Reprint (1956)	4.25	13.00	26.00

MAN AGAINST TIME
May, 1996 - No. 3, June, 1996 ($2.25, limited series)
Image Comics (Motown Machineworks)

1-3: 1-Simonson-c. 2,3-Leon-c.			2.25

MAN-BAT (See Batman Family, Brave & the Bold, & Detective #400)
Dec-Jan, 1975-76 - No. 2, Feb-Mar, 1976; Dec, 1984
National Periodical Publications/DC Comics

1-Ditko-a(p); Aparo-c; Batman app.; 1st app. She-Bat?	1.00	2.60	6.00
2-Aparo-c		1.60	4.00
1 (12/84)-N. Adams-r(3)/Det.(Vs. Batman on-c)		1.60	4.00

MAN-BAT
Feb, 1996 - No. 3, Apr, 1996 ($2.25, limited series)
DC Comics

1-3: Dixon scripts in all. 2-Killer Croc/app.			2.25

MAN CALLED A-X, THE
Nov, 1994 - No. 4, Jun, 1995 ($2.95, limited series)
Malibu Comics (Bravura)

0-4: Marv Wolfman scripts & Shawn McManus-c/a. 0-(2/95). 1-"1A" on cover			
		1.20	3.00

MAN COMICS
Dec, 1949 - No. 28, Sept, 1953 (#1-6: 52 pgs.)
Marvel/Atlas Comics (NPI)

1-Tuska-a	17.00	51.00	120.00
2-Tuska-a	10.00	30.00	60.00
3-6	8.35	25.00	50.00
7,8	7.50	22.50	45.00
9-13,15: 9-Format changes to war	5.00	15.00	30.00
14-Henkel (3 pgs.); Pakula-a	6.70	20.00	40.00
16-21,23-28: 28-Crime issue (Bob Brant)	4.25	13.00	26.00
22-Krigstein-a, 5 pgs.	7.50	22.50	45.00

NOTE: *Berg* a-14, 15, 19. *Colan* a-9, 21. *Everett* a-8, 22; c-22, 25. *Heath* a-11, 17, 21. *Kubertish* a-9. *Maneely* a-11; c-10, 11. *Reinman* a-11. *Robinson* a-7, 10, 14. *Robert Sale* a-9, 11. *Sinnott* a-22, 23. *Tuska* a-14, 23.

MANDRAKE THE MAGICIAN (See Defenders Of The Earth, 123, 46, 52, 55, Giant Comic Album, King Comics, Magic Comics, The Phantom #21, Tiny Tot Funnies & Wow Comics, '36)

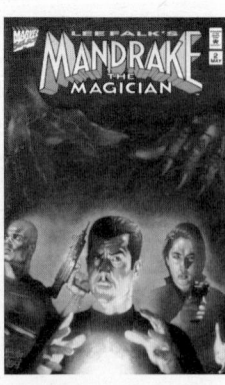

Mandrake the Magician #2 © KFS

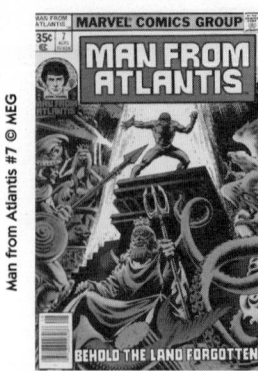

Man from Atlantis #7 © MEG

Manhunter #17 © DC

	GD25	FN65	NM94

MANDRAKE THE MAGICIAN (See Harvey Comics Hits #53)
1938 - 1948; Sept, 1966 - No. 10, Nov, 1967 (Also see Four Color #752)
David McKay Publ./King Comics (All 12¢)

	GD25	FN65	NM94
Feature Books 18,19 (1938)	37.50	112.50	375.00
Feature Books 46	37.00	111.00	260.00
Feature Books 52,55	30.00	90.00	210.00
1-Begin S.O.S. Phantom, ends #3	4.00	12.00	28.00
2-7,9: 4-Girl Phantom app. 5-Flying Saucer-c/story. 5,6-Brick Bradford app.			
7-Origin Lothar. 9-Brick Bradford app.	2.30	6.70	16.00
8-Jeff Jones-a (4 pgs.)	3.25	9.50	22.00
10-Rip Kirby app.; Raymond-a (14 pgs.)	3.9	11.50	27.00

MANDRAKE THE MAGICIAN
Apr, 1995 - No. 2, May, 1995 ($2.95, unfinished limited series)
Marvel Comics

1,2: Mike Barr scripts		1.20	3.00

MAN-EATING COW (See Tick #7,8)
July, 1992 - No. 10, 1994? ($2.75, B&W, limited series)
New England Comics

1-10		1.20	3.00
Man-Eating Cow Bonanza (6/96, $4.95, 128 pgs.)-r/#1-4.			5.00

MAN FROM ATLANTIS (TV)
Feb, 1978 - No. 7, Aug, 1978
Marvel Comics

1-($1.00, 84 pgs.)-Sutton-a(p), Buscema-c; origin			1.20
2-7 (#1: cast photos & origin Mark Harris inside)			1.00

MAN FROM PLANET X, THE
1987 (no price;probably unlicensed)
Planet X Productions

1-Reprints Fawcett Movie Comic			1.00

MAN FROM U.N.C.L.E., THE (TV) (Also see The Girl From Uncle)
Feb, 1965 - No. 22, Apr, 1969 (All photo-c)
Gold Key

1	13.50	40.50	135.00
2-Photo back c-2-8	8.50	25.50	85.00
3-10: 7-Jet Dream begins (1st app., also see Jet Dream) (all new stories)			
	5.50	16.50	55.00
11-22: 21,22-Reprint #10 & 7	4.50	13.50	45.00

MAN FROM U.N.C.L.E., THE (TV)
1987 - No. 11 ($1.50/$1.75, B&W)
Entertainment Publishing

1-7 ($1.50), 8-11 ($1.75)		.80	2.00

MAN FROM WELLS FARGO (TV)
No. 1287, Feb-Apr, 1962 - May-July, 1962 (Photo-c)
Dell Publishing Co.

Four Color 1287, #01-495-207	5.00	15.00	50.00

MANGA ZEN (Also see Zen Intergalactic Ninja)
1996 - Present ($2.50, B&W)
Zen Comics (Fusion Studios)

1			2.50

MANGLE TANGLE TALES
1990 ($2.95, deluxe format)
Innovation Publishing

1-Intro by Harlan Ellison		1.20	3.00

MANHUNT! (Becomes Red Fox #15 on)
Oct, 1947 - No. 14, 1953
Magazine Enterprises

1-Red Fox by L. B. Cole, Undercover Girl by Whitney, Space Ace begin (1st

	GD25	FN65	NM94
app.); negligee panels	40.00	120.00	300.00
2-Electrocution-c	33.00	99.00	230.00
3-6	28.00	84.00	195.00
7-10: 7-Space Ace ends. 8-Trail Colt begins (intro/1st app., 5/48) by			
Guardineer; Trail Colt-c. 10-G. Ingels-a	25.00	75.00	175.00
11(8/48)-Frazetta-a, 7 pgs.; The Duke, Scotland Yard begin			
	34.00	101.00	235.00
12	18.00	54.00	125.00
13(A-1 #63)-Frazetta, r-/Trail Colt #1, 7 pgs.	31.00	94.00	220.00
14(A-1 #77)-Bondage/hypo-c; last L. B. Cole Red Fox; Ingels-a			
	25.00	75.00	175.00

NOTE: *Guardineer* a-1-5; c-8. *Whitney* a-2-14; c-1-6, 10. Red Fox by **L. B. Cole**-#1-14. #15 was advertised but came out as Red Fox #15. Bondage c-6.

MANHUNTER (See Adventure #58, 73, Brave & the Bold, Detective Comics, 1st Issue Special, House of Mystery #143 and Justice League of America)
1984 ($2.50, 76 pgs; high quality paper)
DC Comics

1-Simonson-c/a(r)/Detective; Batman app.		1.00	2.50

MANHUNTER
July, 1988 - No. 24, Apr, 1990 ($1.00)
DC Comics

1-24: 8,9-Flash app. 9-Invasion. 17-Batman-c/sty			1.00

MANHUNTER
No. 0, Nov, 1994 - No. 12, Nov, 1995 ($1.95/$2.25)
DC Comics

0-7		.80	2.00
8-12: 8-Begin $2.25-c		.90	2.25

MAN IN BLACK (See Thrill-O-Rama) (Also see All New Comics, Front Page, Green Hornet #31, Strange Story & Tally-Ho Comics)
Sept, 1957 - No. 4, Mar, 1958
Harvey Publications

1-Bob Powell-c/a	11.50	34.00	80.00
2-4: Powell-c/a	10.00	30.00	60.00

MAN IN BLACK
1990 - No. 2, July, 1991 (B&W)
Lorne-Harvey Publications (Recollections)

1,2		.80	2.00

MAN IN FLIGHT (Disney, TV)
No. 836, Sept, 1957
Dell Publishing Co.

Four Color 836	7.00	21.00	70.00

MAN IN SPACE (Disney, TV, see Dell Giant #27)
No. 716, Aug, 1956 - No. 954, Nov, 1958
Dell Publishing Co.

Four Color 716-A science feat. from Tomorrowland	9.00	27.00	90.00
Four Color 954-Satellites	7.00	21.00	70.00

MAN OF PEACE, POPE PIUS XII
1950 (See Pope Pius XII... & To V2#8)
Catechetical Guild

nn-All Powell-a	4.00	12.00*	24.00

MAN OF STEEL, THE (Also see Superman: The Man of Steel)
1986 (June release) - No. 6, 1986 (75¢, limited series)
DC Comics

1-Silver logo; Byrne-c/a/scripts in all; origin			1.00
1-Alternate-c for newsstand sales			1.00
1-Distr. to toy stores by So Much Fun			1.00
2-6: 2-Intro. Lois Lane, Jimmy Olsen. 3-Intro/origin Magpie; Batman-c/story.			
4-Intro. new Lex Luthor			1.00
1-6-Silver Editions (1993, $1.95)-r/1-6		.80	2.00

Man-Thing #11 © MEG

Mantra #7 © Malibu

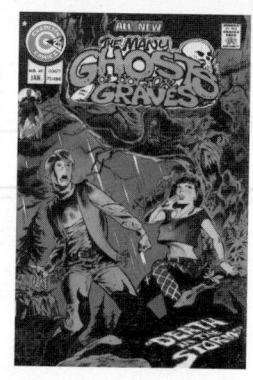

Many Ghosts of Dr. Graves #49 © CC

	GD25	FN65	NM94

...The Complete Saga nn-Contains #1-6, given away in contest .80 2.00
Limited Edition, softcover 4.30 13.00 30.00
NOTE: Issues 1-6 were released between Action #583 (9/86) & Action #584 (1/87) plus Superman #423 (9/86) & Advs. of Superman #424 (1/87).

MAN OF WAR (See Liberty Guards & Liberty Scouts)
Nov, 1941 - No. 2, Jan, 1942
Centaur Publications

1-The Fire-Man, Man of War, The Sentinel, Liberty Guards, & Vapo-Man
begin; Gustavson-c/a; Flag-c 137.00 412.00 1100.00
2-Intro The Ferret; Gustavson-c/a 115.00 346.00 925.00

MAN OF WAR
Aug, 1987 - No. 3, Feb, 1988 ($1.75, Baxter paper)
Eclipse Comics

1-3: Bruce Jones scripts 1.80

MAN OF WAR (See The Protectors)
1993 - No, 8, Feb, 1994 ($1.95/$2.50/$2.25)
Malibu Comics

1-5 ($1.95)-Newsstand Editions w/different-c .80 2.00
1-5 ($2.50)-Collector's Editions w/poster 1.00 2.50
6-8 ($2.25): 6-Polybagged w/Skycap. 8-Vs. Rocket Rangers .90 2.25

MAN O' MARS
1953; 1964
Fiction House Magazines

1-Space Rangers; Whitman-c 36.00 107.00 250.00
I.W. Reprint #1-r/Man O'Mars #1 & Star Pirate; Murphy Anderson-a 7.00 21.00 42.00

MANTECH ROBOT WARRIORS
Sept, 1984 - No. 4, Apr, 1985 (75¢)
Archie Enterprises, Inc.

1-4: Ayers-c/a(p). 1-Buckler-c(i) .80

MAN-THING (See Fear, Giant-Size..., Marvel Comics Presents, Marvel Fanfare, Monsters Unleashed, Power Record Comics & Savage Tales)
Jan, 1974 - No. 22, Oct, 1975; V2#1, Nov, 1979 - V2#11, July, 1981
Marvel Comics Group

1-Howard the Duck(2nd app.) cont'd/Fear #19 2.85 8.50 20.00
2 1.65 4.20 10.00
3-1st app. original Foolkiller 1.20 3.00 7.00
4-Origin Foolkiller; last app. 1st Foolkiller 1.60 4.00
5-11-Ploog-a. 11-Foolkiller cameo (flashback) 1.20 3.00
12-22: 19-1st app. Scavenger. 20-Spidey cameo. 21-Origin Scavenger, Man-Thing. 22-Howard the Duck cameo 1.00 2.50
V2#1(1979) - 11 1.50
NOTE: Alcala a-14. Brunner c-1. J. Buscema a-12p, 13p, 16p. Gil Kane c-4p, 10p, 12-20p, 21. Mooney a-17, 18, 19p, 20-22, V2#1-3p. Ploog Man-Thing-5p, 6p, 7, 8, 9-11p; c-5, 6, 8, 9, 11. Sutton a-13i. No. 19 says #10 in indicia.

MANTRA
July, 1993 - No. 24, Aug, 1995 ($1.95/$2.50)
Malibu Comics (Ultraverse)

1-Polybagged w/trading card & coupon 1.60 4.00
1-Newsstand edition w/o trading card or coupon 1.20 3.00
1-Full cover holographic edition 25.00
1-Ultra-limited silver foil-c 1.65 4.20 10.00
2,3,5,6: 3-Intro Warstrike & Kismet. 6-Break-Thru x-over .90 2.25
2-($2.50- Newsstand edition bagged w/card 1.00 2.50
4-($2.50, 48 pgs.)-Rune flip-c/story by B. Smith (3 pgs.) 1.00 2.50
7-9,11-17: 7-Prime app.; origin Prototype by Jurgens/Austin (2 pgs.). 11-New costume. 17-Intro NecroMantra & Pinnacle; prelude to Godwheel. .80 2.00
10-($3.50, 68 pgs.)-Flip-c w/Ultraverse Premiere #2 1.40 3.50
18-24: 18-Begin $2.50-c 1.00 2.50

Giant Size 1 (7/94, $2.50, 44 pgs.) 1.00 2.50
...Spear of Destiny 1,2 (4/95, $2.50, 36pgs.) 1.00 2.50

MANTRA (2nd Series) (Also See Black September)
Infinity, Sept, 1995 - No. 7, Apr, 1996 ($1.50)
Malibu Comics (Ultraverse)

Infinity (9/95, $1.50)-Black September x-over, Intro new Mantra. 1.50
1-7: 1-(10/95). 5-Return of Eden (original Mantra). 6,7-Rush app. 1.50

MAN WITH THE X-RAY EYES, THE (See X,... under Movie Comics)
MANY GHOSTS OF DR. GRAVES, THE (Doctor Graves #73 on)
5/67 - No. 60, 12/76; No. 61, 9/77 - No. 62, 10/77; No. 63, 2/78 - No. 65, 4/78; No. 66, 6/81 - No. 72, 5/82
Charlton Comics

1-Palais-a; early issues 12¢-c 1.70 4.20 10.00
2-10 1.00 2.00 5.00
11-20 1.40 3.50
21-44,46-72: 47,49-Newton-a .80 2.00
45-1st Newton comic work (8 pgs.); new logo 1.20 3.00
Modern Comics Reprint 12,25 (1978) 1.00
NOTE: Aparo a-4, 5, 7, 8, 66r, 69r; c-8, 14, 19, 66r, 67r. Byrne c-54. Ditko a-1, 7, 9, 11-13, 15-18, 20-22, 24, 26, 27, 35, 37, 38, 40-44, 47, 48, 51-54, 58, 60r-65r, 70, 72; c-11-13, 16-18, 22, 24, 26-35, 38, 40, 55, 58, 62-65. Howard a-45i; c-48. Morisi a-13, 14, 23, 26. Newton a-45, 47p, 49p; c-49, 52. Sutton a-42, 49; c-42, 44, 45; painted c-53.

MANY LOVES OF DOBIE GILLIS (TV)
May-June, 1960 - No. 26, Oct, 1964
National Periodical Publications

1-Most covers by Bob Oskner 30.00 90.00 210.00
2-5 16.00 47.00 110.00
6-10 11.50 34.00 80.00
11-26: 20-Drucker-a 10.00 30.00 70.00

MARAUDER'S MOON (See Luke Short, Four Color #848)
MARCH OF COMICS (Boys' and Girls'...#3-353)
1946 - No. 488, April, 1982 (#1-4 are not numbered)
(K.K. Giveaway) (Founded by Sig Feuchtwanger)
K. K. Publications/Western Publishing Co.

Early issues were full size, 32 pages, and were printed with and without an extra cover of slick stock, just for the advertiser. The binding was stapled if the slick cover was added; otherwise, the pages were glued together at the spine. Most 1948 - 1951 issues were full size,24 pages, pulp covers. Starting in 1952 they were half-size and 32 pages with slick covers.1959 and later issues had only 16 pages plus covers. 1952 -1959 issues read oblong; 1960 and later issues read upright. All have new stories except where noted.

nn (#1, 1946)-Goldilocks; Kelly back-c (16 pgs., stapled) 36.00 107.00 250.00
nn (#2, 1946)-How Santa Got His Red Suit; Kelly-a (11 pgs., r/4-Color #61 from 1944) (16pgs., stapled) 36.00 107.00 250.00
nn (#3, 1947)-Our Gang (Walt Kelly) 46.00 137.00 340.00
nn (#4)-Donald Duck by Carl Barks, "Maharajah Donald", 28 pgs.; Kelly-c? (Disney) 857.00 2571.00 7000.00
5-Andy Panda (Walter Lantz) 20.00 60.00 140.00
6-Popular Fairy Tales; Kelly-c; Noonan-a(2) 24.00 71.00 165.00
7-Oswald the Rabbit 24.00 71.00 165.00
8-Mickey Mouse, 32 pgs. (Disney) 71.00 215.00 500.00
9(nn)-The Story of the Gloomy Bunny 11.00 33.00 75.00
10-Out of Santa's Bag 10.00 30.00 65.00
11-Fun With Santa Claus 8.35 25.00 50.00
12-Santa's Toys 8.35 25.00 50.00
13-Santa's Surprise 8.35 25.00 50.00
14-Santa's Candy Kitchen 8.35 25.00 50.00
15-Hip-It-Ty Hop & the Big Bass Viol 8.35 25.00 50.00
16-Woody Woodpecker (1947)(Walter Lantz) 15.00 45.00 105.00
17-Roy Rogers (1948) 26.00 79.00 185.00

March of Comics #27 © WDC

LOBEL'S
MARCH OF COMICS
Featuring
WALT DISNEY'S
MICKEY MOUSE

March of Comics #56 © WDC

Boys' and Girls'
MARCH OF COMICS
Featuring
WALT DISNEY'S
DONALD DUCK

March of Comics #75 © Warner Bros.

Edwards
MARCH OF COMICS
Featuring
Warner Brothers'
BUGS BUNNY

	GD25	FN65	NM94		GD25	FN65	NM94
18-Popular Fairy Tales	13.00	39.00	90.00	77-Roy Rogers	16.00	47.00	110.00
19-Uncle Wiggily	11.00	33.00	75.00	78-Gene Autry (1951); last regular size issue	14.00	43.00	100.00
20-Donald Duck by Carl Barks, "Darkest Africa", 22 pgs.; Kelly-c (Disney)				79-Andy Panda (1952, 5x7" size)	4.25	13.00	28.00
	500.00	1500.00	4000.00	80-Popeye	11.50	34.00	80.00
21-Tom and Jerry	12.00	36.00	85.00	81-Oswald the Rabbit	5.00	15.00	30.00
22-Andy Panda (Lantz)	11.00	33.00	75.00	82-Tarzan; Lex Barker photo-c	19.00	58.00	135.00
23-Raggedy Ann & Andy; Kerr-a	17.00	49.00	115.00	83-Bugs Bunny	6.70	20.00	40.00
24-Felix the Cat, 1932 daily strip reprints by Otto Messmer				84-Henry	4.00	12.00	24.00
	27.00	81.00	190.00	85-Woody Woodpecker	4.00	12.00	24.00
25-Gene Autry	25.00	75.00	175.00	86-Roy Rogers	13.50	41.00	95.00
26-Our Gang; Walt Kelly	26.00	77.00	180.00	87-Krazy Kat	8.70	26.00	52.00
27-Mickey Mouse; r/in M. M. #240 (Disney)	50.00	150.00	350.00	88-Tom and Jerry	5.70	17.00	34.00
28-Gene Autry	25.00	75.00	175.00	89-Porky Pig	4.00	12.00	24.00
29-Easter Bonnet Shop	5.85	17.50	35.00	90-Gene Autry	13.00	39.00	90.00
30-Here Comes Santa	4.25	13.00	28.00	91-Roy Rogers & Santa	13.00	39.00	90.00
31-Santa's Busy Corner	4.25	13.00	28.00	92-Christmas with Santa	4.00	10.00	20.00
32-No book produced				93-Woody Woodpecker (1953)	4.00	12.00	24.00
33-A Christmas Carol (12/48)	4.25	13.00	28.00	94-Indian Chief	10.00	30.00	65.00
34-Woody Woodpecker	11.00	33.00	75.00	95-Oswald the Rabbit	4.00	12.00	24.00
35-Roy Rogers (1948)	26.00	77.00	180.00	96-Popeye	10.00	30.00	68.00
36-Felix the Cat(1949); by Messmer; 1934 daily strip-r				97-Bugs Bunny	5.70	17.00	34.00
	24.00	71.00	165.00	98-Tarzan; Lex Barker photo-c	21.00	62.00	145.00
37-Popeye	18.00	54.00	125.00	99-Porky Pig	4.00	12.00	24.00
38-Oswald the Rabbit	10.00	30.00	58.00	100-Roy Rogers	10.00	30.00	68.00
39-Gene Autry	25.00	75.00	175.00	101-Henry	4.00	11.00	22.00
40-Andy and Woody	10.00	30.00	58.00	102-Tom Corbett (TV)('53, early app.); painted-c	17.00	49.00	115.00
41-Donald Duck by Carl Barks, "Race to the South Seas", 22 pgs.; Kelly-c				103-Tom and Jerry	4.00	12.00	24.00
	500.00	1500.00	3500.00	104-Gene Autry	11.00	33.00	75.00
42-Porky Pig	10.00	30.00	58.00	105-Roy Rogers	11.00	33.00	75.00
43-Henry	8.00	24.00	48.00	106-Santa's Helpers	4.00	10.00	20.00
44-Bugs Bunny	11.00	33.00	75.00	107-Santa's Christmas Book - not published			
45-Mickey Mouse (Disney)	39.00	116.00	270.00	108-Fun with Santa (1953)	4.00	10.00	20.00
46-Tom and Jerry	11.00	33.00	75.00	109-Woody Woodpecker (1954)	4.00	11.00	22.00
47-Roy Rogers	22.00	66.00	155.00	110-Indian Chief	5.70	17.00	34.00
48-Greetings from Santa	4.00	12.00	24.00	111-Oswald the Rabbit	4.00	11.00	22.00
49-Santa Is Here	4.00	12.00	24.00	112-Henry	4.00	10.00	20.00
50-Santa Claus' Workshop (1949)	4.00	12.00	24.00	113-Porky Pig	4.00	11.00	22.00
51-Felix the Cat (1950) by Messmer	19.00	58.00	135.00	114-Tarzan; Russ Manning-a	21.00	62.00	145.00
52-Popeye	15.00	45.00	105.00	115-Bugs Bunny	4.25	13.00	28.00
53-Oswald the Rabbit	10.00	30.00	58.00	116-Roy Rogers	11.00	33.00	75.00
54-Gene Autry	21.00	62.00	145.00	117-Popeye	10.00	30.00	68.00
55-Andy and Woody	8.70	26.00	52.00	118-Flash Gordon; painted-c	13.50	41.00	95.00
56-Donald Duck; not by Barks; Barks art on back-c (Disney)				119-Tom and Jerry	4.00	11.00	22.00
	36.00	109.00	255.00	120-Gene Autry	11.00	33.00	75.00
57-Porky Pig	8.70	26.00	52.00	121-Roy Rogers	11.00	33.00	75.00
58-Henry	6.35	19.00	38.00	122-Santa's Surprise (1954)	3.00	7.50	15.00
59-Bugs Bunny	10.00	30.00	65.00	123-Santa's Christmas Book	3.00	7.50	15.00
60-Mickey Mouse (Disney)	35.00	105.00	245.00	124-Woody Woodpecker (1955)	4.00	10.00	20.00
61-Tom and Jerry	8.70	26.00	52.00	125-Tarzan; Lex Barker photo-c	19.00	58.00	135.00
62-Roy Rogers	21.00	62.00	145.00	126-Oswald the Rabbit	4.00	10.00	20.00
63-Welcome Santa (1/2-size, oblong)	4.00	12.00	24.00	127-Indian Chief	5.00	15.00	30.00
64(nn)-Santa's Helpers (1/2-size, oblong)	4.00	12.00	24.00	128-Tom and Jerry	4.00	10.00	20.00
65(nn)-Jingle Bells (1950) (1/2-size, oblong)	4.00	12.00	24.00	129-Henry	3.40	8.50	17.00
66-Popeye (1951)	13.00	39.00	90.00	130-Porky Pig	4.00	10.00	20.00
67-Oswald the Rabbit	8.00	24.00	48.00	131-Roy Rogers	11.00	33.00	75.00
68-Roy Rogers	19.00	58.00	135.00	132-Bugs Bunny	4.00	12.00	24.00
69-Donald Duck; Barks-a on back-c (Disney)	31.00	94.00	220.00	133-Flash Gordon; painted-c	12.00	36.00	85.00
70-Tom and Jerry	8.00	24.00	48.00	134-Popeye	8.00	24.00	48.00
71-Porky Pig	8.00	24.00	48.00	135-Gene Autry	10.00	30.00	68.00
72-Krazy Kat	10.00	30.00	65.00	136-Roy Rogers	10.00	30.00	68.00
73-Roy Rogers	17.00	49.00	115.00	137-Gifts from Santa	2.40	6.00	12.00
74-Mickey Mouse (1951)(Disney)	29.00	86.00	200.00	138-Fun at Christmas (1955)	2.40	6.00	12.00
75-Bugs Bunny	8.70	26.00	52.00	139-Woody Woodpecker (1956)	4.00	10.00	20.00
76-Andy and Woody	8.00	24.00	48.00	140-Indian Chief	5.00	15.00	30.00

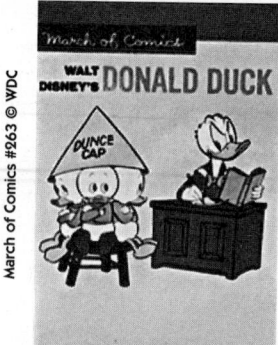

March of Comics #155 © ERB

March of Comics #185 © ERB

March of Comics #263 © WDC

	GD25	FN65	NM94
141-Oswald the Rabbit	4.00	10.00	20.00
142-Flash Gordon	12.00	36.00	85.00
143-Porky Pig	4.00	10.00	20.00
144-Tarzan; Russ Manning-a; painted-c	18.00	54.00	125.00
145-Tom and Jerry	4.00	10.00	20.00
146-Roy Rogers; photo-c	11.00	33.00	75.00
147-Henry	3.00	7.50	15.00
148-Popeye	8.00	24.00	48.00
149-Bugs Bunny	4.00	11.00	22.00
150-Gene Autry	10.00	30.00	68.00
151-Roy Rogers	10.00	30.00	68.00
152-The Night Before Christmas	2.40	6.00	12.00
153-Merry Christmas (1956)	2.40	6.00	12.00
154-Tom and Jerry (1957)	4.00	10.00	20.00
155-Tarzan; photo-c	18.00	54.00	125.00
156-Oswald the Rabbit	4.00	10.00	20.00
157-Popeye	6.70	20.00	40.00
158-Woody Woodpecker	4.00	10.00	20.00
159-Indian Chief	5.00	15.00	30.00
160-Bugs Bunny	4.00	11.00	22.00
161-Roy Rogers	10.00	30.00	58.00
162-Henry	3.00	7.50	15.00
163-Rin Tin Tin (TV)	7.50	22.50	45.00
164-Porky Pig	4.00	10.00	20.00
165-The Lone Ranger	10.00	30.00	65.00
166-Santa and His Reindeer	2.40	6.00	12.00
167-Roy Rogers and Santa	10.00	30.00	58.00
168-Santa Claus' Workshop (1957)	2.40	6.00	12.00
169-Popeye (1958)	6.70	20.00	40.00
170-Indian Chief	5.00	15.00	30.00
171-Oswald the Rabbit	3.60	9.00	18.00
172-Tarzan	13.50	41.00	95.00
173-Tom and Jerry	3.60	9.00	18.00
174-The Lone Ranger	10.00	30.00	65.00
175-Porky Pig	3.60	9.00	18.00
176-Roy Rogers	9.15	27.00	55.00
177-Woody Woodpecker	3.60	9.00	18.00
178-Henry	3.00	7.50	15.00
179-Bugs Bunny	3.60	9.00	18.00
180-Rin Tin Tin (TV)	6.35	19.00	38.00
181-Happy Holiday	2.00	5.00	10.00
182-Happi Tim	3.20	8.00	16.00
183-Welcome Santa (1958)	2.00	5.00	10.00
184-Woody Woodpecker (1959)	3.20	8.00	16.00
185-Tarzan; photo-c	13.00	39.00	90.00
186-Oswald the Rabbit	3.20	8.00	16.00
187-Indian Chief	4.70	14.00	28.00
188-Bugs Bunny	3.20	8.00	16.00
189-Henry	2.80	7.00	14.00
190-Tom and Jerry	3.20	8.00	16.00
191-Roy Rogers	8.35	25.00	50.00
192-Porky Pig	3.20	8.00	16.00
193-The Lone Ranger	10.00	30.00	60.00
194-Popeye	5.85	17.50	35.00
195-Rin Tin Tin (TV)	5.85	17.50	35.00
196-Sears Special - not published			
197-Santa Is Coming	2.00	5.00	10.00
198-Santa's Helpers (1959)	2.00	5.00	10.00
199-Huckleberry Hound (TV)(1960, early app.)	6.70	20.00	40.00
200-Fury (TV)	5.35	16.00	32.00
201-Bugs Bunny	3.20	8.00	16.00
202-Space Explorer	9.15	27.50	55.00
203-Woody Woodpecker	2.80	7.00	14.00
204-Tarzan	10.00	30.00	70.00

	GD25	FN65	NM94
205-Mighty Mouse	6.35	19.00	38.00
206-Roy Rogers; photo-c	8.35	25.00	50.00
207-Tom and Jerry	2.80	7.00	14.00
208-The Lone Ranger; Clayton Moore photo-c	12.00	36.00	85.00
209-Porky Pig	2.80	7.00	14.00
210-Lassie (TV)	6.35	19.00	38.00
211-Sears Special - not published			
212-Christmas Eve	2.00	5.00	10.00
213-Here Comes Santa (1960)	2.00	5.00	10.00
214-Huckleberry Hound (TV)(1961)	5.85	17.50	35.00
215-Hi Yo Silver	6.35	19.00	38.00
216-Rocky & His Friends (TV)(1961); predates Rocky and His Fiendish Friends #1 (see Four Color #1128)	10.00	30.00	70.00
217-Lassie (TV)	5.00	15.00	30.00
218-Porky Pig	2.80	7.00	14.00
219-Journey to the Sun	5.35	16.00	32.00
220-Bugs Bunny	3.20	8.00	16.00
221-Roy and Dale; photo-c	7.50	22.50	45.00
222-Woody Woodpecker	2.80	7.00	14.00
223-Tarzan	10.00	30.00	70.00
224-Tom and Jerry	2.80	7.00	14.00
225-The Lone Ranger	7.50	22.50	45.00
226-Christmas Treasury (1961)	2.00	5.00	10.00
227-Sears Special - not published?			
228-Letters to Santa (1961)	2.00	5.00	10.00
229-The Flintstones (TV)(1962); early app.; predates 1st Flintstones Gold Key issue (#7)	10.00	30.00	60.00
230-Lassie (TV)	5.00	15.00	30.00
231-Bugs Bunny	3.20	8.00	16.00
232-The Three Stooges	10.00	30.00	65.00
233-Bullwinkle (TV) (1962, very early app.)	11.00	32.00	75.00
234-Smokey the Bear	4.00	10.00	20.00
235-Huckleberry Hound (TV)	5.85	17.50	35.00
236-Roy and Dale	5.85	17.50	35.00
237-Mighty Mouse	4.70	14.00	28.00
238-The Lone Ranger	7.50	22.50	45.00
239-Woody Woodpecker	2.80	7.00	14.00
240-Tarzan	9.15	27.50	55.00
241-Santa Claus Around the World	2.00	5.00	10.00
242-Santa's Toyland (1962)	2.00	5.00	10.00
243-The Flintstones (TV)(1963)	9.15	27.50	55.00
244-Mister Ed (TV); early app.; photo-c	5.85	17.50	35.00
245-Bugs Bunny	3.20	8.00	16.00
246-Popeye	4.35	13.00	26.00
247-Mighty Mouse	4.70	14.00	28.00
248-The Three Stooges	10.00	30.00	65.00
249-Woody Woodpecker	2.80	7.00	14.00
250-Roy and Dale	5.85	17.50	35.00
251-Little Lulu & Witch Hazel	14.00	43.00	100.00
252-Tarzan; painted-c	9.15	27.50	55.00
253-Yogi Bear (TV)	6.35	19.00	38.00
254-Lassie (TV)	5.35	16.00	32.00
255-Santa's Christmas List	2.00	5.00	10.00
256-Christmas Party (1963)	2.00	5.00	10.00
257-Mighty Mouse	4.70	14.00	28.00
258-The Sword in the Stone (Disney)	9.15	27.50	55.00
259-Bugs Bunny	3.20	8.00	16.00
260-Mister Ed (TV)	4.70	14.00	28.00
261-Woody Woodpecker	2.80	7.00	14.00
262-Tarzan	8.35	25.00	50.00
263-Donald Duck; not by Barks (Disney)	10.00	30.00	65.00
264-Popeye	4.35	13.00	26.00
265-Yogi Bear (TV)	4.70	14.00	28.00
266-Lassie (TV)	4.15	12.50	25.00

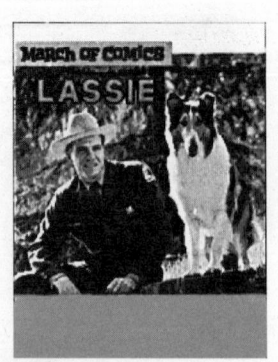

March of Comics #308 © WEST

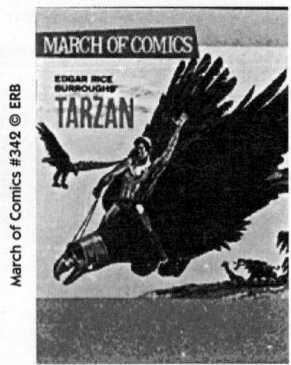

March of Comics #342 © ERB

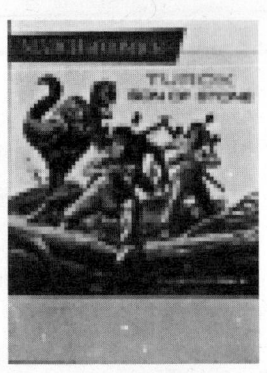

March of Comics #378 © WEST

	GD25	FN65	NM94		GD25	FN65	NM94
267-Little Lulu; Irving Tripp-a	11.50	34.00	80.00	331-Daffy Duck	2.00	5.00	10.00
268-The Three Stooges	10.00	30.00	60.00	332-Tarzan	5.35	16.00	32.00
269-A Jolly Christmas	2.00	5.00	10.00	333-Tom and Jerry	2.00	5.00	10.00
270-Santa's Little Helpers	2.00	5.00	10.00	334-Lassie (TV)	4.00	10.00	20.00
271-The Three Flintstones (TV)(1965)	9.15	27.50	55.00	335-Little Lulu	4.35	13.00	26.00
272-Tarzan	8.35	25.00	50.00	336-The Three Stooges	7.50	22.50	45.00
273-Bugs Bunny	3.20	8.00	16.00	337-Yogi Bear (TV)	4.00	11.00	22.00
274-Popeye	4.35	13.00	26.00	338-The Lone Ranger	6.70	20.00	40.00
275-Little Lulu; Irving Tripp-a	10.00	30.00	65.00	339-(Was not published)			
276-The Jetsons (TV)	14.00	43.00	100.00	340-Here Comes Santa (1969)	2.00	5.00	10.00
277-Daffy Duck	3.20	8.00	16.00	341-The Flintstones (TV)	6.70	20.00	40.00
278-Lassie (TV)	4.15	12.50	25.00	342-Tarzan	5.35	16.00	32.00
279-Yogi Bear (TV)	4.70	14.00	28.00	343-Bugs Bunny	2.40	6.00	12.00
280-The Three Stooges; photo-c	10.00	30.00	60.00	344-Yogi Bear (TV)	4.00	10.00	20.00
281-Tom and Jerry	2.40	6.00	12.00	345-Tom and Jerry	2.00	5.00	10.00
282-Mister Ed (TV)	4.70	14.00	28.00	346-Lassie (TV)	4.00	10.00	20.00
283-Santa's Visit	2.00	5.00	10.00	347-Daffy Duck	2.00	5.00	10.00
284-Christmas Parade (1965)	2.00	5.00	10.00	348-The Jetsons (TV)	10.00	30.00	60.00
285-Astro Boy (TV); 2nd app. Astro Boy	36.00	107.00	250.00	349-Little Lulu; not by Stanley	4.00	11.00	22.00
286-Tarzan	7.50	22.50	45.00	350-The Lone Ranger	5.00	15.00	30.00
287-Bugs Bunny	3.20	8.00	16.00	351-Beep-Beep, the Road Runner (TV)	2.80	7.00	14.00
288-Daffy Duck	2.80	7.00	14.00	352-Space Family Robinson (TV); Spiegle-a	13.00	40.00	90.00
289-The Flintstones (TV)	8.35	25.00	50.00	353-Beep-Beep, the Road Runner (1971) (TV)	2.80	7.00	14.00
290-Mister Ed (TV); photo-c	4.00	12.00	24.00	354-Tarzan (1971)	4.70	14.00	28.00
291-Yogi Bear (TV)	4.00	12.00	24.00	355-Little Lulu; not by Stanley	4.00	11.00	22.00
292-The Three Stooges; photo-c	10.00	30.00	60.00	356-Scooby Doo, Where Are You? (TV)	4.00	11.00	22.00
293-Little Lulu; Irving Tripp-a	9.15	27.50	55.00	357-Daffy Duck & Porky Pig	2.00	5.00	10.00
294-Popeye	4.35	13.00	26.00	358-Lassie (TV)	4.00	10.00	20.00
295-Tom and Jerry	2.40	6.00	12.00	359-Baby Snoots	2.80	7.00	14.00
296-Lassie (TV); photo-c	4.00	11.00	22.00	360-H. R. Pufnstuf (TV); photo-c	4.00	10.00	20.00
297-Christmas Bells	2.00	5.00	10.00	361-Tom and Jerry	2.00	5.00	10.00
298-Santa's Sleigh (1966)	2.00	5.00	10.00	362-Smokey the Bear (TV)	2.00	5.00	10.00
299-The Flintstones (TV)(1967)	8.35	25.00	50.00	363-Bugs Bunny & Yosemite Sam	2.40	6.00	12.00
300-Tarzan	7.50	22.50	45.00	364-The Banana Splits (TV); photo-c	2.40	6.00	12.00
301-Bugs Bunny	2.80	7.00	14.00	365-Tom and Jerry (1972)	2.00	5.00	10.00
302-Laurel and Hardy (TV); photo-c	5.00	15.00	30.00	366-Tarzan	4.35	13.00	26.00
303-Daffy Duck	2.00	5.00	10.00	367-Bugs Bunny & Porky Pig	2.40	6.00	12.00
304-The Three Stooges; photo-c	9.15	27.50	55.00	368-Scooby Doo (TV)(4/72)	4.00	10.00	20.00
305-Tom and Jerry	2.00	5.00	10.00	369-Little Lulu; not by Stanley	3.60	9.00	18.00
306-Daniel Boone (TV); Fess Parker photo-c	5.85	17.50	35.00	370-Lassie (TV); photo-c	4.00	10.00	20.00
307-Little Lulu; Irving Tripp-a	7.50	22.50	45.00	371-Baby Snoots	2.40	6.00	12.00
308-Lassie (TV); photo-c	4.00	11.00	22.00	372-Smokey the Bear (TV)	2.00	5.00	10.00
309-Yogi Bear (TV)	4.00	11.00	22.00	373-The Three Stooges	6.70	20.00	40.00
310-The Lone Ranger; Clayton Moore photo-c	12.00	36.00	85.00	374-Wacky Witch	2.00	5.00	10.00
311-Santa's Show	2.00	5.00	10.00	375-Beep-Beep & Daffy Duck (TV)	2.00	5.00	10.00
312-Christmas Album (1967)	2.00	5.00	10.00	376-The Pink Panther (1972) (TV)	2.80	7.00	14.00
313-Daffy Duck (1968)	2.00	5.00	10.00	377-Baby Snoots (1973)	2.40	6.00	12.00
314-Laurel and Hardy (TV)	4.70	14.00	28.00	378-Turok, Son of Stone; new-a	14.00	43.00	100.00
315-Bugs Bunny	2.80	7.00	14.00	379-Heckle & Jeckle New Terrytoons (TV)	2.00	5.00	10.00
316-The Three Stooges	7.50	22.50	45.00	380-Bugs Bunny & Yosemite Sam	2.00	5.00	10.00
317-The Flintstones (TV)	6.70	20.00	40.00	381-Lassie (TV)	3.20	8.00	16.00
318-Tarzan	6.70	20.00	40.00	382-Scooby Doo, Where Are You? (TV)	3.60	9.00	18.00
319-Yogi Bear (TV)	4.00	11.00	22.00	383-Smokey the Bear (TV)	1.60	4.00	8.00
320-Space Family Robinson (TV); Spiegle-a	13.00	40.00	90.00	384-Pink Panther (TV)	2.00	5.00	10.00
321-Tom and Jerry	2.00	5.00	10.00	385-Little Lulu	3.00	7.50	15.00
322-The Lone Ranger	6.70	20.00	40.00	386-Wacky Witch	1.60	4.00	8.00
323-Little Lulu; not by Stanley	4.35	13.00	26.00	387-Beep-Beep & Daffy Duck (TV)	1.60	4.00	8.00
324-Lassie (TV); photo-c	4.00	11.00	22.00	388-Tom and Jerry (1973)	1.60	4.00	8.00
325-Fun with Santa	2.00	5.00	10.00	389-Little Lulu; not by Stanley	3.00	7.50	15.00
326-Christmas Story (1968)	2.00	5.00	10.00	390-Pink Panther (TV)	1.60	4.00	8.00
327-The Flintstones (TV)(1969)	6.70	20.00	40.00	391-Scooby Doo (TV)	3.20	8.00	16.00
328-Space Family Robinson (TV); Spiegle-a	13.00	40.00	90.00	392-Bugs Bunny & Yosemite Sam	1.20	3.00	6.00
329-Bugs Bunny	2.80	7.00	14.00	393-New Terrytoons (Heckle & Jeckle) (TV)	1.20	3.00	6.00
330-The Jetsons (TV)	10.00	30.00	70.00	394-Lassie (TV)	2.40	6.00	12.00

March of Crime #3 © FOX

Marco Polo © CC

Marc Spector: Moon Knight #13 © MEG

MA

	GD25	FN65	NM94
95-Woodsy Owl	1.20	3.00	6.00
96-Baby Snoots	1.60	4.00	8.00
97-Beep-Beep & Daffy Duck (TV)	1.20	3.00	6.00
98-Wacky Witch	1.20	3.00	6.00
99-Turok, Son of Stone; new-a	11.00	32.00	75.00
00-Tom and Jerry	1.20	3.00	6.00
01-Baby Snoots (1975) (r/#371)	1.60	4.00	8.00
02-Daffy Duck (r/#313)	1.00	2.50	5.00
03-Bugs Bunny (r/#343)	1.20	3.00	6.00
04-Space Family Robinson (TV)(r/#328)	10.00	30.00	65.00
05-Cracky	1.00	2.50	5.00
06-Little Lulu (r/#355)	2.40	6.00	12.00
07-Smokey the Bear (TV)(r/#362)	1.20	3.00	6.00
08-Turok, Son of Stone; c-r/Turok #20 w/changes; new-a			
	8.35	25.00	55.00
09-Pink Panther (TV)	1.00	2.50	5.00
10-Wacky Witch	.80	2.00	4.00
11-Lassie (TV)(r/#324)	2.40	6.00	12.00
12-New Terrytoons (1975) (TV)	.80	2.00	4.00
13-Daffy Duck (1976)(r/#331)	.80	2.00	4.00
14-Space Family Robinson (r/#328)	8.35	25.00	55.00
15-Bugs Bunny (r/#329)	.80	2.00	4.00
16-Beep-Beep, the Road Runner (r/#353)(TV)	.80	2.00	4.00
17-Little Lulu (r/#323)	2.40	6.00	12.00
18-Pink Panther (r/#384) (TV)	.80	2.00	4.00
19-Baby Snoots (r/#377)	1.00	2.50	5.00
20-Woody Woodpecker	.80	2.00	4.00
21-Tweety & Sylvester	.80	2.00	4.00
22-Wacky Witch (r/#386)	.80	2.00	4.00
23-Little Monsters	1.00	2.50	5.00
24-Cracky (12/76)	.80	2.00	4.00
25-Daffy Duck	.80	2.00	4.00
26-Underdog (TV)	3.00	7.50	15.00
27-Little Lulu (r/#335)	1.60	4.00	8.00
28-Bugs Bunny	.60	1.50	3.00
29-The Pink Panther (TV)	.60	1.50	3.00
30-Beep-Beep, the Road Runner (TV)	.60	1.50	3.00
31-Baby Snoots	.80	2.00	4.00
32-Lassie	1.20	3.00	6.00
33-437: 433-Tweety & Sylvester. 434-Wacky Witch. 435-New Terrytoons (TV).			
436-Wacky Advs. of Cracky. 437-Daffy Duck	.60	1.50	3.00
38-Underdog (TV)	3.00	7.50	15.00
39-Little Lulu (r/#349)	1.60	4.00	8.00
40-442,444-446: 440-Bugs Bunny. 441-The Pink Panther (TV). 442-Beep-Beep, the Road Runner (TV). 444-Tom and Jerry. 445-Tweety and			
Sylvester. 446-Wacky Witch	.60	1.50	3.00
43-Baby Snoots	.80	2.00	4.00
47-Mighty Mouse	1.20	3.00	6.00
48-455,457,458: 448-Cracky. 449-Pink Panther. 450-Baby Snoots. 451-Tom and Jerry. 452-Bugs Bunny. 453-Popeye. 454-Woody Woodpecker. 455-Beep-Beep, the Road Runner (TV). 457-Tweety & Sylvester. 458-Wacky Witch	.60	1.50	3.00
56-Little Lulu (r/#369)	1.20	3.00	6.00
59-Mighty Mouse	1.20	3.00	6.00
60-466: 460-Daffy Duck. 461-The Pink Panther (TV). 462-Baby Snoots. 463-Tom and Jerry. 464-Bugs Bunny. 465-Popeye. 466-Woody Woodpecker	.60	1.50	3.00
67-Underdog (TV)	2.40	6.00	12.00
68-Little Lulu (r/#385)	.80	2.00	4.00
69-Tweety & Sylvester	.60	1.50	3.00
70-Wacky Witch	.60	1.50	3.00
71-Mighty Mouse	.80	2.50	5.00
72-474,476-478: 472-Heckle & Jeckle(12/80). 473-Pink Panther(1/81)(TV). 474-Baby Snoots. 476-Bugs Bunny. 477-Popeye. 478-Woody Woodpecker			

	GD25	FN65	NM94
	.60	1.50	3.00
475-Little Lulu (r/#323)	.80	2.00	4.00
479-Underdog (TV)	2.00	5.00	10.00
480-482: 480-Tom and Jerry. 481-Tweety and Sylvester. 482-Wacky Witch			
	.60	1.50	3.00
483-Mighty Mouse	.80	2.00	5.00
484-487: 484-Heckle & Jeckle. 485-Baby Snoots. 486-The Pink Panther (TV).			
487-Bugs Bunny	.60	1.50	3.00
488-Little Lulu (4/82) (r/#335)	.80	2.00	4.00

MARCH OF CRIME (Formerly My Love Affair #1-6) (See Fox Giants)
No. 7, July, 1950 - No. 2, Sept, 1950; No. 3, Sept, 1951
Fox Features Syndicate

	GD25	FN65	NM94
7(#1)(7/50)-True crime stories; Wood-a	31.00	94.00	220.00
2(9/50)-Wood-a (exceptional)	31.00	94.00	220.00
3(9/51)	13.00	39.00	90.00

MARCO POLO
1962 (Movie classic)
Charlton Comics Group

	GD25	FN65	NM94
nn (Scarce)-Glanzman-c/a (25 pgs.)	13.50	41.00	95.00

MARC SPECTOR: MOON KNIGHT (Also see Moon Knight)
June, 1989 - No. 60, Mar, 1994 ($1.50/$1.75, direct sales)
Marvel Comics

	GD25	FN65	NM94
1		1.20	3.00
2-7: 4-Intro new Midnight		.80	2.00
8,9-Punisher app.		1.20	3.00
10-18: 15-Silver Sable app. 20-Guice-c. 21-23-Cowan-c(p)		.80	2.00
19-21-Spider-Man & Punisher app.		1.20	3.00
22-24,26-31,34: 34-Last $1.50-c		.70	1.75
25-($2.50, 52 pgs.)-Ghost Rider app.		1.20	3.00
32,33-Hobgoblin II (Macendale) & Spider-Man (in black costume) app.			
		1.20	3.00
35-38-Punisher story		.80	2.00
39-49,51-54: 42-44-Infinity War x-over. 46-Demogoblin app. 51,53-Gambit app.			
		.70	1.75
50-($2.95, 56 pgs.)-Special die-cut cover		1.30	3.25
55-New look & Stephen Platt-c/a begin		1.20	3.00
56,57-Platt-c/a. 57-Spider-Man-c/story		1.60	4.00
58-60: 58,59-S. Platt-c only. 60-S.Platt-c/a; Moon Knight dies.			
		.80	2.00
...: Divided We Fall ($4.95, 52 pgs.)	1.00	2.00	5.00
Special 1 (1992, $2.50)		1.00	2.50

NOTE: Heath c/a-4. Platt c-a

MARGARET O'BRIEN (See The Adventures of...)

MARGE'S LITTLE LULU (Little Lulu #207 on)
No. 74, 6/45 - No. 164, 7-9/62; No. 165, 10/62 - No. 206, 8/72
Dell Publishing Co./Gold Key #165-206

Marjorie Henderson Buell, born in Philadelphia, Pa., in 1904, created Little Lulu, a cartoon character that appeared weekly in the Saturday Evening Post from Feb. 23, 1935 through Dec. 30, 1944. She was not responsible for any of the comic books. John Stanley did pencils only on all Little Lulu comics through at least #135 (1959). He did pencils and inks on Four Color #74 & 97. Irving Tripp began inking stories from #1 on, and remained the comic's illustrator throughout its entire run. Stanley did storyboards (layouts), pencils, and scripts in all cases and inking only on covers. His word balloons were written in cursive. Tripp and occasionally other artists at Western Publ. in Poughkeepsie, N.Y. blew up the pencilled pages, inked the blowups, and lettered them. Arnold Drake did storyboards, pencils and scripts starting with #197 (1970) on, amidst reprinted issues. Buell sold her rights exclusively to Western Publ. in Dec., 1971. The earlier issues had to be approved by Buell prior to publication.

	GD25	FN65	NM94
Four Color 74('45)-Intro Lulu, Tubby & Alvin	96.00	288.00	960.00
Four Color 97(2/46)	45.00	135.00	450.00
(Above two books are all John Stanley - cover, pencils, and inks.)			
Four Color 110('46)-1st Alvin Story Telling Time; 1st app. Willy			
	33.00	99.00	325.00
Four Color 115-1st app. Boys' Clubhouse	33.00	99.00	325.00

Marines In Action #1 © ATLAS

Marines In Battle #3 © ATLAS

Mark #2 © DH

	GD25	FN65	NM94
Four Color 120, 131: 120-1st app. Eddie	28.00	84.00	280.00
Four Color 139('47),146,158	26.00	78.00	260.00
Four Color 165 (10/47)-Smokes doll hair & has wild hallucinations. 1st Tubby			
detective story	26.00	78.00	260.00
1(1-2/48)-Lulu's Diary feature begins	55.00	165.00	550.00
2-1st app. Gloria; 1st Tubby story in a L.L. comic; 1st app. Miss Feeny			
	28.00	84.00	280.00
3-5	25.00	75.00	250.00
6-10: 7-1st app. Annie; Xmas-c	18.00	54.00	180.00
11-20: 18-X-Mas-c. 19-1st app. Wilbur. 20-1st app. Mr. McNabbem			
	16.00	48.00	160.00
21-30: 26-r/F.C. 110. 30-Xmas-c	13.00	40.00	125.00
31-38,40: 35-1st Mumday story	10.00	30.00	100.00
39-Intro. Witch Hazel in "That Awful Witch Hazel"	12.00	36.00	115.00
41-60: 42-Xmas-c. 45-2nd Witch Hazel app. 49-Gives Stanley & others credit			
	10.00	30.00	100.00
61-80: 63-1st app. Chubby (Tubby's cousin). 68-1st app. Prof. Cleff.			
78-Xmas-c. 80-Intro. Little Itch (2/55)	7.00	21.00	70.00
81-99: 90-Xmas-c	5.00	15.00	50.00
100	6.00	18.00	60.00
101-130: 123-1st app. Fifi	5.00	15.00	50.00
131-164: 135-Last Stanley-p	4.00	12.00	40.00
165-Giant; ...in Paris ('62)	12.00	36.00	120.00
166-Giant; ...Christmas Diary (1962 - '63)	12.00	36.00	120.00
167-169	3.00	9.00	30.00
170,172,175,176,178-196,198-200-Stanley-r. 182-1st app. Little Scarecrow			
Boy	2.80	7.00	14.00
171,173,174,177,197	1.60	4.00	8.00
201,203,206-Last issue to carry Marge's name	1.20	3.00	6.00
202,204,205-Stanley-r	1.80	4.50	9.00
...& Tubby in Japan (12¢)(5-7/62) 01476-207	10.00	30.00	60.00
...Summer Camp 1(8/67-G.K.-Giant) '57-58-r	7.00	21.00	42.00
...Trick 'N' Treat 1(12¢)(12/62-Gold Key)	8.35	25.00	50.00

NOTE: See Dell Giant Comics #23, 29, 36, 42, 50, & Dell Giants for annuals. All Giants not by Stanley from L.L. on Vacation (7/54) on. Irving Tripp a-#1-on. Christmas c-7, 18, 30, 42, 78, 90, 126, 166, 250. Summer Camp issues #173, 177, 181, 189, 197, 201, 206.

MARGE'S LITTLE LULU (See Golden Comics Digest #19, 23, 27, 29, 33, 36, 40, 43, 46, & March of Comics #251, 267, 275, 293, 307, 323, 335, 349, 355, 369, 385, 406, 417, 427, 439, 456, 468, 475, 488)

MARGE'S TUBBY (Little Lulu)(See Dell Giants)
No. 381, Aug, 1952 - No. 49, Dec-Feb, 1961-62
Dell Publishing Co./Gold Key

Four Color 381(#1)-Stanley script; Irving Tripp-a	17.50	52.50	175.00
Four Color 430,444-Stanley-a	10.00	30.00	100.00
Four Color 461 (4/53)-1st Tubby & Men From Mars story; Stanley-a			
	9.00	27.00	90.00
5 (7-9/53)-Stanley-a	7.00	21.00	70.00
6-10	5.00	15.00	50.00
11-20	4.00	12.00	40.00
21-30	4.00	11.00	32.00
31-49	3.00	9.00	27.00
...& the Little Men From Mars No. 30020-410(10/64-G.K.)-25¢, 68 pgs.			
	8.00	24.00	70.00

NOTE: John Stanley did all storyboards & scripts through at least #35 (1959). Lloyd White did all art except F.C. 381, 430, 444, 461 & #5.

MARGIE (See My Little...)

MARGIE (TV)
No. 1307, Mar-May, 1962 - No. 2, July-Sept, 1962 (Photo-c)
Dell Publishing Co.

Four Color 1307(#1), 2	4.00	12.00	40.00

MARGIE COMICS (Formerly Comedy Comics; Reno Browne #50 on)
(Also see Cindy Comics & Teen Comics)
No. 35, Winter, 1946-47 - No. 49, Dec, 1949

	GD25	FN65	NM94

Marvel Comics (ACI)

35	10.00	30.00	70.0
36-38,42,45,47-49	6.35	19.00	38.0
39,41,43(2),44,46-Kurtzman's "Hey Look"	9.15	27.00	55.0
40-Three "Hey Looks", three "Giggles 'n' Grins" by Kurtzman			
	10.00	30.00	65.0

MARINES (See Tell It to the...)

MARINES ATTACK
Aug, 1964 - No. 9, Feb-Mar, 1966
Charlton Comics

1	2.00	6.00	14.0
2-9	1.20	3.00	7.0

MARINES AT WAR (Formerly Tales of the Marines #4)
No. 5, Apr, 1957 - No. 7, Aug, 1957
Atlas Comics (OPI)

5-7	5.00	15.00	30.0

NOTE: Colan a-5. Drucker a-5. Everett a-5. Maneely a-5. Orlando a-7. Severin c-5.

MARINES IN ACTION
June, 1955 - No. 14, Sept, 1957
Atlas News Co.

1-Rock Murdock, Boot Camp Brady begin	8.00	24.00	48.0
2-14	4.25	13.00	28.0

NOTE: Berg a-2, 8, 9, 11, 14. Heath c-2, 9. Maneely c-1. Severin a-4; c-7-11, 14.

MARINES IN BATTLE
Aug, 1954 - No. 25, Sept, 1958
Atlas Comics (ACI No. 1-12/WPI No. 13-25)

1-Heath-c; Iron Mike McGraw by Heath; history of U.S. Marine Corps. begins			
	13.00	39.00	90.0
2-Heath-c	8.35	25.00	50.0
3-6,8-10: 4-Last precode (2/55)	5.85	17.50	35.0
7-Kubert/Moskowitz-a (6 pgs.)	7.00	21.00	42.0
11-16,18-21,24	4.25	13.00	28.0
17-Williamson-a (3 pgs.)	8.00	24.00	48.0
22,25-Torres-a	5.85	17.50	35.0
23-Crandall-a; Mark Murdock app.	7.00	21.00	42.0

NOTE: Berg a-22. G. Colan a-22, 23. Drucker a-6. Everett a-4, 15; c-21. Heath c-1, 2, 4. Maneely c-23, 24. Orlando a-14. Pakula a-6, 23. Powell a-16. Severin a-22; c-12. Sinnott a-23. Tuska a-15.

MARINE WAR HEROES (Charlton Premiere #19 on)
Jan, 1964 - No. 18, Mar, 1967
Charlton Comics

1-Montes/Bache-c/a	2.00	6.00	14.
2-18: 14,18-Montes/Bache-a	1.20	3.00	7.

MARK, THE (Also see Mayhem)
Dec, 1993 - No. 4, Mar, 1994 ($2.50, limited series)
Dark Horse Comics

1-4		1.00	2.

MARK HAZZARD: MERC
Nov, 1986 - No. 12, Oct, 1987 (75¢)
Marvel Comics Group

1-12: Morrow-a			..
Annual 1 (11/87, $1.25)			1..

MARK OF ZORRO (See Zorro, Four Color #228)

MARKSMAN, THE (Also see Champions)
Jan, 1988 - No. 5, 1988 ($1.95)
Hero Comics

1-5: 1-Rose begins. 1-3-Origin The Marksman		.80	2..
Annual 1 ('88, $2.75, 52pgs)-Champions app.		1.10	2..

MARK STEEL

Mark Trail #5 © STD

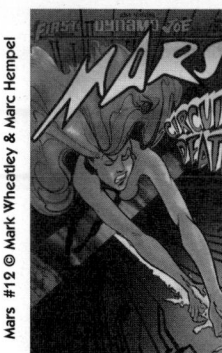

Mars #12 © Mark Wheatley & Marc Hempel

Martha Washington Goes to War #2 © Frank Miller & Dave Gibbons

67, 1968, 1972 (Giveaway) (24 pgs.)			
merican Iron & Steel Institute			
67,1968- "Journey of Discovery with…"; Neal Adams art			
	3.60	9.00	18.00
72- "…Fights Pollution"; N. Adams-a	1.50	3.75	9.00

ARK TRAIL
ct, 1955; No. 5, Summer, 1959
andard Magazines (Hall Syndicate)/Fawcett Publ. No. 5

(1955)-Sunday strip-r	5.85	17.50	35.00
(1959)	4.00	10.00	20.00
Adventure Book of Nature 1 (Summer, 1958, 25¢, Pines)-100 pg. Giant;			
Special Camp Issue; contains 78 Sunday strip-r	8.35	25.00	50.00

ARMADUKE MONK
date; 1963 (10¢)
V. Enterprises/Super Comics

V. Reprint 1 (nd)	1.00	2.60	6.00
per Reprint 14 (1963)-r/Monkeyshines Comics #?	1.00	2.60	6.00

ARMADUKE MOUSE
ring, 1946 - No. 65, Dec, 1956 (Early issues: 52 pgs.)
ality Comics Group (Arnold Publ.)

-Funny animal	14.00	43.00	100.00
	8.35	25.00	50.00
-10	6.35	19.00	38.00
-30	4.25	13.00	28.00
-65: Later issues are 36 pgs.	4.00	11.00	22.00
per Reprint #14(1963)	1.65	4.20	10.00

ARRIED … WITH CHILDREN (TV)
ne, 1990 - No. 7, Feb, 1991(12/90 inside) ($1.75)
#1, Sept, 1991 - No. 12, 1992 ($1.95)
ow Comics

-Based on Fox TV show		.80	2.00
-2nd printing ($1.75)		.70	1.75
-Photo-c		.80	2.00
-2nd printing ($1.75)		.70	1.75
-7		.70	1.75
#1-12: 1,4,5,9-Photo-c		.80	2.00
Buck's Tale (6/94, $1.95)		.80	2.00
1994 Annual nn (2/94, $2.50, 52 pgs.)-Flip book format	1.00	2.50
ecial 1 (7/92, $1.95)-Kelly Bundy photo-c/poster		.80	2.00

ARRIED … WITH CHILDREN: KELLY BUNDY
g, 1992 - No. 3, Oct, 1992 ($1.95, limited series)
ow Comics

-3: Kelly Bundy photo-c & poster in each		.80	2.00

ARRIED … WITH CHILDREN: QUANTUM QUARTET
ct, 1993 - No. 4, 1994, ($1.95, limited series)
ow Comics

-4: Fantastic Four parody		.80	2.00

ARRIED … WITH CHILDREN: 2099
ne, 1993 - No. 3, Aug, 1993 (limited series)
w Comics

-3		.80	2.00

ARS
n, 1984 - No. 12, Jan, 1985 ($1.00, Mando paper)
st Comics

: 1-12: Marc Hempel & Mark Wheatley story & art. 2-The Black Flame begins.
10-Dynamo Joe begins 1.00

ARS & BEYOND (Disney, TV)
. 866, Dec, 1957

Dell Publishing Co.

Four Color 866-A Science feat. from Tomorrowland 10.00		30.00	90.00

MARS ATTACKS
May, 1994 - No. 5, Sept, 1994 ($2.95, limited series)
Topps Comics

1-5-Giffen story; flip books		1.60	4.00
Special Edition	2.15	6.50	15.00
Trade paperback (12/94, $12.95)-r/limited series plus new 8 pg. story			
			13.00

MARS ATTACKS
V2#1, 8/95 - V2#3, 10/95; V2#4, 1/96 - Present ($2.95, bi-monthly #6 on)
Topps Comics

V2#1-7: 1-Counterstrike storyline begins. 4-(1/96). 5-(1/96). 5,7-Brereton-c.			
6-(3/96)-Simonson-c. 7-Story leads into Baseball Special #1.			
		1.20	3.00
Baseball Special 1 (6/96, $2.95)-Bisley-c.		1.20	3.00

MARSHAL BLUEBERRY (See Blueberry)
1991 (14.95, graphic novel)
Marvel Comics (Epic Comics)

1-Moebius-a	2.15	6.50	15.00

MARSHAL LAW (Also see Crime And Punishment: Marshall Law…)
Oct, 1987 - No. 6, May, 1989 ($1.95, mature readers) (See Pinhead Vs….)
Marvel Comics (Epic Comics)

1-6		.80	2.00

M.A.R.S. PATROL TOTAL WAR (Formerly Total War #1,2)
No. 3, Sept, 1966 - No. 10, Aug, 1969 (All-Painted-c except #7)
Gold Key

3-Wood-a	5.50	17.00	45.00
4-10	3.25	9.50	22.00

MARTHA WASHINGTON (Also see Dark Horse Presents Fifth Anniversary Special, Dark
Horse Presents #100-4, Give Me Liberty, Happy Birthday Martha Washington & San Diego
Comicon Comics #2)

MARTHA WASHINGTON GOES TO WAR
May, 1994 - No. 5, Sept, 1994 ($2.95, limited series)
Dark Horse Comics (Legend)

1-5-Miller scripts; Gibbons-c/a		1.20	3.00

MARTHA WASHINGTON STRANDED IN SPACE
Nov, 1995 ($2.95, one-shot)
Dark Horse Comics (Legend)

nn-Miller-s/Gibbons-a; Big Guy app.		1.20	3.00

MARTHA WAYNE (See The Story of…)

MARTIAN MANHUNTER (See Detective Comics & Showcase '95 #9)
May, 1988 - No. 4, Aug,. 1988 ($1.25, limited series)
DC Comics

1-4: 1,4-Batman app. 2-Batman cameo			1.25
Special 1-(1996, $3.50)			3.50

MARTIN KANE (William Gargan as… Private Eye)(Stage/Screen/Radio/TV)
No. 4, June, 1950 - No. 2, Aug, 1950 (Formerly My Secret Affair)
Fox Features Syndicate (Hero Books)

4(#1)-True crime stories; Wood-c/a(2); used in **SOTI**, pg. 160; photo back-c			
	25.00	75.00	175.00
2-Wood/Orlando story, 5 pgs; Wood-a(2)	19.00	58.00	135.00

MARTY MOUSE
No date (1958?) (10¢)
I. W. Enterprises

1-Reprint	1.00	2.60	6.00

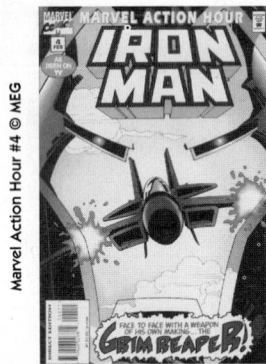
Marvel Action Hour #4 © MEG

Marvel Adventures #2 © MEG

Marvel Chillers #3 © MEG

GD25 FN65 NM94   **GD25 FN65 NM94**

MARVEL ACTION HOUR FEATURING IRON MAN (TV cartoon)
Nov, 1994 - No. 8, June, 1995 ($1.50/$2.95)
Marvel Comics

1-8: Based on cartoon series		1.50
1 ($2.95)-Polybagged w/16 pg Marvel Action Hour Preview & acetate print		
	1.20	3.00

MARVEL ACTION HOUR FEATURING THE FANTASTIC FOUR (TV cartoon)
Nov, 1994 - No. 8, June, 1995 ($1.50/$2.95)
Marvel Comics

1-8: Based on cartoon series		1.50
1-($2.95)-Polybagged w/ 16 pg. Marvel Action Hour Preview & acetate print		
	1.20	3.00

MARVEL ACTION UNIVERSE (TV cartoon)
Jan, 1989 ($1.00, one-shot)
Marvel Comics

1-r/Spider-Man And His Amazing Friends		1.00

MARVEL ADVENTURES STARRING DAREDEVIL (...Adventure #4 on)
Dec, 1975 - No. 6, Oct, 1976
Marvel Comics Group

1-6-r/Daredevil #22-27 by Colan	.80	2.00

MARVEL AND DC PRESENT FEATURING THE UNCANNY X-MEN AND THE NEW TEEN TITANS
1982 ($2.00, 68 pgs., one-shot, Baxter paper)
Marvel Comics Group/DC Comics

1-3rd app. Deathstroke the Terminator; Darkseid app.; Simonson/Austin-c/a		
	1.70	12.00

MARVEL BOY (Astonishing #3 on; see Marvel Super Action #4)
Dec, 1950 - No. 2, Feb, 1951
Marvel Comics (MPC)

1-Origin Marvel Boy by Russ Heath	78.00	234.00	625.00
2-Everett-a	62.00	187.00	500.00

MARVEL CHILLERS (Also see Giant-Size Chillers)
Oct, 1975 - No. 7, Oct, 1976 (All 25¢ issues)
Marvel Comics Group

1,2-Intro. Modred the Mystic, ends #2; Kane-c(p)		1.30	3.25
3-Tigra, the Were-Woman begins (origin), ends #7 (see Giant-Size Creatures #1). Chaykin/Wrightson-c.	1.00	2.00	5.00
4-7: 4-Kraven app. 5,6-Red Wolf app. 6-Byrne-a(p); Buckler-c(p). 7-Kirby-c; Tuska-p		.90	2.25
NOTE: *Bolle* a-1. *Buckler* c-2.

MARVEL CLASSICS COMICS SERIES FEATURING... (Also see Pendulum Illustrated Classics)
1976 - No. 36, Dec, 1978 (52 pgs., no ads)
Marvel Comics Group

1-Dr. Jekyll and Mr. Hyde		1.60	4.00
2-27,29-36		1.10	2.75
28-1st Golden-c/a; The Pit and the Pendulum	1.10	2.70	6.50
NOTE: *Adkins* c-1i, 4i, 12i. *Alcala* a-34i; c-34. *Bolle* a-35. *Buscema* c-17p, 19p, 26p. *Golden* c/a-28. *Gil Kane* c-1-16p, 21p, 22p, 24p, 32p. *Nebres* a-5; c-24i. *Nino* a-2, 8, 12. *Redondo* a-1, 9. No. 1-12 were reprinted from Pendulum Illustrated Classics.

MARVEL COLLECTOR'S EDITION
1992 (Ordered thru mail with Charleston Chew candy wrapper)
Marvel Comics

1-Flip-book format; Spider-Man, Silver Surfer, Wolverine (by Sam Kieth), & Ghost Rider stories; Wolverine back-c by Kieth	.90	2.25

MARVEL COLLECTOR'S EDITION: X-MEN
1993 (3-3/4x6-1/2")
Marvel Comics

1-4-Pizza Hut giveaways	.80	2.00

MARVEL COLLECTORS' ITEM CLASSICS (Marvel's Greatest #23 on)
Feb, 1965 - No. 22, Aug, 1969 (25¢, 68 pgs.)
Marvel Comics Group(ATF)

1-Fantastic Four, Spider-Man, Thor, Hulk, Iron Man-r begin			
	8.00	23.50	55.
2 (4/66) - 4	4.50	14.00	32
5-22: 22-r/The Man in the Ant Hill/TTA #27	2.60	7.50	18
NOTE: All reprints; *Ditko, Kirby* art in all.

MARVEL COMICS (Marvel Mystery Comics #2 on)
October, November, 1939
Timely Comics (Funnies, Inc.)

NOTE: The first issue was originally dated October 1939. Most copies have a black o stamped over the date (on cover and inside) with "November" printed over it. However, s copies do not have the November overprint and could have a higher value. Most No. 1's h printing defects, i.e., light-colored area which caused trimming into the panels usually on right side bottom. Covers exist with and without gloss finish.

	GD25	FN65	VF82	NM
1-Origin Sub-Mariner by Bill Everett(1st newsstand app.); 1st 8 pgs. were pr duced for Motion Picture Funnies Weekly #1 which was probably not distri buted outside of advance copies; intro Human Torch by Carl Burgos, Kaza the Great (1st Tarzan clone), & Jungle Terror(only app.); intro. The Angel l Gustavson, The Masked Raider & his horse Lightning (ends #12); cover b sci/fi pulp illustrator Frank R. Paul				
	10,222.00	30,667.00	61,333.00	98,000
(Estimated up to 50 total copies exist, 4 in NM/Mint)				

MARVEL COMICS PRESENTS
Early Sept, 1988 - No. 175, Feb, 1995 ($1.25/$1.50/$1.75, bi-weekly)
Marvel Comics (Midnight Sons imprint #143 on)

	GD25	FN65	NM
1-Wolverine by Buscema in #1-10	1.65	4.20	10
2-5	1.00	2.00	5
6-10: 6-Sub-Mariner app. 10-Colossus begins		1.20	3
11-32,34-37: 17-Cyclops begins. 19-1st app. Damage Control. 24-Havok begins. 25-Origin/1st app. Nth Man. 26-Hulk begins by Rogers. 29-Quasar app. 31-Excalibur begins by Austin (i). 32-McFarlane-a(p). 37-Devil-Slayer app.		.80	2
33-Capt. America; Jim Lee-a		1.10	2
38-Wolverine begins by Buscema; Hulk app.	1.00	2.00	5
39-47,51-53: 39-Spider-Man app. 46-Liefeld Wolverine-c. 51-53-Wolverine b Rob Liefeld		1.10	2
48-50-Wolverine & Spider-Man team-up by Erik Larsen-c/a. 48-Wasp app. 49 50-Savage Dragon prototype app. by Larsen. 50-Silver Surfer. 50-53-Con Man; Bill Mumy scripts	1.00	2.00	5
54-61-Wolverine/Hulk story. 54-Werewolf by Night begins; The Shroud by Di 58-Iron Man by Ditko. 59-Punisher	1.00	2.00	5
62-Deathlok & Wolverine stories	1.00	2.00	5
63-Wolverine		1.50	3
64-71-Wolverine/Ghost Rider 8-part story. 70-Liefeld Ghost Rider/ Wolverine-c		1.60	4
72-Begin 13-part Weapon-X story (Wolverine origin) by B. Windsor-Smith (prologue)	1.25	3.00	7
73-Weapon-X part 1; Black Knight, Sub-Mariner	1.00	2.00	7
74-Weapon-X part 2; Black Knight, Sub-Mariner		1.50	3
75-80: 76-Death's Head story. 77-Mr. Fantastic story. 78-Iron Man by Steacy 80,81-Capt. America by Ditko/Austin		1.10	2
81-84: 81-Daredevil by Rogers/Williamson. 82-Power Man. 83-Human Torch by Ditko(a&scripts); $1.00-c direct, $1.25 newsstand. 84-Last Weapon-X (24 pg. conclusion)		.90	2
85-Begin 8-part Wolverine story by Sam Kieth (c/a); 1st Kieth-a on Wolverine begin 8-part Beast story by Jae Lee(p) with Liefeld part pencils 85,86; 1st Jae Lee-a (assisted w/Liefeld, 1991)	1.20	3.00	7
86-89-Wolverine, Beast stories continue		1.50	3
90-Begin 8-part Ghost Rider & Cable story, ends #97; begin flip book format with two covers		1.90	4
91-94: 93-Begin 6-part Wolverine story, ends #98		1.10	2

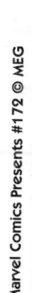
Marvel Comics Presents #95 © MEG

Marvel Comics Presents #172 © MEG

Marvel Fanfare #58 © MEG

	GD25	FN65	NM94

95-98: 95-Begin price \$1.50-c. 98-Begin 2-part Ghost Rider story .70 1.80
99,101-107,112-116: 99-Spider-Man story. 101-Begin 6-part Ghost Rider/Dr. Strange story & begin 8-part Wolverine/Nightcrawler story by Colan/Williamson; Punisher story. 107-Begin 6-part Ghost Rider/Werewolf by Night story. 112-Demogoblin story by Colan/Williamson; Pip the Troll story w/Starlin scripts & Gamora cameo. 113-Begin 6-part Giant-Man & begin 6-part Ghost Rider/Iron Fist stories .65 1.60
100-Full-length Ghost Rider/Wolverine story by Sam Kieth w/Tim Vigil assists; anniversary issue, non flip-book 1.00 2.50
108-111: 108-Begin 4 part Thanos story; Starlin scripts. 109-Begin 8 part Wolverine/Typhoid Mary story. 111-Iron Fist .80 2.00
117-Preview of Ravage 2099 (1st app.); begin 6 part Wolverine/Venom story w/Kieth-a 1.00 2.50
118-Preview of Doom 2099 (1st app.) 1.00 2.50
119-142,147-152: 119-Begin Ghost Rider/Cloak & Dagger story by Colan. 120,136,138-Spider-Man. 123-Begin 6-part Ghost Rider/Typhoid Mary story; begin 4-part She Hulk story; begin 8-partWolverine/Lynx story. 125-Begin 6-part Iron Fist story. 129-Jae Lee back-c. 130-Begin 6-part Ghost Rider/Cage story. 131-Begin 6-part Ghost Rider/Cage story. 132-Begin 5-part Wolverine story. 133-136-Iron Fist vs. Sabretooth. 136-Daredevil. 137-Begin 6-part Wolverine story & 6-part Ghost Rider story. 147-Begin 2-part Vengeance-c/story w/new Ghost Rider. 149-Vengeance-c/story w/new Ghost Rider. 150-Silver ink-c; begin 2-part Bloody Mary story w/Typhoid Mary, Wolverine, Daredevil, new Ghost Rider; intro Steel Raven. 152-Begin 4-part Wolverine, 4-part War Machine, 4-part Vengeance, 3-part Moon Knight stories; same date as War Machine #1 .70 1.80
143-146: (\$1.75)-Siege of Darkness parts 3,6,11,14; all have spot-varnished covers. 143-Ghost Rider/Scarlet Witch; intro new Werewolf. 144-Begin 2-part Morbius story. 145-Begin 2-part Nightstalkers story. .70 1.75
153-175: 153-\$1.75-c begins. 153-155-Bound-in Spider-Man trading card sheet 1.00 1.75
NOTE: *Austin* a-31-37i; c(i)-48, 50, 99, 122. *Buscema* a-1-10, 38-47; c-6. *Byrne* a-79; c-71. *Colan* a(p)-36, 37. *Colan/Williamson* a-101-108. *Ditko* a-7p, 10, 56p, 58, 80, 81, 83. *Guice* a-*Sam Kieth* a-85-92, 117-122; c-85-98, 99p, 100-108, 117, 118, 120-122; back-c-109-113, 7. *Jae Lee* c-129(back). *Liefeld* a-51, 52, 53p(2), 85p; c-46, 70. *McFarlane* c-32. *Mooney* a-*Rogers* a-26, 38, 46i, 81p. *Russell* a-10i; c-4i. *Saltares* a-8p(early), 38-45p. *Simonson* c-1. *Smith* a-72-84; c-72-84. *P. Smith* c-34. *Sparling* a-33. *Starlin* a-89i. *Staton* a-74. *Steacy* a-*Sutton* a-101-105. *Williamson* c-62i. Two Gun Kid by Gil Kane in #116, 122.

MARVEL COMICS SUPER SPECIAL, A (Marvel Super Special #5 on)
Sept, 1977 - No. 41(?), Nov, 1986 (nn 7) (\$1.50, magazine)
Marvel Comics Group

Kiss, 40 pgs. comics plus photos & features; Simonson-a(p); also see Howard the Duck #12 8.30 25.00 58.00
1-Conan (1978) 1.50
2-Close Encounters of the Third Kind (1978); Simonson-a 1.50
3-The Beatles Story (1978)-Perez/Janson-a; has photos & articles 1.65 4.70 11.00
4-Kiss (1978)-Includes poster 4.70 14.00 33.00
5-Jaws II (1978) 1.50
6-Sgt. Pepper; Beatles movie adaptation; withdrawn from U.S. distribution 1.50
7-Battlestar Galactica; tabloid size (\$1.50, 1978); adapts TV show 1.50
7-Battlestar Galactica; publ. in regular magazine format; low distribution (\$1.50, 8-1/2x11") 1.50
8,10: 9-Conan. 10-Star-Lord 1.50
11-Weirdworld begins #11; 25 copy special press run of each with gold seal and signed by artists (Proof quality), Spring-June, 1979 8.00 24.00 55.00
11-Weirdworld (regular issues): 11-Fold-out centerfold 1.50
15-Miller-c(p); adapts movie "Meteor." 1.20
16-Star Trek with photos & pin-ups(\$1.50) 1.20
16-With \$2.00 price (scarce); the price was changed at tail end of a 200,000 press run .80 1.75
17-20 (Movie adaptations): 16-Empire Strikes Back; Williamson-a. 17-Xanadu. 18-Raiders of the Lost Ark. 19-For Your Eyes Only (James Bond). 20-Dragonslayer .70 1.75

21-41 (Movie adaptations): 21-Conan. 22-Bladerunner; Williamson-a; Steranko-c. 23-Annie. 24-The Dark Crystal. 25-Rock and Rule-w/photos; artwork is from movie. 26-Octopussy (James Bond). 27-Return of the Jedi. 28-Krull; photo-c. 29-Tarzan of the Apes (Greystoke movie). 30-Indiana Jones and the Temple of Doom. 31-The Last Star Fighter. 32-The Muppets Take Manhattan. 33-Buckaroo Bonzai. 34-Sheena. 35-Conan The Destroyer. 36-Dune. 37-2010. 38-Red Sonja. 39-Santa Claus: The Movie. 40-Labyrinth. 41-Howard The Duck .70 1.75
NOTE: *J. Buscema* a-1, 2, 9, 11-13, 18p, 21, 35, 40; c-11(part), 12. *Chaykin* a-9, 19p; c-18, 19. *Colan* a(p)-6, 10, 14. *Morrow* a-34; c-1i, 34. *Nebres* a-11. *Spiegle* a-29. *Stevens* a-27. *Williamson* a-27. #22-28 contain photos from movies.

MARVEL DOUBLE FEATURE
Dec, 1973 - No. 21, Mar, 1977
Marvel Comics Group

1-Capt. America, Iron Man-r/T.O.S. begin 1.00 2.00 5.00
2-16,20,21: 3-Last 20¢ issue. 17-Last 25¢ issue 1.20 3.00
17-Reprints story/Iron Man & Sub-Mariner #1 1.60 4.00
18,19-Colan/Craig-r from Iron Man #1 in both 1.00 2.00 5.00
NOTE: *Colan* r-1-19p. *Craig* r-17-19i. *G. Kane* r-15p; c-15p. *Kirby* r-1-16p, 20, 21; c-17-20.

MARVEL FAMILY (Also see Captain Marvel Adventures No. 18)
Dec, 1945 - No. 89, Jan, 1954
Fawcett Publications

1-Origin Captain Marvel, Captain Marvel Jr., Mary Marvel, & Uncle Marvel retold; origin/1st app. Black Adam 137.00 412.00 1100.00
2-The 3 Lt. Marvels & Uncle Marvel app. 64.00 193.00 515.00
3 45.00 135.00 360.00
4,5 40.00 120.00 290.00
6-10: 7-Shazam app. 33.00 99.00 230.00
11-20 25.00 75.00 175.00
21-30 20.00 60.00 140.00
31-40 17.00 49.00 115.00
41-46,48-50 13.50 41.00 95.00
47-Flying Saucer-c/story (5/50) 18.00 54.00 125.00
51-76,79,80,82-89: 79-Horror satire-c 12.00 36.00 85.00
77-Communist Threat-c 19.00 58.00 135.00
78,81-Used in POP, pg. 92,93. 14.00 43.00 100.00

MARVEL FANFARE (1st Series)
March, 1982 - No. 60, Jan, 1992 (\$1.25/\$2.25, slick paper, direct sales)
Marvel Comics Group

1-Spider-Man/Angel team-up; 1st Paul Smith-a (1st full story; see King Conan #7); Daredevil story 1.30 3.25 8.00
2-Spider-Man, Ka-Zar, The Angel. F.F. origin retold .90 2.30 5.50
3,4-X-Men & Ka-Zar. 4-Deathlok, Spidey app. 1.00 2.00 5.00
5-Dr. Strange, Capt. America 1.20 3.00
6-15: 6-Spider-Man, Scarlet Witch. 7-Incredible Hulk; D.D. back-up(also 15). 8-Dr. Strange; Wolf Boy begins. 9-Man-Thing. 10-13-Black Widow. 14-The Vision. 15-The Thing by Barry Smith, c/a 1.00 2.50
16-32,34-50: 16,17-Skywolf. 16-Sub-Mariner back-up. 17-Hulk back-up. 18-Capt. America by Miller. 19-Cloak and Dagger. 20-Thing/Dr. Strange. 21-Thing/Dr. Strange/Hulk. 22,23-Iron Man vs. Dr. Octopus. 24-26-Weird-world. 26-Wolverine back-up. 27-Daredevil/Spider-Man. 28-Alpha Flight. 29-Hulk. 30-Moon Knight. 31,32-Captain America. 34-37-Warriors Three. 38-Moon Knight/Dazzler. 39-Moon Knight/Hawkeye. 40-Angel/Rogue & Storm. 41-Dr. Strange. 42-Spider-Man. 43-Sub-Mariner/Human Torch. 44-Iron Man vs. Dr. Doom by Ken Steacy. 45-All pin-up issue by Steacy, Art Adams & others. 46-Fantastic Four. 47-She-Hulk/Vision. 49-Dr. Strange/Nick Fury. 50-X-Factor; begin \$2.25-c 1.00 2.50
33-X-Men, Wolverine app.; Punisher pin-up 1.00 2.00 5.00
51-(\$2.95, 52 pgs.)-Silver Surfer; Fantastic Four & Capt. Marvel app.; 51,52-Colan/Williamson back-up (Dr. Strange) 1.20 3.00
52,53: 52-54-Black Knight. 53-Iron Man back up 1.00 2.50
54,55-Wolverine back-ups. 55-Power Pack 1.20 3.00
56-60: 56-59-Shanna the She-Devil. 58-Vision & Scarlet Witch back-up. 60-

Marvel Fanfare #2 (2nd Series) © MEG

Marvel Feature #6 © MEG

Marvel Holiday Special #1 © MEG

Black Panther/Rogue/Daredevil stories 1.00 2.50
NOTE: **Art Adams** c-13. **Austin** a-1i, 4i, 33i, 38i; c-8i, 33i. **Buscema** a-51p. **Byrne** a-1p, 29, 48; c-29. **Chiodo** painted c-56-59. **Colan** a-51p. **Cowan/Simonson** c/a-60. **Golden** a-1, 2, 4p, 47; c-1, 2, 47. **Infantino** c/a(p)-8. **Gil Kane** a-8-11p. **Miller** a-18; c-1(Back-c), 18. **Perez** a-10, 11p, 12, 13p; c-10-13p. **Rogers** a-5p; c-5p. **Russell** a-5i, 6i, 8-11i, 43i; c-5i, 6. **Paul Smith** a-1p, 4p, 32, 60; c-4p. **Staton** c/a-50(p). **Williamson** a-30i, 51i.

MARVEL FANFARE (2nd Series)
Sept, 1996 - Present (99¢)
Marvel Comics

1-6: 1-Capt. America & The Falcon-c/story; Deathlok app. 2-Wolverine & Hulk-c/app. 3-Ghost Rider & Spider-Man-c/app. 1.00

MARVEL FEATURE (See Marvel Two-In-One)
Dec, 1971 - No. 12, Nov, 1973 (1,2: 25¢ giants)(#1-3: quarterly)
Marvel Comics Group

1-Origin/1st app. The Defenders (Sub-Mariner, Hulk & Dr. Strange); see Sub-Mariner #34,35 for prequel; Dr. Strange solo story (predates D.S. #1) plus 1950s Sub-Mariner-r; Neal Adams-c 11.00 33.00 75.00
2-2nd app. Defenders; 1950s Sub-Mariner-r 4.70 14.00 33.00
3-Defenders ends 4.70 14.00 33.00
4-Re-intro Antman (1st app. since 1960s), begin series; brief origin; Spider-Man app. 1.85 5.50 13.00
5-10: 6-Wasp app. & begins team-ups. 8-Origin Antman & Wasp-r/TTA #44. 9-Iron Man app. 10-Last Antman 1.00 2.50 5.50
10-(7/73)-Variant w/4 extra pgs. ads on slick paper 1.00 2.50 6.00
11-Thing vs. Hulk; 1st Thing solo book (9/73); origin Fantastic Four retold 1.50 3.75 9.00
12-Thing/Iron Man; early Thanos app.; occurs after Capt. Marvel #33; Starlin-a(p) 1.65 4.00 10.00
NOTE: **Bolle** a-9i. **Everett** a-1i, 3i. **Hartley** a-10. **Kane** c-3p, 7p. **Russell** a-7-10p. **Starlin** a-8, 11, 12; c-8.

MARVEL FEATURE (Also see Red Sonja)
Nov, 1975 - No. 7, Nov, 1976 (Story continues in Conan #68)
Marvel Comics Group

1-Red Sonja begins (pre-dates Red Sonja #1); adapts Howard short story; Adams-r/Savage Sword of Conan #1 1.60 4.00
2-7: Thorne-c/a in #2-7. 7-Battles Conan .90 2.25

MARVEL FRONTIER COMICS UNLIMITED
Jan, 1994 ($2.95, 68 pgs.)
Marvel Frontier Comics

1-Dances with Demons, Immortalis, Children of the Voyager, Evil Eye, The Fallen stories 1.20 3.00

MARVEL FUMETTI BOOK
Apr, 1984 ($1.00, one-shot)
Marvel Comics Group

1-All photos; Stan Lee photo-c; Art Adams touch-ups 1.00

MARVEL GRAPHIC NOVEL
1982 - No. 38, 1990? ($5.95/$6.95)
Marvel Comics Group (Epic Comics)

1-Death of Captain Marvel (1st Marvel graphic novel); Capt. Marvel battles Thanos by Jim Starlin (c/a/scripts) 2.85 8.50 20.00
1 (2nd & 3rd printings) 1.00 2.00 5.00
2-Elric: The Dreaming City 1.50 3.75 9.00
3-Dreadstar; Starlin-c/a, 52 pgs. 1.40 3.50 7.50
4-Origin/1st app. The New Mutants (1982) 1.65 4.20 10.00
4,5-2nd printings 1.20 3.00 5.50
5-X-Men; book-length story (1982) 2.40 6.00 13.00
6-18: 6-The Star Slammers. 7-Killraven. 8-Super Boxers; Byrne scripts. 9-The Futurians. 10-Heartburst. 11-Void Indigo. 12-The Dazzler. 13-Starstruck. 14-The Swords Of The Swashbucklers. 15-The Raven Banner (Asgard). 16-The Aladdin Effect. 17-Revenge Of The Living Monolith. 18-She Hulk 1.20 3.00 5.50
19-32: 19-The Witch Queen of Acheron (Conan). 20-Greenberg the Vampire.

21-Marada the She-Wolf. 22-Amaz. Spider-Man in Hooky by Wrightson. 23-Dr. Strange. 24-Love and War (Daredevil); Miller scripts. 25-Alien Legio 26-Dracula. 27-Avengers (Emperor Doom). 28-Conan the Reaver. 29-The Big Chance (Thing vs. Hulk). 30-A Sailor's Story. 31-Wolfpack. 32-Death of Groo 1.40 3.50 7.
32-2nd printing ($5.95) 1.20 3.00 6.
33,34,36,37: 33-Thor. 34-Predator & Prey (Cloak & Dagger). 36-Willow (movie adapt.). 37-Hercules 1.40 3.50 7.
35-Hitler's Astrologer (The Shadow, $12.95, hard-c) 1.85 5.50 13.
35-Soft-c reprint (1990, $10.95) 1.65 4.70 11.
38-Silver Surfer (Judgement Day)($14.95) 2.15 6.50 15.
nn-Inhumans (1988, $7.95)-Williamson-i 1.30 3.25 8.
nn-Last of the Dragons (1988, $6.95) 1.20 3.00 7.
nn-Who Framed Roger Rabbit (1989, $6.95) 1.20 3.00 7.
nn-Roger Rabbit In The Resurrection Of Doom (1989, $8.95) 1.50 3.75 9.
nn-Arena by Bruce Jones ($5.95) 1.00 2.50 6.
NOTE: **Aragones** a-27, 32. **Buscema** a-38. **Byrne** c/a-18. **Heath** a-35i. **Kaluta** a-13, 35p; c-1 **Miller** a-24p. **Simonson** a-6; c-6. **Starlin** c/a-1,3. **Williamson** a-34. **Wrightson** c-29i.

MARVEL-HEROES & LEGENDS
Oct, 1996 ($2.95, one-shot)
Marvel Comics

nn-Wraparound-c 3.

MARVEL HOLIDAY SPECIAL
No. 1, 1991 ($2.25, 84 pgs.); nn, Jan, 1993 ($2.95, 68 pgs.)
Marvel Comics

1-X-Men, Fantastic Four, Punisher, Thor, Capt. America, Ghost Rider, Capt. Ultra, Spidey stories; Art Adams-c/a .90 2
nn (1/93)-Wolverine, Thanos (by Starlin/Lim/Austin) 1.20 3
NOTE: **Art Adams** c-nn. **Golden** a-nn.

MARVEL ILLUSTRATED: SWIMSUIT ISSUE (See Marvel Swimsuit Spec.)
1991 ($3.95, magazine, 52 pgs.)

V1#1-Parody of Sports Illustrated swimsuit issue; Mary Jane Parker centerfold pin-up by Jusko; 2nd print exists 1.60 4

MARVEL MASTERPIECES COLLECTION, THE
May, 1993 - No. 4, Aug, 1993 ($2.95, coated paper, limited series)
Marvel Comics

1-4-Reprints Marvel Masterpieces trading cards w/ new Jusko paintings in each; Jusko painted-c/a 1.20 3

MARVEL MASTERPIECES 2 COLLECTION, THE
July, 1994 - No. 3, Sept, 1994 ($2.95, limited series)
Marvel Comics

1-3: 1-Kaluta-c; r/trading cards; new Steranko centerfold 1.20 3

MARVEL MILESTONE EDITION
1991 - 1995 ($2.95, coated stock)(r/originals with original ads w/silver ink-c)
Marvel Comics

...: X-Men #1-Reprints X-Men #1 (1991) 1.20 3
...: Giant Size X-Men #1-(1991, $3.95, 68 pgs.) 1.60 3
...: Fantastic Four #1 (11/91) 1.20 3
...: Incredible Hulk #1 (3/92, says 3/91 by error) 1.20 3
...: Amazing Fantasy #15 (3/92) 1.20 3
...: Fantastic Four #5 (11/92) 1.20 3
...: Amazing Spider-Man #129 (11/92) 1.20 3
...: Iron Man #55 (11/92) 1.20 3
...: Iron Fist #14 (11/92) 1.20 3
...: Amazing Spider-Man #1 (1/93) 1.20 3
...: Tales of Suspense #39 (3/93) 1.20 3
...: Avengers #1 (9/93) 1.20 3
...: X-Men #9 (10/93) 1.20 3
...: Avengers #16 (10/93) 1.20 3

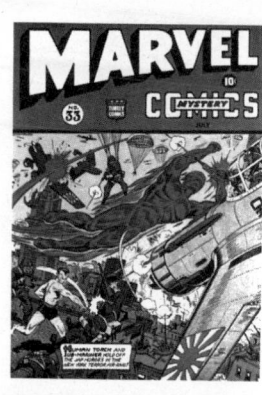

Marvel Mystery Comics #33 © MEG

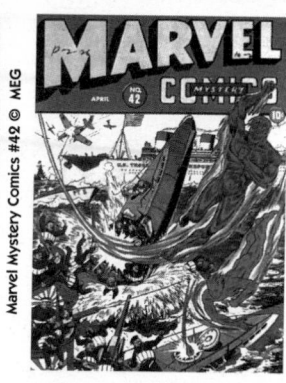

Marvel Mystery Comics #42 © MEG

Marvel Mystery Comics #83 © MEG

	GD25	FN65	NM94
...:Amazing Spider-Man #149 (11/94, $2.95)	1.20	3.00	
...:X-Men #28 (11/94, $2.95)	1.20	3.00	
...:Captain America #1 (3/95, $3.95)	1.60	4.00	
...:Amazing Spider-Man #3 (3/95, $2.95)	1.20	3.00	
...:Avengers #4 (3/95, $2.95)	1.20	3.00	
...:Strange Tales-r/Dr. Strange stories from #110, 111, 114, & 115.			
	1.20	3.00	

MARVEL MINI-BOOKS
1966 (50 pgs., B&W; 5/8x7/8") (6 different issues)
Marvel Comics Group (Smallest comics ever published)

Captain America, Spider-Man, Sgt. Fury, Hulk, Thor	5.50	17.00	45.00
Millie the Model	5.50	17.00	45.00

NOTE: Each came in six different color covers, usually one color: Pink, yellow, green, etc.

MARVEL MOVIE PREMIERE (Magazine)
Sept, 1975 (B&W, one-shot)
Marvel Comics Group

1-Burroughs' "The Land That Time Forgot" adaptation	.80	2.00	

MARVEL MOVIE SHOWCASE FEATURING STAR WARS
Nov, 1982 - No. 2, Dec, 1982 ($1.25, 68 pgs.)
Marvel Comics Group

1,2-Star Wars movie adaptation; reprints Star Wars #1-6 by Chaykin;
1-Reprints-c to Star Wars #1. 2-Stevens-r   1.20   3.00

MARVEL MOVIE SPOTLIGHT FEATURING RAIDERS OF THE LOST ARK
Nov, 1982 ($1.25, 68 pgs.)
Marvel Comics Group

1-Edited-r/Raiders of the Lost Ark #1-3; Buscema-c/a(p); movie adaptation
    1.25

MARVEL MYSTERY COMICS (Formerly Marvel Comics) (Becomes Marvel Tales No. 93 on)
No. 2, Dec, 1939 - No. 92, June, 1949
Timely /Marvel Comics (TP #2-17/TCI #18-54/MCI #55-92)

	GD25	VF82	NM94
2-American Ace begins, ends #3; Human Torch (blue costume) by Burgos, Sub-Mariner by Everett continue; 2 pg. origin recap of Human Torch	1800.00	5400.00 12,200.00	19,000.00
	GD25	FN65	NM94
3-New logo from Marvel pulp begins	840.00	2520.00	8400.00
4-Intro. Electro, the Marvel of the Age (ends #19), The Ferret, Mystery Detective (ends #9); 1st Nazi war-c on a comic book & 1st German flag (Swastika) on-c of a comic (2/40)	680.00	2040.00	6800.00
	GD25	FN65	VF82
5 (Scarce)	1400.00	4200.00	8400.00 14,000.00
(Estimated up to 75 total copies exist, 3 in NM/Mint)			
	GD25	FN65	NM94
7: 6-Gustavson Angel story	460.00	1380.00	4600.00
8-1st Human Torch & Sub-Mariner battle(6/40)	680.00	2040.00	6800.00
	GD25	FN65	VF82
9 (Scarce)-Human Torch & Sub-Mariner battle (cover/story); 1st Television in comics?; classic-c	1600.00	4800.00	9600.00 16,000.00
(Estimated up to 75 total copies exist, 6 in NM/Mint)			
	GD25	FN65	NM94
10-Human Torch & Sub-Mariner battle, conclusion; Terry Vance, the Schoolboy Sleuth begins, ends #57	470.00	1400.00	4700.00
11	288.00	862.00	2500.00
12-Classic Kirby-c	325.00	975.00	2800.00
13-Intro. & 1st app. The Vision by S&K (11/40); Sub-Mariner dons new costume, ends #15	333.00	1000.00	3300.00
14-16: 14-Shows-c to Human Torch #1 on-c (12/40). 15-S&K Vision, Gustavson Angel story	200.00	600.00	1600.00
17-Human Torch/Sub-Mariner team-up by Burgos/Everett; pin-up on back-c; shows-c to Human Torch #2 on-c	225.00	675.00	1800.00

	GD25	FN65	NM94
18	181.00	543.00	1450.00
19-Origin Toro in text; shows-c to Sub-Mariner #1 on-c	200.00	600.00	1600.00
20-Origin The Angel in text	200.00	600.00	1600.00
21-Intro. & 1st app. The Patriot (7/41); not in #46-48; pin-up on back-c	181.00	543.00	1450.00
22-25: 23-Last Gustavson Angel; origin The Vision in text. 24-Injury-to-eye story	156.00	468.00	1250.00
26-30: 27-Ka-Zar ends; last S&K Vision who battles Satan. 28-Jimmy Jupiter in the Land of Nowhere begins, ends #48; Sub-Mariner vs. The Flying Dutchman. 30-1st Japanese war-c	143.00	431.00	1150.00
31-Sub-Mariner by Everett ends, begins again #84	125.00	375.00	1000.00
32-1st app. The Boobos	125.00	375.00	1000.00
33,35-40: 40-Zeppelin-c	125.00	375.00	1000.00
34-Everett, Burgos, Martin Goodman, Funnies, Inc. office appear in story & battles Hitler; last Burgos Human Torch	143.00	431.00	1150.00
41-43,45-48: 46-Hitler-c. 48-Last Vision; flag-c	109.00	328.00	875.00
44-Classic Super Plane-c	109.00	328.00	875.00
49-Origin Miss America	143.00	431.00	1150.00
50-Mary becomes Miss Patriot (origin)	115.00	346.00	925.00
51-60: 53-Bondage-c. 60-Last Japanese war-c	101.00	305.00	815.00
61,62,64-Last German war-c	96.00	290.00	775.00
63-Classic Hitler War-c; The Villainess Cat-Woman only app.	103.00	309.00	825.00
65,66-Last Japanese War-c	96.00	290.00	775.00
67-75: 74-Last Patriot. 75-Young Allies begin	87.00	262.00	700.00
76-78: 76-Ten Chapter Miss America serial begins, ends #85	87.00	262.00	700.00
79-New cover format; Super Villains begin on cover; last Angel	87.00	262.00	700.00
80-1st app. Capt. America in Marvel Comics	115.00	346.00	925.00
81-Captain America app.	87.00	262.00	700.00
82-Origin & 1st app. Namora (5/47); 1st Sub-Mariner/Namora team-up; Captain America app.	200.00	600.00	1600.00
83,85: 83-Last Young Allies. 85-Last Miss America. Blonde Phantom app.	84.00	253.00	675.00
84-Blonde Phantom begins (on-c of #84,88,89); Sub-Mariner by Everett begins; Captain America app.	115.00	346.00	925.00
86-Blonde Phantom i.d. revealed; Captain America app.; last Bucky app.	95.00	286.00	765.00
87-1st Capt. America/Golden Girl team-up	101.00	305.00	815.00
88-Golden Girl, Namora, & Sun Girl (1st in Marvel Comics) x-over; Captain America, Blonde Phantom app.; last Toro	96.00	290.00	775.00
89-1st Human Torch/Sun Girl team-up; 1st Captain America solo; Blonde Phantom app.	95.00	286.00	765.00
90-Blonde Phantom un-masked; Captain America app.	101.00	305.00	815.00
91-Capt. America app.; Blonde Phantom & Sub-Mariner end; early Venus app. (4/49)	101.00	305.00	815.00
92-Feature story on the birth of the Human Torch and the death of Professor Horton (his creator); 1st app. The Witness in Marvel Comics; Captain America app.	231.00	693.00	1850.00
132 Pg. issue, B&W, 25¢ (1943-44)-printed in N. Y.; square binding, blank inside covers; has Marvel No. 33-c in color; contains Capt. America #18 & Marvel Mystery Comics #33; same contents as Captain America Annual			
	GD25	FN65	VF82
(Less than 5 copies known to exist)	2285.00	6857.00 16,000.00	

NOTE: **Brodsky** c-49, 72, 86, 88-92. **Crandall** a-26i. **Everett** c-7-9, 27, 84. **Gabrielle** c-30-32. **Schomburg** c-3-11, 13-29, 33-36, 39-48, 50-59, 63-69, 74, 76, 132 pg. issue. **Shores** c-37, 38, 75p, 77, 78p, 79p, 80, 81p, 82-84, 85p, 87p. **Sekowsky** c-73. Bondage covers-3, 4, 7, 12, 28, 29, 49, 50, 52, 56, 57, 58, 59, 65. Angel c-2, 3, 8, 12. Remember Pearl Harbor issues-#30-32.

MARVEL NO-PRIZE BOOK, THE (The Official... on-c)
Jan, 1983 (one-shot, direct sales only)
Marvel Comics Group

	GD25	FN65	NM94

Marvel Premiere #30 © MEG

Marvel Presents #8 © MEG

Marvels #4 © MEG

	GD25	FN65	NM94

1-Golden-c   1.00

MARVEL PREMIERE
April, 1972 - No. 61, Aug, 1981 (A tryout book for new characters)
Marvel Comics Group

1-Origin Warlock (pre-#1) by Gil Kane/Adkins; origin Counter-Earth; Hulk & Thor cameo (#1-14 are 20¢-c)	6.50	19.50	45.00
2-Warlock ends; Kirby Yellow Claw-r	3.60	11.00	25.00
3-Dr. Strange series begins (pre #1, 7/72), B. Smith-a(p); Smith-c?	3.90	11.50	27.00
4-Smith/Brunner-a	1.65	4.70	11.00
5-9: 8-Starlin-c/a(p)	1.10	2.70	6.50
10-Death of the Ancient One	1.50	3.75	9.00
11-14: 11-Dr. Strange origin-r by Ditko. 14-Last Dr. Strange (3/74); gets own title 3 months later		1.80	4.50
15-Origin/1st app. Iron Fist (5/74), ends #25	6.50	19.00	45.00
16-2nd app. Iron Fist; origin cont'd from #15; Hama's 1st Marvel-a	2.10	6.40	15.00
17-24: Iron Fist in all	1.85	5.50	13.00
25-1st Byrne Iron Fist (moves to own title next)	2.30	6.75	16.00
26,27: 26-Hercules. 27-Satana	1.80	4.50
28-Legion of Monsters (Ghost Rider, Man-Thing, Morbius, Werewolf)	1.70	5.00	12.00
29-49,51-56,61: 29,30-The Liberty Legion. 29-1st modern app. Patriot. 31-1st app. Woodgod; last 25¢ issue. 32-1st app. Monark Starstalker. 33,34-1st color app. Solomon Kane (Robert E. Howard adaptation "Red Shadows". 35-Origin/1st app. 3-D Man. 36,37-3-D Man. 38-1st Weirdworld. 39,40-Torpedo. 41-1st Seeker 3001! 42-Tigra. 43-Paladin. 44-Jack of Hearts (1st solo book, 10/78). 45,46-Man-Wolf. 47-Origin/1st app. new Ant-Man. 48-Ant-Man. 49-The Falcon (1st solo book, 8/79). 51-53-Black Panther. 54-1st Caleb Hammer. 55-Wonder Man. 56-1st color app. Dominic Fortune. 61-Star Lord		.80	2.00
50-1st app. Alice Cooper; co-plotted by Alice	1.00	2.50	5.50
57-Dr. Who (2nd U.S. app.-see Movie Classics)		1.40	3.50
58-60-Dr. Who		.90	2.25

NOTE: **N. Adams** (Crusty Bunkers) parts 10, 12, 13. **Austin** a-50i, 56i; c-46i, 50i, 56i, 58. **Brunner** a-4i, 6p, 9-14p; c-9-14. **Byrne** a-47p, 48p. **Chaykin** a-32-34; c-32, 33, 56. **Giffen** a-31p, 44p; c-44. **Gil Kane** a(p)-1, 2, 15; c(p)-1, 2, 15, 16, 22-24, 27, 36, 37. **Kirby** c-26, 29-31, 35. **Layton** a-47i, 48i; c-47. **McWilliams** a-25i. **Miller** c-49p, 53p, 58p. **Nebres** a-44i; c-38i. **Nino** a-38i. **Perez** c(a-38p, 45p, 46p. **Ploog** a-38; c-5-7. **Russell** a-7p. **Simonson** a-60(2pgs.); c-57. **Starlin** a-8p; c-8. **Sutton** a-41, 43, 50p, 61; c-50p, 61. #57-60 published w/two different prices on-c.

MARVEL PRESENTS
October, 1975 - No. 12, Aug, 1977 (#1-5 are 25¢ issues)
Marvel Comics Group

1,2: 1-Origin & 1st app. Bloodstone. 2-Origin Bloodstone continued; Kirby-c		1.60	4.00
3-Guardians of the Galaxy (1st solo book, 2/76) begins, ends #12	2.15	6.50	15.00
4-7,9-12: 9,10-Origin Starhawk	1.65	4.20	10.00
8-r/story from Silver Surfer #2 plus 4 pgs. new-a	1.70	5.00	12.00

NOTE: **Austin** a-6i. **Buscema** r-8p. **Chaykin** a-5p. **Kane** c-1p. **Starlin** layouts-10.

MARVEL PREVIEW (Magazine) (Bizarre Adventures #25 on)
Feb (no month), 1975 - No. 24, Winter, 1980 (B&W) ($1.00)
Marvel Comics Group

1-Man-Gods From Beyond the Stars; Crusty Bunkers (Neal Adams)-a(i) & cover; Nino-a		.80	2.00
2-1st origin The Punisher (see Amaz. Spider-Man #129 & Classic Punisher); 1st app. Dominic Fortune	18.00	54.00	125.00
3-7,9,10: 3-Blade the Vampire Slayer. 4-Star-Lord & Sword in the Star (origins & 1st app.). 5,6-Sherlock Holmes. 6-N. Adams frontispiece. 7-Satana, Sword in the star app. 9-Man-God! origin Star Hawk, ends #20. 10-Thor the Mighty. 10,11-Starlin frontispiece in each		.80	2.00
8-Legion of Monsters; Morbius app.	1.30	3.30	8.00
11-20,22-24: 11-Star-Lord; Byrne-a. 12-Haunt of Horror. 14,15-Star-Lord.			

14-Starlin painted-c. 16-Masters of Terror. 17-Blackmark by G. Kane (see SSOC #1-3). 18-Star-Lord. 19-Kull. 20-Bizarre Advs. 22-King Arthur. 23-Bizarre Advs.; Miller-a. 24-Debut Paradox		.80	2.
21-Moon Knight (Spr/80)-Predates Moon Knight #1; The Shroud by Ditko		1.00	2.00	5.

NOTE: **N. Adams** (C. Bunkers) r-20i. **Buscema** a-22, 23. **Byrne** a-11. **Chaykin** a-20r; c-20 (new). **Colan** a-8, 16p(3), 18p, 23p; c-16p. **Elias** a-18. **Giffen** a-7. **Infantino** a-14p. **Kaluta** a-c-15. **Miller** a-23. **Morrow** a-8i; c-2-4. **Perez** a-20p. **Ploog** a-8. **Starlin** c-13, 14. Nudity in som issues

MARVEL RIOT
Dec, 1995 ($1.95, one-shot)
Marvel Comics

1-"Age of Apocalypse" spoof; Lobdell script		.80	2.

MARVELS
Jan, 1994 - No. 4, Apr, 1994 ($5.95, painted limited series, 52 pgs.)
No. 1 (2nd Printing), Apr, 1996 - No. 4 (2nd Printing), July, 1996 ($2.95, painte limited series)
Marvel Comics

1-4: Kurt Busiek scripts & Alex Ross painted-c/a in all; double-c w/acetate overlay		1.00	2.50	6.
Marvel Classic Collectors Pack ($11.90)-Issues #1 & 2 boxed (1st printings).		1.70	5.00	12.
0-(8/94, $2.95)-no acetate overlay.		1.20	3.
1-4-(2nd printing): r/original limited series w/o acetate overlay			3.
Hardcover (1994, $49.95)-r/#0-4; w/intros by Stan Lee, John Romita, Sr., Kurt Busiek & Scott McCloud.			50.
Trade paperback ($19.95)			20.

MARVEL SAGA, THE
Dec, 1985 - No. 25, Dec, 1987
Marvel Comics Group

1			1.
2-25			1.

NOTE: **Williamson** a(i)-9, 10; c(i)-7, 10-12, 14, 16.

MARVEL'S GREATEST COMICS (Marvel Collectors' Item Classics #1-22)
No. 23, Oct, 1969 - No. 96, Jan, 1981
Marvel Comics Group

23-30: Begin Fantastic Four-r/#30s?-116		1.20	3.
31-34,38-96: 42-Silver Surfer-r/F.F.(others?)		.80	2.
35-37-Silver Surfer-r/Fantastic Four #48-50		.80	2.

NOTE: **Dr. Strange**, Fantastic Four, Iron Man, Watcher-#23, 24. Capt. America, Dr. Strange, I Man, Fantastic Four-#25-28. Fantastic Four-#38-96. **Buscema** r-85-92; c-87-92p. **Ditko** r-23-**Kirby** r-23-52; c-75, 77p, 80p. #81 reprints Fantastic Four #100.

MARVELS OF SCIENCE
March, 1946 - No. 4, June, 1946
Charlton Comics

1-A-Bomb story	17.00	51.00	120.
2-4	11.50	34.00	80.

MARVEL SPECIAL EDITION FEATURING... (Also see Special Collectors' E
1975 - 1978 (84 pgs.) (Oversized)
Marvel Comics Group

1-The Spectacular Spider-Man ($1.50); r/Amazing Spider-Man #6,35, Annual 1; Ditko-a(r)		.80	2.
1-Star Wars (1977, $1.00); r/Star Wars #1-3		1.20	3.
2-Star Wars (1978, $1.00); r/Star Wars #4-6		1.20	3.
3-Star Wars ('78, $2.50, 116pgs.); r/S. Wars #1-6		1.20	4.
3-Close Encounters of the Third Kind (1978, $1.50, 56 pgs.)-Movie adaptation; Simonson-a(p)		1.20	3.
V2#2(Spring, 1980, $2.00, oversized)- "Star Wars: The Empire Strikes Back"; r/Marvel Comics Super Special #16		1.60	4.

NOTE: **Chaykin** c/a(r)-1(1977), 2, 3. **Stevens** a(r)-2i, 3i. **Williamson** a(r)-V2#2.

MARVEL SPECTACULAR

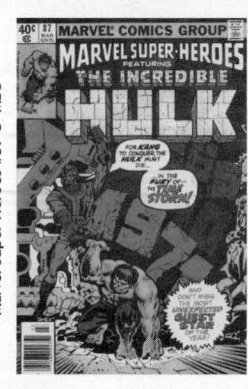

Marvel Spectacular #2 © MEG

Marvel Super Action #16 © MEG

Marvel Super-Heroes #87 © MEG

| | GD25 | FN65 | NM94 | | | GD25 | FN65 | NM94 |

...ug, 1973 - No. 19, Nov, 1975
Marvel Comics Group

1-Thor-r from mid-sixties begin by Kirby	1.00	2.50
2-19	.80	2.00

...ARVELS: PORTRAITS
...ar, 1995 - No. 4, June, 1995 ($2.95, limited series)
Marvel Comics

1-4:Different artists renditions of Marvel characters.		
	1.20	3.00

...ARVEL SPOTLIGHT (...& Son of Satan #19, 20, 23, 24)
...ov, 1971 - No. 33, Apr, 1977; V2#1, July, 1979 - V2#11, Mar, 1981
Marvel Comics Group (A try-out book for new characters)

1-Origin Red Wolf (western hero)(1st solo book, pre-#1); Wood inks, Neal Adams-c; only 15¢ issue	2.85	8.50	20.00
2-(25¢, 52 pgs.)-Venus-r by Everett; origin/1st app. Werewolf By Night (begins) by Ploog; N. Adams-c	7.50	22.50	60.00
3,4: 4-Werewolf By Night ends (6/72); gets own title 9/72			
	1.70	5.00	12.00
5-Origin/1st app. Ghost Rider (8/72) & begins	16.00	50.00	110.00
6-8: 6-Origin G.R. retold. 8-Last Ploog issue	7.00	21.00	50.00
9-11-Last Ghost Rider (gets own title next mo.)	5.50	17.00	40.00
2-Origin & 2nd full app. The Son of Satan (10/73); story cont'd from Ghost Rider #2 & into #3; series begins, ends #24	1.65	4.20	10.00
2-Variant w/4 extra pgs. of ads on slick paper plus a Mark Jeweler pull-out centerfold ad	1.65	4.20	10.00
3-21,23,24: 13-Partial origin Son of Satan. 14-Last 20¢ issue. 24-Last Son of Satan (10/75); gets own title 12/75	1.60	4.00	
2-Ghost Rider-c & cameo (5 panels)	1.50	3.75	9.00
5-27,30,31: 25-Sinbad; contains pull-out Mark Jewelers ad. 26-Scarecrow. 27-Sub-Mariner. 30-The Warriors Three. 31-Nick Fury			
	1.20	3.00	
...8,29: Moon Knight. 28-1st solo Moon Knight app., (6/76). 29-Last 25¢ issue	1.65	4.20	10.00
2-1st app./partial origin Spider-Woman (2/77); Nick Fury app.	1.30	3.25	8.00
3-Deathlok; 1st app. Devil-Slayer	1.30	3.25	8.00
2#1-11: 1-4,8-Capt. Marvel. 5-Dragon Lord. 6,7-StarLord; origin 6. 9-11-Capt. Universe (see Micronauts #8)			1.00

..OTE: **Austin** c-V2#2i, 8. **J. Buscema** c/a-30p. **Chaykin** a-31; c-26, 31. **Colan** a-18p, 19p. ..tko a-V2#4, 5, 9-11; c-V2#4, 9-11. **Kane** c-21p, 32p. **Kirby** c-29p. **McWilliams** a-20i. **Miller** a-..2#8p; c(p)-V2#2, 5, 7, 8. **Mooney** a-8i, 10i, 14p, 15, 16p, 17p, 24p, 27, 32i. **Nasser** a-33p. ..loog a-2-5, 6-8p; c-3-9. **Romita** c-13. **Sutton** a-9-11p, V2#6, 7. #29-25¢ & 30¢ issues exist.

...ARVEL SUPER ACTION (Magazine)
...an, 1976 (B&W, 76 pgs.)
...arvel Comics Group

1-Origin/2nd app. Dominic Fortune(see Marv. Preview); early Punisher app.; Weird World & The Huntress; Evans, Ploog-a	8.50	26.00	60.00

...ARVEL SUPER ACTION
...ay, 1977 - No. 37, Nov, 1981
...arvel Comics Group

1-Reprints Capt. America #100 by Kirby		1.20	3.00
2,3,5-13: r/Capt. America #101,102,103-111. 11-Origin-r. 12,13-Classic Steranko-c/a(r)		.80	2.00
4-Marvel Boy-r(origin)/M. Boy #1		.80	2.00
4-37: r/Avengers #55,56, Annual 2, others. 30-r/Hulk #6 from U.K.			1.00

..OTE: **Buscema** a(r)-14p, 15p; c-18-20, 22, 35r-37. **Everett** a-4. **Heath** a-4r. **Kirby** r-1-3, 5-11. **Smith** a-27r, 28r. **Steranko** a(r)-12p, 13p; c-12r, 13r.

...ARVEL SUPER HERO CONTEST OF CHAMPIONS
...une, 1982 - No. 3, Aug, 1982 (Limited series)
...arvel Comics Group

...-3: Features nearly all Marvel characters currently appearing in their comics; 1st Marvel limited series		1.60	4.00

MARVEL SUPER HEROES
October, 1966 (25¢, 68 pgs.) (1st Marvel one-shot)
Marvel Comics Group

1-r/origin Daredevil from D.D. #1; r/Avengers #2; G.A. Sub-Mariner-r/Marvel Mystery #8 (Human Torch app.)	10.00	30.00	70.00

MARVEL SUPER-HEROES (Formerly Fantasy Masterpieces #1-11)
(Also see Giant-Size Super Heroes) (#12-20: 25¢, 68 pgs.)
No. 12, 12/67 - No. 31, 11/71; No. 32, 9/72 - No. 105, 1/82
Marvel Comics Group

12-Origin & 1st app. Capt. Marvel of the Kree; G.A. Human Torch, Destroyer, Capt. America, Black Knight, Sub-Mariner-r (#12-20 all contain new stories and reprints)	14.00	43.00	100.00
13-2nd app. Capt. Marvel; G.A. Black Knight, Torch, Vision, Capt. America, Sub-Mariner-r	7.00	21.50	50.00
14-Amazing Spider-Man (5/68, new-a by Andru/Everett); G.A. Sub-Mariner, Torch, Mercury (1st Kirby-a at Marvel), Black Knight, Capt. America reprints	15.00	45.00	105.00
15-Black Bolt cameo in Medusa (new-a); Black Knight, Sub-Mariner, Black Marvel, Capt. America-r	2.15	6.50	15.00
16-Origin & 1st app. S. A. Phantom Eagle; G.A. Torch, Capt. America, Black Knight, Patriot, Sub-Mariner-r	2.15	6.50	15.00
17-Origin Black Knight (new-a); G.A. Torch, Sub-Mariner-r; reprint from All-Winners Squad #21 (cover & story)	2.15	6.50	15.00
18-Origin/1st app. Guardians of the Galaxy (1/69); G.A. Sub-Mariner, All-Winners Squad-r	8.50	26.00	60.00
19-Ka-Zar (new-a); G.A. Torch, Marvel Boy, Black Knight, Sub-Mariner reprints; Smith-c(p); Tuska-a(r)	1.70	5.00	12.00
20-Doctor Doom (5/69); r/Young Men #24 w/-c	1.70	5.00	20.00
21-31: All-r issues. 21-X-Men, Daredevil, Iron Man-r begin, end #31. 31-Last Giant issue	1.00	2.00	5.00
32-105: Sub-Mariner-r begin from TTA. 56-r/origin Hulk/Inc. Hulk #102; Hulk-r begin			1.00

NOTE: **Austin** a-104. **Colan** a(p)-12, 13, 15, 18; c-12, 13, 15, 18. **Everett** a-14i(new); r-14, 15i, 18, 19, 33; c-85(!). New **Kirby** c-22, 27, 54. **Maneely** r-14, 15, 19. **Severin** r-83-85i, 100-102; c-100-102r. **Starlin** c-47. **Tuska** a-19p. Black Knight-r by **Maneely** in 12-16, 19. Sub-Mariner-r by **Everett** in 12-20.

MARVEL SUPER-HEROES
May, 1990 - V2#15, Oct, 1993 ($2.95/$2.25/$2.50, quarterly, 68-84 pgs.)
Marvel Comics

1-Moon Knight, Hercules, Black Panther, Magik, Brother Voodoo, Speedball (by Ditko) & Hellcat; Hembeck-a		1.20	3.00
2,4,5: 2-Summer Special(7/90); Rogue, Speedball (by Ditko), Iron Man, Falcon, Tigra & Daredevil. 4-Spider-Man/Nick Fury, Daredevil, Speedball, Wonder Man, Spitfire & Black Knight; Byrne-c. 5-Thor, Dr. Strange, Thing & She-Hulk; Speedball by Ditko(p)		1.20	3.00
V2#3-Retells origin Capt. America w/new facts; Blue Shield, Capt. Marvel, Speedball, Wasp; Hulk by Ditko/Rogers		1.20	3.00
V2#6-9: 6-8-$2.25-c. 6,7-X-Men, Cloak & Dagger, The Shroud (by Ditko) & Marvel Boy in each. 8-X-Men, Namor & Iron Man (by Ditko); Larsen-c. 9-W.C Avengers, Iron Man app.; Kieth-c(p); begin $2.50-c		1.00	2.50
V2#10-Ms. Marvel/Sabretooth-c/story (intended for Ms. Marvel #24; shows-c to #24); Namor, Vision, Scarlet Witch stories		1.00	2.50
V2#11,12 ($2.50): 11-Original Ghost Rider-c/story; Giant-Man, Ms. Marvel stories. 12-Dr. Strange, Falcon, Iron Man		1.00	2.50
V2#13-15 ($2.75, 84 pgs.): 13-All Iron Man issue; 30th anniversary. 15-Iron Man/Thor/Volstagg/Dr. Druid		1.10	2.75

MARVEL SUPER-HEROES MEGAZINE
Oct, 1994 - No. 6, Mar, 1995 ($2.95, 100 pgs.)
Marvel Comics

1-6: 1-r/FF #232, DD #159, Iron Man #115, Incred. Hulk #314	1.20		3.00

MARVEL SUPER-HEROES SECRET WARS (See Secret Wars II)
May, 1984 - No. 12, Apr, 1985 (limited series)

Marvel Tales #115 © MEG

Marvel Tales #128 © MEG

Marvel Tales #108 © MEG

	GD25	FN65	NM94

Marvel Comics Group

		GD25	FN65	NM94
1		1.20		3.00
1-3-2nd printings (sold in multi-packs)				1.00
2-7,9-12: 6-The Wasp dies. 7-Intro. new Spider-Woman. 12-($1.00, 52 pgs.)		.80		2.00
8-Spider-Man's new black costume explained as alien costume (1st app. Venom as alien costume)		2.90	8.60	20.00

NOTE: *Zeck* a-1-12; c-13, 8-12.

MARVEL SUPER SPECIAL A (See Marvel Comics Super...)

MARVEL SWIMSUIT SPECIAL (Also see Marvel Illustrated...)
1992 ($3.95/$4.50, magazine, 52 pgs.)
Marvel Comics

1-Silvestri; pin-ups by many good artists		1.60		4.00
2-Jusko painted-c; all pin-ups		1.80		4.50

MARVEL TAILS STARRING PETER PORKER THE SPECTACULAR SPIDER-HAM (Also see Peter Porker...)
Nov, 1983 (one-shot)
Marvel Comics Group

1-Peter Porker, the Spectacular Spider-Ham, Captain Americat, Goose Rider, Hulk Bunny app.			1.50

MARVEL TALES (Formerly Marvel Mystery Comics #1-92)
No. 93, Aug, 1949 - No. 159, Aug, 1957
Marvel/Atlas Comics (MCI)

93-Horror/weird stories begin	112.00	338.00	900.00
94-Everett-a	78.00	234.00	625.00
95,96,99,101,103,105: 95-New logo	58.00	174.00	465.00
97-Sun Girl, 2 pgs; Kirbyish-a; one story used in N.Y. State Legislative document	65.00	195.00	520.00
98-Krigstein-a	55.00	165.00	440.00
100	55.00	165.00	440.00
102-Wolverton-a "The End of the World", (6 pgs.)	75.00	225.00	600.00
104-Wolverton-a "Gateway to Horror", (6 pgs.)	71.00	215.00	575.00
106,107-Krigstein-a. 106-Decapitation story	44.00	130.00	345.00
108-120: 118-Hypo-c/panels in End of World story. 120-Jack Katz-a	33.00	99.00	230.00
121,123-131: 128-Flying Saucer-c. 131-Last precode (2/55)	26.00	79.00	185.00
122-Kubert-a	29.00	84.00	195.00
132,133,135-141,143,145	16.00	47.00	110.00
134-Krigstein, Kubert-a; flying saucer-c	18.00	54.00	125.00
142-Krigstein-a	16.00	47.00	110.00
144-Williamson/Krenkel-a, 3 pgs.	16.00	47.00	110.00
146,148-151,154-156,158: 150-1st S.A. issue. 156-Torres-a	12.00	36.00	85.00
147-Ditko-a	16.00	47.00	110.00
152-Wood, Morrow-a	16.00	47.00	110.00
153-Everett End of World c/story	17.00	49.00	115.00
157,159-Krigstein-a	13.50	41.00	95.00

NOTE: *Andru* a-103. *Briefer* a-118. *Check* a-147. *Colan* a-105, 107, 118, 120, 121, 127, 131. *Drucker* a-127, 135, 141, 146, 150. *Everett* a-98, 104, 106(2), 108(2), 131, 148, 151, 153, 155; c-107, 109, 111, 112, 114, 117, 127, 143, 147-151, 153, 155, 156. *Forte* a-119, 125, 130. *Heath* a-110, 113, 118, 119; c-104-106, 110, 130. *Gil Kane* a-117. *Lawrence* a-130. *Maneely* a-111, 126, 129; c-108, 116, 120, 129, 152. *Mooney* a-114. *Morisi* a-153. *Morrow* a-150, 152, 156. *Orlando* a-149, 151, 157. *Pakula* a-119, 121, 135, 144, 150, 152, 156. *Powell* a-136, 137, 150, 154. *Ravielli* a-157. *Rico* a-97, 99. *Romita* a-108. *Sekowsky* a-96-98. *Shores* a-110; c-96. *Sinnott* a-105, 116. *Tuska* a-114. *Whitney* a-107. *Wildey* a-126, 138.

MARVEL TALES (...Annual #1,2; ...Starring Spider-Man #123 on)
1964 - No. 291, Nov, 1994 (No. 1-32: 72 pgs.)
Marvel Comics Group (NPP earlier issues)

1-Reprints origins of Spider-Man/Amazing Fantasy #15, Hulk/Inc. Hulk#1, Ant-Man/T.T.A. #35, Giant Man/T.T.A. #49, Iron Man/T.O.S. #39,48, Thor/ J.I.M. #83 & r/Sgt. Fury #1	36.00	109.00	255.00
2 ('65)-r/X-Men #1(origin), Avengers #1(origin), origin Dr. Strange-r/Strange			

		GD25	FN65	NM94
Tales #115 & origin Hulk(Hulk #3)		11.50	34.00	80.0
3 (7/66)-Spider-Man, Strange Tales (H. Torch), Journey into Mystery (Thor), Tales to Astonish (Ant-Man)-r begin (r/Strange Tales #101)		5.30	16.00	37.0
4,5		2.60	7.50	18.0
6-8,10: 10-Reprints 1st Kraven/Amaz. S-M #15		1.70	4.20	10.0
9-r/Amazing Spider-Man #14 w/cover		1.70	5.00	12.0
11-32: 11-Spider-Man battles Daredevil-r/Amaz. Spider-Man #16. 13-Origin Marvel Boy-r/M. Boy #1. 22-Green Goblin-c/story-r/Amaz. Spider-Man #27. 30-New Angel story. 32-Last 72 pg. issue		1.10	2.70	6.5
33-105: 33-(52 pgs.)-Kraven-r. 34-Begin regular size issues. 75-Origin Spider-Man-r. 77-79-Drug issues/r/A. Spider-Man #96-98. 98-Death of Gwen Stacy-r/A. Spider-Man #121 (Green Goblin). 99-Death Green Goblin-r/A. Spider-Man #122. 100-(52 pgs.)-New Hawkeye/Two Gun Kid story. 101-105-All Spider-Man-r				1.5
106-1st Punisher-r/Amazing Spider-Man #129		1.30	3.25	8.0
107-133-All Spider-Man-r. 111,112-r/Spider-Man #134,135 (Punisher). 113, 114-r/Spider-Man #136,137(Green Goblin). 126-128-r/clone story from Amazing Spider-Man #149-151				1.0
134-136-Dr. Strange-r begin; SpM stories continue. 134-Dr. Strange-r/ Strange Tales #110				1.0
137-Origin r Dr. Strange; shows original unprinted-c & origin Spider-Man/ Amazing Fantasy #15		1.80		4.5
137-Nabisco giveaway				1.0
138-Reprints all Amazing Spider-Man #1; begin reprints of Spider-Man with covers similar to originals		1.80		4.5
139-144: r/Amazing Spider-Man #2-7 continue		.80		2.0
145-191,193-199: Spider-Man continue w/#8 on. 149-Contains skin "Tattooz" decals. 150-($1.00, 52pgs.)-r/Spider-Man Annual 1(Kraven app.). 153-r/1st Kraven/Spider-Man #15. 159-r/2nd Green Goblin/Spider-Man #17. 161,164,165-Gr. Goblin-c/stories-r/Spider-Man #23,26,27. 178,179-Green Goblin-c/story-r/Spider-Man #39,40. 187,189-Kraven-r. 191-($1.50, 68 pgs.) r/Spider-Man #96-98. 193-Byrne-r/Marvel Team-Up begin w/scripts				1.2
192-($1.25, 52 pgs.)-r/Spider-Man #121,122		.80		1.5
200-Double size ($1.25)-Miller-c & r/Annual #14				1.5
201-208,210-222: 208-Last Byrne-r. 210,211-r/Spidey #134,135. 212,213-r/ Giant-Size Spidey #4. 213-r/1st solo Silver Surfer story/F.F. Annual #5. 214, 215-r/Spidey #161,162. Green Goblin-c/stories-r/Spectacular Spider-Man #83; last Punisher reprint				1.0
209-Reprints 1st app. The Punisher/Amazing Spider-Man #129; Punisher reprints begin, end #222		1.00		2.5
223-McFarlane-c begins, end #239				1.5
224-249,251,252,254-257: 233-Spider-Man/X-Men team-ups begin; r/X-Men #35. 234-r/Marvel Team-Up #4. 235,236-r/M. Team-Up Annual #1. 237, 238-r/M. Team-Up #150. 239,240-r/M. Team-Up #38,90(Beast). 242-r/M. Team-Up #89. 243-r/M. Team-Up #117(Wolverine). 251-r/M. Team-Up #100 (Green Goblin-c/story). 252-r/1st app. Morbius/Amaz. Spider-Man #101. 254-r/M. Team-Up #15(Ghost Rider); new painted-c. 255,256-Spider-Man & Ghost Rider/Marvel Team-Up #58,51. 257-Hobgoblin-r begin(r/Amazing Spider-Man #238); last $1.00-c				1.0
250-($1.50, 52pgs.)-r/1st Karma/M. Team-Up #100				1.5
253-($1.50, 52 pgs.)-r/Amaz. S-M #102				1.5
258-289: 258-261-r/A. Spider-Man #239,249-251(Hobgoblin). 262,263-r/Marv. Team-Up #53,54. 262-New X-Men vs. Sunstroke story. 263-New Woodgod origin story. 264,265-r/A. Spider-Man Annual 5. 266-273-Reprints alien costume stories/A. S-M 252-259. 277-r/1st Silver Sable/A. S-M 265. 283-r/ A. S-M 275 (Hobgoblin). 284-r/A. S-M 276 (Hobgoblin)				1.2
285-variant w/Wonder-Con logo on c-no price-giveaway				1.0
286-($2.95)-p/bagged w/16 page insert & animation print		1.20		3.0
290, 291: 290-Begin $1.50-c				1.5

NOTE: *All contain reprints; some have new art. #89-97-r/Amazing Spider-Man #110-118; #98-136-r/#121-159; #137-150-r/Amazing Fantasy #15, #1-12 & Annual 1; #151-167-r/#13-28 & Annual 2; #168-186-r/#29-46. Austin* a-100i; c-272i, 273i. *Byrne* a(r)-193-198p, 201-208p. *Ditko*

372

Marvel Team-Up #23 © MEG

Marvel Team-Up #62 © MEG

Marvel Team-Up #80 © MEG

GD25 FN65 NM94

GD25 FN65 NM94

a-1-30, 83, 100, 137-155. **G. Kane** *a-71, 81, 98-101p, 249r; c-125-127p, 130p, 137-155.* **Sam Kieth** *c-255, 262, 263.* **Ron Lim** *c-266p-281p, 283p-285p.* **McFarlane** *c-223-239.* **Mooney** *a-63, 95-97i, 103(i).* **Nasser** *a-100p.* **Nebres** *a-242i.* **Perez** *c-259-261.* **Rogers** *c-240, 241, 243-252.*

MARVEL TEAM-UP (See Marvel Treasury Edition #18 & Official Marvel Index To...) (Replaced by Web of Spider-Man)
March, 1972 - No. 150, Feb, 1985
Marvel Comics Group
NOTE: *Spider-Man team-ups in all but Nos. 18, 23, 26, 29, 32, 35, 97, 104, 105, 137.*

1-Human Torch	11.00	34.00	90.00
2-Human Torch	4.30	13.00	30.00
3-Spider-Man/Human Torch vs. Morbius (part 1); 3rd app. of Morbius (7/72)			
	6.00	18.00	42.00
4-Spider-Man/X-Men vs. Morbius (part 2 of story); 4th app. of Morbius			
	7.50	22.00	52.00
5-10: 5-Vision. 6-Thing. 7-Thor. 8-The Cat (4/73, came out between The Cat #3 & 4). 9-Iron Man. 10-H-T			
	2.50	6.30	15.00
11,13,14,16-20: 11-Inhumans. 13-Capt. America. 14-Sub-Mariner. 16-Capt. Marvel. 17-Mr. Fantastic. 18-H-T/Hulk. 19-Ka-Zar. 20-Black Panther; last 20¢ issue			
	1.70	4.20	10.00
12-Werewolf (8/73, 1 month before Werewolf #1)	1.65	4.70	11.00
15-1st Spider-Man/Ghost Rider team-up (11/73)	2.40	7.20	17.00
21-30: 21-Dr. Strange. 22-Hawkeye. 23-H-T/Iceman (X-Men cameo). 24-Brother Voodoo. 25-Daredevil. 26-H-T/Thor. 27-Hulk. 28-Hercules. 29-H-T/Iron Man. 30-Falcon			
	1.00	2.50	6.00
31-45,47-50: 31-Iron Fist. 32-H-T/Son of Satan. 33-Nighthawk. 34-Valkyrie. 35-H-T/Dr. Strange. 36-Frankenstein. 37-Man-Wolf. 38-Beast. 39-H-T. 40-Sons of the Tiger/H-T. 41-Scarlet Witch. 42-The Vision. 43-Dr. Doom; retells origin. 44-Moondragon. 45-Killraven. 47-Thing. 48-Iron Man; last 25¢ issue. 49-Dr. Strange; Iron Man app. 50-Iron Man; Dr. Strange app.			
	1.00	2.00	5.00
46-Spider-Man/Deathlok team-up	1.70	5.00	12.00
51,52,56,57: 51-Iron Man; Dr. Strange app. 52-Capt. America. 56-Daredevil. 57-Black Widow		1.60	4.00
53-Hulk; Woodgod & X-Men app., 1st Byrne-a on X-Men (1/77)			
	2.40	7.20	17.00
54,59,60: 54-Hulk; Woodgod app. 59-Yellowjacket/The Wasp (Byrne-a in all)	1.00	2.50	6.00
55-Warlock-c/story; Byrne-a	1.30	3.30	8.00
58-Ghost Rider	1.00	2.50	6.00
61-70: All Byrne-a; 61-H-T. 62-Ms. Marvel; last 30¢ issue. 63-Iron Fist. 64-Daughters of the Dragon. 65-Capt. Britain (1st U.S. app.). 66-Capt. Britain; 1st app. Arcade. 67-Tigra; Kraven the Hunter app. 68-Man-Thing. 69-Havok (X-Men app.). 70-Thor			
	1.20	3.00	
71-74,76-78,80: 71-Falcon. 72-Iron Man. 73-Daredevil. 74-Not Ready for Prime Time Players (Belushi). 76-Dr. Strange. 77-Ms. Marvel. 78-Wonder Man. 80-Dr. Strange/Clea; last 35¢ issue		1.20	3.00
75,79: Byrne-a(p). 75-Power Man; Cage app. 79-Mary Jane Watson as Red Sonja; Clark Kent cameo (1 panel, 3/79)		1.20	3.00
81-85,87,88,90,92-99: 81-Satana. 82-Black Widow. 83-Nick Fury. 84-Shang-Chi. 92-Hawkeye. 93-Werewolf by Night. 94-SpM vs. The Shroud. 95-Mockingbird (intro.); Nick Fury app. 96-Howard the Duck; last 40¢ issue. 97-Spider-Woman/Hulk. 98-Black Widow. 99-Machine Man. 85-Shang-Chi/Black Widow/Nick Fury. 87-Black Panther. 88-Invisible Girl. 90-Beast			
		.80	2.00
86-Guardians of the Galaxy		1.20	3.00
89-Nightcrawler (from X-Men)		1.20	3.00
91-Ghost Rider		1.60	4.00
100-(Double-size)-Fantastic Four/Storm/Black Panther; origin/1st app. Karma, one of the New Mutants; origin Storm; X-Men x-over; Miller-c/a(p); Byrne-a (X-Men app. only)	1.30	3.25	8.00
101-116: 101-Nighthawk(Ditko-a). 102-Doc Samson. 103-Ant-Man. 104-Hulk/Ka-Zar. 105-Hulk/Powerman/Iron Fist. 106-Capt. America. 107-She-Hulk. 108-Paladin; Dazzler cameo. 109-Dazzler; Paladin app. 110-Iron Man. 111-Devil-Slayer. 112-King Kull; last 50¢ issue. 113-Quasar. 114-Falcon.			

115-Thor. 116-Valkyrie			1.50
117-Wolverine-c/story		1.70	5.00	12.00
118-140,142-149: 118-Professor X; Wolverine app. (4 pgs.); X-Men cameo. 119-Gargoyle. 120-Dominic Fortune. 121-Human Torch. 122-Man-Thing. 123-Daredevil. 124-The Beast. 125-Tigra. 126-Hulk & Powerman/Son of Satan. 127-The Watcher. 128-Capt. America; Spider-Man/Capt. America photo-c. 129-The Vision. 130-Scarlet Witch. 131-Frogman. 132-Mr. Fantastic. 133-Fantastic Four. 134-Jack of Hearts. 135-Kitty Pryde; X-Men cameo. 136-Wonder Man. 137-Aunt May/Franklin Richards. 138-Sandman. 139-Nick Fury. 140-Black Widow. 142-Capt. Marvel. 143-Starfox. 144-Moon Knight. 145-Iron Man. 146-Nomad. 147-Human Torch; SpM back to old costume. 148-Thor. 149-Cannonball			1.50
141-Daredevil; SpM/Black Widow app. (Spidey in new black costume; ties w/ Amaz. S-M #252 for 1st black costume)		1.20	3.00
150-X-Men ($1.00, double-size); B. Smith-c		1.60	4.00
Annual 1(1976)-SpM/X-Men (early app.)	2.00	6.00	15.00
Annuals 2-7: 2(1979)-SpM/Hulk. 3(1980)-Hulk/Power Man/Machine Man/Iron Fist; Miller-c(p). 4(1981)-SpM/Daredevil/Moon Knight/Power Man/Iron Fist; brief origins of each; Miller-c; Miller scripts on Daredevil. 5(1982)-SpM/The Thing/Scarlet Witch/Dr. Strange/Quasar. 6(1983)-SpM/New Mutants (early app.), Cloak & Dagger. 7(1984)-Alpha Flight; Byrne-c(i)		.80	2.00

NOTE: **Art Adams** *c-141p.* **Austin** *a-79i; c-76i, 79i, 96i, 101i, 112i, 130i.* **Bolle** *a-9i.* **Byrne** *a(p)-53-55, 59-70, 75, 79, 100; c-68p, 70p, 72p, 75, 76p, 79p, 129i, 133i.* **Colan** *a-87p.* **Ditko** *a-101.* **Kane** *a(p)-4-6, 13, 14, 16-19, 23; c(p)-4, 13, 14, 17-19, 23, 25, 26, 32-35, 37, 41, 44, 45, 47, 53, 54.* **Miller** *a-100p; c-95p, 99p, 100p, 102p, 106.* **Mooney** *a-2i, 7i, 8, 10p, 11p, 16r.* **Nasser** *a-89p; c-101p.* **Simonson** *c-99i, 148.* **Paul Smith** *c-131, 132.* **Starlin** *c-27.* **Sutton** *a-93p. "H-T" means Human Torch; "SpM" means Spider-Man; "S-M" means Sub-Mariner.*

MARVEL TREASURY EDITION
1974; #2, Dec, 1974 - #28, 1981 ($1.50/$2.50, 100 pgs., oversized, new-a &-r)
Marvel Comics Group

1-Spectacular Spider-Man; story-r/Marvel Super-Heroes #14; Romita-c/a(r); G. Kane, Ditko-r; Green Goblin/Hulk-r	1.30	3.25	8.00
1-1,000 numbered copies signed by Stan Lee & John Romita on front-c & sold thru mail for $5.00; 1st 1,000 copies off the press	1.70	5.00	12.00
2-28: 2-Fantastic Four-r/F.F. 6,11,48-50(Silver Surfer). 3-The Mighty Thor-r/Thor #125-130. 4-Conan the Barbarian; Barry Smith-c/a(r)/Conan #11. 5-The Hulk (origin-r/Hulk #3). 6-Dr. Strange. 7-Mighty Avengers. 8-Giant Superhero Holidy Grab-Bag; Spider-Man, Hulk, Nick Fury. 9-Giant; Super-hero Team-up. 10-Thor; r/Thor #154-157. 11-Fantastic Four. 12-Howard the Duck (r/#H. the Duck #1 & G.S. Man-Thing #4,5) plus new Defenders story. 13-Giant Super-Hero Holiday Grab-Bag. 14-The Sensational Spider-Man; r/1st Morbius from Amazing S-M #101,102 plus #100 & r/Not Brand Echh #6. 15-Conan; B. Smith, Neal Adams-i; r/Conan #24. 16-The Defenders (origin) & Valkyrie; r/Defenders #1,4,13,14. 17-The Hulk. 18-The Astonishing Spider-Man; r/Spider-Man's 1st team-ups with Iron Fist, The X-Men, Ghost Rider & Werewolf by Night; inside back-c has photos from 1978 Spider-Man TV show. 19-Conan the Barbarian. 20-Hulk. 21-Fantastic Four. 22-Spider-Man. 23-Conan. 24-Rampaging Hulk. 25-Spider-Man vs. The Hulk. 26-The Hulk; Wolverine app. 27-Spider-Man. 28-Spider-Man/Superman; (origin of each)	1.00	2.60	6.00

NOTE: *Reprints-2, 3, 5, 7-9, 13, 14, 16, 17.* **Neal Adams** *a(i)-6, 15.* **Brunner** *a-6, 12; c-6.* **Buscema** *a-15, 19, 28; c-28.* **Colan** *a-6r; c-12p.* **Ditko** *a-1, 6.* **Gil Kane** *c-16p.* **Kirby** *a-2, 10, 11; c-7.* **Romita** *c-1, 5.* **B. Smith** *a-4, 15, 19; c-4, 19.*

MARVEL TREASURY OF OZ FEATURING THE MARVELOUS LAND OF OZ
1975 ($1.50, oversized) (See MGM's Marvelous...)
Marvel Comics Group

1-Buscema; Romita-c	1.00	2.00	5.00

MARVEL TREASURY SPECIAL (Also see 2001: A Space Odyssey)
1974; 1976 ($1.50, oversized, 84 pgs.)
Marvel Comics Group

Vol. 1-Spider-Man, Torch, Sub-Mariner, Avengers "Giant Superhero Holiday Grab-Bag"; Wood, Colan/Everett, plus 2 Kirby-r; reprints Hulk vs. Thing from Fantastic Four #25,26	1.00	2.60	6.00

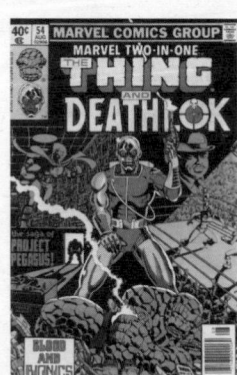

Marvel Two-In-One #54 © MEG

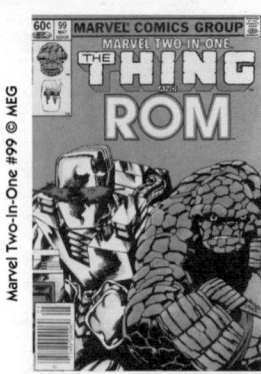

Marvel Two-In-One #99 © MEG

Mask #2 © DH

	GD25	FN65	NM94

Vol. 1-... Featuring Captain America's Bicentennial Battles (6/76)-Kirby-a;
B. Smith inks, 11 pgs. ... 1.65 ... 4.20 ... 10.00

MARVEL TRIPLE ACTION (See Giant-Size...)
Feb, 1972 - No. 24, Mar, 1975; No. 25, Aug, 1975 - No. 47, Apr, 1979
Marvel Comics Group

1-(25¢ giant, 52 pgs.)-Dr. Doom, Silver Surfer, The Thing begin, end #4
('66 reprints from Fantastic Four) ... 1.20 ... 3.00
2-47: 45-r/X-Men #45. 46-r/Avengers #53(X-Men) ... 1.00
NOTE: #5-44, 46, 47 reprint Avengers #11 thru ?. #40-r/Avengers #48(1st Black Knight).
Buscema a(r)-35p, 36p, 38p, 39p, 41, 42, 43p, 44p, 46p, 47p. **Ditko** a-2r; c-47. **Kirby** a(r)-1-4p.
Starlin c-7. **Tuska** a(r)-40p, 43i, 46i, 47i. #2 through at least #17 are 20¢-c.

MARVEL TWO-IN-ONE (...Featuring ... #82? on; also see The Thing)
January, 1974 - No. 100, June, 1983
Marvel Comics Group

1-Thing team-ups begin; Man-Thing ... 4.30 ... 13.00 ... 30.00
2-4: 2-Sub-Mariner; last 20¢ issue. 3-Daredevil. 4-Capt. America
... 1.80 ... 5.00 ... 11.00
5-Guardians of the Galaxy (9/74, 2nd app.?) ... 2.15 ... 6.50 ... 15.00
6-Dr. Strange (11/74) ... 2.40 ... 7.30 ... 17.00
7,9,10 ... 1.20 ... 2.90 ... 7.00
8-Early Ghost Rider app. (3/75) ... 1.70 ... 5.00 ... 12.00
11-20: 13-Power Man. 14-Son of Satan (early app.). 17-Spider-Man. 18-Last
25¢ issue ... 1.80 ... 4.50
21-26,28,29,31-40: 29-Master of Kung Fu; Spider-Woman cameo. 39-Vision
... 1.40 ... 3.50
27-Deathlok ... 1.00 ... 2.00 ... 5.00
30-2nd full app. Spider-Woman (see Marvel Spotlight #32 for 1st app.)
... .90 ... 2.30 ... 5.50
41,42,44-49: 42-Capt. America. 45-Capt. Marvel. 46-Thing battles Hulk-c/story
... .80 ... 2.00
43,50,53,55-Byrne-a(p). 53-Quasar(7/79, 2nd app.) ... 1.00 ... 2.50
51-The Beast, Nick Fury, Ms. Marvel; Miller-p ... 1.20 ... 3.00
52-Moon Knight app. ... 1.20 ... 3.00
54-Death of Deathlok: Byrne-a ... 1.65 ... 4.20 ... 10.00
56-60,64-68,70-79,81,82: 60-Intro. Impossible Woman. 68-Angel. 71-1st app.
Maelstrom. 75-Avengers (52 pgs.). 76-Iceman ... 1.50
61-63: 61-Starhawk (from Guardians); "The Coming of Her" storyline begins,
ends #63; cover similar to F.F. #67 (Him-c). 62-Moondragon; Thanos &
Warlock cameo in flashback; Starhawk app. 63-Warlock?; Warlock revived
shortly; Starhawk & Moondragon app. ... .80 ... 2.00
69-Guardians of the Galaxy ... 1.60 ... 4.00
80-Ghost Rider ... 1.00 ... 2.00 ... 5.00
83,84: 83-Sasquatch. 84-Alpha Flight app. ... .80 ... 2.00
85-99: 90-Spider-Man. 93-Jocasta dies. 96-X-Men-c & cameo ... 1.00
100-Double size, Byrne scripts ... 1.50
Annual 1 (1976, 52 pgs.)-Thing/Liberty Legion ... .80 ... 2.00
Annual 2(1977, 52 pgs.)-Thing/Spider-Man; 2nd death of Thanos; end of
Thanos saga; Warlock app.; Starlin-c/a ... 1.70 ... 5.00 ... 12.00
Annual 3,4 (1978-79, 52 pgs.): 3-Nova. 4-Black Bolt ... 1.50
Annual 5-7 (1980-82, 52 pgs.): 5-Hulk. 6-1st app. American Eagle. 7-The Thing/
Champion; Sasquatch, Colossus app.; X-Men cameo (1 pg.) ... 1.00
NOTE: **Austin** c(i)-42, 54, 56, 58, 61, 63, 66. **John Buscema** a-30p, 45; c-30p. **Byrne** (p)-43, 50,
53-55; c-43, 53p, 56p, 98i, 99i. **Gil Kane** a-1p, 2p; c(p)-1-3, 9, 11, 14, 28. **Kirby** c-10, 12, 19p,
20, 25, 27. **Mooney** a-18i, 38i, 90i. **Nasser** a-70p. **Perez** a(p)-56-58, 60, 64, 65; c(p)-32, 33, 42,
50-52, 54, 55, 57, 58, 61-66, 70. **Roussos** a-Annual 1i. **Simonson** c-43i, 97p, Annual 6i. **Starlin**
c-6, Annual 1. **Tuska** a-6p.

MARVEL UNIVERSE (See Official Handbook Of The...)

MARVEL VERSUS DC (See DC Versus Marvel) (Also see Amazon,
Assassins, Bruce Wayne: Agent of S.H.I.E.L.D., Bullets & Bracelets, Doctor
Strangefate, JLX, Legend of the Dark Claw, Magneto & The Magnetic Men,
Speed Demon, Spider-Boy, Super Soldier, & X-Patrol)
No. 2, 1996 - No. 3, 1996 ($3.95, limited series)
Marvel Comics

2,3: 2-Peter David script. 3-Ron Marz script; Dan Jurgens-a(p). 1st app. of

Super Soldier, Spider-Boy, Dr. Doomsday, Doctor Strangefate, The Dark
Claw, Nightcreeper, Amazon, Wraith & others. Storyline continues in
Amalgam books. ... .80 ... 1.60 ... 4.C

MARVEL X-MEN COLLECTION, THE
Jan, 1994 - No. 3, Mar, 1994 ($2.95, limited series)
Marvel Comics

1-3-r/X-Men trading cards by Jim Lee ... 1.20 ... 3.C

MARVIN MOUSE
September, 1957
Atlas Comics (BPC)

1-Everett-c/a; Maneely-a ... 10.00 ... 30.00 ... 65.C

MARY JANE & SNIFFLES (See Looney Tunes)
No. 402, June, 1952 - No. 474, June, 1953
Dell Publishing Co.

Four Color 402 (#1) ... 9.00 ... 27.00 ... 90.
Four Color 474 ... 8.00 ... 24.00 ... 80.C

MARY MARVEL COMICS (Monte Hale #29 on) (Also see Captain Marvel #18,
Marvel Family, Shazam, & Wow Comics)
Dec, 1945 - No. 28, Sept, 1948
Fawcett Publications

1-Captain Marvel introduces Mary on-c; intro/origin Georgia Sivana
... 150.00 ... 450.00 ... 1200.C
2 ... 62.00 ... 187.00 ... 500.C
3,4: 3-New logo ... 41.00 ... 124.00 ... 330.C
5-8: 8-Bulletgirl x-over in Mary Marvel; X-Mas-c ... 33.00 ... 99.00 ... 230.C
9,10 ... 29.00 ... 86.00 ... 200.C
11-20 ... 19.00 ... 58.00 ... 135.C
21-28: 28-Western-c ... 17.00 ... 49.00 ... 115.C

MARY POPPINS (See Movie Comics & Walt Disney Showcase No. 17)

MARY'S GREATEST APOSTLE (St. Louis Grignion de Montfort)
No date (16 pgs.; paper cover)
Catechetical Guild (Topix) (Giveaway)

nn ... 2.40 ... 6.00 ... 12.

MARY SHELLEY'S FRANKENSTEIN
Oct, 1994 - Jan, 1995 ($2.95, limited series)
Topps Comics

1-4-polybagged w/3 trading cards ... 1.20 ... 3.
1-4 ($2.50)-Newsstand ed. ... 1.00 ... 2.

MARY WORTH (See Harvey Comics Hits #55 & Love Stories of...)
March, 1956 (Also see Romantic Picture Novelettes)
Argo

1 ... 6.70 ... 20.00 ... 40.

MASK (TV)
Dec, 1985 - No. 4, Mar, 1986; Feb, 1987 - No. 9, Oct, 1987 (limited series)
DC Comics

1-Sat. morning TV show. ... .80 ... 2.
2-4 ... 1.4
1-(2nd series) ... 1.2
2-9

MASK, THE
Aug, 1991 - No. 4, Oct, 1991; No. 0, Dec, 1991 ($2.50, 36 pgs., limited series)
Dark Horse Comics

1-4: 1-1st app. Lt. Kellaway as The Mask ... 1.00 ... 2.00 ... 5.
0-(12/91, B&W, 56 pgs.)-r/Mayhem #1-4 ... 1.00 ... 2.00 ... 5.

MASK: HUNT FOR GREEN OCTOBER
July, 1995 - Oct, 1995 ($2.50, limited series)
Dark Horse Comics

Mask Returns #4 © DH

Mask Southern Discomfort #3 © DH

Master Comics #29 © FAW

	GD25	FN65	NM94
1-4-Evan Dorkin scripts		1.00	2.50

MASK: OFFICIAL MOVIE ADAPTATION
July, 1994 - Aug, 1994 ($2.50, limited series)
Dark Horse Comics

		GD25	FN65	NM94
1,2			1.00	2.50

MASK RETURNS
Oct, 1992 - Mar, 1993 ($2.50, limited series)
Dark Horse Comics

	GD25	FN65	NM94
1-4		1.60	4.00

MASK SOUTHERN DISCOMFORT
Mar, 1996 - July, 1996 ($2.50, limited series)
Dark Horse Comics

	GD25	FN65	NM94
1-4		1.00	2.50

MASK STRIKES BACK
Feb, 1995 - Jun, 1995 ($2.50, limited series)
Dark Horse Comics

	GD25	FN65	NM94
1-5		1.00	2.50

MASK SUMMER VACATION
July, 1995 ($10.95, one shot, hard-c)

	GD25	FN65	NM94
1-nn-Rick Geary-c/a	1.65	4.70	11.00

MASK WORLD TOUR
Dec, 1995 - Mar, 1996 ($2.50, limited series)
Dark Horse Comics

	GD25	FN65	NM94
1-4-3-X & Ghost-c/app.		1.00	2.50

MASK COMICS
Feb-Mar, 1945 - No. 2, Apr-May, 1945; No. 2, Fall, 1945
Rural Home Publications

	GD25	FN65	NM94
1-Classic L. B. Cole Satan-c/a; Palais-a	187.00	562.00	1500.00
2-(Scarce)-Classic L. B. Cole Satan-c; Black Rider, The Boy Magician, & The Collector app.	125.00	375.00	1000.00
2-(Fall, 1945)-No publ.-same as regular #2; L. B. Cole-c	100.00	300.00	800.00

MASKED BANDIT, THE
1952
Avon Periodicals

	GD25	FN65	NM94
1-Kinstler-a	13.00	39.00	90.00

MASKED MAN, THE
2/84 - #10, 4/86; #11, 10/87; #12, 4/88 ($1.75/$2.00, color/B&W #9 on, Baxter paper)
Eclipse Comics

	GD25	FN65	NM94
1-Origin retold		.80	2.00
2-12: 3-Origin Aphid-Man; begin $2.00-c		.75	1.80

MASKED MARVEL (See Keen Detective Funnies)
Sept, 1940 - No. 3, Dec, 1940
Centaur Publications

	GD25	FN65	NM94
1-The Masked Marvel begins	150.00	450.00	1200.00
2,3: 2-Gustavson, Tarpe Mills-a	103.00	309.00	825.00

MASKED PILOT, THE (See Popular Comics #43)
1939 (7-1/2x5-1/4", 16 pgs., premium, non-slick-c)
U.S. Callender

	GD25	FN65	NM94
nn-Bob Jenney-a			

MASKED RAIDER, THE (Billy The Kid #9 on; Frontier Scout, Daniel Boone #10-13) (Also see Blue Bird)
June, 1955 - No. 8, July, 1957; No. 14, Aug, 1958 - No. 30, June, 1961
Charlton Comics

	GD25	FN65	NM94
1-Masked Raider & Talon the Golden Eagle begin; painted-c	10.00	30.00	70.00

	GD25	FN65	NM94
2	6.70	20.00	40.00
3-8: 8-Billy The Kid app.	4.25	13.00	28.00
14,16-30: 22-Rocky Lane app.	4.00	11.00	22.00
15-Williamson-a, 7 pgs.	4.25	13.00	28.00

MASKED RANGER
Apr, 1954 - No. 9, Aug, 1955
Premier Magazines

	GD25	FN65	NM94
1-The Masked Ranger, his horse Streak, & The Crimson Avenger (origin) begin, end #9; Woodbridge/Frazetta-a	34.00	101.00	235.00
2,3	10.00	30.00	70.00
4-8-All Woodbridge-a. 5-Jesse James by Woodbridge. 6-Billy The Kid by Woodbridge. 7-Wild Bill Hickok by Woodbridge. 8-Jim Bowie's Life Story	11.50	34.00	80.00
9-Torres-a; Wyatt Earp by Woodbridge; Says Death of Masked Ranger on-c	12.00	36.00	85.00

NOTE: **Check** a-1. **Woodbridge** c/a-1, 4-9.

MASK OF DR. FU MANCHU, THE (See Dr. Fu Manchu)
1951
Avon Periodicals

	GD25	FN65	NM94
1-Sax Rohmer adapt.; Wood-c/a (26 pgs.); Hollingsworth-a	78.00	234.00	625.00

MASQUE OF THE RED DEATH (See Movie Classics)

MASTER COMICS (Combined with Slam Bang Comics #7 on)
Mar, 1940 - No. 133, Apr, 1953 (No. 1-6: oversized issues)
(#1-3: 15¢, 52 pgs.; #4-6: 10¢, 36 pgs.; #7-Begin 68 pg. issues)
Fawcett Publications

	GD25	FN65	VF82	NM94
1-Origin & 1st app. Master Man; The Devil's Dagger, El Carim, Master of Magic, Rick O'Say, Morton Murch, White Rajah, Shipwreck Roberts, Frontier Marshal, Streak Sloan, Mr. Clue begin (all features end #6)	670.00	2010.00	4020.00	6700.00

(Estimated up to 100 total copies exist, 4 in NM/Mint)

	GD25	FN65	NM94
2	200.00	600.00	1600.00
3-5	156.00	468.00	1250.00
6-Last Master Man	156.00	468.00	1250.00

NOTE: #1-6 rarely found in near mint to mint condition due to large-size format.

	GD25	FN65	NM94
7-(10/40)-Bulletman, Zoro, the Mystery Man (ends #22), Lee Granger, Jungle King, & Buck Jones begin; only app. The War Bird & Mark Swift & the Time Retarder; Zoro, Lee Granger, Jungle King & Mark Swift all continue from Slam Bang; Bulletman moves from Nickel	250.00	750.00	2000.00
8-The Red Gaucho (ends #13), Captain Venture (ends #22) & The Planet Princess begin	131.00	393.00	1050.00
9,10: 10-Lee Granger ends	106.00	318.00	850.00
11-Origin & 1st app. Minute-Man (2/41)	237.00	712.00	1900.00
12	118.00	356.00	950.00
13-Origin & 1st app. Bulletgirl; Hitler-c	181.00	543.00	1450.00
14-16: 14-Companions Three begins, ends #31	96.00	290.00	775.00
17-20: 17-Raboy-a on Bulletman begins. 20-Captain Marvel cameo app. in Bulletman	91.00	275.00	735.00

	GD25	FN65	VF82	NM94
21-(12/41; Scarce)-Captain Marvel & Bulletman team up against Capt. Nazi; origin & 1st app. Capt. Marvel Jr.'s most famous nemesis Captain Nazi who will cause creation of Capt. Marvel Jr. in Whiz #25. Part I of trilogy origin of Capt. Marvel Jr.; 1st Mac Raboy-c for Fawcett; Capt. Nazi-c	422.00	1267.00	2533.00	4200.00

(Estimated up to 110 total copies exist, 6 in NM/Mint)

22-(1/42)-Captain Marvel Jr. moves over from Whiz #25 & teams up with Bulletman against Captain Nazi; part II of trilogy origin of Capt. Marvel Jr. & his 1st cover and adventure	378.00	1133.00	2267.00	3800.00

(Estimated up to 135 total copies exist, 7 in NM/Mint)

	GD25	FN65	NM94
23-Capt. Marvel Jr. c/stories begin (1st solo story); fights Capt. Nazi by himself.			

Master Comics #45 © FAW

Master of Kung-Fu #64 © MEG

Masters of the Universe #2 © Mattel

	GD25	FN65	NM94
	225.00	675.00	2000.00
24,25,29: 29-Hitler & Hirohito-c	90.00	271.00	725.00
26-28,30-Captain Marvel Jr. vs. Capt. Nazi. 30-Flag-c			
	82.00	247.00	660.00
31,32: 32-Last El Carim & Buck Jones; intro Balbo, the Boy Magician in El Carim story	58.00	176.00	470.00
33-Balbo, the Boy Magician (ends #47), Hopalong Cassidy (ends #49) begins	58.00	176.00	470.00
34-Capt. Marvel Jr. vs. Capt. Nazi-c/story	65.00	195.00	525.00
35	58.00	176.00	470.00
36-40: 40-Flag-c	53.00	159.00	425.00
41-Bulletman, Capt. Marvel Jr. & Bulletgirl x-over in Minute-Man; only app. Crime Crusaders Club (Capt. Marvel Jr., Minute-Man, Bulletman & Bulletgirl); only team in Fawcett Comics	58.00	176.00	470.00
42-47,49: 47-Hitler becomes Corpl. Hitler Jr. 49-Last Minute-Man	38.00	114.00	265.00
48-Intro. Bulletboy; Capt. Marvel cameo in Minute-Man	40.00	120.00	310.00
50-Intro Radar & Nyoka the Jungle Girl & begin series (5/44); Radar also intro in Captain Marvel #35 (same date); Capt. Marvel x-over in Radar; origin Radar; Capt. Marvel & Capt. Marvel, Jr. introduce Radar on-c	29.00	86.00	200.00
51-58	19.00	56.00	135.00
59-62: Nyoka serial "Terrible Tiara" in all; 61-Capt. Marvel Jr. 1st meets Uncle Marvel	22.00	66.00	155.00
63-80	15.00	45.00	105.00
81,83-87,89-91,95-99: 88-Hopalong Cassidy begins (ends #94). 95-Tom Mix begins (ends #133)	13.50	41.00	95.00
82,88,92-94-Krigstein-a	15.00	45.00	105.00
100	13.50	41.00	95.00
101-106-Last Bulletman	12.00	36.00	85.00
107-131	11.00	33.00	75.00
132-B&W and color illos in POP	11.50	34.00	80.00
133-Bill Battle app.	13.50	41.00	95.00

NOTE: Mac Raboy a-15-39, 40(part), 42, 58. c-21-49, 51, 52, 54, 56, 58, 68(part), 69(part). Bulletman c-7-11, 13(half), 15, 18(part), 19, 20, 21(w/Capt. Marvel & Capt. Nazi), 22(w/Capt. Marvel, Jr.). Capt. Marvel, Jr. c-23-133. Master Man c-1-6. Minute Man c-12, 13(half), 14, 16, 17, 18(part).

MASTER DETECTIVE
1964 (Reprints)
Super Comics

17-r/Criminals on the Loose V4 #2; r/Young King Cole #?; McWilliams-r	1.30	3.25	8.00

MASTER OF KUNG FU (Formerly Special Marvel Edition; see Deadly Hands of Kung Fu & Giant-Size…)
No. 17, April, 1974 - No. 125, June, 1983
Marvel Comics Group

17-Starlin-a; intro Black Jack Tarr; 3rd Shang-Chi (ties w/Deadly Hands #1)	2.15	6.50	15.00
18-20: 19-Man-Thing-c/story	1.30	3.25	8.00
21-23,25-30	1.00	2.00	5.00
24-Starlin, Simonson-a	1.00	2.60	6.00
31-99: 33-1st Leiko Wu. 43-Last 25¢ issue		1.20	3.00
100-Double size		1.60	4.00
101-117,119-124		1.00	2.50
118,125-Double size issues		1.40	3.50
Annual 1(4/76)-Iron Fist app.	1.00	2.00	5.00

NOTE: Austin c-63i, 74i. Buscema c-44p. Gulacy a(p)-18-20, 22, 25, 29-31, 33-35, 38, 39, 40(p&i), 42-50, 53r(#20); c-51, 55, 64, 67. Gil Kane c(p)-20, 38, 39, 42, 45, 59, 63. Nebres c-73i. Starlin a-17p, 24; c-54. Sutton a-42i. #53 reprints #20.

MASTER OF KUNG-FU: BLEEDING BLACK
Feb, 1991 ($2.95, 84 pgs., one-shot)
Marvel Comics

	GD25	FN65	NM94
1-The Return of Shang-Chi		1.20	3.

MASTER OF THE WORLD
No. 1157, July, 1961
Dell Publishing Co.

Four Color 1157-Movie	6.00	18.00	60.

MASTERS OF TERROR (Magazine)
July, 1975 - No. 2, Sept, 1975 (B&W) (All reprints)
Marvel Comics Group

1-Brunner, Barry Smith-a; Morrow/Steranko-c; Starlin-a(p); Gil Kane-a		.70	1.
2-Reese, Kane, Mayerik-a; Adkins/Steranko-c			1.

MASTERS OF THE UNIVERSE
Dec, 1982 - No. 3, Feb, 1983 (Mini-series)
DC Comics

1-3: 2-Origin He-Man & Ceril			1.

NOTE: Alcala a-1i,, 2i. Tuska a-1-3p; c-1-3p. #2 has 75 & 95 cent cover price.

MASTERS OF THE UNIVERSE (Comic Album)
1984 (8-1/2x11", $2.95, 64 pgs.)
Western Publishing Co.

11362-Based on Mattel toy & cartoon		1.20	3.

MASTERS OF THE UNIVERSE
May 1986 - No. 12, March, 1988 (75¢/$1.00)
Star Comics/Marvel #7 on

1-12: 8-Begin $1.00-c			1.
The Motion Picture (11/87, $2.00)-Tuska-p		.80	2.

MASTERWORKS SERIES OF GREAT COMIC BOOK ARTISTS, THE
May, 1983 - No. 3, Dec, 1983 (Baxter paper)
Sea Gate Distributors/DC Comics

1-3: 1,2-Shining Knight by Frazetta r-/Adventure. 2-Tomahawk by Frazetta-r. 3-Wrightson-c/a(r)		.80	2.

MATT SLADE GUNFIGHTER (Kid Slade Gunfighter #5 on; See Western Gunfighters)
May, 1956 - No. 4, Nov, 1956
Atlas Comics (SPI)

1-Intro Matt & horse Eagle; Williamson/Torres-a	16.00	47.00	110.
2-Williamson-a	10.00	30.00	60.
3,4	7.50	22.50	45.

NOTE: Maneely a-1, 3, 4; c-1, 2, 4. Roth a-2-4. Severin a-1, 3, 4. Maneely c/a-1.

MAVERICK (TV)
No. 892, 4/58 - No. 19, 4-6/62 (All have photo-c)
Dell Publishing Co.

Four Color 892 (#1)-James Garner photo-c begin	25.00	75.00	250.
Four Color 930,945,962,980,1005 (6-8/59): 945-James Garner/Jack Kelly photo-c begin	11.00	33.00	110.
7 (10-12/59) - 14: Last Garner/Kelly-c	8.50	25.50	85.
15-18: Jack Kelly/Roger Moore photo-c	7.20	21.60	72.
19-Jack Kelly photo-c	7.20	21.60	72.

MAVERICK MARSHAL
Nov, 1958 - No. 7, May, 1960
Charlton Comics

1	4.00	12.00	24.
2-7	2.80	7.00	14.

MAVERICKS
Jan, 1994 - No. 5, 1994 ($2.50)
Daggar Comics Group

1-($2.75)		1.00	2
1-Bronze		1.00	2
1-Gold		1.00	2

Maximage #3 © rob Liefeld

Maxx #13 © I Before E

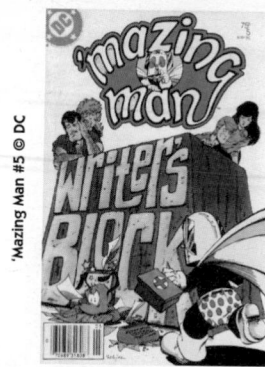

'Mazing Man #5 © DC

	GD25	FN65	NM94

	GD25	FN65	NM94
1-Silver		1.00	2.50
2-5		1.00	2.50

MAX BRAND (See Silvertip)

MAXIMAGE
Dec, 1995 - Present ($2.50)
Image Comics (Extreme Studios)

1-7: 1-Liefeld-c. 2-Extreme Destroyer Pt. 2; polybagged w/card. 4-Angela & Glory-c/app.			2.50

MAXX (Also see Darker Image & Primer #5)
Mar, 1993 - Present ($1.95)
Image Comics (I Before E)

1/2	1.65	4.20	10.00
1/2 (Gold)	1.65	4.20	10.00
1-Sam Kieth-c/a/scripts	1.00	2.00	5.00
1-Glow-in-the-dark variant	1.65	4.20	10.00
2-10: 6-Savage Dragon cameo(1 pg.). 7,8-Pitt-c & story	1.20	3.00	
11-33	.80	2.00	

MAYA (See Movie Classics)
Mar, 1968
Gold Key

1 (10218-803)(TV)	1.70	5.00	12.00

MAYHEM
May, 1989 - No. 4, Sept, 1989 ($2.50, B&W, 52 pgs.)
Dark Horse Comics

1- 4-part Stanley Ipkiss/Mask story begins; Mask-c	2.85	8.50	20.00
2-4: 2-Mask 1/2 back-c. 4-Mask-c	1.70	5.00	12.00

MAZE AGENCY, THE
Dec, 1988 - No. 20, 1991 ($1.95-$2.50, color)
Comico/Innovation Publishing #8 on

1-6,8-15 ($1.95): 9-Ellery Queen app.	.80	2.00	
7 ($2.50)-Last Comico issue	1.00	2.50	
16-20 ($2.50)	1.00	2.50	
Annual 1 (1990, $2.75)-Ploog-c; Spirit tribute ish	1.10	2.80	
Special 1 (1989, $2.75)-Staton-p (Innovation)	1.10	2.80	

MAZIE (...& Her Friends) (See Flat-Top, Mortie, Stevie & Tastee-Freez)
1953 - #12, 1954; #13, 12/54 - #22, 9/56; #23, 9/57 - #28, 8/58
Mazie Comics(Magazine Publ.)/Harvey Publ. No. 13-on

1-(Teen-age)-Stevie's girl friend	6.35	19.00	38.00
2	3.60	9.00	18.00
3-10	2.80	7.00	14.00
11-28	1.80	4.50	9.00

MAZIE
1950 - No. 7, 1951 (5¢) (5x7-1/4"-miniature)(52 pgs.)
Nation Wide Publishers

1-Teen-age	11.50	34.00	80.00
2-7	6.70	20.00	40.00

MAZINGER (See First Comics Graphic Novel #17)

'MAZING MAN
Jan, 1986 - No. 12, Dec, 1986
DC Comics

1-12: 7,8-Hembeck-a. 12-Dark Knight part-c by Miller			.80
Special 1 ('87), 2 (4/88), 3 ('90)-All $2.00, 52pgs.		.80	2.00

McCRORY'S CHRISTMAS BOOK
1955 (36 pgs., slick-c)
Western Printing Co. (McCrory Stores Corp. giveaway)

nn-Painted-c	3.20	8.00	16.00

McCRORY'S TOYLAND BRINGS YOU SANTA'S PRIVATE EYES

1956 (16 pgs.)
Promotional Publ. Co. (Giveaway)

nn-Has 9 pg. story plus 7 pgs. toy ads	2.40	6.00	12.00

McCRORY'S WONDERFUL CHRISTMAS
1954 (20 pgs., slick-c)
Promotional Publ. Co. (Giveaway)

nn	3.20	8.00	16.00

McHALE'S NAVY (TV) (See Movie Classics)
May-July, 1963 - No. 3, Nov-Jan, 1963-64 (All have photo-c)
Dell Publishing Co.

1	5.00	15.00	50.00
2,3	4.00	12.00	40.00

McKEEVER & THE COLONEL (TV)
Feb-Apr, 1963 - No. 3, Aug-Oct, 1963
Dell Publishing Co.

1-Photo-c	5.00	15.00	50.00
2,3	4.00	12.00	40.00

McLINTOCK (See Movie Comics)

MD
Apr-May, 1955 - No. 5, Dec-Jan, 1955-56
E. C. Comics

1-Not approved by code	12.00	36.00	85.00
2-5	10.00	30.00	65.00

NOTE: *Crandall, Evans, Ingels, Orlando* art in all issues; *Craig c-1-5.*

M.D. GEIST
1995, 2 and 3, 1995 (Limited series)
CPM Comics

1-3		1.20	3.00

M.D. GEIST DATA ALBUM
June, 1996 ($9.95, trade paperback)
CPM Comics

1			10.00

M.D. GEIST: GROUND ZERO
Mar, 1996 - Present ($2.95, limited series)
CPM Comics

1,2			3.00

MEAT CAKE
1992 (B&W)
Iconographix

1			1.00

MEAT CAKE
No. 1, Oct, 1993 - Present (B&W)
Fantagraphics Books

0-5: 3-Sal Buscema-a. 0 (1996)-reprints Meat Cake #1 from Iconographix.		.80	2.50

MECHA (Also see Mayhem)
June, 1987 - No. 6, 1988 ($1.50/$1.95, color/B&W)
Dark Horse Comics

1-6: 1,2 ($1.95, color), 3,4-($1.75, B&W), 5,6-($1.50, B&W)	.80	2.00	

MECHA SPECIAL
May, 1995 ($2.95, one-shot)
Dark Horse Comics

1		1.20	3.00

MEDAL FOR BOWZER, A
1966 (8 pgs.)
American Visuals

Megalith Deathwatch 2000 #2 © Continuity

Megaton #7 © Megaton

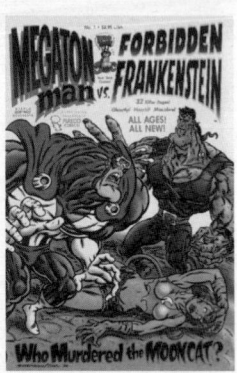

Megaton Man Vs. Forbidden Frankenstein #1 © Donald Simpson

	GD25	FN65	NM94
nn-Eisner-c/script	29.00	86.00	200.00

MEDAL OF HONOR COMICS
Spring, 1946
A. S. Curtis

1-War stories	10.00	30.00	65.00

MEDAL OF HONOR SPECIAL
1994 ($2.50, one-shot)
Dark Horse Comics

1-Kubert-c/a (first story)		1.00	2.50

MEDIA STARR
July, 1989 - No. 3, Sept, 1989 ($1.95, color, mini-series, 28pgs.)
Innovation Publishing

1-3: Deluxe format		.80	2.00

MEDIEVAL SPAWN/WITCHBLADE
May, 1996 - No. 3, June, 1996 ($2.95, limited series)
Image Comics (Top Cow Productions)

1-3: Garth Ennis scripts			3.00

MEET ANGEL (Formerly Angel & the Ape)
No. 7, Nov-Dec, 1969
National Periodical Publications

7-Wood-a(i)	1.65	4.20	10.00

MEET CORLISS ARCHER (Radio/Movie)(My Life #4 on)
Mar, 1948 - No. 3, July, 1948
Fox Features Syndicate

1-(Teen-age)-Feldstein-c/a; headlight-c	58.00	174.00	465.00
2-Feldstein-c only	45.00	136.00	365.00
3-Part Feldstein-c only	40.00	120.00	285.00

NOTE: No. 1-3 used in Seduction of the Innocent, pg. 39.

MEET HERCULES (See Three Stooges)

MEET HIYA A FRIEND OF SANTA CLAUS
1949 (18 pgs.?, paper-c)
Julian J. Proskauer/Sundial Shoe Stores, etc. (Giveaway)

nn	5.85	17.50	35.00

MEET MERTON
Dec, 1953 - No. 4, June, 1954
Toby Press

1-(Teen-age)-Dave Berg-c/a	7.00	21.00	42.00
2-Dave Berg-c/a	4.25	13.00	26.00
3,4-Dave Berg-c/a	4.00	12.00	24.00
I.W. Reprint #9	1.00	2.60	6.00
Super Reprint #11('63), 18	1.00	2.60	6.00

MEET MISS BLISS (Becomes Stories Of Romance #5 on)
May, 1955 - No. 4, Nov, 1955
Atlas Comics (LMC)

1-Al Hartley-c/a	10.00	30.00	65.00
2-4	6.70	20.00	40.00

MEET MISS PEPPER (Formerly Lucy, The Real Gone Gal)
No. 5, April, 1954 - No. 6, June, 1954
St. John Publishing Co.

5-Kubert/Maurer-a	16.00	47.00	110.00
6-Kubert/Maurer-a; Kubert-c	13.00	39.00	90.00

MEET THE NEW POST GAZETTE SUNDAY FUNNIES
3/12/49 (7-1/4x10-1/4", 16 pgs., paper-c)
Commercial Comics (insert in newspaper)
Pittsburgh Post Gazette

Dick Tracy by Gould, Gasoline Alley, Terry & the Pirates, Brenda Starr, Buck Rogers by Yager, The Gumps, Peter Rabbit by Fago, Superman, Funnyman by Siegel & Shuster, The Saint,

Archie, & others done especially for this book. A fine copy sold at auction in 1985 for $276.00.

Estimated value....			$300 – $800

MEGALITH DEATHWATCH 2000 (Megalith #3 on)
Apr, 1993 - No. 7, Jan, 1994 ($2.50)
Continuity

0-Foil-c; no c-price, giveaway; Adams plot		1.00	2.5...
1-3-Bagged w/card: 1-Gatefold-c by Nebres; Adams plot. 2-Fold-out-c; Adam... plot. 3-Indestructible-c		1.00	2.5...
4-7-Embossed-c: 4-Adams/Nebres-c; Adams part-i. 5-Sienkiewicz-i. 6-Adams part-i. 7-Adams-c(p); Adams plot		1.00	2....

MEGATON (A super hero)
Nov, 1983; No. 2, Oct, 1985 - No. 8, Aug, 1987 (B&W)
Megaton Publ. (#3: 44 pgs.; #4: 52 pgs.)

1-($2.00, 68 pgs.)-Erik Larsen's 1st pro work; Vanguard by Larsen begins (1st app.), ends #4; 1st app. Megaton, Berzerker, & Ethrian; Guice-c/a(p); Gustovich-a(p) in #1,2	1.65	4.20	10....
2-($2.00, 68 pgs.)-The Dragon cameo (1 pg.) by Larsen (later The Savage Dragon in Image Comics); Guice-c/a(p)	1.30	3.25	8....
3-1st full app. Savage Dragon-c/story by Larsen; 1st comic book work by Angel Medina (pin-up)	2.15	6.50	15....
4-2nd full app. Savage Dragon by Larsen; 4,5-Wildman by Grass Green	1.70	5.00	12....
5-1st Liefeld published-a (inside f/c, 6/86)	1.00	2.00	5....
6,7: 6-Larsen-c		1.20	3....
8-1st Liefeld story-a (7 pg. super hero story) plus 1 pg. Youngblood ad	1.20	3....
...Explosion (6/87, 16 pg. color giveaway)-1st app. Youngblood by Rob Liefeld (2 pg. spread); shows Megaton heroes	2.85	8.50	20....
...Holiday Special 1 (1994, $2.95, color, 40 pgs., publ. by Entity Comics)-Gold foil logo; bagged w/Kelley Jones card; Vanguard, Megaton plus shows unpublished-c to 1987 Youngblood #1 by Liefeld/Ordway	1.20	3....

NOTE: Copies of Megaton Explosion were also released in early 1992 all signed by Rob Liefel and were made available to retailers.

MEGATON MAN (See Don Simpson's Bizarre Heroes)
Nov, 1984 - No. 10, 1986
Kitchen Sink Enterprises

1-10		.80	2....
1-2nd printing (1989)		.80	2....
...Meets The Uncategorizable X-Thems 1 (4/89, $2.00)		.80	2....

MEGATON MAN VS. FORBIDDEN FRANKENSTEIN
Apr, 1996 ($2.95, B&W, one-shot)
Fiasco Comics

1-Intro The Tomb Team (Forbidden Frankenstein, Drekula, Bride of the Monster, & Moon Wolf)			3....

MEL ALLEN SPORTS COMICS (The Voice of the Yankees)
No. 5, Nov, 1949 - No. 6, June, 1950
Standard Comics

5(#1 on inside)-Tuska-a	17.00	51.00	120....
6(#2)-Lou Gehrig story	12.00	36.00	85....

MELTING POT
Dec, 1993 - No. 4, Sept, 1994 ($2.95)
Kitchen Sink Press

1-4: Bisley-painted-c		1.20	3....

MELVIN MONSTER (See Peter, the Little Pest)
Apr-June, 1965 - No. 10, Oct, 1969
Dell Publishing Co.

1-By John Stanley	11.00	33.00	110....
2-10-All by Stanley. #10-r/#1	7.50	22.50	75....

MELVIN THE MONSTER (Dexter The Demon #7)
July, 1956 - No. 6, July, 1957

Menace #4 © MEG

Men of War #1 © DC

Men's Adventures #12 © MEG

	GD25	FN65	NM94

Atlas Comics (HPC)

1-Maneely-c/a	10.00	30.00	70.00
2-6: 4-Maneely-c/a	7.50	22.50	45.00

MENACE
Mar, 1953 - No. 11, May, 1954
Atlas Comics (HPC)

1-Horror & sci/fi stories begin; Everett-c/a	50.00	150.00	400.00
2-Post-atom bomb disaster by Everett; anti-Communist propaganda/torture scenes; Sinnott sci/fi story "Rocket to the Moon"	38.00	114.00	265.00
3,4,6-Everett-a. 4-Sci/fi story "Escape to the Moon." 6-Romita sci/fi story "Science Fiction"	29.00	86.00	200.00
5-Origin & 1st app. The Zombie by Everett (reprinted in Tales of the Zombie #1)(7/53); 5-Sci/fi story "Rocket Ship"	40.00	120.00	300.00
7,8,10,11: 7-Frankenstein story. 8-End of world story; Heath 3-D art(3 pgs.). 10-H-Bomb panels	21.00	62.00	145.00
9-Everett-a r-in Vampire Tales #1	25.00	75.00	175.00

NOTE: **Brodsky** c-7, 8, 11. **Colan** a-6; c-9. **Everett** a-1-6, 9; c-1-6. **Heath** a-8; c-10. **Katz** a-11. **Maneely** a-3, 5, 7-9. **Powell** a-11. **Romita** a-3, 6, 8, 11. **Shelly** a-10. **Shores** a-7. **Sinnott** a-2, 7. **Tuska** a-1, 2, 5.

MEN AGAINST CRIME (Formerly Mr. Risk; Hand of Fate #8 on)
No. 3, Feb, 1951 - No. 7, Oct, 1951
Ace Magazines

3-Mr. Risk app.	8.35	25.00	50.00
4-7: 4-Colan-a; entire book-r as Trapped! #4	4.25	13.00	28.00

MEN, GUNS, & CATTLE (See Classics Illustrated Special Issue)

MEN IN ACTION (Battle Brady #10 on)
April, 1952 - No. 9, Dec, 1952 (War stories)
Atlas Comics (IPS)

1-Berg, Reinman-a	11.50	34.00	80.00
2	7.50	22.50	45.00
3-6,8,9: 3-Heath-c/a	5.85	17.50	35.00
7-Krigstein-a; Heath-c	9.15	27.00	55.00

NOTE: **Brodsky** c-1, 4-6. **Maneely** c-5. **Pakula** a-1, 6. **Robinson** c-8. **Shores** c-9.

MEN IN ACTION
April, 1957 - No. 9, 1958
Ajax/Farrell Publications

1	7.50	22.50	45.00
2	4.25	13.00	26.00
3-9	4.00	11.00	22.00

MEN INTO SPACE
No. 1083, Feb-Apr, 1960
Dell Publishing Co.

Four Color 1083-Anderson-a, photo-c	6.00	18.00	60.00

MEN OF BATTLE (Also see New Men of Battle)
#5, March, 1943 (Hardcover)
Catechetical Guild

#5-Topix reprints	3.60	9.00	18.00

MEN OF COURAGE
1949
Catechetical Guild

Bound Topix comics-V7#2,4,6,8,10,16,18,20	3.60	9.00	18.00

MEN OF WAR
August, 1977 - No. 26, March, 1980 (#9,10: 44 pgs.)
DC Comics, Inc.

1-Enemy Ace, Gravedigger (origin #1,2) begin		1.60	4.00
2-26: 9-Unknown Soldier app.			1.00

NOTE: **Chaykin** a-9, 10, 12-14, 19, 20. **Evans** c-25. **Kubert** c-2-23, 24p, 26.

MEN'S ADVENTURES (Formerly True Adventures)
No. 4, Aug, 1950 - No. 28, July, 1954

Marvel/Atlas Comics (CCC)

4(#1)(52 pgs.)	23.00	69.00	160.00
5-Flying Saucer story	13.00	39.00	90.00
6-8: 7-Buried alive story. 8-Sci/fic story	10.00	30.00	70.00
9-20: All war format	8.35	25.00	50.00
21,22,24-26: 25-Shrunken head-c	10.00	30.00	65.00
23-Crandall-a; Fox-a(i); horror format	11.00	33.00	75.00
27,28-Human Torch & Toro-c/stories; Captain America & Sub-Mariner stories in each (also see Young Men #24-28)	90.00	271.00	725.00

NOTE: **Ayers** a-27(H. Torch). **Berg** a-15, 16. **Brodsky** c-4-9, 11, 12, 16-18, 24. **Burgos** c-27, 28(Human Torch). **Colan** a-14, 19. **Everett** a-10, 14, 22, 25, 28; c-14, 21-23. **Heath** a-8, 11, 24; c-13, 20, 26. **Lawrence** a-23; 27(Captain America). **Maneely** a-24; c-10, 15. **Mac Pakula** a-15, 25. **Post** a-23. **Powell** a-27(Sub-Mariner). **Reinman** a-11, 12. **Robinson** c-19. **Romita** a-22. **Shores** c-25. **Sinnott** a-21. **Tuska** a-24. Adventure-#4-8; War-#9-20; Weird/Horror-#21-26.

MEN WHO MOVE THE NATION
(Giveaway) (B&W)
Publisher unknown

nn-Neal Adams-a	4.25	13.00	26.00

MEPHISTO VS... (See Silver Surfer #3)
Apr, 1987 - No. 4, July, 1987 ($1.50, mini-series)
Marvel Comics Group

1-4: 1-Fantastic Four; Austin-i. 2-X-Factor. 3-X-Men. 4-Avengers		.70	1.75

MERC (See Mark Hazzard: Merc)

MERCHANTS OF DEATH
July, 1988 - No. 4, Nov, 1988 ($3.50, B&W/16pgs. color, 44pg. mag.)
Acme Press (Eclipse)

1-4: 4-Toth-c		1.40	3.50

MERCY
1993 ($5.95, 68 pgs., mature)
DC Comics (Vertigo)

nn	1.00	2.60	6.00

MERLIN JONES AS THE MONKEY'S UNCLE (See Movie Comics and The Misadventures of... under Movie Comics)

MERRILL'S MARAUDERS (See Movie Classics)

MERRY CHRISTMAS (See A Christmas Adventure, Donald Duck..., Dell Giant #39, & March of Comics #153)

MERRY CHRISTMAS, A
1948 (Giveaway)
K. K. Publications (Child Life Shoes)

nn	4.35	13.00	26.00

MERRY CHRISTMAS
1956 (7-1/4x5-1/4")
K. K. Publications (Blue Bird Shoes Giveaway)

nn	1.80	4.50	9.00

MERRY CHRISTMAS FROM MICKEY MOUSE
1939 (16 pgs.) (Color & B&W)
K. K. Publications (Shoe store giveaway)

nn-Donald Duck & Pluto app.; text with art (Rare); c-reprint/Mickey Mouse Mag. V3#3 (12/37)(Rare)	200.00	800.00	1600.00

MERRY CHRISTMAS FROM SEARS TOYLAND
1939 (16 pgs.) (Color)
Sears Roebuck Giveaway

nn-Dick Tracy, Little Orphan Annie, The Gumps, Terry & the Pirates	100.00	400.00	800.00

MERRY COMICS
Dec, 1945 (No cover price)
Carlton Publishing Co.

Meta 4 #1 © FC

Metal Men #2 © DC

Metaphysique #6 © Norm Breyfogle

	GD25	FN65	NM94
nn-Boogeyman app.	17.00	49.00	115.00

MERRY COMICS
1947
Four Star Publications

1	11.00	33.00	75.00

MERRY-GO-ROUND COMICS
1944 (25¢, 132 pgs.); 1946; 9-10/47 - No. 2, 1948
LaSalle Publ. Co./Croyden Publ./Rotary Litho.

nn(1944)(LaSalle)-Funny animal; 29 new features	16.00	47.00	110.00
21	5.85	17.50	35.00
1(1946)(Croyden)-Al Fago-c; funny animal	9.15	27.00	55.00
V1#1,2(1947-48; 52 pgs.)(Rotary Litho. Co. Ltd., Canada); Ken Hultgren-a			
	6.70	20.00	40.00

MERRY MAILMAN (See Fawcett's Funny Animals #87-89)

MERRY MOUSE (Also see Funny Tunes & Space Comics)
June, 1953 - No. 4, Jan-Feb, 1954
Avon Periodicals

1-1st app.; funny animal; Frank Carin-c/a	7.00	21.00	42.00
2-4	4.25	13.00	26.00

META-4
Feb, 1991 - No. 4, 1991 ($2.25)
First Comics

1-($3.95, 52pgs.)		1.60	4.00
2-4		.90	2.25

METAL MEN (See Brave & the Bold, DC Comics Presents, and
Showcase #37-40)
4-5/63 - No. 41, 12-1/69-70; No. 42, 2-3/73 - No. 44, 7-8/73;
No. 45, 4-5/76 - No. 56, 2-3/78
National Periodical Publications/DC Comics

1-(4-5/63)-5th app. Metal Men	53.00	160.00	425.00
2	20.00	60.00	140.00
3-5	14.00	43.00	100.00
6-10	9.30	28.00	65.00
11-20: 12-Beatles cameo (12/65)	7.00	21.50	50.00
21-26,28-30: 21-Batman, Robin & Flash x-over	5.70	17.00	40.00
27-Origin Metal Men retold	8.50	26.00	60.00
31-41(1968-70): 38-Last 12¢ issue. 41-Last 15¢	5.00	15.00	35.00
42-44(1973)-Reprints	1.70	5.00	12.00
45('76)-49-Simonson-a in all: 48,49-Re-intro Eclipso	1.65	4.70	11.00
50-56: 50-Part-r. 54,55-Green Lantern x-over	1.65	4.70	11.00

NOTE: *Andru/Esposito* c-1-29. *Aparo* c-53-56. *Giordano* c-45, 46. *Kane* a-30, 31p; c-31.
Simonson a-45-49; c-47-52. *Staton* a-50-56.

METAL MEN
Oct, 1993 - No. 4, Jan, 1994 ($1.25, mini-series)
DC Comics

1-($2.50)-Multi-colored foil-c		1.00	2.50
2-4: 2-Origin			1.25

METAMORPHO (See Action Comics #413, Brave & the Bold #57,58, 1st Issue
Special,& World's Finest #217)
July-Aug, 1965 - No. 17, Mar-Apr, 1968 (All 12¢ issues)
National Periodical Publications

1-(7-8/65)-3rd app. Metamorpho	13.00	39.00	90.00
2,3	8.00	23.50	55.00
4-6	5.70	17.00	40.00
7-9	5.00	15.00	35.00
10-Origin & 1st app. Element Girl (1-2/67)	5.70	17.00	40.00
11-17	3.60	11.00	25.00

NOTE: *Ramona Fraden* a-B&B 57, 58, 1-4. *Orlando* a-5, 6; c-5-9, 11. *Sal Trapani* a-7-16.

METAMORPHO
Aug, 1993 - No. 4, Nov, 1993 ($1.50, mini-series)

	GD25	FN65	NM94
DC Comics			
1-4			1

METAPHYSIQUE
Apr, 1995 - No. 6, Oct, 1995 ($2.95, limited series)
Malibu Comics (Bravura)

1-6: Norm Breyfogle-c/a/scripts		1.20	3.

METEOR COMICS
Nov, 1945
L. L. Baird (Croyden)

1-Captain Wizard, Impossible Man, Race Wilkins app.; origin Baldy Bean, Capt. Wizard's sidekick; bare-breasted mermaids story			
	33.00	99.00	230

METEOR MAN
Aug, 1993 - No. 6, Jan, 1994 ($1.25, limited series)
Marvel Comics

1-6: 1-Polybagged w/button & rap newspaper. 4-Night Thrasher-c/story. 6-Terry Austin-c(i)			1

METROPOL (See Ted McKeever's...)

METROPOL A.D. (See Ted McKeever's...)

METROPOLIS S.C.U. (Also see Showcase '96 #1)
Nov, 1995 - No. 4, Feb, 1996 ($1.50, limited series)
DC Comics

1-4:1-Superman-c & app.			1

MEZZ: GALACTIC TOUR 2494 (Also See Nexus)
May, 1994 ($2.50, one-shot)
Dark Horse Comics

1		1.00	2

MGM'S MARVELOUS WIZARD OF OZ (See Marvel Treasury of Oz)
1975 ($1.50, 84 pgs.; oversize)
Marvel Comics Group/National Periodical Publications

1-Adaptation of MGM's movie; J. Buscema-a		1.60	4

M.G.M'S MOUSE MUSKETEERS (Formerly M.G.M.'s The Two Mouseketeers)
No. 670, Jan, 1956 - No. 1290, Mar-May, 1962
Dell Publishing Co.

Four Color 670 (#4)	3.00	9.00	30.
Four Color 711,728,764	2.00	6.00	20
8 (4-6/57) - 21 (3-5/60)	1.80	5.50	18
Four Color 1135,1175,1290	2.00	6.00	20

M.G.M.'S SPIKE AND TYKE
No. 499, Sept, 1953 - No. 1266, Dec-Feb, 1961-62
Dell Publishing Co.

Four Color 499 (#1)	3.00	9.00	30
Four Color 577,638	2.00	6.00	20
4(12-2/55-56)-10	1.80	5.50	18
11-24(12-2/60-61)	1.50	4.50	15
Four Color 1266	1.80	5.50	18

M.G.M.'S THE TWO MOUSEKETEERS
No. 475, June, 1953 - No. 642, July, 1955
Dell Publishing Co.

Four Color 475 (#1)	7.00	21.00	70
Four Color 603 (11/54), 642	4.00	12.00	40

MICHAELANGELO CHRISTMAS SPECIAL (See Teenage Mutant Ninja Turtles
Christmas Special)

MICHAELANGELO, TEENAGE MUTANT NINJA TURTLE
1986 (One shot) ($1.50, B&W)
Mirage Studios

1		1.00	2.00	5

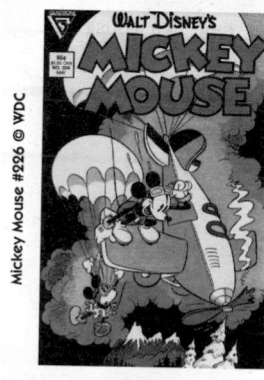

Mickey Mouse #226 © WDC

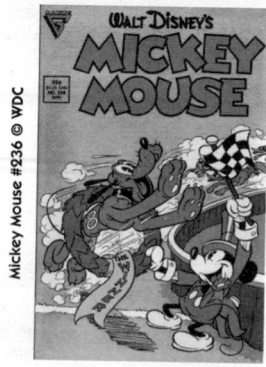

Mickey Mouse #236 © WDC

Mickey Mouse #252 © WDC

	GD25	FN65	NM94
1-2nd printing ('89, $1.75)-Reprint plus new-a		1.20	3.00

MICKEY AND DONALD (See Walt Disney's…)

MICKEY AND DONALD IN VACATIONLAND (See Dell Giant No. 47)

MICKEY & THE BEANSTALK (See Story Hour Series)

MICKEY & THE SLEUTH (See Walt Disney Showcase #38, 39, 42)

MICKEY FINN (Also see Big Shot Comics #74 & Feature Funnies)
Nov?, 1942 - V3#2, May, 1952
Eastern Color 1-4/McNaught Synd. #5 on (Columbia)/Headline V3#2

1	29.00	86.00	200.00
2	14.00	43.00	100.00
3-Charlie Chan story	10.00	30.00	70.00
4	8.35	25.00	50.00
5-10	6.35	19.00	38.00
11-15(1949): 12-Sparky Watts app.	4.25	13.00	28.00
V3#1,2(1952)	4.00	11.00	22.00

MICKEY MALONE
1936 (Color, punchout-c) (B&W-a on back)
Hale Nass Corp.

	GD	FN	VF
nn-1pg. of comics	125.00	250.00	400.00

MICKEY MANTLE (See Baseball's Greatest Heroes #1)

MICKEY MOUSE (See Adventures of Mickey Mouse, The Best of Walt Disney Comics, Cheerios giveaways, Donald Duck and …, Dynabrite Comics, 40 Big Pages…, Gladstone Comic Album, Merry Christmas From…, Walt Disney's Mickey and Donald, Walt Disney's Comics & Stories, Walt Disney's…, & Wheaties)

MICKEY MOUSE (…Secret Agent #107-109; Walt Disney's… #148-205?)
(See Dell Giants for annuals)
#16, 1941 - #84, 7/9-62; #85, 11/62 - #218, 7/84; #219, 10/86 - #256, 4/90
Dell Publ. Co./Gold Key #85-204/Whitman #205-218/Gladstone #219 on

	GD25	FN65	VF82
Four Color 16(1941)-1st Mickey Mouse comic book; "…vs. the Phantom Blot" by Gottfredson	800.00	2400.00	8500.00
(Estimated up to 200 total copies exist, 5 in VF-NM)			

	GD25	FN65	NM94
Four Color 27(1943)- "7 Colored Terror"	85.00	255.00	850.00
Four Color 79(1945)-By Carl Barks (1 story)	105.00	315.00	1050.00
Four Color 116(1946)	24.00	72.00	235.00
Four Color 141,157(1947)	21.00	63.00	200.00
Four Color 170,181,194('48)	16.00	48.00	160.00
Four Color 214('49),231,248,261	14.00	43.00	140.00
Four Color 268-Reprints/WDC&S #22-24 by Gottfredson ("Surprise Visitor")	14.00	43.00	140.00
Four Color 279,286,296	11.00	33.00	110.00
Four Color 304,313(#1),325(#2),334	9.00	27.00	90.00
Four Color 343,352,362,371,387	7.00	21.00	70.00
Four Color 401,411,427(10-11/52)	5.00	15.00	50.00
Four Color 819-Mickey Mouse in Magicland	4.00	12.00	40.00
Four Color 1057,1151,1246(1959-61)-Album	3.50	10.50	35.00
28(12-1/52-53)-32,34	3.00	9.00	30.00
33-(Exists with 2 dates, 10-11/53 & 12-1/54)	3.00	9.00	30.00
35-50	2.00	7.50	18.00
51-73,75-80	1.70	5.00	12.00
74-Story swipe "The Rare Stamp Search" from 4-Color #422- "The Gilded Man"	2.00	6.00	14.00
81-99: 93,95-titled "Mickey Mouse Club Album"	1.70	5.00	12.00
100-105: Reprint 4-Color #427,194,279,170,343,214 in that order			
	1.70	5.00	12.00
106-120	1.65	4.20	10.00
121-130	1.50	3.75	9.00
131-146	1.20	3.00	7.00
147,148: 147-Reprints "The Phantom Fires" from WDC&S #200-202. 148-Reprints "The Mystery of Lonely Valley" from WDC&S #208-210			
	1.20	3.00	7.00

	GD25	FN65	NM94
149-158	1.00	2.00	5.00
159-Reprints "The Sunken City" from WDC&S #205-207			
	1.00	2.00	5.00
160-170: 162-170-r		2.60	6.00
171-178,180-218: 200-r/Four Color #371		1.60	4.00
179-(52 pgs.)		.80	2.00
219-1st Gladstone issue; The Seven Ghosts serial-r begins by Gottfredson		.80	2.00
	2.15	6.50	15.00
220,221	1.30	3.25	8.00
222-225: 222-Editor-in Grief strip-r		1.20	3.00
226-230		1.20	3.00
231-243,245-254: 240-r/March of Comics #27. 245-r/F.C. #279. 250-r/ F.C. #248		1.20	3.00
244 (1/89, $2.95, 100 pgs.)-Squarebound 60th anniversary issue; gives history of Mickey		1.60	4.00
245, 256: 245-r/F.C. #279. 256-$1.95, 68 pgs.		1.60-	4.00
255 ($1.95, 68 pgs.)		.80	2.00

NOTE: Reprints #195-197, 198(2/3), 199(1/3), 200-208, 211(1/2), 212, 213, 215(1/3), 216-on.
Gottfredson Mickey Mouse serials in #219-239, 241-244, 246-249, 251-253, 255.

Album 01-518-210(Dell), 1(10082-309)(9/63-Gold Key)			
	2.40	6.00	12.00
…& Goofy "Bicep Bungle"(1952, 16 pgs., 3-1/4x7") Fritos giveaway, soft-c (also see Donald Duck & Ludwig Von Drake)	5.35	16.00	32.00
…& Goofy Explore Business(1978)		.80	2.00
…& Goofy Explore Energy(1976-1978, 36 pgs.); Exxon giveaway in color; regular size		.80	2.00
…& Goofy Explore Energy Conservation(1976-1978)-Exxon			
		.80	2.00
…& Goofy Explore The Universe of Energy(1985, 20 pgs.); Exxon giveaway in color; regular size		.80	2.00
…Club 1(1/64-Gold Key)(TV)	4.00	10.00	20.00
Mini Comic 1(1976)(3-1/4x6-1/2")-Reprints 158		.80	2.00
New Mickey Mouse Club Fun Book 11190 (Golden Press, 1977, $1.95, 224 pgs.)		1.20	3.00
The Perils of Mickey nn (1993, 5-1/4x7-1/4", 16 pgs.)-Nabisco giveaway w/ games, Nabisco coupons & 6 pgs. of stories; Phantom Blot app.			
			1.00
Surprise Party 1(30037-901, G.K.)(1/69)-40th Anniversary (see Walt Disney Showcase #40)	4.00	10.00	20.00
Surprise Party 1(1979)-r/1969 issue		1.00	2.50

MICKEY MOUSE ADVENTURES
June, 1990 - No. 18, Nov, 1991 ($1.50)
Disney Comics

1-18: 1-Bradbury, Murry-r/M.M. #45,73 plus new-a. 2-Begin all new stories. 8-Byrne-c. 9-Fantasia 50th ann. issue w/new adapt. of movie. 10-r/F.C. #214			
			1.50

MICKEY MOUSE
ca. 1933-1934 (10"x8-3/4", 34 pgs., cardboard-c)
Whitman Publishing Co.

948-1932 & 1933 Sunday strips in color, printed from the same plates as Mickey Mouse Book #3 by David McKay, but only pages 5-17 & 32-48 (including all of the "Wolf Barker" continuity)	131.00	395.00	1050.00

NOTE: Some copies bound with back cover upside down. Variance doesn't affect value. Some art appears on front and back covers of all copies. Height of Whitman reissue of McKay book trimmed 1/2 inch.

MICKEY MOUSE CLUB MAGAZINE (See Walt Disney…)

MICKEY MOUSE CLUB SPECIAL (See The New Mickey Mouse…)

MICKEY MOUSE COMICS DIGEST
1986 - No. 5, 1987 (96 pgs.)
Gladstone

1,2 ($1.25)	1.00	2.00	5.00
3-5 ($1.50)		1.20	3.00

Mickey Mouse Magazine V3#12 ©WDC

Mickey Mouse Magazine V4#5 © WDC

Mickey Mouse Magazine V5#2 © WDC

	GD25	FN65	NM94

MICKEY MOUSE IN COLOR
1988 (Deluxe, 13"x17", hard-c, $250.00)(Trade, 9-7/8"x11-1/2", hard-c, $39.95)
Another Rainbow/Pantheon

Deluxe limited edition of 3,000 copies signed by Floyd Gottfredson and Carl Barks, designated as the "Official Mickey Mouse 60th Anniversary" book. Mickey Sunday and daily reprints, plus Barks "Riddle of the Red Hat" from Four Color #79. Comes with 45 r.p.m. record interview with Gottfredson and Barks. 240 pgs.

	36.00	107.00	250.00

Deluxe, limited to 100 copies, as above, but with a unique colored pencil original drawing of Mickey Mouse by Carl Barks. Add value of art to book price.
750.00

Pantheon trade edition, edited down & without Barks, 192 pgs.
5.50   17.00   40.00

MICKEY MOUSE MAGAZINE
V1#1, Jan, 1933 - V1#9, Sept, 1933 (5-1/4x7-1/4")
No. 1-3 published by Kamen-Blair (Kay Kamen, Inc.)
Walt Disney Productions

	GD25	FN65	VF82

(Scarce)-Distributed by dairies and leading stores through their local theatres. First few issues had 5¢ listed on cover, later ones had no price.

V1#1	357.00	1071.00	3000.00
2-9	117.00	350.00	900.00

MICKEY MOUSE MAGAZINE
V1#1, 11/33 - V2#12, 10/35 (Mills giveaways issued by different dairies)
Walt Disney Productions

	GD25	FN65	NM94
V1#1	125.00	375.00	1000.00
2-12: 2-X-mas issue	44.00	132.00	350.00
V2#1-12: 2-X-mas issue. 4-St. Valentine-c	34.00	101.00	235.00

MICKEY MOUSE MAGAZINE (Becomes Walt Disney's Comics & Stories)
(No V3#1, /V4#6)
Summer, 1935 (June-Aug, indicia) - V5#12, Sept, 1940
V1#1-5, V3#11,12, V4#1-3 are 44 pgs.; V2#3-100 pgs; V5#12-68 pgs;
rest are 36 pgs.
K. K. Publ./Western Publishing Co.

	GD25	FN65	VF82	NM94
V1#1 (Large size, 13-1/4x10-1/4"; 25¢)-Contains puzzles, games, cels, stories & comics of Disney characters. Promotional magazine for Disney cartoon movies and paraphernalia	1100.00	3300.00	7150.00	11000.00

(Estimated up to 100 total copies exist, 3 in NM/Mint)
Note: Some copies were autographed by the editors & given away with all early one year subscriptions.

	GD25	FN65	VF82	
2 (Size change, 11-1/2x8-1/2"; 10/35; 10¢)-High quality paper begins; Messmer-a	131.00	395.00	1050.00	
3,4: 3-Messmer-a	72.00	216.00	575.00	
5-1st Donald Duck solo-c; last 44 pg. & high quality paper issue	81.00	244.00	650.00	
6-9: 6-36 pg. issues begin; Donald becomes editor. 8-2nd Donald solo-c.				
9-1st Mickey/Minnie-c	64.00	193.00	525.00	
10-12, V2#1,2: 11-1st Pluto/Mickey-c; Donald fires himself and appoints Mickey as editor	61.00	182.00	475.00	
V2#3-Special 100 pg. Christmas issue (25¢); Messmer-a; Donald becomes editor of Wise Quacks	287.00	862.00	2300.00	
4-Mickey Mouse Comics & Roy Ranger (adventure strip) begin; both end V2#9; Messmer-a	54.00	160.00	420.00	

	GD25	FN65	NM94
5-Ted True (adventure strip, ends V2#9) & Silly Symphony Comics (ends V3#3) begin	43.00	130.00	330.00
6-9: 6-1st solo Minnie-c. 6-9-Mickey Mouse Movies cut-out in each	43.00	130.00	330.00
10-1st full color issue; Mickey Mouse (by Gottfredson; ends V3#12) & Silly Symphony (ends V3#3) full color Sunday-r, Peter The Farm Detective (ends V3#3) & Ole Of The North (ends V3#3) begins	67.00	200.00	525.00
11-13: 12-Hiawatha-c & feature story	43.00	130.00	330.00

	GD25	FN65	NM94
V3#2-Big Bad Wolf Halloween-c	52.00	155.00	410.00
3 (12/37)-1st app. Snow White & The Seven Dwarfs (before release of movie)(possibly 1st in print); Mickey X-mas-c	90.00	270.00	675.00
4 (1/38)-Snow White & The Seven Dwarfs serial begins (on stands before release of movie); Ducky Symphony (ends V3#11) begins	72.00	215.00	550.00
5-1st Snow White & Seven Dwarfs-c (St. Valentine's Day)	93.00	280.00	700.00
6-Snow White serial ends; Lonesome Ghosts app. (2 pp.)	50.00	150.00	390.00
7-Seven Dwarfs Easter-c	49.00	145.00	375.00
8-10: 9-Dopey-c. 10-1st solo Goofy-c	40.00	120.00	310.00
11,12 (44 pgs; 8 more pgs. color added). 11-Mickey the Sheriff serial (ends V4#3) & Donald Duck strip-r (ends V3#12) begin. Color feature on Snow White's Forest Friends	43.00	130.00	330.00
V4#1 (10/38; 44 pgs.)-Brave Little Tailor-c/feature story, nominated for Academy Award; Bobby & Chip by Otto Messmer (ends V4#2) & The Practical Pig (ends V4#2) begin	43.00	130.00	330.00
2 (44 pgs.)-1st Huey, Dewey & Louie-c	43.00	130.00	330.00
3 (12/38, 44 pgs.)-Ferdinand The Bull-c/feature story, Academy Award winner; Mickey Mouse & The Whalers serial begins, ends V4#12	43.00	130.00	330.00
4-Spotty, Mother Pluto strip-r begin, end V4#8	40.00	120.00	310.00
5-St. Valentine's day-c. 1st Pluto solo-c	47.00	141.00	360.00
7 (3/39)-The Ugly Duckling-c/feature story, Academy Award winner	43.00	130.00	330.00
7 (4/39)-Goofy & Wilbur The Grasshopper classic-c/feature story from 1st Goofy solo cartoon movie; Timid Elmer begins, ends V5#5	43.00	130.00	330.00
8-Big Bad Wolf-c from Practical Pig movie poster; Practical Pig feature story	43.00	130.00	330.00
9-Donald Duck & Mickey Mouse Sunday-r begin; The Pointer feature story, nominated for Academy Award	43.00	130.00	330.00
10-Classic July 4th drum & fife-c; last Donald Sunday-r	54.00	160.00	425.00
11-1st slick-c; last over-sized issue	40.00	120.00	310.00
12 (9/39; format change, 10-1/4x8-1/4")-1st full color, cover to cover issue; Donald's Penguin-c/feature story	48.00	145.00	375.00
V5#1-Black Pete-c; Officer Duck-c/feature story; Autograph Hound feature story; Robinson Crusoe serial begins	48.00	145.00	375.00
2-Goofy-c; 1st app. Pinocchio (cameo)	64.00	195.00	500.00
3 (12/39)-Pinocchio Christmas-c (Before movie release). 1st app. Jiminy Cricket; Pinocchio serial begins	72.00	215.00	550.00
4,5: 5-Jiminy Cricket-c; Pinocchio serial ends; Donald's Dog Laundry feature story	48.00	145.00	375.00
6-Tugboat Mickey feature story; Rip Van Winkle feature begins, ends V5#8	47.00	140.00	360.00
7-2nd Huey, Dewey & Louie-c	47.00	140.00	360.00
8-Last magazine size issue; 2nd solo Pluto-c; Figaro & Cleo feature story	47.00	140.00	360.00
9 (6/40; change to comic book size)-Jiminy Cricket feature story; Donald-c & Sunday-r begin	52.00	155.00	400.00
10-Special Independence Day issue	52.00	155.00	400.00
11-Hawaiian Holiday & Mickey's Trailer feature stories; last 36 pg. issue	52.00	155.00	400.00
12 (Format change)-The transition issue (68 pgs.) becoming a comic book. With only a title change to follow, becomes Walt Disney's Comics & Stories #1 with the next issue	411.00	1233.00	3700.00
V4#1 (Giveaway)	38.00	114.00	265.00

NOTE: **Otto Messmer**-a is in many issues of the first two-three years. The following story titles and issues have gags created by **Carl Barks**: V4#3(12/38)-'Donald's Better Self' & 'Donald's Game;' V4#4(1/39)-'Donald's Lucky Day;' V4#7(3/39)-'Hockey Champ;' V4#7(4/39)-'Donald's Cousin Gus;' V4#9(6/39)-'Sea Scouts;' V4#12(9/39)-'Donald's Penguin;' V5#9 (6/40)-'Donald's Vacation;' V5#10(7/40)-'Bone Trouble;' V5#12(9/40)-'Window Cleaners.'

MICKEY MOUSE MARCH OF COMICS (See March of Comics #8,27,45,60,74)

Micronauts #13 © MEG

Midnight Sons Unlimited #9 © MEG

Mighty Crusaders #5 © AP

	GD25	FN65	NM94

MICKEY MOUSE SUMMER FUN (See Dell Giants)

MICKEY MOUSE'S SUMMER VACATION (See Story Hour Series)

MICKEY SPILLANE'S MIKE DANGER
Sept, 1995 - No. 11, May, 1996 ($1.95)
Tekno Comix

	GD25	FN65	NM94
1-11: 1-Frank Miller-c. 7-polybagged; Simonson-c. 8,9-Simonson-c. .80			2.00

MICKEY SPILLANE'S MIKE DANGER
V2#1, June, 1996 - Present ($2.25)
Big Entertainment

V2#1-6: Max Allan Collins scripts			2.25

MICROBOTS, THE
Dec, 1971 (one-shot)
Gold Key

1 (10271-112)	1.20	3.00	7.00

MICRONAUTS (Toys)
Jan, 1979 - No. 59, Aug, 1984 (Mando paper #53 on)
Marvel Comics Group

1-Intro/1st app. Baron Karza	.90		2.20
2-5			1.20
6-36,39-59: 7-Man-Thing app. 8-1st app. Capt. Universe (8/79). 9-1st app. Cilicia. 13-1st app. Jasmine. 15-Death of Microtron. 15-17-Fantastic Four app. 17-Death of Jasmine. 20-Ant-Man app. 21-Microverse series begins. 25-Origin Baron Karza. 25-29-Nick Fury app. 27-Death of Biotron. 34,35-Dr. Strange app. 35-Double size; origin Microverse; intro Death Squad. 40-Fantastic Four app. 57-(52 pgs.). 59-Golden painted-c			1.00
37-Nightcrawler app.; X-Men cameo (2 pgs.)	.80		2.00
38-First direct sale	.65		1.60
nn-Reprints #1-3; blank UPC; diamond on top			.40
Annual 1(12/79)-Ditko-c/a	1.00		2.50
Annual 2(10/80)-Ditko-c/a	.80		2.00

NOTE: #38-on distributed only through comic shops. *N. Adams* a-7i. *Chaykin* a-13-18p. *Ditko* a-39p. *Giffen* a-36p, 37p(part). *Golden* a-1-12p; c-2-7p, 8-23, 24p, 38, 39, 59. *Guice* a-48-58p; c-49-58. *Gil Kane* a-38, 40-45p; c0-45. *Layton* c-33-37. *Miller* c-31.

MICRONAUTS (Toys)
Oct, 1984 - No. 20, May, 1986
Marvel Comics Group

V2#1-20			.75

NOTE: *Kelley Jones* a-1; c-1, 6. *Guice* a-4p; c-2p.

MICRONAUTS SPECIAL EDITION
Dec, 1983 - No. 5, Apr, 1984 ($2.00, limited series, Baxter paper)
Marvel Comics Group

1-5: r-/original series 1-12; Guice-c(p)-all	.80		2.00

MIDGET COMICS (Fighting Indian Stories)
Feb, 1950 - No. 2, Apr, 1950 (5-3/8x7-3/8", 68 pgs.)
St. John Publishng Co.

1-Fighting Indian Stories; Matt Baker-c	14.00	43.00	100.00
2-Tex West, Cowboy Marshal (also in #1)	7.50	22.50	45.00

MIDNIGHT (See Smash Comics #18)

MIDNIGHT
Apr, 1957 - No. 6, June, 1958
Ajax/Farrell Publ. (Four Star Comic Corp.)

1-Reprints from Voodoo & Strange Fantasy with some changes	10.00	30.00	70.00
2-6	6.35	19.00	38.00

MIDNIGHT EYE
1991 - No. 6, 1992 ($4.95, 44 pgs., mature)
Viz Premiere Comics

1-6: Japanese stories translated into English	1.00	2.00	5.00

MIDNIGHT MEN
June, 1993 - No. 4, Sept, 1993 ($2.50/$1.95, limited series)
Marvel Comics (Epic Comics/Heavy Hitters)

1-($2.50)-Embossed-c; Chaykin-c/a & scripts in all.		1.00	2.50
2-4		.80	2.00

MIDNIGHT MYSTERY
Jan-Feb, 1961 - No. 7, Oct, 1961
American Comics Group

1-Sci/Fi story	11.00	33.00	75.00
2-7: 7-Gustavson-a	6.35	19.00	38.00

NOTE: *Reinman* a-1, 3. *Whitney* a-1, 4-6; c-1-3, 5, 7.

MIDNIGHT SONS UNLIMITED
Apr, 1993 - No. 9, May, 1995 ($3.95, 68 pgs.)
Marvel Comics (Midnight Sons imprint #4 on)

1-9: Blaze, Darkhold (by Quesada #1), Ghost Rider, Morbius & Nightstalkers in all. 1-Painted-c. 3-Spider-Man app. 4-Siege of Darkness part 17; new Dr. Strange & new Ghost Rider app.; spot varnish-c	1.60		4.00

NOTE: *Sears* a-2.

MIDNIGHT TALES
Dec, 1972 - No. 18, May, 1976
Charlton Press

V1#1	1.30	3.25	8.00
2-18: 11-14-Newton-a(p)		1.20	3.00
12,17(Modern Comics reprint, 1977)			1.00

NOTE: *Adkins* a-13i. *Ditko* a-12. *Howard* (Wood imitator) a-1-15, 17, 18; c-1-18. *Don Newton* a-11-14p. *Staton* a-1, 3-11, 13. *Sutton* a-3-10.

MIGHTY ATOM, THE (...& the Pixies #6) (Formerly The Pixies #1-5)
No. 6, 1949; Nov, 1957 - No. 6, Aug-Sept, 1958
Magazine Enterprises

6(1949-M.E.)-no month (1st Series)	4.70	14.00	28.00
1-6(2nd Series)-Pixies-r	3.20	8.00	16.00
I.W. Reprint #1(nd)		1.20	3.00
Giveaway(1959, '63, Whitman)-Evans-a	1.60	4.00	8.00
Giveaway ('64r, '65r, '66r, '67r, '68r, '73r, '76r)-Evans-r		.50	1.00

MIGHTY BEAR (Formerly Fun Comics; becomes Unsane #15)
No. 13, Jan, 1954 - No. 14, Mar, 1954; 9/57 - No. 3, 2/58
Star Publ. No. 13,14/Ajax-Farrell (Four Star)

13,14-L. B. Cole-c	12.00	36.00	85.00
1-3('57-58)Four Star; becomes Mighty Ghost #4	4.00	12.00	24.00

MIGHTY COMICS (...Presents) (Formerly Flyman)
No. 40, Nov, 1966 - No. 50, Oct, 1967 (All 12¢ issues)
Radio Comics (Archie)

40-Web	2.15	6.50	15.00
41-50: 41-Shield, Black Hood. 42-Black Hood. 43-Shield, Web & Black Hood. 44-Black Hood, Steel Sterling & The Shield. 45-Shield & Hangman; origin Web retold. 46-Steel Sterling, Web & Black Hood. 47-Black Hood & Mr. Justice. 48-Shield & Hangman; Wizard x-over in Shield. 49-Steel Sterling & Fox; Black Hood x-over in Steel Sterling. 50-Black Hood & Web; Inferno x-over in Web	1.85	5.50	13.00

NOTE: *Paul Reinman* a-40-50.

MIGHTY CRUSADERS, THE (Also see Adventures of the Fly, The Crusaders & Fly Man)
Nov, 1965 - No. 7, Oct, 1966 (All 12¢ issues)
Mighty Comics Group (Radio Comics)

1-Origin The Shield	4.30	13.00	30.00
2-Origin Comet	2.40	7.20	17.00
3-Origin Fly-Man	2.15	6.50	15.00
4-1st S.A. app. Fireball, Inferno & Fox; Firefly, Web, Bob Phantom, Blackjack, Hangman, Zambini, Kardak, Steel Sterling, Mr. Justice, Wizard, Capt. Flag,			

Mighty Heroes #1 © Spotlight Comics

Mighty Marvel Western #22 © MEG

Mighty Mouse #5 © Viacom

	GD25	FN65	NM94

	GD25	FN65	NM94
Jaguar x-over	2.60	7.50	18.00
5-Intro. Ultra-Men (Fox, Web, Capt. Flag) & Terrific Three (Jaguar, Mr. Justice, Steel Sterling)	2.15	6.50	15.00
6,7: 7-Steel Sterling feature; origin Fly-Girl	2.15	6.50	15.00

NOTE: *Reinman a-6.*

MIGHTY CRUSADERS, THE (All New Advs. of…#2)
Mar, 1983 - No. 13, Sept, 1985 ($1.00, 36 pgs, Mando paper)
Red Circle Prod./Archie Ent. No. 6 on

1-13: 1-Origin Black Hood, The Fly, Fly Girl, The Shield, The Wizard, The Jaguar, Pvt. Strong & The Web. 2-Mister Midnight begins. 4-Darkling replaces Shield. 5-Origin Jaguar, Shield begins. 7-Untold origin Jaguar			1.00

NOTE: *Buckler a-1-3, 4i, 5p, 7p, 8i, 9i; c-1-10p.*

MIGHTY GHOST (Formerly Mighty Bear #1-3)
No. 4, June, 1958
Ajax/Farrell Publ.

4	4.00	11.00	22.00

MIGHTY HERCULES, THE (TV)
July, 1963 - No. 2, Nov, 1963
Gold Key

1,2(10072-307, 10072-311)	11.00	33.00	110.00

MIGHTY HEROES, THE (TV) (Funny)
Mar, 1967 - No. 4, July, 1967
Dell Publishing Co.

1-Also has a 1957 Heckle & Jeckle-r	13.00	39.00	130.00
2-4: 4-Has two 1958 Mighty Mouse-r	9.50	28.50	95.00

MIGHTY HEROES
1987 (B&W, one-shot)
Spotlight Comics

1-Heckle & Jeckle backup			1.00

MIGHTY MARVEL WESTERN, THE
Oct, 1968 - No. 46, Sept, 1976 (#1-14: 68 pgs.; #15,16: 52 pgs.)
Marvel Comics Group (LMC earlier issues)

1-Begin Kid Colt, Rawhide Kid, Two-Gun Kid-r	1.20	3.00	7.00
2-10		1.20	3.00
11-20		.80	2.00
21-46: 24-Kid Colt-r end. 25-Matt Slade-r begin. 31-Baker-r. 32-Origin-r/ Rawhide Kid #23; Williamson-r/Kid Slade #7. 37-Williamson, Kirby-r/ Two-Gun Kid 51			1.25

NOTE: *Jack Davis a(r)-21-24. Keller r-1-13, 22. Kirby a(r)-1-3, 6, 9, 12-14, 16, 26, 29, 32, 36, 41, 43, 44; c-29. Maneely a(r)-22. Severin c-3i, 9. No Matt Slade-r#43.*

MIGHTY MIDGET COMICS, THE (Miniature)
No date; circa 1942-1943 (Sold 2 for 5¢, B&W and red, 36 pgs, approx. 5x4")
Samuel E. Lowe & Co.

Bulletman #11(1943)-r/cover/Bulletman #3	14.00	43.00	100.00
Captain Marvel Adventures #11	14.00	43.00	100.00
	GD25	FN65	–
Captain Marvel #11 (Same as above except for full color ad on back cover; this issue was glued to cover of Captain Marvel #20 and is not found in fine-mint condition)	225.00	675.00	–
	GD25	FN65	NM94
Captain Marvel Jr. #11 (Same-c as Master #27	14.00	43.00	100.00
	GD25	FN65	–
Captain Marvel Jr. #11 (Same as above except for full color ad on back-c; this issue was glued to cover of Captain Marvel #21 and is not found in fine-mint condition)	225.00	675.00	–
	GD25	FN65	NM94
Golden Arrow #11	13.00	39.00	90.00
Ibis the Invincible #11(1942)-Origin; reprints cover to Ibis #1 (Predates Fawcett's Ibis the Invincible #1).			

Spy Smasher #11(1942)	14.00	43.00	100.00

NOTE: *The above books came in a box called "box full of books" and was distributed with oth* *Samuel Lowe puzzles, paper dolls, coloring books, etc. They are not titled Mighty Midget Comi* *All have a war bond seal on back cover which is otherwise blank. These books came in a "Mig* *Midget" flat cardboard counter display rack.*

Balbo, the Boy Magician #12 (1943)-1st book devoted entirely to character.	5.00	15.00	30.00
Bulletman #12	10.00	30.00	70.00
Commando Yank #12 (1943)-Only comic devoted entirely to character.	7.50	22.50	45.00
Dr. Voltz the Human Generator (1943)-Only comic devoted entirely to character	5.00	15.00	30.00
Lance O'Casey #12 (1943)-1st comic devoted entirely to character (Predates Fawcett's Lance O'Casey #1).	5.00	15.00	30.00
Leatherneck the Marine (1943)-Only comic devoted entirely to character.	5.00	15.00	30.00
Minute Man #12	10.00	30.00	70.00
Mister "Q" (1943)-Only comic devoted entirely to character.	5.00	15.00	30.00
Mr. Scarlet and Pinky #12 (1943)-Only comic devoted entirely to character.	9.15	27.00	55.00
Pat Wilton and His Flying Fortress (1943)-1st comic devoted entirely to character.	5.00	15.00	30.00
The Phantom Eagle #12 (1943)-Only comic devoted entirely to character.	5.85	17.50	35.00
State Trooper Stops Crime (1943)-Only comic devoted entirely to character.	5.00	15.00	30.00
Tornado Tom (1943)-Origin, r/from Cyclone #1-3; only comic devoted entirely to character.	5.00	15.00	30.00

MIGHTY MORPHIN' POWER RANGERS: THE MOVIE (Also see Saban's
Mighty Morphin' Power Rangers)
Sept, 1995 ($3.95, one-shot)
Marvel Comics

nn-adaptation of movie		1.60	4.00

MIGHTY MOUSE (See Adventures of..., Dell Giant #43, Giant Comics Edition, March of Comics #205, 237, 247, 257, 447, 459, 471, 483, Oxydol-Dreft, Paul Terry's, & Terry-Toons Comics)

MIGHTY MOUSE (1st Series)
Fall, 1946 - No. 4, Summer, 1947
Timely/Marvel Comics (20th Century Fox)

1	100.00	300.00	800.00
2	48.00	144.00	385.00
3,4	38.00	114.00	265.00

MIGHTY MOUSE (2nd Series) (Paul Terry's... #62-71)
Aug, 1947 - No. 67, 11/55; No. 68, 3/56 - No. 83, 6/59
St. John Publishing Co./Pines No. 68 (3/56) on (TV issues #72 on)

5(#1)	36.00	107.00	250.00
6-10	18.00	54.00	125.00
11-19	11.50	34.00	80.00
20 (11/50) - 25-(52 pg. editions)	10.00	30.00	60.00
20-25-(36 pg. editions)	8.35	25.00	50.00
26-37: 35-Flying saucer-c	6.70	20.00	40.00
38-45-(100 pgs.)	17.00	51.00	120.00
46-83: 62-64,67-Painted-c. 82-Infinity-c	6.35	19.00	38.00
Album 1(10/52, 25¢, 100 pgs., St. John)-Gandy Goose app.	26.00	79.00	185.00
Album 2,3(11/52 & 12/52, St. John) (100 pgs.)	21.00	64.00	150.00
Fun Club Magazine 1(Fall, 1957-Pines, 25¢, 100 pgs.) (CBS TV)-Tom Terrific, Heckle & Jeckle, Dinky Duck, Gandy Goose	15.00	45.00	105.00
Fun Club Magazine 2-6(Winter, 1958-Pines)	10.00	30.00	65.00
3-D 1-(1st printing-9/53, 25¢)(St. John)-Came w/glasses; stiff covers; says World's First! on-c; 1st 3-D comic	29.00	86.00	200.00

Mike Barnett, Man Against Crime #4 © FAW

Mike Grell's Sable #7 © Mike Grell

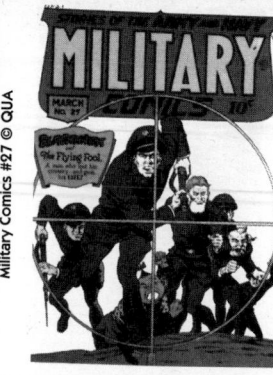

Military Comics #27 © QUA

	GD25	FN65	NM94

3-D 1-(2nd printing-10/53, 25¢)-Came w/glasses; slick, glossy covers, slightly
smaller — 26.00 / 77.00 / 180.00
3-D 2,3(11/53, 12/53, 25¢)-(St. John)-With glasses 24.00 / 73.00 / 170.00

MIGHTY MOUSE (TV)(3rd Series)(Formerly Adventures of Mighty Mouse)
No. 161, Oct, 1964 - No. 172, Oct, 1968
Gold Key/Dell Publishing Co. No. 166-on

161(10/64)-165(9/65)-(Becomes Adventures of... No. 166 on)
— 3.50 / 10.50 / 35.00
166(3/66), 167(6/66)-172 — 2.40 / 7.20 / 24.00

MIGHTY MOUSE (TV)
1987 - No. 2, 1987 ($1.50, color)
Spotlight Comics

1,2-New stories — — / — / 1.50
...And Friends Holiday Special (11/87, $1.75) — .70 / 1.75

MIGHTY MOUSE (TV)
Oct, 1990 - No. 10, July, 1991 ($1.00)(Based on Sat. cartoon)
Marvel Comics

1-10: 1-Dark Knight-c parody. 2-10: 3-Intro Bat-Bat; Byrne-c. 4,5-Crisis-c/
story parodies w/Perez-c. 6-Spider-Man-c parody. 7-Origin Bat-Bat
— — / — / 1.00

MIGHT MOUSE ADVENTURE MAGAZINE
1987 ($2.00, B&W, 52 pgs., magazine size, one-shot)
Spotlight Comics

1-Deputy Dawg, Heckle & Jeckle backup stories — .80 / 2.00

MIGHTY MOUSE ADVENTURES (Adventures of... #2 on)
November, 1951
St. John Publishing Co.

1 — 31.00 / 94.00 / 220.00
2-5 — — / — / —

MIGHTY MOUSE ADVENTURE STORIES (Paul Terry's... on-c only)
1953 (50¢, 384 pgs.)
St. John Publishing Co.

nn-Rebound issues — 40.00 / 120.00 / 325.00

MIGHTY MUTANIMALS (See Teenage Mutant Ninja Turtles Adventures #19)
May, 1991 - No. 3, July, 1991 ($1.00, limited series)
Apr, 1992 - Present ($1.25)
Archie Comics

1-3: 1-Story cont'd from TMNT Advs. #19 — — / 1.00
1-8 (1992): 7-1st app. Merdude — — / 1.25

MIGHTY SAMSON (Also see Gold Key Champion)
7/64 - #20, 11/69; #21, 8/72; #22, 12/73 - #31, 3/76; #32, 8/82
Gold Key (Painted c-1-31)

1-Origin/1st app.; Thorne-a begins — 5.00 / 15.00 / 40.00
6-10: 7-Tom Morrow begins, ends #20 — 2.85 / 8.50 / 20.00
11-20 — 2.30 / 6.75 / 16.00
21-32: 21,22,32-r — 1.70 / 5.00 / 12.00
— 1.20 / 3.00 / 7.00

MIGHTY THOR (See Thor)

MIKE BARNETT, MAN AGAINST CRIME (TV)
Dec, 1951 - No. 6, Oct, 1952
Fawcett Publications

1 — 14.00 / 43.00 / 100.00
2 — 9.15 / 27.00 / 55.00
3,4,6 — 7.50 / 22.50 / 45.00
5- "Market for Morphine" cover/story — 10.00 / 30.00 / 60.00

MIKE DANGER (See Mickey Spillane's...)

MIKE DEODATO'S FALLOUT 3000
1996 ($2.95, B&W, one-shot)

Caliber

1 — — / — / 3.00

MIKE DEODATO'S PRIME CUTS
1996 - Present ($2.95, B&W, magazine size, limited series)
Caliber

1 — — / — / 3.00

MIKE DEODATO'S PROTHEUS
1996 - No. 2, 1996 ($2.95, B&W, limited series)
Caliber

1,2 — — / — / 3.00

MIKE DEODATO'S RAMTHAR
1996 ($2.95, B&W, one-shot)
Caliber

1 — — / — / 3.00

MIKE DEODATO'S RAZOR NIGHTS
1996 ($2.95, B&W, one-shot)
Caliber

1 — — / — / 3.00

MIKE GRELL'S SABLE (Also see Jon Sable & Sable)
Mar, 1990 - No. 10, Dec, 1990 ($1.75)
First Comics

1-10: r/Jon Sable Freelance #1-10 by Grell — .75 / 1.80

MIKE MIST MINUTE MIST-ERIES (See Ms. Tree/Mike Mist in 3-D)
April, 1981 ($1.25, B&W, one-shot)
Eclipse Comics

1 — — / — / 1.25

MIKE SHAYNE PRIVATE EYE
Nov-Jan, 1962 - No. 3, Sept-Nov, 1962
Dell Publishing Co.

1 — 2.60 / 7.50 / 18.00
2,3 — 1.70 / 5.00 / 12.00

MILITARY COMICS (Becomes Modern Comics #44 on)
Aug, 1941 - No. 43, Oct, 1945
Quality Comics Group

	GD25	FN65	VF82	NM94

1-Origin/1st app. Blackhawk by C. Cuidera (Eisner scripts); Miss America,
The Death Patrol by Jack Cole (also #2-7,27-30), & The Blue Tracer by
Guardineer; X of the Underground, The Yankee Eagle, Q-Boat & Shot &
Shell, Archie Atkins, Loops & Banks by Bud Ernest (Bob Powell)(ends #13)
begin — 750.00 / 2250.00 / 4500.00 / 7500.00
(Estimated up to 160 total copies exist, 9 in NM/Mint)

	GD25	FN65		NM94

2-Secret War News begins (by McWilliams #2-16); Cole-a; new uniform with
yellow circle & hawk's head for Blackhawk — 231.00 / 693.00 / 1850.00
3-Origin/1st app. Chop Chop — 200.00 / 600.00 / 1600.00
4 — 156.00 / 468.00 / 1250.00
5-The Sniper begins; Miss America in costume #4-7
— 131.00 / 393.00 / 1050.00
6-9: 8-X of the Underground begins (ends #13). 9-The Phantom Clipper
begins (ends #16) — 100.00 / 300.00 / 800.00
10-Classic Eisner-c — 106.00 / 318.00 / 850.00
11-Flag-c — 81.00 / 243.00 / 650.00
12-Blackhawk by Crandall begins, ends #22 — 106.00 / 318.00 / 850.00
13-15: 14-Private Dogtag begins (ends #83) — 78.00 / 234.00 / 625.00
16-20: 16-Blue Tracer ends. 17-P.T. Boat begins — 68.00 / 206.00 / 550.00
21-31: 22-Last Crandall Blackhawk. 23-Shrunken head-c. 27-Death Patrol
revived — 58.00 / 174.00 / 465.00
32-43 — 51.00 / 153.00 / 410.00
NOTE: *Berg* a-6. *Al Bryant* c-31-34, 38, 40-43. *J. Cole* a-1-3, 27-32. *Crandall* a-12-22; c-13-20.
Cuidera c-2-9. *Eisner* c-1, 2(part), 9, 10. *Kotsky* c-21-29, 35, 37, 39. *McWilliams* a-2-16.

Millennium Fever #4 © Nick Abadzis & Duncan Fegredo

Miracleman #22 © ECL

Miracleman: Apocrypha #2 © ECL

Powell a-1-13. Ward Blackhawk-30, 31(15 pgs. each); c-30.

MILK AND CHEESE
1991 - Present ($2.50, B&W)
Slave Labor

1, Other #1, Third #1, Fourth #1, First Second Issue, #666-Evan Dorkin story & art in all.	1.00	2.50

NOTE: Multiple printings of all issues exist and are worth cover price.

MILLENNIUM
Jan, 1988 - No. 6, Feb, 1988 (Weekly limited series)
DC Comics

1-Staton c/a(p) begins	1.00	2.50
2-8		1.60

MILLENNIUM FEVER
Oct, 1995 - No.4, Jan, 1996 ($2.50, limited series)
DC Comics (Vertigo)

1-4: Duncan Fegredo-c/a	1.00	2.50

MILLENNIUM INDEX
Mar, 1988 - No. 2, Mar, 1988 ($2.00)
Independent Comics Group

1,2	.80	2.00

MILLIE, THE LOVABLE MONSTER
Sept-Nov, 1962 - No. 6, Jan, 1973
Dell Publishing Co.

12-523-211, 2(8-10/63)	3.50	10.50	35.00
3(8-10/64)	2.60	7.80	26.00
4(7/72), 5(10/72), 6(1/73)	1.40	4.20	14.00

NOTE: Woggon a-3-6; c-3-6. 4 reprints 1; 5 reprints 2; 6 reprints 3.

MILLIE THE MODEL (See Comedy Comics, A Date With..., Joker Comics #28, Life With..., Mad About..., Marvel Mini-Books & Modeling With...)
1945 - No. 207, December, 1973
Marvel/Atlas/Marvel Comics (CnPC #1)(SPI/Male/VPI)

1-Origin	59.00	178.00	475.00
2 (10/46)-Millie becomes The Blonde Phantom to sell Blonde Phantom perfume; a pre-Blonde Phantom app. (see All-Select #11, Fall, 1946)			
	36.00	107.00	250.00
3-7: 4-7- Willie app. 7-Willie smokes extra strong tobacco	21.00	64.00	150.00
8,10-Kurtzman's "Hey Look". 8-Willie & Rusty app.21.00		64.00	150.00
9-Powerhouse Pepper by Wolverton, 4 pgs.	26.00	77.00	180.00
11-Kurtzman-a, "Giggles 'n' Grins"	14.00	43.00	100.00
12,15,17-20: 12-Rusty & Hedy Devine app.	10.00	30.00	70.00
13,14,16-Kurtzman's "Hey Look". 13-Hedy Devine app.			
	12.00	36.00	85.00
21-30	7.50	22.50	45.00
31-60	4.50	14.00	32.00
61-99	3.40	10.00	24.00
100	4.50	14.00	32.00
101-153,155-190: 107-Jack Kirby app. in story	2.30	6.70	16.00
154-New Millie begins (10/67)	2.85	8.50	20.00
191-207: 192-(52 pgs.)	1.50	3.75	9.00
Annual 1(1962)-Early Marvel annual (2nd?)	19.00	58.00	135.00
Annual 2(1963)	16.00	47.00	110.00
Annual 3-5 (1964-1966)	9.15	27.50	55.00
Annual 6-10(1967-11/71)	6.35	19.00	38.00
Queen-Size 11(9/74), 12(1975)	4.70	14.00	28.00

NOTE: Dan DeCarlo a-18-93.

MILLION DOLLAR DIGEST (Richie Rich... #23 on; also see Richie Rich...)
11/86 - No. 7, 11/87; No. 8, 4/88 - No. 34, Nov, 1994 ($1.25/$1.75, digest size)
Harvey Publications

1-8: 8-(68 pgs.)			1.25

9-34: 9-Begin $1.75-c. 14-May not exist		.70	1.75

MILT GROSS FUNNIES (Also see Picture News #1)
Aug, 1947 - No. 2, Sept, 1947
Milt Gross, Inc. (ACG?)

1,2	11.00	33.00	75.00

MILTON THE MONSTER & FEARLESS FLY (TV)
May, 1966
Gold Key

1 (10175-605)	7.00	21.00	70.00

MINIMUM WAGE
V1#1, July, 1995 ($9.95, B&W, graphic novel, mature)
V2#1, 1995 - Present ($2.95, B&W, mature)
Fantagraphics Books

V1#1-Bob Fingerman story & art	1.65	4.20	10.00
V2#1-4($2.95): Bob Fingerman story & art. 2-Kevin Nowlan back-c. 4-w/pin-ups			
		1.20	3.00

MINUTE MAN (See Master Comics & Mighty Midget Comics)
Summer, 1941 - No. 3, Spring, 1942 (68 pgs.)
Fawcett Publications

1	137.00	412.00	1100.00
2,3	96.00	288.00	770.00

MINUTE MAN
No date (16 pgs.B&W, paper-c blue & red)
Sovereign Service Station giveaway

nn-American history	1.20	3.00	6.00

MINUTE MAN ANSWERS THE CALL, THE
1942 (4 pgs.)
By M. C. Gaines (Giveaway inserted in Jr. JSA Membership Kit)

nn-Sheldon Moldoff-a	10.00	30.00	65.00

MIRACLE COMICS
Feb, 1940 - No. 4, Mar, 1941
Hillman Periodicals

1-Sky Wizard Master of Space, Dash Dixon, Man of Might, Pinkie Parker, Dusty Doyle, The Kid Cop, K-7, Secret Agent, The Scorpion, & Blandu, Jungle Queen begin; Masked Angel only app. (all 1st app.)			
	150.00	450.00	1200.00
2	75.00	225.00	600.00
3,4: 3-Bill Colt, the Ghost Rider begins. 4-The Veiled Prophet & Bullet Bob (by Burnley) app.	68.00	206.00	550.00

MIRACLEMAN
Aug, 1985 - No. 15, Nov, 1988; No. 16, Dec, 1989 - No. 24, 1994
Eclipse Comics

1-r/British Marvelman series; Alan Moore scripts in #1-16	1.20	3.00
1-Gold & Silver editions		.80	2.00
2-12: 8-Airboy preview. 9,10-Origin Miracleman. 9-Shows graphic scenes of childbirth. 10-Snyder-c			1.20
13-15-($1.75)		.70	1.75
16-18-($1.95): 17-"The Golden Age" begins, ends #22. Dave McKean-c begins end #22; Neil Gaiman scripts in #17-24	.80	2.00
19-24-($2.50): 23-"The Silver Age" begins. 23,24-B. Smith-c.	1.00	2.50
3-D 1 (12/85)		1.00	2.50

NOTE: Chaykin c-3. Gulacy c-7. McKean c-17-22. B. Smith c-23, 24. Starlin c-4. Totleben a-11-13; c-9, 11-13. Truman c-6.

MIRACLEMAN: APOCRYPHA
Nov, 1991 - No. 3, Feb, 1992 ($2.50, limited series)
Eclipse Comics

1-3: 1-Stories by Neil Gaiman, Mark Buckingham, Alex Ross & others. 3-Stories by James Robinson, Kelley Jones, Matt Wagner, Neil Gaiman, Mark Buckingham & others			2.50

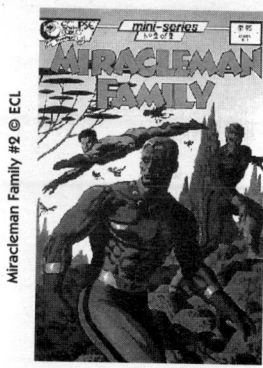

Miracleman Family #2 © ECL

Miss America Magazine #5 © MEG

Mission Impossible #1 © Paramount

MI

	GD25	FN65	NM94

MIRACLEMAN FAMILY
May, 1988 - No. 2, Sept, 1988 ($1.95, limited series, Baxter paper)
Eclipse Comics

1,2: 2-Gulacy-c		.80	2.00

MIRACLE OF THE WHITE STALLIONS, THE (See Movie Comics)

MIRACLE ON BROADWAY
Dec, 1995 (Giveaway)
Broadway Comics

1-Ernie Colon-c/a; Jim Shooter &Co. story; 1st known digitally printed comic
book; 1st app. Spire & Knights on Broadway (1150 print run)   20.00
NOTE: *Miracle on Broadway was a limited edition comic given to 1100 VIPs in the entertainment
industry for the 1995 Holiday Season.*

MIRACLE SQUAD, THE
Aug, 1986 - No. 4, 1987 ($2.00, limited series)
Upshot Graphics (Fantagraphics Books)

1-4		.80	2.00

MIRACLE SQUAD: BLOOD AND DUST, THE
Jan, 1989 - No. 4, July, 1989 ($1.95, B&W, limited series)
Apple Comics

1-4		.80	2.00

MISADVENTURES OF MERLIN JONES, THE (See Movie Comics & Merlin Jones
as the Monkey's Uncle under Movie Comics)

MISS AMERICA COMICS (Miss America Magazine #2 on; also see Blonde
Phantom & Marvel Mystery Comics)
1944 (one-shot)
Marvel Comics (20CC)

1-2 pgs. pin-ups	137.00	412.00	1100.00

MISS AMERICA MAGAZINE (Formerly Miss America; Miss America #51 on)
V1#2, Nov, 1944 - No. 93, Nov, 1958
Miss America Publ. Corp./Marvel/Atlas (MAP)

V1#2-Photo-c of teenage girl in Miss America costume; Miss America, Patsy
Walker (intro.) comic stories plus movie reviews & stories; intro. Buzz
Baxter & Hedy Wolfe; 1 pg. origin Miss America

	118.00	356.00	950.00
3-5-Miss America & Patsy Walker stories	44.00	132.00	350.00
6-Patsy Walker only	10.00	30.00	60.00
V2#1(4/45)-6(9/45)-Patsy Walker continues	5.00	15.00	30.00
V3#1(10/45)-6(4/46)	5.00	15.00	30.00
V4#1(5/46),2,5(9/46)	4.70	14.00	28.00
V4#3(7/46)-Liz Taylor photo-c	8.35	25.00	50.00
V4#4 (8/46; 68 pgs.)	4.35	13.00	26.00
V4#6 (10/46; 92 pgs.)	4.35	13.00	26.00
V5#1(11/46)-6(4/47), V6#1(5/47)-3(7/47)	4.35	13.00	26.00
V7#1(8/47)-14,16-23(#56, 6/49)	4.00	11.00	22.00
V7#15-All comics	4.35	13.00	26.00
V7#24(#57, 7/49)-Kamen-a (becomes Best Western #58 on?)			
	4.00	12.00	24.00
V7#25(8/49), 27-44(3/52), VII,nn(5/52)	4.00	10.00	20.00
V7#26(9/49)-All comics	4.35	13.00	26.00
V1,nn(7/52)-V1,nn(1/53)(#46-49)	4.00	10.00	20.00
V7#50(Spring '53), V1#51-V7?#54(7/53)	4.00	10.00	20.00
55-93	4.00	10.00	20.00

NOTE: *Photo-c #1, 4, V2#1, 4, 5, V3#5, V4#3, 4, 6, V7#15, 16, 24, 26, 34, 37, 38. Painted c-3.
Powell a-V7#31.*

MISS BEVERLY HILLS OF HOLLYWOOD (See Adventures of Bob Hope)
Mar-Apr, 1949 - No. 9, July-Aug, 1950 (52 pgs.)
National Periodical Publications

1 (Meets Alan Ladd)	51.00	155.00	415.00
2-William Holden photo on-c	40.00	120.00	300.00
3-5: 2-9-Part photo-c. 5-Bob Hope photo on-c	34.00	101.00	235.00
6,7,9: 6-Lucille Ball photo on-c	31.00	94.00	220.00

	GD25	FN65	NM94

8-Reagan photo on-c	39.00	118.00	275.00

NOTE: *Beverly meets Alan Ladd in #1, Eve Arden #2, Betty Hutton #4, Bob Hope #5.*

MISS CAIRO JONES
1945
Croyden Publishers

1-Bob Oksner daily newspaper-r (1st strip story); lingerie panels			
	19.00	58.00	135.00

MISS FURY COMICS (Newspaper strip reprints)
Winter, 1942-43 - No. 8, Winter, 1946 (Published quarterly)
Timely Comics (NPI 1/CmPI 2/MPC 3-8)

1-Origin Miss Fury by Tarpe' Mills (68 pgs.) in costume w/pin-ups			
	300.00	900.00	2400.00
2-(60 pgs.)-In costume w/pin-ups	137.00	412.00	1100.00
3-(60 pgs.)-In costume w/pin-ups; Hitler-c	112.00	338.00	900.00
4-(52 pgs.)-In costume, 2 pgs. w/pin-ups	87.00	262.00	700.00
5-(52 pgs.)-In costume w/pin-ups	81.00	243.00	650.00
6-(52 pgs.)-Not in costume in inside stories, w/pin-ups			
	75.00	225.00	600.00
7,8-(36 pgs.)-In costume 1 pg. each; no pin-ups	70.00	211.00	565.00

NOTE: *Schomburg c-1, 5, 6.*

MISS FURY
1991 - No. 4, 1991 ($2.50, limited series)
Adventure Comics

1-4: 1-Origin; granddaughter of original Miss Fury		1.00	2.50
1-Limited ed. ($4.95)	1.00	2.00	5.00

MISSION IMPOSSIBLE (TV)
May, 1967 - No. 4, Oct, 1968; No. 5, Oct, 1969 (All have photo-c)
Dell Publishing Co.

1	9.00	27.00	90.00
2-5: 5-Reprints #1	6.00	18.00	60.00

MISSION IMPOSSIBLE (Movie)
May, 1996 ($2.95, one-shot) (1st Paramount Comics book)
Marvel Comics (Paramount Comics)

1-Liefeld-c & back-up story			3.00

MISS LIBERTY (Becomes Liberty Comics)
1945 (MLJ reprints)
Burten Publishing Co.

1-The Shield & Dusty, The Wizard, & Roy, the Super Boy app.; r/Shield-Wizard #13	27.00	81.00	190.00

MISS MELODY LANE OF BROADWAY (See The Adventures of Bob Hope)
Feb-Mar, 1950 - No. 3, June-July, 1950 (52 pgs.)
National Periodical Publications

1-Movie stars photos app. on all-c	50.00	150.00	400.00
2,3: 3-Ed Sullivan photo on-c	36.00	107.00	250.00

MISS PEACH
Oct-Dec, 1963; 1969
Dell Publishing Co.

1-Jack Mendelsohn-a/script	7.00	21.00	70.00
...Tells You How to Grow (1969; 25¢)-Mel Lazarus-a; also given away (36 pgs.)			
	4.00	12.00	40.00

MISS PEPPER (See Meet Miss Pepper)
MISS SUNBEAM (See Little Miss...)
MISS VICTORY (See Captain Fearless #1,2, Holyoke One-Shot #3, Veri Best Sure Fire &
Veri Best Sure Shot Comics)

MISTER AMERICA
Apr, 1994 - No. 2, May, 1994 ($2.95, limited series)
Endeavor Comics

1,2		1.20	3.00

Mister Miracle #3 © DC

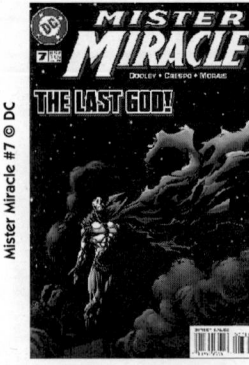

Mister Miracle #7 © DC

Mr. Monster #10 © Michael T. Gilbert

MR. & MRS. BEANS
No. 11, 1939
United Features Syndicate

Single Series 11	30.00	90.00	210.00

MR. & MRS. J. EVIL SCIENTIST (TV)(See The Flintstones & Hanna-Barbera
Band Wagon #3)
Nov, 1963 - No. 4, Sept, 1966 (Hanna-Barbera, all 12¢)
Gold Key

1-From The Flintstones	5.50	16.50	55.00
2-4	3.00	9.00	30.00

MR. ANTHONY'S LOVE CLINIC (Based on radio show)
Nov, 1949 - No. 5, Apr-May, 1950 (52 pgs.)
Hillman Periodicals

1-Photo-c	10.00	30.00	70.00
2	6.70	20.00	40.00
3-5: 5-Photo-c	5.85	17.50	35.00

MR. BUG GOES TO TOWN (See Cinema Comics Herald)
1941 (Giveaway, 52 pgs.)
K.K. Publications

nn-Cartoon movie (scarce)	56.00	168.00	450.00

MR. DISTRICT ATTORNEY (Radio/TV)
Jan-Feb, 1948 - No. 67, Jan-Feb, 1959 (1-23: 52 pgs.)
National Periodical Publications

1-Howard Purcell c-5-23 (most)	90.00	271.00	725.00
2	40.00	120.00	315.00
3-5	30.00	90.00	210.00
6-10	23.00	69.00	160.00
11-20	18.00	54.00	125.00
21-43: 43-Last pre-code (1-2/55)	13.50	41.00	95.00
44-67	11.00	33.00	75.00

MR. DISTRICT ATTORNEY (SeeThe Funnies #35)
No. 13, 1942
Dell Publishing Co.

Four Color 13-See The Funnies #35 for 1st app.	28.00	84.00	280.00

MISTER E (Also see Books of Magic limited series)
Jun, 1991- No. 4, Sept, 1991($1.75, limited series)
DC Comics

1-4-Snyder III-c/a; follow-up to Books of Magic limited series.			
	0.40	0.80	2.00

MISTER ED, THE TALKING HORSE (TV)
Mar-May, 1962 - No. 6, Feb, 1964 (All photo-c; photo back-c: 1-6)
Dell Publishing Co./Gold Key

Four Color 1295	13.00	40.00	130.00
1(11/62) (Gold Key)-Photo-c	10.00	30.00	100.00
2-6: Photo-c	5.00	15.00	50.00
(See March of Comics #244, 260, 282, 290)			

MR. HERO, THE NEWMATIC MAN (See Neil Gaiman's...)

MR. MAGOO (TV) (The Nearsighted..., ...& Gerald McBoing Boing 1954
issues; formerly Gerald McBoing-Boing And ...)
No. 6, Nov-Jan, 1953-54; 5/54 - 3-5/62; 9-11/63 - 3-5/65
Dell Publishing Co.

6	10.00	30.00	100.00
Four Color 561(5/54),602(11/54)	10.00	30.00	100.00
Four Color 1235(#1, 12-2/62),1305(#2, 3-5/62)	9.00	27.00	90.00
3(9-11/63) - 5	8.00	24.00	80.00
Four Color 1235(12-536-505)(3-5/65)-2nd Printing	5.00	15.00	50.00

MISTER MIRACLE (1st series) (See Cancelled Comic Cavalcade)
3-4/71 - V4#18, 2-3/74; V5#19, 9/77 - V6#25, 8-9/78; 1987 (Fourth World)

National Periodical Publications/DC Comics

1-1st app. Mr. Miracle (#1-3 are 15¢)	4.30	13.00	30.00
2,3	2.15	6.50	15.00
4-8: 4-Boy Commandos-r begin; all 52 pgs.	1.85	5.50	13.00
9,10: 9-Origin Mr. Miracle; Darkseid cameo	1.65	4.20	10.00
11-18: 15-Intro/1st app. Shilo Norman. 18-Barda & Scott Free wed; New			
Gods app. & Darkseid cameo; Last Kirby issue.	1.65	4.20	10.00
19-25 (1977-78)	1.00	2.00	5.00
Special 1(1987, $1.25, 52 pgs.)		1.20	3.00

NOTE: *Austin a-19i. Ditko a-6r. Golden a-23-25p; c-25p. Heath a-24i, 25i; c-25i. Kirby a(p)/c-
1-18. Nasser a-19i. Rogers a-19-22p; c-19, 20p, 21p, 22-24. 4-8 contain Simon & Kirby Boy
Commandos reprints from Detective 82,76, Boy Commandos 1, 3 & Detective 64 in that order.*

MISTER MIRACLE (2nd Series) (See Justice League)
Jan, 1989 - No. 28, June, 1991 ($1.00)
DC Comics

1-28: 13,14-Lobo app. 22-1st new Mr. Miracle w/new costume			1.00

MISTER MIRACLE (3rd Series)
Apr, 1996 - No. 7, Oct, 1996 ($1.95)
DC Comics

1-7: 2-Vs. JLA.			2.00

MR. MIRACLE (See Capt. Fearless #1 & Holyoke One-Shot #4)

MR. MONSTER (1st Series)(Doc Stearn... #7 on; See Airboy-Mr. Monster
Special, Dark Horse Presents, Super Duper Comics & Vanguard Illustrated #7)
Jan, 1985 - No. 10, June, 1987 ($1.75, color, Baxter paper)
Eclipse Comics

1-1st story-r from Vanguard Ill. #7(1st app.)	1.00	2.00	5.00
2-Dave Stevens-c		1.20	3.00
3-10: 3-Alan Moore scripts; Wolverton-r/Weird Mysteries #5. 6-Ditko-r/Fan-			
tastic Fears #5 plus new Giffen-a 10 6-D issue	.80	2.00

MR. MONSTER
Feb, 1988 - No. 8, July, 1991 ($1.75, B&W)
Dark Horse Comics

1-7		.70	1.75
8-($4.95, 60 pgs.)-Origins conclusion	1.00	2.00	5.00

MR. MONSTER'S SUPER-DUPER SPECIAL
May, 1986 - No. 8, July, 1987
Eclipse Comics

1-(5/86)...3-D High Octane Horror #1		1.20	3.00
1-(5/86)...2-D version, 100 copies		2.30	5.50
2-(8/86)...High Octane Horror #1		.80	2.00
3-(9/86)...True Crime #1		.80	2.00
4-(11/86)...True Crime #2		.80	2.00
5-(1/87)...Hi-Voltage Super Science #1		.80	2.00
6-(3/87)...High Shock Schlock #1		.80	2.00
7-(5/87)...High Shock Schlock #2		.80	2.00
8-(7/87)...Weird Tales Of The Future #1		.80	2.00

NOTE: *Jack Cole r-3, 4. Evans a-2r. Kubert a-1r. Powell a-5r. Wolverton a-2r, 7r, 8r.*

MR. MUSCLES (Formerly Blue Beetle #18-21)
No. 22, Mar, 1956; No. 23, Aug, 1956
Charlton Comics

22,23	5.35	16.00	32.00

MISTER MYSTERY (Tales of Horror and Suspense)
Sept, 1951 - No. 19, Oct, 1954
Mr. Publ. (Media Publ.) No. 1-3/SPM Publ./Stanmore (Aragon)

1-Kurtzmanesque horror story	62.00	187.00	500.00
2,3-Kurtzmanesque story. 3-Anti-Wertham edit.	41.00	124.00	330.00
4,6: Bondage-c; 6-Torture	41.00	124.00	330.00
5,8,10	39.00	116.00	270.00
7- "The Brain Bats of Venus" by Wolverton; partially re-used in Weird Tales			
of the Future #7	87.00	262.00	700.00

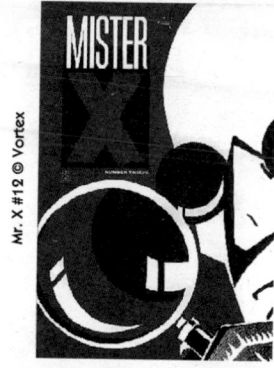

Mr. T and the T-Force #2 © Now Comics

Mr. X #12 © Vortex

Mobfire #2 © DC

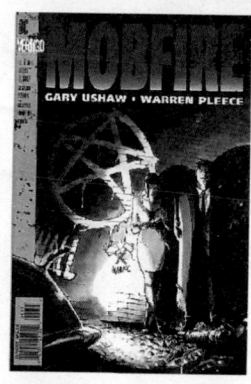

	GD25	FN65	NM94

	GD25	FN65	NM94
9-Nostrand-a	39.00	116.00	270.00
11-Wolverton "Robot Woman" story/Weird Mysteries #2, cut up, rewritten & partially redrawn	59.00	178.00	475.00
12-Classic injury to eye-c	87.00	262.00	700.00
13,14,17,19: 17-Severed heads-c. 19-Reprints	26.00	77.00	180.00
15- "Living Dead" junkie story	26.00	77.00	180.00
16-Bondage-c	26.00	77.00	180.00
18- "Robot Woman" by Wolverton reprinted from Weird Mysteries #2; decapitation, bondage-c	44.00	135.00	360.00

NOTE: Andru a-1, 2p, 3p. Andru/Esposito c-1-3. Baily c-10-18(most). Mortellaro c-5-7. Bondage c-7. Some issues have graphic dismemberment scenes.

MR. MYSTIC (See Will Eisner Presents)

MR. PUNCH
1994 ($24.95, one-shot)
DC Comics (Vertigo)

nn (Hard-c)-Gaiman scripts; McKean-c/a	3.60	11.00	25.00
nn (Soft-c)	2.15	6.50	15.00

MISTER Q (See Mighty Midget Comics & Our Flag Comics #5)

MR. RISK (Formerly All Romances; Men Against Crime #3 on)(Also see Our Flag Comics & Super-Mystery Comics)
No. 7, Oct, 1950 - No. 2, Dec, 1950
Ace Magazines

7,2	6.35	19.00	38.00

MR. SCARLET & PINKY (See Mighty Midget Comics)

MR. T AND THE T-FORCE
June, 1993 - No. 10, May, 1994 ($1.95, color)
Now Comics

1-10-Newsstand editions: 1-7-polybagged with photo trading card in each. 1,2-Neal Adams-c/a(p). 3-Dave Dorman painted-c		.80	2.00
1-10-Direct Sale editions polybagged w/line drawn trading cards. 1-Contains gold foil trading card by Neal Adams		.80	2.00

MISTER UNIVERSE (Professional wrestler)
July, 1951; No. 2, Oct, 1951 - No. 5, April, 1952
Mr. Publications Media Publ. (Stanmor, Aragon)

1	17.00	49.00	115.00
2- "Jungle That Time Forgot", (24 pg. story); Andru/Esposito-c	11.00	33.00	75.00
3-Marijuana story	11.00	33.00	75.00
4,5- "Goes to War" cover/stories	8.35	25.00	50.00

MISTER X (See Vortex)
6/84 - No. 14, 8/88 ($1.50/$2.25, direct sales, coated paper)
V2#1, Apr, 1989 - V2#12, Mar, 1990 ($2.00/$2.50, B&W, newsprint)
V3#1, 1996 - Present ($2.95, B&W)
Mr. Publications/Vortex Comics / Caliber V3#1 on

1		1.70	4.00
2		1.00	2.50
3-14: 11-Dave McKean story & art (6 pgs.)		.80	2.00
V2#1-11 (Second Coming, $2.00, B&W): 1-Four different covers. 10-Photo-c		.80	2.00
V2#12 ($2.50)		1.00	2.50
V3#1-3(2.95, B&W): 1-1st Caliber issue			3.00
Return of... ($11.95, graphic novel)-r/1-4	1.70	5.00	12.00
Return of... ($34.95, hardcover limited edition)-r/1-4	5.00	15.00	35.00
Special (no date, 1990?)		.80	2.00

MISTY
Dec, 1985 - No. 6, May, 1986 (Limited series)
Marvel Comics (Star Comics)

1-6: Millie The Model's niece			.80

MITZI COMICS (Becomes Mitzi's Boy Friend #2 on)(See All Teen)
Spring, 1948 (one-shot)

Timely Comics

1-Kurtzman's "Hey Look" plus 3 pgs. "Giggles 'n' Grins"	17.00	49.00	115.00

MITZI'S BOY FRIEND (Formerly Mitzi Comics; becomes Mitzi's Romances)
No. 2, June, 1948 - No. 7, April, 1949
Marvel Comics (TCI)

2	9.15	27.00	55.00
3-7	6.70	20.00	40.00

MITZI'S ROMANCES (Formerly Mitzi's Boy Friend)
No. 8, June, 1949 - No. 10, Dec, 1949
Timely/Marvel Comics (TCI)

8-Becomes True Life Tales #8 (10/49) on?	9.15	27.00	55.00
9,10: 10-Painted-c	6.70	20.00	40.00

MOBFIRE
Dec, 1994 - No. 6, May, 1995 ($2.50, limited series)
DC Comics (Vertigo)

1-6		1.00	2.50

MOBY DICK (See Feature Presentations #6, and King Classics)
No. 717, Aug, 1956
Dell Publishing Co.

Four Color 717-Movie, Gregory Peck photo-c	9.00	27.00	90.00

MOBY DUCK (See Donald Duck #112 & Walt Disney Showcase #2,11)
Oct, 1967 - No. 11, Oct, 1970; No. 12, Jan, 1974 - No. 30, Feb, 1978
Gold Key (Disney)

1	1.70	5.00	12.00
2-5	1.20	2.90	7.00
6-11		1.60	4.00
12-30: 21,30-r		.80	2.00

MODEL FUN (With Bobby Benson)
No. 3, Winter, 1954-55 - No. 5, July, 1955
Harle Publications

3-Bobby Benson	6.35	19.00	38.00
4,5-Bobby Benson	4.00	12.00	24.00

MODELING WITH MILLIE (Formerly Life With Millie)
No. 21, Feb, 1963 - No. 54, June, 1967
Atlas/Marvel Comics Group (Male Publ.)

21	10.00	30.00	60.00
22-30	5.85	17.50	35.00
31-54	4.00	12.00	24.00

MODERN COMICS (Formerly Military Comics #1-43)
No. 44, Nov, 1945 - No. 102, Oct, 1950
Quality Comics Group

44-Blackhawk continues	50.00	150.00	400.00
45-52: 49-1st app. Fear, Lady Adventuress	40.00	120.00	285.00
53-Torchy by Ward begins (9/46)	40.00	120.00	315.00
54-60: 55-J. Cole-a	34.00	101.00	235.00
61-77,79,80: 73-J. Cole-a	30.00	90.00	210.00
78-1st app. Madame Butterfly	34.00	101.00	235.00
81-99,101: 82,83-One pg. J. Cole-a. 83-The Spirit app.; last 52 pg. issue?	30.00	90.00	210.00
99-Blackhawks on the moon-c/story	30.00	90.00	210.00
100	30.00	90.00	210.00
102-(Scarce)-J. Cole-a; Spirit by Eisner app.	35.00	105.00	245.00

NOTE: Al Bryant c-44-51, 54, 55, 66, 69. Jack Cole a-55, 73. Crandall Blackhawk-46, 47, 50, 51, 54, 56, 58-60, 64, 67-70, 73, 74, 76-78, 80-83; c-60-65, 67, 68, 70-95. Crandall/Cuidera c-56-59, 96-102. Gustavson a-47. Ward Blackhawk-52, 53, 55 (15 pgs. each). Torchy in #53-102; by Ward only in #53-89(9/49); by Gil Fox #93, 102.

MODERN LOVE
June-July, 1949 - No. 8, Aug-Sept, 1950
E. C. Comics

Moebius #2 © Moebius

The Monster #2 © FH

Monster Hunters #1 © CC

	GD25	FN65	NM94
1	50.00	150.00	400.00
2-Craig/Feldstein-c	40.00	120.00	300.00
3-Spanking panel	36.00	107.00	250.00
4-6 (Scarce): 4-Bra/panties panels	47.00	141.00	375.00
7,8	39.00	118.00	275.00

NOTE: **Craig** a-3. **Feldstein** a-in most issues; c-1, 2i, 3-8. **Harrison** a-4. **Iger** a-6-8. **Ingels** a-1, 2, 4-7. **Palais** a-5. **Wood** a-7. **Wood/Harrison** a-5-7. (Canadian reprints known; see Table of Contents.)

MOD LOVE
1967 (50¢, 36 pgs.)
Western Publishing Co.

1	3.40	10.00	24.00

MODNIKS, THE
Aug, 1967 - No. 2, Aug, 1970
Gold Key

10206-708(#1), 2	1.70	5.00	12.00

MOD SQUAD (TV)
Jan, 1969 - No. 3, Oct, 1969 - No. 8, April, 1971
Dell Publishing Co.

1-Photo-c	4.50	14.00	45.00
2-8: 2-4-Photo-c. 8-Photo-c; Reprints #2	2.30	6.70	23.00

MOD WHEELS
Mar, 1971 - No. 19, Jan, 1976
Gold Key

1	1.70	5.00	12.00
2-19: 11,15-Extra 16 pgs. ads	1.00	2.60	6.00

MOE & SHMOE COMICS
Spring, 1948 - No. 2, Summer, 1948
O. S. Publ. Co.

1	7.00	21.00	42.00
2	5.35	16.00	32.00

MOEBIUS (Graphic novel)
Oct, 1987 - No. 6, 1988; No. 7, 1990; No. 8, 1991 ($9.95, 8x11", mature)
Marvel Comics (Epic Comics)

1,2,4-6,8: (#2, 2nd printing, $9.95)	1.65	4.00	10.00
3,7: 3-(1st & 2nd printings, $12.95)	1.85	5.50	13.00
0 (1990, $12.95)	1.85	5.50	13.00
Moebius I-Signed & numbered hard-c ($45.95, Graphitti Designs, 1,500 copies printed)-r/#1-3	7.00	21.50	50.00

MOEBIUS COMICS
May, 1996 - Present ($2.95, B&W)
Caliber

1,2: Moebius-c/a. 1-William Stout-a			3.00

MOEBIUS: THE MAN FROM CIGURI
1996 ($7.95, digest-size)
Dark Horse Comics

nn-Moebius-c/a			8.00

MOLLY MANTON'S ROMANCES (Romantic Affairs #3)
Sept, 1949 - No. 2, Dec, 1949 (52 pgs.)
Marvel Comics (SePl)

1-Photo-c (becomes Blaze the Wonder Collie #2 (10/49) on? & Molly Manton's Romances #2	10.00	30.00	70.00
2-Titled "Romances of..."; photo-c	8.00	24.00	48.00

MOLLY O'DAY (Super Sleuth)
February, 1945 (1st Avon comic)
Avon Periodicals

1-Molly O'Day, The Enchanted Dagger by Tuska (r/Yankee #1), Capt'n Courage, Corporal Grant app.	40.00	120.00	300.00

MONKEES, THE (TV)(Also see Circus Boy, Groovy, Not Brand Echh #3, Teen-Age Talk, Teen Beam & Teen Beat)
March, 1967 - No. 17, Oct, 1969 (#1-4,6,7,9,10,12,15,16 have photo-c)
Dell Publishing Co.

1-Photo-c	9.00	27.00	90.00
2-4,6,7,9,10,12,15,16: All photo-c	5.50	16.50	55.00
5,8,11,13,14,17-No photo-c: 17-Reprints #1	3.80	11.50	38.00

MONKEY AND THE BEAR, THE
Sept, 1953 - No. 3, Jan, 1954
Atlas Comics (ZPC)

1-Howie Post-c/a in all; funny animal	5.85	17.50	35.00
2,3	4.00	11.00	22.00

MONKEYMAN AND O'BRIEN (Also see Dark Horse Presents #80, 100-5, Hellboy: Seed of Destruction, & San Diego Comic Con #2)
July, 1996 - No. 3, Sept, 1996 ($2.95, limited series)
Dark Horse Comics (Legend)

1-3: New stories; Art Adams-c/a/scripts		1.20	3.00
nn-(2/96, $2.95)-r/back-up stories from Hellboy: Seed of Destruction; Adams-c/a/scripts		1.20	3.00

MONKEYSHINES COMICS
Summer, 1944 - No. 27, July, 1949
Ace Periodicals/Publishers Specialists/Current Books/Unity Publ.

1-Funny animal	10.00	30.00	65.00
2-(Aut/44)	5.35	16.00	32.00
3-10: 3-(Win/44)	4.25	13.00	26.00
11-27: 23,24-Fago-c/a	4.00	11.00	22.00

MONKEY'S UNCLE, THE (See Merlin Jones As... under Movie Comics)

MONROES, THE (TV)
Apr, 1967
Dell Publishing Co.

1-Photo-c	2.00	6.00	20.00

MONSTER
1953 - No. 2, 1953
Fiction House Magazines

1-Dr. Drew by Grandenetti; reprint from Rangers Comics #48; Whitman-c	40.00	120.00	300.00
2-Whitman-c	32.00	96.00	225.00

MONSTER CRIME COMICS (Also see Crime Must Stop)
Oct, 1952 (15¢, 52 pgs.)
Hillman Periodicals

1 (Scarce)	75.00	225.00	600.00

MONSTER HOWLS (Magazine)
December, 1966 (Satire) (35¢, 68 pgs.)
Humor-Vision

1	3.60	11.00	25.00

MONSTER HUNTERS
Aug, 1975 - No. 9, Jan, 1977; No. 10, Oct, 1977 - No. 18, Feb, 1979
Charlton Comics

1,2: 1-Howard-a; Newton-c. 2-Ditko-a	1.00	2.60	6.00
3-13,15-18		1.00	2.50
14-Special all-Ditko issue		1.60	4.00
1,2(Modern Comics reprints, 1977)			1.00

NOTE: **Ditko** a-2, 6, 8, 10, 13-15r, 18r; c-13-15, 18. **Howard** r-13. **Morisi** a-1. **Staton** a-1, 13. **Sutton** a-2, 4; c-2, 4. Reprints in #12-18.

MONSTER MADNESS (Magazine)
1973 - #3, 1973? (60¢, B&W)
Marvel Comics

1-3: Stories by "Sinister" Stan Lee

Monster Menace #2 © MEG

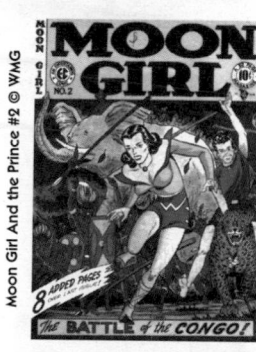

Moon Girl And the Prince #2 © WMG

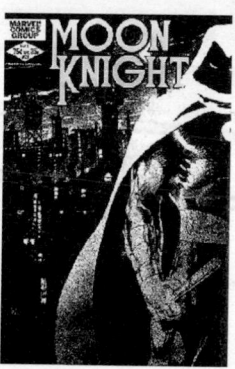

Moon Knight #23 © MEG

	GD25	FN65	NM94

MONSTER MENACE
Dec, 1993 - No. 4, Mar, 1994 ($1.25, limited series)
Marvel Comics

1-4: Pre-code Atlas horror reprints.   1.25
NOTE: *Ditko-r* & *Kirby-r* in all.

MONSTER OF FRANKENSTEIN (See Frankenstein)

MONSTERS ON THE PROWL (Chamber of Darkness #1-8)
No. 9, 2/71 - No. 27, 11/73; No. 28, 6/74 - No. 30, 10/74
Marvel Comics Group (No. 13,14: 52 pgs.)

9-Barry Smith inks	1.00	2.00	5.00
10-30: 16-(4/72)-2nd app. King Kull; see Creatures on the Loose #10 (3/71);			
Severin-c	1.20		3.00
NOTE: *Ditko r-5, 9, 14, 16. Gil Kane c-7. Kirby r-10-17, 21, 23, 25, 27, 28, 30; c-9, 25. Kirby/Ditko r-14, 17-20, 22, 24, 26, 29. Reinman r-5. Marie/John Severin a-16(Kull). 9-13, 15 contain one new story. Woodish art by Reese-11. King Kull created by Robert E. Howard.*

MONSTERS UNLEASHED (Magazine)
July, 1973 - No. 11, Apr, 1975; Summer, 1975 (B&W)
Marvel Comics Group

1	1.65	4.20	10.00
2,3,5-11: 2-The Frankenstein Monster begins. 3-Neal Adams-c/a; The Man-Thing begins (origin-r). 7-Williamson-a(r). 8-N. Adams-c. 9-Wendigo app.			
10-Origin Tigra		1.60	4.00
4-Intro. Satana, the Devil's daughter	1.00	2.60	6.00
Annual 1 (Summer,1975)-Kane-a	1.20		3.00
NOTE: *Boris c-2, 6. Brunner a-2; c-11. J. Buscema a-2p, 4p, 5p. Colan a-1, 4r. Davis a-3r. Everett a-2r. G. Kane a-3. Krigstein r-4. Morrow a-3; c-1. Perez a-8. Ploog a-6. Reese a-1, 2. Tuska a-3p. Wildey a-1r.*

MONTANA KID, THE (See Kid Montana)

MONTE HALE WESTERN (Movie star; Formerly Mary Marvel #1-28; also see Fawcett Movie Comic, Motion Picture Comics, Picture News #8, Real Western Hero, Six-Gun Heroes, Western Hero & XMas Comics)
No. 29, Oct, 1948 - No. 88, Jan, 1956
Fawcett Publications/Charlton No. 83 on

29-(#1, 52 pgs.)-Photo-c begin, end #82; Monte Hale & his horse Pardner begin	44.00	132.00	350.00
30-(52 pgs.)-Big Bow and Little Arrow begin, end #34; Captain Tootsie by Beck	23.00	69.00	160.00
31-36,38-40-(52 pgs.): 34-Gabby Hayes begins, ends #80. 39-Captain Tootsie by Beck	17.00	51.00	120.00
37,41,45,49-(36 pgs.)	11.50	34.00	80.00
42-44,46-48,50-(52 pgs.): 47-Big Bow & Little Arrow app.	12.00	36.00	85.00
51,52,54-56,58,59-(52 pgs.)	10.00	30.00	68.00
53,57-(36 pgs.): 53-Slim Pickens app.	8.70	26.00	52.00
60-81: 36 pgs. #60-on. 80-Gabby Hayes ends	8.70	26.00	52.00
82-Last Fawcett issue (6/53)	10.00	30.00	68.00
83-1st Charlton issue (2/55); B&W photo back-c begin. Gabby Hayes returns, ends #86	10.00	30.00	68.00
84 (4/55)	8.70	26.00	52.00
85-86	8.00	24.00	48.00
87-Wolverton-r, 1/2 pg.	8.70	26.00	52.00
88-Last issue	8.70	26.00	52.00
NOTE: *Gil Kane a-33?, 34? Rocky Lane -1 pg. (Carnation ad)-38, 40, 41, 43, 44, 46, 55.*

MONTY HALL OF THE U.S. MARINES (See With the Marines…)
Aug, 1951 - No. 11, Apr, 1953
Toby Press

1	9.15	27.00	55.00
2	5.85	17.50	35.00
3-5	5.00	15.00	30.00
6-11	4.25	13.00	26.00
NOTE: *Full page pin-ups (Pin-Up Pete) by Jack Sparling in #1-9.*

MOON, A GIRL…ROMANCE, A (Becomes Weird Fantasy #13 on; formerly

	GD25	FN65	NM94

Moon Girl #1-8)
No. 9, Sept-Oct, 1949 - No. 12, Mar-Apr, 1950
E. C. Comics

9-Moon Girl cameo; spanking panel	60.00	180.00	460.00
10,11	45.00	135.00	350.00
12-(Scarce)	63.00	190.00	475.00
NOTE: *Feldstein, Ingels art in all. Feldstein c-9-12. Wood/Harrison a-10-12. Canadian reprints known; see Table of Contents.*

MOON GIRL AND THE PRINCE (#1) (Moon Girl #2-6; Moon Girl Fights Crime #7, 8; becomes A Moon, A Girl, Romance #9 on)(Also see Animal Fables #7 and Happy Houlihans)
Fall, 1947 - No. 8, Summer, 1949
E. C. Comics

1-Origin Moon Girl (see Happy Houlihans #1)	75.00	225.00	600.00
2	41.00	122.00	315.00
3,4: 4-Moon Girl vs. a vampire	39.00	116.00	270.00
5-E.C.'s 1st horror story, "Zombie Terror"	96.00	290.00	735.00
6-8-(Scarce): 7-Origin Star (Moongirl's sidekick)	45.00	135.00	350.00
NOTE: *Craig a-2, 5. Moldoff a-1-8; c-2-6. Wheelan's Fat and Slat app. in #3, 4, 6. #2 & #3 are 52 pgs., #4 on, 36 pgs. Canadian reprints known; (see Table of Contents).*

MOON KNIGHT (Also see The Hulk, Marc Spector…, Marvel Preview #21, Marvel Spotlight & Werewolf by Night #32)
November, 1980 - No. 38, July, 1984 (Mando paper No. 33 on)
Marvel Comics Group

1-Origin resumed in #4; begin Sienkiewicz-c/a	1.20		3.00
2-34,36-38: 4-Intro Midnight Man. 16-The Thing app. 25-Double size			1.50
35-($1.00, 52 pgs.)-X-men app.; F.F. cameo			1.50
NOTE: *Austin c-27, 31i. Cowan a-16; c-16, 17. Kaluta c-36-38. Miller c-9, 12p, 13p, 15p, 27p. Ploog back-c-35. Sienkiewicz a-1-15, 17-20, 22-26, 28-30, 33i, 36(4), 37; c-1-5, 7, 8, 10, 11, 14-16, 18-26, 28-30, 31p, 33, 34.*

MOON KNIGHT
June, 1985 - V2#6, Dec, 1985
Marvel Comics Group

V2#1-6: 1-Double size; new costume. 6-Sienkiewicz painted-c.			1.00

MOON KNIGHT: DIVIDED WE FALL
1992 ($4.95, 52 pgs.)
Marvel Comics

nn-Denys Cowan-c/a(p)	1.00	2.00	5.00

MOON KNIGHT SPECIAL
Oct, 1992 ($2.50, 52 pgs.)
Marvel Comics

1-Shang Chi, Master of Kung Fu-c/story	1.00		2.50

MOON KNIGHT SPECIAL EDITION
Nov, 1983 - No. 3, Jan, 1984 ($2.00, limited series, Baxter paper)
Marvel Comics Group

1-3: Reprints from Hulk mag. by Sienkiewicz		.80	2.00

MOON MULLINS (See Popular Comics, Super Book #3 & Super Comics)
1941 - 1945
Dell Publishing Co.

Four Color 14(1941)	35.00	105.00	350.00
Large Feature Comic 29(1941)	25.00	75.00	250.00
Four Color 31(1943)	18.00	54.00	180.00
Four Color 81(1945)	10.00	30.00	100.00

MOON MULLINS
Dec-Jan, 1947-48 - No. 8, 1949 (52 pgs.)
Michel Publ. (American Comics Group)

1-Alternating Sunday & daily strip-r	20.00	60.00	140.00
2	10.00	30.00	70.00
3-8: 8-…Featuring Kayo on-c	9.15	27.50	55.00

Moonshadow #5 © DC

Morbid Angel #1 © London Night

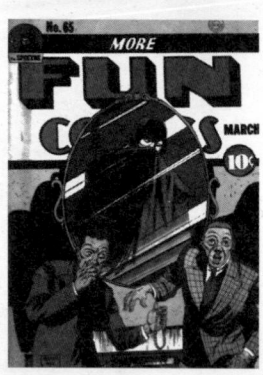
More Fun Comics #65 © DC

	GD25	FN65	NM94

NOTE: *Milt Gross a-2-6, 8. Frank Willard r-all.*

MOON PILOT
No. 1313, Mar-May, 1962
Dell Publishing Co.

	GD25	FN65	NM94
Four Color 1313-Movie, photo-c	7.00	21.00	70.00

MOONSHADOW
5/85 - #12, 2/87 ($1.50/$1.75, mature)(1st fully painted comic book)
Marvel Comics (Epic Comics)

1-Origin; J. M. DeMatteis scripts & Jon J. Muth painted-c/a.		2.00	5.00
		1.20	3.00
2-12: 11-Origin		1.20	3.00
Trade paperback (1987?)-r/#1-12	2.00	6.00	14.00
Signed & numbered hard-c ($39.95, 1,200 copies)-r/#1-12	11.00	33.00	75.00

MOONSHADOW
Oct, 1994 - No. 12, Aug, 1995 ($2.25/$2.95, painted limited series, mature)
DC Comics

1-11: Reprints Epic series.		.90	2.25
12 ($2.95)		1.20	3.00

MOON-SPINNERS, THE (See Movie Comics)

MOPSY (See Pageant of Comics & TV Teens)
Feb, 1948 - No. 19, Sept, 1953
St. John Publ. Co.

1-Part-r; reprints "Some Punkins" by Neher	16.00	47.00	110.00
2	10.00	30.00	60.00
3-10(1953): 8-Lingerie panels	7.50	22.50	45.00
11-19-Lingerie-c	6.35	19.00	38.00

NOTE: #1, 3-6, 13, 18, 19 have paper dolls.

MORBID ANGEL
Oct, 1995 ($3.00, B&W)
London Night Studios

1-Hartsoe-c		1.20	3.00

MORBID ANGEL
July, 1996 - Present ($3.00)
London Night Studios

1/2-($9.95)-Angel Tear Edition; foil logo			10.00
1			3.00
1-Penance-c			4.00

MORBID ANGEL-TO HELL AND BACK
Oct, 1996 - Present ($3.00, B&W)
London Night Studios

1			3.00

MORBIUS REVISITED
Aug, 1993 - No. 5 Dec, 1993 ($1.95, mini-series)
Marvel Comic

1-5-Reprints Fear #27-31		.80	2.00

MORBIUS: THE LIVING VAMPIRE (Also see Amazing Spider-Man #101, 102, Fear #20, Marvel Team-Up #3, 4, Midnight Sons Unl. & Vampire Tales)
Sept, 1992 - No. 32, Apr, 1995 ($1.75/$1.95)
Marvel Comics (Midnight Sons imprint #16 on)

1-($2.75, 52 pgs.)-Polybagged w/poster; Ghost Rider & Johnny Blaze x-over (part 3 of Rise of the Midnight Sons)		1.20	3.00
2-5: 3,4-Vs. Spider-Man-c/story		.80	2.00
6-11,13-20: 15-Ghost Rider app. 16-Spot varnish-c. 16,17-Siege of Darkness parts 5 &13. 18-Deathlok app.		.70	1.75
12-($2.25)-Outer-c is a Darkhold envelope made of black parchment w/gold ink; Midnight Massacre x-over		.90	2.25
21-24,26-32: 21-Begin $1.95-c; bound-in Spider-Man trading card sheet; S-M app.		.80	2.00

	GD25	FN65	NM94
25-($2.50, 52 pgs.)-Gold foil logo		1.00	2.50

MORE FUN COMICS (Formerly New Fun Comics #1-6)
No. 7, Jan, 1936 - No. 127, Nov-Dec, 1947 (No. 7,9-11: paper-c)
National Periodical Publications

	GD25	FN65	VF82
7(1/36)-Oversized, paper-c; 1 pg. Kelly-a	766.00	2300.00	4600.00
(Estimated up to 15 total copies exist, none in NM/Mint)			
8(2/36)-Oversized (10x12"), slick-c; 1 pg. Kelly-a	766.00	2300.00	4600.00
9(3-4/36)(Very rare, 1st comic-sized issue)-Last multiple panel-c	950.00	2850.00	5700.00
10,11(7/36): 10-Last Henri Duval by Siegel & Shuster. 11-1st "Calling All Cars" by Siegel & Shuster; new classic logo begins	533.00	1600.00	3200.00
12(8/36)-Slick-c begin	416.00	1250.00	2500.00
V2#1(9/36, #13)	383.00	1150.00	2300.00
2(10/36, #14)-Dr. Occult in costume (1st in color)(Superman proto-type); 1st DC appearance) continues from The Comics Magazine, ends #17	1915.00	5750.00	11,500.00
(Estimated up to 10 total copies exist, none in NM/Mint)			
V2#3(11/36, #15), 16(V2#4), 17(V2#5): 16-Cover numbering begins; Xmas-c; last Superman tryout issue	750.00	2250.00	4500.00
18-20(V2#8, 5/37)	283.00	850.00	1700.00

	GD25	FN65	NM94
21(V2#9)-24(V2#12, 9/37)	283.00	850.00	1700.00
25(V3#1, 10/37)-27(V3#3, 12/37): 27-Xmas-c	283.00	850.00	1700.00
28-30: 30-1st non-funny cover	250.00	750.00	1500.00
31-Has ad for Action #1	266.00	800.00	1600.00
32-35: 32-Last Dr. Occult	250.00	750.00	1500.00
36-40: 36-(10/38)-The Masked Ranger & sidekick Pedro begins; Ginger Snap by Bob Kane (2 pgs.; 1st-a?). 39-Xmas-c	250.00	750.00	1500.00
41-50: 41-Last Masked Ranger	191.00	575.00	1150.00
51-The Spectre app. (in costume) in one panel ad at end of Buccaneer story	733.00	2200.00	4400.00

	GD25	FN65	VF82	NM94
52-(2/40)-Origin/1st app. The Spectre (in costume splash panel only), part 1 by Bernard Baily (parts 1 & 2 written by Jerry Siegel); Spectre's costume changes color from purple & blue to green & grey; last Wing Brady	4889.00	14,667.00	29,333.00	47,000.00
(Estimated up to 60 total copies exist, 3 in NM/Mint)				
53-Origin The Spectre (in costume at end of story), part 2; Capt. Desmo begins	3000.00	9000.00	19,500.00	32,000.00
(Estimated up to 60 total copies exist, 3 in NM/Mint)				
54-The Spectre in costume; last King Carter; classic-c	867.00	2600.00	5200.00	8000.00
55-(Scarce, 5/40)-Dr. Fate begins (Intro & 1st app.); last Bulldog Martin	1222.00	3667.00	7333.00	11,500.00
(Estimated up to 100 total copies exist, 6 in NM/Mint)				

	GD25	FN65	NM94
56-Congo Bill begins (6/40), 1st app.; 1st Dr. Fate-c (classic), origin continues.	444.00	1333.00	4200.00
57,59,60	325.00	975.00	2700.00
58-Classic Spectre-c	325.00	975.00	2900.00
62-64,66: 63-Last St. Bob Neal. 64-Lance Larkin begins.	275.00	825.00	2200.00
61,65: 61-Classic Dr. Fate-c. 65-Classic Spectre-c	288.00	862.00	2400.00

	GD25	FN65	VF82	NM94
67-(5/41)-Origin (1st) Dr. Fate; last Congo Bill & Biff Bronson (C.B. continues in Action Comics #37 (6/41)	667.00	2000.00	4000.00	6300.00
(Estimated up to 105 total copies exist, 6 in NM/Mint)				

	GD25	FN65	NM94
68-70: 68-Clip Carson begins. 70-Last Lance Larkin	212.00	637.00	1700.00

	GD25	FN65	VF82	NM94
71-Origin & 1st app. Johnny Quick by Mort Weisinger (9/41); sci/fi-c	522.00	1567.00	3133.00	4900.00

Morlock 2001 #1 © ATLAS

Morningstar Special #1 © Comico

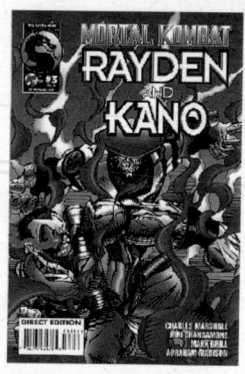

Mortal Kombat: Raydon & Kano #3 © Midway

GD25 FN65 NM94

(Estimated up to 90 total copies exist, 6 in NM/Mint)

	GD25	FN65	NM94
72-Dr. Fate's new helmet; last Sgt. Carey, Sgt. O'Malley & Captain Desmo; German submarine-c (only German war-c)	175.00	525.00	1400.00

	GD25	FN65	VF82	NM94
73-Origin & 1st app. Aquaman (11/41) & begins; intro. Green Arrow & Speedy	1111.00	3333.00	6667.00	10,500.00

(Estimated up to 85 total copies exist, 5 in NM/Mint)

	GD25	FN65	NM94
74-2nd Aquaman	231.00	693.00	1850.00
75-80: 76-Last Clip Carson; Johnny Quick (by Meskin #76-97) begins, ends #107. 80-Last large logo	200.00	600.00	1600.00
81-88: 82-1st small logo. 84-Only Japanese war-c. 87-Last Radio Squad	115.00	346.00	925.00
89-Origin Green Arrow & Speedy Team-up	131.00	393.00	1050.00
90-99: 91-1st bi-monthly issue. 93-Dover & Clover begin (1st app., 9-10/43). 97-Kubert-a. 98-Last Dr. Fate	84.00	253.00	675.00
100	115.00	346.00	925.00

	GD25	FN65	VF82	NM94
101-Origin & 1st app. Superboy (1-2/45)(not by Siegel & Shuster); last Spectre issue	711.00	2133.00	4266.00	7000.00

(Estimated up to 200 total copies exist, 9 in NM/Mint)

	GD25	FN65	NM94
102-2nd Superboy	116.00	347.00	925.00
103-3rd Superboy	88.00	262.00	700.00
104-107: 107-Last Johnny Quick & Superboy	73.00	220.00	585.00
108-120: 108-Genius Jones begins (3-4/46; cont'd from Adventure Comics #102)	19.00	56.00	130.00
121-124,126: 121-123,126-Post-c (Jimminy-c)	13.50	41.00	95.00
125-Superman on cover	66.00	197.00	525.00
127-(Scarce)-Post c/a	30.00	90.00	210.00

NOTE: All issues are scarce to rare. Cover features: The Spectre-#52-55, 57-60, 62-67. Dr. Fate-#56, 61, 68-76. The Green Arrow & Speedy-#77-85, 88-97, 99, 101 (w/Dover & Clover-#98, 103). Johnny Quick-#86, 87, 100. Dover & Clover-#102, (104, 106 w/Superboy), 107, 108(w/Genius Jones), 110, 112, 114, 117, 119. Genius Jones-#109, 111, 113, 115, 118, 120. **Baily** a-45, 52-on; c-52-55, 57-60, 62-67. **Ellsworth** c-7. **Creig Flessel** c-30, 31, 35-48(most). **Guardineer** c-47, 49, 50. **Kiefer** a-20. **Meskin** c-86, 87, 100? **Moldoff** c-51. **George Papp** c-77-85. **Post** c-121-127. **Vincent Sullivan** c-8-28, 32-34.

MORE SEYMOUR (See Seymour My Son)
Oct, 1963
Archie Publications

1	2.40	6.00	12.00

MORE TRASH FROM MAD (Annual)
1958 - No. 12, 1969
E. C. Comics

nn(1958)-8 pgs. color Mad reprint from #20	25.00	75.00	175.00
2(1959)-Market Product Labels	17.00	51.00	120.00
3(1960)-Text book covers	16.00	47.00	110.00
4(1961)-Sing Along with Mad booklet	16.00	47.00	110.00
5(1962)-Window Stickers; r/from Mad #39	11.00	33.00	75.00
6(1963)-TV Guise booklet	12.00	36.00	85.00
7(1964)-Alfred E. Neuman commemorative stamps	10.00	30.00	60.00
8(1965)-Life size poster-Alfred E. Neuman	6.70	20.00	40.00
9,10(1966-67)-Mischief Sticker	5.85	17.50	35.00
11(1968)-Campaign poster & bumper sticker	5.85	17.50	35.00
12(1969)-Pocket medals	5.85	17.50	35.00

NOTE: **Kelly Freas** c-1, 2, 4. **Mingo** c-3, 5-9, 12.

MORGAN THE PIRATE (Movie)
No. 1227, Sept-Nov, 1961
Dell Publishing Co.

Four Color 1227-Photo-c	10.00	30.00	100.00

MORLOCK 2001
Feb, 1975 - No. 3, July, 1975

Atlas/Seaboard Publ.

1,2: 1-(Super-hero)-Origin & 1st app.			1.00
3-Ditko/Wrightson-a; origin The Midnight Man & The Midnight Men			1.25

MORNINGSTAR SPECIAL
Apr, 1990 ($2.50)
Comico

1-From the Elementals; Willingham-c/a/scripts		1.00	2.50

MORRIGAN
Aug, 1993 ($2.75, B&W)
Dimension X

1-Foil stamped-c		1.10	2.75

MORTAL KOMBAT
July, 1994 - No. 6, Dec, 1994 ($2.95)
Malibu Comics

1-6: 1-Two variant covers exist		1.20	3.00
1-Limited edition gold foil embossed-c	1.00	2.00	5.00
0 (12/94), Special Edition 1 (11/94)		1.20	3.00
Tournament Edition (12/94, $3.95)		1.60	4.00
Tournament Edition II (1995, $3.95)		1.60	4.00

MORTAL KOMBAT: BARAKA
June, 1995 ($2.95, one-shot)
Malibu Comics

1		1.20	3.00

MORTAL KOMBAT: BATTLEWAVE
Feb, 1995 - No. 6, July, 1995 ($2.95)
Malibu Comics

1-6		1.20	3.00

MORTAL KOMBAT: GORO, PRINCE OF PAIN
Sept, 1994 - No. 3, Nov, 1994 ($2.95, limited series)
Malibu Comics

1-3		1.20	3.00

MORTAL KOMBAT: KITANA AND MILEENA
Aug, 1995 ($2.95, one-shot)
Malibu Comics

1		1.20	3.00

MORTAL KOMBAT: KUNG LAO
July, 1995 ($2.95, one shot)
Malibu Comics

1		1.20	3.00

MORTAL KOMBAT: RAYDON & KANO
Mar, 1995 - No. 3, May, 1995 ($2.95, limited series)
Malibu Comics

1-3		1.20	3.00

MORTAL KOMBAT: U.S. SPECIAL FORCES
Jan, 1995 - No. 2, Feb, 1995 ($3.50, limited series)
Malibu Comics

1,2		1.20	3.50

MORTIE (Mazie's Friend; also see Flat-Top)
Dec, 1952 - No. 4, June, 1953?
Magazine Publishers

1	5.85	17.50	35.00
2-4	4.00	10.00	20.00

MORTIGAN GOTH: IMMORTALIS (See Marvel Frontier Comics Unlimited)
Sept, 1993 - No. 4, Mar, 1994 ($1.95, mini-series)
Marvel Comics

1-($2.95)-Foil-c		1.20	3.00

Mort the Dead Teenager #4 © MEG

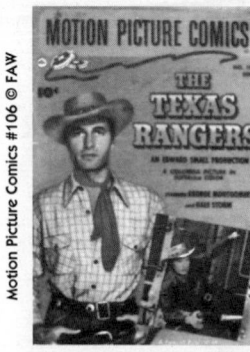

Motion Picture Comics #106 © FAW

Motorhead #3 © DH

	GD25	FN65	NM94

	GD25	FN65	NM94

2-4		.80	2.00

MORT THE DEAD TEENAGER
Nov, 1993 - No. 4, Mar, 1994 ($1.75, mini-series)
Marvel Comics

1-4		.70	1.75

MORTY MEEKLE
No. 793, May, 1957
Dell Publishing Co.

Four Color 793	3.00	9.00	30.00

MOSES & THE TEN COMMANDMENTS (See Dell Giants)

MOTHER GOOSE AND NURSERY RHYME COMICS (See Christmas With Mother Goose)
No. 41, 1944 - No. 862, Nov, 1957
Dell Publishing Co.

Four Color 41-Walt Kelly-c/a	22.00	65.00	220.00
Four Color 59, 68-Kelly c/a	19.00	57.00	190.00
Four Color 862-The Truth About..., Movie (Disney)	8.00	24.00	80.00

MOTHER OF US ALL
1950? (32 pgs.)
Catechetical Guild Giveaway

nn	1.60	4.00	8.00

MOTHER TERESA OF CALCUTTA
1984
Marvel Comics Group

1			1.25

MOTION PICTURE COMICS (See Fawcett Movie Comics)
No. 101, 1950 - No. 114, Jan, 1953 (All-photo-c)
Fawcett Publications

101- "Vanishing Westerner"; Monte Hale (1950)	29.00	88.00	205.00
102- "Code of the Silver Sage"; Rocky Lane (1/51)	27.00	81.00	190.00
103- "Covered Wagon Raid"; Rocky Lane (3/51)	27.00	81.00	190.00
104- "Vigilante Hideout"; Rocky Lane (5/51)-Book length Powell-a			
	27.00	81.00	190.00
105- "Red Badge of Courage"; Audie Murphy; Bob Powell-a (7/51)			
	33.00	99.00	230.00
106- "The Texas Rangers"; George Montgomery (9/51)			
	28.00	84.00	195.00
107- "Frisco Tornado"; Rocky Lane (11/51)	24.00	73.00	170.00
108- "Mask of the Avenger"; John Derek	17.00	51.00	120.00
109- "Rough Rider of Durango"; Rocky Lane	25.00	75.00	175.00
110- "When Worlds Collide"; George Evans-a (5/52); Williamson & Evans drew themselves in story; (also see Famous Funnies No. 72-88)			
	84.00	253.00	675.00
111- "The Vanishing Outpost"; Lash LaRue	30.00	90.00	210.00
112- "Brave Warrior"; Jon Hall & Jay Silverheels	17.00	49.00	115.00
113- "Walk East on Beacon"; George Murphy; Shaffenberger-a			
	11.50	34.00	80.00
114- "Cripple Creek"; George Montgomery (1/53)	13.00	39.00	90.00

MOTION PICTURE FUNNIES WEEKLY (Amazing Man #5 on?)
1939 (Giveaway)(B&W, 36 pgs.)
No month given; last panel in Sub-Mariner story dated 4/39
(Also see Colossus, Green Giant & Invaders No. 20)
First Funnies, Inc.

1-Origin & 1st printed app. Sub-Mariner by Bill Everett (8 pgs.); Fred Schwab-c; reprinted in Marvel Mystery #1 with color added over the craft tint which was used to shade the black & white version; Spy Ring, American Ace (reprinted in Marvel Mystery #3) app. (Rare)-only eight (8) known copies,one near mint with white pages, the rest with brown pages.
2600.00 5500.00 15,000.00

Covers only to #2-4 (set)			500.00

NOTE: The only eight known copies (with a ninth suspected) were discovered in 1974 in the estate of the deceased publisher. Covers only to issues No. 2-4 were also found which evidently were printed in advance along with #1. #1 was to be distributed only through motion picture movie houses. However, it is believed that only advanced copies were sent out and the motion picture houses not going for the idea. Possible distribution at local theaters in Boston suspected. The last panel of Sub-Mariner contains a rectangular box with "Continued Next Week" printed in it. When reprinted in Marvel Mystery, the box was left in with lettering omitted.

MOTORHEAD (See Comic's Greatest World)
Aug, 1995 - No. 6, Jan, 1996 ($2.50)
Dark Horse Comics

1-6: Bisley-c on all. 1-Predator app.		1.00	2.50
Special 1 (3/94, $3.95, 52pgs.)-Jae Lee-c; Barb Wire, The Machine & Wolf Gang app.		1.60	4.00

MOTORMOUTH (... & Killpower #7? on)
June, 1992 - No. 13, June, 1993 ($1.75)
Marvel Comics UK

1-13: 1,2-Nick Fury app. 3-Punisher-c/story. 5,6-Nick Fury & Punisher app. 6-Cable cameo. 7-9-Cable app.		.70	1.80

MOUNTAIN MEN (See Ben Bowie)

MOUSE MUSKETEERS (See M.G.M.'s...)

MOUSE ON THE MOON, THE (See Movie Classics)

MOVIE CLASSICS
Jan, 1963 - Dec, 1969
Dell Publishing Co.

(Before 1963, most movie adaptations were part of the 4-Color series)
(Disney movie adaptations after 1970 are in Walt Disney Showcase)

Around the World Under the Sea 12-030-612 (12/66)	3.60	11.00	25.00
Bambi 3(4/56)-Disney; r/4-Color #186	4.00	12.00	28.00
Battle of the Bulge 12-056-606 (6/66)	3.70	11.00	26.00
Beach Blanket Bingo 12-058-509	10.00	30.00	62.00
Bon Voyage 01-068-212 (12/62)-Disney; photo-c	4.00	12.00	28.00
Castilian, The 12-110-401	4.00	12.00	28.00
Cat, The 12-109-612 (12/66)	3.25	9.50	22.00
Cheyenne Autumn 12-112-506 (4-6/65)	7.50	22.00	52.00
Circus World, Samuel Bronston's 12-115-411; John Wayne app.; John Wayne photo-c	12.00	36.00	85.00
Countdown 12-150-710 (10/67)-James Caan photo-c	4.00	12.00	28.00
Creature, The 1 (12-142-302) (12-2/62-63)	5.70	17.00	40.00
Creature, The 12-142-410 (10/64)	3.40	10.00	24.00
David Ladd's Life Story 12-173-212 (10-12/62)-Photo-c			
	11.00	33.00	75.00
Die, Monster, Die 12-175-603 (3/66)-Photo-c	5.70	17.00	40.00
Dirty Dozen 12-180-710 (10/67)	5.30	16.00	37.00
Dr. Who & the Daleks 12-190-610 (12/66)-Peter Cushing photo-c; 1st U.S. app. of Dr. Who	13.50	41.00	95.00
Dracula 12-231-212 (10/62)-Photo-c	5.85	17.50	35.00
El Dorado 12-240-710 (10/67)-John Wayne; photo-c	16.00	47.00	115.00
Ensign Pulver 12-257-410 (8-10/64)	3.40	10.00	24.00
Frankenstein 12-283-305 (3-5/63)	4.70	14.00	33.00
Great Race, The 12-299-603 (3/66)-Natallie Wood, Tony Curtis photo-c			
	5.00	15.00	35.00
Hallelujah Trail, The 12-307-602 (2/66) (Shows 1/66 inside); Burt Lancaster, Lee Remick photo-c	5.70	17.00	40.00
Hatari 12-340-301 (1/63)-John Wayne	10.00	30.00	70.00
Horizontal Lieutenant, The 01-348-210 (10/62)	3.40	10.00	24.00
Incredible Mr. Limpet, The 12-370-408; Don Knotts photo-c			
	4.70	14.00	33.00
Jack the Giant Killer 12-374-301 (1/63)	11.00	33.00	75.00
Jason & the Argonauts 12-376-310 (8-10/63)-Photo-c			
	11.50	34.00	80.00
Lancelot & Guinevere 12-416-310 (10/63)	7.50	22.00	52.00
Lawrence 12-426-308 (8/63)-Story of Lawrence of Arabia; movie ad on back-c;			

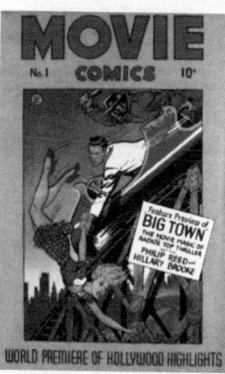

Movie Comics #1 © FH

Movie Comics #2 © FH

Movie comics #3 © FH

	GD25	FN65	NM94
not exactly like movie	7.00	21.50	50.00
Lion of Sparta 12-439-301 (1/63)	3.40	10.00	24.00
Mad Monster Party 12-460-801 (9/67)-Based on Kurtzman's screenplay			
	7.50	22.00	52.00
Magic Sword, The 01-496-209 (9/62)	7.00	21.50	50.00
Masque of the Red Death 12-490-410 (8-10/64)-Vincent Price photo-c			
	5.70	17.00	40.00
Maya 12-495-612 (12/66)-Clint Walker & Jay North part photo-c			
	5.30	16.00	37.00
McHale's Navy 12-500-412 (10-12/64)	3.70	11.00	26.00
Merrill's Marauders 12-510-301 (1/63)-Photo-c	4.00	10.00	24.00
Mouse on the Moon, The 12-530-312 (10/12/63)-Photo-c			
	3.70	11.00	26.00
Mummy, The 12-537-211 (9-11/62) 2 versions with different back-c			
	5.30	16.00	37.00
Music Man, The 12-538-301 (1/63)	3.40	10.00	24.00
Naked Prey, The 12-545-612 (12/66)-Photo-c	8.00	24.00	56.00
Night of the Grizzly, The 12-558-612 (12/66)-Photo-c	5.00	15.00	35.00
None But the Brave 12-565-506 (4-6/65)	8.00	24.00	56.00
Operation Bikini 12-597-310 (10/63)-Photo-c	4.00	12.00	28.00
Operation Crossbow 12-590-512 (10-12/65)	4.00	12.00	28.00
Prince & the Pauper, The 01-654-207 (5-7/62)-Disney			
	5.00	15.00	35.00
Raven, The 12-680-309 (9/63)-Vincent Price photo-c	5.70	17.00	40.00
Ring of Bright Water 01-701-910 (10/69) (inside shows #12-701-909)			
	5.00	15.00	35.00
Runaway, The 12-707-412 (10-12/64)	3.60	11.00	25.00
Santa Claus Conquers the Martians #? (1964)-Photo-c			
	10.00	30.00	70.00
Santa Claus Conquers the Martians 12-725-603 (3/66, 12¢)-Reprints 1964 issue; photo-c			
	8.30	25.00	58.00
Another version given away with a Golden Record, SLP 170, nn, no price (3/66)-Complete with record	19.00	56.00	130.00
Six Black Horses 12-750-301 (1/63)-Photo-c	4.00	12.00	28.00
Ski Party 12-743-511 (9-11/65)-Frankie Avalon photo-c			
	5.70	17.00	40.00
Smoky 12-746-702 (2/67)	3.40	10.00	25.00
Sons of Katie Elder 12-748-511 (9-11/65); John Wayne app.; photo-c			
	17.00	51.00	120.00
Tales of Terror 12-793-302 (2/63)-Evans-a	3.40	10.00	24.00
Three Stooges Meet Hercules 01-828-208 (8/62)-Photo-c			
	10.00	30.00	70.00
Tomb of Ligeia 12-830-506 (4-6/65)	3.40	10.00	24.00
Treasure Island 01-845-211 (7-9/62)-Disney; r/4-Color #624			
	4.00	12.00	28.00
Twice Told Tales (Nathaniel Hawthorne) 12-840-401 (11-1/63-64); Vincent Price photo-c	4.70	14.00	33.00
Two on a Guillotine 12-850-506 (4-6/65)	3.40	10.00	24.00
Valley of Gwangi 01-880-912 (12/69)	11.00	33.00	75.00
War Gods of the Deep 12-900-509 (7-9/65)	3.70	11.00	26.00
War Wagon, The 12-533-709 (9/67); John Wayne app.			
	11.00	33.00	75.00
Who's Minding the Mint? 12-924-708 (8/67)	3.40	10.00	24.00
Wolfman, The 12-922-308 (6-8/63)	3.70	11.00	26.00
Wolfman, The 1(12-922-410)(8-10/64)-2nd printing; r/#12-922-308			
	3.70	11.00	26.00
Zulu 12-950-410 (8-10/64)-Photo-c	10.00	30.00	70.00

MOVIE COMICS (See Cinema Comics Herald & Fawcett Movie Comics)

MOVIE COMICS
April, 1939 - No. 6, Sept-Oct, 1939 (Most all photo-c)
National Periodical Publications/Picture Comics

1- "Gunga Din", "Son of Frankenstein", "The Great Man Votes", "Fisherman's Wharf", & "Scouts to the Rescue" part 1; Wheelan "Minute Movies" begin	281.00	845.00	2500.00
2- "Stagecoach", "The Saint Strikes Back", "King of the Turf","Scouts to the Rescue" part 2, "Arizona Legion", Andy Devine photo-c	200.00	600.00	1600.00
3- "East Side of Heaven", "Mystery in the White Room", "Four Feathers", "Mexican Rose" with Gene Autry, "Spirit of Culver", "Many Secrets", "The Mikado"	156.00	468.00	1250.00
4- "Captain Fury", Gene Autry in "Blue Montana Skies", "Streets of N.Y." with Jackie Cooper, "Oregon Trail" part 1 with Johnny Mack Brown, "Big Town Czar" with Barton MacLane, & "Star Reporter" with Warren Hull	120.00	361.00	965.00
5- "The Man in the Iron Mask", "Five Came Back", "Wolf Call", "The Girl & the Gambler", "The House of Fear", "The Family Next Door", "Oregon Trail" part 2	133.00	399.00	1065.00
6- "The Phantom Creeps", "Chumps at Oxford", & "The Oregon Trail" part 3; 2nd Robot-c	156.00	468.00	1250.00

NOTE: Above books contain many original movie stills with dialogue from movie scripts. All issues are scarce. 2-Andy Devine photo-c.

MOVIE COMICS
Dec, 1946 - No. 4, 1947
Fiction House Magazines

1-Big Town (by Lubbers), Johnny Danger begin; Celardo-a; Mitzi of the Movies by Fran Hopper	48.00	144.00	385.00
2-(2/47)- "White Tie & Tails" with William Bendix; Mitzi of the Movies begins by Matt Baker, ends #4	39.00	118.00	275.00
3-(6/47)-Andy Hardy starring Mickey Rooney	39.00	118.00	275.00
4-Mitzi in Hollywood by Matt Baker; Merton of the Movies with Red Skelton; Yvonne DeCarlo & George Brent in "Slave Girl"	44.00	132.00	350.00

MOVIE COMICS
Oct, 1962 - Mar, 1972
Gold Key/Whitman

Alice in Wonderland 10144-503 (3/65)-Disney; partial reprint of 4-Color #331	4.00	12.00	28.00
Aristocats, The 1 (30045-103)(3/71)-Disney; with pull-out poster (25¢)			
	10.00	30.00	65.00
Bambi 1 (10087-309)(9/63)-Disney; r/4-C #186	4.00	12.00	28.00
Bambi 2 (10087-607)(7/66)-Disney; r/4-C #186	3.40	10.00	24.00
Beneath the Planet of the Apes 30044-012 (12/70)-with pull-out poster; photo-c	5.30	16.00	37.00
Big Red 10026-211 (11/62)-Disney; photo-c	3.60	11.00	25.00
Big Red 10026-503 (3/65)-Disney; reprints 10026-211; photo-c			
	3.60	11.00	25.00
Blackbeard's Ghost 10222-806 (6/68)-Disney	3.40	10.00	24.00
Bullwhip Griffin 10181-706 (6/67)-Disney; Manning-a; photo-c			
	4.70	14.00	33.00
Captain Sindbad 10077-309 (9/63)-Manning-a; photo-c			
	7.50	22.00	52.00
Chitty Chitty Bang Bang 1 (30038-902)(2/69)-with pull-out poster; Disney; photo-c	6.00	18.00	42.00
Cinderella 10152-508 (8/65)-Disney; r/4-C #786	3.40	10.00	24.00
Darby O'Gill & the Little People 10251-001(1/70)-Disney; reprints 4-Color #1024 (Toth-a); photo-c	6.00	18.00	42.00
Dumbo 1 (10090-310)(10/63)-Disney; r/4-C #668	3.40	10.00	24.00
Emil & the Detectives 10120-502 (2/65)-Disney; photo-c			
	4.30	13.00	30.00
Escapade in Florence 1 (10043-301)(1/63)-Disney; starring Annette Funicello	10.00	30.00	70.00
Fall of the Roman Empire 10118-407 (7/64); Sophia Loren photo-c			
	4.00	12.00	28.00
Fantastic Voyage 10178-702 (2/67)-Wood/Adkins-a; photo-c			
	5.70	17.00	40.00
55 Days at Peking 10081-309 (9/63)-Photo-c	4.00	12.00	28.00
Fighting Prince of Donegal, The 10193-701 (1/67)-Disney			

Movie lLove #2 © FF

Movie love #5 © FF

Movie love #13 © FF

	GD25	FN65	NM94
	3.40	10.00	24.00
First Men in the Moon 10132-503 (3/65)-Fred Fredericks-a; photo-c	3.70	11.00	26.00
Gay Purr-ee 30017-301(1/63, 84 pgs.)	5.00	15.00	35.00
Gnome Mobile, The 10207-710 (10/67)-Disney	4.30	13.00	30.00
Goodbye, Mr. Chips 10246-006 (6/70)-Peter O'Toole photo-c	4.00	12.00	28.00
Happiest Millionaire, The 10221-804 (4/68)-Disney	3.60	11.00	25.00
Hey There, It's Yogi Bear 10122-409 (9/64)-Hanna-Barbera	5.30	16.00	37.00
Horse Without a Head, The 10109-401 (1/64)-Disney	3.40	10.00	24.00
How the West Was Won 10074-307 (7/63)-Tufts-a	5.00	15.00	35.00
In Search of the Castaways 10048-303 (3/63)-Disney; Hayley Mills photo-c	8.30	25.00	58.00
Jungle Book, The (6022-801)(1/68-Whitman)-Disney; large size (10x13-1/2"); 59¢	4.30	13.00	30.00
Jungle Book, The 1 (30033-803)(3/68, 68 pgs.)-Disney; same contents as Whitman #1	3.25	9.50	22.00
Jungle Book, The 1 (6/78, $1.00 tabloid)			1.20
Jungle Book (1984)-r/Giant			1.00
Kidnapped 10080-306 (6/63)-Disney; reprints 4-Color #1101; photo-c	3.60	11.00	25.00
King Kong 30036-809(9/68-68 pgs.)-painted-c	3.40	10.00	24.00
King Kong nn-Whitman Treasury($1.00, 68 pgs.,1968), same cover as Gold Key issue	1.00	2.60	6.00
King Kong 11299(#1-786, 10x13-1/4", 68 pgs., $1.00, 1978)			1.00
Lady and the Tramp 10042-301 (1/63)-Disney; r/4-Color #629	3.70	11.00	26.00
Lady and the Tramp 1 (1967-Giant; 25¢)-Disney; reprints part of Dell #1	6.00	18.00	42.00
Lady and the Tramp 2 (10042-203)(3/72)-Disney; r/4-Color #629	2.70	8.00	19.00
Legend of Lobo, The 1 (10059-303)(3/63)-Disney; photo-c	3.60	11.00	25.00
Lt. Robin Crusoe, U.S.N. 10191-610 (10/66)-Disney; Dick Van Dyke photo-c	3.25	9.50	22.00
Lion, The 10035-301 (1/63)-Photo-c	2.70	8.00	19.00
Lord Jim 10156-509 (9/65)-Photo-c	3.60	11.00	25.00
Love Bug, The 10237-906 (6/69)-Disney; Buddy Hackett photo-c	3.40	10.00	24.00
Mary Poppins 10136-501 (1/65)-Disney; photo-c	6.00	18.00	42.00
Mary Poppins 30023-501 (1/65-68 pgs.)-Disney; photo-c	8.50	26.00	60.00
McLintock 10110-403 (3/64); John Wayne app.; John Wayne & Maureen O'Hara photo-c	16.00	47.00	110.00
Merlin Jones as the Monkey's Uncle 10115-510 (10/65)-Disney; Annette Funicello front/back photo-c	6.00	18.00	42.00
Miracle of the White Stallions, The 10065-306 (6/63)-Disney	3.70	11.00	26.00
Misadventures of Merlin Jones, The 10115-405 (5/64)-Disney; Annette Funicello photo front/back-c	6.00	18.00	42.00
Moon-Spinners, The 10124-410 (10/64)-Disney; Haley Mills photo-c	8.30	25.00	58.00
Mutiny on the Bounty 1 (10040-302)(2/63)-Marlon Brando photo-c	4.00	12.00	28.00
Nikki, Wild Dog of the North 10141-412 (12/64)-Disney; reprints 4-Color #1226	3.25	9.50	22.00
Old Yeller 10168-601 (1/66)-Disney; reprints 4-Color #869; photo-c	3.25	9.50	22.00
One Hundred & One Dalmations 1 (10247-002) (2/70)-Disney; reprints Four Color #1183	3.40	10.00	24.00
Peter Pan 1 (10086-309)(9/63)-Disney; reprints Four Color #442	4.30	13.00	30.00
Peter Pan 2 (10086-909)(9/69)-Disney; reprints Four Color #442			

	GD25	FN65	NM94
	3.25	9.50	22.00
Peter Pan 1 ('83)-r/4-Color #442			1.00
P.T. 109 10123-409 (9/64)-John F. Kennedy	5.70	17.00	40.00
Rio Conchos 10143-503(3/65)	5.30	16.00	37.00
Robin Hood 10163-506 (6/65)-Disney; reprints Four Color #413	3.40	10.00	24.00
Shaggy Dog & the Absent-Minded Professor 30032-708 (8/67-Giant, 68 pgs.)-Disney; reprints 4-Color #985,1199	6.00	18.00	42.00
Sleeping Beauty 1 (30042-009)(9/70)-Disney; reprints Four Color #973; with pull-out poster	5.70	17.00	40.00
Snow White & the Seven Dwarfs 1 (10091-310)(10/63)-Disney; reprints Four Color #382	3.40	10.00	24.00
Snow White & the Seven Dwarfs 10091-709 (9/67)-Disney; reprints Four Color #382	3.60	11.00	25.00
Snow White & the Seven Dwarfs 90091-204 (2/84)-Reprints Four Color #382			1.00
Son of Flubber 1 (10057-304)(4/63)-Disney; sequel to "The Absent-Minded Professor"	3.40	10.00	24.00
Summer Magic 10076-309 (9/63)-Disney; Hayley Mills photo-c; Manning-a	8.30	25.00	58.00
Swiss Family Robinson 10236-904 (4/69)-Disney; reprints Four Color #1156; photo-c	3.40	10.00	24.00
Sword in the Stone, The 30019-402 (2/64-Giant, 68 pgs.)-Disney (see March of Comics #258 & Wart and the Wizard	6.70	20.00	47.00
That Darn Cat 10171-602 (2/66)-Disney; Hayley Mills photo-c	7.50	22.00	52.00
Those Magnificent Men in Their Flying Machines 10162-510 (10/65); photo-c	3.40	10.00	24.00
Three Stooges in Orbit 30016-211 (11/62-Giant, 32 pgs.)-All photos from movie; stiff-photo-c	11.50	34.00	80.00
Tiger Walks, A 10117-406 (6/64)-Disney; Torres?, Tufts-a; photo-c	6.00	18.00	42.00
Toby Tyler 10142-502 (2/65)-Disney; reprints Four Color #1092; photo-c	3.40	10.00	24.00
Treasure Island 1 (10200-703)(3/67)-Disney; reprints Four Color #624; photo-c	3.25	9.50	22.00
20,000 Leagues Under the Sea 1 (10095-312)(12/63)-Disney; reprints Four Color #614	3.25	9.50	22.00
Wonderful Adventures of Pinocchio, The 1 (10089-310)(10/63)-Disney; reprints Four Color #545 (see Wonderful Advs. of...)	3.25	9.50	22.00
Wonderful Adventures of Pinocchio, The 10089-109 (9/71)-Disney; reprints Four Color #545	3.25	9.50	22.00
Wonderful World of the Brothers Grimm 1 (10008-210)(10/62)	5.00	15.00	40.00
X, the Man with the X-Ray Eyes 10083-309 (9/63)-Ray Milland photo on-c	8.30	25.00	62.00
Yellow Submarine 35000-902 (2/69-Giant, 68 pgs.)-With pull-out poster; The Beatles cartoon movie	29.00	86.00	200.00
Without poster	7.00	21.50	50.00

MOVIE LOVE (Also see Personal Love)
Feb, 1950 - No. 22, Aug, 1953
Famous Funnies

	GD25	FN65	NM94
1-Dick Powell, Evelyn Keyes, & Mickey Rooney photo-c	11.00	33.00	75.00
2-Myrna Loy photo-c	6.35	19.00	38.00
3-7,9: 6-Ricardo Montalban photo-c. 9-Gene Tierney, John Lund, Glenn Ford, & Rhonda Fleming photo-c.	5.00	15.00	30.00
8-Williamson/Frazetta-a, 6 pgs.	30.00	90.00	210.00
10-Frazetta-a, 6 pgs.	36.00	107.00	250.00
11,14-16: 14-Janet Leigh photo-c	4.25	13.00	26.00
12-Dean Martin & Jerry Lewis photo-c (12/51, pre-dates Advs. of Dean Martin & Jerry Lewis comic)	6.35	19.00	38.00
13-Ronald Reagan photo-c with 1 pg. biog.	18.00	54.00	125.00
17-Leslie Caron & Ralph Meeker photo-c; 1 pg. Frazetta ad			

Ms. Marvel #23 © MEG

Ms. Mystic #3 © Continuity

Ms. Tree #21 © Max collins & Terry Beatty

	GD25	FN65	NM94

	4.25	13.00	26.00
18-22: 19-John Derek photo-c. 21-Paul Henreid & Patricia Medina photo-c.			
22-John Payne & Coleen Gray photo-c	4.00	12.00	24.00

NOTE: Each issue has a full-length movie adaptation with photo covers.

MOVIE THRILLERS (Movie)
1949
Magazine Enterprises

1-Adaptation of "Rope of Sand" w/Burt Lancaster; Burt Lancaster photo-c	27.00	81.00	190.00

MOVIE TOWN ANIMAL ANTICS (Formerly Animal Antics; becomes Raccoon Kids #52 on)
No. 24, Jan-Feb, 1950 - No. 51, July-Aug, 1954
National Periodical Publications

24-Raccoon Kids continue	10.00	30.00	72.00
25-51	10.00	30.00	62.00

NOTE: Sheldon Mayer a-28-33, 35, 37-41, 43, 44, 47, 49-51.

MOVIE TUNES COMICS (Formerly Animated...; Frankie No. 4 on)
No. 3, Fall, 1946
Marvel Comics (MgPC)

3-Super Rabbit, Krazy Krow, Silly Seal & Ziggy Pig	10.00	30.00	68.00

MOWGLI JUNGLE BOOK
No. 487, Aug-Oct, 1953 - No. 620, Apr, 1955 (Rudyard Kipling's..)
Dell Publishing Co.

Four Color 487 (#1)	5.00	15.00	50.00
Four Color 582 (8/54), 620	4.00	12.00	40.00

MOXI
July, 1996 - Present ($3.00)
Lightning Comics

1-Flip book w/Hellina; two covers			3.00
1-($9.95)-Commemorative Edition; polybagged			10.00

MOXI'S FRIENDS...BOBBY JOE & NITRO
Sept, 1996 - Present ($2.75, B&W)
Lightning Comics

1-Regular Edition			2.75
1($9.95)-Commemorative Edition			10.00

MR. (See Mister)

MS. CYANIDE & ICE
June, 1995 - No. 1, 1995 ($2.95, B&W)
Blackout Comics

0,1		1.20	3.00

MS. MARVEL (Also see The Avengers #183)
Jan, 1977 - No. 23, Apr, 1979
Marvel Comics Group

1-1st app. Ms. Marvel; Scorpion app. in #1,2		1.60	4.00
2-Origin		1.00	2.50
3-10: 5-Vision app. 10-Last 30¢ issue		.80	2.00
11-15,19-23: 19-Capt. Marvel app. 20-New costume. 23-Vance Astro (leader of the Guardians) app.			1.50
6,17-Mystique cameo	1.65	4.20	10.00
8-1st full Mystique; Avengers x-over	2.15	6.50	15.00

NOTE: Austin c-14i, 16i, 17i, 22i. Buscema a-1-3p; c(p)-2, 4, 6, 7, 15. Infantino a-14p, 19p. Gil Kane c-8. Mooney a-4-8p, 13p, 15-18p. Starlin c-12.

MS. MYSTIC
Oct, 1982 - No. 2, Feb, 1984 ($1.00/$1.50)
Pacific Comics

1-Origin; intro Erth, Ayre, Fyre & Watr; Neal Adams-c/a/script			1.50
2 ($1.50)-N. Adams-c/a/script			1.50

MS. MYSTIC

MS. MYSTIC (continued)
V2#1, Oct, 1993 - V2#4, Jan?, 1994 ($2.50)
Continuity Comics

V2#1-4: 1-Adams-c(i)/part-i. 2-4-Embossed-c. 2-Nebres part-i. 3-Adams-c(i)/plot. 4-Adams-c(p)/plot		1.00	2.50

MS. MYSTIC DEATHWATCH 2000 (Ms. Mystic #3)
May, 1993 - No. 3, Aug, 1993 ($2.50)
Continuity

1-Bagged w/card; Adams-c & plot		1.00	2.50
2-Bagged w/card; Adams plot		1.00	2.50
3-Bagged w/card; wraparound indestructible-c by Golden/Cory; Adams plot		1.00	2.50

MS. TREE QUARTERLY/SPECIAL
Summer, 1990 -No. 10, 1992 ($3.95/$3.50, 84 pgs, mature)
DC Comics

1-Midnight story; Batman text story, Grell-a.		1.60	4.00
2-9: 2,3-Midnight stories; The Butcher text stories.		1.60	4.00
10 ($3.50)			3.50

NOTE: Cowan c-2. Grell c-1, 6. Infantino a-8.

MS. TREE'S THRILLING DETECTIVE ADVS (Ms. Tree #4 on; also see The Best of Ms. Tree)(Baxter paper #4-9)
2/83 - #9, 7/84; #10, 8/84 - #18, 5/85; #19, 6/85 - #50, 6/89
Eclipse Comics/Aardvark-Vanaheim 10-18/Renegade Press 19 on

1		1.60	4.00
2-8: 2-Scythe begins		.75	1.80
9-Last Eclipse & last color issue		.75	1.80
10-49: 10,11-2-tone; ($1.70; $2.00 #34 on)		.75	1.80
50-Contains flexi-disc ($3.95, 52pgs.)		1.60	4.00
Summer Special 1 (8/86)		1.20	3.00
1950s 3-D Crime (7/87, no glasses)-Johnny Dynamite in 3-D		1.00	2.50
Mike Mist in 3-D (8/85)-With glasses		1.20	3.00

NOTE: Miller pin-up 1-4. Johnny Dynamite-r begin #36 by Morisi.

MS. VICTORY SPECIAL (Also see Capt. Paragon & Femforce)
Jan, 1985 (nd)
Americomics

1			1.70

MUGGSY MOUSE (Also see Tick Tock Tales)
1951 - No. 3, 1951; No. 4, 1954 - No. 5, 1954; 1963
Magazine Enterprises

1(A-1 #33)	5.85	17.50	35.00
2(A-1 #36)-Racist-c	8.35	25.00	50.00
3(A-1 #39), 4(A-1 #95), 5(A-1 #99)	4.00	10.00	20.00
Super Reprint #14(1963)	1.00	2.60	6.00
I.W. Reprint #1,2 (nd)	1.00	2.60	6.00

MUGGY-DOO, BOY CAT
July, 1953 - No. 4, Jan, 1954
Stanhall Publ.

1-Funny animal; Irving Spector-a	6.70	20.00	40.00
2-4	4.70	14.00	28.00
Super Reprint #12('63), 16('64)	1.00	2.60	6.00

MULLKON EMPIRE (See John Jake's...)

MUMMY, THE (See Universal Presents... under Dell Giants & Movie Classics)

MUNDEN'S BAR ANNUAL
Apr, 1988 ($2.95, 52 pgs.)
First Comics

1-r/from Grimjack; Fish Police story		1.20	3.00

MUNSTERS, THE (TV)
Jan, 1965 - No. 16, Jan, 1968 (All photo-c)
Gold Key

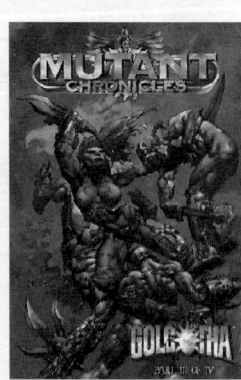
Mutant Chronicles #3 © Acclaim

Mutants Vs. Ultras #1 © MEG/ Malibu

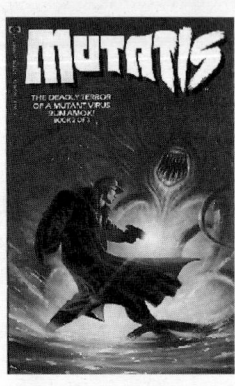
Mutatis #2 © MEG

	GD25	FN65	NM94
1 (10134-501)	19.00	57.00	190.00
2	9.00	27.00	90.00
3-5	7.00	21.00	70.00
6-16	6.00	18.00	60.00

MUPPET BABIES, THE (TV)(See Star Comics Magazine)
Aug, 1985 - No. 26, July, 1989 (Children's book)
Marvel Comics (Star Comics)/Marvel #18 on

1-13 (75¢)			.75
14-26 ($1.00)			1.00

MUPPETS TAKE MANHATTAN, THE
Nov, 1984 - No. 3, Jan, 1985
Marvel Comics (Star Comics)

1-3-Movie adapt. r-/Marvel Super Special			.60

MURCIELAGA, SHE-BAT
Jan, 1993 - No. 2, 1993 (B&W)
Heroic Publishing

1-($1.50, 28 pgs.)			1.50
2-($2.95, 36 pgs.)-Coated-c		1.20	3.00

MURDER INCORPORATED (My Private Life #16 on)
1/48 - No. 15, 12/49; (2 No.9's); 6/50 - No. 3, 8/51
Fox Feature Syndicate

1 (1st Series); 1,2 have 'For Adults Only' on-c	40.00	120.00	300.00
2-Electrocution story	32.00	96.00	225.00
3-7,9(4/49),10(5/49),11-15	17.00	51.00	120.00
8-Used in SOTI, pg. 160	19.00	58.00	135.00
9(3/49)-Possible use in SOTI, pg. 145; r/Blue Beetle #56('48)	19.00	56.00	130.00
5(#1, 6/50)(2nd Series)-Formerly My Desire #4; bondage-c.	11.50	34.00	85.00
2(8/50)-Morisi-a	11.00	33.00	75.00
3(8/51)-Used in POP, pg. 81; Rico-a; lingerie-c/panels	13.00	39.00	90.00

MURDEROUS GANGSTERS
July, 1951; No. 2, Dec, 1951 - No. 4, June, 1952
Avon Periodicals/Realistic No. 3 on

1-Pretty Boy Floyd, Leggs Diamond; 1 pg. Wood-a	39.00	118.00	275.00
2-Baby-Face Nelson; 1 pg. Wood-a; painted-c	24.00	71.00	165.00
3-Painted-c	18.00	54.00	125.00
4- "Murder by Needle" drug story; Mort Lawrence-a; Kinstler-c	24.00	71.00	165.00

MURDER TALES (Magazine)
V1#10, Nov, 1970 - V1#11, Jan, 1971 (52 pgs.)
World Famous Publications

V1#10-One pg. Frazetta ad	2.85	8.50	20.00
11-Guardineer-r; bondage-c	1.70	5.00	12.00

MUSHMOUSE AND PUNKIN PUSS (TV)
September, 1965 (Hanna-Barbera)
Gold Key

1 (10153-509)	6.50	19.50	65.00

MUSIC MAN, THE (See Movie Classics)

MUTANT CHRONICLES (Video game)
May, 1996 - No. 4, Aug, 1996 ($2.95, limited series)
Acclaim Comics (Armada)

1-4: Simon Bisley-c on all			3.00
Sourcebook (#5)			3.00

MUTANT MISADVENTURES OF CLOAK AND DAGGER, THE (Becomes
Cloak and Dagger #14 on)
Oct, 1988 - No. 19, Aug, 1991 ($1.25/$1.50)

Marvel Comics

1-8,10-18: 1-$.25-c. X-Factor app. 2-Begin $1.50-c. 9,10-Painted-c. 12-Dr. Doom app. 14-Begin new direction. 16-18-Spider-Man x-over. 18-Infinity Gauntlet x-over; Thanos cameo; Ghost Rider app.			1.5◆
9-($2.50, 52 pgs.)-The Avengers x-over		1.00	2.5◆
19-($2.50, 52 pgs.)-Origin Cloak & Dagger		1.00	2.5◆

NOTE: **Austin** a-12i; c(i)-4, 12, 13; scripts-all. **Russell** a-2i. **Williamson** a-14i-16i; c-15i.

MUTANTS & MISFITS
1987 - No. 3, 1987 ($1.95)
Silverline Comics (Solson)

1-3		.80	2.0◆

MUTANTS VS. ULTRAS
Nov, 1995 ($6.95, one-shot)
Malibu Comics (Ultraverse)

1-r/Exiles vs. X-Men, Night Man vs. Wolverine, Prime vs. Hulk	1.20	3.00	7.0◆

MUTATIS
1992 - No. 3, 1992 ($2.25, mini-series)
Marvel Comics (Epic Comics)

1-3: Painted-c		.90	2.2◆

MUTINY (Stormy Tales of the Seven Seas)
Oct, 1954 - No. 3, Feb, 1955
Aragon Magazines

1	13.00	39.00	90.0◆
2,3: 2-Capt. Mutiny. 3-Bondage-c	10.00	30.00	65.0◆

MUTINY ON THE BOUNTY (See Classics Illustrated #100 & Movie Comics)

MUTT AND JEFF (See All-American, All-Flash #18, Cicero's Cat, Comic
Cavalcade, Famous Feature Stories, The Funnies, Popular & Xmas Comics)
Summer, 1939 (nd) - No. 148, Nov, 1965
All American/National 1-103(6/58)/Dell 104(10/58)-115 (10-12/59)/
Harvey 116(2/60)-148

	GD25	FN65	NM94
1(nn)-Lost Wheels	143.00	431.00	1150.0◆
2(nn)-Charging Bull (Summer, 1940, nd; on sale 6/20/40)	78.00	234.00	625.0◆
3(nn)-Bucking Broncos (Summer, 1941, nd)	56.00	168.00	450.0◆
4(Winter, '41), 5(Summer, '42)	50.00	150.00	400.0◆
6-10	26.00	79.00	185.0◆
11-20: 20-X-Mas-c	17.00	49.00	115.0◆
21-30	12.00	36.00	85.0◆
31-50: 32-X-Mas-c	10.00	30.00	60.0◆
51-75-Last Fisher issue. 53-Last 52 pgs.	7.50	22.50	45.0◆
76-99,101-103: 76-Last precode issue(1/55)	5.35	16.00	32.0◆
100	6.35	19.00	38.0◆
104-148: 116-131-Richie Rich app.	3.25	9.50	22.0◆
...Jokes 1-3(8/60-61, Harvey)-84 pgs.; Richie Rich in all; Little Dot in #2,3	3.70	11.00	26.0◆
...New Jokes 1-4(10/63-11/65, Harvey)-68 pgs.; Richie Rich in #1-3; Stumbo in #1	2.30	6.70	16.0◆

NOTE: Most all issues by **Al Smith**. Issues from 1963 on have **Fisher** reprints. Clarification:
early issues signed by Fisher are mostly drawn by Smith.

MY BROTHERS' KEEPER
1973 (35/49¢, 36 pgs.)
Spire Christian Comics (Fleming H. Revell Co.)

nn			1.0◆

MY CONFESSIONS (My Confession #7&8; formerly Western True Crime; A
Spectacular Feature Magazine #11)
No. 7, Aug, 1949 - No. 10, Jan-Feb, 1950
Fox Feature Syndicate

7-Wood-a (10 pgs.)	16.00	47.00	110.0◆
8,9: 8-Harrison/Wood-a (19 pgs.). 9-Wood-a	14.00	43.00	100.0◆

My Date Comics #3 © HILL

My Desire Comics #31 © FOX

My Diary #2 © MEG

	GD25	FN65	NM94
10	7.50	22.50	45.00

MY DATE COMICS (Teen-age)
July, 1947 - V1No.4, Jan, 1948 (2nd Romance comic; see Young Romance)
Hillman Periodicals

1-S&K-c/a	26.00	79.00	185.00
2-4-S&K-c/a; Dan Barry-a	17.00	51.00	120.00

MY DESIRE (Formerly Jo-Jo Comics; becomes Murder, Inc. #5 on)
No. 30, Aug, 1949 - No. 4, April, 1950
Fox Feature Syndicate

30(#1)	10.00	30.00	70.00
31 (#2, 10/49),3(2/50),4	7.50	22.50	45.00
31 (Canadian edition)	5.00	15.00	30.00
32(12/49)-Wood-a	14.00	43.00	100.00

MY DIARY (Becomes My Friend Irma #3 on?)
Dec, 1949 - No. 2, Mar, 1950
Marvel Comics (A Lovers Mag.)

1,2-Photo-c	10.00	30.00	70.00

MY DOG TIGE (Buster Brown's Dog)
1957 (Giveaway)
Buster Brown Shoes

nn	4.00	11.00	22.00

MY EXPERIENCE (Formerly All Top; becomes Judy Canova #23 on)
No. 19, Sept, 1949 - No. 22, Mar, 1950
Fox Feature Syndicate

19-Wood-a	17.00	49.00	115.00
20	7.50	22.50	45.00
21-Wood-a(2)	17.00	51.00	120.00
22-Wood-a (9 pgs.)	14.00	43.00	100.00

MY FAVORITE MARTIAN (TV)
1/64; No.2, 7/64 - No. 9, 10/66 (No. 1,3-9 have photo-c)
Gold Key

1-Russ Manning-a	13.00	39.00	130.00
2	6.50	19.50	65.00
3-9	5.50	16.50	55.00

MY FRIEND IRMA (Radio/TV) (Formerly My Diary? and/or Western Life Romances?)
No. 3, June, 1950 - No. 47, Dec, 1954; No. 48, Feb, 1955
Marvel/Atlas Comics (BFP)

3-Dan DeCarlo-a in all; 52 pgs. begin, end ?	11.00	33.00	75.00
4-Kurtzman-a (10 pgs.)	13.50	41.00	95.00
5- "Egghead Doodle" by Kurtzman (4 pgs.)	10.00	30.00	70.00
6,8-10: 9-paper dolls, 1 pg; Millie app. (5 pgs.)	6.70	20.00	40.00
7-One pg. Kurtzman-a	7.00	21.00	42.00
1-23: 23-One pg. Frazetta-a	4.35	13.00	26.00
24-48	4.00	10.00	20.00

MY GIRL PEARL
2/55 - #4, 10/55; #5, 7/57 - #6, 9/57; #7, 8/60 - #11, ?/61
Atlas Comics

1-Dan DeCarlo-c/a in #1-6	10.00	30.00	70.00
2	5.85	17.50	35.00
3-6	4.00	10.00	20.00
7-11	3.20	8.00	16.00

MY GREATEST ADVENTURE (Doom Patrol on #86 on)
Jan-Feb, 1955 - No. 85, Feb, 1964
National Periodical Publications

1-Before CCA	137.00	412.00	1100.00
2	65.00	195.00	525.00
3-5	41.00	124.00	330.00

	GD25	FN65	NM94
6-10: 6-Science fiction format begins	40.00	120.00	285.00
11-15: 12-1st S.A. issue	29.00	86.00	200.00
16-18: Kirby-a in all. 18-Kirby-c	32.00	96.00	225.00
19,22-25	25.00	75.00	175.00
20,21,28-Kirby-a	29.00	86.00	200.00
26,27,29,30	18.00	54.00	125.00
31-40	14.00	43.00	100.00
41-61: 58,60,61-Toth-a; Last 10¢ issue	10.00	30.00	75.00
62-79: 77-Toth-a	5.70	17.00	42.00
80-(6/63)-Intro/origin Doom Patrol and begin series; origin & 1st app. Negative Man, Elasti-Girl & S.A. Robotman	44.00	132.00	350.00
81-85: 81,85-Toth-a	20.00	60.00	140.00

NOTE: **Anderson** a-42. **Cameron** a-24. **Colan** a-77. **Meskin** a-25, 26, 32, 39, 45, 50, 56, 57, 61, 64, 70, 73, 74, 76, 79; c-76. **Moreira** a-11, 12, 15, 17, 20, 23, 25, 27, 37, 40-43, 46, 48, 55-57, 59, 60, 62-65, 67, 69, 70; c-1-4, 7-10. **Roussos** c/a-71-73. **Wildey** a-32.

MY GREATEST THRILLS IN BASEBALL
Date? (16 pg. Giveaway)
Mission of California

nn-By Mickey Mantle	47.00	142.00	380.00

MY GREAT LOVE (Becomes Will Rogers Western #5)
Oct, 1949 - No. 4, Apr, 1950
Fox Feature Syndicate

1	10.00	30.00	70.00
2-4	6.35	19.00	38.00

MY INTIMATE AFFAIR (Inside Crime #3)
Mar, 1950 - No. 2, May, 1950
Fox Feature Syndicate

1	10.00	30.00	70.00
2	6.35	19.00	38.00

MY LIFE (Formerly Meet Corliss Archer)
No. 4, Sept, 1948 - No. 15, July, 1950
Fox Feature Syndicate

4-Used in SOTI, pg. 39; Kamen/Feldstein-a	31.00	94.00	220.00
5-Kamen-a	15.00	45.00	105.00
6-Kamen/Feldstein-a	16.00	47.00	110.00
7-Wood-a; wash cover	14.00	43.00	100.00
8,9,11-15	6.35	19.00	38.00
10-Wood-a	13.00	39.00	90.00

MY LITTLE MARGIE (TV)
July, 1954 - No. 54, Nov, 1964
Charlton Comics

1-Photo front/back-c	25.00	75.00	175.00
2-Photo front/back-c	11.50	34.00	80.00
3-7,10	7.00	21.00	42.00
8,9-Infinity-c	7.50	22.50	45.00
11-14: Part-photo-c (#13, 8/56)	6.35	19.00	38.00
15-19	3.75	11.25	28.00
20-(25¢, 100 pg. issue)	10.00	30.00	68.00
21-38-Last 10¢ issue?	4.00	12.00	24.00
39-53	2.60	7.50	18.00
54-Beatles on cover; lead story spoofs the Beatle haircut craze of the 1960's	15.00	45.00	105.00

NOTE: Doll cut-outs in 32, 33, 40, 45, 50.

MY LITTLE MARGIE'S BOY FRIENDS (TV) (Freddy V2#12 on)
Aug, 1955 - No. 11, Apr?, 1958
Charlton Comics

1-Has several Archie swipes	10.00	30.00	70.00
2	7.00	21.00	42.00
3-11	4.25	13.00	28.00

MY LITTLE MARGIE'S FASHIONS (TV)
Feb, 1959 - No. 5, Nov, 1959

My Love #2 © MEG

My Love Affair #2 © FOX

I HAD MY HOUR • MY DREADFUL SECRET • THEY SAID I WAS GUILTY

My Name is...Holocaust #5 © Milestone Media

	GD25	FN65	NM94
Charlton Comics			
1	10.00	30.00	65.00
2-5	6.70	20.00	40.00
MY LOVE (Becomes Two Gun Western #5 (11/50) on?)			
July, 1949 - No. 4, Apr, 1950 (All photo-c)			
Marvel Comics (CLDS)			
1	10.00	30.00	65.00
2,3	6.70	20.00	40.00
4-Betty Page photo-c (see Cupid #2)	24.00	73.00	170.00
MY LOVE			
Sept, 1969 - No. 39, Mar, 1976			
Marvel Comics Group			
1	1.70	5.00	12.00
2-9: 4-6-Colan-a	1.00	2.50	6.00
10-Williamson-r/My Own Romance #71; Kirby-a	1.20	2.90	7.00
11-20: 14-Morrow-c/a; Kirby/Colletta-r		1.60	4.00
21,22,24-39: 38,39-Reprints		1.50	3.00
23-Steranko-r/Our Love Story #5	1.00	2.00	5.00
Special(12/71)	1.00	2.00	5.00
NOTE: **John Buscema** a-1-7, 10, 22r(2), 24r, 25r, 29r, 34r, 36r, 37r, Spec. (r)(4); c-13, 15, 25, 27, Spec. **Colan** a-16, 22, 24r, 35r, 39r. **Colan/Everett** a-13, 15, 16, 27(r/r#13).			
MY LOVE AFFAIR (March of Crime #7 on)			
July, 1949 - No. 6, May, 1950			
Fox Feature Syndicate			
1	10.00	30.00	70.00
2	6.70	20.00	40.00
3-6-Wood-a. 5-(3/50)-Becomes Love Stories #6	13.00	39.00	90.00
MY LOVE LIFE (Formerly Zegra)			
No. 6, June, 1949 - No. 13, Aug, 1950; No. 13, Sept, 1951			
Fox Feature Syndicate			
6-Kamenish-a	11.50	34.00	80.00
7-13	6.70	20.00	40.00
13 (9/51)	5.85	17.50	35.00
MY LOVE MEMOIRS (Formerly Women Outlaws; Hunted #13 on)			
No. 9, Nov, 1949 - No. 12, May, 1950			
Fox Feature Syndicate			
9,11,12-Wood-a	12.00	36.00	85.00
10	6.70	20.00	40.00
MY LOVE SECRET (Formerly Phantom Lady; Animal Crackers #31)			
No. 24, June, 1949 - No. 30, June, 1950; No. 53, 1954			
Fox Feature Syndicate/M. S. Distr.			
24-Kamen/Feldstein-a	11.50	34.00	80.00
25-Possible caricature of Wood on-c?	7.50	22.50	45.00
26,28-Wood-a	12.00	36.00	85.00
27,29,30: 30-Photo-c	5.85	17.50	35.00
53-(Reprint, M.S. Distr.) 1954? nd given; formerly Western Thrillers; becomes			
Crimes by Women #54; photo-c	4.00	12.00	24.00
MY LOVE STORY (Hoot Gibson Western #5 on)			
Sept, 1949 - No. 4, Mar, 1950			
Fox Feature Syndicate			
1	10.00	30.00	70.00
2	6.35	19.00	38.00
3,4-Wood-a	13.00	39.00	90.00
MY LOVE STORY			
April, 1956 - No. 9, Aug, 1957			
Atlas Comics (GPS)			
1	9.15	27.50	55.00
2	4.35	13.00	26.00
3-Matt Baker-a	6.35	19.00	38.00

	GD25	FN65	NM94
4-6,8,9	4.00	12.00	24.
7-Matt Baker, Toth-a	6.35	19.00	38.
NOTE: **Brewster** a-3. **Colletta** a-1(2), 3, 4(2), 5; c-3.			
MY NAME IS CHAOS			
1992 - No. 4, 1992 ($4.95, limited series, 52 pgs.)			
DC Comics			
Book 1-4: Tom Veitch scripts; painted-c	1.00	2.00	5.0
MY NAME IS HOLOCAUST			
May, 1995 - No. 5, Sept, 1995 ($2.50, limited series)			
DC Comics			
1-5		1.00	2.5
MY ONLY LOVE			
July, 1975 - No. 9, Nov, 1976			
Charlton Comics			
1,2,4-9		1.20	3.0
3-Toth-a		1.60	4.0
MY OWN ROMANCE (Formerly My Romance; Teen-Age Romance #77 on)			
No. 4, Mar, 1949 - No. 76, July, 1960			
Marvel/Atlas (MjPC/RCM No. 4-59/ZPC No. 60-76)			
4-Photo-c	10.00	30.00	70.0
5-10: 5,6,8-10-Photo-c	5.00	15.00	30.0
11-20: 14-Powell-a	4.25	13.00	26.0
21-42: 42-Last precode (2/55)	4.00	12.00	24.0
43-54,56-60	4.00	10.00	20.0
55-Toth-a	5.00	15.00	30.
61-70,72-76	3.20	8.00	16.
71-Williamson-a	5.35	16.00	32.
NOTE: **Brewster** a-59. **Colletta** a-45(2), 48, 50, 55, 57(2), 59; c-58, 59, 61. **Everett** a-25; c-5 **Morisi** a-18. **Orlando** a-61. **Romita** a-36. **Tuska** a-10.			
MY PAL DIZZY (See Comic Books, Series I)			
MY PAST (...Confessions) (Formerly Western Thrillers)			
No. 7, Aug, 1949 - No. 11, April, 1950 (Crimes Inc. #12)			
Fox Feature Syndicate			
7	10.00	30.00	65.
8-10	6.35	19.00	38.
11-Wood-a	12.00	36.00	85.
MY PERSONAL PROBLEM			
11/55; No. 2, 2/56; No. 3, 9/56 - No. 4, 11/56; 10/57 - No. 3, 5/58			
Ajax/Farrell/Steinway Comic			
1	7.50	22.50	45.
2-4	4.25	13.00	28.
1-3('57-'58)-Steinway	4.00	12.00	24.
MY PRIVATE LIFE (Formerly Murder, Inc.; becomes Pedro #18)			
No. 16, Feb, 1950 - No. 17, April, 1950			
Fox Feature Syndicate			
16,17	9.15	27.00	55.
MYRA NORTH (See The Comics, Crackajack Funnies & Red Ryder)			
No. 3, Jan, 1940			
Dell Publishing Co.			
Four Color 3	72.00	216.00	725.
MY REAL LOVE			
No. 5, June, 1952 (Photo-c)			
Standard Comics			
5-Toth-a, 3 pgs.; Tuska, Cardy, Vern Greene-a	10.00	30.00	65.
MY ROMANCE (Becomes My Own Romance #4 on)			
Sept, 1948 - No. 3, Jan, 1949			
Marvel Comics (RCM)			
1	10.00	30.00	70.

My Secret Life #24 © CC

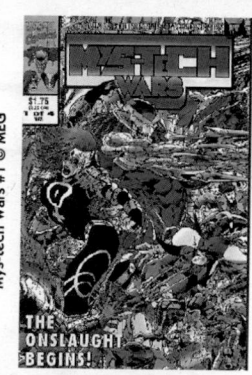
Mys-tech Wars #1 © MEG

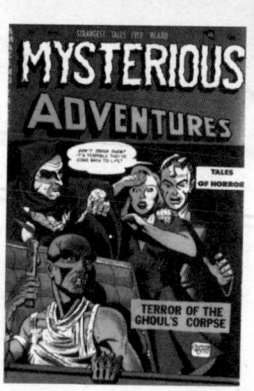
Mysterious Adventures #2 © Story Comics

MY

	GD25	FN65	NM94
2,3: 2-Anti-Wertham editorial (11/48)	6.35	19.00	38.00

MY ROMANTIC ADVENTURES (Formerly Romantic Adventures)
No. 68, 8/56 - No. 115, 12/60; No. 116, 7/61 - No. 138, 3/64
American Comics Group

	GD25	FN65	NM94
68	6.70	20.00	40.00
69-85	4.00	11.00	22.00
86-Three pg. Williamson-a (2/58)	5.85	17.50	35.00
87-100	3.00	7.50	15.00
101-138	1.50	3.75	9.00

NOTE: *Whitney art in most issues.*

MY SECRET (Becomes Our Secret #4 on)
Aug, 1949 - No. 3, Oct, 1949
Superior Comics, Ltd.

1	10.00	30.00	70.00
2,3	7.50	22.50	45.00

MY SECRET AFFAIR (Becomes Martin Kane #4)
Dec, 1949 - No. 3, April, 1950
Hero Book (Fox Feature Syndicate)

1-Harrison/Wood-a (10 pgs.)	14.00	43.00	100.00
2-Wood-a (poor)	10.00	30.00	65.00
3-Wood-a	12.00	36.00	85.00

MY SECRET CONFESSION
September, 1955
Sterling Comics

1-Sekowsky-a	6.70	20.00	40.00

MY SECRET LIFE (Formerly Western Outlaws; Romeo Tubbs #26 on)
No. 22, July, 1949 - No. 27, May, 1950
Fox Feature Syndicate

22	8.35	25.00	50.00
23,26-Wood-a, 6 pgs.	12.00	36.00	85.00
24,25,27	5.85	17.50	35.00

NOTE: *The title was changed to Romeo Tubbs after #25 even though #26 & 27 did come out.*

MY SECRET LIFE (Formerly Young Lovers; Sue & Sally Smith #48)
No. 19, Aug, 1957 - No. 47, Sept, 1962
Charlton Comics

19	3.20	8.00	16.00
20-35	1.60	4.00	8.00
36-47: 44-Last 10¢ issue	1.00	2.50	5.00

MY SECRET MARRIAGE
May, 1953 - No. 24, July, 1956
Superior Comics, Ltd.

1	9.15	27.00	55.00
2-24	4.25	13.00	26.00
	3.60	9.00	18.00
W. Reprint #9	1.00	2.00	5.00

NOTE: *Many issues contain Kamenish art.*

MY SECRET ROMANCE (Becomes A Star Presentation #3)
Jan, 1950 - No. 2, March, 1950
Hero Book (Fox Feature Syndicate)

1-Wood-a	9.15	27.00	55.00
2	12.00	36.00	85.00

MY SECRET STORY (Formerly Captain Kidd #25; Sabu #30 on)
No. 26, Oct, 1949 - No. 29, April, 1950
Fox Feature Syndicate

26	10.00	30.00	65.00
27-29	6.70	20.00	40.00

MYS-TECH WARS
Mar, 1993 - No. 4, June, 1993 ($1.75, mini-series)
Marvel Comics UK

	GD25	FN65	NM94
1-4: 1-Gatefold-c		.70	1.75

MYSTERIES (...Weird & Strange)
May, 1953 - No. 11, Jan, 1955
Superior/Dynamic Publ. (Randall Publ. Ltd.)

1	26.00	79.00	185.00
2-A-Bomb blast story	14.00	43.00	100.00
3-9,11	11.50	34.00	80.00
10-Kamenish-c/a reprinted from Strange Mysteries #2; cover is from a panel in Strange Mysteries #2	12.00	36.00	85.00

MYSTERIES OF SCOTLAND YARD (Also see A-1 Comics)
No. 121, 1954 (one shot)
Magazine Enterprises

A-1 121-Reprinted from Manhunt (5 stories)	13.00	39.00	90.00

MYSTERIES OF UNEXPLORED WORLDS (See Blue Bird) (Becomes Son of Vulcan V2#49 on)
Aug, 1956; No. 2, Jan, 1957 - No. 48, Sept, 1965
Charlton Comics

1	29.00	86.00	200.00
2-No Ditko	10.00	30.00	70.00
3,4,8,9 Ditko-a. 3-Diko c/a (4). 4-Ditko c/a (2).	19.00	58.00	135.00
5-7,10,11: 5,6-Ditko-c/a (all). 7-(2/58, 68 pgs.); Ditko-a(4). 10-Ditko-c/a(4). 11-Ditko-c/a(3); signed J. Kotdi	21.00	64.00	150.00
12,19,21-24,26-Ditko-a. 12-Ditko sty (3); Baker story "The Charm Bracelet."	14.00	43.00	100.00
13-18,20	3.75	11.25	28.00
25,27-30	2.60	7.50	18.00
31-45	1.70	5.00	12.00
46(5/65)-Son of Vulcan begins (origin/1st app.)	3.40	10.00	24.00
47,48	1.70	5.00	12.00

NOTE: *Ditko c-3-6, 10, 11, 19, 21-24. Covers to #19, 21-24 reprint story panels.*

MYSTERIOUS ADVENTURES
March, 1951 - No. 24, Mar, 1955; No. 25, Aug, 1955
Story Comics

1-All horror stories	40.00	120.00	285.00
2	21.00	64.00	150.00
3,4,6,10	18.00	54.00	125.00
5-Bondage-c	21.00	64.00	150.00
7-Daggar in eye panel	30.00	90.00	210.00
8-Eyeball story	31.00	94.00	220.00
9-Extreme violence	24.00	73.00	170.00
11(12/52)-Used in SOTI, pg. 84	24.00	73.00	170.00
12,13	21.00	64.00	150.00
14-E.C. Old Witch swipe	20.00	60.00	140.00
15-21: 18-Used in Senate Investigative report, pgs. 5,6; E.C. swipe/TFTC #35; The Coffin-Keeper & Corpse (hosts). 20-Used by Wertham in the Senate hearings. 21-Bondage/beheading-c	30.00	90.00	210.00
22- "Cinderella" parody	20.00	60.00	140.00
23-Disbrow-a (6 pgs.); E.C. swipe "The Mystery Keeper's Tale" (host) and "Mother Ghoul's Nursery Tale"	19.00	58.00	135.00
24,25	15.00	45.00	105.00

NOTE: *Tothish art by Ross Andru-#22, 23. Bache a-8. Cameron a-5-7. Harrison a-12. Hollingsworth a-3-8, 12. Schaffenberger a-24, 25. Wildey a-15, 17.*

MYSTERIOUS ISLAND
No. 1213, July-Sept, 1961
Dell Publishing Co.

Four Color 1213-Movie, photo-c	9.00	27.00	90.00

MYSTERIOUS ISLE
Nov-Jan, 1963/64 (Jules Verne)
Dell Publishing Co.

1	2.40	6.00	12.00

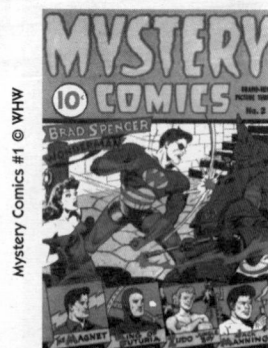
Mystery Comics #1 © WHW

Mystery In Space #116 © DC

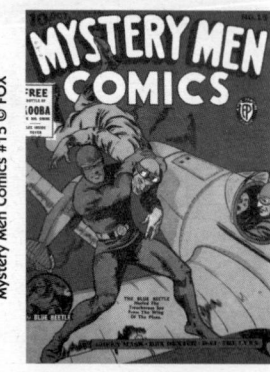
Mystery Men Comics #15 © FOX

	GD25	FN65	NM94

MYSTERIOUS RIDER, THE (See Zane Grey, 4-Color 301)

MYSTERIOUS STORIES (Formerly Horror From the Tomb #1)
No. 2, Dec-Jan, 1954-1955 - No. 7, Dec, 1955
Premier Magazines

2-Woodbridge-c; last pre-code issue	29.00	86.00	200.00
3-Woodbridge-c/a	19.00	58.00	135.00
4-7: 5-Cinderella parody. 6-Woodbridge-c	18.00	54.00	125.00

NOTE: *Hollingsworth a-2, 4.*

MYSTERIOUS SUSPENSE
Oct, 1968 (12¢)
Charlton Comics

1-Return of the Question by Ditko (c/a)	4.30	13.00	30.00

MYSTERIOUS TRAVELER (See Tales of the...)

MYSTERIOUS TRAVELER COMICS (Radio)
Nov, 1948
Trans-World Publications

1-Powell-c/a(2); Poe adaptation, "Tell Tale Heart"	47.00	141.00	375.00

MYSTERY COMICS
1944 - No. 4, 1944 (No months given)
William H. Wise & Co.

1-The Magnet, The Silver Knight, Brad Spencer, Wonderman, Dick Devins, King of Futuria, & Zudo the Jungle Boy begin (all 1st app.); Schomburg-c on all	87.00	262.00	700.00
2-Bondage-c	59.00	178.00	475.00
3-Lance Lewis, Space Detective begins (1st app.); Robot-c	52.00	157.00	420.00
4(V2#1 inside)	52.00	157.00	420.00

MYSTERY COMICS DIGEST
Mar, 1972 - No. 26, Oct, 1975
Gold Key

1-Ripley's Believe It or Not; reprint of Ripley's #1 origin Ra-Ka-Tep the Mummy; Wood-a	1.00	2.00	5.00
2-9: 2-Boris Karloff Tales of Mystery; Wood-a; 1st app. Werewolf Count Wulfstein 3-Twilight Zone (TV); Crandall, Toth & George Evans-a; 1st app. Tragg & Simbar the Lion Lord; (2) Crandall/Frazetta-r/Twilight Zone 4-Ripley's Believe It or Not; 1st app. Baron Tibor, the Vampire. 5-Boris Karloff Tales of Mystery; 1st app. Dr. Spektor. 6-Twilight Zone (TV); 1st app. U.S. Marshal Reid & Sir Duane; Evans-r. 7-Ripley's Believe It or Not; origin The Lurker in the Swamp; 1st app. Duroc. 8-Boris Karloff Tales of Mystery; McWilliams-r; Orlando-r. 9-Twilight Zone (TV); Williamson, Crandall, McWilliams-a; 2nd Tragg app.;Torres, Evans, Heck/Tuska-r	1.00		2.50
10-26: 10,13-Ripley's Believe It or Not: 13-Orlando-r. 11,14-Boris Karloff Tales of Mystery. 14-1st app. Xorkon. 12,15-Twilight Zone (TV). 16,19,22,25-Ripley's Believe It or Not. 17-Boris Karloff Tales of Mystery; Williamson-r; Orlando-r. 18,21,24-Twilight Zone (TV). 20,23,26-Boris Karloff Tales of Mystery			1.00

NOTE: *Dr. Spektor app.-#5, 10-12, 21. Durak app.-#15. Duroc app.-#14 (later called Durak). King George 1st app.-#8.*

MYSTERY IN SPACE
4-5/51 - No. 110, 9/66; No. 111, 9/80 - No. 117, 3/81 (#1-3: 52 pgs.)
National Periodical Publications

1-Frazetta-a, 8 pgs.; Knights of the Galaxy begins, ends #8	275.00	825.00	2500.00
2	118.00	356.00	950.00
3	96.00	290.00	775.00
4,5	78.00	234.00	625.00
6-10: 7-Toth-a	65.00	195.00	520.00
11-15: 13-Toth-a	45.00	135.00	360.00
16-18,20-25: Interplanetary Insurance feature by Infantino in all. 21-1st app. Space Cabbie. 24-Last pre-code issue	41.00	124.00	330.00

	GD25	FN65	NM94
19-Virgil Finlay-a	45.00	135.00	360.
26-40: 26-Space Cabbie feature begins. 34-1st S.A. issue	39.00	118.00	275.
41-52: 47-Space Cabbie feature ends	29.00	88.00	205.

	GD25	FN65	VF82	NM9
53-Adam Strange begins (8/59, 10pg. sty)	150.00	450.00	900.00	1500.

	GD25	FN65		NM9
54	44.00	132.00		385.
55-Grey tone-c	32.00	96.00		250.
56-60: 59-Kane/Anderson-a	24.00	71.00		180.
61-71: 61-1st app. Adam Strange foe Ulthoon. 62-1st app. A.S. foe Mortan. 63-Origin Vandor. 66-Star Rovers begin (1st app.). 68-1st app. Dust Devils (6/61). 69-1st Mailbag. 70-2nd app. Dust Devils.				
71-Last 10¢ issue	18.00	54.00		140.
72-74,76-80	12.00	36.00		95.
75-JLA x-over in Adam Strange (5/62)(sequel to JLA #3)	30.00	90.00		210.
81-86	8.50	26.00		65.
87-(11/63)-Adam Strange/Hawkman double feat begins; 3rd Hawkman tryout series	24.00	73.00		170.
88-Adam Strange & Hawkman stories	20.00	60.00		150
89-Adam Strange & Hawkman stories	19.00	56.00		140
90-Adam Strange & Hawkman team-up for 1st time (3/64); Hawkman moves to own title next month	22.00	66.00		160
91-103: 91-End Infantino art on Adam Strange; double-length Adam Strange story. 92-Space Ranger begins (6/64), ends #103. 92-94,96,98-Space Ranger-c. 94,98-Adam Strange/Space Ranger team-up. 102-Adam Strange ends (no Space Ranger). 103-Origin Ultra, the Multi-Alien; last Space Ranger	4.30	13.00		33
104-110: 110-(9/66)-Last 12¢ issue	2.15	6.50		15
V17#111(9/80)-117: 1.00-Newton-a(3 pgs.)	1.00	2.00		5

NOTE: *Anderson a-2, 4, 8-10, 12-17, 19, 45-48, 51, 57, 59i, 61-64, 70, 76, 87-91; c-9, 10, 15, 25, 87, 89, 105-108, 110. Aparo a-111. Austin a-112i. Bolland a-115. Craig a-114, 116. Ditko a-111, 114-116. Drucker a-13, 14. Elias a-98, 102, 103. Golden a-113p. Sid Greene a-78, 9 Infantino a-1-8, 11, 14-25, 27-46, 48, 49, 51, 53-91, 103; c-60-86, 88, 90, 91, 105, 107. Kane a-14p, 15p, 18p, 19p, 26p, 29-59p(most), 100-102; c-52, 101. Kubert a-113; c-111-115 Moriera c-27, 28. Rogers a-111. Sekowsky a-52. Simon & Kirby a-4(2 pgs.). Spiegle a-111 114. Starlin c-116. Sutton a-112. Tuska a-115p, 117p.*

MYSTERY MEN COMICS
Aug, 1939 - No. 31, Feb, 1942
Fox Features Syndicate

1-Intro. & app. The Blue Beetle, The Green Mask, Rex Dexter of Mars by Briefer, Zanzibar by Tuska, Lt. Drake, D-13-Secret Agent by Powell, Chen Chang, Wing Turner, & Captain Denny Scott	944.00	2833.00	9400
2-Robot & sci/fi-c (Wolverton; w/Movie #6)	288.00	862.00	2400
3 (10/39)-Classic Lou Fine-c	333.00	999.00	3000
4,5: 4-Capt. Savage begins (11/39)	225.00	675.00	1800
6-Tuska-c	188.00	562.00	1500
7-1st Blue Beetle-c app.	225.00	675.00	1800
8-Lou Fine-c	200.00	600.00	1600
9-The Moth begins; Lou Fine-c	100.00	300.00	800
10-12: All Joe Simon-c. 10-Wing Turner by Kirby. 11-Intro. Domino	87.00	262.00	700
13-Intro. Lynx & sidekick Blackie (8/40)	58.00	174.00	465
14-18	55.00	165.00	440
19-Intro. & 1st app. Miss X (ends #21)	57.00	172.00	460
20-31: 26-The Wraith begins	50.00	150.00	400

NOTE: *Briefer a-1-15, 20, 24; c-9. Cuidera a-22. Lou Fine c-1-5,8,9. Powell a-1-15, 24. Sim c-10-12. Tuska a-1-16, 22, 24, 27; c-6. Bondage-c 1, 3, 7, 8, 25, 27-29, 31. Blue Beetle c-7, # 10-31. D-13 Secret Agent c-6. Green Mask c-1, 3-5. Rex Dexter of Mars c-2, 9.*

MYSTERY TALES
Mar, 1952 - No. 54, Aug, 1957
Atlas Comics (20CC)

1-Horror/weird stories in all	65.00	195.00	525.

Mystic #11 © MEG

Mystique & Sabretooth #3 © MEG

The 'Nam #41 © MEG

	GD25	FN65	NM94
2-Krigstein-a	40.00	120.00	290.00
3-10: 6-A-Bomb panel. 10-Story similar to "The Assassin" from Shock SuspenStories	29.00	88.00	205.00
11,13-21: 14-Maneely s/f story. 20-Electric chair issue. 21-Matt Fox-a; decapitation story	21.00	64.00	150.00
12,22: 12-Matt Fox-a. 22-Forte/Matt Fox-c; a(i)	23.00	69.00	160.00
23-26 (2/55)-Last precode issue	17.00	51.00	120.00
27,29-35,37,38,41-43,48,49: 43-Morisi story contains Frazetta art swipes from Untamed Love	13.50	41.00	95.00
28,36,39,40,45: 28-Jack Katz-a. 36,39-Krigstein-a. 40,45-Ditko-a (#45 is 3 pgs. only)	14.00	43.00	100.00
44,46,47,51: 44,51-Williamson/Krenkel-a	15.00	45.00	105.00
46-Williamson/Krenkel-a; Crandall text illos	15.00	45.00	105.00
47-Crandall, Ditko, Powell-a	15.00	45.00	105.00
50-Torres, Morrow-a	14.00	43.00	100.00
52,53	12.00	36.00	85.00
54-Crandall, Check-a	13.50	41.00	95.00

NOTE: Ayers a-18, 49, 52. Berg a-17, 51. Colan a-1, 3, 18, 35, 43. Colletta a-18. Drucker a-41. Everett a-29, 33, 35, 41; c-8-11, 14, 38, 39, 41, 43, 44, 46, 48-51, 53. Fass a-16. Forte a-21, 22, 45, 46. Matt Fox a-127, 21, 22; c-22. Heath a-3; c-3, 15, 17, 26. Heck a-25. Kinstler a-15. Mort Lawrence a-26, 32, 34. Maneely a-1, 9, 14, 22; c-12, 23, 24, 27. Mooney a-3, 40. Morisi a-43, 49, 52. Morrow a-50. Orlando a-51. Pakula a-16. Powell a-21, 29, 37, 38, 47. Reinman a-11, 14, 17. Robinson a-7p, 42. Romita a-37. Roussos a-4, 44. R.Q. Sale a-45, 46, 49. Severin c-52. Shores a-17, 45. Tuska a-10, 12, 14. Whitney a-2. Wildey a-37.

MYSTERY TALES
1964
Super Comics

Super Reprint #16,17('64): 16-r/Tales of Horror #2. 17-r/Eerie #14(Avon)			
	1.50	3.75	9.00
Super Reprint #18-Kubert-r/Strange Terrors #4	1.50	3.75	9.00

MYSTIC (3rd Series)
March, 1951 - No. 61, Aug, 1957
Marvel/Atlas Comics (CLDS 1/CSI 2-21/OMC 22-35/CSI 35-61)

	GD25	FN65	NM94
1-Atom bomb panels; horror/weird stories in all	68.00	206.00	550.00
2	40.00	120.00	305.00
3-Eyes torn out	34.00	103.00	240.00
4- "The Devil Birds" by Wolverton (6 pgs.)	60.00	180.00	480.00
5,7-10	25.00	75.00	175.00
6- "The Eye of Doom" by Wolverton (7 pgs.)	60.00	180.00	480.00
11-20: 16-Bondage/torture c/story	22.00	66.00	155.00
21-25,27-36-Last precode (3/55). 25-E.C. swipe	17.00	49.00	115.00
26-Atomic War, severed head stories	17.00	51.00	120.00
37-51,53-57,61: 57-Story "Trapped in the Ant-Hill" (1957) is very similar to "The Man in the Ant Hill" in TTA #27	13.50	41.00	95.00
52-Wood-a; Crandall-a?	16.00	47.00	110.00
58,59-Krigstein-a	14.00	43.00	100.00
60-Williamson/Mayo-a (4 pgs.)	14.00	43.00	100.00

NOTE: Andru a-23, 49. Ayers a-35, 53; c-8. Berg a-49. Cameron a-49, 51. Check a-31, 60. Colan a-3, 7, 12, 21, 37, 60. Colletta a-29. Drucker a-46, 52, 56. Everett a-8, 9, 17, 40, 44, 57; c-13, 18, 21, 41, 47, 49, 51-55, 57-59, 61. Forte a-35, 52, 58. Fox a-24i. Al Hartley a-35. Heath a-10; c-10, 20, 22, 23, 25, 30. Infantino a-12. Kane a-8, 24p. Jack Katz a-31, 33. Mort Lawrence a-19, 37. Maneely a-22, 24, 58; c-7, 15, 28, 29, 31. Moldoff a-29. Morisi a-48, 49, 52. Morrow a-51. Orlando a-57, 61. Pakula a-52, 57, 59. Powell a-52, 54-56. Robinson a-5. Romita a-11, 15. R.Q. Sale a-35, 53, 58. Sekowsky a-1, 2, 4, 5. Severin c-56, 60. Tuska a-15. Whitney a-33. Wildey a-28, 30. Ed Win a-17, 20. Canadian reprints known-title 'Startling.'

MYSTICAL TALES
June, 1956 - No. 8, Aug, 1957
Atlas Comics (CCC 1/EPI 2-8)

1-Everett-c/a	37.00	111.00	260.00
2,4: 2-Berg-a	20.00	60.00	140.00
3,5: 3,4-Crandall-a. 5-Williamson-a (4 pgs.)	21.00	62.00	145.00
6-Torres, Krigstein-a	19.00	58.00	135.00
7-Bolle, Forte, Torres, Orlando-a	19.00	56.00	130.00
8-Krigstein, Check-a	17.00	49.00	115.00

NOTE: Everett a-1; c-1-4, 6, 7. Orlando a-1, 2, 7. Pakula a-3. Powell a-1, 4.

MYSTIC COMICS (1st Series)
March, 1940 - No. 10, Aug, 1942
Timely Comics (TPI 1-5/TCI 8-10)

	GD25	FN65	VF82	NM94
1-Origin The Blue Blaze, The Dynamic Man, & Flexo the Rubber Robot; Zephyr Jones, 3X's & Deep Sea Demon app.; The Magician begins (all 1st app.); c-from Spider pulp V18#1, 6/39	1222.00	3667.00	7333.00	12,000.00

(Estimated up to 110 total copies exist, 4 in NM/Mint)

	GD25	FN65	NM94
2-The Invisible Man & Master Mind Excello begin; Space Rangers, Zara of the Jungle, Taxi Taylor app.	338.00	1012.00	3000.00
3-Origin Hercules, who last appears in #4	262.00	788.00	2400.00
4-Origin The Thin Man & The Black Widow; Merzak the Mystic app.; last Flexo, Dynamic Man, Invisible Man & Blue Blaze (some issues have date sticker on cover; others have July w/August overprint in silver color); Roosevelt assassination-c	288.00	862.,00	2600.00
5-(3/41)-Origin The Black Marvel, The Blazing Skull, The Sub-Earth Man, Super Slave & The Terror; The Moon Man & Black Widow app.; 5-German war-c begin; and #10	262.00	788.00	2400.00
6-(10/41)-Origin The Challenger & The Destroyer (1st app.?; also see All-Winners #2, Fall, 1941)	288.00	862.0	2600.00
7-The Witness begins (12/41, origin & 1st app.); origin Davey & the Demon; last Black Widow; Hitler opens his trunk of terror-c by Simon & Kirby (classic-c)	300.00	900.00	2700.00
8,9: 9-Gary Gaunt app.; last Black Marvel, Mystic & Blazing Skull; Hitler-c	175.00	525.00	1400.00
10-Father Time, World of Wonder, & Red Skeleton app.; last Challenger & Terror	175.00	525.00	1400.00

NOTE: Gabrielle c-8-10. Kirby/Schomburg c-6. Rico a-9(2). Schomburg a-1-4; c-1-5. Sekowsky a-9. Sekowsky/Klein a-8(Challenger). Bondage c-1, 2, 9.

MYSTIC COMICS (2nd Series)
Oct, 1944 - No. 3, Win, 1944-45; No. 4, Mar, 1945
Timely Comics (ANC)

1-The Angel, The Destroyer, The Human Torch, Terry Vance the Schoolboy Sleuth, & Tommy Tyme begin	193.00	581.00	1550.00
2-(Fall/44)-Last Human Torch & Terry Vance; bondage/hypo-c	106.00	318.00	850.00
3-Last Angel (two stories) & Tommy Tyme	103.00	309.00	825.00
4-The Young Allies-c & app.; Schomburg-c	96.00	290.00	775.00

MYSTIQUE & SABRETOOTH (Sabretooth and Mystique on-c)
Dec, 1996 - No. 4, Mar, 1997 ($1.95, limited series)
Marvel Comics

1-4: Characters from X-Men			2.00

MY STORY (…True Romances in Pictures #5,6) (Formerly Zago)
No. 5, May, 1949 - No. 12, Aug, 1950
Hero Books (Fox Features Syndicate)

5-Kamen/Feldstein-a	14.00	43.00	100.00
6-8,11,12: 12-Photo-c	7.50	22.50	45.00
9,10-Wood-a	13.00	39.00	90.00

MY TRUE LOVE (Formerly Western Killers #64; Frank Buck #70 on)
No. 65, July, 1949 - No. 69, March, 1950
Fox Features Syndicate

65	10.00	30.00	65.00
66,68,69: 69-Morisi-a	7.50	22.50	45.00
67-Wood-a	13.50	41.00	95.00

NAKED PREY, THE (See Movie Classics)

'NAM, THE (See Savage Tales #1, 2nd series)
Dec, 1986 - No. 84, Sept, 1993
Marvel Comics Group

1-Golden a(p)/c begins, ends #13		1.00	2.50
1 (2nd printing)			1.00
2-7: 7 Golden-a (2 pgs.)			1.50

Namora #3 © MEG

Namor, The Sub-Mariner #12 © MEG

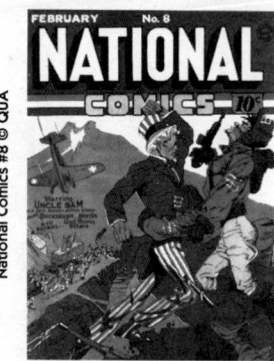
National Comics #8 © QUA

	GD25	FN65	NM94
8-51,54-64: 32-Death R. Kennedy. 58-Silver logo			1.25
52-Frank Castle (The Punisher) app.		1.00	2.50
53-Frank Castle (The Punisher) app.			1.50
52,53-Gold 2nd printings			1.25
65-74,76-84: 65-Heath-c/a; begin $1.75-c. 67-69-Punisher 3 part story.			
70-Lomax scripts begin			1.50
75-($2.25, 52 pgs.)		.90	2.25
Trade Paperback 1-r/#1-4		1.80	4.50
Trade Paperback 2-r/#5-8		1.90	4.50

'NAM MAGAZINE, THE
Aug, 1988 - No. 10, May, 1989 ($2.00, B&W, 52pgs.)
Marvel Comics

	GD25	FN65	NM94
1-10: Each issue reprints 2 of the comic		.80	2.00

NAMORA (See Marvel Mystery Comics #82 & Sub-Mariner Comics)
Fall, 1948 - No. 3, Dec, 1948
Marvel Comics (PrPI)

	GD25	FN65	NM94
1-Sub-Mariner x-over in Namora; Namora by Everett(2), Sub-Mariner by Rico (10 pgs.)	193.00	581.00	1550.00
2-The Blonde Phantom & Sub-Mariner story; Everett-a	118.00	356.00	950.00
3-(Scarce)-Sub-Mariner app.; Everett-a	118.00	356.00	950.00

NAMOR, THE SUB-MARINER (See Prince Namor & Sub-Mariner)
Apr, 1990 - No. 62, May, 1995 ($1.00/1.25/$1.50)
Marvel Comics

	GD25	FN65	NM94
1-Byrne-c/a/scripts in 1-25 (scripts only #26-32)		1.20	3.00
2-5: 5-Iron Man app.			1.50
6-11: 8,10,16-Re-intro Iron Fist (8-cameo only)			1.25
12-($1.50, 52 pgs.)-Re-intro. The Invaders		.70	1.75
13-22: 18-Punisher cameo (1 panel); 21-23,25-Wolverine cameos. 22-Last $1.00-c. 22,23-Iron Fist app.		1.00	
23-25: 24-Namor vs. Wolverine			1.00
26-New look for Namor w/new costume; 1st Jae Lee-c/a this title (5/92) & begins		1.20	3.00
27-30: 28-Iron Fist-c/story		.80	2.00
31-36,38,49: 31-Dr. Doom-c/story. 33,34-Iron Fist cameo. 35-New Tiger Shark-c/story. 48-The Thing app.		.60	1.25
37-($2.00)-Aqua holo-grafx foil-c		.90	2.25
50-($1.75, 52 pgs.)-Newsstand edition; w/bound-in S-M trading card sheet (both versions)		.70	1.75
50-($2.95, 52 pgs.)-Collector edition w/foil-c		1.20	3.00
51-62: 51-Begin $1.50-c			1.50
Annual 1 (1991, $2.00, 68 pgs.)-3 pg. origin recap		.80	2.00
Annual 2 (1992, $2.25, 68 pgs.)-Return/Defenders		.90	2.25
Annual 3 (1993, $2.95, 68 pgs.)-Bagged w/card		1.20	3.00
Annual 4 (1994, $2.95, 68 pgs.)-Painted-c		1.20	3.00

NOTE: *Jae Lee* a-26-30p, 31-37, 38p, 39, 40; c-26-40.

NANCY AND SLUGGO (See Comics On Parade & Sparkle Comics)
No. 16, 1949 - No. 23, 1954
United Features Syndicate

	GD25	FN65	NM94
16(#1)	7.50	22.50	45.00
17-23	4.25	13.00	28.00

NANCY & SLUGGO (Nancy #146-173; formerly Sparkler Comics)
No. 121, Apr, 1955 - No. 192, Oct, 1963
St. John/Dell #146-187/Gold Key #188 on

	GD25	FN65	NM94
121(4/55)(St. John)	5.85	17.50	35.00
122-145(7/57)(St. John)	4.25	13.00	26.00
146(9/57)-Peanuts begins, ends #192 (Dell)	3.80	11.40	38.00
147-161 (Dell)	3.00	9.00	30.00
162-165,177-180-John Stanley-a	7.00	21.00	70.00
166-176-Oona & Her Haunted House series; Stanley-a	8.00	24.00	80.00

	GD25	FN65	NM94
181-187(3-5/62)(Dell)	3.00	9.00	30.00
188(10/62)-192 (Gold Key)	3.00	9.00	30.00
Four Color 1034(9-11/59)-Summer Camp	3.00	9.00	30.00
(See Dell Giant #34, 45 & Dell Giants)

NANNY AND THE PROFESSOR (TV)
Aug, 1970 - No. 2, Oct, 1970 (Photo-c)
Dell Publishing Co.

	GD25	FN65	NM94
1(01-546-008), 2	3.50	10.50	35.00

NAPOLEON
No. 526, Dec, 1953
Dell Publishing Co.

	GD25	FN65	NM94
Four Color 526	2.35	7.00	23.00

NAPOLEON & SAMANTHA (See Walt Disney Showcase No. 10)

NAPOLEON & UNCLE ELBY (See Clifford McBride's...)
July, 1942 (68 pgs.) (One Shot)
Eastern Color Printing Co.

	GD25	FN65	NM94
1	36.00	107.00	250.00
1945-American Book-Strafford Press (128 pgs.) (8x10-1/2"; B&W reprints; hardcover)	13.00	39.00	90.00

NARRATIVE ILLUSTRATION, THE STORY OF THE COMICS
Summer, 1942 (32 pgs., 7-1/4"x10", B&W w/color inserts)
M.C. Gaines

	GD25	FN65	NM94
nn-16pgs. text with illustrations of ancient art, strips and comic covers; 4 pg. WWII War Bond promo, "The Minute Man Answers the Call" color comic drawn by Shelly and a special 8-page color comic insert of "The Story of Saul" from Picture Stories from the Bible #1 or soon to appear in PS #1. Insert has special title page indicating it was No. 10 of a Sunday newspaper supplement insert series that had already run in a New England "Sunday Herald." (very rare; only one known copy.) Estimated value...			1,000.00

NATHANIEL DUSK
Feb, 1984 - No. 4, May, 1984 ($1.25, mini-series, direct sales, Baxter paper)
DC Comics

	GD25	FN65	NM94
1-4: 1-Intro/origin; Gene Colan-c/a in all			1.25

NATHANIEL DUSK II
Oct, 1985 - No. 4, Jan, 1986 ($2.00, mini-series, Baxter paper)
DC Comics

	GD25	FN65	NM94
1-4: Gene Colan-c/a in all		.80	2.00

NATIONAL COMICS
July, 1940 - No. 75, Nov, 1949
Quality Comics Group

	GD25	FN65	NM94
1-Uncle Sam begins (1st app.); origin sidekick Buddy by Eisner; origin Wonder Boy & Kid Dixon; Merlin the Magician (ends #45); Cyclone, Kid Patrol, Sally O'Neil Policewoman, Pen Miller (by Klaus Nordling; ends #22), Prop Powers (ends #26), & Paul Bunyan (ends #22)	422.00	1267.00	4200.00
2	200.00	600.00	1600.00
3-Last Eisner Uncle Sam	137.00	412.00	1100.00
4-Last Cyclone	110.00	330.00	880.00
5-(11/40)-Quicksilver begins (1st app.)(3rd w/lightning speed?); origin Uncle Sam; bondage-c	125.00	375.00	1000.00
6,8-11: 8-Jack & Jill begins (ends #22). 9-Flag-c	110.00	330.00	880.00
7-Classic Lou Fine-c	137.00	412.00	1100.00
12	82.00	247.00	660.00
13-16-Lou Fine-a	73.00	221.00	590.00
17,19-22: 22-Last Pen Miller (moves to Crack #23)	55.00	165.00	440.00
18-(12/41)-Shows orientals attacking Pearl Harbor; on stands one month before actual event	96.00	290.00	775.00
23-The Unknown & Destroyer 171 begin	56.00	168.00	450.00
24-Japanese War-c	54.00	163.00	435.00
25,26,28,30: 26-Wonder Boy ends	40.00	120.00	310.00

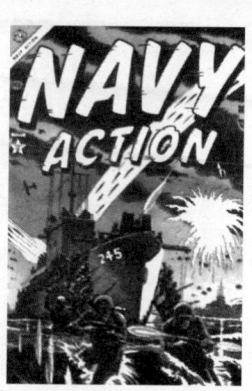
Navy Action #2 © ATLAS

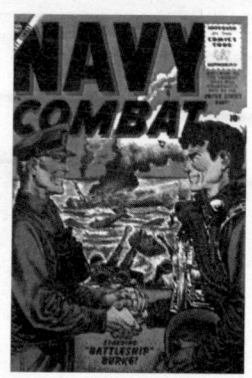
Navy Combat #6 © ATLAS

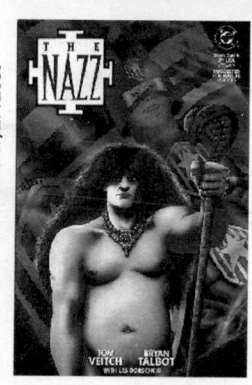
Nazz #3 © Tom Veitch & Bryan Talbot

	GD25	FN65	NM94
27-G-2 the Unknown begins (ends #46)	40.00	120.00	310.00
29-Origin The Unknown	40.00	120.00	310.00
31-33: 33-Chic Carter begins (ends #47)	44.00	132.00	350.00
34-40: 35-Last Kid Patrol. 39-Hitler-c	30.00	90.00	210.00
41-50: 42-The Barker begins (1st app?, 5/44); The Barker covers begin.			
48-Origin The Whistler	18.00	54.00	125.00
51-Sally O'Neil by Ward, 8 pgs. (12/45)	24.00	73.00	170.00
52-60	14.00	43.00	100.00
61-67: 67-Format change; Quicksilver app.	11.00	33.00	75.00
68-75: The Barker ends	9.15	27.50	55.00

NOTE: *Cole* Quicksilver-13; Barker-43; c-43, 46, 47, 49-51. *Crandall* Uncle Sam-11-13 (with *Fine*), 25, 26; c-24-26, 30-33, 43. *Crandall* Paul Bunyan-10-13. *Fine* Uncle Sam-13 (w/*Crandall*), 17, 18; c-1-14, 16, 18, 21. *Gill Fox* c-69-74. *Guardineer* Quicksilver-27, 35. *Gustavson* Quicksilver-14-26. *McWilliams* a-23-28, 55, 57. Uncle Sam c-1-41. Barker c-42-75.

NATIONAL CRUMB, THE (Magazine-Size)
August, 1975 (52 pgs.) (Satire)
Mayfair Publications

1	1.30	3.25	8.00

NATIONAL VELVET (TV)
May-July, 1961 - No. 2, March, 1963 (All photo-c)
Dell Publishing Co./Gold Key

Four Color 1195 (#1)	7.00	21.00	70.00
Four Color 1312	4.00	12.00	40.00
01-556-207, 12-556-210 (Dell)	4.00	12.00	40.00
1(12/62), 2(3/63) (Gold Key)	4.00	12.00	40.00

NATION OF SNITCHES
1990 ($4.95, color, 52 pgs.)
Piranha Press (DC)

1	1.00	2.00	5.00

NATURE BOY (Formerly Danny Blaze; Li'l Rascal Twins #6 on)
No. 3, March, 1956 - No. 5, Feb, 1957
Charlton Comics

3-Origin; Blue Beetle story; Buscema-c/a	21.00	62.00	145.00
4,5	16.00	47.00	110.00

NOTE: *John Buscema* a-3, 4p, 5; c-3. *Powell* a-4.

NATURE OF THINGS (Disney, TV/Movie)
No. 727, Sept, 1956 - No. 842, Sept, 1957
Dell Publishing Co.

Four Color 727 (#1, 842)-Jesse Marsh-a	7.00	21.00	70.00

NAUSICAA OF THE VALLEY OF WIND
1988 - No. 7, 1989; 1989 - No. 4, 1990 ($2.50-$2.95, B&W, 68pgs.)
Viz Comics

Book 1-7: ($2.50) 1-Contains Moebius poster		1.00	2.50
Part II, Book 1-3 ($2.95)		1.20	3.00
Part II, Book 4 ($3.25)		1.30	3.25

NAVY ACTION (Sailor Sweeney #12-14)
Aug, 1954 - No. 11, Apr, 1956; No. 15, 1/57 - No. 18, 8/57
Atlas Comics (CDS)

1-Powell-a	13.00	39.00	90.00
2-Lawrence-a	8.00	24.00	48.00
3-11: 4-Last precode (2/55)	5.00	15.00	30.00
15-18	4.15	12.50	25.00

NOTE: *Berg* a-7, 9. *Colan* a-8. *Drucker* a-7, 17. *Everett* a-3, 7, 16; c-16, 17. *Heath* c-1, 2, 6. *Maneely* a-7, 8, 18; c-9, 11. *Pakula* a-2, 3, 9. *Reinman* a-17.

NAVY COMBAT
June, 1955 - No. 20, Oct, 1958
Atlas Comics (MPI)

1-Torpedo Taylor begins by Don Heck	13.00	39.00	90.00
2	8.00	24.00	48.00
3-10	5.00	15.00	30.00

	GD25	FN65	NM94
11,13,15,16,18-20	4.25	13.00	28.00
12-Crandall-a	7.50	22.50	45.00
14-Torres-a	5.85	17.50	35.00
17-Williamson-a, 4 pgs.; Torres-a	6.35	19.00	38.00

NOTE: *Berg* a-10, 11. *Colan* a-11. *Drucker* a-7. *Everett* a-3, 20; c-8 & 9 w/*Tuska*, 10, 13-16. *Heck* a-11(2). *Maneely* c-1, 6, 11, 17. *Morisi* a-8. *Pakula* a-7. *Powell* a-20.

NAVY HEROES
1945
Almanac Publishing Co.

1-Heavy in propaganda	10.00	30.00	65.00

NAVY: HISTORY & TRADITION
1958 - 1961 (nn) (Giveaway)
Stokes Walesby Co./Dept. of Navy

1772-1778, 1778-1782, 1782-1817, 1817-1865, 1865-1936, 1940-1945:			
1772-1778-16 pg. in color	4.70	14.00	28.00
1861: Naval Actions of the Civil War: 1865-36 pg. in color; flag-c			
	4.70	14.00	28.00

NAVY PATROL
May, 1955 - No. 4, Nov, 1955
Key Publications

1	5.85	17.50	35.00
2-4	4.00	10.00	20.00

NAVY TALES
Jan, 1957 - No. 4, July, 1957
Atlas Comics (CDS)

1-Everett-c; Berg, Powell-a	11.00	33.00	75.00
2-Williamson/Mayo-a(5 pgs); Crandall-a	10.00	30.00	65.00
3,4-Reinman-a; Severin-c. 4-Crandall-a	9.15	27.50	55.00

NOTE: *Colan* a-4. *Maneely* c-2. *Sinnott* a-4.

NAVY TASK FORCE
Feb, 1954 - No. 8, April, 1956
Stanmor Publications/Aragon Mag. No. 4-8

1	6.35	19.00	38.00
2	4.00	10.00	20.00
3-8: #8-r/Navy Patrol #1	3.20	8.00	16.00

NAVY WAR HEROES
Jan, 1964 - No. 7, Mar-Apr, 1965
Charlton Comics

1	1.60	4.00	8.00
2-7	.60	1.50	3.00

NAZA (Stone Age Warrior)
Nov-Jan, 1963-64 - No. 9, March, 1966
Dell Publishing Co.

12-555-401 (#1)-Painted-c	2.00	6.00	20.00
2-9: 2-4-Painted-c	1.70	4.20	14.00

NAZZ, THE
1990 - No. 4, 1991 ($4.95, 52 pgs., mature)
DC Comics

1-4	1.00	2.00	5.00

NEBBS, THE (Also see Crackajack Funnies)
1941; 1945
Dell Publishing Co./Croydon Publishing Co.

Large Feature Comic 23(1941)	14.00	42.00	145.00
1(1945, 36 pgs.)-Reprints	7.50	22.50	75.00

NECROMANCER: THE GRAPHIC NOVEL
1989 ($8.95)
Marvel Comics (Epic Comics)

nn	1.50	3.75	9.00

Neil Gaiman's Mr. Hero #14 © BIG Entertainment

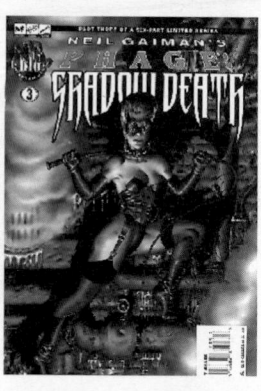

Neil Gaiman's Phage-Shadowdeath #3 © BIG Entertainment

Neil Gaiman's Wheel of Worlds #1 © BIG Entertainment

	GD25	FN65	NM94

NEGATIVE BURN
1993 - Present ($2.95, B&W, anthology)
Caliber

1,2,4-12,26-30,32-35: Anthology by various including Bolland, Burden, Doran, Gaiman, Moebius, Moore, & Pope		1.20	3.00
3-Bone story	1.65	4.20	10.00
13-Strangers in Paradise story	1.65	4.20	10.00
25,31,36,37-($3.95): 25-Gaiman, Moore & Pope		1.60	4.00

NEGRO (See All-Negro)

NEGRO HEROES (Calling All Girls, Real Heroes, & True Comics reprints)
Spring, 1947 - No. 2, Summer, 1948
Parents' Magazine Institute

1	68.00	206.00	550.00
2-Jackie Robinson-c/story	75.00	225.00	600.00

NEGRO ROMANCE (Negro Romances #4)
June, 1950 - No. 3, Oct, 1950 (All photo-c)
Fawcett Publications

1-Evans-a	96.00	290.00	775.00
2,3	75.00	225.00	600.00

NEGRO ROMANCES (Formerly Negro Romance; Romantic Secrets #5 on)
No. 4, May, 1955
Charlton Comics

4-Reprints Fawcett #2	59.00	178.00	475.00

NEIL GAIMAN'S LADY JUSTICE
Sept, 1995 - No. 11, May, 1996 ($1.95/$2.25)
Tekno Comix

1-($2.25)-Sienkiewicz-c; pin-ups		.90	2.25
1-5-($1.95): Brereton-c in all.		.80	2.00
6-11: 6-Begin $2.25-c. 7-polybagged. 11-Includes The Big Bang Pt. 7			2.25

NEIL GAIMAN'S LADY JUSTICE
V2#1, June, 1996 - Present ($2.25)
BIG Entertainment

V2#1-6: Dan Brereton-c on all. 6-Dan Brereton script			2.25

NEIL GAIMAN'S MR. HERO-THE NEWMATIC MAN
Mar, 1995 - No. 17, May, 1996 ($1.95/$2.25)
Tekno Comix

1-Intro Mr. Hero & Teknophage; bound-in game piece and trading card		.80	2.50
2-11: 4-w/Steel edition Neil Gaiman's Teknophage #1 coupon.			2.00
12-17: 12-Begin $2.25-c. 13-polybagged.		.80	2.25

NEIL GAIMAN'S MR. HERO-THE NEWMATIC MAN
V2#1, June, 1996 ($2.25)
BIG Entertainment

V2#1-Teknophage destroys Mr. Hero; includes The Big Bang Pt. 10		.80	2.25

NEIL GAIMAN'S PHAGE-SHADOWDEATH
June, 1996 - No. 6, Nov, 1996 ($2.25, limited series)
BIG Entertainment

1-6: Bryan Talbot-c & scripts in all. 1-1st app. Orlando Holmes			2.25

NEIL GAIMAN'S TEKNOPHAGE
Aug, 1995 - No. 10, Mar, 1996 ($1.95/$2.25)
Tekno Comix

1-6-Rick Veitch scripts & Bryan Talbot-c/a.			2.00
1-Steel Edition	1.00	2.00	5.00
7-10: Paul Jenkins scripts in all. 7-$2.25-c begins. 8-polybagged.			

	GD25	FN65	NM94
		.80	2.00

NEIL GAIMAN'S WHEEL OF WORLDS
Apr, 1995 - No. 1, May, 1996 ($2.95/$3.25)
Tekno Comix

0-1st app. Lady Justice; 48 pgs.; bound-in poster		1.20	3.00
0-Regular edition		.80	2.00
1 ($3.25, 5/96)-Bruce Jones scripts; Lady Justice & Teknophage app.; computer-generated photo-c.			3.25

NEIL THE HORSE (See Charlton Bullseye #2)
2/83 - No. 10, 12/84; No. 11, 4/85 - #15, 1985 (B&W)
Aardvark-Vanaheim #1-10/Renegade Press #11 on

1($1.40)		.80	2.00
1-2nd print			1.50
2-13: 13-Double size; 11,13-w/paperdolls		.80	2.00
14,15: Double size ($3.00). 15 is a flip book(2-c)		1.20	3.00

NELLIE THE NURSE (Also see Gay Comics & Joker Comics)
1945 - No. 36, Oct, 1952; 1957
Marvel/Atlas Comics (SPI/LMC)

1-(1945)	31.00	94.00	220.00
2-(Spring/46)	14.00	43.00	100.00
3,4: 3-New logo (9/46)	11.00	33.00	75.00
5-Kurtzman's "Hey Look" (3); Georgie app.	13.00	39.00	90.00
6-8,10: 7,8-Georgie app. 10-Millie app.	10.00	30.00	65.00
9-Wolverton-a (1 pg.); Mille the Model app.	10.00	30.00	70.00
11,14-16,18-Kurtzman's "Hey Look"	11.00	33.00	75.00
12- "Giggles 'n' Grins" by Kurtzman	10.00	30.00	65.00
13,17,19,20: 17-Annie Oakley app.	8.00	24.00	48.00
21-27,29,30	6.35	19.00	38.00
28-Mr. Nexdoor-r (3 pgs.) by Kurtzman/Rusty #22	7.00	21.00	42.00
31-36: 36-Post-c	5.35	16.00	32.00
1('57)-Leading Mag. (Atlas)-Everett-a, 20 pgs	7.00	21.00	42.00

NELLIE THE NURSE
No. 1304, Mar-May, 1962
Dell Publishing Co.

Four Color 1304-Stanley-a	10.00	30.00	90.00

NEMESIS THE WARLOCK (Also see Spellbinders)
Sept, 1984 - No. 7, Mar, 1985 (36 pgs, limited series)
Eagle Comics (Baxter paper)

1-7: 2000 A.D. reprints			1.50

NEMESIS THE WARLOCK
1989 - No. 10, 1990 ($1.95, B&W)
Quality Comics/Fleetway Quality #2 on

1-10		.80	2.00

NEURO JACK
Aug, 1996 - Present ($2.25)
BIG Entertainment Interactive

1-Digital art			2.25

NEUTRO
Jan, 1967
Dell Publishing Co.

1-Jack Sparling-c/a (super hero)	2.20	6.60	22.00

NEVADA (See Zane Grey's Four Color 412, 996 & Zane Grey's Stories of the West #1)

NEVER AGAIN (War stories; becomes Soldier & Marine V2#9)
Aug, 1955 - No. 2, Oct?, 1955; No. 8, July, 1956 (No #3-7)
Charlton Comics

1	6.70	20.00	40.00
2-(Becomes Fightin' Air Force #3), 8-(Formerly Foxhole?)	4.00	12.00	24.00

New Adventures of Speed Racer #6 © Golden Books

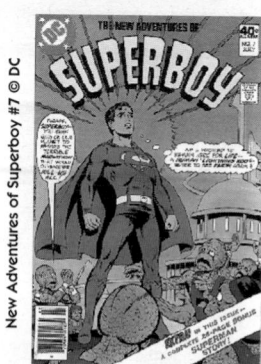
New Adventures of Superboy #7 © DC

New Force #1 © Rob Liefeld

NE

	GD25	FN65	NM94

NEW ADVENTURE COMICS (Formerly New Comics; becomes Adventure Comics #32 on; V1#12 indicia says NEW COMICS #12)
V1#12, Jan, 1937 - No. 31, Oct, 1938
National Periodical Publications

	GD25	FN65	VF82	NM94
V1#12-Federal Men by Siegel & Shuster continues; Jor-L mentioned; Whitney Ellsworth-c begin, end #14	483.00	1450.00	2900.00	–
V2#1(2/37, #13)-(Rare)	450.00	1350.00	2700.00	–
V2#2 (#14)	400.00	1200.00	2400.00	–

	GD25	FN65	NM94
15(V2#3)-20(V2#8): 15-1st Adventure logo; Creig Flessel-c begin, end #31.			
16-1st Shuster-c; 1st non-funny cover. 17-Nadir, Master of Magic begins, ends #30	400.00	1200.00	2400.00
21(V2#9),22(V2#10, 2/37): 22-X-Mas-c	366.00	1100.00	2200.00
23-31	308.00	924.00	1850.00

NEW ADVENTURE OF WALT DISNEY'S SNOW WHITE AND THE SEVEN DWARFS, A (See Snow White Bendix Giveaway)

NEW ADVENTURES OF CHARLIE CHAN, THE (TV)
May-June, 1958 - No. 6, Mar-Apr, 1959

	GD25	FN65	NM94
1 (Scarce)-Gil Kane/Sid Greene-a in all	56.00	168.00	450.00
2 (Scarce)	40.00	120.00	300.00
3-6 (Scarce)-Greene/Giella-a	36.00	107.00	250.00

NEW ADVENTURES OF HUCK FINN, THE (TV)
December, 1968 (Hanna-Barbera)
Gold Key

1- "The Curse of Thut"; part photo-c	2.40	7.20	24.00

NEW ADVENTURES OF PETER PAN (Disney)
1953 (5x7-1/4", 36 pgs.) (Admiral giveaway)
Western Publishing Co.

nn	10.00	30.00	70.00

NEW ADVENTURES OF PINOCCHIO (TV)
Oct-Dec, 1962 - No. 3, Sept-Nov, 1963
Dell Publishing Co.

12-562-212(#1)	8.50	25.50	85.00
2,3	5.50	16.50	55.00

NEW ADVENTURES OF ROBIN HOOD (See Robin Hood)

NEW ADVENTURES OF SHERLOCK HOLMES (Also see Sherlock Holmes)
No. 1169, Mar-May, 1961 - No. 1245, Nov-Jan, 1961/62
Dell Publishing Co.

Four Color 1169(#1), 1245	16.00	48.00	160.00

NEW ADVENTURES OF SPEED RACER
Dec, 1993 - No. 7, 1994? ($1.95)
Now Comics

1-7		.80	2.00
0-(Premiere)-3-D cover		1.60	4.00

NEW ADVENTURES OF SUPERBOY, THE (Also see Superboy)
Jan, 1980 - No. 54, June, 1984
DC Comics

1-54: 7-Has extra story "The Computers That Saved Metropolis" by Starlin (Radio Shack giveaway w/indicia). 11-Superboy gets new power. 14-Lex Luthor app. 15-Superboy gets new parents. 28-Dial "H" For Hero begins, ends #49. 45-47-1st app. Sunburst. 48-Begin 75¢-c. 50-Legion app.			1.00

NOTE: *Buckler* a-9p; c-36p. *Giffen* a-50; c-50. 40i. *Gil Kane* c-32p, 33p, 35, 39, 41-49. *Miller* c-51. *Starlin* a-7. Krypto back-ups in 17, 22. Superbaby in 11, 14, 19, 24.

NEW ADVENTURES OF THE PHANTOM BLOT, THE (See The Phantom Blot)

NEW AMERICA
Nov, 1987 - No. 4, Feb, 1988 ($1.75, Baxter paper)
Eclipse Comics

1-4: Scout limited series		.75	1.80

NEW ARCHIES, THE (TV)
Oct, 1987 - No. 22, May, 1990 (75¢)
Archie Comic Publications

1-22: 3-Xmas issue; 17-22 (.95-$1.00): 21-Xmas issue			1.00

NEW ARCHIES DIGEST (TV)(…Comics Digest Magazine #4?-10; …Digest Magazine #11 on)
May, 1988 - No. 14, July, 1991 ($1.35/$1.50, digest-size, quarterly)
Archie Comics

1-14: 6-Begin $1.50-c			1.50

NEW BOOK OF COMICS (Also see Big Book Of Fun)
1937; No. 2, Spring, 1938 (100 pgs. each) (Reprints)
National Periodical Publ.

	GD25	FN65	VF82	NM94
1(Rare)-1st regular size comic annual; 2nd DC annual; contains r/New Comics #1-4 & More Fun #9; r/Federal Men (8 pgs.), Henri Duval (1 pg.), & Dr. Occult in costume (1 pg.) by Siegel & Shuster; Moldoff, Sheldon Mayer (15 pgs.)-a	1833.00	5500.00	11,000.00	–
(Estimated up to 50 total copies exist, none in NM/Mint)				

	GD25	FN65	VF82	NM94
2-Contains-r/More Fun #15 & 16; r/Dr. Occult in costume (a Superman prototype), & Calling All Cars (4 pgs.) by Siegel & Shuster	916.00	2750.00	5500.00	–

NEW COMICS (New Adventure #12 on)
12/35 - No. 11, 12/36 (No. 1-6: paper cover) (No. 1-5: 84 pgs.)
National Periodical Publ.

	GD25	FN65	VF82	NM94
V1#1-Billy the Kid, Sagebrush 'n' Cactus, Jibby Jones, Needles, The Vikings, Sir Loin of Beef, Now-When I was a Boy, & other 1-2 pg. strips; 2 pgs. Kelly art(1st)-(Gulliver's Travels); Sheldon Mayer-a(1st)(2 pg. strips); Vincent Sullivan-c(1st)	2417.00	7250.00	14,500.00	–
(Estimated up to 50 total copies exist, none in NM/Mint)				
2-1st app. Federal Men by Siegel & Shuster & begins (also see The Comics Magazine #2); Mayer, Kelly-a (Rare)(1/36)	916.00	2750.00	5500.00	–
3-6: 3,4-Sheldon Mayer-a which continues in The Comics Magazine #1. 3-Vincent Sullivan-c. 4-Dickens' "A Tale of Two Cities" adaptation begins. 5-Junior Federal Men Club; Kiefer-a. 6- "She" adaptation begins	550.00	1650.00	3300.00	–
7-11: 11-Christmas-c	433.00	1300.00	2600.00	–

NOTE: #1-6 rarely occur in mint condition. *Whitney Ellsworth* c-4-11.

NEW DEFENDERS (See Defenders)

NEW DNAGENTS, THE (Formerly DNAgents)
V2#1, Oct, 1985 - V2#17, Mar, 1987 (Whole #s 25-40; Mando paper)
Eclipse Comics

V2#1-12: 1-Origin recap. 7-Begin 95 cent-c. 9,10-Airboy preview			1.00
13-17 ($1.25)			1.25
3-D 1 (1/86, $2.25)		.90	2.25
2-D 1 (1/86)-Limited ed. (100 copies)		1.60	4.00

NEWFORCE (Also see Newmen)
Jan, 1996 - No. 4, Apr, 1996 ($2.50, limited series)
Image Comics (Extreme Studios)

1-4: 1-"Extreme Destroyer" Pt. 8; polybagged w/gaming card. 4-Newforce disbands.			2.50

NEW FUN COMICS (More Fun #7 on; see Big Book of Fun Comics)
Feb, 1935 - No. 6, Oct, 1935 (10x15", No. 1-4,: slick-c)
(No. 1-5: 36 pgs; No. 6, No. 6)
National Periodical Publications

	GD25	FN65	VF82	NM94
V1#1 (1st DC comic); 1st app. Oswald The Rabbit; Jack Woods (cowboy) begins	6170.00	18,500.00	37,000.00	–

New Gods #12 © DC

New Man #4 © Rob Liefeld

THE SHADOWHUNT ENDS HERE!

New Men #21 © Rob Liefeld

	GD25	FN65	NM94

(Estimated up to 10 copies exist, 1 in VF/NM)
2(3/35)-(Very Rare) 2590.00 7750.00 15,500.00 –
(Estimated up to 5 total copies exist)
3-5(8/35): 3-Don Drake on the Planet Soro-c/story (sci/fi, 4/35). 5-Soft-c
1300.00 3900.00 7800.00 –
6(10/35)-1st Dr. Occult by Siegel & Shuster (Leger & Reuths); last "New
Fun" title. "New Comics" #1 begins in Dec. which is reason for title
change to More Fun; Henri Duval (ends #10) by Siegel & Shuster begins;
paper-c 2917.00 8750.00 17,500.00 –
(Estimated up to 10 total copies exist)

NEW FUNNIES (The Funnies #1-64; Walter Lantz...#109 on; New TV... #259,
260, 272, 273; TV Funnies #261-271)
No. 65, July, 1942 - No. 288, Mar-Apr, 1962
Dell Publishing Co. **GD25 FN65 NM94**
65(#1)-Andy Panda in a world of real people, Raggedy Ann & Andy, Oswald
the Rabbit (with Woody Woodpecker x-overs), Li'l Eight Ball & Peter Rabbit
begin 61.00 182.00 610.00
66-70: 66-Felix the Cat begins. 67-Billy & Bonnie Bee by Frank Willard
begins. 69-Kelly-a (2 pgs.); The Brownies begin (not by Kelly)
30.00 90.00 300.00
71-75: 72-Kelly illos. 75-Brownies by Kelly? 18.00 54.00 180.00
76-Andy Panda (Carl Barks & Pabian-a); Woody Woodpecker x-over in
Oswald ends 100.00 300.00 1000.00
77,78: 77-Kelly-c. 78-Andy Panda in a world with real people ends
18.00 54.00 180.00
79-81 13.00 40.00 130.00
82-Brownies by Kelly begins; Homer Pigeon begins 14.00 43.00 140.00
83-85-Brownies by Kelly in ea. 83-X-mas-c. 85-Woody Woodpecker, 1 pg.
strip begins 14.00 43.00 140.00
86-90: 87-Woody Woodpecker stories begin 10.00 30.00 100.00
91-99 6.00 18.00 60.00
100 (6/45) 7.00 21.00 70.00
101-110 4.00 12.00 40.00
111-120: 119-X-Mas-c 3.50 10.50 35.00
121-150: 131,143-X-Mas-c 3.00 9.00 30.00
151-200: 155-X-Mas-c. 168-X-Mas-c. 182-Origin & 1st app. Knothead &
Splinter. 191-X-Mas-c 2.60 7.50 18.00
201-240 1.65 4.20 10.00
241-288: 270,271-Walter Lantz c-app. 281-1st story swipes/WDC&S #100
1.20 3.00 7.00
NOTE: Early issues written by **John Stanley**.

NEW GODS, THE (New Gods #12 on)(See Adventure #459, DC Graphic Novel
#4, 1st Issue Special #13 & Super-Team Family)(1st series)
2-3/71 - V2#11, 10-11/72; V3#12, 7/77 - V3#19, 7-8/78 (Fourth World)
National Periodical Publications/DC Comics
1-Intro/1st app. Orion; 4th app. Darkseid (cameo; 3 weeks after Forever People
#1) (#1-3 are 15¢ issues) 6.50 19.50 45.00
2-Darkseid-c/story (2nd full app., 4-5/71) 3.60 11.00 25.00
3-1st app. Black Racer 2.60 7.50 18.00
4-9: (25¢, 52 pg. giants): 4-Darkseid cameo; origin Manhunter-r. 5,7,8-
Young Gods feature. 7-Darkseid app. (2-3/72); origin Orion; 1st origin of all
New Gods as a group. 9-1st app. Bug 2.00 6.00 14.00
10,11: 11-Last Kirby issue. 1.70 5.00 12.00
12-19: Darkseid storyline w/minor apps. 12-New costume Orion (see 1st Issue
Special #13 for 1st new costume). 19-Story continued in Adventure Comics
#459,460 1.20 3.00 7.00
NOTE: #4-9(25¢, 52 pgs.) contain Manhunter-r by **Simon & Kirby** from Adventure #73, 74, 75,
76, 77, 78 with covers in that order. **Adkins** i-12-14, 17-19. **Buckler** a(p)-15. **Kirby** c/a-1-11p.
Newton a(p)-12-14, 16-19. **Starlin** c-17. **Staton** c-19p.

NEW GODS (Also see DC Graphic Novel #4)
May, 1984 - No. 6, Nov, 1984 ($2.00, Baxter paper)
DC Comics
1-6: 1-5: New Kirby-c; r/New Gods #1-10. 6-Reprints New Gods #11 w/48 pgs

of new Kirby story & art; leads into DC Graphic Novel #4
.90 2.25

NEW GODS (2nd Series)
Feb, 1989 - No. 28, Aug, 1991 ($1.50)
DC Comics
1-28 1.50

NEW GODS (3rd Series) (Also see Showcase '94 #1 & Showcase '95 #7)
Oct, 1995 - No. 15, Feb, 1997 ($1.95)
DC Comics
1-11,13-15: 9-Giffen-a(p). 10,11-Superman app. 13-Takion, Mr. Miracle & Big
Barda app. 13-15-Byrne-c/a/scripts & Simonson-c .80 2.00
12-(11/96, 99¢)-Byrne-a(p)/scripts & Simonson-c begin; Takion cameo; indicia
reads October 1996 1.00

NEW GUARDIANS, THE
Sept, 1988 - No. 12, Sept, 1989 ($1.25)
DC Comics
1-($2.00, 52pgs)-Staton-c/a in #1-9 .80 2.00
2-12 1.25

NEW HEROIC (See Heroic)

NEW JUSTICE MACHINE, THE (Also see The Justice Machine)
1989 - No. 3, 1989 ($1.95, limited series)
Innovation Publishing
1-3 .80 2.00

NEW KIDS ON THE BLOCK, THE (Also see Richie Rich and...)
Dec, 1990 -1991 ($1.25)
Harvey Comics
1-5 1.25
...Backstage Pass 1 (12/90, $1.25) - 5 1.25
Chillin' 1 (12/90, $1.25) - 5: 1-Photo-c 1.25
Comics Tour '90/91 1 (12/90, $1.25) - 5 1.25
Hanging Tough 1 (2/91, $1.25) - 3 1.25
Live 1 (2/91, $1.25) - 3 1.25
Magic Summer Tour 1 (Fall/90, $1.25, one-shot) 1.25
Step By Step 1 (Fall/90, $1.25, one-shot) 1.25
Valentine Girl 1 (Fall/90, $1.25, one-shot)-Photo-c 1.25

NEWMAN
Jan, 1996 - No. 4, Apr, 1996 ($2.50, limited series)
Image Comics (Extreme Studios)
1-4: 1-Extreme Destroyer Pt. 3; polybagged w/card. 4-Shadowhunt tie-in;
Eddie Collins becomes new Shadowhawk 2.50

NEWMEN (Also see Newforce)
Apr, 1994 - No. 20, Nov, 1995; No. 21, Nov, 1996 ($1.95/$2.50)
Image Comics (Extreme Studios)
1-5: Matsuda-c/a. 1-Liefeld/Matsuda plot .80 2.00
6-21: 6 (9/94)-Begin $2.50-c. 10-Polybagged w/trading card. 11-Polybagged.
20-Variant-c; Babewatch! x-over. 21-(11/96)-Series relaunch; Chris
Sprouse-a begins; pin-up 1.00 2.50
16-Quesada & Palmiotti variant-c 1.20 3.00

NEW MEN OF BATTLE, THE
1949 (nn) (Carboard-c)
Catechetical Guild
nn(V8#1-3,5,6)-192 pgs.; contains 5 issues of Topix rebound
4.70 14.00 28.00
nn(V8#7-V8#11)-160 pgs.; contains 5 iss. of Topix 4.70 14.00 28.00

NEW MUTANTS, THE (See Marvel Graphic Novel #4 for 1st app.)(Also see
X-Force & Uncanny X-Men #167)
Mar, 1983 - No. 100, Apr, 1991
Marvel Comics Group

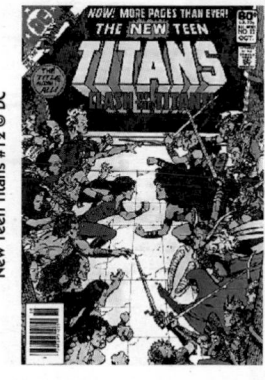

New Nexus #4 © Mike Baron & Steve Rude

New Mutants #99 © MEG

New Shadowhawk #5 © Jim Valentino

New Teen Titans #12 © DC

NE

	GD25	FN65	NM94

NEW YORK GI

NEW YORK ST
PUBLICATION
1951, 1955
N.Y. State Legi

This document wa
numerous repros fi
1955 version (196

NEW YORK WO
1939, 1940 (100
National Periodi

1939-Scoop Sc
Zatara, Slam
app. The Sa
Sullivan-c; c

(E

1940-Batman, H
(by Creig Fle
appear togeth

NOTE: The 1939 e
25¢, and was first s
copies were adverti
price was dropped t
Superman #1 or a t
price. Four variation
and was priced at 15

NEW YORK: YE
July, 1988 - No. 4
Eclipse Comics

1-4

NEXT MAN
Mar, 1985 - No. 3
Comico

1-5

NEXT MEN (See J

NEXT NEXUS, TH
an, 1989 - No. 4,
First Comics

1-4: Mike Baron s

NEXUS (See First
une, 1981 - No. 6
Direct sales only,
Capital Comics/Firs

1-B&W version; m
1-B&W 1981 limit
except this vers
Rude
2-B&W, magazine
3-B&W, magazine

2#1-Color version
2-80: 2-Nexus
$2.25-c
NOTE: Bissette c-V2#
OTE: Portacio a(i)-
ide c-3(B&W), V2#1
Simonson
2#37, 38, 43, 44, 51

NEXUS: ALIEN JU
ec., 1992 - No. 3,
ark Horse Comics

1	1.20	3.00	7.00
2,3; 3,4-Ties into X-Men #167		1.60	4.00
4-10: 10-1st app. Magma		1.20	3.00
11-17,19,20: 13-Kitty Pryde app. 16-1st app. Warpath (w/out costume); see			
X-Men #193		1.00	2.50
18-Intro. new Warlock	1.00	2.00	5.00
21-Double size; origin new Warlock; newsstand version has cover price			
written in by Sienkiewicz	1.00	2.00	5.00
22-24,29,30: 23-25-Cloak & Dagger app.		1.00	2.50
25-Legion app. (cameo)	1.30	3.25	8.00
26-1st full Legion app.	1.30	3.25	8.00
27,28	1.00	2.00	5.00
31-58: 35-Magneto intro'd as new headmaster. 43-Portacio-i. 50-Double size.			
58-Contains pull-out mutant registration form		.80	2.00
59-Fall of The Mutants begins, ends #61		1.40	3.50
60-($1.25, 52 pgs.)		1.00	2.50
61-Fall of The Mutants ends		.80	2.00
62,64-72,74-85: 68-Intro Spyder. 76-X-Factor & X-Terminator app. 85-			
Liefeld-c begin			1.25
63-X-Men & Wolverine clones app.; begin $1.00-c		1.40	3.50
73-($1.50, 52 pgs.)		.80	2.00
86-Rob Liefeld begins; McFarlane-c(i) swiped from Ditko splash pg.;			
Cable cameo (last page teaser)	2.15	6.50	15.00
87-1st full app. Cable (3/90)	4.50	13.00	35.00
87-2nd printing; gold metallic ink-c ($1.00)		.80	2.00
88-2nd app. Cable	2.10	6.40	15.00
89-3rd app. Cable	1.70	5.00	12.00
90,91: 90-New costumes. 90,91-Sabretooth app.	1.65	4.70	11.00
92-No Liefeld-a; Liefeld-c	1.00	2.00	5.00
93,94-Cable vs. Wolverine	1.50	3.75	9.00
95-97-X-Tinction Agenda x-over. 95-Death of new Warlock. 97-Wolverine &			
Cable-c, but no app.	1.30	3.25	8.00
95-Gold 2nd printing		1.00	2.50
98-1st app. Deadpool, Gideon & Domino (2/91); 2nd Shatterstar (cameo)			
	2.15	6.50	15.00
99-1st app. of Feral (of X-Force); Byrne-c/swipe (X-Men, 1st Series #138)			
	1.20	2.90	7.00
100-($1.50, 52 pgs.)-1st app. X-Force (cameo)		1.20	3.00
100-Gold 2nd printing		1.20	3.00
100-Silver ink 3rd printing			1.50
Annual 1 (1984)		1.20	3.00
Annual 2 (1986, $1.25)-1st Psylocke	2.15	6.50	15.00
Annual 3 (1987, $1.25)		.80	2.00
Annual 4 (1988, $1.75)-Evolutionary War x-over		.80	2.00
Annual 5 (1989, $2.00, 68 pgs.)-Atlantis Attacks; 1st Liefeld-a on New Mutants			
	1.65	4.20	10.00
Annual 6 (1990, $2.00, 68 pgs.)-1st new costumes by Liefeld (3 pgs.); 1st			
app. (cameo) Shatterstar (of X-Force)	.40	1.00	2.00
Annual 7 (1991, $2.00, 68 pgs.)-Liefeld pin-up only; X-Terminators back-up			
story; 2nd app. X-Force (continued in New Warriors Annual #1)			
	.40	1.00	2.00
Special 1-Special Edition ('85, 68 pgs.)-Ties in w/X-Men Alpha Flight limited			
series; cont'd in X-Men Annual #9; Art Adams/Austin-a			
	1.00	2.00	5.00
Summer Special 1(Sum/90, $2.95, 84 pgs.)		1.20	3.00

NOTE: Art Adams c-38, 39. Austin c-57i. Byrne c/a-75p. Liefeld a-86-91p, 93-96p, 98-100p, Annual 5p, 6(3 pgs.); c-85-91p, 92, 93p, 94, 95, 96p, 97-100, Annual 5, 6p. McFarlane c-85-89i, Portacio a(i)-43. Russell a-48i. Sienkiewicz a-18-31, 35-38i; c-17-31, 35i, 37i, Annual 1. B. Smith c-36, 40-48. Williamson a(i)-69, 71-73, 78-80, 82, 83; c(i)-69, 72, 73i, 78i.

NEW ORDER, THE
Nov, 1994 ($2.95)
FCFD Publishing

1		1.20	3.00

NEW PEOPLE, THE (TV)
Jan, 1970 - No. 2, May, 1970
Dell Publishing Co.

1,2	1.70	5.00	12.00

NEW ROMANCES
No. 5, May, 1951 - No. 21, Apr?, 1954
Standard Comics

5-Photo-c	10.00	30.00	60.00
6-9: 6-Barbara Bel Geddes, Richard Basehart "Fourteen Hours" photo-c.			
7-Ray Milland & Joan Fontaine photo-c. 9-Photo-c from '50s movie			
	5.35	16.00	32.00
10,14,16,17-Toth-a	6.70	20.00	40.00
11-Toth-a; Liz Taylor, Montgomery Cliff photo-c	11.50	34.00	80.00
12,13,15,18-21	4.00	12.00	24.00

NOTE: Celardo a-9. Moreira a-6. Tuska a-7, 20. Photo c-5-16.

NEW SHADOWHAWK, THE (Also see Shadowhawk & Shadowhunt)
June, 1995 - No. 7, Mar, 1996 ($2.50)
Image Comics (Shadowline Ink)

1-7: Kurt Busiek scripts in all		1.00	2.50

NEW STATESMEN, THE
1989 - No. 5, 1990 ($3.95, limited series, mature readers, 52pgs.)
Fleetway Publications (Quality Comics)

1-5: Futuristic; squarebound; 3-Photo-c		1.60	4.00

NEWSTRALIA
July, 1989 - No. 5, 1989 ($1.75, color)(#2 on, $2.25,, B&W)
Innovation Publishing

1,2: Timothy Truman-c/a; Gustovich-a		.80	2.00
3-5 ($2.25, B&W)		.90	2.25

NEW TALENT SHOWCASE (Talent Showcase #16 on)
Jan, 1984 - No. 19, Oct, 1985 (Direct sales only)
DC Comics

1-10: Features new strips & artists			.70
11-19 ($1.25): 18-Williamson-c(i)			1.25

NEW TEEN TITANS, THE (See DC Comics Presents 26, Marvel and DC
Present & Teen Titans; Tales of the Teen Titans #41 on)
Nov, 1980 - No. 40, Mar, 1984
DC Comics

1-Robin, Kid Flash, Wonder Girl, The Changeling (1st app.), Starfire, The			
Raven, Cyborg begin; partial origin	1.65	4.20	10.00
2-1st app. Deathstroke the Terminator	1.65	4.20	10.00
3-9: 3-Origin Starfire; Intro The Fearsome Five. 4-Origin continues; J.L.A. app.			
6-Origin Raven. 7-Cyborg origin. 8-Origin Kid Flash retold. 9-Minor cameo			
Deathstroke on last pg.		1.60	4.00
10-2nd app. Deathstroke the Terminator (see Marvel & DC Present for 3rd			
app.); origin Changeling retold	1.30	3.30	8.00
11-20: 13-Return of Madame Rouge & Capt. Zahl; Robotman revived. 14-			
Return of Mento; origin Doom Patrol. 15-Death of Madame Rouge & Capt.			
Zahl; intro. new Brotherhood of Evil. 16-1st app. Captain Carrot (free 16 pg.			
preview). 18-Return of Starfire. 19-Hawkman teams-up			
			1.50
21-30: 21-Intro Night Force in free 16 pg. insert; intro Brother Blood. 23-1st			
app. Vigilante (not in costume), & Blackfire. 24-Omega Men app. 25-Omega			
Men cameo; free 16 pg. preview Masters of the Universe. 26-1st app. Terra.			
27-Free 16 pg. preview Atari Force. 29-The New Brotherhood of Evil &			
Speedy app. 30-Terra joins the Titans			1.00
31-33,35-38,40: 37-Batman & The Outsiders x-over. 38-Origin Wonder Girl			
			1.00
34-4th app. Deathstroke the Terminator	1.20	3.00	
39-Last Dick Grayson as Robin; Kid Flash quits	.80	2.00	
Annual 1(11/82)-Omega Men app.			1.50

Night Force #6 © DC

Night Man V2#3 © Malibu

Nightmare #2 © MEG

New New Teen Titans Annual #3 © DC

Marvel Comics			
V2#1-26: 10-Capt. America app. 13-Return of The Yellow Claw. 15-Fantastic			
Four app.			1.50
27-29-Wolverine-c/stories		.80	2.00
30-47: 30,31-Deathlok app. 32-Begin $1.75-c. 36-Cage app. 37-Woodgod			
c/story. 38-41-Flashes back to pre-Shield days after WWII. 44-Capt.			
America-c/s. 45-Viper-c/s. 46-Gideon x-over		.70	1.75
NOTE: **Alan Grant** scripts-11. Guice a(p)-20-23, 25, 26; c-20-28.			

NICK FURY VS. S.H.I.E.L.D.
June, 1988 - No. 6, Nov, 1988 ($3.50, 52 pgs, deluxe format)
Marvel Comics

1-Steranko-c		1.60	4.00
2-(Low print run) Sienkiewicz-c	1.00	2.00	5.00
3-6		1.20	3.00

NICK HALIDAY (Thrill of the Sea)
May, 1956
Argo

1-Daily & Sunday strip-r by Petree	7.50	22.50	45.00

NIGHT AND THE ENEMY (Graphic Novel)
1988 (8-1/2x11") ($11.95, color, 80 pgs.)
Comico

1-Harlan Ellison scripts/Ken Steacy-c/a; r/Epic Illustrated & new-a			
(1st and 2nd printings)	1.70	5.00	12.00
1-Limited edition ($39.95)	5.50	17.00	40.00

NIGHT BEFORE CHRISTMAS, THE (See March of Comics No. 152)

NIGHT BEFORE CHRISTMASK, THE
Nov, 1994 ($9.95, one-shot)
Dark Horse Comics

nn-Hardcover book; Rick Geary -c/a	1.65	4.20	10.00

NIGHTBREED (See Clive Barker's Nightbreed)

NIGHTCRAWLER
Nov, 1985 - No. 4, Feb, 1986 (Mini-series from X-Men)
Marvel Comics Group

1-4: 1-Cockrum-c/a		.80	2.00

NIGHT FORCE, THE (See New Teen Titans #21)
Aug, 1982, No. 14, Sept, 1983 (60¢)
DC Comics

1		1.20	3.00
2-14: 13-Origin Baron Winter. 14-Nudity panels		.80	2.00
NOTE: **Colan** c/a-1-14p. Giordano c-1i, 2i, 4i, 5i, 7i, 12i.			

NIGHT GLIDER
April, 1993 ($2.95, one-shot)
Topps Comics (Kirbyverse)

1-Kirby c-1, Heck-a; polybagged w/Kirbychrome trading card.			
		1.20	3.00

NIGHTINGALE, THE
1948 (10¢, 7-1/4x10-1/4", 14 pgs., 1/2 B&W)
Henry H. Stansbury Once-Upon-A-Time Press, Inc.

(Very Rare)-Low distribution; distributed to Westchester County & Bronx, N.Y. only; used in Seduction of the Innocent, pg. 312,313 as the 1st and only "good" comic book ever published.
Ill. by Dong Kingman; 1,500 words of text, printed on high quality paper & no word balloons.
Copyright registered 10/22/48, distributed week of 12/5/48. (By Hans Christian Andersen)
Estimated value........$200

NIGHT MAN, THE (See Sludge #1)
Oct, 1993 - No. 23, Aug, 1995 ($1.95/$2.50)
Malibu Comics (Ultraverse)

1-($2.50, 48 pgs.)-Rune flip-c/story by B. Smith (3 pgs.)		1.00	2.50
1-Ultra-Limited silver foil-c		1.65	4.20	10.00
2-15, 17: 3-Break-Thru x-over; Freex app. 4-Origin Firearm (2 pgs.) by			

Chaykin. 6-TNTNT app. 8-1st app. Teknight		.80	2.00
16 ($3.50)-flip book (Ultraverse Premiere #11)		1.40	3.50
...:the Pilgrim Conundrum Saga (1/95, $3.95, 68 pgs.)-Strangers app.			
		1.60	4.00
18-23: 22-Loki-c/a		1.00	2.50
Infinity ($1.50)			1.50
...Vs. Wolverine #0-Kelley Jones-c; mail in offer	1.65	4.20	10.00
NOTE: **Zeck** a-16.			

NIGHT MAN, THE
Sept, 1995 - No.4, Dec, 1995 ($1.50, limited series)
Malibu Comics (Ultraverse)

1-4: Post Black September storyline			1.50

NIGHT MAN, THE/GAMBIT
Mar, 1996 - No. 3, May, 1996 ($1.95, limited series)
Malibu Comics (Ultraverse)

1-3: David Quinn scripts in all. 3-Rhiannon discovered to be The Night Man's			
mother			2.00

NIGHTMARE
Summer, 1952 - No. 3, Winter, 1952, 53 (Painted-c)
Ziff-Davis (Approved Comics)/St. John No. 3,4

1-1 pg. Kinstler-a; Tuska-a(2)	43.00	128.00	340.00
2-Kinstler-a-Poe's "Pit & the Pendulum"	34.00	101.00	235.00
3-Kinstler-a	27.00	81.00	190.00

NIGHTMARE (Weird Horrors #1-9) (Amazing Ghost Stories #14 on)
No. 10, Dec, 1953 - No. 13, Aug, 1954
St. John Publishing Co.

10-Reprints Ziff-Davis Weird Thrillers #2 w/new Kubert-c plus 2 pgs.			
Kinstler-a; Anderson, Colan & Toth-a	44.00	132.00	350.00
11-Krigstein-a; painted-c; Poe adapt., "Hop Frog"	36.00	107.00	250.00
12-Kubert bondage-c; adaptation of Poe's "The Black Cat"; Cannibalism story			
	29.00	86.00	200.00
13-Reprints Z-D Weird Thrillers #3 with new cover; Powell-a(2), Tuska-a;			
Baker-c	22.00	66.00	155.00

NIGHTMARE (Magazine)
Dec, 1970 - No. 23, Feb, 1975 (B&W, 68 pgs.)
Skywald Publishing Corp.

1-Everett-a	3.60	11.00	25.00
2-5: 4-Decapitation story	1.65	4.20	10.00
6-Kaluta-a; Jeff Jones photo & interview	1.70	5.00	12.00
7,9,10: 9-Wrightson-a	1.50	3.75	9.00
8-Features E. C. movie "Tales From the Crypt"; reprints some E.C. comics			
panels	1.70	5.00	12.00
11-23: 12-Excessive gore, severed heads. 20-Byrne's 1st artwork (8/74);			
severed head-c. 21-(1974 Summer Special)-Kaluta-a. 22-Tomb of Horror			
issue. 23-(1975 Winter Special)	1.20	3.00	7.00
Annual 1(1972)-B. Jones-a	1.65	4.20	10.00
Winter Special 1(1973)	1.20	3.00	7.00
Yearbook nn(1974)	1.00	2.60	6.00
NOTE: **Adkins** a-5. **Boris** c-2, 3, 5 (#4 is not by Boris). **Byrne** a-20p. **Everett** a-4, 5. **Jeff Jones** a-6, 21(Psycho #6); c-6. **Katz** a-5. **Reese** a-4, 5. **Wildey** a-5, 6, 21, '74 Yearbook.			

NIGHTMARE (Alex Nino's)
1989 ($1.95)
Innovation Publishing

1-Alex Nino-a		.80	2.00

NIGHTMARE
Dec, 1994 - No. 4, Mar, 1995 ($1.95, limited series)
Marvel Comics

1-4		.80	2.0

NIGHTMARE & CASPER (See Harvey Hits #71) (Casper & Nightmare #6 on)
(See Casper The Friendly Ghost #19)

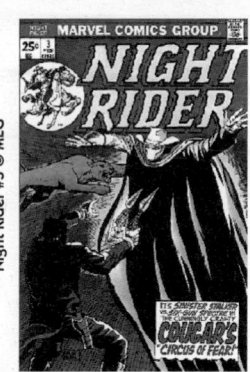

Night Rider #3 © MEG

Nightstalkers #3 © MEG

Nightwatch #7 © MEG

	GD25	FN65	NM94

ug, 1963 - No. 5, Aug, 1964 (25¢)
arvey Publications

-All reprints?	4.80	14.40	48.00
-5: All reprints?	3.00	9.00	30.00

IGHTMARE ON ELM STREET, A (See Freddy Krueger's...)

IGHTMARES (See Do You Believe in Nightmares)

IGHTMARES
ay, 1985 - No. 2, May, 1985 ($1.75, Baxter paper)
clipse Comics

,2		.70	1.75

IGHTMARK: BLOOD & HONOR
94 - No. 3, 1994 ($2.50, B&W, mini-series)
pha Productions

,2		1.00	2.50

IGHTMARK MYSTERY SPECIAL
n, 1994 ($2.50, B&W)
pha Productions

		1.00	2.50

IGHTMASK
ov, 1986 - No. 12, Oct, 1987
arvel Comics Group

-12			.75

IGHT MASTER
b, 1987 ($1.50, B&W)
verwolf

-Tim Vigil-c/a			1.50

IGHT MUSIC (See Exlispe Graphic Album Series, The Magic Flute)
ec, 1984 - No. 7, Feb, 1988 ($1.75, Baxter paper)
clipse Comics

-7: 3-Russell's Jungle Book adapt. 4,5-Pelleas And Melisande (double titled)			
6-Salome' (double titled). 7-Red Dog #1		.70	1.75

IGHT NURSE
ov, 1972 - No. 4, May, 1973
arvel Comics Group

	3.60	11.00	25.00
-4	1.65	4.20	10.00

IGHT OF MYSTERY
53 (no month) (one-shot)
on Periodicals

-1 pg. Kinstler-a, Hollingsworth-c	36.00	107.00	250.00

IGHT OF THE GRIZZLY, THE (See Movie Classics)

IGHTRAVEN: THE COLLECTED STORIES
91 ($9.95, graphic novel)
arvel Comics UK, Ltd.

-Bolton-r/British Hulk mag.; David Lloyd-c/a	1.65	4.00	10.00

IGHT RIDER (Western)
ct, 1974 - No. 6, Aug, 1975
arvel Comics Group

: 1-6 reprint Ghost Rider #1-6 (#1-origin)		.80	2.00
-6			1.25

IGHT'S CHILDREN: THE VAMPIRE
ly, 1995 - No. 2, Aug, 1995 ($2.95, B&W)
ilenium

,2: Wendy Snow-Lang story & art		1.20	3.00

IGHTSTALKERS (Also see Midnight Sons Unlimited)

Nov, 1992 - No. 21, Apr, 1994 ($1.75)
Marvel Comics (Midnight Sons imprint #14 on)

1-($2.75, 52 pgs.)-Polybagged w/poster; part 5 of Rise of the Midnight Sons			
storyline; Garney/Palmer-c/a begins; Hannibal King, Blade & Frank Drake			
begin (see Tomb of Dracula for & Dr. Strange)		1.10	2.75
2-9,11-21: 5-Punisher app. 7-Ghost Rider app. 8,9-Morbius app. 14-Spot			
varnish-c. 14,15-Siege of Darkness Pts 1 & 9		.70	1.75
10-($2.25)-Outer-c is a Darkhold envelope made of black parchment w/gold			
ink; Midnight Massacre part 1		.90	2.25

NIGHT THRASHER (Also see The New Warriors)
Aug, 1993 - No. 21, Apr, 1995 ($1.75/$1.95)
Marvel Comics

1-($2.95, 52 pgs.)-Red holo-grafx foil-c; origin		1.20	3.00
2-9: 2-Intro Tantrum. 3-Gideon (of X-Force) app.		.70	1.75
10-21: 10-Begin $1.95-c; bound-in trading card sheet; Iron Man app. 15-Hulk			
app.		.80	2.00

NIGHT THRASHER: FOUR CONTROL
Oct, 1992 - No. 4, Jan, 1993 ($2.00, limited series)
Marvel Comics

1-4: 1-Hero from New Warriors. 2-Intro Tantrum. 3-Gideon (of X-Force) app.			
		.80	2.00

NIGHTVEIL (Also see Femforce)
Nov, 1984 - No. 7, 1985 ($1.75)
Americomics/AC Comics

1-7		.80	2.00
...'s Cauldron Of Horror 1 (1989, B&W)-Kubert, Powell, Wood-r plus new			
Nightveil story		1.00	2.50
...'s Cauldron Of Horror 2 (1990, $2.95, B&W, 44pgs)-Pre-code horror-r by			
Kubert & Powell		1.20	3.00
Special 1 ('88, $1.95)-Kaluta-c		.80	2.00

NIGHTWATCH
Apr, 1994 - No. 12, Mar, 1995 ($1.50)
Marvel Comics

1-($2.95)-Collectors edition; foil-c; Ron Lim-c/a begins; Spider-Man app.			
		1.20	3.00
1-($1.50)-Regular edition			1.50
2-12: 2-Bound-in S-M trading card sheet; 5,6-Venom-c & app. 7,11-Cardiac			
app.			1.50

NIGHTWING (Also see New Teen Titans, New Titans, Showcase '93 #11,12,
Tales of the New Teen Titans & Teen Titans Spotlight)
Sept, 1995 - No. 4, Dec, 1995 ($2.25, limited series)
DC Comics

1-4-Dennis O'Neil story		.90	2.25

NIGHTWING
Oct, 1996 - Present ($1.95)
DC Comics

1-12: Chuck Dixon scripts & Scott McDaniel-c/a			2.00

NIGHTWING: ALFRED'S RETURN
July, 1995 ($3.50, one-shot)
DC Comics

1		1.40	3.50

NIGHTWINGS (See DC Science Fiction Graphic Novel)

NIKKI, WILD DOG OF THE NORTH (Disney, see Movie Comics)
No. 1226, Sept, 1961
Dell Publishing Co.

Four Color 1226-Movie, photo-c	6.00	18.00	60.00

1963
Apr, 1993 - No. 6, Oct, 1993 ($1.95, limited series)

Ninjak #5 © Voyager Comm.

Nocturnals #3 © Dan Brereton

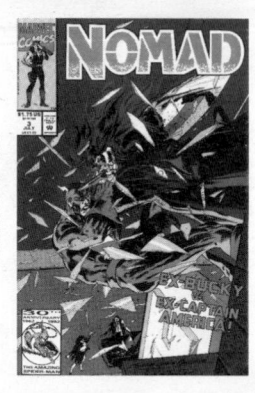

Nomad #3 © MEG

	GD25	FN65	NM94

Image Comics (Shadowline Ink)

		GD25	FN65	NM94
1-6: Alan Moore scripts; Veitch, Bissette & Gibbons-a(p)			.80	2.00
1-Gold		1.00	2.00	5.00

NOTE: *Bissette a-2-4; Gibbons a-1i, 2i, 6i; c-2.*

1984 (Magazine) (1994 #11 on)
June, 1978 - No. 10, Jan, 1980 ($1.50)
Warren Publishing Co.

			GD25	FN65	NM94
1-Nino-a in all				1.60	4.00
2-10				.80	2.00

NOTE: *Alacla a-1-3, 5i. Corben a-1-8; c-1, 2. Thorne a-7-10. Wood a-1, 2, 5i.*

1994 (Formerly 1984) (Magazine)
No. 11, Feb, 1980 - No. 29, Feb, 1983
Warren Publishing Co.

	GD25	FN65	NM94
11-29: 27-The Warhawks return		.80	2.00

NOTE: *Corben a-11-19, 20(2), 21, 25, 26, 28; c-21. Redondo c-20. Thorne a-11-14, 17-21, 25, 26, 28, 29.*

NINJAK (See Bloodshot #6, 7 & Deathmate)
Feb, 1994 - No. 26, Nov. 1995 ($2.25/$2.50)
Valiant/Acclaim Comics (Valiant) No. 16 on

		GD25	FN65	NM94
1 ($3.50)-Chromium-c; Quesada-c/a(p) in #1-3			1.40	3.50
1-Gold	1.30		3.25	8.00
2-14: 3-Batman, Spawn & Random (from X-Factor) app. as costumes at party				
(cameo). 4-w/bound-in trading card. 5,6-X-O app			.90	2.25
15-26 ($2.50)			1.00	2.50
0 ($6.95)			1.00	2.50
00 (6/95, $2.50)			1.00	2.50
Yearbook 1 (1994, $3.95)			1.60	4.00

NINTENDO COMICS SYSTEM
1990 - No. 3, 1990 ($4.95, card stock-c, 68pgs.)
Valiant Comics

	GD25	FN65	NM94
1-3: 3-Layton-c (features 8 stories each)	1.00	2.00	5.00

NIRA X: CYBERANGEL
Dec, 1994 - No. 4, 1995 ($2.95, limited series)
Entity Comics

		GD25	FN65	NM94
1-Foil logo			1.20	3.00
2-4 ($2.50)			1.00	2.50
4-($6.95)-bagged w/PC Game	1.20		3.00	7.00

NIRA X: CYBERANGEL SERIES II
1995 - No. 4, 1995 ($2.50, limited series)
Entity Comics

	GD25	FN65	NM94
1-4			2.50

NIRA X: CYBERANGEL SERIES III
1995 - No. 3, 1995 ($2.50/$2.95, limited series)
Entity Comics

	GD25	FN65	NM94
1,2-($2.50)			2.50
3-($2.95)			3.00
1-($6.95)-Bagged w/PC Game			7.00

NIRA X-CYNDER: ENDANGERED SPECIES
Feb, 1996 ($2.95, one-shot)
Entity Comics

	GD25	FN65	NM94
1-Maus-a(p)/scripts			3.00
1-($12.95)-Commemorative			13.00

NIRA X: HELLINA
Aug, 1996 ($2.95, one-shot)
Entity Comics

	GD25	FN65	NM94
1-Two covers (1 gold foil & 1 red foil)			3.00
1-($12.95)-Platinum Edition; polybagged w/certificate			13.00

NIRA X UNLIMITED SERIES

No. 0, Mar, 1996 - No. 4, Aug, 1996 ($2.75, B&W)
Entity Comics

	GD25	FN65	NM94
0-4			2.7
Annual 1-($2.75)			2.7

NOAH'S ARK
1973 (35/49¢)
Spire Christian Comics/Fleming H. Revell Co.

	GD25	FN65	NM94
nn-By Al Hartley			1.0

NOCTURNALS, THE
Jan, 1995 - No. 6, Aug, 1995 ($2.95, painted limited series)
Malibu Comics (Bravura)

		GD25	FN65	NM94
1-6: Dan Brereton painted-c/a & scripts			1.20	3.0
1-Glow-in-the-Dark premium edition	1.65		4.20	10.0

NOCTURNE
June, 1995 - No. 4, Sept. 1995 ($1.50, limited series)
Marvel Comics

	GD25	FN65	NM94
1-4			1.5

NO ESCAPE (Movie)
June, 1994 - No. 3, Aug, 1994 ($1.50)
Marvel Comics

	GD25	FN65	NM94
1-3: Based on movie			1.5

NOMAD (See Captain America #180)
Nov, 1990 - No. 4, Feb, 1991 ($1.50, limited series)
Marvel Comics

	GD25	FN65	NM94
1-4: 1,4-Captain America app.			1.5

NOMAD
V2#1, May, 1992 - No. 25, May, 1994 ($1.75)
Marvel Comics

		GD25	FN65	NM94
V2#1-($2.00)-Has gatefold-c w/map/wanted poster			1.00	2.5
2-5: 4-Deadpool x-over. 5-Punisher vs. Nomad-c/story			.75	1.8
6-25: 6-Punisher & Daredevil-c/story cont'd in Punisher War Journal #48.				
7-Gambit-c/story. 10-Red Wolf app. 21-Man-Thing-c/story. 25-Bound-in				
trading card sheet			.70	1.7

NOMAN (See Thunder Agents)
Nov, 1966 - No. 2, March, 1967 (25¢, 68 pgs.)
Tower Comics

		GD25	FN65	NM94
1-Wood/Williamson-c; Lightning begins; Dynamo cameo; Kane-a(p) &				
Whitney-a	6.50	19.50	50.0
2-Wood-c only; Dynamo x-over; Whitney-a	4.50	14.00	35.0

NONE BUT THE BRAVE (See Movie Classics)

NOODNIK COMICS (See Pinky the Egghead)
Dec, 1953; No. 2, Feb, 1954 - No. 5, Aug, 1954
Comic Media/Mystery/Biltmore

		GD25	FN65	NM94
3-D(1953, 25¢; Comic Media)(#1)-Came w/glasses	32.00	96.00	225.0
2-5	5.85	17.50	35.0

NORMALMAN (See Cerebus the Aardvark #55, 56)
Jan, 1984 - No. 12, Dec, 1985 ($1.70/$2.00)
Aardvark-Vanaheim/Renegade Press #6 on

		GD25	FN65	NM94
1-5 ($1.70, color)-Jim Valentino-c/a in all			.70	1.7
6-12 ($2.00, B&W): 10-Cerebus cameo; Sim-a (2 pgs.)			.80	2.0
...3-D 1 (Annual, 1986, $2.25)			.90	2.2

NORMALMAN-MEGATON MAN SPECIAL
Aug, 1994 ($2.50, color)
Image Comics

	GD25	FN65	NM94
1		1.00	2.5

NORTH AVENUE IRREGULARS (See Walt Disney Showcase #49)

Northstar #2 © MEG

Nova #4 © MEG

Nth the Ultimate Man #8 © MEG

NU

	GD25	FN65	NM94

NORTHSTAR
Apr, 1994 - No. 4, July, 1994 ($1.75, mini-series)
Marvel Comics

| 1-4: Character from Alpha Flight | | .70 | 1.75 |

NORTH TO ALASKA
No. 1155, Dec, 1960
Dell Publishing Co.

| Four Color 1155-Movie, John Wayne photo-c | 16.00 | 48.00 | 160.00 |

NORTHWEST MOUNTIES (Also see Approved Comics #12)
Oct, 1948 - No. 4, July, 1949
Jubilee Publications/St. John

1-Rose of the Yukon by Matt Baker; Walter Johnson-a; Lubbers-c			
	40.00	120.00	315.00
2-Baker-a; Lubbers-c. Ventrilo app.	33.00	99.00	230.00
3-Bondage-c, Baker-a; Sky Chief, K-9 app.	34.00	103.00	240.00
4-Baker-c/a(2 pgs.); Blue Monk & The Desperado app.			
	34.00	103.00	240.00

NO SLEEP 'TIL DAWN
No. 831, Aug, 1957
Dell Publishing Co.

| Four Color 831-Movie, Karl Malden photo-c | 7.00 | 21.00 | 70.00 |

NOT BRAND ECHH (Brand Echh #1-4; See Crazy, 1973)
Aug, 1967 - No. 13, May, 1969 (1st Marvel parody book)
Marvel Comics Group (LMC)

1: 1-8 are 12¢ issues	4.30	13.00	30.00
2-4: 3-Origin Thor, Hulk & Capt. America; Monkees, Alfred E. Neuman cameo. 4-X-Men app.	2.15	6.50	15.00
5-8: 5-Origin/intro. Forbush Man. 7-Origin Fantastical-4 & Stuporman. 8-Beatles cameo; X-Men satire	2.15	6.50	15.00
9-13 (25¢, 68 pgs., all Giants) 9-Beatles cameo. 10-All-r; The Old Witch, Crypt Keeper & Vault Keeper cameos. 12,13-Beatles cameo			
	2.30	6.70	16.00

NOTE: **Colan** a(p)-4, 5, 8, 9, 13. **Everett** a-1i. **Kirby** a(p)-1, 3, 5-7, 10r; c-1p. **J. Severin** a-1c, 6-8, 11. **M. Severin** a-1-13; c-2, 9, 10, 12, 13. **Sutton** a-3, 4, 5i, 6i, 8, 9, 10r, 11-13; c-5. Archie satire in #9. Avengers satire in #8, 12.

NOTHING CAN STOP THE JUGGERNAUT
1989 ($3.95)
Marvel Comics

| 1-r/Amazing Spider-Man #229 & 230 | | 1.60 | 4.00 |

NO TIME FOR SERGEANTS (TV)
No. 914, July, 1958; Feb-Apr, 1965 - No. 3, Aug-Oct, 1965
Dell Publishing Co.

| Four Color 914 (Movie)-Toth-a; Andy Griffith photo-c | 10.00 | 30.00 | 100.00 |
| 1(2-4/65)-3 (TV): Photo-c | 4.00 | 12.00 | 40.00 |

NOVA (The Man Called... No. 22-25)(See New Warriors)
Sept, 1976 - No. 25, May, 1979
Marvel Comics Group

1-Origin/1st app. Nova	1.00	2.00	5.00
2-11: 4-Thor x-over		1.00	2.50
12-Spider-Man x-over		1.60	4.00
13-25: 13-Intro Crime-Buster. 14-Last 30¢ issue. 18-Yellow Claw app. 19-Wally West (Kid Flash) cameo		.70	1.80

NOTE: **Austin** c-21i, 23i. **John Buscema** a(p)-1-3, 8, 21; c-1p, 2, 15. **Infantino** a(p)-15-20, 22-25; c-17-20, 21p, 23p, 24p. **Kirby** c-4p, 5, 7. **Nebres** c-25i. **Simonson** a-23i.

NOVA
Jan, 1994 - June, 1995 ($1.75/$1.95)(Started as 4-part mini-series)
Marvel Comics

1-($2.95, 52 pgs.)-Collector's Edition w/gold foil-c; new costume for Nova			
		1.20	3.00
1-($2.25, 52 pgs.)-Newsstand Edition w/o foil-c		.90	2.25

	GD25	FN65	NM94

| 2-4: 3-Spider-Man-c/story. 5-Stan Lee app. | | .70 | 1.75 |
| 5-18: 5-Begin $1.95-c; bound-in card sheet. 13-Firestar & Night Thrasher app.14-Darkhawk | .40 | 1.00 | 2.00 |

NOW AGE ILLUSTRATED (See Pendulum Illustrated Classics)

NTH MAN THE ULTIMATE NINJA (See Marvel Comics Presents 25)
Aug, 1989 - No. 16, Sept, 1990 ($1.00)
Marvel Comics

| 1-7,9-16-Ninja mercenary | | | 1.00 |
| 8-Dale Keown's 1st Marvel work (1/90, pencils) | | .80 | 2.00 |

NUCLEUS (Also see Cerebus)
May, 1979 ($1.50, B&W, adult fanzine)
Heiro-Graphic Publications

| 1-Contains "Demonhorn" by Dave Sim; early app. of Cerebus The Aardvark (4 pg. story) | 4.00 | 12.00 | 28.00 |

NUKLA
Oct-Dec, 1965 - No. 4, Sept, 1966
Dell Publishing Co.

1-Origin & 1st app. Nukla (super hero)	2.80	8.50	28.00
2,3	2.15	6.50	15.00
4-Ditko-a, c(p)	2.60	8.00	26.00

NURSE BETSY CRANE (Formerly Teen Secret Diary)
V2#12, Aug, 1961 - V2#27, Mar, 1964 (See Soap Opera Romances)
Charlton Comics

| V2#12-27 | .80 | 2.00 | 4.00 |

NURSE HELEN GRANT (See The Romances of...)
NURSE LINDA LARK (See Linda Lark)

NURSERY RHYMES
No. 10, July-Aug, 1951 - No. 2, Winter, 1951 (Painted-c)
Ziff-Davis Publ. Co. (Approved Comics)

| 10 (#1), 2: 10-Howie Post-a | 11.50 | 34.00 | 80.00 |

NURSES, THE (TV)
April, 1963 - No. 3, Oct, 1963 (Photo-c: #1,2)
Gold Key

| 1 | 2.60 | 7.50 | 18.00 |
| 2,3 | 1.70 | 5.00 | 12.00 |

NUTS! (Satire)
March, 1954 - No. 5, Nov, 1954
Premiere Comics Group

1-Hollingsworth-a	25.00	75.00	175.00
2,4,5: 5-Capt. Marvel parody	18.00	54.00	125.00
3-Drug "reefers" mentioned	19.00	56.00	130.00

NUTS (Magazine) (Satire)
Feb, 1958 - No. 2, April, 1958
Health Knowledge

| 1 | 7.50 | 22.50 | 45.00 |
| 2 | 5.85 | 17.50 | 35.00 |

NUTS & JOLTS
No. 22, 1941
Dell Publishing Co.

| Large Feature Comic 22 | 9.50 | 28.50 | 95.00 |

NUTSY SQUIRREL (Formerly Hollywood Funny Folks)(See Comic Cavalcade)
#61, 9-10/54 - #69, 1-2/56; #70, 8-9/56 - #71, 10-11/56; #72, 11/57
National Periodical Publications

| 61-Mayer-a; Grossman-a in all | 12.00 | 36.00 | 85.00 |
| 62-72: Mayer a-62,65,67-72 | 9.15 | 27.00 | 55.00 |

NUTTY COMICS
Winter, 1946 (Funny animal)

415

Oblivion #1 © Comico

Obnoxio the Clown #1 © MEG

Official Hawkman Index #1 © DC

	GD25	FN65	NM94

Fawcett Publications

	GD25	FN65	NM94
1-Capt. Kidd story; 1 pg. Wolverton-a	11.50	34.00	80.00

NUTTY COMICS
1945 - No. 8, June-July, 1947
Home Comics (Harvey Publications)

nn-Helpful Hank, Bozo Bear & others (funny animal)	7.50	22.50	45.00
2-4	4.25	13.00	28.00
5-8: 5-Rags Rabbit begins(1st app.); infinity-c	4.00	11.00	22.00

NUTTY LIFE (Formerly Krazy Life #1; becomes Wotalife Comics #3 on)
No. 2, Summer, 1946
Fox Features Syndicate

2	8.70	26.00	52.00

NYOKA, THE JUNGLE GIRL (Formerly Jungle Girl; see The Further Adventures of..., Master Comics #50 & XMas Comics)
No. 2, Winter, 1945 - No. 77, June, 1953 (Movie serial)
Fawcett Publications

2	50.00	150.00	400.00
3	28.00	84.00	195.00
4,5	24.00	71.00	165.00
6-10	17.00	51.00	120.00
11,13,14,16-18-Krigstein-a: 17-Sam Spade ad by Lou Fine	17.00	51.00	120.00
12,15,19,20	15.00	45.00	105.00
21-30: 25-Clayton Moore photo-c?	10.00	30.00	60.00
31-40	8.00	24.00	48.00
41-50	6.35	19.00	38.00
51-60	4.25	13.00	28.00
61-77	4.00	12.00	24.00

NOTE: Photo-c from movies 25, 30-70, 72, 75-77. Bondage c-4, 5, 7, 8, 14, 24.

NYOKA, THE JUNGLE GIRL (Formerly Zoo Funnies; Space Adventures #23 on)
No. 14, Nov, 1955 - No. 22, Nov, 1957
Charlton Comics

14	8.35	25.00	50.00
15-22	6.35	19.00	38.00

OAKLAND PRESS FUNNYBOOK, THE
9/17/78 - 4/13/80 (16 pgs.) (Weekly)
Full color in comic book form; changes to tabloid size 4/20/80-on
The Oakland Press

Contains Tarzan by Manning, Marmaduke, Bugs Bunny, etc. (low distribution);

9/23/79 - 4/13/80 contain Buck Rogers by Gray Morrow & Jim Lawrence		.80	2.00

OAKY DOAKS (See Famous Funnies #190)
July, 1942 (One Shot)
Eastern Color Printing Co.

1	30.00	90.00	210.00

OBIE
1953 (6¢)
Store Comics

1	.80	2.00	4.00

OBLIVION
Aug, 1995 - Present ($2.50)
Comico

1-3: 1-Art Adams-c. 2-(1/96)-Polybagged w/gaming card. 3-(5/96)-Darrow-c		1.00	2.50

OBNOXIO THE CLOWN
April, 1983 (one-shot) (Character from Crazy Magazine)
Marvel Comics Group

	GD25	FN65	NM94
1-Vs. the X-Men			1.0

OCCULT FILES OF DR. SPEKTOR, THE
Apr, 1973 - No. 24, Feb, 1977; No. 25, May, 1982 (Painted-c #1-24)
Gold Key/Whitman No. 25

1-1st app. Lakota; Baron Tibor begins	1.50	3.80	9.0
2-5		1.80	4.5
6-10: 8-Dracula app.		1.20	3.0
11-13,15-25: 11-1st app. Spektor as Werewolf. 25-Reprints		1.00	2.5
14-Dr. Solar app.	1.65	4.20	10.0
9(Modern Comics reprint, 1977)			1.5

NOTE: Also see Dan Curtis, Golden Comics Digest 33, Gold Key Spotlight, Mystery Comics Digest 5, & Spine Tingling Tales.

ODELL'S ADVENTURES IN 3-D (See Adventures in 3-D)

OFFICIAL CRISIS ON INFINITE EARTHS INDEX, THE
Marcg, 1986 ($1.75)
Independent Comics Group (Eclipse)

1		.70	1.7

OFFICIAL CRISIS ON INFINITE EARTHS CROSSOVER INDEX, THE
July, 1986 ($1.75)
Independent Comics Group (Eclipse)

1-Perez-c.		.70	1.7

OFFICIAL DOOM PATROL INDEX, THE
Feb, 1986 - No. 2, Mar, 1986 ($1.50, limited series)
Independent Comics Group (Eclipse)

1,2: Byrne-c.			1.5

OFFICIAL HANDBOOK OF THE CONAN UNIVERSE (See Handbook of...)

OFFICIAL HANDBOOK OF THE MARVEL UNIVERSE, THE
Jan, 1983 - No. 15, May, 1984 (Limited series)
Marvel Comics Group

1-Lists Marvel heroes & villains (letter A)		1.60	4.0
2 (B-C)		1.20	3.0
3-5: 3-(C-D). 4-(D-G). 5-(H-J)		1.10	2.7
6-9: 6-(K-L). 7-(M). 8-(N-P); Punisher-c. 9-(Q-S)		.90	2.2
10-15: 10-(S). 11-(S-U). 12-(V-Z); Wolverine-c. 13,14-Book of the Dead.			
15-Weaponry catalogue		.80	2.0

NOTE: Bolland a-8. Byrne c/a(p)-1-14; c-15p. Grell a-6, 9. Kirby a-1, 3. Layton a-2, 5, 7. Mignola a-3, 4, 5, 6, 8, 12. Miller a-4-6, 8, 10. Nebres a-3, 4, 8. Redondo a-3, 4, 8, 13, 14. Simonson a-1, 4, 6-13. Paul Smith a-1-12. Starlin a-5, 7, 8, 10, 13, 14. Steranko a-8p. Zeck 14.

OFFICIAL HANDBOOK OF THE MARVEL UNIVERSE, THE
Dec, 1985 - No. 20, Feb, 1988 ($1.50, maxi-series)
Marvel Comics Group

V2#1-Byrne-c		1.20	3.0
2-5: 2,3-Byrne-c		1.00	2.5
6-10		.80	2.0
11-20		.60	1.5
Trade paperback Vol. 1-10 ($6.95)	1.20	3.00	7.0

NOTE: Art Adams a-7, 8, 11, 12, 14. Bolland a-8, 10, 13. Buckler a-1, 3, 5, 10. Buscema a-1, 5, 8, 9, 10, 13, 14. Byrne a-1-14; c-1-11. Ditko a-1, 2, 4, 6, 7, 11, 13. a-7, 11. Mignola a-2, 4, 11, 13. Miller a-2, 4, 12. Simonson a-1, 2, 4-13, 15. Paul Smith a-1-5, 7-12, 14. Starlin a-6, 8, 9, 12, 16. Zeck a-1-4, 6, 7, 9-14, 16.

OFFICIAL HANDBOOK OF THE MARVEL UNIVERSE, THE
July, 1989 - No. 8, Mid-Dec, 1990 ($1.50, limited series, 52 pgs.)
Marvel Comics

V3#1-8: 1-McFarlane-a(2 pgs.)			1.5

OFFICIAL HAWKMAN INDEX, THE
Nov, 1986 - No. 2, Dec, 1986 ($2.00)
Independent Comics Group

1,2		.80	2.0

Official JLA Index © DC

Official Marvel Index to X-Men #5 © MEG

OMAC #6 © DC

OM

	GD25	FN65	NM94

OFFICIAL JUSTICE LEAGUE OF AMERICA INDEX, THE
April, 1986 - No. 8, Mar, 1987 ($2.00, Baxter)
Independent Comics Group (Eclipse)

		GD25	FN65	NM94
1-8: 1,2-Perez-c.			.80	2.00

OFFICIAL LEGION OF SUPER-HEROES INDEX, THE
Dec, 1986 - No. 5, 1987 ($2.00, limited series)(No Official in Title #2 on)
Independent Comics Group (Eclipse)

1-5: 4-Mooney-c.	.80	2.00

OFFICIAL MARVEL INDEX TO MARVEL TEAM-UP
Jan, 1986 - No. 6, 1986 ($1.25, limited series)
Marvel Comics Group

1-6	1.30

OFFICIAL MARVEL INDEX TO THE AMAZING SPIDER-MAN
Apr, 1985 - No. 9, Dec, 1985 ($1.25, limited series)
Marvel Comics Group

1 ($1.00)-Byrne-c.	1.00	2.50
2-9: 5,6,8,9-Punisher-c.	.80	2.00

OFFICIAL MARVEL INDEX TO THE AVENGERS, THE
V2#1, Oct, 1994 - V2#6, 1995 ($1.95, limited series)
Marvel Comics

V2#1-#6	.80	2.00

OFFICIAL MARVEL INDEX TO THE FANTASTIC FOUR
Dec, 1985 - No. 5, 1986 ($1.25, limited series)
Marvel Comics Group

1-5: 1-Byrne-c.	1.50

OFFICIAL MARVEL INDEX TO THE X-MEN, THE
V2#1, Apr, 1994 - V2#5, 1994 ($1.95, limited series)
Marvel Comics

V2#1-5: 1-Covers X-Men #1-51. 2-Covers #52-122,Special #1,2,Giant-Size #1,2.
3-Byrne-c; covers #123-177, Annuals 3-7, Spec. Ed. #1. 4-Covers Uncanny
X-Men #178-234, Annuals 8-12. 5-Covers #235-287, Annuals 13-15

	.80	2.00

OFFICIAL SOUPY SALES COMIC (See Soupy Sales)

OFFICIAL TEEN TITANS INDEX, THE
Aug, 1985 - No. 5, 1986 ($1.50, limited series)
Independent Comics Group (Eclipse)

1-5	1.50

OFFICIAL TRUE CRIME CASES (Formerly Sub-Mariner #23; All-True Crime
Cases #26 on)
No. 24, Fall, 1947 - No. 25, Winter, 1947-48
Marvel Comics (OCI)

24(#1)-Burgos-a; Syd Shores-c	19.00	58.00	135.00
25-Syd Shores-c; Kurtzman's "Hey Look"	16.00	47.00	110.00

OF SUCH IS THE KINGDOM
1955 (15¢, 36 pgs.)
George A. Pflaum

nn-Reprints from 1951 Treasure Chest	2.00	5.00	10.00

O.G. WHIZ (See Gold Key Spotlight #10)
2/71 - No. 6, 5/72; No. 7, 5/78 - No. 11, 1/79 (No. 7: 52 pgs.)
Gold Key

1,2-John Stanley scripts	5.50	16.50	55.00
3-6(1972)	2.80	8.40	28.00
7-11(1978-79)-Part-r: 9-Tubby app.	1.50	3.75	9.00

OH, BROTHER! (Teen Comedy)
Jan, 1953 - No. 5, Oct, 1953
Stanhall Publ.

1-By Bill Williams	5.85	17.50	35.00
2-5	4.00	11.00	22.00

OH MY GODDESS! (Manga)
Aug, 1994 - No. 6, Jan, 1995($2.50, B&W, limited series)
Dark Horse Comics

1-6	1.00	2.50

OH MY GODDESS! PART II (Manga)
Feb, 1995 - No. 9, Sept, 1995 ($2.50, B&W, limited series)
Dark Horse Comics

1-9	1.00	2.50

OH MY GODDESS! PART III (Manga)
Nov, 1995 - No. 11, Sept, 1996 ($2.95, B&W, limited series)
Dark Horse Comics

1-11	1.20	3.00

OH SUSANNA (TV)
No. 1105, June-Aug, 1960 (Gale Storm)
Dell Publishing Co.

Four Color 1105-Toth-a, photo-c	12.50	37.50	125.00

OKAY COMICS
July, 1940
United Features Syndicate

1-Captain & the Kids & Hawkshaw the Detective reprints			
	40.00	120.00	290.00

OK COMICS
July, 1940 - No. 2, Oct, 1940
United Features Syndicate

1-Little Giant, Phantom Knight, Sunset Smith, & The Teller Twins begin			
	67.00	202.00	540.00
2 (Rare)-Origin Mister Mist	67.00	202.00	540.00

OKLAHOMA KID
June, 1957 - No. 4, 1958
Ajax/Farrell Publ.

1	9.15	27.00	55.00
2-4	5.35	16.00	32.00

OKLAHOMAN, THE
No. 820, July, 1957
Dell Publishing Co.

Four Color 820-Movie, photo-c	10.00	30.00	100.00

OKTANE
Aug, 1995 - Nov, 1995($2.50, color, limited series)
Dark Horse Comics

1-4-Gene Ha-a	1.00	2.50

OLD GLORY COMICS
1944 (Giveaway)
Chesapeake & Ohio Railway

nn-Capt. Fearless reprint	5.85	17.50	35.00

OLD IRONSIDES (Disney)
No. 874, 1958
Dell Publishing Co.

Four Color 874-Movie w/Johnny Tremain	7.00	21.00	70.00

OLD YELLER (Disney, see Movie Comics, and Walt Disney Showcase #25)
No. 869, Jan, 1958
Dell Publishing Co.

Four Color 869-Movie, photo-c	7.00	21.00	70.00

OMAC (One Man Army; ...Corps. #4 on; also see Kamandi #59 & Warlord)
Sept-Oct, 1974 - No. 8, Nov-Dec, 1975

100 Pages of Comics © DELL

Omega Men #16 © DC

Onslaught: Marvel #1 © MEG

	GD25	FN65	NM94

National Periodical Publications

1-Origin	1.70	5.00	12.00
2-8: 8-2 pg. Neal Adams ad	1.20	3.00	7.00

NOTE: *Kirby* a-1-8p; c-1-7p. *Kubert* c-8. See Cancelled Comic Cavalcade.

OMAC: ONE MAN ARMY CORPS
1991 - No. 4, 1991 ($3.95, B&W, mini-series, mature readers, 52 pgs.)
DC Comics

Book One - Four: John Byrne-c/a & scripts	1.60		4.00

O'MALLEY AND THE ALLEY CATS
April, 1971 - No. 9, Jan, 1974 (Disney)
Gold Key

1	2.00	6.00	14.00
2-9	1.50	3.80	9.00

OMEGA ELITE
1987 ($1.25)
Blackthorne Publishing

1-Starlin-c			1.25

OMEGA MEN, THE (See Green Lantern #141)
Dec, 1982 - No. 38, May, 1986 ($1.00/$1.50; Baxter paper)
DC Comics

1			1.50
2,4,6-8,11-18,21-36,38: 2-Origin Broot. 7-Origin The Citadel. 26,27-Alan Moore scripts. 30-Intro new Primus. 31-Crisis x-over. 34,35-Teen Titans x-over			1.00
3-1st app. Lobo (5 pgs.)(6/83); Lobo-c	1.00	2.00	5.00
5,9-2nd & 3rd app. Lobo (cameo, 2 pgs. each)		1.20	3.00
10-1st full Lobo story	1.00	2.00	5.00
19-Lobo cameo			1.50
20-2nd full Lobo story		1.60	4.00
37-1st solo Lobo story (8 pg. back-up by Giffen)	1.00		2.50
Annual 1(11/84, 52 pgs.), 2(11/85)			1.50

NOTE: *Giffen* c/a-1-6p. *Morrow* a-24r. *Nino* c/a-16, 21; a-Annual 1i.

OMEGA THE UNKNOWN
March, 1976 - No. 10, Oct, 1977
Marvel Comics Group

1-1st app. Omega		1.20	3.00
2-7,10: 2-Hulk-c/story. 3-Electro-c/story		.70	1.80
8-1st app. 2nd Foolkiller (Greg Salinger), 1 panel only (cameo)			1.50
9-1st full app. 2nd Foolkiller		.80	2.00

NOTE: *Kane* c(p)-3, 5, 8, 9. *Mooney* a-1-3, 4p, 5, 6p, 7, 8i, 9, 10.

OMEN
1989 - No. 3?, 1989 ($2.00, B&W, mature)
Northstar Publishing

1-Tim Vigil-c/a in all	1.00	2.00	5.00
1-2nd printing		.80	2.00
2,3		.80	2.00

OMNI MEN
1987 - No. 3, 1987 ($1.25)
Blackthorne Publishing

1-3			1.25

ONE, THE
July, 1985 - No. 6, Feb, 1986 (Limited series, mature)
Marvel Comics (Epic Comics)

1-Post nuclear holocaust super-hero			1.50
2-6: 2-Intro The Other			1.50

ONE-ARM SWORDSMAN, THE
1987 - No. 12, 1990 ($2.75/$1.80, 52pgs.)
Victory Prod./Leung's Publications #4 on

1-3 ($2.75)		1.10	2.75
4-12: 4-6-$1.80-c. 7-12-$2.00-c			1.80

ONE HUNDRED AND ONE DALMATIANS (Disney, see Cartoon Tales, Movie Comics, and Walt Disney Showcase #9, 51)
No. 1183, Mar, 1961
Dell Publishing Co.

Four Color 1183-Movie	10.00	30.00	100.00

101 DALMATIONS (Movie)
1991 (52 pgs., graphic novel)
Disney Comics

nn-($4.95, direct sales)-r/movie adaptation & more	1.00	2.00	5.00
1-($2.95, newsstand edition)		1.20	3.00

100 PAGES OF COMICS
1937 (Stiff covers, square binding)
Dell Publishing Co.

101(Found on back cover)-Alley Oop, Wash Tubbs, Capt. Easy, Og Son of Fire, Apple Mary, Tom Mix, Dan Dunn, Tailspin Tommy, Doctor Doom	143.00	431.00	1150.00

100 PAGE SUPER SPECTACULAR (See DC 100 Page...)

100% TRUE?
Summer 1996 ($4.95, B&W)
DC Comics (Paradox Press)

1-Reprints stories from various Paradox Press books.			5.00

$1,000,000 DUCK (See Walt Disney Showcase #5)

ONE MILLION YEARS AGO (Tor #2 on)
Sept, 1953
St. John Publishing Co.

1-Origin & 1st app. Tor; Kubert-c/a; Kubert photo inside front cover	18.00	54.00	125.00

ONE SHOT (See Four Color...)

1001 HOURS OF FUN
No. 13, 1943
Dell Publishing Co.

Large Feature Comic 13 (nn)-Puzzles & games; by A.W. Nugent. This book was bound as #13 w/Large Feature Comics in publisher's files	18.00	54.00	180.00

ONSLAUGHT: MARVEL
Oct, 1996 ($3.95, one-shot)
Marvel Comics

1-Conclusion to Onslaught x-over; wraparound-c	1.00	2.00	5.00

ONSLAUGHT: X-MEN
Aug, 1996 ($3.95, one-shot)
Marvel Comics

1-Mark Waid & Scott Lobdell script; Fantastic Four & Avengers app.; Xavier as Onslaught	1.00	2.00	5.00
1-Variant-c			12.00

ON STAGE
No. 1336, Apr-June, 1962
Dell Publishing Co.

Four Color 1336-Not by Leonard Starr	5.00	15.00	50.00

ON THE AIR
1947 (Giveaway, paper-c)
NBC Network Comic

nn-(Rare)	23.00	69.00	160.00

ON THE DOUBLE (Movie)
No. 1232, Sept-Nov, 1961

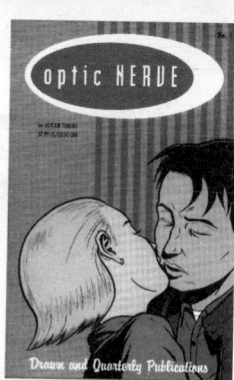
Optic Nerve #1 © Adrian Tomine

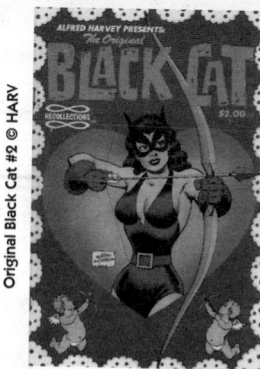
Original Black Cat #2 © HARV

Origin of Galactus #1 © MEG

	GD25	FN65	NM94
Dell Publishing Co.			
Four Color 1232	5.00	15.00	50.00
ON THE ROAD WITH ANDRAE CROUCH			
1973, 1977 (39¢)			
Spire Christian Comics (Fleming H. Revell)			
nn			1.00
ON THE SPOT (Pretty Boy Floyd...)			
Fall, 1948			
Fawcett Publications			
nn-Pretty Boy Floyd photo on-c; bondage-c	27.00	81.00	190.00
ONYX OVERLORD			
Oct., 1992 - No. 4, Jan, 1993 ($2.75, mini-series)			
Marvel Comics (Epic Comics)			
1-4: Moebius scripts		1.10	2.75
OPEN SPACE			
Mid-Dec, 1989 - No. 4, Aug, 1990 ($4.95, bi-monthly, 68 pgs.)			
Marvel Comics			
1-4: 1-Bill Wray-a; Freas-c	1.00	2.00	5.00
OPERATION BIKINI (See Movie Classics)			
OPERATION BUCHAREST (See The Crusaders)			
OPERATION CROSSBOW (See Movie Classics)			
OPERATION: KNIGHTSTRIKE (See Knightstrike)			
May, 1995 - No.3, July, 1995 ($2.50)			
Image Comics (Extreme Studios)			
1-3		1.00	2.50
OPERATION PERIL			
Oct-Nov, 1950 - No. 16, Apr-May, 1953 (#1-5: 52 pgs.)			
American Comics Group (Michel Publ.)			
1-Time Travelers, Danny Danger (by Leonard Starr) & Typhoon Tyler (by Ogden Whitney) begin	33.00	99.00	230.00
2	20.00	60.00	140.00
3-5: 3-Horror story. 5-Sci/fi-c/story	17.00	51.00	120.00
6-12-Last Time Travelers. 6,8,9-Sci/fi-c	14.00	43.00	100.00
13-16: All war format	7.50	22.50	45.00
NOTE: *Starr* a-2, 5. *Whitney* a-1, 2, 5-10, 12; c-1, 3, 5, 8, 9.			
OPTIC NERVE			
Apr, 1995 - Present ($2.95, bi-annual)			
Drawn and Quarterly			
1-3: Adrian Tomine-c/a/scripts	1.00	2.00	5.00
32 Stories-($9.95, trade paperback)-r/Optic Nerve mini-comics			10.00
32 Stories-($29.95, hardcover)-r/Optic Nerve mini-comics; signed & numbered			30.00
ORAL ROBERTS' TRUE STORIES (Junior Partners #120 on)			
1956 (no month) - No. 119, 7/59 (15¢)(No #102: 25¢)			
TelePix Publ. (Oral Roberts' Evangelistic Assoc./Healing Waters)			
V1#1(1956)-(Not code approved)- "The Miracle Touch"	18.00	54.00	125.00
102-(Only issue approved by code, 10/56)	11.00	33.00	75.00
103-119: 115-(114 on inside)	7.50	22.50	45.00
NOTE: *Also see Happiness & Healing For You.*			
ORANGE BIRD, THE			
No date (1980) (36 pgs.; in color; slick cover)			
Walt Disney Educational Media Co.			
nn-Included with educational kit on foods			1.00
..in Nutrition Adventures nn (1980)			.60
..and the Nutrition Know-How Revue nn (1983)			.60

	GD25	FN65	NM94
ORBIT			
1990 - No. 3, 1990 ($4.95, 52 pgs., squarebound)			
Eclipse Books			
1-3: Reprints from Isaac Asimov's Science Fiction Magazine; 1-Dave Stevens-c; Bolton-a. 3-Bolton-c/a, Yeates-a	1.00	2.00	5.00
ORIENTAL HEROES			
Aug, 1988 - No. 26, 1991 ($1.50/$1.95, 68pgs.)			
Jademan Comics			
1-9 ($1.50)			1.5
10-26 ($1.95)		.80	2.00
ORIGINAL ASTRO BOY, THE			
Sept, 1987 - No. 19, 1989 ($1.50/$1.75)			
Now Comics			
1-All have Ken Steacy painted-c/a		1.20	3.00
2,3: 3-Begin $1.75-c		.80	2.00
4-19			1.50
ORIGINAL BLACK CAT, THE			
Oct. 6, 1988 - No. 3, 1989 ($2.00, limited series)			
Recollections			
1-3: Elias-r; 1-Bondage-c. 2-M. Anderson-c		.80	2.00
ORIGINAL DICK TRACY, THE			
Sept, 1990 - No. 5, 1991 ($1.95, bi-monthly, 68pgs.)			
Gladstone Publishing			
1-5: 1-Vs. Pruneface. 2-& the Evil influence; begin $2.00-c		.80	2.00
NOTE: #1 reprints strips 7/16/43 - 9/30/43. #2 reprints strips 12/1/46 - 2/2/47. #3 reprints 8/31/46 - 11/14/46. #4 reprints 9/17/45 - 12/23/45. #5 reprints 6/10/46 - 8/28/46.			
ORIGINAL E-MAN AND MICHAEL MAUSER, THE			
Oct, 1985 - No. 7, April, 1986 ($1.75, Baxter paper)			
First Comics			
1-Has r/Charlton's E-Man, Vengeance Squad		.80	2.00
2-6: 2-Shows #4 in indicia by mistake		.75	1.80
7 ($2.00, 44pgs.)-Staton-a		.80	2.00
ORIGINAL GHOST RIDER, THE			
July, 1992 - No. 20, Feb, 1994 ($1.75)			
Marvel Comics			
1-20: 1-7-r/Marvel Spotlight #5-11 by Ploog w/new-c. 3-New Phantom Rider (former Night Rider) back-ups begin by Ayers. 4-Quesada-c(p). 8-Ploog-c. 8,9-r/Ghost Rider #1,2. 10-r/Marvel Spotlight #12. 11-18,20-r/Ghost Rider #3-12. 19-r/Marvel Two-in-One #8		.70	1.75
ORIGINAL GHOST RIDER RIDES AGAIN, THE			
July, 1991 - No. 7, Jan, 1992, ($1.50, limited series, 52 pgs.)			
Marvel Comics			
1-Reprints Ghost Rider #68(origin),69 w/covers			1.50
2-7: Reprints G.R. #70-81 w/covers			1.50
ORIGINAL NEXUS GRAPHIC NOVEL (See First Comics Graphic Novel #19)			
ORIGINAL SHIELD, THE			
Apr, 1984 - No. 4, Oct, 1984			
Archie Enterprises, Inc.			
1-4: 1,2-Origin Shield; Ayers p-1-4, Nebres c-1,2			1.00
ORIGINAL SWAMP THING SAGA, THE (See DC Special Series #2, 14, 17, 20)			
ORIGIN OF GALACTUS (See Fantastic Four #48-50)			
Feb, 1996 ($2.50, one-shot)			
Marvel Comics			
1-Lee & Kirby reprints w/pin-ups			2.50
ORIGIN OF THE DEFIANT UNIVERSE, THE			
Feb, 1994 ($1.50, 20 pgs., one-shot)			

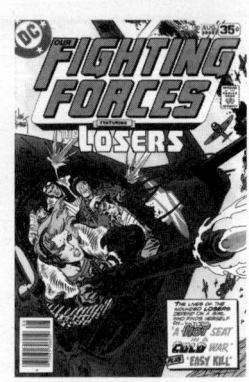
	GD25	FN65	NM94

Defiant Comics

1-David Lapham, Adam Pollina & Alan Weiss-a; Weiss-c ... 1.50

NOTE: *The comic was originally published as Defiant Genesis and was distributed at the 1994 Philadelphia ComicCon.*

OSCAR COMICS (Formerly Funny Tunes; Awful…#11 & 12)
(Also see Cindy Comics)
No. 24, Spring, 1947 - No. 10, Apr, 1949; No. 13, Oct, 1949
Marvel Comics

	GD25	FN65	NM94
24(#1, Spring, 1947)	11.50	34.00	80.00
25(#2, Sum, 1947)-Wolverton-a plus Kurtzman's "Hey Look"			
	14.00	43.00	100.00
26(#3)-Same as regular #3 except #26 was printed over in black ink with #3 appearing on-c below the over print	9.15	27.50	55.00
3-9,13: 8-Margie app.	9.15	27.50	55.00
10-Kurtzman's "Hey Look"	10.00	30.00	70.00

OSWALD THE RABBIT (Also see New Fun Comics #1)
No. 21, 1943 - No. 1268, 12-2/61-62 (Walter Lantz)
Dell Publishing Co.

	GD25	FN65	NM94
Four Color 21(1943)	50.00	150.00	500.00
Four Color 39(1943)	35.00	105.00	350.00
Four Color 67(1944)	17.00	52.00	170.00
Four Color 102(1946)-Kelly-a, 1 pg.	15.00	45.00	150.00
Four Color 143,183	9.00	27.00	90.00
Four Color 225,273	5.00	15.00	50.00
Four Color 315,388	4.00	12.00	40.00
Four Color 458,507,549,593	3.00	9.00	30.00
Four Color 623,697,792,894,979,1268	2.00	6.00	20.00

OSWALD THE RABBIT (See The Funnies, March of Comics #7, 38, 53, 67, 81, 95, 111, 126, 141, 156, 171, 186, New Funnies & Super Book #8, 20)

OTHERS, THE
1995 - No. 3, 1995 ($2.50)
Image Comics (Shadowline Ink)

0 ($1.00)-16 pg. preview			1.00
1-3		1.00	2.50

OUTCAST, THE
Dec, 1995 ($2.50, one-shot)
Valiant

1-Breyfogle-a		1.00	2.50

OUR ARMY AT WAR (Becomes Sgt. Rock #302 on; also see Army At War)
Aug, 1952 - No. 301, Feb, 1977
National Periodical Publications

	GD25	FN65	NM94
1	143.00	431.00	1150.00
2	65.00	195.00	525.00
3,4: 4-Krigstein-a	48.00	146.00	390.00
5-7	40.00	120.00	320.00
8-11,14-Krigstein-a	40.00	120.00	290.00
12,15-20	34.00	103.00	240.00
13-Krigstein-c/a; flag-c	36.00	109.00	255.00
21-31: Last precode (2/55)	24.00	71.00	165.00
32-40	19.00	58.00	135.00
41-60: 51-1st S.A. issue	17.00	49.00	115.00
61-70	13.50	41.00	95.00
71-80	11.50	34.00	80.00
81-1st Sgt. Rock app. (4/59) by Andru & Esposito in Easy Co. story			
	167.00	501.00	2000.00
82-Sgt. Rock cameo in Easy Co. story (6 panels)	56.00	168.00	450.00
83-1st Kubert Sgt. Rock (6/59)	93.00	281.00	750.00
84,86-90	26.00	77.00	180.00
85-Origin & 1st app. Ice Cream Soldier	32.00	96.00	225.00
91-All Sgt. Rock issue	58.00	174.00	465.00

92-100: 95-1st app. Bulldozer; 1st app. Zack. 99-Sgt. Rock-c by Kubert

	GD25	FN65	NM94
	14.00	43.00	110.00
101-120: 101-1st app. Buster. 111-1st app. Wee Willie & Sunny. 113-1st app. Wildman & Jackie Johnson. 115-Rock revealed as orphan; 1st x-over Mlle Marie. 118-Sunny dies	8.75	26.00	70.00
121-127,129-150: 126-1st app. Canary; grey tone-c. 127-1st app. Little Sure Shot. 140-All Sgt. Rock issue	5.70	17.00	45.00
128-Training & origin Sgt. Rock	21.00	64.00	165.00
151-Intro. Enemy Ace by Kubert (2/65)	31.00	92.00	275.00
152,154,156,157,159-163,165-170: 157-2 pg. pin-up. 162,163-Viking Prince x-over in Sgt. Rock	5.00	15.00	38.00
153-2nd app. Enemy Ace (4/65)	14.00	43.00	115.00
155-3rd app. Enemy Ace (6/65)(see Showcase)	8.75	26.00	70.00
158-Origin & 1st app. Iron Major(9/65), formerly Iron Captain			
	5.70	17.00	42.00
164-Giant G-19	8.00	23.50	60.00
171-176,178-181	3.75	11.25	28.00
177-(80 pg. Giant G-32)	5.00	15.00	40.00
182,183,186-Neal Adams-a. 186-Origin retold	4.00	12.00	30.00
184,185,187-189,191-199: 184-Wee Willie dies. 189-Intro. The Teen-age Underground Fighters of Unit 3	3.40	10.00	24.00
190-(80 pg. Giant G-44)	3.75	11.25	28.00
200-12 pg. Rock story told in verse; Evans-a	2.85	8.50	20.00
201-Krigstein-r/#14	1.50	3.75	9.00
202,204-215: 204,205-All reprints; no Sgt. Rock	1.20	3.00	7.00
203-(80 pg. Giant G-56)-All-r, Sgt. Rock story	2.60	7.50	18.00
216,229-(80 pg. Giants G-68, G-80): 216-Has G-58 on-c by mistake			
	2.15	6.50	15.00
217-228,230-239,241	1.00	2.60	6.00
240-Neal Adams-a	1.20	3.00	7.00
242-(50¢ issue DC-9)-Kubert-c	1.20	3.00	7.00
243-301: 244-N. Adams-a? 270,275-(100 pgs.). 280-(68 pgs.)-200th app. Sgt. Rock; reprints Our Army at War #81,83	1.00	2.60	6.00

NOTE: **Alcala** a-251. **Drucker** a-27, 67, 68, 79, 82, 83, 96, 164, 177, 203, 212, 243r, 244, 269r, 275r, 280r. **Evans** a-165-175, 200, 266, 269, 270, 274, 278, 280. **Glanzman** a-218, 220, 222, 223, 225, 227, 230-232, 238-241, 244, 247, 248, 256-259, 261, 265-267, 271, 282, 283, 298. **Grandenetti** c-91. **Grell** a-287. **Heath** a-50, 164, & most 176-281. **Kubert** a-38, 59, 67, 68 & most issues from 83-165, 233, 236, 267, 275, 300; c-84, 280. **Maurer** a-233, 237, 239, 240, 45, 280, 284, 288, 290, 291, 295. **Severin** a-236, 252, 265, 267, 269r, 272. **Toth** a-235, 241, 254. **Wildey** a-283-285, 287p. **Wood** a-249.

OUR FIGHTING FORCES
Oct-Nov, 1954 - No. 181, Sept-Oct, 1978
National Periodical Publications/DC Comics

	GD25	FN65	NM94
1-Grandenetti-c/a	85.00	256.00	685.00
2	40.00	120.00	320.00
3-Kubert-c; last precode issue (3/55)	39.00	118.00	275.00
4,5	30.00	90.00	210.00
6-9: 7-1st S.A. issue	24.00	73.00	170.00
10-Wood-a	26.00	77.00	180.00
11-20: 20-Grey tone-c (4/57)	19.00	58.00	135.00
21-30	13.00	39.00	90.00
31-40	12.00	36.00	85.00
41-Unknown Soldier tryout	14.00	43.00	100.00
42-44	11.00	33.00	75.00
45-Gunner & Sarge begins, end #94	37.00	111.00	260.00
46	15.00	45.00	105.00
47	11.00	33.00	75.00
48,50	7.00	21.50	55.00
49-1st Pooch	11.00	33.00	80.00
51-64: 51-Grey tone-c. 64-Last 10¢ issue	6.50	19.50	50.00
65-70	5.00	15.00	38.00
71-80: 71-Grey tone-c	2.85	8.50	20.00
81-90	2.60	7.50	18.00
91-98,100: 95-Devil-Dog begins, ends 98.	1.85	5.50	13.00
99-Capt. Hunter begins, ends #106	2.60	7.50	18.00

101-181: 106-Hunters Hellcats begin. 116-Mlle. Marie app. 121-Intro. Heller.

Outbreed 999 #1 © Blackout Comics

Outcasts #2 © DC

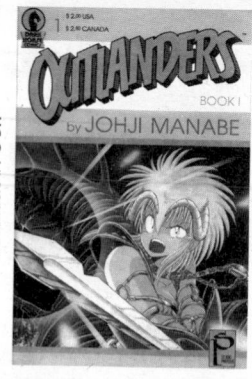

Outlanders #1 © DH

123-Losers (Capt. Storm, Gunner & Sarge, Johnny Cloud) begin by Kirby.
134,146-Toth-a   1.65   4.20   10.00
NOTE: **N. Adams** c-147. **Drucker** a-28, 37, 39, 42-44, 49, 53, 133r. **Evans** a-149, 164-174, 177-181. **Glanzman** a-125-128, 132, 134, 138-141, 143, 144. **Heath** a-2, 16, 18, 28, 41, 44, 49, 114, 135-139r; c-51. **Kirby** a-151-162p; c-152-159. **Kubert** c/a in many issues. **Maurer** a-135. **Redondo** a-166. **Severin** a-123-130, 131i, 132-150.

OUR FIGHTING MEN IN ACTION (See Men In Action)

OUR FLAG COMICS
Aug, 1941 - No. 5, April, 1942
Ace Magazines

1-Captain Victory, The Unknown Soldier (intro.) & The Three Cheers begin
   193.00   581.00   1550.00
2-Origin The Flag (patriotic hero); 1st app?   103.00   309.00   825.00
3-5: 5-Intro & 1st app. Mr. Risk   83.00   249.00   665.00
NOTE: **Anderson** a-1, 4. **Mooney** a-1, 2; c-2.

OUR GANG COMICS (With Tom & Jerry #39-59; becomes Tom & Jerry #60 on; based on film characters)
Sept-Oct, 1942 - No. 59, June, 1949
Dell Publishing Co.

1-Our Gang & Barney Bear by Kelly, Tom & Jerry, Pete Smith, Flip & Dip,
   The Milky Way begin (all 1st app.)   100.00   300.00   800.00
2-Benny Burro begins (#2 by Kelly)   43.00   130.00   430.00
3-5   29.00   86.00   290.00
6-Bumbazine & Albert only app. by Kelly   43.00   130.00   430.00
7-No Kelly story   22.00   65.00   220.00
8-Benny Burro begins by Barks   57.00   171.00   570.00
9-Barks-a(2): Benny Burro & Happy Hound; no Kelly story
   50.00   150.00   500.00
10-Benny Burro by Barks   36.00   107.00   360.00
11-1st Barney Bear & Benny Burro by Barks (5-6/44); Happy Hound by Barks
   50.00   150.00   500.00
12-20   22.00   66.00   220.00
21-30: 30-X-Mas-c   14.00   43.00   140.00
31-36-Last Barks issue   10.00   30.00   100.00
37-40   5.00   15.00   50.00
41-50   4.00   12.00   40.00
51-57   3.00   9.00   30.00
58,59-No Kelly art or Our Gang stories   2.50   7.50   25.00
NOTE: **Barks** art in part only. **Barks** did not write Barney Bear stories #30-34. (See March of Comics #3, 26). Early issues have photo back-c.

OUR LADY OF FATIMA
3/11/55 (15¢) (36 pgs.)
Catechetical Guild Educational Society

395   3.00   7.50   15.00

OUR LOVE (True Secrets #3 on? or Romantic Affairs #3 on?)
Sept, 1949 - No. 2, Jan, 1950
Marvel Comics (SPC)

1-Photo-c   10.00   30.00   70.00
2-Photo-c   6.70   20.00   40.00

OUR LOVE STORY
Oct, 1969 - No. 38, Feb, 1976
Marvel Comics Group

1   1.65   4.20   10.00
2-4,6-13   1.80   4.50
5-Steranko-a   2.00   6.00   14.00
14-New story by Gary Fredrich & Tarpe' Mills   1.00   2.60   6.00
15-38: 27-Colan/Everett-a(r?); Kirby/Colletta-r   1.00   2.00
NOTE: **J. Buscema** a-1-3, 5-7, 9, 13r, 16r, 19r(2), 21r, 22r(2), 23r, 34r, 35r; c-11, 13, 16, 22, 23, 24, 27, 35. **Colan** a-3-6, 21r(#6), 22r, 23r(#3), 24r(#4), 27; c-19. **Katz** a-17. **Weiss** a-16, 17, 29r(#17).

OUR MISS BROOKS
No. 751, Nov, 1956

Dell Publishing Co.

Four Color 751-Photo-c   8.00   24.00   80.00

OUR SECRET (Exciting Love Stories)(Formerly My Secret)
No. 4, Nov, 1949 - No. 8, Jun, 1950
Superior Comics Ltd.

4-Kamen-a; spanking scene   13.00   39.00   90.00
5,6,8   8.00   24.00   48.00
7-Contains 9 pg. story intended for unpublished Ellery Queen #5; lingerie
   panels   10.00   30.00   58.00

OUTBREED 999
May, 1994 - No. 6, 1994 ($2.95)
Blackout Comics

1-6: 4-1st app. of Extreme Violet in 7 pg. backup story
   1.20   3.00

OUTCASTS
Oct, 1987 - No. 12, Sept, 1988 ($1.75, mini-series)
DC Comics

1-12: John Wagner & Alan Grant scripts in all   .75   1.80

OUTER LIMITS, THE (TV)
Jan-Mar, 1964 - No. 18, Oct, 1969 (All painted-c)
Dell Publishing Co.

1   7.00   21.50   70.00
2   4.00   12.00   40.00
3-10   3.00   9.00   30.00
11-18: 17-Reprints #1. 18-r/#2   2.50   7.50   25.00

OUTER SPACE (Formerly This Magazine Is Haunted, 2nd Series)
No. 17, May, 1958 - No. 25, Dec, 1959; Nov, 1968
Charlton Comics

17-Williamson/Wood style art; not by them (Sid Check?)
   11.00   33.00   75.00
18-20-Ditko-a   17.00   49.00   115.00
21-25: 21-Ditko-c   8.50   26.00   65.00
V2#1(11/68)-Ditko-a, Boyette-c   4.30   13.00   35.00

OUTER SPACE BABES, THE
Feb, 1994 ($2.95)
Silhouette Studios

V3#1   1.20   3.00

OUTLANDERS (Manga)
Dec, 1988 - No. 25, 1991 ($2.00-$2.50, B&W, 44pgs.)
Dark Horse Comics

1-7: Japanese Sci-fi manga   .80   2.00
8-21 ($2.25)   .90   2.25
22-25 ($2.50)   1.00   2.50

OUTLAW (See Return of the...)

OUTLAW FIGHTERS
Aug, 1954 - No. 5, Apr, 1955
Atlas Comics (IPC)

1-Tuska-a   10.00   30.00   70.00
2-5: 5-Heath-c/a, 7 pgs.   7.00   21.00   42.00
NOTE: **Heath** c/a-5. **Maneely** c-2. **Pakula** a-2. **Reinman** a-2. **Tuska** a-1, 2.

OUTLAW KID, THE (1st Series; see Wild Western)
Sept, 1954 - No. 19, Sept, 1957
Atlas Comics (CCC No. 1-11/EPI No. 12-29)

1-Origin; The Outlaw Kid & his horse Thunder begin; Black Rider app.
   19.00   58.00   135.00
2-Black Rider app.   10.00   30.00   70.00
3-7,9: 3-Wildey-a(3)   10.00   30.00   65.00
8-Williamson/Woodbridge-a, 4 pgs.   8.00   24.00   48.00

Outlaw Kid #10 © MEG

Outlaws #5 © DC

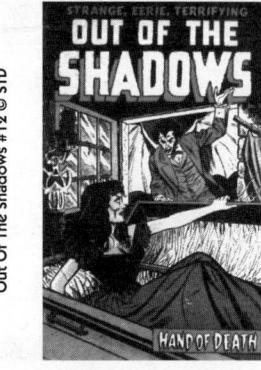

Out Of The Shadows #12 © STD

	GD25	FN65	NM94
10-Williamson-a	8.35	25.00	50.00
11-17,19: 13-Baker text illo (unsigned)			
	5.85	17.50	35.00
18-Williamson/Mayo-a	7.00	21.00	42.00

NOTE: *Berg* a-4, 7, 13. *Maneely* c-1-3, 5-8, 11-13, 15, 16, 18. *Pakula* a-3. *Severin* c-10, 17, 19. *Shores* a-1. *Wildey* a-1(3), 2-8, 10, 11, 12(4), 13(4), 15-19(4 each); c-4.

OUTLAW KID, THE (2nd Series)
Aug, 1970 - No. 30, Oct, 1975
Marvel Comics Group

		GD25	FN65
1,2-Reprints; 1-Orlando-r, Wildey-r(3)		1.60	4.00
3,9-Williamson-a(r)		.80	2.00
4-8: 8-Double size; Crandall-r		.80	2.00
10-30: 10-Origin; new-a in #10-16. 27-Origin-r/#10		.75	1.80

NOTE: *Ayers* a-10, 27r. *Berg* a-7, 25r. *Everett* a-2(2 pgs.). *Gil Kane* c-10, 11, 15, 27r, 28. *Roussos* a-10i, 27i(r). *Severin* c-1, 9, 20, 25. *Wildey* r-1-4, 6-9, 19-22, 25, 26. *Williamson* a-28r. *Woodbridge/Williamson* a-9r.

OUTLAWS
Feb-Mar, 1948 - No. 9, June-July, 1949
D. S. Publishing Co.

	GD25	FN65	NM94
1-Violent & suggestive stories	25.00	75.00	175.00
2-Ingels-a; Baker-a	25.00	75.00	175.00
3,5,6: 3-Not Frazetta. 5-Sky Sheriff by Good app. 6-McWilliams-a			
	11.00	33.00	75.00
4-Orlando-a	13.00	39.00	90.00
7,8-Ingels-a in each	19.00	58.00	135.00
9-(Scarce)-Frazetta-a (7 pgs.)	40.00	120.00	300.00

NOTE: Another #3 was printed in Canada with Frazetta art "Prairie Jinx", 7 pgs.

OUTLAWS, THE (Formerly Western Crime Cases)
No. 10, May, 1952 - No. 13, Sept, 1953; No. 14, April, 1954
Star Publishing Co.

	GD25	FN65	NM94
10-L. B. Cole-c	13.00	39.00	90.00
11-14-L. B. Cole-c. 14-Reprints Western Thrillers #4 (Fox) w/new L.B. Cole-c;			
Kamen, Feldstein-r	10.00	30.00	65.00

OUTLAWS
Sept, 1991 - No. 8, Apr, 1992 ($1.95, limited series)
DC Comics

1-8: Post-apocalyptic Robin Hood.			2.00

OUTLAWS OF THE WEST (Formerly Cody of the Pony Express #10)
No. 11, 7/57 - No. 81, 5/70; No. 82, 7/79 - No. 88, 4/80
Charlton Comics

	GD25	FN65	NM94
11	7.50	22.50	45.00
12,13,15-17,19,20	4.00	11.00	22.00
14-(68 pgs.), 2/58)	4.35	13.00	26.00
18-Ditko-a	8.35	25.00	55.00
21-30	2.30	6.70	16.00
31-50	1.50	3.75	9.00
51-70: 54-Kid Montana app. 64-Captain Doom begins (1st app.)			
	1.00	2.00	5.00
71-81: 73-Origin & 1st app. The Sharp Shooter, last app. #74. 75-Last Capt.			
Doom. 80,81-Ditko-a	1.20		3.00
82-88			1.50
64,79(Modern Comics-r, 1977, '78)			1.00

OUTLAWS OF THE WILD WEST
1952 (25¢, 132 pgs.) (4 rebound comics)
Avon Periodicals

	GD25	FN65	NM94
1-Wood back-c; Kubert-a (3 Jesse James-r)	26.00	79.00	185.00

OUTLAW TRAIL (See Zane Grey 4-Color 511)

OUT OF SANTA'S BAG (See March of Comics #10)

OUT OF THE NIGHT (The Hooded Horseman #18 on)
Feb-Mar, 1952 - No. 17, Oct-Nov, 1954

	GD25	FN65	NM94
American Comics Group (Creston/Scope)			
1-Williamson/LeDoux-a (9 pgs.)	53.00	159.00	425.00
2-Williamson-a (5 pgs.)	44.00	132.00	355.00
3,5-10: 9-Sci/Fic story	21.00	64.00	150.00
4-Williamson-a (7 pgs.)	40.00	120.00	290.00
11-17: 13-Nostrand-a? 17-E.C. Wood swipe	17.00	49.00	115.00

NOTE: *Landau* a-14, 16, 17. *Shelly* a-12.

OUT OF THE PAST A CLUE TO THE FUTURE
1946? (16 pgs.) (paper cover)
E. C. Comics (Public Affairs Comm.)

	GD25	FN65	NM94
nn-Based on public affairs pamphlet "What Foreign Trade Means to You"			
	24.00	71.00	165.00

OUT OF THE SHADOWS
No. 5, July, 1952 - No. 14, Aug, 1954
Standard Comics/Visual Editions

	GD25	FN65	NM94
5-Toth-p; Moreira, Tuska-a; Roussos-c	40.00	120.00	285.00
6-Toth/Celardo-a; Katz-a(2)	29.00	86.00	200.00
7-Jack Katz-c/a(2)	19.00	56.00	130.00
8,10: 8-Katz shrunken head-c. 10-Sekowsky-a	15.00	45.00	105.00
9-Crandall-a(2)	19.00	56.00	130.00
11-Toth-a, 2 pgs.; Katz-a; Andru-c	19.00	56.00	130.00
12-Toth/Peppe-a(2); Katz-a	29.00	86.00	200.00
13-Cannabalism story; Sekowsky-a; Roussos-a	21.00	62.00	145.00
14-Toth-a	21.00	62.00	145.00

OUT OF THE VORTEX (Comics' Greatest World:... #1-4)
Oct., 1993 - No. 12, Oct, 1994 ($2.00, limited series)
Dark Horse Comics

	GD25	FN65	NM94
1-11: 1-Foil logo. 4-Dorman-c(p). 6-Hero Zero x-over		.80	2.00
12 ($2.50)			2.50

NOTE: *Art Adams* c-7. *Golden* c-8. *Mignola* c-2. *Simonson* c-3. *Zeck* c-10.

OUT OF THIS WORLD
Aug, 1956 - No. 16, Dec, 1959
Charlton Comics

	GD25	FN65	NM94
1	19.00	58.00	135.00
2	11.00	33.00	75.00
3-6-Ditko-c/a (3) each	24.00	73.00	170.00
7-(2/58, 15¢, 68 pgs.)-Ditko-c/a(4)	24.00	73.00	170.00
8-(5/58, 15¢, 68 pgs.)-Ditko-a(2)	20.00	60.00	140.00
9,10,12,16-Ditko-a.	17.00	49.00	115.00
11-Ditko c/a (3)	18.00	54.00	125.00
13-15	8.00	24.00	48.00

NOTE: *Ditko* c-3-12, 16. *Reinman* a-10.

OUT OF THIS WORLD (...Adventures #2)
June, 1950; No. 2, Dec, 1950 (25¢ pulp)
Avon Periodicals

	GD25	FN65	NM94
1-Kubert-a(2) (one reprinted/Eerie #1, 1947) plus Crom the Barbarian by			
Gardner Fox & John Giunta (origin); Fawcette-c.; pulp magazine w/comic			
insert	53.00	159.00	425.00
2-Kubert-a plus The Spider God of Akka by Gardner Fox & John Giunta.			
	40.00	120.00	300.00

NOTE: *Out of This World Adventures is a sci-fi pulp magazine w/32 pgs. of color comics.*

OUT OUR WAY WITH WORRY WART
No. 680, Feb, 1956
Dell Publishing Co.

	GD25	FN65	NM94
Four Color 680	3.00	9.00	30.00

OUTPOSTS
June, 1987 - No. 4, 1987 ($1.25)
Blackthorne Publishing

1-4: 1-Kaluta-c(p)			1.25

OUTSIDERS, THE

Outsiders #17 © DC

Over The Edge #4 © MEG

Ozzie & Babs #3 © FAW

	GD25	FN65	NM94

Nov, 1987 - No. 28, Feb, 1988
DC Comics

1			1.50
2-28: 18-26-Batman returns. 21-Intro. Strike Force Kobra. 22-E.C. parody; Orlando-a. 21-1st app. Clayface IV. 25-Atomic Knight app. 27,28-Millennium tie-ins.			1.00
Annual 1 (12/86, $2.50)		.80	2.00
Special 1 (7/87, $1.50)			1.50

NOTE: *Aparo* a-1-7, 9-14, 17-22, 25, 26; c-1-7, 9-14, 17, 19-26. *Byrne* a-11. *Bolland* a-6, 18; c-16. *Ditko* a-13p. *Erik Larsen* a-24, 27 28; c-27, 28. *Morrow* a-12.

OUTSIDERS
Nov, 1993 - No. 24, Nov, 1995 ($1.75/$1.95/$2.25)
DC Comics

1-Alpha; Travis Charest-c		.70	1.75
1-Omega; Travis Charest-c		.70	1.75
2-9: 5-Atomic Knight app. 8-New Batman-c/story		.70	1.75
10,11: 10-Begin $1.95-c. 11-(9/94)-Zero Hour		.80	2.00
0,12-18: 0-(10/94).12-(11/94).		.80	2.00
19-24: 19-Begin $2.25-c. 21-Darkseid cameo. 22-New Gods app.		.90	2.25

OUTSTANDING AMERICAN WAR HEROES
1944 (16 pgs., paper-c)
The Parents' Institute

nn-Reprints from True Comics	4.00	10.00	20.00

OVERSEAS COMICS (Also see G.I. Comics & Jeep Comics)
1944 - No. 105?, 1946 (7-1/4x10-1/4"; 16 pgs. in color)
Giveaway (Distributed to U.S. armed forces)

23-105-Bringing Up Father (by McManus), Popeye, Joe Palooka, Dick Tracy, Superman, Gasoline Alley, Buz Sawyer, Li'l Abner, Blondie, Terry & the Pirates, Out Our Way	5.00	15.00	30.00

OVER THE EDGE
Nov, 1995 - Present (99¢)
Marvel Comics

1-10: 1,6,10-Daredevil-c/story. 2,7-Dr. Strange-c/story. 3-Hulk-c/story. 4,9-Ghost Rider-c/story. 5-Punisher-c/story. 8-Elektra-c/story			1.00

OWL, THE (See Crackajack Funnies #25 & Popular Comics #72)(Also see The Hurricane Kids & Magic Morro
1940 (Giveaway)(7-1/2x5-1/4")(Soft-c, color)
Western Publ. Co./R.S. Callender

nn-Frank Thomas-a	17.00	51.00	120.00

OWL, THE (See Crackajack Funnies #25 & Popular Comics #72)
April, 1967; No. 2, April, 1968
Gold Key

1,2-Written by Jerry Siegel; '40s super hero	2.80	8.40	28.00

OXYDOL-DREFT
1950 (Set of 6 pocket-size giveaways; distributed through the mail as a set)
Oxydol-Dreft (Scarce)

1-3: 1-Li'l Abner. 2-Daisy Mae. 3-Shmoo	10.00	30.00	70.00
4-John Wayne; Williamson/Frazetta from John Wayne #3	15.00	45.00	105.00
5-Archie	11.00	33.00	75.00
6-Terrytoons Mighty Mouse	10.00	30.00	70.00

NOTE: *Set is worth more with original envelope.*

OZ (See First Comics Graphic Novel, Marvel Treaury Of Oz & MGM's Marvelous...)

OZARK IKE
Feb, 1948; Nov, 1948 - No. 24, Dec, 1951; No. 25, Sept, 1952
Dell Publishing Co./Standard Comics B11 on

Four Color 180(1948-Dell)	10.00	30.00	100.00

	GD25	FN65	NM94

B11, B12, 13-15	8.35	25.00	50.00
16-25	6.35	19.00	38.00

OZ SQUAD
1992 - No. 4, 1994 ($2.50/$2.75, B&W)
Brave New Worlds/Patchwork Press (No. 4)

1-3		1.00	2.50
4		1.10	2.75

OZ SQUAD
Dec, 1995 - No. 8?, 1996 ($2.95, B&W)
Patchwork Press

1 ($3.95)		1.60	4.00
2-8		1.20	3.00

OZ-WONDERLAND WARS, THE
Jan, 1986 - No. 3, March, 1986 (Mini-series)
DC Comics

1-3	.40	1.00	2.00

OZZIE & BABS (TV Teens #14 on)
Dec, 1947 - No. 13, Fall, 1949
Fawcett Publications

1-Teen-age	8.35	25.00	50.00
2	4.35	13.00	26.00
3-13	4.00	10.00	20.00

OZZIE & HARRIET (See The Adventures of...)

PACIFIC COMICS GRAPHIC NOVEL (See Image Graphic Novel)

PACIFIC PRESENTS (Also see Starslayer #2, 3)
Oct, 1982 - No. 2, Apr, 1983; No. 3, Mar, 1984 - No. 4, June, 1984
Pacific Comics

1-Chapter 3 of The Rocketeer; Stevens-c/a	1.00	2.00	5.00
2-Chapter 4 of The Rocketeer (4th app.); nudity; Stevens-c/a		1.60	4.00
3,4: 3-1st app. Vanity		.80	2.00

NOTE: *Conrad* a-3, 4; c-3. *Ditko* a-1-3; c-1(1/2). *Dave Stevens* a-1, 2; c-1(1/2), 2.

PACT, THE
Feb, 1994 - No. 3, June, 1994 ($1.95, limited series)
Image Comics

1-3: Valentino co-scripts & layouts		.80	2.00

PADRE OF THE POOR
nd (Giveaway) (16 pgs., paper-c)
Catechetical Guild

nn	2.00	5.00	10.00

PAGEANT OF COMICS (See Jane Arden & Mopsy)
Sept, 1947 - No. 2, Oct, 1947
Archer St. John

1-Mopsy strip-r	8.70	26.00	52.00
2-Jane Arden strip-r	8.70	26.00	52.00

PANCHO VILLA
1950
Avon Periodicals

nn-Kinstler-c	20.00	60.00	140.00

PANHANDLE PETE AND JENNIFER (TV) (See Gene Autry #20)
July, 1951 - No. 3, Nov, 1951
J. Charles Laue Publishing Co.

1	9.15	27.00	55.00
2,3	6.35	19.00	38.00

PANIC (Companion to Mad)
Feb-Mar, 1954 - No. 12, Dec-Jan, 1955-56
E. C. Comics (Tiny Tot Comics)

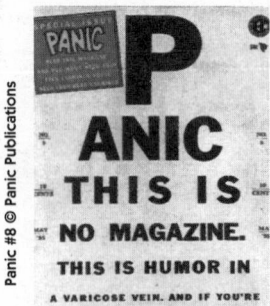

Panic #8 © Panic Publications

Paradax #2 © Vortex

Parts Unknown #1 © Beau Smith & Brad Gorby

1-Used in Senate Investigation hearings; Elder draws entire E. C. staff; Santa
Claus & Mickey Spillane parody ... 24.00 71.00 165.00
2 ... 11.00 33.00 75.00
3,4: 3-Senate Subcommittee parody; Davis draws Gaines, Feldstein & Kelly,
1 pg.; Old King Cole smokes marijuana. 4-Infinity-c; John Wayne parody
... 10.00 30.00 65.00
5-11: 8-Last pre-code issue (5/55). 9-Superman, Smilin' Jack & Dick Tracy
app. on-c; has photo of Walter Winchell on-c ... 9.15 27.50 55.00
12 (Low distribution; thousands were destroyed) ... 11.00 33.00 75.00
NOTE: **Davis** a-1-12; c-12. **Elder** a-1-12. **Feldstein** c-1-3, 5. **Kamen** a-1. **Orlando** a-1-9.
Wolverton c-4, panel-3. **Wood** a-2-9, 11, 12.

PANIC (Magazine) (Satire)
July, 1958 - No. 6, July, 1959; V2#10, Dec, 1965 - V2#12, 1966
Panic Publications
1 ... 10.00 30.00 60.00
2-6 ... 5.00 15.00 30.00
V2#10-12: Reprints earlier issues ... 4.00 11.00 22.00
NOTE: **Davis** a-3(2 pgs.), 4, 5, 10; c-10. **Elder** a-5. **Powell** a-V2#10, 11. **Torres** a-1-5. **Tuska** a-
V2#11.

PARADAX (Also see Strange Days)
1986 (one-shot)
Eclipse Comics
1 ... .80 2.00

PARADAX
April, 1987 - No. 2, Aug, 1987 ($1.75, mature)
Vortex Comics
1,2-Nudity, adult language ... .75 1.80

PARADE (See Hanna-Barbera...)

PARADE COMICS (Frisky Animals on Parade #2 on)
Sept, 1957
Ajax/Farrell Publ. (World Famous Publ.)
1 ... 5.35 16.00 32.00
NOTE: Cover title: Frisky Animals on Parade.

PARADE OF PLEASURE
1954 (192 pgs.) (Hardback book)
Derric Verschoyle Ltd., London, England
By Geoffrey Wagner. Contains section devoted to the censorship of American
comic books with illustrations in color and black and white. (Also see
Seduction of the Innocent). Distributed in USA by Library Publishers,
N. Y. ... 39.00 118.00 275.00
with dust jacket.... 65.00 195.00 525.00

PARADOX
June, 1994 - No. 2, July?, 1994 ($2.95, B&W, mature)
Dark Visions Comics
1,2: 1-Linsner-c. 2-Boris-c. ... 1.00 2.00 5.00

PARALLAX: EMERALD NIGHT (See Final Night)
Nov, 1996 ($2.95, one-shot, 48 pgs.)
DC Comics
1-Final Night tie-in; Green Lantern (Kyle Rayner) app. ... 3.00

PARAMOUNT ANIMATED COMICS (See Harvey Comics Hits #60, 62)
Feb, 1953 - No. 22, July, 1956
Harvey Publications
1-Baby Huey, Herman & Katnip, Buzzy the Crow begin
... 19.00 56.00 130.00
2 ... 10.00 30.00 70.00
3-6 ... 8.35 25.00 50.00
7-Baby Huey becomes permanent cover feature; cover title becomes Baby
Huey with #9 ... 18.00 54.00 125.00
8-10: 9-Infinity-c ... 8.00 24.00 48.00
11-22 ... 5.35 16.00 32.00

PARENT TRAP, THE (Disney)
No. 1210, Oct-Dec, 1961
Dell Publishing Co.
Four Color 1210-Movie, Haley Mills photo-c ... 10.00 30.00 100.00

PARODY
Mar, 1977 - No. 3, Aug, 1977 (B&W humor magazine)
Armour Publishing
1-3 ... .80 2.00

PAROLE BREAKERS
Dec, 1951 - No. 3, July, 1952
Avon Periodicals/Realistic #2 on
1(#2 on inside)-r-c/Avon paperback #283 (painted) 38.00 114.00 265.00
2-Kubert-a; r-c/Avon paperback #114 (photo-c) 26.00 77.00 180.00
3-Kinstler-c ... 24.00 71.00 165.00

PARTRIDGE FAMILY, THE (TV)(Also see David Cassidy)
Mar, 1971 - No. 21, Dec, 1973
Charlton Comics
1 ... 3.40 10.00 24.00
2-4,6-21 ... 1.70 5.00 12.00
5-Partridge Family Summer Special (52 pgs.); The Shadow, Lone Ranger,
Charlie McCarthy, Flash Gordon, Hopalong Cassidy, Gene Autry & others
app. ... 3.75 11.25 28.00

PARTS UNKNOWN
July, 1992 - No. 4, Oct, 1992 ($2.50, B&W, mini-series, mature)
Eclipse Comics/FX
1-4: All contain FX gaming cards ... 1.00 2.50

PASSION, THE
No. 394, 1955
Catechetical Guild
394 ... 2.80 7.00 14.00

PAT BOONE (TV)(Also see Superman's Girlfriend Lois Lane #9)
Sept-Oct, 1959 - No. 5, May-Jun, 1960 (All have photo-c)
National Periodical Publications
1 ... 40.00 120.00 300.00
2-5: 3-Fabian, Connie Francis & Paul Anka photos on-c. 4-Previews "Journey
To The Center Of The Earth". 4-Johnny Mathis & Bobbie Darin photos on-c.
5-Dick Clark & Frankie Avalon photos on-c ... 34.00 103.00 240.00

PATCHES
Mar-Apr, 1945 - No. 11, Nov, 1947
Rural Home/Patches Publ. (Orbit)
1-L. B. Cole-c ... 26.00 77.00 180.00
2 ... 10.00 30.00 70.00
3,4,6,8-11: 6-Henry Aldrich story. 8-Smiley Burnette-c/s (6/47); pre-dates
Smiley Burnette #1. 9-Mr. District Attorney story (radio). Leav/Keigstein-a
(16 pgs.). 9-11-Leav-c. 10-Jack Carson (radio) c/story; Leav-c. 11-Red
Skelton story ... 10.00 30.00 65.00
5-Danny Kaye-c/story; L.B. Cole-c. ... 13.00 39.00 90.00
7-Hopalong Cassidy-c/story ... 11.50 34.00 80.00

PATHWAYS TO FANTASY
July, 1984
Pacific Comics
1-Barry Smith-c/a; Jeff Jones-a (4 pgs.) ... 1.50

PATORUZU (See Adventures of...)

PATSY & HEDY (Teenage)(Also see Hedy Wolfe)
Feb, 1952 - No. 110, Feb, 1967
Atlas Comics/Marvel (GPI/Male)
1-Patsy Walker & Hedy Wolfe; Al Jaffee-c ... 16.00 47.00 110.00
2 ... 9.15 27.00 55.00

Patsy Walker #5 © MEG

Paul the Samurai #2 © Ben Edlund

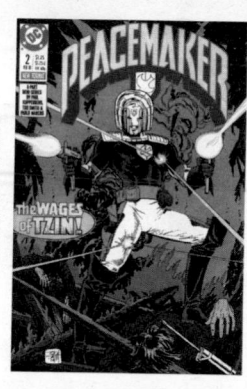

Peacemaker #2 © MEG

	GD25	FN65	NM94
3-10: 3,8-Al Jaffee-c	7.00	21.00	42.00
11-20	5.00	15.00	30.00
21-40	4.00	12.00	24.00
41-60	2.60	7.50	18.00
61-110: 88-Lingerie panel	1.50	3.75	9.00
Annual 1(1963)-Early Marvel annual	6.00	18.00	42.00

PATSY & HER PALS (Teenage)
May, 1953 - No. 29, Aug, 1957
Atlas Comics (PPI)

1-Patsy Walker	13.00	39.00	90.00
2	7.50	22.50	45.00
3-10	5.85	17.50	35.00
11-29: 24-Everett-c	4.25	13.00	26.00

PATSY WALKER (See All Teen, A Date With Patsy, Girls' Life, Miss America Magazine, Patsy & Hedy, Patsy & Her Pals & Teen Comics)
1945 (no month) - No. 124, Dec, 1965
Marvel/Atlas Comics (BPC)

1-Teenage	40.00	120.00	300.00
2	20.00	60.00	140.00
3,4,6-10	14.00	43.00	100.00
5-Injury-to-eye-c; spanking panel	18.00	54.00	125.00
11,12,15,16,18	10.00	30.00	65.00
13,14,17,19-22-Kurtzman's "Hey Look"	11.00	33.00	75.00
23,24	7.50	22.50	45.00
25-Rusty by Kurtzman; painted-c	11.00	33.00	75.00
26-29,31: 26-31: 52 pgs.	5.85	17.50	35.00
30(52 pgs.)-Egghead Doodle by Kurtzman (1 pg.)	8.35	25.00	50.00
32-57: Last precode (3/55)	4.00	12.00	24.00
58-80	3.60	9.00	18.00
81-99: 92,98-Millie x-over	2.00	6.00	14.00
100	2.30	6.70	16.00
101-124	1.50	3.75	9.00
Fashion Parade 1(1966, 68 pgs.)	5.50	16.50	38.00

NOTE: Painted c-25-28. Anti-Wertham editorial in #21. Georgie app. in #8, 11. Millie app. in #10, 92, 98. Mitzi app. in #11. Rusty app. in #12, 25. Willie app. in #12. Al Jaffee c-57, 58.

PAT THE BRAT (Adventures of Pipsqueak #34 on)
June, 1953; Summer, 1955 - No. 4, 5/56; No. 15, 7/56 - No. 33, 7/59
Archie Publications (Radio)

nn(6/53)	11.00	33.00	75.00
1(Summer, 1955)	8.00	24.00	48.00
2-4-(5/56) (#5-14 not published)	4.70	14.00	28.00
15-(7/56)-33	3.20	8.00	16.00

PAT THE BRAT COMICS DIGEST MAGAZINE
October, 1980
Archie Publications

1			1.50

PATTY POWERS (Formerly Della Vision #3)
No. 4, Oct, 1955 - No. 7, Oct, 1956
Atlas Comics

4	7.50	22.50	45.00
5-7	4.00	12.00	24.00

PAT WILTON (See Mighty Midget Comics)

PAUL
1978 (49¢)
Spire Christian Comics (Fleming H. Revell Co.)

nn			1.00

PAULINE PERIL (See The Close Shaves of...)

PAUL REVERE'S RIDE (TV, Disney, see Walt Disney Showcase #34)
No. 822, July, 1957
Dell Publishing Co.

Four Color 822-w/Johnny Tremain, Toth-a	12.50	37.50	125.00

PAUL TERRY'S ADVENTURES OF MIGHTY MOUSE (See Adventures of...)

PAUL TERRY'S COMICS (Formerly Terry-Toons Comics; becomes Adventures of Mighty Mouse No. 126 on)
No. 85, Mar, 1951 - No. 125, May, 1955
St. John Publishing Co.

85,86-Same as Terry-Toons #85, & 86 with only a title change; published at same time?; Mighty Mouse, Heckle & Jeckle & Gandy Goose continue from Terry-Toons

	10.00	30.00	68.00
87-99	6.70	20.00	40.00
100	8.35	25.00	50.00
101-104,107-125: 121,122,125-Painted-c	6.35	19.00	38.00
105,106-Giant Comics Edition (25¢, 100 pgs.) (9/53 & ?). 105-Little Roquefort-c/story	16.00	47.00	110.00

PAUL TERRY'S HOW TO DRAW FUNNY CARTOONS
1940's (14 pgs.) (Black & White)
Terrytoons, Inc. (Giveaway)

nn-Heckle & Jeckle, Mighty Mouse, etc.	12.00	36.00	85.00

PAUL TERRY'S MIGHTY MOUSE (See Mighty Mouse)

PAUL TERRY'S MIGHTY MOUSE ADVENTURE STORIES (See Mighty Mouse Adventure Stories)

PAUL THE SAMURAI (See The Tick #4)
July, 1992 - No. 6, July, 1993 ($2.75, B&W)
New England Comics

1		1.60	4.00
2-6		1.20	3.00

PAWNEE BILL
Feb, 1951 - No. 3, July, 1951
Story Comics (Youthful Magazines?)

1-Bat Masterson, Wyatt Earp app.	10.00	30.00	68.00
2,3: 3-Origin Golden Warrior; Cameron-a	6.70	20.00	40.00

PAY-OFF (This is the..., ...Crime, ...Detective Stories)
July-Aug, 1948 - No. 5, Mar-Apr, 1949 (52 pgs.)
D. S. Publishing Co.

1-True Crime Cases #1,2	19.00	56.00	130.00
2	11.50	34.00	80.00
3-5-Thrilling Detective Stories	10.00	30.00	70.00

PEACEMAKER, THE (Also see Fightin' Five)
V3#1, Mar, 1967 - No. 5, Nov, 1967 (All 12¢ cover price)
Charlton Comics

1-Fightin' Five begins	3.60	11.00	25.00
2,3,5	2.00	6.00	14.00
4-Origin The Peacemaker	3.60	11.00	25.00
1,2(Modern Comics reprint, 1978)			1.00

PEACEMAKER (Also see Crisis On Infinite Earths & Showcase '93 #7,9,10)
Jan, 1988 - No. 4, Apr, 1988 ($1.25, limited series)
DC Comics

1-4			1.25

PEANUTS (Charlie Brown) (See Fritzi Ritz, Nancy & Sluggo, Tip Top, Tip Topper & United Comics)
1953-54; No. 878, 2/58 - No. 13, 5-7/62; 5/63 - No. 4, 2/64
Dell Publishing Co./Gold Key

1(1953-54)-Reprints United Features' Strange As It Seems, Willie, Ferdnand	11.00	33.00	110.00
Four Color 878(#1)	14.00	43.00	135.00
Four Color 969,1015('59)	10.00	30.00	100.00
4(2-4/60)	8.00	24.00	75.00
5-13	5.00	15.00	50.00

Pedro #18 © FOX

Penny #3 © AVON

Penthouse Men's Adventure Comics #5 © Penthouse Int.

	GD25	FN65	NM94
1(Gold Key, 5/63)	9.00	27.00	90.00
2-4	6.00	18.00	60.00

PEBBLES & BAMM BAMM (TV) (See Cave Kids #7, 12)
Jan, 1972 - No. 36, Dec, 1976 (Hanna-Barbera)
Charlton Comics

1-From the Flintstones	4.30	12.90	30.00
2-10	2.10	6.50	15.00
11-36	1.50	3.80	9.00

PEBBLES & BAMM BAMM (TV)
Nov, 1993 - No. 3, Mar, 1994 ($1.50) (Hanna-Barbera)
Harvey Comics

V2#1-3		.80	2.00
...Giant Size 1 (10/93, $2.25, 68 pgs.)("Summer Special" on-c)		1.00	2.50

PEBBLES FLINTSTONE (TV) (See The Flintstones #11)
Sept, 1963 (Hanna-Barbera)
Gold Key

1 (10088-309)-Early Pebbles app.	7.50	22.50	75.00

PEDRO (Formerly My Private Life #17; also see Romeo Tubbs)
No. 18, June, 1950 - No. 2, Aug, 1950?
Fox Features Syndicate

18(#1)-Wood-c/a(p)	19.00	58.00	135.00
2-Wood-a?	15.00	45.00	105.00

PEE-WEE PIXIES (See The Pixies)

PELLEAS AND MELISANDE (See Night Music #4, 5)

PENALTY (See Crime Must Pay the...)

PENDRAGON (Knights of... #5 on; also see Knights of...)
July, 1992 - No. 15, Sept, 1993 ($1.75)
Marvel Comics UK, Ltd.

1-15: 1-4-Iron Man app. 6-8-Spider-Man app.		.70	1.75

PENDULUM ILLUSTRATED BIOGRAPHIES
1979 (B&W)
Pendulum Press
19-355x-George Washington/Thomas Jefferson, 19-3495-Charles Lindbergh/Amelia Earhart, 19-3509-Harry Houdini/Walt Disney, 19-3517-Davy Crockett/Daniel Boone-Redondo-a, 19-3525-Elvis Presley/Beatles, 19-3533-Benjamin Franklin/Martin Luther King Jr, 19-3541-Abraham Lincoln/Franklin D. Roosevelt, 19-3568-Marie Curie/Albert Einstein-Redondo-a, 19-3576-Thomas Edison/Alexander Graham Bell-Redondo-a, 19-3584-Vince Lombardi/Pele, 19-3592-Babe Ruth/Jackie Robinson, 19-3606-Jim Thorpe/Althea Gibson

Softback			1.50
Hardback			4.50

NOTE: *Above books still available from publisher.*

PENDULUM ILLUSTRATED CLASSICS (Now Age Illustrated)
1973 - 1978 (75¢, 62pp, B&W, 5-3/8x8") (Also see Marvel Classics)
Pendulum Press
64-100x(1973)-Dracula-Redondo art, 64-131x-The Invisible Man-Nino art, 64-0968-Dr. Jekyll and Mr. Hyde-Redondo art, 64-1005-Black Beauty, 64-1010-Call of the Wild, 64-1020-Frankenstein, 64-1025-Huckleberry Finn, 64-1030-Moby Dick-Nino-a, 64-1040-Red Badge of Courage, 64-1045-The Time Machine-Nino-a, 64-1050-Tom Sawyer, 64-1055-Twenty Thousand Leagues Under the Sea, 64-1069-Treasure Island, 64-1328(1974)-Kidnapped, 64-1336-Three Musketeers-Nino art, 64-1344-A Tale of Two Cities, 64-1352-Journey to the Center of the Earth, 64-1360-The War of the Worlds-Nino-a, 64-1379-The Greatest Advs. of Sherlock Holmes-Redondo art, 64-1387-Mysterious Island, 64-1395-Hunchback of Notre Dame, 64-1409-Helen Keller-story of my life, 64-1417-Scarlet Letter, 64-1425-Gulliver's Travels, 64-2618(1977)-Around the World in Eighty Days, 64-2626-Captains Courageous, 64-2634-Connecticut Yankee, 64-2642-The Hound of the Baskervilles, 64-2650-The House of Seven Gables, 64-2669-Jane Eyre, 64-2677-The Last of the Mohicans, 64-2685-The Best of O'Henry, 64-2693-The Best of Poe-Redondo-a, 64-2707-Two Years Before the Mast, 64-2715-White Fang, 64-2723-Wuthering Heights, 64-3126(1978)-Ben Hur-Redondo art, 64-3134-A Christmas Carol, 64-3142-The Food of the Gods, 64-3150-Ivanhoe, 64-3169-The Man in the Iron Mask, 64-3177-The Prince and the Pauper, 64-3185-The Prisoner of Zenda, 64-3193-The Return of the Native, 64-3207-Robinson Crusoe, 64-3215-The Scarlet Pimpernel, 64-3223-The Sea Wolf, 64-3231-The Swiss Family Robinson, 64-3851-Billy Budd, 64-386x-Crime and Punishment, 64-3878-Don Quixote, 64-3886-Great Expectations, 64-3894-Heidi, 64-3908-The Iliad, 64-3916-Lord Jim, 64-3924-The Mutiny on Board H.M.S.

Bounty, 64-3932-The Odyssey, 64-3940-Oliver Twist, 64-3959-Pride and Prejudice, 64-3967-The Turn of the Screw

Softback			1.45
Hardback			4.50

NOTE: *All of the above books can be ordered from the publisher; some were reprinted as Marvel Classic Comics #1-12. In 1972 there was another brief series of 12 titles which contained Classics III. artwork. They were entitled **Now Age Books** Illustrated, but can be easily distinguished from later series by the small Classics Illustrated logo at the top of the front cover. The format is the same as the later series. The 48 pg. C.I. art was stretched out to make 62 pgs. After Twin Circle Publ. terminated the Classics III. series in 1971, they made a one year contract with Pendulum Press to print these twelve titles of C.I. art. Pendulum was unhappy with the contract and at the end of 1972 began their own art series, utilizing the talents of the Filipino artist group. One detail which makes this rather confusing is that when they redid the art in 1973, they gave the same identifying no. as the 1972 series. All 12 of the 1972 C.I. editions have new covers taken from internal art panels. In spite of their recent age, all of the 1972 C.I. series are very rare. Near Mint copies would fetch at least $50. Here is a list of the 1972 series, with C.I. title no. counted in part:*

64-1005 (CI#60-A2) 64-1010 (CI#91) 64-1015 (CI-Jr #503) 64-1020 (CI#26) 64-1025 (CI#19-A2) 64-1030 (CI#5-A2) 64-1035 (CI#169) 64-1040 (CI#98) 64-1045 (CI#133) 64-1050 (CI#50-A2) 64-1055 (CI#47) 64-1060 (CI-Jr#535)

PENDULUM ILLUSTRATED ORIGINALS
1979 (In color)
Pendulum Press

94-4254-Solarman: The Beginning		.65	1.60

PENDULUM'S ILLUSTRATED STORIES
1990 - No. 72, 1990? (No cover price ($4.95), squarebound, 68 pgs.)
Pendulum Press

1-72: Reprints Pendulum Ill. Classics series	1.00	2.00	5.00

PENNY
1947 - No. 6, Sept-Oct, 1949 (Newspaper reprints)
Avon Comics

1-Photo & biography of creator	10.00	30.00	68.00
2-5	6.35	19.00	38.00
6-Perry Como photo on-c	7.00	21.00	42.00

PENTHOUSE COMIX
1994 - Present ($4.95, bimonthly, magazine, mature)
General Media International

1	2.85	8.50	20.00
2,3	2.15	6.50	15.00
4-16: 15-Corben-c. 16-Dorman-c	1.00	2.00	5.00

PENTHOUSE MAX
July, 1996 - Present ($4.95, magazine, mature)
General Media International

1,2: 1-Giffen, Sears, Maguire-a. 2-Political satire			5.00

PENTHOUSE MEN'S ADVENTURE COMIX
1995 - No. 7, 1996 ($4.95, magazine, mature)
General Media International

1-7 (Magazine Size): 1-Boris-c	1.00	2.00	5.00
1-5 (Comic Size): 1-Boris-c	1.00	2.00	5.00

PEP COMICS (See Archie Giant Series #576, 589, 601, 614, 624)
Jan, 1940 - No. 411, Mar, 1989
MLJ Magazines/Archie Publications No. 56 (3/46) on

	GD25	FN65	VF82	NM94
1-Intro. The Shield by Irving Novick (1st patriotic hero); origin & 1st app. The Comet by Jack Cole, The Queen of Diamonds & Kayo Ward; The Rocket, The Press Guardian (The Falcon #1 only), Sergeant Boyle, Fu Chang, & Bentley of of Scotland Yard; Robot-c; Shield-c begin	667.00	2000.00	4000.00	6600.00

(Estimated up to 150 total copies exist, 7 in NM/Mint)

	GD25	FN65		NM94
2-Origin The Rocket	193.00	581.00		1550.00
3	137.00	412.00		1100.00

426

Pep Comics #7 © MLJ

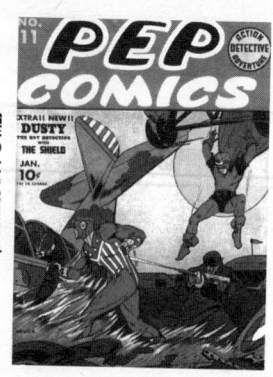

Pep Comics #11 © MLJ

The Perfect Crime #11 © Cross

PE

	GD25	FN65	NM94
4-Wizard cameo	103.00	309.00	825.00
5-Wizard cameo in Shield story	103.00	309.00	825.00
6-10: 8-Last Cole Comet; no Cole-a in #6,7	82.00	247.00	660.00
11-Dusty, Shield's sidekick begins (1st app.); last Press Guardian, Fu Chang	89.00	268.00	715.00
12-Origin & 1st app. Fireball (2/41); last Rocket & Queen of Diamonds; Danny in Wonderland begins	105.00	315.00	840.00
13-15	68.00	206.00	550.00
16-Origin Madam Satan; blood drainage-c	105.00	315.00	840.00
17-Origin/1st app. The Hangman (7/41); death of The Comet; Comet is revealed as Hangman's brother	275.00	825.00	2400.00
18-21: 20-Last Fireball. 21-Last Madam Satan	68.00	206.00	550.00

	GD25	FN65	VF82	NM94
22-Intro. & 1st app. Archie, Betty, & Jughead(12/41); (also see Jackpot)				
	833.00	2500.00	5000.00	8000.00
(Estimated up to 150 total copies exist, 7 in NM/Mint)				

	GD25	FN65	NM94
23	106.00	318.00	850.00
24,25: 24-Coach Kleets app. (unnamed until Archie #94); bondage/torture-c. 25-1st app. Archie's jalopy; 1st skinny Mr. Weatherbee prototype	93.00	281.00	750.00
26-1st app. Veronica Lodge (4/42)	125.00	375.00	1000.00
27-30: 29-Origin Shield retold; 30-Capt. Commando begins; bondage/torture-c; 1st Miss Grundy (definitive version); see Jackpot #4	75.00	225.00	600.00
31-35: 31-MLJ offices & artists are visited in Sgt. Boyle story; 1st app. Mr. Lodge. 32-Shield dons new costume. 34-Bondage/Hypo-c. 33-Pre-Moose tryout (see Jughead #1)	58.00	176.00	470.00
36-1st Archie-c (2/43) w/Shield & Hangman	125.00	375.00	1000.00
37-40	45.00	135.00	360.00
41-50: 41-Archie-c begin. 47-Last Hangman issue; infinity-c. 48-Black Hood begins (5/44); ends #51,59,60	33.00	99.00	230.00
51-60: 52-Suzie begins. 56-Last Capt. Commando. 59-Black Hood not in costume; spanking & lingerie panels; Archie dresses as his aunt; Suzie ends. 60-Katy Keene begins(3/47), ends #154	24.00	71.00	165.00
61-65-Last Shield. 62-1st app. Li'l Jinx (7/47)	19.00	58.00	135.00
66-80: 66-G-Man Club becomes Archie Club (2/48); Nevada Jones by Bill Woggon. 78-1st app. Dilton	11.50	34.00	80.00
81-99	10.00		60.00
100	11.00	33.00	75.00
101-130	5.00		30.00
131-149	2.60	7.50	18.00
150-160-Super-heroes app. in each (see note). 150 (10/61?)-2nd or 3rd app. The Jaguar? 152-157-Sci-Fi-c. 157-Li'l Jinx story	2.85	8.50	20.00
161-167,169-200	1.20	3.00	7.00
168-Jaguar app.	1.30	3.25	8.00
201-260		1.20	3.00
261-411-383-Marvelous Maureen begins (Sci/fi). 393-Thunderbunny begins.			
400-Story featuring Archie staff (DeCarlo-a)			1.00

NOTE: Biro a-2, 4, 5. Jack Cole a-1-5, 8. Al Fagaly c-55-72. Fuje a-39, 45, 47; c-34. Meskin a-4, 5, 11(2). Montana c-30, 32, 33, 36, 73-87(most). Novick c-1-28, 29(w/Schomburg), 31i. Harry Sahle c-35, 39-50. Schomburg c-38. Bob Wood a-2, 4-6, 11. The Fly app. in 151, 154, 160. Flygirl app. in 153, 155, 156, 158. Jaguar app. in 150, 152, 157, 159, 168. Katy Keene by Bill Woggon in many later issues. Bondage c-7, 12, 13, 15, 18, 21, 31, 32. Cover features: Shield #1-16; Shield/Hangman #17-27, 29-41; Hangman #28. Archie #36, 41-on.

PEPE
No. 1194, Apr, 1961
Dell Publishing Co.

Four Color 1194-Movie, photo-c	4.00	12.00	40.00

PERFECT CRIME, THE
Oct, 1949 - No. 33, May, 1953 (#2-12, 52 pgs.)
Cross Publications

1-Powell-a(2)	24.00	71.00	165.00
2(4/50)	13.00	39.00	90.00

	GD25	FN65	NM94
3-10: 7-Steve Duncan begins, ends #30. 10-Flag-c	11.00	33.00	75.00
11-Used in **SOTI**, pg. 159	13.00	39.00	90.00
12-14	10.00	30.00	60.00
15- "The Most Terrible Menace" 2 pg. drug editorial	10.00	30.00	70.00
16,17,19-25,27-29,31-33	7.50	22.50	45.00
18-Drug cover, heroin drug propaganda story, plus 2 pg. anti-drug editorial	17.00	49.00	115.00
26-Drug-c with hypodermic; drug propaganda story	17.00	49.00	115.00
30-Strangulation cover	18.00	54.00	125.00

NOTE: Powell a-No. 1, 2, 4. Wildey a-1, 5. Bondage c-11.

PERFECT LOVE
#10, 8-9/51 (cover date; 5-6/51 indicia date); #2, 10-11/51 - #10, 12/53
Ziff-Davis(Approved Comics)/St. John No. 9 on

10(#1)(8-9/51)-Painted-c	14.00	43.00	100.00
2(10-11/51)	10.00	30.00	65.00
3,5-7: 3-Painted-c. 5-Photo-c	7.50	22.50	45.00
4,8 (Fall, 1952)-Kinstler-a; last Z-D issue	8.35	25.00	50.00
9,10 (10/53, 12/53, St. John): 9-Painted-c. 10-Photo-c	6.70	20.00	40.00

PERG (Also see Hellina)
Oct, 1993 - No. 8, May, 1994 ($2.95)
Lightning Comics

1-($3.50)-Flip-c is glow-in-the-dark by Saltares		1.40	3.50
1-Platinum Edition		1.20	3.00
2-8: 4-Origin Perg		1.40	3.50
2,3-Platinum Edition		1.20	3.00
4-Platinum Edition		1.20	3.00
7-Blue & Pink cover versions		1.20	3.00

PERRI (Disney)
No. 847, Jan, 1958
Dell Publishing Co.

Four Color 847-Movie, w/2 diff-c publ.	8.00	24.00	80.00

PERRY MASON
No. 49, 1946 - No. 50, 1946
David McKay Publications

Feature Books 49, 59-Based on Gardner novels	23.00	69.00	160.00

PERRY MASON MYSTERY MAGAZINE (TV)
June-Aug, 1964 - No. 2, Oct-Dec, 1964
Dell Publishing Co.

1,2: 2-Raymond Burr photo-c	4.00	11.00	22.00

PERSONAL LOVE (Also see Movie Love)
Jan, 1950 - No. 33, June, 1955
Famous Funnies

1	13.00	39.00	90.00
2-Kathryn Grayson & Mario Lanza photo-c	7.50	22.50	45.00
3-7,10: 7-Robert Walker & Joanne Dru photo-c. 10-Loretta Young & Joseph Cotton photo-c	5.85	17.50	35.00
8,9: 8-Esther Williams & Howard Keel photo-c. 9-Debra Paget & Louis Jourdan photo-c	6.35	19.00	38.00
11-Toth-a; Glenn Ford & Gene Tierney photo-c	10.00	30.00	60.00
12,16,17-One pg. Frazetta each. 17-Rock Hudson & Yvonne DeCarlo photo-c	5.85	17.50	35.00
13-15,18-23: 12-Jane Greer & William Lundigan photo-c. 14-Kirk Douglas photo-c. 15-Dale Robertson & Joanne Dru photo-c. 18-Gregory Peck & Susan Hayworth photo-c. 19-Anthony Quinn & Suzan Ball photo-c. 20-Robert Wagner & Kathleen Crowley photo-c. 21-Roberta Peters & Byron Palmer photo-c. 22-Dale Robertson photo-c. 23-Rhonda Fleming-c	5.00	15.00	30.00
24,27,28-Frazetta-a in each (8,8&6 pgs.). 27-Rhonda Fleming & Fernando Lamas photo-c. 28,30-Mitzi Gaynor photo-c	30.00	90.00	210.00
25-Frazetta-a (tribute to Betty Page, 7 pg. story); Tyrone Power/Terry Moore			

Personal Love #17 © PRIZE

Peter Panda #4 © DC

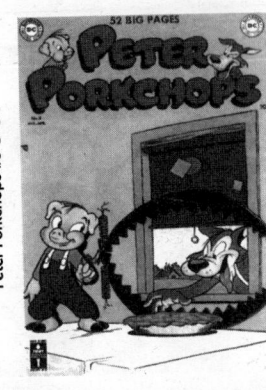

Peter Porkchops #3 © DC

	GD25	FN65	NM94

	GD25	FN65	NM94
photo-c from "King of the Khyber Rifles"	30.00	90.00	210.00
26,29,30,33: 26-Constance Smith & Byron Palmer photo-c. 29-Charlton Heston & Nicol Morey photo-c. 30-Johnny Ray & Mitzi Gaynor photo-c. 33-Dana Andrews & Piper Laurie photo-c	4.25	13.00	28.00
31-Marlon Brando & Jean Simmons photo-c; last pre-code (2/55)	7.50	22.50	45.00
32-Classic Frazetta-a (8 pgs.); Kirk Douglas & Bella Darvi photo-c	41.00	124.00	330.00

NOTE: All have photo-c. Many feature movie stars. **Everett** a-5, 9, 10, 24.

PERSONAL LOVE (Going Steady V3#3 on)
V1#1, Sept, 1957 - V3#2, Nov-Dec, 1959
Prize Publ. (Headline)

V1#1	6.70	20.00	40.00
2	4.00	12.00	24.00
3-6(7-8/58)	4.00	11.00	22.00
V2#1(9-10/58)-V2#6(7-8/59)	3.60	9.00	18.00
V3#1-Wood?/Orlando-a	4.25	13.00	26.00
2	3.20	8.00	16.00

PETER CANNON - THUNDERBOLT (See Crisis on Infinite Earths)(Also see Thunderbolt)
Sept, 1992 - No. 12, Aug, 1993 ($1.25)
DC Comics

1-12			1.25

PETER COTTONTAIL
Jan, 1954; Feb, 1954 - No. 2, Mar, 1954 (Says 3/53 in error)
Key Publications

1(1/54)-Not 3-D	6.35	19.00	38.00
1(2/54)-(3-D, 25¢)-Came w/glasses; written by Bruce Hamilton	20.00	60.00	140.00
2-Reprints 3-D #1 but not in 3-D	5.00	15.00	30.00

PETER GUNN (TV)
No. 1087, Apr-June, 1960
Dell Publishing Co.

Four Color 1087-Photo-c	10.00	30.00	100.00

PETER PAN (Disney) (See Hook, Movie Classics & Comics, New Adventures of... & Walt Disney Showcase #36)
No. 442, Dec, 1952 - No. 926, Aug, 1958
Dell Publishing Co.

Four Color 442 (#1)-Movie	10.00	30.00	100.00
Four Color 926-Reprint of 442	5.00	15.00	50.00

PETER PAN
1991 ($5.95, graphic novel, 68 pgs.)(Celebrates release of video)
Disney Comics

nn-r/Peter Pan Treasure Chest from 1953	1.00	2.60	6.00

PETER PANDA
Aug-Sept, 1953 - No. 31, Aug-Sept, 1958
National Periodical Publications

1-Grossman-c/a in all	37.00	111.00	260.00
2	17.00	49.00	115.00
3-10	12.00	36.00	85.00
11-31	9.15	27.00	55.00

PETER PAN TREASURE CHEST (See Dell Giants)

PETER PARKER (See The Spectacular Spider-Man)

PETER PAT
No. 8, 1939
United Features Syndicate

Single Series 8	29.00	88.00	205.00

PETER PAUL'S 4 IN 1 JUMBO COMIC BOOK

No date (1953)
Capitol Stories (Charlton)

1-Contains 4 comics bound; Space Adventures, Space Western, Crime & Justice, Racket Squad in Action	36.00	109.00	255.

PETER PENNY AND HIS MAGIC DOLLAR
1947 (16 pgs.; paper cover; regular size)
American Bankers Association, N. Y. (Giveaway)

nn-(Scarce)-Used in SOTI, pg. 310, 311	14.00	43.00	100
Diff. version (7-1/4x11")-redrawn, 16 pgs., paper-c	10.00	30.00	60

PETER PIG
No. 5, May, 1953 - No. 6, Aug, 1953
Standard Comics

5,6	4.25	13.00	26

PETER PORKCHOPS (See Leading Comics #23)
11-12/49 - No. 61, 9-11/59; No. 62, 10-12/60 (1-11: 52 pgs.)
National Periodical Publications

1	31.00	92.00	215
2	14.00	43.00	100
3-10: 6- "Peter Rockets to Mars!" c/story	11.00	33.00	75
11-30	9.15	27.00	55
31-62	7.50	22.50	45

NOTE: Otto Feur a-all. **Sheldon Mayer** a-30-38, 40-44, 46-52, 61.

PETER PORKER, THE SPECTACULAR SPIDER-HAM
May, 1985 - No. 17, Sept, 1987 (Also see Marvel Tails)
Star Comics (Marvel)

1-Michael Golden-c		.80	
2-17: 12-Origin/1st app. Bizarro Phil. 13-Halloween issue			

NOTE: Back-up features: 2-X-Bugs. 3-Iron Mouse. 4-Croctor Strange. 5-Thrr, Dog of Thunc

PETER POTAMUS (TV)
Jan, 1965 (Hanna-Barbera)
Gold Key

1	6.00	18.00	6

PETER RABBIT (See New Funnies #65 & Space Comics)
No. 1, 1942
Dell Publishing Co.

Large Feature Comic 1	37.00	111.00	37

PETER RABBIT (Adventures of...; New Advs. of... #9 on)(Also see Funny Tunes & Space Comics)
1947 - No. 34, Aug-Sept, 1956
Avon Periodicals

1(1947)-Reprints 1943-44 Sunday strips; contains a biography & drawing Cady	33.00	99.00	23
2 (4/48)	24.00	73.00	17
3 ('48) - 6(7/49)-Last Cady issue	21.00	64.00	1
7-10(1950-8/51): 9-New logo	5.35	16.00	
11('51)-34('56)-Avon's character	4.00	11.00	
...Easter Parade (1952, 25¢, 132 pgs.)	15.00	45.00	1
...Jumbo Book (1954-Giant Size, 25¢)-Jesse James by Kinstler (6 pgs.); space ship-c	21.00	62.00	

PETER RABBIT
1958
Fago Magazine Co.

1	6.70	20.00	

PETER RABBIT 3-D
April, 1990 ($2.95, with glasses; sealed in plastic bag)
Eternity Comics

1-By Harrison Cady (reprints)		1.20	

PETER, THE LITTLE PEST (#4 titled Petey)

Phantom #69 © KFS

Phantom #1 © KFS

Phantom Force #3 © Jack Kirby

	GD25	FN65	NM94

Nov, 1969 - No. 4, May, 1970
Marvel Comics Group

1	1.30	3.25	8.00
2-4-r-Dexter the Demon & Melvin the Monster	1.00	2.00	5.00

PETER WHEAT (The Adventures of...)
1948 - 1956? (16 pgs. in color) (paper covers)
Bakers Associates Giveaway

nn(No.1)-States on last page, end of 1st Adventure of...; Kelly-a			
	29.00	86.00	200.00
nn(4 issues)-Kelly-a	19.00	57.00	130.00
6-10-All Kelly-a	13.00	40.00	90.00
11-20-All Kelly-a	11.00	32.00	75.00
21-35-All Kelly-a	10.00	30.00	60.00
36-66	6.70	20.00	40.00
...Artist's Workbook ('54, digest size)	6.70	20.00	40.00
...Four-In-One Fun Pack (Vol. 2, '54), oblong, comics w/puzzles			
	8.35	25.00	50.00
..Fun Book ('52, 32 pgs., paper-c, B&W & color, 8-1/2x10-3/4")-Contains cutouts, puzzles, games, magic & pages to color	10.00	30.00	70.00

NOTE: *Al Hubbard* art #36 on; written by Del Connell.

PETER WHEAT NEWS
1948 - No. 30, 1950 (4 pgs. in color)
Bakers Associates

Vol. 1-All have 2 pgs. Peter Wheat by Kelly	24.00	72.00	165.00
2-10	14.00	43.00	100.00
11-20	8.35	25.00	50.00
21-30	5.35	16.00	32.00

NOTE: Early issues have no date & *Kelly* art.

PETE'S DRAGON (See Walt Disney Showcase #43)

PETE THE PANIC
November, 1955
Stanmor Publications

1-Code approved	4.00	10.00	20.00

PETEY (See Peter, the Little Pest)

PETTICOAT JUNCTION (TV)
Oct-Dec, 1964 - No. 5, Oct-Dec, 1965 (#1-3, 5 have photo-c)
Dell Publishing Co.

1	5.50	16.50	55.00
2-5	4.00	12.00	40.00

PETUNIA (Also see Looney Tunes and Porky Pig)
No. 463, Apr, 1953
Dell Publishing Co.

Four Color 463	4.00	12.00	40.00

PHAGE (See Neil Gaiman's Teknophage & Neil Gaiman's Phage-Shadowdeath)

PHANTASMO (See The Funnies #45)
No. 18, 1941
Dell Publishing Co.

Large Feature Comic 18	25.00	75.00	250.00

PHANTOM, THE
1939 - 1949
David McKay Publishing Co.

Feature Books 20	65.00	195.00	650.00
Feature Books 22	55.00	165.00	550.00
Feature Books 39	46.00	137.00	365.00
Feature Books 53,56,57	39.00	118.00	275.00

PHANTOM, THE (See Ace Comics, Defenders Of The Earth, Eat Right to Work and Win, Square Comics, Harvey Comics Hits #51,56, Harvey Hits #1, 6, 12, 15, 26, 36, 44, 48, & King Comics)

	GD25	FN65	NM94

PHANTOM, THE (nn 29-Published overseas only) (Also see Comics Reading Library)
Nov, 1962 - No. 17, July, 1966; No. 18, Sept, 1966 - No. 28, Dec, 1967; No. 30, Feb, 1969 - No. 74, Jan, 1977
Gold Key (#1-17)/King (#18-28)/Charlton (#30 on)

1-Manning-a; origin revealed on inside-c. & back-c.	10.00	30.00	100.00
2-King, Queen & Jack begins, ends #11	5.50	16.50	55.00
3-10	4.00	12.00	40.00
11-17: 12-Track Hunter begins	3.60	11.00	35.00
18-Flash Gordon begins; Wood-a	3.20	9.60	32.00
19,20-Flash Gordon ends (both by Gil Kane)	2.20	6.60	22.00
21-24,26,27: 21-Mandrake begins. 20,24-Girl Phantom app. 26-Brick Bradford app.	3.25	9.50	22.00
25-Jeff Jones-a(4 pgs.); 1 pg. Williamson ad	3.25	9.50	22.00
28(nn)-Brick Bradford app.	2.60	7.50	18.00
30-40: 36,39-Ditko-a	2.00	6.00	14.00
41-46: 46-Intro. The Piranha. 62-Bolle-c	1.65	4.20	10.00
67-71,73-Newton-c/a: 67-Origin retold	1.20	3.00	7.00
72,74: 74-Newton flag-c; Newton-a	1.20	3.00	7.00

NOTE: *Aparo* a-31-34, 36-38; c-31-38, 60, 61. Painted c-1-17.

PHANTOM, THE
May, 1988 - No. 4, Aug, 1988 ($1.25, mini-series)
DC Comics

1-4: Orlando-c/a in all			1.25

PHANTOM, THE
Mar, 1989 - No. 13, Mar, 1990 ($1.50)
DC Comics

1-13: 1-Brief origin			1.50

PHANTOM, THE
1992 - No. 8, 1993? ($2.25)
Wolf Publishing

1-8		.90	2.25

PHANTOM BLOT, THE (#1 titled New Adventures of...)
Oct, 1964 - No. 7, Nov, 1966 (Disney)
Gold Key

1 (Meets The Beagle Boys)	4.00	12.00	40.00
2-1st Super Goof	2.40	7.20	24.00
3-7	1.80	5.40	18.00

PHANTOM EAGLE (See Mighty Midget, Marvel Super Heroes #16 & Wow #6)

PHANTOM FORCE
12/93 - #2, 1994; #0, 3/94; #3, 5/94 - #7, 10/94 ($2.50/$3.50, limited series)
Image Comics/Genesis West #0, 3-7

0 (3/94, $2.50)-Kirby/Jim Lee-c; Kirby-p pgs. 1,5,24-29.	1.00	2.50
1 (12/93, $2.50)-Polybagged w/trading card; Kirby Liefeld-c; Kirby plots/pencils w/inks by Liefeld, McFarlane, Jim Lee, Silvestri, Larsen, Williams, Ordway & Miki.	1.00	2.50
2 ($3.50)-Kirby-a(p); Kirby/Larson-c	1.40	3.50
3-7: 3-(5/94, $2.50)-Kirby/McFarlane 4-(5/94)-Kirby-c(p). 5-(6/94).	1.00	2.50

PHANTOM LADY (1st Series) (My Love Secret #24 on) (Also see All Top, Daring Adventures, Freedom Fighters, Jungle Thrills, & Wonder Boy)
No. 13, Aug, 1947 - No. 23 Apr, 1949
Fox Features Syndicate

13(#1)-Phantom Lady by Matt Baker begins (1st app.); The Blue Beetle story	300.00	900.00	2700.00
14(#2)-Not Baker-c	200.00	600.00	1600.00
15-P.L. injected with experimental drug	200.00	600.00	1600.00
16-Negligee-c, panels; true crime stories begin	200.00	600.00	1600.00
17-Classic bondage cover; used in SOTI, illo "Sexual stimulation by combining 'headlights' with the sadist's dream of tying up a woman"			

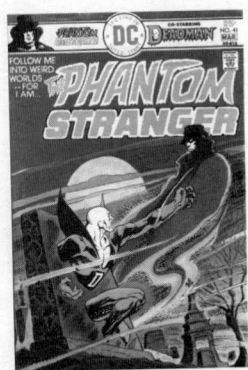

Phantom Stranger #41 © DC

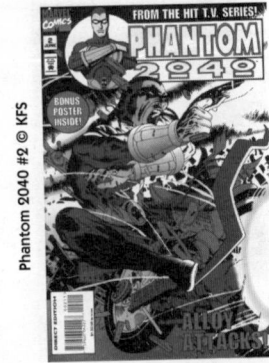

Phantom 2040 #2 © KFS

Phantom Zone #2 © DC

	GD25	FN65	NM94
	422.00	1266.00	3800.00
18,19	143.00	431.00	1150.00
20-23: 23-Bondage-c	112.00	338.00	900.00

NOTE: **Matt Baker** a-in all; c-13, 15-21. **Kamen** a-22, 23.

PHANTOM LADY (2nd Series) (See Terrific Comics) (Formerly Linda)
V1#5, Dec-Jan, 1954/1955 - No. 4, June, 1955
Ajax/Farrell Publ.

	GD25	FN65	NM94
V1#5(#1)-By Matt Baker	87.00	262.00	700.00
V1#2-Last pre-code	73.00	219.00	585.00
3,4-Red Rocket. 3-Heroin story	58.00	174.00	465.00

PHANTOM PLANET, THE
No. 1234, 1961
Dell Publishing Co.

	GD25	FN65	NM94
Four Color 1234-Movie	7.00	21.00	70.00

PHANTOM STRANGER, THE (1st Series)(See Saga of Swamp Thing)
Aug-Sept, 1952 - No. 6, June-July, 1953
National Periodical Publications

	GD25	FN65	NM94
1(Scarce)-1st app.	150.00	450.00	1200.00
2 (Scarce)	100.00	300.00	800.00
3-6 (Scarce)	87.00	262.00	700.00

PHANTOM STRANGER, THE (2nd Series) (See Showcase #80)
May-June, 1969 - No. 41, Feb-Mar, 1976
National Periodical Publications

	GD25	FN65	NM94
1-2nd S.A. app. P. Stranger; only 12¢ issue	8.00	23.50	60.00
2,3	3.60	11.00	25.00
4-1st new look Phantom Stranger; N. Adams-a	3.75	11.25	28.00
5-7	2.60	7.50	18.00
8-14: 14-Last 15¢ issue	2.00	6.00	14.00
15-19: All 25¢ giants (52 pgs.)	1.50	3.75	9.00
20-30,32-41: 20-Dark Circle begins, ends #24. 23-Spawn of Frankenstein begins by Kaluta; series ends #30. 26-Book-length story featuring Ph. Stranger, Dr. 13 & Spawn/Frankenstein. 33-Deadman-c/story. 34-Last 20¢ issue (#35 on are 25¢). 39-41-Deadman app.	1.00	2.60	6.00
31-The Black Orchid begins (6-7/74).	1.65	4.20	10.00

NOTE: **N. Adams** a-4; c-3-19. **Anderson** a-4, 5i. **Aparo** a-7-17, 19-26; c-20-24, 33-41. **B. Bailey** a-27-30. **DeZuniga** a-12-16, 18, 19, 21, 22, 31, 34. **Greil** a-33. **Kaluta** a-23-25; c-26. **Meskin** r-15, 16, 18, 19. **Redondo** a-32, 35, 36. **Sparling** a-20. **Starr** a-17r. **Toth** a-15r. Black Orchid by **Carrilo**-38-41. Dr. 13 solo in-13, 18, 19, 20, 21, 34. Frankenstein by **Kaluta**-23-25; by **Baily**-27-30. No Black Orchid-33, 34, 37.

PHANTOM STRANGER (See Justice League of America #103)
Oct, 1987 - No. 4, Jan, 1988 (75¢, limited series)
DC Comics

	GD25	FN65	NM94
1-Mignola/Russell-c/a & Eclipso app. in all		.80	2.00
2-4: 3,4-Eclipso-c			1.25

PHANTOM: THE GHOST WHO WALKS
Feb, 1995 - No. 3, Apr, 1995 ($2.95, limited series)
Marvel Comics

	GD25	FN65	NM94
1-3		1.20	3.00

PHANTOM 2040 (TV cartoon)
May, 1995 - No. 4, Aug, 1995 ($1.50)
Marvel Comics

	GD25	FN65	NM94
1-4-Based on animated series			1.50

PHANTOM WITCH DOCTOR (Also see Durango Kid #8 & Eerie #8)
1952
Avon Periodicals

	GD25	FN65	NM94
1-Kinstler-c/a (7 pgs.)	40.00	120.00	290.00

PHANTOM ZONE, THE (See Adventure #283 & Superboy #100, 104)
January, 1982 - No. 4, April, 1982
DC Comics

	GD25	FN65	NM94
1-Superman app. in all			1
2-4: Batman, Green Lantern app.			1

NOTE: **Colan** a-1-4p; c-1-4p. **Giordano** c-1-4i.

PHAZE
Apr, 1988 - No. 2, Oct, 1988 ($2.25)
Eclipse Comics

	GD25	FN65	NM94
1,2: 2-Gulacy painted-c		.90	2

PHIL RIZZUTO (Baseball Hero)(See Sport Thrills, Accepted reprint)
1951 (New York Yankees)
Fawcett Publications

	GD25	FN65	NM94
nn-Photo-c	58.00	174.00	465

PHOENIX
Jan, 1975 - No. 4, Oct, 1975
Atlas/Seaboard Publ.

1-Origin
2-4: 3-Origin & only app. The Dark Avenger. 4-New origin/costume The
  Protector (formerly Phoenix)
NOTE: **Infantino** appears in #1, 2. **Austin** a-3i. **Thorne** c-3.

PHOENIX (...The Untold Story)
April, 1984 ($2.00, one-shot)
Marvel Comics Group

	GD25	FN65	NM94
1-Byrne/Austin-r/X-Men #137 with original unpublished ending	1.65	4.20	1

PHOENIX RESURRECTION, THE
1995 - 1996 ($3.95)
Malibu Comics (Ultraverse)
Aftermath #1 (1/96)-X-Men app.
Genesis #1 (12/95)-X-Men app; wraparound-c
Revelations #1 (12/95)-X-Men app; wraparound-c

PICNIC PARTY (See Dell Giants)

PICTORIAL CONFESSIONS (Pictorial Romances #4 on)
Sept, 1949 - No. 3, Dec, 1949
St. John Publishing Co.

	GD25	FN65	NM94
1-Baker-c/a(3)	22.00	66.00	1
2-Baker-a; photo-c	13.50	41.00	
3-Kubert, Baker-a; part Kubert-c	13.50	41.00	

PICTORIAL LOVE STORIES (Formerly Tim McCoy)
No. 22, Oct, 1949 - No. 26, July, 1950 (all photo-c)
Charlton Comics

	GD25	FN65	NM94
22-26: All have "Me-Dan Cupid". 25-Fred Astaire-c	15.00	45.00	1

PICTORIAL LOVE STORIES
October, 1952
St. John Publishing Co.

	GD25	FN65	NM94
1-Baker-c	21.00	64.00	

PICTORIAL ROMANCES (Formerly Pictorial Confessions)
No. 4, Jan, 1950; No. 5, Jan, 1951 - No. 24, Mar, 1954
St. John Publishing Co.

	GD25	FN65	NM94
4-Baker-a; photo-c	21.00	62.00	
5,10-All Matt Baker issues. 5-Reprints all stories from #4 w/new Baker-c	16.00	47.00	
6-9,12,13,15,16-Baker-c, 2-3 stories	11.00	33.00	
11-Baker-c/a(3); Kubert-r/Hollywood Confessions #1	12.00	36.00	
14,21-24: Baker-c/a each. 21,24-Each has signed story by Estrada	10.00	30.00	
17-20(7/53, 25¢, 100 pgs.): Baker-c/a; each has two signed stories by Es	21.00	64.00	

NOTE: **Matt Baker** art in most issues. **Estrada** a-17-20(2), 21, 24.

Pinhead #5

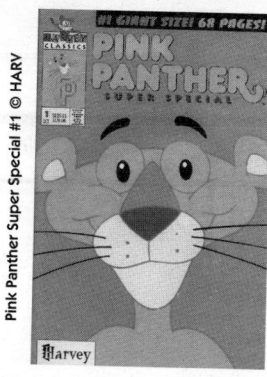

Pink Panther Super Special #1 © HARV

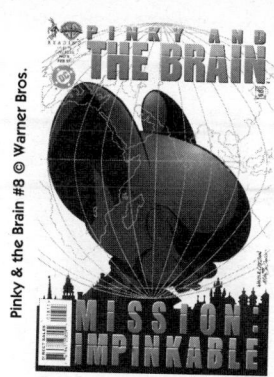

Pinky & the Brain #8 © Warner Bros.

PI

	GD25	FN65	NM94

PICTURE NEWS
Jan, 1946 - No. 10, Jan-Feb, 1947
Lafayette Street Corp.

1-Milt Gross begins, ends No. 6; 4 pg. Kirby-a; A-Bomb-c/story	33.00	99.00	230.00
2-Atomic explosion panels; Frank Sinatra/Perry Como story	16.00	47.00	110.00
3-Atomic explosion panels; Frank Sinatra, June Allyson, Benny Goodman stories	13.00	39.00	90.00
4-Atomic explosion panels; "Caesar and Cleopatra" movie adapt. w/Claude Raines & Vivian Leigh; Jackie Robinson story	15.00	45.00	105.00
5-7: 5-Hank Greenberg story. 6-Joe Louis-c/story	10.00	30.00	65.00
8-Monte Hale story (9-10/46; 1st?)	11.50	34.00	80.00
9-A-Bomb story; "Crooked Mile" movie adaptation; Joe DiMaggio story	11.00	33.00	75.00
10-Dick Quick; A-Bomb story; Krigstein, Gross-a	11.50	34.00	80.00

PICTURE PARADE (Picture Progress #5 on)
Sept, 1953 - V1#4, Dec, 1953 (28 pgs.)
Gilberton Company (Also see A Christmas Adventure)

1-Andy's Atomic Adventures; A-bomb blast-c; (Teachers version distributed to schools exists)	14.00	43.00	100.00
2-Around the World with the United Nations	10.00	30.00	65.00
3-Adventures of the Lost One(The American Indian), 4-A Christmas Adventure (r-under same title in 1969)	10.00	30.00	65.00

PICTURE PROGRESS (Formerly Picture Parade)
#5, Jan, 1954 - V3#2, Oct, 1955 (28-36 pgs.)
Gilberton Corp.

#5-9,V2#1-9: 5-News in Review 1953. 6-The Birth of America. 7-The Four Seasons. 8-Paul Revere's Ride. 9-The Hawaiian Islands(5/54). V2#1-The Story of Flight(9/54). 2-Vote for Crazy River(The Meaning of Elections). 3-Louis Pasteur. 4-The Star Spangled Banner. 5-News in Review 1954. 6-Alaska: The Great Land. 7-Life in the Circus. 8-The Time of the Cave Man. 9-Summer Fun(5/55)	4.25	13.00	26.00
V3#1,2: 1-The Man Who Discovered America. 2-The Lewis & Clark Expedition	4.25	13.00	26.00

PICTURE SCOPE JUNGLE ADVENTURES (See Jungle Thrills)

PICTURE STORIES FROM AMERICAN HISTORY
1945 - No. 4, Sum, 1947 (#1,2: 10¢, 56 pgs.; #3,4: 15¢, 52 pgs.)
National/All-American/E. C. Comics

1,2	24.00	71.00	165.00
3,4	18.00	54.00	125.00

PICTURE STORIES FROM SCIENCE
Spring, 1947 - No. 2, Fall, 1947
E.C. Comics

1,2: 1-(15¢). 2-(10¢)	24.00	71.00	165.00

PICTURE STORIES FROM THE BIBLE (See Narrative Illustration, the Story of the Comics by M.C. Gaines)
1942 - No. 4, Fall, 1943; 1944-46
National/All-American/E.C. Comics

1('42-Fall, '43)-Old Testament (DC)	21.00	62.00	145.00
Complete Old Testament Edition, (12/43-DC, 50¢, 232 pgs.);-1st printing; contains #1-4; 2nd - 8th (1/47) printings exist; later printings by E.C.	25.00	75.00	175.00
Complete Old Testament Edition (1945-publ. by Bible Pictures Ltd.)-232 pgs., cardbound, in color with dust jacket	25.00	75.00	175.00
1(New Test.; 1944-46, DC)-52 pgs. ea.	15.00	45.00	105.00
Complete Life of Christ Edition (1945, 25¢, 96 pgs.)-Contains #1&2 of the New Testament Edition	21.00	62.00	145.00

NOTE: Both Old and New Testaments published in England by Bible Pictures Ltd. in hardback, in color, 376 pgs. (2 vols.: O.T. 232 pgs. & N.T. 144 pgs.) and were also published by Press in 1979 (Old Test., $9.95) and in 1980 (New Test., $7.95)

1,2(Old Testament-r in comic book form)(E.C., 1946; 52 pgs.)	15.00	45.00	105.00
1(DC),2(AA),3(EC)(New Testament-r in comic book form)(E.C., 1946; 52 pgs.)	15.00	45.00	105.00
Complete New Testament Edition (1946-E.C., 50¢, 144 pgs.)-Contains #1-3	21.00	62.00	145.00

NOTE: Another British series entitled The Bible Illustrated from 1947 has recently been discovered, with the same internal artwork. This eight edition series (5-OT, 3-NT) is of particular interest to Classics Ill. collectors because it exactly copied the C.I. logo format. The British publisher was Thorpe & Porter, who in 1951 began publishing the British Classics Ill. series. All editions of The Bible Ill. have new British painted covers. While this market is still new, and not all editions have as yet been found, current market value is about the same as the first U.S. editions of Picture Stories From The Bible.

PICTURE STORIES FROM WORLD HISTORY
Spring, 1947 - No. 2, Summer, 1947 (52, 48 pgs.)
E.C. Comics

1,2: 1-(15¢). 2-(10¢)	24.00	71.00	165.00

PINHEAD
Dec, 1993 - No. 9, 1994 ($2.50)
Marvel Comics (Epic Comics)

1-($2.95)-Embossed foil-c by Kelley Jones; Intro Pinhead & Disciples (Snakeoil, Hangman, Fan Dancer & Dixie)		1.20	3.00
2-9		1.00	2.50

PINHEAD & FOODINI (TV)(Also see Foodini & Jingle Dingle Christmas...)
July, 1951 - No. 4, Jan, 1952 (Early TV comic)
Fawcett Publications

1-(52 pgs.)-Photo-c; based on TV puppet show	28.00	84.00	195.00
2-Photo-c	13.00	39.00	90.00
3,4: 3-Photo-c	10.00	30.00	70.00

PINHEAD VS. MARSHALL LAW (Law in Hell)
Nov, 1993 - No. 2, Dec, 1993 ($2.95, limited series)
Marvel Comics (Epic Comics)

1,2: 1-Embossed red foil-c. 2-Embossed silver foil-c		1.20	3.00

PINK PANTHER, THE (TV)(See The Inspector & Kite Fun Book)
April, 1971 - No. 87, 1984
Gold Key

1-The Inspector begins	3.60	11.00	25.00
2-10	1.65	4.20	10.00
11-30: Warren Tufts-a #16-on	1.30	3.25	8.00
31-60		1.60	4.00
61-87		1.30	3.25
Mini-comic No. 1(1976)(3-1/4x6-1/2")		1.00	2.50

NOTE: Pink Panther began as a movie cartoon. (See Golden Comics Digest #38, 45 and March of Comics #376, 384, 390, 409, 418, 429, 441, 449, 461, 473, 486); #37, 72, 80-85 contain reprints.

PINK PANTHER SUPER SPECIAL (TV)
Oct, 1993 ($2.25, 68 pgs.)
Harvey Comics

V2#1-The Inspector & Wendy Witch stories also		.90	2.25

PINK PANTHER, THE
Nov, 1993 - No. 9, July, 1994 ($1.50)
Harvey Comics

V2#1-9			1.50

PINKY & THE BRAIN (See Animaniacs)
July, 1996 - Present ($1.75)
DC Comics

1-8			1.75
Christmas Special (1/96, $1.50)			1.50

PINKY LEE (See Adventures of...)

PINKY THE EGGHEAD

P.I.'s #2 © FC/Max Collins & Terry Beatty

Pitt #9 © Dale Keown

Pitt in the Blood © Dale Keown

	GD25	FN65	NM94
1963 (Reprints from Noodnik)			
I.W./Super Comics			
I.W. Reprint #1,2(nd)	1.00	2.00	5.00
Super Reprint #14-r/Noodnik Comics #4	1.00	2.00	5.00

PINOCCHIO (See 4-Color #92, 252, 545, 1203, Mickey Mouse Mag. V5#3, Movie Comics under Wonderful Advs. of..., New Advs. of..., Thrilling Comics #2, Walt Disney Showcase, Walt Disney's..., Wonderful Advs. of..., & World's Greatest Stories #2)
No. 92, 1945 - No. 1203, Mar, 1962 (Disney)
Dell Publishing Co.

Four Color 92-The Wonderful Adventures of...; 16 pg. Donald Duck story ;			
entire book by Kelly	60.00	180.00	600.00
Four Color 252 (10/49)-Origin, not by Kelly	10.00	30.00	100.00
Four Color 545 (3/54)-The Wonderful Advs. of...; part-r of 4-Color #92; Disney-			
movie	8.00	24.00	80.00
Four Color 1203 (3/62)	5.85	17.50	58.00

PINOCCHIO
1940 (10 pgs.; linen-like paper)
Cocomalt/Montgomery Ward Co. (Giveaway)

nn-Cocomalt edition	17.00	49.00	115.00
nn-store edition	13.00	40.00	90.00

PINOCCHIO AND THE EMPEROR OF THE NIGHT
Mar, 1988 ($1.25, 52 pgs.)
Marvel Comics

1-Adapts film			1.25

PINOCCHIO LEARNS ABOUT KITES (See Kite Fun Book)

PIN-UP PETE (Also see Great Lover Romances & Monty Hall...)
1952
Toby Press

1-Jack Sparling pin-ups	15.00	45.00	105.00

PIONEER MARSHAL (See Fawcett Movie Comics)

PIONEER PICTURE STORIES
Dec, 1941 - No. 9, Dec, 1943
Street & Smith Publications

1-The Legless Air Ace begins	24.00	73.00	170.00
2 -True life story of Errol Flynn	12.00	36.00	85.00
3-9	10.00	30.00	70.00

PIONEER WEST ROMANCES (Firehair #1,2,7-11)
No. 3, Spring, 1950 - No. 6, Winter, 1950-51
Fiction House Magazines

3-(52 pgs.)-Firehair continues	17.00	49.00	115.00
4-6	17.00	49.00	115.00

PIPSQUEAK (See The Adventures of...)

PIRACY
Oct-Nov, 1954 - No. 7, Oct-Nov, 1955
E. C. Comics

1-Williamson/Torres-a	27.00	81.00	190.00
2-Williamson/Torres-a	17.00	51.00	120.00
3-7	14.00	43.00	100.00

NOTE: *Crandall* a-in all; c-2-4. *Davis* a-1, 2, 6. *Evans* a-3-7; c-7. *Ingels* a-3-7. *Krigstein* a-3-5, 7; c-5, 6. *Wood* a-1, 2; c-1.

PIRANA (See The Phantom #46 & Thrill-O-Rama #2, 3)

PIRATE CORPS, THE
1987 - No. 5, 1988 ($1.95)
Eternity Comics/Slave Labor Graphics

1-5: 3-Color begins		.80	2.00
Special 1 ('89, $1.95, B&W)-Slave Labor Publ.		.80	2.00

PIRATE OF THE GULF, THE (See Superior Stories #2)

PIRATES COMICS
Feb-Mar, 1950 - No. 4, Aug-Sept, 1950 (All 52 pgs.)
Hillman Periodicals

1	20.00	60.00	140
2-Dave Berg-a	14.00	43.00	100
3,4-Berg-a	13.00	39.00	90

P.I.'S: MICHAEL MAUSER AND MS. TREE, THE
Jan, 1985 - No. 3, May, 1985 ($1.25, limited series)
First Comics

1-3: Staton-c/a(p)			

PITT, THE (Also see The Draft & The War)
Mar, 1988 ($3.25, 52 pgs., one-shot)
Marvel Comics

1-Ties into Starbrand, D.P.7		1.40	

PITT (See Youngblood #4 & Gen 13 #3,#4)
Jan, 1993 - Present ($1.95, intended as a four part limited series)
Image Comics #1-9/Full Bleed #1/2,10-on

1/2 (12/95)-1st Full Bleed issue	0.30	0.60	
1-Dale Keown-c/a. 1-1st app. The Pitt	1.00	2.00	
2,4: Dale Keown-c/a		1.60	
3 (Low distribution)		1.20	
5-11: All Dale Keown-c/a. 10 (1/96)-Indicia reads "January 1995"			
		.80	

PITT IN THE BLOOD
Aug, 1996 ($2.50, one-shot)
Full Bleed Studios

nn-Richard Pace-a/script			

PIUS XII MAN OF PEACE
No date (12 pgs.; 5-1/2x8-1/2") (B&W)

nn-Catechetical Guild Giveaway	4.00	10.50	2

PIXIE & DIXIE & MR. JINKS (TV)(See Jinks, Pixie, and Dixie & Whitman Comic Books)
July-Sept, 1960 - Feb, 1963 (Hanna-Barbera)
Dell Publishing Co./Gold Key

Four Color 1112	7.00	21.00	7
Four Color 1196,1264	5.00	15.00	5
01-631-207 (Dell, 7/62), 1(2/63-Gold Key)	5.00	15.00	5

PIXIE PUZZLE ROCKET TO ADVENTURELAND
Nov, 1952
Avon Periodicals

1	11.00	33.00	9

PIXIES, THE (Advs. of...)(The Mighty Atom and ...#6 on)(See A-1 Comics #)
Winter, 1946 - No. 4, Fall?, 1947; No. 5, 1948
Magazine Enterprises

1-Mighty Atom	6.70	20.00	
2-5-Mighty Atom	4.00	11.00	2
I.W. Reprint #1(1958), 8-(Pee-Wee Pixies), 10-I.W. on cover, Super on insid			
	1.30	3.25	

PLANET COMICS
1/40 - No. 62, 9/49; No. 63, Wint, 1949-50; No. 64, Spring, 1950;
No. 65, 1951(nd); No. 66-68, 1952(nd); No. 69, Wint, 1952-53;
No. 70-72, 1953(nd); No. 73, Winter, 1953-54
Fiction House Magazines

	GD25	FN65	VF82	NM
1-Origin Auro, Lord of Jupiter by Briefer (ends #61); Flint Baker & The Red				
Comet begin; Eisner/Fine-c	911.00	2733.00	5466.00	900
(Estimated up to 160 total copies exist, 10 in NM/Mint)				

	GD25	FN65	NM
2-Lou Fine-c (Scarce)	333.00	1000.00	330

Planet of the Apes: Blood of the Apes #1 © Malibu

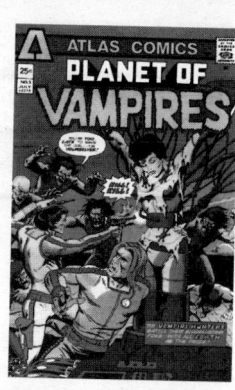
Planet of Vampires #3 © ATLAS

Plastic Man #14 © DC

PL

	GD25	FN65	NM94
3-Eisner-c	262.00	788.00	2300.00
4-Gale Allen and the Girl Squadron begins	231.00	693.00	1850.00
5,6-(Scarce): 5-Eisner/Fine-c	218.00	656.00	1750.00
7-12: 8-Robot-c. 12-The Star Pirate begins	181.00	543.00	1450.00
13-14: 13-Reff Ryan begins	134.00	403.00	1075.00
15-(Scarce)-Mars, God of War begins (11/41); see Jumbo Comics #31 for 1st app.	262.00	787.00	2100.00
16-20,22	125.00	375.00	1000.00
21-The Lost World & Hunt Bowman begin	128.00	384.00	1025.00
23-26: 26-Space Rangers begin (9/43), end #71	115.00	346.00	925.00
27-30	95.00	285.00	760.00
31-35: 33-Origin Star Pirates Wonder Boots, reprinted in #52. 35-Mysta of the Moon begins, ends #62	78.00	234.00	625.00
36-45: 38-1st Mysta of the Moon-c. 41-New origin of "Auro, Lord of Jupiter". 42-Last Gale Allen. 43-Futura begins	71.00	215.00	575.00
46-60: 48-Robot-c. 53-Used in SOTI, pg. 32	56.00	168.00	450.00
61-68,70: 61-Last 68 pg. issue. 64,70-Robot-c. 65-70-All partial-r of earlier issues. 70-r/stories from #41	40.00	120.00	325.00
69-Used in POP, pgs. 101,102	40.00	120.00	325.00
71-73-No series stories. 71-Space Rangers strip	33.00	99.00	230.00
NOTE: Reprint #1(nd)-r/#70; cover-r from Attack on Planet Mars			
NOTE: Reprint #8 (r/#72), 9-r/#73	9.15	27.00	55.00
	9.15	27.00	55.00

NOTE: Anderson a-33-36, 40-51 (Star Pirate). Matt Baker a-53-59 (Mysta of the Moon). Bardo c-12. Bill Discount a-71 (Space Rangers). Elias c-70. Evans a-46-49 (Auro, Lord of Jupiter), 50-64 (Lost World). Fine c-2, 5. Hopper a-31, 35 (Gale Allen), 41, 42, 48, 49 (Mysta of the Moon). Ingels a-24-31 (Lost World), 56-61 (Auro, Lord of Jupiter). Lubbers a-44-47 (Space Rangers); c-40, 41. Moriera a-43, 44 (Mysta of the Moon). Renee a-40-49 (Lost World); c-53, 35, 73. Tuska a-30 (Star Pirate). M. Whitman a-50-52 (Mysta of the Moon), 53-58 (Star Pirate); c-73. Star Rangers a-59. Zolnerwich c-10. 13-25. Bondage c-53.

PLANET COMICS
?, 1988 - No. 3 (2.00, color/B&W #3)
Blackthorne Publishing

1-3: New stories. 1-Dave Stevens-c		.80	2.00

PLANET OF THE APES (Magazine) (Also see Adventures on the... & Power Record Comics)
?, 1974 - No. 29, Feb, 1977 (B&W) (Based on movies)
Marvel Comics Group

1-Ploog-a	2.15	6.50	15.00
2-Ploog-a	1.00	2.00	5.00
3-10		1.60	4.00
11-20		1.20	3.00
21-29		.80	2.00

NOTE: Alcala a-7-11, 17-22, 24. Ploog a-1-4, 6, 8, 11, 13, 14, 19. Sutton a-11, 12, 15, 17, 19, 21, 23, 24, 29. Tuska a-1-6.

PLANET OF THE APES
?, 1990 - No. 24, 1992 ($2.50, B&W)
Adventure Comics

1-New movie tie-in; comes w/outer-c (3 colors)	1.00	2.50	5.50
1-Limited serial numbered edition ($5.00)	1.00	2.50	5.50
1-2nd printing (no outer-c, $2.50)		1.00	2.50
2-24		1.10	2.75
Special 1 ($3.50)		1.50	3.75
Urchak's Folly 1-4 ($2.50, mini-series)		1.10	2.75

PLANET OF VAMPIRES
?, 1975 - No. 3, July, 1975
Seaboard Publications (Atlas)

1-Neal Adams-c(i); 1st Broderick c/a(p)			1.50
2-Neal Adams-c. 3-Heath-c/a			1.00

PLANET TERRY
?, 1985 - No. 12, March, 1986 (Children's comic)
Marvel Comics (Star Comics)/Marvel

			.70

PLASM (See Warriors of Plasm)
June, 1993
Defiant Comics

0-Came bound into Diamond Previews V3#6 (6/93); price is for complete Previews with comic still attached		1.60	4.00
0-Comic only removed from Previews		1.20	3.00

PLASMER
Nov, 1993 - No. 4, Feb, 1994 ($1.95, limited series)
Marvel Comics UK

1-($2.50)-Polybagged w/4 trading cards		1.00	2.50
2-4: Capt. America & Silver Surfer app.		.80	2.00

PLASTIC FORKS
1990 - No. 5, 1990 ($4.95, 68 pgs., limited series, mature)
Marvel Comis (Epic Comics)

Book 1-5: Squarebound	1.00	2.00	5.00

PLASTIC MAN (Also see Police Comics & Smash Comics #17)
Sum, 1943 - No. 64, Nov, 1956
Vital Publ. No. 1,2/Quality Comics No. 3 on

nn(#1)- "In The Game of Death"; Skull-c; Jack Cole begins; ends-#64?	350.00	1050.00	2900.00
nn(#2, 2/44)- "The Gay Nineties Nightmare"	150.00	450.00	1200.00
3 (Spr, '46)	93.00	281.00	750.00
4 (Sum, '46)	76.00	230.00	615.00
5 (Aut, '46)	65.00	195.00	525.00
6-10	51.00	155.00	415.00
11-20	47.00	141.00	375.00
21-30: 26-Last non-r issue?	40.00	120.00	295.00
31-40: 40-Used in POP, pg. 91	32.00	96.00	225.00
41-64: 53-Last precode issue. 54-Robot-c	26.00	79.00	185.00
Super Reprint 11,16,18: 11('63)-r/#16. 16-r/#18 & #21; Cole-a. 18('64)-Spirit-r by Eisner from Police #95	5.70	17.00	40.00

NOTE: Cole r-44, 49, 56, 58, 59 at least. Cuidera c-32-64i.

PLASTIC MAN (See DC Special #15 & House of Mystery #160)
11-12/66 - No. 10, 5-6/68; V4#11, 2-3/76 - No. 20, 10-11/77
National Periodical Publications/DC Comics

1-Real 1st app. Silver Age Plastic Man (House of Mystery #160 is actually tryout); Gil Kane-c/a; 12¢ issues begin	8.20	24.50	57.00
2-5: 4-Infantino-c; Mortimer-a	3.90	11.50	27.00
6-10('68): 7-G.A. Plastic Man & Woozy Winks (1st S.A. app.) app.; origin retold. 10-Sparling-a; last 12¢ issue	2.30	6.70	16.00
V4#11('76)-20: 11-20-Fraden-p. 17-Origin retold	1.00	2.00	5.00

PLASTIC MAN
Nov, 1988 - No. 4, Feb, 1989 ($1.00, mini-series)
DC Comics

1-4: 1-Origin; Woozy Winks app.			1.00

PLASTRON CAFE
Dec, 1992 - 1993 ($2.25, B&W)
Mirage Studios

1-4: 1-Teenage Mutant Ninja Turtles app.; Kelly Freas-c. 2-Hildebrandt painted-c. 4-Spaced & Alien Fire stories		.90	2.25

PLAYFUL LITTLE AUDREY (TV)(Also see Little Audrey #25)
6/57 - No. 110, 11/73; No. 111, 8/74 - No. 121, 4/76
Harvey Publications

1	16.00	48.00	160.00
2	9.00	27.00	90.00
3-5	6.00	18.00	60.00
6-10	3.80	11.40	38.00
11-20	2.60	7.80	26.00
21-40	2.60	7.50	18.00
41-60	2.00	6.00	14.00

Poison Elves #6 © Drew Hayes

Poizon #0 © Everette Hartsoe

Police Action #2 © ATLAS

	GD25	FN65	NM94
61-80	1.65	4.20	10.00
81-99	1.20	3.00	7.00
100-52 pg. Giant	1.65	4.20	10.00
101-103: 52 pg. Giants	1.50	3.75	9.00
104-121		1.60	4.00
...In 3-D (Spring, 1988, $2.25, Blackthorne #66)		.90	2.25

PLOP! (Also see The Best of DC #60)
Sept-Oct, 1973 - No. 24, Nov-Dec, 1976
National Periodical Publications

1-20: Sergio Aragones-a. 1,5-Wrightson-a	1.00	2.00	5.00
21,22,24 (52 pgs.)		1.80	4.50
23-No Aragones-a (52 pgs.)		.80	2.00

NOTE: Alcala a-1-3. Anderson a-5. Aragones a-1-22, 24. Ditko a-16p. Evans a-1. Mayer a-1. Orlando a-21, 22; c-21. Sekowsky a-5, 6p. Toth a-11. Wolverton r-4, 22-24(1 pg.ea.); c-1-12, 14, 17, 18. Wood a-14, 16i, 18-24; c-13, 15, 16, 19.

PLUTO (See Cheerios Premiums, Four Color #537, Mickey Mouse Magazine, Four Color 509, Mickey Mouse Showcase #4, 7, 13, 20, 23, 33 & Wheaties)
No. 7, 1942; No. 429, 10/52 - No. 1248, 11-1/61-62 (Walt Disney)
Dell Publishing Co.

Large Feature Comic 7(1942)-Written by Carl Barks, Jack Hannah, & Nick George (Barks' 1st comic book work)	115.00	345.00	1150.00
Four Color 429 (#1)	9.50	28.50	95.00
Four Color 509	6.00	18.00	60.00
Four Color 595,654,736,853	4.00	12.00	40.00
Four Color 941,1039,1143,1248	3.50	10.00	35.00

POCAHONTAS
1941 - No. 2, 1942
Pocahontas Fuel Company (Coal)

nn(#1), 2	11.00	33.00	75.00

POCKET COMICS (Becomes Super Duper #5?; also see Double Up)
Aug, 1941 - No. 4, Jan, 1942 (Pocket size; 100 pgs.)
Harvey Publications (1st Harvey comic)

1-Origin & 1st app. The Black Cat, Cadet Blakey the Spirit of '76, The Red Blazer, The Phantom, Sphinx, & The Zebra; Phantom Ranger, British Agent #99, Spin Hawkins, Satan, Lord of Evil begin (1st app. of each); Simon-c/a in #1-3	84.00	253.00	675.00
2-Black Cat on-c #2-4	58.00	174.00	465.00
3,4	44.00	132.00	350.00

POGO PARADE (See Dell Giants)

POGO POSSUM (Also see Animal Comics & Special Delivery)
No. 105, 4/46 - No. 148, 5/47; 10-12/49 - No. 16, 4-6/54
Dell Publishing Co.

Four Color 105(1946)-Kelly-c/a	67.50	205.00	675.00
Four Color 148-Kelly-c/a	60.00	180.00	600.00
1-(10-12/49)-Kelly-c/a in all	50.00	150.00	500.00
2	40.00	120.00	400.00
3-5	27.00	81.00	270.00
6-10: 10-Infinity-c	23.00	70.00	230.00
11-16: 11-X-Mas-c	18.00	54.00	180.00

NOTE: #1-4, 9-13: 52 pgs.; #5-8, 14-16: 36 pgs.

POINT BLANK
May, 1989 - No. 2, 1989 ($2.95, B&W, magazine)
Acme Press (Eclipse)

1,2-European-r		1.20	3.00

POISON ELVES (Formerly I, Lusipher)
No. 8, 1993- No. 19, 1995 (B&W, magazine/comic size, mature readers)
Mulehide Graphics

8-Drew Hayes-c/a/scripts.	5.70	17.00	40.00
9,10	4.30	13.00	30.00
11-1st comic size issue	5.00	15.00	35.00

	GD25	FN65	NM94
12-14, 16-18, 20	2.85	8.50	20
15-scarce	4.30	13.00	30
15-2nd print	1.00	2.00	5
19	4.30	13.00	30

POISON ELVES (See I, Lusiphur)
June, 1995 - Present ($2.50, B&W, mature readers)
Sirius Entertainment

1-Linsner-c; Drew Hayesc/a/scripts in all.	1.00	2.00	5
2		1.60	4
3-15: Purple Marauder-c/app.		1.00	2
...Requiem For An Elf (6/96, $14.95, trade paperback)-Reprints I, Lusiphur #1-6			1

POIZON
Oct, 1995 - Present ($3.00)
London NIght Studios

0,1/2-3: 1/2-Razor-c/app. 1-Razor & Stryke app.; wraparound-c. 2-Razor & Stryke app. 3-Razor-c/app.			
0-Gothik Edition			
1-($5.95)-Necro-Nude Edition			6
1-Purple Reign Edition			
1-($15.00)-Green Death Edition; in green envelope w/certificate			1

POLICE ACADEMY (TV)
Nov, 1989 - No. 6, Feb, 1990 ($1.00)
Marvel Comics

1-6: Based on TV cartoon; Post-c/a(p) in all

POLICE ACTION
Jan, 1954 - No. 7, Nov, 1954
Atlas News Co.

1-Violent-a by Robert Q. Sale	16.00	47.00	11
2	9.15	27.00	5
3-7: 7-Powell-a	7.50	22.50	4

NOTE: Ayers a-4, 5. Colan a-1. Forte a-1, 2. Mort Lawrence a-5. Maneely a-3; c-1, 5. Reinman a-6, 7.

POLICE ACTION
Feb, 1975 - No. 3, June, 1975
Atlas/Seaboard Publ.

1-3: 1-Lomax, N.Y.P.D., Luke Malone begin; McWilliams-a. 2-Origin Luke Malone, Manhunter

NOTE: Ploog art in all. Sekowsky/McWilliams a-1-3. Thorne c-3.

POLICE AGAINST CRIME
April, 1954 - No. 9, Aug, 1955
Premiere Magazines

1-Disbrow-a; extreme violence (man's face slashed with knife); Hollingsworth-a	19.00	58.00	13
2-Hollingsworth-a	10.00	30.00	6
3-9	9.15	27.00	5

POLICE BADGE #479 (Formerly Spy Thrillers #1-4)
No. 5, Sept, 1955
Atlas Comics (PrPI)

5-Maneely-c/a (6 pgs.)	9.15	27.00	5

POLICE CASE BOOK (See Giant Comics Editions)

POLICE CASES (See Authentic... & Record Book of...)

POLICE COMICS
Aug, 1941 - No. 127, Oct, 1953
Quality Comics Group (Comic Magazines)

1-Origin/1st app. Plastic Man by Jack Cole (r-in DC Special #15), The Hurr Bomb by Gustavson, & No. 711; intro. Chic Carter by Eisner, The Firebra by Reed Crandall, The Mouthpiece by Guardineer, Phantom Lady, & The

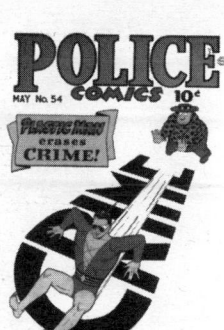

Police Comics #54 © QUA

Police Comics #111 © QUA

Police Line-Up #1 © AVON

	GD25	FN65	NM94
Sword; Firebrand-c 1-4	611.00	1833.00	5800.00
2-Plastic Man smuggles opium	250.00	750.00	2100.00
3	175.00	525.00	1400.00
4	165.00	496.00	1325.00
5-Plastic Man-c begin; Plastic Man forced to smoke marijuana; Plastic Man covers begin, end #102	150.00	450.00	1200.00
6,7	137.00	412.00	1100.00
8-Manhunter begins (origin/1st app.) (3/42)	168.00	506.00	1350.00
9,10	121.00	365.00	975.00
11-The Spirit strip reprints begin by Eisner (origin-strip #1); 1st comic book app. The Spirit & 1st cover begin. (9/42)	193.00	581.00	1550.00
12-Intro. Ebony	121.00	365.00	975.00
13-Intro. Woozy Winks; last Firebrand	121.00	365.00	975.00
14-19: 15-Last No. 711; Destiny begins	81.00	243.00	650.00
20-The Raven x-over in Phantom Lady; features Jack Cole app.	81.00	243.00	650.00
21,22: 21-Raven & Spider Widow x-over in Phantom Lady (cameo in #22)	66.00	200.00	535.00
23-30: 23-Last Phantom Lady. 24-26-Flatfoot Burns by Kurtzman in all	60.00	181.00	485.00
31-41: 37-1st app. Candy by Sahle & begins (12/44). 41-Last Spirit-r by Eisner	40.00	120.00	325.00
42,43-Spirit-r by Eisner/Fine	39.00	116.00	270.00
44-Fine Spirit-r begin, end #88,90,92	34.00	101.00	235.00
45-50: 50-(#50 on-c, #49 on inside, 1/46)	34.00	101.00	235.00
51-60: 58-Last Human Bomb	29.00	84.00	195.00
61-88: 63-(Some issues have #65 printed on cover, but #63 on inside) Kurtzman, 6 pgs.	21.00	64.00	150.00
89,91,93-No Spirit stories	19.00	56.00	130.00
90,92-Spirit by Fine	24.00	71.00	165.00
94-99,101,102: Spirit by Eisner in all; 101-Last Manhunter. 102-Last Spirit & Plastic Man by Jack Cole	30.00	90.00	210.00
100	37.00	111.00	260.00
103-Content change to crime; Ken Shannon & T-Man begin (1st app. of each, 12/50)	21.00	64.00	150.00
104-111,114-127: Crandall-a most issues (not in 104,105,122,125-127). 109-Atomic bomb story	17.00	49.00	115.00
112-Crandall-a	17.00	49.00	115.00
113-Crandall-c/a(2), 9 pgs. each	17.00	51.00	115.00

NOTE: Most Spirit stories signed by Eisner are not by him; all are reprints. Cole c-17, 19-21, 24-26, 28-31, 36-38, 40-42, 45-48, 65-68, 69, 73, 75. Crandall Firebrand-1-8. Spirit by Eisner 1-41, 94-102; by Eisner/Fine-42, 43; by Fine-44-88, 90, 92, 103, 109. Al Bryant c-33, 34. Cole c-17-32, 35-102(most). Crandall c-13, 14. Crandall/Cuidera c-105-127. Eisner c-4i. Gill Fox c-1-3, 4p, 5-12, 15. Bondage c-103, 109, 125.

POLICE LINE-UP
Aug, 1951 - No. 4, July, 1952 (Painted-c #1-3)
Avon Periodicals/Realistic Comics #3,4

1-Wood-a, 1 pg. plus part-c; spanking panel-r/Saint #5	33.00	99.00	230.00
2-Classic story "The Religious Murder Cult", drugs, perversion; c-r/Avon paperback #329	23.00	69.00	160.00
3-Kubert-a(r?)/part-c; Kinstler-a (inside-c only)	17.00	49.00	115.00
4	17.00	49.00	115.00

POLICE TRAP (Public Defender In Action #7 on)
8-9/54 - No. 4, 2-3/55; No. 5, 7/55 - No. 6, 9/55
Mainline No. 1-4/Charlton No. 5,6

1-S&K covers-all issues; Meskin-a; Kirby scripts	21.00	64.00	150.00
2-4	13.00	39.00	90.00
5,6-S&K c/a	19.00	56.00	130.00

POLICE TRAP
No. 11, 1963; No. 16-18, 1964
Super Comics

Reprint #11,16-18: 11-r/Police Trap #3. 16-r/Justice Traps the Guilty #?

17-r/Inside Crime #3 & r/Justice Traps The Guilty #83; 18-r/Inside Crime #3	1.30	3.25	8.00

POLL PARROT
Poll Parrot Shoe Store/International Shoe
1950 - No. 4, 1951; No. 2, 1959 - No. 16, 1962
K. K. Publications (Giveaway)

1 ('50)-Howdy Doody; small size	13.00	39.00	90.00
2-4('51)-Howdy Doody	10.00	30.00	70.00
2('59)-16('62): 2-The Secret of Crumbley Castle. 5-Bandit Busters. 7-The Make-Believe Mummy. 8-Mixed Up Mission('60). 10-The Frightful Flight. 11-Showdown at Sunup. 12-Maniac at Mubu Island. 13-....and the Runaway Genie. 14-Bully for You. 15-Trapped In Tall Timber. 16-...& the Rajah's Ruby('62)	3.60	9.00	18.00

POLLY & HER PALS (See Comic Monthly #1)

POLLYANNA (Disney)
No. 1129, Aug-Oct, 1960
Dell Publishing Co.

Four Color 1129-Movie, Haley Mills photo-c	10.00	30.00	100.00

POLLY PIGTAILS (Girls' Fun & Fashion Magazine #44 on)
Jan, 1946 - V4#43, Oct-Nov, 1949
Parents' Magazine Institute/Polly Pigtails

1-Infinity-c; photo-c	10.00	30.00	65.00
2-Photo-c	5.35	16.00	32.00
3-5: 3,4-Photo-c	4.00	12.00	24.00
6-10: 7-Photo-c	4.00	10.00	20.00
11-30: 22-Photo-c	2.80	7.00	14.00
31-43	2.40	6.00	12.00

PONY EXPRESS (See Tales of the...)

PONYTAIL
7-9/62 - No. 12, 10-12/65; No. 13, 11/69 - No. 20, 1/71
Dell Publishing Co./Charlton No. 13 on

12-641-209(#1)	2.30	6.70	16.00
2-12	1.30	3.25	8.00
13-20	1.00	2.00	5.00

POP COMICS
1955 (36 pgs.; 5x7"; in color) (7¢)
Modern Store Publ.

1-Funny animal	1.00	2.00	5.00

POPEYE (See Comic Album #7, 11, 15, Comics Reading Libraries, Eat Right to Work and Win, Giant Comic Album, King Comics, Kite Fun Book, Magic Comics, March of Comics #37, 52, 66, 80, 96, 117, 134, 148, 157, 169, 194, 246, 264, 274, 294, 453, 465, 477 & Wow Comics, 1st series)

POPEYE (See Thimble Theatre)
1935 (25¢; 52 pgs.; B&W) (By Segar)
David McKay Publications

1-Daily strip serial reprints- "The Gold Mine Thieves"	57.00	172.00	575.00
2-Daily strip-r	45.00	135.00	450.00

NOTE: Popeye first entered Thimble Theatre in 1929.

POPEYE
1937 - 1939 (All by Segar)
David McKay Publications

Feature Books nn (100 pgs.) (Very Rare)	600.00	1800.00	6000.00
Feature Books 2 (52 pgs.)	67.00	200.00	675.00
Feature Books 3 (100 pgs.)-r/nn issue with a new-c	62.00	186.00	625.00
Feature Books 5,10 (76 pgs.)	57.00	171.00	575.00
Feature Books 14 (76 pgs.) (Scarce)	67.00	200.00	675.00

POPEYE (Strip reprints through 4-Color #70)
1941 - 1947: #1, 2-4/48 - #65, 7-9/62; #66, 10/62 - #80, 5/66; #81, 8/66 - #92,

Popeye V2#6 © KFS

Popeye Special #1 © KFS

Popular Comics #14 © DELL

	GD25	FN65	NM94

12/67; #94, 2/69 - #138, 1/77; #139, 5/78 - #171, 7/84 (no #93,160,161)
Dell #1-65/Gold Key #66-80/King #81-92/Charlton #94-138/Gold Key #139-155/
Whitman #156 on

	GD25	FN65	NM94
Large Feature Comic 24('41)-Half by Segar	55.00	165.00	550.00
Four Color 25('41)-by Segar	70.00	210.00	700.00
Large Feature Comic 10('43)	45.00	135.00	450.00
Four Color 17('43),26('43)-by Segar	52.50	157.50	525.00
Four Color 43('44)	31.00	93.00	315.00
Four Color 70('45)-Title: ...& Wimpy	25.00	75.00	255.00
Four Color 113('46-original strips begin),127,145('47),168			
	13.00	39.00	130.00
1(2-4/48)(Dell)-All new stories continue	28.00	84.00	280.00
2	14.00	42.00	140.00
3-10: 5-Popeye on moon w/rocket-c	11.00	33.00	115.00
11-20	10.00	30.00	100.00
21-40	8.00	24.00	80.00
41-45,47-50	5.50	16.50	55.00
46-Origin Swee' Pee	8.00	24.00	80.00
51-60	5.00	15.00	50.00
61-65 (Last Dell issue)	4.00	12.00	40.00
66,67-Both 84 pgs. (Gold Key)	5.50	16.50	55.00
68-80	2.85	8.50	20.00
81-92,94-100	2.00	6.00	14.00
101-130	1.30	3.25	8.00
131-159,162-171: 144-50th Anniversary issue	1.00	2.00	5.00
Bold Detergent giveaway (Same as regular issue #94)	1.20		3.00

NOTE: Reprints-#145, 147, 149, 151, 153, 155, 157, 163-68(1/3), 170.

POPEYE
1972 - 1974 (36 pgs. in color)
Charlton (King Features) (Giveaway)

E-1 to E-15 (Educational comics)		.80	2.00
nn-Popeye Gettin' Better Grades-4 pgs. used as intro. to above giveaways (in color)		.80	2.00

POPEYE
Nov, 1993 - No. 7, Aug, 1994 ($1.50)
Harvey Comics

V2#1-7			1.50
...Summer Special V2#1-(10/93, $2.25, 68 pgs.)-Sagendorf-r & others		.90	2.25

POPEYE CARTOON BOOK
1934 (8-1/2x13", 40 pgs., cardboard-c)
The Saalfield Publ. Co.

2095-(Rare)-1933 strip reprints in color by Segar; each page contains a vertical
half of a Sunday strip, so the continuity reads row by row completely across
each double page spread. If each page is read by itself, the continuity makes
no sense. Each double page spread reprints one complete Sunday page

(from 1933)	130.00	390.00	1300.00
12 Page Version	62.50	187.50	625.00

POPEYE SPECIAL
Summer, 1987 - No. 2, Sept, 1988 ($1.75/$2.00)
Ocean Comics

1-Origin ($1.75)			1.75
2 ($2.00)		.80	2.00

POPPLES (TV, movie)
Dec, 1986 - No. 5, Aug, 1987
Star Comics (Marvel)

1-3-Based on toys			.70
4,5 ($1.00)			1.00

POPPO OF THE POPCORN THEATRE
10/29/55 - No. 13, 1956 (weekly)
Fuller Publishing Co. (Publishers Weekly)

	GD25	FN65	NM94
1	8.00	24.00	48.00
2-5	5.00	15.00	30.00
6-13	4.00	12.00	24.00

NOTE: By Charles Biro. 10¢ cover, given away by supermarkets such as IGA.

POP-POP COMICS
No date (Circa 1945) (52 pgs.)
R. B. Leffingwell Co.

1-Funny animal	8.70	26.00	52.00

POPSICLE PETE FUN BOOK (See All-American Comics #6)
1947, 1948
Joe Lowe Corp.

nn-36 pgs. in color; Sammy 'n' Claras, The King Who Couldn't Sleep & Popsicle Pete stories, games, cut-outs	9.15	27.50	55.00
Adventure Book ('48)-Has Classics ad with checklist to HRN #343 (Great Expectations #43)	7.50	22.50	45.00

POPULAR COMICS
Feb, 1936 - No. 145, July-Sept, 1948
Dell Publishing Co.

	GD25	FN65	VF82
1-Dick Tracy (1st comic book app.), Little Orphan Annie, Terry & the Pirates, Gasoline Alley, Don Winslow (1st app.), Harold Teen, Little Joe, Skippy, Moon Mullins, Mutt & Jeff, Tailspin Tommy, Smitty, Smokey Stover, Winnie Winkle & The Gumps begin (all strip-r)	566.00	1700.00	3400.00
(Estimated up to 90 total copies exist, 4 in NM/Mint)			
2	183.00	550.00	1100.00
3	145.00	437.00	875.00
4,5: 5-Tom Mix begins	119.00	357.00	715.00
6-10: 8,9-Scribbly, Reglar Fellers app.	91.00	275.00	550.00

	GD25	FN65	NM94
11-20: 12-X-Mas-c	78.00	234.00	470.00
21-27: 27-Last Terry & the Pirates, Little Orphan Annie, & Dick Tracy	54.00	162.00	325.00
28-37: 28-Gene Autry app. 31,32-Tim McCoy app. 35-Christmas-c; Tex Ritter app.	45.00	137.00	275.00
38-43: Tarzan in text only. 38-(4/39)-Gang Busters (Radio, 2nd app.) & Zane Grey's Tex Thorne begins? 43-The Masked Pilot app.; 1st non-funny-c?	46.00	138.00	300.00
44,45: 45-Hurricane Kid-c	28.00	84.00	195.00
46-Origin/1st app. Martan, the Marvel Man(12/39)	40.00	120.00	285.00
47-50	26.00	79.00	185.00
51-Origin The Voice (The Invisible Detective) strip begins (5/40)			
	29.00	86.00	200.00
52-59: 55-End of World story	22.00	66.00	155.00
60-Origin/1st app. Professor Supermind and Son (2/41)			
	23.00	69.00	160.00
61-71: 63-Smilin' Jack begins	18.00	54.00	125.00
72-The Owl & Terry & the Pirates begin (2/42); Smokey Stover reprints begin			
	39.00	118.00	275.00
73-75	24.00	73.00	165.00
76-78-Capt. Midnight in all	31.00	94.00	220.00
79-85-Last Owl	21.00	62.00	145.00
86-99: 98-Felix the Cat, Smokey Stover-r begin	16.00	47.00	110.00
100	17.00	49.00	115.00
101-130	10.00	30.00	65.00
131-145: 142-Last Terry & the Pirates	10.00	30.00	60.00

NOTE: Martan, the Marvel Man c-47-49, 52, 57-59. Professor Supermind c-60-63, 64(1/2), 65, 66. The Voice c-53.

POPULAR FAIRY TALES (See March of Comics #6, 18)

POPULAR ROMANCE
No. 5, Dec, 1949 - No. 29, July, 1954
Better-Standard Publications

5	7.50	22.50	45.00
6-9: 7-Palais-a; lingerie panels	4.25	13.00	28.00

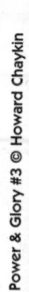

Popular Teen-Agers #8 © STAR

Power & Glory #3 © Howard Chaykin

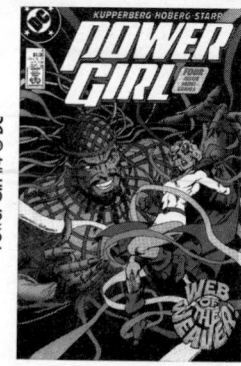

Power Girl #4 © DC

PC

	GD25	FN65	NM94
10-Wood-a (2 pgs.)	7.00	21.00	42.00
11,12,14-16,18-21,28,29	4.00	12.00	24.00
13,17-Severin/Elder-a (3&8 pgs.)	4.25	13.00	28.00
22-27-Toth-a	8.00	24.00	48.00

NOTE: All have photo-c. Tuska art in most issues.

POPULAR TEEN-AGERS (Secrets of Love) (School Day Romances #1-4)
No. 5, Sept, 1950 - No. 23, Nov, 1954
Star Publications

	GD25	FN65	NM94
5-Toni Gay, Midge Martin & Eve Adams continue from School Day Romances; Ginger Bunn (formerly Ginger Snapp & becomes Honey Bunn #6 on) begins; all features end #8	24.00	73.00	165.00
6-8 (7/51)-Honey Bunn begins; all have L. B. Cole-c; 6-Negligee panels	21.00	62.00	145.00
9-(...Romances; 1st romance issue, 10/51)	11.00	33.00	75.00
10-(...Secrets of Love thru #23)	11.00	33.00	75.00
11,16,18,19,22,23	9.15	27.00	55.00
12,13,17,20,21-Disbrow-a	10.00	30.00	65.00
14-Harrison/Wood-a; 2 spanking scenes	18.00	54.00	125.00
15-Wood?, Disbrow-a	13.50	41.00	95.00
Accepted Reprint 5,6 (nd); L.B. Cole-c	5.85	17.50	35.00

NOTE: All have L. B. Cole covers.

PORKY PIG (See Bugs Bunny &..., Kite Fun Book, Looney Tunes, March of Comics #42, 57, 71, 89, 99, 113, 130, 143, 164, 175, 192, 209, 218, 367, and Super Book #6, 18, 30)

PORKY PIG (...& Bugs Bunny #40-69)
No. 16, 1942 - No. 81, Mar-Apr, 1962; Jan, 1965 - No. 109, July, 1984
Dell Publishing Co./Gold Key No. 1-93/Whitman No. 94 on

	GD25	FN65	NM94
Four Color 16(#1, 1942)	78.00	233.00	780.00
Four Color 48(1944)-Carl Barks-a	100.00	300.00	1000.00
Four Color 78(1945)	24.00	72.00	240.00
Four Color 112(7/46)	14.00	43.00	140.00
Four Color 156,182,191('49)	10.00	30.00	100.00
Four Color 226,241('49),260,271,277,284,295	8.00	24.00	80.00
Four Color 303,311,322,330: 322-Sci/fi-c/story	5.00	15.00	50.00
Four Color 342,351,360,370,385,399,410,426	4.00	12.00	40.00
25 (11-12/52)-30	3.00	9.00	30.00
31-40	2.00	6.00	14.00
41-60	1.70	5.00	12.00
61-81(3-4/62)	1.30	3.25	8.00
1(1/65-Gold Key)(2nd Series)	1.70	5.00	12.00
2,4,5-r/4-Color 226,284 & 271 in that order	1.00	2.60	6.00
3,6-10		1.60	4.00
11-50		1.00	2.50
51-109			1.00

NOTE: Reprints-#1-8, 9-35(2/3); 36-46, 58, 67, 69-74, 76, 78, 102-109(1/3-1/2).

PORKY PIG'S DUCK HUNT
1938 (12pgs.)(large size)(heavy linen-like paper)
Saalfield Publishing Co.

	GD25	FN65	NM94
2178-1st app. Porky Pig & Daffy Duck by Leon Schlesinger. Illustrated text story book written in verse.1st book ever devoted to these characters. (see Looney Tunes #1 for their 1st comic book app.)	62.00	188.00	500.00

PORKY'S BOOK OF TRICKS
1942 (8-1/2x5-1/2", 48 pgs.)
K. K. Publications (Giveaway)

	GD25	FN65	NM94
nn-7 pg. comic story, text stories, plus games & puzzles	40.00	120.00	300.00

PORKY PIG'S DUCK HUNT
1938 (12 pgs., heavy linen-like paper)
Saalfield Publishing Co.

	GD25	FN65	NM94
#2178-1st app. Porky Pig & Daffy Duck by Leon Schlesinger; written in verse	62.00	188.00	500.00

PORTIA PRINZ OF THE GLAMAZONS

	GD25	FN65	NM94
Dec, 1986 - No. 6, Oct, 1987 ($2.00, B&W, Baxter paper)			

Eclipse Comics

1-6		.80	2.00

POST GAZETTE (See Meet the New...)

POWDER RIVER RUSTLERS (See Fawcett Movie Comics)

POWER & GLORY (Also See American Flagg! & Howard Chaykin's American Flagg!
Feb, 1994 - No. 4, May, 1994 ($2.50, limited series, mature)
Malibu Comics (Bravura)

	GD25	FN65	NM94
1A, 1B-By Howard Chaykin; w/Bravura stamp		1.00	2.50
1 ($2.95)-Newsstand ed. polybagged w/children's warning on bag; Howard Chaykin-c/a begin		1.20	3.00
1 (Gold ed.)	1.65	4.20	10.00
1 (Silver-foil ed.)	1.30	3.25	8.00
1 (Blue-foil ed.)-print run of 10,000	1.00	2.00	5.00
1 (Serigraph ed.)-print run of 3,000	1.00	2.00	5.00
2-4-Contains Bravura stamp		1.00	2.50
Holiday Special (Win '94, $2.95)		1.20	3.00

POWER COMICS
1944 - No. 4, 1945
Holyoke Publ. Co./Narrative Publ.

	GD25	FN65	NM94
1-L. B. Cole-c	112.00	338.00	900.00
2-Hitler, Hirohito-c (scarce)	112.00	338.00	900.00
3-Classic L.B. Cole-c; Dr. Mephisto begins?	125.00	375.00	1000.00
4-L.B. Cole-c; Miss Espionage app. #3,4; Leav-a	112.00	338.00	900.00

POWER COMICS
1977 - No. 5, Dec, 1977 (B&W)
Power Comics Co.

	GD25	FN65	NM94
1- "A Boy And His Aardvark" by Dave Sim; first Dave Sim aardvark (not Cerebus)	1.30	3.25	8.00
1-Reprint (3/77, black-c)	1.00	2.00	5.00
2-Cobalt Blue by Gustovich		1.00	2.50
3-5: 3-Nightwitch. 4-Northern Light. 5-Bluebird		1.00	2.50

POWER COMICS
Mar, 1988 - No. 4, Sept, 1988 ($2.00, B&W, mini-series)
Eclipse Comics (Acme Press)

1-4: Bolland, Gibbons-r in all		.80	2.00

POWER FACTOR
May, 1987 - No. 3, 1987 ($1.95)
Wonder Color Comics

1-3: Super team. 2-Inantino-c		.80	2.00

POWER FACTOR
Oct, 1990 - No. 3, 1991 ($1.95/$2.25)
Innovation Publishing

1-Reprints 1st story plus new-a		.80	2.00
2,3: 2-Begin $2.25-c; r/2nd story plus new-a. 3-Infantino-a		.90	2.25

POWER GIRL (See All-Star 58, Infinity, Inc., Showcase #97-99)
June, 1988 - No. 4, Sept, 1988 ($1.00, color, limited series)
DC Comics

1-4			1.00

POWERHOUSE PEPPER COMICS (See Gay Comics, Joker Comics & Tessie the Typist)
No. 1, 1943; No. 2, May, 1948 - No. 5, Nov, 1948
Marvel Comics (20CC)

	GD25	FN65	NM94
1-(60 pgs.)-Wolverton-a in all; c-2,3	131.00	393.00	1050.00
2	71.00	215.00	575.00
3,4	65.00	195.00	525.00

Power Man #17 © MEG

Power Of Shazam #19 © DC

Preacher #9 © Garth Ennis & Steve Dillon

	GD25	FN65	NM94
5-(Scarce)	81.00	243.00	650.00

POWER LINE
May, 1988 - No. 8, Sept, 1989 ($1.25/$1.50)
Marvel Comics (Epic Comics)

1-3: 2-Williamson-i. 3-Austin-i, Dr. Zero app.			1.25
4-8: 4-Begin $1.50-c. 4-7-Morrow-a. 8-Williamson-i			1.50

POWER LORDS
Dec, 1983 - No. 3, Feb, 1984 (Limited series, Mando paper)
DC Comics

1-3: Based on Revell toys			.80

POWER MAN (Formerly Hero for Hire; ...& Iron Fist #68 on; see Cage & Giant-Size...)
No. 17, Feb, 1974 - No. 125, Sept, 1986
Marvel Comics Group

17-Luke Cage continues; Iron Man app.	1.50	3.75	9.00
18-20: 18-Last 20¢ issue		1.60	4.00
21-31: 31-Part Neal Adams-i		1.20	3.00
32-47: 34-Last 25¢ issue. 36-r/Hero For Hire #12. 41-1st app. Thunderbolt. 45-Starlin-c.			2.25
48-50-Byrne-a(p); 48-Power Man/Iron Fist 1st meet. 50-Iron Fist joins Cage		.90	2.25
51-56,58-60: 58-Intro El Aguila			1.50
57-New X-Men app. (6/79)		1.50	3.75
61-65,67-77,79-83,85-124: 75-Double size. 77-Daredevil app. 87-Moon Knight app. 90-Unus app. 109-The Reaper app. 100-Double size; origin K'un L'un			1.00
66-2nd app. Sabretooth (see Iron Fist #14)	3.60	11.00	25.00
78-3rd app. Sabretooth (cameo under cloak)	2.15	6.50	15.00
84-4th app. Sabretooth	2.15	6.50	15.00
125-Double size; death of Iron Fist		.80	2.00
Annual 1(1976)-Punisher cameo in flashback		1.20	3.00

NOTE: Austin c-102i. Byrne a-48-50; c-102, 104, 106, 107, 112-116. Kane c(p)-24, 25, 28, 48. Miller a-68, 76(2 pgs.); c-66-68, 70-74, 80i. Mooney a-38i, 53i, 55i. Nebres a-76p. Nino a-42i, 43i. Perez a-27. B. Smith a-47i. Tuska a(p)-17, 20, 24, 26, 28, 29, 36, 47. Painted c-75, 100.

POWER OF PRIME
July, 1995 - No. 4, Nov, 1995 ($2.50, limited series)
Malibu Comics (Ultraverse)

1-4		1.00	2.50

POWER OF SHAZAM!, THE (See SHAZAM!)
1994 (Painted graphic novel) (Prequel to new series)
DC Comics

Hardcover-($19.95)-New origin of Shazam!; Ordway painted-c/a & script			20.00
Softcover-($9.95)-New-c.			10.00

POWER OF SHAZAM!, THE
Mar, 1995 - Present ($1.50/$1.75)
DC Comics

1-Jerry Ordway scripts begin		.80	2.00
2,3			1.50
4-25: 4-Begin $1.75-c. 6:Re-intro of Capt. Nazi. 8-Re-intro of Spy Smasher, Bulletman & Minuteman; Swan-a (7 pgs.). 11-Re-intro of Ibis, Swan-a (2 pgs.). 14-Gil Kane-a(p)		.70	1.75
Annual 1 (1996, $2.95)-Legends of the Dead Earth story; Jerry Ordway-c; Mike Manley-a			3.00

POWER OF STRONGMAN, THE (Also see Strongman)
1989 ($2.95)
AC Comics

1-Powell G.A.-r		1.20	3.00

POWER OF THE ATOM (See Secret Origins #29)
Aug, 1988 - No. 18, Nov, 1989 ($1.00)

DC Comics

1-18: 6-Chronos returns; Byrne-p. 9-JLI app.			1.00

POWER PACHYDERMS
Sept, 1989 ($1.25, one-shot)
Marvel Comics

1-Elephant super-heroes			1.30

POWER PACK
Aug, 1984 - No. 62, Feb, 1991
Marvel Comics Group

1-($1.00, 52 pgs.)-Origin & 1st app. Power Pack			1.50
2-18,20-26,28,30-45,47-62			1.00
19-(52 pgs.)-Cloak & Dagger, Wolverine app.			4.00
27-Mutant massacre; Wolverine & Sabretooth app.	1.00	2.00	5.00
29-Spider-Man & Hobgoblin app.		.80	2.00
46-Punisher app.		1.20	3.00
...Holiday Special 1 (2/92, $2.25, 68 pgs.)		.90	2.25

NOTE: Austin scripts-53. Mignola c-20. Morrow a-51. Spiegle a-55i. Williamson a(i)-43, 50, 52.

POWER RANGERS ZEO (TV)(Saban's...)(Also see Saban's Mighty Morphin Power Rangers)
Aug, 1996 - Present ($2.50)
Image Comics (Extreme Studios)

1-Based on TV show			2.50

POWER RECORD COMICS
1974 - 1978 ($1.49, 7x10" comics, 20 pgs. with 45 R.P.M. record)
Marvel Comics/Power Records

PR10-Spider-Man-r/from #124,125; Man-Wolf app. PR11-Hulk-r. PR12-Captain America-r/#168. PR13-Fantastic Four-r/#126. PR14-Frankenstein-Ploog-r/#1. PR15-Tomb of Dracula-Colan-r/#2. PR16-Man-Thing-Ploog-r/#5. PR17-Werewolf By Night-Ploog-r/Marvel Spotlight #2. PR18-Planet of the Apes-r. PR19-Escape From the Planet of the Apes-r. PR20-Beneath the Planet of the Apes-r. PR21-Battle for the Planet of the Apes-r. PR24-Spider-Man II-New-a begins. PR25-Star Trek "Passage to Moauv". PR26-Star Trek "Crier in Emptiness." PR27-Batman "Stacked Cards"; N. Adams-a(p). PR28-Superman "Alien Creatures". PR29-Space: 1999 "Breakaway". PR30-Batman; N. Adams-r/Det.(7 pgs.). PR31-Conan-N. Adams-a; reprinted in Conan #116. PR32-Space: 1999 "Return to the Beginning". PR33-Superman-G.A. origin, Buckler-a(p). PR34-Superman. PR35-Wonder Woman-Buckler-a(p). PR36-Holo-Man. PR37-Robin Hood. PR39-Huckleberry Finn. PR40-Davy Crockett. PR41-Robinson Crusoe. PR42-20,000 Leagues Under the Sea. PR46-Star Trek "The Robot Masters". PR47-Little Women

With record; each....	2.15	6.50	15.00

POWERS THAT BE (Becomes Star Seed No.7 on)
Nov, 1995 - No. 6, June, 1996 ($2.50)
Broadway Comics

1-5: 1-Intro of Fatale & Star Seed.		1.00	2.50
6-Begin $2.95-c.			3.00
Preview Editions 1-3 (9/95 - 11/95, B&W)		1.00	2.50

POW MAGAZINE (Bob Sproul's) (Satire Magazine)
Aug, 1966 - No. 3, Feb, 1967 (30¢)
Humor-Vision

1-3: 2-Jones-a. 3-Wrightson-a	4.00	11.00	22.00

PREACHER
Apr, 1995 - Present ($2.50, mature)
DC Comics (Vertigo)

1 ($2.95)-Ennis scripts, Dillon-a & Fabry-c in all; 1st app. Jesse, Tulip, & Cassidy			25.00
2,3: 2-1st app. Saint of Killers			20.00
3,4			15.00
5-24-Polybagged w/videogame w/Ennis text. 13-Hunters storyline begins; ends #17		1.00	2.50
Gone To Texas ($14.95, 1996, TPB)-r/#1-7; Fabry-c			15.00

PREACHER SPECIAL: SAINT OF KILLERS
Aug, 1996 - No. 4, Nov, 1996 ($2.50, limited series, mature)

Predator: Dark River #3 © 20th Century Fox

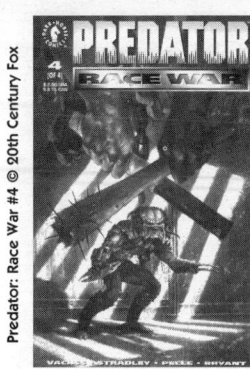

Predator: Race War #4 © 20th Century Fox

Predator Vs. Magnus #1 (Platinum) © 20th Century Fox/WEST

	GD25	FN65	NM94
DC Comics (Vertigo)			
1-4: Ennis-scripts & Fabry-c in all. 1,3,4-Pugh-a			2.50
PREDATOR (Also see Aliens Vs. …, Batman vs. …, Dark Horse Comics, & Dark Horse Presents)			
June, 1989 - No. 4, Mar, 1990 ($2.25, limited series)			
Dark Horse Comics			
1-Based on movie; 1st app. Predator	1.65	4.20	10.00
1-2nd printing	1.00	2.00	5.00
2	1.00	2.00	5.00
3,4		1.20	3.00
Trade paperback (1990, $12.95)-r/#1-4	1.85	5.50	13.00
PREDATOR: BAD BLOOD			
Dec, 1993 - No. 4, 1994 ($2.50, limited series)			
Dark Horse Comics			
1-4		1.00	2.50
PREDATOR: BIG GAME			
Mar, 1991 - No. 4, June, 1991 ($2.50, limited series)			
Dark Horse Comics			
1: 1-3-Contain 2 Dark Horse trading cards		1.20	3.00
2-4		1.10	2.75
PREDATOR BLOODY SANDS OF TIME			
Feb, 1992 - No. 2, Feb, 1992 ($2.50, limited series)			
Dark Horse Comics			
1,2-Dan Barry-c/a(p)/scripts		1.00	2.50
PREDATOR COLD WAR			
Sept, 1991 - No. 4, Dec, 1991 ($2.50, limited series)			
Dark Horse Comics			
1-4: All have painted-c		1.00	2.50
PREDATOR: DARK RIVER			
July, 1996 - No. Oct, 1996 ($2.95, limited series)			
Dark Horse Comics			
1-4: Miran Kim-c			3.00
PREDATOR: INVADERS FROM THE FOURTH DIMENSION			
July, 1994 ($3.95, one-shot, 52 pgs.)			
Dark Horse Comics			
1		1.60	4.00
PREDATOR: JUNGLE TALES			
Mar, 1995 ($2.95, one-shot)			
Dark Horse Comics			
1-r/Dark Horse Comics		1.20	3.00
PREDATOR: RACE WAR (See Dark Horse Presents #67)			
Feb, 1993 - No. 4, Oct, 1993 ($2.50, color, limited series)			
Dark Horse Comics			
1-4-Dorman painted-c #1-4		1.00	2.50
0-(4/93)		1.00	2.50
PREDATOR 2			
Feb, 1991 - No. 2, June, 1991 (2.50, limited series)			
Dark Horse Comics			
1-Adapts movie; 2 trading cards inside; photo-c		1.00	2.50
2-Photo-c; w/2 trading cards inside		1.00	2.50
PREDATOR VS. MAGNUS ROBOT FIGHTER			
Oct, 1992 - No. 2, 1993 ($2.95, mini-series)(1st Dark Horse/Valiant x-over)			
Dark Horse/Valiant			
1 (Regular)-Barry Smith-c; Lee Weeks-a in both	1.00	2.00	5.00
1 (Platinum edition, 11/92)-Barry Smith-c	1.65	4.20	10.00
2-Contains 2 bound-in trading cards; Barry Smith-c.		1.60	4.00

	GD25	FN65	NM94
PREHISTORIC WORLD (See Classics Illustrated Special Issue)			
PREMIERE (See Charlton Premiere)			
PRESTO KID, THE (See Red Mask)			
PRETTY BOY FLOYD (See On the Spot)			
PREZ (See Cancelled Comic Cavalcade & Supergirl #10)			
Aug-Sept, 1973 - No. 4, Feb-Mar, 1974			
National Periodical Publications			
1-Origin; Joe Simon scripts	1.00	2.00	5.00
2-4		1.00	2.50
PRICE, THE (See Eclipse Graphic Album Series)			
PRIDE AND THE PASSION, THE			
No. 824, Aug, 1957			
Dell Publishing Co.			
Four Color 824-Movie, Frank Sinatra & Cary Grant photo-c	9.00	27.00	90.00
PRIDE OF THE YANKEES, THE (See Real Heroes & Sport Comics)			
1949 (The Life of Lou Gehrig)			
Magazine Enterprises			
nn-Photo-c; Ogden Whitney-a	71.00	215.00	575.00
PRIEST (Also see Asylum)			
Aug, 1996 - Present ($2.99)			
Maximum Press			
1-3			3.00
PRIMAL FORCE			
No. 0, Oct, 1994 - No. 14, Dec, 1995 (1.95/2.25)			
DC Comics			
0-8: Red Tornado, Golem, Jack O'Lantern, Meridian & Silver Dragon		.80	2.00
9-14: 9-begin $2.25-c		.80	2.25
PRIMAL MAN (See The Crusaders)			
PRIME (See Break-Thru, Flood Relief & Ultraforce)			
June, 1993 - No. 26, Aug, 1995 ($1.95/$2.50)			
Malibu Comics (Ultraverse)			
1-1st app. Prime; has coupon for Ultraverse Premiere #0	1.00	2.60	6.00
1-With coupon missing			1.50
1-Full cover holographic edition; 1st of kind w/Hardcase #1 & Strangers #1	2.15	6.50	15.00
1-Ultra 5,000 edition w/silver ink-c	1.30	3.25	8.00
2-Polybagged w/card & coupon for U. Premiere #0	1.00	2.00	5.00
3,4-Prototype app. 4-Direct sale w/o card		1.10	2.75
4-($2.50)-Newsstand ed. polybagged w/card		1.20	3.00
5-($2.50, 48 pgs.)-Rune flip-c/story part B by Barry Smith; see Sludge #1 for 1st app. Rune; 3-pg. Night Man preview		1.20	3.00
6-11,14-19: 6-Bill & Chelsea Clinton app. 7-Break-Thru x-over. 8-Mantra app.; 2-pg. origin Freex by Simonson. 10-Firearm app.15-Intro Papa Verite; Perez-c/a. 16-Intro Turbo Charge		.80	2.00
12-($3.50, 68 pgs.)-Flip book w/Ultraverse Premiere #3; silver foil logo		1.40	3.50
13-($2.95, 52 pgs.)-Variant covers		1.20	3.00
20-26: 20-$2.50-c begins.		1.00	2.50
…: Gross and Disgusting 1 (10/94, $3.95)-Boris-c; "Annual" on cover, published monthly in indicia		1.80	4.50
…Month "Ashcan" (8/94, 75¢)-Boris-c			1.00
… Time: A Prime Collection (1994, $9.95)-r/1-4	1.65	4.20	10.00
…Vs. The Incredible Hulk (1995)-mail away limited edition	1.65	4.20	10.00
…Vs. The Incredible Hulk premium edition	2.15	6.50	15.00
NOTE: **Perez** a-15; c-15, 16.			

Prime V2#14 © Malibu

Primer #6 © Comico

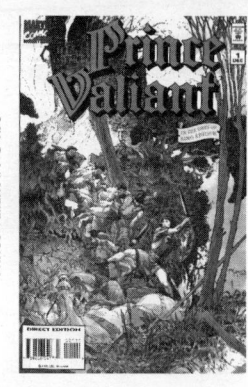

Prince Valiant #1 © KFS

	GD25	FN65	NM94

PRIME (Also see Black September)
Infinity, Sept, 1995 - V2#15, Dec, 1996 ($1.50)
Malibu Comics (Ultraverse)

Infinity, V2#1-8: Post Black September storyline. 6-8-Solitaire app.
9-Breyfogle-c/a. 10-12-Ramos-c. 15-Lord Pumpkin app. 1.50

PRIME/CAPTAIN AMERICA
Mar, 1996 ($3.95, one-shot)
Marvel Comics

1-Norm Breyfogle-a 4.00

PRIMER (Comico…)
Oct (no month), 1982 - No. 6, Feb, 1984 (B&W)
Comico

1 (52 pgs.)	1.00	2.00	5.00
2-1st app. Grendel & Argent by Wagner	11.00	34.00	90.00
3,4	1.00	2.00	5.00
5-1st Sam Kieth art in comics ('83) & 1st The Maxx	5.00	15.00	40.00
6-Intro & 1st app. Evangeline		1.60	4.00

PRIMORTALS (Leonard Nimoy's…)

PRIMUS (TV)
Feb, 1972 - No. 7, Oct, 1972
Charlton Comics

1-Staton-a in all	1.30	3.25	8.00
2-7: 6-Drug propaganda story	1.00	2.00	5.00

PRINCE NAMOR, THE SUB-MARINER (Also see Namor …)
Sept, 1984 - No. 4, Dec, 1984 (Limited-series)
Marvel Comics Group

1		.75	1.80
2-4			1.20

PRINCE NIGHTMARE
1987 ($2.95, 68pgs.)
Aaaargh! Associated Artists

Book 1		1.20	3.00

PRINCE VALIANT (See Ace Comics, Comics Reading Libraries, & King Comics #146, 147)
No. 26, 1941; No. 67, June, 1954 - No. 900, May, 1958
Feature Books 26 ('41)-Harold Foster-c/a; newspaper strips reprinted, pgs.

1-28,30-63; color & 68 pgs; Foster cover is only original comic book artwork by him	88.00	262.00	725.00
Four Color 567 ((6/54)(#1)-By Bob Fuje-Movie, photo-c	10.00	30.00	100.00
Four Color 650 (9/55), 699 (4/56), 719 (8/56),-Fuje-a	6.00	18.00	60.00
Four Color 788 (4/57), 849 (1/58), 900-Fuje-a	6.00	18.00	60.00

PRINCE VALIANT
Dec, 1994 - No. 4, Mar, 1995 ($3.95, limited series)
Marvel Comics

1-4		1.60	4.00

PRINCE VANDAL
Nov, 1993 - Apr?, 1994 ($2.50)
Triumphant Comics

1-6: 1,2-Triumphant Unleashed x-over	1.00		2.50

PRINCESS SALLY (Video game)
Apr, 1995 - No. 3, June, 1995 ($1.50, limited series)
Archie Publications

1-3: Spin-off from Sonic the Hedgehog			1.50

PRIORITY: WHITE HEAT
1986 - No. 2, 1986 ($1.75, mini-series)
AC Comics

1,2-Bill Black-a		.75	1.80

	GD25	FN65	NM94

PRISCILLA'S POP
No. 569, June, 1954 - No. 799, May, 1957
Dell Publishing Co.

Four Color 569 (#1)	4.00	12.00	40.00
Four Color 630 (5/55), 704 (5/56), 799	4.00	12.00	40.00

PRISON BARS (See Behind…)

PRISON BREAK!
Sept, 1951 - No. 5, Sept, 1952 (Painted c-3)
Avon Periodicals/Realistic No. 3 on

1-Wood-c & 1 pg.; has-r/Saint #7 retitled Michael Strong Private Eye	38.00	114.00	265.00
2-Wood-c; Kubert-a; Kinstler inside front-c	24.00	73.00	170.00
3-Orlando, Check-a; c-/Avon paperback 179	21.00	62.00	145.00
4,5: 4-Kinstler-c & inside f/c; Lawrence, Lazarus-a. 5-Kinstler-c; Infantino-a	18.00	54.00	125.00

PRISONER, THE (TV)
1988 - No. 4, 1989 ($3.50, squarebound, mini-series)
DC Comics

1-4 (Books a-d)		1.40	3.50

PRISON RIOT
1952
Avon Periodicals

1-Marijuana Murders-1 pg. text; Kinstler-c; 2 Kubert illos on text pages	24.00	71.00	165.00

PRISON TO PRAISE
1974 (35¢)
Logos International

nn-True Story of Merlin R. Carothers			1.00

PRIVATE BUCK
No. 21, 1941 - No. 12, 1942
Dell Publishing Co.

Large Feature Comic 21 (#1)(1941)(Series I)	9.50	28.50	95.00
Large Feature Comic 22 (1941)(Series I), 12 (1942)(Series II)	9.50	28.50	95.00

PRIVATEERS
Aug, 1987 - No. 2, 1987 ($1.50)
Vanguard Graphics

1,2			1.50

PRIVATE EYE (Cover title: Rocky Jorden…#6-8)
Jan, 1951 - No. 8, March, 1952
Atlas Comics (MCI)

1-Cover title: Crime Cases… #1-5	17.00	51.00	120.00
2,3-Tuska c/a(3)	10.00	30.00	65.00
4-8	9.15	27.00	55.00
NOTE: *Henkel a-6(3), 7; c-7. Sinnott a-6.*

PRIVATE EYE (See Mike Shayne…)

PRIVATE SECRETARY
Dec-Feb, 1962-63 - No. 2, Mar-May, 1963
Dell Publishing Co.

1,2	1.70	5.00	12.00

PRIVATE STRONG (See The Double Life of...)

PRIZE COMICS (…Western #69 on) (Also see Treasure Comics)
March, 1940 - No. 68, Feb-Mar, 1948
Prize Publications

1-Origin Power Nelson, The Futureman & Jupiter, Master Magician; Ted O'Neil, Secret Agent M-11, Jaxon of the Jungle, Bucky Brady & Storm Curtis begin (1st app. of each)	188.00	562.00	1500.00

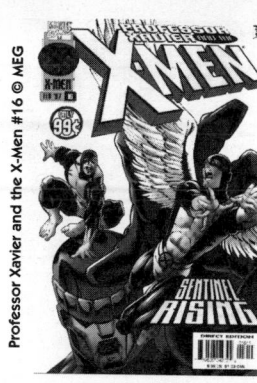
Professor Xavier and the X-Men #16 © MEG

Prophet Annual #1 © Rob Liefeld

Prophet/Chapel: Super Soldiers #1 © Rob Liefeld

	GD25	FN65	NM94
2-The Black Owl begins (1st app.)	87.00	262.00	700.00
3,4: 4-Robot-c	75.00	225.00	600.00
5,6: Dr. Dekkar, Master of Monsters app. in each	68.00	206.00	550.00
7-(Scarce)-Black Owl by S&K; origin/1st app. Dr. Frost & Frankenstein; The Green Lama, Capt. Gallant, The Great Voodini & Twist Turner begin; 1st app. The Green Lama (12/40)	156.00	468.00	1250.00
8,9-Black Owl & Ted O'Neil by S&K	83.00	249.00	665.00
10-12,14-20: 11-Origin Bulldog Denny. 16-Spike Mason begins	58.00	176.00	470.00
13-Yank & Doodle begin (8/41, origin/1st app.)	65.00	195.00	525.00
21-24	40.00	120.00	325.00
25-30	25.00	75.00	175.00
31-33	20.00	60.00	140.00
34-Origin Airmale, Yank & Doodle; The Black Owl joins army, Yank & Doodle's father assumes Black Owl's role	24.00	73.00	170.00
35-36,38-40: 35-Flying Fist & Bingo begin	17.00	49.00	115.00
37-Intro. Stampy, Airmale's sidekick; Hitler-c	24.00	73.00	170.00
41-50: 45-Yank & Doodle learn Black Owl's I.D. (their father). 48-Prince Ra begins	12.00	36.00	85.00
51-62,64,67,68: 53-Transvestism story. 55-No Frankenstein. 57-X-Mas-c.			
64-Black Owl retires	11.00	33.00	75.00
63-Simon & Kirby c/a	13.00	39.00	90.00
65,66-Frankenstein-c by Briefer	11.50	34.00	80.00

NOTE: *Briefer* a 7-on; c-65, 66. *J. Binder* a-16; c-21-29. *Guardineer* a-62. *Kiefer* c-62. *Palais* c-68. *Simon & Kirby* c-63, 75, 83.

PRIZE COMICS WESTERN (Formerly Prize Comics #1-68)
No. 69(V7#2), Apr-May, 1948 - No. 119, Nov-Dec, 1956
Prize Publications (Feature) (No. 69-84: 52 pgs.)

	GD25	FN65	NM94
69(V7#2)	13.00	39.00	90.00
70-75: 74-Kurtzman-a (8 pgs.)	11.00	33.00	75.00
76-Randolph Scott photo-c; "Canadian Pacific" movie adaptation	12.00	36.00	85.00
77-Photo-c; Severin/Elder, Mart Bailey-a; "Streets of Laredo" movie adaptation	11.00	33.00	75.00
78-Photo-c; S&K-a, 10 pgs.; Severin, Mart Bailey-a; "Bullet Code", & "Roughshod" movie adaptations	16.00	47.00	110.00
79-Photo-c; Kurtzman-a, 8 pgs.; Severin/Elder, Severin, Mart Bailey-a; "Stage To Chino" movie adaptation w/George O'Brien	16.00	47.00	110.00
80,81-Photo-c; Severin/Elder-a(2)	11.50	34.00	80.00
82-Photo-c; 1st app. The Preacher by Mart Bailey; Severin/Elder-a(3)	11.50	34.00	80.00
83,84	10.00	30.00	65.00
85-1st app. American Eagle by John Severin & Will (V9#6, 1-2/51)	23.00	69.00	160.00
86,101-105	11.00	33.00	75.00
87-99,110,111-Severin/Elder-a(2-3) each	11.50	34.00	80.00
100	13.00	39.00	90.00
106-108,112	9.15	27.00	55.00
109-Severin/Williamson-a	11.00	33.00	75.00
113-Williamson/Severin-a(2)/Frazetta?	11.50	34.00	80.00
114-119: Drifter begins in all; by Mort Meskin #114-118	6.70	20.00	40.00

NOTE: *Fass* a-81. *Severin & Elder* c-84-99. *Severin* a-72, 75, 77-79, 83-86, 96, 97, 100-105; c-92,100-109(most), 110-119. *Simon & Kirby* c-75, 83.

PRIZE MYSTERY
May, 1955 - No. 3, Sept, 1955
Key Publications

	GD25	FN65	NM94
1	7.50	22.50	45.00
2,3	5.85	17.50	35.00

PROFESSIONAL FOOTBALL (See Charlton Sport Library)

PROFESSOR COFFIN
No. 19, Oct, 1985 - No. 21, Feb, 1986
Charlton Comics

	GD25	FN65	NM94
19-21: Wayne Howard-a(r)			1.00

PROFESSOR OM
May, 1990 - No. 2, 1990 ($2.50, limited series)
Innovation Publishing

1,2-East Meets West spin-off		1.00	2.50

PROFESSOR XAVIER AND THE X-MEN (Also see X-Men, 1st series)
Nov, 1995 - Present (99¢)
Marvel Comics

1-25: Stories featuring the Original X-Men. 2-vs. the Blob. 5-Vs. the Original Brotherhood of Evil Mutants. 10-Vs The Avengers			1.00

PROJECT A-KO (Manga)
Mar, 1994 - No. 4, June, 1994 ($2.95)
Malibu Comics

1-4-Based on anime film		1.20	3.00

PROJECT A-KO 2 (Manga)
May, 1995 - No. 3, Aug, 1995 ($2.95, limited series)
CPM Comics

1-3		1.20	3.00

PROJECT A-KO VERSUS THE UNIVERSE (Manga)
Oct, 1995 - No. 5, June, 1996 ($2.95, limited series, bi-monthly)
CPM Comics

1-5			3.00

PROJECT: HERO
Aug, 1987 ($1.50)
Vanguard Graphics (Canadian)

1			1.50

PROPELLERMAN
Jan, 1993 - No. 8, Mar, 1994 ($2.95, limited series)
Dark Horse Comics

1-8: 2,4,8-Contain 2 trading cards		1.20	3.00

PROPHET (See Youngblood #2)
Oct, 1993 - No. 10, 1995 ($1.95)
Image Comics (Extreme Studios)

1-($2.50)-Liefeld/Panosian-c/a; 1st app. Mary McCormick; Liefeld scripts in 1-4; #1-3 contain coupons for Prophet #0		1.20	3.00
1-Gold foil embossed-c edition rationed to dealers	1.00	2.00	5.00
2-4: 2-Liefeld-c(p). 3-1st app. Judas. 4-1st app. Omen; Black and White Pt. 3 by Thibert		.80	2.00
4-Alternate-c by Stephen Platt		1.20	3.00
5,6-Platt-c/a		.80	2.00
0-(7/94, $2.50)-San Diego Comic Con ed. (2200 copies)	1.00	2.00	5.00
7-10: 7-(9/94, $2.50)-Platt-c/a. 8-Bloodstrike app. 10-Polybagged w/trading card; Platt-c.		1.00	2.50

PROPHET
V2#1, Aug, 1995 - Present ($3.50)
Image Comics (Extreme Studios)

V2#1-8: Dixon scripts in all. 1-4-Platt-a. 1-Boris-c; F. Miller variant-c. 4-Newmen app. 5,6-Wraparound-c		1.40	3.50
Annual 1 (9/95, $2.50)-Bagged w/Youngblood gaming card; Quesada-c		1.00	2.50
Babewatch Special 1 (12/95, $2.50)-Babewatch tie-in			2.50
1995 San Diego Edition-B&W preview of V2#1.	1.00	2.00	5.00

PROPHET/CHAPEL: SUPER SOLDIERS (Manga)
May, 1996 - No. 2, June, 1996 ($2.50, limited series)
Image Comics (Extreme Studios)

1,2: 1-Two covers exist			2.50
1-San Diego Edition; B&W-c			5.00

Prototype #2 © Malibu

Prowler #4 © ECL

Pryde And Wisdom #2 © MEG

	GD25	FN65	NM94

PROTECTORS (Also see The Ferret)
Sept, 1992 - No. 20, May, 1994 ($1.95-$2.50/$2.25/$2.50)
Malibu Comics

1-12 ($2.50, direct sale)-With poster & diff-c: 1-Origin; has 3/4 outer-c			
	1.00		2.50
1-12 ($1.95, newsstand)-Without poster	.80		2.00
13-16 ($2.25): 13-Polybagged w/Skycap	.90		2.25
17-20: 17-Begin $2.50-c	1.00		2.50

PROTOTYPE (Also see Flood Relief & Ultraforce)
Aug, 1993 - No. 18, Feb, 1995 ($1.95/$2.50)
Malibu Comics (Ultraverse)

1,2		.80	2.00
1-Holo-c	1.65	4.20	10.00
1-Ultra Limited silver foil-c	1.30	3.25	8.00
3-($2.50, 48 pgs.)-Rune flip-c/story by B. Smith (3 pgs.)	1.00		2.50
4-12: 4-Intro Wrath. 5-Break-Thru & Strangers x-over. 6-Arena cameo.			
7,8-Arena-c/story. 12-(7/94)		.80	2.00
0-(8/94,$ 2.50, 44 pgs.)	1.00		2.50
13 (8/94, $3.50)-Flip book(Ultraverse Premiere #6)	1.40		3.50
14-17: 14-(10/94)		.80	2.00
18 ($2.50)	1.00		2.50
Giant Size 1 (10/94, $2.50, 44 pgs.)	1.00		2.50

PROWLER (Also see Revenge of the…)
July, 1987 - No. 4, Oct, 1987 ($1.75)
Eclipse Comics

1-4: Snyder-c/a. 3,4-Origin		.75	1.80

PROWLER, THE
Nov, 1994 ($1.75)
Marvel Comics

1-4: 1-Spider-Man app.		.70	1.75

PROWLER IN "WHITE ZOMBIE", THE
Oct, 1988 ($2.00, B&W, Baxter paper)
Eclipse Comics

1-Adapts Bela Lugosi movie White Zombie	.80		2.00

PRUDENCE & CAUTION (Also see Dogs of War & Warriors of Plasm)
May, 1994 - No. 2, June, 1994 ($3.50/$2.50)(Spanish versions exist)
Defiant

1-($3.50, 52 pgs.)-Chris Claremont scripts in all	1.40		3.50
2-($2.50)	1.00		2.50

PRYDE AND WISDOM (Also see Excalibur)
Sept, 1996 - No. 3, Nov, 1996 ($1.95, limited series)
Marvel Comics

1-3: Warren Ellis scripts; Terry Dodson & Karl Story-c/a			2.00

PSI-FORCE
Nov, 1986 - No. 32, June, 1989 (75¢/$1.50)
Marvel Comics Group

1-32: 11-13-Williamson-i			1.25
Annual 1 (10/87)			1.25

PSI-JUDGE ANDERSON
1989 No. 10, 1990 ($1.95, B&W)
Fleetway Publications (Quality)

1-10		1.00	2.50

PSI-LORDS
Sept, 1994 - No. 10, June, 1995 ($2.25)
Valiant

1-($3.50)-Chromium wraparound-c		1.40	3.50
1-Gold	1.00	2.00	5.00
2-10: 3-Chaos Effect Epsilon Pt. 2		.90	2.25

PSYBA-RATS (Also see Showcase '94 #3,4)
Apr, 1995-No. 3, June, 1995 ($2.50, limited series)
DC Comics

1-3		1.00	2.50

PSYCHO (Magazine)
Jan, 1971 - No. 24, Mar, 1975 (68 pgs.; B&W) (No #22?)
Skywald Publishing Corp.

1-All reprints	2.15	6.50	15.00
2-Origin & 1st app. The Heap, & Frankenstein series by Adkins			
	1.70	5.00	12.00
3-24: 13-Cannabalism; 3 pgs of Christopher Lee as Dracula photos. 18-Injury			
to eye-c. 20-Severed Head-c. 24-1975 Winter Special			
	1.20	3.00	7.00
Annual 1(1972)	1.30	3.25	8.00
Fall Special (1974)-Reese, Wildey-a(r)	1.00	2.00	5.00
Winter Special 1 (1975)-Dave Sim scripts	1.00	2.00	5.00
Yearbook(1974-nn)	1.00	2.00	5.00

NOTE: **Boris** c-3, 5. **Buckler** a-4, 5. **Everett** a-3-6. **Jeff Jones** a-7, 9; c-12. **Kaluta** a-13. **Katz/Buckler** a-3. **Morrow** a-1. **Reese** a-5. **Sutton** a-3. **Wildey** a-5.

PSYCHOANALYSIS
Mar-Apr, 1955 - No. 4, Sept-Oct, 1955
E. C. Comics

1-All Kamen-c/a; not approved by code	17.00	49.00	115.00
2-4-Kamen-c/a in all	13.00	39.00	90.00

PSYCHOBLAST
Nov, 1987 - No. 9, July, 19898 ($1.75)
First Comics

1-9		.75	1.80

PSYCHONAUTS
Oct, 1993 - No. 4, Jan, 1994 ($4.95, limited series)
Marvel Comics (Epic Comics)

1-4: American/Japanese co-produced comic	1.00	2.00	5.00

P.T. 109 (See Movie Comics)

PUBLIC DEFENDER IN ACTION (Formerly Police Trap)
No. 7, Mar, 1956 - No. 12, Oct, 1957
Charlton Comics

7	8.35	25.00	50.00
8-12	5.35	16.00	32.00

PUBLIC ENEMIES
1948 - No. 9, June-July, 1949
D. S. Publishing Co.

1-True Crime Stories	17.00	51.00	125.00
2-Used in **SOTI**, pg. 95	19.00	56.00	130.00
3-5: 5-Arrival date of 10/1/48	10.00	30.00	70.00
6,8,9	10.00	30.00	60.00
7-McWilliams-a; injury to eye panel	10.00	30.00	70.00

PUDGY PIG
Sept, 1958 - No. 2, Nov, 1958
Charlton Comics

1,2	4.00	10.00	20.00

PUMA BLUES
1986 - No. 26, 1990 ($1.70-$1.75, B&W)
Aardvark One International/Mirage Studios #21 on

1-19, 21-26: 1-1st & 2nd printings. 25,26-$1.75-c		.80	2.00
20 ($2.25)-By Alan Moore, Miller, Grell, others		1.00	2.50
Trade Paperback (12/88, $14.95)			14.95

PUMPKINHEAD: THE RITES OF EXORCISM (Movie)
1993 - No. 2, 1993 ($2.50, limited series)

Punisher #5 © MEG

Punisher #30 © MEG

Punisher #71 © MEG

	GD25	FN65	NM94
k Horse Comics			
2: Based on movie; painted-c by McManus		1.00	2.50
NCH & JUDY COMICS			
-4; No. 2, Fall, 1944 - V3#2, 12/47; V3#3, 6/51 - V3#9, 12/51			
man Periodicals			
#1-(60 pgs.)	18.00	54.00	125.00
2	10.00	30.00	65.00
3-12(7/46)	7.50	22.50	45.00
#1(8/49),3-9	4.35	13.00	26.00
#2,10-12, V3#1-Kirby-a(2) each	18.00	54.00	125.00
#2-Kirby-a	17.00	49.00	115.00
3-9	4.25	13.00	26.00
NCH COMICS			
41; #2, 2/42; #9, 7/44 - #19, 10/46; #20, 7/47 - #23, 1/48			
ry 'A' Chesler			
Mr. E, The Sky Chief, Hale the Magician, Kitty Kelly begin			
	103.00	309.00	825.00
-Captain Glory app.	68.00	206.00	550.00
-Rocketman & Rocket Girl & The Master Key begin			
	56.00	168.00	450.00
-Sky Chief app.; J. Cole-a; Master Key-r/Scoop #3			
	44.00	132.00	350.00
-Origin Master Key-r/Scoop #1; Sky Chief, Little Nemo app.; Jack Cole-a;			
Fineish art by Sultan	44.00	132.00	350.00
-Rocket Boy & Capt. Glory app; classic Skull-c	81.00	243.00	650.00
-Cover has list of 4 Chesler artists' names on tombstone			
	50.00	150.00	400.00
-17,19	44.00	132.00	350.00
-Bondage-c; hypodermic panels	53.00	159.00	425.00
-Unique cover with bare-breasted women	65.00	195.00	525.00
-Hypo needle story	44.00	132.00	350.00
,23-Little Nemo-not by McCay. 22-Intro Baxter (teenage)			
	24.00	73.00	170.00
NCHY AND THE BLACK CROW			
. 10, Oct, 1985 - No. 12, Feb, 1986			
arlton Comics			
-12: Al Fago funny animal-r			1.00
NISHER (See Amazing Spider-Man #129, Blood and Glory, Captain America #241,			
ssic Punisher, Daredevil #182-184, 257, Daredevil and the..., Ghost Rider V2#5, 6, Marc			
ctor #8 & 9, Marvel Preview #2, Marvel Super Action, Marvel Tales, Power Pack #46,			
ectacular Spider-Man #81-83, 140, 141, 143 & new Strange Tales #13 & 14)			
NISHER (The...)			
n, 1986 - No. 5, May, 1986 (Limited series)			
rvel Comics Group			
Double size	3.60	11.00	25.00
	2.15	6.50	15.00
5: 3-Has 2 diff. cover prices, 75¢ & 95¢(w/UPC)	1.00	2.60	6.00
de Paperback (1988)-r/#1-5	1.65	4.70	11.00
TE: Zeck a-1-4; c-1-5.			
NISHER (The...)			
y, 1987 - No. 104, July, 1995			
rvel Comics			
#1	2.15	6.50	15.00
2-9: 7-Last 75¢ issue. 8-Portacio/Williams-c/a begins, ends #18. 9-Scarcer,			
low distribution	1.00	2.00	5.00
10-Daredevil app.; ties in w/Daredevil #257	1.30	3.25	8.00
11-15: 13-18-Kingpin app.	1.00	2.00	5.00
16-20: 19-Stroman-c/a. 20-Portacio-c(p)		1.20	3.00
21-24,26-30: 24-1st app. Shadowmasters		.70	1.75
25-($1.50, 52 pgs.)-Shadowmasters app.		.80	2.00
31-40			1.50

	GD25	FN65	NM94
41-49 ($1.25)			1.25
50-($1.50, 52 pgs.)			1.50
51-59: 57-Photo-c; came w/outer-c (newsstand ed. w/o outer-c). 59-			
Punisher is severely cut & has skin grafts (has black skin); last $1.00-c			1.00
60-74,76-85,87-89: 60-Begin $1.25-c. 60-62-Luke Cage app. 62-Punisher			
back to white skin. 68-Tarantula-c/story. 85-Prequel to Suicide Run Pt. 0.			
87,88-Suicide Run Pt. 6 & 9			1.00
75-($2.75, 52 pgs.)-Embossed silver foil-c		1.10	2.75
86-($2.95, 52 pgs.)-Embossed & foil stamped-c; Suicide Run part 3			
		1.20	3.00
90-99, 101-104: 90-Begin $1.50-c; bound-in card sheet. 99-Cringe app.			
102-Bullseye.			1.50
100-($2.95, 68 pgs.)		1.20	3.00
100-($3.95, 68 pgs.)-Foil cover		1.60	4.00
"Ashcan" edition (75¢)-Joe Kubert-c			0.75
Annual 1 (1988)-Evolutionary War x-over	1.00	2.00	5.00
Annual 2 (1989, $2.00, 68 pgs.)-Atlantis Attacks x-over; Jim Lee-a(p)			
(back-up story, 6 pgs.); Moon Knight app.		1.20	3.00
Annual 3,4 ('90, '91, $2.00, 68 pgs.): 4-Golden-c(p)		.80	2.00
Annual 5 (1992, $2.25, 68 pgs.)		.90	2.25
Annual 6 (1993, $2.95, 68 pgs.)-Bagged w/card		1.20	3.00
Annual 7 (1994, $2.95)-Rapido app.		1.20	3.00
...: A Man Named Frank (1994, $6.95, TPB)	1.20	2.90	7.00
...and Wolverine in African Saga nn (1989, $5.95, 52 pgs.)-Reprints Punisher			
War Journal #6 & 7; Jim Lee-c/a(r)		2.60	6.00
Back to School Special 1 (11/92, $2.95, 68 pgs.)		1.20	3.00
Back to School Special 2 (10/93, $2.95, 68 pgs.)		1.20	3.00
Back to School Special 3 (10/94, $2.95)		1.20	3.00
.../Batman: Deadly Knights (10/94, $4.95)	1.00	2.00	5.00
...Bloodlines nn (1991, $5.95, 68 pgs.)	1.00	2.50	6.00
...: Die Hard in the Big Easy nn ('92, $4.95, 52 pgs.)			
	1.00	2.00	5.00
...G-Force nn (1992, $4.95, 52 pgs.)-Painted-c	1.00	2.00	5.00
...Holiday Special 1 (1/93, $2.95, 52 pgs.)-Foil-c		1.20	3.00
...Holiday Special 2 (1/94, $2.95, 68 pgs.)		1.20	3.00
...Holiday Special 3 (1/95, $2.95, 68 pgs.)		1.20	3.00
...Invades the 'Nam: Final Invasion nn (2/94, $6.95)-J. Kubert-c & chapter break			
art; reprints The 'Nam #52,53,67-69	1.20	2.90	7.00
...Meets Archie (8/94, $3.95, 52 pgs.)-Die cut-c; no ads; same contents as			
Archie Meets The Punisher		1.60	4.00
...Movie Special 1 (6/90, $5.95, 68 pgs.)	1.00	2.50	6.00
...: No Escape nn (1990, $4.95, 52 pgs.)-New-a	1.00	2.00	5.00
...The Prize nn (1990, $4.95, 68 pgs.)-New-a	1.00	2.00	5.00
Summer Special 1 (8/91, $2.95, 52 pgs.)-No ads		1.20	3.00
Summer Special 2 (8/92, $2.50, 52 pgs.)-Bisley painted-c; Austin-a(i)			
	1.00		2.50
Summer Special 3 (8/93, $2.50, 52 pgs.)-No ads	1.00		2.50
Summer Special 4 (7/94, $2.95, 52 pgs.)	1.00	1.20	3.00
NOTE: Austin c(i)-47, 48. Cowan c-39. Golden c-50, 85, 86, 100. Heath a-26, 27, 89, 90; c-26,			
27. Quesada c-56p, 62p. Sienkiewicz c-Back to School 1.Stroman a-76p(9 pgs.). Williamson			
a(i)-25, 60-62p, 64-70, 74, Annual 5; c(i)-62, 65-68.			
PUNISHER (Also see Double Edge)			
Nov, 1995 - Present ($2.95/$1.95)			
Marvel Comics			
1 ($2.95)-Ostrander scripts begin; foil-c.		1.20	3.00
2-20: 7-Vs. S.H.I.E.L.D. 12,13-X-Cutioner-c/app.		.80	2.00
PUNISHER AND WOLVERINE: DAMAGING EVIDENCE (See Wolverine and...)			
PUNISHER ARMORY, THE			
7/90 ($1.50); No. 2, 6/91; No. 3, 4/92 - 10/94($1.75/$2.00)			
Marvel Comics			
1($1.50)-r/weapons pgs. from War Journal; Jim Lee-c			1.50
2 ($1.75)-Jim Lee-c		.80	2.00
3-10 ($2.00): All new material. 3-Jusko painted-c		.80	2.00

Punisher 2099 #31 © MEG

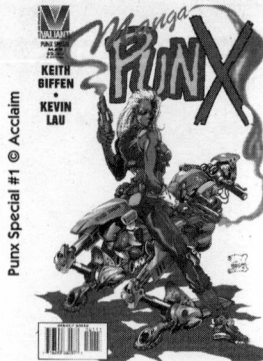

Punx Special #1 © Acclaim

Purgatori Prelude © Chaos! Comics

	GD25	FN65	NM94

PUNISHER KILLS THE MARVEL UNIVERSE
Nov, 1995 ($5.95, one-shot)
Marvel Comics

1-Garth Ennis script 6.00

PUNISHER MAGAZINE, THE
Oct, 1989 - No. 16, Nov, 1990 ($2.25, B&W, Magazine, 52 pgs.)
Marvel Comics

1-3: 1-r/Punisher #1('86). 2,3-r/Punisher 2-5 .... .90 .... 2.25
4-16: 4-7-r/Punisher V2#1-8. 4-Chiodo-c. 8-r/Punisher #10 & Daredevil
#257; Portacio & Lee-r. 14-r/Punisher War Journal #1,2 w/new Lee-c.
16-r/Punisher W. J. #3,8 .... .90 .... 2.25
NOTE: *Chiodo* painted c-4, 7, 16. *Jusko* painted c-6, 8. *Jim Lee* r-8, 14-16; c-14. *Portacio/
Williams* r-7-12.

PUNISHER MOVIE COMIC
Nov, 1989 - No. 3, Dec, 1989 ($1.00, limited series)
Marvel Comics

1-3: Movie adaptation 1.25
1 (1989, $4.95, squarebound)-contains #1-3 ... 1.00 ... 2.00 ... 5.00

PUNISHER: ORIGIN OF MICRO CHIP, THE
July, 1993 - No. 2, Aug, 1993 ($1.75, limited series)
Marvel Comics

1,2 .... .70 .... 1.75

PUNISHER: P.O.V.
1991 - No. 4, 1991 ($4.95, painted, limited series, 52 pgs.)
Marvel Comics

1-4: Starlin scripts & Wrightson painted-c/a in all. 2-Nick Fury app.
.... 1.00 ... 2.00 ... 5.00

PUNISHER: THE GHOSTS OF INNOCENTS
Jan, 1993 - No. 2, Jan, 1993 ($5.95, 52 pgs.)
Marvel Comics

1,2-Starlin scripts .... 1.00 ... 2.50 ... 6.00

PUNISHER 2099 (See Punisher War Journal #50)
Feb, 1993 - No. 34, Nov, 1995 ($1.25/$1.50/$1.95)
Marvel Comics

1-($1.75)-Foil stamped-c .... .80 .... 2.00
1-($1.75)-Second printing .... .70 .... 1.75
2-15: 13-Spider-Man 2099 x-over; Ron Lim-c(p) 1.25
16-24, 26,27: 16-Begin $1.50-c; bound-in card sheet 1.50
25 ($2.95, 52 pgs.)-Deluxe edition; embossed foil-cover
.... 1.20 ... 3.00
25 ($2.25, 52 pgs.) .... .90 .... 2.25
28-34: 28-Begin $1.95-c .... .80 .... 2.00

PUNISHER WAR JOURNAL, THE
Nov, 1988 - No. 80, July, 1995 ($1.50/$1.75/$1.95)
Marvel Comics

1-Origin The Punisher; Matt Murdock cameo; Jim Lee inks begin.
.... 1.65 ... 4.20 ... 10.00
2-5: 2,3-Daredevil x-over; Jim Lee-c(i). 4-Jim Lee c/a begins.
.... 1.20 ... 3.00 ... 7.00
6-Two part Wolverine story begins .... 1.50 ... 3.75 ... 9.00
7-Wolverine-c; story ends .... 1.00 ... 2.00 ... 5.00
8-12,17-19: 19-Last Jim Lee-c/a .... 1.20 .... 3.00
13-16,20-22: No Jim Lee-a. 13-Lee-c only. 13-15-Heath-i. 14,15-Spider-Man
x-over .... .70 .... 1.75
23-28,31-49,51-60,62,63,65: 23-Begin $1.75-c. 31-Andy & Joe Kubert art. 36-
Photo-c. 47,48-Nomad/Daredevil-c/stories; see Nomad. 57,58-Daredevil &
Ghost Rider-c/stories. 62,63-Suicide Run Pt. 4 & 7 .... 1.50
29,30-Ghost Rider app. .... .70 .... 1.75
50-($2.95, 52 pgs.)-Preview of Punisher 2099 (1st app.); embossed-c.
.... 1.20 ... 3.00

61-($2.95, 52 pgs.)-Embossed foil cover; Suicide Run Pt. 1
.... 1.20 ... 3
64-($2.95, 52 pgs.)-Die-cut-c; Suicide Run Pt. 10 ...... 1.20 ... 3
64-($2.25, 52 pgs.)-Regular cover edition .... .90 ... 2
66-74. 76-80: 66-Begin $1.95-c; bound-in card sheet ... .80 ... 2
75 ($2.50, 52 pgs.) .... 1.00 ... 2
NOTE: *Golden* c-25-30, 40, 61, 62. *Jusko* painted c-31, 32. *Jim Lee* a-1i-3i, 4p-13p, 17p-19
c-2i, 3i, 4p-15p, 17p, 18p, 19p. Painted c-40.

PUNISHER: WAR ZONE, THE
Mar, 1992 - No. 40, July, 1995 ($1.75/$1.95)
Marvel Comics

1-($2.25, 40 pgs.)-Die cut-c; Romita, Jr.-c/a begins ... 1.20 ... 3
2 .... .80 ... 2
3-22,24,26: 8-Last Romita, Jr.-c/a. 19-Wolverine app. 24-Suicide Run Pt. 5
.... .70 ... 1
23-($2.95, 52 pgs.)-Embossed foil-c; Suicide Run part 2; Buscema-a(part)
.... 1.20 ... 3
25-($2.25, 52 pgs.)-Suicide Run part 8; painted-c ...... .90 ... 3
27-40: 27-Begin 1.95-c; bound-in card sheet .... .80 ... 2
Annual 1 (1993, $2.95, 68 pgs.)-Bagged w/card; John Buscema-a
.... 1.20 ... 3
Annual 2 (1994, $2.95, 68 pgs.) .... 1.20 ... 3
NOTE: *Golden* c-23. *Romita, Jr.* c/a-1-8.

PUNISHER: YEAR ONE
Dec, 1994 - No. 4, Apr, 1995 ($2.50, limited series)
Marvel Comics

1-4 .... 1.00 ... 2

PUNX
Nov, 1995 - No. 3, Jan, 1996 ($2.50, unfinished limited series)
Acclaim (Valiant)

1-3: Giffen story & art in all. 2-Satirizes Scott McCloud's Understanding
Comics .... 1.00 ... 2
(Manga) Special 1 (3/96, $2.50)-Giffen scripts .... 1.00 ... 2

PUPPET COMICS
Spring, 1946 - No. 2, Summer, 1946
George W. Dougherty Co.

1,2-Funny animal .... 9.15 ... 27.00 ... 55

PUPPETOONS (See George Pal's...)

PURE OIL COMICS (Also see Salerno Carnival of Comics, 24 Pages of
Comics, & Vicks Comics)
Late 1930's (24 pgs., regular size, paper-c)
Pure Oil Giveaway

nn-Contains 1-2 pg. strips; i.e., Hairbreadth Harry, Skyroads, Buck Rogers by
Calkins & Yager, Olly of the Movies, Napoleon, S'Matter Pop, etc.
.... 39.00 ... 118.00 ... 275
Also a 16 pg. 1938 giveaway w/Buck Rogers ... 37.00 ... 111.00 ... 260

PURGATORI
Prelude #-1, 5/96 ($1.50, 16 pgs.); 1996 - Present ($3.50/$2.95, limited series
Chaos! Comics

Prelude #-1-Brian Pulido story; Jim Balent-c/a; contains sketches & interviews
.... 1
1-($3.50)-Wraparound cover; red foil embossed-c; Jim Balent-a
.... 1.40 ... 3
1-($19.95)-Premium Edition (1000 print run) 20
2-($3.00)-Wraparound-c 3
2-Variant-c 5

PURGE
Aug, 1993 ($1.95, unfinished limited series)
ANIA/U.P. Comics

1 .... .80 ... 2

Quasar #18 © MEG

The Question #29 © DC

The Question Quarterly #3 © DC

	GD25	FN65	NM94

PURPLE CLAW, THE (Also see Tales of Horror)
Jan, 1953 - No. 3, May, 1953
Minoan Publishing Co./Toby Press

1-Origin; horror/weird stories in all	24.00	73.00	170.00
2,3: 1-3 r-in Tales of Horror #9-11	18.00	54.00	125.00
I.W. Reprint #8-Reprints #1	3.60	9.000	18.00

PUSSYCAT (Magazine)
Oct, 1968 (B&W reprints from Men's magazines)
Marvel Comics Group

1-(Scarce)-Ward, Everett, Wood-a; Everett-c	19.00	56.00	130.00

PUZZLE FUN COMICS (Also see Jingle Jangle)
Spring, 1946 - No. 2, Summer, 1946 (52 pgs.)
George W. Dougherty Co.

1-Gustavson-a	19.00	58.00	135.00
2	14.00	43.00	100.00

NOTE: #1 & 2('46) each contain a **George Carlson** cover plus a 6 pg. story "Alec in Fumbleland"; also many puzzles in each.

QUACK!
July, 1976 - No. 6, 1977? ($1.25, B&W)
Star Reach Productions

1-Brunner-c/a on Duckaneer (Howard the Duck clone); Dave Stevens, Gilbert, Shaw-a		1.60	4.00
1-2nd printing (10/76)			1.50
2,4,6: 2-Newton the Rabbit Wonder by Aragones/Leialoha; Gilbert, Shaw-a; Leialoha-c. 6-Brunner-a (Duckeneer); Gilbert-a		.80	2.00
3-The Beavers by Dave Sim begin, end #5; Gilbert, Shaw-a; Sim/Leialoha-c		1.60	4.00

QUADRANT
1983 - No. 8, 1986 (B&W, nudity, adults)
Quadrant Publications

1-Peter Hsu-c/a in all	1.00	2.60	6.00
2		1.20	3.00
3-8		.80	1.90

QUAKER OATS (Also see Cap'n Crunch)
1965 (Giveaway) (2-1/2x5-1/2") (16 pgs.)
Quaker Oats Co.

"Plenty of Glutton", starring Quake & Quisp; "Lava Come-Back", "Kite Tale", "A Witch in Time"	2.85	8.50	20.00
		1.60	4.00

QUANTUM LEAP (TV) (See A Nightmare on Elm Street)
Sept, 1991 - No. 12, June?, 1993 ($2.50, color, painted-c)
Innovation Publishing

1-12: Based on TV show; all have painted-c. 8-Has photo gallery		1.00	2.50
Special Edition 1 (10/92)-r/#1 w/8 extra pgs. of photos & articles		1.00	2.50
Time and Space Special 1 (#13) ($2.95)-Foil logo		1.20	3.00

QUASAR (See Avengers #302, Captain America #217, Incredible Hulk #234, Marvel Team-Up #113 & Marvel Two-in-One #53)
Oct, 1989 - July, 1994 ($1.00/$1.25) (Direct sales #17 on)
Marvel Comics

1-Origin; formerly Marvel Boy/Marvel Man		.80	2.00
2-5: 3-Human Torch app.			1.50
6-Venom cameo (2 pgs.)		.80	2.00
7-Cosmic Spidey app.		1.00	2.50
8-15,18-24: 11-Excalibur x-over. 14-McFarlane-c. 20-Fantastic Four app. 23-Ghost Rider x-over			1.20
16-($1.50, 52 pgs.)			1.50
17-Flash parody (Buried Alien)		.80	2.00
25-($1.50, 52 pgs.)-New costume Quasar			1.50
26-Infinity Gauntlet x-over; Thanos-c/story		.80	2.00

	GD25	FN65	NM94

27-Infinity Gauntlet x-over			1.50
28-30: 30-Thanos cameo in flashback; last $1.00-c			1.00
31-49,51-60: 31-Begin $1.25-c; D.P. 7 guest stars. 38-40-Infinity War x-overs. 38-Battles Warlock. 39-Thanos-c & cameo. 40-Thanos app. 42-Punisher-c/story. 53-Warlock & Moondragon app. 58-w/bound-in card sheet		.60	1.25
50-($2.95, 52 pgs.)-Holo-grafx foil-c; Silver Surfer, Man-Thing, Ren & Stimpy app.		1.20	3.00
Special #1-3 ($1.25, newsstand)-Same as #32-34			1.25

QUEEN OF THE WEST, DALE EVANS (TV)(See Dale Evans Comics & Western Roundup under Dell Giants)
No. 479, 7/53 - No. 22, 1-3/59 (All photo-c; photo back c-4-8, 15)
Dell Publishing Co.

Four Color 479(#1, '53)	20.00	60.00	200.00
Four Color 528(#2, '54)	9.00	27.00	90.00
3,4: 3(4-6/54)-Toth-a. 4-Toth, Manning-a	8.00	24.00	80.00
5-10-Manning-a. 5-Marsh-a	6.30	18.90	63.00
11,19,21-No Manning 21-Tufts-a	4.50	13.50	45.00
12-18,20,22-Manning-a	5.40	16.20	54.00

QUENTIN DURWARD
No. 672, Jan, 1956
Dell Publishing Co.

Four Color 672-Movie, photo-c	7.00	21.00	70.00

QUESTAR ILLUSTRATED SCIENCE FICTION CLASSICS
1977 (224 pgs.) ($1.95)
Golden Press

11197-Stories by Asimov, Sturgeon, Silverberg & Niven; Starstream-r		1.20	3.00

QUEST FOR DREAMS LOST (Also see Word Warriors)
July 4, 1987 ($2.00, B&W, 52 pgs.)(Proceeds donated to help illiteracy)
Literacy Volunteers of Chicago

1-Teenage Mutant Ninja Turtles by Eastman/Laird, Trollords, Silent Invasion, The Realm, Wordsmith, Reacto Man, Eb'nn, Aniverse	1.00	2.50	

QUESTION, THE (See Americomics, Blue Beetle (1967), Charlton Bullseye & Mysterious Suspense)

QUESTION, THE (Also see Showcase '95 #3)
Feb, 1987 - No. 36, Mar, 1990 ($1.50)
DC Comics

1-36: Denny O'Neil scripts in all			1.50
Annual 1 (1988, $2.50)		1.00	2.50
Annual 2 (1989, $3.50)		1.40	3.50

QUESTION QUARTERLY, THE
Summer, 1990 - No. 5, Spring, 1992 ($2.50, 52pgs.)
DC Comics

1-5		1.00	2.50

NOTE: **Cowan** a-1, 2, 4, 5; c-1-3, 5. **Mignola** a-5i. **Quesada** a-3-5.

QUESTPROBE
8/84; No. 2, 1/85; No. 3, 11/85 - No. 4, 12/85 (limited series)
Marvel Comics Group

1-4: 1-The Hulk app. by Romita. 2-Spider-Man; Mooney-a(i). 3-Human Torch & Thing			1.00

QUICK-DRAW McGRAW (TV) (Hanna-Barbera)(See Whitman Comic Books)
No. 1040, 12-2/59-60 - No. 11, 7-9/62; No. 12, 11/62; No. 13, 2/63; No. 14, 4/63; No. 15, 6/69 (1st show aired 9/29/59)
Dell Publishing Co./Gold Key No. 12 on

Four Color 1040(#1)	11.00	33.00	110.00
2(4-6/60)-6: 2-Augie Doggie & Snooper & Blabber stories (8 pgs. each); pre-dates both of their #1 issues. 4-Augie Doggie & Snooper & Blabber stories. 5-Early Snagglepuss app.; last 10¢ issue	7.00	21.00	70.00

Rack & Pain #3 © Brian Pulido

Rack & Pain: Killers #1 g Chaos! Comics

Radical Dreamer #4 © Mark Wheatley

	GD25	FN65	NM94
7-11	5.00	15.00	50.00
12,13-Title change to …Fun-Type Roundup (84pgs.)	8.00	24.00	80.00
14,15	4.00	12.00	40.00

QUICK-DRAW McGRAW (TV)(See Spotlight #2)
Nov, 1970 - No. 8, Jan, 1972 (Hanna-Barbera)
Charlton Comics

1	4.50	14.00	32.00
2-8	2.40	7.20	17.00

QUICK-TRIGGER WESTERN (…Action #12; Cowboy Action #5-11)
No. 12, May, 1956 - No. 19, Sept, 1957
Atlas Comics (ACI No. 12/WPI No. 13-19)

12-Baker-a	11.00	33.00	75.00
13-Williamson-a, 5 pgs.	11.50	34.00	80.00
14-Everett, Crandall, Torres-a; Heath-c	10.00	30.00	70.00
15-Torres, Crandall-a	9.15	27.00	55.00
16-Orlando, Kirby-a	8.35	25.00	50.00
17,18: 18-Baker-a	8.35	25.00	50.00
19	5.85	17.50	35.00

NOTE: **Ayers** a-17. **Colan** a-16. **Maneely** a-15, 17; c-15, 18. **Morrow** a-18. **Powell** a-14.
Severin a-19; c-12, 13, 16, 17, 19. **Shores** a-16. **Tuska** a-17.

QUINCY (See Comics Reading Libraries)

Q-UNIT
Dec, 1993 ($2.95)
Harris Comics

1-($2.95)-Polybagged w/trading card version 1.2	1.20		3.00

RABID
1994 ($5.95, B&W)
FantaCo Enterprises

1	1.00	2.50	6.00

RACCOON KIDS, THE (Formerly Movietown Animal Antics)
No. 52, Sept-Oct, 1954 - No. 64, Nov, 1957
National Periodical Publications (Arleigh No. 63,64)

52-Doodles Duck by Mayer	14.00	43.00	100.00
53-64: 53-62-Doodles Duck by Mayer	10.00	30.00	70.00

RACE FOR THE MOON
Mar, 1958 - No. 3, Nov, 1958
Harvey Publications

1-Powell-a(5); 1/2-pg. S&K-a; cover redrawn from Galaxy Science Fiction			
pulp (5/53)	11.50	34.00	80.00
2-Kirby/Williamson-c(r)/a(3); Kirby-p 7 more stys	24.00	71.00	165.00
3-Kirby/Williamson-c/a(4); Kirby-p 6 more stys	25.00	75.00	175.00

RACE OF SCORPIONS
1990 - No. 2, 1990 ($4.50/$4.95, 52pgs.)
Dark Horse Comics

1-r/stories from Dark Horse Presents 23-27		1.80	4.50
2-($4.95-c); r/Dark Horse Presents	1.00	2.00	5.00

RACER-X
8/88 - No. 11, 8/89; V2#1, 9/89 - V2#10, 1990 ($1.75)
Now Comics

0-Deluxe ($3.50)		1.40	3.50
1 (9/88) - 11, V2#1-10		.75	1.80

RACK & PAIN
Mar, 1994 - No. 4, June, 1994 ($2.50, limited series)
Dark Horse Comics

1-4: Brian Pulido scripts in all. 1-Greg Capullo-c	1.20		3.00

RACK & PAIN: KILLERS
Sept, 1996 - No. 4, Jan, 1997 ($2.95, limited series)
Chaos! Comics

	GD25	FN65	NM94
1-4: Brian Pulido scripts; Jae Lee-c			3.00

RACKET SQUAD IN ACTION
May-June, 1952 - No. 29, Mar, 1958
Capitol Stories/Charlton Comics

1	23.00	69.00	160.00
2-4,6: 3,4,6-Dr. Neff, Ghost Breaker app.	11.00	33.00	75.00
5-Dr. Neff, Ghost Breaker app; headlights-c	19.00	47.00	115.00
7-10: 10-Explosion-c	10.00	30.00	65.00
11-Ditko-c/a	22.00	66.00	155.00
12-Ditko explosion-c (classic); Shuster-a(2)	40.00	120.00	280.00
13-Shuster-c(p)/a.	9.15	27.00	55.00
14-Marijuana story "Shakedown"	10.00	30.00	70.00
15-28	8.35	25.00	50.00
29-(15¢, 68 pgs.)	9.15	27.00	55.00

RADIANT LOVE (Formerly Daring Love #1)
No. 2, Dec, 1953 - No. 6, Aug, 1954
Gilmor Magazines

2	5.85	17.50	35.00
3-6	4.00	11.00	22.00

RADICAL DREAMER
No. 0, May, 1994 - No. 1, July, 1994 ($1.99)
Blackball Comics

0,1-($1.99)-Poster format		.80	2.00

RADICAL DREAMER
V2#1, June, 1995 - V2#6, Feb, 1996 ($2.95, B&W, limited series)
Mark's Giant Economy Size Comics

V2#1-6		1.20	3.00
Prime (5/96, $2.95)			3.00

RADIOACTIVE MAN (Simpson's TV show)
1993 - No. 6, Nov, 1994 ($1.95/$2.25, limited series)
Bongo Comics

1-($2.95)-Glow-in-the-dark-c; bound-in jumbo poster; origin Radioactive Man			
(cover dated Nov. 1952)		1.30	3.00
2-Says #88 on-c & inside & dated May 1962; cover parody of Atlas Kirby			
monster-c; Superior Squad app.; origin Fallout Boy		.80	2.00
3-($1.95)-Cover "dated" Aug 1972 #216		.80	2.00
4-($2.25)-Cover "dated" Oct 1980 #412; w/trading card		.90	2.25
5-($2.25)-Cover "dated" Jan 1986 #679; w/trading card		.90	2.25
6-($2.25)-Cover "dated" #1000		.90	2.25

RAGAMUFFINS
Jan, 1985 ($1.75, one shot)
Eclipse Comics

1-Eclipse Magazine-r, w/color		.75	1.80

RAGGEDY ANN AND ANDY (See Dell Giants, March of Comics #23 & New Funnies)
No. 5, 1942 - No. 533, 2/54; 10-12/64 - No. 4, 3/66
Dell Publishing Co.

Four Color 5(1942)	50.00	150.00	500.00
Four Color 23(1943)	37.00	111.00	370.00
Four Color 45(1943)	30.00	90.00	300.00
Four Color 72(1945)	25.00	75.00	250.00
1(6/46)-Billy & Bonnie Bee by Frank Thomas	25.00	75.00	250.00
2,3: 3-Egbert Elephant by Dan Noonan begins	13.00	40.00	130.00
4-Kelly-a, 16 pgs.	14.00	41.00	140.00
5-10: 7-Little Black Sambo, Black Mumbo & Black Jumbo only app;			
Christmas-c	10.00	30.00	100.00
11-21: 21-Alice In Wonderland cover/story	9.00	27.00	90.00
22-27,29-39(8/49), Four Color 262(1/50): 34-"…In Candyland"			
	7.00	21.00	70.00
28-Kelly-c	8.00	24.00	80.00

Ragman #1 © DC

Ragman: Cry of the Dead #6 © DC

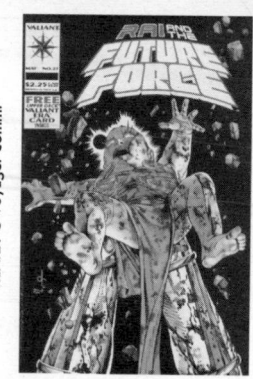

Rai #21 © Voyager Comm.

	GD25	FN65	NM94
Four Color 306,354,380,452,533	5.00	15.00	50.00
1(10-12/64-Dell)	2.70	8.10	27.00
2,3(10-12/65), 4(3/66)	1.70	5.00	12.00

NOTE: Kelly art ("Animal Mother Goose")-#1-34, 36, 37; c-28. Peterkin Pottle by John Stanley in 32-38.

RAGGEDY ANN AND ANDY
Dec, 1971 - No. 6, Sept, 1973
Gold Key

1	1.65	4.20	10.00
2-6	1.00	2.00	5.00

RAGGEDY ANN & THE CAMEL WITH THE WRINKLED KNEES (See Dell Jr. Treasury #8)

RAGMAN (See Batman Family #20, The Brave & The Bold #196 & Cancelled Comic Cavalcade)
Aug-Sept, 1976 - No. 5, June-July, 1977
National Periodical Publications/DC Comics No. 5

1-Origin & 1st app.	1.00	2.00	5.00
2-5: 2-Origin ends; Kubert-c. 4-Drug use story			1.50

NOTE: Kubert a-4, 5; c-1-5. Redondo studios a-1-4.

RAGMAN (2nd Series)
Oct, 1991 - No. 8, May, 1992 ($1.50, limited series)
DC Comics

1-Giffen plots/breakdowns		.80	2.00
2-8: 3-Origin. 8-Batman-c/story			1.50

RAGMAN: CRY OF THE DEAD
Aug, 1993 - No. 6, Jan, 1994 ($1.75, limited series)
DC Comics

1-6: Joe Kubert-c		.70	1.75

RAGS RABBIT (Formerly Babe Ruth Sports #10 or Little Max #10?; also see Harvey Hits #2, Harvey Wiseguys & Tastee Freez)
No. 11, June, 1951 - No. 18, March, 1954 (Written & drawn for little folks)
Harvey Publications

11-(See Nutty Comics #5 for 1st app.)	3.60	9.00	18.00
12-18	3.20	8.00	16.00

RAI (Rai and the Future Force #9-23) (See Magnus #5-8)
3/92 - No. 0,10/92; No. 9, 5/93 - No. 33, 6/95 ($1.95/$2.25)
Valiant

1,2-Valiant's 1st original character	1.30	3.25	8.00
3,4: 4-Low print run; last $1.95-c	1.65	4.20	10.00
5-8: 6,7-Unity x-overs. 7-Death of Rai		1.60	4.00
0-(11/92)-Origin/1st app. new Rai (Rising Spirit) & 1st full app. & partial origin Bloodshot; also see Eternal Warrior #4; tells future of all characters	1.00	2.00	5.00
9-($2.50)-Gatefold-c; story cont'd from Magnus #24; Magnus, Eternal Warrior & X-O app.	1.00	2.50	
10-33: 15-Manowar Armor app. 17-19-Magnus x-over. 21-1st app. The Starwatchers (cameo); bound-in trading card. 22-Death of Rai. 26-Chaos Effect Epsilon Pt. 3		.90	2.25

NOTE: Layton c-2i, 9i. Miller c-6. Simonson c-7.

RAIDERS OF THE LOST ARK (Movie)
Sept, 1981 - No. 3, Nov, 1981 (Movie adaptation)
Marvel Comics Group

1-r/Marvel Comics Super Special #18			1.50
2,3			1.00

NOTE: Buscema a(p)-1-3; c(p)-1. Simonson a-3i; scripts-1-3.

RAINBOW BRITE AND THE STAR STEALER (Movie)
1985
DC Comics

1-Movie adaptation			.80

	GD25	FN65	NM94
RALPH KINER, HOME RUN KING			
1950 (Pittsburgh Pirates)			
Fawcett Publications			
nn-Photo-c; life story	51.00	155.00	415.00

RALPH SNART ADVENTURES
June, 1986 - V2#9, 1987; V3#1 - #26, Feb, 1991; V4#1, 1992 - #4, 1992
Now Comics

1-($1.00, B&W)			1.00
2,3			1.25
V2#1 (11/86, B&W) - 9			1.50
V3#1 (9/88, $1.75)-Color series begins			1.75
2-23,25,26		.70	1.75
24-($2.50)-3-D issue		1.00	2.50
V4#1-4-Direct sale versions w/cards		1.00	2.50
V4#1-4-Newsstand versions w/random cards		.80	2.00
Book 1	1.30	3.30	8.00
3-D Special (11/92, $3.50)-Complete 12-card set w/3-D glasses		1.40	3.50

RAMAR OF THE JUNGLE (TV)
1954 (no month); No. 2, Sept, 1955 - No. 5, Sept, 1956
Toby Press No. 1/Charlton No. 2 on

1-Jon Hall photo-c; last pre-code issue	16.00	47.00	110.00
2-5: 2-Jon Hall photo-c	11.00	33.00	75.00

RAMM
May, 1987 - No. 2, Sept, 1987 ($1.50, B&W)
Megaton Comics

1,2-Both have 1 pg. Youngblood ad by Liefeld			1.50

RAMPAGING HULK (The Hulk #10 on; see Marvel Treasury Edition)
Jan, 1977 - No. 9, June, 1978 ($1.00, B&W magazine)
Marvel Comics Group

1-6,8: Bloodstone story	1.00	2.00	5.00
2-Old X-Men app; origin old & new X-Men in text w/Cockrum illos	1.30	3.25	8.00
3,7,9: 7-Man-Thing story. 9-Thor vs. Hulk battle; Shanna the She-Devil story. 10-Color issue		.90	2.25

NOTE: Alcala a-1-3i, 5i, 8i. Buscema a-1. Giffen a-4. Nino a-4i. Simonson a-1-3p. Starlin a-4(w/Nino), 7; c-4, 5, 7.

RANDOLPH SCOTT (Movie star)(See Crack Western #67, Prize Comics Western #76, Western Hearts #8, Western Love #1 & Western Winners #7)

RANGE BUSTERS
Sept, 1950 - No. 8, 1951
Fox Features Syndicate

1	14.00	43.00	100.00
2	10.00	30.00	60.00
3-8	8.35	25.00	50.00

RANGE BUSTERS (Formerly Cowboy Love?; Wyatt Earp, Frontier Marshall #11 on)
No. 8, May, 1955 - No. 10, Sept, 1955
Charlton Comics

8	6.35	20.00	40.00
9,10	4.15	12.50	25.00

RANGELAND LOVE
Dec, 1949 - No. 2 Mar, 1950 (52 pgs.)
Atlas Comics (CDS)

1-Robert Taylor & Arlene Dahl photo-c	12.00	36.00	85.00
2-Photo-c	11.00	33.00	75.00

RANGER, THE (See Zane Grey, Four Color #255)

RANGE RIDER (See The Flying A's...)

RANGE RIDER, THE (TV)

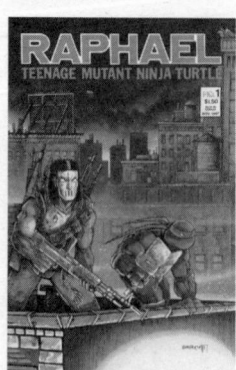
Raphael #1 © Mirage Studios

Ravage 2099 #30 © MEG

The Raven Chronicles #1 © Caliber

	GD25	FN65	NM94

No. 404, June-July, 1952
Dell Publishing Co.

	GD25	FN65	NM94
Four Color 404 (#1)-Photo-c	11.00	33.00	110.00

RANGE ROMANCES
Dec, 1949 - No. 5, Aug, 1950 (#5: 52 pgs.)
Comic Magazines (Quality Comics)

1-Gustavson-c/a	20.00	60.00	140.00
2-Crandall-c/a; "spanking" scene	26.00	77.00	180.00
3-Crandall, Gustavson-a; photo-c	17.00	51.00	120.00
4-Crandall-a; photo-c	14.00	43.00	100.00
5-Gustavson-a; Crandall-a(p); photo-c	15.00	45.00	105.00

RANGERS COMICS (...of Freedom #1-7)
10/41 - No. 67, 10/52; No. 68, Fall, 1952; No. 69, Winter, 1952-53
Fiction House Magazines (Flying stories)

1-Intro. Ranger Girl & The Rangers of Freedom; ends #7, cover app. only #5	188.00	562.00	1500.00
2	71.00	215.00	575.00
3	60.00	181.00	485.00
4,5	54.00	163.00	435.00
6-10: 8-U.S. Rangers begin	43.00	128.00	340.00
11,12-Commando Rangers app.	40.00	120.00	315.00
13-Commando Ranger begins-not same as Commando Rangers	40.00	120.00	295.00
14-20	34.00	103.00	240.00
21-Intro/origin Firehair (begins, 2/45)	38.00	114.00	265.00
22-30: 23-Kazanda begins, ends #28. 28-Tiger Man begins (origin/1st app., 4/46), ends #46. 30-Crusoe Island begins, ends #40	26.00	77.00	180.00
31-40: 33-Hypodermic panels	21.00	64.00	150.00
41-46: 41-Last Werewolf Hunter	17.00	51.00	120.00
47-56- "Eisnerish" Dr. Drew by Grandenetti. 48-Last Glory Forbes. 53-Last 52 pg. issue. 55-Last Sky Rangers	18.00	54.00	125.00
57-60-Straight Dr. Drew by Grandenetti	13.50	41.00	95.00
61,62,64-66: 64-Suicide Smith begins	11.50	34.00	80.00
63-Used in POP, pgs. 85, 99	11.50	34.00	80.00
67-69: 67-Space Rangers begin, end #69	11.50	34.00	80.00

NOTE: Bondage, discipline covers, lingerie panels are common. Crusoe Island by Larsen-#30-36. Firehair by Lubbers-#30-49. Glory Forbes by Baker-#36-45, 47; by Whitman-#34, 35. I Confess in #41-53. Jan of the Jungle in #42-58. King of the Congo in #49-53. Tiger Man by Celardo-#30-39. M. Anderson a-30? Baker a-36-38, 42, 44. John Celardo a-34, 36-39. Lee Elias a-21-28. Evans a-19, 38-46, 48-52. Hopper a-25, 26. Ingels a-13-16. Larsen a-34. Bob Lubbers a-30-38, 40-44; c-40-45. Moreira a-41-47. Tuska a-16, 17, 19, 22. M. Whitman c-61-66. Zolnerwich c-1-17.

RANGO (TV)
Aug, 1967
Dell Publishing Co.

1-Tim Conway photo-c	1.80	5.40	18.00

RAPHAEL (See Teenage Mutant Ninja Turtles)
1985 ($1.50, 7-1/2x11", B&W w/2 color cover, one-shot)
Mirage Studios

1-1st Turtles one-shot spin-off; contains 1st drawing of the Turtles as a group from 1983	1.00	2.00	5.00
1-2nd printing (11/87); new-c & 8 pgs. art	1.20		3.00

RASCALS IN PARADISE
Aug, 1994 - No. 3 Dec, 1994 ($3.95, limited series, magazine size)
Dark Horse Comics

1-3-Jim Silke-a/story		1.60	4.00
Trade paperback-($16.95)-r/#1-3			17.00

RATFINK (See Frantic & Zany)
Oct, 1964
Canrom, Inc.

1-Woodbridge-a	4.00	12.00	24.00

RAT PATROL, THE (TV)
Mar, 1967 - No. 5, Nov, 1967; No. 6, Oct, 1969
Dell Publishing Co.

1-Christopher George photo-c	5.50	16.50	55.00
2	3.50	10.50	35.00
3-6: 3-6-Photo-c	2.80	8.40	28.00

RAVAGE 2099 (See Marvel Comics Presents #117)
Dec, 1992 - No. 33, Aug, 1995($1.25/$1.50)
Marvel Comics

1-($1.75)-Gold foil stamped-c; Stan Lee scripts		.80	2.00
1-($1.75)-2nd printing		.70	1.00
2,3		.70	1.00
4-17: 5-Last Ryan-c. 6-Last Ryan-a. 14-Punisher 2099 x-over. 15-Ron Lim-c			1.00
18-24, 26-30: 18-Begin $1.50-c; bound-in card sheet			1.50
25 ($2.25, 52 pgs.)			2.50
25 ($2.95, 52 pgs.)-Silver foil embossed-c			3.00
31-33: 31-Begin $1.95-c			2.00

RAVEN, THE (See Movie Classics)

RAVEN CHRONICLES
1995 - Present ($2.95, B&W)
Calber (New Worlds)

1-10: 10-Flip book w/Wordsmith #6		1.20	3.00

RAVENS AND RAINBOWS
Dec, 1983 (Baxter paper)(Reprints fanzine work in color)
Pacific Comics

1-Jeff Jones-c/a(r); nudity scenes			1.00

RAWHIDE (TV)
Sept-Nov, 1959 - June-Aug, 1962; July, 1963 - No. 2, Jan, 1964
Dell Publishing Co./Gold Key

Four Color 1028 (#1)	23.00	68.00	225.00
Four Color 1097,1160,1202,1261,1269	15.00	45.00	150.00
01-684-208(8/62-Dell)	13.00	40.00	130.00
1(10071-307, G.K.), 2-(12¢)	12.00	36.00	115.00

NOTE: All have Clint Eastwood photo-c. Tufts a-1028.

RAWHIDE KID
3/55 - No. 16, 9/57; No. 17, 8/60 - No. 151, 5/79
Atlas/Marvel Comics (CnPC No. 1-16/AMI No. 17-30)

1-Rawhide Kid, his horse Apache & sidekick Randy begin; Wyatt Earp app.; #1 was not code approved; Maneely splash pg.	68.00	206.00	550.00
2	30.00	90.00	210.00
3-5	19.00	58.00	135.00
6-10: 7-Williamson-a (4 pgs.)	16.00	47.00	110.00
11-16: 16-Torres-a	13.00	39.00	90.00
17-Origin by Jack Kirby; Kirby-a begins	25.00	75.00	175.00
18-20,24-30	12.00	36.00	85.00
22-Monster-c/story by Kirby/Ayers	13.50	41.00	95.00
23-Origin retold by Jack Kirby	18.00	54.00	125.00
31,32-Kirby-a	10.00	30.00	60.00
33-35-Davis-a. 34-Kirby-a. 35-Intro & death of The Raven	10.00	30.00	60.00
36-41: 38-Red Raven-c/story; Kirby-c (2/64). 40-Two-Gun Kid x-over.	10.00	30.00	60.00
42,43-Kirby-a; 42-1st Larry Lieber issue	10.00	30.00	60.00
44,46: 46-Toth-a	8.35	25.00	50.00
45-Origin retold	10.00	30.00	60.00
47-70: 50-Kid Colt x-over. 64-Kid Colt story. 66-Two-Gun Kid story. 67-Kid Colt story	3.40	10.00	24.00
71-83,85: 79-Williamson-a(r).	2.00	6.00	14.00

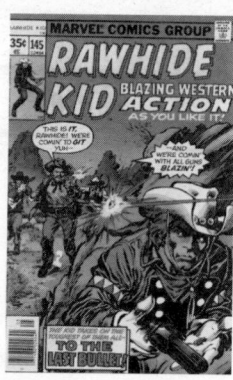

Rawhide Kid #145 © MEG

The Ray #28 © DC

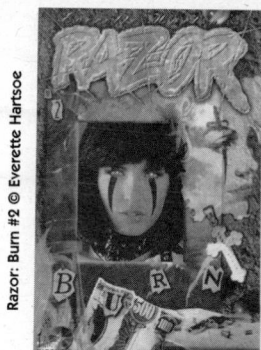

Razor: Burn #2 © Everette Hartsoe

	GD25	FN65	NM94
84,86,92: 86-Origin-r; Williamson-r/Ringo Kid #13 (4 pgs.). 92-Kirby-a	2.30	6.75	16.00
87-91,93-99	1.30	3.25	8.00
100-Origin retold & expanded	1.00	2.60	6.00
101-151: 115-Last new story	1.30	3.25	8.00
Special 1(9/71, 25¢, 68 pgs.)-All Kirby/Ayers-r	1.30	3.25	8.00

NOTE: **Ayers** a-13, 14, 16. **Colan** a-5, 35, 37; c-145p, 148p, 149p. **Davis** a-125r. **Everett** a-54i, 65, 66, 88, 96i, 148i(r). **Gulacy** c-147. **Heath** c-4. **G. Kane** a-101, 144. **Keller** a-5, 144r. **Kirby** a-17-32, 34, 42, 43, 84, 86, 92, 109r, 112r, 137r, Spec. 1; c-17-35, 37, 38, 40, 41, 43-47, 137r. **Maneely** c-1, 2, 5, 6, 14. **Morisi** a-13. **Morrow/Williamson** a-111. **Roussos** r-146i, 147i, 149-151i. **Severin** a-16; c-8, 13. **Torres** a-99r. **Tuska** a-14. **Wildey** r-146-151(Outlaw Kid). **Williamson** r-79, 86, 95.

RAWHIDE KID
Aug, 1985 - No. 4, Nov, 1985 (Mini-series)
Marvel Comics Group

1-4			1.00

RAY, THE (See Freedom Fighters & Smash Comics #14)
Feb, 1992 - No. 6, July, 1992 ($1.00, mini-series)
DC Comics

1-Sienkiewicz-c; Joe Quesada-a(p) in 1-5	1.00	2.60	6.00
2		1.40	3.50
3: 3-6-Quesada-c(p)		1.20	3.00
4-6: 6-Quesada layouts only		.80	2.00
...In a Blaze of Power (1994, $12.95)-r/#1-6 w/new Quesada-c	1.90	5.60	13.00

RAY, THE
May, 1994 - No. 28, Oct, 1996 ($1.75/$1.95/$2.25)
DC Comics

1-3: 1,2-Quesada-c(p); Superboy app.		.70	1.75
1-($2.95)-Collectors Edition w/different Quesada-c; embossed foil-c		1.20	3.00
4,5: 4-Begin $1.95-c. 5-(9/94)		.80	2.00
0,6-12: 0-(10/94)		.80	2.00
13-24, 26-28: 13-Begin $2.25-c		.90	2.25
25-($3.50)-Flash (Bart Allen)-c/app; double size			3.50
Annual 1($3.95, 68 pgs.)-Superman app.	1.60		4.00

RAY BRADBURY COMICS
Feb, 1993 - V4#1, June, 1994 ($2.95)
Topps Comics

1-5-Polybagged w/3 trading cards each. 1-All dinosaur issue; Corben-a; Williamson/Torres/Krenkel-r/Weird Science-Fantasy #25. 3-All dinosaur issue; Steacy painted-c; Stout-a

Special Edition 1 (1994, $2.95)-The Illustrated Man	1.20		3.00
...Trilogy of Terror V3#1 (5/94, $2.50)	1.20		3.00
...Martian Chronicles V4#1 (6/94, $2.50)-Steranko-c	1.00		2.50
	1.00		2.50

NOTE: **Kelley Jones** a-Trilogy of Terror V3#1. **Kaluta** a-Martian Chronicles V4#1. **McKean** c-4. **Mignola** a-4. **Wood** a-Trilogy of Terror V3#1r. **Kurtzman/Matt Wagner** c-2.

RAZOR
May, 1992 - No. 25, Aug, 1996 ($3.95, B&W, mature)
London Night Studios

0 (5/92, $3.95)-Direct market	3.60	11.00	25.00
0 (4/95, $3.00)-London Night edition	1.00	2.00	5.00
1/2 (4/95, mail-in offer)-1st Poizon; Linsner-c	1.65	4.20	10.00
1 (8/92, $2.50)-Fathom Press	3.60	11.00	25.00
1-2nd printing	1.00	2.00	5.00
2 ($2.95)-J. O'Barr-c	2.85	8.50	20.00
2-Limited editions in red & blue	3.60	11.00	25.00
3-Platinum; no price on cover	3.60	11.00	25.00
4-($3.95)-Jim Balent-c	1.70	5.00	12.00
4-w/poster insert	2.15	6.50	15.00
5-Vigil-c	1.30	3.25	8.00
5-w/poster insert	1.65	4.20	10.00

	GD25	FN65	NM94
5-Linsner-c	2.15	6.50	15.00
5-Platinum	2.85	8.50	20.00
6,7	1.00	2.60	6.00
8-10: 10-1st app. Stryke	1.00	2.00	5.00
11,12 ($3.00)-Rituals Pt. 1 & 2		1.20	3.00
13-25-Uncut: 21-Rose & Gunn app. 25-Photo-c		1.20	3.00
25-Uncut ($10.00)-Nude Edition; double-c			10.00
Annual 1 (1993, $2.95)-1st app. Shi	3.75	11.25	30.00
Annual 1-Gold (1200 printed)	7.00	21.50	50.00
Annual 2 (Late 1994, $3.00)	1.00	2.00	5.00
.../Cry No More 1-($3.95)-Origin Razor; variant-c exists			4.00
.../Shi Special 1 (7/94, $3.00)	1.65	4.20	10.00
...: Swimsuit Special-painted-c		1.20	3.00
.../Warrior Nun Areala-Faith-(5/96, $3.95)			4.00
.../Warrior Nun Areala-Faith-(5/96, $3.95)-Virgin-c			10.00

RAZOR: BURN
1994 - No. 5, 1994 ($3.00, limited series, mature)
London Night Studios

1-5			3.00

RAZOR/DARK ANGEL: THE FINAL NAIL
June, 1994 -No. 2, June, 1994 ($2.95, B&W, limited series, mature)
Boneyard Press #1/London Night Studios #2

1,2		1.20	3.00

RAZOR: THE SUFFERING
1994 - No. 3, 1995 ($2.95, limited series, mature)
London Night Studios

1-3 ($2.95): 2-(9/94)			3.00
1-($3.00)-Director's Cut			3.00
1-Platinum			10.00
Trade paperback-($12.95)			13.00

RAZOR: TORTURE
1995 - No. 6, 1995 ($3.00, limited series, mature)
London Night Studios

0-($3.95)-Wraparound, chromium-c; polybagged w/card; alternate-c exists?			4.00
1-6 ($3.00): 3-Error & corrected issues exist			3.00

RAZORLINE
Sept, 1993 (75¢, one-shot)
Marvel Comics

1-Clive Barker super-heroes: Ectokid, Hokum & Hex, Hyperkind & Saint Sinner (all 1st app.)			1.00

REAL ADVENTURE COMICS (Action Adventure #2 on)
Apr, 1955
Gillmor Magazines

1	4.25	13.00	26.00

REAL ADVENTURES OF JONNY QUEST, THE
Sept, 1996 - Present ($2.95)
Dark Horse Comics

1-6			3.00

REAL CLUE CRIME STORIES (Formerly Clue Comics)
V2#4, June, 1947 - V8#3, May, 1953
Hillman Periodicals

V2#4(#1)-S&K c/a(3); Dan Barry-a	39.00	118.00	275.00
5-7-S&K c/a(3-4). 7-Iron Lady app.	29.00	86.00	200.00
8-12	8.35	25.00	50.00
V3#1-8,10-12, V4#1-3,5-8,11,12	6.70	20.00	40.00
V3#9-Used in SOTI, pg. 102	10.00	30.00	65.00
V4#4-S&K-a	10.00	30.00	65.00
V4#9,10-Krigstein-a	9.15	27.00	55.00

Real Fact Comics #16 © DC

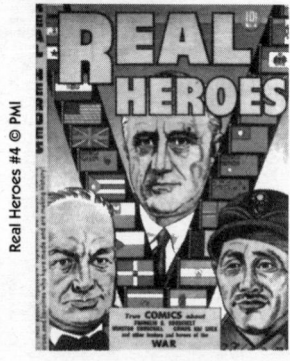

Real Heroes #4 © PMI

R3eal Life Comics #23 © Pictorial Magazine

	GD25	FN65	NM94
V5#1-5,7,8,10,12	5.35	16.00	32.00
6,9,11-Krigstein-a	9.15	27.00	55.00
V6#1-5,8,9,11	4.25	13.00	26.00
6,7,10,12-Krigstein-a. 10-Bondage-c	8.35	25.00	50.00
V7#1-3,5-11, V8#1-3: V7#6-1 pg. Frazetta ad "Prayer" - 1st app.?			
	4.25	13.00	26.00
4,12-Krigstein-a	8.35	25.00	50.00

NOTE: **Barry** a-9, 10; c-V2#8. **Briefer** a-V6#6. **Fuje** a- V2#7(2), 8, 11. **Infantino** a-V2#8; c-V2#11. **Lawrence** a-V3#8, V5#7. **Powell** a-V4#11, 12. V5#4, 5, 7 are 68 pgs.

REAL EXPERIENCES (Formerly Tiny Tessie)
No. 25, Jan, 1950
Atlas Comics (20CC)

25-Virginia Mayo photo-c from movie "Red Light"	5.35	16.00	32.00

REAL FACT COMICS
Mar-Apr, 1946 - No. 21, July-Aug, 1949
National Periodical Publications

1-S&K-c/a; Harry Houdini story; Just Imagine begins (not by Finlay); Fred Ray-a	56.00	168.00	450.00
2-S&K-a; Rin-Tin-Tin & P. T. Barnum stories	40.00	120.00	300.00
3-H.G. Wells, Lon Chaney stories; 1st DC letter column	36.00	107.00	250.00
4-Virgil Finlay-a on 'Just Imagine' begins, ends #12 (2 pgs. each); Jimmy Stewart & Jack London stories; Joe DiMaggio 1 pg. biography	40.00	120.00	300.00
5-Batman/Robin-c taken from cover of Batman #9; 5 pg. story about creation of Batman & Robin; Tom Mix story	175.00	525.00	1400.00
6-Origin & 1st app. Tommy Tomorrow by Finlay (1-2/47); Flag-c; 1st writing by Harlan Ellison (letter column, non-professional); "First Man to Reach Mars" epic-c/story	109.00	328.00	875.00
7-(No. 6 on inside)-Roussos-a; D. Fairbanks sty.	18.00	54.00	125.00
8-2nd app. Tommy Tomorrow by Finlay (5-6/47)	50.00	150.00	450.00
9-S&K-a; Glenn Miller, Indianapolis 500 stories	29.00	86.00	200.00
10-Vigilante by Meskin (based on movie serial); 4 pg. Finlay s/f story	26.00	79.00	185.00
11,12: 11-Annie Oakley, G-Men stories; Kinstler-a	15.00	45.00	105.00
13-Dale Evans and Tommy Tomorrow-c/stories	50.00	150.00	400.00
14,17,18: 14-Will Rogers story	13.50	41.00	95.00
15-Nuclear explosion part-c ("Last War on Earth" story); Clyde Beatty story	18.00	54.00	125.00
16-Tommy Tomorrow app.; 1st Planeteers?	44.00	132.00	350.00
19-Sir Arthur Conan Doyle story	16.00	47.00	110.00
20-Kubert-a, 4 pgs; Daniel Boone story	17.00	51.00	120.00
21-Kubert-a, 2 pgs; Kit Carson story	13.50	41.00	95.00

NOTE: **Barry** c-16. **Virgil Finlay** c-6, 8. **Meskin** c-10. **Roussos** a-1-4, 6.

REAL FUN OF DRIVING!!, THE
1965, 1967 (Regular size)
Chrysler Corp.

nn-Shaffenberger-a (12 pgs.)	1.00	2.50	5.00

REAL FUNNIES
Jan, 1943 - No. 3, June, 1943
Nedor Publishing Co.

1-Funny animal, humor; Black Terrier app. (clone of The Black Terror)	26.00	79.00	185.00
2,3	13.00	39.00	90.00

REAL GHOSTBUSTERS, THE (Also see Slimer)
Aug, 1988 - No. 32, 1991 ($1.75, color)
Now Comics

1-32: 1-Based on Ghostbusters movie. 30-Begin $1.95-c	.80		2.00

REAL HEROES COMICS
Sept, 1941 - No. 16, Oct, 1946
Parents' Magazine Institute

	GD25	FN65	NM94
1-Roosevelt-c/story	28.00	84.00	195.
2-J. Edgar Hoover-c/story	12.00	36.00	85.
3-5,7-10: 4-Churchill, Roosevelt stories	10.00	30.00	70.
6-Lou Gehrig-c/story	17.00	49.00	115.
11-16: 13-Kiefer-a	6.70	20.00	40.

REAL HIT
1944 (Savings Bond premium)
Fox Features Publications

1-Blue Beetle-r	17.00	49.00	115.

NOTE: Two versions exist, with and without covers. The coverless version has the title, No. 1 and price printed at top of splash page.

REALISTIC ROMANCES
July-Aug, 1951 - No. 17, Aug-Sept, 1954 (No #9-14)
Realistic Comics/Avon Periodicals

1-Kinstler-a; c-/Avon paperback #211	16.00	47.00	110.
2	8.35	25.00	50.
3,4	6.70	20.00	40.
5,8-Kinstler-a	7.00	21.00	42.
6-c-/Diversey Prize Novels #6; Kinstler-a	8.00	24.00	48.
7-Evans-a?; c-/Avon paperback #360	8.00	24.00	48.
15,17: 17-Kinstler-c	6.35	19.00	38.
16-Kinstler marijuana story-r/Romantic Love #6	8.00	24.00	48.
I.W. Reprint #1,8,9: #1-r/Realistic Romances #4; Astarita-a. 9-r/Women To Love #1	1.00	2.00	5.

NOTE: **Astarita** a-2-4, 7, 8, 17. Photo c-1, 2. Painted c-3, 4.

REAL LIFE COMICS
Sept, 1941 - No. 59, Sept, 1952
Nedor/Better/Standard Publ./Pictorial Magazine No. 13

1-Uncle Sam-c/story; Daniel Boone story	40.00	120.00	315.
2	18.00	54.00	125.
3-Hitler cover	37.00	111.00	260.
4,5: 4-Story of American flag "Old Glory"	11.50	34.00	80.
6-10: 6-Wild Bill Hickok story	11.00	33.00	75.
11-20: 17-Albert Einstein story	10.00	30.00	60.
21-23,25,26,28,30: 29-A-Bomb story	7.50	22.50	45.
24-Story of Baseball (Babe Ruth)	12.00	36.00	85.
27-Schomburg A-Bomb-c; story of A-Bomb	12.00	36.00	85.
31-33,35,36,42-44,48,49: 49-Baseball issue	5.35	16.00	32.
34,37,41,45-47: 34-Jimmy Stewart story. 37-Story of motion pictures; Bing Crosby story. 38-Jane Froman story. 39- "1,000,000 A.D." story. 40-Bob Feller story. 41-Jimmie Foxx story; "Home Run" Baker story. 45-Story of Olympic games; Burl Ives & Kit Carson story. 46-Douglas Fairbanks Jr. & Sr. story. 47-George Gershwin story	7.50	22.50	45.
50-Frazetta-a (5 pgs.)	21.00	64.00	150.
51-Jules Verne "Journey to the Moon" by Evans	14.00	43.00	100.
52-Frazetta-a (4 pgs.); Severin/Elder-a(2)	21.00	64.00	150.
53-57-Severin/Elder-a. 54-Bat Masterson-c/story	10.00	30.00	65.
58-Severin/Elder-a(2)	10.00	30.00	70.
59-1 pg. Frazetta; Severin/Elder-a	10.00	30.00	60.

NOTE: Some issues had two titles. **Guardineer** a-40(2), 44. **Meskin** a-52. **Roussos** a-50. **Schomburg** c-1, 2, 4, 5, 7, 11, 13-21, 23, 24, 26, 28, 30-32, 34-40, 42, 44-47, 55. **Tuska** a-53. Photo-c 5, 6.

REAL LIFE SECRETS (Real Secrets #2 on)
Sept, 1949 (one-shot)
Ace Periodicals

1-Painted-c	8.00	24.00	48.

REAL LIFE STORY OF FESS PARKER (Magazine)
1955
Dell Publishing Co.

1	13.00	39.00	90.

REAL LIFE TALES OF SUSPENSE (See Suspense)

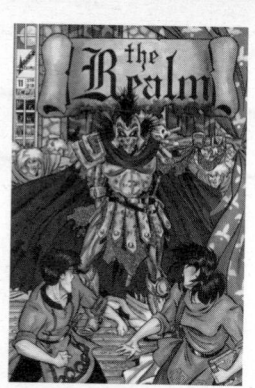

The Realm #11 ©Arrow Comics

R.E.B.E.L.S. '96 © DC

Rebel Sword #4 © DH

	GD25	FN65	NM94

REAL LOVE (Formerly Hap Hazard)
No. 25, April, 1949 - No. 76, Nov, 1956
Ace Periodicals (A. A. Wyn)

25	10.00	30.00	60.00
26	5.35	16.00	32.00
27-L. B. Cole-a	8.35	25.00	55.00
28-35	4.00	12.00	24.00
36-66: 66-Last pre-code (2/55)	4.00	10.00	20.00
67-76	2.60	6.50	13.00

NOTE: Photo c-50-76. Painted c-46.

REALM, THE
Feb, 1986 - No. 20? ($1.50/$1.95/$2.50, B&W)
Arrow Comics/WeeBee Comics #13/Caliber Press #14 on

1		1.60	4.00
2		.80	2.00
3,5-16: 13-Begin $1.95-c			1.25
4-1st app. Deadworld (9/86)	1.20	3.00	7.00
17-20: 17-Begin $2.50-c		1.00	2.50
Book 1 ($4.95, B&W)	1.00	2.00	5.00

REAL McCOYS, THE (TV)
No. 1, 1-3/60 - 5-7/1962 (All have Walter Brennan photo-c)
Dell Publishing Co.

Four Color 1071,1134-Toth-a in both	10.00	30.00	100.00
Four Color 1193,1265	9.00	27.00	90.00
01-689-207 (5-7/62)	8.00	24.00	80.00

REAL SCREEN COMICS (#1 titled Real Screen Funnies; TV Screen Cartoons #129-138)
Spring, 1945 - No. 128, May-June, 1959 (#1-49: 52 pgs.)
National Periodical Publications

1-The Fox & the Crow, Flippity & Flop, Tito & His Burrito begin	100.00	300.00	800.00
2	47.00	141.00	375.00
3-5	31.00	94.00	220.00
6-10 (2-3/47)	21.00	62.00	145.00
11-20 (10-11/48): 13-The Crow x-over in Flippity & Flop	16.00	47.00	110.00
21-30 (6-7/50)	11.50	34.00	80.00
31-50	10.00	30.00	70.00
51-99	8.35	25.00	50.00
100	9.15	27.50	55.00
101-128	6.35	19.00	38.00

REAL SECRETS (Formerly Real Life Secrets)
No. 2, Nov, 1950 - No. 5, May, 1950
Ace Periodicals

2-Painted-c	7.50	22.50	45.00
3-5: 3-Photo-c	4.25	13.00	28.00

REAL SPORTS COMICS (All Sports Comics #2 on)
Oct-Nov, 1948 (52 pgs.)
Hillman Periodicals

1-Powell-a (12 pgs.)	34.00	103.00	240.00

REAL WAR STORIES
July, 1987; No. 2, Jan, 1991 ($2.00, 52 pgs.)
Eclipse Comics

1-Bolland-a(p), Bissette-a, Totleben-a(i); Alan Moore scripts (2nd printing exists, 2/88)		.80	2.00
2-($4.95)	1.00	5.00

REAL WESTERN HERO (Formerly Wow #1-69; Western Hero #76 on)
No. 70, Sept, 1948 - No. 75, Feb, 1949 (All 52 pgs.)
Fawcett Publications

70(#1)-Tom Mix, Monte Hale, Hopalong Cassidy, Young Falcon begin

	GD25	FN65	NM94
	33.00	99.00	230.00
71-75: 71-Gabby Hayes begins. 71,72-Captain Tootsie by Beck. 75-Big Bow and Little Arrow app.	21.00	62.00	145.00

NOTE: Painted/photo c-70-73; painted c-74, 75.

REAL WEST ROMANCES
4-5/49 - V1#6, 3/50; V2#1, Apr-May, 1950 (All 52 pgs. & photo-c)
Crestwood Publishing Co./Prize Publ.

V1#1-S&K-a(p)	17.00	51.00	120.00
2-Spanking panel	13.50	41.00	95.00
3-Kirby-a(p) only	10.00	30.00	60.00
4-S&K-a; Whip Wilson, Reno Browne photo-c	15.00	45.00	105.00
5-Audie Murphy, Gale Storm photo-c; S&K-a	13.50	41.00	95.00
6-Produced by S&K, no S&K-a; Robert Preston & Cathy Downs photo-c	10.00	30.00	70.00
V2#1-Kirby-a(p)	8.35	25.00	50.00

NOTE: Meskin a-V1#5, 6. Severin/Elder a-V1#3-6, V2#1. Meskin a-V1#6. Leonard Starr a-1-3. Photo-c V1#1-6, V2#1.

RE-ANIMATOR IN FULL COLOR
Oct, 1991 - No. 3, 1992 ($2.95, mini-series)
Adventure Comics

1-3: Adapts horror movie. 1-Dorman painted-c		1.20	3.00

REAP THE WILD WIND (See Cinema Comics Herald)

REBEL, THE (TV)
No. 1076, Feb-Apr, 1960 - No. 1262, Dec-Feb, 1961-62
Dell Publishing Co.

Four Color 1076 (#1)-Sekowsky-a, photo-c	10.00	30.00	100.00
Four Color 1138 (9-11/60), 1207 (9-11/61), 1262-Photo-c	9.00	27.00	90.00

R.E.B.E.L.S. '94 (Becomes R.E.B.E.L.S. '95 & R.E.B.E.L.S. '96)
No. 0, Oct, 1994 - No. 17, Mar, 1996 ($1.95/$2.25)
DC Comics

0-7		.80	2.00
8-17: 8-$2.25-c begins. 15-R.E.B.E.L.S '96 begins.		.90	2.25

REBEL SWORD (Manga)
Oct, 1994 - No. 6, Feb, 1995 ($2.50, B&W)
Dark Horse Comics

1-6		1.00	2.50

RECORD BOOK OF FAMOUS POLICE CASES
1949 (25¢, 132 pgs.)
St. John Publishing Co.

nn-Kubert-a(3); r/Son of Sinbad; Baker-c	33.00	99.00	230.00

RED ARROW
May-June, 1951 - No. 3, Oct, 1951
P. L. Publishing Co.

1	9.15	27.00	55.00
2,3	7.50	22.50	45.00

RED BALL COMIC BOOK
1947 (Red Ball Shoes giveaway)
Parents' Magazine Institute

nn-Reprints from True Comics	2.40	6.00	12.00

RED BAND COMICS
Feb, 1945 - No. 4, May, 1945
Enwil Associates

1	29.00	86.00	200.00
2-Origin Bogeyman & Santanas; c-reprint/#1	23.00	69.00	160.00
3,4-Captain Wizard app. in both (1st app.); each has identical contents/cover	21.00	62.00	145.00

REDBLADE

Redblade #1 © DH

Red Circle Sorcery #11 © Archie

Red Dragon Comics #9 © S&S

GD25   FN65   NM94

GD25   FN65   NM94

Apr, 1993 - No. 3, July, 1993 ($2.50, mini-series)
Dark Horse Comics

1-3: 1-Double gatefold-c		1.00	2.50

RED CIRCLE COMICS
Jan, 1945 - No. 4, April, 1945
Rural Home Publications (Enwil)

1-The Prankster & Red Riot begin	26.00	79.00	185.00
2-Starr-a; The Judge (costumed hero) app.	21.00	64.00	150.00
3,4-Starr-c/a. 3-The Prankster not in costume	17.00	49.00	115.00
4-(Dated 4/45)-Leftover covers to #4 were later restapled over early 1950s coverless comics; variations in the coverless comics used are endless; Woman Outlaws, Dorothy Lamour, Crime Does Not Pay, Sabu, Diary Loves, Love Confessions & Young Love V3#3 known	11.00	33.00	75.00

RED CIRCLE SORCERY (Chilling Adventures in Sorcery #1-5)
No. 6, Apr, 1974 - No. 11, Feb, 1975 (All 25¢ issues)
Red Circle Publications (Archie)

6-11: 8-Only app. The Cobra. 10-Wood-a(i)			1.50

NOTE: *Chaykin a-6, 10.* **B. Jones** *a-7(w/Wrightson,* **Kaluta, J. Jones**)*.* **McWilliams** *a-10(2 & 3 pgs.).* **Mooney** *a-11p.* **Morrow** *a-6-8, 9(text illos), 10, 11l; c-6-11.* **Thorne** *a-8, 10.* **Toth** *a-8, 9.*

RED DOG (See Night Music #7)

RED DRAGON
June, 1996 ($2.95)
Comico

1-Bisley-c			3.00

RED DRAGON COMICS (1st Series) (Formerly Trail Blazers; see Super Magician V5#7, 8)
No. 5, Jan, 1943 - No. 9, Jan, 1944
Street & Smith Publications

5-Origin Red Rover, the Crimson Crimebuster; Rex King, Man of Adventure, Captain Jack Commando, & The Minute Man begin; text origin Red Dragon; Binder-c	81.00	243.00	650.00
6-Origin The Black Crusader & Red Dragon (3/43); 1st story app. Red Dragon & 1st cover (classic-c)	137.00	412.00	1100.00
7-Classic-c	93.00	281.00	750.00
8-The Red Knight app.	53.00	159.00	425.00
9-Origin Chuck Magnon, Immortal Man	53.00	159.00	425.00

RED DRAGON COMICS (2nd Series)(See Super Magician V2#8)
Nov, 1947 - No. 6, Jan, 1949; No. 7, July, 1949
Street & Smith Publications

1-Red Dragon begins; Elliman, Nigel app.; Edd Cartier-c/a	75.00	225.00	600.00
2-Cartier-c	56.00	168.00	450.00
3-1st app. Dr. Neff Ghost Breaker by Powell; Elliman, Nigel app.	48.00	144.00	385.00
4-Cartier c/a	62.00	187.00	500.00
5-7	38.00	114.00	265.00

NOTE: *Maneely a-5, 7.* **Powell** *a-2-7; c-3, 5, 7.*

REDDY GOOSE
No #, 1958?; No. 2, Jan, 1959 - No. 16, July, 1962 (Giveaway)
International Shoe Co. (Western Printing)

nn (#1)	6.70	20.00	40.00
2-16	4.00	10.50	21.00

REDDY KILOWATT (5¢) (Also see Story of Edison)
1946 - No. 2, 1947; 1956 - 1960 (no month) (16 pgs., paper-c)
Educational Comics (E. C.)

nn-Reddy Made Magic (1946, 5¢)	12.00	35.00	70.00
nn-Reddy Made Magic (1958)	5.35	16.00	32.00
2-Edison, the Man Who Changed the World (3/4" smaller than #1) (1947, 5¢)	12.00	35.00	70.00
...Comic Book 2 (1954)- "Light's Diamond Jubilee"	6.70	20.00	40.00

...Comic Book 2 (1958, 16 pgs.)- "Wizard of Light"	5.35	16.00	32.00
...Comic Book 3 (1956, 8 pgs.)- "The Space Kite"; Orlando story; regular size	5.35	16.00	32.00
...Comic Book 3 (1960, 8 pgs.)- "The Space Kite"; Orlando story; regular size	4.70	14.00	28.00

NOTE: *Several copies surfaced in 1979.*

REDDY MADE MAGIC
1956, 1958 (16 pgs., paper-c)
Educational Comics (E. C.)

1-Reddy Kilowatt-r (splash panel changed)	8.00	24.00	48.00
1 (1958 edition)	5.00	15.00	30.00

RED EAGLE
No. 16, Aug, 1938
David McKay Publications

Feature Books 16	16.00	48.00	160.00

REDEYE (See Comics Reading Libraries)

RED FOX (Formerly Manhunt! #1-14; also see Extra Comics)
No. 15, 1954
Magazine Enterprises

15(A-1 #108)-Undercover Girl story; L.B. Cole-c/a (Red Fox); r-from Manhunt; Powell-a	14.00	43.00	100.00

RED GOOSE COMIC SELECTIONS (See Comic Selections)

RED HAWK (See A-1 Comics, Bobby Benson's ..#14-16 & Straight Arrow #2)
No. 90, 1953
Magazine Enterprises

A-1 90-Powell-c/a	10.00	30.00	70.00

RED ICEBERG, THE
1960 (10¢, 16 pgs.) (Communist propaganda)
Impact Publ. (Catechetical Guild)

nn-(Rare)- 'We The People" back-c	39.00	116.00	270.00
2nd version- 'Impact Press' back-c	40.00	120.00	300.00

NOTE: *This book was the Guild's last anti-communist propaganda book and had very limited circulation. 3 - 4 copies surfaced in 1979 from the defunct publisher's files. Other copies do turn up.*

RED MASK (Formerly Tim Holt; see Best Comics, Blazing Six-Guns)
No. 42, 6-7/1954 - No. 53, 5/56; No. 54, 9/57
Magazine Enterprises No. 42-53/Sussex No. 54 (M.E. on-c)

42-Ghost Rider by Ayers continues, ends #50; Black Phantom continues; 3-D effect c/stories begin	18.00	56.00	130.00
43-3-D effect-c/stories	17.00	51.00	120.00
44-50: 3-D effect stories only. 47-Last pre-code issue. 50-Last Ghost Rider	16.00	47.00	110.00
51-The Presto Kid begins by Ayers (1st app.); Presto Kid-c begins, ends #54; last 3-D effect story	16.00	47.00	110.00
52-Origin The Presto Kid	16.00	47.00	110.00
53,54-Last Black Phantom	11.50	34.00	80.00
I.W. Reprint #1 (r-/#52). 2 (nd, r/#51 w/diff.-c). 3, 8 (nd; Kinstler-c); 8-r/Red Mask #52	2.60	7.50	18.00

NOTE: *Ayers art on Ghost Rider & Presto Kid.* **Bolle** *art in all (Red Mask); c-43, 44, 49.* **Guardineer** *a-52.* **Black Phantom** *in #42-44, 47-50, 53, 54.*

REDMASK OF THE RIO GRANDE
1990 ($2.50, 28pgs.) (Has photos of movie posters)
AC Comics

1-Bolle-c/a(r); photo inside-c		1.00	2.50

RED MOUNTAIN FEATURING QUANTRELL'S RAIDERS (Movie)(Also see Jesse James #28)
1952
Avon Periodicals

nn-Alan Ladd; Kinstler-c	23.00	69.00	160.00

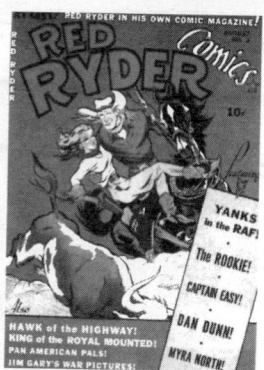
Red Ryder Comics #3 © Hawley

Red Sonja Scavenger Hunt © ERB

Red Tornado #2 © DC

"RED" RABBIT COMICS
Jan, 1947 - No. 22, Aug-Sept, 1951
Dearfield Comic/J. Charles Laue Publ. Co.

1	10.00	30.00	70.00
2	6.35	19.00	38.00
3-10	4.25	13.00	28.00
11-17,19-22	4.00	12.00	24.00
18-Flying Saucer-c (1/51)	5.85	17.50	35.00

RED RAVEN COMICS (Human Torch #2 on)(Also see X-Men #44 &
Sub-Mariner #26, 2nd series)
August, 1940
Timely Comics

	GD25	FN65	VF82	NM94
1-Origin & 1st app. Red Raven; Comet Pierce & Mercury by Kirby, The				
Human Top & The Eternal Brain; intro. Magar, the Mystic & only app.;				
Kirby-c (his 1st signed work)	1000.00	3000.00	6000.00	9400.00
(Estimated up to 50 total copies exist, 6 in NM/Mint)				

RED RYDER COMICS (Hi Spot #2)(Movies, radio)(See Crackajack Funnies)
9/40; No. 3, 8/41 - No. 5, 12/41; No. 6, 4/42 - No. 151, 4-6/57
Hawley Publ. No. 1/Dell Publishing Co.(K.K.) No. 3 on

	GD25	FN65	NM94
1-Red Ryder, his horse Thunder, Little Beaver & his horse Papoose strip			
reprints begin by Fred Harman; 1st meeting of Red & Little Beaver;			
Harman line-drawn-c #1-85	220.00	660.00	2200.00
3-(Scarce)-Alley Oop, King of the Royal Mtd., Capt. Easy, Freckles & His			
Friends, Myra North, Dan Dunn strip-r begin	82.00	246.00	825.00
4,5	40.00	120.00	400.00
6-1st Dell issue (4/42)	40.00	120.00	400.00
7-10	33.00	99.00	330.00
11-20	23.00	69.00	235.00
21-32-Last Alley Oop, Dan Dunn, Capt. Easy, Freckles			
	16.00	48.00	155.00
33-40 (52 pgs.)	10.00	30.00	100.00
41 (52 pgs.)-Rocky Lane photo back-c; photo back-c begin, end #57			
	11.00	33.00	105.00
42-46 (52 pgs.): 46-Last Red Ryder strip-r	8.50	25.50	85.00
47-53 (52 pgs.): 47-New stories on Red Ryder begin. 49,52-Harmon photo			
back-c	8.00	24.00	70.00
54-57 (36 pgs.)	6.00	18.00	54.00
58-73 (36 pgs.)- 59-Harmon photo back-c. 73-Last King of the Royal Mtd; strip-r			
by Jim Gary	6.00	18.00	54.00
74-85,93 (52 pgs.)-Harman line-drawn-c	6.00	18.00	54.00
86-92 (52 pgs.)-Harman painted-c	6.00	18.00	54.00
94-96 (36 pgs.)-Harman painted-c	4.50	13.50	40.00
97,98,107,108 (36 pgs.)-Harman line-drawn-c	4.50	13.50	40.00
99,101-106 (36 pgs.)-Jim Bannon Photo-c	4.50	13.50	40.00
100 (36 pgs.)-Bannon photo-c	5.00	15.00	45.00
109-118 (52 pgs.)-Harman line-drawn-c	3.50	10.50	32.00
119-129 (52 pgs.): 119-Painted-c begin, not by Harman, end #151			
	3.35	10.00	30.00
130-144 (#130 on have 36 pgs.)	3.00	9.00	27.00
145-148: 145-Title change to Red Ryder Ranch Magazine with photos			
	2.50	7.50	22.00
149-151: 149-Title changed to Red Ryder Ranch Comics			
	2.50	7.50	22.00
Four Color 916 (7/58)	3.00	9.00	30.00
Buster Brown Shoes Giveaway (1941, color, soft-c, 32 pgs.)			
	26.00	79.00	185.00
Red Ryder Super Book Of Comics 10 (1944; paper-c; 32 pgs.; blank back-c)-			
Magic Morro app.	26.00	79.00	185.00
Red Ryder Victory Patrol-nn(1944, 32 pgs.)-r-/#43,44; comic has a paper-c & is			
stapled inside a triple cardboard fold-out-c; contains membership card,			
decoder, map of R.R. ranch range, etc. Herky app. (Langendorf Bread give-			
away; sub-titled 'Super Book of Comics')(Rare)	378.00	1133.00	3400.00

Wells Lamont Corp. giveaway (1950)-16 pgs. in color; regular size; paper-c;

1941-r	24.00	73.00	170.00

NOTE: **Fred Harman** a-1-99; c-1-98, 107-118. Don Red Barry, Allan Rocky Lane, Wild Bill Elliott
& Jim Bannon starred as Red Ryder in the movies. Robert Blake starred as Little Beaver.

RED RYDER PAINT BOOK
1941 (8-1/2x11-1/2", 148 pgs.)
Whitman Publishing Co.

nn-Reprints 1940 daily strips	56.00	170.00	450.00

RED SEAL COMICS (Formerly Carnival Comics, and/or Spotlight Comics?)
No. 14, 10/45 - No. 18, 10/46; No. 19, 6/47 - No. 22, 12/47
Harry 'A' Chesler/Superior Publ. No. 19 on

14-The Black Dwarf begins (continued from Spotlight?); Little Nemo app;			
bondage/hypo-c; Tuska-a	53.00	159.00	425.00
15-Torture story; funny-c	40.00	120.00	285.00
16-Used in **SOTI**, pg. 181, illo "Outside the forbidden pages of de Sade, you			
find draining a girl's blood only in children's comics"; drug club story r-later			
in Crime Reporter #1; Veiled Avenger & Barry Kuda app; Tuska-a; funny-c			
	50.00	150.00	400.00
17-Lady Satan, Yankee Girl & Sky Chief app; Tuska-a			
	40.00	120.00	290.00
18,20-Lady Satan & Sky Chief app.	40.00	120.00	290.00
19-No Black Dwarf (on-c only); Zor, El Tigre app.	32.00	96.00	225.00
21-Lady Satan & Black Dwarf app.	27.00	81.00	190.00
22-Zor, Rocketman app. (68 pgs.)	27.00	81.00	190.00

REDSKIN (Thrilling Indian Stories)(Famous Western Badmen #13 on)
Sept, 1950 - No. 12, Oct, 1952
Youthful Magazines

1-Walter Johnson-a (7 pgs.)	11.00	33.00	75.00
2	9.15	27.00	55.00
3-12: 3-Daniel Boone story. 6-Geronimo story	7.50	22.50	45.00

NOTE: **Walter Johnson** c-3, 4. **Palais** a-11. **Wildey** a-5, 11. Bondage c-6, 12.

RED SONJA (Also see Conan #23, Kull & The Barbarians, Marvel Feature &
Savage Sword Of Conan #1)
1/77 - No. 15, 5/79; V1#1, 2/83 - V2#2, 3/83; V3#1, 8/83 - V3#4, 2/84;
V3#5, 1/85 - V3#13, 1986
Marvel Comics Group

1-Created by Robert E. Howard	1.00	2.00	5.00
2-5: 5-Last 30¢ issue		.80	2.00
6-15, V1#1,V2#2: 14-Last 35¢ issue			1.00
V3#1-4 ($1.00, 52 pgs.)			1.20
5-13 (65-75¢)			1.00

NOTE: **Brunner** c-12-14. **J. Buscema** a(p)-12, 13, 15; c-V#1. **Nebres** a-V3#3i(part). **N.
Redondo** a-8i, V3#2i, 3i. **Simonson** a-V3#1. **Thorne** c/a-1-11.

RED SONJA: SCAVENGER HUNT
Dec, 1995 ($2.95, one-shot)
Marvel Comics

1		1.20	3.00

RED SONJA: THE MOVIE
Nov, 1985 - No. 2, Dec, 1985 (Limited-series)
Marvel Comics Group

1,2-Movie adapt-r/Marvel Super Spec. #38			.80

RED TORNADO (See All-American #20 & Justice League of America #64)
July, 1985 - No. 4, Oct, 1985 (Limited series)
DC Comics

1-4: Kurt Busiek scripts in all. 1-3-Superman cameos. 1,3-Batman cameos			
			1.00

RED WARRIOR
Jan, 1951 - No. 6, Dec, 1951
Marvel/Atlas Comics (TCI)

1-Red Warrior & his horse White Wing; Tuska-a	14.00	43.00	100.00

Reg'lar Fellers #5 © STD

Regulators #3 © Jim Valentino

Reid Fleming #3 © ECL

	GD25	FN65	NM94
2-Tuska-c	10.00	30.00	60.00
3-6: 4-Origin White Wing. 6-Maneely-c	8.35	25.00	50.00

RED WOLF (See Avengers #80 & Marvel Spotlight #1)
May, 1972 - No. 9, Sept, 1973
Marvel Comics Group

1-(Western hero); Gil Kane/Severin-c; Shores-a	1.00	2.00	5.00
2-9: 2-Kane-c; Shores-a. 6-Tuska-r in back-up. 7-Red Wolf as super hero			
begins. 9-Origin sidekick, Lobo (wolf)		1.20	3.00

REESE'S PIECES
Oct, 1985 - No.2, Oct, 1985 ($1.75, Baxter paper)
Eclipse Comics

1,2-B&W-r in color		.75	1.80

REFORM SCHOOL GIRL!
1951
Realistic Comics

nn-Used in **SOTI**, pg. 358, & cover ill. with caption "Comic books are supposed			
to be like fairy tales"	106.00	318.00	850.00
(Prices vary widely on this book)			

NOTE: *The cover and title originated from a digest-sized book published by Diversey Publishing Co. of Chicago in 1948. The original book "House of Fury", Doubleday, came out in 1941. The girl's real name which appears on the cover of the digest and comic is Marty Collins, Canadian model and ice skating star who posed for this special color photograph for the Diversey novel.*

REGENTS ILLUSTRATED CLASSICS
1981 (Plus more recent reprintings)
(48 pgs., B&W-a with 14 pgs. of teaching helps)
Prentice Hall Regents, Englewood Cliffs, NJ 07632
NOTE: *This series contains Classics Ill. art, and was produced from the same illegal source as Cassette Books. But when Twin Circle sued to stop the sale of the Cassette Books, they decided to permit this series to continue. This series was produced as a teaching aid. The 20 title series is divided into four levels based upon number of basic words used therein. There is also a teacher's manual for each level. All of the titles are still available from the publisher for about $5 each retail. The number to call for mail order purchases is (201)767-5937. Almost all of the issues have new covers taken from some interior art panel. Here is a list of the series by Regents ident. no. and the Classics Ill. counterpart.*

16770(CI#24-A2)18333(CI#3-A2)21668(CI#13-A2)32224(CI#21)33051(CI#26)
35788(CI#84)37153(CI#16)44460(CI#19-A2)44808(CI#18-A2)52395(CI#4-A2)
58627(CI#5-A2)60067(CI#30)68405(CI#23-A1)70302(CI#29)78192(CI#7-A2)
78193(CI#10-A2)79679(CI#85)92046(CI#1-A2)93062(CI#64)93512(CI#25)

REGGIE (Formerly Archie's Rival...; Reggie & Me #19 on)
No. 15, Sept, 1963 - No. 18, Nov, 1965
Archie Publications

15(9/63), 16(10/64)	4.00	12.00	40.00
17(8/65), 18(11/65)	4.00	12.00	40.00

NOTE: *Cover title No. 15 & 16 is Archie's Rival Reggie.*

REGGIE AND ME (Formerly Reggie)
No. 19, Aug, 1966 - No. 126, Sept, 1980 (No. 50-68: 52 pgs.)
Archie Publications

19-Evilheart app.	2.60	7.50	18.00
20-23-Evilheart app.; with Pureheart #22	1.50	3.75	9.00
24-40		1.20	3.00
41-60			1.50
61-126			1.00

REGGIE'S JOKES (See Reggie's Wise Guy Jokes)

REGGIE'S REVENGE!
Spring, 1994 - Present ($2.00, 52 pgs.)(Published semi-annually)
Archie Comic Publications, Inc.

1-3: 1-Bound-in pull-out poster		.80	2.00

REGGIE'S WISE GUY JOKES
Aug, 1968 - No. 60, Jan, 1982 (#5-28 are Giants)
Archie Publications

1	2.00	6.00	14.00
2-4	1.00	2.50	6.00

	GD25	FN65	NM94
5-10		1.20	3.00
11-28			1.50
29-60			1.00

REGISTERED NURSE
Summer, 1963
Charlton Comics

1-r/Nurse Betsy Crane & Cynthia Doyle	1.00	2.50	5.00

REG'LAR FELLERS
No. 5, Nov, 1947 - No. 6, Mar, 1948
Visual Editions (Standard)

5,6	8.00	24.00	48.00

REG'LAR FELLERS HEROIC (See Heroic Comics)

REGULATORS
June, 1995 - No. 3, Aug, 1995 ($2.50)
Image Comics

1-3: Kurt Busiek scripts		1.00	2.50

REID FLEMING, WORLD'S TOUGHEST MILKMAN
8/86; V2#1, 12/86 - V2#3, 12/88; V2#4, 11/89; V2#5, 11/90 (B&W)
Eclipse Comics

1 (3rd print, large size, 8/86, $2.50)		1.20	3.00
1-4th & 5th printings ($2.50)		1.00	2.50
V2#1 (10/86, regular size, $2.00)		.80	2.00
1-2nd print, 3rd print ($2.00, 2/89)		.80	2.00
2-4 , V2#2-2nd & 3rd printings, V2#4-2nd printing, V2#5 ($2.00)			
		.80	2.00

RELUCTANT DRAGON, THE (Walt Disney's...)
No. 13, 1940
Dell Publishing Co.

Four Color 13-Contains 2 pgs. of photos from film; 2 pg. foreword to Fantasia by			
Leopold Stokowski; Donald Duck, Goofy, Baby Weems & Mickey Mouse (as			
the Sorcerer's Apprentice) app.	160.00	480.00	1600.00

REMEMBER PEARL HARBOR
1942 (68 pgs.) (Illustrated story of the battle)
Street & Smith Publications

nn-Uncle Sam-c; Jack Binder-a	40.00	120.00	290.00

REN & STIMPY SHOW, THE (TV) (Nicklodeon cartoon characters)
Dec, 1992 - No. 44, July, 1996 ($1.75/$1.95)
Marvel Comics

1-($2.25)-Polybagged w/scratch & sniff Ren or Stimpy air fowler (equal			
amounts of each were made)	1.00	2.00	5.00
1-2nd printing; different dialogue on-c		.80	2.00
1-3rd printing; yet different dialogue on-c		.80	2.00
2,3		.80	2.00
4-6: 4-Muddy Mudskipper back-up. 5-Bill Wray painted-c. 6-Spider-Man vs.			
Powered Toast Man		1.20	3.00
7-17: 12-1st solo back-up story w/Tank & Brenner		.70	1.75
18-44: 18-Begin $1.95-c; Powered Toast Man app.			
		.80	2.00
25($2.95) Deluxe edition w/die cut cover		1.20	3.00
...Don't Try This at Home (3/94, $12.95, TPB)-r/#9-121.85		5.50	13.00
...Eenteractive Special ('95, $2.95)		1.20	3.00
...Holiday Special 1994 (2/95, $2.95, 52 pgs.)		1.20	3.00
...Pick of the Litter nn (1993, $12.95, TPB)-r/#1-4	1.85	5.50	13.00
...Running Joke nn (1993, $12.95, TPB)-r/#1-4 plus new-a			
	1.85	5.50	13.00
...Seeek Little Monkeys (1/95, $12.95)-r/#17-20	1.85	5.50	13.00
...Special: Around the World in a Daze ($2.95)			3.00
...Special: Four Swerks (1/95, $2.95, 52 pgs.)-FF #1 cover swipe; cover reads			
"Four Swerks w/5 pg. coloring book."		1.20	3.00
...Special: Powered Toast Man 1 (4/94, $2.95, 52 pgs.)		1.20	3.00

Renfield #3 © Caliber

Replacement God #4 © Amaze ink

Return To Jurassic Park #9 © Universal City Studios /Amblin Entertainment

	GD25	FN65	NM94

..Special: Powdered Toast Man's Cereal Serial (4/95, $2.95)

		1.20	3.00
..Special: Sports (10/95, $2.95)		1.20	3.00
..Tastes Like Chicken nn (11/93,$12.95,TPB)-r/5-8	1.85	5.50	13.00
Special 2 (7/94, $2.95, 52 pgs.)		1.20	3.00
Special 3 (10/94, $2.95, 52 pgs.)-Choose adventure		1.20	3.00
..Your Pals (1994, $12.95, TPB)-r/13-16	1.90	5.60	13.00

RENFIELD
1994 - No. 3, 1995 ($2.95, B&W, limited series)
Caliber Press

1-3		1.20	3.00

RENO BROWNE, HOLLYWOOD'S GREATEST COWGIRL (Formerly
Margie Comics; Apache Kid #53 on; also see Western Hearts, Western Life
Romances & Western Love)
No. 50, April, 1950 - No. 52, Sept, 1950 (52 pgs.)
Marvel Comics (MPC)

50-Reno Browne photo-c on all	27.00	81.00	190.00
51,52	24.00	73.00	170.00

REPLACEMENT GOD
June, 1995 - Present ($2.95, B&W)
Amaze Ink

1-5		1.20	3.00

REPTILICUS (Becomes Reptisaurus #3 on)
Aug, 1961 - No. 2, Oct, 1961
Charlton Comics

1 (Movie)	12.00	36.00	85.00
2	8.00	23.50	55.00

REPTISAURUS (Reptilicus #1,2)
V2#3, Jan, 1962 - No. 8, Dec, 1962; Summer, 1963
Charlton Comics

V2#3-8: 8-Montes/Bache-c/a	5.00	15.00	35.00
Special Edition 1 (Summer, 1963)	4.30	13.00	30.00

REQUIEM FOR DRACULA
Feb, 1993 ($2.00, 52 pgs.)
Marvel Comics

nn-r/Tomb of Dracula #69,70 by Gene Colan		.80	2.00

RESCUERS, THE (See Walt Disney Showcase #40)

RESTAURANT AT THE END OF THE UNIVERSE, THE (See Hitchhiker's
Guide to the Galaxy & Life, the Universe & Everything)
1994 - No. 3, 1994 ($6.95, limited series)
DC Comics

1-3		1.20	3.00	7.00

RESTLESS GUN (TV)
No. 934, Sept, 1958 - No. 1146, Nov-Jan, 1960-61
Dell Publishing Co.

Four Color 934 (#1)-Photo-c	11.00	33.00	110.00
Four Color 986 (5/59), 1045 (11-1/60), 1089 (3/60), 1146-Wildey-a; all photo-c			
	8.00	24.00	80.00

RETIEF (Keith Laumer's)
Dec, 1989 - No.2?, Jan, 1990 ($2.25, B&W)
Adventure Comics (Malibu)

1,2: 2-exist?			2.25
..and The Warlords #1 (1/91)			2.50
..: Diplomatic Immunity #1 (4/91)			2.50
..: Giant Killer #1 (9/91)			2.50
..: Crime & Punishment #1 (11/91)			2.50

RETURN FROM WITCH MOUNTAIN (See Walt Disney Showcase #44)

RETURN OF GORGO, THE (Formerly Gorgo's Revenge)

	GD25	FN65	NM94

No. 2, Aug, 1963; No. 3, Fall, 1964 (12¢)
Charlton Comics

2,3-Ditko-c/a; based on M.G.M. movie	7.00	21.50	50.00

RETURN OF KONGA, THE (Konga's Revenge #2 on)
1962
Charlton Comics

nn	7.00	21.50	50.00

RETURN OF MEGATON MAN
July, 1988 - No. 3, 1988 ($2.00, limited series)
Kitchen Sink Press

1-3: Simpson-c/a		.80	2.00

RETURN OF THE OUTLAW
Feb, 1953 - No. 11, 1955
Toby Press (Minoan)

1-Billy the Kid	8.35	25.00	50.00
2	5.00	15.00	30.00
3-11	4.00	12.00	24.00

RETURN TO JURASSIC PARK
Apr, 1995 - No. 9, Feb, 1996 ($2.50/$2.95)
Topps Comics

1,2		1.00	2.50
3-9: 3-Begin $2.95-c. 9-Artist's Jam issue		1.20	3.00

REVEALING LOVE STORIES (See Fox Giants)

REVEALING ROMANCES
Sept, 1949 - No. 6, Aug, 1950
Ace Magazines

1	7.50	22.50	45.00
2	4.15	12.50	25.00
3-6	4.00	10.00	20.00

REVENGE OF THE PROWLER (Also see The Prowler)
Feb, 1988 - No. 4, June, 1988 ($1.75/$1.95)
Eclipse Comics

1,3,4: 1-$1.75. 3,4-$1.95-c; Snyder III-a(p)		.80	2.00
2 ($2.50)-Contains flexi-disc		1.00	2.50

REVENGERS FEATURING MEGALITH
Sept, 1985; 1987 - No. 5, 1988 ($2.00, Baxter paper)
Continuity Comics

1 (1985)-Origin; Neal Adams-c/a, scripts		.80	2.00
1 (1987, newsstand)- 5		.80	2.00

REX ALLEN COMICS (Movie star)(Also see Four Color #877 & Western
Roundup under Dell Giants)
No. 316, Feb, 1951 - No. 31, Dec-Feb, 1958-59 (All-photo-c)
Dell Publishing Co.

Four Color 316(#1)(52 pgs.)-Rex Allen & his horse Koko begin; Marsh-a			
	16.00	48.00	160.00
2 (9-11/51, 36 pgs.)	9.50	28.50	95.00
3-10	7.00	21.00	70.00
11-20	5.00	15.00	50.00
21-23,25-31	4.70	14.00	47.00
24-Toth-a	5.50	16.50	55.00

NOTE: **Manning** a-20, 27-30. Photo back-c F.C. #316, 2-12, 20, 21.

REX DEXTER OF MARS (See Mystery Men Comics)
Fall, 1940 (68 pgs.)
Fox Features Syndicate

1-Rex Dexter, Patty O'Day, & Zanzibar (Tuska-a) app.; Briefer-c/a			
	168.00	206.00	1350.00

REX HART (Formerly Blaze Carson; Whip Wilson #9 on)
No. 6, Aug, 1949 - No. 8, Feb, 1950 (All photo-c)

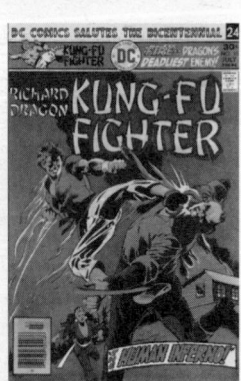

Richard Dragon, Kung-Fu Master #10 © DC

Ribtickler #8 © FOX

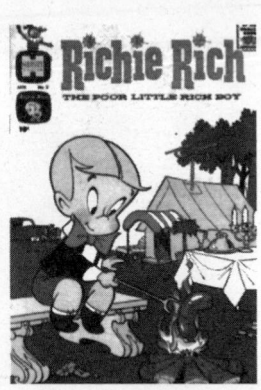

Richie Rich #2 © HARV

	GD25	FN65	NM94

Timely/Marvel Comics (USA)

6-Rex Hart & his horse Warrior begin; Black Rider app; Captain Tootsie by Beck	25.00	75.00	175.00
7,8: 18 pg. Thriller in each. 8-Blaze the Wonder Collie app. in text	17.00	51.00	120.00

REX MORGAN, M.D. (Also see Harvey Comics Library)
Dec, 1955 - No. 3, Apr?, 1956
Argo Publ.

1-r/Rex Morgan daily newspaper strips & daily panel-r of "These Women" by D'Alessio & "Timeout" by Jeff Keate	10.00	30.00	70.00
2,3	8.00	24.00	48.00

REX THE WONDER DOG (See The Adventures of...)

RHUBARB, THE MILLIONAIRE CAT
No. 423, Sept-Oct, 1952 - No. 563, June, 1954
Dell Publishing Co.

Four Color 423 (#1)	5.00	15.00	50.00
Four Color 466(5/53),563	4.00	12.00	40.00

RIBIT!
Jan, 1989 - No. 4, April?, 1989 ($1.95, limited series)
Comico

1-4: Frank Thorne story & art		.80	2.00

RIBTICKLER (Also see Fox Giants)
1945 - No. 9, Aug, 1947; 1957; 1959
Fox Feature Synd./Green Publ. (1957)/Norlen (1959)

1-Funny animal	11.50	34.00	80.00
2-(1946)	6.70	20.00	40.00
3-9: 3,7-Cosmo Cat app.	5.00	15.00	30.00
3,7,8 (Green Publ.-1957)	3.20	8.00	16.00
3,7,8 (Norlen Mag.-1959)	3.20	8.00	16.00

RICHARD DRAGON, KUNG-FU FIGHTER (See Brave & the Bold)
Apr-May, 1975 - No. 18, Nov-Dec, 1977
National Periodical Publications/DC Comics

1,2: 1-Adaptation of novel begins, ends #4. 2-Starlin/Weiss-a	1.20	3.00
3-18: 3-Kirby-a(p). 4-8-Wood inks		1.00

RICHARD THE LION-HEARTED (See Ideal a Classical Comic)

RICHIE RICH (See Harvey Collectors Comics, Harvey Hits, Little Dot, Little Lotta, Little Sad Sack, Million Dollar Digest, Mutt & Jeff, Super Richie, and 3-D Dolly)

RICHIE RICH (...the Poor Little Rich Boy) (See Harvey Hits #3, 9)
Nov, 1960 - #218, Oct, 1982; #219, Oct, 1986 - #254, Jan, 1991
Harvey Publications

1-(See Little Dot for 1st app.)	130.00	390.00	1300.00
2	50.00	150.00	450.00
3-5	28.00	86.00	260.00
6-10: 8-Christmas-c	17.00	53.00	160.00
11-20	10.00	30.00	90.00
21-30	8.80	26.60	80.00
31-40	6.60	20.00	60.00
41-50	4.00	12.00	40.00
51-60: 56-1st app. Super Richie. 59-Buck, prototype of Dollar the Dog	3.90	11.50	30.00
61-80: 65-1st app. Dollar the Dog. 71-Nixon & Robert Kennedy caricatures	2.30	6.70	16.00
81-99	1.65	4.20	10.00
100(12/70)-1st app. Irona the robot maid	2.15	6.50	15.00
101-111,117-120	1.20	3.00	7.00
112-116: All 52 pg. Giants	1.30	3.25	8.00
121-140: 137-1st app. Mr. Cheepers	1.00	2.00	5.00
141-160: 145-Infinity-c. 155-3rd app. The Money Monster	1.30	3.25
161-180		.85	2.10

	GD25	FN65	NM94

181-254: 210-Stone-Age Riches app. 237-Last original material		.65	1.6

RICHIE RICH
Mar, 1991 - No. 28, Nov, 1994 ($1.00, bi-monthly)
Harvey Comics

1-28: Reprints best of Richie Rich			1.0
Giant Size 1 (10/91, $2.25, 68 pgs.)		.90	2.2
Giant Size 2 (1991, $2.25, 68 pgs.)		.90	2.2
Giant Size 3 (1992, $2.25)			2.2
Giant Size 4 (10/93, $2.25)			2.2

RICHIE RICH ADVENTURE DIGEST MAGAZINE
1992 ($1.25, quarterly, digest-size)
Harvey Comics

1			1.2

RICHIE RICH AND...
Oct, 1987 - No. 11, May, 1990 ($1.00)
Harvey Comics

1-11: 1-Professore Keenbean. 2-Casper. 3-Dollar the Dog. 4-Cadbury. 5-Mayda Munny. 6-Irona. 7-Little Dot. 8-Professor Keenbean. 9-Little Audrey. 10-Mayda Munny. 11-Cadbury.			1.0

RICHIE RICH AND BILLY BELLHOPS
Oct, 1977 (52 pgs., one-shot)
Harvey Publications

1		1.20	3.0

RICHIE RICH AND CADBURY
10/77; #2, 9/78 - #23, 7/82; #24, 7/90 - #29, 1/91 (1-10: 52pgs.)
Harvey Publications

1	1.00	2.00	5.0
2-5		1.00	2.5
6-29: 24-Begin $1.00-c			1.0

RICHIE RICH AND CASPER
Aug, 1974 - No. 45, Sept, 1982
Harvey Comics

1	1.65	4.20	10.0
2-5	1.00	2.00	5.0
6-10: 10-Xmas-c		1.00	2.5
11-20		.70	1.7
21-40: 22-Xmas-c			1.5
41-45			1.0

RICHIE RICH AND DOLLAR THE DOG (See Richie Rich #65)
Sept, 1977 - No. 24, Aug, 1982 (#1-10: 52 pgs.)
Harvey Publications

1		1.60	4.0
2-10		.80	2.0
11-24			1.0

RICHIE RICH AND DOT
Oct, 1974 (one-shot)
Harvey Publications

1	1.00	2.60	6.0

RICHIE RICH AND GLORIA
Sept, 1977 - No. 25, Sept, 1982 (#1-11: 52 pgs.)
Harvey Publications

1		1.60	4.0
2-5		.80	2.0
6-25			1.0

RICHIE RICH AND HIS GIRLFRIENDS
April, 1979 - No. 16, Dec, 1982
Harvey Publications

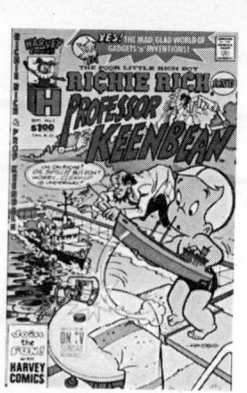
Richie rich & Professor Keenbeam #1 © HARV

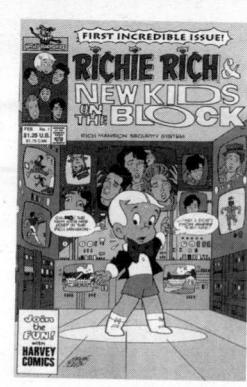
Richie Rich & The New kids On The Block #1 © HARV

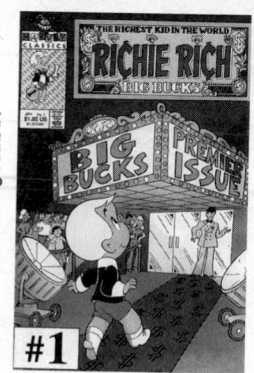
Richie Rich Big Bucks #1

	GD25	FN65	NM94
1-(52 pg. Giant)		1.20	3.00
2-(52 pg. Giant)		1.00	2.40
3-10		.80	2.00
11-16			1.00

RICHIE RICH AND HIS MEAN COUSIN REGGIE
April, 1979 - No. 3, 1980 (50¢) (#1,2: 52 pgs.)
Harvey Publications

	GD25	FN65	NM94
1		1.80	2.00
2-3:			1.50

NOTE: No. 4 was advertised, but never released.

RICHIE RICH AND JACKIE JOKERS (Also see Jackie Jokers)
Nov, 1973 - No. 48, Dec, 1982
Harvey Publications

	GD25	FN65	NM94
1: 52 pg. Giant; contains material from unpublished Jackie Jokers #5	3.25	9.50	22.00
2,3-(52 pg. Giants). 2-R.R. & Jackie 1st meet	1.70	5.00	12.00
4,5	1.00	2.50	6.00
6-10		1.60	4.00
11-20: 11-1st app. Kool Katz		1.20	3.00
21-40: 26-Star Wars parody			1.50
41-48			1.00

RICHIE RICH AND PROFESSOR KEENBEAN
Sept, 1990 - No. 2, Nov, 1990 ($1.00)
Harvey Comics

	GD25	FN65	NM94
1,2			1.00

RICHIE RICH AND THE NEW KIDS ON THE BLOCK
Feb, 1991 - No. 3, June, 1991 ($1.25)
Harvey Publications

	GD25	FN65	NM94
1-3			1.30

RICHIE RICH AND TIMMY TIME
Sept, 1977 (50¢, 52 pgs, one-shot)
Harvey Publications

	GD25	FN65	NM94
1		1.20	3.00

RICHIE RICH BANK BOOKS
Oct, 1972 - No. 59, Sept, 1982
Harvey Publications

	GD25	FN65	NM94
1	3.75	11.25	26.00
2-5: 2-2nd app. The Money Monster	2.15	6.50	15.00
6-10	1.30	3.25	8.00
11-20: 18-Super Richie app.	1.00	2.60	6.00
21-30		1.40	3.50
31-40		.80	2.00
41-59			1.00

RICHIE RICH BEST OF THE YEARS
Oct, 1977 - No. 6, June, 1980 (128 pgs., digest-size)
Harvey Publications

	GD25	FN65	NM94
1(10/77)-Reprints, #2(10/78)-Reprints, #3(6/79, 75¢)		.80	2.00
4-6(11/79-6/80, 95¢)			1.00

RICHIE RICH BIG BUCKS
Apr, 1991 - No. 8, July, 1992 ($1.00, bi-monthly)
Harvey Publications

	GD25	FN65	NM94
1-8			1.00

RICHIE RICH BILLIONS
Oct, 1974 - No. 48, Oct, 1982 (#1-33: 52 pgs.)
Harvey Publications

	GD25	FN65	NM94
1	2.30	6.70	16.00
2-5	1.30	3.25	8.00
6-10	1.00	2.60	6.00

	GD25	FN65	NM94
11-20		1.40	3.50
21-33		.80	2.00
34-48: 35-Onion app.			1.00

RICHIE RICH CASH
Sept, 1974 - No. 47, Aug, 1982
Harvey Publications

	GD25	FN65	NM94
1-1st app. Dr. N-R-Gee	2.60	7.50	18.00
2-5	1.50	3.75	9.00
6-10	1.00	2.60	6.00
11-20		1.40	3.50
21-30		.80	2.00
31-47: 33-Dr. Blemish app.			1.00

RICHIE RICH CASH MONEY
May, 1992 - No. 2, Aug, 1992 ($1.25)
Harvey Comics

	GD25	FN65	NM94
1,2			1.25

RICHIE RICH, CASPER & WENDY NATIONAL LEAGUE
June, 1976 (52 pgs.)
Harvey Publications

	GD25	FN65	NM94
1 (Released-3/76 with 6/76 date)		1.20	3.00
1 (6/76)-2nd version w/San Francisco Giants & KTVU 2 logos; has "Compliments of Giants and Straw Hat Pizza" on-c		1.20	3.00

RICHIE RICH COLLECTORS COMICS (See Harvey Collectors Comics)

RICHIE RICH DIAMONDS
Aug, 1972 - No. 59, Aug, 1982 (#1, 23-45: 52 pgs.)
Harvey Publications

	GD25	FN65	NM94
1-(52 pg. Giant)	3.75	11.25	30.00
2-5	2.00	6.00	14.00
6-10	1.30	3.25	8.00
11-22	1.00	2.60	6.00
23-30		1.40	3.50
31-45: 39-Origin Little Dot			1.50
46-50			1.20
51-59			1.00

RICHIE RICH DIGEST
Oct, 1986 - No. 42, Oct, 1994 ($1.25/$1.75, digest-size)
Harvey Publications

	GD25	FN65	NM94
1-42		.70	1.75

RICHIE RICH DIGEST STORIES (...Magazine #?-on)
Oct, 1977 - No., 17, Oct, 1982 (75¢/95¢, digest-size)
Harvey Publications

	GD25	FN65	NM94
1-Reprints		.80	2.00
2-17: Reprints			1.00

RICHIE RICH DIGEST WINNERS
Dec, 1977 - No. 16, Sept, 1982 (75¢/95¢, 132 pgs., digest-size)
Harvey Publications

	GD25	FN65	NM94
1		.80	2.00
2-16			1.00

RICHIE RICH DOLLARS & CENTS
Aug, 1963 - No. 109, Aug, 1982 (#1-43: 68 pgs.; 44-60, 71-94: 52 pgs.)
Harvey Publications

	GD25	FN65	NM94
1: (#1-64 are all reprint issues)	14.00	43.00	140.00
2	6.50	19.50	65.00
3-5: 5-r/1st app. of R.R. from Little Dot #1	4.00	12.00	40.00
6-10	3.75	11.25	26.00
11-20	3.25	9.50	22.00
21-30: 25-1st app. Nurse Jenny	1.70	5.00	12.00
31-43: 43-Last 68 pg. issue	1.30	3.25	8.00
44-60: All 52 pgs.	1.00	2.00	5.00

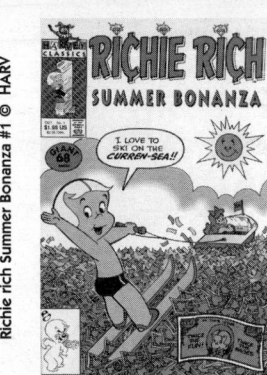

Richie rich Dollars & Cents #1 © HARV

Richie Rich Millions #1 © HARV

Richie rich Summer Bonanza #1 © HARV

	GD25	FN65	NM94
61-71		1.00	2.50
72-94: All 52 pgs.			1.50
95-109: 100-Anniversary issue			1.00

RICHIE RICH FORTUNES
Sept, 1971 - No. 63, July, 1982 (#1-15: 52 pgs.)
Harvey Publications

	GD25	FN65	NM94
1	4.00	12.00	30.00
2-5	2.00	6.00	14.00
6-10	1.30	3.25	8.00
11-15: 11-1st app. The Onion	1.00	2.60	6.00
16-30		1.40	3.50
31-40			1.50
41-63: 62-Onion app.			1.00

RICHIE RICH GEMS
Sept, 1974 - No. 43, Sept, 1982
Harvey Publications

	GD25	FN65	NM94
1	2.30	6.70	16.00
2-5	1.20	3.00	7.00
6-10		1.60	4.00
11-20		1.00	2.50
21-30			1.50
31-43: 36-Dr. Blemish, Onion app. 38-1st app. Stone-Age Riches			1.00

RICHIE RICH GOLD AND SILVER
Sept, 1975 - No. 42, Oct, 1982 (#1-27: 52 pgs.)
Harvey Publications

	GD25	FN65	NM94
1	1.65	4.00	10.00
2-5	1.00	2.00	5.00
6-10		.80	2.00
11-27			1.50
28-42: 34-Stone-Age Riches app.			1.00

RICHIE RICH GOLD NUGGETS DIGEST
Feb., 1991 - No.5, June, 1991 ($1.75, digest-size)
Harvey Publications

	GD25	FN65	NM94
1-5		.70	1.75

RICHIE RICH HOLIDAY DIGEST MAGAZINE (…Digest #4)
Jan, 1980 - #3, Jan, 1982; #4, 3/88; #5, 2/89 (Published annually)
Harvey Publications

	GD25	FN65	NM94
1-3: All X-Mas-c			1.00
4-(3/88, $1.25), 5-(2/89, $1.75)			1.25

RICHIE RICH INVENTIONS
Oct, 1977 - No. 26, Oct, 1982 (#1-11: 52 pgs.)
Harvey Publications

	GD25	FN65	NM94
1	1.00	2.00	5.00
2-5		1.00	2.50
6-11			1.50
12-26			1.00

RICHIE RICH JACKPOTS
Oct, 1972 - No. 58, Aug, 1982 (#41-43: 52 pgs.)
Harvey Publications

	GD25	FN65	NM94
1	4.00	12.00	30.00
2-5	2.30	6.75	16.00
6-10	1.65	4.20	10.00
11-20: 16-Super Richie app.	1.00	2.60	6.00
21-30		1.40	3.50
31-40,44-50: 37-Caricatures of Frank Sinatra, Dean Martin, Sammy Davis, Jr. 45-Dr. Blemish app.		.80	2.00
41-43 (52 pgs.)		1.20	3.00
51-58			1.50

RICHIE RICH MILLION DOLLAR DIGEST (…Magazine #?-on)(See Million Dollar Digest)

Oct, 1980 - No. 10, Oct, 1982 ($1.50)
Harvey Publications

	GD25	FN65	NM94
1-10			1.50

RICHIE RICH MILLIONS
9/61; #2, 9/62 - #113, 10/82 (#1-48: 68 pgs.; 49-64, 85-97: 52 pgs.)
Harvey Publications

	GD25	FN65	NM94
1: (#1-3 are all reprint issues)	16.00	48.00	165.00
2	9.00	27.00	90.00
3-10: All other giants are new & reprints. 5-1st 15 pg. Richie Rich story	7.00	21.00	70.00
11-20	3.20	10.50	32.00
21-30	2.60	7.50	18.00
31-48: 48-Last 68 pg. Giant	1.70	5.00	12.00
49-64: 52 pg. Giants	1.30	3.25	8.00
65-84: 68-1st Super Richie-c (11/74). 74-1st app. Mr. Woody; Super Richie app		1.60	4.00
85-97: 52 pg. Giants		1.60	4.00
98-100			1.50
101-113			1.00

RICHIE RICH MONEY WORLD
Sept, 1972 - No. 59, Sept, 1982
Harvey Publications

	GD25	FN65	NM94
1-(52 pg. Giant)-1st app. Mayda Munny	3.75	11.25	28.00
2-5: 2-Super Richie app.	1.70	5.00	12.00
6-10: 9,10-Richie Rich mistakenly named Little Lotta on covers	1.00	2.60	6.00
11-20: 16,20-Dr. N-R-Gee		1.40	3.50
21-30		.80	2.00
31-50			1.50
51-59			1.00
Digest 1 (2/91, $1.75) - 8 (12/93, $1.75)		.70	1.75

RICHIE RICH PROFITS
Oct, 1974 - No. 47, Sept, 1982
Harvey Publications

	GD25	FN65	NM94
1	2.60	7.50	18.00
2-5	1.50	3.75	9.00
6-10: 10-Origin of Dr. N-R-Gee	1.00	2.00	5.00
11-20: 15-Christmas-c		1.20	3.00
21-30			1.50
31-47			1.00

RICHIE RICH RELICS
Jan, 1988 - No.4, Feb, 1989 (75¢/$1.00, reprints)
Harvey Comics

	GD25	FN65	NM94
1-4			1.00

RICHIE RICH RICHES
July, 1972 - No. 59, Aug, 1982 (#1, 2, 41-45: 52 pgs.)
Harvey Publications

	GD25	FN65	NM94
1-(52 pg. Giant)-1st app. The Money Monster	4.00	12.00	32.00
2-(52 pg. Giant)	2.30	6.75	16.00
3-5	1.50	3.75	9.00
6-10	1.20	3.00	7.00
11-20: 17-Super Richie app. (3/75)		1.60	4.00
21-40		.80	2.00
41-45: 52 pg. Giants		1.20	3.00
46-59: 56-Dr. Blemish app.			1.00

RICHIE RICH SUCCESS STORIES
Nov, 1964 - No. 105, Sept, 1982 (#1-38: 68 pgs., 39-55, 67-90: 52 pgs.)
Harvey Publications

	GD25	FN65	NM94
1	14.00	43.00	140.00
2-5	7.00	21.00	70.00

The Rifleman #2 © DELL

Rima, The Jungle Girl #6 © DC

Ringo Kid Western #2 © MEG

	GD25	FN65	NM94
-10	3.50	10.50	35.00
-30: 27-1st Penny Van Dough (8/69)	2.60	7.50	18.00
-38: 38-Last 68 pg. Giant	1.70	5.00	12.00
-55-(52 pgs.): 44-Super Richie app.	1.65	4.20	10.00
-66	1.00	2.60	6.00
-90: 52 pgs. (Majority of early issues are reprints)	1.20		3.00
-105: 91-Onion app. 101-Dr. Blemish app.			1.50

:HIE RICH SUMMER BONANZA
, 1991 ($1.95, one-shot, 68 pgs.)
vey Comics

Richie Rich, Little Dot, Little Lotta		.80	2.00

:HIE RICH TREASURE CHEST DIGEST (…Magazine #3)
, 1982 - No. 3, Aug, 1982 (95¢, Digest Mag.)(#4 advertised but not publ.)
y Publications

3			1.50

:HIE RICH VACATION DIGEST
, 1991 ($1.75, digest-size)
vey Comics

			1.75

:HIE RICH VACATION DIGEST
, 1992 ($1.75, digest size)
vey Comics

		.70	1.75

:HIE RICH VACATION DIGEST
, 1993 ($1.75, digest-size)
vey Comics

			1.75

:HIE RICH VACATIONS DIGEST
77; No. 2, 10/78 - No. 7, 10/81; No. 8, 8/82; No. 9, 10/82 (Digest, 132 pgs.)
vey Publications

Reprints		.80	2.00
3			1.50

HIE RICH VAULT OF MYSTERY
, 1974 - No. 47, Sept, 1982
y Publications

	2.00	6.00	14.00
0	1.20	3.00	7.00
-20		1.60	4.00
-30		.80	2.00
-47			1.00

HIE RICH ZILLIONZ
, 1976 - No. 33, Sept, 1982 (#1-4: 68 pgs.; #5-18: 52 pgs.)
vey Publications

	1.70	5.00	12.00
4: 4-Last 68 pg. Giant	1.00	2.60	6.00
0		1.20	3.00
-18: 18-Last 52 pg. Giant			1.50
33			1.00

K GEARY'S WONDERS AND ODDITIES
, 1988 ($2.00, B&W, one-shot)
k Horse Comics

		.80	2.00

KY
5, Sept, 1953
dard Comics (Visual Editions)

Teenage humor	4.00	12.00	24.00

KY NELSON (TV)(See Sweethearts V2#42)

	GD25	FN65	NM94

No. 956, Dec, 1958 - No. 1192, June, 1961 (All photo-c)
Dell Publishing Co.

Four Color 956,998	20.00	60.00	200.00
Four Color 1115	15.00	45.00	150.00
Four Color 1192-Manning-a	15.00	45.00	150.00

RIDER, THE (Frontier Trail #6; also see Blazing Sixguns I.W. Reprint #10, 11)
Mar, 1957 - No. 5, 1958
Ajax/Farrell Publ. (Four Star Comic Corp.)

1-Swift Arrow, Lone Rider begin	10.00	30.00	60.00
2-5	5.85	17.50	35.00

RIDERS OF THE PURPLE SAGE (See Zane Grey & Four Color #372)

RIFLEMAN, THE (TV)
No. 1009, 7-9/59 - No. 12, 7-9/62; No. 13, 11/62 - No. 20, 10/64
Dell Publ. Co./Gold Key No. 13 on

Four Color 1009 (#1)	22.00	66.00	220.00
2 (1-3/60)	11.00	33.00	110.00
3-Toth-a (4 pgs.)	13.00	38.00	130.00
4,5,7-10	10.00	30.00	100.00
6-Toth-a (4 pgs.)	10.00	30.00	100.00
11-20	7.50	22.00	75.00

NOTE: *Warren Tufts* a-2-9. All have Chuck Connors photo-c. Photo back c-13-15.

RIMA, THE JUNGLE GIRL
Apr-May, 1974 - No. 7, Apr-May, 1975
National Periodical Publications

1-Origin, part 1 (#1-5: 20¢; 6,7: 25¢)	1.00	2.00	5.00
2-4-Origin, parts 2-4		1.20	3.00
5-6		1.20	3.00
7-Origin & only app. Space Marshal	1.00	2.00	5.00

NOTE: *Kubert* c-1-7. *Nino* a-1-7. *Redondo* a-1-7.

RING OF BRIGHT WATER (See Movie Classics)

RING OF THE NIBELUNG, THE
1989 - No. 4, 1990 ($4.95, squarebound, 52 pgs., mature readers)
DC Comics

1-4: Adapts novel, Gil Kane-c/a	1.00	2.00	5.00

RINGO KID, THE (2nd Series)
Jan, 1970 - No. 23, Nov, 1973; No. 24, Nov, 1975 - No. 30, Nov, 1976
Marvel Comics Group

1-Williamson-a r-from #10, 1956.		1.60	4.00
2-30: 2-Severin-c. 13-Wildey-r. 20-Williamson-r/#1		.80	2.00

RINGO KID WESTERN, THE (1st Series) (See Wild Western & Western Trails)
Aug, 1954 - No. 21, Sept, 1957
Atlas Comics (HPC)/Marvel Comics

1-Origin; The Ringo Kid begins	24.00	73.00	170.00
2-Black Rider app.; origin/1st app. Ringo's Horse Arab	12.00	36.00	85.00
3-5	9.15	27.00	55.00
6-8-Severin-a(3) each	10.00	30.00	65.00
9,11,12,14-21: 12-Orlando-a (4 pgs.)	6.70	20.00	40.00
10,13-Williamson-a (4 pgs.)	8.00	24.00	48.00

NOTE: *Berg* a-8. *Maneely* a-1-5, 15, 16(text illos only), 17(4), 18, 20, 21; c-1-6, 8, 13, 15-18, 20.
J. Severin c-10, 11. *Sinnott* a-1. *Wildey* a-16-18.

RIN TIN TIN (See March of Comics #163,180,195)

RIN TIN TIN (TV) (…& Rusty #21 on; see Western Roundup under Dell Giants)
Nov, 1952 - No. 38, May-July, 1961; Nov, 1963 (All Photo-c)
Dell Publishing Co./Gold Key

Four Color 434 (#1)	15.00	45.00	150.00
Four Color 476,523	8.00	24.00	80.00
4(3-5/54)-10	6.00	18.00	60.00
11-20	5.50	16.50	55.00

Rio At Bay #2 © DH

Riot Gear #1 © Triumphant

Riot Gear #1 © Triumphant

Ripclaw #3 © Top Cow Productions

	GD25	FN65	NM94
21-38: 36-Toth-a (4 pgs.)	4.00	12.00	40.00
... & Rusty 1 (11/63-Gold Key)	5.00	15.00	50.00

RIO (Also see Eclipse Monthly)
June, 1987 ($8.95, 64 pgs.)
Comico

1-Wildey-c/a	1.50	3.75	9.00

RIO AT BAY
July, 1992 - No. 2, Aug, 1992 ($2.95, limited series)
Dark Horse Comics

1,2-Wildey-c/a		1.20	3.00

RIO BRAVO (Movie) (See 4-Color #1018)
June, 1959
Dell Publishing Co.
Four Color #1018-Toth-a; John Wayne, Dean Martin, & Ricky Nelson photo-c.

	20.00	60.00	200.00

RIO CONCHOS (See Movie Comics)

RIOT (Satire)
Apr, 1954 - No. 3, Aug, 1954; No. 4, Feb, 1956 - No. 6, June, 1956
Atlas Comics (ACI No. 1-5/WPI No. 6)

1-Russ Heath-a	23.00	69.00	160.00
2-Li'l Abner satire by Post	18.00	54.00	125.00
3-Last precode (8/54)	16.00	47.00	110.00
4-Infinity-c; Marilyn Monroe "7 Year Itch" movie satire; Mad Rip-off ads	21.00	62.00	145.00
5-Marilyn Monroe, John Wayne parody; part photo-c	21.00	64.00	150.00
6-Lorna of the Jungle satire by Everett; Dennis the Menace satire-c/story; part photo-c	15.00	45.00	105.00

NOTE: **Berg** a-3. **Burgos** c-1, 2. **Colan** a-1. **Everett** a-1, 4, 6. **Heath** a-1. **Maneely** a-1, 2, 4-6; c-3, 4, 6. **Post** a-1-4. **Reinman** a-2. **Severin** a-4-6.

RIOT GEAR
Sept, 1993 - No. 11, July, 1994 ($2.50, serially numbered comics)
Triumphant Comics

1-11: 1-2nd app. Riot Gear. 2-1st app. Rabin. 3,4-Triumphant Unleashed x-over. 3-1st app. Surzar. 4-Death of Captain Tich.		1.00	2.50
Violent Past 1,2: 1-(2/94, $2.50)		1.00	2.50

R.I.P.
1990 - No. 8, 1991 ($2.95, 44 pgs.)
TSR, Inc.

1-8-Based on TSR game		1.20	3.00

RIPCLAW (See Cyberforce)
Apr, 1995 - No. 3, June, 1995 (Limited series)
Image Comics (Top Cow Productions)

1/2-Gold	2.15	6.50	15.00
1/2-San Diego ed.	1.70	5.00	12.00
1/2-Chicago ed.	1.70	5.00	12.00
1-3: Brandon Peterson-a(p)		1.00	2.50

RIPCLAW
V2#1, Dec, 1995 - Present ($2.50)
Image Comics (Top Cow Productions)

V2#1-6: 5-Medieval Spawn/Witchblade Preview		1.00	2.50
Special (10/95, $2.50)		1.00	2.50

RIPCORD (TV)
Mar-May, 1962
Dell Publishing Co.

Four Color 1294	7.00	21.00	70.00

RIPFIRE
No. 0, Apr, 1995 ($2.50, one-shot)

Malibu Comics (Ultraverse)

0		1.00	2

RIP HUNTER TIME MASTER (See Showcase #20, 21, 25, 26 & Time Master)
Mar-Apr, 1961 - No. 29, Nov-Dec, 1965
National Periodical Publications

1-(3-4/61)	56.00	170.00	450
2	30.00	90.00	210
3-5: 5-Last 10¢ issue	17.00	51.00	120
6,7-Toth-a in each	13.50	41.00	95
8-15	10.00	30.00	70
16-20	8.50	26.00	60
21-29: 29-Gil Kane-c	7.00	21.50	50

RIP IN TIME (Also see Teenage Mutant Ninja Turtles #5-7)
Aug, 1986 - No.5, 1987 ($1.50, B&W)
Fantagor Press

1-5: Corben-c/a in all			

RIP KIRBY (Also see Harvey Comics Hits #57, & Street Comix)
1948 David McKay Publications

Feature Books 51,54: Raymond-c; 51-Origin	32.00	96.00	225

RIPLEY'S BELIEVE IT OR NOT! (See Ace Comics, All-American Comics, Mystery Comics Digest #1, 4, 7, 10, 13, 16, 19, 22, 25)

RIPLEY'S BELIEVE IT OR NOT!
Sept, 1953 - No. 4, March, 1954
Harvey Publications

1-Powell-a	10.00	30.00	70
2-4	7.50	22.50	45
J. C. Penney giveaway (1948)	7.50	22.50	4

RIPLEY'S BELIEVE IT OR NOT! (Formerly ...True War Stories)
No. 4, April, 1967 - No. 94, Feb, 1980
Gold Key

4-Photo-c; McWilliams-a	4.00	11.00	2
5-Subtitled "True War Stories"; Evans-a; 1st Jeff Jones-a in comics? (2 pgs	2.80	7.00	1
6-10: 6-McWilliams-a. 10-Evans-a(2)	2.80	7.00	1
11-20: 15-Evans-a	1.80	4.50	1
21-30	1.20	2.90	
31-38,40-60		1.60	
39-Crandall-a	1.00	2.00	
61-94: 74,77-83-(52 pgs.)		1.20	
Story Digest Mag. 1(6/70)-4-3/4x6-1/2"	1.20	3.00	

NOTE: **Evanish** art by **Luiz Dominguez** #22-25, 27, 30, 31, 40. **Jeff Jones** a-5(2 pgs.). **McWilliams** a-65, 66, 70, 89. **Orlando** a-8. **Sparling** c-68. Reprints-74, 77-84, 87 (part); 91 (all). **Williamson, Wood** a-80r/#1.

RIPLEY'S BELIEVE IT OR NOT! TRUE GHOST STORIES (Becomes ...True War Stories) (See Dan Curtis)
June, 1965 - No. 2, Oct, 1966
Gold Key

1-Williamson, Wood & Evans-a; photo-c	4.00	12.00	30
2-Orlando, McWilliams-a; photo-c	2.85	8.50	20
Mini-Comic 1(1976-3-1/4x6-1/2")			
11186(1977)-Golden Press, ($1.95, 224 pgs.)-All-r		1.20	
11401(3/79)-Golden Press; ($1.00, 96 pgs.)-All-r			

RIPLEY'S BELIEVE IT OR NOT! TRUE WAR STORIES (Formerly ...True Ghost Stories; becomes Ripley's Believe It or Not! #4 on)
Nov, 1966
Gold Key

1(#3)-No Williamson-a	3.25	9.50	2

RIPLEY'S BELIEVE IT OR NOT! TRUE WEIRD

Roachmill #10 © DH

Roarin' Rick's Rare Bit Fiends #20 © Rick Veitch

Robin #37 © DC

	GD25	FN65	NM94

June, 1966 - No. 2, Aug, 1966 (B&W Magazine)
Ripley Enterprises

1,2-Comic stories & text	1.20	3.00	6.00

RIPTIDE
Sep, 1995 - No. 2, Oct, 1995 ($2.50, limited series)
Image Comics

1,2: Rob Liefeld-c		1.00	2.50

RISE OF APOCALYPSE
Oct, 1996 - No. 4, Jan, 1997 ($1.95, limited series)
Marvel Comics

1-4: Adam Pollina-c/a			2.00

RIVERDALE HIGH (Archie's... #7,8)
Aug, 1990 - No. 8, Oct, 1991 ($1.00, bi-monthly)
Archie Comics

1-8			1.00

RIVER FEUD (See Zane Grey & Four Color #484)

RIVETS
No. 518, Nov, 1953
Dell Publishing Co.

Four Color 518	3.00	9.00	30.00

RIVETS (A dog)
Jan, 1956 - No. 3, May, 1956
Argo Publ.

1-Reprints Sunday & daily newspaper strips	4.35	13.00	26.00
2,3	3.60	9.00	18.00

ROACHMILL
Dec, 1986 - No. 6, Oct, 1987 ($1.75, B&W)
Blackthorne Publ.

1-6		.70	1.75

ROACHMILL
May, 1988 - No. 10, Dec, 1990 ($1.75, B&W)
Dark Horse Comics

1-10: 10-Contains trading cards		.70	1.75

ROAD RUNNER (See Beep Beep, the...)

ROADWAYS
May, 1994 ($2.75, B&W, limited series)
Cult Press

		1.10	2.75

ROARIN' RICK'S RARE BIT FIENDS
July, 1994 - Present ($2.95, B&W, mature)
King Hell Press

1-21: Rick Veitch-c/a/scripts in all. 20-(5/96). 21-(8/96)-Reads Subtleman #1
   on cover

		1.20	3.00
RABID EYE: THE DREAM ART OF RICK VEITCH ($14.95, B&W, TPB)-r/#1-8 & the appendix from #12			15.00
POCKET UNIVERSE (6/96, $14.95, B&W, TPB)-Reprints			15.00

ROBERT E. HOWARD'S CONAN THE BARBARIAN
1993 ($2.50, 68 pgs., Baxter paper)
Marvel Comics

nn-r/Savage Tales #2,3 by Smith, c-r/Conan #21 by Smith.	1.00	2.50

ROBIN (See Aurora, Detective Comics #38, New Teen Titans, Robin II, Robin III, Robin 3000, Spangled Comics #65 & Teen Titans)

ROBIN (See Batman #457)
Jan, 1991 - No. 5, May, 1991 ($1.00, limited series)
DC Comics

1-Free poster by N. Adams; Bolland-c on all	1.00	2.00	5.00

	GD25	FN65	NM94

1-2nd & 3rd printings (without poster)			1.50
2		.70	1.75
2-2nd printing			1.00
3-5			1.50
Annual 1,2 (1992-93, $2.50, 68 pgs.): 1-Grant/Wagner scripts; Sam Kieth-c.			
2-Intro Razorsharp; Jim Balent-c(p)		1.00	2.50

ROBIN (See Detective #668)
Nov, 1993 - Present ($1.50/$1.95)
DC Comics

1-($2.95)-Collector's edition w/foil embossed-c; 1st app. Robin's car, The Redbird; Azrael as Batman app.		1.40	3.50
1-Newsstand ed.		.70	1.75
0,2-13,15,16-Regular editions: 3-5-The Spoiler app. 6-The Huntress-c/story cont'd from Showcase '94 #5. 7-Knightquest: The Conclusion w/new Batman (Azrael) vs. Bruce Wayne. 8-KnightsEnd Pt. 5. 9-KnightsEnd Aftermath; Batman-c & app. 10-(9/94)-Zero Hour. 0-(10/94). 11-(11/94)			1.50
14 ($2.50)-Embossed-c; Troika Pt. 4		1.00	2.50
17-40: 17-Begin $1.95-c. 25-Green Arrow-c/app. 26-Batman app. 27-Contagion Pt. 3; Catwoman-c/app; Penguin & Azrael app. 28-Contagion Pt. 11. 29-Penguin app. 31-Wildcat-c/app. 32-Legacy Pt. 3. 33-Legacy Pt. 7		.80	2.00
Annual 3-5: 3-(1994, $2.95)-Elseworlds story. 4-(1995, $2.95)-Year One story. 5-(1996, $2.95)-Legends of the Dead Earth story.		1.20	3.00

ROBIN: A HERO REBORN
1991 ($4.95, squarebound, trade paperback)
DC Comics

nn-r/Batman #455-457 & Robin #1-5; Bolland-c	1.00	2.00	5.00

ROBIN HOOD (See the Advs. of..., Brave and the Bold, Four Color #413, 669, King Classics, Movie Comics & Power Record Comics)
ROBIN HOOD (...& His Merry Men, The Illustrated Story of...) (See Classic Comics #7 & Classics Giveaways, 12/44)
ROBIN HOOD (New Adventures of...)
1952 (Flour giveaways, 5x7-1/4", 36 pgs.)
Walt Disney Productions

"New Adventures of Robin Hood", "Ghosts of Waylea Castle", & "The Miller's Ransom" each	4.25	13.00	26.00

ROBIN HOOD (Adventures of... #7, 8)
No. 52, Nov, 1955 - No. 6, June, 1957
Magazine Enterprises (Sussex Publ. Co.)

52 (#1)-Origin Robin Hood & Sir Gallant of the Round Table	14.00	43.00	100.00
53 (#2), 3-6: 6-Richard Greene photo-c (TV)	10.00	30.00	70.00
I.W. Reprint #1,2,9: 1-r/#3. 2-r/#4. 9-r/#52 (1963)	2.00	6.00	14.00
Super Reprint #10,15: 10-r/#53. 15-r/#5	2.00	6.00	14.00

NOTE: **Bolle** a-in all; c-52. **Powell** a-6.

ROBIN HOOD (Not Disney)
May-July, 1963 (one-shot)
Dell Publishing Co.

1	2.60	7.50	18.00

ROBIN HOOD (Disney)
1973 ($1.50, 8-1/2x11", 52 pgs., cardboard-c)
Western Publishing Co.

96151- "Robin Hood", based on movie, 96152- "The Mystery of Sherwood Forest", 96153- "In King Richard's Service", 96154- "The Wizard's Ring" each....	1.60	4.00

ROBIN HOOD
July, 1991 - No. 3, 1991 ($2.50, limited series)
Eclipse Comics

1-3: Timothy Truman layouts		1.00	2.50

Robin III #6 © DC

Robocop #8 © Orion Pictures

Robocop Vs. Terminator #1 © Orion Pictures/Cinema 84

	GD25	FN65	NM94

ROBIN HOOD AND HIS MERRY MEN (Formerly Danger & Adventure)
No. 28, Apr, 1956 - No. 38, Aug, 1958
Charlton Comics

	GD25	FN65	NM94
28	8.35	25.00	50.00
29-37	6.70	20.00	40.00
38-Ditko-a (5 pgs.); Rocke-c	12.00	36.00	85.00

ROBIN HOOD'S FRONTIER DAYS (…Western Tales, Adventures of… #1)
No date (Circa 1955) 20 pgs., slick-c (Seven issues?)
Shoe Store Giveaway (Robin Hood Stores)

nn	4.25	13.00	28.00
nn-Issues with Crandall-a	8.00	24.00	48.00

ROBIN HOOD TALES (Published by National Periodical #7 on)
Feb, 1956 - No. 6, Nov-Dec, 1956
Quality Comics Group (Comic Magazines)

1-All have Baker/Cuidera-c	27.00	81.00	190.00
2-5-Matt Baker-a	27.00	81.00	190.00
6-Baker-a	19.00	56.00	130.00
Frontier Days giveaway (1956)	7.00	21.00	42.00

ROBIN HOOD TALES (Cont'd from Quality series)(See Brave & the Bold #5)
No. 7, Jan-Feb, 1957 - No. 14, Mar-Apr, 1958
National Periodical Publications

7-All have Andru/Esposito-c	33.00	99.00	230.00
8-14	27.00	81.00	190.00

ROBINSON CRUSOE (See King Classics & Power Record Comics)
Nov-Jan, 1963-64
Dell Publishing Co.

1	1.60	4.00	8.00

ROBIN II (The Joker's Wild)
Oct, 1991 - No. 4, Dec, 1991 ($1.50, mini-series)
DC Comics

1-(Direct sales, $1.50)-With 4 different-c; same hologram on each			1.50
1-(Newsstand, $1.00)-No hologram; 1 version			1.00
1-Collector's set ($10.00)-Contains all 5 versions bagged with hologram trading card inside	1.65	4.00	10.00
2-(Direct sales, $1.50)-With 3 different-c			1.50
2-4-(Newsstand, $1.00)-1 version of each			1.00
2-Collector's set ($8.00)-Contains all 4 versions bagged with hologram trading card inside	1.30	3.25	8.00
3-(Direct sale, $1.50)-With 2 different-c			1.50
3-Collector's set ($6.00)-Contains all 3 versions bagged with hologram trading card inside	1.00	2.50	6.00
4-(Direct sales, $1.50)-Only one version			1.50
4-Collector's set ($4.00)-Contains both versions bagged with Bat-Signal hologram trading card		1.60	4.00
Multi-pack (All four issues w/hologram sticker)		1.60	4.00
Deluxe Complete Set ($30.00)-Contains all 14 versions of #1-4 plus a new hologram trading card; numbered & limited to 25,000; comes with slipcase & 2 acid free backing boards	4.30	13.00	30.00

ROBIN III: CRY OF THE HUNTRESS
Dec, 1992 - No. 6, Mar, 1993 (Limited series)
DC Comics

1-6 ($2.50, collector's ed.)-Polybagged w/movement enhanced-c plus mini-poster of newsstand-c by Zeck		1.00	2.50
1-6 ($1.25, newsstand ed.): All have Zeck-c			1.25

ROBIN 3000
1992 - No. 2, 1992 ($4.95, mini-series, 52 pgs.)
DC Comics (Elseworlds)

1,2-Foil logo; Russell-c/a	1.00	2.00	5.00

ROBOCOP
Oct, 1987 ($2.00, B&W, magazine, one-shot)
Marvel Comics

1-Movie adaptation		.80	2

ROBOCOP (Also see Dark Horse Comics)
Mar, 1990 - No. 23, Jan, 1992 ($1.50)
Marvel Comics

1-Based on movie		1.60	4
2		1.20	3
3-6		.80	2
7-23			1
nn (7/90, $4.95, 52 pgs.)-r/B&W magazine in color; adapts 1st movie		1.00	2.00	5

ROBOCOP: MORTAL COILS
Sept, 1993 - No. 4, Dec, 1993 ($2.50, limited series)
Dark Horse Comics

1-4: 1,2-Cago painted-c		1.00	2

ROBOCOP: PRIME SUSPECT
Oct, 1992 - No. 4, Jan, 1993 ($2.50, limited series)
Dark Horse Comics

1-4: 1,3-Nelson painted-c. 2,4-Bolton painted-c		1.00	2

ROBOCOP: ROULETTE
Dec, 1993 - No. 4, 1994 ($2.50, limited series)
Dark Horse Comics

1-4: 1,3-Nelson painted-c. 2,4-Bolton painted-c		1.00	2

ROBOCOP 2
Aug, 1990 ($2.25, B&W, magazine, 68 pgs.)
Marvel Comics

1-Adapts movie sequel		.90	2

ROBOCOP 2
Aug, 1990; Late Aug, 1990 - #3, Late Sept, 1990 ($1.00, limited series)
Marvel Comics

nn-(8/90, $4.95, 68 pgs., color)-Same contents as B&W magazine		1.00	2.00	5
1: #1-3 reprint no number issue			1.20	5
2,3: 2-Guice-c(i)			

ROBOCOP 3
July, 1993 - No. 3, Nov, 1993 ($2.50, limited series)
Dark Horse Comics

1-3: Nelson painted-c; Nguyen-a(p)		1.00	2

ROBOCOP VERSUS THE TERMINATOR
Sept, 1992 - No. 4, 1992 (Dec.) ($2.50, limited series)
Dark Horse Comics

1-4: Miller scripts & Simonson-c/a in all		1.00	2
1-Platinum Edition			1
NOTE: All contain a different Robocop cardboard cut-out stand-up.

ROBO-HUNTER (Also see Sam Slade…)
Apr, 1984 - No. 6, 1984 ($1.00)
Eagle Comics

1-6-2000 A.D.

R.O.B.O.T. BATTALION 2050
Mar, 1988 ($2.00, B&W, one-shot)
Eclipse Comics

1			.80

ROBOT COMICS
No. 0, June, 1987 ($2.00, B&W, one-shot)
Renegade Press

Robotech: The Macross Saga #10 © Comico

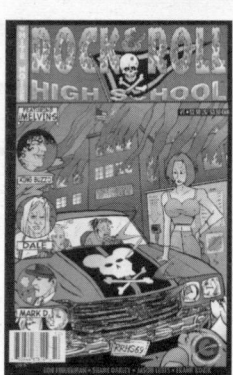
Rock & Roll High School #1 © Roger Corman

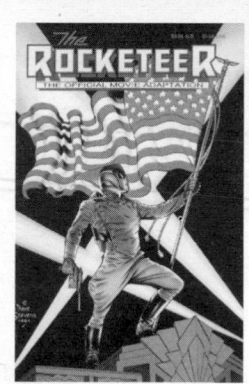
Rocketeer Movie Adaptation © Dave Stevens

	GD25	FN65	NM94
Bob Burden story & art		.80	2.00

ROTECH DEFENDERS
, 1985 - No. 2, Apr, 1985 (Mini-series)
Comics

			1.00

ROTECH IN 3-D (TV)
, 1987 ($2.50)
nico

Steacy painted-c		1.00	2.50

ROTECH MASTERS (TV)
, 1985 - No. 23, Apr, 1988 ($1.50)
nico

		1.00	2.50
3		.80	2.00

ROTECH SPECIAL
, 1988 ($2.50, one-shot, 44 pgs.)
nico

teacy wraparound-c; partial photo-c		1.20	3.00

ROTECH THE GRAPHIC NOVEL
, 1986 ($5.95, 8-1/2x11", 52pgs.)
nico

Origin SDF-1; intro T.R. Edwards, Steacy-c/a; 2nd printing also exists
12/86).

	1.00	2.60	6.00

ROTECH: THE MACROSS SAGA (TV)(Formerly Macross)
2, Feb, 1985 - No. 36, Feb, 1989 ($1.50)
nico

0		1.00	2.50
36: 12,17-Ken Steacy painted-c. 26-Begin $1.75-c. 35,36-($1.95)			
		.80	2.00

ROTECH: THE NEW GENERATION
, 1985 - No. 25, July, 1988
nico

5		.80	2.00

ROTIX
, 1986 (75¢, one-shot)
el Comics

ased on toy			1.00

ROTMEN OF THE LOST PLANET (Also see Space Thrillers)
(Also see Strange Worlds #19)
Periodicals

ccann-a (3 pgs.); Fawcette-a	81.00	243.00	650.00

ROY
(Disney-Movie)
Publishing Co.

Color 544-Manning-a, photo-c	9.00	27.00	90.00

K & ROLL HIGH SCHOOL
, 1995 ($2.50)
er Corman's Cosmic Comics

lob Fingerman scripts		1.00	2.50

K AND ROLLO (Formerly TV Teens)
4, Oct, 1957 - No. 19, Sept, 1958
Iton Comics

4-19	4.00	12.00	24.00

KET COMICS
1940 - No. 3, May, 1940
an Periodicals

	GD25	FN65	NM94
1-Rocket Riley, Red Roberts the Electro Man (origin), The Phantom Ranger, The Steel Shark, The Defender, Buzzard Barnes and his Sky Devils, Lefty Larson, & The Defender, the Man with a Thousand Faces begin (1st app. of each); all have Rocket Riley-c	200.00	600.00	1600.00
2,3	100.00	300.00	800.00

ROCKETEER, THE (See Eclipse Graphic Album Series, Pacific Presents & Starslayer)

ROCKETEER ADVENTURE MAGAZINE, THE
July, 1988 ($2.00); No. 2, July, 1989 ($2.75); No. 3, Jan, 1995 ($2.95)
Comico/Dark Horse Comics No. 3

1-(7/88, $2.00)-Dave Stevens-c/a in all; Kaluta back-up-a; 1st app. Jonas (character based on The Shadow)	1.00	2.00	5.00
2-(6/88, $2.75)-Stevens/Dorman painted-c		1.20	3.00
3-(1/95, $2.95)-Includes pinups by Stevens, Gulacy, Plunkett, & Mignola			
			3.00

ROCKETEER SPECIAL EDITION, THE
Nov, 1984 ($1.50, Baxter paper)(Chapter 5 of Rocketeer serial)
Eclipse Comics

1-Stevens-c/a; Kaluta back-c; pin-ups inside	1.30	3.25	8.00

NOTE: Originally intended to be published in Pacific Presents.

ROCKETEER: THE OFFICIAL MOVIE ADAPTATION, THE
1991
W. D. Publications (Disney)

nn-($5.95, 68 pgs.)-Squarebound deluxe edition	1.00	2.50	6.00
nn-($2.95, 68 pgs.)-Stapled regular edition		1.20	3.00
3-D Comic Book (1991, $7.98, 52 pgs.)	1.30	3.30	8.00

ROCKET KELLY (See The Bouncer, Green Mask #10); becomes Li'l Pan #6)
1944; Fall, 1945 - No. 5, Oct-Nov, 1946
Fox Feature Syndicate

nn (1944)	23.00	69.00	160.00
1	23.00	69.00	160.00
2-The Puppeteer app. (costumed hero)	18.00	54.00	125.00
3-5: 5-(#5 on cover, #4 inside)	17.00	49.00	115.00

ROCKETMAN (Strange Fantasy #2 on) (See Hello Pal & Scoop Comics)
June, 1952 (Strange Stories of the Future)
Ajax/Farrell Publications

1-Rocketman & Cosmo	37.00	111.00	260.00

ROCKET RACCOON
May, 1995 - No. 4, Aug, 1985 (color, limited series)
Marvel Comics

1-4: Mignola-a			1.50

ROCKETS AND RANGE RIDERS
May, 1957 (Giveaway, 16 pgs., soft-c)
Richfield Oil Corp.

nn-Toth-a	17.00	51.00	120.00

ROCKET SHIP X
September, 1951; 1952
Fox Features Syndicate

1	51.00	155.00	415.00
1952 (nn, nd, no publ.)-Edited 1951-a	38.00	114.00	265.00

ROCKET TO ADVENTURE LAND (See Pixie Puzzle...)

ROCKET TO THE MOON
1951
Avon Periodicals

nn-Orlando-c/a; adapts Otis Aldebert Kline's "Maza of the Moon"			
	85.00	256.00	685.00

ROCK FANTASY COMICS
Dec, 1989 - No. 16?, 1991 ($2.25/$3.00, B&W)(No cover price)
Rock Fantasy Comics

Rock N Roll Comics #9 © Revolutionary

Rocko's Modern Life #6 © Nickelodeon

Rocky Horror Picture Show #1 © Caliber

	GD25	FN65	NM94
1-Pink Floyd part 1		1.00	2.50
1-2nd printing ($3.00-c)		1.20	3.00
2,3: 2-Rolling Stones #1. 3-Led Zeppelin #1		1.20	3.00
2,3: 2nd printings ($3.00-c, 1/90 & 2/90)		1.20	3.00
4-Stevie Nicks Not published			
5-Monstrosities of Rock #1; photo back-c		1.00	2.50
5-2nd printing ($3.00, 3/90 indicia, 2/90-c)		1.20	3.00

6-15,17,18: 6-Guns n' Roses #1 (1st & 2nd printings, 3/90)-Begin $3.00-c. 7-Sex Pistols #1. 8-Alice Cooper; not published. 9-Van Halen #1; photo back-c.

| 10-Kiss #1; photo back-c. 11-Jimi Hendrix #1; wraparound-c | | 1.20 | 3.00 |
| 16-($5.00, 68 pgs.)-The Great Gig in the Sky(Floyd) | 1.00 | 2.00 | 5.00 |

ROCK HAPPENING (Harvey Pop Comics:...)(See Bunny)
Sept, 1969 - No. 2, Nov, 1969
Harvey Publications

| 1,2: Featuring Bunny | 2.85 | 8.50 | 20.00 |

ROCK N' ROLL COMICS
June, 1989 - No. 24?, 1992 ($1.50/$1.95, B&W/color #15 on)
Revolutionary Comics

1-Guns N' Roses		.80	2.00
1-2nd thru 6th printings			1.50
1-7th printing (full color w/new-c/a; $1.95)		.80	2.00
2-Metallica		.80	2.00
2-2nd thru 6th printings (6th in color)			1.50
3-Bon Jovi (no reprints)		.80	2.00

4-8,10-24: 4-Motley Crue(2nd printing only, 1st destroyed). 5-Def Leppard (2 printings). 6-Rolling Stones(4 printings). 7-The Who(3 printings). 8-Skid Row; not published. 10-Warrant/Whitesnake(2 printings). 12-3rd printing; rewritten & titled NKOTB Hate Book. 13-Led Zeppelin. 14-Sex Pistols. 15-Poison; 1st color issue. 16-Van Halen. 17-Madonna. 18-Alice Cooper. 19-Public Enemy/2 Live Crew. 20-Queensryche/Tesla. 21-Prince?

22-AC/DC; begin $2.50-c. 23-Living Colour. 24-Anthrax	1.00	2.50
9-Kiss		1.60	4.00
9-2nd & 3rd printings		.80	2.00
NOTE: Most issues were reprinted except #3. Later reprints are in color. #8 was not released.

ROCKO'S MODERN LIFE (TV)
June, 1994 - No. 7, Dec, 1994 ($1.95) (Nickelodeon cartoon)
Marvel Comics

| 1-7 | | .80 | 2.00 |

ROCKY AND HIS FIENDISH FRIENDS (TV)(Bullwinkle)
Oct, 1962 - No. 5, Sept, 1963 (Jay Ward)
Gold Key

1 (25¢, 80 pgs.)	22.00	66.00	220.00
2,3 (25¢, 80 pgs.)	15.00	45.00	155.00
4,5 (Regular size, 12¢)	10.50	30.00	105.00

ROCKY AND HIS FRIENDS (TV) (See Kite Fun Book & March of Comics #216)

ROCKY AND HIS FRIENDS (TV)
No. 1128, 8-10/60 - No.1311,1962 (Jay Ward)
Dell Publishing Co.

| Four Color #1128 (#1) (8-10/60) | 35.00 | 105.00 | 350.00 |
| Four Color #1152 (12-2/61), 1166, 1208, 1275, 1311('62) | 25.00 | 75.00 | 250.00 |

ROCKY HORROR PICTURE SHOW THE COMIC BOOK, THE
July, 1990 - No. 3, 1990 ($2.95, mini-series, 52 pgs.)(Photo-c #1)
Caliber Press

1-Adapts cult film plus photos, etc.		1.60	4.00
1-2nd printing		1.20	3.00
2,3		1.20	3.00
...Collection ($4.95)	1.00	2.00	5.00

ROCKY JONES SPACE RANGER (See Space Adventures #15-18)

	GD25	FN65	NM94

ROCKY JORDEN PRIVATE EYE (See Private Eye)

ROCKY LANE WESTERN (Allan Rocky Lane starred in Republic movies & (for a short time as Allan Lane, Red Ryder & Rocky Lane) (See Black Jack
Fawcett Movie Comics, Motion Picture Comics & Six-Gun Heroes)
May, 1949 - No. 87, Nov, 1959
Fawcett Publications/Charlton No. 56 on

1 (36 pgs.)-Rocky, his stallion Black Jack, & Slim Pickens begin; photo-c begin, end #57; photo back-c	87.00	262.00	700
2 (36 pgs.)-Last photo back-c	39.00	118.00	27
3-5 (52 pgs.): 4-Captain Tootsie by Beck	26.00	77.00	18
6,10 (36 pgs.): 10-Complete western novelette "Badman's Reward"	19.00	58.00	13
7-9 (52 pgs.)	21.00	64.00	15
11-13,15-17 (52 pgs.): 15-Black Jack's Hitching Post begins, ends #25	15.00	45.00	10
14,18 (36 pgs.)	12.00	36.00	8
19-21,23,24 (52 pgs.): 20-Last Slim Pickens. 21-Dee Dickens begins, ends #55,57,65-68	12.00	36.00	8
22,25-28,30 (36 pgs. begin)	11.50	34.00	8
29-Classic complete novel "The Land of Missing Men" with hidden land of ancient temple ruins (r-in #65)	16.00	47.00	11
31-40	10.00	30.00	7
41-54	10.00	30.00	6
55-Last Fawcett issue (1/54)	10.00	30.00	6
56-1st Charlton issue (2/54)-Photo-c	16.00	47.00	11
57,60-Photo-c	10.00	30.00	6
58,59,61-64: 59-Young Falcon app. 64-Slim Pickens app.	7.50	22.50	4
65-r/#29, "The Land of Missing Men"	9.15	27.00	5
66-68: Reprints #30,31,32	7.50	22.50	4
69-78,80-86	7.50	22.50	4
79-Giant Edition (68 pgs.)	10.00	30.00	5
87-Last issue	9.15	27.00	5
NOTE: Complete novels in #10, 14, 18, 22, 25, 30-32, 36, 38, 39, 49. Captain Tootsie in #4, 20. Big Bow and Little Arrow in #11, 28, 63. Black Jack's Hitching Post in #15-25, 64, 73.

ROCKY LANE WESTERN
1989 ($2.50, B&W, one-shot?)
AC Comics

| 1-Photo-c; Giordano reprints | | | |
| Annual 1 (1991, $2.95, B&W, 44 pgs.)-photo front/back & inside-c; reprints. | | | |

ROD CAMERON WESTERN (Movie star)
Feb, 1950 - No. 20, Apr, 1953
Fawcett Publications

1-Rod Cameron, his horse War Paint, & Sam The Sheriff begin; photo front/back-c begin	47.00	141.00	37
2	24.00	73.00	17
3-Novel length story "The Mystery of the Seven Cities of Cibola"	21.00	62.00	14
4-10: 9-Last photo back-c	17.00	49.00	11
11-19	13.00	39.00	9
20-Last issue & photo-c	13.50	41.00	9
NOTE: Novel length stories in No. 1-8, 12-14.

RODEO RYAN (See A-1 Comics #8)
No. 8 (one-shot)
Magazine Enterprises

| A-1 8-Intro Rodeo Ryan | | | 2 |

ROGAN GOSH
1994 ($6.95, one-shot)
DC Comics (Vertigo)

| nn-Peter Milligan scripts | | 1.20 | 3.00 |

ROGER DODGER (Also in Exciting Comics #57 on)

Rogue #2 © MEG

Rogue Trooper #40 © Quality

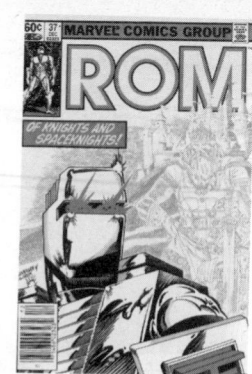

Rom #37 © MEG

	GD25	FN65	NM94

). 5, Aug, 1952
andard Comics

-Teen-age	4.00	12.00	24.00

OGER RABBIT (Also see Marvel Graphic Novel)
ne, 1990 - No. 18, Nov, 1991 ($1.50)
sney Comics

-All new stories	1.20	3.00
3		.80	2.00
-18			1.50
3-D 1 (1992, $2.50)-Sold at Wal-Mart?; w/glasses	1.00	2.50

GER RABBIT'S TOONTOWN
g, 1991 - No. 5, Dec, 1991 ($1.50)
ney Comics

5			1.50

GER ZELANY'S AMBER: THE GUNS OF AVALON
6 - No. 3, 1996 ($6.95, limited series)
Comics

3: Based on novel			7.00

G 2000
e, 1982 ($2.95, one-shot)
ific Comics

Byrne-c/a (r); 2nd printing (7/82) exists	1.20	3.00

G 2000
7 - No. 2, 1987 ($2.00, limited series)
tagraphics Books

-Byrne-r		.80	2.00

UE
1995 - No. 4, Apr, 1995 ($2.95, limited series)
vel Comics

: 1-Gold foil logo	1.40	3.50

UES GALLERY
($3.50, one-shot)
Comics

inups of DC villains by various artists			3.50

UE TROOPER
1986 - No. 49, 1991 ($1.25/$1.50/$1.75)
ty Comics/Fleetway Quality #38-on

:($1.25). 6-Double size			1.25
8- ($1.50): 21,22,25-27-Guice-c			1.50
9 ($1.75): 47,48-Alan Moore scripts		.70	1.75

Y POLY COMIC BOOK
- No. 15, 1946 (MLJ reprints)
n Publishing Co.

ed Rube & Steel Sterling begin; Sahle-c	24.00	73.00	170.00
e Blue Circle & The Steel Fist app.	13.00	39.00	90.00
rigin Red Rube retold; Steel Sterling story (Zip #41)	12.00	36.00	85.00
,14: The Black Hood app. in each. 14-Decapitation-c	14.00	43.00	100.00
e Blue Circle & The Steel Fist app.; cover exact swipe from Fox Blue etle #1	29.00	86.00	200.00

(Based on toy)
979 - No. 75, Feb, 1986
Comics Group

sed on a Parker Bros. toy; origin/1st app.	1.20	3.00
			1.20
13-Saga of the Space Knights begins			1.00

	GD25	FN65	NM94

17,18-X-Men app.	1.00	2.50
19-24,26-30: 19-X-Men cameo. 24-F.F. cameo; Skrulls, Nova & The New Champions app. 26,27-Galactus app.	1.00
25-Double size			1.00
			1.20
31-75: 31,32-Brotherhood of Evil Mutants app. 32-X-Men cameo. 34,35-Sub-Mariner app. 41,42-Dr. Strange app. 50-Skrulls app. (52 pgs.). 56,57-Alpha Flight app. 58,59-Ant-Man app. 65-West Coast Avengers & Beta Ray Bill app. 65,66-X-Men app.	1.00
Annual 1,4: 1(1982, 52 pgs.). 4(1985, 52 pgs.)	1.20
Annual 2,3: 2(1983, 52 pgs.). 3(1984, 52 pgs.)	1.00

NOTE: Austin c-3i, 18i, 61i. Byrne a-74i; c-56, 57, 74. Ditko a-59-75p, Annual 4. Golden c-7-12, 19. Guice a-61i; c-55, 58, 60p, 70p. Layton a-59i, 72i; c-15, 59i, 69. Miller c-2p?, 3p, 17p, 18p. Russell a(i)-64, 65, 67, 69, 71, 75; c-64, 65i, 66, 71i, 75. Severin c-41p. Sienkiewicz a-53i; c-46, 47, 52-54, 68, 71p, Annual 2. Simonson c-18. P. Smith c-59p. Starlin c-67. Zeck c-50.

ROMANCE (See True Stories of...)

ROMANCE AND CONFESSION STORIES (See Giant Comics Edition)
No date (1949) (25¢, 100 pgs.)
St. John Publishing Co.

1-Baker-c/a; remaindered St. John love comics	34.00	101.00	235.00

ROMANCE DIARY
Dec, 1949 - No. 2, Mar, 1950
Marvel Comics (CDS)(CLDS)

1,2	10.00	30.00	68.00

ROMANCE OF FLYING, THE
1942
David McKay Publications

Feature Books 33 (nn)-WW II photos	13.00	39.00	90.00

ROMANCES OF MOLLY MANTON (See Molly Manton)

ROMANCES OF NURSE HELEN GRANT, THE
Aug, 1957
Atlas Comics (VPI)

1	5.35	16.00	32.00

ROMANCES OF THE WEST (Becomes Romantic Affairs #3?)
Nov, 1949 - No. 2, Mar, 1950 (52 pgs.)
Marvel Comics (SPC)

1-Movie photo-c of Yvonne DeCarlo & Howard Duff (Calamity Jane & Sam Bass)	18.00	54.00	125.00
2-Photo-c	12.00	36.00	85.00

ROMANCE STORIES OF TRUE LOVE (Formerly Love Problems & Advice)
No. 45, 5/57 - No. 50, 3/58; No. 51, 9/58 - No. 52, 11/58
Harvey Publications

45-51: 45,46,48-50-Powell-a	3.60	9.00	18.00
52-Matt Baker-a	5.85	17.50	35.00

ROMANCE TALES (Formerly Western Winners #6?)
No. 7, Oct, 1949 - No. 9, Mar, 1950 (7,8: photo-c)
Marvel Comics (CDS)

7	10.00	30.00	65.00
8,9: 8-Everett-a	7.50	22.50	45.00

ROMANCE TRAIL
July-Aug, 1949 - No. 6, May-June, 1950 (All photo-c & 52 pgs.)
National Periodical Publications

1-Kinstler, Toth-a; Jimmy Wakely photo-c	50.00	150.00	400.00
2-Kinstler-a; Jim Bannon photo-c	26.00	79.00	185.00
3-Photo-c; Kinstler, Toth-a	29.00	86.00	200.00
4-Photo-c; Toth-a	22.00	66.00	155.00
5,6: Photo-c on both. 5-Kinstler-a	19.00	56.00	130.00

ROMAN HOLIDAYS, THE (TV)
Feb, 1973 - No. 4, Nov, 1973 (Hanna-Barbera)
Gold Key

Romantic Love #10 © AVON

Romantic Marriage #3 © Z-D

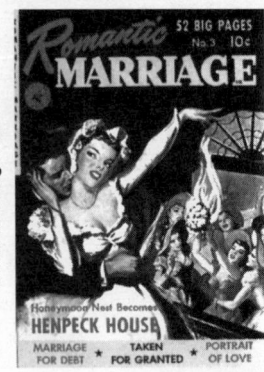

Romantic Secrets #1 © FAW

	GD25	FN65	NM94

	GD25	FN65	NM94
1	2.15	6.50	15.00
2-4	1.70	5.00	12.00

ROMANTIC ADVENTURES (My... #49-67, covers only)
Mar-Apr, 1949 - No. 67, July, 1956 (Becomes My... #68 on)
American Comics Group (B&I Publ. Co.)

1	13.00	39.00	90.00
2	7.50	22.50	45.00
3-10	4.25	13.00	28.00
11-20 (4/52)	4.00	12.00	24.00
21-45,49,51,52: 52-Last Pre-code (2/55)	3.60	9.00	18.00
46-48-3-D effect-c/stories (TrueVision)	9.15	27.00	55.00
50-Classic cover/story "Love of A Lunatic"	6.70	20.00	40.00
53-67	2.40	6.00	12.00

NOTE: #1-23, 52 pgs. **Shelly** a-40. Whitney c/art in many issues.

ROMANTIC AFFAIRS (Formerly Molly Manton's Romances #2 and/or Romances of the West #2 and/or Our Love #2?)
No. 3, Mar, 1950
Marvel Comics (SPC)

3-Photo-c from Molly Manton's Romances #2	6.70	20.00	40.00

ROMANTIC CONFESSIONS
Oct, 1949 - V3#1, Apr-May, 1953
Hillman Periodicals

V1#1-McWilliams-a	11.00	33.00	75.00
2-Briefer-c; negligee panels	7.00	21.00	42.00
3-12	4.25	13.00	28.00
V2#1,2,4-8,10-12: 2-McWilliams-a	4.00	12.00	24.00
3-Krigstein-a	7.00	21.00	42.00
9-One pg. Frazetta ad	4.00	11.00	22.00
V3#1	4.00	11.00	22.00

ROMANTIC HEARTS
Mar, 1951 - No. 10, Oct, 1952; July, 1953 - No. 12, July, 1955
Story Comics/Master/Merit Pubs.

1(3/51) (1st Series)	10.00	30.00	70.00
2	5.85	17.50	35.00
3-10: Cameron-a	4.25	13.00	28.00
1(7/53) (2nd Series)-Some say #11 on-c	6.70	20.00	40.00
2	4.00	12.00	24.00
3-12	4.00	10.00	20.00

ROMANTIC LOVE
9-10/49 - #3, 1-2/50; #4, 2-3/51 - #13, 10/52; #20, 3-4/54 - #23, 9-10/54
Avon Periodicals/Realistic (No #14-19)

1-c-/Avon paperback #252	18.00	54.00	125.00
2-5: 3-c-/paperback Novel Library #12. 4-c-/paperback Diversey Prize Novel #5. 5-c-/paperback Novel Library #34	11.00	33.00	75.00
6- "Thrill Crazy" marijuana story; c-/Avon paperback #207; Kinstler-a	13.50	41.00	95.00
7,8: 8-Astarita-a(2)	10.00	30.00	65.00
9-12: 9-c-/paperback Novel Library #41; Kinstler-a. 10-c-/Avon paperback #212. 11-c-/paperback Novel Library #17; Kinstler-a. 12-c-/paperback Novel Library #13	11.00	33.00	75.00
13,21,22: 22-Kinstler-c	10.00	30.00	65.00
20-Kinstler-c/a	10.00	30.00	65.00
23-Kinstler-c	8.35	25.00	50.00
nn(1-3/53)(Realistic-r)	7.50	22.50	45.00

NOTE: **Astarita** a-7, 10, 11, 21. Painted c-1-3, 5, 7-11, 13. Photo c-4, 6.

ROMANTIC LOVE
No. 4, June, 1950
Quality Comics Group

4 (6/50)(Exist?)	5.00	15.00	30.00
I.W. Reprint #2,3,8: 2-r/Romantic Love #2		1.60	4.00

ROMANTIC MARRIAGE (Cinderella Love #25 on)
#1-3 (1950, no months); #4, 5-6/51 - #17, 9/52; #18, 9/53 - #24, 9/54
Ziff-Davis/St. John No. 18 on (#1-8: 52 pgs.)

1-Photo-c; Cary Grant/Betsy Drake photo back-c.	14.00	43.00	1
2-Painted-c; Anderson-a (also #15)	9.15	27.00	
3-9: 3,4,8,9-Painted-c; 5-7-Photo-c	7.50	22.50	
10-Unusual format; front-c is a painted-c; back-c is a photo-c complete with logo, price, etc.	13.00	39.00	
11-17 13-Photo-c. 15-Signed story by Anderson. 17-(9/52)-Last Z-D issue	6.70	20.00	
18-22,24: 20-Photo-c	6.70	20.00	
23-Baker-c; all stories are reprinted from #15	7.50	22.50	

ROMANTIC PICTURE NOVELETTES
1946
Magazine Enterprises

1-Mary Worth-r; Creig Flessel-c	13.00	39.00	

ROMANTIC SECRETS (Becomes Time For Love)
Sept, 1949 - No. 39, 4/53; No. 5, 10/55 - No. 52, 11/64 (#1-5: photo-c)
Fawcett/Charlton Comics No. 5 (10/55) on

1-(52 pg. issues begin, end #?)	11.50	34.00	
2,3	7.00	21.00	
4,9-Evans-a	8.00	24.00	
5-8,10	4.25	13.00	
11-23	4.25	13.00	
24-Evans-a	5.85	17.50	
25-39('53)	4.00	10.00	
5 (Charlton, 2nd Series)(10/55, formerly Negro Romances #4)			
	6.70	20.00	
6-10	4.00	11.00	
11-20	2.40	6.00	
21-35: Last 10¢ issue?	1.00	2.60	
36-52('64)		1.20	

NOTE: **Bailey** a-20. **Powell** a(1st series)-5, 7, 10, 12, 16, 17, 20, 26, 29, 33, 34, 36, 37. **Sekowsky** a-26. Photo c(1st series)-1-5, 16, 25, 27, 33. **Swayze** a(1st series)-16, 18, 19, 28, 31, 32, 39.

ROMANTIC STORY (Cowboy Love #28 on)
11/49 - #22, Sum, 1953; #23, 5/54 - #27, 12/54; #28, 8/55 - #130, 11/73
Fawcett/Charlton Comics No. 23 on

1-Photo-c begin, end #24; 52 pgs. begins	12.00	36.00	
2	7.00	21.00	
3-5	6.35	19.00	
6-14	4.25	13.00	
15-Evans-a	6.35	19.00	
16-22(Sum, '53; last Fawcett issue). 21-Toth-a?	4.00	10.00	
23-39: 26,29-Wood swipes	4.00	10.00	
40-(100 pgs.)	5.85	17.50	
41-50	2.80	7.00	
51-80: 57-Hypo needle story	1.00	2.50	
81-100		1.20	
101-130		.80	

NOTE: **Jim Aparo** a-94. **Powell** a-7, 8, 16, 20, 30. **Marcus Swayze** a-2, 12, 20, 32.

ROMANTIC THRILLS (See Fox Giants)

ROMANTIC WESTERN
Winter, 1949 - No. 3, June, 1950 (All Photo-c)
Fawcett Publications

1	16.00	47.00	
2-(Spr/50)-Williamson, McWilliams-a	17.00	51.00	
3	11.50	34.00	

ROMEO TUBBS (...That Lovable Teenager; formerly My Secret Life)
No. 26, 5/50 - No. 28, 7/50; No. 1, 1950; No. 27, 12/52
Fox Feature Syndicate/Green Publ. Co. No. 27

Ronin #5 © Frank Miller

Rook #1 © Harris

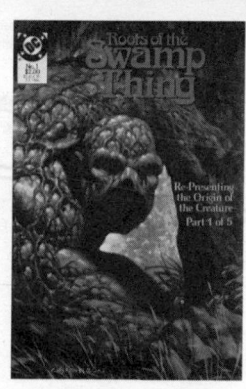

Roots of the Swamp Thing #1 © DC

RO

	GD25	FN65	NM94
26-Teen-age	10.00	30.00	60.00
27-Contains Pedro on inside; Wood-a	13.00	39.00	90.00
28, 1	8.35	25.00	50.00
RONALD McDONALD (TV)			
Sept, 1970 - No. 4, March, 1971			
Charlton Press (King Features Synd.)			
1	1.00	2.60	6.00
2-4		1.20	3.00
RONIN			
July, 1983 - No. 6, Aug, 1984 ($2.50, limited series, 52 pgs.)			
DC Comics			
1-Frank Miller-c/a/scripts in all		1.60	4.00
2-5		1.20	3.00
6-Scarcer; has fold-out poster.		2.50	6.00
Trade paperback (1987, $12.95)-Reprints #1-6	1.85	5.50	13.00
ROOK (See Eerie Magazine & Warren Presents: The Rook)			
Nov, 1979 - No. 14, April, 1982			
Warren Publications			
1-Nino-a		1.20	3.00
2-14: 3,4-Toth-a		.80	2.00
ROOK			
No. 0, Jun, 1995 - No. 4, 1995 ($2.95)			
Harris Comics			
0-4: 0-short stories (3) w/preview. 4-Brereton-c.		1.20	3.00
ROOKIE COP (Formerly Crime and Justice?)			
No. 27, Nov, 1955 - No. 33, Aug, 1957			
Charlton Comics			
27	8.00	24.00	48.00
28-33	5.35	16.00	32.00
ROOM 222 (TV)			
Jan, 1970; No. 2, May, 1970 - No. 4, Jan, 1971			
Dell Publishing Co.			
1	5.00	15.00	50.00
2-4: 2,4-Photo-c. 3-Marijuana story. 4 r/#1	3.00	9.00	30.00
ROOTIE KAZOOTIE (TV)(See 3-D-ell)			
No. 415, Aug, 1952 - No. 6, Oct-Dec, 1954			
Dell Publishing Co.			
Four Color 415 (#1)	11.00	33.00	110.00
Four Color 459,502(#2,3)	7.00	21.00	70.00
4(4-6/54)-6	7.00	21.00	70.00
ROOTS OF THE SWAMP THING			
July, 1986 - No.5, Nov, 1986 ($2.00, Baxter paper, 52 pgs.)			
DC Comics			
1-5: r/Swamp Thing #1-10 by Wrightson & House of Mystery-r. 1-new Wrightson-c (2-5 reprinted covers).		.80	2.00
ROSE N'GUNN			
Jan, 1995 - No. 6, May, 1996 ($2.95, B&W, mature)			
Bishop Press			
1-6		1.20	3.00
Creator's Choice ($2.95)-reprints w/pin-ups		1.20	3.00
ROSE N'GUNN			
June, 1996 - Present ($3.00, B&W, mature)			
London Night Studios			
1			3.00
1-($6.00)-Blood & Glory Edition			6.00
ROSWELL: LITTLE GREEN MAN			
1996 - Present ($2.95, quarterly)			

	GD25	FN65	NM94
Bongo Comics			
1			3.00
ROUND THE WORLD GIFT			
No date (mid 1940's) (4 pgs.)			
National War Fund (Giveaway)			
nn	12.00	36.00	85.00
ROUNDUP (...Western Crime Stories)			
July-Aug, 1948 - No. 5, Mar-Apr, 1949 (All 52 pgs.)			
D. S. Publishing Co.			
1-Kiefer-a	17.00	49.00	115.00
2-5: 2-Marijuana drug mention story	11.00	33.00	75.00
ROYAL ROY			
May, 1985 - No.6, Mar, 1986 (Children's book)			
Marvel Comics (Star Comics)			
1-6			1.00
ROY CAMPANELLA, BASEBALL HERO			
1950 (Brooklyn Dodgers)			
Fawcett Publications			
nn-Photo-c; life story	51.00	155.00	415.00
ROY ROGERS (See March of Comics #17, 35, 47, 62, 68, 73, 77, 86, 91, 100, 105, 116, 121, 131, 136, 146, 151, 161, 167, 176, 191, 206, 221, 236, 250)			
ROY ROGERS AND TRIGGER			
Apr, 1967			
Gold Key			
1-Photo-c; reprints	5.85	17.50	35.00
ROY ROGERS COMICS (See Western Roundup under Dell Giants)			
No. 38, 4/44 - No. 177, 12/47 (#38-166: 52 pgs.)			
Dell Publishing Co.			
Four Color 38 (1944)-49 pg. story; photo front/back-c on all 4-Color issues (1st western comic with photo-c)	160.00	480.00	1600.00
Four Color 63 (1945)-Color photos on all four-c	47.00	141.00	465.00
Four Color 86,95 (1945)	32.00	96.00	325.00
Four Color 109 (1946)	25.00	75.00	255.00
Four Color 117,124,137,144	18.00	54.00	180.00
Four Color 153,160,166: 166-48 pg. story	16.00	48.00	155.00
Four Color 177 (36 pgs.)-32 pg. story	16.00	48.00	155.00
ROY ROGERS COMICS (...& Trigger #92(8/55)-on)(Roy starred in Republic movies, radio & TV) (Singing cowboy) (Also see Dale Evans, It Really Happened #8, Queen of the West Dale Evans, & Roy Rogers' Trigger)			
Jan, 1948 - No. 145, Sept-Oct, 1961 (#1-19: 36 pgs.)			
Dell Publishing Co.			
1-Roy, his horse Trigger, & Chuck Wagon Charley's Tales begin; photo-c begin, end #145	70.00	210.00	700.00
2	25.00	75.00	250.00
3-5	18.00	54.00	180.00
6-10	14.00	43.00	135.00
11-19: 19-Chuck Wagon Charley's Tales ends	10.00	30.00	100.00
20 (52 pgs.)-Trigger feature begins, ends #46	10.00	30.00	100.00
21-30 (52 pgs.)	8.50	25.50	85.00
31-46 (52 pgs.): 37-X-Mas-c	6.50	19.50	65.00
47-56 (36 pgs.): 47-Chuck Wagon Charley's Tales returns, ends #133. 49-X-mas-c. 55-Last photo back-c	4.80	14.40	48.00
57 (52 pgs.)-Heroin drug propaganda story	5.60	16.80	56.00
58-70 (52 pgs.): 58-Heroin drug use/dealing story. 61-X-Mas-c	4.80	14.40	48.00
71-80 (52 pgs.): 73-X-Mas-c	3.80	11.40	38.00
81-91 (36 pgs. #81-on): 85-X-Mas-c	4.25	12.75	34.00
92-99,101-110,112-118: 92-Title changed to Roy Rogers and Trigger (8/55)	4.25	12.75	34.00

Rune #6 © Malibu

Rune V2#6 © Malibu

Rune: Hearts Of Darkness #3 © Malibu

	GD25	FN65	NM94

	GD25	FN65	NM94
100-Trigger feature returns, ends #131	6.00	18.00	48.00
111,119-124-Toth-a	5.50	16.50	50.00
125-131: 125-Toth-a (1 pg.)	4.75	14.25	38.00
132-144-Manning-a. 132-1st Dale Evans-sty by Russ Manning138,144-Dale Evans featured	5.25	15.75	42.00
145-Last issue	7.00	20.50	55.00
...& the Man From Dodge City (Dodge giveaway, 16 pgs., 1954)-Frontier, Inc. (5x7-1/4")	11.50	34.00	80.00
Official Roy Rogers Riders Club Comics (1952; 16 pgs., reg. size, paper-c)	12.00	36.00	180.00

NOTE: **Buscema** a-74-108(2 stories each). **Manning** a-123, 124, 132-144. **Marsh** a-110. Photo back-c No. 1-9, 11-35, 38-55.

ROY ROGERS' TRIGGER (TV)
No. 329, May, 1951 - No. 17, June-Aug, 1955
Dell Publishing Co.

	GD25	FN65	NM94
Four Color 329 (#1)-Painted-c	11.00	33.00	110.00
2 (9-11/51)-Photo-c	9.50	28.50	95.00
3-5: 3-Painted-c begin, end #17, most by S. Savitt	3.80	11.40	38.00
6-17: Title merges with Roy Rogers after #17	2.80	8.40	28.00

ROY ROGERS WESTERN CLASSICS
1989 -Present? ($2.95/$3.95, 44pgs.) (24 pgs in color, 16 pgs. in B&W)
AC Comics

	GD25	FN65	NM94
1-Dale Evans-r by Manning, Trigger-r by Buscema; photo covers & interior photos by Roy & Dale		1.20	3.00
2-Buscema-r (3); photo-c & B&W photos inside		1.20	3.00
3,4 ($3.95): 3-Dale Evans-r by Manning; Trigger-r by Buscemaplus other Buscema-r; photo-c.		1.60	4.00

RUDOLPH, THE RED NOSED REINDEER (See Limited Collectors' Edition #20, 24, 33, 42, 50)

RUDOLPH, THE RED-NOSED REINDEER
1939 (2,400,000 copies printed); Dec, 1951
Montgomery Ward (Giveaway)

	GD25	FN65	NM94
Paper cover-1st app. in print; written by Robert May; ill. by Denver Gillen	11.50	34.00	80.00
Hardcover version	16.00	47.00	110.00
1951 Edition (Has 1939 date)-36 pgs., slick-c printed in red & brown; pulp interior printed in four mixed-ink colors: red, green, blue & brown	7.50	22.50	45.00
1951 Edition with red-spiral promotional booklet printed on high quality stock, 8-1/2"x11", in red & brown, 25 pages composed of 4 fold outs, single sheets and the Rudolph comic book inserted (rare)	50.00	150.00	385.00

RUDOLPH, THE RED-NOSED REINDEER
1950 - No. 13?, Winter, 1962-63 (Issues are not numbered)
National Periodical Publications

	GD25	FN65	NM94
1950 issue (#1); Grossman-c/a begins	13.00	39.00	90.00
1951-54 issues (4 total)	9.15	27.50	55.00
1955-62 issues (8 total)	6.35	19.00	38.00

NOTE: The 1962-63 issue is 84 pages. 13 total issues published. Has games & puzzles also.

RUFF AND REDDY (TV)
No. 937, 9/58 - No. 12, 1-3/62 (Hanna-Barbera)(#9 on: 15¢)
Dell Publishing Co.

	GD25	FN65	NM94
Four Color 937(#1)(1st Hanna-Barbera comic book)	12.00	36.00	120.00
Four Color 981,1038	8.00	24.00	80.00
4(1-3/60)-12: 8-Last 10¢ issue	6.00	18.00	60.00

RUGGED ACTION (Strange Stories of Suspense #5 on)
Dec, 1954 - No. 4, June, 1955
Atlas Comics (CSI)

	GD25	FN65	NM94
1-Brodsky-a	10.00	30.00	65.00
2-4: 2-Last precode (2/55)	6.70	20.00	40.00

NOTE: Ayers a-2, 3. Maneely c-2, 3. Severin a-2.

RUINS

July, 1995 - No. 2, Sept, 1995 ($5.00, painted, limited series)
Marvel Comics (Alterniverse)

	GD25	FN65	NM94
1,2: Phil Sheldon from Marvels; Warren Ellis scripts; acetate-c	1.00	2.00	5.00

RULAH JUNGLE GODDESS (Formerly Zoot; I Loved #28 on) (Also see All Top Comics & Terrors of the Jungle)
No. 17, Aug, 1948 - No. 27, June, 1949
Fox Features Syndicate

	GD25	FN65	NM94
17	71.00	215.00	575.00
18-Classic girl-fight interior splash	54.00	163.00	435.00
19,20	50.00	150.00	400.00
21-Used in SOTI, pg. 388,389	54.00	163.00	435.00
22-Used in SOTI, pg. 22,23	50.00	150.00	400.00
23-27	40.00	120.00	315.00

NOTE: Kamen c-17-19, 21, 22.

RUNAWAY, THE (See Movie Classics)

RUN BABY RUN
1974 (39¢)
Logos International

	GD25	FN65	NM94
nn-By Tony Tallarico from Nicky Cruz's book			1.00

RUN, BUDDY, RUN (TV)
June, 1967 (Photo-c)
Gold Key

	GD25	FN65	NM94
1 (10204-706)	2.60	7.50	18.00

RUNE (See Curse of Rune, Sludge & all other Ultraverse titles for previews)
1994 - No. 9, Apr, 1995 ($1.95)
Malibu Comics (Ultraverse)

	GD25	FN65	NM94
1,2,4-9: 1-Barry Windsor-Smith-c/a/stories begin, ends #6. 5-1st app. of Gemini. 6-Prime & Mantra app.		.80	2.00
1-(1/94)-"Ashcan" edition flip book w/Wrath #1			1.00
1-Ultra 5000 Limited silver foil edition	1.30	3.25	8.00
0-Obtained by sending coupons from 11 comics; came w/Solution #0, poster, temporary tattoo, card	1.70	4.20	10.00
3-(3/94, $3.50, 68 pgs.)-Flip book w/Ultraverse Premiere #1	1.40		3.50
Giant Size 1 ($2.50, 44 pgs.)-B.Smith story & art.	1.00		2.50

RUNE (2nd Series)(Formerly Curse of Rune)(See Ultraverse Unlimited #1)
Infinity, Sept, 1995 - V2#7, Apr, 1996 ($1.50)
Malibu Comics (Ultraverse)

	GD25	FN65	NM94
Infinity, V2#1-7: Infinity-Black September tie-in; black-c & painted-c exist. 1,3-7-Marvel's Adam Warlock app; regular & painted-c exist. 2-Flip book w/"Phoenix Resurrection" Pt. 6.			1.50
...Vs. Venom 1 (12/95, $3.95)			4.00

RUNE: HEARTS OF DARKNESS
Sept, 1996 - No. 3, Nov, 1996 ($1.50, limited series)
Malibu Comics (Ultraverse)

	GD25	FN65	NM94
1-3: Doug Moench scripts & Kyle Hotz-c/a; flip books w/6 pg. Rune story by the Pander Bros.			1.50

RUNE/SILVER SURFER
Apr, 1995 ($5.95/$2.95, one-shot)
Marvel Comics/Malibu Comics (Ultraverse)

	GD25	FN65	NM94
1 ($5.95, direct market)-BWS-c	1.00	2.60	6.00
1 ($2.95, newstand)-BWS-c		1.20	3.00
1-Collector's limited edition	1.00	2.00	5.00

RUST
7/87 - No. 15, 11/88; V2#1, 2/89 - No. 7, 1989 ($1.50/$1.75)
Now Comics

	GD25	FN65	NM94
1-3 ($1.50)			1.50
4-11,13-15, V2#1-7 ($1.75)		.70	1.75
12-(8/88, $1.75)-5 pg. preview of The Terminator (1st app.)			

Saban's Mighty Morphin Power Rangers #5 © Saban

Sabretooth Classics #13 © MEG

Sable #16 © Mike Grell

	GD25	FN65	NM94
	1.00	2.00	5.00

THE RUSTLERS (See Zane Grey Four Color 532)

RUSTY, BOY DETECTIVE
Mar-April, 1955 - No. 5, Nov, 1955
Good Comics/Lev Gleason

1-Bob Wood, Carl Hubbell-a begins	7.50	22.50	45.00
2-5	5.00	15.00	30.00

RUSTY COMICS (Formerly Kid Movie Comics; Rusty and Her Family #21, 22; The Kelleys #23 on; see Millie The Model)
No. 12, Apr, 1947 - No. 22, Sept, 1949
Marvel Comics (HPC)

12-Mitzi app.	11.00	32.00	100.00
13	7.50	22.50	55.00
14-Wolverton's Powerhouse Pepper (4 pgs.) plus Kurtzman's "Hey Look"	17.00	51.00	120.00
15-17-Kurtzman's "Hey Look"	13.50	41.00	95.00
18,19	7.00	21.00	42.00
20-Kurtzman-a (5 pgs.)	13.50	41.00	95.00
21,22-Kurtzman-a (17 & 22 pgs.)	18.00	54.00	125.00

RUSTY DUGAN (See Holyoke One-Shot #2)

RUSTY RILEY
No. 418, Aug, 1952 - No. 554, April, 1954 (Frank Godwin strip reprints)
Dell Publishing Co.

Four Color 418 (...a Boy, a Horse, and a Dog) #1	5.00	15.00	50.00
Four Color #451(2/53), 486 ('53), 554	4.00	12.00	40.00

SAARI ("The Jungle Goddess")
November, 1951
P. L. Publishing Co.

1	39.00	116.00	270.00

SABAN'S MIGHTY MORPHIN POWER RANGERS
Dec, 1994 - No. 6, May, 1995 ($1.95, limited series)
Hamilton Comics

1-6: 1-w/bound-in Power Ranger Barcode Card		.80	2.00

SABAN'S MIGHTY MORPHIN POWER RANGERS (TV)
1995 - No. 8, 1996 ($1.75)
Marvel Comics

1-8		.70	1.75

SABAN'S NINJA RANGERS
Dec, 1995 - No. 4, Mar, 1995 ($1.95, limited series)
Hamilton Comics

1-4: Flip book w/Saban's V.R. Troopers			2.00

SABAN'S V.R. TROOPERS (See Saban's Ninja Rangers)

SABLE (Formerly Jon Sable, Freelance; also see Mike Grell's...)
Mar, 1988 - No. 27, May, 1990 ($1.75/$1.95)
First Comics

1-27: 10-Begin $1.95-c		.80	2.00

SABRE (See Eclipse Graphic Album Series)
Aug, 1982 - No. 14, Aug, 1985 (Baxter paper #4 on)
Eclipse Comics

1 ($1.00)-Sabre & Morrigan Tales begin			1.00
2-14: 4-6-Incredible Seven origin			1.00

SABRETOOTH (See Iron Fist, Power Man, X-Factor #10 & X-Men)
Aug, 1993 - No. 4, Nov, 1993 ($2.95, coated paper)
Marvel Comics

1-4: 1-Die-cut-c. 3-Wolverine app.	1.20		3.00
Trade paperback (12/94, $12.95) r/#1-4			13.00

SABRETOOTH CLASSIC

May, 1994 - No. 15, July, 1995 ($1.50)
Marvel Comics

1-15: 1-3-r/Power Man & Iron Fist #66,78,84. 4-r/Spec. S-M #116. 9-Uncanny X-Men #212, 10-r/Uncanny X-Men #213. 11-0r/ Daredevil #238. 12-r/Classic X-Men #10			1.50

SABRINA'S CHRISTMAS MAGIC (See Archie Giant Series Magazine #196, 207, 220, 231, 243, 455, 467, 479, 491, 503, 515)

SABRINA'S HALLOWEEN SPOOOKTACULAR
1993 ($2.00, 52 pgs.)
Archie Publications

1-Neon orange ink-c; bound-in poster		.80	2.00

SABRINA, THE TEEN-AGE WITCH (TV)(See Archie Giant Series 544, Archie's Madhouse 22, Archie's TV..., Chilling Advs. In Sorcery)
April, 1971 - No. 77, Jan, 1983 (Giants No. 1-17)
Archie Publications

1	4.50	13.50	45.00
2	3.25	9.50	22.00
3-5: 3,4-Archie's Group x-over	1.70	5.00	12.00
6-10	1.20	3.00	7.00
11-20		1.60	4.00
21-77		.80	2.00

SABRINA, THE TEEN-AGE WITCH
1996 ($1.50, 32 pgs., one-shot)
Archie Publications

1-Updated origin			1.50

SABU, "ELEPHANT BOY" (Movie; formerly My Secret Story)
No. 30, June, 1950 - No. 2, Aug, 1950
Fox Features Syndicate

30(#1)-Wood-a; photo-c from movie	21.00	64.00	150.00
2-Photo-c from movie; Kamen-a	15.00	45.00	105.00

SACHS & VIOLENS
Nov, 1993 - No. 4, July, 1994 ($2.25, limited series, mature)
Marvel Comics (Epic Comics)

1-($2.75)-Embossed-c w/bound-in trading card	1.10		2.75
1-($3.50)-Platinum edition (1 for each 10 ordered)			6.00
2-4: Perez-c/a; bound-in trading card: 2-(5/94)		.90	2.25

SACRAMENTS, THE
Oct, 1955 (25¢)
Catechetical Guild Educational Society

304	2.40	6.00	12.00

SACRED AND THE PROFANE, THE (See Eclipse Graphic Album Series #9 & Epic Illustrated #20)

SAD CASE OF WAITING ROOM WILLIE, THE
1950? (nd) (14 pgs. in color; paper covers; regular size)
American Visuals Corp. (For Baltimore Medical Society)

nn-By Will Eisner (Rare)	44.00	132.00	350.00

SADDLE JUSTICE (Happy Houlihans #1,2) (Saddle Romances #9 on)
No. 3, Spring, 1948 - No. 8, Sept-Oct, 1949
E. C. Comics

3-The 1st E.C. by Bill Gaines to break away from M. C. Gaines' old Educational Comics format. Craig, Feldstein, H. C. Kiefer, & Stan Asch-a; mentioned in Love and Death	39.00	118.00	275.00
4-1st Graham Ingels-a for E.C.	39.00	118.00	275.00
5-8-Ingels-a in all	36.00	109.00	255.00

NOTE: *Craig* and *Feldstein* art in most issues. Canadian reprints known; see Table of Contents. *Craig* c-3, 4. *Ingels* c-5-8. #4 contains a biography of *Craig*.

SADDLE ROMANCES (Saddle Justice #3-8; Weird Science #12 on)
No. 9, Nov-Dec, 1949 - No. 11, Mar-Apr, 1950

Sade #0 © Bishop Press

Sad Sack And Sarge #1 © HARV

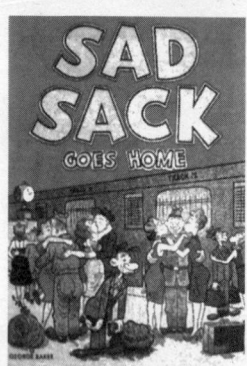

Sad Sack Goe Home © HARV

	GD25	FN65	NM94

E. C. Comics

	GD25	FN65	NM94
9-Ingels-c/a	39.00	118.00	275.00
10-Wood's 1st work at E. C.; Ingels-a; Feldstein-c	40.00	120.00	285.00
11-Ingels-a; Feldstein-c	39.00	118.00	275.00

NOTE: Canadian reprints known; see Table of Contents. **Wood/Harrison** a-10, 11.

SADE
No. 0, May, 1995 - No. 2, 1996 ($2.95, B&W, mature)
Bishop Press/London Night Studios

		GD25	FN65	NM94
0-2: All Bishop Press issues. 1-Razor app; w/pin-ups			1.20	3.00
1($3.00)-London Night Studio's Encore Edition.				3.00
Special 1-Razor app.				3.00
Special 1 ($4.95, limited edition)-Razor app.		1.00	2.00	5.00

SADE
June, 1996 - Present ($3.00, B&W, mature)
London Night Studios

			GD25	NM94
1-4				3.00
1-Balance of Pain Edition				3.00

SADE AND ROSE & GUNN CONFEDERATE MISTS
Mar, 1996 ($3.00, B&W, one-shot, mature)
Bishop Press

				NM94
1-w/pin-ups.				3.00

SADIE SACK (See Harvey Hits #93)

SAD SACK AND THE SARGE
Sept, 1957 - No. 155, June, 1982
Harvey Publications

	GD25	FN65	NM94
1	11.00	33.00	110.00
2	5.00	15.00	50.00
3-10	3.50	10.50	35.00
11-20	3.00	9.00	30.00
21-30	1.80	5.40	18.00
31-50	1.70	5.00	12.00
51-90,97-100	1.00	2.60	6.00
91-96: All 52 pg. Giants	1.20	3.00	7.00
101-155		1.20	3.00

SAD SACK COMICS (See Harvey Collector's Comics #16, Little Sad Sack, Tastee Freez Comics #4 & True Comics #55)
Sept, 1949 - No. 287, Oct, 1982; No. 288, 1992 - No. 293?, 1993
Harvey Publications/Lorne-Harvey Publications (Recollections) (#288 on)

	GD25	FN65	NM94
1-Infinity-c; Little Dot begins (1st app.); civilian issues begin, end #21; based on comic strip	37.00	111.00	375.00
2-Flying Fool by Powell	18.00	54.00	185.00
3	10.00	30.00	100.00
4-10	7.50	22.50	75.00
11-21	5.00	15.00	50.00
22-("Back In The Army Again" on covers #22-36); "The Specialist" story about Sad Sack's return to Army	3.00	9.00	30.00
23-50	2.00	6.00	20.00
51-100: 62-"The Specialist" reprinted	2.00	6.00	14.00
101-150	1.20	3.00	7.00
151-222		1.60	4.00
223-228 (25¢ Giants, 52 pgs.)		1.80	4.50
229-287: 286,287 had limited distribution		1.00	2.50
288,289 ($2.75, 1992): 289-50th anniversary issue		1.10	2.75
290-293 ($1.00, 1993, B&W)			1.00
3-D 1 (1/54, 25¢)-Came with 2 pairs of glasses; titled "Harvey 3-D Hits"	22.00	66.00	155.00
Armed Forces Complimentary copies, HD #1-40 (1957-1962)	1.20	3.00	6.00
...At Home for the Holidays 1 (1993, no-c price)-Publ. by Lorne-Harvey' X-Mas issue		.80	2.00

NOTE: The Sad Sack Comics comic book was a spin-off from a Sunday Newspaper strip

launched through John Wheeler's Bell Syndicate. The previous Sunday page and the first 21 comics depicted the Sad Sack in civvies. Unpopularity caused the Sunday page to be discontin ued in the early '50s. Meanwhile Sad Sack returned to the Army, by popular demand, in issu No. 22, remaining there ever since. Incidentally, relatively few of the first 21 issues were ever co lected and remain scarce due to this.

SAD SACK FUN AROUND THE WORLD
1974 (no month)
Harvey Publications

			GD25	FN65	NM94
1-About Great Britain				1.60	4.00

SAD SACK GOES HOME
1951 (16 pgs. in color, no cover price)
Harvey Publications

	GD25	FN65	NM94
nn-By George Baker	7.00	21.00	42.00

SAD SACK LAUGH SPECIAL
Winter, 1958-59 - No. 93, Feb, 1977 (#1-9: 84 pgs.; #10-60: 68 pgs.; #61-76: 52 pgs.)
Harvey Publications

	GD25	FN65	NM94
1-Giant 25¢ issues begin	8.50	25.50	85.00
2	4.20	12.60	42.00
3-10	3.00	9.00	30.00
11-30	2.60	7.50	18.00
31-60: 31-1st app. Hi-Fi Tweeter. 60-Last 68 pg. Giant	1.65	4.20	10.00
61-76-(All 52 pg. issues)	1.00	2.60	6.00
77-93		1.40	3.50

SAD SACK NAVY, GOBS 'N' GALS
Aug, 1972 - No. 8, Oct, 1973
Harvey Publications

		GD25	FN65	NM94
1: 52 pg. Giant		1.30	3.25	8.00
2-8			1.60	4.00

SAD SACK'S ARMY LIFE (See Harvey Hits #8, 17, 22, 28, 32, 39, 43, 47, 51, 55, 58, 61, 64, 67, 70)

SAD SACK'S ARMY LIFE (...Parade #1-57, ...Today #58 on)
Oct, 1963 - No. 60, Nov, 1975; No. 61, May, 1976
Harvey Publications

	GD25	FN65	NM94
1-(68 pg. issues begin)	4.50	13.50	45.00
2-10	3.25	9.50	22.00
11-20	1.70	5.00	12.00
21-34: Last 68 pg. issue	1.30	3.25	8.00
35-51: All 52 pgs.		1.60	4.00
52-61		.80	2.00

SAD SACK'S FUNNY FRIENDS (See Harvey Hits #75)
Dec, 1955 - No. 75, Oct, 1969
Harvey Publications

	GD25	FN65	NM94
1	7.50	22.50	75.00
2-10	3.80	11.40	38.00
11-20	2.30	6.70	16.00
21-30	1.20	3.00	7.00
31-75	1.00	2.00	5.00

SAD SACK'S MUTTSY (See Harvey Hits #74, 77, 80, 82, 84, 87, 89, 92, 96, 99, 102, 105, 108, 111, 113, 115, 117, 119, 121)

SAD SACK USA (...Vacation #8)
Nov, 1972 - No. 7, Nov, 1973; No. 8, Oct, 1974
Harvey Publications

		GD25	FN65	NM94
1		1.00	2.60	6.00
2-8			1.20	3.00

SAD SACK WITH SARGE & SADIE
Sept, 1972 - No. 8, Nov, 1973
Harvey Publications

		GD25	FN65	NM94
1-(52 pg. Giant)		1.00	2.60	6.00

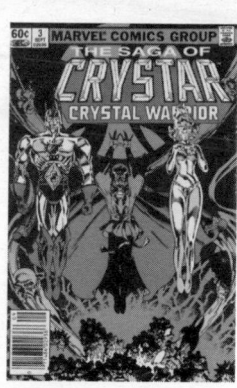
The Saga of Crystar, The Crystal Warrior #3 © Remco

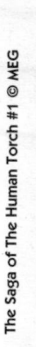
The Saga of The Human Torch #1 © MEG

Saint Sinner #5 © Clive Barker

	GD25	FN65	NM94
2-8		1.20	3.00

SAD SAD SACK WORLD
Oct, 1964 - No. 46, Dec, 1973 (#1-31: 68 pgs.; #32-38: 52 pgs.)
Harvey Publications

1	3.25	9.50	22.00
2-10	1.70	5.00	12.00
11-31: 31-Last 68 pg. issue	1.50	3.75	9.00
32-39-(All 52 pgs)	1.00	2.00	5.00
40-46		1.20	3.00

SAFEST PLACE IN THE WORLD, THE
1993 ($2.50, one-shot)
Dark Horse Comics

1-Steve Ditko-c/a/scripts		1.00	2.50

SAGA OF BIG RED, THE
Sept, 1976 ($1.25) (In color)
Omaha World-Herald
nn-by Win Mumma; story of the Nebraska Cornhuskers (sports)

		.80	2.00

SAGA OF CRYSTAR, CRYSTAL WARRIOR, THE
May, 1983 - No. 11, Feb, 1985 (Remco toy tie-in)
Marvel Comics

1 ($2.00, baxter paper)			2.00
2-5,7-11: 3-Dr. Strange app. 3-11-Golden-c (painted-4,5). 11-Alpha Flight app.			1.00
6-Nightcrawler app; Golden-c.			1.50

SAGA OF RA'S AL GHUL, THE
Jan, 1988 - No. 4, Apr, 1988 ($2.50, limited series)
DC Comics

1-4-r/N. Adams Batman		1.00	2.50

SAGA OF SABAN'S MIGHTY MORPHIN POWER RANGERS (Also see
Saban's Mighty Morphin Power Rangers)
1995 - No. 4, 1995 ($1.95, limited series)
Hamilton Comics

1-4		.80	2.00

SAGA OF THE SWAMP THING, THE (See Swamp Thing)

SAGA OF THE ORIGINAL HUMAN TORCH
Apr, 1990 - No. 4, July, 1990 ($1.50, limited series)
Marvel Comics

1-4: 1-Origin; Buckler-c/a(p). 3-Hitler-c			1.50

SAGA OF THE SUB-MARINER, THE
Nov, 1988 - No. 12, Oct, 1989 ($1.25/$1.50 #5 on)
Marvel Comics

1-12: 9-Original X-Men app.			1.50

SAILOR ON THE SEA OF FATE (See First Comics Graphic Novel #11)

SAILOR SWEENEY (Navy Action #1-11, 15 on)
No. 12, July, 1956 - No. 14, Nov, 1956
Atlas Comics (CDS)

12-14: 12-Shores-a. 13-Severin-c	7.50	22.50	45.00

SAINT, THE (Also see Movie Comics(DC) #2 & Silver Streak #18)
Aug, 1947 - No. 12, Mar, 1952
Avon Periodicals

1-Kamen bondage-c/a	60.00	181.00	485.00
2	38.00	114.00	265.00
3,4: 4-Lingerie panels	28.00	84.00	195.00
5-Spanking panel	35.00	105.00	245.00
6-Miss Fury app. by Tarpe Mills (14 pgs.)	40.00	120.00	295.00
7-c-/Avon paperback #118	23.00	69.00	160.00

	GD25	FN65	NM94
8,9(12/50): Saint strip-r in #8-12; 9-Kinstler-c	20.00	60.00	140.00
10-Wood-a, 1 pg; c-/Avon paperback #289	20.00	60.00	140.00
11	13.50	41.00	95.00
12-c-/Avon paperback #123	17.00	49.00	115.00

NOTE: *Lucky Dale, Girl Detective* in #1,2,4,6. *Hollingsworth* a-4, 6. *Painted-c* 7, 8, 10-12.

ST. GEORGE
June, 1988 - No.8, Oct, 1989 ($1.25,/$1.50)
Marvel Comics (Epic Comics)

1-8: Sienkiewicz-c 3-begin $1.50-c			1.50

SAINT SINNER (See Razorline)
Oct, 1993 - No. 7, Apr, 1994 ($1.75)
Marvel Comics (Razorline)

1-($2.50)-Foil embossed-c; created by Clive Barker		1.00	2.50
2-7: 5-Ectokid x-over		.70	1.75

ST. SWITHIN'S DAY
Apr, 1990 ($2.50, one-shot)
Trident Comics

1-Grant Morrison scripts			2.50

SALERNO CARNIVAL OF COMICS (Also see Pure Oil Comics, 24 Pages of
Comics, & Vicks Comics)
Late 1930s (Giveaway, 16 pgs, paper-c)
Salerno Cookie Co.
nn-Color reprints of Calkins' Buck Rogers & Skyroads, plus other strips from
Famous Funnies

	48.00	144.00	385.00

SALOME' (See Night Music #6)

SAM AND MAX, FREELANCE POLICE SPECIAL
1987 ($1.75, B&W); Jan, 1989 ($2.75, 44 pgs.)
Fishwrap Productions/Comico

1 ($1.75, B&W, Fishwrap)		.70	1.75
2 ($2.75, color, Comico)		1.10	2.75

SAM HILL PRIVATE EYE
1950 - No. 7, 1951
Close-Up (Archie)

1	13.00	39.00	90.00
2	8.35	25.00	50.00
3-7	7.50	22.50	45.00

SAM SLADE ROBOHUNTER
Oct, 1986 - No. 31, 1989 ($1.25/$1.50)
Quality Comics

1-19 ($1.25)			1.25
20-20-31 ($1.50)			1.50

SAMSON (1st Series) (Captain Aero #7 on; see Big 3 Comics)
Fall, 1940 - No. 6, Sept, 1941 (See Fantastic Comics)
Fox Features Syndicate

1-Samson begins, ends #6; Powell-a, a signed 'Rensie;' Wing Turner by Tuska app; Fine-c?	175.00	525.00	1400.00
2-Dr. Fung by Powell; Fine-c?	68.00	206.00	550.00
3-Navy Jones app.; Joe Simon-c	56.00	168.00	450.00
4-Yarko the Great, Master Magician begins	48.00	144.00	385.00
5,6: 6-Origin The Topper	40.00	120.00	300.00

SAMSON (2nd Series) (Formerly Fantastic Comics #10, 11)
No. 12, April, 1955 - No. 14, Aug, 1955
Ajax/Farrell Publications (Four Star)

12-Wonder Boy	24.00	73.00	170.00
13,14: 13-Wonder Boy, Rocket Man	21.00	64.00	150.00

SAMSON (See Mighty Samson)

SAMSON & DELILAH (See A Spectacular Feature Magazine)

Samuree #2 © Continuity

Sandman #75 © DC

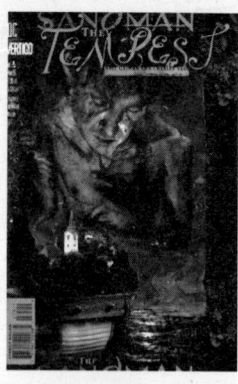

Sandman Mystery Theatre #46 © DC

	GD25	FN65	NM94

SAMUEL BRONSTON'S CIRCUS WORLD (See Circus World under Movie Comics)

SAMURAI (Also see Eclipse Graphic Album Series #14)
1985 - No. 22, 1988? ($1.70, B&W)
Aircel Publications

		GD25	FN65	NM94
1			1.20	3.00
1-2nd & 3rd printings			.70	1.70
2-12,17-22			.70	1.70
2-2nd printing			.70	1.70
13-Dale Keown's 1st published artwork (1987)		1.20	2.90	7.00
14-16-Dale Keown-a		1.00	2.00	5.00

SAMURAI CAT
June, 1991 - No. 3, Sept, 1991 ($2.25, limited series)
Marvel Comics (Epic Comics)

1-3: 3-Darth Vader-c/story parody		.90	2.25

SAMUREE
May, 1987 - No. 12, 1988?
Continuity Comics

1-12		.80	2.00

SAMUREE
V2#1, May, 1993 - V2#4, Jan,1994 ($2.50)
Continuity Comics

V2#1-4-Embossed-c: 2,4-Adams plot, Nebres-i. 3-Nino-c(i)	1.00	2.50

SAMUREE
Oct, 1995 - No. 3, Dec,1995 ($2.50, limited series)
Acclaim Comics (Windjammer)

1-3		1.00	2.50

SAN DIEGO COMIC CON COMICS
1992 - No. 3, 1994 (B&W, promo comic for the San Diego Comic Con)
Dark Horse Comics

1 (1992)-Includes various characters published from Dark Horse including Concrete, The Mask, RoboCop and others; 1st app. of Sprint from John Byrne's Next Men; art by Quesada, Byrne, Rude, Burden, Moebius & others; pin-ups by Rude, Dorkin, Allred & others; Chadwick-c. ... 5.00

2 (1993)-Intro of Legend imprint; 1st app. of John Byrne's Danger Unlimited, Mike Mignola's Hellboy, Art Adam's Monkeyman & O'Brien; contains stories featuring Concrete, Sin City, Martha Washington & others; Grendel, Madman, & Big Guy pin-ups; Don Martin-c. ... 6.00

3 (1994)-Contains stories featuring Barb Wire, The Mask, The Dirty Pair, & Grendel by Matt Wagner; contains pin-ups of Ghost, Predator & Rascals In Paradise; The Mask-c. ... 5.00

SANDMAN, THE (1st Series) (Also see Adventure Comics #40, New York World's Fair & World's Finest #3)
Winter, 1974; No. 2, Apr-May, 1975 - No. 6, Dec-Jan, 1975-76
National Periodical Publications

1-1st app. Bronze Age Sandman by Simon & Kirby (last S&K collaboration) .			
	1.70	5.00	12.00
2-6: 6-Kirby/Wood-c/a	1.00	2.00	5.00

NOTE: *Kirby a-1p, 4-6p; c-1-5, 6p.*

SANDMAN (2nd Series) (See Books of Magic, Vertigo Jam & Vertigo Preview)
Jan, 1989 - No. 75, Mar, 1996 ($1.50/$1.75/$2.50, mature)
DC Comics (Vertigo imprint #47 on)

1 ($2.00, 52 pgs.)-1st app. Modern Age Sandman (Morpheus); Neil Gaiman scripts begin; Sam Kieth-a(p) in #1-5; Wesley Dodds (G.A. Sandman) cameo.	11.50	34.00	80.00
2-Cain & Abel app. (from HOM & HOS)	7.00	21.50	50.00
3-5: 3-John Constantine app.	5.70	17.00	40.00
6,7	4.30	13.00	30.00

8-Regular ed. has Jeanette Kahn publishorial & American Cancer Society ad w/no indicia on inside front-c; Death-c/story (1st app.)

	8.00	23.50	55.00
8-Limited ed. (600+ copies?); has Karen Berger editorial and next issue teaser on inside covers (has indicia)	29.00	86.00	200.00
9-13: 10-Has explanation about #8 mixup; has bound-in Shocker movie poster	2.40	7.20	17.00
14-($2.50, 52 pgs.)-Bound-in Nightbreed fold-out	2.60	7.50	18.00
15-20: 16-Photo-c. 17,18-Kelley Jones-a. 19-Vess-a.	1.65	4.20	10.00
18-Error version w/1st 3 panels on pg. 1 in blue ink	2.85	8.50	20.00
19-Error version w/switched pgs. (no 2 pg. spread)	2.85	8.50	20.00
21,23-27: Seasons of Mist storyline. 22-World Without End preview. 24-Kelley Jones/Russell-a	1.65	4.20	10.00
22-1st Daniel (Later becomes new Sandman)	3.60	11.00	25.00
28-30	1.00	2.60	6.00
31-35,37-48: 41,44-48-Metallic ink on-c. 48-Cerebus appears as a doll		1.60	4.00
36-($2.50, 52 pgs.)	1.00	2.00	5.00
49,51-53,55: 49-Begin $1.95-c		1.20	3.00
50-($2.95, 52 pgs.)-Black-c w/metallic ink by McKean; Russell-a; McFarlane pin-up	1.00	2.00	5.00
50-($2.95)-Signed & limited (5,000) Treasury Edition with sketch of Neil Gaiman	2.15	6.50	15.00
50-Platinum			50.00
54-Re-intro Prez; Death app.; Belushi, Nixon & Wildcat cameos.		1.60	4.00
56-68: 57-Metallic ink on c. 65-w/bound-in trading card		.80	2.00
69-Death of Sandman		1.20	3.00
70-75: 70-73-Zulli-a. 74-Jon J. Muth-a. 75-Vess-a.		1.00	2.50
Annual 1 (10/94, $3.95)		1.60	4.00
Special 1 (1991, $3.50, 68 pgs.)-Glow-in-the-dark-c	1.30	3.25	8.00
....: A Gallery of Dreams ($2.95)-Intro by N. Gaiman		1.20	3.00
....: Preludes & Nocturnes ($29.95, HC)-r/#1-8.			30.00
....: The Doll's House (1990, $29.95, HC)-r/#8-16.			30.00
....: Dream Country ($29.95, HC)-r/#17-20.			30.00
....: Season of Mists ($29.95, Leatherbound HC)-r/21-28.			30.00
....: A Game of You ($29.95, HC)-r/32-37.			30.00
....: Fables and Reflections ($29.95, HC)-r/Vertigo Preview #1, Sandman Special #1, #29-31, #38-40 & #50.			30.00
....: Brief Lives ($29.95, HC)-r/#41-49.			30.00
....: World's End ($29.95, HC)-r/#51-56.			30.00
....: The Kindly Ones (1996, $34.95, HC)-r/#57-69 & Vertigo Jam#1			35.00

NOTE: *Bachalo a-12; Kelley Jones a-17, 18, 22, 23, 26, 27. Vess a-19, 75.*

SANDMAN MIDNIGHT THEATRE
Sept, 1995 ($6.95, squarebound one-shot)
DC Comics (Vertigo)

nn-Modern Age Sandman (Morpheus) meets G.A. Sandman; Gaiman & Wagner story, Kristiansen-a.	1.20	3.00	7.00

SANDMAN MYSTERY THEATRE (Also see Sandman (2nd Series) #1)
Apr, 1993 - Present ($1.95/$2.25, mature)
DC Comics (Vertigo)

1-60: 1-G.A. Sandman advs. begin; Matt Wagner scripts begin. 5-Neon ink logo. 28-Begin $2.25-c. 29-32-Hourman app. 38-Ted Knight (G.A. Starman) app. 42-Jim Corrigan (Spectre) app. 45-48-Blackhawk app.		.90	2.25
Annual 1 (10/94, $3.95, 68 pgs.)-Bolton, Ross & others-a.			
		1.60	4.00

SANDMAN MIDNIGHT THEATRE
Sept, 1995 ($6.95, squarebound, one-shot)
DC Comics (Vertigo)

nn-Modern Age Sandman (Morpheus) meets G.A. Sandman; Gaiman & Wagner story; McKean-c; Kristiansen-a	1.20	3.00	7.00

SANDS OF THE SOUTH PACIFIC
Jan, 1953

Santa Claus Paradfe #1 © Z-D

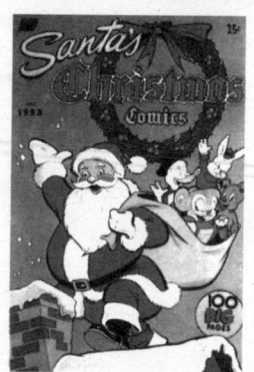

Santa's Christmas Comics © STD

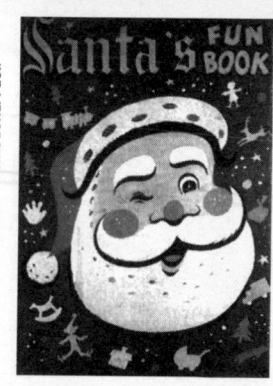

Santa's Fun Book © Promotional Publ.

SA

	GD25	FN65	NM94
Toby Press			
1	18.00	54.00	125.00
SANTA AND HIS REINDEER (See March of Comics #166)			
SANTA AND POLLYANNA PLAY THE GLAD GAME			
Aug, 1960 (16 pgs.) (Disney giveaway)			
Sales Promotion			
nn	2.40	6.00	12.00
SANTA AND THE ANGEL (See Dell Junior Treasury #7)			
Dec, 1949 (Combined w/Santa at the Zoo) (Gollub-a condensed from FC#128)			
Dell Publishing Co.			
Four Color 259	5.00	15.00	50.00
SANTA & THE BUCCANEERS			
1959 (Giveaway)			
Promotional Publ. Co.			
nn-Reprints 1952 Santa & the Pirates	1.80	4.50	9.00
SANTA & THE CHRISTMAS CHICKADEE			
1974 (Giveaway, 20 pgs.)			
Murphy's			
nn	1.00	2.00	5.00
SANTA & THE PIRATES			
1952 (Giveaway)			
Promotional Publ. Co.			
nn-Marv Levy-c/a	2.40	6.00	12.00
SANTA AT THE ZOO			
Dec, 1949 (Combined w/Santa and the Angel) (Gollub-a condensed from #128)			
Dell Publishing Co.			
Four Color 259	5.00	15.00	45.00
SANTA CLAUS AROUND THE WORLD (See March of Comics #241)			
SANTA CLAUS CONQUERS THE MARTIANS (See Movie Classics)			
SANTA CLAUS FUNNIES (Also see The Little Fir Tree)			
nd; 1940 (Giveaway, 8x10") 12 pgs., color & B&W, heavy paper)			
W. T. Grant Co./Whitman Publishing			
nn-(2 versions)	12.00	36.00	85.00
SANTA CLAUS FUNNIES (Also see Dell Giants)			
Dec?, 1942 - No. 1274, Dec, 1961			
Dell Publishing Co.			
nn(#1)(1942)-Kelly-a	39.00	118.00	390.00
2(12/43)-Kelly-a	25.00	75.00	250.00
Four Color 61(1944)-Kelly-a	24.00	72.00	240.00
Four Color 91(1945)-Kelly-a	18.00	54.00	180.00
Four Color 128('46),175('47)-Kelly-a	14.00	43.00	140.00
Four Color 205,254-Kelly-a	13.00	40.00	130.00
Four Color 302,361	4.00	12.00	40.00
Four Color 525,607,666,756,867	4.00	12.00	40.00
Four Color 958,1063,1154,1274	3.50	10.50	35.00
NOTE: Most issues contain only one Kelly story.			
SANTA CLAUS PARADE			
1951; No. 2, Dec, 1952; No. 3, Jan, 1955 (25¢)			
Ziff-Davis (Approved Comics)/St. John Publishing Co.			
1(1951-Ziff-Davis)-116 pgs. (Xmas Special 1,2)	24.00	73.00	170.00
2(12/52-Ziff-Davis)-100 pgs.; Dave Berg-a	19.00	58.00	135.00
1#3(1/55-St. John)-100 pgs.; reprints-c/#1	17.00	49.00	115.00
SANTA CLAUS' WORKSHOP (See March of Comics #50, 168)			
SANTA IS COMING (See March of Comics #197)			
SANTA IS HERE (See March of Comics #49)			
SANTA ON THE JOLLY ROGER			
1965			

	GD25	FN65	NM94
Promotional Publ. Co. (Giveaway)			
nn-Marv Levy-c/a	.80	2.00	4.00
SANTA! SANTA!			
1974 (20 pgs.)			
R. Jackson (Montgomery Ward giveaway)			
nn		1.20	3.00
SANTA'S BUSY CORNER (See March of Comics #31)			
SANTA'S CANDY KITCHEN (See March of Comics #14)			
SANTA'S CHRISTMAS BOOK (See March of Comics #123)			
SANTA'S CHRISTMAS COMICS			
Dec, 1952 (100 pgs.)			
Standard Comics (Best Books)			
nn-Supermouse, Dizzy Duck, Happy Rabbit, etc.	16.00	47.00	110.00
SANTA'S CHRISTMAS COMIC VARIETY SHOW			
1943 (24 pgs.)			
Sears Roebuck & Co.			
Contains puzzles & new comics of Dick Tracy, Little Orphan Annie, Moon Mullins, Terry & the Pirates, etc.	29.00	86.00	200.00
SANTA'S CHRISTMAS LIST (See March of Comics #255)			
SANTA'S CHRISTMAS TIME STORIES			
nd (Late 1940s) (16 pgs., paper-c)			
Premium Sales, Inc. (Giveaway)			
nn	5.00	15.00	30.00
SANTA'S CIRCUS			
1964 (Giveaway, half-size)			
Promotional Publ. Co.			
nn-Marv Levy-c/a	1.20	3.00	6.00
SANTA'S FUN BOOK			
1951, 1952 (Regular size, 16 pgs., paper-c)			
Promotional Publ. Co. (Murphy's giveaway)			
nn	3.00	7.50	15.00
SANTA'S GIFT BOOK			
No date (16 pgs.)			
No Publisher			
nn-Puzzles, games only	2.40	6.00	12.00
SANTA'S HELPERS (See March of Comics #64, 106, 198)			
SANTA'S LITTLE HELPERS (See March of Comics #270)			
SANTA'S NEW STORY BOOK			
1949 (16 pgs., paper-c)			
Wallace Hamilton Campbell (Giveaway)			
nn	5.00	15.00	30.00
SANTA'S REAL STORY BOOK			
1948, 1952 (Giveaway, 16 pgs.)			
Wallace Hamilton Campbell/W. W. Orris			
nn	4.70	14./00	28.00
SANTA'S RIDE			
1959 (Giveaway)			
W. T. Grant Co.			
nn	2.80	7.00	14.00
SANTA'S RODEO			
1964 (Giveaway, half-size)			
Promotional Publ. Co.			
nn-Marv Levy-a	1.00	2.00	5.00
SANTA'S SECRETS			
1951, 1952? (16 pgs., paper-c)			

Satanika #1 © Verotik

Savage Dragon #31 © Erik Larsen

Savage Dragon/Teenage Mutant Ninja Turtles #1 © Erik Larsen/Mirage Studios

Sam B. Anson Christmas giveaway

nn-Has games, stories & pictures to color	3.20	8.00	16.00

SANTA'S SHOW (See March of Comics #311)
SANTA'S SLEIGH (See March of Comics #298)
SANTA'S STORIES
1953 (Regular size, paper-c)
K. K. Publications (Klines Dept. Store)

nn-Kelly-a	16.00	47.00	110.00
nn-Another version (1953, glossy-c, half-size, 7-1/4x5-1/4")-Kelly-a	11.00	33.00	75.00

SANTA'S SURPRISE (See March of Comics #13)
SANTA'S SURPRISE
1947 (Giveaway, 36 pgs., slick-c)
K. K. Publications

nn	5.00	15.00	30.00

SANTA'S TINKER TOTS
1958
Charlton Comics

1-Based on "The Tinker Tots Keep Christmas"	2.80	7.00	14.00

SANTA'S TOYLAND (See March of Comics #242)
SANTA'S TOYS (See March of Comics #12)
SANTA'S TOYTOWN FUN BOOK
1953 (Giveaway)
Promotional Publ. Co.

nn-Marv Levy-c	1.40	3.50	7.00

SANTA'S VISIT (See March of Comics #283)
SANTIAGO (Movie)
Sept, 1956 (Alan Ladd photo-c)
Dell Publishing Co.

Four Color 723-Kinstler-a	11.00	33.00	110.00

SARGE SNORKEL (Beetle Bailey)
Oct, 1973 - No. 17, Dec, 1976
Charlton Comics

1	1.00	2.00	5.00
2-17		.80	2.00

SARGE STEEL (Becomes Secret Agent #9 on; also see Judomaster)
Dec, 1964 - No. 8, Mar-Apr, 1966 (All 12¢ issues)
Charlton Comics

1-Origin & 1st app.	2.15	6.50	15.00
2-5,7,8	1.20	3.00	7.00
6-2nd app. Judomaster	1.65	4.20	10.00

SATANIKA
Jan, 1995 - No. 2, 1995 ($2.95, limited series, mature)
Verotik

0-2: Danzig story in all. 0-(7/95)-Frazetta-c; 1-Bisley-c.			
	1.00	2.60	6.00
The Brimstone Trail (1996, $9.95, TPB)-r/#0-2.			10.00

SATANIKA
Feb, 1996 - Present ($2.95, mature)
Verotik

1-3: Danzig story in all. 2-Igrat cameo; indicia reads "Satanika #1."			
			3.00

SATANIKA X
Feb, 1996 ($4.95, one-shot, mature)
Verotik

1-Embossed-c.			5.00

SATAN'S SIX
Apr, 1993 - No. 4, July, 1993 ($2.95, limited series)
Topps Comics (Kirbyverse)

1-Polybagged w/Kirbychrome trading card; Kirby/McFarlane-c plus 8 pgs.
Kirby-a(p); has coupon for Kirbychrome ed. of Secret City Saga #0

	1.20		3
2-4-Polybagged w/3 cards. 4-Teenagents preview	1.20		3

NOTE: *Ditko* a-1. *Miller* a-1.

SATAN'S SIX: HELLSPAWN
June, 1994 - No. 3, July, 1994 ($2.50, limited series)
Topps Comics (Kirbyverse)

1-3: 1-(6/94)-Indicia incorrectly shows "Vol 1 #2". 2-(6/94)	1.00		2

SAVAGE COMBAT TALES
Feb, 1975 - No. 3, July, 1975
Atlas/Seaboard Publ.

1-3: 1-Sgt. Stryker's Death Squad begins (origin). 2-Only app. Warhawk			
			1.

NOTE: *Buckler* c-3. *McWilliams* a-1-3; c-1. *Sparling* a-1, 3. *Toth* a-2.

SAVAGE DRAGON, THE (See Megaton #3 & 4)
July, 1992 - No. 3, Dec, 1992 ($1.95, limited series)
Image Comics (Highbrow Entertainment)

1-Erik Larsen-c/a/scripts & bound-in poster in all; 4 cover color variations w/4
different posters; 1st Highbrow Entertainment title.

	1.60		4.
2-Intro SuperPatriot-c/story (10/92)	1.60		4.
3-Contains coupon for Image Comics #0	1.00		2.
3-With coupon missing	.80		2.
...Vs. Savage Megaton Man 1 (3/93, $1.95)-Larsen & Simpson-c/a.			
	.80		2.

SAVAGE DRAGON, THE
June, 1993 - Present ($1.95/$2.50)
Image Comics (Highbrow Entertainment)

1-Erik Larsen-c/a/scripts	1.20		3.
3-7: Erik Larsen-c/a/scripts. 3-Mighty Man back-up story w/Austin-a(i). 4-Flip book w/Ricochet. 5-Mighty Man flip-c & back-up plus poster. 6-Jae Lee poster. 7-Vanguard poster	.90		2.
2,27-(Wondercon Exclusive): 2-($2.95, 52 pgs.)-Teenage Mutant Ninja Turtles-c/story; flip book features Vanguard #0 (See Megaton for 1st app.). 27 (Wondercon Exclusive)-new-c.	1.20		3.
8-12,13B,14-15: 8-Deadly Duo poster by Larsen. 13B (6/95)-Larsen story. 15-Dragon poster by Larsen.	.80		2.
13A,16-24,26-38: 13A (10/94)-Jim Lee-c/a; 1st app. Max Cash (Condition Red). 16-$2.50-c begins. 22-TMNT-c/a; Bisley pin-up. 28-Maxx-c/app. 29-Wildstar-c/app. 30-Spawn app. 31-God vs. The Devil; alternate version exists w/o expletives (has "God Is Good" inside Image log	1.00		2.
25 ($3.95)-variant-c exists.			4.

SAVAGE DRAGON/TEENAGE MUTANT NINJA TURTLES CROSSOVER
Sept, 1993 ($2.75, one-shot)
Mirage Studios

1-Erik Larsen-c(i) only	1.10		2.

SAVAGE HENRY
Jan, 1987 - No. 16?, 1990 ($1.75/$2.00, B&W, mature)
Vortex Comics

1-9 ($1.75)	.70		1.
10-15 ($2.00)	.80		2.
16-Begin $2.50-c	1.00		2.

SAVAGE HULK, THE (Also see Incredible Hulk)
Jan, 1996 ($6.95, one-shot)
Marvel Comics

The Savage Hulk #1 © MEG

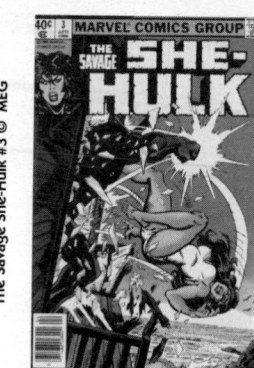
The Savage She-Hulk #3 © MEG

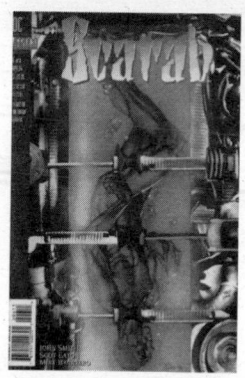
Scarab #6 © DC

	GD25	FN65	NM94

1-Bisley-c; David, Lobdell, Wagner, Loeb, Gibbons, Messner-Loebs scripts; McKone, Kieth, Ramos & Sale-a.   7.00

SAVAGE RAIDS OF GERONIMO (See Geronimo #4)

SAVAGE RANGE (See Luke Short, Four Color 807)

SAVAGE RETURN OF DRACULA
1992 ($2.00, 52 pgs.)
Marvel Comics

1-r/Tomb of Dracula #1,2 by Gene Colan   .80   2.00

SAVAGE SHE-HULK, THE (See The Avengers, Marvel Graphic Novel #18 & The Sensational She-Hulk)
Feb, 1980 - No. 25, Feb, 1982
Marvel Comics Group

1-Origin & 1st app. She-Hulk	1.20	3.00	7.00
2-10		1.20	3.00
11-25: 25-(52 pgs.)		.90	2.25

NOTE: Austin a-25i; c-23i-25i. J. Buscema a-1p; c-1, 2p. Golden c-8-11.

SAVAGE SWORD OF CONAN (The... #41 on; ...The Barbarian #175 on)
Aug, 1974 - No. 235, July, 1995 ($1.00/$1.25/$2.25, B&W magazine, mature)
Marvel Comics Group

1-Smith-r; J. Buscema/N. Adams/Krenkel; origin Blackmark by Gil Kane (part 1, ends #3); Blackmark's 1st app. in magazine form-r/from paperback) & Red Sonja (3rd app.)	11.50	34.00	80.00
2-Neal Adams-c; Chaykin/N. Adams-a	5.00	15.00	35.00
3-Severin/B. Smith-a; N. Adams-a	2.90	8.60	20.00
4-Neal Adams/Kane-a(r)	2.10	6.40	15.00
5-10: 5-Jeff Jones frontispiece (r)	1.70	5.00	12.00
11-20	1.50	3.80	9.00
21-50: 34-3 pg. preview of Conan newspaper strip. 35-Cover similar to Savage Tales #1. 45-Red Sonja returns; begin $1.25-c	1.30	3.00	8.00
51-100: 63-Toth frontispiece. 65-Kane-a w/Chaykin/Miller/Simonson/Sherman finishes. 70-Article on movie. 83-Red Sonja-r by Neal Adams from #1	1.00	2.00	5.00
101-176: 163-Begin $2.25-c. 169-King Kull story. 171-Soloman Kane by Williamson (i). 172-Red Sonja story	1.40		3.50
177-235: 179,187,192-Red Sonja story. 190-193-4 part King Kull story. 196, 202-King Kull story. 200-New Buscema-a; Robert E. Howard app. with Conan in story. 204-60th anniversary (1932-92). 211-Rafael Kayanan's 1st Conan-a. 214-Sequel to Red Nails by Robert E. Howard	.90		2.25
Special 1(1975, B&W)-B. Smith-r/Conan #10,13	1.65	4.20	10.00

NOTE: N. Adams a-14p, 60, 83p(r). Alcala a-2, 4, 7, 12, 15-20, 23, 24, 28, 59, 67, 69, 75, 76i, 80i, 82i, 83i, 89, 180i, 184i, 187i, 189i, 216p. Austin a-89i. Boris painted c-1, 4, 5, 7, 9, 10, 12, 15. Brunner a-30; c-8, 30. Buscema a-1-5, 7, 10-12, 15-24, 26-28, 31, 32, 36-43, 45, 47-58p, 60-67p, 70, 71-74p, 76-81p, 87-96p, 98, 99-101p, 190-204p; painted c-40. Chaykin c-31. Chiodo painted c-71, 76, 79, 81, 84, 85, 178. Conrad c-215, 217. Corben a-4, 16, 29. Finlay a-6. Golden a-98, 101; c-98, 101, 105, 106, 117, 124. Kaluta a-11, 18; c-3, 91, 93. Gil Kane a-2, 3, 8, 13r, 29, 47, 64, 65, 67, 85p, 86p. Rafael Kayanan a-211-213, 215, 217. Krenkel a-9, 11, 14, 16, 24. Morrow a-7. Nebres a-93i, 101i, 107, 114. Newton c/a-6. Redondo painted c-48-50, 52, 56, 57, 85i, 90, 96i. Marie & John Severin a-Special 1. Simonson a-7, 8, 12, 15-17. Barry Smith a-7, 16, 24, 82r, Special 1r. Starlin c-26. Toth a-64. Williamson a(i)-162, 171, 186. No. 8, 16 & 16 contain a Robert E. Howard Conan adaptation.

SAVAGE TALES (...Featuring Conan #4 on)(Magazine)
May, 1971; No. 2, 10/73; No. 3, 2/74 - No. 12, Summer, 1975 (B&W)
Marvel Comics Group

1-Origin/1st app. The Man-Thing by Morrow; Conan the Barbarian by Barry Smith (1st Conan x-over outside his own title); Femizons by Romita-r/in #3; Ka-Zar story by Buscema	19.00	58.00	135.00
2-B. Smith, Brunner, Morrow, Williamson-a; Wrightson King Kull reprint/Creatures on the Loose #10	6.00	19.00	45.00
3-B. Smith, Brunner, Steranko, Williamson-a	4.30	12.90	30.00
4,5-N. Adams-c; last Conan (Smith-r/#4) plus Kane/N. Adams-a. 5-Brak the Barbarian begins, ends #8	2.90	8.60	20.00
6-Ka-Zar begins; Williamson-r; N. Adams-c	1.10	2.70	6.50
7-N. Adams-i	1.00	2.00	5.00

8-Shanna, the She-Devil app. thru #10; Williamson-r	1.80		4.50
9,11		1.40	3.50
10-Neal Adams-a(i), Williamson-r	1.80		4.50
...Featuring Ka-Zar Annual 1 (Summer, '75, B&W)(#12 on inside)-Ka-Zar origin by G. Kane; B. Smith-r/Astonishing Tales	.90	2.30	5.50

NOTE: Boris a-7, 10. Buscema a-5r, 6p, 8p; c-2. Colan a-1p. Fabian c-8. Golden a-1, 4; c-1. Heath a-10p, 11p. Kaluta c-9. Maneely r-2, 4(The Crusader in both). Morrow a-1, 2, Annual 1. Reese a-2. Severin a-1-7. Starlin a-5. Robert E. Howard adaptations-1-4.

SAVAGE TALES
Nov, 1985 - No. 9, Mar, 1987 ($1.50, B&W, magazine, mature)
Marvel Comics Group

1-1st app. The Nam; Golden, Morrow-a	1.00	2.00	5.00
2-9: 2,7-Morrow-a. 4-2nd Nam story; Golden-a			1.50

SAVED BY THE BELL (TV)
Mar, 1992 - No. 4, Aug, 1992? ($1.25, limited series)
Harvey Comics

1-4			1.25
Special 1 (9/92, $1.50)-photo-c			1.50

SCAMP (Walt Disney)(See Walt Disney's Comics & Stories #204)
No. 703, 5/56 - No. 1204, 8-10/61; 11/67 - No. 45, 1/79
Dell Publishing Co./Gold Key

Four Color 703(#1)	9.00	27.00	90.00
Four Color 777,806('57),833	7.00	21.00	70.00
5(3-5/58)-10(6-8/59)	5.00	15.00	50.00
11-16(12-2/60-61)	3.50	10.50	35.00
Four Color 1204(1961)	3.50	10.50	35.00
1(12/67-Gold Key)-Reprints begin	3.00	9.00	30.00
2(3/69)-10	1.70	5.00	12.00
11-20	1.30	3.25	8.00
21-45	1.00	2.60	6.00

NOTE: New stories-#20(in part), 22-25, 27, 29-31, 34, 36-40, 42-45. New covers-#11, 12, 14, 15, 17-25, 27, 29-31, 34, 36-38.

SCARAB
Nov, 1993 - No. 8, June, 1994 ($1.95, limited series)
DC Comics (Vertigo)

1-8-Glenn Fabry painted-c: 1-Silver ink-c. 2-Phantom Stranger app.	.80		2.00

SCAR FACE (See The Crusaders)

SCARECROW OF ROMNEY MARSH, THE (See W. Disney Showcase #53)
April, 1964 - No. 3, Oct, 1965 (Disney TV Show)
Gold Key

10124-404 (#1)	3.40	10.00	24.00
2,3	2.60	7.50	18.00

SCARLET O'NEIL (See Harvey Comics Hits #59 & Invisible...)

SCARLET SPIDER
Nov, 1995 - No. 4, Feb, 1996 ($1.95)
Marvel Comics

1-4: Replaces Spider-Man		.80	2.00

SCARLET SPIDER UNLIMITED
Nov, 1995 ($3.95, one-shot)
Marvel Comics

1-Replaces Spider-Man Unlimited	1.60		4.00

SCARLETT
Jan, 1993 - No. 14, Feb, 1994 (1.75)
DC Comics

1-($2.95)	1.20		3.00
2-14	.70		1.75

SCARLET THUNDER
Nov, 1995, - Present ($1.50, B&W)

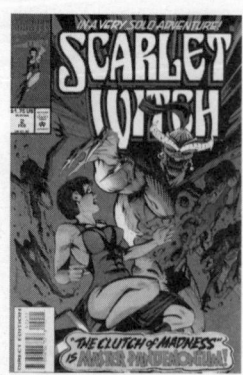

Scarlet Witch #2 © MEG

Scary Tales #1 © Charlton

Scavengers #1 © Quality

	GD25	FN65	NM94

Amaze Ink

1-3: 3-(5/96)			1.50

SCARLET WITCH (See Avengers #16, Vision &... & X-Men #4)
Jan, 1994 - No. 4, Apr, 1994 ($1.75, limited series)
Marvel Comics

1-4		.70	1.75

SCARY TALES
8/75 - #9, 1/77; #10, 9/77 - #20, 6/79; #21, 8/80 - #46, 10/84
Charlton Comics

1-Origin/1st app. Countess Von Bludd, not in #2	1.20		3.00
2-11: 3-Sutton painted-c			1.50
12-36,39,46-All reprints			1.50
37,38,40-45-New-a. 38-Mr. Jigsaw app.			1.50
1(Modern Comics reprint, 1977)			1.00

NOTE: **Adkins** a-31i; c-31i. **Ditko** a-3, 5, 7, 8(2), 11, 12, 14-16r, 18(3)r, 19r, 21r, 30r, 32, 39r; c-5, 11, 14, 18, 30, 32. **Newton** a-31p; c-31p. **Powell** a-18r. **Staton** a-1(2 pgs.), 4, 20r; c-1, 20. **Sutton** a-9; c-4, 9.

SCAVENGERS
Feb, 1988 - No. 14, 1989 ($1.25/$1.50)
Quality Comics

1-7 ($1.25)			1.25
8-14 ($1.50): 9-13-Guice-c			1.50

SCAVENGERS
1993(nd, July) - No. 11, May, 1994 ($2.50, serially numbered)
Triumphant Comics

1-9: 5,6-Triumphant Unleashed x-over. 9-(3/94)	1.00		2.50
0-Retail edition (3/94, $2.50, 36 pgs.)	1.00		2.50
0-Giveaway edition (3/94, 20 pgs.)	1.00		2.50
0-Coupon redemption edition	1.00		2.50
10,11: 10-(4/94)	1.00		2.50

SCHOOL DAY ROMANCES (...of Teen-Agers #4; Popular Teen-Agers #5 on)
Nov-Dec, 1949 - No. 4, May-June, 1950 (Teenage)
Star Publications

1-Toni Gayle (later Toni Gay), Ginger Snapp, Midge Martin & Eve Adams begin	20.00	60.00	140.00
2,3: 3-Jane Powell photo on-c & true life story	13.00	39.00	90.00
4-Ronald Reagan photo on-c; L.B. Cole-c	22.00	66.00	155.00

NOTE: All have **L. B. Cole** covers.

SCHWINN BICYCLE BOOK (...Bike Thrills, 1959)
1949; 1952; 1959 (10¢)
Schwinn Bicycle Co.

1949	5.00	15.00	30.00
1952-Believe It or Not facts; comic format; 36 pgs.	4.00	10.00	20.00
1959	2.00	5.00	10.00

SCIENCE COMICS (1st Series)
Feb, 1940 - No. 8, Sept, 1940
Fox Features Syndicate

1-Origin Dynamo (1st app., called Electro in #1), The Eagle (1st app.), & Navy Jones; Marga, The Panther Woman (1st app.), Cosmic Carson & Perisphere Payne, Dr. Doom begin; bondage/hypo-c; Electro-c	338.00	1012.00	3000.00
2-Lou Fine Dynamo-c	175.00	525.00	1400.00
3-Classic Lou Fine Dynamo-c	150.00	450.00	1200.00
4-Kirby-a; Cosmic Carson-c by Joe Simon	131.00	393.00	1050.00
5-8: 5,8-Eagle-c. 6,7-Dynamo-c	81.00	243.00	650.00

NOTE: Cosmic Carson by **Tuska**-#1-3; by **Kirby**-#4. **Lou Fine** c-1-3 only.

SCIENCE COMICS (2nd Series)
Jan, 1946 - No. 5, 1946
Humor Publications (Ace Magazines?)

1-Palais-c/a in #1-3; A-Bomb-c	12.00	36.00	85.00

	GD25	FN65	NM94

2	6.70	20.00	40
3-Feldstein-a (6 pgs.)	12.00	36.00	85
4,5: 4-Palais-c	5.35	16.00	32

SCIENCE COMICS
May, 1947 (8 pgs. in color)
Ziff-Davis Publ. Co.

nn-Could be ordered by mail for 10¢; like the nn Amazing Adventures (1950) & Boy Cowboy (1950); used to test the market	36.00	107.00	250

SCIENCE COMICS (True Science Illustrated)
Mar, 1951
Export Publication Ent., Toronto, Canada
Distr. in U.S. by Kable News Co.

1-Science Adventure stories plus some true science features; man on moon story	8.00	24.00	48

SCIENCE FICTION SPACE ADVENTURES (See Space Adventures)

SCOOBY DOO (TV)(...Where are you? #1-16,26; ...Mystery Comics #17-25, 27 on)(See March Of Comics #356, 368, 382, 391)
Mar, 1970 - No. 30, Feb, 1975 (Hanna-Barbera)
Gold Key

1	4.00	12.00	40
2-5	2.50	7.50	25
6-10	2.00	6.00	20
11-20: 11-Tufts-a	1.85	5.50	13.
21-30	1.50	3.75	9.

SCOOBY DOO (TV)
Apr, 1975 - No. 11, Dec, 1976 (Hanna-Barbera)
Charlton Comics

1	2.30	6.90	16.
2-5	1.30	3.25	8.
6-11	1.00	2.60	6.

SCOOBY-DOO (TV)
Oct, 1977 - No. 9, Feb, 1979 (Hanna-Barbera)
Marvel Comics Group

1-Dyno-Mutt begins		1.20	3.
2-9			1.

SCOOBY-DOO (TV)
Sept, 1992 - No. 3, May, 1993 ($1.25)
Harvey Comics

V2#1,2			1.
Big Book 1,2 (11/92, 4/93, $1.95, 52 pgs.)		.80	2.
Giant Size 1,2 (10/92, 3/93, $2.25, 68 pgs.)		.90	2.

SCOOBY DOO (TV)
Oct, 1995 - Present ($1.50)
Archie Comics

1-12: 12-Cover by Scooby Doo creative designer Iwao Takamoto			1.

SCOOP COMICS (Becomes Yankee Comics #4-7, a digest sized cartoon boo not listed in this guide; becomes Snap #9)
November, 1941 - No. 3, Mar, 1943; No. 8, 1944
Harry 'A' Chesler (Holyoke)

1-Intro. Rocketman & Rocketgirl & begins; origin The Master Key & begins; Dan Hastings begins; Charles Sultan-c/a	109.00	328.00	875.
2-Rocket Boy begins; injury to eye story (reprinted in Spotlight #3); classic-c	109.00	328.00	875.
3-Injury to eye story-r from #2; Rocket Boy	56.00	168.00	450.
8-Formerly Yankee Comics; becomes Snap	36.00	107.00	250.

SCOOTER (See Swing With...)

SCOOTER COMICS

The Scorpion #3 © ATLAS

Scout #11 © ECL

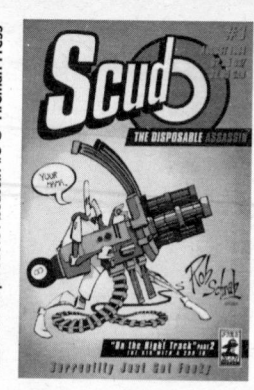

Scud The Disposable Assassin #3 © Fireman Press

SE

	GD25	FN65	NM94

Apr, 1946
Rucker Publ. Ltd. (Canadian)

1-Teen-age/funny animal	8.70	26.00	52.00

SCORCHED EARTH
Apr, 1991 - No. 6, 1991 ($2.95, stiff-c)
Tundra Publishing

1-6		1.20	3.00

SCORE, THE
1989 - No. 4, 1990 ($4.95, 52 pgs, squarebound, mature)
DC Comics (Piranha Press)

Books One - Four		1.20	3.00

SCORPION
Feb, 1975 - No. 3, July, 1975
Atlas/Seaboard Publ.

1-Intro.; bondage-c by Chaykin			1.20
2,3: 2-Chaykin-a w/Wrightson, Kaluta, Simonson assists(p)			1.00
NOTE: *Chaykin a-1, 2; c-1. Colon c-2. Craig c/a-3.*

SCORPION CORPS
Nov, 1993 - No. 7, May, 1994? ($2.75/$2.50)
Dagger Comics Group

1,2-($2.75): 1-Intro Angel Dust, Shellcase, Tork, Feedback & Magnon			
		1.10	2.75
2-Bronze		1.10	2.75
2-Gold		1.10	2.75
2-Silver		1.10	2.75
3-7-($2.50)		1.00	2.50

SCORPIO ROSE
Jan, 1983 - No. 2, Oct, 1983 ($1.25, Baxter paper)
Eclipse Comics

1,2: Dr. Orient back-up story begins. 2-origin.			1.25

SCOTLAND YARD (Inspector Farnsworth of)(Texas Rangers in Action #5 on?)
June, 1955 - No. 4, Mar, 1956
Charlton Comics Group

1-Tothish-a	12.00	36.00	85.00
2-4: 2-Tothish-a	10.00	30.00	58.00

SCOUT (See Eclipse Graphic Album #16, New America & Swords of
Texas)(Becomes Scout: War Shaman)
Dec, 1985 - No. 27, Oct, 1987($1.75/$1.25, Baxter paper)
Eclipse Comics

1-8,11,12: 11-Monday, the Eliminator begins		.75	1.80
9,10 ($1.25): 9-Airboy preview. 10-Bissette-a			1.25
13-15,17,18,20-24 ($1.75): 15-Swords of Texas		.75	1.80
16-Scout 3-D Special ($2.50)		1.00	2.50
16-Scout 2-D Limited Edition		1.00	2.50
19-contains flexi-disk ($2.50)		1.00	2.50
Handbook 1 (8/87, $1.75, B&W)		.70	1.75

SCOUT: WAR SHAMAN (Formerly Scout)
Mar, 1988 - No. 16, Dec, 1989 ($1.95)
Eclipse Comics

1-16		.80	2.00

SCREAM (...Comics) (Andy Comics #20 on)
Autumn, 1944 - No. 19, Apr, 1948
Humor Publications/Current Books(Ace Magazines)

1-Teenage humor	13.50	41.00	95.00
	8.00	24.00	48.00
2-16: 11-Racist humor (Indians). 16-Intro. Lily-Belle	6.70	20.00	40.00
17,19	5.00	15.00	30.00
18-Hypo needle story	6.70	20.00	40.00

	GD25	FN65	NM94

SCREAM
Aug, 1973 - No. 11, Feb, 1975 (68 pgs., B&W, magazine)
Skywald Publishing Corp.

1	1.70	5.00	12.00
2-5: 2-Origin Lady Satan. 3 (12/73)-#3 found on pg. 22			
	1.20	3.00	7.00
6-11: 6-Origin The Victims. 9-Severed head-c. 11- "Mr. Poe and the Raven" story	1.00	2.60	6.00

SCREWBALL SQIRREL
July, 1995 - No. 3, Sept, 1995 ($2.50, limited series)
Dark Horse Comics

1-3: Characters created by Tex Avery		1.00	2.50

SCRIBBLY (See All-American Comics, Buzzy, The Funnies, Leave It To Binky
& Popular Comics)
8-9/48 - No. 13, 8-9/50; No. 14, 10-11/51 - No. 15, 12-1/51-52
National Periodical Publications

1-Sheldon Mayer-c/a in all; 52 pgs. begin	93.00	281.00	750.00
2	61.00	183.00	490.00
3-5	48.00	146.00	390.00
6-10	37.00	111.00	260.00
11-15: 13-Last 52 pgs.	33.00	99.00	230.00

SCUD: THE DISPOSABLE ASSASSIN
Feb, 1994 - Present ($2.95, B&W)
Fireman Press

1	1.20	3.00	7.00
2,3	1.00	2.00	5.00
4-13: 13-(7/96)		1.20	3.00

SEA DEVILS (See Limited Collectors' Edition #39,45, & Showcase #27-29)
Sept-Oct, 1961 - No. 35, May-June, 1967
National Periodical Publications

1-(9-10/61)	56.00	169.00	475.00
2-Last 10¢ issue	30.00	90.00	230.00
3-Begin 12¢ issues thru #35	19.00	58.00	145.00
4,5	18.00	54.00	135.00
6-10	10.00	30.00	75.00
11,12,14-20	8.00	23.50	60.00
13-Kubert, Colan-a; Joe Kubert app. in story	8.00	24.50	65.00
21-35: 22-Intro. International Sea Devils; origin & 1st app. Capt. X & Man Fish	5.50	17.00	40.00
NOTE: *Heath a-B&B 27-29, 1-10; c-B&B 27-29, 1-10, 14-16. Moldoff a-16i.*

SEADRAGON (Also see the Epsilion Wave)
May, 1986 - No. 8, 1987 ($1.75)
Elite Comics

1-8: 1-1st & 2nd printings exist		.70	1.75

SEA HOUND, THE (Captain Silver's Log Of The...)
1945 (no month) - No. 2, Sept-Oct, 1945
Avon Periodicals

nn (#1)-29 pg. novel length sty-"The Esmeralda's Treasure"			
	12.00	36.00	85.00
2	10.00	30.00	65.00

SEA HOUND, THE (Radio)
No. 3, July, 1949 - No. 4, Sept, 1949
Capt. Silver Syndicate

3,4	8.00	24.00	48.00

SEA HUNT (TV)
No. 928, 8/58 - No. 1041, 10-12/59; No. 4, 1-3/60 - No. 13, 4-6/62
Dell Publishing Co. (All have Lloyd Bridges photo-c)

Four Color 928(#1)	12.00	36.00	120.00
Four Color 994(#2), 4-13: Manning-a #4-6,8-11,13	8.50	26.00	85.00

Sebastian O #3 © Grant Morrison

Second Life of Doctor Mirage #10 © Voyager Comm.

Secret Defenders #9 © MEG

	GD25	FN65	NM94
Four Color 1041(#3)-Toth-a	9.00	27.00	90.00
SEAQUEST (TV)			
Mar, 1994 ($2.25)			
Nemesis Comics			
1-Has 2 diff-c stocks (slick & cardboard); Alcala-i		.90	2.25
SEARCH FOR LOVE			
Feb-Mar, 1950 - No. 2, Apr-May, 1950 (52 pgs.)			
American Comics Group			
1	10.00	30.00	60.00
2,3(6-7/50): 3-Exist?	6.70	20.00	40.00
SEARCHERS, THE (Movie)			
No. 709, 1956			
Dell Publishing Co.			
Four Color 709-John Wayne photo-c	26.00	78.00	260.00
SEARS (See Merry Christmas From...)			
SEASON'S GREETINGS			
1935 (6-1/4x5-1/4", 32 pgs. in color)			
Hallmark (King Features)			
nn-Cover features Mickey Mouse, Popeye, Jiggs & Skippy. "The Night Before			
Christmas" told one panel per page, each panel by a famous artist featuring			
their character. Art by Alex Raymond, Gottfredson, Swinnerton, Segar, Chic			
Young, Milt Gross, Sullivan (Messmer), Herriman, McManus, Percy Crosby			
& others (22 artists in all)			
Estimated value...		500.00	
SEBASTION O			
May, 1993 - No. 3, July, 1993 ($1.95, limited series)			
DC Comics (Vertigo)			
1-3-Grant Morrison scripts		.80	2.00
SECOND LIFE OF DOCTOR MIRAGE, THE (See Shadowman #16)			
Nov, 1993 - No. 18, May, 1995 ($2.50)			
Valiant			
1-18: 1-With bound-in poster. 5-Shadowman x-over. 7-Bound-in trading card		1.00	2.50
1-Gold ink logo edition; no price on-c	1.00	2.00	5.00
SECRET AGENT (Formerly Sarge Steel)			
V2#9, Oct, 1966; V2#10, Oct, 1967			
Charlton Comics			
V2#9-Sarge Steel part-r begins	1.65	4.20	10.00
10-Tiffany Sinn, CIA app. (from Career Girl Romances #39); Aparo-a	1.00	2.00	5.00
SECRET AGENT (TV) (See Four Color #1231)			
Nov, 1966; No. 2, Jan, 1968			
Gold Key			
1-Photo-c	17.00	49.00	115.00
2-Photo-c	9.50	28.00	75.00
SECRET AGENT X-9 (See Flash Gordon #4 by King)			
1934 (Book 1: 84 pgs.; Book 2: 124 pgs.) (8x7-1/2")			
David McKay Publications			
Book 1-Contains reprints of the first 13 weeks of the strip by Alex Raymond;			
complete except for 2 dailies	40.00	120.00	315.00
Book 2-Contains reprints immediately following contents of Book 1, for 20			
weeks by Alex Raymond; complete except for two dailies. Note: Raymond			
mis-dated the last five strips from 6/34, and while the dating sequence is			
confusing, the continuity is correct	39.00	116.00	270.00
SECRET AGENT X-9 (See Magic Comics)			
Dec, 1937 (Not by Raymond)			
Dell Publishing Co.			
Feature Books 8	38.00	114.00	380.00

	GD25	FN65	NM94
SECRET AGENT Z-2 (See Holyoke One-Shot No. 7)			
SECRET CITY SAGA (See Jack Kirby's Secret City Saga)			
SECRET DEFENDERS (Also see The Defenders & Fantastic Four #374)			
Mar, 1993 - No. 25, Mar, 1995 ($1.75/$1.95)			
Marvel Comics			
1-($2.50)-Red foil stamped-c; Dr. Strange, Nomad, Wolverine, Spider Woman			
& Darkhawk begin		1.00	2
2-11,13,14: 9-New team w/Silver Surfer, Thunderstrike, Dr. Strange & War			
Machine. 13-Thanos replaces Dr. Strange as leader; leads into Cosmic			
Powers limited series; 14-Dr. Druid		.70	1
12-($2.50)-Prismatic foil-c		1.00	2
15-24: 15-Begin $1.95-c.; bound-in card sheet. 18-Giant Man & Iron Fist app.		.80	2
25 ($2.50, 52 pgs.)			2
SECRET DIARY OF EERIE ADVENTURES			
1953 (25¢ giant, 100 pgs., one-shot)			
Avon Periodicals			
nn-(Rare)-Kubert-a; Hollingsworth-c; Sid Check back-c	125.00	375.00	1000
SECRET HEARTS			
9-10/49 - No. 6, 7-8/50; No. 7, 12-1/51-52 - No. 153, 7/71 (All 52 pgs.)			
National Periodical Publications (Beverly)(Arleigh No. 50-113)			
1-Kinstler-a; photo-c begin, end #6	44.00	132.00	350
2-Toth-a (1 pg.); Kinstler-a	23.00	69.00	165
3,6 (1950)	21.00	62.00	145
4,5-Toth-a	21.00	64.00	150
7(12-1/51-52) (Rare)	29.00	86.00	200
8-10 (1952)	13.50	41.00	95
11-20	11.50	34.00	80
21-26: 26-Last precode (2-3/55)	10.00	30.00	65
27-40	7.50	22.50	45
41-50	5.85	17.50	35
51-60	4.25	13.00	28
61-75: 75-Last 10¢ issue	4.00	17.00	22
76-109	2.30	6.75	16
110- "Reach for Happiness" serial begins, ends #138	1.70	5.00	12
111-119,121-126,128-133,135-138-140	1.30	3.25	8
120,134-Neal Adams-c	1.65	4.20	10
127 (4/68)-Beatles cameo	2.00	6.00	14
141,142- "20 Miles to Heartbreak", Chapter 2 & 3 (see Young Love for			
Chapters 1 & 4); Toth, Colletta-a	1.65	4.20	10
143-148,150-153: 144-Morrow-a. 153-Kirby-i	1.20	3.00	7
149-Toth-a	1.30	3.25	8
SECRET ISLAND OF OZ, THE (See First Comics Graphic Novel)			
SECRET LOVE (See Fox Giants & Sinister House of...)			
SECRET LOVE			
12/55 - No. 3, 8/56; 4/57 - No. 5, 2/58; No. 6, 6/58			
Ajax-Farrell/Four Star Comic Corp. No. 2 on			
1(12/55-Ajax, 1st series)	7.50	22.50	45
2,3	4.25	13.00	28
1(4/57-Ajax, 2nd series)	5.85	17.50	35
2-6: 5-Bakerish-a	4.00	11.00	22
SECRET LOVES			
Nov, 1949 - No. 6, Sept, 1950 (#5: photo-c)			
Comic Magazines/Quality Comics Group			
1-Ward-c	18.00	54.00	125
2-Ward-c	16.00	47.00	110
3-Crandall-a	10.00	30.00	75
4,6	7.00	21.00	42
5-Suggestive art "Boom Town Babe"	10.00	30.00	60

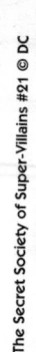
Secret Origins #7 © DC

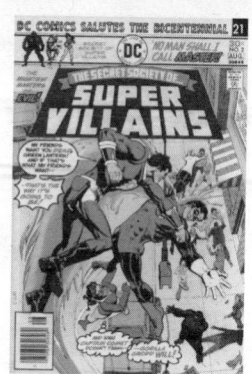
The Secret Society of Super-Villains #21 © DC

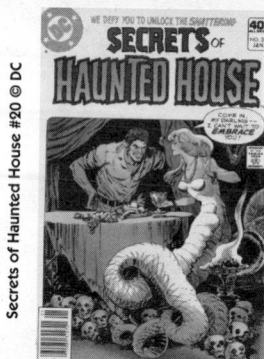
Secrets of Haunted House #20 © DC

	GD25	FN65	NM94

SECRET LOVE STORIES (See Fox Giants)

SECRET MISSIONS (Admiral Zacharia's…)
February, 1950
St. John Publishing Co.

1-Joe Kubert-c; stories of U.S. foreign agents	17.00	49.00	115.00

SECRET MYSTERIES (Formerly Crime Mysteries & Crime Smashers)
No. 16, Nov, 1954 - No. 19, July, 1955
Ribage/Merit Publications No. 17 on

16-Horror, Palais-a; Myron Fass-c	19.00	56.00	130.00
17-19-Horror. 17-Fass-c; mis-dated 3/54?	12.00	36.00	85.00

SECRET ORIGINS (1st Series) (See 80 Page Giant #8)
Aug-Oct, 1961 (Annual) (Reprints)
National Periodical Publications

1-Origin Adam Strange (Showcase #17), Green Lantern (Green Lantern #1), Challengers (partial-r/Showcase #6, 6 pgs. Kirby-a), J'onn J'onzz (Det. #225), The Flash (Showcase #4), Green Arrow (1 pg. text), Superman-Batman team (W. Finest #94), Wonder Woman (Wonder Woman #105)	62.00	187.00	500.00

SECRET ORIGINS (2nd Series)
Feb-Mar, 1973 - No. 6, Jan-Feb, 1974; No. 7, Oct-Nov, 1974 (All 20¢ issues)
National Periodical Publications (All origin reprints)

1-Superman(r/1 pg. origin/Action #1, 1st time since G.A.), Batman(Det. #33), Ghost(Flash #88), The Flash(Showcase #4)	2.00	5.00	12.00
2-4: 2-Green Lantern & The Atom(Showcase #22 & 34), Supergirl(Action #252). 3-Wonder Woman(W.W. #1), Wildcat(Sensation #1). 4-Vigilante (Action #42) by Meskin, Kid Eternity(Hit #25)	1.00	2.60	6.00
5-7: 5-The Spectre by Baily (More Fun #52,53). 6-Blackhawk(Military #1) & Legion of Super-Heroes(Superboy #147). 7-Robin(Detective #38), Aquaman (More Fun #73)	1.00	2.00	5.00

NOTE: *Infantino a-1. Kane a-2. Kubert a-1.*

SECRET ORIGINS (3rd Series)
4/86 - No. 50, 8/90 (All origins)(52 pgs. #6 on)(#27 on: $1.50)
DC Comics

1-Origin Superman	1.00	2.00	5.00
2-Blue Beetle		1.60	4.00
3-5: 3-Shazam. 4-Firestorm. 5-Crimson Avenger		1.60	4.00
6-Halo/G.A. Batman		1.80	5.00
7-12,14-26: 7-Green Lantern(Guy Gardner)/G.A. Sandman. 8-Shadow Lass/Doll Man. 9-G.A. Flash/Skyman. 10-Phantom Stranger w/Alan Moore scripts; Legends spin-off. 11-G.A. Hawkman/Power Girl. 12-Challengers of Unknown/G.A. Fury (2nd modern app.). 14-Suicide Squad; Legends spin-off. 15-Spectre/Deadman. 16-G.A. Hourman/Warlord. 17-Adam Strange story by Carmine infantino; Dr. Occult. 18-G.A. Gr. Lantern/The Creeper. 19-Uncle Sam/The Guardian. 20-Batgirl/G.A. Dr. Mid-Nite. 21-Jonah Hex/Black Condor. 22-Manhunters. 23-Floronic Man/Guardians of the Universe. 24-Blue Devil/Dr. Fate. 25-LSH/Atom. 26-Black Lightning/Miss America		1.20	3.00
3-Origin Nightwing; Johnny Thunder app.	1.00	2.00	5.00
7-38,40-44: 27-Zatara/Zatanna. 28-Midnight/Nightshade. 29-Power of the Atom/Mr. America; new 3 pg. Red Tornado story by Mayer (last app. of Scribbly, 8/88). 30-Plastic Man/Elongated Man. 31-JSA. 32-JLA. 33-35-JLI. 36-Poison Ivy by Neil Gaiman & Mark Buckingham/Green Lantern. 37-Legion Of Substitute Heroes/Doctor Light. 38-Green Arrow/Speedy; Grell scripts. 40-All Ape issue. 41-Rogues Gallery of Flash. 42-Phantom Girl/Grim Ghost. 43-Original Hawk & Dove/Cave Carson/Chris KL-99. 44-Batman app.; story based on Det. #40		1.00	2.50
3-Animal Man-c/story continued in Animal Man #10; Grant Morrison scripts; Batman app.		1.20	3.00
5-49: 45-Blackhawk/El Diablo. 46-JLA/LSH/New Titans. 47-LSH. 48-Ambush Bug/Stanley & His Monster/Rex the Wonder Dog/Trigger Twins. 49-Newsboy Legion/Silent Knight/brief origin Bouncing Boy		.80	2.00

50-($3.95, 100 pgs.)-Batman & Robin in text, Flash of Two Worlds, Johnny Thunder, Dolphin, Black Canary & Space Museum	1.00	2.00	5.00
Annual 1 (8/87)-Capt. Comet/Doom Patrol		.90	2.25
Annual 2 ('88, $2.00)-Origin Flash II & Flash III		.90	2.25
Annual 3 ('89, $2.95, 84 pgs.)-Teen Titans; 1st app. new Flamebird who replaces original Bat-Girl		1.40	3.50
Special 1 (10/89, $2.00)-Batman villains: Penguin, Riddler, & Two-Face; Bolland-c; Sam Kieth-a; Neil Gaiman scripts(2)	1.00	2.00	5.00

NOTE: *Art Adams a-33i(part). M. Anderson 8, 19, 21, 25i; c-19(part). Aparo c/a-10. Bissette c-23. Bolland c-7. Byrne c/a-Annual 1. Colan c/a-5p. Forte a-37. Giffen a-18p, 44p, 48. Infantino a-17, 50p. Kaluta c-39. Gil Kane a-2, 28; c-2p. Kirby c-19(part). Erik Larsen a-13. Mayer a-29. Morrow a-21. Orlando a-10. Perez a-50i, Annual 3i; c- Annual 3. Rogers a-6p. Russell a-27i. Simonson c-22. Staton a-36, 50p. Steacy a-35. Tuska a-4p, 9p.*

SECRET ORIGINS OF SUPER-HEROES (See DC Special Series #10, 19)

SECRET ORIGINS OF THE WORLD'S GREATEST SUPER-HEROES
1989 ($4.95, 148 pgs.)
DC Comics

nn-Reprints Batman, Superman, JLA.origins; Bolland-c.	.90	2.30	5.50

SECRET ROMANCE
Oct, 1968 - No. 41, Nov, 1976; No. 42, Mar, 1979 - No. 48, Feb, 1980
Charlton Comics

1-Begin 12¢ issues, ends #?	1.60	4.00	8.00
2-10: 9-Reese-a	.80	2.00	4.00
11-48	.40	1.00	2.00

NOTE: *Beyond the Stars app.-No. 9, 11, 12, 14.*

SECRET ROMANCES (Exciting Love Stories)
Apr, 1951 - No. 27, July, 1955
Superior Publications Ltd.

1	10.00	30.00	70.00
2	6.70	20.00	40.00
3-10	5.00	15.00	30.00
11-13,15-18,20-27	4.00	11.00	22.00
14,19-Lingerie panels	4.25	13.00	28.00

SECRET SERVICE (See Kent Blake of the…)

SECRET SIX (See Action Comics Weekly)
Apr-May, 1968 - No. 7, Apr-May, 1969 (12¢)
National Periodical Publications

1-Origin/1st app.	5.70	17.00	40.00
2-7	3.60	11.00	25.00

SECRET SOCIETY OF SUPER-VILLAINS
May-June, 1976 - No. 15, June-July, 1978
National Periodical Publications/DC Comics

1-Origin; JLA cameo & Capt. Cold app.		1.60	4.00
2-5: 2-Re-intro/origin Capt. Comet; Green Lantern x-over. 5-Green Lantern, Hawkman x-over; Darkseid app.		1.20	3.00
6-15: 9,10-Creeper x-over. 11-Capt. Comet; Orlando-i. 15-G.A. Atom, Dr. Midnite, & JSA app.		.80	2.00

SECRET SOCIETY OF SUPER-VILLAINS SPECIAL (See DC Special Series #6)

SECRETS OF HAUNTED HOUSE
4-5/75 - #5, 12-1/75-76; #6, 6-7/77 - #14, 10-11/78; #15, 8/79 - #46, 3/82
National Periodical Publications/DC Comics

1	1.00	2.00	5.00
2-10		1.00	2.50
11-46: 31-Mr. E series begins, ends #41		.70	1.75

NOTE: *Aparo c-7. Aragones a-1. B. Bailey a-8. Bissette a-46. Buckler c-32-40p. Ditko a-9, 12, 41, 45. Golden a-10. Howard a-13i. Kaluta c-8, 10, 11, 14, 16, 29. Kubert c-41, 42. Sheldon Mayer a-43p. McWilliams a-35. Nasser a-24. Newton a-30p. Nino a-1, 13, 19. Orlando c-13, 30, 43, 45i. N. Redondo a-4, 5, 29. Rogers c-26. Spiegle a-31-41i. Wrightson c-5, 44.*

SECRETS OF HAUNTED HOUSE SPECIAL (See DC Special Series #12)

Secret Story Romances #1 © ATLAS

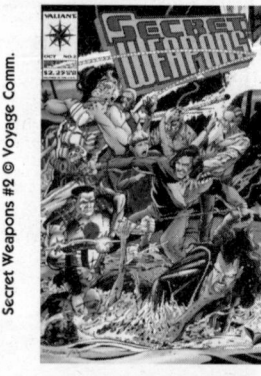
Secret Weapons #2 © Voyage Comm.

Select Detective #1 © D. S. Publ.

	GD25	FN65	NM94

SECRETS OF LIFE (Movie)
1956 (Disney)
Dell Publishing Co.

Four Color 749-Photo-c	6.00	18.00	60.00

SECRETS OF LOVE (See Popular Teen-Agers...)

SECRETS OF LOVE AND MARRIAGE
V2#1, Aug, 1956 - V2#25, June, 1961
Charlton Comics

V2#1	4.00	10.00	20.00
V2#2-6	2.40	6.00	12.00
V2#7-9-(All 68 pgs.)	1.80	4.50	9.00
10-25	1.20	3.00	6.00

SECRETS OF MAGIC (See Wisco)

SECRETS OF SINISTER HOUSE (Sinister House of Secret Love #1-4)
No. 5, June-July, 1972 - No. 18, June-July, 1974
National Periodical Publications

5-9: 5-(52 pgs.). 7-Redondo-a	1.20	3.00	7.00
10-Neal Adams-a(i)	1.50	3.75	9.00
11-18: 15-Redondo-a. 17-Barry-a; early Chaykin 1 pg. strip	1.00	2.00	5.00

NOTE: Alcala a-6, 13, 14. Glanzman a-7. Kaluta c-6, 7. Nino a-8, 11-13. Ambrose Bierce adapt.-#14.

SECRETS OF THE LEGION OF SUPER-HEROES
Jan, 1981 - No. 3, Mar, 1981 (Limited series)
DC Comics

1-3: 1-Origin of the Legion. 2-Retells origins of Brainiac 5, Shrinking Violet, Sun-Boy, Bouncing Boy, Ultra-Boy, Matter-Eater Lad, Mon-El, Karate Kid, & Dream Girl			1.00

SECRETS OF TRUE LOVE
Feb, 1958
St. John Publishing Co.

1	4.00	12.00	24.00

SECRETS OF YOUNG BRIDES
No. 5, Sept, 1957 - No. 44, Oct, 1964; July, 1975 - No. 9, Nov, 1976
Charlton Comics

5	4.25	13.00	26.00
6-10: 8-Negligee panel	3.00	7.50	15.00
11-20	2.00	5.00	10.00
21-30: Last 10¢ issue?	1.20	3.00	7.00
31-44		1.60	4.00
1-9 (2nd series)			1.50

SECRET SQUIRREL (TV)(See Kite Fun Book)
Oct, 1966 (12¢) (Hanna-Barbera)
Gold Key

1	9.50	28.50	95.00

SECRET STORY ROMANCES (Becomes True Tales of Love)
Nov, 1953 - No. 21, Mar, 1956
Atlas Comics (TCI)

1-Everett-a; Jay Scott Pike-c	10.00	30.00	70.00
2	5.85	17.50	35.00
3-11: 11-Last pre-code (2/55)	4.25	13.00	28.00
12-21	4.00	12.00	24.00

NOTE: Colletta a-10, 14, 15, 17, 21; c-10, 14, 17.

SECRET VOICE, THE (See Great American Comics Presents...)

SECRET WARS II (Also see Marvel Super Heroes...)
July, 1985 - No. 9, Mar, 1986 (Maxi-series)
Marvel Comics Group

1-9: 2-1st app. Boom Boom. 2,8,9-X-Men app. 5,8,9-Spider-Man app.

9-(75¢, 52 pgs.)			1

SECRET WEAPONS
Sept, 1993 - No. 21, May, 1995 ($2.25)
Valiant

1-10,12-21: 3-Reese-a(i). 5-Ninjak app. 9-Bound-in trading card. 12-Bloodshi app.		.90	2
11-(Sept. on envelope, Aug on-c, $2.50)-Enclosed in manilla envelope; Blootshot app; intro new team.		1.00	2

SECTAURS
June, 1985 - No. 10?, 1986 (75¢) (Based on Coleco Toys)
Marvel Comics

1-10			1
1-Coleco giveaway; different-c			1

SEDUCTION OF THE INNOCENT (Also see New York State Joint Legislative Committee to Study...)
1953, 1954 (400 pgs.) (Hardback, $4.00)(Written by Fredric Wertham, M.D.)
Rinehart & Co., Inc., N. Y. (Also printed in Canada by Clarke, Irwin & Co. Ltd. Toronto)

(1st Version)-with bibliographical note intact (pages 399 & 400)(several copies got out before the comic publishers forced the removal of this page)	45.00	136.00	365
Dust jacket only	34.00	103.00	240
(1st Version)-without bibliographical note	27.00	81.00	190
Dust jacket only	14.00	43.00	100
(2nd Version)-Published in England by Kennikat Press, 1954, 399 pgs. has bibliographical page	10.00	30.00	60
1972 r-/of 2nd version; 400 pgs. w/bibliography page; Kennikat Press	4.00	12.00	24

NOTE: Material from this book appeared in the November, 1953(Vol.70, pp50-53,214) issue the Ladies' Home Journal under the title "What Parents Don't Know About Comic Books". the release of this book, Dr. Wertham reveals seven years of research attempting to link juve delinquency to comic books. Many illustrations showing excessive violence, sex, sadism, torture are shown. This book was used at the Kefauver Senate hearings which led to the Co Code Authority. Because of the influence this book had on the comic in dustry and the collec interest in it, we feel this listing is justified. Also see Parade of Pleasure.

SEDUCTION OF THE INNOCENT! (Also see Halloween Horror)
Nov, 1985 - 3-D#2, Apr, 1986 ($1.75)
Eclipse Comics

1-6: Double listed under cover title from #7 on			1
3-D 1 (10/85, $2.25, 36 pgs.)-contains unpublished Advs. Into Darkness #15 (pre-code);Dave Stevens-c		.90	2
2D 1 (100 copy limited signed & numbered edition)(B&W)		1.00	2.00	5
3-D 2 (4/86)-Baker, Toth, Wrightson-c		1.00	2
2-D 2 (100 copy limited signed & numbered edition)(B&W)		1.00	2.00	5

NOTE: Anderson r-2, 3. Crandall c/a(r)-1. Meskin c/a(r)-3, 3-D 1. Moreira r-2. Toth a-1-6r; 4r. Tuska r-6.

SEEKER
Apr, 1994 ($2.50, one-shot)
Sky Comics

1		1.00	2

SELECT DETECTIVE (Exciting New Mystery Cases)
Aug-Sept, 1948 - No. 3, Dec-Jan, 1948-49
D. S. Publishing Co.

1-Matt Baker-a	21.00	62.00	145
2-Baker, McWilliams-a	13.00	39.00	90
3	11.00	33.00	75

SELF-LOATHING COMICS
Feb, 1995 ($2.95, B&W)
Fantagraphics Books

Sensational She-Hulk #92

Sensation Comics #18 © DC

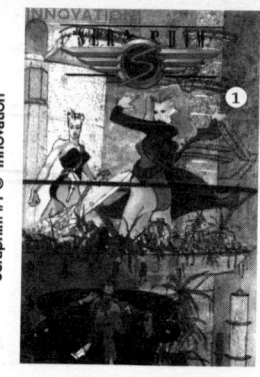

Seraphim #1 © Innovation

	GD25	FN65	NM94

	GD25	FN65	NM94
1-Crumb		1.20	3.00

SEMPER FI (Tales of the Marine Corp)
Dec, 1988- No.9, Aug, 1989 (75¢)
Marvel Comics

1-9: Severin-c/a			1.00

SENSATIONAL POLICE CASES (Becomes Captain Steve Savage, 2nd Series)
1952; 1954 - No. 4, July-Aug, 1954
Avon Periodicals

nn-(1952, 25¢, 100 pgs.)-Kubert-a?; Check, Larsen, Lawrence & McCann-a; Kinstler-c	36.00	107.00	250.00
1 (1954)-Exists?	12.00	36.00	85.00
2-4: 2-Kirbyish-a (3-4/54). 4-Reprint/Saint #5; spanking panel	10.00	30.00	65.00
I.W. Reprint #5-(1963?, nd)-Reprints Prison Break #5(1952-Realistic); Infantino-a	2.60	7.50	18.00

SENSATIONAL SHE-HULK, THE (She-Hulk #21-23) (See Savage She-Hulk)
V2#1, 5/89 - No. 60, Feb, 1994 ($1.50/$1.75, deluxe format)
Marvel Comics

V2#1-Byrne-c/a(p)/scripts begin, end #8	1.20		3.00
2-8: 3-Spidey. 4-Reintro G.A. Blonde Phantom	.90		2.25
9-49,51-60: 14-17-Howard the Duck app. 21-23-Return of the Blonde Phantom. 22-All Winners Squad app. 25-Thor app. 26-Excalibur app.; Guice-c. 29-Wolverine app. (3 pgs.). 30-Hobgoblin-c & cameo. 31-Byrne-c/a/scripts begin again. 35-Last $1.50-c. 37-Wolverine/Punisher/Spidey-c, but no app. 39-Thing app. 56-War Zone app. 57-Vs. Hulk-c/story. 58-Electro-c/story. 59-Jack O'Lantern app.	.80		2.00
50-($2.95, 52 pgs.)-Embossed green foil-c; Byrne app.; last Byrne-c/a; Austin, Chaykin, Simonson-a; Miller-a(2 pgs.)	1.30		3.25

NOTE: **Dale Keown** a(p)-13, 15-22.

SENSATIONAL SHE-HULK IN CEREMONY, THE
1989 - No. 2, 1989 ($3.95, squarebound, 52 pgs.)
Marvel Comics

nn-Part 1, nn-Part 2		1.60	4.00

SENSATIONAL SPIDER-MAN
Apr, 1989 ($5.95, squarebound, 80 pgs.)
Marvel Comics

1-r/Amazing Spider-Man Annual #14,15 by Miller & Annual #8 by Kirby & Ditko.	1.00	2.60	6.00

SENSATIONAL SPIDER-MAN, THE
Jan, 1996 - Present ($1.95)
Marvel Comics

0 ($4.95)-Linticular-c; Jurgens-a/scripts	1.00	2.00	5.00
1-15: 2-Kaine & Rhino app. 3-Giant-Man app. 9-Onslaught tie-in; revealed that Peter & Mary Jane's unborn baby is a girl. 11-Revelations	.80		2.00

SENSATION COMICS (Sensation Mystery #110 on)
Jan, 1942 - No. 109, May-June, 1952
National Per. Publ./All-American

	GD25	FN65	VF82	NM94
1-Origin Mr. Terrific(1st app.), Wildcat(1st app.), The Gray Ghost, & Little Boy Blue; Wonder Woman(cont'd from All Star #8), The Black Pirate begin; intro. Justice & Fair Play Club	2000.00	6000.00	13,000.00	20,000.00

(Estimated up to 150 total copies exist, 7 in NM/Mint)

	GD25	FN65	NM94
1-Reprint, Oversize 13-1/2x10". WARNING: This comic is an exact duplicate reprint of the original except for its size. DC published it in 1974 with a second cover titling it as a Famous First Edition. There have been many reported cases of the outer cover being removed and the interior sold as the original edition. The reprint with the new outer cover removed is practically worthless. See Famous First Edition for value.			
2-Etta Candy begins	333.00	1000.00	3300.00
3-W. Woman gets secretary's job	212.00	637.00	1700.00
4-1st app. Stretch Skinner in Wildcat	156.00	468.00	1250.00

	GD25	FN65	NM94
5-Intro. Justin, Black Pirate's son	125.00	375.00	1000.00
6-Origin/1st app. Wonder Woman's magic lasso	125.00	375.00	1000.00
7-10	90.00	271.00	725.00
11,12,14-20	79.00	238.00	635.00
13-Hitler, Tojo, Mussolini-c (as bowling pins)	98.00	296.00	790.00
21-30	62.00	187.00	500.00
31-33	48.00	144.00	385.00
34-Sargon, the Sorcerer begins (10/44), ends #36; begins again #52	50.00	150.00	400.00
35-40: 38-X-Mas-c	41.00	124.00	330.00
41-50: 43-The Whip app.	39.00	118.00	275.00
51-60: 51-Last Black Pirate. 56,57-Sargon by Kubert	34.00	103.00	240.00
61-67,69-80: 63-Last Mr. Terrific. 66-Wildcat by Kubert	34.00	103.00	240.00
68-Origin & 1st app.Huntress (8/47)	36.00	107.00	250.00
81-Used in SOTI, pg. 33,34; Krigstein-a	36.00	107.00	250.00
82-90: 83-Last Sargon. 86-The Atom app. 90-Last Wildcat	26.00	77.00	180.00
91-Streak begins by Alex Toth	26.00	79.00	185.00
92,93: 92-Toth-a (2 pgs.)	26.00	79.00	185.00
94-1st all girl issue	39.00	118.00	275.00
95-99,101-106: 95-Unmasking of Wonder Woman-c/story. 99-1st app. Astra, Girl of the Future, ends #106. 103-Robot-c. 105-Last 52 pgs. 106-Wonder Woman ends	37.00	111.00	260.00
100-(11-12/50)	45.00	136.00	365.00
107-(Scarce, 1-2/52)-1st mystery issue; Johnny Peril by Toth(p), 8 pgs. & begins; continues from Danger Trail #5 (3-4/51)(see Comic Cavalcade #15 for 1st app.)	51.00	155.00	415.00
108-(Scarce)-Johnny Peril by Toth(p)	44.00	132.00	350.00
109-(Scarce)-Johnny Peril by Toth(p)	51.00	155.00	415.00

NOTE: **Krigstein** a-(Wildcat)-81, 83, 84. **Moldoff** Black Pirate-1-25; Black Pirate not in 34-36, 43-48. **Oskner** c(i)-89-91, 94-106. Wonder Woman by **H. G. Peter**, all issues except #8, 17-19, 21; c-4-7, 9-18, 20-88, 92, 93. **Toth** a-91, 98; c-107. Wonder Woman c-1-109.

SENSATION MYSTERY (Formerly Sensation Comics #1-109)
No. 110, July-Aug, 1952 - No. 116, July-Aug, 1953
National Periodical Publications

110-Johnny Peril continues	34.00	103.00	240.00
111-116-Johnny Peril in all. 116-M. Anderson-a	34.00	103.00	240.00

NOTE: **M. Anderson** c-110. **Colan** a-114p. **Giunta** a-112. **G. Kane** c(p)-108, 109, 111-115.

SENTINELS OF JUSTICE, THE (See Americomics & Captain Paragon &...)

SENTRY SPECIAL
1991 ($2.75, one-shot)(Hero Alliance spin-off)
Innovation Publishing

1-Lost in Space preview (3 pgs.)		1.10	2.75

SERAPHIM
May, 1990 ($2.50, mature readers)
Innovation Publishing

1		1.00	2.50

SERGEANT BARNEY BARKER (Becomes G. I. Tales #4 on)
Aug, 1956 - No. 3, Dec, 1956
Atlas Comics (MCI)

1-Severin-c/a(4)	17.00	49.00	115.00
2,3: 2-Severin-c/a(4). 3-Severin-c/a(5)	11.50	34.00	80.00

SERGEANT BILKO (Phil Silvers Starring as...) (TV)
May-June, 1957 - No. 18, Mar-Apr, 1960
National Periodical Publications

1-All have Bob Oskner-c	62.00	187.00	500.00
2	37.00	111.00	260.00
3-5	30.00	90.00	210.00
6-18: 11,12,15,17-Photo-c	24.00	73.00	170.00

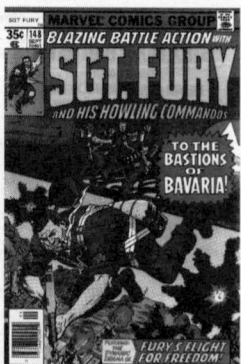
Sgt. Fury #148 © MEG

Sgt. Rock #339 © DC

Sgt. Rock Special #3 © DC

	GD25	FN65	NM94

SGT. BILKO'S PVT. DOBERMAN (TV)
June-July, 1958 - No. 11, Feb-Mar, 1960
National Periodical Publications

	GD25	FN65	NM94
1-Bob Oskner c-1-4,7,11	40.00	120.00	280.00
2	24.00	73.00	170.00
3-5: 5-Photo-c	17.00	51.00	120.00
6-11: 6,9-Photo-c	13.00	39.00	90.00

SGT. DICK CARTER OF THE U.S. BORDER PATROL (See Holyoke One-Shot)

SGT. FURY (& His Howling Commandos)(See Fury & Special Marvel Edition)
May, 1963 - No. 167, Dec, 1981
Marvel Comics Group (BPC earlier issues)

1-1st app. Sgt. Nick Fury (becomes agent of Shield in Strange Tales #135); Kirby/Ayers-c/a; 1st Dum-Dum Dugan & the Howlers	112.00	338.00	900.00
2-Kirby-a	39.00	118.00	275.00
3-5: 3-Reed Richards x-over. 4-Death of Junior Juniper. 5-1st Baron Strucker app.; Kirby-a	21.00	64.00	160.00
6-10: 8-Baron Zemo, 1st Percival Pinkerton app. 9-Hitler-c & app. 10-1st app. Capt. Savage (the Skipper)(9/64)	14.00	43.00	110.00
11,12,14-20: 14-1st Blitz Squad. 18-Death of Pamela Hawley	8.50	26.00	65.00
13-Captain America & Bucky app.(12/64); 2nd solo Capt. America x-over outside The Avengers; Kirby-a	36.00	109.00	255.00
21-30: 25-Red Skull app. 27-1st app. Eric Koenig; origin Fury's eye patch	5.70	17.00	45.00
31-50: 34-Origin Howling Commandos. 35-Eric Koenig joins Howlers. 43-Bob Hope, Glen Miller app. 44-Flashback on Howlers 1st mission	3.60	11.00	25.00
51-60	2.60	7.50	18.00
61-80: 64-Capt. Savage & Raiders x-over. 76-Fury's Father app. in WWI story	2.15	6.50	15.00
81-100: 98-Deadly Dozen x-over. 100-Capt. America, Fantastic 4 cameos; Stan Lee, Martin Goodman & others app.	1.65	4.70	11.00
101-120: 101-Origin retold	1.20	3.00	7.00
121-130: 121-123-r/#19-21	1.00	2.60	6.00
131-167: 167-Reprints (from 1963)	1.00	2.00	5.00
Annual 1(1965, 25¢, 72 pgs.)-r/#4,5 & new-a	17.00	51.00	120.00
Special 2(1966)	6.50	19.50	45.00
Special 3(1967)	4.00	12.00	28.00
Special 4(1968)	2.60	7.50	18.00
Special 5-7(1969-11/71)	1.65	4.20	10.00

NOTE: **Ayers** a-8, Annual 1. **Ditko** a-15i. **Gil Kane** c-37, 96. **Kirby** a-1-7, 13p, 167p(r). Special 5; c-1-20, 25, 167p. **Severin** a-44-46, 48, 162, 164; inks-49-79, Special 4, 5, 6, 44, 46, 110, 149i, 155i, 162-166. **Sutton** a-57p. Reprints in #80, 82, 85, 87, 89, 91, 93, 95, 99, 101, 103, 105, 107, 109, 111, 121-123, 148-155, 167.

SGT. FURY AND HIS HOWLING DEFENDERS (See The Defenders #147)

SERGEANT PRESTON OF THE YUKON (TV)
No. 344, Aug, 1951 - No. 29, Nov-Jan, 1958-59
Dell Publishing Co.

Four Color 344(#1)-Sergeant Preston & his dog Yukon King begin; painted-c begin, end #18	11.00	33.00	110.00
Four Color 373,397,419('52)	7.00	21.00	70.00
5(11-1/52-53)-10(2-4/54): 6-Bondage-c.	5.00	15.00	50.00
11,12,14-17	4.00	12.00	40.00
13-Origin Sgt. Preston	5.00	15.00	50.00
18-Origin Yukon King; last painted-c	5.00	15.00	50.00
19-29: All photo-c	6.00	18.00	60.00

SERGEANT PRESTON OF THE YUKON
1956 (4 comic booklets) (Soft-c, 16 pgs., 7x2-1/2" & 5x2-1/2")
Giveaways with Quaker Cereals

"How He Found Yukon King", "The Case That Made Him A Sergeant", "How Yukon King Saved Him From The Wolves", "How He Became A Mountie"

each...	8.35	25.00	50.

SGT. ROCK (Formerly Our Army at War; see Brave & the Bold #52 & Showcase #45)
No. 302, Mar, 1977 - No. 422, July, 1988 (See G.I. Combat #108)
National Periodical Publications/DC Comics

302	2.60	7.50	18.
303-310	1.70	5.00	12.0
311-320: 318-Reprints	1.30	3.25	8.0
321-350	1.20	3.00	7.0
351-422: 422-1st Joe, Adam, Andy Kubert-a team		1.60	4.0
Annual 2-4: 2(1982)-Formerly Sgt. Rock's Prize Battle Tales #1. 3(1983). 4(1984)		1.60	4.0

NOTE: **Estrada** a-322, 327, 331, 336, 337, 341, 342i. **Glanzman** a-384, 421. **Kubert** a-302, 303, 305r, 306, 328, 351, 356, 368, 373, 422; c-317, 318r, 319-323, 325-333-on, Annual 2, 3. **Severin** a-382, Annual 2, 3. **Thorne** a-384. **Toth** a-385r. **Wildey** a-307, 311, 313, 314.

SGT. ROCK SPECIAL (Sgt. Rock #14 on; see DC Special Series #3)
Oct, 1988 - No. 21, Feb, 1992; No. 1, 1992 ($2.00, quarterly, 52 pgs.)
DC Comics

1		1.10	2.7
2-8,10-21: All-r; 5-r/1st Sgt. Rock/Our Army at War #81. 7-Tomahawk-r by Thorne. 10-All Rock issue. 11-r/1st Haunted Tank story. 12-All Kubert issue begins monthly. 13-Dinosaur story by Heath(r). 14-Enemy Ace-r (22 pgs.) by Adams/Kubert. 15-Enemy Ace (22 pgs.) by Kubert. 16-Iron Major-c/story. 16,17-Enemy Ace-r. 19-r/Batman/Sgt. Rock team-up/B&B #108 by Aparo		.90	2.2
9-Enemy Ace by Kubert		1.20	3.0
1,2: 1 (1992, $2.95, 68 pgs.)-Simonson-c; unpubbed Kubert-a; Glanzman, Russell, Pratt, & Wagner-a		1.40	3.5

NOTE: **Neal Adams** r-1, 8, 14p. **Chaykin** a-2; r-3, 9(2pgs.); c-3. **Drucker** r-6. **Glanzman** r-20. **Golden** a-1. **Heath** a-2; r-5, 9-13, 16, 19, 21. **Krigstein** r-4, 8. **Kubert** r-1-17, 20, 21; c-1p, 2, 8, 14-21. **Miller** r-6p. **Severin** r-3, 6, 10. **Simonson** r-2, 4; c-4. **Thorne** r-7. **Toth** r-2, 8, 11. **Wood** 4.

SGT. ROCK SPECTACULAR (See DC Special Series #13)

SGT. ROCK'S PRIZE BATTLE TALES (Becomes Sgt. Rock Annual #2 on; see DC Special Series #18 & 80 Page Giant #7)
Winter, 1964 (Giant - 80 pgs., one-shot)
National Periodical Publications

1-Kubert, Heath-r; new Kubert-c	36.00	107.00	250.0

SGT. STRYKER'S DEATH SQUAD (See Savage Combat Tales)

SERGIO ARAGONES DESTROYS DC
June, 1996 ($3.50, one-shot)
DC Comics

1-DC Superhero parody book; Aragones-c/a; Evanier scripts.			3.5

SERGIO ARAGONES MASSACRES MARVEL
June, 1996 ($3.50, one-shot)
Marvel Comics

1-Marvel Superhero parody book; Aragones-c/a; Evanier scripts.			3.5

SERGIO ARAGONES' GROO THE WANDERER (See Groo...)

SERRA ANGEL ON THE WORLDS OF MAGIC THE GATHERING
Aug, 1996 ($5.95, one-shot)
Acclaim Comics (Armada)

1			6.0

SERINA
Mar, 1996 - Present ($2.95)
Antarctic Press

1,2: Warrior Nun app.			3.0

SEVEN BLOCK

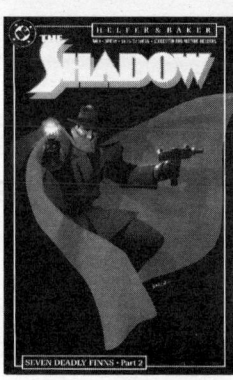
	GD25	FN65	NM94

	GD25	FN65	NM94

1990 ($4.50, one-shot, 52 pgs.)
Marvel Comics (Epic Comics)

1		1.80	4.50

SEVEN DEAD MEN (See Complete Mystery #1)

SEVEN DWARFS (Also see Snow White)
No. 227, 1949 (Disney-Movie)
Dell Publishing Co.

Four Color #227	11.00	33.00	110.00

SEVEN SAMUROID, THE (See Image Graphic Novel)

SEVEN SEAS COMICS
Apr, 1946 - No. 6, 1947 (no month)
Universal Phoenix Features/Leader No. 6

1-South Sea Girl by Matt Baker, Capt. Cutlass begin; Tugboat Tessie by			
Baker app.	66.00	200.00	535.00
2	58.00	174.00	465.00
3-6: 3-Six pg. Feldstein-a	51.00	153.00	410.00

NOTE: *Baker a-1-6; c-3-6.*

1776 (See Charlton Classic Library)

7TH VOYAGE OF SINBAD, THE (Movie)
Sept, 1958 (photo-c)
Dell Publishing Co.

Four Color 944-Buscema-a	13.00	40.00	130.00

77 SUNSET STRIP (TV)
No. 1066, Jan-Mar, 1960 - No. 2, Feb, 1963 (All photo-c)
Dell Publ. Co./Gold Key

Four Color 1066-Toth-a	11.00	33.00	110.00
Four Color 1106,1159-Toth-a	10.00	30.00	100.00
Four Color 1211,1263,1291, 01-742-209(7-9/62)-Manning-a in all			
	9.00	27.00	90.00
1(11/62-G.K.), 2-Manning-a in each	9.00	27.00	90.00

77TH BENGAL LANCERS, THE (TV)
May, 1957
Dell Publications

Four Color 791-Photo-c	7.00	21.00	70.00

SEYMOUR, MY SON (See More Seymour)
Sept, 1963
Archie Publications (Radio Comics)

1	4.00	11.00	22.00

SHADE, THE CHANGING MAN (See Cancelled Comic Cavalcade)
June-July, 1977 - No. 8, Aug-Sept, 1978
National Periodical Publications/DC Comics

1-1st app. Shade; Ditko-c/a in all	1.00	2.00	5.00
2-8		1.20	3.00

SHADE, THE CHANGING MAN (2nd series) (Also see Suicide Squad #16)
July, 1990 - No.70, 1996 ($1.50/$1.75/$1.95/$2.25, mature)
DC Comics (Vertigo imprint #33 on)

1-($2.50, 52 pgs.)-Peter Milligan scripts in all	1.60	4.00
2-49,51-59: 6-Preview of World Without End. 17-Begin $1.75-c. 33-Metallic ink			
on-c. 41-Begin $1.95-c. 42-44-John Constantine app.	.80	2.00
50-($2.95, 52 pgs.)	1.40	3.50
60-70: 60-begin $2.25-c	.90	2.25

NOTE: *Bachalo a-1-9, 11-13, 15-21, 23-26, 33-39, 42-45, 47-50; c-30, 33-39.*

SHADO: SONG OF THE DRAGON (See Green Arrow #63-66)
1992 - No. 4, 1992 ($4.95, limited series, 52 pgs.)
DC Comics

Book One - Four: Grell scripts; Morrow-a(i)	1.00	2.00	5.00

SHADOW, THE (See Batman #253, 259 & Marvel Graphic Novel #35)

SHADOW, THE (Pulp, radio)
Aug, 1964 - No. 8, Sept, 1965 (All 12¢)
Archie Comics (Radio Comics)

1-Jerrry Siegel scripts in all; Shadow-c.	6.70	20.00	40.00
2-8: 2-App. in super-hero costume on-c only; Reinman-a(backup). 3-Superhero			
begins; Reinman-a (book-length novel). 3,4,6,7-The Fly 1 pg. strips. 4-8-			
Reinman-a. 5-8-Jerry Siegel scripts. 7-Shield app.	3.25	9.50	22.00

SHADOW, THE
Oct-Nov, 1973 - No. 12, Aug-Sept, 1975
National Periodical Publications

1-Kaluta-a begins	3.60	11.00	25.00
2	2.15	6.50	15.00
3-Kaluta/Wrightson-a	2.60	7.50	18.00
4,6-Kaluta-a ends. 4-Chaykin, Wrightson part-i	1.70	5.00	12.00
5,7-12: 11-The Avenger (pulp character) x-over	1.20	3.00	7.00

NOTE: *Craig a-10. Cruz a-10-12. Kaluta a-1, 3p, 4, 6; c-1-4, 6, 10-12. Kubert c-9. Robbins a-5, 7-9; c-5, 7, 8.*

SHADOW, THE
May, 1986 - No. 4, Aug, 1986 (limited series)
DC Comics

1-4: Howard Chaykin art in all		.80	2.00
Blood & Judgement ($12.95)-r/1-4	1.85	5.50	13.00

SHADOW, THE
Aug, 1987 - No. 19, Jan, 1989 ($1.50)
DC Comics

1-19: Andrew Helfer scripts in all.			1.50
Annual 1 (12/87, $2.25)		.90	2.25
Annual 2 (1988, $2.50)-The Shadow dies; origin retold (story inspired by the			
movie "Citizen Kane").			2.50

NOTE: *Kyle Baker a-7i, 8-19, Annual 2. Chaykin c-Annual 1. Helfer scripts in all. Orlando a-Annual 1. Rogers c/a-7. Sienkiewicz c/a-1-6.*

SHADOW, THE (Movie)
June, 1994 - No. 2, July, 1994 ($2.50, limited series)
Dark Horse Comics

1,2-Adaptation from Universal Pictures film	1.00	2.50

NOTE: *Kaluta c/a-1, 2.*

SHADOW AND DOC SAVAGE, THE
July, 1995 - No. 2, Aug, 1995 ($2.95, limited series)
Dark Horse Comics

1,2		1.20	3.00

SHADOW AND THE MYSTERIOUS 3, THE
Sept, 1994 ($2.95, one-shot)
Dark Horse Comics

1-Kaluta co-scripts.		1.20	3.00

NOTE: *Stevens c-1.*

SHADOW CABINET (See Heroes)
Jan, 1994 - No. 17, Oct, 1995 ($1.75/$2.50)
DC Comics (Milestone)

0-($2.50, 52 pgs.)-Silver ink-c; Simonson-c	1.00	2.50
1-13: 1-Byrne-c	.70	1.75
14-17: 14-begin $2.50-c	1.00	2.50

SHADOW COMICS (Pulp, radio)
March, 1940 - V9#5, Aug-Sept, 1949
Street & Smith Publications

NOTE: *The Shadow first appeared on radio in 1929 and was featured in pulps beginning in April, 1931, written by Walter Gibson. The early covers of this series were reprinted from the pulp covers.*

V1#1-Shadow, Doc Savage, Bill Barnes, Nick Carter (radio), Frank Merriwell,			
Iron Munro, the Astonishing Man begin	389.00	1167.00	3800.00
2-The Avenger begins, ends #6; Capt. Fury only app.			
	162.00	487.00	1300.00

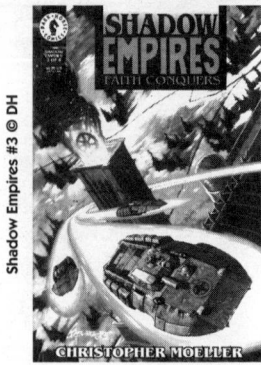

Shadow Comics #6 © S&S

Shadow Empires #3 © DH

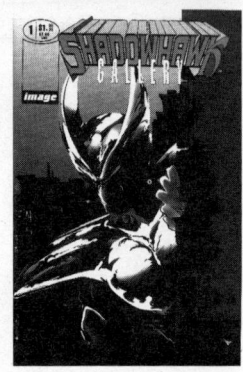

Shadowhawk Gallery #1 © Jim Valentino

	GD25	FN65	NM94

3(nn-5/40)-Norgil the Magician app.; cover is exact swipe of Shadow pulp
from 1/33 — 112.00 / 338.00 / 900.00
4,5: 4-The Three Musketeers begins, ends #8. 5-Doc Savage ends
— 93.00 / 281.00 / 750.00
6,8,9: 9-Norgil the Magician app. — 81.00 / 243.00 / 650.00
7-Origin/1st app. The Hooded Wasp & Wasplet (11/40); series ends V3#8;
Hooded Wasp/Wasplet app. on-c thru #9 — 87.00 / 262.00 / 700.00
10-Origin The Iron Ghost, ends #11; The Dead End Kids begins, ends #14
— 81.00 / 243.00 / 650.00
11-Origin Hooded Wasp & Wasplet retold — 81.00 / 243.00 / 650.00
12-Dead End Kids app. — 62.00 / 187.00 / 500.00
V2#1,2(11/41): 2-Dead End Kids story — 56.00 / 168.00 / 450.00
3-Origin & 1st app. Supersnipe (3/42); series begins; Little Nemo story
— 81.00 / 243.00 / 650.00
4,5: 4,8-Little Nemo story — 50.00 / 150.00 / 400.00
6-9: 6-Blackstone the Magician story — 44.00 / 132.00 / 350.00
10-12: 10-Supersnipe app. — 44.00 / 132.00 / 350.00
V3#1-12: 10-Doc Savage begins, not in V5#5, V6#10-12, V8#4
— 40.00 / 120.00 / 325.00
V4#1-12 — 40.00 / 120.00 / 300.00
V5#1-12 — 39.00 / 118.00 / 275.00
V6#1-11: 9-Intro. Shadow, Jr. (12/46) — 34.00 / 103.00 / 240.00
12-Powell-c/a; atom bomb panels — 39.00 / 118.00 / 275.00
V7#1,2,5,7-9,12: 2,5-Shadow, Jr. app.; Powell-a — 40.00 / 120.00 / 300.00
3,6,11-Powell-c/a — 41.00 / 125.00 / 335.00
4-Powell-c/a; Atom bomb panels — 44.00 / 133.00 / 355.00
10(1/48)-Flying Saucer-c/story (2nd of this theme; see The Spirit 9/28/47);
Powell-c/a — 50.00 / 150.00 / 400.00
V8#1-12-Powell-a. 8-Powell Spider-c/a — 41.00 / 125.00 / 335.00
V9#1,5-Powell-a — 40.00 / 120.00 / 300.00
2-4-Powell-c/a — 41.00 / 125.00 / 335.00
NOTE: Binder c-V3#1. Powell in most issues beginning V6#12. Painted c-1-6.

SHADOWDRAGON
1995 ($3.50, annual)
DC Comics

Annual 1-Year One story — 1.40 / 3.50

SHADOW EMPIRES: FAITH CONQUERS
Aug, 1994 - No. 4, Nov, 1994 ($2.95, limited series)
Dark Horse Comics

1-4 — 1.20 / 3.00

SHADOWHAWK (See Images of Shadowhawk, New Shadowhawk, Shadowhawk II, Shadowhawk III & Youngblood #2)
8/92 - No. 4, 3/93; No. 12, 8/94 - No. 18, 5/95 ($1.95/$2.50)
Image Comics (Shadowline Ink)

1-($2.50)-Embossed silver foil stamped-c; Valentino/Liefeld-c; Valentino-c/a/
scripts in all; has coupon for Image #0; 1st Shadowline Ink title.
— 1.00 / 2.00 / 5.00
1-With coupon missing — 1.20 / 3.00
1-($1.95)-Newsstand version w/o foil stamp — 1.20 / 2.50
2-Shadowhawk poster w/McFarlane-i; brief Spawn app.; wraparound-c
w/silver ink highlights — 1.20 / 3.00
3-($2.50)-Glow-in-the-dark-c — 1.00 / 2.50
4-($1.95)-Savage Dragon-c/story; Valentino/Larsen-c — .80 / 2.00
12,13;12-Cont'd from Shadowhawk III; pull-out poster by Texeira.
13-w/ShadowBone poster; WildC.A.T.s app. — .80 / 2.00
0 (10/94)-Liefeld c/a/story; ShadowBart poster. — .80 / 2.00
14-18: 14-(10/94, $2.50)-The Others app. 16-Supreme app. 17-Spawn app.;
story cont'd from Badrock & Co. #6. 18-Shadowhawk dies; Savage Dragon &
Brigade app. — 1.00 / 2.50
Special 1(12/94, $3.50, 52 pgs.)-Silver Age Shadowhawk flip book
— 1.40 / 3.50
Gallery (4/94, $1.95) — .80 / 2.00
Out of the Shadows ($19.95)-r/Youngblood #2, Shadowhawk #1-4, Image

Zero #0, Operation :Urban Storm (Never published)2.85 / 8.50 / 20.00
.../Vampirella (2/95, $4.95)-Pt.2 of x-over (See Vampirella/Shadowhawk for
Pt. 1) — 1.00 / 2.00 / 5.00
NOTE: Shadowhawk was originally a four issue limited series. The story continued in
Shadowhawk II, Shadowhawk III & then became Shadowhawk again with issue #12.

SHADOWHAWK II
V2#1, May, 1993 - V2#3, Aug, 1993 ($3.50/$1.95/$2.95, limited series)
Image Comics (Shadowline Ink)

V2#1 ($3.50)-Cont'd from Shadowhawk #4; die-cut mirricard-c.
— 1.40 / 3.50
2 ($1.95)-Foil embossed logo; reveals identity; gold-c variant exists
— .80 / 2.00
3 ($2.95)-Pop-up-c w/Pact ashcan insert — 1.20 / 3.00

SHADOWHAWK III
V3#1, Nov, 1993 - V3#4, Mar, 1994 ($1.95, limited series);
Image Comics (Shadowline Ink)

V3#1-4: 1-Cont'd from Shadowhawk II; intro Valentine; gold foil & red foil
stamped-c variations. 2-(52 pgs.)-Shadowhawk contracts HIV virus; U.S.
Male by M. Anderson (p) in free 16 pg.insert. 4-Continues in Shadowhawk
#12. — .80 / 2.00

SHADOWHAWKS OF LEGEND
Nov, 1995 ($4.95, one-shot)
Image Comics (Shadowline Ink)

nn-Stories of past Shadowhawks by Kurt Busiek, Beau Smith & Alan Moore.
— 5.00

SHADOW, THE: HELL'S HEAT WAVE (Movie, pulp, radio)
Apr, 1995 - No. 3, June, 1995 ($2.95, limited series)
Dark Horse Comics

1-3: Kaluta story — 1.20 / 3.00

SHADOWHUNT SPECIAL
Apr, 1996 ($2.50)
Image Comics (Extreme Studios)

1-Retells origin of past Shadowhawks; Jim Valentino script; Chapel app.
— 2.50

SHADOW, THE: IN THE COILS OF THE LEVIATHAN (Movie, pulp, radio)
Oct, 1993 - No. 4, Apr, 1994 ($2.95, limited series)
Dark Horse Comics

1-4-Kaluta-c & co-scripter — 1.20 / 3.00
Trade paperback (10/94, $13.95)-r/1-4 — 14.00

SHADOWLINE SAGA: CRITICAL MASS, A
Jan, 1990 - No. 7, July, 1990 ($4.95, limited series, 68 pgs.)
Marvel Comics (Epic)

1-6: Dr. Zero, Powerline, St. George — 1.00 / 2.00 / 5.00
7 ($5.95, 84 pgs.)-Morrow-a, Williamson-c(i) — 1.00 / 2.60 / 6.00

SHADOWMAN (See X-O Manowar #4)
May, 1992 - No. 43, Dec, 1995 ($2.50)
Valiant/Acclaim Comics (Valiant)

1-partial origin — 1.00 / 2.60 / 6.00
2-5: 3-1st app. Sousa the Soul Eater — 1.00 / 2.00 / 5.00
6-15,17: 8-1st app. Master Darque — 1.60 / 4.00
16-1st app. Dr. Mirage (8/93) — 1.20 / 3.00
18-43: 15-Minor Turok app. 17,18-Archer & Armstrong x-over. 19-Aerosmith-
c/story. 23-Dr. Mirage x-over. 24-(4/94). 25-Bound-in trading card.
29-Chaos Effect. 43-Shadowman jumps to his death. — 1.00 / 2.50
0-($2.50, 4/94)-Regular edition — 1.00 / 2.50
0-($3.50)-Wraparound chromium-c edition — 1.40 / 3.50
0-Gold — 1.65 / 4.20 / 10.00
Yearbook 1 (12/94, $3.95) — 1.65 / 4.00

SHADOWMASTERS

Shadow of the Batman #3 © DC

Shadows Fall #2 © DC

Shadow Strikes #7 © Conde Nast

SH

10/89 - No.4, 1/90 ($3.95, squarebound, limited series, 52 pgs.)
Marvel Comics

1-Jim Lee-c; Heath-a(i); story cont'd from Punisher	1.60	4.00
2-4: Heath-a(i)	1.60	4.00

SHADOW OF THE BATMAN
Dec, 1985 - No. 5, Apr, 1986 ($1.75, limited series)
DC Comics

1-Detective-r (all have wraparound-c)	1.00	2.50	5.50
2,3,5: 3-Penguin-c & cameo. 5-Clayface app.	1.40	3.50	
4-Joker-c/story	1.90	4.75	

NOTE: *Austin* a(new)-2i, 3i; r-2-4i. *Rogers* a(new)-1, 2p, 3p, 4, 5; r-1-5p; c-1-5. *Simonson* a-1r.

SHADOW OF THE TORTURER, THE
July, 1991 - No. 6, 1992 ($2.50, limited series)
Innovation

1-6: Based on Pocket Books novel	1.00	2.50

SHADOW ON THE TRAIL (See Zane Grey & Four Color #604)

SHADOW PLAY (Tales of the Supernatural)
June, 1982
Whitman Publications

1-Painted-c	1.00

SHADOW RIDERS
June, 1993 - No. 4, Sept, 1993 ($1.75, limited series)
Marvel Comics UK, Ltd.

1-($2.50)-Embossed-c; Cable-c/story	1.00	2.50
2-4-Cable app. 2-Ghost Rider app.	.70	1.75

SHADOWS FROM BEYOND (Formerly Unusual Tales)
V2#50, October, 1966
Charlton Comics

V2#50-Ditko-c	1.20	3.00	7.00

SHADOW SLASHER
No. 0, 1994 - No. 6, 1995? ($2.50, B&W)
Pocket Change Comics

0-6	1.00	2.50

SHADOW'S FALL
Nov, 1994 - No. 6, Apr, 1995 ($2.95, limited series)
DC Comics (Vertigo)

1-6: Van Fleet-c/a in all.	1.20	3.00

SHADOW STATE
Dec, 1995 - No. 5, Apr, 1996 ($2.50)
Broadway Comics

1-5: 1,2-Fatale back-up story; Cockrum-a(i)	1.00	2.50
Preview Edition 1,2 (10-11/95, $2.50, B&W)	1.00	2.50

SHADOW STRIKES!, THE (Pulp, radio)
Sept, 1989 - No.31, May, 1992 ($1.75)
DC Comics

1-18: 5,6-Doc Savage x-over	.75	1.80
19-31: 19-begin $2.00-c. 31-Mignola-c.	1.00	2.00
Annual 1 (1989, $3.50, 68 pgs.)-Spiegle a; Kaluta-c	1.40	3.50

SHADOW WAR OF HAWKMAN
May, 1985 - No. 4, Aug, 1985 (limited series)
DC Comics

1-4		1.00

SHAGGY DOG & THE ABSENT-MINDED PROFESSOR (See Movie Comics &
Walt Disney Showcase #46)(Disney-Movie)
No. 985, May, 1959 (photo-all four covers; Annette on back-c)
Dell Publishing Co.

Four Color 985	7.00	21.00	70.00

SHALOMAN
Aug, 1988 - V2#5, 1994? (B&W)
Al Wiesner

V1#1-9	.70	1.75
V2#1	.80	2.00
2-4	1.00	2.50
5 (Color)-Shows Vol 2, No. 4 in indicia	1.20	3.00

SHAMAN'S TEARS (Also see Maggie the Cat)
5/93 - No. 2, 8/93; No. 3, 11/94 - No. 0, 1/96 ($2.50/$1.95)
Image Comics (Creative Fire Studio)

0-2: 0-(DEC-, 1/96)-Last Issue. 1-(5/93)-Embossed red foil stamped-c; Mike Grell-c/a & scripts in all. 2-Cover unfolds into poster (8/93-c, 7/93 inside).	1.00	2.50
3-12: 3-Begin $1.95-c. 5-Re-intro Jon Sable. 12-Re-intro Maggie the Cat (1 pg)		2.00

SHANNA, THE SHE-DEVIL (See Savage Tales #8)
Dec, 1972 - No. 5, Aug, 1973 (All are 20¢ issues)
Marvel Comics Group

1-1st app. Shanna; Steranko-c; Tuska-a(p)	1.00	2.60	6.00
2-Steranko-c; heroin drug story	1.60	4.00	
3-5	1.20	3.00	

SHARDS
Apr, 1994 ($2.50, B&W, unfinished limited series)
Ascension Comics

1-Flip-c.	1.00	2.50

SHARK FIGHTERS, THE (Movie)
Jan, 1957
Dell Publishing Co.

Four Color 762-Buscema-a; photo-c	10.00	30.00	100.00

SHARP COMICS (Slightly large size)
Winter, 1945-46 - V1#2, Spring, 1946 (52 pgs.)
H. C. Blackerby

V1#1-Origin Dick Royce Planetarian	36.00	107.00	250.00
2-Origin The Pioneer; Michael Morgan, Dick Royce, Sir Gallagher, Planetarian, Steve Hagen, Weeny and Pop app.	33.00	99.00	230.00

SHARPY FOX (See Comic Capers & Funny Frolics)
1958; 1963
I. W. Enterprises/Super Comics

1,2-I.W. Reprint (1958): 2-r/Kiddie Kapers #1	1.30	3.25	8.00
14-Super Reprint (1963)	1.30	3.25	8.00

SHATTER (See Jon Sable #25-30)
June, 1985; Dec, 1985 - No. 14, Apr, 1988. ($1.75, Baxter paper/deluxe paper)
First Comics

1 (6/85)-1st computer gernerated-a in a comic book (1st & 2nd printings)	.70	1.75
1-14: computer-generated-a & lettering in all. 1-(12/85)	.70	1.75

SHATTERED IMAGE
Aug, 1996 - No. 4, Dec, 1996 ($2.50, limited series)
Image Comics (Wildstorm Productions)

1-4: 1st Image company-wide x-over; Kurt Busiek scripts in all. 1-Tony Daniel-c/a(p). 2-Alex Ross-c/swipe (Kingdom Come) by Ryan Benjamin & Travis Charest	2.50

SHAZAM (See Giant Comics to Color & Limited Collectors' Edition)

SHAZAM! (TV)(See World's Finest #253)
Feb, 1973 - No. 35, May-June, 1978
National Periodical Publications/DC Comics

1-1st revival of original Captain Marvel since G.A. (origin retold), by Beck; Captain Marvel Jr. & Mary Marvel x-over; Superman-c.

Shazam! #15 © DC

Sheena 3-D Special © ECL

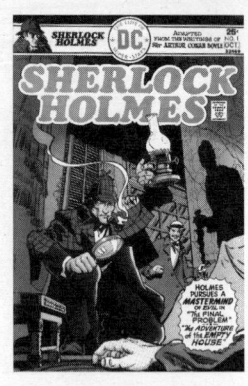

Sherlock Holmes #1 © DC

	GD25	FN65	NM94
	1.00	2.60	6.00

2-35: 2,6-Infinity photo-c. 2-Re-intro Mr. Mind & Tawney. 3-Capt. Marvel-r. (10/46, 8 pgs.). 4-Origin retold; Capt. Marvel-r. (1949, 6 pgs.). 5-Capt. Marvel Jr. origin retold; Capt. Marvel-r. (1948, 7 pgs.). 6-photo-c; Capt. Marvel-r (1950, 6 pgs.). 8-(100 pgs.)-r/Capt. Marvel Jr. by Raboy; origin/C.M. #80; origin Mary Marvel/C.M. #18; origin Mr. Tawny/C.M. #79. 9-Mr. Mind app. 10-Last C.C. Beck issue. 11-Shaffenberger-a begins. 12-17-(All 100 pgs.). 15-vs. Lex Luthor & Mr. Mind. 21-24-All reprints. 25-1st app. Isis. 26-Sivana app. (10/76). 27-Kid Eternity teams up w/Capt. Marvel. 28-1st S.A. app. of Black Adam. 30-1st DC app. 3 Lt. Marvels. 31-1st DC app. Minuteman.

34-Origin Capt. Nazi & Capt. Marvel Jr. retold.   1.20   3.00
NOTE: Reprints in #1-8, 10, 12-17, 21-24. **Beck** a-1-10, 12-17r, 21-24r; c-1, 3-9. **Nasser** c-35p. **Newton** a-35p. **Raboy** a-5r, 8r, 17r. **Shaffenberger** a-11, 14-20, 25, 26, 27p, 28, 29-31p, 33l, 35l; c-20, 22, 23, 25, 26l, 27l, 28-33.

SHAZAM: THE NEW BEGINNING
Apr, 1987 - No. 4, July, 1987 (Legends spin-off) (Limited series)
DC Comics

1-4: 1-New origin & 1st modern app. Captain Marvel; Marvel Family cameo.			
2-4-Sivana & Black Adam app.			1.00

SHEA THEATRE COMICS (Also see Theatre Comics)
No date (1940's) (32 pgs.)
Shea Theatre

nn-Contains Rocket Comics; MLJ cover in one color	10.00	30.00	60.00

SHE-BAT (See Murcielaga, She-Bat & Valeria the She-Bat)

SHEENA (Movie)
Dec, 1984 - No. 2, Feb, 1985 (limited series)
Marvel Comics

1,2-r/Marvel Comics Super Special #34			1.00

SHEENA, QUEEN OF THE JUNGLE (See Jerry Iger's Classic…, Jumbo Comics, & 3-D Sheena)
Spring, 1942; No. 2, Wint, 1942-43; No. 3, Spring, 1943; No. 4, Fall, 1948; No. 5, Sum, 1949; No. 6, Spring, 1950; No. 7-10, 1950(nd); No. 11, Spring, 1951 - No. 18, Winter, 1952-53 (#1-3: 68 pgs.; #4-7: 52 pgs.)
Fiction House Magazines

1-Sheena begins	206.00	618.00	1650.00
2 (Winter, 1942-43)	93.00	281.00	750.00
3 (Spring, 1943)	68.00	206.00	550.00
4,5 (Fall, 1948, Sum, 1949): 4-New logo; cover swipe from Jumbo #20	41.00	124.00	330.00
6,7 (Spring, 1950, 1950)	40.00	120.00	280.00
8-10 (1950 - Win/50, 36 pgs.)	37.00	111.00	260.00
11-18: 15-Cover swipe from Jumbo #43. 18-Used in **POP**, pg. 98	30.00	90.00	210.00
I.W. Reprint #9-r/#18; c-r/White Princess #3	6.35	19.00	38.00

NOTE: **Baker** c-5-10? **Whitman** c-11-18(most).

SHEENA 3-D SPECIAL (Also see Blackthorne 3-D Series #1)
Jan, 1985 ($2.00)
Eclipse Comics

1-Dave Stevens-c		.80	2.00

SHE-HULK (See The Savage She-Hulk & The Sensational She-Hulk)

SHERIFF BOB DIXON'S CHUCK WAGON (TV) (See Wild Bill Hickok #22)
Nov, 1950
Avon Periodicals

1-Kinstler-c/a(3)	11.00	33.00	75.00

SHERIFF OF COCHISE, THE (TV)
1957 (16 pgs.)
Mobil Giveaway

nn-Shaffenberger-a	2.40	6.00	12.00

SHERIFF OF TOMBSTONE
Nov, 1958 - No. 17, Sept, 1961

	GD25	FN65	NM94

Charlton Comics

V1#1-Giordano-c; Severin-a	10.00	30.00	60.00
2	5.85	17.50	35.00
3-17	4.00	11.00	22.00

SHERLOCK HOLMES (See Marvel Preview, New Adventures of..., & Spectacular Stories)

SHERLOCK HOLMES (All New Baffling Adventures of…)(Young Eagle #3 on?)
Oct, 1955 - No. 2, Mar, 1956
Charlton Comics

1-Dr. Neff, Ghost Breaker app.	40.00	120.00	290.00
2	34.00	103.00	240.00

SHERLOCK HOLMES (Also see The Joker)
Sept-Oct, 1975
National Periodical Publications

1-Cruz-a; Simonson-c			1.50

SHERRY THE SHOWGIRL (Showgirls #4)
July, 1956 - No. 3, Dec, 1956; No. 5, Apr, 1957 - No. 7, Aug, 1957
Atlas Comics

1-Dan DeCarlo-c/a in all	10.00	30.00	70.00
2	7.50	22.50	45.00
3,5-7	5.85	17.50	35.00

SHE'S JOSIE (See Josie)

SHI/CYBLADE: THE BATTLE FOR THE INDEPENDENTS
Sept, 1995 ($2.95)
Crusade Comics

1-Tucci c; features Cerebus, Bone, Hellboy, as well as others.			
	1.00	2.00	5.00
1-Silvestri variant-c	1.65	4.20	10.00

S.H.I.E.L.D. (Nick Fury & His Agents of…) (Also see Nick Fury)
Feb, 1973 - No. 5, Oct, 1973 (All 20¢ issues)
Marvel Comics Group

1-Steranko-c	1.00	2.00	5.00
2-5: 2-Steranko flag-c. 1-5 all contain-r from Str. Tales #146-155. 3-5-are cover-r; 3-Kirby/Steranko-c(r). 4-Steranko-c(r)		1.20	3.00

NOTE: **Buscema** a-3p(r). **Kirby** layouts 1-5; c-3 (w/Steranko). **Steranko** a-3r, 4r(2).

SHIELD, THE (Becomes Shield-Steel Sterling #3; #1 titled Lancelot Strong; also see Advs. of the Fly, Double Life of Private Strong, Fly Man, Mighty Comics, The Mighty Crusaders, The Original… & Pep Comics #1)
June, 1983 - No. 2, Aug, 1983
Archie Enterprises, Inc.

1,2: Steel Sterling app.			1.00

SHIELD-STEEL STERLING (Formerly The Shield)
No. 3, Dec, 1983 (Becomes Steel Sterling No. 4)
Archie Enterprises, Inc.

3-Nino-a			1.00

SHIELD WIZARD COMICS (Also see Pep Comics & Top-Notch Comics)
Summer, 1940 - No. 13, Spring, 1944
MLJ Magazines

1-(V1#5 on inside)-Origin The Shield by Irving Novick & The Wizard by Ed Ashe, Jr; Flag-c	338.00	1012.00	3000.00
2-(Winter/40)-Origin The Shield retold; Wizard's sidekick, Roy the Super Boy begins (see Top-Notch #8 for 1st app.)	162.00	487.00	1300.00
3,4	103.00	309.00	825.00
5-Dusty, the Boy Detective begins	93.00	281.00	750.00
6-8: 6-Roy the Super Boy begins. 7-Shield dons new costume (Summer, 1942 S & K-c?	85.00	256.00	685.00
9-13: 13-Bondage-c	71.00	215.00	575.00

NOTE: **Bob Montana** c-13. **Novick** c-1-6,8-11. **Harry Sahle** c-12.

Shi: Senryaku #3 © William Tucci

Shi: The Way of the Warrior #11 © William Tucci

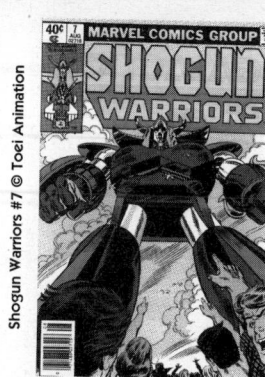
Shogun Warriors #7 © Toei Animation

	GD25	FN65	NM94

SHINING KNIGHT (See Adventure Comics #66)

SHIP AHOY
Nov, 1944 (52 pgs.)
Spotlight Publishers

1-L. B. Cole-c	12.00	39.00	90.00

SHIPWRECKED! (Disney-Movie)
1990 ($5.95, graphic novel, 68 pgs.)
Disney Comics

nn-adaptation; Spiegle-a	1.00	2.60	6.00

SHI: SENRYAKU
Aug, 1995 - No. 3, Nov, 1995 ($2.95, limited series)
Crusade Comics

1-3: 1-Tucci-c; Quesada, Darrow, Sim, Lee, Smith-a. 2-Tucci-c; Silvestri,
Balent, Perez, Mack-a. 3-Jusko-c; Hughes, Ramos, Bell, Moore-a.

	1.00	2.00	5.00
1-variant-c (no logo)	1.65	4.20	10.00
Hardcover ($24.95)-r/#1-3; Frazetta-c.			25.00
Trade Paperback ($13.95)-r/#1-3; Frazetta-c.			14.00

SHI: THE WAY OF THE WARRIOR (See Razor Annual #1 for 1st app.)
Mar, 1994 - Present ($2.50/$2.95)
Crusade Comics

1	5.70	17.00	40.00
1-Commemorative ed., B&W, new-c; given out at 1994 San Diego Comic Con			
	7.00	21.50	50.00
1-Fan appreciation edition -r/#1	1.00	2.00	5.00
1-Fan appreciation edition (variant)	2.15	6.50	15.00
2	3.60	11.00	25.00
2-Commemorative edition (3,000)	5.70	17.00	40.00
3	1.65	4.20	10.00
4-7: 4-Silvestri poster		1.60	4.00
5-Silvestri variant-c	2.85	8.50	20.00
6-Tomeo #1 variant-c	2.85	8.50	20.00
7-Tomoe app.			2.50
8-12: 8-Begin $2.95-c			3.00
8-Signed Edition-(5000)			5.00
Trade paperback (1995, $12.95)-r/#1-4			13.00
Trade paperback (1995, $14.95)-r/#1-4 revised; Julie Bell-c			15.00

SHI VS. TOMOE
Aug, 1996 ($3.95, one-shot)
Crusade Comics

1-Tucci-a/scripts; wraparound foil-c			4.00
1-(6/96, $5.00. B&W)-Preview Edition; sold at San Diego Comic Con			
			5.00

SHMOO (See Al Capp's... & Washable Jones &...)

SHOCK (Magazine)
May, 1969 - V3#4, Sept, 1971 (B&W)(Reprints from horror comics)
Stanley Publications

V1#1-Cover-r/Weird Tales of the Future #7 by Bernard Baily; r/Weird Chills #1			
	4.00	12.00	28.00
2-Wolverton-r/Weird Mysteries 5; r-Weird Mysteries #7 used in **SOTI**; cover reprints cover to Weird Mysteries #1	3.40	10.00	24.00
3,5,6	2.15	6.50	15.00
4-Harrison/Williamson-r/Forbid. Worlds #6	2.60	7.50	18.00
V2#2, V1#8, V2#4-6, V3#1-c: V2#4-Cover swipe from Weird Mysteries #6			
	2.15	6.50	15.00

NOTE: *Disbrow*-r-V2#4; *Bondage* c-V1#4, V2#6, V3#1.

SHOCK DETECTIVE CASES (Formerly Crime Fighting Detective)
Becomes Spook Detective Cases #22)
No. 20, Sept, 1952 - No. 21, Nov, 1952
Star Publications

	GD25	FN65	NM94

20,21-L.B. Cole-c; based on true crime cases	16.00	47.00	110.00

NOTE: *Palais* a-19. No. 21-Fox-r.

SHOCK ILLUSTRATED (...Adult Crime Stories; Magazine format)
Sept-Oct, 1955 - No. 3, Spring, 1956 (Adult Entertainment on-c 1,2)(All 25¢)
E. C. Comics

1-All by Kamen; drugs, prostitution, wife swapping	6.70	20.00	40.00
2-Williamson-a redrawn from Crime SuspenStories #13 plus Ingels, Crandall, Evans & part Torres-i; painted-c	7.50	22.50	45.00
3-Only 100 known copies bound & given away at E.C. office; Crandall, Evans-a; painted-c; shows May, 1956 on-c	100.00	300.00	700.00

SHOCKING MYSTERY CASES (Formerly Thrilling Crime Cases)
No. 50, Sept, 1952 - No. 60, Oct, 1954 (All crime reprints?)
Star Publications

50-Disbrow "Frankenstein" story	31.00	94.00	220.00
51-Disbrow-a	17.00	51.00	120.00
52-60: 56-Drug use story	16.00	47.00	110.00

NOTE: *L. B. Cole* covers on all; a-60(2 pgs.). *Hollingsworth* a-52. *Morisi* a-55.

SHOCKING TALES DIGEST MAGAZINE
Oct, 1981 (95¢)
Harvey Publications

1-1957-58-r; Powell, Kirby, Nostrand-a		.80	2.00

SHOCK SUSPENSTORIES
Feb-Mar, 1952 - No. 18, Dec-Jan, 1954-55
E. C. Comics

1-Classic Feldstein electrocution-c	68.00	206.00	550.00
2	40.00	120.00	315.00
3,4: 4-Used in **SOTI**, pg. 387,388	29.00	86.00	200.00
5-Hanging-c	29.00	86.00	200.00
6,7: 6-Classic bondage-c. 7-Classic face melting-c	34.00	103.00	240.00
8-Williamson-a	29.00	86.00	200.00
9-11: 9-Injury to eye panel. 10-Junkie story	24.00	71.00	165.00
12- "The Monkey" classic junkie cover/story; anti-drug propaganda issue			
	27.00	81.00	200.00
13-Frazetta's only solo story for E.C., 7 pgs.	34.00	103.00	240.00
14-Used in Senate Investigation hearings	18.00	54.00	125.00
15-Used in 1954 Reader's Digest article, "For the Kiddies to Read"; Bill Gaines stars in prose story "The EC Caper"	18.00	54.00	125.00
16- "Red Dupe" editorial; rape story	17.00	49.00	115.00
17,18	17.00	49.00	115.00

NOTE: *Ray Bradbury* adaptations-1, 7, 9. *Craig* a-11; c-11. *Crandall* a-9-13, 15-18. *Davis* a-1-5. *Evans* a-7, 8, 14-18; c-16-18. *Feldstein* c-1, 3-9, 12. *Ingels* a-1, 2, 6. *Kamen* a-in all; c-10, 13, 15. *Krigstein* a-14, 18. *Orlando* a-1, 3-7, 9, 10, 12, 16, 17. *Wood* a-2-15; c-2-6, 14.

SHOCK SUSPENSTORIES
Sept, 1992 - Present ($1.50/$2.00/$2.50, quarterly)
Russ Cochran/Gemstone Publishing

1,2-r/#1,2 above with original-c			1.50
3-16: 3-r/#3-7 above with original-c		.80	2.00
17-20: 17-r/HOF #17			2.50

SHOGUN WARRIORS
Feb, 1979 - No. 20, Sept, 1980 (Based on Mattel toys)
Marvel Comics Group (1-3: 35¢; 4-19: 40¢; 20: 50¢)

1-Raydeen, Combatra, & Dangard Ace begin		.80	2.00
2-20: 11-Austin-i. 12-Simonson-c. 19,20-FF x-over			1.50

SHOOK UP (Magazine) (Satire)
Nov, 1958
Dodsworth Publ. Co.

V1#1	4.00	10.00	20.00

SHORT RIBS
No. 1333, Apr - June, 1962
Dell Publishing Co.

Shotgun Mary #1 © Ben Dunn

Showcase #8 © DC

Showcase #15 © DC

	GD25	FN65	NM94
Four Color 1333	5.00	15.00	50.00

SHORT STORY COMICS (See Hello Pal,...)

SHORTY SHINER (The Five-Foot Fighter in the Ten Gallon Hat)
June, 1956 - No. 3, Oct, 1956
Dandy Magazine (Charles Biro)

	GD25	FN65	NM94
1	5.35	16.00	32.00
2,3	4.00	11.00	22.00

SHOTGUN MARY
Sep, 1995 - Present ($2.95)
Antarctic Press

	GD25	FN65	NM94
1,2-w/pin-ups	1.20		3.00
1-($8.95)-Bagged w/CD			9.00
...Deviltown-(7/96, $2.95)			3.00
...Shooting Gallery-(6/96, $2.95)			3.00

SHOTGUN SLADE (TV)
No. 1111, July-Sept, 1960
Dell Publishing Co.

	GD25	FN65	NM94
Four Color 1111-Photo-c	6.00	18.00	60.00

SHOWCASE (See Cancelled Comic Cavalcade & New Talent...)
3-4/56 - No. 93, 9/70; No. 94, 8-9/77 - No. 104, 9/78
National Per. Publ./DC Comics

	GD25	FN65	VF82	NM94
1-Fire Fighters; w/Fireman Farrell	260.00	780.00	1690.00	2800.00

	GD25	FN65		NM94
2-King of the Wild; Kubert-a (animal stories)	78.00	233.00		770.00
3-The Frogmen by Russ Heath; Heath greytone-c (early DC example, 7-8/56)	76.00	228.00		750.00

	GD25	FN65	VF82	NM94
4-Origin/1st app. The Flash (1st DC S.A. hero, Sept-Oct, 1956) & The Turtle; Kubert-a; r/in Secret Origins #1 ('61 & '73); Flash shown reading G.A. Flash #13; Infantino/Kubert-c	1633.00	4900.00	14,700.00	25,000.00

	GD25	FN65		NM94
5-Manhunters	89.00	268.00		900.00

	GD25	FN65		NM94
6-Origin/1st app. Challengers of the Unknown by Kirby, partly r/in Secret Origins #1 & Challengers #64,65 (1st S.A. super-hero team & 1st original concept S.A. series)(1-2/56)	290.00	870.00	1885.00	3200.00

	GD25	FN65		NM94
7-Challengers of the Unknown by Kirby (2nd app.) reprinted in Challengers of the Unknown #75	155.00	465.00		1550.00

	GD25	FN65	VF82	NM94
8-The Flash (5-6/57, 2nd app.); origin & 1st app. Capt. Cold	1167.00	3500.00		7500.00
9-Lois Lane (Pre-#1, 7-8/57) (1st Showcase character to win own series) Superman app. on-c	533.00	1600.00	3500.00	–

	GD25	FN65		NM94
10-Lois Lane; Jor-el cameo; Superman app. on-c	210.00	630.00		2300.00
11-Challengers of the Unknown by Kirby (3rd)	140.00	420.00		1400.00
12-Challengers of the Unknown by Kirby (4th)	150.00	450.00		1500.00
13-The Flash (3rd app.); origin Mr. Element	320.00	960.00		3400.00
14-The Flash (4th app.); origin Dr. Alchemy, former Mr. Element	330.00	990.00		4300.00

	GD25	FN65	VF82	NM94
15-Space Ranger (7-8/58, 1st app.)	150.00	450.00	900.00	1550.00

	GD25	FN65		NM94
16-Space Ranger (9-10/58, 2nd app.)	86.00	258.00		850.00

	GD25	FN65	VF82	NM94
17-(11-12/58)-Adventures on Other Worlds; origin/1st app. Adam Strange by Gardner Fox & Mike Sekowsky	180.00	540.00	1170.00	1950.00
18-Adventures on Other Worlds (2nd A. Strange)	105.00	315.00		1025.00
19-Adam Strange; 1st Adam Strange logo	116.00	348.00		1160.00
20-Rip Hunter; origin & 1st app. (5-6/59); Moriera-a	82.00	245.00		800.00
21-Rip Hunter (7-8/59, 2nd app.); Sekowsky-c/a	52.00	156.00		460.00

	GD25	FN65	VF82	NM94
22-Origin & 1st app. Silver Age Green Lantern by Gil Kane (9-10/59); reprinted in Secret Origins #2	367.00	1100.00	2750.00	4600.00
23-Green Lantern (3-4.60, 2nd app.); nuclear explosion-c	145.00	435.00	942.00	1450.00
24-Green Lantern (1-2/60, 3rd app.)	147.00	442.00	883.00	1475.00

	GD25	FN65		NM94
25,26-Rip Hunter by Kubert. 25-Grey tone-c	40.00	120.00		280.00
27-Sea Devils (7-8/60, 1st app.); Heath-c/a	78.00	233.00		700.00
28-Sea Devils (9-10/60, 2nd app.); Heath-c/a	46.00	137.00		365.00
29-Sea Devils; Heath-c/a; grey tone c-27-29	45.00	135.00		360.00
30-Origin Silver Age Aquaman (1-2/61) (see Adventure #260 for 1st S.A. origin	75.00	225.00		680.00
31,32-Aquaman	46.00	137.00		370.00
33-Aquaman	51.00	152.00		415.00

	GD25	FN65	VF82	NM94
34-Origin & 1st app. Silver Age Atom by Kane & Anderson (9-10/61); reprinted in Secret Origins #2	120.00	360.00	780.00	1300.00

	GD25	FN65		NM94
35-The Atom by Gil Kane (2nd); last 10¢ issue	81.00	242.00		725.00
36-The Atom by Gil Kane (1-2/62, 3rd app.)	68.00	204.00		545.00
37-Metal Men (3-4/62, 1st app.)	67.00	200.00		535.00
38-Metal Men (5-6/62, 2nd app.)	52.00	156.00		415.00
39-Metal Men (7-8/62, 3rd app.)	40.00	120.00		315.00
40-Metal Men (9-10/62, 4th app.)	40.00	120.00		285.00
41,42-Tommy Tomorrow (parts 1 & 2). 42-Origin	21.00	62.00		150.00
43-Dr. No (James Bond); Nodel-a; originally published as British Classics Illustrated #158A as #6 in a European Detective series, all with diff. painted-c. This Showcase #43 version is actually censored, deleting all racial skin color and dialogue thought to be racially demeaning (1st DC S.A. movie adaptation)(based on Ian Fleming novel & movie)	44.00	132.00		375.00
44-Tommy Tomorrow	14.00	43.00		100.00
45-Sgt. Rock (7-8/63); pre-dates B&B #52; origin retold; Heath-c	26.00	79.00		200.00
46,47-Tommy Tomorrow	12.00	36.00		85.00
48,49-Cave Carson (3rd tryout series; see B&B)	9.30	28.00		65.00
50,51-I Spy (Danger Trail-r by Infantino), King Farady story (#50 has new 4 pg. story)	8.00	24.50		65.00
52-Cave Carson	7.00	21.50		50.00
53,54-G.I. Joe (11-12/64, 1-2/65); Heath-a	8.50	26.00		60.00
55-Dr. Fate & Hourman (3-4/65); origin of each in text; 1st solo app. G.A. Green Lantern in Silver Age (pre-dates Gr. Lantern #40); 1st S.A. app. Solomon Grundy	31.00	92.00		215.00
56-Dr. Fate & Hourman	20.00	60.00		150.00
57-Enemy Ace by Kubert (7-8/65, 4th app. after Our Army at War #155)	18.00	54.00		130.00
58-Enemy Ace by Kubert (5th app.)	13.00	39.00		90.00
59-Teen Titans (11-12/65, 3rd app.)	30.00	90.00		220.00
60-1st S. A. app. The Spectre; Anderson-a (1-2/66); origin in text	18.00	54.00		125.00
61-The Spectre by Anderson (2nd app.)	10.00	30.00		80.00
62-Origin & 1st app. Inferior Five (5-6/66)	5.70	17.00		40.00
63,65-Inferior Five. 65-X-Men parody (11-12/66)	17.00	49.00		120.00
64-The Spectre by Anderson (5th app.)	3.60	11.00		25.00
66,67-B'wana Beast	3.60	11.00		25.00
68,69,71-Maniaks	3.40	10.00		24.00
70-Binky (9-10/67)-Tryout issue	3.40	10.00		24.00
72-Top Gun (Johnny Thunder-r)-Toth-a	14.00	43.00		100.00
73-Origin/1st app. Creeper; Ditko-c/a (3-4/68)	9.30	28.00		65.00
74-Intro/1st app. Anthro; Post-c/a (5/68)	12.00	36.00		85.00
76-1st app. Bat Lash (8/68)	6.50	19.50		45.00
77-1st app. Angel & The Ape (9/68)	6.50	19.50		45.00
78-1st app. Jonny Double (11/68)	3.70	11.00		26.00

Showcase '94 #7 © DC

Showcase '95 #8 © DC

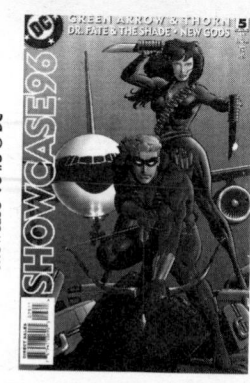

Showcase '96 #5 © DC

	GD25	FN65	NM94
79-1st app. Dolphin (12/68); Aqualad origin-r	5.70	17.00	40.00
80-1st S.A. app. Phantom Stranger (1/69); Neal Adams-c			
	3.60	11.00	25.00
81-Windy & Willy	3.25	9.50	22.00
82-1st app. Nightmaster (5/69) by Grandenetti & Giordano; Kubert-c			
	7.00	21.50	50.00
83,84-Nightmaster by Wrightson w/Jones/Kaluta ink assist in each; Kubert-c			
83-Last 12¢ issue 84-Origin retold; begin 15¢	6.50	19.50	45.00
85-87-Firehair; Kubert-a	2.15	6.50	15.00
88-90-Jason's Quest: 90-Manhunter 2070 app.	1.30	3.25	8.00
91-93-Manhunter 2070: 92-Origin	1.30	3.25	8.00
94-Intro/origin new Doom Patrol & Robotman	1.50	3.75	9.00
95,96-The Doom Patrol. 95-Origin Celsius	1.30	3.25	8.00
97-99-Power Girl; origin-97,98; JSA cameos	1.30	3.25	8.00
100-(52 pgs.)-Most Showcase characters featured	1.30	3.25	8.00
101-103-Hawkman; Adam Strange x-over	1.30	3.25	8.00
104-(52 pgs.)-O.S.S. Spies at War	1.30	3.25	8.00

NOTE: *Anderson* a-22-(44), 34-36l, 55, 56, 60, 61, 64, 101-103l; c-50l, 51l, 55, 56, 60, 61, 64. *Aparo* c-94-96. *Boring* c-10. *Estrada* a-104. *Fraden* c(p)-30, 31, 33. *Heath* c-3, 27-29. *Infantino* c/a(p)-4, 8, 13, 14; c-50p, 51p. *Gil Kane* a-22-24p, 34-36p; c-17-19, 22-24p(w/Giella), 31. *Kane/Anderson* a-34-36. *Kirby* c-11, 12. *Kirby/Stein* c-6, 7. *Kubert* a-2, 4l, 25, 26, 45, 53, 54, 72; c-25, 26, 53, 54, 57, 58, 82-87, 101-104; c-2, 4l. *Moriera* c-5. *Orlando* a-62p, 63p, 97l; c-62, 63, 97l. *Sekowsky* a-65p. *Sparling* a-78. *Staton* a-94, 95-99p, 100; c-97-100p.

SHOWCASE '93
Jan, 1993 - No. 12, Dec, 1993 ($1.95, limited series, 52 pgs.)

1-12: 1-Begin 4 part Catwoman story & 6 part Blue Devil story; begin Cyborg story; Art Adams/Austin-c. 2-Flash by Travis Charest (p) 6-Azrael in Bat-costume (2 pgs.). 7,8-Knightfall parts 13 & 14. 6-10-Deathstroke app. (6,10-cameo). 9,10-Austin-i. 10-Azrael as Batman in new costume app.; Gulacy-c. 11-Perez-c. 12-Creeper app.; Alan Grant scripts.
| | | .80 | 2.00 |

NOTE: *Chaykin* c-8. *Fabry* c-8. *Giffen* a-12. *Golden* c-3. *Zeck* c-6.

SHOWCASE '94
Jan, 1994 - No. 12, Dec, 1994 ($1.95, limited series, 52 pgs.)
DC Comics

1-12: 1,2-Joker & Gunfire stories. 1-New Gods. 4-Riddler story. 5-Huntress-c/story w/app. new Batman. 6-Huntress-c/story w/app. Robin; Atom story. 7-Penguin story.by Peter David, P. Craig Russell, & Michael T. Gilbert; Penguin-c by Jae Lee. 8,9-Scarface origin story by Alan Grant, John Wagner,& Teddy Kristiansen; Prelude to Zero Hour. 10-Zero Hour tie-in story. 11-Man-Bat.
| | | .80 | 2.00 |

NOTE: *Alan Grant* scripts-3, 4. *Kelley Jones* c-12. *Mignola* c-3. *Nebres* a(i)-2. *Quesada* c-10. *Russell* a-7p. *Simonson* c-5.

SHOWCASE '95
Jan, 1995 - No. 12, Dec, 1995 ($2.50/$2.95, limited series)
DC Comics

1-4-Supergirl story. 3-Eradicator-c.; The Question story. 4-Thorn c/story
| | | 1.00 | 2.50 |
5-12: 5-Thorn-c/story; begin $2.95-c. 8-Spectre story. 12-The Shade story by James Robinson & Wade Von Grawbadger; Maitresse story by Chris Claremont & Alan Davis.
| | | 1.20 | 3.00 |

SHOWCASE '96
Jan, 1996 - No. 12, Dec, 1996 ($2.95, limited series)
DC Comics

1-12: 1-Steve Geppi cameo. 3-Black Canary & Lois Lane-c/story; Deadman story by Jamie Delano & Wade Von Grawbadger, Gary Frank-c. 4-Firebrand & Guardian-c/story; The Shade & Dr. Fate "Times Past" story by James Robinson & Matt Smith begins, ends #5.
| | | 1.20 | 3.00 |

SHOWGIRLS (Formerly Sherry the Showgirl #3)
No. 4, 2/57; June, 1957 - No. 2, Aug, 1957
Atlas Comics (MPC No. 2)

4-Dan DeCarlo c/a begins | 8.35 | 25.00 | 50.00 |

	GD25	FN65	NM94
1-Millie, Sherry, Chili, Pearl & Hazel begin	10.00	30.00	60.00
2	7.50	22.50	45.00

SHROUD, THE (See Super-Villain Team-Up #5)
Mar, 1994 - No. 4, June, 1994 ($1.75, mini-series)
Marvel Comics

1-4: 1,2,4-Spider-Man & Scorpion app. | | .70 | 1.75 |

SHROUD OF MYSTERY
June, 1982
Whitman Publications

1 | | | 1.00 |

SICK (Sick Special #131) (Magazine) (Satire)
Aug, 1960 - No. 131, Feb, 1980
Feature Publ./Headline Publ./Crestwood Publ. Co./Hewfred Publ./
Pyramid Comm./Charlton Publ. No. 109 (4/76) on

	GD25	FN65	NM94
V1#1-Jack Paar photo on-c; Torres-a	17.00	51.00	120.00
2-5-Torres-a in all	8.50	26.00	60.00
6	5.50	16.50	38.00
V2#1-8(#7-14)	4.30	13.00	30.00
V3#1-8 (#15-22)	3.40	10.00	24.00
V4#1-5 (#23-27)	2.60	7.50	18.00
28-32,34-40: 29-Beatles-c by Jack Davis	1.70	5.00	12.00
33-Ringo Starr photo-c & spoof on "A Hard Day's Night"; inside-c has Beatles photos	3.75	11.25	28.00
41-131: 45 has #44 on-c & #45 on inside. 70-John & Yoko-c. 128-Superman-c/movie parody. 131-Superman parody	1.00	2.60	6.00
Annual 1969, 1970, 1971	2.15	6.50	15.00
Annual 2-4(1980)	1.20	3.00	7.00
Big Sick Laff-in (1968)-w/psychedelic posters	2.60	7.50	18.00
Birthday Annual (1967)-3 pg. Huckleberry Fink fold out			
	2.60	7.50	18.00
7th Annual Yearbook (1967)-Davis-c, 2 pg. glossy poster insert			
	2.60	7.50	18.00
Special 2 (1978)	1.00	2.00	5.00
Yearbook 14(1974), 15(1975, 84 pgs.)	1.00	2.50	6.00

NOTE: *Davis* c-42, 87; c-22, 23, 25, 29, 31, 32. *Powell* a-7, 31, 57. *Simon* a-1-3, 10, 41, 42, 87, 99; c-1, 47, 57, 59, 69, 91, 95-97, 99, 100, 102, 107, 112. *Torres* a-1-3, 29, 31, 47, 49. *Tuska* a-14, 41-43. Civil War Blackouts-23, 24. #42 has biography of Bob Powell.

SIDESHOW
1949 (one-shot)
Avon Periodicals

1-(Rare)-Similar to Bachelor's Diary | 26.00 | 79.00 | 185.00 |

SIEGEL AND SHUSTER: DATELINE 1930s
Nov, 1984 - No. 2, Sept, 1985 ($1.50/$1.75, Baxter paper #1)
Eclipse Comics

1-Unpublished samples of strips from the '30s; includes 'Interplanetary Police'; Shuster-c | | | 1.50 |
2 ($1.75, B&W)-unpublished strips; Shuster-c | | .70 | 1.75 |

SILENT INVASION, THE
Apr, 1986 - No.12, Mar, 1988 ($1.70/$2.00, B&W)
Rengade Press

1-UFO sightings of the '50's		1.20	3.00
2		1.00	2.50
3-12		.80	2.00
Book 1- reprints ($7.95)	1.30	3.25	8.00

SILENT MOBIUS
1991 - No. 5, 1992 ($4.95, color, squarebound, 44 pgs.)
Viz Select Comics

1-5: Japanese stories translated to English | 1.00 | 2.00 | 5.00 |

SILLY PILLY (See Frank Luther's...)

SILLY SYMPHONIES (See Dell Giants)

Silver Sable and the Wild Pack #3 © MEG

Silver Star #1 © Jack Kirby

Silver Surfer #33 © MEG

	GD25	FN65	NM94

SILLY TUNES
Fall, 1945 - No. 7, June, 1947
Timely Comics

	GD25	FN65	NM94
1-Silly Seal, Ziggy Pig begin	16.00	47.00	110.00
2-(2/46)	10.00	30.00	60.00
3-7: 6-New logo	8.00	24.00	48.00

SILVER (See Lone Ranger's Famous Horse...)

SILVERBACK
1989 - No. 3, 1990 ($2.50, color, limited series, mature readers)
Comico

1-3: Character from Grendel: Matt Wagner-a		1.20	3.00

SILVERBLADE
Sept, 1987 - No. 12, Sept, 1988
DC Comics

1-12: Colan -c/a in all			1.50

SILVERHAWKS
Aug, 1987 - No. 6, June, 1988 ($1.00)
Star Comics/Marvel Comics #6

1-6			1.00

SILVERHEELS
Dec, 1983 - No. 3, May, 1984 ($1.50)
Pacific Comics

1-3			1.50

SILVER KID WESTERN
Oct, 1954 - No. 5, July?, 1955
Key/Stanmor Publications

	GD25	FN65	NM94
1	9.15	27.00	55.00
2	4.25	13.00	28.00
3-5	4.25	13.00	26.00
I.W. Reprint #1,2-Severin-c: 1-r/#? 2-r/#1	1.50	3.75	9.00

SILVER SABLE AND THE WILD PACK (See Amazing Spider-Man #265)
June, 1992 - No. 35, Apr, 1995 ($1.25/$1.50)
Marvel Comics

1-($2.00)-Embossed & foil stamped-c; Spider-Man app.		1.00	2.50
2-4: 4,5-Dr. Doom-c/story		.70	1.75
5-23: 6,7-Deathlok-c/story. 9-Origin Silver Sable. 15-Punisher-c/s. 15-Capt. America-c/s. 16,17-Intruders app. 18,19-Venom-c/s. 19-Siege of Darkness x-over. 23-Daredevil (in new costume) & Deadpool app.			1.25
24,26-35: 24-Begin $1.50-c; bound-in card sheet. Li'l Sylvie backup story			1.50
25-($2.00, 52 pgs.)-Li'l Sylvie backup story		.80	2.00

SILVER STAR (Also see Jack Kirby's...)
Feb, 1983 - No. Jan, 1984 ($1.00)
Pacific Comics

1-6: 1-1st app. Last of the Viking Heroes. 1-5-Kirby-c/a. 2-Ditko-a			1.00

SILVER STREAK COMICS (Crime Does Not Pay #22 on)
Dec, 1939 - No. 21, May, 1942; No. 22-24, 1946 (Silver logo-#1-5)
Your Guide Publs. No. 1-7/New Friday Publs. No. 8-17/Comic House Publ./Newsbook Publ.

	GD25	FN65	VF82	NM94
1-(Scarce)-Intro The Claw by Cole (r-/in Daredevil #21), Red Reeves, Boy Magician, & Captain Fearless begin; The Wasp, Mister Midnight begin; Spirit Man app. Silver metallic-c begin, end #5; Claw c-1,2,6-8	950.00	2850.00	5700.00	9500.00

(Estimated up to 100 total copies exist, 6 in NM/Mint)

	GD25	FN65	NM94
2-The Claw by Cole; Simon-c/a	338.00	999.00	3000.00

3-1st app. & origin Silver Streak (2nd with lightning speed); Dickie Dean the Boy Inventor, Lance Hale, Ace Powers, Bill Wayne, & The Planet Patrol begin   288.00   862.00   2550.

	GD25	FN65	NM94
4-Sky Wolf begins; Silver Streak by Jack Cole (new costume); 1st app. Jackie, Lance Hale's sidekick	143.00	431.00	1150.0
5-Jack Cole c/a(2)	168.00	506.00	1350.

	GD25	FN65	VF82	NM9
6-(Scarce, 9/40)-Origin & 1st app. Daredevil (blue & yellow costume) by Jack Binder; The Claw returns; classic Cole Claw-c	1056.00	3167.00	6333.00	10,500.
7-Claw vs. Daredevil (new costume-blue & red) by Jack Cole & 3 other Cole stories (38 pgs.)	667.00	2000.00	4000.00	6600.

(#6, 7-Estimated up to 120 total copies of each exist, 7-10 in NM/Mint)

	GD25	FN65	NM9
8-Claw vs. Daredevil by Cole; last Cole Silver Streak	250.00	750.00	2000.
9-Claw vs. Daredevil by Cole	162.00	487.00	1300.
10-Origin & 1st app. Captain Battle (5/41); Claw vs. Daredevil by Cole; Robot-c	137.00	412.00	1100.
11-Intro. Mercury by Bob Wood, Silver Streak's sidekick; conclusion Claw vs. Daredevil by Rico; in 'Presto Martin,' 2nd pg., newspaper says 'Roussos does it again'	96.00	290.00	775.
12-14: 13-Origin Thun-Dohr	75.00	225.00	600.
15, 17-Last Daredevil issue.	68.00	206.00	550.
16-Hitler-c	75.00	225.00	600.
18-The Saint begins (2/42, 1st app.) by Leslie Charteris (see Movie Comics #2 by DC); The Saint-c	57.00	172.00	460.
19-21(1942): 20,21 have Wolverton's Scoop Scuttle. 21-Hitler app. in strip on cover	44.00	132.00	350.
22,24(1946)-Reprints	29.00	86.00	200.
23-Reprints?; bondage-c	29.00	86.00	200.
nn(11/46)(Newsbook Publ.)-R-/S.S. story from #4-7 plus 2 Captain Fearless stories, all in color; bondage/torture-c	40.00	120.00	325.

NOTE: **Binder** c-3, 4, 13-15, 17. **Jack Cole** a-(Daredevil)-#6-10, (Dickie Dean)-#3-10, (Pirate Prince)-#7, (Silver Streak)-#4-8, nn; c-5 (Silver Streak), 6 (Claw), 7, 8 (Daredevil). **Everett** Reed begins #20. **Guardineer** a-#8-13. **Don Rico** a-11-17 (Daredevil); c-11, 12, 16. **Simon** a (Silver Streak), **Bob Wood** a-13 (Silver Streak); c-9, 10. Captain Battle c-11, 13-15, 17. Claw c-#1, 2, 6-8. Daredevil c-7, 8, 12. Dickie Dean c-19. Ned of the Navy c-20 (war). The Saint c-18. Silver Streak c-5, 9, 10, 16, 23.

SILVER SURFER (See Fantastic Four, Fantasy Masterpieces V2#1, Marvel Graphic Novel, Marvel Presents #8, Marvel's Greatest Comics & Tales To Astonish #92)

SILVER SURFER, THE
Aug, 1968 - No. 18, Sept, 1970; June, 1982 (No. 1-7: 25¢, 68 pgs.)
Marvel Comics Group

	GD25	FN65	NM94
1-More detailed origin by John Buscema (p); The Watcher back-up stories begin (origin), end #7	52.00	156.00	415.
2	23.00	69.00	160.
3-1st app. Mephisto	19.00	56.00	130.
4-Low distribution; Thor & Loki app.	49.00	146.00	390.
5-7-Last giant size. 5-The Stranger app.; Fantastic Four app. 6-Brunner inks. (8/69)-1st app. Frankenstein's monster (cameo)	11.00	33.00	77.
8-10: 8-18-(15¢ issues)	8.00	24.00	60.
11-13,15-18: 15-Silver Surfer vs. Human Torch; Fantastic Four app. 17-Nick Fury app. 18-Vs. The Inhumans; Kirby-c/a	6.20	18.50	45.
14-Spider-Man x-over	9.30	28.00	65.
V2#1 (6/82, 52 pgs.)-Byrne-c/a	1.50	3.75	9.

NOTE: **Adkins** c-3, 4, 13-15. **Brunner** a-6i. **J. Buscema** a-1-17p. **Colan** a-1-3p. **Reinman** a-1-4i. #14 were reprinted in Fantasy Masterpieces V2#1-14.

SILVER SURFER (See Marvel Graphic Novel #38)
V3#1, July, 1987 - Present
Marvel Comics Group

V3#1-Double size ($1.25)	1.00	2.00	5.
2		1.20	3.
3-17: 15-Ron Lim-c/a begins (9/88)		1.60	4.
18-20		1.20	3.

Silver Surfer: Dangerous Artifacts © MEG

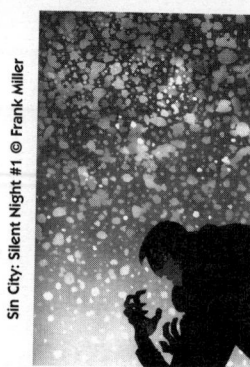

Sin City: Silent Night #1 © Frank Miller

Sin City: That Yellow Bastard #4 © Frank Miller

	GD25	FN65	NM94

21-33,39-43: 25,31 ($1.50, 52 pgs.). 25-Skrulls app. 32,39-No Ron Lim-c/a.

39-Alan Grant scripts		.80	2.00
34-Thanos returns (cameo); Starlin scripts begin	1.00	2.60	6.00

35-1st full Thanos app. in Silver Surfer (3/90); reintro Drax the Destroyer on
| last pg. (cameo) | 1.20 | 3.00 | 7.00 |

36-38: 36-Recaps history of Thanos; Capt. Marvel & Warlock app. in recap
37-1st full app. Drax the Destroyer; Drax-c. 38-Silver Surfer battles
Thanos	1.00	2.00	5.00
44,45,49-Thanos stories (c-44,45)			
46,47: 46-Return of Adam Warlock (2/91); re-intro Gamora & Pip the Troll.			
47-Warlock battles Drax	1.00	2.00	5.00
48-Last Starlin scripts (also #50)		.80	2.00

50-($1.50, 52 pgs.)-Embossed & silver foil-c; Silver Surfer has brief battle
w/Thanos; story cont'd in Infinity Gauntlet #1	1.00	2.00	5.00
50-2nd & 3rd printings		.80	2.00
51-53: Infinity Gauntlet x-over		1.00	2.50

54-57: Infinity Gauntlet x-overs. 54-Rhino app. 55,56-Thanos-c & app.
| 57-Thanos-c & cameo | | .80 | 2.00 |
58,59-Infinity Gauntlet x-overs; 58-Ron Lim only. 59-Thanos battles
Silver Surfer-c/story; Thanos joins	1.20		3.00
60-66: 61-Last $1.00-c. 63-Capt. Marvel app.			1.50
67-69-Infinity War x-overs		.80	2.00

70-74,76-81,83-91: 76-78-Jack of Hearts-c/s. 83-85-Infinity Crusade x-over;
83,84-Thanos cameo. 85-Storm, Wonder Man x-over. 86-Thor-c/s. 87-Dr.
Strange & Warlock app. 88-Thanos-c/s		.60	1.25
75-($2.50, 52 pgs.)-Embossed foil-c; Lim-c/a	.70	1.75	3.50
82-($1.75, 52 pgs.)	.35	.90	1.75

92-99; 101-109: 92-Begin $1.50-c; bound-in card stock sheet. 95-FF app. 96-Hulk
& FF app. 97-Terrax & Nova app. 106-Doc Doom app.			1.50
110-117: 110-Begin $1.95-c			2.00
118-130: 118-Begin $1.50-c. 121-Quasar & Beta Ray Bill app.			1.50
100 ($2.25, 52 pgs.)-Wraparound-c		.90	2.25
100 ($3.95, 52 pgs.)-Enhanced-c		1.60	4.00

Annual 1 (1988, $1.75)-Evolutionary War app.; 1st Ron Lim-a on Silver Surfer
| (20 pg. back-up story & pin-ups) | 1.00 | 2.00 | 5.00 |
Annual 2-4 (1989-91, $2.00, 68 pgs.): 2-Atlantis Attacks. 4-3 pg. origin story;
| Silver Surfer battles Guardians of the Galaxy | 1.00 | | 2.50 |
Annual 5 (1992, $2.25, 68 pgs.)-Return of the Defenders, part 3; Lim-c/a
| (3 pgs. of pin-ups only) | 1.00 | | 2.50 |
Annual 6 (1993, $2.95, 68 pgs.)-Polybagged w/trading card; 1st app. Legacy;
card is by Lim/Austin	1.20		3.00
Annual 7 (1994, $2.95)	1.20		3.00
Graphic Novel (Hardcover, $14.95)	2.10	6.00	15.00
Graphic Novel (The Enslavers, $16.95)	2.40	7.00	17.00
.Dangerous Artifacts-(1996, $3.95)-Ron Marz scripts; Galactus-c/app.			
			4.00

.: The First Coming of Galactus nn (11/92, $5.95, 68 pgs.)-Reprints Fantastic
| Four #48-50 with new Lim-c | 1.00 | 2.50 | 6.00 |
NOTE: Austin c(i)-71, 73, 74, 76, 79. Cully Hamner a-83p. Ron Lim a(p)-15-31, 33-38, 40-55,
56, 57-part-p), 60-65, 73-82; c(p)-15-31, 32-38, 40-84, 86-92, Annual 5, 6. M. Rogers a-1-10,
2, 19, 21; c-1-12, 21.

LVER SURFER, THE
ec, 1988 - No. 2, Jan, 1989 ($1.00, limited series)
arvel Comics (Epic Comics)
| 1,2: By Stan Lee scripts & Moebius-c/a | | 1.00 | 2.50 |

LVER SURFER VS. DRACULA
b, 1994 ($1.75, one-shot)
arvel Comics

-r/Tomb of Dracula #50; Everett Vampire-r/Venus #19; Howard the Duck
| back-up by Brunner; Lim-c(p) | | .70 | 1.75 |

LVER SURFER/WARLOCK: RESURRECTION
ar, 1993 - No. 4, June, 1993 ($2.50, limited series)
arvel Comics

	GD25	FN65	NM94
1-4: Starlin-c/a & scripts		1.00	2.50

SILVERTIP (Max Brand)
No. 491, Aug, 1953 - No. 898, May, 1958
Dell Publishing Co.

Four Color 491 (#1)	10.00	30.00	100.00
Four Color 572,608,637,667,731,789,898-Kinstler-a; all painted-c			
	5.00	15.00	50.00
Four Color 835	4.00	12.00	40.00

SIMPSONS COMICS (See Bartman, Itchy & Scratchy & Radioactive Man)
1993 - Present ($1.95, color)
Bongo Comics Group

| 1-($2.25)-FF#1-c swipe; pull-out poster; flip book | 1.60 | | 4.00 |
2,3-($1.95): 2-Patty & Selma on flip side. 3-Krusty, Agent of K.L.O.W.N. flip-c/
story		1.00	2.50
4-($2.25)-Infinity-c; flip-c of Busman #1; w/trading card	.90		2.25
5-Wraparound-c w/trading card		.90	2.25
6-24: All Flip books. 6-w/Chief Wiggums "Crime Comics". 7-w/McBain
Comics". 8-w/Edna, Queen of the Congo". 9-w/"Barney Gumble". 10-
w/"Apu". 11-w/"Homer". 12-w/"White Knuckled War Stories". 13-w/"Jimbo
Jones' Wedgie Comics". 14-w/"Grampa". 15-w/"Itchy & Scratchy".
16-w/"Bongo Grab Bag". 17-w/"Headlight Comics". 18-w."Milhouse".
19-22-w."Roswell". 23-w/Hellfire Comics". 24-w/"Lil' Honey"	.90		2.25
...Extravaganza (1994, $10.00)-r/#1-4; infinity-c			10.00
...Simpsorama (1996, $10.95)-r/#11-14			11.00

SIMPSONS COMICS AND STORIES
1993 ($2.95, one-shot)
Welsh Publishing Group

| 1-(Direct Sale)-Polybagged w/Bartman poster | 1.20 | | 3.00 |
| 1-(Newsstand Edition)-Without poster | 1.20 | | 3.00 |

SIMULATORS, THE
1991 ($2.50, stiff-c)
Neatly Chiseled Features

| 1-Super hero group | | 1.00 | 2.50 |

SINBAD, JR (TV Cartoon)
Sept-Nov, 1965 - No. 3, May, 1966
Dell Publishing Co.

| 1 | 2.30 | 6.70 | 16.00 |
| 2,3 | 1.70 | 5.00 | 12.00 |

SINDBAD (See Capt. Sindbad under Movie Comics, and Fantastic Voyages of Sindbad)

SIN CITY (See Dark Horse Presents, Decade of Dark Horse, A & San Diego Comic Con
Comics #2)

SIN CITY: A DAME TO KILL FOR
Nov, 1993 - No. 6, May, 1994 ($2.95, B&W, limited series)
Dark Horse Comics (Legend)

1-6: Frank Miller-c/a & story in all. 1-1st app. Dwight.	1.20		3.00
Limited Edition Hardcover			100.00
Hardcover			25.00

SIN CITY: SILENT NIGHT
Dec, 1995 ($2.95, B&W, one-shot)
Dark Horse Comics (Legend)

| 1-Miller-c/a & story; Marv app. | 1.20 | | 3.00 |

SIN CITY: THAT YELLOW BASTARD
Feb, 1996 - No. 6, July, 1996 ($2.95, B&W and yellow, limited series)
Dark Horse Comics (Legend)

| 1-4: Miller-c/a & story in all. 1-1st app. Hartigan. | | | 3.00 |

SIN CITY: THE BABE WORE RED AND OTHER STORIES
Nov, 1994 ($2.95, B&W and red, one-shot)
Dark Horse Comics (Legend)

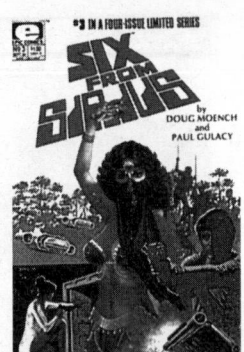

	GD25	FN65	NM94

	GD25	FN65	NM94

1-r/serial run in Previews as well as other stories; Miller-c/a & scripts; Dwight app.   1.20   3.00

SIN CITY: THE BIG FAT KILL
Nov, 1994 - No. 5, Mar, 1995 ($2.95, B&W, limited series)
Dark Horse Comics (Legend)

1-4-Miller story & art in all; Dwight app.		1.20	3.00
5 ($3.50)-Dwight app.		1.40	3.50
Hardcover			25.00

SINGING GUNS (See Fawcett Movie Comics)

SINGLE SERIES (Comics on Parade #30 on)(Also see John Hix…)
1938 - No. 28, 1942 (All 68 pgs.)
United Features Syndicate

Note: See Individual Alphabetical Listings for prices

1-Captain and the Kids (#1)	2-Broncho Bill (1939) (#1)
3-Ella Cinders (1939)	4-Li'l Abner (1939) (#1)
5-Fritzi Ritz (#1)	6-Jim Hardy by Dick Moores (#1)
7-Frankie Doodle	8-Peter Pat (On sale 7/14/39)
9-Strange As It Seems	10-Little Mary Mixup
11-Mr. and Mrs. Beans	12-Joe Jinks
13-Looy Dot Dope	14-Billy Make Believe
15-How It Began (1939)	16-Illustrated Gags (1940)-Has ad
17-Danny Dingle	for Captain and the Kids #1
18-Li'l Abner (#2 on-c)	reprint listed below
19-Broncho Bill (#2 on-c)	20-Tarzan by Hal Foster
21-Ella Cinders (#2 on-c; on sale 3/19/40)	22-Iron Vic
23-Tailspin Tommy by Hal Forrest (#1)	24-Alice in Wonderland (#1)
25-Abbie and Slats	26-Little Mary Mixup (#2 on-c, 1940)
27-Jim Hardy by Dick Moores (1942)	28-Ella Cinders & Abbie and Slats
1-Captain and the Kids (1939 reprint)-2nd	(1942)
Edition	1-Fritzi Ritz (1939 reprint)-2nd ed.

NOTE: Some issues given away at the 1939-40 New York World's Fair (#6).

SINISTER HOUSE OF SECRET LOVE, THE (Becomes Secrets of Sinister House No. 5 on)
Oct-Nov, 1971 - No. 4, Apr-May, 1972 (52 pgs.)
National Periodical Publications

1	2.30	6.75	16.00
2-4: 2-Jeff Jones-c. 3-Toth-a (36 pgs.)	1.50	3.75	9.00

SIR CHARLES BARKLEY AND THE REFEREE MURDERS
1993 ($9.95, 8-1/2" x 11", 52 pgs.)
Hamilton Comics

nn-Photo-c; Sports fantasy comic book fiction (uses real names of NBA super stars). Scipt by Alan Dean Foster, art by Joe Staton. Comes with bound-in sheet of 35 gummed "Moods of Charles Barkley" stamps. Photo/story on Barkley   2.00   5.00   10.00

Special Edition of 100 copies for charity signed on an affixed book plate by Barkley, Foster & Staton   150.00

Ashcan edition given away to dealers, distributors & promoters (low distribution). Four pages in color, balance of story in b&w   1.65   4.20   10.00

SIREN (Also see Eliminator & Ultraforce)
Sept, 1995 - No. 3, Dec, 1995 ($1.50)
Malibu Comics (Ultraverse)

Infinity, 1-3: Infinity-Black-c & painted-c exists. 1-Regular-c & painted-c; War Machine app. 2-Flip book w/Phoenix Ressurection Pt. 3   1.50

Special 1-(2/96, $1.95, 28 pgs.)-Origin Siren; Marvel Comic's Juggernaut-c/app.   2.00

SIR LANCELOT (TV)
No. 606, Dec, 1954 - No. 775, Mar, 1957
Dell Publishing Co.

Four Color 606 (not TV)	9.00	27.00	90.00
Four Color 775 (…and Brian)-Buscema-a; photo-c	10.00	30.00	100.00

SIR WALTER RALEIGH (Movie)
May, 1955 (Based on movie "The Virgin Queen")
Dell Publishing Co.

Four Color 644-Photo-c	7.00	21.00	70.

SISTERHOOD OF STEEL (See Eclipse Graphic Novel #13)
Dec, 1984 -No. 8, Feb, 1986 ($1.50, Baxter paper, mature)
Marvel Comics (Epic Comics)

1-8			1.

SISTERS OF MERCY
Dec, 1995 - Present ($2.50)
Maximum Press/No Mercy Comics No. 3 on

1-5: 1-Liefeld variant-c exists			2

6 BLACK HORSES (See Movie Classics)

SIX FROM SIRIUS
July, 1984 - No. 4, Oct, 1984 ($1.50, limited series, mature)
Marvel Comics (Epic Comics)

1-4: Moench scripts; Gulacy-c/a in all			1

SIX FROM SIRIUS II
Feb, 1986 - No. 4, May, 1986 ($1.50, limited series, mature)
Marvel Comics (Epic Comics)

1-4: Moench scripts; Gulacy-c/a in all			1

SIX-GUN HEROES
March, 1950 - No. 23, Nov, 1953 (Photo-c #1-23)
Fawcett Publications

1-Rocky Lane, Hopalong Cassidy, Smiley Burnette begin (same date as Smiley Burnette #1)	40.00	120.00	315
2	25.00	75.00	175
3-5: 5-Lash LaRue begins	16.00	47.00	110
6-15	13.00	39.00	90.
16-22: 17-Last Smiley Burnette. 18-Monte Hale begins	11.00	33.00	75
23-Last Fawcett issue	12.00	36.00	85

NOTE: Hopalong Cassidy photo c-1-3. Monte Hale photo c-18. Rocky Lane photo c-4, 5, 7, 9 11, 13, 15, 17, 20, 21, 23. Lash LaRue photo c-6, 8, 10, 12, 14, 16, 19, 22.

SIX-GUN HEROES (Continued from Fawcett; Gunmasters #84 on)
No. 24, Jan, 1954 - No. 83, Mar-Apr, 1965 (All Vol. 4)(See Blue Bird)
Charlton Comics

24-Lash LaRue, Hopalong Cassidy, Rocky Lane & Tex Ritter begin; photo-c	17.00	51.00	120
25	10.00	30.00	58
26-30: 26-Rod Cameron story. 28-Tom Mix begins?	8.00	24.00	48
31-40: 38-Jingles & Wild Bill Hickok (TV)	6.70	20.00	40
41-46,48,50	6.35	19.00	38
47-Williamson-a, 2 pgs; Torres-a	7.00	21.00	42
49-Williamson-a in both	7.00	21.00	42
51-56,58-60: 58-Gunmaster app.	4.00	12.00	24
57-Origin & 1st app. Gunmaster	5.00	15.00	30
61-70: 62-Origin Gunmaster	3.60	9.00	18
71-83: 76-Gunmaster begins. 79-1st app. & origin of Bullet, the Gun-Boy	2.60	6.50	13

SIXGUN RANCH (See Luke Short & Four Color #580)

SIX-GUN WESTERN
Jan, 1957 - No. 4, July, 1957
Atlas Comics (CDS)

1-Crandall-a; two Williamson text illos	16.00	47.00	110
2,3-Williamson-a in both	12.00	36.00	85
4-Woodbridge-a	8.00	24.00	48

NOTE: Ayers a-2, 3. Maneely a-1; c-2, 3. Orlando a-2. Pakula a-2. Powell a-3. Romita a-1. Severin c-1, 4. Shores a-2.

Skreemer #4 © DC

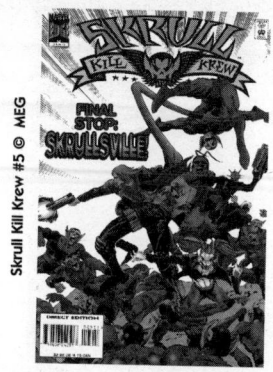

Skull Kill Krew #5 © MEG

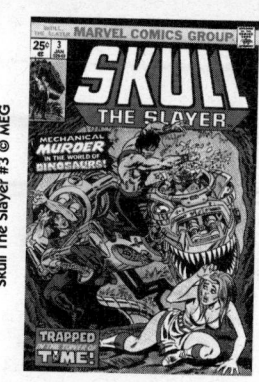

Skull The Slayer #3 © MEG

SL

	GD25	FN65	NM94

SIX MILLION DOLLAR MAN, THE (TV)
6/76 - No. 4, 12/76; No. 5, 10/77; No. 6, 2/78 - No. 9, 6/78
Charlton Comics
| 1-Staton-c/a; Lee Majors photo on-c | 1.20 | 3.00 |
| 2-9: 2-Neal Adams-c; Staton-a | .80 | 2.00 |

SIX MILLION DOLLAR MAN, THE (TV)(Magazine)
July, 1976 - No. 7, Nov, 1977 (B&W)
Charlton Comics
1-Neal Adams-c/a	1.20	3.00
2-Neal Adams-c		1.20
3-7: 3-N. Adams part inks; Chaykin-a		1.20

67 SECONDS
1992 ($15.95, 54 pgs., graphic novel)
Marvel Comics (Epic Comics)
| nn-James Robinson scripts; Steve Yeowell-c/a | | 16.00 |

SKATEMAN
Nov, 1983 (Baxter paper, one-shot)
Pacific Comics
| 1-Adams-c/a | | 1.50 |

SKATING SKILLS (...In Secrets of the Supernatural)
1957 (36 & 12 pgs.; 5x7", two versions) (10¢)
Custom Comics, Inc./Chicago Roller Skates
| nn-Resembles old ACG cover plus interior art | 3.20 | 8.00 | 16.00 |

SKELETON HAND (...In Secrets of the Supernatural)
Sept-Oct, 1952 - No. 6, July-Aug, 1953
American Comics Group (B&M Dist. Co.)
1	37.00	111.00	260.00
2	25.00	75.00	175.00
3-6	21.00	62.00	145.00

SKELETON KEY
July, 1995 - Present ($1.25/$1.50/$1.75)
Amaze Ink
1-9: 2-Begin $1.50		1.25
		1.50
10-14: 10-Begin $1.75		1.75
Beyond The Threshold (6/96. $11.95, trade paperback)-r/#1-6		12.00

SKELETON WARRIORS
Mar, 1995 - No. 4, July, 1995 ($1.50)
Marvel Comics
| 1-4: Based on animated series. | | 1.50 |

SKIN GRAFT: THE ADVENTURES OF A TATTOOED MAN
July, 1993 - No. 4, Oct, 1993 ($2.50, limited series, mature)
DC Comics (Vertigo)
| 1-4 | | 1.00 | 2.50 |

SKIP PARTY (See Movie Classics)

SKIPPY'S OWN BOOK OF COMICS (See Popular Comics)
1934 (Giveaway, 52 pgs., strip reprints)
no publisher listed
| 1(Scarce)-By Percy Crosby | 500.00 | 1500.00 | 5000.00 |
(Estimated up to 40 total copies exist, 2 in NM/Mint)
Published by Max C. Gaines for Phillip's Dental Magnesia to be advertised on the Skippy Radio show and given away with the purchase of a tube of Phillip's Tooth Paste. This is the first four-color comic book of reprints about one character.

SKREEMER
Nov, 1989 - No. 6, Oct, 1989 ($2.00, limited series, mature)
DC Comics
| 6: Contains graphic violence | | .80 | 2.00 |

	GD25	FN65	NM94

SKRULL KILL KREW
Sept, 1995 - No. 5, Dec, 1995 ($2.95, limited series)
Marvel Comics
| 1-5: Grant Morrison scripts. 2,3-Cap America app. | | 1.20 | 3.00 |

SKULL & BONES
1992 - No. 3, 1992 ($4.95, limited series, 52 pgs.)
DC Comics
| Book 1-3: 1-1st app. | 1.00 | 2.00 | 5.00 |

SKULL, THE SLAYER
Aug, 1975 - No. 8, Nov, 1976 (20¢/25¢)
Marvel Comics Group
| 1-Origin & 1st app.; Gil Kane-c | | .80 | 2.00 |
| 2-8: 2-Gil Kane-c. 8-Kirby-c | | | 1.25 |

SKY BLAZERS (CBS Radio)
Sept, 1940 - No. 2, Nov, 1940
Hawley Publications
| 1-Sky Pirates, Ace Archer, Flying Aces begin | 50.00 | 150.00 | 400.00 |
| 2 | 36.00 | 107.00 | 250.00 |

SKY KING "RUNAWAY TRAIN" (TV)
1964 (Regular size, 16 pgs.)
National Biscuit Co.
| nn | 3.60 | 9.00 | 18.00 |

SKYMAN (See Big Shot Comics & Sparky Watts)
Fall?, 1941 - No. 2, 1941; No. 3, 1948 - No. 4, 1948
Columbia Comics
1-Origin Skyman, The Face, Sparky Watts app.; Whitney-c/a; 3rd story-r from Big Shot #1; Whitney c-1-4	81.00	243.00	650.00
2 (1941)-Yankee Doodle	44.00	132.00	350.00
3,4 (1948)	32.00	96.00	225.00

SKYPILOT
No. 10, 1950(nd) - No. 11, Apr-May, 1951 (Saunders painted-c)
Ziff-Davis Publ. Co.
| 10,11-Frank Borth-a | 11.00 | 33.00 | 75.00 |

SKY RANGER (See Johnny Law...)

SKYROCKET
1944
Harry 'A' Chesler
| nn-Alias the Dragon, Dr. Vampire, Skyrocket & The Desperado app. | 23.00 | 69.00 | 160.00 |

SKY SHERIFF (Breeze Lawson...) (Also see Exposed & Outlaws)
Summer, 1948
D. S. Publishing Co.
| 1-Edmond Good-c/a | 10.00 | 30.00 | 65.00 |

SKY WOLF (Also see Airboy)
Mar, 1988 - No. 3, Oct, 1988 ($1.25/$1.50/$1.95, limited series)
Eclipse Comics
| 1,2-($1.75) | | .70 | 1.75 |
| 3-($1.95) | | .80 | 1.95 |

SLACKER COMICS
Aug, 1994 - Present ($2.95, B&W, quarterly)
Slave Labor Graphics
| 1-9 | | 1.20 | 3.00 |
| 1 (2nd printing)-Reads "2nd print" in indicia | | 1.20 | 3.00 |

SLAINE, THE BERSERKER (Slaine the King #21 on)
July, 1987 - No. 28, 1989 ($1.25/$1.50)
Quality

Slash Maraud #6 © DC

Sliders: Darkest Hour #3 © 20th Century Fox

Sliders: Ultimatum #2 © 20th Century Fox

	GD25	FN65	NM94
1-12			1.25
13-28: 13-Begin $1.50-c			1.50

SLAM BANG COMICS (Western Desperado #8)
Mar, 1940 - No. 7, Sept, 1940 (Combined with Master Comics #7)
Fawcett Publications

	GD25	FN65	NM94
1-Diamond Jack, Mark Swift & The Time Retarder, Lee Granger, Jungle King begin & continue in Master	162.00	487.00	1300.00
2	68.00	206.00	550.00
3-Classic-c	90.00	271.00	725.00
4-7: 6-Intro Zoro, the Mystery Man (also in #7).	56.00	168.00	450.00

SLAM BANG COMICS
No. 9, No date
Post Cereal Giveaway

	GD25	FN65	NM94
9-Dynamic Man, Echo, Mr. E, Yankee Boy app.	4.00	11.00	22.00

SLAPSTICK
Nov, 1992 - No. 4, Feb, 1993 ($1.25, limited series)
Marvel Comics

1-4: Fry/Austin-c/a. 4-Ghost Rider, D.D., F.F. app.			1.25

SLAPSTICK COMICS
nd (1946?) (36 pgs.)
Comic Magazines Distributors

	GD25	FN65	NM94
nn-Firetop feature; Post-a(2)	19.00	56.00	130.00

SLASH-D DOUBLECROSS
1950 (Pocket-size, 132 pgs.)
St. John Publishing Co.

	GD25	FN65	NM94
nn-Western comics	18.00	54.00	125.00

SLASH MARAUD
Nov, 1987 - No. 6, Apr, 1988 ($1.75, limited series)
DC Comics

1-6		.70	1.75

SLAUGHTERMAN
Feb, 1983 - No. 2, 1983 ($1.50, B&W)
Comico

1,2			1.50

SLAVE GIRL COMICS (See Malu... & White Princess of the Jungle #2)
Feb, 1949 - No. 2, Apr, 1949 (52 pgs.); Mar, 1989 (B&W, 44 pgs)
Avon Periodicals/Eternity Comics (1989)

	GD25	FN65	NM94
1-Larsen-c/a	73.00	221.00	590.00
2-Larsen-i	55.00	165.00	440.00
1-(3/89, $2.25, B&W, 44 pgs.)-r/#1		.90	2.25

SLEDGE HAMMER (TV)
Feb, 1988 - No. 2, Mar,1988 ($1.00, limited series)
Marvel Comics

1,2			1.00

SLEEPING BEAUTY (See Dell Giants & Movie Comics)
No. 973, May, 1959 - No. 984, June, 1959 (Disney)
Dell Publishing Co.

	GD25	FN65	NM94
Four Color 973 (...and the Prince)	13.00	40.00	130.00
Four Color 984 (...Fairy Godmother's)	10.00	30.00	100.00

SLEEPWALKER
June, 1991 - No. 33, Feb, 1994 ($1.00/$1.25)
Marvel Comics

1-1st app. Sleepwalker			1.50
2-5: 4-Williamson-i. 5-Spider-Man-c/story			1.50
6-10: 7-Infinity Gauntlet x-over. 8-Vs. Deathlok-c/story			1.50
11-18,20-24,26-33: 11-Ghost Rider-c/story. 12-Quesada-c/a(p) 14-Intro Spectra. 15-F.F.-c/story. 17-Darkhawk & Spider-Man x-over. 18-Infinity			

War x-over; Quesada/Williamson-c. 21,22-Hobgoblin app.

	GD25	FN65	NM94
19-($2.00)-Die-cut Sleepwalker mask cover		.80	1
25-($2.95, 52 pgs.)-Holo-grafx foil-c; origin		1.20	3
Holiday Special 1 (1/93, $2.00, 52 pgs.)-Quesada-c(p)		.80	2

SLEEZE BROTHERS, THE
Aug, 1989 - No. 6, Jan, 1990 ($1.75, mature)
Marvel Comics (Epic Comics)

1-6: 4-6 (9/89 - 11/89 indicia dates)			1
nn-(1991, $3.95, 52 pgs.)		1.60	4

SLICK CHICK COMICS
1947(nd) - No. 3, 1947(nd)
Leader Enterprises

	GD25	FN65	NM94
1-Teenage humor	10.00	30.00	65
2,3	8.00	24.00	48

SLIDERS (TV)
June, 1996 - No. 2, July, 1996 ($2.50, limited series)
Acclaim Comics (Armada)

1,2: D.G. Chichester scripts; Dick Giordano-a.			2

SLIDERS: DARKEST HOUR (TV)
Oct, 1996 - No. 3, Dec, 1996 ($2.50, limited series)
Acclaim Comics (Armada)

1-3			2

SLIDERS SPECIAL
Nov, 1996 ($3.95, one-shot)
Acclaim Comics (Armada)

1			4

SLIDERS: ULTIMATUM (TV)
Sept, 1996 - No. 2, Sept, 1996 ($2.50, limited series)
Acclaim Comics (Armada)

1,2			2

SLIMER! (TV cartoon) (Also see the Real Ghostbusters)
1989 - No. 19, Feb?, 1991 ($1.75)
Now Comics

1-19: Based on animated cartoon		.70	1

SLIM MORGAN (See Wisco)

SLUDGE
Oct, 1993 - No. 12, Dec, 1994 ($2.50/$1.95)
Malibu Comics (Ultraverse)

1-($2.50, 48 pgs.)-Intro/1st app. Sludge; Rune flip-c/story Pt. 1 (1st app., 3 pgs.) by Barry Smith; The Night Man app. (3 pg. preview); The Mighty Magnor 1 pg strip begins by Aragones (cont. in other titles)			1.00
1-Ultra 5000 Limited silver foil		1.30	3.25
2-11: 3-Break-Thru x-over. 4-2 pg. Mantra origin. 8-Bloodstorm app.			.80
12 ($3.50)-Ultravenire Premiere #8 flip book; Alex Ross poster.		1.40	
...:Red Xmas (12/94, $2.50, 44 pgs.)			1.00

SLUGGER (Little Wise Guys Starring...)(Also see Daredevil Comics)
April, 1956
Lev Gleason Publications

	GD25	FN65	NM94
1-Biro-c	5.35	16.00	3

SMASH COMICS (Becomes Lady Luck #86 on)
Aug, 1939 - No. 85, Oct, 1949
Quality Comics Group

1-Origin Hugh Hazard & His Iron Man, Bozo the Robot, Espionage, Starring Black X by Eisner, & Hooded Justice (Invisible Justice #2 on); Chic Carter & Wings Wendall begin; 1st Robot on the cover of a comic book (Bozo)

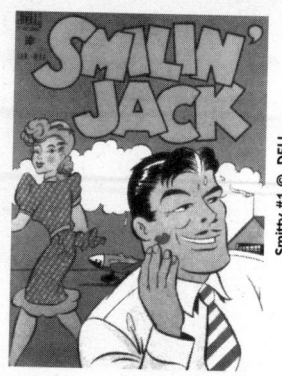

Smash Comics #40 © QUA

Smilin' Jack #1 © DELL

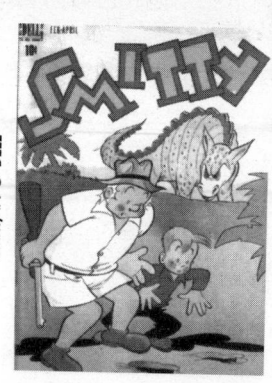

Smitty #1 © DELL

	GD25	FN65	NM94
2-The Lone Star Rider app; Invisible Hood gains power of invisibility	206.00	618.00	1650.00
	81.00	243.00	650.00
3-Captain Cook & Eisner's John Law begin	50.00	150.00	400.00
4,5- 4-Flash Fulton begins	47.00	140.00	370.00
6-12- 12-One pg. Fine-a	40.00	120.00	315.00
3-Magno begins (8/40); last Eisner issue; The Ray app. in full page ad; The Purple Trio begins	40.00	120.00	325.00
4-Intro. The Ray (9/40) by Lou Fine & others	225.00	675.00	1800.00
5,16- 16-The Scarlet Seal begins	106.00	318.00	850.00
7-Wun Cloo becomes plastic super-hero by Jack Cole (9-months before Plastic Man)	112.00	338.00	900.00
8-Midnight by Jack Cole begins (origin & 1st app., 1/41)	131.00	393.00	1050.00
9-22- Last Fine Ray; The Jester begins-#22	71.00	213.00	570.00
3,24- 24-The Sword app.; last Chic Carter; Wings Wendall dons new costume #24,25	57.00	172.00	460.00
5-Origin/1st app. Wildfire; Rookie Rankin begins	71.00	213.00	570.00
6-30- 28-Midnight-c begins, end #85	53.00	159.00	425.00
1,32,34- Ray by Rudy Palais; also #33	40.00	120.00	315.00
3-Origin The Marksman	53.00	159.00	425.00
5-37	40.00	120.00	315.00
3-The Yankee Eagle begins; last Midnight by Jack Cole	44.00	132.00	350.00
0,40-Last Ray issue	40.00	120.00	300.00
43-50	26.00	77.00	180.00
2-Lady Luck begins by Klaus Nordling	40.00	120.00	325.00
-60	19.00	56.00	130.00
-70	16.00	47.00	110.00
-85- 79-Midnight battles the Men from Mars-c/s	15.00	45.00	105.00

TE: Al Bryant c-54, 63-68. Cole a-17-38, 68, 69, 72, 73, 78, 80, 83, 85; c-38, 60-62, 69-84.
andall a-(Ray)-23-29, 35-38; c-36, 39, 40, 42-44, 46. Fine a-(Ray)-14, 15, 16(w/Tuska), 17-22.
x c-24-35. Fuje Ray-30. Gil Fox a-6-7, 9, 11-13. Guardineer a-(The Marksman)-39-?, 49, 52.
stavson a-4-7, 9, 11-13 (The Jester)-22-46; (Magno)-13-21; (Midnight)-39(Cole inks), 49, 52,
65. Kotzky a-(Espionage)-33-38; c-45, 47-53. Nordling a-49, 52, 63-65. Powell a-11, 12,
dul (the Arab)-13-24.Black X c-2, 6, 9, 11, 13, 16. Bozo the Robot c-1, 3, 5, 8, 10, 12, 14, 18,
22, 24, 26. Midnight c-28-85. The Ray c-15, 17, 19, 21, 23, 25, 27. Wings Wendall c-4, 7.

ASH HIT SPORTS COMICS
#1, Jan, 1949
sankay Publications

	GD25	FN65	NM94
#1-L.B. Cole-c/a	24.00	71.00	165.00

ILE COMICS (Also see Gay Comics, Tickle, & Whee)
5 (52 pgs.; 5x7-1/4") (7¢)
dern Store Publ.

	.60	1.50	3.00

LEY BURNETTE WESTERN (Also see Patches #8 & Six-Gun Heroes)
ch, 1950 - No. 4, Oct, 1950 (All photo front & back-c)
cett Publications

	GD25	FN65	NM94
Red Eagle begins	40.00	120.00	325.00
4	31.00	92.00	215.00

LIN' JACK (See Famous Feature Stories, Popular Comics, Super Book
2, 7, 19 & Super Comics)
5, 1940 - No. 8, Oct-Dec, 1949
Publishing Co.

	GD25	FN65	NM94
rColor 5	58.00	174.00	585.00
Color 10 (1940)	52.00	156.00	525.00
e Feature Comic 12,14,25 (1941)	51.00	153.00	515.00
Color 4 (1942)	43.00	129.00	435.00
Color 14 (1943)	34.00	102.00	345.00
Color 36,58 (1943-44)	22.00	66.00	225.00
Color 80 (1945)	15.00	45.00	155.00
Color 149 (1947)	10.00	30.00	100.00
-3(48)	10.00	30.00	100.00

	GD25	FN65	NM94
2	6.00	18.00	54.00
3-8 (10-12/49)	4.00	12.00	36.00

Popped Wheat Giveaway (1947)-1938 strip reprints; 16 pgs. in full color

	1.00	2.00	5.00
Shoe Store Giveaway-1938 strip reprints; 16 pgs.	4.25	13.00	28.00
Sparked Wheat Giveaway (1942)-16 pgs. in full color	4.25	13.00	28.00

SMILING SPOOK SPUNKY (See Spunky)

SMITTY (See Popular Comics, Super Book #2, 4 & Super Comics)
No. 11, 1940 - No. 7, Aug-Oct, 1949; No. 909, Apr, 1958
Dell Publishing Co.

	GD25	FN65	NM94
Four Color 11 (1940)	36.00	108.00	360.00
Large Feature Comic 26 (1941)	26.00	78.00	260.00
Four Color 6 (1942)	21.00	63.00	210.00
Four Color 32 (1943)	15.00	45.00	155.00
Four Color 65 (1945)	12.00	36.00	120.00
Four Color 99 (1946)	10.50	31.50	105.00
Four Color 138 (1947)	9.00	27.00	90.00
1 (2-4/48)	9.00	27.00	90.00
2-(5-7/48)	5.00	15.00	45.00
3,4; 3-(8-10/48), 4-(11-1/48-49)	4.00	12.00	36.00
5-7, Four Color 909 (4/58)	3.00	9.00	30.00

SMOKEY BEAR (TV) (See March Of Comics #234, 362, 372, 383, 407)
Feb, 1970 - No. 13, Mar, 1973
Gold Key

1	1.00	2.50	6.00
2-13		1.20	3.00

SMOKEY STOVER (See Popular Comics, Super Book #5, 17, 29 & Super
Comics)
No. 7, 1942 - No. 827, Aug, 1957
Dell Publishing Co.

	GD25	FN65	NM94
Four Color 7 (1942)-Reprints	32.00	96.00	320.00
Four Color 35 (1943)	16.00	48.00	160.00
Four Color 64 (1944)	12.00	36.00	120.00
Four Color 229 (1949)	5.00	15.00	50.00
Four Color 730,827	3.80	11.40	38.00
General Motors giveaway (1953)	5.00	15.00	30.00
National Fire Protection giveaway(1953 & 1954)-16 pgs., paper-c	5.00	15.00	30.00

SMOKEY THE BEAR (See Forest Fire for 1st app.)
No. 653, 10/55 - No. 1214, 8/61 (See March of Comics #234)
Dell Publishing Co.

	GD25	FN65	NM94
Four Color 653 (#1)	10.00	30.00	100.00
Four Color 708,754,818,932	5.00	15.00	50.00
Four Color 1016,1119,1214	4.00	12.00	40.00

True Story of…, The('59)-U.S. Forest Service giveaway-Publ. by Western
Printing Co. (reprinted in 1964 & 1969)-Reprints 1st 16 pgs. of Four Color

932	3.20	8.00	16.00

SMOKY (See Movie Classics)

SMURFS (TV)
1982 (Dec) - No. 3, 1983
Marvel Comics

1-3			1.00
…Treasury Edition 1 (64 pgs.)-r/#1-3		1.00	2.50

SNAFU (Magazine)
Nov, 1955 - V2#2, Mar, 1956 (B&W)
Atlas Comics (RCM)

	GD25	FN65	NM94
V1#1-Heath/Severin-a; Everett, Maneely-a	11.00	33.00	75.00
V2#1,2-Severin-a	9.15	27.50	55.00

SNAGGLEPUSS (TV)(See Hanna-Barbera Band Wagon #3, Quick-Draw

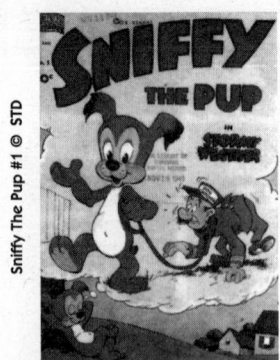
Sniffy The Pup #1 © STD

Solar #9 © WEST

Solarman #2 © MEG

	GD25	FN65	NM94

McGraw & Spotlight #4)
Oct, 1962 - No. 4, Sept, 1963 (Hanna-Barbera)
Gold Key

1	7.00	21.00	70.00
2-4	5.00	15.00	50.00

SNAP (Formerly Scoop #8; becomes Jest #10,11 & Komik Pages #10)
No. 9, 1944
Harry 'A' Chesler

9-Manhunter, The Voice	15.00	45.00	105.00

SNAPPY COMICS
1945
Cima Publ. Co. (Prize Publ.)

1-Airmale app.; 9 pg. Sorcerer's Apprentice adapt; Kiefer-a	24.00	73.00	170.00

SNARKY PARKER (See Life With...)

SNIFFY THE PUP
No. 5, Nov, 1949 - No. 18, Sept, 1953
Standard Publications (Animated Cartoons)

5-Two Frazetta text illos	10.00	30.00	60.00
6-10	4.00	11.00	22.00
11-18	3.20	8.00	16.00

SNOOPER AND BLABBER DETECTIVES (TV) (See Whitman Comic Books)
Nov, 1962 - No. 3, May, 1963 (Hanna-Barbera)
Gold Key

1	7.00	21.00	70.00
2,3	5.50	16.50	55.00

SNOW FOR CHRISTMAS
1957 (16 pgs.) (Giveaway)
W. T. Grant Co.

nn	3.20	8.00	16.00

SNOW WHITE (See Christmas With..., Mickey Mouse Mag., Movie Comics &
Seven Dwarfs)
No. 49, July, 1944 - No. 382, Mar, 1952 (Disney-Movie)
Dell Publishing Co.

Four Color 49 (...& the Seven Dearfs)	60.00	180.00	600.00
Four Color 382 (1952)-origin; partial reprint of Four Color 49	13.00	40.00	130.00

SNOW WHITE
Jan, 1995 ($1.95, one-shot)
Marvel Comics

1-r/1937 Sunday newspaper pages		.80	2.00

SNOW WHITE AND THE SEVEN DWARFS
1952 (32 pgs., 5x7-1/4", soft-c) (Disney)
Bendix Washing Machines

nn	11.00	32.00	75.00

SNOW WHITE AND THE SEVEN DWARFS
1957 (Small size)
Promotional Publ. Co.

nn	4.00	10.50	21.00

SNOW WHITE AND THE SEVEN DWARFS
1958 (16 pgs, 5x7-1/4", soft-c) (Disney premium)
Western Printing Co.

nn- "Mystery of the Missing Magic"	6.70	20.00	40.00

SNOW WHITE AND THE SEVEN DWARFS
April, 1982 (60¢)
Whitman Publications

nn-r/Four Color 49		1.20	3.00

SNOW WHITE AND THE SEVEN DWARFS GOLDEN ANNIVERSARY
Fall, 1987 ($2.95, magazine size, 52 pgs.)
Gladstone

1-Contains poster		1.30	3.25

SNOW WHITE AND THE 7 DWARFS IN "MILKY WAY"
1955 (16 pgs., soft-c, 5x7-1/4") (Disney premium)
American Dairy Association

nn		11.00	32.00	7

SOAP OPERA LOVE
Feb, 1983 - No. 3, June, 1983
Charlton Comics

1-3

SOAP OPERA ROMANCES
July, 1982 - No. 5, March, 1983
Charlton Comics

1-5-Nurse Betsy Crane-r

SO DARK THE ROSE
Oct, 1995 ($2.95)
CFD Productions

1-Wrightson-c			1.20

SOJOURN
Sept, 1977 - No. 2, 1978 ($1.50, B&W & color, full tabloid size)
White Cliffs Publ. Co.

1,2: 1-Tor by Kubert, Eagle by Severin, E. V. Race, Private Investigator by
Doug Wildey, T. C. Mars by Aragones begin plus other strips   .70

SOLAR (...Man of the Atom) (Also see Doctor Solar)
Sept, 1991 - No. 60, Apr, 1996 ($1.75/$1.95/$2.50, 44 pgs.)
Valiant/Acclaim Comics (Valiant)

1-Layton-a(i) on Solar; Barry Windsor-Smith-c/a	1.65	4.20	
2,3: 2-Layton-a(i) on Solar, B. Smith-a. 3-1st app. Harada (11/91)		1.30	3.25
4-9: 7-vs. X-O Armor; last 8-$2.25-c begins			1.20
10-(6/92, $3.95)-1st app. Eternal Warrior (6 pgs.); black embossed-c; origin 1st app. Geoff McHenry (Geomancer)	1.65	4.20	
10-($3.95)-2nd printing		1.60	
11-15: 11-1st full app. Eternal Warrior. 12,13-Unity x-overs. 14-1st app. Fred Bender (becomes Dr. Eclipse). 15-2nd Dr. Eclipse			1.20
16-45: 17-X-O Manowar app. 23-Solar splits. 29-1st Valiant Vision book. 3 Valiant Vision; bound-in trading card. 38-Chaos Effect Epsilion Pt.1			.90
46-60: 46-$2.50-c begins. 46-52-Dan Jurgens-a(p)/scripts w/Giordano-i. 53,54-Jurgens scripts only. 60-Keith Giffen scripts; Jeff Johnson-a(p)			1.00
0-($9.95, trade paperback)-Alpha and Omega r/origin story; polybagged w/poster			10.00

...:Second Death (1994, $9.95)-r/issues #1-4.
NOTE: #1-10 all have free 8 pg. insert "Alpha and Omega" which is a 10 chapter Solar orig
story. All 10 centerfolds can pieced together to show climax of story. **Ditko** a-11p, 14p.
Giordano a-46, 47, 48, 49, 50, 51, 52i. **Johnson** a-60p. **Jurgens** a-46, 47, 48, 49, 50 , 51
Layton a-13i; c-2i, 11i, 17i, 25i. **Miller** c-12. **Quesada** a-17p, 20-23p, 29p. **Simonson** c-
Smith a-1-10; c-1, 3, 5, 7, 19i. **Thibert** c-22i, 23i.

SOLARMAN
Jan, 1989 - No. 2, May, 1990 ($1.00, limited series)
Marvel Comics

1,2

SOLDIER & MARINE COMICS (Fightin' Army #16 on)
No. 11, Dec, 1954 - No. 15, Aug, 1955; V2#9, Dec, 1956
Charlton Comics (Toby Press of Conn. V1#11)

V1#11 (12/54)-Bob Powell-a	5.35	16.00	

Solitaire #4 © Malibu

Solo #3 © MEG

Solution #8 © Malibu

	GD25	FN65	NM94
12(2/55)-15: 12-Photo-c	4.00	10.00	20.00
9(Formerly Never Again; Jerry Drummer V2#10 on)	4.00	10.00	20.00

DIER COMICS
1952 - No. 11, Sept, 1953
cett Publications

	10.00	30.00	65.00
	5.35	16.00	32.00
	4.25	13.00	26.00
1: 8-Illo. in POP	4.00	11.00	22.00

DIERS OF FORTUNE
Apr, 1951 - No. 13, Feb-Mar, 1953
rican Comics Group (Creston Publ. Corp.)

Capt. Crossbones by Shelly, Ace Carter, Lance Larson begin			
	20.00	60.00	140.00
	11.50	34.00	80.00
0: 6-Bondage-c	10.00	30.00	70.00
13 (War format)	5.00	15.00	30.00
E: Shelly a-1-3, 5. Whitney a-6, 8-11, 13; c-1-3, 5, 6.			

DIERS OF FREEDOM
7 - No. 2? ($1.75)
ricomics

		.75	1.80

ITAIRE (Also See Prime V2#6-8)
1993 - No. 12, Dec, 1994 ($1.95)
ou Comics (Ultraverse)

$2.50)-Collector's edition bagged w/playing card	1.00	2.50
2: 1-Regular edition w/o playing card. 2,4-Break-Thru x-over. 3-2 pg. origin		
he Night Man. 4-Gatefold-c. 5-Two pg. origin the Strangers	.80	2.00

O
, 1994 - No. 4, Dec, 1994 ($1.75, limited series)
vel Comics

Spider-Man app.	.70	1.75

O (Movie)
1996 - No. 2, Aug, 1996 ($2.50, limited series)
Horse Comics

Adaptation of film; photo-c		2.50

O AVENGERS (Becomes Avenger Spotlight #21 on)
1987 - No. 20, July, 1989 (75¢/$1.00)
el Comics

m Lee-a on back-up story	1.00	2.50
		1.50
0: 11-Intro Bobcat		1.00

OMON AND SHEBA (Movie)
1070, Jan-Mar, 1960
Publishing Co.

Color 1070-Sekowsky-a; photo-c	10.00	30.00	100.00

OMON KANE (Also see Blackthorne 3-D Series #60 & Marvel Premiere)
, 1985 - No. 6, July, 1986 (Limited series)
el Comics

1-Double size. 3-6-Williamson-a(i)		1.00

UTION, THE
, 1993 - No. 17, Feb, 1995 ($1.95)
ou Comics (Ultraverse)

-13: 1-Intro Meathook, Deathdance, Black Tiger, Tech. 4-Break-Thru x-over;		
atefold-c. 5-2 pg. origin The Strangers. 11-Brereton-c	.80	2.00
$2.50)-Newsstand ed. polybagged with trading card	1.00	2.50
ltra 5000 Limited silver foil	2.15	6.50	15.00

	GD25	FN65	NM94
0-Obtained w/Rune #0 by sending coupons from 11 comics			
	1.50	3.75	9.00
2-($2.50, 48 pgs.)-Rune flip-c/story by B. Smith; The Mighty Magnor 1 pg. strip			
by Aragones		1.00	2.50
11-15: 11-Brereton-c		.80	2.00
16 ($3.50)-Flip-c Ultraverse Premiere #10			
		1.40	3.50
17 ($2.50)		1.00	2.50

SOMERSET HOLMES (See Eclipse Graphic Novel Series)
Sept, 1983 - No. 6, Dec, 1984 ($1.50, Baxter paper)
Pacific Comics/ Eclipse Comics No. 5, 6

1-Brent Anderson-c/a. Cliff Hanger by Williamson begins, ends #6.		
		1.50
2-6		1.50

SONG OF THE SOUTH (See Brer Rabbit)
No. 693, Mar, 1956 (Disney)
Dell Publishing Co.

Four Color 693-Partial-r/Four Color 129	10.00	30.00	100.00

SONIC & KNUCKLES
Aug, 1995 ($2.00)
Archie Comics

1		.80	2.00

SONIC DISRUPTORS
Dec, 1987 - No. 7, July, 1988 ($1.75, limited series, mature)
DC Comics

1-7		.70	1.75

SONIC THE HEDGEHOG (TV, video game)
Feb, 1993 - No. 3, May, 1993 ($1.25, mini-series)
July, 1993 - Present ($1.25/$1.50)
Archie Comics

0(2/93),1-3: Shaw-a(p) & covers		1.25
1-20: 8-Neon ink-c.		1.25
20-36 ($1.50): 25-Silver ink-c		1.50
Triple Trouble Special (10/95, $2.00, 48 pgs.)	.80	2.00

SONIC'S FRIENDLY NEMESIS KNUCKLES
July, 1996 - No. 3, Sept, 1996 ($1.50, limited series)
Archie Publications

1-3		1.50

SON OF AMBUSH BUG (See Ambush Bug)
July, 1986 - No. 6, Dec, 1986 (75¢)
DC Comics

1-6: Giffen-c/a in all. 5-Bissette-a.		.75

SON OF BLACK BEAUTY (Also see Black Beauty)
No. 510, Oct, 1953 - No. 566, June, 1954
Dell Publishing Co.

Four Color 510, 566	4.00	12.00	40.00

SON OF FLUBBER (See Movie Comics)

SON OF MUTANT WORLD
1990 - No. 5, 1990? ($2.00, bi-monthly)
Fantagor Press

1-3: Corben-c/a		.80	2.00
4,5 ($1.75, B&W)		.70	1.75

SON OF SATAN (Also see Ghost Rider #1 & Marvel Spotlight #12)
Dec, 1975 - No. 8, Feb, 1977 (25¢)
Marvel Comics Group

1-Mooney-a; Kane-c(p), Starlin splash(p)	1.70	5.00	12.00
2-8: 2-Origin The Possessor. 5-Russell-p. 8-Heath-a	1.30	3.25	8.00

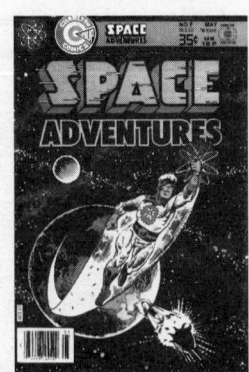

	GD25	FN65	NM94		GD25	FN65	NM94

SON OF SINBAD (Also see Abbott & Costello & Daring Adventures)
Feb, 1950
St. John Publishing Co.

1-Kubert-c/a	37.00	111.00	260.00

SON OF TOMAHAWK (See Tomahawk)

SON OF VULCAN (Formerly Mysteries of Unexplored Worlds #1-48;
Thunderbolt V3#51 on)
V2#49, Nov, 1965 - V2#50, Jan, 1966
Charlton Comics

V2#49,50: 50-Roy Thomas scripts (1st pro work)	2.15	6.50	15.00

SON OF YUPPIES FROM HELL (See Yuppies From Hell)
1990 ($3.50, B&W, squarebound, 52 pgs.)
Marvel Comics

nn		1.40	3.50

SONS OF KATIE ELDER (See Movie Classics)

SORCERY (See Chilling Adventures in... & Red Circle...)

SORORITY SECRETS
July, 1954
Toby Press

1	6.35	19.00	38.00

SOULSEARCHERS AND COMPANY
June, 1995 - Present ($2.50, B&W)
Claypool Comics

1-20: Peter David scripts	1.00		2.50

SOULQUEST
Apr, 1989 ($3.95, squarebound, 52 pgs.)
Innovation

1-Blackshard app.		1.60	4.00

SOUPY SALES COMIC BOOK (TV)(The Official...)
1965
Archie Publications

1	8.00	24.00	80.00

SOUTHERN KNIGHTS, THE (See Crusaders #1)
1983 - No. 34? (B&W)
Guild Publ/Fictioneer Books

2-Magazine size			1.50
3-34			1.50
Dread Halloween Special 1		.90	2.25
Special 1 (Spring, 1989, $2.25)		.90	2.25
Graphic Novels #1-4	1.00	2.00	5.00

SOVEREIGN SEVEN (Also see Showcase '95 #12)
July, 1995 - Present ($1.95) (1st creator-owned mainstream DC comic)
DC Comics

1-Gold	1.30	3.25	8.00

1-24: 1-1st app. Sovereign Seven (Reflex, Indigo, Cascade, Finale, Cruiser,
Network & Rampart); 1st app. Maitresse; Darkseid app.; Chris Claremont
scripts & Dwayne Turner-c/a begins. 2-Wolverine cameo. 4-Neil Gaiman
cameo. 5,8-Batman app. 7-Ramirez cameo (from the movie Highlander).
9-Humphrey Bogart cameo from Casablanca. 10-Impulse app; Manoli
Wetherell & Neal Conan cameo from Uncanny X-Men #226. 11-Robin app.

16-Final Night x-over		.80	2.00
Annual 1 (1995, $3.95)-Year One story; Big Barda & Lobo app.; Jeff Johnson-c/a.		1.60	4.00
Annual 2 (1996, $2.95)-Legends of the Dead Earth; Rick Leonardi-c/a			3.00

SPACE: ABOVE AND BEYOND (TV)
Jan, 1996 - No. 3, Mar, 1996 ($2.95, limited series)

Topps Comics

1-3: Adaptation of pilot episode; Steacy-c.

SPACE: ABOVE AND BEYOND--THE GAUNTLET (TV)
May, 1996 -No. 2, June, 1996 ($2.95, limited series)
Topps Comics

1,2

SPACE ACE (Also see Manhunt!)
No. 5, 1952
Magazine Enterprises

5(A-1 #61)-Guardineer-a	40.00	120.00	31

SPACE ACTION
June, 1952 - No. 3, Oct, 1952
Ace Magazines (Junior Books)

1-Cameron-a in all (1 story)	57.00	172.00	46
2,3	47.00	141.00	37

SPACE ADVENTURES (War At Sea #22 on)
7/52 - No. 21, 8/56; No. 23, 5/58 - No. 59, 11/64; V3#60, 10/67;
V1#2, 7/68 - V1#8, 7/69; No. 9, 5/78 - No. 13, 3/79
Capitol Stories/Charlton Comics

1	40.00	120.00	30
2	21.00	62.00	14
3-5: 4,6-Flying saucer-c/stories	17.00	49.00	1
6-9: 7-Sex change story "Transformation". 9-A-Bomb panel	14.00	43.00	10
10,11-Ditko-c/a; 11-Two Ditko stories	39.00	118.00	27
12-Ditko-c (classic)	40.00	120.00	32
13-(Fox-r, 10-11/54); Blue Beetle-c/story	17.00	49.00	11
14-Blue Beetle-c/story; Fox-r (12-1/54-55, last pre-code)	15.00	45.00	1
15,17,18-Rocky Jones-c/s.(TV); 15-Part photo-c	16.00	47.00	1
16-Krigstein-a; Rocky Jones-c/story (TV)	18.00	54.00	12
19	11.00	33.00	7
20-Reprints Fawcett's "Destination Moon"	24.00	71.00	16
21-(8/56) (no #22)(Becomes War At Sea)	11.00	33.00	7
23-(5/58; formerly Nyoka, The Jungle Girl)-Reprints Fawcett's "Destination Moon"	19.00	56.00	13
24,25,31,32-Ditko-a. 24-Severin-a(signed "LePoer")	16.00	47.00	1
26,27-Ditko-a(4) each. 26,28-Flying saucer-c	17.00	51.00	1
28-30	6.35	19.00	3
33-Origin/1st app. Capt. Atom by Ditko (3/60)	40.00	120.00	32
34-40,42-All Captain Atom by Ditko	17.00	51.00	12
41,43-59: 44-1st app. Mercury Man; also in #45	2.85	8.50	1
V3#60(#1, 10/67)-Origin & 1st app. Paul Mann & The Saucers From the Fu	3.60	11.00	
2-8(1968-69)-2,5,6,8-Ditko-a; 2,4-Aparo-c/a	1.65	4.70	
9-13(1978-79)-Capt. Atom-r/Space Adventures by Ditko; 9-Reprints origin/1st app. Capt. Atom from #33			.80

NOTE: *Aparo* a-V3#60. c-V3#8. *Ditko* c-12, 31-42. *Giordano* c-3, 4, 7-9, 18p. *Krigstein* c
Shuster a-11. Issues 13 & 14 have Blue Beetle logos; #15-18 have Rocky Jones logos.

SPACE ARK
June, 1985 - No. 5, Sept, 1987 ($1.75)
Americomics (AC Comics)/ Apple Comics #3 on

1-5: Funny animal (#1,2-color; #3-5-B&W)			.75

SPACE BUSTERS
Spring, 1952 - No. 2, Fall, 1952 (Painted-c by Norman Saunders)
Ziff-Davis Publ. Co.

1-Krigstein-a(3)	68.00	206.00	5
2-Kinstler-a(2 pgs.)	55.00	165.00	4

NOTE: *Anderson* a-2. Bondage c-2.

SPACE CADET (See Tom Corbett,...)

Space Detective #3 © AVON

Spaceman #1 © ATLAS

Space: 1999 #5 © CC

	GD25	FN65	NM94

SPACE COMICS (Formerly Funny Tunes)
No. 4, Mar-Apr, 1954 - No. 5, May-June, 1954
Avon Periodicals

	GD25	FN65	NM94
4,5-Space Mouse, Peter Rabbit, Super Pup (formerly Spotty the Pup), & Merry Mouse continue from Funny Tunes	5.35	16.00	32.00
I.W. Reprint #8 (nd)-Space Mouse-r	1.30	3.25	8.00

SPACED
1982 - No. 13, 1988 ($1.25/$1.50, B&W, quarterly)
Anthony Smith Publ. #1,2/Unbridled Ambition/Eclipse Comics #10 on

1-($1.25-c)	1.65	4.20	10.00
2-($1.25-c)	1.20	3.00	7.00
3,4: 3-Begin $1.50-c	1.00	2.00	5.00
5,6		1.20	3.00
7-13			1.50
Special Edition (1983, Mimeo)	1.00	2.50	6.00

SPACE DETECTIVE
July, 1951 - No. 4, July, 1952
Avon Periodicals

1-Rod Hathway, Space Detective begins, ends #4; Wood-c/a(3)-23 pgs.; "Opium Smugglers of Venus" drug story; Lucky Dale-r/Saint #4	86.00	260.00	695.00
2-Tales from the Shadow Squad story; Wood/Orlando-c; Wood inside layouts; "Slave Ship of Saturn" story	56.00	168.00	450.00
3-Kinstler-c	34.00	103.00	240.00
4-Kinstlerish-a by McCann	34.00	103.00	240.00
I.W. Reprint #1(Reprints #2), 8(Reprints cover #1 & part Famous Funnies #191)	4.25	13.00	26.00
I.W. Reprint #9-Exist?	4.25	13.00	26.00

SPACE EXPLORER (See March of Comics #202)

SPACE FAMILY ROBINSON (TV)(...Lost in Space #15-37, ...Lost in Space On Space Station One #38 on)(See Gold Key Champion)
Dec, 1962 - No. 36, Oct, 1969; No. 37, 10/73 - No. 54, 11/78; No. 55, 3/81 - No. 59, 5/82 (All painted covers)
Gold Key

1-(Low distribution); Spiegle-a in all	31.00	92.00	240.00
2(3/63)-Family becomes lost in space	13.00	39.00	110.00
3-10: 6-Captain Venture back-up stories begin	7.00	21.00	60.00
11-20: 14-(10/65). 15-Title change (1/66)	5.35	16.00	40.00
21-36: 28-Last 12¢ issue. 36-Captain Venture ends	2.85	8.50	25.00
37-48: 37-Origin retold	1.00	2.00	5.00
49-59: Reprints #49,50,55-59		1.00	2.50

NOTE: The TV show first aired on 9/15/65. Title changed after TV show debuted.

SPACE FAMILY ROBINSON (See March of Comics #320, 328, 352, 404, 414)

SPACE GHOST (TV) (Also see Golden Comics Digest #2 & Hanna-Barbera Super TV Heroes #3-7)
March, 1967 (Hanna-Barbera) (TV debut was 9/10/66)
Gold Key

1 (10199-703)-Spiegle-a	30.00	90.00	300.00

SPACE GHOST (TV cartoon)
Mar, 1987 ($3.50, deluxe format, one-shot)(Hanna-Barbera)
Comico

1-Steve Rude-c/a		1.60	4.00

SPACE GIANTS, THE (TV cartoon)
1979 ($1.00, B&W, one-shots)
FBN Publications

1-Based on Japanese TV series		1.60	4.00

SPACEHAWK
1989 - No. 3, 1990 ($2.00, B&W)
Dark Horse Comics

	GD25	FN65	NM94
1-3-Wolverton-c/a(r) plus new stories by others.		.80	2.00

SPACE KAT-ETS (...in 3-D)
Dec, 1953 (25¢, came w/glasses)
Power Publishing Co.

1	31.00	92.00	215.00

SPACEMAN (Speed Carter...)
Sept, 1953 - No. 6, July, 1954
Atlas Comics (CnPC)

1-Grey tone-c	52.00	157.00	420.00
2	37.00	111.00	260.00
3-6: 4-A-Bomb explosion-c	33.00	99.00	230.00

NOTE: Everett c-1, 3. Heath a-1. Maneely a-1(3), 2(4), 3(3), 4-6; c-5, 6. Romita a-1. Sekowsky c-4. Sekowsky/Abel a-4(3). Tuska a-5(3).

SPACE MAN
No. 1253, 1-3/62 - No. 8, 3-5/64; No. 9, 7/72 - No. 10, 10/72
Dell Publishing Co.

Four Color 1253 (#1)(1-3/62)	8.00	24.00	80.00
2,3	4.00	12.00	36.00
4-8	3.00	9.00	27.00
9,10: 9-Reprints #1253. 10-Reprints #2	1.20	3.00	6.00

SPACE MOUSE (Also see Funny Tunes & Space Comics)
April, 1953 - No. 5, Apr-May, 1954
Avon Periodicals

1	8.35	25.00	50.00
2	5.35	16.00	32.00
3-5	4.00	11.00	22.00

SPACE MOUSE (Walter Lantz...#1; see Comic Album #17)
No. 1132, Aug-Oct, 1960 - No. 5, Nov, 1963 (Walter Lantz)
Dell Publishing Co./Gold Key

Four Color 1132,1244	4.00	12.00	40.00
1(11/62)(G.K.)	4.00	14.00	40.00
2-5	3.00	9.00	30.00

SPACE MYSTERIES
1964 (Reprints)
I.W. Enterprises

1-r/Journey Into Unknown Worlds #4 w/new-c	1.65	4.20	10.00
8,9: 9-r/Planet Comics #73	1.70	5.00	12.00

SPACE: 1999 (TV) (Also see Power Record Comics)
Nov, 1975 - No. 7, Nov, 1976
Charlton Comics

1-Origin Moonbase Alpha; Staton-c/a		1.40	3.50
2,7: 2-Staton-a		1.00	2.50
3-6: All Byrne-a; c-3,5,6		1.80	4.50

SPACE: 1999 (TV)(Magazine)
Nov, 1975 - No. 8, Nov, 1976 (B&W)(#7 shows #6 on inside)
Charlton Comics

1-Origin Moonbase Alpha; Morrow-c/a	1.00	2.60	6.00
2-8: 2,3-Morrow-a. 4-6-Morrow-c. 5,8-Morrow-a		1.20	3.00

SPACE PATROL (TV)
Summer, 1952 - No. 2, Oct-Nov, 1952 (Painted-c by Norman Saunders)
Ziff-Davis Publishing Co. (Approved Comics)

1-Krigstein-a	71.00	215.00	575.00
2-Krigstein-a(3)	53.00	159.00	425.00
...'s Special Mission (8 pgs., B&W, Giveaway)	59.00	178.00	475.00

SPACE PIRATES (See Archie Giant Series #533)

SPACE RANGER (See Mystery in Space #92, Showcase #15 & Tales of the Unexpected)

SPACE SQUADRON (In the Days of the Rockets)(Becomes Space Worlds #6)
June, 1951 - No. 5, Feb, 1952

Space Usagi #2

Spanner's Galaxy #4

Sparkler Comics #1 © UFS

Marvel/Atlas Comics (ACI)

	GD25	FN65	NM94
1-Space team; Brodsky c-1,5	52.00	157.00	420.00
2: Tuska c-2-4	45.00	136.00	365.00
3-5: 3-Capt. Jet Dixon by Tuska(3). 4-Weird advs. begin	40.00	120.00	295.00

SPACE THRILLERS
1954 (25¢ Giant)
Avon Periodicals

nn-(Scarce)-Robotmen of the Lost Planet; contains 3 rebound comics of The Saint & Strange Worlds. Contents could vary	93.00	281.00	750.00

SPACE TRIP TO THE MOON (See Space Adventures #23)

SPACE USAGI
June, 1992 - No. 3, 1992 ($2.00, B&W, mini-series)
V2#1, Nov, 1993 - V2#3, Jan, 1994 ($2.75)
Mirage Studios

1-3: Stan Sakai-c/a/scripts		.80	2.00
V2#1-3		1.10	2.75

SPACE USAGI
Jan, 1996 - No. 3, Mar, 1996 ($2.00, B&W, limited series)
Dark Horse Comics

1-3: Stan Sakai-c/a/scripts			2.00

SPACE WAR (Fightin' Five #28 on)
Oct, 1959 - No. 27, Mar, 1964; No. 28, Mar, 1978 - No. 34, 3/79
Charlton Comics

V1#1-Giordano-c begin, end #3	16.00	47.00	110.00
2,3	7.00	21.50	50.00
4-6,8,10-Ditko-c/a	16.00	47.00	110.00
7,9,11-15: Last 10¢ issue?	3.40	10.00	24.00
16-27	3.00	9.00	21.00
28,29,33,34-Ditko-c/a(r)	5.50	16.50	38.00
30-Ditko-c/a(r); Staton, Sutton/Wood-a	6.00	18.00	42.00
31-Ditko-c/a(3); same-c as Strange Suspense Stories #2 (1968); atom blast-c	6.50	19.50	45.00
32-r/Charlton Premiere V2#2; Sutton-a	1.20		3.00

SPACE WESTERN (Formerly Cowboy Western Comics; becomes Cowboy Western Comics #46 on)
No. 40, Oct, 1952 - No. 45, Aug, 1953
Charlton Comics (Capitol Stories)

40-Intro Spurs Jackson & His Space Vigilantes; flying saucer story	47.00	141.00	375.00
41,43-45: 41-Flying saucer-c. 45-Hitler app.	39.00	116.00	270.00
42-Atom bomb explosion-c	40.00	120.00	300.00

SPACE WORLDS (Formerly Space Squadron #1-5)
No. 6, April, 1952
Atlas Comics (Male)

6-Sol Brodsky-c	39.00	116.00	270.00

SPANKY & ALFALFA & THE LITTLE RASCALS (See The Little Rascals)

SPANNER'S GALAXY
Dec, 1984 - No. 6, May, 1985 (limited series)
DC Comics

1-6: Mandrake-c/a in all.			1.00

SPARKIE, RADIO PIXIE (Radio)(Becomes Big Jon & Sparkie #4)
Winter, 1951 - No. 3, July-Aug, 1952 (Painted-c)(Sparkie #2,3; #1?)
Ziff-Davis Publ. Co.

1-Based on children's radio program	19.00	58.00	135.00
2,3: 3-Big Jon and Sparkie on-c only	14.00	43.00	100.00

SPARKLE COMICS
Oct-Nov, 1948 - No. 33, Dec-Jan, 1953-54 (#1-3: 52 pgs.)

United Features Syndicate

	GD25	FN65	NM94
1-Li'l Abner, Nancy, Captain & the Kids, Ella Cinders	12.00	36.00	85.00
2	7.00	21.00	42.00
3-10	5.35	16.00	32.00
11-20	4.25	13.00	28.00
21-33	4.00	11.00	22.00

SPARKLE PLENTY (See Harvey Comics Library #2)
No. 215, 1949 (Dick Tracy reprint by Gould)
Dell Publishing Co.

Four Color 215	10.00	30.00	100.00

SPARKLER COMICS (1st series)
July, 1940 - No. 2, 1940
United Feature Comic Group

1-Jim Hardy	34.00	103.00	240.00
2-Frankie Doodle	26.00	79.00	185.00

SPARKLER COMICS (2nd series)(Nancy & Sluggo #121 on)(Cover title becomes Nancy and Sluggo #101? on)
July, 1941 - No. 120, Jan, 1955
United Features Syndicate

1-Origin 1st app. Sparkman; Tarzan (by Hogarth in all issues), Captain & the Kids, Ella Cinders, Danny Dingle, Dynamite Dunn, Nancy, Abbie & Slats, Broncho Bill, Frankie Doodle, begin; Sparkman c-1-9,11,12; Hap Hopper c-10,13	187.00	562.00	1500.00
2	68.00	206.00	550.00
3,4	53.00	159.00	425.00
5-10: 9-Sparkman's new costume	48.00	144.00	385.00
11-13,15-20: 12-Sparkman's new costume (color change). 19-1st Race Riley and the Commandos plus-c	40.00	120.00	300.00
14-Tarzan-c by Hogarth	44.00	132.00	350.00
21,25,28,31,34,37,39-Tarzan-c by Hogarth	40.00	120.00	290.00
22-24,26,27,29,30: 22-Race Riley & the Commandos strips begin, ends #44	31.00	94.00	220.00
32,33,35,36,38,40	17.00	51.00	120.00
41,43,45,46,48,49	12.00	36.00	85.00
42,44,47,50-Tarzan-c (42,47,50 by Hogarth)	23.00	69.00	160.00
51,52,54-70: 57-Li'l Abner begins (not in #58); Fearless Fosdick app. in #58	10.00	30.00	70.00
53-Tarzan-c by Hogarth	19.00	56.00	130.00
71-80	7.50	22.50	45.00
81,82,84-90: 85-Li'l Abner ends. 86-Lingerie panels	6.70	20.00	40.00
83-Tarzan-c	10.00	30.00	70.00
91-96,98-99	6.70	20.00	40.00
97-Origin Casey Ruggles by Warren Tufts	11.50	34.00	80.00
100	8.35	25.00	50.00
101-107,109-112,114-120	4.25	13.00	28.00
108,113-Toth-a	8.35	25.00	50.00

SPARKLING LOVE
June, 1950; 1953
Avon Periodicals/Realistic (1953)

1-(Avon)-Kubert-a; photo-c	17.00	51.00	120.00
nn(1953)-Reprint; Kubert-a	7.50	22.50	45.00

SPARKLING STARS
June, 1944 - No. 33, March, 1948
Holyoke Publishing Co.

1-Hell's Angels, FBI, Boxie Weaver, Petey & Pop, & Ali Baba begin	13.00	39.00	90.00
2-Speed Spaulding story	9.15	27.00	55.00
3-Actual FBI case photos & war photos	6.70	20.00	40.00
4-10: 7-X-Mas-c	5.85	17.50	35.00
11-19: 13-Origin/1st app. Jungo the Man-Beast-c/s	5.00	15.00	30.00

Spartan: Warrior Spirit #2 © Aegis Entertainment.

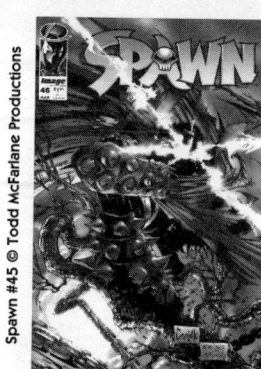

Spawn #45 © Todd McFarlane Productions

Spawn/WildC.A.T.S. #3 © Aegis Entertainment.

	GD25	FN65	NM94
20-Intro Fangs the Wolf Boy	5.85	17.50	35.00
21-29,32,33: 29-Bondage-c	5.00	15.00	30.00
31-Sid Greene-a	5.85	17.50	35.00

SPARK MAN (See Sparkler Comics)
1945 (36 pgs., one-shot)
Frances M. McQueeny

| 1-Origin Spark Man r/Sparkler #1-3; female torture story; cover redrawn from Sparkler #1 | 27.00 | 81.00 | 190.00 |

SPARKY WATTS (Also see Big Shot Comics & Columbia Comics)
Nov?, 1942 - No. 10, 1949
Columbia Comic Corp.

1(1942)-Skyman & The Face app; Hitler-c	40.00	120.00	285.00
2(1943)	21.00	64.00	150.00
3(1944)	15.00	45.00	105.00
4(1944)-Origin	13.50	41.00	95.00
5(1947)-Skyman app.; Boody Rogers-c/a	11.00	33.00	75.00
6,7,9,10: 6(1947),10(1949)	8.00	24.00	48.00
8(1948)-Surrealistic-c	11.00	33.00	75.00

NOTE: *Boody Rogers* c-1-8.

SPARTACUS (Movie)
No. 1139, Nov. 1960 (Kirk Douglas photo-c)
Dell Publishing Co.

| Four Color 1139-Buscema-a | 12.00 | 36.00 | 120.00 |

SPARTAN: WARRIOR SPIRIT (Also see WildC.A.T.S: Covert Action Teams)
July, 1995 - No. 4, Nov. 1995 ($2.50, limited series)
Image Comics (Wildstorm Productions)

| 1-4: Kurt Busiek scripts; Mike McKone-c/a | | 1.00 | 2.50 |

SPAWN
May, 1992 - Present ($1.95)
Image Comics (Todd McFarlane Productions)

1-1st app. Spawn; McFarlane-c/a begins; McFarlane/Steacy-c; 1st Todd McFarlane Productions title.	2.40	7.20	17.00
2,3: 2-1st app. Violator; McFarlane/Steacy-c	1.70	5.00	12.00
4-Contains coupon for Image Comics #0	1.70	5.00	12.00
4-With coupon missing		1.60	4.00
4-Newsstand edition w/o poster or coupon	1.00	2.00	5.00
5-Cerebus cameo (1 pg.) as stuffed animal; Spawn mobile poster #1	1.20	3.00	7.00
6-8,10: 7-Spawn Mobile poster #2. 8-Alan Moore scripts; Miller poster. 10-Cerebus app.; Dave Sim scripts; 1 pg. cameo app. by Superman.	1.00	2.60	6.00
9-Neil Gaiman scripts; Jim Lee poster; 1st Angela.	1.30	3.25	8.00
11-17,19,20,22-30: 11-Miller script; Darrow poster. 12-Bloodwulf poster by Liefeld. 14,15-Violator app. 16,17-Grant Morrison scripts; Capullo-c/a(p). 23,24-McFarlane-a/stories. 25-(10/94). 19-(10/94). 20-(11/94)	1.00	2.00	5.00
18,21: 18-Grant Morrison script, Capullo-c/a(p); low distribution.	2.00	6.00	14.00
31-49, 51-60: 31-1st app. The Redeemer; new costume cameo. 32-1st full app new costume. 38-40,42,44,46,48-Tony Daniel-c/a(p). 38-1st app. Cy-Gor. 40,41-Cy-Gor & Curse app. 52-Savage Dragon app.		.80	2.00
50-($3.95, 48 pgs.)		1.60	4.00
..Bible-(8/96, $1.95)-Character bios			2.00

NOTE: *Capullo* a-16p-18p; c-16p-18p. *Daniel* a-38-40, 42, 44, 46. *McFarlane* a-1-15; c-1-15p. *Thibert* a-16(part). Posters come with issues 1, 4, 7-9, 11, 12. #25 was released before #19 & 20.

SPAWN-BATMAN (Also see Batman/Spawn: War Devil under Batman: One-Shots)
1994 ($3.95, one-shot)
Image Comics (Todd McFarlane Productions)

| 1-Miller scripts; McFarlane-c/a | | 1.60 | 4.00 |

	GD25	FN65	NM94

SPAWN: BLOOD FEUD
June, 1995 - No. 3, Sept. 1995 ($2.25, limited series)
Image Comics (Todd McFarlane Productions)

| 1-3-Alan Moore scripts, Tony Daniel-a | | .90 | 2.25 |

SPAWN FAN EDITON
Aug, 1996 - No. 3, Oct, 1996 (Giveaway, 12 pgs.)
(Polybagged w/Overstreet's FAN)
Image Comics (Todd McFarlane Productions)

1-3: Beau Smith scripts; Brad Gorby-a(p). 1-1st app. Nordik, the Norse Hellspawn. 2-1st app. McFallon, the Dragon Master. 3-1st app. Mercy			5.00
1-3-(Gold): All retailer incentives			15.00
2-(Platinum)-Retailer incentive			25.00

SPAWN/WILDC.A.T.S
Jan, 1996 - No. 4, Apr, 1996 ($2.50, limited series)
Image Comics (Wildstorm Productions)

| 1-4: Alan Moore scripts in all. | | | 2.50 |

SPECIAL AGENT (Steve Saunders...)(Also see True Comics #68)
Dec, 1947 - No. 8, Sept, 1949 (Based on true FBI cases)
Parents' Magazine Institute (Commended Comics No. 2)

1-J. Edgar Hoover photo on-c	10.00	30.00	65.00
2	5.85	17.50	35.00
3-8	4.25	13.00	28.00

SPECIAL COLLECTORS' EDITION
Dec, 1975 (No month given) (10-1/4x13-1/2")
Marvel Comics Group

| 1-Kung Fu, Iron Fist (early), Sons of the Tiger | | 1.30 | 3.25 |

SPECIAL COMICS (Becomes Hangman #2 on)
Winter, 1941-42
MLJ Magazines

| 1-Origin The Boy Buddies (Shield & Wizard x-over); death of The Comet; origin The Hangman retold; Hangman-c | 225.00 | 675.00 | 1800.00 |

SPECIAL DELIVERY
1951 (32 pgs., B&W)
Post Hall Synd. (Giveaway)

| nn-Origin of Pogo, Swamp, etc.; 2 pg. biog. on Walt Kelly (One copy sold in 1980 for $150.00) | | | |

SPECIAL EDITION (See Gorgo and Reptisaurus)

SPECIAL EDITION (U. S. Navy Giveaways)
1944 - 1945 (Regular comic format with wording simplified, 52 pgs.)
National Periodical Publications

1-Action (1944)-Reprints Action #80	62.00	187.00	500.00
2-Action (1944)-Reprints Action #81	62.00	187.00	500.00
3-Superman (1944)-Reprints Superman #33	62.00	187.00	500.00
4-Detective (1944)-Reprints Detective #97	65.00	195.00	525.00
5-Superman (1945)-Reprints Superman #34	62.00	187.00	500.00
6-Action (1945)-Reprints Action #84	62.00	187.00	500.00

NOTE: *Wayne Boring* c-1, 2, 6. *Dick Sprang* c-4.

SPECIAL EDITION COMICS
1940 (August) (68 pgs.), one-shot)
Fawcett Publications

	GD25	FN65	VF82	NM94
1-1st book devoted entirely to Captain Marvel; C.C. Beck-c/a; only app. of Capt. Marvel with belt buckle; Capt. Marvel appears with button-down flap; 1st story (came out before Captain Marvel #1)	800.00	2400.00	4800.00	8000.00
(Estimated up to 150 total copies exist, 7 in NM/Mint)				

NOTE: Prices vary widely on this book. Since this book is actually a pre-Captain Marvel #1. There is speculation that this book almost became *Captain Marvel #1*. After *Special Edition* was published, there was an editor change at Fawcett. The new editor commissioned Kirby to do a nn *Captain Marvel* book early in 1941. This book was followed by a 2nd book several months later. This 2nd book was advertised as a #3 (making Special Edition

Species #2 © 20th Century Fox

Spectacular Spider-Man #79 © MEG

Spectacular Spider-Man #222 © MEG

	GD25	FN65	NM94

the #1, & the nn issue the #2). However, the 2nd book did come out as a #2.

SPECIAL EDITION: SPIDER-MAN VS. THE HULK (See listing under The Amazing Spider-Man)

SPECIAL EDITION X-MEN
Feb, 1983 ($2.00, one-shot, Baxter paper)
Marvel Comics Group

	GD25	FN65	NM94
1-r/Giant-Size X-Men #1 plus one new story	2.15	6.50	15.00

SPECIAL MARVEL EDITION (Master of Kung Fu #17 on)
Jan, 1971 - No. 16, Feb, 1974 (#1-4: 25¢, 68 pgs.; #5-16: 20¢, regular ed.)
Marvel Comics Group

1-Thor-r by Kirby; 68 pgs.	1.20	3.00	7.00
2-4: Thor-r by Kirby; 68 pg. Giant	1.00	2.00	5.00
5-14: Sgt. Fury-r; 11-r/Sgt. Fury #13 (Capt. America)		1.60	4.00
15-Master of Kung Fu (Shang-Chi) begins (1st app., 12/73); Starlin-a; origin/ 1st app. Nayland Smith & Dr. Petric	5.00	15.00	40.00
16-1st app. Midnight; Starlin-a (2nd Shang-Chi)	2.85	8.50	20.00

SPECIAL MISSIONS (See G.I. Joe...)

SPECIAL WAR SERIES (Attack V4#3 on?)
Aug, 1965 - No. 4, Nov, 1965
Charlton Comics

V4#1-D-Day (also see D-Day listing)	2.00	6.00	14.00
2-Attack!	1.50	3.75	9.00
3-War & Attack (also see War & Attack)	1.50	3.75	9.00
4-Judomaster (intro/1st app.; see Sarge Steel)	4.30	13.00	32.00

SPECIES (Movie)
June, 1995 - No. 4, Sept, 1995 ($2.50, limited series)
Dark Horse Comics

1-4: Adaptation of film		1.00	2.50

SPECTACULAR ADVENTURES (See Adventures)

SPECTACULAR FEATURE MAGAZINE, A (Formerly My Confessions)
(Spectacular Features Magazine #12)
No. 11, April, 1950
Fox Feature Syndicate

11 (#1)-Samson and Delilah	26.00	77.00	180.00

SPECTACULAR FEATURES MAGAZINE (Formerly A Spectacular Feature Magazine)
No. 12, June, 1950 - No. 3, Aug, 1950
Fox Feature Syndicate

12 (#2)-Iwo Jima; photo flag-c	26.00	77.00	180.00
3-True Crime Cases From Police Files	19.00	56.00	130.00

SPECTACULAR SCARLET SPIDER
Nov, 1995 - No. 2, Dec, 1995 ($1.95, limited series)
Marvel Comics

1,2: Replaces Spectacular Spider-Man		.80	2.00

SPECTACULAR SPIDER-MAN, THE (See Marvel Special Edition and Marvel Treasury Edition)

SPECTACULAR SPIDER-MAN, THE (Magazine)
July, 1968 - No. 2, Nov, 1968 (35¢)
Marvel Comics Group

1-(B&W)-Romita/Mooney 52 pg. story plus updated origin story with Everett-a(i)	9.30	28.00	65.00
2-(Color)-Green Goblin-c & 58 pg. story; Romita painted-c (story reprinted in King Size Spider-Man #9); Romita/Mooney-a	12.00	36.00	85.00

SPECTACULAR SPIDER-MAN, THE (Peter Parker...#54-132, 134)
Dec, 1976 - Present
Marvel Comics Group

1-Origin recap in text; return of Tarantula	8.00	23.50	55.00
2-Kraven the Hunter app.	3.30	10.00	23.00

3-5: 3-Intro Lightmaster. 4-Vulture app.	2.15	6.50	15.0
6-8-Morbius app.; 6-r/Marvel Team-Up #3 w/Morbius	3.25	9.50	22.
9-20: White Tiger app. 11-Last 30¢-c. 17,18-Angel & Iceman app. (from Champions); Ghost Rider cameo in flashback	1.20	3.00	7.
21,24-26: 21-Scorpion app. 26-Daredevil app.	1.00	2.60	6.
22,23-Moon Knight app.	1.65	4.20	10.0
27-Miller's 1st art on Daredevil (2/79); also see Captain America #235	2.15	6.50	15.0
28-Miller Daredevil (p)	1.65	4.70	11.0
29-55,57,59: 33-Origin Iguana. 38-Morbius app.	1.00	2.00	5.0
56-2nd app. Jack O'Lantern (Macendale) & 1st Spidey/Jack O'Lantern battle (7/81)	1.65	4.20	10.0
58-Punisher app.	1.00	2.00	5.0
60-Double size; origin retold with new facts revealed	1.00	2.60	6.0
61-63,65-68,71-74: 65-Kraven the Hunter app.		1.60	4.0
64-1st app. Cloak & Dagger (3/82)	1.00	2.00	5.0
69,70-Cloak & Dagger app.		1.60	4.0
75-Double size	1.00	2.00	5.0
76-80: 78,79-Punisher cameo		1.60	4.0
81,82-Punisher, Cloak & Dagger app.	1.20	3.00	7.0
83-Origin Punisher retold (10/83)	2.15	6.50	15.0
84,86-99: 90-Spider-man's new black costume, last panel(ties w/Amazing Spider-Man #252 & Marvel Team-Up #141 for 1st app.). 94-96-Cloak & Dagger app. 98-Intro The Spot		1.60	4.0
85-Hobgoblin (Ned Leeds) app. (12/83); gains powers of original Green Goblin (see Amazing Spider-Man #238)	3.60	11.00	25.0
100-(3/85)-Double size	1.00	2.00	5.0
101-115,117,118,120-129: 107-110-Death of Jean DeWolff. 111-Secret Wars II tie-in. 128-Black Cat new costume		1.40	3.5
116,119-Sabretooth-c/story	1.20	3.00	7.0
130-Hobgoblin app.	1.00	2.00	5.0
131-Six part Kraven tie-in	1.20	3.00	7.0
132-Kraven tie-in	1.00	2.60	6.0
133-139: 138-1st full app. Tombstone (origin #139)		1.00	2.5
140-Punisher cameo app.		1.20	3.0
141-Punisher app.	1.00	2.00	5.0
142,143-Punisher app.		1.60	4.0
144-146,148-157: 151-Tombstone returns		.90	2.2
147-1st app. new Hobgoblin (Macendale) in 1 pg. cameo; continued in Web of Spider-Man #48	2.85	8.50	20.0
158-Spider-Man gets new powers (1st Cosmic Spidey, cont'd in Web of Spider-Man #59)	1.00	2.00	5.0
159-Cosmic Spider-Man app.	1.30	3.25	8.0
160-170: 161-163-Hobgoblin app. 168-170-Avengers x-over. 169-1st app. The Outlaws		.80	2.0
171-184: 180,181,183,184-Green Goblin app.			1.5
185-188,190-199: 197-199-Original X-Men-c/story			1.5
189-($2.95, 52 pgs.)-Silver hologram on-c; battles Green Goblin; origin retold; Vess poster w/Spidey & Hobgoblin	1.30	3.25	8.0
189-(2nd printing)-Gold hologram on-c		1.20	3.0
195-(Deluxe ed.)-Polybagged w/audio cassette		1.20	3.0
200-($2.95)-Holo-grafx foil-c; Green Goblin-c/story		1.20	3.0
201-211: 203-Maximum Carnage x-over. 204-Begin 4 part death of Tombstone story. 207,208-The Shroud-c/story. 208-Siege of Darkness x-over (#207 is a tie-in). 209-Black Cat back-up			1.5
212-219,221,222,224,226-228,230-250: 212-Begin $1.50-c; bound-in card sheet. 215,216-Scorpion app. 217-Power & Responsibility Pt. 4. 231-Return of Kaine; Spider-Man corpse discovered. 232-New Doc Octopus app. 233-Carnage-c/app. 235-Dragon Man cameo. 236-Dragon Man-c/app; Lizard app.; Peter Parker regains powers. 238,239-Lizard app. 239-w/card insert. 240-Revelations storyline begins			1.5
213-Collectors ed. polybagged w/16 pg. preview & animation cel; foil-c; 1st meeting Spidey & Typhoid Mary		1.20	3.0

Spectacular Storie Magazine #4 © FOX

Spectre #46 © DC

Speed Comics #2 © Brookwood Publ.

SHOCK GIBSON - BIG DOUBLE-LENGTH FEATURE

	GD25	FN65	NM94

213-Version polybagged w/Gamepro #7; no-c date, price 1.50
217 ($2.95)-Deluxe edition foil-c; flip book 1.20 3.00
219-($2.95)-Deluxe edition foil-c; flip book 1.20 3.00
220 ($2.25, 52 pgs.)-Flip book, Mary Jane reveals pregnancy 1.20 3.00
223 ($2.50) 1.00 2.50
223 ($2.95)-Die Cut-c 1.20 3.00
225 ($3.95)-Direct Market Holodisk-c (Green Goblin) 1.60 4.00
225 ($2.95)-Newsstand-Green Goblin 1.20 3.00
229 ($3.95)-Acetate-c, Spidey quits 1.60 4.00
229 ($2.50)-Spidey quits 1.00 2.50
Annual 1 (1979)-Doc Octopus-c & 46 pg. story 1.20 3.00 7.00
Annual 2 (1980)-Origin/1st app. Rapier 1.00 2.00 5.00
Annual 3-7: 3(1981)-Last Man-Wolf. 4(1984). 5(1985). 6(10/86). 7(1987) 1.40 3.50
Annual 8 (1988,$ 1.75)-Evolutionary War x-over; Daydreamer returns Gwen Stacy "clone" back to real self (not Gwen Stacy) 1.60 4.00
Annual 9 (1989, $2.00, 68 pgs.)-Atlantis Attacks 1.20 3.00
Annual 10 (1990, $2.00, 68 pgs.)-McFarlane-a 1.00 2.50
Annual 11 (1991, $2.00, 68 pgs.)-Iron Man app. .80 2.00
Annual 12 (1992, $2.25, 68 pgs.)-Venom solo story cont'd from Amazing Spider-Man Annual #26 .90 2.25
Annual 13 (1993, $2.95, 68 pgs.)-Polybagged w/trading card; John Romita, Sr. back-up-a 1.20 3.00
Annual 14 (1994, $2.95) 1.20 3.00
Special 1 (1995, $3.95)-Flip book 1.60 4.00
NOTE: Austin c-21i, Annual 11. Buckler a-203, 107-111, 116, 117, 119, 122, Annual 1, Annual 10; c-103, 107-111, 113, 116-119, 122, Annual 1. Buscema c-121. Byrne c(p)-17, 43, 58, 101, 102. Giffen a-120p. Hembeck c/a-86p. Larsen c-Annual 11p. Miller c-46p, 48p, 50, 51p, 52p, 54p, 55, 56p, 57, 60. Mooney a-7i, 11i, 21p, 23p, 25p, 26p, 29-34p, 36p, 37p, 39i, 41, 42i, 49p, 50i, 51i, 53p, 54-57i, 59-66i, 68i, 71i, 73-79i, 81-83i, 85i, 87-99i, 102i, 125p, Annual 1i, 2p. Nasser c-37p. Perez c-10. Simonson c-54i. Zeck a-118, 131, 132; c-131, 132.

SPECTACULAR STORIES MAGAZINE (Formerly A Star Presentation)
No. 4, July, 1950 - No. 3, Sept, 1950
Fox Feature Sydicate (Hero Books)
4-Sherlock Holmes (true crime stories) 34.00 101.00 235.00
3-The St. Valentine's Day Massacre (true crime) 22.00 66.00 155.00

SPECTRE, THE (1st Series) (See Adventure Comics #431, More Fun & Showcase)
Nov-Dec, 1967 - No. 10, May-June, 1969 (All 12¢)
National Periodical Publications
1-(11-12/67)-Anderson-c/a 13.20 39.60 92.00
2-5-Neal Adams-c/a; 3-Wildcat x-over 9.60 28.75 67.00
6-8,10: 6-8-Anderson inks. 7-Hourman app. 6.00 18.00 42.00
9-Wrightson-a 6.00 18.00 42.00

SPECTRE, THE (2nd Series) (See Saga of the Swamp Thing #58, Showcase '95 #8 & Wrath of the...)
Apr, 1987 - Oct, 1989 ($1.00, new format)
DC Comics
1-31: 1-Colan-a begins. 9-Nudity panels. 10-Batman cameo. 10,11-Millennium tie-ins 1.50
Annual 1 (1988, $2.00)-Deadman app. .90 2.25
NOTE: Art Adams c-Annual 1. Colan a-1-6. Kaluta c-1-3. Mignola c-7-9. Morrow a-9-15. Sears c/a-22. Vess c-13-15.

SPECTRE, THE (3rd Series) (Also see Brave and the Bold #72, 75, 116, 180, 199 & Showcase '95 #8)
Dec, 1992 - Present ($1.75/$1.95/$2.25)
DC Comics
1-($1.95)-Glow-in-the-dark-c; Mandrake-a begins 1.00 2.00 5.00
2,3 1.20 3.00
4-7,9-12,14-20: 10-Kaluta-c. 11-Hildebrandt painted-c. 16-Aparo/K. Jones-a. 20-Sienkiewicz-c .80 2.00
8,13-($2.50)-Glow-in-the-dark-c 1.20 3.00

	GD25	FN65	NM94

21,22: 21-Begin $1.95-c. 22-(9/94)-Superman-c & app. .80 2.00
0,23-29: 0-(10/94). 23-(11/94) .80 2.00
30-55: 30-Begin-$2.25-c. 42-Kent Williams-c. 44-Kaluta-c. 47-Final Night x-over .90 2.25
Annual 1 (1995, $3.95)-Year One story 1.60 4.00
NOTE: Bisley c-27. Fabry c-2. Kelley Jones c-31. Vess c-5.

SPEEDBALL (See Amazing Spider-Man Annual #12, Marvel Super-Heroes & The New Warriors)
Sept, 1988(10/88-inside) - No. 11, July, 1989 (75¢)
Marvel Comics
1-11: Ditko/Guice a-1-4, c-1; Ditko a-1-10; c-1-11p 1.00

SPEED BUGGY (TV)(Also see Fun-In #12, 15)
July, 1975 - No. 9, Nov, 1976 (Hanna-Barbera)
Charlton Comics
1 1.20 3.00
2-9 .80 2.00

SPEED CARTER SPACEMAN (See Spaceman)

SPEED COMICS (New Speed)(Also see Double Up)
10/39 - #11, 8/40; #12, 3/41 - #44, 1-2/47 (#14-16: pocket size, 100 pgs.)
Brookwood Publ./Speed Publ./Harvey Publications No. 14 on
1-Origin & 1st app. Shock Gibson; Ted Parrish, the Man with 1000 Faces begins; Powell-a; becomes Champion #2 on? 275.00 825.00 2200.00
2-Powell-a 87.00 262.00 700.00
3 47.00 142.00 380.00
4,5: 4-Powell-a?5-Dinosaur-c 41.00 124.00 330.00
6-11: 7-Mars Mason begins, ends #11 40.00 120.00 290.00
12 (3/41; shows #11 in indicia)-The Wasp begins; Major Colt app. (Capt. Colt #12) 41.00 124.00 330.00
13-Intro. Captain Freedom & Young Defenders; Girl Commandos, Pat Parker (costumed heroine), War Nurse begins; Major Colt app. 47.00 142.00 380.00
14-16 (100 pg. pocket size, 1941): 14-2nd Harvey comic (See Pocket); Shock Gibson dons new costume. 15-Pat Parker dons new costume, last in costume #23; no Girl Commandos 51.00 153.00 410.00
17-Black Cat begins (4/42, early app.; see Pocket #1); origin Black Cat-r/Pocket #1; not in #40,41; S&K-c 59.00 178.00 475.00
18-20-S&K-c 44.00 132.00 350.00
21,22-Kirby-c 44.00 132.00 350.00
23-Origin Girl Commandos; Kirby-c 47.00 141.00 375.00
24-Pat Parker team-up with Girl Commandos 34.00 103.00 240.00
25-30: 26-Flag-c 36.00 107.00 250.00
31-Schomburg Hitler & Hirohito-c 40.00 120.00 300.00
32-36-Schomburg-c 40.00 120.00 300.00
37,39-42, 44 36.00 107.00 250.00
38-Iwo-Jima Flag-c 38.00 114.00 265.00
43-Robot-c 39.00 118.00 275.00
NOTE: Al Avison c-14-16, 30, 43. Briefer a-6, 7. Jon Henri (Kirbyesque) c-17-20. Kubert a-7-11(Mars Mason), 37, 38, 42-44. Kirby/Caseneuve c-21-23. Palais c-37, 39-42. Powell a-1-2, 4-7, 28, 31, 44. Schomburg c-31-36. Tuska a-3, 6, 7. Bondage c-18, 35. Captain Freedom c-16-24, 25(part), 26-44(Black Cat #27, 29, 31, 32-40). Shock Gibson c-1-15.

SPEED DEMON (Also see Marvel Versus DC #3 & DC Versus Marvel #4)
Apr, 1996 ($1.95, one-shot)
Marvel Comics (Amalgam)
1 2.00

SPEED DEMONS (Formerly Frank Merriwell at Yale #1-4?; Submarine Attack #11 on)
No. 5, Feb, 1957 - No. 10, 1958
Charlton Comics
5-10 2.80 7.00 14.00

SPEED RACER (Also see The New Adventures of...)
July, 1987 - No. 38, Nov, 1990 ($1.75)

Speed Racer #6 © Golden Books

Spelljammer #11 © TSR

Spider-Man #45 © MEG

	GD25	FN65	NM94

	GD25	FN65	NM94

Now Comics

1-38		.80	2.00
1-2nd printing		.80	2.00
Special 1 (1988, $2.00)		.80	2.00
Special 2 (1988, $3.50)		1.40	3.50

SPEED RACER FEATURING NINJA HIGH SCHOOL
Aug, 1993 - No. 2, 1993 ($2.50, mini-series)
Now Comics

1,2: 1-Polybagged w/card. 2-Exists?		1.00	2.50

SPEED RACER: RETURN OF THE GRX
Mar, 1994 - No. 2, Apr, 1994 ($1.95, limited series)
Now Comics

1,2		.90	2.25

SPEED SMITH-THE HOT ROD KING (Also see Hot Rod King)
Spring, 1952
Ziff-Davis Publishing Co.

1-Saunders painted-c	18.00	54.00	125.00

SPEEDY GONZALES
No. 1084, Mar, 1960
Dell Publishing Co.

Four Color 1084	3.00	9.00	30.00

SPEEDY RABBIT (See Television Puppet Show)
nd (1953); 1963
Realistic/I. W. Enterprises/Super Comics

nn (1953)-Realistic Reprint?	1.65	4.20	10.00
I.W. Reprint #1 (2 versions w/diff. c/stories exist)-Peter Cottontail #?			
	1.00	2.00	5.00
Super Reprint #14(1963)	1.00	2.00	5.00

SPELLBINDERS
Dec, 1986 - No. 12, Jan, 1988 ($1.25)
Quality

1-12: Nemesis the Warlock, Amadeus Wolf			1.25

SPELLBOUND (See The Crusaders)

SPELLBOUND (Tales to Hold You… #1, Stories to Hold You…)
Mar, 1952 - #23, June, 1954; #24, Oct, 1955 - #34, June, 1957
Atlas Comics (ACI 1-15/Male 16-23/BPC 24-34)

1-Horror/weird stories in all	50.00	150.00	400.00
2-Edgar A. Poe app.	31.00	92.00	215.00
3-5: 3-Whitney-a; cannibalism story	26.00	77.00	180.00
6-Krigstein-a	26.00	77.00	180.00
7-10: 8-Ayers-a	21.00	62.00	145.00
11-16,18-20: 14-Ed Win-a	17.00	49.00	115.00
17-Krigstein-a	18.00	54.00	125.00
21-23: 23-Last precode (6/54)	15.00	45.00	105.00
24-28,30,31,34: 25-Orlando-a	13.50	41.00	95.00
29-Ditko-a (4 pgs.)	15.00	45.00	105.00
32,33-Torres-a	13.50	41.00	95.00

NOTE: **Brodsky** a-5; c-1, 5-7, 10, 11, 13, 15, 25-27, 32. **Colan** a-17. **Everett** a-2, 5, 7, 10, 16, 28, 31; c-2, 8, 9, 14, 17-19, 28, 30. **Forgione/Abel** a-29. **Forte/Fox** a-16. **Al Hartley** a-2. **Heath** a-2, 4, 8, 9, 12, 14, 16; c-3, 4, 12, 16, 20, 21. **Infantino** a-15. **Keller** a-5. **Kida** a-2, 14. **Maneely** a-7, 14, 27; c-24, 29, 31. **Mooney** a-5, 13, 18. **Mac Pakula** a-22, 32. **Post** a-8. **Powell** a-19, 20, 32. **Robinson** a-1. **Romita** a-24, 26, 27. **R.Q. Sale** a-29. **Sekowsky** a-5. **Severin** c-29. **Sinnott** a-8, 16, 17.

SPELLBOUND
Jan, 1988 - Apr, 1988 ($1.50, bi-weekly, Baxter paper)
Marvel Comics

1-5			1.50
6 ($2.25, 52 pgs.)		.90	2.25

SPELLJAMMER (Also see TSR Worlds Comics Annual)

Sept, 1990 - Feb, 1992 ($1.75)
DC Comics

1-18: Based on TSR game. 11-Heck-a.		.75	1.

SPENCER SPOOK (Formerly Giggle Comics; see Adventures of…)
No. 100, Mar-Apr, 1955 - No. 101, May-June, 1955
American Comics Group

100,101	5.70	17.00	34.

SPIDER, THE
1991 - Book 3, 1991 ($4.95, 52 pgs., limited series)
Eclipse Books

Book 1-3-Truman-c/a	1.00	2.00	5.

SPIDER-BOY (Also see Marvel Versus DC #3)
Apr, 1996 ($1.95)
Marvel Comics (Amalgam)

1-Mike Wieringo-c/a; Karl Kesel story; 1st app. of Bizarnage, Insect Queen, Challengers of the Fantastic, Sue Storm: Agent of S.H.I.E.L. D., & King Lizard.		.80	2.

SPIDER-MAN (See Amazing…, Giant-Size…, Marvel Tales, Marvel Team-Up, Spectacular…, Spidey Super Stories, Venom, & Web Of…)

SPIDER-MAN
Aug, 1990 - Present ($1.75)
Marvel Comics

1-Silver edition, direct sale only (unbagged)	1.00	2.60	6.
1-Silver bagged edition; direct sale, no price on comic, but $2.00 on plastic bag (125,000 print run)	2.15	6.50	15.
1-Regular edition w/Spidey face in UPC area (unbagged); green-c			
	1.00	2.00	5.
1-Regular bagged edition w/Spidey face in UPC area; green cover (125,000)			
	1.65	4.20	10.
1-Newsstand bagged w/UPC code	1.00	2.00	5.
1-Gold edition, 2nd printing (unbagged) with Spider-Man in box (400,000-450,000)	1.00	2.00	5.
1-Gold 2nd printing w/UPC code; sold in Wal-Mart; not scarce			
	1.20	3.00	7.
1-Platinum ed. mailed to retailers only (10,000 print run); has new McFarlane & editorial material instead of ads; stiff-c, no cover price			200.
2-McFarlane-c/a/scripts continue		1.80	4.
3-5		1.10	2.
6,7-Ghost Rider & Hobgoblin app.	1.00	2.00	5.
	1.00	2.50	
8-12: 8-Wolverine cameo; Wolverine storyline begins. 12-Wolverine storyline ends		1.20	3.
13-Spidey's black costume returns; Morbius app.	1.00	2.00	5.
14,15: 14-Morbius app. 15-Erik Larsen-c/a; Beast c/s		.90	2.
16,17: 16-X-Force-c/story w/Liefeld assists; continues in X-Force #4; reads sideways; last McFarlane issue. 17-Thanos-c/story; Leonardi/Williamson-c/a		1.00	2.
18-23,25: 13,14-Spidey in black costume. 18-Ghost Rider-c/story. 18-23-Sinister Six storyline w/Erik Larsen-c/a/scripts. 19-Hulk & Hobgoblin-c & app. 20-22-Deathlok app. 22,23-Ghost Rider, Hulk, Hobgoblin app. 23-Wrap-around gatefold-c. 24-Infinity War x-over w/Demogoblin & Hobgoblin-c/story		.80	2.
24-Demogoblin dons new costume & battles Hobgoblin-c/story			
	.40	1.00	2.
26-($3.50, 52 pgs.)-Silver hologram on-c w/gatefold poster by Ron Lim; Spider-Man retells his origin		1.60	4.
26-2nd printing; gold hologram on-c		1.60	4.
27-45: 32-34-Punisher-c/story. 37-Maximum Carnage x-over. 39,40-Electro-c/s (cameo #38). 41-41-Iron Fist-c/stories w/Jae Lee-c/a. 42-Intro Platoon. 44-Hobgoblin app		.70	1.
46-49,51-53, 55, 56,58-80: 46-Begin $1.95-c; bound-in card sheet. 51-Power &			

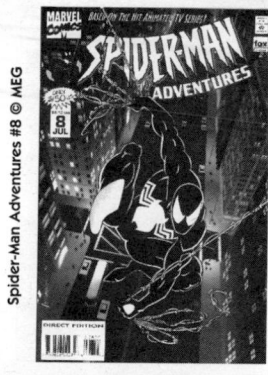

Spider-Man Adventures #8 © MEG

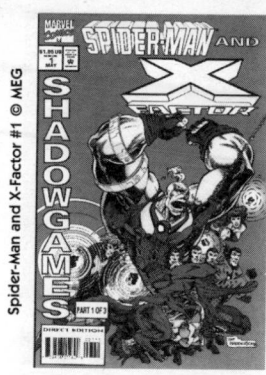

Spider-Man and X-Factor #1 © MEG

Spider-Man: Redemption #2 © MEG

	GD25	FN65	NM94

Responsibility Pt. 3. 52,53-Venom app. 60-Kaine revealed. 61-Origin Kaine.
65-Mysterio app. 66-Kaine-c/app.; Peter Parker app. 67-Carnage-c/app.
68,69-Hobgoblin-c/app. 72-Onslaught x-over; Spidey vs. Sentinels.
74-Daredevil-c/app.

			2.25
46-($2.95)-Polybagged; silver ink-c w/16 pg. preview of cartoon series & animation style print; bound-in trading card sheet	1.20	3.00	
50-($2.50)-Newsstand edition	1.00	2.50	
50-($3.95)-Collectors edition w/holographic-c	.80	1.60	4.00
51-($2.95)-Deluxe edition foil-c; flip book	1.20	3.00	
54 ($2.75, 52 pgs.)-Flip book	1.10	2.75	
57 ($2.50)	1.00	2.50	
57 ($2.95)-Die cut-c	1.20	3.00	
65-($2.95)-Variant-c; polybagged w/cassette			3.00
Super Special (7/95, $3.95)-Planet of the Symbiotes			4.00
...: Carnage nn (6/93, $6.95, TPB)-r/Amazing S-M #344,345,359-363; spot varnish-c	1.20	3.00	7.00
.../Dr. Strange: "The Way to Dusty Death" nn (1992, $6.95, 68 pgs.)	1.20	3.00	7.00
Special Edition 1 (12/92-c, 11/92 inside)-The Trial of Venom; ordered thru mail with $5.00 donation or more to UNICEF; embossed metallic ink; came bagged w/bound-in poster; Daredevil app.	1.65	4.00	10.00
...Vs. Venom nn (1990, $8.95, TPB)-r/Amaz. S-M #300,315-317 w/new McFarlane-c	1.50	3.80	9.00

NOTE: **Erik Larsen** c/a-15, 18-23. **M. Rogers/Keith Williams** c/a-27, 28.

SPIDER-MAN ADVENTURES
Dec, 1994 - No. 15, Mar, 1996 ($1.50)
Marvel Comics

1-15 ($1.50)-Based on animated series			1.50
1-($2.95)-Foil embossed-c	1.20	3.00	

SPIDER-MAN AND BATMAN
1995 ($5.95, one-shot)
Marvel Comics

nn-DeMatteis-s; Joker, Carnage app.	1.00	2.60	6.00

SPIDER-MAN AND DAREDEVIL
Mar, 1984 ($2.00, one-shot, deluxe paper)
Marvel Comics Group

1-r/Spectacular Spider-Man #26-28 by Miller	1.20	3.00	

SPIDER-MAN AND HIS AMAZING FRIENDS (See Marvel Action Universe)
Dec, 1981 (one-shot)
Marvel Comics Group

1-Adapted from NBC TV cartoon show; Green Goblin-c/story; 1st Spidey, Firestar, Iceman team-up; Spiegle-a	1.20	3.00	

SPIDER-MAN AND THE INCREDIBLE HULK (See listing under Amazing...)

SPIDER-MAN AND THE UNCANNY X-MEN
Mar, 1996 ($16.95, trade paperback)
Marvel Comics

nn-r/Uncanny X-Men #27, Uncanny X-men #35, Amazing Spider-Man #92, Marvel Team-Up Annual #1, Marvel Team-Up #150, & Spectacular Spider-Man #197-199			17.00

SPIDER-MAN AND X-FACTOR
May, 1994 - No. 3, July, 1994 ($1.95, limited series)
Marvel Comics

1-3		.80	2.00

SPIDER-MAN CLASSICS
Apr, 1993 - No. 16, July, 1994 ($1.25)
Marvel Comics

1-14,16: 1-r/Amaz. Fantasy #15 & Strange Tales #115. 2-16-r/Amaz. Spider-Man #1-15. 6-Austin-c(i)			1.25
15-($2.95)-Polybagged w/16 pg. insert & animation style print; r/Amazing S-M #14 (1st Green Goblin)	1.20	3.00	

	GD25	FN65	NM94

SPIDER-MAN COLLECTOR'S PREVIEW
Dec, 1994 ($1.50, 100 pgs., one-shot)
Marvel Comics

1-wraparound-c; no comics			1.50

SPIDER-MAN COMICS MAGAZINE
Jan, 1987 - No. 13, 1988 ($1.50, digest-size)
Marvel Comics Group

1-13-Reprints			1.50

SPIDER-MAN: FRIENDS AND ENEMIES
Jan, 1995 - No. 4, Apr, 1995 ($1.95, limited series)
Marvel Comics

1-4-Darkhawk, Nova & Speedball app.		.80	2.00

SPIDER-MAN: FUNERAL FOR AN OCTOPUS
Mar, 1995 - No. 3, May, 1995 ($1.50, limited series)
Marvel Comics

1-3			1.50

SPIDER-MAN: HOT SHOTS
Jan, 1996 ($2.95, one-shot)
Marvel Comics

nn-fold out posters by various, inc. Vess and Ross	1.20	3.00	

SPIDER-MAN: LEGACY OF EVIL
June, 1996 ($3.95, one-shot)
Marvel Comics

1-Kurt Busiek script & Mark Texiera-c/a			4.00

SPIDER-MAN MAGAZINE
1994 - No. 3, 1994 ($1.95, magazine)
Marvel Comics

1-Contains 4 S-M promo cards & 4 X-Men Ultra Fleer cards; Spider-Man story by Romita, Sr.; X-Men story; puzzles & games		.80	2.00
2,3: 2-Doc Octopus & X-Men stories		.80	2.00

SPIDER-MAN: MAXIMUM CLONAGE
1995 ($4.95)
Marvel Comics

Alpha #1-Acetate-c.	1.00	2.00	5.00
Omega #1-Chromium-c.	1.00	2.00	5.00

SPIDER-MAN MEGAZINE
Oct, 1994 - No. 6, Mar, 1995 ($2.95, 100 pgs.)
Marvel Comics

1-6: 1-r/ASM #16,224,225, Marvel Team-Up #1	1.20	3.00	

SPIDER-MAN: POWER OF TERROR
Jan, 1995 - No. 4, Apr, 1995 ($1.95, limited series)
Marvel Comics

1-4-Silvermane & Deathlok app.		.80	2.00

SPIDER-MAN: REDEMPTION
Sept, 1996 - No. 4, Dec, 1996 ($1.50, limited series)
Marvel Comics

1-4: Dematteis scripts; Zeck-a			1.50

SPIDER-MAN SAGA
Nov, 1991 - No. 4, Feb, 1992 ($2.95, limited series)
Marvel Comics

1-4: Gives history of Spider-Man: text & illustrations	1.20	3.00	

SPIDER-MAN TEAM-UP
Dec, 1995 - No. 4, Mar, 1996 ($2.95)
Marvel Comics

1-4: 1-w/ X-Men. 2-w/ Silver Surfer. 3-w/Fantastic Four. 4-w/Avengers.	1.20	3.00	

Spider-Man 2099 #46 © MEG

Spider-Man Unlimited #12 © MEG

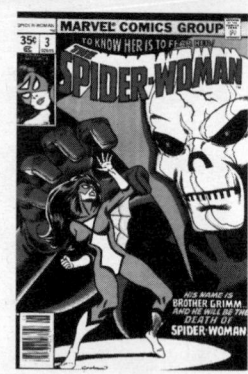

Spider-Woman #3 © MEG

GD25   FN65   NM94   GD25   FN65   NM94

SPIDER-MAN: THE ARACHNIS PROJECT
Aug, 1994 - No. 6, Jan, 1995 ($1.75, limited series)
Marvel Comics

1-6-Venom, Styx, Stone & Jury app.	.70	1.75

SPIDER-MAN: THE CLONE JOURNAL
Mar, 1995 ($2.95, one-shot)
Marvel Comics

1	1.20	3.00

SPIDER-MAN: THE FINAL ADVENTURE
Nov, 1995 - No. 4, Feb, 1996 ($2.95, limited series)
Marvel Comics

1-4: 1-Nicieza scripts; foil-c	1.20	3.00

SPIDER-MAN: THE JACKAL FILES
Aug, 1995 ($1.95, one-shot)
Marvel Comics

1	.80	2.00

SPIDER-MAN: THE LOST YEARS
Aug, 1995 - No. 3, Oct, 1995; No. 0, 1996 ($2.95/$3.95, limited series)
Marvel Comics

0-(1/96, $3.95)-Reprints.		
1-3-DeMatteis scripts, Romita, Jr.-c/a	1.20	3.00

NOTE: *Romita c-0i. Romita, Jr. a-0r, 1-3p. c-0-3p. Sharp a-0r.*

SPIDER-MAN: THE MUTANT AGENDA
No. 0, Feb, 1994; No. 1, Mar, 1994 - No. 3, May, 1994 ($1.75, limited series)
Marvel Comics

0-(2/94, $1.25, 52 pgs.)-Crosses over w/newspaper strip; has empty pages to paste in newspaper strips; gives origin of Spidey		1.25
1-3: Beast & Hobgoblin app. 1-X-Men cameo.	.70	1.75

SPIDER-MAN: THE PARKER YEARS
Nov, 1995 ($2.50, one-shot)
Marvel Comics

1	1.00	2.50

SPIDER-MAN 2099 (See Amazing Spider-Man #365)
Nov, 1992 - No. 46, Aug, 1996 ($1.25/$1.50/$1.95)
Marvel Comics

1-($1.75, stiff-c)-Red foil stamped-c; begins origin of Miguel O'Hara (Spider-Man 2099); Leonardi/Williamson-c/a begins	1.00	2.50
1-2nd printing ($1.75)	.70	1.75
2-Origin continued, ends #3	.90	2.25
3,4: 4-Doom 2099 app.	.80	2.00
5-18: 13-Extra 16 pg. insert on Midnight Sons		1.25
19-24,26-31: 19-Begins 1.50-c; bound-in trading card sheet		1.50
25-($2.25, 52 pgs.)-Newsstand edition	.90	2.25
25-($2.95, 52 pgs.)-Deluxe edition w/embossed foil-c	1.20	3.00
32-46: 32-Begin $1.95-c. 35-variant-c. 36-two-c; Jae Lee-a. 37,38-two-c. 46-The Vulture app; Mike McKone-a(p).	.80	2.00
Annual 1 (1994, $2.95, 68 pgs.)	1.20	3.00
Special 1 (1995, $3.95)	1.60	4.00

NOTE: *Chaykin c-37. Ron Lim a(p)-18; c(p)-13, 16, 18. Kelley Jones a-c/a-9. Leonardi/Williamson a-1-8, 10-13, 15-17, 19, 20, 22-25; c-1-13, 15, 17-19, 20, 22-25, 35.*

SPIDER-MAN 2099 MEETS SPIDER-MAN
1995 ($5.95, one-shot)
Marvel Comics

nn-Peter David script; Leonardi/Williamson-c/a.	1.00	2.60	6.00

SPIDER-MAN UNLIMITED
May, 1993 - Present ($3.95, quarterly, 68 pgs.)
Marvel Comics

1-Begin Maximum Carnage storyline, ends; Carnage-c/story.	1.00	2.00	5.00

2-17: 2-Venom & Carnage-c/story; Ron Lim-c/a(p) in #2-6. 10-Vulture app., McManus-a	1.60	4

SPIDER-MAN VS. DRACULA
Jan, 1994 ($1.75, 52 pgs., one-shot)
Marvel Comics

1-r/Giant-Size Spider-Man #1 plus new Matt Fox-a	.70	1.

SPIDER-MAN VS. WOLVERINE
Feb, 1987; V2#1, 1990 (68 pgs.)
Marvel Comics Group

1-Williamson-c/a(i); intro Charlemagne; death of Ned Leeds (old Hobgoblin)	2.85	8.50	20
V2#1 (1990, $4.95)-Reprints #1 (2/87)	1.00	2.00	5.

SPIDER-MAN: WEB OF DOOM
Aug, 1994 - No. 3, Oct, 1994 ($1.75, limited series)
Marvel Comics

1-3	.70	1

SPIDER REIGN OF THE VAMPIRE KING, THE (Also see The Spider)
1992 - No. 3, 1992 ($4.95, limited series, coated stock, 52 pgs.)
Eclipse Books

Book One - Three: Truman scripts & painted-c	1.00	2.00	5

SPIDER'S WEB, THE (See G-8 and His Battle Aces)

SPIDER-WOMAN (Also see The Avengers #240, Marvel Spotlight #32, Marvel Super Heroes Secret Wars #7 & Marvel Two-In-One #29)
April, 1978 - No. 50, June, 1983 (New logo #47 on)
Marvel Comics Group

1-New complete origin & mask added	1.00	2.00	5
2-36,39-49: 6,19-Werewolf by Night-c/stories. 13,15-The Shroud-c/s. 20,28,2 Spider-Man app. 46-Kingpin app. 49-Tigra-c/story.	.70	1
37,38-X-Men x-over; 37-1st app. Siryn of X-Force; origin retold		1.60	4
50-(52 pgs.)-Death of Spider-Woman; photo-c	1.60	4

NOTE: *Austin a-37i. Byrne c-26p. Layton c-19. Miller c-32p.*

SPIDER-WOMAN
Nov, 1993 - No. 4, Feb, 1994 ($1.75, mini-series)
Marvel Comics

V2#1-4: 1,2-Origin; U.S. Agent app.	.70	1

SPIDEY SUPER STORIES (Spider-Man)
Oct, 1974 - No. 57, Mar, 1982 (35¢, no ads)
Marvel/Children's TV Workshop

1-Origin (stories simplified)	1.20	3
2-12: 2-Kraven. 6-Iceman	.80	2
13-38,40-44,46-57: 31-Moondragon-c/story; Dr. Doom app. 33-Hulk. 34-Sub-Mariner. 38-F.F. 44-Vision. 56-Battles Jack O'Lantern-c/story (exactly one year after 1st app. in Machine Man #19)	.80	2
39-Thanos-c/story	1.20	3
45-Silver Surfer & Dr. Doom app.	.80	2

SPIKE AND TYKE (See M.G.M.'s...)

SPIKE AND TYKE (See M.G.M.'s...)

SPIN & MARTY (TV) (Walt Disney's)(See Walt Disney Showcase #32)
No. 714, June, 1956 - No. 1082, Mar-May, 1960 (All photo-c)
Dell Publishing Co. (Mickey Mouse Club)

Four Color 714 (#1)	11.00	33.00	110
Four Color 767,808 (#2,3)	10.00	30.00	100
Four Color 826 (#4)-Annette Funicello photo-c	24.00	72.00	240
5(3-5/58) - 9(6-8/59)	7.50	22.50	75
Four Color 1026,1082	7.50	22.50	75

SPINE-TINGLING TALES (Doctor Spektor Presents...)
May, 1975 - No. 4, Jan, 1976 (All 25¢ issues)
Gold Key

The Spirit 6/9/40 © Will Eisner

The Spirit 7/14/40 © Will Eisner

The Spirit 8/5/40 © Will Eisner

SP

	GD25	FN65	NM94

1-4: 1-1st Tragg-r/Mystery Comics Digest #3. 2-Origin Ra-Ka-Tep-r/Mystery
Comics Digest #1; Dr. Spektor #12. 3-All Durak-r issue; 4-Baron Tibor's 1st
app.-r/Mystery Comics Digest #4; painted-c 1.00

SPIRAL PATH, THE
July, 1986 - No. 2 ($1.75, Baxter paper, limited series)
Eclipse Comics

		GD25	FN65	NM94
1,2			.75	1.80

SPIRAL ZONE
Feb, 1988 - No. 4, May, 1988 ($1.00, mini-series)
DC Comics

			GD25	FN65	NM94
1-4-Based on Tonka toys					1.00

SPIRIT, THE (Weekly Comic Book)
6/2/40 - 10/5/52 (16 pgs.; 8 pgs.) (no cover) (in color)
(Distributed through various newspapers and other sources)
Will Eisner
NOTE: **Eisner** script, pencils/inks for the most part from 6/2/40-4/26/42; a few stories
assisted by Jack Cole, Fine, Powell and Kotsky.

	GD25	FN65	NM94
6/2/40(#1)-Origin/1st app. The Spirit; reprinted in Police #11; Lady Luck (Brenda Banks)(1st app.) by Chuck Mazoujian & Mr. Mystic (1st. app.) by S. R. (Bob) Powell begin	65.00	195.00	525.00
6/9/40(#2)	31.00	92.00	215.00
6/16/40(#3)-Black Queen app. in Spirit	18.00	54.00	125.00
6/23/40(#4)-Mr. Mystic receives magical necklace	15.00	45.00	105.00
6/30/40(#5)	15.00	45.00	105.00
7/7/40(#6)-1st app.: Spirit carplane; Black Queen app. in Spirit	15.00	45.00	105.00
7/14/40(#7)-8/4/40(#10): 7/21/40-Spirit becomes fugitive wanted for murder	12.00	36.00	85.00
8/11/40-9/22/40	11.00	33.00	75.00
9/29/40-Ellen drops engagement with Homer Creep	10.00	30.00	65.00
10/6/40-11/3/40	10.00	30.00	65.00
11/10/40-The Black Queen app.	10.00	30.00	65.00
11/17/40, 11/24/40	10.00	30.00	65.00
12/1/40-Ellen spanking by Spirit on cover & inside; Eisner-1st 3 pgs., J. Cole rest	14.00	43.00	100.00
2/8/40-3/9/41	8.35	25.00	50.00
3/16/41-Intro. & 1st app. Silk Satin	13.00	39.00	90.00
3/23/41-6/1/41: 5/11/41-Last Lady Luck by Mazoujian; 5/18/41-Lady Luck by Nick Viscardi begins, ends 2/22/42	8.35	25.00	50.00
6/8/41-2nd app. Satin; Spirit learns Satin is also a British agent	10.00	30.00	70.00
6/15/41-1st app. Twilight	10.00	30.00	60.00
6/22/41-Hitler app. in Spirit	8.35	25.00	50.00
6/29/41-1/25/42,2/8/42	6.70	20.00	40.00
2/1/42-1st app. Duchess	10.00	30.00	60.00
3/15/42-4/26/42-Lady Luck by Klaus Nordling begins 3/1/42	7.50	22.50	45.00
5/3/42-8/16/42-Eisner/Fine/Quality staff assists on Spirit	5.00	15.00	30.00
8/23/42-Satin cover splash; Spirit by Eisner/Fine although signed by Fine	9.30	28.00	65.00
8/30/42,9/27/42-10/11/42,10/25/42-11/8/42-Eisner/Fine/Quality staff assists on Spirit	5.00	15.00	30.00
9/6/42-9/20/42,10/18/42-Fine/Belfi art on Spirit; scripts by Manly Wade Wellman	3.00	9.00	21.00
11/15/42-12/6/42,12/20/42,12/27/42,1/17/43-4/18/43,5/9/43-8/8/43-Wellman/ Woolfolk scripts, Fine pencils, Quality staff inks	3.00	9.00	21.00
12/13/42,1/3/43,1/10/43,4/25/43,5/2/43-Eisner scripts/layouts; Fine pencils, Quality staff inks	3.75	11.25	26.00
5/23/43-Eisner script/layout; pencils/inks by Quality staff; Jack Cole-a	2.30	6.75	16.00
12/2/43-12/12/43-Wellman/Woolfolk scripts, Fine pencils, Quality staff inks; Mr. Mystic by Guardineer-10/10/43-10/24/43	2.30	6.75	16.00

	GD25	FN65	NM94
12/19/43-8/13/44-Wellman/Woolfolk/Jack Cole scripts; Cole, Fine & Robin King-a; Last Mr. Mystic-5/14/44	2.00	6.00	14.00
8/20/44-12/16/45-Wellman/Woolfolk scripts; Fine art with unknown staff assists	2.00	6.00	14.00

NOTE: Scripts/layouts by Eisner, or Eisner/Nordling, Eisner/Mercer or Spranger/Eisner;
inks by Eisner or Eisner/Spranger in issues 12/23/45-2/2/47.

	GD25	FN65	NM94
12/23/45-1/6/46: 12/23/45-Christmas-c	3.75	11.25	28.00
1/13/46-Origin Spirit retold	6.00	18.00	45.00
1/20/46-1st postwar Satin app.	5.00	15.00	38.00
1/27/46-3/10/46: 3/3/46-Last Lady Luck by Nordling	3.70	11.00	28.00
3/17/46-Intro. & 1st app. Nylon	5.00	15.00	38.00
3/24/46,3/31/46,4/14/46	3.70	11.00	28.00
4/7/46-2nd app. Nylon	4.30	13.00	32.00
4/21/46-Intro. & 1st app. Mr. Carrion & His Pet Buzzard Julia	5.70	17.00	45.00
4/28/46-5/12/46,5/26/46-6/30/46: Lady Luck by Fred Schwab in issues 5/5/46-11/3/46	3.70	11.00	28.00
5/19/46-2nd app. Mr. Carrion	4.30	13.00	32.00
7/7/46-Intro. & 1st app. Dulcet Tone & Skinny	5.50	16.50	40.00
7/14/46-9/29/46	3.70	11.00	28.00
10/6/46-Intro. & 1st app. P'Gell	6.00	18.00	45.00
10/13/46-11/3/46,11/16/46-11/24/46	3.70	11.00	28.00
11/10/46-2nd app. P'Gell	4.50	14.00	35.00
12/1/46-3rd app. P'Gell	4.30	13.00	32.00
12/8/46-2/2/47	4.00	12.00	24.00

NOTE: Scripts, pencils/inks by Eisner except where noted in issues 2/9/47-12/19/48.

	GD25	FN65	NM94
2/9/47-7/6/47: 6/8/47-Eisner self satire	3.40	10.00	24.00
7/13/47- "Hansel & Gretel" fairy tales	5.00	15.00	38.00
7/20/47-Li'L Abner, Daddy Warbucks, Dick Tracy, Fearless Fosdick parody; A-Bomb blast-c	5.50	16.50	40.00
7/27/47-9/14/47	3.40	10.00	24.00
9/21/47-Pearl Harbor flashback	4.00	12.00	30.00
9/28/47-1st mention of Flying Saucers in comics-3 months after 1st sighting in Idaho on 6/25/47	9.30	28.00	65.00
10/5/47- "Cinderella" fairy tales	5.00	15.00	38.00
10/12/47-11/30/47	3.40	10.00	24.00
12/7/47-Intro. & 1st app. Powder Pouf	5.70	17.00	45.00
12/14/47-12/28/47	3.40	10.00	24.00
1/4/48-2nd app. Powder Pouf	4.30	13.00	32.00
1/11/48-1st app. Sparrow Fallon; Powder Pouf app.	4.30	13.00	32.00
1/18/48-He-Man ad cover; satire issue	4.30	13.00	32.00
1/25/48-Intro. & 1st app. Castanet	5.50	16.50	40.00
2/1/48-2nd app. Castanet	3.70	11.00	28.00
2/8/48-3/7/48	3.40	10.00	24.00
3/14/48-Only app. Kretchma	3.70	11.00	28.00
3/21/48,3/28/48,4/11/48-4/25/48	3.40	10.00	24.00
4/4/48-Only app. Wild Rice	3.70	11.00	28.00
5/2/48-2nd app. Sparrow	3.40	10.00	24.00
5/9/48-6/27/48,7/11/48,7/18/48: 6/13/48-Television issue	3.40	10.00	24.00
7/4/48-Spirit by Andre Le Blanc	2.60	7.50	18.00
7/25/48-Ambrose Bierce's "The Thing" adaptation classic by Eisner/ Grandenetti	9.30	28.00	65.00
8/1/48-8/15/48,8/29/48-9/12/48	3.40	10.00	24.00
8/22/48-Poe's "Fall of the House of Usher" classic by Eisner/Grandinetti	9.30	28.00	65.00
9/19/48-Only app. Lorelei	4.50	14.00	35.00
9/26/48-10/31/48	3.40	10.00	24.00
11/7/48-Only app. Plaster of Paris	4.50	14.00	35.00
11/14/48-12/19/48	3.40	10.00	24.00

NOTE: Scripts by Eisner or Feiffer or Eisner/Feiffer or Eisner or Nordling. Art by Eisner with backgrounds
by Eisner, Grandenetti, Le Blanc, Stallman, Nordling, Dixon and/or others in issues 12/26/48-
4/1/51 except where noted.

	GD25	FN65	NM94
12/26/48-Reprints some covers of 1948 with flashbacks	3.40	10.00	24.00

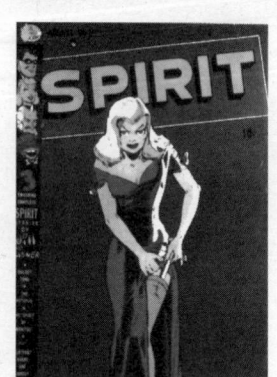
The Spirit #22 © Will Eisner

The Spirit #4 © Will Eisner

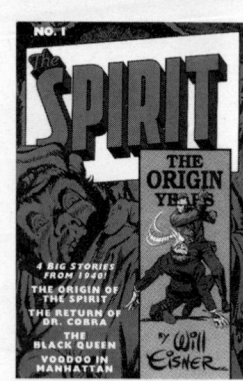
Spirit: The Origin Years #1 © Will Eisner

	GD25	FN65	NM94
1/2/49-1/16/49	3.40	10.00	24.00
1/23/49,1/30/49-1st & 2nd app. Thorne	4.50	14.00	35.00
2/6/49-8/14/49	3.40	10.00	24.00
8/21/49,8/28/49-1st & 2nd app. Monica Veto	4.50	14.00	35.00
9/4/49,9/11/49	3.40	10.00	24.00
9/18/49-Love comic cover; has gag love comic ads on inside	4.50	14.00	35.00
9/25/49-Only app. Ice	4.00	12.00	30.00
10/2/49,10/9/49-Autumn News appears & dies in 10/9 issue	4.00	12.00	30.00
10/16/49,11/27/49,12/18/49,12/25/49	3.40	10.00	24.00
12/4/49,12/11/49-1st & 2nd app. Flaxen	3.70	11.00	28.00
1/1/50-Flashbacks to all of the Spirit girls-Thorne, Ellen, Satin, & Monica	6.00	18.00	45.00
1/8/50-Intro. & 1st app. Sand Saref	8.50	26.00	65.00
1/15/50-2nd app. Saref	5.70	17.00	45.00
1/22/50-2/5/50	3.40	10.00	24.00
2/12/50-Roller Derby issue	4.30	13.00	32.00
2/19/50-Half Dead Mr. Lox - Classic horror	4.30	13.00	32.00
2/26/50-4/23/50,5/14/50,5/28/50,7/23/50-9/3/50	3.40	10.00	24.00
4/30/50-Script/art by Le Blanc with Eisner framing	1.70	5.00	12.00
5/7/50,6/4/50-7/16/50-Abe Kanegson-a	1.70	5.00	12.00
5/21/50-Script by Feiffer/Eisner, art by Blaisdell, Eisner framing	1.70	5.00	12.00
9/10/50-P'Gell returns	4.50	14.00	35.00
9/17/50-1/7/51	3.40	10.00	24.00
1/14/51-Life Magazine cover; brief biography of Comm. Dolan, Sand Saref, Silk Satin, P'Gell, Sammy & Willum, Darling O'Shea, & Mr. Carrion & His Pet Buzzard Julia, with pin-ups by Eisner	4.50	14.00	35.00
1/21/51,2/4/51-4/1/51	3.40	10.00	24.00
1/28/51- "The Meanest Man in the World" classic by Eisner	4.50	14.00	35.00
4/8/51-7/29/51,8/12/51-Last Eisner issue	3.40	10.00	24.00
8/5/51,8/19/51-7/20/52-Not Eisner	1.70	5.00	12.00
7/27/52-(Rare)-Denny Colt in Outer Space by Wally Wood; 7 pg. S/F story of E.C. vintage	32.00	95.00	225.00
8/3/52-(Rare)- "Mission…The Moon" by Wood	32.00	95.00	225.00
8/10/52-(Rare)- "A DP On The Moon" by Wood	32.00	95.00	225.00
8/17/52-(Rare)- "Heart" by Wood/Eisner	27.00	81.00	190.00
8/24/52-(Rare)- "Rescue" by Wood	32.00	95.00	225.00
8/31/52-(Rare)- "The Last Man" by Wood	32.00	95.00	225.00
9/7/52-(Rare)- "The Man in The Moon" by Wood	32.00	95.00	225.00
9/14/52-(Rare)-Eisner/Wenzel-a	8.50	26.00	60.00
9/21/52-(Rare)- "Denny Colt, Alias The Spirit/Space Report" by Eisner/Wenzel	11.50	34.00	80.00
9/28/52-(Rare)- "Return From The Moon" by Wood	32.00	95.00	225.00
10/5/52-(Rare)- "The Last Story" by Eisner	11.50	34.00	80.00

Large Tabloid pages from 1946 on (Eisner) - Price 200 percent over listed prices.
NOTE: Spirit sections came out in both large and small format. Some newspapers went to the 8-pg. format months before others. Some printed the pages so they cannot be folded into a small comic book section; these are worth less. (Also see Three Comics & Spiritman)

SPIRIT, THE (1st Series)(Also see Police Comics #11)
1944 - No. 22, Aug, 1950
Quality Comics Group (Vital)

	GD25	FN65	NM94
nn(#1)- "Wanted Dead or Alive"	61.00	185.00	495.00
nn(#2)- "Crime Doesn't Pay"	40.00	120.00	285.00
nn(#3)- "Murder Runs Wild"	31.00	92.00	215.00
4,5: 4-Flatfoot Burns begins, ends #22. 5-Wertham app.	25.00	75.00	175.00
6-10	21.00	64.00	150.00
11	19.00	56.00	130.00
12-17-Eisner-c. 19-Honeybun app.	30.00	90.00	210.00
18-21-Strip-r by Eisner; Eisner-c	40.00	120.00	280.00

	GD25	FN65	NM94
22-Used by N.Y. Legis. Comm; classic Eisner-c	49.00	146.00	390
Super Reprint #11-r/Quality Spirit #19 by Eisner	3.25	9.50	22
Super Reprint #12-r/Spirit #17 by Fine; Sol Brodsky-c	2.85	8.50	20

SPIRIT, THE (2nd Series)
Spring, 1952 - No. 5, 1954
Fiction House Magazines

	GD25	FN65	NM94
1-Not Eisner	34.00	103.00	240
2-Eisner-c/a(2)	32.00	96.00	225
3-Eisner/Grandenetti-c	22.00	66.00	155
4-Eisner/Grandenetti-c; Eisner-a	25.00	75.00	175
5-Eisner-c/a(4)	31.00	92.00	215

SPIRIT, THE
Oct, 1966 - No. 2, Mar, 1967 (Giant Size, 25¢, 68 pgs.)
Harvey Publications

	GD25	FN65	NM94
1-Eisner-r plus 9 new pgs.(origin Denny Colt, Take 3, plus 2 filler pgs.) (#3 was advertised, but never published)	6.50	19.50	45
2-Eisner-r plus 9 new pgs.(origin of the Octopus)	6.50	19.50	45

SPIRIT, THE (Underground)
Jan, 1973 - No. 2, Sept, 1973 (Black & White)
Kitchen Sink Enterprises (Krupp Comics)

	GD25	FN65	NM94
1-New Eisner-c & 4 pgs. new Eisner-a plus-r (titled Crime Convention)	1.65	4.20	10
2-New Eisner-c & 4 pgs. new Eisner-a plus-r (titled Meets P'Gell)	1.70	5.00	12

SPIRIT, THE (Magazine)
4/74 - No. 16, 10/76; No. 17, Winter, 1977 - No. 41, 6/83 (B&W w/color)
Warren Publ. Co./Krupp Comic Works No. 17 on

	GD25	FN65	NM94
1-Eisner-r begin	1.20	3.00	
2-5	1.00	2.00	
6-9,11-16: 7-All Ebony issue. 8-Female Foes issue. 12-X-Mas issue. 16-Gia Summer Special ($1.50)			1.20
10-Giant Summer Special ($1.50)-Origin			1.20
17,18(8/78): 17-Lady Luck-r. 20-Outer Space-r			.80
19-21-New Eisner-a. 20,21-Wood-r (#21-r/A DP on the Moon by Wood)			
22,23-Wood-r (#22-r/Mission the Moon by Wood)			
24-29,31-35: 28-r/last story (10/5/52)			
30-(7/81)-Special Spirit Jam issue w/Caniff, Corben, Bolland, Byrne, Miller, Kurtzman, Rogers, Sienkiewicz-a & 40 others			.80
36-Begin Spirit Section-r; r/1st story (6/2/40) in color; new Eisner-c/a (18 pgs.)($2.95)			1.40
37-41: 37-r/2nd story in color plus 18 pgs. new Eisner-a. 38-41: r/3rd - 6th stories in color. 41-Lady Luck Mr. Mystic in color			1.40
Special 1(1975)-All Eisner-a			.80

NOTE: Covers pencilled/inked by Eisner only #1-9,12-16; painted by Eisner & Ken Kelly #1 11; painted by Eisner #17-up; one color story reprinted in #1-10. **Austin** -a30i. **Byrne** -a30p. **Miller** -a30p.

SPIRIT, THE (See Will Eisner's 3-D Classics Featuring...)
Oct, 1983 - No. 87, Jan, 1992 (Baxter paper) ($2.00)
Kitchen Sink Enterprises

	GD25	FN65	NM94
1-4: 1-Origin-r/12/23/45 Spirit Section. 2-r/sections 1/20/46. 3-r/ 2/17/46-3/10/46. 4-r/3/17/46-4/7/46			1.00
5-11 ($2.95 cover): 11-Last color issue			1.00
12-87 ($1.95/$2.00, B&W): 54-r/section 2/19/50. 85-87-Reprint the Outer Space Spirit stories by Wood. 86-r/A DP on the Moon by Wood from 1952			1.00

SPIRIT: THE ORIGIN YEARS
May, 1992 - No. 4, Aug, 1992 ($2.95, B&W, high quality paper)
Kitchen Sink Press

	GD25	FN65	NM94
1-4: 1-r/sections 6/2/40(origin)-6/23/40 (all 1940s)			1.20

Spirit of Wonder #5 © DH

Splitting Image #1 © Image

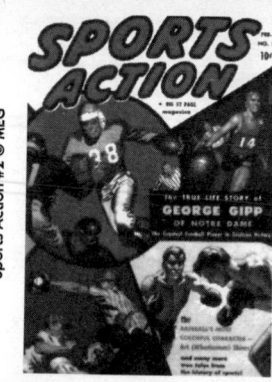
Sports Action #2 © MEG

GD25　FN65　NM94

SPIRITMAN (Also see Three Comics)
No date (1944) (10¢)
(Triangle Sales Co. ad on back cover)
No publisher listed

1-Three 16pg. Spirit sections bound together, (1944, 10¢, 52 pgs.)		19.00	58.00	135.00
2-Two Spirit sections (3/26/44, 4/2/44) bound together; by Lou Fine		17.00	49.00	115.00

SPIRIT OF THE BORDER (See Zane Grey & Four Color #197)

SPIRIT OF WONDER (Manga)
Apr, 1996 - No. 5, Aug, 1996 ($2.95, B&W, limited series)
Dark Horse Comics

1-5			3.00

SPIRIT WORLD (Magazine)
Fall, 1971 (B&W)
National Periodical Publications

1-Kirby-a; Neal Adams-c	1.00	2.60	6.00

SPITFIRE
No. 132, 1944 (Aug) - No. 133, 1945 (Female undercover agent)
Malverne Herald (Elliot)(J. R. Mahon)

132,133: Both have Classics Gift Box ads on b/c with checklist to #20		20.00	60.00	140.00

SPITFIRE AND THE TROUBLESHOOTERS
Oct, 1986 - No. 9, June, 1987 (Codename: Spitfire #10 on)
Marvel Comics

1-9: 4-McFarlane-a			1.00

SPITFIRE COMICS (Also see Double Up)
Aug, 1941 - No. 2, Oct, 1941 (Pocket size; 100 pgs.)
Harvey Publications

1-Origin The Clown, The Fly-Man, The Spitfire & The Magician From Bagdad		53.00	159.00	425.00
2		45.00	135.00	360.00

SPLITTING IMAGE
Mar, 1993 - No. 2, 1993 ($1.95)
Image Comics

1,2-Simpson-c/a; parody comic		.80	2.00

SPOOF
Oct, 1970; No. 2, Nov, 1972 - No. 5, May, 1973
Marvel Comics Group

1-Infinity-c; Dark Shadows-c & parody	1.00	2.00	5.00
2-5: 3-Beatles, Osmond's, Jackson 5, David Cassidy, Nixon & Agnew-c.			
5-Rod Serling, Woody Allen, Ted Kennedy-c		1.20	3.00

SPOOK (Formerly Shock Detective Cases)
No. 22, Jan, 1953 - No. 30, Oct, 1954
Star Publications

22-Sgt. Spook-r; acid in face story; hanging-c	27.00	81.00	190.00
23,25,27: 25-Jungle Lil-r. 27-Two Sgt. Spook-r	17.00	51.00	120.00
24-Used in SOTI, pgs. 182,183-r/Inside Crime #2; Transvestism story			
	20.00	60.00	140.00
26-Disbrow-a	17.00	51.00	120.00
28,29-Rulah app. 29-Jo-Jo app.	17.00	51.00	120.00
30-Disbrow-c/a(2); only Star-r	17.00	51.00	120.00
NOTE: **L. B. Cole** covers-all issues; a-28(1 pg.). **Disbrow** a-26(2), 28, 29(2), 30(2); No. 30 blue Bolt Weird Tales #114.				

SPOOK COMICS
1946
Baily Publications/Star

1-Mr. Lucifer story	24.00	71.00	165.00

GD25　FN65　NM94

SPOOKY (The Tuff Little Ghost; see Casper The Friendly Ghost)
11/55 - 139, 11/73; 7/74 - No. 155, 3/77; No. 156, 12/77 - No. 158,
4/78; No. 159, 9/78; No. 160, 10/79; No. 161, 9/80
Harvey Publications

1-Nightmare begins (see Casper #19)	25.00	75.00	250.00
2	13.00	40.00	125.00
3-10(1956-57)	7.00	21.00	70.00
11-20(1957-58)	3.50	10.50	35.00
21-40(1958-59)	2.00	6.00	20.00
41-60	2.00	6.00	14.00
61-80	1.50	3.75	9.00
81-120	1.00	2.60	6.00
121-126,133-140		1.40	3.50
127-132: All 52 pg. Giants	1.00	2.00	5.00
141-161		.65	1.60

SPOOKY
Nov, 1991 - No. 4, Sept, 1992 ($1.00/$1.25)
Harvey Comics

1-4: 3-Begin $1.25-c			1.25
...Digest 1-3 (10/92, 6/93, 10/93, $1.75, 100 pgs.)-Casper, Wendy, etc.			
		.70	1.75

SPOOKY HAUNTED HOUSE
Oct, 1972 - No. 15, Feb, 1975
Harvey Publications

1	2.15	6.50	15.00
2-5	1.20	3.00	7.00
6-10		1.40	3.50
11-15			1.50

SPOOKY MYSTERIES
No date (1946) (10¢)
Your Guide Publ. Co.

1-Mr. Spooky, Super Snooper, Pinky, Girl Detective app.		13.50	41.00	95.00

SPOOKY SPOOKTOWN
9/61; No. 2, 9/62 - No. 52, 12/73; No. 53, 10/74 - No. 66, Dec, 1976
Harvey Publications

1-Casper, Spooky; 68 pgs. begin	11.00	33.00	110.00
2	6.00	18.00	60.00
3-5	3.80	11.40	38.00
6-10	3.40	10.00	24.00
11-20	2.15	6.50	15.00
21-39: 39-Last 68 pg. issue	1.50	3.75	9.00
40-45: All 52 pgs.		1.80	4.50
46-66: 61-Hot Stuff/Spooky team-up story		1.20	3.00

SPORT COMICS (Becomes True Sport Picture Stories #5 on)
Oct, 1940(No mo.) - No. 4, Nov, 1941
Street & Smith Publications

1-Life story of Lou Gehrig	44.00	132.00	350.00
2	25.00	75.00	175.00
3,4	21.00	64.00	150.00

SPORT LIBRARY (See Charlton Sport Library)

SPORTS ACTION (Formerly Sport Stars)
No. 2, Feb, 1950 - No. 14, Sept, 1952
Marvel/Atlas Comics (ACI No. 2,3/SAI No. 4-14)

2-Powell painted-c; George Gipp life story	29.00	86.00	200.00
3-Everett-a	18.00	54.00	125.00
4-11,14: Weiss-a	17.00	49.00	115.00
12,13: 12-Everett-c. 13-Krigstein-a	18.00	54.00	125.00
NOTE: Title may have changed after No. 3, to Crime Must Lose No. 4 on, due to publisher change. **Sol Brodsky** c-4-7, 13, 14. **Maneely** c-3, 8-11.				

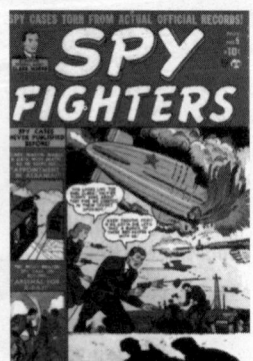

Spy Fighters #5 © MEG

Spy Smasher #7 © FAW

Spy Thrillers #2 © ATLAS

	GD25	FN65	NM94

SPORT STARS
Feb-Mar, 1946 - No. 4, Aug-Sept, 1946 (Half comic, half photo magazine)
Parents' Magazine Institute (Sport Stars)

1- "How Tarzan Got That Way" story of Johnny Weissmuller			
	34.00	101.00	235.00
2-Baseball greats	21.00	64.00	150.00
3,4	18.00	54.00	125.00

SPORT STARS (Becomes Sports Action #2 on)
Nov, 1949 (52 pgs.)
Marvel Comics (ACI)

1-Knute Rockne; painted-c	31.00	92.00	215.00

SPORT THRILLS (Formerly Dick Cole; becomes Jungle Thrills #16)
No. 11, Nov, 1950 - No. 15, Nov, 1951
Star Publications

11-Dick Cole begins, ends #13?; Ted Williams & Ty Cobb life stories			
	24.00	71.00	165.00
12-Joe DiMaggio, Phil Rizzuto stories & photos on-c; L.B. Cole-c/a			
	17.00	51.00	120.00
13-15-All L. B. Cole-c. 13-Jackie Robinson, Pee Wee Reese stories & photo			
on-c. 14-Johnny Weissmuler life story	17.00	51.00	120.00
Accepted Reprint #11 (#15 on-c, nd); L.B. Cole-cover			
	5.35	16.00	32.00
Accepted Reprint #12 (nd); L.B. Cole-c; Joe DiMaggio & Phil Rizzuto life			
stories-r/#12	5.35	16.00	32.00

SPOTLIGHT (TV)
Sept, 1978 - No. 4, Mar, 1979 (Hanna-Barbera)
Marvel Comics Group

1-4: 1-Huckleberry Hound, Yogi Bear; Shaw-a. 2-Quick Draw McGraw, Augie			
Doggie, Snooper & Blabber. 3-The Jetsons, Yakky Doodle. 4-Magilla Gorilla,			
Snagglepuss		.80	2.00

SPOTLIGHT COMICS (Becomes Red Seal Comics #14 on?)
Nov, 1944 - No. 3, 1945
Harry 'A' Chesler (Our Army, Inc.)

1-The Black Dwarf (cont'd in Red Seal?), The Veiled Avenger, & Barry Kuda			
begin; Tuska-c	47.00	141.00	375.00
2	42.00	126.00	335.00
3-Injury to eye story (reprinted from Scoop #3)	44.00	132.00	350.00

SPOTTY THE PUP (Becomes Super Pup #4, see Television Puppet Show)
No. 2, Oct-Nov, 1953 - No. 3, Dec-Jan, 1953-54 (Also see Funny Tunes)
Avon Periodicals/Realistic Comics

2,3	4.00	12.00	24.00
nn (1953, Realistic-r)	2.80	7.00	14.00

SPUNKY (...Junior Cowboy)(...Comics #2 on)
April, 1949 - No. 7, Nov, 1951
Standard Comics

1,2-Text illos by Frazetta	8.00	24.00	48.00
3-7	4.00	11.00	22.00

SPUNKY THE SMILING SPOOK
Aug, 1957 - No. 4, May, 1958
Ajax/Farrell (World Famous Comics/Four Star Comic Corp.)

1-Reprints from Frisky Fables	7.00	21.00	42.00
2-4	4.25	13.00	26.00

SPY AND COUNTERSPY (Becomes Spy Hunters #3 on)
Aug-Sept, 1949 - No. 2, Oct-Nov, 1949 (52 pgs.)
American Comics Group

1-Origin, 1st app. Jonathan Kent, Counterspy	18.00	56.00	130.00
2	12.00	36.00	85.00

SPY CASES (Formerly The Kellys)

No. 26, Sept, 1950 - No. 19, Oct, 1953
Marvel/Atlas Comics (Hercules Publ.)

26 (#1)	17.00	51.00	120.
27(#2),28(#3, 2/51): 27-Everett-a; bondage-c	10.00	30.00	70.
4(4/51) - 7,9,10	9.15	27.00	55.
8-A-Bomb-c/story	10.00	30.00	65.
11-19: 10-14-War format	7.50	22.50	45.

NOTE: *Sol Brodsky* c-1-5, 8, 9, 11-14, 17, 18. *Maneely* a-8; c-7, 10. *Tuska* a-7.

SPY FIGHTERS
March, 1951 - No. 15, July, 1953 (Cases from official records)
Marvel/Atlas Comics (CSI)

1-Clark Mason begins; Tuska-a; Brodsky-c	19.00	56.00	130.
2-Tuska-a	10.00	30.00	65.
3-13: 3-5-Brodsky-c. 7-Heath-c	9.15	27.00	55.
14,15-Pakula-a(3), Ed Win-a. 15-Brodsky-c	10.00	30.00	60.

SPY-HUNTERS (Formerly Spy & Counterspy)
No. 3, Dec-Jan, 1949-50 - No. 24, June-July, 1953 (#3-14: 52 pgs.)
American Comics Group

3-Jonathan Kent continues, ends #10	19.00	56.00	130.
4-10: 4,8,10-Starr-a	11.00	33.00	75.
11-15,17-22,24: 18-War-c begin. 21-War-c/stories begin			
	9.15	27.00	55.
16-Williamson-a (9 pgs.)	13.00	39.00	90.
23-Graphic torture, injury to eye panel	17.00	51.00	120.

NOTE: *Drucker* a-12. *Whitney* a-many issues; c-7, 8, 10-12, 15, 16.

SPYMAN (Top Secret Adventures on cover)
Sept, 1966 - No. 3, Feb, 1967 (12¢ issues)
Harvey Publications (Illustrated Humor)

1-Origin and 1st app. of Spyman. Steranko-a(p)-1st pro work; 1 pg. Neal			
Adams ad; Tuska-c/a; Crandall-a(i)	4.50	14.00	35
2,3: Simon-c. 2-Steranko-a(p)	3.40	10.00	24

SPY SMASHER (See Mighty Midget, Whiz & Xmas Comics) (Also see Crime Smasher)
Fall, 1941 - No. 11, Feb, 1943
Fawcett Publications

1-Spy Smasher begins; silver metallic-c	288.00	862.00	2500
2-Raboy-c	137.00	412.00	1100
3,4: 3-Bondage-c	96.00	290.00	775
5-7: Raboy-a; 6-Raboy-c/a. 7-Part photo-c (movie).			
	87.00	262.00	700
8,11	71.00	215.00	575
9-Hitler, Tojo, Mussolini-c.	78.00	234.00	625
10-Hitler-c	75.00	225.00	600
Well Known Comics (1944, 12 pgs., 8-1/2x10-1/2"), paper-c, glued binding,			
printed in green; Bestmaid/Samuel Lowe giveaway			
	15.00	45.00	105

SPY THRILLERS (Police Badge No. 479 #5)
Nov, 1954 - No. 4, May, 1955
Atlas Comics (PrPI)

1-Brodsky c-1,2	16.00	47.00	110
2-Last precode (1/55)	10.00	30.00	60
3,4	8.35	25.00	50

SQUADRON SUPREME
Aug, 1985 - No. 12, Aug, 1986 (Maxi-series)
Marvel Comics Group

1-Double size			1
2-12			1

SQUALOR
Dec, 1989 - Aug, 1990 ($2.75, limited series)
First Comics

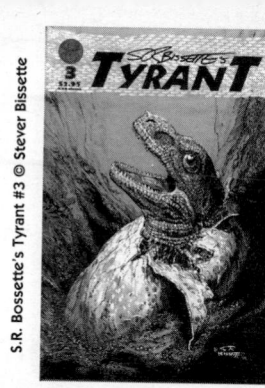

S.R. Bossette's Tyrant #3 © Steven Bissette

Stalkker #4 © DC

Stalkers #1 © MEG

	GD25	FN65	NM94

1-4: Sutton-a — | 1.10 | | 2.75

SQUEEKS (Also see Boy Comics)
Oct, 1953 - No. 5, June, 1954
Lev Gleason Publications

1-Funny animal; Biro-c; Crimebuster's pet monkey "Squeeks" begins

	6.70	20.00	40.00
2-Biro-c	4.00	11.00	22.00
3-5: 3-Biro-c	3.60	9.00	18.00

S.R. BISSETTE'S SPIDERBABY COMIX
Aug, 1996 - Present ($3.95, B&W, magazine size)
SpiderBaby Grafix

Preview-(8/96, $3.95)-Graphic violence & nudity; Laurel & Hardy app.
| | | | 4.00 |

S.R. BISSETTE'S TYRANT
Sept, 1994 - Present ($2.95, B&W)
SpiderBaby Grafix

1-4		1.20	3.00

STAINLESS STEEL RAT
Oct, 1985 - No. 6, Mar, 1986 (Limited series)
Eagle Comics

1 (52 pgs.; $2.25-c)			2.25
2-6 ($1.50)			1.50

STALKER
June-July, 1975 - No. 4, Dec-Jan, 1975-76
National Periodical Publications

1-Origin & 1st app; Ditko/Wood-c/a	1.00	2.00	5.00
2-4-Ditko/Wood-c/a		1.20	3.00

STALKERS
Apr, 1990 - No. 12, Mar, 1991 ($1.50)
Marvel Comics (Epic Comics)

1-12: 1-Chadwick-c			1.50

STAMP COMICS (Stamps... on-c; Thrilling Adventures In...#8)
Oct, 1951 - No. 7, Oct, 1952 (No. 1: 15¢)
Youthful Magazines/Stamp Comics, Inc.

1-('Stamps' on indicia No. 1-3,5,7)	29.00	86.00	200.00
2	16.00	47.00	110.00
3-6: 3,4-Kiefer, Wildey-a	14.00	43.00	100.00
7-Roy Krenkel (4 pgs.)	17.00	51.00	120.00

NOTE: Promotes stamp collecting; gives stories behind various commemorative stamps. No. 2, 10¢ printed over 15¢ c-price. Kiefer a-1-7. Kirkel a-1-6. Napoli a-2-7. Palais a-2-4, 7.

STANLEY & HIS MONSTER (Formerly The Fox & the Crow)
No. 109, Apr-May, 1968 - No. 112, Oct-Nov, 1968
National Periodical Publications

109-112	2.15	6.50	15.00

STANLEY & HIS MONSTER
Feb, 1993 - No. 4, May, 1993 ($1.50, limited series)
DC Comics

1-4			1.50

STAN SHAW'S BEAUTY & THE BEAST
Nov, 1993 ($4.95, one-shot)
Dark Horse Comics

1	1.00	2.00	5.00

STAR
June, 1995 - No. 4, Oct, 1995 ($2.50, limited series)
Image Comics (Highbrow Entertainment)

1-4		1.00	2.50

STARBLAST

	GD25	FN65	NM94

Jan, 1994 - No. 4, Apr, 1994 ($1.75, limited series)
Marvel Comics

1-($2.00, 52 pgs.)-Nova, Quasar, Black Bolt; painted-c	.80	2.00
2-4	.70	1.75

STAR BLAZERS
Apr, 1987 - No. 4, July, 1987 ($1.75, limited series)
Comico

1-4	.70	1.75

STAR BLAZERS
1989 ($1.95/$2.50, limited series)
Comico

1 ($1.95)- Steacy wraparound painted-c on all	.80	2.00
2-5 ($2.50)	1.00	2.50

STAR BLAZERS (The Magazine of Space Battleship Yamato)
No. 0, Aug, 1995 - No. 3, Dec, 1995 ($2.95)
Argo Press

0-3	1.20	3.00

STAR BRAND
Oct, 1986 - No. 19, May, 1989 (75¢/$1.25)
Marvel Comics (New Universe)

1-19: 14-begin $1.25-c. 16-19-Byrne story & art.		1.00
Annual 1 (10/87)		1.25

STARCHILD
1992 - Present ($2.25/$2.50, B&W)
Tailspin Press

1,2-(1992)	1.00	2.50
0-(4/93)-Illos by Chadwick, Eisner, Sim, M. Wagner; $2.50-c begins	1.10	2.75
3-12: 3-(7/93). 4-(11/93). 6-(2/94)	1.10	2.75

STAR COMICS
Feb, 1937 - V2#7 (No. 23), Aug, 1939 (#1-6: large size)
Ultem Publ. (Harry `A' Chesler)/Centaur Publications

V1#1-Dan Hastings (s/f) begins	118.00	356.00	950.00
2	59.00	178.00	475.00
3-6 (#6, 9/37): 4,5-Little Nemo-c/stories	55.00	165.00	440.00
7-9: 8-Severed head centerspread; Impy & Little Nemo by Winsor McCay Jr, Popeye app. by Bob Wood; Mickey Mouse & Popeye app. as toys in Santa's bag on-c; X-Mas-c	48.00	146.00	390.00
10 (1st Centaur; 3/38)-Impy by Winsor McCay Jr; Don Marlow by Guardineer begins	70.00	211.00	565.00
11-1st Jack Cole comic-a, 1 pg. (4/38)	48.00	146.00	390.00
12-15: 12-Riders of the Golden West begins; Little Nemo app. 15-Speed Silvers by Gustavson & The Last Pirate by Burgos begins	43.00	128.00	340.00
16 (12/38)-The Phantom Rider & his horse Thunder begins, ends V2#6	43.00	128.00	340.00
V2#1(#17, 2/39)-Phantom Rider-c (only non-funny-c)	43.00	128.00	340.00
2-7(#18-23): 2-Diana Deane by Tarpe Mills app. 3-Drama of Hollywood by Mills begins. 7-Jungle Queen app.	40.00	120.00	310.00

NOTE: Biro c-6, 9, 10. Burgos a-15, 16, V2#1-7. Ken Ernst a-10, 12, 14. Filchock c-15, 18, 22. Gill Fox c-14, 19. Guardineer a-6, 8-14. Gustavson a-13-16, V2#1-7. Winsor McCay c-4, 5. Tarpe Mills a-15, V2#1-7. Schwab c-20, 23. Bob Wood a-10, 12, 13; c-7, 8.

STAR COMICS MAGAZINE
Dec, 1986 - No. 13, 1988 ($1.50, digest-size)
Marvel Comics (Star Comics)

1-13		1.50

S.T.A.R. CORPS
Nov, 1993 - No. 6, Apr, 1994 ($1.50, limited series)
DC Comics

Starfire #3 © DC

Starman #7 © DC

Starman #4 © DC

	GD25	FN65	NM94

	GD25	FN65	NM94

1-6: 1,2-Austin-c(i). 1-Superman app.   1.50

STAR FEATURE COMICS
1963
I. W. Enterprises

Reprint #9-Stunt-Man Stetson-r/Feat. Comics #141   1.00   2.50   5.00

STARFIRE (See New Teen Titans & Teen Titans #18)
Aug-Sept, 1976 - No. 8, Oct-Nov, 1977
National Periodical Publications/DC Comics

1-Origin (CCA stamp fell off cover art; so it was approved by code)
   .75   1.80
2-8   1.30

STARGATE (Movie)
July, 1996 - No. 4, Oct, 1996 ($2.95, limited series)
Entity Comics

1-4: Based on film   3.00
1-4-($3.50): Special Edition foil-c   3.50

STAR HUNTERS (See DC Super Stars #16)
Oct-Nov, 1977 - No. 7, Oct-Nov, 1978
National Periodical Publications/DC Comics

1-7: 1-Newton-a(p). 7-Giant   1.10
NOTE: **Buckler** a-4-7p; c-1-7p. **Layton** a-1-5i; c-1-6i. **Nasser** a-3p. **Sutton** a-6i.

STARJAMMERS (See X-Men Spotlight on Starjammers)

STARJAMMERS (Also see Uncanny X-Men)
Oct, 1995 - No. 4, Jan, 1996 ($2.95, limited series)
Marvel Comics

1-4: Foil-c; Ellis scripts   1.20   3.00

STARK TERROR
Dec, 1970 - No. 5, Aug, 1971 (B&W, magazine, 52 pgs.)
Stanley Publications

1-Bondage, torture-c   2.60   7.50   18.00
2-4 (Gillmor/Aragon-r)   1.65   4.20   10.00
5 (ACG-r)   1.30   3.25   8.00

STARLET O'HARA IN HOLLYWOOD (Teen-age) (Also see Cookie)
Dec, 1948 - No. 4, Sept, 1949
Standard Comics

1-Owen Fitzgerald-a in all   16.00   47.00   110.00
2   11.00   33.00   75.00
3,4   10.00   30.00   65.00

STAR-LORD THE SPECIAL EDITION (Also see Marvel Comics Super
Special #10, Marvel Premiere & Preview & Marvel Spotlight V2#6,7)
Feb, 1982 (one-shot, direct sales) (1st Baxter paper comic)
Marvel Comics Group

1-Byrne/Austin-a; Austin-c; 8 pgs. of new-a by Golden (p); Dr. Who story by
Dave Gibbons; 1st deluxe format comic   1.00   2.00   5.00

STARLORD MEGAZINE
Nov, 1996 ($2.95, one-shot)
Marvel Comics

1-Reprints w/preview of new series   3.00

STARMAN (1st Series) (Also see Justice League & War of the Gods)
Oct, 1988 - No. 45, Apr, 1992 ($1.00)
DC Comics

1-25,27-45: 1-Origin. 4-Intro The Power Elite. 9,10,34-Batman app.
14-Superman app. 17-Power Girl app. 27-Starman (David Knight) app.
28-Starman disguised as Superman; leads into Superman #50. 38-
War of the Gods x-over. 42-Lobo cameo.42-45-Eclipso-c/stories (#43,44
with Lobo)   .80   2.00
26-1st app. David Knight (G.A.Starman's son).   1.20   3.00

STARMAN (2nd Series) (Also see The Golden Age, Showcase 95 #12,
Showcase 96 #4,5)
No. 0, Oct, 1994 - Present ($1.95/$2.25)
DC Comics

0,1: 0-James Robinson scripts, Tony Harris-c/a(p) & Wade Von
Grawbadger-a(i) begins; Sins of the Father storyline begins, ends #3; 1st
app. new Starman (Jack Knight); reintro of the G.A. Mist & G.A. Shade;
1st app. Nash; David Knight dies   1.20   3.00   7
2-8: 2-Reintro/2nd
app "Blue" Starman (1st app. in 1st Issue Special #12); Will Payton
app. (both cameos). 5-David Knight app. 6-The Shade "Times Past" story;
Teddy Kristiansen-a. 7-The Black Pirate cameo   1.20   3.
9-33: 9-Begin $2.25-c. 10-1st app. new Mist.(Nash) 11-JSA "Times Past" sto
Matt Smith-a. 12-Sins of the Child storyline begins, ends #16. 17-The Blac
Pirate app. 18-G.A. Starman "Times Past" story; John Watkiss-a. 19-Davi
Knight app. 20-23-G.A. Sandman app. 24-26-Demon Quest; all 3 covers
make-up triptych   .90   2.
Annual 1(1996, $3.50)-Legends of the Dead Earth story; Prince Gavyn & G.A.
Starman stories; J.H. Williams III, Bret Blevins, Craig Hamilton-c/a(p)
   3
Sins of the Father-($12.95, trade paperback)-r/#0-5   13

STARMASTERS
Mar, 1984 ($1.50, one-shot)
Americomics

1-Origin The Women of W.O.S.P. & Breed   1.

STAR PRESENTATION, A (Formerly My Secret Romance #1,2;
Spectacular Stories #4 on) (Also see This Is Suspense)
No. 3, May, 1950
Fox Features Syndicate (Hero Books)

3-Dr. Jekyll & Mr. Hyde by Wood & Harrison (reprinted in Startling Terror Tal
#10); "The Repulsing Dwarf" by Wood; Wood-c   44.00   132.00   350.

STAR QUEST COMIX (Warren Presents... on cover)
Oct, 1978
Warren Publications

1-Corben, Maroto, Neary-a   1.

STAR RAIDERS (See DC Graphic Novel #1)

STAR RANGER (Cowboy Comics #13 on)
Feb, 1937 - No. 12, May, 1938 (Large size: No. 1-6)
Ultem Publ./Centaur Publications

1-(1st Western comic)-Ace & Deuce, Air Plunder; Creig Flessel-a
   125.00   375.00   1000.
2   58.00   174.00   465.
3-6   50.00   150.00   400.
7-9: 8-Christmas-c   40.00   120.00   325.
V2#10 (1st Centaur; 3/38)   70.00   211.00   565.
11,12   53.00   159.00   425.
NOTE: **J. Cole** a-10, 12; c-12. **Ken Ernst** a-11. **Gill Fox** a-8(illo), 9, 10. **Guardineer** a-1, 3, 6,
8(illus), 9, 10, 12. **Gustavson** a-8-10, 12. **Fred Schwab** c-2-11. **Bob Wood** a-8-10.

STAR RANGER FUNNIES (Formerly Cowboy Comics)
V1#15, Oct, 1938 - V2#5, Oct, 1939
Centaur Publications

V1#15-Eisner, Gustavson-a   80.00   241.00   645.
V2#1 (1/39)   58.00   174.00   465.
2-5: 2-Night Hawk by Gustavson. 4-Kit Carson app.
   50.00   150.00   400.
NOTE: **Jack Cole** a-V2#1, 3; c-V2#1. **Filchock** c-V2#2, 3. **Guardineer** a-V2#3. **Gustavson** a
V2#2. **Pinajian** c/a-V2#5.

STAR REACH CLASSICS
Mar, 1984 - No. 6, Aug, 1984 ($1.50, Baxter paper)
Eclipse Comics

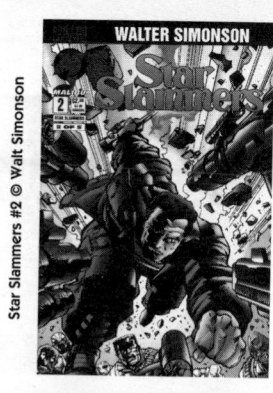
Star Slammers #2 © Walt Simonson

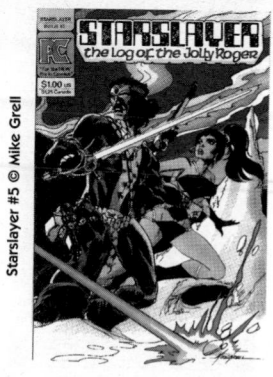
Starslayer #5 © Mike Grell

Star Spangled Cokmics #50 © DC

	GD25	FN65	NM94
1-6: Neal Adams-r/Star Reach #1			1.50

NOTE: *Dave Sim* a-1. *Starlin* a-1.

STARR FLAGG, UNDERCOVER GIRL (See Undercover...)

STARRIORS
Aug, 1984 - Feb, 1985 (Limited series) (Based on Tomy toys)
Marvel Comics

1-4			1.00

STARS AND STRIPES COMICS
No. 2, May, 1941 - No. 6, Dec, 1941
Centaur Publications

	GD25	FN65	NM94
2(#1)-The Shark, The Iron Skull, A-Man, The Amazing Man, Mighty Man, Minimidget begin; The Voice & Dash Dartwell, the Human Meteor, Reef Kinkaid app.; Gustavson Flag-c	193.00	581.00	1550.00
3-Origin Dr. Synthe; The Black Panther app.	115.00	346.00	925.00
4-Origin/1st app. The Stars and Stripes; injury to eye-c	103.00	309.00	825.00
5(#5 on cover & inside)	71.00	215.00	575.00
5(#6)-(#5 on cover, #6 on inside)	71.00	215.00	575.00

NOTE: *Gustavson* c/a-3. *Myron Strauss* c-4, 5(#5), 5(#6).

STAR SEED (Formerly Powers That Be)
No. 7, 1996 - Present ($2.95)
Broadway Comics

7-9			3.00

STAR SLAMMERS (See Marvel Graphic Novel #6)
May, 1994 - No. 4, Aug, 1994 ($2.50, unfinished limited series)
Malibu Comics (Bravura)

1-4: W. Simonson-a/stories; contain Bravura stamps		1.00	2.50

STAR SLAMMERS SPECIAL
June, 1996 ($2.95, one-shot)
Dark Horse Comics (Legend)

nn-Simonson-c/a/scripts; concludes Bravura limited series.

			3.00

STARSLAYER
Feb, 1982 - No. 6, Apr, 1983; No. 7, Aug, 1983 - No. 34, Nov, 1985
Pacific Comics/First Comics No. 7 on

1-Origin & 1st app.; excessive blood & gore; 1 pg. Rocketeer cameo which continues in #2		1.20	3.00
2-Origin/1st full app. the Rocketeer (4/82) by Dave Stevens (Chapter 1 of Rocketeer saga; see Pacific Presents #1,2)	1.65	4.20	10.00
3-Chapter 2 of Rocketeer saga by Stevens	1.20	3.00	7.00
4		.80	2.00
5-2nd app. Groo the Wanderer by Aragones	1.30	3.25	8.00
6,7: 7-Grell-a ends		.80	2.00
8-34: 10:1st app. Grimjack (11/83, ends #17. 18-Starslayer meets Grimjack. 20-The Black Flame begins (9/84, 1st app.), ends #33. 27-Book length Black Flame story			1.00

NOTE: *Grell* a-1-7; c-1-8. *Stevens* back c-2, 3. *Sutton* a-17p, 20-22p, 24-27p, 29-33p.

STARSLAYER (The Director's Cut)
June, 1994 - No. 8, Dec, 1995 ($2.50)
Acclaim Comics (Windjammer)

1-8: Mike Grell-c/a/scripts		1.00	2.50

STAR SPANGLED COMICS (Star Spangled War Stories #131 on)
Oct, 1941 - No. 130, July, 1952
National Periodical Publications

1-Origin/1st app. Tarantula; Captain X of the R.A.F., Star Spangled Kid (see Action #40), Armstrong of the Army begin; Robot-c	366.00	1100.00	3300.00
2	137.00	412.00	1100.00
3-5	90.00	271.00	725.00

	GD25	FN65	NM94
6-Last Armstrong/Army; Penniless Palmer begins	58.00	174.00	465.00

	GD25	FN65	VF82	NM94
7-(4/42)-Origin/1st app. The Guardian by S&K, & Robotman (by Paul Cassidy & created by Siegel);The Newsboy Legion (1st app.), Robotman & TNT begin; last Captain X	555.00	1667.00	3333.00	5500.00

(Estimated up to 100 total copies exist, 5 in NM/Mint)

	GD25	FN65	NM94
8-Origin TNT & Dan the Dyna-Mite	193.00	581.00	1550.00
9,10	162.00	487.00	1300.00
11-17	118.00	356.00	950.00
18-Origin Star Spangled Kid	150.00	450.00	1200.00
19-Last Tarantula	116.00	350.00	935.00
20-Liberty Belle begins (5/43)	116.00	350.00	935.00
21-29-Last S&K issue; 23-Last TNT. 25-Robotman by Jimmy Thompson begins. 29-Intro Robbie the Robotdog	96.00	290.00	775.00
30-40: 31-S&K-c	48.00	144.00	385.00
41-50: 41,49,-Kirby-c. 50-1st S.A. issue	44.00	132.00	350.00
51-64: Last Newsboy Legion & The Guardian; last Liberty Belle? 51-Kirby-c. 53 by S&K	44.00	132.00	350.00
65-Robin begins with c/app. (2/47); Batman cameo in 1 panel; Robin-c begins, end #95	125.00	375.00	1000.00
66-Batman cameo in Robin story	81.00	243.00	650.00
67,68,70-80: 72-Burnley Robin-c	65.00	195.00	525.00
69-Origin/1st app. Tomahawk by F. Ray (6/47)	100.00	300.00	800.00
81-Origin Merry, Girl of 1000 Gimmicks in Star Spangled Kid story	49.00	146.00	390.00
82,85: 82-Last Robotman?	49.00	146.00	390.00
83-Tomahawk enters the lost valley, a land of dinosaurs; Capt. Compass begins, ends #130	49.00	146.00	390.00
84,87: 87-Batman cameo in Robin	75.00	225.00	600.00
86-Batman cameo in Robin story; last Star Spangled Kid	54.00	163.00	435.00
88(1/49)-94: Batman-c/stories in all. 91-Federal Men begin, end #93. 94-Manhunters Around the World begin, end #121	58.00	175.00	465.00
95-Batman story; last Robin-c	53.00	160.00	425.00
96,98-Batman cameo in Robin stories. 96-1st Tomahawk-c (also #97-121)	39.00	116.00	270.00
97,99	32.00	96.00	225.00
100 (1/50)-Pre-Bat-Hound tryout in Robin story (pre-dates Batman #92).	40.00	120.00	280.00
101-109,118,119,121: 121-Last Tomahawk-c	30.00	90.00	210.00
110,111,120-Batman cameo in Robin stories. 120-Last 52 pg. issue			
112-Batman & Robin story	31.00	94.00	220.00
113-Frazetta-a (10 pgs.)	34.00	101.00	235.00
114-Retells Robin's origin (3/51); Batman & Robin story	40.00	120.00	300.00
115,117-Batman app. in Robin stories	40.00	120.00	325.00
116-Flag-c	32.00	96.00	225.00
122-(11/51)-Ghost Breaker-c/stories begin (origin/1st app.), ends #130 (Ghost Breaker covers #122-130)	31.00	94.00	220.00
123-126,128,129	34.00	101.00	235.00
127-Batman cameo	23.00	69.00	160.00
130-Batman cameo in Robin story	25.00	75.00	175.00
	26.00	79.00	185.00

NOTE: Most all issues after #29 signed by Simon & Kirby are not by them. *Bill Ely* c-122-130. *Mortimer* c-65-74(most), 76-95(most). *Fred Ray* c-96-106, 109, 110, 112, 113, 115-120. *S&K* c-7-31, 33, 34, 36, 37, 39, 40, 48, 49, 50-54, 56-58. *Hal Sherman* c-1-6. *Dick Sprang* c-75.

STAR SPANGLED KID (See Action #40, Leading Comics & Star Spangled Comics)

STAR SPANGLED WAR STORIES (Formerly Star Spangled Comics #1-130; Becomes The Unknown Soldier #205 on) (See Showcase)
No. 131, 8/52 - No. 133, 10/52; No. 3, 11/52 - No. 204, 2-3/77
National Periodical Publications

	GD25	FN65	NM94
131(#1)	90.00	271.00	725.00
132	65.00	195.00	520.00

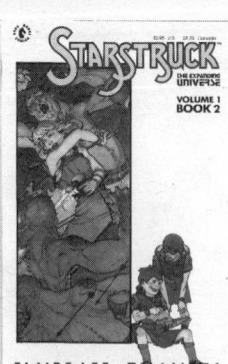

Starstruck #2 © Elaine Lee & M.W. Kaluta

Startling Comics #49 © NEDOR

Startling Terror Tales #11 © STAR

	GD25	FN65	NM94
133-Used in **POP**, pg. 94	58.00	173.00	460.00
3-6: 4-Devil Dog Dugan app. 6-Evans-a	34.00	103.00	240.00
7-10	26.00	79.00	185.00
11-20	24.00	71.00	165.00
21-30: 30-Last precode (2/55)	21.00	62.00	140.00
31-33,35-40	13.50	41.00	95.00
34-Krigstein-a	14.00	43.00	100.00
41-50: 45-1st DC grey tone-c (5/56)	12.00	36.00	85.00
51-83: 67-Easy Co. story without Sgt. Rock	10.00	30.00	65.00
84-Origin Mlle. Marie	19.00	58.00	135.00
85-89-Mlle. Marie in all	10.00	30.00	70.00
90-1st dinosaur issue-c/story (4-5/60)	41.00	124.00	340.00
91,93-No dinosaur stories	7.00	21.50	55.00
92,95-99: All dinosaur-c/s.	17.00	49.00	115.00
94 (12/60)- "Ghost Ace" story; Baron Von Richter as The Enemy Ace (pre-dates Our Army... #151)	18.00	54.00	125.00
100-Dinosaur-c/story.	19.00	58.00	135.00
101-115: All dinosaur issues	11.50	34.00	80.00
116-125,127-133,135-137-Last dinosaur story; Heath Birdman-#129,131	10.00	30.00	70.00
126-No dinosaur story	6.50	19.50	45.00
134-Dinosaur story; Neal Adams-a	11.50	34.00	80.00
138-New Enemy Ace-c/stories begin by Joe Kubert (4-5/68), end #150 (also see Our Army at War #151 and Showcase #57)	12.00	36.00	85.00
139-Origin Enemy Ace (7/68)	9.50	28.00	75.00
140-143,145: 145-Last 12¢ issue (6-7/69)	7.00	21.00	50.00
144-Neal Adams/Kubert-a	7.50	22.00	55.00
146-Enemy Ace-c only	4.30	13.00	33.00
147,148-New Enemy Ace stories	5.50	16.50	40.00
149,150-Last new Enemy Ace by Kubert. Viking Prince by Kubert	4.50	14.00	35.00
151-1st Unknown Soldier (6-7/70); Enemy Ace-r begin (from Our Army at War, Showcase & SSWS); end #161	11.00	32.00	85.00
152,153,155-Enemy Ace reprints	2.15	6.50	15.00
154-Origin Unknown Soldier	7.50	22.50	60.00
156-1st Battle Album; Unknown Soldier story; Kubert-c/a	2.60	7.50	18.00
157-Sgt. Rock x-over in Unknown Soldier story.	1.65	4.20	10.00
158-161: 160-Unknown Soldier story; Kubert-c/a. 161-Last Enemy Ace-r	1.65	4.20	10.00
162-204: 181-183-Enemy Ace vs. Balloon Buster serial app; Frank Thorne-a. 200-Enemy Ace back-up.	1.00	2.00	5.00

NOTE: **Chaykin** a-167. **Drucker** a-59, 61, 64, 66, 67, 73-84. **Estrada** a-149. **John Giunta** a-72. **Glanzman** a-167, 171, 172, 174. **Heath** a-122, 132, 133; c-67, 122, 132-134. **Kaluta** a-197; c-167. **G. Kane** a-169. **Kubert** a-6-163(most later issues), 200. **Maurer** a-160, 165. **Severin** a-65, 162. **S&K** c-7-31, 33, 34, 37, 40. **Simonson** a-170, 172, 174, 180. **Sutton** a-168. **Thorne** a-183. **Toth** a-164. **Wildey** a-161. Suicide Squad in 110, 116-118, 120, 121, 127.

STARSTREAM (Adventures in Science Fiction)(See Questar illustrated)
1976 (79¢, 68 pgs., cardboard-c)
Whitman/Western Publishing Co.

1-Bolle-a			1.60
2-4-McWilliams & Bolle-a			1.20

STARSTRUCK
Feb, 1985 - No. 6, Feb, 1986 ($1.50, mature)
Marvel Comics (Epic Comics)

1-6: Kaluta-a.		1.20	3.00

STARSTRUCK
Aug, 1990 - No. 4, Nov?, 1990 ($2.95, B&W, limited series, 52pgs.)
Dark Horse Comics

1-3:Kaluta-c/r(epic series plus new-c/a in all		1.20	3.00
4 (68, pgs.)-contains 2 trading cards		1.20	3.00

STAR STUDDED

1945 (25¢, 132 pgs.); 1945 (196 pgs.)
Cambridge House/Superior Publishers

	GD25	FN65	NM94
nn-Captain Combat by Giunta, Ghost Woman, Commandette, & Red Rogue app.; Infantino-a	25.00	75.00	175.
nn-The Cadet, Edison Bell, Hoot Gibson, Jungle Lil (196 pgs.); copies vary; Blue Beetle in some	20.00	60.00	140.

STAR TEAM
1977 (6-1/2x5", 20 pgs.)
Marvel Comics Group (Ideal Toy Giveaway)

nn			1.

STARTLING COMICS
June, 1940 - No. 53, May, 1948
Better Publications (Nedor)

1-Origin Captain Future-Man Of Tomorrow, Mystico (By Eisner/Fine), The Wonder Man; The Masked Rider & his horse Pinto begins; Masked Rider formerly in pulps; drug use story	175.00	525.00	1400.
2 -Don Davis, Espionage Ace begins	71.00	215.00	575.
3	58.00	174.00	465.
4	44.00	132.00	350.
5-9	40.00	120.00	290.
10-The Fighting Yank begins (9/41, origin/1st app.)	275.00	825.00	2200.
11-2nd app. Fighting Yank	85.00	255.00	680.
12-Hitler, Hirohito, Mussolini-c	59.00	178.00	475.
13-15	44.00	132.00	350.
16-Origin The Four Comrades; not in #32,35	50.00	150.00	400.
17-Last Masked Rider & Mystico	39.00	118.00	275.
18-Pyroman begins (12/42, origin)(also see America's Best Comics #3 for 1st app., 11/42)	81.00	243.00	650.
19	40.00	120.00	285.
20-The Oracle begins (3/43); not in issues 26,28,33,34	40.00	120.00	285.
21-Origin The Ape, Oracle's enemy	40.00	120.00	315.
22-33	40.00	120.00	285.
34-Origin The Scarab & only app.	40.00	120.00	285.
35-Hypodermic syringe attacks Fighting Yank in drug story	40.00	120.00	285.
36-43: 36-Last Four Comrades. 38-Bondage/torture-c. 40-Last Capt. Future & Oracle. 41-Front Page Peggy begins; A-Bomb-c. 43-Last Pyroman	36.00	107.00	250.
44-Lance Lewis, Space Detective begins; Ingels-c; sci/fi-c begin	47.00	142.00	380.
45-Tygra begins (intro/origin, 5/47); Ingels-c/a (splash pg. & inside f/c B&W ad)	47.00	142.00	380.
46-Ingels-c/a	47.00	142.00	380.
47,48,50-53: 50,51-Sea-Eagle app.	44.00	132.00	350.
49-Classic Schomburg Robot-c; last Fighting Yank	250.00	750.00	2000.

NOTE: **Ingels** a-44, 45; c-44, 45, 46(wash). **Schomburg (Xela)** c-21-43; 47-53 (airbrush). **Tus** c-45? Bondage c-16, 21, 37, 46-49. Captain Future c-1-9, 13, 14. Fighting Yank c-10-12, 15-1 21, 22, 24, 26, 28, 30, 32, 34, 36, 38, 40, 42. Pyroman c-18-20, 23, 25, 27, 29, 31, 33, 35, 37, 39, 41, 43.

STARTLING TERROR TALES
No. 10, May, 1952 - No. 14, Feb, 1953; No. 4, Apr, 1953 - No. 11, 1954
Star Publications

10-(1st Series)-Wood/Harrison-a (r/A Star Presentation #3) Disbrow/Cole-c; becomes 4 different titles after #10; becomes Confessions of Love #11 on, The Horrors #11, Terrifying Tales #11 on, Terrors of the Jungle #11 on & continues w/Startling Terror #11	51.00	155.00	415.
11-(#1a, 8/52)-L. B. Cole Spider-c; r-Fox's "A Feature Presentation" #5	38.00	114.00	265.
12(#1b),14(#3)	15.00	45.00	105.

514

Star Trek #17 © Paramount

Star Trek Annual #6 © Paramount

Star Trek: Deep Space Nine #12 © Paramount

	GD25	FN65	NM94
13(#2)-Jo-Jo-r; Disbrow-a	17.00	49.00	115.00
4-7,9,11(1953-54) (2nd Series): 11-New logo	13.50	41.00	95.00
8-Spanking scene-r from inside front-c of All Famous Crime Stories (Fox Giant) (1949)	13.50	41.00	95.00
10-Disbrow-a	15.00	45.00	105.00

NOTE: *L. B. Cole* covers-all issues. *Palais*-a-V2#8r, V2#11r.

STAR TREK (TV) (See Dan Curtis Giveaways, Dynabrite Comics & Power Record Comics)
7/67; No. 2, 6/68; No. 3, 12/68; No. 4, 6/69 - No. 61, 3/79
Gold Key

1-Photo-c begin, end #9	60.00	182.00	450.00
2	36.00	107.00	275.00
3-5	25.00	75.00	185.00
6-9	20.00	60.00	150.00
10-20	11.00	33.00	75.00
21-30	8.00	23.50	55.00
31-40	5.70	17.00	40.00
41-61: 52-Drug propaganda story	3.60	11.00	25.00
...the Enterprise Logs nn (8/76)-Golden Press, ($1.95, 224 pgs.)-r/#1-8 plus 7 pgs. by McWilliams (#11185)-Photo-c	1.70	5.00	12.00
...the Enterprise Logs Vol. 2 ('76)-r/#9-17 (#11187)-Photo-c	1.70	5.00	12.00
...the Enterprise Logs Vol. 3 ('77)-r/#18-26 (#11188); McWilliams-a (4 pgs.)- Photo-c	1.20	3.00	7.00
Star Trek Vol. 4 (Winter '77)-Reprints #27,28,30-34,36,38 (#11189) plus 3 pgs. new art	1.20	3.00	7.00

NOTE: *McWilliams*-a-38, 40-44, 46-61. #29 reprints #1; #35 reprints #4; #37 reprints #5; #45 reprints #7. The tabloids all have photo covers and blank inside covers. Painted covers #10-44, 46-59.

STAR TREK
April, 1980 - No. 18, Feb, 1982
Marvel Comics Group

1: 1-3-r/Marvel Super Special; movie adapt.	1.00	2.50	5.50
2-18: 5-Miller-a		1.60	4.00

NOTE: *Austin* c-18i. *Buscema* a-13. *Gil Kane* a-15. *Nasser* c/a-7. *Simonson* c-17.

STAR TREK (Also see Who's Who In Star Trek)
Feb, 1984 - No. 56, Nov, 1988 (75¢, Mando paper)
DC Comics

1-Sutton-a(p) begins	1.70	5.00	12.00
2-5	1.30	3.25	8.00
6-10: 7-Origin Saavik	1.00	2.60	6.00
11-20: 19-Walter Koenig story		1.60	4.00
21-32		1.20	3.00
33-($1.25, 52 pgs.)-20th anniversary issue	1.80	4.50	
34-49: 37-Painted-c. 49-Begin $1.00-c	.90	2.25	
50-($1.50, 52 pgs.)	.80	2.00	
51-56	.70	1.75	
Annual 1-3: 1(1985). 2(1986). 3(1988, $1.50)	1.40	3.50	

NOTE: *Morrow* a-28, 35, 36, 56. *Orlando* c-8i. *Perez* c-1-3. *Spiegle* a-19. *Starlin* c-24, 25. *Sutton* a-1-6p, 8-18p, 20-27p, 29p, 31-34p, 39-52p, 55p; c-4-6p, 8-22p, 46p.

STAR TREK
Oct, 1989 - No. 80, Jan, 1996 ($1.50/$1.75/$1.95/$2.50)
DC Comics

1-Capt. Kirk and crew	1.30	3.25	8.00
2,3		1.60	4.00
4-23,25-30: 10-12-The Trial of James T. Kirk. 21-Begin $1.75-c		1.20	3.00
24-($2.95, 68 pgs.)-40 pg. epic w/pin-ups	1.40	3.50	
31-49,51-60	.80	2.00	
50-($3.50, 68 pgs.)-Painted-c	1.60	4.00	
61-70: 61-Begin $1.95-c	.90	2.25	
71-74, 76-80: 71-begin $2.50-c	1.00	2.50	
75 ($3.95)	1.60	4.00	

	GD25	FN65	NM94
Annual 1,2('90, '91, $2.95, 68 pgs.): 1-Morrow-a	1.40		3.50
Annual 3,4 ('92,93, $3.50, 68 pgs.): 3-Painted-c	1.60		4.00
Annual 5 (1994, $3.95)	1.60		4.00
Annual 6 (1995, $3.95)	1.60		4.00
Special 1 (1994, $3.50, 68 pgs.)-Sutton-a.	1.40		3.50
Special 2 (1995, $3.50, 68 pgs.)	1.40		3.50
Special 3 (1995, $3.95)			4.00
...: The Ashes of Eden (1995, $14.95, 100 pgs.)-Shatner story	2.15	6.50	15.00
...Generations (1994, $3.95, 68 pgs.)-Movie adaptation	1.60		4.00
...Generations (1994, $5.95, 68 pgs.)-Squarebound	1.00	2.60	6.00

STAR TREK: DEEP SPACE NINE (TV)
Aug, 1993 - No. 32, Jan, 1996 ($2.50)
Malibu Comics

1-Direct Sale Edition w/line drawn-c	1.20		3.00
1-Newsstand Edition with photo-c	1.20		3.00
0 (1/95, $2.95)-Terok Nor	1.20		3.00
2-32: 2-Polybagged w/trading card. 9-4 pg. prelude to Hearts & Minds	1.00		2.50
Annual 1 (1/95, $3.95, 68 pgs.)	1.00		2.50
Special 1 (1995, $3.50)	1.60		4.00
Ultimate Annual 1 (12/95, $5.95)	1.40		3.50
			6.00
...:Lightstorm (12/94, $3.50)	1.40		3.50

STAR TREK DEEP SPACE NINE (TV)
Nov, 1996 - Present ($1.95)
Marvel Comics (Paramount Comics)

1-6			2.00

STAR TREK DEEP SPACE NINE-THE CELEBRITY SERIES; BLOOD AND HONOR
May, 1995 ($2.95)
Malibu Comics

1-Mark Lenard script	1.20		3.00
1-Aron Eisenberg script			3.00

STAR TREK: DEEP SPACE NINE HEARTS AND MINDS
June, 1994 - No. 4, Sept, 1994 ($2.50, limited series)
Malibu Comics

1-4		1.00	2.50
1-Holographic-c	1.00	2.00	5.00

STAR TREK: DEEP SPACE NINE, THE MAQUIS
Feb, 1995 - No. 3, Apr, 1995 ($2.50, limited series)
Malibu Comics

1-Newsstand-c		1.00	2.50
1-Photo-c		1.00	2.50
2,3		1.00	2.50

STAR TREK: DEEP SPACE NINE/THE NEXT GENERATION
Oct, 1994 - No. 2, Nov, 1994 ($2.50, limited series)
Malibu Comics

1,2: Parts 2 & 4 of "Prophet & Losses."	1.00		2.50

STAR TREK: DEEP SPACE NINE WORF SPECIAL
Dec, 1995 ($3.95, one-shot)
Marvel Comics

1-Includes pinups			4.00

STAR TREK MOVIE SPECIAL
1984 (June) - No. 2, 1987 ($1.50, 68 pgs); No. 1, 1989 ($2.00, 52 pgs.)
DC Comics

nn-(#1)-Adapts Star Trek III; Sutton-p (68 pgs.)	.70		1.75
2-Adapts Star Trek IV; Sutton-a; Chaykin-c. (68 pgs.)	.70		1.75
1 (1989)-Adapts Star Trek V; painted-c	.90		2.25

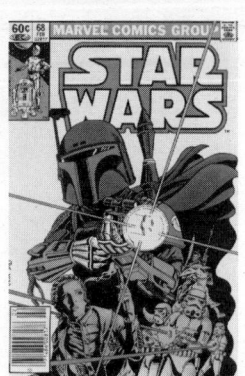

Star Trek: The Next Generation-Ill Wind #3 © Paramount

Star Trek: Voyager #3 © Paramount

Star Wars #68 © Lucasfilm

	GD25	FN65	NM94		GD25	FN65	NM94

STAR TREK VI: THE UNDISCOVERED COUNTRY (Movie)
1992
DC Comics

1-($2.95, regular edition, 68 pgs.)-Adaptation of film	1.20		3.00
nn-($5.95, prestige edition)-Has photos of movie not included in regular edition; painted-c by Palmer; photo back-c	1.00	2.50	6.00

STAR TREK - THE ASHES OF EDEN
1995 ($14.95, 100 pgs., one-shot)
DC Comics

nn-Shatner scripts			15.00

STAR TREK - THE MODALA IMPERATIVE
Late July, 1991 - No. 4, Late Sept, 1991 ($1.75, limited series)
DC Comics

1		1.00	2.50
2-4		.80	2.00

STAR TREK: THE NEXT GENERATION (TV)
Feb, 1988 - No. 6, July, 1988 (limited series)
DC Comics

1 ($1.50, 52 pgs.)-Sienkiewicz painted-c	1.85	5.50	13.00
2-6 ($1.00)	1.25	3.00	7.50

STAR TREK: THE NEXT GENERATION (TV)
Oct, 1989 -No. 80, 1995 ($1.50/$1.75/$1.95)
DC Comics

1-Capt. Picard and crew from TV show	1.65	4.20	10.00
2,3	1.30	3.25	8.00
4,5	1.00	2.50	5.50
6-10		1.60	4.00
11-23,25-30: 21-Begin $1.75-c	1.00	2.50	
24-($2.50, 52 pgs.)	1.20	3.00	
31-49,51-60	.80	2.00	
50-($3.50, 68 pgs.)-Painted-c	1.60	4.00	
61-70: 61-Begins $1.95-c	.90	2.25	
71-74,76-80: 71-begin $2.50-c	1.00	2.50	
75-($3.95, 50 pgs.)	1.60	4.00	
Annual 1 (1990, $2.95, 68 pgs.)	1.60	4.00	
Annual 2-4 (1991-93, $3.50, 68 pgs.)	1.80	4.50	
Annual 5 (1994, $3.95, 68 pgs.)	1.60	4.00	
Annual 6 (1995, $3.95)	1.60	4.00	
Special 1 (1993, $3.50, 68 pgs.)-Contains 3 stories	1.60	4.00	
Special 2 (Sum/94, $3.95, 68 pgs.)	1.60	4.00	
Special 3 ('95, $3.95)	1.60	4.00	
...-The Series Finale (1994, $3.95, 68 pgs.)	1.60	4.00	

STAR TREK: THE NEXT GENERATION/DEEP SPACE NINE (TV)
Dec, 1994 - No. 2, Jan, 1995 ($2.50, limited series)
DC Comics

1,2-Parts 1 & 3 of "Prophets & Losses"	1.00	2.50	

STAR TREK: THE NEXT GENERATION - ILL WIND
Nov, 1995 - Present ($2.50, limited series)
DC Comics

1-3		1.00	2.50

STAR TREK: THE NEXT GENERATION - THE MODALA IMPERATIVE
Early Sept, 1991 - No. 4, Late Oct, 1991 ($1.75, limited series)
DC Comics

1		1.00	2.50
2-4		.80	2.00

STAR TREK: THE NEXT GENERATION-SHADOWHEART
Dec, 1994 - No. 4, Mar, 1995 ($1.95, limited series)
DC Comics

1-4		.80	2.00

STAR TREK: VOYAGER
Nov, 1996 - Present ($1.95)
Marvel Comics (Paramount Comics)

1-6			2.0

STAR WARS (Movie) (See Classic..., Contemporary Motivators, Dark Horse Comics, The Droids, The Ewoks, Marvel Movie Showcase, Marvel Special Ed.)
July, 1977 - No. 107, Sept, 1986
Marvel Comics Group

1-(Regular 30¢ edition)-Price in square w/UPC code; #1-6 adapt first movie	7.50	22.50	60.0
1-(35¢-c; limited distribution - 1500 copies?)- Price in square w/UPC code (see note below)	50.00	150.00	450.0
2-6: 2-4-30¢ issues. 4-Battle with Darth Vader. 6-Dave Stevens-a(i).	3.40	10.00	24.0
2,5-35¢ with UPC code; not reprints	3.40	10.00	24.0
7-20	2.60	7.50	18.0
21-91, 93-99: 39-44-The Empire Strikes Back-r by Al Williamson in all. 81-Reintro Boba Fett. 98-Williamson-a.	2.15	6.50	15.
92,100-106: 92,100-($1.00, 52 pgs.).	2.85	8.50	20.
107	5.00	15.00	40.
1-9: Reprints; has "reprint" in upper lefthand corner of cover or on inside of price and number inside a diamond with no date or UPC on cover; 30¢ and 35¢ issues published	1.60		4.
Annual 1 (12/79, 52 pgs.)-Simonson-c	1.50	3.75	9.
Annual 2 (11/82, 52 pgs.), 3(12/83, 52 pgs.)	1.50	3.75	9.

NOTE: The rare 35¢ edition has the cover price in a square box, and the UPC box in the lower left hand corner has the UPC code lines running through it. **Austin** c-11-15i, 21i, 38; c-12-15i, 21i. **Byrne** c-13p. **Chaykin** a-1-10p; c-1. **Golden** c/a-38. **Miller** c-47p; pin-up-43. **Nebres** c/a-Annual 2i. **Portacio** a-107i. **Sienkiewicz** c-92i, 98. **Simonson** a-16p, 49p, 51-63p, 65p, 66p; c-16, 49-51, 52p, 53-62, Annual 1. **Steacy** painted a-105i, 106i; c-105. **Williamson** a-39-44p, 56, 98; c-39, 40, 41-44p. Painted c-81, 87, 92, 95, 98, 100, 105.

STAR WARS: BOBA FETT
Dec, 1995 - Present ($3.95) (Originally intended as a one-shot)
Dark Horse Comics

1-Kennedy-c/a			5.0
2			4.0

STAR WARS: DARK EMPIRE
Dec, 1991 - No. 6, Oct, 1992 ($2.95, limited series)
Dark Horse Comics

1-All have Dorman painted-c	2.15	6.50	15.
1-2nd printing	1.00	2.00	5.
2-Low print run	2.85	8.50	20.
2,3-2nd printings	1.00	2.00	5.
3	1.30	3.25	8.
4-6		1.60	4.
Gold Embossed Set (#1-6)-With gold embossed foil logo (price is for set)	14.00	43.00	100.
Platinum Embossed Set (#1-6)	25.00	75.00	175.
... (4/93, $16.95, TPB)	2.40	7.20	17.
Trade paperback (4/93, 16.95)	2.40	7.20	17.

STAR WARS: DARK EMPIRE II
Dec, 1994 - No. 6, May, 1995 ($2.95, limited series)
Dark Horse Comics

1-Dave Dorman painted-c		1.60	4.
2-6: Dorman-c in all.		1.20	3.
Platinum Embossed Set (#1-6)			35.
Trade paperback ($17.95)			18.

STARS WARS: DROIDS (See Dark Horse Comics #17-19)
Apr, 1994 - #6, Sept, 1994; V2#1, Apr, 1995 - V2#8, Dec, 1995 ($2.50, limited series)
Dark Horse Comics

1-($2.95)-Embossed-c		1.20	3.

Star War: Shadows Of The Empire #5 © Lucasfilm

Steel #35 © DC

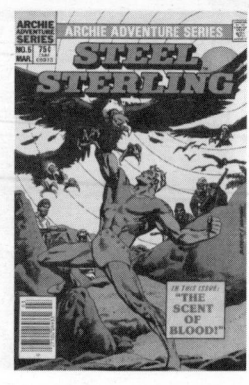

Steel Sterling #5 © AP

	GD25	FN65	NM94
Weath...			
1-3-Ind			
3-1st a			
0-($2.50			
9-(4/94,			
10-17: 10			
10-Alterna			
18-36,38-			
Wildsto			
1995 or			
22-($1.95)			
37-(7/96,			
Er Jack Ha			
#1-c/sw			
Special 1 (			
Se Special 2 (			
Su Sourcebool			
1 STORMWA			
2 Apr, 1989 -			
3 Eclipse Cor			
6-			
9-			
10 1-4			
11 STORMY (D			
19 No. 537, Fe			
Dell Publishi			
Four Color 5			
20, bottom 1			
STISTORY HOI			
961948, 1949;			
WGiven away			
w Whitman Pul			
upnn(1948)-Mi			
hn(1948)-Mi			
hn(1948)-Mir			
upnn(1949)-The			
TRhn(1949)-Da			
95300(1948)-D			
W. 1953 editi			
301(1948)-M			
W. 1951, 195			
02(1948)-B			
W. 103(1948)-Bo			
Sh04(1948)-Mi			
or06-15(1949)			
upe05-15(1949)			
upe948, 1949 H			
TORY OF E			
upei956 (16 pgs.			
upei ducational C			
upein-Reprint of F			
Ex948 (Giveaw			
RAemocratic Na			
ne, n-Gives biogr			
alibu			
-4,6			
#0;7-ETORY OF JE			
wra o. 851, Jan, 1			

	GD25	FN65	NM94
2-($2.25)	1.00		2.50
3-6	1.00		2.50
Special 1 (1/95, $2.50)			2.50
V2#1-8			2.50

STAR WARS: EMPIRE'S END
Oct, 1995 - No. 2, Nov, 1995 ($2.95, limited series)
Dark Horse Comics

1,2-Dorman-c	1.20		3.00

STAR WARS : HEIR TO THE EMPIRE
Oct, 1995 - No.6, Apr, 1996 ($2.95, limited series)
Dark Horse Comics

1-6: Adaptation of Zahn novel	1.20		3.00

STAR WARS: JABBA THE HUTT
Apr, 1995 ($2.50, one-shots)
Dark Horse Comics

nn	1.00		2.50
...The Betrayal			2.50
...The Dynasty Trap	1.00		2.50
...The Hunger of Princess Nampi	1.00		2.50

STAR WARS: RETURN OF THE JEDI (Movie)
Oct, 1983 - No. 4, Jan, 1984 (Limited series)
Marvel Comics Group

1-4-Williamson-p in all; r/Marvel Super Special #27	1.00	2.00	5.00
Oversized issue (1983, 2.95, 10-3/4x8-1/4", 68 pgs., cardboard-c)-r/#1-4		1.20	3.00

STAR WARS: RIVER OF CHAOS
June, 1995 - No. 4, Sept, 1995 (limited series)
Dark Horse Comics

1-4: Louise Simonson scripts	1.00		2.50

STAR WARS: SHADOWS OF THE EMPIRE
May, 1996 - No. 6, Oct, 1996 ($2.95, limited series)

1-6: Story details events between The Empire Strikes Back & Return of the Jedi; Russell-a(i).			3.00

STAR WARS: TALES FROM MOS EISLY
Mar, 1996 ($2.95, one-shot)
Dark Horse Comics

1-Bret Blevins-a.			3.00

STAR WARS: TALES OF THE JEDI (See Dark Horse Comics #7)
Oct, 1993 - No. 5, Feb, 1994 ($2.50, limited series)
Dark Horse Comics

1-5: All have Dave Dorman painted-c. 3-r/Dark Horse Comics #7-9 w/new coloring & some panels redrawn	1.20	3.00	
1-5-Gold foil embossed logo; limited # printed-7500	7.00	21.50	50.00

STAR WARS: TALES OF THE JEDI-DARK LORDS OF THE SITH
Oct, 1994 - No. 6, Mar, 1995 (limited series)
Dark Horse Comics

1-6: 1-Polybagged w/trading card	1.20		3.00

STAR WARS: TALES OF THE JEDI-THE FREEDOM NADD UPRISING
Aug, 1994 - No. 2, Sept, 1994 ($2.50, limited series)
Dark Horse Comics

1,2	1.00		2.50

STAR WARS: TALES OF THE JEDI-THE SITH WAR
Aug, 1995 - No. 6, Jan, 1996 ($2.50, limited series)
Dark Horse Comics

1-6: Anderson scripts	1.00		2.50

STAR WARS: X-WING ROGUE SQUADRON (Star Wars: X-Wing Rogue

Squadron-The Phantom Affair #5-8 appears on cover only))
July, 1995 - Present ($2.95)
Dark Horse Comics

1-12: 1-4-Baron scripts. 5-10-Stackpole scripts	1.20		3.00

S.T.A.T.
Dec, 1993 ($2.25)
Majestic Entertainment

1	.90		2.25

STATIC (Also see Eclipse Monthly)
No, 11, Oct, 1985 - No. 12, Dec, 1985
Charlton Comics

11,12-Ditko-c/a			1.00

STATIC (See Heroes)
June, 1993 - Present ($1.50/$1.75/$2.50)
DC Comics (Milestone)

1-($2.95)-Collector's Edition; polybagged w/poster & trading card & backing board (direct sales only)		1.20	3.00
1-13: 2-Origin. 8-Shadow War; Simonson silver ink-c			1.50
14-($2.50, 52 pgs.)-Worlds Collide Pt. 14		1.00	2.50
15-24: 15-Begin $1.75-c		.70	1.75
25 ($3.95)		1.60	4.00
26-30,32-50: 26-Begin $2.50-c. 27-Kent Williams-c		1.00	2.50
31-(99¢)			1.00

STEALTH SQUAD
Sept, 1993 ($2.50, unfinished limited series)
Petra Comics

1-Super hero team		1.00	2.50

STEED AND MRS. PEEL (TV)(Also see The Avengers)
1990 - No. 3, 1991 ($4.95, limited series)
Eclipse Books/ ACME Press

Books One - Three: Grant Morrison scripts	1.00	2.00	5.00

STEEL
Feb, 1994 - Present ($1.50/$1.95)
DC Comics

1-8: 1-From Reign of the Superman storyline. 6,7-Worlds Collide Pt. 5 & 12. 8-(9/94)			1.50
0,9-15: 0-(10/94). 9-(11/94)			1.50
16-22: 16-Begin $1.95-c		.80	2.00
Annual 1 (1994, $2.95)-Elseworlds story		1.20	3.00
Annual 2 (1995, $3.95)-Year One story		1.60	4.00

STEELGRIP STARKEY
June, 1990 - No. 6, July, 1987 ($1.50, limited series, Baxter paper)
Marvel Comics (Epic Comics)

1-6			1.50

STEEL STERLING (Formerly Shield-Steel Sterling; see Blue Ribbon, Jackpot, Mighty Comics, Mighty Crusaders, Roly Poly & Zip Comics)
No. 4, Jan, 1984 - No. 7, July, 1984
Archie Enterprises, Inc.

4-7: 6-McWilliams-a			1.00

STEEL, THE INDESTRUCTIBLE MAN (See All-Star Squadron #8)
Mar, 1978 - No. 5, Oct-Nov, 1978
DC Comics

1			1.20
2-5: 5-Giant			1.00

STEELTOWN ROCKERS
Apr, 1987 - No. 6, Sept, 1990 ($1.00, limited series)
Marvel Comics

1-6: Small town teens form rock band			1.00

	GD25	FN65	NM94

STRANGE SUSPENSE STORIES (Lawbreakers Suspense Stories #10-15; This Is Suspense #23-26; Captain Atom V1#78 on)
6/52 - No. 5, 2/53; No. 16, 1/54 - No. 22, 11/54; No. 27, 10/55 - No. 77, 10/65; V3#1, 10/67 - V1#9, 9/69
Fawcett Publications/Charlton Comics No. 16 on

1-(Fawcett)-Powell, Sekowsky-a	58.00	174.00	465.00
2-George Evans horror story	40.00	120.00	280.00
3-5 (2/53)-George Evans horror stories	36.00	107.00	250.00
16(1-2/54)-Formerly Lawbreakers S.S.	21.00	64.00	150.00
17,21: 21-Shuster-a	17.00	49.00	115.00
18-E.C. swipe/HOF 7; Ditko-c/a(2)	30.00	90.00	210.00
19-Ditko electric chair-c; Ditko-a	38.00	114.00	265.00
20-Ditko-c/a(2)	29.00	84.00	195.00
22(11/54)-Ditko-c, Shuster-a; last pre-code issue; becomes This Is Suspense	25.00	75.00	175.00
27(10/55)-(Formerly This Is Suspense #26)	10.00	30.00	70.00
28-30,38	5.35	16.00	45.00
31-33,35,37,40-Ditko-c/a(2-3 each)	16.00	47.00	110.00
34-Story of ruthless business man, Wm. B. Gaines; Ditko-c/a	28.00	83.00	250.00
36-(15¢, 68 pgs.); Ditko-a(4)	15.00	45.00	120.00
39,41,52,53-Ditko-a	12.00	36.00	95.00
42-44,46,49,54-60	4.20	12.50	30.00
45,47,48,50,51-Ditko-c/a	11.00	33.00	75.00
61-74	2.00	5.00	14.00
75(6/65)-Reprints origin/1st app. Captain Atom by Ditko from Space Advs. #33; r/Severin-a/Space Advs. #24 (75-77: 12¢ issues)	13.00	39.00	90.00
76,77-Captain Atom-r by Ditko/Space Advs.	5.70	17.00	40.00
V3#1(10/67)-4: All 12¢ issues	1.70	5.00	12.00
V1#2-9: All 12¢ issues. 2-Ditko-c/a; atom bomb-c	.90	2.30	5.50

NOTE: *Alascia* a-19. *Aparo* a-60, V3#1, 2, 4; c-V1#4, 8. *Baily* a-1-3; c-2, 5. *Evans* c-3, 4. *Giordano* c-16, 17p, 24p, 25p. *Montes/Bache* c-66. *Powell* a-4. *Shuster* a-19, 21. *Marcus Swayze* a-27.

STRANGE TALES (...Featuring Warlock #178-181; Doctor Strange #169 on)
June, 1951 - #168, May, 1968; #169, Sept, 1973 - #188, Nov, 1976
Atlas (CCPC #1-67/ZPC #68-79/VPI #80-85)/Marvel #86(7/61) on

1-Horror/weird stories begin	288.00	862.00	2300.00
2	95.00	286.00	765.00
3,5: 3-Atom bomb panels	70.00	211.00	565.00
4-Cosmic eyeball story "The Evil Eye"	76.00	230.00	615.00
6-9: 6-Heath-c/a	53.00	159.00	425.00
10-Krigstein-a	58.00	172.00	460.00
11-14,16-20	38.00	114.00	265.00
15-Krigstein-a	39.00	118.00	275.00
21,23-27,29-34: 27-Atom bomb panels. 33-Davis-a. 34-Last pre-code issue (2/55)	30.00	90.00	210.00
22-Krigstein, Forte/Fox-a	31.00	92.00	215.00
28-Jack Katz story used in Senate Investigation report, pgs. 7 & 169	31.00	94.00	220.00
35-41,43,44: 37-Vampire story by Colan	24.00	71.00	165.00
42,45,59,61-Krigstein-a; #61 (2/58)	24.00	73.00	170.00
46-57,60: 51-1st S.A. issue. 53,56-Crandall-a. 60-(8/57)	20.00	60.00	140.00
58,64-Williamson-a in each, with Mayo-a/#58	21.00	62.00	145.00
62,63,65,66: 62-Torres-a. 66-Crandall-a	19.00	58.00	135.00
67-Prototype ish. (Quicksilver)	25.00	75.00	175.00
68,71,72,74,77,80: Ditko/Kirby-a in #67-80	21.00	64.00	150.00
69-Prototype ish. (Prof. X)	30.00	90.00	210.00
70-Prototype ish. (Giant Man)	30.00	90.00	210.00
73-Prototype ish. (Ant-Man)	30.00	90.00	210.00
75-Prototype ish. (Iron Man)	30.00	90.00	210.00
76-Prototype ish. (Human Torch)	30.00	90.00	210.00
78-Prototype ish. (Ant-Man)	30.00	90.00	210.00
79-Prototype ish. (Dr. Strange) (12/60)	30.00	90.00	210.00

81-83,85-88,90,91-Ditko/Kirby-a in all: 90-(11/61)-Atom bomb blast panel	19.00	56.00	130.00
84-Prototype ish. (Magneto)(5/61); has powers like Magneto of X-Men over two years later; Ditko/Kirby-a	26.00	77.00	180.00
89-1st app. Fin Fang Foom (10/61) by Kirby	47.00	141.00	375.00
92-Prototype ish. (Ancient One); last 10¢ issue	20.00	60.00	140.00
93,95,96,98-100: Kirby-a	17.00	51.00	120.00
94-Prototype ish. (The Thing); Kirby-a	20.00	60.00	140.00
97-1st app. Aunt May & Uncle Ben by Ditko (6/62), before Amazing Fantasy #15; Kirby-a	40.00	120.00	325.00

	GD25	FN65	NM94
101-Human Torch begins by Kirby (10/62); origin recap Fantastic Four & Human Torch; H. Torch-c begin	89.00	267.00	533.00	850.00

	GD25	FN65	NM94
102-1st app. Wizard	40.00	120.00	280.00
103-105: 104-1st app. Trapster. 105-2nd Wizard	34.00	101.00	235.00
106,108,109: 106-Fantastic Four guests (3/63)	21.00	64.00	150.00
107-(4/63)-Human Torch/Sub-Mariner battle; 4th S.A. Sub-Mariner app. & 1st x-over outside of Fantastic Four	26.00	77.00	180.00

	GD25	FN65	VF82	NM94
110-(7/63)-Intro Doctor Strange, Ancient One & Wong by Ditko	95.00	285.00	585.00	950.00

	GD25	FN65	NM94
111-2nd Dr. Strange	40.00	120.00	300.00
112,113	14.00	43.00	100.00
114-Acrobat disguised as Captain America, 1st app. since the G.A.; intro. & 1st app. Victoria Bentley; 3rd Dr. Strange app. & begin series (11/63)	40.00	120.00	350.00
115-Origin Dr. Strange; Human Torch vs. Sandman (Spidey villain); 2nd app. & brief origin); early Spider-Man x-over (12/63)	53.00	160.00	450.00
116-(1/64)-Human Torch battles The Thing; 1st Thing x-over	14.00	43.00	100.00
117,118,120: 120-1st Iceman x-over (from X-Men)	9.30	28.00	65.00
119-Spider-Man x-over (2 panel cameo)	17.00	49.00	115.00
121,122,124,126-134: Thing/Torch team-up in 121-134. 126-Intro Clea. 128-Quicksilver & Scarlet Witch app. (1/65). 130-The Beatles cameo. 134-Last Human Torch; The Watcher-c/story; Wood-a(i)	8.00	23.50	55.00
123-1st app. The Beetle (see Amazing Spider-Man #21 for next app.); 1st Thor x-over (8/64); Loki app.	8.50	26.00	60.00
125-Torch & Thing battle Sub-Mariner (10/64)	8.00	23.50	55.00
135-Col. (formerly Sgt.) Nick Fury becomes Nick Fury Agent of Shield (origin/1st app.) by Kirby (8/65); series begins	13.50	41.00	95.00
136-147,149: 138-Intro Eternity. 145-Begins alternating-c features w/Nick Fury (odd #'s) & Dr. Strange (even #'s). 146-Only Ditko Dr. Strange who is in consecutive stories since #113. 146-Only Ditko Dr. Strange-c this title.	8.00	23.50	55.00
147-Dr. Strange (by Everett #147-152) continues thru #168, then Dr. Strange #169	5.70	17.00	40.00
	9.30	28.00	65.00
148-Origin Ancient One	5.70	17.00	40.00
150(11/66)-John Buscema's 1st work at Marvel	7.50	22.00	52.00
151-Kirby/Steranko-a; 1st Marvel work by Steranko	5.00	15.00	35.00
152,153-Kirby/Steranko-a	5.00	15.00	35.00
154-158-Steranko-a/script	5.30	16.00	37.00
159-Origin Nick Fury retold; Intro Val; Captain America-c/story; Steranko-a	5.30	16.00	37.00
160-162-Steranko-a/scripts; Capt. America app.	4.30	13.00	30.00
163-166,168-Steranko-a(p). 168-Last Nick Fury (gets own book next month) & last Dr. Strange who also gets own book	4.30	13.00	30.00
167-Steranko pen/script; classic flag-c	6.50	19.50	45.00
169-177: 169-1st app. Brother Voodoo(origin in 169,170) & begin series, ends #173. 174-Origin Golem. 177-Brunner-a	1.60	4.00
178-(2/75)-Warlock by Starlin begins; origin Warlock & Him retold; 1st app. Magus; Starlin-c/a/scripts in 178-181 (all before Warlock #9)	2.90	8.60	20.00
179-181-All Warlock. 179-Intro/1st app. Pip the Troll. 180-Intro Gamora. 181-			

Strange Tales V3#1 © MEG

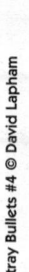
Stray Bullets #4 © David Lapham

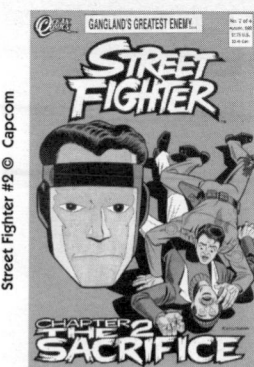
Street Fighter #2 © Capcom

	GD25	FN65	NM94

(8/75)-Warlock story continued in Warlock #9 ... 1.50 ... 3.75 ... 9.00
-188 ... 1.40 ... 3.50
ual 1(1962)-Reprints from Strange Tales #73,76,78, Tales of Suspense
#7,9, Tales to Astonish #1,6,7, & Journey Into Mystery #53,55,59; (1st Marvel
annual?) ... 47.00 ... 141.00 ... 400.00
ual 2(7/63)-Reprints from Strange Tales #67, Strange Worlds (Atlas) #1-3,
World of Fantasy #16; new Human Torch vs. Spider-Man story by Kirby/
Ditko (1st Spidey x-over; tied for 6th app. with Amazing Spider-Man #5);
Kirby-c ... 55.00 ... 165.00 ... 440.00
E: Briefer a-17. Burgos a-123p. J. Buscema a-174p. Colan a-11, 20, 37, 53, 169-173p.
o. Davis c-71. Ditko a-46, 50, 67-122, 123-125p, 126-146, 175r, 182-188r; c-51, 93, 115,
146. Everett a-4, 21, 40-42, 73, 147-152, 164i; c-8, 10, 11, 13, 15, 24, 45, 49-54, 56, 58,
61, 63, 148, 150, 152, 158i. Forte a-27, 43, 50, 53, 54, 60. Heath a-6; c-6, 18-20. Kamen a-
G. Kane c-170-173, 182p. Kirby Human Torch-101-105, 108, 109, 114, 120; Nick Fury-
, 141-143p; (Layouts)-135-153; other Kirby a-67-100p; c-68-70, 72-74, 76-92, 94, 95, 101-
116-123, 125-130, 132-135, 136p, 138-145, 147, 149, 151p. Kirby/Ayers c-101-106, 108-
Kirby/Ditko a-80, 88, 121; c-75, 93, 97, 100. . Lawrence a-29. Leiber/ Fox a-110, 111,
Maneely a-3, 37, 42; c-33, 40. Moldoff a-20. Mooney a-174i. Morisi a-53, 56. Morrow a-
Orlando a-41, 44, 46, 49, 52. Powell a-42, 44, 49, 54, 130-134p; c-131p. Reinman a-11, 50,
88, 91, 95, 104, 106, 112i, 124-127i. Robinson a-17. Romita c-169. Roussos a-201i. R.Q.
a-56; c-16. Sekowski a-3, 11. Severin a(i)-136-138; c-137. Starlin a-178, 179, 180p, 181p;
-180, 181p. Steranko a-151-161, 162-168p; c-151i, 153, 155, 157, 159, 161, 163, 165,
Torres a-53, 62. Tuska a-14, 166p. Whitney a-149. Wildey a-42, 56. Woodbridge a-59.
astic Four cameos #101-134. Jack Katz app.-26.

RANGE TALES
, 1987 - No. 19, Oct, 1988
vel Comics Group
#1-19 ... 1.00

RANGE TALES
, 1994 ($6.95, one-shots)
vel Comics
1-acetate-c ... 1.20 ... 3.00 ... 7.00

RANGE TALES OF THE UNUSUAL
, 1955 - No. 11, Aug, 1957
s Comics (ACI No. 1-4/WPI No. 5-11)
Powell-a ... 38.00 ... 114.00 ... 265.00
... 21.00 ... 62.00 ... 145.00
Williamson-a (4 pgs.) ... 21.00 ... 64.00 ... 150.00
,8,11 ... 13.50 ... 41.00 ... 95.00
Crandall, Ditko-a ... 18.00 ... 54.00 ... 125.00
: 7-Kirby, Orlando-a. 9-Krigstein-a ... 15.00 ... 45.00 ... 105.00
Torres, Morrow-a ... 13.50 ... 41.00 ... 95.00
E: Baily a-6. Brodsky c-2-4. Everett a-2, 6; c-6, 9, 11. Heck a-1. Maneely c-1. Orlando a-
akula a-10. Romita a-1. R.Q. Sale a-3. Wildey a-3.

RANGE TERRORS
e, 1952 - No. 7, Mar, 1953
John Publishing Co.
Bondage-c; Zombies spelled Zoombies on-c; Fineesque-a ... 39.00 ... 118.00 ... 275.00
... 21.00 ... 64.00 ... 150.00
Kubert-a; painted-c ... 28.00 ... 84.00 ... 195.00
Kubert-a (reprinted in Mystery Tales #18); Ekgren painted-a;
Jerry Iger caricature ... 38.00 ... 114.00 ... 265.00
Kubert-a; painted-c ... 28.00 ... 84.00 ... 195.00
Giant (25¢, 100 pgs.)(1/53); bondage-c ... 38.00 ... 114.00 ... 265.00
Giant (25¢, 100 pgs.); Kubert-c/a ... 40.00 ... 120.00 ... 300.00
E: Cameron a-6, 7. Morisi a-6.

RANGE WORLD OF YOUR DREAMS
, 1952 - No. 4, Jan-Feb, 1953
e Publications
Simon & Kirby-a ... 50.00 ... 150.00 ... 400.00
-Simon & Kirby-a. 2-Meskin-a ... 40.00 ... 120.00 ... 325.00
-&K-c; Meskin-a ... 38.00 ... 114.00 ... 265.00

RANGE WORLDS (#18 continued from Avon's Eerie #1-17)

11/50 - No. 9, 11/52; No. 18, 10-11/54 - No. 22, 9-10/55 (No #11-17)
Avon Periodicals
1-Kenton of the Star Patrol by Kubert (r/Eerie #1 from 1947); Crom the
Barbarian by John Giunta ... 68.00 ... 206.00 ... 550.00
2-Wood-a; Crom the Barbarian by Giunta; Dara of the Vikings app.; used
in SOTI, pg. 112; injury to eye panel ... 65.00 ... 195.00 ... 525.00
3-Wood/Orlando-a (Kenton), Wood/Williamson/Frazetta/Krenkel/Orlando-a
(7 pgs.); Malu Slave Girl Princess app.; Kinstler-c ... 131.00 ... 393.00 ... 1050.00
4-Wood-c/a (Kenton); Orlando-a; origin The Enchanted Daggar; Sultan-a ... 62.00 ... 187.00 ... 500.00
5-Orlando/Wood-a (Kenton); Wood-c ... 44.00 ... 130.00 ... 345.00
6-Kinstler-a(2); Orlando/Wood-c; Check-a ... 34.00 ... 101.00 ... 235.00
7-Fawcette & Becker/Alascia-a ... 26.00 ... 79.00 ... 185.00
8-Kubert, Kinstler, Hollingsworth & Lazarus-a; Lazarus Robot-c ... 29.00 ... 86.00 ... 200.00
9-Kinstler, Fawcette, Alascia-a ... 25.00 ... 75.00 ... 175.00
18-(Formerly Eerie #17)-Reprints "Attack on Planet Mars" by Kubert ... 25.00 ... 75.00 ... 175.00
19-r/Avon's "Robotmen of the Lost Planet"; last pre-code issue; Robot-c ... 25.00 ... 75.00 ... 175.00
20-War-c/story; Wood-c(r)/U.S. Paratroops #1 ... 7.50 ... 22.50 ... 45.00
21,22-War-c/stories. 22-New logo ... 5.85 ... 17.50 ... 35.00
I.W. Reprint #5-Kinstler-a(r)/Avon's #9 ... 2.00 ... 6.00 ... 14.00

STRANGE WORLDS
Dec, 1958 - No. 5, Aug, 1959
Marvel Comics (MPI No. 1,2/Male No. 3,5)
1-Kirby & Ditko-a; flying saucer issue ... 68.00 ... 206.00 ... 550.00
2-Ditko-c/a ... 40.00 ... 120.00 ... 300.00
3-Kirby-a(2) ... 33.00 ... 99.00 ... 230.00
4-Williamson-a ... 31.00 ... 94.00 ... 220.00
5-Ditko-a ... 26.00 ... 77.00 ... 180.00
NOTE: Buscema a-3, 4. Ditko a-1-5; c-2.. Heck a-2. Kirby a-1, 3. Kirby/Brodsky c-1, 3-5.

STRAWBERRY SHORTCAKE
June, 1985 - No. 7, Apr, 1986 (Children's comic)
Marvel Comics (Star Comics)
1-7: Howie Post-a ... 1.00

STRAY BULLETS
1995 - Present ($2.95, B&W, mature readers)
El Capitan Books
1-David Lapham-c/a/scripts ... 1.20 ... 3.00 ... 7.00
2,3 ... 1.60 ... 4.00
4,6-8 ... 1.20 ... 3.00
5 ($3.50) ... 1.40 ... 3.50
9,10: Begin $2.95-c ... 3.00
Volume 1 ($29.95, hardcover) ... 30.00
NOTE: Multiple issues of all issues exist & are worth cover price.

STRAY TOASTERS
Jan, 1988 - No. 4, April, 1989 ($3.50, squarebound, limited series)
Marvel Comics (Epic Comics)
1-4: Sienkiewicz-c/a/scripts ... 1.75 ... 3.50

STREET COMIX
1973 (50¢, B&W, 36 pgs.) (20,000 print run)
Street Enterprises/King Features
1,2: 1-Rip Kirby. 2-Flash Gordon ... 1.50

STREETFIGHTER
Aug, 1986 - No. 4, Spr, 1987 ($1.75, limited series)
Ocean Comics
1-4: 2-Origin begins ... .90 ... 1.80

STREET FIGHTER

	GD25	FN65	NM94

Street Fighter II #7 © Capcom

Strike! #1 © ECL

Stryke #0 © Everette Hartsoe

	GD25	FN65	NM94
Sept, 1993 - No. 3, Nov, 1993 ($2.95)			
Malibu Comics			
1-3: 3-Includes poster; Ferret x-over		1.20	3.00
STREET FIGHTER: THE BATTLE FOR SHADALOO			
1995 ($3.95, one-shot)			
DC Comics/CAP Co. Ltd.			
1-polybagged w/trading card & Tattoo		1.60	4.00
STREET FIGHTER II			
Apr, 1994 - No. 8, Nov, 1994 ($2.95, limited series)			
Tokuma Comics (Viz)			
1-8		1.20	3.00
STREET POET RAY			
Spring, 1989; 1990 - No. 4, 1990 ($2.95, B&W, squarebound)			
Blackthorne Publ./Marvel Comics			
1 (Blackthorne, $2.00)		1.00	2.00
1-4 (Marvel, $2.95, thick-c & paper)		1.50	3.00
STREETS			
1993 - No. 3, 1993 ($4.95, limited series, 52 pgs.)			
DC Comics			
Book 1-3-Estes painted-c	1.00	2.00	5.00
STREET SHARKS			
Jan, 1996 - No. 3, Mar, 1996 ($1.50, limited series)			
Archie Publications			
1-3			1.50
STREET SHARKS			
May, 1996 - Present ($1.50, published 8 times a year)			
Archie Publications			
1-6			1.50
STRICTLY PRIVATE (You're in the Army Now)			
July, 1942 (#1 on sale 6/15/42)			
Eastern Color Printing Co.			
1,2: Private Peter Plink. 2-Says 128 pgs. on-c	21.00	62.00	145.00
STRIKE!			
Aug, 1987 - No. 6, Jan, 1988 ($1.75)			
Eclipse Comics			
1-6		.90	1.80
...Vs. Sgt. Strike Special 1 (5/88, $1.95)		1.00	2.00
STRIKEBACK! (The Hunt For Nikita)			
Oct, 1994 - No. 3, Jan, 1995 ($2.95, unfinished limited series)			
Malibu Comics (Bravura)			
1-3: Jonathon Peterson script, Kevin Maguire-c/a		1.20	3.00
1-Gold foil embossed-c	1.30	3.25	8.00
STRIKEBACK!			
Jan, 1996 - No. 5, May, 1996 ($2.50, limited series)			
Image Comics (Wildstorm Productions)			
1-6: Reprints original Bravura series w/additional story & art by Kevin Maguire			
& Jonathon Peterson; new Maguire-c in all. 4,5-New story & art.			
			2.50
STRIKEFORCE: MORITURI			
Dec, 1986 - No. 31, July, 1989			
Marvel Comics Group			
1-12, 14: 14-Williamson-i			1.00
13-Double size			1.50
15-23 ($1.00-$1.25)			1.25
24-31 ($1.50): 25-Heath-c			1.50
STRIKEFORCE MORITURI: ELECTRIC UNDERTOW			

	GD25	FN65	NM94	
Dec, 1989 - No. 5, Mar, 1990 ($3.95, 52 pgs., limited series)				
Marvel Comics				
1-5 Squarebound			2.00	4
STRONG MAN (Also see Complimentary Comics & Power of...)				
Mar-Apr, 1955 - No. 4, Sept-Oct, 1955				
Magazine Enterprises				
1(A-1 #130)-Powell-c/a	20.00	60.00	14(	
2-4: (A-1 #132,134,139)-Powell-a. 2-Powell-c	17.00	49.00	11!	
STRONTIUM DOG				
Dec, 1985 - No. 4, Mar, 1986 ($1.25, limited series)				
Eagle Comics				
1-4: 4-Moore scripts.				
Special 1 (1986)-Moore scripts				
STRYFE'S STRIKE FILE				
Jan, 1993 ($1.75, one-shot, no ads)				
Marvel Comics				
1-Stroman, Capullo, Andy Kubert, Brandon Peterson-a; silver metallic ink-c;				
X-Men tie-in to X-Cutioner's Song			.70	
1-Gold metallic ink 2nd printing			.70	
STRYKE				
1995 ($3.00)				
London Night Studios				
0			1.20	
0-Alternate-c		1.00	2.00	
STUMBO THE GIANT (See Harvey Hits #49, 54, 57, 60, 63, 66, 69, 72, 78, 88 & Hot Stuff #2)				
STUMBO TINYTOWN				
Oct, 1963 - No. 13, Nov, 1966 (All 25¢ giants)				
Harvey Publications				
1-Stumbo, Hot Stuff & others begin	12.00	36.00	12	
2	7.00	21.00	7(	
3-5	5.00	15.00	4	
6-13	4.00	12.00	3(	
STUNT DAWGS				
Mar, 1993 ($1.25, one-shot)				
Harvey Comics				
1				
STUNTMAN COMICS (Also see Thrills Of Tomorrow)				
Apr-May, 1946 - No. 2, June-July, 1946; No. 3, Oct-Nov, 1946				
Harvey Publications				
1-Origin Stuntman by S&K reprinted in Black Cat #9; S&K-c	87.00	262.00	70	
2-S&K-c/a; The Duke of Broadway story	59.00	178.00	47	
3-Small size (5-1/2x8-1/2"; B&W; 32 pgs.); distributed to mail subscribers only; S&K-a; Kid Adonis by S&K reprinted in Green Hornet #37				
Estimated value...			$250.00-$400.(	
(Also see All-New #15, Boy Explorers #2, Flash Gordon #5 & Thrills of Tomorrow)				
STUPID HEROES				
Sept, 1993 ($2.75, unfinished limited series)				
Mirage Studios				
1-Laird-c/a & scripts; 2 trading cards bound in			1.10	
STYGMATA				
No. 0, July, 1994 - No. 3, Oct, 1994 ($2.95, B&W, limited series)				
Entity Comics				
0-Foil-c			1.20	
1-3: 1-Foil-c. 3-Silver foil logo			1.20	
Yearbook 1 (1995, $2.95)			1.20	
SUBMARINE ATTACK (Formerly Speed Demons)				

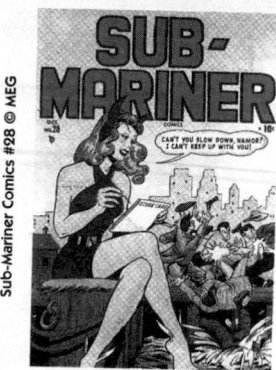

Sub-Mariner #9 © MEG

Sub-Mariner Comics #98 © MEG

Subtle Violents #1 © CFD Productions

	GD25	FN65	NM94

No. 11, May, 1958 - No. 54, Feb-Mar, 1966
Charlton Comics

11	3.25	9.50	22.00
12-20	2.15	6.50	15.00
21-54	1.65	4.20	10.00

NOTE: Glanzman c/a-25. Montes/Bache a-38, 40, 41.

SUB-MARINER (See All-Select, All-Winners, Blonde Phantom, Daring, The Defenders, Fantastic Four #4, Human Torch, The Invaders, Iron Man &..., Marvel Mystery, Marvel Spotlight #27, Men's Adventures, Motion Picture Funnies Weekly, Namora, Namor, The..., Prince Namor, The Sub-Mariner, Saga Of The..., Tales to Astonish #70 & 2nd series, USA Young Men)

SUB-MARINER, THE (2nd Series)(Sub-Mariner #31 on)
May, 1968 - No. 72, Sept, 1974 (No. 43: 52 pgs.)
Marvel Comics Group

1-Origin Sub-Mariner; story continued from Iron Man & Sub-Mariner #1	19.00	56.00	130.00
2-Triton app.	7.60	22.75	55.00
3-10: 5-1st Tiger Shark (9/68). 6-Tiger Shark-c & 2nd app., cont'd from #5. 7-Photo-c. (1968). 8-Sub-Mariner vs. Thing. 9-1st app. Serpent Crown (origin in #10 & 12)	4.50	14.00	35.00
11-13,15: 15-Last 12¢ issue	3.60	11.00	25.00
14-Sub-Mariner vs. G.A. Human Torch; death of Toro (1st modern app. & only app. Toro, 6/69)	5.30	16.00	40.00
16-20: 19-1st Sting Ray (11/69); Stan Lee, Romita, Heck, Thomas, Everett & Kirby cameos. 20-Dr. Doom app.	1.85	5.50	13.00
21-33,36-40: 22-Dr. Strange x-over. 25-Origin Atlantis. 30-Capt. Marvel x-over. 37-Death of Lady Dorma. 38-Origin retold. 40-Spider-Man x-over	1.50	3.75	9.00
34,35-Prelude to 1st Defenders story. 34-Hulk & Silver Surfer x-over. 35-Namor-Hulk/Silver Surfer team-up to battle The Avengers-c/story (3/71); hints at teaming up again	2.40	7.30	17.00
41-49,56,62,64-72: 42-Last 15¢ issue. 43-King Size Special (52 pgs.). 44,45-Sub-Mariner vs. H. Torch. 47,48-Dr. Doom app. 49-Cosmic Cube story. 62-1st Tales of Atlantis, ends #66. 64-Hitler cameo. 67-New costume; F.F. x-over. 69-Spider-Man x-over (6 panels)	1.00	2.00	5.00
-1st app. Nita, Namor's niece (later Namorita in New Warriors)	1.20	3.00	7.00
50-55,57-61,63-Everett issues: 59-1st battle with Thor. 61-Last artwork by Everett; 1st 4 pgs. completed by Mortimer; pgs. 5-20 by Mooney.	1.25	3.00	7.50
Special 1,2: 1(1/71)-r/Tales to Astonish #70-73. 2(1/72)-r/T.T.A. #74-76; Everett-a	1.25	3.00	7.50

NOTE: Bolle a-67i. Buscema a(p)-1-8, 20, 24. Colan a(p)-10, 11, 40, 43, 46-49, Special 1, 2; 10, 11, 40. Craig a-17i, 19-23i. Everett a-45r, 50-55, 57, 58, 59-61(plot); c-47, 48i, 57-59i, 61, Spec. 2. G. Kane c(p)-42-52, 58, 66, 70, 71. Mooney a-24i, 25i, 32-35i, 39i, 42i, 45i, 60i, 61i, 65p, 66p, 68i, Severin c/a-38i. Starlin c-59p. Tuska a-41p, 42p, 69-71p. Johnson a-36i. #53, 54-r/stories Sub-Mariner Comics #41 & 39.

SUB-MARINER COMICS (1st Series) (The Sub-Mariner #1, 2, 33-42)(Official True Crime Cases #24 on; Amazing Mysteries #32 on; Best Love #33 on)
Spring, 1941 - No. 23, Sum, 1947; No. 24, Wint, 1947 - No. 31, 4/49; No. 32, 7/49; No. 33, 4/54 - No. 42, 10/55
Timely/Marvel Comics (TCI 1-7/SePI 8/MPI 9-32/Atlas Comics (CCC 33-42))

	GD25	FN65	VF82	NM94
1-The Sub-Mariner by Everett & The Angel begin	2000.00	6000.00	12,000.00	20,000.00

(Estimated up to 190 total copies exist, 8 in NM/Mint)

	GD25	FN65	NM94
2-Everett-a	422.00	1267.00	4200.00
3-Churchill assassination-c; 40 pg. Sub-Mariner story	325.00	975.00	2900.00
4-Everett-a, 40 pgs.; 1 pg. Wolverton-a	275.00	825.00	2450.00
5,8-Gabrielle/Klein-c	206.00	618.00	1650.00
6,7,10: 9-Wolverton-a, 3 pgs.; flag-c	168.00	506.00	1350.00
9	125.00	375.00	1000.00

	GD25	FN65	NM94
16-20	112.00	338.00	900.00
21-Last Angel; Everett-a	90.00	271.00	725.00
22-Young Allies app.	90.00	271.00	725.00
23-The Human Torch, Namora x-over (Sum/47); 2nd app. Namora after Marvel Mystery #82	90.00	271.00	725.00
24-Namora x-over (3rd app.)	90.00	271.00	725.00
25-The Blonde Phantom begins (Spr/48), ends No. 31; Kurtzman-a; Namora x-over; last quarterly issue	112.00	338.00	900.00
26-28: 28-Namora cover; Everett-a	90.00	271.00	725.00
29-31 (4/49): 29-The Human Torch app. 31-Capt. America app.	90.00	271.00	725.00
32 (7/49, Scarce)-Origin Sub-Mariner	150.00	450.00	1200.00
33 (4/54)-Origin Sub-Mariner; The Human Torch app.; Namora x-over in Sub-Mariner #33-42	82.00	247.00	660.00
34,35-Human Torch in each	65.00	195.00	525.00
36,37,39-41: 36,39-41-Namora app.	65.00	195.00	525.00
38-Origin Sub-Mariner's wings; Namora app.; last pre-code (2/55)	75.00	225.00	600.00
42-Last issue	78.00	234.00	625.00

NOTE: Angel by Gustavson-#1, 8. Brodsky c-34-36, 42. Everett a-1-4, 22-24, 26-42; c-32, 33, 40. Maneely a-38; c-37, 39-41. Rico c-27-31. Schomburg c-1-4, 6, 8-18, 20. Sekowsky c-24, 25, 26(w/Rico). Shores c-21-23, 38. Bondage c-13, 22, 24, 25, 34.

SUBSPECIES
May, 1991 - No. 4, Aug, 1991 ($2.50, limited series)
Eternity Comics

1-4: New stories based on horror movie		1.00	2.50

SUBTLE VIOLENTS
1991 ($2.50, B&W, mature)
CFD Productions

1-Linsner-c & story	2.85	8.50	20.00
San Diego Limited Edition			95.00

SUE & SALLY SMITH (Formerly My Secret Life)
V2#48, Nov, 1962 - No. 54, Nov, 1963 (Flying Nurses)
Charlton Comics

V2#48	1.20	3.00	6.00
49-54	.80	2.00	4.00

SUGAR & SPIKE (Also see The Best of DC & DC Silver Age Classics)
Apr-May, 1956 - No. 98, Oct-Nov, 1971
National Periodical Publications

1 (Scarce)	131.00	393.00	1050.00
2	58.00	174.00	465.00
3-5: 3-Letter column begins	50.00	150.00	400.00
6-10	34.00	103.00	240.00
11-20	30.00	90.00	210.00
21-29,31-40: 26-Christmas-c	17.00	51.00	120.00
30-Scribbly & Scribbly, Jr. x-over	19.00	56.00	130.00
41-60	9.30	28.00	70.00
61-80: 69-1st app. Tornado-Tot-c/story. 72-Origin & 1st app. Bernie the Brain	6.50	19.50	48.00
81-98: 84-Bernie the Brain apps. as Superman in 1 panel (9/69). 85-(68 pgs.); r-#72. 96-(68 pgs.). 97,98-(52 pgs.)	4.50	14.00	32.00

NOTE: All written and drawn by Sheldon Mayer.

SUGAR BEAR
No date, circa 1975? (2-1/2x4-1/2", 16 pgs.)
Post Cereal Giveaway

"The Almost Take Over of the Post Office", "The Race Across the Atlantic", "The Zoo Goes Wild" each...			1.00

SUGAR BOWL COMICS (Teen-age)
May, 1948 - No. 5, Jan, 1949
Famous Funnies

1-Toth-c/a	13.00	39.00	90.00

Suicide Squad #4 © DC

Summer Fun #1 © WDC

Sunglasses #3 © Nancy Collins

	GD25	FN65	NM94
2,4,5	5.85	17.50	35.00
3-Toth-a	10.00	30.00	60.00

SUGARFOOT (TV)
No. 907, May, 1958 - No. 1209, Oct-Dec, 1961
Dell Publishing Co.

	GD25	FN65	NM94
Four Color 907 (#1)-Toth-a, photo-c	13.00	40.00	125.00
Four Color 992 (5-7/59), Toth-a, photo-c	13.00	40.00	125.00
Four Color 1059 (11-1/60), 1098 (5-7/60), 1147 (11-1/61), 1209-all photo-c			
	9.00	27.00	90.00

SUICIDE SQUAD (See Brave & the Bold and Doom Patrol &Suicide Squad Spec., Legends #3 & note under Star Spangled War stories)
May, 1987 - No. 44, 1991 (Direct sales only #32 on)
DC Comics

1-44: 9-Millennium x-over. 10-Batman-c/story. 13-JLI app. (Batman). 16-Re-intro Shade The Changing Man. 27-34-Snyder-a. 36,37-Snyder-a. 40-43-"The Phoenix Gambit" Batman storyline. 40-Free Batman/Suicide Squad poster			1.00
Annual 1 (1988, $1.50)-Manhunter x-over			1.50

NOTE: *Chaykin c-1.*

SUMMER FUN (See Dell Giants)

SUMMER FUN (Formerly Li'l Genius; Holiday Surprise #55)
No. 54, Oct, 1966 (Giant)
Charlton Comics

54	1.65	4.20	10.00

SUMMER FUN (Walt Disney's...)
Summer, 1991 ($2.95, annual, 68 pgs.)
Disney Comics

1-D. Duck, M. Mouse, Brer Rabbit, Chip 'n' Dale & Pluto, Li'l Bad Wolf, Super Goof, Scamp stories		1.20	3.00

SUMMER LOVE (Formerly Brides in Love?)
V2#46, Oct, 1965; V2#47, Oct, 1966; V2#48, Nov, 1968
Charlton Comics

V2#46-Beatles-c/story	8.50	26.00	65.00
47-Beatles story	8.50	26.00	65.00
48	.80	2.00	4.00

SUMMER MAGIC (See Movie Comics)

SUNDANCE (See Hotel Deparee...)

SUNDANCE KID (Also see Blazing Six-Guns)
June, 1971 - No. 3, Sept, 1971 (52 pgs.)
Skywald Publications

1-Durango Kid; Two Kirby Bullseye-r		1.20	3.00
2-Swift Arrow, Durango Kid, Bullseye by S&K; Meskin plus 1 pg. origin		1.00	2.50
3-Durango Kid, Billy the Kid, Red Hawk-r		.80	2.00

SUNDAY FUNNIES
1950
Harvey Publications

1	4.00	11.00	22.00

SUN DEVILS
July, 1984 - No. 12, June, 1985 ($1.25, maxi series)
DC Comics

1-12: 6-Death of Sun Devil			1.25

SUN FUN KOMIKS
1939 (15¢, B&W & red)
Sun Publications

1-Satire on comics	26.00	79.00	185.00

SUN GIRL (See The Human Torch & Marvel Mystery Comics #88)
Aug, 1948 - No. 3, Dec, 1948

Marvel Comics (CCC)

	GD25	FN65	NM94
1-Sun Girl begins; Miss America app.	137.00	412.00	1100
2,3: 2-The Blonde Phantom begins	103.00	309.00	825

SUNGLASSES
Nov, 1995 - Present ($2.95, limited series, mature)
Verotik

1-4: Nancy Collins scripts; adaptation of "Sunglasses after Dark"

SUNNY, AMERICA'S SWEETHEART (Formerly Cosmo Cat #1-10)
No. 11, Dec, 1947 - No. 14, June, 1948
Fox Features Syndicate

11-Feldstein-c/a	56.00	168.00	450
12-14-Feldstein-c/a; 14-Lingerie panels	47.00	141.00	375
I.W. Reprint #8-Feldstein-a; r/Fox issue	13.50	41.00	90

SUN-RUNNERS (Also see Tales of the...)
2/84 - No. 3, 5/84; No. 4, 11/84 - No. 6, 1986 (Baxter paper)
Pacific Comics/Eclipse Comics/Amazing Comics

1-6: P. Smith-a in some			.80
Christmas Special 1 (1987, $1.95)-By Amazing			1.00

SUNSET CARSON (Also see Cowboy Western)
Feb, 1951 - No. 4, 1951 (No month) (Sunset Carson photo on-c of each)
Charlton Comics

1-Photo/retouched-c (Scarce, all issues)	75.00	225.00	600
2-Kit Carson story; adapts "Kansas Raiders" w/Brian Donlevy, Audie Murphy & Margaret Chapman	57.00	172.00	460
3,4	44.00	132.00	350

SUNSET PASS (See Zane Grey & 4-Color #230)

SUPER ANIMALS PRESENTS PIDGY & THE MAGIC GLASSES
Dec, 1953 (25¢, came w/glasses)
Star Publications

1-(3-D Comics)-L. B. Cole-c	40.00	120.00	300

SUPER BOOK OF COMICS
nd (1943?) (Soft-c, 32 pgs.) (Pan-Am/Gilmore Oil/Kelloggs premiums)
Western Publishing Co.

nn-Dick Tracy (Gilmore)-Magic Morro app.	40.00	120.00	290
1-Dick Tracy & The Smuggling Ring; Stratosphere Jim app. (Rare) (Pan-Am)			
	35.00	105.00	240
1-Smilin' Jack, Magic Morro (Pan-Am)	11.00	33.00	75
2-Smilin' Jack, Stratosphere Jim (Pan-Am)	11.00	33.00	75
2-Smitty, Magic Morro (Pan-Am)	11.00	33.00	75
3-Captain Midnight, Magic Morro (Pan-Am)	17.00	51.00	125
3-Moon Mullins?	10.00	30.00	60
4-Red Ryder, Magic Morro (Pan-Am)	10.00	30.00	60
4-Smitty, Stratosphere Jim (Pan-Am)	10.00	30.00	60
5-Don Winslow, Magic Morro (Gilmore)	10.00	30.00	70
5-Don Winslow, Stratosphere Jim (Pan-Am)	10.00	30.00	70
5-Terry & the Pirates	16.00	47.00	110
6-Don Winslow, Stratosphere Jim (Pan-Am)-McWilliams-a			
	11.50	34.00	80
6-King of the Royal Mounted, Magic Morro (Pan-Am)			
	11.00	33.00	70
7-Dick Tracy, Magic Morro (Pan-Am)	17.00	51.00	125
7-Little Orphan Annie	11.00	33.00	70
8-Dick Tracy, Stratosphere Jim (Pan-Am)	17.00	51.00	125
8-Dan Dunn, Magic Morro (Pan-Am)	11.00	33.00	70
9-Terry & the Pirates, Magic Morro (Pan-Am)	14.00	43.00	100
10-Red Ryder, Magic Morro (Pan-Am)	10.00	30.00	60

SUPER-BOOK OF COMICS
(Omar Bread & Hancock Oil Co. giveaways)
1944 - No. 30, 1947 (Omar); 1947 - 1948 (Hancock) (16 pgs.)

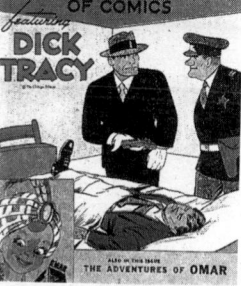

Super Book Of Comics #13 © WEST

Superboy #3 © DC

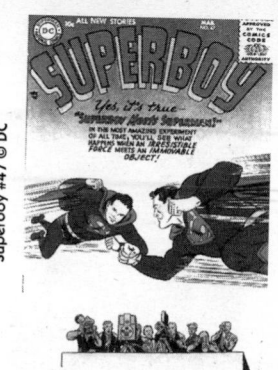

Superboy #47 © DC

SU

Western Publishing Co.

Note: The Hancock issues are all exact reprints of the earlier Omar issues.
The issue numbers were removed in some of the reprints.

-Dick Tracy (Omar, 1944)	21.00	64.00	150.00
-Dick Tracy (Hancock, 1947)	16.00	47.00	110.00
-Bugs Bunny (Omar, 1944)	7.50	22.50	45.00
-Bugs Bunny (Hancock, 1947)	5.85	17.50	35.00
-Terry & the Pirates (Omar, 1944)	12.00	36.00	85.00
-Terry & the Pirates (Hancock, 1947)	11.00	33.00	75.00
-Andy Panda (Omar, 1944)	7.50	22.50	45.00
-Andy Panda (Hancock, 1947)	5.85	17.50	35.00
-Smokey Stover (Omar, 1945)	5.85	17.50	35.00
-Smokey Stover (Hancock, 1947)	5.85	17.50	35.00
Porky Pig (Omar, 1945)	7.50	22.50	45.00
Porky Pig (Hancock, 1947)	5.85	17.50	35.00
-Smilin' Jack (Omar, 1945)	7.50	22.50	45.00
-Smilin' Jack (Hancock, 1947)	5.85	17.50	35.00
Oswald the Rabbit (Omar, 1945)	5.85	17.50	35.00
Oswald the Rabbit (Hancock, 1947)	4.15	12.50	25.00
Alley Oop (Omar, 1945)	13.00	39.00	90.00
Alley Oop (Hancock, 1947)	11.50	34.00	80.00
-Elmer Fudd (Omar, 1945)	5.85	17.50	35.00
-Elmer Fudd (Hancock, 1947)	4.15	12.50	25.00
-Little Orphan Annie (Omar, 1945)	8.35	25.00	50.00
-Little Orphan Annie (Hancock, 1947)	6.35	19.00	38.00
Woody Woodpecker (Omar, 1945)	5.85	17.50	35.00
Woody Woodpecker (Hancock, 1947)	4.15	12.50	25.00
Dick Tracy (Omar, 1945)	13.00	39.00	90.00
Dick Tracy (Hancock, 1947)	11.50	34.00	80.00
Bugs Bunny (Omar, 1945)	5.85	17.50	35.00
Bugs Bunny (Hancock, 1947)	4.15	12.50	25.00
Andy Panda (Omar, 1945)	5.00	15.00	30.00
Andy Panda (Hancock, 1947)	4.15	12.50	25.00
Terry & the Pirates (Omar, 1945)	11.50	34.00	80.00
Terry & the Pirates (Hancock, 1947)	10.00	30.00	65.00
Smokey Stover (Omar, 1946)	5.85	17.50	35.00
Smokey Stover (Hancock, 1948?)	4.15	12.50	25.00
Porky Pig (Omar, 1946)	5.00	15.00	30.00
Porky Pig (Hancock, 1948?)	4.15	12.50	25.00
Smilin' Jack (Omar, 1946)	5.85	17.50	35.00
Smilin' Jack (Hancock, 1948)	4.15	12.50	25.00
Oswald the Rabbit (Omar, 1946)	5.00	15.00	30.00
Oswald the Rabbit (Hancock, 1948)	4.00	12.00	24.00
Gasoline Alley (Omar, 1946)	8.35	25.00	50.00
Gasoline Alley (Hancock, 1948)	6.35	19.00	38.00
Elmer Fudd (Omar, 1946)	5.00	15.00	30.00
Elmer Fudd (Hancock, 1948)	4.00	12.00	24.00
Little Orphan Annie (Omar, 1946)	7.50	22.50	45.00
Little Orphan Annie (Hancock, 1948)	5.85	17.50	35.00
Woody Woodpecker (Omar, 1946)	5.00	15.00	30.00
Woody Woodpecker (Hancock, 1948)	4.00	12.00	24.00
Dick Tracy (Omar, 1946)	11.50	34.00	80.00
Dick Tracy (Hancock, 1948)	10.00	30.00	60.00
Bugs Bunny (Hancock, 1946))	5.00	15.00	30.00
Andy Panda (Omar, 1946)	5.00	15.00	30.00
Andy Panda (Hancock, 1946)	4.00	12.00	24.00
Terry & the Pirates (Omar, 1946)	11.50	34.00	80.00
Terry & the Pirates (Hancock, 1948)	10.00	30.00	60.00
Smokey Stover (Hancock, 1947)	5.00	15.00	30.00
Smokey Stover (Omar, 1947)	4.00	12.00	24.00
Porky Pig (Omar, 1947)	5.00	15.00	30.00
Porky Pig (Hancock, 1948)	4.00	12.00	24.00
Bugs Bunny (Hancock, 1948)-Does not match any Omar book			

	4.00	12.00	24.00

SUPERBOY (See Adventure, Aurora, DC Super Stars, DC Comics Presents, DC 100 Page Super Spectacular #15, DC Super Stars, 80 Page Giant #10, More Fun Comics, The New Advs. of... & Superman Family #191)

SUPERBOY (1st Series)(...& the Legion of Super-Heroes with #231)(Becomes The Legion of Super-Heroes No. 259 on)
Mar-Apr, 1949 - No. 258, Dec, 1979 (#1-16: 52 pgs.)
National Periodical Publications/DC Comics

	GD25	FN65	VF82	NM94
1-Superman cover	620.00	1860.00	3720.00	6200.00

(Estimated up to 275 total copies exist, 15 in NM/Mint)

	GD25	FN65	NM94
2-Used in **SOTI**, pg. 35-36,226	168.00	506.00	1350.00
3	131.00	393.00	1050.00
4,5: 5-1st pre-Supergirl tryout (c/story, 11-12/49)	90.00	271.00	725.00
6-10: 8-1st Superbaby. 10-1st app. Lana Lang	78.00	234.00	625.00
11-15	59.00	178.00	475.00
16-20	40.00	120.00	300.00
21-26,28-30: 21-Lana Lang app.	34.00	103.00	240.00
27-Low distribution	36.00	107.00	250.00
31-38: 38-Last pre-code issue (1/55)	25.00	75.00	175.00
39-48,50 (7/56)	22.00	66.00	155.00
49 (6/56)-1st app. Metallo (Jor-El's robot)	26.00	77.00	180.00
51-60: 52-1st S.A. issue	17.00	51.00	120.00
61-67	14.00	43.00	100.00
68-Origin/1st app. original Bizarro (10-11/58)	55.00	165.00	440.00
69-77,79: 75-Spanking-c. 76-1st Supermonkey. 77-Pre-Pete Ross tryout			
	11.00	33.00	75.00
78-Origin Mr. Mxyzptlk & Superboy's costume	20.00	60.00	140.00
80-1st meeting Superboy/Supergirl (4/60)	17.00	49.00	115.00
81,83-85,87,88: 83-Origin/1st app. Kryptonite Kid	9.30	28.00	65.00
82-1st Bizarro Krypto	10.00	30.00	70.00
86-(1/61)-4th Legion app.	16.00	47.00	120.00
89-(6/61)-1st app. Mon-el; 2nd Phantom Zone	32.00	96.00	225.00
90-92: 90-Pete Ross learns Superboy's I.D. 92-Last 10¢ issue			
	9.30	28.00	65.00
93-10th Legion app.(12/61); Chameleon Boy app.	9.50	28.00	75.00
94-97,99	5.70	17.00	40.00
98-(7/62)-18th Legion app; origin & 1st app. Ultra Boy; Pete Ross joins Legion	10.50	32.00	85.00
100-(10/62)-Ultra Boy app; 1st app. Phantom Zone villains, Dr. Xadu & Erndine. 2 pg. map of Krypton; origin Superboy retold; r-cover of Superman #1			
	24.00	71.00	165.00
101-120: 104-Origin Phantom Zone. 115-Atomic bomb-c. 117-Legion app.			
	4.30	13.00	33.00
121-128: 124-(10/65)-1st app. Insect Queen (Lana Lang). 125-Legion cameo. 126-Origin Krypto the Super Dog retold with new facts			
	3.75	11.25	30.00
129-(80-pg. Giant G-22)-Reprints origin Mon-el	4.50	14.00	32.00
130-137,139,140: 131-Legion statues cameo in Dog Legionnaires story. 132-1st app. Supremo. 133-Superboy meets Robin	3.60	9.00	18.00
138 (80-pg. Giant G-35)	4.50	14.00	35.00
141-146,148-155,157-164,166-173,175,176: 145-Superboy's parents regain their youth. 171-1st app. Aquaboy? 172,173,176-Legion app.; 172-Origin Yango (Super Ape). 176-Partial photo-c	1.70	5.00	12.00
147(6/68)-Giant G-47; 1st origin of L.S.H. (Saturn Girl, Lightning Lad, Cosmic Boy); origin Legion of Super-Pets-r/Adv. (#293?	2.85	8.50	20.00
156,165,174 (Giants G-59,71,83): 165-r/1st app. Krypto the Superdog from Adventure Comics #210	1.85	5.50	13.00
177-184,186,187 (All 52 pgs.): 182-All new origin of the classic World's Finest team (Superman & Batman) as teenagers (2/72, 22pgs.). 184-Origin Dial H for Hero-r.	1.00	2.00	5.00
185-DC 100 Pg. Super Spectacular #12; Legion-c/story; Teen Titans, Kid Eternity(r/Hit #46), Star Spangled Kid-r(S.S. 55)	1.70	5.00	12.00

Superboy #258 © DC

Superboy #1 © DC

Supercops #1 © Now Comics

	GD25	FN65	NM94

188-196: 188-Origin Karkan. 191-Origin Sunboy retold; Legion app. 193-Chameleon Boy & Shrinking Violet get new costumes. 195-1st app. Erg/Wildfire; Phantom Girl gets new costume. 196-Last Superboy solo story
.90 2.25

197-Legion series begins; Lightning Lad's new costume
1.30 3.25 8.00

198,199: 198-Element Lad & Princess Projectra get new costumes
1.00 2.50

200-Bouncing Boy & Duo Damsel marry; J'onn J'onzz cameo
1.20 3.00 7.00

201,204,206,207,209: 201-Re-intro Erg as Wildfire. 204-Supergirl resigns from Legion. 206-Ferro Lad & Invisible Kid app. 209-Karate Kid's new costume
1.10 2.75

202,205-(100 pgs.): 202-Light Lass gets new costume; Mike Grell's 1st comic work-i (5-6/74)
1.30 3.25

203-Invisible Kid dies
1.50 3.75

208,210: 208-(68 pgs.). 210-Origin Karate Kid
1.30 3.25

211-220: 212-Matter-Eater Lad resigns. 216-1st app. Tyroc who joins Legion in #218
1.00 2.50

221-249: 226-Intro. Dawnstar. 228-Death of Chemical King. 240-Origin Dawnstar. 242-(52 pgs.). 243-Legion of Substitute Heroes app.

243-245-(44 pgs.)
.80 2.00

250-258: 253-Intro Blok. 257-Return of Bouncing Boy & Duo Damsel by Ditko
.80 2.00

Annual 1(Sum/64, 84 pgs.)-Origin Krypto-r 19.00 56.00 150.00

Spectacular 1(1980, Giant)-Distr. through comic stores; mostly-r
.80 2.00

NOTE: **Neal Adams** c-143, 145, 146, 148-155, 157-161, 163, 164, 166-168, 172, 173, 175, 176, 178. **M. Anderson** a-245i. **Ditko** a-257r. **Grell** a-202i, 203-219, 220-224p, 235p; c-207-232, 235, 236p, 237, 239p, 240p, 243p, 246, 258. **Nasser** a(p)-222, 225, 226, 230, 231, 233, 236. **Simonson** a-237p. **Starlin** a(p)-239, 250, 251; c-238. **Staton** a-227p, 243-249p, 252-258p; c-247-251p. **Swan/Moldoff** c-109. **Tuska** a-172, 173, 176, 183, 235p. **Wood** inks-153-155, 157-161. Legion app.-172, 173, 176, 177, 183, 184, 188, 190, 191, 193, 195.

SUPERBOY (TV)(The Adventures of...#19 on) (2nd Series)
Feb, 1990 - No. 22, Dec, 1991 ($1.00/$1.25)
DC Comics

1-15: Mooney-a(p) in 1-8,18-20; 1-Photo-c from TV show. 8-Bizarro-c/story; Arthur Adams-a(i). 9-12,14-17-Swan-p
1.00

16-22: 16-Begin $1.25-c
1.30

SUPERBOY (3rd Series)
Feb, 1994 - Present ($1.50/$1.95)
DC Comics

1-5-Metropolis Kid from Reign of the Supermen
1.50

6-8: 6,7-Worlds Collide Pts. 3 & 8. 8-(9/94)-Zero Hour x-over
1.50

0, 9-15: 0-(10/94). 9-(11/94)-King Shark app.
1.50

16-24,26-34: 16-$1.95-c begins. 21-Legion app. 28-Supergirl-c/app.
.80 2.00

25-($2.95)-New Gods & Female Furies app.; w/pin-ups
1.20 3.00

Annual 1 (1994, $2.95, 68 pgs.)-Elseworlds story, Pt. 2 of The Super Seven (see Adventures Of Superman Annual #6)
1.20 3.00

Annual 2 (1995, $3.95)-Year One story
1.60 4.00

Annual 3 (1996, $2.95)-Legends of the Dead Earth
1.20 3.00

SUPER BRAT
Jan, 1954 - No. 4, July, 1954
Toby Press

1
5.35 16.00 32.00

2-4: 4-Li'l Teevy by Mel Lazarus
4.00 10.00 20.00

I.W. Reprint #1,2,3,7,8('58): 1-r/#1
1.60 4.00

I.W. (Super) Reprint #10('63)
1.60 4.00

SUPERCAR (TV)
Nov, 1962 - No. 4, Aug, 1963 (All painted-c)

Gold Key

1
31.00 92.00 21

2,3
15.00 45.00 10

4
21.00 62.00 14

SUPER CAT (Formerly Frisky Animals; also see Animal Crackers)
No. 56, Nov, 1953 - No. 58, May, 1954; Sept, 1957 - No. 4, May, 1958
Star Publications #56-58/Ajax/Farrell Publ. (Four Star Comic Corp.)

56-58-L.B. Cole-c on all
16.00 47.00 11

1(1957-Ajax)- "The Adventures of…"
7.50 22.50 4

2-4
5.00 15.00 3

SUPER CIRCUS (TV)
Jan, 1951 - No. 5, Sept, 1951 (Mary Hartline)
Cross Publishing Co.

1-(52 pgs.)-Cast photos on-c
10.00 30.00 6

2-Cast photos on-c
8.00 24.00 4

3-5
6.35 19.00 3

SUPER CIRCUS (TV)
No. 542, March, 1954 - No. 694, Mar, 1956 (Featuring Mary Hartline)
Dell Publishing Co.

Four Color 542,592,694: Mary Hartline photo-c
6.00 18.00 4

SUPER COMICS
May, 1938 - No. 121, Feb-Mar, 1949
Dell Publishing Co.

1-Terry & The Pirates, The Gumps, Dick Tracy, Little Orphan Annie, Little Joe, Gasoline Alley, Smilin' Jack, Smokey Stover, Smitty, Tiny Tim, Moon Mullins, Harold Teen, Winnie Winkle begin
266.00 800.00 16

2
100.00 300.00 6

3
91.00 275.00 5

4,5: 4-Dick Tracy-c; also #8-10,17,26(part),31
73.00 219.00 4

6-10
58.00 174.00 3

11-20: 20-Smilin' Jack-c (also #29,32)
45.00 137.00 2

21-29: 21-Magic Morro begins (origin & 1st app., 2/40). 22,27-Ken Ernst-c (also #257); Magic Morro c-22,25,27,34
36.00 107.00 2

30- "Sea Hawk" movie adaptation-c/story with Errol Flynn
36.00 107.00 20

31-40: 34-Ken Ernst. 35-Dick Tracy-c begin
28.00 84.00 10

41-50: 41-Intro Lightning Jim. 43-Terry & The Pirates ends
23.00 69.00 1

51-60
17.00 49.00 1

61-70: 62-Flag-c. 65-Brenda Starr-r begin? 67-X-Mas-c
14.00 43.00 1

71-80
11.50 34.00

81-99
10.00 30.00

100
11.00 33.00

101-115-Last Dick Tracy (moves to own title)
7.00 21.00

116,118-All Smokey Stover
5.85 17.50

117-All Gasoline Alley
5.85 17.50

119-121-Terry & The Pirates app. in all
5.85 17.50

SUPER COPS, THE
July, 1974 (one-shot)
Red Circle Productions (Archie)

1-Morrow-c/a

SUPER COPS
Sept, 1990 - No. 4, Dec?, 1990 ($1.75)
Now Comics

1-($2.75, 52 pgs.)-Dave Dorman painted-c
1.40

1-2nd printing ($2.75)
1.40

2-4
.90

SUPER CRACKED (See Cracked)

Super Friends #1 © DC

Supergirl #3 © DC

Supergirl /Lex Luthor Special #1 © DC

	GD25	FN65	NM94

UPER DC GIANT (25-50¢, all 68-52 pg. Giants)
., 13, 9-10/70 - No. 26, 7-8/71; V3#27, Summer, 1976 (No #1-12)
ational Periodical Publications

	GD25	FN65	NM94
13-Binky	2.15	6.50	15.00
14-Top Guns of the West; Kubert-c; Trigger Twins, Johnny Thunder, Wyoming Kid-r; Moreira-r (9-10/70)	1.00	2.60	6.00
15-Western Comics; Kubert-c; Pow Wow Smith, Vigilante, Buffalo Bill-r; new Gil Kane-a (9-10/70)	1.20	3.00	7.00
16-Best of the Brave & the Bold; Batman-r & Metamorpho origin-r from Brave & the Bold; Spectre pin-up.	1.00	2.60	6.00
17-Love 1970	1.65	4.20	10.00
18-Three Mouseketeers; Dizzy Dog, Doodles Duck, Bo Bunny-r; Sheldon Mayer-a	1.00	2.60	6.00
19-Jerry Lewis; no Neal Adams-a	1.65	4.20	10.00
20-House of Mystery; N. Adams-c; Kirby-r(3)	1.65	4.20	10.00
21-Love 1971	1.50	3.75	9.00
22-Top Guns of the West	1.00	2.00	5.00
23-The Unexpected	1.50	3.75	9.00
24-Supergirl	1.00	2.60	6.00
25-Challengers of the Unknown; all Kirby/Wood-r	1.00	2.00	5.00
26-Aquaman (1971)	1.00	2.00	5.00
Strange Flying Saucers Adventures (Sum, 1976)	1.00	2.00	5.00

NOTE: *Sid Greene r-27p(2), Heath r-27. G. Kane a-14r(2), 15, 27r(p). Kubert r-16.*

PER-DOOPER COMICS
6 - No. 8, 1946 (10¢, 32 pgs., paper-c)(#1-4 exist?)
 Manufacturing Co.

he Clock, Gangbuster app.	14.00	43.00	100.00
	10.00	30.00	60.00
,6	8.35	25.00	50.00
-Capt. Freedom & Shock Gibson	10.00	30.00	65.00
hock Gibson, Sam Hill	10.00	30.00	65.00

ER DUCK COMICS (The Cockeyed Wonder) (See Jolly Jingles)
1944 - No. 94, Dec, 1960 (Also see Laugh #24)(#1-5 are quarterly)
Mag. No. 1-4(9/45)/Close-Up No. 5 on (in Archie)

rigin; Hitler & Hirohito-c	40.00	120.00	290.00
ll Vigoda-c	19.00	58.00	135.00
4-20-Al Fagaly-c (most)	14.00	43.00	100.00
	11.50	34.00	80.00
	10.00	30.00	60.00
3-40	8.35	25.00	50.00
sed in SOTI, pg. 35,307,308	9.15	27.50	55.00
	5.85	17.50	35.00
	4.00	12.00	24.00

R DUPER (Formerly Pocket Comics #1-4?)
1941 - No. 11, 1941
y Publications

aptain Freedom & Shock Gibson app.	25.00	75.00	175.00
	14.00	43.00	100.00

R DUPER COMICS (Formerly Latest Comics?)
May-June, 1947
oward Publ.

app. Mr. Monster	9.15	27.00	55.00

R FRIENDS (TV) (Also see Best of DC & Limited Collectors' Edition)
976 - No. 47, Aug, 1981 (#14 is 44 pgs.)
al Periodical Publications/DC Comics

erman, Batman, Robin, Wonder Woman, Aquaman, Atom, Wendy, rvin & Wonder Dog begin (1st Super Friends)		1.20	3.00

2-Penguin-c/story. 7-1st app. Wonder Twins & The Seraph. 8-1st app.
k O'Lantern. 9-1st app. Icemaiden. 13-1st app. Dr. Mist. 14-Origin
nder Twins. 25-1st app. Fire & Green Fury. 28-Bizarro app. 31-Black
hid app. 36,43-Plastic Man app. 47-Origin Fire & Green Fury

	GD25	FN65	NM94

...Special 1 (1981, giveaway, no ads, no code or price)-r/Super Friends #19		1.00	2.50
& 36		.80	2.00

NOTE: *Estrada a-1p, 2p. Orlando a-1p. Staton a-43, 45.*

SUPER FUN
Jan, 1956 (By A.W. Nugent)
Gillmor Magazines

1-Comics, puzzles, cut-outs by A.W. Nugent	3.20	8.00	16.00

SUPER FUNNIES (...Western Funnies #3,4)
Dec, 1953 - No. 4, Sept, 1954
Superior Comics Publishers Ltd. (Canada)

1-(3-D, 10¢)...Presents Dopey Duck; make your own 3-D glasses cut-out inside front-c; did not come w/glasses	36.00	107.00	250.00
2-Horror & crime satire	10.00	30.00	60.00
3-Phantom Ranger-c/s; Geronimo, Billy the Kid app.	5.00	15.00	30.00
4-Phantom Ranger-c/story	5.00	15.00	30.00

SUPERGEAR COMICS
1976 (Giveaway, 4 pgs. in color, slick paper)
Jacobs Corp.

nn-(Rare)-Superman, Lois Lane; Steve Lombard app. (500 copies printed, over half destroyed?)	1.00	2.50	6.00

SUPERGIRL (See Action, Adventure #281, Brave & the Bold, Crisis on Infinite Earths #7, Daring New Advs. of..., Super DC Giant, Superman Family, & Super-Team Family)

SUPERGIRL
Nov, 1972 - No. 9, Dec-Jan, 1973-74; No. 10, Sept-Oct, 1974 (1st solo title)(20¢)
National Periodical Publications

1-Zatanna back-up stories begin, end #5	2.15	6.50	15.00
2-10: 5-Zatanna origin-r. 8-JLA x-over; Batman cameo	1.00	2.00	5.00

NOTE: *Zatanna in #1-5, 7(Guest); Prez app. in #10. #1-10 are 20¢ issues.*

SUPERGIRL (Formerly Daring New Adventures of...)
No. 14, Dec, 1983 - No. 23, Sept, 1984
DC Comics

14-23: 16-Ambush Bug app. 20-JLA and New Teen Titans app.			1.00
...Movie Special (1985)-Adapts movie; Morrow-a; photo back-c			1.25
Giveaway ('84, '86 Baxter, nn)(American Honda/U.S. Dept. Transportation)-Torres-c/a			1.25

SUPERGIRL
Feb, 1994 - No. 4, May, 1994 ($1.50, limited series)
DC Comics

1-4: Guice-a(i)			1.50

SUPERGIRL (See Showcase '96 #8)
Sept, 1996 - Present ($1.95)
DC Comics

1-8: Peter David scripts & Gary Frank-c/a			2.00
Annual 1 (1996, $2.95)-Legends of the Dead Earth; Dixon & Lansdale scripts			3.00

SUPERGIRL/LEX LUTHOR SPECIAL (Supergirl and Team Luthor on-c)
1993 ($2.50, 68 pgs., one-shot)
DC Comics

1-Pin-ups by Byrne & Thibert		1.00	2.50

SUPER GOOF (Walt Disney) (See Dynabrite & The Phantom Blot)
Oct, 1965 - No. 74, 1982
Gold Key No. 1-57/Whitman No. 58 on

1	3.60	9.00	20.00
2-5	2.00	5.00	10.00
6-10	1.60	4.00	8.00
11-20	1.20	3.00	6.00
21-30		1.20	3.00

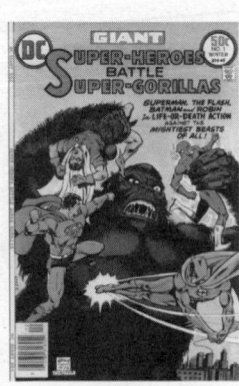
Super-Heroes Battle Super-Gorillas #1 © DC

Superman #11 © DC

Superman #16 © DC

	GD25	FN65	NM94
31-50		.80	2.00
51-74			1.00

NOTE: *Reprints in #16, 24, 28, 29, 37, 38, 43, 45, 46, 54(1/2), 56-58, 65(1/2), 72(r-#2).*

SUPER GREEN BERET (Tod Holton…)
April, 1967 - No. 2, June, 1967 (25¢, 68 pgs.)
Lightning Comics (Milson Publ. Co.)

1,2	2.85	8.50	20.00

SUPER HEROES (See Giant-Size… & Marvel…)

SUPER HEROES
Jan, 1967 - No. 4, June, 1967
Dell Publishing Co.

1-Origin & 1st app. Fab 4	3.60	11.00	25.00
2-4	2.30	6.75	16.00

SUPER-HEROES BATTLE SUPER-GORILLAS (See DC Special #16)
Winter, 1976 (52 pgs., all reprints, one-shot)
National Periodical Publications

1-Superman, Batman, Flash stories; Infantino-a(p)		.80	2.00

SUPER HEROES PUZZLES AND GAMES
1979 (32 pgs., regular size)
General Mills Giveaway (Marvel Comics Group)

nn-Four 2-pg. origin stories of Spider-Man, Captain America, The Hulk, & Spider-Woman	1.00	2.00	5.00

SUPER HEROES VERSUS SUPER VILLAINS
July, 1966 (no month given)(68 pgs.)
Archie Publications (Radio Comics)

1-Flyman, Black Hood, Web, Shield-r; Reinman-a	5.70	17.00	40.00

SUPERICHIE (Formerly Super Richie)
No. 5, Oct, 1976 - No. 18, Jan, 1979 (52 pgs. giants)
Harvey Publications

5-18: 5-Origin/1st app. new costumes for Rippy & Crashman			1.00

SUPERIOR STORIES
May-June, 1955 - No. 4, Nov-Dec, 1955
Nesbit Publishing Co.

1-The Invisible Man by H.G. Wells	15.00	45.00	105.00
2-The Pirate of the Gulf by J.H. Ingrahams	8.70	26.00	52.00
3-Wreck of the Grosvenor by William Clark Russell	8.70	26.00	52.00
4-The Texas Rangers by O'Henry	8.70	26.00	52.00

NOTE: *Morisi c/a in all. Kiwanis stories in #3 & 4. #4 has photo of Gene Autry on-c.*

SUPER MAGIC (Super Magician Comics #2 on)
May, 1941
Street & Smith Publications

V1#1-Blackstone the Magician-c/story; origin/1st app. Rex King (Black Fury); Charles Sultan-c; Blackstone-c begin	106.00	318.00	850.00

SUPER MAGICIAN COMICS (Super Magic #1)
No. 2, Sept, 1941 - V5#8, Feb-Mar, 1947
Street & Smith Publications

V1#2-Blackstone the Magician continues; Rex King, Man of Adventure app.	45.00	135.00	360.00
3-Tao-Anwar, Boy Magician begins	31.00	94.00	220.00
4-Origin Transo	29.00	86.00	200.00
5-7,9-12: 11-Supersnipe app.	29.00	86.00	200.00
8-Abbott & Costello story (1st app?, 11/42)	31.00	94.00	220.00
V2#1-The Shadow app.	34.00	103.00	240.00
2-12: 5-Origin Tigerman. 8-Red Dragon begins	13.50	41.00	95.00
V3#1-12: 5-Origin Mr. Twilight	13.50	41.00	95.00
V4#1-12: 11-Nigel Elliman begins	11.50	34.00	80.00
V5#1-6	11.50	34.00	80.00
7,8-Red Dragon by Edd Cartier-c/a	30.00	90.00	210.00

NOTE: *Jack Binder c-1-14(most). Red Dragon c-V5#7, 8.*

SUPERMAN (See Action Comics, Advs. of…, All-New Coll. Ed., All-Star Comics, Best of DC, Brave & the Bold, Cosmic Odyssey, DC Comics Presents, Heroes Against Hunger, Krµ Chronicles, Limited Coll. Ed., Man of Steel, Phantom Zone, Power Record Comics, Special Edition, Steel, Super Friends, Superman: The Man of Steel, Taylor's Christmas Tabloid, Th Dimension Advs., World of Krypton, World Of Metropolis, World of Smallville & World's Fir**

SUPERMAN (Becomes Adventures of…#424 on)
Summer, 1939 - No. 423, Sept, 1986 (#1-5 are quarterly)
National Periodical Publications/DC Comics

	GD25	FN65	VF82	N
1(nn)-1st four Action stories reprinted; origin Superman by Siegel & Shuste has a new 2 pg. origin plus 4 pgs. omitted in Action story; see The Comi Magazine #1 & More Fun #14-17 for Superman proto-type app.; cover r/splash page from Action #10; 1st pin-up Superman on back-c - 1st pin-comics	12,500.00	37,500.00	70,000.00	110,00

(Estimated up to 190 total copies exist, 3 in NM/Mint)

1-Reprint, Oversize 13-1/2x10". WARNING: This comic is an exact duplicate reprint original except for its size. DC published it in 1978 with a second cover titling it as a Famo Edition. There have been many reported cases of the outer cover being removed and the sold as the original edition. The reprint with the new outer cover removed is practically wo See Famous First Edition for value.

	GD25	FN65	N
2-All daily strip-r; full pg. ad for N.Y. World's Fair	967.00	2900.00	920
3-2nd story-r from Action #5; 3rd story-r from Action #6	620.00	1860.00	620
4-2nd mention of Daily Planet (Spr/40); also see Action #23; 2nd & 3rd Luthor (red-headed; also see Action #23)	489.00	1467.00	46
5-4th Luthor app. (red hair)	355.00	1066.00	32
6,7: 6-1st splash pg. in a Superman comic. 7-1st Perry White? (11-12/40)	281.00	843.00	22
8-10: 10-5th app. Luthor (1st bald Luthor, 5-6/41)	243.00	731.00	19
11-13,15: 13-Jimmy Olsen & Luthor app.	175.00	525.00	14
14-Patriotic Shield-c by Fred Ray	281.00	843.00	22
16,18-20: 16-1st Lois Lane-c this title (5-6/42); 2nd Lois-c after Action #29	150.00	450.00	12
17-Hitler, Hirohito-c	162.00	487.00	13
21-23,25: 25-Clark Kent's only military service; Fred Ray's only super-hero	112.00	338.00	9
24-Jack Burnley flag-c	143.00	431.00	11
26-29: 27,29-31-Lois Lane-c. 28-Lois Lane Girl Reporter series begins, en #40,42	103.00	309.00	8
28-Overseas edition for Armed Forces; same as reg. #28	103.00	309.00	8
30-Origin & 1st app. Mr. Mxyztplk (9-10/44)(pronounced "Mix-it-plk") in co books; name later became Mxyzptlk ("Mix-yez-pit-l-ick"); the character w inspired by a combination of Al Capp's Joe Blyfstyk (the littl man with the black cloud over his head) & the devilish antics of Bugs Bu he 1st app. in newspapers 3/7/44	162.00	487.00	13
31-40: 33-(3-4/45)-3rd app. Mxyzptlk. 35,36-Lois Lane-c. 38-Atomic bomb story (1-2/46); delayed because of gov't cencorship; Superman shown reading Batman #32 on cover	90.00	271.00	7
41-50: 42-Lois Lane-c. 45-Lois Lane as Superwoman (see Action #60 for app.). 46-(5-6/47)-1st app. Superboy this title? 48-1st time Superman tr thru time	68.00	206.00	5
51,52: 51-Lois Lane-c	56.00	168.00	4
53-Origin Superman retold; 10th anniversary ('48)	237.00	712.00	19
54,56-60: 58-Intro Tiny Trix	56.00	168.00	4
55-Used in SOTI, pg. 33	60.00	181.00	4
61-Origin Superman retold; origin Green Kryptonite (1st Kryptonite story); Superman returns to Krypton to save it & sees his parents for 1st time since infancy, discovers he's not earth man	112.00	338.00	9
62-65,67-70: 62-Orson Welles-c/story. 65-1st Krypton Foes: Mala, K120, & U-Ban. 67-Perry Como-c/story. 68-1st Luthor-c this title (see Action Cor	56.00	168.00	4
66-2nd Superbaby story	56.00	168.00	4
71-75: 74-2nd Luthor-c this title. 75-Some have #74 on-c	53.00	159.00	4

Superman #301 © DC

Superman #408 © DC

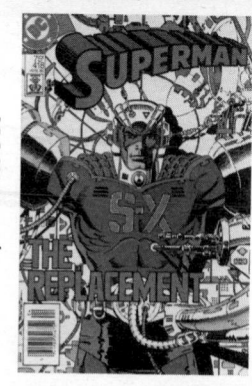

Superman #418 © DC

SU

	GD25	FN65	NM94
72-Giveaway(9-10/51)-(Rare)-Price blackened out; came with banner wrapped around book; without banner	64.00	193.00	515.00
72-Giveaway with banner	93.00	281.00	750.00
76-Batman x-over; Superman & Batman learn each other's I.D. for the 1st time (5-6/52)(also see World's Finest #71)	153.00	459.00	1225.00
77-81: 78-Last 52 pg. issue. 81-Used in POP, pg. 88	50.00	150.00	400.00
82-87,89,90	46.00	138.00	370.00
88-Prankster, Toyman & Luthor team-up	48.00	146.00	390.00
91-95: 95-Last precode issue (2/55)	40.00	120.00	320.00
96-99: 96-Mr. Mxyztplk-c/story	39.00	116.00	270.00

	GD25	FN65	VF82	NM94
100 (9-10/55)-Shows cover to #1 on-c	150.00	450.00	910.00	1500.00

	GD25	FN65	NM94
101-105,107-110: 109-1st S.A. issue	36.00	107.00	250.00
106 (7/56)-Retells origin	39.00	118.00	275.00
111-120	30.00	90.00	210.00
121-130: 123-Pre-Supergirl tryout-c/story (8/58). 127-Origin/1st app. Titano. 128-Red Kryptonite used (4/59). 129-Intro/origin Lori Lemaris, The Mermaid	26.00	77.00	180.00
131-139: 139-Lori Lemaris app.; "Untold Story of Red Kryptonite" back-up story	20.00	60.00	140.00
140-1st Blue Kryptonite & Bizarro Supergirl; origin Bizarro Jr. #1	22.00	66.00	155.00
141-145,148: 142-2nd Batman x-over	16.00	47.00	110.00
146-(7/61)-Superman's life story; back-up hints at Earth II	19.00	58.00	135.00
147(8/61)-7th Legion app; 1st app. Legion of Super-Villains; 1st app. Adult Legion; swipes-c to Adv. #247	18.00	54.00	125.00
149(11/61)-9th Legion app. (cameo); "The Death of Superman" imaginary story; last 10¢ issue	16.00	47.00	110.00
150-162: 152(4/62)-15th Legion app. 155-(8/62)-19th Legion app; Lightning Man & Cosmic Man, & Adult Legion app. 156,162-Legion app. 157-Gold Kryptonite used (see Adv. 299); Mon-el app.; Lightning Lad cameo (11/62). 158-1st app. Flamebird & Nightwing & Nor-Kan of Kandor (12/62). 161-1st told death of Pa and Pa Kent	8.00	24.50	65.00
161-2nd printing (1987, $1.25)-New DC logo; sold thru So Much Fun Toy Stores (reprint title: Superman Classic)	.90		2.25
163-166,168-180: 166-XMas-c. 168-All Luthor issue; JFK tribute/memorial. 169-Bizarro Invasion of Earth-c/story; last Sally Selwyn. 170-Pres. Kennedy story is finally published after delay from #169 due to assassination. 172,173-Legion cameos. 174-Super-Mxyztplk; Bizarro app.	6.50	19.50	48.00
167-New origin Brainiac & Brainiac 5; intro Tixarla (later Luthor's wife)	11.00	33.00	78.00
181,182,184-186,188-192,194-196,198,200: 181-1st 2965 story/series. 182-1st S.A. app. of The Toyman (1/66). 189-Origin/destruction of Krypton II.	5.00	15.00	40.00
183,187,193,197 (Giants G-18,G-23,G-31,G-36)	5.70	17.00	45.00
199-1st Superman/Flash race (8/67); also see Flash #175 & World's Finest #198,199 (r-in Limited Coll. Ed. #48)	26.00	79.00	190.00
201,203-206,208-211,213-216: 213-Brainiac-5 app.	3.60	11.00	25.00
202 (80-pg. Giant G-42)-All Bizarro issue	4.00	12.00	30.00
207,212,217,222,239 (Giants G-48,G-54,G-60,G-66,G-84): 207-Legion app.; 30th anniversary Superman (6/68)	4.00	12.00	30.00
218-221,223-226,228-231	2.85	8.50	20.00
227,232(Giants, G-72,G-78)-All Krypton issues	4.00	12.50	33.00
233-2nd app. Morgan Edge; Clark Kent switches from newspaper reporter to TV newscaster; all Kryptonite on earth destroyed	3.75	11.25	30.00
234-238	2.15	6.50	15.00
240-Kaluta-a	1.20	3.00	7.00
241-244 (All 52 pgs.): 243-G.A.-r/#38	1.00	2.60	6.00
245-DC 100 Pg. Super Spectacular #7; Air Wave, Kid Eternity, Hawkman-r; Atom-r/Atom #3	1.65	4.20	12.00

	GD25	FN65	NM94
246-248,250,251,253 (All 52 pgs.): 246-G.A.-r/#40. 248-World of Krypton story. 251-G.A.-r/#45. 253-Finlay-a, 2 pgs., G.A.-r/#1	1.00	2.00	7.00
249,254-Neal Adams-a. 249-(52 pgs.); origin & 1st app. Terra-Man by Neal Adams (inks)	1.65	4.20	10.00
252-DC 100 Pg. Super Spectacular #13; Ray(r/Smash #17), Black Condor, (r/Crack #18), Hawkman(r/Flash #24); Starman-r/Adv. #67; Dr. Fate & Spectre-r/More Fun #57; N. Adams-c	1.70	5.00	12.00
255-271,273-277,279-283: 263-Photo-c. 264-1st app. Steve Lombard. 276-Intro Capt. Thunder. 279-Batman, Batgirl app.	1.00		2.50
272,278,284-All 100 pgs. G.A.-r in all. 272-r/2nd app. Mr. Mxyztplk from Action #80	1.65	4.20	10.00
285-299: 289-Partial photo-c. 292-Origin Lex Luthor retold	1.00		2.50
300-Retells origin (6/76)	1.30	3.25	8.00
301-399: 301,320-Solomon Grundy app. 323-Intro. Atomic Skull. 327-329-(44 pgs.). 330-More facts revealed about I. D. 338-The bottled city of Kandor enlarged. 344-Frankenstein & Dracula app. 353-Brief origin. 354,355,357-Superman 2020 stories (354-Debut of Superman III). 356-World of Krypton story (also #360,367,375). 366-Fan letter by Todd McFarlane. 372-Superman 2021 story. 376-Free 16 pg. preview Daring New Advs. of Supergirl. 377-Free 16 pg. preview Masters of the Universe	1.00		2.50
400 (10/84, $1.50, 68 pgs.)-Many top artists featured; Chaykin painted cover, Miller back-c	1.00	2.00	5.00
401-422: 405-Super-Batman story. 408-Nuclear Holocaust-c/story. 411-Special Julius Schwartz tribute issue. 414,415-Crisis x-over. 422-Horror-c	1.00		2.50
423-Alan Moore scripts; Perez-a(i); last Earth I Superman story, cont'd in Action #583	1.65	4.20	10.00
Annual 1(10/60, 84 pgs.)-Reprints 1st Supergirl story/Action #252; r/Lois Lane #1; Krypto-r (1st Silver Age DC annual)	82.00	246.00	825.00
Annual 2(Win, 1960-61)-Super-villain issue; Brainiac, Titano, Metallo, Bizarro origin-r	39.00	117.00	375.00
Annual 3(Sum, 1961)-Strange Lives of Superman	31.00	92.00	275.00
Annual 4(Win, 1961-62)-11th Legion app; 1st Legion origins (text & pictures); advs. in time, space & on alien worlds	25.00	75.00	225.00
Annual 5(Sum, 1962)-All Krypton issue	20.00	60.00	180.00
Annual 6(Win, 1962-63)-Legion-r/Adv. #247	19.00	58.00	165.00
Annual 7(Sum, 1963)-Origin-r/Superman-Batman team/Adv. 275; r/1955 Superman dailies	15.00	45.00	120.00
Annual 8(Win, 1963-64)-All origins issue	13.00	39.00	105.00
Annual 9(8/64)-Was advertised but came out as 80 Page Giant #1 instead			
Annual 9(1983)-Toth/Austin-a	1.00	2.50	6.00
Annuals 10-12(1984, $1.25)-M. Anderson inks. 11(1985)-Moore scripts. 12(1986)-Bolland-c	1.00	2.00	5.00
Special 1(1983)-G. Kane-c/a; contains German-r	1.00	2.00	5.00
Special 2,3(1984, 1985, $1.25, 52 pgs.)	1.00	2.00	5.00
The Amazing World of Superman "Official Metropolis Edition" (1973, $2.00, 14x10-1/2")-Origin retold; Wood-r(i) from Superboy #153,161	1.65	4.20	10.00
Kelloggs Giveaway-(2/3 normal size, 1954)-r-two stories/Superman #55	33.00	100.00	230.00
...Meets the Quik Bunny (1987, Nestles Quik premium, 36 pgs.)			1.50
Pizza Hut Premiums (12/77)-Exact reprints of 1950s comics except for paid ads (set of 6 exist?); Vol. 1-r#97 (#113-r also known)			2.00
Radio Shack Giveaway-36 page series (7/80) "The Computers That Saved Metropolis", Starlin/Giordano-a; advertising insert in Action #509, New Advs. of Superboy #7, Legion of Super-Heroes #265, & House of Mystery #282. (All comics were 68 pgs.) Cover of inserts printed on newsprint. Giveaway contains 4 extra pgs. of Radio Shack advertising that inserts do not	.80		2.00
Radio Shack Giveaway-(7/81) "Victory by Computer"	.80		2.00
Radio Shack Giveaway-(7/82) "Computer Masters of Metropolis"	.80		2.00
11195 (2/79, $1.95, $1.25, 52 pgs.)-Golden Press	1.00		2.50

NOTE: **N. Adams** a-249i, 254p; c-204-208, 210, 212-215, 219, 231, 233-237, 240-243, 249-252, 254, 263, 307, 308, 313, 314, 317. **Adkins** a-323i. **Austin** c-368i. **Wayne Boring** art-late 1940's to early 1960's. **Buckler** a(p)-352, 363, 364, 369; c(p)-324-327, 356, 363, 368, 369, 373, 376, 378. **Burnley** a-252r; c-19-25, 30, 33, 34, 35p, 38p, 39p, 45p. **Fine** a-252r. **Kaluta** a-400. **Gil**

531

Superman #53 © DC

Superman #115 © DC

Superman Adventures #4 © DC

	GD25	FN65	NM94

Kane a-272r, 367, 372, 375, Special 2; c-374p, 375p, 377, 381, 382, 384-390, 392, Annual 9, Special 2. Joe Kubert a-216. Miller-pin-up. Morrow a-238. Mortimer a-250r. Perez c-364p. Fred Ray a-25; c-6, 8-18. Starlin c-355. Staton a-354l, 355l. Swan/Moldoff c-149. Williamson a(i)-408-410, 412-416; c-408l, 409l. Wrightson a-400, 416.

SUPERMAN (2nd Series)
Jan, 1987 - Present (75¢/$1.00/$1.25/$1.50/$1.95)
DC Comics

1-Byrne-c/a begins; intro new Metallo		1.20	3.00
2-8,10: 3-Legends x-over; Darkseid-c & app. 7-Origin/1st app. Rampage.			
8-Legion app.		.80	2.00
9-Joker-c		1.60	4.00
11-49,51,52,54-56,58-67: 11-1st new Mr. Mxyzptlk. 12-Lori Lemaris revived. 13-1st app. new Toyman. 13,14-Millennium x-over. 16-1st app. new Supergirl (4/88). 20-Doom Patrol app.; Supergirl cameo. 21-Supergirl-c/story; 1st app. Matrix who becomes new Supergirl. 31-Mr. Mxyzptlk app. 37-Newsboy Legion app. 41-Lobo app. 44-Batman storyline, part 1. 45-Free extra 8 pgs. 54-Newsboy Legion story. 63-Aquaman x-over.			
67-Last $1.00-c		.80	2.00
50-($1.50, 52 pgs.)-Clark Kent proposes to Lois		1.80	4.50
50-2nd printing		.70	1.75
53-Clark reveals i.d. to Lois (Cont'd from Action #662)		1.20	3.00
53-2nd printing			1.50
57-($1.75, 52 pgs.)		.70	1.75
68-72: 65,66,68-Deathstroke-c/stories. 70-Superman & Robin team-up			1.50
73-Doomsday cameo		1.60	4.00
74-Doomsday Pt. 2 (Cont'd from Justice League #69); Superman battles Doomsday	1.00	2.00	5.00
73,74-2nd printings		.80	2.00
75-($2.50)-Collector's Ed.; Doomsday Pt. 6; Superman dies; polybagged w/poster of funeral, obituary from Daily Planet, postage stamp & armband premiums (direct inks only)	2.15	6.50	15.00
75-Direct sales copy (no upc code, 1st print)		1.60	4.00
75-Direct sales copy (no upc code, 2nd print)			1.25
75-Direct sales copy (no upc code, 3rd, 4th prints)			1.25
75-Newsstand copy w/upc code		1.60	4.00
75-Platinum Edition; given away to retailers	7.00	21.50	50.00
76,77-Funeral for a friend parts 4 & 8		.90	2.25
78-($1.95)-Collector's Edition with die-cut outer-c & bound-in mini poster; Doomsday cameo		.90	2.25
78-($1.50)-Newsstand Edition w/poster and different-c; Doomsday-c & cameo		.80	2.00
79-81,83-89: 83-Funeral for a Friend epilogue; new Batman (Azrael) cameo. 87,88-Bizarro-c/story		.80	2.00
82-($3.50)-Collector's Edition w/all chromium-c; real Superman revealed; Green Lantern x-over from G.L. #46; no ads		1.40	3.50
82-($2.00, 44 pgs.)-Regular Edition w/different-c		.80	2.00
90-93: 93-(9/94)-Zero Hour			1.50
0, 94-99: 0-(10/94). 94-(11/94). 95-Atom app. 96-Return of Brainiac.			1.50
100-Death of Clark Kent foil-c		1.60	4.00
100-Newsstand		1.20	3.00
101-115: 101-Begin $1.95-c; Black Adam app. 105-Green Lantern app. 110-Plastic Man-c/app. 114-Brainiac app; Dwyer-c. 115-Lois leaves Metropolis. 116-(10/96)-1st app. Teen Titans by Dan Jurgens & George Perez in 8 pg. preview		.80	2.00
Annual 1,2: 1 (1987)-No Byrne-a. 2 (1988)-Byrne-a; Newsboy Legion; return of the Guardian		.80	2.00
Annual 3 (1991, $2.00, 68 pgs.)-Armageddon 2001 x-over; Batman app.; Austin-c(i) & part inks		.90	2.25
Annual 3-2nd & 3rd printings; 3rd has silver ink		.80	2.00
Annual 4 (1992, $2.50, 68 pgs.)-Eclipso app.		1.00	2.50
Annual 5 (1993, $2.50, 68 pgs.)		1.00	2.50
Annual 6 (1994, $2.95, 68 pgs.)-Elseworlds story		1.20	3.00

	GD25	FN65	NM94

Annual 7 (1995, $3.95, 69 pgs.)-Year One story		1.40	3.50
Annual 8 (1996, $2.95)-Legends of the Dead Earth story			3.00
Special 1 (1992, $3.50, 68 pgs.)-Simonson-c/a		1.40	3.50
...: TIME AND TIME AGAIN (1994, $7.50)-Reprints	1.30	3.10	7.50
THE DEATH OF SUPERMAN TPB nn (1993, $4.95)-Reprints Man of Steel #17-19, Superman #73-75, Advs. of Superman #496,497, Action #683,684 & Justice League #69			6.00
THE DEATH OF SUPERMAN, 2nd & 3rd printings		2.00	5.00
THE DEATH OF SUPERMAN Platinum Edition	2.85	6.50	15.00

NOTE: Austin a(i)-1-3. Byrne a-1-16p, 17, 19-21p, 22; c-1-17, 20-22; scripts-1-22. Guice c/a-64. Kirby c-37p. Joe Quesada c-Annual 4. Russell c/a-23l. Simonson c-69l. #19-21 2nd printings sold in multi-packs.

SUPERMAN (one-shots)
DAILY NEWS MAGAZINE PRESENTS DC COMICS' SUPERMAN
nn-(1987, 8 pgs.)-Supplement to New York Daily News; Perez-c/a

			1.50
...: AT EARTH'S END (1995, $4.95)-Elseworlds story			3.00
... FOR EARTH (1991, $4.95, 52 pgs, printed on recycled paper)-Ordway wraparound-c	1.00	2.00	5.00
...IV MOVIE SPECIAL (1987, $2.00)-Movie adaptation; Heck-a			5.00
...GALLERY, THE 1 (1993, $2.95)-Poster-a		.80	2.00
...: KAL (1995, $5.95)-Elseworlds story		1.20	3.00
...MOVIE SPECIAL-(9/83)-Adaptation of Superman III; other versions exist with store logos on bottom 1/3 of-c	1.00	2.60	6.00
...: SPEEDING BULLETS-(1993, $4.95, 52 pgs.)-Elseworlds			1.00
.../SPIDER-MAN-(1995, $3.95)-r/DC and Marvel Presents...			5.00
...: THE EARTH STEALERS 1-(1988, $2.95, 52 pgs, prestige format) 1-Byrne script; painted-c		1.40	3.50
...: THE EARTH STEALERS 1-2nd printing		1.20	3.00
...: THE LEGACY OF SUPERMAN #1 (3/93, $2.50, 68 pgs.)-Art Adams-c; Simonson-a		1.00	2.50
.../TOYMAN-(1996, $1.95)			2.00
...: UNDER A YELLOW SUN nn (1994, $5.95, 68 pgs.)-A Novel by Clark Kent; embossed-c	1.00	2.50	6.00

SUPERMAN ADVENTURES, THE (TV)
Oct, 1996 - Present ($1.75) (Based on animated series)
DC Comics

1-6: 1-Rick Burchett-c/a begins; Paul Dini script; Lex Luthor app.; silver ink, wraparound-c. 2-Scott McCloud scripts begin; Metallo-c/app. 3-Brainiac-c/app.			1.75

SUPERMAN AND THE GREAT CLEVELAND FIRE
1948 (Giveaway, 4 pgs., no cover) (Hospital Fund)
National Periodical Publications

nn-In full color	59.00	178.00	475.00

SUPERMAN/BATMAN: ALTERNATE HISTORIES
1996 ($14.95, trade paperback)
DC Comics

nn-Reprints Detective Comics Annual #7, Action Comics Annual #6, Steel Annual #1, Legends of the Dark Knight Annual #4			15.00

SUPERMAN/DOOMSDAY: HUNTER/PREY
1994 - No. 3, 1994 ($4.95, limited series, 52 pgs.)
DC Comics

1-3		1.00	2.00	5.00

SUPERMAN FAMILY, THE (Formerly Superman's Pal Jimmy Olsen)
No. 164, Apr-May, 1974 - No. 222, Sept, 1982
National Periodical Publications/DC Comics

164-Jimmy Olsen, Supergirl, Lois Lane begin		1.60	4.00
165-176 (100-68 pgs.)		1.20	3.00

Superman's Christmas Adventure © DC

Superman's Girlfriend Lois Lane #21 © DC

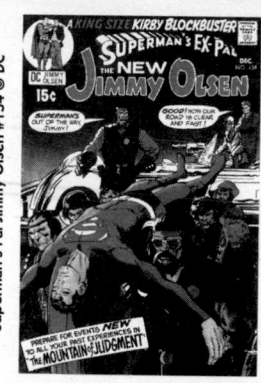

Superman's Pal Jimmy Olsen #134 © DC

	GD25	FN65	NM94
177-181 (52 pgs.)		1.00	2.50
182,194: Marshall Rogers-a in each. 182-$1.00 issues begin; Krypto begins, ends #192		1.20	3.00

183-193,195-222: 183-Nightwing-Flamebird begins, ends #194. 189-Brainiac 5, Mon-el app. 191-Superboy begins, ends #198. 200-Book length story. 211-Earth II Batman & Catwoman marry .80 2.00

NOTE: *N. Adams* a-182-185. *Anderson* a-186i. *Buckler* c(p)-190, 191, 209, 210, 215, 217, 220. *Jones* a-191-193. *Gil Kane* c(p)-221, 222. *Mortimer* a(p)-191-193, 199, 201-222. *Orlando* a(i)-186, 187. *Rogers* a-182, 194. *Staton* a-191-194, 196p. *Tuska* a(p)-203, 207-209.

SUPERMAN FOR EARTH (See Superman one-shots)

SUPERMAN (Miniature)
1942; 1955 - 1956 (3 issues, no #'s, 32 pgs.)
The pages are numbered in the 1st issue: 1-32; 2nd: 1A-32A, and 3rd: 1B-32B
National Periodical Publications

No date-Py-Co-Pay Tooth Powder giveaway (8 pgs.; circa 1942)
82.00 245.00 625.00
1-The Superman Time Capsule (Kellogg's Sugar Smacks)(1955)
50.00 150.00 400.00
1A-Duel in Space (1955) 40.00 120.00 300.00
1B-The Super Show of Metropolis (also #1-32, no B)(1955)
40.00 120.00 300.00
NOTE: Numbering variations exist. Each title could have any combination-#1, 1A, or 1B.

SUPERMAN RECORD COMIC
1966 (Golden Records)
National Periodical Publications

(With record)-Record reads origin of Superman from comic; came with iron-on patch, decoder, membership card & button; comic-r/Superman #125,146
18.00 54.00 125.00
Comic only 11.50 34.00 80.00

SUPERMAN'S BUDDY (Costume Comic)
1954 (4 pgs., slick paper-c; one-shot) (Came in box w/costume)
National Periodical Publications

1-w/box & costume 142.00 428.00 1000.00
Comic only 56.00 170.00 450.00
1-(1958 edition)-Printed in 2 colors 16.00 47.00 110.00

SUPERMAN'S CHRISTMAS ADVENTURE
1940, 1944 (Giveaway, 16 pgs.)
Distributed by Nehi drinks, Bailey Store, Ivey-Keith Co., Kennedy's Boys Shop, Macy's Store, Boston Store
National Periodical Publications

1(1940)-Burnley-a; F. Ray-c/r from Superman #6 (Scarce)-Superman saves Santa Claus. Santa makes real Superman Toys offered in 1940. 1st merchandising story 388.00 1166.00 3500.00
nn(1944) w/Santa Claus & X-mas tree-c 97.00 291.00 775.00
nn(1944) w/Candy cane & Superman-c 84.00 253.00 675.00

SUPERMAN SCRAPBOOK (Has blank pages; contains no comics)

SUPERMAN'S GIRLFRIEND LOIS LANE (See Action Comics #1, 80 Page Giant #3, #14, Lois Lane, Showcase #9,10, Superman #28 & Superman Family)

SUPERMAN'S GIRLFRIEND LOIS LANE (See Showcase #9,10)
Mar-Apr, 1958 - No. 136, Jan-Feb, 1974; No. 137, Sept-Oct, 1974
National Periodical Publ.

	GD25	FN65	VF82	NM94
1-(3-4/58)	190.00	570.00	1235.00	2200.00

	GD25	FN65		NM94
2	69.00	209.00		675.00
3	53.00	160.00		450.00
4,5	40.00	120.00		350.00
6,7	39.00	116.00		285.00
8-10: 9-Pat Boone-c/story	32.00	96.00		240.00
11-20: 12-(10/59)-Aquaman app. 14-Supergirl x-over; Batman app? 20-Supergirl-c/sty	19.00	56.00		140.00

	GD25	FN65	NM94
21-29: 23-1st app. Lena Thorul, Lex Luthor's sister. 27-Bizarro-c/story. 29-Aquaman, Batman, Green Arrow cameo; last 10¢ issue	14.00	43.00	105.00
30-32,34-46,48,49	7.00	21.50	55.00
33(5/62)-Mon-el app.	8.30	25.00	60.00
47-Legion app.	8.00	23.50	58.00
50(7/64)-Triplicate Girl, Phantom Girl & Shrinking Violet app.	6.50	19.50	45.00
51-55,57-67,69: 59-Jor-el app.; Batman back-up sty	5.50	16.50	38.00
56-Saturn Girl app.	5.50	16.50	38.00
68-(Giant G-26)	5.70	17.00	40.00
70-Penguin & Catwoman app. (1st S.A. Catwoman, 11/66; also see Detective #369 for 3rd app.); Batman & Robin cameo	29.00	86.00	200.00
71-Batman & Robin cameos (3 panels); Catwoman story cont'd from #70 app.); see Detective #369 for 3rd app	17.00	51.00	120.00
72,73,75,76,78	2.85	8.50	20.00
74-1st Bizarro Flash (5/67); JLA cameo	4.30	13.00	30.00
77-(Giant G-39)	3.40	10.00	24.00
79-Neal Adams-c begin, end #95,108	1.50	3.75	9.00
80-85,87-94: 89-Batman x-over; all N. Adams-c. 93-Wonder Woman-c/story	1.20	3.00	7.00
86,95: (Giants G-51,G-63)-Both have Neal Adams-c. 95-Wonder Woman x-over	2.40	7.20	17.00
96-103,106-111: 108-Neal Adams-c. 111-Morrow-a	1.00	2.50	5.50
104,113-(Giants G-75,87): 113-Kubert-a (previously unpublished G.A. story)	2.40	7.20	17.00
105-Origin/1st app. The Rose & the Thorn.	1.65	4.20	10.00
112,114-123 (52 pgs.): 122-G.A. Lois Lane-r/Superman #30. 123-G.A. Batman-r/Batman #35 (w/Catwoman)	1.20	3.00	7.00
124-137: 130-Last Rose & The Thorn. 132-New Zatanna story. 136-Wonder Woman x-over	1.20		3.00
Annual 1(Sum, 1962)-r/L. Lane #12; Aquaman app.	19.00	58.00	160.00
Annual 2(Sum, 1963)	13.00	38.00	100.00

NOTE: *Buckler* a-117-121p. *Curt Swan* (or *Kurt Schaffenberger*) a-1-50(most); c(p)-1-15.

SUPERMAN'S PAL JIMMY OLSEN (Superman Family #164 on)
(See Action Comics #6 for 1st app. & 80 Page Giant)
Sept-Oct, 1954 - No. 163, Feb-Mar, 1974 (Fourth World #133-148)
National Periodical Publ.

	GD25	FN65	VF82	NM94
1	300.00	900.00	2100.00	3400.00

	GD25	FN65		NM94
2	110.00	330.00		1100.00
3-Last pre-code issue	75.00	225.00		600.00
4,5	47.00	141.00		425.00
6-10	39.00	116.00		285.00
11-20: 15-1st S.A. issue	25.00	75.00		185.00
21-30: 29-1st app. Krypto in Jimmy Olsen	17.00	49.00		125.00
31-40: 31-Origin & 1st app.Elastic Lad (Jimmy Olsen). 33-One pg. biography of Jack Larson (TV Jimmy Olsen). 36-Intro Lucy Lane. 37-2nd app. Elastic Lad & 1st cover app.	12.00	36.00		90.00
41-50: 41-1st J.O. Robot. 48-Intro/origin Superman Emergency Squad	9.30	28.00		70.00
51-56: 56-Last 10¢ issue	8.00	23.50		55.00
57-62,64-70: 57-Olsen marries Supergirl. 62-Mon-el & Elastic Lad app. but not as Legionnaires. 70-Element Lad app.	3.75	11.25		30.00
63(9/62)-Legion of Super-Villains app.	4.50	13.00		35.00
71,74,75,78,80-84,86,89,90: 86-Jimmy Olsen Robot becomes Congorilla	3.60	11.00		25.00
72(10/63)-Legion app; Elastic Lad (Olsen) joins	3.75	11.25		28.00
73-Ultra Boy app.	3.75	11.25		28.00
76,85-Legion app.	3.75	11.25		28.00
77,79: 77-Olsen with Colossal Boy's powers & costume; origin Titano retold. 79-(9/64)-Titled The Red-headed Beatle of 1000 B.C.	3.75	11.25		26.00
87-Legion of Super-Villains app.	3.75	11.25		30.00

SL

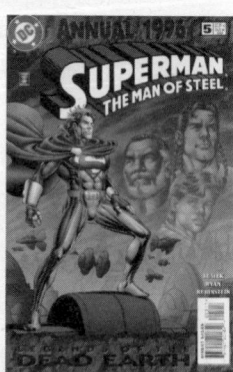

Superman: The Man of Steel Annual #5 © DC

Superman: The Man of Tomorrow #7 © DC

Superman Vs. Aliens #1 © DC/20th Century Fox

	GD25	FN65	NM94
88-Star Boy app.	3.75	11.25	26.00
91-94,96-99: 99-Olsen w/powers & costumes of Lightning Lad, Sun Boy &			
Star Boy	2.85	8.50	20.00
95,104 (Giants G-25,G-38)	3.60	11.00	25.00
100-Legion cameo	2.85	8.50	20.00
101-103,105-112,114-121,123-130,132: 106-Legion app. 110-Infinity-c.			
117-Batman & Legion cameo	1.50	3.75	9.00
113,122,131,140 (Giants G-50,G-62,G-74,G-86): 113-Unpublished G.A.			
Kubert-a (2 pgs.)	2.85	8.50	20.00
133-(10/70)-Re-intro Newsboy Legion; Kirby story & art begins; 1st app. Morgan			
Edge.	3.60	11.00	25.00
134-1st app. Darkseid (1 panel, 12/70)	6.25	19.00	50.00
135-35-2nd app. Darkseid (1 pg. cameo; see New Gods & Forever People);			
G.A. Guardian app.	2.15	6.50	15.00
136-139,141-163: 136-Origin new Guardian. 138-Partial photo-c. 139-Last 15¢			
issue. 141-Photo-c. 139-Last 15¢ issue; Newsboy Legion-r by S&K begin; full pg. self-portrait			
Kirby; Don Rickles cameo. 141-150-(25¢, 52 pgs.). 149, 150-G.A. Plastic			
Man-r in both; last 52 pg. issue. 150-Newsboy Legion app.			
	1.00	2.60	6.00

NOTE: Issues #141-148 contain *Simon & Kirby* Newsboy Legion reprints from Star Spangled #7, 8, 9, 10, 11, 12, 13, 14 in that order. **N. Adams** c-109-112, 115, 117, 118, 120, 121, 132, 134-136, 147, 148. **Kirby** a-133-139p, 141-148p; c-133, 137, 139, 142, 145p. **Kirby/N. Adams** c-137, 138, 141-144, 146. **Curt Swan** c-1-14(most).

SUPERMAN SPECTACULAR (Also see DC Special Series #5)
1982 (Magazine size, square binding)
DC Comics

1		.80	2.00

SUPERMAN: THE MAN OF STEEL (Also see The Man of Steel)
July, 1991 - Present ($1.00/$1.25/$1.50/$1.95)
DC Comics

1-($1.75, 52 pgs.)-Painted-c		1.20	3.00
2-16: 3-War of the Gods x-over. 5-Reads sideways. 10-Last $1.00-c. 14-			
Superman & Robin team-up			1.25
17-1st app. Doomsday (cameo)	1.00	2.00	5.00
17-2nd printing			1.25
18-1st full app. Doomsday	1.30	3.25	8.00
18-2nd & 3rd printings			1.25
19-Doomsday battle issue (c/story)		1.00	2.00
20,21-Funeral for a Friend		.80	2.00
22-($1.95)-Collector's Edition w/die-cut outer-c & bound-in poster; Steel-c/story			
	.40	1.00	2.00
22-($1.50)-Newsstand Ed. w/poster & different-c			1.50
23-37: 23-$1.50-c begins. 30-Regular edition. 32-Bizarro-c/story. 35,36-Worlds			
Collide Pt. 1. 10. 37-(9/94)-Zero Hour x-over			1.50
30-($2.50)-Collector's Edition; polybagged with Superman & Lobo vinyl clings			
that stick to wraparound-c; Lobo-c/story		1.00	2.50
0, 38-44(1994). 58-(11/94)			1.50
45-49,51-60: 45-$1.95-c begins. 48-Aquaman app. 54-Spectre-c/app; Lex			
Luthor app. 56-Mxyzptlk-c/story. 57-G.A. Flash app. 58-Supergirl app.			
59-Parasite-c/app.; Steel app. 60-Reintro Bottled City of Kandor			
			1.50
50 ($2.95)-The Trial of Superman			
Annual 1,2 (1992-93, $2.50, 68 pgs.): 1-Eclipso app.; Joe Quesada-c(p).			
2-Intro Edge		1.00	2.50
Annual 3 (1994, $2.95, 68 pgs.)-Elseworlds story; Mignola-c; Batman app.			
	1.20	3.00	
Annual 4 (1995, $2.95)-Year One story	1.20	3.00	

SUPERMAN: THE MAN OF TOMORROW
1995 -Present ($1.95, quarterly)
DC Comics

1-7: 1-Lex Luthor app. 3-Lex Luthor-c/app; Joker app. 4-Shazam! app.			
5-Wedding of Lex Luthor.		.80	2.00

SUPERMAN: THE SECRET YEARS

	GD25	FN65	NM94
Feb, 1985 - No. 4, May, 1985 (limited series)			
DC Comics			
1-Miller-c on all			1.5
2-4			1.0

SUPERMAN 3-D (See Three-Dimension Adventures)

SUPERMAN-TIM (Becomes Tim)
Aug, 1942 - May, 1950 (Half size) (B&W Giveaway w/2 color covers)
Superman-Tim Stores/National Periodical Publications

8/42(#1)	75.00	225.00	600.0
2/43(#2)-Two pg. Superman illo	36.00	109.00	255.0
3/43, 6/43, 8/43, 9/43(#6)-Two pg. Superman illo	26.00	79.00	185.0
3/44, 2/45, 11/49 issues-Two pg. Superman illos	19.00	56.00	130.0
10/43, 12/43, 2/44-no Superman	18.00	54.00	125.0
4/44-1/45, 3/45, 4/45, 4/46, 5/46, 6/46, 7/46, 8/46 issues-no Superman			
	16.00	47.00	110.0
9/46-1st stamp album issue (worth more if complete with Superman stamps)			
	38.00	114.00	265.0
10/46-1st Superman story	26.00	79.00	185.0
11/46, 12/46, 1/47, 2/47, 3/47, 4/47, 5/47-8/47 issues-Superman story in each;			
2/47-Infinity-c	26.00	79.00	185.0
9/47-Stamp album issue & Superman story	34.00	103.00	240.0
10/47, 11/47, 12/47-Superman stories	26.00	79.00	185.0
1/48, 2/48, 4/48, 8/48, 10/48, 11/48, 2/49-10/49 issues-no Superman			
	19.00	58.00	135.0
9/48-Stamp album issue	21.00	62.00	145.0
12/49-5/50 Superman stories	24.00	71.00	165.0

NOTE: 16 pgs. through 9/47; 8 pgs. 10/47 on? The stamp album issues (3) may contain Superman stamps that were made to glue in these books. Books with the stamps included would be worth more, and the value would depend upon completeness of the album. There is no stamp album in the 9/49 issue.

SUPERMAN VS. ALIENS
July, 1995 - No. 3, Sept, 1995 ($4.95, limited series)
DC Comics/Dark Horse Comics

1-3: Jurgens/Nowlan-a	1.00	2.00	5.0

SUPERMAN VS. THE AMAZING SPIDER-MAN (Also see Marvel Treasury Edition No. 28)
1976 ($2.00, over-sized, 100 pgs.)
National Periodical Publications/Marvel Comics Group

1-Andru/Giordano-a; 1st Marvel/DC x-over.	2.85	8.50	20.0
1-2nd printing; 5000 numbered copies signed by Stan Lee & Carmine			
Infantino on front cover & sold through mail	3.60	11.00	25.0
nn-(1995, $5.95)-r/#1			6.0

SUPERMAN WORKBOOK
1945 (B&W, one-shot, reprints, 68 pgs)
National Periodical Publ./Juvenile Group Foundation

nn-Cover-r/Superman #14	125.00	375.00	1000.0

SUPER MARIO BROS. (Also see Adventures of the...)
1990 - No. 5?, 1991 ($1.95, slick-c)
V2#1, 1991 - No. 5, 1991 ($1.50)
Valiant Comics

1-5: 1-Wildman-a		.80	2.0
V2#1-5			1.5
Special Edition 1 (1990, $1.95)-Wildman-a		.80	2.0

SUPERMOUSE (...the Big Cheese; see Coo Coo Comics)
Dec, 1948 - No. 34, Sept, 1955; No. 35, Apr, 1956 - No. 45, Fall, 1958
Standard Comics/Pines No. 35 on (Literary Ent.)

1-Frazetta text illos (3)	26.00	79.00	185.0
2-Frazetta text illos	13.50	41.00	95.0
3,5,6-Text illos by Frazetta in all	11.00	33.00	75.0
4-Two pg. text illos by Frazetta	11.50	34.00	80.0

Supernatural Thrillers #3 © MEG

Supersnipe V8#3 @ S&S

Super Soldier #1 © DC/MEG

SL

	GD25	FN65	NM94
7-10	4.70	14.00	28.00
11-20: 13-Racist humor (Indians)	4.00	11.00	22.00
21-45	3.20	8.00	16.00
1-Summer Holiday issue (Summer, 1957, 25¢, 100 pgs.)-Pines	11.00	33.00	75.00
2-Giant Summer issue (Summer, 1958, 25¢, 100 pgs.)-Pines; has games, puzzles & stories	9.15	27.00	55.00

SUPER-MYSTERY COMICS
July, 1940 - V8#6, July, 1949
Ace Magazines (Periodical House)

	GD25	FN65	NM94
V1#1-Magno, the Magnetic Man & Vulcan begins (1st app.); Q-13, Corp. Flint, & Sky Smith begin	150.00	450.00	1200.00
2	71.00	215.00	575.00
3-The Black Spider begins (1st app.)	62.00	187.00	500.00
4-Origin Davy	48.00	144.00	385.00
5-Intro. The Clown & begin series (12/40)	48.00	144.00	385.00
6(2/41)	40.00	120.00	315.00
V2#1(4/41)-Origin Buckskin	40.00	120.00	315.00
2-6(4/42): 6-Vulcan begins again	40.00	120.00	285.00
V3#1(4/42),2: 1-Black Ace begins	36.00	107.00	250.00
3-Intro. The Lancer; Dr. Nemesis & The Sword begin; Kurtzman-c/a(2) (Mr. Risk & Paul Revere Jr.); Robot-c	41.00	124.00	340.00
4-Kurtzman-c/a	40.00	120.00	285.00
5-Kurtzman-a(2); L.B. Cole-a; Mr. Risk app.	41.00	124.00	340.00
6(10/43)-Mr. Risk app.; Kurtzman's Paul Revere Jr.; L.B. Cole-a	41.00	124.00	340.00
V4#1(1/44)-L.B. Cole-a	40.00	120.00	280.00
2-6(4/45): 2,5,6-Mr. Risk app.	15.00	75.00	175.00
V5#1(7/45)-6	26.00	79.00	185.00
V6#1-6: 3-Torture story. 4-Last Magno. Mr. Risk app. in #2,4-6. 6-New logo	20.00	60.00	140.00
V7#1-6, V8#1-4,6	20.00	60.00	140.00
V8#5-Meskin, Tuska, Sid Greene-a	21.00	64.00	150.00

NOTE: **Sid Greene** a-V7#4. **Mooney** c-V1#5, 6, V2#1-6. **Palais** a-V5#3, 4; c-V4#6-V5#4, V6#2, V8#4. Bondage c-V2#5, 6, V3#2, 5. Magno c-V1#1-V3#6, V4#2-V5#5, V6#2. The Sword c-V4#1, 6(w/Magno).

SUPERNATURAL THRILLERS
Dec, 1972 - No. 6, Nov, 1973; No. 7, July, 1974 - No. 15, Oct, 1975
Marvel Comics Group

1-3: 1-Itl!; Sturgeon adaptation. 2-The Invisible Man; H.G. Wells adapt. 3-The Valley of the Worm; R.E. Howard adapt.		1.10	2.75
4-15: 4-Dr. Jekyll & Mr. Hyde; R.L. Stevenson adapt. 5-1st app. The Living Mummy. 6-The Headless Horseman; last 20¢ issue. 7-The Living Mummy begins			2.50

NOTE: **Brunner** c-11. **Buckler** a-5p. **Ditko** a-8r, 9r. **G. Kane** a-3p; c-3, 9p, 15p. **Mayerik** a-2p, 7, 8, 9p, 10p, 11. **McWilliams** a-14i. **Mortimer** a-4. **Steranko** c-1, 2. **Sutton** a-15. **Tuska** a-6p.

SUPERPATRIOT (Also see Freak Force & Savage Dragon #2)
July, 1993 - No. 4, Dec, 1993 ($1.95, limited series)
Image Comics (Highbrow Entertainment)

1-4: Dave Johnson-c/a; Larsen scripts; Giffen plots		.80	2.00

SUPERPATRIOT: LIBERTY & JUSTICE
July, 1995 - No. 4, Oct, 1995 ($2.50, limited series)
Image Comics (Highbrow Entertainment)

1-4: Dave Johnson-c/a. 1-1st app. Liberty & Justice		1.00	2.50

SUPER POWERS (1st Series)
July, 1984 - No. 5, Nov, 1984
DC Comics

1-Joker/Penguin-c/story; Batman app.			1.30
2-5: 1-5-Kirby-c; 5-Kirby-c/a			1.20

SUPER POWERS (2nd Series)
Sept, 1985 - No. 6, Feb, 1986
DC Comics

	GD25	FN65	NM94
1-Kirby-c/a in all; Capt. Marvel & Firestorm join; Batman cameo; Darkseid storyline in #1-6		.80	2.00
2-6: 4-Batman cameo. 5,6-Batman app.		.80	2.00

SUPER POWERS (3rd Series)
Sept, 1986 - No. 4, Dec, 1986
DC Comics

1-4: 1-Cyborg joins; 1st app. Samurai from Super Friends TV show. 1-4-Batman cameos; Darkseid storyline in #1-4		.80	2.00

SUPER PUP (Formerly Spotty The Pup) (See Space Comics)
No. 4, Mar-Apr, 1954 - No. 5, 1954
Avon Periodicals

	GD25	FN65	NM94
4,5: 5-Robot-c	4.25	13.00	26.00

SUPER RABBIT (See All Surprise, Animated Movie Tunes, Comedy Comics, Comic Capers, Ideal Comics, It's A Duck's Life, Movie Tunes & Wisco)
Fall, 1944 - No. 14, Nov, 1948
Timely Comics (CmPI)

	GD25	FN65	NM94
1-Hitler & Hirohito-c; war effort paper recycling PSA by S&K; Ziggy Pig & Silly begin?	58.00	174.00	465.00
2	31.00	94.00	220.00
3-5	20.00	60.00	140.00
6-Origin	21.00	64.00	150.00
7-10: 9-Infinity-c	12.00	36.00	85.00
11-Kurtzman's "Hey Look"	13.50	41.00	95.00
12-14	11.50	34.00	80.00
I.W. Reprint #1,2('58),7,10('63): 1-r/#13. 2-r/#10.	1.70	5.00	12.00

SUPER RICHIE (Superichie #5 on) (See Richie Rich Millions #68)
Sept, 1975 - No. 4, Mar, 1976 (All 52 pg. Giants)
Harvey Publications

1		1.20	3.00
2-4		.80	2.00

SUPERSNIPE COMICS (Formerly Army & Navy #1-5)
V1#6, Oct, 1942 - V5#1, Aug-Sept, 1949 (See Shadow Comics V2#3)
Street & Smith Publications

	GD25	FN65	NM94
V1#6-Rex King - Man of Adventure (costumed hero, see Super Magic/ Magician) by Jack Binder begins; Supersnipe by George Marcoux continues from Army & Navy #5; Bill Ward-a	68.00	206.00	550.00
7,10-12: 10,11-Little Nemo app.	40.00	120.00	325.00
.8-Hitler, Tojo, Mussolini in Hell with Devil-c	44.00	132.00	350.00
9-Doc Savage x-over in Supersnipe; Hitler-c	56.00	168.00	450.00
V2#1-12: Both V2#1(2/44) & V2#2(4/44) has V2#1 on outside-c. 1-Huck Finn by Clare Dwiggins begins, ends V3#5; V2#2 shows V2#1 on cover	31.00	94.00	220.00
V3#1-12: 8-Bobby Crusoe by Dwiggins begins, ends V3#12. 9-X-Mas-c	28.00	84.00	195.00
V4#1-12, V5#1: V4#10-X-Mas-c	20.00	60.00	140.00

NOTE: **George Marcoux** c-V1#6-V3#4. Doc Savage app. in some issues.

SUPER SOLDIER (See Marvel Versus DC #3)
Apr, 1996 ($1.95, one-shot)
DC Comics (Amalgam)

1-Mark Waid script & Dave Gibbons-c/a.			2.00

SUPER SOLDIERS
Apr, 1993 - No. 8, Nov, 1993 ($1.75)
Marvel Comics UK

1-($2.50)-Embossed silver foil logo		1.00	2.50
2-8: 5-Capt. America app. 6-Origin; Nick Fury app.; neon ink-c		.70	1.75

SUPERSPOOK (Formerly Frisky Animals on Parade)
No. 4, June, 1958
Ajax/Farrell Publications

	GD25	FN65	NM94
4	6.35	19.00	38.00

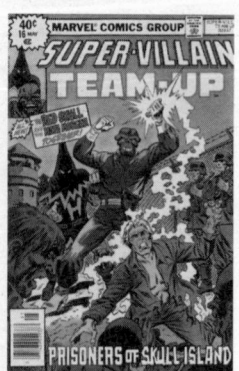
Super-Villain Team-Up #16 © MEG

Supreme: Glory Days #1 © Rob Liefeld

Surge #2 © ECL

SUPER SPY (See Wham Comics)
Oct, 1940 - No. 2, Nov, 1940 (Reprints)
Centaur Publications

	GD25	FN65	NM94
1-Origin The Sparkler	106.00	318.00	850.00
2-The Inner Circle, Dean Denton, Tim Blain, The Drew Ghost, The Night Hawk by Gustavson, & S.S. Swanson by Glanz app.	65.00	195.00	525.00

SUPER STAR HOLIDAY SPECIAL (See DC Special Series #21)

SUPER-TEAM FAMILY
Oct-Nov, 1975 - No. 15, Mar-Apr, 1978
National Periodical Publications/DC Comics

1-Reprints by Neal Adams & Kane/Wood; 68 pgs. begin, ends #4		.90	2.25
2,3: New stories		.60	1.60
4-7: Reprints. 4-G.A. JSA-r & Superman/Batman/Robin-r from World's Finest. 5-52 pgs. begin			1.10
8-10: New Challengers of the Unknown stories		.90	2.25
11-15: New stories			1.30

NOTE: *Neal Adams* r-1-3. *Brunner* c-3. *Buckler* c-8p. *Tuska* a-7r. *Wood* a-1i(r), 3.

SUPER TV HEROES (See Hanna-Barbera...)

SUPER-VILLAIN CLASSICS
May, 1983
Marvel Comics Group

1-Galactus - The Origin			1.00

SUPER-VILLAIN TEAM-UP (See Fantastic Four #6 & Giant-Size...)
8/75 - No. 14, 10/77; No. 15, 11/78; No. 16, 5/79; No. 17, 6/80
Marvel Comics Group

1-Giant-Size Super-Villian Team-Up #2; Sub-Mariner & Dr. Doom begin, end #10	1.00	2.00	5.00
2-17: 5-1st app. The Shroud. 6-F.F., Shroud app. 7-Origin Shroud. 9-Avengers app. 11-15-Dr. Doom & Red Skull app.	1.00		2.50

NOTE: *Buckler* c-4p, 5p, 7p. *Buscema* c-1. *Byrne/Austin* c-14. *Evans* a-1p. *Everett* a-1p. *Giffen* a-8p, 13p; c-13p. *Kane* c-2p, 9p. *Mooney* a-4i. *Starlin* c-6. *Tuska* r-1p, 15p. *Wood* r-15p.

SUPER WESTERN COMICS (Also see Buffalo Bill)
Aug, 1950 - No. 4, Mar, 1951
Youthful Magazines

1-Buffalo Bill begins; Wyatt Earp, Calamity Jane & Sam Slade app; Powell-c/a	10.00	30.00	70.00
2-4	6.70	20.00	40.00

SUPER WESTERN FUNNIES (See Super Funnies)

SUPERWORLD COMICS
Apr, 1940 - No. 3, Aug, 1940 (All have 68 pgs.)
Hugo Gernsback (Komos Publ.)

1-Origin & 1st app. Hip Knox, Super Hypnotist; Mitey Powers & Buzz Allen, the Invisible Avenger, Little Nemo begin; cover by Frank R. Paul (all have sci/fi-c)(Scarce)	400.00	1200.00	4000.00
2-Marvo 1-2 Go+, the Super Boy of the Year 2680 (1st app.); Paul-c (Scarce)	288.00	862.00	2400.00
3 (Scarce)	212.00	637.00	1700.00

SUPREME (Becomes ...The New Adventures #43)(See Youngblood #3)(Also see Bloodwulf Special, Legend of Supreme, & Trencher #3)
V2#1, Nov, 1992 - V2#42, Sept, 1996 ($1.95/$2.50)
Image Comics (Extreme Studios)

V2#1-Liefeld-a(i) & scripts; embossed foil logo		1.40	3.50
1-Gold Edition	1.30	3.25	8.00
2-(3/93)-Liefeld co-plots & inks; 1st app. Grizlock		.80	2.00
3-12,25: 3-Intro Bloodstrike; 1st app. Khrome. 5-1st app. Thor. 6-The Starguard cameo. 7-1st full app. The Starguard. 10-Black and White Pt 1 (1st app.) by Art Thibert (2 pgs. ea. installment). 25-(5/94)-Platt-c		.80	2.00

13-24, 26-42: 11-Coupon #4 for Extreme Prejudice #0; Black and White Pt 7 by Thibert. 12-(4/94)-Platt-c. 13,14-(6/94). 15 (7/94). 16 (7/94)-Stormwatch app. 18-Kid Supreme Sneak Preview; Pitt app. 19,20-Polybagged w/trading card. 20-1st app. Woden & Loki (as a dog); Overtkill app. 21-1st app. Loki (in true form). 21-23-Polybagged trading card. 32-Lady Supreme cameo. 33-Origin & 1st full app. of Lady Supreme (Probe from the Starguard); Babewatch! tie-in. 37-Intro Loki; Fraga-c. 40-Retells Supreme's past advs. 41-Alan Moore scripts begin; Supreme revised; intro The Supremacy; Jerry Ordway-c (Joe Bennett variant-c exists). 42-New origin w/Rick Veitch-a; intro Radar, The Hound Supreme & The League of Infinity

		1.00	2.5
Annual 1-(1995, $2.95)		1.20	3.0

NOTE: *Rob Liefeld* a(i)-1, 2; co-plots-2-4; scripts-1, 5, 6. *Ordway* c-41. *Platt* c-12, 25. *Thib.* c(i)-7-9.

SUPREME: GLORY DAYS
Oct, 1994 - No. 2 Dec, 1994 ($2.95/$2.50, limited series)
Image Comics (Extreme Studios)

1		1.20	3.0
2-Diehard, Roman, Superpatriot, & Glory app.		1.00	2.5

SUPREME: THE NEW ADVENTURES (Formerly Supreme)
V3#43, Oct, 1996 - Present ($2.50)
Maximum Press

V3#43-50: 43-Alan Moore scripts begin; Joe Bennett-a; Rick Veitch-a (8 pgs.) Dan Jurgens-a (1 pg.); intro Citadel Supreme & Suprematons; 1st app. Allied Supermen of America			2.5

SURE-FIRE COMICS (Lightning Comics #4 on)
June, 1940 - No. 4, Oct, 1940 (Two No. 3's)
Ace Magazines

V1#1-Origin Flash Lightning & begins; X-The Phantom Fed, Ace McCoy, Buck Steele, Marvo the Magician, The Raven, Whiz Wilson (Time Traveler) begin (all 1st app.); Flash Lightning c-1-4	125.00	375.00	1000.0
2	68.00	206.00	550.0
3(9/40)	55.00	165.00	440.0
3(#4)(10/40)-nn on-c, #3 on inside	55.00	165.00	440.0

SURF 'N' WHEELS
Nov, 1969 - No. 6, Sept, 1970
Charlton Comics

1	2.30	6.75	16.0
2-6	1.65	4.20	10.0

SURGE
July, 1984 - No. 4, Jan, 1985 ($1.50, limited series, Baxter paper)
Eclipse Comics

1-4 Ties into DNAgents series			1.5

SURPRISE ADVENTURES (Formerly Tormented)
No. 3, Mar, 1955 - No. 5, July, 1955
Sterling Comic Group

3-5: 3,5-Sekowsky-a	5.35	16.00	32.0

SUSIE Q. SMITH
No. 323, Mar, 1951 - No. 553, Apr, 1954
Dell Publishing Co.

Four Color 323 (#1)	4.00	12.00	40.0
Four Color 377, 453 (2/53), 553	3.50	10.50	35.0

SUSPENSE (Radio/TV issues #1-11; Real Life Tales of... #1-4) (Amazing Detective Cases #3 on?)
Dec, 1949 - No. 29, Apr, 1953 (#1-8,17-23: 52 pgs.)
Marvel/Atlas Comics (CnPC No. 1-10/BFP No. 11-29)

1-Powell-a; Peter Lorre, Sidney Greenstreet photo-c from Hammett's "The Verdict"	47.00	141.00	375.0

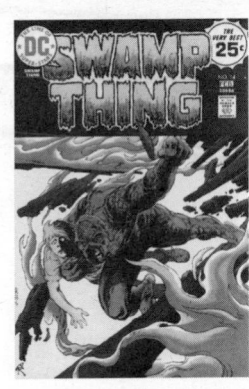
Swamp Thing #14 (1st Series) © DC

Swampt Thing #46 (2nd Series) © DC

Swamp Thing #129 (2nd Series) © DC

	GD25	FN65	NM94
2-Crime stories; Dennis O'Keefe & Gale Storm photo-c from Universal movie			
"Abandoned"	26.00	77.00	180.00
3-Change to horror	27.00	81.00	190.00
4,7-10: 7-Dracula-sty	21.00	62.00	145.00
5-Krigstein, Tuska, Everett-a	22.00	66.00	155.00
6-Tuska, Everett, Morisi-a	21.00	62.00	145.00
11-17,19,20: 14-Hypo-c; A-Bomb panels	15.00	45.00	105.00
18,22-Krigstein-a	18.00	54.00	125.00
21,23,26-29	14.00	43.00	100.00
24-Tuska-a	15.00	45.00	105.00
25-Electric chair-c/story	20.00	60.00	140.00

NOTE: **Ayers** a-20. **Briefer** a-5, 7, 27. **Brodsky** c-4, 6-9, 11, 16, 17, 25. **Colan** a-8(2), 9. **Everett** a-5, 6(2), 19, 23, 28; c-21-23, 26. **Fuje** a-29. **Heath** a-5, 6, 8, 10, 12, 14; c-14, 19, 24. **Kaneely** a-12, 23, 24, 28, 29; c-5, 6p, 10, 13, 15, 18. **Mooney** a-24, 28. **Morisi** a-6, 12. **Palais** a-10. **Rico** a-7-9. **Robinson** a-29. **Romita** a-20(2), 25. **Sekowsky** a-11, 13, 14. **Sinnott** a-23, 25. **Tuska** a-5, 6(2), 12; c-12. **Whitney** a-15, 16, 22. **Ed Win** a-27.

SUSPENSE COMICS
Dec, 1943 - No. 12, Sept, 1946
Continental Magazines

	GD25	FN65	NM94
1-The Grey Mask begins; bondage/torture-c; L. B. Cole-a (7 pgs.)			
	288.00	866.00	2600.00
2-Intro. The Mask; Rico, Giunta, L. B. Cole-a (7 pgs.)			
	238.00	712.00	1900.00
3-L.B. Cole-a; classic Schomburg-c (Scarce)	900.00	2700.00	9000.00
4-6: 5-L. B. Cole-c begin	175.00	525.00	1400.00
7,9,10,12: 9-L.B. Cole eyeball-c	143.00	431.00	1150.00
8-Classic L. B. Cole spider-c	312.00	938.00	2800.00
11-Classic Devil-c	255.00	766.00	2300.00

NOTE: **L. B. Cole** c-5-12. **Fuje** a-8. **Larsen** a-11. **Palais** a-10, 11. **Bondage** c-1, 3, 4.

SUSPENSE DETECTIVE
June, 1952 - No. 5, Mar, 1953
Fawcett Publications

	GD25	FN65	NM94
1-Evans-a (11 pgs); Baily-c/a	36.00	107.00	250.00
2-Evans-a (10 pgs.)	21.00	64.00	150.00
3-5	17.00	51.00	120.00

NOTE: **Baily** a-4, 5; c-1-3. **Sekowsky** a-2, 4, 5; c-5.

SUSPENSE STORIES (See Strange Suspense Stories)

SUSSEX VAMPIRE, THE (Sherlock Holmes)
1996 ($2.95, 32 pgs., B&W, one-shot)
Caliber Comics

	GD25	FN65	NM94
1-Adapts Sir Arthur Conan Doyle's story; Warren Ellis scripts			
			3.00

SUZIE COMICS (Formerly Laugh Comix; see Laugh Comics, Liberty Comics #10, Pep Comics & Top-Notch Comics #28)
No. 49, Spring, 1945 - No. 100, Aug, 1954
(Close-Up No. 49,50/MLJ Mag./Archie No. 51 on)

	GD25	FN65	NM94
49-Ginger begins	23.00	69.00	160.00
50-55: 54-Transvestism story	14.00	43.00	100.00
56-Katy Keene begins by Woggon	13.00	39.00	90.00
57-65	10.00	30.00	65.00
66-80	10.00	30.00	60.00
81-87,89-100: 100-Last Katy Keene	9.15	27.00	55.00
88-Used in POP, pgs. 76,77; Bill Woggon draws himself in story			
	10.00	30.00	60.00

NOTE: **Al Fagaly** c-49-67. Katy Keene app. in 53-82, 85-100.

SWAMP FOX, THE (TV, Disney)(See Walt Disney Presents #2)
No. 1179, Dec, 1960
Dell Publishing Co.

	GD25	FN65	NM94
Four Color 1179-Leslie Nielson photo-c	9.00	27.00	90.00

SWAMP FOX, THE
1960 (14 pgs, small size) (Canada Dry Premiums)
Walt Disney Productions

	GD25	FN65	NM94
Titles: (A)-Tory Masquerade, (B)-Rindau Rampage, (C)-Turnabout Tactics;			
each came in paper sleeve, books 1,2 & 3;			
Set with sleeves	5.00	15.00	30.00
Comic only	1.80	4.50	9.00

SWAMP THING (See Brave & the Bold, Challengers of the Unknown #82, DC Comics Presents #8 & 85, DC Special Series #2, 14, 17, 20, House of Secrets #92, Limited Collectors' Edition C-59, & Roots of the...)

SWAMP THING
Oct-Nov, 1972 - No. 24, Aug-Sept, 1976
National Periodical Publications/DC Comics

	GD25	FN65	NM94
1-Wrightson-c/a begins; origin	9.30	28.00	65.00
2-1st app. Patchwork Man (1 panel cameo)	5.30	16.00	37.00
3-1st full app. Patchwork Man	3.25	9.50	22.00
4-6,8-10: 10-Last Wrightson issue	2.60	7.50	18.00
7-Batman-c/story	3.60	11.00	25.00
11-24-Redondo-a. 13-Origin retold (1 pg.). 23-Swamp Thing reverts back to			
Dr. Holland. 23,24-New logo	1.00	2.00	5.00

NOTE: **J. Jones** a-9i(assist). **Kaluta** a-9i. **Redondo** c-12-19, 21. **Wrightson** issues (#1-10) reprinted in DC Special Series #2, 14, 17, 20 & Roots of the Swampthing.

SWAMP THING (Saga Of The... #1-38,42-45)
May, 1982 - No. 171, Oct, 1996 (Direct sales #65 on)
DC Comics (Vertigo imprint #129 on)

	GD25	FN65	NM94
1-Origin retold; Phantom Stranger series begins; ends #13; Yeates-c/a begins			
		.80	2.00
2-15: 2-Photo-c from movie			1.50
16-19: Bissette-a. 13-Last Yeates-a		1.00	2.50
20-1st app. Alan Moore issue	2.60	7.50	18.00
21-New wrap	2.15	6.50	15.00
22-25: 24-JLA x-over; Last Yeates-c	1.20	2.90	7.00
26-30	1.00	2.00	5.00
31-33: 33-r/1st app. from House of Secrets #92		1.20	3.00
34	1.70	4.20	10.00
35,36		1.20	3.00
37-1st app. John Constantine (Hellblazer) (6/85)	2.85	8.50	20.00
38-40: John Constantine app.	1.30	3.25	8.00
41-51: 44-Batman cameo. 44-51-John Constantine app. 46-Crisis x-over;			
Batman cameo. 49-Spectre app. 50-($1.25, 52 pgs.)-Deadman, Dr. Fate,			
Demon		.80	2.00
52-Arkham Asylum-c/story; Joker-c/cameo		1.60	4.00
53-($1.25, 52 pgs.)-Arkham Asylum; Batman-c/story	1.00	2.00	5.00
54-64: 58-Spectre preview. 64-Last Moore issue		.80	2.00
65-83,85-99,101-124,126-130: 65-Direct sales only begins. 66-Batman &			
Arkham Asylum story. 70,76-John Constantine x-over; 76-X-over			
w/Hellblazer #9. 79-Superman-c/story. 85-Jonah Hex app. 102-Preview of			
World Without End. 116-Photo-c. 129-Metallic ink on-c			
		.80	2.00
84-Sandman (Morpheus) cameo.	1.20	3.00	7.00
100 ($2.50, 52 pgs.)		1.10	2.75
125-($2.95, 52 pgs.)-20th anniversary issue		1.40	3.50
131-149, 151-154: 131-$1.95-c begins. 140-Millar scripts begin, end #171.			
		.80	2.00
150 ($2.95, 52 pgs.)-Anniversary issue		1.20	3.00
155-171: 155-$2.25-c begins. 165-Curt Swan-a(p). 166,169,171-John			
Constantine & Phantom Stranger app. 168-Arcane returns	.90		2.25
Annual 1(1982, $1.00)-Movie Adaptation; painted-c			1.00
Annual 2(1985)-Alan Moore scripts; Bissette-a(p); Spectre app.			
		1.20	3.00
Annual 3(1987, $2.00)-New format; Bolland-c		.90	2.25
Annual 4(1988, $2.00)-Batman-c/story		1.20	3.00
Annual 5(1989, $2.95, 68 pgs.)-Batman cameo; re-intro Brother Power (Geek),			
1st app. since 1968		1.20	3.00
Annual 6(1991, $2.95, 68 pgs.)		1.20	3.00
Annual 7(1993, $3.95)-Children's Crusade		1.60	4.00

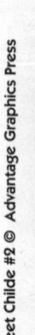

Swarm #1 © Mushroom Comics Sweet Childe #2 © Advantage Graphics Press

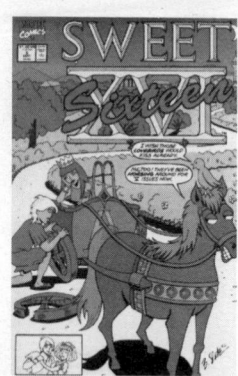

Sweet XVI #5 © MEG

	GD25	FN65	NM94

Saga of the Swamp Thing (1987, $10.95)-r/#21-27 1.65 4.70 11.00
Saga of the Swamp Thing (1989, $12.95, 2nd Printing)
    1.85 5.50 13.00
...Love and Death (1990, $17.95)-r/#28-34 & Annual #2; Totleben painted-c
    2.60 7.50 18.00
NOTE: **Bissette** a(p)-16-19, 21-27, 29, 30, 34-36, 39-42, 44, 46, 50, 64; c-17i, 24-32p, 35-37p, 40p, 44p, 46-50p, 51-58, 61, 62, 63p. **Kaluta** c/a-74. **Spiegle** a-1-3, 6. **Sutton** a-98p. **Totleben** a(i)-10, 16-27, 29, 31, 34-40, 42, 44, 46, 48, 50, 53, 55i; c-25-32i, 33, 35-40i, 42i, 44i, 46-50i, 53, 55i, 59p, 64, 65, 68, 73, 76, 80, 82, 84, 89, 91-100, Annual 4, 5. **Vess** painted c-121, 129-139, Annual 7. **Williamson** 86i. **Wrightson** a-18i(r), 33r. John Constantine appears in #37-40, 44-51, 65-67, 70-77, 80-90, 99, 114, 115, 130, 134-138.

SWARM (See Futuretech)
Jan, 1996 - Present ($2.50, limited series)
Mushroom Comics
  1-Flip book w/Futuretech #1   2.50

SWAT MALONE (America's Home Run King)
Sept, 1955
Swat Malone Enterprises
  V1#1-Hy Fleishman-a 9.15 27.00 55.00

SWEENEY (Formerly Buz Sawyer)
No. 4, June, 1949 - No. 5, Sept, 1949
Standard Comics
  4,5: 5-Crane-a 8.00 24.00 48.00

SWEE'PEA (Also see Popeye #46)
No. 219, Mar, 1949
Dell Publishing Co.
  Four Color 219 9.00 27.00 90.00

SWEET CHILDE
1995 - No. 2, 1995 ($2.95, B&W, limited series, mature)
Advantage Graphics Press
  1,2   1.20 3.00

SWEETHEART DIARY (Cynthia Doyle #66-on)
Wint, 1949; #2, Spr, 1950; #3, 6/50 - #5, 10/50; #6, 1951(nd); #7, 9/51 - #14, 1/53; #32, 10/55; #33, 4/56 - #65, 8/62 (#1-14: photo-c)
Fawcett Publications/Charlton Comics No. 32 on
  1 12.00 36.00 85.00
  2 7.50 22.50 45.00
  3,4-Wood-a 13.00 39.00 90.00
  5-10: 8-Bailey-a 6.35 19.00 38.00
  11-14: 13-Swayze-a. 14-Last Fawcett issue 4.00 12.00 24.00
  32 (10/55; 1st Charlton issue)(Formerly Cowboy Love #31)
    5.00 15.00 30.00
  33-40: 34-Swayze-a 3.00 7.50 15.00
  41-60 1.40 3.50 7.00
  61-65   1.40 3.50

SWEETHEARTS (Formerly Captain Midnight)
#68, 10/48 - #121, 5/53; #122, 3/54; V2#23, 5/54 - #137, 12/73
Fawcett Publications/Charlton No. 122 on
  68-Photo-c begin 12.00 36.00 85.00
  69-80 5.00 15.00 30.00
  81-84,86-93,95-99,105 4.00 12.00 24.00
  85,94,103,110,117-George Evans-a 6.35 19.00 38.00
  100 4.25 13.00 28.00
  101,107-Powell-a 4.25 13.00 26.00
  102,104,106,108,109,112-116,118 3.60 9.00 18.00
  111-1 pg. Ronald Reagan biography 6.35 19.00 38.00
  119-Marilyn Monroe & Richard Widmark photo-c (1/47); also appears in story; part Wood-a 33.00 99.00 230.00
  120-Atom Bomb story 8.35 25.00 50.00
  121-Liz Taylor/Fernando Lamas photo-c 6.35 19.00 38.00
  122-(1st Charlton? 3/54)-Marijuana story 7.50 22.50 45.00

V2#23 (5/54)-28: 28-Last precode issue (2/55) 3.60 9.00 18.00
  29-39,41,43-45,47-50 2.00 5.00 10.00
  40-Photo-c; Tommy Sands story 4.00 10.00 20.00
  42-Ricky Nelson photo-c/story 9.15 27.00 55.00
  46-Jimmy Rodgers photo-c/story 4.00 10.00 20.00
  51-60 2.00 5.00 10.00
  61-80 1.40 3.50 7.00
  81-100   1.20 3.00
  101-110   .80 2.00
  111-137   1.5
NOTE: Photo c-68-121(Fawcett), 40, 42, 46(Charlton). **Swayze** a(Fawcett)-70-118(most).

SWEETHEART SCANDALS (See Fox Giants)

SWEETIE PIE
No. 1185, May-July, 1961 - No. 1241, Nov-Jan, 1961/62
Dell Publishing Co.
  Four Color 1185 (#1), 1241 4.00 12.00 40.00

SWEETIE PIE
Dec, 1955 - No. 15, Fall, 1957
Ajax-Farrell/Pines (Literary Ent.)
  1-By Nadine Seltzer 5.35 16.00 32.00
  2 (5/56; last Ajax?) 4.00 10.00 20.00
  3-15 (#3-10, exist?) 2.40 6.00 12.00

SWEET LOVE
Sept, 1949 - No. 5, May, 1950 (All photo-c)
Home Comics (Harvey)
  1 7.50 22.50 45.00
  2 4.25 13.00 26.00
  3,4: 3-Powell-a 4.00 10.00 20.00
  5-Kamen, Powell-a 5.85 17.50 35.00

SWEET ROMANCE
Oct, 1968
Charlton Comics
  1   1.60 4.00

SWEET SIXTEEN (...Comics and Stories for Girls)
Aug-Sept, 1946 - No. 13, Jan, 1948 (All have movie stars photos on covers)
Parents' Magazine Institute
  1-Van Johnson's life story; Dorothy Dare, Queen of Hollywood Stunt Artists begins (in all issues); part photo-c 15.00 45.00 105.00
  2-Jane Powell, Roddy McDowall "Holiday in Mexico" photo on-c; Alan Ladd story 10.00 30.00 70.00
  3-6,8-11: 4-Elizabeth Taylor photo on-c. 5-Ann Francis photo on-c; Gregory Peck story. 6-Dick Haymes story. 8-Shirley Jones photo on-c. 10-Jean Simmons photo on-c; James Stewart story 8.35 25.00 50.00
  7-Ronald Reagan's life story 16.00 47.00 110.00
  12-Bob Cummings, Vic Damone story 8.35 25.00 50.00
  13-Robert Mitchum's life story 9.15 27.50 55.00

SWEET XVI
May, 1991 - No. 5, Sept, 1991($1.00, color)
Marvel Comics
  ..1-5: Barbara Slate story & art 1.00

SWIFT ARROW (Also see Lone Rider & The Rider)
Feb-Mar, 1954 - No. 5, Oct-Nov, 1954; Apr, 1957 - No. 3, Sept, 1957
Ajax-Farrell
  1(1954) (1st Series) 11.00 33.00 75.00
  2 7.00 21.00 42.00
  3-5: 5-Lone Rider story 5.35 16.00 32.00
  1 (2nd Series) (Swift Arrow's Gunfighters #4) 5.85 17.50 35.00
  2,3: 2-Lone Rider begins 4.25 13.00 26.00

SWIFT ARROW'S GUNFIGHTERS (Formerly Swift Arrow)

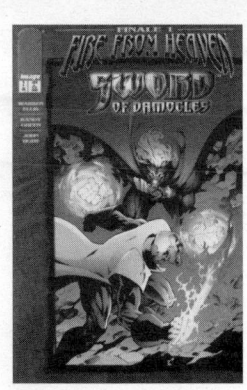

Sword of Damocles #2 © Aegis Entertainment

Tailgunner Jo #3 © DC

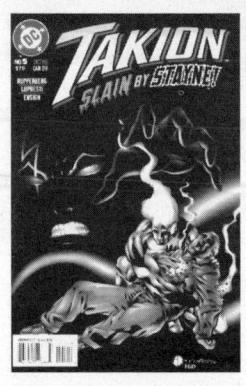

Takion #5 © DC

TA

, Nov, 1957
Farrell Publ. (Four Star Comic Corp.)

| | 5.35 | 16.00 | 32.00 |

G WITH SCOOTER
July, 1966 - No. 35, Aug-Sept, 1971; No. 36, Oct-Nov, 1972
nal Periodical Publications

	3.60	9.00	18.00
: 9-Alfred E. Newman swipe in last panel	2.00	5.00	10.00
)	1.60	4.00	8.00
6: 33-Interview with David Cassidy. 34-Interview with Ron Ely (Doc			
avage)	1.00	2.50	6.00

Orlando a-1-11; c-1-11, 13. #20, 33, 34: 68 pgs.; #35: 52 pgs.

S FAMILY ROBINSON (Walt Disney's..; see King Classics & Movie
cs)
156, Dec, 1960
Publishing Co.

| Color 1156-Movie-photo-c | 7.00 | 21.00 | 70.00 |

RD & THE DRAGON, THE
118, June, 1960
Publishing Co.

| Color 1118-Movie, photo-c | 8.00 | 24.00 | 80.00 |

RD & THE ROSE, THE (Disney)
05, Oct, 1953 - No. 682, Feb, 1956
Publishing Co.

Color 505-Movie, photo-c	9.00	27.00	90.00
Color 682-When Knighthood Was in Flower-Movie, reprint of #505;			
enamed the Sword & the Rose for the novel; photo-c			
	7.00	21.00	70.00

RD IN THE STONE, THE (See March of Comics #258 & Movie Comics & Wart
e Wizard)

RD OF DAMOCLES
1996 - No. 2, Apr, 1996 ($2.50, limited series)
e Comics (Wildstorm Productions)

| Warren Ellis scripts. 1-Prelude to "Fire From Heaven" x-over; 1st app. | | | |
| vord | | | 2.50 |

RD OF SORCERY
Mar, 1973 - No. 5, Nov-Dec, 1973 (20¢)
nal Periodical Publications

eiber Fafhrd & The Grey Mouser; Chaykin/Neal Adams (Crusty Bunkers)			
t; Kaluta-c	1.00	2.00	5.00
ightson-c(i); Neal Adams-a(i)		1.20	3.00
3-Wrightson-i(5 pgs.). 5-Starlin-a(p); Conan cameo	1.00	2.50

Chaykin a-1-4p; c-2p, 3-5. Kaluta a-3l. Simonson a-3i, 4i, 5p; c-5.

RD OF THE ATOM
1983 - No. 4, Dec, 1983 (Limited series)
omics

Kane-c/a in all			1.50
al 1(1984), 2(1985): Kane-c/a each			1.50
al 3(1988, $1.50)			1.50

RDS OF TEXAS (See Scout #15)
987 - No. 4, Jan, 1988 ($1.75, color, Baxter paper)
se Comics

| Scout app. | | .90 | 1.80 |

RDS OF THE SWASHBUCKLERS (See Marvel Graphic Novel)
1985 - No. 12, June, 1987 ($1.50; Mature readers)
el Comics (Epic Comics)

| :-Butch Guice-c/a (Cont'd from Marvel G.N.) | | | 1.60 |

RN TO PROTECT

Sept, 1995 ($1.95) (Based on card game)
Marvel Comics

| nn-Overpower Game Guide; Jubilee story | | .80 | 2.00 |

SYNDICATE FEATURES (Sci/fi)
V1#3, 11/15/37 (Tabloid size, 3 colors, 4 pgs.) (Editors premium)
Harry A. Chesler Syndicate

| V1#3-Dan Hastings daily strips-Guardineer-a | 315.00 | 945.00 | 2200.00 |

SYPHONS
V2#1, May, 1994 - V2#3, 1994 ($2.50, limited series)
Now Comics

| V2#1-3: 1-Stardancer, Knightfire, Raze & Brigade begin | 1.00 | 2.50 |

SYSTEM, THE
May, 1996 - No. 3, July, 1996 ($2.95, limited series)
DC Comics (Vertigo Verite)

| 1-3: Kuper-c/a | | | 3.00 |

TAFFY COMICS
Mar-Apr, 1945 - No. 12, 1948
Rural Home/Orbit Publ.

1-L.B. Cole-c; origin & 1st app. of Wiggles The Wonderworm plus 7 chapter			
WWII funny animal adventures	36.00	107.00	250.00
2-L.B. Cole-c; Wiggles-c/stories in #1-4	17.00	51.00	120.00
3,4,6-12: 6-Perry Como-c/story. 7-Duke Ellington, 2 pgs. 8-Glenn Ford-c/			
story. 9-Lon McCallister part photo-c & story. 10-Mort Leav-c. 11-Mickey			
Rooney-c/story	9.15	27.00	55.00
5-L.B. Cole-c; Van Johnson-c/story	13.50	41.00	95.00

TAILGUNNER JO
Sept, 1988 - No. 6, Jan, 1989 ($1.25)
DC Comics

| 1-6 | | | 1.25 |

TAILS
Dec, 1995 - No. 3, Feb, 1996 ($1.50, limited series)
Archie Publications

| 1-3: Based on Sonic, the Hedgehog video game | | | 1.50 |

TAILSPIN
November, 1944
Spotlight Publishers

| nn-Firebird app.; L.B. Cole-c | 20.00 | 60.00 | 140.00 |

TAILSPIN TOMMY (Also see Popular Comics)
1940; 1946
United Features Syndicate/Service Publ. Co.

| Single Series 23(1940) | 34.00 | 103.00 | 240.00 |
| Best Seller (nd, 1946)-Service Publ. Co. | 13.00 | 39.00 | 90.00 |

TAINTED
Jan, 1995 ($4.95, one-shot)
DC Comics (Vertigo)

| 1-Jamie Delano scripts; Al Davison-c/a; reads February '95 on-c | | | |
| | | | 5.00 |

TAKION
June, 1996 - No. 7, Dec, 1996 ($1.75)
DC Comics

| 1-7: Aaron Lopresti-c/a(p). 1-Origin; Green Lantern app. 6-Final Night x-over | | | |
| | | | 1.75 |

TALENT SHOWCASE (See New Talent Showcase)

TALE OF ONE BAD RAT, THE
Oct, 1994 - No. 4, Jan, 1995 ($2.95, limited series)
Dark Horse Comics

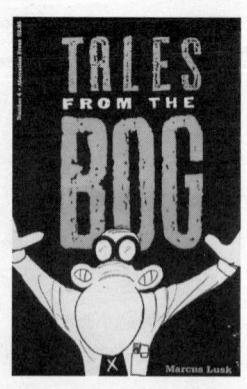
Tales From The Bog #3 © Aberration Press

Tales From The Crypt #4 © WMG

Tales From The Tomb #1 © DELL

		GD25	FN65	NM94
1-4: Bryan Talbot-c/a/scripts			1.20	3.00

TALES CALCULATED TO DRIVE YOU BATS
Nov, 1961 - No. 7, Nov, 1962; 1966 (Satire)
Archie Publications

	GD25	FN65	NM94
1-Only 10¢ issue; has cut-out Werewolf mask (price includes mask)			
	11.00	33.00	75.00
2-Begin 12¢ issues	5.70	17.00	42.00
3-6	4.30	13.00	32.00
7-Storyline change	3.75	11.25	28.00
1(1966, 25¢, 44 pgs.)-r/#1	4.30	13.00	30.00

TALES FROM THE BOG
Nov, 1995 - No. 4, 1996 ($2.95, B&W)
Aberration Press

1-4			3.00

TALES FROM THE CRYPT (Formerly The Crypt Of Terror; see Three Dimensional...)
No. 20, Oct-Nov, 1950 - No. 46, Feb-Mar, 1955
E.C. Comics

	GD25	FN65	NM94
20-See Crime Patrol #15 for 1st Crypt Keeper	106.00	320.00	850.00
21-Kurtzman-r/Haunt of Fear #15(#1)	88.00	262.00	700.00
22-Moon Girl costume at costume party, one panel	69.00	206.00	550.00
23-25: 24-E. A. Poe adaptation	52.00	156.00	415.00
26-30	40.00	120.00	315.00
31-Williamson-a(1st at E.C.); B&W and color illos. in POP; Kamen draws himself, Gaines & Feldstein; Ingels, Craig & Davis draw themselves in his story	42.00	128.00	340.00
32,35-39: 38-Censored-c	36.00	109.00	255.00
33-Origin The Crypt Keeper	59.00	178.00	475.00
34-Used in POP, pg. 83; lingerie panels	36.00	109.00	255.00
40-Used in Senate hearings & in Hartford Cournat anti-comics editorials-1954	36.00	109.00	255.00
41-45: 45-2 pgs. showing E.C. staff	36.00	109.00	255.00
46-Low distribution; pre-advertised cover for unpublished 4th horror title "Crypt of Terror" used on this book	40.00	120.00	290.00

NOTE: *Ray Bradbury* adaptations-34, 36. *Craig* a-20, 22-24; c-20. *Crandall* a-38, 44. *Davis* a-24-46; c-29-46. *Elder* a-37, 38. *Evans* a-32-34, 36, 40, 41, 43, 46. *Feldstein* a-20-23; c-21-25, 28. *Ingels* a-in all. *Kamen* a-20, 22, 25, 27-31, 33-36, 39, 41-45. *Krigstein* a-40, 42, 45. *Kurtzman* a-21. *Orlando* a-27-30, 35, 37, 39, 41-45. *Wood* a-21, 24, 25; c-26, 27. Canadian reprints known; see Table of Contents.

TALES FROM THE CRYPT (Magazine)
No. 10, July, 1968 (35¢, B&W)
Eerie Publications

	GD25	FN65	NM94
10-Contains Farrell reprints from 1950s	3.25	9.50	22.00

TALES FROM THE CRYPT
July, 1990 - No. 6, May, 1991 ($1.95/$2.00, 68 pgs.)
Gladstone Publishing

1-r/TFTC #33 & Crime S.S. #17; Davis-c(r)		.80	2.00
2-6: 2,3,5,6-Davis-c(r). 4-Begin $2.00-c; Craig-c(r)		.80	2.00

TALES FROM THE CRYPT
July, 1991 - Present ($3.95, 10 1/4 x13 1/4", 68 pgs.)
Extra-Large Comics (Russ Cochran)/Gemstone Publishing

1-Davis-c(r); Craig back-c(r); E.C. reprints		2.00	4.00
2-6 ($2.00, comic sized)		1.00	2.00

TALES FROM THE CRYPT
Sept, 1992 - Present ($1.50, quarterly)
Russ Cochran/Gemstone Publishing

1-4-r/Crypt of Terror #17-19, TFTC #20 w/original-c			1.50
5-15 ($2.00)-r/TFTC #21-23 w/original-c		.80	2.00
16-20($2.50)			2.50

TALES FROM THE GREAT BOOK

	GD25	FN65	NM94
Feb, 1955 - No. 4, Jan, 1956
Famous Funnies

	GD25	FN65	NM94
1-Story of Samson; John Lehti-a in all	6.70	20.00	
2-4: 2-Joshua. 3-Joash the Boy King. 4-David	4.00	12.00	

TALES FROM THE HEART OF AFRICA (The Temporary Natives)
Aug, 1990 ($3.95, 52 pgs.)
Marvel Comics (Epic Comics)

1			1.60

TALES FROM THE TOMB (Also see Dell Giants)
Oct, 1962 (25¢ giant)
Dell Publishing Co.

	GD	FN	VF	N
1(02-810-210)-All stories written by John Stanley				
	11.50	34.00	79.00	1

TALES FROM THE TOMB (Magazine)
V1#6, July, 1969 - V7#1, Feb, 1975 (52 pgs.)
Eerie Publications

V1#6-8		3.25	9.50
V2#1-3,5,6: 6-Rulah-r		2.15	6.50
4-LSD story-r/Weird V3#5		2.15	6.50
V3#1-Rulah-r		2.15	6.50
2-6('70),V4#1-5('72),V5#1-6('73),V6#1-6('74),V7#1('75)		1.70	5.00

TALES OF ASGARD
Oct, 1968 (25¢, 68 pgs.); Feb, 1984 ($1.25, 52 pgs.)
Marvel Comics Group

1-Reprints Tales of Asgard (Thor) back-up stories from Journey into Myste #97-106; new Kirby-c		4.00	12.00
V2#1 (2/84)-Thor-r; Simonson-c			

TALES OF DEMON DICK & BUNKER BILL
1934 (B&W, 5x10-1/2", hardcover, 78 pgs.)
Whitman Publishing Co.

	GD25	FN65	NM94
793-By Dick Spencer	23.00	69.00	1

TALES OF EVIL
Feb, 1975 - No. 3, July, 1975 (All 25¢ issues)
Atlas/Seaboard Publ.

1-3: 2-Intro. The Bog Beast; Sparling-a. 3-Origin The Man-Monster; Buckler-a(p)			

NOTE: *Grandenetti* a-1, 2. *Lieber* c-1. *Sekowsky* a-1. *Sutton* a-2. *Thorne* c-2.

TALES OF GHOST CASTLE
May-June, 1975 - No. 3, Sept-Oct, 1975 (All 25¢ issues)
National Periodical Publications

1-3: 1,3-Redondo-a. 2-Nino-a			

TALES OF G.I. JOE
Jan, 1988 - No. 15, Mar, 1989
Marvel Comics

1 ($2.25, 52 pgs.)			.90
2-15 ($1.50): 1-15-r/G.I. Joe #1-15			

TALES OF HORROR
June, 1952 - No. 13, Oct, 1954
Toby Press/Minoan Publ. Corp.

	GD25	FN65	NM94
1	30.00	90.00	2
2-Torture scenes	24.00	73.00	1
3-8,13	15.00	45.00	1
9-11-Reprints Purple Claw #1-3	16.00	47.00	1
12-Myron Fass-c/a; torture scenes	17.00	49.00	1

NOTE: *Andru* a-5. *Baily* a-5. *Myron Fass* a-2, 3, 12; c-1-3, 12. *Hollingsworth* a-2. *Sparli* 6, 9; c-9.

TALES OF JUSTICE

Tales Of Suspense #2 © MEG

Tales Of Suspense #49 © MEG

Tales Of The Beanworld #5 © Larry Marder

	GD25	FN65	NM94

No. 53, May, 1955 - No. 67, Aug, 1957
Atlas Comics(MjMC No. 53-66/Male No. 67)

53	12.00	36.00	85.00
54-57: 54-Powell-a	9.15	27.50	55.00
58,59-Krigstein-a	10.00	30.00	65.00
60-63,65: 60-Powell-a	7.50	22.50	45.00
64,67-Crandall-a	9.15	27.50	55.00
66-Torres, Orlando-a	9.15	27.50	55.00

NOTE: *Everett* a-53, 60. *Orlando* a-65, 66. *Severin* a-64; c-58, 60, 65. *Wildey* a-64, 67.

TALES OF SUSPENSE (Becomes Captain America #100 on)
Jan, 1959 - No. 99, Mar, 1968
Atlas (WPI No. 1,2/Male No. 3-12/VPI No. 13-18)/Marvel No. 19 on

1-Williamson-a (5 pgs.); Heck-c; #1-4 have sci/fi-c	168.00	506.00	1350.00
2,3: 3-Flying saucer-c/story	65.00	195.00	525.00
4-Williamson-a (4 pgs.); Kirby/Everett-c/a	56.00	168.00	450.00
5,6,8,10: 5-Kirby monster-c begin	40.00	120.00	300.00
7-Prototype ish. (Lava Man)	43.00	128.00	340.00
9-Prototype ish. (Iron Man)	46.00	138.00	370.00
11,12,15,17-19: 12-Crandall-a.	33.00	99.00	230.00
13,14: 13-Elektro-c/story. 14-Intro/1st app. Colossus-c/sty.	40.00	120.00	300.00
16-1st Metallo-c/story (4/61, Iron Man prototype)	40.00	120.00	290.00
20-Colossus-c/story (2nd app.)	36.00	107.00	250.00
21-25: 25-Last 10¢ issue	24.00	73.00	170.00
26,27,29,30,33,34,36-38: 33-(9/62)-Hulk 1st x-over cameo (picture on wall)	22.00	66.00	155.00
28-Prototype ish. (Stone Men)	24.00	71.00	165.00
31-Prototype ish. (Dr. Doom)	29.00	86.00	200.00
32-Prototype ish. (Dr. Strange)(8/62)-Sazzik The Sorcerer app.; "The Man and the Beehive" story, 1 month before TTA #35 (2nd Antman), came out after "The Man in the Ant Hill" in TTA #27 (1/62) (1st Antman)-Characters from both stories were tested to see which got best fan response	40.00	120.00	300.00
39-Prototype issue (The Watcher)	29.00	86.00	200.00

	GD25	FN65	VF82	NM94
39 (3/63)-Origin/1st app. Iron Man & begin series; 1st Iron Man story has Kirby layouts	340.00	1020.00	2210.00	3800.00

	GD25	FN65	NM94
40-2nd app. Iron Man (in new armor)	130.00	390.00	1300.00
41-3rd app. Iron Man; Dr. Strange (villain) app.	67.00	200.00	650.00
45: 45-Intro. & 1st app. Happy & Pepper	40.00	120.00	300.00
47: 46-1st app. Crimson Dynamo	24.00	73.00	185.00
New Iron Man armor by Ditko	30.00	90.00	220.00
1st X-Men x-over (same date as X-Men #3, 1/64); 1st Avengers x-over (w/o Captain America); 1st Tales of the Watcher back-up story & begins 2nd app. Watcher; see F.F. #13	21.00	62.00	160.00
1st Scarecrow	16.00	47.00	120.00
1st app. Mandarin	13.00	39.00	100.00
1st app. The Black Widow (4/64)	17.00	51.00	130.00
Origin The Watcher; 2nd Black Widow app.	16.00	47.00	120.00
1st Unicorn; 4th Avengers x-over	10.00	30.00	70.00
Origin/1st app. Hawkeye (9/64)	21.00	64.00	150.00
Captain America battles Iron Man (10/64)-Classic-c; 2nd Kraven app. Captain America plus Iron Man double feature begins (11/64); 1st S.A. Captain America solo story; intro Jarvis, Avenger's butler; classic-c	37.00	111.00	260.00
2nd app. Hawkeye (#64 is 3rd app.)	37.00	111.00	260.00
62,64: 62-Origin Mandarin (2/65)	17.00	51.00	120.00
1st Silver Age origin Captain America (3/65)	10.00	30.00	70.00
66-G.A. Red Skull in WWII stories: 65-1st Silver-Age Red Skull (5/65). 66-Origin Red Skull	29.00	86.00	200.00
78,81-98: 69-1st app. Titanium Man. 70-Begin alternating-c features w/Capt. America (even #'s) & Iron Man (odd #'s). 75-1st app. Agent 13 later named	18.00	54.00	135.00

Sharon Carter. 76-Intro Batroc & Sharon Carter, Agent 13 of Shield. 78-Col. Nick Fury app. 81-Intro the Adaptoid by Kirby (also in #82-84). 88-Mole Man app. in Iron Man story. 92-1st Nick Fury x-over (cameo, as Agent of Shield, 8/67). 94-Intro Modok. 95-Capt. America's i.d. revealed. 98-1st app. new Zemo (son?) in cameo (#99 is 1st full app.)

	7.00	21.50	50.00
79-Begin 3 part Iron Man Sub-Mariner battle story; Sub-mariner-c & cameo; 1st app. Cosmic Cube; 1st modern Red Skull	8.00	24.50	65.00
80-Iron Man battles Sub-Mariner story cont'd in Tales to Astonish #82	7.50	22.50	60.00
99-Captain America story cont'd in Captain America #100; Iron Man story cont'd in Iron Man & Sub-Mariner #1	8.00	24.50	65.00

NOTE: *J. Buscema* a-1; c-3. *Colan* a-39, 73-99p; c(p)-73, 75, 77, 79, 81, 83, 85-87, 89, 91, 93, 95, 97, 99. *Craig* a-73-83i(as Gary Michaels), 99i. *Crandall* a-12. *Davis* a-38. *Ditko* a-1-15, 17-44, 46, 47-49p; c-2, 10i, 13i, 23i. *Kirby/Ditko* a-7; c-10, 13, 22, 28, 34. *Everett* a-8. *Forte* a-5, 9. *Heath* a-2; 10. *Gil Kane* a-88p, 89-91; c-88, 89-91p. *Kirby* a(p)-2-4, 6-35, 40, 41, 43, 59-75, 77-86, 92-99; layouts-69-75, 77; c(p)4-28(most), 29-56, 58-72, 74, 76, 78, 80, 82, 84, 86, 92, 94, 96, 98. *Leiber/Fox* a-42, 43, 45, 51. *Reinman* a-26, 44i, 49i, 52i, 53i. *Tuska* a-58, 70-74. *Wood* c/a-71i.

TALES OF SUSPENSE
V2#1, Jan, 1995 ($6.95, one-shot)
Marvel Comics

V2#1-James Robinson script; acetate-c.	1.20	3.00	7.00

TALES OF SWORD & SORCERY (See Dagar)

TALES OF TERROR
1952 (no month)
Toby Press Publications

1-Fawcette-c; Ravielli-a	18.00	54.00	125.00

NOTE: *This title was cancelled due to similarity to the E.C. title.*

TALES OF TERROR (See Movie Classics)

TALES OF TERROR (Magazine)
Summer, 1964
Eerie Publications

1	2.85	8.50	20.00

TALES OF TERROR
July, 1985 - No. 13, July, 1987 ($2.00, Baxter paper, mature)
Eclipse Comics

1-8 ($1.75-c): 5-1st Lee Weeks-a. 7-Sam Kieth-a		.90	1.80
9-13 ($2.00-c): 10-Snyder-a. 12-Vampire story		1.00	2.00

TALES OF TERROR ANNUAL
1951 - No. 3, 1953 (25¢, 132 pgs., 16 stories each)
E.C. Comics

	GD25	FN65	VF82
nn(1951)(Scarce)-Feldstein infinity-c	371.00	1115.00	3000.00

(Estimated up to 35 total copies exist, 3 in NM/Mint)

	GD25	FN65	NM94
2(1952)-Feldstein-c	162.00	488.00	1300.00
3(1953)-Feldstein bondage/torture-c	125.00	375.00	1000.00

NOTE: *No. 1 contains three horror and one science fiction comic which came out in 1950. No. 2 contains a horror, crime, and science fiction book which generally had cover dates in 1951, and No. 3 had horror, crime, and shock books that generally appeared in 1952. All E.C. annuals contain four complete books that did not sell on the stands which were rebound in the annual format, minus the covers, and sold from the E.C. office and on the stands in key cities. The contents of each annual may vary in the same year. Crypt Keeper, Vault Keeper, Old Witch app. on all-c.*

TALES OF TERROR ILLUSTRATED (See Terror Illustrated)

TALES OF TEXAS JOHN SLAUGHTER (See Walt Disney Presents, 4-Color #997)

TALES OF THE BEANWORLD
Feb, 1985 - No. 19, 1991; No. 20, 1993 - No. 21, 1993 ($1.50/$2.00, B&W)
Beanworld Press/Eclipse Comics

1	1.00	2.00	5.00
2-19		1.20	3.00
20 ($2.50)		1.20	3.00
21 ($2.95)		1.60	4.00

Tales Of The Green Lantern Corps #3 © DC

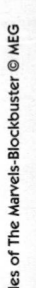
Tales of The Marvels-Blockbuster © MEG

Tales of The Teen Titans #91 © DC

	GD25	FN65	NM94		GD25	FN65	NM94

TALES OF THE GREEN BERET
Jan, 1967 - No. 5, Oct, 1969
Dell Publishing Co.

	GD25	FN65	NM94
1-Glanzman-a in 1-4 & 5r	2.85	8.50	20.00
2-5: 5-Reprints #1	2.00	6.00	14.00

TALES OF THE GREEN HORNET
Sept, 1990 - No. 2, 1990 ($1.75); V3#1, Sept, 1992 - No. 3, Nov, 1992
Now Comics

1,2			1.75
V3#1 ($2.75)-Polybagged w/hologram trading card		1.10	2.75
V3#2,3 ($2.50)		1.00	2.50

TALES OF THE GREEN LANTERN CORPS (See Green Lantern #107)
May, 1981 - No. 3, July, 1981 (Limited series)
DC Comics

1-3: 1-Origin of G.L. & the Guardians			1.50
Annual 1 (1/85)-Gil Kane-c/a		.70	1.75
Annual 2 (1986)-Alan Moore script			1.75

TALES OF THE INVISIBLE SCARLET O'NEIL (See Harvey Comics Hits #59)

TALES OF THE KILLERS (Magazine)
V1#10, Dec, 1970 - V1#11, Feb, 1971 (B&W, 52 pgs.)
World Famous Periodicals

	GD25	FN65	NM94
V1#10-One pg. Frazetta; contains r/Crime Does Not Pay	2.85	8.50	20.00
11-similar cover to Crime Does Not Pay #47; contains r/Crime Does Not Pay	2.00	6.00	14.00

TALES OF THE LEGION (Formerly Legion of Super-Heroes)
No. 314, Aug, 1984 - No. 354, Dec, 1987
DC Comics

314-354: 321-Reprints begin			1.25
Annual 4,5 (1986, 1987)-Formerly LSH Annual			1.40

TALES OF THE MARINES (Formerly Devil-Dog Dugan #1-3)
No. 4, Feb, 1957 (Marines At War #5 on)
Atlas Comics (OPI)

	GD25	FN65	NM94
4-Powell-a; Severin-c	4.25	13.00	28.00

TALES OF THE MARVELS
1995/1996
Marvel Comics

....BLOCKBUSTER 1 (1995, $5.95, one-shot)-acetate, painted-c.	1.00	2.60	6.00
INNER DEMONS 1 (1996, $5.95, one shot)-acetate, painted-c.	1.00	2.60	6.00
....WONDER YEARS 1,2 (1995, $4.95, limited series)-acetate, painted-c.	1.00	2.00	5.00

TALES OF THE MYSTERIOUS TRAVELER (See Mysterious...)
Aug, 1956 - No. 13, June, 1959; V2#14, Oct, 1985 - No. 15, Dec, 1985
Charlton Comics

	GD25	FN65	NM94
1-No Ditko-a; Giordano/Alascia-c	39.00	116.00	270.00
2-Ditko-a(1)	33.00	99.00	230.00
3-Ditko-c/a(1)	33.00	99.00	230.00
4-6-Ditko-c/a(3-4 stories each)	38.00	114.00	265.00
7-9-Ditko-a(1-2 each). 8-Rocke-c	31.00	94.00	220.00
10,11-Ditko-c/a(3-4 each)	34.00	103.00	240.00
12	11.50	34.00	80.00
13-Baker-a (r?)	14.00	43.00	100.00
V2#14,15 (1985)-Ditko-c/a			1.00

TALES OF THE NEW TEEN TITANS
June, 1982 - No. 4, Sept, 1982 (Limited series)
DC Comics

1-4			1

TALES OF THE PONY EXPRESS (TV)
No. 829, Aug, 1957 - No. 942, Oct, 1958
Dell Publishing Co.

	GD25	FN65	NM94
Four Color 829 (#1)--Painted-c	5.00	15.00	50
Four Color 942-Title -Pony Express	5.00	15.00	50

TALES OF THE SUN RUNNERS
V2#1, July, 1986 - V2#3, 1986? ($1.50)
Sirius Comics/Amazing Comics No. 3

V2#1			1
V2#2,3 ($1.95)		1.00	2
Christmas Special 1(12/86)			1

TALES OF THE TEENAGE MUTANT NINJA TURTLES
May, 1987 - No. 7, Aug (Apr-c), 1989 (B&W, $1.50)(See Teenage Mutant...)
Mirage Studios

1			1.20
2-7: Title merges w/Teenage Mutant Ninja...			.80

TALES OF THE TEEN TITANS (Formerly The New Teen Titans)
No. 41, Apr, 1984 - No. 91, July, 1988 (75¢)
DC Comics

41,45-59: 46-Aqualad & Aquagirl join. 50-Double size; app. Betty Kane (Bat-Girl) out of costume. 52-1st app. Azrael in cameo (not same as newer character). 53-1st full app. Azrael; Deathstroke cameo (1 panel). 54,55-Deathstroke-c/stories. 56-Intro Jinx. 57-Neutron app. 59-r/DC Com Presents #26			
42-44: The Judas Contract part 1-3 with Deathstroke the Terminator in all; concludes in Annual #3. 44-Dick Grayson becomes Nightwing (3rd to be Nightwing) & joins Titans; Jericho (Deathstroke's son) joins; origin Deathstroke			1.20
60-91-r/New Teen Titans Baxter series. 68-B. Smith-c. 70-Origin Kole. 83-91 are $1.00 cover			
Annual 3(1984, $1.25)-Part 4 of The Judas Contract; Deathstroke-c/story; Death of Terra; indicia says Teen Titans Annual; formerly New Teen Titan Annual #1,2			1.20
Annual 4,5: 4-(1986, $1.25)-Reprints. 5-(1987)			

TALES OF THE TEXAS RANGERS (See Jace Pearson...)

TALES OF THE UNEXPECTED (Becomes The Unexpected #105 on)(See Adventure #75, Super DC Giant)
Feb-Mar, 1956 - No. 104, Dec-Jan, 1967-68
National Periodical Publications

	GD25	FN65	NM94
1	97.00	292.00	97
2	53.00	160.00	47
3-5	40.00	120.00	32
6-10: 6-1st Silver Age issue	31.00	94.00	24
11,14,19,20	19.00	56.00	14
12,13,15-18,21-24: All have Kirby-a. 15,17-Grey tone-c. 16-Character name 'Thor' with a magic hammer by Kirby (8/57, not like later Thor)	23.00	69.00	18
25-30	19.00	56.00	15
31-39	15.00	45.00	11
40-Space Ranger begins (8/59, 3rd ap.), ends #82	89.00	267.00	85
41,42-Space Ranger stories	36.00	107.00	27
43-1st Space Ranger-c this title; grey tone-c	67.00	200.00	65
44-46	26.00	79.00	20
47-50	19.00	56.00	14
51-60: 54-Dinosaur-c/story	17.00	49.00	12
61-67: 67-Last 10¢ issue	13.50	41.00	11
68-82: 82-Last Space Ranger	8.00	23.50	5
83-100: 91-1st Automan (also in #94,97)	5.70	17.00	4
101-104	4.50	14.00	3

NOTE: **Neal Adams** c-104. **Anderson** a-50. **Brown** a-50-82(Space Ranger); c-19, 40, & m

TA

	GD25	FN65	NM94

Space Ranger-c. **Cameron** a-24, 27, 29; c-24. **Heath** a-49. **Bob Kane** a-24, 48. **Kirby** a-12, 13, 15-18, 21-24; c-13, 18, 22. **Meskin** a-15, 18, 26, 27, 35, 66. **Moreira** a-16, 20, 29, 38, 44, 62, 71; -38. **Roussos** c-10. **Wildey** a-31.

TALES OF THE WEST (See 3-D...)

TALES OF THE WIZARD OF OZ (See Wizard of OZ, 4-Color #1308)

TALES OF THE ZOMBIE (Magazine)
Aug, 1973 - No. 10, Mar, 1975 (75¢, B&W)
Marvel Comics Group

1#1-Reprint/Menace #5; origin	2.60	7.50	18.00
2,3: 2-Everett biography & memorial	1.65	4.20	10.00
2#1(#4)-Photos & text of James Bond movie "Live & Let Die"	1.65	4.20	10.00
5-10: 8-Kaluta-a	1.65	4.20	10.00
nnual 1(Summer,'75)(#11)-B&W; Everett, Buscema-a	1.00	2.60	6.00

OTE: Alcala a-7-9. Boris c-1-4. Colan a-2r, 6. Heath a-5r. Reese a-2. Tuska a-2r.

TALES OF THUNDER
ar, 1985
eluxe Comics

-Dynamo, Iron Maiden, Menthor app.; Giffen-a.35		.80	2.00

TALES OF VOODOO
#11, Nov, 1968 - V7#6, Nov, 1974 (Magazine)
erie Publications

#11	3.20	8.00	20.00
2#1(3/69)-V2#4(9/69)	2.15	6.50	15.00
#1-6('70): 4- "Claws of the Cat" redrawn from Climax #1	1.70	5.00	12.00
#1-6('71), V5#1-7('72), V6#1-6('73), V7#1-6('74)	1.70	5.00	12.00
nual 1	1.70	5.00	12.00

OTE: Bondage-c-V1#10, V2#4, V3#4.

LES OF WELLS FARGO (TV)(See Western Roundup under Dell Giants)
. 876, Feb, 1958 - No. 1215, Oct-Dec, 1961
ll Publishing Co.

ur Color 876 (#1)-Photo-c	10.00	30.00	100.00
ur Color 968, 1023, 1075 (3/60), 1113 (7-9/60)-All photo-c	9.00	27.00	90.00
ur Color 1167 (3-5/61), 1215-Photo-c	8.00	24.00	80.00

LESPIN (Also see Cartoon Tales & Disney's Talespin Limited Series)
ne, 1991 - No. 7, Dec, 1991 ($1.50)
ney Comics

7			1.50

LES TO ASTONISH (Becomes The Incredible Hulk #102 on)
, 1959 - No. 101, Mar, 1968
is (MAP No. 1/ZPC No. 2-14/VPI No. 15-21/Marvel No. 22 on

Jack Davis-a; monster-c.	140.00	420.00	1400.00
Ditko flying saucer-c (Martians); #2-4 have sci/fi-a.	71.00	215.00	575.00
	47.00	141.00	375.00
Prototype issue (Stone Men); Williamson-a (4 pgs.); Kirby monster-c begin	50.00	150.00	400.00
Prototype issue (Stone Men)	43.00	128.00	340.00
Prototype issue (Toad Men)	41.00	124.00	330.00
0	40.00	120.00	300.00
14,17-20: 13-Swipes story from Menace #8	31.00	92.00	215.00
Prototype issue (Electro)	44.00	132.00	350.00
Prototype issue (Stone Men)	36.00	107.00	250.00
(7/61)-Hulk prototype	36.00	107.00	250.00
26,28-34	24.00	71.00	165.00

	GD25	FN65	VF82	NM94
1st Ant-Man app. (1/62); last 10¢ issue (see Strange Tales #73,78 & Tales f Suspense #32)	290.00	870.00	1885.00	3100.00

35-(9/62)-2nd app. Ant-Man, 1st in costume; begin series & Ant-Man-c

	150.00	450.00	900.00	1500.00
		GD25	FN65	NM94
36-3rd app. Ant-Man		66.00	197.00	550.00
37-40: 38-1st app. Egghead		40.00	120.00	350.00
41-43		28.00	84.00	215.00
44-Origin & 1st app. The Wasp (6/63)		31.00	94.00	240.00
45-48: Origin & 1st app. The Porcupine		18.00	54.00	135.00
49-Ant-Man becomes Giant Man (11/63)		22.00	66.00	165.00

50-56,58: 50-Origin/1st app. Human Top (alias Whirlwind). 52-Origin/1st app.
Black Knight (2/64). 53-Origin Colossus   13.00   39.00   100.00

57-Early Spider-Man app. (7/64)		17.00	51.00	130.00

59-Giant Man vs. Hulk feature story (9/64); Hulk's 1st app. this title
20.00   60.00   150.00

60-Giant Man & Hulk double feature begins   23.00   69.00   170.00
61-69: 61-All Ditko issue; 1st mailbag. 62-1st app./origin The Leader; new Wasp
costume. 63-Origin Leader; 65-New Giant Man costume. 68-New Human
Top costume. 69-Last Giant Man.   8.50   26.00   65.00
70-Sub-Mariner & Incredible Hulk begins (8/65)   11.50   34.00   85.00
71-81,83-91,94-99: 72-Begin alternating-c features w/Sub-Mariner (even #'s) &
Hulk (odd #'s). 79-Hulk vs. Hercules-c/story. 81-1st app. Boomerang. 90-1st
app. The Abomination. 97-X-Men cameo (brief)   6.50   19.50   50.00
82-Iron Man battles Sub-Mariner (1st Iron Man x-over outside The Avengers &
TOS); story cont'd from Tales of Suspense #80   8.50   26.00   65.00
92-1st Silver Surfer x-over (outside of Fantastic Four, 4/67); 1 panel cameo
only   8.00   24.50   60.00
93-Hulk battles Silver Surfer-c/story (1st full x-over)   8.50   26.00   65.00
100-Hulk battles Sub-Mariner full-length story   8.00   23.50   60.00
101-Hulk story cont'd in Incredible Hulk #102; Sub-Mariner story continued in
Iron Man & Sub-Mariner #1   10.00   30.00   75.00
NOTE: **Ayers** c(i)-9-12, 16, 18, 19. **Berg** a-1. **Burgos** a-62-64p. **Buscema** a-85-87p. **Colan**
a(p)-70-76, 78-82, 84, 85, 101; c(p)-71-76, 78, 80, 82, 84, 86, 88, 90. **Ditko** a-1, 3-48, 50i, 60-
67p; c-2, 7i, 8i, 14i, 17i. **Everett** a-78, 79, 80-84, 85-90i, 94i, 95, 96; c(i)-79-81, 83, 86, 88. **Forte**
a-6. **Kane** a-76, 88-91; c-89, 91. **Kirby** a(p)-1, 5-34-40, 44, 49-51, 68-70, 82, 83; layouts-71-84;
c(p)-1, 3-48, 50-70, 72, 73, 75, 77, 78, 79, 81, 85, 90. **Kirby/Ditko** a-7, 8, 12, 13, 50; c-7, 8, 10,
13. **Leiber/Fox** a-47, 48, 50, 51. **Powell** a-65-69p, 73, 74. **Reinman** a-6, 36, 45, 46, 54i, 56-60i.

TALES TO ASTONISH (2nd Series)
Dec, 1979 - No. 14, Jan, 1981
Marvel Comics Group

V1#1-Reprints Sub-Mariner #1 by Buscema			1.50
2-14: Reprints Sub-Mariner #2-14			1.50

TALES TO ASTONISH
V3#1, Oct, 1994 ($6.95, one-shot)
Marvel Comics

V3#1-Peter David scripts; acetate, painted-c	1.20	3.00	7.00

TALES TO HOLD YOU SPELLBOUND (See Spellbound)

TALKING KOMICS
1947 (20 pgs, slick-c)
Belda Record & Publ. Co.

Each comic contained a record that followed the story - much like the Golden
Record sets. Known titles: Chirpy Cricket, Lonesome Octopus, Sleepy
Santa, Grumpy Shark, Flying Turtle, Happy Grasshopper
with records...   2.00   5.00   10.00

TALLY-HO COMICS
Dec, 1944
Swappers Quarterly (Baily Publ. Co.)

nn-Frazetta's 1st work as Giunta's assistant; Man in Black horror story;
violence; Giunta-c   31.00   94.00   220.00

TALOS OF THE WILDERNESS SEA
Aug, 1987 ($2.00, one-shot)
DC Comics

1		.80	2.00

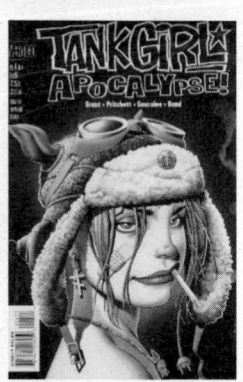

Tank Girl: Apocalypse #4 © Deadline

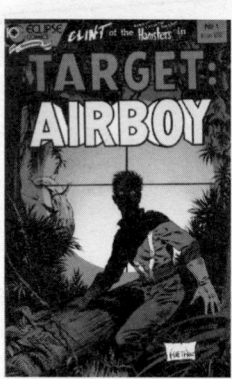

Target: Airboy #1 © ECL

Targitt #1 © ATLAS

	GD25	FN65	NM94

TALULLAH (See Comic Books Series I)

TAMMY, TELL ME TRUE
No. 1233, 1961
Dell Publishing Co.

Four Color 1233-Movie	7.00	21.00	70.00

TANK GIRL
May, 1991 - No. 4, Aug, 1991 ($2.25, B&W, mini-series)
Dark Horse Comics

1-4: 1-Contains Dark Horse trading cards		1.20	3.00

TANK GIRL: APOCALYPSE
Nov, 1995 - No. 4, Feb, 1996 ($2.25, limited series)
DC Comics

1-4		.90	2.25

TANK GIRL: MOVIE ADAPTATION
1995 ($5.95, 68 pgs., one-shot)
DC Comics

nn-Peter Milligan scripts	1.00	2.60	6.00

TANK GIRL: THE ODYSSEY
May, 1995 - No.4, Oct, 1995 ($2.25, limited series)
DC Comics

1-4: Peter Milligan scripts; Hewlett-a		.90	2.25

TANK GIRL 2
Feb, 1996 ($17.95, one-shot, mature)
Dark Horse Comics

1	2.60	7.50	18.00

TAPPAN'S BURRO (See Zane Grey & 4-Color #449)

TAPPING THE VEIN (Clive Barker's...)
1989 - No. 4, 1990 ($6.95, squarebound, mature readers, 68 pgs.)
Eclipse Comics

Book 1-4: 1-Russell-a, Bolton-c. 2-Bolton-a. 4-Die-cut-c			
	1.20	3.00	7.00

TARANTULA (See Weird Suspense)

TARGET: AIRBOY
Mar, 1988 ($1.95)
Eclipse Comics

1		.80	2.00

TARGET COMICS (...Western Romances #106 on)
Feb, 1940 - V10#3 (#105), Aug-Sept, 1949
Funnies, Inc./Novelty Publications/Star Publications

V1#1-Origin & 1st app. Manowar, The White Streak by Burgos, & Bulls-Eye Bill by Everett; City Editor (ends #5), High Grass Twins by Jack Cole (ends #4), T-Men by Joe Simon(ends #9), Rip Rory (ends #4), Fantastic Feature Films by Tarpe Mills (ends #39), & Calling 2-R (ends #14) begin; marijuana use story	366.00	1100.00	3300.00
2	206.00	618.00	1650.00
3,4	112.00	338.00	900.00
5-Origin The White Streak in text; Space Hawk by Wolverton begins (6/40) (see Blue Bolt & Circus)	311.00	933.00	2800.00
6-The Chameleon by Everett begins (7/40, 1st app.); White Streak origin cont'd. in text; early mention of comic collecting in letter column; 1st letter column in comics (7/40)	143.00	431.00	1150.00
7-Wolverton Spacehawk-c/story (Scarce)	377.00	1133.00	3400.00
8,9,12: 12-(1/41)	112.00	338.00	900.00
10-Intro/1st app. The Target (11/40); Simon-c	143.00	431.00	1150.00
11-Origin The Target & The Targeteers	131.00	393.00	1050.00
V2#1-Target by Bob Wood; Uncle Sam flag-c	70.00	211.00	565.00
2-Ten part Treasure Island serial begins; Harold Delay-a; reprinted in Catholic Comics V3#1-10 (see Key Comics #5)	61.00	185.00	495.00

3-5: 4-Kit Carter, The Cadet begins	46.00	138.00	37█
6-9: Red Seal with White Streak in #6-10	46.00	138.00	37█
10-Classic-c	79.00	238.00	63█
11,12: 12-10-part Last of the Mohicans serial begins; Delay-a			
	45.00	136.00	365█
V3#1-10: 8-Flag-c; 6-part Gulliver Travels serial begins; Delay-a. 10-Last Wolverton issue	45.00	136.00	365█
11,12	11.00	33.00	75█
V4#1-12: 6-Targetoons by Wolverton (1 pg.). 8-X-Mas-c			
	10.00	30.00	58█
V5#1-8	8.70	26.00	52█
V6#1-10, V7#1-12	8.00	24.00	48█
V8#1,3-5,8,9,11,12	7.50	22.50	42█
2,6,7-Krigstein-a	8.00	24.00	48█
10-L.B. Cole-c	25.00	75.00	175█
V9#1,4,6,8,10,12, V10#2,3-L.B. Cole-c	25.00	75.00	175█
V9#2,3,5,7,9,11, V10#1	6.35	19.00	3█

NOTE: **Certa** c-V8#9, 11, 12, V9#5, 9, 11, V10#1. **Jack Cole** a-1-8. **Everett** a-1-9; c(signed Blake)-1, 2. **Al Fago** c-V6#8. **Sid Greene** c-V9#9, 12, V3#3. **Walter Johnson** c-V5#6, V6#█. **Tarpe Mills** a-1-4, 6, 8, 11, V3#1. **Rico** a-V7#4, 10, V8#5, 6, V9#3; c-V7#6, 8, 10, V8#2, 4, █. **Simon** a-1, 2. **Bob Wood** c-V2#2, 3, 5, 6.

TARGET: THE CORRUPTORS (TV)
No. 1306, Mar-May, 1962 - No. 3, Oct-Dec, 1962 (All have photo-c)
Dell Publishing Co.

Four Color 1306(#1), #2,3	5.00	15.00	5█

TARGET WESTERN ROMANCES (Formerly Target Comics; becomes Flam█ Western Romances #3)
No. 106, Oct-Nov, 1949 - No. 107, Dec-Jan, 1949-50
Star Publications

106(#1)-Silhouette nudity panel; L.B. Cole-c	30.00	90.00	21█
107(#2)-L.B. Cole-c; lingerie panels	25.00	75.00	175█

TARGITT
March, 1975 - No. 3, July, 1975
Atlas/Seaboard Publ.

1-3: 1-Origin; Nostrand-a in all. 2-1st in costume			

TARZAN (See Aurora, Comics on Parade, Crackajack, DC 100-Page Super Spec., Famo█ Feature Stories #1, Golden Comics Digest #4, 9, Jungle Tales of..., Lir █ Collectors' Edition, Popular, Sparkler, Sport Stars #1, Tip Top & Top Comics)

TARZAN
No. 5, 1939 - No. 161, Aug, 1947
Dell Publishing Co./United Features Syndicate

Large Feature Comic 5('39)-(Scarce)-By Hal Foster; reprints 1st dailies from 1929	120.00	360.00	120█
Single Series 20(:40)-By Hal Foster	95.00	285.00	95█
Four Color 134(2/47)-Marsh-c/a	60.00	180.00	60█
Four Color 161(8/47)-Marsh-c/a	52.50	157.50	52█

TARZAN (...of the Apes #138 on)
1-2/48 - No. 131, 7-8/62; No. 132, 11/62 - No. 206, 2/72
Dell Publishing Co./Gold Key No. 132 on

1-Jesse Marsh-a begins	100.00	300.00	850█
2	55.00	165.00	475█
3-5	41.00	124.00	340█
6-10: 6-1st Tantor the Elephant. 7-1st Valley of the Monsters			
	32.00	96.00	27█
11-15: 11-Two Against the Jungle begins, ends #24. 13-Lex Barker photo-c begin	27.00	80.00	22█
16-20	21.00	63.00	17█
21-24,26-30	16.00	48.00	13█
25-1st "Brothers of the Spear" episode; series ends #156,160,161,196-206			
	19.00	58.00	16█
31-40	10.00	30.00	8█
41-54: Last Barker photo-c	7.00	21.00	6█

Tarzan #212 © ERB

Tarzan #6 © ERB

Tarzan: The Warrior #2 © ERB

	GD25	FN65	NM94
55-60: 56-Eight pg. Boy story	5.50	16.00	40.00
61,62,64-70	4.30	13.00	32.00
63-Two Tarzan stories, 1 by Manning	4.60	13.70	35.00
71-79	3.40	10.00	24.00
80-99: 80-Gordon Scott photo-c begin	3.70	11.00	26.00
00	4.60	13.70	32.00
01-109	3.10	9.00	22.00
10 (Scarce)-Last photo-c	4.00	12.00	28.00
11-120	2.60	7.70	18.00
21-131: Last Dell issue	2.00	6.00	14.00
32-1st Gold Key issue	3.00	9.00	30.00
33-154: 139-(12/63)-1st app. Korak (Boy); leaves Tarzan & gets own book			
1/64	2.40	7.20	24.00
55-Origin Tarzan	2.85	8.50	28.00
56-161: 157-Banlu, Dog of the Arande begins, ends #159, 195. 169-Leopard			
Girl app.	1.80	5.40	18.00
62,165,168,171 (TV)-Ron Ely photo covers	2.40	7.20	24.00
63,164,166,167,169,170: 169-Leopard Girl app.	1.65	4.20	16.00
72-199,201-206: 178-Tarzan origin-r/#155; Leopard Girl app., also in #179,			
190-193	1.50	4.50	15.00
00 (Scarce)	2.00	6.00	20.00
tory Digest 1-(6/70, G.K.)	1.80	5.40	18.00

OTE: #182, 165, 168, 171 are TV issues. #1-153 all have *Marsh* art on Tarzan. #154-161, 163, 14, 166, 167, 172-177 all have *Manning* art on Tarzan. #178, 202 have *Manning* Tarzan prints. No "Brothers of the Spear" in #1-24, 157-159, 162-195. #39-126, 128-156 all have *Russ Manning* art on "Brothers of the Spear". #196-201, 203-205 all have *Manning* B.O.T.S. reprints; 5-38, 127 all have Jesse Marsh art on B.O.T.S. #206 has a Marsh B.O.T.S. reprint. *Golub c-12. Marsh c-1-7. Doug Wildey a-162, 179-187. Many issues have front and back photo cov-*

ARZAN (Continuation of Gold Key series)
. 207, Apr, 1972 - No. 258, Feb, 1977
ational Periodical Publications

7-Origin Tarzan by Joe Kubert, part 1; John Carter begins (origin); 52 pg.			
issues thru #209	1.70	5.00	12.00
8,209: 208-210-Parts 2-4 of origin. 209-Last John Carter			
	1.50	3.75	9.00
0-229,236-258: 210-Kubert-a. 211-Hogarth, Kubert-a. 212-214: Adaptations			

from "Jungle Tales of Tarzan". 213-Beyond the Farthest Star begins, ends #218. 215-218,224,225-All by Kubert. 215-part Foster-r. 219-223: Adapts "The Return of Tarzan" by Kubert. 226-Manning-a. 238-(68 pgs.). 240-243 adapts "Tarzan & the Castaways". 250-256 adapts "Tarzan the Untamed".

252,253-r/#213	1.30	3.25	8.00
0-DC 100 Page Super Spectacular; Kubert, Kaluta-a(p); Korak begins, ends			
#234; Carson of Venus app.	1.65	4.20	10.00
4-235-New Kubert-a.: 231-234-(All 100 pgs.)-Adapts "Tarzan and the Lion			

Man"; Rex, the Wonder Dog r-#232, 233. 235-(100 pgs.)-Last Kubert issue.

	1.65	4.20	10.00
mic Digest 1-(Fall, 1972, 50¢, 160 pgs.)(DC)-Digest size; Kubert-c;			
Manning-a	1.30	3.25	8.00

E: *Anderson a-207, 209, 217, 218. Chaykin a-216. Finlay a(r)-212. Foster strip-r #207-, 211, 212, 221. Heath a-230l. G. Kane a(r)-232p, 233p. Kubert a-207-225, 227-235, 257r, r, c-207-249, 253. Lopez a-250-255p; c-250p, 251, 252, 254. Manning strip-r 230-235, 238. row a-208. Nino a-231-234. Sparling a-230, 231. Starr a-233r.*

RZAN
e, 1977 - No. 29, Oct, 1979
vel Comics Group

		1.20	3.00
29: 2-Origin by John Buscema		.80	2.00
ual 1-3: 1-(1977). 2-(1978). 3-(1979)		.80	2.00

E: *N. Adams c-11l, 12l. Alcala a-9l, 10l; c-8l, 9l. Buckler c-25-27p, Annual 3p. John cema a-1-3, 4-18p, Annual 1; c-1-7, 8p, 9p, 10, 11p, 12p, 13, 14-19p, 21p, 22, 23p, 24p, Annual 1. Mooney a-22l. Nebres a-29l. Russell a-29l.*

RZAN
, 1996 - Present ($2.95)
k Horse Comics

	GD25	FN65	NM94
1-6: All Suydam-c			3.00

TARZAN FAMILY, THE (Formerly Korak, Son of Tarzan)
No. 60, Nov-Dec, 1975 - No. 66, Nov-Dec, 1976
(#60-62: 68 pgs.; #63 on: 52 pgs.)
National Periodical Publications

60-66: 60-Korak begins; Kaluta-r	.80	2.00	

NOTE: *Carson of Venus-r 60-65. New John Carter-62-64, 65r, 66r. New Korak-60-66. Pellucidar feature-66. Foster strip r-60(9/4/32-10/16/32), 62(6/29/32-7/31/32), 63(10/11/31-12/13/31). Kaluta Carson of Venus-60-65. Kubert a-61, 64; c-60-64. Manning strip-r 60-62, 64. Morrow a-66r.*

TARZAN/JOHN CARTER: WARLORDS OF MARS
Jan, 1996 - No. 4, June, 1996 ($2.50, limited series)
Dark Horse Comics

1-4: Bruce Jones scripts in all. 1,2,4-Bret Blevins-c/a. 2-(4/96)-Indicia reads #3			
			2.50

TARZAN KING OF THE JUNGLE (See Dell Giant #37, 51)

TARZAN, LORD OF THE JUNGLE
Sept, 1965 (Giant) (25¢, soft paper-c)
Gold Key

1-Marsh-r	6.00	18.00	70.00

TARZAN: LOVE, LIES AND THE LOST CITY (See Tarzan the Warrior)
Aug. 10, 1992 - No. 3, Sept, 1992 ($2.50, limited series)
Malibu Comics

1-($3.95, 68 pgs.)-Flip book format; Simonson & Wagner scripts			
	1.00	2.00	5.00
2,3-No Simonson or Wagner scripts		1.20	3.00

TARZAN MARCH OF COMICS (See March of Comics #82, 98, 114, 125, 144, 155, 172, 185, 204, 223, 240, 252, 262, 272, 286, 300, 332, 342, 354, 366)

TARZAN OF THE APES
1934? (Hardcover, 4x12", 68 pgs.)
Metropolitan Newspaper Service

1-Strip reprints	20.00	60.00	140.00

TARZAN OF THE APES
July, 1984 - No. 2, Aug, 1984 (Movie adaptation)
Marvel Comics Group

1,2: Origin-r/Marvel Super Spec.			1.50

TARZAN'S JUNGLE ANNUAL (See Dell Giants)

TARZAN'S JUNGLE WORLD (See Dell Giants #25)

TARZAN THE WARRIOR (Also see Tarzan: Love, Lies and the Lost City)
Mar, 19, 1992 - No. 5, 1992 ($2.50, limited series)
Malibu Comics

1-5: 1-Bisley painted pack-c (flip book format-c)		1.20	3.00
1-2nd printing w/o flip-c by Bisley		1.00	2.50

TARZAN VS. PREDATOR AT THE EARTH'S CORE
Jan, 1996 - No. 4, June, 1996 ($2.50, limited series)
Dark Horse Comics

1-4: Lee Weeks-c/a; Walt Simonson scripts		1.00	2.50

TASMANIAN DEVIL & HIS TASTY FRIENDS
Nov, 1962 (12¢)
Gold Key

1-Bugs Bunny & Elmer Fudd x-over	9.50	28.50	95.00

TASTEE-FREEZ COMICS
1957 (10¢, 36 pgs.)(6 different issues given away)
Harvey Comics

1,3: 1-Little Dot. 3-Casper	6.35	19.00	38.00
2,4,5: 2-Rags Rabbit. 4-Sad Sack. 5-Mazie	4.00	12.00	24.00
6-Dick Tracy	5.85	17.50	35.00

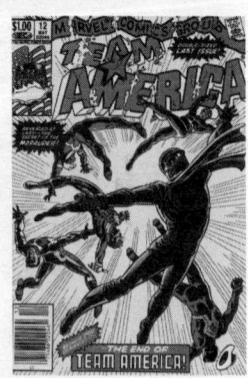
Team America #12 © MEG

Team Anarchy #1 © Dagger Comics

Team 7: Dead Reckoning #3 © Aegis Entertainment

	GD25	FN65	NM94

TAYLOR'S CHRISTMAS TABLOID
Mid 1930s, Cleveland, Ohio
Dept. Store Giveaway (Tabloid size; in color)

nn-(Very Rare)-Among the earliest pro work of Siegel & Shuster; one full color page called "The Battle in the Stratosphere", with a pre-Superman look; Shuster art thoughout. (Only 1 known copy)
Estimated value… 2800.00

TEAM AMERICA (See Captain America #269)
June, 1982 - No. 12, May, 1983
Marvel Comics Group

	GD25	FN65	NM94
1-Origin; Ideal Toy motorcycle characters			1.00
2-10: 9-Iron man app.			1.00
11-Ghost Rider app.		1.20	3.00
12-Double size		.80	2.00

TEAM ANARCHY
Oct, 1993 - No.8, 1994? ($2.50)
Dagger Comics

	GD25	FN65	NM94
1-($2.75)-Red foil logo; intro Team Anarchy		1.10	2.75
1-Platinum		1.10	2.75
2-8		1.10	2.75
3-Bronze		1.10	2.75
3-Gold		1.10	2.75
3-Silver		1.10	2.75

TEAM HELIX
Jan, 1993 - No. 4, Apr, 1993 ($1.75, limited series)
Marvel Comics

	GD25	FN65	NM94
1-4: Teen Super Group. 1,2-Wolverine app.		.70	1.75

TEAM ONE: STORMWATCH (Also see StormWatch)
June, 1995 - No. 2, Aug, 1995 ($2.50, limited series)
Image Comics (Wildstorm Productions)

	GD25	FN65	NM94
1,2: Steven T. Seagle scripts		1.00	2.50

TEAM ONE: WILDC.A.T.S (Also see WildC.A.T.S)
July, 1995 - No. 2, Aug, 1995 ($2.50, limited series)
Image Comics (Wildstorm Productions)

	GD25	FN65	NM94
1,2: James Robinson scripts		1.00	2.50

TEAM 7
Oct, 1994 - No.4, Feb, 1995 ($2.50, limited series)
Image Comics (Wildstorm Productions)

	GD25	FN65	NM94
1-Dixon scripts in all		1.60	4.00
1-Portaclo variant-c	1.00	2.60	6.00
2-4		1.00	2.50

TEAM 7-DEAD RECKONING (limited series)
Jan, 1996 - No. 4, Apr, 1996 ($2.50, limited series)
Image Comics (Wildstorm Productions)

	GD25	FN65	NM94
1-4: Dixon scripts in all			2.50

TEAM 7-OBJECTIVE HELL
May, 1995 - No. 3, July, 1995 ($1.95/$2.50, limited series)
Image Comics (Wildstorm Productions)

	GD25	FN65	NM94
1-($1.95)-Newstand; Dixon scripts in all; Barry Smith-c		.80	2.00
1-($2.50)-Direct Market; Barry Smith-c, bound-in card		1.00	2.50
2,3-($2.50)		1.00	2.50

TEAM TITANS (See Deathstroke & New Titans Annual #7)
Sept, 1992 - No. 24, Sept, 1994 ($1.75/$1.95)
DC Comics

1-Five different #1s exist w/origins in 1st half & the same 2nd story in each: Kilowat, Mirage, Nightrider w/Netzer/Perez-a, Redwing, & Terra w/part Perez-p; Total Chaos Pt 3 .90 2.25

	GD25	FN65	NM94
2-Total Chaos Pt 6		.80	2.00
3-21: 11-Metallik app.		.70	1.75
22-24: 22-$1.95-c begins. 24-Zero Hour x-over		.80	2.00
Annual 1 (1993, $3.50, 68 pgs.)		1.40	3.50
Annual 2 (1994, $3.50, 68 pgs.)-Elseworlds story		1.40	3.50

TEAM YANKEE
Jan, 1989 - No. 6, Feb, 1989 ($1.95, weekly limited series)
First Comics

	GD25	FN65	NM94
1-6		1.00	2.00

TEAM YOUNGBLOOD (Also see Youngblood)
Sept, 1993 - No. 22, Sept, 1995 ($1.95/$2.50)
Image Comics (Extreme Studios)

1-9-Liefeld scripts in all: 1,2,4-6,8-Thibert-c(i). 1-1st app. Dutch & Masada. 3-Spawn cameo. 5-1st app. Lynx. 7,8-Coupons 1 & 4 for Extreme Prejudice #0; Black and White Pt. 4 & 8 by Thibert. 8-Coupon #4 for E. P. #0. 9-Liefeld wraparound-c(p)/a(p) on Pt. I .80 2.0
10-22: 10-$2.50-c begin; Liefeld-c(p). 16-Polybagged w/trading card 17-Polybagged w/trading card. 18-Extreme 3000 Prelude. 19-Cruz-a. 21-Angela & Glory-app. 22-Shadowhawk-c/app 1.00 2.5

TEDDY ROOSEVELT & HIS ROUGH RIDERS (See Real Heroes #1)
1950
Avon Periodicals

	GD25	FN65	NM94
1-Kinstler-c; Palais-a; Flag-c	15.00	45.00	105.0

TEDDY ROOSEVELT ROUGH RIDER (See Battlefield #22 & Classics Illustrated Special Issue)

TED McKEEVER'S METROPOL
Mar, 1991 - No. 12, Mar, 1992 ($2.95, limited series)
Marvel Comics (Epic Comics)

	GD25	FN65	NM94
V1#1-12: Ted McKeever-c/a/scripts		1.50	3.0

TED McKEEVER'S METROPOL A.D.
Oct, 1992 - No. 3, Dec, 1992 ($3.50, limited series)
Marvel Comics (Epic Comics)

	GD25	FN65	NM94
V2#1-3: Ted McKeever-c/a/scripts			3.

TEE AND VEE CROSLEY IN TELEVISION LAND COMICS
(Also see Crosley's House of Fun)
1951 (52 pgs.; 8x11"; paper cover; in color)
Crosley Division, Avco Mfg. Corp. (Giveaway)

	GD25	FN65	NM94
Many stories, puzzles, cut-outs, games, etc.	4.70	14.00	28

TEENA
No. 11, 1948 - No. 15, 1948; No. 20, Aug, 1949 - No. 22, Oct, 1950
Magazine Enterprises/Standard Comics No. 20 on

	GD25	FN65	NM94
A-1 #11-Teen-age; Ogden Whitney-c	7.00	21.00	42
A-1 #12, 15	6.35	19.00	38
20-22 (Standard)	4.00	11.00	22

TEEN-AGE BRIDES (True Bride's Experiences #8 on)
Aug, 1953 - No. 7, Aug, 1954
Harvey/Home Comics

	GD25	FN65	NM94
1-Powell-a	10.00	30.00	58
2-Powell-a	6.35	19.00	38
3-7: 3,6-Powell-a	5.00	15.00	30

TEEN-AGE CONFESSIONS (See Teen Confessions)

TEEN-AGE CONFIDENTIAL CONFESSIONS
July, 1960 - No. 22, 1964
Charlton Comics

	GD25	FN65	NM94
1	4.00	11.00	22
2-10	2.00	5.00	10
11-22	1.20	3.00	6

TEEN-AGE DIARY SECRETS (Formerly Blue Ribbon Comics; becomes Dia

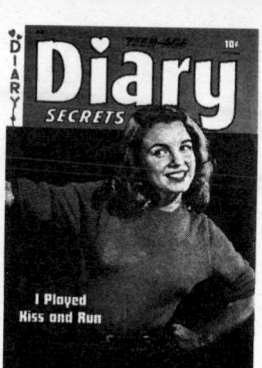
Teen-Age Diary Secrets #6 © STJ

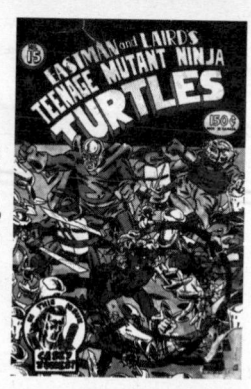
Teenage Mutant Ninja Turtles #15 © Mirage Studios

Teenage Mutant Ninja Turtles #4 © Mirage Studios

	GD25	FN65	NM94
Secrets #10 on)			
No. 4, 9/49; nn (#5), 9/49 - No. 7, 11/49; No. 8, 2/50; No. 9, 8/50			
St. John Publishing Co.			
4(4/49)-Oversized; part mag., part comic	21.00	62.00	145.00
nn(#5),6,8: 6,8-Photo-c; Baker-a(2-3) in each	16.00	47.00	110.00
7,9-Digest size	19.00	58.00	135.00
TEEN-AGE DOPE SLAVES (See Harvey Comics Library #1)			
TEENAGE HOTRODDERS (Top Eliminator #25 on; see Blue Bird)			
Apr, 1963 - No. 24, July, 1967			
Charlton Comics			
1	3.75	11.25	30.00
2-10	2.60	7.50	18.00
11-24	2.00	6.00	14.00
TEEN-AGE LOVE (See Fox Giants)			
TEEN-AGE LOVE (Formerly Intimate)			
V2#4, July, 1958 - No. 96, Dec, 1973			
Charlton Comics			
V2#4	3.25	9.50	22.00
5-9	1.70	5.00	12.00
10(9/59)-20	1.50	3.75	9.00
21-35	1.00	2.60	6.00
36-70		1.20	3.00
71-96: 61&62-Jonnie Love begins (origin)			1.20
TEENAGE MUTANT NINJA TURTLES (Also see Anything Goes, Donatello, First Comics Graphic Novel, Gobbledygook, Grimjack #26, Leonardo, Michaelangelo, Raphael & Tales Of The...)			
1984 - No. 62, Aug, 1993 (1.50/$1.75, B&W; all 44-52 pgs.)			
Mirage Studios			
1-1st printing (3000 copies)-Only printing to have ad for Gobbledygook #1 & 2; Shredder app. (#1-4: 7-1/2x11")	29.00	86.00	200.00
1-2nd printing (6/84)(15,000 copies)	3.60	11.00	25.00
1-3rd printing (2/85)(36,000 copies)	1.30	3.25	8.00
1-4th printing (50,000 copies)	1.00	2.50	5.00
1-5th printing, new-c (8/88-c, 11/88 inside)		.80	2.00
1-Counterfeit. **Note:** Most counterfeit copies have a half inch wide white streak or scratch marks across the center of back cover. Black part of cover is a bluish black instead of a deep black. Inside paper is very white & inside cover is bright white. These counterfeit the 1st printings (no value).			
2-1st printing (1984; 15,000 copies)	9.00	28.00	65.00
2-2nd printing	1.30	3.30	8.00
2-3rd printing; new Corben-c/a (2/85)		1.10	2.75
2-Counterfeit with glossy cover stock (no value).			
3-1st printing (1985, 44 pgs.)	3.60	10.70	25.00
3-Variant, 500 copies, given away in NYC. Has 'Laird's Photo' in white rather than light blue	11.00	32.00	75.00
3-2nd printing; contains new back-up story		1.10	2.75
4-1st printing (1985, 44 pgs.)	1.60	4.70	11.00
4-2nd printing (5/87)		.70	1.75
5-Fugitoid begins, ends #7; 1st full color-c (1985)	1.50	4.00	9.00
5-2nd printing (11/87)		.70	1.75
6-1st printing (1986)	1.25	3.00	7.50
6-2nd printing (4/88-c, 5/88 inside)		.70	1.75
7-4 pg. Eastman/Corben color insert; 1st color TMNT (1986, $1.75-c); Bade Biker back-up story	1.25	3.00	7.50
7-2nd printing (1/89) w/o color insert		.70	1.75
8-Cerebus-c/story with Dave Sim-a (1986)	1.00	2.60	6.00
9,10: 9 (9/86)-Rip In Time by Corben		1.90	4.75
11-15		1.30	3.25
16-18: 18-Mark Bode'-a		1.10	2.75
18-2nd printing ($2.25, color, 44 pgs.)-New-c		.90	2.25
19-51: 19-Begin $1.75-c. 24-26-Veitch-c/a. 35-Begin $2.00-c. 50-Features			
pin-ups by Larsen, McFarlane, Simonson, etc.		.70	1.8
32-2nd printing ($2.75, 52 pgs., full color)		1.00	2.5
52-62: 52-Begin $2.25-c		.90	2.2
Book 1,2($1.50, B&W): 2-Corben-c			1.5
...Christmas Special 1 (12/90, $1.75, B&W, 52 pgs.)-Cover title: Michaelangelo Christmas Special; r/Michaelangelo one-shot plus new Raphael story		.70	1.75
...Special (The Maltese Turtle) nn (1/93, $2.95, color, 44 pgs.)		1.20	3.00
...Special: "Times" Pipeline nn (9/92, $2.95, color, 44 pgs.)-Mark Bode-c/a		1.20	3.00
Hardcover ($100)-r/#1-10 plus one-shots w/dust jackets - limited to 1000 w/letter of authenticity	14.00	43.00	100.00
Softcover ($40)-r/#1-10	6.70	20.00	40.00
TEENAGE MUTANT NINJA TURTLES			
V2#1, Oct, 1993 - V2#10, July, 1994? ($2.75)			
Mirage Studios			
V2#1-10: 1-Wraparound-c		1.10	2.75
TEENAGE MUTANT NINJA TURTLES ADVENTURES (TV)			
8/88 - No. 3, 12/88; 3/89 - No. 62, 1995? ($1.00/$1.25/$1.50/$1.75)			
Archie Comics			
1-Adapts TV cartoon; not by Eastman/Laird		1.20	3.00
2,3 (Mini-series)		.80	2.00
1 (2nd on going series)		1.00	2.50
2-5: 5-Begins original stories not based on TV		.80	2.00
1-11: 2nd printings			1.00
6-49,51-58: 14-Simpson-a(p). 19-31 Mighty Mutanimals (also in #20, 51-54). 20-Begin $1.25-c. 22-Gene Colan-c/a			1.25
50-(1990)-Poster by Eastman/Laird			1.50
59-61,63-73: 59-Begin $1.50-c			1.50
62 ($1.75)-w/poster		.70	1.75
nn (1990, $5.95)-Movie adaptation	1.00	2.50	6.00
nn (Spring, 1991, $2.50, 68 pgs.)-(Meet Archie)		1.00	2.50
nn (Sum, 1991, $2.50, 68 pgs.)-(Movie II)-Adapts movie sequel		1.00	2.50
...Meet the Conservation Corps 1 (1992, $2.50, 68 pgs.)		1.00	2.50
...III The Movie: The Turtles are Back...In Time (1993, $2.50, 68 pgs.)		1.00	2.50
Special 1 (Sum/92, $2.50, 68 pgs.)-Bill Wray-c		1.00	2.50
Special 4 (Spr/93, $2.50, 68 pgs.)		1.00	2.50
Special 5 (Sum/93, $2.50, 68 pgs.)		1.00	2.50
Giant Size Special 6 (Fall/93, $1.95, 52 pgs.)		.80	2.00
Special 7,8 (Win/93, Spr/94, $1.95, 52 pgs.)		.80	2.00
Special 9 (Sum/94, $1.95, 52 pgs.)-Jeff Smith-c		.80	2.00
Special 10 (Fall/94, $2.00, 52 pgs.)		.80	2.00
NOTE: There are 2nd printings of #1-11 w/B&W inside covers. Originals are color.			
TEENAGE MUTANT NINJA TURTLES (Adventures)			
Jan, 1996 - No. 3, Mar, 1996 ($1.50, limited series)			
Archie Publications			
1-3			1.50
TEENAGE MUTANT NINJA TURTLES			
June, 1996 - Present ($1.95)			
Image Comics (Highbrow Entertainment)			
1-4: Eric Larsen-c(i) on all			2.00
TEENAGE MUTANT NINJA TURTLES CLASSICS DIGEST (TV)			
Aug, 1993 - No. 8, Mar, 1995? ($1.75)			
Archie Comics			
1-8: Reprints TMNT Advs.		.70	1.75
TEENAGE MUTANT NINJA TURTLES/FLAMING CARROT CROSSOVER			
Nov, 1993 - No. 4, Feb, 1994 ($2.75, limited series)			
Mirage Publishing			
1-4: Bob Burden story		1.10	2.75

547

Teen-Age Romances #4 © STJ

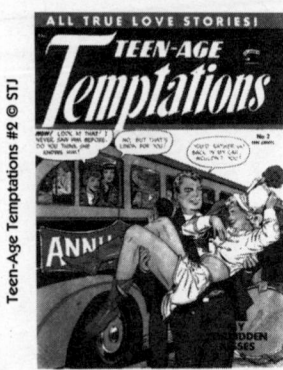

Teen-Age Temptations #2 © STJ

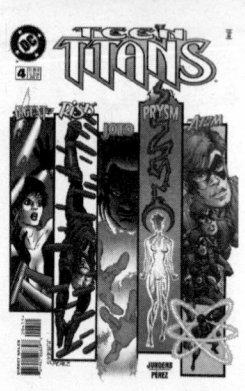

Teen Titans #4 © DC

	GD25	FN65	NM94

TEENAGE MUTANT NINJA TURTLES PRESENTS: APRIL O'NEIL
Mar, 1993 - No. 3, June, 1993 ($1.25, limited series)
Archie Comics

1-3		.60	1.25

TEENAGE MUTANT NINJA TURTLES PRESENTS: DONATELLO AND LEATHERHEAD
July, 1993 - No. 3, Sept, 1993 ($1.25, limited series)
Archie Comics

1-3		.60	1.25

TEENAGE MUTANT NINJA TURTLES PRESENTS: MERDUDE
Oct, 1993 - No. 3, Dec, 1993 ($1.25, limited series)
Archie Comics

1-3-See Mighty Mutanimals #7 for 1st app. Merdude		.60	1.25

TEENAGE MUTANT NINJA TURTLES/SAVAGE DRAGON CROSSOVER
Aug, 1995 ($2.75, one-shot)
Mirage Studios

1		1.10	2.75

TEEN-AGE ROMANCE (Formerly My Own Romance)
No. 77, Sept, 1960 - No. 86, Mar, 1962
Marvel Comics (ZPC)

77-86	2.30	6.70	16.00

TEEN-AGE ROMANCES
Jan, 1949 - No. 45, Dec, 1955
St. John Publ. co. (Approved Comics)

1-Baker-c/a(1)	31.00	94.00	220.00
2-Baker-c/a	17.00	51.00	120.00
3-Baker-c/a(3); spanking panel	19.00	56.00	130.00
4,5,7,8-Photo-c; Baker-a(2-3) each	13.50	41.00	95.00
6-Slightly large size; photo-c; part magazine; Baker-a (10/49)			
	15.00	45.00	105.00
9-Baker-c/a; Kubert-a	18.00	54.00	125.00
10-12,20-Baker-c/a(2-3) each	13.00	39.00	90.00
13-19,21,22-Complete issues by Baker	18.00	54.00	125.00
23-25-Baker-c/a(2-3) each	11.50	34.00	80.00
26,27,33,34,36-40,42: Baker-a. 33-Signed story by Estrada. 38-Suggestive-c.			
42-r/Cinderella Love #9; Last pre-code (3/55)	8.35	25.00	50.00
28-30-No Baker-a	4.00	10.00	20.00
31-Baker-c	4.25	13.00	28.00
32-Baker-c	4.25	13.00	28.00
35-Baker-c/a (16 pgs.)	7.00	21.00	42.00
41-Baker-c; Infantino-a(r); all stories are Ziff-Davis-r	7.00	21.00	42.00
43-45-Baker-a	5.35	16.00	32.00

TEEN-AGE TALK
1964
I.W. Enterprises

Reprint #1	1.70	5.00	12.00
Reprint #5,8,9: 5-r/Hector #? 9-Punch Comics #?; L.B. Cole-c reprint from School Day Romances #1	1.00	2.00	5.00

TEEN-AGE TEMPTATIONS (Going Steady #10 on)(See True Love Pictorial)
Oct, 1952 - No. 9, Aug, 1954
St. John Publishing co.

1-Baker-c/a; has story "Reform School Girl" by Estrada			
	38.00	114.00	265.00
2,4-Baker-c	11.50	34.00	80.00
3,5-7,9-Baker-c/a	17.00	51.00	120.00
8-Teenagers smoke reefers; Baker-c/a	18.00	54.00	125.00
NOTE: *Estrada* a-1, 3-5.			

TEEN BEAM (Formerly Teen Beat #1)
No. 2, Jan-Feb, 1968
National Periodical Publications

2-Orlando, Drucker-a(r); Monkees photo-c	2.85	8.50	20.00

TEEN BEAT (Becomes Teen Beam #2)
Nov-Dec, 1967
National Periodical Publications

1-Photos & text only; Monkees photo-c	3.60	11.00	25.00

TEEN COMICS (Formerly All Teen; Journey Into Unknown Worlds #36 on)
No. 21, April, 1947 - No. 35, May, 1950
Marvel comics (WFP)

21-Kurtzman's "Hey Look"; Patsy Walker, Cindy (1st app.?), Georgie, Margie app.; Syd Shores-a begins, end #23	10.00	30.00	70.00
22,23,25,27,29,31-35: 22-(6/47)-Becomes Hedy Devine #22 (8/47) on?			
	7.50	22.50	45.00
24,26,28,30-Kurtzman's "Hey Look"	10.00	30.00	70.00

TEEN CONFESSIONS
Aug, 1959 - No. 97, Nov, 1976
Charlton Comics

1	9.15	27.00	55.00
2	3.75	11.25	28.00
3-10	2.30	6.70	16.00
11-30	1.65	4.20	10.00
31-Beatles-c	8.00	23.50	55.00
32-36,38-55	1.00	2.60	6.00
37 (1/66)-Beatles Fan Club story; Beatles-c	8.00	23.50	60.00
56-58,60-97: 89,90-Newton-c			1.00
59-Kaluta's 1st pro work? (12/69)	1.20	3.00	7.00

TEENIE WEENIES, THE (America's Favorite Kiddie Comic)
No. 10, 1950 - No. 11, Apr-May, 1951 (Newspaper reprints)
Ziff-Davis Publishing Co.

10,11-Painted-c	16.00	47.00	110.00

TEEN-IN (Tippy Teen)
Summer, 1968 - No. 4, Fall, 1969
Tower Comics

nn(#1, Summer, 1968), nn(#2, Spring, 1969),3,4	2.60	7.50	18.00

TEEN LIFE (Formerly Young Life)
No. 3, Winter, 1945 - No. 5, Fall, 1945 (Teenage magazine)
New Age/Quality Comics Group

3-June Allyson photo on-c & story	10.00	30.00	60.00
4-Duke Ellington photo on-c & story	7.50	22.50	45.00
5-Van Johnson, Woody Herman & Jackie Robinson articles; Van Johnson & Woody Herman photos on-c	10.00	30.00	65.00

TEEN ROMANCES
1964
Super Comics

10,11,15-17-Reprints	.60	1.50	3.00

TEEN SECRET DIARY (Nurse Betsy Crane #12 on)
Oct, 1959 - No. 11, June, 1961; No. 1, 1972
Charlton Comics

1	3.25	9.50	22.00
2	1.70	5.00	12.00
3-11	1.20	3.00	7.00
1 (1972)		1.20	3.00

TEEN TALK (See Teen)

TEEN TITANS(See Brave & the Bold #54,60, DC Super-Stars #1, Marvel & DC Present, New Teen Titans, New Titans, Official...Index and Showcase #59)
1-2/66 - No. 43, 1-2/73; No. 44, 11/76 - No. 53, 2/78
National Periodical Publications/DC Comics

1-(1-2/66)-Titans join Peace Corps; Batman, Flash, Aquaman, Wonder			

	GD25	FN65	NM94
Woman cameos	24.00	71.00	175.00
2	12.00	36.00	85.00
3-5: 4-Speedy app.	7.00	21.00	50.00
6-10: 6-Doom Patrol app.; Beast Boy x-over; readers polled on him joining Titans	5.70	17.00	40.00
11-19: 11-Speedy app. 13-X-Mas-c. 18-1st app. Starfire (11-12/68). 19-Wood-i; Speedy begins as regular	4.30	13.00	32.00
20-22: All Neal Adams-a. 21-Hawk & Dove app.; last 12¢ issue. 22-Origin Wonder Girl	4.70	14.00	35.00
23-30: 23-Wonder Girl dons new costume. 25-Flash, Aquaman, Batman, Green Arrow, Green Lantern, Superman, & Hawk & Dove guests; 1st app. Lilith who joins T.T. West in #50. 29-Hawk & Dove & Ocean Master app. 30-Aquagirl app.	2.15	6.50	15.00
31-35,40-43: 31-Hawk & Dove app.	1.65	4.20	10.00
36-39-52 pgs.: 36,37-Superboy-r. 38-Green Arrow/Speedy-r; Aquaman/ Aqualad story. 39-Hawk & Dove-r.	1.70	5.00	12.00
44,45,47,49,51,52: 44-Mal becomes the Guardian	1.00	2.00	5.00
46-Joker's daughter begins (see Batman Family)	1.65	4.70	11.00
48-Intro Bumblebee; Joker's daughter becomes Harlequin	1.65	4.70	11.00
50-1st revival original Bat-Girl; intro. Teen Titans West	2.85	8.50	20.00
53-Origin retold	1.00	2.50	5.50

NOTE: *Aparo* a-36. *Buckler* c-46-53. *Cardy* c-1-16. *Kane* a(p)-19, 22-24, 39r. *Tuska* a(p)-31, 36, 38, 39. DC Super-Stars #1 (3/76) was released before #44.

TEEN TITANS
Oct, 1995 - Present ($1.95)
DC Comics

1-8: 1-Dan Jurgens-c/a(p)/scripts & George Perez-c/a(i) begin; Atom forms new team (Risk, Argent, Prysm, & Joto); 1st app.Loren Jupiter & Omen; no indicia. 1-3-Origin.			2.00

TEEN TITANS SPOTLIGHT
Aug, 1986 - No. 21, Apr, 1988
DC Comics

1-21: 7-Guice's 1st work at DC. 14-Nightwing; Batman app. 15-Austin-c(i). 18,19-Millenium x-over. 21-($1.00-c)-Original Teen Titans; Spiegle-a			1.00

Note: *Guice* a-7p, 8p; c-7,8. *Orlando* c/a-11p. *Perez* c-1, 17i, 19. *Sienkiewicz* c-10

TEEPEE TIM (...Heap Funny Indian Boy)(Formerly Ha Ha Comics)
No. 100, Feb-Mar, 1955 - No. 102, June-July, 1955
American Comics Group

100-102	3.60	9.00	18.00

TEGRA JUNGLE EMPRESS (Zegra Jungle Empress #2 on)
August, 1948
Fox Features Syndicate

1-Blue Beetle, Rocket Kelly app.; used in **SOTI**, pg. 31	43.00	128.00	340.00

TEKNO COMIX HANDBOOK
May, 1996 ($3.95, one-shot)
Tekno Comix

1-Guide to the Tekno Universe			4.00

TEKNOPHAGE (See Neil Gaiman's...)

TEKNOPHAGE VERSUS ZEERUS
July, 1996 ($3.25, one-shot)
BIG Entertainment

1-Paul Jenkins script			3.25

TEKWORLD (William Shatner's... on-c only)
Sept, 1992 - Aug, 1994 ($1.75)
Epic Comics (Marvel)

	GD25	FN65	NM94
1-Based on Shatner's novel, TekWar, set in L.A. in the year 2120		1.00	2.50
2-24		.70	1.75

TELEVISION (See TV)

TELEVISION COMICS
No. 5, Feb, 1950 - No. 8, Nov, 1950
Standard Comics (Animated Cartoons)

5-1st app. Willy Nilly	8.70	26.00	52.00
6-8: 6 has #2 on inside	6.70	20.00	40.00

TELEVISION PUPPET SHOW (See Spotty the Pup)
1950 - No. 2, Nov, 1950
Avon Periodicals

1,2: 1st app. Speedy Rabbit, Spotty The Pup	13.50	41.00	95.00

TELEVISION TEENS MOPSY (See TV Teens)

TELL IT TO THE MARINES
Mar, 1952 - No. 15, July, 1955
Toby Press Publications

1-Lover O'Leary and His Liberty Belles (with pin-ups), ends #6; Spike & Bat begin, end #6	16.00	47.00	110.00
2-Madame Cobra-c/story	9.15	27.00	55.00
3-5	6.35	19.00	38.00
6-12,14,15: 7-9,14,15-Photo-c	4.25	13.00	28.00
13-John Wayne photo-c	10.00	30.00	65.00
I.W. Reprint #9-r/#1 above	1.00	2.60	6.00
Super Reprint #16(1964)-r/#4 above	1.00	2.60	6.00

TEMPEST (See Aquaman, 3rd Series)
Nov, 1996 - No. 4, Feb, 1996 ($1.75, limited series)
DC Comics

1-4: Formerly Aqualad; Phil Jimenez-c/a/scripts in all			1.75

TEMPUS FUGITIVE
1990 - No. 4, 1991 ($4.95, squarebound, 52 pgs.)
DC Comics

Book 1,2: Ken Steacy painted-c/a & scripts	.85	2.50	5.00
Book 3,4-($5.95-c)	1.00	3.00	6.00

TEN COMMANDMENTS (See Moses the... and Classics Illustrated Special)

TENDER LOVE STORIES
Feb, 1971 - No. 4, July, 1971 (All 25¢, 52 pgs.)
Skywald Publ. Corp.

1-4	.60	1.50	3.00

TENDER ROMANCE (Ideal Romance #3 on)
Dec, 1953 - No. 2, Feb, 1954
Key Publications (Gilmour Magazines)

1-Headlight & lingerie panels; B. Baily-c	12.00	36.00	85.00
2-Bernard Baily-c	7.50	22.50	45.00

TENNESSEE JED (Radio)
nd (1945) (16 pgs.; paper cover; regular size; giveaway)
Fox Syndicate? (Wm. C. Popper & Co.)

nn	16.00	47.00	110.00

TENNIS (...For Speed, Stamina, Strength, Skill)
1956 (16 pgs.; soft cover; 10¢)
Tennis Educational Foundation

Book 1-Endorsed by Gene Tunney, Ralph Kiner, etc. showing how tennis has helped them	4.00	12.00	24.00

TENSE SUSPENSE
Dec, 1958 - No. 2, Feb, 1959
Fago Publications

1,2	6.70	20.00	40.00

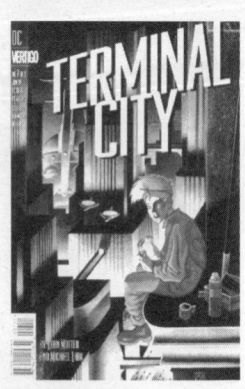
Terminal City #7 © Dean Motter

Terranauts #1 © Fantasy General Comics

Terrific Comics #4 © AJAX

TEN STORY LOVE (Formerly a pulp magazine with same title)
V29#3, June-July, 1951 - V36#5(#209), Sept, 1956 (#3-6: 52 pgs.)
Ace Periodicals

V29#3(#177)-Part comic, part text; painted-c	9.15	27.00	55.00
4-6(1/52)	4.25	13.00	28.00
V30#1(3/52)-6(1/53)	4.00	12.00	24.00
V31#1(2/53),V32#2(4/53)-6(12/53)	3.60	9.00	18.00
V33#1(1/54)-3(5#54, #195), V34#4(7/54, #196)-6(10/54, #198)	3.60	9.00	18.00
V35#1(12/54, #199)-3(4/55, #201)-Last precode	2.80	7.00	14.00
V35#4-6(9/55, #201-204), V36#1(11/55, #205)-3, 5(9/56, #209)	2.40	6.00	12.00
V36#4-L.B. Cole-a	5.85	17.50	35.00

TEN WHO DARED (Disney)
No. 1178, Dec, 1960
Dell Publishing Co.

Four Color 1178-Movie, painted-c; cast member photo on back-c	7.00	21.00	70.00

TERMINAL CITY
July, 1996 - No. 9, Mar, 1997 ($2.50, limited series)
DC Comics (Vertigo)

1-9: Dean Motter scripts		2.50

TERMINATOR, THE (See Robocop vs. ... & Rust #12 for 1st app.)
Sept, 1988 - No. 17, 1989 ($1.75, Baxter paper)
Now Comics

1-Based on movie	1.30	3.25	8.00
2-5		1.20	3.00
6-10		1.60	4.00
11,13-17		.80	2.00
12 ($2.95, 52 pgs.)-Intro. John Connor		1.20	3.00
Trade paperback (1989, $9.95)	1.65	4.00	10.00

TERMINATOR, THE
Aug, 1990 - No. 4, Nov, 1990 ($2.50, limited series)
Dark Horse Comics

1-Set 39 years later than the movie	1.60	4.00
2-4	1.00	2.50

TERMINATOR, THE: ALL MY FUTURES PAST
V3#1, Aug, 1990 - V3#2, Sept, 1990 ($1.75, limited series)
Now Comics

V3#1,2	.70	1.75

TERMINATOR, THE: ENDGAME
Sept, 1992 - No. 3, Nov, 1992 ($2.50, limited series)
Dark Horse Comics

1-3: Guice-a(p); painted-c	1.00	2.50

TERMINATOR, THE: HUNTERS AND KILLERS
Mar, 1992 - No. 3, May, 1992 ($2.50, limited series)
Dark Horse Comics

1-3	1.00	2.50

TERMINATOR, THE: ONE SHOT
July, 1991 ($5.95, 56 pgs.)
Dark Horse Comics

nn-Matt Wagner-a; contains stiff pop-up inside	1.00	2.60	6.00

TERMINATOR, THE: SECONDARY OBJECTIVES
July, 1991 - No. 4, Oct, 1991 ($2.50, limited series)
Dark Horse Comics

1-Gulacy-c/a(p) in all	1.00	2.50
2-4	1.00	2.50

TERMINATOR, THE: THE BURNING EARTH

V2#1, Mar, 1990 - V2#5, July, 1990 ($1.75, limited series)
Now Comics

V2#1-5		.70	1.75
Trade paperback (1990, $9.95)-Reprints V2#1-5	1.65	4.00	10.00

TERMINATOR: THE ENEMY WITHIN, THE
Nov, 1991 - No. 4, Feb, 1992 ($2.50, limited series)
Dark Horse Comics

1-4: All have Simon Bisley painted-c	1.00	2.50

TERMINATOR 2: CYBERNETIC DAWN
Nov, 1995 - No.4, Feb, 1996; No. 0. Apr, 1996 ($2.50, limited series)
Malibu Comics

0-4: Continuation of film. 0 (4/96)-flip book w/Terminator 2: Nuclear Twilight.	1.00	2.50

TERMINATOR 2: JUDGEMENT DAY
Early Sept, 1991 - No. 3, Early Oct, 1991 ($1.00, limited series)
Marvel Comics

1-3: Based on movie sequel; 1-3-Same as nn issues			1.00
nn (1991, $4.95, squarebound, 68 pgs.)-Photo-c	1.00	2.00	5.00
nn (1991, $2.25, B&W, magazine, 68 pgs.)		.90	2.25

TERMINATOR 2: NUCLEAR TWILIGHT
Nov, 1995 - No.4, Feb, 1996; No. 0, Apr, 1996 ($2.50, limited series)
Malibu Comics

0-4:Continuation of film. 0 (4/96)-Gary Erskine-c/a; flip book w/Terminator 2: Cybernetic Dawn.	1.00	2.50

TERRAFORMERS
April, 1987 - No. 2, 1987 ($1.95, limited series)
Wonder Color Comics

1,2-Kelley Jones-a	1.00	2.00

TERRANAUTS
Aug, 1986 - No. 2, 1986 ($1.75, limited series)
Fantasy General Comics

1,2	.75	1.85

TERRARISTS
Nov, 1993 - No. 4, Feb, 1994 ($2.50, limited series)
Marvel Comics (Epic Comics)

1-4-Bound-in trading cards in all	1.00	2.50

TERRIFIC COMICS (Also see Suspense Comics)
Jan, 1944 - No. 6, Nov, 1944
Continental Magazines

1-Kid Terrific; opium story	262.00	787.00	2100.00
2-1st app. The Boomerang by L.B. Cole & Ed Wheelan's "Comics" McCormick called the world's #1 comic book fan begins	200.00	600.00	1600.00
3-Diana becomes Boomerang's costumed aide; L.B. Cole-c	200.00	600.00	1600.00
4-Classic war-c (Scarce)	288.00	862.00	2500.00
5-The Reckoner begins; Boomerang & Diana by L.B. Cole; Schomburg bondage-c (Scarce)	370.00	1110.00	3700.00
6-L.B. Cole-c/a	188.00	562.00	1500.00
NOTE: *L.B. Cole* a-1, 2(2), 3-6. *Fuje* a-5, 6. *Rico* a-2; c-1. *Schomburg* c-2, 5.			

TERRIFIC COMICS (Formerly Horrific; Wonder Boy #17 on)
No. 14, Dec, 1954; No. 16, Mar, 1955 (No #15)
Mystery Publ.(Comic Media)/(Ajax/Farrell)

14-Art swipe/Advs. into the Unknown #37; injury-to-eye-c; pg. 2, panel 5 swiped from Phantom Stranger #4; surrealistic Palais-a; Human Cross story	21.00	64.00	150.00
16-Wonder Boy-c/story (last pre-code)	14.00	43.00	100.00

TERRIFYING TALES (Formerly Startling Terror Tales #10)
No. 11, Jan, 1953 - No. 15, Apr, 1954

Terror, Inc. #11 © MEG

PREY ON HEROES!

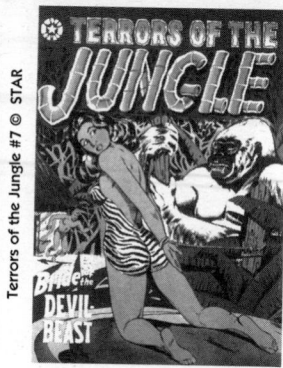

Terrors of the Jungle #7 © STAR

Terry & the Pirates #21 © DELL

	GD25	FN65	NM94

Star Publications

11-Used in **POP**, pgs. 99,100; all Jo-Jo-r	40.00	120.00	285.00
12-Reprints Jo-Jo #19 entirely; L.B. Cole splash	37.00	111.00	260.00
13-All Rulah-r; classic devil-c	40.00	120.00	310.00
14-All Rulah reprints	37.00	111.00	260.00
15-Rulah, Zago-r; used in **SOTI**-r/Rulah #22	37.00	111.00	260.00

NOTE: All issues have **L.B. Cole** covers; bondage covers-No. 12-14.

TERROR ILLUSTRATED (Adult Tales of...)
Nov-Dec, 1955 - No. 2, Spring (April on-c), 1956 (Magazine, 25¢)
E.C. Comics

1-Adult Entertainment on-c	11.50	34.00	80.00
2-Charles Sultan-a	10.00	30.00	65.00

NOTE: **Craig, Evans, Ingels, Orlando** art in each. **Crandall** c-1, 2.

TERROR INC. (See A Shadowline Saga #3)
July, 1992 - No. 13, July, 1993 ($1.75)
Marvel Comics

1-13: 6;7-Punisher-c/story. 9,10-Wolverine-c/story. 13-Ghost Rider app.			
		.70	1.75

TERRORS OF THE JUNGLE (Formerly Jungle Thrills)
No. 17, 5/52 - No. 21, 2/53; No. 4, 4/53 - No. 10, 9/54
Star Publications

17-Reprints Rulah #21, used in **SOTI**; L.B. Cole bondage-c			
	40.00	120.00	290.00
18-Jo-Jo-r	26.00	77.00	180.00
19,20(1952)-Jo-Jo-r; Disbrow-a	24.00	73.00	170.00
21-Jungle Jo, Tangi-r; used in **POP**, pg. 100 & color illos.; shrunken heads on-c	27.00	81.00	190.00
4-10: All Disbrow-a. 5-Jo-Jo-r. 8-Rulah, Jo-Jo-r. 9-Jo-Jo-r; Disbrow-a; Tangi by Orlando10-Rulah-r	24.00	73.00	170.00

NOTE: **L.B. Cole** c-all; bondage c-17, 19, 21, 5, 7.

TERROR TALES (See Beware Terror Tales)

TERROR TALES (Magazine)
V1#7, 1969 - V6#6, Dec, 1974; V7#1, Apr, 1976 - V10, 1979?
(V1-V6: 52 pgs.; V7 on: 68 pgs.)
Eerie Publications

V1#7	3.25	9.50	22.00
V1#8-11('69): 9-Bondage-c	2.15	6.50	15.00
V2#1-6('70), V3#1-6('71), V4#1-7('72), V5#1-6('73), V6#1-6('74)			
	1.70	5.00	12.00
V7#1,4(no V7#2), V8#1-3('77), V9, V10	1.70	5.00	12.00
V7#3-LSD story-r/Weird V3#5	1.70	5.00	12.00

TERRY AND THE PIRATES (See Famous Feature Stories, Merry Christmas From Sears Toyland, Popular Comics, Super Book #3,5,9,16,28, & Super Comics)

TERRY AND THE PIRATES
1939 - 1953 (By Milton Caniff)
Dell Publishing Co.

Large Feature Comic 2(1939)	63.00	189.00	630.00
Large Feature Comic 6(1939)-r/1936 dailies	63.00	189.00	630.00
Four Color 9(1940)	58.00	174.00	580.00
Large Feature Comic 27('41), 6('42)	52.00	156.00	520.00
Four Color 44('43)	39.50	118.50	395.00
Four Color 101('45)	27.00	81.00	270.00
Buster Brown Shoes giveaway(1938)-32 pgs.; in color			
	29.00	86.00	200.00
Canada Dry Premiums-Books #1-3(1953, 36 pgs.; 2x5")-Harvey			
	13.50	41.00	95.00
Family Album(1942)	16.00	48.00	130.00
Gambles Giveaway (1938, 16 pgs.)	9.15	27.50	55.00
Gillmore Giveaway (1938, 24 pgs.)	10.00	30.00	60.00
Popped Wheat Giveaway(1938)-Strip reprints in full color; Caniff-a			
	1.00	2.00	5.00

	GD25	FN65	NM94

Shoe Store giveaway (Weatherbird)(1938, 16 pgs., soft-c)(2-diff.)			
	9.15	27.50	55.00
Sparked Wheat Giveaway(1942, 16 pgs.)-In color	9.15	27.50	55.00

TERRY AND THE PIRATES
1941 (16 pgs.; regular size)(shipped folded in the mail)
Libby's Radio Premiu

	GD	FN	VF
"Adventure of the Ruby of Genghis Khan" - Each pg. is a puzzle that must be completed to read the story	212.00	637.00	1700.00

TERRY AND THE PIRATES (Formerly Boy Explorers; Long John Silver & the Pirates #30 on) (Daily strip-r) (Two #26's)
No. 3, 4/47 - No. 26, 4/51; No. 26, 6/55 - No. 28, 10/55
Harvey Publications/Charlton No. 26-28

	GD	FN	NM
3(#1)-Boy Explorers by S&K; Terry & the Pirates begin by Caniff; 1st app. The Dragon Lady	37.00	111.00	260.00
4-S&K Boy Explorers	20.00	60.00	140.00
5-11: 11-Man in Black app. by Powell	10.00	30.00	65.00
12-20: 16-Girl threatened with red hot poker	8.35	25.00	50.00
21-26(4/51)-Last Caniff issue & last pre-code issue	7.50	22.50	45.00
26-28('55)(Formerly This Is Suspense)-No Caniff-a	5.85	17.50	35.00

NOTE: **Powell** a (Tommy Tween)-5-10, 12, 14; 15-17(1/2 to 2 pgs. each).

TERRY BEARS COMICS (TerryToons, The... #4)
June, 1952 - No. 3, Mar, 1953
St. John Publishing Co.

1-By Paul Terry	6.35	19.00	38.00
2,3	4.25	13.00	28.00

TERRY-TOONS ALBUM (See Giant Comics Edition)

TERRY-TOONS COMICS (1st Series) (Becomes Paul Terry's Comics #85 on; later issues titled "Paul Terry's...")
Oct, 1942 - No. 86, May, 1951
Timely/Marvel No. 1-59 (8/47)(Becomes Best Western No. 58 on?, Marvel)/
St. John No. 60 (9/47) on

1 (Scarce)-Features characters that 1st app. on movie screen; Gandy Goose & Sourpuss begin; war-c; Gandy Goose c-1-37	125.00	375.00	1000.00
2	51.00	155.00	415.00
3-5	39.00	116.00	270.00
6,8-10	27.00	81.00	190.00
7-Hitler, Hirohito, Mussolini-c	33.00	99.00	230.00
11-20	17.00	51.00	120.00
21-37	12.00	36.00	85.00
38-Mighty Mouse begins (1st app., 11/45); Mighty Mouse-c begin, end #86; Gandy, Sourpuss welcome Mighty Mouse on-c	93.00	281.00	750.00
39-2nd app. Mighty Mouse	30.00	90.00	210.00
40-49: 43-Infinity-c	14.00	43.00	100.00
50-1st app. Heckle & Jeckle (11/46)	32.00	96.00	225.00
51-60: 55-Infinity-c. 60-(9/47)-Atomic explosion panel; 1st St. John issue	10.00	30.00	68.00
61-84	8.70	26.00	52.00
85,86-Same book as Paul Terry's Comics #85,86 with only a title change; published at same time?	8.70	26.00	52.00

TERRY-TOONS COMICS (2nd Series)
June, 1952 - No. 9, Nov, 1953; 1957; 1958
St. John Publishing Co./Pines

1-Gandy Goose & Sourpuss begin by Paul Terry	14.00	43.00	100.00
2	8.00	24.00	48.00
3-9	6.70	20.00	40.00
Giant Summer Fun Book 101,102-(Sum, 1957, Sum, 1958, 25¢, Pines)(TV) CBS Television Presents...; Tom Terrific, Mighty Mouse, Heckle & Jeckle Gandy Goose app.	11.00	33.00	75.00

TERRYTOONS, THE TERRY BEARS (Formerly Terry Bears Comics)
No. 4, Summer, 1958 (CBS Television Presents...)
Pines Comics

Tessie the Typist #10 © MEG

Tex Dawson, Gun Slinger #1 © MEG

Tex Ritter Western #5 © FAW

	GD25	FN65	NM94
4	4.25	13.00	26.00

TESSIE THE TYPIST (Tiny Tessie #24; see Comedy Comics, Gay Comics & Joker Comics)
Summer, 1944 - No. 23, Aug, 1949
Timely/Marvel Comics (20CC)

	GD25	FN65	NM94
1-Doc Rockblock & others by Wolverton	50.00	150.00	400.00
2-Wolverton's Powerhouse Pepper	31.00	94.00	220.00
3-(3/45)-No Wolverton	10.00	30.00	65.00
4,5,7,8-Wolverton-a. 4-(Fall/45)	20.00	60.00	140.00
6-Kurtzman's "Hey Look", 2 pgs. Wolverton-a	21.00	62.00	145.00
9-Wolverton's Powerhouse Pepper (8 pgs.) & 1 pg. Kurtzman's "Hey Look"	24.00	71.00	165.00
10-Wolverton's Powerhouse Pepper (4 pgs.)	22.00	66.00	155.00
11-Wolverton's Powerhouse Pepper (8 pgs.)	24.00	71.00	165.00
12-Wolverton's Powerhouse Pepper (4 pgs.) & 1 pg. Kurtzman's "Hey Look"	22.00	66.00	155.00
13-Wolverton's Powerhouse Pepper (4 pgs.)	21.00	64.00	150.00
14-Wolverton's Dr. Whackyhack (1 pg.); 1-1/2 pgs. Kurtzman's "Hey Look"	17.00	49.00	115.00
15-Kurtzman's "Hey Look" (3 pgs.) & 3 pgs. Giggles 'n' Grins	17.00	51.00	120.00
16-18-Kurtzman's "Hey Look" (?, 2 & 1 pg.)	11.50	34.00	80.00
19-Annie Oakley story (8 pgs.)	9.15	27.00	55.00
20-23: 20-Anti-Wertham editorial (2/49)	8.35	25.00	50.00

NOTE: Lana app.-21. Millie The Model app.-13, 15, 17, 21. Rusty app.-10, 11, 13, 15, 17.

TEXAN, THE (Fightin' Marines #15 on; Fightin' Texan #16 on)
Aug, 1948 - No. 15, Oct, 1951
St. John Publishing Co.

	GD25	FN65	NM94
1-Buckskin Belle	13.00	39.00	90.00
2	7.50	22.50	45.00
3,10: 10-Oversized issue	7.00	21.00	42.00
4,5,7,15-Baker-c/a	11.50	34.00	80.00
6,9-Baker-c	8.35	25.00	50.00
8,11,13,14-Baker-c/a(2-3) each	11.50	34.00	80.00
12-All Matt Baker-c/a; Peyote story	16.00	47.00	110.00

NOTE: Matt Baker c-4-9, 11-15. Larsen a-4-6, 8-10, 15. Tuska a-1, 2, 7-9.

TEXAN, THE (TV)
No. 1027, Sept-Nov, 1959 - No. 1096, May-July, 1960
Dell Publishing Co.

	GD25	FN65	NM94
Four Color 1027 (#1)-Photo-c	8.00	24.00	80.00
Four Color 1096-Rory Calhoun photo-c	8.00	24.00	80.00

TEXAS JOHN SLAUGHTER (See Walt Disney Presents, 4-Color #997, 1181 & #2)

TEXAS KID (See Two-Gun Western, Wild Western)
Jan, 1951 - No. 10, July, 1952
Marvel/Atlas Comics (LMC)

	GD25	FN65	NM94
1-Origin; Texas Kid (alias Lance Temple) & his horse Thunder begin; Tuska-a	18.00	54.00	125.00
2	10.00	30.00	68.00
3-10	8.70	26.00	52.00

NOTE: Maneely a-1-4; c-1, 3, 5-10.

TEXAS RANGERS, THE (See Jace Pearson of... and Superior Stories #4)

TEXAS RANGERS IN ACTION (Formerly Captain Gallant or Scotland Yard?)
No. 5, July, 1956 - No. 79, Aug, 1970 (See Blue Bird Comics)
Charlton Comics

	GD25	FN65	NM94
5	7.50	22.50	45.00
6,7,9,10	4.25	13.00	26.00
8-Ditko-a (signed)	6.70	20.00	40.00
11-Williamson-a(5&8 pgs.); Torres/Williamson-a (5 pgs.)	7.50	22.50	45.00
12,14-20	3.60	9.00	18.00
13-Williamson-a (5 pgs); Torres, Morisi-a	6.35	19.00	38.00

	GD25	FN65	NM94
21-30: 31-Last 10¢ issue?	3.20	8.00	16.00
31-59	1.70	5.00	12.00
60-Riley's Rangers begin	1.20	3.00	7.00
61-70: 65-1st app. The Man Called Loco, origin in #67	1.60	4.00	
71-79	.80		2.00
76(Modern Comics-r, 1977)			1.00

TEXAS SLIM (Also see A-1 Comics)
No. 2, 1947 - No.10, 1948
Magazine Enterprises

	GD25	FN65	NM94
A-1 2-8,10: Texas Slim & Dirty Dalton, The corsair, Teddy Rich, Dotty Dripple, Inca Iinca, Tommy Tinker, Little Mexico & Tugboat Tim, The Masqu'rader & others. 7-Corsair-c/s. 8-Intro Rodeo Ryan	4.25	13.00	28.00
A-1 9-All Texas Slim	5.00	15.00	30.00

TEX DAWSON, GUN-SLINGER (Gunslinger #2 on)
January, 1973 (20¢)(Also see Western Kid, 1st series)
Marvel Comics Group

	GD25	FN65	NM94
1-Steranko-c; Williamson-r (4 pgs.); Tex Dawson-r by Romita(3) from 1955; Tuska-r			1.50

TEX FARNUM (See Wisco)

TEX FARRELL (...Pride of the Wild West)
Mar-Apr, 1948
D. S. Publishing Co.

	GD25	FN65	NM94
1-Tex Farrell & his horse Lightning; Shelly-c	11.00	33.00	75.00

TEX GRANGER (Formerly Calling All Boys; see True Comics)
No. 18, June, 1948 - No. 24, Sept, 1949
Parents' Magazine Institute/Commended

	GD25	FN65	NM94
18-Tex Granger & his horse Bullet begin	10.00	30.00	65.00
19	8.00	24.00	48.00
20-24: 22-Wild Bill Hickok story. 23-Vs. Billy the kid; Tim Holt app.	6.35	19.00	38.00

TEX MORGAN (See Blaze Carson and Wild Western)
Aug, 1948 - No. 9, Feb, 1950
Marvel Comics (CCC)

	GD25	FN65	NM94
1-Tex Morgan, his horse Lightning & sidekick Lobo begin	22.00	66.00	155.00
2	16.00	47.00	110.00
3-6: 3,4-Arizona Annie app.	10.00	30.00	70.00
7-9: All photo-c. 7-Captain Tootsie by Beck. 8-18 pg. story "The Terror of Rimrock Valley"; Diablo app.	16.00	47.00	110.00

NOTE: Tex Taylor app.-6, 7, 9. Brodsky c-6. Syd Shores c-2, 5.

TEX RITTER WESTERN (Movie star; singing cowboy; see Six-Gun Heroes and Western Hero)
Oct, 1950 - No. 46, May, 1959 (Photo-c: 1-21)
Fawcett No. 1-20 (1/54)/Charlton No. 21 on

	GD25	FN65	NM94
1-Tex Ritter, his stallion White Flash & dog Fury begin; photo front/back-c begin	62.00	188.00	500.00
2	29.00	86.00	200.00
3-5: 5-Last photo back-c	21.00	64.00	150.00
6-10	17.00	51.00	120.00
11-19	11.50	34.00	80.00
20-Last Fawcett issue (1/54)	13.00	39.00	90.00
21-1st Charlton issue; photo-c (3/54)	14.00	43.00	100.00
22-B&W photo back-c begin, end #32	10.00	30.00	60.00
23-30: 23-25-Young Falcon app.	8.35	25.00	50.00
31-38,40-45	7.00	21.00	42.00
39-Williamson-a; Whitman-c (1/58)	9.15	27.50	55.00
46-Last issue	8.35	25.00	50.00

TEX TAYLOR (...The Fighting Cowboy on-c #1, 2)(See Blaze Carson, Kid Colt, Tex Morgan, Wild West, Wild Western, & Wisco)
Sept, 1948 - No. 9, March, 1950

Thart Chemical Reflex #1 © CFD Productions

Thieves & Kings #14 © I Box

The Thing #12 © MEG

	GD25	FN65	NM94

Marvel Comics (HPC)

1-Tex Taylor & his horse Fury begin	24.00	71.00	165.00
2	13.50	41.00	95.00
3	12.00	36.00	85.00
4-6: All photo-c. 4-Anti-Wertham editorial. 5,6-Blaze Carson app.			
	14.00	43.00	100.00
7-Photo-c; 18 pg. Movie-Length Thriller "Trapped in Time's Lost Land!" with sabre toothed tigers, dinosaurs; Diablo app.	16.00	47.00	110.00
8-Photo-c; 18 pg. Movie-Length Thriller "The Mystery of Devil-Tree Plateau!" with dwarf horses, dwarf people & a lost miniature Inca type village; Diablo app.	16.00	47.00	110.00
9-Photo-c; 18 pg. Movie-Length Thriller "Guns Along the Border!" Captain Tootsie by Schreiber; Nimo the Mountain Lion app.	16.00	47.00	110.00

THANE OF BAGARTH (Also see Hercules, 1967 series)
No. 24, Oct, 1985 - No. 25, Dec, 1985
Charlton Comics

24,25			1.00

THANOS QUEST, THE (See Capt. Marvel #25, Infinity Gauntlet, Iron Man #55, Logan's Run, Marvel Feature #12, Silver Surfer #34 & Warlock #9)
1990 - No. 2, 1990 ($4.95, squarebound, 52 pgs.)
Marvel Comics

1,2-Both have Starlin scripts & covers	1.00	2.00	5.00
1,2-($4.95, 2nd printings)	1.00	2.00	5.00

THAT CHEMICAL REFLEX
1994 ($2.50, B&W, one-shot, mature)
CFD Productions

1-Dan Brereton-c/a		1.00	2.50

THAT DARN CAT (See Movie Comics & Walt Disney Showcase #19)

THAT'S MY POP! GOES NUTS FOR FAIR
1939 (76 pgs., B&W)
Bystander Press

nn-by Milt Gross	23.00	69.00	160.00

THAT THE WORLD MAY BELIEVE
No date (16 pgs.) (Graymoor Friars distr.)
Catechetical Guild Giveaway

nn	1.60	4.00	8.00

THAT WILKIN BOY (Meet Bingo...)
Jan, 1969 - No. 52, Oct, 1982
Archie Publications

1	3.00	7.50	15.00
2-10	1.60	4.00	8.00
11-26: 12-26-Giants	1.00	2.00	5.00
27-52		.80	2.00

THB
Oct, 1994 - Present ($5.50/$2.50/$2.95, B&W)
Horse Press

1 ($5.50)	1.70	5.00	12.00
1 (2nd Printing)-r/#1 w/new material			2.50
2 ($2.50)	1.65	4.20	10.00
3-5		1.60	4.00
69 (1995, no price, low distribution, 12 pgs.)-story reprinted in #1 (2nd Printing).			3.00

T.H.E. CAT (TV)
Mar, 1967 - No. 4, Oct, 1967 (All have photo-c)
Dell Publishing Co.

1	3.25	9.50	22.00

	GD25	FN65	NM94
2-4	2.30	6.75	16.00

THERE'S A NEW WORLD COMING
1973 (35/49¢)
Spire Christian Comics/Fleming H. Revell Co.

nn			1.00

THEY ALL KISSED THE BRIDE (See Cinema Comics Herald)

THEY RING THE BELL
1946
Fox Feature Syndicate

1	10.00	30.00	70.00

THIEF OF BAGHDAD
No. 1229, Oct-Dec, 1961 (one-shot)
Dell Publishing Co.

Four Color 1229-Movie, Crandall/Evans-a, photo-c	6.00	18.00	60.00

THIEVES & KINGS
1994 - Present ($2.35, B&W, bi-monthly)
I Box

1-13		.90	2.35
NOTE: 2nd printings exist of No. 1.			

THIMK (Magazine) (Satire)
May, 1958 - No. 6, May, 1959
Counterpoint

1	6.35	19.00	38.00
2-6	4.00	12.00	24.00

THING!, THE (Blue Beetle #18 on)
Feb, 1952 - No. 17, Nov, 1954
Song Hits No. 1,2/Capitol Stories/Charlton

1-Weird/horror stories in all; shrunken head-c	61.00	183.00	490.00
2,3	43.00	129.00	345.00
4-6,8,10: 5-Severed head-c; headlights	40.00	120.00	290.00
7-Injury to eye-c & inside panel; E.C. swipes from Vault of Horror #28	53.00	159.00	425.00
9-Used in SOTI, pg. 388 & illo "Stomping on the face is a form of brutality which modern children learn early"	60.00	181.00	485.00
11-Necronomicon story; Hansel & Gretel parody; Injury-to-eye-panel; Check-a	47.00	141.00	375.00
12-1st published Ditko-c; "Cinderella" parody; lingerie panels. Ditko-a	62.00	187.00	500.00
13,15-Ditko-c/a(3 & 5); 13-Ditko E.C. swipe/Haunt of Fear #15(#1) "House of Horror"	62.00	187.00	500.00
14-Extreme violence/torture; Rumpelstiltskin story; Ditko-c/a(4)	62.00	187.00	500.00
16-Injury to eye panel	40.00	120.00	315.00
17-Ditko-c; classic parody "Through the Looking Glass"; Powell-r/Beware Terror Tales #1 & recolored	58.00	174.00	465.00
NOTE: Excessive violence, severed heads, injury to eye are common No. 5 on. Al Fago c-4. Forgione c-1i, 2, 6, 8, 9. Palais c-16. All Ditko issues #14, 15.			

THING, THE (See Fantastic Four, Marvel Fanfare, Marvel Feature #11, 12 & Marvel Two-In-One)
July, 1983 - No. 36, June, 1986
Marvel Comics Group

1-Life story of Ben Grimm; Byrne scripts begin		.90	2.25
2-36: 5-Spider-Man, She-Hulk app.			1.30
NOTE: Byrne a-2i, 7; c-1, 7, 36i; scripts-1-13, 19-22. Sienkiewicz c-13i.			

THING, THE (From Another World)
1991 - No. 2, 1992 ($2.95, mini-series, stiff-c)
Dark Horse Comics

1,2-Based on Universal movie; painted-c/a		1.20	3.00

THING FROM ANOTHER WORLD: CLIMATE OF FEAR, THE

Third World War #5 © Fleetway

13: Assassin #1 © TSR

Thor #269 © MEG

	GD25	FN65	NM94

July, 1992 - No. 4, Dec, 1992 ($2.50, mini-series)
Dark Horse Comics

		GD25	FN65	NM94
1-4: Painted-c			1.00	2.50

THING FROM ANOTHER WORLD: ETERNAL VOWS
Dec, 1993 - No. 4, 1994 ($2.50, mini-series)
Dark Horse Comics

1-4-Gulacy-c/a	1.00	2.50

THIRD WORLD WAR
1990 - No. 6, 1991 ($2.50, high quality, thick-c, mature)
Fleetway Publications (Quality)

1-6	1.25	2.50

THIRTEEN (...Going on 18)
11-1/61-62 - No. 25, 12/67; No. 26, 7/69 - No. 29, 1/71
Dell Publishing Co.

1	5.85	17.50	35.00
2-10	4.70	14.00	28.00
11-29: 26-29-r	3.20	8.00	20.00

NOTE: *John Stanley* script-No. 3-29; art?

13: ASSASSIN
1990 - No. 8, 1991 ($2.95, 44 pgs.)
TSR, Inc.

1-8: Agent 13; Alcala-a(i); Springer back-up-a	1.20	3.00

THIRTY SECONDS OVER TOKYO (See American Library)

THIS IS SUSPENSE! (Formerly Strange Suspense Stories; Strange Suspense Stories #27 on)
No. 23, Feb, 1955 - No. 26, Aug, 1955
Charlton Comics

23-Wood-a(r)/A Star Presentation #3 "Dr. Jekyll & Mr. Hyde"; last pre-code issue	21.00	64.00	150.00
24-Censored Fawcett-r; Evans-a (r/Suspense Detective #1)	11.50	34.00	80.00
25,26: 26-Marcus Swayze-a	8.00	24.00	48.00

THIS IS THE PAYOFF (See Pay-Off)

THIS IS WAR
No. 5, July, 1952 - No. 9, May, 1953
Standard Comics

5-Toth-a	11.50	34.00	80.00
6,9-Toth-a	10.00	30.00	65.00
7,8: 8-Ross Andru-c	4.00	12.00	24.00

THIS IS YOUR LIFE, DONALD DUCK (See Donald Duck..., Four Color #1109)

THIS MAGAZINE IS CRAZY (Crazy #? on)
V3#2, July, 1957 - V4#8, Feb, 1959 (25¢, magazine, 68 pgs.)
Charlton Publ. (Humor Magazines)

V3#2-V4#7: V4#5-Russian Sputnik-c parody	5.00	15.00	30.00
V4#8-Davis-a (8 pgs.)	6.35	19.00	38.00

THIS MAGAZINE IS HAUNTED (Danger and Adventure #22 on)
Oct, 1951 - No. 14, 12/53; No. 15, 2/54 - V3#21, Nov, 1954
Fawcett Publications/Charlton No. 15(2/54) on

1-Evans-a; Dr. Death as host begins	46.00	138.00	370.00
2,5-Evans-a	35.00	105.00	245.00
3,4: 3-Vampire-c/story	21.00	64.00	150.00
6-9,11,12,14	17.00	49.00	115.00
10-Severed head-c	24.00	73.00	170.00
13-Severed head-c/story	24.00	71.00	165.00
15,20: 15-Dick Giordano-c. 20-Cover is swiped from panel in The Thing #16	13.50	41.00	95.00
16,19-Ditko-c. 19-Injury-to-eye panel; story-r/#1	29.00	86.00	200.00
17-Ditko-c/a(4); blood drainage story	36.00	107.00	250.00
18-Ditko-c/a(1 story); E.C. swipe/Haunt of Fear #5; injury-to-eye panel; reprints "Caretaker of the Dead" from Beware Terror Tales & recolored	30.00	90.00	210.00
21-Ditko-c, Evans-r/This Magazine Is Haunted #1	27.00	81.00	190.00

NOTE: *Baily* a-1, 3, 4, 21r/#1. *Moldoff* c/a-1-13. *Powell* a-3-5, 11, 12, 17. *Shuster* a-18-20. Issues 19-21 have reprints which have been recolored from This Magazine is Haunted #1.

THIS MAGAZINE IS HAUNTED (2nd Series) (Formerly Zaza the Mystic; Outer Space #17 on)
V2#12, July, 1957 - V2#16, May, 1958
Charlton Comics

V2#12-14-Ditko-c/a in all	30.00	90.00	210.00
15-No Ditko-c/a	4.70	14.00	28.00
16-Ditko-a	19.00	58.00	135.00

THIS MAGAZINE IS WILD (See Wild)

THIS WAS YOUR LIFE (Religious)
1964 (3 1/2 x 5 1/2", 40 pgs., B&W and red)
Jack T. Chick Publ.

nn	1.00
Another version (5x2 3/4", 26 pgs.)	1.20

THOR (See Avengers #1, Giant-Size..., Marvel Collectors Item Classics, Marvel Graphic Novel #33, Marvel Preview, Marvel Spectacular, Marvel Treasury Edition, Special Marvel Edition & Tales of Asgard)

THOR (Journey Into Mystery #1-125, 503-on)(The Mighty Thor #413-490)
No. 126, Mar, 1966 - No. 502, Sept, 1996
Marvel Comics Group

126-Thor continues (#125-130 Thor vs. Hercules)	18.00	54.00	125.00
127-133,135-140: 127-1st app. Pluto	6.50	19.50	45.00
134-Intro High Evolutionary	8.00	24.00	56.00
141-157,159,160: 146-Inhumans begin (early app.), end #151 (see Fantastic Four #45 for 1st app.). 146,147-Origin The Inhumans. 148,149-Origin Black Bolt in each. 149-Origin Medusa, Crystal, Maximus, Gorgon, Kornak	4.30	13.00	30.00
158-Origin-r/#83; 158,159-Origin Dr. Blake (Thor)	9.00	26.50	62.00
161,167,170-179: 179-Last Kirby issue	2.85	8.50	20.00
162,168,169-Origin Galactus; Kirby-a	4.50	14.00	32.00
163,164-2nd & 3th brief cameo Warlock (Him)	2.85	8.50	20.00
165-1st full app. Warlock (Him) (6/69, see Fantastic Four #67); last 12¢ issue; Kirby-a	7.00	21.00	55.00
166-2nd full app. Warlock (Him); battles Thor	6.00	18.00	42.00
180,181-Neal Adams-a	2.00	6.00	14.00
182-192,194-200	1.20	3.00	7.00
193-(25¢, 52 pgs.); Silver Surfer x-over	5.00	15.00	40.00
201-250: 225-Intro. Firelord	1.00	2.00	5.00
251-280: 271-Iron Man x-over. 274-Death of Balder the Brave		1.30	3.2
281-299: 294-Origin Asgard & Odin		1.10	2.5
300-(12/80)-End of Asgard; origin of Odin & The Destroyer	1.00	2.50	6.0
301-336: 316-Iron Man x-over		.80	2.0
337-Simonson-c/a begins, ends #382; Beta Ray Bill becomes new Thor	1.30	3.25	8.0
338-Two variants exist, 60¢ & 75¢ cover price	1.40	3.5
339,340: 340-Donald Blake returns as Thor	.80	2.0
341-373,375-381,383: 341-Clark Kent & Lois Lane cameo. 373-X-Factor tie-in		1.5
374-Mutant Massacre; X-Factor app.	1.00	2.60	6.0
382-($1.25)-Anniversary issue; last Simonson-a	1.00	2.5
384-Intro. new Thor	.90	2.2
385-399,401-410,413-428: 385-Hulk x-over. 391-Spider-Man x-over; 1st Eric Masterson. 395-Intro Earth Force. 408-Eric Masterson becomes Thor. 427, 428-Excalibur x-over		1.2
400-($1.75, 68 pgs.)-Origin Loki	1.00	2.5

Thor #502 © MEG

Thor Corps #4 © MEG

3-D Alien Terror #1 © ECL

	GD25	FN65	NM94

ntro New Warriors (appears in costume in last panel); Juggernaut-c/story
1.20   3.00
st full app. New Warriors (Marvel Boy, Kid Nova, Namorita, Night
hrasher, Firestar & Speedball)   1.00   2.00   5.00
430-Ghost Rider x-over   1.20   3.00
434-443: 434-Capt. America x-over. 437-Thor vs. Quasar; Hercules app.;
ales of Asgard back-up stories begin. 443-Dr. Strange & Silver Surfer
over; last $1.00-c   1.50
$1.50, 52 pgs.)-Thor's 300th app. (vs. Loki); reprints origin & 1st app.
om Journey into Mystery #83   1.30   3.25
ntro new Thor   1.00   2.00   5.00
449,451-473: 448-Spider-Man-c/story. 455,456-Dr. Strange back-up. 457-
'd Thor returns (3 pgs.). 459-Intro Thunderstrike. 460-Starlin scripts begin.
65-Super Skrull app. 466-Drax app. 469,470-Infinity Watch x-over.
72-Intro the Godlings   1.50
$2.50, 68 pgs.)-Flip-book format; r/story JIM #87 (1st Loki) plus-c plus a
allery of past-c; gatefold-c   1.20   3.00
76-481,483-499,501,502: 474-Begin $1.50-c; bound-in trading card sheet.
59-Intro Thunderstrike, 460-Starlin scripts begin. 472-Intro the Godlings.
The Absorbing Man app. 491-Warren Ellis scripts begins, ends #494;
eodato-c/a begins. 492-Reintro The Enchantress; Beta Ray Bill dies.
5-Wm. Messner-Loebs scripts begin; Isherwood-c/a. 501-Reintro Red
orvell. 502-Onslaught tie-in; Red Norvell, Jane Foster & Hela app.
1.50
$2.00, 52 pgs.)-Regular edition   .80   2.00
$2.50, 68 pgs.)-Collectors edition w/foil embossed-c   1.00   2.50
$2.95, 84 pgs.)-400th issue   1.20   3.00
$2.50)-Double-size; wraparound-c; Deodato-c/a; Dr. Strange app.
2.50
al 2(9/66)-See Journey Into Mystery for 1st annual
7.00   21.50   50.00
Size Special 3(1/71)   1.65   4.20   10.00
al 4(12/71)-r/Thor #131,132 & JIM #113   1.65   4.20   10.00
al 5-8: 5(11/76). 6(10/77)-Guardians of the Galaxy app. 7(1978). 8(1979)-
or vs. Zeus-c/story   1.20   2.90   7.00
a-9-12: 9('81). 10('82). 11('83). 12('84)   1.40   3.50
al 13-16: 13(1985). 14('89, $2.00, 68 pgs.)-Atlantis Attacks. 15('90, $2.00,
pgs.). 16('91, $2.00, 68 pgs.)-3 pg. origin; Guardians of the Galaxy x-over
.80   2.00
al 17 (1992, $2.25, 68 pgs.)   .90   2.25
al 18 (1993, $2.95, 68 pgs.)-Polybagged w/card   1.20   3.00
al 19 (1994, $2.95, 68 pgs.)   1.20   3.00
ne Against the Celestials nn (6/92, $5.95)-r/Thor #387-389
1.00   2.50   6.00
orldengine (8/96, $9.95)-r/#491-494; Deodato-c/a; story & new intermission
Warren Ellis.
Neal Adams a-180,181; c-179-181. Austin a-342i, 346i; c-312i. Buscema a(p)-178,
3, 215-226, 231-238, 241-253, 254r, 256-259, 272-278, 283-285, 370, Annual 6, 8, 11i;
5, 182-196, 198-200, 202-204, 206, 211, 212, 215, 219, 221, 226, 256, 259, 261, 262,
'8, 283, 289, 370, Annual 6. Everett a(i)-143, 170-175; c(i)-171, 172, 174, 176, 241. Gil
a-318p; c(p)-201, 205, 207-210, 216, 220, 222, 223, 231, 233-240, 242, 243, 318. Kirby
26-177, 179, 194r, 254r; c(p)-126-169, 171-174, 176-178, 249-253, 255, 257, 258, Annual
cial 1-4. Mooney a(i)-201, 204, 214-216, 218, 322i, 324i, 325i, 327i. Sienkiewicz c-332,
35. Simonson a-260-271p, 337-354, 357-367, 380, Annual 7p; c-260, 263-271, 337-355,
9, 371, 373-382, Annual 7. Starlin c-213.

R CORPS
1993 - No. 4, Jan, 1994 ($1.75, limited series)
el Comics
1-Invaders cameo. 2-Invaders app. 3-Spider-Man 2099, Rawhide Kid,
vo-Gun Kid & Kid Colt app. 4-Painted-c   .70   1.75

R: THE LEGEND
1996 ($3.95, one-shot)
el Comics
bute issue   4.00

	GD25	FN65	NM94

THOSE MAGNIFICENT MEN IN THEIR FLYING MACHINES (See Movie Comics)
THREE CABALLEROS (Walt Disney's...)
No. 71, 1945
Dell Publishing Co.
Four Color 71-by Walt Kelly, c/a   79.00   237.00   790.00
THREE CHIPMUNKS, THE (TV)
No. 1042, Oct-Dec, 1959
Dell Publishing Co.
Four Color 1042 (#1)-(Alvin, Simon & Theodore)   3.60   10.80   36.00
THREE COMICS (Also see Spiritman)
1944 (10¢, 52 pgs.) (2 different covers exist)
The Penny King Co.
1,3,4-Lady Luck, Mr. Mystic, The Spirit app. (3 Spirit sections bound together);
Lou Fine-a   21.00   64.00   150.00
NOTE: No. 1 contains Spirit Sections 4/9/44 - 4/23/44, and No. 4 is also from 4/44.
3-D (NOTE: The prices of all the 3-D comics listed include glasses. Deduct 40-50 percent if
glasses are missing, and reduce slightly if glasses are loose.)
3-D ACTION
Jan, 1954 (Oversized, 15¢)(2 pairs of glasses included)
Atlas Comics (ACI)
1-Battle Brady; Sol Brodsky-c   36.00   107.00   250.00
3-D ADVENTURE COMICS
Aug, 1986 (one shot)
Stats, Etc.
1-Promo material   1.50
3-D ALIEN TERROR
June, 1986 ($2.50)
Eclipse Comics
1-Old Witch, Crypt-Keeper, Vault Keeper cameo; Morrow, John
Pound-a, Yeates-c   1.25   2.50
...in 2-D: 100 copies signed, numbered(B&W)   .85   2.50   5.00
3-D ANIMAL FUN (See Animal Fun)
3-D BATMAN (Also see Batman 3-D)
1953 (Reprinted in 1966)
National Periodical Publications
1953-(25¢)-Reprints Batman #42 & 48 (Penguin-c/story); Tommy Tomorrow
app.; came with pair of 3-D Bat glasses   100.00   300.00   800.00
1966-Tommy Tomorrow app.; Penguin-c/story(r); has inside-c photos of
Batman & Robin from TV show (50¢)   36.00   107.00   250.00
3-D CIRCUS
1953 (25¢, came w/glasses)
Fiction House Magazines (Real Adventures Publ.)
1   37.00   111.00   260.00
3-D COMICS (See Mighty Mouse, Tor and Western Fighters)
3-D DOLLY
December, 1953 (25¢, came with 2 pairs of glasses)
Harvey Publications
1-Richie Rich story redrawn from his 1st app. in Little Dot #1; shows cover in
3-D on inside   21.00   64.00   150.00
3-D-ELL
1953 - No. 3, 1953 (3-D comics) (25¢, came w/glasses)
Dell Publishing Co.
1,2-Rootie Kazootie   40.00   120.00   280.00
3-Flukey Luke   36.00   109.00   255.00
3-D EXOTIC BEAUTIES
Nov, 1990 ($2.95, 28 pgs.)
The 3-D Zone

Three-Dimensional DNAgents © ECL

3-D Three Stooges #3 © ECL

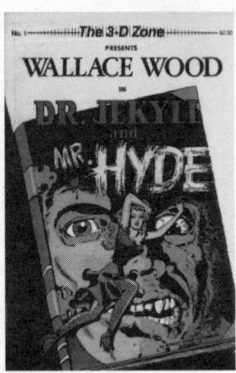

The 3-D Zone #1 © Renegade Press

	GD25	FN65	NM94
1-L.B. Cole-c		1.50	3.00

3-D FEATURES PRESENTS JET PUP
Oct-Dec (Winter on-c), 1953 (25¢, came w/glasses)
Dimensions Publications

	GD25	FN65	NM94
1-Irving Spector-a(2)	37.00	111.00	260.00

3-D FUNNY MOVIES
1953 (25¢, came w/glasses)
Comic Media

1-Bugsey Bear & Paddy Pelican	37.00	111.00	260.00

THREE-DIMENSION ADVENTURES (Superman)
1953 (25¢, large size, came w/glasses)
National Periodical Publications

nn-Origin Superman (new art)	100.00	300.00	800.00

THREE DIMENSIONAL ALIEN WORLDS (See Alien Worlds)
July, 1984 (1st Ray Zone 3-D book)(one-shot)
Pacific Comics

1-Bolton-p(a); Stevens-p(i); Art Adams 1st published-p(a)	.85	2.50	5.00

THREE DIMENSIONAL DNAGENTS (See New DNAgents)

THREE DIMENSIONAL E. C. CLASSICS (Three Dimensional Tales From the Crypt No. 2)
Spring, 1954 (Prices include glasses; came with 2 pair)
E. C. Comics

1-Stories by Wood (Mad #3), Krigstein (W.S. #7), Evans (F.C. #13), & Ingels (CSS #5); Kurtzman-c(a)(r) (rare in high grade due to unstable paper)	75.00	225.00	600.00

NOTE: Stories redrawn to 3-D format. Original stories not necessarily by artists listed.
CSS: Crime SuspenStories; F.C.: Frontline Combat; W.S.: Weird Science.

THREE DIMENSIONAL TALES FROM THE CRYPT (Formerly Three Dimensional E. C. Classics)(Cover title: ...From the Crypt of Terror)
No. 2, Spring, 1954 (Prices include glasses; came with 2 pair)
E. C. Comics

2-Davis (TFTC #25), Elder (VOH #14), Craig (TFTC #24), & Orlando (TFTC #22) stories; Feldstein-c (rare in high grade due to unstable paper)	78.00	235.00	625.00

NOTE: Stories redrawn to 3-D format. Original stories not necessarily by artists listed.
TFTC: Tales From the Crypt; VOH: Vault of Horror.

3-D LOVE
Dec, 1953 (25¢, came w/glasses)
Steriographic Publ. (Mikeross Publ.)

1	37.00	111.00	260.00

3-D NOODNICK (See Noodnick)

3-D ROMANCE
Jan, 1954 (25¢, came w/glasses)
Steriographic Publ. (Mikeross Publ.)

1	37.00	111.00	260.00

3-D SHEENA, JUNGLE QUEEN (Also see Sheena 3-D)
1953 (25¢, came w/glasses)
Fiction House Magazines

1-Maurice Whitman-c	62.00	187.00	500.00

3-D SUBSTANCE
July, 1990 ($2.95, 28 pgs.)
The 3-D Zone

1-Ditko-c/a(r)		1.50	3.00

3-D TALES OF THE WEST
Jan, 1954 (Oversized) (15¢, came with 2 pair of glasses)
Atlas Comics (CPS)

	GD25	FN65	NM94
1 (3-D)-Sol Brodsky-c	39.00	118.00	27

3-D THREE STOOGES (Also see Three Stooges)
Sept, 1986 - No. 2, Nov, 1986; No. 3, Oct, 1987; No. 4, 1989 ($2.50)
Eclipse Comics

1-3 (10/87)-Maurer-r			1.25
4 (1989, $3.50)-Reprints "Three Missing Links"			1.75
1-3 (2-D)		.85	2.50

3-D WHACK (See Whack)

3-D ZONE, THE
Feb, 1987 - No. 20, 1989 ($2.50)
The 3-D Zone (Renegade Press)/Ray Zone

1-10: 1-r/A Star Presentation, 2-Wolverton-r, 3-Picture Scope Jungle Advs., 4-Electric Fear, 5-Krazy Kat-r, 6-Ratfink, 7-Hollywood 3-D Jayne Mansfield photo-c, 8-High Seas 3-D, 9-Redmask-r, 10-Jet 3-D; Powell & Williamson-r			1.25
11-20: 11-Danse MAcabre; Matt Fox c/a(r). 12-3-D Presidents. 13-Flash Gordon. 14-Tyranostar. 15-3-Dementia Comics; Kurtzman-c, Kubert, Maurer-a. 16-Space Vixens; Dave Stevens-c/a. 17-Thrilling Love. 18-Spacehawk; Wolverton-r. 19-Cracked Classics. 20-Commande Battle and His Atomic Submarine			1.25

NOTE: Davis r-19. Ditko r-19. Elder r-19. Everett r-19. Feldstein r-17. Frazetta r-17. Kamen r-19. Kamen r-17. Severin r-19. Ward r-17,19. Wolverton r-2,18,19. Wood r-1,17. Photo c-

3 LITTLE PIGS (Disney)(...and the Wonderful Magic Lamp)
No. 218, Mar, 1949
Dell Publishing Co.

Four Color 218 (#1)	12.00	36.00	12

3 LITTLE PIGS, THE (See Walt Disney Showcase #15 & 21)
May, 1964; No. 2, Sept, 1968 (Walt Disney)
Gold Key

1-Reprints Four Color #218	4.00	10.00	2
2	2.40	6.00	

THREE MOUSEKETEERS, THE (1st Series)(See Funny Stuff #1)
3-4/56 - No. 24, 9-10/59; No. 25, 8-9/60 - No. 26, 10-12/60
National Periodical Publications

1	24.00	71.00	1
2	12.00	36.00	
3-10: 6,8-Grey tone-c	10.00	30.00	
11-26: 24-Cover says 11/59, inside says 9-10/59	8.70	26.00	

NOTE: Rube Grossman a-1-26. Sheldon Mayer a-1-8; c-1-7.

THREE MOUSEKETEERS, THE (2nd Series) (See Super DC Giant)
May-June, 1970 - No. 7, May-June, 1971 (#5-7: 68 pgs.)
National Periodical Publications

1-Mayer-r in all	2.60	7.50	
2-7: 5-Dodo & the Frog, Bo Bunny & Doodles Duck begin	1.65	4.20	

THREE MUSKETEERS, THE (See Disney's The Three Musketeers)

THREE NURSES (Confidential Diary #12-17; Career Girl Romances #24 o
V3#18, May, 1963 - V3#23, Mar, 1964
Charlton Comics

V3#18-23	1.00	2.00	

THREE RASCALS
1958; 1963
I. W. Enterprises

I.W. Reprint #1,2,10: 1-(Says Super Comics on inside)-(M.E.'s Clubhouse Rascals). #2-(1958). 10-(1963)-r/#1	1.00	2.00	

THREE RING COMICS
March, 1945
Spotlight Publishers

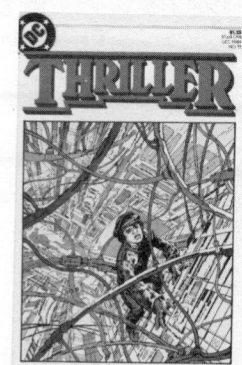

Thriller #11 © DC

Thrilling Comics #34 © Nedor

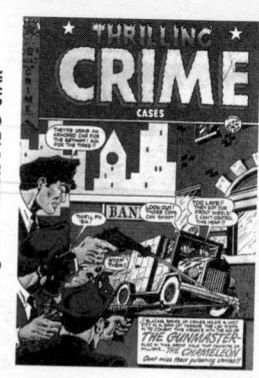

Thrilling Crime Comics #42 © STAR

	GD25	FN65	NM94
1-Funny animal	12.00	36.00	85.00

THREE RING COMICS (Also see Captain Wizard & Meteor Comics)
April, 1946
Century Publications

1-Prankster-c; Captain Wizard, Impossible Man, Race Wilkins, King O'Leary, & Dr. Mercy app.	30.00	90.00	210.00

THREE ROCKETEERS (See Blast-Off)

THREE STOOGES (See Comic Album #18, Top Comics, The Little Stooges, March of Comics #232, 248, 268, 280, 292, 304, 316, 336, 373, Movie Classics & Comics & 3-D Three Stooges)
Feb, 1949 - No. 2, May, 1949; Sept, 1953 - No. 7, Oct, 1954
Jubilee No. 1/St. John No. 1 (9/53) on

1-(Scarce, 1949)-Kubert-a; infinity-c	87.00	262.00	700.00
2-(Scarce)-Kubert, Maurer-a	68.00	206.00	550.00
1(9/53)-Hollywood Stunt Girl by Kubert (7 pgs.)	60.00	181.00	485.00
2-3-D, 10/53, 25¢)-Came w/glasses; Stunt Girl story by Kubert	40.00	120.00	320.00
3(3-D, 10/53, 25¢)-Came w/glasses; has 3-D-c	40.00	120.00	320.00
4(3/54)-7(10/54): 4-1st app. Li'l Stooge?	35.00	105.00	245.00

NOTE: All issues have Kubert-Maurer art & Maurer covers. 6, 7-Partial photo-c.

THREE STOOGES
No. 1043, Oct-Dec, 1959 - No. 55, June, 1972
Dell Publishing Co./Gold Key No. 10 (10/62) on

Four Color 1043 (#1)	18.00	54.00	180.00
Four Color 1078,1127,1170,1187	10.00	30.00	100.00
3(1-9/61) - 10: 6-Professor Putter begins; ends #16	9.00	27.00	90.00
11,14,16-20: 17-The Little Monsters begin (5/64)(1st app.?)	7.00	21.00	70.00
Go Around the World in a Daze (movie scenes)	8.00	24.00	80.00
12-23-30	6.00	18.00	60.00
55-Movie scenes from "The Outlaws Is Coming"	7.00	21.00	70.00
55	5.00	15.00	50.00

NOTE: All Four Colors, 6-50, 52-55 have photo-c.

THREE STOOGES IN 3-D, THE
1 ($3.95, high quality paper, w/glasses)
Eternity Comics

1-Reprints Three Stooges by Gold Key; photo-c	1.00	2.00	5.00

3 WORLDS OF GULLIVER
F.C. 1158, July, 1961 (2 issues exist with diff. covers)
Dell Publishing Co.

Four Color 1158-Movie, photo-c	6.00	18.00	60.00

THRILL COMICS (See Flash Comics, Fawcett)

THRILLER
1983 - No. 12, Nov, 1984 ($1.25, Baxter paper)
DC Comics

11,12: 1-Intro Seven Seconds; Von Eeden-c/a begins. 2-Origin. 5,6-Elvis satire.			1.30
(#2.00)		1.00	2.00

THRILLING ADVENTURES IN STAMPS COMICS (Formerly Stamp Comics)
#7, Jan, 1953 (25¢, 100 pgs.)
P.L. Comics, Inc. (Very Rare)

7-Harrison, Wildey, Kiefer, Napoli-a	66.00	200.00	535.00

THRILLING ADVENTURE STORIES (See Tigerman)
#1, 1975 - No. 2, Aug, 1975 (B&W, 68 pgs.)
Seaboard Publ.

1-Tigerman, Kromag the Killer begin; Heath, Thorne-a. 2-Heath, Toth,

	GD25	FN65	NM94
Severin, Simonson-a; Neal Adams-c		1.00	2.40

THRILLING COMICS
Feb, 1940 - No. 80, April, 1951
Better Publ./Nedor/Standard Comics

1-Origin & 1st app. Dr. Strange (37 pgs.), ends #?; Nickie Norton of the Secret Service begins	200.00	600.00	1600.00
2-The Rio Kid, The Woman in Red, Pinocchio begins	93.00	281.00	750.00
3-The Ghost & Lone Eagle begin	58.00	174.00	465.00
4-10: 5-Dr. Strange changed to Doc Strange	50.00	150.00	400.00
11-18,20	44.00	132.00	350.00
19-Origin & 1st app. The American Crusader (8/41), ends #39,41	50.00	151.00	405.00
21-30: 24-Intro. Mike, Doc Strange's sidekick (1/42). 29-Last Rio Kid	40.00	120.00	285.00
31-41: 36-Commando Cubs begin (7/43, 1st app.)	34.00	101.00	235.00
42,43,45-52: 52-The Ghost ends	23.00	69.00	160.00
44-Hitler-c	35.00	105.00	245.00
53-The Phantom Detective begins; The Cavalier app.; no Commando Cubs	25.00	75.00	175.00
54-The Cavalier app.; no Commando Cubs	25.00	75.00	175.00
55-Lone Eagle ends	25.00	75.00	175.00
56-Princess Pantha begins (10/46, 1st app.)	40.00	120.00	290.00
57-66: 61-Ingels-a; The Lone Eagle app. 65-Last Phantom Detective & Commando Cubs. 66-Frazetta text illo	34.00	101.00	235.00
67,70-73: Frazetta-a(5-7 pgs.) in each. 72-Sea Eagle app.; Buck Ranger, Cowboy Detective begins	40.00	120.00	290.00
68,69-Frazetta-a(2), 8 & 6 pgs.; 9 & 7 pgs.	40.00	120.00	295.00
74-Last Princess Pantha; Tara app.	25.00	75.00	175.00
75-78: 75-All western format begins	11.50	34.00	80.00
79-Krigstein-a	12.00	36.00	85.00
80-Severin & Elder, Celardo, Moreira-a	12.00	36.00	85.00

NOTE: Bondage c-5, 9, 13, 20, 22, 27-30, 38, 41, 52, 54, 70. Kinstler a-45. Leo Morey a-7. Schomburg (Xela) c-7, 9-19, 36-80 (airbrush 62-71). Tuska a-62, 63. Woman in Red not in #19, 23, 31-33, 39-45. No. 45 exists as a Canadian reprint but numbered #48. No. 72 exists as a Canadian reprint with no Frazetta story.American Crusader c-20-24. Buck Ranger c-72-80. Commando Cubs c-37, 39, 41, 43, 45, 47, 49, 51. Doc Strange c-1-19, 25-36, 38, 40, 42, 44, 46, 48, 50, 52-57, 59. Princess Pantha c-58, 60-71.

THRILLING CRIME CASES (Formerly 4Most; becomes Shocking Mystery Cases #50 on)
No. 41, June-July, 1950 - No. 49, July, 1952
Star Publications

41	20.00	60.00	140.00
42-45: 42-L. B. Cole-c/a (1); Chameleon story (Fox-r)	17.00	51.00	120.00
46-48: 47-Used in POP, pg. 84	16.00	47.00	110.00
49-(7/52)-Classic L. B. Cole-c	34.00	103.00	240.00

NOTE: L. B. Cole c-all; a-43p, 45p, 46p, 49(2 pgs.). Disbrow a-48. Hollingsworth a-48.

THRILLING ROMANCES
No. 5, Dec, 1949 - No. 26, June, 1954
Standard Comics

5	10.00	30.00	60.00
6,8	4.25	13.00	28.00
7-Severin/Elder-a (7 pgs.)	7.50	22.50	45.00
9,10-Severin/Elder-a; photo-c	6.35	19.00	38.00
11,14-21,26: 12-Tyrone Power/ Susan Hayward photo-c.14-Gene Tierney & Danny Kaye photo-c from movie "On the Riviera". 15-Tony Martin/Janet Leigh photo-c	4.00	12.00	24.00
12-Wood-a (2 pgs.)	9.15	27.00	55.00
13-Severin-a	5.35	16.00	32.00
22-25-Toth-a	7.00	21.00	42.00

NOTE: All photo-c. Celardo a-9, 16. Colletta a-23, 24(2). Toth text illos-19. Tuska a-9.

THRILLING SCIENCE TALES

Thrilling Science Tales #1 © AC

Thundeercats #1 © MEG

Thundergod #2 © William Tucci

	GD25	FN65	NM94

1989 - No. 2? ($3.50, 2/3 color, 52 pgs.)
AC Comics

1-r/Bob Colt #6(saucer); Frazetta, Guardineer (Space Ace), Wood,
Krenkel, Orlando, WIlliamson-r; Kaluta-c   1.75   3.50
2-Capt. Video-r by Evans, Capt. Science-r by Wood, Star Pirate-r by
Whitman & Mysta of the Moon-r by Moreira   1.75   3.50

THRILLING TRUE STORY OF THE BASEBALL...
1952 (Photo-c, each)
Fawcett Publications

...Giants-photo-c; has Willie Mays rookie photo-biography; Willie Mays, Eddie
Stanky & others photos on-c   60.00   180.00   480.00
...Yankees-photo-c; Yogi Berra, Joe DiMaggio, Mickey Mantle & others photos
on-c   55.00   165.00   440.00

THRILLOGY
Jan, 1984 (One-shot, color)
Pacific Comics

1-Conrad-c/a   1.00

THRILL-O-RAMA
Oct, 1965 - No. 3, Dec, 1966
Harvey Publications (Fun Films)

1-Fate (Man in Black) by Powell app.; Doug Wildey-a(2); Simon-c
   2.85   8.50   20.00
2-Pirana begins (see Phantom #46); Williamson 2 pgs.; Fate (Man in Black)
app.; Tuska/Simon-c   2.00   6.00   14.00
3-Fate (Man in Black) app.; Sparling-c   1.70   5.00   12.00

THRILLS OF TOMORROW (Formerly Tomb of Terror)
No. 17, Oct, 1954 - No. 20, April, 1955
Harvey Publications

17-Powell-a (horror); r/Witches Tales #7   8.00   24.50   65.00
18-Powell-a (horror); r/Tomb of Terror #1   6.25   19.00   50.00
19,20-Stuntman-c/stories by S&K (r/from Stuntman #1 & 2); 19 has origin &
   is last pre-code (2/55)   19.00   60.00   180.00
NOTE: *Kirby* c-19, 20. *Palais* a-17. *Simon* c-18?

THROBBING LOVE (See Fox Giants)

THROUGH GATES OF SPLENDOR
1973, 1974 (36 pages) (39-49 cents)
Spire Christian Comics (Flemming H. Revell Co.)

nn   1.00

THUMPER (Disney)
No, 19, 1942 - No. 243, Sept, 1949
Dell Publishing Co.

Four Color 19-Walt Disney's...Meets the Seven Dwarfs; reprinted in Silly
Symphonies   55.00   165.00   550.00
Four Color 243-...Follows His Nose   10.00   30.00   100.00

THUMPER (Disney)
1942 (50 cents, 32pgs., hardcover book, 7"x8-1/2" w/dust jacket)
Grosset & Dunlap

nn-Given away (along with a copy of Bambi) for a $2.00, 2-year subscription to
WDC&S in 1942. (Xmas offer). Book only   16.00   47.00   110.00
Dust jacket only   9.15   27.50   55.00

THUN'DA (...King of the Congo)
1952 - No. 6, 1953
Magazine Enterprises

1(A-1 #47)-Origin; Frazetta c/a; only comic done entirely by Frazetta; all
Thun'da stories, no Cave Girl   94.00   281.00   750.00
2(A-1 #56)-Powell-c/a begins, ends #6; Intro/1st app. Cave Girl in filler strip
(also app. in 3-6)   16.00   47.00   110.00
3(A-1 #73), 4(A-1 #78)   11.50   34.00   80.00
5(A-1 #83), 6(A-1 #86)   10.00   30.00   70.00

	GD25	FN65	NM9

THUN'DA TALES (See Frank Frazetta's...)

THUNDER AGENTS (See Dynamo, Noman & Tales Of Thunder)
11/65 - No. 17, 12/67; No. 18, 9/68, No. 19, 11/68, No. 20, 11/69
(No. 1-16: 68 pgs.; No. 17 on: 52 pgs.)(All are 25¢)
Tower Comics

1-Origin & 1st app. Dynamo, Noman, Menthor, & The Thunder Squad; 1st
app. The Iron Maiden   14.00   43.00   1
2-Death of Egghead; A-bomb blast panel   8.50   26.00   4
3-5: 4-Guy Gilbert becomes Lightning who joins Thunder Squad; Iron Maiden
app.   5.70   17.00   4
6-10: 7-Death of Menthor. 8-Origin & 1st app. The Raven
   4.30   13.00
11-15: 13-Undersea Agent app.; no Raven story   2.85   8.50
16-19   2.30   6.70
20-Special Collectors Edition; all reprints   1.30   3.25
NOTE: *Crandall* a-1, 4p, 5p, 18, 20r; c-18. *Ditko* a-6, 7p, 12p, 13?, 14p, 16, 18. *Giunta* a
Kane a-1, 5p, 6p?, 14, 16p; c-14, 15. *Reinman* a-13. *Sekowsky* a-6. *Tuska* a-1p, 7, 8, 10
17, 19. *Whitney* a-9p, 10, 13, 15, 17, 18; c-17. *Wood* a-1-11, 15(w/Ditko-12, 18), (inks-#9
14, 16, 17), 19i, 20r; c-1-8, 9i, 10-13(#10 w/Williamson(p)), 16.

T.H.U.N.D.E.R. AGENTS (See Blue Ribbon Comics, Hall of Fame
Featuring the..., JCP Features & Wally Wood's...)
May, 1983 - No. 2, Jan, 1984
JC Comics (Archie Publications)

1,2-New material   1.20

THUNDER BIRDS (See Cinema Comics Herald)

THUNDERBOLT (See The Atomic...)

THUNDERBOLT (Peter Cannon...; see Crisis on Infinite Earths & Peter...)
Jan, 1966; No. 51, Mar-Apr, 1966 - No. 60, Nov, 1967
Charlton Comics

1-Origin & 1st app. Thunderbolt   1.70   5.00
51-(Formerly Son of Vulcan #50)   1.30   3.25
52-59: 54-Sentinels begin. 59-Last Thunderbolt & Sentinels (back-up story
   1.00   2.00
60-Prankster app.   1.30   3.25
57,58 ('77)-Modern Comics-r
NOTE: *Aparo* a-60. *Morisi* a-1, 51-56, 58; c-1, 51-56, 58, 59.

THUNDERBUNNY (Also see Blue Ribbon Comics #13, Charlton Bullseye &
Comics #393)
Jan, 1984 (Direct sale only)
Red Circle Comics

1-Origin

THUNDERCATS (TV)
Dec, 1985 - No. 24, June, 1988 (75¢)
Marvel Comics (Star Comics)/Marvel #22 on

1-Mooney-c/a begins
2-24: 2-(65 & 75 cent cover exists). 12-Begin $1.00-c. 18-20-Williamson-i
23-Williamson-c(i)

THUNDERGOD
July, 1996 - Present ($2.95, B&W)
Crusade Entertainment

1,2: Painted-c

THUNDER MOUNTAIN (See Zane Grey, Four Color #246)

THUNDERSTRIKE (See Thor #459)
June, 1993 - No. 24, July, 1995 ($1.25)
Marvel Comics

1-($2.95, 52 pgs.)-Holo-grafx lightning patterned foil-c; Bloodaxe returns
   1.20
2-7: 2-Juggernaut-c/s. 4-Capt. America app. 4-6-Spider-Man app.
8-24: 8-Begin $1.50-c; bound-in trading card sheet. 18-Bloodaxe app. 24
of Thunderstrike.

The Tick #12 © Ben Edlund

Tigerman #2 © ATLAS

Timber Wolf #4 © DC

	GD25	FN65	NM94

	GD25	FN65	NM94
l Double Feature...Thunderstrike/Code Blue #13 ($2.50)-Same as			
understrike #13 w/Code Blue flip book	1.00		2.50
THE (Also see The Chroma-Tick)			
1988 - No. 12, May, 1993 ($1.75/$1.95/$2.25; B&W, over-sized)			
England Comics Press			
al Edition 1-1st comic book app. serially numbered & limited to 5,000			
pies	7.00	21.50	50.00
al Edition 1-(5/96, $5.95)-Double-c; foil-c; serially numbered (5,001 thru			
,000) & limited to 9,000 copies			6.00
al Edition 2-Serially numbered and limited to 3000 copies	7.00	21.50	50.00
al Edition 2-(8/96, $5.95)-Double-c; foil-c; serially numbered (5,001 thru			
000) & limited to 9,000 copies			6.00
prints Special Ed. 1 w/minor changes	5.70	17.00	40.00
d printing	1.00	2.00	5.00
printing ($1.95, 6/89)		1.20	3.00
printing ($2.25)		1.00	2.50
printing ($2.75)		1.20	3.00
prints Special Ed. 2 w/minor changes	4.30	13.00	30.00
d printing ($1.95)	1.00	2.00	5.00
& 4th printings ($2.25)		1.00	2.50
printing ($2.75)		1.20	3.00
51.95): 4-1st app. Paul the Samurai	1.00	2.00	5.00
d & 3rd printings ($2.25)		1.00	2.50
printing ($2.75)		1.20	3.00
d printing ($2.25)		1.00	2.50
- 5th printings ($2.75)		1.20	3.00
2.25): 7-1st app. Man-Eating Cow.		1.60	4.00
nd printings ($2.75)		1.20	3.00
printing ($2.75)		1.20	3.00
iant with no logo, price, issue number or company logos.			
	2.85	8.50	20.00
($2.75)		1.20	3.00
ecial Edition; card-stock, virgin foil-c; numbered edition			
			30.00
Sampler-(1990)-Tick-c/story			15.00
S GIANT CIRCUS OF THE MIGHTY, THE			
er, 1992 - No. 3, Fall, 1993 ($2.75, B&W, magazine size)			
ngland Comics			
0). 2-(P-Z). 3-1993 Update		1.20	3.00
KARMA TORNADO, THE			
993 - No. 9, 1994? ($2.75)			
ngland Comics Press			
.25)		1.40	3.50
2-$2.75-c begins		1.20	3.00
E COMICS (Also see Gay, Smile, & Whee Comics)			
7¢, 5x7-1/4", 52 pgs)			
n Store Publ.			
	.50	1.25	2.50
OCK TALES			
946 - V3#33, Jan-Feb, 1951			
ine Enterprises			
ko & Kola begin	10.00	30.00	68.00
	5.70	17.00	34.00
	4.25	13.00	28.00
19-Flag-c. 23-Muggsy Mouse, The Pixies & Tom-Tom the Jungle Boy			
. 25-The Pixies & Tom-Tom app.	4.00	10.00	20.00
(Also see Comics Reading Libraries)			
970 - No. 6, Jan, 1971 (15¢)			
n Press (King Features)			

	GD25	FN65	NM94
1	1.00	2.00	5.00
2-6		1.20	3.00
TIGER BOY (See Unearthly Spectaculars)			
TIGER GIRL			
Sept, 1968 (15¢)			
Gold Key			
1(10227-809)-Sparling-c/a; Jerry Siegel scripts	3.60	11.00	25.00
TIGERMAN (Also see Thrilling Adventure Stories)			
Apr, 1975 - No. 3, Sept, 1975 (All 25¢ issues)			
Seaboard Periodicals (Atlas)			
1-3: 2,3-Ditko-p in each			1.50
TIGER WALKS, A (See Movie Comics)			
TIGRESS, THE			
Aug, 1992 - No. 6?, July, 1993 ($3.95/$2.95/$3.95, B&W)			
Hero Graphics			
1-Tigress vs. Flare		1.40	3.50
2-5: 2-$2.95-c begins		1.20	3.00
6-(6/93, $3.95, 44 pgs.)		1.60	4.00
TILLIE THE TOILER (See Comic Monthly)			
No. 15, 1941 - No. 237, July, 1949			
Dell Publishing Co.			
Four Color 15(1941)	35.00	105.00	350.00
Large Feature Comic 30(1941)	22.00	66.00	220.00
Four Color 8(1942)	22.00	66.00	220.00
Four Color 22(1943)	17.00	52.00	170.00
Four Color 55(1944), 89(1945)	13.00	40.00	130.00
Four Color 106('45),132('46): 132-New stories begin	10.00	30.00	100.00
Four Color 150,176,184	9.00	27.00	90.00
Four Color 195,213,237	6.00	18.00	60.00
TILLY AND TED-TINKERTOTLAND			
1945 (Giveaway, 20 pgs.)			
W. T. Grant Co.			
nn-Christmas comic	6.35	19.00	38.00
TIM (Formerly Superman-Tim; becomes Gene Autry-Tim)			
June, 1950 - Oct, 1950 (B&W, half-size)			
Tim Stores			
4 issues; 6/50, 9/50, 10/50 known	7.00	21.00	42.00
TIMBER WOLF (See Action Comics #372, & Legion of Super-Heroes)			
Nov, 1992 - No. 5, Mar, 1993 ($1.25, limited series)			
DC Comics			
1-5			1.25
TIME BANDITS			
Feb, 1982 (one-shot)			
Marvel Comics Group			
1-Movie adaptation			1.00
TIME BEAVERS (See First Comics Graphic Novel #2)			
TIMECOP (Movie)			
Sept, 1994 - No. 2, Nov, 1994 ($2.50, limited series)			
Dark Horse Comics			
1,2-Adaptation of film		1.00	2.50
TIME FOR LOVE (Formerly Romantic Secrets)			
V2#53, Oct, 1966; Oct, 1967 - No. 47, May, 1976			
Charlton Comics			
V2#53(10/66), 1(10/67), 2(12/67)-20	1.00	2.00	5.00
21-47: 30-(10/72)-Full-length portrait of David Cassidy		1.20	3.00
TIMELESS TOPIX (See Topix)			

Time Masters #8 © DC

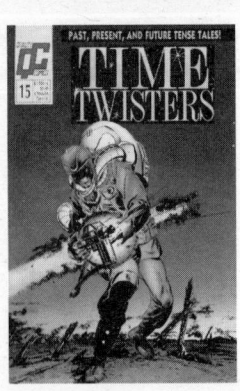
Time Twisters #15 © Fleetway

Timewalker #7 © Voyager Comm.

	GD25	FN65	NM94

	GD25	FN65	NM9

TIME MACHINE, THE
No. 1085, Mar, 1960 (H.G. Wells)
Dell Publishing Co.

Four Color 1085-Movie, Alex Toth-a; Rod Taylor photo-c
| | 15.00 | 45.00 | 150.00 |

TIME MASTERS
Feb, 1990 - No. 8, Sept, 1990 ($1.75, mini-series)
DC Comics

1-8: New Rip Hunter series. 5-Cave Carson, Viking Prince app. 6-
Dr. Fate app.
| | | .90 | 1.80 |

TIMESPIRITS
Oct, 1984 - No. 8, Mar, 1986 ($1.50, Baxter paper, direct sales)
Marvel Comics (Epic Comics)

1-8: 4-Williamson-a
| | | | 1.50 |

TIME TUNNEL, THE (TV)
Feb, 1967 - No. 2, July, 1967 (12¢)
Gold Key

1,2-Photo back-c
| | 4.00 | 12.00 | 40.00 |

TIME TWISTERS
Sept, 1987 - No. 21, 1989 ($1.25/$1.50)
Quality Comics

1-10: Alan Moore scripts in 1-4, 6-9, 14 (2 pg.).
| | | | 1.25 |
11-21 ($1.50): 14-Bolland-a (2 pg.). 15,16 Guice-c
| | | | 1.50 |

TIME 2: THE EPIPHANY (See First Comics Graphic Novel #9)

TIMEWALKER (Also see Archer & Armstrong)
Jan, 1994 - No. 15, Oct, 1995 ($2.50)
Valiant

1-15: 2-"JAN" on-c, February, 1995 in indicia.
| | 1.00 | | 2.50 |
Yearbook 1 (5/95, $2.95)
| | 1.20 | | 3.00 |

TIME WARP (See The Unexpected #210)
Oct-Nov, 1979 - No. 5, June-July, 1980 ($1.00, 68 pgs.)
DC Comics, Inc.

1-5
| | | | 1.00 |
NOTE: *Aparo* a-1. *Buckler* a-1p. *Chaykin* a-2. *Ditko* a-1-4. *Kaluta* c-1-5. *G. Kane* a-1.
Nasser a-4. *Newton* a-1-5p. *Orlando* a-2. *Sutton* a-1-3.

TIME WARRIORS THE BEGINNING
1986 (Aug) - No. 2, 1986? ($1.50)
Fantasy General Comics

1,2-Alpha Track/Skellon Empire
| | | | 1.50 |

TIM HOLT (Movie star) (Becomes Red Mask #42 on; also see Crack Western #72, & Great Western)
1948 - No. 41, April-May, 1954 (All 36 pgs.)
Magazine Enterprises

1-(A-1 #14)-Line drawn-c w/Tim Holt photo on-c; Tim Holt, His horse Lightning
& sidekick Chito begin
| | 56.00 | 168.00 | 450.00 |
2-(A-1 #17)(9-10/48)-Photo-c begin, end #18
| | 32.00 | 96.00 | 225.00 |
3-(A-1 #19)-Photo back-c
| | 24.00 | 73.00 | 170.00 |
4(1-2/49),5: 5-Photo front/back-c
| | 19.00 | 56.00 | 130.00 |
6(5/49)-1st app. The Calico Kid (alias Rex Fury), his horse Ebony & Sidekick
Sing-Song (begin series)
| | 31.00 | 94.00 | 220.00 |
7-10: 7-Calico Kid by Ayers. 8-Calico Kid by Guardineer (r-in/Great Western
#10). 9-Map of Tim's Home Range
| | 15.00 | 45.00 | 105.00 |
11-The Calico Kid becomes The Ghost Rider (origin & 1st app.) by Dick Ayers
(r-in/Great Western I.W. #8); his horse Spectre & sidekick Sing-Song begin
series
| | 40.00 | 120.00 | 300.00 |
12-16,18-Last photo-c
| | 11.50 | 34.00 | 80.00 |
17-Frazetta Ghost Rider-c
| | 31.00 | 92.00 | 215.00 |
19,22,24: 19-Last Tim Holt-c; Bolle line-drawn-c begin; Tim Holt photo on

covers #19-28,30-41. 22-interior photo-c
| | 10.00 | 30.00 | |
20-Tim Holt becomes Redmask (origin); begin series; Redmask-c #20-on
| | 14.00 | 43.00 | |
21-Frazetta Ghost Rider/Redmask-c
| | 27.00 | 81.00 | |
23-Frazetta Redmask-c
| | 23.00 | 69.00 | |
25-1st app. Black Phantom
| | 17.00 | 51.00 | |
26-30: 28-Wild Bill Hickok, Bat Masterson team up with Redmask. 29-B&W
photo-c
| | 9.15 | 27.00 | |
31-33-Ghost Rider ends
| | 8.35 | 25.00 | |
34-Tales of the Ghost Rider begins (horror)-Classic "The Flower Women"
& "Hard Boiled Harry!"
| | 10.00 | 30.00 | |
35-Last Tales of the Ghost Rider
| | 9.15 | 27.00 | |
36-The Ghost Rider returns, ends #41; liquid hallucinogenic drug story
| | 10.00 | 30.00 | |
37-Ghost Rider classic "To Touch Is to Die!", about Inca treasure
| | 10.00 | 30.00 | |
38-The Black Phantom begins (not in #39); classic Ghost Rider "The Phan
Guns of Feather Gap!"
| | 10.00 | 30.00 | |
39-41: All 3-D effect c/stories
| | 13.00 | 39.00 | |
NOTE: *Dick Ayers* a-7, 9-41. *Bolle* a-1-41; c-19, 20, 22, 24-28, 30-41.

TIM IN SPACE (Formerly Gene Autry Tim; becomes Tim Tomorrow)
1950 (1/2 size giveaway) (B&W)
Tim Stores

nn
| | 4.00 | | 11.00 |

TIM McCOY (Formerly Zoo Funnies; Pictorial Love Stories #22 on)
No. 16, Oct, 1948 - No. 21, Aug, 1949 (Western Movie Stories)
Charlton Comics

16-John Wayne, Montgomery Clift app. in "Red River"; photo back-c
| | 40.00 | 120.00 | |
17-21: 17-Allan "Rocky" Lane guest stars. 18-Rod Cameron guest stars.
Whip Wilson, Andy Clyde guest star; Jesse James story. 20-Jimmy Wa
guest stars. 21-Johnny Mack Brown guest stars
| | 38.00 | 114.00 | |

TIM McCOY, POLICE CAR 17
No. 674, 1934 (32 pgs.) (11x14-3/4") (B&W) (Like Feature Books)
Whitman Publishing Co.

674-1933 movie ill.
| | 25.00 | 75.00 | |

TIMMY
No. 715, Aug, 1956 - No. 1022, Aug-Oct, 1959
Dell Publishing Co.

Four Color 715 (#1)
| | 4.00 | | 12.00 |
Four Color 823 (8/57), 923 (8/58), 1022
| | 3.00 | | 9.00 |

TIMMY THE TIMID GHOST (Formerly Win-A-Prize?; see Blue Bird)
No. 3, 2/56 - No. 44, 10/64; No. 45, 9/66; 10/67 - No. 23, 7/71; V4#24,
9/85 - No. 26, 1/86
Charlton Comics

3(1956) (1st Series)
| | 7.50 | | 22.50 |
4,5
| | 4.00 | | 12.00 |
6-10
| | 2.80 | | 7.00 |
11,12(4/58,10/58)(100 pgs.)
| | 5.00 | | 15.00 |
13-20
| | 2.00 | | 5.00 |
21-45(1966)
| | 1.00 | | 2.50 |
1(10/67, 2nd series)
| | 1.00 | | 2.50 |
2-23
| | | | 1.00 |
24-26 (1985-86): Fago-r

TIM TOMORROW (Formerly Tim In Space)
8/51, 9/51, 10/51, Christmas, 1951 (5x7-3/4")
Tim Stores

nn-Prof. Fumble & Captain Kit Comet in all
| | 4.35 | | 13.00 |

TIM TYLER (See Harvey Comics Hits #54)

TIM TYLER (Also see Comics Reading Libraries)

Tim Tyler #13 © STD

Tip Top Comics #1 © UFS

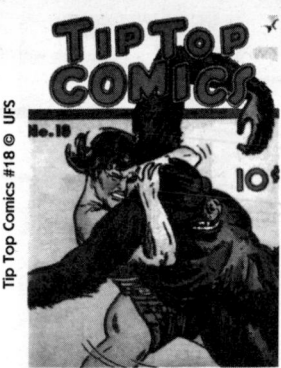
Tip Top Comics #18 © UFS

	GD25	FN65	NM94
Publications			
	11.50	34.00	80.00
..YLER COWBOY			
.., Nov, 1948 - No. 18, 1950			
...ard Comics (King Features Synd.)			
.. Lyman Young	8.00	24.00	48.00
.. 13-15-Full length western adventures	5.70	17.00	34.00
..R BELL (Disney, TV)(See Walt Disney Showcase #37)			
..6, Mar, 1958 - No. 982, Apr-June, 1959			
..ublishing Co.			
...olor 896 (#1)-The Adventures of...	8.00	24.00	80.00
...olor 982-The New Advs. of...	8.00	24.00	80.00
..FOLKS FUNNIES			
.., 1944			
..ublishing Co.			
...olor 60	14.00	43.00	140.00
..ESSIE (Tessie #1-23; Real Experiences #25)			
.., Oct, 1949 (52 pgs.)			
.. Comics (20CC)			
	7.00	21.00	42.00
..IM (Also see Super Comics)			
..1941 - No. 235, July, 1949			
..ublishing Co.			
..Feature Comic 4('41)	32.00	96.00	320.00
...olor 20(1941)	29.00	87.00	290.00
...olor 42(1943)	16.00	48.00	160.00
...olor 235	5.00	15.00	50.00
..OT COMICS			
..946 - No. 10, Nov-Dec, 1947 (For younger readers)			
..omics			
..52 pg. issues begin, end #4	29.00	86.00	200.00
..6)	17.00	51.00	120.00
..10-Christmas-c	14.00	43.00	100.00
..OT FUNNIES (Formerly Family Funnies; becomes Junior Funnies)			
..June, 1951			
.. Publ. (King Features Synd.)			
..sh Gordon, Mandrake, Dagwood, Daisy, etc.	5.00	15.00	30.00
..OTS COMICS			
..Not reprints)			
..ublishing Co.			
..y-a(2); fairy tales	39.00	118.00	275.00
..& CAP STUBBS (See Popular Comics)			
..0, Jan, 1949 - No. 242, Aug, 1949			
..blishing Co.			
...olor 210 (#1)	4.00	12.00	40.00
...olor 242	4.00	12.00	40.00
..S FRIENDS GO-GO & ANIMAL			
..966 - No. 15, Oct, 1969 (25¢)			
..Comics			
	3.60	9.00	18.00
..9-15: 12-15 titled "Tippy's Friend Go-Go"	2.40	6.00	12.00
.. Monkees photo-c	5.00	15.00	30.00
..tles app. on front/back-c	7.50	22.50	45.00
..TEEN (See Vicki)			
..65 - No. 27, Feb, 1970 (25¢)			
..Comics			

	GD25	FN65	NM94
1	2.15	6.50	15.00
2-4,6-27: 16-Twiggy photo-c	1.30	3.25	8.00
5-1 pg. Beatles pin-up	1.70	5.00	12.00
Special Collectors' Editions nn-(1969, 25¢)	1.30	3.25	8.00
TIPPY TERRY			
1963			
Super/I. W. Enterprises			
Super Reprint #14('63)-r/Little Groucho #1	1.00	2.00	5.00
I.W. Reprint #1 (nd)-r/Little Groucho #1	1.00	2.00	5.00
TIP TOP COMICS			
4/36 - No. 210, 1957; No. 211, 11-1/57-58 - No. 225, 5-7/61			
United Features #1-187/St. John #188-210/Dell Publishing Co. #211 on			

	GD25	FN65	VF82	NM94
1-Tarzan by Hal Foster, Li'l Abner, Broncho Bill, Fritzi Ritz, Ella Cinders, Capt. & The Kids begin; strip-r (1st comic book app. of each)				
	916.00	2750.00	4122.00	5500.00
(Estimated up to 80 total copies exist, 4 in NM/Mint)				

	GD25	FN65	VF82	
2	200.00	600.00	1200.00	
3-Tarzan-c	183.00	549.00	1100.00	
4	108.00	324.00	650.00	
5-8,10: 7-Photo & biography of Edgar Rice Burroughs. 8-Christmas-c				
	79.00	237.00	475.00	
9-Tarzan-c	100.00	300.00	600.00	

	GD25	FN65	NM94
11,13,16,18-Tarzan-c: 11-Has Tarzan pin-up	79.00	237.00	475.00
12,14,15,17,19,20: 20-Christmas-c	64.00	192.00	385.00
21,24,27,30-Tarzan-c	47.00	141.00	375.00
22,23,25,26,28,29	40.00	120.00	300.00
31,35,38,40	39.00	118.00	275.00
32,36-Tarzan-c: 32-1st published Jack Davis-a (cartoon). 36-Kurtzman panel (1st published comic work)	47.00	141.00	375.00
33,34,37,39-Tarzan-c	44.00	132.00	350.00
41-Reprints 1st Tarzan Sunday; Tarzan-c	47.00	141.00	375.00
42-50: 43-Mort Walker panel	37.00	111.00	260.00
51,53	31.00	94.00	220.00
52-Tarzan-c	39.00	118.00	275.00
54-Origin Mirror Man & Triple Terror, also featured on cover	39.00	116.00	270.00
55,56,58,60: 56-Last Tarzan by Foster	24.00	73.00	170.00
57,59,61,62-Tarzan by Hogarth	31.00	92.00	215.00
63-80: 65,67-70,72-74,77,78-No Tarzan	15.00	45.00	105.00
81-90	13.50	41.00	95.00
91-99	11.00	33.00	75.00
100	12.00	36.00	85.00
101-140: 110-Gordo story. 111-Li'l Abner app. 118, 132-No Tarzan. 137-Sadie Hawkins Day story	8.00	24.00	48.00
141-170: 145,151-Gordo stories. 157-Last Li'l Abner; lingerie panels	5.35	16.00	32.00
171-188-Tarzan reprints by B. Lubbers in all. 177-Peanuts by Schulz begins?; no Peanuts in #178,179,181-183	5.85	17.50	35.00
189-225	4.00	12.00	24.00
Bound Volumes (Very Rare) sold at 1939 World's Fair; bound by publisher in pictorial comic boards (also see Comics on Parade)			
Bound issues 1-12	214.00	643.00	1650.00
Bound issues 13-24	143.00	430.00	1100.00
Bound issues 25-36	121.00	365.00	950.00

NOTE: Tarzan covers-#1(part), 2(part), 3, 9, 11, 13, 16, 18, 21, 24, 27, 30, 32-34, 36, 37, 39, 41, 43, 45, 47, 50, 52 (all worth 10-20 percent more). Tarzan by Foster-#1-40, 44-50; by Rex Maxon-#41-43; by Burne Hogarth-#57, 59, 62.

TIP TOPPER COMICS
Oct-Nov, 1949 - No. 28, 1954
United Features Syndicate

Titan Special #1 © DH

Titans Sell-Out #1 © DC

Tomahawk #10 © DC

	GD25	FN65	NM94
1-Li'l Abner, Abbie & Slats	9.15	27.50	55.00
2	5.35	16.00	32.00
3-5: 5-Fearless Fosdick app.	4.70	14.00	28.00
6-10: 6-Fearless Fosdick app.	4.00	12.00	24.00
11-25: 17-22,24,26-Peanuts app. (2 pgs.)	3.60	9.00	18.00
26-28-Twin Earths	4.70	14.00	28.00

NOTE: Many lingerie panels in Fritzi Ritz stories.

TITAN SPECIAL
June, 1994 ($3.95, one-shot)
Dark Horse Comics

1-($3.95, 52 pgs.)		1.60	4.00

TITANS SELL-OUT SPECIAL
Nov, 1992 ($3.50, 52 pgs., one-shot)
DC Comics

1-Fold-out Nightwing poster; 1st Teeny Titans		1.40	3.50

T-MAN (Also see Police Comics #103)
Sept, 1951 - No. 38, Dec, 1956
Quality Comics Group

1-Pete Trask, T-Man begins; Jack Cole-a	34.00	103.00	240.00
2-Crandall-c	18.00	54.00	125.00
3,7,8: All Crandall-c	15.00	45.00	105.00
4,5-Crandall-c/a each	16.00	47.00	110.00
6-"The Man Who Could Be Hitler" c/story; Crandall-c.	17.00	51.00	120.00
9,10-Crandall-c	13.00	39.00	90.00
11-Used in POP, pg. 95 & color illo.	10.00	30.00	65.00
12-19,21,22-26: 21- "The Return of Mussolini" c/story. 23-H-Bomb panel.			
24-Last pre-code issue (4/55). 25-Not Crandall-a	8.35	25.00	50.00
20-H-Bomb explosion-c/story	11.00	33.00	75.00
27-38	7.50	22.50	45.00

NOTE: Anti-communist stories common. Crandall c-2-10p. Cuidera c(i)-1-38. Bondage c-15.

TMNT MUTANT UNIVERSE SOURCEBOOK
1992 - No. 3, 1992? ($1.95, 52 pgs.)(Lists characters from A-Z)
Archie Comics

1-3: 3-New characters; fold-out poster		.80	2.00

TNT COMICS
Feb, 1946 (36 pgs.)
Charles Publishing Co.

1-Yellowjacket app.	22.00	66.00	155.00

TOBY TYLER (Disney, see Movie Comics)
No. 1092, Apr-June, 1960
Dell Publishing Co.

Four Color 1092-Movie, photo-c	7.00	21.00	70.00

TODAY'S BRIDES
Nov, 1955; No. 2, Feb, 1956; No. 3, Sept, 1956; No. 4, Nov, 1956
Ajax/Farrell Publishing Co.

1	6.35	19.00	38.00
2-4	4.00	12.00	24.00

TODAY'S ROMANCE
No. 5, March, 1952 - No. 8, Sept, 1952 (All photo-c?)
Standard Comics

5-Photo-c	6.35	19.00	38.00
6-Photo-c; Toth-a	7.00	21.00	42.00
7,8	4.00	11.00	22.00

TOKA (Jungle King)
Aug-Oct, 1964 - No. 10, Jan, 1967 (Painted-c #1,2)
Dell Publishing Co.

1	2.60	7.50	18.00
2	1.65	4.20	10.00

	GD25	FN65	NM9
3-10	1.30	3.25	

TOMAHAWK (Son of... on-c of #131-140; see Star Spangled Comics #69
World's Finest Comics #65)
Sept-Oct, 1950 - No. 140, May-June, 1972
National Periodical Publications

1-Tomahawk & boy sidekick Dan Hunter begin by Fred Ray	143.00	431.00	1
2-Frazetta/Williamson-a (4 pgs.)	56.00	168.00	
3-5	40.00	120.00	
6-10: 7-Last 52 pg. issue	29.00	86.00	
11-20	21.00	62.00	
21-27,30: 30-Last precode (2/55)	16.00	47.00	
28-1st app. Lord Shilling (arch-foe)	17.00	51.00	
29-Frazetta-r/Jimmy Wakely #3 (3 pgs.)	23.00	69.00	
31-40	13.50	41.00	
41-50	11.00	33.00	
51-56,58-60	8.70	26.00	
57-Frazetta-r/Jimmy Wakely #6 (3 pgs.)	12.00	36.00	
61-77: 77-Last 10¢ issue	5.70	17.00	
78-85: 81-1st app. Miss Liberty. 83-Origin Tomahawk's Rangers	4.00	12.00	
86-100: 96-Origin/1st app. The Hood, alias Lady Shilling	2.30	6.70	
101-110: 107-Origin/1st app. Thunder-Man	1.65	4.20	
111-130,132-138,140	1.00	2.60	
131-Frazetta-r/Jimmy Wakely #7 (3 pgs.); origin Firehair retold	1.20	3.00	
139-Frazetta-r/Star Spangled #113	1.00	2.00	

NOTE: Neal Adams c-116-119, 121, 123-130. Fred Ray c-1, 2, 8, 11, 30, 34, 35, 40-43
82. Firehair by Kubert-131-134, 136. Maurer a-138. Severin a-135. Starr a-5. Thorne a
140.

TOM AND JERRY (See Comic Album #4, 8, 12, Dell Giant #21, Dell Giants, Golden
Digest #1, 5, 8, 13, 15, 18, 22, 25, 28, 35, Kite fun Book & March of Comics #21, 46, 61,
103, 119, 128, 145, 154, 173, 190, 207, 224, 281, 295, 305, 321,333, 345, 361, 365, 38
444, 451, 463, 480)

TOM AND JERRY (...Comics, early issues) (M.G.M.)
(Formerly Our Gang No. 1-59) (See Dell Giants for annuals)
No. 193, 6/48; No. 60, 7/49 - No. 212, 7-9/62; No. 213, 11/62 - No. 291, 2
No. 292, 3/77 - No. 342, 5/82 - No. 344, 1982?
Dell Publishing Co./Gold Key 213-327/Whitman No. 328 on

Four Color 193 (#1)-Titled "M.G.M. Presents..."	14.00	43.00	
60-Barney Bear, Benny Burro cont. from Our Gang	8.00	24.00	
61	7.00	21.00	
62-70: 66-X-Mas-c	5.00	15.00	
71-80: 77,90-X-Mas-c	4.00	12.00	
81-99: 81-Spike & Tyke begin? 84-Droopy begins?	3.50	10.00	
100	3.60	11.00	
101-120	3.40	10.00	
121-140: 126-X-Mas-c	3.25	9.50	
141-160	2.30	6.70	
161-200	2.00	6.00	
201-212(7-9/62)(Last Dell issue)	1.50	3.75	
213,214-(84 pgs.)-Titled "...Funhouse"	3.70	11.00	
215-240: 215-Titled "...Funhouse"	1.30	3.25	
241-270	1.20	3.00	
271-300: 286- "Tom & Jerry"		1.60	
301-344		.80	
Mouse From T.R.A.P. 1(7/66)-Giant, G. K.	3.70	11.00	
Summer Fun 1(7/67, 68 pgs.)(Gold Key)-Reprints Barks' Droopy from			
Summer Fun #1	3.70	11.00	

NOTE: #60-87, 98-121, 268, 277, 289, 302 are 52 pgs.. Reprints-#225, 241, 245, 247, 2
266, 268, 270, 292-327, 329-342, 344.

TOM & JERRY
Sept, 1991 - No. 4, 1992 ($1.25)

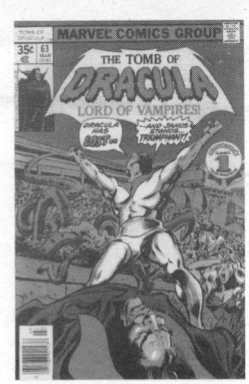

Tomb of Dracula #63 © MEG

Tommi Gunn #2 © Everette Hartsoe

Tom Mix Western #1 © FAW

	GD25	FN65	NM94

⬝rvey Comics

4: 1-Tom & Jerry, Barney Bear-r by Barks ... 1.30

h Anniversary Special 1 (10/91, $2.50, 68 pgs.)-Benny the Lone-
some Burro-r by Barks (story/a)/Our Gang #9 1.00 2.50

⬝MB OF DARKNESS (Formerly Beware)
⬝ 9, July, 1974 - No. 23, Nov, 1976
⬝rvel Comics Group

⬝3: 15,19-Ditko-r. 17-Woodbridge-r/Astonishing #62; Powell-r. 20-Everett
Venus-r/Venus #19. 22-r/Venus #19. 23-Everett-r 1.50

⬝MB OF DRACULA (See Giant-Size Dracula, Dracula Lives, Nightstalkers,
⬝wer Record Comics & Requiem for Dracula)
⬝, 1972 - No. 70, Aug, 1979
⬝rvel Comics Group

⬝-1st app. Dracula & Frank Drake; Colan-p in all 10.00 30.00 80.00
6.00 18.00 42.00
⬝5: 3-Intro. Dr. Rachel Van Helsing & Inspector Chelm
4.00 12.00 30.00
⬝10: 10-1st app. Blade the Vampire Slayer 3.60 11.00 25.00
⬝-20: 12-Brunner-c(p). 13-Origin Blade 2.15 6.50 15.00
⬝-40: 25-1st app. & origin Hannibal King 1.70 5.00 12.00
⬝-49,51-60 1.00 2.50 6.00
⬝-Silver Surfer app. 1.70 5.00 12.00
⬝-70: 70-Double size 1.00 2.00 5.00
⬝TE: *N. Adams* c-1, 6. *Colan* a-1-70p; c(p)-8, 38-42, 44-56, 58-70. *Wrightson* c-43.

⬝MB OF DRACULA, THE (Magazine)
⬝t, 1979 - No. 6, Aug, 1980 (B&W)
⬝rvel Comics Group

⬝4-6 1.60 4.00
⬝3: 2-Ditko-a (36 pgs.). 3-Miller-a(2 pg. sketch) 1.00 2.00 5.00
⬝TE: *Buscema* a-4p, 5p. *Chaykin* c-5, 6. *Colan* a(p)-1, 3-6. *Miller* a-3. *Romita* a-2p.

⬝MB OF DRACULA
⬝91 - No. 4, 1992 ($4.95, 52 pgs., squarebound, mini-series)
⬝rvel Comics (Epic Comics)

⬝ok 1-4: Colan/Williamson-a; Colan painted-c 1.00 2.00 5.00

⬝MB OF LEGEIA (See Movie Classics)

⬝MB OF TERROR (Thrills of Tomorrow #17 on)
⬝ne, 1952 - No. 16, July, 1954
⬝rvey Publications

31.00 94.00 220.00
17.00 49.00 115.00
⬝-Bondage-c; atomic disaster story 18.00 54.00 125.00
⬝12: 4-Heart ripped out. 8-12-Nostrand-a 17.00 49.00 115.00
⬝,14-Special S/F issues. 14-Check-a 20.00 60.00 140.00
⬝-S/F issue; c-shows head exploding 24.00 73.00 170.00
⬝-Special S/F issue; Nostrand-a 20.00 60.00 140.00
⬝TE: *Edd Cartier* a-13? *Elias* c-2, 5-16. *Kremer* a-1, 7; c-1. *Nostrand* a-8-12, 15r 16. *Palais*
⬝, 3, 5-7. *Powell* a-1, 3, 5, 9-16. *Sparling* a-12, 13, 15.

⬝MBSTONE TERRITORY (See Four Color #1123)

⬝M CAT (Formerly Bo; Atom The Cat #9 on)
⬝. 4, Apr, 1956 - No. 8, July, 1957
⬝arlton Comics

⬝-Al Fago-c/a 6.35 19.00 38.00
⬝-8 4.25 13.00 26.00

⬝M CORBETT, SPACE CADET (TV)
⬝. 378, Jan-Feb, 1952 - No. 11, Sept-Nov, 1954 (All painted covers)
⬝ll Publishing Co.

⬝ur Color 378 (#1)-McWilliams-a 16.00 48.00 160.00
⬝ur Color 400,421-McWilliams-a 10.00 30.00 100.00
⬝(11-1/53) - 11 7.00 21.00 70.00

	GD25	FN65	NM94

TOM CORBETT SPACE CADET (See March of Comics #102)

TOM CORBETT SPACE CADET (TV)
V2#1, May-June, 1955 - V2#3, Sept-Oct, 1955
Prize Publications

V2#1 24.00 73.00 170.00
2,3-Meskin-c 21.00 64.00 150.00

TOM, DICK & HARRIET (See Gold Key Spotlight)

TOM LANDRY AND THE DALLAS COWBOYS
1973 (35/49¢)
Spire Christian Comics/Fleming H. Revell Co.

nn 1.00

TOMMI GUNN
May, 1996 - No. 3, Aug, 1996 ($3.00, limited series, mature)
London Night Studios

1/2,1-3: W/J.J. North centerfold 3.00
1/2-($10.00)-Naughty Edition; photo-c 10.00
1-Naughty Platinum; embossed nude-c w/nude J.J. North centerfold inside 10.00
2-Variant nude-c 5.00

TOM MIX (...Commandos Comics #10-12)
Sept, 1940 - No. 12, Nov, 1942 (36 pgs.); 1983 (one-shot)
Given away for two Ralston box-tops; 1983 came in cereal box
Ralston-Purina Co.

1-Origin (life) Tom Mix; Fred Meagher-a 275.00 825.00 2500.00
2 93.00 281.00 750.00
3-9 59.00 178.00 475.00
10-12: 10-Origin Tom Mix Commando Unit; Speed O'Dare begins; Japanese
sub-c. 12-Sci/fi-c 45.00 136.00 365.00
1983- "Taking of Grizzly Grebb", Toth-a; 16 pg. miniature
1.20 3.00 6.00

TOM MIX WESTERN (Movie, radio star) (Also see The Comics, Crackajack
Funnies, Master Comics, 100 Pages Of Comics, Popular Comics, Real
Western Hero, Six Gun Heroes, Western Hero & XMas Comics)
Jan, 1948 - No. 61, May, 1953 (1-17: 52 pgs.)
Fawcett Publications

1 (Photo-c, 52 pgs.)-Tom Mix & his horse Tony begin; Tumbleweed Jr.
begins, ends #52,54,55 87.00 262.00 700.00
2 (Photo-c) 40.00 120.00 300.00
3-5 (Painted/photo-c): 5-Billy the Kid & Oscar app. 31.00 94.00 220.00
6,7 (Painted/photo-c) 26.00 77.00 180.00
8-Kinstler tempera-c 26.00 77.00 180.00
9,10 (Painted/photo-c)-Used in **SOTI**, pgs. 323-25 24.00 71.00 165.00
11-Kinstler oil-c 21.00 64.00 150.00
12 (Painted/photo-c) 18.00 56.00 130.00
13-17 (Painted-c, 52 pgs.) 18.00 56.00 130.00
18,22 (Painted-c, 36 pgs.) 16.00 47.00 110.00
19 (Photo-c, 52 pgs.) 17.00 49.00 115.00
20,21,23 (Painted-c, 52 pgs.) 13.50 41.00 95.00
24,25,27-29 (52 pgs.): 24-Photo-c begin, end #61. 29-Slim Pickens app.
13.50 41.00 95.00
26,30 (36 pgs.) 12.00 36.00 85.00
31-33,35-37,39,40,42 (52 pgs.): 39-Red Eagle app. 11.50 34.00 80.00
34,38 (36 pgs. begin) 10.00 30.00 70.00
41,43-60: 57-(9/52)-Dope smuggling story 8.35 25.00 50.00
61-Last issue 10.00 30.00 65.00
NOTE: Photo-c from 1930s Tom Mix movies (he died in 1940). Many issues contain ads for Tom
Mix, Rocky Lane, Space Patrol and other premiums. Captain Tootsie by *C.C. Beck* in #6-11, 20.

TOM MIX WESTERN
1988 - No. 2, 1989? ($2.95, B&W w/16 pgs. color, 44 pgs.)
AC Comics

Tomoe #2 © Crusade

Tongue Lash #2 © DH

Top Comics #5 © Warner Bros.

	GD25	FN65	NM94

1-Tom Mix-r/Master #124,128,131,102 plus Billy the Kid-r by Severin; photo
front/back/inside-c 1.20 3.00
2-($2.50, B&W)-Gabby Hayes-r; photo covers 1.00 2.50
...Holiday Album 1 (1990, $3.50, B&W, one-shot, 44 pgs.)-Contains photos &
1950s Tom Mix-r; photo inside-c 1.40 3.50

TOMMY OF THE BIG TOP (Thrilling Circus Adventures)
No. 10, Sept, 1948 - No. 12, Mar, 1949
King Features Syndicate/Standard Comics

10-By John Lehti 5.35 16.00 32.00
11,12 4.00 10.00 20.00

TOMMY TOMORROW (See Action Comics #127, Real Fact #6, Showcase #41,42,44,46,47 & World's Finest #102)

TOMOE (Also see Shi: The Way Of the Warrior #6)
July, 1995 - Present ($2.95)
Crusade Comics

0-3: 2-B&W Dogs o' War preview. 3-B&W Demon Gun preview.
  3.00
0 (3/96, $2.95)-variant-c. 3.00
0-Commemorative edition (5,000) 17.00
1-Commemorative edition (5,000) 2.85 8.50 20.00

TOMOE-WITCHBLADE/MANGA SHI PREVIEW EDITION
July, 1996 ($5.00, B&W)
Crusade Comics

nn-San Diego Preview Edition 5.00

TOMORROW KNIGHTS
June, 1990 - No. 6, Mar, 1991 ($1.50)
Marvel Comics (Epic Comics)

1-($1.95, 52 pgs.) .80 2.00
2-6 1.50

TOM SAWYER (See Adventures of... & Famous Stories)

TOM SAWYER COMICS
1951? (Paper cover)
Giveaway

nn-Contains a coverless Hopalong Cassidy from 1951; other combinations
known 2.00 5.00 10.00

TOM SKINNER-UP FROM HARLEM (See Up From Harlem)

TOM TERRIFIC! (TV)(See Mighty Mouse Fun Club Magazine #1)
Summer, 1957 - No. 6, Fall, 1958 (See Terry Toons Giant Summer Fun Book)
Pines Comics (Paul Terry)

1-1st app.?; CBS Television Presents... 19.00 56.00 130.00
2-6 13.50 41.00 95.00

TOM THUMB
No. 972, Jan, 1959
Dell Publishing Co.

Four Color 972-Movie, George Pal 10.00 30.00 100.00

TOM-TOM, THE JUNGLE BOY (See A-1 Comics & Tick Tock Tales)
1947 - No. 3, 1947; Nov, 1957 - No. 3, Mar, 1958
Magazine Enterprises

1-Funny animal 7.50 22.50 45.00
2,3(1947): 3-Christmas issue 5.35 16.00 32.00
Tom-Tom & Itchi the Monk 1(11/57) - 3(3/58) 2.80 7.00 14.00
I.W. Reprint No. 1,2,8,10: 1,2,8-r/Koko & Kola #? 1.00 2.60 6.00

TONGUE LASH
Aug, 1996 - No. 2, Sept, 1996 ($2.95, limited series, mature)
Dark Horse Comics

1,2: Taylor-c/a 3.00

TONKA (Disney)

No. 966, Jan, 1959
Dell Publishing Co.

Four Color 966-Movie (Starring Sal Mineo)-photo-c 9.00 27.00 90

TONTO (See The Lone Ranger's Companion...)

TONY TRENT (The Face #1,2)
No. 3, 1948 - No. 4, 1949
Big Shot/Columbia Comics Group

3,4: 3-The Face app. by Mart Bailey 12.00 36.00 85

TOODLES, THE (The Toodle Twins with #1)
No. 10, July-Aug, 1951; Mar, 1956 (Newspaper-r)
Ziff-Davis (Approved Comics)/Argo

10-Newspaper-r by the Baers 8.00 24.00 48
...Twins 1(Argo, 3/56)-Reprints by The Baers 5.70 17.00 34

TOO MUCH COFFEE MAN
July, 1993 - Present ($2.50, B&W)
Adhesive Comics

1-Shannon Wheeler tory & art 1.20 3
2-5 1.00 2
Full Color Special-($2.95) 3

TOOTS & CASPER
No. 5, 1942
Dell Publishing Co.

Large Feature Comic 5 11.00 33.00 110

TOP ADVENTURE COMICS
1964 (Reprints)
I. W. Enterprises

1-r/High Adv. (Explorer Joe #2); Krigstein-r 2.15 6.50 15
2-Black Dwarf-r/Red Seal #22; Kinstler-c 2.15 6.50 15

TOP CAT (TV) (Hanna-Barbera)(See Kite Fun Book)
12-2/61-62 - No. 3, 6-8/62; No. 4, 10/62 - No. 31, 9/70
Dell Publishing Co./Gold Key No. 4 on

1 (TV show debuted 9/27/61) 16.00 48.00 145
2-Augie Doggie back-ups in 1-4 8.75 26.50 80
3-5: 3-Last 15¢ issue. 4-Begin 12¢ issues; 1st app. Yakky Doodle in 1 pg.
strip. 5-1st app. Touche' Turtle 6.00 18.00 55
6-10 4.50 13.50 36
11-20 3.40 10.00 24
21-31: 21,24,25,29-Reprints 2.60 7.50 18

TOP CAT (TV) (Hanna-Barbera)(See TV Stars #4)
Nov, 1970 - No. 20, Nov, 1973
Charlton Comics

1 4.00 12.00 32
2-10 2.60 7.50 18
11-20 1.70 5.00 12
NOTE: #8 (1/72) went on sale late in 1972 between #14 and #15 with the 1/73 issues.

TOP COMICS
July, 1967 (All reprints)
K. K. Publications/Gold Key

nn-The Gnome-Mobile (Disney-movie) 1.60 4.00 8
1-Beagle Boys (#7), Beep Beep the Road Runner (#5), Bugs Bunny, Chip 'n'
Dale, Daffy Duck (#50), Flipper, Huckleberry Hound, Huey, Dewey & Louie
Junior Woodchucks, Lassie, The Little Monsters (#71), Moby Duck, Porky
Pig (has Gold Key label - says Top Comics on inside), Scamp, Super Goof,
Tarzan of the Apes (#169), Three Stooges (#35), Tom & Jerry Top Cat (#2),
Tweety & Sylvester (#7), Walt Disney C&S (#322), Woody Woodpecker,
Yogi Bear, Zorro (r/G.K. Zorro #7 w/Toth-a; says 2nd printing) known; each
character given own book 1.60 4.00 8
1-Uncle Scrooge (#70) 2.40 6.00 12
1-Donald Duck (not Barks), Mickey Mouse 2.00 5.00 10

564

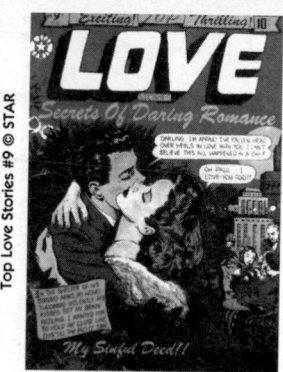

Topix V5#1 © Catechetical Guild Educational Society

Top Love Stories #9 © STAR

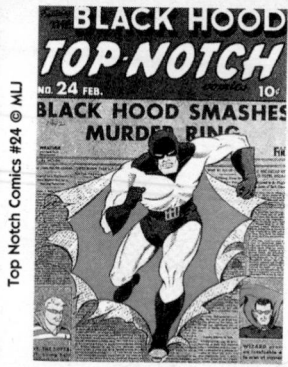

Top Notch Comics #24 © MLJ

	GD25	FN65	NM94
1-Flintstones	4.20	12.50	25.00
1-The Jetsons	5.85	17.50	35.00
2-Bugs Bunny, Daffy Duck, Donald Duck (not Barks), Mickey Mouse (#114), Porky Pig, Super Goof, Three Stooges, Tom & Jerry, Tweety & Sylvester, Uncle Scrooge (#71)-Barks-c, Walt Disney's C&S (r/#325), Woody Wood-			
pecker, Yogi Bear (#30), Zorro (r/#8; Toth-a)	1.60	4.00	8.00
2-Snow White & 7 Dwarfs(6/67)(1944-r)	2.00	5.00	10.00
3-Donald Duck	1.80	4.50	9.00
3-Uncle Scrooge (#72)	2.00	6.00	12.00
3,4-The Flintstones	4.20	12.50	25.00
3-Mickey Mouse (r/#115), Tom & Jerry, Woody Woodpecker, Yogi Bear			
	1.60	4.00	8.00
4-Mickey Mouse, Woody Woodpecker	1.60	4.00	8.00

NOTE: Each book in this series is identical to its counterpart except for cover, and came out at same time. The number in parentheses is the original issue it contains.

TOP COW PRODUCTIONS, INC./BALLISTIC STUDIOS SWIMSUIT SPECIAL
May, 1995 ($2.95, one-shot)
Image Comics (Top Cow Productions)

1	1.00	2.00	5.00

TOP COW SECRETS:SPECIAL WINTER LINGERIE EDITION
Jan, 1996 ($2.95, one-shot)
Image Comics (Top Cow Productions)

1-Pin-ups			3.00

TOP DETECTIVE COMICS
1964 (Reprints)
I. W. Enterprises

9-r/Young King Cole #14; Dr. Drew (not Grandenetti)			
	1.65	4.20	10.00

TOP DOG (See Star Comics Magazine, 75¢)
Apr, 1985 - No. 14, June, 1987 (Children's book)
Star Comics (Marvel)

1-14: 10-Peter Parker & J. Jonah Jameson cameo			1.00

TOP ELIMINATOR (Teenage Hotrodders #1-24; Drag 'n' Wheels #30 on)
No. 25, Sept, 1967 - No. 29, July, 1968
Charlton Comics

25-29	1.30	3.25	8.00

TOP FLIGHT COMICS
1947; July, 1949
Four Star Publications/St. John Publishing Co.

1(1947)	10.00	30.00	65.00
1(7/49, St. John)-Hector the Inspector; funny animal	7.00	21.00	42.00

TOP GUN (See Luke Short, 4-Color #927 & Showcase #72)

TOP GUNS OF THE WEST (See Super DC Giant)

TOPIX (...Comics) (Timeless Topix-early issues) (Also see Men of Battle, Men of Courage & Treasure Chest)(V1-V5#1,V7#1-20-paper-c)
1/42 - V10#15, 1/28/52 (Weekly - later issues)
Catechetical Guild Educational Society

1#1(8 pgs.,8x11")	16.00	47.00	110.00
2,3(8 pgs.,8x11")	10.00	30.00	65.00
4-8(16 pgs.,8x11")	8.00	24.00	48.00
2#1-10(16 pgs.,8x11"): V2#8-Pope Pius XII	5.35	16.00	32.00
3#1-10(16 pgs.,8x11")	5.35	16.00	32.00
4#1-10	4.25	13.00	28.00
5#1(10/46,52 pgs.)-9,12-15(12/47): 13-Lists V5#4	4.00	11.00	22.00
10,11-Life of Christ editions	5.70	17.00	34.00
6#1-14	3.20	8.00	16.00
7#1(9/1/48)-20(6/15/49), 32 pgs.	3.20	8.00	16.00
8#1(9/19/49)-3,5-11,13-30(5/15/50)	3.20	8.00	16.00
4-Dagwood Splits the Atom(10/10/49)-Magazine format			
	4.00	10.00	20.00

	GD25	FN65	NM94
12-Ingels-a	5.85	17.50	35.00
V9#1(9/25/50)-11,13-30(5/14/51)	2.80	7.00	14.00
12-Special 36 pg. Xmas issue, text illos format	3.20	8.00	16.00
V10#1(10/1/51)-15: 14-Hollingsworth-a	2.80	7.00	14.00

TOP JUNGLE COMICS
1964 (Reprint)
I. W. Enterprises

1(nd)-Reprints White Princess of the Jungle #3, minus cover; Kinstler-a			
	2.60	7.50	18.00

TOP LOVE STORIES (Formerly Gasoline Alley #2)
No. 3, 5/51 - No. 19, 3/54
Star Publications

3(#1)	16.00	47.00	110.00
4,5,7-9: 8-Wood story	12.00	36.00	85.00
6-Wood-a	19.00	56.00	130.00
10-16,18,19-Disbrow-a	12.00	36.00	85.00
17-Wood art (Fox-r)	14.00	43.00	100.00

NOTE: All have L. B. Cole covers.

TOP-NOTCH COMICS (...Laugh #28-45; Laugh Comix #46 on)
Dec, 1939 - No. 45, June, 1944
MLJ Magazines

1-Origin/1st app. The Wizard; Kardak the Mystic Magician, Swift of the Secret Service (ends #8), Air Patrol, The Westpointer, Manhunters (by J. Cole), Mystic (ends #2) & Scott Rand (ends #3) begin; Wizard covers begin, end #8			
	422.00	1267.00	4200.00
2-Dick Storm (ends #8), Stacy Knight M.D. (ends #4) begin; Jack Cole-a			
	187.00	562.00	1500.00
3-Bob Phantom, Scott Rand on Mars begin; J. Cole-a			
	131.00	393.00	1050.00
4-Origin/1st app. Streak Chandler on Mars; Moore of the Mounted only app.; J. Cole-a			
	106.00	318.00	850.00
5-Flag-c; origin/1st app. Galahad; Shanghai Sheridan begins (ends #8); Shield cameo; Novick-a; classic-c			
	112.00	338.00	900.00
6-Meskin-a	85.00	256.00	685.00
7-The Shield x-over in Wizard; The Wizard dons new costume			
	103.00	309.00	825.00
8-Origin/1st app. The Firefly & Roy, the Super Boy (9/40, 2nd costumed boy hero after Robin?; also see Toro in Human Torch #1 (Fall/40)			
	116.00	350.00	935.00
9-Origin & 1st app. The Black Hood; 1st Black Hood-c & logo (10/40); Fran Frazier begins (Scarce)			
	390.00	1170.00	3900.00
10-2nd app. Black Hood	131.00	393.00	1050.00
11-15	78.00	234.00	625.00
16-20	70.00	211.00	565.00
21-30: 23-26-Roy app. 24-No Wizard. 25-Last Bob Phantom. 27-Last Firefly. 28-Suzie, Pokey Oakey begin. 29-Last Kardak			
	56.00	168.00	450.00
31-44: 33-Dotty & Ditto by Woggon begins (2/43, 1st app.). 44-Black Hood series ends			
	37.00	111.00	260.00
45-Last issue	40.00	120.00	285.00

NOTE: J. Binder a-1-3. Meskin a-2, 3, 6, 15. Bob Montana a-30; c-28-31. Harry Sahle c-42-45. Woggon a-33-40, 42. Bondage c-17, 19. Black Hood also appeared on radio in 1944.Black Hood app. on c-9-34, 41-44. Roy the Super Boy app. on c-8, 9, 11-27. The Wizard app. on c-1-8, 11-13, 15-22, 24, 25, 27. Pokey Oakey app. on c-28-43. Suzie app. on c-44-on.

TOPPER & NEIL (TV)
No. 859, Nov, 1957
Dell Publishing Co.

Four Color 859	4.00	12.00	40.00

TOPPS COMICS
1947
Four Star Publications

1-L. B. Cole-c	17.00	49.00	115.00

TOPPS COMICS PRESENTS

Tor #6 © Joe Kubert

Torch of Liberty Special © John Byrne

Torchy #4 © QUA

No. 0, 1993 (Giveaway, B&W, 36 pgs.)
Topps Comics

0-Dracula vs. Zorro, Teenagents, Silver Star, & Bill the Galactic Hero stories

  1.00

TOPS
July, 1949 - No. 2, Sept, 1949 (25¢, 10-1/4x13-1/4", 68 pgs.)
(Large size-magazine format; for the adult reader)
Tops Magazine, Inc. (Lev Gleason)

1 (Rare)-Story by Dashiell Hammett; Crandall/Lubbers, Tuska, Dan Barry, Fuje-a; Biro painted-c	93.00	281.00	750.00
2 (Rare)-Crandall/Lubbers, Biro, Kida, Fuje, Guardineer-a	87.00	262.00	700.00

TOPS COMICS
1944 (10¢, 132 pgs.)
Consolidated Book Publishers

2000-(Color-c, inside in red shade & some in full color)-Ace Kelly by Rick Yager, Black Orchid, Don on the Farm, Dinky Dinkerton (Rare)	26.00	77.00	180.00

NOTE: This book is printed in such a way that when the staple is removed, the strips on the left side of the book correspond with the same strips on the right side. Therefore, if strips are removed from the book, each strip can be folded into a complete comic section of its own.

TOPS COMICS (See Tops in Humor)
1944 (7-1/4x5", 32 pgs.)
Consolidated Book (Lev Gleason)

2001-The Jack of Spades (costumed hero)	13.50	41.00	95.00
2002-Rip Raider	8.70	26.00	52.00
2003-Red Birch (gag cartoons)	2.00	5.00	10.00

TOP SECRET
Jan, 1952
Hillman Publ.

1	17.00	49.00	115.00

TOP SECRET ADVENTURES (See Spyman)

TOP SECRETS (...of the F.B.I.)
Nov, 1947 - No. 10, July-Aug, 1949
Street & Smith Publications

1-Powell-c/a	29.00	86.00	200.00
2-Powell-c/a	21.00	62.00	145.00
3-6,8,10-Powell-a	18.00	54.00	125.00
9-Powell-c/a	19.00	56.00	130.00
7-Used in SOTI, pg. 90 & illo. "How to hurt people"; used by N.Y. Legis. Comm.; Powell c/a	29.00	86.00	200.00

NOTE: Powell c-1-3, 5-10.

TOPS IN ADVENTURE
Fall, 1952 (25¢, 132 pgs.)
Ziff-Davis Publishing Co.

1-Crusader from Mars, The Hawk, Football Thrills, He-Man; Powell-a; painted-c	40.00	120.00	290.00

TOPS IN HUMOR (See Tops Comics?)
1944 (7-1/4x5")
Consolidated Book Publ. (Lev Gleason)

2001(#1)-Origin The Jack of Spades, Ace Kelly by Rick Yager, Black Orchid (female crime fighter) app.	15.00	45.00	105.00
2	10.00	30.00	65.00

TOP SPOT COMICS
1945
Top Spot Publ. Co.

1-The Menace, Duke of Darkness app.	24.00	73.00	170.00

TOPSY-TURVY
Apr, 1945

R. B. Leffingwell Publ.

1-1st app. Cookie	9.15	27.00	55.00

TOR (Prehistoric Life on Earth) (Formerly One Million Years Ago)
No. 2, Oct, 1953; No. 3, May, 1954 - No. 5, Oct, 1954
St. John Publishing Co.

3-D 2(10/53)-Kubert-c/a	12.00	36.00	85.00
3-D 2(10/53)-Oversized, otherwise same contents	11.00	33.00	75.00
3-D 2(11/53)-Kubert-c/a; has 3-D cover	11.00	33.00	75.00
3-5-Kubert-c/a: 3-Danny Dreams by Toth; Kubert 1 pg. story (w/self portrait)	12.00	36.00	85.00

NOTE: The two October 3-D's have same contents and Powell art; the October & November issues are titled 3-D Comics. All 3-D issues are 25¢ and came with 3-D glasses.

TOR (See Sojourn)
May-June, 1975 - No. 6, Mar-Apr, 1976
National Periodical Publications

1-6: 1-New origin by Kubert. 2-Origin-r/St. John #1			1.50

NOTE: Kubert a-1, 2-6r; c-1-6. Toth a(p)-3r.

TOR (3-D)
July, 1986 - No. 2, Aug, 1987 ($2.50)
Eclipse Comics

1,2: 1-r/One.Million Years Ago. 2-r/Tor 3-D #2		1.25	2.50
...2-D: 1,2-Limited signed & numbered editions		1.25	2.50

TOR
June, 1993 - No. 4, 1993 ($5.95, limited series)
Marvel Comics (Epic Comics/Heavy Hitters)

1-4: Joe Kubert-c/a/scripts	1.00	2.50	6.00

TORCH OF LIBERTY SPECIAL
Jan, 1995 ($2.50, one-shot)
Dark Horse Comics (Legend)

1-Byrne scripts		1.20	3.00

TORCHY (...Blonde Bombshell) (See Dollman, Military, & Modern)
Nov, 1949 - No. 6, Sept, 1950
Quality Comics Group

1-Bill Ward-c, Gil Fox-a	110.00	331.00	885.00
2,3-Fox-c/a	53.00	159.00	425.00
4-Fox-c/a(3), Ward-a (9 pgs.)	67.00	202.00	540.00
5,6-Ward-c/a, 9 pgs; Fox-a(3) each	90.00	271.00	725.00
Super Reprint #16(1964)-r/#4 with new-c	8.75	26.00	70.00

TO RIVERDALE AND BACK AGAIN (Archie Comics Presents...)
1990 ($2.50, 68 pgs.)
Archie Comics

nn-Byrne-c, Colan-a(p); adapts NBC TV movie		1.00	2.50

TORMENTED, THE (Becomes Surprise Adventures #3 on)
July, 1954 - No. 2, Sept, 1954
Sterling Comics

1,2: Weird/horror stories	17.00	51.00	120.00

TORNADO TOM (See Mighty Midget Comics)

TOTAL ECLIPSE
May, 1988 - No. 5, Apr, 1989 ($3.95, 52 pgs., deluxe size)
Eclipse Comics

Book 1-5: 3-Intro/1st app. new Black Terror		1.60	4.00

TOTAL ECLIPSE: THE SERAPHIM OBJECTIVE
Nov, 1988 ($1.95, one-shot, Baxter paper)
Eclipse Comics

1-Airboy, Valkyrie, The Heap app.		.80	2.00

TOTAL JUSTICE
Oct, 1996 - No. 3, Nov, 1996 ($2.25, bi-weekly limited series)(Based on toyline)

Tour of Torture '96 © Everette Hartsoe

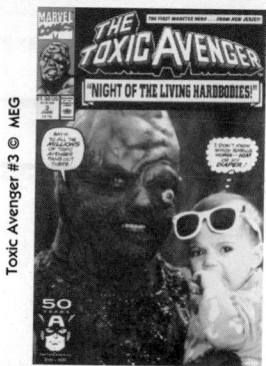

Toxic Avenger #3 © MEG

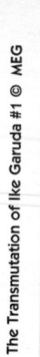

The Transmutation of Ike Garuda #1 © MEG

ELAINE LEE & JAMES SHERMAN

	GD25	FN65	NM94

DC Comics

	GD25	FN65	NM94
1-3			2.25

TOTAL RECALL (Movie)
1990 ($2.95, 68 pgs., movie adaptation, one-shot)
DC Comics

1-Arnold Schwarzenegger photo-c		1.20	3.00

TOTAL WAR (M.A.R.S. Patrol #3 on)
July, 1965 - No. 2, Oct, 1965 (Painted-c)
Gold Key

1,2: Wood-a in each	4.00	12.00	40.00

TO THE LAST MAN (See Zane Grey Four Color #616)

TOUGH KID SQUAD COMICS
Timely Comics (TCI)

	GD25	FN65	VF82	NM94
1-(Scarce)-Origin & 1st app.The Human Top & The Tough Kid Squad; The Flying Flame app.	778.00	2333.00	4667.00	7700.00

(Estimated up to 100 total copies exist, 6 in NM/Mint)

TOUR OF TORTURE
June, 1996 ($10.00, one-shot)
London Night Studios

nn-Photo-c			10.00

TOWER OF SHADOWS (Creatures on the Loose #10 on)
Sept, 1969 - No. 9, Jan, 1971
Marvel Comics Group

	GD25	FN65	NM94
1-Steranko, Craig-a(p)	3.60	11.00	25.00
2-Neal Adams-a	1.70	5.00	12.00
3-Barry Smith, Tuska-a	1.70	5.00	12.00
4-Marie Severin-c	1.20	3.00	7.00
5,7-B. Smith-a(p), Wood-a. 5-Wood draws himself (1st pg., 1st panel)			
	1.70	5.00	12.00
6-9: 6,8-Wood-a; 8-Wrightson-c. 9-Wrightson-c; Roy Thomas app.			
	1.30	3.25	8.00
Special 1(12/71)-Neal Adams-a	1.30	3.25	8.00

NOTE: J. Buscema a-1p, 2p, Special 1r. Colan a-3p, 6p, Special 1. J. Craig a(r)-1p. Ditko a-6, 9r, Special 1. Everett a-9(i)r; c-5i. Kirby a-9(p)r. Severin c-5p, 6. Steranko a-1p. Tuska a-3. Wood a-5-8. Issues 1-9 contain new stories with some pre-Marvel age reprints in 6-9. H. P. Lovecraft adaptation-9.

TOWN & COUNTRY
May, 1940
Publisher?

nn-Origin The Falcon	40.00	120.00	300.00

TOWN THAT FORGOT SANTA, THE
1961 (Giveaway, 24 pgs.)
W. T. Grant Co.

nn	3.20	8.00	16.00

TOXIC AVENGER (Movie)
Apr, 1991 - No. 11, Feb, 1992 ($1.50)
Marvel Comics

1-10: Based on movie character. 3,10-Photo-c			1.50
11-($1.75)		.90	1.80

TOXIC CRUSADERS (TV)
May, 1992 - No. 8, Dec, 1992 ($1.25)
Marvel Comics

1-3-Sam Kieth-c; based on USA network cartoon			1.50
4-8: 8-Kieth-c(i)			1.25

TOYBOY
Oct, 1986 - No. 7?, 1991 ($2.00, Baxter paper)
Continuity Comics

	GD25	FN65	NM94
1-7	1.00		2.00

NOTE: N. Adams a-1; c-1, 2,5. Golden a-7p; c-6,7. Nebres a(i)-1,2.

TOYLAND COMICS
Jan, No. 2, Mar, 1947; No. 3, July, 1947 - No. 4, 1947
Fiction House Magazines

1-Wizard of the Moon begins	21.00	64.00	150.00
2-4: 2,3-Bob Lubbers-c. 3-Tuska-a	13.50	39.00	90.00
148 pg. issue	24.00	71.00	165.00

NOTE: All above contain strips by Al Walker.

TOY TOWN COMICS
1945 - No. 7, May, 1947
Toytown/Orbit Publ./B. Antin/Swapper Quarterly

1-Mertie Mouse; L. B. Cole-c/a; funny animal	27.00	81.00	190.00
2-L. B. Cole-a	18.00	54.00	125.00
3-7-L. B. Cole-a. 5-Wiggles the Wonderworm-c	15.00	45.00	105.00

TRAGG AND THE SKY GODS (See Gold Key Spotlight, Mystery Comics Digest #3,9 & Spine Tingling Tales)
June, 1975 - No. 8, Feb, 1977; No. 9, May, 1982 (Painted-c #3-8)
Gold Key/Whitman No. 9

1-Origin		1.00	2.50
2-9: 4-Sabre-Fang app. 8-Ostellon app.; 9-r/#1			1.50

NOTE: Santos a-1, 2, 9r; c-3-7. Spiegel a-3-8.

TRAIL BLAZERS (Red Dragon #5 on)
1941; No. 2, Apr, 1942 - No. 4, Oct, 1942 (True stories of American heroes)
Street & Smith Publications

1-Life story of Jack Dempsey & Wright Brothers	30.00	90.00	210.00
2-Brooklyn Dodgers-c/story; Ben Franklin story	18.00	54.00	125.00
3,4: 3-Fred Allen, Red Barber, Yankees stories	17.00	49.00	115.00

TRAIL COLT (Also see Extra Comics & Manhunt!)
1949 - No. 2, 1949
Magazine Enterprises

nn(A-1 #24)-7 pg. Frazetta-a r-in Manhunt #13; Undercover Girl app.; The Red Fox by L. B. Cole; Ingels-c; Whitney-a (Scarce)	36.00	107.00	250.00
2(A-1 #26)-Undercover Girl; Ingels-c; L. B. Cole-a (6 pgs.)			
	30.00	90.00	210.00

TRANSFORMERS, THE (TV)(See G.I. Joe and...)
Sept, 1984 - No. 80, July, 1991 (75¢/$1.00)
Marvel Comics Group

1-Based on Hasbro Toys		1.25	2.50
2,3		.90	1.80
4-10,75: 75-($1.50, 52 pgs.)			1.50
11-74,76-80: 21-Intro Aerialbots. 54-Intro Micromasters			1.00

NOTE: Second and third printings of all issues exist and are worth less than originals. Was originally planned as a four issue mini-series. Wrightson a-64i(4 pgs.).

TRANSFORMERS: GENERATION 2
Nov, 1993 - No. 12, Oct, 1994 ($1.75)
Marvel Comics

1-($2.95, 68 pgs.)-Collector's ed. w/bi-fold metallic-c		1.20	3.00
1-11: 1-Newsstand edition (68 pgs.)		.70	1.75
12-($2.25, 52 pgs.)		.90	2.25

TRANSMUTATION OF IKE GARUDA, THE
July, 1991 - No. 2, 1991 ($3.95, 52 pgs.)
Marvel Comics (Epic Comics)

1,2		2.00	4.00

TRAPMAN
June, 1994 - No. 2, 1994? ($2.95, quarterly, unfinished limited series)
Phantom Comics

1,2		1.20	3.00

TRAPPED

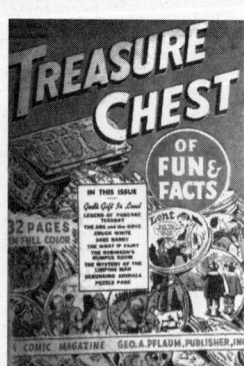

Treasure Chest #1 © George A. Pflaum

Treasure Comics #4 © PRIZE

Treasury of Comics #2 © STJ

	GD25	FN65	NM94

1951 (Giveaway, soft-c, 16 pgs.)
Harvey Publications (Columbia University Press)

nn-Drug education comic (30,000 printed?) distributed to schools.; mentioned in **SOTI**, pgs. 256,350	1.60	4.00	8.00

NOTE: Many copies surfaced in 1979 causing a setback in price; beware of trimmed edges, because many copies have a brittle edge.

TRAPPED!
Oct, 1954 - No. 5, June?, 1955
Periodical House Magazines (Ace)

1 (All reprints)	8.70	26.00	52.00
2-5: 4-r/Men Against Crime #4 in its entirety	5.70	17.00	34.00

NOTE: Colan a-1, 4. Sekowsky a-1.

TRASH
Mar, 1978 - No. 2, June, 1978 (B&W, magazine)
Trash Publ. Co.

1,2		1.00	2.00

TRAVELS OF JAIMIE McPHEETERS, THE (TV)
Dec, 1963
Gold Key

1-Kurt Russell photo on-c plus photo back-c	3.25	9.50	22.00

TREASURE CHEST (Catholic Guild; also see Topix)
3/12/46 - V27#8, July, 1972 (Educational comics)
George A. Pflaum (not publ. during Summer)

V1#1	19.00	56.00	130.00
2-6 (5/21/46): 5-Dr. Styx app. by Baily	9.15	27.00	55.00
V2#1-20 (9/3/46-5/27/47)	6.70	20.00	40.00
V3#1-5,7-20 (1st slick cover)	5.00	15.00	30.00
V3#6-Jules Verne's "Voyage to the Moon"	7.50	22.50	45.00
V4#1-20 (9/9/48-5/31/49)	4.00	11.00	22.00
V5#1-20 (9/6/49-5/31/50)	3.60	9.00	18.00
V6#1-20 (9/14/50-5/31/51)	3.60	9.00	18.00
V7#1-20 (9/13/51-6/5/52)	2.80	7.00	14.00
V8#1-20 (9/11/52-6/4/53)	2.40	6.00	12.00
V9#1-20 ('53-'54)	2.00	5.00	10.00
V10#1-20 ('54-'55)	2.00	5.00	10.00
V11('55-'56), 7/12('56-'57)	1.30	3.25	8.00
V13#1,3-5,7,9-V17#1 ('57-'63)	1.20	3.00	6.00
V13#2,6,8-Ingels-a	5.00	15.00	35.00
V17#2- "This Godless Communism" series begins(not in odd #'d issues); cover shows hammer & sickle over Statue of Liberty; 8 pg. Crandall-a-of family life under communism	16.00	47.00	110.00
V17#3,5,7,9,11,13,15,17,19	1.00	2.00	5.00
V17#4,6,14- "This Godless Communism" stories	10.00	30.00	70.00
V17#8-Shows red octopus encompassing Earth, firing squad; 8 pgs. Crandall-a	11.50	34.00	80.00
V17#10- "This Godless Communism" - how Stalin came to power, part I; Crandall-a	11.00	33.00	75.00
V17#12-Stalin in WWII, forced labor, death by exhaustion; Crandall-a	11.00	33.00	75.00
V17#16-Kruschev takes over; de-Stalinization	11.00	33.00	75.00
V17#18-Kruschev's control; murder of revolters, brainwash, space race by Crandall	11.00	33.00	75.00
V17#20-End of series; Kruschev-people are puppets, firing squads hammer & sickle over Statue of Liberty, snake around communist manifesto by Crandall	11.00	33.00	75.00
V18#1-20, V19#11-20, V20#1-20(1964-65): V18#11-Crandall draws himself & 13 other artists on cover	1.00	2.00	5.00
V18#5- "What About Red China?" - describes how communists took over China	4.50	14.00	32.00
V19#1-10- "Red Victim" anti-communist series in all	4.50	14.00	32.00
V21-V25(1965-70)-(two V24#5's 11/7/68 & 11/21/68) (no V24#6)			
	1.60	4.00	

V26, V27#1-8 (V26,27-68 pgs.)	.80	2.	
Summer Edition V1#1-6('66), V2#1-6('67)	.80	2.	

NOTE: **Anderson** a-V18#13. **Borth** a-V7#10-19 (serial), V8#8-17 (serial), V9#1-10 (serial), V13#2, 6, 11, V14-V25 (except V22#1-3, 11-13), Summer Ed. V1#3-6. **Crandall** a-V16#7, 9, 14, 16-18, 20; V17#1, 2, 4-6, 10, 12, 14-16, 18, 20; V18#1, 2, 3(2 pg.), 7, 9-20; V19#4, 11, 13, 16, 19, 20; V20#1, 2, 4, 6, 8-10, 12, 14-16, 18, 20; V21#1-5, 8-11, 13, 16-18; V22#8, 7, 9-11, V23#3, 6, 9, 16, 18; V24#7, 8, 10, 13, 16; V25#8, 16; V27#1-7r, 8r(2 pg.), Summer Ed. V1#3-V2#3; c-V16#7, V18#2(part), 7, 11, V19#4, 19, 20, V20#15, V21#5, 9, V22#3, 7, 9, 11, V23#9, 16, V24#13, 16, V25#8, Summer Ed. V1#2 (back c-V1#2-5). **Powell** a-V10#11. V19#11, 15, V10#13, V13#6, 8 all have wraparound covers. All the above Crandall issues should be priced by condition from $4-8.00 in mint unless already priced.

TREASURE CHEST OF THE WORLD'S BEST COMICS
1945 (500 pgs., hard-c)
Superior, Toronto, Canada

Contains Blue Beetle, Captain Combat, John Wayne, Dynamic Man, Nemo, Li'l Abner; contents can vary - represents random binding of extra books; Capt. America on-c	81.00	243.00	650

TREASURE COMICS
No date (1943) (50¢, 324 pgs., cardboard-c)
Prize Publications? (no publisher listed)

1-(Rare)-Contains rebound Prize Comics #7-11 from 1942 (blank inside-c)			
	187.00	562.00	1500

TREASURE COMICS
June-July, 1945 - No. 12, Fall, 1947
Prize Publications (American Boys' Comics)

1-Paul Bunyan & Marco Polo begin; Highwayman & Carrot Topp only app.; Kiefer-a	24.00	73.00	170.
2-Arabian Knight, Gorilla King, Dr. Styx begin	13.00	39.00	90.
3,4,9,12: 9-Kiefer-a	10.00	30.00	65.
5-Marco Polo-c; Krigstein-a	17.00	49.00	115.
6,11-Krigstein-a; 11-Krigstein-a	14.00	43.00	100.
7,8-Frazetta-a (5 pgs. each). 7-Capt. Kidd Jr. app.	29.00	88.00	205.
10-Simon & Kirby-c/a	24.00	73.00	170.

NOTE: **Barry** a-9-11; c12. **Kiefer** a-3, 5, 7; c-2, 6, 7. **Roussos** a-11.

TREASURE ISLAND (See Classics Illustrated #64, Doc Savage Comics #1, King Classics, Movie Classics & Movie Comics)
No. 624, Apr, 1955 (Disney)
Dell Publishing Co.

Four Color 624-Movie, photo-c	9.00	27.00	90.

TREASURY OF COMICS
1947; No. 2, July, 1947 - No. 4, Sept, 1947; No. 5, Jan, 1948
St. John Publishing Co.

nn(#1)-Abbie an' Slats (nn on-c, #1 on inside)	14.00	43.00	100.
2-Jim Hardy Comics; featuring Windy & Paddles	10.00	30.00	70.
3-Bill Bumlin	8.35	25.00	50.
4-Abbie an' Slats	10.00	30.00	70.
5-Jim Hardy Comics #1	10.00	30.00	70.

TREASURY OF COMICS
Mar, 1948 - No. 5, 1948 (Reg. size); 1948-1950 (Over 500 pgs., $1.00)
St. John Publishing Co.

1	18.00	54.00	125.
2(#2 on-c, #1 on inside)	10.00	30.00	70.
3-5	10.00	30.00	60.
1-(1948, 500 pgs., hard-c)-Abbie & Slats, Abbott & Costello, Casper, Little Annie Rooney, Little Audrey, Jim Hardy, Ella Cinders (16 books bound together) (Rare)	107.00	321.00	800.
1(1949, 500 pgs.)-Same format as above	107.00	321.00	800.
1(1950, 500 pgs.)-Same format as above; different-c; (also see Little Audrey Yearbook) (Rare)	107.00	321.00	800.

TREASURY OF DOGS, A (See Dell Giants)

TREASURY OF HORSES, A (See Dell Giants)

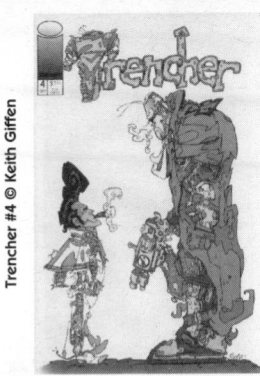
Trencher #4 © Keith Giffen

Triple X #1 © DH

The Trouble with Girls #1 © Gerard Jones

	GD25	FN65	NM94

EEHOUSE OF HORROR (Bart Simpson's...)
5 -Present ($2.95, annual)
ngo Comics

		GD25	FN65	NM94
2: 1-(1995)-Groening-c; Allred, Robinson & Smith stories. 2-(1996)-Stories by Paul Dini & Peter Bagge; infinity-c by Groening			1.20	3.00

EKKER (See Dark Horse Presents #6)
y, 1987 - No. 9?, 1988 ($1.50, B&W)
rk Horse Comics

9: Sci/Fi stories				1.50
or Special 1 (1989, $2.95, 52 pgs.)			1.50	3.00
lection ($5.95, B&W)		1.00	3.00	6.00

ENCHER (See Blackball Comics)
y, 1993 - No. 4, Oct, 1993 ($1.95, unfinished limited series)
age Comics

4: Keith Giffen-c/a/scripts. 3-Supreme-c/story			.80	2.00

BAL FORCE
g, 1996 - Present ($2.50)
stic Comics

Reads "Special Edition" on-c				2.50

B COMIC BOOK, THE
ot. 24, 1977 - Vol.2, #10, Mar. 11, 1978 (8-1/2"x11", 24 pgs., weekly)
nnipeg Tribune

Color pages (Sunday strips)-Spiderman, Asterix, Disney's Scamp, Wizard of Id, Doonesbury, Inside Woody Allen, Mary Worth, & others (similar to Spirit sections)

sections)		2.00	6.00	14.00
up		1.65	4.20	10.00

IBE (See WildC.A.T.S #4)
, 1993; No. 2, Sept, 1993 - No. 3, 1994 ($2.50/$1.95)
age Comics/Axis Comics No. 2 on

By Johnson & Stroman; gold foil & embossed on black-c

By Johnson & Stroman; gold foil & embossed on black-c		1.00		2.50
($2.50)-Ivory Edition; gold foil & embossed on white-c; available only through the creators		1.60		4.00
3: 2-1st Axis Comics issue. 3-Savage Dragon app.		.80		2.00

IGGER (See Roy Rogers'...)

IGGER TWINS
r-Apr, 1973 (20¢, one-shot)
ional Periodical Publications

Trigger Twins & Pow Wow Smith-r/All-Star Western #94,103 & Western Comics #81; Infantino-r(p)			1.20	3.00

NITY (See DC Universe: Trinity)

PLE GIANT COMICS (See Archie All-Star Specials under Archie Comics)

PLE THREAT
nter, 1945
ecial Action/Holyoke/Gerona Publ.

Duke of Darkness, King O'Leary		16.00	47.00	110.00

IPLE-X
c, 1994 - No. 7, June, 1995 ($3.95, B&W, limited series)
rk Horse Comics

7			1.60	4.00

IP WITH SANTA ON CHRISTMAS EVE, A
date (Early 1950s) (Giveaway, 16 pgs., paper-c)
ckford Dry Goods Co.

		3.60	9.00	18.00

IUMPH (Also see Justice League Task Force & Zero Hour)
ne, 1995 - No. 4, Sept, 1995 ($1.75, limited series)
Comics

	GD25	FN65	NM94
1-4: 3-Hourman, JLA app.		.70	1.75

TRIUMPHANT UNLEASHED
No. 0, Nov, 1993 - No. 1, Nov, 1993 ($2.50, limited series)
Triumphant Comics

0-Serially numbered			1.00	2.50
0-Red logo			1.00	2.50
0-White logo (no cover price; giveaway)			1.00	2.50
1-Cover is negative & reverse of #0-c			1.00	2.50

TROLL (Also see Brigade)
Dec, 1993 ($2.50, one-shot, 44 pgs.)
Image Comics (Extreme Studios)

1-1st app. Troll; Liefeld scripts; Matsuda-c/a(p)			1.00	2.50
Halloween Special (1994, $2.95)-Maxx app.				3.00
...Once A Hero (8/94, $2.50)				2.50

TROLLORDS
2/86 - No. 15, 1988; V2#1, 11/88 - V2#4, 1989 (1-15: $1.50, B&W)
Tru Studios/Comico V2#1 on

1-1st & 2nd printings				1.50
2-15: 6-Christmas issue; silver logo				1.50
V2#1 ($1.75, color, Comico)				1.80
V2#2,3 ($1.95, color)			.80	2.00
4 ($2.50, color)			1.00	2.50
Special 1 ($1.75, 2/87, color)-Jerry's Big Fun Bk.				1.80

TROLLORDS
July, 1989 - No. 6, 1990 ($2.25, B&W, limited series)
Apple Comics

1-6: 1-"The Big Batman Movie Parody"			.90	2.30

TROLL PATROL
Jan, 1993 ($1.95, 52 pgs.)
Harvey Comics

1			.80	2.00

TROLL II (Also see Brigade)
July, 1994 ($3.95, one-shot)
Image Comics (Extreme Studios)

1			1.60	4.00

TROUBLED SOULS
1990 ($9.95, trade paperback)
Fleetway

nn-Garth Ennis scripts & John McCrea painted-c/a.				10.00

TROUBLEMAN
June, 1996 - No. 3, Aug, 1996 ($2.25, limited series)
Image Comics (Motown Machineworks)

1-3				2.25

TROUBLE SHOOTERS, THE (TV)
No. 1108, Jun-Aug, 1960
Dell Publishing Co.

Four Color 1108-Keenan Wynn photo-c		6.00	18.00	60.00

TROUBLE WITH GIRLS, THE
8/87 - #14, 1988; V2#1, 2/89 - V2#10, 1990? ($1.95, B&W/color)
Malibu Comics (Eternity Comics) #7-14/Comico V2#1-4/Eternity V2#5 on

1-14 ($1.95, Eternity)-Gerard Jones scripts & Tim Hamilton-c/a in all.			1.00	2.00
V2#1-4 ($1.95, color, Comico)-Jones scripts, Hamilton-c/a.			1.00	2.00
5-10 ($1.95, B&W, Eternity)-Jones scripts, Hamilton-c/a.			1.00	2.00
Annual 1 (1988, $2.95)			1.50	3.00
Christmas Special 1 (12/91, $2.95, B&W, Eternity)-Jones scripts, Hamilton-c/a.				

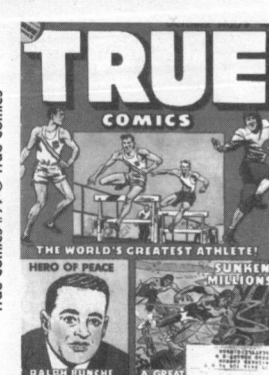

True Comics #79 © True Comics

True Confidences #3 © FAW

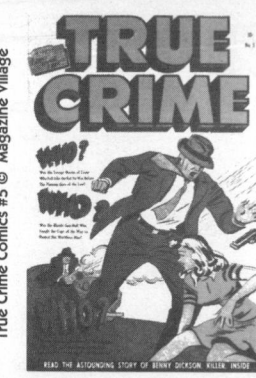

True Crime Comics #5 © Magazine Village

	GD25	FN65	NM94
			3.00
Graphic Novel 1 (7/88, $6.95, B&W)-r/#1-3	1.15	3.50	7.00
Graphic Novel 2 (1989, $7.95, B&W)-r/#4-6	1.35	4.00	8.00

TROUBLE WITH GIRLS, THE: NIGHT OF THE LIZARD
1993 - No. 4, 1993 ($2.50/$1.95, limited series)
Marvel Comics (Epic Comics/Heavy Hitters)

	GD25	FN65	NM94
1-Embossed-c; Gerard Jones scripts & Bret Blevins-c/a in all.			2.50
2-4: 2-Begin $1.95-c.			2.00

TRUE ADVENTURES (Formerly True Western)(Men's Adventures #4 on)
No. 3, May, 1950 (52 pgs.)
Marvel Comics (CCC)

	GD25	FN65	NM94
3-Powell, Sekowsky-a; Brodsky-c	13.00	39.00	90.00

TRUE ANIMAL PICTURE STORIES
Winter, 1947 - No. 2, Spring-Summer, 1947
True Comics Press

	GD25	FN65	NM94
1,2	8.35	25.00	50.00

TRUE AVIATION PICTURE STORIES (Becomes Aviation Adventures & Model Building #16 on)
1942; No. 2, Jan-Feb, 1943 - No. 15, Sept-Oct, 1946
Parents' Magazine Institute

	GD25	FN65	NM94
1-(#1 & 2 titled ...Aviation Comics Digest)(not digest size)	12.00	36.00	85.00
2	8.00	24.00	48.00
3-14: 3-10-Plane photos on-c. 11,13-Photo-c	6.70	20.00	40.00
15-(Titled "True Aviation Adventures & Model Building")	5.85	17.50	35.00

TRUE BRIDE'S EXPERIENCES (Formerly Teen-Age Brides)
(True Bride-To-Be Romances No. 17 on)
No. 8, Oct, 1954 - No. 16, Feb, 1956
True Love (Harvey Publications)

	GD25	FN65	NM94
8	6.35	19.00	38.00
9,10: 10-Last pre-code (2/55)	3.40	10.00	24.00
11-15	2.30	6.75	16.00
16-Spanking panels (3)	5.85	17.50	35.00

NOTE: **Powell** a-8-10, 12, 13.

TRUE BRIDE-TO-BE ROMANCES (Formerly True Bride's Experiences)
No. 17, Apr, 1956 - No. 30, Nov, 1958
Home Comics/True Love (Harvey)

	GD25	FN65	NM94
17-S&K-c, Powell-a	5.50	16.50	50.00
18-20,22,25-28,30	2.25	6.75	20.00
21,23,24,29-Powell-a. 29-Baker-a (1 pg.)	2.60	8.00	24.00

TRUE COMICS (Also see Outstanding American War Heroes)
April, 1941 - No. 84, Aug, 1950
True Comics/Parents' Magazine Press

	GD25	FN65	NM94
1-Marathon run story; life story Winston Churchill	29.00	86.00	200.00
2-Red Cross story; Everett-a	14.00	43.00	100.00
3-Baseball Hall of Fame story	17.00	49.00	115.00
4,5: 4-Story of American flag "Old Glory". 5-Life story of Joe Louis	11.50	34.00	80.00
6-Baseball World Series story	16.00	47.00	110.00
7-10: 7-Buffalo Bill story. 10,11-Teddy Roosevelt	9.15	27.50	55.00
11-16,18-20: 11-Thomas Edison, Douglas MacArthur stories. 13-Harry Houdini story. 14-Charlie McCarthy story. 15-Flag-c; Bob Feller story. 18-Story of America begins, ends #26. 19-Eisenhower-c/s	8.35	25.00	50.00
17-Brooklyn Dodgers story	10.00	30.00	60.00
21-30: 24-Marco Polo story	7.00	21.00	42.00
31-Red Grange "Galloping Ghost" story	5.00	15.00	30.00
32-46: 33-Origin/1st app. Steve Saunders, Special Agent. 39-FDR story. 46-George Gershwin story	4.35	13.00	26.00

	GD25	FN65	NM94
47-Atomic bomb issue (c/story, 3/46)	9.15	27.50	55
48-66: 55-(12/46)-1st app. Sad Sack by Baker (1/2 pg.). 58-Jim Jeffries (box story; Harry Houdini story. 59-Bob Hope story. 60-Speedway Speed Deme c/story. 66-Will Rogers-c/story	4.00	12.00	24
67-1st oversized issue (12/47); Steve Saunders, Special Agent begins	5.85	17.50	35
68-70,72,74-79: 68-70,72,74-78-Features True FBI advs. 69-Jack Benny sto 72-Jackie Robinson story. 74-Amos 'n' Andy story. 78-Stan Musial-c/story	4.00	12.00	24
71-Joe DiMaggio-c/story.	5.00	15.00	30
73-Walt Disney's life story	5.85	17.50	35
80-84 (Scarce)-All distr. to subscribers through mail only; paper-c. 80-Rocke trip to the moon story. 81-Red Grange story	16.00	48.00	110
(Prices vary widely on issues 80-84)			

NOTE: **Bob Kane** a-7. Palais a-80. **Powell** c/a-80. 80-84 have soft covers and combined v Tex Granger, Jack Armstrong, and Calling All Kids. #68-78 featured true FBI adventures.

TRUE COMICS AND ADVENTURE STORIES
1965 (Giant) (25¢)
Parents' Magazine Institute

	GD25	FN65	NM94
1,2: 1-Fighting Hero of Viet Nam; LBJ on-c	1.40	3.50	7

TRUE COMPLETE MYSTERY (Formerly Complete Mystery)
No. 5, Apr, 1949 - No. 8, Oct, 1949
Marvel Comics (PrPI)

	GD25	FN65	NM94
5	20.00	60.00	140
6-8: 6-8-Photo-c	16.00	47.00	110

TRUE CONFIDENCES
1949 (Fall) - No. 4, June, 1950 (All photo-c)
Fawcett Publications

	GD25	FN65	NM94
1-Has ad for Fawcett Love Adventures #1, but publ. as Love Memoirs #1 as Marvel published the title first; Swayze-a	13.00	39.00	90
2-4: 3-Swayze-a. 4-Powell-a	9.15	27.00	55

TRUE CRIME CASES (...From Official Police Files)
1944 (25¢, 100 pg. Giant)
St. John Publishing Co.

	GD25	FN65	NM94
nn-Matt Baker-c	38.00	114.00	265

TRUE CRIME COMICS (Also see Complete Book of...)
No. 2, May, 1947; No. 3, July-Aug, 1948 - No. 6, June-July, 1949;
V2#1, Aug-Sept, 1949 (52 pgs.)
Magazine Village

	GD25	FN65	NM94
2-Jack Cole-c/a; used in SOTI, pgs. 81,82 plus illo. "A sample of the injury-t eye motif" & illo. "Dragging living people to death"; used in POP, pg. 105; "Murder, Morphine and Me" classic drug propaganda story used by N.Y. Legis. Comm.	115.00	346.00	925
3-Classic Kane-c/a; drug story with hypo, opium den & with drawing addict	84.00	253.00	675
4-Jack Cole-c/a; c-taken from a story panel in #3 (r-(2) SOTI & POP stories/#2?)	76.00	228.00	610
5-Jack Cole-c, Marijuana racket story (Canadian ed. w/cover similar to #3 exists w/out drug story)	48.00	146.00	390
6-Not a reprint, original story (Canadian ed. reprints #4 w/different coloring on-c)	40.00	120.00	295
V2#1-Used in SOTI, pgs. 81,82 & illo. "Dragging living people to death"; Toth, Wood (3 pgs.), Roussos-a; Cole-r from #2	68.00	206.00	550

NOTE: V2#1 was reprinted in Canada as V2#9 (12/49); same-c & contents minus Wood-a.

TRUE FAITH
1990 ($9.95, graphic novel)
Fleetway

	GD25	FN65	NM94
nn-Garth Ennis scripts	1.65	4.20	10

TRUE GHOST STORIES (See Ripley's...)

TRUE LIFE ROMANCES (...Romance on cover)

True Love #2 © ECL

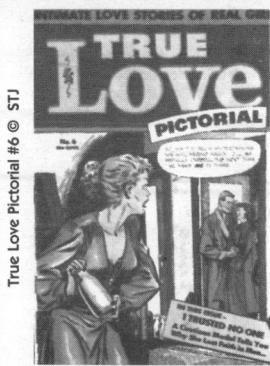
True Love Pictorial #6 © STJ

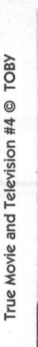
True Movie and Television #4 © TOBY

	GD25	FN65	NM94

·, 1955 - No. 3, Aug, 1956
k/Farrell Publications

	GD25	FN65	NM94
	9.15	27.00	55.00
	5.00	15.00	30.00
Disbrow-a	6.00	18.00	36.00

JE LIFE SECRETS
-April, 1951 - No. 28, Sept, 1955; No. 29, Jan, 1956
nantic Love Stories/Charlton

	GD25	FN65	NM94
Photo-c begin, end #3?	10.00	30.00	65.00
	5.35	16.00	32.00
9	4.00	12.00	24.00
29: 25-Last precode(3/55)	4.00	10.00	20.00

JE LIFE TALES (Formerly Mitzi's Romances #8?)
8, Oct, 1949 - No. 2, Jan, 1950 (52 pgs.)
vel Comics (CCC)

	GD25	FN65	NM94
#1, 10/49), 2-Both have photo-c	8.00	24.00	48.00

JE LOVE
, 1986 - No. 2, Jan, 1986 ($2.00, Baxter paper)
ose Comics

	GD25	FN65	NM94
2-Love stories reprinted from pre-code Standard Comics; Toth-a(p)			
n both; 1-Dave Stevens-a. 2-Mayo-a		1.00	2.00

JE LOVE CONFESSIONS
v, 1954 - No. 11, Jan, 1956
mier Magazines

	GD25	FN65	NM94
Marijuana story	9.15	27.00	55.00
	4.25	13.00	26.00
1	4.00	11.00	22.00

JE LOVE PICTORIAL
2 - No. 11, Aug, 1954
John Publishing Co.

	GD25	FN65	NM94
Only photo-c	12.00	36.00	85.00
Baker-c/a	8.35	25.00	50.00
5(All 25¢, 100 pgs.): 4-Signed story by Estrada. 5-(4/53)-Formerly Teen-Age			
Temptations; Kubert-a in #3; Baker-a in #3-5	26.00	77.00	180.00
7: Baker-c/a. 7-Signed story by Estrada	13.00	39.00	90.00
10,11-Baker-c/a	12.00	36.00	85.00
Baker-a	10.00	30.00	60.00

JE MOVIE AND TELEVISION (Part teenage magazine)
, 1950 - No. 3, Nov, 1950; No. 4, Mar, 1951 (52 pgs.) (1-3: 10¢)
y Press

	GD25	FN65	NM94
Elizabeth Taylor photo-c; Gene Autry, Shirley Temple, Li'l Abner app.			
	37.00	111.00	260.00
9/50)-Janet Leigh/Liz Taylor/Ava Gardner & others photo-c; Frazetta John			
Wayne illo from J.Wayne Adv. Comics #2 (4/50)	27.00	81.00	190.00
June Allyson photo-c; Montgomery Cliff, Esther Williams, Andrews Sisters			
app; Li'l Abner featured; Sadie Hawkins' Day	24.00	73.00	170.00
Jane Powell photo-c (15¢)	11.00	33.00	75.00

E: 16 pgs. in color, rest movie material in black & white.

JE SECRETS (Formerly Our Love?)
3, Mar, 1950; No. 4, Feb, 1951 - No. 40, Sept, 1956
vel (IPS)/Atlas Comics (MPI) #4 on

	GD25	FN65	NM94
52 pgs.)(IPS one-shot)	10.00	30.00	65.00
,7-10	5.35	16.00	32.00
2-Everett-a	7.00	21.00	42.00
20	4.25	13.00	28.00
23-28: 28-Last pre-code (2/55)	4.00	10.00	20.00
40: 24-Colletta-c. 34,36-Colletta-a	3.60	9.00	18.00

JE SPORT PICTURE STORIES (Formerly Sport Comics)
5, Feb, 1942 - V5#2, July-Aug, 1949

Street & Smith Publications

	GD25	FN65	NM94
V1#5-Joe DiMaggio-c/story	29.00	86.00	200.00
6-12 (1942-43): 12-Jack Dempsey story	15.00	45.00	105.00
V2#1-12 (1944-45): 7-Stan Musial-c/story; photo story of the New York Yankees			
	13.00	39.00	90.00
V3#1-12 (1946-47): 7-Joe DiMaggio, Stan Musial, Bob Feller & others back			
from the armed service story. 8-Billy Conn vs. Joe Louis-c/story			
	11.50	34.00	80.00
V4#1-12 (1948-49), V5#1,2	10.00	30.00	70.00

NOTE: Powell a-V3#10, V4#1-4, 6-8, 10-12; V5#1, 2; c-V3#11, V4#3-7, 9-12. **Ravielli** c-V5#2.

TRUE STORIES OF ROMANCE
Jan, 1950 - No. 3, May, 1950 (All photo-c)
Fawcett Publications

	GD25	FN65	NM94
1	10.00	30.00	65.00
2,3: 3-Marcus Swayze-a	7.50	22.50	45.00

TRUE STORY OF JESSE JAMES, THE (See Jesse James, Four Color 757)

TRUE SWEETHEART SECRETS
5/50; No. 2, 7/50; No. 3, 1951(nd); No. 4, 9/51 - No. 11, 1/53
Fawcett Publications (All photo-c)

	GD25	FN65	NM94
1-Photo-c; Debbie Reynolds?	10.00	30.00	70.00
2-Wood-a (11 pgs.)	14.00	43.00	100.00
3-11: 4,5-Powell-a. 8-Marcus Swayze-a. 11-Evans-a			
	7.50	22.50	45.00

TRUE TALES OF LOVE (Formerly Secret Story Romances)
No. 22, April, 1956 - No. 31, Sept, 1957
Atlas Comics (TCI)

	GD25	FN65	NM94
22	6.35	19.00	38.00
23-24,26-31-Colletta-a in most:	4.00	10.00	20.00
25-Everett-a; Colletta-a	4.15	12.50	25.00

TRUE TALES OF ROMANCE
No. 4, June, 1950
Fawcett Publications

	GD25	FN65	NM94
4-Photo-c	6.70	20.00	40.00

TRUE 3-D
Dec, 1953 - No. 2, Feb, 1954 (25¢)(Both came with 2 pair of glasses)
Harvey Publications

	GD25	FN65	NM94
1-Nostrand, Powell-a	5.00	15.00	50.00
2-Powell-a	5.00	15.00	50.00

NOTE: Many copies of #1 surfaced in 1984.

TRUE-TO-LIFE ROMANCES (Formerly Guns Against Gangsters)
#8, 11-12/49; #9, 1-2/50; #3, 4/50 - #5, 9/50; #6, 1/51 - #23, 10/54
Star Publications

	GD25	FN65	NM94
8(#1, 1949)	17.00	49.00	115.00
9(#2),4-10	12.00	36.00	85.00
3-Janet Leigh/Glenn Ford photo on-c plus true life story of each			
	13.50	41.00	95.00
11,22,23	10.00	30.00	70.00
12-14,17-21-Disbrow-a	12.00	36.00	85.00
15,16-Wood & Disbrow-a in each	14.00	43.00	100.00

NOTE: Kamen a-13. Kamen/Feldstein a-14. All have **L.B. Cole** covers.

TRUE WAR EXPERIENCES
Aug, 1952 - No. 4, Dec, 1952
Harvey Publications

	GD25	FN65	NM94
1	7.00	21.00	70.00
2-4	3.00	9.00	30.00

TRUE WAR ROMANCES (Becomes Exotic Romances #22 on)
Sept, 1952 - No. 21, June, 1955
Quality Comics Group

	GD25	FN65	NM94
1-Photo-c	10.00	30.00	65.00

TSR Worlds Annual #1 © TSR

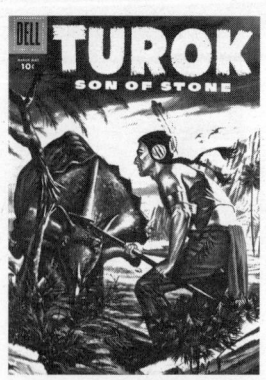

Turok, Son Of Stone #3 © WEST

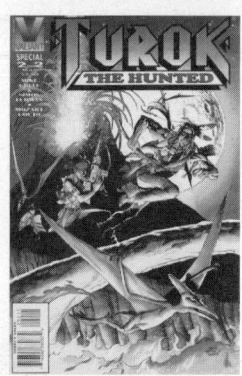

Turok the Hunted #2 © WEST

	GD25	FN65	NM94
2	5.35	16.00	32.00
3-10: 9-Whitney-a	4.00	12.00	24.00
11-21: 20-Last precode (4/55). 14-Whitney-a	4.00	10.00	20.00

TRUE WAR STORIES (See Ripley's...)

TRUE WESTERN (True Adventures #3)
Dec, 1949 - No. 2, March, 1950
Marvel Comics (MMC)

1-Photo-c; Billy The Kid story	13.50	41.00	95.00
2: Alan Ladd photo-c	18.00	54.00	125.00

TRUMP
Jan, 1957 - No. 2, Mar, 1957 (50¢, magazine)
HMH Publishing Co.

1-Harvey Kurtzman satire	21.00	62.00	145.00
2-Harvey Kurtzman satire	17.00	51.00	120.00
NOTE: *Davis, Elder, Heath, Jaffee art-#1,2; Wood a-1. Article by Mel Brooks in #2.*

TRUMPETS WEST (See Luke Short, Four Color #875)

TRUTH ABOUT CRIME (See Fox Giants)

TRUTH ABOUT MOTHER GOOSE (See Mother Goose, Four Color #862)

TRUTH BEHIND THE TRIAL OF CARDINAL MINDSZENTY, THE (See Cardinal Mindszenty)

TRUTHFUL LOVE (Formerly Youthful Love)
No. 2, July, 1950
Youthful Magazines

2-Ingrid Bergman's true life story	7.50	22.50	45.00

TRY-OUT WINNER BOOK
Mar, 1988
Marvel Comics

1-Spider-Man vs. Doc Octopus			1.25

TSR WORLD (...Annual on cover only)
1990 ($3.95, 84 pgs.)
DC Comics

1-Advanced D&D, ForgottenReals, Dragonlance & 1st app. Spelljammer		1.60	4.00

TUBBY (See Marge's...)

TUFF GHOSTS STARRING SPOOKY
July, 1962 - No. 39, Nov, 1970; No. 40, Sept, 1971 - No. 43, Oct, 1972
Harvey Publications

1-12¢ issues begin	7.00	21.00	70.00
2-5	3.60	10.80	36.00
6-10	2.85	8.50	20.00
11-20	2.00	6.00	14.00
21-30: 29-Hot Stuff/Spooky team-up story	1.50	3.75	9.00
31-39,43	1.00	2.00	5.00
40-42: 52 pg. Giants	1.00	2.60	6.00

TUFFY
No. 5, July, 1949 - No. 9, Oct, 1950
Standard Comics

5-All by Sid Hoff	4.35	13.00	26.00
6-9	3.20	8.00	16.00

TUFFY TURTLE
No date
I. W. Enterprises

1-Reprint	1.00	2.00	5.00

TUG & BUSTER
Nov, 1995 - Present ($2.95, B&W, bi-monthly)
Art & Soul Comics

1-5: Marc Hempel--c/a/scripts		1.20	3.00

TUROK, DINOSAUR HUNTER (See Magnus Robot Fighter #12 & Archer & Armstrong #2)
June, 1993 - No. 47, Aug, 1996 ($2.50)
Valiant/Acclaim Comics

1-($3.50)-Chromium & foil-c		1.40	
1-Gold foil-c variant	1.30	3.25	
0, 2-47: 4-Andar app. 5-Death of Andar. 7-9-Truman/Glanzman-a. 11-Bound trading card. 16-Chaos Effect		1.00	
Yearbook 1 (1994, $3.95, 52 pgs.)		1.60	

TUROK, SON OF STONE (See Dan Curtis, Golden Comics Digest #31 & March of Comics #378, 399, 408)
No. 596, 12/54 - No. 29, 9/62; No. 30, 12/62 - No. 91, 7/74; No. 92, 9/74 - No. 125, 1/80; No. 126, 3/81 - No. 130, 4/82
Dell Publ. Co. #1-29(9/62)/Gold Key #30(12/62)-85(7/73)/Gold Key or Whitman #86(9/73)-125(1/80)/Whitman #126(3/81) on

Four Color 596 (12/54)(#1)-1st app./origin Turok & Andar; dinosaur-c. Created by Matthew H. Murphy; written by Alberto Giolitti	67.00	201.00	670
Four Color 656 (10/55)(#2)-1st mention of Lanok	42.00	126.00	420
3(3-5/56)-5: 3-Cave men	23.00	70.00	230
6-10: 8-Dinosaur of the deep; Turok enters Lost Valley; series begins	16.00	48.00	160
11-20: 17-Prehistoric Pygmies	10.00	30.00	100
21-30: 30-33-Painted back-c pin-ups	7.00	21.00	60
31-Drug use story	7.00	21.00	60
32-40	5.50	17.00	50
41-50	4.20	13.00	30
51-60: 58-Flying Saucer c/story	4.00	12.00	30
61-70: 62-12 & 15¢-c. 63-Only line drawn-c	3.60	11.00	20
71-84: 84-Origin & 1st app. Hutec	2.30	6.70	10
85-129:93-r-c/#19 w/changes. 94-r-c/#28 w/changes. 97-r-c/#31 w/changes. 98-r-c/#58 w/o spaceship & spacemen on-c. 99-r-c/#52 w/changes. 114,11 (52 pgs.)	1.40	3.50	
130-Last issue	1.65	4.20	10
Giant 1(30031-611) (11/66)-Slick-c; r/#10-12 & 16 plus cover to #11	11.00	34.00	90
Giant 1-Same as above but with paper-c	13.00	39.00	100
NOTE: *Most painted-c; line-drawn #63 & 130. Alberto Gioletti a-24-27, 30-119, 123; painte No. 30-129. Sparling a-117, 120-130. Reprints-#36, 54, 57, 75, 112, 114(1/3), 115(1/3), 11 121, 125, 127(1/3), 128, 129(1/3), 130(1/3), Giant 1. Cover r-93, 94, 97-99, 126(all different original covers.*

TUROK THE HUNTED
Feb, 1996 - No. 2, Mar, 1996 ($2.50, limited series)
Acclaim Comics (Valiant)

1,2-Mike Grell story		1.00	

TURTLE SOUP
Sept, 1987 ($2.00, 76 pgs., B&W, one-shot)
Mirage Studios

1-Featuring Teenage Mutant Ninja Turtles		1.20	

TURTLE SOUP
Nov, 1991 - No. 4, 1992 ($2.50, limited series, coated paper)
Mirage Studios

1-4: Features the Teenage Mutant Ninja Turtles		1.00	

TV CASPER & COMPANY
Aug, 1963 - No. 46, April, 1974 (25¢ Giants)
Harvey Publications

1: 68 pg. Giants begin; Casper, Little Audrey, Baby Huey, Herman & Catnip, Buzzy the Crow begin	8.50	25.50	85
2-5	4.00	12.00	30
6-10	3.00	9.00	30
11-20	2.30	6.75	10
21-31: 31-Last 68 pg. issue	1.65	4.20	10
32-46: All 52 pgs.	1.00	2.60	6

TV Stars #1 © H-B

2099 World of Tomorrow #2 © MEG

22 Brides #3 © Joe Quesada & Jimmy Palmiotti

TW

	GD25	FN65	NM94

NOTE: Many issues contain reprints.

TV FUNDAY FUNNIES (See Famous TV...)

TV FUNNIES (See New Funnies)

TV FUNTIME (See Little Audrey)

TV LAUGHOUT (See Archie's...)

TV SCREEN CARTOONS (Formerly Real Screen)
No. 129, July-Aug, 1959 - No. 138, Jan-Feb, 1961
National Periodical Publications

129-138 (Scarce)	10.00	30.00	70.00

TV STARS (TV)
Aug, 1978 - No. 4, Feb, 1979 (Hanna-Barbera)
Marvel Comics Group

1-Great Grape Ape app.	1.20	3.00	7.00
2,4: 4-Top Cat app.		1.60	4.00
3-Toth-c/a; Dave Stevens inks	1.00	2.60	6.00

TV TEENS (Formerly Ozzie & Babs; Rock and Rollo #14 on)
#14, Feb, 1954 - V2#13, July, 1956
Charlton Comics

#14 (#1)-Ozzie & Babs	7.50	22.50	45.00
15 (#2)	4.00	12.00	24.00
2#3(6/54) - 6-Don Winslow	4.35	13.00	26.00
7-13-Mopsy. 8(7/55)	4.00	12.00	24.00

TWEETY AND SYLVESTER (1st Series)
No. 406, June, 1952 - No. 37, June-Aug, 1962
Dell Publishing Co.

Four Color 406 (#1)-1st app.?	7.00	21.00	70.00
Four Color 489,524	3.50	10.00	35.00
4 (3-5/54) - 20	2.60	7.50	18.00
1-37	1.65	4.20	10.00
(See March of Comics #421, 433, 445, 457, 469, 481)			

TWEETY AND SYLVESTER (2nd Series)(See Kite Fun Book)
Nov, 1963; No. 2, Nov, 1965 - No. 121, July, 1984
Gold Key No. 1-102/Whitman No. 103 on

1-10	3.00	7.50	15.00
11-30	1.40	3.50	7.00
31-70		1.60	4.00
71-121: 99,119-r(1/3)		.80	2.00
Mini Comic No. 1(1976, 3-1/4x6-1/2")			1.00
			1.00

12 O'CLOCK HIGH (TV)
Jan-Mar, 1965 - No. 2, Apr-June, 1965 (Photo-c)
Dell Publishing Co.

1,2	4.50	14.00	40.00

16 PAGES OF COMICS (No title) (Also see Pure Oil Comics, Salerno Carnival Comics, & Vicks Comics)
Late 1930s
Giveaway by various outlets including Sears

Contains strip reprints-Buck Rogers, Napoleon, Sky Roads, War on Crime			
	34.00	101.00	235.00

1999 A.D.
May, 1995 ($3.95, one-shot)
Marvel Comics

Acetate-c by Quesada & Palmiotti.	1.60	4.00

1999 APOCALYPSE
, 1995 ($4.95, one-shot)
Marvel Comics

Chromium wraparound-c; Ellis script	1.00	2.00	5.00

1999 GENESIS

Jan, 1996 ($4.95, one-shot)
Marvel Comics

1-Chromium wraparound-c; Ellis script	1.00	2.00	5.00

2099 UNLIMITED
Sept, 1993 - No. 10, 1996 ($3.95, 68 pgs.)
Marvel Comics

1-10: 1st app. Hulk 2099 & begins. 1-3-Spider-Man 2099 app. 9-Joe Kubert-c; Len Wein & Nancy Collins scripts	1.60	4.00

2099 WORLD OF DOOM SPECIAL
May, 1995 ($2.25, one-shot)
Marvel Comics

1-Doom's "Contract w/America"	.90	2.25

2099 WORLD OF TOMORROW
Sept, 1996 - Present ($2.50) (Replaces 2099 titles)
Marvel Comics

1-3: 1-Wraparound-c	2.50

21
Feb, 1996 - No. 3, Apr, 1996 ($2.50)
Image Comics (Top Cow Productions)

1-3: Len Wein scripts	2.50
1-Variant-c	5.00

20,000 LEAGUES UNDER THE SEA (Movie)(See King Classics, Movie Comics & Power Record Comics)
No. 614, Feb, 1955 (Disney)
Dell Publishing Co.

Four Color 614-Movie, painted-c	9.00	27.00	90.00

22 BRIDES
Mar, 1996 - Present ($2.95)
Event Comics

1-3: Fabian Nicieza scripts	3.00
2-Variant-c	5.00
3-Variant-c	4.00

TWICE TOLD TALES (See Movie Classics)

TWILIGHT
1990 - No. 3, 1991 ($4.95, 52 pgs, limited series, squarebound, mature)
DC Comics

1-3: Tommy Tomorrow app; Chaykin scripts, Garcia-Lopez-c/a.	.85	2.50	5.00

TWILIGHT AVENGER, THE
July, 1986 - No. 2, 1987 ($1.75, 28 pgs, limited series)
Elite Comics

1,2	.90	1.80

TWILIGHT MAN
June, 1989 - No. 4, Sept, 1989 ($2.75, limited series)
First Publishing

1-4	1.40	2.80

TWILIGHT ZONE, THE (TV) (See Dan Curtis)
No. 1173, 3-5/61 - No. 91, 4/79; No. 92, 5/82
Dell Publishing Co./Gold Key/Whitman No. 92

Four Color 1173 (#1)-Crandall-c/a	19.00	58.00	190.00
Four Color 1288-Crandall/Evans-c/a	11.00	34.00	115.00
01-860-207 (5-7/62-Dell, 15¢)	8.00	24.00	80.00
12-860-210 on-c; 01-860-210 on inside(8-10/62-Dell)-Evans-c/a (3 stories)			
	8.00	24.00	80.00
1(11/62-Gold Key)-Crandall/Frazetta-a (10 & 11 pgs.); Evans-a			
	9.50	28.50	95.00
2	6.50	19.50	65.00

Twilight Zone #11 © Now Comics

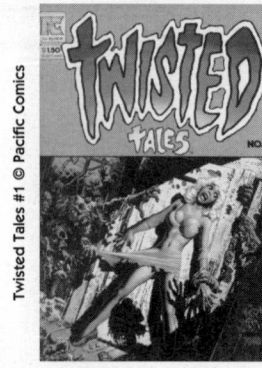

Twisted Tales #1 © Pacific Comics

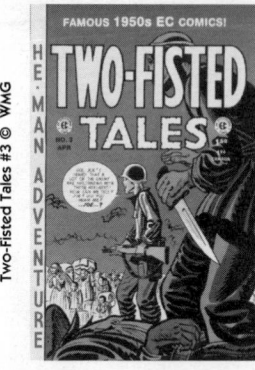

Two-Fisted Tales #3 © WMG

	GD25	FN65	NM94

	GD25	FN65	NM94
3-11: 3(11 pgs.),4(10 pgs.),9-Toth-a	4.50	13.50	45.00
12-15: 12-Williamson-a. 13,15-Crandall/Torres-a			
	3.20	9.60	32.00
16-20	2.85	8.50	20.00
21-27: 21-Crandall-a(r). 25-Evans/Crandall-a(r); Toth-r/#4. 26-Flying Saucer-c/ story; Crandall, Evans-a(r). 27-Evans-r(2)	2.15	6.50	15.00
28-32: 32-Evans-a(r)	1.20	3.00	7.00
33-51: 43-Celardo-a. 51-Williamson-a	1.00	2.00	5.00
52-70		1.20	3.00
71-91: 71-Reprint. 83,84-(52 pgs.). 84-Frank Miller's 1st comic book work.			
	.60	1.60	
92-Last issue; r/#1.		1.60	4.00
Mini Comic #1(1976, 3-1/4x6-1/2")	.60	1.60	

NOTE: **Bolle** a-13(w/**McWilliams**), 50, 55, 57, 59, 77, 78, 80, 83, 84. **McWilliams** a-59, 78, 80, 82, 84. **Miller** a-84, 85. **Orlando** a-15, 19, 20, 22, 23. **Sekowsky** a-50, 54, 55, 83r. **Weiss** a-39, 79r(#39). (See Mystery Comics Digest 3, 6, 9, 12, 15, 18, 21, 24). Reprints-26(1/3), 71, 73, 79, 83, 84, 86, 92. Painted c-91.

TWILIGHT ZONE, THE (TV)
Nov, 1990 ($2.95)
Oct, 1991; V2#1, Nov, 1991 - No. 14? 1992 ($1.95)
V3#1, 1993 - No. 4, 1993 ($2.50)
Now Comics

	GD25	FN65	NM94
1-(11/90, $2.95, 52 pgs.)-Direct sale edition; Neal Adams-a, Sienkiewicz-c; Harlan Ellison scripts	1.00	2.00	5.00
1-(11/90, $1.75)-Newsstand ed. w/N. Adams-c		.80	2.00
1-Prestige Format (10/91, $4.95)-Reprints above with extra Harlan Ellison short story	1.00	2.00	5.00
1-Collector's Edition (10/91, $2.50)-None-code approved and polybagged; reprints 11/90 issue; gold logo	1.00	2.00	5.00
1-Reprint ($2.50)-r/direct sale 11/90 version		1.00	2.50
1-Reprint ($2.50)-r/newsstand 11/90 version		1.00	2.50
V2#1-Direct sale & newsstand ed. w/different-c		.80	2.00
V2#2-8,10-14		.80	2.00
V2#9-($2.95)-3-D Special; polybagged w/glasses & hologram on-c	1.20		3.00
V2#9-($4.95)-Prestige Edition; contains 2 extra stories & a different hologram on-c; polybagged w/glasses	1.00	2.00	5.00
V3#1-4		1.00	2.50
Anniversary Special 1 (1992, $2.50)		1.00	2.50
Annual 1 (4/93, $2.50)-No ads		1.00	2.50

TWINKLE COMICS
May, 1945
Spotlight Publishers

	GD25	FN65	NM94
1	19.00	56.00	130.00

TWIST, THE
July-Sept, 1962
Dell Publishing Co.

	GD25	FN65	NM94
01-864-209-Painted-c	4.30	13.00	30.00

TWISTED TALES (See Eclipse Graphic Album Series #15)
11/82 - No. 8, 5/84; No. 9, 11/84; No. 10, 12/84 (Baxter paper)
Pacific Comics/Independent Comics Group (Eclipse) #9,10

	GD25	FN65	NM94
1-B. Jones/Corben-c; nudity/violence in all	1.40		3.50
2-10	.80		2.00

NOTE: **Alcala** a-1. **Bolton** painted c-4, 6, 7; a-7. **Conrad** a-1, 3, 5; c-1i, 3, 5. **Guice** a-8. **Morrow** a-10. **Ploog** a-3. **Wildey** a-3. **Wrightson** a(Painted)-10; c-2.

TWISTED TALES
Nov, 1982 - No. 10, Dec, 1984
Pacific Comics

	GD25	FN65	NM94
1-10			1.50

TWO BIT THE WACKY WOODPECKER (See Wacky...)
1951 - No. 3, May, 1953
Toby Press

	GD25	FN65	NM94
1	6.70	20.00	40
2,3	4.00	11.00	22

TWO FACES OF COMMUNISM (Also see Double Talk)
1961 (Giveaway, paper-c, 36 pgs.)
Christian Anti-Communism Crusade, Houston, Texas

	GD25	FN65	NM94
nn	12.00	36.00	85

TWO-FISTED TALES (Formerly Haunt of Fear #15-17)
No. 18, Nov-Dec, 1950 - No. 41, Feb-Mar, 1955
E. C. Comics

	GD25	FN65	NM94
18(#1)-Kurtzman-c	79.00	235.00	600
19-Kurtzman-c	57.00	171.00	450
20-Kurtzman-c	38.00	114.00	265
21,22-Kurtzman-c	29.00	86.00	200
23-25-Kurtzman-c	22.00	66.00	155
26-35: 33- "Atom Bomb" by Wood	16.00	47.00	110
36-41	11.50	34.00	80
Two-Fisted Annual (1952, 25¢, 132 pgs.)	70.00	210.00	525
Two-Fisted Annual (1953, 25¢, 132 pgs.)	52.00	156.00	385

NOTE: **Berg** a-29. **Colan** a-39p. **Craig** a-18, 19, 32. **Crandall** a-35, 36. **Davis** a-20-36, 40; c-34, 35, 41, Annual 2. **Evans** a-34, 40, 41; c-40. **Feldstein** a-18. **Krigstein** a-41. **Kubert** a-33. **Kurtzman** a-18-25; c-18-29, 31, Annual 1. **Severin** a-26, 28, 29, 31, 34-41 (No. 37-39 all-**Severin** issues); c-36-39. **Severin/Elder** a-19-29, 31, 33, 36. **Wood** a-18-28, 30-35, 41; 33. Special issues: #26 (Chan,Jin Reservoir), 31 (Civil War), 35 (Civil War). Canadian reprint known; see Table of Contents. #25-Davis biog. #27-Wood biog. #28-Kurtzman biog.

TWO-FISTED TALES
Oct, 1992 - Present ($1.50/$2.00/$2.50)
Russ Cochran/Gemstone Publishing

	GD25	FN65	NM94
1-15: 1-4r/Two-Fisted Tales #18-21 w/original-c			2
16-19			2

TWO-GUN KID (Also see All Western Winners, Best Western, Black Rider, Blaze Carson, Kid Colt, Western Winners, Wild West, & Wild Western)
3/48(No mo.) - No. 10, 11/49; No. 11, 12/53 - No. 59, 4/61; No. 60, 11/62 - No. 92, 3/68; No. 93, 7/70 - No. 136, 4/77
Marvel/Atlas (MCI No. 1-10/HPC No. 11-59/Marvel No. 60 on)

	GD25	FN65	NM94
1-Two-Gun Kid & his horse Cyclone begin; The Sheriff begins	81.00	243.00	650
2	38.00	114.00	265
3,4: 3-Annie Oakley app.	29.00	86.00	200
5-Pre-Black Rider app. (Wint. 48/49); spanking panel; Anti-Wertham editorial (1st?)	36.00	107.00	250
6-10(11/49): 8-Blaze Carson app. 9-Black Rider app.	23.00	69.00	160
11(12/53)-Black Rider app.; explains how Kid Colt became an outlaw	18.00	54.00	125
12-Black Rider app.	18.00	54.00	125
13-20: 13-1st to have Atlas globe on-c. 14-Opium story	13.00	39.00	90
21-24,26-29	11.50	34.00	80
25,30: 25-Williamson-a (5 pgs.). 30-Williamson/Torres-a (4 pgs.)	12.00	36.00	85
31-33,35,37-40	9.15	27.00	55
34-Crandall-a	10.00	30.00	60
36,41,42,48-Origin in all	10.00	30.00	60
43,44,47	7.00	21.00	42
45,46-Davis-a	8.00	24.00	48
49,50,52,55,57-Severin-a(2) in each	6.35	19.00	38
51-Williamson-a (5 pgs.)	8.00	24.00	48
53,54-Severin-a(3) in each	7.00	21.00	42
56,59: 59-Last 10¢ issue (4/61)	2.85	8.50	20
58,60-New origin. 58-Kirby/Ayers-c/a "The Monster of Hidden Valley" cover/ story (Kirby monster-c)	3.25	9.50	22
61-80: 64-Intro. Boom-Boom	1.65	4.20	10
81-92: 92-Last new story; last 12¢ issue		1.60	4

2000 AD Showcase #27/28 © Fleetway

Typhoid #1 © MEG

Ultra Cybernetic Dolphin Droids #1 © Polestar

	GD25	FN65	NM94

-100,102-136 .... 1.50
-Origin retold/#58 .... 1.20 .... 3.00
E: Ayers a-26, 27. Davis c-45-47. Drucker a-23. Everett a-82, 91. Fuje a-13. Heath a-
, 4(3), 5(2), 7; c-13, 21, 23, 53. Keller a-16, 19, 28. Kirby a-54, 55, 57-62, 75-77, 90, 95,
119, 120, 129; c-10, 52, 54-65, 67-72, 74-76, 116. Maneely a-20; c-11, 12, 16, 19, 20, 25-
35, 49. Powell a-38, 102, 104. Severin a-9, 29, 51, 55, 57, 99r(3); c-9, 51, 99. Shores c-1-8,
Tuska a-11, 12. Whitney a-87, 89-91, 98-113, 124, 129; c-87, 89, 91, 113. Wildey a-21.
iamson a-110r. Kid Colt in #13, 14, 16-21.

O GUN KID:SUNSET RIDERS
", 1995 - No. 2, Dec, 1995 ($6.95, squarebound, limited series)
rvel Comics
2: Fabian Nicieza scripts in all. 1-painted-c. .... 1.20 .... 3.00 .... 7.00

O GUN WESTERN (1st Series) (Formerly Casey Crime Photographer
4? or My Love #1-4?)
5, Nov, 1950 - No. 14, June, 1952
rvel/Atlas Comics (MPC)
The Apache Kid (Intro & origin) & his horse Nightwind begin by Buscema .... 21.00 .... 64.00 .... 150.00
10: 8-Kid Colt, The Texas Kid & his horse Thunder begin? .... 14.00 .... 43.00 .... 100.00
-14: 13-Black Rider app. .... 10.00 .... 30.00 .... 70.00
E: Maneely a-6, 7, 9; c-6, 11-13. Morrow a-9. Romita a-8. Wildey a-8.

UN WESTERN (2nd Series) (Formerly Billy Buckskin #1-3; Two-Gun
stern #5 on)
4, May, 1956
s Comics (MgPC)
Colan, Ditko, Severin, Sinnott-a; Maneely-c .... 13.00 .... 39.00 .... 90.00

O-GUN WESTERN (Formerly 2-Gun Western)
5, July, 1956 - No. 12, Sept, 1957
s Comics (MgPC)
Return of the Gun-Hawk-c/story; Black Rider app. 11.00 .... 33.00 .... 75.00
7 .... 8.35 .... 25.00 .... 50.00
0,12-Crandall-a .... 10.00 .... 30.00 .... 60.00
1-Williamson-a in both (5 pgs. each) .... 10.00 .... 30.00 .... 60.00
E: Ayers a-9. Colan a-5. Everett c-12. Forgione a-5, 6. Kirby a-12. Maneely a-6, 8, 12; c-
8, 11. Morrow a-9, 10. Powell a-7, 11. Severin c-10. Sinnott a-5. Wildey a-5.

O MOUSEKETEERS, THE (See 4-Color #475, 603, 642 under M.G.M.'s...;
O ON A GUILLOTINE (See Movie Classics)

O A.D. MONTHLY/PRESENTS (Showcase #25 on)
5 - #6, 9/85; 4/86 - #54, 1991 ($1.25-$1.50, Mando paper)
gle Comics/Quality Comics No. 5 on
6 ($1.25): 1-4 r/British series featuring Judge Dredd; Alan Moore
scripts begin .... .80 .... 2.00
25 ($1.25)-Reprints from British 2000 AD .... .80 .... 2.00
27/28, 29/30, 31-44: 27/28, 29/30,31-Guice-c .... .80 .... 2.00
54: 45-Begin $1.75-c .... .80 .... 2.00

1, A SPACE ODYSSEY (Movie)
, 1976 - No. 10, Sept, 1977 (30¢)
rvel Comics Group
Adaptation of film; Kirby-c/a in all .... 1.20 .... 3.00
10: 8-Original/1st app. Machine Man (called Mr. Machine) .... .80 .... 2.00
ward Johnson giveaway (1968, 8pp); 6 pg. movie adaptation, 2 pg.
games, puzzles; McWilliams-a .... .80 .... 2.00

1 NIGHTS
0 - No. 10, 1991 ($3.75, B&W, limited series, mature readers, 84 pgs.)
Premiere Comics
5: Japanese sci-fi. 1-Wraparound-c .... 1.90 .... 3.80
10: 6-Begin $4.25-c .... 2.15 .... 4.30
0 (Movie)

	GD25	FN65	NM94

Apr, 1985 - No. 2, May, 1985
Marvel Comics Group
1,2-r/Marvel Super Special movie adaptation. 1.00

TYPHOID (Also see Daredevil)
Nov, 1995 - No. 4, Feb, 1996 ($3.95, squarebound, limited series)
Marvel Comics
1-4: Van Fleet-c/a .... 1.60 .... 4.00

UFO & ALIEN COMIX
Jan, 1978 (one-shot)
Warren Publishing Co.
nn-Toth, Severin-a(r) .... 1.00 .... 2.50

UFO & OUTER SPACE (Formerly UFO Flying Saucers)
No. 14, June, 1978 - No. 25, Feb, 1980 (All painted covers)
Gold Key
14-Reprints UFO Flying Saucers #3 .... 1.00 .... 2.60 .... 6.00
15,16-Reprints .... 1.60 .... 4.00
17-20-New material .... 1.00 .... 2.00 .... 5.00
21-25: 23-McWilliams-a. 24-(3 pg.-r). 25-Reprints UFO Flying Saucers #2
w/cover .... 1.60 .... 4.00

UFO ENCOUNTERS
May, 1978 ($1.95, 228 pgs.)
Western Publishing Co.
11192-Reprints UFO Flying Saucers .... 1.00 .... 2.60 .... 6.00
11404-Vol.1 (128 pgs.)-See UFO Mysteries for Vol.2 .... 1.60 .... 4.00

UFO FLYING SAUCERS (UFO & Outer Space #14 on)
Oct, 1968 - No. 13, Jan, 1977 (No. 2 on, 36 pgs.)
Gold Key
1(30035-810) (68 pgs.) .... 3.60 .... 11.00 .... 25.00
2(11/70), 3(11/72), 4(11/74) .... 1.70 .... 5.00 .... 12.00
5(2/75)-13: Bolle-a #4 on .... 1.50 .... 3.75 .... 9.00

UFO MYSTERIES
1978 ($1.00, reprints, 96 pgs.)
Western Publishing Co.
11400($1.00, 96 pgs.) .... 1.60 .... 4.00
11404(Vol.2)-Cont'd from UFO Encounters, pgs. 129-224 .... 1.60 .... 4.00

ULTRACYBERNETIC DOLPHINDROIDS, THE
Dec, 1993 ($2.50, unfinished limited series)
Polestar Comics
1 .... 1.00 .... 2.50

ULTRAFORCE (1st Series) (Also see Avengers/Ultraforce #1)
Aug, 1994 - No. 10, Aug, 1995 ($1.95/$2.50)
Malibu Comics (Ultraverse)
0 (9/94, $2.50)-Perez-c/a. .... 1.00 .... 2.50
1-($2.50, 44 pgs.)-Bound-in trading card; team consisting of Prime, Prototype,
Hardcase, Pixx, Ghoul, Contrary & Topaz; Gerard Jones scripts begin, ends
#6; Perez-c/a begins. .... 1.00 .... 2.50
1-Ultra 5000 Limited Silver Foil Edition .... 1.30 .... 3.25 .... 8.00
1-Holographic-c, no price .... 1.65 .... 4.20 .... 10.00
2-5: Perez-c/a in all. 2 (10/94, $1.95)-Prime quits, Strangers cameo. 3-Origin of
Topaz; Prime rejoins. 5-Pixx dies. .... .80 .... 2.00
2 ($2.50)-Flourescent logo; limited edition stamp on-c .... 1.20 .... 3.00
6-10: 6-Begin $2.50-c, Perez-c/a. 7-Ghoul story, Steve Erwin-a. 8-Marvel's
Black Knight enters the Ultraverse (last seen in Avengers #375); Perez-c/a.
9,10-Black Knight app.; Perez-c. 10-Leads into Ultraforce/Avengers Prelude.
.... 1.00 .... 2.50
Malibu "Ashcan ": Ultraforce (6/94) 0.75
.../Avengers Prelude 1 (8/95, $2.50)-Perez-c. .... 1.00 .... 2.50
.../Avengers 1 (8/95, $3.95)-Warren Ellis script; Perez-c/a; foil-c.

Ultraforce Infinity © Malibu

Uncanny Origins #3 © MEG

Uncanny X-Men #159 © MEG

		1.60	4.00

ULTRAFORCE (2nd Series)(Also see Black September)
Infinity, Sept, 1995 - V2#15, Dec, 1996 ($1.50)
Malibu Comics (Ultraverse)

Infinity, V2#1-15: Infinity-Team consists of Marvel's Black Knight, Ghoul, Topaz, Prime & redesigned Prototype; Warren Ellis scripts begin, ends #3; variant-c exists. 1-1st app.Cromwell, Lament & Wreckage. 2-Contains free encore presentation of Ultraforce #1; flip book "Phoenix Resurrection" Pt. 7. 7-Darick Robertson, Jeff Johnson & others-a. 8,9-Intro. Future Ultraforce (Prime, Hellblade, Angel of Destruction, Painkiller & Whipslash); Gary Erskine-c/a. 9-Foxfire app. 10-Len Wein scripts & Deodato Studios-c/a begin. 10-Lament back-up story. 11-Ghoul back-up story by Pander Bros.
12-Ultraforce vs. Maxis (cont'd in Ultraforce Unlimited #2); Exiles & Iron Clad app. 13-Prime leaves; Hardcase returns 1.50

Infinity (2000 signed)	1.65	4.20	10.00

...Spider-Man ($3.95)-Marv Wolfman script; Green Goblin app; 2 covers exist. 4.00

ULTRA KLUTZ
1981; 6/86 - #27, 1/89, #28, 4/90 - #31, 1990? ($1.50/$1.75/$2.00, B&W)
Onward Comics

1 (1981)-Re-released after 2nd #1		1.50
1-22: 1-(6/86)		1.50
23-30: 23-$2.00-c begins. 27-Photo back-c	1.00	2.00
31-($2.95, 52 pgs.)	1.50	3.00

ULTRAMAN
Mar, 1994 - No. 4, 1995? ($1.75/$1.95)
Nemesis Comics

1-($2.25)-Collector's edition; foil-c; special 3/4 wraparound-c	.90	2.25
1-($1.75)-Newsstand edition	.70	1.75
2-4: 3-$1.95-c begins	.80	2.00

ULTRAVERSE DOUBLE FEATURE
Jan, 1995 ($3.95, one-shot, 68 pgs.)
Malibu Comics (Ultraverse)

1-Flip-c featuring Prime & Solitaire.	1.60	4.00

ULTRAVERSE ORIGINS
Jan, 1994 (99¢, one-shot)
Malibu Comics (Ultraverse)

1-Gatefold-c; 2 pg. origins all characters		1.00
1-Newsstand edition; different-c, no gatefold		1.00

ULTRAVERSE PREMIERE
1994 (one-shot)
Malibu Comics (Ultraverse)

0-Ordered thru mail w/coupons	-	2.10	5.00

ULTRAVERSE UNLIMITED
June, 1996; No. 2, Sept, 1996 ($2.50)
Malibu Comics (Ultraverse)

1,2: 1-Adam Warlock returns to the Marvel Universe; Rune-c/app. 2-Black Knight, Reaper & Sierra Blaze return to the Marvel Universe 2.50

ULTRAVERSE YEAR ONE
1994 ($4.95, one-shot)
Malibu Comics (Ultraverse)

nn-In-depth synopsis of the first year's titles & stories.	1.00	2.00	5.00

ULTRAVERSE YEAR TWO
Aug, 1995 ($4.95, one-shot)
Malibu Comics (Ultraverse)

nn-In-depth synopsis of second year's titles & stories	1.00	2.00	5

ULTRAVERSE YEAR ZERO: THE DEATH OF THE SQUAD
Apr, 1995 - No. 4, July, 1995 ($2.95, limited series)
Malibu Comics (Ultraverse)

1-4: 3-Codename: Firearm back-up story.		1.20	3

UNBIRTHDAY PARTY WITH ALICE IN WONDERLAND (See Alice In Wonderla
Four Color #341)

UNCANNY ORIGINS
Sept, 1996 - Present (99¢)
Marvel Comics

1-6: 1-Cyclops. 2-Quicksilver. 3-Archangel. 4-Firelord	1

UNCANNY TALES
June, 1952 - No. 56, Sept, 1957
Atlas Comics (PrPI/PPI)

1-Heath-a; horror/weird stories begin	68.00	206.00	550
2	40.00	120.00	290
3-5	34.00	103.00	240
6-Wolvertonish-a by Matt Fox	34.00	103.00	240
7-10: 8-Atom bomb story; Tothish-a (by Sekowsky?). 9-Crandall-a	29.00	88.00	205
11-20: 17-Atom bomb panels; anti-communist story; Hitler story. 19-Krenkel-a	23.00	69.00	160
21-27: 25-Nostrand-a?	19.00	56.00	130
28-Last precode issue (1/55); Kubert-a; #1-28 contain 2-3 sci/fi stories each	20.00	60.00	140
29-41,43-49,51,52: 52-Oldest? Iron Man prototype (2/57)	12.00	36.00	85
42,54,56-Krigstein-a	13.50	41.00	95
50,53,55-Torres-a	12.00	36.00	85

NOTE: **Andru** a-15, 27. **Ayers** a-22. **Bailey** a-51. **Briefer** a-19, 20. **Brodsky** c-1, 3, 4, 6, 8, 16, 19. **Brodsky/Everett** c-9. **Cameron** a-47. **Colan** a-11, 16, 17, 52. **Drucker** a-37, 42, 45. **Everett** a-2, 9, 12, 32, 36, 39, 48; c-7, 11, 17, 39, 41, 50, 52, 53. **Fass** a-9, 10, 15, 24. Forte 18, 27, 34, 52, 53. **Heath** a-13, 14; c-5, 10, 18. **Keller** a-3. **Lawrence** a-14, 17, 19, 23, 27, 2 35. **Maneely** a-4, 8, 10, 16, 29, 35; c-2, 22, 26, 33, 38. **Moldoff** a-23. **Morisi** a-48, 52. **Morro** a-46, 51. **Orlando** a-49, 50, 53. **Powell** a-12, 18, 34, 36, 38, 43, 50, 56. **Robinson** a-3, 13. **Reinman** a-12. **Romita** a-10. **Roussos** a-8. **Sale** a-47, 53; c-20. **Sekowsky** a-25. **Sinnott** a 52. **Torres** a-53. **Tothish**-a by **Andru**-27. **Wildey** a-22, 48.

UNCANNY TALES
Dec, 1973 - No. 12, Oct, 1975
Marvel Comics Group

1-Crandall-r/Uncanny Tales #9('50s)		1.60	4
2-12		1.00	2

NOTE: **Ditko** reprints-#4, 6-8, 10-12.

UNCANNY X-MEN, THE (Formerly The X-Men))
No. 142, Feb, 1981 - Present
Marvel Comics Group

142-Rachel app.; deaths of alt. future Wolverine, Storm & Colossus	3.25	9.50	22
143-Last Byrne issue	1.50	3.80	9
144-150: 144-Man-Thing app. 145-Old X-Men app. 148-Spider-Woman, Dazzler app. 150-Double size	1.30	3.00	7
151-157,159-161,163,164: 161-Origin Magneto. 163-Origin Binary. 164-1st a Binary as Carol Danvers	1.00	2.00	5
158-1st app. Rogue in X-Men (6/82, see Avengers Annual #10)	2.15	6.50	15
162-Wolverine solo story	1.65	4.20	10
165-Paul Smith-c/a begins, ends #175	1.50	3.75	9
166-Double size; Paul Smith-a	1.20	3.00	7
167-170: 167-New Mutants app. (3/83); same date as New Mutants #1; 1st meeting w/X-Men; ties into N.M. #3,4; Starjammers app.; contains skin "Tattooz" decals. 168-1st app. Madelyne Pryor (last pg. cameo) in X-Men (see Avengers Annual #10)	.90	2.30	5

Uncanny X-Men #200 © MEG

Uncanny X-Men #299 © MEG

Uncanny X-Men #337 © MEG

	GD25	FN65	NM94
171-Rogue joins X-Men; Simonson-c/a	2.15	6.50	15.00
172-174: 172,173-Two part Wolverine solo story. 173-Two cover variations, blue & black. 174-Phoenix cameo	1.00	2.00	5.00
175-(52 pgs.)-Anniversary issue; Phoenix returns	1.65	4.20	10.00
176-185: 181-Sunfire app. 182-Rogue solo story. 184-1st app. Forge (8/84)	1.00	2.00	5.00
186-Double-size; Barry Smith/Austin-a	1.00	2.00	5.00
187-192,194-199: 190,191-Spider-Man & Avengers x-over. 195-Power Pack x-over		1.60	4.00
193-Double size; 100th app. New X-Men; 1st app. Warpath in costume (see New Mutants #16)	1.30	3.25	8.00
200-(12/85, $1.25, 52 pgs.)	1.65	4.20	10.00
201-(1/86)-1st app. Cable? (as baby Nathan; see X-Factor #1); 1st Whilce Portacio-c/a(i) on X-Men (guest artist)	3.60	10.70	25.00
202-204,206-209: 204-Nightcrawler solo story; 2nd Portacio-a(i) on X-Men. 207-Wolverine/Phoenix story	1.00	2.50	6.00
205-Wolverine solo story by Barry Smith	2.40	7.30	17.00
210,211-Mutant Massacre begins	2.90	9.00	20.00
212,213-Wolverine vs. Sabretooth (Mutant Mass.)	5.00	15.00	35.00
214-221,223,224: 219-Havok joins (7/87); brief app. Sabretooth	1.00	2.00	5.00
222-Wolverine battles Sabretooth-c/story	2.40	7.30	17.00
225-227: Fall Of The Mutants. 226-Double size	1.50	3.80	9.00
228-239,241: 229-$1.00 begins	1.00	2.00	5.00
240-Sabretooth app.	1.00	2.50	6.00
242-Double size, X-Factor app., Inferno tie-in	1.00	2.00	5.00
243,245-247: 245-Rob Liefeld-a(p)		1.60	4.00
244-1st app. Jubilee	3.60	11.00	25.00
248-1st Jim Lee art on X-Men (1989)	3.60	11.00	25.00
248-2nd printing (1992, $1.25)			1.25
249-252: 252-Lee-c		1.00	2.50
253-255: 253-All new X-Men begin. 254-Lee-c		1.80	4.50
256,257-Jim Lee-c/a begins	1.70	5.10	12.00
258-Wolverine solo story; Lee-c/a	2.00	6.00	14.00
259-Silvestri-c/a; no Lee-a	1.00	2.50	6.00
260-265-No Lee-a. 260,261,264-Lee-c		1.00	2.50
266-1st full app. Gambit (see Ann. #14)-No Lee-a	5.70	17.00	40.00
267-Jim Lee-c/a resumes; 2nd full Gambit app.	2.15	6.50	15.00
268-Capt. America, Black Widow & Wolverine team-up; Lee-a	3.30	9.90	23.00
269-Lee-a	1.00	2.90	7.00
270-X-Tinction Agenda begins	1.70	5.10	12.00
270-Gold 2nd printing		1.60	4.00
271,272-X-Tinction Agenda	1.30	3.00	8.00
273-New Mutants (Cable) & X-Factor x-over; Golden, Byrne & Lee part pencils	1.20	2.90	7.00
274	1.00	2.50	6.00
275-($1.50, 52 pgs.)-Tri-fold-c by Jim Lee (p); Prof. X	1.20	2.90	7.00
275-Gold 2nd printing		1.00	2.50
276-280-Last Lee-c/a. 280-X-Factor x-over		.80	2.00
281-(10/91)-1st new team begins (Storm, Archangel, Colossus, Iceman & Marvel Girl); Whilce Portacio-c/a begins; Byrne scripts begin; wraparound-c (white logo)	1.10	2.70	6.50
281-2nd printing with red metallic ink logo w/o UPC box ($1.00-c); does not say 2nd printing inside			1.25
282-1st app. Bishop (cover & 1 pg. cameo)	2.15	6.50	15.00
282-Gold ink 2nd printing			1.00
283-1st full app. Bishop (12/91)	2.40	7.20	15.00
284-293,297-299: 284-Last $1.00-c. 286,287-Lee plots. 287-Bishop joins team. 288-Lee/Portacio plots. 294-Brandon Peterson-a(p) begins (#292 is 1st Peterson-c)			1.25
294-296 ($1.50)-Polybagged w/trading card in each; X-Cutioner's Song x-overs; all have Peterson/Austin-c/a		.80	2.00
300-($3.95, 68 pgs.)-Holo-grafx foil-c; Magneto app.	1.00	2.00	5.00

	GD25	FN65	NM94
301-303,305-309,311			1.25
304-($3.95, 68 pgs.)-Wraparound-c with Magneto hologram on-c; 30th anniversary issue; Jae Lee-a (4 pgs.)	1.00	2.00	5.00
310-($1.95)-Bound-in trading card sheet		.80	2.00
312-321: 312-$1.50-c begins; bound-in card sheet			1.50
316,317-($2.95)-Foil enhanced editions		1.20	3.00
318-322-($1.95)-Deluxe editions		.80	2.00
323,324,326-349: 323-Return from Age of Apocalypse. 328-Sabretooth-c. 329,330-Dr. Strange app. 331-White Queen-c/app. 334-Juggernaut app.; w/Onslaught Update. 335-Onslaught, Avengers, Apocalypse, & X-Man app. 336-Onslaught. 338-Archangel's wings return to normal. 339-Havok vs. Cyclops; Spider-Man app.		.80	2.00
325-($3.95)-Anniverary issue; gatefold-c		1.60	4.00
Special 1(12/70)-Kirby-c/a; origin The Stranger	8.50	26.00	60.00
Special 2(11/71)	7.00	21.50	50.00
Annual 3(1979, 52 pgs.)-New story; Miller/Austin-c; Wolverine still in old yellow costume	2.40	7.30	17.00
Annual 4(1980, 52 pgs.)-Dr. Strange guest stars	1.30	3.00	7.50
Annual 5(1981, 52 pgs.)	1.00	2.50	6.00
Annual 6(1982, 52 pgs.)-Dracula app.	1.00	2.00	5.00
Annual 7,8: 7-(1983, 52 pgs.). 8-(1984, 52 pgs.)	1.00	2.00	5.00
Annual 9(1985)-New Mutants x-over cont'd from New Mutants Special Ed. #1; Art Adams-a	1.85	5.50	13.00
Annual 10(1986)-Art Adams-a	1.65	4.70	11.00
Annual 11(1987)		1.20	3.00
Annual 12(1988, $1.75)-Evolutionary War; A.Adams-a(p)		1.60	4.00
Annual 13(1989, $2.00)-Atlantis Attacks		1.20	3.00
Annual 14(1990, $2.00, 68 pgs.)-1st app. Gambit (minor app., 5 pgs.); Fantastic Four, New Mutants (Cable) & X-Factor x-over; Arthur Adams-c/a(p)	1.70	5.00	12.00
Annual 15 (1991, $2.00, 68 pgs.)-4 pg. origin; New Mutants x-over; 4 pg. Wolverine solo back-up story; 4th app. X-Force cont'd from New Warriors Annual #1		1.60	4.00
Annual 16 (1992, $2.25, 68 pgs.)-Jae Lee-c/a(p)(2)		.90	2.25
Annual 17 (1993, $2.95, 68 pgs.)-Bagged w/card		1.20	3.00
Annual 18 (1994, $2.95, 68 pgs.)		1.20	3.00
…'95-(11/95, $3.95)-Wraparound-c			4.00
…'96-(1996, $2.95)-Wraparound-c			3.00
…: THE DARK PHOENIX SAGA (1990, $12.95, trade paperback)	1.90	5.60	13.00
…IN THE DAYS OF FUTURE PAST (1989, $3.95, trade paperback, 52 pgs.)			4.00

NOTE: Art Adams a-Annual 9, 10, 12p, 14p; c-218p. Neal Adams a-56-63p, 65p; c-56-63. Adkins a-34, 35p; c-31, 34, 35. Austin a-108i, 109i, 111-117i, 119-143i, 186i, 204i, 228i, 294-297i, Annual 3i, 7i, 9i, 13; c-109-111i, 114-122i, 123, 124-141i, 142, 143, 196i, 204i, 228i, 294-297i, Annual 3i. J. Buscema c-42, 43, 45. Buscema/Tuska a-45. Byrne a(p)-108, 109, 111-143, 273; c(p)-113-116, 127, 129, 131-141. Capullo c-14. Ditko r-86, 89-91, 93. Everett c-73. Golden a-273, Annual 7p. Guice a-216p, 217p. G. Kane c(p)-33, 74-76, 79, 80, 94, 95. Kirby a(p)-1-17 (#12-17, 49-57-layouts); c(p)-1-17, 25, 30 (18, 26-parts). Layton a-105i; c-112i, 113i. Jim Lee a(p)-248, 256-258, 267-277; c(p)-252, 254, 256-261, 264, 267, 270, 275-277, 286. Perez a-Annual 3p; c(p)-112, 128, Annual 3. Peterson a(p)-294-300, 304(part); c(p)-294-299. Whilce Portacio a(p)-281-286, 289, 290; a(i)-267; c-281-285p, 289p, 290; c(i)-267. Romita, Jr. a-300; c-300. Roussos a-84i. Simonson a-171p; c-171, 217. B. Smith a-53, 186p, 198p, 205, 214; c-53-55, 186p, 198, 205, 212, 214, 216. Paul Smith a(p)-165-170, 172-175, 278; c-165-170, 172-175, 278. Sparling a-78p. Steranko a-50p, 51p; c-49-51. Sutton a-106i. Art Thibert a(i)-281-286; c(i)-281, 282, 284, 285. Toth a-12p, 67p(r). Tuska a-40-42i, 43-46p, 88i(r); c-39-41, 77p, 78p. Williamson a-202i, 203i, 211i; c-202i, 203i, 206i. Wood c-14i.

UNCANNY X-MEN AND THE NEW TEEN TITANS (See Marvel and DC Present…)

UNCANNY X-MEN AT THE STATE FAIR OF TEXAS, THE
1983 (36 pgs., one-shot)
Marvel Comics Group

nn-Supplement to the Dallas Times Herald	1.65	4.20	10.00

UNCENSORED MOUSE, THE
Apr, 1989 - No. 2, Apr, 1989 ($1.95, B&W)(Came sealed in plastic bag)
Eternity Comics

Uncle Sam Quarterly #6 © QUA

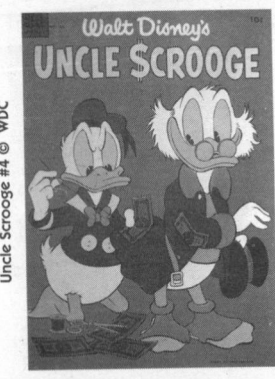

Uncle Scrooge #4 © WDC

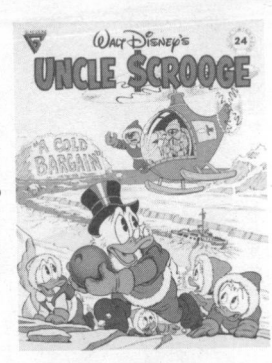

Uncle Scrooge #24 © WDC

	GD25	FN65	NM94
1-Early Gottfredson strip-r in each		1.20	3.00
2-Both contain racial stereotyping & violence	1.00	2.00	5.00

NOTE: *Both issues contain unauthorized reprints. Series was cancelled. Win Smith r-1, 2.*

UNCLE CHARLIE'S FABLES
Jan, 1952 - No. 5, Sept, 1952 (All have Biro painted-c)
Lev Gleason Publications

	GD25	FN65	NM94
1-Norman Maurer-a; has Biro's picture	10.00	30.00	70.00
2-Fuje-a; Biro photo	7.50	22.50	45.00
3-5	6.35	19.00	38.00

UNCLE DONALD & HIS NEPHEWS DUDE RANCH (See Dell Giant #52)
UNCLE DONALD & HIS NEPHEWS FAMILY FUN (See Dell Giant #38)

UNCLE JOE'S FUNNIES
1938 (B&W)
Centaur Publications

	GD25	FN65	NM94
1-Games, puzzles & magic tricks, some interior art; Bill Everett-c	40.00	120.00	295.00

UNCLE MILTY (TV)
Dec, 1950 - No. 4, July, 1951 (52 pgs.)(Early TV comic)
Victoria Publications/True Cross

	GD25	FN65	NM94
1-Milton Berle photo on-c of #1,2	40.00	120.00	325.00
2	26.00	77.00	180.00
3,4	21.00	64.00	150.00

UNCLE REMUS & HIS TALES OF BRER RABBIT (See Brer Rabbit, 4-Color #129, 208, 693)

UNCLE SAM QUARTERLY (Blackhawk 9 on)(See Freedom Fighters)
Autumn, 1941 - No. 8, Fall, 1943 (Also see National Comics)
Quality Comics Group

	GD25	FN65	NM94
1-Origin Uncle Sam; Fine/Eisner-c, chapter headings, 2 pgs. by Eisner; (2 versions: dark cover, no price; light cover with price sticker); Jack Cole-a	277.00	833.00	2500.00
2-Cameos by The Ray, Black Condor, Quicksilver, The Red Bee, Alias the Spider, Hercules & Neon the Unknown; Eisner, Fine-c/a	110.00	330.00	880.00
3-Tuska-c/a; Eisner-a(2)	82.00	247.00	660.00
4	73.00	221.00	590.00
5,7-Hitler, Mussolini & Tojo-c	75.00	225.00	600.00
6,8	58.00	176.00	470.00

NOTE: *Kotzky (or Tuska) a-3-8.*

UNCLE SAM'S CHRISTMAS STORY
1958 (Giveaway)
Promotional Publ. Co.

	GD25	FN65	NM94
nn-Reprints 1956 Christmas USA	2.40	6.00	12.00

UNCLE SCROOGE (Disney) (Becomes Walt Disney's... #210 on) (See Cartoon Tales, Dell Giants #33, 55, Disney Comic Album, Donald and Scrooge, Dynabrite, Four Color #178, Gladstone Comic Album, Walt Disney's Comics & Stories #98, Walt Disney's ...)
No. 386, 3/52 - No. 39, 8-10/62, No. 40, 12/62 - No. 209, 1984
Dell #1-39/Gold Key #40-173/Whitman #174-209

	GD25	FN65	NM94
Four Color 386(#1)-in "Only a Poor Old Man" by Carl Barks; r-in Uncle Scrooge & Donald Duck #1('65) & The Best of Walt Disney Comics (1974)	100.00	300.00	900.00
1-(1986)-Reprints F.C. #386; given away with lithograph "Dam Disaster at Money Lake" & as a subscription offer giveaway to Gladstone subscribers	2.60	7.50	18.00
Four Color 456(#2)-in "Back to the Klondike" by Carl Barks; r-in Best of U.S. & D.D. #1('66) & Gladstone C.A. #4	61.00	183.00	550.00
Four Color 495(#3)-r-in #105	50.00	150.00	450.00
4(12-2/53-54)-r-in Gladstone Comic Album #11	39.00	117.00	350.00
5-r-in Gladstone Special #2 & W.D. Digest #1	32.00	96.00	290.00
6-r-in U.S. #106,165,233 & Best of U.S. & D.D. #1('66)			
	25.00	75.00	220.00
7-The Seven Cities of Cibola by Barks; r-in #217 & Best of D.D. & U.S. #2 ('67)	22.00	65.00	200.00
8-10: 8-r-in #111,222. 9-r-in #104,214. 10-r-in #67	18.00	54.00	165.00
11-20: 11-r-in #237. 17-r-in #215. 19-r-in Gladstone C.A. #1. 20-r-in #213	16.00	48.00	150.00
21-30: 24-X-Mas-c. 26-r-in #211	14.00	42.00	125.00
31-35,37-40: 34-r-in #228. 40-X-Mas-c	11.00	32.00	105.00
36-1st app. Magica De Spell; Number one dime 1st identified by name	13.00	40.00	115.00
41-60: 48-Magica De Spell-c/story (3/64). 49-Sci/fi-c. 51-Beagle Boys-c/story (8/64)	9.50	28.00	85.00
61-63,65,66,68-71:71-Last Barks issue w/original story (#71-he only storyboarded the script)	8.00	24.00	70.00
64-Barks Vietnam War story "Treasure of Marco Polo" banned for reprints by Disney because of its third world revolutionary war theme	13.00	38.00	100.00
67,72,73: 67,72,73-Barks-r	8.00	24.00	70.00
74-84: 74-Barks-r(1pg.). 75-81,83-Not by Barks. 82,84-Barks-r begin	5.00	15.00	45.00
85-110	4.00	12.00	36.00
111-141,143-152,154-157	2.60	7.50	18.00
142-Reprints Four Color #456 with-c	3.25	9.50	22.00
153,158,162-164,166,168-170,178,180: No Barks	1.20	3.00	7.00
159-160,165,167,172-176-Barks-a	1.65	4.20	10.00
161(r/#14), 171(r/#11), 177(r/#16), 179(r/#9), 183(r/#6)-Barks-r	1.65	4.20	10.00
181(r/4-Color #495), 195(r/4-Color #386)	1.65	4.20	10.00
182,186,191-194,197-202,204-206: No Barks	1.00	2.60	6.00
184,185,187,188-Barks-a	1.30	3.25	8.00
189(r/#5), 190(r/#4), 196(r/#13), 203(r/#12), 207(r/#93,92), 208(r/U.S. #18), 209(r/U.S. #21)-Barks-r	1.30	3.25	8.00
Uncle Scrooge & Money(G.K.)-Barks-r/from WDC&S #130 (3/67)	4.00	12.00	35.00
Mini Comic #1(1976)(3-1/4x4-6-1/2")-r/U.S. #115; Barks-c			1.0

NOTE: *Barks c-Four Color 386, 456, 495, #4-37, 39, 40, 43-71.*

UNCLE SCROOGE & DONALD DUCK
June, 1965 (25¢, paper cover)
Gold Key

	GD25	FN65	NM94
1-Reprint of Four Color #386(#1) & lead story from Four Color #29	7.00	21.00	70.0

UNCLE SCROOGE COMICS DIGEST
Dec, 1986 - No. 5, Aug, 1987 ($1.25, Digest-size)
Gladstone Publishing

	GD25	FN65	NM94
1,3	1.00	2.00	5.0
2,4		1.20	3.0
5 (scarce)	1.00	2.60	6.0

UNCLE SCROOGE GOES TO DISNEYLAND (See Dell Giants)
Aug, 1985 ($2.50)
Gladstone Publishing Ltd.

	GD25	FN65	NM94
1-Reprints Dell Giant w/new-c by Mel Crawford, based on old cover	1.65	4.20	10.
...Comics Digest 1 ($1.50, digest size)	1.70	5.00	12.

UNCLE SCROOGE IN COLOR
1987 ($29.95, Hardcover, 9-1/4"X12-1/4", 96 Pgs.)
Gladstone Publishing

	GD25	FN65	NM94
nn-Reprints "Christmas on Bear Mountain" from Four Color 178 by Barks; Uncle Scrooge's Christmas Carol (published as Donald Duck & the Christmas Carol, A Little Golden Book), reproduced from the original art as adapted by Norman McGary from pencils by Barks; and Uncle Scrooge the Lemonade King, reproduced from the original art, plus Barks' original pencils	8.35	25.00	50.

Underworld #3 © DC

Underworld Unleashed #2 © DC

Unexpected #198 © DC

	GD25	FN65	NM94

nn-Slipcase edition of 750, signed by Barks, issued at $79.95
| | 45.00 | 135.00 | 300.00 |

UNCLE SCROOGE THE LEMONADE KING
1960 (A Top Top Tales Book, 6-3/8"x7-5/8", 32 pgs.)
Whitman Publishing Co.

2465-Storybook pencilled by Carl Barks, finished art adapted by Norman
McGary | 60.00 | 180.00 | 400.00

UNCLE WIGGILY (See March of Comics #19)
No. 179, Dec, 1947 - No. 543, Mar, 1954
Dell Publishing Co.

Four Color 179 (#1)-Walt Kelly-c	16.00	48.00	160.00
Four Color 221 (3/49)-Part Kelly-c	10.00	30.00	100.00
Four Color 276 (5/50), 320 (#1, 3/51)	8.00	24.00	80.00
Four Color 349 (9-10/51), 391 (4-5/52)	7.00	21.00	70.00
Four Color 428 (10/52), 503 (10/53), 543	5.00	15.00	50.00

UNDERCOVER GIRL (Starr Flagg) (See Extra Comics & Manhunt!)
No. 5, 1952 - No. 7, 1954
Magazine Enterprises

| 5(#1)(A-1 #62)-Fallon of the F.B.I. in all | 36.00 | 107.00 | 250.00 |
| 6(A-1 #98), 7(A-1 #118)-All have Starr Flagg | 33.00 | 99.00 | 230.00 |
NOTE: *Powell* c-6, 7. *Whitney* a-5-7.

UNDERDOG (TV)(See Kite Fun Book, March of Comics #426, 438, 467, 479)
July, 1970 - No. 10, Jan, 1972; Mar, 1975 - No. 23, Feb, 1979
Charlton Comics/Gold Key

1 (1st series, Charlton)-1st app. Underdog	8.50	26.00	60.00
2-10	5.00	15.00	35.00
1 (2nd series, Gold Key)	5.70	17.00	45.00
2-10	3.75	11.25	28.00
11-23: 13-1st app. Shack of Solitude	2.60	7.50	18.00

UNDERDOG
1987 - No. 3?, 1987 ($1.50)
Spotlight Comics

| 1-3 | | | 1.50 |

UNDERDOG SUMMER SPECIAL (TV)
Oct, 1993 ($2.25, 68 pgs.)
Harvey Comics

| 1 | | .90 | 2.25 |

UNDERSEA AGENT
Jan, 1966 - No. 6, Mar, 1967 (25¢, 68 pgs.)
Tower Comics

1-Davy Jones, Undersea Agent begins	6.50	19.50	45.00
2-6: 2-Jones gains magnetic powers. 5-Origin & 1st app. of Merman.			
6-Kane/Wood-c(r)	4.30	13.00	30.00
NOTE: *Gil Kane* a-3-6; c-4, 5. *Moldoff* a-2i.

UNDERSEA FIGHTING COMMANDOS (See Fighting Undersea...)
1964
W. Enterprises

| W. Reprint #1,2('64): 1-r/#? 2-r/#1; Severin-c | 1.30 | 3.25 | 8.00 |

UNDERWATER CITY, THE
No. 1328, 1961
Dell Publishing Co.

| Four Color 1328-Movie, Evans-a | 7.00 | 21.00 | 70.00 |

UNDERWORLD (...True Crime Stories)
Feb-Mar, 1948 - No. 9, June-July, 1949 (52 pgs.)
D. S. Publishing Co.

| 1-Moldoff (Shelly)-c; excessive violence | 38.00 | 114.00 | 265.00 |
| 2-Moldoff (Shelly)-c; Ma Barker story used in **SOTI**, pg. 95; female electrocution panel; lingerie art | 39.00 | 116.00 | 270.00 |

	GD25	FN65	NM94

3-McWilliams-c/a; extreme violence, mutilation	32.00	96.00	225.00
4-Used in Love and Death by Legman; Ingels-a	24.00	73.00	170.00
5-Ingels-a	18.00	54.00	125.00
6-9: 8-Ravielli-a	13.50	41.00	95.00

UNDERWORLD
Dec, 1987 - No. 4, Mar, 1988 ($1.00, limited series, mature)
DC Comics

| 1-4 | | | 1.00 |

UNDERWORLD CRIME
June, 1952 - No. 9, Oct, 1953
Fawcett Publications

1	24.00	73.00	170.00
2	16.00	47.00	110.00
3-6,8,9 (8,9-exist?)	13.50	41.00	95.00
7-(6/53)-Bondage/torture-c	23.00	69.00	160.00

UNDERWORLD STORY, THE (Movie)
1950
Avon Periodicals

| nn-(Scarce)-Ravielli-c | 24.00 | 71.00 | 165.00 |

UNDERWORLD UNLEASHED
Nov, 1995 - No. 3, Jan, 1996 ($2.95, limited series)
DC Comics

1-3: Mark Waid scripts & Howard Porter-c/a(p)		1.20	3.00
...: Abyss: Hell's Sentinel 1-($2.95)-Alan Scott, Phantom Stranger, Zatanna app.		1.20	3.00
...: Apokolips-Dark Uprising 1 ($1.95)		.80	2.00
...: Batman-Devil's Asylum 1-($2.95)-Batman app.		1.20	3.00
...: Patterns of Fear-($2.95)		1.20	3.00

UNEARTHLY SPECTACULARS
Oct, 1965 - No. 3, Mar, 1967
Harvey Publications

1-(12¢)-Tiger Boy; Simon-c	2.60	7.50	18.00
2-(25¢ giants)-Jack Q. Frost, Tiger Boy & Three Rocketeers app.; Williamson, Wood, Kane-a; r-1 story/Thrill-O-Rama #2	3.75	11.25	28.00
3-(25¢ giants)-Jack Q. Frost app.; Williamson/Crandall-a; r-from Alarming Advs. #1,1962	3.75	11.25	28.00
NOTE: *Crandall* a-3r. *G. Kane* a-2. *Orlando* a-3. *Simon, Sparling, Wood* c-2. *Simon/Kirby* a-3r. *Torres* a-1?. *Wildey* a-1(3). *Williamson* a-2, 3r. *Wood* a-2(2).

UNEXPECTED, THE (Formerly Tales of the...)
No. 105, Feb-Mar, 1968 - No. 222, May, 1982
National Periodical Publications/DC Comics

105-Begin 12¢ cover price	3.25	9.50	22.00
106-113: 113-Last 12¢ issue (6-7/69)	2.60	7.50	18.00
114,115,117,118,120,122-127	1.30	3.25	8.00
116,119,121,128-Wrightson-a	1.65	4.20	10.00
129-131,137-156		1.60	4.00
132-136-(52 pgs.)	1.00	2.60	6.00
157-162-(100 pgs.)	1.65	4.20	10.00
163-188: 187,188-(44 pgs.)		1.00	2.50
189,190,192-195 ($1.00, 68 pgs.): 189 on are combined with House of Secrets & The Witching Hour		.80	2.00
191-Rogers-a(p) ($1.00, 68 pgs.)		1.20	3.00
196-221: 200-Return of Johnny Peril by Tuska. 205-213-Johnny Peril app.			
210-Time Warp story			1.40
NOTE: *Neal Adams* c-110, 112-118, 121, 124. *J. Craig* a-195. *Ditko* a-189, 221p, 222p; c-222. *Drucker* a-107r, 132r. *Giffen* a-219, 222. *Kaluta* c-203, 212. *Kirby* a-127r, 162. *Kubert* c-204, 214-216, 219-221. *Mayer* a-217p, 220, 221p. *Moldoff* a-136r. *Moreira* a-133. *Mortimer* a-212p. *Newton* a-204p. *Orlando* a-202; c-191. *Perez* a-217p. *Redondo* a-155, 166, 195. *Reese* a-145. *Sparling* a-107, 205-209p, 212p. *Spiegle* a-217. *Starlin* c-198. *Toth* a-126r, 127r. *Tuska* a-127, 132, 134, 136, 139, 152, 180, 200p. *Wildey* a-128r, 193. *Wood* a-122i, 133i, 137i, 138i. *Wrightson* a-161r(2 pgs.). Johnny Peril in #106-114, 116, 117, 200, 205-213.

UNEXPECTED ANNUAL, THE (See DC Special Series #4)

Union #9 © Aegis Entertainment

Unknown Soldier #235 © DC

Unknown Soldier #7 (Limited Series) © DC

UNIDENTIFIED FLYING ODDBALL (See Walt Disney Showcase #52)

UNION
June, 1993 - No. 0, July, 1994 ($1.95, limited series)
Image Comics (Wildstorm Productions)

0-(7/94, $2.50)		1.00	2.50
0-Alternate Portacio-c (See Deathblow #5)	1.65	4.20	10.00
1-($2.50)-Embossed foil-c; Texeira-c/a in all		1.00	2.50
1-($1.95)-Newsstand edition w/o foil-c		.80	2.00
2-4: 4-(7/94)		.80	2.00

UNION
Feb, 1995 - No. 9, Dec, 1995 ($2.50)
Image Comics (Wildstorm Productions)

1-3,5-9: 3-Savage Dragon app. 6-Fairchild from Gen 13 app.	1.00	2.50
4-($1.95, Newsstand)-Wildstorm Rising Pt. 3	.80	2.00
4-($2.50, Direct Market)-Wildstorm Rising Pt. 3, bound-in card	..80	2.50

UNITED COMICS (Formerly Fritzi Ritz #7; has Fritzi Ritz logo)
Aug, 1940 - No. 8, 1950 - No. 26, Jan-Feb, 1953
United Features Syndicate

1(68 pgs.)-Fritzi Ritz & Phil Fumble	21.00	64.00	150.00
8-Fritzi Ritz, Abbie & Slats	4.25	13.00	28.00
9-26: 20-Strange As It Seems; Russell Patterson Cheesecake-a. 22,25-			
Peanuts app.	4.00	12.00	24.00

NOTE: Abbie & Slats reprinted from Tip Top.

UNITED NATIONS, THE (See Classics Illustrated Special Issue)

UNITED STATES AIR FORCE PRESENTS: THE HIDDEN CREW
1964 (36 pgs.)
U.S. Air Force

nn-Shaffenberger-a	.80	2.00	4.00

UNITED STATES FIGHTING AIR FORCE (Also see U.S. Fighting Air Force)
Sept, 1952 - No. 29, Oct, 1956
Superior Comics Ltd.

1	7.50	22.50	45.00
2	4.00	12.00	24.00
3-10	2.80	7.00	14.00
11-29	2.40	6.00	12.00

UNITED STATES MARINES
1943 - No. 4, 1944; No. 5, 1952 - No. 8, 1952; No. 7 - No. 11, 1953
William H. Wise/Life's Romances Publ. Co./Magazine Enterprises #5-8/
Toby Press #7-11

nn-Mart Bailey-a	10.00	30.00	65.00
2-Bailey-a; Tojo classic-c	10.00	30.00	70.00
3-Tojo-c	8.35	25.00	50.00
4	6.35	19.00	38.00
5(A-1 #55)-Bailey-a, 6(A-1 #60), 7(A-1 #68), 8(A-1 #72)			
	5.00	15.00	30.00
7-11 (Toby)	3.20	8.00	16.00

NOTE: Powell a-5-7.

UNITY
No. 0, Aug, 1992 - No. 1, 1992 (Free comics w/limited distribution, 20 pgs.)
Valiant

0 (Blue)-Prequel to Unity x-overs in all Valiant titles; B. Smith-c/a. (Free to			
everyone that bought all 8 titles that month.)		1.60	4.00
0 (Red)-Same as above, but w/red logo (5,000).			
	1.65	4.20	10.00
0 (Gold)-Promotional copy.	1.30	3.25	8.00
1-Epilogue to Unity x-overs; B. Smith-c/a. (1 copy available for every 8 Valiant			
books ordered by dealers.)		1.60	4.00
1 (Gold)-Promotional copy.	1.30	3.25	8.00
1 (Platinum)-Promotional copy.	1.65	4.20	10.00
Yearbook 1 (2/95, $3.95)-"1994" in indicia.		1.60	4.00

UNIVERSAL MONSTERS
1993 ($4.95/$5.95, 52 pgs.)(All adapt original movies)
Dark Horse Comics

		GD	FN	NM
Frankenstein nn-($3.95)-Painted-c/a			1.60	4.00
Dracula nn-($4.95)		1.00	2.00	5.00
The Mummy nn-($4.95)-Painted-c		1.00	2.00	5.00
Creature From the Black Lagoon nn-($4.95)-Art Adams/Austin-c/a				
		1.00	2.00	5.00

UNIVERSAL PRESENTS DRACULA-THE MUMMY& OTHER STORIES
Sept-Nov, 1963 (one-shot, 84 pgs.) (Also see Dell Giants)
Dell Publishing Co.

	GD	FN	VF	NM
02-530-311-r/Dracula 12-231-212, The Mummy 12-437-211 & part of Ghost				
Stories No. 1	14.00	42.00	98.00	210.00

UNIVERSAL SOLDIER (Movie)
Sept, 1992 - No. 3, Nov, 1992 (Limited series, polybagged, mature)
Now Comics

1-3 ($2.50, Direct Sales) 1-Movie adapatation; hologram on-c (all direct sales			
editions have painted-c)		1.00	2.50
1-3 ($1.95, Newstand)-Rewritten & redrawn code approved version;			
all newsstand editions have photo-c		.80	2.00

UNKEPT PROMISE
1949 (Giveaway, 24 pgs.)
Legion of Truth

nn-Anti-alcohol	7.50	22.50	45.00

UNKNOWN MAN, THE (Movie)
1951
Avon Periodicals

nn-Kinstler-c	24.00	71.00	165.00

UNKNOWN SOLDIER (Formerly Star-Spangled War Stories)
No. 205, Apr-May, 1977 - No. 268, Oct, 1982
National Periodical Publications/DC Comics

205-268: 219-221-(44 pgs.). 248,249-Origin. 251-Enemy Ace begins.265-267-			
Enemy Ace vs. Balloon Buster. 268-Death of Unknown Soldier			
	1.00	2.00	5.00

NOTE: Chaykin a-234. Evans a-265-267; c-235. Kubert c-Most. Miller a-219p. Severin a-251, 253, 260, 261, 265-267. Simonson a-254-256. Spiegle a-258, 259, 262-264.

UNKNOWN SOLDIER, THE (Also see Brave &the Bold #146)
Winter, 1988-'89 - No. 12, Dec, 1989 ($1.50, maxi-series, mature)
DC Comics

1-12: 8-Begin $1.75-c			1.5

UNKNOWN WORLD (Strange Stories From Another World #2 on)
June, 1952
Fawcett Publications

1-Norman Saunders painted-c	36.00	107.00	250.00

UNKNOWN WORLDS (See Journey Into...)

UNKNOWN WORLDS
Aug, 1960 - No. 57, Aug, 1967
American Comics Group/Best Synd. Features

1-Schaffenberger-c	18.00	54.00	140.00
2-5: 2-Dinosaur-c/story	10.00	30.00	80.00
6-11: 9-Dinosaur-c/story. 11-Last 10¢ issue	7.00	21.50	55.00
12-19: 12-Begin 12¢ issues?; ends #57	5.70	17.00	45.00
20-Herbie cameo (12-1/62-63)	6.50	19.50	50.00
21-35	3.75	11.25	28.00
36- "The People vs. Hendricks" by Craig; most popular ACG story ever			
	4.50	14.00	35.00
37-46	3.75	11.25	26.00
47-Williamson-a r-from Adventures Into the Unknown #96, 3 pgs.; Craig-a			
	3.75	11.25	28.00

Untamed #3 © MEG

Untold Legend of the Batman #2 © DC

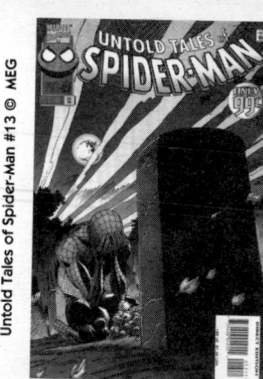

Untold Tales of Spider-Man #13 © MEG

	GD25	FN65	NM94

48-57: 53-Frankenstein app. 3.30 10.00 23.00
NOTE: *Ditko* a-49, 50p, 54. *Forte* a-3, 6, 11. *Landau* a-56(2). *Reinman* a-3, 9, 13, 20, 22, 23, 36, 38, 54. *Whitney* c/a-most issues. *John Force, Magic Agent* app.-35, 36, 48, 50, 52, 54, 56.

UNKNOWN WORLDS OF FRANK BRUNNER
Aug, 1985 - No. 2, Aug, 1985 ($1.75)
Eclipse Comics

1,2-B&W-r in color .90 1.80

UNKNOWN WORLDS OF SCIENCE FICTION
Jan, 1975 - No. 6, Nov, 1975; 1976 ($1.00, B&W Magazine)
Marvel Comics Group

1-Williamson/Krenkel/Torres/Frazetta-r/Witzend #1, Neal Adams-r/Phase 1;
  Brunner & Kaluta-r; Freas/Romita-c 1.60 4.00
2-6: 5-Kaluta text illos 1.20 3.00
Special 1(1976,100 pgs.)-Newton painted-c 1.20 3.00
NOTE: *Brunner* a-2; c-4, 6. *Buscema* a-Special 1p. *Chaykin* a-5. *Colan* a(p)-1, 3, 5, 6. *Corben* a-4. *Kaluta* a-2, Special 1(ext illos); c-2. *Morrow* a-3, 5. *Nino* a-3, 6, Special 1. *Perez* a-2, 3. Ray Bradbury interview in #1.

UNSANE (Formerly Mighty Bear #13, 14? or The Outlaws #10-14?)
No. 15, June, 1954
Star Publications

15-Disbrow-a(2); L. B. Cole-c 30.00 90.00 210.00

UNSEEN, THE
No. 5, 1952 - No. 15, July, 1954
Visual Editions/Standard Comics

5-Horror stories in all; Toth-a 30.00 90.00 210.00
6,7,9,10-Jack Katz-a 21.00 62.00 145.00
8,11,13,14 13.50 41.00 95.00
12,15-Toth-a. 12-Tuska-a 21.00 62.00 145.00
NOTE: *Nick Cardy* c-12. *Fawcette* a-13, 14. *Sekowsky* a-7, 8(2), 10, 13, 15.

UNTAMED
June, 1993 - No. 3, Aug, 1993 ($1.95, limited series)
Marvel Comics (Epic Comics/Heavy Hitters)

1-($2.50)-Embossed-c 1.00 2.50
2,3 .80 2.00

UNTAMED LOVE (Also see Frank Frazetta's Untamed Love)
Jan, 1950 - No. 5, Sept, 1950
Quality Comics Group (Comic Magazines)

1-Ward-c, Gustavson-a 20.00 60.00 140.00
2,4: 2-5-Photo-c 11.50 34.00 80.00
3,5-Gustavson-a 13.00 39.00 90.00

UNTOLD LEGEND OF THE BATMAN, THE
July, 1980 - No. 3, Sept, 1980 (Limited series)
DC Comics

1-Origin; Joker-c; Byrne's 1st work at DC 1.60 4.00
2,3 1.20 3.00
1-3: Batman cereal premiums (1989, 28 pgs., 6X9"); 1st & 2nd printings
  known 1.00 2.50
NOTE: *Aparo* a-1i, 2, 3. *Byrne* a-1p.

UNTOLD ORIGIN OF THE FEMFORCE, THE (Also see Femforce)
1989 ($4.95, 68 pgs.)
AC Comics

1-Origin Femforce; Bill Black-a(i) & scripts .85 2.50 5.00

UNTOLD TALES OF SPIDER-MAN (Also see Amazing Fantasy #16-18)
Sept, 1995 - Present (99¢)
Marvel Comics

1-23: Kurt Busiek scripts begin; Pat Olliffe-c/a in all (except #9). 2-1st app.
  Batwing. 4-1st app. The Spacemen (Gantry, Orbit, Satellite & Vacuum).
  8-1st app. The Headsman; The Enforcers (The Big Man, Montana, The Ox &
  Fancy Dan) app. 9-Ron Frenz-a. 10-1st app. Commanda. 16-Reintro Mary
  Jane Watson 1.00

...'96-(1996, $1.95, 46 pgs.)-Kurt Busiek scripts; Mike Allred-c/a; Kurt Busiek &
  Pat Oliffe app. in back-up story; contains pin-ups 2.00

UNTOUCHABLES, THE (TV)
No. 1237, 10-12/61 - No. 4, 8-10/62 (All have Robert Stack photo-c)
Dell Publishing Co.

Four Color 1237(#1) 20.00 60.00 200.00
Four Color 1286 15.00 45.00 150.00
01-879-207, 12-879-210(01879-210 on inside) 10.00 30.00 90.00
  Topps Bubblegum premiums produced by Leaf Brands, Inc.-2-1/2x4-1/2", 8
  pgs. (3 diff. issues) "The Organization, Jamaica Ginger, The Otto Frick Story
  (drug), 3000 Suspects, The Antidote, Mexican Stakeout, Little Egypt, Purple
  Gang, Bugs Moran Story, & Lily Dallas Story" 2.30 6.70 16.00

UNUSUAL TALES (Blue Beetle & Shadows From Beyond #50 on)
Nov, 1955 - No. 49, Mar-Apr, 1965
Charlton Comics

1 20.00 60.00 140.00
2 10.00 30.00 70.00
3-5 5.70 17.00 45.00
6-Ditko-c only 7.00 21.50 55.00
7,8-Ditko-c/a 17.00 49.00 125.00
9-Ditko-c/a (20 pgs.) 17.00 51.00 130.00
10-Ditko-c/a(4) 21.00 62.00 155.00
11-(3/58, 68 pgs.)-Ditko-a(4) 19.00 58.00 145.00
12,14-Ditko-a 12.00 36.00 95.00
13,16-20 4.30 13.00 32.00
15-Ditko-c/a 13.00 39.00 100.00
21,24,28 3.25 9.50 22.00
22,23,25-27,29-Ditko-a 8.50 26.00 65.00
30-49 2.60 7.50 18.00
NOTE: *Colan* a-11. *Ditko* c-22, 23, 25-27, 31(part).

UP FROM HARLEM (Tom Skinner...)
1973 (35/49¢)
Spire Christian Comics (Fleming H. Revell Co.)

nn 1.00

UP-TO-DATE COMICS
No date (1938) (36 pgs.; B&W cover) (10¢)
King Features Syndicate

nn-Popeye & Henry cover; The Phantom, Jungle Jim & Flash Gordon by
  Raymond, The Katzenjammer Kids, Curley Harper & others. Note: Variations
  in content exist. 23.00 69.00 160.00

UP YOUR NOSE AND OUT YOUR EAR (Satire)
Apr, 1972 - No. 2, June, 1972 (52 pgs., magazine)
Klevart Enterprises

V1#1,2 1.20 3.00

URBAN
1994 ($1.75, B&W)
Moving Target Entertainment

1 .70 1.75

URTH 4
1990 - No. 4, 1990 ($2.00, deluxe format)
Continuity Comics

1-4: Ms. Mystic characters. 2-Neal Adams-c(i) 1.00 2.00

URZA-MISHRA WAR ON THE WORLD OF MAGIC THE GATHERING
1996 - No. 2, 1996 ($5.95, limited series)
Acclaim Comics (Armada)

1,2 6.00

USA COMICS
Aug, 1941 - No. 17, Fall, 1945
Timely Comics (USA)

	GD25	FN65	VF82	NM94

USA #5 © MEG

Usagi Yojimbo #4 © Stan Sakai

U.S. Jones #1 © FOX

	GD25	FN65	NM94

1-Origin Major Liberty (called Mr. Liberty #1), Rockman by Wolverton, & The Whizzer by Avison; The Defender with sidekick Rusty & Jack Frost begin; The Young Avenger only app.; S&K-c plus 1 pg. art

	900.00	2700.00	9000.00

(Estimated up to 145 total copies exist, 7 in NM/Mint)

	GD25	FN65	NM94

2-Origin Captain Terror & The Vagabond; last Wolverton Rockman

	294.00	881.00	2600.00
3-No Whizzer	237.00	712.00	1900.00

4-Last Rockman, Major Liberty, Defender, Jack Frost, & Capt. Terror; Corporal Dix app.

	200.00	600.00	1600.00

5-Origin American Avenger & Roko the Amazing; The Blue Blade, The Black Widow & Victory Boys; Gypo the Gypsy Giant & Hills of Horror only app.; Sergeant Dix begins; no Whizzer; Hitler, Mussolini & Tojo-c

	181.00	543.00	1450.00

6-Captain America (ends #17), The Destroyer, Jap Buster Johnson, Jeep Jones begin; Terror Squad only app.

	237.00	712.00	1900.00

7-Captain Daring, Disk-Eyes the Detective by Wolverton app.; origin & only app. Marvel Boy (3/43); Secret Stamp begins; no Whizzer, Sergeant Dix

	200.00	600.00	1600.00

8-10: 9-Last Secret Stamp. 10-The Thunderbird only app.

	156.00	468.00	1250.00
11,12: 11-No Jeep Jones	131.00	393.00	1050.00

13-17: 13-No Whizzer; Jeep Jones ends. 15-No Destroyer; Jap Buster Johnson ends

	100.00	300.00	800.00

NOTE: **Brodsky** c-14. **Gabrielle** c-4, 8. **Schomburg** c-6-8, 10, 12, 13, 15-17. **Shores** a-1, 4; c-9, 11. **Ed Win** a-4. Cover features: 1-The Defender; 2, 3-Captain Terror; 4-Major Liberty; 5-Victory Boys; 6-17-Captain America & Bucky.

U.S. AGENT (See Jeff Jordan...)

U.S. AGENT (See Captain America #354)
June, 1993 - No. 4, Sept, 1993 ($1.75, limited series)
Marvel Comics

1-4		.70	1.75

USAGI YOJIMBO (See Albedo, Doomsday Squad #3 & Space Usagi)
July, 1987 - No. 36? ($2.00, B&W)
Fantagraphics Books

1		1.20	3.00
1,8,10-2nd printings		.80	2.00
2-9,11-28: 11-Aragones-a		.80	2.00
10-Leonardo app. (TMNT)		1.20	3.00
29-36: 29-Begin $2.25-c		.90	2.25
Color Special 1 (11/89, $2.95, 68 pgs.)-new & r		1.20	3.00
Color Special 2 (10/91, $3.50)		1.40	3.50

Color Special #3 (10/92, $3.50)-Jeff Smith's Bone promo on inside cover

		1.40	3.50

Summer Special 1 (1986, B&W, $2.75)-r/early Albedo issues

		1.00	2.60	6.00

USAGI YOJIMBO
V2#1, Mar, 1993 - No. 16, 1994 ($2.75)
Mirage Studios

V2#1-16: 1-Teenage Mutant Ninja Turtles app.		1.10	2.75

USAGI YOJIMBO
V3#1, Apr, 1996 - V3#6, Sept, 1996 ($2.95, B&W, limited series)
Dark Horse Comics

V3#1-6: Stan Sakai-c/a			3.00

U.S. AIR FORCE COMICS (Army Attack #38 on)
Oct, 1958 - No. 37, Mar-Apr, 1965
Charlton Comics

1	4.50	14.00	36.00
2	2.85	8.50	20.00
3-10	1.85	5.50	13.00

	GD25	FN65	NM94
11-20	1.30	3.25	8.0
21-37	1.00	2.00	5.0

NOTE: **Glanzman** c/a-9, 10, 12. **Montes/Bache** a-33.

USA IS READY
1941 (68 pgs., one-shot)
Dell Publishing Co.

1-War propaganda	36.00	107.00	250.

U.S. BORDER PATROL COMICS (Sgt. Dick Carter of the...) (See Holyoke One Shot)

U.S. FIGHTING AIR FORCE (Also see United States Fighting Air Force)
No date (1960s?)
I. W. Enterprises

1,9(nd): 1-r/United States Fighting...#?. 9-r/#1		1.60	4.0

U.S. FIGHTING MEN
1963 - 1964 (Reprints)
Super Comics

10-r/With the U.S. Paratroops #4(Avon)	1.20	3.00	7.0

11,12,15-18: 11-r/Monty Hall #10. 12,16,17,18-r/U.S. Fighting Air Force #10,3,?&? 15-r/Man Comics #11

	1.00	2.00	5.0

U.S. JONES (Also see Wonderworld Comics #28)
Nov, 1941 - No. 2, Jan, 1942
Fox Features Syndicate

1-U.S. Jones & The Topper begin; Nazi-c	106.00	318.00	850.0
2-Nazi-c	79.00	238.00	635.0

U.S. MARINES
Fall, 1964 (12¢, one-shot)
Charlton Comics

1	1.00	2.50	5.0

U.S. MARINES IN ACTION
Aug, 1952 - No. 3, Dec, 1952
Avon Periodicals

1-Louis Ravielli-c/a	6.70	20.00	40.
2,3: 3-Kinstler-c	4.00	12.00	24.

U.S. 1
May, 1983 - No. 12, Oct, 1984 (7,8: painted-c)
Marvel Comics Group

1-12: 2-Sienkiewicz-c. 3-12-Michael Golden-c			1.

U.S. PARATROOPS (See With the...)

U.S. PARATROOPS
1964?
I. W. Enterprises

1,8: 1-r/With the U.S. Paratroops #1; Wood-c. 8-r/With the U.S. Paratroops #6; Kinstler-c

	1.20	3.00	7.0

U.S. TANK COMMANDOS
June, 1952 - No. 4, Mar, 1953
Avon Periodicals

1-Kinstler-c	8.00	24.00	48.0
2-4: Kinstler-c	5.35	16.00	32.0
I.W. Reprint #1,8: 1-r/#1. 8-r/#3	1.30	3.25	8.0

NOTE: **Kinstler** a-I.W. #1; c-1-4, I.W. #1, 8.

"V" (TV)
Feb, 1985 - No. 18, July, 1986
DC Comics

1-Based on TV movie & series (Sci/Fi)			1.5
2-18: 17,18-Denys Cowan-c/a			1.0

VACATION COMICS (Also see A-1 Comics)
No. 16, 1948 (one-shot)
Magazine Enterprises

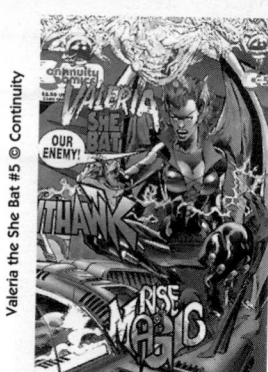

Valeria the She Bat #5 © Continuity

Valor #3 © WMG

Valor #7 © DC

	GD25	FN65	NM94

	GD25	FN65	NM94

A-1 16-The Pixies, Tom Tom, Flying Fredd & Koko & Kola

| | 4.00 | 12.00 | 24.00 |

VACATION DIGEST
Sept, 1987 ($1.25, digest size)
Harvey Comics

| 1 | | | 1.25 |

VACATION IN DISNEYLAND (Also see Dell Giants)
Aug-Oct, 1959; May, 1965 (Walt Disney)
Dell Publishing Co./Gold Key (1965)

| Four Color 1025-Barks-a | 20.00 | 60.00 | 200.00 |
| 1(30024-508)(G.K., 5/65, 25¢)-r/Dell Giant #30 & cover to #1 ('58); celebrates |
| Disneyland's 10th anniversary | 4.00 | 12.00 | 40.00 |

VACATION PARADE (See Dell Giants)

VALERIA THE SHE BAT
May, 1993 - No. 5, Nov, 1993
Continuity Comics

| 1-Premium; glow-in-the-dark-c; N. Adams-a/scripts; given as gift to retailers |
| | 1.30 | 3.25 | 8.00 |
| 2-5: 5 (11/93)-Embossed-c; N. Adams-a/scripts | | 1.00 | 2.50 |
NOTE: Due to lack of continuity, #2-4 do not exist.

VALERIA THE SHE BAT
Sept, 1995 - No.2, Oct, 1995 ($2.50, limited series)
Acclaim Comics (Windjammer)

| 1,2 | | 1.00 | 2.50 |

VALKYRIE (See Airboy)
May,1987 - No. 3, July, 1987 ($1.75, limited series)
Eclipse Comics

| 1-3: 2-Holly becomes new Black Angel | | 1.25 | 2.50 |

VALKYRIE!
July, 1988 - No. 3, Sept, 1988 ($1.95, limited series)
Eclipse Comics

| 1-3 | | .80 | 2.00 |

VALLEY OF THE DINOSAURS (TV)
Apr, 1975 - No. 11, Dec, 1976 (Hanna-Barbera)
Charlton Comics

| 1 | | 1.20 | 3.00 |
| 2-11: 3-Byrne text illos (early work, 7/75) | | | 1.50 |

VALLEY OF GWANGI (See Movie Classics)

VALOR
Mar-Apr, 1955 - No. 5, Nov-Dec, 1955
E. C. Comics

1-Williamson/Torres-a; Wood-c/a	27.00	81.00	190.00
2-Williamson-c/a; Wood-a	24.00	73.00	170.00
3,4: 3-Williamson, Crandall-a. 4-Wood-c	17.00	49.00	115.00
5-Wood-c/a; Williamson/Evans-a	15.00	45.00	105.00
NOTE: Crandall a-3, 4. Ingels a-1, 2, 4, 5. Krigstein a-1-5. Orlando a-3, 4; c-3. Wood a-1, 2, 5; c-1, 4, 5.

VALOR (Also see Legion of Super-Heroes & Legionnaires)
Nov, 1992 - No. 23, Sept, 1994 ($1.25/$1.50)
DC Comics

| 1-12: 1-Eclipso The Darkness Within aftermath. 2-Vs. Supergirl. 4-Vs. Lobo. |
| 12-Lobo cameo | | | 1.25 |
| 13-22: 13-Begin $1.50-c. 14-Legionnaires, JLA app. 17-Austin-c(i); death of |
| Valor. 18-22-Build-up to Zero Hour | | | 1.50 |
| 23-Zero Hour tie-in | | .70 | 1.75 |

VALOR THUNDERSTAR AND HIS FIREFLIES
Dec, 1986 ($1.50)
Now Comics

| 1-Ordway-c(p) | | | 1.50 |

VAMPIRE BITES
May, 1995 ($2.95, B&W)
Brainstorm Comics

| 1-Color pin-up | | 1.20 | 3.00 |

VAMPIRE GIRLS: CALIFORNIA 1969
May, 1969 - Present ($2.95, B&W)
Angel Entertainment

0,1			3.00
0-($10.00)-Nude-c			10.00
0-($20.00)-3-D Platinum; embossed-c			20.00
1-($10.00)-Nude Edition			10.00

VAMPIRE LESTAT, THE
Jan, 1990 - No. 12, 1991 ($2.50, painted limited series)
Innovation Publishing

1-Adapts novel; Bolton painted-c on all	5.00	15.00	35.00
1-2nd printing (has UPC code, 1st prints don't)	1.00	2.00	5.00
1-3rd & 4th printings		1.00	2.50
2-1st printing	2.15	6.50	15.00
2-2nd & 3rd printings		1.00	2.50
3-5	1.65	4.20	10.00
3-6,9-2nd printings		1.00	2.50
6-12	1.00	2.00	5.00

VAMPIRELLA (Magazine)(See Warren Presents)
Sept, 1969 - No. 112, Feb, 1983; No. 113, Jan, 1988? (B&W)
Warren Publishing Co./Harris Publications #113

1-Intro. Vampirella	44.00	132.00	385.00
2-Amazonia series begins, ends #12	19.00	56.00	145.00
3 (Low distribution)	40.00	120.00	330.00
4-7	11.50	34.00	90.00
8-Vampi begins by Tom Sutton as serious strip (early issues-gag line)
	13.00	39.00	100.00
9-Barry Smith-a; Boris-c	10.00	30.00	80.00
10-No Vampi story	4.50	13.00	35.00
11-15: 11-Origin & 1st app. Pendragon. 12-Vampi by Gonzales begins
	7.00	21.50	55.00
16-18,20-25: 17-Tomb of the Gods begins, ends #22. 25-Begin partial color
issues	5.50	17.00	45.00
19 (1973 Annual)	6.50	19.50	50.00
26,28-36,38-40: 30-Intro. Pantha; Corben-a(color). 31-Origin Luana, the Beast
Girl. 33-Pantha ends	4.00	12.00	30.00
27 (1974 Annual)	5.00	15.00	38.00
37 (1975 Annual)	4.30	13.00	33.00
41-45,47-50: 49-1st app. The Blood Red Queen of Hearts. 50-Spirit cameo by
Eisner	3.25	9.50	22.00
46-Origin retold (10/75)	3.75	11.25	28.00
51-66,68,70,72,73,75-99: 60-62,65,66-The Blood Red Queen of Hearts app.
93-Cassandra St. Knight begins, ends #103; new Pantha series begins,
ends #108	2.30	6.75	16.00
67,69,71,74-photo-c	2.85	8.50	20.00
100 (96 pg. r-special)-Origin reprinted	6.50	19.50	50.00
101-110,112: 101,102-The Blood Red Queen of Hearts app. 108-Torpedo series
by Toth begins	4.30	13.00	32.00
111-Giant Collector's Edition ($2.50)	5.00	15.00	38.00
113 (1988)-1st Harris Issue	25.00	75.00	175.00
Annual 1(1972)-New origin Vampirella by Gonzales; reprints by Neal Adams
(from #1), Wood (from #9)	36.00	107.00	250.00
Special 1 (1977; large-square bound)	3.75	11.25	28.00
NOTE: Neal Adams a-1, 19p, 19p(r/#10). Alcala a-90, 93i. Bode/Todd c-3. Bode/Jones c-4. Boris a-9, Brunner a-10, 12(1 pg.). Corben a-30, 31, 33, 54. Crandall a-1, 19(r/#1). Frazetta c-1, 5, 7, 11, 31. Heath a-76-78, 83. Jones a-5, 9, 12, 27, 32, 33(2 pg.), 34, 50i, 83r. Nino a-59i, 61i, 67, 76, 85, 90. Ploog a-14. Barry Smith a-9. Starlin a-78. Sutton a-11. Toth a-90i, 108, 110. Wood a-9, 10, 12, 19(r/#12), 27r, c-9. Wrightson a-33(w/Jones), 63r. All reprint issues-37,

Vampirella #5 © Harris

Vampirella of Drakulon #3 © Harris

Vamps: Hollywood & Vein #4 © DC

	GD25	FN65	NM94

74, 83, 87, 91, 105, 107, 109, 111. Annuals from 1973 on are included in regular numbering. Later annuals are same format as regular issues.

VAMPIRELLA (Also see Cain/… & Vengeance of…)
Nov, 1992 - No. 5, Nov, 1993 ($2.95)
Harris Publications

0		1.60	4.00
0-Gold	6.50	19.50	45.00
1-Jim Balent inks in #1-3; Adam Hughes c-1-3	5.70	17.00	40.00
1-2nd printing	1.20	3.00	7.00
2	4.30	13.00	30.00
3-5: 4-Snyder III-c. 5-Brereton painted-c	1.20	3.00	7.00
Trade paperback nn (10/93, $5.95)-r/#1-4; Jusko-c			6.00

NOTE: Issues 1-5 contain certificates for free Dave Stevens Vampirella poster.

VAMPIRELLA & THE BLOOD RED QUEEN OF HEARTS
Sept, 1996 ($9.95, 96 pgs., B&W, squarebound, one-shot)
Harris Publications

nn-r/Vampirella #49,60-62,65,66,101,102; John Bolton-c; Michael Bair back-c			10.00

VAMPIRELLA CLASSICS
Feb, 1995 - No. 5, Nov, 1995 ($2.95, limited series)
Harris Publications

1-5: Reprints Archie Goodwin stories.		1.20	3.00

VAMPIRELLA: DEATH & DESTRUCTION
July, 1996 - No. 3, Sept, 1996 ($2.95, limited series)
Harris Publications

1-3: Amanda Conner-a(p) in all. 1-Tucci-c. 2-Hughes-c. 3-Jusko-c		1.20	3.00

VAMPIRELLA: MORNING IN AMERICA
1991 - No. 4, 1992 ($3.95, B&W, limited series, 52 pgs.)
Harris Publications/Dark Horse Comics

1-All have Kaluta painted-c	1.20	3.00	7.00
2-4	1.00	2.00	5.00

VAMPIRELLA OF DRAKULON
Jan, 1996 - Present ($2.95)
Harris Publications

1-5: All reprints. 3-Polybagged w/card. 4-Texiera-c			3.00

VAMPIRELLA PIN-UP SPECIAL
Oct, 1995 ($2.95, one-shot)
Harris Publications

1-Hughes-c, pin-ups by various		1.20	3.00
1-Variant-c			3.00

VAMPIRELLA: SAD WINGS OF DESTINY
Sept, 1996 ($3.95, one-shot)
Harris Publications

1-Jusko-c			4.00

VAMPIRELLA/SHADOWHAWK: CREATURES OF THE NIGHT (Also see Shadowhawk)
1995 ($4.95, one-shot)
Harris Publications

1	1.00	2.00	5.00

VAMPIRELLA STRIKES
Sept, 1995 - Present ($2.95, limited series)
Harris Publications

1-8: 1-Photo-c. 2-Deodato-c; polybagged w/card. 5-Eudaemon-c/app; wraparound-c; alternate-c exists. 6-(6/96)-Mark Millar script; Texeira-c; alternate-c exists. 7-Flip book		1.20	3.00
1-Newsstand Edition; different photo-c.			3.00
1-Limited Edition; different photo-c.			3.00

VAMPIRELLA: 25TH ANNIVERSARY SPECIAL
Oct, 1996 ($5.95, squarebound, one-shot)
Harris Publications

nn-Reintro The Blood Red Queen of Hearts; James Robinson, Grant Morrison Warren Ellis scripts; Mark Texeira, Michael Bair & Amanda Connor-a(p); Frank Frazetta-c			6.00

VAMPIRE TALES
Aug, 1973 - No. 11, June, 1975 (75¢, B&W, magazine)
Marvel Comics Group

1-Morbius, the Living Vampire begins by Pablo Marcos (1st solo Morbius series & 5th Morbius app.)	3.60	11.00	25.00
2-Intro. Satana; Steranko-r	1.65	4.20	10.00
3,4,6-11: 3-Satana app. 6-1st Lilith app. 8-Blade app. (see Tomb of Dracula)	1.00	2.00	5.00
5-Origin Morbius	1.30	3.25	8.00
Annual 1(10/75)-Heath-r/#9		1.20	3.00

NOTE: Alcala a-6, 8, 9i. Boris c-4, 6. Chaykin a-7. Everett a-1r. Gulacy a-7p. Heath a-9. Infantino a-3r. Gil Kane a-4, 5r.

VAMPIRE VERSES, THE
Aug, 1995 - No. 3, 1995 ($2.95, B&W, mature)
CFD Productions

1-3		1.20	3.00

VAMPRESS LUXURA, THE
Feb, 1996 - Present ($2.95)
Brainstorm Comics

1-Lindo-c/a/scripts			3.00
1-($10.00, Gold edition)-Gold foil logo			10.00

VAMPS
Aug, 1994 - No. 6, Jan, 1995 ($1.95, limited series, mature)
DC Comics (Vertigo)

1-Bolland-c	1.00	2.00	5.00
2-6: Bolland-c in all		1.20	3.00
Trade paperback ($9.95)-r/#1-6			10.00

VAMPS: HOLLYWOOD & VEIN
Feb, 1996 - No. 6, July, 1996 ($2.25, limited series, mature)
DC Comics (Vertigo)

1-6: Winslade-c			2.00

VANGUARD (…Outpost: Earth) (See Megaton)
1987 ($1.50)
Megaton Comics

1-Erik Larsen-c(p)		1.20	3.00

VANGUARD (See Savage Dragon #2)
Oct, 1993 - No.6, 1994 ($1.95)
Image Comics (Highbrow Entertainment)

1-6: 1-Wraparound gatefold-c; Erik Larsen back-up-a; Supreme x-over. 3-(12/93)-Indicia says December 1994. 4-Berzerker back-up. 5-Angel Medina a(p).		.80	2.00

VANGUARD ILLUSTRATED
Nov, 1983 - No. 11, Oct, 1984 (Baxter paper)(Direct sales only)
Pacific Comics

1-6,8-11: 1,7-Nudity scenes. 2-1st app. Stargrazers (see Legends of the Stargrazers; Dave Stevens-c			1.00
7-1st app. Mr. Monster (r-in Mr. Monster #1)	1.00	2.00	5.00

NOTE: Evans a-7. Kaluta c-5, 7p. Perez a-6; c-6. Rude a-1-4; c-4. Williamson c-3.

VANITY (See Pacific Presents #3)
Jun, 1984 - No. 2, Aug, 1984 ($1.50, direct sales)
Pacific Comics

1,2: Origin			1.00

Vault of Evil #1 © MEG

V...Comics #1 © FOX

Velocity #3 © Top Cow Productions

VE

ARIETY COMICS (The Spice of Comics)
944 - No. 2, 1945; No. 3, 1946
ural Home Publications/Croyden Publ. Co.

...1-Origin Captain Valiant	17.00	49.00	115.00
...2-Captain Valiant	10.00	30.00	65.00
...3(1946-Croyden)-Captain Valiant	8.35	25.00	55.00

ARIETY COMICS (See Fox Giants)

ARIOGENESIS
...ne, 1994 ($3.50)
...agger Comics Group

		1.40	3.50

ARSITY
...#45
...arents' Magazine Institute

		6.70	20.00	40.00

AULT OF EVIL
...eb, 1973 - No. 23, Nov, 1975
...arvel Comics Group

...1 (1950s reprints begin)	1.00	2.00	5.00	
...2-23: 3,4-Brunner-c		.70	1.75	

OTE: **Ditko** a-14r, 15r, 20-22r. **Drucker** a-10r(Mystic #52), 13r(Uncanny Tales #42). **Everett** a-r(Menace #2), 13r(Menace #4); c-10. **Heath** a-5r. **Gil Kane** c-1, 6. **Krigstein** a-20r(Uncanny les #54). **Reinman** r-1. **Tuska** a-6r.

AULT OF HORROR (Formerly War Against Crime #1-11)
...o. 12, Apr-May, 1950 - No. 40, Dec-Jan, 1954-55
...C. Comics

...2 (Scarce)	389.00	1167.00	3500.00	
...3-Morphine story	88.00	265.00	675.00	
...4	81.00	242.00	600.00	
...5- "Terror in the Swamp" is same story w/minor changes as "The Thing in the				
Swamp" from Haunt of Fear #15	66.00	197.00	500.00	
...6	48.00	145.00	385.00	
...7-19	40.00	120.00	280.00	
...0-25: 22-Frankenstein-c & adaptation. 23-Used in POP, pg. 84; Davis-a(2). 24-				
Craig biography	33.00	99.00	230.00	
...6-B&W & color illos in POP	33.00	99.00	230.00	
...7-35: 30-Dismemberment-c. 31-Ray Bradbury biog. 32-Censored-c.				
35-X-Mas-c	24.00	73.00	170.00	
...6- "Pipe Dream" classic opium addict story by Krigstein; "Twin Bill" cited in				
articles by T.E. Murphy, Wertham	24.00	73.00	170.00	
...7-1st app. Drusilla, a Vampirella look alike; Williamson-a				
	24.00	73.00	170.00	
...8-39: 39-Bondage-c	20.00	60.00	140.00	
...0-Low distribution	24.00	73.00	170.00	

OTE: **Craig** art in all but No. 13 & 33; c-12-40. **Crandall** a-33, 34, 39. **Davis** a-17-38. **Evans** a-...28, 30, 32, 33. **Feldstein** a-12-16. **Ingels** a-13-20, 22-40. **Kamen** a-15-22, 25, 29, 35. ...igstein a-36, 38-40. **Kurtzman** a-12, 13. **Orlando** a-24, 31, 40. **Wood** a-12-14. #22, 29 & 31 ...ve Ray Bradbury adaptations. #16 & 17 have H. P. Lovecraft adaptations.

AULT OF HORROR, THE
...g, 1990 - No. 6, June, 1991 ($1.95, 68 pgs.)(#4 on: $2.00)
...adstone Publishing

...-Craig-c(r); all contain EC reprints		1.60	4.00	
...-6: 2,4-6-Craig-c(r). 3-Ingels-c(r)		.80	2.00	

AULT OF HORROR
...pt, 1991 - No. 5, May, 1992? ($2.00); Oct, 1992 - Present ($1.50)
...ss Cochran/Gemstone Publishing

...-5: E.C reprints		.80	2.00	
...-16: 1-4r/VOH #12-15 w/original-c			1.50	

..-COMICS (Morse code for "V" - 3 dots, 1 dash)
...n, 1942 - No. 2, Mar-Apr, 1942
...x Features Syndicate

1-Origin V-Man & the Boys; The Banshee & The Black Fury, The Queen of				
Evil, & V-Agents begin; Nazi-c	108.00	324.00	865.00	
2-Nazi bondage/torture-c	84.00	253.00	675.00	

VECTOR
1986 - No. 4, 1986? ($1.50, 1st color comic by Now Comics)
Now Comics

1-4: Computer-generated art			1.50

VEGAS KNIGHTS
1989 ($1.95, one-shot)
Pioneer Comics

1		.80	2.00

VELOCITY (Also see Cyberforce)
Nov, 1995 - No. 3, Jan, 1996 ($2.50, limited series)
Image Comics (Top Cow Productions)

1-3: Kurt Busiek scripts in all. 2-Savage Dragon-c/app.	1.00	2.50

VENGEANCE OF VAMPIRELLA (Becomes Vampirella: Death & Destruction)
Apr, 1994 - No. 25, Apr, 1996 ($2.95)
Harris Comics

1-($3.50)-Quesada/Palmiotti "bloodfoil" wraparound-c			
	2.85	8.50	20.00
1-2nd printing; blue foil-c	1.00	2.00	5.00
1-Gold	5.70	17.00	40.00
2	1.70	5.00	12.00
3,4	1.20	3.00	7.00
5-25: 8-Polybagged w/trading card; 10-w/coupon for Hyde -25 poster.			
11, 19-Polybagged w/ trading card. 25-Quesada & Palmiotti red foil-c.			
...: Bloodshed (1995, $6.95)	1.20	3.00	7.00

VENGEANCE OF VAMPIRELLA: THE MYSTERY WALK
Nov, 1995 ($2.95, one-shot)
Harris Comics

0		1.20	3.00

VENGEANCE SQUAD
July, 1975 - No. 6, May, 1976 (#1-3 are 25¢ issues)
Charlton Comics

1-Mike Mauser, Private Eye begins by Staton		.80	2.00
2-6: Morisi-a in all		.60	1.60
5,6(Modern Comics-r, 1977)			1.40

VENOM: ALONG CAME A SPIDER (See Amazing Spider-Man #298 & Marvel
Comics Presents)
Jan, 1996 - No. 4, Apr, 1996 ($2.95, limited series)
Marvel Comics

1-4:Spider-Man & Carnage app.			3.00

VENOM: CARNAGE UNLEASHED
Apr, 1995 - No. 4, July, 1995 ($2.95, limited series)
Marvel Comics

1-4		1.20	3.00

VENOM: FUNERAL PYRE
Aug, 1993 - No. 3, Oct, 1993 ($2.95, limited series)
Marvel Comics

1-3: 1-Holo-grafx foil-c; Punisher app. in all		1.20	3.00

VENOM: LETHAL PROTECTOR
Feb, 1993 - No. 6, July, 1993 ($2.95, limited series)
Marvel Comics

1-Red holo-grafx foil-c; Bagley-c/a in all	1.00	2.00	5.00
1-Gold variant sold to retailers	2.85	8.50	20.00
1-Black-c	21.00	64.00	150.00
2-6: Spider-Man app. in all		1.20	3.00

Venom: The Hunger #1 © MEG

Venus Wars #13 © DH

Vermillion #4 © Lucius Shepard

	GD25	FN65	NM94

VENOM: NIGHTS OF VENGEANCE
Aug, 1994 - No. 4, Nov, 1994 ($2.95, limited series)
Marvel Comics

1-4: 1-Red foil-c	1.20	3.00

VENOM: SEPERATION ANXIETY
Dec, 1994 - No. 4, Mar, 1995 ($2.95, limited series)
Marvel Comics

1-4: 1-Embossed-c	1.20	3.00

VENOM: SINNER TAKES ALL
Aug, 1995 - No. 5, Oct, 1995 ($2.95, limited series)
Marvel Comics

1-5	1.20	3.00

VENOM: SUPER SPECIAL
Aug, 1995 ($3.95, one-shot)
Marvel Comics

1-Flip book	1.60	4.00

VENOM: THE ENEMY WITHIN
Feb, 1994 - No. 3, Apr, 1994 ($2.95, limited series)
Marvel Comics

1-3: Demogoblin & Morbius app. 1-Glow-in-the-dark-c.	1.20	3.00

VENOM: THE HUNGER
Aug, 1996 - No. 4, Nov, 1996 ($1.95, limited series)
Marvel Comics

1-4		2.00

VENOM: THE HUNTED
May, 1996 -No. 3, July, 1996 ($2.95, limited series)
Marvel Comics

1-3		3.00

VENOM: THE MACE
May, 1994 - No. 3, July, 1994 ($2.95, limited series)
Marvel Comics

1-3: 1-Embossed-c	1.20	3.00

VENOM: THE MADNESS
Nov, 1993 - No. 3, Jan, 1994 ($2.95, limited series)
Marvel Comics

1-3: Kelley Jones-c/a(p). 1-Embossed-c; Juggernaut app.	1.20	3.00

VENTURE
Aug, 1986 - No. 3, 1986? ($1.75)
AC Comics (Americomics)

1-3: 1-3-Bolt. 1-Astron. 2-Femforce. 3-Fazers	.90	1.80

VENUS (See Marvel Spotlight #2 & Weird Wonder Tales)
Aug, 1948 - No. 19, Apr, 1952 (Also see Marvel Mystery #91)
Marvel/Atlas Comics (CMC 1-9/LCC 10-19)

1-Venus & Hedy Devine begin; 1st app. Venus; Kurtzman's "Hey Look"			
	106.00	318.00	850.00
2	61.00	185.00	495.00
3,5	52.00	157.00	420.00
4-Kurtzman's "Hey Look"	53.00	161.00	430.00
6-9: 6-Loki app. 7,8-Painted-c. 9-Begin 52 pg.; book-length feature "Whom			
the Gods Destroy!"	47.00	142.00	380.00
10-S/F-horror issues begin (7/50)	52.00	157.00	420.00
11-S/F end of the world (11/50)	65.00	195.00	520.00
12-Colan-a	41.00	124.00	330.00
13-19-Venus by Everett, 2-3 stories each; covers-#13,15-19; 14-Everett part			
cover (Venus). 17-Bondage-c	65.00	195.00	520.00

NOTE: Berg s/f story-13. Everett c-13, 14(part; Venus only), 15-19. Heath s/f story-11. Maneely s/f story-10(3pg.), 16. Morisi a-19. Syd Shores c-6.

VENUS DOMINA
July, 1996 - Present ($2.95/$4.95, mature)
Verotik

1-($4.95)-Embossed-c w/nudity by Dave Stevens	5
1-($2.95, San Diego Edition)-Wing Bird-c/a	3

VENUS WARS, THE (Manga)
Apr, 1991 - No.14, May, 1992 ($2.25, B&W)
Dark Horse Comics

1-6,8,9,11-14: 1-3 Contain 2 Dark Horse trading cards	1.15	2
7,10 ($2.50): 1,3,7,10-(44 pgs.)	1.25	2

VERI BEST SURE FIRE COMICS
No date (circa 1945) (Reprints Holyoke one-shots)
Holyoke Publishing Co.

1-Captain Aero, Alias X, Miss Victory, Commandos of the Devil Dogs, Red			
Cross, Hammerhead Hawley, Capt. Aero's Sky Scouts, Flagman app.;			
same-c as Veri Best Sure Shot #1	34.00	103.00	240

VERI BEST SURE SHOT COMICS
No date (circa 1945) (Reprints Holyoke one-shots)
Holyoke Publishing Co.

1-Capt. Aero, Miss Victory by Quinlan, Alias X, The Red Cross, Flagman,			
Commandos of the Devil Dogs, Hammerhead Hawley, Capt. Aero's Sky			
Scouts; same-c as Veri Best Sure Fire #1	34.00	103.00	240

VERMILLION
Oct, 1996 - Present ($2.25)
DC Comics (Helix)

1-6: Lucius Shepard scripts	2

VERONICA (Also see Archie's Girls, Betty &…)
Apr, 1989 - Present
Archie Comics

1-21: 1,2-(75¢). 3-30-(95¢-$1.00)	1
21-36: 21-Begin $1.25-c. 34-Neon ink-c	1
36-60	1

VERONICA'S PASSPORT DIGEST MAGAZINE (Becomes Veronica's Digest
Magazine #3 on)
Nov, 1992 - Present ($1.50, digest size)
Archie Comics

1-15	1

VERONICA'S SUMMER SPECIAL (See Archie Giant Series Magazine #615, 625)

VEROTIKA
Mar, 1995 - Present ($2.95, mature) (1st Verotik title)
Verotik

1,2	1.30	3.25	8
3-115: 9-Adam Pollina-a. 10-Nudity-c		1.20	3

VERTIGO GALLERY, THE: DREAMS AND NIGHTMARES
1995 ($3.50, one-shot)
DC Comics (Vertigo)

1-Pin-ups of Vertigo characters by Sienkiewicz, Toth, Van Fleet & others; Da		
McKean-c		1.60	4

VERTIGO JAM
Aug, 1993 ($3.95, one-shot, 68 pgs.)(Painted-c by Fabry)
DC Comics (Vertigo)

1-Sandman by Neil Gaiman, Hellblazer, Animal Man, Doom Patrol, Swamp		
Thing, Kid Eternity & Shade the Changing Man	1.00	2.00	5

VERTIGO PREVIEW
1992 (75¢, one-shot, 36 pgs.)
DC Comics (Vertigo)

1-Vertigo previews; Sandman story by Neil Gaiman		.80	2

Vertigo Verite: The Unseen Hand #2 © Terry LaBan

V For Vendetta #7 © DC

Victory #1 © Jack Kirby

	GD25	FN65	NM94

	GD25	FN65	NM94

ERTIGO VERITE: THE UNSEEN HAND
pt, 1996 - No. 4, Dec, 1996 ($2.50, limited series)
C Comics (Vertigo)

-4: Terry LaBan scripts in all			2.50

ERTIGO VISIONS
ne, 1993 - Present (68 pgs.)
C Comics (Vertigo)

e Geek 1 (6/93, $3.95)		1.60	4.00
e Eaters ($4.95, 1995)-Milligan story.			5.00
e Phantom Stranger 1 (10/93, $3.50)		1.40	3.50
Occult 1 (7/94, $3.95)		1.60	4.00
ez 1 (7/95, $3.95)		1.60	4.00

RY BEST OF DENNIS THE MENACE, THE
y, 1979 - No. 2, Apr, 1980 (95¢/$1.00, digest-size, 132 pgs.)
wcett Publications

,2-Reprints		.80	2.00

RY BEST OF DENNIS THE MENACE, THE
r, 1982 - No. 3, Aug, 1982 ($1.25, digest-size)
arvel Comics Group

-3: Reprints			1.25

TE: *Hank Ketcham c-all. A few thousand of #1 & 2 were printed with DC emblem.*

RY VICKY
93? - No. 8, 1995 ($2.50, B&W)
eet Danny Ocean

-8		1.00	2.50
Calling All Hillbillies (1995, $2.50)		1.00	2.50

FOR VENDETTA
pt, 1988 - No. 10, May, 1989 ($2.00, maxi-series)
C Comics

-10: Alan Moore scripts in all		.80	2.00
ade paperback (1990, $14.95)			15.00

C BRIDGES FAZERS SKETCHBOOK AND FACT FILE
v, 1986 ($1.75)
Comics

		.75	1.80

C FLINT(Crime Buster…)(See Authentic Police Cases #10-14 & Fugitives
om Justice #2)
gust, 1948 - No. 5, April, 1949 (Newspaper reprints; NEA Service)
John Publishing Co.

	10.00	30.00	70.00
	7.50	22.50	45.00
5	5.85	17.50	35.00

C FLINT (Crime Buster…)
o, 1956 - No. 2, May, 1956 (Newspaper reprints)
go Publ.

2	6.70	20.00	40.00

C JORDAN (Also see Big Shot Comics #32)
il, 1945
il Service Publ.

1944 daily newspaper-r	11.50	34.00	80.00

CKI (Humor)
, 1975 - No. 4, Aug, 1975 (No. 1,2: 68 pgs.)
as/Seaboard Publ.

Reprints Tippy Teen		1.20	3.00
4		.65	1.60

CKI VALENTINE (…Summer Special #1)
r, 1985 - No. 4, July, 1986 ($1.70, B&W)

Renegade Press

1-4: Woggon, Rausch-a; all have paper dolls. 2-Christmas issue .85			1.70

VICKS COMICS (See Pure Oil Comics, Salerno Carnival of Comics & 24 Pages
of Comics)
nd (circa 1938) (Giveaway, 68 pgs. in color)
Eastern Color Printing Co. (Vicks Chemical Co.)

nn-Famous Funnies-r (before #40); contains 5 pgs. Buck Rogers (4 pgs. from F.F. #15, & 1 pg. from #16) Joe Palooka, Napoleon, etc. app.	68.00	206.00	550.00
nn-16 loose, untrimmed page giveaway; paper-c; r/Famous Funnies #14; Buck Rogers, Joe Palooka app.	26.00	79.00	185.00

VICKY
Oct, 1948 - No. 5, June, 1949
Ace Magazine

nn(10/48)-Teenage humor	5.35	16.00	32.00
4(12/48), nn(2/49), 4(4/49), 5(6/49): 5-Dotty app.	4.25	13.00	26.00

VIC TORRY & HIS FLYING SAUCER (Also see Mr. Monster's…#5)
1950 (one-shot)
Fawcett Publications

nn-Book-length saucer story by Powell; photo/painted-c	47.00	141.00	375.00

VICTORY
June, 1994 ($2.50, unfinished limited series)
Topps Comics

1-Kurt Busiek script; Giffen-c/a; Rob Liefeld variant-c exists	1.00		2.50

VICTORY COMICS
Aug, 1941 - No. 4, Dec, 1941 (#1 by Funnies, Inc.)
Hillman Periodicals

1-The Conqueror by Bill Everett, The Crusader, & Bomber Burns begin; Conqueror's origin in text; Everett-c	250.00	750.00	2000.00
2-Everett-c/a	112.00	338.00	900.00
3,4	75.00	225.00	600.00

VIC VERITY MAGAZINE
1945; No. 2, Jan?, 1947 - No. 7, Sept, 1946 (A comic book)
Vic Verity Publications

1-C. C. Beck-c/a	14.00	43.00	100.00
2-Beck-c	9.15	27.00	55.00
3-7: 6-Beck-a. 7-Beck-c	7.50	22.50	45.00

VIDEO JACK
Nov, 1987 - No. 6, Nov, 1988 ($1.25)
Marvel Comics (Epic Comics)

1-6: 6-Neal Adams, Keith Giffen, Wrightson, others-a			1.30

VIETNAM JOURNAL
Nov, 1987 - No. 11, July, 1989 ($1.75/$1.95, B&W)
Apple Comics

1-Don Lomax-c/a/scripts in all		.80	2.00
1-2nd print		.80	2.00
2-11: 10,11-$2.00/$2.25-c		.80	2.00
…: Indian Country Vol. 1 (1990, $12.95)-r/#1-4 plus one new story		1.85	5.50	13.00

VIETNAM JOURNAL: VALLEY OF DEATH
June, 1994 - No. 2, Aug, 1994 ($2.75, B&W, limited series)
Apple Comics

1,2: By Don Lomax		1.10	2.75

VIGILANTE, THE (Also see New Teen Titans #23 & Annual V2#2)
Oct, 1983 - No. 50, Feb, 1988 ($1.25, Baxter paper)
DC Comics

Vigilante #28 © DC

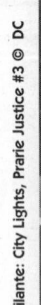

Vigilante: City Lights, Prarie Justice #3 © DC

Violator Vs. Badrock #3 ©
Todd McFarlane/Rob Liefeld

	GD25	FN65	NM94
1-Origin		1.20	3.00
2-10: 3-Cyborg app. 4-1st app. The Exterminator; Newton-a(p). 6,7-Origin			1.50
11-50: 17,18-Alan Moore scripts. 20,21-Nightwing app. 35-Origin Mad Bomber. 47-Batman-c/story. 50-Ken Steacy painted-c			1.25
Annual (1985)		1.00	2.50
Annual 2 (1986)		.80	2.00

VIGILANTE: CITY LIGHTS, PRARIE JUSTICE (Also see Action Comics #42,
Justice League of America #78, Leading Comics & World's Finest #244)
Nov, 1995 - No. 4, Feb, 1995 ($2.50, limited series)
DC Comics

1-4: James Robinson scripts in all		1.00	2.50

VIGILANTES, THE
No. 839, Sept, 1957
Dell Publishging Col.

Four Color 839-Movie	7.00	21.00	70.00

VIKINGS, THE (Movie)
No. 910, May, 1958
Dell Publishing Co.

Four Color 910-Buscema-a, Kirk Douglas photo-c	9.00	27.00	90.00

VILLAINS AND VIGILANTES
Dec, 1986 - No. 4, May, 1987 ($1.50/$1.75, limited series, Baxter paper)
Eclipse Comics

1-4: Based on role-playing game. 2-4 ($1.75-c)		.90	1.75

VINTAGE MAGNUS (...Robot Fighter)
Jan, 1992 - No. 4, Apr, 1992 ($2.25, limited series)
Valiant

1-4: 1-Layton-c; r/origin from Magnus R.F. #22		1.20	3.00

VIOLATOR (Also see Spawn #2)
May, 1994 - No. 3, Aug, 1994 ($1.95, limited series)
Image Comics (Todd McFarlane Productions)

1-Alan Moore scripts in all	1.00	2.00	5.00
2,3: Bart Sears-c(p)/a(p)		1.60	4.00

VIOLATOR VS. BADROCK
May, 1995 - No. 4, Aug, 1995 ($2.50, limited series)
Image Comics (Extreme Studios)

1-4: Alan Moore scripts in all. 1-1st app Celestine; variant-c (3?)		1.00	2.50

VIPER (TV)
Aug, 1994 - No. 4, Nov, 1994 ($1.95, limited series)
DC Comics

1-4-Adaptation of television show		.80	2.00

VIRGINIAN, THE (TV)
June, 1963
Gold Key

1(10060-306)-Part photo-c of James Drury plus photo back-c	3.00	9.00	30.00

VIRTUA FIGHTER (Video Game)
Aug, 1995 (2.95, one-shot)
Marvel Comics

1-Sega Saturn game		1.20	3.00

VIRUS (Manga)
1993 - No. 4, 1993 ($2.50, limited series)
Dark Horse Comics

1-4: Ploog-c		1.00	2.50

VISION, THE
Nov, 1994 - No. 4, Feb, 1995 ($1.75, limited series)

	GD25	FN65	NM94
Marvel Comics			
1-4		.70	1

VISION AND THE SCARLET WITCH, THE (See Marvel Fanfare)
Nov, 1982 - No. 4, Feb, 1983 (Limited series)
Marvel Comics Group

1		.90	1
2-4: 2-Nuklo & Future Man app.			

VISION AND THE SCARLET WITCH, THE
Oct, 1985 - No. 12, Sept, 1986 (Maxi-series)
Marvel Comics Group

V2#1-Origin; 1st app. in Avengers #57		.90	1
2-5: 2-West Coast Avengers x-over			
6-12			

VISIONARIES
Nov, 1987 - No. 6, Sept, 1988
Marvel Comics (Star Comics)/Marvel Comics #3 on

1-6			

VISIONS
1979 - No. 5, 1983 (B&W, fanzine)
Vision Publications

1-Flaming Carrot begins(1st app?); N. Adams-c	5.00	15.00	3
2-N. Adams, Rogers-a; Gulacy back-c; signed & numbered to 2000	4.30	13.00	3
3-Williamson-c(p); Steranko back-c	2.15	6.50	1
4-Flaming Carrot-c & info.	2.85	8.50	2
5-1 pg. Flaming Carrot	1.20	3.00	

NOTE: *Eisner* a-4. *Miller* a-4. *Starlin* a-3. *Williamson* a-5. After #4, Visions became an ann
publication of The Atlanta Fantasy Fair.

VISITOR, THE
Apr, 1995 - No. 13, Nov, 1995 ($2.50)
Valiant/Acclaim Comics (Valiant)

1-13: 8-Harbinger revealed. 13-Visitor revealed to be Sting from Harbinger.		1.00	1

VISITOR, VS. THE VALIANT UNIVERSE, THE
Feb, 1995 - No. 2, Mar, 1995 ($2.95, limited series)
Valiant

1,2		1.20	4

VOGUE (Also see Youngblood)
Oct, 1995 - No.3, Jan, 1996 ($2.50, limited series)
Image Comics (Extreme Studios)

1-3: 1-Liefeld-c		1.00	
1-Variant-c		1.20	

VOID INDIGO (Also see Marvel Graphic Novel)
11/84 - No. 2, 3/85 ($1.50, direct sales, unfinished series, mature)
Marvel Comics (Epic Comics)

1,2: Cont'd from Marvel G.N.; graphic sex & violence			

VOLTRON (TV)
1985 - No. 3, 1985 (75¢, limited series)
Modern Publishing

1-3: Ayers-a in all			

VOODA (Jungle Princess) (Formerly Voodoo)
No. 20, April, 1955 - No. 22, Aug, 1955
Ajax-Farrell (Four Star Publications)

20-Baker-c/a (r/Seven Seas #6)	28.00	84.00	19
21,22-Baker-a plus Kamen/Baker story, Kimbo Boy of Jungle, & Baker-c (p)			
in all. 22-Censored Jo-Jo-r (name Powaa)	24.00	73.00	17

NOTE: #20-22 each contain one heavily censored-r of South Sea Girl by *Baker* from Seven
Seas Comics with name changed to Vooda. #20-r/Seven Seas #6; #21-r/#4; #22-4/#3.

Voodoo #9 © AJAX

Voodoo-Zealot: Skin Trade #1 © Aegis Entertainment

Vortex #13 © Vortex

WA

	GD25	FN65	NM94

VOODOO (Weird Fantastic Tales) (Vooda #20 on)
May, 1952 - No. 19, Jan-Feb, 1955
Ajax-Farrell (Four Star Publ.)

1-South Sea Girl-r by Baker	40.00	120.00	320.00
2-Rulah story-r plus South Sea Girl from Seven Seas #2 by Baker (name changed from Alani to El'nee)	37.00	111.00	260.00
3-Bakerish-a; man stabbed in face	25.00	75.00	175.00
4,8-Baker-r. 8-Severed head panels	25.00	75.00	175.00
5-7,9,10: 5-Nazi death camp story (flaying alive). 6-Severed head panels	20.00	60.00	140.00
11-14,16-18: 14-Zombies take over America. 16-Post nuclear world story. 17-Electric chair panels	17.00	51.00	120.00
15-Opium drug story-r/Ellery Queen #3	19.00	56.00	130.00
19-Bondage-c; Baker-r(2)/Seven Seas #5 w/minor changes & #1, heavily modified; last pre-code; contents & covers chane to jungle theme	23.00	69.00	160.00
nnual 1(1952, 25¢, 100 pgs.)-Baker-a (scarce)	50.00	150.00	400.00

VOODOO (See Tales of...)

VOODOO-ZEALOT: SKIN TRADE (See WildC.A.T.S: Covert Action Teams)
ug, 1995 ($4.95, one-shot)
mage Comics (Wildstorm Productions)

1	1.00	2.00	5.00

VORTEX
ov, 1982 - No. 15, 1988 (No month) ($1.50/$1.75, B&W)
ortex Publs.

1 ($1.95)-Peter Hsu-a; Ken Steacy-c; nudity	1.65	4.20	10.00
2-1st app. Mister X (on-c only)	1.00	2.00	5.00
		1.20	3.00
4-15: 12-Sam Kieth-a		.80	2.00

VORTEX
91 - No. 2? ($2.50, limited series)
mico

1,2: Heroes from The Elementals	1.00	2.50	

VORTEX
96 - Present ($2.95)
tity Comics

1b: 1b-Kaniuga-c			3.00

YAGE TO THE BOTTOM OF THE SEA (Movie, TV)
1230, Sept-Nov, 1961; Dec, 1964 - #16, Apr, 1970 (Painted-c)
l Publishing Co./Gold Key

ur Color 1230 (1961)	10.00	30.00	100.00
(#33-412(#1, 12/64)(Gold Key)	6.00	18.00	60.00
7/65) - 5: Photo back-c, 1-5	4.00	12.00	40.00
14	3.15	10.00	31.00
16-Reprints	2.30	6.70	16.00

YAGE TO THE DEEP
t-Nov, 1962 - No. 4, Nov-Jan, 1964 (Painted-c)
Publishing Co.

	5.50	16.50	38.00
	4.00	12.00	28.00

CKO
t, 1980 - No. 3, Oct, 1981 (84 pgs., B&W, magazine)
l Publ. Corp.

		.80	2.00

CKY ADVENTURES OF CRACKY (Also see Gold Key Spotlight)
1972 - No. 12, Sept, 1975
Key

	1.65	4.20	10.00

	GD25	FN65	NM94

2	1.00	2.00	5.00
3-12		1.20	3.00

(See March of Comics #405, 424, 436, 448)

WACKY DUCK (...Comics #3-6; formerly Dopey Duck; Justice Comics #7 on)
(See Film Funnies)
No. 3, Fall, 1946 - No. 6, Summer, 1947; Aug, 1948 - No. 2, Oct, 1948
Marvel Comics (NPP)

3	14.00	43.00	100.00
4-Infinity-c	17.00	49.00	115.00
5,6(1947)-Becomes Justice comics	12.00	36.00	85.00
1,2(1948)	9.15	27.00	55.00
I.W. Reprint #1,2,7('58): 1-r/Wacky Duck #6	1.30	3.25	8.00
Super Reprint #10(I.W. on-c, Super-inside)	1.30	3.25	8.00

WACKY QUACKY (See Wisco)

WACKY RACES (TV)
Aug, 1969 - No. 7, Apr, 1972 (Hanna-Barbera)
Gold Key

1	2.15	6.50	15.00
2-7	1.30	3.25	8.00

WACKY SQUIRREL (Also see Dark Horse Presents)
Oct, 1987 - No. 4, 1988 ($1.75, B&W)
Dark Horse Comics

1-4: 4-Superman parody		.70	1.75
Halloween Adventure Special 1 (1987, $2.00)		.80	2.00
Summer Fun Special 1 (1988, $2.00)		.80	2.00

WACKY WITCH (Also see Gold Key Spotlight)
March, 1971 - No. 21, Dec, 1975
Gold Key

1	2.15	6.50	15.00
2	1.30	3.25	8.00
3-10	1.00	2.00	5.00
11-21		1.20	3.00

(See March of Comics #374, 398, 410, 422, 434, 446, 458, 470, 482)

WACKY WOODPECKER (See Two Bit the...)
1958; 1963
I. W. Enterprises/Super Comics

I.W. Reprint #1,2,7 (nd-reprints Two Bit...): 7-r/Two-Bit, the Wacky Woodpecker #1.	1.00	2.60	6.00
Super Reprint #10('63): 10-r/Two-Bit, The Wacky Woodpecker #?	1.00	2.60	6.00

WAGON TRAIN (1st Series) (TV) (See Western Roundup under Dell Giants)
No. 895, Mar, 1958 - No. 13, Apr-June, 1962 (All photo-c)
Dell Publishing Co.

Four Color 895 (#1)	12.00	36.00	120.00
Four Color 971(#2), 1019(#3)	6.50	19.50	65.00
4(1-3/60), 6-13	5.50	16.50	55.00
5-Toth-a	6.00	18.00	60.00

WAGON TRAIN (2nd Series)(TV)
Jan, 1964 - No. 4, Oct, 1964 (All front & back photo-c)
Gold Key

1-Tufts-a in all	4.50	13.50	45.00
2-4	3.00	9.00	30.00

WAITING ROOM WILLIE (See Sad Case of...)

WALLY (Teen-age)
Dec, 1962 - No. 4, Sept, 1963
Gold Key

1	2.60	7.50	18.00
2-4	1.65	4.20	10.00

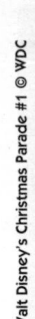

Walt Disney Giant #6 © WDC

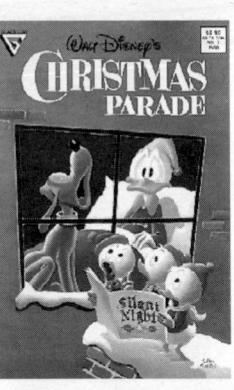

Walt Disney's Christmas Parade #1 © WDC

Walt Disney Comics & Stories #18 © WDC

	GD25	FN65	NM94

WALLY THE WIZARD
Apr, 1985 - No. 12, Mar, 1986 (Children's comic)
Marvel Comics (Star Comics)

1-12: Bob Bolling a-1,3; c-1,9,11,12		1.00

WALLY WOOD'S T.H.U.N.D.E.R. AGENTS (See Thunder Agents)
Nov, 1984 - No. 5, Oct, 1986 ($2.00, 52 pgs.)
Deluxe Comics

1-5: 5-Jerry Ordway-c/a in Wood style	1.20	3.00

NOTE: *Anderson* a-2i, 3i. *Buckler* a-4. *Ditko* a-3, 4. *Giffen* a-1p-4p. *Perez* a-1p, 2, 4; c-1-4.

WALT DISNEY CHRISTMAS PARADE (Also see Christmas Parade)
Winter, 1977 ($1.95, cardboard covers, 224 pgs.)
Whitman Publishing Co. (Golden Press)

11191-Barks-r/Christmas in Disneyland #1, Dell Christmas Parade #9 & Dell Giant #53	1.20	3.00

WALT DISNEY COMICS DIGEST
June, 1968 - No. 57, Feb, 1976 (50¢, digest size)
Gold Key

	GD25	FN65	NM94
1-Reprints Uncle Scrooge #5; 192 pgs.	3.50	10.50	35.00
2-4-Barks-r	2.00	6.00	20.00
5-Daisy Duck by Barks (8 pgs.); last published story by Barks (art only) plus 21 pg. Scrooge-r by Barks	4.00	12.00	40.00
6-13-All Barks-r	2.10	6.50	15.00
14,15	1.30	3.25	8.00
16-Reprints Donald Duck #26 by Barks	2.10	6.50	15.00
17-20-Barks-r	1.70	5.00	12.00
21-31,33,35-37-Barks-r; 24-Toth Zorro	1.70	4.20	10.00
32,41,45,47-49	1.00	2.50	6.00
34-Reprints 4-Color #318	1.70	4.20	10.00
38-Reprints Christmas in Disneyland #1	1.70	4.20	10.00
39-Two Barks-r/WDC&S #272, 4-Color #1073 plus Toth Zorro-r	1.70	4.20	10.00
40-Mickey Mouse-r by Gottfredson	1.20	2.90	7.00
42,43-Barks-r	1.20	2.90	7.00
44-(Has Gold Key emblem, 50¢)-Reprints 1st story of 4-Color #29,256,275,282	2.85	8.00	20.00
44-Republished in 1976 by Whitman; not identical to original; a bit smaller, blank back-c, 69¢	1.30	3.25	8.00
46,50,52-Barks-r. 52-Barks-r/WDC&S #161,132	1.00	2.50	6.00
51-Reprints 4-Color #71	1.70	4.20	10.00
53-55: 53-Reprints Dell Giant #30. 54-Reprints Donald Duck Beach Party #2. 55-Reprints Dell Giant #49	1.00	2.00	5.00
56-r/Uncle Scrooge #32 (Barks)	1.20	2.90	7.00
57-r/Mickey Mouse Almanac('57) & two Barks stories	1.00	2.50	6.00

NOTE: *Toth* a-52r. #1-10, 196 pgs.; #11-41, 164 pgs.; #42 on, 132 pgs. Old issues were being reprinted & distributed by Whitman in 1976.

WALT DISNEY GIANT (Disney)
Sept, 1995 - No. 7, Sept, 1996 ($2.95, bi-monthly, 48 pgs.)
Bruce Hamilton Company (Gladstone)

1-7: 1-Scrooge McDuck in the Yukon; Rosa-c/a/scripts plus r/F.C. #218. 2-Uncle Scrooge-r by Barks plus 17 pg. text story. 3-Donald the Mighty Duck; Rosa-c/a; Barks & Rosa-r. 4-Mickey and Goofy; new-a (story actually stars Goofy. Mickey Mouse by Caesar Ferioli; Donald Duck by Giorgio Cavazzano (1st in U.S.). 6-Uncle Scrooge & the Jr. Woodchucks; new-a and Barks-r. 7-Uncle Scrooge-r by Barks plus new-a		.90	2.25

NOTE: Series was initially solicited as Uncle Walt's Collectory. Issue #8 was advertised, but later cancelled.

WALT DISNEY PRESENTS (TV)(Disney)
No. 997, 6-8/59 - No. 6, 12-2/1960-61; No. 1181, 4-5/61 (All photo-c)
Dell Publishing Co.

Four Color 997 (#1)	7.00	21.00	70.00
2(12-2/60)-The Swamp Fox(origin), Elfego Baca, Texas John Slaughter			

	GD25	FN65	NM94
(Disney TV show) begin	4.50	13.50	45
3-6: 5-Swamp Fox by Warren Tufts	4.00	12.00	4
Four Color 1181-Texas John Slaughter	7.00	21.00	7

WALT DISNEY'S CHRISTMAS PARADE (Also see Christmas Parade)
Winter, 1988; No. 2, Winter, 1989 ($2.95, 100 pgs.)
Gladstone

1-Barks-r/painted-c	1.65	4.20	1
2-Barks-r	1.30	3.25	

WALT DISNEY'S COMICS AND STORIES (Cont. of Mickey Mouse Magazir (#1-30 contain Donald Duck newspaper reprints) (Titled "Comics And Stories" #264 to #?; titled "Walt Disney's Comics And Stories" #511 on)
10/40 - #263, 8/62; #264, 10/62 - #510, 1984; #511, 10/86 - Present
Dell Publishing Co./Gold Key #264-473/Whitman #474-510/Gladstone #511-547(4/90)/Disney Comics #548(6/90)-#585/Gladstone #586(8/93) on

NOTE: The whole number can always be found at the bottom of the title pag in the lower left-hand or right hand panel.

	GD25	FN65	VF82	NM
1(V1#1-c; V2#1-indicia)-Donald Duck strip-r by Al Taliaferro & Gottfredson's Mickey Mouse begin	1500.00	4500.00	9750.00	16,00
(Estimated up to 245 total copies exist, 12 in NM/Mint)				

	GD25	FN65	NM
2	550.00	1650.00	600
3	219.00	656.00	185
4-X-Mas-c; 1st Huey, Dewey & Louie-c this title (See Mickey Mouse Magaz V4#2 for 1st-c ever)	150.00	450.00	130
4-Special promotional, complimentary issue; cover same except one corne was blanked out & boxed in to identify the giveaway (not a paste-over). special pressing was probably sent out to former subscribers to Mickey Mouse Mag. whose subscriptions had expired. (Very rare-5 known copie	250.00	750.00	220
5-Goofy-c	112.00	338.00	100
6-10: 8-Only Clarabelle Cow-c. 9-Taliaferro-c (1st)	94.00	281.00	85
11-14: 11-Huey, Dewey & Louie-c/app.	81.00	245.00	70
15-17: 15-The 3 Little Kittens (17 pgs.). 16-The 3 Little Pigs (29 pgs.); X-Ma 17-The Ugly Duckling (14 pgs.)	72.00	216.00	64
18-21	59.00	178.00	52
22-30: 22-Flag-c. 24-The Flying Gauchito (1st original comic book story dor WDC&S). 27-Jose Carioca by Carl Buettner (2nd original story in WDC&	52.00	156.00	48
31-New Donald Duck stories by Carl Barks begin (See F.C. #9 for 1st Barks Donald Duck)	300.00	900.00	290
32-Barks-a	128.00	383.00	125
33-Barks-a; infinity-c	94.00	283.00	90
34-Gremlins by Walt Kelly begin, end #41; Barks-a	77.00	233.00	75
35,36-Barks-a	70.00	210.00	67
37-Donald Duck by Jack Hannah	36.00	108.00	34
38-40-Barks-a. 39-X-Mas-c. 40,41-Gremlins by Kelly	47.00	140.00	45
41-50-Barks-a. 43-Seven Dwarfs-c app. (4/44). 45-50-Nazis in Gottfredson's Mickey Mouse Stories	38.00	112.00	36
51-60-Barks-a. 51-X-Mas-c. 52-Li'l Bad Wolf begins, ends #203 (not in #55 58-Kelly flag-c	25.00	75.00	*
61-70: Barks-a. 61-Dumbo story. 63,64-Pinocchio stories. 63-Cover swipe New Funnies #94. 64-X-Mas-c. 65-Pluto story. 66-Infinity-c. 67,68-Mickey Mouse Sunday-r by Bill Wright	22.00	65.00	2
71-80: Barks-a. 75-77-Brer Rabbit stories, no Mickey Mouse. 76-X-Mas-c	16.00	48.00	15
81-87,89,90: Barks-a. 82-Goofy-c. 82-84-Bongo stories. 86-90-Goofy & Ag app. 89-Chip 'n' Dale story	14.00	43.00	14
88-1st app. Gladstone Gander by Barks (1/48)	19.00	58.00	18
91-97,99: Barks-a. 95-1st WDC&S Barks-c. 96-No Mickey Mouse; Little To begins, ends #97. 99-X-Mas-c	12.00	37.00	12
98-1st Uncle Scrooge app. in WDC&S (11/48)	25.00	75.00	24

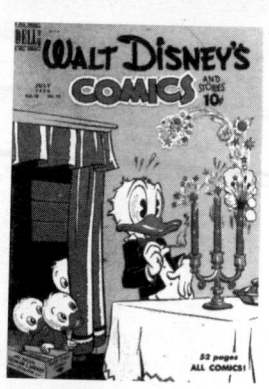
Walt Disney's Comics & Stories #118 © WDC

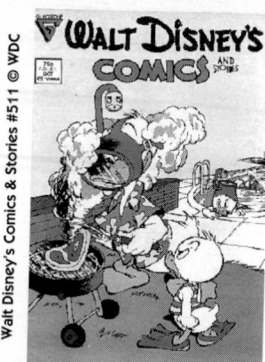
Walt Disney's Comics & Stories #511 © WDC

Walt Disney's Comics & Stories #603 © WDC

WA

	GD25	FN65	NM94

00-(1/49)-Barks-a 15.50 47.00 150.00
01-110-Barks-a. 107-Taliaferro-c; Donald acquires super powers
11.00 33.00 110.00
11,114,117-All Barks 9.50 28.00 85.00
12-Drug (ether) issue (Donald Duck) 9.50 28.00 85.00
13,115,116,118-123: No Barks. 116-Dumbo x-over. 121-Grandma Duck
begins, ends #168; not in #135,142,146,155 4.00 12.00 38.00
24,126-130-All Barks. 124-X-Mas-c 7.50 22.50 70.00
25-1st app. Junior Woodchucks (2/51); Barks-a 11.50 35.00 105.00
31,133,135-137,139-All Barks 7.50 22.50 70.00
32-Barks-a(2) (D. Duck & Grandma Duck) 8.50 25.00 75.00
34-Intro. & 1st app. The Beagle Boys (11/51) 18.00 53.00 160.00
38-Classic Scrooge money story 13.00 40.00 120.00
40-1st app. Gyro Gearloose by Barks (5/52) 18.00 53.00 160.00
41-150-All Barks. 143-Little Hiawatha begins, ends #151,159
5.50 16.50 50.00
51-170-All Barks 4.50 13.50 40.00
71-199-All Barks 4.50 11.00 35.00
90 5.00 11.00 45.00
71-240: All Barks. 204-Chip 'n' Dale & Scamp begin 4.00 11.00 35.00
71-283: Barks-a. 241-Dumbo x-over. 247-Gyro Gearloose begins, ends #274.
256-Ludwig Von Drake begins, ends #274 3.00 9.00 26.00
84,285,287,290,295,296,309-311-Not by Barks 4.50 12.00
86,288,289,291-294,297,298,308-All Barks stories; 293-Grandma Duck's Farm
Friends. 297-Gyro Gearloose. 298-Daisy Duck's Diary-r
6.00 16.00
299-307-All contain early Barks-r (#43-117). 305-Gyro Gearloose
2.25 6.75 18.00
312-Last Barks issue with original story 2.25 6.75 18.00
313-315,317-327,329-334,336-341 1.50 4.50 12.00
335-Last issue published during life of Walt Disney 1.50 4.50 12.00
335,342-350-Barks-r 1.50 4.50 12.00
351-360-With posters inside; Barks reprints (2 versions of each with & without
posters)-without posters… 1.50 4.50 12.00
351-360-With posters… 2.25 6.75 18.00
361-400-Barks-r 1.50 4.50 12.00
401-429-Barks-r 1.50 4.50 12.00
430,433,437,438,441,444,445,466,506-No Barks 1.00 2.50 6.00
431,432,434,436,439,440,442,443-Barks-r 1.00 2.50 6.00
435-465,467-505,507-510: All Barks-r. 494-r/WDC&S #98
1.00 2.00 5.00
511-Donald Duck by Daan Jippes (1st in U.S.; in all through #518); Gyro
Gearloose Barks-r begins (in most through #547); Wuzzles by Disney studio
(1st by Gladstone) 2.85 8.50 20.00
512,513 1.70 5.00 12.00
514-516,520,523: 523-1st Rosa 10 pager 1.20 3.00 7.00
517,519,521,522,524-547: 518-Infinity-c. 522-r/1st app. Huey, Dewey & Louie
from D. Duck Sunday. 535-546-Barks-r. 537-1st Donald Duck by William Van
Horn in WDC&S. 541-545-52 pgs. 546,547-68 pgs. 546-Kelly-c. 547-Rosa-a
1.20 3.00
548 ($1.50, 6/90)-1st Disney issue; new-a; no M. Mouse .70 1.75
549-570,572,573,577-579,581,584 ($1.50): 549-Barks-r begin, ends #585,
not in #555, 556, & 564. 551-r/1 story from F.C. #29. 556,578-r/Mickey
Mouse Cheerios Premium by Dick Moores. 562,563,568-570, 572,
581-Taliaferro strip-r. 570-Valentine issue; has Mickey/Minnie
centerfold. 584-Taliaferro strip-r .65 1.60
571 ($2.25, 52 pgs.)-Donald Duck by Barks; previously only printed in The
Netherlands (1st time in U.S.); also r/Chip 'n Dale & Scamp from #204
1.00 2.50
574-r/Donald Duck's Atomic Bomb by Barks from 1947 Cheerios
Premium 1.60 4.00
575,576,580,582,583 ($2.95, 68 pgs.): 574-r/1st Pinocchio Sunday strip (1939-
40). 575-Gottfredson-r, Pinocchio-r/WDC&S #64. 580-r/Donald Duck's 1st
app. from Silly Symphony strip 12/16/34 by Taliaferro; Gottfredson strip-r

	GD25	FN65	NM94

begin; not in #584 & 600. 582,583-r/Mickey Mouse on Sky Island from
WDC&S #1,2 1.30 3.25
585 ($2.50, 52 pgs.)-r/#140; Barks-r/WDC&S #140 1.30 3.25
586,587: 586-Gladstone issues begin again; begin $1.50-c; Gottfredson-r begins
(not in #600). 587-Donald Duck by William Van Horn begins
2.00
588-597: 588,591-599-Donald Duck by William Van Horn 1.50
598,599 ($1.95, 36 pgs.): 598-r/1st drawings of Mickey Mouse by Ub Iwerks
2.00
600 ($2.95, 48 pgs.)-L.B. Cole-c(r)/WDC&S #1; Barks-r/WDC&S #32 plus Rosa,
Jippes, Van Horn-r and new Rosa centerspread 3.00
601-606 ($5.95, 64 pgs., squarebound, bi-monthly): 601-Barks-c, r/Mickey
Mouse V1#1, Rosa-a/scripts. 602-Rosa-c. 604-Taliaferro strip-r/1st Silly
Symphony Sundays from 1932. 604,605-Jippes-a. 605-Walt Kelly-c;
Gottfredson "Mickey Mouse Outwits the Phantom Blot" r/F.C. #16
6.00
NOTE: (#1-38, 68 pgs.; #39-42, 60 pgs.; #43-57, 61-134, 143-168, 446, 447, 52 pgs.; #58-60,
135-142, 169-540, 36 pgs.)
NOTE: Barks art in all issues #31 on, except where noted; c-95, 96, 104, 108, 109, 130-172,
174-178, 183, 198-200, 204, 206-209, 212-216, 218, 220, 226, 228-233, 235-238, 240-243, 247,
250, 253, 256, 260, 261, 276-283, 288-292, 295-298, 301, 303, 304, 306, 307, 309, 310, 313-
316, 319, 321, 322, 324, 326, 328, 329, 331, 332, 334, 341, 342, 350, 351, 527r, 530r,
540(never before published), 546r, 557-586r(most), 596b, 601p. Kelly a-24p, 34-41, 43; r-522-
524, 546, 547, 582, 583; covers(most)-34-118, 531r, 537r, 541r-543r, 562r, 571r, 605r. Walt
Disney's Comics & Stories featured Mickey Mouse serials which were in practically every issue
from #1 through #941 and #511 to date. The titles of the serials, along with the issues they are
in, are listed in previous editions of this price guide. Floyd Gottfredson Mickey Mouse serials in
issues #1-14, 18-66, 69-74, 78-100, 128, 562, 563, 568-572, 582, 583, 586-599, 601-603, 605-
present , plus "Service with a Smile" in #13; "Mickey Mouse in a Warplant" (3 pgs.), and "Pluto
Catches a Nazi Spy" (3 pgs.) in #62; "Mystery Next Door", #93; "Sunken Treasure", #94; "Aunt
Marissa", #95 (r in #575); "Gangland", #98 (r in #562); "Thanksgiving Dinner", #99 (r in #567);
and "The Talking Dog", #100 (r in #563); "Morty's Escapade", #128. "The Brave Little Tailor",
#580; "Introducing Mickey Mouse Movies" , #581; Circus Roustabout, #585; "Rumplewatt the
Giant", #604. Mickey Mouse by Paul Murry #152-547 except 155-57 (Dick Moore), 327-29
(Tony Strobl), 348-50 (Jack Manning), 533 (Bill Wright). Don Rosa story-a-523, 524, 526,
528, 531, 547, 601-present. Al Taliaferro Silly Symphonies in #5-"Three Little Pigs"; #13-"Birds
of a Feather"; #14-"The Boarding School Mystery"; #15-"Cookieland" and "Three Little Kittens";
#16-"The Practical Pig"; #17-"The Ugly Duckling"; "The Wise Little Hen" in #580; and "Ambrose
the Robber Kitten"; #19-"Penguin Isle"; and "Bucky Bug" in #20-23, 25, 26, 28 (one continuous
story from 1932-34; first 2 pgs. not Taliaferro). Gottfredson strip r-562, 563, 568-572, 581, 585,
586, 590. Taliaferro strip r-584, 580. Van Horn a-537, 545, 561, 574, 587, 588, 591-present.

WALT DISNEY'S COMICS & STORIES
1943 (36 pgs.) (Dept. store Xmas giveaway)
Walt Disney Productions
nn-X-Mas-c with Donald & the Boys; Donald Duck by Jack Hannah; Thumper
by Ken Hultgren 39.00 117.00 390.00

WALT DISNEY'S COMICS & STORIES
1942-1963 known (7-1/3"x10-1/4", 4 pgs. in color, slick paper)
(folded horizontally once or twice as mailers)
K.K. Publications (Xmas subscription offer)
1942 mailer-r/Kelly cover to WDC&S 25; 2-year subscription + two Grosset &
Dunlap hardcover books (32-pages each), of Bambi and of Thumper, offered
for $2.00; came in an illustrated C&S envelope with an enclosed postage
paid envelope (Rare) Mailer only 16.00 48.00 165.00
with envelopes 23.00 69.00 230.00
1949 mailer-A rare Barks item: Same WDC&S cover as 1942 mailer, but with art
changed so that newphew is handing teacher Donald a comic book rather
than an apple, as originally drawn by Kelly. The tiny, 7/8"x1-1/4" cover shown
was a rejected cover by Barks that was intended for C&S 110, but was
redrawn by Kelly for C&S 111. The original art has been lost and this is its
only app. (Rare) 32.00 96.00 320.00
1950 mailer-P.1 r/Kelly cover to Dell Xmas Parade 1 (without title); p.2 r/Kelly
cover to C&S 101 (w/o title), but with the art altered to show Donald reading
C&S 122 (by Kelly); hardcover book, "Donald Duck in Bringing Up the Boys"
given with a $1.00 one-year subscription. P.4 r/full Kelly Xmas cover to C&S
99 (Rare) 11.00 33.00 115.00
1953 mailer-P.1 r/cover Dell Xmas Parade 4 (w/o title); insides offer "Donald

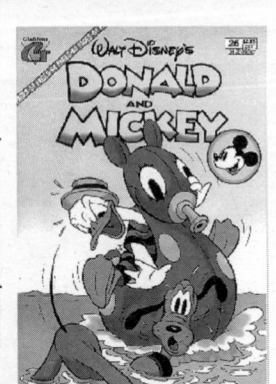

Walt Disney's Donald and Mickey #25 © WDC

Walt Disney's Donald Duck Adventures (2nd Series) #27 © WDC

Walt Disney's Donald Duck Adventures (2nd Series) #31 © WDC

	GD25	FN65	NM94

Duck Full Speed Ahead," a 28-page, color, 5-5/8"x6-5/8" book, not of the Story Hour series; P.4 r/full Barks C&S 148 cover (Rare)

| | 7.00 | 21.00 | 70.00 |

1963 mailer-Pgs. 1,2 & 4 r/GK Xmas art; P.3 r/a 1963 C&S cover (Scarce)

| | 4.00 | 12.00 | 40.00 |

NOTE: It is assumed a different mailer was printed each Xmas for at least twenty years. A 1952 mailer is known.

WALT DISNEY'S COMICS DIGEST
Dec, 1986 - No. 7, Sept, 1987
Gladstone

| 1 | .60 | 1.80 | 6.00 |
| 2-7 | | 1.60 | 4.00 |

WALT DISNEY'S DONALD AND MICKEY (Formerly Walt Disney's Mickey and Donald)
No. 19, Sept, 1993 - No. 30, 1995 ($1.50, 36 & 68 pgs.)
Gladstone (Bruce Hamilton Company)

19,21-24,26-30: New & reprints. 19,21,23,24-Barks-r. 19,26-Murry-r. 22-Barks "Omelet" story r/WDC&S #146. 27-Mickey Mouse story by Caesar Ferioli (1st U.S work). 29-Rosa-c; Mickey Mouse story actually starring Goofy (does not include Mickey except on title page).

| | | 1.60 | 4.00 |
| 20,25-($2.95, 68 pgs.): 20-Barks, Gottfredson-r | .50 | 1.50 | 5.00 |

NOTE: Donald Duck stories were all reprints.

WALT DISNEY'S DONALD DUCK ADVENTURES (D.D. Adv. #1-3)
11/87-No. 20, 4/90 (1st Series); No. 21, 8/93-Present (3rd Series)
Gladstone

| 1 | 1.20 | 3.00 | 7.00 |
| 2-r/F.C. #308 | | 1.20 | 3.00 |

3,4,6,7,9-11,13,15-18: 3-r/F.C. #223. 4-r/F.C. #62. 9-r/F.C. #159, "Ghost of the Grotto". 11-r/F.C. #159, "Adventure Down Under." 16-r/F.C. #291; Rosa-c.

18-r/FC #318; Rosa-c	1.00	2.50
5,8-Don Rosa-c/a	1.60	4.00
12($1.50, 52pgs)-Rosa-c/a w/Barks poster	1.60	4.00
14-r/F.C. #29, "Mummy's Ring"	1.20	3.00
19($1.95, 68 pgs.)-Barks-r/F.C. #199 (1 pg.)	1.20	3.00

20($1.95, 68 pgs.)-Barks-r/F.C. #189 & cover-r; William Van Horn-a

| | | 1.20 | 3.00 |
| 21,22: 21-r/D.D. #46. 22-r/F.C. #282 | | .90 | 2.25 |

23-27,29,31,32-($1.50, 36 pgs.): 21,23,29-Rosa-c. 23-Intro/1st app. Andold Wild Duck by Marco Rota. 24-Van Horn-a. 27-1st Pat Block-a, "Mystery of Widow's Gap." 31,32-Block-c.

| | | .80 | 2.00 |

26,28($2.95, 68 pgs.): 26-Barks-r/F.C. #108, "Terror of the River".

28-Barks r-r/F.C. #199, "Sheriff of Bullet Valley"	1.60	4.00
30($2.95,68 pgs.)-r/F.C. #367, Barks' "Christmas for Shacktown"		
	1.60	4.00
34-40: 34-Begin $1.50-c. 34,35,37-Block-a/scripts. 38-Van Horn-c/a		
		1.50

NOTE: Barks a-1-22r, 26r, 28r, 33r, 36c; c-10r, 14r, 20r. Block a-27, 30, 34, 35, 37; c-27, 30-32, 34, 35, 37; c-27, 30, 31, 32, 34, 35, 37. Rosa a-5, 8, 12; c-13, 16-18, 21, 23.

WALT DISNEY'S DONALD DUCK ADVENTURES (2nd Series)
June, 1990 - No. 38, July, 1993 ($1.50)
Disney Comics

| 1-Rosa-a & scripts | 1.20 | 3.00 |

2-38: 2-Barks-r/WDC&S #35; William Van Horn-a begins, ends #20. 9-Barks-r/F.C. #178. 9,11,14,17-No Van Horn-a. 11-Mad #1 cover parody. 14-Barks-r. 17-Barks-r. 21-r/FC #203 by Barks. 22-Rosa-a (10 pgs.) & scripts. 24-Rosa-a & scripts. 26-r/March of Comics #41 by Barks. 29-r/MOC #20 by Barks. 34-Rosa-c/a. 37-Rosa-a; Barks-r

| | | .80 | 2.00 |

NOTE: Barks r-2, 4, 9(F.C. #178), 14,(D.D. #45), 17, 21, 26, 27, 29 , 35, 36(D.D #60)-38. Taliaferro a-34r, 36r.

WALT DISNEY'S DONALD DUCK AND MICKEY MOUSE (Formerly Walt Disney's Donald and Mickey)
Sept, 1995 - No. 7, Sept, 1996 ($1.50, 32 pgs.)
Gladstone (Bruce Hamilton Company)

1-7: 1-Barks-r and new Mickey Mouse stories in all. 5,6-Mickey Mouse story by Caesar Ferioli. 7-New Donald Duck and Mickey Mouse x-over story; Barks-r/WDC&S #51

NOTE: Issue #8 was advertised, but cancelled.

WALT DISNEY SHOWCASE
Oct, 1970 - No. 54, Jan, 1980 (No. 44-48: 68pgs., 49-54: 52pgs.)
Gold Key

1-Boatniks (Movie)-Photo-c	2.60	7.70	
2-Moby Duck	1.70	4.20	
3,4,7: 3-Bongo & Lumpjaw-r. 4,7-Pluto-r	1.30	3.25	
5-$1,000,000 Duck (Movie)-Photo-c	1.70	5.00	
6-Bedknobs & Broomsticks (Movie)	1.70	5.00	
8-Daisy & Donald	1.30	3.25	
9-101 Dalmatians (cartoon feat.); r/F.C. #1183	1.70	4.20	
10-Napoleon & Samantha (Movie)-Photo-c	1.70	5.00	
11-Moby Duck-r	1.20	2.90	
12-Dumbo-r/Four Color #668	1.30	3.25	
13-Pluto-r	1.20	2.90	
14-World's Greatest Athlete (Movie)-Photo-c	1.70	5.00	
15-3 Little Pigs-r	1.30	3.25	
16-Aristocats (cartoon feature); r/Aristocats #1	1.70	5.00	
17-Mary Poppins; r/M.P. #10136-501-Photo-c	1.70	5.00	
18-Gyro Gearloose; Barks-r/F.C. #1047,1184	2.60	7.70	

19-That Darn Cat; r/That Darn Cat #10171-602-Hayley Mills photo-c

	1.70	5.00	
20,23-Pluto-r	1.30	3.25	
21-Li'l Bad Wolf & The Three Little Pigs	1.20	2.90	

22-Unbirthday Party with Alice in Wonderland; r/Four Color #341

| | 1.70 | 4.20 | |

24-26: 24-Herbie Rides Again (Movie); sequel to "The Love Bug"; photo-c. Old Yeller (Movie); r/F.C. #869; Photo-c. 26-Lt. Robin Crusoe USN (Movie) r/Lt. Robin Crusoe USN #10191-601; photo-c

	1.30	3.25	
27-Island at the Top of the World (Movie)-Photo-c	1.70	4.20	
28-Brer Rabbit, Bucky Bug-r/WDC&S #58	1.30	3.25	

29-Escape to Witch Mountain (Movie)-Photo-c

	1.70	4.20	
30-Magica De Spell; Barks-r/Uncle Scrooge #36 & WDC&S #258		
	3.10	9.00	
31-Bambi (cartoon feature); r/Four Color #186	1.70	4.20	

32-Spin & Marty-r/F.C. #1026; Mickey Mouse Club (TV)-Photo-c

| | 1.70 | 5.00 | |

33-39: 33-Pluto-r/F.C. #1143. 34-Paul Revere's Ride with Johnny Tremain (TV); r/F.C. #822. 35-Goofy-r/F.C. #952. 36-Peter Pan-r/F.C. #442. 37-Tinker Bell & Jiminy Cricket-r/F.C. #982,989. 38,39-Mickey & the Sleuth Parts 1 & 2

| | 1.00 | 2.50 | |
| 40-The Rescuers (cartoon feature) | 1.20 | 2.90 | |

41-Herbie Goes to Monte Carlo (Movie); sequel to "Herbie Rides Again"; photo-c

	1.30	3.25	
42-Mickey & the Sleuth	1.00	2.50	
43-Pete's Dragon (Movie)-Photo-c	1.70	4.20	

44-Return From Witch Mountain (new) & In Search of the Castaways-r (Movies)-Photo-c; 68 pg. giants begin

| | 1.70 | 4.20 | |
| 45-The Jungle Book (Movie); r/#30033-803 | 1.70 | 4.20 | |

46-The Cat From Outer Space (Movie)(new), & The Shaggy Dog (Movie)-r/F.C. #985; photo-c

| | 1.20 | 2.90 | |
| 47-Mickey Mouse Surprise Party-r | 1.20 | 2.90 | |

48-The Wonderful Advs. of Pinocchio-r/F.C. #1203; last 68 pg. issue

| | 1.70 | 4.20 | |

49-54: 49-North Avenue Irregulars (Movie); Zorro-r/Zorro #11; 52 pgs. begin photo-c. 50-Bedknobs & Broomsticks-r/#6; Mooncussers-r/World of Advt photo-c. 51-101 Dalmatians-r. 52-Unidentified Flying Oddball (Movie); r/Picnic Party #8; photo-c. 53-The Scarecrow-r (TV). 54-The Black Hole (Movie)-Photo-c (predates Black Hole #1)

| | 1.00 | 2.00 | |

WALT DISNEY'S MAGAZINE (TV)(Formerly Walt Disney's Mickey Mouse Club Magazine) (50¢, bi-monthly)

Walt Disney's Mickey and Donald #3 © WDC

Walt Disney's Uncle Scrooge #302 © WDC

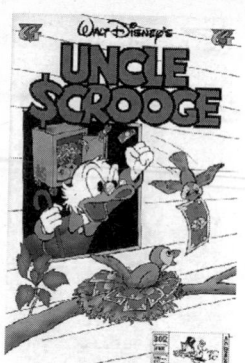

Walt Disney's Uncle Scrooge Adventures #41 © WDC

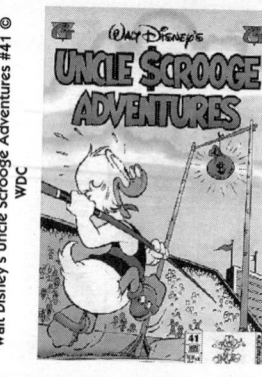

GD25 FN65 NM94

V2#4, June, 1957 - V4#6, Oct, 1959
Western Publishing Co.

V2#4-Stories & articles on the Mouseketeers, Zorro, & Goofy and other
Disney characters & people 4.50   13.50   45.00
V2#5, V2#6(10/57) 3.50   10.50   35.00
V3#1(12/57), V3#3-6(10/58) 2.80   8.40   28.00
V3#2-Annette Funicello photo-c 9.00   27.00   90.00
V4#1(12/58) - V4#2-4,6(10/59) 2.80   8.40   28.00
V4#5-Annette Funicello photo-c, w/ 2-photo articles 9.00   27.00   90.00
NOTE: V2#4-V3#6 were 11-1/2x8-1/2", 48 pgs.; V4#1 on were 10x8", 52 pgs. (Peak circulation 400,000).

WALT DISNEY'S MERRY CHRISTMAS (See Dell Giant #39)

WALT DISNEY'S MICKEY AND DONALD(M & D #1,2)(Becomes Walt Disney's Donald & Mickey #19 on)
Mar, 1988 - No. 18, May, 1990 (95¢)
Gladstone

1-Don Rosa-a; r/1949 Firestone giveaway 1.00   2.60   6.00
2-8: 3-Infinity-c. 4-8-Barks-r 1.20   3.00
9-15: 9-r/1948 Firestone giveaway; X-Mas-c 1.20   3.00
16($1.50, 52 pgs.)-r/FC #157 .... 1.00   2.00   5.00
17,18($1.95, 68 pgs.): 17-Barks M.M.-r/FC #79 plus Barks D.D.-r; Rosa-a; X-Mas-c. 18-Gottfredson-r/WDC&S #13,72-74; Kelly-c(r); Barks-r 1.00   2.00   5.00
NOTE: Barks reprints in 1-15, 17, 18. Kelly c-13r, 14 (r/Walt Disney's C&S #58), 18r.

WALT DISNEY'S MICKEY MOUSE CLUB MAGAZINE (TV)(Becomes Walt Disney's Magazine)
Winter, 1956 - V2#3, Apr, 1957 (11-1/2x8-1/2", quarterly, 48 pgs.)
Western Publishing Co.

#1 .... 12.00   36.00   120.00
#2-4 .... 6.00   18.00   60.00
V2#1-3 .... 4.50   13.50   45.00
nn-ual(1956)-Two different issues; ($1.50-Whitman); 120 pgs., cardboard covers, 11-3/4x8-3/4"; reprints 13.00   39.00   130.00
nn-ual(1957)-Same as above 11.00   33.00   115.00

WALT DISNEY'S PINOCCHIO SPECIAL
Spring, 1990 ($1.00)
Gladstone

50th anniversary edition; Kelly-r/F.C. #92 .... 1.20   3.00

WALT DISNEY'S SEBASTIAN (See Sebastian)

WALT DISNEY'S THE JUNGLE BOOK
nn ($5.95, graphic novel, 68 pgs.)
W.D. Publications (Disney Comics)

Movie adaptation; movie rereleased in 1990 .... 1.00   3.00   6.00
nn($2.95, 68 pgs.)-Comic edition; wraparound-c 1.50   3.00

WALT DISNEY'S UNCLE SCROOGE (Formerly Uncle Scrooge #1-209)
#210, 10/86 - No. 242, 4/90; No. 243, 6/90 - Present
Gladstone #210-242/Disney Comics #243-280/Gladstone #281 on
1st Gladstone issue; r/WDC&S #134 (1st Beagle Boys)
.... 2.15   6.50   15.00
211-218: 216-New story ("Go Slowly Sands of Time") plotted and partly scripted by Barks. 217-r/U.S. #7, "Seven Cities of Cibola" 1.50   4.50   15.00
219-"Son Of The Sun" by Rosa 2.50   7.50   25.00
220-Don Rosa-a/scripts 1.00   2.00   5.00
221-240: 235-Rosa-a/scripts 1.20   3.00
236-($1.95, 68 pgs.)-Rosa finishes over Barks-r 1.20   3.00
237-($1.95, 68 pgs.)-Barks-r; Rosa-a(1 pg.) 1.20   3.00
238-249,251-280,282-284-($1.50): 243-1st by Disney Comics. 261-263, 276-Don Rosa-c/a. 274-All Barks issue. 275-Contains poster by Rosa.
250-r/WDC&S #98 .... .90   2.25
281-($2.25, 52 pgs.)-Barks-r; wraparound-c 1.20   3.00

281-Gladstone issues start again; Rosa-c 1.00   2.00   5.00
285-The Life and Times of Scrooge McDuck Pt. 1; Rosa-c/a/scripts 1.65   4.20   10.00
286-292: The Life and Times of Scrooge McDuck Pt. 2-8; Rosa-c/a/scripts 1.00   2.00   5.00
293-($1.95, 36 pgs.)-The Life and Times of Scrooge McDuck Pt. 9
294-299-($1.50, 32 pgs.): 294-296-The Life and Times of Scrooge McDuck Pt. 10-12. 297-The Life and Times of Uncle Scrooge Pt. 0; Rosa-c/a/scripts 1.50
300-($2.25, 48 pgs.)-Rosa-a; Barks-r/WDC&S #104 and U.S. #216; r/U.S. #220; includes new centerfold. .... .90   2.25
NOTE: Barks r-210-218, 220-223, 224(2pg.), 225-234, 236-242, 245, 246, 250-253, 255, 256, 258, 261(2 pg.) 265, 267, 268, 270(2), 272-284, 299-present; c(r)-210, 212, 221, 228, 229, 232, 233, 284. scripts-287, 293. Rosa a-219, 220, 224, 226, 227, 235, 261-263, 268, 275-277, 285-289; c-219, 224, 231, 261-263, 276, 278-281, 285-289; scripts-219, 220, 224, 235, 261-263, 268, 276, 285-289.

WALT DISNEY'S UNCLE SCROOGE ADVENTURES (U. Scrooge Advs. #1-3)
Nov, 1987 - No. 21, May, 1990; No. 22, Sept, 1993 - Present
Gladstone Publishing

1-Barks-r begin, ends #26 .... 1.30   3.25   8.00
2-5: 5-Rosa-c/a; no Barks-r 1.60   4.00
6-19: 9,14-Rosa-a. 10-r/U.S. #18(all Barks) 1.20   3.00
20,21 ($1.95, 68 pgs.) 20-Rosa-c/a. 21-Rosa-a 1.20   3.00
22 ($1.50)-Rosa-c; r/U.S. #26 .... 1.00   2.00   5.00
23-($2.95, 68 pgs.)-Vs. The Phantom Blot-r/P.B. #3; Barks-r 1.60   4.00
24-26,29,31,32,34-36: 24,25,29,31,32-Rosa-c. 25-r/U.S. #21 .... .80   2.00
27-Guardians of the Lost Library - Rosa-c/a/story; origin of Junior Woodchuck Guidebook 1.20   3.00
28-($2.95, 68 pgs.)-r/U.S. #13 w/restored missing panels 1.60   4.00
30-($2.95, 68 pgs.)-r/U.S. #12; Rosa-c 4.00
33-($2.95, 64 pgs.)-New Barks story 3.00
37-40: 37-Begin $1.50-c 1.50
NOTE: Barks r-1-4, 6-8, 10-13, 15-21, 23, 24; c(r)-15, 16, 17, 21. Rosa a-5, 9, 14, 20, 21, 27; c-5, 13, 14, 17(finishes), 20, 22, 24, 25, 27, 28; scripts-5, 9, 14, 27.

WALT DISNEY'S WHEATIES PREMIUMS (See Wheaties)

WALTER (Campaign of Terror) (Also see The Mask)
Feb, 1996 - No. 4, May, 1996 ($2.50, limited series)
Dark Horse Comics

1-4 .... 2.50

WALTER LANTZ ANDY PANDA (Also see Andy Panda)
Aug, 1973 - No. 23, Jan, 1978 (Walter Lantz)
Gold Key

1-Reprints 1.00   2.00   5.00
2-10-All reprints .... .80   2.00
11-23: 15,17-19,22-Reprints 1.50

WALT KELLY'S...
Dec, 1987; Apr, 1988 ($1.75/$2.50, Baxter paper)
Eclipse Comics

...Christmas Classics 1 (12/87, $1.75)-Kelly-r/Peter Wheat & Santa Claus Funnies .... .70   1.75
...Springtime Tales 1 (4/88, $2.50)-Kelly-r 1.00   2.50

WALTONS, THE (See Kite Fun Book)

WALT SCOTT (See Little People)

WALT SCOTT'S CHRISTMAS STORIES (See Christmas Stories, 4-Color #959, 1062)

WAMBI, JUNGLE BOY (See Jungle Comics)
Spr, 1942; No. 2, Win, 1942-43; No. 3, Spr, 1943; No. 4, Fall, 1948; No. 5, Sum, 1949; No. 6, Spr, 1950; No. 7-10, 1950(nd); No. 11, Spr, 1951 - No. 18, Win, 1952-53 (#1-3: 68 pgs.)
Fiction House Magazines

1-Wambi, the Jungle Boy begins 81.00   243.00   650.00
2 (1942)-Kiefer-c 44.00   132.00   350.00

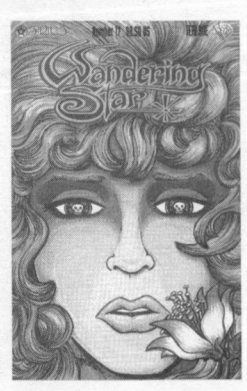
Wandering Star #17 © Teri S. Wood

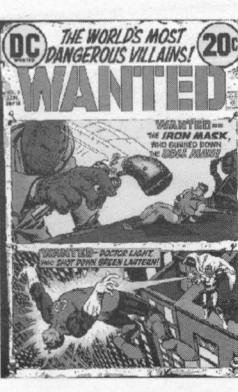
Wanted, The World's Most Dangerous Villains #5 © DC

War Action #14 © ATLAS

	GD25	FN65	NM94
3 (1943)-Kiefer-c/a	31.00	94.00	220.00
4 (1948)-Origin in text	19.00	58.00	135.00
5 (Fall, 1949, 36 pgs.)-Kiefer-c/a	16.00	47.00	110.00
6-10: 7-(52 pgs.)-New logo	14.00	43.00	100.00
11-18	10.00	30.00	70.00
I.W. Reprint #8('64)-r/#12 with new-c	2.30	6.70	16.00

NOTE: *Alex Blum* c-8. *Kiefer* c-1-5. *Whitman* c-11-18.

WANDERERS (See Adventure Comics #375, 376)
June, 1988 - No. 13, Apr, 1989 ($1.25) (Legion of Super-Heroes spin off)
DC Comics

1-13: 1,2-Steacy-c. 3-Legion app.			1.30

WANDERING STAR
1993 - No. 21, March, 1997 ($2.50/$2.75, B&W)
Pen & Ink Comics/Sirius Entertainment No. 12 on

1-1st printing; Teri Sue Wood c/a/scripts in all	1.00	2.00	5.00
1-2nd and 3rd printings		1.00	2.50
2-1st printing		1.20	3.00
2-2nd printing		1.00	2.50
3-6: 1st and 2nd printings exist		1.00	2.50
7-9		1.00	2.50
10-11: 10-$2.75-c begins		1.10	2.75
12-21: 12-(1/96)-1st Sirius issue; $2.50-c begins		1.00	2.50
Trade paperback ($11.95)-r/1-7; 1st printing of 1000, signed and numbered			15.00
Trade paperback-2nd printing, 2000 signed			12.00

WANTED COMICS
No. 9, Sept-Oct, 1947 - No. 53, April, 1953 (#9-33: 52 pgs.)
Toytown Publications/Patches/Orbit Publ.

9-True crime cases; radio's Mr. D. A. app.	14.00	43.00	100.00
10,11: 10-Giunta-a; radio's Mr. D. A. app.	10.00	30.00	60.00
12-Used in **SOTI**, pg. 277	10.00	30.00	70.00
13-Heroin drug propaganda story	9.15	27.00	55.00
14-Marijuana drug mention story (2 pgs.)	7.50	22.50	45.00
15-17,19,20	5.85	17.50	35.00
18-Marijuana story, "Satan's Cigarettes"; r-in #45 & retitled	19.00	47.00	110.00
21,22: 21-Krigstein-a. 22-Extreme violence	7.50	22.50	45.00
23,25-34,36-38,40-44,46-48,53	4.00	12.00	24.00
24-Krigstein-a; "The Dope King", marijuana mention story	7.50	22.50	45.00
35-Used in **SOTI**, pg. 160	7.50	22.50	45.00
39-Drug propaganda story "The Horror Weed"	10.00	30.00	65.00
45-Marijuana story from #18	6.35	19.00	38.00
49-Has unstable pink-c that fades easily; rare in mint condition	5.00	15.00	30.00
50-Has unstable pink-c like #49; surrealist-c by Buscema; horror stories	10.00	30.00	60.00
51- "Holiday of Horror" junkie story; drug-c	7.00	21.00	42.00
52-Classic "Cult of Killers" opium use story	7.00	21.00	42.00

NOTE: *Buscema* c-50, 51. *Lawrence* and *Leav* c/a most issues. *Syd Shores* c/a-48; c-37. Issues 9-46 have wanted criminals with their descriptions & drawn picture on cover.

WANTED: DEAD OR ALIVE (TV)
No. 1102, May-July, 1960 - No. 1164, Mar-May, 1961
Dell Publishing Co.

Four Color 1102 (#1)-Steve McQueen photo-c	12.00	36.00	125.00
Four Color 1164-Steve McQueen photo-c	10.00	30.00	100.00

WANTED, THE WORLD'S MOST DANGEROUS VILLAINS (See DC Special)
July-Aug, 1972 - No. 9, Aug-Sept, 1973 (All reprints & 20¢ issues)
National Periodical Publications

1-Batman, Green Lantern (story r-from G.L. #1), & Green Arrow	1.30	3.25	8.00

	GD25	FN65	NM94
2-Batman/Joker/Penguin-c/story r-from Batman #25; plus Flash story (r-from Flash #121)		1.50	3.75
3-9: 3-Dr. Fate(r/More Fun #65), Hawkman(r/Flash #100), & Vigilante(r/Ac #69). 4-Gr. Lantern(r/All-American #61) & Kid Eternity(r/Kid Eternity #15 Dollman/Green Lantern. 6-Burnley Starman; Wildcat/Sargon. 7-Johnny Quick(r/More fun #76), Hawkman(r/Flash #90), Hourman by Baily(r/Adv. #72). 8-Dr. Fate/Flash(r/Flash #114). 9-S&K Sandman/Superman			1.80

NOTE: *B. Bailey* a-7r. *Infantino* a-2r. *Kane* r-1, 5. *Kubert* r-3i, 6, 7. *Meskin* r-3, 7. *Reinm 6.

WAR
July, 1975 - No. 9, Nov, 1976; No. 10, Sept, 1978 - No. 49?, 1984
Charlton Comics

1-49: 47-Reprints			
7,9 (Modern Comics-r, 1977)			

WAR, THE (See The Draft & The Pitt)
1989 - No. 4, 1990 ($3.50, squarebound, 52 pgs.)
Marvel Comics

1-4: Characters from New Universe			1.75

WAR ACTION (Korean War)
April, 1952 - No. 14, June, 1953
Atlas Comics (CPS)

1	13.50	41.00	
2	10.00	30.00	
3-10,14: 7-Pakula-a	6.70	20.00	
11-13-Krigstein-a	8.35	25.00	

NOTE: *Brodsky* c-1-4. *Heath* a-1; c-7, 14. *Keller* a-6. *Maneely* a-1. *Tuska* a-2, 8.

WAR ADVENTURES
Jan, 1952 - No. 13, Feb, 1953
Atlas Comics (HPC)

1-Tuska-a	12.00	36.00	
2	7.50	22.50	
3-7,9-13: 3-Pakula-a. 7-Maneely-c	5.35	16.00	
8-Krigstein-a	8.35	25.00	

NOTE: *Brodsky* c-1-3, 6, 8, 11, 12. *Heath* a-5, 7, 10; c-4, 5, 9, 13. *Robinson* a-3; c-10.

WAR ADVENTURES ON THE BATTLEFIELD (See Battlefield)

WAR AGAINST CRIME! (Becomes Vault of Horror #12 on)
Spring, 1948 - No. 11, Feb-Mar, 1950
E. C. Comics

1-Real Stories From Police Records on-c #1-9	56.00	170.00	
2,3	33.00	99.00	
4-9	30.00	90.00	
10-1st Vault Keeper app. & 1st Vault of Horror	169.00	506.00	13
11-2nd Vault Keeper app.; 1st horror-c	96.00	290.00	7

NOTE: *All have Johnny Craig* covers. *Feldstein* a-4, 7-9. *Harrison/Wood* a-11. *Ingels* 8. *Palais* a-8. Changes to horror with #10.

WAR AND ATTACK (Also see Special War Series #3)
Fall, 1964; V2#54, June, 1966 - V2#63, Dec, 1967
Charlton Comics

1-Wood-a	2.60	7.50	
V2#54(6/66)-#63 (Formerly Fightin' Air Force)	1.20	3.00	

NOTE: *Montes/Bache* a-55, 56, 60, 63.

WAR AT SEA (Formerly Space Adventures)
No. 22, Nov, 1957 - No. 42, June, 1961
Charlton Comics

22	4.00	11.00	
23-30	1.70	5.00	
31-42	1.30	3.25	

WAR BATTLES
Feb, 1952 - No. 9, Dec, 1953

Warblade: Endangered Species #2 © Aegis Entertainment

War Dancer #6 © EEP

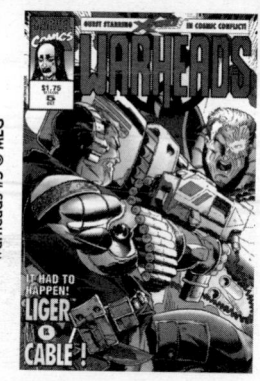

Warheads #5 © MEG

	GD25	FN65	NM94
Harvey Publications			
1-Powell-a; Elias-c	8.00	24.00	80.00
2-Powell-a	4.00	12.00	40.00
3-5,7-9: 3,7-Powell-a	3.50	10.50	35.00
6-Nostrand-a	5.00	15.00	50.00
WAR BIRDS			
1952(nd) - No. 3, Winter, 1952-53			
Fiction House Magazines			
1	12.00	36.00	85.00
2,3	8.00	25.00	50.00
WARBLADE: ENDANGERED SPECIES (Also see WildC.A.T.S: Covert Action Teams)			
Jan, 1995 - No. 4, Apr, 1995 ($2.50, limited series)			
Image Comics (Wildstorm Productions)			
1-4: 1-Gatefold wraparound-c		1.00	2.50
WARCHILD			
Jan. 1995 - No. 4, Aug, 1995 ($2.50)			
Maximum Press			
1-4-Rob Liefeld-c/a/scripts		1.00	2.50
1-4: Variant-c		1.20	3.00
Trade paperback (1/96, $12.95)-r/#1-4.			13.00
WAR COMBAT (Becomes Combat Casey #6 on)			
March, 1952 - No. 5, Nov, 1952			
Atlas Comics (LBI No. 1/SAI No. 2-5)			
1	10.00	30.00	70.00
2	6.70	20.00	40.00
3-5	4.25	13.00	28.00
NOTE: Berg a-2, 4, 5. Brodsky c-1, 2, 4, 5. Henkel a-5. Maneely a-1, 4; c-3.			
WAR COMICS (War Stories #5 on)(See Key Ring Comics)			
May, 1940 (No mo. given) - No. 4, Sept, 1941?			
Dell Publishing Co.			
1-Sikandur the Robot Master, Sky Hawk, Scoop Mason, War Correspondent begin; McWilliams-c; 1st war comic	48.00	144.00	385.00
2-Origin Greg Gilday (5/41)	30.00	90.00	210.00
3-Joan becomes Greg Gilday's aide	19.00	58.00	135.00
4-Origin Night Devils	23.00	69.00	160.00
WAR COMICS			
Dec, 1950 - No. 49, Sept, 1957			
Marvel/Atlas (USA No. 1-41/JPI No. 42-49)			
1	19.00	58.00	135.00
2	10.00	30.00	70.00
3-10	9.15	27.00	55.00
11-Flame thrower w/burning bodies on-c	10.00	30.00	60.00
12-20	7.50	22.50	45.00
21,23-32: 26-Valley Forge story. 32-Last precode issue (2/55)			
	5.35	16.00	32.00
22-Krigstein-a	9.15	27.50	55.00
33-37,39-42,44,45,47,48	5.35	16.00	32.00
38-Kubert/Moskowitz-a	7.50	22.50	45.00
43,49-Torres-a. 43-Severin/Elder E.C. swipe from Two-Fisted Tales #31			
	7.50	22.50	45.00
46-Crandall-a	7.50	22.50	45.00
NOTE: Colan a-4, 36, 48, 49. Drucker a-37, 43, 48. Everett a-17. Heath a-7-9, 16, 19, 25, 30; -11, 16, 19, 25, 26, 29-31, 36. G. Kane a-19. Lawrence a-36. Maneely a-7, 9; c-6, 27, 37. Orlando a-42, 48. Pakula a-26. Ravielli a-27. Reinman a-26. Robinson a-15; c-13. Severin a- -6, 27; c-48.			
WAR DANCER (Also see Charlemagne, Doctor Chaos #2 & Warriors of Plasm)			
Feb, 1994 - No. 6, July, 1994 ($2.50)			
Defiant			
1-3,5,6: 1-Intro War Dancer; Weiss-c/a begins. 1-3-Weiss-a(p). 6-Pre-Schism			

	GD25	FN65	NM94
issue		1.00	2.50
4-($3.25, 52 pgs.)-Charlemagne app.		1.30	3.25
WAR DOGS OF THE U.S. ARMY			
1952			
Avon Periodicals			
1-Kinstler-c/a	11.50	34.00	80.00
WARFRONT			
9/51 - #35, 11/58; #36, 10/65; #39, 2/67			
Harvey Publications			
1-Korean War	8.00	24.00	80.00
2	4.00	12.00	40.00
3-10	3.00	9.00	30.00
11,12,14,16-20	2.00	6.00	20.00
13,15,22-Nostrand-a	4.80	14.40	48.00
21,23-27,29,31-33,35	2.00	6.00	20.00
28,30,34-Kirby-c	4.00	12.00	40.00
36-Dynamite Joe begins, ends #39; Williamson-a	3.00	9.00	30.00
37-Wood-a (17 pgs.)	3.00	9.00	30.00
38,39-Wood-a, 2-3 pgs.; Lone Tiger app.	2.00	6.00	20.00
NOTE: Powell a-1-6, 9-11, 14, 17, 20, 23, 25-28, 30, 31, 34, 36. Powell/Nostrand a-12, 13, 15. Simon c-36?, 38.			
WAR FURY			
Sept, 1952 - No. 4, Mar, 1953			
Comic Media/Harwell (Allen Hardy Associates)			
1-Heck-c/a in all; Palais-a; bullet hole in forehead-c; all issues are very violent	9.15	27.00	55.00
2-4: 4-Morisi-a	5.35	16.00	32.00
WAR GODS OF THE DEEP (See Movie Classics)			
WARHAWKS			
1990 - No. 10, 1991 ($2.95, 44 pgs.)			
TSR, Inc.			
1-10-Based on TSR game, Spiegle a-1-6		1.50	3.00
WARHEADS			
June, 1992 - No. 14, Aug, 1993 ($1.75)			
Marvel Comics UK			
1-Wolverine-c/story; indicia says #2 by mistake	.80	2.00	
2-14: 2-Nick Fury app. 3-Iron Man-c/story. 4,5-X-Force. 5-Liger vs. Cable. 6,7-Death's Head II app. (#6 is cameo)	.70	1.75	
WAR HEROES (See Marine War Heroes)			
WAR HEROES			
7-9/42 (no month); No. 2, 10-12/42 - No. 11, 3/45			
Dell Publishing Co. (Published quarterly)			
1-General Douglas MacArthur-c	23.00	69.00	160.00
2	12.00	36.00	85.00
3,5: 3-Pro-Russian back-c	10.00	30.00	65.00
4-Disney's Gremlins app.	17.00	49.00	115.00
6-11: 6-Tothish-a by Discount	8.70	26.00	52.00
NOTE: No. 1 was to be released in July, but was delayed. Painted c-4, 6-9.			
WAR HEROES			
May, 1952 - No. 8, Apr, 1953			
Ace Magazines			
1	9.15	27.00	55.00
2-Lou Cameron-a	5.35	16.00	32.00
3-8: 6,7-Cameron-a	4.00	12.00	24.00
WAR HEROES (Also see Blue Bird Comics)			
Feb, 1963 - No. 27, Nov, 1967			
Charlton Comics			
1	3.00	7.50	15.00
2-10: 2-John F. Kennedy story	1.60	4.00	8.00

Warlock and the Infinity Watch #1 © MEG

Warlock Chronicles #8 © MEG

Warlord #56 © DC

	GD25	FN65	NM94

11-27: 27-1st Devils Brigade by Glanzman 1.00 2.50 5.00
NOTE: *Montes/Bache* a-3-7, 21, 25, 27; c-3-7.

WAR IS HELL
Jan, 1973 - No. 15, Oct, 1975
Marvel Comics Group

1-Williamson-a(r), 5 pgs.; Ayers-a 1.50
2-15: 2-9-All reprints 1.00
NOTE: *Bolle* a-3r. *Powell* a-1. *Woodbridge* a-1. Sgt. Fury reprints-7, 8.

WARLOCK (The Power of...)(Also see Fantastic Four #66, 67, Incredible Hulk #178, Infinity Crusade, Infinity Gauntlet, Infinity War, Marvel Premiere #1, Silver Surfer V3#46, Strange Tales #178-181 & Thor #165)
Aug, 1972 - No. 8, Oct, 1973; No. 9, 1975 - No. 15, Nov, 1976
Marvel Comics Group

1-Origin by Kane 3.60 11.00 25.00
2,3 1.40 4.00 10.00
4-8: 4-Death of Eddie Roberts 1.30 3.10 7.50
9-Starlin's 2nd Thanos saga begins, ends #15; new costume Warlock; Thanos cameo only; story cont'd from Strange Tales #178-181; Starlin-c/a in #9-15 1.50 4.00 9.00
10-Origin Thanos & Gamora; recaps events from Capt. Marvel #25-34. Thanos vs.The Magus-c/story 4.30 13.00 30.00
11-Thanos app.; Warlock dies 3.60 11.00 25.00
12-14: 14-Origin Star Thief; last 25¢ issue 1.70 4.00 10.00
15-Thanos-c/story 2.85 8.50 20.00
NOTE: *Buscema* a-2p; c-8p. *G. Kane* a-1p, 3-5p; c-1p, 2, 3, 4p, 5p, 7p. *Starlin* a-9-14p, 15; c-9, 10, 11p, 12p, 13-15. *Sutton* a-1-8i.

WARLOCK (...Special Edition on-c)
Dec, 1982 - No. 6, May, 1983 ($2.00, slick paper, 52 pgs.)
Marvel Comics Group

1-6: 1-Warlock-r/Strange Tales #178-180. 2-r/Str. Tales #180,181 & Warlock #9. 3-r/Warlock #10-12(Thanos origin recap). 4-r/Warlock #12-15. 5-r/Warlock #15, Marvel Team-Up #55 & Avengers Ann. #7. 6-r/2nd half Avengers Annual #7 & Marvel Two-in-One Annual #2 1.00 5.00
Special Edition #1(12/83) .90 2.25
NOTE: *Byrne* a-5r. *Starlin* a-1-6r; c-1-6(new). Direct sale only.

WARLOCK
V2#1, May, 1992 - No. 6, Oct, 1992 ($2.50, limited series)
Marvel Comics

V2#1-6: 1-Reprints 1982 reprint series w/Thanos 1.00 2.50

WARLOCK AND THE INFINITY WATCH (Also see Infinity Gauntlet)
Feb, 1992 - No. 42, July, 1995 ($1.75) (Sequel to Infinity Gauntlet)
Marvel Comics

1-Starlin scripts begin; brief origin recap Warlock; sequel to Infinity Gauntlet 1.20 3.00
2-Reintro Moondragon 1.00 2.50
3 .80 2.00
4-24,26: 7-Reintro The Magus; Moondragon app.; Thanos cameo on last 2 pgs. 8,9-Thanos battles Gamora-c/story. 8-Magus & Moondragon app. 10-Thanos-c/story; Magus app. 13-Hulk x-over. 21-Drax vs. Thor 1.75
25-($2.95, 52 pgs.)-Die-cut & embossed double-c; Thor & Thanos app. 1.20 3.00
28-42: 28-$1.95-c begins; bound-in card sheet .80 2.00
NOTE: *Austin* c/a-1-4i, 7i. *Leonardi* a(p)-3, 4. *Medina* c/a(p)-1, 2, 5; 6, 9, 10, 14, 15, 20. *Williams* a(i)-8, 12, 13, 16-19.

WARLOCK CHRONICLES
June, 1993 - No. 8, Feb, 1994 ($2.00, limited series)
Marvel Comics

1-($2.95)-Holo-grafx foil & embossed-c; origin retold; Starlin scripts begin; Keith Williams-a(i) in all 1.20 3.00
2-8: 3-Thanos & Mephisto-c/story. 4-Vs. Magus-c/s. 8-Contains free 16 pg. Razorline insert .80 2.00

WARLOCK 5
11/86 - No. 22, 5/89; V2#1, June, 1989 - V2#5?, 1989 ($1.70, B&W)
Aircel Publishing

1-All issues by Barry Blair 1.60 4.
2 1.20 3.
3 1.00 2.60 6.
4-6: 5-Green Cyborg on-c. 6-Misnumbered; Blue Girl on-c. 1.60 4.
7-9 1.60 4.
10-22: 18-$1.95-c begins .80 2.
V2#1-5 ($2.00, B&W) .80 2.
Compilation 1-r/#1-5 (1988, $5.95) 1.00 2.60 6.
Compilation 2-r/#6-9 ($5.95) 1.00 2.60 6.

WARLORD (See 1st Issue Special #8)
1-2/76; No.2, 3-4/76; No.3, 10-11/76 - No. 133, Win, 1988-89
National Periodical Publications/DC Comics #123 on

1-Story cont'd from 1st Issue Special #8 2.15 6.50 15.
2-Intro. Machiste 1.30 3.25 8.
3-5 1.00 2.00 5.
6-10: 6-Intro Mariah. 7-Origin Machiste. 9-Dons new costume 1.60 4.
11-20: 11-Origin-r. 12-Intro Aton. 15-Tara returns; Warlord has son 1.20 3.
21-40: 28-New facts about origin. 28-1st app. Wizard World. 32-Intro Shakira. 37,38-Origin Omac by Starlin. 39-Intro Jennifer Morgan, Warlord's daughter. 39-Omac ends. 40-Warlord gets new costume .80 2.
41-47,49-52: 42-47-Omac back-up series. 49-Claw The Unconquered app. 50-Death of Aton. 51-Reprints #1 1.
48-($2.00, 52 pgs.)-1st app. Arak; contains free 14 pg. Arak Son of Thunder; Claw The Unconquered app. .80 2.
53-130,132: 55-Arion Lord of Atlantis begins, ends #62. 63-The Barren Earth begins; free 16pg. Masters of the Universe preview. 91-Origin w/new facts. 114,115-Legends x-over. 100-($1.25, 52 pgs.). 125-Death of Tara 1.
131-1st DC work by Rob Liefield (9/88) 1.20 3.
133-($1.50, 52 pgs.) 1.
Remco Toy Giveaway (2-3/4x4") 1.
Annual 1(1982)-Grell-c/a(p) .80 2.
Annual 2-6: 2(1983). 3(1984). 4(1985). 5(1986). 6(1987, $1.25)-New Gods app. 1.
NOTE: *Grell* a-1-15, 16-50p, 51r, 52p, 59p, Annual 1p; c-1-70, 100-104, 112, 116, 117, Annua 1, 5. *Wayne Howard* a-64i. *Starlin* a-37-39p.

WARLORD
Jan, 1992 - No. 6, June, 1992 ($1.75, limited series)
DC Comics

1-6: Grell-c & scripts in all .70 1.

WARLORDS (See DC Graphic Novel #2)

WAR MAN
Nov, 1993 - No. 2, Dec, 1993 ($2.50, limited series)
Marvel Comics (Epic Comics)

1,2 1.00 2.

WAR MACHINE (Also see Iron Man #281,282 & Marvel Comics Presents #15)
Apr, 1994 - No. 25, Apr, 1996 ($1.50)
Marvel Comics

"Ashcan" edition (nd, 75¢, B&W, 16 pgs.) 1.
1-($2.00, 52 pgs.)-Newsstand edition; Cable app. .80 2.
1-($2.95, 52 pgs.)-Collectors ed.; embossed foil-c 1.20 3.
2-14, 16-25: 2-Bound-in trading card sheet; Cable app. 2,3-Deathlok app. 8-red logo 1.
8-($2.95)-Polybagged w/16 pg. Marvel Action Hour preview & acetate print; yellow logo 1.20 3.
15 ($2.50)-Flip book 1.00 2.

WAR OF THE GODS
Sept, 1991 - No. 4, Dec, 1991 ($1.75, limited series)

Warp #9 © FC

Warrior #2 © Ultimate Creations

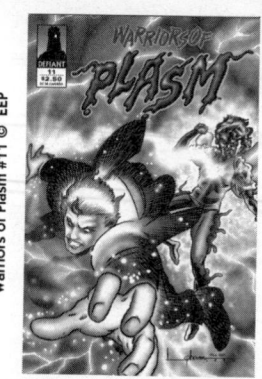

Warriors of Plasm #11 © EEP

DC Comics
1-4: Perez layouts, scripts & covers. 1-Contains free mini posters (Robin, Deathstroke). 2-4-Direct sale versions include 4 pin-ups printed on cover stock plus different-c .90 1.80

WAR OF THE WORLDS, THE
1996 - Present ($2.95, B&W, 32 pgs.)(Based on H. G. Wells novel)
Caliber
1-Randy Zimmerman scripts begin 3.00

WARP
Mar, 1983 - No. 19, Feb, 1985 ($1.00/$1.25, Mando paper)
First Comics
1-Sargon-Mistress of War app. .80 2.00
2-19: 2-Faceless Ones begin. 10-New Warp advs., & Outrider begin 1.25
Special 1-3: 1(7/83, 36 pgs.)-Origin Chaos-Prince of Madness; origin of Warp Universe begins, ends #3. 2(1/84)-Lord Cumulus vs. Sargon Mistress of War ($1.00). 3(6/84)-Chaos-Prince of Madness 1.00

WAR PARTY
Oct, 1994 (2.95, B&W)
Lightning Comics
1-1st app. Deathmark 1.20 3.00

WARPED
June, 1990 - No. 2, Oct-Nov, 1990 (B&W magazine)
Empire Entertainment (Solson)
1,2 .80 2.00

WARPATH (Indians on the...)
Nov, 1954 - No. 3, Apr, 1955
Key Publications/Stanmor
1 10.00 30.00 58.00
2,3 5.70 17.00 34.00

WARP GRAPHICS ANNUAL
Dec, 1985; 1988 ($2.50)
WaRP Graphics
1-Elfquest, Blood of the Innocent, Thunderbunny & Myth Adventures app. 1.00 2.50
1 (1988) 1.00 2.50

WARREN PRESENTS
Jan, 1979 - No. 14, Nov, 1981
Warren Publications
1-14-Eerie, Creepy, & Vampirella-r 1.00 2.00 5.00
...The Rook 1 (5/79)-r/Eerie #82-85 1.00 2.00 5.00

WAR REPORT
Sept, 1952 - No. 5, May, 1953
Ajax/Farrell Publications (Excellent Publ.)
1 10.00 30.00 58.00
2 5.35 16.00 32.00
3-5: 4-Used in POP, pg. 94 4.25 13.00 28.00

WARRIOR (Wrestling star)
May, 1996 - Present ($2.95)
Ultimate Creations
1-3: Warrior scripts; Callahan-c/a. 3.00
1-Variant-c. 7.00

WARRIOR COMICS
1945 (1930s DC reprints)
H.C. Blackerby
1-Wing Brady, The Iron Man, Mark Markon 17.00 49.00 115.00

WARRIOR NUN AREALA

Dec, 1994 - No. 3, Apr, 1995 ($2.95, limited series)
Antarctic Press
1 1.00 2.00 5.00
1-Special Edition (5000) 10.00
2-3 1.20 3.00
3-Bagged w/CD 1.00 2.60 6.00

WARRIOR NUN AREALA: PORTRAITS
Mar, 1996 ($3.95, one-shot)
Antarctic Press
1-Pin-ups 4.00

WARRIOR NUN AREALA: RITUALS
July, 1995 - No. 6, June, 1996 ($2.95)
Antarctic Press
1-5 3.00
6-($3.50) 3.50

WARRIOR NUN AREALA VS. RAZOR (See Razor/...)
May, 1996 ($3.95, one-shot)
Antarctic Press
1-Dunn-c/a 4.00
1-($9.95)-Comic polybagged w/CD 10.00

WARRIORS
1993 (B&W, one-shot)
CFD Productions
1-Linsner, Dark One-a 25.00

WARRIORS OF PLASM (Also see Plasm)
Aug, 1993 - No. 13, Aug, 1995 ($2.95/$2.50)
Defiant
1-4: Shooter-scripts; Lapham-c/a: 1-1st app. Glory. 4-Bound-in fold-out poster 1.20 3.00
5-7,10-13: 5-Begin $2.50-c. 13-Schism issue 1.00 2.50
8,9-($2.75, 44 pgs.) 1.10 2.75
The Collected Edition (2/94, $9.95)-r/Plasm #0, WOP #1-4 & Splatterball 1.70 4.20 10.00

WAR ROMANCES (See True...)

WAR SHIPS
1942 (36 pgs.)(Similar to Large Feature Comics)
Dell Publishing Co.
nn-Cover by McWilliams; contains photos & drawings of U.S. war ships 14.00 43.00 100.00

WAR STORIES (Formerly War Comics)
No. 5, 1942(nd); No. 6, Aug-Oct, 1942 - No. 8, Feb-Apr, 1943
Dell Publishing Co.
5-Origin The Whistler 24.00 71.00 165.00
6-8: 6-8-Night Devils app. 8-Painted-c 17.00 51.00 120.00

WAR STORIES (Korea)
Sept, 1952 - No. 5, May, 1953
Ajax/Farrell Publications (Excellent Publ.)
1 9.15 27.00 55.00
2 4.25 13.00 28.00
3-5 4.00 12.00 24.00

WAR STORIES (See Star Spangled...)

WARSTRIKE
May, 1994 - No. 7, Nov, 1995 ($1.95)
Malibu Comics (Ultraverse)
1-7: 1-Simonson-c .80 2.00
1-Ultra 5000 Limited silver foil 1.65 4.20 10.00
Giant Size 1 (12/94, 2.50, 44pgs.)-Prelude to Godwheel 1.00 2.50

Wasteland #2 © DC

Watchmen #1 © DC

Weapon Zero #2 © Top Cow Productions

WART AND THE WIZARD (See The Sword & the Stone under Movie Comics)
Feb, 1964 (Walt Disney)(Characters from Sword in the Stone movie)
Gold Key

1 (10102-402)	3.40	8.50	17.00

WARTIME ROMANCES
July, 1951 - No. 18, Nov, 1953
St. John Publishing Co.

1-All Baker-c/a	24.00	73.00	170.00
2-All Baker-c/a	17.00	49.00	115.00
3,4-All Baker-c/a	15.00	45.00	105.00
5-8-Baker-c/a(2-3) each	12.00	36.00	85.00
9,11,12,16,18: Baker-c/a each. 9-Two signed stories by Estrada			
	10.00	30.00	65.00
10,13-15,17-Baker-c only	5.85	17.50	35.00

WAR VICTORY ADVENTURES (#1 titled War Victory Comics)
Summer, 1942 - No. 3, Winter, 1943-44 (5¢)
U.S. Treasury Dept./War Victory/Harvey Publ.

1-(Promotion of Savings Bonds)-Featuring America's greatest comic art by
top syndicated cartoonists; Blondie, Joe Palooka, Green Hornet, Dick Tracy,
Superman, Gumps, etc.; (36 pgs.); all profits were contributed to U.S.O. &
Army/Navy relief funds

	34.00	103.00	240.00
2-Battle of Stalingrad story; Powell-a (8/43); flag-c	17.00	51.00	120.00
3-Capt. Red Cross-c & text only; Powell-a	16.00	47.00	110.00

WAR WAGON, THE (See Movie Classics)

WAR WINGS
Oct, 1968
Charlton Comics

1		1.60	4.00

WARWORLD!
Feb, 1989 ($1.75, B&W, one-shot)
Dark Horse Comics

1-Gary Davis sci/fi art in Moebius style		.75	1.80

WARZONE
1995 ($2.95, B&W)
Entity Comics

1-3		1.20	3.00

WASHABLE JONES AND THE SHMOO (Also see Al Capp's Shmoo)
June, 1953
Toby Press

1- "Super-Shmoo"	17.00	51.00	120.00

WASH TUBBS (See The Comics, Crackajack Funnies)
No. 11, 1942 - No. 53, 1944
Dell Publishing Co.

Four Color 11 (#1)	29.00	87.00	290.00
Four Color 28 (1943)	21.00	63.00	210.00
Four Color 53	15.50	46.50	155.00

WASTELAND
Dec, 1987 - No. 18, May, 1989 ($1.75-$2.00 #13 on, mature)
DC Comics

1-5(4/88), 5(5/88), 6(5/88)-18: 13,15-Orlando-a		.90	2.25

NOTE: **Orlando** a-12, 13, 15. **Truman** a-10; c-13.

WATCHMEN
Sept, 1986 - No. 12, Oct, 1987 (maxi-series)
DC Comics

1-12-Alan Moore scripts & Dave Gibbons-c/a in all		1.60	4.00
Hardcover Collection-Slip-cased-r/#1-12 w/new material; produced by Graphitti Designs			50.00
Trade paperback (1987, $14.95)-r/#1-12			15.00

WATCH OUT FOR BIG TALK
1950
Giveaway

nn-Dan Barry-a; about crooked politicians	4.00	12.00	24.00

WATER BIRDS AND THE OLYMPIC ELK (Disney)
No. 700, Apr, 1956
Dell Publishing Co.

Four Color 700-Movie	6.00	18.00	60.00

WEAPON X
Apr, 1994 ($12.95, one-shot)
Marvel Comics

nn-r/Marvel Comics Presents #72-84	1.90	6.00	13.00

WEAPON X
Mar, 1995 - No. 4, June, 1995 ($1.95)
Marvel Comics

1-Age of Apocalypse		1.60	4.20
2-4		.80	2.00

WEAPON ZERO
No. T-4(#1), June, 1995 - No. T-0(#5), Dec, 1995 ($2.50, limited series)
Image Comics (Top Cow Productions)

T-4(#1)-T-0(#5): Walt Simonson scripts in all.		1.00	2.50

WEAPON ZERO
V2#1, Mar, 1996 - Present ($2.50)
Image Comics (Top Cow Productions)

V2#1-7: Walt Simonson scripts			2.50

WEASEL PATROL SPECIAL, THE (Also see Fusion #17)
Apr, 1989 ($2.00, B&W, one-shot)
Eclipse Comics

1-Funny animal		.80	2.00

WEATHER-BIRD (See Comics From..., Dick Tracy, Free Comics to You... &
Terry and the Pirates)
1958 - No. 16, July, 1962 (Shoe store giveaway)
International Shoe Co./Western Printing Co.

1	3.25	9.50	22.00
2-16	1.70	5.00	12.00

NOTE: The numbers are located in the lower bottom panel, pg. 1. All feature a character called
Weather-Bird.

WEATHER BIRD COMICS (See Comics From Weather Bird)
1957 (Giveaway)
Weather Bird Shoes

nn-Contains a comic bound with new cover. Several combinations possible;
contents determines price (40 - 60 percent of contents).

WEAVEWORLD
Dec, 1991 - No. 3, 1992 ($4.95, limited series, 68 pgs.)
Marvel Comics (Epic Comics)

1-3: Clive Barker adaptation		1.00	2.00	5.00

WEB, THE (Also see Mighty Comics & Mighty Crusaders)
Sept, 1991 - No. 14, Oct, 1992 ($1.00)
DC Comics (Impact Comics)

1-14: 5-The Fly x-over 9-Trading card inside			1.00
Annual 1 (1992, $2.50, 68 pgs.)-With Trading card		1.00	2.50

NOTE: **Gil Kane** c-5, 9, 10, 12-14. **Bill Wray** a(i)-1-9, 10(part).

WEB OF EVIL
Nov, 1952 - No. 21, Dec, 1954
Comic Magazines/Quality Comics Group

1-Used in SOTI, pg. 388. Jack Cole-a; morphine use story		43.00	128.00	340.00

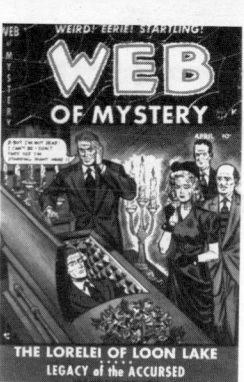
Web of Mystery #2 © ACE

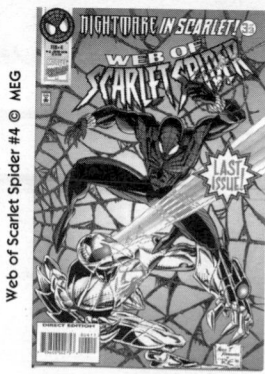
Web of Scarlet Spider #4 © MEG

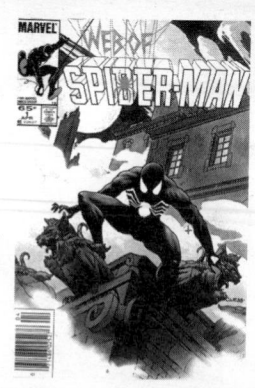
Web of Spider-Man #1 © MEG

	GD25	FN65	NM94
2-4,6,7: 2,3-Jack Cole-a. 4,6,7-Jack Cole-c/a	33.00	99.00	230.00
5-Electrocution-c/story; Jack Cole-c/a	37.00	111.00	260.00
8-11-Jack Cole-a	28.00	84.00	195.00
12,13,15,16,19-21	13.50	41.00	95.00
14-Part Crandall-c; Old Witch swipe	15.00	45.00	105.00
17-Opium drug propaganda story	13.50	41.00	95.00
18-Acid-in-face story	17.00	49.00	115.00

NOTE: *Jack Cole* a(2 each)-2, 6, 8, 9. *Cuidera* c-1-21i. *Ravielli* a-13.

WEB OF HORROR
Dec, 1969 - No. 3, Apr, 1970 (Magazine)
Major Magazines

1-Jeff Jones painted-c; Wrightson-a	5.00	15.00	40.00
2-Jones painted-c; Wrightson-a(2), Kaluta-a	3.75	11.25	28.00
3-Wrightson-c/a (1st published-c); Brunner, Kaluta, Bruce Jones-a	3.75	11.25	28.00

WEB OF MYSTERY
Feb, 1951 - No. 29, Sept, 1955
Ace Magazines (A. A. Wyn)

1	40.00	120.00	285.00
2-Bakerish-a	21.00	62.00	145.00
3-10: 4-Colan-a	19.00	58.00	135.00
11-18,20-26: 12-John Chilly's 1st cover art. 13-Surrealistic-a. 20-r/The Beyond #1	17.00	49.00	115.00
19-Reprints Challenge of the Unknown #6 used in N.Y. Legislative Committee	17.00	49.00	115.00
27-Bakerish-a(r/The Beyond #2); last pre-code ish	16.00	47.00	110.00
28,29: 28-All-r	11.50	34.00	80.00

NOTE: *This series was to appear as "Creepy Stories", but title was changed before publication.* *Cameron* a-6, 8, 11-13, 17-20, 22, 24, 25, 27; c-8, 13, 17. *Palais* a-28r. *Sekowsky* a-1-3, 7, 8, 11, 14, 21, 29. *Tothish* a-by *Bill Discount* #16. 29-all-r, 19-28-partial-r.

WEB OF SCARLET SPIDER
Oct, 1995 - No. 4, Jan, 1996 ($1.95, limited series)
Marvel Comics

1-4: Replaces "Web of Spider-Man"		.80	2.00

WEB OF SPIDER-MAN (Replaces Marvel Team-Up)
Apr, 1985 - No. 129, Sept, 1995
Marvel Comics Group

1-Painted-c (5th app. black costume?)	5.70	17.00	40.00
2,3	1.70	5.00	12.00
4-8: 7-Hulk x-over; Wolverine splash	1.50	3.75	9.00
9-13: 10-Dominic Fortune guest stars; painted-c	1.30	3.25	8.00
14-28: 18-1st app. Venom (behind the scenes, 9/86). 19-Intro Humbug & Solo	1.00	2.00	5.00
29-Wolverine, new Hobgoblin (Macendale) app.	2.15	6.50	15.00
30-Origin recap The Rose & Hobgoblin I (entire book is flashback story); Punisher & Wolverine cameo	2.15	6.50	15.00
31,32-Six part Kraven storyline begins	1.70	4.20	10.00
33-37,39-47,49: 36-1st app. Tombstone (cameo)		1.20	3.00
38-Hobgoblin app.; begin $1.00-c	1.20	3.00	7.00
48-Origin Hobgoblin II(Demogoblin) cont'd from Spectacular Spider-Man #147; Kingpin app.	3.60	11.00	25.00
50-($1.50, 52 pgs.)		1.00	2.50
51-58		.80	2.00
59-Cosmic Spidey cont'd from Spect. Spider-Man	1.65	4.00	10.00
60-65,68-85,87-89,91-94: 69,70-Hulk x-over. 74-76-Austin-c(i). 76-Fantastic Four x-over. 78-Cloak & Dagger app. 81-Origin/1st app. Bloodshed. 84-Begin 6 part Rose & Hobgoblin II storyline; last $1.00-c. 93-Gives brief history of Hobgoblin. 93,94-Hobgoblin (Macendale) Reborn-c/story, parts 1,2; Moon Knight app. 94-Venom cameo		.80	2.00
66,67-Green Goblin (Norman Osborn) app. as a super-hero	1.20	3.00	
86-Demon leaves Hobgoblin; 1st Demogoblin	1.20	3.00	
90-($2.95, 52 pgs.)-Polybagged w/silver hologram-c, gatefold poster showing			

	GD25	FN65	NM94
Spider-Man & Spider-Man 2099 (Williamson-i)	.80	2.10	5.00
90-2nd printing; gold hologram-c		1.20	3.00
95-Begin 4 part x-over w/Spirits of Venom w/Ghost Rider/Blaze/Spidey vs. Venom & Demogoblin (cont'd in Ghost Rider/Blaze #5,6)	1.20	3.00	
96-99,101-106: 96-Spirits of Venom part 3; painted-c. 101,103-Maximum Carnage x-over. 103-Venom & Carnage app. 104-106-Nightwatch back-up stories		.80	2.00
100-($2.95, 52 pgs.)-Holo-grafx foil-c; intro new Spider-Armor		1.30	3.25
107-111: 107-Intro Sandstorm; Sand & Quicksand app.			1.25
112,-116, 118, 119, 121-124, 126-129: 112-Begin $1.50-c; bound-in trading card sheet. 113-Gambit & Black Cat app. 117-Flip book; Power & Responsibility Pt. 1. 118-1st solo cover story; Venom app			1.50
113 ($2.95)-Collector's ed. polybagged w/foil-c; 16 pg. preview of Spider-Man cartoon & animation cel		1.20	3.00
117 ($1.50)-Flip book; Power & Responsibility Pt.1			1.50
117 ($2.95)-Collector's edition; foil-c; flip book		1.20	3.00
119 ($6.45)-Direct market edition; polybagged w/ Marvel Milestone Amazing Spider-Man #150 & coupon for Amazing Spider-Man #396, Spider-Man #53, & Spectacular Spider-Man #219.	1.10	2.70	6.50
120 ($2.95)-Flip book w/ preview of the Ultimate Spider-Man.		.90	2.25
125 ($3.95)-Holodisk-c; Gwen Stacy clone		1.60	4.00
125 ($2.95)-Newsstand		1.20	3.00
Annual 1 (1985)		1.20	3.00
Annual 2 (1986)-New Mutants; Art Adams-a	1.00	2.60	6.00
Annual 3 (1987)		1.20	3.00
Annual 4 (1988, $1.75)-Evolutionary War x-over		1.20	3.00
Annual 5 (1989, $2.00, 68 pgs.)-Atlantis Attacks; Captain Universe by Ditko (p) & Silver Sable stories (s); F.F. app.		1.10	2.75
Annual 6 ('90, $2.00, 68 pgs.)-Punisher back-up plus Capt. Universe by Ditko; G. Kane-a		1.10	2.75
Annual 7 (1991, $2.00, 68 pgs.)-Origins of Hobgoblin I, Hobgoblin II, Green Goblin I & II w/pinups; Larsen/Austin-c		1.10	2.75
Annual 8 (1992, $2.25, 68 pgs.)-Part 3 of Venom story; New Warriors x-over; Black Cat back-up story		1.10	2.75
Annual 9 (1993, $2.95, 68 pgs.)-Bagged w/card		1.20	3.00
Annual 10 (1994, $2.95, 68 pgs.)		1.20	3.00
Super Special 1 (1995, $3.95)-flip book		1.60	4.00

NOTE: *Art Adams* a-Annual 2. *Byrne* c-3-6. *Chaykin* c-10. *Mignola* a-Annual 2. *Vess* c-1, 8, Annual 1, 2. *Zeck* a-6i, 31, 32; c-31, 32.

WEDDING BELLS
Feb, 1954 - No. 19, Nov, 1956
Quality Comics Group

1-Whitney-a	11.50	34.00	80.00
2	7.00	21.00	42.00
3-9: 8-Last precode (4/55)	4.25	13.00	28.00
10-Ward-a (9 pgs.)	10.00	30.00	68.00
11-14,17	4.00	11.00	22.00
15-Baker-c	4.15	12.50	25.00
16-Baker-a	6.70	20.00	40.00
18,19-Baker-a each	5.85	17.50	35.00

WEDDING OF DRACULA
Jan, 1993 ($2.00, 52 pgs.)
Marvel Comics

1-Reprints Tomb of Dracula #30,45,46		.80	2.00

WEEKENDER, THE (Illustrated...)
V1#3, Sept, 1945 - V1#4, Nov, 1945; V2#1, Jan, 1946 (52 pgs.)
Rucker Publ. Co.

V1#3,4: 3-Super hero-c. 4-Same-c as Punch Comics #10 (9/44); r/Hale the Magician (7 pgs.) & r/Mr. E (8 pgs.-Lou Fine? or Gustavson?) plus 3 humor strips & many B&W photos & r/newspaper articles plus cheesecake photos of Hollywood stars	13.00	39.00	90.00

Weird #4 © DC

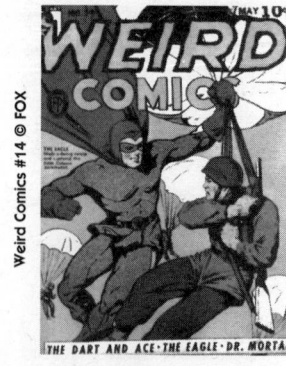

Weird Comics #14 © FOX

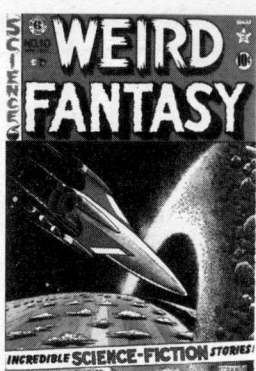

Weird Fantasy #10 © WMG

V2#1-36 pgs. comics, 16 in newspaper format with photos; partial Dynamic
Comics reprints; 4 pgs. of cels from the Disney film Pinocchio; Little Nemo
story by Winsor McCay, Jr.; Jack Cole-a; same-c as Dynamic #11

	16.00	47.00	110.00

WEEKLY COMIC MAGAZINE
May 12, 1940 (16 pgs.) (Others exist w/o super-heroes)
Fox Publications

(1st Version)-8 pg. Blue Beetle story, 7 pg. Patty O'Day story; two copies
  known to exist. Estimated value… 500.00
(2nd Version)-7 two-pg. adventures of Blue Beetle, Patty O'Day, Yarko,
  Dr. Fung, Green Mask, Spark Stevens, & Rex Dexter; one copy known to
  exist. Estimated value… 400.00
Discovered with business papers, letters and exploitation material promoting **Weekly Comic
Magazine** for use by newspapers in the same manner of **The Spirit** weeklies. Interesting note:
these are dated three weeks before the first Spirit comic. Letters indicate that samples may have
been sent to a few newspapers. These sections were actually 15-1/2x22" pages which will fold
down to an approximate 8x10" comic booklet. Other various comic sections were found with the
above, but were more like the Sunday comic sections in format.

WEEZUL
Aug, 1996 - Present ($2.75/$3.00, B&W)
Lightning Comics

1-($2.75)			2.75
1b-($3.00)			3.00
1-($9.95) Commemorative Edition			10.00

WEIRD
V1#1, 1/66 - V8#6, 12/74; V9#1, 1/75 - V11#4, Dec, 1978 (Magazine)
(V1-V8: 52 pgs.; V9 on: 68 pgs.)
Eerie Publications

V1#10(#1)-Intro. Morris the Caretaker of Weird (ends V2#10); Burgos-a

	3.60	11.00	25.00
11,12	2.15	6.50	15.00
V2#1-4 (10/67), V3#1(1/68), V2#6(4/68)-V2#7,9,10(12/68), V3#1(2/69)-V3#4			
	2.15	6.50	15.00
V2#8-r/Ditko's 1st story/Fantastic Fears #5	2.85	8.50	20.00
5(12/69)-Rulah reprint; "Rulah" changed to "Pulah", LSD story reprinted in			
Horror Tales V4#4, Tales From the Tomb V2#4, & Terror Tales V7#3			
	2.15	6.50	15.00
V4#1-6('70), V5#1-6('71), V6#1-7('72), V7#1-7('73), V8#1-6('74), V9#1-4			
(1/75-'76)(no V9#1), V10#1-3('77), V11#1-4	2.15	6.50	15.00

NOTE: V9#4 (12/76) has a cover swipe from Horror Tales V5#1 (2/73).

WEIRD, THE
Apr, 1988 - No. 4, July, 1988 ($1.50, limited series)
DC Comics

1-4: Wrightson-c/a in all	.80		2.00

WEIRD ADVENTURES
May-June, 1951 - No. 3, Sept-Oct, 1951
P. L. Publishing Co. (Canada)

1- "The She-Wolf Killer" by Matt Baker (6 pgs.)	40.00	120.00	285.00
2-Bondage/hypodermic panel	33.00	99.00	230.00
3-Male bondage/torture-c; severed head story	29.00	86.00	200.00

WEIRD ADVENTURES
No. 10, July-Aug, 1951
Ziff-Davis Publishing Co.

10-Painted-c	33.00	99.00	230.00

WEIRD CHILLS
July, 1954 - No. 3, Nov, 1954
Key Publications

1-Wolverton-r/Weird Mysteries No. 4; blood transfusion-c by Baily

	50.00	150.00	400.00

2-Extremely violent injury to eye-c by Baily; Hitler story

	50.00	150.00	400.00

3-Bondage E.C. swipe-c by Baily	35.00	105.00	245.00

WEIRD COMICS
Apr, 1940 - No. 20, Jan, 1942
Fox Features Syndicate

1-The Birdman, Thor, God of Thunder (ends #5), The Sorceress of Zoom,
  Blast Bennett, Typhon, Voodoo Man, & Dr. Mortal begin; Lou Fine
  bondage-c

	355.00	1066.00	3200.
2-Lou Fine-c	175.00	525.00	1400.
3,4: 3-Simon-c. 4-Torture-c	100.00	300.00	800.
5-Intro. Dart & sidekick Ace (8/40) (ends #20); bondage/hypo-c			
	103.00	309.00	825.
6,7-Dynamite Thor app. in each. 6-Super hero covers begin			
	86.00	258.00	690.
8-Dynamo, the Eagle (11/40, early app.; see Science #1) & sidekick Buddy &			
Marga, the Panther Woman begin	86.00	258.00	690.
9,10: 10-Navy Jones app.	71.00	215.00	575.
11-19: 16-Flag-c. 17-Origin The Black Rider.	53.00	159.00	425.
20-Origin The Rapier; Swoop Curtis app; Churchill & Hitler-c			
	57.00	172.00	460.

NOTE: Cover features: Sorceress of Zoom-4; Dr. Mortal-5; Dart & Ace-6-13, 15; Eagle-14, 16-

WEIRD FANTASY (Formerly A Moon, A Girl, Romance; becomes Weird
Science-Fantasy #23 on)
No. 13, May-June, 1950 - No. 22, Nov-Dec, 1953
E. C. Comics

13(#1) (1950)	162.00	488.00	1300.
14-Necronomicon story; cosmic ray bomb explosion-c			
	62.00	188.00	500.
15,16: 16-Used in **SOTI**, pg. 144	50.00	150.00	400.
17 (1951)	44.00	132.00	350.
6-10: 6-Robot-c	36.00	107.00	250.
11-13 (1952): 12-E.C. artists cameo. 13-Anti-Wertham "Cosmic			
Correspondence"	29.00	86.00	200.
14-Frazetta/Williamson(1st team-up at E.C.)/Krenkel-a (7 pgs.); Orlando draws			
E.C. staff; "Cosmic Ray Bomb Explosion" by Feldstein stars Gaines &			
Feldstein	40.00	120.00	300.
15-Williamson/Evans-a(3), 4,3,&7 pgs.	29.00	86.00	200.
16-19-Williamson/Krenkel-a in all. 18-Williamson/Feldstein-a			
	27.00	81.00	190.
20-Frazetta/Williamson-a (7 pgs.)	29.00	86.00	200.
21-Frazetta/Williamson-c & Williamson/Krenkel-a	40.00	120.00	300.
22-Bradbury adaptation	20.00	60.00	140.

NOTE: Ray Bradbury adaptations-13, 17-20, 22. Crandall a-22. Elder a-17. Feldstein a-
13(#1)-8; c-13(#1)-18 (#18 w/Williamson), 20. Harrison/Wood a-13. Kamen a-13(#1)-16, 18,
22. Krigstein a-22. Kurtzman a-13(#1)-17(#5), 6. Orlando a-9-22 (2 stories in #16); c-19, 22.
Severin/Elder a-18-21. Wood a-13(#1)-14, 17(2 stories ea. in #10-13). Ray Bradbury adaptations in #17-19, 22. Canadian reprints exist; see Table of Contents.

WEIRD FANTASY
Oct, 1992 - Present ($1.50)
Russ Cochran/Gemstone Publishing

1,2: 1,2-r/Weird Fantasy #13,14; Feldstein-c	.80		2.
3-17: 3-5-r/Weird Fantasy #15-17	1.00		2.

WEIRD HORRORS (Nightmare #10 on)
June, 1952 - No. 9, Oct, 1953
St. John Publishing Co.

1-Tuska-a	40.00	120.00	290.
2,3: 3-Hashish story	23.00	69.00	160.
4,5	20.00	60.00	140.
6-Ekgren-c; atomic bomb story	34.00	103.00	240.
7-Ekgren-c; Kubert, Cameron-a	39.00	116.00	270.
8,9-Kubert-c/a	31.00	92.00	215.

NOTE: Cameron a-7, 9. Finesque a-1-5. Forgione a-6. Morisi a-3. Bondage c-8.

WEIRD MYSTERIES
Oct, 1952 - No. 12, Sept, 1954

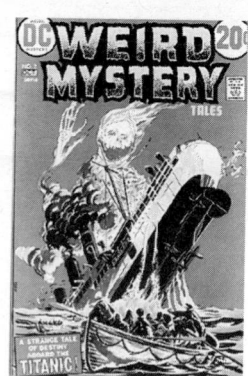

Weird Mystery Tales #2 © DC

Weird Science #18 © WMG

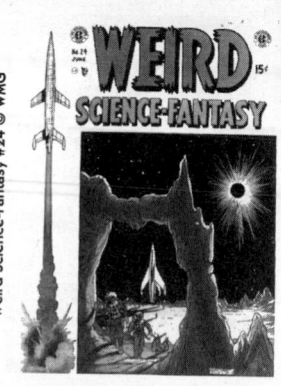

Weird Science-Fantasy #24 © WMG

WE

GD25   FN65   NM94   GD25   FN65   NM94

Gillmore Publications

1-Partial Wolverton-c swiped from splash page "Flight to the Future" in Weird
Tales of the Future #2; "Eternity" has an Ingels swipe
                                   53.00   161.00   430.00
2- "Robot Woman" by Wolverton; Bernard Baily-c reprinted in Mister Mystery
#18; acid in face panel   75.00   225.00   600.00
3,6; Both have decapitation-c   40.00   120.00   290.00
4- "The Man Who Never Smiled" (3 pgs.) by Wolverton; B. Baily skull-c
                                   64.00   193.00   515.00
5-Wolverton story "Swamp Monster" (6 pgs.) 64.00 193.00 515.00
7-Used in SOTI, illo "Indeed", illo "Sex and blood" 57.00 172.00 460.00
8-Wolverton-c panel-r/#5; used in a '54 Readers Digest anti-comics article by
T. E. Murphy entitled "For the Kiddies to Read" 40.00 120.00 290.00
9-Excessive violence, gore & torture 40.00 120.00 280.00
10-Silhouetted nudity panel   34.00   103.00   240.00
11,12: 12-r/Mr. Mystery #8(2), Weird Mysteries #3 & Weird Tales of the Future
#6   31.00   92.00   215.00
NOTE: Baily c-2-12. Anti-Wertham column in #5. #1-12 all have 'The Ghoul Teacher' (host).

WEIRD MYSTERIES (Magazine)
Mar-Apr, 1959 (35¢, B&W, 68 pgs.)
Pastime Publications

1-Torres-a; E. C. swipe from Tales From the Crypt #46 by Tuska "The
Ragman"   6.00   18.00   36.00

WEIRD MYSTERY TALES (See DC 100 Page Super Spectacular)

WEIRD MYSTERY TALES (See Cancelled Comic Cavalcade)
July-Aug, 1972 - No. 24, Nov, 1975
National Periodical Publications

1-Kirby-a; Wrightson splash pg.   1.65   4.20   10.00
2-24: 21-Wrightson-a   1.00   2.00   5.00
NOTE: Alcala a-5, 10, 13, 14. Aparo a-8. Bailey a-8. Bolle a-8?. Howard a-4. Kaluta a-4, 24;
-1. G. Kane a-10. Kirby a-1, 2p, 3p. Nino a-5, 6, 9, 13, 16, 21. Redondo a-9. 17. Sparling c-6.
Starlin a-3?, 4. Wood a-23.

WEIRD ROMANCE (Seduction of the Innocent #9)
Feb, 1988 ($2.00, B&W)
Eclipse Comics

1-Pre-code horror-r; Lou Cameron-r(2)   .80   2.00

WEIRD SCIENCE (Formerly Saddle Romances) (Becomes Weird
Science-Fantasy #23 on)
No. 12, May-June, 1950 - No. 22, Nov-Dec, 1953
E. C. Comics

12(#1) (1950)-"Lost in the Microcosm" classic-c/story by Kurtzman
                                  162.00   488.00   1300.00
3-Flying saucers over Washington-c/story, 2 years before the actual event
                                   69.00   206.00   550.00
4-Robot-c/story by Feldstein   69.00   206.00   550.00
5 (1950)   62.00   188.00   500.00
5-10: 5-Atomic explosion-c   40.00   120.00   300.00
1-14 (1952): 12- "Dream of Doom" stars Gaines & E.C. artists
                                   29.00   86.00   200.00
15-18-Williamson/Krenkel-a in each; 15-Williamson-a. 17-Used in POP, pgs.
81,82. 18-Bill Gaines doll app. in story 31.00 92.00 215.00
19,20-Williamson/Frazetta-a (7 pgs. each). 19-Used in SOTI, illo "A young girl
on her wedding night stabs her sleeping husband to death with a hatpin…"
                                   40.00   120.00   285.00
1-Williamson/Frazetta-a (6 pgs.); Wood draws E.C. staff; Gaines & Feldstein
app. in story   40.00   120.00   285.00
2-Williamson/Frazetta/Krenkel/Krigstein-a (8 pgs.); Wood draws himself in
his story (last pg. & panel)   40.00   120.00   285.00
NOTE: Elder a-14, 19. Evans a-20. Feldstein a-12(#1)-8; c-12(#1)-8, 11. Ingels a-15. Kamen
12(#1)-13, 15-18, 20, 21. Kurtzman a-12(#1)-7. Orlando a-10-22. Wood a-12(#1), 13(#2), 5-
(#9, 10, 12, 13 all have 2 Wood stories); c-9, 10, 12-22. Canadian reprints exist; see Table of
Contents. Ray Bradbury adaptations in #17-20.

WEIRD SCIENCE
Sept, 1990 - No. 4, Mar, 1991 ($1.95/$2.00, 68 pgs.)
Gladstone Publishing

1-4: Wood-c(r); all reprints in each   1.20   3.00

WEIRD SCIENCE
Sept, 1992 - Present ($1.50/$2.00/$2.50)
Russ Cochran/Gemstone Publishing

1,2: r/Weird Science #12,13 w/original-c   .80   2.00
3-18: 3,4-r/#14,15. 5-7-w/original-c   1.00   2.50

WEIRD SCIENCE-FANTASY (Formerly Weird Science & Weird Fantasy)
(Becomes Incredible Science Fiction #30)
No. 23 Mar, 1954 - No. 29, May-June, 1955 (#23,24: 15¢)
E. C. Comics

23-Williamson, Wood-a; Bradbury adaptation 29.00 86.00 200.00
24-Williamson & Wood-a; Harlan Ellison's 1st professional story, "Upheaval",
later adapted into a short story as "Mealtime", and then into a TV episode of
Voyage to the Bottom of the Sea as "The Price of Doom"
                                   29.00   86.00   200.00
25-Williamson-c; Williamson/Torres/Krenkel-a plus Wood-a; Bradbury
adaptation; cover price back to 10¢ 33.00 99.00 230.00
26-Flying Saucer Report; Wood, Crandall-a; A-bomb panels
                                   27.00   81.00   190.00
27-Adam Link/I Robot series begins? 29.00   86.00   200.00
28-Williamson/Krenkel/Torres-a; Wood-a 31.00 94.00 220.00
29-Frazetta-c; Williamson/Krenkel & Wood-a; last pre-code issue; new logo
                                   45.00   135.00   360.00
NOTE: Crandall a-26, 27, 29. Evans a-26. Feldstein c-24, 26, 28. Kamen a-27, 28. Krigstein
a-23-25. Orlando a-in all. Wood a-in all; c-23, 27. The cover to #29 was originally intended for
Famous Funnies #217 (Buck Rogers), but was rejected for being "too violent."

WEIRD SCIENCE-FANTASY
Nov, 1992 - Present ($1.50/$2.00/$2.50)
Russ Cochran/Gemstone Publishing

1,2: r/Weird Science-Fantasy #23,24   .80   2.00
3-18: r/#25-27   1.00   2.50

WEIRD SCIENCE-FANTASY ANNUAL
1952, 1953 (Sold thru the E. C. office & on the stands in some major cities)
(25¢, 132 pgs.)
E. C. Comics

1952-Feldstein-c   162.00   488.00   1300.00
1953-Feldstein-c   94.00   283.00   850.00
NOTE: The 1952 annual contains books cover-dated in 1951 & 1952, and the 1953 annual from
1952 & 1953. Contents of each annual may vary in same year.

WEIRD SUSPENSE
Feb, 1975 - No. 3, July, 1975
Atlas/Seaboard Publ.

1-3: 1-Tarantula begins.   1.50
NOTE: Buckler c-1, 3.

WEIRD SUSPENSE STORIES (Canadian reprint of Crime SuspenStories #1-3; see
Table of Contents)

WEIRD TALES ILLUSTRATED
1992 - No. 2, 1994 ($2.95, high quality paper)
Millennium Publications

1,2-Bolton painted-c. 1-Adapts E.A. Poe & Harlan Ellison stories. 2-E.A. Poe &
H.P. Lovecraft adaptations   1.40   3.50
1-($4.95, 52 pgs.)-Deluxe edition w/Tim Vigil a not in regular #1; stiff-c;
Bolton painted-c   1.00   2.00   5.00

WEIRD TALES OF THE FUTURE
Mar, 1952 - No. 8, July-Aug, 1953
S.P.M. Publ. No. 1-4/Aragon Publ. No. 5-8

1-Andru-a(2); Wolverton partial-c   60.00   181.00   485.00

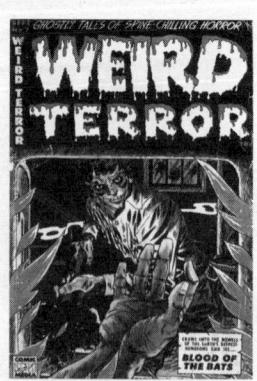

Weird Terror #7 © Comic Media

Weird Wonder Tales #1 © MEG

Weird Worlds #10 © DC

2,3-Wolverton-c/a(3) each. 2- "Jumpin Jupiter" satire by Wolverton begins,
ends #5   96.00   290.00   775.00
4- "Jumpin Jupiter" satire & "The Man From the Moon" by Wolverton; partial
Wolverton-c   60.00   180.00   480.00
5-Wolverton-c/a(2); "Jumpin Jupiter" satire   96.00   290.00   775.00
6-Bernard Baily-c   40.00   120.00   300.00
7- "The Mind Movers" from the art to Wolverton's "Brain Bats of Venus" from
Mr. Mystery #7 which was cut apart, pasted up, partially redrawn, and
rewritten by Harry Kantor, the editor; Baily-c   57.00   172.00   460.00
8-Reprints Weird Mysteries #1(10/52) minus cover; gory cover showing heart
ripped out by B. Baily   40.00   120.00   280.00

WEIRD TALES OF THE MACABRE (Magazine)
Jan, 1975 - No. 2, Mar, 1975 (75¢, B&W)
Atlas/Seaboard Publ.

1-Jeff Jones painted-c   1.00   2.00   5.00
2-Boris Vallejo painted-c; Severin-a   1.00   2.00   5.00

WEIRD TERROR (Also see Horrific)
Sept, 1952 - No. 13, Sept, 1954
Allen Hardy Associates (Comic Media)

1- "Portrait of Death", adapted from Lovecraft's "Pickman's Model"; lingerie
panels, Hitler story   37.00   111.00   260.00
2-Text on Marquis DeSade, Torture, Demonology, & St. Elmo's Fire
                                                   25.00   75.00   175.00
3-Extreme violence, whipping, torture; article on sin eating, dowsing
                                                   25.00   75.00   175.00
4-Dismemberment, decapitation, article on human flesh for sale, Devil,
whipping   29.00   86.00   200.00
5-Article on body snatching, mutilation; cannibalism story
                                                   23.00   69.00   160.00
6-Dismemberment, decapitation, man hit by lightning
                                                   27.00   81.00   190.00
7,9,10   21.00   62.00   145.00
8-Decapitation story; Ambrose Bierce adapt.   26.00   77.00   180.00
11-End of the world story with atomic blast panels; Tothish-a by Bill Discount
                                                   26.00   77.00   180.00
12-Discount-a   19.00   58.00   135.00
13-Severed head panels   21.00   62.00   145.00
NOTE: *Don Heck* a-most issues; c-1-13. *Landau* a-6. *Morisi* a-2-5, 7, 9, 12. *Palais* a-1, 5, 6, 8(2), 10, 12. *Powell* a-10. *Ravielli* a-11, 20.

WEIRD THRILLERS
Sept-Oct, 1951 - No. 5, Oct-Nov, 1952 (#2-5: painted-c)
Ziff-Davis Publ. Co. (Approved Comics)

1-Rondo Hatton photo-c   53.00   159.00   425.00
2-Toth, Anderson, Colan-a   40.00   120.00   300.00
3-Two Powell, Tuska-a; classic-c   47.00   141.00   375.00
4-Kubert, Tuska-a   39.00   118.00   275.00
5-Powell-a   36.00   107.00   250.00
NOTE: *M. Anderson* a-2, 3. *Roussos* a-4. #2, 3 reprinted in Nightmare #10 & 13; #4, 5 reprinted in Amazing Ghost Stories #16 & #15.

WEIRD WAR TALES
Sept-Oct, 1971 - No. 124, June, 1983 (#1-5: 52 pgs.)
National Periodical Publications/DC Comics

1-Kubert-a in #1-4,7; c-1-7   6.25   19.00   50.00
2,3-Drucker-a: 2-Crandall-a. 3-Heath-a   2.15   6.50   15.00
4-7,9,10: 5,6,10-Toth-a. 5,7-Heath-a   1.20   3.00   7.00
8-Neal Adams-c/a(i)   1.65   4.20   10.00
11-50: 36-(68 pgs.)-Crandall & Kubert-r/#2; Heath-r/#3. 36,38-Kubert-c
                                                    1.60   4.00
51-63,65-67,69-124: 93-Intro/origin Creature Commandos. 101-Intro/origin
G.I. Robot   1.20   3.00
64,68-Frank Miller-a in both. 64-Miller's 1st DC work. 1.60   4.00

WEIRD WESTERN TALES (Formerly All-Star Western)

No. 12, June-July, 1972 - No. 70, Aug, 1980
National Periodical Publications/DC Comics

12-(52 pgs.)-3rd app. Jonah Hex; Bat Lash, Pow Wow Smith reprints;
El Diablo by Neal Adams/Wrightson   3.75   11.25   30
13-Jonah Hex-c (1st?) & 4th app.; Neal Adams-a 3.60   11.00   25
14-Toth-a   2.00   6.00   14
15-Neal Adams-c/a; no Jonah Hex   1.70   5.00   12
16,17,19-28,30-38: Jonah Hex in all. 38-Last Jonah Hex
                                              1.00   2.60   6
18,29: 18-1st all Jonah Hex issue (7-8/73) & begins. 29-Origin Jonah Hex
                                              2.15   6.50   15
39-70: 39-Origin/1st app. Scalphunter & begins. 64-Bat Lash-c/story
                                                      1.40   3
NOTE: *Alcala* a-16, 17. *Evans* inks-39-48; c-39i, 40, 47. *G. Kane* a-15, 20. *Kubert* c-12, 33. *Starlin* c-44, 45. *Wildey* a-26. 48 & 49 are 44 pgs..

WEIRD WONDER TALES
Dec, 1973 - No. 22, May, 1977
Marvel Comics Group

1-Wolverton-r/Mystic #6 (Eye of Doom)   1.60   4
2-22: 16-18-Venus-r by Everett from Venus #19,18 & 17. 19-22-Dr. Druid
(Droom)-r   1.20   3
NOTE: *All 1950s & early 1960s reprints. Check* r-1. *Colan* a-17. *Ditko* r-4, 5, 10-13, 19-21. *Drucker* r-12, 20. *Everett* r-3(Spellbound #16), 6(Astonishing #10), 9(Adv. into Mystery #5). *Heath* a-13r. *Heck* a-14r, 14r. *Gil Kane* c-1, 2, 10. *Kirby* r-6, 11, 13, 16-22; c-17, 19, 20. *Krigstein* r-19. *Kubert* r-22. *Maneely* r-8. *Mooney* r-7p. *Powell* r-3, 7. *Torres* r-7. *Wildey* r-7.

WEIRD WORLDS (See Adventures Into...)

WEIRD WORLDS (Magazine)
V1#10(12/70), V2#1(2/71) - No. 4, Aug, 1971 (52 pgs.)
Eerie Publications

V1#10   2.15   6.50   15
V2#1-4   1.70   5.00   12

WEIRD WORLDS (Also see Ironwolf: Fires of the Revolution)
Aug-Sept, 1972 - No. 9, Jan-Feb, 1974; No. 10, Oct-Nov, 1974 (All 20¢ issues)
National Periodical Publications

1-Edgar Rice Burrough's John Carter Warlord of Mars & David Innes begin
(1st DC app.); Kubert-c   1.80   4
2-7: 2-Infantino/Orlando-c. 3-Murphy Anderson-c. 3-7-Last John Carter.
4-Kaluta-c. 5-Kaluta-c.   1.00   2
8-10: 8-Iron Wolf begins by Chaykin (1st app.)   .70   1
NOTE: *Neal Adams* a-2i, 3i. *John Carter* by *Andersonin* #1-3. *Chaykin* c-7, 8. *Kaluta* a-4; c-6, 10. *Orlando* a-4i; c-2, 3, 4i. *Wrightson* a-2i, 4i.

WELCOME BACK, KOTTER (TV) (See Limited Collectors' Edition #57)
Nov, 1976 - No. 10, Mar-Apr, 1978
National Periodical Publications/DC Comics

1-Sparling-a(p)   1.20   3
2-10: 3-Estrada-a.   1

WELCOME SANTA (See March of Comics #63,183)

WELCOME TO THE LITTLE SHOP OF HORRORS
May, 1995 -No. 3, July, 1995 ($2.50, 4-limited series)
Roger Corman's Cosmic Comics

1-3   1.00   2

WELLS FARGO (See Tales of...)

WENDY AND THE NEW KIDS ON THE BLOCK
Mar?, 1991 - No. 4, 1991 ($1.25/$1.50)
Harvey Comics

1-4: 4-$1.50-c   1

WENDY DIGEST
Oct, 1990 - No. 2, Nov, 1990 ($1.75, digest size)
Harvey Comics

West Coast Avengers Annual #7 MEG

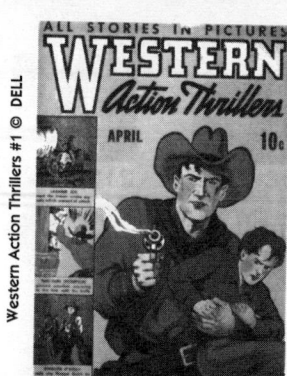
Western Action Thrillers #1 © DELL

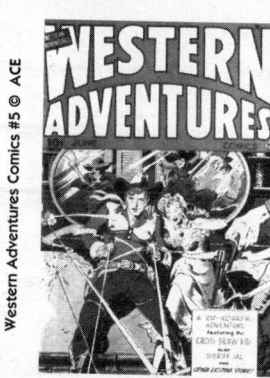
Western Adventures Comics #5 © ACE

WE

	GD25	FN65	NM94

1,2   .90   1.80

WENDY PARKER COMICS
July, 1953 - No. 8, July, 1954
Atlas Comics (OMC)

	GD25	FN65	NM94
1	10.00	30.00	58.00
2	5.70	17.00	34.00
3-8	4.25	13.00	28.00

WENDY, THE GOOD LITTLE WITCH (TV)
3/60 - #82, 11/73; #83, 8/74 - #93, 4/76; #94, 9/90 - #97, 12/90
Harvey Publications

1-Wendy & Casper the Friendly Ghost begins	13.00	40.00	130.00
2	6.00	18.00	60.00
3-5	4.50	13.50	45.00
6-10	3.50	10.50	35.00
11-20	2.00	6.00	20.00
21-30	1.80	5.40	14.00
31-50	1.65	4.20	10.00
51-69: 65 (2/71)-Wendy origin.	1.30	3.25	8.00
70-74: All 52 pg. Giants	1.70	5.00	12.00
75-93		1.60	4.00
94-97 (1990, $1.00-c): 94-Has #194 on-c			1.50

(See Casper the Friendly Ghost #20 & Harvey Hits #7, 16, 21, 23, 27, 30, 33)

WENDY THE GOOD LITTLE WITCH (2nd Series)
Apr, 1991 - No. 15, Aug, 1994 ($1.00/$1.25 #7-11/$1.50 #12-15)
Harvey Comics

1-15-Reprints Wendy & Casper stories. 12-Bunny app.   1.00

WENDY WITCH WORLD
10/61; No. 2, 9/62 - No. 52, 12/73; No. 53, 9/74
Harvey Publications

1-(25¢, 68 pg. Giants begin)	8.50	25.50	85.00
2-5	4.00	12.00	40.00
6-10	3.40	10.00	24.00
1-20	2.60	7.50	18.00
1-30	1.50	3.75	9.00
1-39: 39-Last 68 pg. issue	1.30	3.25	8.00
40-45: 52 pg. issues	1.00	2.60	6.00
46-53		1.40	3.50

WEREWOLF (Super Hero) (Also see Dracula & Frankenstein)
Dec, 1966 - No. 3, April, 1967
Dell Publishing Co.

1-1st app.	1.20	3.00	7.00
2,3		1.60	4.00

WEREWOLF BY NIGHT (See Giant-Size..., Marvel Spotlight #2-4 & Power
Record Comics)
Sept, 1972 - No. 43, Mar, 1977
Marvel Comics Group

1-Ploog-a cont'd. from Marvel Spotlight #4	6.50	19.50	50.00
2	6.50	19.50	50.00
3-5	2.40	7.20	17.00
6-10	1.70	5.00	12.00
11-20: 15-New origin Werewolf; Dracula-c/story cont'd from Tomb of Dracula			
#18	1.65	4.20	10.00
21-31	1.20	3.00	7.00
32-Origin & 1st app. Moon Knight (8/75)	8.00	24.50	65.00
33-2nd app. Moon Knight	4.60	14.00	32.00
34-36,38-43: 35-Starlin/Wrightson-c		1.60	4.00
37-Moon Knight app; part Wrightson-c	1.30	3.00	8.00

NOTE: Bolle a-6i. G. Kane a-11p, 12p; c-21, 22, 24-30, 34p. Mooney a-7i. Ploog 1-4p, 5, 6p,
13-16p; c-5-8, 13-16. Reinman a-8i. Sutton a(i)-9, 11, 16, 35.

WEREWOLVES & VAMPIRES (Magazine)
1982 (One Shot)

Charlton Comics

1   6.00   18.00   45.00

WEST COAST AVENGERS
Sept, 1984 - No. 4, Dec, 1984 (limited series, Mando paper)
Marvel Comics Group

1-Origin & 1st app. W.C. Avengers (Hawkeye, Iron Man, Mockingbird & Tigra)		.80	2.00
2-4			1.50

WEST COAST AVENGERS (Becomes Avengers West Coast #48 on)
Oct, 1985 - No. 47, Aug, 1989
Marvel Comics Group

V2#1-20			1.50
21-41			1.00
42-Byrne-a(p)/scripts begin		.80	2.00
43-102: 46-Byrne-c; 1st app. Great Lakes Avengers			1.00
Annual 1 (1986)			2.00
Annual 2 (1987)		.80	2.00
Annual 3 (1988, $1.75)-Evolutionary War app.		.80	2.00
Annual V2#4 (1989, $2.00, 68 pgs.)-Atlantis Attacks; Byrne/Austin-a			
		.80	2.00
Annual V2#5,6 (1990, 1991, $2.00, 68 pgs.)		.80	2.00
Annual V2#7 (1992, $2.25, 68 pgs.)-Darkhawk app.		.90	2.25

WESTERN ACTION
No. 7, 1964
I. W. Enterprises

7-Reprints Cow Puncher #? by Avon   1.00   2.60   6.00

WESTERN ACTION
Feb, 1975
Atlas/Seaboard Publ.

1-Kid Cody by Wildey & The Comanche Kid stories; intro. The Renegade
                                                                         1.00

WESTERN ACTION THRILLERS
Apr, 1937 (10¢, square binding; 100 pgs.)
Dell Publishers

1-Buffalo Bill, The Texas Kid, Laramie Joe, Two-Gun Thompson, & Wild West
Bill app.   70.00   211.00   565.00

WESTERN ADVENTURES COMICS (Western Love Trails #7 on)
Oct, 1948 - No. 6, Aug, 1949
Ace Magazines

nn(#1)-Sheriff Sal, The Cross-Draw Kid, Sam Bass begin			
	18.00	54.00	125.00
nn(#2)(12/48)	10.00	30.00	65.00
nn(#3)(2/49)-Used in **SOTI**, pgs. 30,31	11.00	33.00	75.00
4-6	9.15	27.00	55.00

WESTERN BANDITS
1952 (Painted-c)
Avon Periodicals

1-Butch Cassidy, The Daltons by Larsen; Kinstler-a; c-part-r/paperback
Avon Western Novel #1   13.00   39.00   90.00

WESTERN BANDIT TRAILS (See Approved Comics)
Jan, 1949 - No. 3, July, 1949
St. John Publishing Co.

1-Tuska-a; Baker-c; Blue Monk, Ventrilo app.	20.00	60.00	140.00
2-Baker-c	15.00	45.00	105.00
3-Baker-c/a; Tuska-a	18.00	54.00	125.00

WESTERN COMICS (See Super DC Giant #15)
Jan-Feb, 1948 - No. 85, Jan-Feb, 1961 (1-27: 52pgs.)
National Periodical Publications

Western Crime Busters #7 © TM

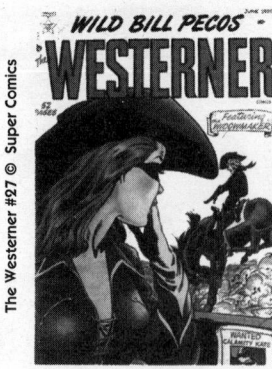
The Westerner #27 © Super Comics

Western Fighters #12 © HILL

	GD25	FN65	NM94

	GD25	FN65	NM94
1-Wyoming Kid & his horse Racer, The Vigilante in "Jesse James Rides Again" (Meskin-a), Cowboy Marshal, Rodeo Rick begin	68.00	206.00	550.00
2	39.00	118.00	275.00
3,4-Last Vigilante	31.00	94.00	220.00
5-Nighthawk & his horse Nightwind begin (not in #6); Captain Tootsie by Beck	27.00	81.00	190.00
6,7,9,10	21.00	62.00	145.00
8-Origin Wyoming Kid; 2 pg. pin-ups of rodeo queens	29.00	86.00	200.00
11-20	17.00	51.00	120.00
21-40: 24-Starr-a. 27-Last 52 pgs. 28-Flag-c	13.00	39.00	90.00
41-49: Last precode issue (2/55). 43-Pow Wow Smith begins, ends #85	11.50	34.00	80.00
50-60	10.00	30.00	70.00
61-85-Last Wyoming Kid. 77-Origin Matt Savage Trail Boss. 82-1st app. Fleetfoot, Pow Wow's girlfriend	9.15	27.00	55.00

NOTE: **G. Kane, Infantino** art in most. **Meskin** a-1-4. **Moreira** a-28-39. **Post** a-3-5.

WESTERN CRIME BUSTERS
Sept, 1950 - No. 10, Mar-Apr, 1952
Trojan Magazines

1-Six-Gun Smith, Wilma West, K-Bar-Kate, & Fighting Bob Dale begin; headlight-a	26.00	79.00	185.00
2	13.50	41.00	95.00
3-5: 3-Myron Fass-c	12.00	36.00	85.00
6-Wood-a	26.00	79.00	185.00
7-Six-Gun Smith by Wood	26.00	79.00	185.00
8	12.00	36.00	85.00
9-Tex Gordon & Wilma West by Wood; Lariat Lucy app.	26.00	79.00	185.00
10-Wood-a	25.00	75.00	175.00

WESTERN CRIME CASES (Formerly Indian Warriors #7,8; becomes The Outlaws #10 on)
No. 9, Dec, 1951
Star Publications

9-White Rider & Super Horse; L. B. Cole-c	13.00	39.00	90.00

WESTERN DESPERADO COMICS (Formerly Slam Bang Comics)
No. 8, 1940 (Oct.?)
Fawcett Publications

8-(Rare)	62.00	187.00	500.00

WESTERNER, THE (Wild Bill Pecos)
No. 14, June, 1948 - No. 41, Dec, 1951 (#14-31: 52 pgs.)
"Wanted" Comic Group/Toytown/Patches

14	10.00	30.00	70.00
15-17,19-21: 19-Meskin-a	5.35	16.00	32.00
18,22-25-Krigstein-a	10.00	30.00	58.00
26(4/50)-Origin & 1st app. Calamity Kate, series ends #32; Krigstein-a	10.00	30.00	70.00
27-Krigstein-a(2)	11.00	33.00	75.00
28-41: 33-Quest app. 37-Lobo, the Wolf Boy begins	4.25	13.00	26.00

NOTE: **Mort Lawrence** a-20-27, 29, 37, 39; c-19, 22-24, 26, 27. **Leav** c-14-18, 20, 31. **Syd Shores** a-39; c-34, 35, 37-41.

WESTERNER, THE
1964
Super Comics

Super Reprint 15-17: 15-r/Oklahoma Kid #? 16-r/Crack West. #65; Severin-c; Crandall-r. 17-r/Blazing Western #2; Severin-c	1.00	2.00	5.00

WESTERN FIGHTERS
Apr-May, 1948 - V4#7, Mar-Apr, 1953 (#1-V3#2: 52 pgs.)
Hillman Periodicals/Star Publ.

V1#1-Simon & Kirby-c	31.00	94.00	220.00
2-Not Kirby-a	9.15	27.50	55.00

3-Fuje-c	8.35	25.00	5
4-Krigstein, Ingels, Fuje-a	10.00	30.00	6
5,6,8,9,12	5.85	17.50	3
7,10-Krigstein-a	10.00	30.00	6
11-Williamson/Frazetta-a	25.00	75.00	17
V2#1-Krigstein-a	10.00	30.00	6
2-12: 4-Berg-a	4.00	12.00	2
V3#1-11	4.00	11.00	2
12-Krigstein-a	9.15	27.50	5
V4#1,4-7	4.00	11.00	2
2,3-Krigstein-a	9.15	27.50	5
3-D 1(12/53, 25¢, Star Publ.)-Came w/glasses; L. B. Cole-c	34.00	103.00	24

NOTE: **Kinstlerish** a-V2#6, 8, 9, 12; V3#2, 5-7, 11, 12; V4#1(plus cover). **McWilliams** a-1 **Powell** a-V2#2. **Reinman** a-1-12, V4#3. **Rowich** c-5, 6i. **Starr** a-5.

WESTERN FRONTIER
Apr-May, 1951 - No. 7, 1952
P. L. Publishers

1	10.00	30.00	6
2	6.35	19.00	3
3-7	4.25	13.00	3

WESTERN GUNFIGHTERS (1st Series) (Apache Kid #11-19)
No. 20, June, 1956 - No. 27, Aug, 1957
Atlas Comics (CPS)

20	10.00	30.00	6
21-Crandall-a	10.00	30.00	6
22-Wood & Powell-a	15.00	45.00	10
23,24: 23-Williamson-a. 24-Toth-a	10.00	30.00	6
25-27	8.00	24.00	4

NOTE: **Berg** a-20. **Colan** a-20, 26, 27. **Crandall** a-21. **Heath** a-25. **Maneely** a-24, 25; c-22 25. **Morisi** a-24. **Morrow** a-26. **Pakula** a-23. **Severin** c-20, 27. **Torres** a-26. **Woodbridge**

WESTERN GUNFIGHTERS (2nd Series)
Aug, 1970 - No. 33, Nov, 1975 (#1-6: 25¢, 68 pgs.)
Marvel Comics Group

1-Ghost Rider begins; Fort Rango, Renegades & Gunhawk app.		1.00	2.60
2-33: 2-Origin Nightwind (Apache Kid's horse). 7-Origin Ghost Rider retold 52 pgs. 10-Origin Black Rider. 12-Origin Matt Slade			1.60

NOTE: **Baker** r-2, 3. **Colan** r-2. **Drucker** r-3. **Everett** a-6i. **G. Kane** c-29, 31. **Kirby** a-1p(r), 11. **Kubert** r-2. **Maneely** r-2, 10. **Morrow** r-29. **Severin** c-10. **Shores** a-3, 4. **Barry Smith** a **Steranko** c-14. **Sutton** a-1, 2i, 5, 4. **Torres** r-26('57). **Wildey** r-8, 9. **Williamson** r-2, 18. **Woodbridge** r-27('57). Renegades in #4, 5; Ghost Rider in #1-7.

WESTERN HEARTS
Dec, 1949 - No. 10, Mar, 1952 (All photo-c)
Standard Comics

1-Severin-a; Whip Wilson & Reno Browne photo-c	17.00	51.00	12
2-Beverly Tyler & Jerome Courtland photo-c from movie "Palomino"; Williamson/Frazetta-a (2 pgs.)	17.00	49.00	11
3-Rex Allen photo-c	10.00	30.00	6
4-7,10-Severin & Elder, Al Carreno-a. 5-Ray Milland & Hedy Lamarr photo from movie "Copper Canyon". 6-Fred MacMurray & Irene Dunn photo-c from movie "Never a Dull Moment". 7-Jock Mahoney photo-c. 10-Bill Williams & Jane Nigh photo-c	10.00	30.00	6
8-Randolph Scott & Janis Carter photo-c from "Santa Fe"; Severin & Elder	10.00	30.00	6
9-Whip Wilson & Reno Browne photo-c; Severin & Elder-a	11.00	33.00	7

WESTERN HERO (Wow Comics #1-69; Real Western Hero #70-75)
No. 76, Mar, 1949 - No. 112, Mar, 1952
Fawcett Publications

76(#1, 52 pgs.)-Tom Mix, Hopalong Cassidy, Monte Hale, Gabby Hayes, Young Falcon (ends #78,80), & Big Bow and Little Arrow (ends #102,105			

Western Kid #4 © ATLAS

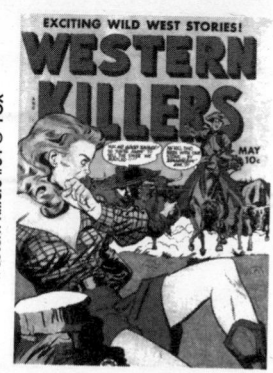

Western Killers #64 © FOX

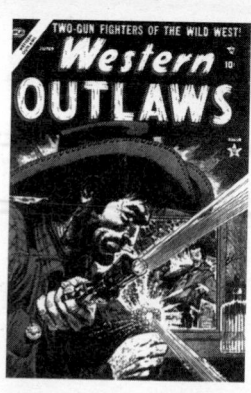

Western Outlaws #3 © ATLAS

	GD25	FN65	NM94

	GD25	FN65	NM94
begin; painted-c begin	26.00	79.00	185.00
77 (52 pgs.)	14.00	43.00	100.00
78,80-82 (52 pgs.): 81-Capt. Tootsie by Beck	14.00	43.00	100.00
79,83 (36 pgs.): 83-Last painted-c	12.00	36.00	85.00
84-86,88-90 (52 pgs.): 84-Photo-c begin, end #112. 86-Last Hopalong Cassidy	13.00	39.00	90.00
87,91,95,99 (36 pgs.): 87-Bill Boyd begins, ends #95	11.00	33.00	75.00
92-94,96-98,101 (52 pgs.): 96-Tex Ritter begins. 101-Red Eagle app.	12.00	36.00	85.00
100 (52 pgs.)	13.00	39.00	90.00
102-111: 102-Begin 36 pg. issues	11.00	33.00	75.00
112-Last issue	12.00	36.00	85.00

NOTE: 1/2 to 1 pg. Rocky Lane (Carnation) in 80-83, 86, 88, 97. Photo covers feature Hopalong Cassidy #84, 86, 89; Tom Mix #85, 87, 90, 92, 94, 97; Monte Hale #88, 91, 93, 95, 98, 100, 104, 107, 110; Tex Ritter #96, 99, 101, 105, 108, 111; Gabby Hayes #103.

WESTERN KID (1st Series)
Dec, 1954 - No. 17, Aug, 1957
Atlas Comics (CPC)

1-Origin; The Western Kid (Tex Dawson), his stallion Whirlwind & dog Lightning begin	16.00	47.00	110.00
2 (2/55)-Last pre-code	9.15	27.00	55.00
3-8	8.35	25.00	50.00
9,10-Williamson-a in both (4 pgs. each)	9.15	27.00	55.00
11-17	5.85	17.50	35.00

NOTE: Ayers a-6, 7. Maneely a-c2-7, 10, 14. Romita a-1-17; c-1, 12. Severin c-17.

WESTERN KID, THE (2nd Series)
Dec, 1971 - No. 5, Aug, 1972 (All 20¢ issues)
Marvel Comics Group

1-Reprints; Romita-c/a(3)	1.00	2.60	6.00
2-5: 2-Romita-a; Severin-c. 3-Williamson-r. 4-Everett-r	1.40		3.50

WESTERN KILLERS
No. 57?, July, 1948; No. 60, Sept, 1948 - No. 64, May, 1949; No. 6, July, 1949
Fox Features Syndicate

57? (#59?)(nd, F&J Trading Co.)-Range Busters; formerly Blue Beetle #57?	19.00	56.00	130.00
60 (#1, 9/48)-Extreme violence; lingerie panel	21.00	64.00	150.00
61-Jack Cole, Starr-a	17.00	49.00	115.00
62-64, 6	15.00	45.00	105.00

WESTERN LIFE ROMANCES (My Friend Irma #3 on?)
Dec, 1949 - No. 2, Mar, 1950 (52 pgs.)
Marvel Comics (IPP)

1-Whip Wilson & Reno Browne photo-c	16.00	47.00	110.00
2-Audie Murphy & Gale Storm photo-c; spanking scene	13.00	39.00	90.00

WESTERN LOVE
July-Aug, 1949 - No. 5, Mar-Apr, 1950 (All photo-c & 52 pgs.)
Prize Publications

1-S&K-a; Randolph Scott photo-c from movie "Canadian Pacific" (see Prize Comics #76)	24.00	73.00	170.00
2,5-S&K-a: 2-Whip Wilson & Reno Browne photo-c. 5-Dale Robertson photo-c	21.00	62.00	140.00
3,4: 3-Reno Browne? photo-c	11.50	34.00	80.00

NOTE: Meskin & Severin/Elder a-2-5.

WESTERN LOVE TRAILS (Formerly Western Adventures)
No. 7, Nov, 1949 - No. 9, Mar, 1950
Magazines (A. A. Wyn)

7	10.00	30.00	65.00
8,9	8.35	25.00	50.00

WESTERN MARSHAL (See Steve Donovan...)
No. 534, 2-4/54 - No. 640, 7/55 (Based on Ernest Haycox's "Trailtown")

Dell Publishing Co.

Four Color 534 (#1)-Kinstler-a	6.00	18.00	60.00
Four Color 591 (10/54), 613 (2/55), 640-All Kinstler-a	6.00	18.00	60.00

WESTERN OUTLAWS (Junior Comics #9-16; My Secret Life #22 on)
No. 17, Sept, 1948 - No. 21, May, 1949
Fox Features Syndicate

17-Kamen-a; Iger shop-a in all; 1 pg. "Death and the Devil Pills" r-in Ghostly Weird #122	29.00	86.00	200.00
18-21	17.00	49.00	115.00

WESTERN OUTLAWS
Feb, 1954 - No. 21, Aug, 1957
Atlas Comics (ACI No. 1-14/WPI No. 15-21)

1-Heath, Powell-a; Maneely hanging-c	17.00	49.00	110.00
2	10.00	30.00	60.00
3-10: 7-Violent-a by R.Q. Sale	7.50	22.50	45.00
11,14-Williamson-a in both (6 pgs. each)	9.15	27.00	55.00
12,18,20,21: Severin covers	6.70	20.00	40.00
13-Baker-a	7.00	21.00	42.00
15-Torres-a	7.50	22.50	45.00
16-Williamson text illo	5.85	17.50	35.00
17,19-Crandall-a. 17-Williamson text illo	7.50	22.50	45.00

NOTE: Ayers a-7, 10, 18, 20. Bolle a-21. Colan a-5, 10, 11, 17. Drucker a-11. Everett a-9, 10. Heath a-1; c-3, 4, 8, 16. Kubert a-9p. Maneely a-13, 16, 17, 19; c-1, 5, 7, 9, 10, 13. Morisi a-18. Powell a-3, 16. Romita a-7, 13. Severin a-8, 16, 19; c-17, 18, 20, 21. Tuska a-6, 15.

WESTERN OUTLAWS & SHERIFFS (Formerly Best Western)
No. 60, Dec, 1949 - No. 73, June, 1952
Marvel/Atlas Comics (IPC)

60 (52 pgs.)	19.00	58.00	135.00
61-65: 61-Photo-c	17.00	49.00	115.00
66-Story contains 5 hangings	13.00	39.00	90.00
68-72	11.50	34.00	80.00
67-Cannibalism story	14.00	43.00	100.00
73-Black Rider story; Everett-c	12.00	36.00	85.00

NOTE: Maneely a-62, 67; c-62, 69-73. Robinson a-68. Sinnott a-70. Tuska a-69-71.

WESTERN PICTURE STORIES (1st Western comic)
Feb, 1937 - No. 4, June, 1937
Comics Magazine Company

1-Will Eisner-a	150.00	450.00	1200.00
2-Will Eisner-a	93.00	281.00	750.00
3,4: 3-Eisner-a. 4-Caveman Cowboy story	75.00	225.00	600.00

WESTERN PICTURE STORIES (See Giant Comics Edition #6, 11)

WESTERN ROMANCES (See Target...)

WESTERN ROUGH RIDERS
Nov, 1954 - No. 4, May, 1955
Gillmor Magazines No. 1,4 (Stanmor Publications)

1	7.00	21.00	42.00
2-4	4.25	13.00	28.00

WESTERN ROUNDUP (See Dell Giants & Fox Giants)

WESTERN TALES (Formerly Witches...)
No. 31, Oct, 1955 - No. 33, July-Sept, 1956
Harvey Publications

31,32-All S&K-a; Davy Crockett app. in each	17.00	49.00	115.00
33-S&K-a; Jim Bowie app.	17.00	49.00	115.00

NOTE: #32 & 33 contain Boy's Ranch reprints. Kirby c-31.

WESTERN TALES OF BLACK RIDER (Formerly Black Rider; Gunsmoke Western #33 on)
No. 28, May, 1955 - No. 31, Nov, 1955
Atlas Comics (CPS)

28 (#1): The Spider (a villain) dies	14.00	43.00	100.00

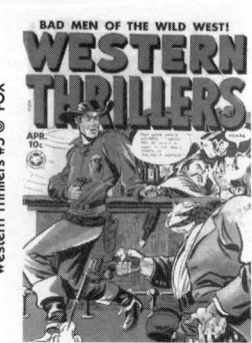

Western Thrillers #5 © FOX

Wetworks #5 © Aegis Entertainment

What If? #8 (1st Series) © MEG

29-31	10.00	30.00	70.00				

NOTE: *Lawrence* a-30. *Maneely* c-28-30. *Severin* a-28. *Shores* c-31.

WESTERN TEAM-UP
Nov, 1973 (20¢)
Marvel Comics Group

1-Origin & 1st app. The Dakota Kid; Rawhide Kid-r; Gunsmoke Kid-r by Jack Davis		1.20	3.00

WESTERN THRILLERS (My Past Confessions #7 on)
Aug, 1948 - No. 6, June, 1949; No. 52, 1954?
Fox Features Syndicate/M.S. Distr. No. 52

1- "Velvet Rose" (Kamenish-a); "Two-Gun Sal", "Striker Sisters" (all women outlaws issue); Brodsky-c	40.00	120.00	315.00
2	17.00	49.00	115.00
3,6	14.00	43.00	100.00
4,5-Bakerish-a; 5-Butch Cassidy app.	17.00	49.00	115.00
52-(Reprint, M.S. Dist.)-1954? No date given (becomes My Love Secret #53)	7.00	21.00	42.00

WESTERN THRILLERS (Cowboy Action #5 on)
Nov, 1954 - No. 4, Feb, 1955 (All-r/Western Outlaws & Sheriffs)
Atlas Comics (ACI)

1	12.00	36.00	85.00
2-4	8.00	24.00	48.00

NOTE: *Heath* c-3. *Maneely* a-1; c-2. *Powell* a-4. *Robinson* a-4. *Romita* c-4. *Tuska* a-2.

WESTERN TRAILS (Ringo Kid Starring in...)
May, 1957 - No. 2, July, 1957
Atlas Comics (SAI)

1-Ringo Kid app.; Severin-c	10.00	30.00	65.00
2-Severin-c	7.00	21.00	42.00

NOTE: *Bolle* a-1, 2. *Maneely* a-1; *Severin* c-1, 2.

WESTERN TRUE CRIME (Becomes My Confessions)
No. 15, Aug, 1948 - No. 6, June, 1949
Fox Features Syndicate

15(#1)-Kamen-a; formerly Zoot #14 (5/48)?	23.00	69.00	160.00
16(#2)-Kamenish-a; headlight panels, violence	21.00	62.00	145.00
3,4: 3-Kamen-a. 4-Johnny Craig-a	17.00	51.00	120.00
5,6	11.00	33.00	75.00

WESTERN WINNERS (Formerly All-Western Winners; becomes Black Rider #8 on & Romance Tales #7 on?)
No. 5, June, 1949 - No. 7, Dec, 1949
Marvel Comics (CDS)

5-Two-Gun Kid, Kid Colt, Black Rider; Shores-c	28.00	84.00	195.00
6-Two-Gun Kid, Black Rider, Heath Kid Colt story; Captain Tootsie by C.C. Beck	24.00	71.00	165.00
7-Randolph Scott Photo-c w/true stories about the West	24.00	71.00	165.00

WEST OF THE PECOS (See Zane Grey, 4-Color #222)

WESTWARD HO, THE WAGONS (Disney)
No. 738, Sept, 1956 (Movie)
Dell Publishing Co.

Four Color 738-Fess Parker photo-c	10.00	30.00	100.00

WETWORKS (See WildC.A.T.S: Covert Action Teams #2)
June, 1994 - Present ($1.95/$2.50)
Image Comics (Wildstorm Productions)

1-"July" on-c; gatefold wraparound-c; Portacio/Williams-c/a	1.00	2.00	5.00
1-Chicago Comicon edition	1.65	4.20	10.00
2-4		1.20	3.00
2-Alternate Portacio-c, see Deathblow #5	1.65	4.20	10.00

5-7,9-25: 5-($2.50). 13-Portacio-c. 16-Fire From Heaven Pt. 4. 17-Fire From

Heaven Pt. 11			1.00
8 ($1.95)-Newstand, Wildstorm Rising Pt. 7			.80
8 ($2.50)-Direct Market, Wildstorm Rising Pt. 7			1.00
Sourcebook 1 (10/94, $2.50)-Text & illustrations (no comics)			1.00

WHACK (Satire)
Oct, 1953 - No. 3, May, 1954
St. John Publishing Co. (Jubilee Publ.)

1-(3-D, 25¢)-Kubert-a; Maurer-c; came w/glasses	27.00	81.00	1
2,3-Kubert-a in each. 2-Bing Crosby on-c; Mighty Mouse & Steve Canyon parodies. 3-Li'l Orphan Annie parody; Maurer-c	15.00	45.00	1

WHACKY (See Wacky)

WHAM COMICS (See Super Spy)
Nov, 1940 - No. 2, Dec, 1940
Centaur Publications

1-The Sparkler, The Phantom Rider, Craig Carter and his Magic Ring, Detecto, Copper Slug, Speed Silvers by Gustavson, Speed Centaur & Jon Linton (s/f) begin	125.00	375.00	10
2-Origin Blue Fire & Solarman; The Buzzard app.	87.00	262.00	7

WHAM-O GIANT COMICS
April, 1967 (98¢, newspaper size, one-shot)
Wham-O Mfg. Co. (Six issue subscription was advertised)

1-Radian & Goody Bumpkin by Wood; 1 pg. Stanley-a; Fine, Tufts-a; flying saucer reports; wraparound-c	5.00	15.00	

WHAT DO YOU KNOW ABOUT THIS COMICS SEAL OF APPROVAL?
nd (1955) (4 pgs., slick paper-c)
No publisher listed (DC Comics Giveaway)

nn-(Rare)	54.00	160.00	4

WHAT IF? (1st Series) (What If? Featuring... #13 & #7-33)
Feb, 1977 - No. 47, Oct, 1984; June, 1988 (All 52 pgs.)
Marvel Comics Group

1-Brief origin Spider-Man, Fantastic Four	3.60	11.00	
2-Origin The Hulk retold	1.70	5.00	
3-5: 3-Avengers. 4-Invaders. 5-Capt. America	1.30	3.25	
6-10: 8-Daredevil; Spidey parody. 9-Origins Venus, Marvel Boy, Human Robot, 3-D Man. 11-Marvel Bullpen as F. F.	1.20	3.00	
11,12	1.00	2.00	
13-Conan app.; John Buscema-c/a(p)	1.20	2.90	
14-16		1.80	
17-Ghost Rider & Son of Satan app.	1.30	3.00	
18-26,29: 18-Begin 75¢-c; Dr. Strange. 19-Spider-Man. 22-Origin Dr. Doom retold		1.60	
27-X-Men app.; Miller-c	1.65	4.20	
28-Daredevil by Miller; Ghost Rider app.	1.65	4.20	
30-"What If...Spider-Man's Clone Had Lived?"	2.15	6.50	
31-Begin $1.00-c; featuring Wolverine & the Hulk; X-Men app.; death of Hu Wolverine & Magneto	2.15	6.50	
32-47: 32,36-Byrne-a. 34-Marvel crew each draw themselves. 35-What if Elektra had lived?; Miller/Austin-a. 37-Old X-Men & Silver Surfer app. 39-Thor battles Conan	1.20		
Special 1 ($1.50, 6/88)-Iron Man, F.F., Thor app.		.80	

NOTE: *Austin* a-27p, 32i, 34, 35i; c-35i, 36i. *J. Buscema* a-13p, 15p; c-10, 13p, 13p. *Byr* 32i, 36; c-36p. *Colan* a-21p; c-17p, 18p, 21p. *Ditko* a-35, Special 1. *Golden* c-29, 40-42. a-40p. *Gil Kane* a-3p, 24p; c(p)-2-4, 7, 8. *Kirby* a-11p; c-9p, 11p. *Layton* a-32i, 33i; c-30, 33i, 34. *Mignola* c-39i. *Miller* a-28p, 32i, 34(1), 35p; c-27, 28p. *Mooney* a-8i, 30i. *Perez* a Robbins a-24p. *Sienkiewicz* c-43-46. *Simonson* a-15p, 32i. *Starlin* a-32i. *Stevens* a-8, 16i(part). *Sutton* a-2i, 18p, 28. *Tuska* a-5p. *Weiss* a-37p.

WHAT IF...? (2nd Series)
V2#1, July, 1989 - Present ($1.25/$1.50)
Marvel Comics

V2#1-...The Avengers Had Lost the Evol. War			1.60
2-5: 2-Daredevil, Punisher app.			1.10

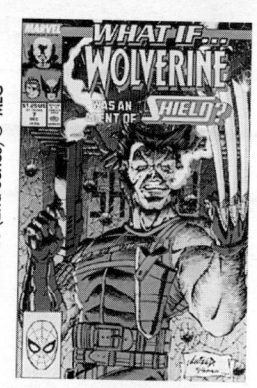

What If? #7 (2nd Series) © MEG

What The--?! #11 © MEG

Where In The World Is Carmen Sandiego #3 © DC

	GD25	FN65	NM94

6-X-Men app. / 1.60 / 4.00
7-Wolverine app.; Liefeld-c/a(1st on Wolvie?) 1.00 / 2.00 / 5.00
8,11: 11-Fantastic Four app.; McFarlane-c(i) / .90 / 2.25
9,12-X-Men / 1.20 / 3.00
10-Punisher / 1.20 / 3.00
13-15,17-21,23,27-29: 13-Prof. X; Jim Lee-c. 14-Capt. Marvel; Lim/Austin-c. 15-F.F.; Capullo-c/a(p). 17-Spider-Man/Kraven. 18-F.F. 19-Vision. 20,21-Spider-Man. 23-X-Men. 27-Namor/F.F. 28,29-Capt. America. 29-Swipes cover to Avengers #4 / / 1.50
16-Wolverine battles Conan; Red Sonja app.; X-Men cameo 1.80 / 4.50
22-Silver Surfer by Lim/Austin-c/a / 1.20 / 3.00
24-Wolverine; Punisher app. / 1.10 / 2.75
25-($1.50, 52 pgs.)-Wolverine app. / 1.20 / 3.00
26-Punisher app. / .80 / 2.00
30-($1.75, 52 pgs.)-Sue Richards/F.F. / .70 / 1.75
31-40: 31-Cosmic Spider-Man & Venom app.; Hobgoblin cameo. 32,33-Phoenix; X-Men app. 35-Fantastic Five (w/Spidey). 36-Avengers vs. Guardians of the Galaxy. 37-Wolverine; Thibert-c(i). 38-Thor; Rogers-p (part). 40-Storm; X-Men app. / / 1.50
41-($1.75, 52 pgs.)-Avengers vs. Galactus / .70 / 1.75
42-49,51-60: 42-Spider-Man. 43-Wolverine. 44-Venom/Punisher. 45-Ghost Rider. 46-Cable. 47-Magneto. 49-Infinity Gauntlet w/Silver Surfer & Thanos. 52-Dr. Doom. 54-Death's Head. 57-Punisher as Shield. 58-"What if Punisher Had Killed Spider-Man" w/cover similar to Amazing S-M #129. 59-...Wolverine led Alpha Flight. 60-X-Men Wedding Album 1.25
50-($2.95, 52 pgs.)-Foil embossed-c; "What If Hulk Had Killed Wolverine" / 1.20 / 3.00
61-99: 61-$1.50-c begins; bound-in card sheet. 61,86,88-Spider-Man. 74,77,81,84,85-X-Men. 76-Last app. Watcher in title. 78-Bisley-c. 80-Hulk. 87-Sabretooth. 89-Fantastic Four. 90-Cyclops & Havok. 91-The Hulk / / 1.50

HAT'S BEHIND THESE HEADLINES
48 (16 pgs.)
lliam C. Popper Co.
-Comic insert "The Plot to Steal the World" 4.25 / 13.00 / 26.00

HAT'S NEW? - THE COLLECTED ADVENTURES OF PHIL & DIXIE'
t, 1991 - No. 2, 1991? ($5.95, mostly color, squarebound, 52 pgs.)
lliard Press
2-By Phil Foglio 1.00 / 2.50 / 6.00

HAT THE--?!
g, 1988 - No. 26, 1993 ($1.25/$1.50/$2.50, semi-annually #5 on)
rvel Comics
All contain parodies / 1.00 / 2.50
4,5: 5-Punisher/Wolverine parody; Jim Lee-a / / 1.50
X-Men parody; Todd McFarlane-a / 1.20 / 3.00
25: 6-($1.00)-Punisher, Wolverine, Alpha Flight. 9-Wolverine. 16-EC back-c parody. 17-Wolverine/Punisher parody. 18-Star Trek parody w/Wolverine. 19-Punisher, Wolverine, Ghost Rider. 21-Weapon X parody. 22-Punisher/Wolverine parody / / 1.25
Fall Special ($2.50, 68 pgs.)-Spider-Ham 2099-c/story; origin Silver Surfer; Hulk & Doomsday parody; indicia reads "Winter Special." / .90 / 2.50
mmer Special 1 (1993, $2.50)-X-Men parody / .90 / 2.50
E: Austin a-6i. Byrne a-2, 6, 10; c-2, 6-8, 10, 12, 13. Golden a-22. Dale Keown a-8p(8). McFarlane a-3. Rogers c-15i, 16p. Severin a-2. Staton a-21p. Williamson a-2i.

EATIES (Premiums)
0 & 1951 (32 titles, pocket-size, 32 pgs.)
t Disney Productions
(Set A-1 to A-8, 1950)
Mickey Mouse & the Disappearing Island, A-2-Grandma Duck, Homespun Detective, A-3-Donald Duck & the Haunted Jewels, A-4-Donald Duck & the Giant Ape, A-5-Mickey Mouse, Roving Reporter, A-6-Li'l Bad Wolf, Forest

Ranger, A-7-Goofy, Tightrope Acrobat, A-8-Pluto & the Bogus Money each... / 4.20 / 12.50 / 25.00
(Set B-1 to B-8, 1950)
B-1-Mickey Mouse & the Pharoah's Curse, B-2-Pluto, Canine Cowpoke, B-3-Donald Duck & the Buccaneers, B-4-Mickey Mouse & the Mystery Sea Monster, B-5-Li'l Bad Wolf in the Hollow Tree Hideout, B-6-Donald Duck, Trail Blazer, B-7-Goofy & the Gangsters, B-8 Donald Duck, Klondike Kid each... / 4.20 / 12.50 / 25.00
(Set C-1 to C-8, 1951)
C-1-Donald Duck & the Inca Idol, C-2-Mickey Mouse & the Magic Mountain, C-3-Li'l Bad Wolf, Fire Fighter, C-4-Gus & Jaq Save the Ship, C-5-Donald Duck in the Lost Lakes, C-6-Mickey Mouse & the Stagecoach Bandits, C-7-Goofy, Big Game Hunter, C-8-Donald Duck Deep-Sea Diver each... / 4.20 / 12.50 / 25.00
(Set D-1 to D-8, 1951)
D-1-Donald Duck in Indian Country, D-2-Mickey Mouse and the Abandoned Mine, D-3-Pluto & the Mysterious Package, D-4-Bre'r Rabbit's Sunken Treasure, D-5-Donald Duck, Mighty Mystic, D-6-Mickey Mouse & the Medicine Man, D-7-Li'l Bad Wolf and the Secret of the Woods, D-8-Minnie Mouse, Girl Explorer each... / 4.20 / 12.50 / 25.00
NOTE: Some copies lack the Wheaties ad.

WHEE COMICS (Also see Gay, Smile & Tickle Comics)
1955 (7¢, 5x7-1/4", 52 pgs.)
Modern Store Publications
1-Funny animal / .80 / 2.00 / 4.00

WHEELIE AND THE CHOPPER BUNCH (TV)
July, 1975 - No. 7, July, 1976 (Hanna-Barbera)
Charlton Comics
1,2: 1-Byrne text illo (see Nightmare for 1st art); Staton-a. 2-Byrne-c/a. / 1.30 / 3.00 / 8.00
3-7-Staton-a. 3-Byrne-c/a / 1.70 / 4.25

WHEN KNIGHTHOOD WAS IN FLOWER (See The Sword & the Rose, 4-Color #505, 682)

WHEN SCHOOL IS OUT (See Wisco)

WHERE CREATURES ROAM
July, 1970 - No. 8, Sept, 1971
Marvel Comics Group
1-Kirby/Ayers-r / 1.30 / 3.25 / 8.00
2-8-Kirby-r / 1.60 / 4.00
NOTE: Ditko r-1-6, 7. Heck r-2, 5. Kirby r-2-5. All contain pre super-hero reprints.

WHERE MONSTERS DWELL
Jan, 1970 - No. 38, Oct, 1975
Marvel Comics Group
1-Kirby/Ditko-r; all contain pre super-hero-r / 2.15 / 6.50 / 15.00
2-10,12: 4-Crandall-a(r). 12-Giant size / 1.30 / 3.25 / 8.00
11,13-37: 18,20-Starlin-c / 1.20 / 3.00
38-Williamson-r/World of Suspense #3 / 1.60 / 4.00
NOTE: Colan r-12. Ditko a(r)-4, 6, 8, 10, 12, 17-19, 23-25, 37. Kirby r-1-6; c-12? Reinman a-3r, 4r, 12r. Severin c-15.

WHERE'S HUDDLES? (TV) (See Fun-In #9)
Jan, 1971 - No. 3, Dec, 1971 (Hanna-Barbera)
Gold Key
1 / 1.65 / 4.20 / 10.00
2,3: 3-r/most #1 / 1.00 / 2.60 / 6.00

WHERE IN THE WORLD IS CARMEN SANDIEGO (TV)
June, 1996 - No. 4, Dec, 1996 ($1.75)
DC Comics
1-4: Adaptation of TV show / / 1.75

WHIP WILSON (Movie star) (Formerly Rex Hart; Gunhawk #12 on; see

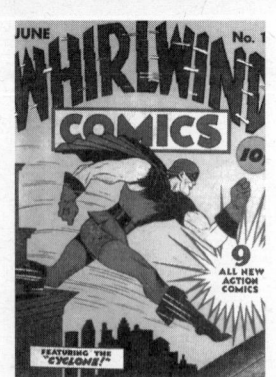

Whirlwind Comics #1 © Nita Publication

White Princess Of The Jungle #2 © AVON

Whiz Comics #23 © FAW

	GD25	FN65	NM94

Western Hearts, Western Life Romances, Western Love)
No. 9, April, 1950 - No. 11, Sept, 1950 (#9,10: 52 pgs.)
Marvel Comics

9-Photo-c; Whip Wilson & his horse Bullet begin; origin Bullet; issue #23 listed on splash page; cover changed to #9	51.00	155.00	415.00
10,11: Both have photo-c. 11-36 pgs.	32.00	96.00	225.00
I.W. Reprint #1(1964)-Kinstler-c; r-Marvel #11	2.85	8.50	20.00

WHIRLWIND COMICS (Also see Cyclone Comics)
June, 1940 - No. 3, Sept, 1940
Nita Publication

1-Origin & 1st app. Cyclone; Cyclone-c	125.00	375.00	1000.00
2,3: Cyclone-c	87.00	262.00	700.00

WHIRLYBIRDS (TV)
No. 1124, Aug, 1961 - No. 1216, Oct-Dec, 1961
Dell Publishing Co.

Four Color 1124 (#1)-Photo-c	9.00	27.00	90.00
Four Color 1216-Photo-c	8.00	24.00	80.00

WHISPER (Female Ninja)
Dec, 1983 - No. 2, 1984 ($1.75, Baxter paper)
Capital Comics

1,2: 1-Origin; Golden-c	1.00	2.00	5.00

WHITE CHIEF OF THE PAWNEE INDIANS
1951
Avon Periodicals

nn-Kit West app.; Kinstler-c	13.00	39.00	90.00

WHITE EAGLE INDIAN CHIEF (See Indian Chief)

WHITE FANG
1990 ($5.95, 68 pgs.)
Disney Comics

nn-Graphic novel adapting new Disney movie	1.00	3.00	6.00

WHITE INDIAN
No. 11, July, 1953 - No. 15, 1954
Magazine Enterprises

11(A-1 94), 12(A-1 101), 13(A-1 104)-Frazetta-r(Dan Brand) in all from Durango Kid. 11-Powell-c	21.00	62.00	145.00
14(A-1 117), 15(A-1 135)-Check-a; Torres-a-#15	10.00	30.00	70.00

NOTE: #11 contains reprints from Durango Kid #1-4; #12 from #5, 9, 10, 11; #13 from #7, 12, 13, 16. #14 & 15 contain all new stories.

WHITE PRINCESS OF THE JUNGLE (Also see Jungle Adventures & Top Jungle Comics)
July, 1951 - No. 5, Nov, 1952
Avon Periodicals

1-Origin of White Princess (Taanda) & Capt'n Courage (r); Kinstler-c	40.00	120.00	325.00
2-Reprints origin of Malu, Slave Girl Princess from Avon's Slave Girl Comics #1 w/Malu changed to Zora; Kinstler-c/a(2)	36.00	107.00	250.00
3-Origin Blue Gorilla; Kinstler-c/a	29.00	86.00	200.00
4-Jack Barnum, White Hunter app.; r/Sheena #9	26.00	77.00	180.00
5-Blue Gorilla by McCann?; Kinstler inside-c; Fawcette/Alascia-a(3)	26.00	77.00	180.00

WHITE RIDER AND SUPER HORSE (Formerly Humdinger V2#2; Indian Warriors #7 on; also see Blue Bolt #1, 4Most & Western Crime Cases)
1950 - No. 6, Mar, 1951
Novelty-Star Publications/Accepted Publ.

1: 1-3-Exist?	16.00	47.00	110.00
2,3	13.00	39.00	90.00
4-6-Adapts "The Last of the Mohicans". 4-(9/50)-Says #11 on inside	13.00	39.00	90.00
Accepted Reprint #5(r/#5),6 (nd); L.B. Cole-c	7.00	21.00	42.00

NOTE: All have **L. B. Cole** covers.

WHITE WILDERNESS (Disney)
No. 943, Oct, 1958
Dell Publishing Co.

Four Color 943-Movie		7.00	21.00

WHITMAN COMIC BOOK, A
Sept., 1962 (136 pgs.; 7-3/4x5-3/4; hardcover) (B&W)
Whitman Publishing Co.

1-7: 1-Yogi Bear. 2-Huckleberry Hound. 3-Mr. Jinks and Pixie & Dixie. 4-The Flintstones. 5-Augie Doggie & Loopy de Loop. 6-Snooper & Blabbr Fearless Detectives/Quick DrawMcGraw of the Wild West. 7-Bugs Bunny from #47,51,53,54 & 55	1.00	3.00	
8-Donald Duck-reprints most of WDC&S #209-213. Includes 5 Barks stories 1 complete Mickey Mouse serial by Paul Murry & 1 Mickey Mouse serial missing the 1st episode	10.00	30.00	

NOTE: Hanna-Barbera #1-4,6,8(TV), original stories. Dell reprints-#5, 7.

WHIZ COMICS (Formerly Flash Comics & Thrill Comics #1)
No. 2, Feb, 1940 - No. 155, June, 1953
Fawcett Publications

	GD25	FN65	VF82	N
1-(nn on cover, #2 inside)-Origin & 1st newsstand app. Captain Marvel (formerly Captain Thunder) by C. C. Beck (created by Bill Parker), Spy Smasher, Golden Arrow, Ibis the Invincible, Dan Dare, Scoop Smith, Sivana, & Lance O'Casey begin	7,857.00	23,571.00	39,285.00	60,00
(Estimated up to 100 total copies exist, 3 in NM/Mint)				
(The only Mint copy sold in 1995 for $176,000 cash)				

1-Reprint, oversize 13-1/2x10". **WARNING:** This comic is an exact duplicate (except for dropping "Gangway for Captain Marvel" from-c) of the original except for its size published in 1974 with a second cover titling it as a Famous First Edition. There have many reported cases of the outer cover being removed and the interior sold as the original tion. The reprint with the new outer cover removed is practically worthless. See Famous First Edition for value.

	GD25	FN65	N
2-(3/40, nn on cover, #3 inside); cover to Flash #1 redrawn, pg. 12, panel Spy Smasher reveals I.D. to Eve	400.00	1200.00	38
3-(4/40, #3 on-c, #4 inside)-1st app. Beautia	288.00	862.00	23
4-(5/40, #4 on cover, #5 inside)-Brief origin Capt. Marvel retold	237.00	712.00	19
5-Captain Marvel wears button-down flap on splash page only	200.00	600.00	16
6-10: 7-Dr. Voodoo begins (by Raboy-#9-22)	150.00	450.00	12
11-14: 12-Capt. Marvel does not wear cape	106.00	318.00	8
15-Origin Sivana; Dr. Voodoo by Raboy	115.00	346.00	9
16-18-Spy Smasher battles Captain Marvel	115.00	346.00	9
19,20	73.00	219.00	5
21-Origin & 1st app. Lt. Marvels	78.00	234.00	6
22-24: 23-Only Dr. Voodoo by Tuska	60.00	181.00	4
25-(12/41)-Captain Nazi jumps from Master Comics #21 to take on Capt. Marvel solo after being beaten by Capt. Marvel/Bulletman team, causing the creation of Capt. Marvel Jr.; 1st app./origin of Capt. Marvel Jr. (part trilogy origin by CC. Beck & Mac Raboy); Captain Marvel sends Jr. back Master #22 to aid Bulletman against Capt. Nazi; origin Old Shazam in te	450.00	1350.00	45
26-30	53.00	159.00	4
31,32: 32-1st app. The Trolls; Hitler/Mussolini satire by Beck	45.00	136.00	3
33-Spy Smasher, Captain Marvel x-over on cover and inside	53.00	159.00	4
34,36-40: 37-The Trolls app. by Swayze	40.00	120.00	2
35-Captain Marvel & Spy Smasher-c	42.00	126.00	3
41-50: 43-Spy Smasher, Ibis, Golden Arrow x-over in Capt. Marvel. 44-Flash 47-Origin recap (1 pg.)	28.00	84.00	1
51-60: 52-Capt. Marvel x-over in Ibis. 57-Spy Smasher, Golden Arrow, Ibis cameo	25.00	75.00	1
61-70	22.00	66.00	1

608

Whoa, Nellie! #2 © Jaime Hernandez

Whodunnit? #2 © ECL

Who's Who in Star Trek #2 © Paramount

	GD25	FN65	NM94
71,77-80	20.00	60.00	140.00
72-76-Two Captain Marvel stories in each; 76-Spy Smasher becomes Crime Smasher	21.00	62.00	145.00
81-99: 86-Captain Marvel battles Sivana Family. 91-Infinity-c	20.00	60.00	140.00
100-(8/48)-Anniversary issue	24.00	71.00	165.00
101-106: 102-Commando Yank app. 106-Bulletman app.	19.00	58.00	135.00
107-152: 107-White House photo-c. 108-Brooklyn Bridge photo-c. 112-Photo-c 139-Infinity-c. 140-Flag-c. 142-Used in **POP**, pg. 89	19.00	58.00	135.00
153-155-(Scarce):154,155-1st/2nd Dr. Death stories	24.00	73.00	170.00

Wheaties Giveaway(1946, Miniature, 6-1/2x8-1/4", 32 pgs.); all copies were taped at each corner to a box of Wheaties and are never found in fine or mint condition; "Capt. Marvel & the Water Thieves", plus Golden Arrow, Ibis, Crime Smasher stories 70.00 280.00 –

NOTE: **C.C. Beck** *Captain Marvel-No. 25(part).* **Krigstein** *Golden Arrow-No. 75, 78, 91, 95, 96, 98-100.* **Mac Raboy** *Dr. Voodoo-No. 9-22. Captain Marvel-No. 25(part).* **M.Swayze** *a-37, 38, 59; c-38.* **Schaffenberger** *c-138-158(most).* **Wolverton** *1/2 pg. "Culture Corner"-No. 65-67, 68(2 1/2 pgs), 70-85, 87-96, 98-100, 102-109, 112-121, 123, 125, 126, 128-131, 133, 134, 136, 142, 143, 146.*

WHOA, NELLIE (Also see Love & Rockets)
July, 1996 - No. 3, Sept, 1996 ($2.95, B&W, limited series)
Fantagraphics Books

1-3: Jamie Hernandez-c/a/scripts			3.00

WHODUNIT
Aug-Sept, 1948 - No. 3, Dec-Jan, 1948-49 (#1,2: 52 pgs.)
D.S. Publishing Co.

1-Baker-a (7 pgs.)	20.00	60.00	140.00
2,3	10.00	30.00	70.00

WHODUNNIT?
June, 1986 - No. 3, Apr, 1987 ($2.00, limited series)
Eclipse Comics

1-3: Spiegle-a. 2-Gulacy-c		1.00	2.00

WHO FRAMED ROGER RABBIT (See Marvel Graphic Novel)

WHO IS NEXT?
No. 5, Jan, 1953
Standard Comics

5-Toth, Sekowsky, Andru-a	17.00	49.00	115.00

WHO IS THE CROOKED MAN?
Sept, 1996 - Present ($3.50, B&W, 40 pgs.)
Crusade

1-Intro The Martyr, Scarlet 7 & Garrison			3.50

WHO'S MINDING THE MINT? (See Movie Classics)

WHO'S WHO IN STAR TREK
Mar, 1987 - #2, Apr, 1987 ($1.50, limited series)
DC Comics

1,2	1.00	2.00	5.00

NOTE: **Byrne** *a-1, 2.* **Chaykin** *c-1, 2.* **Morrow** *a-1, 2.* **McFarlane** *a-2.* **Perez** *a-1, 2. Sutton a-1, 2.*

WHO'S WHO IN THE LEGION OF SUPER-HEROES
Apr, 1987 - No. 7, Nov, 1988 ($1.25, limited series)
DC Comics

1-7			1.30

WHO'S WHO: THE DEFINITIVE DIRECTORY OF THE DC UNIVERSE
Mar, 1985 - No. 26, Apr, 1987 (Maxi-series, no ads)
DC Comics

1-DC heroes from A-Z	1.00	2.00	
1-26: All have 1-2 pgs-a by most DC artists			1.50

NOTE: **Art Adams** *a-4, 11, 18, 20.* **Anderson** *a-1-5, 7-12, 14, 15, 19, 21, 23-25.* **Aparo** *a-2, 3,*

9, 10, 12, 13, 14, 15, 17, 18, 21, 23. **Byrne** *a-4, 7, 14, 16, 18i, 19, 22i, 24; c-22.* **Cowan** *a-3-5, 8, 10-13, 16-18, 22-25.* **Ditko** *a-19-22.* **Evans** *a-20.* **Giffen** *a-1, 3-6, 8, 13, 15, 17, 18, 23.* **Grell** *a-6, 9, 14, 20, 23, 25, 26.* **Infantino** *a-1-10, 12, 15, 17-22, 24, 25.* **Kaluta** *a-14, 21.* **Gil Kane** *a-1-11, 13, 14, 16, 19, 21-23, 25.* **Kirby** *a-2-6, 8-18, 20, 22, 25.* **Kubert** *a-2, 3, 7-11, 19, 20, 25.* **Erik Larsen** *a-24.* **McFarlane** *a-10-12, 17, 19, 25, 26.* **Morrow** *a-4, 7, 25, 26.* **Orlando** *a-1, 4, 10, 11, 21i.* **Perez** *a-1-5, 8-19, 22-26; c-1-4, 13-18.* **Rogers** *a-1, 2, 5-7, 11, 12, 15, 24.* **Starlin** *a-13, 14, 16.* **Stevens** *a-4, 7, 18.*

WHO'S WHO UPDATE '87
Aug, 1987 - No. 5, Dec, 1987 ($1.25, limited series)
DC Comics

1-5: Contains art by most DC artists			1.50

NOTE: **Giffen** *a-1.* **McFarlane** *a-1-4; c-4.* **Perez** *a-1-4.*

WHO'S WHO UPDATE '88
Aug, 1988 - No. 4, Nov, 1988 ($1.25, limited series)
DC Comics

1-4: Contains art by most DC artists			1.25

NOTE: **Giffen** *a-1.* **Erik Larsen** *a-1.*

WIDOW: BOUND BY BLOOD
Aug, 1996 - No. 5, 1996 ($3.50/$3.00, B&W/color, limited series, mature)
Ground Zero Comics

1-(B&W, $3.50)			3.50
3-5: 2-Begin $3.00-c & color			3.00
Platinum Edition-(4/96, B&W)-Complete 1st issue preview			10.00

WIDOW: METAL GYPSIES
Aug, 1995 - No. 2, 1995 ($3.00)
London Night Studios

1,2		1.20	3.00
1-Platinum	1.00	2.00	5.00

WILBUR COMICS (Teen-age) (Also see Laugh Comics, Laugh Comix, Liberty Comics #10 & Zip Comics)
Sum', 1944 - No. 87, 11/59; No. 88, 9/63; No. 89, 10/64; No. 90, 10/65 (No. 1-46: 52 pgs.)(#1-11 are quarterly)
MLJ Magazines/Archie Publ. No. 8, Spring, 1946 on

1	43.00	128.00	340.00
2(Fall, 1944)	25.00	75.00	175.00
3,4(Wint, '44-45; Spr, '45)	18.00	54.00	125.00
5-1st app. Katy Keene (Sum, '45) & begin series; Wilbur story same as Archie story in Archie #1 except Wilbur replaces Archie	54.00	163.00	435.00
6-10: 10-(Fall, 1946)	16.00	47.00	110.00
11-20	10.00	30.00	65.00
21-30: 30-(4/50)	6.70	20.00	40.00
31-50	4.70	14.00	28.00
51-70	4.00	10.00	20.00
71-90: 88-Last 10¢ issue (9/63)	1.65	4.20	10.00

NOTE: Katy Keene in No. 5-56, 58-69. **Al Fagaly** *c-6-9, 12-24 at least.* **Vigoda** *c-2.*

WILD
Feb, 1954 - No. 5, Aug, 1954
Atlas Comics (IPC)

1	21.00	64.00	150.00
2	13.00	39.00	90.00
3-5	10.00	30.00	70.00

NOTE: **Berg** *a-5; c-4.* **Burgos** *c-3.* **Colan** *a-4.* **Everett** *a-1-3.* **Heath** *a-2, 3, 5.* **Maneely** *a-1-3, 5; c-1, 5.* **Post** *a-2, 5.* **Ed Win** *a-1, 3.*

WILD (This Magazine Is...) (Satire)
Jan, 1968 - No. 3, 1968 (Magazine, 52 pgs.)
Dell Publishing Co.

1-3	1.00	2.50	6.00

WILD ANIMALS
Dec, 1982 ($1.00, one-shot, direct sales)
Pacific Comics

WildC.A.T.S. #29 © Aegis Entertainment

WildC.A.T.S. Adventures #6 © Aegis Entertainment

Wild Dog #3 © DC

	GD25	FN65	NM94

1-Funny animal; Sergio Aragones-a; Shaw-c/a ... 1.00

WILD BILL ELLIOTT (Also see Western Roundup under Dell Giants)
No. 278, 5/50 - No. 643, 7/55 (No #11,12) (All photo-c)
Dell Publishing Co.

Four Color 278(#1, 52pgs.)-Titled "Bill Elliott"; Bill & his horse Stormy begin; photo front/back-c begin	13.00	40.00	130.00
2 (11/50), 3 (52 pgs.)	7.00	21.00	70.00
4-10(10-12/52)	5.00	15.00	50.00
Four Color 472(6/53),520(12/53)-Last photo back-c	5.00	15.00	50.00
13(4-6/54) - 17(4-6/55)	4.00	12.00	40.00
Four Color 643 (7/55)	4.00	12.00	40.00

WILD BILL HICKOK (Also see Blazing Sixguns)
Sept-Oct, 1949 - No. 28, May-June, 1956
Avon Periodicals

1-Ingels-c	19.00	56.00	130.00
2-Painted-c; Kit West app.	10.00	30.00	58.00
3-5-Painted-c (4-Cover by Howard Winfield)	5.35	16.00	32.00
6-10,12: 8-10-Painted-c. 12-Kinsler-c?	5.35	16.00	32.00
11,13,14-Kinstler-c/a (#11-c & inside-f/c only)	5.70	17.00	34.00
15,17,18,20: 18-Kit West story. 20-Kit West by Larsen	4.00	12.00	24.00
16-Kamen-a; r-3 stories/King of the Badmen of Deadwood	5.00	15.00	30.00
19-Meskin-a	4.00	12.00	24.00
21-Reprints 2 stories/Chief Crazy Horse	4.00	12.00	24.00
22-McCann-a?; r/Sheriff Bob Dixon's...	4.00	12.00	24.00
23-27: 23-Kinstler. 24-27-Kinstler-c/a(r) (24,25-r?)	4.25	13.00	28.00
28-Kinstler-c/a (new); r-/Last of the Comanches	4.25	13.00	28.00
I.W. Reprint #1-r/#2; Kinstler-c	1.30	3.25	8.00
Super Reprint #10-12: 10-r/#18. 11-r/#?. 12-r/#8	1.30	3.25	8.00

NOTE: #23, 25 contain numerous editing deletions in both art and script due to code. **Kinstler** c-6, 7, 11-14, 17, 18, 20-22, 24-28. **Howard Larsen** a-1, 2, 4, 5, 6(3), 7-9, 11, 12, 17, 18, 20-24, 26. **Meskin** a-7. **Reinman** a-6, 11.

WILD BILL HICKOK AND JINGLES (TV)(Formerly Cowboy Western) (Also see Blue Bird)
No. 68, Aug, 1958 - No. 75, Dec, 1959
Charlton Comics

68,69-Williamson-a (all are 10¢ issues)	10.00	30.00	60.00
70-Two pgs. Williamson-a	6.35	19.00	38.00
71-75 (#76, exist?)	4.00	12.00	24.00

WILD BILL PECOS WESTERN (Also see The Westerner)
1989 ($3.50, 1/2 color/1/2 B&W, 52 pgs.)
AC Comics

1-Syd Shores-c/a(r)/Westerner; photo back-c ... 1.75 ... 3.50

WILD BOY OF THE CONGO (Also see Approved Comics)
No. 10, 2-3/51 - No. 12, 8-9/51; No. 4, 10-11/51 - No. 15, 6/55
Ziff-Davis No. 10-12,4-8/St. John No. 9 on

10(#1)(2-3/51)-Origin; bondage-c by Saunders (painted); used in **SOTI**, pg. 189; painted-c begin, end #9	17.00	51.00	120.00
11(4-5/51),12(8-9/51)-Norman Saunders painted-c	10.00	30.00	65.00
4(10-11/51)-Saunders painted bondage-c	10.00	30.00	65.00
5(Winter, '51)-Saunders painted-c	9.15	27.00	55.00
6,8,9(10/53),10: 6-Saunders c. 8,9-Painted-c	9.15	27.00	55.00
7(8-9/52)-Kinstler-a	10.00	30.00	65.00
11-13-Baker-c. 11-r/#7 w/new Baker-c; Kinstler-a (2 pgs.)	10.00	30.00	70.00
14(4/55)-Baker-c; r-#12('51)	10.00	30.00	70.00
15(6/55)	7.50	22.50	45.00

WILD CARDS
Sept, 1990 - No. 4, 1990 ($4.50, limited series, 52 pgs.)
Marvel Comics (Epic Comics)

1-4 ... 2.25 ... 4
NOTE: **Guice** a-1; c-1-4p. **Morrow** a-4. **Rogers** a-1, 4. **Williamson** a-3.

WILDCAT (See Sensation Comics #1)

WILDC.A.T.S ADVENTURES (TV cartoon)
Sept, 1994 - No. 10, June, 1995 ($1.95/$2.50)
Image Comics (Wildstorm Productions)

1-5		.80	2
6-10: 6-$2.50-c begins		1.00	2
Sourcebook 1 (1/95, $2.95)		1.20	3

WILDC.A.T.S: COVERT ACTION TEAMS
Aug, 1992 - No. 4, Mar, 1993; No. 5, Nov, 1993 - Present ($1.95/$2.50)
Image Comics (Wildstorm Productions)

1-1st app; Jim Lee/Williams-c/a & Lee scripts begin; contains 2 trading cards (Two diff versions of cards inside); 1st Wildstorm Productions title.	1.00	2.00	5
1-All gold foil signed edition	3.60	11.00	25
1-All gold foil unsigned edition	1.30	3.25	8
1-Newsstand edition w/o cards		1.20	
2-($2.50)-Prism foil stamped-c; contains coupon for Image Comics #0 & 4 pg preview to Portacio's Wetworks (back-up)	1.00	2.00	
2-With coupon missing		.80	2
2-Direct sale misprint w/o foil-c		1.20	2
2-Newsstand ed., no prism or coupon		1.20	2
3-Lee/Liefeld-c (1/93-c, 12/92 inside)	1.00	2.00	5
4-($2.50)-Polybagged w/Topps trading card; 1st app. Tribe by Johnson & Stroman; Youngblood cameo	1.00	2.00	5
4-variant w/red card	1.30	3.25	8
5-7-Jim Lee/Williams-c/a; Lee script		1.60	4
8-12: 8-Begin $2.50-c; X-Men's Jean Grey & Scott Summers cameos. 10-1st app. Huntsman & Soldier; Claremont scripts begin, ends #13. 11-1st app. Savant, Tapestry & Mr. Majestic.		1.60	4
11-Alternate Portacio-c, see Deathblow #5	1.65	4.20	10
13-19,21-24,26-45: 15-James Robinson scripts begin, ends #20. 15,16-Black Razor story. 21-Alan Moore scripts begin, end #34; intro Tao & Ladytron; WildC.A.T.S team comes (Mr. Majestic, Savant, Condition Red (Max Cash Tao & Ladytron). 22-Maguire-a. 29-(5/96)-Fire From Heaven Pt 7; reads A on-c. 30-(6/96)-Fire From Heaven Pt. 13; Spartan revealed to have transplanted personality of John Colt (from Team One: WildC.A.T.S). 31-(9/96)-Grifter rejoins team; Ladytron dies		1.00	2
20-($2.50)-Direct Market, Wildstorm Rising Pt. 2 w/bound-in card		1.00	2
20-($1.95)-Newsstand, Wildstorm Rising Part 2		1.00	2
25-($4.95)-Alan Moore script; wraparound foil-c.			5
Compendium (1993, $9.95)-r/#1-4; bagged w/#0	1.65	4.00	10
Sourcebook 1 (9/93, $2.50)-Foil embossed-c		1.00	2
Sourcebook 1-($1.95)-Newsstand ed. w/o foil embossed-c		.80	2
Sourcebook 2 (11/94, $2.50)-wraparound-c		1.00	2
Special 1 (11/93, $3.50, 52 pgs.)-1st Travis Charest WildC.A.T.S-a.		1.40	3

WILDC.A.T.S TRILOGY
June, 1993 - No. 3, Dec, 1993 ($1.95, limited series)
Image Comics (Wildstorm Productions)

1-($2.50)-Multi-color foil-c; Jae Lee-c/a in all		1.00	2
1-($1.95)-Newsstand ed. w/o foil-c		.80	2
2,3-($1.95)-Jae Lee-c/a		.80	2

WILD DOG
Sept, 1987 - No. 4, Dec, 1987 (75¢, limited series)
DC Comics

1-4 ... 1
Special 1 (1989, $2.50, 52 pgs.) ... 1.00 ... 1

WILDERNESS TREK (See Zane Grey, Four Color 333)

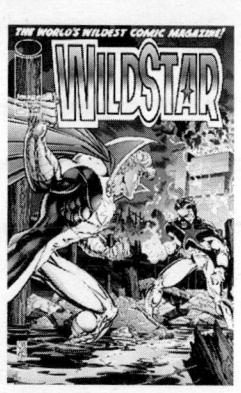

Wildstar #2 © Al Gordon & Jerry Ordway

Wildstorm #3 © Aegis Entertainment

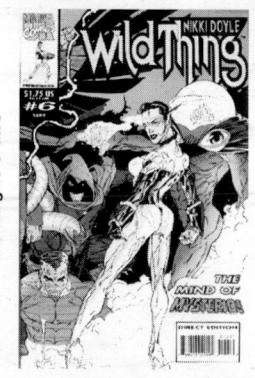

Wild Thing #6 © MEG

	GD25	FN65	NM94

WILDFIRE (See Zane Grey, FourColor 433)

WILD FRONTIER (Cheyenne Kid #8 on)
Oct, 1955 - No. 7, Apr, 1957
Charlton Comics

1-Davy Crockett	7.50	22.50	45.00
2-6-Davy Crockett in all	4.25	13.00	28.00
7-Origin & 1st app. Cheyenne Kid	5.00	15.00	30.00

WILD KINGDOM (TV)
1965 (Giveaway, regular size, slick-c, 16 pgs.)
Western Printing Co.

nn-Mutual of Omaha's...	2.00	6.00	14.00

WILDSTAR (Also see The Dragon & The Savage Dragon)
Sept, 1995 - No. 3, Jan, 1996 ($2.50, limited series)
Image Comics (Highbrow Entertainment)

1-3: Al Gordon scripts; Jerry Ordway-c/a	1.00		2.50

WILDSTAR: SKY ZERO
Mar, 1993 - No. 4, Nov, 1993 ($1.95, limited series)
Image Comics (Highbrow Entertainment)

1-($2.50)-Embossed-c w/silver ink; Ordway-c/a in all	1.00		2.50
1-($1.95)-Newsstand ed. w/silver ink-c, not embossed		.80	2.00
1-Gold variant	1.30	3.25	8.00
2-4		.80	2.00

WILDSTORM
1994/1995 ($2.50/$2.95/$4.95)
Image Comics (Wildstorm Publishing)

...Chamber of Horrors (10/95, $3.50)-Bisley-c	1.40		3.50
...Rarities 1(12/94, $4.95, 52 pgs.)-r/Gen 13 1/2 & other stories			
	1.30	3.25	8.00
...Swimsuit Special 1 (12/94, $2.95)	1.60		4.00
...Swimsuit Special 2 (1995, $2.50)	1.40		3.50
...Universe Sourcebook (5/95, $2.50)			2.50

WILDSTORM!
Aug, 1995 - No. 4, Nov, 1995 ($2.50, B&W/color, anthology)
Image Comics (Wildstorm Publishing)

1-4: 1-Simonson-a	1.00		2.50

WILDSTORM RISING
May, 1995 - No.2, June, 1995 ($1.95/$2.50)
Image Comics (Wildstorm Publishing)

1 ($2.50)-Direct Market, Wildstorm Rising Pt. 1 w/bound-in card			
	1.00		2.50
1 ($1.95)-Newsstand, Wildstorm Rising Pt. 1		.80	2.00
2 ($2.50)-Direct Market, Wildstorm Rising Pt. 10 w/bound-in card; continues in WildC.A.T.S #21.	1.00		2.50
2 ($1.95)-Newsstand, Wildstorm Rising Pt. 10		.80	2.00
Trade paperback (1996, $19.95)-Collects x-over; B. Smith-c			20.00

WILDTHING
Apr, 1993 - No. 7, Oct, 1993 ($1.75)
Marvel Comics UK

1-($2.50)-Embossed-c; Venom & Carnage cameo	1.00		2.50
2-7: 2-Spider-Man & Venom. 6-Mysterio app.		.70	1.75

WILD WEST (Wild Western #3 on)
Spring, 1948 - No. 2, July, 1948
Marvel Comics (WFP)

1-Two-Gun Kid, Arizona Annie, & Tex Taylor begin; Shores-c			
	29.00	86.00	200.00
2-Captain Tootsie by Beck; Shores-c	20.00	60.00	140.00

WILD WEST (Black Fury #1-57)
V2#58, Nov, 1966

Charlton Comics

V2#58		.80	2.

WILD WEST C.O.W.-BOYS OF MOO MESA (TV)
Dec, 1992 - No. 3, Feb, 1993 (limited series)
V2#1, Mar, 1993 - No. 3, July, 1993 ($1.25)
Archie Comics

1-3			1.2
V2#1-3			1.2

WILD WESTERN (Formerly Wild West #1,2)
No. 3, 9/48 - No. 57, 9/57 (3-11: 52 pgs, 12-on: 36 pgs)
Marvel/Atlas Comics (WFP)

3(#1)-Tex Morgan begins; Two-Gun Kid, Tex Taylor, & Arizona Annie continue from Wild West	23.00	69.00	160.
4-Last Arizona Annie; Captain Tootsie by Beck; Kid Colt app.	17.00	51.00	120.
5-2nd app. Black Rider (1/49); Blaze Carson, Captain Tootsie (by Beck) app.	19.00	58.00	135.0
6-8: 6-Blaze Carson app; anti-Wertham editorial	12.00	36.00	85.0
9-Photo-c; Black Rider, ends #19	17.00	49.00	115.0
10-Charles Starrett photo-c	19.00	56.00	130.0
11-(Last 52 pg. issue)	11.50	34.00	80.0
12-14,16-19: All Black Rider-c/stories. 12-14-The Prairie Kid & his horse Fury app.	10.00	30.00	70.0
15-Red Larabee, Gunhawk (origin), his horse Blaze, & Apache Kid begin, end #22; Black Rider-c/story	11.00	33.00	75.0
20-29: 20-Kid Colt-c begin. 24-Has 2 Kid Colt stories. 26-1st app. The Ringo Kid? (2/53); 4 pg. story	10.00	30.00	60.0
30-Katz-a	10.00	30.00	58.0
31-40	7.00	21.00	42.0
41-47,49-51,53,57	5.35	16.00	32.0
48-Williamson/Torres-a (4 pgs); Drucker-a	8.70	26.00	52.0
52-Crandall-a	8.70	26.00	52.0
54,55-Williamson-a in both (5 & 4 pgs.), #54 with Mayo plus 2 text illos			
	8.35	25.00	50.0
56-Baker-a?	5.35	16.00	32.0

NOTE: *Annie Oakley in #46, 47. Apache Kid in #15-22, 39. Arizona Kid in #21, 23. Arrowhead-a #34-39. Black Rider in #5, 9-19, 33-44. Fighting Texan in #17. Kid Colt in #4-6, 9-11, 20-47, 52, 54-56. Outlaw Kid in #43. Red Hawkins in #13, 14. Ringo Kid in #26, 39, 41, 43, 44, 46, 47, 50, 52-56. Tex Morgan in #3, 4, 6, 9, 11. Tex Taylor in #3-6, 9, 11. Texas Kid in #23-25. Two-Gun Kid in #3-6. 9, 11, 12, 33-39, 41. Wyatt Earp in #47. Ayers a-41, 42. Berg a-26; c-24. Colan a-49. Forte a-28, 30. Al Hartley a-16. Heath a-4, 5, 8; c-34, 44. Keller a-24, 26(2), 29-40, 44-46, 48, 52. Maneely a-10, 12, 15, 16, 28, 35, 38, 40-45; c-18-22, 33, 35, 36, 38, 39, 41, 42, 45. Morisi a-23, 52. Pakula a-42, 52. Powell a-51. Romita a-24(2). Severin a-46, 47; c-48. Shores a-3, 5, 30, 31, 33, 35, 38, 41; c-3-5. Sinnott a-34-39. Wildey a-43. Bondage c-19.*

WILD WESTERN ACTION (Also see The Bravados)
Mar, 1971 - No. 3, June, 1971 (25¢, reprints, 52 pgs.)
Skywald Publishing Corp.

1-Durango Kid, Straight Arrow-r; with all references to "Straight" in story relettered to "Swift"; Bravados begin; Shores-a (new)		.80	2.0
2-Billy Nevada, Durango Kid			1.5
3-Red Mask, Durango Kid			1.5

WILD WESTERN ROUNDUP
Oct, 1957; 1960-'61
Red Top/Decker Publications/I. W. Enterprises

1(1957)-Kid Cowboy-r	3.60	9.00	18.0
I.W. Reprint #1('60-61)-r/#1 by Red Top	1.00	2.60	6.0

WILD WEST RODEO
1953 (15¢)
Star Publications

1-A comic book coloring book with regular full color cover & B&W inside			
	5.35	16.00	32.0

WILD WILD WEST, THE (TV)

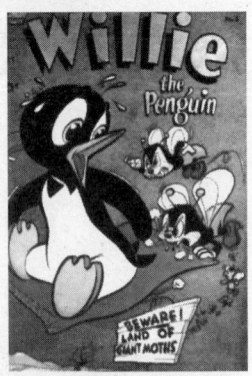

Willie The Penguin #6 © STD

Willow #0 © Angel Entertainment

Will To Power #5 © DH

	GD25	FN65	NM94

June, 1966 - No. 7, Oct, 1969 (Robert Conrad photo-c)
Gold Key

	GD25	FN65	NM94
1-McWilliams-a; photo back-c	11.50	34.50	115.00
2-McWilliams-a; photo back-c	8.50	25.50	85.00
3-7	6.50	19.50	65.00

WILD, WILD WEST, THE (TV)
Oct, 1990 - No. 4, Jan?, 1991 ($2.95, limited series)
Millennium Publications

1-4-Based on TV show		1.50	3.00

WILKIN BOY (See That...)

WILLIE COMICS (Formerly Ideal #1-4; Crime Cases #24 on; Li'l Willie #20 & 21) (See Gay Comics, Laugh, Millie The Model & Wisco)
#5, Fall, 1946 - #19, 4/49; #22, 1/50 - #23, 5/50 (No #20 & 21)
Marvel Comics (MgPC)

5(#1)-George, Margie, Nellie the Nurse & Willie begin	13.50	41.00	95.00
6,8,9	8.00	24.00	48.00
7(1),10,11-Kurtzman's "Hey Look"	10.00	30.00	60.00
12,14-18,22,23	6.35	19.00	38.00
13,19-Kurtzman's "Hey Look" (#19-last by Kurtzman?)	9.15	27.00	55.00

NOTE: Cindy app. in #17. Jeanie app. in #17. Little Lizzie app. in #22.

WILLIE MAYS (See The Amazing...)

WILLIE THE PENGUIN
Apr, 1951 - No. 6, Apr, 1952
Standard Comics

1-Funny animal	5.85	17.50	35.00
2-6	4.00	11.00	22.00

WILLIE THE WISE-GUY (Also see Cartoon Kids)
Sept, 1957
Atlas Comics (NPP)

1-Kida, Maneely-a	6.70	20.00	40.00

WILLOW
Aug, 1988 - No. 3, Oct, 1988 ($1.00)
Marvel Comics

1-3-R/Marvel Graphic Novel #36 (movie adaptation)			1.00

WILLOW
June, 1996 - Present ($2.95, B&W)
Angel Entertainment

0			3.00
0-($5.95)-Black Magic Foil			3.00
0-($10.00)-Nude Edition			10.00

WILL ROGERS WESTERN (Formerly My Great Love #1-4; see Blazing & True Comics #66)
No. 5, June, 1950 - No. 2, Aug, 1950
Fox Features Syndicate

5(#1)	32.00	96.00	225.00
2: Photo-c	28.00	84.00	195.00

WILL TO POWER (Also see Comic's Greatest World)
June, 1994 - No. 12, Aug, 1994 ($1.00, weekly limited series, 20 pgs.)
Dark Horse Comics

1-12: 12-Vortex kills Titan.			1.25

NOTE: Mignola c-10-12. Sears c-1-3.

WILL-YUM!
No. 676, Feb, 1956 - No. 902, May, 1958
Dell Publishing Co.

Four Color 676 (#1))	2.70	8.00	27.00
Four Color 765 (1/57), 902	2.70	8.00	27.00

WIN A PRIZE COMICS (Timmy The Timid Ghost #3 on?)
Feb, 1955 - No. 2, Apr, 1955
Charlton Comics

V1#1-S&K-a; Poe adapt; E.C. War swipe	59.00	178.00	475.0□
2-S&K-a	44.00	132.00	350.0□

WINDY & WILLY
May-June, 1969 - No. 4, Nov-Dec, 1969
National Periodical Publications

1-4: r/Dobie Gillis with some art changes		1.60	4.0□

WINGS COMICS
9/40 - No. 109, 9/49; No. 110, Wint, 1949-50; No. 111, Spring, 1950; No. 112, 1950(nd); No. 113 - No. 115, 1950(nd); No. 116, 1952(nd); No. 117, Fall, 1952 No. 122, Wint, 1953-54; No. 123 - No. 124, 1954(nd)
Fiction House Magazines

1-Skull Squad, Clipper Kirk, Suicide Smith, Jane Martin, War Nurse, Phantom Falcons, Greasemonkey Griffin, Parachute Patrol & Powder Burns begin	193.00	581.00	1550.0□
2	84.00	253.00	675.0□
3-5	56.00	168.00	450.0□
6-10	48.00	144.00	385.0□
11-15	41.00	124.00	330.0□
16-Origin & 1st app. Captain Wings & begin series	48.00	144.00	385.0□
17-20	39.00	118.00	275.0□
21-30	36.00	107.00	250.0□
31-40	28.00	84.00	195.0□
41-50	22.00	66.00	155.□
51-60: 60-Last Skull Squad	19.00	56.00	130.□
61-67: 66-Ghost Patrol begins (becomes Ghost Squadron #71 on), ends #112	19.00	56.00	130.□
68,69: 68-Clipper Kirk becomes The Phantom Falcon-origin, Part 1; part 2 in #69	19.00	56.00	130.□
70-72: 70-1st app. The Phantom Falcon in costume, origin-Part 3; Capt. Wings battles Col. Kamikaze in all	16.00	47.00	110.□
73-99: 80-Phantom Falcon by Larsen. 99-King of the Congo begins?	16.00	47.00	110.□
100-(12/48)	17.00	51.00	120.□
101-124: 111-Last Jane Martin. 112-Flying Saucer-c/story (1950). 115-Used in **POP**, pg. 89	14.00	43.00	100.□

NOTE: Bondage covers are common. Captain Wings battles Sky Hag-#75, 76; ...Mr. Atlantis-#85-92; ...Mr. Pupin(Red Agent)-#98-103. Capt. Wings by Elias-#52-64, 68, 69; by Lubbers-#29-32, 70-111; by Renee-#33-46. Evans a-85-106, 108-111(Jane Martin); text illos-72-84. Larsen a-52, 59, 64, 73-77. Jane Martin by Fran Hopper-#68-84; Suicide Smith by John Celardo-#72, 74, 76, 80-104; by Hollingsworth-#68-70, 105-109, 111; Ghost Squadron by Astarita-#67-79; by Maurice Whitman-#80-111. King of the Congo by Moreira-#99, 100. Sku Squad by M. Baker-#52-60; Clipper Kirk by Baker-#60, 61; by Colan-#53; by Ingels-(some issues?). Phantom Falcon by Larsen-#73-84. Elias c-58-72. Fawcette c-3-12, 16, 17, 19, 22-Lubbers c-74-109. Tuska a-5. Whitman c-74-109, 112-124. Zolnerwich c-15, 21.

WINGS OF THE EAGLES, THE
No. 790, Apr, 1957 (10¢ & 15¢ editions exist)
Dell Publishing Co.

Four Color 790-Movie; John Wayne photo-c; Toth-a	14.50	43.50	145.□

WINKY DINK (Adventures of...)
No. 75, Mar, 1957 (one-shot)
Pines Comics

75-Marv Levy-c/a	4.00	12.00	24.□

WINKY DINK (TV)
No. 663, Nov, 1955
Dell Publishing Co.

Four Color 663 (#1)	7.00	21.00	70.□

WINNIE-THE-POOH (Also see Dynabrite Comics)
January, 1977 - No. 33, 1984 (Walt Disney)
(Winnie-The-Pooh began as Edward Bear in 1926 by Milne)

Winterworld #1 © ECL

Witchblade #10 © Top Cow Productions

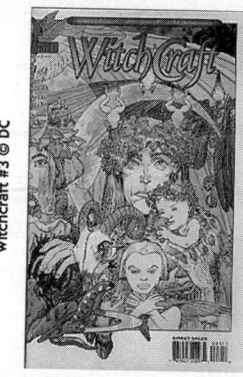

Witchcraft #3 © DC

	GD25	FN65	NM94

Gold Key No. 1-17/Whitman No. 18 on

1-New art		.80	2.00
2-33: 5,12-33-New material			1.50

WINNIE WINKLE (See Popular Comics & Super Comics)
1941 - No. 7, Sept-Nov, 1949
Dell Publishing Co.

Large Feature Comic 2 (1941)	18.00	54.00	180.00
Four Color 94 (1945)	12.00	36.00	120.00
Four Color 174	7.00	21.00	70.00
1(3-5/48)-Contains daily & Sunday newspaper-r from 1939-1941			
	7.00	21.00	63.00
2 (6-8/48)	4.00	12.00	36.00
3-7	3.00	9.00	25.00

WINTERWORLD
Sept, 1987 - No. 3, Mar, 1988 ($1.75, limited series)
Eclipse Comics

1-3		.90	1.80

WISCO/KLARER COMIC BOOK (Miniature)
1948 - 1964 (3-1/2x6-3/4", 24 pgs.)
Marvel Comics/Vital Publications/Fawcett Publications

Given away by Wisco "99" Service Stations, Carnation Malted Milk, Klarer Health Wieners, Fleers Dubble Bubble Gum, Rodeo All-Meat Wieners, Perfect Potato Chips, & others; see ad in Tom Mix #21

Blackstone & the Gold Medal Mystery (1948)	6.70	20.00	40.00
Blackstone "Solves the Sealed Vault Mystery" (1950)	6.70	20.00	40.00
Blaze Carson in "The Sheriff Shoots It Out" (1950)	6.70	20.00	40.00
Captain Marvel & Billy's Big Game (r/Capt. Marvel Adv. #76)			
	29.00	85.00	200.00
(Prices vary widely on this book)			
China Boy in "A Trip to the Zoo" #10 (1948)	4.00	12.00	24.00
Indoors-Outdoors Game Book	2.00	5.00	10.00
Jim Solar Space Sheriff in "Battle for Mars", "Between Two Worlds", "Conquers Outer Space", "The Creatures on the Comet", "Defeats the Moon Missile Men", "Encounter Creatures on Comet", "Meet the Jupiter Jumpers", "Meets the Man From Mars", "On Traffic Duty", "Outlaws of the Spaceways", "Pirates of the Planet X", "Protects Space Lanes", "Raiders From the Sun", "Ring Around Saturn", "Robots of Rhea", "The Sky Ruby", "Spacetts of the Sky", "Spidermen of Venus", "Trouble on Mercury"	5.85	17.50	35.00
Johnny Starbrand & the Underseas Pirates (1948)	3.60	9.00	18.00
Kid Colt in "He Lived by His Guns" (1950)	6.70	20.00	40.00
Little Aspirin as "Crook Catcher" #2 (1950)	2.00	5.00	10.00
Little Aspirin in "Naughty But Nice" #6 (1950)	2.00	5.00	10.00
Return of the Black Phantom (not M.E. character)(Roy Dare)(1948)			
	4.35	13.00	26.00
Secrets of Magic	2.40	6.00	12.00
Slim Morgan "Brings Justice to Mesa City" #3	2.40	6.00	12.00
Super Rabbit(1950)-Cuts Red Tape, Stops Crime Wave!			
	10.00	30.00	60.00
Tex Farnum, Frontiersman (1948)	2.80	14.00	14.00
Tex Taylor in "Draw or Die, Cowpoke!" (1950)	4.70	14.00	28.00
Tex Taylor in "An Exciting Adventure at the Gold Mine" (1950)			
	4.35	13.00	26.00
Wacky Quacky in "All-Aboard"	1.20	3.00	6.00
When School Is Out	1.20	3.00	6.00
Willie in a "Comic-Comic Book Fall" #1	1.60	4.00	8.00
Wonder Duck "An Adventure at the Rodeo of the Fearless Quacker!" (1950)			
	8.35	25.00	50.00
Rare uncut version of three; includes Capt. Marvel, Tex Farnum, Black Phantom Estimated value…			$300.00
Rare uncut version of three; includes China Boy, Blackstone, Johnny Starbrand & the Underseas Pirates Estimated value…			$82.00

WISE GUYS (See Harvey...)

WISE LITTLE HEN, THE
1935 (c.1934)(48 pgs.); 1937 (Story book)
David McKay Publ./Whitman

nn-(1935 edition w/dust jacket)(48 pgs. with color, 8-3/4x9-3/4") -Debut of Donald Duck (see Advs. of Mickey Mouse); Donald app. on cover with Wise Little Hen & Practical Pig; painted cover; same artist as the B&W's from Silly Symphony Cartoon, The Wise Little Hen (1934) (McKay)			
Book w/dust jacket	133.00	400.00	800.00
Dust jacket only	36.00	107.00	250.00
888(1937)(9-1/2x13", 12 pgs.)(Whitman) Donald Duck app.			
	24.00	73.00	170.00

WISE SON: THE WHITE WOLF
Nov, 1996 - No. 4, Feb, 1996 ($2.50, limited series)
DC Comics (Milestone)

1-4: Ho Che Anderson-c/a			2.50

WITCHBLADE (Also see Cyblade/Shi)
Nov, 1995 - Present ($2.50)
Image Comics (Top Cow Productions)

1/2-Mike Turner/Marc Silvestri-c.			25.00
1-Mike Turner-a(p) in all.			15.00
2			10.00
3			7.00
4-12: 8-Wraparound-c. 9-Tony Daniel-a(p). 10-Darkness #0 variant-c exists			2.50
9-Variant-c			5.00

WITCHBLADE COLLECTED EDITION
July, 1996 - No. 4, Oct, 1996 ($4.95, squarebound, limited series)
Image Comics (Top Cow Productions)

1-4: 1-r/#1,2. 2-r/#3,4. 3-r/#5,6. 4-r/#7,8			5.00
4-(10/96, $10.95)-Packaged w/slipcase			11.00

WITCHCRAFT (See Strange Mysteries, Super Reprint #18)
Mar-Apr, 1952 - No. 6, Mar, 1953
Avon Periodicals

1-Kubert-a; 1 pg. Check-a	51.00	155.00	415.00
2-Kubert & Check-a	40.00	120.00	300.00
3,6: 5-Lawrence-a; Kinstler inside-c	29.00	88.00	205.00
4-People cooked alive c/story	34.00	103.00	240.00
5-Kelly Freas painted-c	39.00	118.00	275.00
NOTE: *Hollingsworth* a-4-6; c-4, 6. *McCann* a-3?			

WITCHCRAFT
June, 1994 - No. 3, Aug, 1994 ($2.95, limited series)
DC Comics (Vertigo)

1-3: James Robinson scripts & Kaluta-c in all	1.00	2.00	5.00
1-Platinum Edition	2.60	7.50	18.00
Trade paperback-(1996, $14.95)-r/#1-3; Kaluta-c			15.00

WITCHES TALES (Witches Western Tales #29,30)
Jan, 1951 - No. 28, Dec, 1954 (date misprinted as 4/55)
Witches Tales/Harvey Publications

1-Powell-a (1 pg.)	39.00	118.00	275.00
2-Eye injury panel	21.00	62.00	145.00
3-7,9,10	13.50	41.00	95.00
8-Eye injury panels	15.00	45.00	105.00
11-13,15,16: 12-Acid in face story	12.00	36.00	85.00
14,17-Powell/Nostrand-a. 17-Atomic disaster story	15.00	45.00	105.00
18-Nostrand-a; E.C. swipe/Shock S.S.	15.00	45.00	105.00
19-Nostrand-a; E.C. swipe/ "Glutton"; Devil-c	15.00	45.00	105.00
20-24-Nostrand-a. 21-E.C. swipe; rape story. 23-Wood E.C. swipes/Two-Fisted Tales #34	15.00	45.00	105.00
25-Nostrand-a; E.C. swipe/Mad Barber; decapitation-c			
	15.00	45.00	105.00

Witching Hour #83 © DC

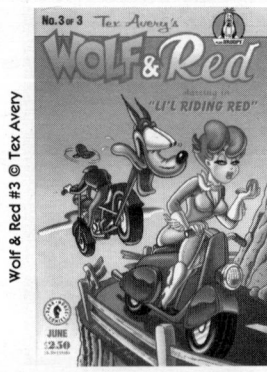

Wolf & Red #3 © Tex Avery

Wolverine #4 © MEG

	GD25	FN65	NM94

26-28: 27-r/#6 with diff.-c. 28-r/#8 with diff.-c   11.00   33.00   75.00
NOTE: *Check* a-24. *Elias* c-8, 10, 16-27. *Kremer* a-18; c-25. *Nostrand* a-17-25; 14, 17(w/*Powell*). *Palais* a-1, 2, 4(2), 7-9, 12, 14, 15, 17. *Powell* a-3-7, 10, 11, 19-27. *Bondage-*c 1, 3, 5, 6, 8, 9.

WITCHES TALES (Magazine)
V1#7, July, 1969 - V7#1, Feb, 1975 (B&W, 52 pgs.)
Eerie Publications

V1#7(7/69) - 9(11/69)	2.85	8.50	20.00
V2#1-6('70), V3#1-6('71)	2.15	6.50	15.00
V4#1-6('72), V5#1-6('73), V6#1-6('74), V7#1	1.70	5.00	12.00

NOTE: *Ajax/Farrell reprints in early issues.*

WITCHES' WESTERN TALES (Formerly Witches Tales)(Western Tales #31on)
No. 29, Feb, 1955 - No. 30, Apr, 1955
Harvey Publications

29,30-Featuring Clay Duncan & Boys' Ranch; S&K-r/from Boys' Ranch			
including-c. 29-Last pre-code	13.00	40.00	120.00

WITCH HUNTER
Apr, 1996 ($2.50, one-shot)
Malibu Comics (Ultraverse)

1			2.50

WITCHING HOUR ("The ..." in later issues)
Feb-Mar, 1969 - No. 85, Oct, 1978
National Periodical Publications/DC Comics

1-Toth-a, plus Neal Adams-a (2 pgs.)	4.50	13.00	35.00
2,6: 6-Toth-a	2.30	6.75	16.00
3,5-Wrightson-a; Toth-p. 3-Last 12¢ issue	2.00	6.00	14.00
4,7-12: Toth-a in all. 8-Toth, Neal Adams-a	1.65	4.20	10.00
13-Neal Adams-c/a, 2pgs.	1.20	3.00	7.00
14-Williamson/Garzon, Jones-a; N. Adams-c	1.50	3.75	9.00
15-20		1.60	4.00
21-40		1.40	3.50
38-(100 pgs.)	1.20	3.00	7.00
41-85: 84-(44 pgs.)		1.00	2.50

NOTE: *Combined with The Unexpected with #189. Neal Adams* c-7-11, 13, 14. *Alcala* a-24, 27, 33, 41, 43. *Anderson* a-9, 38. *Cardy* c-4, 5. *Kaluta* a-7. *Kane* a-12p. *Morrow* a-10, 13, 15, 16. *Nino* a-31, 40, 45, 47. *Redondo* a-20, 23, 24, 34, 65; c-53. *Reese* a-23. *Sparling* a-1. *Toth* a-1, 3-12, 38r. *Tuska* a-11, 12. *Wood* a-15.

WITHIN OUR REACH
1991 ($7.95, 84 pgs.)
Star Reach Productions

nn-Spider-Man, Concrete by Chadwick, Gift of the Magi by Russell;			
X-mas stories; Chadwick-c; Spidey back-c	1.35	4.00	8.00

WITH THE MARINES ON THE BATTLEFRONTS OF THE WORLD
1953 (no month) - No. 2, Mar, 1954 (Photo covers)
Toby Press

1-John Wayne story	27.00	81.00	190.00
2-Monty Hall in #1,2	6.70	20.00	40.00

WITH THE U.S. PARATROOPS BEHIND ENEMY LINES (Also see U.S. Paratroops...; #2-6 titled U.S. Paratroops...)
1951 - No. 6, Dec, 1952
Avon Periodicals

1-Wood-c & inside f/c	13.50	41.00	95.00
2-Kinstler-c & inside f/c only	8.00	24.00	48.00
3-6-Kinstler-c & inside f/c only	6.70	20.00	40.00

NOTE: *Kinstler* c-2, 4-6.

WITNESS, THE (Also see Amazing Mysteries, Captain America #71, Ideal #4, Marvel Mystery #92 & Mystic #7)
Sept, 1948
Marvel Comics (MjMe)

1(Scarce)-Rico-c?	137.00	412.00	1100.00

WITTY COMICS
1945 - No. 7, 1945
Irwin H. Rubin Publ./Chicago Nite Life News No. 2

1-The Pioneer, Junior Patrol; war-c	16.00	47.00	110.00
2-The Pioneer, Junior Patrol	10.00	30.00	60.00
3-7-Skyhawk	7.50	22.50	45.00

WIZARD OF FOURTH STREET, THE
Dec, 1988 - No. 2, 1988 ($1.75, B&W, limited series)
Dark Horse Comics

1,2: Adapts novel by S/F author Simon Hawke		.90	1.80

WIZARD OF OZ (See Classics Illustrated Jr. 535, Dell Jr. Treasury No. 5, First Comics Graphic Novel, Marvelous..., & Marvel Treasury of Oz)
No. 1308, Mar-May, 1962 (TV)
Dell Publishing Co.

Four Color 1308	10.00	30.00	100.00

WOLF & RED
Apr, 1995 - No. 3, June, 1995 ($2.50, limited series)
Dark Horse Comics

1-3: Characters created by Tex Avery		1.00	2.50

WOLFF & BYRD, COUNSELORS OF THE MACABRE
May, 1994 - Present ($2.50, B&W)
Exhibit A Press

1-10		1.00	2.50

WOLF GAL (See Al Capp's...)
WOLFMAN, THE (See Movie Classics)
WOLFPACK
Feb, 1988 ($7.95); Aug, 1988 - No. 12, July, 1989 (Limited series)
Marvel Comics

1-1st app./origin (Marvel Graphic Novel #31)	1.35	4.00	8.00
1-12			1.00

WOLVERINE (See Alpha Flight, Daredevil #196, 249, Ghost Rider; Wolverine; Punisher, Havok &..., Incredible Hulk #180, Incredible Hulk &..., Kitty Pryde And..., Marvel Comics Presents, Power Pack, Punisher and..., Spider-Man vs... & X-Men #94)

WOLVERINE
Sept, 1982 - No. 4, Dec, 1982 (limited series)
Marvel Comics Group

1-Frank Miller-c/a(p) in all	5.00	15.00	35.00
2,3	3.60	11.00	25.00
4	3.90	11.50	27.00
Trade paperback 1(7/87, $4.95)-Reprints #1-4 with new Miller-c.			
	1.30	3.25	8.00
Trade paperback nn (2nd printing, $9.95)-r/#1-4	1.65	4.20	10.00

WOLVERINE
Nov, 1988 - Present ($1.50/$1.75, Baxter paper)
Marvel Comics

1-Buscema a-1-16, c-1-10; Williamson a(i)-1,4-8	5.00	15.00	35.00
2	2.40	7.20	17.00
3-5: 4-BWS back-c	2.00	6.00	14.00
6-9: 6-McFarlane back-c. 7,8-Hulk app.	1.70	5.00	12.00
10-1st battle with Sabretooth (before Wolverine had his claws)			
	3.60	11.00	25.00
11-16: 11-New costume	1.20	3.00	7.00
17-20: 17-Byrne-c/a(p) begins, ends #23	1.00	2.00	5.00
21-30: 24,25,27-Jim Lee-c. 26-Begin $1.75-c		1.60	4.00
31-40,44,47		1.20	3.00
41-Sabretooth claims to be Wolverine's father; Cable cameo			
	1.00	2.60	6.00
41-Gold 2nd printing ($1.75)		.80	2.00
42-Sabretooth, Cable & Nick Fury app.; Sabretooth proven not to be			

Wolverine '95 © MEG · Wolverine #66 © MEG

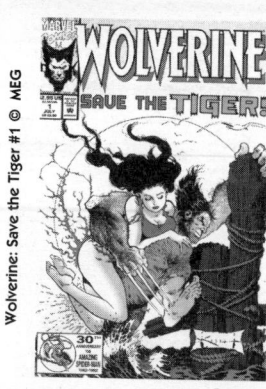

Wolverine: Save the Tiger #1 © MEG

	GD25	FN65	NM94
Wolverine's father	1.00	2.60	6.00
42-Gold ink 2nd printing ($1.75)		.80	2.00
43-Sabretooth cameo (2 panels); saga ends	1.00	2.00	5.00
45,46-Sabretooth-c/stories		1.60	4.00
48,49-Sabretooth app. 48-Begin 3 part Weapon X sequel		1.20	3.00
50-($2.50, 64 pgs.)-Die cut-c; Wolverine back to old yellow costume; Forge, Cyclops, Jubilee, Jean Grey & Nick Fury app.	1.00	2.00	5.00
51-74,76-80: 51-Sabretooth-c & app. 54-Shatterstar (from X-Force) app. 55-Gambit, Jubilee, Sunfire-c/story. 55-57,73-Gambit app. 57-Mariko Yashida dies (Late 7/92). 58,59-Terror, Inc. x-over. 60-64-Sabretooth storyline (60,62,64-c).		.80	2.00
75-($3.95, 68 pgs.)-Wolverine hologram on-c	1.00	2.00	5.00
81-84,86: 81-Begin $1.95-c; bound-in card sheet		.90	2.25
85-($2.50)-Newsstand edition		1.00	2.50
85-($3.50)-Collectors edition		1.60	4.00
87-90 ($1.95)-Deluxe edition		.80	2.00
87-90 ($1.50)-Regular edition			1.50
91-99,101-110: 91-Return from "Age of Apocalypse", 93-Juggernaut app. 94-Gen X app. 101-104-Elektra app. 104-Origin of Onslaught. 105-Onslaught x-over		.80	2.00
100 ($3.95)-Hologram-c; Wolverine loses humanity.	1.20	3.25	8.00
100 ($2.95)-Regular-c.		1.20	3.00
Annual nn (1990, $4.50, squarebound, 52 pgs.)-The Jungle Adventure; Simonson scripts; Mignola-c/a		1.80	4.50
Annual 2 (12/90, $4.95, squarebound, 52 pgs.)-Bloodlust	1.00	2.00	5.00
Annual nn (#3, 8/91, $5.95, 68 pgs.)-Rahne of Terror; Cable & The New Mutants app.; Andy Kubert-c/a (2nd print exists)	1.00	2.50	6.00
...'95 (1995, $3.95, annual)		1.60	4.00
...BATTLES THE INCREDIBLE HULK nn (1989, $4.95, squarebound, 52 pg.) r/Incredible Hulk #180,181	1.00	2.00	5.00
...BLOOD HUNGRY nn (1993, $6.95, 68 pgs.)-Kieth-r/Marvel Comics Presents #85-92 w/ new Kieth-c	1.20	3.00	7.00
...: BLOODY CHOICES nn (1993, $7.95, 68 pgs.)-r/Graphic Novel; Nick Fury app.	1.20	3.00	6.00
...EVILUTION (9/94, $5.95)	1.30	3.25	8.00
...: GLOBAL JEOPARDY 1 (12/93, $2.95, one-shot)-Embossed-c; Sub-Mariner, Zabu, Ka-Zar, Shanna & Wolverine app.; produced in cooperation with World Wildlife Fund	1.20	3.00	
...:INNER FURY nn (1992, $5.95, 52 pgs.)-Sienkiewicz-c/a	1.00	2.50	6.00
...: KNIGHT OF TERRA (1995, $6.95)-Ostrander script			7.00
...: SAVE THE TIGER 1 (7/92, $2.95, 84 pgs.)-Reprints Wolverine stories from Marvel Comics Presents #1-10 w/new Kieth-c	1.20	3.00	
...TRIUMPHS AND TRAGEDIES (1995, $16.95, trade paperback)-r/Uncanny X-Men #109,172,173, Wolverine limited series #4, & Wolverine #41,42,75			17.00
...TYPHOID'S KISS (6/94, $6.95)-r/Wolverine stories from Marvel Comics Presents #109-116	1.20	2.90	7.00

NOTE: **Austin** c-3i. **Bolton** c(back)-5. **Buscema** 25, 27p. **Byrne** a-17-22p, 23; c-1(back), 17-22, 23p. **Colan** a-24. **Andy Kubert** c/a-51. **Jim Lee** c-24, 25, 27. **Silvestri** a(p)-31-43, 45, 46, 48-50, 52, 53, 55-57, c-31-42p, 43, 45p, 46p, 48, 49p, 50p, 52p, 53p, 55-57p. **Stroman** a-44p; c-60p.

WOLVERINE AND THE PUNISHER: DAMAGING EVIDENCE
Oct, 1993 - No. 3, Dec, 1993 ($2.00, limited series)
Marvel Comics

1-3: 2,3-Indicia says "The Punisher and Wolverine…"		.80	2.00

WOLVERINE/GAMBIT: VICTIMS
Sept, 1995 - No. 3, 1995 (2.95, limited series)
Marvel Comics

1-3: Jeph Loeb scripts; Tim Sale-a; foil-c		1.20	3.00

WOLVERINE SAGA
Sept, 1989 - No. 4, Mid-Dec, 1989 ($3.95, limited series, 52 pgs.)

	GD25	FN65	NM94
Marvel Comics			
1-Gives history; Liefeld/Austin-c (front & back)	1.00	2.00	5.00
2-4: 2-Romita, Jr.-Austin-c. 4-Kaluta-c	1.00	2.00	5.00

WOLVERINE VS. SPIDER-MAN
Mar, 1995 (2.50, one-shot)
Marvel Comics

1-r/Marvel Comics Presents #48 - 50		1.00	2.50

WOMAN OF THE PROMISE, THE
1950 (General Distr.) (Paper cover, 32 pgs.)
Catechetical Guild

nn	3.00	7.50	15.00

WOMEN IN LOVE (A Feature Presentation #5)
Aug, 1949 - No. 4, Feb, 1950
Fox Features Synd./Hero Books

1	23.00	69.00	160.00
2-Kamen/Feldstein-c	19.00	58.00	135.00
3	12.00	36.00	85.00
4-Wood-a	16.00	47.00	110.00

WOMEN IN LOVE (Thrilling Romances for Adults)
Winter, 1952 (25¢, 100 pgs.)
Ziff-Davis Publishing Co.

nn-(Scarce)-Kinstler-a; painted-c	40.00	120.00	325.00

WOMEN OUTLAWS (My Love Memories #9 on)(Also see Red Circle)
July, 1948 - No. 8, Sept, 1949
Fox Features Syndicate

1-Used in SOTI, illo "Giving children an image of American womanhood"; negligee panels	58.00	174.00	465.00
2-Spanking panel	53.00	161.00	430.00
3-Kamenish-a	50.00	150.00	400.00
4-8	40.00	120.00	290.00
nn(nd)-Contains Cody of the Pony Express; same cover as #7	29.00	86.00	200.00

WOMEN TO LOVE
No date (1953)
Realistic

nn-(Scarce)-Reprints Complete Romance #1; c-/Avon paperback #165	34.00	103.00	240.00

WONDER BOY (Formerly Terrific Comics) (See Blue Bolt, Bomber Comics & Samson)
No. 17, May, 1955 - No. 18, July, 1955 (Code approved)
Ajax/Farrell Publ.

17-Phantom Lady app. Bakerish-c/a	39.00	118.00	275.00
18-Phantom Lady app.	36.00	107.00	250.00

NOTE: *Phantom Lady not by Matt Baker.*

WONDER COMICS (Wonderworld #3 on)
May, 1939 - No. 2, June, 1939 (68 pgs.)
Fox Features Syndicate

	GD25	FN65	VF82	NM94
1-(Scarce)-Wonder Man app. by Will Eisner; Dr. Fung (by Powell), K-51 begins; Bob Kane-a; Eisner-c	1350.00	4050.00	8100.00	13,500.00

(Estimated up to 70 total copies exist, 3 in NM/Mint)

	GD25	FN65		NM94
2-(Scarce)-Yarko the Great, Master Magician (see Samson) by Eisner begins; 'Spark' Stevens by Bob Kane, Patty O'Day, Tex Mason app. Lou Fine's 1st-c; Fine-a (2 pgs.); Yarko-c (see Wonder Man-c #1)	420.00	12,600.00		4200.00

WONDER COMICS
May, 1944 - No. 20, Oct, 1948
Great/Nedor/Better Publications

1-The Grim Reaper & Spectro, the Mind Reader begin; Hitler/Hirohito

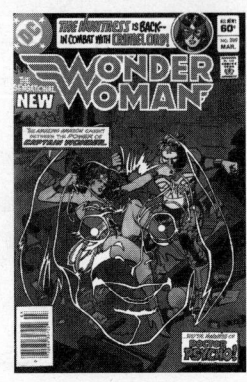

Wonder Man #2 © MEG

Wonder Woman #33 © DC

Wonder Woman #289 © DC

	GD25	FN65	NM94
bondage-c	93.00	281.00	750.00
2-Origin The Grim Reaper; Super Sleuths begin, end #8,17	54.00	163.00	435.00
3-5	50.00	150.00	400.00
6-10: 6-Flag-c. 8-Last Spectro. 9-Wonderman begins	40.00	120.00	315.00
11-14: 11-Dick Devens, King of Futuria begins, ends #14. 11,12-Ingels-c & splash pg.	45.00	135.00	360.00
15-Tara begins (origin), ends #20	54.00	163.00	435.00
16,18: 16-Spectro app.; last Grim Reaper. 18-The Silver Knight begins	45.00	135.00	360.00
17-Wonderman with Frazetta panels; Jill Trent with all Frazetta inks	48.00	146.00	390.00
19-Frazetta panels	45.00	135.00	360.00
20-Most of Silver Knight by Frazetta	54.00	163.00	435.00

NOTE: **Ingels** c-11, 12. **Roussos** a-19. **Schomburg (Xela)** c-1-10; (airbrush)-13-20. Bondage c-12, 13, 15. Cover features: Grim Reaper #1-8; Wonder Man #9-15; Tara #16-20.

WONDER DUCK (See Wisco)
Sept, 1949 - No. 3, Mar, 1950
Marvel Comics (CDS)

1-Funny animal	12.00	36.00	85.00
2,3	10.00	30.00	60.00

WONDERFUL ADVENTURES OF PINOCCHIO, THE (See Movie Comics & Walt Disney Showcase #48)
No. 3, April, 1982 (Walt Disney)
Whitman Publishing Co.

3-(Continuation of Movie Comics?); r/FC #92	1.20		3.00

WONDERFUL WORLD OF DUCKS (See Golden Picture Story Book)
1975
Colgate Palmolive Co.

1-Mostly-r			1.00

WONDERFUL WORLD OF THE BROTHERS GRIMM (See Movie Comics)

WONDERLAND COMICS
Summer, 1945 - No. 9, Feb-Mar, 1947
Feature Publications/Prize

1-Alex in Wonderland begins; Howard Post-c	10.00	30.00	70.00
2-Howard Post-c/a(2)	6.70	20.00	40.00
3-9: 3,4-Post-c	5.00	15.00	30.00

WONDER MAN (See The Avengers #9, 151)
Mar, 1986 ($1.25, one-shot, 52 pgs.)
Marvel Comics Group

1			1.30

WONDER MAN
Sept, 1991 - No. 29, Jan, 1994 ($1.00)
Marvel Comics Group

1-5: 1-Free fold out poster by Johnson/Austin. 1-3-Johnson/Austin-c/a.			1.00
2-Avengers West Coast x-over. 4 Austin-c(i)			1.25
6-29: 6-begin 1.25-c			1.25
Annual 1 (1992, $2.25)-Immonen-a (10 pgs.)	.90		2.25

WONDERS OF ALADDIN, THE
No. 1255, Feb-Apr, 1962
Dell Publishing Co.

Four Color 1255-Movie	6.30	19.00	63.00

WONDER WOMAN (See Adventure Comics #459, All-Star Comics, Brave & the Bold, DC Comics Presents, Justice League of America, Legend of..., Power Record Comics, Sensation Comics, Super Friends and World's Finest Comics #244)

WONDER WOMAN
Summer, 1942 - No. 329, Feb, 1986
National Periodical Publications/All-American Publ./DC Comics

	GD25	FN65	VF82	NM94

	GD25	FN65	NM94
1-Origin Wonder Woman retold (more detailed than All-Star #8); H. G. Peter-c/a begins	1650.00 4950.00	9900.00	16,500.00

(Estimated up to 150 total copies exist, 8 in NM/Mint)

1-Reprint, Oversize 13-1/2x10". **WARNING:** This comic is an exact reprint of the original except for its size. DC published it in 1974 with a second cover titling it as a Famous Fi Edition. There have been many reported cases of the outer cover being removed and the inter sold as the original edition. The reprint with the new outer cover removed is practically worthle See Famous First Edition for value.

	GD25	FN65	NM94
2-Origin/1st app. Mars; Duke of Deception app.	262.00	787.00	2100.00
3	168.00	506.00	1350.00
4,5: 5-1st Dr. Psycho app.	137.00	412.00	1100.00
6-10: 6-1st Cheetah app. 10-Invasion from Saturn	112.00	338.00	900.00
11-20	84.00	253.00	675.00
21-30: 23-Story from Wonder Woman's childhood	71.00	215.00	575.00
31-40: 38-Last H.G. Peter-c	48.00	146.00	390.00
41-44,46-49: 49-Used in **SOTI**, pgs. 234,236; last 52 pg. issue	39.00	118.00	275.00
45-Origin retold	65.00	195.00	525.00
50-(44 pgs.)-Used in **POP**, pg. 97	34.00	103.00	240.00
51-60: 60-New logo	25.00	75.00	175.00
61-72: 62-Origin of W.W. i.d. 64-Story about 3-D movies. 70-1st Angle Man app. 72-Last pre-code (2/55)	21.00	62.00	145.00
73-90: 80-Origin The Invisible Plane. 85-1st S.A. issue. 89-Flying saucer-c/story	19.00	58.00	135.00
91-94,96,97,99: 97-Last H. G. Peter-a	13.50	41.00	95.00
95-A-Bomb-c	14.00	43.00	100.00
98-New origin & new art team (Andru & Esposito) begin (5/58); origin W.W. id w/new facts	15.00	105.00	
100-(8/58)	17.00	49.00	115.00
101-104,106,108-110	12.00	36.00	85.
107-1st advs. of Wonder Girl; 1st Merboy; tells how Wonder Woman won her costume	13.50	41.00	95.
105-(Scarce, 4/59)-W. W.'s secret origin; W. W. appears as girl (no costume ye (called Wonder Girl - see DC Super-Stars #1)	56.00	168.00	450.
111-120	8.00	23.50	60.
121-126: 122-1st app. Wonder Tot. 124-1st app. Wonder Woman Family. 126-Last 10¢ issue	5.70	17.00	45.
127-130: 128-Origin The Invisible Plane retold. 129-2nd app. Wonder Woman Family (#133 is 3rd app.)	3.75	11.25	30.
131-150: 132-Flying saucer-c	3.60	11.00	25.
151-155,157,158,160-170 (1967): 151-Wonder Girl solo issue	3.25	9.50	22.
156-(8/65)-Early mention of a comic book shop & comic collecting; mentions DCs selling for $100 a copy	3.25	9.50	22.
159-Origin retold (1/66); 1st S.A. origin?	3.75	11.25	30.
171-178	1.70	5.00	12.
179-195: 179-Wears no costume to issue #203. 180-Death of Steve Trevor. 195-Wood inks	1.30	3.25	8.
196 (52 pgs.)-Origin-r/All-Star #8 (6 out of 9 pgs.)	1.30	3.25	8.
197,198 (52 pgs.)-Reprints	1.30	3.25	8.
199,200 (5-6/72)-Jeff Jones-c; 52 pgs.	1.30	3.25	8.
201-204: 201,202-Catwoman app. 202-Fafhrd & The Grey Mouser debut. 204-Return to old costume; death of I Ching.	1.00	2.60	6.
205-210			1.5
211-230,233-240: 211,214-(100 pgs.). 212-The Cavalier app. 217-(68 pgs.). 220-N. Adams assist. 223-Steve Trevor revived as Steve Howard & learns W.W.'s I.D. 228-Both Wonder Women team up & new World War II stories begin, end #243. 237-Origin retold. 243-Both W. Women team-up again		.80	2.
231,232: JSA app.	1.00		2.5
241-266,269-280,284-286: 241-Intro Bouncer; Spectre app. 247-249-(44 pgs.). 248-Steve Trevor Howard dies. 249-Hawkgirl app. 250-Origin/1st app. Orana, the new W. Woman. 251-Orana dies. 269-Last Wood a(i) for DC? (7/80). 271-Huntress & 3rd Life of Steve Trevor begin			1.
267,268-Re-intro Animal Man (5/80 & 6/80)	1.70	5.00	12.

Wonder Woman #92 © DC

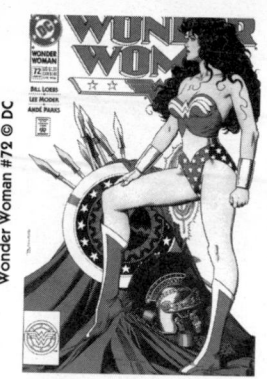
Wonder Woman #72 © DC

Wonderworld Comics #25 © FOX

	GD25	FN65	NM94
281-283: Joker-c/stories in Huntress back-ups		1.20	3.00
287-New Teen Titans x-over			1.50
288-299,301-328: 288-New costume & logo. 291-293-Three part epic with Super-Heroines			1.00
300-($1.50, 76 pgs.)-Anniv. issue; Giffen-a; New Teen Titans, Bronze Age Sandman, JLA & G.A. Wonder Woman app.; 1st app. Lyta Trevor who becomes Fury in All-Star Squadron #25; G.A. W.W. & Steve Trevor revealed as married.			1.50
329 (Double size)-S.A. W.W. & Steve Trevor wed.			1.50
Pizza Hut Giveaways (12/77)-Reprints #60,62			1.00

NOTE: **Andru/Esposito** c-66-160(most). **Buckler** a-300. **Colan** a-288-305p; c-288-290p. **Giffen** a-300p. **Grell** c-217. **Kaluta** c-297. **Gil Kane** c-294p, 303-305, 307, 312, 314. **Miller** c-298p. **Morrow** c-233. **Nasser** a-232p; c-231p, 232p. **Bob Oskner** c(i)-39-65(most). **Perez** c-283p, 284p. **Spiegle** a-312. **Staton** a(p)-241, 271-287, 289, 290, 294-299; c(p)-241, 245, 246. Huntress back-up stories 271-287, 289, 290, 294-299, 301-321.

WONDER WOMAN
Feb, 1987 - Present (75¢/$1.00/$1.25/$1.95)
DC Comics

	GD25	FN65	NM94
1-New origin; Perez-c/a begins		1.20	3.00
2-20: 8-Origin Cheetah. 12,13-Millennium x-over. 18,26-Free 16 pg. story			1.25
21-49,51-62: 24-Last Perez-a; scripts continue thru #62. 60-Vs. Lobo; last Perez-c. 62-Last $1.00-c			1.00
50-($1.50, 52 pgs.)-New Titans, Justice League			1.50
63-81: 63-New direction & Bolland-c begin; Deathstroke story continued from Wonder Woman Special #1			1.25
82-84: 82-Begin $1.50-c			.80	2.00
85-1st Deodato-a; ends #100		1.65	4.20	10.00
86,87			1.20	3.00
88-93: 88-Superman-c & app. 90-(9/94)-1st Artemis. 91-(11/94). 93-Hawkman app.		1.60	4.00
0-(10/94)		1.00	2.00	5.00
94-97: 96-Joker-c			.80	2.00
98,99: 98-Begin $1.75-c			.70	1.75
101-124: 101-Begin $1.95-c; Byrne-c/a/scripts begin. 101-104-Darkseid app. 105-Phantom Stranger cameo. 106-108-Phantom Stranger & Demon app. 107,108-Arion app. 111-1st app.new Wonder Girl. 111,112-Vs.Doomsday. 112-Superman app. 113-Wonder Girl-c/app; Sugar & Spike app.			1.95
00 ($2.95, Newsstand)-Death of Artemis; Bolland-c ends.		1.20	3.00
00 ($3.95, Direct Market)-Death of Artemis; foil-c.		1.60	4.00
nnual 1,2: 1 ('88, $1.50)-Art Adams-c. 2 ('89, $2.00, 68 pgs.)-All women artists issue; Perez-c(i)/a.			.80	2.00
nnual 3 (1992, $2.50, 68 pgs.)-Quesada-c(p)		1.00	2.50
nnual 4 (1995, $3.50)-Year One			1.40	3.50
nnual 5 (1996, $2.95)-Legends of the Dead Earth story; Byrne scripts; Cockrum-a		1.20	3.00
pecial 1 (1992, $1.75, 52 pgs.)-Deathstroke-c/story continued in Wonder Woman #63			.80	2.00
HE CHALLENGE OF ARTEMIS (1996, $9.95)-r/#94-100; Deodato-c/a			10.00

TE: **Art Adams** a-Annual 1. **Byrne** c/a 101-107. **Bolton** a-Annual 1. **Deodato** a-85-100. erez a-Annual 1; c-Annual 1(i). **Quesada** c(p)-Annual 3.

ONDER WOMAN SPECTACULAR (See DC Special Series #9)

ONDER WORKER OF PERU
o date (5x7", 16 pgs.), B&W, giveaway)
atechetical Guild

	GD25	FN65	NM94
		3.60	9.00	18.00

ONDERWORLD COMICS (Formerly Wonder Comics)
o. 3, July, 1939 - No. 33, Jan, 1942
x Features Syndicate

-Intro The Flame by Fine; Dr. Fung (Powell-a), K-51 (Powell-a?), & Yarko

	GD25	FN65	NM94
the Great, Master Magician (Eisner-a) continues; Eisner/Fine-c	570.00	1710.00	5700.00
4-Lou Fine-c	275.00	825.00	2200.00
5-7,9,10: Lou Fine-c	150.00	450.00	1200.00
8-Classic Lou Fine-c	175.00	525.00	1400.00
11-Origin The Flame	125.00	375.00	1000.00
12-15:13-Dr. Fung ends; last Fine-c	100.00	300.00	800.00
16-20:	75.00	225.00	600.00
21-Origin The Black Lion & Cub	68.00	206.00	550.00
22-27: 22,25-Dr. Fung app.	55.00	165.00	440.00
28-Origin & 1st app. U.S. Jones (8/41); Lu-Nar, the Moon Man begins	71.00	215.00	575.00
29,31,33	41.00	124.00	330.00
30-Intro & Origin Flame Girl	82.00	247.00	660.00
32-Hitler-c	47.00	141.00	375.00

NOTE: **Spies at War** by **Eisner** in #13, 17. Yarko by **Eisner** in #3-11. **Eisner** text illos-3. **Lou Fine** a-3-11; c-3-13, 15; text illos-4. **Nordling** a-4-14. **Powell** a-3-12. **Tuska** a-5-9. Bondage-c 14, 15, 28, 31, 32. Cover features: The Flame-#3, 5-31; U.S. Jones-#32, 33.

WONDERWORLDS
1992 ($3.50, squarebound, 100 pgs.)
Innovation Publishing

	GD25	FN65	NM94
1-Rebound super-hero comics, contents may vary; Hero Alliance, Terraformers, etc.		1.40	3.50

WOODSY OWL (See March of Comics #395)
Nov, 1973 - No. 10, Feb, 1976
Gold Key

	GD25	FN65	NM94
1	1.00	2.00	5.00
2-10		1.20	3.00

WOODY WOODPECKER (Walter Lantz... #73 on?)(See Dell Giants for annuals)(Also see The Funnies, Jolly Jingles, Kite Fun Book, New Funnies)
No. 169, 10/47 - No. 72, 5-7/62; No. 73, 10/62 - No. 201, 4/84 (nn 192)
Dell Publishing Co./Gold Key No. 73-187/Whitman No. 188 on

Four Color 169(#1)-Drug turns Woody into a Mr. Hyde

	GD25	FN65	NM94
	14.50	43.50	145.00
Four Color 188	10.00	30.00	100.00
Four Color 202,232,249,264,288	6.30	18.90	63.00
Four Color 305,336,350	3.60	10.80	36.00
Four Color 364,374,390,405,416,431('52)	3.40	10.20	34.00
16 (12-1/52-53) - 30('55)	2.60	7.50	18.00
31-50	2.30	6.70	16.00
51-72 (Last Dell)	1.65	4.70	11.00
73-75 (Giants, 84 pgs., Gold Key)	3.50	10.50	35.00
76-80	1.50	3.75	9.00
81-100	1.20	3.00	7.00
101-120	1.00	2.00	5.00
121-191,193-201 (No #192)		1.00	2.50
Christmas Parade 1(11/68-Giant)(G.K.)	3.60	11.00	25.00
Clover Stamp-Newspaper Boy Contest('56)-9 pg. story-(Giveaway)	3.60	9.00	18.00
In Chevrolet Wonderland(1954-Giveaway)(Western Publ.)-20 pgs., full story line; Chilly Willy app.	17.00	51.00	120.00
...Meets Scotty McTape(1953-Scotch Tape giveaway)-16 pgs., full size	17.00	51.00	120.00
Summer Fun 1(6/66-G.K.)(84 pgs.)	4.50	14.00	32.00

NOTE: 15¢ editions exist. Reprints-No. 92, 102, 103, 105, 106, 124, 125, 152, 153, 157, 162, 165, 194(1/3)-200(1/3).

WOODY WOODPECKER (See Comic Album #5,9,13, Dell Giant #24, 40, 54, Dell Giants, The Funnies, Golden Comics Digest #1, 3, 5, 8, 15, 16, 20, 24, 32, 37, 44, March of Comics #16, 34, 85, 93, 109, 124, 139, 158, 177, 184, 203, 222, 239, 249, 261, 420, 454, 466, 478, New Funnies & Super Book #12, 24)

WOODY WOODPECKER
Sept, 1991 - No. 7, 1993 ($1.25)
Harvey Comics

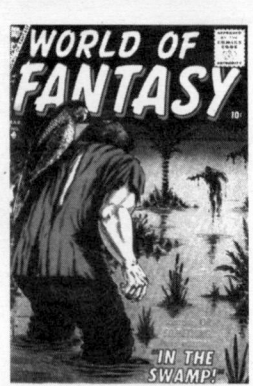

Wordsmith #3 © R. G. Taylor

World Around Us #24 © GIL

World of Fantasy #6 © MEG

	GD25	FN65	NM94
1-7: 1-r/W.W. #53			1.30
50th Anniversary Special 1 (10/91, $2.50, 68 pgs.)		1.25	2.50

WOODY WOODPECKER AND FRIENDS
Dec, 1991 - No. 4, 1992 ($1.25)
Harvey Comics

1-4			1.30

WOOLWORTH'S CHRISTMAS STORY BOOK
1952 - 1954 (16 pgs., paper-c) (See Jolly Christmas Book)
Promotional Publ. Co.(Western Printing Co.)

nn	4.35	13.00	26.00

NOTE: *1952 issue-Marv Levy c/a.*

WOOLWORTH'S HAPPY TIME CHRISTMAS BOOK
1952 (Christmas giveaway, 36 pgs.)
F. W. Woolworth Co.(Whitman Publ. Co.)

nn	4.35	13.00	26.00

WORDSMITH (1st Series)
Aug, 1985 - No. 12, Jan, 1988 ($1.70/$2.00, B&W, bi-monthly)
Renegade Press

1-6: R. G. Taylor-c/a			1.70
7-12: 7-Begin 2.00-c. R. G. Taylor-c/a in all.			2.00

WORDSMITH (2nd Series)
1996 - No. 6, 1996 ($2.95, B&W, limited series)
Caliber

1-6: Reprints in all. 1-Contains 3 pg. sketchbook. 6-Flip book w/Raven Chronicles #10			3.00

WORD WARRIORS (Also see Quest for Dreams Lost)
1987 ($1.50, B&W)(Proceeds donated to help illiteracy)
Literacy Volunteers of Chicago

1-Jon Sable by Grell, Ms. Tree, Streetwolf; Chaykin-c			1.50

WORLD AROUND US, THE (Illustrated Story of...)
Sept, 1958 - No. 36, Oct, 1961 (25¢)
Gilberton Publishers (Classics Illustrated)

1-Dogs; Evans-a	5.00	15.00	30.00
2-4: 2-Indians; Check-a. 3-Horses; L. B. Cole-c. 4-Railroads; L. B. Cole-a (5 pgs.)	5.00	15.00	30.00
5-Space; Ingels-a	6.70	20.00	40.00
6-The F.B.I.; Disbrow, Evans, Ingels-a	6.70	20.00	40.00
7-Pirates; Disbrow, Ingels, Kinstler-a	5.35	16.00	32.00
8-Flight; Evans, Ingels, Crandall-a	5.85	17.50	35.00
9-Army; Disbrow, Ingels, Orlando-a	5.00	15.00	30.00
10-13: 10-Navy; Disbrow, Kinstler-a. 11-Marine Corps. 12-Coast Guard; Ingels-a (9 pgs.). 13-Air Force; L.B. Cole-a	4.35	13.00	28.00
14-French Revolution; Crandall, Evans, Kinstler-a	6.70	20.00	40.00
15-Prehistoric Animals; Al Williamson-a, 6 & 10 pgs. plus Morrow-a	7.50	22.50	45.00
16-18: 16-Crusades; Kinstler-a. 17-Festivals; Evans, Crandall-a. 18-Great Scientists; Crandall, Evans, Torres, Williamson, Morrow-a	5.85	17.50	35.00
19-Jungle; Crandall, Williamson, Morrow-a	7.50	22.50	45.00
20-Communications; Crandall, Evans, Torres-a	6.70	20.00	40.00
21-American Presidents; Crandall/Evans, Morrow-a	6.70	20.00	40.00
22-Boating; Morrow-a	4.25	13.00	26.00
23-Great Explorers; Crandall, Evans-a	5.35	16.00	32.00
24-Ghosts; Morrow, Evans-a	6.70	20.00	40.00
25-Magic; Evans, Morrow-a	6.70	20.00	40.00
26-The Civil War	9.15	25.00	55.00
27-Mountains (High Advs.); Crandall/Evans, Morrow, Torres-a	6.35	19.00	38.00
28-Whaling; Crandall, Evans, Morrow, Torres, Wildey-a; L.B. Cole-c	5.85	17.50	35.00

	GD25	FN65	NM94
29-Vikings; Crandall, Evans, Torres, Morrow-a	7.00	21.00	42
30-Undersea Adventure; Crandall/Evans, Kirby, Morrow, Torres-a	6.70	20.00	40
31-Hunting; Crandall/Evans, Ingels, Kinstler, Kirby-a	5.85	17.50	35
32,33: 32-For Gold & Glory; Morrow, Kirby, Crandall, Evans-a. 33-Famous Teens; Torres, Crandall, Evans-a	6.35	19.00	38
34-36: 34-Fishing; Crandall/Evans-a. 35-Spies; Kirby, Morrow?, Evans-a. 36-Fight for Life (Medicine); Kirby-a	5.35	16.00	32

NOTE: See Classics Illustrated Special Edition. Another *World Around Us* issue entitled *The* had been prepared in 1962 but was never published in the U.S. It was published in British/European *World Around Us* series. Those series then continued with seven additi WAU titles not in the U.S. series.

WORLD FAMOUS HEROES MAGAZINE
Oct, 1941 - No. 4, Apr, 1942 (A comic book)
Comic Corp. of America (Centaur)

1-Gustavson-c; Lubbers, Glanzman-a; Davy Crockett, Paul Revere, Lewis & Clark, John Paul Jones stories; Flag-c	106.00	318.00	850
2-Lou Gehrig life story; Lubbers-a	47.00	141.00	375
3,4-Lubbers-a. 4-Wild Bill Hickok story; 2 pg. Marlene Dietrich story	40.00	120.00	325

WORLD FAMOUS STORIES
1945
Croyden Publishers

1-Ali Baba, Hansel & Gretel, Rip Van Winkle, Mid-Summer Night's Dream	11.00	33.00	75

WORLD IS HIS PARISH, THE
1953 (15¢)
George A. Pflaum

nn-The story of Pope Pius XII	4.00	11.00	22

WORLD OF ADVENTURE (Walt Disney's...)(TV)
Apr, 1963 - No. 3, Oct, 1963 (12¢)
Gold Key

1-3-Disney TV characters; Savage Sam, Johnny Shiloh, Capt. Nemo, The Mooncussers	1.20	3.00	6

WORLD OF ARCHIE, THE (See Archie Giant Series Mag. #148, 151, 156, 160, 165, 177, 182, 188, 193, 200, 208, 213, 225, 232, 237, 244, 249, 456, 461, 468, 473, 480, 485, 497, 504, 509, 516, 521, 532, 543, 554, 565, 574, 587, 599, 612, 627)

WORLD OF ARCHIE
Aug, 1992 - Present ($1.25/$1.50)
Archie Comics

1-11: 9-Neon ink-c			1
12-26			1

WORLD OF FANTASY
May, 1956 - No. 19, Aug, 1959
Atlas Comics (CPC No. 1-15/ZPC No. 16-19)

1	38.00	114.00	265
2-Williamson-a (4 pgs.)	24.00	71.00	165
3-Sid Check, Roussos-a	21.00	64.00	150
4-7	16.00	47.00	110
8-Matt Fox, Orlando, Berg-a	17.00	49.00	115
9-Krigstein-a	16.00	47.00	110
10,12-15	12.00	36.00	85
11-Torres-a	13.50	41.00	95
16-Williamson-a (4 pgs.); Ditko, Kirby-a	17.00	49.00	115
17-19-Ditko, Kirby-a	17.00	49.00	115

NOTE: *Ayers a-3. B. Baily a-4. Berg a-5, 6, 8. Brodsky c-3. Check a-3. Ditko a-17, 19. Everett a-2; c-4-7, 9, 12, 13. Forte a-4. Infantino a-14. Kirby c-15, 17-19. Krigstein a-9. Maneely c-2, 14. Mooney a-14. Morrow a-7. Orlando a-8, 13, 14. Pakula a-9. Powell a-4, R.Q. Sale a-3, 9. Severin c-1.*

WORLD OF GIANT COMICS, THE (See Archie All-Star Specials under Archie Comic

WORLD OF GINGER FOX, THE (Also see Ginger Fox)

World of Krypton #2 © DC

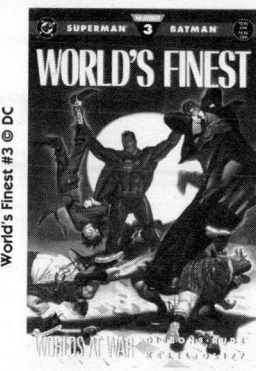

World's Finest #3 © DC

World's Finest Comics #29 © DC

	GD25	FN65	NM94

Nov, 1986 ($6.95, 8 1/2 x 11", 68 pgs., mature)
Comico

Graphic Novel ($6.95)	1.15	3.50	7.00
Hardcover ($27.95)	4.70	14.00	28.00

WORLD OF JUGHEAD, THE (See Archie Giant Series Mag. #9, 14, 19, 24, 30, 136, 143, 149, 152, 157, 161, 166, 172, 178, 183, 189, 194, 202, 209, 215, 227, 233, 239, 245, 251, 457, 463, 469, 475, 481, 487, 493, 499, 505, 511, 517, 523, 531, 542, 553, 564, 577, 590, 602)

WORLD OF KRYPTON, THE (World of...#3) (See Superman #248)
7/79 - No. 3, 9/79; 12/87 - No. 4, 3/88 (Both are limited series)
DC Comics, Inc.

1-3 (1979, 40¢; 1st comic book mini-series): 1-Jor-El marries Lara. 3-Baby Superman sent to Earth; Krypton explodes; Mon-el app.			1.00
1-4 (75¢)-Byrne scripts; Byrne/Simonson-c			1.00

WORLD OF METROPOLIS, THE
Aug, 1988 - No. 4, July, 1988 ($1.00, limited series)
DC Comics

1-4: Byrne scripts			1.00

WORLD OF MYSTERY
June, 1956 - No. 7, July, 1957
Atlas Comics (GPI)

1-Torres, Orlando-a; Powell-a?	37.00	111.00	260.00
2-Woodish-a	13.50	41.00	95.00
3-Torres, Davis, Ditko-a	17.00	51.00	120.00
4-Pakula, Powell-a	18.00	54.00	125.00
5,7: 5-Orlando-a	13.50	41.00	95.00
6-Williamson/Mayo-a (4 pgs.); Ditko-a; Crandall text illo	18.00	54.00	125.00

NOTE: Brodsky c-2. Colan a-7. Everett c-1, 3. Pakula a-4, 6. Romita a-2. Severin c-7.

WORLD OF SMALLVILLE
Apr, 1988 - No. 4, July, 1988 (75¢, limited series)
DC Comics

1-4: Byrne scripts			1.00

WORLD OF SUSPENSE
Apr, 1956 - No. 8, July, 1957
Atlas News Co.

	30.00	90.00	210.00
2-Ditko-a (4 pgs.)	17.00	49.00	115.00
3-7-Williamson-a in both (4 pgs. each); #7-with Mayo	17.00	49.00	115.00
6,8	13.00	39.00	90.00

NOTE: Berg a-6. Cameron a-2. Ditko a-2. Drucker a-1. Everett a-1, 5; c-6. Heck a-5. Maneely c-1-3. Orlando a-5. Powell a-6. Reinman a-4. Roussos a-3. Shores a-1.

WORLD OF WHEELS (Formerly Dragstrip Hotrodders)
No. 17, Oct, 1967 - No. 32, June, 1970
Charlton Comics

17-20-Features Ken King	1.70	5.00	12.00
21-32-Features Ken King	1.20	3.00	7.00
Modern Comics Reprint 23(1978)		1.20	3.00

WORLD OF WOOD
No. 6 - No. 4, 1987; No. 5, 2/89 ($1.75, limited series)
Eclipse Comics

1-4:1-Dave Stevens-c. 2-Wood/Stevens-c		.75	1.80
5($2.00, B&W)-r/Avon's Flying Saucers		.80	2.00

WORLD'S BEST COMICS (World's Finest Comics #2 on)
Spring, 1941 (Cardboard-c)(DC's 6th annual format comic)
National Per. Publications (100 pgs.)

	GD25	FN65	VF82	NM94
1-The Batman, Superman, Crimson Avenger, Johnny Thunder, The King, Young Dr. Davis, Zatara, Lando, Man of Magic, & Red, White & Blue begin; Superman, Batman & Robin covers begin (inside-c is blank); Fred Ray-c;				

15¢ cover price	1388.00	4166.00	8333.00	12,500.00

(Estimated up to 185 total copies exist, 6 in NM/Mint)

WORLDS BEYOND (Stories of Weird Adventure)(Worlds of Fear #2 on)
Nov, 1951
Fawcett Publications

	GD25	FN65	NM94
1-Powell, Bailey-a; Moldoff-c	36.00	109.00	255.00

WORLDS COLLIDE
July, 1994 ($2.50, one-shot)
DC Comics

1-($2.50, 52 pgs.)-Milestone & Superman titles x-over		1.00	2.50
1-($3.95, 52 pgs.)-Polybagged w/vinyl clings		1.60	4.00

WORLD'S FAIR COMICS (See New York...)

WORLD'S FINEST (Also see Legends of World Finest)
1990 - No. 3, 1990 ($3.95, squarebound, limited series, 52 pgs.)
DC Comics

1-3: Batman & Superman team-up against The Joker and Lex Luthor; Dave Gibbons scripts & Steve Rude-c/a. 2,3-Joker/Luthor painted-c by Steve Rude	1.00	2.00	5.00

WORLD'S FINEST COMICS (Formerly World's Best Comics #1)
No. 2, Sum, 1941 - No. 323, Jan, 1986 (#1-17 have cardboard covers) (#2-9 have 100 pgs.)
National Periodical Publ./DC Comics

2 (100 pgs.)-Superman, Batman & Robin covers continue from World's Best; (cover price 15¢ #2-70)	356.00	1067.00	3500.00
3-The Sandman begins; last Johnny Thunder; origin & 1st app. The Scarecrow	300.00	900.00	2600.00
4-Hop Harrigan app.; last Young Dr. Davis	231.00	693.00	1850.00
5-Intro. TNT & Dan the Dyna-Mite; last King & Crimson Avenger	231.00	693.00	1850.00
6-Star Spangled Kid begins (Sum/42); Aquaman app.; S&K Sandman with Sandy in new costume begins, ends #7	162.00	487.00	1300.00
7-Green Arrow begins (Fall/42); last Lando, King, & Red, White & Blue; S&K art	162.00	487.00	1300.00
8-Boy Commandos begin (by Simon(p) #12)	150.00	450.00	1200.00
9-Batman cameo in Star Spangled Kid; S&K-a; last 100 pg. issue; Hitler, Mussolini, Tojo-c	156.00	468.00	1250.00
10-S&K-a; 76 pg. issues begin	131.00	393.00	1050.00
11-17-Last cardboard cover issue	125.00	375.00	1000.00
18-20: 18-Paper covers begin; last Star Spangled Kid. 20-Last quarterly issue	106.00	318.00	850.00
21-30: 21-Begin bi-monthly. 30-Johnny Everyman app.	75.00	225.00	600.00
31-40: 33-35-Tomahawk app.	64.00	193.00	515.00
41-50: 41-Boy Commandos end. 42-Intro The Wyoming Kid & begins (9-10/49), ends #63. 43-Full Steam Foley begins, ends #48. 48-Last square binding. 49-Tom Sparks, Boy Inventor begins	48.00	144.00	385.00
51-60: 51-Zatara ends. 54-Last 76 pg. issue. 59-Manhunters Around the World begins (7-8/52), ends #62	48.00	144.00	385.00
61-64: 61-Joker story. 63-Capt. Compass app.	26.00	77.00	180.00
65-Origin Superman; Tomahawk begins (7-8/53), ends #101	65.00	195.00	525.00
66-70-(15¢ issues, scarce)-Last 15¢, 68pg. issue	45.00	136.00	365.00
71-(10¢ issue, scarce)-Superman & Batman begin as team (7-8/54); were in separate stories until now; Superman & Batman exchange identities; 10¢ issues begin	92.00	277.00	740.00
72-(10¢ issue, scarce)	65.00	195.00	525.00
73-(10¢ issue, scarce)	68.00	206.00	550.00
74-Last pre-code issue	52.00	157.00	420.00
75-(1st code approved, 3-4/55)	48.00	144.00	385.00
76-80: 77-Superman loses powers & Batman obtains them this issue only	40.00	120.00	280.00

World's Finest Comics #267 © DC

Worlds Unknown #7 © MEG

World Without End #5 © DC

	GD25	FN65	NM94

81-90: 84-1st S.A. issue. 88-1st Joker/Luthor team-up. 89-2nd Batmen of All Nations (aka Club of Heroes). 90-Batwoman's 1st app. in World's Finest (10/57, 3rd app. anywhere) plus-c app.

	32.00	96.00	225.00
91-93,95-99: 96-99-Kirby Green Arrow	22.00	66.00	155.00
94-Origin Superman/Batman team retold	62.00	187.00	500.00
100 (3/59)	40.00	120.00	280.00

101-110: 102-Tommy Tomorrow begins, ends #124 16.00   47.00   110.00

111-121: 111-1st app. The Clock King. 113-Intro. Miss Arrowette in Green Arrow; 1st Bat-Mite/Mr. Mxyzptlk team-up (11/60). 121-Last 10¢ issue

  13.00   39.00   90.00

122-128,130-142: 123-2nd Bat-Mite/Mr. Mxyzptlk team-up (2/62). 125-Aquaman begins (5/62), ends #139 (Aquaman #1 is dated 1-2/62). 135-Last Dick Sprang story. 140-Last Green Arrow; last Clayface until Action #443. 142-Origin The Composite Superman (villain); Legion app.

	6.00	18.00	45.00
129-Joker/Luthor team-up-c/story	9.15	27.50	60.00
143-150: 143-1st Mailbag	4.50	14.00	35.00

151-153,155,157-160: 156-Intro of Bizarro Batman. 157-2nd Super Sons story; last app. Kathy Kane (Bat-woman) until Batman Family #10

	3.75	11.25	26.00
154-1st Super Sons story; last Bat-woman in costume until Batman Family #10.	3.75	11.25	30.00
156-1st Bizarro Batman; Joker-c/story	12.00	36.00	85.00
161,170 (80-Pg. Giants G-28,G-40)	3.75	11.25	30.00

162-165,167-169,171-174: 168,172-Adult Legion app. 169-3rd app. new Batgirl (9/67)(cover and 1 panel cameo); 3rd Bat-Mite/Mr. Mxyzptlk team-up.

	2.85	8.50	20.00
166-Joker-c/story	3.25	9.50	22.00

175,176-Neal Adams-a; both reprint J'onn J'onzz origin/Detective #225,226

	2.60	7.50	18.00
177-Joker/Luthor team-up-c/story	2.60	7.50	18.00

178,180-187: 182-Silent Knight-r/Brave & Bold #6. 185-Johnny Quick-r. 187-Green Arrow origin-r by Kirby (Adv. #256) 1.30   3.25   8.00

179,188 (80-Pg. Giants G-52,G-64): 179-r/#94	2.60	7.50	18.00
189-196: 190-193-Robin-r	1.00	2.60	6.00
197-(80 Pg. Giant G-76)	2.60	7.50	18.00

198,199-3rd Superman/Flash race (see Flash #175 & Superman #199)

	11.00	33.00	75.00
200-204: 203-Last 15¢ issue.		1.60	4.00

205-(52 pgs.)-Shining Knight-r (6 pgs.) by Frazetta/Adv. #153; Teen Titans x-over 1.20   3.00   7.00

206 (80-Pg. Giant G-88)	1.65	4.20	10.00

207-212-(25¢, 52 pgs.). 208-Origin Robotman-r/Det. #138.

	1.20	3.00	7.00

213-222,229-248: 215-Intro. Batman Jr. & Superman Jr. 217-Metamorpho begins, ends #220; Batman/Superman team-ups begin. 229-r/origin Superman-Batman team. 242-Super Sons. 244-Green Arrow, Black Canary, Wonder Woman, Vigilante begin; $1.00, 84 pg. issues begin. 246-Death of Stuff in Vigilante; origin Vigilante retold. 248-Last Vigilante

  1.70   4.25

223-228-(100 pgs.). 223-N. Adams-r. 223-Deadman origin. 226-N. Adams, S&K, Toth-r; Manhunter part origin-r/Det. #225,226. 227-Deadman app.

	1.30	3.25	8.00
249-The Creeper begins by Ditko, ends #255	1.00	2.50	5.50

250-270,272-299: 250-The Creeper origin retold by Ditko. 252-Last 84 pg. issue. 253-Capt. Marvel begins; 68 pgs. begin, end #265. 255-Last Creeper. 256-Hawkman begins. 257-Black Lightning begins. 263-Super Sons. 266-282-(52 pgs.). 264-Clay Face app. 267-Challengers of the Unknown app. 268-Capt. Marvel Jr. origin retold. 274-Zatanna begins. 279, 280-Capt. Marvel Jr. & Kid Eternity learn they are brothers. 284-Legion app.

  .90   2.25

271-Origin Superman/Batman team retold		1.00	2.50

300-($1.25, 52pgs.)-Justice League of America, New Teen Titans & The Outsiders app.; Perez-a (3 pgs.) 1.30   3.25

301-323: 304-Origin Null and Void. 309,319-Free 16 pg. story in each (309-Flash Force 2000, 319-Mask preview)   .80   2.00

Giveaway (c. 1944-45, 8 pgs., in color, paper-c)-Johnny Everyman-r/World's Finest   18.00   54.00   125.00

Giveaway (c. 1949, 8 pgs., in color, paper-c)- "Make Way For Youth" r/World's Finest; based on film of same name   13.50   41.00   95.00

NOTE: Neal Adams a-230ir; c-174-176, 178-180, 182, 183, 185, 186, 199-205, 208-211, 244-246, 258. Austin a-244-246i. Burnley a-8, 10; c-7-9, 11-14, 15p?, 16-18p, 20-31p. Colan a-274p, 297, 299. Ditko a-249-255. Giffen a-322; c-284p, 322. G. Kane a-38, 174r, 282, 283; c-281, 282, 289. Kirby a-187. Kubert Zatara-40-44. Miller c-285p. Mooney c-134. Morrow a-245, 248. Mortimer c-16-21, 26-71. Nasser a(p)-244-246, 259, 260. Newton a-253-281p. Orlando a-224r. Perez a-300i; c-271, 276, 277p, 278p. Fred Ray c-1-5. Fred Ray/Robinson c-13-16. Robinson a-2, 9, 13-15; c-6. Rogers a-259p. Roussos a-212r. Simonson c-291. Spiegle a-275-278, 284. Staton a-262p, 273p. Swan/Moldoff c-126. Swan/Mortimer c-79-82. Toth a-228r. Tuska a-230r, 250p, 252p, 254p, 257p, 283p, 284p, 308p. Boy Commandos by Infantino #39-41.

(Also see 80 Page Giant #15)

WORLD'S FINEST COMICS DIGEST (See DC Special Series #23)

WORLD'S GREATEST ATHLETE (See Walt Disney Showcase #14)

WORLD'S GREATEST SONGS
Sept, 1954
Atlas Comics (Male)

1-(Scarce)-Heath & Harry Anderson-a; Eddie Fisher life story plus-c; gives lyrics to Frank Sinatra song "Young at Heart"   34.00   103.00   240.00

WORLD'S GREATEST STORIES
Jan, 1949 - No. 2, May, 1949
Jubilee Publications

1-Alice in Wonderland; Lewis Carroll adapt.	24.00	73.00	170.00
2-Pinocchio	23.00	69.00	160.00

WORLD'S GREATEST SUPER HEROES
1977 (Giveaway, 3-3/4x3-3/4", 24 pgs.)
DC Comics (Nutra Comics) (Child Vitamins, Inc.)

nn-Batman & Robin app.; health tips   .80   2.00

WORLDS OF FEAR (Stories of Weird Adventure)(Formerly Worlds Beyond #1)
V1#2, Jan, 1952 - V2#10, June, 1953
Fawcett Publications

V1#2	34.00	103.00	240.00
3-Evans-a	29.00	86.00	200.00
4-6(9/52)	23.00	69.00	160.00
V2#7-9	21.00	62.00	145.00

10-Saunders painted-c; man with no eyes surrounded by eyeballs-c plus eyes ripped out story   38.00   114.00   265.00

NOTE: Moldoff c-2-8. Powell a-2, 4, 5. Sekowsky a-4, 5.

WORLDS UNKNOWN
May, 1973 - No. 8, Aug, 1974
Marvel Comics Group

1-r/from Astonishing #54; Torres, Reese-a		1.60	4.00
2-8		1.20	3.00

NOTE: Adkins/Mooney a-5. Buscema c/a-4p. W. Howard c/a-3i. Kane a(p)-1,2; c(p)-5, 6, 8. Sutton a-2. Tuska a(p)-7, 8; c-7p. No. 7, 8 has Golden Voyage of Sinbad movie adaptation.

WORLD WAR STORIES
Apr-June, 1965 - No. 3, Dec, 1965
Dell Publishing Co.

1-Glanzman-a in all	3.75	11.25	26.00
2,3	2.30	6.75	16.00

WORLD WAR II (See Classics Illustrated Special Issue)

WORLD WAR III
Mar, 1953 - No. 2, May, 1953
Ace Periodicals

1-(Scarce)-Atomic bomb blast-c; Cameron-a   49.00   148.00   395.00

2-Used in POP, pg. 78 & B&W & color illos; Cameron-a

Wow Comics #42 © FAW

Wrath #6 © Malibu

Wrath of the Spectre #4 © DC

	GD25	FN65	NM94
	45.00	136.00	365.00

WORLD WITHOUT END
990 - No. 6, 1991 ($2.50, limited series, mature, stiff-c)
DC Comics

1-6: Horror/fantasy; all painted-c/a		1.25	2.50

WORLD WRESTLING FEDERATION BATTLEMANIA
991 - No. 5?, 1991 ($2.50, magazine size, 68 pgs.)
aliant

1-5: 5-Includes 2 free pull-out posters		1.00	2.50

WORST FROM MAD, THE (Annual)
958 - No. 12, 1969 (Each annual cover is reprinted from the cover of the
ad issues being reprinted)
C. Comics

1(1958)-Bonus; record labels & travel stickers; 1st Mad annual; r/Mad #29-34	39.00	118.00	275.00
2(1959)-Bonus is small 33⅓ rpm record entitled "Meet the Staff of Mad"; r/Mad #35-40	40.00	120.00	315.00
3(1960)-Has 20x30" campaign poster "Alfred E. Neuman for President"; r/Mad #41-46	26.00	79.00	185.00
4(1961)-Sunday comics section; r/Mad #47-54	24.00	73.00	170.00
5(1962)-Has 33-1/3 record; r/Mad #55-62	38.00	114.00	265.00
6(1963)-Has 33-1/3 record; r/Mad #63-70	40.00	120.00	280.00
7(1964)-Mad protest signs; r/Mad #71-76	13.50	41.00	95.00
8(1965)-Build a Mad Zeppelin	17.00	51.00	120.00
9(1966)-33-1/3 rpm record	27.00	81.00	190.00
(1967)-Mad bumper sticker	8.50	26.00	60.00
(1968)-Mad cover window stickers	8.00	23.50	55.00
(1969)-Mad picture postcards; Orlando-a	8.00	23.50	55.00

E: Covers: **Bob Clarke**-#8. **Mingo**-#7, 9-12.

TALIFE COMICS (Formerly Nutty Life #2; Phantom Lady #13 on)
3, Aug-Sept, 1946 - No. 12, July, 1947; 1959
Features Syndicate/Norlen Mag.

-Cosmo Cat, Li'l Pan, others begin	10.00	30.00	58.00
2-Cosmo Cat, Li'l Pan in all	6.35	19.00	38.00
1959-Norlen)-Atomic Rabbit, Atomic Mouse; reprints cover to #6; reprints entire book?	5.85	17.50	35.00

TALIFE COMICS
7 - No. 5, 1957
en Publications

	4.00	12.00	24.00
	3.60	9.00	18.00

W COMICS
, 1936 - No. 4, Nov, 1936 (52 pgs., magazine size)
le Publishing Co.

uck Jones in "The Phantom Rider" (1st app. in comics), Fu Manchu; Capt. cott Dalton begins; Eisner-a; Briefer-c	225.00	675.00	1800.00
en Maynard, Fu Manchu, Popeye by Segar plus article on Popeye; isner-a	150.00	450.00	1200.00
isner-c/a(3); Popeye by Segar, Fu Manchu, Hiram Hick by Bob Kane; pace Limited app.; Jimmy Dempsey talks about Popeye's punch; Bob ipley Believe it or Not begins; Briefer-a	150.00	450.00	1200.00
ash Gordon by Raymond, Mandrake, Popeye by Segar, Tillie The Toiler, Hiram Hick by Bob Kane; Eisner-a(3); Briefer-c/a	188.00	562.00	1500.00

W COMICS (Real Western Hero #70 on)(See XMas Comics)
, 1940-41; No. 2, Summer, 1941 - No. 69, Fall, 1948
ett Publications

	GD25	FN65	VF82	NM94
)-Origin Mr. Scarlet by S&K; Atom Blake, Boy Wizard, Jim Dolan, & Rick Shay begin; Diamond Jack, The White Rajah, & Shipwreck Roberts, only p.; 1st mention of Gotham City in comics; the cover was printed on				

---

unstable paper stock and is rarely found in fine or mint condition; blank
inside-c; bondage-c by Beck

	GD25	FN65	NM94	
	1250.00	3750.00	7500.00	12,500.00

(Estimated up to 100 total copies exist, 3 in NM/Mint)

	GD25	FN65	NM94
2 (Scarce)-The Hunchback begins	200.00	600.00	1600.00
3 (Fall, 1941)	93.00	281.00	750.00
4-Origin & 1st app. Pinky	100.00	300.00	800.00
5	62.00	187.00	500.00
6-Origin & 1st app. The Phantom Eagle (7/15/42); Commando Yank begins			
7,8,10: 10-Swayze-c/a on Mary Marvel	62.00	187.00	500.00
	50.00	150.00	400.00
9 (1/6/43)-Capt. Marvel, Capt. Marvel Jr., Shazam app.; Mary Marvel-c/stories begin (cameo #9)	106.00	318.00	850.00
11-17,19,20: 15-Flag-c	39.00	118.00	275.00
18-1st app. Uncle Marvel (10/43); infinity-c	40.00	120.00	300.00
21-30: 29-Pinky x-over	21.00	64.00	150.00
31-40: 32-68-Phantom Eagle by Swayze	14.00	43.00	100.00
41-50	13.00	39.00	90.00
51-58: Last Mary Marvel	11.50	34.00	80.00
59-69: 59-Ozzie (teenage) begins. 62-Flying Saucer gag-c (1/48). 65-69-Tom Mix stories (cont'd in Real Western Hero	10.00	30.00	70.00

NOTE: *Cover features: Mr. Scarlet-#1-5; Commando Yank-#6, 7, (w/Mr. Scarlet #8) Mary Marvel-#9-56, (w/Commando Yank-#46-50), (w/Mr. Scarlet & Commando Yank-#51), (w/Mr. Scarlet & Pinky #53), (w/Phantom Eagle #54, 56), (w/Commando Yank & Phantom Eagle #58); Ozzie-#59, 65.*

WRATH (Also see Prototype #4)
Jan, 1994 - No. 9, Nov, 1995 ($1.95)
Malibu Comics

1-9: 2-Mantra x-over. 3-Intro/1st app. Slayer. 4,5-Freex app. 8-Mantra & Warstrike app. 9-Prime app.		.80	2.00
1-Ultra 5000 Limited silver foil	1.30	3.25	8.00
Giant Size 1 (2.50, 44 pgs.)		1.00	2.50

WRATH OF THE SPECTRE, THE
May, 1988 - No. 4, Aug, 1988 ($2.50, limited series)
DC Comics

1-4: Aparo-r/Adventure #431-440		1.20	3.00

WRECK OF GROSVENOR (See Superior Stories #3)

WRETCH (1996 ($2.95, B&W)
Caliber

1-Phillip Hester-a/scripts			3.00

WRINGLE WRANGLE (Disney)
No. 821, July, 1957
Dell Publishing Co.

Four Color 821-Based on movie "Westward Ho, the Wagons"; Marsh-a; Fess Parker photo-c	9.00	27.00	90.00

WULF THE BARBARIAN
Feb, 1975 - No. 4, Sept, 1975
Atlas/Seaboard Publ.

1-4: 1-Origin. 2-Intro. Berithe the Swordswoman; Neal Adams, Wood, Reese-a assists			1.00

WYATT EARP
Nov, 1955 - #29, June, 1960; #30, Oct, 1972 - #34, June, 1973
Atlas Comics/Marvel No. 23 on (IPC)

1	18.00	54.00	125.00
2-Williamson-a (4 pgs.)	10.00	30.00	70.00
3-6,8-11: 3-Black Bart app. 8-Wild Bill Hickok app	9.15	27.00	55.00
7,12-Williamson-a, 4 pgs. ea.; #12 with Mayo	9.15	27.00	55.00
13-20: 17-1st app. Wyatt's deputy, Grizzly Grant	7.50	22.50	45.00
21-Davis-c	5.85	17.50	35.00
22-24,26-29: 22-Ringo Kid app. 23-Kid From Texas app. 29-Last 10¢ issue			

X #20 © DH

X-Calibre #1 © MEG

X-Factor #90 © MEG

	GD25	FN65	NM94

	4.25	13.00	26.00
25-Davis-a	4.25	13.00	28.00
30-Williamson-r (1972)		.80	2.00
31-34-Reprints. 32-Torres-a(r)			1.00

NOTE: **Ayers** a-8, 10(2), 17, 20(4). **Berg** a-9. **Everett** c-6. **Kirby** c-25, 29. **Maneely** a-1; c-1-4, 8, 12, 17, 20. **Maurer** a-2(2), 3(4), 4(4), 8(4). **Severin** a-4, 9(4), 10; c-2, 9, 10, 14. **Wildey** a-5, 17, 24, 28.

WYATT EARP (TV) (Hugh O'Brian Famous Marshal)
No. 860, Nov, 1957 - No. 13, Dec-Feb, 1960-61 (Hugh O'Brian photo-c)
Dell Publishing Co.

Four Color 860 (#1)-Manning-a	11.00	33.00	110.00
Four Color 890,921(6/58)-All Manning-a	7.50	23.00	75.00
4 (9-11/58) - 12-Manning-a. 5-Photo back-c	5.00	15.00	50.00
13-Toth-a	5.50	16.50	55.00

WYATT EARP FRONTIER MARSHAL (Formerly Range Busters) (Also see
Blue Bird)
No. 12, Jan, 1956 - No. 72, Dec, 1967
Charlton Comics

12	7.50	22.50	45.00
13-19	4.00	12.00	24.00
20-(68 pgs.)-Williamson-a(4), 8,5,5,& 7 pgs.	9.15	27.00	55.00
21-30	2.30	6.75	16.00
31-50	1.50	3.75	9.00
51-72	1.00	2.00	5.00

X (Comics' Greatest World: X #1 only) (Also see Comics' Greatest World & Dark
Horse Comics #8)
Feb, 1994 - No. 25, Apr, 1996 ($2.00/$2.50)
Dark Horse Comics

1-7: 3-Pit Bulls x-over		.80	2.00
8-25: 8 ($2.50)-Ghost-c & app. 18-Miller-c.; Predator app. 19-22-Miller-c.		1.00	2.50
Hero Illustrated Special #1,2 (1994, $1.00, 20 pgs.)			1.00
One Shot to the Head (1994, $2.50, 36 pgs.)-Miller-c.		1.00	2.50

NOTE: Miller c-18-22. Quesada c-6. Russell a-6.

XANADU COLOR SPECIAL
Dec, 1988 ($2.00, one-shot)
Eclipse Comics

1-Reprints Xanadu from Thoughts & Images		.80	2.00

X-CALIBRE
Mar, 1995 - No. 4, July, 1995 ($1.95, limited series)
Marvel Comics

1-4-Age of Apocalypse		.80	2.00

XENOBROOD
No. 0, Oct, 1994 - No. 6, Apr, 1995 ($1.50, limited series)
DC Comics

0-6: 0-Indicia says "Xenobroods"			1.50

XENON
Dec, 1987 - No. 23, Nov. 1, 1988 ($1.50, B&W, bi-weekly)
Eclipse Comics

1-23			1.50

XENOTECH
Sept, 1993 - No. 3, Dec, 1994 ($2.75)
Mirage Studios

1-3: Bound with 2 trading cards. 2-(10/94)		1.10	2.75

XENOZOIC TALES (Also see Cadillacs & Dinosaurs, Death Rattle #8)
Feb, 1986 - No. 11?
Kitchen Sink Press

1-11: 1-2nd printing exists (1/89)		.80	2.00

XENYA

	GD25	FN65	NM9

Apr, 1994 - Present ($2.95)
Sanctuary Press

1-3: 1-Hildebrandt-c; intro Xenya			1.20

X-FACTOR (Also see The Avengers #263 & Fantastic Four #286)
Feb, 1986 - Present
Marvel Comics Group

1-($1.25, 52 pgs)-Story recaps 1st app. from Avengers #263; story cont'd from F.F. #286; return of original X-Men (now X-Factor); Guice/Layton-a. Baby Nathan app. (2nd after X-Men #201)	2.15	6.50	
2-4	1.00	2.60	
5-1st app. Apocalypse (2-pg. cameo)	1.65	4.20	
6-1st full app. Apocalypse	3.60	11.00	
7-10: 10-Sabretooth app. (11/86, 3 pgs.) cont'd in X-Men #212; 1st app. in X-Men comic book		1.60	
11-20: 13-Baby Nathan app. in flashback. 15-Intro wingless Angel		1.20	
21,22		1.00	
23: 23-1st app. Archangel (2 pg. cameo)	1.70	5.00	
24-1st full app. Archangel (now in Uncanny X-Men); Fall Of The Mutants begins; origin Apocalypse	3.25	9.50	
25,26: Fall Of The Mutants; 26-New outfits		1.60	
27-30		.80	
31-37,39,41-49: 35-Origin Cyclops			
38,50-($1.50, 52 pgs.): 50-Liefeld/McFarlane-c		.80	
40-Rob Liefeld-c/a (4/89, 1st at Marvel?)	1.00	2.00	
51-53-Sabretooth app. 52-Liefeld-c(p)	1.00	2.00	
54-59: 54-Intro Crimson; Silvestri-c/a(p)			
60-X-Tinction Agenda x-over; New Mutants (w/Cable) x-over in #60-62; Wolverine in #62	1.30	3.25	
60-Gold ink 2nd printing		1.00	
61,62-X-Tinction Agenda. 62-Jim Lee-c	1.00	2.50	
63-Portacio/Thibert-c/a(p) begins, ends #69	1.00	2.50	
64-67,69,70: 65-68-Lee co-plots. 65-The Apocalypse Files begins, ends # 66,67-Baby Nathan app. 67-Inhumans app. 69,70-X-Men (w/Wolverine x-over		.80	
68-Baby Nathan is sent into future to save his life	1.00	2.00	
71-New team begins (Havok, Polaris, Strong Guy, Wolfsbane & Madrox); Stroman-c/a begins	1.00	2.50	
71-2nd printing ($1.25)			
72-74: 74-Last $1.00-c		.70	
75-($1.75, 52 pgs.)			
76-83,87-91,93-99,101: 77-Cannonball (of X-Force) app. 87-Quesada-c/a; monthly comic begins, ends #92. 88-1st app. Random.		.80	
84-86 ($1.50)-Polybagged with trading card in each; X-Cutioner's Song x 84-86-Jae Lee-a(p). 85,86-Jae Lee-c		.80	
92-($3.50, 68 pgs.)-Wraparound-c by Quesada w/Havok hologram on-c; X-Men 30th anniversary issues; Quesada-a.	1.00	2.00	
92-2nd printing	.70	1.75	
100-($2.95, 52 pgs.)-Embossed foil-c; Multiple Man dies.	1.00	2.00	
100-($1.75, 52 pgs.)-Regular edition		.80	
102-105,107: 102-Begin $1.50-c; bound-in card sheet			
106-($2.00)-Newsstand edition		.80	
106-($2.95)-Collectors edition		1.20	
108-124,126: 108-Begin $1.95-c. 112-Return from Age of Apocalypse. 115-card insert. 119-123-Sabretooth app. 123-Hound app. 124-w/Ons. Update. 126-Onslaught x-over; Beast vs. Dark Beast		.80	
Annual 1-6: 1-(10/86). 2-(10/87). 3-(1988, $1.75)-Evolutionary War x-over 4-(1989, $2.00, 68 pgs.)-Atlantis Attacks; Byrne/Simonson-a; Byrne-c, 5-(1990, $2.00, 68 pgs.)-Fantastic Four, New Mutants x-over; Keown a pin-up. 6-(1991, $2.00, 68 pgs.)-New Warriors app.; 5th app. X-Force from X-Men Annual #15		1.00	
Annual 7 (1992, $2.25, 68 pgs.)-1st Quesada-a(p) on X-Factor plus-c(p)			

X-Files #9 © 20th Century Fox

X-Force #55 © MEG

X-Man #17 © MEG

XM

	GD25	FN65	NM94

	GD25	FN65	NM94

nual 8 (1993, $2.95, 68 pgs.)-Bagged w/trading card	.90	2.25
nual 9 (1994, $2.95, 68 pgs.)-Austin-a(i)	1.20	3.00
PRISONER OF LOVE nn (1990, $4.95, 52 pgs.)-Starlin scripts; Guice-a	1.20	3.00

TE: **Art Adams** a-41p, 42p. **Buckler** a-50p. **Liefeld** a-40; c-40, 50i, 52p. **McFarlane** c-50i. **gnola** c-70. **Brandon Peterson** a-78p(part). **Whilce Portacio** c/a(p)-63-69. **Quesada** a(p)-92, Annual 7. c(p)-78, 79, 82, Annual 7. **Simonson** c/a-10, 11, 13-15, 17-19, 21, 23-31, 33, 36-39; c-12, 16. **Paul Smith** a-44-48; c-43. **Stroman** a(p)-71-75, 77, 78(part), 80, 81; c(p)-77, 80, 81, 84. **Zeck** c-2.

FILES, THE (TV)
n, 1995 - Present ($2.50)
ps Comics

2-W/certificate		3.60	11.00	25.00
Adaptation of TV show; direct market & newsstand editions; Miran Kim-c on all		5.50	17.00	45.00
4	4.30	13.00	30.00
10	2.00	6.00	14.00
25: 11-Begin $2.95-c	1.00	2.00	5.00
ual 1 ($3.95)			3.00
Illustrated Giveaway		1.60	4.00
cial Edition 1 ($4.95)-r/#1-3.	2.15	6.50	15.00
cial Edition 2 ($4.95)-r/#4-6.		1.60	5.00
cial Edition 3 ($4.95)-r/#7-9			5.00
Wars Galaxy Magazine Giveaway (B&W)	1.65	4.20	10.00
de paperback ($19.95)			20.00

LES COMICS DIGEST, THE
1995 - Present ($3.50, quarterly, digest-size)
s Comics

New X-Files stories w/Ray Bradbury Comics-r
E: **Adlard** a-1, 2. **Jack Davis** a-2r. **Russell** a-1r. 3.50

RCE (Also see The New Mutants #100 & 1992 X-Men Annuals)
1991 - Present ($1.00/$1.25/$1.50/$1.95)

1.50, 52 pgs.)-Polybagged with 1 of 5 diff. Marvel Universe trading cards side (each); 6th app. of X-Force; Liefeld-c/a begins		1.80	4.50
st printing with Cable trading card inside	1.00	2.60	6.00
nd print; metallic ink-c (no bag or card)			1.50
2-Deadpool-c/story.-3-New Brotherhood of Evil Mutants app.		1.20	3.00
pider-Man x-over; cont'd from Spider-Man #16; reads sideways		1.20	3.00
6-Last $1.00-c. 7,9-Weapon X back-ups. 8-Intro The Wild Pack (Cable, ane, Domino, Hammer, G.W. Bridge, & Grizzly); Liefeld-c/a (4); Mignola-a. -Weapon X full-length story (part 3). 11-1st Weapon Prime (cameo); eadpool-c/story.		.80	2.00
5,19-24,26-33: 15-Cable leaves X-Force			1.50
($1.50)-Polybagged with trading card in each; X-Cutioner's Song x-overs		.80	2.00
3.50, 52 pgs.)-Wraparound-c w/Cable hologram on-c; Cable returns	1.00	2.00	5.00
,39-45: 34-Begin $1.50-c; bound-in card sheet			1.50
2.00)-Newsstand edition		.80	2.00
2.95)-Collectors edition	1.00	2.00	5.00
(1.95)-Deluxe edition		.80	2.00
,51-65: 44-Return from Age of Apocalypse. 45-Sabretooth app. Sebastian Shaw app. 52-Blob app., Onslaught cameo. 55-Vs. S.H.I.E.L.D. Deadpool app. 57-Mr. Sinister & X-Man-c/app; Onslaught x-over.			2.00
3.95)-Gatefold wrap-around foil-c		1.60	4.00
.95)-Liefeld variant-c	2.15	6.50	15.00

Annual 1 (1992, $2.25, 68 pgs.)-1st Greg Capullo-a(p) on X-Force			
Annual 2 (1993, $2.95, 68 pgs.)-Polybagged w/trading card; intro X-Treme & Neurtap		.90	2.25
Annual 3 (1994, $2.95)		1.20	3.00
...AND CABLE '95 (12/95, $3.95)-Impossible Man app.			4.00
...AND SPIDER-MAN: SABOTAGE nn (11/92, $6.95)-Reprints X-Force #3,4 & Spider-Man #16		1.20	3.00	7.00

NOTE: **Capullo** a(p)-15-25, Annual 1; c(p)-14-27. **Rob Liefeld** a-1-7, 9p; c-1-9, 11p; plots-1-12. **Mignola** a-8p.

X-FORCE MEGAZINE
Nov, 1996 ($3.95, one-shot)
Marvel Comics

1-Reprints   4.00

XIMOS: VIOLENT PAST
Mar, 1994 - No. 2, Mar, 1994 ($2.50, limited series)
Triumphant Comics

1,2   1.10   2.75

X-MAN (Also see X-Men Omega & X-Men Prime)
Mar, 1995 - Present ($1.95)
Marvel Comics

1-Age of Apocalypse	1.20	3.00
1-2nd print	.80	2.00
2-4	.80	2.00
5-30: 5-Post Age of Apocalypse stories begin. 5-7-Madelyne Pryor app. 10-Professor X app. 12-vs. Excalibur. 13-Marauders, Cable app. 14-Vs. Cable; Onslaught app. 15-17-Vs. Holocaust. 17-w/Onslaught Update. 18-Onslaught x-over; X-Force-c/app; Marauders app. 19-Onslaught x-over. 20-Abomination-c/app.; w/card insert	.80	2.00

XMAS COMICS
12?/1941 - No. 2, 12?/1942 (50¢, 324 pgs.)
No. 3, 12?/1943 - No. 7, 12?/1947 (25¢, 132 pgs.)
Fawcett Publications

	GD25	FN65	VF82	NM94
1-Contains Whiz #21, Capt. Marvel #3, Bulletman #2, Wow #3, & Master #18; Raboy back-c. Not rebound, remaindered comics; printed at same time as originals	300.00	900.00	1800.00	3000.00
(Estimated up to 110 total copies exist, 5 in NM/Mint)				

	GD25	FN65	NM94
2-Capt. Marvel, Bulletman, Spy Smasher	100.00	300.00	1000.00
3-7-Funny animals (Hoppy, Billy the Kid & Oscar)	40.00	120.00	400.00

XMAS COMICS
No. 4, Dec, 1949 - No. 7, Dec, 1952 (50¢, 196 pgs.)
Fawcett Publications

4-Contains Whiz, Master, Tom Mix, Captain Marvel, Nyoka, Capt. Video, Bob Colt, Monte Hale, Hot Rod Comics, & Battle Stories. Not rebound, remaindered comics; printed at the same time as originals	44.00	132.00	440.00
5-7-Same as above. 7-Bill Boyd app.; stocking on cover is made of green felt (novelty cover)	36.00	108.00	360.00

XMAS FUNNIES
No date (Giveaway, paper cover, 36 pgs.?)
Kinney Shoes

Contains 1933 color strip-r; Mutt & Jeff, etc.   36.00   107.00   250.00

X-MEN, THE (See Adventures of Cyclops and Phoenix, Amazing Adventures, Archangel, Capt. America #172, Classic X-Men, Further Adventures of Cyclops & Phoenix, Gambit, Giant-Size..., Heroes For Hope..., Kitty Pryde & Wolverine, Marvel & DC Present, Marvel Collector's Edition:..., Marvel Fanfare, Marvel Graphic Novel, Marvel Super Heroes, Marvel Team-Up, Marvel Triple Action, The Marvel X-Men Collection, New Mutants, Nightcrawler, Official Marvel Index To..., Rogue, Special Edition..., The Uncanny..., Wolverine, X-Factor, X-Force, X-Terminators)

X-MEN, THE (Becomes Uncanny X-Men with #142)(The X-Men #1-93; X-Men

X-Men #82 (1st Series) © MEG

X-Men #105 (1st Series) © MEG

X-Men #55 (2nd Series) © MEG

	GD25	FN65	NM94

#94-141; The Uncanny X-Men on-c only #114-141)
Sept, 1963 - No. 66, Mar, 1970; No. 67, Dec, 1970 - No. 141, Jan, 1981
Marvel Comics Group

	GD25	FN65	VF82	NM94
1-Origin/1st app. X-Men (Angel, Beast, Cyclops, Iceman & Marvel Girl); 1st app. Magneto & Professor X	385.00	1155.00	2812.00	5000.00

	GD25	FN65		NM94
2-1st app. The Vanisher	150.00	480.00		1600.00
3-1st app. The Blob (1/64)	69.00	206.00		600.00
4-1st Quick Silver & Scarlet Witch & Brotherhood of the Evil Mutants (3/64); 1st app. Toad; 2nd app. Magneto	60.00	182.00		550.00
5-Magneto & Evil Mutants-c/story	43.00	129.00		375.00
6-10: 6-Sub-Mariner app. 7-Magneto app. 8-1st Unus the Untouchable. 9-Early Avengers app. (1/65); 1st Lucifer. 10-1st S.A. app. Ka-Zar & Zabu the sabertooth (3/65)	36.00	107.00		275.00
11,13-15: 11-1st app. The Stranger. 14-1st app. Sentinels. 15-Origin Beast	29.00	86.00		225.00
12-Origin Prof. X; Origin/1st app. Juggernaut	38.00	114.00		290.00
16-20: 19-1st app. The Mimic (4/66)	13.00	39.00		100.00
21-27,29,30: 27-Re-enter The Mimic (r-in #75); Spider-Man cameo	11.00	33.00		85.00
28-1st app. The Banshee (1/67)(r-in #76)	16.00	49.00		130.00
31-34,36,37,39,40: 34-Adkins-c/a. 39-New costumes	8.00	23.50		60.00
35-Spider-Man x-over (8/67)(r-in #83); 1st app. Changeling	13.00	39.00		100.00
38-Origins of the X-Men series begins, ends #57	11.00	33.00		80.00
41-49: 42-Death of Prof. X (Changeling disguised as). 44-1st S.A. app. G.A. Red Raven. 49-Steranko-c; 1st Polaris	7.00	21.50		55.00
50,51-Steranko-c/a	8.00	23.50		60.00
52	5.00	15.00		40.00
53-Barry Smith-c/a (his 1st comic book work)	8.00	23.50		60.00
54,55-B. Smith-c. 54-1st app. Alex Summers who later becomes Havok. 55-Summers discovers he has mutant powers	8.00	24.50		65.00
56,57,59-63,65-Neal Adams-a(p). 56-Intro Havok w/o costume. 65-Return of Professor X	7.00	21.00		52.00
58-1st app. Havok in costume; N. Adams-a(p)	10.50	32.00		85.00
64-1st app. Sunfire	8.00	23.50		60.00
66-Last new story w/original X-Men; battles Hulk	5.70	17.00		45.00
67-70,72: (52 pgs.). 67-Reprints begin, end #93	3.75	11.25		26.00
71,73-93: 71-Last 15¢ issue. 73-86-r/#25-38 w/new-c. 83-Spider-Man-c/story. 87-93-r/#39-45 with covers	3.25	9.50		22.00
94 (8/75)-New X-Men begin (see Giant-Size X-Men for 1st app.); Colossus, Nightcrawler, Thunderbird, Storm, Wolverine, & Banshee join; Angel, Marvel Girl, & Iceman resign	44.00	132.00		400.00
94-Variant w/Mark Jewelers pull-out ad	44.00	132.00		400.00
95-Death of Thunderbird	10.50	32.00		85.00
96-99: 98,99-25¢ & 30¢ versions exist	8.00	24.50		65.00
100-Old vs. New X-Men; part origin Phoenix; last 25¢ issue (8/76)	8.00	24.50		65.00
101-Phoenix origin concludes	7.00	20.50		55.00
102-107: 102-Origin Storm. 104-1st app. Starjammers (brief cameo); Magneto-c/story. 106-Old vs. New X-Men; 30¢ & 35¢ issues exist. 107-1st full app. Starjammers; last 30¢ issue	3.75	11.25		28.00
108-Byrne-a begins (see Marvel Team-Up #53)	7.00	20.50		55.00
109-1st app. Weapon Alpha (becomes Vindicator)	5.25	15.75		42.00
110,111: 110-Phoenix joins	3.75	11.25		28.00
112-119: 117-Origin Professor X	3.40	10.00		24.00
120-1st app. Alpha Flight (cameo), story line begins (4/79); 1st app. Vindicator (formerly Weapon Alpha); last 35¢ issue	5.70	17.00		45.00
121-1st full Alpha Flight app.	6.50	19.50		50.00
122-128: 123-Spider-Man x-over. 124-Colossus becomes Proletarian	3.25	9.50		22.00
129-Intro Kitty Pryde (1/80); last Banshee; Dark Phoenix saga begins	3.75	11.25		28.00

	GD25	FN65	NM9•
130-1st app. The Dazzler by Byrne (2/80)	3.40	10.00	
131-135: 131-Dazzler app. 132-1st White Queen. 133-Wolverine app. 134-Phoenix becomes Dark Phoenix	2.30	6.70	
136,138: 138-Dazzler app.; Cyclops leaves	2.00	6.00	
137-Giant; death of Phoenix	2.60	7.50	
139-Alpha Flight app.; Kitty Pryde joins; new costume for Wolverine	4.30	13.00	
140-Alpha Flight app.	4.00	12.00	
141-Intro Future X-Men & The New Brotherhood of Evil Mutants; 1st app. Rachel (Phoenix II); Death of Franklin Richards	4.30	13.00	

X-MEN (2nd Series)
Oct, 1991 - Present ($1.00/$1.25/$1.95)
Marvel Comics

	GD25	FN65	NM
1 a-d ($1.50, 52 pgs.)-Jim Lee-c/a begins, ends #11; new team begins (Cyclops, Beast, Wolverine, Gambit, Psylocke & Rogue); new Uncanny X-Men & Magneto app.; four different covers exist	1.00	2.60	
1 e ($3.95)-Double gate-fold-c consisting of all four covers from 1a-d by Lee; contains all pin-ups from #1a-d plus inside-c foldout poster; no ad printed on coated stock	1.20	3.00	
2-7: 4-Wolverine back to old yellow costume (same date as Wolverine #8); last $1.00-c. 5-Byrne scripts. 6-Sabretooth-c/story	1.00	2.60	
8-10: 8-Gambit vs. Bishop-c/story; last Lee-a; Ghost Rider cameo cont'd Ghost Rider #26. 9-Wolverine vs. Ghost Rider; cont'd/G.R. #26. 10-Return of Longshot		1.60	
11-13,17-24,26-29,31: 12,13-Art Thibert-c/a. 28,29-Sabretooth-c/story		.80	
11-Silver ink 2nd printing; came with X-Men board game	2.85	8.50	
14-16-($1.50)-Polybagged with trading card in each; X-Cutioner's Song x-14-Andy Kubert-c/a begins		.80	
25-($3.50, 52 pgs.)-Wraparound-c with Gambit hologram on-c; Professor erases Magneto's mind..	2.15	6.50	
25-30th anniversary issue w/B&W-c with Magneto in color & Magneto holo & no price on-c	3.60	11.00	
25-Gold	4.30	13.00	
30-($3.50)-Wedding issue w/bound-in trading card sheet		1.60	
32-35: 32-Begin $1.50-c; bound-in card sheet. 33-Gambit & Sabretooth-c			
36,37-($2.95)-Collectors editions	1.00	2.00	
38-44,46-49,51-60: 42,43- Paul Smith-a. 46,49,53-56-Onslaught app. 51 scripts begin, end #56. 54-(Regular edition)-Onslaught revealed as Pr X. 55, 56-Onslaught x-over; Avengers, FF & Sentinels app. 56-Dr. Do app. 57-Xavier taken into custody; Byrne-c/swipe (X-Men, 1st Series #1		.80	
45 ($3.95)-Annual issue; gatefold-c		1.60	
50 ($2.95)-Vs. Onslaught, wraparound-c.		1.60	
50 ($3.95)-Vs. Onslaught, wraparound foil-c.	1.00	2.00	
50 ($2.95)-Variant-c.	1.30	3.25	
54-(Limited edition)-Embossed variant-c; Onslaught revealed as Professo			
Annual 1 (1992, $2.25, 68 pgs.)-Lee-c & layouts		1.00	
Annual 2 (1993, $2.95, 68 pgs.)-Bagged w/card		1.60	
Annual 3 (1994, $2.95)		1.60	
Ashcan #1			
Special '95 ($3.95)		1.60	
....FATAL ATTRACTIONS ('94, $17.95)-r/x-Factor #92, X-Force #25, Un X-Men #304, X-Men #25, Wolverine #75, & Excalibur #71			
....GOD LOVES, MAN KILLS (8/94, $6.95)-r/Marvel Graphic Novel #5	1.20	3.00	
...PREMIUM EDITION #1 (1993)-Cover says "Toys 'R' Us Limited Editio X-Men"			
...RARITIES (1995, $5.95)-Reprints	1.00	2.60	

624

X-Men: Clandestine #2 © MEG

X-Men Classic #76 © MEG

X-Men: The Early Years #16 © MEG

..: THE COMING OF BISHOP ('95, $12.95)-r/Uncanny X-Men #282-285,287,
288   13.00
OTE: *Jim Lee* a-1-11p; c-1-6p, 7, 8, 9p, 10, 11p. *Art Thibert* a-6-9i, 12, 13; c-6i, 12, 13.

-MEN ADVENTURES (TV)
ov, 1992 - No. 15, Jan, 1994 ($1.25)(Based on animated series)
arvel Comics

-Wolverine, Cyclops, Jubilee, Rogue, Gambit	.80	2.00
2-5: 3-Magneto-c/story	.80	2.00
6-10: 6-Sabretooth-c/story. 7-Cable-c/story. 10-Archangel guest star	.80	2.00
1-14: 11-Cable-c/story		1.25
5-($1.75, 52 pgs.)		.70	1.75

MEN ADVENTURES II (TV)
eb, 1994 - No. 13, Feb, 1995 ($1.25/$1.50)(Based on 2nd TV season)
arvel Comics

-8: 4-Bound-in trading card sheet. 5-Alpha Flight app.		1.25
-13: 9-Begin $1.50-c		1.50
Captive Hearts/Slave Island (TPB, $4.95)-r/X-Men Adventures #5-8	1.00	2.00	5.00
The Irresistible Force, The Muir Island Saga (5.95, 10/94, Trade Paperback)-r/X-Men Adventures #9-12	1.00	2.60	6.00

MEN ADVENTURES III (TV)(See Adventures of the X-Men)
r, 1995 - No. 13, Mar, 1996 ($1.50) (Based on 3rd TV season)
rvel Comics

13		1.50

MEN ALPHA
4 ($3.95, one-shot)
rvel Comics

Age of Apocalypse; wraparound chromium-c	1.20	3.00	7.00
$49.95)-Gold logo	7.00	21.50	50.00

MEN/ALPHA FLIGHT
, 1985 - No. 2, Dec, 1985 ($1.50, limited series)
vel Comics Group

2: 1-Intro The Berserkers; Paul Smith-a	1.00	2.00	5.00

EN AND THE MICRONAUTS, THE
1984 - No. 4, Apr, 1984 (Limited series)
vel Comics Group

: Guice-c/a(p) in all	.80	2.00

EN ARCHIVES
1995 - No. 4, Apr, 1995 ($2.25, limited series)
rvel Comics

: Reprints Legion stories from New Mutants	.90	2.25
Magneto app.	.90	2.25

EN ARCHIVES FEATURING CAPTAIN BRITAIN
1995 - No. 7, 1996 ($2.95, limited series)
el Comics

Reprints early Capt. Britain stories	1.20	3.00

N BOOKS OF ASKANI
($2.95, one-shot)
el Comics

ainted pin-ups w/text		3.00

N CHRONICLES
1995 (3.95, one-shot)
l Comics

Age of Apocalypse x-over: 1-wraparound-c	1.00	2.00	5.00

N: CLANDESTINE
996 - No. 2, Nov, 1996 ($2.95, limited series, 48 pgs.)

Marvel Comics

1,2: Alan Davis-c(p)/a(p)/scripts & Mark Farmer-c(i)/a(i) in all; wraparound-c		3.00

X-MEN CLASSIC (Formerly Classic X-Men)
No. 46, Apr, 1990 - No. 110, Aug, 1995 ($1.25/$1.50)
Marvel Comics

46-69,71-78,80-89,91-96,98,99: Reprints from X-Men. 54-($1.25, 52 pgs.). 57, 60-63,65-Russell-c(i); 62-r/X-Men #158(Rogue). 66-r/#162(Wolverine). 69-Begins-r of Paul Smith issues (#165 on)		1.50
70,79,90,97-($1.75, 52 pgs.). 70-r/X-Men #166. 90-r/#186		.80	2.00
100-110: 100-($1.50). 104-r/X-Men #200.		.70	1.75

X-MEN CLASSICS
Dec, 1983 - No. 3, Feb, 1984 ($2.00, Baxter paper)
Marvel Comics Group

1-3: X-Men-r by Neal Adams	1.20	3.00

NOTE: *Zeck* c-1-3.

X-MEN: EARTHFALL
Sept, 1996 ($2.95, one-shot)
Marvel Comics

1-r/Uncanny X-Men #232-234; wraparound-c		3.00

X-MEN OMEGA
June, 1995 ($3.95, one-shot)
Marvel Comics

nn-Age of Apocalypse finale	1.00	2.00	5.00
nn-($49.95)-Gold edition	7.00	21.50	50.00

X-MEN PRIME
July, 1995 ($4.95, one-shot)
Marvel Comics

nn-Post Age of Apocalypse begins	1.00	2.00	5.00

X-MEN RARITIES
1995 ($5.95, one-shot)
Marvel Comics

nn-Reprints hard-to-find stories	1.00	2.60	6.00

X-MEN ROAD TO ONSLAUGHT
Oct, 1996 ($2.50, one-shot)
Marvel Comics

nn-Retells Onslaught Saga		2.50

X-MEN SPOTLIGHT ON... STARJAMMERS (Also see X-Men #104)
1990 - No. 2, 1990 ($4.50, 52 pgs.)
Marvel Comics

1,2: Features Starjammers		1.80	4.50

X-MEN SURVIVAL GUIDE TO THE MANSION
Aug, 1993 ($6.95, spiralbound)
Marvel Comics

1	1.65	4.20	10.00

X-MEN: THE EARLY YEARS
May, 1994 - No. 17, Sept, 1995 ($1.50/$2.50)
Marvel Comics

1-16: r/X-Men #1-8 w/new-c		1.50
17-$2.50-c; r/X-Men #17,18		1.00	2.50

X-MEN: THE ULTRA COLLECTION
Dec, 1994 - No. 5, Apr, 1995 ($2.95, limited series)
Marvel Comics

1-5: Pin-ups; no scripts		1.20	3.00

X-MEN: THE WEDDING ALBUM
1994 ($2.95, magazine size, one-shot)
Marvel Comics

X-O Manowar #64 (1st Series) © Acclaim

X-O Manowar #2 (2nd Series) © Acclaim

XSE #3 © MEG

	GD25	FN65	NM94
1-Wedding of Scott Summers & Jean Grey		1.20	3.00

X-MEN 2099 (Also see 2099: World of Tomorrow)
Oct, 1993 - No. 35, Aug, 1996 ($1.25/$1.50/$1.95)
Marvel Comics

	GD25	FN65	NM94
1-($1.75)-Foil-c; Ron Lim/Adam Kubert-a begins		.80	2.00
1-2nd printing ($1.75)		.70	1.75
1-Gold edition (15,000 made); sold thru Diamond for $19.40	2.85	8.00	20.00
2-7: 3-Death of Tina; Lim-c/a(p) in #1-8			1.25
8-19: 8-Begin $1.50-c; bound-in trading card sheet			1.50
20-24,26-35: 20-$1.95-c begins. 35-Nostromo (from X-Nation) app; storyline cont'd in 2099: World of Tomorrow.		.80	2.00
25 ($2.50)-Double sized		1.00	2.50
Special 1 (3.95)		1.60	4.00

X-MEN ULTRA III PREVIEW
1995 ($2.95)
Marvel Comics

	GD25	FN65	NM94
nn-Kubert-a		1.20	3.00

X-MEN UNLIMITED
1993 - Present ($3.95, 68 pgs.)
Marvel Comics

	GD25	FN65	NM94
1-Chris Bachalo-c/a; Quesada-a.	1.30	3.25	8.00
2,4-9: 2-Origin of Magneto. script.		1.60	4.00
3-Sabretooth-c/story	1.20	3.00	7.00
10-Dark Beast vs. Beast; Mark Waid script			6.50
11,12: 11-Magneto & Rogue. 12-Onslaught x-over; Juggernaut-c/app.			

NOTE: *Bachalo c/a-1. Quesada a-1. Waid scripts-10*

X-MEN VS. DRACULA
Dec, 1993 ($1.75)
Marvel Comics

	GD25	FN65	NM94
1-r/X-Men Annual #6; Austin-c(i)		.70	1.75

X-MEN VS. THE AVENGERS, THE
Apr, 1987 - No. 4, July, 1987 ($1.50, limited series, Baxter paper)
Marvel Comics Group

	GD25	FN65	NM94
1		1.60	4.00
2-4		1.20	3.00

X-MEN VISIONARIES
1995 ($8.95, trade paperback)
Marvel Comics

	GD25	FN65	NM94
nn-Reprints X-Men stories; Adam & Andy Kubert-a			9.00

X-NATION 2099
Mar, 1996 - No. 6, Aug, 1996 ($1.95)
Marvel Comics

	GD25	FN65	NM94
1-($3.95)-Humberto Ramos-a(p); wraparound, foil-c			4.00
2-6: 2,3-Ramos-a. 4-Exodus-c/app. 5-Exodus cameo. 6-Reed Richards app			2.00

X-O MANOWAR (1st Series)
Feb, 1992 - No. 68, Sept, 1996 ($1.95/$2.25/$2.50, high quality)
Valiant/Acclaim (Valiant) No. 43 on

	GD25	FN65	NM94
0-(8/93, $3.50)-Wraparound embossed chromium-c by Quesada; Solar app.; origin Aric (X-O Manowar)		1.60	4.00
0-Gold variant		4.20	10.00
1-Intro/1st app. & partial origin of Aric (X-O Manowar); Barry Smith/Layton-a	1.65	4.20	10.00
2-4: 2-B. Smith/Layton-c; Layton part inks. 3-Layton-c(i). 4-1st app. Shadowman (cameo)	1.30	3.25	8.00
5-8: 5-B. Smith-c. 6-Begin $2.25-c; Ditko-a(p). 7,8-Unity x-overs. 7-Miller-c.			

	GD25	FN65	NM9
8-Simonson-c		1.00	2.00
9-13: 12-1st app. Randy Calder			1.20
14,15-Turok-c/stories		.80	1.60
15-Hot pink logo variant; came with Ultra Pro Rigid Comic Sleeves box; no price on cover		1.00	2.00
16-24,26-43: 20-Serial number contest insert. 27-29-Turok x-over. 28-Bou trading card. 30-1st app. new "good skin"; Solar app. 33-Chaos Effect Delta Pt. 3. 42-Shadowman app.; includes X-O Manowar Birthquake! Prequel			.90
25-($3.50)-Has 16 pg. Armorines #0 bound-in w/origin			1.40
44-68: 44-Begin $2.50-c. 50-X, 50-O, 51, 52, 63-Bart Sears-c/a/scripts. 68-Revealed that Aric's past stories were premonitions of his future			1.00

	GD25	FN65	NM9
Trade paperback nn (1993, $9.95)-Polybagged with copy of X-O Database inside	1.65	4.00	
Yearbook 1 (4/95, $2.95)			1.20

NOTE: *Layton a-1i, 2i(part); c-1, 2i, 3i, 6i, 21i. Reese a-4i(part); c-26i.*

X-O MANOWAR (2nd Series)
V2#1, Oct, 1996 - Present ($2.50)
Acclaim Comics (Valiant Heroes)

	GD25	FN65	NM9
V2#1-6: 1-Mark Waid & Brian Augustyn scripts begin; Rand Banion dies; p variant-c exists			

X-O MANOWAR/IRON MAN: IN HEAVY METAL (See Iron Man/X-O Mar Heavy Metal)
Sept, 1996 ($2.50, one-shot)
Acclaim Comics (Valiant Heroes)

	GD25	FN65	NM9
1-Pt 1 of X-O Manowar/Iron Man x-over; Arnim Zola app.; Fabian Nicieza scripts; Andy Smith-a			

XOMBI
Jan, 1994 - No. 21, Feb, 1996 ($1.75/$2.50)
DC Comics (Milestone)

	GD25	FN65	NM9
0-($1.95)-Shadow War x-over; Simonson silver ink varnish-c			.80
1-13: 1-John Byrne-a			.70
14-21: 14-Begin $2.50-c			1.00

X-PATROL
Apr, 1996 ($1.95, one-shot)
Marvel Comics (Amalgam)

	GD25	FN65	NM9
1-Cruz-a(p)			

XSE
Nov, 1996 - No. 4, Feb, 1997 ($1.95, limited series)
Marvel Comics

	GD25	FN65	NM9
1-4: 1-Bishop & Shard app.			
1-Variant-c			

X-TERMINATORS
Oct, 1988 - No. 4, Jan, 1989 ($1.00, limited series)
Marvel Comics

	GD25	FN65	NM9
1-1st app.; X-Men/X-Factor tie-in; Williamson-i			1.20
2			.70
3,4			

X, THE MAN WITH THE X-RAY EYES (See Movie Comics)

X-UNIVERSE
May, 1995 - No. 2, June, 1995 ($3.50, limited series)
Marvel Comics

	GD25	FN65	NM9
1,2: Age of Apocalypse		1.00	2.00

X-VENTURE (Super Heroes)
July, 1947 - No. 2, Nov, 1947
Victory Magazines Corp.

	GD25	FN65	NM9
1-Atom Wizard, Mystery Shadow, Lester Trumble begin	65.00	195.00	

Yankee Comics 32 © CHES

Yanks In Battle #1 © QUA

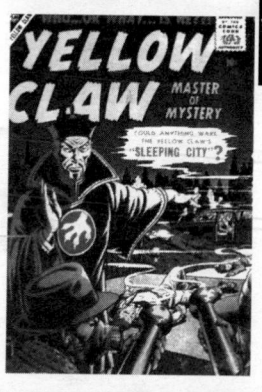
Yellow Claw #3 © ATLAS

	GD25	FN65	NM94
2	40.00	120.00	325.00

XYR (See Eclipse Graphic Album Series #21)

YAK YAK
No. 1186, May-July, 1961 - No. 1348, Apr-June, 1962
Dell Publishing Co.

Four Color 1186 (#1)- Jack Davis-c/a; 2 versions, one minus 3pgs.			
	9.00	27.00	90.00
Four Color 1348 (#2)-Davis c/a	9.00	27.00	90.00

YAKKY DOODLE & CHOPPER (TV) (Also see Spotlight #3 & Top Cat #4)
Dec, 1962 (Hanna-Barbera)
Gold Key

1	4.50	13.50	45.00

YALTA TO KOREA (Also see Korea My Home)
1952 (Giveaway, paper cover, 8 pgs.)
M. Phillip Corp. (Republican National Committee)

nn-Anti-communist propaganda book	19.00	58.00	135.00

YANG (See House of Yang)
Nov, 1973 - No. 13, May, 1976; V14#14, Sept, 1985 - No. 17, Jan, 1986
Charlton Comics

1-Origin		1.60	4.00
2-13(1976)		.80	2.00
14-17(1986)			1.00
3,10,11(Modern Comics-r, 1977)			1.00

YANKEE COMICS
Sept, 1941 - No. 5, 1942?
Harry 'A' Chesler

1-Origin The Echo, The Enchanted Dagger, Yankee Doodle Jones, The Firebrand, & The Scarlet Sentry; Black Satan app.; Yankee Doodle Jones app. on all covers
| | 112.00 | 338.00 | 900.00 |

2-Origin Johnny Rebel; Major Victory app.; Barry Kuda begins
| | 56.00 | 168.00 | 450.00 |

3,4: 4-(3/42)	44.00	132.00	350.00

4 (nd, 1940s; 7-1/4x5", 68 pgs, distr. to the service)-Foxy Grandpa, Tom, Dick & Harry, Impy, Ace & Deuce, Dot & Dash, Ima Slooth by Jack Cole (Remington Morse publ.)
| | 1.70 | 5.00 | 12.00 |

5-(nd; 10¢, 7-1/4x5", 68 pgs.)(Remington Morse publ.)-urges readers to send their copies to servicemen.

YANKS IN BATTLE
Sept, 1956 - No. 4, Dec, 1956; 1963
Quality Comics Group

1-Cuidera-c(i)	8.00	24.00	48.00
2-4: Cuidera-c(i)	4.25	13.00	28.00
.W. Reprint #3(1963)-r/#?; exist?	1.30	3.25	8.00

YARDBIRDS, THE (G. I. Joe's Sidekicks)
Summer, 1952
Ziff-Davis Publishing Co.

1-By Bob Oskner	8.70	26.00	52.00

YARN MAN (See Megaton Man)
Oct, 1989 ($2.00, B&W, one-shot)
Kitchen Sink

1-Donald Simpson-c/a/scripts		.80	2.00

YARNS OF YELLOWSTONE
1972 (50¢, 36 pgs.)
World Color Press

nn-Illustrated by Bill Chapman	1.00	2.00	5.00

YELLOW CLAW (Also see Giant Size Master of Kung Fu)
Oct, 1956 - No. 4, Apr, 1957
Atlas Comics (MjMC)

1-Origin by Joe Maneely	75.00	225.00	600.00
2-Kirby-a	62.00	187.00	500.00
3,4-Kirby-a; 4-Kirby/Severin-a	59.00	178.00	475.00

NOTE: Everett c-3. Maneely c-1. Reinman a-2i, 3. Severin c-2, 4.

YELLOWJACKET COMICS (Jack in the Box #11 on)(See TNT Comics)
Sept, 1944 - No. 10, June, 1946
E. Levy/Frank Comunale/Charlton

1-Intro & origin Yellowjacket; Diana, the Huntress begins; E.A. Poe's "The Black Cat" adaptation	47.00	141.00	375.00
2-Yellowjacket-c begin, end #10	29.00	86.00	200.00
3,5	27.00	81.00	190.00
4-E.A. Poe's "Fall of the House Of Usher" adaptation; Palais-a	28.00	84.00	195.00
6-10: 1,3,4,6-10-Have stories narrated by old witch in "Tales of Terror"	24.00	73.00	170.00

YELLOWSTONE KELLY (Movie)
No. 1056, Nov-Jan, 1959/60
Dell Publishing Co.

Four Color 1056-Clint Walker photo-c	5.40	16.00	54.00

YELLOW SUBMARINE (See Movie Comics)

YIN FEI THE CHINESE NINJA
1988 - No. 12?, 1990 ($1.80/$2.00, 52 pgs.)
Leung's Publications

1-6: 1-Begin $1.80-c		.90	1.80
7-12: 7-Begin $2.00-c		1.00	2.00

YOGI BEAR (See Dell Giant #41, Golden Comics Digest, Kite Fun Book, March of Comics #253, 265, 279, 291, 309, 319, 337, 344, Movie Comics under "Hey There It's…" & Whitman Comic Books)

YOGI BEAR (TV) (Hanna-Barbera) (See Four Color #990)
No. 1067, 12-2/59-60 - No. 9, 7-9/62; No. 10, 10/62 - No. 42, 10/70
Dell Publishing Co./Gold Key No. 10 on

Four Color 1067 (#1)-TV show debuted 1/30/61	10.00	30.00	100.00
Four Color 1104,1162 (5-7/61)	7.00	21.00	70.00
4(8-9/61) - 6(12-1/61-62)	4.50	13.50	45.00
Four Color 1271(11/61)	4.50	13.50	45.00
Four Color 1349(1/62)-Photo-c	9.00	27.00	90.00
7(2-3/62) - 9(7-9/62)-Last Dell	4.50	13.50	45.00
10(10/62-G.K.), 11(1/63)-titled "Yogi Bear Jellystone Jollies" (80 pgs.); 11-X-mas-c	5.00	15.00	50.00
12(4/63), 14-20	3.20	9.60	32.00
13(7/63, 68 pgs.)-Surprise Party	4.50	13.50	45.00
21-30	2.00	6.00	20.00
31-42	1.20	3.60	12.00
Giveaway ('84, '86)-City of Los Angeles, "Creative First Aid" & "Earthquake Preparedness for Children"	.80	2.00	

YOGI BEAR (TV)
Nov, 1970 - No. 35, Jan, 1976 (Hanna-Barbera)
Charlton Comics

1	3.25	9.50	22.00
2-6,8-10	1.70	5.00	12.00
7-Summer Fun (Giant, 52 pgs.)	2.30	6.75	16.00
11-35: 28-31-partial-r	1.30	3.25	8.00

YOGI BEAR (TV)(See The Flintstones, 3rd series & Spotlight #1)
Nov, 1977 - No. 9, Mar, 1979 (Hanna-Barbera)
Marvel Comics Group

1-Flintstones begin		.80	2.00
2-9			1.50

YOGI BEAR (TV)
Sept, 1992 - No. 6, Mar, 1994 ($1.25/$1.50) (Hanna-Barbera)
Harvey Comics

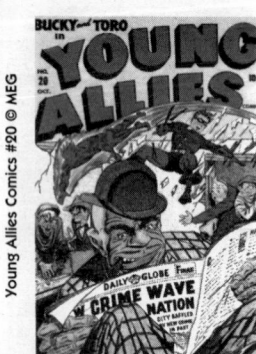

Young Allies Comics #20 © MEG

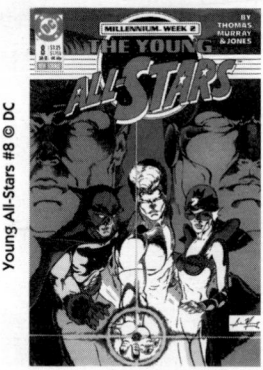

Young All-Stars #8 © DC

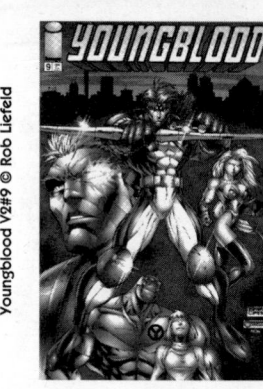

Youngblood V2#9 © Rob Liefeld

	GD25	FN65	NM94
V2#1-4			1.25
5,6: 5-Begin $1.50-c			1.50
...Big Book V2#1,2 ($1.95, 52 pgs): 1-(11/92). 2-(3/93)		.80	2.00
...Giant Size V2#1,2 ($2.25, 68 pgs.): 1-(10/92). 2-(4/93)		.90	2.25

YOGI BEAR'S EASTER PARADE (See The Funtastic World of Hanna-Barbera #2)

YOGI BERRA (Baseball hero)
1951 (Yankee catcher)
Fawcett Publications

	GD25	FN65	NM94
nn-Photo-c	56.00	168.00	450.00

YOSEMITE SAM (...& Bugs Bunny)
Dec, 1970 - No. 81, Feb, 1984
Gold Key/Whitman

	GD25	FN65	NM94
1	1.70	5.00	12.00
2-10	1.00	2.00	5.00
11-30		1.20	3.00
31-81: 81-(1/3-r)		.80	2.00

(See March of Comics #363, 380, 392)

YOUNG ALLIES COMICS (All-Winners #21; see Kid Komics #2)
Summer, 1941 - No. 20, Oct, 1946
Timely Comics (USA 1-7/NPI 8,9/YAI 10-20)

	GD25	FN65	VF82	NM94
1-Origin/1st app. The Young Allies (Bucky, Toro, others); 1st meeting of Captain America & Human Torch; Red Skull-c & app.; S&K-c/splash; Hitler-c	920.00	2760.00	5520.00	9200.00

(Estimated up to 165 total copies exist, 9 in NM/Mint)

	GD25	FN65	NM94
2-(Winter, 1941)-Captain America & Human Torch app.; Simon & Kirby-c	255.00	766.00	2300.00
3-Fathertime, Captain America & Human Torch app.; Remember Pearl Harbor issue (Spring, 1942); Stan Lee scripts; Vs. Japs-c/full-length story	206.00	618.00	1650.00
4-The Vagabond & Red Skull, Capt. America, Human Torch app. Classic Red Skull-c	288.00	862.00	2600.00
5-Captain America & Human Torch app.	125.00	375.00	1000.00
6-8,10: 10-Origin Tommy Tyme & Clock of Ages; ends #19	90.00	271.00	725.00
9-Hitler, Tojo, Mussolini-c.	96.00	290.00	775.00
11-20: 12-Classic decapitation story	75.00	225.00	600.00

NOTE: **Brodsky** c-15. **Gabrielle** a-3; c-3, 4. **S&K** c-1, 2. **Schomburg** c-5-14, 16-19. **Shores** c-20.

YOUNG ALL-STARS
June, 1987 - No. 31, Nov, 1989 ($1.00, deluxe format)
DC Comics

	GD25	FN65	NM94
1-31: 1-1st app. Iron Munro & The Flying Fox. 7-18-$1.25. 8,9-Millennium tie-ins. 19-23-$1.50. 24-Begin $1.75-c		.80	2.00
Annual 1 (1988, $2.00)		.80	2.00

YOUNGBLOOD (See Brigade #4, Megaton Explosion & Team Youngblood)
Apr, 1992 - No. 4, Feb, 1993 (limited series);
No. 6, June, 1994 (No #5) - No. 10, Dec, 1994 ($1.95/$2.50)
Image Comics (Extreme Studios)

	GD25	FN65	NM94
1-Liefeld-c/a/scripts in all; flip book format with 2 trading cards; 1st Image/Extreme Studios title.	1.00	2.00	5.00
1-2nd printing		1.20	3.00
2-(JUN-c, July 1992 indicia)-1st app. Shadowhawk in solo back-up story; 2 trading cards inside; flip book format; 1st app. Prophet, Kirby, Berzerkers, Darkthorn		1.20	3.00
2-2nd printing (1.95)		.80	2.00
3-(OCT-c, August 1992 indicia)-Contains 2 trading cards inside (flip book); 1st app. Supreme in back-up story; 1st app. Showdown	1.00		2.50
0-(12/92, $1.95)-Contains 2 trading cards; 2 cover variations exist, green or beige logo; w/Image #0 coupon		.80	2.00
4, 5:4-(2/93)-Glow-in-the-dark-c w/2 trading cards; 2nd app. Dale Keown's The			

	GD25	FN65	NM94
Pitt; Bloodstrike app.		1.00	2.5
6-($3.50, 52 pgs.)-Wraparound-c		1.40	3.
7-10: 7, 8-Liefeld-c(p)/a(p)/story. 8,9-(9/94) 9-Valentino story & art		1.00	2.5
Battlezone 1 (MAY-c, 4/93 inside, $1.95)-Arsenal book; Liefeld-c(p)		.80	2.
Battlezone 2 (7/94, $2.95)-Wraparound-c		1.20	3.
Yearbook 1 (7/93, $2.50)-Fold out panel; 1st app. Tyrax & Kanan		1.00	2.
Trade paperback (1996, $16.95)-r/Team Youngblood #8-10 & Youngblood #6-10			17.

YOUNGBLOOD
V2#1, Sept, 1995 - Present ($2.50)
Image Comics (Extreme Studios)/Maximum Press No. 14 on

	GD25	FN65	NM94
V2#1-10,14: Roger Cruz-a in all. 4-Extreme Destroyer Pt. 4 w/gaming card. 5-Variant-c exists. 6-Angela & Glory. 7-Shadowhawk Pt. 3; Shadowhawk a 8,10-Thor (from Supreme) app. 10-(7/96). 14-(12/96)-1st Maximum Press issue		1.00	2.5

YOUNGBLOOD: STRIKEFILE
Apr, 1993 - No. 11, Feb, 1995 ($1.95/$2.50/$2.95)
Image Comics (Extreme)

	GD25	FN65	NM94
1-($1.95)-Flip book w/Jae Lee-c/a & Liefeld-c/a in #1-3; 1st app. The Allies, Giger, & Glory		.80	2.
2-4,11: 2-Begin $2.50. 3-Thibert-i asisst. 4-Liefeld-c(p); no Lee-a		1.00	2.5
5-10: 5-Begin $2.95-c; Liefeld-c(p). 8-Platt-c		1.20	3.

NOTE: Youngblood: Strikefile began as a four issue limited series.

YOUNGBLOOD/X-FORCE
July, 1996 ($4.95, one-shot)
Image Comics (Extreme Studios)

	GD25	FN65	NM94
1-Cruz-a(p); two covers exist			5.

YOUNG BRIDES (True Love Secrets)
Sept-Oct, 1952 - No. 30, Nov-Dec, 1956 (Photo-c: 1-4)
Feature/Prize Publications

	GD25	FN65	NM94
V1#1-Simon & Kirby-a	24.00	71.00	165.
2-S&K-a	12.00	36.00	85.
3-6-S&K-a	11.00	33.00	75.
V2#1,3,7-10,12 (#7-18)-S&K-a	10.00	30.00	70.
2,8,9-No S&K-a	4.00	10.00	20.
V3#1-3(#19-21)-Last precode (3-4/55)	3.20	8.00	16.
4,6(#22,24), V4#1,3(#25,27)	2.40	6.00	12.
V3#5(#23)-Meskin-c	3.60	9.00	18.
V4#2(#26)-All S&K issue	9.15	27.00	55.
V4#4(#28)-S&K-a	7.50	22.50	45.
V4#5,6(#29,30)	4.00	11.00	22.

YOUNG DR. MASTERS (See The Adventures of Young Dr. Masters)

YOUNG DOCTORS, THE
Jan, 1963 - No. 6, Nov, 1963
Charlton Comics

	GD25	FN65	NM94
V1#1	1.20	3.00	6.
2-6	.60	1.50	3.

YOUNG EAGLE
12/50 - No. 10, 6/52; No. 3, 7/56 - No. 5, 4/57 (Photo-c: 1-10)
Fawcett Publications/Charlton

	GD25	FN65	NM94
1-Intro Young Eagle	15.00	45.00	105.
2-Complete picture novelette "The Mystery of Thunder Canyon"	8.35	25.00	50.
3-9	7.50	22.50	45.
10-Origin Thunder, Young Eagle's Horse	5.35	16.00	32.
3-5(Charlton)-Formerly Sherlock Holmes?	4.00	11.00	22.

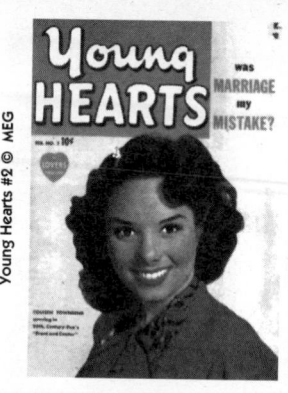
Young Hearts #2 © MEG

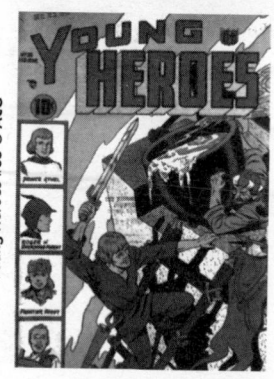
Young Heroes #35 © ACG

Young King Cole #3 © NP

YO

	GD25	FN65	NM94

YOUNG HEARTS
Nov, 1949 - No. 2, Feb, 1950
Marvel Comics (SPC)

1-Photo-c	10.00	30.00	60.00
2-Colleen Townsend photo-c from movie	6.35	19.00	38.00

YOUNG HEARTS IN LOVE
1964
Super Comics

17,18: 17-r/Young Love V5#6 (4-5/62)	1.00	2.60	6.00

YOUNG HEROES (Formerly Forbidden Worlds #34)
No. 35, Feb-Mar, 1955 - No. 37, June-July, 1955
American Comics Group (Titan)

35-37-Frontier Scout	8.00	24.00	48.00

YOUNG INDIANA JONES CHRONICLES, THE
Feb, 1992 - No. 12, Feb, 1993 ($2.50)
Dark Horse Comics

1-12: Dan Barry scripts in all	1.00		2.50

NOTE: **Dan Barry** a(p)-1, 2, 5, 6, 10; c-1-10. **Morrow** a-3, 4, 5p, 6p. **Springer** a-1i, 2i.

YOUNG INDIANA JONES CHRONICLES, THE
1992 ($3.95, squarebound, 68 pgs.)
Hollywood Comics (Disney)

1-3: 1-r/YIJC #1,2 by D. Horse. 2-r/#3,4. 3-r/#5,6	1.60		4.00

YOUNG KING COLE (...Detective Tales)(Becomes Criminals on the Run)
Fall, 1945 - V3#12, July, 1948
Premium Group/Novelty Press

V1#1-Toni Gayle begins	214.00	73.00	170.00
2	11.00	33.00	75.00
3-4	10.00	30.00	65.00
V2#1-7(8-9/46-7/47): 6,7-Certa-c	7.50	22.50	45.00
V3#1,3-6,8,9,12: 3-Certa-c. 5-McWilliams-c/a. 8,9-Harmon-c			
	6.70	20.00	40.00
2-L.B. Cole-a; Certa-c	10.00	30.00	70.00
7-L.B. Cole-c/a	13.00	39.00	90.00
10,11-L.B. Cole-c	11.00	33.00	75.00

YOUNG LAWYERS, THE (TV)
Jan, 1971 - No. 2, Apr, 1971
Dell Publishing co.

1,2	1.70	5.00	12.00

YOUNG LIFE (Teen Life #3 on)
Summer, 1945 - No. 2, Fall, 1945
New Age Publ./Quality Comics Group

1-Skip Homeier, Louis Prima stories	11.00	33.00	75.00
2-Frank Sinatra photo on-c plus story	11.00	33.00	75.00

YOUNG LOVE (Sister title to Young Romance)
2/49 - No. 73, 12-1/56-57; V3#5, 2-3/60 - V7#1, 6-7/63
Prize(Feature)Publ.(Crestwood)

V1#1-S&K-c/a(2)	37.00	111.00	260.00
2-Photo-c begin; S&K-a(2)	18.00	54.00	125.00
3-S&K-a	13.50	41.00	95.00
4-5-Minor S&K-a	9.15	27.00	55.00
V2#1(#7)-S&K-a(2)	13.50	41.00	95.00
2-5(#8-11)-Minor S&K-a	6.70	20.00	40.00
6,8(#12,14)-S&K-c only. 14-S&K 1 pg. art	9.15	27.00	55.00
7,9-12(#13,15-18)-S&K-c/a	12.00	36.00	85.00
V3#1-4(#19-22)-S&K-c/a	11.00	33.00	75.00
5,7-9,12(#23-25,27-30)-Photo-c resume; S&K-a	10.00	30.00	65.00
8(#26)-No S&K-a	4.00	10.00	20.00
V4#1,6(#31,36)-S&K-a	10.00	30.00	60.00
2-5,7-12(#32-35,37-42)-Minor S&K-a	6.70	20.00	40.00

V5#1-12(#43-54), V6#1-9(#55-63)-Last precode; S&K-a in some

	4.00	11.00	22.00
V6#10-12(#64-66)	3.00	7.50	15.00
V7#1-7(#67-73)	2.40	6.00	12.00
V3#5(2-3/60),6(4-5/60)(Formerly All For Love)	1.80	4.50	9.00
V4#1(6-7/60)-6(4-5/61)	1.60	4.00	8.00
V5#1(6-7/61)-6(4-5/62)	1.60	4.00	8.00
V6#1(6-7/62)-6(4-5/63), V7#1	1.20	3.00	6.00

NOTE: **Meskin** a-14(2), 27, 42. **Powell** a-V4#6. **Severin/Elder** a-V1#3. S&K art not in #53, 57, 58, 61, 63-65. Photo c-V3#5-V5#11.

YOUNG LOVE
#39, 9-10/63 - #120, Wint./75-76; #121, 10/76 - #126, 7/77
National Periodical Publ.(Arleigh Publ. Corp #49-60)/DC Comics

39	5.00	15.00	30.00
40-50	3.20	8.00	16.00
51-63,65-70	2.80	7.00	14.00
64-Simon & Kirby-a	3.60	9.00	18.00
71,72,74-77,80	1.50	3.75	9.00
73,78,79-Toth-a		1.60	4.00
81-126: 107-114-(100 pgs.): 107-DC 100 Pg. Super Spect.	.80		2.00

NOTE: **Bolle** a-117. **Colan** a-107r. **Nasser** a-123, 124. **Orlando** a-122. **Simonson** c-125. **Toth** a-73, 78, 79, 122-125r. **Wood** a-109(4 pgs.).

YOUNG LOVER ROMANCES (Formerly & becomes Great Lover...)
No. 4, June, 1952 - No. 5, Aug, 1952
Toby Press

4,5-Photo-c	4.25	13.00	28.00

YOUNG LOVERS (My Secret Life #19 on)(Formerly Brenda Starr?)
No. 16, July, 1956 - No. 18, May, 1957
Charlton Comics

16,17('56): 16-Marcus Swayze-a	4.00	12.00	24.00
18-Elvis Presley picture-c, text story (biography)(Scarce)			
	47.00	141.00	375.00

YOUNG MARRIAGE
June, 1950
Fawcett Publications

1-Powell-a; photo-c	10.00	30.00	60.00

YOUNG MEN (Formerly Cowboy Romances)(...on the Battlefield #12-20
(4/53); ...In Action #21)
No. 4, 6/50 - No. 11, 10/51; No. 12, 12/51 - No. 28, 6/54
Marvel/Atlas Comics (IPC)

4-(52 pgs.)	13.50	41.00	95.00
5-11	9.15	27.00	55.00
12-23: 12-20-War format. 21-23-Hot Rod issues starring Flash Foster			
	8.00	24.00	48.00
24-(12/53)-Origin Captain America, Human Torch, & Sub-Mariner which are revived thru #28; Red Skull app.	121.00	365.00	975.00
25-28: 25-Romita-c/a (see Men's Advs.)	87.00	262.00	700.00

NOTE: **Berg** a-7, 14, 17, 18, 20; c-17? **Brodsky** c-4-9, 13, 14, 16, 17, 21-25. **Burgos** a-26-28. **Colan** a-14, 15. **Everett** a-18-20. **Heath** a-13, 14. **Maneely** c-10, 12, 15. **Pakula** a-14, 15. **Robinson** a-18. Captain America by **Romita**-#24?, 25, 26?, 27, 28. Human Torch by **Burgos**-#25, 27, 28. Sub-Mariner by **Everett**-#24-28.

YOUNG REBELS, THE (TV)
Jan, 1971
Dell Publishing Co.

1-Photo-c	1.65	4.00	10.00

YOUNG ROMANCE COMICS (The 1st romance comic)
Sept-Oct, 1947 - V16#4, June-July, 1963 (#1-33: 52 pgs.)
Prize/Headline Feature Publ. (Crestwood)

V1#1-S&K-c/a(2)	39.00	116.00	270.00
2-S&K-c/a(2-3)	24.00	71.00	165.00
3-6-S&K-c/a(2-3) each	21.00	64.00	150.00

Youthful Romances #1 © YM

Zago, Jungle Prince #2 © FOX

Zatanna #3 © DC

	GD25	FN65	NM94
V2#1-6(#7-12)-S&K-c/a(2-3) each	18.00	54.00	125.00
V3#1-3(#13-15): V3#1-Photo-c begin; S&K-a	11.50	34.00	80.00
4-12(#16-24)-Photo-c; S&K-a	11.50	34.00	80.00
V4#1-11(#25-35)-S&K-a	11.00	33.00	75.00
12(#36)-S&K, Toth-a	13.50	41.00	95.00
V5#1-12(#37-48), V6#4-12(#52-60)-S&K-a	11.00	33.00	75.00
V6#1-3(#49-51)-No S&K-a	4.00	12.00	24.00
V7#1-11(#61-71)-S&K-a in most	10.00	30.00	60.00
V7#12(#72), V8#1-3(#73-75)-Last precode (12-1/54-55)-No S&K-a			
	3.20	8.00	16.00
V8#1(#76, 4-5/55), 5(#77)-No S&K-a	2.80	7.00	14.00
V8#6-8(#78-80, 12-1/55-56)-S&K-a	6.70	20.00	40.00
V9#3,5,6(#81, 2-3/56, 83,84)-S&K-a	6.70	20.00	40.00
4, V10#1(#82,85)-All S&K-a	8.35	25.00	50.00
V10#2-6(#86-90, 10-11/57)-S&K-a	6.70	20.00	40.00
V11#1,2,5,6(#91,92,95,96)-S&K-a	6.70	20.00	40.00
3,4(#93,94), V12#2,4,5(#98,100,101)-No S&K	1.70	5.00	12.00
V12#1,3,6(#97,99,102)-S&K-a	6.70	20.00	40.00
V13#1(#103)-Powell-a; S&K's last-a for Crestwood	6.70	20.00	40.00
2-6(#104-108)	1.30	3.25	8.00
V14#1-6, V15#1-6, V16#1-4(#109-124)	1.00	2.60	6.00

NOTE: **Meskin**-a-16, 24(2), 33, 47, 50. **Robinson/Meskin**-a-6. **Leonard Starr**-a-11. Photo c-13-32, 34-65. Issues 1-3 say "Designed for the More **Adult** Readers of **Comics**" on cover.

YOUNG ROMANCE COMICS (Continued from Prize series)
No. 125, Aug-Sept, 1963 - No. 208, Nov-Dec, 1975
National Periodical Publ.(Arleigh Publ. Corp. No. 127)

125	4.30	13.00	35.00
126-162: 154-Neal Adams-c	2.60	7.50	18.00
163,164-Toth-a	2.00	6.00	14.00
165-196: 170-Michell from Young Love ends; Lily Martin, the Swinger begins			
	1.20	3.00	7.00
197-208: 197-204-(100 pgs.)		1.60	4.00

YOUNG ZEN: CITY OF DEATH
Late 1994 ($3.25, B&W)
Entity Comics

1		1.30	3.25

YOUNG ZEN INTERGALACTIC NINJA (Also see Zen…)
1993 - No. 3, 1994 ($2.95, B&W)
Entity Comics

1-($3.50)-Polybagged w/Sam Kieth chromium trading card; gold foil logo			
		1.40	3.50
2,3-($2.95)-Gold foil logo		1.20	3.00

YOUR DREAMS (See Strange World of…)

YOU'RE UNDER ARREST (Manga)
Dec, 1995 - No. 8, July, 1996 ($2.95, limited series)
Dark Horse Comics

1-8			3.00

YOUR TRIP TO NEWSPAPERLAND
June, 1955 (14x11-1/2", 12 pgs.)
Philadelphia Evening Bulletin (Printed by Harvey Press)

nn-Joe Palooka takes kids on newspaper tour	4.00	11.00	22.00

YOUR UNITED STATES
1946
Lloyd Jacquet Studios

nn-Used in **SOTI**, pg. 309,310; Sid Greene-a	22.00	66.00	155.00

YOUTHFUL HEARTS (Daring Confessions #4 on)
May, 1952 - No. 3, Sept, 1952
Youthful Magazines

1- "Monkey on Her Back" swipes E.C. drug story/Shock SuspenStories #12; Frankie Laine photo on-c; Doug Wildey-a in all	21.00	62.00	145.00

	GD25	FN65	NM94
2,3: 2-Vic Damone photo on-c. 3-Johnny Raye photo on-c			
	14.00	43.00	100

YOUTHFUL LOVE (Truthful Love #2)
May, 1950
Youthful Magazines

1	8.70	26.00	52

YOUTHFUL ROMANCES
8-9/49 - No. 5, 4/50; No. 6, 2/51; No. 7, 5/51 - #14, 10/52; #15, 1/53 - #18, 7/53; No. 5, 9/53 - No. 9, 8/54
Pix-Parade #1-14/Ribage #15 on

1-(1st series)-Titled Youthful Love-Romances	18.00	54.00	125
2-Walter Johnson c-1-4	10.00	30.00	70
3-5	9.15	27.00	55
6,7,9-14(10/52, Pix-Parade; becomes Daring Love)			
photo-c. 10(1/52)-Mel Torme photo-c/story. 13-Richard Hayes (singer) ph			
c/story; Bob & Ray photo/text story.	7.50	22.50	45
8-Wood-c	13.00	39.00	90
15-18 (Ribage)-All have photos on-c. 15-Spike Jones photo-c/story			
	5.85	17.50	35
5(9/53, Ribage)-Les Paul & Mary Ford photo-c/story; Charlton Heston			
photo/text story	5.00	15.00	30
6-9: 6-Bobby Wayne (singer) photo-c/story; Debbie Reynolds photo/text sto			
7(2/54)-Tony Martin photo-c/story; Cyd Charise photo/text story. 8(5/54)-			
Gordon McCrae photo-c/story. 9(8/54)-Ralph Flanagan (band leader) ph			
c/story; Audrey Hepburn photo/text story.	4.00	12.00	24

YUPPIES FROM HELL (Also see Son of…)
1989 ($2.95, B&W, one-shot, direct sales, 52 pgs.)
Marvel Comics

1-Satire		1.20	3

ZAGO, JUNGLE PRINCE (My Story #5 on)
Sept, 1948 - No. 4, Mar, 1949
Fox Features Syndicate

1-Blue Beetle app.; partial-r/Atomic #4 (Toni Luck)	48.00	144.00	385
2,3-Kamen-a	39.00	116.00	270
4-Baker-c	33.00	99.00	230

ZANE GREY'S STORIES OF THE WEST
No. 197, 9/48 - No. 996, 5-7/59, 11/64 (All painted-c)
Dell Publishing Co./Gold Key 11/64

Four Color 197(#1)(9/48)	11.50	34.50	115
Four Color 222,230,236('49)	7.00	21.00	70
Four Color 246,255,270,301,314,333,346	4.50	13.50	36
Four Color 357,372,395,412,433,449,467,484	3.60	10.80	36
Four Color 511-Kinstler-a; Kubert-a	4.50	13.50	45
Four Color 532,555,583,604,616,632(5/55)	3.60	10.80	36
27(9-11/55) - 39(9-11/58)	3.20	9.60	32
Four Color 996(5-7/59)	3.20	9.60	32
10131-411-(11/64-G.K.)-Nevada; r/4-Color #996	1.80	5.40	18

ZANY (Magazine)(Satire)(See Frantic & Ratfink)
Sept, 1958 - No. 4, May, 1959
Candor Publ. Co.

1-Bill Everett-c	8.35	25.00	50
2-4: 4-Everett-c	5.85	17.50	35

ZATANNA (See Adv. Comics #413, JLA #161, Supergirl #1, World's Finest Comics #274)
July, 1993 - No. 4, Oct, 1993 ($1.95, limited series)
DC Comics

1-4		.80	2
Special 1(1987, $2.00)-Gray Morrow-c/a		1.00	2

ZAZA, THE MYSTIC (Formerly Charlie Chan; This Magazine Is Haunted

Zealot #3 © Aegis Entertainment

Zero Hour #3 © DC

Zip Comics #22 © MLJ

	GD25	FN65	NM94

V2#12 on)
No. 10, Apr, 1956 - No. 11, Sept, 1956
Charlton Comics

10,11	10.00	30.00	60.00

ZEALOT (Also see WildC.A.T.S: Covert Action Teams)
Aug, 1995 - No. 3, Nov, 1995 ($2.50, limited series)
Image Comics

1-3		1.00	2.50

ZEGRA JUNGLE EMPRESS (Formerly Tegra)(My Love Life #6 on)
No. 2, Oct, 1948 - No. 5, April, 1949
Fox Features Syndicate

2	50.00	150.00	400.00
3-5	40.00	120.00	290.00

ZEN INTERGALACTIC NINJA
1987 ($1.75, B&W)
No Publisher

1,2: Copyright-Stern & Cote	1.00	2.50	5.00

ZEN, INTERGALACTIC NINJA (Also see Young Zen...)
Sept, 1992 - No. 4, 1993? ($1.25)(Formerly a B&W comic by Zen Comics)
Zen Comics/Archie Comics

1-4: 1-Origin Zen; contains mini-poster			1.25

ZEN INTERGALACTIC NINJA
No. 0, June-July, 1993 - No. 3, 1994 ($2.95, B&W, limited series)
Entity Comics

0-Gold foil stamped-c; photo-c of Zen model		1.20	3.00
1-3: Gold foil stamped-c; Bill Maus-c/a		1.20	3.00
0-(1993, $3.50, color)-Chromium-c by Jae Lee		1.40	3.50

ZEN INTERGALACTIC NINJA: APRIL FOOL'S SPECIAL
1994 ($2.50, B&W)
Parody Press

1-w/flip story of Renn Intergalactic Chihuahua		1.00	2.50

ZEN INTERGALACTIC NINJA COLOR
1994 - No. 7, 1995? ($2.25)
Entity Comics

1-($3.95)-Chromium die cut-c		1.60	4.00
1-($2.25)		.90	2.25
1-($2.25)-Newsstand; Jae Lee-c; r/...All New Color Special #0		.90	2.25
2-($2.50)-Flip book		1.00	2.50
2-($3.50)-Flip book, polybagged w/chromium trading card		1.40	3.50
3-5: 3-Begin $2.50-c		1.00	2.50
6,7: 6-Begin $2.95-c		1.20	3.00
Yearbook: Hazardous Duty 1 (1995)		1.20	3.00

ZEN INTERGALACTIC NINJA MILESTONE
1994 - No. 3, 1994 ($2.95, limited series)
Entity Comics

1-3: Gold foil logo; r/Defend the Earth		1.20	3.00

ZEN INTERGALATIC NINJA SPRING SPECTACULAR
1994 ($2.95, B&W, one-shot)
Entity Comics

1-Gold foil logo		1.20	3.00

ZEN INTERGALACTIC NINJA STARQUEST
1994 - No. 7, 1995? ($2.95, B&W)
Entity Comics

1-7: Gold foil logo		1.20	3.00

ZEN, INTERGALACTIC NINJA: THE HUNTED
1993 - No. 3, 1994 ($2.95, B&W, limited series)
Entity Comics

	GD25	FN65	NM94

1-3: Newsstand Edition; foil logo		1.20	3.00
1-($3.50)-Polybagged w/chromium card by Kieth; foil logo		1.40	3.50

ZERO HOUR: CRISIS IN TIME (Also see Showcase '94 #8-10)
No. 4(#1), Sept, 1994 - No. 0(#5), Oct, 1994 ($1.50, limited series)
DC Comics

4(#1)-0(#5)		.80	2.00
"Ashcan"-(1994, free, B&W, 8 pgs.)			1.00

ZERO PATROL, THE
Nov, 1984 - No. 2; 1987 - No. 5, 1989? ($2.00)
Continuity Comics

1,2: Neal Adams-c/a; Megalith begins		.80	2.00
1-5 (#1,2-reprints above, 1987)		.80	2.00

ZERO TOLERANCE
Oct, 1990 - No. 4, Jan, 1991 ($2.25, limited series)
First Comics

1-4: Tim Vigil-c/a(p) (his 1st color limited series)		.90	2.25

ZERO ZERO
Mar, 1995 - Present ($3.95, B&W, anthology, mature)
Fantagraphics

1-10		1.60	4.00

ZIGGY PIG-SILLY SEAL COMICS (See Animal Fun, Animated Movie-Tunes,
Comic Capers, Krazy Komics, Silly Tunes & Super Rabbit)
Fall, 1944 - No. 6, Fall, 1946
Timely Comics (CmPL)

1-Vs. the Japs	19.00	56.00	130.00
2	10.00	30.00	65.00
3-5	9.15	27.00	55.00
6-Infinity-c	10.00	30.00	70.00
I.W. Reprint #1(1958)-r/Krazy Komics	1.20	3.00	7.00
I.W. Reprint #2,7,8	1.00	2.60	6.00

ZIP COMICS
Feb, 1940 - No. 47, Summer, 1944 (#1-7?: 68 pgs.)
MLJ Magazines

1-Origin Kalathar the Giant Man, The Scarlet Avenger, & Steel Sterling; Mr. Satan (by Edd Ashe), Nevada Jones (masked hero) & Zambini, the Miracle Man, War Eagle, Captain Valor begins	350.00	1050.00	3200.00
2-Nevada Jones adds mask & horse Blaze	168.00	506.00	1350.00
3	118.00	356.00	950.00
4,5	96.00	290.00	775.00
6-8	83.00	249.00	665.00
9-Last Kalathar & Mr. Satan; classic-c	93.00	281.00	750.00
10-Inferno, the Flame Breather begins, ends #13	89.00	268.00	715.00
11,12: 11-Inferno without costume	68.00	206.00	550.00
13-17,19: 17-Last Scarlet Avenger	68.00	206.00	550.00
18-Wilbur begins (9/41, 1st app.)	71.00	215.00	575.00
20-Origin & 1st app. Black Jack (11/41); Hitler-c	106.00	318.00	850.00
21-26: 25-Last Nevada Jones. 26-Black Witch begins; last Captain Valor	62.00	187.00	500.00
27-Intro. Web (7/42) plus-c app.	110.00	330.00	880.00
28-Origin Web	103.00	309.00	825.00
29,30: 29-The Hyena app.	90.00	150.00	400.00
31-38: 34-1st Applejack app. 35-Last Zambini, Black Jack. 38-Last Web issue	40.00	120.00	300.00
39-Red Rube begins (origin, 8/43)	40.00	120.00	300.00
40-47: 45-Wilbur ends	33.00	99.00	230.00

NOTE: Biro a-5, 9, 17; c-3-17. Meskin a-1-3, 5-7, 9, 10, 12, 13, 15, 16 at least. Montana c-29, 30, 32-35. Novick c-18-28, 31. Sahle c-37, 38, 40-46. Bondage c-8, 9, 33, 34. Cover features: Steel Sterling 1-43, 47; (w/Blackjack-20-27 & Web-27-35), 28-39; (w/Red Rube-40-43); Red Rube-44-47.

ZIP-JET (Hero)
Feb, 1953 - No. 2, Apr-May, 1953

Zoot Comics #10 © FOX

Zorro #3 © Johnston McCulley

Zot #24 © Scott McCloud

	GD25	FN65	NM94

St. John Publishing Co.
1-Rocketman-r from Punch Comics; #1-c from splash in Punch #10

		GD25	FN65	NM94
		50.00	150.00	400.00
2		40.00	120.00	300.00

ZIPPY THE CHIMP (CBS TV Presents…)
No. 50, March, 1957; No. 51, Aug, 1957
Pines (Literary Ent.)

50,51	5.00	15.00	30.00

ZODY, THE MOD ROB
July, 1970
Gold Key

1	1.20	3.00	7.00

ZONE (Also see Dark Horse Presents)
1990 ($1.95, B&W)
Dark Horse Comics

1-Character from Dark Horse Presents	.80	2.00

ZONE CONTINUM, THE
1994 ($2.95, B&W)
Caliber Press

1	1.20	3.00

ZOO ANIMALS
No. 8, 1954 (15¢, 36 pgs.)
Star Publications

8-(B&W for coloring)	4.00	12.00	24.00

ZOO FUNNIES (Tim McCoy #16 on)
Nov, 1945 - No. 15, 1947
Charlton Comics/Children Comics Publ.

101(#1)(11/45, 1st Charlton comic book)-Funny animal; Al Fago-c			
	16.00	47.00	110.00
2(12/45, 52 pgs.)	9.15	27.00	55.00
3-5	7.50	22.50	45.00
6-15: 8-Diana the Huntress app.	5.35	16.00	32.00

ZOO FUNNIES (Becomes Nyoka, The Jungle Girl #14 on?)
July, 1953 - No. 13, Sept, 1955; Dec, 1984
Capitol Stories/Charlton Comics

1-1st app.? Timothy The Ghost; Fago-c/a	9.15	27.00	55.00
2	5.35	16.00	32.00
3-7 (8/46)	4.25	13.00	26.00
8-13-Nyoka app.	7.00	21.00	42.00
1(1984)			1.00

ZOONIVERSE
8/86 - No. 6, 6/87 ($1.25/$1.75, limited series, Mando paper)
Eclipse Comics

1-5 ($1.25)		1.30
6 ($1.75)	.90	1.80

ZOO PARADE (TV)
#662, 1955 (Marlin Perkins)
Dell Publishing Co.

Four Color 662	4.50	13.50	45.00

ZOOM COMICS
Dec, 1945 (one-shot)
Carlton Publishing Co.

nn-Dr. Mercy, Satannas, from Red Band Comics; Capt. Milksop origin retold			
	37.00	111.00	260.00

ZOOT (Rulah Jungle Goddess #17 on)
nd (1946) - No. 16, July, 1948 (Two #13s & 14s)
Fox Features Syndicate

nn-Funny animal only	14.00	43.00	100.00

	GD25	FN65	NM94
2-The Jaguar app.	13.00	39.00	90
3(Fall, 1946) - 6-Funny animals & teen-age	8.35	25.00	50
7-(6/47)-Rulah, Jungle Goddess begins (origin & 1st app.)			
	75.00	225.00	600
8-10	54.00	163.00	435
11-Kamen bondage-c	58.00	174.00	465
12-Injury-to-eye panels, torture scene	40.00	120.00	290
13(2/48)	40.00	120.00	290

14(3/48)-Used in SOTI, pg. 104, "One picture showing a girl nailed by her wrists to trees with blood flowing from the wounds, might be taken straight from an ill. ed. of the Marquis deSade"

	47.00	141.00	375
13(4/48),14(5/48)-Western True Crime #15 on?	40.00	120.00	290
15,16	40.00	120.00	290

ZORRO (Walt Disney with #882)(TV)(See Eclipse Graphic Album)
May, 1949 - No. 15, Sept-Nov, 1961 (Photo-c 882 on)
Dell Publishing Co.
(Zorro first appeared in a pulp story Aug 19, 1919 - 1994 was 75th anniversa

Four Color 228 (#1)	21.00	63.00	210
Four Color 425,617,732	12.50	37.50	125
Four Color 497,538,574-Kinstler-a	13.50	40.50	135
Four Color 882-Photo-c begin; Toth-a	18.00	54.00	180
Four Color 920,933,960,976-Toth-a in all	12.50	37.50	125
Four Color 1003('59)-Toth-a	12.50	37.50	125
Four Color 1037-Annette Funicello photo-c	16.00	48.00	160
8(12-2/59-60)	8.00	24.00	80
9,12-Toth-a. 12-Last 10¢ issue	8.50	25.50	85
10,11,13-15-Last photo-c	7.00	21.00	70

NOTE: Warren Tufts a-4-Color 1037, 8, 9, 10, 13.

ZORRO (Walt Disney)(TV)
Jan, 1966 - No. 9, Mar, 1968 (All photo-c)
Gold Key

1-Toth-a	7.00	21.00	70
2,4,5,7,9-Toth-a. 5-r/F.C. #1003 by Toth	4.00	12.00	40
3,6-Tufts-a	3.50	10.50	35

NOTE: #1-9 are reprinted from Dell issues. Tufts a-3, 4. #1-r/F.C. #882. #2-r/F.C. #960. #3-r/#12-c & #8 inside. #4-r/#9-c & insides. #6-r/#11(all); #7-r/#14-c. #8-r/F.C. #933 inside & ba & #976-c. #9-r/F.C. #920.

ZORRO (TV)
Dec, 1990 - No. 12, Nov, 1991 ($1.00)
Marvel Comics

1-12: Based on TV show. 12-Toth-c			1

ZORRO
Nov, 1993 - No. 11, Nov, 1994 ($2.50/$2.95)
Topps Comics

0-(11/93, $1.00, 20 pgs.)-Painted-c; collector's ed.			1

1,4,6-9,11-15: 1-Miller-c. 4-Mike Grell-c. 6-Mignola-c. 7-Lady Rawhide-c by Gulacy. 8-Perez-c. 10-Julie Bell-c. 11-Lady Rawhide-c.

		1.20	3
2--Lady Rawhide-app. (not in costume)	1.65	4.20	10

3-1st app. Lady Rawhide in costume, 3-Lady Rawhide-c by Adam Hughes

	1.70	5.00	12
5-Lady Rawhide app.	1.00	2.00	5
10 ($2.95)-Lady Rawhide-c/app.		1.60	4

ZOT! (Also see Adventures of Zot)
4/84 - No. 10, 7/85; No. 11, 1/87 - No. 35 3/91 ($1.50, Baxter paper)
Eclipse Comics

1	1.00	2.00	5
2,3		1.20	3
4-10: 4-Origin. 10-Last color issue		.80	2
11-35: 11-Begin $2.00-c, B&W issues		.80	2

Z-2 COMICS (Secret Agent…)(See Holyoke One-Shot #7)

ZULU (See Movie Classics)

636

CONTINUED FROM LAST PAGE

641

651

GRAB THE BEST IN GOLD
AND SILVER AGE COMICS
AT

BEDROCK CITY
COMIC COMPANY

6521 Westheimer
(at Hillcroft)
Houston, Texas 77057
(713) 780-0675

2204-D FM 1960 W.
(at Kuykendahl)
Houston, Texas 77090
(713) 444-9763

Fax (713) 780-2366

Red Bee © 1995 D.C. Comics

655

658

ART RESTORATION
Matthew Wilson, Conservator

MASTERPIECES

P.O. BOX 881 / KELSO, WA 98626 / (360) 577-0351

FANTASY MASTERPIECES is a business dedicated to the art of paper conservation. It is our philosophy that art restoration should take the *whole* item into account. That means that not only should your item look as good as possible but that it should be made as structurally sound as possible. What good is a restored work of art if it disintegrates two years later? For that reason, I have developed various methods and techniques of paper art restoration unmatched anywhere else.

I am familiar with the construction of 19th & 20th century papers and have worked extensively on the most valuable of the Golden and Silver aged books from Action #1 to Amazing Fantasy #15.

When it comes to your paper art collection, whether it's a Superman #1 or a rare paper document that is priceless to you, why take a risk with anyone else? **FANTASY MASTERPIECES** is the answer.

Before

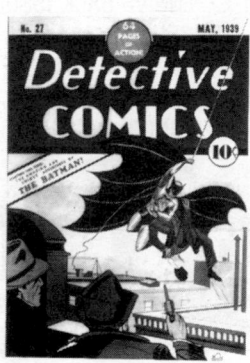

After

Our rate is $55.00 per hour. Estimates are free & questions are always welcome. Items to be restored should be worth at least $125.00 in their present condition.

We perform the following services with expert precision:

1) Cleaning
2) Whitening
3) Tape Removal
4) Piece Replacement
5) Repair Tears
6) Spine Roll Removal
7) Deacidification
8) Color Retouching
9) Staple Replacement
10) Page Lightening

All the Best to You from Diamond

Established in 1982, Diamond Comic Distributors has grown from a single warehouse in Baltimore, Maryland, to become the world's largest distributor of English-language comics and related merchandise.

But size alone isn't what's made Diamond the industry leader. Our growth is a direct result of our commitment to delivering one thing to comic book specialty retailers: **the best.**

The Best Products and Discounts

Our *Previews* catalog offers retailers and consumers comics from hundreds of suppliers every month. Plus, Diamond is comic book specialty retailers' exclusive source of products from DC Comics, Image, Dark Horse, Acclaim, Wizard Press, Gemstone Publishing and a host of other fine suppliers.

We also offer a wide variety of comics-related merchandise including graphic novels, trading cards, toys, models, collectible card games, apparel, and more — all at highly competitive discounts!

The Best Systems

Every product we sell is backed by our fast, accurate, and reliable industry-leading distribution network. Strategically located throughout the world, every facility is fully staffed with knowledgeable and friendly service professionals trained to deliver your shipments with maximum speed and efficiency.

The Best Service

Whenever you need us, Diamond's "One Call Does It All" Customer Service ensures that the products you want, the answers you need, and the attention you deserve are always available to you with just a toll-free phone call or fax to your personal Diamond Customer Service/Inside Sales Rep!

The Best Business Partner

At Diamond, we understand that our success has always depended upon the success of our customers. That's why we always invite you to share your questions, comments, and opinions with us — and we listen to them. Your feedback helps us refine and add to the ever-growing roster of services which help our customers bring the best to their customers.

You can depend on us because we depend on you.

RETAILERS: To find out more about Diamond, contact our Customer Service Department today!

Diamond
Comic Distributors, Inc.

1966 Greenspring Drive, Suite 300
Timonium, MD USA 21093
Phone: (410) 560-7100 • Fax: (410) 560-7148
E-mail: service@diamdcom.com
Internet: www.diamdcom.com

SPAWN

ASTRO CITY

GEN13

WITCHBLADE

SAVAGE DRAGON

TOUCH OF SILVER

THERE'S NEVER BEEN ANYTHING LIKE US BEFORE!

image COMICS

STRANGERS IN PARADISE

DARKCHYLDE

THE MAXX

THE TENTH

HELLSHOCK

LABMAN

OVER 40,000 DIFFERENT COMICS IN STOCK

BUY – SELL with Marty Hay or I'll SMASH YA!!!

Enclose 1 stamp each for Buying or Selling List!

I PAY BIG CASH FOR QUALITY COMICS

FAST CASH SINGLE BOOKS AND LARGE COLLECTIONS. I WANT ALL EARLY MARVELS, SILVER-AGE DCs, GOLDEN AGE, DISNEY POSTERS & MISC. ANY CONDITION. 50% TO 400% OF GUIDE FOR ITEMS NEEDED! WHY TAKE LESS FOR YOUR VALUED COLLECTIBLES? I SELL QUALITY COMICS AT REASONABLE PRICES. **SEND YOUR LIST FOR FAST CASH OFFER!!! NO RECENT COMICS PLEASE!**

SAMPLE BUYING PRICES (SUBJECT ONLY TO INCREASE)

FLASH #105...UP TO $8,000 FOR TOP QUALITY
BRAVE & BOLD #1-43,50,61...N-MINTS ARE WORTH 110%-300%
JUSTICE LEAGUE #1..PERFECTION CAN BE WORTH $7,000
SHOWCASE #1-45,55,60..CHOICE ISSUES 110%-300% PAID
OUR ARMY AT WAR #81...CASH PERHAPS TO $1,600
CAPT. AMERICA #1-78..VG OR BETTER 75%-125% OFFERED
MORE FUN #1-107..VG OR BETTER 70%-150% PAID
ACTION #1-252..VG OR BETTER 65%-150% PAID
DETECTIVE #1-233..VG OR BETTER 70%-150% PAID
SUSPENSE COMICS...ANY CONDITION UP TO 10X GUIDE (#3)
"BIG CASH FOR OTHER DC, TIMELYS, OTHER GOLD OR SILVER AGE."

MARTY HAY
P.O. BOX 359
329 E. MAIN
SPRINGERVILLE, AZ 85938
WORK (520) 333-2222
HOME (520) 333-2255

SERVING FANDOM FOR OVER 26 YEARS

SERVING FANDOM FOR OVER 26 YEARS

I WILL PAY MORE THAN ANY BUYING PRICES OFFERED IN THIS GUIDE!

Archie COMICS

AMERICA'S #1 HUMOR PUBLISHER FOR OVER 55 YEARS!

ASK YOUR LOCAL COMICS OUTLET FOR SUCH TOP-SELLING TITLES AS:

★ARCHIE ★BETTY ★VERONICA ★JUGHEAD
★BETTY & VERONICA ★CHERYL BLOSSOM
★SABRINA THE TEENAGE WITCH
★THE ARCHIE DIGEST LIBRARY

...AND SUCH HOT LICENSED PROPERTIES AS:

★SONIC THE HEDGEHOG ★KNUCKLES

... AND MUCH, MUCH MORE!

ARCHIE COMIC PUBLICATIONS, INC.
325 Fayette Ave., Mamaroneck, NY 10543.
PHONE: (914) 381-5155. FAX: (914) 381-2335.
Email: ArchieCom@aol.com

Capital City Comics

1910 Monroe Street
Madison, WI 53711
Mon–Fri: 11–7
Sat: 10–5
Phone (608) 251-8445

2565 N. Downer Ave.
Milwaukee, WI 53211
Mon–Fri: 11–7
Sat: 10–5
Phone (414) 332-8199

689

693

Take a trip to another World.

COMIC BOOK WORLD

7130 Turfway Rd · Florence, KY 41042 · 606-371-9562
Just off I-75 at exit 182/Turfway Road

4016 Harrison Ave · Cincinnati, OH 45211 · 513-661-6300
Four miles from I-75 at exit 2/Harrison Avenue

6905 Shepherdsville Rd · Louisville, KY 40219 · 502-964-5500
On Shepherdsville between Fern Valley & Outer Loop

699

STEVE SIBRA
PO Box 9055, Missoula MT 59807
Phone: (406) 542-8270

PREMIERE COMIC DEALER OF THE PLAINS STATES

Actively Buying Old Comics Throughout The Plains, Pacific NW, And SW Canada

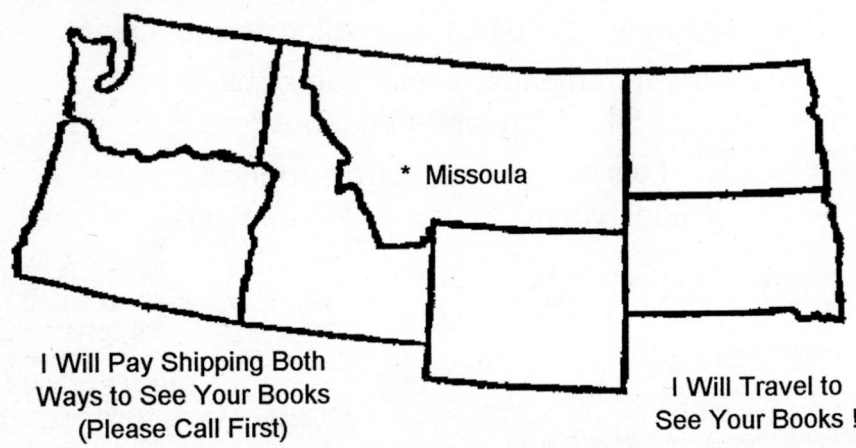

* Missoula

I Will Pay Shipping Both
Ways to See Your Books
(Please Call First)

I Will Travel to
See Your Books !

I PAY TOP DOLLAR FOR GOLD & SILVER AGE
COMICS 1933-1966

Nobody can pay the most every time for every collection; however, I have successfully outbid other major dealers in the purchase of many significant collections. I will gladly provide references from satisfied customers whose collections I have purchased.

* Immediate Cash Available
* Over 15 Years Experience
  Buying & Selling Gold &
  Silver Age Comics
* Honest, Friendly Service
* Accurate Grading
* Competitive Pricing

* Many Years Experience as an
  Overstreet Advisor
* Founder and Former Owner of
  Rocket Comics in Seattle, WA.
* Contributing Author to Comic
  Book Marketplace Magazine
  Since Its Inception

706

CLASSIFIED ADS

DIRECTORY OF COMIC AND NOSTALGIA SHOPS
(PAID ADVERTISING - STORE LISTINGS)

You can have your store listed here for very reasonable rates. Send for details for next year's Guide. The following list of stores have paid to be included in this list. We cannot assume any responsibility in your dealings with these shops. This list is provided for your information only. When planning trips, it would be advisable to make appointment's in advance. Remember, to get your shop included in the next edition, call, fax or write us for rates. **Gemstone Publishing, Inc., 1966 Greenspring Dr., Suite 405, Timonium, MD 21093. PH 888-375-9800 or 410-560-5806, FAX 410-560-6107.**

Items stocked by these shops are listed just after the telephone number and are coded as follows:

(a) Golden Age Comics
(b) Silver Age Comics
(c) New Comics, magazines
(d) Pulps
(e) Paperbacks
(f) Big Little Books
(g) Magazines

(h) Books (old)
(i) Movie Posters
(j) Original Art
(k) Toys
(l) Records/CDs,Video Tapes
(m) Trading Cards
(n) Underground Comics

(o) Premiums(rings,decoders,etc.)
(p) Comic Related Posters
(q) Comic Supplies
(r) Role Playing Games
(s) Star Trek Items
(t) Dr. Who Items
(u) Japanimation Items

ALABAMA

Campbell's Collectibles
1221 Littlebrook Ln.
Birmingham, AL 35235
PH: (205) 853-8227
(a,d-h,k,m,o)

Wizard's Comics
324 North Court
Florence, AL 35630
PH: (205) 766-6821
(a-c,q-u)

Jennings Collectibles
2120 Metro Circle
Huntsville, AL 35801
PH: (205) 881-6222
(b,c,g,i,k,m,p,q,s)

Sincere Comics
4667 Airport Blvd.
Mobile, AL 36608
PH: (334) 342-2603
(a-c,e,m,p-s,u)

ARIZONA

Atomic Comics III
5965 West Ray Road #14
Chandler, AZ 85226
PH: (602) 940-6061
(b,c,g,i-k,m-u)

Atomic Comics
1318 West Southern #1
Mesa, AZ 85202
PH: (602) 649-0807
(a-c,f,g,j,k,m,n,p-u)

Greg's Comics
2722 South Alma
School Rd. #8
Mesa, AZ 85210
PH: (602) 752-1881
(a-c,k,m,q-s)

All About Books & Comics
517 E. Camelback
Phoenix, AZ 85021
PH: (602) 277-0757
(a-c,e,g,h,k-n,p-u)

Atomic Comics II
3029 West Peoria #CC
Phoenix, AZ 85021
PH: (602) 395-1066
(a-c,f,g,j,k,m,n,p-u)

Dirt Cheap Comics & Toys
5811 N. 7th. St.
Phoenix, AZ 85014
PH: (602) 279-5855
(a,b,k,m,q,r)

Lost Dutchman Comics
747 W. Camelback Rd.
Phoenix, AZ 85013
PH: (602) 263-5249
(a,b,d,f,g,h,n)

Key Comics:Discount Back-Issues
P. O. Box 3855
Scottsdale, AZ 85271
Ph: (602) 949-8499
(a-c,j)

All About Books & Comics
810 S. Ash
Tempe, AZ 85281
PH: (602) 858-9447
(b,c,g,k,m,n,p-u)

ARKANSAS

Alternate Worlds
Boardwalk Village
3812 Central Ave. Suite G
Hot Springs, AR 71913
PH: (501) 525-8999
(a-c,m,o,q,r-u)

Comic Book Store
9307 Treasure Hill
Little Rock, AR 72227
PH: (501) 227-9777
(a-c,g,m,p-u)

Collector's Book Store
3217 John F.
Kennedy Blvd.
North Little Rock, AR 72116
PH: (501) 791-4222
(a-c,g,m,p-u)

CALIFORNIA

It Came From the Basement
2308 Encinal Ave.
Alameda, CA 94501
PH: (510) 521-5840
(c,e,k-m,p-s,u)

Galactic Archives
5219 East
Orangethrope Ave.
Anaheim Hills, CA 92807
PH: (714) 693-0673
(b-i,k-m,q-u)

Comic Relief Berkeley
2138 University Avenue
Berkeley, CA 94704
PH: (510) 843-5002
(a-d,f-h,j,n,p,q,u)

Astounding Fantasy Art Books and Comics
2319-A West Olive Ave.
Burbank, CA 91506
PH: (818) 953-7234
(a-d,f,g,i,k-m,q-u)

Crush Comics And Cards
2869 Castro Valley Blvd.
Castro Valley, CA 94546
PH: (510) 581-4779
(b,c,g,k,m,p,q,s)

Collectors Ink
932-A West 8th Ave.
Chico, CA 95926
PH: (916) 345-0958
(a-c,e,g,k-n,p-u)

Comic Bookie
415 West Foothill Blvd.
#318
Claremont, CA 91711
PH: (909) 399-0228
(b,c,g,k-n,p,q,s-u)

Flying Colors Comics & Other Cool Stuff
2980 Treat Blvd.
Oak Grove Plaza
Concord, CA 94518
PH: (510) 835-5410
(a-c,j,k,m,p,q,s,u)

Superior Comics
1970 Newport Blvd.
Costa Mesa, CA 92627
PH: (714) 631-3933
(a-c,f,g,j,k,m,n,p-r,u)

High Quality Comics
(mail order only)
1106 2nd St. Suite #110
Encinitas, CA 92024
PH: (619) 723-7269
(b,c,g,j,n)

Comic Gallery
322-J West El
Norte Pkwy.
Escondido, CA 92026
PH: (619) 745-5660
(b,c,m,n,p-s,u)

Comicmania!
124 W. Commonwealth
Fullerton, CA 92832
PH: (714) 992-6649
(a-c,f,g,i-k,m-q,s,u)

Mile High Comics
12041 Harbor Blvd.
Garden Grove, CA
92840
PH: (714) 748-7091
(a-c,f-u)

Geoffrey's Comics
15530 Crenshaw Blvd.
Gardena, CA 90249
PH: (888) 538-3198
(a-c,l,n,q,u)

Shooting Star Comics
618 E. Colorado Blvd.
Glendale, CA 91205
PH: (818) 502-1535
(b,c,k,m,n,p,q,u)

Bud Plant Comic Art
P. O. Box 1689-OSP
Grass Valley, CA 95945
PH: (800) 242-6642
(c,h,l,m,p,q,u)

Treasures Of Youth
1201 C St.
Hayward, CA 94541
PH: (510) 888-9675
(a,b,d,e-g,i-k,m,o)

**Amazing Comics &
Cards**
5555 Stearns St. #103
Long Beach, CA 90815
PH: (310) 493-4427
(b,c,e,g,k-m,p,q,s-u)

**Another World Comics
& Books**
1615 Colorado Blvd.
Los Angeles, CA 90041
PH: (213) 257-7757
(a-g,i,m,p,t,u)

Golden Apple Comics
7711 Melrose Ave.
Los Angeles, CA 90046
PH: (213) 658-6047
http://www.goldenapple-
comics.com
(a-c,l-n,p,q,t)

**Meltdown Comics And
Collectibles**
7529 Sunset Blvd.
Los Angeles, CA 90046
PH: (213) 851-7223
(b,c,g,i-r ,u)

**Pacific Comic
Exchange, Inc.**
(by appointment only)
P. O. Box 34849
Los Angeles, CA 90034
PH: (310) 836-7234
(PCEI)
http://www.pcei.com/
email:sales@pcei.com
(a, b)

Brians Books
73 North Milpitas Blvd.
Milpitas, CA 95035
PH: (408) 942-6903
(a-c,g,m,p,q,s,u)

Pegasus Hobbies
5505 Moreno Blvd.
Montclair, CA 91763
PH: (909) 931-4872
(a-c,g,k,m,q-s,u)

The Big Guy's Comics
167 El Camino East
Mountain View,
CA 94040
PH: (415) 965-8272
(a-c,m,n,q,s)

Golden Apple Comics
8962 Reseda Blvd.
Northridge, CA 91324
PH: (818) 993-7804
http://www.goldenapple-
comics.com
(a-c,e,l-n,p,q,u)

**Dr. Comics & Mr.
Games**
4014 Piedmont Ave.
Oakland, CA 94611
PH: (510) 601-7800
(a-c,g,k,m,n,p-s,u)

Lee's Comics, Inc.
3783 El Camino Real
Palo Alto, CA 94306
PH: (415) 493-3957
e mail
lee@lcomics.com
(a-c,f,g,i,k,m,n,p-u)

**Gotham Comics &
Games**
248 Golf Club Rd.
Pleasant Hill, CA 94523
PH: (510) 682-1891
(c,e,k-m,p-s,u)

A-1 Comics
5800 Madison Avenue
Sacramento, CA 95841
PH: (916) 331-9203
(a-g,i,k-m,p-s,u)

Comic Gallery
4224 Balboa Ave.
San Diego, CA 92117
PH: (619) 483-4853
(b,c,m,n,p-s,u)

Comic Gallery
9460-G Mira
Mesa Blvd.
San Diego, CA 92126
PH: (619) 578-9444
(b,c,m,n,p-s,u)

**San Diego Comics &
Collectibles**
6937 El Cajon Blvd.
San Diego, CA 92115
PH: (619) 698-1177
(a-c,k,m)

Amazing Adventures
3800 Noriega
San Francisco,
CA 94122
PH: (415) 661-1344
(a-c,g,i-k,m,n,q,r)

The Funny Pages
5957 Geary Blvd. at
24th Ave.
San Francisco,
CA 94121
PH: (415) 752-1914
(a-e,g-m,o-s,u)

**Captain Nemo Comics
& Games**
797 Marsh St.
San Luis Obispo,
CA 93401
PH: (805) 544-6366
(a-c,e,g,i,k,m-u)

Lee's Comics, Inc.
2222 S. El Camino Real
San Mateo, CA 94403
PH: (415) 571-1489
e mail
lee@lcomics.com
(a-c,f,g,i,k,m,n,p-s,u)

**Metro Comics &
Games**
15 West Anapamu
Santa Barbara,
CA 93101
PH: (805) 963-2168
metrocomix@aol.com
(a-c,e,g,k,m,n,p-s,u)

Brains Books
2767 El Camino
Santa Clara, CA 95051
PH: (408) 985-7481
(a-c,g,m,p,q,s,u)

**What's Hot Comics &
Cards**
1061 Lafayette St.
Santa Clara, CA 95050
PH: (408) 241-8212
(b,c,g,k,m,p-r,u)

Atlantis Fantasyworld
1020 Cedar St.
Santa Cruz, CA 95060
PH: (408) 426-0158
(b,c,g,i,k,m,n,p-s,u)

**Hi De Ho Comics &
Fantasy**
525 Santa Monica Blvd.
Santa Monica,
CA 90401
PH: (310) 394-2820
(a-n,p-u)

Mega City Comics
2955 B-2 Cochran St.
Simi Valley, CA 93065
PH: (805) 583-3027
(b,c,e,g,i-k,m,n,p-s,u)

Comicmania!
815 S. Fair Oaks Ave.
South Pasadena,
CA 91030
PH: (818) 441-8052
(a-c,g,j,k,m,p,q,s,u)

Ralph's Comic Corner
2377 E. Main Street
Ventura, CA 93003
PH: (805) 653-2732
(a-c,g,m,n.p-s,u)

Pegasus Hobbies
6554 Greenleaf
Whittier, CA 90601
PH: (310) 907-4663
(a-c,g,k,m,q-s,u)

COLORADO

All C's Collectibles
1113 So. Abilene St.
#104
Aurora, CO 80012
PH: (303) 751-6882
(a-d,g,i-s,u)

Castaway Comics
648 Peoria St.
Aurora, CO 80011
PH: (303) 341-1958
(a-k,m,n,p,q,u)

**Time Warp Comics &
Cards, Inc.**
1631 28th Street
Boulder, CO 80301
PH: (303) 443-4500
(a-c,g,n,q-s)

Bargain Comics
21 1/2 E. Bijou
Colorado Springs,
CO 80903
PH: (719) 578-8847
(a-c,g,n,p-r)

Comic Vault
929 North Murray Blvd.
Colorado Springs,
CO 80915
PH: (719) 596-2155
(a-c,e,g-k,o-u)

Mile High Comics
760 South
Colorado Blvd.
Denver, CO 81221
PH: (303) 691-2212
(a-c,f-u)

Mile High Comics
Tabor Center
16th & Lawrence,
3rd Floor
Denver, CO 80202
PH: (303) 446-8250
(a-c,f-u)

Blue Coyote Comics
P. O. Box 2163
Evergreen, CO 80439
PH: (303) 670-8386
(a,b,n)

J. R. R. Comix
P. O. Box 2163
3869 Evergreen Pkwy.
Evergreen,
CO 80437-2163
PH: (303) 670-8386
(a-e,g,k-n,p-u)

Mile High Comics
1st & Wadsworth
Lakewood, CO 80226
PH: (303) 238-8125
(a-c,f-u)

RTS Unlimited Inc.
P. O. Box 150412
Lakewood, CO
80215-0412
PH: (303) 279-0946
(a,b,g,q)

Mile High Comics
50 West Littleton Blvd.
Littleton, CO 80120
PH: (303) 730-8160
(a-c,f-u)

Outer Limits Comic Books
614 West 29th Street
Pueblo, CO 81008
PH: (719) 583-2750
(c,e,i,k,m,p,q,s,t)

Mile High Comics
9201 North Washington
Thornton, CO 80229
PH: (303) 457-2612
(a-c,f-u)

CONNECTICUT

Sarge's Comics
325 Route 12
Groton, CT 06340
PH: (860) 445-2646
(b,c,g,k-n,p,q,s,u)

D. J.'s Comics, Cards, Games
303 East Main St.
Meriden, CT 06450
PH: (203) 235-7300
(a-c,g,k,n,r)

Collector's Dream
20 Prospect Street
Moosup, CT 06354
PH: (860) 564-8857
(a-c,g,k,p-u)

Sarge's Comics
52 State St.
New London, CT 06320
PH: (860) 443-2004
(a-c,e,g,k-n,p,q,s-u)

DELAWARE

Captain Blue Hen Comics & Cards
280 E. Main St. #1
Newark, DE 19711
PH: (302) 737-3434
(a-c,g,k-q,s,u)

FLORIDA

Past Present Future Superstore-Boca Raton
23066 Sandlefoot
Plaza Drive
Boca Raton, FL 33428
PH: (561) 470-5700
(b,c,e,g,j,k,m,n,p-s,u)

Emerald City Too Comics & Collectables, Inc.
2475-L Mc Mullen
Booth Road
Clearwater, FL 34619
PH: (813) 797-0664
(a-c,g,j-u)

SMRC Comics
6927 Red Road
Coral Gables, FL 33143
PH: (800) 826-3089
(a,b,q)

Tropic Comics East
5439 North
Federal Highway
Ft. Lauderdale,
FL 33308
PH: (954) 351-0001
(a-g,i-k,m,n,p,q,s-u)

Phil's Comic Shoppe
6512 W. Atlantic Blvd.
Margate, FL 33063
PH: (954) 977-6947
(a-c,j,k,q)

Tropic Comics South
742 NE 167th. St.
N. Miami Beach,
FL 33162
PH: (305) 940-8700
(a-g,i-k,m,n,p,q,s-u)

Bay Hill Comics & Used Book Exchange
7657 Turkey Lake Rd.
Orlando, FL 32819
PH: (407) 363-0040
(b,c,e,g,m,o,p,s)

Starbase K-7
829 Sand Lake Road
Orlando, FL 32809
PH: (407) 240-7989
(a-c,e,g,i-m,p-u)

Sincere Comics
40 West 9 Mile Rd.
Pensacola, FL 32534
PH: (904) 476-9944
(a-c,e,f,m,p-s,u)

Tropic Comics
313 S. State Road 7
Plantation, FL 33317
PH: (954) 587-8878
(a-g,i-k,m,n,p,q,s-u)

Emerald City Comics & Collectables, Inc.
9249
Seminole Boulevard
Seminole, FL 33772
PH: (813) 398-2665
(a-c,e,g,j-u)

Past Present Future Superstore-Sunrise
8432 W. Oakland
Park Blvd.
Sunrise, FL 33351
PH: (954) 742-0777
(b,c,e,g,j,k,m,n,p-u)

The Comics Club, Inc.
8126 N. University Dr.
Tamarac, FL 33321
PH: (954) 726-2121
(a-c,e,g,i,k,m,q-s)

Past Present Future Superstore-West Palm Beach
1387 N. Military Trail
West Palm Beach,
FL 33409
PH: (561) 697-2554
(b,c-g,j,k,m,n,p-u)

GEORGIA

Oxford Comics Inc.
2855 Piedmont Rd. NE
Atlanta, GA 30305
Ph: (404) 233-8682
(a-u)

Titan Games & Comics VI
2000 Cheshire
Bridge Rd.
Atlanta, GA 30324
PH: (404) 982-0227
(a-c,e,g,k-m,p-u)

Titan Games & Comics
5436 Riverdale Rd.
College Park,
GA 30349
PH: (770) 996-9129
(a-c,e,g,k-m,p-u)

Comic Company
1058 Mistletoe Rd.
Decatur, GA 30033
PH: (404) 248-9846
(a-c,g,m,n,p,q)

Dark Adventure Comics/Dark Adventure Comics International,Inc.
2785 Buford Hwy.,
Ste. 102B
Duluth, GA 30136
Ph: (770) 623 - 3675
(a-e,g,k,m-s)

Titan Games & Comics IV
2131 Pleasant Hill Rd.
Duluth, GA 30136
PH: (770) 497-0202
(a-c,e,g,k-m,p-u)

Heroes Ink
2500 Cobb Parkway
NW (U.S.41)
Kennesaw, GA 30152
Ph: (770) 428-3033
(b,c,e,g,h,k,m,o-s)

Odin's Cosmic Bookshelf
Killian Hill Crossing
4760 Hwy. 29, Suite A-1
Lilburn, GA 30247
PH: (770) 923-0123
(a-c,e,g,h,m,o-s,u)

Titan Games & Comics III
2585 Spring Rd.
Smyrna, GA 30080
PH: (770) 433-8223
(a-c,e,g,k-m,p-u)

Odin's Cosmic Bookshelf
Stone Mountain Festival
1825 Rockbridge
Rd. S.W.
Stone Mountain,
GA 30087
PH: (770) 413-0123
(a-c,g,k,m,o-s,u)

Titan Games & Comics II
3853 Lawrenceville
Hwy.
Tucker, GA 30084
PH: (770) 491-8067
(a-c,e,g,k-m,p-u)

HAWAII

Compleat Comics Company
1728-E Kaahumanu
Avenue
Wailuku, HI 96793
PH: (808) 242-5875
(c,k,m,n,p-s,u)

ILLINOIS

Graham Crackers Comics, Ltd.
261 East Indian
Trail Rd.
Aurora, IL 60505
PH: (630) 897-6622
(b,c,g,k,m,o,p,r)

Graham Crackers Comics, Ltd.
369 West Army
Trail Rd.
Bloomingdale, IL 60108
PH: (630) 894-8810
(b,c,g,k,m-p-s,u)

Graham Crackers Comics, Ltd.
120 North
Bolingbrook Dr. (Rt.53)
Bolingbrook, IL 60515
PH: (630) 739-6810
(b,c,g,k,m,o,p,r-u)

Amazing Fantasy Books & Comics
582 Torrence Ave.
Calumet City, IL 60409
PH: (708) 891-2260
(b,c,e,g,l-n,p-u)

Chicago Comics
3244 North Clark St.
Chicago, IL 60657
PH: (773) 528-1983
(a-c,g,k,m,n,p,q,u)

Independence Comics & Cards
3955 W. Irving Pk. Rd.
Chicago, IL 60618
PH: (773) 539-6720
(a-c,i,k,m,o-s,u)

Joe Sarno's Comic Kingdom
5941 West Irving
Park Road
Chicago, IL 60634
PH: (773) 545-2231
(a-d,j,q)

Larry Laws
(Appointment Only)
831 Cornelia
Chicago, IL 60657
PH: (773) 477-9247
(e,g,h,m,o)

Larry's Comic Book Store
1219 W. Devon Ave.
Chicago, IL 60660
PH: (773) 274-1832
(a-c,q,t,u)

Yesterday
1143 West Addison St.
Chicago, IL 60613
PH: (773) 248-8087
(a,b,d-g,l-n,q,s)

Graham Crackers Comics, Ltd.
7511 Lemont Rd. #190
(75th & Lemont Rd.)
Darien, IL 60561
PH: (630) 910-5059
(b,c,g,k,m,o,p,r)

Titan Comics, Inc.
1452 Miner St.
Des Plaines, IL 60016
PH: (847) 298-6322
(a-c,f,k,m,p,q,s,u)

The Paper Escape
205 West First St.
Dixon, IL 61021
PH: (815) 284-7567
(c,e,m,p,r,s)

Graham Crackers Comics, Ltd.
5232 South Main St.
Downers Grove,
IL 60515
PH: (630) 852-1810
(b,c,g,k,m,p-r,t,u)

GEM Comics
156 N. York Rd.
Elmhurst, IL 60126
PH: (630) 833-8787
(b,c,g,m,p-r)

Amazing Fantasy Books & Comics
47 E. Lincoln Hwy.
Frankfort, IL 60423
PH: (815) 469-5092
(b,c,e,g,l-n,p-u)

Graham Crackers Comics, Ltd.
650 Roosevelt Rd. #102
Glen Ellyn, IL 60137
PH: (630) 469-6141
(b,c,g,k,m,o,p,r)

Rob's Comics
1301 N. Raynor
Joliet, IL 60435
PH: (815) 722-0673
(g)

Amazing Fantasy Books & Comics
1211 E. 9th St.
Lockport, IL 60441
PH: (815) 834-1658
(b,c,e,g,l-n,p-u)

Graham Crackers Comics, Ltd.
5 East Chicago Ave.
Naperville, IL 60540
PH: (630) 355-4310
(a-c,g,j-n,p-u)

M & M Comic Service
13617 Southwest Hwy.
Orland Park, IL 60462
PH: (708) 349-2486
(c,g,i,p,q,u)

Tomorrow is Yesterday, Inc.
5600 N. 2nd St.
Rockford, IL 61111
PH: (815) 633-0330
(a-n,p-u)

Graham Crackers Comics, Ltd.
108 East Main St.
(Rt.64)
St. Charles, IL 60174
PH: (630) 584-0610
(b,c,g,k,m,o,p,r,s,u)

Keith's Komix, Inc.
528 S. Roselle Rd.
Schaumburg, IL 60193
PH: (847) 534-9436
(b,c,e,g,j-m,p-u)

Webs Comics
4644 Oakton
Skokie, IL 60076
PH: (847) 982-9327
(c,m,p-r)

Amazing Fantasy Books & Comics
15948 S. Harlem
Tinley Park, IL 60477
PH: (708) 633-0837
(b,c,e,g,l-n,p-u)

Unicorn Comics & Cards
216 S. Villa Avenue
Villa Park, IL 60181
PH: (630) 279-5777
(a-e,g-n,p,q)

Graham Crackers Comics, Ltd.
1207 East
Butterfield Rd.
Wheaton, IL 60187
PH: (630) 668-1350
(b,c,g,k,m,o,p,r)

Igor's Comic Book Emporium
123 N. Main St.
Wheaton, IL 60187
PH: (630) 260-8787
(b,c,g,m,p,q,r)

INDIANA

Comic Cave
3221 E. 17th Street
Columbus, IN 47201
PH: (812) 372-8430
(b,c,k,m,p,q,s)

The Book Broker
2127 S. Weinbach
Evansville, IN 47714
PH: (812) 479-5647
(a-h,k-n,p-u)

Books Comics and Things
2212 Maplecrest Rd.
Fort Wayne, IN 46815
PH: (219) 446-0025
(a-c,e,g,m,p-u)

Books Comics and Things
5936 West
Jefferson Blvd.
Fort Wayne, IN 46804
PH: (219) 436-0159
(a-c,e,g,m,p-u)

Comic Carnival
6265 North
Carrollton Ave.
Indianapolis, IN 46220
PH: (317) 253-8882
(a-j,l-t)

Comic Carnival
7311 U.S. 31 South
Indianapolis, IN 46227
PH: (317) 889-889
((a-j,l-t)

Comic Carnival
3837 North High
School Rd.
Indianapolis, IN 46254
PH: (317) 293-4386
(a-j,l-t)

Comic Carnival
9729 East
Washington St.
Indianapolis, IN 46229
PH: (317) 898-5010
(a-j,l-t)

Downtown Comics
111 N. Pennsylvania St.
Indianapolis, IN 46204
PH: (317) 237-0397
(a-u)

Downtown Comics - Carmel
13682 N. Meridian St.
Indianapolis, IN 46032
PH: (317) 848-2305
(a-u)

Downtown Comics - Castleton
5767 E. 86th St.
Indianapolis, IN 46258
PH: (317) 845-9991
(a-u)

Downtown Comics - Greenwood
8925 S. Meridian St.
Indianapolis, IN 46227
PH: (317) 885-6395
(a-u)

Downtown Comics - West
8336 W. 10th St.
Indianapolis, IN 46234
PH: (317) 271-7610
(a-u)

Galactic Greg's
1407 East Lincolnway
Valparaiso, IN 46383
PH: (219) 464-0119
(b,c,g,m,n,p-r,u)

IOWA

Oak Leaf Comics
1926 Valley Park Drive
Cedar Falls, IA 50613
PH: (319) 277-1835
(a-c,f,k,m,n,p-s,u)

Comic World
1626 Central Ave.
Dubuque, IA 52001
PH: (319) 557-1897
(b,c,m,q,r)

Oak Leaf Comics
23-5th St. S.W.
Mason City, IA 50401
PH: (515) 424-0333
(a-c,f,i,k-s,u)

KANSAS

Prairie Dog Comics
Main Store
7130 West Maple
Wichita, KS 67207
PH: (316) 942-3456
(a-u)

KENTUCKY

Pac-Rat's, Inc.
1051 Bryant Way
Bowling Green,
KY 42103
PH: (502) 782-8092
(a-c,e,g,l-n,p-r)

Comic Book World,
Inc
7130 Turfway Rd.
Florence, KY 41042
PH: (606) 371-9562
(a-c,g,m,q-u)

Collectibles Etc
115 Locust Hill Dr.
Suite 106
Lexington, KY 40509
PH: (606) 269-6633
(a-c,g,j,k,m,p-r,u)

Collectibles Etc
200 Bolivar Street
Lexington, KY 40508
PH: (606) 225-4639
(a-c,g,k,m,n,p-s,u)

Red Rock
Collectables
929 Liberty Road
Lexington, KY 40505
PH: (606) 225-5452
(b-e,g,i-s,u)

Comic Book World,
Inc.
6905
Shepherdsville Rd.
Louisville, KY 40219
PH: (502) 964-5500
(a-c,g,m,q-u)

The Great Escape
2433 Bardstown Rd.
Louisville, KY 40205
PH: (502) 456-2216
(a-c,e,g,i-n,p-u)

LOUISIANA

The Phoenix
3200 Jackson Street
Alexandria, LA 71301
PH: (318) 487-1246
(c,g,h,m,q,r)

B.T. & W.D. Giles
P. O. Box 271
Keithville, LA 71047
PH: (318) 925-6654
(a,b,d-f,h,l)

More Fun Comics
8200 Oak Street
New Orleans, LA 70118
PH: (504) 865-1800
(b,c,e,g,k,m,n,q,r)

MAINE

Top Shelf Comics
34 Main St.
Bangor, ME 04401
PH: (207) 947-4939
(a-c,g,k,m,q-s)

Moonshadow Comics
215 US Route 1
Falmouth, ME 04105
PH: (207) 781-8902
(a-c,g,i,m,n,q-u)

All About Comics &
Hobbies
49 Topsham
Fair Mall Road
Suite 7
Topsham, ME 04086
PH: (207) 729-9255
(b,c,g,m,o-s)

MARYLAND

Comic Book
Kingdom, Inc
4307 Harford Rd
P. O. Box 3679
Baltimore,
MD 21214-0679
PH: (410) 426-4529
(a-c,e-h,k,m,p,q)

Geppi's Comic World
1000 Lancaster St.
Baltimore, MD 21231
PH: (410) 547-0910
(a-c,k-m,q,s,t)

Geppi's Comic World
1722 North Rolling Rd.
Baltimore, MD 21244
PH: (410) 298-1758
(a-c,k-m,q,s,t)

Alternate Worlds
72 Cranbrook Rd.
Yorktowne Plaza
Cockeysville, MD 21030
PH: (410) 666-3290
(b,c,e,g,k-n,p-u)

The Closet of Comics
7315 Baltimore Ave.
College Park,
MD 20740
PH: (301) 699-0498
(b-d,l-n,p,q)

Comics To Astonish
9400 Snowden
River Pkwy.
Columbia, MD 21045
PH: (410) 381-2732
(a-c,j,k,m,p-r)

Comic Classics
203 East Main St.
Frostburg, MD 21532
PH: (301) 689-1823
(a-c,m,n,p,q,s)

Comic Classics
365 Main St.
Laurel, MD 20707
PH: (301) 490-9811
(410) 792-4744
(a-c,k,m,n,p,q,s-u)

Cards Comics And
Collectibles
513 Main St.
Reisterstown,
MD 21136
PH: (410) 526-7410
(a-c,f,g,j,k,m,p,q)

Adventure Comics
1055 Rockville Pike
Rockville, MD 20852
PH: (301) 251-2888
(a-d,j,q)

Geppi's Comic World
Silver Spring
8317 Fenton St.
Silver Spring,
MD 20910
PH: (301) 588-2546
(a-c,k-m,q,s,t)

MASSACHUSETTS

New England Comics
131 Harvard Ave.
Allston, MA 02134
PH: (617) 783-1848
NEC@necomics.com
(a-c,e,g,k-n,p-u)

New England Comics
1840 Centre St.
West Roxbury
Boston, MA 02132
PH: (617) 325-1848
(a-c,e,g,k-n,p-u)

New England Comics
744 Crescent St.
East Crossing Plaza
Brockton, MA 02402
PH: (508) 559-5068
(a-c,e,g,k-n,p-u)

New England Comics
316 Harvard St.
Coolidge Corner
Brookline, MA 02146
PH: (617) 566-0115
(a-c,e,g,k-n,p-u)

New England Comics
14A Eliot St.
Cambridge, MA 02138
PH: (617) 354-5352
(a-c,e,g,k-n,p-u)

That's Entertainment
371 John Fitch Highway
Fitchburg, MA 01420
PH: (508) 342-8607
(a-u)

Bop City Comics
Framingham Mall
400 Cochituate Rd.
(Route 30)
Framingham, MA 01701
PH: (508) 872-2317
(a-u)

Jams Comic
Connection
435 King St.
(Rt. 110/2A)
Littleton, MA 01460
PH: (508) 486-1099
(c,e,g,k,m,p-s)

New England Comics
18 Pleasant St.
Malden, MA 02148
PH: (617) 322-2404
(a-c,e,g,k-n,p-u)

New England Comics
732 Washington St.
Norwood Center
Norwood, MA 02062
PH: (617) 769-4552
(a-c,e,g,k-n,p-u)

Imagine That
Bookstore
58 Dalton Ave.
Pittsfield, MA 01201
PH: (413) 445-5934
(a-n,p-u)

New England Comics
1511 Hancock St.
Quincy Center
Quincy, MA 02169
PH: (617) 770-1848
(a-c,e,g,k-n,p-u)

Megaverse City
Comics & Collectibles
608 Dorchester Ave.
So. Boston, MA 02127
PH: (888) 675-4857
(b,c,e,g,k-n,p-s,u)

Web-Head Enterprises
Ltd.
353 Main St.
Wakefield, MA 01880
PH: (617) 246-1797
(a-g,m,n,q,s,t)

The Outer Limits
463 Moody St.
Waltham, MA 02154
PH: (617) 891-0444
(a-u)

That's Entertainment
244 Park Avenue
Worcester, MA 01609
PH: (508) 755-4207
(a-u)

MICHIGAN

**Cashman's Comics &
Collectibles**
1018 S. Madison Ave.
Bay City,
MI 48708-7261
PH: (517) 895-1113
(a-c,g,k-u)

Comics North!
108 E. State Street
Cheboygan,
MI 49721-1752
PH: (616) 627-3740
(b,c,g,p-u)

Campus Comics
541 East Grand River
Campus Town Mall
East Lansing, MI 48823
PH: (517) 351-4513
(b,c,g,m,n,q,r)

Curious Book
307 East Grand River
East Lansing, MI 48823
PH: (517) 332-0112
(d-k,m,o,s,u)

Curious Comic Shop
210 M. A. C. Ave.
East Lansing, MI 48823
PH: (517) 332-0222
(a-c,l-u)

**Amazing Book
Store, Inc.**
3718 Richfield Rd.
Flint, MI 48506
PH: (810) 736-3025
(a-c,n,q)

Argos Book Shop
1405
Robinson Rd. S.E.
Grand Rapids,
MI 49506
PH: (616) 454-0111
(a-k,o-u)

**Tardy's Collector's
Corner, Inc. I**
2009 Eastern Ave., S.E.
Grand Rapids,
MI 49507
Ph: (616) 247-7828
(a-c,g,n,p,q)

Galaxy Comics
1319 S. Mission
Mt. Pleasant, MI 48858
PH: (517) 775-7838
(b,c,k,m,p,q,s)

Coy's Comics
301 South Hamilton
Saginaw, MI 48602
PH: (517) 790-1810
(a-c,f,g,k-s,u)

Galaxy Comics
3089 Bay Plaza
Saginaw, MI 48604
PH: (517) 799-6334
(a-c,g,k,m,n,p,q,s)

**Tardy's Discount
Comics II**
4158 Lake Michigan
Dr. N. W.
Walker, MI 49504
PH: (616) 791-4575
(c,g,p-s,u)

**Tardy's Collector's
Corner III**
2313 Lee St. S. W.
Wyoming, MI 49509
PH: (616) 531-5161
(b,c,e,g,m,n,p,q)

MINNESOTA

**John Mlachnik,
Overstreet Advisor**
P. O. Box 69
Chisholm, MN 55719
PH: (218) 254-3763
(a,b,g,l)

Nostalgia Zone
3149 1/2 Hennepin
Ave. S.
Minneapolis, MN 55408
PH: (612) 822-2806
(a,b,d-n,p,q)

**Nostalgia Zone (By
Appointment Only)**
3825 East Lake Street
Minneapolis, MN 55406
PH: (612) 721-7200
(a,b,d-q,u)

Midway Book & Comic
1579 University Ave.
St Paul, MN 55104
PH: (612) 644-7605
(a-h,n,q)

MISSOURI

**Betty's Books and
Collectible Comics**
1520 B Gravois Rd.
High Ridge, MO 63049
PH: (314) 677-3197
(a,b,e,h)

**Antiquarium Books &
Collectibles**
504 East High St.
Jefferson City,
MO 65101
PH: (573) 636-8995
(a-h,k-m,p-s)

Paperback Rack
126 E. 69 Highway
Kansas City, MO 64119
PH: (816) 452-7478
(b,c,e,p,q)

Not Just Comix
339 West Main St.
Park Hills, MO 63601
PH: (314) 431-4587
(b,c,g,m,p-s,u)

**MO's Comics &
Stories**
4573 Gravois
St. Louis, MO 63116
PH: (314) 353-9500
(a-d,f,g,o,q)

MONTANA

Starbase Comics
710 Grand Ave. #10
Billings, MT 59101
PH: (406) 245-2537
(a-c,k,m,q-s)

The Book Exchange
2335 Brooks St.
Tremper's
Shopping Ctr.
Missoula, MT 59801
PH: (406) 728-6342
(b,c,e,h,q-s)

NEBRASKA

Just Comics, Inc.
11814 South 25th St.
Omaha, NE 68123
PH: (402) 292-3337
(b,c,k,n,p,q,s,u)

NEVADA

Comic Zone
5020 E. Tropicana Ave.
Las Vegas, NV 89122
PH: (702) 435-2525
(a-c,g,m,n,p-s,u)

**Fandom's Comicworld
& Gallery of Reno, Inc.**
2001 East Second St.
Reno, NV 89502
PH: (702) 786-7977
(b,c,i,j,m,p-r,u)

NEW HAMPSHIRE

James F. Payette
P. O. Box 750
Bethlehem, NH 03574
PH: (603) 869-2097
(a,b,d-h)

Collectibles Unlimited
30A Warren St.
Concord, NH 03301
PH: (603) 228-3712
(b,c,m,q,s)

NEW JERSEY

The Hobby Shop
Route 34
Strathmore
Shopping Center
Aberdeen, NJ 07747
PH: (908) 583-0505
(a-c,k,m,q-s)

Comics Plus
Laurel Square,
Hwy. 70 &88
Brick, NJ 08723
PH: (908) 206-1070
(a-c,g,h,k,m,p,q)

Excellent Adventures
900 High Street
Burlington, NJ 08016
PH: (609) 386-7195
(a-c,f,g,k,m,p-s,u)

Eldorado Comics
2110 E. Rt. 70
P. O. Box 3630
Cherry Hill, NJ 08034
PH: (609) 489-1199
(a-g,i-k,m,n,p-u)

**Cantina Comics and
Collectibles**
116 East White
Horse Pike
Clementon,
NJ 08021-4225
PH: (609) 783-5141
(a,b,c,k,n,q,s)

Legends
2E-13 Deptford Mall
300 North
Almonesson Rd.
Deptford, NJ 08096
PH: (609) 845-8055

**Thunder Road
Sportscards
and Comics**
1973 North Olden Ave.
Ewing, NJ 08618
PH: (609) 771-1055
(a,b,k,m,q)

**A Time Lost.....
And Found**
310 East Evesham Rd.
Glendora, NJ 08029
PH: (609) 939-1909
(a-c,k,m,n,p,s,t)

**Thunder Road
Sportscards
and Comics**
1637 Route 33
Hamilton Square,
NJ 08690
PH: (609) 587-5353
(a,b,k,m,q)

The Comic Store
5174 Route 9 South
Howell, NJ 07731
PH: (908) 905-0001
(c,k,l,q-s)

Comics Plus
Middletown Plaza
1383 Hwy. 35
Middletown, NJ 07748
PH: (908) 706-0102
(a-c,g,h,k,m,p,q)

One Flight Up Books
63 MainSt.
Millburn, NJ 07041
PH: (201) 467-9288
(b,c,g,i,k-r)

Main St. Hobbies Inc.
74 N. Main St.
Milltown, NJ 08850
PH: (908) 828-7886
(a-c,k,m,q)

Montclair Book Center
221 Glenridge Ave.
Montclair, NJ 07042
PH: (201) 783-3630
(a-h,m,n,p-t)

Fat Jack's Comicrypt
521 White Horse Pike
Oaklyn, NJ 08107
PH: (609) 858-3877
(a-c,g,m,n,p,q,u)

MC Comics Inc.
54 Old Matawan Rd.
Old Bridge, NJ 08857
PH: (908) 238-5969
(a-c,g,k,m,n,p,q,s)

Zapp! Comics, Cards & Toys
2909 Washington Rd.
Suite 145
Parlin, NJ 08859
PH: (908) 727-4700
(a-c,g,k,m,n,p-u)

Passaic Book Center Inc.
594-96 Main Ave.
Dept. FP5
Passaic, NJ 07055
PH: (201) 778-6646
(a-u)

Excellent Adventures
72 Hanover St.
Pemberton, NJ 08068
PH: (609) 894-0255
(a-c,f,g,k,m,p-s,u)

Comics Plus
Ocean Plaza
Hwy. 35 & Sunset Ave.
Wanamassa, NJ 07712
PH: (908) 922-3308
(a-c,g,h,k,m,p,q)

Zapp! Comics, Cards & Toys
574 Valley Rd.
Wayne, NJ 07470
PH: (201) 628-4500
(a-c,g,k,m,n,p-u)

Frankenstein Comics
845 Mantua Pike
Route 45
Woodbury, NJ 08096
PH: (609) 848-6347
(b,c,g,k,m,q,r)

JHV Associates
By Appointment Only
P. O. Box 317
Woodbury Heights, NJ 08097
PH: (609) 845-4010
(a,b,d)

NEW YORK

FantaCo
21 Central Avenue
Albany, NY 12210-1305
PH: (518) 463-1400
(c,e,g,k-n,p-u)

Long Island Comics
1675 Sunrise Highway
Bay Shore, NY 11706
PH: (516) 665-4342
(b,c,r)

Wow Comics
2084 White
Plains Road
Bronx, NY 10462
PH: (718) 829-0461
(a-c,e,g,k,m,p-u)

Comic Shop At Pinocchio
1814 McDonald Ave.
Brooklyn, NY 11223
PH: (718) 645-2573
(b,c,g,k,m,q,s)

Comic Shop At Pinocchio
6914 20th Ave.
Brooklyn, NY 11204
PH: (718) 256-7832
(b,c,g,k,m,q,s)

Comic Quest
57-10 Hoffman Drive
Elmhurst, NY 11373
PH: (718) 205-8174
(c,d,e,g,k,m,n,q,r)

Golden Memories
250 Broadway
Hicksville, NY 11801
PH: (516) 932-8581
(a-c,k,m,q)

Comics & Hobbies
156 Mamaroneck Ave.
Mamaroneck,
NY 10543
(c,h,m,q,r)

47th Street Comics
326 W. 47th Street
New York, NY 10036
PH: (212) 664-0472
(b,c,g,i,k,m,n,p,q,s,u)

Action Comics
1551 Second Ave.
New York, NY 10028
PH: (212) 639-1976
(a-c,g,j,k,m,p-s,u)

Alex's MVP Cards & Comics
256 East 89th St.
New York, NY 10128
PH: (212) 831-2273
(a-c,g,j,k,m,n,p-s)

Comic Art Gallery
940 Third Avenue
New York, NY 10022
PH: (212) 759-6255
(b,c,g,i,k,m,n,p,q,s,u)

Four Color Comics
115 West 27th St.
New York, NY 10007
PH: (212) 675-6990

Funny Business Comics, Ltd.
660 B Amsterdam Ave.
at 92nd St.
New York, NY 10025
PH: (212) 799-9477
(b,c,l-n,q)

Jerry Ohlinger's Movie Material Store, Inc.
242 West 14 Street
New York, NY 10011
PH: (212) 989-0869
(i)

Jim Hanley's Universe
14 West 33rd Street
(Opposite the Empire State Building)
New York, NY 10001
PH: (212) 268-7088
(a-c,g,m,n,p-u)

Manhattan Comics & Cards
228 West 23rd. St.
New York, NY 10011
PH: (212) 243-9349
(a-c,g,j-n,q,u)

Metropolis Collectibles
873 Broadway,
Suite 201
New York, NY 10003
PH: (212) 260-4147
(a,b,k,i,j)

Village Comics
214 Sullivan Street
New York, NY 10012
PH: (212) 777-2770
(b,c,g,i,k,m,n,p,q,s,u)

Fantastic Planet
24 Oak St.
Plattsburgh, NY 12901
PH: (518) 563-2946
(a-c,e,g,m,p-u)

Dragon's Den
Poughkeepsie
Plaza Mall
Poughkeepsie,
NY 12601
PH: (914) 471-1401
(b,c,e,g,m,p-s,u)

Empire® Comics
1176 Mt. Hope Ave.
Rochester, NY 14620
PH: (716) 442-0371
(a-c,f,h,k,m,q-s,u)

Empire® Comics
375 Stone Rd.
Rochester, NY 14616
PH: (716) 663-6877
(a-c,f,h,k,m,q-s,u)

Jim Hanley's Universe
325 New Dorp Lane
Staten Island,
NY 10306
PH: (718) 351-6299
(a-c,g,m,n,p-u)

Krypton Comics of Staten Island, Inc.
2143 Hylan Blvd.
Staten Island,
NY 10306
PH: (718) 667-7695
(b,c,g,k,m,p,r,s)

Twilight Book & Game
1401 North Salina St.
Syracuse, NY 13208
PH: (315) 471-3139
(a-c,e,g,k,m,n,p-u)

Ravenswood, Inc.
263 Genesee St.
Utica, NY 13501
PH: (315) 735-3699
(a-c,g,m,p-t)

NORTH CAROLINA

Super Giant Comics
697 Brevard Rd.
Asheville, NC 28806
PH: (704) 665-2800
(a-c,j,l,n,q)

Heroes Aren't Hard To Find
Corner Central Ave.
& The Plaza
P. O. Box 9181
Charlotte, NC 28299
PH: (704) 375-7462
(a-c,g,j-n,p,s,u)

Heroes Are Here
208 South
Berkeley Blvd.
Goldsboro, NC 27534
PH: (919) 751-3131
(a-c,m,p,q)

Acme Comics
3808-C High Point Rd.
Greensboro, NC 27407
PH: (910) 855-0217
(b,c,g,i,k-n,p,q,s,u)

Acme Comics
2150 Lawndale Dr.
Greensboro, NC 27408
PH: (910) 574-2263
(b,c,g,i,k-n,p,q,s,u)

Parts Unknown, The Comic Book Store
551 South
Mendenhall Street
Greensboro, NC 27403
PH: (910) 272-0191
(a-c,g,n,p,q)

Heroes Are Here, Too
116 East Fifth St.
Greenville, NC 27834
PH: (919) 757-0948
(a-c,m,p,q)

Capitol Comics of Raleigh
3027-A
Hillsborough Street
Raleigh, NC 27607
PH: (919) 832-4600
(a-c,m,p,q)

Capitol Comics II
5212 Hollyridge Drive
Raleigh, NC 27612
PH: (919) 781-9500
(a-c,k,m,p,q,s)

Tales Resold
3936 Atlantic Ave.
Raleigh, NC 27604
PH: (919) 878-8551
(a-c,e,g,h,j,q)

Comics & Cards Unlimited
506 Waynesville Plaza
Waynesville, NC 28786
PH: (704) 456-8787
(a-c,g,k,l,m,q,r)

NORTH DAKOTA

Barry's Collector's Corner
8 S. 3rd. St.
City Center Mall
Grand Forks, ND 58201
PH: (701) 772-2518
(a-c,f-u)

Tom's Coin Stamp Gem Baseball & Comic Shop
#2 1st Street S.W.
Minot, ND 58701
PH: (701) 852-4522
(a-q,s,u)

OHIO

Kenmore Komics & Games
1020 Kenmore Blvd.
Akron, OH 44314
PH: (330) 745-5530
(b,c,m,p-u)

Dark Star III Books & Comics
1273 North Fairfield Rd.
Beavercreek, OH 45432
PH: (513) 427-3213
(b,c,e,g,k,m,p-s)

Comic Book World, Inc.
4016 Harrison Ave.
Cincinnati, OH 45211
PH: (513) 661-6300
(a-c,g,m,q-u)

Funny Books N Stuff
5063 Glenway Ave.
Cincinnati, OH 45238
PH: (513) 921-5720
(a-c,e-g,i,k,m,p,q,s,u)

Collectors Warehouse, Inc.
5437 Pearl Rd.
Cleveland, OH 44129
PH: (216) 842-2896
(a-g,i,k,m,n,q-t)

Bookery Fantasy & Comics
16 W. Main St.
Fairborn, OH 45324
PH: (937) 879-1408
(a-i,k-m,p-u)

Bookie Parlor
2778 Wilmington Pike
Kettering, OH 45419
PH: (937) 293-2243
(a-c,g,i,k,m,p,q,s)

Levit's Westside Market
Collectibles Division-
Neil Levit
4274 Oberlin Ave.
Lorain, OH 44053
PH: (216) 960-2601
(i,k,m,p)

Parker's Records & Comics
1222 Suite C Route 28
Milford, OH 45150
PH: (513) 575-3665
(a-c,g,i,m,n,p-r)

Collectible Comcs & Cards
30 W. Columbus St.
Pickerington, OH 43147
PH: (614) 833-3773
(a-c,g,j-n,p-s,u)

Dark Star Books & Comics
237 Xenia Ave. (Rt. 68)
Yellow Springs,
OH 45387
PH: (513) 767-9400
(b,c,e-h,k-n,p,q,s-u)

OKLAHOMA

Planet Comics & SF #1
918 West Main
Norman, OK 73069
PH: (405) 329-9695
(c,g,i,k-m,p-u)

New World Comics & Games
6219 N. Meridian
Oklahoma City,
OK 73112
PH: (405) 721-7634
(a-c,g,p-u)

New World Comics & Games
4420 SE 44th St.
Oklahoma City,
OK 73135
PH: (405) 677-2559
(a-c,g,p-u)

Comic Empire of Tulsa
3122 S. Mingo
Tulsa, OK 74146
PH: (918) 664-5808
(a-c,m,n,p,q)

Starbase 21
2130 So. Sheridan Rd.
Tulsa, OK 74129
PH: (918) 838-3388
(a-c,e,g,i-m,p-u)

Want List Comics
(Appointment Only)
P. O. Box 701932
Tulsa, OK 74170-1932
PH: (918)299-0440
(a,b,f,h-k,m)

OREGON

Emerald City Comics
770 E 13th
Eugene, OR 97401
PH: (541) 345-2568
(c,e,g,l-n,q,r,u)

Emerald City Comics III
3135 West 11th-G-1
Eugene, OR 97402
PH: (541) 342-5243
(c,l,m,q,r,u)

Nostalgia Collectibles
527 Willamette
Eugene, OR 97401
PH: (541) 484-9202
(a-g,k-n,p,q,s)

Beyond Comics
322 East Main
Medford, OR 97501
PH: (541) 779-9543
(a-c,p,q,s)

Future Dream East Burnside
1800 East Burnside
Portland,
OR 97214-1599
PH: (503) 231-8311
(a-c,e-j,m,n,p-u)

Future Dreams Gateway
1424 NE 103rd
Portland, OR 97220
PH: (503) 255-5245
(b,c,e,g,m,n,p,q)

Heroes Haven
627 S.E. Jackson St.
Roseburg, OR 97470
PH: (541) 673-5004
(a-c,f,g,k,m,p-s,u)

Ancient Wonders
19060 SW Boones Fy
Tualatin, OR 97062
PH: (503) 692-0753
(b,c,l,m,p-s)

PENNSYLVANIA

Cap's Comic Cavalcade
1894 Catasauqua Rd.
Allentown, PA 18103
PH: (610) 264-5540
(a-c,g,k,m-u)

Dreamscape Comics
310 West Broad St.
Bethlehem, PA 18018
PH: (610) 867-1178
(a-c,m,n,p-r)

Showcase Comics
874 West
Lancaster Ave.
Bryn Mawr, PA 19010
PH: (610) 527-6236
(a-c,k,m,n,p-s,u)

Comix Connection - Camp Hill
604 Camp Hill Mall
Camp Hill, PA 17011
PH: (800) 730-0994
(a-c,k,m,n,q-s,u)

Time Tunnel Collectibles
1001 Castle
Shannon Blvd.
Castle Shannon,
PA 15234
PH: (412) 531-8833
(a-c,g,h,m,p-s,u)

New Dimension Comics
20550 Route 19
Piazza Plaza
Cranberry Township,
PA 16066-7520
PH: (412) 776-0433
(a-c,k,m,q-s)

720

Dreamscape Comics
25th Street
Shopping Center
Easton, PA 18045
PH: (610) 250-9818
(a-c,m,n,p-r)

New Dimension Comics
508 Lawrence Avenue
Ellwood City, PA 16117
PH: (412) 758-2324
(a-c,k,m,q-s)

Comic Collection and Compact Discs
931 Bustleton Pike
Feasterville, PA 19053
PH: (215) 357-3332
(a-c,g,k-m,p-s,u)

The Comic Store
28 McGovern Ave.
Lancaster, PA 17602
PH: (717) 397-8737
(a-d,g,m,n,p-s,u)

Hobbies & Heroes
1107 Ligonier Street
Latrobe, PA 15650
PH: (412) 539-1101
(b,c,g,m,p-s,u)

Showcase Comics
Granite Run Mall
1067
West Baltimore Pike
Media, PA 19063
PH: (610) 891-9229
(a-c,k,m,n,p-s,u)

Fat Jack's Comicrypt I
2006 Sansom St.
Philadelphia, PA 19103
PH: (215) 963-0788
(a-c,g,m,n,p,q,u)

Fat Jack's Comicrypt II
7596 Haverford Ave.
Philadelphia, PA 17151
PH: (215) 473-6333
(a-c,g,m,n,p,q,u)

Fat Jack's Comicrypt III
5506 North 5th St.
Philadelphia, PA 19120
PH: (215) 924-8210
(a-c,g,m,n,p,q,u)

Showcase Comics
424 South St.
Philadelphia, PA 19147
PH: (215) 625-9613
(a-c,k,m,n,p-s,u)

Duncan Comics, Books, and Accessories
1047 Perry Highway
Pittsburgh (North Hills),
PA 15237
PH: (412) 635-0886
(a-e,g,h,k,m,n,p-s)

Eide's Entertainment
1111 Penn Ave.
Pittsburgh, PA 15222
PH: (412) 261-0900
(a-u)

Legends
2600 Plymouth
Meeting Mall
Plymouth Meeting, PA
19462
PH: (610) 828-5848
(a-c,g,k,m,n,p-s,u)

Comic Swap
110 South Fraser Street
State College,
PA 16801
PH: (814) 234-6005
(b,c,g,m,n,p-r,u)

Legends
3009 Willow Grove Mall
Willow Grove, PA 19090
PH: (215) 657-6141
(a-c,g,j,k,m,n,p-s,u)

Comic Store West
351 Loucks Rd.
York, PA 17404
PH: (717) 845-9198
(b,c,m,n,p-s,u)

Comix Connection - York
1201 Carlisle Rd.
York, PA 17404
PH: (717) 843-6516
(a-c,k,m,n,q-s,u)

RHODE ISLAND

The Annex
314 Broadway
Newport, RI 02840
PH: (401) 847-4607
(b,c,g,k,m,n,q-s,u)

Time Capsule Comics
2737 Post Rd.
Warwick, RI 02886
PH: (401) 732-8007
(a-c,g,j-u)

SOUTH CAROLINA

Heroes & Dragons Mega-Store
Boozer Shopping Ctr.
1563-B Broad River Rd.
Columbia, SC 29210
PH: (803) 731-4376
(a-c,g,k-n,p-s,u)

Planet Comics
3448 Cinema Center
Anderson, SC 29621
PH: (864) 261-3578
(a-c,g,j-n,p-u)

TENNESSEE

Funny Pages
325 East Bernard Ave.
Greeneville, TN 37745
PH: (423) 636-1028
(a-c,g,i-k,m,p,q)

The Great Escape
111-B
North Gallatin Rd.
Madison, TN 37115
PH: (615) 865-8052
(a-c,e,g,i,k-m,o-u)

The Great Escape
1925 Broadway
Nashville, TN 37203
PH: (615) 327-0646
(a-u)

TEXAS

Lone Star Comics Books & Games
504 East Abram St.
Arlington, TX 76010
PH: (817) METRO
265-0491
(a-c,e,g,k,m,p-u)

Lone Star Comics Books & Games
3415 South Cooper St.,
#141
Arlington, TX 76015
PH: (817) 557-5252
(a-c,e,g,k,m,p-u)

Austin Books & Sports Cards
5002 N. Lamar
Austin, TX 78751
PH: (512) 454-4197
(a-e,g-i,k,m,n,p,q,s-u)

Lone Star Comics Books & Games
11661 Preston
Forest Village
Dallas, TX 75230
PH: (214) 373-0934
(a-c,e,g,k,m,p-u)

Remember When
2431 Valwood Pkwy.
Dallas, TX 75234
PH: (972) 243-3439
(a-c,g,i,j,m,p,q,s,t)

Titan Comics
9444 Marsh Lane
Dallas, TX 75220
PH: (214) 350-4420
(b,c,n,p,q,u)

Lone Star Comics Books & Games
6312 Hulen Bend Blvd.
Ft. Worth, TX 76132
PH: (817) 346-7773
(a-c,e,g,k,m,p-u)

Bedrock City Comic Co.
6521 Westheimer
Houston, TX 77057
PH: (713) 780-0675
(a-g,j,k,m-u)

Bedrock City Comic Co.
2204-D FM 1960 W.
Houston, TX 77090
PH: (713) 444-9763
(a-g,j,k,m-u)

Phoenix Comics & Games
2424 Montrose
Houston, TX 77006
PH: (713) 524-1150
(c,e,g,m,p-r,u)

Third Planet Sci-Fi Superstore
2718
Southwest Freeway
Houston, TX 77098
PH: (713) 528-1067
(a-u)

Lone Star Comics Books & Games
931 Melbourne
Hurst, TX 76053
PH: (817) 595-4375
(a-c,e,g,k,m,p-u)

Lone Star Comics Books & Games
2550 N. Beltine Rd.
Irving, TX 75062
PH: (972) 659-0317
(a-c,e,g,k,m,p-u)

Lone Star Comics Books & Games
3600 Gus Thomasson
Suite 107
Mesquite, TX 75150
PH: (972) 681-2040
(a-c,e,g,k,m,p-u)

Lone Star Comics Books & Games
3100 Independence
Pkwy Suite 219
Plano, TX 75075
PH: (972) 985-1953
(a-c,e,g,k,m,p-u)

Ground Zero Comics
1700 SSE Loop 323
Suite 302
Tyler, TX 75701
PH: (903) 566-1185
(c,e,g,l,m,p-s,u)

Bankston's Comics
1321 S. Valley Mills Dr.
Waco, TX 76711
PH: (817) 755-0070
(b,c,f,i,k,m,p,q,s)

VIRGINIA

Comic and Card Collectorama
2008 Mt. Vernon Ave.
Alexandria, VA 22301
(Greater D. C. area)
PH: (703) 548-3466
(a-c,e,f,h,m,p,q,s,t)

Geppi's Comic World
Crystal City
1606 Crystal
Square Arcade
Arlington, VA 22202
PH: (703) 413-0618
(a-c,k-m,q,s,t)

Atlas Comics & Games
1691 Seminole Trail
Charlottesville,
VA 22901
PH: (804) 974-7512
(a-c,e,g,k,m,n,p-s,u)

Hole in the Wall Books
905 W. Broad St.
Falls Church, VA 22046
PH: (703) 536-2511
(b-e,g,h,l,n,p-u)

Marie's Books And Things
1701 Princess
Anne Street
Fredericksburg,
VA 22401-1344
PH: (540) 373-5196
(a-c,e-h,k,p,q,s)

Trilogy Shop #2
700 E. Little Creek Rd.
Norfolk, VA 23518
PH: (757) 587-2540
(c,e,g,m,q-u)

Nostalgia Plus
1601 Willow Lawn Drive
Richmond, VA 23230
PH: (804) 282-5532
(a-c,g,m,n,p,q)

B & D Comic Shop
802 Elm Avenue SW
Roanoke, VA 24016
PH: (540) 342-6642
(b,c,g,m,p-s)

Big Planet Comics
426 Maple Ave. East
Vienna, VA 22180
PH: (703) 242-9412
(b,c,p,q,m)

Comics & Things
4406 Holland Rd.
Virginia Beach,
VA 23452
PH: (757) 486-5870
(a-c,e,g,h,k,m,p-s,u)

Trilogy Shop #1
5773 Princess
Anne Rd.
Virginia Beach,
VA 23462
PH: (757) 490-2205
(a-c,e,g-i,k,m,n,p-s,u)

Trilogy Shop #4
857 S. Lynnhaven Rd.
Virginia Beach,
VA 23452
PH: (757) 468-0412
(c,e,g,m,q,r)

WASHINGTON

Everett Comics and Cards
2936 Colby Ave.
Everett, WA 98201
PH: (206) 252-8181
(a-c,k,m,r-u)

The Comic Character Shop
Old Firehouse
Antique Mall
110 Alaskan Way South
Seattle, WA 98104
PH: (206) 283-0532
(b,h-k,p)

Comic Dungeon
1622 1/2 North 45th St.
Seattle, WA 98103
PH: (206) 545-8373
(a-c,f,g,k,m-q,s)

Golden Age Collectables LTD
1501 Pike Place Market
401 Lower Level
Seattle, WA 98101
PH: (206) 622-9799
(a-g,l-n,p-q)

Rocket Comics
8408 Greenwood
Ave. N
Seattle, WA 98103
PH: (206) 784-7300
(a-h, p,q)

Digital Heroes
13 Boyer Ave.
Walla Walla, WA 99362
PH: (888) DHEROES
e mail
dighero@bmi.net
web http://www.digital-heroes.com
(b,c,g,k,m-u)

North Star Comics
917 South 2nd Ave. #B
Walla Walla, WA 99362
PH: (509) 522-9891
(c,e,i,k-m,p-s)

WEST VIRGINIA

Comic Castle
314 Neville St.
Beckley, WV 25801
PH: (304) 253-1974
(b,c,m,n,p,q,s)

WISCONSIN

Discount Comics
P. O. Box 112
Cottage Grove,
WI 53527
PH: (608) 764-8410
(c,i,k-u)

Clairemont Comics
2543
E. Clairemont Pkwy.
Eau Claire, WI 54701
PH: (715) 831-2112
(a-c,g,m,p-s,u)

20th Century Books
108 King St.
Madison, WI 53703
PH: (608) 251-6226
(c,e,g,h,m,n,q,t,u)

Capital City Comics
1910 Monroe St.
Madison, WI 53711
PH: (608) 251-8445
(a-d,f,j,m,n,p,q,u)

Westfield's Comics, Etc.
676 S. Whitney Way
Madison, WI 53711
PH: (608) 277-1280
(b,c,e,g,k-m,o-u)

Capital City Comics
2565 North
Downer Ave.
Milwaukee, WI 53211
PH: (414) 332-8199
(a-d,f,j,m,n,p,q,u)

CANADA

ALBERTA

Amazing Heroes Ltd.
1008 MacLeod TRSE
Calgary, AB T2G 2M7
PH: (403) 262-0366
(c,k,m,o,p,r,s)

Another Dimension Comics
324-10 St. N.W.
Calgary, AB T2N 1V8
PH: (403) 283-7078
(a-c,e,g,k,m,n,p-s,u)

Redd Skull Comics & CD's
720 A Edmonton
Trail N. E.
Calgary, AB T2E 3J4
PH: (403) 230-2716
(a-c,k-r,u)

Beyond Fantasy the Comic Store
16205 Stony Plain Rd.
Edm., Alberta T5P 4A3
PH: (403) 483-2669
(b,c,e,g-i,k,m,n,p-s,u)

Comic Fever
11338-132 ave.
Edmonton, AB
T5E 1A1
PH: (403) 452-6324
(b,c,g,i-k,m,p-s)

BRITISH COLUMBIA

Page After Page
1795 Harvey Ave.
Kelowna, BC V1Y 6G4
PH: (250) 860-6554
(b,c,q,r,u)

Golden Age Collectables
830 Granville Street
Vancouver, BC
V6Z 1K3
PH: (604) 683-2819
(a-c,i,k,m,n,q-s,u)

MANITOBA

The Collector's Slave
156 Imperial Ave.
Winnipeg, Manitoba
R2M 0K8
PH: (204) 237-4428
(a-c,e-g,k-n,s)

ONTARIO

3RD Quadrant
226 Queen St. W. UPR
Toronto, ON M5V 1Z6
PH: (416) 974-9211
(b,c,k,m,p-s)

B.A.'s Comics & Nostalgia
121 Oxford St. East
London, Ontario
N6A 1T4
PH: (519) 439-9636
(b,c,g,m,n,p,q,u)

Paradise Comics
3278 Yonge Ave.
Toronto, ONT M4N 2L6
PH: (416) 487-9807
(a-c,g,j,k,m,n,p-r)

The Final Stop
381 McArthur Avenue
Vanier, ON K1L 6N5
PH: (613) 749-1247
(c,g,k,m,n,p,q)

QUEBEC

Komico Inc.
4210 Decarie
Montreal, Quebec
H4A 3K3
PH: (514) 489-4009
(b,c,p,q)

Les Comiques St Martin Inc.
1654 St Martin West
Laval, QC H7S 1M9
PH: (514) 681-2339
(c,e,m,q-s,u)

QUICK REFERENCE LISTS

The following lists were compiled to give our readers more detailed information about their favorite comic books. We invite your criticism, comments, and suggestions for omitted entries.

SILVER & MODERN AGE INDEX

Below is a complete listing of all titles published by the ten most popular comic book companies today. Where several titles exist by the same name, we have listed the title once for space considerations. index compiled by Arnold T. Blumberg & Scott Braden

Gravestone
Hardcase
Lord Pumpkin
.../Necromantra
Malibu Ashcan: Rafferty
Man Called A-X, The
Man of War
Mantra
Metaphysique
Mortal Kombat
...: Baraka
...: Battlewave
...: Goro, Prince of Pain
...: Kitana and Mileena
...: Kung Lao
...: Raydon & Kano
...: U. S. Special Forces
Mutants Vs. Ultras
Night Man, The
Nocturnals, The
Power & Glory
Power of Prime
Prime
Project A-KO
Protectors
Prototype
Ripfire
Rune
.../Silver Surfer
Siren
Sludge
Solitaire
Solution, The
Star Slammers
Star Trek: Deep Space Nine
...-The Celebrity Series: Blood and Honor
...Hearts and Minds
..., The Maquis
.../The Next Generation
Strangers, The

Street Fighter
Strikeback!
Tarzan: Love, Lies and the Lost City
...the Warrior
Terminator 2: Cybernetic Dawn
...: Nuclear Twilight
Ultraforce
Ultraverse Double Feature
...Origins
...Premiere
...Year One
...Year Two
...Year Zero: The Death of the Squad
Warstrike
Wrath

Marvel UK
Action Force
Battletide
...II
Captain Britain
Codename: Genetix
Dark Angel
...Guard
Death Metal
...Vs. Genetix
Death's Head
...II
...II & the Origin of Die-Cut
Death 3
...Wreck
Die-Cut
...Vs. G-Force
Digitek
Dragon's Claws
Gene Dogs
Genetix
Gun Runner
Hell's Angel
Incomplete Death's Head

Killpower: The Early Years
King Arthur and the Knights of Justice
Knights of Pendragon, The
Motormouth
Mys-Tech Wars
Nightraven: The Collected Stories
Pendragon
Plasmer
Shadow Riders
Super Soldiers
Warheads
Wildthing

Star Comics
Air Raiders
Animax
Bullwinkle and Rocky
Care Bears
Chuck Norris
Defenders of the Earth
Droids
Ewoks
Flintstone Kids, The
Flintstones, The
Foofur
Fraggle Rock
Getalong Gang, The
Heathcliff
...'s Funhouse
Hugga Bunch
Inhumanoids, The
Madballs
Masters of the Universe
Misty
Muppet Babies, The
Muppets Take Manhattan, The
Peter Porker the Spectacular Spider-Ham
Planet Terry

Popples
Royal Roy
Silverhawks
Star Comics Magazine
Strawberry Shortcake
Thundercats
Top Dog
Visionaries
Wally the Wizard

SIRIUS
Against Blackshard 3-D
Akiko
Animal Mystic
Crypt of Dawn
Dawn
Dolls
Drama
Eleven or One
Greylore
Hero Alliance, The
Poison Elves
Tales of the Sun Runners
Wandering Star

TEKNO COMIX/BIG ENT.
Gene Roddenberry's Lost Universe
...Xander in Lost Universe
Isaac Asimov's I-Bots
John Jakes' Mullkon Empire
Leonard Nimoy's Primortals
...Origins
Mickey Spillane's Mike Danger
Neil Gaiman's Lady Justice
...Mr. Hero - The Newmatic Man
...Teknophage
...Wheel of Worlds

TOPPS COMICS
Barbi Twins, The
Bombast
Bram Stoker's Dracula
Cadillacs and Dinosaurs
Captain Glory
Dracula Chronicles
...Versus Zorro
...: Vlad the Impaler
Duckman
...: The Mob Frog Saga
Exosquad
Frankenstein/Dracula War
Jack Kirby's Secret City Saga
...Silver Star
...Teenagents
Jason Goes to Hell: The Final Friday
...Vs. Leatherface
Jurassic Park
...: Raptor
...: Raptors Attack
...: Raptors Hijack
Lady Rawhide
Lone Ranger and Tonto
Mars Attacks
Mary Shelley's Frankenstein
Night Glider
Ray Bradbury Comics
Return to Jurassic Park
Satan's Six
...: Hellspawn
Topps Comics Presents
Victory
X-Files, The
Zorro

1ST APPEARANCES

A-Man the Amazing Man - Amazing-Man Comics #5, 9/39

Adam Strange - Showcase #17, 11-12/58

Adult Legion - Superman #147, 8/61

Agent Liberty - Superman #60 (2nd Series), 10/91

Air Man - (Hawkman imitator) Keen Detective Funnies #23, 8/40

Air Wave - Detective Comics #60, 2/42

Air Wave II - Green Lantern #100, 1/78

Airboy - Air Fighters Comics V1#2, 11/42

Airwave I - Detective Comics #60, 2/42

Alex Summers - (becomes Havok) X-Men #54, 3/69

Alfred - Batman #16 4-5/43; (1st skinny Alfred) Detective Comics #83, 1/44

Alice Cooper - Marvel Premiere #50, 10/79

Alicia Masters - Fantastic Four #8, 11/62

Aliens - Aliens #1 May '88; Magnus, Robot Fighter #1, 2/63

Alley Oop - Funnies #1, 10/36

Alpha Flight - X-Men #120, 4/78

Amazing Man - All Star Squadron #23, 7/83

American Ace - (1st newsstand app.) Marvel Mystery Comics #2, 12/39

American Crusader - Thrilling Comics #19, 8/41

American Eagle - Marvel Two-In-One Annual #6, 1981; (1st published app.) Motion Picture Funnies Weekly #1, 1939

Ancient One - Strange Tales #110, 7/63

Andy Panda - Crackajack Funnies #39, 9/41

Angel - Marvel Comics #1, 10-11/39

Angel (now Archangel) **-** X-Men #1, 9/63

Angel & the Ape - Showcase #77, 9/68

Animal Man - (in costume) Strange Adventures #190, 7/66; (no costume) Strange Adventures #180, 9/65; (re-intro) Wonder Woman #267, 5/80

Ant-Man - (costume) Tales to Astonish #35, 9/62; (new) Marvel Premiere #47, 4/79; (no costume) Tales to Astonish #27, 1/62; (re-intro) Avengers #46, 11/67

Anthro - Showcase #74, 5/68

Apache Kid - Two Gun Western #5, 11/50

Ape, The - Startling Comics #21, 5/43

Aqua-Girl - Aquaman #33, 5-6/67

Aquababy - Aquaman #23, 9-10/65

Aquaboy - Superboy #171

Aquagirl - (try out, not same as other) Adventure Comics #266, 11/59

Aquagirl - Aquaman #33, 5-6/67

Aqualad - Adventure Comics #269, 2/60

Aquarian (Wundarr) **-** Adventure Into Fear #17, '73

Aquaman - More Fun Comics #73, 11/41

Arak - Warlord #48, 8/81

Archangel - (cameo) (formerly Angel) X-Factor #23, 12/87; (full app.) X-Factor #24, 1/88

Archie Andrews - Pep Comics #22, 12/41

Arion - Warlord #55

Arrow - Funny Pages V2#10, 9/38

Arthur Stacy - Amazing Spider-Man #93, 2/71

Asbestos Lady - Captain America Comics #63, 7/47

Astro Boy - Astro Boy #1, 8/65

Atom - All-American Comics #19, 10/40; (S.A.) Showcase #34, 9-10/61

Atoman - Atoman #1, 2/46

Atomaster - Comic Books #1, 1950

Atomic Mouse - Atomic Mouse #1, 3/53

Atomic Rabbit - Atomic Rabbit #1, 8/55

Atomic Thunderbolt - Atomic Thunderbolt #1, 2/46

Aunt May - Amazing Fantasy #15, 8-9/62; (prototype) Strange Tales #92, 6/62

Aurora - X-Men #120

Avenger - Shadow Comics #2, 4/40

Azrael - (cameo) Tales of the Teen Titans #52, 4/85; (full app.) Tales of the Teen Titans #53, 5/85

Baby Huey - Casper, the Friendly Ghost #1, 9/49; (1st Harvey app.) Harvey Comics Hits #60, 9/52

Badger - Badger #1, 12/83

Balbo, the Boy Magician - Master Comics #32, 11/42

Bamm Bamm - (Flintstones) Flintstones #16, 1/64

Barker - National Comics #42, 5/44

Barney Bear - Our Gang Comics #1, 9-10/42

Baron Strucker - Sgt. Fury #5, 1/64

Bat Lash - Showcase #76, 8/68

Bat-Girl - Batman #139, 4/61; (new) Detective #359, 1/67

Batgirl - Detective Comics #359, 1/67

Batman - Detective Comics #27, May

'39; (new look w/new costume) Detective Comics #327, 5/64

Batman, Jr. - World's Finest Comics #215, 10/72

Batmite - Detective Comics #267, 5/59

Batwoman - Detective Comics #233, 7/56; (1st modern app. G.A. Batwoman) Brave and the Bold #182, 1/82; (new) Detective Comics #624, 12/90; (re-intro) Batman Family #10, 3-4/77

Beast - X-Men #1, 9/63; (new) (1st in mutated form) Amazing Adventures #11, 3/72

Beast Boy - (becomes Changeling) Doom Patrol #99, 11/65

Belit - Giant-Size Conan #1, 9/74

Bennett Brant - Amazing Spider-Man #11, 4/64

Bernie the Brain - Sugar & Spike #72, ?, '68

Berserkers, The - X-Men/Alpha Flight #1, 12/85

Betty - Pep Comics #22, 12/41

Betty Brant - Amazing Spider-Man #4, 9/63

Bill Barnes - (Air Ace) Shadow Comics #1, 3/40

Binary - (formerly Ms. Marvel) X-Men #164, 12/82

Birdman, The - Weird Comics #1, 4/40

Bishop - (cameo) X-Men #282, 11/91; (full app.) X-Men #283, 12/91

Bizarro Jimmy Olsen - Adventure Comics #287, 8/61

Bizarro Lana Lang - Adventure Comics #292, 1/62

Bizarro Lois Lane - Action Comics #255, 8/59

Bizarro Lucy Lane - Adventure Comics #292, 1/62

Bizarro Marilyn Monroe - Adventure Comics #294, 3/62

Bizarro Perry White - Adventure Comics #287, 8/61

Bizarro President Kennedy - Adventure Comics #294, 3/62

Black Bolt - (1st full app.) Fantastic Four #46, 1/66 (cameo) (from Inhumans) Fantastic Four #45, 12/65

Black Canary - Flash Comics #86, 8/47; (Silver Age) Justice League of America #74; (1st modern app.) Detective Comics #554, 9/85; (1st solo story) Flash Comics #92, 2/48

Black Cat - Pocket Comics #1, 8/41

Black Cobra - Captain Flight Comics #8 ?, '46

Black Condor - Crack Comics #1, 5/40

Black Dwarf - Spotlight Comics #1, 11/44

Black Flame - Starslayer #20 9/84; Action Comics #304, 9/63

Black Fury - Fantastic Comics #18, 5/41

Black Goliath - Black Goliath #1, 2/76

BlackHawk - Military Comics #1, 8/41

Black Hood - Top-Notch Comics #9, 10/40; (S.A.) Adventures of the Fly #7, 7/60

Black Jack - Zip Comics #20, 11/41

Black Knight - Black Knight #1, 5/55

Black Knight - Tales to Astonish #52, 2/64

Black Knight II - Avengers #48, 1/68

Black Lightning - Black Lightning #1, 4/77

Black Marvel - Mystic Comics #5, 3/41

Black Orchid - Adventure Comics #428, 6-7/73; (new) Black Orchid #1, 12/88

Black Owl - Prize Comics #2, 4/40

Black Panther - Stars & Stripes #3, 7/41

Black Panther - Fantastic Four #52, 7/66

Black Phantom - Tim Holt #25, 9/51

Black Pirate - Sensation Comics #1, 1/42

Black Rider - All Western Winners #2, Win '48-49

Black Spider - Super-Mystery Comics V1#3, 10/40

Black Terror - Exciting Comics #9, 5/41

Black Widow - Mystic Comics #4, 7-8/40

Black Widow - Tales of Suspense #52, 4/64

Blackie the Hawk - Blackhawk #75, 4/54

Blackie the Hawk - (re-intro) Blackhawk #108, 1/57

Blade the Vampire Slayer - Tomb of Dracula #10, ?/73?

Blok - (Legion) Superboy #253, 7/79

Blonde Phantom - All-Select Comics #11, Fall '46; (re-intro) Sensational She-Hulk #4, 8/89

Blondie - Ace Comics #1, 4/37

Bloodshot - (cameo) Eternal Warrior #4, 11/92; (1st full app.) Rai #0, 11/92

Bloodstone - Marvel Presents #1, 10/75

Blue Beetle - (G.A.) Mystery Men Comics #1, 8/39; (Charlton) Blue Beetle #18, 2/55; (Ted Kord) Captain Atom #83, 11/66; (1st DC app.) Crisis on Infinite Earths #1, 4/85

Blue Blade - USA Comics #5, Sum '42

Blue Blaze - Mystic Comics #1, 3/40

Blue Bolt - Blue Bolt #1, 6/40

Blue Circle - Blue Circle Comics #1, 6/44

Blue Devil - Fury of Firestorm #24, 6/84

Blue Streak - Crash Comics #1, 5/40

Bo Bunny - Funny Stuff #70, 1-2?/53

Bobby Benson - Bobby Benson's B-Bar-B Riders #1, 5-6/50

Boboes - Marvel Mystery Comics #32, 6/42

Bomba - Bomba, the Jungle Boy #1, 9-10/67

Bombshell - Boy Comics #3, 4/42

Booster Gold - Booster Gold #1, 2/86

Bouncer - Bouncer nn, 1944

Bouncing Boy - (Legion) Action Comics #276, 5/61

Boy Commandos - Detective Comics #64, 6/42

Bozo the Robot - Smash Comics #1, 8/39

Braniac 5 - Action Comics #276, 5/61

Brick Bradford - King Comics #1, 4/36

Broncho Bill - Tip Top Comics #1, 4/36

Brother Power - Brother Power, the Geek #1, 9-10/68; (re-intro) Saga of Swamp Thing Annual #5, 1989

Buck Rogers - (in comics) Famous Funnies #3, 9/34

Buckskin - Super Mystery V2#1, 4/41

Bucky - (Captain America's sidekick) Captain America Comics #1, 3/41;(Silver Age) Avengers #4, 3/64;

Bugs Bunny - Looney Tunes & Merrie Melodies #1, 1941

Bullet - Amazing Mystery Funnies V3#1, 1/40

Bulletboy - Master Comics #48, 3/44

Bulletman - Nickel Comics #1, 5/40

Bumblebee - Teen Titans (1st series) #48, 1977

Buzzy - All Funny Comics #1, Win '43-44

Buzzy the Crow - Harvey Comics Hits #60, 9/52

B'Wanna Beast - Showcase #66

Cable - (1st full app.) New Mutants #87, 3/90; (cameo) New Mutants #86, 2/90

Cain - (House of Mystery host) House of Mystery #176, 10/67

Calico Kid - (becomes Ghost Rider) Tim Holt #6, 5/49

Camilla - Jungle Comics #1, 1/40

Candy - Police Comics #37, 12/44

Captain & the Kids - Famous Comics Cartoon Books #1200, 1934; Tip Top Comics #1, 4/36

Captain Action - Captain Action & Action Boy nn, 1967

Captain Aero - Captain Aero Comics V1#7, 12/41

Captain America - Captain America Comics #1, 3/41; (Silver Age) Strange Tales #114, 11/63; (Acrobat disguised as) Avengers #4, 3/64; (fomerly Super Patriot) Captain America #333, 9/87; (new) Captain America #181, 1/75; (new) (formerly Nomad) Captain America #183, 3/75

Captain Atom - (1st DC app.) Crisis on Infinite Earths #9, 9/85; (new) Captain Atom #84, 1/67; (new) Captain Atom #1 3/87; (S.A.) Space Adventures #33, 3/60

Captain Battle - Silver Streak Comics #10, 5/41

Captain Britain - Captain Britain #1, 3/87; (1st U.S. app.) Marvel Team-Up #65, 1/78

Captain Comet - Strange Adventures #9, 6/51; (re-intro) Secret Society of Super-Villains #2, 7-8/76

Captain Commando - Pep Comics #30, 8/42

Captain Courageous - Banner Comics #3, 9/41

Captain Daring - Buccaneers #19, 1/50; Daring Mystery Comics #7, 4/41

Captain Desmo - Adventure Comics #32, 11/38

Captain Easy - Funnies #1, 10/36; Famous Comics Cartoon Books #1202, 1934

Captain Fearless - Silver Streak Comics #1, 12/39

Captain Fight - Fight Comics #16, 12/41

Captain Flag - Blue Ribbon Comics #16, 9/41

Captain Flash - Captain Flash #1, 11/54

Captain Freedom - Speed Comics #13, 5/41

Captain Future - Man of Tomorrow - Startling Comics #1, 6/40

Captain George Stacy - Amazing Spider-Man #56, 1/68

Captain Marvel (Shazam) - Whiz Comics #1, 2/40; (M.F.Enterprises) Captain Marvel #1, 4/66; (modern) Shazam: the New Beginning #1, 4/87; (new) Legends #1, 11/86;(re-intro) Shazam! #1, 2/73

Captain Marvel (female) - Amazing Spider-Man Annual #14, 1982

Captain Marvel of the Kree - Marvel Super-Heroes #12, 12/67

Captain Marvel, Jr. - Whiz Comics #25, 12/41

Captain Midnight - Funnies #57, 7/41

Captain Savage - Mystery Men Comics #4, 11/39

Captain Storm - Captain Storm #1, 5-6/64

Captain Strong - Action Comics #421, 3/73

Captain Terror - U.S.A. #2, 11/41

Captain Terry Thunder - Jungle Comics #1, 1/40

Captain Thunder - Flash Comics (Fawcett) #1, 1/40

Captain Thunder - Superman #276, ?'74

Captain Triumph - Crack Comics #27, 1/43

Captain Universe - Micronauts #8, 8/79

Captain Victory - Our Flag Comics #1, 8/41

Captain Wizard - Red Band Comics #3, ?'45

Captain Wonder - Kid Komics #1, 2/43

Captain Yank - Big Shot Comics #29, 11/42

Casper the Friendly Ghost - (1st Harvey app.) Harvey Comics Hits #60, 9/52; Casper #1, 9/49

Cat - The Cat #1, 11/72

Cat Girl - Adventures of the Fly #9, 11/60

Catman - Crash Comics #5, 11/40

Cave Carson - Brave and the Bold #31, 8-9/60

Cerebus - Cerebus the Aardvark #1, 12/77

Challenger - Mystic Comics #6, 10/41

Chameleon - Target Comics V1#6, 7/40

Chameleon Boy - (Legion) Action Comics #267, 8/60

Champ - Champion Comics #2, 12/39

Changeling - (formerly Beast Boy) New Teen Titans #1, 11/80; (X-Men) X-Men #35, 8/67

Charlie Chan - Feature Comics #23, 8/39

Charlie-27 - Marvel Super Heroes

Fighting Yank - Startling Comics #10, 9/41

Fin - Daring Mystery Comics #7, 4/41

Fin Fang Foom - Strange Tales #89, 10/61

Fire - Super Friends #25

Fireball - Pep Comics #12, 2/41; (S.A.) Mighty Crusaders #4, 5?/66

Firebrand - Police Comics #1, 8/41

Firefist - Blue Beetle #1, 6/86

Firefly - Top-Notch Comics #8, 9/40

Firehair - Rangers Comics #21, 2/45

Firehawk - Fury of Firestorm #17, 10/83

Fire Lad - Adventure Comics #306, 2/63

Firelord - Thor #225, 7/74

FireStar - X-Men #193, 4/85

Firestorm - Firestorm,the Nuclear Man #1, 3/78; (new) Firestorm, the Nuclear Man Annual #5, 10/87

Flag, The - Our Flag Comics #2, 10/41

Flame, The - Wonderworld Comics #3, 7/39

Flamebird - (Jimmy Olsen as) Superman #158, 12/62; (new) Secret Origins Annual #3, 1989

Flaming Carrot - Visions #1, 1979

Flash - Flash Comics #1, 1/40; (G.A.) (1st app. in S.A.) Flash #123, 9/61

Flash - Showcase #4, 9-10/56

Flash Gordon - King Comics #1, 4/36

Flash Lightning - (becomes Lash Lightning) Sure-Fire Comics #1, 6/40

Flash Rabbit - All Top Comics #1, 1945

Flexo the Rubber Man - Mystic Comics #1, 3/40

Flintstones - Dell Giant #48, 7/61

Fly - Double Life of Private Strong #1, 6/59

Fly Girl - (1st in costume) Adventures of the Fly #14, 9?/61; (w/o costume) Adventures of the Fly #13, 7?/61

Fly-Man, The - Spitfire Comics #1, 8/41

Forbush Man - Not Brand Echh #5, 12/67

Forge - (X-Force) X-Men #184, 8/84

Fox - Blue Ribbon Comics #4, 6/40; (new) Black Hood #11, 11/92

Frankenstein - Prize Comics #7, 12/40; Frankenstein #2, 9/66

Frankenstein's monster - (cameo) Silver Surfer #7, 8/69

Freckles & His Friends - Famous Comics Cartoon Books #1204, 1934

Fred Bender - (becomes Dr. Eclipse) Solar #14, 10/92

Freezum - Blue Bolt V2#5, 10/41

Fritzi Ritz - Tip Top Comics #1, 4/36

Fu Manchu - (1st in Detective) Detective Comics #17, 7/38; (1st cvr.) Det. #1, 3/37

G. I. Robot - Weird War Tales #101, 7/81

Gambit - (cameo) X-Men Annual #14, 1990; (full app.) X-Men #266, 8/90

Gandy Goose - Terry-Toons Comics #1, 10/42

Gangbuster - Adventures of Superman #434, 11/87

Gargoyle - Defenders #94, 4/80

Gary Concord - (Ultra Man) All-American Comics #8, 11/39

Genius Jones - All Funny Comics #1, Win '43-44

Gentleman Ghost - Atom & Hawkman #43, 6-7/69

Ghost Breaker - Star Spangled Comics #122, 11/51

Ghost Patrol - Flash Comics #29, 5/42

Ghost Patrol - Wings #66, 2/46

Ghost Rider - (formerly Calico Kid) Tim Holt #11, ?/49

Ghost Rider - (western) Ghost Rider #1, 2/67; (Johnny Blaze) Marvel Spotlight #5, 8/72; (new-Daniel Ketch) Ghost Rider V2#1, 5/90

Giant-Man - (formerly Ant-Man) Tales to Astonish #49, 11/63

Gideon - New Mutants #98, 2/91

Gladstone Gander - Walt Disney's Comics and Stories #88, 1/48

Glory Grant - Amazing Spider-Man #140, 1/75

Gnort - Justice League International #10

God Of Thunder, The - Weird Comics #1, 4/40

Godiva - New Teen Titans Annual #3, 11/87

Golden Arrow - Whiz Comics #1, 2/40

Golden Dragon - Adventure Comics #32, 11/38

Golden Girl - Golden Lad #5, 6/46

Golden Gladiator - Brave and the Bold #1, 8-9/55

Golden Gorilla - Action Comics #224, 1/57

Golden Lad - Golden Lad #1, 7/45

Golem - Strange Tales #174, 2/74

Goliath - (formerly Giant-Man) Avengers #28, 5/66 (formerly Hawkeye) Avengers #63, 4/69

Grandma Duck - Donald and Mickey Merry Christmas nn, 1945

Gray Ghost - Sensation Comics #1, 1/42

Great Gazoo - (Flintstones) Flintstones #34

Green Arrow - More Fun Comics #73, 11/41

Green Falcon - Blue Ribbon Comics #4, 6/40

Green Flame - Super Friends #42, 3/81

Green Fury - (formerly Green Flame) Infinity, Inc. #32, 11/86

Green Hornet - (1st in comics) Green Hornet Comics #1, 12/40; (Silver Age) Green Hornet #1, 2/67

Green Lama - Prize Comics #7, 12/40

Green Lantern - All-American Comics #16, 7/40; (S.A.) Showcase #22, 9-10/59

Green Mask - Mystery Men Comics #1, 8/39

Green Turtle - Blazing Comics #1, 6/44

Grendel - Primer #2, 2/83

Grey Mask - Suspense Comics #1, 12/43

Grimjack - Starslayer #10, 11/83

Grim Reaper, The - Wonder Comics #1, 5/44

Groo the Wanderer - Destroyer Duck #1, 1982

Gruesomes - (Flintstones) Flintstones #24

Guardian - Star Spangled Comics #7, 4/42; (formerly Vindicator) Alpha Flight #2, 9/83

Guardian Angel - (formerly Hop Harrigan) All-American Comics #25, 4/41

Guardsman I - Iron Man #43, 11?/71?

Guardsman II - Iron Man #96, 3/77

Gunner & Sarge - All-American Men of War #57, ? '58?; Our Fighting Forces #45, 5/59

Guy Gardner - (later a Green Lantern)Green Lantern #59, 3/68; (1st app. as a Green Lantern) Green Lantern #116, 5/79

Gwen Stacy - Amazing Spider-Man #31, 12/65

Gyro Gearloose - Walt Disney's Comics and Stories #140, 5/52

Halo - Blue Beetle #24, 8/43

Hangman - Pep Comics #17, 7/41

Hangman - (re-intro) Comet #6, 12/91; (S.A.) Fly Man #33, 9/65

Happy Houlihans - Blackstone, the Magician Detective #1, Fall '47

Harada - Solar #3, 11/91

Harbinger - Harbinger #1, 1/92

Harlequin - (Joker's Daughter) Teen Titans #48, '77

Harry Osborn - (later becomes Green Goblin II) Amazing Spider-Man #31, 12/65

Harvey Bullock - Batman #361, 7/83

Havok - (no costume) X-Men #56, 5/69; (with costume) X-Men #58, 7/69

Hawk & Dove - Showcase #75, 7-8/67

Hawkeye - Tales of Suspense #57, 9/64; (formerly Goliath) Avengers #98, 4/72

Hawkgirl - (formerly Shiera Sanders) All Star Comics #5, 6-7/41; (Silver Age) Brave & the Bold #34, 2-3/61

Hawkman - Flash Comics #1, 1/40; (S.A.) Brave and the Bold #34, 2-3/61; (modern) Hawkworld: Book #1, 1989

Heap - Air Fighters Comics V1#3, 12/42

Heckle & Jeckle - Terry-Toons Comics #50, 11/46

Hedy Devine - Hedy Devine Comics #22, 8/47

Hedy Wolfe - Miss America Magazine #2, 11/44

Heimdall - Journey Into Mystery #85, 10/62

Hellblazer - (John Constantine) Saga of Swamp Thing #37, 6/85

Hellcat - Avengers #144, 2/76

Her - (formerly Paragon) Marvel Two-In-One #61, 3/80

Herbie - Forbidden Worlds #73, ? '59?

Hercules - Blue Ribbon Comics #4, 6/40; Incredible Hulk #3, 9/62; Hit Comics #1 7/40; Mystic Comics #3, 6/40

Herman & Catnip - Harvey Comics Hits #60, 9/52

High Evolutionary - Thor #134, 11/66

Him - (Warlock) (cameo) Fantastic

Four #67, 10/67 (Warlock) (full app.) Thor #165, 6/69

Hocus & Pocus - Action Comics #83, 4/45

Hooded Horseman - Blazing West #14, 11-12/50

Hooded Wasp - Shadow Comics #7, 11/40

Hop Harrigan - All-American Comics #1, 4/39

Hoppy the Marvel Bunny - Fawcett's Funny Animals #1, 12/42

Hourman - Adventure Comics #48, 3/40; (1st app. in S.A.) Justice League of America #21, 8/63

Hourman - (new) Infinity, Inc. #21, 12/85

Howard the Duck - Fear #19, 12/73

Huey, Dewey and Louie - Donald Duck nn (bubble pipe cover)

Hulk - (green skin) Incredible Hulk #2, 7/62; (grey skin) Incredible Hulk #1, 5/62; (new) Incredible Hulk #377, 1/91; (re-intro with grey skin) Incredible Hulk #324, 10/86

Hulk 2099 - 2099 Unlimited #1, 9/93

Human Target - Action Comics #419, 1/73

Human Top - Red Raven Comics #1, 8/40; Tough Kid Squad #1, 3/42

Human Torch - Marvel Comics #1, 10-11/39; (Johnny Storm) Fantastic Four #1, 11/61; (re-intro G.A.) Avengers West Coast #50, 97/89

Humphrey - Joe Palooka #15, 12/47

Hunchback, The - Wow Comics #2, Spr, 1941

Huntress - (G.A.) Sensation Comics #68, 8/47; (1st S.A. app. of G.A. Huntress) Brave and the Bold #62, 10-11/65; (modern) All Star Comics #69, 11-12/77

Hurricane - Captain America Comics #1, 3/41

Hydroman - Heroic Comics #1, 8/40

Hyper, the Phenomenal - Hyper Mystery Comics #1, 5/40

Ibis the Invincible - Whiz Comics #1, 2/40

Ice - Super Friends #9

Ice Cream Soldier - Our Army at War #85, 8/59

Iceman - X-Men #1, 9/63

Imp - Captain America Comics #12, 3/42

Impossible Man - Fantastic Four #11, 2/63; (re-intro) Fantastic Four #176, 11/76

Impossible Woman - Marvel Two-In-One #60, 2/80

Inferno - (S.A.) Mighty Crusaders #4, 5?/66

Inferno, the Flame Breather - Zip Comics #10, 1/41

Insect Queen - (Lana Lang) (Legion) Superboy #124, 10/65

Invisible Girl - (Sue Storm) Fantastic Four #1, 11/61

Invisible Kid - (Legion) Action Comics #267, 8/60 (new) Legion of Super-Heroes Annual #1, 1982

Invisible Scarlett O'Neil - Famous Funnies #81, 4/42

Iron Fist - Marvel Premiere #15, 5/74; (re-intro, cameo) Namor, the

Sub-Mariner #8, 11/90; (re-intro, full app.) Namor, the Sub-Mariner #10, 1/91

Iron Major - Our Army at War #158, 9/65

Iron Man - (Tony Starks) Tales of Suspense #39, 3/63; (new armor) Tales of Suspense #40, 4/63; (new) (Jim Rhodes) Iron Man #231, 6/88

Iron Wolf - Weird Worlds #8, 11-12/73

Isis - Shazam! #25, ? '76

Jack Monroe - (1st full app.) Captain America #154, 10/72; (cameo) Captain America #153, 9/72

Jack of Hearts - Deadly Hands of Kung-Fu #22, 4?/76; (1st solo book) Marvel Premiere #44, 10/78

Jack Q. Frost - Unearthly Spectaculars #1, 10/65

Jack Woods - Adventure Comics #39, 1/39

Jaguar - Adventures of the Jaguar #1, 9/61

Jarella (Hulk's love) - The Incredible Hulk #140, 6/71

Jason Bard - (becomes Robin) Detective Comics #392, 10/69

Jason Todd - Batman #357, 3/83; (1st in Robin costume) Batman #366, 12/83

Jean DeWolf - Marvel Team Up #48, 8/76

Jester - Smash Comics #22, 5/41

Jigsaw - Jigsaw #1, 9/66

Jiminy Cricket - Mickey Mouse Magazine V5#3, 12/39

Jimmy "Minuteman" Martin - Adventure Comics #53, 8/40

Jimmy Martin as Hourman's aide - Adventure Comics #71, 2/42

Jimmy Olsen - Action Comics #6, 11/38; (new) Man of Steel #2, 10/86

Jo-Jo, Congo King - Jo-Jo Comics #7, 7/47

Joe Palooka - Joe Palooka nn, 1933; (1st in comic book format) Feature Funnies #1, 10/37

Joe Robertson - Amazing Spider-Man #52, 9/67

John Carter of Mars - Funnies #30, 4/39

John Carter, Warlord of Mars - Weird Worlds #1, 8-9/72

John Connor - Terminator #12, ?/89

John Constantine - (Hellblazer) Saga of Swamp Thing #37, 6/85

John Force - (Magic Agent) Magic Agent #1, 1-2/62

John Jameson - Amazing Spider-Man #1, 3/63

John Law - Smash Comics #3, 10/39

John Stewart - (later a Green Lantern) Green Lantern #87, 12-1/71-72

Johnny Blaze - (re-intro) Ghost Rider V2#10, 2/91; (Ghost Rider) Marvel Spotlight #5, 8/72

Johnny Cloud - All-American Men of War #82

Johnny Dynamite - Dynamite #3, 9/53

Johnny Peril - Comic Cavalcade #15, 6-7/46

Johnny Quick - More Fun Comics #71, 9/41

Johnny Thunder - All-American Comics #100, 8/48; Flash Comics #1, 1/40; (1st S.A. app.) Flash #137, ?/63

Jon Linton - Amazing Mystery Funnies V2#11, 11/39

Jonah Hex - All Star Western #10, 2-3/72

J'onn J'onzz (See Martian Manhunter)

Jonni Thunder - (Thunderbolt) Jonni Thunder #1, 2/85

Jonny Double - Showcase #78, 11/68

Jordan Brothers - Green Lantern #9, 11-12/61

Jose Delgado - (becomes Gangbuster) Adventures of Superman #432, 9/87

Jubilee - X-Men #244, 2?/89

Judomaster - Special War Series V4#4, 11/65; (1st DC app.) Crisis on Infinite Earths #6, 9/85

Jughead Jones - Pep Comics #22, 12/41

Julie Madison - Detective Comics #31, 9/39

Jungle Jim - Ace Comics #1, 4/37

Junior Woodchucks - Walt Disney's Comics and Stories #125, 2/51

Kaanga, Lord of the Jungle - Jungle Comics #1, 1/40

Kamandi - Kamandi, the Last Boy on Earth #1, 10-11/72

Karate Kid - (Legion) Adventure Comics #346, 7/66

Karma - (New Mutants) Marvel Team-Up #100, 12/80

Katy Keene - Wilbur Comics #5, Sum '45

Kazar the Great - Marvel Comics #1, 10-11/39; (Silver Age) X-men #10, 6/64

Ken Shannon - Police Comics #103, 12/50

Kid Eternity - Hit Comics #25, 12/42

Kid Flash - (later becomes Flash) Flash #110, 12-1/59-60

Killer Frost - Firestorm, the Nuclear Man #3, 6-7/78

King Kull - Creatures on the Loose #10, 3/71

Kit - (Black Cat's sidekick) Black Cat Comics #28, 4/51

Kitty Pryde - (Ariel) (X-Men) X-Men #129, 1/80

Kobra - Kobra #1, 2-3/76

Kole - (New Teen Titan) New Teen Titans #8, 5?/85

Kong the Untamed - Kong the Untamed #1, 6-7/75

Kraven - (War of the Worlds) Amazing Adventures #18, 5/73

Krazy Kat - Ace Comics #1, 4/37

Krypto - Adventure Comics #210, 3/55

Kryptonite (Blue) - Superman #128, 4/59

Kryptonite (Gold) - Superman #140, 4/60

Kryptonite (Red) - Adventure #299, 8/62

Kryptonite Kid - Superboy #83, ?/60

Lady Blackhawk - Blackhawk #133, 2/58

Lady Luck - Spirit nn, 6/2/40

Lana Lang - (becomes Insect Queen) Superboy #10, 9-10/50

Lance Hale - Silver Streak Comics #3, 3/40

Lance O'Casey - Whiz Comics #1, 2/40

Lancer - Super-Mystery Comics V3#3, 1/43

Lash Lightning - (formerly Flash Lightning) Lightning Comics V2#2, 8/41

Lassie - Adventures of Lassie nn, ?/49

Lemonade Kid - Bobby Benson's B-Bar-B Riders #15, 6/50

Leopard Girl - Jungle Action #1, 10/54

Li'l Abner - Tip Top Comics #1, 4/36

Li'l Jinx - Pep Comics #62, 7/47

Liberator - Exciting Comics #15, 12/41

Liberty Belle - Star Spangled #20, 5/43

Light Lass - (formerly Lightning Lass) Adventure Comics #317, 2/64

Lightning - Thunder Agents #4, 4/66

Lightning - (cover only) Jumbo Comics #14, 4/40; (1st story app.) Jumbo Comics #15, 5/40

Lightning Boy - (Legion) Adventure Comics #247, 4/58

Lightning Girl - Lightning Comics V3#1, 6/42

Lightning Lad - (formerly Lightning Boy) Adventure Comics #267, 12/59

Lightning Lass - (Legion) Adventure Comics #308, 5/63

Lilith - Vampire Tales #6, ?/74; (Dracula's daughter) Giant-Size Chillers #1, 6/74; (re-intro) New Teen Titans #2, 9/84; (Teen Titans) Teen Titans #2, 1-2/70

Little Audrey - Little Audrey #1, 4/48

Little Dot - Sad Sack Comics #1, 9/49

Little Dynamite - Boy Comics #6, 10/42

Little Lotta - Little Dot #1, 9/53

Little Lulu - Marge's Little Lulu 4-Color #74, 6/45; (as text illo) King Comics #46, 2/40

Little Max - Joe Palooka #27, 12/48

Little Orphan Annie - Popular Comics #1, 2/36

Little Wise Guys - Daredevil Comics #13, 10/42

Living Mummy - Supernatural Thrillers #5, 8/73

Liz Allen - Amazing Spider-Man #4, 9/63

Lobo - (1st full story) Omega Men #10, 1/84; (1st solo story, back-up) Omega Men #37, 4/86; (cameo) Omega Men #3, 6/83

Lockheed - X-Men #166, 2/83

Lois Lane - Action Comics #1, 6/38; (new) Man of Steel #2, 10/86

Lois Lane as Superwoman - Action Comics #60, 5/43

Lone Warrior - Banner Comics #3, 9/41

Longshot - Longshot #1, 9/85

Lori Lemaris the Mermaid - Superman #129, 5/59

Lt. Marvels - Whiz Comics #21, 9/41

Lucy Lane - Superman's Pal Jimmy Olsen #36, 2?/62

Luke Cage - (Hero for Hire) Hero For

Hire #1, 6/72

Lynx & sidekick Blackie - Mystery Men Comics #13, 8/40

Mad Hatter - Mad Hatter #1, 1-2/46

Madame Satan - Pep Comics #16, 6/41

Madame Web - Amazing Spider-Man #210, 11/80

Madelyne Pryor - (of X-Men) Avengers Annual #10, 1981

Madrox - Giant-Size Fantastic Four #4, 2/75

Mage - (re-intro) Grendel #16, 1/88

Magic Morro - Super Comics #21, 2/40

Magician from Mars - Amazing-Man Comics #7, 11/39

Magicman - Forbidden Worlds #125

Magma - New Mutants #10, 12/83

Magno the Magnetic Man & Davey -Super-Mystery Comics V1#1, 7/40

Magnus, Robot Fighter - Magnus, Robot Fighter #1, 2/63

Major Mynah - Atom #37, 6-7/68

Man Bat - Detective #400, 6/70

Man in Black - Front Page Comic Book #1, 1945

Man of War - Man of War #1, 11/41

Manowar - Target Comics #1, 2/40

Man-Thing - Savage Tales #1, 5/71; (1st full story) Fear #15, 8/73

Mandrake the Magician - King Comics #1, 4/36

Manhunter - Police Comics #8, 3/42; (1st in new costume) Detective Comics #437, 10-11/73; (Paul Kirk) Adventure Comics #58, 1/41; (new) Adventure Comics #73, 4/42

Mantis - Avengers #112, 6/73

Margie - Comedy Comics #34, Fall '46

Mark Merlin - House of Secrets #23, 8/59

Marshal Law - Marshal Law #1, 10/87

Martan, the Marvel Man - Popular Comics #46, 12/39

Martian Manhunter - (J'onn J'onzz) Detective Comics #225, 11/55; (re-intro) Justice League of America #228, 7/84

Marvel Boy - (1st & only app.) Daring Mystery Comics #6, 9/40

Marvel Girl - (becomes Phoenix) X-Men #1, 9/63

Marvel Man - (later Quasar) Captain America #217, 1/78

Mary Jane & Sniffles - Looney Tunes & Merrie Melodies #1, 1941

Mary Jane Watson - (1st mention) Amazing Spider-Man #15, 8/64; (cameo, face not shown) Amazing Spider-Man #25, 6/65; (cameo, face shown) Amazing Spider-Man #42, 11/66; (cameo, not shown) Amazing Spider-Man #38, 7/66; (re-intro) Amazing Spider-Man #243, 8/83

Mary Marvel - Captain Marvel Adventures #18, 12/42

Mask, The - Exciting Comics #1, 4/40

Mask, The - Suspense Comics #2, 1944

Masked Marvel - Keen Detective Funnies V2#7, 7/39

Masked Raider - Marvel Comics #1, 10-11/39

Master Key - Scoop Comics #1, 11/41

Master Man - Master Comics #1, 3/40

Master of Kung-Fu - (Shang-Chi) Special Marvel Edition #15, 12/73

Matter Eater Lad - (Legion) Adventure Comics #303, 12/62

Maximillian O'Leary - (Sargon's aide) All-American Comics #70, 1-2/46

Maya - Atom #1, 6-7/62

Megaton - Megaton #1, 11/83

Menthor - Thunder Agents #1, 11/65

Mento - (non-member) Doom Patrol #91, 11/64

Mentor - Iron Man #55, 2/73

Mera - Aquaman #11, 9-10/63

Merboy - Wonder Woman #107

Mercury - (Silver Streak's sidekick) Silver Streak Comics #11, 6/41

Mercury Man - Space Adventures #44, ?/61?

Metal Men - Showcase #37, 3-4/62

Metallo - (Jor-El's robot) Superboy #49, 6/56

Metamorpho - Brave and the Bold #57, 12-1/64-65

Mickey Finn - (1st comic book app.) Feature Funnies #1, 10/37

Mickey Mouse - Mickey Mouse Book nn, '30

Midnight - Smash Comics #18, 1/41

Mighty Girl - Adventure Comics #453,9-10/77

Mighty Mouse - Terry-Toons Comics #38, 11/45

Mighty Samson - Mighty Samson #1, 7/64

Millie the Model - Gay Comics #1, 3/44

Milton Berle - Uncle Milty #1, 12/50

Minnie Mouse - Mickey Mouse Book nn, 1930

Minute Man - Master Comics #11, 2/41

Minuteman - (re-intro) Shazam! #31,9-10/77

Miss Arrowette - World's Finest #113, 4/60

Miss America - (modern) Giant-Size Avengers #1, 8/74

Miss Masque - Exciting Comics #51, 9/46; America's Best Comics #23, 9/47

Miss Patriot - Marvel Mystery Comics #50, 12/43

Miss Victory - Captain Fearless Comics #1, 8/41

Mister Miracle - Mister Miracle #1, 3-4/71

Mister X - (on cover only) Vortex #2

Moby Duck - Donald Duck #112

Mockingbird - Marvel Team-Up #95, 7/80

Modred the Mystic - Marvel Chillers #1, 10/75

Molly O'Day - Molly O'Day #1, 2/45

Mon-El - (Legion) Superboy #89, 6/61

Monarch Starstalker - Marvel Premiere #32, 10/76

Moon Girl - Happy Houlihans #1, Fall '47; Moon Girl and the Prince #1, Fall '47

Moon Knight - Werewolf by Night #32, 8/75; (1st solo book) Marvel Spotlight #28, 6/76

Moondragon - Iron Man #54, 1/73; (re-intro) Warlock and the Infinity Watch #2, 3/92

Morbius - Amaz. Spider-Man #101, 10/71

Morgan Edge - (cameo) Superman's Pal Jimmy Olsen #133, 10/70

Morlock 2001 - Morlock 2001 #1, 2/75

Morty and Ferdie - (Mickey Mouse's nephews) Mickey Mouse #3, 1933

Moth Man - Mystery Men Comics #9, 4/40

Mr. America - (formerly Tex Thompson) Action Comics #33, 2/41

Mr. Fantastic - (Reed Richards) Fantastic Four #1, 11/61

Mr. Justice - Blue Ribbon Comics #9, 2/41

Mr. Miracle - Captain Fearless Comics #1, 8/41

Mr. Monster - Super Duper Comics #3, 5-6/47; (new) Vanguard Illustrated #7, 5/84

Mr. Mystic - Spirit nn, 6/2/40

Mr. Satan - Zip Comics #1, 2/40

Mr. Scarlet - Wow Comics #1, Win '40-41

Mr. Tawny - Captain Marvel #79, 12/47; (Silver Age) Shazam! #2, 4/73

Mr. Terrific - Sensation Comics #1, 1/42; (1st app. in S.A.) Justice League of America #37, 8?/65

Ms. Marvel - (becomes Binary) Ms. Marvel #1, 1/77

Ms. Victory - Femforce Special #1, Fall '84; (new) Femforce #25

Mutt & Jeff - (1st in comic book for mat) Funnies #1, 10/36

Mutt & Jeff - Mutt & Jeff #1, 1910

Mystery Men of Mars - All-American Comics #1, 4/39

Nam - Savage Tales #1, 11/85

Namora - Marvel Mystery Comics #82, 5/47

Ned Leeds - (later becomes Hobgoblin) Amazing Spider-Man #18, 11/64

Negative Man - My Greatest Adventure #80, 6/63

Neil the Horse - Charlton Bullseye #2, 8?/81

Nemesis - Adventures into the Unknown #154, 2/66?

Nemesis Kid - (Legion) Adventure Comics #346, 7/66

Neon the Unknown - Hit Comics #1, 7/40

Neuman, Alfred E. - (cover only, fake ad) Mad #21, 3/55

Nevada Jones - Zip Comics #1, 2/40

New Gods - New Gods #1, 2-3/71

Nick Fury - (formerly Sgt. Fury) Strange Tales #135, 8/65

Night Hawk - All-New Comics #1, 1/43

Nightcrawler - Giant-Size X-Men #1, Sum '75

Nightgirl - Adventure Comics #306, 11/63

Nighthawk - Avengers #71, 12/69

Nightmare - (Casper's horse) Casper, the Friendly Ghost #19, 4/54

Nightmaster - Showcase #82, 5/69

Nightshade - Amazing-Man Comics #24, 10/41; Captain Atom #82,

9/66; (1st DC app.) Crisis on Infinite Earths #6, 9/85

Night Thrasher - Thor #412

Nightwing - (Dick Grayson) Tales of the Teen Titans #44, 7/84; (Superman as) Superman #158, 12/62; (Van-Zee) Superman Family #183, 5-6/77

Nita - (later Namorita in New Warriors) Sub-Mariner #50

Nomad - (formerly Steve Rogers) Captain America #180, 12/74

Noman - Thunder Agents #1, 11/65

Norman Osborn - (Green Goblin I) Amazing Spider-Man #37, 6/66

Nova - Nova #1, 9/76

Nth Man - Marvel Comics Presents #25, 7/89

Nukla - Nukla #1, 10-12/65

Nutsy Squirrel - Funny Folks #1, 4-5/46

Nyoka, the Jungle Girl - Master Comics #50, 5/44

Ocean Master - Aquaman #25, 1-2/66

Odin - (1st full app.) Journey Into Myst. #86, 11/62; (cameo) Journey Into Mystery #85,10/62

Omac - Omac #1, 9-10/74

Omega - Omega the Unknown #1, 3/76

Oracle, The - Startling Comics #20, 2/43

Orion - (New Gods) New Gods #1, 2-3/71; (of New Gods) (1st new costume) First Issue Special #13, 4/76

Oswald the Rabbit - New Fun Comics #1, 2/35

Outlaw Kid - Outlaw Kid #1, 9/54

Owl - Crackajack Funnies #25, 7/40

Pantha - (New Titan) New Titans #74, 3/91

Paragon - (becomes Her) Incredible Hulk Annual #6, 1977

Pat Parker - (in costume) Speed Comics #15, 11/41; (no costume) Speed Comics #13, 5/41

Pat, Patsy & Pete - Looney Tunes & Merrie Melodies #1, 1941

Patchwork Man - (cameo) Swamp Thing #2, 12-1/72-73; (full app.) Swamp Thing #3, 2-3/73

Patriot - Marvel Mystery Comics #21, 7/41; (modern age) Marvel Premiere #29, 4/76

Patsy Walker - Miss America Magazine #2, 11/44

Peacemaker - Fightin' Five V2#40, ?/66; (1st DC app.) Crisis on Infinite Earths #6, 9/85

Pebbles - (Flintstones) Flintstones #11, 6/63

Perry White - Superman #7, 11-12/40

Pete Ross - (Legion) Superboy #86, 1/61; (tryout only) Superboy #77, 9?/59

Peter Parker's parents - Amazing Spider-Man Annual #5, 11/68; (re-intro) Amazing Spider-Man #365,8/92

Peter Porkchops - Leading Comics #23,2-3/47

Phantasmo, Master of the World -Funnies #45, 7/40

Phantom - Ace Comics #11, 2/38

Phantom Eagle - (S.A.) Marvel

Super-Heroes #16, 9/68; (G.A.) Wow Comics #6, 7/42

Phantom Falcon - Wings #68, 4/46

Phantom Girl - (Legion) Action Comics #276, 5/61

Phantom Lady - Police Comics #1, 8/41

Phantom Lady - Phantom Lady #13, 8/47

Phantom of the Fair - Amazing Mystery Funnies V2#7, 7/39

Phantom Rider - Star Comics #16, 12/38

Phantom Stranger - Phantom Stranger #1, 5-6/69

Phoenix - (formerly Marvel Girl) X-Men #101, 10/76

Phoenix II - (Rachel) X-Men #141, 1/81

Pinocchio - (cameo) Mickey Mouse Mag.V5#2, 11/39; (full app.) Mickey Mouse Magazine V5#3, 12/39

Pip the Troll - Strange Tales #179, 4/75

Plastic Man - Police Comics #1, 8/41; (S.A. tryout) House of Mystery #160, 7/66; (S.A.) Plastic Man #1, 11-12/66

Pluto - Thor #127, 4/66

Pluto - (Disney) Mickey Mouse #2, 1932

Pogo - Animal Comics #1, 12-1/41-42

Polar Boy - Adventure #306, 11/63

Polaris - (X-Men) X-Men #44, 5/68

Popside Pete - All-American Comics #6, 9/39

Porky Pig - Looney Tunes & Merrie Melodies #1, '41

Pow Wow Smith - Detective Comics #151, 9/49

Power Girl - All Star Comics #58, 1-2/76

Power Man - (Rip Regan) Fight Comics #3, 3/40

Power Nelson the Future Man - Prize Comics #1, 3/40

Powerhouse Pepper - Joker Comics #1, 4/42

Predator - Predator #1, 6/89

Presto Kid - Red Mask #51, 9/55

Prince Ra-Man - (formerly Mark Merlin) House of Secrets #73, 7-8/65

Prince Valiant - Ace Comics #26, 5/39

Princess Pantha - Thrilling Comics #56, 10/46

Princess Projectra - (Legion) Adventure Comics #346, 7/66

Professor Supermind & Son - Popular Comics #60, 2/41

Professor Warren - Amazing Spider-Man #31, 12/65

Professor X - X-Men #1, 9/63

Psylocke - New Mutants Annual #2, 10/86

Punisher - Amaz. Spider-Man #129, 2/74

Punisher 2099 - Punisher War Journal #50, 1/93

Pureheart the Powerful - Archie as Pureheart the Powerful #1, 9/66

Purple Mask - Daring Mystery Comics #3, 4/40

Pyroman - America's Best Comics

734

V1#1, 7/40

Wagon Train - Four Color #895, 3/58

Wambi, Jungle Boy - Jungle Comics #1, 1/40

Warlock - (Him) (cameo) Fantastic Four #67, 10/67; (Him) (full app.) Thor #165, 6/69; (new) New Mutants #18, 8/84; (re-intro) Silver Surfer #46, 2/91

Warlord - First Issue Special #8, 11/75

Warpath - (with costume) X-Men #193, 5/85; (without costume) New Mutants #16, 6/84

Wash Tubbs - Famous Comics Cartoon Books #1202, 1934

Wasp, The - Speed Comics #12, 3/41

Wasp - Tales to Astonish #44, 6/63

Wasplet - (Hooded Wasp's sidekick) Shadow Comics #7, 11/40

Watcher - Fantastic Four #13, 4/63

Waverider - Armageddon 2001 #1, 5/91

Weapon Alpha - (becomes Vindicator) X-Men #109, 2/78

Web - Zip Comics #27, 7/42; (S.A.) Fly Man #36, 3/66

Wendigo - Incredible Hulk #162, 4/73

Wendy the Good Little Witch - Casper, the Friendly Ghost #20, ?/54

Werewolf - Werewolf #1, 12/66

Werewolf by Night - Marvel Spotlight #2, 1?/72

Whirlybats - Detective Comics #257, 7/58

White Rider & Super Horse - Blue Bolt #1, 6/40

White Streak - Target Comics V1#1, 2/40

White Tiger - Deadly Hands of Kung-Fu #19, 1?/76

White Witch - (Legion) Adventure Comics #351, 12/66

Whizzer, The - USA Comics #1, 8/41; (modern) Giant-Size Avengers #1, 8/74

Whizzer McGee - (Phantasmo's side kick) Funnies #45, 7/40

Wiggles the Wonderworm - Taffy Comics #1, 3/45

Wilbur - Zip Comics #18, 9/41

Wild Bill Elliott - Four Color #278, 5/50

Wildcat - Sensation Comics #1, 1/42; (S.A.) Brave and the Bold #62, 10-11/65

Wildfire - (formerly Erg) Superboy #201, '74

Will O' the Wisp - Amazing Spider-Man #167, 4/77

Willie - Gay Comics #1, Mar '44

Winky, Blinky & Noddy - All-Flash #5, Sum '42

Witch Hazel - Marge's Little Lulu #39, 9/51

Witness - Mystic Comics #7, 12/40

Wizard - Top-Notch Comics #1, 12/39; (S.A.) Fly Man #33, 9/65

Wizard - Strange Tales #102, 11/62

Wolverine - (1st full app.) Incredible Hulk #181, 11/74; (cameo) Incredible Hulk #180, 10/74

Wonder Boy - Blue Bolt #1, 6/40; National Comics #1, 7/40

Wonder Boy - Bomber Comics #1, 3/44

Wonder Duck - Wonder Duck #1, 9/49

Wonder Girl - Wonder Woman #107, 7/61; (new) (Teen Titan) Brave and the Bold #60, 6-7/65

Wonder Man - Startling Comics #1, 6/40

Wonderman - Wonder Comics #9, 1945

Wonder Man - Avengers #9, 10/64; Wonder Comics #1, 5/39; (re-intro) Avengers #151, 9/76

Wonder Tot - Wonder Woman #122

Wonder Woman - All Star Comics #8, 12-1/41-42; (Orana) Wonder Woman #250, 12/78

Wonder Woman Family - Wonder Woman #124, 12/62

Wonderman - (Brad Spencer) Mystery Comics #1, 1944

Wong - Strange Tales #110, 7/63

Woodgod - Marvel Premiere #31, 8/76

Woody Woodpecker - Funnies #64, 5/42

Woozy Winks - Police Comics #13, 11/42 ˙

X-O Manowar - X-O Manowar #1, 2/92

X-Terminators - X-Terminators #1, 10/88

Yank and Doodle - Prize Comics #13, 8/41

Yankee Doodle Jones - Yankee Comics #1, 9/41

Yarko the Great, Master Magician - Wonder Comics #2, 6/39

Yellow Claw - Yellow Claw #1, 10/56

Yellowjacket - Yellowjacket #1, 9/44

Yellowjacket - Avengers #59, 12/68; (formerly Goliath) Avengers #63, 4/69

Yogi Bear - Four Color #1067, 12-2/59-60

Yosemite Sam - Yosemite Sam #1, 12/70

Zanzibar - Mystery Men Comics #1, 8/39

Zardi, the Eternal Man - Amazing-Man Comics #11, 4/40

Zatanna - Hawkman #4, 10-11/64

Zatara - Action Comics #1, 6/38

Zebra - All-New Comics #7, 3/44; Pocket Comics #1, 8/41

Zegra, Jungle Empress - Zegra #2, 10/48

Ziggy Pig - Krazy Komics #1, 7/42

Zombie - Menace #5, 7/53

Zorro - Zorro Four Color #228, 5/49

1ST APPEARANCES: VILLAINS

Abomination - Tales to Astonish #90, 4/67

Abra Kadabra - Flash #128, 2?/62

Absorbing Man - Journey Into Mystery #114, 3/65

Amazo The Android - Brave & The Bold #30, 6-7/60

Angle Man - Wonder Woman #70, 11/54

Annihilus - Fantastic Four Annual #6, 11/68

Apocalypse - (cameo) X-Factor #5, 6/86; (full app.) X-Factor #6, 7/86

Arcade - Marvel Team-Up #66, 2/78

Atomic Skull - Superman #323, 5/78

Attuma - Fantastic Four #33, 12/64

Bane - Batman: Vengeance of Bane Special #1, '92

Banshee - X-Men #28, 1/67

Baron Blood - Invaders #7, 7/76

Baron Mordo - Strange Tales #111, 8/63

Baron Strucker - Sgt. Fury #5, 1963

Baron Zemo - Captain America #276

Batmite - Detective #267, 5/59

Batroc - Tales of Suspense #76, 4/66

Beetle - Strange Tales #123, 8/64

Bengal - Daredevil #258, 9/88

Beyonder - Marvel Two-In-One #63, 1986

Big Man - Amazing Spider-Man #10, 3/64

Bizarro - Superboy #68, 10-11/56

Bizarro Batman - World's Finest Comics #156

Bizarro Flash - Superman's Girlfriend Lois Lane #74, 5/67

Bizarro Krypto - Superboy #82, ?/60

Bizarro Lana Lang - Adventure Comics #292, 1/62

Bizarro Lucy Lane -Adventure Comics #292, 1/62

Bizarro Lex Luthor - Adventure Comics #293, 2/62

Bizarro Lois Lane - Action Comics #255, 8/59

Bizarro Mxyzptlk - Adventure Comics #286, 7/61

Bizarro Supergirl - Superman #140, 10/60

Bizarro Titano - Adventure Comics #295, 4/62

Black Cat - Amazing Spider-Man #194, 7/79

Black Mask - Batman #386, 8/85

Blackout - Ghost Rider #2, 6/90

Black Racer - New Gods #3, 6-7/71

Black Spider - Detective Comics #463

Blastarr - Fantastic Four #62, 5/67

Blizzard - Iron Man #86, ?/76?

Blob - X-Men #3, 1/64

Blockbuster - Detective Comics #345, 11/65

Boomerang - Tales to Astonish #81, 7/66

Brain Storm - Justice League of America #32, 12/64

Brain Wave - All Star Comics #15, 2-3/43

Brainiac - Action Comics #242, 7/58; (modern) Adventures of Superman #438, 2/88

Brainwasher - (Kingpin) Amazing Spider-Man #59, 4/68

Brother Blood - New Teen Titans #21, 7/82

Brother Voodoo - Strange Tales #169, 9/73

Bullet - Daredevil #250, 12/88

Bullseye - Nick Fury Agent of Shield #15, 11/69

Calypso - Amazing Spider-Man #209, 10/80

Captain Boomerang - Flash #117, 12/60

Captain Cold - Showcase #8, 5-6/57

Captain Fear - Adventure Comics #425, 12-1/72-73

Captain Nazi - Master Comics #21, 12/41

Cardinal - New Warriors #28, 10/92

Carnage - (1st full app.) Amazing Spider-Man #361, 4/92; (cameo) Amazing Spider-Man #360, 3/92

Carrion - Spectacular Spider-Man #25, 12/78

Cat-Man - Detective Comics #311, 1/63

Catwoman - (1st in costume) Batman #3, Fall '40; (1st time called Catwoman) Batman #2, Sum '40; (modern, Selina Kyle) Batman #404, 2/87; (new costume w/o cat-head mask) Batman #35, 5-6/46; (new) Detective Comics #624, 12/90; (S.A.) Superman's Girlfriend Lois Lane #70, 11/66; (The Cat) Batman #1, Spr '40

Cavalier - Detective Comics #81, 11/43

Chameleon - Amazing Spider-Man #1, 3/63

Changeling - X-Men #35, 8/67

Cheetah - Wonder Woman #6, Fall '43; (new) Wonder Woman #274, 12/80; (new) (full app.) Wonder Woman #275, 1/81

Chronos - Atom #3, 10-11/62

Chunk - Flash #9, 2/88

Claw - Silver Streak Comics #1, 12/39

Clayface I - (Basil Karlo) Detective Comics #40, 6/40

Clayface II - (Matt Hagen) Detective Comics #298, 12/61

Clayface III - (Preston Payne) Detective Comics #478, 7-8/78

Clock King - World's Finest Comics #111, 8/60

Clown - Flash #270, 2/79

Cobra (see Human Cobra)

Colonel Computron - Flash #304, 12/81

Composite Superman - World's Finest #142

Computo - Adventure Comics #340, 1/66

Constrictor - Incredible Hulk #212, 6/77

Copperhead - Daredevil #124, 6?/75

Crime Master - Amazing Spider-Man #26, 7/65

Crimson Dynamo - (Anton Vanko) Tales of Suspense #46, 10/63

Crimson Dynamo II - (Boris Turgenov) Tales of Suspense #52, 4/64

Crimson Dynamo III - (Alex Nevsky) Iron Man #21, 3/78

Crimson Dynamo IV - (Yuri Petrovich) Champions #8, 10/76

Crimson Dynamo V - (Dimitri Bukharin) Iron Man #109, 4/78

Cyclone - Amazing Spider-Man #143, 4/75

Dark Phoenix - X-Men #134

Darkseid - (1st full app.) Forever People #1, 2-3/71; (cameo) Superman's Pal

737

#129, 2/74
Puppet Master - Batman #3, Fall '40; Fantastic Four #8, 11/62
Rainbow Raider - Flash #286, 6/80
Rama-Tut - Fantastic Four #19, 10/63
Rampage - Superman #7, 7/87
Rancor - (1st full app.) Guardians of the Galaxy #9, 2/91; (cameo) (descendant of Wolverine) Guardians of the Galaxy #8, 1/91
Ras Al Ghul - Batman #232, 7/71
Reaper - Batman #237, 12/71
Red Ghost - Fantastic Four #13, 4/63
Red Skull - Captain America Comics #1, 3/41; (S.A.) Tales of Suspense #65, 5/65
Rhino - Amazing Spider-Man #41, 10/66
Riddler - Detective Comics #140, 10/48; (S.A.) Batman #171, 5/65
Ringmaster - Incredible Hulk #3, 9/62
Rose - Amazing Spider-Man #253, 6/84
Rose and the Thorn - Flash Comics #89, 11/47; (new) Superman's Girlfriend Lois Lane #105
Saber-Tooth - Flash #291, 11/80
Sabretooth - Iron Fist #14, 8/77
Sandman - Amazing Spider-Man #4, 9/63
Sandstorm - Web of Spider-Man #107, 12/93
Sargon - (re-intro) Flash #186, 8?/69
Sargon the Sorcerer - (1st story app.) All-American Comics #26, 5/41; (text only) All-American Comics #24, 3/41
Sauron - X-Men #60
Scarecrow - Tales of Suspense #51, 3/64; World's Finest Comics #3, Fall '41; Dead of Night #11, 8/75; (S.A.) Batman #189, ? '67?
Schemer - Amazing Spider-Man #83, 4/70

Scorpion - Amazing Spider-Man #20, 1/65
Serpent Crown - Sub-Mariner #9, 1/69
Sha-Shan - Amazing Spider-Man #108, 5/72
Shade - (modern) Flash #298, 6/81
Shadow Thief - Brave and the Bold #36,6-7/61
Shaper - Incredible Hulk #155, 9/72
Shark - Amazing-Man Comics #6, 10/39; Green Lantern #24, 10/63
Shocker - Amazing Spider-Man #46, 3/67
Shotgun - Daredevil #272, 9?/89
Shroud - Super-Villain Team-Up #5, 4/76
Signalman - Batman #112, 12/57; (S.A.) Detective Comics #466
Silvermane - Amazing Spider-Man #73, 6/69
Silver Samurai - Daredevil #111, 6/74
Sinestro - Green Lantern #7, 7-8/61
Sivana - Whiz Comics #1, 2/40
Sivana, Jr. - Captain Marvel Adventures #52, 1/46
Sky Pirate - Green Lantern #27, 8-9/47
Solarr - Captain America #160, 4/73
Solo - Web of Spider-Man #19, 10/86
Solomon Grundy - All-American Comics #61, 11/44; (S.A.) Showcase #55, 3-4/65
Sonar - Green Lantern #14, 7/62
Sorcerer - Alpha Flight #71, 5/89
Speed McGee - Flash #5, 10/87
Spirit of Vengeance - (futuristic Ghost Rider) Guardians of the Galaxy #13, 6/91
Spyder - New Mutants #68, 10/88
Star Thief - Warlock #14, 10/76
Stilt-Man - Daredevil #8, 6/65
Sting Ray - Sub-Mariner #19, 11/69
Stranger - X-Men #11, 5/65

Sub-Mariner - (S.A) Fantastic Four #4, 5/62
Sunburst - New Adventures of Superboy #45, 9/83
Super Skrull - Fantastic Four #18, 9/63
Supremo - Superboy #132, ?/66
Swordsman - Avengers #19, 8/65
Tantrum - Night Thrasher: Four Control #2, 11/92
Tarantula - Amazing Spider-Man #134, 7/74
Taskmaster - Avengers #119, 1/80
Tattooed Man - Green Lantern #23, 9?/63
Terra-Man - Superman #249, 4/72
Terrax - Fantastic Four #211, 10/79
Terrible Tinkerer - Amazing Spider-Man #2, 5/63
Thanos - Iron Man #55, 2/73; (re-intro) (cameo) Silver Surfer #34, 2/90; (re-intro) (full app.) Silver Surfer #35, 3/90
Thinker - All-Flash #12, Fall '43
Thundra - Fantastic Four #129, 12/72
Tiger Shark - (new) Namor, the Sub-Mariner #35, 2/93; (S.A.) Sub-Mariner #5, 9/68
Time Trapper - Adventure Comics #321, 6/64
Titanium Man - Tales of Suspense #69, 9/65
Titano - Superman #127, 2/59
Toad - X-Men #4, 3/64
Tombstone - Web of Spider-Man #36, 3/88; (full app.) Spectacular Spider-Man #138, 5/88
Top - Flash #122, 6-7?/61
Torpedo - Daredevil #126, 8?/75
Toyman - Action Comics #64, 9/43; (new) Superman #13, 1/88; (S.A.) Action Comics #432, 2/74
Trapster - Strange Tales #104, 1/63
Trauma - Incredible Hulk #394, 6/92
Trickster - Flash #113, 6-7/60

Turtle - Showcase #4, 9-10/56
Tweedledum & Tweedledee - Detective Comics #74, 4/43
Two-Face - Detective Comics #66, 8/42; (S.A.) Batman #234, 9/71
Typhoid Mary - Daredevil #254, 5/88
Ulik - Thor #137
Ultron - Avengers #54
Ulthoon - (Adam Strange foe) Mystery In Space #61,
Umar - Strange Tales #150, 11/66
Unicorn - Tales of Suspense #56, 8/64
Universo - Adventure Comics #349, 10/66
Unus the Untouchable - X-Men #8, 11/64
U. S. Jones - Wonderworld Comics #28, 8/41
Vandall Savage - Green Lantern #10 ,Win '43; (S.A.) Flash #137, ?/63
Vanisher - X-Men #2, 11/63
Venom - (1st full app.) Amazing Spider-Man #300, 5/88; (cameo w/costume) Amazing Spider-Man #298; (cameo, no costume), #299, 4/88
Vindicator - X-Men #109, 5/78
Viper - Captain America #110, 2/69
Vulture - Amazing Spider-Man #2, 5/63
Warpath - X-Men #193, 5/85
Watcher - Fantastic Four #13, 4/63
Weapon Omega - Alpha Flight #102, 11/81
Weather Wizard - Flash #110, 12-1/59-60
Whirlwind - (Human Top) Tales to Astonish #50, 12/63
White Queen - X-Men #132, 4/80
Wizard - Strange Tales #102, 11/62
Zemo - Avengers #6, 7/64
Zzzax - Incredible Hulk #166, 8/73

1ST APPEARANCES: GROUPS

Adult Legion - Superman #147, 8/61
All Star Squadron - Justice League of America #193, 8/81
All Winners Squad - All Winners Comics #19, Fall, 1946
Alpha Flight -(cameo) X-Men #120, 4/79; (full app.) X-Men #121, 5/79
Atari Force - New Teen Titans #27, 1/83
Atomic Knights - Strange Adventures #117, 6/60
Avengers - Avengers #1, 9/63
Avengers new line up - Avengers #16, 5/65; Avengers #150, 8/76; Avengers #181, 3/79; Avengers #211, 9/81
Avengers West Coast - West Coast Avengers #1, 9/84
Big-3 - (Blue Beetle/Flame/ Samson) Big-3 #1, Fall, 1940
Bizarro Legionnaires - Adventure Comics #329, 2/65
Boy Commandos - Detective Comics #64, 6/42
Brainiac 5 - Action Comics #276, 5/61
Challengers of the Unknown -

Showcase #6, 1-2/57
Champions - Champions #1, 10/75
Creature Commandos - Weird War Tales #93, 11/80
Damage Control - Marvel Comics Presents #19, 5/89
Darkstars - Dark Stars #1, 10/92
Defenders - Marvel Feature #1, 12/71; (new) Defenders #125, 11/83; (pre-lude) Sub-Mariner #34, 2/71
Doom Patrol - My Greatest Adventure #80, 6/63; (new) Showcase #94, 8-9/77
Easy Company - Our Army At War #81, 4/59
Elementals, The - Justice Machine Annual #1, 1/84
Eternals - Eternals #1, 7/76
Excalibur - Excalibur Special Edition nn, 1987
Explorers - Boy Explorers #1, 5-6/46
Fab 4 - Super Heroes #1, 1/67
Fantastic Four - Fantastic Four #1, 11/61; (1st in costumes) Fantastic Four #3, 3/62; (new team) Fantastic Four #306, 9/87
Federal Men - New Comics #2,

1/36
Femforce - Femforce Special #1, Fall, 1984
Fightin' Five - Fightin' Five V2#28, 7/64
Forever People - Forever People #1,2-3/71
Freedom Fighters - Justice League of America #107, 1975
Frightful Four - Fantastic Four #36, 10/64
Future X-Men - X-Men #141, 1/81
Ghost Patrol - Flash Comics #29, 5/42
Girl Commandos - Speed Comics #13, 4/41
Great Lakes Avengers - West Coast Avengers #46, 7/89
Green Lantern Corp. - Green Lantern #130
Guardians of the Galaxy - Marvel Super-Heroes #18, 1/69; (1st solo book) Marvel Presents #3, 2/76
Guardians of the Universe - Green Lantern #1, 7-8/60
H.A.R.D. Corps - Harbinger #10, 10/92
Inferior Five - Showcase #62, 5-

6/66
Infinity, Inc. - All Star Squadron #25,9/83
Inhumans - Fantastic Four #45, 12/65
Injustice Society Of The World - All Star Comics #37, 10-11/47
Intergalactic Vigilante Squadron - Adventure Comics #237, 6/57
International Sea Devils - Sea Devils #22, 3-4/66
Invaders - Avengers #71, 12/69; (re-intro) Namor, the Sub-Mariner #12, 3/91
Justice League Europe - Justice League International #24, 2/89; (new) Justice League Spectacular #1, 1992
Justice League International - (new) Justice League Spectacular #1, 1992
Justice League of America - Brave and the Bold #28, 2-3/60; Legends #6, 4/87; (new team) Justice Leagueof America Annual #2, 1984
Justice Society of America - All Star Comics #3, Win, '40-41; (1st

739

S.A. cameo) Flash #137, ?/63
Kiss - (1st full app.) Howard the Duck #13, 6/77; (cameo) Howard the Duck #12, 3/77
Knights of the Galaxy - Mystery In Space #1, 4-5/51
Legion of Monsters - (Ghost Rider, Man-Thing, Morbius, Werewolf) Marvel Premiere #28, 1975
Legion of Substitute Heroes - Adventure Comics #306, 3/63
Legion of Super Heroes - Adventure Comics #247, 4/58
Legion Of Super Pets - Adventure Comics #293, 2/62
Liberators - Avengers #83, 12/70
Liberty Legion - Marvel Premiere #29, 1975
Losers - (Storm/Gunner/Sarge/J. Cloud) G. I. Combat #138, 10-11/69
Lt. Marvels - Whiz Comics #21, 9/41
Marvel Family - Captain Marvel Adventures #18, 12/42
Masters Of Evil - Avengers #6, 2/64
Masters of the Universe - New Teen Titans #25, 11/82
Mercenaries - G.I. Combat #244, 1982
Metal Men - Showcase #37, 3-4/62
Mighty Crusaders - Mighty

Crusaders #1, 11/65
New Gods - New Gods #1, 2-3/71
New Mutants - Marvel Graphic Novel #4, 1982
New Teen Titans - DC Comics Presents #26, 10/80
New Warriors - (cameo) Thor #411, 12/89; (full app.) Thor #412, 12/89
Newsboy Legion - Star Spangled Comics #7, 4/42; (re-intro) Superman's Pal Jimmy Olsen #133, 10/70
Next Men - Dark Horse Presents #54, 9/91
Night Force - New Teen Titans #21, 7/82
Omega Men - Green Lantern #141, 6/81
Our Gang - Our Gang Comics #1, 9-10/42
Outsiders - Brave and the Bold #200, 7/83
Planeteers - Real Fact Comics #16, 9-10/48
Power Elite - Starman #4, Win '88
Power Pack - Power Pack #1, 8/84
Sea Devils - Showcase #27, 7-8/60
Secret Six - Secret Six #1, 4-5/68; (re-intro) Action Comics #601, 6/88
Sentinels - X-Men #14, 11/65
Seven Soldiers of Victory - Leading Comics #1, Wint. '41-42

Shadowmaster - Punisher #24, ?/89
S.H.I.E.L.D. - Nick Fury Agent of Shield #1, 6/68
Stargazers - Vanguard III. #2, 12/83
Starjammers - (cameo) X-Men #104, 4/77; (full app.) X-Men #107, 10/77
Star Rovers - Mystery In Space #66, 1961
Stargrazers - Vanguard Illustrated #2, 12/83
Suicide Squad - Brave and the Bold #25, 8-9/59; (new) Legends #3, 1/87
Super Friends - Super Friends #1, 11/76
Team America - Captain America #269, 5/82
Team Titans - (Teen Titans) New Titans Annual #7, 1991
Teenage Mutant Ninja Turtles - Gobbledygook #1, 1984
Teen Titans - Brave and the Bold #54, 6-7/64; (re-intro.) DC Super Stars #1, 3/76
Terrific Three - (Jaguar, Mr. Justice, Steel Sterling) Mighty Crusaders #5, 9/66
Three Mouseketeers - Funny Stuff #1, Sum '44
Thunder Agents - Thunder Agents #1, 11/65
Tiger Squadron - Blue Beetle #20,

4/43
Toxic Crusaders - Toxic Crusaders #1, 5/92
Tough Kid Squad - Tough Kid Squad #1, 3/42
Transformers - Transformers #1, 9/84
Tribe - WILDC.A.T.s: Covert Action Teams #4, 3/93
Ultra-Men - (Fox, Web, Capt. Flag) Mighty Crusaders #5, 9/66
Wanderers - Adventure Comics #375, 12/68
Warlords - West Coast Avengers - West Coast Avengers #1, 9/84
Wildcats - WILDC.A.T.s: Covert Action Teams #1, 8/92
X-Factor - Avengers #263, 1/86; (new team) X-Factor #71, 10/91
X-Force - (cameo) New Mutants #100, 4/91
X-Men - X-Men #1, 9/63; X-Men #1, 10/91; (new team) X-Men #253, 1989; (new team) X-Men #281, 10/91; (new) Giant-Size X-Men #1, Sum, '75
X-Terminators - X-Terminators #1, 10/88
Young Allies - Young Allies #1, Sum '41
Youngblood - (1 pg. ad) Megaton #8, 8/87; (2pgs.) Megaton Explosion nn, 6/87

1ST APPEARANCES: VILLAIN GROUPS

Beagle Boys - Walt Disney's Comics and Stories #134, 11/51
Blue Trinity - Flash #7, 12/87
Brotherhood of Evil - (new) New Teen Titans #15, 1/82
Brotherhood of Evil Mutants - X-Men #4, 3/64; (new) X-Men #141, 1/81
Citadel - Green Lantern #136, 1/81
Enforcers - Amazing Spider-Man

#10, 3/64
Fearsome Five - New Teen Titans #3, 1/81
Frightful Four - (Sandman/Wizard/P.P. Pete) Fantastic Four #36, 3/65
Injustice Society - All Star Comics #37, 10-11/47
Krypton Foes - Superman #65, 7-8/50

Legion of Super-Villains - Superman #147, 8/61
Masters of Evil - Avengers #6, 7/64; (new) Avengers #54, 7/68
Phantom Zone Villains - (Dr. Zadu & Emdine) - Superboy #100, 10/62
Royal Flush Gang - Justice League of America #43, 7/66; (new) Justice League of America #203,

6/82
Secret Society of Super-Villains - Secret Society of Super-Villains #1, 5-6/76
Sinister Six - Amazing Spider-Man Annual #1, 1964
Skrulls - Fantastic Four #2, 1/62
Toad Men - Incredible Hulk #2, 7/62

1ST CROSSOVERS

Ant-Man - Fantastic Four #16, 7/63
Avengers - Tales of Suspense #49, 1/64
Capt. America - (outside of Avengers) Sgt. Fury #13
Conan - Savage Tales #1, 5/71
Daredevil - Amazing Spider-Man #16, 9/64
Doctor Strange - Fantastic Four #27, 6/64

Fantastic Four - Amazing Spider-Man #1, 3/63
Hulk - Fantastic Four #12, 3/63
G.A. Green Lantern x-over in S.A. - Showcase #55, 3-4/65
Iceman - Strange Tales #120, 5/64
Iron Man - (x-over outside Avengers) Tales to Astonish #82, 8/66
Magneto - Journey Into Mystery

#109, 10/64
Nick Fury - (as agent of Shield) Tales of Suspense #92, 8/67
S.A. Capt. America - Sgt. Fury #13, 12/64
Sgt. Fury - Fantastic Four #21, 12/63
Silver Surfer - (cameo) Tales to Astonish #92, 6/67; (full app.) Tales to Astonish #93, 7/67

Spider-Man - Strange Tales Annual #2, 7/63
Sub-Mariner - (outside Fantastic Four) Strange Tales #107, (4/63)
Thing - Strange Tales #116, 1/64
Thor - Strange Tales #123, 8/64
X-Men - Tales of Suspense #49, 1/64

1ST SUPERPETS

Bat-Hound - Batman #92, 6/55
Captain Carrot - New Teen Titans #16, 2/82
Comet - (Superhorse) Adventure Comics #293, 2/62
Cosmo - (Challengers Spacepet)

Challengers of the Unknown #18, 9-10/60
Krypto the Super Dog - Adventure Comics #210, 3/55
Legion of Super Pets - Adventure Comics #293, 2/62

Rang-A-Tang the Wonder Dog - Blue Ribbon Comics #1, 11/39
Streak the Wonder Dog - Green Lantern #30, 2-3/48
Streaky the Super Cat - Action Comics #261, 2/60

Supermonkey - Superboy #76, 8?/59
Wolf - (Boy Commandos mascot) Boy Commandos #34, 7-8/49

1ST OF A PUBLISHER

Ace Magazines - Sure-Fire #1, 6/40
American Comics Group - Giggle

#1 & Ha Ha #1, 10/43
Atlas Comics - All Winners #11, Wint. '43/44

Avon Comics -Molly O'Day #1, 2/45
Better Publications (Standard) - Best Comics #1, 11/39

Bilbara Publishing Co. - Cyclone #1, 6/40
Brookwood Publications - Speed

Comics #1, 10/39

Carlton Publishing Co. - Zoom Comics #1, 12/45

Catechetical Guild - Topix #1, 11/42

Centaur Publications -Funny Pages V2#6, 3/38; Funny Picture Stories V2#6, 3/38; Star Comics #10, 3/38; Star Ranger V2#10, 3/38

Charlton Comics -Zoo Funnies #1, 11/45

Columbia Comics Group - Big Shot #1, 5/40

Comico - Primer #1, 10/82

Comics Magazine - Comics Magazine #1, 5/36

Dark Horse - Dark Horse Presents #1, 7/86

David McKay Publ. - King Comics #1, 4/36

DC Comics - New Fun Comics #1, 2/35

Defiant Comics - Warriors Of Plasm #1, 8/93

Dell Publishing Co. - Popular Comics #1, 2/36

Eastern Color - Funnies On Parade nn, 1933

Elliot Publications - Double Comics, 1940

Fawcett Publications - Whiz Comics #2 (#1), 2/40

Fiction House - Jumbo Comics #1, 9/38

Flying Cadet - Flying Cadet #1, 1/43

Fox Features Syndicate - Wonder Comics #1, 5/39

Funnies, Inc. - Motion Picture Funnies Weekly #1, 1939

Gilberton Publ. - Classic Comics #1, 10/41

Gladstone - Disneyland Birthday Party, 8/85; Uncle Scrooge Goes To Disneyland, 8/85

Globe Syndicate - Circus Comics #1, 6/38

Great Publications - Great Comics #1, 11/41

Harry 'A' Chesler - Star Comics #1, 2/37

Harvey Comics - Pocket Comics #1, 8/41

Hawley Publications - Captain Easy nn, 1939

Hillman Periodicals - Miracle Comics #1, 2/40

Holyoke (Continental) - Crash Comics #1, 5/40

Hugo Gernsback - Superworld #1, 4/40

Hyper Publications - Hyper Mystery #1, 5/40

Image Comics - Youngblood #1, 4/92

K.K. Publications - Mickey Mouse Magazine #1, Sum, 1935

Lev Gleason - Silver Streak #1, 12/39

Mirage Studios - Gobbledygook #1, no month '84

MLJ Magazines - Blue Ribbon Comics #1, 11/39

Nita Publications - Whirlwind Comics #1, 6/40

Novelty Publications - Target Comics #1, 6/40

Parents' Magazine Institute - True Comics #1, 4/41

Prize Publications - Prize Comics #1, 3/40

Progressive Publishers - Feature Comics #21, 6/39

Quality Comics Group - Feature Comics #21, 6/39

Ralston-Purina Co. - Tom Mix #1, 9/40

Standard Comics (Better Publ.) - Best Comics #1, 11/39

Street and Smith Publications - Shadow Comics #1, 3/40

Sun Publications - Colossus Comics #1, 3/40

Timely Comics - Marvel Mystery #1, 11/39

United Features Syndicate - Tip Top Comics #1, 4/36

Valiant Comics - (hero) Magnus Robot Fighter, 5/91

Warren all comics magazine - Creepy #1, no month '64

Whitman Publishing Co. - Mammoth Comics #1, 1937

Will Eisner - Spirit #1, 6/2/40

William H. Wise - Columbia Comics #1, 1943

1ST PROTOTYPES

Some of today's popular super hero characters were developed from or after earlier forms or prototypes. These prototype characters sometimes were introduced to test new ideas and concepts which later developed into full fledged super heros, or old material sometimes would inspire new characters. Below is a list of all known prototypes. The Marvel/Atlas issues have been verified by Stan Lee, Steve Ditko and Jack Kirby.

Ancient One - Strange Tales #92, 1/62

Ant-Man - Strange Tales #73, 2/60; Strange Tales #78, 11/60

Aunt May - Strange Tales #97, 6/62

Doctor Doom - Tales of Suspense #31, 7/62

Doctor Strange - Journey Into Mystery #78, 3/62; Strange Tales #79, 12/60; Tales of Suspense #32, 8/62

Electro - Tales To Astonish #15, 1/61

Giant-Man - Strange Tales #70,

8/59

Hulk - Journey Into Mystery #62, 11/60; Journey Into Mystery #66, 3/61

Human Torch - Strange Tales #76, 8/60

Iron Man - Strange Tales #75, 6/60; Tales of Suspense #9, 5/60; Tales of Suspense #16, 4/61

Kamandi - Alarming Tales #1, 9/57

Lava Men - Tales of Suspense #7, 1/60

Magneto - Strange Tales #84, 5/61

Mr. Hyde - Journey Into Mystery

#79, 4/62

Professor X - Amazing Adult Fantasy #14, 7/62; Strange Tales #69, 6/59

Quicksilver - Strange Tales #67, 2/59

Red Tornado - House Of Mystery #155, 9-10/65

Sandman - Journey Into Mystery #70, 7/61

Savage Dragon - Marvel Comics Presents #50, 1990

Spider-Man - Journey Into Mystery

#73, 10/61

Stone Men - Tales of Suspense #28, 4/62; Tales to Astonish #5, 9/59; Tales to Astonish #16, 2/61

Superman - (Dr. Mystic) Comics Magazine #1, 5/36; More Fun Comics #14, 10/36; New Book of Comics #2, Spr '38

Toad Men - Tales to Astonish #7, 1/60

Uncle Ben - Strange Tales #97, 6/62

Watcher - Tales of Suspense #35, 11/62

Lost without your comics?

If you can't find a comic shop, you need this number...

PREVIEWS

Your Monthly Quota of Cool!

Discover the excitement inside **PREVIEWS** every month, with **informative, full-color advance information** on the latest upcoming ...

▼ Comics
▼ Magazines
▼ Books
▼ Trading

▼ Cards
▼ Games
▼ Toys
▼ Models
▼ Videos
... and **More!**

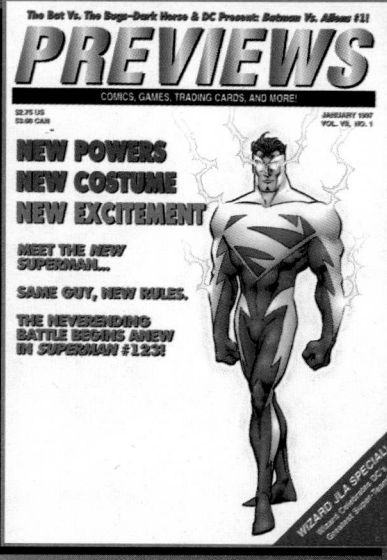

Plus:

▼ *The Splash Page*—Full-color news on the hottest comics and interviews with the industry's top creators!

▼ *Under the Reading Lamp* and *Small Press Spotlight*—Closer looks at promising new publishers and their hits-in-progress!

▼ **PREVIEWS** Contests—Your chance to win original art, limited-edition comics, and more incredible prizes!

▼ **PREVIEWS** Comics—Exclusive full-color comics serials <u>available</u> <u>nowhere</u> <u>else</u>!

▼ **Editorial Highlights** from major publishers!

▼ **Promotional Inserts** showcasing the coolest trading cards to come!

▼ **Gems of the Month** — <u>in</u> <u>full</u> <u>color</u>!

PREVIEWS

Nothing so hot was ever so cool!

PREVIEWS is a publication of Diamond Comic Distributors, Inc., the industry's leading distributor of new comics and related merchandise.

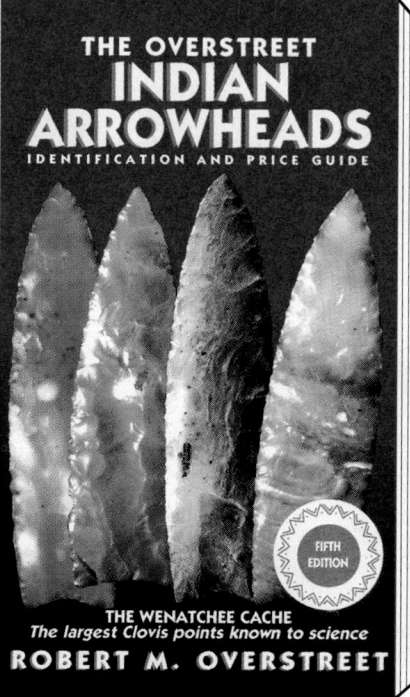

Overstreet's Back Issue Price Guide

The Overstreet® Comic Book Price Guide has held the record for being the longest running annual comic book publication. We are now celebrating our 27th anniversary and comic book collectors are as interested in putting together complete sets of these books as they are in collecting the old comics. The demand for the Overstreet® price guides is extremely strong and the collectors have created a legitimate market for them. They have consistantly been bringing record prices each year. Besides the price consideration, collectors also have a record of comic book prices going back further than any other source in comic fandom. The prices listed below are for near mint condition only. The other grades can be determined as follows: Good - 25% and Fine - 50% of the near mint value. Canadian editions exist for a couple of the early issues.
Abbreviations used: SC = soft cover; HC = hard cover, L = leather bound.

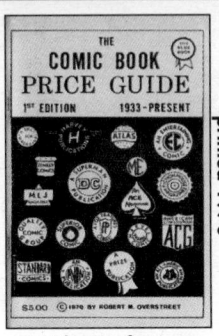

printed 1970

#1 White Soft Cover
$1200.00

#1 Blue Soft Cover
(2nd Printing)
$1000.00

printed 1972

#2 SC $600.00
#2 HC $800.00

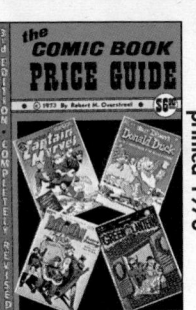

printed 1973

#3 SC $250.00
#3 HC $600.00

printed 1974

#4 SC $100.00
#4 HC $150.00

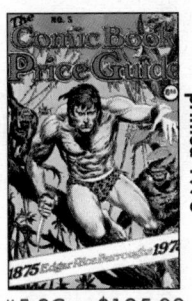

printed 1975

#5 SC $125.00
#5 HC $175.00

printed 1976

#6 SC $100.00
#6 HC $125.00

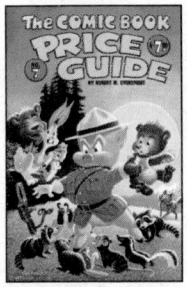

printed 1977

#7 SC $125.00
#7 HC $175.00

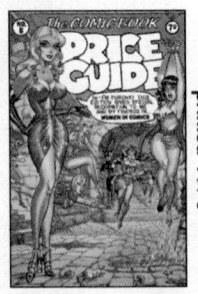

printed 1978

#8 SC $100.00
#8 HC $125.00

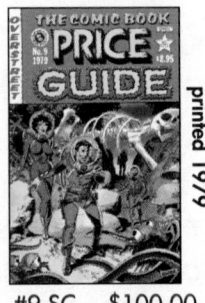

printed 1979

#9 SC $100.00
#9 HC $150.00

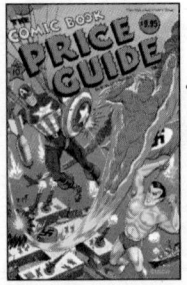

printed 1980

#10 SC $100.00
#10 HC $150.00

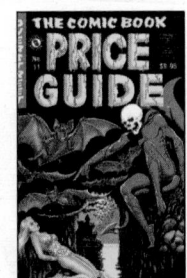

printed 1981

#11 SC $75.00
#11 HC $100.00

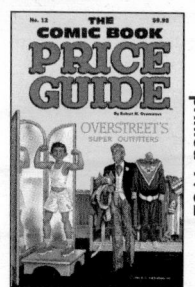

printed 1982

#12 SC $75.00
#12 HC $100.00

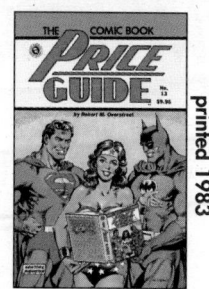

printed 1983

#13 SC $75.00
#13 HC $100.00

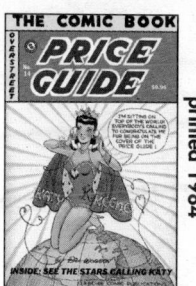

printed 1984

#14 SC $50.00
#14 HC $100.00

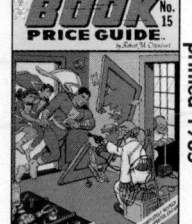

printed 1985

#15 SC $50.00
#15 HC $75.00
#15 L $150.00

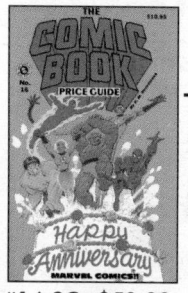

printed 1986

#16 SC $50.00
#16 HC $75.00
#16 L $150.00

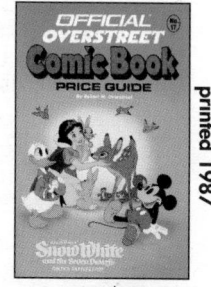

printed 1987

#17 SC $50.00
#17 HC $100.00
#17 L $150.00

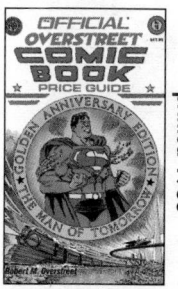

printed 1988

#18 SC $40.00
#18 HC $60.00
#18 L $150.00

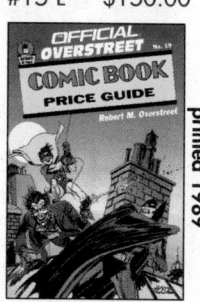

printed 1989

#19 SC $40.00
#19 HC $50.00
#19 L $150.00

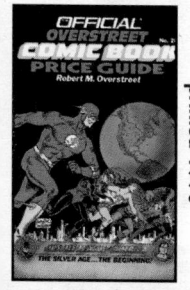

printed 1990

#20 SC $30.00
#20 HC $45.00
#20 L $125.00

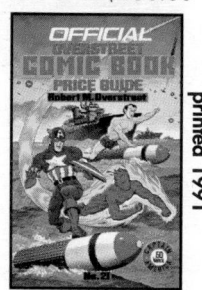

printed 1991

#21 SC $30.00
#21 HC $45.00
#21 L $125.00

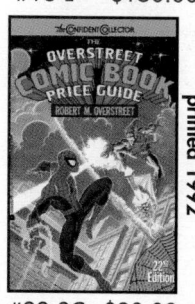

printed 1992

#22 SC $30.00
#22 HC $45.00

printed 1993

#23 SC $30.00
#23 HC $45.00

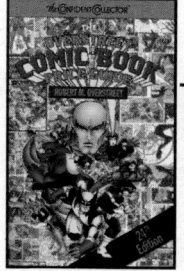

printed 1994

#24 SC $20.00
#24 HC $30.00

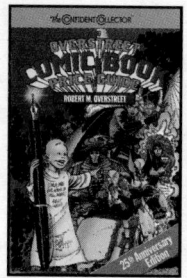

printed 1995

#25 SC $20.00
#25 HC $30.00
#25 L $100.00

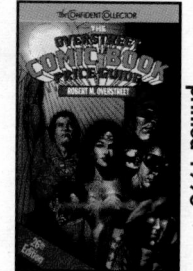

printed 1996

#26 SC $16.00
#26 HC $30.00
#26 L $100.00

PLATINUM AGE

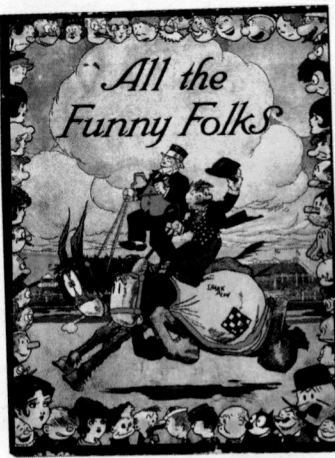

ALL THE FUNNY FOLKS
© 1926 World Press Today, Inc.

BARNEY GOOGLE #2
© 1924 C&L

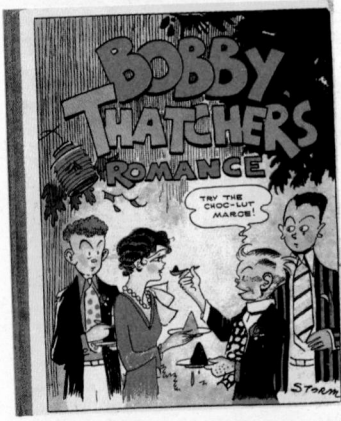

BOBBY THATCHER'S ROMANCE
© 1931 Henry Altemus Co.

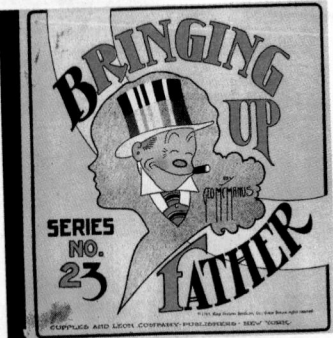

BRINGING UP FATHER #23
© 1933 C&L

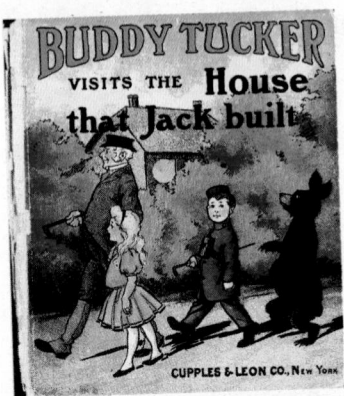

BUDDY TUCKER VISITS...
© 1907 C&L

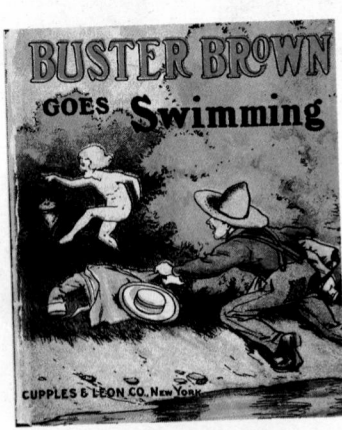

**BUSTER BROWN
GOES SWIMMING**
© 1907 C&L

COVER GALLERY

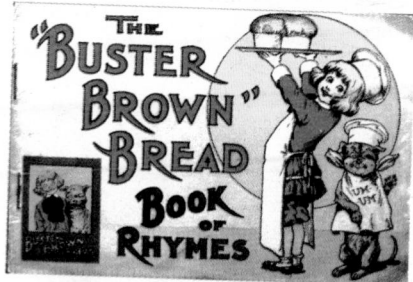

BUSTER BROWN BREAD BOOK
© 1904 Buster Brown Bread Co.

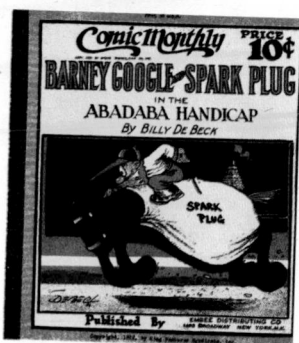

COMICS MONTHLY #11
© 1922 Embee Dist. Co.

BUSTER BROWN'S AMUSING CAPERS
© 1908 C&L

FOXY GRANDPA'S TRIUMPHS
© 1908 Bunny Publ.

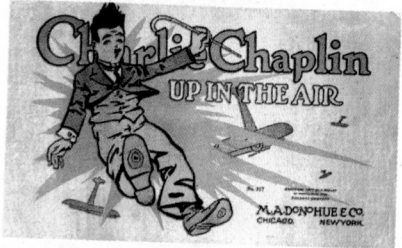

CHARLIE CHAPLIN UP IN THE AIR #317
© 1917 Essanay

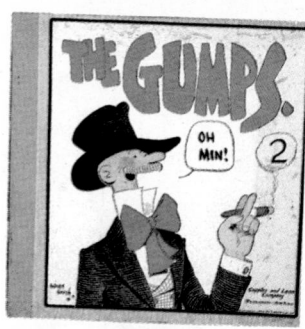

GUMPS #2
© 1925 C&L

COMICS MONTHLY #1
© 1922 Embee Dist. Co.

GUMPS #6
© 1921 C&L

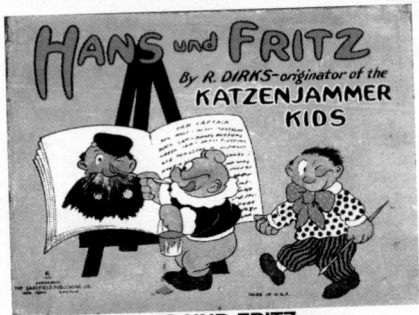

HANS UND FRITZ
© 1929 Saalfield

THE KATZENJAMMER KIDS
© 1905 NY American & Journal

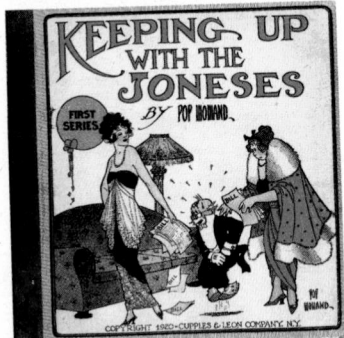

KEEPING UP WITH THE JONESES #1
© 1920 C&L

LITTLE NEMO IN SLUMBERLAND
© 1906 Duffield & Co.

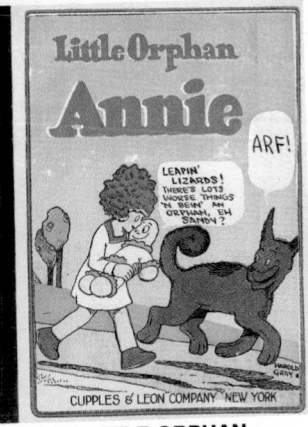

**LITTLE ORPHAN
ANNIE #1**
© 1926 C&L

MAUD
© 1906 Frederick A. Stokes

MOON MULLINS #1
© 1927 C&L

750

MUTT & JEFF #1
© 1910 Ball Publ.

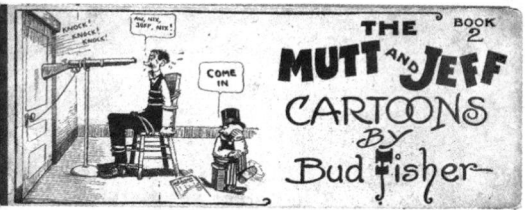

MUTT & JEFF #2
© 1911 Ball Publ.

**SMITTY IN THE
NORTH WOODS**
© 1932 C&L

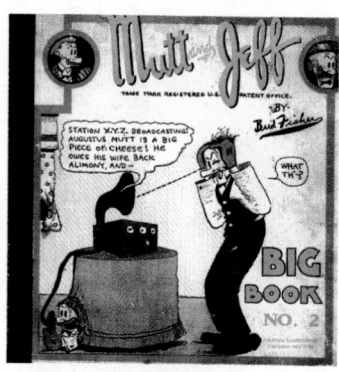

MUTT & JEFF BIG BOOK #2
© 1929 C&L

TILLIE THE TOILER #7
© 1932 C&L

**PORE LIL MOSE
HIS LETTERS TO HIS MAMMY**
© 1902 WHIT

WILLIE WESTINGHOUSE
© 1906 William A. Stokes

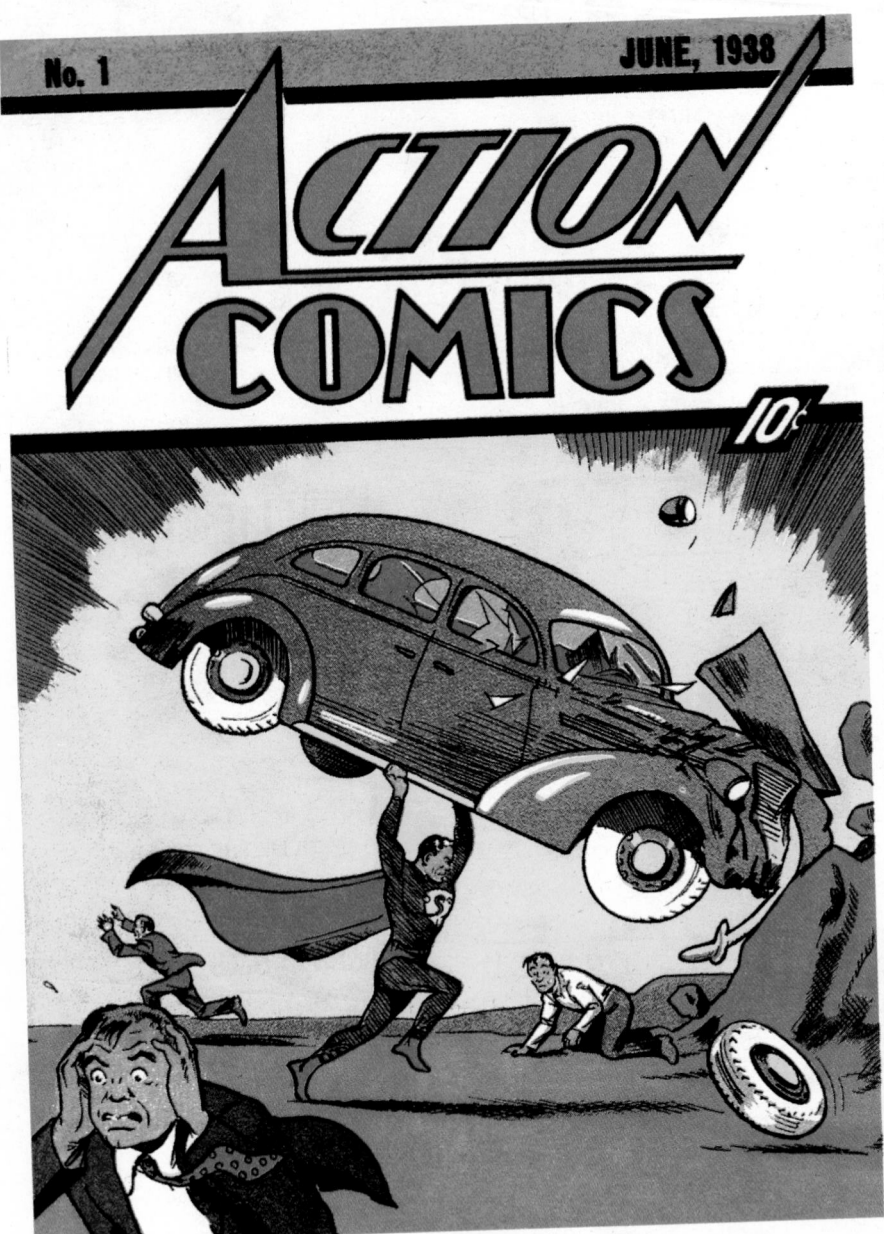

ACTION COMICS #1
© DC

COVER GALLERY

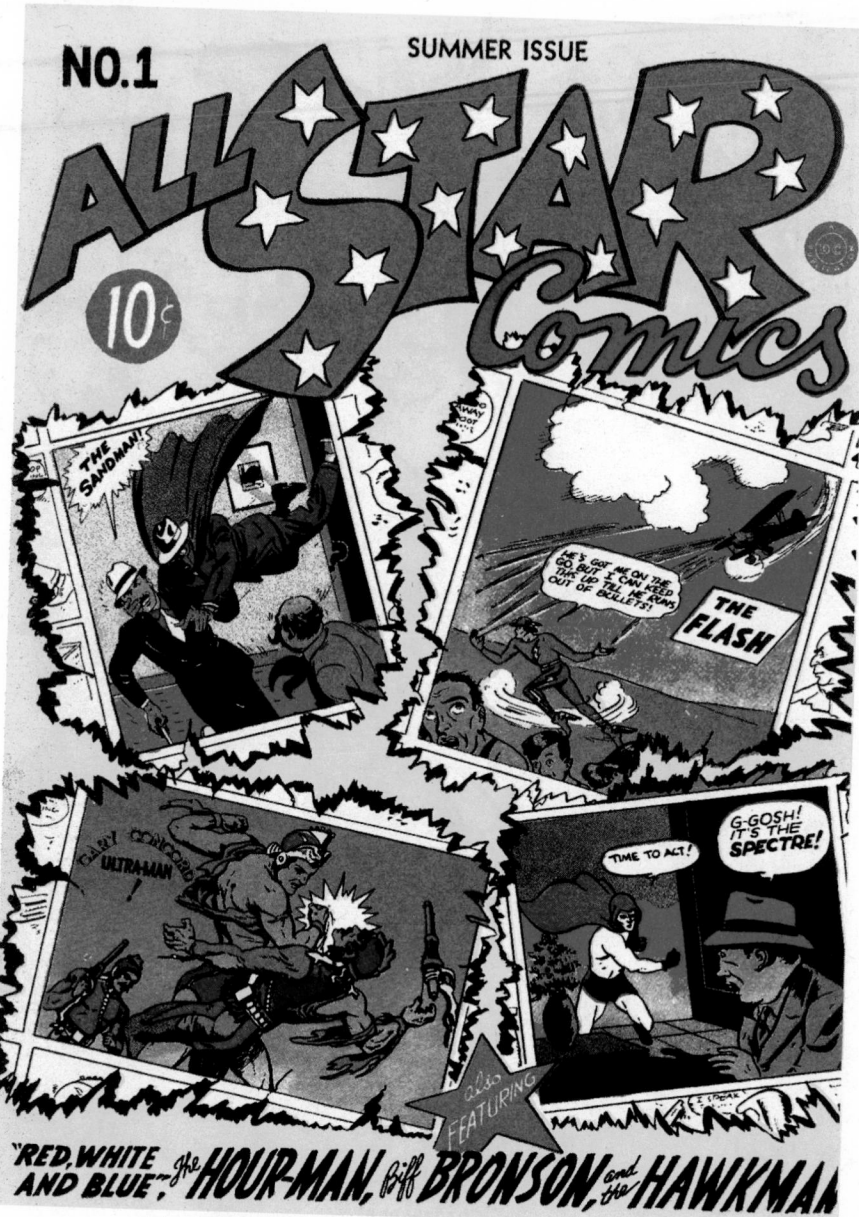

ALL-STAR COMICS #1 (From the Mile High Collection)
© DC

BATMAN #1
© DC

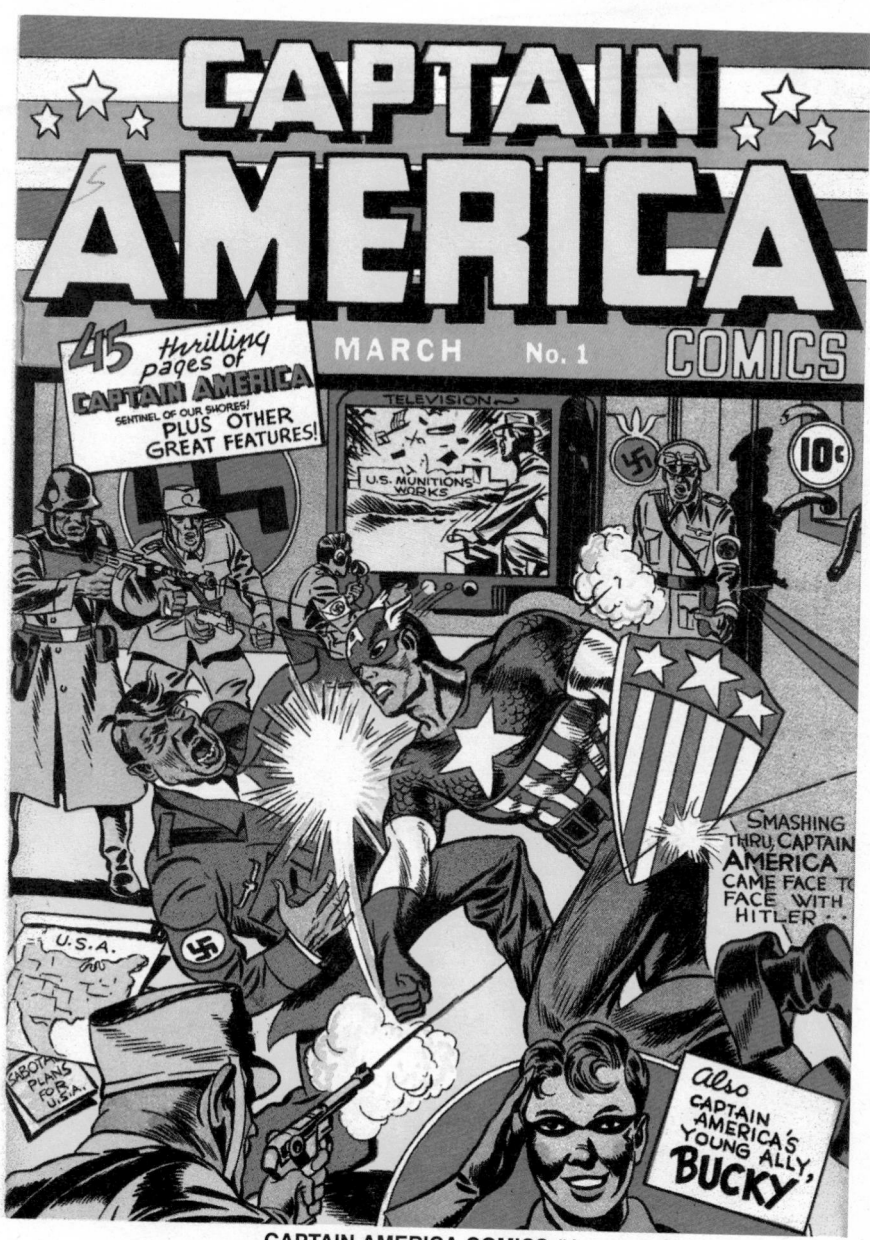

CAPTAIN AMERICA COMICS #1
© MEG

MARVEL COMICS #1 (Publisher's Pay Copy)
© MEG

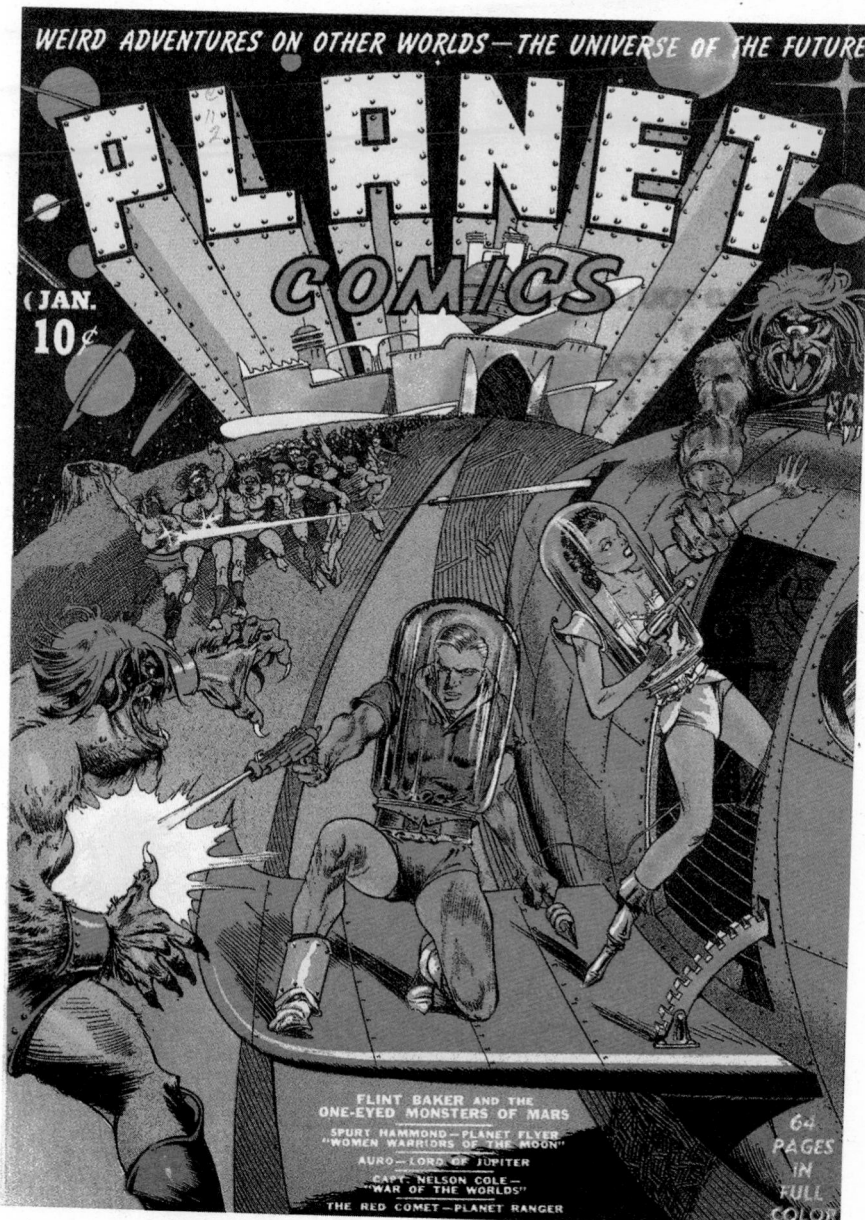

PLANET COMICS #1 (From the Mile High Collection)
© FH

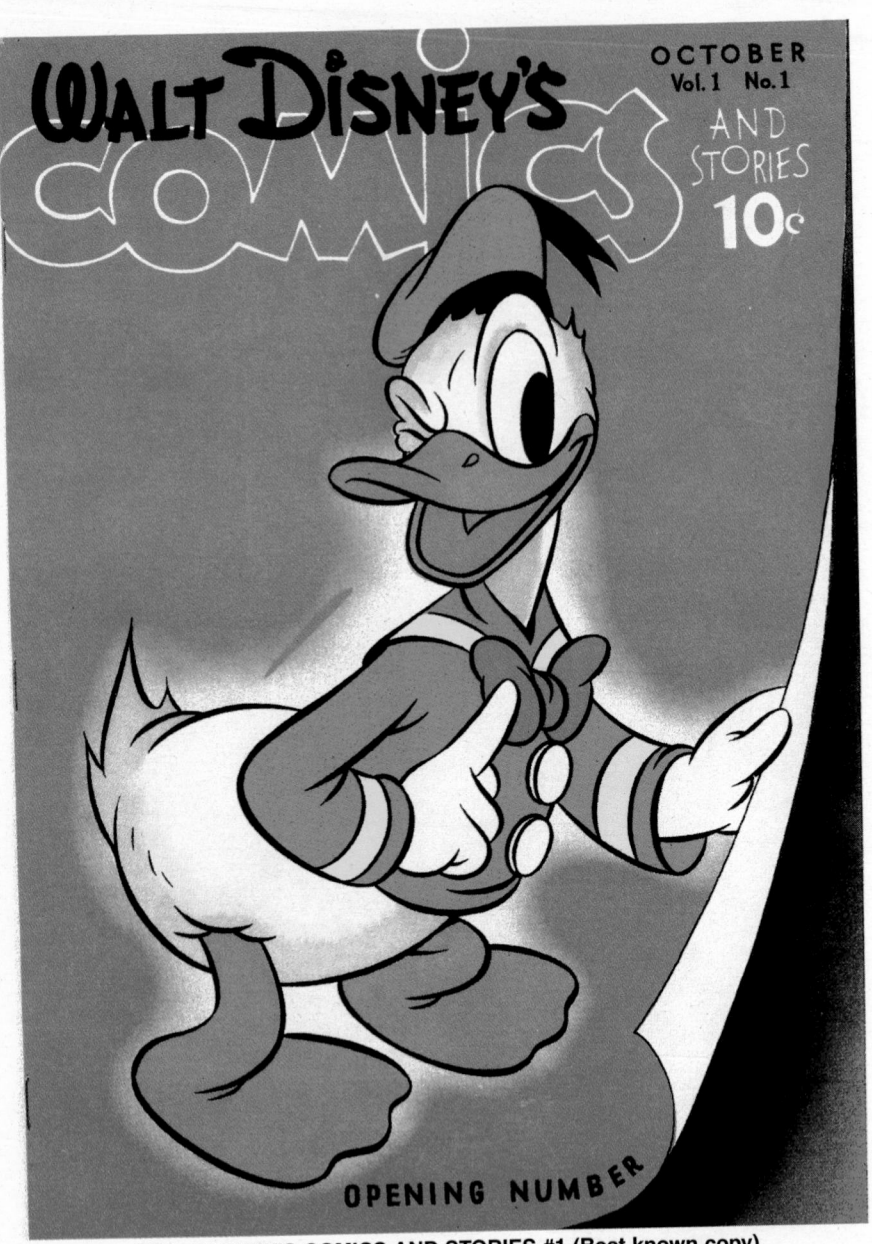

WALT DISNEY'S COMICS AND STORIES #1 (Best known copy)
© WDC

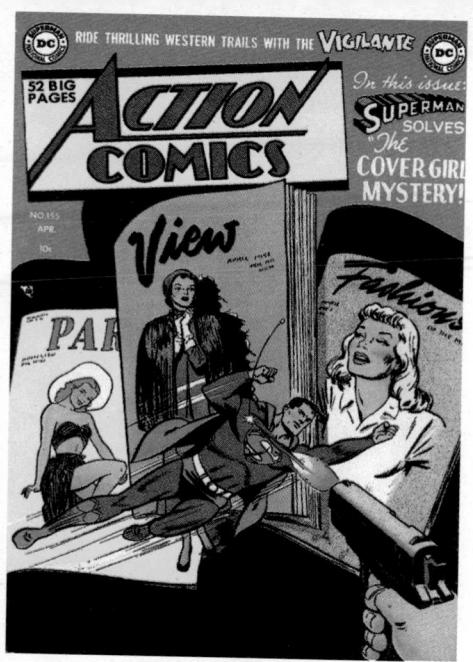

ACTION COMICS #155
© DC

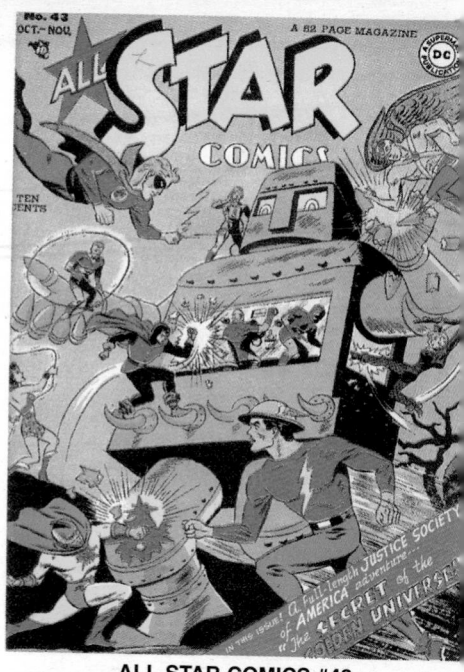

ALL STAR COMICS #43
© DC

ALL TOP COMICS #10
© FOX

ALL-AMERICAN COMICS #52
© DC

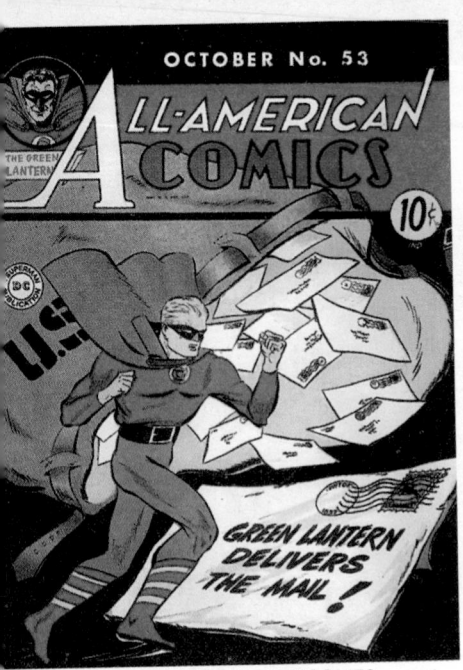

ALL-AMERICAN COMICS #53
© DC

ALL-AMERICAN COMICS #54
© DC

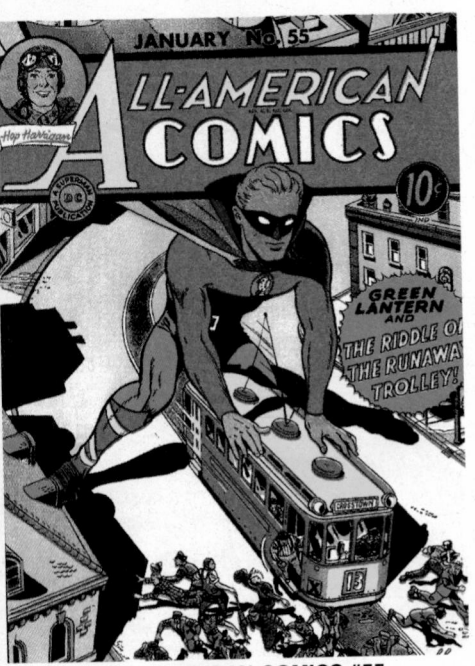

ALL-AMERICAN COMICS #55
© DC

BAFFLING MYSTERIES #8
© Periodical House

BLACKHAWK #71
© QUA

BLOOD IS THE HARVEST
© Catechetical Guild

BLUE RIBBON COMICS #22
© MLJ

BRENDA STARR #14
© SUPR

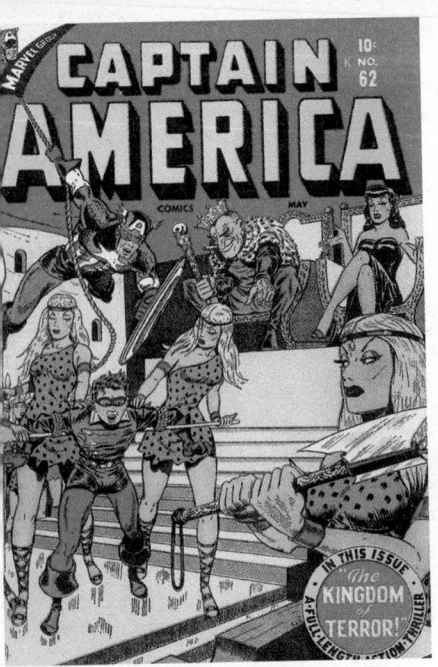

CAPTAIN AMERICA COMICS #62
© MEG

CASPER #3
© Paramount

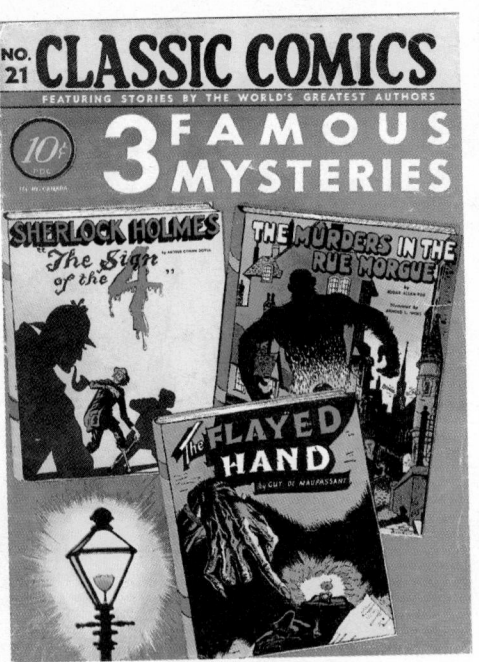

CLASSIC COMICS #21
© GIL

COLOSSUS COMICS #1
© Sun Publ.

COOKIE #12
© ACG

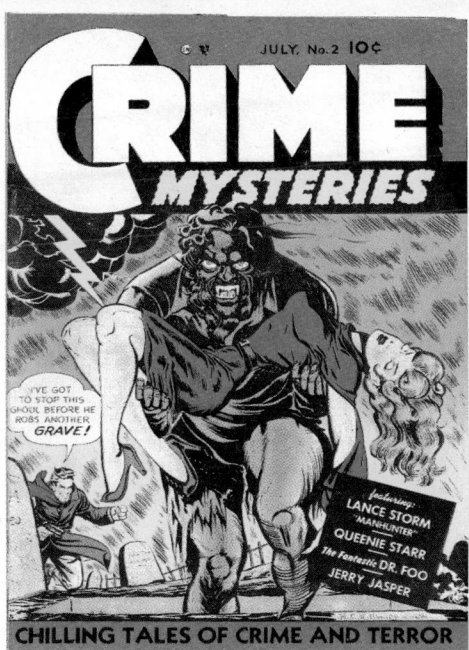

CRIME MYSTERIES #2
© TM

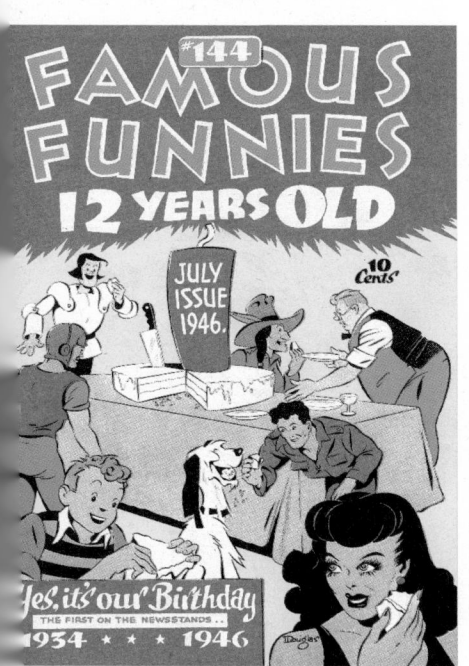

FAMOUS FUNNIES #144
© EAS

FANTASTIC FOUR #1
© MEG

FORBIDDEN WORLDS #3
© ACG

FRANKENSTEIN COMICS #8
© PRIZE

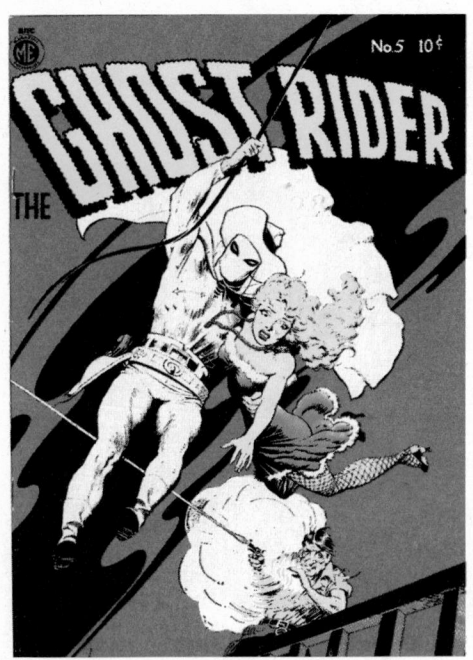

GHOST RIDER #5
© ME

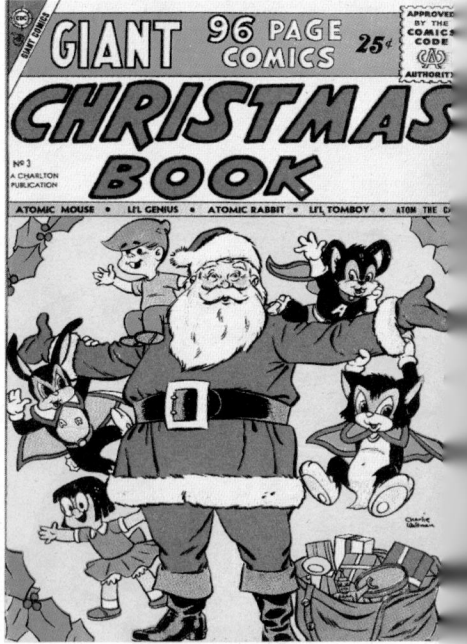

GIANT COMICS #3
© CC

GREEN LANTERN #33
© DC

HAND OF FATE #13
© ACE

HI-HO #1
2/46, © HOKE

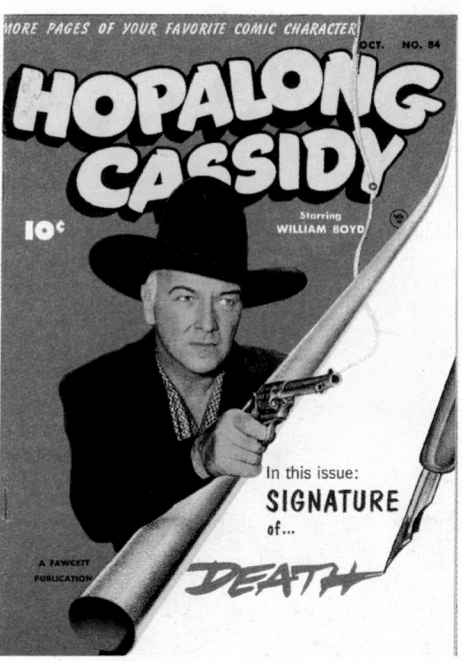

HOPALONG CASSIDY #84
10/53, © FAW

HOUSE OF MYSTERY #64
© DC

IBIS #1
© FAW

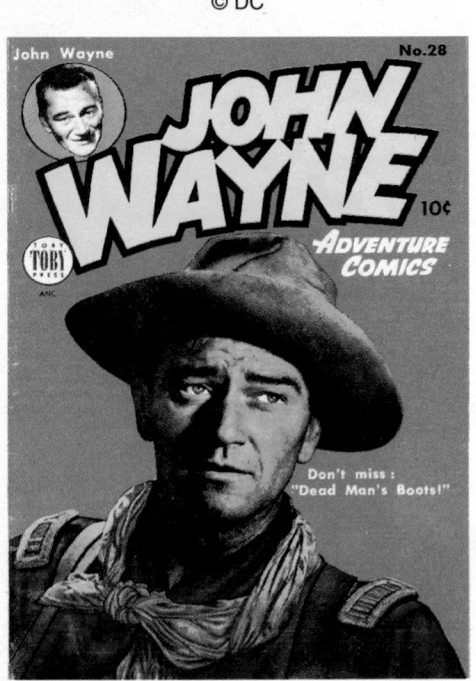

JOHN WAYNE ADVENTURE COMICS #28 ©
TOBY

JUMBO #123
© FH

LEGENDS OF DANIEL BOONE #5
© DC

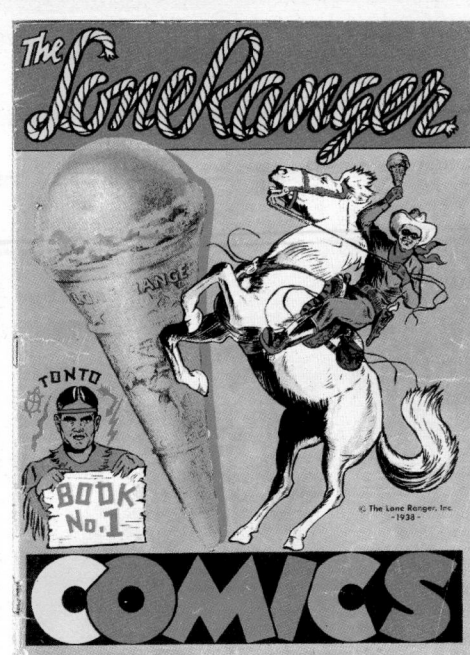

LONE RANGER ICE CREAM BOOK #1
© Lone Ranger, Inc.

MILLIE THE MODEL ANNUAL #1
© MEG

MISS FURY #4
© MEG

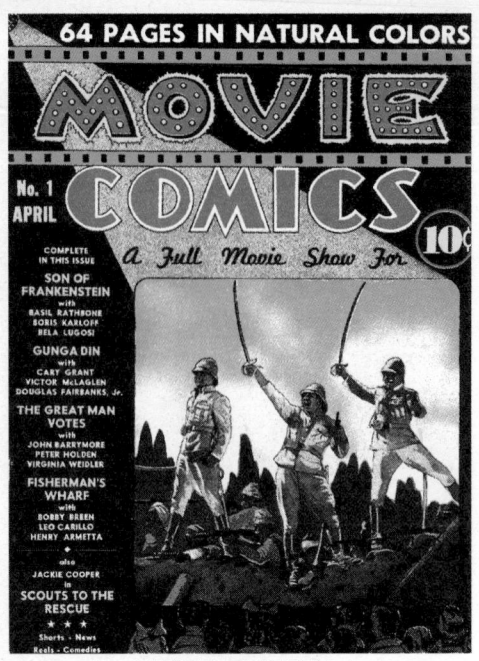

MOVIE COMICS #1
© DC

MYSTERIOUS ADVENTURES #2
© Story Comics

NATIONAL COMICS #16
© QUA

NELLIE THE NURSE #10
© DELL

OUT OF THE NIGHT #7
© ACG

PERFECT CRIME #28
© Cross Publ.

PLASTIC MAN #61
© QUA

POLICE AGAINST CRIME #2
© Premiere Magazines

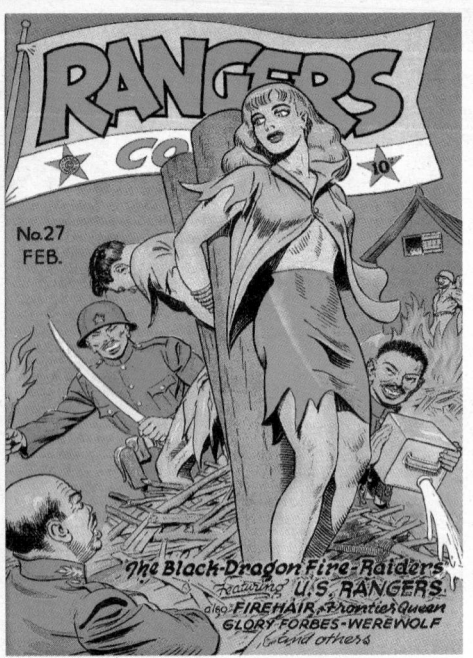

RANGERS COMICS #27
© FH

RED RYDER COMICS #3
© Hawley Publ.

RICHIE RICH #4
© HARV

SECRET MYSTERIES #16
© Merit Publ.

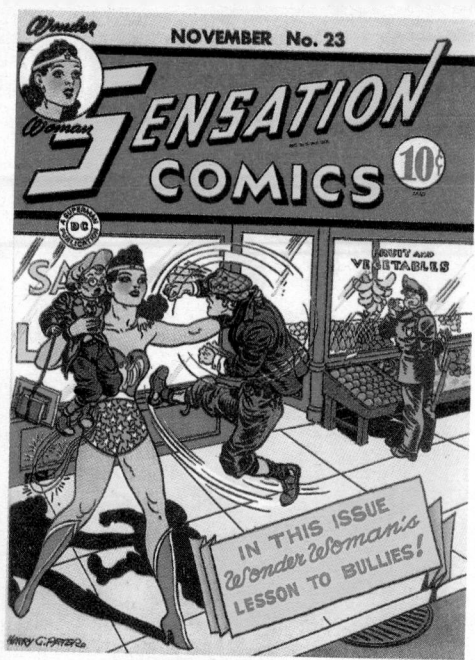

SENSATION COMICS #23
© DC

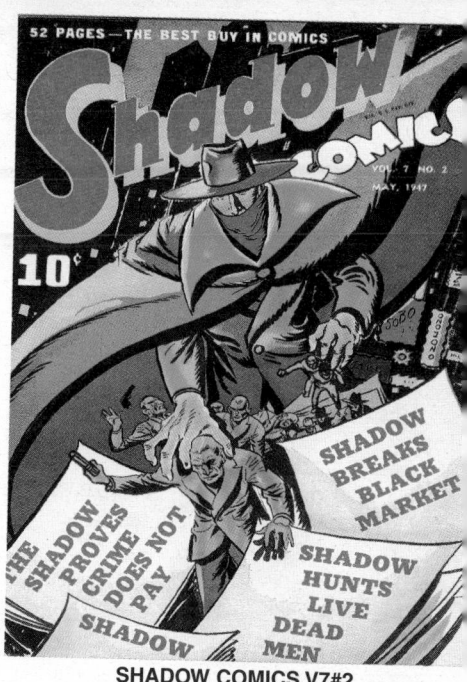

SHADOW COMICS V7#2
© S&S

SHOWCASE #8
© DC

SPACE ADVENTURES #15
© CC

STAR SPANGLED WAR COMICS #38
© DC

STRAIGHT ARROW #20
© ME

STRANGE ADVENTURES #78
© DC

SUPERMAN #70
© DC

TERRY-TOONS #10
© STJ

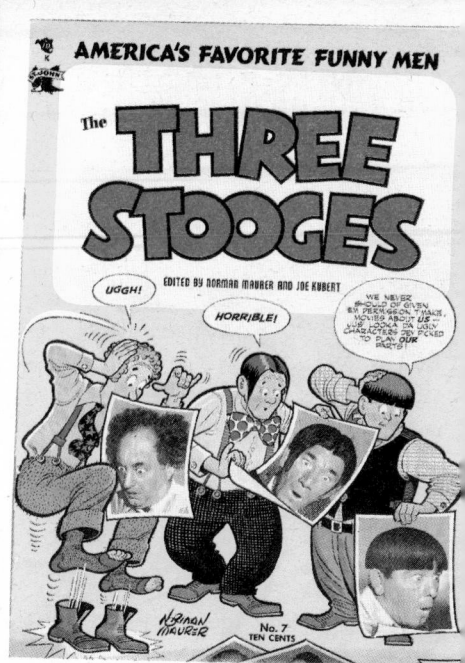

THREE STOOGES #7
© DELL

WAR COMICS #26
© MEG

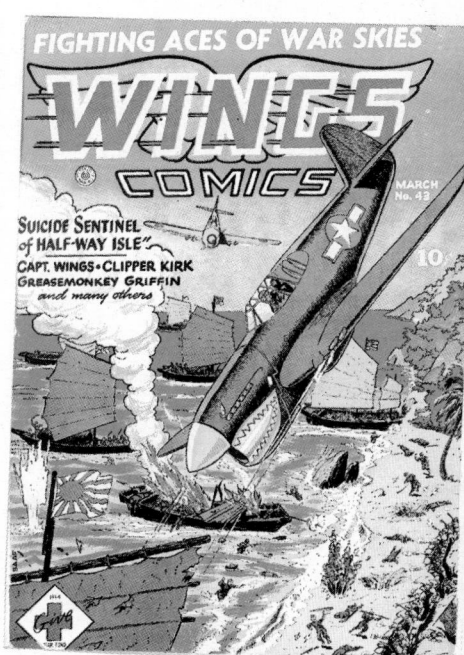

WINGS COMICS #43
© FH

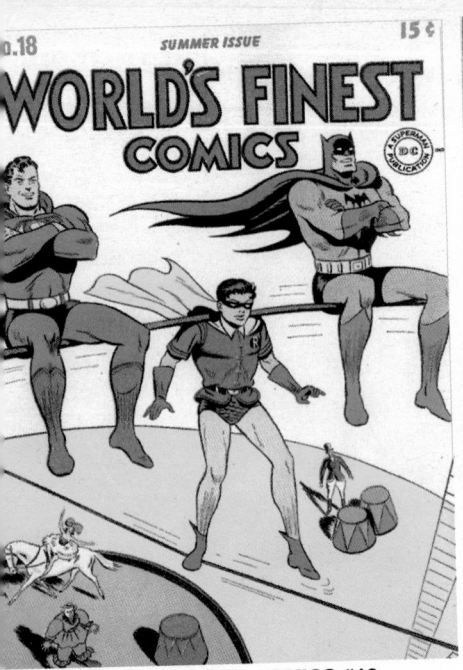

WORLD'S FINEST COMICS #18
© DC

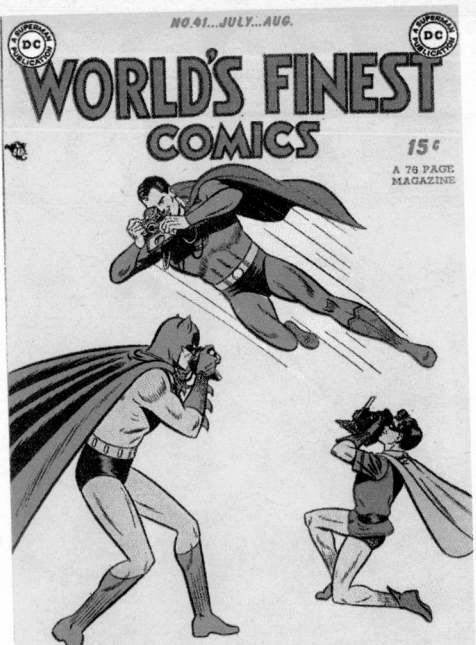

WORLD'S FINEST COMICS #41
© DC

YOUNG LOVERS #18
© CC

YOUNG ROMANCE COMICS #11
© PRIZE

THE REVIEWS ARE IN!

Overstreet Presents:

Hake's Price Guide to

Character Toy Premiums

including Comic Books, T.V., Movies, Radio, Cereal items and More

No. 1
$24.95 US
$34.50 CAN

A PEP BUTTON IN EVERY BOX!

GI JOE • DISNEYANA • UNDER... • ROY...
...ALONG CASSIDY • SPIDE...
BUCK ROGERS • BATMAN • FLINT...

ICY-FROST TWINS

premiums · toys · giveaways

OVERSTREET ADVISORS

DAVID T. ALEXANDER
David Alexander Comics
Tampa, FL

JON BERK, Attorney
President AACBC
Hartford, CT

GARY CARTER
Editor, CBM
Coronado, CA

JOHN CHRUSCINSKI
Tropic Comics
Plantation, FL

LARRY CURCIO
Avalon Comics
Medford, MA

GARY DOLGOFF
Gary Dolgoff Comics
Brooklyn, NY

BRUCE ELLSWORTH
Tropic Comics
Plantation, FL

RICHARD EVANS
Bedrock City Comics
Houston, TX

STEVE FISHLER
Metropolis Collectibles
New York, NY

STEVEN GENTNER
Golden Age Specialist
Portland, OR

MICHAEL GOLDMAN
Motor City Comics
Southfield, MI

JAMIE GRAHAM
Graham Crackers
Chicago, IL

DANIEL GREENHALGH
Showcase New England
Wallingford, CT

ERIC J. GROVES
Collector
Oklahoma City, OK

BRUCE HAMILTON
Hamilton Comics
Prescott, AZ

JOHN HAUSER
Dealer/Collector
New Berlin, WI

BILL HUGHES
Executive Collectibles
Beverly Hills, CA

ROB HUGHES
Archangels
Manhattan Beach, CA

JOSEPH KOCH
Dealer/Collector
Brooklyn, NY

PHIL LEVINE
Dealer/Collector
Three Bridges, NJ

HARRY MATETSKY
Collector
Middletown, NJ

MICHAEL NAIMAN
Silver Age Specialist
San Diego, CA

RICHARD OLSON
Dealer/Collector
Slidell, LA

JIM PAYETTE
Golden Age Specialist
Bethlehem, NH

RON PUSSELL
Redbeard's Book Den
Crystal Bay, NV

TODD REZNIK
Pacific Comic Exchange
Los Angeles, CA

ROBERT ROGOVIN
Four Color Comics
New York, NY

RORY ROOT
Comic Relief
Berkeley, CA

ROBERT ROTER
Pacific Comic Exchange
Los Angeles, CA

CHUCK ROZANSKI
Mile High Comics
Denver, CO

JOHN SNYDER
Diamond Int. Galleries
Timonium, MD

MATT SCHIFFMAN
Bronze Age Specialist
Wilsonville, OR

CRAIG SOIFER
Comic Shop Owner
Brooklyn, NY

TONY STARKS
Silver Age Specialist
Newburgh, IN

TERRY STROUD
Dealer/Collector
Santa Monica, CA

JOE VERENAULT
Golden Age Specialist
Woodbury Heights, NJ

JERRY WEIST
Sotheby's
New York, NY

HARLEY YEE
Dealer/Collector
Detroit, MI

VINCENT ZURZOLO, JR.
Vincent's Collectibles
Belle Harbor, NY

Thanks to all our advisors for their assistance in the completion of this 27th Edition of the Overstreet Comic Book Price Guide.

ADVERTISERS DIRECTORY

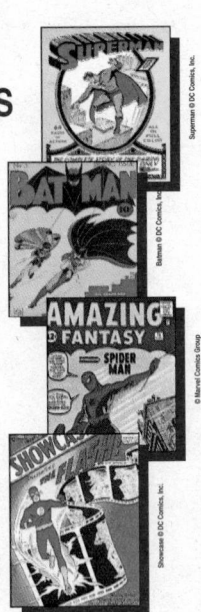